shakespearean criticism

"Thou art a Monument without a tomb,
And art alive still while thy Book doth
live
And we have wits to read and praise to
give."

*Ben Jonson, from the preface
to the First Folio, 1623.*

Mr. WILLIAM

SHAKESPEARES

COMEDIES,
HISTORIES, &
TRAGEDIES.

Published according to the True Originall Copies.

Martin Droeshout sculpsit London.

LONDON
Printed by Isaac Iaggard, and Ed. Blount. 1623.

Frontispiece to the First Folio (1623). By permission of the Folger Shakespeare Library.

ISSN 0883-9123

Volume 6

shakespearean criticism

Excerpts from the Criticism of
William Shakespeare's Plays and Poetry,
from the First Published Appraisals
to Current Evaluations

Mark W. Scott
Editor

Sandra L. Williamson
Associate Editor

Gale Research Company
Book Tower
Detroit, Michigan 48226

STAFF

Mark W. Scott, *Editor*

Sandra L. Williamson, *Associate Editor*

Kathleen M. Aro, Cappy Beins, K. R. Krolicki, *Assistant Editors*

Carolyn Bancroft, Phyllis Carmel Mendelson, *Contributing Editors*

Denise Michlewicz Broderick, Joyce A. Davis, Melissa Reiff Hug, Debra A. Wells,
Contributing Assistant Editors

Jeanne A. Gough, *Permissions & Production Manager*
Lizbeth A. Purdy, *Production Supervisor*
Kathleen M. Cook, *Assistant Production Coordinator*
Suzanne Powers, Jani Prescott, Lee Ann Welsh, *Editorial Assistants*
Linda M. Pugliese, *Manuscript Coordinator*
Donna Craft, *Assistant Manuscript Coordinator*
Jennifer E. Gale, Maureen A. Puhl, Rosetta Irene Simms, *Manuscript Assistants*

Victoria B. Cariappa, *Research Supervisor*
Maureen R. Richards, *Research Coordinator*
Mary D. Wise, *Senior Research Assistant*
Joyce E. Doyle, Kent Graham, Kevin B. Hillstrom, Karen D. Kaus, Eric Priehs, Filomena
Sgambati, Laura B. Standley, *Research Assistants*

Janice M. Mach, *Text Permissions Supervisor*
Kathy Grell, *Permissions Coordinator, Text*
Susan D. Battista, *Assistant Permissions Coordinator*
Mabel E. Gurney, Josephine M. Keene, *Senior Permissions Assistants*
H. Diane Cooper, *Permissions Assistant*
Eileen H. Baehr, Martha A. Mulder, Anita Lorraine Ransom, Kimberly F. Smilay, Lisa M.
Wimmer, *Permissions Clerks*

Patricia A. Seefelt, *Picture Permissions Supervisor*
Margaret A. Chamberlain, *Permissions Coordinator, Pictures*
Colleen M. Crane, *Permissions Assistant*
Pamela A. Hayes, Lillian Tyus, *Permissions Clerk*

ISBN 0-8103-6130-2
ISSN 0883-9123

Computerized photocomposition by
Typographics, Incorporated
Kansas City, Missouri

Printed in the United States

Contents

Preface

The works of William Shakespeare have delighted audiences and inspired scholars for nearly four hundred years. Shakespeare's appeal is universal, for in its depth and breadth his work evokes a timeless insight into the human condition.

The vast amount of Shakespearean criticism is a testament to his enduring popularity. Critics of each epoch have contributed to this critical legacy, responding to the comments of their forebears, bringing the moral and intellectual atmosphere of their own era to the works, and suggesting interpretations that continue to inspire critics of today. Thus, to chart the history of criticism of Shakespeare is to note the changing aesthetic philosophies of the past four centuries.

The Scope of the Work

The success of Gale's four existing literary series, *Contemporary Literary Criticism (CLC), Twentieth-Century Literary Criticism (TCLC), Nineteenth-Century Literature Criticism (NCLC),* and *Children's Literature Review (CLR),* suggested an equivalent need among students and teachers of Shakespeare. Moreover, since the criticism of Shakespeare's works spans four centuries and is larger in size and scope than that of any author, a prodigious amount of critical material confronts the student.

Shakespearean Criticism (SC) presents significant passages from published criticism on the works of Shakespeare. Nine volumes of the series will be devoted to aesthetic criticism of the plays. Performance criticism will be treated in separate special volumes. Other special volumes will be devoted to such topics as Shakespeare's sonnets and nondramatic poems, the authorship controversy and the apocrypha, stage history of the plays, and other general subjects, such as Shakespeare's language, religious and philosophical thought, and characterization. The first nine volumes will each contain criticism on three to six plays, with an equal balance of genres and an equal balance of plays based on their critical importance. Thus, Volume 6 contains criticism on one major tragedy *(Antony and Cleopatra),* one history *(Richard II),* and one minor comedy *(The Two Gentlemen of Verona).*

The length of each entry is intended to represent the amount of critical attention the play has received from critics writing in English and from foreign criticism in translation. The editors have tried to identify only the major critics and lines of inquiry for each play. Each entry represents a historical overview of the critical response to the play: early criticism is presented to indicate initial responses and later selections represent significant trends in the history of criticism of the play. We have also attempted to identify and include excerpts from the seminal essays on each play by the most important Shakespearean critics. We have directed our series to students in late high school and early college who are beginning their study of Shakespeare. Thus, ours is not a work for the specialist, but an introduction for the researcher newly acquainted with the works of Shakespeare.

The Organization of the Book

Each entry consists of the following elements: play heading, an introduction, excerpts of criticism (each followed by a bibliographical citation), and an additional bibliography for further reading.

The *introduction* begins with a discussion of the date, text, and sources of the play. This section is followed by a critical history, which outlines the major critical trends and identifies the prominent commentators on the play.

Criticism is arranged chronologically within each play entry to provide a perspective on the changes in critical evaluation over the years. For purposes of easier identification, the critic's name and the date of the essay are given at the beginning of each piece. For an anonymous essay later attributed to a critic, the critic's name appears in brackets at the beginning of the excerpt and in the bibliographical citation. Within the text, all act, scene, and line designations have been changed to conform to *The Riverside*

Shakespeare, published by Houghton Mifflin Company, which is a standard text used in many high school and college English classes. All of the individual essays are prefaced with *explanatory notes* as an additional aid to students using *SC.* The explanatory notes provide several types of useful information, including: the importance of the critics in literary history, the critical schools with which they are identified, if any, and the importance of their comments on Shakespeare and the play discussed. The explanatory notes also identify the main issues in the commentary on each play and provide previous publication information, such as original title and date, for reprinted and translated publications.

A complete *bibliographical citation* designed to facilitate the location of the original essay or book follows each piece of criticism.

Within each play entry are *illustrations,* such as facsimiles of title pages taken from the quarto and First Folio editions of the plays as well as pictures drawn from such sources as early editions of the collected works and artists' renderings of some of the famous scenes and characters. The captions following each illustration indicate act, scene, characters, and the artist and date, if known. The illustrations are arranged chronologically and, as a complement to the criticism, provide a historical perspective on Shakespeare throughout the centuries.

The *additional bibliography* appearing at the end of each play entry suggests further reading on the play. This section includes references to the major discussions of the date, the text, and the sources of each play.

A *list of plays* covered in the series follows the Preface. This listing indicates which works of the canon are treated in each existing or future volume.

To help students locate essays by certain commentators, *SC* includes a *cumulative index to critics;* under each critic's name are listed the plays on which the critic has written and the volume and page where the criticism appears. *SC* also provides a *cumulative index to topics.* This feature identifies the principal topics of debate in the criticism of each play; the topics are arranged alphabetically and indicate the initial page number of each excerpt that offers substantial commentary on that topic.

As an additional aid to students, *SC* offers a *glossary* of terms relating to date, text, and source information frequently mentioned by critics and used throughout the introductions to the plays. The glossed terms and source names are identified by small capital letters when they first appear in the introductions.

An *appendix* is also included that lists the sources from which the material in the volume is reprinted. It does not, however, list every book or periodical consulted for the volume.

Acknowledgments

No work of this scope can be accomplished without the cooperation of many people. The editors wish to thank the copyright holders of the excerpts included in this volume, the permissions managers of the book and magazine publishing companies for assisting us in securing reprint rights, and the staffs of the Detroit Public Library, the University of Michigan libraries, and the Wayne State University Library for making their resources available to us. We would especially like to thank the staff of the Rare Book Room of the University of Michigan Library for their research assistance and the Folger Shakespeare Library for their help in picture research. We would also like to thank Anthony J. Bogucki for assistance with copyright research.

Suggestions Are Welcome

The editors welcome the comments and suggestions of readers to expand the coverage and enhance the usefulness of the series. For example, in response to various recommendations, several features have been added to *SC* since the series began, including: the list of plays covered in each volume; the glossary; and the topic index.

List of Plays Covered in *SC*

[The year or years in parentheses indicate the composition date of the play as determined by G. Blakemore Evans in *The Riverside Shakespeare*]

Volume 1

The Comedy of Errors (1592-94)
Hamlet (1600-01)
1 and *2 Henry IV* (1596-98)
Timon of Athens (1607-08)
Twelfth Night (1601-02)

Volume 2

Henry VIII (1612-13)
King Lear (1605)
Love's Labour's Lost (1594-95)
Measure for Measure (1604)
Pericles (1607-08)

Volume 3

1, 2, and *3 Henry VI* (1589-91)
Macbeth (1606)
A Midsummer Night's Dream (1595-96)
Troilus and Cressida (1601-02)

Volume 4

Cymbeline (1609-10)
The Merchant of Venice (1596-97)
Othello (1604)
Titus Andronicus (1593-94)

Volume 5

As You Like It (1599)
Henry V (1599)
The Merry Wives of Windsor (1597)
Romeo and Juliet (1595-96)

Volume 6

Antony and Cleopatra (1606-07)
Richard II (1595)
The Two Gentlemen of Verona (1594)

In Forthcoming Volumes:

All's Well That Ends Well (1602-03)
Coriolanus (1607-08)
Julius Caesar (1599)
King John (1594-96)
Much Ado about Nothing (1598-99)
Richard III (1592-93)
The Taming of the Shrew (1593-94)
The Tempest (1611)
The Two Noble Kinsmen (1613)
The Winter's Tale (1610-11)

Antony and Cleopatra

DATE: *Antony and Cleopatra* was entered in the STATIONERS' REGISTER on May 20, 1608, but there is convincing external evidence to support the theory that the play was written and first performed at least one, and probably two years earlier. This evidence rests primarily on Samuel Daniel's publication in 1607 of a revision of his dramatic poem *Cleopatra*. Critics have identified many striking similarities between this work and Shakespeare's *Antony and Cleopatra;* importantly, however, they have also noted that none of these echoes can be found in the five earlier editions of Daniel's play published between 1594 and 1605. For many scholars, Daniel's revision—especially in light of the earlier unaltered reprintings—suggests that between 1605 and 1607 something induced the author to make significant changes in his original work; this impetus, they claim, was the recent production of Shakespeare's drama. If true, this theory would place the composition of *Antony and Cleopatra* prior to the publication of Daniel's revised dramatic poem, most likely in 1606 or early 1607. A few authorities, however, have contended that Shakespeare, not Daniel, was the borrower, thus making the composition date of *Antony and Cleopatra* fall after the appearance of Daniel's revised work, perhaps as early as 1607 but no later than 1608. Another piece of external evidence exists that supports the earlier of these two dates, for in Barnabe Barnes's *The Devil's Charter,* also published in 1607, there is a scene in which two boys are fatally poisoned with asps—an incident, some scholars suggest, possibly drawn from Act V of Shakespeare's play. Again in support of the earlier composition date, certain critics have discovered echoes of *Antony and Cleopatra* in *Macbeth,* which is generally believed to have been written in 1606, thus indicating that Shakespeare had begun work on—or at least had given considerable thought to—the later Roman play at this time.

TEXT: No evidence exists to indicate that *Antony and Cleopatra* appeared in print before its inclusion in the FIRST FOLIO of 1623, and thus this text is generally considered authoritative. Most scholars maintain that it is based on Shakespeare's own manuscript of the play or on a FAIR COPY. Because of the extraordinary length of the Folio text and its unusually precise stage directions, critics posit that it was not set from a PROMPT-BOOK used for actual performances. Except for such errors as mislineations or misspellings that textual scholars have attributed to the COMPOSITORS, the Folio text is judged to be a good one, and most modern editors of the play rely heavily upon it. Although the First Folio version contains no act or scene divisions, editors from the eighteenth century to the present have interpolated them, and modern editions of *Antony and Cleopatra* indicate as many as forty-two scenes. Harley Granville-Barker, however, has argued that these divisions are arbitrary and disjunctive, interrupting the flow of dramatic events in a way never intended by Shakespeare.

SOURCES: The principal source for *Antony and Cleopatra* is Thomas North's translation (1579) of ''The Life of Antonius'' in PLUTARCH's *The Lives of the Noble Grecianes and Romans compared together.* Scholars have noted Shakespeare's heavy indebtedness to Plutarch for many incidents in the play, but they have commented most particularly on the several verbal parallels between the drama and North's version. It has often

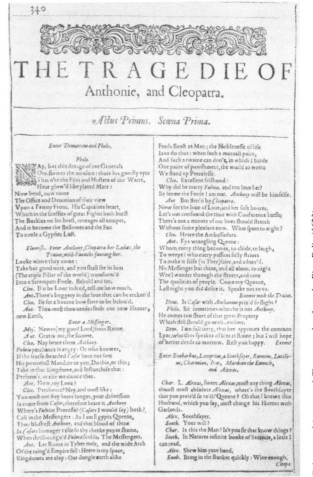

Title page of Antony and Cleopatra taken from the First Folio (1623).

been noted that Enobarbus's famous description of Cleopatra's barge (II. ii. 191ff.) represents a close poetic rendering of North's prose passage on this subject, and there is a strong correspondence in word choice in many other passages as well. Critics are divided, however, over the extent of similarities in characterization and authorial attitude between Shakespeare and Plutarch. Some commentators see Plutarch's condemnation of Antony's conduct replicated in Shakespeare's play, while others do not. Similarly, several critics maintain that Shakespeare's Cleopatra is a more complex, vital, and sympathetic character than her counterpart in the source, but others note that while Plutarch censured the queen for contributing to Antony's downfall, he also credited her with such favorable traits as skillful diplomacy, knowledge of many languages, and maternal devotion, all of which Shakespeare either only hints at or omits entirely. Further, the dramatist makes no mention of the children born to Antony and Octavia, compresses the dramatic action so that events which actually transpired over ten years appear to be more closely connected, and only briefly refers to Antony's unsuccessful Parthian campaign, to which the Greek historian devotes a significant portion of his ''Life of Antonius.'' Finally, many critics hold that the antithesis between Rome and Egypt and the opposition of conflicting values in *Antony and Cleopatra* are not strictly Shakespeare's conception, but have their origin in Plutarch's account.

In addition to North's translation of Plutarch, it has been proposed that Shakespeare drew upon the work of several other writers for the composition of his play. M. W. MacCallum (see Additional Bibliography) was the first to hypothesize that in Appian's *Civil Wars* (translated by "W. B." in 1578) Shakespeare found the material for the dramatic events involving Sextus Pompeius, Fulvia, and Antony's brother. Whereas a few scholars have suggested that there are minor resemblances between Shakespeare's tragedy and Robert Garnier's *Marc-Antoine* (1578), a French work translated into English by the Countess of Pembroke in 1590, many more commentators have remarked on the similarities between the play and Samuel Daniel's *Cleopatra* (1594), which takes up the story after the death of Antony and was written as a companion piece to the Countess's translation. As with Plutarch, there is no general agreement over the nature and extent of Shakespeare's indebtedness to Daniel. Some critics see only a few traces of *Cleopatra* in Shakespeare's play, while others argue that both dramatists included incidents not found in Plutarch. Geoffrey Bullough (see Additional Bibliography), for example, noted that the two plays share elements not available in any previous treatment of the story; Bullough included among these new elements the contrast between "the authority of Rome" and "the luxury of Egypt," the portrayal of Cleopatra as a waning beauty, and the suggestion that the queen's fear of Octavia's scorn is a motive for her suicide. He also argued that Cleopatra's preparations for death are very similar in these two dramas. Another possible source consulted by Shakespeare is Daniel's "Letter from Octavia," printed in his *Poetical Essayes* (1599), which is, in Bullough's words, a "dignified protest" against Antony's mistreatment of his wife.

CRITICAL HISTORY: The principal issues in the criticism of *Antony and Cleopatra* include the dotage and nobility of Antony; Cleopatra's various and contradictory behavior, as well as the significance of her death; the nature of the lovers' passion for each other; and what judgment—if any—is evoked by their conduct. The opposition or correlation of Rome and Egypt, the play's language and imagery, its structure, and the political context are also important questions and are frequently discussed in connection with the most central ones. Commentators have identified a variety of thematic interests in the play as well, including the relationship between reason and imagination or passion, the nature of love, the choice between love and empire, and political or social disintegration. In addition, there are a number of secondary concerns in the criticism of *Antony and Cleopatra,* such as the importance of irony, paradox, and ambiguity in the play; the character of Octavius; the presence of religious or supernatural elements; and whether this tragedy deserves to be considered equal in artistic merit to *Hamlet, Othello, King Lear,* and *Macbeth.* Relatively minor questions also include the character of Enobarbus; the significance of the Seleucus episode (Act V, Scene ii); the purpose of the drama's comic or realistic elements; the motif of regeneration or reconciliation; the relative merits of *Antony and Cleopatra* and John Dryden's *All for Love* (1677); and the identification of Shakespeare's sources.

From the first substantial commentary to the beginning of the nineteenth century, the central critical interests in Shakespeare's tragedy were the character of Cleopatra and the play's structure, although during this period several commentators

also offered explications of other characters and addressed certain issues peculiar to the era. In 1691, Gerard Langbaine noted Shakespeare's reliance on classical historians, especially Plutarch, for the dramatic material of the play. Early in the eighteenth century, Charles Gildon, too, remarked upon Shakespeare's indebtedness to Plutarch, and he pointed out that Dryden also drew many of the particulars of his *All for Love* from that source. Gildon was the first to allude to the structure of *Antony and Cleopatra,* citing the large number of scenes, the unusual brevity of some of these, and the frequent movements back and forth between Rome and Egypt. Two mid-eighteenth-century commentators, John Hill and an anonymous writer, followed Gildon in comparing Shakespeare's play with Dryden's. The anonymous critic judged *Antony and Cleopatra* superior to the later work, despite its flouting of the Neoclassical rules of dramatic decorum, especially for its power to rouse the reader's or spectator's emotions. Hill, however, discerned in *All for Love* a dramatic style more in keeping with the portrayal of the lovers' passion, and he also charged that Shakespeare's play is too lengthy to be staged as written. In 1750, Thomas Seward remarked briefly on the quality of the play's poetic language, noting the rapidness and boldness of Shakespeare's metaphors. More than a decade later, Samuel Johnson returned to the issue of dramatic structure; he argued that audience attention is closely held by the frequent alternation of dramatic setting, the rapid pace of dramatic events, "the variety of incidents," and the successive change in focus from one character to another. Johnson added, however, that the events of the play are neither carefully disposed nor skillfully unified. He also considered Cleopatra the only distinctively drawn character in the play, although he claimed that, in some instances, the "feminine arts" she practices are "too low." Francis Gentleman emphasized the queen's cunning and vanity and regarded Antony's love for her as excessive. He further maintained that the structure of *Antony and Cleopatra* is faulty and confused, questioning why Antony's death does not occur in the fifth act rather than the fourth and charging that Enobarbus's remorse is not clearly presented. On the other hand, Elizabeth Griffith asserted that before he dies Enobarbus fully acknowledges that he has compromised his honor and acted basely in deserting Antony. She also contended that Antony's generosity toward Enobarbus is consistent with the hero's inherent nobility, which she held to be in bold contrast to the worthlessness, jealousy, and vengefulness of Octavius. Thomas Davies, too, remarked on Antony's magnanimity toward Enobarbus and on his doting love for Cleopatra. Furthermore, Davies was the earliest commentator to assert that Cleopatra, though noteworthy for her "feminine arts," displays a noble spirit as well in choosing to die rather than be publicly humiliated in Rome, and he argued that her manner of preparing for death elevates her in our esteem. Near the close of the eighteenth century, George Steevens commented on Cleopatra's "variety of accomplishments" and intellectual acumen, urging his female readers to develop similar talents and erudition if they wished to capture and hold a man's heart.

The increasing critical interest in Cleopatra continued into the nineteenth century, but from 1800 to 1850 commentators also focused on the play's structure and examined for the first time such concerns as Shakespeare's ambiguous presentation of events, the series of oppositions in the tragedy, and the appropriateness of judging the lovers and their conduct. Early in the century, August Wilhelm Schlegel emphasized Cleopatra's contradictory nature, noting that she is by turns regal, vain, inconstant, and devoted to Antony. Like earlier critics, Schlegel also compared Antony's generosity to Octavius's small-mindedness and found fault with the structure of the play, charging that allusions to events outside the dramatic action bewilder the audience, that some historically important figures receive only scant attention, and that the link between "preparatory and concurring circumstances" is not always clearly established. By contrast, Samuel Taylor Coleridge judged *Antony and Cleopatra* "the most wonderful" of Shakespeare's dramas, and he was the first critic to suggest that the tragedy might be classified with *Hamlet, Othello, King Lear,* and *Macbeth* as one of Shakespeare's major works. What is most distinctive about this play, Coleridge contended, is its "happy valiancy of style"; this phrase is perhaps the most famous in the critical history of *Antony and Cleopatra.* On other matters, Coleridge explicated the nature of the queen's passion for Antony, noting that although it requires repeated stimulation and enhancement, its "depth and energy" extenuate its illicit quality. William Hazlitt described Cleopatra as a masterpiece; he contended that the queen is essentially a voluptuary, motivated by "the love of pleasure and the power of giving it," but, like Davies in the previous century and many critics thereafter, Hazlitt maintained that the magnificent manner of her death mitigates the effect of her earlier behavior. He also addressed the issue of dramatic structure, comparing the movement of events to the revolution of fortune's wheel.

Well into the nineteenth century, Anna Brownell Jameson offered an extensive and provocative analysis of Cleopatra. Her judgment that the heroine is chiefly motivated by "the love of pleasure, the love of power, and the love of self" resembles Hazlitt's appraisal; but Jameson additionally discovered warm affection and sincerity in the queen's passion for Antony. In her assessment of Cleopatra's inherent contradictions, Jameson further developed the remarks of earlier critics and foreshadowed some significant twentieth-century views of the character. Although a few later commentators continued to regard the inconsistencies in the queen's persona as a dramatic flaw, Jameson presaged the majority view and judged them as both consonant with human nature and the chief source of her power to fascinate. The critic also focused on Cleopatra's preparations for death, acknowledging that fear and vanity make her recoil from the idea of public humiliation in Rome, but concluding that her suicide is noble. Also, in a brief aside, Jameson became the first commentator to describe Enobarbus as an ironist.

Three significant discussions of *Antony and Cleopatra* in the first half of the nineteenth century treated concerns other than the character of the queen, including questions of the play's structure, its moral judgment, the character of Antony, and Shakespeare's principal themes. In 1839, Hermann Ulrici contended that the central idea of the play is the preservation of Rome from social and political disintegration. Octavius's moderate, prudent, and foresighted nature make him particularly suited for this task, the critic argued, but he is petty and mean-spirited as well, and therefore not an admirable figure. Ulrici also asserted that Antony combines elements of the old Roman order with those of the new and less noble one typified by Octavius; in the critic's estimation, it is these baser elements that lead to Antony's downfall and link him with the eastern corruption of Cleopatra. Hartley Coleridge—Samuel Taylor's son—argued that audience response to both Antony and Cleopatra is ambivalent, for their heroic stature prohibits us from pitying their weaknesses while their vicious foolishness limits our admiration of their heroism. Coleridge also found fault with Shakespeare's dramatic construction, claiming that there are too many episodes of only passing interest and that the many short scenes impede the movement of the action. Ulrici's

contemporary, G. G. Gervinus, also contended that the continuity of *Antony and Cleopatra* is frequently disrupted, and he dispraised the play on several other counts as well, most notably for its lack of a central figure of ethical excellence and for its "morally repulsive" subject. Gervinus further maintained that the principal thematic idea of the play is the conflict between the world of action and politics and the world of sensuality and enjoyment. In choosing the latter, Antony becomes guilty of both moral and political profligacy, the critic asserted, concluding that Shakespeare portrays his protagonist as a hollow man of only "seeming greatness and seeming nobleness."

From 1850 until the end of the nineteenth century, several critics examined the question of whether Shakespeare intended his audience to pass an unfavorable judgment on Antony—or on Cleopatra—such as that voiced by Gervinus. J. A. Heraud, for example, maintained that because Shakespeare portrays the lovers as superhuman figures, the question of their moral guilt or innocence is irrelevant. Paul Heyse argued that Antony's warmth and vigor counterbalance his sin of self-indulgence, and he thus concluded that *Antony and Cleopatra* is not intended to demonstrate a moralistic warning against intemperance or dissipation. In his study of 1881, Edward Dowden proposed that although Shakespeare is not a stern moralist, the spirit of the play is "essentially severe," underscoring as it does the temporal limitations of power and beauty as well as the pageantry and splendor that surround the lovers. Arthur Symons declared that although Shakespeare portrays Antony as essentially noble and Cleopatra as supremely fascinating, he demonstrates that it is morally wrong to abandon "everything to the claim of love." Near the close of the century, William Winter expressed a similar view, contending that the implicit moral of the drama is that "mortal delight in mortal love" is inevitably doomed.

Those nineteenth-century commentators who addressed the issue of judgment in the play generally offered character analyses of Antony and Cleopatra as well, as did several other critics during this period. The noted French poet and novelist Victor Hugo maintained that although she is characterized as a strumpet, Cleopatra is transformed by her love for Antony and thus claims the sympathy which would ordinarily belong to Octavia. As mentioned above, Heraud suggested—the first critic to do so—that Antony and Cleopatra are superhuman figures whose creator shared their view of themselves as "the very deities of love." Heyse described the queen as a masterpiece of characterization, but he doubted whether her fascination can be wholly represented in the theater; unless we are convinced of her incomparable magnetism, he claimed, we disbelieve that she is worth what Antony forsakes, and we further regard the triumvir's following her from the battle of Actium as supreme folly. Karl Frenzel emphasized Cleopatra's irascibility, especially dispraising her behavior in the scenes with the messenger and her treasurer Seleucus. Richard Chenevix Trench pointed out the differences between Plutarch's Antony and Shakespeare's, asserting that Shakespeare idealized his hero by ignoring or glossing over many negative elements in the historian's account. Algernon Charles Swinburne regarded Cleopatra, too, as an ideal figure, describing her as "the perfect and the everlasting woman." Dowden, however, regarded the queen as a combination of unattractive as well as enchanting features, judging that as she prepares to die she exhibits sensuousness, artifice, and coquetry as well as splendor. Near the end of the century, Denton J. Snider emphasized Cleopatra's magnetism and sensuality, but he also asserted that her suffering ennobles her and that in the final scenes of the play "she shows signs of a better nature." Symons described the queen as "the most wonderful of Shakespeare's women," but he also remarked on her cunning, capriciousness, volatility, and cruelty. He further contended that Antony's total absorption in Cleopatra poisons his essentially noble nature and that he is inclined to self-dramatizing and posturing. Like Heraud, Winter regarded the lovers as larger than life; their elevated stature and many-sidedness fascinate us, he declared, and their glorious and tumultuous world provides a striking contrast to normalcy and convention. Proposing, like some earlier commentators, that Cleopatra may be Shakespeare's masterpiece of female characterization, Bernhard Ten Brink coined the often-noted phrase "courtesan of genius" to describe her.

Two of these commentators on the protagonists of *Antony and Cleopatra*—Frenzel and Snider—also discussed such other questions as the play's style, its dramatic structure, the character of Octavius, and the series of oppositions. Frenzel charged that the tragedy is more narrative than dramatic and that it includes material and historical figures which Shakespeare should have eliminated. He further judged that many of the speeches are bombastic and complained that "the perpetual love-making of the hero and heroine," though initially comic, is eventually tedious. Snider argued that the structure of *Antony and Cleopatra* is based on the opposition of conflicting principles represented in several characters, especially the opposition between Antony's hedonism and Octavius's pursuit of historic destiny. Snider further maintained that Octavius's fixity of purpose, his talent for discerning the most politically effective course, and his ability to resist the fascination of Cleopatra make him eminently qualified to perpetuate Roman principles and imperial destiny.

The nineteenth-century critical focus on Antony and Cleopatra and their passion for each other continued throughout the first fifty years of the twentieth century, with increasing debate over whether or not Shakespeare portrays the protagonists' love as transcendent over worldly considerations. The issue of dramatic structure also continued to receive considerable attention. But during and after the 1930s, modern critics began to concentrate more and more on the language and imagery of the play, as well as on its historical or political aspects. During this period, scholars also further compared *Antony and Cleopatra* with Shakespeare's four major tragedies and examined such other issues as the question of its moral judgment, the significance of the Egypt-Rome opposition, and the characterization of Octavius.

From 1900 through 1949, critics were apparently more concerned with analyzing the character of Cleopatra than of Antony, although both received significant commentary. In 1900, Bernard Shaw charged that Shakespeare's transfiguration of Cleopatra from a harlot, which she appears to be throughout most of the play, into a tragic figure at her death is fraudulent. A few years later, A. C. Bradley stressed the queen's inexhaustible variety, her compulsion to mesmerize every man who comes into her presence, and, most importantly, "her spirit of fire and air" that "makes her wonderful and sovereign." Bradley further contended that Cleopatra does not become a tragic figure until after the death of Antony, when she becomes transformed by her love for him. In the following year, the Arden editor R. H. Case examined the issue of Cleopatra's suicide, arguing that the queen's motives in choosing to die are not clearly presented but that her love for Antony and her desire not to live without him are more significant than her fear of

public humiliation in Rome. In one of the harshest evaluations of Cleopatra ever written, E. K. Chambers viewed the queen as the primary agent in Antony's downfall, contending that she exerts a "baleful influence" over the triumvir, is chiefly responsible for his loss of reputation, and—through her cowardice in battle—causes the military defeat of his forces. Horace Howard Furness rebutted the charge that Cleopatra behaves dishonestly and viciously in the scene with Seleucus and Octavius (Act V, Scene ii). He endorsed the proposal of an earlier German critic, Adolf Stahr (see Additional Bibliography), that the incident was prearranged by the queen and her treasurer in order to conceal her intended suicide from Octavius. In 1919, Levin L. Schucking generated a controversy over Shakespeare's characterization of Cleopatra. Echoing Jameson some eighty years earlier, Schucking maintained that in Acts I through III Cleopatra is vulgar, immoral, vain, calculating, and absolutely inconsistent with the regal, thoughtful, and tender queen of Acts IV and V. Responding to Schucking's evaluation, C. H. Herford denied that Cleopatra becomes a wholly different person in the final acts of the play. By endowing her with both noble and ignoble qualities, he declared, Shakespeare creates a figure of psychological verisimilitude; Herford further contended that even in her dying moments Cleopatra occasionally behaves more like a courtesan than a queen, and he stressed that her "infinite variety" must not be equated with inconsistency of character. Elmer Edgar Stoll also disputed Schucking's claim of Cleopatra's inconsistent characterization, arguing that she is a coherent figure from beginning to end. He asserted that she is sometimes regal in the early scenes as well as at the close, an erotic coquette not only in Acts I through III, but even as she confronts death, and essentially capricious throughout the drama. The question of Cleopatra's contradictory nature, as distinguished from the consistency of her characterization, was examined by D. A. Traversi and S. L. Bethell. Traversi argued that her imperfections serve as the very bases for the true nobility she ultimately achieves. Bethell described Cleopatra as a paradoxical figure in whom seemingly opposite qualities are fused, and he also emphasized her role as a symbolic representation of immortal love and beauty. In his essay published after Traversi's but before Bethell's, Mark Van Doren likewise noted the serpentine, changeable, and emotive aspects of Cleopatra's nature, remarking that she embodies the very aura of Egypt.

During the first fifty years of the twentieth century there were similarly conflicting estimations of the character of Antony. Shaw denounced Antony's progression from debauched sensualist to tragic hero, claiming that Shakespeare thus implies that sexual infatuation "alone makes our life worth living." Bradley held that Antony is both a "strumpet's fool" and a figure of tragic stature, born not to govern, but to love Cleopatra. Chambers contended that both Antony's greatness and his degradation stem from his inexhaustible capacity for life and his exuberant energies. Furness emphasized the depth and sincerity of Antony's love and his godlike qualities that captivate the Egyptian queen. Arthur Quiller-Couch maintained that Antony and Cleopatra are transcendent figures, "great as the gods are great" in their careless audacity and aloofness from events of the world. Similarly, Caroline F. E. Spurgeon regarded Antony as a superhuman figure, beyond comparison with anything except the whole universe. In 1936, John Middleton Murry argued that Antony's essential quality is spiritual royalty. Murry was also the earliest critic to discover specific Christian analogies in the play, suggesting that on the eve of the second battle (Act IV, Scene ii) Antony and his attendants resemble Christ and the disciples at the Last Supper; he further compared Enobarbus's desertion and remorse with the biblical account of Judas's betrayal of Christ. E. M. W. Tillyard, however, remarked that Antony possesses several negative qualities which Shakespeare never reconciles with the nobler aspects of his nature; indeed, the critic contended, Shakespeare merely ignores these unfavorable traits when he portrays the protagonists as transfigured by their deaths. In 1940, James Emerson Phillips, Jr., maintained that Antony's downfall ensues from his lack of self-rule and his failure to control excessive passion with reason. Also writing in the 1940s, G. S. Griffiths distinguished Antony from Shakespeare's other tragic heroes, stating that unlike his dramatic predecessors the triumvir dies without gaining enlightenment, self-discipline, or moral insight as a result of his suffering.

Besides these general character analyses, assessments of Antony and Cleopatra's love for each other comprise a further share of modern criticism of the play. Chambers declared that "passion as the ruin of greatness" is the central thematic idea in the tragedy, asserting that Antony's unfortunate dotage is matched by Cleopatra's foolish infatuation for him. Furness, however, claimed that the lovers' passion is deep and sincere, not dominated by either sensuality or sexual appetite. As in his interpretation of Cleopatra's inconsistent characterization, Schucking contended that the queen's love for Antony is equally incoherent, principally characterized in the first three acts by eroticism and self-gratification, but depicted in Acts IV and V as a genuinely tender, devoted, and unselfish passion. According to Quiller-Couch, the dominant concept in Antony and Cleopatra is the universal impact of the protagonists' passion for each other, for Shakespeare emphasizes the far-reaching implications of their love. The critic contended, in fact, that the theme of the play is love in its most destructive, feral, voluptuous, and superhuman manifestation. Herford, on the other hand, described Antony and Cleopatra's love for each other as a "light liaison" that develops into a fierce passion, with "moments of self-forgetting devotion." Stoll declared that Antony and Cleopatra clearly love each other and their passion deserves the prerogative and title of the word "love." In a seminal essay on the play, G. Wilson Knight asserted that Antony and Cleopatra offers a visionary and idealized view of love. Its primary vision of "transcendental and ethereal humanism," he contended, develops from the dramatization of Antony's sacrifice of power, military honor, and imperial glory for his union with Cleopatra, and furthermore from the treatment of love as a conjunction of physical and transcendental qualities.

Other critics of this period who discussed the nature of Antony and Cleopatra's love include D. A. Traversi, John F. Danby, and L. C. Knights. Traversi, like G. Wilson Knight, argued that Shakespeare endows the final scene of Antony and Cleopatra with an aura of triumphant love. The dramatist, however, does not ignore the imperfections of the lovers, Traversi acknowledged, but instead makes these flaws serve as the bases for their ultimate ascendancy over earthly faults and limitations. Contrary to the position of such commentators as Knight and Traversi, Danby maintained that although the play demonstrates the glories of the flesh and the enchantment of passion, the love of Antony and Cleopatra is neither redemptive nor transcendent, and thus is not presented as a "final value." Commending Danby's essay as a much-needed corrective to romantic assessments of the play, Knights contended that Shakespeare treats the love of Antony and Cleopatra with clear-eyed realism. According to the critic, their passion consists of monotony and artifice as well as variety and vitality, an impulse toward both self-destruction and regeneration. Knights held that after the second battle Antony discovers the immateriality of their love, and he concluded that the pathos of the final scene stems from our appreciation of the possibilities that have not been realized.

As mentioned earlier, the language and imagery of Antony and Cleopatra generated a substantial amount of criticism during the first half of the twentieth century. In the first decade, Chambers called attention to the language of the closing scenes, declaring that because of the "austere and lucid simplicity" of the passages there, the tragedy concludes on a "note of awe and reverence." In 1930, Granville-Barker offered a close analysis of the play's poetic language; he especially emphasized its idiosyncratic "rhythm and music," noted that Shakespeare takes unusual liberties with meter and grammar in order to achieve certain dramatic effects, and identified a unique combination of simplicity, concentration, power, and clarity as the cardinal virtue of the play's verse. Knight offered an extended analysis of the metaphorical patterns in Antony and Cleopatra. He identified an ascending scale of allusions that proceed from the concrete and sensuous to the "elemental and ethereal" as the love of the protagonists becomes more rarified. He also described the language throughout as tightly compressed, subtle but powerful, and possessing an abundance of intellectual conceptions. Spurgeon asserted that the most significant metaphorical pattern is composed of universal images—the world, the sky, the oceans, and "vastness generally." Traversi examined the way in which poetic images of rottenness and fertility, opulence and royalty, mirror the assimilative growth of Antony and Cleopatra's passion from infatuation to transcendent love. He further contended that Rome is closely associated with images of opulence, overripeness, decay, and disorder, thereby not only characterizing that world as mean and decadent, but also linking the lovers and Rome "in a single poetic creation." Van Doren held that the dramatic style of Antony and Cleopatra is discontinuous and flexible, aptly suitable for a world which is uniquely luminous, vast, watery, and mercurial.

Several critics prior to 1950 were concerned with the issue of structural discontinuity or unity in Antony and Cleopatra as well. Case judged the dramatic structure as flawed because it offers no "rousing incident" until the play is well advanced. Schucking iterated the view of most nineteenth-century critics on the subject, charging that there is no unity of dramatic action, that individual scenes lack a context to measure their import, and that the progress of events is repeatedly slowed and interrupted. In an essay frequently cited by subsequent critics, however, Granville-Barker provided a detailed justification of the play's construction. Noting that an Elizabethan production of the play would not have been divided into the more than forty scenes which most modern editions include, he demonstrated that the structure of Antony and Cleopatra is taut and well-balanced and its dramatic episodes carefully woven together into a unified pattern. David Cecil maintained that because Shakespeare presents the dramatic action as predestined, making it clear from the beginning that Antony will sacrifice his political eminence for Cleopatra and be defeated by Octavius, the structure of the play lacks dramatic suspense. Danby declared that a dialectic in which contrary principles are juxtaposed, then merge, and ultimately dissolve controls the structure of Antony and Cleopatra. He contended that conflicts between opposing perspectives are central to the drama, identifying such recurring oppositions as the world and the flesh, Rome and Egypt, and Octavius and Cleopatra.

The opposition between Egyptian and Roman values as a principal conflict in *Antony and Cleopatra* was also addressed during this period by such critics as Hamilton Wright Mabie, Mark Van Doren, and S. L. Bethell, among others. Near the beginning of the century, Mabie stated that *Antony and Cleopatra* dramatizes a fatal collision between East and West, with the West triumphant because of its superior moral fiber and organization. Van Doren, however, assessed the world of Egypt as greater and more expansive than its Roman counterpart, arguing that before his death Antony recognizes the value of Egypt's immobility and timelessness. In one of the most extensive analyses of the opposition of Roman and Egyptian value systems, Bethell maintained that Shakespeare invests both worlds with equal measures of dignity and grandeur. The play affirms Antony's choice of the Egyptian virtues, he concluded, for these provide the basis for "the good life"; however, Shakespeare also demonstrates that it is through "such better Roman qualities" as "deprivation and denial" that Antony and Cleopatra attain a state of eternal grace.

Shakespeare's portrayal of Roman imperialism and the significance of historical or political elements in the play—other important concerns during the early twentieth century—were examined by Case, Quiller-Couch, Granville-Barker, Traversi, Phillips, and Cecil. Case declared that the sense of political catastrophe in *Antony and Cleopatra* is only minimal. Quiller-Couch, on the other hand, identified the world-wide impact of the protagonists' passion for each other as the dominant chord in the play. Similarly, Granville-Barker averred that the principal theme of *Antony and Cleopatra* is "the wider ruin" in the Roman world precipitated by Antony's personal downfall; unlike Quiller-Couch, however, Granville-Barker contended that the tragic love between the triumvir and the queen becomes an issue only after the second major battle of the play, when the state of the Empire is determined. As previously mentioned, Traversi posited that Rome is characterized as mean and decadent through its close associations with images of opulence, overripeness, decay, and disorder. Although Phillips concluded that the political events are of secondary interest, he identified two important precepts of Renaissance political theory as underlying the dramatic action: that monarchy is the natural organization of political entities and that a ruler's passion must be governed by reason. Cecil asserted that the historical-political aspect—that is, the rivalry between Antony and Octavius—is the premier element in the play. The central thematic question, he argued, is what kind of man will succeed in the political sphere; but with regard to whether the attainment of worldly success is worth the cost, he determined, Shakespeare remains profoundly doubtful and ironic.

Whether the dramatist himself passes judgment on the protagonists or whether he invites us to do so became a major critical question in the second half of the twentieth century. But from 1900 to 1949, such commentators as Chambers, Stoll, Cecil, and Danby provided early reactions to this issue. As mentioned above, Chambers maintained that Cleopatra is the agent of Antony's downfall, asserting that she is responsible for his loss of reputation and—through her cowardice—the principal cause of his disastrous military losses to Octavius. Stoll, on the other hand, argued for the suspension of moral judgment, since Shakespeare clearly demonstrates the sincerity and value of Antony and Cleopatra's love. A generation later, Cecil asserted that Shakespeare is intentionally ambiguous as to what judgment should be made of Antony's conduct, leaving us to decide for ourselves whether his sacrifice of political power for love was right or wrong. Noting the unusually high incidence of

judgments for and against Antony and Cleopatra offered by the other characters, Danby foreshadowed the views of more recent critics by contending that the nature of judgment itself is a central concern in the play.

Finally, a measure of critical commentary during the first five decades of the twentieth century treated the characters of Octavius and Enobarbus. A. C. Bradley characterized Octavius as an agent of the forces of tragic destiny, against which ordinary men cannot hope to prevail. Horace Howard Furness offered a strong defense of the future emperor, insisting that he is generous-hearted and sympathetic and that we are meant to believe his love for Antony is sincere and profound. Many years later, Phillips, too, defended Octavius. Acknowledging that he may not be a dramatically interesting figure, the critic declared that Octavius does possess the requisite qualities of a ruler: self-control, a measure of nobility and magnanimity, and the sincere conviction that a divine destiny directs him in the interests of Rome's highest good. In his often-cited study of 1945, G. S. Griffiths assessed the role of Enobarbus, noting that while he acts to censor Antony's behavior and judge his tragic errors, his principal function is to direct the hero's and our attention to the dangerous implications of Cleopatra's demonic energy. Also worth noting is the detailed analysis of Enobarbus made by Elkin Calhoun Wilson (see Additional Bibliography). Wilson maintained that while Enobarbus acts as a choric figure—helping to bridge gaps in dramatic time and space, serving as "a credible reporter of off-stage events," presciently foreshadowing the tragic outcome, and guiding audience sympathies—his detached and judicious commentary is infused with intimate revelations of his own nature as well.

From 1950 to the present, commentators have, for the most part, continued to debate those issues addressed by earlier critics; but there has also been a noticeably greater concern with the importance of irony, paradox, and ambiguity in *Antony and Cleopatra*, with the series of oppositions dramatized by Shakespeare, and with the question of moral judgment concerning the protagonists. Still, the portrayals of the Egyptian queen and her Roman lover, together with the quality of their love for each other, have remained leading issues in recent commentary on the play. Such critics as Willard Farnham, Harold C. Goddard, Daniel Stempel, Brents Stirling, Maurice Charney, William Rosen, Northrop Frye, Julian Markels, Roy W. Battenhouse, and A. L. French have all provided analyses of both of the lovers. In his study of 1950, Farnham argued that Shakespeare endowed each of his protagonists with serious flaws as well as high nobility, treating them with an unusual combination of detachment and sympathy. This balanced treatment is also evident in the presentation of Cleopatra's death, he contended, for there is both evidence that she kills herself over Antony's loss and that she chooses suicide to escape public humiliation in Rome. Maintaining that the play dramatizes the superiority and eventual triumph of spiritual power over worldly might, Goddard (see Additional Bibliography) asserted that Antony's military losses are followed by his transubstantiation into a figure of "true divinity." The critic further claimed that Antony's devotion quickens the birth of a new Cleopatra as well. In what is perhaps the most radical reading of *Antony and Cleopatra*, Stempel declared that the queen is motivated by eroticism and a love of power, adding that her domination of Antony is an unnatural reversal of sexual roles that perilously endangers the body politic. By allowing his will to overrule his reason, Stempel contended, Antony similarly violates a cardinal principle of political order and hierarchy, which he compounds by his disruptive contention against Octavius. The critic averred that Cleopatra chooses death because she has failed to subvert Octavius, and he concluded that her suicide signals the removal of "the morbid disease" that ruined Antony and threatened the safety of the state.

In contrast to Stempel, though like Farnham, Stirling postulated that Shakespeare presents Antony in various lights: sometimes comical, sometimes absurdly self-conscious, occasionally worldly wise and dignified; but the critic held that before his death, Antony forgoes his tendency to "strain at sublimity" and achieves a truly elevated stature. Stirling discerned a similarly balanced view of Cleopatra in the play's closing scene, maintaining that the satirical episode with Seleucus in Act V is offset by the seriousness of Octavius's final praise of the dead queen. In 1957, in the first of two essays on the play, Charney demonstrated how Antony's downward movement after the battle of Actium and his final elevation at his death are mirrored in the play's imagery. In his second essay two years later, the critic analyzed the way in which the language of the play contributes to the double characterization of Cleopatra—even in her death—as both whore and monarch. Rosen contended that *Antony and Cleopatra* is principally concerned with the struggle between Antony's two personalities—"the illustrious public figure of the past and the decadent private figure of the present." Because of the pernicious influence of Cleopatra, the critic argued, Antony fails to regain his heroic stature, and although they each die with noble dignity, neither is altered or transfigured in the final scenes of the play. Frye employed the model of "the wheel of fortune and history" to trace Antony's disastrous wavering between Rome and Egypt and his eventual falling away from the political stage, but he asserted that in exchange for preeminence in the temporal realm the hero achieves an incomparable vision of a world that can never be ordered or controlled. Offering yet another perspective, Markels claimed that Antony gradually perceives the mutual relevance of both Roman and Egyptian values and reconciles the two systems in his own life; according to the critic, he thereafter submits to the vacillations of fortune, progresses from endurance to magnanimity, and introduces new possibilities of correct behavior to other characters in *Antony and Cleopatra*. It is not until after the battle of Actium, Markels added, that Cleopatra begins to understand, as her lover does, the relevance of public values to her private life; but as she reenacts Antony's suffering and apotheosis in her own prelude to death, he contended, she achieves a full appreciation of Antony's reconciling vision. Battenhouse maintained that Antony and Cleopatra's passion for each other and their deluded view of themselves as deities are parodied by allusions to the Christian religion and by the play's comic elements. He discovered these parodic effects even in the death of Cleopatra, and he further argued that although both protagonists achieve some self-understanding before they die, neither one repents or experiences a change of conduct. Finally, French—arguing that the dramatic mode of *Antony and Cleopatra* is one of genial detachment—identified elements of hollowness, sanctimony, indignation, and a desperate need for admiration in Antony, thus styling him as "an illusory hero." In a similarly unfavorable assessment, the critic stated that Cleopatra, after Antony's death, forgoes her previous honesty, shrewdness, and pragmatism for the inflated style of her lover; French cautioned that while her speeches from that point on are superlative verse, they convey a vision that is "poignantly untrue for us."

In addition to the preceding analyses of both protagonists, a number of commentators have focused their discussions on one lover or the other. In her essay of 1972, Phyllis Rackin emphasized Cleopatra's artistry in seeming and showing, noting that these activities link her to her dramatic creator. She also evaluated the play's final scene, maintaining that Shakespeare here undermines his earlier comic portrayal of Cleopatra when he depicts her renouncing all her weaknesses, demonstrating her greatness, and reincarnating her love for Antony in the golden world of the imagination. In a similar vein, Anne Barton asserted that by her flawless death as tragic queen Cleopatra defeats any attempt by Octavius or the "quick comedians" to cheapen the story of the lovers. Also, the critic declared, in her dream of Antony, Cleopatra endows her lover with a colossal identity that is both heroic and beyond the reach of time and history. Eugene M. Waith evaluated Antony as a tragic, Herculean hero, contending that his furious rages, his struggle against Rome, and his extravagant nature are all characteristic of the Renaissance Herculean protagonist. Additionally, the critic argued, Antony further resembles the typical Herculean hero in his deep sense of shame at the loss of honor, his eventual recovery of that honor and rediscovery of himself, and his fortitude when facing death, but he represents a departure from the archetype in his final assertion of personal integrity and the value of love. Robert B. Heilman averred that from the time Antony leaves for Rome until the close of the drama, his self-knowledge continually dissolves in delights and passion. According to the critic, Antony is momentarily jolted into self-understanding after the two disastrous battles, but on neither occasion is there a deep and final achievement of self-judgment. Heilman further characterized Antony as a hero of unusual charm and charisma, and he questioned whether such a figure is even capable of reflection and inner-directedness. In her seminal study of the play discussed more fully below, Janet Adelman focused on Antony's Nile-like "mingled abundance," noting its association with Herculean excess; these allusions to the god who is a model for achieved hyperbole, she observed, lead us to believe in the impossible. Adelman further averred that the play affirms the protagonists' assertions of love and union in death, adding that their paradoxical loss of identities in order to achieve them again suggests that sometimes truth may only be revealed through lies.

In addition to Adelman, many other critics since 1950—including John Dover Wilson, Willard Farnham, Norman Holmes Pearson, Brents Stirling, Maynard Mack, William Rosen, Norman Rabkin, and Roy W. Battenhouse—have analyzed the nature and thematic importance of Antony and Cleopatra's love. Dover Wilson asserted that the play affirms the choice of love over "the world and the kingdoms thereof" in portraying Antony and Cleopatra's triumph over those who lack their vitality and imagination. The critic considered the play a celebration of the warmth and vigor of human nature, in effect, Shakespeare's "Hymn to Man." Farnham, however, contended that the lovers' passion has an ambiguous nobility, for our admiration of it is tempered by our appreciation that Antony falls because of it. The critic further maintained that although Cleopatra's love for Antony is never comparable to his for her, she does comprehend what such a passion would be like before she dies. Pearson perceived a different pattern of development in the lovers' emotions, asserting that before their deaths both come to understand that the essential harmony of marriage springs from the conjunction of love and honor, intuition and reason, two hearts and two minds. Stirling noted the play's recurrent questioning of the protagonists' love as a truly tragic passion and remarked upon the diversity of responses this generates from various characters; he discovered no final affirmation or rejection of their passion, but emphasized that Shakespeare alternates between sympathetic and satirical or realistic treatments of Antony, Cleopatra, and their love. Mack argued that the love of Antony and Cleopatra is clearly unstable and self-destructive throughout most of the play, but he claimed that the evidence of the final scenes is ambiguous as to whether or not this passion becomes exalted and the lovers transcendent. We are in no doubt about what they have lost for love, he concluded, but we remain uncertain over what "if anything, has been won." Rosen was more emphatic in his estimation of the question of the lovers' transcendence, maintaining that it is a misperception to view them as ultimately transfigured by their love for each other. He declared that without such an intermediary as Enobarbus in the final scenes to maintain the proper perspective, and because the language and imagery of the drama are so overwhelming, we mistakenly view the play as an exaltation of Antony and Cleopatra's love. Rabkin asserted that Shakespeare emphasizes the paradoxical nature of love in *Antony and Cleopatra,* for the passion of the protagonists is simultaneously shown as liberating and demanding, merging spirituality with sensuality and finding its most complete expression in "the finality of death." Battenhouse argued that Shakespeare parodies Antony and Cleopatra's passion and their deluded view of themselves as deities by references to the distinction between *eros* and *agape* and by "dark analogy to Christian legend." The critic maintained that through a deeply ironic perspective on the transcendence of the lovers, Shakespeare reveals the "true view" of dramatic events.

Critical interest in whether *Antony and Cleopatra* invites or directs us to a judgment of the protagonists has grown steadily since 1950. In his introduction to the 1954 Arden edition of the play, M. R. Ridley held that although the protagonists' passion for each other is not the most laudable form of love, it is idle to attempt to judge its morality or immorality, for in this drama such disputes are meaningless. Similarly, Maynard Mack asserted that everything in *Antony and Cleopatra* is in motion. Because "nothing is stable, fixed, or sure," he contended—"not even ultimate values"—there can be no certainties in Shakespeare's dramatic world. Robert B. Heilman claimed that Antony's personal attractiveness is so great that it almost leads us to renounce any "judgment of character." Indeed, he pronounced, the world of the play is a glittering one, where all elements invite us, if we wish, to join the lovers in "brilliant unconcern." A. P. Riemer contended that Shakespeare establishes an emotional detachment between characters and audience, enabling us to understand the protagonists, but—because we are unlikely to identify ourselves with them—inhibiting us from judging their conduct. A. L. French maintained that instead of structuring the play as either a "lyrical tragedy" or a pitiless exposure of human weakness, Shakespeare's perspective on dramatic events is amused rather than censorious. Like John F. Danby, Adelman posited that in reading or viewing *Antony and Cleopatra* we are forced to experience the same concern with "right judgment" that so obsesses all the characters and to recognize—as the lovers do—"the folly of judgment" itself; according to the critic, we must realize, again like the lovers, that the only alternative when faced by ambiguities is an existential "leap of faith."

The question of judgment concerning the protagonists is closely linked to the issue of ambiguity or ambivalence in *Antony and Cleopatra.* Although commented on by a number of modern critics at different times, the topic has been most fully addressed by Maurice Charney, Maynard Mack, Norman Rabkin, and Ronald R. MacDonald. In his study of 1959, Charney contended that both Cleopatra's "infinite variety" and her death are presented ambiguously. The hyperbolical portrayal of the

queen is constantly being undermined, he argued, so that our attention is drawn to the artificiality and ennui of a compulsively sensual life; concerning her suicide, Charney noted that hints of violence are evident beneath her regal splendor in Act V, Scene ii as she approaches death. Mack proposed that Shakespeare's ambivalence toward the lovers, discussed above, is apparent not only in the pervasive ambiguity of their characterization, but in virtually every other facet of the play as well. Rabkin deemed *Antony and Cleopatra* a "profoundly dualistic" play in both its presentation of the nature of love and its depiction of Rome. MacDonald posited that Shakespeare is chiefly concerned with the ambiguous relation between reality, meaning, and language. He argued that through active command of language and imagination, Antony and Cleopatra create identities for themselves and each other that go beyond the bounds of meaning imposed on them by Rome or "'reality,' whatever that is."

In the decades since 1950, several other commentators have examined the related issue of the role of paradox and irony in *Antony and Cleopatra.* Daniel Stempel discerned many ironic elements in the play and related these to the characterization of the lovers, which he maintained was principally satiric and only secondarily tragic. In 1958, Benjamin T. Spencer related Shakespeare's use of paradox in the drama to the conflict between Egyptian and Roman values and to the irrationality or contradictions inherent in human love as demonstrated by the protagonists. The play offers "an undefined synthesis" of the two cultures, Spencer contended, expressed in a style that emphasizes bafflement and the discrepancies between appearance and reality. As mentioned above, Roy W. Battenhouse argued that the transcendence of the lovers is undermined by a deeply ironic perspective, based on symbolism and diction, that gives us the "true view" of dramatic events. Remarking on the discrepancy between poetry and dramatic events throughout the play, Janet Adelman contended that this gap is heightened by Shakespeare's pervasive use of paradox and hyperbole. Andrew Fichter discovered deep irony in the characters' unawareness of the impending birth of Christ and the enormity of the changes that would ensue in the world. But he also contended that Antony's tragically unattainable aspiration of "new heaven, new earth" (I. i. 17) prefigures the Christian vision of true transcendence.

Another prominent issue that has continued to interest post-1950 scholars is the opposition of Rome and Egypt in the play. In 1954, Norman Holmes Pearson argued that *Antony and Cleopatra* gradually progresses toward a triumphant demonstration that the values exemplified by Rome and Egypt are complementary, not mutually exclusive, for harmony is achieved when the lovers discern the interdependency of seemingly opposite qualities. In a similar vein, as previously noted, Spencer urged that the resolution does not demonstrate Shakespeare's predilection for one value system over another, but offers "an undefined synthesis" of the two. Northrop Frye, however, focused on the disparities between the Roman or western "day world of history"—with its emphasis on measure, rule, and order—and "the Egyptian night world of passion," Dionysian and overflowing all measure. Rabkin discerned two opposing but equally valid views of Rome in the play. On the one hand, he remarked, Shakespeare emphasizes its honor, fame, and colossal military achievements, while on the other he depicts its viciousness, treachery, and hollowness. Like Pearson and Spencer, Julian Markels asserted that Rome and Egypt are mutually relevant value systems, and he maintained that by refusing to choose one over the other, Antony reconciles the two systems in his own life, making them coexistent and conditional on each other. Phyllis Rackin examined the opposition between Roman reliance on quantitative measurement ''as an index of truth'' and the poet's imaginative vision that produces unquantifiable veracities. Like Frye, Adelman held that the play focuses on excess and Antony's propensity to ''overflow the measure.'' The Roman idea of measure and graceless temperance is exemplified by Octavius, she argued, while Egypt provides a scale against which Antony's Nile-like ''mingled abundance'' may be more appropriately assessed.

Interest in the language and imagery of *Antony and Cleopatra*—initiated in the present century by such critics as G. Wilson Knight, Caroline F. E. Spurgeon, and D. A. Traversi—has also increased since 1950. In his earlier study of 1957, Maurice Charney remarked on the frequent allusions to swords in the tragedy and held that, on one hand, they emphasize Antony's role as a Roman commander, but on the other, they have sexual or phallic connotations. He demonstrated that metaphors of powerless swords refer not only to Antony's military losses and his dereliction of military responsibilities, but also to his emasculation that results from Cleopatra's domination. Charney further noted persistent images of ''vertical dimension and dissolution'' that he claimed underscore both Antony's downward progress and his eventual elevation at his death. In his second essay on the language of *Antony and Cleopatra*, Charney focused on Shakespeare's use of hyperbole to convey a sense of spaciousness and to express ideas or experiences conceivable in the imagination but beyond nature or reality. He also noted, however, that these hyperboles are continually undercut, resulting in an ambiguous presentation of characters and themes. William Rosen argued that the language and imagery, especially the extravagant treatment of Cleopatra, Egypt, and passion itself, are frequently at odds with the dramatic action. A. P. Riemer maintained that the play's language and imagery distance the audience from the dramatic figures. Even passages of swelling verse, he contended, are frequently characterized by punning and hyperbole and are often surrounded by ironic commentary or action that deter our emotional involvement. And, as mentioned above, Adelman asserted that the discrepancy between poetry and dramatic events is heightened by Shakespeare's use of paradox and hyperbole.

In addition to these more prominent concerns, such issues as the meaning of the play's religious allusions, the significance of the episode between Cleopatra and her treasurer Seleucus in Act V, Scene ii, the dramatic structure, and *Antony and Cleopatra*'s relation to Shakespeare's four major tragedies have also been addressed by a number of commentators since 1950. Examining the last of these issues, Riemer contended that Shakespeare's tragedy is markedly different from the four major works, especially since it lacks both evil and an implicit metaphysical world with which the temporal world may interact. *Antony and Cleopatra* exists solely on the plane of politics, humanity, and society, he argued, and ''deals with issues intrinsically much less important than those of the great tragedies.'' Battenhouse discussed the allusions in the play to the Christian concepts of *eros* and *agape* and the analogies to Christian legend. As discussed earlier, he contended that these references parody Antony and Cleopatra's passion for each other and ironically undermine their deluded view of themselves as deities. Andrew Fichter argued that Christian allusions in the play direct us to see the imperfections and limitations of ''tragic vision itself.'' Although the Christian perspective on dramatic events is a retrospective one, he held,

its promise of redemption offers a bold contrast to the impoverished world we find at the close of the drama.

John Dover Wilson, M. R. Ridley, and Brents Stirling (see Additional Bibliography) have all discussed the implications of the episode with Seleucus, which first attracted critical attention in the nineteenth century. Dover Wilson followed earlier commentators in contending that the scene demonstrates Cleopatra's firm resolve for death and presents her successful attempt to mislead Octavius about her intentions. Ridley, however, asserted that after she expresses her resolution to die, in Act IV, Scene xv, Cleopatra subsequently wavers and does, indeed, explore the possibility of preserving her life. Ridley examined in turn the episode with Seleucus and the queen's conversation with Proculeius and speculated on what may have transpired during the interval between Act IV, Scene xv and the beginning of Act V, Scene ii; he concluded that Cleopatra would have negotiated ''terms with Caesar if she could make her own,'' but that Dolabella convinces her of Octavius's humiliating intentions. Brents Stirling maintained that in the Seleucus episode Cleopatra is acting on her own, playing for time until she finds the resolution to carry out her carefully planned suicide. It is not the evidence of concealed wealth that leads Octavius to believe that Cleopatra means to live on, the critic held, but the queen's furious and bizarre demonstration of ''combative pride'' in attacking Seleucus.

Finally, both Anne Barton and Michael Long have recently considered the dramatic structure of *Antony and Cleopatra*, and A. L. French—like a number of earlier critics—evaluated the play in relation to Shakespeare's major tragedies. Barton analyzed *Antony* in terms of its ''divided catastrophe,'' assessing the impact of Shakespeare's decision not to end his drama with the death of the hero, but to continue it through more than four hundred lines which principally focus on Cleopatra and her death. This unusual structure, she determined, achieves several effects: it imposes a new perspective on earlier dramatic events, modifying our response to them; it subdues and transfigures the ambiguities that have persisted throughout the play; it redeems Antony's bungled suicide by associating it with Cleopatra's ''own flawless farewell''; and it ''makes us understand something about historical process.'' Long argued that *Antony and Cleopatra* is constructed in terms of a Dionysian vision, with the first half of the play presenting the lyrical, ribald, expansive, and festive aspects of the song of Dionysus and the second half the volatile, chaotic, and tumultuous elements of that vision. He further maintained that the second half of the drama demonstrates the paradoxical nature of the Dionysian vision, for, under both pressure from Rome and ''the intrinsic pressures of the Dionysiac,'' Antony and Cleopatra respond with hysteria and panic, alternating in the final scenes between humiliation and exaltation, grotesquerie and magnificence, dejection and spiritual triumph. French maintained that unlike Shakespeare's major tragedies, *Antony and Cleopatra* forces on us no profound emotional disturbance or potentially threatening insights into the human condition.

A review of the critical history of *Antony and Cleopatra* indicates that while pre-1950 commentators consistently stressed Shakespeare's antithetical presentation of characters, themes, and other dramatic elements, critics since have discerned a more balanced or complementary treatment. Recent scholars have urged that Shakespeare is here questioning whether Rome and Egypt do indeed represent mutually exclusive value systems, as previously proposed. Even more emphatically, they have called into question whether the play invites or requires us to judge the validity of Antony and Cleopatra's conduct, and there appears to be a growing consensus that the dramatic events are purposely ambiguous. Moreover, even those critics who caution against succumbing to what Coleridge described as the "happy valiancy" of the play's style admit with its defenders the incomparable versification of *Antony and Cleopatra*. And while few critics esteem it the equal of *Hamlet*, *Othello*, *King Lear*, and *Macbeth*, several have shared Arthur Quiller-Couch's estimation that *Antony and Cleopatra* is "among the very greatest, and in some ways the most wonderful, of Shakespeare's triumphs."

SAMUEL WESLEY   (poem date 1685)

[*A clergyman and poet, Wesley is principally remembered as the father of John and Charles Wesley, the founders of Methodism in England. The following excerpt is from a volume of verse entitled* Maggots: or, Poems on Several Subjects Never Before Handled (1685). *The line "I come she cryed . . ." appears to be an echo of "Husband, I Come!" at V. ii. 287 of* Antony and Cleopatra.]

> 'Twas I *brought down* that Rampant *Gypsie*
> Whose *Love* and *Pearls* made Tony tipsie:
> And, when she him no more could clasp,
> The *Maggot* bit, as well's the *Asp*.
> I stood at the *Beds-feet*, Intent
> On her *Last Will*, and *Testament*:
> I come she cryed, I com' dear *Hony*!
> And then kickt up with *Tony! Tony*:

> > Samuel Wesley, in an extract in The Shakspere Allusion-Book: A Collection of Allusions to Shakspere from 1591-1700, Vol. II, edited by John Munro, revised edition, 1932. Reprint by Books for Libraries Press, 1970; distributed by Arno Press, Inc., p. 311.

GERARD LANGBAINE   (essay date 1691)

[*Langbaine is generally acknowledged as the first historian of the English theater. He wrote several catalogues of dramatic history, including* An Account of the English Dramatick Poets (1691), *in which he provided biographical sketches of playwrights, lists of their works, and possible sources for the plots of their plays. In the excerpt below from that work, Langbaine is the earliest commentator to remark upon Shakespeare's indebtedness to Roman and Greek historians, especially Plutarch, for the dramatic material of* Antony and Cleopatra.]

Antony and Cleopatra, a Tragedy. The ground of this play is founded on History: see Plutarch's Life of *Antony: Appian, Dion Cassius, Diodorus, Florus* &c. (p. 361)

> > Gerard Langbaine, in an extract in The Shakspere Allusion-Book: A Collection of Allusions to Shakspere from 1591-1700, Vol. II, edited by John Munro, revised edition, 1932. Reprint by Books for Libraries Press, 1970; distributed by Arno Press, Inc., pp. 359-61.

[CHARLES GILDON]   (essay date 1710)

[*Gildon was the first critic to write an extended commentary on the entire Shakespearean dramatic canon. Like many other Neoclassicists, he regarded Shakespeare as an imaginative playwright who nevertheless frequently violated the dramatic "rules" necessary for correct writing. In the following excerpt, Gildon draws attention to one of the most celebrated passages in* Antony and Cleopatra: *Enobarbus's description of Cleopatra's barge (II. ii. 191-218) and invites a comparison with the parallel lines in Dryden's* All for Love (1677), *where the speech is given to Antony rather than Enobarbus. He is the first critic to note that both dramatists drew the particulars of their descriptions from Plutarch. Gildon is also the earliest commentator to allude to the dramatic construction of* Antony and Cleopatra, *citing the unusually large number of scenes, the remarkable brevity of some of these episodes, and the repeated alternation of setting between Rome and Egypt.*]

This Play is the History of *Anthony* and *Cleopatra* from the Death of *Fulvia* to the taking of *Alexandria*, and the Death of *Cleopatra*. The Scene is sometimes at *Rome* sometimes in *Ægypt*, sometimes at Sea and sometimes at Land, and seldom a Line allow'd for a Passage to so great a Distance and the Play is full of Scenes strangely broken: many of which exceed not ten Lines. It is needless to write the Story since it is so known to every Body. . . . (p. 413)

Augustus gives *Anthony* his true Character . . . , *When thou wert beaten from* Mutina, &c [I. iv. 56-7]. And the concern and care of *Cleopatra* in the next [scene] is not unnatural—*Oh! Chairman! where think' st thou he is now?* [I. v. 18-19]. *Pompey's* Wish against *Anthony* [II. i. 20-1] . . . is very apt and pretty. *But all the Charms of Love, salt* Cleopatra, *soften thy wand Lips*, &c.

I must not omit the Description *Enobarbus* gives of *Cleopatra's* Sailing down the *Cydnos*, because Mr. *Dryden* has given us one of the same in his *All for Love*, which I shall here compare together and leave the Decision of the Victory to the impartial Reader.

> The Barge she sate in, like a burnish'd Throne,
> Burnt on the Water; the Poop was beaten Gold,
> Purple the Sails, and so perfumed, that
> The Winds were Lovesick
> With them; the Oars were silver,
> Which to the Tune of Flutes kept Stroke, and made
> The Water which they beat, to follow faster,
> As amorous of their Strokes. . . .
> > > From the Barge
> A strange invisible Perfume hits the Sense
> Of the adjacent Wharfs. The City cast her
> People out upon her, and *Antony*
> Enthron'd in th' Market-place did sit alone
> Whistling to the Air, which but for Vacancy
> Had gone to gaze on *Cleopatra* too,
> And make a Gap in Nature.
> > > [II. ii. 191-97, 211-18]

Mr. *Dryden* in his *All for Love* Act third, where *Antony* gives it to *Dolabella* in these Words.

> Her Gally down the silver *Cydnos* row'd
> The Tackling Silk, the Streamers wav'd with Gold
> The gentle Winds were lodg'd in Purple Sails. . . .
> > > To soft Flutes
> The silver Oars kept time, and while they played
> The Hearing gave new Pleasure to the Sight
> And both to Thought. 'Twas Heaven or somewhat more
> For she so charm'd all Hearts, that gazing Crowds
> Stood panting on the Shore, and wanted Breath
> To give their welcome Voice———

Both Poets are a little beholding to the *Historian* for at least the Groundwork of this Description. (pp. 413-15)

> [*Charles Gildon*], *"Remarks on the Plays of Shakespear," in* The Works of William Shakespear, Vol. 7, 1710. Reprint by AMS Press, Inc., 1967, pp. 257-444.

ANONYMOUS (essay date 1747)

[*The following excerpt is reprinted from an unsigned work,* An Examen of the New Comedy, Call'd 'The Suspicious Husband'. With Some Observations Upon our Dramatick Poetry and Authors, *first published in 1747. The author compares* Antony and Cleopatra *with* All for Love, *asserting that Shakespeare's play, although "incorrect and careless," is superior to Dryden's. The critic further remarks that although* Antony and Cleopatra *flaunts the Neoclassical rules of construction, it nevertheless evokes strong emotional responses from us.*]

All for Love is esteemed [Dryden's] Master-piece, and has been generally look'd upon as a perfect Performance; I have seen it more than once represented to the greatest Advantage by *Booth, Oldfield, &c.* And tho' my Ears have been delighted with the Poetry, and my Mind charm'd with the Sentiments, yet my Eyes have been dry, and my Heart quiet. Read *Antony and Cleopatra,* from which the other is taken, tho' one of the most incorrect and careless of *Shakespeare's* Plays, and you will soon *feel* the Difference. *Dryden's* Play is most correctly poetical with the Unities; *Shakespeare's* is most pathetically Natural without 'em. The first is the finish'd Performance of a great Poet, the last the hasty Production of a true Dramatick Genius. (pp. 269-70)

> *From an extract in* Shakespeare, the Critical Heritage: 1733-1752, Vol. 3, *edited by Brian Vickers, Routledge & Kegan Paul, 1975, pp. 269-70.*

THOMAS SEWARD (essay date 1750)

[*Seward was a clergyman who coedited* The Works of Mr Francis Beaumont, and Mr John Fletcher *(1750). The excerpt below is from the preface to that work. Seward's brief remark on the nature of the poetic language of* Antony and Cleopatra—*especially his use of the phrase "a Rapidity and Boldness of Metaphors"—anticipates Samuel Taylor Coleridge's famous description of the play's "happy valiancy of style" (see excerpt below, 1813-34).*]

[Shakespeare] has given both *Antony* and *Cleopatra* a Rapidity and Boldness of Metaphors that approaches even to Phrensy, which was peculiarly proper to their Characters.

> *Thomas Seward, in an extract in* Shakespeare, the Critical Heritage: 1733-1752, Vol. 3, *edited by Brian Vickers, Routledge & Kegan Paul, 1975, p. 388.*

[SIR JOHN HILL] (essay date 1759)

[*Editor of* The British Magazine *and contributor to* The London Advertiser and Literary Gazette, *Hill also wrote* The Actor: A Treatise on the Art of Playing *(1750). The excerpt below is from an essay entitled "Some Remarks on the new-revised Play of 'Antony and Cleopatra'" (1759) and ascribed to Hill. The adaptation referred to is one prepared the previous year by David Garrick and Edward Capell, who omitted several individual speeches and deleted nine entire scenes from Shakespeare's text. Hill argues that* Antony and Cleopatra *is too lengthy for staging in its entirety and commends the adapters for making it "less tedious." He also considers Dryden's* All for Love *to be stylist-*

ically more harmonious with "the tender passion" of the lovers' story.]

As the length of [*Antony and Cleopatra*] was certainly an obstacle to its exhibition we are of opinion [Garrick and Capell's] alterations are so much for the better as they have rendered it less tedious, as well for the audience as the actors. I cannot, however, but be of opinion that this piece is inferior to most of Shakespeare's productions, and that it even gives way to Dryden's *All for Love, or the World well lost,* which is founded upon the same historical event. I do not mean by this to give the preference to Dryden as a greater dramatic poet in general than Shakespeare, but must own that his soft flowing numbers are more sympathetic to the tender passion which this story is so particularly animated with than the general language of Shakespeare's *Antony.* (pp. 402-03)

> [*Sir John Hill*], *in an extract in* Shakespeare, The Critical Heritage: 1753-1765, Vol. 4, *edited by Brian Vickers, Routledge & Kegan Paul, 1976, pp. 402-04.*

SAMUEL JOHNSON (essay date 1765)

[*Johnson has long held an important place in the history of Shakespearean criticism. He is considered the foremost representative*

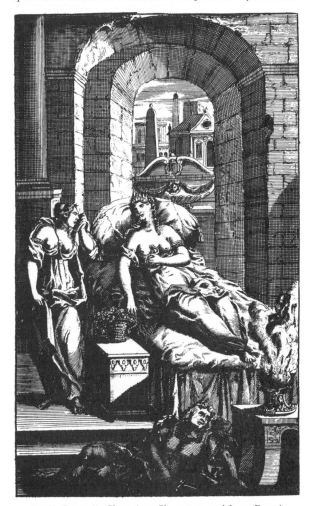

Act V. Scene ii. Charmian, Cleopatra, and Iras. Frontispiece to the Rowe edition (1709). By permission of the Folger Shakespeare Library.

*of moderate English Neoclassicism and is credited by some lit-
erary historians with freeing Shakespeare from the strictures of
the three unities valued by strict Neoclassicists: that dramas should
have a single setting, take place in less than twenty-four hours,
and have a causally connected plot. More recent scholars portray
him as a critic who was able to synthesize existing critical theory
rather than as an innovative theoretician. Johnson was a master
of Augustan prose style and a personality who dominated the
literary world of his epoch. In the excerpt below, taken from his
end note to* Antony and Cleopatra *in his 1765 edition of Shakespeare's plays, Johnson expresses a limited admiration of the
play. He states that audience attention is held "from first to last"
by the rapid pace of dramatic events, "the variety of incidents,"
the successive change in focus from one character to another,
and, especially, by the frequent alteration of dramatic setting.
Johnson further contends that dramatic events are neither carefully disposed nor artfully linked together. He finds Cleopatra the
only distinctively drawn figure in the drama, but he also judges
that in some places the "feminine arts" she practices are "too
low."*]

[*Antony and Cleopatra*] keeps curiosity always busy, and the
passions always interested. The continual hurry of the action,
the variety of incidents, and the quick succession of one personage to another, call the mind forward without intermission
from the first act to the last. But the power of delighting is
derived principally from the frequent changes of the scene; for,
except the feminine arts, some of which are too low, which
distinguish Cleopatra, no character is very strongly discriminated. Upton, who did not easily miss what he desired to find,
has discovered that the language of Antony is, with great skill
and learning, made pompous and superb, according to his real
practice [in his *Critical Observations on Shakespeare*]. But I
think his diction not distinguishable from that of others: the
most tumid speech in the play is that which Caesar makes to
Octavia.

The events, of which the principal are described according to
history, are produced without any art of connection or care of
disposition. (p. 873)

*Samuel Johnson, "Notes on Shakespeare's Plays:
'Antony and Cleopatra'," in his* The Yale Edition
of the Works of Samuel Johnson: Johnson on Shakespeare, Vol. VIII, *edited by Arthur Sherbo, Yale
University Press, 1968, pp. 837-73.*

[FRANCIS GENTLEMAN]   (essay date 1774)

[*Gentleman, an Irish actor and playwright, was the author of* The
Dramatic Censor; or Critical Companion *(1770) and contributed
introductions and commentary to John Bell's 1774 edition of
Shakespeare's plays. In his comments on various aspects of* Antony and Cleopatra *taken from the latter work and excerpted
below, Gentleman describes Cleopatra as "a tinsel pattern of
vanity and female cunning." He judges that Antony's love for her
is excessive and asserts that he is undone by "indolence and
dissipation." Gentleman strongly condemns Octavius for his conduct towards Cleopatra, accusing him of equivocation, treachery,
and "double-dealing." He also finds fault with Shakespeare's
artistry, questioning whether Enobarbus's remorse is clearly demonstrated and why Antony's death does not occur in the final act
rather than the previous one. Gentleman concludes that the play
as a whole is "rather too incorrect and confused" in its dramatic
action.*]

Whether this play, tho' excellently wrote, has any chance for
long existence on the stage, is very doubtful. Twenty years
since, that very able and successful Dramatic Modeller, *Mr.
Garrick,* produced it under the most probable state of refor-

mation; yet, tho' elegantly decorated, and finely performed, it
too soon languished. *Antony* and *Cleopatra* are the chief marked
characters in it: he is a flighty infatuated slave to an excess of
love and luxury; she a tinsel pattern of vanity and female
cunning, which work the downfal of both. A double moral
may be inferred, namely, That indolence and dissipation may
undo the greatest of men; and that beauty, under the direction
of vanity, will not only ruin the possessor, but admirer also.
(p. 261)

When we meet two such celebrated names, and consider our
author's great abilities, we are naturally led to expect a very
capital piece. Those characters are accordingly very greatly
supported; but the whole piece, as it stands here, seems rather
too incorrect and confused for action. (p. 263)

The whole of [Act I, Scene ii] might well be spared in representation: it has a blameable relish of indecency. (p. 265)

The luxury of *Antony* is well pointed out by *Enobarbus,* and
the description he gives shortly after of her meeting *Antony* is
admirably poetical. *Dryden,* in *All for Love,* has boldly ventured a comparison upon the identical circumstance; but, though
capital, we think him inferior to *Shakespeare,* though he has
disposed the description better, by putting it in *Antony's* mouth.
(p. 288)

[Act II] does not contain much matter for representation, any
more than the former; but the description of *Cleopatra* by
Enobarbus will, to a judicious reader, atone for greater deficiencies. (p. 305)

If we can suppose, and we have no other intimation, that
Enobarbus dies through sheer grief of his ingratitude to *Antony,*
it shows great and sensible feeling; though the corrective part
of it should, no doubt, have appeared sooner, and to more
effect. (p. 340)

[In Act V, Scene i], *Caesar* . . . shews double-dealing, ambition, and much more of the politician than the honest man.
(p. 354)

Cleopatra, in [V. ii. 49-62], displays great and becoming magnanimity of spirit, finely opposed to the equivocal treacherous
behaviour of *Octavius.* (p. 356)

Notwithstanding the fifth Act wants the assistance of *Antony,*
who, as a main pillar, should not have been cast down so soon,
yet it is rather the most regular and affecting of the whole:
Cleopatra in it is very consistent; and supported by an actress
possessing grace, power, and feeling, must work very tragic
effects. (p. 366)

[*Francis Gentleman], in his notes on "Antony and
Cleopatra," in* Bell's Edition of Shakespeare's Plays,
*Vol. 6, 1774. Reprint by Cornmarket Press, 1969,
pp. 261-366.*

ELIZABETH GRIFFITH   (essay date 1775)

[*Griffith exemplifies the seventeenth- and eighteenth-century
preoccupation with searching through Shakespeare's plays for set
speeches and passages that could be read out of dramatic context
for their own sake. Griffith, however, avoided the more usual
practice of collecting and commenting on poetic "beauties" and
concentrated instead on the "moral" subjects treated in the text.
In the following excerpt, she focuses on Enobarbus's desertion
of Antony. She marvels that a figure of such "treachery and
vileness" could yet be sincerely contrite, but she maintains that
in his final words Enobarbus fully acknowledges that he has com-*

promised his honor and acted basely. Griffith also applauds Antony's magnanimity towards Enobarbus. She considers him a much nobler figure than Octavius, whom she castigates as "worthless, mean, jealous, and vengeful."]

In [Act III, Scene xiii], Enobarbus, seeing the downfal of his master's fortunes, enters into debate with himself, whether he shall preserve his fidelity to him still, or shift about, and take part with the conqueror; in which soliloquy he seems fairly to give the preference to the nobler side of the question, in his argument, though he afterwards determines against it, in his conduct.

But 'tis usually so, in all deliberations of this sort; for virtue and vice are of such opposite natures, that there is no possibility of bringing them at all into comparison by any sophister whose judgment has not before been rendered partial and corrupt. So that in such cases one may venture generally to pronounce, as the Poet does of women, that *they who deliberate are lost.*

> *Enobarbus.* Mine honesty and I begin to square;
>   The loyalty well held to fools, does make
>   Our faith mere folly—Yet he that can endure
>   To follow with allegiance a fall'n lord,
>   Does conquer him that did his master conquer,
>   And earns a place i' th' story.
>   [III. xiii. 41-6]

When Antony is told that Enobarbus had gone over to the enemy, but left his chests and effects behind him, he says,

> Go, Eros, send his treasure after—Do it—
> Detain no jot, I charge thee—Write to him—
> I will subscribe gentle adieus and greetings—
> Say that I wish he never find more cause
> To change a master. Oh, my fortunes have
> Corrupted honest men! Dispatch, my Eros.
>   [IV. v. 12-17]

There is such an heroic liberality of soul expressed here, as must make one lament the misfortunes of the unhappy Antony, even at this distance of time—for the fact here represented, is taken from historical record. We may justly say of him, as the soldier does here, upon delivering the message to Enobarbus,

> *Your emperor continues still a Jove.*
>   [IV. vi. 27-8]

Antony was not only a braver and a greater, but a better man than his competitor for empire. Augustus was of a worthless, mean, jealous, and vengeful nature; though poets, and *some historians,* have deified him. (pp. 472-73)

[In Act IV, Scene vi] Enobarbus appears to have been equally struck with the generosity of his master, and his own vileness; upon which joint reflection he passes a very just sentence on himself.

> I am alone the villain of the earth,
> And feel I am so most. O, Antony,
> Thou mine of bounty, how wouldst thou have paid
> My better service, when my turpitude
> Thou dost so crown with gold! This blows my heart;
> If swift thought break it not, a swifter mean
> Shall out-strike thought—But thought will do't, I feel.
> I fight against thee!—*No, I will go seek
> Some ditch, where I may die; the foul'st best fits
> My latter part of life.*
>   [IV. vi. 29-38]

The contrition of Enobarbus was sincere; for here the strong sense of his baseness bursts his swoln heart:

> O bear me witness, night! . . .
> Be witness to me, O thou blessed moon!
> When men revolted shall upon record
> Bear hateful memory, poor Enobarbus did
> Before thy face repent! . . .
> O sovereign mistress of true melancholy,
> The poisonous damp of night dispunge upon me,
> That life, a very rebel to my will,
> May hang no longer on me! O Antony,
> Nobler than my revolt is infamous,
> Forgive me in thine own particular;
> But let the world rank me in register,
> A master-leaver, and a fugitive—
> Oh Antony! Oh Antony!
>   [*Dies.*]
>   [IV. ix, 5, 7-10, 12-15, 18-23]

I shall not pretend to dispute a knowledge of human nature with Shakespeare, but, if he had not given us a representation of this character, I should hardly have been brought to imagine that a breast capable of harbouring such treachery and vileness, could ever, at the same time, have contained a spirit of so much honour, and so strong a sense of shame.

One of the centinels, upon seeing him sink down on the ground, says to his companion, that he has fallen asleep; but the other, who had overheard his soliloquy, replies, very justly,

> Swoons, rather; *for so bad a prayer as his,
> Was never yet for sleep.*
>   [IV. ix. 26-7]
>   (pp. 473-74)

Elizabeth Griffith, " 'Antony and Cleopatra'," in her The Morality of Shakespeare's Drama Illustrated, *1775. Reprint by Frank Cass & Co. Ltd., 1971, pp. 465-75.*

THOMAS DAVIES (essay date 1784)

[*A bookseller and an actor, Davies was also an associate of Samuel Johnson, who encouraged him to compose his very successful* Life of David Garrick *(1780). In the following excerpt, taken from* Dramatic Miscellanies: consisting of Critical Observations on several Plays of Shakespeare *(1784), he gently disputes the statement posited by Johnson (see excerpt above, 1765) that none of the characters in* Antony and Cleopatra *is "strongly discriminated." Davies contends that in addition to being "conspicuous for feminine arts," Cleopatra displays nobility of spirit in choosing death rather than public humiliation in Rome. He judges that her conduct as she prepares to die elevates her in our esteem. Davies further notes that Antony exhibits a "variety of passion," ranging from liberality towards Enobarbus to doting love for Cleopatra. Of Enobarbus himself, Davies remarks that he demonstrates shrewdness, humor, and "plain-dealing."*]

Admidst all the folly, profligacy, and mad flights of Mark Antony, some bright beams of a great and generous soul break forth with inimitable lustre. [At IV. v. 16-17, instead] of reproaching his officer for desertion and treachery, he lays the blame on his own adverse fortune, which had unhappily overthrown the principles of the best and worthiest men. This is one of our author's characteristical strokes, and perfectly suited to Mark Antony. (pp. 379-80)

Cleopatra's preparation for death is animated to a degree of sublimity which greatly raises the character of the Egyptian princess, and makes us lament her in death whom living we could not praise, though it was impossible not to admire her. . . .

I cannot help thinking that Dr. Johnson has been rather precipitate in deciding upon the merit of *Antony and Cleopatra* [see excerpt above, 1765].—How can I submit to that sentence which pronounces that there is no discrimination of character in this play, except in Cleopatra, whom he considers only as conspicuous for feminine arts? Those she has in abundance, it is true; but her generous resolution to die rather than submit to embrace life upon ignoble terms is surely also worth remembering. But is not Antony highly discriminated by variety of passion, by boundless generosity as well as unexampled dotage? What does this truly great writer think of Enobarbus, the rough old warrior, shrewd in his remarks and humorous in his plain-dealing? I shall say nothing of Octavius or Lepidus, though they are certainly separated from other parts. The simplicity of the fable is necessarily destroyed by exhibiting such a croud of events happening in distant periods of time, a fault common to historical plays. But, in spite of all irregularities this tragedy remains unequalled by any that have been written on the same subject. (p. 380)

> *Thomas Davies, in an extract from* Shakespeare, the Critical Heritage: 1774-1801, Vol. 6, *edited by Brian Vickers, Routledge & Kegan Paul, 1981, pp. 379-80.*

GEORGE STEEVENS   (essay date 1793)

[*Steevens was an English scholar who collaborated with Samuel Johnson on a ten-volume edition of Shakespeare's dramatic works in 1773. The subsequent revision of this collection, along with Steevens's own edition of 1793, formed the textual basis for the first two Variorum editions of Shakespeare's plays. In the excerpt below, taken from his 1793 edition of* The Plays of William Shakespeare, *Steevens invites his "female readers" to consider that Cleopatra's magnetism had its source in her "infinite variety," not her physical appearance. If you wish to capture and hold a man's heart, he counsels, emulate her by developing a "variety of accomplishments" and "mental attractions."*]

> Age cannot wither her, nor custom *stale*
> Her *infinite variety*:
>
> [II. ii. 234-35]

Such is the praise bestowed by Shakespeare on his heroine; a praise that well deserves the consideration of our female readers. Cleopatra, as appears from the tetradrachms of Antony, was no Venus; and indeed the majority of ladies who most successfully enslaved the hearts of princes are known to have been less remarkable for personal than mental attractions. The reign of insipid beauty is seldom lasting; but permanent must be the rule of a woman who can diversify the sameness of life by an inexhausted variety of accomplishments.

> *George Steevens, in an extract from* Shakespeare, the Critical Heritage: 1774-1801, Vol. 6, *edited by Brian Vickers, Routledge & Kegan Paul, 1981, p. 596.*

AUGUST WILHELM SCHLEGEL   (essay date 1811)

[*A prominent German Romantic critic, Schlegel holds a key place in the history of Shakespeare's reputation in European criticism. His translations of sixteen of the plays are still considered the best German editions of Shakespeare. Schlegel was also a leading spokesman for the Romantic movement, which permanently over-*

threw the Neoclassical contention that Shakespeare was a child of nature whose plays lacked artistic form. The excerpt below is taken from his Course of Lectures on Dramatic Art and Literature, *originally published in German in 1811. Schlegel judges that the characters of Antony and Cleopatra are vividly depicted and "powerfully arrest the imagination." He maintains that Cleopatra's essential ambiguity is evidenced by her "royal pride, female vanity, luxury, inconstancy, and true attachment." Remarking that Antony also displays both noble and ignoble qualities, Schlegel contends that "the heartless littleness" of Octavius serves as a foil to Antony's generosity of spirit. Additionally, Schlegel suggests that* Antony and Cleopatra *is flawed in three significant ways: one, it contains bewildering allusions to events outside the dramatic action; two, "[many] persons of historical importance" receive scant attention; and three, connections are not always clearly established between "preparatory and concurring circumstances."*]

In the three Roman pieces, *Coriolanus, Julius Caesar,* and *Antony and Cleopatra,* the moderation with which Shakespeare excludes foreign appendages and arbitrary suppositions, and yet fully satisfies the wants of the stage, is particularly deserving of admiration. These plays are the very thing itself; and under the apparent artlessness of adhering closely to history as he found it, an uncommon degree of art is concealed. Of every historical transaction Shakspeare knows how to seize the true poetical point of view, and to give unity and rounding to a series of events detached from the immeasurable extent of history without in any degree changing them. The public life of ancient Rome is called up from its grave, and exhibited before our eyes with the utmost grandeur and freedom of the dramatic form, and the heroes of Plutarch are ennobled by the most eloquent poetry. (p. 414)

Antony and Cleopatra may, in some measure, be considered as a continuation of *Julius Caesar:* the two principal characters of *Antony and Augustus* are equally sustained in both pieces. *Antony and Cleopatra* is a play of great extent; the progress is less simple than in *Julius Caesar.* The fulness and variety of political and warlike events, to which the union of the three divisions of the Roman world under one master necessarily gave rise, were perhaps too great to admit of being clearly exhibited in one dramatic picture. In this consists the great difficulty of the historical drama:—it must be a crowded extract, and a living development of history;—the difficulty, however, has generally been successfully overcome by Shakspeare. But now many things, which are transacted in the background, are here merely alluded to, in a manner which supposes an intimate acquaintance with the history; but a work of art should contain, within itself, every thing necessary for its being fully understood. Many persons of historical importance are merely introduced in passing; the preparatory and concurring circumstances are not sufficiently collected into masses to avoid distracting our attention. The principal personages, however, are most emphatically distinguished by lineament and colouring, and powerfully arrest the imagination. In Antony we observe a mixture of great qualities, weaknesses, and vices; violent ambition and ebullitions of magnanimity; we see him now sinking into luxurious enjoyment and then nobly ashamed of his own aberrations,—manning himself to resolutions not unworthy of himself, which are always shipwrecked against the seductions of an artful woman. It is Hercules in the chains of Omphale, drawn from the fabulous heroic ages into history, and invested with the Roman costume. The seductive arts of Cleopatra are in no respect veiled over; she is an ambiguous being made up of royal pride, female vanity, luxury, inconstancy, and true attachment. Although the mutual passion of herself and Antony is without moral dignity, it still excites our sympathy as an insurmountable fascination:—they seem formed for each other, and Cleopatra is as remarkable for her seductive charms as Antony for the splendour of his deeds. As they die for each other, we forgive them for having lived for each other. The open and lavish character of Antony is admirably contrasted with the heartless littleness of Octavius, whom Shakspeare seems to have completely seen through, without allowing himself to be led astray by the fortune and the fame of Augustus. (pp. 416-17)

August Wilhelm Schlegel, "Criticisms on Shakespeare's Historical Dramas," in his A Course of Lectures on Dramatic Art and Literature, *edited by Rev. A. J. W. Morrison, translated by John Black, revised edition, Henry G. Bohn, 1846, pp. 414-45.*

SAMUEL TAYLOR COLERIDGE   (essay date 1813-34?)

[*Coleridge's lectures and writings on Shakespeare form a major chapter in the history of English Shakespearean criticism. As the channel for the critical ideas of the German Romantics and as an original interpreter of Shakespeare in the new spirit of Romanticism, Coleridge played a strategic role in overthrowing the last remains of the Neoclassical approach to Shakespeare and in establishing the modern view of the dramatist as a conscious artist and masterful portrayer of human character. Coleridge's remarks on Shakespeare come down to posterity largely as fragmentary notes, marginalia, and reports by auditors on the lectures, rather than in polished essays. The following excerpt is taken from undated notes made by Coleridge sometime between 1813 and his death in 1834. Concerning* Antony and Cleopatra, *he is the earliest critic to question whether in its display of "strength and vigor of maturity," the play should not be considered "a formidable rival" of Shakespeare's four major tragedies. Coleridge terms it "the most wonderful" in the canon and—coining a phrase that has been frequently cited by subsequent critics—distinguishes this work from all the others by its "happy valiancy of style." He singles out for praise Shakespeare's representation of Cleopatra, arguing that the "depth and energy" of her passion mitigate our awareness of its illicit quality; he also holds that her passion is not instinctive or spontaneous, but "springs out of the habitual cravings of a licentious nature" and requires repeated stimulation and enhancement by artifice and stratagem.*]

The highest praise or rather form of praise, of [*Antony and Cleopatra*] which I can offer in my own mind, is the doubt which its perusal always occasions in me, whether it is not in all exhibitions of a giant power in its strength and vigor of maturity, a formidable rival of the *Macbeth, Lear, Othello,* and *Hamlet. Feliciter audax* [happy valiancy] is the motto for its style comparatively with his other works, even as it is the general motto of all his works compared with those of other poets. Be it remembered too, that this happy valiancy of style is but the representative and result of all the material excellencies so exprest.

This play should be perused in mental contrast with Romeo and Juliet;—as the love of passion and appetite opposed to the love of affection and instinct. But the art displayed in the character of Cleopatra is profound in this, especially, that the sense of criminality in her passion is lessened by our insight into its depth and energy, at the very moment that we cannot but perceive that the passion itself springs out of the habitual craving of a licentious nature, and that it is supported and reinforced by voluntary stimulus and sought-for associations, instead of blossoming out of spontaneous emotion.

But of all perhaps of Shakespeare's plays the most wonderful is the *Antony and Cleopatra*. [There are] scarcely any in which he has followed history more minutely, and yet few even of his own in which he impresses the notion of giant strength so much, perhaps none in which he impresses it more strongly. This [is] owing to the manner in which it is sustained throughout—that he *lives* in and through the play—to the numerous momentary flashes of nature counteracting the historic abstraction, in which take as a specimen the [death of Cleopatra]. (pp. 76-7)

Samuel Taylor Coleridge, "Notes on the Tragedies of Shakespeare: 'Antony and Cleopatra'," in his Shakespearean Criticism, Vol. 1, *edited by Thomas Middleton Raysor, second edition, Dutton, 1960, pp. 76-9.*

WILLIAM HAZLITT   (essay date 1817)

[*Hazlitt is considered a leading Shakespearean critic of the English Romantic movement. A prolific essayist and commentator on a wide range of subjects, Hazlitt remarked in the preface to his* Characters of Shakespear's Plays, *first published in 1817, that he was inspired by the German critic August Wilhelm Schlegel and was determined to supplant what he considered the pernicious influence of Samuel Johnson's Shakespearean criticism. Hazlitt's criticism is typically Romantic in its emphasis on character studies. His experience as a drama critic was an important factor in shaping his descriptive, as opposed to analytical, interpretations of Shakespeare. In the following excerpt, taken from the work mentioned above, Hazlitt esteems the character of Cleopatra as "a masterpiece." She is essentially a voluptuary, he contends, whose principal consideration is "the love of pleasure and the power of giving it," and he proposes that the magnificent manner of her death comes near to atoning for her "great and unpardonable faults." Hazlitt is the first critic to link the pattern of the play's dramatic action to the revolution of fortune's wheel, noting that in the second half of* Antony and Cleopatra *the pattern of alternating defeats and successes is repeated at a rate that is almost frenzied. He is also the earliest to comment at some length on Antony's kaleidoscopic cloud speech (IV. xiv. 1-13), which he praises for its imagery and its evocation of the evanescence, uncertainty, and mutability of human existence.*]

This is a very noble play. Though not in the first class of Shakespear's productions, it stands next to them, and is, we think, the finest of his historical plays, that is, of those in which he made poetry the organ of history, and assumed a certain tone of character and sentiment, in conformity to known facts, instead of trusting to his observations of general nature or to the unlimited indulgence of his own fancy. What he has added to the actual story, is upon a par with it. His genius was, as it were, a match for history as well as nature, and could grapple at will with either. The play is full of that pervading comprehensive power by which the poet could always make himself master of time and circumstances. It presents a fine picture of Roman pride and Eastern magnificence: and in the struggle between the two, the empire of the world seems suspended, "like the swan's downfeather,

> That stands upon the swell at full of tide,
> And neither way inclines.
>
> [III. ii. 48-50]

The characters breathe, move, and live. Shakespear does not stand reasoning on what his characters would do or say, but at once *becomes* them, and speaks and acts for them. He does not present us with groups of stage-puppets of poetical machines making set speeches on human life, and acting from a calculation of problematical motives, but he brings living men and women on the scene, who speak and act from real feelings, according to the ebbs and flows of passion, without the least tincture of pedantry of logic or rhetoric. Nothing is made out by inference and analogy, by climax and antithesis, but every thing takes place just as it would have done in reality, according to the occasion.—The character of Cleopatra is a master-piece. What an extreme contrast it affords to Imogen [in *Cymbeline*]! One would think it almost impossible for the same person to have drawn both. She is voluptuous, ostentatious, conscious, boastful of her charms, haughty, tyrannical, fickle. The luxurious pomp and gorgeous extravagance of the Egyptian queen are displayed in all their force and lustre, as well as the irregular grandeur of the soul of Mark Antony. Take only the first four lines that they speak as an example of the regal style of lovemaking.

> *Cleopatra.* If it be love indeed, tell me how much?
> *Antony.* There's beggary in the love that can be
>   reckon'd.
> *Cleopatra.* I'll set a bourn how far to be belov'd.
> *Antony.* Then must thou needs find out new heav'n,
>   new earth.
>
> [I. i. 14-17]

The rich and poetical description of her person beginning—

> The barge she sat in, like a burnish'd throne,
> Burnt on the water; the poop was beaten gold,
> Purple the sails, and so perfumed, that
> The winds were love-sick—
>
> [II. ii. 191-94]

seems to prepare the way for, and almost to justify the subsequent infatuation of Antony when in the sea-fight at Actium, he leaves the battle, and "like a doating mallard" [III. x. 19] follows her flying sails.

Few things in Shakespear (and we know of nothing in any other author like them) have more of that local truth of imagination and character than the passage in which Cleopatra is represented conjecturing what were the employments of Antony in his absence—"He's speaking now, or murmuring—*Where's my serpent of old Nile?*" [I. v. 24-5]. Or again, when she says to Antony, after the defeat at Actium, and his summoning up resolution to risk another fight—"It is my birth-day; I had thought to have held it poor; but since my lord is Antony again, I will be Cleopatra" [III. xiii. 184-86]. Perhaps the finest burst of all is Antony's rage after his final defeat when he comes in, and surprises the messenger of Caesar kissing her hand—

> To let a fellow that will take rewards,
> And say God quit you, be familiar with,
> My play-fellow, your hand; this kingly seal,
> And plighter of high hearts.
>
> [III. xiii. 123-26]

It is no wonder that he orders him to be whipped; but his low condition is not the true reason: there is another feeling which lies deeper, though Antony's pride would not let him shew it, except by his rage; he suspects the fellow to be Caesar's proxy.

Cleopatra's whole character is the triumph of the voluptuous, of the love of pleasure and the power of giving it, over every other consideration. Octavia is a dull foil to her, and Fulvia a

shrew and shrill-tongued. What a picture do those lines give of her—

> Age cannot wither her, nor custom steal
> Her infinite variety. Other women cloy
> The appetites they feed, but she makes hungry
> Where most she satisfies.
>
> [II. ii. 234-37]

What a spirit and fire in her conversation with Antony's messenger who brings her the unwelcome news of his marriage with Octavia! How all the pride of beauty and of high rank breaks out in her promised reward to him—

> ————There's gold, and here
> My bluest veins to kiss!—
>
> [II. v. 28-9]

She had great and unpardonable faults, but the grandeur of her death almost redeems them. She learns from the depth of despair the strength of her affections. She keeps her queen-like state in the last disgrace, and her sense of the pleasurable in the last moments of her life. She tastes a luxury in death. After applying the asp, she says with fondness—

> Dost thou not see my baby at my breast,
> That sucks the nurse asleep? . . .
> As sweet as balm, as soft as air, as gentle.
> Oh Antony!
>
> [V. ii. 309-10, 311-12]

It is worth while to observe that Shakespear has contrasted the extreme magnificence of the descriptions in this play with pictures of extreme suffering and physical horror, not less striking—partly perhaps to place the effeminate charcter of Mark Antony in a more favourable light, and at the same time to preserve a certain balance of feeling in the mind. Caesar says, hearing of his rival's conduct at the court of Cleopatra,

> ————Antony,
> Leave thy lascivious wassels. When thou once
> Wert beaten from Mutina, where thou slew'st
> Hirtius and Pansa, consuls, at thy heel
> Did famine follow, whom thou fought'st against,
> Though daintily brought up, with patience more
> Than savages could suffer. Thou did'st drink
> The stale of horses, and the gilded puddle
> Which beast would cough at. Thy palate then did deign
> The roughest berry on the rudest hedge,
> Yea, like the stag, when snow the pasture sheets,
> The barks of trees thou browsed'st. On the Alps,
> It is reported, thou didst eat strange flesh,
> Which some did die to look on: and all this,
> It wounds thine honour, that I speak it now,
> Was borne so like a soldier, that thy cheek
> So much as lank'd not.
>
> [I. iv. 55-71]

The passage after Antony's defeat by Augustus, where he is made to say—

> Yes, yes; he at Philippi kept
> His sword e'en like a dancer; while I struck
> The lean and wrinkled Cassius, and 'twas I
> That the mad Brutus ended.
>
> [III. xi. 35-8]

is one of those fine retrospections which shew us the winding and eventful march of human life. The jealous attention which has been paid to the unities both of time and place has taken away the principle of perspective in the drama, and all the interest which objects derive from distance, from contrast, from privation, from change of fortune, from long-cherished passion; and contrasts our view of life from a strange and romantic dream, long, obscure, and infinite, into a smartly contested, three hours' inaugural disputation on its merits by the different candidates for theatrical applause.

The latter scenes of *Antony and Cleopatra* are full of the changes of accident and passion. Success and defeat follow one another with startling rapidity. Fortune sits upon her wheel more blind and giddy than usual. This precarious state and the approaching dissolution of his greatness are strikingly displayed in the dialogue of Antony with Eros.

> *Antony.* Eros, thou yet behold'st me?
> *Eros.* Ay, noble lord.
> *Antony.* Sometime we see a cloud that's
>   dragonish,
> A vapour sometime, like a bear or lion,
> A towered citadel, a pendant rock.
> A forked mountain, or blue promontory
> With trees upon't, that nod unto the world
> And mock our eyes with air. Thou hast seen these
>   signs,
> They are black vesper's pageants.
> *Eros.* Ay, my lord.
> *Antony.* That which is now a horse, even with a
>   thought
> The rack dislimns, and makes it indistinct
> As water is in water.
> *Eros.* It does, my lord.
> *Antony.* My good knave, Eros, now thy captain is
> Even such a body, &c.
>
> [IV. xiv. 1-13]

This is, without doubt, one of the finest pieces of poetry in Shakespear. The splendour of the imagery, the semblance of reality, the lofty range of picturesque objects hanging over the world, their evanescent nature, the total uncertainty of what is left behind, are just like the mouldering schemes of human greatness. It is finer than Cleopatra's passionate lamentation over his fallen grandeur, because it is more dim, unstable, unsubstantial. Antony's headstrong presumption and infatuated determination to yield to Cleopatra's wishes to fight by sea instead of land, meet a merited punishment; and the extravagance of his resolutions, increasing with the desperateness of his circumstances, is well commented upon by Enobarbus.

> ———I see men's judgments are
> A parcel of their fortunes, and things outward
> Do draw the inward quality after them
> To suffer all alike.
>
> [III. xiii. 31-4]

The repentance of Enobarbus after his treachery to his master is the most affecting part of the play. He cannot recover from the blow which Antony's generosity gives him, and he dies broken-hearted, ''a master-leaver and a fugitive'' [IV. ix. 22].

Shakespear's genius has spread over the whole play a richness like the overflowing of the Nile. (pp. 58-63)

> William Hazlitt, ''Characters of Shakespear's Plays: 'Antony and Cleopatra','' in his Characters of Shakespear's Plays & Lectures on the English Poets, The Macmillan Company, 1903, pp. 58-63.

ANNA BROWNELL JAMESON   (essay date 1833)

[*Jameson was a well-known nineteenth-century essayist. Her essays and criticism span the end of the Romantic age and the beginning of Victorian realism, reflecting elements from both periods. She is best remembered for her study* Characteristics of Women: Moral, Poetical, and Historical, *originally published in 1832 but revised one year later. This work demonstrates both her historical interests and her sympathetic appreciation of Shakespeare's female characters. In the excerpt below, taken from the 1833 edition of her book, Jameson emphasizes Cleopatra's many-sided nature, describing her as ''a brilliant antithesis, a compound of contradictions,'' and celebrating the inconsistencies in her demeanor as both ''perfectly natural'' and the source of our fascination with her. The critic argues that the Egyptian queen's love for Antony is compounded of sincere attachment and—in a phrase reminiscent of Hazlitt (see excerpt above, 1817)—''the love of pleasure, the love of power, and the love of self.'' Jameson regards the scene in which the messenger brings Cleopatra the news of Antony's marriage to Octavia (Act II, Scene ii) as neither vulgar nor comic, but instead considers it a powerful and truthful exposition of the queen's complex nature. She also focuses on Cleopatra's preparations for death, maintaining that ''our respect and interest'' are not diminished by either her evident timidity or the vanity which makes her shrink from the prospect of public humiliation in Rome; indeed, Jameson concludes that her death is a heroic one.*]

Of all Shakspeare's female characters, Miranda [in *The Tempest*] and Cleopatra appear to me the most wonderful. The first, unequalled as a poetic conception; the latter, miraculous as a work of art. If we could make a regular classification of his characters, these would form the two extremes of simplicity and complexity; and all his other characters would be found to fill up some shade or gradation between these two.

Great crimes, springing from high passions, grafted on high qualities, are the legitimate source of tragic poetry. But to make the extreme of littleness produce an effect like grandeur, to make the excess of frailty produce an effect like power, to heap up together all that is most unsubstantial, frivolous, vain, contemptible, and variable till the worthlessness be lost in the magnitude and a sense of the sublime spring from the very elements of littleness—to do this belonged only to Shakspeare, that worker of miracles. Cleopatra is a brilliant antithesis, a compound of contradictions, of all that we most hate with what we most admire. The whole character is the triumph of the external over the innate; and yet, like one of her country's hieroglyphics, though she present at first view a splendid and perplexing anomaly, there is deep meaning and wondrous skill in the apparent enigma when we come to analyse and decipher it. But how are we to arrive at the solution of this glorious riddle, whose dazzling complexity continually mocks and eludes us? What is most astonishing in the character of Cleopatra is its antithetical construction—its *consistent inconsistency*, if I may use such an expression—which renders it quite impossible to reduce it to any elementary principles. It will, perhaps, be found, on the whole that vanity and the love of power predominate; but I dare not say it *is* so, for these qualities and a hundred others mingle into each other, and shift and change and glance away like the colours in a peacock's train.

In some others of Shakspeare's female characters, also remarkable for their complexity (Portia and Juliet, for instance), we are struck with the delightful sense of harmony in the midst of contrast, so that the idea of unity and simplicity of effect is produced in the midst of variety. But in Cleopatra it is the absence of unity and simplicity which strikes us; the impression is that of perpetual and irreconcileable contrast. The continual approximation of whatever is most opposite in character, in situation, in sentiment, would be fatiguing were it not so perfectly natural; the woman herself would be distracting if she were not so enchanting.

I have not the slightest doubt that Shakspeare's Cleopatra is the real historical Cleopatra—the "rare Egyptian"—individualised and placed before us. Her mental accomplishments, her unequalled grace, her woman's wit and woman's wiles, her irresistible allurements, her starts of irregular grandeur, her bursts of ungovernable temper, her vivacity of imagination, her petulant caprice, her fickleness and her falsehood, her tenderness and her truth, her childish susceptibility to flattery, her magnificent spirit, her royal pride, the gorgeous eastern colouring of the character—all these contradictory elements has Shakspeare seized, mingled them in their extremes, and fused them into one brilliant impersonation of classical elegance, Oriental voluptuousness and gipsy sorcery.

What better proof can we have of the individual truth of the character than the admission that Shakspeare's Cleopatra produces exactly the same effect on us that is recorded of the real Cleopatra? She dazzles our faculties, perplexes our judgment, bewilders and bewitches our fancy; from the beginning to the end of the drama we are conscious of a kind of fascination against which our moral sense rebels, but from which there is no escape. The epithets applied to her perpetually by Antony and others confirm this impression; "enchanting queen"—"witch"—"spell"—"great fairy"—"cockatrice"—"serpent of old Nile"—"thou grave charm!" [I. v. 25; IV. xii. 25] are only a few of them, and who does not know by heart the famous quotations in which this Egyptian Circe is described, with all her infinite seductions?—

> Fie! wrangling queen!
> Whom every thing becomes, to chide, to laugh,
> To weep; whose every passion fully strives
> To make itself, in thee, fair and admir'd.
>
> [I. i. 48-51]

> Age cannot wither her, nor custom stale
> Her infinite variety: . . .
> . . . for vilest things
> Become themselves in her.
>
> [II. ii. 234-35, 237-38]

And the pungent irony of Enobarbus has well exposed her feminine arts when he says, on the occasion of Antony's intended departure—

> Cleopatra, catching but the least noise of this,
> dies instantly; I have seen her die twenty times
> upon far poorer moment.
> *Antony.* She is cunning past man's thought.
> *Enobarbus.* Alack, sir, no! her passions are
> made of nothing but the finest part of pure love.
> We cannot call her winds and waters, sighs and
> tears; they are greater storms and tempests than
> almanacks can report; this cannot be cunning
> in her; if it be, she makes a shower of rain as
> well as Jove.
>
> [I. ii. 140-51]

The whole secret of her absolute dominion over the facile Antony may be found in one little speech—

> See where he is—who's with him—what he does:—
> (I did not send you). If you find him sad,
> Say I am dancing; if in mirth, report
> That I am sudden sick; Quick! and return.

> *Charmian.* Madam, methinks, if you did love him
> dearly,
> You do not hold the method to enforce
> The like from him.
> *Cleopatra.*   What should I do I do
> not?
> *Charmian.* In each thing give him way; cross him in
> nothing.
> *Cleopatra.* Thou teachest like a fool, the way to lose
> him.
> *Charmian.* Tempt him not so too far.
>
> [I. iii. 2-11]

But Cleopatra is a mistress of her art, and knows better; and what a picture of her triumphant petulance, her imperious and imperial coquetry, is given in her own words!—

> That time—O, times!—
> I laugh'd him out of patience; and that night
> I laugh'd him into patience: and next morn,
> Ere the ninth hour, I drunk him to his bed;
> Then put my tires and mantles on him, whilst
> I wore his sword, Philippan.
>
> [II. v. 18-23]

When Antony enters, full of some serious purpose which he is about to impart, the woman's perverseness and the tyrannical waywardness with which she taunts him and plays upon his temper are admirably depicted—

> I know, by that same eye, there's some good news.
> What says the married woman?—You may go;
> 'Would she had never given you leave to come! . . .
> Why should I think, you can be mine, and true,
> Though you in swearing shake the throned gods,
> Who have been false to Fulvia? Riotous madness,
> To be entangled with those mouth-made vows,
> Which break themselves in swearing!
> *Antony.*   Most sweet queen!
> *Cleopatra.* Nay, pray you, seek no colour for your
> going.
> But bid farewell, and go.
>
> [I. iii. 19-21, 27-33]

She recovers her dignity for a moment at the news of Fulvia's death, as if roused by a blow—

> Though age from folly could not give me freedom,
> It does from childishness:—Can Fulvia die?
>
> [I. iii. 57-8]

And then follows the artful mockery with which she tempts and provokes him, in order to discover whether he regrets his wife—

> O most false love!
> Where be the sacred vials thou shouldst fill
> With sorrowful water? Now I see, I see
> In Fulvia's death, how mine receiv'd shall be. . . .
> I pr'ythee, turn aside, and weep for her;
> Then bid adieu to me, and say, the tears
> Belong to Egypt: Good now, play one scene
> Of excellent dissembling; and let it look
> Like perfect honour.
> *Antony.*   You'll heat my blood; no more.
> *Cleopatra.* You can do better yet; but this is meetly.
> *Antony.* Now, by my sword—
> *Cleopatra.*   And target—still he mends;

But this is not the best. Look, pr'ythee, Charmian,
How this Herculean Roman does become
The carriage of his chafe.

                                        [I. iii. 62-5, 76-85]

This is, indeed, most "excellent dissembling"; but when she
has fooled and chafed the Herculean Roman to the verge of
danger, then comes that return of tenderness which secures the
power she has tried to the utmost, and we have all the elegant,
the poetical Cleopatra, in her beautiful farewell—

                    Forgive me!
Since my becomings kill me when they do not
Eye well to you. Your honour calls you hence,
Therefore be deaf to my unpitied folly,
And all the gods go with you! Upon your sword
Sit laurell'd victory; and smooth success
Be strew'd before your feet!

                                        [I. iii. 95-101]

Finer still are the workings of her variable mind and lively
imagination after Antony's departure; her fond repining at his
absence, her violent spirit, her right royal wilfulness and impatience, as if it were a wrong to her majesty, an insult to her
sceptre, that there should exist in her despite such things as
space and time, and high treason to her sovereign power to
dare to remember what she chooses to forget—

Give me to drink mandragora. . . .
That I might sleep out this great gap of time
My Antony is away. . . .
                    O Charmian!
Where think'st thou he is now? Stands he, or sits he,
Or does he walk? or is he on his horse?
O happy horse to bear the weight of Antony!
Do bravely, horse! for wot'st thou whom thou mov'st?
The demi-Atlas of this earth—the arm
And burgonet of men. . . .
                    But, come, away,
Get me ink and paper: he shall have every day
A several greeting, or I'll unpeople Egypt.
                                        [I. v. 4, 5-6, 18-24, 75-7]

We learn from Plutarch, that it was a favourite amusement
with Antony and Cleopatra to ramble through the streets at
night, and bandy ribald jests with the populace of Alexandria.
From the same authority we know that they were accustomed
to live on the most familiar terms with their attendants and the
companions of their revels. To these traits we must add that,
with all her violence, perverseness, egotism, and caprice, Cleopatra mingled a capability for warm affections and kindly feeling, or, rather, what we should call in these days a constitutional *good-nature;* and was lavishly generous to her favourites
and dependants. These characteristics we find scattered through
the play; they are not only faithfully rendered by Shakspeare,
but he has made the finest use of them in his delineation of
manners. Hence the occasional freedom of her women and her
attendants, in the midst of their fears and flatteries, becomes
most natural and consistent; hence, too, their devoted attachment and fidelity, proved even in death. But, as illustrative of
Cleopatra's disposition, perhaps the finest and most characteristic scene in the whole play is that in which the messenger
arrives from Rome with the tidings of Antony's marriage with
Octavia. She perceives at once with quickness that all is not
well, and she hastens to anticipate the worst, that she may
have the pleasure of being disappointed. Her impatience to
know what she fears to learn, the vivacity with which she

gradually works herself up into a state of excitement, and at
length into fury, is wrought out with a force of truth which
makes us recoil. . . . (pp. 217-24)

I know nothing comparable to [this scene]. The pride and
arrogance of the Egyptian queen, the blandishment of the woman,
the unexpected but natural transitions of temper and feeling,
the contest of various passions, and at length—when the wild
hurricane has spent its fury—the melting into tears, faintness,
and languishment, are portrayed with the most astonishing power,
and truth, and skill in feminine nature. More wonderful still
is the splendour and force of colouring which is shed over this
extraordinary scene. The mere idea of an angry woman beating
her menial presents something ridiculous or disgusting to the
mind; in a queen or a tragedy heroine it is still more indecorous;
yet this scene is as far as possible from the vulgar or the comic.
Cleopatra seems privileged to "touch the brink of all we hate"
with impunity. This imperial termagant, this "wrangling queen,
whom everything becomes," becomes even her fury. We know
not by what strange power it is, that, in the midst of all these
unruly passions and childish caprices, the poetry of the character and the fanciful and sparkling grace of the delineation
are sustained and still rule in the imagination; but we feel that
it is so.

I need hardly observe, that we have historical authority for the
excessive violence of Cleopatra's temper: witness the story of
her boxing the ears of her treasurer, in presence of Octavius,
as related by Plutarch. Shakspeare has made a fine use of this
anecdote also towards the conclusion of the drama, but it is
not equal in power to this scene with the messenger.

The man is afterwards brought back, almost by force, to satisfy
Cleopatra's jealous anxiety by a description of Octavia:—but
this time, made wise by experience, he takes care to adapt his
information to the humours of his imperious mistress, and gives
her a satirical picture of her rival. The scene which follows,
in which Cleopatra—artful, acute, and penetrating as she is—
becomes the dupe of her feminine spite and jealousy, nay,
assists in duping herself; and after having cuffed the messenger
for telling her truths which are offensive, rewards him for the
falsehood which flatters her weakness; is not only an admirable
exhibition of character, but a fine moral lesson.

She concludes, after dismissing the messenger with gold and
thanks—

                    I repent me much
That so I harried him. Why, methinks, by him
This creature's no such thing.
   Charmian.   Nothing, madam.
   *Cleopatra.*The man hath some majesty, and should
      know

                                        [III. iii. 39-42]

Do we not fancy Cleopatra drawing herself up with all the vain
consciousness of rank and beauty, as she pronounces this last
line? and is not this the very woman who celebrated her own
apotheosis, who arrayed herself in the robe and diadem of the
goddess Isis, and could find no titles magnificent enough for
her children but those of *the Sun* and *the Moon?* (pp. 226-28)

There was no room left in this amazing picture for the display
of that passionate maternal tenderness which was a strong and
redeeming feature in Cleopatra's historical character; but it is
not left untouched; for when she is imprecating mischiefs on
herself she wishes, as the last and worst of possible evils, that
"thunder may smite Caesarion!"

In representing the mutual passion of Antony and Cleopatra as real and fervent, Shakspear has adhered to the truth of history as well as to general nature. On Antony's side it is a species of infatuation, a single and engrossing feeling: it is, in short, the love of a man declined in years for a woman very much younger than himself, and who has subjected him by every species of female enchantment. In Cleopatra the passion is of a mixed nature, made up of real attachment, combined with the love of pleasure, the love of power, and the love of self. Not only is the character most complicated, but no one sentiment could have existed pure and unvarying in such a mind as hers: her passion in itself is true, fixed to one centre; but, like the pennon streaming from the mast, it flutters and veers with every breath of her variable temper: yet in the midst of all her caprices, follies, and even vices, womanly feeling is still predominant in Cleopatra, and the change which takes place in her deportment towards Antony, when their evil fortune darkens round them, is as beautiful and interesting in itself as it is striking and natural. Instead of the airy caprice and provoking petulance she displays in the first scenes, we have a mixture of tenderness, and artifice, and fear, and submissive blandishment. Her behaviour, for instance, after the battle of Actium, when she quails before the noble and tender rebuke of her lover, is partly female subtlety and partly natural feeling—

> *Cleopatra.*　　　　O my lord, my lord,
> Forgive my fearful sails! I little thought
> You would have follow'd.
> 　　*Antony.*　　　　Egypt, thou knew'st too well,
> My heart was to thy rudder tied by th' strings,
> And thou should'st tow me after. . . .
> 　　　　　　　　　　You did know
> How much you were my conqueror; and that
> My sword, made weak by my affection, would
> Obey it on all cause.
> 　　*Cleopatra.*　　　　Pardon, pardon!
> 　　*Antony.* Fall not a tear, I say; one of them rates
> All that is won or lost. Give me a kiss
> Even this repays me.
>
> 　　　　　　　　　　[III. xi. 54-8, 65-71]

It is perfectly in keeping with the individual character, that Cleopatra, alike destitute of moral strength and physical courage, should cower, terrified and subdued, before the masculine spirit of her lover, when once she has fairly roused it. (pp. 229-31)

The character of Mark Antony, as delinated by Shakespeare, reminds me of the Farnese Hercules. There is an ostentatious display of power, an exaggerated grandeur, a colossal effect in the whole conception, sustained throughout in the pomp of the language, which seems, as it flows along, to resound with the clang of arms and the music of the revel. The coarseness and violence of the historic portrait are a little kept down; but every word which Antony utters is characteristic of the arrogant but magnanimous Roman, who "with half the bulk o' the world play'd as he pleased" [III. xi. 64], and was himself the sport of a host of mad (and bad) passions, and the slave of a woman.

History is followed closely in all the details of the catastrophe, and there is something wonderfully grand in the hurried march of events towards the conclusion. As disasters hem her round, Cleopatra gathers up her faculties to meet them, not with the calm fortitude of a great soul, but the haughty, tameless spirit of a wilful woman unused to reverse or contradiction.

Her speech, after Antony has expired in her arms, I have always regarded as one of the most wonderful in Shakspeare. Cleopatra is not a woman to grieve silently. The contrast between the violence of her passions and the weakness of her sex, between her regal grandeur and her excess of misery, her impetuous, unavailing struggles with the fearful destiny which has compassed her, and the mixture of wild impatience and pathos in her agony, are really magnificent. She faints on the body of Antony, and is recalled to life by the cries of her women—

> *Iras.*　　　　　　Royal Egypt—empress!. . .
> *Cleopatra.* No more, but e'en a woman; and commanded
> By such poor passion as the maid that milks
> And does the meanest chares.—It were for me
> To throw my sceptre at the injurious gods;
> To tell them, that this world did equal theirs
> Till they had stolen our jewel. All's but nought;
> Patience is sottish; and impatience does
> Become a dog that's mad; Then is it sin
> To rush into the secret house of death,
> Ere death dare come to us? How do you, women?
> What, what? good cheer! why how now, Charmian?
> My noble girls!—ah, women, women! look
> Our lamp is spent, it's out.
> We'll bury him; and then, what's brave, what's noble,
> Let's do it after the high Roman fashion,
> And make death proud to take us.
>
> 　　　　　　　　　　[IV. xv. 70-1, 73-88]

But although Cleopatra talks of dying "after the high Roman fashion," she fears what she most desires, and cannot perform with simplicity what costs her such an effort. That extreme physical cowardice which was so strong a trait in her historical character, which led to the defeat of Actium, which made her delay the execution of a fatal resolve till she had "tried conclusions infinite of *easy* ways to die" [V. ii. 335-36], Shakspeare has rendered with the finest possible effect, and in a manner which heightens instead of diminishing our respect and interest. Timid by nature, she is courageous by the mere force of will, and she lashes herself up with high-sounding words into a kind of false daring. Her lively imagination suggests every incentive which can spur her on to the deed she has resolved, yet trembles to contemplate. She pictures to herself all the degradations which must attend her captivity; and let it be observed, that those which she anticipates are precisely such as a vain, luxurious, and haughty woman would especially dread, and which only true virtue and magnanimity could despise. Cleopatra could have endured the loss of freedom; but to be led in triumph through the streets of Rome is insufferable. She could stoop to Caesar with dissembling courtesy, and meet duplicity with superior art; but "to be chastised" by the scornful or upbraiding glance of the injured Octavia—"rather a ditch in Egypt!" [V. ii. 57]. (pp. 231-33)

The idea of this frail, timid, wayward woman dying with heroism, from the mere force of passion and will, takes us by surprise. The Attic elegance of her mind, her poetical imagination, the pride of beauty and royalty predominating to the last, and the sumptuous and picturesque accompaniments with which she surrounds herself in death, carry to its extreme height that effect of contrast which prevails through her life and character. No arts, no invention, could add to the real circumstances of Cleopatra's closing scene. Shakspeare has shown profound judgment and feeling in adhering closely to the classical authorities; and to say that the language and sentiments worthily fill up the outline is the most magnificent praise that can be given. The magical play of fancy and the overpowering fascination of the character are kept up to the last: and when

Cleopatra, on applying the asp, silences the lamentations on her women—

> Peace! peace!
> Dost thou not see my baby at my breast
> That sucks the nurse asleep?—
>
> [V. ii. 308-10]

These few words—the contrast between the tender beauty of the image and the horror of the situation—produce an effect more intensely mournful than all the ranting in the world. The generous devotion of her women adds the moral charm which alone was wanting: and when Octavius hurries in too late to save his victim, and exclaims, when gazing on her—

> She looks like sleep—
> As she would catch another Antony
> In her strong toil of grace—
>
> [V. ii. 346-48]

the image of her beauty and her irresistible arts triumphant even in death, is at once brought before us, and one masterly and comprehensive stroke consummates this most wonderful, most dazzling delineation.

I am not here the apologist of Cleopatra's historical character, nor of such women as resemble her: I am considering her merely as a dramatic portrait of astonishing beauty, spirit, and originality. She has furnished the subject of two Latin, sixteen French, six English, and at least four Italian tragedies; yet Shakspeare alone has availed himself of all the interest of the story without falsifying the character. He alone has dared to exhibit the Egyptian queen with all her greatness and all her littleness—all her frailties of temper, all her paltry arts and dissolute passions, yet preserved the dramatic propriety and poetical colouring of the character, and awakened our pity for fallen grandeur without once beguiling us into sympathy with guilt and error. (pp. 234-36)

Shakspeare's Cleopatra is like one of those graceful and fantastic pieces of antique Arabesque, in which all anomalous shapes and impossible and wild combinations of form are woven together in regular confusion and harmonious discord; and such we have reason to believe, was the living woman herself, when she existed upon this earth.

I do not understand the observation of a late critic, that in this play "Octavia is only a dull foil to Cleopatra" [see excerpt above by William Hazlitt, 1817]. Cleopatra requires no foil, and Octavia is not dull, though in a moment of jealous spleen her accomplished rival gives her that epithet. It is possible that her beautiful character, if brought more forward and coloured up to the historic portrait, would still be eclipsed by the dazzling splendour of Cleopatra's; for so I have seen a flight of fireworks blot out for a while the silver moon and ever-burning stars. But here, the subject of the drama being the love of Antony and Cleopatra, Octavia is very properly kept in the background, and far from any competition with her rival; the interest would otherwise have been unpleasantly divided, or rather, Cleopatra herself must have served but as a foil to the tender, virtuous, dignified, and generous Octavia, the very *beau ideal* of a noble Roman lady—

> Admired Octavia, whose beauty claims
> No worse a husband than the best of men;
> Whose virtue and whose general graces speak
> That which none else can utter.
>
> [II. ii. 127-30]
> (pp. 241-42)

The character of Octavia is merely indicated in a few touches, but every stroke tells. We see her with "downcast eyes sedate and sweet, and looks demure"—with her modest tenderness and dignified submission—the very antipodes of her rival! Nor should we forget that she has furnished one of the most graceful similes in the whole compass of poetry, where her soft equanimity in the midst of grief is compared to—

> The swan's down feather
> That stands upon the swell at flood of tide,
> And neither way inclines.
>
> [III. ii. 48-50]

The fear which seems to haunt the mind of Cleopatra lest she should be "chastised by the sober eye" [V. ii. 54] of Octavia, is exceedingly characteristic of the two women; it betrays the jealous pride of her who was conscious that she had forfeited all real claim to respect; and it places Octavia before us in all the majesty of that virtue which could strike a kind of envying and remorseful awe even into the bosom of Cleopatra. (pp. 242-43)

Anna Brownell Jameson, "Cleopatra" and "Octavia," in her Shakespeare's Heroines: Characteristics of Women, Moral, Poetical, & Historical, *George Newnes, Limited, 1897, pp. 216-40, 241-43.*

HERMANN ULRICI   (essay date 1839)

[*A German scholar, Ulrici was a professor of philosophy and the author of works on Greek poetry and Shakespeare. The following excerpt is from an English translation of his* Über Shakespeares dramatische Kunst, und sein Verhältniss zu Calderon und Göthe, *a work first published in 1839. This study exemplifies the "philosophical criticism" developed in Germany during the nineteenth century. The immediate sources for Ulrici's critical approach appear to be August Wilhelm Schlegel's conception of the play as an organic, interconnected whole and George Wilhelm Friedrich Hegel's view of drama as an embodiment of the conflict of historical forces and ideas. Unlike his fellow German Shakespearean critic G. G. Gervinus, Ulrici sought to develop a specifically Christian aesthetics, but one which, as he carefully points out in the introduction to the work mentioned above, in no way intrudes on "that unity of idea, which preeminently constitutes a work of art a living creation in the world of beauty." In the excerpt reprinted below, Ulrici asserts that the central thematic idea of* Antony and Cleopatra *is that "moderation, prudence, and forethought" are the requisite "half-virtues" which can temporarily preserve Rome from social and political disintegration. Octavius possesses these qualities, the critic argues, and therefore he achieves political leadership, while all whom he supplants or defeats—Antony, Lepidus, Pompey, and Cleopatra—are notably deficient in them and are thus overcome by the course of history. Although Ulrici regards Octavius as the appropriate man for the times, he does not admire him, but rather views him as petty and mean-spirited. The critic also contends that Antony combines many virtues reminiscent of the old Roman system with vices typical of "the new order of things"; he adds that it is these vices which lead to Antony's downfall and yoke him with the eastern corruption of "Cleopatra, the spotted and slimy 'serpent of old Nile'" (I. v. 25).*]

Antony and Cleopatra . . . is evidently to be regarded as the continuation of *Julius Caesar;* if for no other reason, yet for the obvious affinity of their fundamental ideas. In the former we have the olden times at war with the new, and in the latter the same elements are arranged in hostile conflict with each other.

The straight-forward and noble Antony, with his love of truth, personal bravery, and admiration for all true greatness and virtue (as displayed in his funeral oration over the dead body of Brutus in the former piece), is here the representative of the olden spirit, but still not in its absoluteness and purity; in Antony it has already entered into and adopted many of the sentiments of the new order of things. For these olden virtues are united in his character with the chief vices of the latter; such as avarice, lust of power, inconstancy, voluptuousness, and immorality. On his side are Lepidus and Sextus Pompeius; the former virtuous, but weak, and without mental or physical energy; the latter a rash enterprising youth, alike destitute of prudence and experience. They all pass away; their brightness pales before the lucky star of Octavian. Compared with Antony, Octavius appears without vigour and depth of mind, and even as a general without skill or courage, and supported by nothing but his cunning and moderation. And yet he is the conqueror of all! And why?—because the times pre-eminently called for prudence and moderation. When all true moral principle and virtue in a state or people are dead, then is their place to be supplied by such half virtues, if the nation is to be preserved from complete and immediate disorganization. The final fall of Rome was not as yet the purpose of history, and therefore was Octavius to be raised to the empire of the world. But even in other circumstances it requires—what is itself action—moderation, prudence, and forethought. Whoever does not possess these qualities,—whether like Antony he is unable to command himself, or like Lepidus with the sceptre in his hand sleeps off his drunken debauches, or dreaming of the crocodiles of Egypt, or, like Sextus Pompeius hopes by a sentiment to leap at once into the empire of the world,—must keep aloof from the machinery of the history, or else it will but draw him in to crush him to pieces. This well-known but widely neglected lesson, which all history, and all historical dramas, loudly proclaim, pervades every part of *Antony and Cleopatra* as its leading and fundamental idea. History is here . . . depicted in its unlimited power; but at the same time we are taught that even because it is thus despotic, it requires of the ministers of its development that they should be men energetic of will and deed, and above all else, moderate, forecasting, and self-possessed.

The same theme is re-echoed in the fall of Ænobarbus and Fulvia. In their lives and characters they stand in the same relation to Octavia, Mecænas, and Agrippa, as Antony does to Octavius. But Cleopatra, the spotted and slimy "serpent of old Nile" [I. v. 25]—the representative of a corrupt oriental luxury, which has already made its inroads on the Roman world—raised so high by her grace and beauty, her talents and her wit—so womanish and yet so unwomanly—she who clothes all her inmost purposes, and yet thinks with mere outward clothing, with paint and spangles, to cheat history—she pays the penalty of her temerity which hurried her out of the nursery and boudoir into the council-chamber, and into the midst of wars and battles. With all her shrewdness and cunning, she is as little possessed of true prudence as of moderation, and all her machinations are frustrated by the cool, calculating Octavius. Before the tribunal of history he gains his cause, simply because he has more of intrinsic moral rectitude on his side. He is no doubt ambitious and greedy of power, but so also are his opponents. The moderation, however, which he alone possesses is the first principle of virtue, since in its truth it involves self-control. And because history, in its ultimate end reaches far beyond this earthly existence, it demands of man before all things the controul of himself, in order that when he shall have

stripped off his earthly body, he may be fit and able to live in another and better world.

And yet how poor does Octavius appear in this his meagre virtue, and which, when he employs it for the sole purpose of his own earthly aggrandizement, sinks at once into mere worldly cunning. In his character, as laid open to us by Shakespeare, we already read the whole story of his long unworthy life—those arts of the actor—the tacks and doubles with which he sought to steer in safety, through the troubled waves of the times, the ship of state freighted with the precious burthen of his own ascendancy. Like history, true poetry exhibits the future in the present; while it paints the earthly success which accompanies historical justice, it yet lays bare the foul worm-eaten kernel of such prosperity, when in its motives and feelings it rises not above earth. The real victory, therefore, rests neither with Antony nor with Augustus: tried by a higher standard, both alike are in the wrong. But the degraded Roman people could no longer endure sterling justice and truth. The great and noble-minded Julius falls to make room for the little and mean-spirited Augustus. Such is the tragic fate of man, to which his own sinfulness has doomed him, and out of which God's grace alone can deliver him. In this, therefore, as in all his other pieces, the ground-idea of the single drama thus rises to the universal historical view of the world itself. (pp. 357-59)

Hermann Ulrici, "Histories: 'Antony and Cleopatra'," in his Shakespeare's Dramatic Art: And His Relation to Calderon and Goethe, *translated by A. J. W. Morrison, Chapman, Brothers, 1846, pp. 357-59.*

HARTLEY COLERIDGE   (essay date 1849?)

[*Hartley Coleridge, the eldest son of Samuel Taylor Coleridge, was a minor English poet and essayist. The following excerpt is taken from a collection of his poems, criticism, and marginal notations assembled by his brother Derwent after Hartley's death in 1849 and published as* Essays and Marginalia *(1851). Coleridge argues that there are too many episodes of only tangential interest in* Antony and Cleopatra *and that the progress of the dramatic action is impeded by the profusion of short scenes. He also suggests that, while the play's language and characterization are masterful, our response to Antony and Cleopatra themselves is ambivalent, for they are "too heroic to be pitied for weakness and too viciously foolish to be admired for their heroism."*]

The general neglect of "Antony and Cleopatra" by all but students of Shakspeare, and the preference long given to Dryden's play on the same subject, prove the danger of protracting the interest of a plot, in order to introduce a greater variety of incidents. The scenes, for example, wherein Pompey figures, though well-written, are wholly inconclusive; they form a part of the biography of Antony, not of his tragedy. Nor is it easy to conjecture Shakspeare's reason for introducing so many short scenes, which serve no purpose but to let the auditor know the news. They form a sort of back-ground to the picture, but they detain the action. For poetry and character, there are few dramas superior; nor is there any want of deep and grand pathos; but perhaps both Antony and Cleopatra are too heroic to be pitied for weakness, and too viciously foolish to be admired for their heroism. Seldom has unlawful love been rendered so interesting; but the interest, though not dangerous, is not perfectly agreeable.

I'll set a bourne how far to be beloved.

[I. i. 16]

If Antony owed to Cleopatra the loss of empire, he is indebted to her for less hateful renown than would else have clung to him. Shakspeare and Dryden make the Phillipics forgotten, and the murderer of Cicero is lost in the lover of Cleopatra. (pp. 183-84)

> Hartley Coleridge, "Notes on Shakspeare: 'Antony and Cleopatra'," in his Essays and Marginalia, Vol. II, edited by Derwent Coleridge, Edward Moxon, 1851, pp. 183-84.

G. G. GERVINUS (essay date 1849-50)

[One of the most widely read Shakespearean critics of the latter half of the nineteenth century, the German critic Gervinus was praised by such eminent contemporaries as Edward Dowden, F. J. Furnivall, and James Russell Lowell; however, he is little known in the English-speaking world today. Like his predecessor Hermann Ulrici, Gervinus wrote in the tradition of the "philosophical criticism" developed in Germany in the mid-nineteenth century. Under the influence of August Wilhelm Schlegel's literary theory and Georg Wilhelm Friedrich Hegel's philosophy, such German critics as Gervinus tended to focus their analyses around a search for the literary work's organic unity and ethical import. Gervinus believed that Shakespeare's work contained a rational ethical system independent of any religion—in contrast to Ulrici, for whom Shakespeare's morality was basically Christian. The following excerpt is reprinted from an English translation of his Shakespeare, first published in German in 1849-50. Gervinus contends that the conflict between the world of action and politics, on the one hand, and "the calm sensual life of enjoyment," on the other, is the principal thematic idea in Antony and Cleopatra. Antony possesses the potential for political greatness, the critic argues, but as a result of choosing Cleopatra's "intoxication of delight" over "the sober communion of rule with Octavius" he becomes a figure of "splendid nothingness." Gervinus further maintains that Antony's desertion of Octavia marks "the tragic turning point of his fortune," because in this one act he becomes guilty of both moral and political profligacy. The critic also finds fault with the play on several points, asserting that Shakespeare: one, impaired the clarity of the play's dramatic vision by focusing too much interest on the relationship between Antony and Cleopatra in what is ostensibly a historical drama; two, provided in this work "no great and noble character" of ethical excellence to "comfort and elevate us amid so much degradation"; three, erred in his choice of a "morally repulsive" subject; and four, destroyed the structural continuity by "too numerous and too discordant interruptions."]

Coleridge . . . placed Antony in the highest class of Shakespeare's writings [see excerpt above, 1813-34]. He considered this play as a powerful rival to Lear and all the best dramas of our poet; he saw in it a gigantic power in its ripest prime, and contrasted it with Romeo and Juliet, because here the love of lust and passion is depicted, as there that of inclination and instinct. Among the historical plays of Shakespeare he declared it to be by far the most remarkable. This judgment, however, will not have found much support; we will try to place it in a more just and striking light. It is true this play is full and rich; we can scarcely name another like it in these respects. The diction is very forced, often short and obscure; the crowd of matter creates a crowd of ideas; important affairs are disposed of in a few sentences, great events recorded in a few words, historical names and references presumed to be known are left unexplained in the play itself. . . . A wanton multiplicity of incidents and personages pass before our eyes; political and warlike occurrences run parallel with the most intimate affairs of domestic life and of the affections; the interest is fettered to the passion of a single pair, and yet the scene of it is the wide world from Parthia to Cape Misenum. For the historical character this is indeed highly expressive and striking, but it does no little damage to the dramatic clearness. Therefore it is that, perhaps, no play of Shakespeare's is so difficult to retain in the memory as this. With this one other cause is combined, or, at least, it co-operates with it, why this drama is seldom brought on the stage, and is little admired in representation. By the too numerous and discordant interruptions, that psychical continuity is destroyed which is necessary to the development of such a remarkable connection of the innermost affections as that between Antony and Cleopatra. Let the reader think over the purport of the various historical plays of our poet; he will nowhere find the external actual material of history impregnated with a sensible or sensual connection of so much importance. Let him look over the purely psychological dramas, and nowhere will he find a connection of the affections so incessantly crossed by external public affairs of such an opposite nature. This contrast is closely and profoundly connected with the plan and idea of the play. If Goethe understood the matter rightly when he said, 'Here everything declares with a thousand tongues that enjoyment and activity exclude one another' [in his "Shakespeare ad Infinitum"], we then perceive that the poet felt it incumbent on him to show the contradiction between the excited, busy, historical world, and the calm, sensual life of enjoyment. The way in which he understood, and, as it were, explained the given history, deserves the highest praise of Coleridge and all others; it is a master-work full of deep thought, from which every writer of history may learn to extract the spirit out of chronicles. But whether the theme, æsthetically considered, might not have been better carried out, whether large dramatic groups might not have been cut out of the complete history, which would have better satisfied the Aristotelian requirement of being easily surveyed as a whole, whether many of the inferior characters unnecessary to the aim of the play might not have been omitted, and all the acting personages thus concentrated upon the main point of the piece after Shakespeare's usual method—this remains a subject of doubt much easier for us to express than it could have been for the poet to remove. If, then, we are willing to subscribe to Coleridge's opinion concerning the apprehension of the historical matter and the description of character in the chief personages, we shall find it harder in an æsthetic view to rank this drama so high as he does. For there arises an ethical objection also, which will make most readers opponents to this piece and to Coleridge's opinion of it. There is no great and noble character among the personages; no really elevating feature in the actions of this drama, either in its politics or its love affairs. This play seems to evince to us how much we should lose in Shakespeare if, with his ever great knowledge of men and nature, there did not go hand in hand on one side that æsthetic excellence (the ideal concentration of the actors and actions), and on the other side that ethical excellence (the ideal elevation of the representation of manhood). The poet had to represent a debased period in Antony and Cleopatra; he did this in obedience to historical truth; but this ought not to have prevented him from casting a glance at a better state of human nature, which might comfort and elevate us amid so much degradation. If we recall to mind the historical plays in which Shakespeare had to depict for the most part degenerate and ruined races, we shall recollect that in Richard II. there was not wanting a Gaunt and a Carlisle to make amends, and even in Richard III. the few strokes that described the sons of Edward are an agreeable compensation for the universal wickedness. Here, however, there is nothing of the kind, and we may even say the opportunity for such a counterbalance has been obviously neglected. It would surely have been easy, in the character of Octavia at least, to keep in view before us some higher human nature, which by a few traits only might have *exhibited* her to us in action, such as she now is merely spoken of in words. (pp. 723-25)

As regards what is morally repulsive in *Antony and Cleopatra,* it is only fair to confess that if an error has been committed it is evidently in the choice of the subject; and that the poet, being unwilling to alter historical truth, has done all he could, nay, perhaps too much, to ennoble the matter, and to make it worthy of a place in the realm of poetry. . . . We might imagine he had put the characters of Antony and Cleopatra in a better light than he ought to have done, and clothed the voluptuaries with a certain lofty splendour, as if betraying a preference for them. But what he did in this respect was done undoubtedly for æsthetic purposes, and not from lightness of morality. If Shakespeare had taken Antony exactly as he found him in Plutarch, he would never have been able to give him a tragic character, he could never have excited an interest in him precisely in his relations with Cleopatra. A man who had grown up in the wild companionship of a Curio and a Clodius, who had gone through the high school of debauchery in Greece and Asia, who had shocked everybody in Rome under Cæsar's dictatorship by his vulgar conduct, who had made himself popular among the soldiers by drinking and encouraging their low amours, a man upon whom the hatred of the proscriptions under the rule of the triumvirate especially fell, who displayed a cannibal pleasure over Cicero's bloody head and hand, who afterwards renewed in the East the wanton life of his youth, and robbed in grand style to maintain the vilest brood of parasites and jugglers—such a man, depicted finally as the prey of an old and artful courtesan, could not possibly have been made an object of dramatic interest. It is wonderful how Shakespeare preserved the historical features of Antony's character so as on the one side not to make him unrecognisable, and yet how he contrived on the other hand to render him an attractive personage.

We are inclined to designate the ennobling transformation which the poet undertook by one word; he refined the rough features of Mark Antony into the character of an Alcibiades. He passes silently over the youth of his hero, he took from him his tendency to cruelty, covered the misdeeds of the triumvirate with a veil, showed only the best side of his rapacity and lavish prodigality, spoke loudly of his warlike past, his victory over Brutus and Cassius, his heroic endurance of hunger and want after his defeat at Modena, and strove especially to make his hero interesting on the score of brilliant natural gifts. It is not to be disputed that Shakespeare, by these touches, brought out the most attractive side of Antony. Even in the voluptuary and the profligate there is an alluring charm in the ready versatility, the natural superiority, the variety of talent, the abundance of resources, and in the natural aptness to fill any part. (pp. 726-28)

It is sufficiently evident how well fitted was a man so gifted as Antony to be placed in the great conflict between activity and enjoyment, between the government of the world, and the being governed by a common, but powerful passion. If the active power conquers in such a nature, in such a position, the result will be an Alexandrian gift of political organisation, impulsion, and new creation in all the ramifications of life, a ready understanding and furtherance of the most manifold arrangements of all practical and theoretical matters. If such a nature turns to laxness and repose, there will then be the most extraordinary waste of external and internal riches on the mea-

nest gratifications; a master of enjoyment will be formed; because that many-sidedness will now be displayed in the art of varying pleasures and spicing them with ever new ingenuity. Now, with regard to the active power of Antony, we [may see], in *Julius Cæsar,* the proofs of his diplomatic skill, demagogic eloquence, and warlike readiness. In this sphere of life, however, he was placed beside a man, the young Octavius, who even then treated him, the elder in politics and war, with haughtiness; in whose vicinity his genius (that is, the practical, actively disposed part of his genius) felt itself oppressed, and before whom his courage, his nobility, his magnanimity, bowed, although unwillingly. An inward misgiving warned the more profound Julius Cæsar against Cassius; it needed a soothsayer to warn this superficial being against Octavius; as Caesar in his pride disclaims fear, so Antony pays no attention to the loud voice within him, when his presumption and self-conceit return, as soon as he is absent from Octavius. With regard, on the other side, to the repose and love of enjoyment in Antony, we find him, at the very beginning of our play, at the court of Cleopatra entangled in voluptuousness and luxury, and we have an opportunity of observing how he moves in this sphere. We see him placed beside a woman who, in contrast to the sober communion of rule with Octavius, offered him an intoxication of delight, who rivalled him in the rarest attractions and perfections, in whose society his genius (of course that part of his genius devoted to enjoyment) felt itself stimulated and shook its wings. If originally Antony's activity and laxness, 'his taints and honours,' as Mæcenas said at his death, 'waged equal with him' [V. i. 30-1], this connection alone would have given preponderance to the bad side.

We will leave it undetermined whether Shakespeare himself asserted this original balance of opposite gifts in Antony; from his words it might seem that he did; from the facts the preponderance seems everywhere on the weak side. From the beginning, even in *Julius Caesar,* we see him everywhere needing a prop, a supporter, never able to stand alone. . . . His imitation of Hercules or Bacchus refers to this trait; he leans against a tutelar god, who, according to Shakespeare and to Plutarch, turns from him when he is to perish. With a nature thus ever needing support, he encounters this paragon of female weakness, Cleopatra, like ivy leaning on ivy. He knows her nature, and is aware that it can yield him no support but he is soon so entwined by the parasitical plant—his senses, his inclinations, his humours are so entangled—that he, who should sustain the world as 'a triple pillar' [I. i. 12], loses his own strength, nay, even the inclination to seek a *firm* support, and soon sinks together with the creeping plant upon the ground, and with the woman he becomes a woman. (pp. 729-30)

At the commencement of our play, Antony is balancing between his political vocation and his joy in Egypt; but his inclination is already perfectly decided. It is a torment to him to hear of Rome, he neglects the messages of Octavius; for all that he cares 'Rome may in Tiber melt, and the wide arch of the rang'd empire may fall;—here is his space' [I. i. 33-4]. But he neglected the messengers of Octavius only from a passing emotion of shame, because Cleopatra taunted him with his subjection to Octavius; he then makes amends for his fault in diplomatic style without derogating from his dignity. The news from Rome arouses him. His wife Fulvia had taken the heroic step of stirring up a war against Octavius to force him out of his Eastern bondage; she played the man whilst he played the woman; in Asia, Parthia was lost through his indolence; a new rival for the world's dominion was rising up in Sextus Pompeius. Antony hears this heavy news with composure and tranquillity; he still has feelings of shame and honour, and an abhorrence of disgrace; he still retains enough ambition to assert himself in the triumvirate with Octavius against the new rival; he rouses himself to break Cleopatra's chains, that he may not be quite lost in the delirium of love. . . . Antony arms himself against Cleopatra's attacks and her artifices; he calmly explains his affairs to her; he shows that he also has not forgotten his old art of persuasion, he uses the death of Fulvia to make his going away easier and less suspicious. The call of honour and manly resolution so far triumphs that he actually goes, to the astonishment of Pompey, who had expected that his voluptuous life would be his ruin. And Antony really was so entangled already, that he departs with the promise to make all his plans dependent upon *her; she* is to decide for peace or war. He sends a message to assure her that he will lay the whole of the East at her feet; and whilst the statesmanlike Octavius receives news every hour concerning the state of the political world, Antony establishes a chain of daily messages to Cleopatra in Egypt. The impression is that he goes away only to pacify the storm of disturbances, and to make way for the peaceful enjoyment of his pleasures in the East; as if his inroad into the world of action were only to ensure for him the world of enjoyment. And this is confirmed by the whole course of his affairs in the West.

The scene of his conference with Octavius (Act. ii. sc. 2) is excellently managed. . . . Plutarch's declaration that Antony's genius always bowed to that of Octavius could not be evidenced more finely than it is here. The attempt of the former to assert his dignity and equality is evident throughout, yet he entirely submits in the material points of the transaction; he confesses the point in dispute and 'plays the penitent' [II. ii. 92], although in a reserved manner; by this confession he will do no prejudice to his 'greatness,' and he calls his confessions by the more honourable name of 'honesty;' gladly and without objection he falls in with the highly critical offer of Octavius' sister in marriage. In all this he is not premeditatedly false and deceitful, any more than when in the presence of Brutus he stood with deep emotion over Caesar's corpse; then he acted with involuntary tact, cleverly and boldly, according to the state of things; here, in presence of his all-powerful rival, he acts also, but not with tact, not cleverly, not boldly, but over-mastered by yielding weakness. And here there was no honourable motive for his acting a part, as his undissembled love for Caesar had impelled him then—here there was only a longing to return to his coquettish friend in Egypt. His blunt follower Enobarbus, whose plain truths Antony bears in private but will not listen to before others, who follows everywhere the deep dissembler, the hypocrite disguised even to himself, this man discovers immediately that this peace is only patched up for a time, until the two triumvirs have got rid of Pompey; he perceives as clearly that Antony has only married Octavia for the sake of his interest, that this marriage will not loosen his connection with Cleopatra, but will be 'the very strangler of his amity' [II. vi. 121-22] with the Cæsarian family. Antony himself makes the blunt confession that he only concluded this marriage for the sake of peace and tranquillity; his pleasure lies in Egypt. He had snatched himself thence in an effervescence of honourable feeling; but it was only an apparent victory over his passion. The relapse is all the more shocking, and the dissolution of his remaining strength the more certain and paralysing now that an evil conscience reproaches him for the flagitious conduct with which he breaks the ties of friendship and marriage, formed under the mask of repentance and honour.

He picks a quarrel with Octavius; he sends his sister, whose heart is painfully divided between husband and brother, coldly

and heartlessly to Rome; deludes her with intentional falsehood, and dismisses her with the venomous words, 'Let your best love draw to that point which seeks best to preserve it' [III. iv. 21-2]. Not to him, therefore, who hastens, as soon as she has left him, back to Egypt! With extraordinary thoughtlessness he makes himself guilty of deceit, perjury, and adultery, thus offending his powerful rival; nay, he even attacks the honour of the state and of the gods. He places his children with Cleopatra as monarchs in Egypt, and bestows upon them the kingdoms of the East; sitting publicly beside Cleopatra, in the habiliments of the goddess Isis, criminally sporting with everything sacred.

Here then is the tragic turning point of his fortune; here vengeance overtakes him. The very means by which he hoped to secure peace caused discord and led to his fall. Warned in vain by Octavius, he made 'the cement' of their new love 'the ram to batter the fortress of it' [III. ii. 30-1]. A double profligacy, a moral and a political one, lay at this turning point in this political marriage and its results, and it drew down upon Antony his fate. The political profligacy belongs to the intellectual idea of the play, and consequently a greater emphasis is laid upon it. If Antony (and it is his rival who makes this remark) incurred moral responsibility alone, if he 'only filled his vacancy with his voluptuousness,' the natural consequences would 'call on him for it;' but to 'confound such time' and his high calling makes him deserve

> to be chid
> As we rate boys; who, being mature in knowledge,
> Pawn their experience to their present pleasure,
> And so rebel to judgment.
> [I. iv. 25-6, 28, 30-3]

In these words the emphasis is laid chiefly on Antony's political sins, and the contrast aimed at between the active life of the world and the corrupt seeking for enjoyment is brought out strongly. . . . The poet makes political ruin follow closely on Antony's political crime; immediately, stroke upon stroke. Octavius gets rid of Lepidus and Pompey, and suddenly appears as an all-powerful adversary before the helpless Antony, who has no one to fight on his side but the coquettish woman. She 'takes,' as Enobarbus says, 'from his heart, from his brain, and from his time, what should not then be spared' [III. vii. 11-12]; crime and presumption ruin his understanding; his want of understanding ruins his fortune; he offers single combat and a battle on land to Octavius at Pharsalia, which Octavius prudently declines; and he foolishly accepts Octavius' challenge to a sea-fight, in which his talents did not lie, and from which all skilful warriors endeavour to dissuade him: all but Cleopatra, who flees while the fight is still undecided, and whom he 'like a doting mallard' [III. x. 19] follows. Experience, manhood, honour, never were so shamefully violated as here; 'the greater cantle of the world is lost, with very ignorance' [III. x. 6-7]; kingdoms and provinces are 'kissed away!' Thus the warriors think, who desert from Antony. He himself is so altered by shame that he fancies the very earth is ashamed to bear him.

And yet, in this degradation, he thinks a tear of Cleopatra's 'rates all that is won and lost' [III. xi. 69-70]; a kiss would repay him for everything. He now would be content if Octavius would 'let him breathe . . . a private man in Athens' [III. xii. 14-15]. But his enjoyment and repose are to be embittered not only in the disputes of the world, but in their very spring. Military glory and dominion were lost in the battle of Actium; in Egypt the last traces of equanimity and the shadow of his fortune with Cleopatra are to disappear. We return, therefore, in the last two acts, exclusively to the personal relations between these two, in which, under all the varnish of happiness, there was from the beginning a dark tinge of dissatisfaction, through all their harmony a creeping discord, through all their love mistrust and suspicion, in all their idleness 'sweating labour,' and in all their enjoyments a root of discontent. And this for the simple reason that in spite of all the ornament of exterior grace and the evident arts of pleasing, that inner adornment and worth of character was lacking, on which alone true love, true fidelity, and true happiness can be founded. Great princes before Antony had trembled, 'kissing' the charming hand of Cleopatra; Cæsar had been in her toils; Pompey had looked into her eyes. Antony knew this. She had angled for him with cunning skill in her declining days; he knew her to be artful beyond men's thoughts, and called her his 'serpent,' but he had allowed her to enchant him, and to vanquish him, well knowing that he too was a conqueror in that warfare. So she knows him too to be infirm of purpose, and a deep dissembler; she knows he did not love Fulvia, and, therefore, does not trust in his love for herself; she wished to separate him from his lawful spouse, and when the first is dead he takes a second. If on one side he is 'painted like a Mars' to her, 't'other way he's a Gorgon' [II. v. 117, 116]. Thus they both know each other to be unworthy of confidence, and yet they trust each other and then find reason for upbraidings; they know of each other that faithlessness and changeableness are natural to them, but they entangle each other more and more with the tendrils of their passion, in order that, though faithless to others, they may be the more true to one another; in the hour of trial, however, they have no faith in each other. The very trouble which they take to fix what they know to be untrue incites them mutually to raise their fidelity even to passionateness and frightful jealousy, in which they again nourish suspicion against each other's truth. The poet has woven a wonderful psychological web out of this rare and yet most natural contradiction, and there is great art and knowledge in the manner in which he displays how the passion of both increases by this ever-recurring mistrust; how they ennoble an ignoble connection by this straining and strengthening of their fidelity, how their personal nobleness sometimes rises and sometimes sinks by it, and how, when they make the greatest sacrifice in their unblessed union, it drags them down to destruction. (pp. 732-37)

The death of both is, according to the opinion of their enemies, the best in them. Nevertheless, we cannot dwell upon it with elevated feelings. The fate of Brutus has revengingly befallen Antony; he utters many lofty words about his design, a Roman vanquished by a Roman; his page is to slay him like Brutus, and the boy prefers falling on his own sword, *without one word,* thus showing himself 'thrice nobler' than he who now must kill himself, and strikes with no certain aim. In like manner Iras precedes her mistress, setting the example of self-destruction, an action by which Cleopatra also finds herself shamed. Her death, like her love, her jealousy, her life, is notoriously studied, calculated, prepared, planned; even the separation from life made an enjoyment; painlessly the asp sucks her breast, as a babe 'that sucks the nurse asleep' [V. ii. 310]. Charmian emulates her in this 'noble weakness,' when she, already poisoned, tremblingly stood trimming up the diadem on her dead mistress.

In this our exposition of the issue of the pair, according to the play, everyone must be aware that the strictest justice is satisfied in the events. According to the expressions it might

indeed appear as if too much light were cast upon Antony; as if the aesthetic object of elevating somewhat the principal character had led to a conflict with the ethical truth. We might imagine that Shakespeare, in laying the foundation of this character, had, contrary to his usual view of life, laid too much stress upon the passive being and natural disposition of man, instead of on activity, on the man in motion, and on the use of innate gifts, since it sometimes seems as if Antony's hereditary good qualities were to be reckoned as meritorious virtues, while his evil ones on the contrary were designated as pardonable weaknesses. It is necessary, therefore, for us to observe in whose mouth the various opinions concerning him are placed. We shall certainly not listen to Cleopatra, when she sees him stride over land and sea like a god, when she praises his power, his goodness, and above all his bounty, and when she says that of him which is the most evident untruth, that his delights in which he perished like dolphins showed their backs above the element they lived in. The weak Lepidus, who made the best of everything, says of him that 'there are not evils enough to darken all his goodness' [I. iv. 10-11]. At his death, at the moment when even his conqueror Octavius is touched, the noble enemies Maecenas and Aggrippa express this mild judgment:—

> His taints and honours
> Waged equal with him. A rarer spirit never
> Did steer humanity: but you, gods, will give us
> Some faults to make us men.
>
> [V. i. 30-3]

Antony's sub-officers, among them Ventidius, designate the weaknesses of his petty ambition, and spare him. Others of his soldiers, like Philo, mention unreservedly the disgraceful situation of the triumvir, who has become the fool and the paramour of the gipsy. Pompey expects and wishes that

> Sleep and feeding may prorogue his honour,
> Even till a Lethe'd dulness.
>
> [II. i. 26-7]

One of his dependants, Canidius, deserts him early; the other, Enobarbus, does not leave him until his tutelar god has forsaken him; the third, Eros, is true to him until death. Thus this man of many sides and many meanings makes a different impression upon everyone; it may be asked on whom he makes the most correct one. His enemy Octavius, who knows him best, does not judge him worst. He speaks of him as 'the abstract of all faults that all men follow' [I. iv. 22]; he accepts unwillingly but yieldingly that praise of Antony, that everything becomes him; that man's 'composure must be rare indeed' whom the low pleasures to which he was addicted could not blemish. He glances disapprovingly but forbearingly at the moral shadows that fall upon him. But he finds his whole conduct unpardonable when he looks upon his political vocation. If this lays open to us the main point of view in reference to Antony, in so far as we see him in relation to his position in the world, Antony himself, on the other hand, furnishes in a remarkable manner the ultimatum concerning his personality, his character in itself; and in this we must recognise the poet's own judgment upon him. And this was surprisingly well comprehended in a nature not inaccessible to truth, which assumed involuntarily a dissembling exterior, and consequently appeared different to different people; a nature which equally involuntarily received glimpses of knowledge from without, and unintentionally displayed the result of this self-knowledge in various situations. In the first scene (Act I.) in his intoxication he uttered the opinion that refinement in the pleasures of love made the sole difference between man and beast; in the second scene, when he has come to himself and has been 'eared' by bad news from Rome, he utters on the contrary what strongly condemns his pleasures; 'we bring forth weeds when our quiet winds lie still' [I. ii. 109-10]. When he has trifled away his fortune, and lost all the healthy tact and instinct of action which was once peculiar to him, he indicates in his rage against Cleopatra his wretched fall by these bitter words:—

When we in our viciousness grow hard,
(O misery on't) the wise gods seal our eyes;
In our own filth drop our clear judgments; make us
Adore our errors; laugh at us, while we strut
To our confusion.

[III. xiii. 111-15]

And at last, just before his death, looking upon his situation, he compares it with the evening clouds, which deceive the eye first with one shape, then another, and then vanish into nothing. And by nothing more striking than this poetical image could the poet, in full accordance with Plutarch, comprise his judgment respecting the whole life of this man, who astonished and deceived the world with his splendid nothingness, with his seeming greatness and seeming nobleness, in a thousand changing forms. (pp. 739-41)

> G. G. Gervinus, "Third Period of Shakespeare's Dramatic Poetry: 'Antony and Cleopatra'," in his Shakespeare Commentaries, translated by F. E. Bunnètt, revised edition, 1877. Reprint by AMS Press, Inc., 1971, pp. 722-45.

VICTOR HUGO (essay date 1859-66)

[Hugo was the leading poet and novelist of French Romanticism. In his study William Shakespeare, first published in 1864, he groups Shakespeare with such other "immovable giants of the human mind" as Aeschylus, Juvenal, Dante, and Cervantes and regards the poet as a genius who explored the limits of human experience. Hugo was also interested in Shakespeare's use of the supernatural; he claimed that the dramatist "believed profoundly in the mystery of things." From 1859 to 1866 Hugo published an eighteen-volume translation into French of the complete works of Shakespeare, prefacing each volume with an introductory essay. The excerpt below is from his introduction to Antoine et Cléopatre, which appeared in volume seven. Hugo asserts that Cleopatra's love for Antony is constant and genuine, transforming her in the eyes of the audience. In a triumph of dramatic artistry, he argues, Shakespeare has redirected the sympathy we would ordinarily extend to Octavia to a figure whom he unequivocally characterizes as a strumpet. Hugo also argues that the union of Antony and Cleopatra is portrayed as legitimized—even sanctified—by the intensity of their passion for each other.]

Shakespeare for ever brings back the interest to [the] sovereign figure which gives to [Antony and Cleopatra] its unity. Present or absent, Cleopatra pervades the entire drama. Even at the feast which the young Pompey spreads for the Triumvirs aboard his galley, even at that monstrous orgy where wine turns the head of the noblest, where Lepidus rolls under the table, where Antony staggers and where Caesar stammers, it is Cleopatra who, unperceived, presides. Cleopatra is the fatal enchantress who initiated Rome into the startling mysteries of oriental voluptuousness. She is the invisible sorceress who sweeps the masters of the globe into the dizzy whirl of an Egyptian bacchanal. . . . Cleopatra is the supreme type of seduction. The spell which she weaves is the greatest triumph of feminine magic. Her sisters, the other heroines of Shakespeare, attract us only by their virtues and by their qualities; she, she enchants

us by her very faults, her very weaknesses. . . . Fully assured of the irresistible charm of his heroine, the poet does not, for a single instant, suffer us to be under any illusion. From the very beginning of the drama, at the moment when she enters on the arm of her lover, he tells us what she is with the utmost frankness. 'Look,' he cries, 'and you shall see in him The triple pillar of the world transform'd 'Into a strumpet's fool' [I. i. 11-13]. Away with reticence, away with ambiguity! Shakespeare has neither the timidity of Corneille nor that of Dryden; he does not evade the subject, he faces it full front. He does not deny his heroine, he proclaims her. It is a 'strumpet' that he installs on the scene; it is to a 'strumpet' that he attracts our interest; it is for a 'strumpet' that he demands our pity; it is for the death of a 'strumpet' and her lover that he exacts our tears. Omnipotence of genius! In this drama, where an outraged wife reclaims her rights from a courtesan, it is not the wife who enlists our sympathy, it is the courtesan! She whom we compassionate, is not Octavia, the austere, the chaste; it is this light o' love whom Antony had found as a 'morsel cold upon dead Caesar's trencher' [III. xiii. 116-17]. But by what means has the poet been enabled to produce such a change in the consciences of the spectators, and to concentrate on Cleopatra all the sympathy that should be due to Octavia? To work this miracle Shakespeare needed to tell nothing but the truth; he had merely to reveal to us the profound sentiment which inspired his heroine. Cleopatra had in her heart the flame that purifies everything: she loves. It is by love that the royal courtesan stands revealed; it is by love that she is rehabilitated. Ay, this Antony whom she teases, whom she torments, whom she maddens, this Antony whom at one moment she abjures and unscrupulously deceives with Thyreus, she loves him, she loves him to distraction. Do you doubt? Listen. The minute that Antony is absent, Cleopatra is utterly desolate. She thinks only of him, she speaks only of him; she intoxicates herself with mandragora to sleep out the great gap of his absence. (pp. 497-98)

In Plutarch Antony lives long with Octavia, in Shakespeare the marriage was a mere formality. Who does not see in this perversion of history, by the hand of genius, a feature of exquisite delicacy? The poet would not suffer his hero to be for a single instant unfaithful to his heroine; he has not permitted a single treason, even if legalised, to profane this sanctified adultery. To Shakespeare, the union of Antony and Octavia was never aught else than an ephemeral bargain arranged by policy; but his union with Cleopatra is an everlasting compact, sealed by devotion. Thus the poet does not hesitate to sacrifice the first to the second. In his eyes, that which sanctifies the relations between man and woman is less social convention than the natural law. Let two beings love each other, let them live the one for the other, that is sufficient; they are affianced for ever, all other engagements to the contrary notwithstanding. In the eyes of posterity, as in Shakespeare's, the spouse of Antony is no longer Octavia, it is Cleopatra. The intensity of the passion is its legitimacy. (p. 498)

> Victor Hugo, in an essay, translated by Horace Howard Furness, in A New Variorum Edition of Shakespeare: The Tragedie of Anthonie, and Cleopatra, edited by Horace Howard Furness, J. B. Lippincott Company, 1907, pp. 496-99.

J. A. HERAUD (essay date 1865)

[Heraud was an English poet, dramatist, and journalist. The following excerpt is taken from his Shakspere, his Inner Life as intimated in his Works *(1865). Heraud is the earliest commentator to propose that Antony and Cleopatra are superhuman figures— not merely persons of superior rank, but "the very deities of love." Not only do they view each other this way, he contends, but Shakespeare shared their perspective and intended that they not be held accountable to ordinary standards of conduct. Thus, Heraud maintains, there can be no question of their being guilty of violating moral laws, for they "absolutely transcend all relative conventions."]*

In closing his cycle of Roman plays, Shakspere's ambition manifested itself in the highest form. His intellectual energies had already blended with and modified his imaginative, his passionate, and his creative power and impulses; but they were now to be identified at the acme of their manifestations, in his sublime and wonderful tragedy of *Antony and Cleopatra.* We have already witnessed the poet looking down, as a superior intelligence, on the loves of *Troilus and Cressida,* and sporting as an equal with those of *Venus and Adonis.* We have now to see him identify himself with two mortals at the height of fortune, who, in a species of heroic madness, had conceived themselves to be in the position of Divine Powers, exempt from all laws except that of their own wills. This is the elevation at which Shakespere sustains his argument, and thus prevents it from becoming immoral, as it does in the hands of Dryden, who paints his heroine and hero as mere human persons, of great rank indeed, indulging in voluptuous and licentious habits. No notion of guilt attaches to the conduct of Shakspere's *Antony and Cleopatra* either in the poet's opinion or their own. They absolutely transcend all relative conventions, all possible forms of manners. They consciously acknowledge, and therefore transgress, no law. They live in an ideal region, far above the reach of a moral code, and justify their acts on the warranty of their own nature. They swear by and recognise no higher power than themselves. That this is a false position there is no doubt; and the poet, by the catastrophe of his tragedy shows it to have been such. But while the divine revels last, the actors in them fully believe that they are the divinities whom they would represent. Antony and Cleopatra surrender themselves without reserve to the inspirations with which they are filled, and are no less in their own estimation than the very deities of love. They suffer no vulgar criticism, no every-day cares, to come near them, and hold themselves aloof from the customary and the common. They sit on thrones outside the circle of the round globe, and repose on couches which float in air-like clouds, and never touch the surface of the planet. . . . There is a poetic valour as well as a personal one, and it required a brave poet to conceive and execute such a design. With a happy audacity, Shakspere rises from the beginning to the height of his theme. The love of his heroic pair, they assume to be boundless. To set a bourne to it, would require the discovery of a new heaven, new earth. The manner in which Antony suffers the imperial Egyptian to overbear his very manhood shows at any rate that his is without limits. No consideration or interest, however solemn or serious, can prevent its extension. (pp. 480-81)

J. A. Heraud, in an essay in A New Variorum Edition of Shakespeare: The Tragedie of Anthonie, and Cleopatra, *edited by Horace Howard Furness, J. B. Lippincott Company, 1907, pp. 480-81.*

PAUL HEYSE (essay date 1867)

[*A German poet, dramatist, and novelist, Heyse was an important member of the Munich group of mid-nineteenth-century poets who actively opposed the beginnings of realism and naturalism in German literature. He was awarded the Nobel Prize in Literature in 1910. The following excerpt is taken from his introduction to Friedrich Bodenstedt's edition of* Antonius and Kleopatra, *published in 1867. Although Heyse describes Cleopatra as "the very greatest masterpiece of female characterisation," he doubts whether any actress could incarnate that mystifying power of her love necessary to convince an audience that Antony is justifiably indifferent to "the gain or loss of a hemisphere in comparison with separation from his enchantment." The critic maintains that unless we can wholly believe in the incomparable magnetism of Cleopatra, Antony loses "all claim to any tragic sympathy." Heyse, however, also argues that even though Antony is guilty of the sin of self-indulgence, by his warmth and vigor he "overshadows the discreet, cool, [and] efficient" Octavius, and he concludes that the play is not meant to be a moralistic warning against intemperance and dissipation.*]

Two natures are here brought in contact, which, in good qualities as well as bad, are as completely complemental to each other, as their elevation is high above the average of mankind. A ruler of the universe, who has tasted to the last drop all that the world offers both of toil and of self-indulgence, meets a queen who can also say that nothing human is alien to her. Both stand at the very highest hey-day of life, and are in complete fullness of their powers. Long before reaching this point, both would have been, in modern phrase, *blasés,* had not the inexhaustible, classic life of the senses endowed each of them with eternal youth. Thus nature, by a species of necessity, binds them to each other; each beholds a recognised counterpart in the opposite sex. It is in both a final passion, which, because it is the last, blazes up with all the intensity of a first love; in a moment, it makes these two mature, world-worn beings, children again, and, with the same lightheartedness, as ever a Romeo or a Juliet, wafts them above all dangers of their time, and all duties of their station. The only difference between them and those two young lovers is that they were *conscious* of their state and had reduced their intoxicating revel to a system, and diversified their enjoyments with all the refinement of an exquisite art of living. (p. 492)

Up to [the] point [where Antony leaves Octavia and returns to Cleopatra] the general public will understand the hero, and follow his conduct with sympathy. . . . But when, at the very crisis of his fate, he leaves the naval battle because his mistress from womanish timidity sets sail and flies,—from that moment he forfeits, in the opinion of the majority, all claim to any tragic sympathy, and it is doubtful if, throughout the rest of the play, he ever quite regains it. Here is a point, where, in my opinion, the psychological problem becomes too fine, too exceptional, too deep for a dramatic performance. The conception of a woman, with a power so demoniacal that it mystifies both sense and reason . . . will rarely find on the stage an incarnation, which, even to a certain extent, will justify the hero, in holding indifferent the gain or loss of a hemisphere in comparison with separation from his enchantress. When we can be brought to believe in such an elemental power of this passion, then and then only can we face the shame of this hero, not with a disapproving shrug, but with that tragic shock, which the horror of every inexorable fate always awakens in us. I must deny myself the illustration by separate examples of that lavish exuberance of characteristics wherewith the hand of genius has set forth the figure of the Egyptian Queen. I honestly believe it to be the very greatest masterpiece of female characterisation; alongside of which there can be placed no more richly devised figure in the whole literature of modern romance, whereof the strength lies in psychologic analysis and vivid contrasts. With equal poetic power and depth is the character of Antony depicted to the very last; both are to be measured separately, just as both separately are overtaken by a fate so completely interwoven that the flame of passion, which transfigures them at the close with a wondrous glory, reflects its glow back to the beginning of the play and illumines many a shadow. The scholastic view, which turns Shakespeare into a conscientious moralist, above all things anxious to display, in the fate of mortals, the equipoise of guilt and expiation, appears, as it seems to me, in no single play in such embarrassing perplexity as in the presence of this tragedy; which undoubtedly preaches with a hundred tongues the lesson, in Goethe's striking words, that 'self-indulgence and achievement are incompatible' [in his "Shakespeare ad Infinitum"]. But a single principle, founded on experience, and, among others, objectively contained in a poem, cannot on that account claim to be considered the soul of the whole work. If the poet had chosen this material in order to warn the world against being fooled by self-indulgence, because it disables the power of achievement, he would have devised the development very differently. In spite of the gross stain wherewith this hero of self-indulgence, this heroic *roué*, has defiled himself, his character decidedly overshadows the discreet, cool, efficient, and, in fact, victorious rival. Extremely few readers will waver in their choice as to which they would give the preference, to the cold-blooded Cæsar or to the warm-blooded Marc Antony. And even an audience of women would not remain insensible to Cleopatra's charm. But if a majority could be really found, who, in spite of the tragic downfall, did not cease to deem the aristocratic autocracy of these natures as criminal, the minority could console themselves that they had on their own side the poet himself. There arose before him the dazzling apparition of such a pair, that 'stood up peerless' [I. i. 40], and it stimulated his creative power. Whatsoever was holy and unholy in such a tie, everything that an average morality could plead against it, was undoubtedly as ever present to him as to his critics of today. And although it may not have stood written in history, his higher comprehension and knowledge of the world taught him the inflexible law that even the most highly endowed man must succumb as soon as he 'would make his will Lord of his reason' [III. xiii. 3-4]. Shakespeare, with his incorruptible honesty, neither concealed all this, nor adorned it. Nay, there are traces of even a certain defiance in the sharp prominence given to what is hateful and mean. He allows it freely to unfold itself in sharp realistic features of every-day life. In his heart, however, he is aware that he has but to await the propitious moment to melt all this dross into an irresistible glow and refine it. He could not have been the poet that he is, the richly endowed son of Mother Nature, had he not known himself to be a blood relation to whatsoever of nobility she had brought forth. When he saw, in this pair, the powers of a luxurious life bloom forth and wither in obedience to the law of all earthly things, a tragic pain broke from his heart, which had no rest until he had adorned their grave with all the treasures of poesy, and, by the most affecting funeral ceremony, rendered their death immortal. (pp. 492-93)

> *Paul Heyse, in an essay, translated by Horace Howard Furness, in* A New Variorum Edition of Shakespeare: The Tragedie of Anthonie, and Cleopatra, *edited by Horace Howard Furness, J. B. Lippincott Company, 1907, pp. 492-93.*

KARL FRENZEL (essay date 1871)

[*Frenzel was a German journalist, novelist, and short story writer. In the excerpt below, taken from an essay which first appeared in* Berliner Dramaturgie *in May, 1871, Frenzel offers a negative appraisal of* Antony and Cleopatra. *The critic charges that the play is more narrative than dramatic and includes material and historic figures that should have been eliminated. Frenzel also judges that a large percentage of the characters' speeches are bombastic. He further castigates "the perpetual love-making of the hero and heroine," describing it as "at first comic, but at last tedious," and he styles Cleopatra as an unremittingly "quarrelsome woman," particularly disapproving of her conduct in the scenes with the messenger and her treasurer.*]

Cleopatra is of the race of Semiramis and of Zenobia, between her and Antony there is enacted not merely a love-story but a great political undertaking. Along side of the riotous festivities of Alexandria there was advancing a powerful political and social movement which was to shake the world. On this rock, of which he was only dimly conscious, rather than clearly perceiving it, Shakespeare's poetry was wrecked. It is not the continuous shifting of the scene, whereby we are chased as though by a storm from Alexandria to Rome on board of Pompey's galley, from Rome to Actium, and back to Alexandria; it is not the messengers, the servants, the guards, who necessarily, by their news, spin out the thread of the action, that break up and shatter the dramatic unity; it is the material itself, as Shakespeare has comprehended it, which has remained in the epic form of a chronicle. The poet has neither known how, out of the numberless persons, to select the most important, nor, out of the superabundance of circumstances, to eliminate the weightiest; consequently the drama lacks genuine core and deliquesces like pap. . . . In not a single instance is the contrast between Antony and Octavius sharply defined, and the perpetual love-making of the hero and heroine, which rises and falls in a monotonous alternation from tender cooing to furious execrations, is at first comic, but at last tedious. Very possibly, admirers of Shakespeare may accept it differently, but to my taste, a good third of the speeches of Antony and of Cleopatra trenches close on the bombast of the weaker tragedy of Corneille. There is no attempt at a development of character in the grand style; from the beginning to the end, Cleopatra is a quarrelsome woman, who, in the scenes with the messenger and with Seleucus, strikingly proves that, on the old English stage such *rôles* of Furies and fish-wives could have been played only by young men, for whom they were written.

> *Karl Frenzel, in an essay, translated by Horace Howard Furness, in* A New Variorum Edition of Shakespeare: The Tragedie of Anthonie, and Cleopatra, *edited by Horace Howard Furness, J. B. Lippincott Company, 1907, p. 495.*

RICHARD CHENEVIX TRENCH (essay date 1873)

[*Trench was an English poet, scholar, and theologian. In the excerpt below from* Plutarch: His Life, His "Lives" and His "Morals" *(1873), he comments upon Shakespeare's departures from his principal source in developing the character of Antony. According to Trench, the dramatist has given us an idealized Antony with only touches of the actual historical figure, ignoring the triumvir's cruelty and wickedness and glossing over his coarseness. The critic maintains that "the whole range of poetry offers no more tragical figure" than that of Antony in his degradation, and "few that arouse a deeper pity."*]

[Shakespeare's] three great Roman plays, reproducing the ancient Roman world as no other modern poetry has ever done— I refer to *Coriolanus, Julius Caesar,* and *Antony and Cleopatra*—would never have existed, or, had Shakespeare lighted by chance on these arguments, would have existed in forms altogether different from those in which they now appear, if Plutarch had not written, and Sir Thomas North, or some other in his place, had not translated. We have in Plutarch not the framework or skeleton only of the story, no, nor yet merely the ligaments and sinews, but very much also of the flesh and blood wherewith these are covered and clothed. (p. 51)

In *Antony and Cleopatra,* and in the adaptation of the story, as it lay before him in the pages of Plutarch, to the needs of his art, Shakespeare had a much harder problem to solve than any which *Julius Caesar* offered; and his solution of this problem, when we realize what it was, may well fill us with unbounded admiration. The Brutus of Plutarch was a character ready made to his hands. Here and there a melancholy grace, a touch of gentleness and of beauty has been added by him, but hardly more than this; while if in Cassius the lines are deepened and the character more sharply delineated, this is all that Shakespeare has done, even as it was all that was needed. But it was otherwise with Antony. The Antony of history, of Plutarch himself, would have been no subject for poetry. Splendidly endowed by nature as he was, it would yet have been impossible to claim or create a sympathy for one so cruel, dyed so deeply in the noblest blood of Rome, the wholesale plunderer of peaceful cities and provinces that he might squander their spoils on the vilest ministers of his pleasures; himself of orgies so shameless, sunken in such a mire of sin; in whom met the ugliest features, and what one would have counted beforehand as the irreconcilable contradictions, of an Oriental despot and a Roman gladiator. And yet, transformed, we may say transfigured by that marvellous touch, the Antony of Shakespeare, if not the veritable Antony of history, has not so broken with him as not to be recognizable still.

The play, starting from a late period of Antony's career, enables Shakespeare to leave wholly out of sight, and this with no violation of historic truth, much in the life of the triumvir which was wickedest and worst. For the rest, what was coarse is refined, what would take no colour of goodness is ignored, what had any fair side on which it could be shown is shown on that side alone. He appears from the first as not himself, but as under the spells of that potent Eastern enchantress who had once held by these spells a Caesar himself. There are followers who cleave to him in his lowest estate, even as there are fitful gleams and glimpses of generosity about him which explain this fidelity of theirs; and when at the last we behold him standing amid the wreck of fortunes and the waste of gifts, all wrecked and wasted by himself, penetrated through and through with the infinite shame and sadness of such a close to such a life, the whole range of poetry offers no more tragical figure than he is, few that arouse a deeper pity; while yet, ideal as this Antony of Shakespeare is, he is connected by innumerable subtle bands and finest touches with the real historical Antony, at once another and the same. (pp. 55-7)

> *Richard Chenevix Trench, "Plutarch's Parallel Lives," in his* Plutarch: His Life, His "Lives" and His "Morals," *Macmillan and Co., 1873, pp. 29-72.*

ALGERNON CHARLES SWINBURNE (essay date 1880)

[*Swinburne was an English poet, dramatist, and critic who devoted much of his literary career to the study of Shakespeare and other Elizabethan writers. His three books on Shakespeare—*A Study of Shakespeare *(1880),* Shakespeare *(1909), and* Three Plays of Shakespeare *(1909)—all demonstrate his keen interest in Shakespeare's poetic talents and, especially, his major tragedies. Swinburne's literary commentary is frequently conveyed in*

a style that is markedly intense and effusive. In the excerpt below, the critic descants on the incomparable nature of Shakespeare's Cleopatra, concluding that she is "the perfect and the everlasting woman."]

[The] one fit and crowning epithet for [*Antony and Cleopatra*] is that bestowed by Coleridge—"the most wonderful" [see excerpt above, 1813-34]. It would seem a sign or birthmark of only the greatest among poets that they should be sure to rise instantly for awhile above the very highest of their native height at the touch of a thought of Cleopatra. So was it, as we all know, with William Shakespeare. . . . [From] her first imperial dawn on the stage of Shakespeare to the setting of that eastern star behind a pall of undissolving cloud we feel the charm and the terror and the mystery of her absolute and royal soul. (pp. 188-89)

Never has [Shakespeare] given such proof of his incomparable instinct for abstinence from the wrong thing as well as achievement of the right. He has utterly rejected and disdained all occasion of setting her off by means of any lesser foil than all the glory of the world with all its empires. And we need not Antony's example to show us that these are less than straws in the balance. . . . Even as that Roman grasp relaxed and let fall the world, so has Shakespeare's self let go for awhile his greater world of imagination, with all its all but infinite variety of life and thought and action, for love of that more infinite

Act V. Scene ii. Iras, Charmian, Cleopatra, and Clown. Frontispiece to the Hanmer edition by Francis Hayman (1744). By permission of the Folger Shakespeare Library.

variety which custom could not stale. Himself a second and a yet more fortunate Antony, he has once more laid a world, and a world more wonderful than ever, at her feet. He has put aside for her sake all other forms and figures of womanhood; he, father or creator of Rosalind, of Cordelia, of Desdemona, and of Imogen [in *As You Like It, King Lear, Othello,* and *Cymbeline,* respectively], he too, like the sun-god and sender of all song, has anchored his eyes on her whom "Phoebus' amorous pinches" could not leave "black," nor "wrinkled deep in time" [I. v. 28-9] on that incarnate and imperishable "spirit of sense," to whom at the very last

> The stroke of death is as a lover's pinch,
> That hurts, and is desired.
>
> [V. ii. 295-96]

To him, as to the dying husband of Octavia, this creature of his own hand might have boasted herself that the loveliest and purest among all her sisters of his begetting,

> with her modest eyes
> And still conclusion, shall acquire no honour,
> Demurring upon me.
>
> [I. v. 28-9]

To sum up, Shakespeare has elsewhere given us in ideal incarnation the perfect mother, the perfect wife, the perfect daughter, the perfect mistress, or the perfect maiden: here only once for all he has given us the perfect and the everlasting woman. (pp. 189-91)

> *Algernon Charles Swinburne, "Third Period: Tragic and Romantic," in his* A Study of Shakespeare, *R. Worthington, 1880, pp. 170-227.*

EDWARD DOWDEN   (essay date 1881)

[*Dowden was an Irish critic and biographer whose* Shakspere: A Critical Study of His Mind and Art, *first published in 1875 and revised in 1881, was the leading example of the biographical criticism popular in the English-speaking world near the end of the nineteenth century. Biographical critics sought in the plays and poems a record of Shakespeare's personal development. As that approach gave way in the twentieth century to aesthetic theories with greater emphasis on the constructed, formal nature of literary works, the biographical analysis of Dowden and other critics came to be regarded as limited and often misleading. In the following excerpt, Dowden contends that although Shakespeare is not a stern moralist, the spirit of* Antony and Cleopatra *"is essentially severe," for the play depicts not only "the visible pomp of the earth, and the splendor of sensuous passion," but also the temporal limitations inherent in strength and beauty. Both* Antony and Cleopatra *are victims of their "sensuous imaginations," the critic asserts, through which they misperceive the quality of their lives together and are led to destruction. Further, Dowden argues that the reference to Hercules withdrawing his favor from Antony (IV. iii. 16-17) marks the moment at which Antony's downfall becomes irreversible. Finally, the critic judges Cleopatra's attempt to conceal a portion of her jewels from Cæsar as "right and natural" and her death as exhibiting "something dazzling and splendid, something sensuous, something theatrical, something magnificently coquettish, and nothing stern."*]

The transition from the *Julius Cæsar* of Shakspere to his *Antony and Cleopatra* produces in us the change of pulse and temper experienced in passing from a gallery of antique sculpture to a room splendid with the colors of Titian and Paul Veronese. In the characters of the *Julius Cæsar* there is a severity of outline; they impose themselves with strict authority upon the imagination; subordinated to the great spirit of Cæsar, the con-

spirators appear as figures of life-size, but they impress us as no larger than life. The demand which they make is exact; such and such tribute must be rendered by the soul to each. The characters of the *Antony and Cleopatra* insinuate themselves through the senses, trouble the blood, ensnare the imagination, invade our whole being, like color or like music. The figures dilate to proportions greater than human, and are seen through a golden haze of sensuous splendor. *Julius Cæsar* and *Antony and Cleopatra* are related as works of art rather by points of contrast than by points of resemblance. In the one an ideal of duty is dominant; the other is a divinization of pleasure followed by the remorseless Nemesis of eternal law. Brutus, the Stoic, constant, loyal to his ideas, studious of moral perfection, bent upon gaining self-mastery, unsullied and untarnished to the end, stands over against Antony, swayed hither and thither by appetites, interests, imagination, careless of his own moral being, incapable of self-control, soiled with the stains of passion and decay. And of Cleopatra what shall be said? Is she a creature of the same breed as Cato's daughter, Portia [in *Julius Cæsar*]? Does the one word woman include natures so diverse? Or is Cleopatra—Antony's "serpent of old Nile" [I. v. 25]—no mortal woman, but Lilith, who ensnared Adam before the making of Eve? Shakspere has made the one as truly woman as the other—Portia, the ideal of moral loveliness, heroic and feminine; Cleopatra, the ideal of sensual attractiveness, feminine also:

> A bliss in proof, and proved, a very woe;
> Before, a joy proposed; behind, a dream.
>
> [Sonnet 129]

We do not once see the lips of Brutus laid on Portia's lips as seal of perfect union, but we know that their beings and their lives had embraced in flawless confidence and perfect mutual service. Antony, embracing Cleopatra, exclaims,

> The nobleness of life
> Is to do thus; when such a mutual pair
> And such a twain can do't, in which I bind,
> On pain of punishment, the world to weet
> We stand up peerless.
>
> [I. i. 36-40]

Yet this "mutual pair," made each to fill the body and soul of the other with voluptuous delight, are made also each for the other's torment. Antony is haunted by suspicion that Cleopatra will betray him; he believes it possible that she could degrade herself to familiarity with Cæsar's menials. And Cleopatra is aware that she must weave her snares with endless variety, or Antony will escape.

The spirit of the play, though superficially it appear voluptuous, is essentially severe. That is to say, Shakspere is faithful to the fact. The fascination exercised by Cleopatra over Antony, and hardly less by Antony over Cleopatra, is not so much that of the senses as of the sensuous imagination. A third of the world is theirs. They have left youth behind with its slight melodious raptures and despairs. Theirs is the deeper intoxication of middle age, when death has become a reality; when the world is limited and positive; when life is urged to yield up quickly its utmost treasures of delight. What may they not achieve of joy who have power and beauty, and pomp and pleasure, all their own? How shall they fill every minute of their time with the quintessence of enjoyment and of glory?

> Let Rome in Tiber melt! and the wide arch
> Of the ranged empire fall? here is my space.
>
> [I. i. 33-4]

Only *one* thing they had not allowed for—that over and above power and beauty, and pleasure and pomp, there is a certain inevitable fact—a law—which cannot be evaded. Pleasure sits enthroned as queen; there is a revel, and the lords of the earth, crowned with roses, dance before her to the sound of lascivious flutes. But presently the scene changes; the hall of revel is transformed to an arena; the dancers are armed gladiators; and as they advance to combat they pay the last homage to their queen with the words *Morituri te salutant* [We who are about to die salute you].

The pathos of *Antony and Cleopatra* resembles the pathos of *Macbeth*. But Shakspere, like Dante, allows the soul of the perjurer and murderer to drop into a lower, blacker, and more lonely circle of Hell than the soul of the man who has sinned through voluptuous self-indulgence. Yet none the less Antony is daily dropping away farther from all that is sound, strong, and enduring. His judgment wanes with his fortune. He challenges to a combat with swords his clear-sighted and unimpassioned rival, into whose hands the empire of the world is about to fall. He abandons himself to a senseless exasperation:

> I will be treble-sinew'd, hearted, breathed,
> And fight maliciously; for when mine hours
> Were nice and lucky, men did ransom lives
> Of me with jests; but now I'll set my teeth,
> And send to darkness all that stop me.
>
> [III. xiii. 177-81]

He sees his fate closing in upon him; he will sell his life dearly; and, meantime, like a man condemned to execution upon the morrow, he will have one more night of pleasure:

> Come,
> Let's have one other gaudy night: call to me
> All my sad captains; fill our bowls once more;
> Let's mock the midnight bell.
>   *Cleo.*   It is my birthday.
>
> [III. xiii. 181-84]

But Antony's struggle after boisterous mirth proves a piteous mockery. The banquet is a valediction; the great leader's followers are transformed to women; Enobarbus turns away "onion-eyed." Antony makes one rude effort to lift himself up above the damps and depression which have fallen on his spirit; one effort to fling aside the consciousness of the failure of his life, which yet clings to him:

> Ho, ho, ho!
> Now the witch take me, if I meant it thus!
> Grace grow where those drops fall! My hearty friends,
> You take me in too dolorous a sense;
> For I spake to you for your comfort; did desire you
> To burn this night with torches: know, my hearts,
> I hope well of to-morrow; and will lead you
> Where rather I'll expect victorious life
> Than death and honor. Let's to supper, come,
> And drown consideration.
>
> [IV. ii. 36-45]

Hercules, the generous wielder of strength, whom Antony loved, is departing from him; music heard at midnight by the sentinels warn them of the withdrawal of the favor of the divinity. Experience, manhood, honor, more and more violate themselves in Antony. Cleopatra's ship turns the rudder and flies from the sea-fight. Antony, regardless of fortune and of shame,

> Claps on the sea-wing and, like a doting mallard,
> Leaving the fight in height, flies after her.
>
> [III. x. 19-20]

He is, indeed, the ruin of Cleopatra's magic; yet he is a lordly and eminent ruin; and before all sinks in blackness and ashes there is a last leaping-up of the flame of his fortune, by which we see the figure of Antony, still majestic, pathetically illuminated by a glory that passes away. He is made glad with one hour's victory. Though deserted by Enobarbus, Scarus has been faithful, and is at his side, red from honorable wounds:

> Give me thy hand;
> [*Enter Cleopatra, attended.*]
> To this great fairy I'll commend thy acts,
> Make her thanks bless thee.—[*To Cleo.*] O thou day o'
>   the world,
> Chain mine arm'd neck; leap thou, attire and all,
> Through proof of harness to my heart, and there
> Ride on the pants triumphing!
>   *Cleo.*   Lord of lords!
> O infinite virtue, comest thou smiling from
> The world's great snare uncaught?
>   *Ant.*   My nightingale,
> We have beat them to their beds. What, girl! though
>   gray
> Do something mingle with our younger brown,
> Yet ha' we a brain that nourishes our nerves,
> And can get goal for goal of youth.
>
> [IV. viii. 11-22]

Measure things only by the sensuous imagination, and everything in the world of Oriental voluptuousness, in which Antony lies bewitched, is great. The passion and the pleasure of the Egyptian queen and of her paramour toil after the infinite. The Herculean strength of Antony, the grandeur and prodigal power of his nature, inflate and buoy up the imagination of Cleopatra:

> The demi-Atlas of this earth, the arm
> And burgonet of men.
>
> [I. v. 23-4]

While he is absent, Cleopatra would, if it were possible, annihilate time—

> *Charmian.*   Why, madam?
> *Cleo.*That I might sleep out this great gap of time.
> My Antony is away.
>
> [I. v. 4-6]

When Antony dies, the only eminent thing in the earth is gone, and a universal flatness, an equality of insignificances, remains:

> Young boys and girls
> Are level now with men; the odds is gone,
> And there is nothing left remarkable
> Beneath the visiting moon.
>
> [IV. xv. 65-8]

We do not mistake this feeling of Cleopatra towards Antony for love; but he has been for her (who had known Cæsar and Pompey) the supreme sensation. She is neither faithful to him nor faithless; in her complex nature, beneath each fold or layer of sincerity lies one of insincerity, and we cannot tell which is the last and innermost. Her imagination is stimulated and nourished by Antony's presence. And he, in his turn, finds in the beauty and witchcraft of the Egyptian something no less incommensurable and incomprehensible. Yet no one felt more profoundly than Shakspere—as his *Sonnets* abundantly testify—that the glory of strength and of beauty is subject to limit and to time. What he would seem to say to us in this play, not in the manner of a doctrinaire or a moralist, but wholly as an artist, is that this sensuous infinite is but a dream, a deceit, a snare. The miserable change comes upon Antony. The remorseless practice of Cleopatra upon his heart has done him to death. And among things which the barren world offers to the Queen she now finds death—a painless death—the least hateful. Shakspere, in his high impartiality to fact, denies none of the glory of the lust of the eye and the pride of life. He compels us to acknowledge these to the utmost. But he adds that there is another demonstrable fact of the world which tests the visible pomp of the earth, and the splendor of sensuous passion, and finds them wanting. The glory of the royal festival is not dulled by Shakspere or diminished; but, also, he shows us, in letters of flame, the handwriting upon the wall.

This Shakspere effects, however, not merely or chiefly by means of a catastrophe. He does not deal in precepts or moral reflections, or practical applications. He is an artist, but an artist who grasps truth largely. The ethical truth lives and breathes in every part of his work as artist, no less than the truth to things sensible and presentable to the imagination. At every moment in this play we assist at a catastrophe—the decline of a lordly nature. At every moment we are necessarily aware of the gross, the mean, the disorderly womanhood in Cleopatra, no less than of the witchery and wonder which excite and charm and subdue. We see her a dissembler, a termagant, a coward; and yet "vilest things become her." The presence of a spirit of *life* in Cleopatra, quick, shifting, multitudinous, incalculable, fascinates the eye, and would, if it could, lull the moral sense to sleep, as the sea does with its endless snake-like motions in the sun and shade. She is a wonder of the world, which we would travel far to look upon. (pp. 272-78)

If we would know how an artist devoted to high moral ideals would treat such a character as that of the fleshly enchantress, we have but to turn to the *Samson Agonistes*. Milton exposes Dalila only to drive her explosively from the stage. Shakspere would have studied her with equal delight and detestation. Yet the severity of Shakspere, in his own dramatic fashion, is as absolute as that of Milton. Antony is dead. The supreme sensation of Cleopatra's life is ended, and she seems, in the first passionate burst of chagrin, to have no longer interest in anything but death. By-and-by she is in the presence of Cæsar, and hands over to him a document, the "brief of money, plate, and jewels" [V. ii. 138] of which she is possessed. She calls on her treasurer, Seleucus, to vouch for its accuracy:

> Speak the truth, Seleucus.
> *Sel.* Madam,
> I had rather seal my lips than to my peril
> Speak that which is not.
> *Cleo.*   What have I kept back?
> *Sel.* Enough to purchase what you have made known.
> *Cæs.* Nay, blush not, Cleopatra; I approve
> Your wisdom in the deed.
>
> [V. ii. 144-50]

In her despair, while declaring that she will die "in the high Roman fashion" [IV. xv. 87], Cleopatra yet clings to her plate and jewels. And the cold approval of Cæsar, who never gains the power which passion supplies, nor loses the power which passion withdraws and dissipates—the approval of Cæsar is confirmed by the judgment of the spectator. It is right and natural that Cleopatra should love her jewels, and practise a fraud upon her conqueror.

Nor is her death quite in that "high Roman fashion" which she had announced. She dreads physical pain, and is fearful of the ravage which death might commit upon her beauty; under

her physician's direction, she has "pursued conclusions infinite of easy ways to die" [V. ii. 355-56]. And now to die painlessly is better than to grace the triumph of Octavius. In her death there is something dazzling and splendid, something sensuous, something theatrical, something magnificently coquettish, and nothing stern. Yet Shakspere does not play the rude moralist; he needs no chorus of Israelite captives to utter invective against this Dalila. Let her possess all her grandeur and her charm. Shakspere can show us more excellent things which will make us proof against the fascination of these.

> *Cleo.* Give me my robe, put on my crown; I have
> Immortal longings in me: now no more
> The juice of Egypt's grape shall moist this lip:—
> Yare, yare, good Iras; quick.—Methinks I hear
> Antony call: I see him rouse himself
> To praise my noble act; I hear him mock
> The luck of Cæsar, which the gods give men
> To excuse their after-wrath. Husband, I come:
> Now to that name my courage prove my title!
> I am fire and air; my other elements
> I give to baser life. . . .
>   Come, thou mortal wretch:
>   [*To an asp, which she applies to her breast.*]
> With thy sharp teeth this knot intrinsicate
> Of life at once untie: poor venomous fool,
> Be angry and despatch. O, couldst thou speak,
> That I might hear thee call great Cæsar ass
> Unpolicied!
> *Char.*   O eastern star!
> *Cleo.*   Peace, peace.!
> Dost thou not see my baby at my breast
> That sucks the nurse asleep?
> *Char.*   O, break! O, break!
> *Cleo.* As sweet as balm, as soft as air, as gentle—
> O Antony!—Nay, I will take thee too:
>   [*Applying another asp to her arm*]
> What should I say   [*Dies*]
> *Char.* In this vile world? So, fare thee well.
> Now boast thee, Death! in thy possession lies
> A lass unparallel'd. Downy windows, close;
> And golden Phœbus never be beheld
> Of eyes again so royal.
>   [V. ii. 280-90, 303-18]
>   (pp. 279-82)

Edward Dowden, "The Roman Plays," in his Shakspere: A Critical Study of His Mind and Art, *third edition, Harper & Brothers Publishers, 1881, pp. 245-99.*

DENTON J. SNIDER   (essay date 1890)

[*Snider was an American scholar, philosopher, and poet who closely followed the precepts of the German philosopher Georg Wilhelm Friedrich Hegel and contributed greatly to the dissemination of his dialectical philosophy in America. Snider's critical writings include studies on Homer, Dante, and Goethe, as well as Shakespeare. Like Hermann Ulrici and G. G. Gervinus, Snider sought the dramatic unity and ethical import in Shakespeare's plays, but he adopted a more rigorous Hegelian approach than either of these German philosophical critics. In the introduction to his three-volume work* The Shakespearian Drama: A Commentary *(1887-90), Snider states that Shakespeare's plays present various ethical principles which, in their differences, come into "Dramatic Collision," but are ultimately resolved and brought into harmony. He claims that these collisions can be traced in the plays' various "Dramatic Threads" of action and thought, which together form a "Dramatic Movement," and that the analysis of these threads and movements—"the structural elements of the drama"—reveals the organic unity of Shakespeare's art. Snider observes two basic movements in the tragedies—guilt and retribution—and three in the comedies—separation, mediation, and return. The excerpt below is taken from his* The Shakespearian Drama, a Commentary: The Histories, *first published in 1890. Snider maintains that the structure of* Antony and Cleopatra *is based on an opposition of conflicting principles represented in several of the characters, particularly the opposition between Octavius's relentless pursuit of Rome's historic destiny and Antony's hedonism. In the critic's judgment, Octavius's fixity of purpose, his talent for perceiving the most political course to achieve his goal, and his ability to "resist the fascination of the Orient" make him eminently qualified to maintain and perpetuate "the Roman principle and the Roman empire." Further, Snider emphasizes Cleopatra's "power of fascination" and her inability to fascinate Octavius, arguing that "sensual intensity" is her dominant characteristic and that her suffering so ennobles her that "she shows signs of a better nature" in the final scenes of the play. In addition, the critic discusses such secondary characters as Enobarbus, the Soothsayer, Lepidus, Pompey, and Menas.*]

The universal complaint is that *Antony and Cleopatra* is wanting in dramatic simplicity, and the complaint is certainly well founded. To the less careful reader or spectator its movement seems confused—at times chaotic—and there is hardly a doubt but that the Poet has undertaken to compass too much in the limits of one drama. Still, it has his language, his thought, and his characterization in their highest potence. We shall . . . consider the organization of the play as a whole, and attempt to unfold its various parts, stating their meaning and relation.

There are manifestly two main movements, though other divisions are possible, according to the stand-point of the critic. The first movement exhibits the various conflicting elements of the Roman World, and ends in their apparent reconciliation. It has three distinct threads or groups of characters, each of which has a locality of its own. The central figures of these groups are, respectively, Antony and Cleopatra, Octavius, Pompey. The second movement shows the disruption of the truce and the struggle of the hostile principles and individuals, till their final and complete subordination to one man—Octavius. Here there are essentially two threads—that of Antony and Cleopatra on the one hand, and that of Octavius on the other; the minor groups are more or less intimately connected with these leading personages. The elaboration of this scheme will show all the elements of the work in their proper order and signification.

There is a general sweep forward from a threatened breach between the parties—Antony, Pompey, Octavius—to a patched-up reconciliation. The Triumvirate is showing its seams, and the whole Roman world is about to break into warring fragments, but a temporary truce holds it together, which truce, however, breaks the love-bond between Antony and Cleopatra.

The first thread of the first movement may be called the Egyptian thread, and is the fullest in its portraiture, as well as the most interesting. The first speaker is an old Roman soldier, who strikes at once the key-note of the drama. He complains in bitter scorn that the illustrious warrior, the "triple pillar of the world" [I. i. 12], has sacrificed his great historical destiny to sensuality. But here come the pair; what is their conversation? They are talking of love, whose power Antony expresses in the strongest language. It is illimitable—subdues all; it demands "a new heaven and a new earth" [I. i. 17]. Note must

be taken that this is not the ethical affection of the Family, but sensual love. Here is indicated the strongest principle of Antony's nature; he will often fluctuate between his contradictory impulses, but in the end will always return to the "Egyptian dish." Just now he is feeling some satiety and shame, which he seeks to disguise carefully from Cleopatra.

She, however, with a true instinct of the situation, suspects him, and we shall now behold the successive waves of jealousy, anger, affection, despair, which heave and surge through her breast. The fundamental trait of Cleopatra is passion—passion in all its forms and in its fullest intensity. As love, as hate, as irascibility, as jealousy, it has the same colossal manifestation. There is absolutely no ethical subordination in the woman. She recognizes no duty, submits to no institution. She seems to have admiration for the heroic element of Antony's character, and, with the true instinct of her sex, she adores his courage; but her love for him springs mainly from his boundless capacity for revelry and sensual indulgence, in which she participates along with him. Corresponding quite to the degree and intensity of her passion, the Poet has portrayed her power of fascination—indeed, the one arises from the other. It is curious to note how some of the greatest personages of Roman history have, in turn, submitted to her spell: Pompey, Julius Caesar, and now Antony. The contrast is apparent; it would seem as if the adamantine Roman character must always sink before this gorgeous Oriental enchantress. But she is destined to meet with her master. The cool and wary Octavius sees her; she tries her sorcery upon him without success, and then—dies. It is her destiny that, if her charm be once withstood, she, like the Sirens of old, will destroy herself. Her attractiveness does not consist in youth, in grace, in figure, in personal beauty; it lies in the sensual intensity of her whole being, which appears to set on fire all who dare look into her eyes. Such is the central principle of her character. (pp. 238-42)

[But] she is something more than this person merely. She is the representative of a whole people. She belongs to Egypt, the land of the sphinx, she is herself the sphinx. She has the head of the human being attached to the body of the animal; the rational and the sensuous elements are in her conjoined to one shape, in which, however, they are distinct and unreconciled, nay, contradictory. She is the riddle of Egypt propounded to Roman Antony, which he cannot solve, but Octavius can. The image of the sphinx is the utterance in stone of the Egyptian by the Egyptian, who was not able to harmonize, either in spirit or in art, the dual and contradictory nature of man. Cleopatra is not the classic beauty, though she has in her veins Greek blood which has lapsed to the Orient; she is rather the reincarnation of the old Egyptian spirit which has somehow wandered into her Hellenic body—of the spirit that hewed out the sphinx as its artistic representation. The poet does not, indeed, say this, but he has caught the true historic character of Egypt from Plutarch, and made it live in a person.

We must not dismiss the political side from the delineation of Cleopatra. She is queen, and her game is kings of men, the greatest of the time, though uncrowned. She has political, nay, military ambition; love-craft and state-craft are coupled in her nature so intimately that they cannot be separated. Still she remains the grand enchantress of the world; that is, her power over the senses of men is so great and immediate, that it cannot be resisted. She puts all under her charm, but in doing so, she becomes herself the victim of her own spell. At last, however, the Circe of Egypt finds her Ulysses.

Still another trait must not be left out of the picture. Coupled with this demonic sensuous power, is the intellect of Cleopatra; she has mental culture of a certain kind, she has a good deal of insight into character; she possesses, above all, subtlety in adjusting herself to men. In fact her intelligence is always looking out for her advantage, and in a certain degree directs her passions. But the human head is on the animal body.

We can now go back and take up the second thread of the first movement. The two colleagues of Antony are at Rome, the true center of the nations at that time; their conversation turns upon the man who has sacrificed his Roman destiny to Oriental indulgence. We catch a glimpse of the Triumvirate, with the relation and character of its three members.

Octavius is the man of cold understanding, who has grasped his ultimate end with clearness, and who pursues it in politic disguise, but with inflexible determination. Already we can see his grand purpose looming up in the future; we also see that he plainly comprehends the conflict which he must pass through in order to attain his object. His great obstacle is Antony, who surpasses him in every quality except the greatest, namely, the mind to grasp, and the will to accomplish, the world-historical destiny of Rome. This is for Octavius the highest end; to it everything else has to yield. For this reason his character has often excited moral aversion. He sacrifices his colleague; his sister, whom he seems really to have loved, is thrust by him into a short and unhappy marriage to further his policy; he disregards the most sacred promises; in fine, all the emotions of man, and all the scruples of conscience, he subordinates to his great purpose—the union of the nations in one empire. He himself says in one place that he is seeking universal peace—the harmony of the whole world in a single government. He is one of those world-historical characters whose fate it is to be always condemned for trampling upon moral considerations when they collided, not merely with his own subjective purpose, but with the absolute movement of humanity, which he represented.

But Antony, in this fundamental trait, is the contrast to Octavius. He is one of the triumvirs; he is a great soldier, with heroic elements of character; he was the victor at Philippi; he was the friend and supporter of Julius Caesar. His opportunity is really greater than that of Octavius. But he has not the clear ultimate end; he is not at one with himself; his controlling principle is enjoyment—gratification of the senses—though he is capable of enduring the most terrible hardships of war. Hence he falls into the lap of Orientalism, yet struggles to return to his Roman life and destiny; but he finally relapses completely, and thus loses the great opportunity. Between these two men—Antony and Octavius—the struggle must arise. The question is: Which one will unify the Triumvirate? From the very beginning the Poet has elaborated the dramatic motives so forcibly that the result is plainly foreseen.

Now there remains the third triumvir—Lepidus. He is the peacemaker, though peace is impossible; he tries to compromise two contradictory principles which are on the point of embracing in a death-struggle. Conciliation is possible between individuals, but not between principles. If one principle be truer—that is, more universal than another—the former must subordinate the latter; for, otherwise, it is not more universal. The higher truth must realize itself—must make its superiority valid in the world; this means always the subsumption of what is lower. Lepidus, therefore, has no perception of what is going on around him; he placed himself between the two jaws of the world, and is speedily ground to death. His basis is the peaceful

continuance of the present condition of affairs—of the Triumvirate—which is in reality a fleeting phase of the great transition to imperialism. A man with good intentions, but with a weak head amid a revolution—what is in store for him but annihilation?

Lepidus is one of those peculiar characters whom we may designate as an important nobody. Such people seem to be needed at times; they rise and assert a place by virtue of being at the point of indifference where two great opposites meet, and call forth a neutral third person. Lepidus shows the neutral color, which has also the advantage of being reflected in the mirror of Enobarbus' sarcasm. It is hinted in Plutarch that Antony and Octavius, two strong characters took Lepidus, the third weak character, to turn the edge of envy and suspicion, by sharing thus their power.

The first utterance of Octavius is a complaint against Antony; he is disgracing his office and his country by his conduct in Egypt; he has insulted his colleagues; but, above all, he has permitted, through his inactivity, the enemies of the Triumvirate again to muster their forces and threaten Italy. In other words, he is faithless to his high calling and to the destiny of Rome, which is the most serious thought of Octavius. Here is seen plainly the difference of their characters and their ends. But Antony has shaken off the Egyptian enchantress—has come to Rome; the two rivals are brought face to face in order to settle their quarrel. Antony answers the complaints of Octavius with such success that they are seen to be mere pretexts for the most part; still the old veteran asks pardon of his youthful confederate, and thus tacitly points out the superior to whom he acknowledges responsibility and submission. In this act the destinies of the two men are truthfully foreshadowed. But Octavius is not yet ready to strike the final blow; he must first unify all the rest of the Roman world against his antagonist. He, therefore, consents to conciliation; and, to tie the hands of Antony for a time, he gives his sister in marriage to the latter, as suggested by his wily counselor, Agrippa. The tether works well; it holds Antony till both Lepidus and Pompey are overwhelmed, and their territory absorbed by Octavius. But now they, Antony and Octavius, are reconciled, and hasten to unite their powers against the common foe of the Triumvirate.

Such are the transactions of Antony at Rome; their nature and consequences are now foreshadowed in two very different ways, through two very different characters—through Enobarbus and the Soothsayer. Enobarbus is a wonderful delineation; he is the mirror which reflects the results of the deeds which are enacted by the high personages of the drama; in particular, he adumbrates the conduct of Antony, his friend and companion. His chief trait is intellectual sagacity; he foresees with the clearest vision and foretells with the most logical precision. But he possesses at the same time the reverse side of human nature in colossal magnitude; glutton, debauchee, sensualist, he seems immersed in the very dregs of Egyptian license, and when he is absent his memory is filled with Egyptian orgies. The two extremes meet in him—the keenest intelligence and the grossest sensuality; the mediating principle between them—namely, moral subordination—seems not to exist. He is the peculiar product of an age of corruption, in which even mental cultivation aids in blasting the character. He appears to have anticipated the main consequences from the beginning; he tried to keep Antony in Egypt; then he sought to prevent the reconciliation with Octavius. He also intimates that the marriage will in the end intensify the enmity which it was intended to forestall. For he knows that Antony will return to the Egyptian Queen; his highly-colored account of her appearance when "she pursed up his heart upon the river Cydnus" [II. ii. 186-87] indicates the power of fascination over the senses, and the deep hold which she must consequently retain upon Antony. Enobarbus manifestly thinks that his master ought to go back at once to Egypt, though his appetite seems to favor such a decision quite as strongly as his judgment.

Such is the intellectual reflection of Antony's conduct and destiny; now follows a second reflection of the same through a wholly different medium, namely, through the prophetic emotion. Its bearer is the Soothsayer. This man, too, urges very strongly the return to Egypt—the reason whereof he says he has not in his tongue, but in his feeling, in his instinctive perception of the future. Antony is warned that the demon, "thy spirit that keeps thee" [II. iii. 20], cannot resist the might of Caesar; it becomes afraid in the presence of the latter. Antony feels the truth of the declaration, resolves to go back to Egypt, and gives the true ground—"in the East my pleasure lies" [II. iii. 41]. The Soothsayer thus utters in his peculiar form that which has already been told; the principle of Antony is subordinate to the principle of Octavius—the higher end must vindicate its superior power. This is not only known, but is now felt; the Poet has indicated the same result both through intelligence and through feeling. The Triumvirate is, however, reconciled within itself, and must turn its attention to its external foe.

This is Pompey, who is the central figure of the third thread of the first movement, which thread may now be taken up and traced. Pompey, from the first, exhibits no great strength of purpose, no firm reliance on his principle. He stands as the representation of the old republican constitution of Rome, in opposition to the tendency to imperialism; he cites as examples of admiration those "courtiers of beauteous freedom" [II. vi. 17], pale Cassius and honest Brutus, who drenched the capitol,

—That they would
Have one man but a man. And that is it
Hath made me rig my navy—etc.

[II. vi. 18-20]

He has also a personal ground—to avenge the fate of his father. But he is clearly not the man to be at the head of a great political movement. He has, moreover, a scrupulosity which makes him sacrifice his cause to a moral punctilio. Such a man ought never to begin a rebellion whose success is not his highest principle. His main hope is that Antony will remain in the East; but, when the latter returns and is reconciled with Octavius, Pompey becomes frightened at their hostile preparation and compromises for a certain territory—that is, he really joins the Triumvirate in the division of the world, and thus utterly abandons the principle which he represented. Logically, he is now absorbed in the new idea by his own action, and he disappears as a factor of the drama.

His position is wholly due to the fact that he was the son of the great Pompey; birth, the most external of grounds, makes him leader. But by the side of him is seen the genuine old Roman republican, to whom the cause means everything, though he is called a pirate by his enemies. This is Menas, who sees and condemns the folly of the new treaty; who reflects the weakness of Pompey as Enobarbus reflects the weakness of Antony. Now comes the supreme moment of Pompey's career. All three of the triumvirs are on board of his galley, holding high festival in honor of the peace; the rulers of the world, the enemies of his principle, are, as it were, bagged and placed at his disposition. Menas urges upon him immediate action with

the greatest vehemence; but no, his "honor" will not let him, the nature of which honor is seen in his declaration that he cannot advise the doing of the deed, but he would applaud it if it were done. Menas now deserts, for he to whom the good old cause is the highest principle of existence cannot endure to see the destiny of Rome and of the world sacrificed to a moral scruple. However great may be our admiration of Pompey's motive, it destroys his world-historical character; both he and Antony are, therefore, alike in surrendering their grand opportunity, though the one yields it to sensual love and the other to conscience. Pompey, accordingly, keeps his agreement, but Octavius, who subordinates both emotion and morality to his great political purpose, breaks that same agreement when his plan is ripe, and slays his confederate in return for the latter's fidelity and conscientiousness. (pp. 245-55)

In the final scene of this thread, where the banquet is portrayed, we behold the fate of all the leading characters foreshadowed in the most subtle manner. Here are collected the representatives of the main conflicting principles of the drama—Antony, Pompey, Lepidus, Octavius, with their chief subordinates. They indulge in a drunken carousal, symbolical of the mad confusion of the period. Truly the world is on a spree. Who will keep his head clear and retain his senses amid the wild revel? Lepidus first yields to the wine, and is carried out; the others sink into an Egyptian debauch; but the cool-headed Octavius never for a moment loses his self-control, and when he finds himself touched with the wine he hastens away from the company. No sensual pleasure can conquer his understanding; he will remain master. The symbolism of this scene is complete on every side, and doubtless was intended by the poet.

Such is the first general movement of the play, ending in the reconciliation of all the colliding characters. The Triumvirate is restored to internal harmony; Pompey is admitted to a share of its authority; Antony is restored to the Roman Family and State. Even external conquest breathes for a moment. Nothing is settled, however; principles have been compromised, but they are as antagonistic as before.

Suddenly comes the disruption. The Poet does not portray it in full—he merely indicates the result. Caesar and Lepidus united to destroy Pompey, then Caesar turned upon Lepidus; which important events are all announced in one short scene. Antony leaves Octavia; next we find him with Cleopatra. Such is this rapid separation which introduces the second general movement of the drama. There are now essentially but two threads, namely, the two antagonists, with their respective adherents. Of this last movement there are three distinct phases or groupings—the first defeat of Antony, his second defeat and death, the death of Cleopatra. The structure of this second movement proceeds not by threads, but by groupings, which we shall follow out in order.

Antony, when he fully comprehends the inexorable purpose of Octavius to subordinate him also, takes his departure from Octavia. She is the true Roman wife, who is by no means devoid of deep emotion, but it is the quiet, pure emotion of the Family; her feeling is confined to the bounds of an ethical relation, and herein she is the direct contrast to Cleopatra, whose passion is hampered by no limitations. She tried to perform her duty to both husband and brother; but that husband had as his deepest impulse sensual, instead of conjugal love, and that brother had as his strongest principle political supremacy, instead of fraternal affection, even if he possessed the latter also. Octavia, with the most beautiful devotion, tried to conciliate the conflicting individuals, but was sacrificed by both. Thus the Family sank before the thirst of passion and before the thirst for power.

The Poet, having elaborated the motives of all that is to follow, passes at once to the scene of the struggle which is to decide the fate of the two colliding personages. The infatuation of Antony is brought out in the strongest colors; he fights a naval battle against the advice of all his soldiers, from the commanding officer down to the common private in the ranks. The ground of his conduct is the control exercised over him by Cleopatra. Then during the crisis of the fight she flies; Antony follows. The result is utter defeat by sea, universal desertion by land. His Oriental connection has thus brought to ruin his world-historical opportunity; he has sacrificed everything Roman—even his Roman courage. The internal struggle now begins. He feels the deep degradation of his behavior; the memories of his Roman life again awake in him; he seems ready to reproach the cause of his fatuity; but the weeping enchantress by her presence subdues him more completely than Octavius had done in the battle just fought, and again his deepest trait asserts itself:—

> Fall not a tear, I say; one of them rates
> All that is won and lost; give me a kiss—
> Even this repays me.
>
> [III. xi. 69-71]

But even a stronger evidence of his love is given. He suddenly comes upon Thyreus, the messenger of Caesar, toying with the hand of Cleopatra. There ensues a fit of jealousy so violent that he totally forgets his generous nature and orders the man to be whipped. The thought of her infidelity crazes him; he has loved her more than the whole world in the literal sense of the expression, since he has sacrificed the world for her sake. What if another shares with him the possession? The strongest element of his nature revolts. But a declaration of Cleopatra lulls his wrath; again harmony prevails. Now, however, their union is threatened from without by the approach of the victorious Octavius—a conflict which must arouse all his dormant energy.

Octavius is true to his aim throughout these scenes; his cool calculation is never disturbed by a whiff of passion—his politic cunning is everywhere paramount. His enemy is surrounded by a net-work of espionage, while his own movements are artfully concealed. He acts with a celerity and secrecy which are incomprehensible to Antony; his insight into the real situation is never clouded for a moment. He orders the battle to be fought at sea, with every advantage in his favor. His imperturbable understanding, which grasps clearly the end in view and the means to reach the same, shines through all his actions. After the victory he will grant no terms to Antony, who must be entirely eliminated from the world in order to produce unity. But Cleopatra he attempts to detach by specious promises; he has no faith in her fidelity, and but little trust in women under the most favorable circumstances. She seems to listen to his proposals; her conduct is at least ambiguous; two opposite impulses divide her purpose.

We pass on to the second phase of the second movement, embraced in the Fourth Act. Antony now has a new motive for action—his union with Cleopatra is in jeopardy. His heroic character returns in its fullest intensity; he fights, not to save an empire, but to preserve his relation to the Egyptian Queen. It will be noticed that the deepest principle of his nature is assailed; he might dally away the world, but he cannot surrender the tie to Cleopatra. Again we behold all the noble

elements of his nature in full play—his generosity, his warm-heartedness, even to servants—his activity, his heroism. Nor is the other side of his character omitted; there must be a final debauch before departure for the battle-field. Still, there is the dark reflection of the future; music in the air is heard by the common soldiers, who express their feelings in ominous words; their belief is that the god Hercules, tutelar deity of Antony, is now leaving him—his cause is lost beyond hope.

A second battle is fought; a temporary advantage is gained on land, but the Egyptian fleet yields to the foe—traitorously as Antony supposes, and as also we may suppose. The internal conflict now arises more fiercely than ever; she to whom he has sacrificed a world has betrayed him. What agony could be more intense? She appears before him, but neither her presence nor her language can assuage his revengeful anger this time; she has to leave him. But is his love entirely gone—that which was the strongest principle of his nature? She will put the matter to proof, the test being death—absolute separation. Accordingly word is sent to him that she is no more; that she dies with his name on her lips. He answers the test in the fullest degree—separation from her means death, which he at once proceeds to inflict upon himself. Other motives, too, influence his resolution—as the sense of shame, the fear of dishonor, the loss of his opportunity; but the main impelling power which drove the last blow was the thought of being forever disjoined from Cleopatra. Thus his deepest principle asserts itself with an absolute supremacy. He had already sacrificed an empire and a world-historical destiny for his love; it is easy and consistent now to give his life in addition. His career is made up of a series of external conflicts on account of his passion, and internal conflicts with his passion.

The third phase of the second movement is embraced in the last Act. Cleopatra is now the central figure. The difference between her and Antony is seen in the fact that she is willing to survive him, but he was not willing to survive her; separation does not mean death in her case. There is, however, no doubt about her love for Antony, but there is as little doubt about her readiness to transfer it to another person. She has been making provision for the future—she has been laying plans to catch Octavius in her toils. He comes into her presence; but he is not charmed; his cool head cannot be turned by sensuous enchantment. This seals her fate. She has met her master; she has found the man who is able to resist her spell. The proof is manifest—she learns that Octavius intends to take her to Rome to grace his triumph. This secret is confided to her by Dolabella, who seems to be the last victim of her magical power. That power is now broken; nothing remains except to die. Still, she shows signs of a better nature in this latter part—misfortune has ennobled her character:—

> My desolation begins to make a better life.
>
> [V. ii. 1-2]

The heroic qualities of Antony, now that he is gone and she can captivate no new hero, fill her imagination; she will go and join him in the world beyond. Her sensual life seems purified and exalted as she gives expression to her "immortal longings." Her deepest trait is, however, conquest through sensual love; she will live as long as she can conquer; when her spell is once overcome she will die, dwelling in imagination upon the greatest victory of her principle and upon its most illustrious victim.

The manner of her death corresponds to the manner of her life. She had thought on her final passage beyond: "Her physicians tell me she has pursued conclusions infinite of easy ways to die'' [V. ii. 354-56]. No hard struggle with the grim King of Terrors she seeks; a sleep, an unconscious gliding out of life is her choice—a soft lulling of the senses, which will not wake again. She finds in the bite of the asp her longed-for euthanasia:—

> She looks like sleep,
> As she would catch another Antony
> In her strong toil of grace.

Thus it is said of her, as she lay in her last appearance; she had seemingly fascinated death. The fate of the immediate personal dependents of Antony and Cleopatra is connected with that of their master and mistress. The relation is so intimate that they die together; the devotion of the servants will not permit them to survive. But Enobarbus is the most interesting of all these subordinate personages; his character, too, undergoes a change in this second part. His sharp intellect has foreseen, and tried to avert, the consequences of Antony's folly, but without avail. Now begins his internal conflict. Should he follow interest and desert a fool, or preserve fidelity and cling to his fallen master? It does not surprise us that he goes over to Caesar; that he was led by his sagacity and not by his moral feeling. He saw the rising star of Octavius, and followed—but bitter is his disappointment. The conqueror will not trust a traitor. Enobarbus finds out thathe has ''done ill;'' his intelligence has failed utterly. But this is not all. The generous Antony sends his treasure after him with kindly greetings. Now he calls himself, not fool, but villian; the moral elements—as honor, gratitude, fidelity, conscience—burst up in his soul with terrific force. This principle of morality, which was previously so inert, is now supreme, asserting itself over both pleasure and intellect. He repents of his conduct, but is not reconciled; he slays himself—an irrational act, but one which shows that remorse was stronger than existence. So intense is his anguish that he will not retain a life without moral devotion.

Octavius has passed his final and supreme conflict, which the Poet seems to make the most difficult, as well as the most glorious, of all the conflicts in the drama. This victory is greater than the victory over Antony, who had already been subdued by Cleopatra; now the mighty conqueress is herself conquered. The man who can resist the fascination of the Orient is the true Roman—is the ruler capable of maintaining and perpetuating the Roman principle and the Roman empire. Even Alexander was absorbed by the East, and his realm passed away like a dream. Octavius can spend a tear of pity over his illustrious foes, but his emotions never clouded his judgment or hindered the clear, definite pursuit of his political end. When the play terminates we feel that a great epoch, with its external and internal throes, with its weak men and mighty heroes, has passed away. All the struggles are overcome, not by temporary compromises, but by the subordination of the lower to the higher principle. The world finds unity, peace and law in the Empire. This epoch is, therefore, the true date of Imperialism. (pp. 257-66)

> *Denton J. Snider, '' 'Antony and Cleopatra','' in his* Shakespearian Drama, a Commentary: The Histories, *1890. Reprint by Indiana Publishing Co., 1894, pp. 229-68.*

ARTHUR SYMONS (essay date 1892)

[*An English poet, literary critic, dramatist, and short story writer, Symons is regarded as one of the most important critics of the modern era. His* The Symbolist Movement in Literature *(1899)*

introduced his English-speaking contemporaries to the French symbolist poets, and his aesthetic theories had a significant influence on such writers as T. S. Eliot, W. B. Yeats, James Joyce, and Ezra Pound. The following excerpt is taken from the introduction to Antony and Cleopatra *in the* Henry Irving Shakespeare *(1892); it was later reprinted in Symons'* Studies in the Elizabethan Drama *(1919). Symons maintains that Antony's noble nature has been poisoned by his total absorption in Cleopatra, and he contends that while the hero reproaches himself for his ignoble conduct—particularly after the battle of Actium—he clearly bears no malice toward the queen and refuses to blame her for ruining his life. The critic also notes that Antony is inclined to self-dramatization, and he comments that this is especially evident in Act IV, Scene ii, where ''he cannot help posturing a little before his servants, exerting himself to win their tears.'' Symons describes Cleopatra as ''the most wonderful of Shakespeare's women,'' yet he also views her as cunning, capricious, emotionally volatile, cruel, and overly conscious of her effect on others; he argues that her love for Antony is genuine enough, but wholly sensual and selfish. The critic concludes that although Shakespeare has portrayed Antony as essentially noble and Cleopatra as supremely fascinating despite her contemptible conduct, he intended us to share his own conviction that it is morally wrong to abandon ''everything to the claim of love.''*]

Antony and Cleopatra is the most wonderful, I think, of all Shakespeare's plays, and it is so mainly because the figure of Cleopatra is the most wonderful of Shakespeare's women.... Before the thought of Cleopatra every man is an Antony, Shakespeare no less than another, though in the play he holds the balance quite steadily.... [Unless] we adopt the surely untenable theory that the Sonnets, with their passionate sincerity of utterance, the curiously individual note of their complex harmonies, are merely passion according to the Italian Opera, is it not possible that the dark woman, the ''woman coloured ill'' [Sonnet 144], of whom they show us such significant hints of outline, may have turned his thoughts in the direction of Plutarch's story of Antony and Cleopatra? It is possible; and if so, Shakespeare must have felt a singular satisfaction in putting thus to use an experience bought so sorrowfully, with so much ''expense of spirit'' [Sonnet 129]; must have felt that he was repaid, more than repaid.

In the conduct of this play, dealing with so typical a story of passion, and with lovers so unrestrained, it is curious to note how much there is of restraint, of coolness, how carefully the style everywhere is heightened, and how much of gravity, in the scenes of political moment, comes to hinder us from any sense of surfeit in those scenes, the central ones of action and interest, in which the heady passion of Cleopatra spends itself. Never was a play fuller of contrasts, of romantic elements, of variety. The stage is turbulent with movement; messengers come and go incessantly, troops are passing over, engaging, and now in flight; the scene shifts, carrying us backward and forward with a surprising rapidity. But one has a feeling that contrast is of the essence of the piece, and that surprise is to be expected; and not even the variety of the play is more evident than its perfect congruity. (pp. 119-20)

While the main interest of the play is of course centred in the personages who give it name, Shakespeare has not here adopted the device, used in *Macbeth*, for instance, of carefully subordinating all the other characters, leaving the two principal ones under a strong light, and in a salient isolation. He has rather developed these characters through the medium of a crowd of persons and incidents, giving us, not a small corner of existence burningly alive with tremendous issues, but a lover's tragic comedy played out in the sight of the world, on an eminence, and with the fate of nations depending upon it;

a tragic comedy in whose fortunes the arrival of a messenger may make a difference, and whose scenes are timed by interviews with generals and rulers. It is the eternal tragedy of love and ambition, and here, for once, it is the love which holds by the baser nature of the man who is the subject of it, the ambition which is really the prompting of his nobler side. Thus the power of Cleopatra is never more really visible than in the scenes in which she does not appear, and in which Antony seems to have forgotten her. For by the tremendous influences which in these scenes are felt to be drawing him away from her, by all that we see and hear of the incitements to heroic action and manly life, we can measure the force of that magic which brings him back always; from Caesar, who might be a friend, from Octavia, who would be a wife, from Pompey, a rival; to her feet. Such scenes are, besides, a running comment of moral interpretation, and impress upon us a sane and weighty criticism of that flushed and feverish existence, with what is certainly so tempting in it, which is being led by these imperial lovers on terms of such absolute abandonment of everything to the claims of love. This criticism is singularly definite, leaving us in no doubt as to the moral Shakespeare intended to draw, a moral still further emphasized by the reticent quietude of Octavia, the counterpoise to Cleopatra; a character of delicate invention, surprising us by the precise and attractive image she leaves upon a play where she is mainly silent. The ambiguous character of Enobarbus is still further useful in giving the point of irony which appears in all really true and fine studies of a world in which irony seems, after all, to be the final word with the disinterested observer. Enobarbus acts the part of chorus. He is neither for nor against virtue; and by seeming to confound moral judgments he serves the part of artistic equity.

"Antonius being thus inclined, the last and extremest mischief of all other (to wit, the love of Cleopatra) lighted upon him, who did waken and stir up many vices yet hidden in him, and were never seen of any: and if any spark of goodness or hope of rising were left him, Cleopatra quenched it straight, and made it worse than before." So Plutarch, in the picturesque version of Sir Thomas North, "Shakespeare's Plutarch," gives the first distinct sign of the finally downward course of Antony. Of Antony as he had been, we read a little above [in Plutarch]: "Howbeit he was of such a strong nature, that by patience he would overcome any adversity: and the heavier fortune lay upon him, the more constant showed he himself." When the play opens, this Antony of the past is past indeed; the first words strike the keynote: "Nay, but this dotage of our general's" [I.i.1]. Yet in the character as it comes before us, one finds, broken indeed yet there though in ruins, the potent nature of the man, standing out now and again suddenly, though with but little result in action. See, for example, in the second scene, the scarcely perceptible flash, in the jesting colloquy with Enobarbus: "No more light words!" [I. ii. 176] and the sudden change which comes about. He can still, when Antony is Antony, command. And observe again, in the meeting between the jarring triumvirs, how gravely and well he holds his own, and especially that scrupulous care of his honour, evidently so dear to him, and by no means a matter of words only. But the man, as we see him, is wrecked; he has given himself wholly over into the hands of a woman, "being so ravished and enchanted of the sweet poison of her love, that he had no other thought but of her." It is in studying Cleopatra that we shall best see all that is important for us to see of Antony.

In the short scene which serves for prelude to the play, we get a significant glimpse of the kind of power wielded by Cleopatra, and the manner in which she wields it. We see her taming with an inflection of frivolous irony the man who has conquered kingdoms; and we see, too, the unerring and very feminine skill, the finesse of light words veiling a strong purpose, by which she works the charm. From the second scene we perceive something of the tremors incident to a conquest held on such terms: the fear of that "Roman thought" which has taken Antony, the little touch of anxiety at his leaving her for a moment. So long as the man is in her presence she knows he is safe. But she has always to dread the hour of departure. . . . Antony is not yet dead to honour; he feels his strength, feels that he can break away from the enchantress, as Tannhäuser breaks away from Venus. But Cleopatra knows well that, like Tannhäuser, her lover must come back and be hers for ever.

One sees from the scene which follows how deeply Cleopatra loves, not alone her conquest, but her lover. Hers is a real passion, the passion of a woman whose Greek blood is heated by the suns of Egypt, who knows, too, how much greater is the intoxication of loving than of being loved. . . . Love is a "trade" in which she never calculates; wily by nature, and as a loving woman is wily who has to humour her lover, she follows her blood, follows it to distraction, and her fits and starts are not alone played for a purpose, before Antony, but are native to her, and break out with the same violence before her women. She is a woman who must have a lover, but she is satisfied with one, with one at a time; and in Antony she finds her ideal, whom she can call, in her pride, and truly:

> The demi-Atlas of this earth, the arm
> And burgonet of men.
>
> [I. v. 23-4]

And she loves him with passion real of its kind, an intense, an exacting, an oppressive and overwhelming passion, wholly of the senses and wholly selfish: the love which requires possession, and to absorb the loved one. Before Antony she is never demonstrative: "the way to lose him!" [I.iii.10]. She knows that a man like Antony is not to be taken with snares of mere sweetness, that neither for her beauty nor for her love would he love her continuously. She knows how to interest him, to be to him everything he would have in woman, to change with or before every mood of his as it changes. And this is her secret, as it is the secret of success in her kind of love. "So sweet was her company and conversation that a man could not possibly but be taken," we read in Plutarch. And Shakespeare has expressed it monumentally in the lines which bring the whole woman before us:

> Age cannot wither her nor custom stale
> Her infinite variety: other women cloy
> The appetite they feed; but she makes hungry
> Where most she satisfies: for vilest things
> Become themselves in her.
>
> [I. ii. 234-38]

In the fifth scene of the second act we have what is perhaps the most wonderful revelation that literature gives us of the essentially feminine; not necessarily of woman in the general, but of that which radically, in looking at human nature, seems to differentiate the woman from the man. It is a scene with the infinite variety of Cleopatra: it is as miraculous as she: it proves to us that the woman who was "cunning past man's thought" [I. ii. 145] could not be cunning past the thought of Shakespeare. We realize from this scene, more clearly than from anything else in the play, the boundless empire of her caprice, the incalculable instability of her moods, and how natural to her, how entirely instinctive, is the spirit of change and movement by which, partly, she fascinates her lover. The scene brings out the tiger element in her, the union, which we find so often, of cruelty with voluptuousness. It shows us, too, that even in the most violent shock of real emotion she never quite loses the consciousness of self, that she cannot be quite simple. Even at the moment when the blow strikes her, the news of the marriage with Octavia, she has still the posing instinct: "I am pale, Charmian!" [II. v. 59]. Then what a world of meaning, how subtle a touch of insight into the secrets of the hearts of women, there is in that avowal:

> In praising Antony, I have dispraised Caesar. . . .
> I am paid for 't now.
>
> [II. v. 107, 108]

But when at last, exhausted by the violence of her battling and uncontrollable emotions, she surprises us by those humble words, so full of real pathos:

> Pity me, Charmian,
> But do not speak to me;
>
> [II. v. 118-19]

one becomes aware of how deeply the blow has struck, how much there is in her to feel such a blow. Certainly, in this as in everything, she can never be quite simple. There is wounded vanity as well as wounded love in her cry. But it is the proudest as well as the most pitiless of women who asks for pity; and one can refuse her nothing, not even that.

It is significant of the magic charm of the "queen, whom everything becomes" [I. i. 48-9], and of the magic of Shakespeare's art, that she fascinates us even in her weakness, dominating derision, and winning an extorted admiration from the very borders of contempt. In the scene which follows the flight from Actium, Shakespeare puts forth his full power. There are few more effective groupings than this of Cleopatra sitting silent over against Antony, neither daring to approach the other; he, crushed into an unspeakable shame which can never be redeemed; she, incapable of shame, but seeing it in the eyes of Antony, and conscious that she has done him a deed which can never be forgiven. She is here, as ever, cunning. Excuses can but be useless, and she attempts none, none but the faintest murmur:

> I never thought
> You would have followed!
>
> [III. xi. 55-6]

It is a mere broken sob of "Pardon, pardon!" The tears are at hand, tears being with her the last weapon of all her armoury. They cannot but conquer, and the lover, who has given the world for love, says, not without the saddest of irony, as he takes her kiss: "Even this repays me" [III. xi. 71].

It is in the recoil from a reconciliation felt to be ignoble that Antony bursts out into such coarse and furious abuse, the first really angry reproaches he has addressed to her, at the mere sight of Caesar's messenger kissing her hand. Despair and self-reproach have pricked him into a state of smarting sensitiveness. One sees that, as Enobarbus says, "valour preys on reason"; he is "frighted out of fear" [III. xiii. 198, 195]. Well may Caesar exclaim: "Poor Antony!" Is there really a cause for his suspicion of Cleopatra? Did she really betray him to Caesar? Plutarch is silent, and Shakespeare seems intentionally to leave it a little vague. But I think the suspicion wrongs her. Merely on the ground of worldly prudence she had more to hope from Antony than from Caesar. And there is nothing in

all she says to Antony which comes with a more genuine sound than that reproachful question: "Not know me yet?" and then, "Ah, dear, if I be so!" [III. xiii. 157, 158].

I have said that Cleopatra has the instinct of posing. But in Antony, too, there is almost always something showy, an element of somewhat theatrical sentiment. Now, preparing for his last battle, and really moved himself, he cannot help posturing a little before his servants, exerting himself to win their tears. It is not a simple leave-taking; it comes as if prepared beforehand. And next morning, how stagily, and yet with what a real exhilaration of spirits, does he arm himself and go forth, going forth gallantly, indeed, as Cleopatra says of him! Experience has taught him so little that he thinks even now that he may conquer. It has been so much his habit, as it has been Cleopatra's (caught perhaps from her) to believe what he pleases! His treatment of Enobarbus shows him still capable of a generous act; a little ostentatious, as it may perhaps be. And the effect of that generous and forbearing tolerance shows that his fascination has not left him even in his evil fortune. He can still conquer hearts. And Cleopatra's? His, certainly, is still hers; and when, raging against the woman who has wrought all his miseries, he learns the news of her pretended death, it is with words full of the quiet of despair that he takes the blow which releases him:

> Unarm me, Eros; the long day's task is done,
> And we must sleep.
>
> [IV. xiv. 35-6]

Love, as it does always when death has freed us from what we had felt to be a burden, returns; and he stabs himself with the sole thought of rejoining her. When, this side of the grave, he does rejoin her, not a syllable of regret or reproach falls from his lips. In the presence of death he becomes gentle: the true sweetness of the man's nature, long poisoned, comes back again at last. Nothing now is left him but his love for Cleopatra, love refined to an oblivious tenderness; that, and the thought that death is upon him, and that he falls not ignobly:

> a Roman by a Roman
> Valiantly vanquished.
>
> [IV. xv. 57-8]

And so the fourth act ends on the magnificent words of Cleopatra over the dead body of the lord of the world and of her. The thought and the spectacle of death, of such a death, call out in her a far-thoughted reflection on the blindness of Fate, the general hazard of the world's course, with a vivid sense of the emptiness of all for which one takes thought. Death takes Antony as a mean man is taken; her, too, he leaves unqueened, a mere woman who has lost her lover. Then "all's but nought," the world is left poor, the light of it gone out; and it is with real sincerity, with a feeling of overwhelming disaster now irretrievably upon her, that she looks to "the briefest end" [IV. xv. 78, 91].

In her last days Cleopatra touches a certain elevation: the thought of the death she prepares for herself intoxicates (while it still frights) her reason. It gives her still a triumphant sense of her mastery over even Caesar, whom she will conquer by eluding; over even Destiny, from which she will escape by the way of death. After all, the keenest incitement to her choice comes from the thought of being led in triumph to Rome; of appearing there, little and conquered, before Octavia. She has lived a queen; in all her fortunes there has been, as she conceived it, no dishonour. She will die now, she would die a thousand times, rather than live to be a mockery and a scorn in men's mouths. How significant is her ceaseless and panging remembrance of Octavia! a touch of almost petty spite, the spite of a jealous woman. Petty, too (but, inexhaustible as she is in resources, turned, with the frank audacity of genius, into a final triumph) is the keeping back of the treasures. But craft is as natural to her as breath. It is by craft that she is to attain her end of dying. The means of that attainment, a poor man bringing death in his basket of figs, the very homeliness of the fact, comes with an added effect of irony in the passing of this imperial creature. She is a woman to the last, and it is in no heroic frame of mind that she commends the easiness of the death by which she is to die. Yet, too, all her greatness gathers itself, her love of Antony (the one thing that had ever been real and steadfast in the deadly quicksand of her mind) her pride and her tenderness, and, at the last, her resolution.

> I am fire and air; my other elements
> I give to baser life.
>
> [V. ii. 289-90]

So she dies, undisfigured in death, the signs of death barely perceptible, lying

> As she would catch another Antony
> In her strong toil of grace.
>
> [V. ii. 347-48]

And the play ends with a touch of grave pity over "a pair so famous" [V. ii. 360], cut off after a life so full of glory and of dishonour, and taking with them, in their passing out of it, so much of the warmth and colour of the world. (pp. 120-24)

> *Arthur Symons, in an introduction to "Antony and Cleopatra," in* The Works of William Shakespeare, *Vol. VI, edited by Henry Irving and Frank A. Marshall, Blackie & Son, Limited, 1892, pp. 113-24.*

WILLIAM WINTER (essay date 1892)

[*Winter was an American drama critic who wrote the three-volume* Shakespeare on the Stage *(1911-16) as well as biographies of several nineteenth- and early twentieth-century English and American actors and producers. Winter disparaged the rise of realism in the theater during the 1880s, and he forfeited much of his earlier influence as a critic by insisting that morality should be the paramount element in all drama. In the following excerpt from* Old Shrines and Ivy, *originally published in 1892, Winter argues that it is the larger-than-life quality of Antony and Cleopatra, their "splendid stature and infinite variety" that fascinates us. Their glorious and tumultuous world, he contends, offers a vivid contrast to normalcy and convention. Although Shakespeare has vivified their passion, Winter asserts, he has also implied a moral: that "nothing is more inevitably doomed than mortal delight in mortal love."*]

Whatever else may be said as to the drift of the tragedy of *Antony and Cleopatra* this certainly may with truth be said, that to strong natures that sicken under the weight of convention and are weary with looking upon the littleness of human nature in its ordinary forms, it affords a great and splendid, howsoever temporary, relief and refreshment. The winds of power blow through it; the strong meridian sunshine blazes over it; the colours of morning burn around it; the trumpet blares in its music; and its fragrance is the scent of a wilderness of roses. Shakespeare's vast imagination was here loosed upon colossal images and imperial splendours. The passions that clash or mingle in this piece are like the ocean surges—fierce, glittering, terrible, glorious. The theme is the ruin of a demigod. The adjuncts are empires. Wealth of every sort is poured forth

with regal and limitless profusion. The language glows with a prodigal emotion and towers to a superb height of eloquence. It does not signify, as modifying the effect of all this tumult and glory, that the stern truth of mortal evanescence is suggested all the way and simply disclosed at last in a tragical wreck of honour, love, and life. While the pageant endures it endures in diamond light, and when it fades and crumbles the change is instantaneous to darkness and death.

> The odds is gone,
> And there is nothing left remarkable
> Beneath the visiting moon.
>
> [IV. xv. 66-8]

There is no need to inquire whether Shakespeare—who closely followed Plutarch, in telling the Roman and Egyptian story—has been true to the historical fact. His characters declare themselves with absolute precision and they are not to be mistaken. Antony and Cleopatra are in middle life, and the only possible or admissible ideal of them is that which separates them at once and forever from the gentle, puny, experimental emotions of youth, and invests them with the developed powers and fearless and exultant passions of men and women to whom the world and life are a fact and not a dream. They do not palter. For them there is but one hour, which is the present, and one life, which they will entirely and absolutely fulfil. They have passed out of the mere instinctive life of the senses, into that more intense and thrilling life wherein the senses are fed and governed by the imagination. Shakespeare has filled this wonderful play with lines that tell unerringly his grand meaning in this respect—lines that, to Shakespearean scholars, are in the alphabet of memory:—

> There's beggary in the love that can be reckoned.
>
> [I. i. 15]

> There's not a minute of our lives should stretch
> Without some pleasure now.
>
> [I. i. 46-7]

> Let Rome in Tiber melt and the wide arch
> Of the ranged empire fall! Here is my space!
>
> [I. i. 33-4]

> O, thou day of the world,
> Chain mine armed neck! Leap thou, attire and all,
> Through proof of harness, to my heart and there
> Ride on the pants triumphant.
>
> [IV. viii. 13-16]

> Fall not a tear, I say! one of them rates
> All that is won and lost. Give me a kiss;
> Even this repays me.
>
> [III. xi. 69-71]

Here is no Orsino [in *Twelfth Night*], sighing for the music that is the food of love; no Romeo, taking the measure of an unmade grave; no Hamlet lover, bidding his mistress go to a nunnery. You may indeed, if you possess the subtle, poetic sense, hear, through this voluptuous story, the faint, far-off rustle of the garments of the coming Nemesis; the low moan of the funeral music that will sing those imperial lovers to their rest—for nothing is more inevitably doomed than mortal delight in mortal love, and no moralist ever taught his lesson of truth with more inexorable purpose than Shakespeare uses here. But in the meantime it is the present vitality and not the moral implication of the subject that actors must be concerned to show, and observers to recognise and comprehend, upon the stage, if this tragedy is to be rightly acted and rightly seen.

Antony and Cleopatra are lovers, but not lovers only. It is the splendid stature and infinite variety of character in them that render them puissant in fascination. Each of them speaks great thoughts in great language. Each displays noble imagination. Each becomes majestic in the hour of danger and pathetically heroic in the hour of death. The dying speeches of Antony are in the highest vein that Shakespeare ever reached; and, when you consider what is implied as well as what is said, there is nowhere in him a more lofty line than Cleopatra's

> Give me my robe, put on my crown; I have
> Immortal longings in me!
>
> [V. ii. 280-81]

Antony at the last is a ruin, and like a ruin—dark, weird, grim, lonely, haggard—he seems to stand beneath a cold and lurid sunset sky, wherein the black clouds gather, while the rising wind blows merciless and terrible over an intervening waste of rock and desert. Those images indicate the spirit and atmosphere of Shakespeare's conception. (pp. 219-23)

> William Winter, "A Mad World: 'Antony and Cleo-patra'," in his Old Shrines and Ivy, Macmillan and Company, 1892, pp. 219-23.

BERNHARD TEN BRINK   (lecture date 1893?)

[*A German of Dutch origin, Brink was a critic, philologist, and professor of English literature. His publications on* Beowulf *and* Chaucer *led to a revival of interest in these works in England as well as in Germany. Brink is best known for his two-volume* History of English Literature *(1883-96), originally published in German as* Geschichte der englischen Literatur *(1877-95). The following excerpt is taken from his* Shakspere *(1893), which comprises material he first delivered in a series of five lectures on the dramatist. Brink focuses on Cleopatra, coining the phrase "a courtesan of genius" to describe her and judging that she may be Shakespeare's masterpiece of female characterization. He is one of the earliest commentators to assert that Cleopatra and Antony are equally pivotal to the dramatic action of the play.*]

In "Antony and Cleopatra," the third in the series of Roman dramas, we see, for the first time since "Romeo and Juliet," a woman share on an equal footing with the principal character in the action of a Shakesperean tragedy. But what a contrast between Juliet and Cleopatra: one, a young girl, scarce more than a child, whom the might of a pure and unselfish passion transforms into a woman, whose whole being is absorbed by this love which consummates her character and her life; the other, a courtesan of genius, if I may say so, with experience of life and the world, devoted to pleasure, practiced in all the arts of seduction, endowed by nature with an alluring witchery, to whom the fire of her love for Antony alone lends a glimmer of womanly dignity. Artistically considered, Cleopatra is, perhaps, the masterpiece among Shakespeare's female characters; given the problem, Shakespeare has solved it as no one else could have done. But what conflicts must his soul have endured, what bitter experiences must he have passed through, to have set himself such a problem, to have created a woman so widely different from all those he had pictured before—a woman so devoid of the ideal womanly graces, yet so irresistible, for whose sake Antony sacrifices the dominion of the world. (pp. 90-1)

> Bernhard Ten Brink, "The Chronology of Shake-speare's Works," in his Five Lectures on Shake-speare, translated by Julia Franklin, Henry Holt and Company, 1895, pp. 49-101.

BERNARD SHAW   (essay date 1900)

[*Shaw, an Irish dramatist and critic, was the major English play-wright of his generation. In his Shakespearean criticism, he con-sistently attacked what he considered Shakespeare's inflated rep-utation as a dramatist. Shaw did not hesitate to judge the characters in the plays by the standards of his own values and prejudices, and much of his commentary is presented—as the prominent Shaw critic Edwin Wilson once remarked—"with an impudence that had not been seen before, nor is likely to be seen again." Shaw's hostility towards Shakespeare's work was due in large measure to his belief that it was interfering with the acceptance of Henrik Ibsen and the new social theater he so strongly advocated. The following excerpt is taken from the preface to Shaw's* Caesar and Cleopatra; *it was written in 1900 and first published in a collection entitled* Three Plays for Puritans *(1901). Shaw charges that it is intellectually dishonest to conclude the realistic portrayal of An-tony's debauched life and Cleopatra's wantonness with scenes that lend "a theatrical sublimity to the wretched end of the busi-ness." The transfiguration of Antony and Cleopatra into heroic, tragic figures, he asserts, is a perversion of truth. Shaw also argues that "sexual infatuation" is a comic theme, rather than a tragic one, and he censures Shakespeare for implying "that it alone makes our life worth living."*]

The very name of Cleopatra suggests at once a tragedy of Circe, with the horrible difference that whereas the ancient myth rightly represents Circe as turning heroes into hogs, the modern ro-mantic convention would represent her as turning hogs into heroes. Shakespear's *Antony and Cleopatra* must needs be as intolerable to the true Puritan as it is vaguely distressing to the ordinary healthy citizen, because, after giving a faithful picture of the soldier broken down by debauchery, and the typical wanton in whose arms such men perish, Shakespear finally strains all his huge command of rhetoric and stage pathos to give a theatrical sublimity to the wretched end of the business, and to persuade foolish spectators that the world was well lost by the twain. Such falsehood is not to be borne except by the real Cleopatras and Antonys (they are to be found in every public house) who would no doubt be glad enough to be trans-figured by some poet as immortal lovers. Woe to the poet who stoops to such folly! The lot of the man who sees life truly and thinks about it romantically is Despair. How well we know the cries of that despair! Vanity of vanities, all is vanity! moans the Preacher, when life has at last taught him that Nature will not dance to his moralist-made tunes. Thackeray, scores of centuries later, is still baying the moon in the same terms. Out, out, brief candle! cries Shakespear, in his tragedy of the modern literary man as murderer and witch consulter [*MacBeth*, V. v. 23]. Surely the time is past for patience with writers who, having to choose between giving up life in despair and dis-carding the trumpery moral kitchen scales in which they try to weigh the universe, superstitiously stick to the scales, and spend the rest of the lives they pretend to despise in breaking men's spirits. But even in pessimism there is a choice between intellectual honesty and dishonesty. . . . [When] your Shake-spears and Thackerays huddle up the matter at the end by killing somebody and covering your eyes with the undertaker's hand-kerchief, duly onioned with some pathetic phrase, as The flight of angels sing thee to thy rest [*Hamlet*, V. ii. 360], or Adsum, or the like, I have no respect for them at all: such maudlin tricks may impose on tea-drunkards, not on me.

Besides, I have a technical objection to making sexual infa-tuation a tragic theme. Experience proves that it is only effec-tive in the comic spirit. We can bear to see Mrs. Quickly pawning her plate for love of Falstaff, but not Antony running away from the battle of Actium for love of Cleopatra. Let realism have its demonstration, comedy its criticism, or even bawdry its horselaugh at the expense of sexual infatuation, if it must; but to ask us to subject our souls to its ruinous glamor, to worship it, deify it, and imply that it alone makes our life worth living, is nothing but folly gone mad erotically—a thing compared to which Falstaff's unbeglamored drinking and drabbing is respectable and rightminded. (pp. xxviii-xxix)

Bernard Shaw, ''Better than Shakespear?'' in his Three Plays for Puritans, Vol. 3, *1901. Reprint by Brentano's, 1906, pp. xxvii-xxxvii.*

HAMILTON WRIGHT MABIE   (essay date 1901)

[*Mabie was an American essayist and associate editor of* The Outlook. *His* William Shakespeare: Poet, Dramatist, and Man, *from which the following excerpt is taken, was originally published in 1900 and reprinted in a third, revised edition in 1901. Mabie views* Antony and Cleopatra *symbolically as dramatizing a ''moral collision'' of East and West, with the East eventually yielding to ''the superior fibre and more highly organized character of the West.'' He discovers an analogous opposition in Antony's innate ''Roman capacity for action and . . . [his] Eastern passion for pleasure.'' Mabie also praises the brilliance and energy of the play and Cleopatra's ''infinite variety.''*]

[*Antony and Cleopatra* is] a tragedy almost incredibly rich in variety and range of character and in splendour of setting. [Shakespeare] had recourse . . . to Plutarch's ''Life of Antonius,'' fastening . . . upon the nature and fate of one of the most fascinating figures on the stage of the antique world. That world he re-created in its strength and weakness, in its luxury and magnificence, in a drama which brought before the imagination with equal firmness of touch the power of Rome, personified in the disciplined and far-seeing Octavius, the voluptuous temperament of the East in Cleopatra, and the tragic collision of two great opposing conceptions of life in Mark Antony—a man born with the Roman capacity for action and the Eastern passion for pleasure. In Caesar's house in Rome, in newly contracted alliance with Octavius, Antony's heart is in Egypt:

I' the East my pleasure lies.

[II. iii. 41]

The style marks the transition to the poet's latest manner; rhyme almost disappears, and ''weak endings,'' or the use of weak monosyllables at the end of the lines, become very numerous. The poet had secured such conscious mastery of his art that he trusted entirely to his instinct and taste. The story in Plutarch's hands has a noble breadth and beauty, and is full of insight into the ethical relations of the chief actors in this world-drama. The full splendour of Shakespeare's genius has hardly done more than bring out dramatically the significance of these great words of the Greek biographer:

Antonius being thus inclined, the last and extremest mischief of all other (to wit, the love of Cleopatra) lighted on him, who did waken and stir up many vices yet hidden in him, and were never seen to any; and if any spark of goodness or hope of rising were left him, Cleopatra quenched it straight and made it worse than before.

Again and again Shakespeare touched upon this great theme and showed how tragic disaster issues out of unregulated passion and infects the coolest nature with madness; but nowhere else is that tragedy set on so great a stage and so magnificently

enriched with splendid gifts of nature, noble possessions, and almost limitless opportunities of achievement.

It is the drama of the East and West in mortal collision of ideals and motives, and the East succumbs to the superior fibre and more highly organized character of the West. Cleopatra is the greatest of the enchantresses. She has wit, grace, humour; the intoxication of sex breathes from her; she unites the passion of a great temperament with the fathomless coquetry of a courtesan of genius. She is passionately alive, avid of sensation, consumed with love of pleasure, imperious in her demands for that absolute homage which slays honour and saps manhood at the very springs of its power. This superb embodiment of femininity, untouched by pity and untroubled by conscience, has a compelling charm, born in the mystery of passion and taking on the radiance of a thousand moods which melt into one another in endless succession, as if there were no limit to the resources of her temperament and the sorceries of her beauty. Of her alone has the greatest of poets dared to declare that ''age cannot wither her, nor custom stale her infinite variety'' [II. ii. 234-35]. It is this magnificence which invests Cleopatra's criminality with a kind of sublimity, so vast is the scale of her being and so tremendous the force of her passions.

The depth of Shakespeare's poetic art and the power of his imagination are displayed in their full compass in ''Antony and Cleopatra.'' The play is vitalized as by fire, so radiant is it in energy and beauty of expression. Not only are the chief figures realized with historical fidelity, but they breathe the very atmosphere of the East. (pp. 335-38)

Hamilton Wright Mabie, ''The Later Tragedies,'' in his William Shakespeare: Poet, Dramatist, and Man, *third edition, The Macmillan Company, 1901, pp. 314-41.*

A. C. BRADLEY   (lecture date 1905)

[*Bradley was a major Shakespearean critic whose work culminated the method of character analysis initiated in the Romantic era. He is best known for his* Shakespearean Tragedy (1904), *a close analysis of* Hamlet, Othello, King Lear, *and* Macbeth. *Bradley concentrated on Shakespeare as a dramatist, and particularly on his characters, excluding not only the biographical questions so prevalent in the works of his immediate predecessors but also the questions of poetic structure, symbolism, and thematics which became prominent in later criticism. He thus may be seen as a pivotal figure in the transition in Shakespearean studies from the nineteenth to the twentieth century. He has been a major target for critics reacting against Romantic criticism, but he has continued to be widely read to the present day. Bradley's commentary on Antony and Cleopatra, excerpted below, was originally presented in a lecture at Oxford in 1905; in addition to its publication in* The Quarterly Review *in 1906, it was later reprinted in his* Oxford Lectures on Poetry (1909). *Bradley argues that although the play is a masterful achievement, it should not be regarded as a rival of* Hamlet, Othello, Macbeth, *and* King Lear, *principally because its purpose is not to arouse feelings of terror and pity and because it leaves us with sensations of ''triumph and pleasure'' rather than overwhelming sadness. The critic maintains that Antony is both a ''strumpet's fool'' and a figure of tragic stature, one who was born not to govern but to love Cleopatra, for she ''is his heart's desire made perfect.'' Bradley contends that it is not until Act V that Cleopatra becomes a tragic figure, attaining this status through her love for Antony; the critic emphasizes her inexhaustible variety, her compulsion to mesmerize every man she meets, and, most importantly, ''the spirit of fire and air in her'' that ''makes her wonderful and sovereign.'' Finally, he notes several glimmers of the supernatural in the*

Coleridge's one page of general criticism on 'Antony and Cleopatra' contains some notable remarks.

> Of all Shakespeare's historical plays (he writes), "Antony and Cleopatra" is by far the most wonderful. There is not one in which he has followed history so minutely, and yet there are few in which he impresses the notion of angelic strength so much—perhaps none in which he impresses it more strongly. This is greatly owing to the manner in which the fiery force is sustained throughout.

In a later sentence he refers to the play as 'this astonishing drama.' In another he describes the style: '*feliciter audax* is the motto for its style comparatively with that of Shakespeare's other works.' And he translates this motto in the phrase 'happy valiancy of style' [see excerpt above, 1813-34].

Coleridge's assertion that in 'Antony and Cleopatra' Shakespeare followed history more minutely than in any other play might well be disputed; and his statement about the style of this drama requires some qualification in view of the results of later criticism as to the order of Shakespeare's works. The style is less individual than he imagined. On the whole it is the style of all the dramas subsequent to 'Macbeth,' though in 'Antony and Cleopatra,' which probably followed that tragedy, the development of this style is not yet quite complete. And we must add that this style has certain marked defects, unmentioned by Coleridge, as well as the quality which he points out in it. But it is true that here that quality is almost continuously present; and in the phrase by which he describes it, as in his other phrases, he has signalised once for all some of the most salient features of the drama.

It is curious to notice, for example, alike in books and in conversation, how often the first epithets used in reference to 'Antony and Cleopatra' are 'wonderful' and 'astonishing.' And the main source of the feeling thus expressed seems to be the 'angelic strength' or 'fiery force' of which Coleridge wrote. The first of these two phrases is, I think, the more entirely happy. Except perhaps towards the close, one is not so conscious of fiery force as in certain other tragedies; but one is astonished at the apparent ease with which extraordinary effects are produced, the ease, if I may paraphrase Coleridge, of an angel moving with a wave of the hand that heavy matter which men find so intractable. (pp. 329-30)

I have still another sentence to quote from Coleridge.

> The highest praise, or rather form of praise, of this play which I can offer in my own mind (he writes), is the doubt which the perusal always occasions in me, whether the 'Antony and Cleopatra' is not, in all exhibitions of a giant power in its strength and vigour of maturity, a formidable rival of 'Macbeth,' 'Lear,' 'Hamlet,' and 'Othello.'

Unless the clause here about the 'giant power' may be taken to restrict the rivalry to the quality of angelic strength, Coleridge's doubt seems to show a lapse in critical judgment. To regard this tragedy as a rival of the famous four, whether on the stage or in the study, is surely an error. The world certainly has not so regarded it; and, though the world's reasons for its

verdicts on works of art may be worth little, its mere verdict is worth much. Here, it seems to me, it must be accepted. One may notice that, in calling 'Antony and Cleopatra' wonderful or astonishing, we appear to be thinking first of the artist and his activity, while in the case of the four famous tragedies it is the product of this activity, the thing presented, that first engrosses us. I know that I am stating this difference too sharply, but I believe that it is often felt; and, if this is so, the fact is significant. It implies that, although 'Antony and Cleopatra' may be for us as wonderful an achievement as the greatest of Shakespeare's plays, it has not an equal value. Besides, in the attempt to rank it with them there is involved something more, and more important, than an error in valuation. There is a failure to discriminate the peculiar marks of 'Antony and Cleopatra' itself, marks which, whether or no it be the equal of 'Hamlet' or 'Lear,' make it decidedly different. If I proceed to speak of some of these differences it is because they thus go to make the individuality of the play, and because in criticism they seem often not to be distinctly apprehended. (pp. 330-31)

Most of Shakespeare's tragedies are dramatic in a special sense of the word, as well as in its general sense, from beginning to end. The story is not merely exciting and impressive from the movement of conflicting forces towards a terrible issue; but from time to time there come situations and events which, even apart from their bearing on the future, appeal most powerfully to the dramatic feelings—scenes of action or passion which agitate the audience with alarm, horror, painful expectation, or absorbing sympathies and antipathies. Think of the street fights in 'Romeo and Juliet,' the killing of Mercutio and Tybalt, the rapture of the lovers, and their despair when Romeo is banished. Think of the ghost-scenes in the first Act of 'Hamlet,' the passion of the early soliloquies, the scene between Hamlet and Ophelia, the play-scene, the sparing of the King at prayer, the killing of Polonius. Is not 'Hamlet,' if you choose so to regard it, the best melodrama in the world? Think at your leisure of 'Othello,' 'Lear,' and 'Macbeth' from the same point of view; but consider here and now even the two tragedies which, as dealing with Roman history, are companions of 'Antony and Cleopatra.' Consider in 'Julius Caesar' the first suggestion of the murder, the preparation for it in a 'tempest dropping fire' [*Julius Caesar*, I. iii. 10], the murder itself, the speech of Antony over the corpse, and the tumult of the furious crowd; in 'Coriolanus' the bloody battles on the stage, the scene in which the hero attains the consulship, the scene of rage in which he is banished. And remember that all this, in each of those seven cases, comes before the third Act is finished.

In the first three Acts of our play what is there resembling this? Almost nothing. People converse, discuss, accuse one another, excuse themselves, mock, describe, drink together, arrange a marriage, meet and part; but they do not kill, do not even tremble or weep. We see hardly one violent movement; until the battle of Actium is over we witness scarcely any vehement passion; and that battle, as it is a naval action, we do not see. Even later, Enobarbus, when he dies, simply dies; he does not kill himself. We hear wonderful talk; but it is not talk, like that of Macbeth and Lady Macbeth, or Othello and Iago, at which we hold our breath. The scenes that we remember first are those that portray Cleopatra; Cleopatra coquetting, tormenting, beguiling her lover to stay; Cleopatra left with her women and longing for him; Cleopatra receiving the news of his marriage; Cleopatra questioning the messenger about Octavia's personal appearance. But this is to say that the scenes we remember first are the least indispensable to the plot. One at least is not essential to it at all. And this, the astonishing scene where she storms at the messenger, strikes him, and draws her dagger on him, is the one passage in the first half of the drama that contains either an explosion of passion or an exciting bodily action. Nor is this all. The first half of the play, though it forebodes tragedy, is not definitely tragic in tone. Certainly the Cleopatra scenes, even the one just referred to, are not so. We read them, and we should witness them, in delighted wonder and even with amusement. The only scene that can vie with them, that of the revel on Pompey's ship, is in great part humorous. Enobarbus, in this part of the play, is always humorous. Even later, when the tragic tone is deepening, the whipping of Thyreus, in spite of Antony's rage, moves mirth. A play of which all this can truly be said may well be as masterly as 'Othello' or 'Macbeth,' and more delightful; but, in the greater part of its course, it cannot possibly excite the same emotions. It does not attempt to do so; and to regard it as though it made this attempt is to miss its specific character and the intention of its author.

That character depends only in part on Shakespeare's fidelity to his historical authority. This fidelity (I may remark) is often greatly exaggerated; for Shakespeare did not merely present the story of ten years as though it occupied perhaps one fifth of that time, nor did he merely invent freely, but in critical places he made startling changes in the order and combination of events. Still it may be said that, dealing with a history so famous, he could not well make the first half of his play very exciting, moving, or tragic. And this is true so far as mere situations and events are concerned. But, if he had chosen, he might easily have heightened the tone and tension in another way. He might have made the story of Antony's attempt to break his bondage, and the story of his relapse, extremely exciting, by portraying with all his force the severity of the struggle and the magnitude of the fatal step. And the structure of the play might seem at first to suggest this intention. At the opening, Antony is shown almost in the beginning of his infatuation; for Cleopatra is not sure of her power over him, exerts all her fascination to detain him, and plays the part of the innocent victim who has yielded to passion and must now expect to be deserted by her seducer. Alarmed and ashamed at the news of the results of his inaction, he rouses himself, tears himself away, and speeds to Italy. His very coming is enough to frighten Pompey into peace. He reconciles himself with Octavius, and, by his marriage with the good and beautiful Octavia, seems to have knit a bond of lasting amity with her brother, and to have guarded himself against the passion that threatened him with ruin. At this point his power, the world's peace, and his own peace, appear to be secured; his fortune has mounted to its apex. But soon (very much sooner than in Plutarch's story) comes the downward turn or counter-stroke. New causes of offence arise between the brothers-in-law. To remove them Octavia leaves her husband in Athens and hurries to Rome. Immediately Antony returns to Cleopatra and, falling at once into a far more abject slavery than before, is quickly driven to his doom.

Now Shakespeare, I say, with his matchless power of depicting an inward struggle, might have made this story, even where it could not furnish him with thrilling incidents, the source of powerful tragic emotions; and, in doing so, he would have departed from his authority merely in his conception of the hero's character. But he does no such thing till the catastrophe is near. Antony breaks away from Cleopatra without any strenuous conflict. In a variety of ways we are prevented from feeling any real doubt of his return—through the impression made on us by Octavius, through occasional glimpses into Antony's mind, through the absence of any doubt in Enobarbus, through scenes in Alexandria which display Cleopatra and display her irresistible. And finally, the downward turn itself, the fatal step of Antony's return, is shown without the slightest emphasis. Nay, it is not shown, it is only reported; and not a line portrays any inward struggle preceding it. On this side also, then, the drama makes no attempt to rival the other tragedies; and it was essential to its own peculiar character and its most transcendent effects that this attempt should not be made, but that Antony's passion should be represented as a force which he could hardly even desire to resist. By the very scheme of the work, therefore, tragic impressions of any great volume or depth were reserved for the last stage of the conflict; while the main interest, down to the battle of Actium, was directed to matters exceedingly interesting and even, in the wider sense, dramatic, but neither terrible nor piteous—on the one hand, the political aspect of the story; on the other, the personal causes which helped to make the issue inevitable.

The political situation and its development are simple. The story is taken up almost where it was left, years before, in 'Julius Caesar.' There Brutus and Cassius, to prevent the rule of one man, assassinate Caesar. Their purpose is condemned to failure, not merely because they make mistakes, but because that political necessity which Napoleon identified with destiny requires the rule of one man. They spill Caesar's blood, but his spirit walks abroad and turns their swords against their own breasts; and the world is left divided among three men, his friends and his heir. Here 'Antony and Cleopatra' takes up the tale; and its business, from this point of view, is to show the reduction of these three to one. That Lepidus will not be this one was clear already in 'Julius Caesar'; it must be Octavius or Antony. Both ambitious, they are also men of such opposite tempers that they would scarcely long agree even if they wished to, and even if destiny were not stronger than they. As it is, one of them has fixed his eyes on the end, sacrifices everything for it, uses everything as a means to it. The other, though far the greater soldier and worshipped by his followers, has no such singleness of aim; nor yet is power, however desirable to him, the most desirable thing in the world. At the beginning he is risking it for love; at the end he has lost his half of the world, and lost his life, and Octavius rules alone. Whether Shakespeare had this clearly in his mind is a question neither answerable nor important; this is what came out of his mind.

Shakespeare, I think, took little interest in the character of Octavius, and he has not made it wholly clear. It is not distinct in Plutarch's 'Life of Antony'; and I have not found traces that the poet studied closely the 'Life of Octavius,' included in North's volume. To Shakespeare he is one of those men, like Bolingbroke, [in *1* and *2 Henry IV* and *Henry V*] and Ulysses [in *Troilus and Cressida*], who have plenty of 'judgment' and not much 'blood.' Victory in the world, according to the poet, almost always goes to such men; and he makes us respect, fear, and dislike them. His Octavius is very formidable, His cold determination half paralyses Antony; it is so even in 'Julius Caesar.' In 'Antony and Cleopatra' Octavius is more than once in the wrong, but he never admits it; he silently pushes his rival a step backward; and, when he ceases to fear, he shows contempt. He neither enjoys war nor is great in it; at first, therefore, he is anxious about the power of Pompey, and stands in need of Antony. As soon as Antony's presence has served his turn, and he has patched up a union with him and seen him safely off to Athens, he destroys first Pompey and next Lepidus. Then, dexterously using Antony's faithlessness to Octavia and excesses in the East in order to put himself in the right, he makes for his victim with admirable celerity while he is still drunk with the joy of reunion with Cleopatra. For his ends Octavius is perfectly efficient, but he is so partly from his limitations. One phrase of his is exceedingly characteristic. When Antony in rage and desperation challenges him to single combat, Octavius calls him 'the old ruffian.' There is a horrid aptness in the phrase, but it disgusts us. It is shameful in this boy, as hard and smooth as polished steel, to feel at such a time nothing of the greatness of his victim and the tragedy of his victim's fall. Though the challenge of Antony is absurd, we would give much to see them sword to sword. And, when Cleopatra by her death cheats the conqueror of his prize, we feel unmixed delight.

The doubtful point in the character is this. Plutarch says that Octavius was reported to love his sister Octavia dearly; and in the drama he several times expresses such love. When, then, he proposed her marriage with Antony (for of course it was he who spoke through Agrippa), was he honest, or was he laying a trap and, in doing so, sacrificing his sister? . . . If I were forced to choose, I should take the view that Octavius was, at any rate, not wholly honest; partly because I think this view best suits Shakespeare's usual way of conceiving a character of this kind; partly because Plutarch construed in this manner Octavius's behaviour in regard to his sister at a later time, and this hint might naturally influence the poet's way of imagining his earlier action.

Though the character of Octavius is neither attractive nor wholly clear, his figure is invested with a certain tragic dignity, because he is felt to be the Man of Destiny, the agent of forces against which the intentions of an individual would avail nothing. He is represented as having himself some feeling of this kind. His lament over Antony, his grief that their stars were irreconcilable, may be genuine, though we should be surer if it were uttered in soliloquy. His austere words to Octavia again may speak his true mind:—

> Be you not troubled with the time, which drives
> O'er your content these strong necessities;
> But let determined things to destiny
> Hold unbewailed their way.

>   [III. vi. 82-5]

In any case the feeling of destiny comes through to us. It is aided by slight touches of supernatural effect; first in the Soothsayer's warning to Antony that his genius or angel is overpowered whenever he is near Octavius; then in the strangely effective scene where Antony's soldiers, in the night before his last battle, hear music in the air or under the earth:

> 'Tis the god Hercules, whom Antony loved,
> Now leaves him.

>   [IV. iii. 16-17]

And to the influence of this feeling in giving impressiveness to the story is added that of the immense scale and world-wide issue of the conflict. Even the distances traversed by fleets and armies enhance this effect.

And yet there seems to be something half-hearted in Shakespeare's appeal here, something even ironical in his presentation of this conflict. Its external magnitude, like Antony's magnificence in lavishing realms and gathering the kings of the East in his support, fails to uplift or dilate the imagination. The struggle in Lear's little island seems to us to have an infinitely wider scope. It is here that we are sometimes reminded of 'Troilus and Cressida,' and the cold and disenchanting light that is there cast on the Trojan War. The spectacle which he portrays leaves Shakespeare quite undazzled; he even makes it appear inwardly small. The lordship of the world, we ask ourselves, what is it worth, and in what spirit do these 'world-sharers' contend for it? They are no champions of their country like Henry V. The conqueror knows not even the glory of battle. Their aims, for all we see, are as personal as if they were captains of banditti; and they are followed merely from self-interest or private attachment. The scene on Pompey's galley is full of this irony. One 'third part of the world' [II. vii. 90] is carried drunk to bed. In the midst of this mock boon-companionship the pirate whispers to his leader to cut first the cable of his ship and then the throats of the other two Emperors; and we should not greatly care if Pompey took the advice. Later, a short scene, totally useless to the plot, and purely satiric in its purport, is slipped in to show Ventidius afraid to pursue his Parthian conquests because it is not safe for Antony's lieutenant to outdo his master. A painful sense of hollowness oppresses us. We know too well what must happen in a world so splendid, so false, and so petty. We turn for relief from the political game to those who are sure to lose it; to those who love some human being better than a prize, to Eros and Charmian and Iras; to Enobarbus, whom the world corrupts, but who has a heart that can break with shame; to the lovers, who seem to us to find in death something better than their victor's life.

This presentation of the outward conflict has two results. First, it blunts our feeling of the greatness of Antony's fall from prosperity. Indeed this feeling, which we might expect to be unusually acute, is not so; it is less acute, for example, than the like feeling in the case of Richard II, who loses so much smaller a realm. Our deeper sympathies are focussed rather on Antony's heart, on the inward fall to which the enchantment of passion leads him, and the inward greatness which succeeds it. And the second result is this. The greatness of Antony and Cleopatra in their fall is so much heightened by contrast with the world they lose and the conqueror who wins it, that the positive element in the final tragic impression, the element of reconciliation, is strongly emphasised. The peculiar effect of the drama depends partly, as we have seen, on the absence of definitely tragic scenes and events in its first half, but it depends quite as much on this emphasis. In any Shakespearean tragedy we watch some elect spirit colliding, through its error and defect, with a superhuman power which bears it down; and yet we feel that this spirit, even in the error and defect, rises by its greatness into ideal union with the power that overwhelms it. In some tragedies this latter feeling is relatively weak. In 'Antony and Cleopatra' it is unusually strong; stronger, with some readers at least, than the fear and grief and pity with which they contemplate the tragic error and the advance of doom.

The two aspects of the tragedy are presented together in the opening scene. Here is the first. In Cleopatra's palace one friend of Antony is describing to another, just arrived from Rome, the dotage of their great general; and, as the lovers enter, he exclaims:—

>   Look, where they come:
> Take but good note, and you shall see in him
> The triple pillar of the world transformed
> Into a strumpet's fool: behold and see.

>   [I. i. 10-13]

With the next words the other aspect appears:—

Cleo.	If it be love indeed, tell me how much.
Ant.	There's beggary in the love that can be reckoned.
Cleo.	I'll set a bourne how far to be beloved.
Ant.	Then must thou needs find out new heaven, new earth.

[I. i. 14-17]

And directly after, when he is provoked by reminders of the news from Rome:—

> Let Rome in Tiber melt, and the wide arch
> Of the ranged empire fall! Here is my space.
> Kingdoms are clay: our dungy earth alike
> Feeds beast as man: the nobleness of life
> Is to do thus.

[I. i. 33-7]

Here is the tragic excess, and with it the tragic greatness, the capacity of finding in something the infinite, and of pursuing it into the jaws of death.

The two aspects are shown here with the exaggeration proper in dramatic characters. Neither the phrase 'a strumpet's fool,' nor the assertion 'the nobleness of life is to do thus,' answers to the total effect of the play. But the truths they exaggerate are equally essential; and the commoner mistake in criticism is to understate the second. It is plain that the love of Antony and Cleopatra is destructive; that in some way it clashes with the nature of things; that, while they are sitting in their paradise like gods, its walls move inward and crush them at last to death. This is no invention of moralising critics; it is in the play; and any one familiar with Shakespeare would expect beforehand to find it there. But then to forget because of it the other side, to deny the name of love to this ruinous passion, to speak as though the lovers had utterly missed the good of life, is to mutilate the tragedy and to ignore a great part of its effect upon us. For we sympathise with them in their passion; we feel in it the infinity there is in man; even while we acquiesce in their defeat we are exulting in their victory; and when they have vanished we say,

> the odds is gone,
> And there is nothing left remarkable
> Beneath the visiting moon.

[IV. xv. 66-8]

Though we hear nothing from Shakespeare of the cruelty of Plutarch's Antony, or of the misery caused by his boundless profusion, we do not feel the hero of the tragedy to be a man of the noblest type, like Brutus, Hamlet, or Othello. He seeks power merely for himself and uses it for his own pleasure. He is in some respects unscrupulous; and, while it would be unjust to regard his marriage exactly as if it were one in private life, we resent his treatment of Octavia, whose character Shakespeare was obliged to leave a mere sketch, lest our feeling for the hero and heroine should be too much chilled. Yet, for all this, we sympathise warmly with Antony, are greatly drawn to him, and are inclined to regard him as a noble nature half spoiled by his time.

It is a large, open, generous, expansive nature, quite free from envy, capable of great magnanimity, even of entire devotion. Antony is unreserved, naturally straight-forward, we may almost say simple. He can admit faults, accept advice and even reproof, take a jest against himself with good-humour. He is courteous (to Lepidus, for example, whom Octavius treats with cold contempt); and, though he can be exceedingly dignified, he seems to prefer a blunt though sympathetic plainness, which is one cause of the attachment of his soldiers. He has none of the faults of the brooder, the sentimentalist, or the man of principle; his nature tends to splendid action and lusty enjoyment. But he is neither a mere soldier nor a mere sensualist. He has imagination, the temper of an artist who revels in abundant and rejoicing appetites, feasts his senses on the glow and richness of life, flings himself into its mirth and revelry, yet feels the poetry in all this, and is able also to put it by and be more than content with the hardships of adventure. Such a man could never have sought a crown by a murder like Macbeth's, or, like Brutus, have killed on principle the man who loved him, or have lost the world for a Cressida.

Beside this strain of poetry he has a keen intellect, a swift perception of the lie of things, and much quickness in shaping a course to suit them. In 'Julius Caesar' he shows this after the assassination, when he appears as a dexterous politician as well as a warm-hearted friend. . . . Full of genuine grief, he uses his grief like an artist to work on others, and greets his success with the glee of a successful adventurer. In the earlier play he proves himself a master of eloquence, and especially of pathos; and he does so again in the later. With a few words about his fall, he draws tears from his followers and even from the caustic humorist Enobarbus. Like Richard II, he sees his own fall with the eyes of a poet, but a poet much greater than the young Shakespeare, who could never have written Antony's wonderful speech about the sunset clouds. But we listen to Antony, as we do not to Richard, with entire sympathy, partly because he is never unmanly, partly because he himself is sympathetic and longs for sympathy.

The first of living soldiers, an able politician, a most persuasive orator, Antony nevertheless was not born to rule the world. He enjoys being a great man, but he has not the love of rule for rule's sake. Power for him is chiefly a means to pleasure. The pleasure he wants is so huge that he needs a huge power; but half the world, even a third of it, would suffice. He will not pocket wrongs, but he shows not the slightest wish to get rid of his fellow Triumvirs and reign alone. He never minded being subordinate to Julius Caesar. By women he is not only attracted but governed; from the effect of Cleopatra's taunts we can see that he had been governed by Fulvia. Nor has he either the patience or the steadfastness of a born ruler. He contends fitfully, and is prone to take the step that is easiest at the moment. This is the reason why he consents to marry Octavia. It seems the shortest way out of an awkward situation. He does not intend even to try to be true to her. He will not think of the distant consequences.

A man who loved power even as thousands of insignificant people love it would have made a sterner struggle than Antony's against his enchantment. He can hardly be said to struggle at all. He brings himself to leave Cleopatra only because he knows he will return. In every moment of his absence, whether he wake or sleep, a siren music in his blood is singing him back to her and to this music, however he may be occupied, the soul within his soul leans and listens. The joy of life had always culminated for him in the love of women: he could say 'no' to none of them: of Octavia herself he speaks like a poet. When he meets Cleopatra he finds his Absolute. She satisfies, nay glorifies, his whole being. She intoxicates his senses. Her wiles, her taunts, her furies and meltings, her laughter and tears, bewitch him all alike. She loves what he loves, and she surpasses him. She can drink him to his bed, out-jest his practical jokes, out-act the best actress who ever amused him, out-dazzle his own magnificence. She is his playfellow, and yet a great queen. Angling in the river, playing billiards, flourishing the sword he used at Philippi, hopping forty paces in a public street, she remains an enchantress. Her spirit is made of wind and flame, and the poet in him worships her no less than the man. He is under no illusion about her, knows all her faults, sees through her wiles, believes her capable of betraying him. It makes no difference. She is his heart's desire made perfect. To love her is what he was born for. What have the gods in heaven to say against it? To imagine heaven is to imagine her; to die is to rejoin her. To deny that this is love is the madness of morality. He gives her every atom of his heart.

She destroys him. Shakespeare, availing himself of the historic fact, portrays, on Antony's return to her, the suddenness and depth of his descent. In spite of his own knowledge, the protests of his captains, the entreaties even of a private soldier, he fights by sea simply and solely because she wishes it. Then in mid-battle, when she flies, he deserts navy and army and his faithful thousands and follows her. 'I never saw an action of such shame,' cries Scarus [III. x. 20]; and we feel the dishonour of the hero keenly. Then Shakespeare begins to raise him again. First, his own overwhelming sense of shame redeems him. Next, we watch the rage of the dying lion. Then the mere sally before the final defeat—a sally dismissed by Plutarch in three lines—is magnified into a battle, in which Antony displays to us, and himself feels for the last time, the glory of his soldiership. And, throughout, the magnanimity and gentleness which shine through his desperation endear him to us. How beautiful is his affection for his followers and even for his servants, and the devotion they return! How noble his reception of the news that Enobarbus has deserted him! How touchingly significant the refusal of Eros either to kill him or survive him! How pathetic and even sublime the completeness of his love for Cleopatra! His anger is born and dies in an hour. One tear, one kiss, outweighs his ruin. He believes she has sold him to his enemy, yet he kills himself because he hears that she is dead. When, dying, he learns that she has deceived him once more, no thought of reproach crosses his mind: he simply asks to be carried to her. He knows well that she is not capable of dying because he dies, but that does not sting him; he only calls back his last breath to advise her for the days to come. Shakespeare borrowed from Plutarch the final speech of Antony. It is fine, but it is not miraculous. The miraculous speeches belong only to his own hero:—

> I am dying, Egypt, dying; only
> I here importune death awhile, until
> Of many thousand kisses the poor last
> I lay upon thy lips.
>
> [IV. xv. 18-21]

or the first words he utters when he hears of Cleopatra's death:—

> Unarm, Eros, the long day's task is done,
> And we must sleep.
>
> [IV. xiv. 35-6]

If he meant the task of statesman and warrior, that is not what his words mean to us. They remind us of words more familiar and less great—

> No rest but the grave for the pilgrim of love.

And he is more than love's pilgrim; he is love's martyr. (pp. 332-45)

The hero dies in the fourth Act, and the whole of the fifth is devoted to the heroine. In that Act she becomes unquestionably

a tragic character, but, it appears to me, not till then. This, no doubt, is a heresy, but, as I cannot help holding it, and as it is connected with the remarks already made on the first half of the play, I will state it more fully. Cleopatra stands in a group with Hamlet and Falstaff. We might join with them Iago, but that he is decidedly their inferior in one particular quality. They are inexhaustible. You feel that, if they were alive and you spent your whole life with them, their infinite variety could never be staled by custom; they would continue every day to surprise, perplex, and delight you. Shakespeare has bestowed on each of them, though they differ so much, his own originality, his genius. He has given it most fully to Hamlet, to whom none of the chambers of experience is shut, and perhaps more of it to Cleopatra than to Falstaff. Nevertheless, if we ask whether Cleopatra, in the first four Acts, is a tragic figure like Hamlet, we surely cannot answer 'yes.' Naturally it does not follow that she is a comic figure like Falstaff. This would be absurd; for, even if she were ridiculous like Falstaff, she is not ridiculous to herself; she is no humorist. And yet there is a certain likeness. She shares a weakness with Falstaff— vanity; and when she displays it, as she does quite naïvely (for instance, in the second interview with the Messenger), she does become comic. Again, though like Falstaff she is irresistible, and carries us away no less than the people around her, we are secretly aware, in the midst of our delight, that her empire is built on sand. And finally, as his love for the Prince gives dignity and pathos to Falstaff in his overthrow, so what raises Cleopatra at last into tragedy is, in part, that which some critics have denied her, her love for Antony.

Many unpleasant things can be said of Cleopatra; and the more are said the more wonderful she appears. The exercise of sexual attraction is the element of her life; and she has developed nature into a consummate art. When she cannot exert it on the present lover she imagines its effects on him in absence. Longing for the living, she remembers with pride and joy the dead; and the past which the furious Antony holds up to her as a picture of shame is, for her, glory. She cannot see an ambassador, scarcely even a messenger, without desiring to bewitch him. Her mind is saturated with this element. If she is dark, it is because the sun himself has been amorous of her. Even when death is close at hand she imagines his touch as a lover's. She embraces him that she may overtake Iras and gain Antony's first kiss in the other world.

She lives for feeling. Her feelings are, so to speak, sacred, and pain must not come near her. She has tried numberless experiments to discover the easiest way to die. Her body is exquisitely sensitive, and her emotions marvellously swift. They are really so; but she exaggerates them so much, and exhibits them so continually for effect, that some readers fancy them merely feigned. (pp. 346-47)

Some of her feelings are violent, and, unless for a purpose, she does not dream of restraining them; her sighs and tears are winds and waters, storms and tempests. At times, as when she threatens to give Charmian bloody teeth, or hales the luckless Messenger up and down by the hair, strikes him and draws her knife on him, she resembles (if I dare say it) Doll Tearsheet [in *2 Henry IV*] sublimated. She is a mother; but the threat of Octavius to destroy her children if she takes her own life passes by her like the wind (a point where Shakespeare contradicts Plutarch). She ruins a great man, but shows no sense of the tragedy of his ruin. The anguish of spirit that appears in his language to his servants is beyond her; she has to ask Enobarbus what he means. Can we feel sure that she would not have

Act III. Scene xiii. Enobarbus, Antony, Thidias, Iras, Cleopatra and Charmian. Frontispiece to the Bell edition by E. Edwards (1774).

sacrificed him if she could have saved herself by doing so? It is not even certain that she did not attempt it. Antony himself believes that she did—that the fleet went over to Octavius by her orders. That she and her people deny the charge proves nothing. The best we can say is that, if it were true, Shakespeare would have made that clear. She is willing also to survive her lover. Her first thought, to follow him after the high Roman fashion, is too great for her. She would live on if she could, and would cheat her victor too of the best part of her fortune. The thing that drives her to die is the certainty that she will be carried to Rome to grace his triumph. That alone decides her.

The marvellous thing is that the knowledge of all this makes hardly more difference to us than it did to Antony. It seems to us perfectly natural, nay, in a sense perfectly right, that her lover should be her slave; that her women should adore her and die with her; that Enobarbus, who foresaw what must happen, and who opposes her wishes and braves her anger, should talk of her with rapture and feel no bitterness against her; that Dolabella, after a minute's conversation, should betray to her his master's intention and enable her to frustrate it. And when Octavius shows himself proof against her fascination, instead of admiring him, we turn from him with disgust and think him a disgrace to his species. Why? It is not that we

consider him bound to fall in love with her. Enobarbus did not; Dolabella did not; we ourselves do not. The feeling she inspires was felt then, and is felt now, by women no less than men, and would have been shared by Octavia herself. Doubtless she wrought magic on the senses, but she had not extraordinary beauty, like Helen's, such beauty as seems divine. Plutarch says so. The man who wrote the sonnets to the dark lady would have known it for himself. He goes out of his way to add to her age, and tells us of her wrinkles and the waning of her lip. But Enobarbus, in his very mockery, calls her a wonderful piece of work. Dolabella interrupts her with the cry, 'Most sovereign creature' [V. ii. 81], and we echo it. And yet Octavius, face to face with her, and listening to her voice, can think only how best to trap her and drag her to public dishonour in the streets of Rome. We forgive him only for his words when he sees her dead:—

> She looks like sleep,
> As she would catch another Antony
> In her strong toil of grace.
>
> 　　　　　　　　[V. ii. 346-48]

And the words, I confess, sound to me more like Shakespeare's than his.

That which makes her wonderful and sovereign laughs at definition, but she herself came nearest naming it when, in the final speech (a passage surpassed in poetry, if at all, only by the final speech of Othello), she cries—

> I am fire and air; my other elements
> I give to baser life.
>
> 　　　　　　　　[V. ii. 289-90]

The fire and air which at death break from union with those other elements, transfigured them during her life, and still convert into engines of enchantment the very things for which she is condemned. I can refer only to one. She loves Antony. We should marvel at her less and love her more if she loved him more—loved him well enough to follow him at once to death; but it is to blunder strangely to doubt that she loved him, or that her glorious description of him (though it was also meant to work on Dolabella) came from her heart. Only the spirit of fire and air within her refuses to be trammelled or extinguished, burns its way through the obstacles of fortune, even through the resistance of her love and grief, and would lead her undaunted to fresh life and the conquest of new worlds. It is this which makes her 'strong toil of grace' unbreakable; speaks in her brows' bent and every tone and movement; glorifies the arts and the rages which in another would merely disgust or amuse us; and, in the final scenes of her life, flames into such brilliance that we watch her entranced as she struggles for freedom, and thrilled with triumph as, conquered, she puts her conqueror to scorn and goes to meet her lover in the splendour that crowned and robed her long ago, when her barge burnt on the water like a burnished throne, and she floated to Cydnus on the enamoured stream to take him captive for ever.

Why is it that, although we close the book in a triumph which is more than reconciliation, this is mingled, as we look back on the story, with a sadness so peculiar, almost the sadness of disenchantment? Is it that, when the glow has faded, Cleopatra's ecstasy comes to appear, I would not say factitious, but an effort strained and prodigious as well as glorious, not, like Othello's last speech, the final expression of character, of thoughts and emotions which have dominated a whole life? Perhaps this is so, but there is something more, something that sounds paradoxical: we are saddened by the very fact that the catastrophe saddens us so little; it pains us that we should feel so much triumph and pleasure. In 'Romeo and Juliet,' 'Hamlet,' 'Othello,' though in a sense we accept the deaths of hero and heroine, we feel a keen sorrow. We look back, think how noble or beautiful they were, wish that fate had opposed to them a weaker enemy, dream possibly of the life they might then have led. Here we can hardly do this. With all our admiration and sympathy for the lovers we do not wish them to gain the world. It is better for the world's sake, and not less for their own, that they should fail and die. At the very first they came before us, unlike those others, unlike Coriolanus and even Macbeth, in a glory already tarnished, half-ruined by their past. Indeed one source of strange and most unusual effect in their story is that this marvellous passion comes to adepts in the experience and art of passion, who might be expected to have worn its charm away. Its splendour dazzles us; but, when the splendour vanishes, we do not mourn, as we mourn for the love of Romeo or Othello, that a thing so bright and good should die. And the fact that we mourn so little saddens us.

A comparison of Shakespearean tragedies seems to prove that the tragic emotions are stirred in the fullest possible measure only when such beauty or nobility of character is displayed as commands unreserved admiration or love; or when, in default of this, the forces which move the agents, and the conflict which results from these forces, attain a terrifying and overwhelming power. The four most famous tragedies satisfy one or both of these conditions; 'Antony and Cleopatra,' though a great tragedy, satisfies neither of them completely. But to say this is not to criticise it. It does not attempt to satisfy these conditions, and then fail in the attempt. It attempts something different, and succeeds as triumphantly as 'Othello' itself. In doing so it gives us what no other tragedy can give, and it leaves us, no less than any other, lost in astonishment at the powers which created it. (pp. 347-51)

> *A. C. Bradley, ''Shakespeare's 'Antony and Cleopatra','' in* The Quarterly Review, *Vol. 204, No. 407, April, 1906, pp. 329-51.*

R. H. CASE (essay date 1906)

[*Case was the editor of the first Arden edition of* Antony and Cleopatra, *published in 1906. In the excerpt below, he asserts that while the play is as dramatically masterful as* Hamlet, Othello, Macbeth, *and* King Lear, *it differs from these works in several important ways. Case argues that ''profundities of tragic feeling'' are absent in* Antony and Cleopatra, *that the deaths of the protagonists represent their most triumphant rather than despairing moments, that the sense of political catastrophe is only minimal, and that the dramatic structure is flawed because it offers no ''rousing incident till the play is far advanced.'' Additionally, the critic regards Cleopatra as ''a problem.'' Particularly unclear, Case maintains, is the reason why she elects to kill herself, but he concludes that her love for Antony and her desire not to live without him are more significant, in this regard, than her fear of public humiliation in Rome.*]

Since Coleridge's famous criticism of *Antony and Cleopatra* in his *Notes and Lectures,* there has been no danger of the play's being under-rated, and the impression received from many examens in which this criticism is cited is that there is a tendency for its doubt to be ignored and its limitations obscured. Coleridge expressed a ''doubt . . . whether the *Antony and Cleopatra* is not, in all exhibitions of a giant power in its strength and vigour of maturity, a formidable rival of the *Macbeth, Lear, Hamlet,* and *Othello*'' [see excerpt above, 1813-34];

but even if we replace the doubt by an absolute certainty, there remains the fact that a special point of comparison is indicated, viz. ''all exhibitions of a giant power in its strength and vigour of maturity.'' It is in this respect only that comparison is possible with the other plays named by Coleridge, for, in the first place, *Antony and Cleopatra* belongs to a type of play defective in construction and absorbing centre of interest. The Chronicle play has its compensations: we see in *Antony and Cleopatra* vivid presentation of the earlier processes which lead to tragedy, set before us in a series of significant pictures; but historical fact is lopped and telescoped only so far as is indispensable to a stage-plot, and it does not in this case provide any rousing incident till the play is far advanced. Secondly, there is in the theme at its intensest, and the characters at their deepest, a defect of tragedy in comparison with that of the greater plays. The world-tragedy . . . is here too little insistently obvious, and depends too much for its effect on the constitution of a reader's mind, to surround the sufferers with a deeper gloom than their destiny can bestow. The magnanimity of Antony sets him above fate at last, and the death of Cleopatra is her triumph. We see these lovers hasten to reunion ''where souls do couch on flowers'' [IV. xiv. 51]; there is what meeting for Othello and Desdemona?

> O ill-starr'd wench!
> Pale as thy smock! when we shall meet at compt,
> This look of thine will hurl my soul from heaven
> And fiends will snatch at it.
>
> [*Othello,* V. ii. 272-75]

The appalling situations of Macbeth or Othello, set between retrospect and prospect of horror, have no parallel here, and the despairs of Antony and Cleopatra are never as theirs: the profundities of tragic feeling which awe us in their words belong to an abyss of which the two who have been erected to rivalry with them know nothing. The utterance of the latter, for all its magnificence of poetry and pathos, is more conscious, and has in it something of the luxury of woe: it is of their own plane of enchantment, where ''all the haunt'' [IV. xiv. 54] is indeed theirs; it is not humanly heart-rending, nor language of despair fit for a Hall of Eblis.

An extraordinarily vivid presentment in Elizabethan terms of events and characters of the ancient world, with truth to life as its one restraining condition, *Antony and Cleopatra* is almost as far removed from the tragedies as it is from the decorous treatment of the same theme by the Senecan school of poets. The ethical value of that theme is considerable, and has its due weight. Events enforce it, and draw from Enobarbus witty sarcasms, from Antony many a bitter reflection on his own folly. But this is all: the riotous life of pleasure betrays its charm beside its cost, and the ultimate effects of all the moralist would condemn are moral and not immoral. There is a temporary ''diminution in our captain's brain'' [III. xiii. 197] as a permanent one in his fortunes, but all that is great in him, his heart-winning magnanimity in its various manifestations, is conspicuous as ever, and to this is now added the capacity for devotion and self-forgetfulness which he pitifully lacked before. It is absurd to shake our heads over Antony's love because, in the sharp reversal of the situation of himself and Cleopatra with respect to one another, he pays for the mortifications and distresses he had once inflicted on her, in frenzied doubts of a fidelity suspiciously unstable in our eyes as well as his. It must be tested by the unselfish devotion at the supreme hour which renders it incapable of differentiation from a virtuous passion, and which (at first sight, at any rate) is in such striking contrast with Cleopatra's care for her own safety when love and pity should have exiled every other thought.

It is said that Shakespeare softened or suppressed Antony's worst traits as he found them in North; but his instanced cruelties and oppressions precede as much of the story as is retold in the play, and a dramatist must have gone out of his way to reveal in him anything beyond what we gather from his treacherous and cold-blooded treatment of Octavia. It is even questionable whether his good qualities are not more conspicuous in Shakespeare than in Plutarch only because of the diminished size of the canvas; but the former certainly gives them full dramatic effect, and from the first we are attracted by glimpses of the "noble minde," "the rare and singular gifts," with which Plutarch loves to "soften to the heart" Antonius' story.

In this play, as in life, things extraneous to passion strengthen its hold for good or evil. In all probability, Antony must have returned to Cleopatra, but two factors besides infatuation are assigned, the "holy cold and still conversation" [II. vi. 122-23] of Octavia, and, very definitely, the supposed subjection of his genius to Caesar's. Similarly, something *apparently* stronger than her love for Antony, yet, perhaps, connected with it—her royal determination to endure no bonds nor ignominy—seem to transform Cleopatra after his death and to allow that passion to gain depth and dignity under its powerful shelter. She deceives Caesar with exultant cunning, and throughout, in her unswerving purpose, in the tolerance with which she suffers the garrulous clown, in the wonderful language of her exultation, free now from all suspicious notes, she exerts, in this dilation to a tragic figure, a fascination which some may have so far heard more about than felt.

To create his Cleopatra, Shakespeare to some extent forsook Plutarch. His Queen of Egypt is a figure of coarser fibre than that which moves in the prose narrative, even allowing for the strong lights of dialogue; and the arts of irritating perverseness employed in I. iii, where Cleopatra's conduct is not indicated in Plutarch, are of harder cast than "the flickering enticements" with which, at a later time, the latter shows her seeking to keep Antony from Octavia; when she seemed to languish for love, contrived that Antony should often find her weeping, and then made show of hiding her tears, "as if she were unwilling that he should see her weepe" [Plutarch]. The original, with its subtlety preserved or augmented, is outgone in this draught of a type of the sex as well vehement and full-blooded as full of wiles and caprices, in whom qualities of brain and energetic life strike more than "the courteous nature that tempered her words and deeds," and the gift of "words . . . marvelous pleasant" less than its reverse; but the wondrous charm for which the character in its earlier manifestations is praised so unstintedly, seems, in the main, to be unconsciously transferred from the incomparable descriptions of Enobarbus. Of course it does not matter how the illusion is produced, except as a question for the critic; but Cleopatra, as self-revealed merely, does not, I venture to think, altogether justify the somewhat Lepidian "kneel down, kneel down, and wonder" [III. ii. 19] attitude of her admirers. Johnson spoke of "the feminine arts, some of which are too low, which distinguish Cleopatra" [see excerpt above, 1765], but an earlier and kinder critic has set the tune of comment, and the most fastidious almost outvie his "vilest things become themselves in her" [II. ii. 237-38].

If we apply to Cleopatra, and extend, her own metaphor for Antony, one way we look on majesty ("Isis else defend!"' [III. iii. 43]), the other way is painted in hues that belong to

Madam Caesarean's; but full front she is "a very woman," and the question suggests itself: did Shakespeare intend to leave her a problem for this excellent reason? or was he unable to make up his own mind about her? We may probably dismiss from consideration any idea of the play's being incomplete as it stands, or even of vagueness due to haste.

We do not even know whether Cleopatra paltered with Caesar after Actium, and there are ill-sounding notes in her protestations like the tuneless strings in a neglected instrument. We undoubtedly receive an impression, which I hinted at just now, and which seems to go unquestioned, that Shakespeare intentionally represented Cleopatra less favourably than Plutarch in dealing with the motive of her death. Such an impression goes for much, and the fewer the touches that produce it, the greater the writer's art; but even if the inquiry be narrowed to this last respect, it is worth making.

In Plutarch, there is no direct mention of what is so strongly enforced in Shakespeare, and previously in Daniel, Cleopatra's dread of being made part of Caesar's triumph in Rome. He merely states the fact that Cleopatra would not open the gates of the monument, and later, that Dolabella, as she had requested him, informed her that Caesar would within three days send her away before him with her children. In a moving speech as Antony's tomb, she lays stress on her preservation by Caesar only that he may triumph over Antony: there is no word of her own fear of ignominy, and she implores Antony to help her to foil this attempt to triumph over him, and to save her from the misery she endures in living without him. Before this, Plutarch has already told us of her self-disfigurement for grief and her attempt to make the resulting fever fatal by the aid of starvation, from which she was only deterred by Caesar's threat of slaying her children—a threat as little permanently effective as in Shakespeare, however, for Dolabella's news determines her action in Plutarch as in him.

Shakespeare's omissions throw into strong relief his development of the mere hint of a second motive for self-destruction, but it is not absolutely certain that he meant us to infer that this second motive was the only efficient one, and that Cleopatra would gladly have survived. He inserts in the final scene with Antony [IV. xv. 49-50] and after his death [IV. xv. 80ff.] expressions on the part of Cleopatra of determination to die, which rest as much or more on the desire not to outlive Antony as on the unwillingness to endure ignominy. He gives us no right to judge this determination weakened, for it is her first thought when we meet her next, and she reveals then, and in the ensuing scene with Proculeius, no incipient hope of life with grace at Caesar's hands. She has her dagger ready when she is seized, her thought of starvation leaps to her lips, and the fact that, on such an occasion, what she naturally bursts out with is her dread and hatred of the triumph, does not exclude the continuance of her unwillingness to outlive Antony. Caesar's lies cause her no hesitation, as they might be expected to do if she really cared to survive, or was only moved by fear of disgrace: her directions are at once given to Charmian [V. ii. 192], and this *precedes* Dolabella's final and positive information of Caesar's purpose. Here, if anywhere, there is token of omission or confusion. Dolabella had previously assured her that Caesar would lead her in triumph, and he had not, as he now says, been either commanded or sworn to obtain confirmation of that intention.

We have now once more a recurrence to the theme of Caesar's triumph, this time partly to stimulate Iras (as Antony himself had used it to induce Eros to kill him), and it would be the height of absurdity to underrate the force of the desire to escape it as a motive in Cleopatra. I am only endeavouring to ascertain how far we are justified in regarding this, and this only, as what enabled her to "be noble" to herself; and perhaps the best plea I can put in for her love is an appeal to the first appearance of these "triumph" passages. It seems as if Shakespeare felt the necessity of accounting for Cleopatra's refusal to open the gates of the monument, and did so in a way which we interpret adversely to her; but let us recollect the lovers' last previous parting, and admit a doubt whether we should not, like Antony, "weep for" our "pardon." In language as forcible as he could make it, which has not the remotest suggestion in Plutarch, Antony had at once declared his belief in Cleopatra's willingness to grace Caesar's triumph, and the miserable part she would play in it. Such words would surely haunt her; and by her action and the echo of them now, even of the reference to Octavia—a feminine touch, which, if it were not an echo, would go far to overthrow my plea—she took the readiest way to prove their untruth, and to assure Antony that she would help no triumph over him, nor let what he had so jealously engrossed suffer ignominy. If it were so, all was indeed—

> well done, and fitting for a princess
> Descended of so many royal kings.
>
> [V. ii. 326-27]
> (pp. xxxii-xxxvii)

R. H. Case, in an introduction to Antony and Cleopatra *by William Shakespeare, edited by M. R. Ridley, revised edition, Harvard University Press, 1956, pp. xxv-xlvi.*

HORACE HOWARD FURNESS   (essay date 1907)

[*Furness was an American lawyer who abandoned law to devote his life to Shakespearean studies. In 1871 he became the first editor of the New Variorum edition of Shakespeare's works with the publication of* Romeo and Juliet. *Eighteen volumes appeared under his editorship, all of which drew heavily on the First Folio of 1623. The value of Furness's work rests on his extensive textual, critical, and annotative notes derived from the best authorities of the time. In the following excerpt, Furness asserts that Cleopatra loves Antony as deeply and sincerely as he loves her, but with even greater fidelity. Their love is not characterized by sensuality or sexual appetite, the critic argues, and he discerns in Cleopatra's dream speech (V. ii. 76ff.) Shakespeare's revelation of "the qualities of the god-like Antony which had won and kept the Egyptian Queen's heart." Rebutting the charge that Cleopatra behaves dishonestly and viciously in the scene with Octavius and Seleucus, Furness endorses the proposal of an earlier German critic, Adolf Stahr (see Additional Bibliography), that the entire incident was prearranged by the queen and her treasurer in order to conceal her intended suicide from Octavius. The critic also offers a strong defense of Octavius, contending that he is generous-hearted and sympathetic and that Shakespeare intended us to regard his love for Antony as "perfectly sincere and very deepseated."*]

[Possibly] we may scrutinize too closely the sources whence Shakespeare drew his plots, especially in the *Historical Plays*. We learn too much, and bring our knowledge to the interpretation of the plays. It is possible that, thus biased, our judgement becomes warped, and we read into a character somewhat that Shakespeare may not, possibly, have intended. It seems to me that we should accept these plays with our mind the proverbial *tabula rasa*, whence every previous record has been wiped away, and all the light we have comes, untinted, direct

from Shakespeare. In [*Antony and Cleopatra*] I think two characters, at least, have suffered from this extrinsic knowledge on our part: Cæsar is one and Cleopatra,—yes, even Cleopatra,—is another. All that Cæsar says or does we regard as said or done by the Cæsar whom we have known aforetime. We shut our eyes to noble traits which Shakespeare offers us, and open them only on the crafty image of our school-days. Throughout the play, I believe Shakespeare intends us to accept Cæsar's love for Anthony as perfectly sincere and very deepseated. Witness the Scene where Cæsar learns of Anthony's personal challenge and of his brutal conduct in having Cæsar's own ambassador most disgracefully whipt. With justifiable heat Cæsar breaks out, and calls Anthony 'that old Ruffian' [IV. i. 4]; but has he leaves, after giving instructions for the disposition of his army, a flood of memories of old days comes over him, recalling the echoes of Anthony's sole voice which drove Julius Cæsar's murderers in a mad gallop from Rome, and when Anthony had been to him as a protecting elder brother,—and with ineffable pity he sighs forth 'Poor Anthony!' That man is not to be envied who can read this without emotion. From no cold, calculating heart did that bitter sigh break forth. Even Cæsar's affection for his 'dearest sister,' as he names her, has been questioned; and the very fervour of his expressions of love, as she stands pitifully before him after she has been deserted by Anthony, has been cast up to him as a proof of his insincerity. When, as Anthony's bride, Octavia bade farewell to her brother, all the number of the stars had been invoked to give light to her fair way. She returns a solitary, unattended, deserted wife. If ever there were a time when a brother should lavish on a sister all the treasure of his fondest love, surely it was then. What end could be gained in such an hour by 'insincerity'? Would not Octavia have detected an insincere ring in her brother's words instantly?

On Cæsar's first appearance, when Shakespeare so frequently gives us the key to a character, he rehearses with bitterness all Anthony's misdoings in Egypt, and yet before the Scene closes, as though to show how genuinely he loved Anthony, and how true he was to his own fine nature, he recalls with fervour what a grand, noble soldier Anthony was, what bitter hardships he had borne upon the march, and while sharing the lowest lot of the commonest of the host, had even drank the gilded puddle that beasts would cough at. And with what anguish wrung from his heart of heart does Cæsar hear of Anthony's death! His first words are almost of self-reproach, as if he himself had partly been the cause, 'Oh, Anthony, I have followed thee to this!' and then, with 'tears as sovereign as the blood of hearts,' he calls him

> my Brother, my Competitor
> In top of all design, my mate in empire,
> Friend and Companion in the front of War,
> The Arm of mine own Body, and the Heart
> Where mine his thoughts did kindle.
>
> [V. i. 35-6, 41, 42-6]

And yet we are told that his man was cold, crafty, and self-seeking, and that these words were uttered for effect! Much learning has made us mad!

Moreover, does it not injure the tragedy as a work of art that the Power, representing Justice, which is to crush Anthony should be of a character no more elevated than Anthony's own? Anthony deserved to be crushed; he was false to what he knew to be right. But should not the Power that punishes him be more exalted than he? 'He who the sword of Heaven would bear Should be as holy as severe.' A man who is pure craft and selfishness ought not to be entrusted with the sword of Heaven.

Even with more reason than in Cæsar's character, is it necessary that we should accept Cleopatra, at Shakespeare's hands, with minds unbiased by history. We should know no more of her than what we hear on the stage. Of her past, of her salad days, we should know nothing but what we are told. The first words that she and Anthony utter tell of boundless, illimitable love, and this love is maintained to the last throb of life in each of them. Although Cleopatra then says that she'll set a bourne how far to be beloved, and Anthony replies that then she must needs find out a new heaven and a new earth, yet it is not Anthony, but Cleopatra, who sets no bourne to it. Twice Anthony touches this bourne, and twice Cleopatra surmounts and spurns it. Never does Cleopatra waver in her wild and passionate love for Anthony. Even in the Scene with Cæsar's ambassador, Thidias, who comes to Cleopatra with overtures of peace and favour on condition that she will give up Anthony, we knowing ones, crammed with history as pigeons are with peas, tip each other the wink and lay our fingers on our shrewd noses at Cleopatra's evident treachery when she sends word that she kisses Cæsar's conquering hand, and kneels, with her crown, at his feet. But those who read the Queen only by the light thrown by Shakespeare, see clearly enough that at this lowest ebb of Anthony's fortunes this was the only course she could prudently take; to gain time for him she must temporise with Cæsar. And when Anthony surprises Thidias kissing her hand and rages 'like a thousand hurricanes,' she patiently waits until the tumult of the earth and skies abates, and then calmly asks, 'Not know me yet?' [III. xiii. 156]. Are we blind that we do not see that Shakespeare here means to show that Cleopatra has been throughout as true as steel to Anthony, 'her mailed Captain,' and that her protest that, if she be cold-hearted toward him, let heaven 'the *next* Cæsarion smite,' is as sincere as it is tender and pathetic. From this deep, enduring, passionate love she never swerves, and in the very last moments of life she calls to Anthony, '*Husband*, I come' [V. ii. 287], thus sanctifying her love by the holiest of bonds. In accepting her right to claim this relationship our hearts bow down before Shakespeare, not Plutarch. In this expression I find the loftiest note in the tragedy. Amid the 'infinite variety' which was hers, the love for Anthony burned with the unflickering flame of wifely devotion.

It is not until nigh the close that we are shown, in the 'dream' which Cleopatra told to Dolabella, the qualities of the god-like Anthony which had won and kept the Egyptian Queen's heart. On the other hand, the fascination wherewith Cleopatra enslaved Anthony is revealed to us early in the play, and is the key-note of her character. Enobarbus (who herein fulfills the office of a Greek Chorus, like the Fool in *Lear*, and, to a lesser degree, Feste in *Twelfth Night*) says of Cleopatra, in words that are become imbedded in the language,

> Age cannot wither her, nor custom stale
> Her infinite variety.
>
> [II. ii. 234-35]

It is the irresistible potency of this infinite variety which, in the very first Scene, Anthony vows, when he exclaims,

> Fie wrangling queen;
> Whom everything becomes, to chide, to laugh,
> To weep; whose every passion fully strives
> To make itself, in thee, fair and admired.
>
> [I. i. 48-51]

When Mrs Jameson remarks that Anthony's love for Cleopatra is that 'of a man declined in years for a woman very much younger than himself' [see excerpt above, 1833], was it necessary to restrict the infatuation to declining years? Does manhood, however long its span, hold a single year when subjection to the highest earthly ideal is not most welcome, and when the privilege would not be eagerly claimed, of echoing Anthony's

> O'er my spirit
> The full supremacy thou knew'st; and that
> Thy beck might from the bidding of the gods
> Command me?
>
> [III. xi. 58-61]

One Scene there is, however, which must, I think, severely grate every reader. It is the Scene,—the last of all,—where Cleopatra falls into a towering rage with her Treasurer, Seleucus, for his honesty in refusing to countenance the dishonesty of her brief of all she is possessed of, in money, plate, and jewels. That she should descend to low, unqueenly dishonesty is sordid enough, but that she should attempt, while showering opprobrious epithets on her Treasurer, to scratch out his very eyes with her nails is a lower depth to which no admiration, however ardent, can follow her. Of course, ingenuity has been taxed to find excuses for her. We accept her own feeble attempts at apology, and sadly acknowledge, the while, that it is the last flickering of her tempestuous, ungoverned temper which once more flames up, through the 'ashes of her chance' [V. ii. 174], before it dies down for ever,—and the excuse is inadequate enough.

It was reserved to Adolf Stahr, the learned German historian of Cleopatra. so to interpret this Scene as to convert our humiliation into approval [see Additional Bibliography]. Be it remembered that Cleopatra's last words, as Anthony's dead body is borne away, are

> Ah, women, women! Come we have no friend
> But resolution, and the briefest end!
>
> [IV. xv. 90-1]

And from this resolution to compass the briefest end, she never for one minute departs. Before she could even begin her plans she was taken prisoner, and her scheme for procuring an asp demanded the closest secrecy. What she had most to fear was that Cæsar should get some inkling of her design. It was, therefore, of the very highest importance that Cæsar's mind should be utterly disabused of any suspicion of her suicidal intent, and that, instead thereof, he should be firmly convinced, not only that she intended to live, but that she was becoming reconciled to the thought of going to Rome. To give Cæsar a list of her possessions was obligatory; but what proof that she intended to live could Cæsar have greater than the withholding, from her list, treasure sufficient to maintain her hereafter in regal state? This whole Scene, then, with Seleucus was prearranged in order to deceive Cæsar. The rage, the fury, the virago were all assumed. One exquisite touch there is which must have extinguished, in Cæsar's mind, the last spark of suspicion that she intended to destroy herself. In pleading her excuse for thus retaining some of her treasure, she slights to the uttermost its value, calling it 'immoment toys,' 'lady trifles,' etc., and then with infinite cunning she refers to 'some nobler token' which she had kept apart 'for Livia and Octavia' as a friendly greeting,—in Rome, of course [V. ii. 118, 169]. In this last of all her encounters Cleopatra triumphed, and Cæsar was the ass unpolicied.

Of course, as is known to every one who has studied the play, Shakespeare derived this Scene with Seleucus from North's translation of Plutarch, and has here and there used North's very words and phrases, even to the gifts which Cleopatra intended to give Octavia and Livia, and, moreover, Plutarch says that Cæsar was 'glad to hear her say so, persuading himself thereby that she yet had a desire to save her life.' All that is claimed for Stahr's interpretation is the suggestion that the display of honesty by Seleucus, and Cleopatra's violent behaviour, had been pre-arranged between the two for effect. If Cæsar was deceived by it, the guile becomes finer by its having deceived even Plutarch.

Coleridge says that this play should be perused in mental contrast with *Romeo and Juliet*,—as the love of passion and appetite opposed to the love of affection and instinct [see excerpt above, 1813-34]. It is with unfeigned regret that I dissent from our finest Shakespeare critic,—not on the score of the contrast between these two tragedies, but that this play is one involving the love of passion and appetite. Where in the play is there any proof of it? Where is there any scene of passion? Where is there a word which, had it been addressed by a husband to a wife, we should not approve? And because they were not married is that love to be changed at once into sensuality? . . . Is wandering through the streets and noting the quality of the people sensual? Is fishing sensual? Is teasing past endurance sensual? Such are the glimpses that we get into the common life of this 'sensual' pair. If these pastimes be sensual, then are tennis and cricket sensual. All the extravagant terms of love, such as the demi-Atlas of the world, the paragon of men, the great Fairy, and so forth, cannot turn love into passion and appetite. When Cleopatra asks for 'music, moody food of us that trade in love' [II. v. 1-2], she has no thought of trafficking, mercenary love; such love demands no music to sustain it. She and Orsino, in *Twelfth Night,* were fellow-traders in love. With them, Love was the sole thought, the business of their lives, as it is with all true lovers. Was it not Cleopatra's 'infinite variety' that enthralled and held Anthony's heart? His love for her was not of the senses; for, be it remembered, Cleopatra was not beautiful; she had no physical allurements; but she could laugh Anthony out of patience and then laugh him into patience, and dress him up in women's clothes and laugh consumedly at him. And he never knew at what instant her mood would change from imperial scorn to humble, irresistible tenderness. These are some of the charms of infinite variety which are attractive to a man whose grey hairs do something mingle with the brown.

If we read it aright, the whole of the *Fifth Act* is a vindication of Cleopatra. The very first words in it from her lips reveal the change which Anthony's death had wrought:

> My desolation does begin to make
> A better life.
>
> [V. ii. 1-2]

And this better life reveals to her that greatness is merely relative,—that true greatness consists in rising so superior to life that life can be cast off with indifference,—

> To do that thing that ends all other deeds,
> Which shackles accidents, and bolts up change.
>
> [V. ii. 5-6]

From now on, to her last hour, her resolution never falters. Of course, she wishes to make the best terms for her children, and it is of importance to know how Cæsar proposes to treat her. If he is to leave her in Egypt her plans can be completed at will after his departure, but if he is to send her to Rome immediately, no time is to be lost. But before she has any interview with Cæsar, she describes to Dolabella, under the guise of a dream, the proportions and qualities of the man she worshipped as Anthony. Every word springs to her lips, hot from the heart. We see her rapt, upturned gaze, and mark the sensitive, quivering mouth as she describes the man whom she adored:

> His face was as the heavens; and therein stuck
> A sun and moon, which kept their course, and lighted
> The little O, the earth. . . .
> His legs bestrid the ocean; his rear'd arm
> Crested the world; his voice was propertied
> As all the tuned spheres, and that to friends;
> But when he meant to quail and shake the orb,
> He was as rattling thunder. For his bounty
> There was no winter in't; an Anthony it was
> That grew the more by reaping.
>
> [V. ii. 79-81, 82-8]

Where in this description is there a trace of 'passion or appetite' or 'sensuality'? It is cruel to ask the question. But to those who ascribe to her love these debasing qualities it is right that the question should be brought home. (pp. x-xvi)

Of all the stories that History has transmitted, none possesses, it would appear, such universal interest as a theme for dramatic tragedy as the loves of Anthony and Cleopatra. (p. xvii)

In other lands and in other tongues tragedy after tragedy on this theme has been written, and may still be written, but, for those whose mother-tongue is English, the tragedy of *Anthony and Cleopatra* has been written once and for all time. (p. xx)

Horace Howard Furness, in a preface to A New Variorum Edition of Shakespeare: The Tragedie of Anthonie and Cleopatra, Vol. 15, *edited by Horace Howard Furness, J. B. Lippincott Company, 1907, pp. v-xx.*

E. K. CHAMBERS (essay date 1907)

[*Chambers occupies a transitional position in Shakespearean criticism, one which connects the biographical sketches and character analyses of the nineteenth century with the historical, technical, and textual criticism of the twentieth. While a member of the education department at Oxford University, Chambers earned his reputation as a scholar with his multivolume works,* The Medieval Stage *(1903) and* The Elizabethan Stage *(1923); he also edited* The Red Letter Shakespeare *from 1904 to 1908. Chambers investigated both the purpose and limitations of each dramatic genre as Shakespeare presented it and speculated on how the dramatist's work was influenced by contemporary historical issues and his own frame of mind. In the excerpt below, taken from his preface to the Red Letter edition of* Antony and Cleopatra *(1907), Chambers maintains that the portrayal of "passion as the ruin of greatness" is the central thematic idea in the play. He views Cleopatra as the principal agent in Antony's downfall, referring to "her baleful influence" over him, blaming her for his loss of reputation, and contending that her cowardice was the chief element in "the twin defeats of Actium and Alexandria." Chambers believes that Antony's inexhaustible capacity for life and his exuberant energies are the source of both his greatness and his degradation. In addition, the critic calls attention to the language of the closing scenes, declaring that through the "austere and lucid simplicity" of the "monumental phrases" that accompany the deaths of Antony and Cleopatra, the tragedy concludes on a "note of awe and reverence."*]

In the course of his tragic analysis of man and of man's splendid impotence beneath the unpitying stars, Shakespeare reaches two plays, wherein he handles the great ideals which the incurable sentiment of the race is wont to set up as a screen between itself and its destiny, and shows that these also are but tragic stuff. It is honour of chivalry and love of woman, the twin beacons of romance throughout the ages, that must stand their arraignment in *Coriolanus* and in *Antony and Cleopatra*. One may turn back over the pages, and find in this later treatment something of deliberate palinode to the exaltation of triumphant honour in *Henry the Fifth* and of love as, even when vanquished, the blossom and fruitage of life in *Romeo and Juliet*. Already the ideals had been questioned in that comedy of disillusions, *Troilus and Cressida,* where Cressid's love is writ in water, and honour hardly holds up its head amongst the treachery and bickerings of the Greeks. And now, without any question at all, Shakespeare returns to the double theme, to strip the mask of worship from the spectre of egoism, and to indict passion as the ruin of greatness, magnificent and devastating as Attila and his Huns.

Antony is resumed, after a fashion not customary with Shakespeare, except in the historical plays and in the doubtful case of the resurrected Falstaff of *The Merry Wives of Windsor*, from *Julius Cæsar*. Here, as against Brutus, he is the inheritor of the tradition of victorious efficiency, which else would have fallen with Cæsar himself. In *Antony and Cleopatra* this function, which has become the background rather than the motive of the play, is transferred to the hard and passionless Octavius. Antony, who even in *Julius Cæsar* had been 'gamesome' and 'loved plays,' is developed upon more generous lines. The great composition of the man finds room for the most diverse potentialities. He rejects nothing and will drink to the full of every cup that life proffers. He is a mighty warrior and is able to inspire enthusiasms, not only in such poor folk as Lepidus, for whom

His faults, in him, seem as the spots of heaven,

[I. iv. 12]

but also in his own followers and captains. He outdoes his greatest rivals, alike in the nights of revelry and on the field of battle. He drinks the other triumvirs from the deck of Pompey's vessel. At Philippi it was he who struck the lean and wrinkled Cassius, while the boy Octavius kept his sword e'en like a dancer. And so he has won his way to be a triple pillar of the world, and may speak of himself in his downfall as one—

Which had superfluous kings for messengers
Not many moons gone by.

[III. xii. 5-6]

His very capacity is his undoing. The exuberance of his vitality overflows into sensuousness as well as into resource and endurance. The palate that at need—

Did deign
The roughest berry on the rudest hedge,

[I. iv. 63-4]

is not proof against the temptations of 'lascivious wassails' or the stimulating excitements of a 'gaudy night'. And Antony would not be Antony if, to whatever he gave himself, he did not give himself wholly and without reserve. He, who—

With half the bulk of the world played as I pleased,

[III. xi. 64]

is also 'the ne'er lust-wearied Antony' [II. i. 38].

In an evil day Antony crosses the path of the amorous Cleopatra, and is entangled in the strong toils of a passion which for him at least, whatever the dreams of the sentimentalists, makes no contribution towards a strenuous life. His captain's heart reneges all temper, and alliances and empires slip away while he becomes the bellows and the fan to cool a gipsy's lust. There is a struggle, of course. The instinct of domination and the instinct of sex are at odds in him; and if he chooses the worser course, it is not without clear consciousness on his part of the issues at stake. He knows well how Cleopatra is called in Rome, and that he must break the strong Egyptian fetters, if he is ever to recapture his proper place in the counsels of the nations. Once, under the shock of Fulvia's sudden death, he does break them; and his return to activity disconcerts the calculations of Pompey, and obliges even Octavius himself to play the second fiddle. But Cleopatra nods him to her again, and the crisis of Actium, determined by her cowardice, leaves him little more than 'the noble ruin of her magic' [III. x. 18]. Octavius may not affect to speak of one who had quartered the world as no more than an 'old ruffian' and a 'sworder'; and the epitaph of the past he has squandered is in his own mouth—

We have kissed away
Kingdoms and provinces.

[III. x. 7-8]

It is to be observed that it is no part of Shakespeare's scheme to belittle passion. Tragedy lies in the incompatibility and clash of greatnesses, and love that is to be the scourge of the world, even if it is rooted in sensuality, must possess the attributes of majesty. And therefore Cleopatra is so conceived that she is fit to mate with her lover. Even in those, such as Enobarbus, who most deplore her baleful influence, she awakes amazement—

Age cannot wither her, nor custom stale
Her infinite variety.

[II. ii. 234-35]

She is 'a wonderful piece of work' [I. ii. 153-54], one—

Whom everything becomes, to chide, to laugh,
To weep.

[I. i. 49-50]

And thus her relations with Antony take on something of the sublime. He is hardly alone in thinking Rome well lost for her sake, and that the nobleness of life is to be found in a kiss—

When such a mutual pair
And such a twain can do it, in which I bind,
On pain of punishment, the world to weet,
We stand up peerless.

[I. i. 37-40]

And she is no Cressida. A marvellous psychology, wrought surely out of bitter experience, has gone to the making of this subtle princess. She is half a courtesan and half a *grande amoureuse*. Certainly she has at her command all the resources of that most ancient art of those who angle for the souls of men. She plays on Antony like an instrument, ever twitching the sentimental string, and knowing well how to renew her influence, just at the moment when it is upon the wane, with nicely simulated outbursts of pathos or upbraiding. And yet these are not all simulated. 'I have seen her die twenty times upon far poorer moment,' says Enobarbus; and when Antony judges that 'She is cunning past man's thought,' replies, 'Alack, sir, no! Her passions are made of nothing but the finest part of pure love' [I. ii. 141-42, 145, 146-47]. Her art is indeed instinctive, and does but utilize the ebbs and flows of her own wayward and uncertain nature. She is at no time wholly mistress of herself, but lives in that unstable equilibrium of nerves and emotions which is the temperament of such a woman. Characteristically she drugs herself with mandragora and with music—

> Give me some music; music, moody food
> Of us that trade in love.
>
> > [II. v. 1-2]

She has the courtesan's bitter resentment against the respectable members of her sex; against 'shrill-tongued' Fulvia, Fulvia 'the married woman' [I. iii. 20], and later against Octavia 'with her modest eyes and still conclusion' [IV. xv. 27-8]. Even in the unbalanced fury of the scene in which she receives the news of Antony's secret marriage, she recovers herself sufficiently for a quick appraisement of her own personality against that of her new rival; and the admission of the messenger that Octavia is low-voiced and less tall than Cleopatra is turned with naive spite into a conviction that she is 'dull of tongue and dwarfish' [III. iii. 19]. Obviously Cleopatra has had lovers before Antony. She admits that she was a morsel for Cæsar in her salad days when she was green in judgment, and how great Pompey would stand and make his eyes grow in her brow. Since then the Roman world has rung with her gallant adventures. But, though Antony has come late into her life, he now possesses it wholly. She would but sleep out the great gap of time, when he is away. When they met—

> Eternity was in our lips and eyes,
>
> > [I. iii. 35]

and the love that then came into being is to endure, through the wreck of empires, to the close of all time. She is at least as much hypnotized by Antony as he is by her, and the very intensity of this sentiment, baleful as it is, invests it with sufficient dignity to make it worthy of the tragedy.

And so, when Cleopatra has dragged the good name of Antony through the mire and has brought him by cowardice unworthy of a queen to the twin defeats of Actium and Alexandria, the play, which throughout has been written on Shakespeare's highest level of pregnant metaphor and melodious phrase, swells into the organ-notes of a magnificent dirge. I do not know where to turn for anything to surpass the haunting splendour of the two great scenes in which it culminates. In the Fourth Act, Antony, beaten and disgraced, receives a lying message from Cleopatra, who fears the reaction of his mood, that she is dead. For him too it is time to make an end, and he calls upon his freedman to take off his armour with words of double meaning—

> Unarm, Eros! the long day's task is done,
> And we must sleep.
>
> > [IV. xiv. 35-6]

Cleopatra has gone before, and calls upon him to o'ertake her—

> Eros!—I come, my queen.—Eros!—Stay for me!
> Where souls do couch on flowers, we'll hand in hand,
> And with our sprightly port make the ghosts gaze.
> Dido and her Æneas shall want troops,
> And all the haunt be ours.
>
> > [IV. xiv. 50-4]

Presently, taught by Eros, he gives himself a mortal wound, and then learns that he has been misled and that Cleopatra yet lives and is in the monument. He is carried to the foot of it, and Cleopatra beholds what has occurred—

> *Cleopatra.*   O sun,
> Burn the great sphere thou movest in; darkling stand
> The varying shore of the world. O, Antony,
> Antony, Antony! Help, Charmian! help, Iras, help!
> Help, friends below!—let's draw him hither!
> *Antony.*   Peace!
> Not Cæsar's valour hat o'erthrown Antony,
> But Antony's hath triumphed on itself.
> *Cleopatra.* So it should be, that none but Antony
> Should conquer Antony; but woe 't is so.
> *Antony.* I am dying, Egypt, dying; only
> I here importune death awhile, until
> Of many thousand kisses the poor last
> I lay upon thy lips.
>
> > [IV. xv. 9-21]

So he is drawn up, and dies; and Cleopatra says—

> O, see, my women,
> The crown of the earth doth melt. My lord! my lord!—
> O, withered is the garland of the war;
> The soldier's pole is fallen; young boys and girls
> Are level now with men; the odds is gone,
> And there is nothing left remarkable
> Beneath the visiting moon.
>
> > [IV. xv. 62-8]

And then—

> Our lamp is spent; it's out.—Good sirs, take heart!
> We'll bury him; and then, what's brave, what's noble,
> Let's do it after the high Roman fashion,
> And make death proud to take us.
>
> > [IV. xv. 85-8]

In the Fifth Act, Cleopatra's own turn has come. She has played through her interview with Cæsar, but Cæsar's promises cannot stay her. Even the wild bedfellows, her hand-maidens, Iras and Charmian, rise to the height of the great argument. It is Iras who says—

> Finish, good lady; the bright day is done,
> And we are for the dark.
>
> > [V. ii. 193-94]

The countryman with his figs is introduced and wishes her joy o' the worm. Now she has immortal longings in her, but Iras is the first to die. It is as a rebuke to delay—

> This proves me base.
> If she first meet the curled Antony,
> He'll make demand of her, and spend that kiss
> Which is my heaven to have.
>
> > [V. ii. 300-03]

Then, as the eastern star breaks, the asps are applied, and Cleopatra's speech falters, and Charmian pronounces her elegy—

> Now boast thee, Death, in thy possession lies
> A lass unparalleled.
>
> > [V. ii. 315-16]

And the soldiers of Cæsar break in upon the silence with their question—

> What work is here? Charmian, is this well done?
>
> > [V. ii. 325]

And Charmian, before she too falls, makes reply—

> It is well done, and fitting for a princess
> Descended of so many royal kings.
>
> [V. ii. 326-27]

The might of language can hardly go further than in such monumental phrases as these, which with their austere and lucid simplicity bring this most poignent tragedy to a close upon that note of awe and reverence which is the fitting accompaniment of the sublimest art. (pp. 249-57)

> *E. K. Chambers, "'Antony and Cleopatra'," in his*
> Shakespeare: A Survey, *1925. Reprint by Hill and*
> *Wang, 1958, pp. 249-57.*

LEVIN L. SCHUCKING (essay date 1919)

[*A German educator and critic, Schucking adopted a historical approach to the study of Shakespearean drama. In the introduction to his* Character Problems in Shakespeare's Plays: A Guide to the Better Understanding of the Dramatist *(1922), originally published in German in 1919, he attacked the subjective analysis typical of the Romantic movement, proposing that accurate interpretations of the characters could be achieved only by taking into account Elizabethan dramatic conventions and the probable attitudes of Shakespeare's contemporaries toward his dramatic figures. In the excerpt below from this work, Schucking maintains that Cleopatra in Acts I through III is vulgar, immoral, vain, calculating, and absolutely irreconcilable with the regal, thoughtful, and tender woman of Acts IV and V. The critic denies that Shakespeare intended to show any psychological development in her character, arguing that there is no coherence between the two portraits because the dramatist's primary interest was in the effectiveness of individual scenes, not in creating connections between them. Schucking further distinguishes between Cleopatra's love for Antony in the first three acts—where, he contends, eroticism and self-gratification are its principal characteristics—and in Acts IV and V—where, in his words, "she is all tenderness, all passionate devotion, all genuine, unselfish love." The critic also charges that there is no unity of dramatic action in* Antony and Cleopatra, *declaring that individual scenes are detached "from the context of the whole," and therefore the progress of events is frequently slowed and interrupted.*]

[In] the peculiar creative processes of Shakespeare's art various elements are contained which offer a more or less energetic resistance to the establishment of perfect harmony. One of the most effective of these is the tendency to split up the action into a number of independent scenes. In dealing with it we must never lost sight of the fact that the Shakespearean drama still bears distinct traces of its medieval origin; it had grown out of a view of art in which the sense of form, in architecture as well as in epic art, favoured a juxtaposition of identical or similar elements, whereas the following period, under the influence of classical antiquity, demanded the subordination of the parts to a comprehensive idea. The definition of beauty as the "relation of the parts to the whole and the whole to the parts" is as inapplicable to Chaucer's *Canterbury Tales* as to the mystery plays, in the primitive art-form of which many essential details of the later drama, especially the historical drama, originated. This kind of literature is sufficiently loose in structure to admit the insertion of much inartistic matter consisting largely of anachronisms and topical allusions. . . . Still more noticeable is the interruption of the action by comic scenes . . . , which occur even in places where there is apparently no intention to produce a higher unity through contrast. In these we clearly see to what extent the Shakespearean drama can occasionally dispense with internal coherence. But we must

not suppose that we are dealing here with exceptional cases. In reality this practice is nothing but a symptom of Shakespeare's supreme interest in the single scene, which all his knowledge of dramatic art cannot induce him to subordinate to the interest of the whole to the extent that is demanded by a later period. We may even conclude that possibly Shakespeare's peculiar manner of dramatic construction was very different from what we generally imagine it to have been. Grillparzer somewhere says that Shakespeare had the habit of working, so to speak, "step by step". . . . It is true this opinion has been hotly contested . . . , and indeed the bulk and variety of Shakespeare's work renders it almost impossible to apply a judgment of this kind to the whole of his writings without modification. But there can be no doubt . . . that the number of scenes which are intelligible only from the context of the whole play is infinitely greater in the modern than in the Shakespearean drama. (pp. 111-13)

More important, however, is the question to what extent the want of connexion in the scenes may occasionally influence the drawing of the characters, whether Shakespeare's method of work, in spite of his unique ability consistently to work out a complex character, may not at times give rise to contradictions, so that a practised eye can discern a change of physiognomy between the appearance of a character in one scene and another. In general, of course, this question will have to be answered in the negative, because otherwise we should be denying Shakespeare's greatest merit, which undoubtedly is his power of creating consistent characters. In a number of cases, however, we shall not be able altogether to neglect the possibility that there may be contradictions. Of these the most remarkable is perhaps his treatment of the figure of Cleopatra.

Shakespeare's play of *Antony and Cleopatra* is founded upon North's translation of Plutarch. Naturally this author does not regard Cleopatra in a favorable light. The idea pervading the whole of his narrative is that she was the cause of Antony's misfortune. But he has too great a knowledge of human nature, he is too conscientious an historian, to be unjust to the unique qualities of this woman, who united to all the refined sensuality of the Orient a good deal of the culture of the Western world. (pp. 119-20)

If we . . . regard the Cleopatra of Shakespeare's drama we are astonished to find how inferior she is to the original. It is true that Plutarch gives us no clearly outlined picture of her character, but she certainly is not the great courtesan whom Shakespeare shows us in the first acts of his play. The first thing we miss is her culture. We are told nothing about her ability to negotiate with foreign peoples in their own language. As a matter of fact, we never see her acting as queen at all. Nobody would suspect that this woman, as Plutarch informs us, has for years, quite unaided, ruled a great kingdom. She never gives audience, never exercises the functions of her high office. Love seems to be her only aim in life. If the object of her passion is absent we must imagine her (I, v; II, v) reclining drowsily on her couch, yawning and wishing to sleep away the time until her lover returns, and, as this is impossible, tormenting her attendants, who are infected with her voluptuousness and frivolity. Her laziness is equalled by her sensuality. That her thoughts are continually occupied with the enjoyment of love we see from the pleasure she takes in using equivocal language, giving an equivocal meaning to her words even when she speaks of Antony sitting on horseback or of a piece of news entering her ear. This side of her character is brought to our notice by the contemptuous expressions—"'a gipsy's lust'' [I. i. 10] and ''a strumpet''—which Philo uses in the first scene of the first act. . . . [In] the exposition Shakespeare always means the reflection of a character in the minds of subsidiary figures to be taken quite seriously. Further on in the same act (I, ii) she is described by Enobarbus, who throughout the play acts the part of chorus, as consisting ''of nothing but the finest part of pure love'' [I. ii. 146-47]. That here we have to understand the word ''love'' in a purely erotic sense is confirmed by a remark of the same observer, who ironically declares that he can explain her constant threats to kill herself only by her belief that in death she will find a new erotic enjoyment. He evidently regards her as incapable of being attracted or charmed by anything except love. This is certainly an exaggeration, tending to ridicule her weakness, yet there can be no doubt that she is meant to appear as the type of the ''artist in love.'' This conception, as experience proves, implies a certain amount of vulgarity, which comes out in her jesting with the eunuch and in her amusement at his answers to her question, ''Hast thou affections?'' [I. v. 12]. Still more vulgar is her behaviour when, talking to her maids, she makes coarse jokes about having Antony on her hook, and allows her attendants to lose all sense of social distinctions. She even shares in the truly feminine interest which her maids, always craving for erotic excitement, take in the messenger (''A proper man''—''Indeed, he is so'' [III. iii. 38, 39]). The very next moment, however, like a servant who has become a mistress, she turns against those with whom she has just been so familiar, and threatens them with corporal punishment. This vulgar trait, which separates irreconcilably the Cleopatra of Shakespeare from that of Plutarch, reaches its culminating point in the hysterical fits which are so excellently represented. When she hears of the marriage of Antony and Octavia she gets into such a rage that, in the manner of hysterical harlots, she loses all self-control, and mad with fury beats and stabs the messenger and would like to dash everything around her to pieces: ''Melt Egypt into Nile'' [II. v. 78]. (pp. 121-23)

The essential vulgarity of her character is also shown by the pride which, like every courtesan, she takes in having had so many distinguished lovers. The remembrance that among them have been the great Cæsar and the famous Pompey still gives her satisfaction, although now she ought to be thinking only of Mark Antony. But this thought flatters her vanity, a quality which is strongly developed in her. She exercises her trade with the clearest consciousness of her worth, knowing the high price that men are willing to pay for her. ''Here are,'' she says proudly,

> My bluest veins to kiss, a hand that kings
> Have lipp'd, and trembled kissing.
>
> [II. v. 28-30]

But of a truly regal deportment we can find so little trace in her (though she has some touches of that dignity of which none of Shakespeare's royal personages are entirely devoid) that it sounds merely like ridiculous self-conceit when, wishing to exalt herself, she says of her messenger:

> The man hath seen some majesty, and should know.
>
> [III. iii. 42]

Her whole behaviour toward Antony is dominated by an element of calculation. Here again the reflection of her character in the exposition shows us the way. ''She is cunning past man's thought,'' says Antony of her [I. ii. 145]. And, indeed, the little feminine tricks related by Plutarch are harmless in comparison with the marvellous astuteness and proficiency of this

thoroughbred courtesan. Years of intercourse with men since her earliest youth—she now smiles at her naïve innocence in those days—have given her a mastery of all the arts of love that amazes even her frivolous attendants; she knows and successfully uses every means of combating the surfeit of mere sensual enjoyment in her lover which is her greatest danger. This woman is different from Plutarch's heroine in that she does not merge her being into his and make all his interests her own, but, on the contrary, is always on the point of evading him, and continually keeps him running after her. When he comes she goes, and when he is away she charges her maid:

> See where he is, who's with him, what he does:
> I did not send you: if you find him sad,
> Say I am dancing; if in mirth, report
> That I am sudden sick.
>
> [I. iii. 2-5]

This power of falling ill at the right time, of being seized by swoons and fits, so that she must have her dress unlaced, is always at her disposal, and helps her to render Antony helpless by completely disarming him. It is always she who is suffering through him, and in every case her cleverness puts him in the wrong. If he is not sad at the death of his wife it is a sign of what a loving woman may expect of him, and if he is sad he shows that his real love belonged to the other woman and not to her (I, iii). She carries the art of sulking to perfection, and torments him in order to be the more assured of possessing him. At the same time there is a certain amount of cruelty in her joy at seeing him floundering so helplessly in her net. Yet her great cleverness always makes her recognize the moment when, his endurance being near the breaking-point, he might grow tired of the eternal war and begin to break away from her. Nevertheless, she loves him after her fashion, though the selfish and superficial character of her love is clearly revealed in the vain remark she addresses to Charmian:

> Did I, Charmian,
> Ever love Cæsar so?
>
> [I. v. 66-7]

Her feeling is indeed a complex mixture of various emotions. On the one hand she is merely craving for erotic excitement and more enamoured of Antony's love than of himself; on the other it flatters her vanity and gives her a sense of triumph to see the great hero her obedient slave. Her pride in having conquered him naturally allows us to suppose that she admires him, but this need not be a sign, as some have believed, that she also loves him. It is rather a proof of her cleverness that her long intimacy with him has not produced in her case what, according to the proverb, familiarity usually breeds in ordinary people, viz., contempt. That Antony's love means much to her we can easily believe, knowing her calculating nature. But not only upon such motives does her affection rest. Her behaviour, especially her excitement in the scene with the messenger coming from him, reveals a remarkable degree of passion. We should be wrong, however, in assuming that his love would render her capable of sacrificing aught for his sake. She never regards anything from his point of view. For this reason we should not feel inclined to prophesy that this love would be of long duration, especially in view of her heartlessness, which reveals itself distinctly in her indifference to the fate of Cæsar's messenger. Antony finds her flirting with him, and in his indignation orders him to be whipped, without her putting in a word for him.

This is Cleopatra as she appears in the first acts of the play. There is a world of difference between her and the queen of

Plutarch's narrative. What we have before us is a wonderful portrait, drawn with Shakespeare's consummate skill, of an intelligent, passionate, astute, heartless, essentially vulgar, and profoundly immoral creature, but by no means a remarkable or "nobly planned" woman. . . . A number of critics . . . have thought that Shakespeare has merely omitted, by an oversight, to insert a scene in which Cleopatra's grace, wit, or any other of her attractions were actually shown. This omission, however, is not at all unintentional; it is the natural result of his conception. That Shakespeare regarded the purely sensual attraction which Cleopatra possessed for Antony as the principal cause of her power over him we can see from the reflection of her character in the mind of Enobarbus, which is of such great technical importance:

> Age cannot wither her, nor custom stale
> Her infinite variety: other women cloy
> The appetites they feed: but she makes hungry
> Where most she satisfies; for vilest things
> Become themselves in her, that the holy priests
> Bless her when she is riggish.
>
> [II. ii. 234-39]

And in another passage (II, vi), wishing to emphasize the purely physical nature of the bond which holds them together, he designates her quite briefly and contemptuously as Mark Antony's "Egyptian dish."

The contradiction between this picture of Cleopatra and the character Shakespeare gives her in the last two acts, after the position of Antony has become hopeless, is astonishing. The consistent development of the character Shakespeare has put before us in the first part would require that she should endeavour to extricate herself from the fate that threatens Antony. But she does not make any attempt to do so, if we except the insignificant flirtation with Thyreus, the messenger of Octavius. That her ships go over to the enemy and thereby accelerate his downfall is at the time regarded by the suspicious Antony as a piece of treachery on her part, but a number of critics . . . do her grave injustice in thinking her really guilty. This accusation is conclusively proved to be unjust by the express assurance which Cleopatra sends to the dying Antony through Diomedes that he is wrong in suspecting her of having conspired with the enemy against him. Supposing the intention had merely been to throw dust in Antony's eyes, an 'aside' would have been necessary in order to enlighten the spectators.

We may be quite certain, however, that Cleopatra is not faithless to Antony. In this case there is no suspicion of treachery even in the original. If in the beginning of the play Shakespeare appears to have deprived her of some of the good qualities she possesses in Plutarch, he makes up for this by raising her at this stage of the action actually above Plutarch's estimate. . . . All the clamorous and pretentious part of her has now disappeared, and for a while she is nothing but a thoughtful and motherly woman. There is a touch of soft conjugal tenderness in all she says or does. When helping him to arm for the fight, and in parting with him (IV, iv), she almost reminds us of the way in which Desdemona speaks to Othello. At the same time her cleverness makes her recognize quite clearly how hopeless his position is in face of the vastly superior forces which the enemy has brought against the city. Though her heart does not break with woe, yet she is filled with regret and sorrow, and almost forgets her own fate in his. Then the going over of her fleet brings about the collapse; Antony for the first time completely loses his confidence in her. So far he had deliberately shut his eyes to the inevitable approach of catastrophe. Now,

however, the thought that Cleopatra's supposed betrayal has been the cause of his ruin, though in reality it has only accelerated it a little, makes him behave like a madman; he thrusts her from him, and is even prepared to give the order for her death. Then, rightly afraid of him, she takes refuge in her so-called monument and, in order to bring him to his senses, sends him word that she has killed herself. When it is too late she recognizes with horror that the means employed by her have been too dangerous. The messenger whom she sends out in her terrible anxiety confirms her fears: Antony has concluded that his duty is to follow her, and the message that she is still alive is brought to a dying man. (pp. 123-29)

[There] are no traces of the actress to be found in her in these scenes, no sign of frivolity or exaggeration. On the contrary, she is frightened and depressed during the whole time. . . . [We] have . . . the remark expressly made by Cleopatra's messenger that she had been seized with fear of the consequences *after* despatching the message of her death ("fearing since . . ." [IV. xiv. 125]). There is no valid reason for doubting this statement. The dying Antony has himself conveyed to her, and now Cleopatra suddenly appears in a light in which we have never seen her before. Juliet at the bier of Romeo could not have thrown herself on her lover with a more profound, more serious, and more passionate grief than Cleopatra now shows. With her own delicate hands, that are unused to any kind of work, she helps to draw the heavy load of his body up to the monument, and embraces him with the fervour of despair. Now, in her grief, she is all tenderness, all passionate devotion, all genuine, unselfish love. There is no false note in the expression of her feeling, no pettiness in her thoughts. The touching advice of the dying man, to "seek her honour with her safety" at the hands of Cæsar, his adversary, she refuses with the magnificent words: "They do not go together" [IV. xv. 46, 47]. When he dies in her arms she utters the woeful cry of a human being forced to surrender the very core of its existence.

From this moment life for her has ceased to be worth living. The wife of Brutus could not find more magnificent words for defying and wrangling with Fate than are uttered by this unfortunate woman after her servants have recalled her from her swoon:

> No more but e'en a woman, and commanded
> By such poor passion as the maid that milks
> And does the meanest chares. . . .
>   Ah, women, women, look,
> Our lamp is spent, it's out! Good sirs, take heart:
> We'll bury him; and then, what's brave, what's noble,
> Let's do it after the high Roman fashion,
> And make death proud to take us. Come, away:
> This case of that huge spirit now is cold:
> Ah, women, women! come; we have no friend
> But resolution, and the briefest end.
>
> [IV. xv. 73-5, 84-91]

We see that she has acquired an iron strength with the calm of the resolution she has taken in these last words. Now for the first time, when she feels her loss so deeply that it makes her as poor as any peasant girl, does she really look like a queen, and a queen she remains during the negotiations of the last act. There is something truly sublime in her attitude, which resembles that of a Thusnelda in chains, when, having been disarmed by the victors, she goes back in her musings to the past and, staring in front of her with suppressed passion, conjures up the image of Mark Antony in superhuman dimensions:

> His face was as the heavens: and therein stuck
> A sun and moon, which kept their course and lighted
> The little O, the earth. . . .
>   For his bounty,
> There was no winter in't; an autumn 'twas
> That grew the more by reaping; his delights
> Were dolphin-like; they show'd his back above
> The element they lived in: in his livery
> Walk'd crowns and crownets; realms and islands were
> As plates dropp'd from his pocket.
>   [V. ii. 79-81, 86-92]

This impression cannot be diminished even by the scene with Seleucus, her treasurer. . . . Shakespeare . . . in this scene has so far taken into account the general conception of Cleopatra in this part of the play as to restrict the outburst of her temper to a few very violent words addressed to the faithless servant. For Cleopatra now is always the captive queen. No wonder that she finds her 'Mortimer' [in *1 Henry IV*] in Dolabella, the Roman officer who betrays to her the secret plan of Octavius to make her walk in his triumphal procession. Against this humiliation, however, her pride rebels. (pp. 129-31)

Donning her regal garments and placing her crown upon her head, she chooses rather to die with her majesty unsullied.

It cannot well be doubted that this woman, who now is inwardly as well as outwardly a queen, has but little in common with the harlot of the first part. The Cleopatra whom we see in the time of Antony's good fortune gives us no indication of that moral substructure on which alone the fortitude she shows in adversity can rest. We know her well enough to foresee that she will vent her disappointment in endless and vociferous lamentations and, like old Capulet after receiving the news of Juliet's death, first of all and principally bewail her own sad lot. There was far too much calculation in her love to make it possible for her, at a moment when her own existence was in such imminent danger, to mourn so passionately and exclusively for another being. In her nature there was so much pettiness and vulgarity that she was quite unable to acknowledge and express in such sublime language the greatness of the fallen hero. Her life had rendered her far too aimless, undisciplined, and enervated to be capable now of seizing the helm in such an iron grip, and without repining steering straight on to the rocks. By means of that self-characterization which . . . gives us the most valuable key with which to unlock the problems of Shakespeare's characters, she informs us that in her last resolutions she wanted to do "what's brave, what's noble" (V, ii). This point is decisive. The character of Cleopatra in the first acts has hardly a trace of nobility. (p. 132)

This lack of consistency in the development of Cleopatra's character has not been overlooked by all the critics. Most of them have tried to explain it away either by taking a more favourable view of her in the first part, or making her out to be worse than she really is in the second part, or maybe both at the same time. (pp. 132-33)

The attempts to prove that the Cleopatra of the last two acts bears the same physiognomy as that of the first part of the play must . . . be regarded, for the most part, as failures. We are dealing here with a dramatic peculiarity which we shall find again in many parts of Shakespeare's work. (p. 134)

The question now remains to be answered how these contradictions, which are so very remarkable and disturbing, arise. The simplest explanation is found in the method of work described at the beginning of this chapter. There are many other things in *Antony and Cleopatra* which create the impression that it more than any other was composed according to the 'single-scene' method. The way in which Shakespeare has cut up Plutarch's narrative into a succession of co-ordinated scenes is not a sign, despite the great mastery of characterization shown, of a careful mental digestion and welding together of the materials found in the original source. When contrasted with the firm handling of the plot that we find in *Julius Cæsar* or *Macbeth,* this play on the whole shows a decided falling off. Considerable portions must be regarded as dramatically ineffective from the point of view of progressive action. We see, for instance, in the second act the Triumvirs coming to an understanding with Sextus Pompeius, their enemy, and celebrating the event on board his galley with a great banquet. The poet seems to have taken a great delight in depicting this feast. At the end almost the whole company are drunk; they join hands, dance, and, as was the custom at Egyptian revels, unite their hoarse voices in an attempt to sing the burden of a song. This may be productive of a certain stage effect, but it completely *isolates the scene,* detaching it from the context of the whole in a manner which is unequalled even in Shakespeare. There are other cases of the procedure employed in the second part of that act, in which the whole action is made to follow the example of the dancers and keep turning round on the same spot. (pp. 134-35)

But quite apart from the form chosen or the intended dramatic formlessness, there are to be clearly discerned many isolated signs of a rapid and careless workmanship. In numerous places it becomes imperative to look up the corresponding passage in Plutarch in order to understand what is meant. (p. 136)

In one instance one cannot help suspecting that Shakespeare so quickly ran over the text of the original source that he read only the gloss on the margin, which gave an abstract of the contents, not the text itself, the result of which was a curious misunderstanding in the drama. In [IV, xii], we read:

>   Swallows have built
> In Cleopatra's sails their nests: the augurers
> Say they know not, they cannot tell; look grimly
> And dare not speak their knowledge.
>   [IV. xii. 3-6]

The source says: "Swallows had bred under the poope of her shippe and there came others after them that drave away the first and plucked down their neasts." The gloss abbreviates: "An ill signe, foreshewed by swallowes breding in Cleopatraes shippe." This summary, however, reverses the sense; for not the fact that swallows were nesting in the ship, but that they were driven thence by other swallows, was the bad omen. Shakespeare read so carelessly that he transcribed the sense of the marginal gloss instead of the sense of the text. . . . One would like to ask now whether even in these mistakes a wise intention will be seen, or how the orthodox Shakespeareans who discover the profoundest artistic purpose precisely in those places where the master's "brush has slipped" will explain such passages. As the case stands, the most obvious way to explain it is to trace the contradiction in the character back to the general technique of the play and to the tendency toward making the scenes independent. The Cleopatra who treats Antony, the heir of Hercules, as Omphale treated her hero is an independent conception, and the Cleopatra who refuses to accept an unworthy end of her life's tragedy has also been created as a complete and separate individual.

An explanation of the fact that Shakespeare has given the first Cleopatra a character so inferior to that of Plutarch's heroine may be found in the traditional view of her as the great courtesan. He had to deal with a public whose thinking was so much fettered by conventional standards with regard to female virtue that he was obliged to represent a woman who was liable to be charged with adultery as morally deficient in other respects also.

Lastly, a special circumstance may have influenced the characterization of Cleopatra in the first acts, viz., that in her case Shakespeare was probably drawing from the life to an extent so far unknown in his work. The striking resemblance of some of her principal traits to the features of the 'Dark Lady' in the Sonnets, which makes us incline to accept his view, has often been noticed. . . . But even apart from this we occasionally find in the play that special graphic details are used for characterizing her which are manifestly derived from the observation of some definite person to an extent that is found in few other plays of Shakespeare. A description of the peculiar sensual attraction which she exercises, given by Enobarbus, is clearly founded on an individual impression received by a fully attentive observer from a living person. He says:

> I saw her once
> Hop forty paces through the public street;
> And having lost her breath, she spoke, and panted,
> That she did make defect perfection,
> And, breathless, power breathe forth.
>
> [II. ii. 228-32]

This is an unconnected statement quite irrelevant to the action, and of course there is no hint of it in Plutarch. By a combination of such single realistic touches he produces a masterpiece of portraiture, a clearly outlined drawing from the life, very different from the second Cleopatra, who is an ideal figure, like Imogen [in *Cymbeline*] or Desdemona, and several degrees farther removed from reality.

To a certain extent he may have become conscious of this dualism. So we hear it stated that Cleopatra's character has undergone a process of development. Like Macbeth, who at the end of his career says that he has become a different man from what he was before . . . , Cleopatra feels that she has changed completely:

> I have nothing
> Of woman in me: now from head to foot
> I am marble-constant; now the fleeting moon
> No planet is of mine.
>
> [V. ii. 238-41]

Here a difficulty arises. If Shakespeare in this passage explicitly refers to a development of Cleopatra's character, can we still say that he is inconsistent in his characterization? This question must be answered in the affirmative, inasmuch as the Cleopatra of the first part has been designed without regard to the mental and moral physiognomy which the historical facts in Shakespeare's source make it imperative for Cleopatra to possess toward the end of the play. So the reference to the development of her character is merely a kind of afterthought. Had Shakespeare conceived Cleopatra as a consistent character from the very beginning of the work, which he apparently omitted to

do, just as he failed to create a unity of action, there would have been at least some slight indications of the traits which were to come out in the later development. . . . We may find it easier to regard the absence of unity in the character as a sign of development if we consider certain rather unconvincing developments of female characters in famous dramas of the time, and we may even imagine that, in one detail, Shakespeare was slightly influenced by them. In Thomas Dekker's *Honest Whore* we are shown how a common prostitute is reformed by love and changed into an honest woman. This oldest predecessor of the Lady of the Camellias receives the first impulse that awakens in her the desire for regeneration from a speech in which a man to whom she is making love at the time casts in her face his extreme disgust of her trade and her person. . . . It almost seems as if there were a similar crisis in the life of Cleopatra. For here too there comes a moment when Antony's wrath surges fiercely up, and vents itself in a flood of moral invective. It is the scene [III, xiii] where Antony finds her flirting with Cæsar's messenger, through whom she is about to open conversations with his master, the critical moment in which she appears to be going over to the opposite side. He then inveighs with inexpressible indignation against the woman for the sake of whose love he has sacrificed a world, and who now desires to cast him off in order to make friends with his inexorable enemy:

> You were half blasted ere I knew you: ha! . . .
> I found you as a morsel cold upon
> Dead Cæsar's trencher; nay, you were a fragment
> Of Cneius Pompey's; besides what hotter hours,
> Unregister'd in vulgar fame, you have
> Luxuriously pick'd out: for, I am sure,
> Though you can guess what temperance should be,
> You know not what it is.
>
> [III. xiii. 105, 116-22]

The effect of this moral chastisement is astonishing. No word of contradiction betrays that the woman whom he reprimands so severely feels herself insulted. On the contrary, like a child that has been punished, she gives him henceforth no occasion for anger. If a development of her character were to be admitted its crisis would lie in this passage. But the comparison with a proper drama of character development like *The Honest Whore* shows clearly that the resemblance is only apparent and the problem of an essentially different kind. If Shakespeare had really wished to show development he would doubtless . . . have made the woman at the decisive moment become aware of her conversion and openly confess it. Of this, however, there is not the slightest indication in the play. It is not a question of a coherent plan of psychological development in the mind of the dramatist, but of the ''step by step'' method of dramatization, as Grillparzer styles it. This is the reason . . . why the two physiognomies, at the beginning and at the end of the play, are so irreconcilable. (pp. 136-41)

Levin L. Schucking, ''Character and Action,'' in his Character Problems in Shakespeare's Plays: A Guide to the Better Understanding of the Dramatist, *1922. Reprint by Peter Smith, 1959, pp. 111-202.*

SIR ARTHUR QUILLER-COUCH   (lecture date 1922)

[*Quiller-Couch was editor with J. Dover Wilson of the New Cambridge edition of Shakespeare's works. In his study* Shakespeare's

*Workmanship (1918), and in his Cambridge lectures on Shake-
speare, Quiller-Couch based his interpretations on the assumption
that Shakespeare was mainly a craftsman attempting, with the
tools and materials at hand, to solve particular problems central
to his plays. His remarks on* Antony and Cleopatra, *excerpted
below, were originally delivered in a series of lectures at Cambridge and subsequently collected in* Studies in Literature: Second
Series (1922). *Quiller-Couch believes that the play is "in some
ways the most wonderful of Shakespeare's triumphs," worthy of
being ranked with* Hamlet, King Lear, Macbeth, *and* Othello. *The
dominant chord, he contends, is the universal impact of Antony
and Cleopatra's passion for each other, and he asserts that Shakespeare intended both to accentuate the world-wide impact of their
love and to make us feel that we are "the stake this pair are
dicing away." Quiller-Couch maintains that the theme of the play
is love in its most destructive, feral, voluptuous, and superhuman
manifestation. He concludes that Antony and Cleopatra are god-
like figures—audacious, aloof from events, and "great as the
gods are great, high-heartedly, [and] carelessly."]*

I do most ardently desire [*Antony and Cleopatra*] to be reckoned—as it has never been reckoned yet, but I am sure it
deserves to be—among the very greatest, and in some ways
the most wonderful, of Shakespeare's triumphs. I want it to
stand at length—in your estimation at any rate—as a compeer
of *Hamlet, Macbeth, Lear, Othello:* no less.

"Wonderful" is at any rate the word; and Coleridge gives it
to me. "The highest praise," he says, "or rather form of
praise," of this play

> —which I can offer in my own mind, is the
> doubt which the perusal always occasions in
> me, whether the *Antony and Cleopatra* is not,
> in all exhibitions of a giant power in its strength
> and vigour of maturity, a formidable rival of
> *Macbeth, Lear, Hamlet* and *Othello. Feliciter
> audax* is the motto for its style comparatively
> with that of Shakespeare's other works, even
> as it is the general motto of all his works com-
> pared with those of other poets. Be it remem-
> bered, too, that this happy valiancy of style is
> but the representative and result of all the ma-
> terial excellencies so expressed.

He goes on—

> Of all Shakespeare's historical plays, *Antony
> and Cleopatra* is by far the most wonderful.
> There is not one in which he has followed his-
> tory so minutely, and yet there are few in which
> he impresses the notion of angelic strength so
> much;—perhaps none in which he impresses it
> more strongly. This is greatly owing to the
> manner in which the fiery force is sustained
> throughout, and to the numerous momentary
> flashes of nature counteracting the historic ab-
> straction. As a wonderful specimen of the way
> in which Shakespeare lives up to the very end
> of this play, read the last part of the concluding
> scene. And if you would feel the judgment as
> well as the genius of Shakespeare in your heart's
> core, compare this astonishing drama with Dry-
> den's *All for Love* [see excerpt above, 1813-34].

Now, when Coleridge wrote, Dryden's *All for Love* had been
acted at least ten times to *Antony and Cleopatra*'s once. And

so we may forgive him that, groping toward the truth by instinct, he hesitates and just misses to declare it. "The highest
praise . . . which I can offer in my own mind, is the doubt
which the perusal always occasions in me." "Of all Shakespeare's *historical* plays, *Antony and Cleopatra* is by far the
most wonderful." Upon that he pauses. After admitting that
the audacity of its style distinguishes it above Shakespeare's
other works even as that audacity is Shakespeare's general
distinction above other poets, he trails off to admit the "numerous momentary flashes of nature counteracting the historic
abstraction." What he means by "historic abstraction" heaven
knows. History is not abstract, but particular; as Aristotle long
ago pointed out. It narrates what Alcibiades did or suffered.
Coleridge is talking cotton-wool. Hazlitt shows himself no less
cautious—

> This is a very noble play. Though not in the
> first class of Shakespeare's productions, it stands
> next to them, and is, we think, the finest of his
> *historical* plays . . . [see excerpt above, 1817].

He goes on: "What he has added to the actual story, is on a
par with it," but promptly admits that which really means
everything—

> His genius was, as it were [why "as it were"?],
> a match for history as well as nature, and could
> grapple at will with either. The play is full of
> that pervading comprehensive power by which
> the poet could always make himself master of
> time and circumstances—

and, with that, Hazlitt too, having like them that dwelt in
Zebulon and the land of Naphtah seen a glimmer, wanders off
to remark, "The character of Cleopatra is a master-piece. What
an extreme contrast it affords to Imogen!" O yes—and as the
Victorian lady in the stalls observed to her companion when
Sir Herbert Tree presented this very play, "How different, my
dear, from the home life of *our* beloved Queen!"

And then comes along Gervinus, solemnly between his little
finger and his enormous useful thumb measuring out the play
against history and condemning it. "The crowd of matter,"
murmurs Gervinus, checking it, "creates a crowd of ideas."
Vengeance on a crowd of ideas!

"A wanton multiplicity of incidents and personages pass before
our eyes; political and warlike occurrences run parallel with
the most intimate affairs of domestic life and of the affections":
and, as if all this were not sufficiently shocking, "the interest
is fettered to the passion of a single pair, and yet the scene of
it is the wide world from Parthia to Cape Misenum" [see
excerpt above, 1849-50].

But if you are setting out to show how the passion between
one man and one woman can crack the pillars of a wide world
and bring down the roof in ruin (which is precisely what this
play does), surely the grander the sense of that world's extent
you can induce upon your audience's mind, the grander your
effect! Surely for dramatic purpose Shakespeare could have
extended Parthia to China and Cape Misenum to Peru, and
with advantage, if those remoter regions had happened just
then to be discovered and included in the Roman Empire.

In a previous lecture, speaking to you of Aristotle's dictum
that the tragic hero in drama should preferably be a person of

high worldly estate, I suggested that the chief reason for this was a very simple one, and indeed none other than Newton's Law of Gravitation—the higher the eminence from which a man falls the harder he hits the ground—and our imagination. (pp. 179-82)

We must not press this too far, or in every play. For, as Sir Walter Raleigh points out, in *Hamlet* (for example) the issue of the events upon the State of Denmark scarcely concerns us. "The State of Denmark," says he, "is not regarded at all, except as a topical and picturesque interest. The tragedy is a tragedy of private life, made conspicuous by the royal station of the chief actors in it." Yes: but in all *historical* drama, may be, and in *Antony and Cleopatra* most certainly, most eminently, the sense of reacting far-reaching issues *is* a necessary part of our concern. We are not sympathetic merely to the extent of having our emotions swayed by Cleopatra and Antony in turn. We are the world, the stake this pair are dicing away. We watch not only for their catastrophe but for ours, involved in it. Philo gives the thematic phrase in the twelfth and thirteenth lines of the first scene of the first act:

> The triple pillar of the world transform'd
> Into a strumpet's fool.
>
> [I. i. 12-13]

—Every word important, and "world" not the least important, since, if and when the pillar cracks, the roof of a world must fall. I put it to you that anyone insensitive to this dominant, struck by Shakespeare so early in the play and insistent to the end through all that crowding of great affairs which so afflicts the good Gervinus, must miss, roughly speaking, some two-thirds of its meaning. For Gervinus, "by these too numerous and discordant interruptions that psychical continuity is destroyed which is necessary to the development of such a remarkable connection of the innermost affections as that between Antony and Cleopatra."

Pro-digious!

But indeed the theme itself is overpoweringly too much for our poor commentator, as it has ever been too strong for all but the elect. For it is of Love: not the pretty amorous ritual played, on a time, by troubadours and courtiers; not the delicate sighing languishment which the Elizabethans called Fancy; not the business as understood by eighteenth century sentimentalists: but Love the invincible destroyer . . .—destroying the world for itself—itself, too, at the last: Love voluptuous, savage, perfidious, true to itself though rooted in dishonour, extreme, wild, divine, merciless as a panther on its prey. (pp. 182-84)

And I would have you note by the way, and even though it lead us off our track for a moment, that the future fate of the world—whether the West should conquer the East, or the East the West—did actually and historically hang on the embraces of Cleopatra and Antony, as delicately as it had once hung balanced on the issues of Marathon. I do not urge that we are, any of us, the better off because the cold priggish mind of Octavius prevailed over the splendid whoredoms of Egypt: though I think it probable. But it was—for the second time—a great crisis between Europe and Asia; and again, in the second bout, as in the first, Europe won. And I do not say—as I hardly believe—that Shakespeare realised the full weight of the argument that rested on his "triple pillar of the world," or that he realised what a stupendous roof came down with its fall. I only note here that Shakespeare, with superlative skill, sets all

this fate of a world rocking in the embrace of one man and one woman, both fatally loving. . . . (pp. 189-90)

How then, of such a pair, shall Shakespeare make a tragedy of high seriousness? how can he compel us to follow either of such a pair—nay, but he will have us follow both—sympathetically? How can he bring them both to end so nobly that, all contempt forgotten, even our pity is purged into a sense of human majesty? How from the orts and ravages of this sensual banquet shall he dismiss us with "an awed surmise" that man is, after all, master of circumstance and far greater than he knows?

Shakespeare had Plutarch: and Plutarch has the story: but with Shakespeare the story is never the secret. He will take, in his own large indolent way, any man's story and make it his property; nor does he care how the facts may seem to damn hero or heroine, so only that he have the handling of their motives. Many excellent persons profess themselves shocked by the scene where, close on the end, Cleopatra plays the cheat, handing Caesar a false schedule of her wealth, and is detected in the lie. . . . Shakespeare found this in Plutarch and used it, because it is truth; not mere truth of fact, but truth of that universal quality which (as Aristotle noted) makes Poetry a more philosophical thing than History. Cleopatra did not tell that falsehood by chance. She told it naturally, because she was courtesan in grain: born a liar and born also royal Egypt, she cannot sentimentalise one half of her character away at the end, to catch our tears. We must accept her, without paltering, for the naked, conscienceless, absolute, royal she-animal that she is. Cover the courtesan in mistaken truth, and by so much you hide out of sight the secret of her majesty—with her no secret at all, for she is regnant, rather, by virtue of being shameless. (pp. 193-94)

Shakespeare can get plenty of description out of Plutarch to help the impression of Cleopatra's magnificent luxury. I quoted in my last lecture the famous description of her barge upon Cydnus. But all that is *description*: of externals, accessories; helpful but quite undramatic. Getting nearer to the woman, he can make an observer tell us, and truly, that

> Age cannot wither her, nor custom stale
> Her infinite variety: other women cloy
> The appetites they feed, but she makes hungry
> Where most she satisfies.
>
> [II. ii. 34-7]

And that (mark you) is superbly said: we turn back to it as to a last word. But, still, it is somebody's description. It is not the flashing, the revealing, word, that can only, in a drama, be spoken by the person, spoken here by Cleopatra herself. . . .

Cleopatra.	If it be love indeed, tell me how much.
Antony.	There's beggary in the love that can be reckon'd.
Cleopatra.	I'll set a bourn how far to be beloved.
Antony.	Then must thou needs find out new heaven, new earth.
	Enter an Attendant.
Attendant.	News, my good lord, from Rome.
Antony.	Grates me: the sum.
Cleopatra.	Nay, hear them, Antony: Fulvia perchance is angry; or, who knows If the scarce-bearded Caesar have not sent

His powerful mandate to you, ''Do this, or
this;
Take in that kingdom, and enfranchise that;
Perform't, or else we damn thee.''
Antony.   How, my love?
Cleopatra.   Perchance! nay, and most like:
You must not stay here longer, your
dismission
Is come from Caesar; therefore hear it,
Antony.
Where's Fulvia's process? Caesar's I would
say? both?
Call in the messengers. As I am Egypt's
queen,
Thou blushest, Antony, and that blood of
thine
Is Caesar's homager: else so thy cheek pays
shame
When shrill-tongued Fulvia scolds. The
messengers!
Antony.   Let Rome in Tiber melt, and the wide arch
Of the ranged empire fall! Here is my
space.
Kingdoms are clay: our dungy earth alike
Feeds beast as man: the nobleness of life
Is to do thus; when such a mutual pair
And such a twain can do't.
                                          [I. i. 14-38]

There you have the lists set, and the play not 40 lines gone!
Into those 40 lines is already compressed the issue as the world
sees it, critical but well-wishing, through the eyes of Philo:
the issue as Antony sees it—

                    Here is my space.
       Kingdoms are clay . . .

and the hints of half-a-dozen coils through which, entangled
in jealousies, Cleopatra's mind is working.

I shall say nothing of the minor characters of the play save
this—that the true normal, or *punctum indifferens* [standard of
the normal man]—which you always find somewhere in any
tragedy of Shakespeare's—is to be sought, not in Octavius,
but in some spectator such as Philo or even the loose-moralled
Enobarbus. Caesar Octavius represents rather the cool enemy,
blameless, priggish, who, as this world is ordered, inevitably
overthrows Armida's palace—but is none the more lovable for
the feat. . . . The whole point of Octavius—and of Octavia
(upon whom Gervinus, recognising the abstract German housewife in a wilderness of Latins, expends so many tears)—is that
they are ministers of fate precisely because incapable of understanding what it is all *about*. Precisely because he has not
the ghost of a notion of anyone's being such a fool as to lose
the world for love, we see this politician predestined to win.
Nor—the beauty of it!—will he ever divine the sting in Cleopatra's word to the asp, as she applies it to her breast—

              O, couldst thou speak,
       That I might hear thee call great Caesar ass
       Unpolicied!
                                          [V. ii. 306-08]

It is not only, of course, by direct representation of Cleopatra
in her gusts of passion—now real, now simulated—that Shakespeare weaves the spell. The talk exchanged among Iras, Charmian, Alexas and the Soothsayer is as deft and witty an intro-

duction to Venusberg as ever playwright could invent: and,
after that, ''Let Rome in Tiber melt!'' ''Melt Egypt into Nile!''
[II. v. 78].

Gervinus writes out a long laboured estimate of Antony's character. It is all idle; because, the lists being those of passion,
all we want is, of Antony that he should be generous and lusty
and great; all we want of Cleopatra is that she shall be subtle
and lustful and great: both lustful, both unmistakably great.
With all his detailed portraiture of ''my serpent of old Nile''
[I. v. 25] Shakespeare triumphs in this play, the closer you
examine it, by a very sublime simplicity: he triumphs by making this pair royal *because* elemental; *because* they obey impulses greater even than Rome, though it stretch from Parthia
to Cape Misenum. I do not deny that Shakespeare has spent
pains in making Mark Antony lovable to us, so that Dryden
and every playwright who makes him a soft voluptuary must
necessarily fail. But truly this is a woman's play, in which the
man has to be noble in order that the woman may win a high
triumph and perish in it. I would even call it the paradox of
Antony and Cleopatra that it at once is the most wayward of
Shakespeare's tragedies, dependent from scene to scene on the
will of a wanton, and withal one of the most heavily charged
with fate and the expectancy of fate. Who can forget the hushed
talk of the guards and the low rumbling of earth underfoot that
preludes the arming of Antony, when Cleopatra misarrays him?

Antony.   Eros! mine armour, Eros!
Cleopatra.   Sleep a little.
Antony.   No, my chuck. Eros, come; mine armour,
Eros!
                    Enter Eros *with armour.*
Come, good fellow, put mine iron on:
If fortune be not ours to-day, it is
Because we brave her: come.
Cleopatra.   Nay, I'll help too.
What's this for?
Antony.   Ah, let be, let be! thou art
The armourer of my heart: false, false; this,
this. . . .
                                          [IV. iv. 1-7]

and if any object that the supernatural prelude to this is out of
place in tragedy, I am content to answer him with a word from
an early page of Plutarch. ''There be some,'' says Plutarch,
''who think these things to be but fables and tales devised of
pleasure. But methinks, for all that, they are not to be rejected
or discredited, if we will consider Fortune's strange effects
upon times, and of the greatness also of the Roman empire;
which had never achieved to her present possessed power and
authority if the gods had not from the beginning been workers
of the same, and if there had not also been some strange cause
and wonderful foundation.''

But I marvel in this play most of all, and whenever I read it,
at the incomparable life-likeness of Cleopatra, which follows
her through every bewildering trick and turn, caprice or gust
of passion, equally when she queens it, or fools it, modulates
her voice to true or to false passion, or beats her servants and
curses like a drab—and she can do all within any given two
minutes. It is not lime-lantern that follows Cleopatra about the
stage: she carries everywhere with her the light—her own light—
of a convincing if almost blinding realism. I am not, as you
know, overfond of those critics who read Mary Fitton, or some
other ''dark lady'' into everything Shakespeare wrote: but I
must make them the handsome admission that if Shakespeare

did not take some actual particular woman for his Cleopatra, I am clean at a loss to imagine how he created this wonder.

It surprises me—to take up a small point—that the most insistent of these critics, Mr. Frank Harris, should boggle, all of a sudden, over Cleopatra's

> Here's sport indeed!
>
> [IV. xv. 32]

when she and her women are drawing Antony aloft.

This, says Mr. Harris,

> Seems to me a terrible fault, an inexcusable lapse of taste. I should like to think it a misprint, or a misreading; but it is unfortunately like Shakespeare in a certain mood, possible to him, here as elsewhere.

Yes, yes, Mr. Harris! It is shockingly bad taste. But it seems to me mighty fine hysteria.

Let me read the whole passage, not to controvert Mr. Harris, but as leading up to a word upon which I shall conclude because it seems to me the *last* word upon this play.

> *Enter, below,* Antony, *borne by the* Guard.
>
> Cleopatra.   O sun,
> Burn the great sphere thou movest in! darkling stand
> The varying shore o' the world. O Antony, Antony, Antony! . . .
> Help me, my women,—we must draw thee up;
> Assist, good friends.
>
> Antony.   O, quick, or I am gone.

Act I. Scene ii. Iras, Charmian, Soothsayer, and attendants. By Matthew W. Peters.

> Cleopatra.   Here's sport indeed! How heavy weighs my lord!
> Our strength is all gone into heaviness;
> That makes the weight. . . .
> Noblest of men, woo't die?
> Hast thou no care of me? shall I abide
> In this dull world, which in thy absence is
> No better than a sty? O, see, my women,
>   [*Antony dies.*
> The crown o' the earth doth melt. My lord!
> O, wither'd is the garland of the war,
> The soldier's pole is fall'n: young boys and girls
> Are level now with men; the odds is gone,
> And there is nothing left remarkable
> Beneath the visiting moon. . . .
>   Ah, women, women, look,
> Our lamp is spent, it's out! Good sirs, take heart:
> We'll bury him; and then, what's brave, what's noble,
> Let's do it after the high Roman fashion,
> And make death proud to take us.
>
> [IV. xv. 9-12, 30-4, 59-68, 84-8]

After that will you refuse to consent with me that the last word upon this play should be of its greatness? All these people, whatever of righteousness they lack, are great. They have the very aura of greatness.

And they are great, of course, not in their dealing with affairs, with the destinies of Rome or of Egypt—for it is by their neglect or misprision or mishandling of these that they come to misfortune and allow meaner men, calculators, to rise by their downfall: but great as the gods are great, high-heartedly, carelessly. Note how finely, when the whole stake has been thrown and lost, they sit down to their last earthly banquet. They seem in their passion to stand remote above circumstance. They are indifferent to consistency. . . . Like the gods too, these people are exempt of shame: as absolutely above it as Zeus, father of gods and men, who could be ridiculous enough in his amours and yet, when all is said, remains a very grand gentleman. They are heroic souls in this disorderly house of Alexandria—even to pretty mischievous Charmian. Hear her, as she closes Cleopatra's eyes and stands up herself, as the Guard bursts in, to take the stroke. Hear her and mark her last word—

> Charmian.   So, fare thee well.
> Now boast thee, death, in thy possession lies
> A lass unparallel'd. Downy windows, close;
> And golden Phoebus never be beheld
> Of eyes again so royal! Your crown's awry;
> I'll mend it, and then play. . . .
>
> First Guard.   What work is here! Charmian, is this well done?
>
> Charmian.   It is well done, and fitting for a princess
> Descended of so many royal kings.
> Ah, soldier!   [*Dies*
>   [V. ii. 314-19, 325-28]
>   (pp. 195-205)

Sir Arthur Quiller-Couch, " 'Antony and Cleopatra'," in his Studies in Literature, second series, *G. P. Putnam's Sons, 1922, pp. 168-207.*

C. H. HERFORD (essay date 1923)

[*A distinguished English scholar and critic, Herford published commentary on Renaissance and nineteenth-century literature in England and also championed the works of such European writers as Goethe, Ibsen, and Pushkin. His works include a ten-volume edition of the plays and poems of* Shakespeare *(1899-1904),* Shakespeare's Treatment of Love and Marriage *(1921),* A Sketch of Recent Shakespearean Investigation, 1893-1923 *(1923), and A* Sketch of the History of Shakespeare's Influence on the Continent *(1925). In the following excerpt, Herford describes alternative critical methods of explicating apparent inconsistencies in Shakespearean characters, charging that the approach of Levin L. Schucking (see excerpt above, 1919), especially with regard to Cleopatra, betrays a "rather elementary conception of coherence." Whereas Schucking argues that there are, in effect, two Cleopatras in the play—so very different that they are mutually irreconcilable—Herford contends that by portraying her with both noble and ignoble qualities, Shakespeare has given us a character of psychological verisimilitude. Opposing Schucking, the critic denies that Cleopatra becomes a wholly different person in the final acts of the play, contending that even in her dying moments she occasionally behaves more like a courtesan than a queen, and he insists that her "infinite variety" should not be equated with inconsistency of character. Herford also argues that during the course of* Antony and Cleopatra, *Shakespeare depicts the protagonists' love for each other as developing from a "light liaison" into "a fierce though fitful passion which has moments of self-forgetting devotion."*]

[A] dramatic character, like a man, is to be interpreted by the whole of his utterances. . . . But plainly, we are on more dangerous ground when dealing . . . with an imagined character than with that of a living man. A man may be inconsistent or incoherent, he may have conflicting, even contradictory, moods, and yet remain indefeasibly himself. Whereas the seeming inconsistencies of an imagined character may merely betray the artist's fluctuating intention, or uncertain hand, or the capricious accesses and lulls of inspiration; and only subjective criteria are at present usually available to distinguish a character thus inconsistently imagined or drawn from one in which real inconsistencies are veraciously reproduced.

There is thus an opening, in such cases, for at least two types of solution, and the choice serves to discriminate two schools of character-interpretation. For the older idealists, of the Ulrici-Gervinus school, real inconsistency, of either kind, in Shakesperean character, did not exist; they found their way infallibly through all the variations of dramatic mood and utterance to the unifying "idea" discernible in them all. Modern psychology, by its disclosure of the phenomena of dual and multiple personality, has eased the path of those who find real inconsistency in any of Shakespeare's characters; their inconsistency need not detract from their psychological truth. (p. 48)

On the other hand, the modern realist of the more mechanical type lays hands upon every appearance of inconsistency in the character as a sign of incongruity or incoherence in the art. "What is to be made of this heap of contradictions!" exclaims Professor E. E. Stoll after a summary of the demeanour of Othello [in his *"Othello": A Historical and Comparative Study*]. Professor Lewin Schücking [in his *Character Problems in Shakespeare's Plays*] measures coherence by still more rigid standards. When Bottom, for instance, jests with Titania's elves (iii. 1):—"Good Master Mustardseed, . . . that same cowardly giant-like ox-beef hath devoured many a gentleman of your house", &c. [*A Midsummer Night's Dream*, III. i. 191, 192-93ff.]—he is witty, whereas "his ass-head shows that he is meant to be a fool". No one before, I imagine, ever

thought the resourceful Bottom incapable of this homely wit. But Bottom's tether is at best short; he cannot move far in any direction from his base. Schücking, however flies later at a far more elusive quarry—of all Shakespeare's characters the one to whom his rather elementary conception of coherence is the hardest to apply—the mistress of caprice, Cleopatra herself, of whose "infinite variety" we are expressly told, for it is a part of the exquisite charm which fascinated all men from Caesars and triumvirs downward. Such she already appears in Plutarch; but Schücking finds her, in Shakespeare, not merely "various" but divided against herself—a heartless coquette in the first half, a devoted lover, even a wife, in the second [see excerpt above, 1919]. "When she helps to arm him for battle (iv. 4), she might almost be Desdemona with Othello." We are here concerned only to describe a critical method, not to discuss its results; but it is obvious to note, first, that the drama describes precisely a growth of the light liaison between the triumvir and the queen into a fierce though fitful passion which has moments of self-forgetting devotion (when no serious sacrifice is involved); and second, that even in this second phase the coquette, even the hard and brutal woman, flashes out at moments too; in her consummate dying speech, lover and actress, the jealous woman and the magnificent queen, the mistress of a Roman, who wished to die like him "after the high Roman fashion" [IV. xv. 87], and the Oriental weakling who experimented first in "easy ways to die" [V. ii. 356]—all are intermingled. The test of Cleopatra's coherence is not that a rather wooden mind may not discover inconsistency in the play of her "infinite variety", but that she impresses our imagination, not in spite of her variety but by and through it, as a personality superbly real and one. Schücking has thrown much light on the traces of "primitive" technique in Shakespeare's art; but he has not reckoned sufficiently with the fact that Shakespeare's way was not to discard the crude features of dramaturgical art that he found, but to turn them into "something rich and strange" [*The Tempest*, I. ii. 402]. And this is not merely a trait of the artist but a trait of the mind and of the man. (pp. 49-50)

> C. H. Herford, "Critical Interpretation: The Interpretation of the Characters," in his *A Sketch of Recent Shakesperean Investigation: 1893-1923, Blackie & Son Limited, 1923, pp. 46-55.*

E. E. STOLL (essay date 1928)

[*Stoll was one of the earliest critics to attack the method of character analysis that had dominated nineteenth-century Shakespearean criticism. Instead, he maintained that Shakespeare was primarily a man of the professional theater and that his works had to be interpreted in the light of Elizabethan stage conventions and understood for their theatrical effects, rather than their psychological insight. Stoll has in turn been criticized for seeing only one dimension of Shakespeare's art. In the excerpt below, Stoll asserts that Cleopatra is a coherent character from beginning to end, claiming that she is occasionally regal in the early scenes as well as at the close; erotic and coquettish not only in Acts I through III, but even as she confronts death; and essentially capricious throughout the drama. The critic disputes the claim of Levin L. Schucking (see excerpt above, 1919) that in the final scenes only Cleopatra's gentler and nobler qualities are evident; he contends instead that in these scenes she repeatedly exhibits touches of vanity, sensuousness, jealousy, and, most significantly, an unquenchable sense of humor. Stoll further maintains that although* Antony and Cleopatra *is not a "glorification, in the mediaeval style, of illicit love at the expense of the married state," Shakespeare has clearly meant to show that "this man and woman*]

*love each other''; thus, even though their relationship may be
morally wrong their passion truly merits ''love's title [and]
prerogative.''*]

Poets, from Boccaccio to Hérédia, have sung of [Cleopatra];
but since Shakespeare put her into a play she has been his: and
Swinburne and Heine have chosen to write, not of the person
but of the character, not poems but rapturous prose. Shakespeare himself keeps his head. . . . [He] looks upon Cleopatra
both as what she ought to be and as what she ought not to be,
a very vulnerable heroine, a quite mingled blessing unto her
lord, though saved and saving at the last.

Though no character of Shakespeare's is more of an imaginative
success, there is difficulty and disagreement about the interpretation. Professor Schücking has of late declared that as a
whole the character is inconsistent, with a great cleft in the
middle, being that of a vulgar hysterical harlot at first and of
a sublimely devoted lover at the end [see excerpt above, 1919].
And discussion of all sorts has arisen about Cleopatra's intentions in her flight from Actium, in her dealings with Thyreus,
and in her attempt to cheat Caesar out of her treasure before
her death. Did she think of betraying Antony? Did she conceal
the treasure to deck herself out for her final triumphal exit, or
was it all a little game with Seleucus, and her rage a mere feint
to make Caesar think she intended to live? All these questions
are interesting to us not only for their own sakes but also
because of their involving Shakespeare's methods of presentation in general. (pp. 145-46)

With him the main thing is action, says Mr Symons [in his
Introduction to the Study of Browning], what the characters
do. But Shakespeare's characters have, above all, much to say.
It is not the internal organism that concerns him but the man
as he appears—as he acts and speaks, and as (in a sense) he
externally thinks and feels. The speeches . . . are much longer
than in the stage plays of our time, and are far more developed
than the action requires. They present the thoughts and emotions, the fancies and imaginations, of the moment, and serve
both to reveal character and to give the action significance and
force. (p. 147)

In the place of psychology, with its analyses and subtleties,
the poet had an infinite tact, the artist's delicate, plastic, life-
giving touch. 'The Shakespearean delineation of character owes
all its magic,' says Mr Shaw, 'to the turn of the line, which
lets you into the secret of its utterer's mood and temperament,
not by its commonplace meaning, but by some subtle exaltation, or stultification, or shyness, or delicacy, or hesitation, or
what not in the sound of it.' (p. 148)

Shakespeare's characters are much larger than the business in
which they engage, often are superior to it, sometimes . . . are
in a sense contrasted with it. . . . They have better natures, and
bigger thoughts, than their conduct betrays. But that is not all.
We have a more vivid and intimate impression of their personality . . . than in the case of other dramatists. This is produced, not indirectly, by the action, but by means quite direct
and immediate. And that, I think, is, above all, by [the] abundant and (so far as the requirements of the action are concerned)
somewhat superfluous speech. The characters are 'oversize,'
are (though intended to serve the action) in the upshot presented
somewhat for their own sake, and are so real that they project
from the scene, stand out upon the page. Or rather, they seem
so real because they do that.

Now this plastic power is the decisive thing, as it seems to
me, in the question regarding Cleopatra. Not that I accept

Professor Schücking's opinion that Cleopatra is artistically inconsistent. On the stage as in life a character has a right to
change—in Cleopatra's case, to cease from changing—under
stress of love and in the presence of death; and of this Shakespeare takes due account when the mercurial lady cries,

> now from head to foot
> I am marble-constant; now the fleeting moon
> No planet is of mine.
>
> [V. ii. 239-41]

And Professor Schücking, as so many of us do, exaggerates
to make his point. She is no Doll Tearsheet [in *2 Henry IV*]
or Doll Common [in Ben Jonson's *The Alchemist*], in the early
scenes, nor a sublime Queen . . . in the later ones. She is vain
and voluptuous, cunning and intriguing, wrangling and voluble, humorous and vindictive, to the end. Her petulance and
violence when she gets the news of Antony's marriage is not
her then prevailing mood, and yet it reappears when she rails
against fate and fortune at Antony's death and against Seleucus
in his treason. She had been elegant and queenly enough before
the news, and so she is afterwards; in a moment she recovers
herself and makes amends; and she had but used the licence—
exercised the divine right—of a queen. She is a monarch, a
maker of manners, after the similitude of Elizabeth, who raged
and stormed on occasion, but did that, like everything else,
with an air. Shakespeare keeps 'decorum,' but not like Corneille and Racine; his kings and queens are given greater range
and latitude, and are such by what they do rather than by what
they do not. They are human nature enlarged, not enchained.
And her caprice, why, it is the premise with which the poet,
as in Enobarbus' and Antony's own description of her 'infinite
variety,' begins. Caprice, conscious and unconscious, is her
nature, as to be queen and coquette is her station in life. *La
donna è mobile* [Woman is changeable], and she is quintessential woman. It is so that she lives—so that she delights
and attracts the men. In her inconsistency she is consistent.
But the chief means by which the dramatist makes her so is
the identity, through all her changes, of her tone and manner.
She changes as a vivacious, amorous, designing woman changes,
not so as to lose her identity, like Proteus.

When she first appears she is languishing:

Cleo.	If it be love indeed, tell me how much.
Ant.	There's beggary in the love that can be reckon'd.
Cleo.	*I'll set a bourn how far to be beloved.*
Ant.	Then must thou needs find out new heaven, new earth.

> [I. i. 14-17]

And these first words in the delectable colloquy are like her,
time and again. It is love but also 'the love of love and her
soft hours' [I. i. 44]. This phrase is Antony's, who for the
moment is in her mood: but it is she who is most settled in it,
as at the nucleus or centre of her emotional vortex. The voluptuous invitation of the first line—as if it would coax the
very soul out of his body—is, both in its sentiment and its
rhythm, in keeping with the beginning of a later scene, when
Antony is gone:

> Give me some music; music, moody food
> Of us that trade in love.
>
> [II. v. 1-2]

That is the sensuous murmur of one who in retrospect or in
prospect tells the moments over and over, and whose mood

craves music for company, rather than a fire flickering on the hearth or a flowing stream. But a lover's imagination is necessarily dramatic in form, though wholly lyrical in substance. *He* now is murmuring:

> He's speaking now,
> Or murmuring, 'Where's my Serpent of old Nile?'
> For so he calls me: now I feed myself
> With most delicious poison.
>
> [I. v. 24-7]

The last phrase, with its figure, is it not exactly—poetically—fitted to her lips? They know every pulse of passion, but no touch of restraint, every refinement but that of propriety. She is the serpent, which twines and charms, lovelier than lamb or dove. And in the same audacious, sensuous key, for all her exaltation, she expresses herself on her deathbed. She is tenderer with her women, and stronger and more constant, than she had ever been: but her thoughts of Antony, now an inviolable shade, are not celestial or Platonic. They are steeped in amorousness, and she is waiting, coiled on her couch. She loves him more than at the beginning; but neither now nor at his death is she, as Professor Schücking declares, 'all tenderness, all passionate devotion and unselfish love'; nor does she quit life because it is not worth the living. On life she really never loosens her greedy grip. Her beauty she clutches to her dying bosom as the miser does his gold. Her robe and jewels are, even in death, assumed to heighten the impression of it upon Caesar—though only to show him what he had missed. She hears Antony mock him now, from over the bitter wave; and at the outset she had cried,

> go fetch
> My best attires; I am again for Cydnus—
>
> [V. ii. 227-28]

as one who, to please both him and herself, would fain die at her best, reviving all the glories of that triumph. To an ugly death she could scarcely have brought herself: and it is an admirable example of the dramatic touch and tact and mere instinctive choice of what belongs together... that a little before she should have vowed to Proculeius, as she spoke of going to Rome:

> Rather a ditch in Egypt
> Be gentle grave unto me! rather on Nilus' mud
> Lay me stark-nak'd, and let waterflies
> Blow me into abhorring.
>
> [V. ii. 57-60]

The death which even then she is choosing and devising, is not to be like that, but well-nigh an amour. When she sees Iras fall and pass away so quietly, she thinks the stroke of death is as a lover's pinch, which hurts and is desired. And what nerves her up to make haste and apply the asp? Pride, fear to be made a show of at Rome, and—something deeper. 'Love is enough,' but not enough for her.

> If she first meet the curlèd Antony,
> He'll make demand of her and spend that kiss
> Which is my heaven to have.
>
> [V. ii. 301-03]

Without kissing what would heaven be—nay, without jealousy? The vanity and coquetry of her lightly clear the grave. Of all these, her truly 'immortal longings,' Plutarch, the philosopher, says nothing, and makes her apply the cobra, as if it were a leech in a clinic, to her *arm*.

> Peace, peace!
> Dost thou not see my baby at my breast
> That sucks the nurse asleep?
>   *Charmian.*   O, break, O, break!
>   *Cleo.* As sweet as balm, as soft as air, as gentle—
> O Antony—Nay, I will take thee too;
> What should I stay—   [*Dies*
>
> [V. ii. 308-13]

No Freudian is needed to defend the change. For a woman this in itself is a sensation, turning the poison all to balm; and she is wrapped and folded up in sensuous imaginations to the end.

The above indication of her vanity and amorous indulgence is the nearest approach in the character to what we should call psychology. But this is simple, concrete, for the popular stage. Not analysed, it is variously, abundantly presented, and, with the phrase 'of us that trade in love,' is plainly labelled. And it is in harmony with her luxurious, coquetting spirit throughout. She lives for pleasure and neglects the state. She deals affably with Caesar's ambassador, Thyreus, and vouchsafes him her hand; and is demure and complaisant and even apologetic with Caesar himself when she meets him, and when, long before that, she begs good news of the messenger who has none but that of Antony's marriage. As his supreme reward, she proffers him her bluest veins to kiss, a hand (quoth she) that kings have lipp'd and trembled kissing. . . . This coquetry and eroticism, Professor Schücking thinks, is vulgar, but the point is that it continues to the last. She makes eyes at Caesar and Thyreus, and though uplifted by the situation, she speaks when facing death in the same vein. (pp. 152-55)

The death scene . . . , though queenly and elevated through Cleopatra's dignity and tenderness, is quite true to her earlier self; and though glorified by the poetry shed upon it, is not sublime. . . . Indeed, she now shows still other traits of her earlier self—her jealousy of Octavia as well as of Iras, her pride of place and achievement, her spirit of intrigue and emulation, *camaraderie* with her maids, her sense of humour. To Octavia she had paid her compliments (and not for the first time, either) the moment before, as she vowed she would not go to Rome:

> Nor once be chastised with the sober eye
> Of dull Octavia.
>
> [V. ii. 54-5]

Now, at the supreme moment, she would rob the legitimate one even of her title. She would have everything, not only fame but name—the despoiler. She has always remembered that she was a queen; she remembers it still, with robe and crown, but by virtue of her more than conjugal courage puts in the still higher claim. And with Iras and Charmian she is mellower but not different. It is like her inconsistent, inconsiderate spirit to be tart with them when they cross her, and yet make them companions, and kiss them both before they die. She does not sentimentalise; they are not foremost in her heart:

> Come, then, and take the last warmth of my lips.
> Farewell, kind Charmian; Iras, long farewell.
>
> [V. ii. 291-92]

But the pre-eminently felicitous touch, I think, which links her most unmistakably with all her earlier self, and thus effectually contradicts any impression of sublimity, is her sense of humour. Seldom does a tragic dramatist—even Shakespeare—let his characters keep this faculty to the last. Mercutio does [in

Romeo and Juliet], and Edmund, the cynical bastard [in *King Lear*]; Juliet shows a single faint flicker of her earlier gaiety; but Cleopatra, the tameless and reckless, keeps more of hers. Juliet, speaking to Romeo, though dead before her, cannot help doing it—out of the simple fullness of her love—a little as she had always done, as if he were alive. Cleopatra is not so lost in love or in sorrow either; but she is still less concerned to preserve propriety and decorum. Even as they are about to lift up Antony into the monument, she cries, with something like mirth, out of her excitement and rebelliousness:

> Here's sport indeed! How heavy weighs my lord!
> Our strength is all gone into heaviness,
> That makes the weight: had I great Juno's power,
> The strong-wing'd Mercury should fetch thee up,
> And set thee by Jove's side. Yet come a little.—
> Wishes were ever fools—O, come, come, come.
> *[They heave Antony aloft to Cleopatra*
>   [IV. v. 32-7]

And when, afterwards, she receives the country-fellow with the basket, she draws him out, and then, for the curious fun of it, asks him abruptly, upon his praying her to give the asp nothing, because it is not worth the feeding. 'Will it eat me?' [V. ii. 271]. She is playing with her thought, as with her man. But though it takes nerve to do this, she strikes no heroical attitude; and, just before that she asks him, like the very woman, the coquette and coward that she really is, who had fled from Actium,

> Hast thou the pretty worm of Nilus there
> That kills and pains not?
>   [V. ii. 243-44]

For she would do it prettily, painlessly, by a poisoned bouquet if she could. And she is half in jest with Charmian when she utters her fears of Iras stealing a march upon her in the purlieus of Paradise. And then, in the moment that she is nerving herself up, and gritting her own teeth, as the sound of the verse betrays:

> With thy sharp teeth this knot intrinsicate
> Of life at once untie—
>   [V. ii. 304-05]

she laughs out, as one who has played cleverly and won:

> O could'st thou speak
> That I might hear thee call great Caesar ass
> Unpolicied.
>   [V. ii. 306-08]
>   (pp. 156-57)

Apostrophes generally seem rhetorical and artificial, but they have a root in nature, and never was there one more appropriate and dramatic than this. The contrast between 'great Caesar' and the worm, which scorns him—a feeling which is but her own playfully transferred, a boast which rebounds delightfully as a compliment! All her life has been a game, the asp is her last little unexpected trump, and even though now Caesar cannot hear her, she cannot but cry, 'Ah, ha!' (p. 157)

Her vivacity and volubility, another trait which she never loses, it would take pages to illustrate. When in the earlier scenes Antony is trying to break to her his purpose of setting out for Rome she will not let him have more than a word at a time, and she catches him up and twits him, rallies and teases him, without mercy or remorse. So with the messenger of his marriage—she interrupts and anticipates, wheedles and deprecates, bullies and cajoles. And when baffled by Fate at Antony's

death and by Seleucus in the presence of Caesar, she rails almost as volubly as ever. . . . And . . . she is given to repetition, in a way that is not quite like that trait in any other Shakespearean character. 'Note him,' she says of Antony to Charmian in the first Act, 'Note him, good Charmian; 'tis the man; but note him' [I. v. 53-4]. It is the language of exuberant glee. And nothing so much gives us an impression of the identity of her character as the appearance of this trait in the midst of her grief:

> What, what, good cheer! Why how now, Charmian.
> My noble girls! Ah women, women, look,
> Our lamp is spent.
>   [IV. xv. 83-5]

> He words me, girls, he words me, that I should not
> Be noble to myself.
>   [V. ii. 191-92]

> Ah! women, women! come; we have no friend
> But resolution and the briefest end.
>   [IV. xv. 90-1]

Here it is really not the language of grief but of her bearing up against grief—or rather it is the essential utterance of Cleopatra. For she is alive, every inch of her, to her finger-tips; and her speech has the undulation of a bird's flight, or of a thoroughbred woman's gait of her own time, ere woman had heard of heels. Only it is not a walk, but a dance—or rather, a flight, which is, no doubt, more satisfying and exhilarating for one who is equal to it than either.

Surely, then, this character holds together, as a living thing. There are matters left unexplained, but none that cannot be explained—which is Shakespeare's method. Why did Cleopatra conceal the treasure and pretend that she had given a full account? It may have been to make use of this for her supreme, ultimate toilet, or it may even have been in order to be detected in the fraud and convince Cæsar that she had no thought of death. Either explanation would be in keeping with her sinuous, elusive nature, but neither (without some hint to the audience) with Shakespeare's popular art. What fits both his art and the character is that she should have endeavoured to deceive and defraud Caesar for the game's own sake, without material profit, as indeed she does again presently, with her asp. (pp. 158-59)

However it be, her conduct at this juncture—her lie and her rage against Seleucus for not bearing her out in it—is, though quite like her, unbecoming; it is vulgar, though Professor Schücking does not call it so. But her vulgarity here, where she is supposed to be a sublime queen, like the other vulgarity when she is only the harlot, should not offend us, whether artistically or morally. Vulgarity has a place in great art; and we suffer, Professor Schücking and some others of us, from a Victorian, or a petty French, decorum. No lady, no Cornelian or Racinian queen, would act so: but neither the one nor the other could interest us so much. (pp. 159-60)

And morally, too, the vulgarity, and above all the voluptuousness, need not touch us nearly. The dramatist has despite his sympathy 'held the balance even.' He has secured our interest without prejudicing the moral cause. He takes care, indeed, that the virtuous woman Octavia should be kept in the background, and that the simple beauty of the homely and civic duties should not enter into competition with the dark and dubious beauty of an abandoned passion. But he shrewdly remembers its illicit basis, its suspicions, jealousies, and resentments; and at her best Cleopatra is fain to call herself a wife. Here is no glorification, in mediaeval style, of illicit love at the expense of the married state, whether on the part of the lovers or their friends. These are no Lancelot and Guenevere, Tristram and Iseult. For that matter, there are none such in Shakespeare.

And, most remarkable of all, the poet restrains himself in the matter of voluptuousness and erotic colouring. This is suggested rather than presented and expressed. We are made to see that Cleopatra and Antony indulge their sensuous imaginations but are not told them: Cleopatra feeds herself on most delicious poison but pours very little of it into our ear. . . . Though real enough, these Egyptian passions are not near and nude, but keep the cool, serene distance of art. They are as if in a picture or a song, not as if heard and seen through a cranny in a bedroom wall. And Cleopatra's words are sweet as her woman's lips, soft as her breast, sharp on occasion as her teeth and nails, but in the lines her alluring person or Antony's overmastering one scarcely appears, and troubles no innocent spirit.

But the main reason is—that this man and woman love each other. There is more in it all than mere body and beauty. Their imaginations are fired, even their hearts are touched. There can be no question of this at the end—the words of Antony and Cleopatra at his death are among the immortal utterances of sexual tenderness. But this appears also elsewhere, particularly after Actium, in the quarrel about Thyreus, and at the time of Cleopatra's birthday, as well as at the beginning of the play. In Cleopatra it is another vein of unity and continuity in her nature. Though afterwards deepened through trial, her feeling at the outset is more than mere vanity and sense. She knows Antony and has with him a community of tastes. Like true lovers they *like* each other, and that is partly because they like the same things. They are comrades and companions. (pp. 160-61)

Here again [Shakespeare] holds the balance even. He disapproves of their relation and yet does not refuse it love's title or prerogative. He makes the lovers jealous and suspicious, and yet glorifies them with poetry and elicits our sympathy. This is not a contradiction save as it is a contradiction in life . . . and as it must be (still more) in art. A character in a drama or a novel is not quite the same as in reality, and far more than in life must we be made to sympathise as we disapprove. . . . All art is a compromise, an accommodation; all art, even the noblest and truest, must needs please or interest, must in a measure sacrifice truth to effect. . . . And seldom can a character in a drama or even in a novel bear the full stark light of common day. It is a product of a fine labour of simplification and intensification, of projection or subordination, of parallel or contrast. So the love of Antony and Cleopatra is in a sense incompatible with their lives and their natures. The poet puts words of censure in the mouths of Antony's friends and respectable enemies at the beginning; but more and more suppresses these, and instead makes much of their servants' devotion, as he seeks to elicit our sympathy towards the end. He is careful to put Octavia and her children, and the legitimate claims of society, in the play (indeed) but in the background; and to touch on no note of pathos in connexion with hearth and home. As in most people, the love of the famous paramours is the noblest thing about them; but by the licence of exaggeration in art their love is made greater than they. That licence we instinctively allow: all this paltering with the truth we warrant. Yet here, and here only, as it seems to me, is there cause to cavil at the unity of Cleopatra's character;—as we carelessly

forget that she is a figure in a drama and look upon her as but a bit of life. (pp. 162-63)

E. E. Stoll, "Cleopatra," in The Modern Language Review, *Vol. XXIII, No. 2, April, 1928, pp. 145-63.*

HARLEY GRANVILLE-BARKER   (essay date 1930)

[*Granville-Barker was a noted actor, playwright, director, and critic. His work as a Shakespearean critic is at all times informed by his experience as a director, for he treats Shakespeare's plays not as works of literature better understood divorced from the theater, as did many Romantic critics, but as pieces meant for the stage. As a director, he emphasized simplicity in staging, set design, and costuming. He believed that elaborate scenery obscured the poetry which was of central importance to Shakespeare's plays. Granville-Barker also eschewed the approach of directors who scrupulously reconstructed a production based upon Elizabethan stage techniques; he felt that this, too, detracted from the play's meaning. In the following excerpt, Granville-Barker offers a close analysis of the poetic language of* Antony and Cleopatra, *especially emphasizing its idiosyncratic "rhythm and music." He declares that in this play Shakespeare takes unusual liberties with meter and even sacrifices "grammar now and then, and at a pinch, if need be, sheer sense, too" in order to attain the desired "dramatic emphasis." The cardinal virtue of the writing here, Granville-Barker maintains, is its unique combination of "concentration, clarity, strength, [and] simplicity." The critic also contends that the principal theme of the play is "the wider ruin" in the Roman world precipitated by Antony's personal downfall, asserting that the "love-tragedy" of Antony and Cleopatra only becomes an issue after the state of the Empire is decided by the second battle between Octavius's and Antony's forces. Additionally, in a section of his commentary on* Antony and Cleopatra *not excerpted here, Granville-Barker provides a detailed examination of the play's construction, demonstrating that its structure is taut and well-balanced and that the dramatic episodes are carefully woven together into a unified pattern.*]

Here is the most spacious of the plays. It may lack the spiritual intimacy of *Hamlet*, the mysterious power of *Macbeth*, the nobilities of *Othello*, may reach neither to the heights nor depths of *King Lear*; but it has a magnificence and a magic all its own, and Shakespeare's eyes swept no wider horizon.

Eight years or so earlier he had written *Julius Cæsar*. There already are these rivals Antony and Octavius, comrades then; and the main clash of fortune and character is between Antony and Brutus, between the man of action and the idealist. Antony comes from it victorious; the tragedy is the soul's tragedy of Brutus. Thereafter Shakespeare gives us play after play upon this theme of the self-torturing soul. Hamlet (its chief exemplar), Othello, Macbeth, Lear are all concerned with the world within themselves. Now he returns to the world of great affairs, and, almost as if for emphasis, to the very pair that he left standing over the dead body of the idealist in defeat.

We have a play of action, then, not of spiritual insight; that is the first thing to mark. Of a large field of action too. For if with *Julius Cæsar* the insularity of the earlier Histories was left behind, we are shown now not Rome in her might only, but the whole range of the Empire, eastward to Athens, Egypt and the Parthian bounds. Antony, the once-triumphant man of action, is hero; we are to watch his defeat by his subtler sometime pupil. Truly it is his passion for Cleopatra that is his ruin, and the action pulses to this; but the wider issue dictates form, method, and the bulk of the play's content. (pp. 111-12)

Bradley will not place the play with the four great tragedies, because, he says, Antony and Cleopatra themselves do not kindle pity and admiration to the full [see excerpt above, 1905]. He admits, though, that their passion and its ending is by no means the whole of the story. Certainly it is not. What are we shown to begin with? Far less a pair of tragic lovers in the making than—through the indignant Roman eyes of Philo and Demetrius—a doting general, effeminate in Egyptian finery, ignoring Cæsar's messengers, capable of a

> Let Rome in Tiber melt, and the wide arch
> Of the ranged Empire fall.
>
> [I. i. 33-4]

(whoever will may hear it!), and a debauched Eastern queen, mocking at things Roman, battening on his apostasy. Here at once is the larger theme emphasised, the discord which is to be resolved at last to a full close in the elaborate confusions of their defeat and death. The love-tragedy, we might almost say, is not made the main question till no other question is left, till the ruin wreaked by Triumvir and Queen is accomplished. And the action of the play is schemed throughout for the picturing of this wider ruin. Hence its diffuseness; and hence, if this is not understood, much misunderstanding of its artistry. (pp. 114-15)

[Shakespeare] is apt to lay the main lines of his story very firmly and simply, and to let us see where we are going from the start, to cut the complexities from borrowed plots, and if any side-issue later promises distraction, to make (literally) short work of it. Here he reduces the actual story to simplicity itself. Antony breaks from Cleopatra to patch up an insincere peace with Cæsar, since Pompey threatens them both; he marries Octavia, and deserts her to return to Cleopatra; war breaks out, Cæsar defeats them and they kill themselves. That is the plot; and every character is concerned with it and hardly a line is spoken that does not relate to it. There is no under-plot, nor any such obvious relief as Falstaff, Nym, Bardolph, Pistol and Fluellen give to the heroics of the Henriad.

But, for a broad picturesque contrast, Roman and Egyptian are set against each other; and this opposition braces the whole body of the play. (p. 117)

The story is simple, but the tributary threads of it are manifold, and the interweaving conflicts of purpose complex enough. Its theme (once again) is not merely Antony's love for Cleopatra, but his ruin as general and statesman, the final ascension of Octavious, and the true end of

> . . . that work the ides of March begun.
>
> [*Julius Caesar*, V. i. 113]
> (p. 138)

Rome and its Empire are ever a clarion call to Shakespeare's imagination; and the strength of his answer to it lies in his power to make the alien characters his own. For he leaves them in no classic immunity, casting his care upon their impressive reputations. They must be sifted through his dramatist's conscience; he brings them to terms on the ground of common humanity. What is Cleopatra's passport to tragic heights?

> No more but e'en a woman, and commanded
> By such poor passion as the maid that milks
> And does the meanest chares. . . .
>
> [IV. xv. 73-5]

With this, of course, they risk the loss of their conventionally heroic stature. But it is preserved for them by the magic of poetry.

This is literally a sort of magic, by which the vibrations of emotion that the sound of the poetry sets up seem to enlarge its sense, and break the bounds of the stage to carry us into the lost world of romantic history. Conceive such a story and such characters so familiarly, and then tie their expression to plain prose—Dido will be in danger of becoming a dowdy indeed, and Cleopatra a gipsy; unless some other magic can be found. Shakespeare, however, has travelled far since Mercutio could thus mock Romeo's poetic prowess, and is now himself by no means 'for the numbers that Petrarch flowed in' [*Romeo and Juliet*, II. iv. 38-9]. He has another choice. He has come to the writing of a verse which combines actuality and power, and is malleable to every diversity of character and mood. He is at the apogee of his art in this kind; possibly a shade past it already. (pp. 171-72)

Nevertheless, here and there we may feel a strain; sometimes emotion will not quite vivify thought, which stays constricted or confused; or a too constant repetition of effect or an over-simplifying of simplicity may show fatigue. But Shakespeare has always had the tact to seize on the subject that will best fit his artist's mood, or to adapt mood and method to subject—which, it is not our business to inquire. In its qualities and defects alike his present method, resourceful, audacious yet still spontaneous, ripe if to over-ripeness, fits this subject most consummately well.

Big as it is, he feels no need at all to economise strength. He begins at what a pitch!

> Nay, but this dotage of our general's
> O'erflows the measure; those his goodly eyes,
> That o'er the files and musters of the war
> Have glow'd like plated Mars, now bend, now turn,
> The office and devotion of their view
> Upon a tawny front: his captain's heart,
> Which in the scuffles of great fights hath burst
> The buckles on his breast, reneges all temper,
> And is become the bellows and the fan
> To cool a gipsy's lust.
>
> [I. i. 1-10]

This is as ample and virile in substance, as luminous and as consonant in its music as anything well could be. One tremendous sentence, the ends of the lines not answering to pauses either; these, such as they are, fall midway (but a bare four of them in nine lines and more, though), so that fresh impulse may overleap the formal division, and the force be the force of the whole. Note, too, the placing of the dominant 'o'erflows the measure' and its complement 'reneges all temper' with the doubled parenthesis between them, and how the 'now bend, now turn' saves this from slackness; how 'files and musters' and 'office and devotion' strengthen the beat of the verse, with 'plated Mars' coming like the sudden blare of a trumpet, and 'burst the buckles on his breast' to sound the exploding indignation which culminates in the deadly

> And is become the bellows and the fan
> To cool a gipsy's lust.

A fairly opulent dramatic allowance for this Philo, of whom we know nothing, are never to see again. But throughout the play we shall find the least considered characters, and on no special occasion, with as meaty stuff—is there a better term for it?—in their mouths. Mæcenas greets Octavia, upon her disillusioned return, with

> Welcome, dear Madam.
> Each heart in Rome does love and pity you:
> Only the adulterous Antony, most large
> In his abominations, turns you off;
> And gives his potent regiment to a trull,
> That noises it against us.
>
> [III. vi. 91-6]

The anonymous legionary, even, has no less vivid and stirring a moment to his share than

> O noble emperor, do not fight by sea;
> Trust not to rotten planks. . . .
>   [We]
> Have used to conquer, standing on the earth,
> And fighting foot to foot.
>
> [III. vii. 61-2, 64-6]

And from Pompey in his first scene (Shakespeare himself well into his stride by this!) comes the full enrichment of

> . . . But all the charms of love,
> Salt Cleopatra, soften thy waned lip!
> Let witchcraft join with beauty, lust with both!
> Tie up the libertine in a field of feasts,
> Keep his brain fuming; Epicurean cooks
> Sharpen with cloyless sauce his appetite;
> That sleep and feeding may prorogue his honour
> Even till a Lethe'd dullness.
>
> [II. i. 20-7]

Too much rich writing of this sort would be like Cleopatra's feasts, and clog the march of the action. But when mere argument is in hand we fall back to nothing less pedestrian than Antony's

> Sir,
> He fell upon me ere admitted: then
> Three kings I had newly feasted, and did want
> Of what I was i' the morning: but, next day,
> I told him of myself; which was as much
> As to have asked him pardon. Let this fellow
> Be nothing of our strife: if we contend
> Out of our question wipe him.
>
> [II. ii. 74-81]

This, and such a passage as Cæsar's somewhat smug

> Let's grant it is not
> Amiss to tumble in the bed of Ptolemy;
> To give a kingdom for a mirth . . .
>   —yet must Antony
> No way excuse his foils, when we do bear
> So great weight in his lightness.
>
> [I. iv. 16-18, 23-5]

or as Pompey's

> To you all three,
> The senators alone of this great world,
> Chief factors for the gods,—I do not know
> Wherefore my father should revengers want,
> Having a son and friends, since Julius Cæsar,
> Who at Philippi the good Brutus ghosted,
> There saw you labouring for him.
>
> [II. vi. 8-14]

may be taken as the norm of the play's poetic method, upon which its potencies are built up. And it is upon this norm, of course, that the actors must model their own style.

The elemental oratory of this verse needs for its speaking a sense of rhythm that asks no help of strict rule. Shakespeare is so secure by now in the spirit of its laws that the letter may go. He does not commonly stray far. A cæsura may fall oddly or there may be none distinguishable, a syllable or so may splash over at the end. Dramatic emphasis is the thing, first and last; to get that right he will sacrifice strict metre—yet never music—grammar now and then, and at a pinch, if need be, sheer sense too.

These freedoms gain in effect as the play's temper heightens. Cæsar's calculated indignation is sounded in the two swelling catalogues:

> I'the common show place where they exercise,
> His sons he there proclaimed the kings of kings.
> Great Media, Parthia and Armenia
> He gave to Alexander; to Ptolemy he assign'd
> Syria, Cilicia and Phoenicia. . . .
>   . . . he hath assembled
> Bocchus the king of Libya; Archelaus
> Of Cappadocia. . . .
>
> [III. vi. 12-16, 68-70]

The . . . scansion is highly individual.

But no Cleopatra, with an ear, can miss the shrill arrogance of

> Sink Rome, and their tongues rot
> That speak against us! A charge we bear i' the war,
> And, as the president of my kingdom, will
> Appear there for a man. Speak not against it;
> I will not stay behind.
>
> [III. vii. 15-19]

The upward run of semi-quavers in 'A charge we bear i' the war' is as plain as any musical stave could make it; and the pauses seem to mark so many snaps of the jaw. The lines are not, of course, here or elsewhere to be reckoned by syllables, but by beat.

Listen, on the other hand, to the weary descent to depression's depths in Antony's

> Fall not a tear, I say; one of them rates
> All that is won and lost: give me a kiss;
> Even this repays me. We sent our schoolmaster;
> Is 'a come back? Love, I am full of lead.
>
> [III. xi. 69-72]

—given us by a regular cæsura, followed by an irregular one, followed by a mid-line full stop; the line then finished with an effort by the banal 'We sent our schoolmaster' (who could get anything but exhaustion out of that 'schoolmaster'?); the next line with its dead monosyllables dragging after, the pause in the middle made the longer because of them. Then comes a sudden rally in the rhymed couplet:

> Some wine, within there, and our viands! Fortune knows
> We scorn her most when most she offers blows.
>
> [III. xi. 73-4]

—its irregular first line just saving it from sounding mechanical.

The violence of Antony's anger when he finds Thidias kissing Cleopatra's hand has its own notation and tune.

> Approach there! Ah, you kite! Now, gods and devils!
> Authority melts from me. Of late, when I cried 'Ho!',
> Like boys unto a muss, kings would start forth
> And cry 'Your will?' Have you no ears?
> I am Antony yet. Take hence this jack and whip him.
>
> [III. xiii. 89-93]

Long lines, giving a sense of great strength. Exclamatory phrases, prefacing and setting off the powerful centre-phrase, with its ringing 'kings' for a top note. The cæsura-pause of two beats that the short line allows is followed by the repeated crack of two more short phrases, the first with its upward lift, the second with its nasal snarl and the sharp click of its ending; the last line lengthens out, and the business finishes with the bitten *staccato* of

> Take hence this jack and whip him.

Note the deadly flick of the last two words!

The sense apart, what an almost wilful pathos we feel in the smoothly sustained, one- and two-syllable worded, predominantly thin-vowelled speech of Antony's to the weeping servants!

> Tend me to-night;
> Maybe it is the period of your duty:
> Haply you shall not see me more; or if,
> A mangled shadow: perchance to-morrow
> You'll serve another master. I look on you
> As one that takes his leave. Mine honest friends,
> I turn you not away; but like a master
> Married to your good service, stay till death.
> Tend me to-night two hours. I ask no more;
> And the gods yield you for 't.
>
> [IV. ii. 24-33]

Note in particular the importance given to 'A mangled shadow' by the sustaining tripled consonant, and the two-beat pause that follows ('to-morrow,' with its weak ending, ranking for a dissyllable), and how the repeated, 'Tend me tonight' rounds in the speech a trifle artificially.

Throughout these scenes, throughout the play indeed, one can so analyse the verse, find its rhythm and music, often transcending rule, but always close fitted to mood and meaning. The best moments need no analysis, and seem to defy it. One must not appear to be praising

> I am dying, Egypt, dying; only
> I here importune death awhile, until
> Of many thousand kisses the poor last
> I lay upon thy lips.
>   I dare not, dear—,
> Dear, my lord, pardon,—I dare not,
> Lest I be taken:
>
> [IV. xv. 18-23]

merely for the way in which a short first line allows for the two silent breaths that will show Antony's flagging strength, nor for the infallible accenting of Cleopatra's fear, first upon the 'dare,' and then, with repetition, upon the 'not.' But actors have to concern themselves with such impertinences.

The passionate hysteria of her

> Where art thou, death?
> Come hither, come, come, come, and take a queen
> Worth many babes and beggars.
> *Proculeius.*   O, temperance, lady!
> *Cleopatra.* Sir, I will eat no meat, I'll not drink, sir—
>   If idle talk will once be necessary—
>   I'll not sleep neither: this mortal house
>   I'll ruin . . .
>
> [V. ii. 46-51]

asks neither comment nor analysis. Why waste time trying to scan the last line? It is right, and not the extremest perversity could speak it wrongly, one would suppose. Nor will much more be gained by trying to extract meaning from the last line but one. If it has any in particular (which seems doubtful) no audience could be made to grasp it. But as a setting of hysterical gibbering to verbal music, it is perfect.

But one technical excellence among many it is hard to pass by. As Shakespeare nears the last great moment, that of Cleopatra's death, he wants to give his verse solid strength and dignity; and the pulse of it now throbs with a steady intensity, goes processionally forward, as it were.

> Give me my robe, put on my crown, I have
> Immortal longings in me: now no more
> The juice of Egypt's grape shall moist this lip.
> Yare, yare, good Iras: quick. Methinks I hear
> Antony call; I see him rouse himself
> To praise my noble act; I hear him mock
> The luck of Cæsar, which the gods give men
> To excuse their after wrath. . . .
>
> [V. ii. 280-87]

Regular metre, saved from formality by the subtle variety of the mid-line stopping; the whole welded into unity by the constant carrying on of the sentences from line to line. But, lest the effect grow all too set, Charmian is let interpose, a little later, not a single line but one and a half. Then, lest life die out of it, we have—after the added emphasis of an irregular line, in which Cleopatra lays hands on the asp with a heavily accentuated 'Come . . .'—the words clipped, the pace quickened. Twice more Charmian interrupts, but now with phrases that sustain rather than break the rhythm.

> *Cleopatra.*   . . . Come, thou mortal wretch,
>   With thy sharp teeth this knot intrinsicate
>   Of life at once untie; poor venomous fool,
>   Be angry, and despatch. O, could'st thou speak,
>   That I might hear thee call great Cæsar ass
>   Unpolicied!
> *Charmian.*   O Eastern star!
> *Cleopatra.*   Peace, peace!
>   Dost thou not see my baby at my breast,
>   That sucks the nurse asleep?
> *Charmian.*   O break! O break!
> *Cleopatra.* As sweet as balm, as soft as air, as gentle!
>   O, Antony! Nay, I will take thee too:
>   What should I stay—?
>
> [V. ii. 303-13]

Not one beat has been missed till her dying breaks the last line; yet we have been no more conscious of the form than when the verse was at its loosest, only of the added power.

Shakespeare no longer divides his characters into speakers of verse and speakers of prose, nor makes this distinction regularly between scenes. The freedom and variety of his verse writing allow him to pass almost imperceptibly from poetry to prose and back again. Thus he ranges an unbroken scale, from a pedestrian exactitude in stating plain fact at one end of it to the conventional flourish of the rhymed couplet at the other. But he can still make the sharp contrast of a change effective between scene and scene; or in the midst of a scene he can bring passion or pretentiousness down to earth—and prose, or as suddenly restore force and dignity with rhythm and tone. And he can go to work more subtly than that. . . . [In] his play's actual writing, exploiting freedom to the full, he has forged a weapon of extraordinary suppleness and resource.

For instance, in the ostensibly prose scene that follows the play's more formal opening, we have the Soothsayer countering Charmian's impudent chatter with single lines of verse. Their recurrence lends him peculiarity and a slight portentousness; but the surrounding prose is so subtly adjusted that the device itself passes unnoticed. Later, upon Cleopatra's entrance, the scene is suddenly braced to forcefulness by half a dozen consecutive lines of (not too regular, lest the effect be too noticeable) verse. Later still, with a strong dose of prose, Enobarbus turns Antony's philosophic realism very much the seamy side out.

Enobarbus (he in particular) speaks now verse, now prose, either as the scene requires it of him for harmony or contrast, or as his humours dictate; his character being just such a compound of contrasts. Antony only occasionally relapses to prose, and his verse is regular on the whole. Cleopatra hardly touches prose at all; her verse is apt to be a little freer. Cæsar speaks only verse; it is fairly formal, and expressive of his calculated dignity.

But the supreme virtue of the writing lies in its peculiar combination of delicacy and strength, of richness with simplicity. (pp. 172-81)

[We] have concentration, clarity, strength, simplicity all combined in the swift exchange between Alexas and Cleopatra when he brings her the first news of the absent Antony with

> His speech sticks in my heart.
> Mine ear must pluck it thence.
>
> [I. v. 41-2]

she answers; and in her dark misgiving as the unlucky second messenger faces her:

> But, sirrah, mark, we use
> To say the dead are well: bring it to that,
> The gold I give thee I will melt and pour
> Down thy ill-uttering throat.
>
> [II. v. 32-5]

and in the primitive

> Call the slave again:
> Though I am mad I will not bite him: call!
>
> [II. v. 79-80]

Such things seem easy only when they are done—and well done.

Again, there is artistry of the subtlest in the freedom and apparent ease of this (the same wretched messenger is now atoning for his fault by disparaging Octavia, Charmian abetting him):

Messenger.   She creeps:
> Her motion and her station are as one;
> She shows a body rather than a life,
> A statue than a breather.
Cleopatra.   Is this certain?
Messenger. Or I have no observance.
Charmian.   Three in Egypt
> Cannot make better note.
Cleopatra.   He's very knowing;
> I do perceive't: there's nothing in her yet;
> The fellow has good judgment.
Charmian.   Excellent.
Cleopatra. Guess at her years, I prithee.
Messenger.   Madam,
> She was a widow.—
Cleopatra.   Widow, Charmian; hark!
>
> [III. iii. 18-27]

—in the way the continuing swing of the verse keeps the dialogue swift while the dividing of the lines gives spontaneity.

Note how actual incoherence—kept within bounds by the strict rhythm of the verse—leads up to, and trebles the nobility of a culminating phrase. (She and her women surround the dead Antony.)

> How do you, women?
> What, what, good cheer? Why, how now, Charmian!
> My noble girls! Ah women, women, look!
> Our lamp is spent, it's out. Good sirs, take heart:
> We'll bury him; and then, what's brave, what's noble,
> Let's do it after the high Roman fashion,
> And make death proud to take us. . . .
>
> [IV. xv. 82-8]

The compelled swiftness of the beginning, the change without check when she turns to the soldiers, the accordant discipline of the line which follows, so that the last two lines can come out clarion-clear; here, again, is dramatic music exactly scored. In like fashion Antony's mixed metaphors (when he has been told she is dead), which include something very like a pun, lead up to and enhance a luminous close.

> I will o'ertake thee, Cleopatra, and
> Weep for my pardon. So it must be, for now
> All length is torture: since the torch is out,
> Lie down and stray no further: now all labour
> Mars what it does: yea, very force entangles
> Itself with strength: seal then, and all is done.
> Eros.—I come, my queen: Eros!—Stay for me
> Where souls do couch on flowers, we'll hand in hand,
> And with our sprightly port make the ghosts gaze:
> Dido and her Æneas shall want troops,
> And all the haunt be ours.
>
> [IV. xiv. 44-54]

While, for a glorious and famous passage that is music itself—but what more?—take:

> O see, my women,
> The crown o' the earth doth melt. My Lord!
> O, withered is the garland of the war,
> The soldier's pole is fall'n: young boys and girls
> Are level now with men; the odds is gone,
> And there is nothing left remarkable
> Beneath the visiting moon.
>
> [IV. xv. 62-8]

This, in analysis, is little better than ecstatic nonsense; and it is meant to sound so. It has just enough meaning in it for us to feel as we hear it that it may possibly have a little more. Art must by so much at least improve on nature; in nature it would probably have none. But it gives us to perfection the reeling agony of Cleopatra's mind; therefore, in its dramatic setting, it ranks as supreme poetry.

Utterly sure of himself, Shakespeare has, in fine, reached in the writing as in the shaping of this play limits of freedom and daring that he will not, but for the worse, overpass. (pp. 184-88)

> Harley Granville-Barker, '''Antony and Cleopatra','' in his Prefaces to Shakespeare, second series, Sidgwick & Jackson, Ltd., 1930, pp. 111-233.

G. WILSON KNIGHT (essay date 1931)

[*Knight was one of the most influential Shakespearean critics of the twentieth century; he helped shape a new interpretive approach to Shakespeare's work and promoted a greater appreciation of many of the plays. In his studies* The Wheel of Fire *(1930) and* The Shakespearian Tempest *(1932), Knight rejected criticism which emphasizes sources, character analysis, psychology, and ethics and outlined his principles of interpretation which, he claimed, would "replace that chaos by drawing attention to the true Shakespearian unity." Knight argued that this unity lay in Shakespeare's poetic use of images and symbols—particularly in the opposition of "tempests" and "music." He also maintained that a play's spatial aspects, or "atmosphere," should be as closely considered as the temporal elements of the plot if one is "to see the whole play in space as well as time." In the excerpt below from* The Imperial Theme *(1931), Knight identifies two principal thematic issues in* Antony and Cleopatra: *Antony's sacrifice of power, military honor, and "imperial magnificence" for love; and love as a conjunction of physical and transcendental qualities. These twin themes, he contends, are reflected in the two dominant metaphorical patterns of war and love. Knight also discovers an ascending scale of allusions—such as those to gold, empire, feasting, animals, nature's bounty, water, melting or dissolving, weather, air, fire, and music—which he claims moves from the concrete and sensuous to the "elemental and ethereal" as the love of Antony and Cleopatra becomes more rarified. In addition, the critic remarks on the play's dramatic style, describing the language as tightly compressed, subtle yet powerful, possessing an abundance of "intellectual content," and, "like a thin, blazing, electric filament, steadily instinct with keenest fire." Finally, Knight asserts that while* Antony and Cleopatra *offers a visionary and idealized view of love as a potentially transcendent experience, the play also contains elements of realism, coarseness, and "tragic pathos." In another chapter from* The Imperial Theme *not excerpted here, he examines the drama's painful and malevolent aspects, but he insists that "transcendental and ethereal humanism" is the primary vision of the play.*]

[*Antony and Cleopatra*] is probably the subtlest and greatest play in Shakespeare, or, at least, paragoned only by *The Tempest*. The action compasses the Mediterranean and its citied shores; the Roman empire is revivified at its climacteric of grandeur and shown as something of so boundless and rich a magnificence that the princes who sway its destiny appear comparable only to heroes of myth, or divine beings. Yet the persons here are human enough too, and the events sharply realized. Although the play presents, as a whole, a visionary and idealistic optimism, there is no absence of realistic, and, indeed, coarse essences, or of tragic pathos. . . . In *Lear* we have a copious realism within a pessimistic and limited vision; here we have a similar wealth within a correspondingly optimistic and unlimited vision. *Lear* extends a view eminently naturalistic, its scope is bounded by 'nature' and our world.

Antony and Cleopatra discloses a vision rather 'universalistic': nature itself is here transfigured, and our view is directed not to the material alone, nor to the earth alone, but rather to the universal elements of earth, water, air, fire, and music, and beyond these to the all-transcending visionary humanism which endows man with a supernatural glory. The vision is eminently a life-vision and a love-vision: and our love-theme ranges from purely sensuous delights to the rarefied heights . . . of intense spiritual contemplation. But throughout, all is subdued to a single rare poetic quality of an especial kind. The sensuous is not presented sensuously; the poet's medium purifies all it touches, as though all were thinned yet clarified from a new visionary height. Since this quality is most important for our general understanding I will first offer some remarks on the play's style: and afterwards pass to a comprehensive analysis of the varying imaginative themes, the interweaving colours of its design.

This poetry is both metaphysical and emotional: but the emotion is ever thrice-distilled, like Troilus' love, a 'thrice-repured nectar'' [*Troilus and Cressida*, III. ii. 22]; so finely wrought in delicate yet vividly dynamic phrase or word that we find a maximum of power within a minimum of sense-appeal, either visual or aural. There are sense-effects, and they are powerful: but they are always so refined, visually and aurally, that we must recognize them to possess only a secondary delight. We do not find those floods of emotion that surge in *Othello* and *Timon*, nor the violent impactuous image or passion that strikes wonder in *Macbeth* and *Lear*. Here the most tremendous image is thrown off carelessly, or dreamily: an accessory, but not an essential. Yet there is a certain sharpness, keenness in these poetic effects, like the biting air on a mountain height; thence we have a panoramic view not blurred by clouds of sense or passion, nor twilit in any sunset emotion, but clean, crystal-clear, in a medium washed by bright sunlight, where phrases are sharp and brittle as icicles gleaming.

There is a pre-eminence of thin or feminine vowel-sounds, 'e' and 'i'; and a certain lightness and under-emphasis of passion, which yet robs it of no intrinsic power; a refusal of the resonant and reverberating stress, an absence of any direct or prolonged sensuous pleasure in phrase, word, or syllable. It is not easy to speak it: nothing short of intensest intellectual and imaginative concentration can do its delicate subtleties justice. Its quick changes keep the intellect awake; to speak it is to think it as well as feel it, for there is no easy overriding the intellectual content, while leaving all to the emotional cadence. Tragic poetry is rather like a tidal river. The river of logic is lost in the opposing passionate tide: it is often enough to remember and submit to the passion. Here the tide ebbs; intellect and emotion flow together. Nor is that all: there are dotted islets dividing the stream into diverging and rejoining channels, and a light wind ruffles aslant the surface, stirring it into a myriad criss-cross ripples which sparkle in the sun above the moving deeps.

This insistence on thin vowels, especially 'i's, this reluctance to luxuriate in the emotional and colourous phrase, as in *Othello*, or to loose any violent flood of passion, as in *Lear* and *Timon*, is evident throughout. . . . The effects are vastly different from Othello's throbbing, pulsing floods of emotion: in Othello's language, in Timon's, there is blood in its veins, coursing, throbbing. Cleopatra's is veined with a more tenuous and fiery elixir. There is no sonority, nor, in fact, any deep notes at all in the play. Tragedy is taken lightly, almost playfully: yet this lilting merriment of diction holds, strangely, a more intense fire than the solemn cadences or curbless passions of the sombre plays. All feeling here is more subtle: pure emotion but one strand twisted in a more complex pattern. . . . In despising all normal emotional and sensuous associations, working outside the organ cadences of ordinary tragedy, this poetry yet catches the most evanescent tragic essence on the wing:

> O infinite virtue, comest thou smiling from
> The world's great snare uncaught?
>
> [IV. viii. 17-18]

The 'snare' image is at first sight strangely inapposite: the completed association miraculous. Again:

> Here's sport indeed! How heavy weighs my lord!
> Our strength is all gone into heaviness.
>
> [IV. xv. 32-3]

This is rare music. Often the soaring tragic emotion is, paradoxically, closely pinned to earth: witness the sharp realism in:

> No more, but e'en a woman, and commanded
> By such poor passion as the maid that milks
> And does the meanest chares.
>
> [IV. xv. 73-5]

The most powerful phrases are often colourless. Antony is a 'workman' in the 'royal occupation' of fighting [IV. iv. 17]. A world of meaning is compressed in the simplest phrase: 'a Roman thought hath struck him' [I. ii. 83]. Where else in our literature could the commonplace word 'husband' unfurl such starry wells of light as in Cleopatra's simple phrase:

> . . . Husband, I come.
>
> [V. ii. 287]

Then, when it chooses, this style, like some diaphanous-winged and shimmering dragon-fly of the spirit, outsoars the more 'emotional' kinds, outdistances them with a fine ease. Though ever despising the sensuous and sentimental, it yet dares and accomplishes so sweeping a miracle as:

> His face was as the heavens: and therein stuck
> A sun and moon, which kept their course, and lighted
> The little O, the earth.
>
> [V. ii. 79-81]

However 'unemotional' it may have appeared, it yet holds in it a more dynamic and intense power, and emotion, than any other: words and phrases here are as atoms compressing an infinite force and energy. This emotional fibre may be tenuous: but it is tough as wire. The style of *Othello* is like a large glowing coal; that of *Macbeth* like the sparks from an anvil; *Lear,* like a rocket; *Timon,* like phosphorus churned to flame in a tropic ocean. That of *Antony and Cleopatra* is like a thin, blazing, electric filament, steadily instinct with keenest fire.

We thus find a strangely keen yet somewhat unemotional vision. Whatever our elements—whether of feasting and drinking, passionate lust, or military splendour—they are transformed by this peculiar alchemy into essences intensely spiritual, rarefied. This is the process of all poetry: but here it is carried farther. Here, where our subject is one very largely sensuous, our medium is peculiarly desensualized. But the subject-matter is itself various: it ranges from the material and sensuous, through the grand and magnificent, to the more purely spiritual. There is an ascending scale. The style, the poetic vision of the whole, endorses this movement: it views its world as one rising

from matter to spirit, and hence, seeing all things in terms not of their immediate appeal, but rather their potential significance, we find that all here is from the first finely gilded with the tinct of spiritual apprehension. I shall now attempt an analysis of this ascending scale. There are a variety of themes to be noticed, and I . . . deliberately stress the more optimistic and glorious effects: there are others, but they are subsidiary. In selecting certain veins of imagery, suggestion, and symbol for special analysis I do not limit their significance to any one immediate meaning. And we must realize that my 'ascending scale' is a purely intellectual arrangement of imaginative essences, its only justification being its purpose to enrich our imaginative vision of a complex whole. The complexity is amazing. One image may serve numerous purposes. Antony and Cleopatra, we are told, were publicly enthroned in chairs of gold. Now this gold-reference has a varied content. It angers Caesar and precipitates the action; it emphasizes the riotous extravagance of Antony's nature; it illustrates the world-power of our protagonists, their imperial eminence; and it shows them symbolically throned in a rich setting worthy of their opulent and infinite love. Empire-imagery throughout serves at least a dual purpose: suggesting both the material magnificence which Antony loses, and shadowing symbolically the finer spiritual magnificence of love for which he sacrifices it. 'Crowns' occur in both connexions. Hence certain repetitions are unavoidable: and any exact definition of symbolic content is, as always, impossible. The mass-effect is somewhat like a bird's glistening plumage, glinting variously as you change your viewpoint. The imagery is ever-shifting, dazzling, iridescent. But a purposive attention to these varied, interrelated strands in the play's texture will help us to rise to the height of its theme and understand its peculiarly transcendental realism. In my middle sections I will note: first, the theme of imperial magnificence, the imperial power and warrior-honour Antony sacrifices for love; second, the more physical and sensuous love-themes and love-imagery in dialogue and suggestion; third, the natural and elemental symbolisms, in their suggestion of the mating of elements, and also, in their varying ascent from the material to the ethereal, reflecting and blending with our love-theme; and, finally, the more spiritual and transcendental elements in this love-theme itself. (pp. 199-206)

[The] thick-scattered 'world' references . . . suggest imperial magnificence and human grandeur—of the men, Antony in particular is idealized beyond all natural limits. In this play human nature is given no limited framework, as in *Lear.* The imperial setting is brilliant, strongly idealized, a world resplendent and magnificent. Human excellence in all its potential beauty and excelling power rides proudly here. Naturalism is transcended. The earth itself, with its sea and land, is a little thing, a bauble in comparison with such heroes. The setting is not, in fact, our little world at all: it is either (i) the Mediterranean empire idealized beyond all rational limits; or (ii) the universe. A new 'universalism', to coin the term, replaces the Lear-naturalism: the latter views man in relation to his 'natural' setting, the former sees man as he is transfigured under the intense ray of love and keenest poetic vision. Here 'the gods' of orthodox paganism—like those in *Lear,* conceived but faintly—are insignificant beside the human drama. The imagery and suggestion throughout is pointing the transcendental, not the natural, qualities in man, or even in 'nature'. We are subdued by it not to the ethnologist's, but rather the lover's apprehension. Now this general elevation of humanity is related to two main streams of imagery: those of (i) War, and (ii) Love. . . . These two Shakespearian values are vividly present. The first is twined with the empire-theme: the second rises from out that theme, is both blended and contrasted with it. The brilliant love-vision rises from this magnificent dream of imperial Roman splendour. Though these two values clash in the play's action, yet the differing victories of each point the other's peculiar essence: Antony sells a warrior's honour and an emperor's sway for the Imperial Theme which is Cleopatra's love. Each theme wins a victory; one spiritual, the other material. (p. 210)

Antony's passion is variously depicted as lust and high spiritual love. Both aspects are stressed, but not equally: the passion theme as a whole is clearly raised above mere animal desire, though that desire is yet closely inwoven with it. First, we must note this 'lower' element of physical passion and physical indulgence generally. Feasting is constantly referred to. Antony's life with Cleopatra is composed chiefly of love and feasting. And feasting, we must remember, is in Shakespeare not only a matter of sensuous pleasure, but a life-force. Its relevance in a play of sexual love is clear. (p. 219)

[However, the] poetry itself always escapes direct sensuous appeal, nor does the wider technique in scene arrangement and dialogue allow any one sensuous suggestion to develop far enough to give delight unchecked. The sensuous element is always part of a patterning itself far from sensuous. We are given a view of physical delights and passions from the poetic height of a rarefied vision, missing nothing, over-emphasizing nothing, aware of all significances and relations, mapped out below, juxtaposed, understood. The vision is too crystal-clear to under-emphasize the physical, yet ever too spiritually and keenly awake to allow itself to become subdued to what it works in. It is a chaste vision of unchastity: we feel the poet's mind alive before us, as, in exquisite purity and profound insight, it delights in its creation of love and lust intrinsicate. The clear avoidance of direct sensuous delight may be illustrated simply enough. I quote a few lines from *Romeo and Juliet:*

> Spread thy close curtain, love-performing night,
> That runaway's eyes may wink, and Romeo
> Leap to these arms, untalk'd of and unseen.
> Lovers can see to do their amorous rites
> By their own beauties; or, if love be blind,
> It best agrees with night. Come, civil night,
> Thou sober-suited matron, all in black,
> And learn me how to lose a winning match,
> Play'd for a pair of stainless maidenhoods:
> Hood my unmann'd blood, bating in my cheeks,
> With thy black mantle; till strange love, grown bold,
> Think true love acted simple modesty.
>
> [*Romeo and Juliet,* III. ii. 5-16]

There is nothing like that about *Antony and Cleopatra.* The sensuously beautiful is never developed for its own sake: it is a necessary accompaniment to a spiritual love—but that love itself, at its finest moments, so far transcends the sensuous that all sensuous suggestion melts, like morning mist, to nothingness in its sun. Set beside Juliet's words Cleopatra's:

> By Isis, I will give thee bloody teeth,
> If thou with Caesar paragon again
> My man of men.
>
> [I. v. 70-2]

So far from being couched in a luxurious bedding of soft undulating emotions, our last phrase here stands next to that first violent petulancy, 'bloody teeth', and all our emotion is compressed into that gem of love poetry, 'my man of men': phrase

hard as a little piece of grit, as colourless, as ordinary—yet alive with a universe of electronic passions. There is no treacle in this style.

There is another strand in the eroticism here . . . : recurrent references to personal and physical, especially facial, details. . . . [This] concrete and visual eroticism . . . is close-woven, naturally, in such a play: part of the rich interplay here of body and spirit. Our vision here shows us a sheen of purest light playing on a rugged land of matter, touching its crags with startling fire, lighting those lakes that interlace it till they burn themselves refulgent as the heavenly origin itself. To this point I shall now direct my analysis, where the imagery advances beyond the solid and sensuous to suggestions more elemental and ethereal: the imagery of water, air, fire. Then, returning to the love-theme, I will finally notice in that connexion the themes of music, and stress again the peculiarly transcendental humanism of the play. Thus we shall advance towards knowledge why and in what sense this play is not merely a story of a soldier's fall, but rather a spelled land of romance achieved and victorious: a paradisal vision expressed in terms of humanity's quest of love.

As in *Julius Caesar, Macbeth,* and *Lear,* it is important to observe the animal references scattered through the play. There is no direct symbolism: animal images are always implicit in their context, serving a direct purpose apart from their cumulative suggestion. This is true throughout: there is little straining after symbolic effects—all tends to be implicit, probable, realistic, and yet instinct with visionary fire. . . . 'Serpents' and 'snakes' are often mentioned. This image suggests sinuous grace and fascination joined to danger: its aptitude in connexion with Cleopatra is evident. Thus she is the 'Serpent of old Nile' [I. v. 25]. But again, that phrase points us to another force: one suggesting life in an element less material than earth. And, indeed, this play stresses particularly two kinds of life: aquatic and aerial.

First, there is the Serpent, often associated with the Nile. Which river is often here in our imaginations. The name 'Nile', with its tenuous soft vowel-sound, brims with the very emotional colour of the river itself sinuously winding through the rich desert ooze, and both suggest the serpent to which it gives birth, the 'serpent of old Nile' . . . , the 'pretty worm of the Nilus' [V. ii. 243]. . . . Water-flies and sea-birds occur, the aquatic blending with the aerial suggestion. . . . [This] animal-imagery . . . helps to define the watery and ethereal quality which interpenetrates our vision. There is continued suggestion of immaterial life-modes, beautiful and volatile, swimming free in ocean or air. . . . Though ethereal, our life-images are to be related to our erotic theme. They are physical and ethereal at once. In this play nature is ever at work, blending, mingling, dissolving element in element, to produce new strangeness, new beauty. The natural imagery thus reflects our love-theme: the blending of elements reflects the blending of sexes in love. Hence our earth is here fruitful, and many references to life-processes occur, throwing the sex-talk of Cleopatra's girls into a new light: for human and physical love is, to a pure vision, itself pure as the dissolving of clouds in rain. I will next observe such references.

There is imagery of trees, flowers, fruits; the benison of earth's foison, harvest fruitfulness, picturesque cultivation, and flowery joy. Nature is kindly and productive: the mating of sun and earth is an apt setting for the mating of our protagonists. . . .

The earth's fruitfulness is often stressed. We have a reference to the mild, fruitful seasons of spring and autumn:

> Like to the time o' the year between the extremes
> Of hot and cold, he was nor sad nor merry.
>
> [I. v. 51-2]

We have mention also of wheat [II. vi. 37], of reapers [III. vii. 35], of 'death' as a 'scythe' [III. xiii. 193]. 'Grace' is to 'grow' where tears fall [IV. ii. 38]. Again,

> O, then we bring forth weeds,
> When our quick minds lie still; and our ills told us
> Is as our earing.
>
> [I. ii. 109-11]

There is Antony's fine description of the Nile's fertility:

> *Antony (To Caesar).* Thus do they, sir: they take the
>   flow o' the Nile
>   By certain scales i' the pyramid; they know
>   By the height, the lowness, or the mean, if dearth
>   Or foison follow: the higher Nilus swells,
>   The more it promises: as it ebbs, the seedsman
>   Upon the slime and ooze scatters his grain,
>   And shortly comes to harvest.
> *Lepidus.* You've strange serpents there.
> *Antony.* Ay, Lepidus.
> *Lepidus.* Your serpent of Egypt is bred now of your
>   mud by the operation of your sun: so is your
>   crocodile.
> *Antony.* They are so.
>
> [II. vii. 17-28]

Notice the rich watery suggestion—land and water blended in 'slime and ooze'. Elsewhere we hear of 'the fire that quickens Nilus' slime' [I. iii. 68-9], and of 'the o'er-flowing Nilus' humorously suggested to 'presage famine' [I. ii. 50]. The fitness of this 'fruitfulness' imagery in a play whose theme is one of vivid life and love may be seen from Agrippa's words on Cleopatra:

> Royal wench!
> She made great Caesar lay his sword to bed:
> He plough'd her, and she cropp'd.
>
> [II. ii. 226-28]

Such 'nature' . . .—earth's fecundity and flowery delight, the swift forms of sea and air life, interpenetrates our theme of human splendour, human love. The magnificence and glory of human love is set within a picturesque and fruitful universe: it is all, like the fruitful season 'between the extremes of hot and cold' a 'heavenly mingle' [I. v. 59]. Earth and sun are mated to produce rich harvests, and this blends with the richer harvest of our protagonists' love, and, finally, the mating of life and death, where, in passion's ecstasy, the 'strength' of 'death' is 'entangled' with the 'force' of life [IV. xiv. 48-9]. I will now pass to the actual elements of water and air apart from that life they breed.

There is a certain liquidity, a 'melting' and 'dissolving' of element in element throughout the play. It is finely apparent in the passage just quoted of the Nile basin, the river ebbing to leave rich tracts of 'slime and ooze'. It is one form of the mating-theme apparent throughout. Another characteristic image occurs a little later, in Antony's mock-description of the crocodile to satisfy the drunken Lepidus:

> *Lepidus.* What manner o' thing is your crocodile?
> *Antony.* It is shaped, sir, like itself; and it is as broad as
>   it hath breadth: it is just so high as it is, and moves
>   with it own organs: it lives by that which nourisheth
>   it; and the elements once out of it, it transmigrates.
> *Lepidus.* What colour is it of?
> *Antony.* Of it own colour too.
> *Lepidus.* 'Tis a strange serpent.
> *Antony.* 'Tis so. And the tears of it are wet.
>
> [II. vii. 41-9]

An amusing image: the 'strange' beast, creature of water and land, pictorially dropping its liquid tears into the ooze and slime of Nile. A typical suggestion of 'strange' life and liquidity. Throughout we are reminded of 'strange' life-forms. Antony is reported to have eaten 'strange flesh which some did die to look on' [I. iv. 67-8]: hence our aerial and aquatic animals, creatures of element strange to man, and the frequent serpents; serpents of all being the most remote from human understanding, so vividly peculiar and picturesquely dangerous that their very strangeness and sinuous unreality strikes more fear than the strength of lions.

Water-imagery occurs continually. We are often reminded of the Nile. We also continually meet the ideas of 'sea' and 'land' in juxtaposition. . . . Sea-imagery here is not used tempestuously as so often in Shakespeare: the sea is rather static, often the playground of warring navies, navies that threaten 'most sea-like' [III. xiii. 171], but itself not hostile. Hence a ship here may be 'leaky' to suggest human tragedy [III. xiii. 63], but not, as in *Macbeth,* 'tempest-toss'd'. There is a certain stillness interpenetrating the drama's activity throughout: and water-imagery blends with this effect. It is as a still sheen of level quicksilver interlacing and interpenetrating earth's surface: ocean surrounding islands and touching coasts, rivers cutting the land. (pp. 225-34)

Now the suggestion of 'water' juxtaposed with 'land' is important. The two are frequently associated and contrasted. 'Water' appears to suggest something more free and unfettered than earth's solidity: its presence is apt to this peculiar vision. Antony fights beside Cleopatra by sea, strongly as he is warned against it: it thus becomes almost a symbol of his love, opposing the solid prudence of his soldiership. The suggestion cannot be formalized, however: there is no allegory. Yet we might observe that it is further suggested by a soldier's speech to Antony:

> Let the Egyptians
> And the Phoenicians go a-ducking: we
> Have used to conquer, standing on the earth,
> And fighting foot to foot.
>
> [III. vii. 63-6]

The sea is associated clearly with femininity, softness, and the East as opposed to manly strength. Shakespeare's love-imagery often takes him East. And his supreme love-vision takes here the form of West conflicting with East. But throughout we notice a certain diffusing of one element over the other, or interspacing it. We are reminded of the Mediterranean, its islands, the shore and its rivers gleaming through the land and flooding out their tenuous silver in the glistening expanse. Sometimes the two elements are imaged as at war, the finer one victorious: again, reflecting the vast theme of East and West, or Love and Empire, opposed:

> Let Rome in Tiber melt, and the wide arch
> Of the ranged empire fall!
>
> [I. i. 33-4]

cries Antony . . . ; and Cleopatra echoes the thought:

> Sink Rome, and their tongues rot
> That speak against us!
>
> [III. vii. 15-16]

Cleopatra is fond of the image. She cries:

> Melt Egypt into Nile! and kindly creatures
> Turn all to serpents!
>
> [II. v. 78-9]

and again:

> . . . O, I would thou didst,
> So half my Egypt were submerged and made
> A cistern for scaled snakes!
>
> [II. v. 93-5]

These 'melting' images obviously blend with the detailed description of the Nile in flood, the 'ooze and slime' of its bed. The 'melting' idea is frequent. I notice more uses of 'melt' later: the word occurs in two out of these four quotations, and the suggestion is present in all of them. Element 'melts' in element. Thus metal may 'melt' in fire: and Cleopatra uses the image when she threatens to 'melt' the gold she gave the messenger and pour it down his 'ill-uttering throat' [II. v. 34-5]. Authority 'melts' from Antony [III. xiii. 90]. But more usually we have a blending of earth and water, or water and air. We hear of 'quicksands'—again, as in our Nile descriptions, an image of earth melted into liquid:

> These quick-sands, Lepidus,
> Keep off them, for you sink.
>
> [II. vii. 59-60]

The poet equally stresses the union of water and air. It is finely present in one very concrete image:

> Swallows have built
> In Cleopatra's sails their nests.
>
> [IV. xii. 3-4]

Generally it is presented in terms of vapour: and I will next notice this weather-suggestion: everywhere we should observe especially the idea of 'melting', 'dissolving'—it is a crucial theme in the play. For the blending of elements is similar to that blending of the sexes in love which is our main story: and from that we pass, even farther, to a blending of life and death. Often we find the word 'mingle', as well as 'melt'. Gray and brown 'mingle' in Antony's hair [IV. viii. 20]; his disposition, 'nor sad nor merry', is a 'heavenly mingle' [I. v. 59]; and Antony tells his followers to 'make mingle' with their 'rattling tabourines' [IV. viii. 37]. The word can apply to love as well as music: Cleopatra 'loved' Antony and 'her fortunes mingled' with his 'entirely', even to death [IV. xiv. 24-5]. I have already observed how earth and water, and elsewhere earth and sun, fecundate, in this play's imagery, the Nile basin, so that it brings forth crops and strange creatures. Now, in our weather-imagery, we shall again find a suggestion of earth's fruitfulness very often: 'showers' or 'dew', for instance, expressed as symbols of refreshing moisture. But there is also reference to other elemental forms, hail, snow, clouds, wind. All these are important, suggesting both ethereality and a blending of element with element to produce new beauty.

There is little violent storm-suggestion: *Antony and Cleopatra* here diverges clearly from *Macbeth, Lear,* or *Julius Caesar.* Air-imagery is here peaceful. Even Cleopatra's passion, though its 'tempestuous' nature is once—and only once—suggested,

is yet also likened to gentle 'showers'. . . . There are also references to pure air, 'wind'.

> Some o' their plants are ill-rooted already; the least
> wind i' the world will blow them down. . . .
>
> [II. vii. 1-3]

Enobarbus' reason 'sits in the wind' against him [III. x. 36]. Antony's affairs come to Caesar 'on the wind' [III. vi. 63]. Cleopatra, at her death, is 'fire and air' [V. ii. 289], and almost her last words are:

> As sweet as balm, as soft as air, as gentle . . .
>
> [V. ii. 311]

Her death is imaged as a dissolution, a melting from bodily existence into some more fiery and spiritual mode; and we remember her earlier cry—'dissolve my life' [III. xiii. 162]. Hence, too, Charmian's choric utterance at Cleopatra's dying:

> Dissolve, thick cloud, and rain; that I may say,
> The gods themselves do weep!
>
> [V. ii. 299-300]

The 'soft' and 'gentle' of Cleopatra's speech are typical words. Cleopatra wonders that Iras 'and nature can so gently part' in death [V. ii. 294]. Antony's life with Cleopatra is 'soft': 'the beds i' the east are soft', says Antony [II. vi. 50]. Antony and Cleopatra live 'for the love of Love and her soft hours' [I. i. 44]. Wine 'steeps the sense in soft and delicate Lethe' [II. vii. 107-08]. Death is here soft as 'a lover's bed' [IV. xiv. 101], sweet as 'a lover's pinch' [V. ii. 295]. . . . Cleopatra's dying is a soft melting, a dissolving, a blending of essence with essence. Also at Antony's death Cleopatra cries: 'The crown o' the earth doth melt' [IV. xv. 63]. Hence, too, Antony's dialogue with Eros:

> *Antony.* Eros, thou yet behold'st me?
> *Eros.*   Ay, noble lord.
> *Antony.* Sometime we see a cloud that 's dragonish;
>   A vapour sometime like a bear or lion,
>   A tower'd citadel, a pendent rock,
>   A forked mountain, or blue promontory
>   With trees upon 't, that nod unto the world,
>   And mock our eyes with air: thou hast seen these
>   signs;
>   They are black vesper's pageants.
> *Eros.*   Ay, my lord.
> *Antony.* That which is now a horse, even with a thought
>   The rack dislimns, and makes it indistinct,
>   As water is in water.
> *Eros.*   It does, my lord.
> *Antony.* My good knave Eros, now thy captain is
>   Even such a body: here I am Antony;
>   Yet cannot hold this visible shape, my knave.
>
> [IV. xiv. 1-14]

Death is thus a change of mode, a melting, a dissolving and, perhaps, a reforming in some newer fashion of this 'visible shape': an indistinct union, as of 'water in water'. Enobarbus prays likewise that the moon may 'the poisonous damp of night disponge' upon him [IV. ix. 13]. We may observe how all our massed 'air' and 'water' imagery bears relevance to the death-theme in this vision. Death is a soft, changeful dissolution: like the crocodile, the elements once out, man 'transmigrates' [II. vii. 45]. There is a unity-suggestion, quite different from the earlier dualism of life and death in *Hamlet* or *Timon,* where death was hideous or a 'nothing'. The positive element in Antony's death is repeated and further developed, in Cleopatra's: where . . . death is a casting-off of 'baser elements', an entry into modes 'sweet as balm, soft as air' [V. ii. 311].

Thus we now ascend from water and air to air and fire. I will note our fire-imagery, which includes 'sun' and 'moon' references, and may also be related to that glittering brilliance of gold and other precious metals. . . . In *Othello* and *Timon* this imagery replaces human love: the loved one lost, the hero's yearning cries to the heavenly lamps, to sun, moon, or star. . . . Here heaven's fire drops benediction from its empyrean: love is blended with the universe. It is as though the great God absorbs human emotions as the sun drinks the sea, to shower them down afresh in newer life. In this happy vision all dark negations but serve to emphasize a positive brilliance: 'the spots of heaven, more fiery by night's blackness' [I. iv. 12-13]. . . . [The] whole theme of our play is a mating of element with element. There is a clinging mesh of cohering elements, blended in love, to frame our picture of man blending with woman in love, of life dissolved in the other element of death. The mating of sun and Nile is thus important. So, too, the sun woos Cleopatra herself: she is 'with Phoebus' amorous pinches black' [I. v. 28]—a phrase recalling that wherein 'the stroke of death' is 'as a lover's pinch'—a passionate mating of life with death, life surrendered to death's mastering passion [V. ii. 295]; so, too, Antony runs to death 'as to a lover's bed' [IV. xiv. 101]. But there are other passages, where such images are contrasted with love. 'Moon and stars!' cries Antony, when he finds Cleopatra false [III. xiii. 95]. He will 'lodge Lichas on the horns o' the moon [IV. xii. 45]. Enobarbus recognizes his iniquitous fall from loyalty's faith. The night is 'shiny': in bitterness of his own love's failure . . . , he cries out to the moon, heaven's bending eye whose lovelight keeps eternal faith with earth:

> Be witness to me, O thou blessed moon,
> When men revolted shall upon record
> Bear hateful memory, poor Enobarbus did
> Before thy face repent!
>
> [IV. ix. 7-10]

Antony, knowing he must shortly die, speaks farewell to the sun:

> O sun, thy uprise shall I see no more:
> Fortune and Antony part here; even here
> Do we shake hands.
>
> [IV. xii. 18-20]

In these, whatever direct relation they bear to the theme of prosperous love is one of contrast: man, in his tragic pain, cries out to sun or moon, who know no failure, whose station is firm based and faith unfaltering. . . . Elsewhere sun, moon, or star are themselves but love-symbols: they burn or fade as love's torch flickers uncertain. Stars are the vestal priestesses to idealized humanity:

> Let all the number of the stars give light
> To thy fair way! . . .
>
> [III. ii. 65-6]

Cleopatra is 'thou day o' the world' [IV. viii. 13]. As Antony is brought dying to Cleopatra, she cries:

> O sun,
> Burn the great sphere thou movest in! darkling stand
> The varying shore o' the world.
>
> [IV. xv. 9-10]

Now love is itself the sun and moon and stars; itself the universe. Cleopatra's death is to Antony as a light extinguished:

> Since the torch is out,
> Lie down, and stray no farther.
>
> [IV. xiv. 46-7]

So is his death to her:

> Ah, women, women, look,
> Our lamp is spent, it's out!
>
> [IV. xv. 84-5]

Now

> there is nothing left remarkable
> Beneath the visiting moon. . . .
>
> [IV. xv. 67-8]

This 'sun', 'moon', and 'star' imagery elevates the love-theme to universal stature: it lights the whole play with a glitter and a brilliance, merging with the gold-imagery and the watery sheen already observed, so that the vision is seen as through a dropping shower of fire; and it adds the fourth empyreal element to our ascending scale—earth, water, air.

There is, however, darkness in the play: darkness by which these lamps are the richer, a soft velvet darkness, from which the lamps of heaven burn brilliant, 'the spots of heaven more fiery by night's blackness' [I. iv. 13]. Or again, a darkness lit by revelry and feast. 'We made the night light with drinking' [II. ii. 178] says Enobarbus, and, at the end, Antony would 'have one other gaudy night' [III. xiii. 182]. He would 'burn this night with torches' [IV. ii. 41]. Nights here are rich, gaudy, with an Orient fire beautiful as day. The lovers wander through the streets of Alexandria by night [I. i. 53]. Fire is also to be related . . . to man's 'spirit'. Spirit is fiery. This fire-imagery is one with that erotic brilliance and spiritual fire of love which 'gilds' Antony's messenger 'with his tinct' [I. v. 37]. . . . Spirit is fire, and love in Shakespeare 'a spirit all compact of fire' [*Venus and Adonis*, I. 149]. Therefore, dying into love, crowned with its aureole blaze, Cleopatra knows:

> I am fire and air; my other elements
> I give to baser life.
>
> [V. ii. 289-90]

Thus our spiralling and visionary ascent demands no paltry earth alone, no limited naturalism, but rather a universal stage. Such images are recurrent:

> To be called into a huge sphere, and not to be
> seen to move in 't, are the holes where eyes
> should be, which pitifully disaster the cheeks.
>
> [II. vii. 14-16]

The wide universe is our stage, all elements our actors. 'The elements be kind to thee' [III. ii. 40] prays Caesar. The quadruple elemental system is stressed here:

> *Antony.* Their preparation is to-day by sea;
>   We please them not by land.
> *Scarus.*   For both, my lord.
> *Antony.* I would they 'ld fight i' the fire or i' the air;
>   We 'ld fight there too.
>
> [IV. x. 1-4]

Yet higher, beyond all material and visual symbols, like the lark's ascending flight, ever higher, to blend his song with the sun's blaze of fire, we leave the 'elements' and notice, finally, our highest love-accompaniment: music. (pp. 234-44)

Music sounds often in the play. At the start of the banquet on Pompey's galley, 'music plays' (II. vii). It recurs again for the Bacchic song:

> *Enobarbus.*   All take hands.
>   Make battery to our ears with the loud music.
>   [II. vii. 109-10]

'Trumpets' and 'flutes' bid 'a loud farewell' to Neptune at the end [II. vii. 132]. Here, as often elsewhere, the action takes place at night: but it is a 'gaudy night'. This is riotous music, a clash and blare of sensuous enjoyment. So, too, is that which Antony calls for later to celebrate his victorious entry into Alexandria:

>   Trumpeters,
> With brazen din blast you the city's ear;
> Make mingle with our rattling tabourines;
> That heaven and earth may strike their sounds together,
> Applauding our approach.
>   [IV. viii. 35-9]

But there is other music: more soft, more finely tuned to the highest vision which this play discloses from beyond its melting clouds. Cleopatra . . . assuages her love-loneliness with music. Mardian 'sings' to her [I. v. 9]. Again:

> *Cleopatra.* Give me some music; music, moody food
>   Of us that trade in love.
> *Attendant.*   The music, ho!
>   [II. v. 1-2]

Cleopatra describes how she will fish, her 'music playing far off' [II. v. 11]. So, too, in Enobarbus' description of Cleopatra in her barge, which I notice in detail later, we hear that 'flutes' sounded to the strokes of the oars [II. ii. 195]. Finally, there is the fine symbolic effect where mysterious music from beneath 'the earth' or 'i' the air' [IV. iii. 13] sounds an ethereal prelude to the final love-sacrifice; our protagonists' fall, or rise, from earthly splendour, their ascent to love's empyrean. . . . Even earth vibrates in this transcendent play, its myriad whirling atoms alive, burning, dancing, quiring the immortal theme. The world glows with love's fire. Here the disparity between matter and spirit, the human and divine, are ever mingled, blended, melted into unity: so the little earth itself 'makes mingle' [IV. viii. 37] with its orchestra of elements, responds in magic harmony to that spheral music wherein a human death and life and love strike together one single chord in the melodic silences of the Divine.

The wide magnificence and suffusing and spirited glory that this play bodies forth are as laurel-leaves to cluster the brows of our human protagonists: a divine humanism is here. Thus the persons are often compared to gods and heroes. . . . Most such comparisons are used to engild Antony. . . . Cleopatra is credited with supernatural power, too—sometimes in an evil sense. In her 'witchcraft joins with beauty' [II. i. 22]—she fascinates mysteriously though her lip is 'waned' by years. . . . Cleopatra's personality radiates royalty and magic; Antony's, warriorship and Herculean heroism. The value of these suggestions is most evident in a fine passage remarkably enclosing Antony and Cleopatra, emperor and empress of an Oriental kingdom of love, in an imaginative setting, opulent, regal, divine:

> *Caesar.* Contemning Rome, he has done all this, and
>   more,
>   In Alexandria: here 's the manner of 't:
>   I' the market-place, on a tribunal silver'd,

> Cleopatra and himself in chairs of gold
> Were publicly enthroned: at the feet sat
> Caesarion, whom they call my father's son,
> And all the unlawful issue that their lust
> Since then hath made between them. Unto her
> He gave the stablishment of Egypt; made her
> Of lower Syria, Cyprus, Lydia,
> Absolute queen.
> *Mecaenas.*   This in the public eye?
> *Caesar.* I' the common show-place, where they
>   exercise.
>   His sons he there proclaimed the kings of kings:
>   Great Media, Parthia, and Armenia,
>   He gave to Alexander; to Ptolemy he assign'd
>   Syria, Cilicia, and Phoenicia: she
>   In the habiliments of the goddess Isis
>   That day appear'd; and oft before gave audience,
>   As 'tis reported, so.
>   [III. vi. 1-19]

Notice the life-theme of birth [III. xiii. 159-60], heavily exaggerated, like feasting and all our other effects: the natural is expanded to its farthest limits and beyond, to infinity itself. The exaggeration here is the measure of its implicit artistic importance: we have our vision continually thus directed to some strange transfiguration of man. There is lust and showiness in this picture: but they are overweighted by love's resplendence, love's fruitfulness. So, throughout the play, far-flung kingdoms, gold and silver, power and pomp and vainglory, all are but too unworthy caparisons to a love more strangely gold, which encompasses not alone earth's tinsel royalties; to which death is but a purifying flame; and which, Phoenix-like, can rise with pinions that outsoar the empyrean. To that imperial theme our imperial magnificence directs our gaze. Antony and Cleopatra are here symbolically enthroned in love's regality: which blending of earthly and spiritual royalty, of West and East, of empire and love, is throughout the core and heart of our vision. The protagonists change a crown of gold for the more sparkling and ethereal diadem of love. (pp. 244-48)

To conclude, I quote two passages which finely illustrate [the] welding of imaginative 'atmosphere' with the individual protagonist: though, of course, there is really no 'welding' except to intellectual analysis, since the two are not originally distinct. . . . First there is Enobarbus' description of Cleopatra's meeting with Antony:

> *Enobarbus.* I will tell you.
>   The barge she sat in, like a burnish'd throne,
>   Burn'd on the water: the poop was beaten gold;
>   Purple the sails, and so perfumed that
>   The winds were love-sick with them. . . .
>   From the barge
>   A strange invisible perfume hits the sense
>   Of the adjacent wharfs. The city cast
>   Her people out upon her; and Antony,
>   Enthroned i' the market-place, did sit alone,
>   Whistling to the air; which, but for vacancy,
>   Had gone to gaze on Cleopatra too
>   And made a gap in nature.
>   [II. ii. 190-94, 211-18]

Here is a microcosm of the play's peculiar vision, crystal clear. Nearly all the veins of imagery I have noticed recur. We have a sensuous languor and beauty, a richness and splendour, fabric of purple and gold, 'silken tackle', 'divers-colour'd fans', metals gold and silver; an emphasis on human features, 'dimpled boys', 'flower-soft hands'—again reference to flowers and the idea of 'softness'—the 'delicate cheeks' of Cleopatra; the emphasis on ships, and water, and nautical terms—the poop, sails, tackle, oars, wharfs; the still, lake-like surface reflecting the barge, whose gold thus melts into the liquid deeps, still water, its further blue just stirred into silver by the feathering strokes of silver oars; the 'air' and 'wind' suggestion, the 'love-sick' winds, the 'sense' hit by 'a strange invisible perfume'—again 'strange'; and Antony, enthroned, 'whistling to the air'; the thought of 'nature' transcended, or nature thrall to love—the very winds, usually in Shakespeare things of senseless cruelty, enemies of love, are 'love-sick', the water 'amorous', the air 'but for vacancy' had made a gap in 'nature' to gaze on Cleopatra. Nature transcended we noticed in the play merging into human art, 'music': here Cleopatra is like a work of art where 'fancy' outworks 'nature'. In that higher vision, known in love or art, she is beyond 'nature', a goddess, a Venus; again the divine association—so, also, her handmaids surpass humanity, spirits of water-element, 'Nereides', 'mermaids'; her boys are 'Cupids'. Finally, there is again music, 'the tune of flutes'. There is motion in this description; but, as in a picture, it is a motion within stillness. There is mystery and something beyond 'nature'; yet it is crystal clear. Like our whole vision, it is set in a limpid, translucent medium, like strange and lovely flowerings seen swaying lazily through solid, transparent deeps of water.

The other passage gives us Cleopatra's dream-vision of Antony. Again, our recurrent themes of imagery blend in an exquisite poetic unit. She speaks as in a trance, unheeding:

Cleopatra. I dream'd there was an Emperor Antony:
    O, such another sleep, that I might see
    But such another man! . . .
            Think you there was, or might be, such a man
    As this I dream'd of?
Dolabella.   Gentle madam, no.
Cleopatra. You lie, up to the hearing of the gods.
    But, if there be, or ever were, one such,
    It's past the size of dreaming: nature wants stuff
    To vie strange forms with fancy; yet, to imagine
    An Antony, were nature's piece 'gainst fancy,
    Condemning shadows quite.
                              [V. ii. 76-8, 93-100]

In *Othello* and *Timon* a vast universal symbolism replaced the lost human love: here the human love and the wide symbolism, which throughout the play were interlaced in the clinging mesh of our pattern, are now blended to the last, inseparate, unified. Antony is 'dead'. But Cleopatra dreams yet an Antony himself a universe, a universe itself an Antony. Love has transcended human limits, its fire lit man with such emblazonry that sun and moon and earth are but elements of his glory: or, conversely, the wide universe becomes personal, a lover. (pp. 256-59)

In death man is triumphant, a 'conqueror' [IV. xiv. 62]. Eros, Iras, Charmian, Enobarbus, Antony, and Cleopatra—all die in the full flood and blaze of loyalty or love, so that 'death' is no more a 'nothing' as in *Timon*, but rather the blue seas and teeming earth, the winds and gleaming clouds, the languorous beauties of a tropic night, the silver and gold of moon and sun, all intermeshed to the bridal music of the spheres, and, at the last, all indistinguishable from a human voice, a human form. We see the protagonists, in love and war and sport, in death or life or that mystery containing both, transfigured in a trans-

figured universe, themselves that universe and more, outspacing the wheeling orbs of earth and heaven. . . . So Cleopatra and Antony find not death but life. This is the high metaphysic of love which melts life and death into a final oneness; which reality is indeed no pulseless abstraction, but rather blends its single design and petalled excellence from all life and all death, all imperial splendour and sensuous delight, all strange and ethereal forms, all elements and heavenly stars; all that is natural, human, and divine; all brilliance and all glory. (p. 262)

G. Wilson Knight, "The Transcendental Humanism of 'Antony and Cleopatra'," in his The Imperial Theme: Further Interpretations of Shakespeare's Tragedies Including the Roman Plays, *Oxford University Press, London, 1931, pp. 199-262.*

CAROLINE F. E. SPURGEON (essay date 1935)

[Spurgeon's Shakespeare's Imagery and What It Tells Us *(1935) inaugurated the "image-pattern analysis" method of studying Shakespeare's plays, one of the most widely used methods of the mid-twentieth century. In this work, she interprets the thematic structure of the plays through an examination of patterns in the imagery. Spurgeon also sought to learn about Shakespeare's personality from a study of his images, a course which few of her disciples followed. Since publication of her book, earlier works on image patterns in Shakespeare have been discovered, but none was so important in the history of Shakespearean criticism as Spurgeon's. In the following excerpt from the above-mentioned work, she declares that the most significant metaphorical pattern in* Antony and Cleopatra *is composed of "images of the world, the firmament, the ocean and vastness generally." The effect of these images, Spurgeon contends, is to underscore the idea of Antony as a superhuman figure and to make us see that "nothing short of the whole universe suffices for comparison with Antony."]*

In *Antony and Cleopatra* we find ourselves emotionally in another world, in an entirely different atmosphere from that of [*Julius Caesar* and *Coriolanus*]. The difference in poetic fire between *Coriolanus* and *Antony and Cleopatra* is as if, in the one case, the poet's imagination had caught alight three or four times only, and in burning had scattered sparks in the neighbourhood, while, in the other, it is a pure flame driving throughout, fanned by emotion, whose heat purifies, fuses and transmutes into gold all kinds of material, and it is this fierce atmospheric heat which creates the pictures, dominating and directing them.

The group of images in *Antony and Cleopatra* which, on analysis, immediately attracts attention as peculiar to this play, consists of images of the world, the firmament, the ocean and vastness generally. That is the dominating note in the play, magnificence and grandeur, expressed in many ways, and pictured by continually stimulating our imaginations to see the colossal figure of Antony, 'demi-Atlas of this earth', 'triple pillar of the world', built on so vast a scale that the whole habitable globe is but a toy to him, as it were a ball or apple which he quarters with his sword, playing with 'half the bulk of it' as he pleases, 'making and marring fortunes' [I. v. 23; I. i. 12; III. xi. 64].

Antony himself touches this note at once in his royal lovemaking, when he tells Cleopatra that if she would put a bourn to the measure of his love, she must 'needs find out new heaven, new earth' [I. i. 17].

Indeed, nothing short of the whole universe suffices for comparison with Antony, and in Cleopatra's lyrical elegies, wherein is concentrated all the passion and poetry of the most passionate

Act III. Scene xi. Charmian, Iras, Cleopatra, Enobarbus, and Antony. By Henry Tresham. The Department of Rare Books and Special Collections, The University of Michigan Library.

and poetical of the plays, she likens him to one whose face was as the heavens,

> and therein stuck
> A sun and moon, which kept their course and lighted
> The little O, the earth.
>
> [V. ii. 79-81]

In these soaring love laments she sees him and makes us see him as a stupendous super-being, the 'crown o' the earth', whose 'legs bestrid the ocean', whose 'rear'd arm crested the world', and whose qualities can be compared only to the vast elemental forces of nature [IV. xv. 63; V. ii. 82, 82-3]; his voice, to friends,

> was propertied
> As all the tuned spheres, . . .
> But when he meant to quail and shake the orb,
> He was as rattling thunder.
>
> [V. ii. 83-4, 85-6]

Even the verbs used of his aspect are such as are applicable to the sun and planets; when he smiles, he should *shine* on those

> That make their looks by his;
>
> [I. v. 56]

and Alexas, lately come from him, is *gilded* with his *tinct.*

The perennial seasons themselves, with their wealth of association, become as mere adjectives to express the magnificence and scale of his bounty:

> There was no winter in't; an autumn 'twas
> That grew the more by reaping.
>
> [V. ii. 87-8]

When, mortally wounded, he is borne aloft to her, Cleopatra calls on the sun to burn up the sphere in which it is fixed and so plunge the earth in darkness, and, when he dies, she knows there is

> nothing left remarkable
> Beneath the visiting moon.
>
> [IV. xv. 67-8]

Not only Cleopatra thinks of him thus; by a common instinct all who know him compare him to great natural phenomena. He is a 'mine of bounty', says Enobarbus [IV. vi. 31]; in temper, reports Alexas,

> Like to the time o' the year between the extremes
> Of hot and cold, he was nor sad nor merry;
>
> [I. v. 21-2]

his faults in him, cries Lepidus,

seem as the spots of heaven,
More fiery by night's blackness;

[I. iv. 12-13]

and his messenger, Euphronius, is so conscious of his inferiority to his master, that he avows he was

of late as petty to his ends
As is the morn-dew on the myrtle-leaf
To his grand sea.

[III. xii. 8-10]

When the battle goes against him, Scarus remarks,

The greater cantle of the world is lost,
. . . . . . we have kissed away
Kingdoms and provinces;

[III. x. 6, 7-8]

and when he dies, so great a convulsion of nature is it that Caesar declares,

the round world
Should have shook lions into civil streets,
And citizens to their dens. The death of Antony
Is not a single doom; in the name lay
A moiety of the world.

[V. i. 15-19]

This vastness of scale is kept constantly before us by the use of the word 'world', which occurs forty-two times, nearly double, or more than double, as often as in most other plays, and it is continually employed in a way which increases the sense of grandeur, power and space, and which fills the imagination with the conception of beings so great that physical size is annihilated and the whole habitable globe shrinks in comparison with them. Caesar, lamenting his differences with Antony, cries,

if I knew
What hoop should hold us stanch, from edge to edge
O' the world I would pursue it;

[II. ii. 114-16]

and Octavia declares that wars between these two mighty ones, her husband and her brother, would be

As if the world should cleave, and that slain men
Should solder up the rift.

[III. iv. 31-2]

The emotional effect of such a simile as this is incalculable, with its amazing picture of the gigantic gaping fissures in the round globe packed tight with the bodies of the dead. Were the feeling in it not so intense, it would verge on the grotesque, as do some others among these vast world images. Such, for instance, is the kind of huge gargoyle depicted by the saturnine Enobarbus when he hears that Caesar has deposed Lepidus, thus leaving only Antony and himself in power. He imagines them as the two mighty jaws in the world's face, grinding and destroying everything that comes between them, and exclaims,

Then, world, thou hast a pair of chaps, no more;
And throw between them all the food thou hast,
They'll grind the one the other.

[III. v. 13-15]

Antony's imagination moves on this same vast plane, and the pictures that he draws stimulate our vision and keep us ever conscious of the puny size of even the greatest of worldly princes, powers and spaces compared to his stupendous force.

Especially is this so when power is slipping from him, when the old lion is dying, and the tragedy is thus increased by contrast. With what a sublime sweep of simple words he sums up his earlier activities:

I, that with my sword
Quarter'd the world, and o'er green Neptune's back
With ships made cities;

[IV. xiv. 57-9]

and how vivid is the picture of the kings of the earth starting forth at his call, like small boys in a scramble, crying out to know what is his will! When he is angry, the insolent magnificence of his images surpasses that of all others in Shakespeare. Thus, after his defeat at sea, when, furious with Caesar's messenger, he has him soundly whipped and bids him get back to his master, he gives a characteristic picture in style and scale of the reason why it is particularly easy just then to anger him, for his 'good stars' that were his 'former guides'

Have empty left their orbs and shot their fires
Into the abysm of hell;

[III. xiii. 146-47]

and when earlier, Cleopatra mischievously suggests that Caesar has sent for him, the thunder of his reply in majestic sweep and cadence still comes echoing down the centuries:

Let Rome in Tiber melt, and the wide arch
Of the ranged empire fall! Here is my space.

[I. i. 33-4]
(pp. 345-54)

Caroline F. E. Spurgeon, "Leading Motives in the Tragedies," in her Shakespeare's Imagery and What it Tells Us, *1935. Reprint by Cambridge at the University Press, 1971, pp. 309-56.*

JOHN MIDDLETON MURRY   (essay date 1936)

[*A twentieth-century English editor and critic, Murry has been called the most "level-headed" of Shakespeare's major biographical critics. Unlike other proponents of the biographical approach, such as Frank Harris and Edward Dowden, Murry refused to attribute to Shakespeare a definite personality or creative neurosis which determined all of his work, but regarded the poet as a man of powerful insights rather than character, an individual possessing Keats's negative capability, in the sense that he was able to withstand "uncertainties, mysteries, doubts, without any irritable reaching after fact and reason." What Murry considered Shakespeare's greatest gift was his ability to uncover the true spirit of Elizabethan England, to fuse "not merely the poet and dramatist in himself," but to establish "a unique creative relation between himself, his dramatic material, his audience, and his actors." In the following excerpt, Murry contends that* Antony and Cleopatra *dramatizes the precept that true royalty is achieved through loyalty. In Act IV, Scene ii, he argues, Antony's colloquy with his servants on the night before the second battle vividly demonstrates his "'royal' essence," and while this spiritual quality is recognized by Enobarbus and the attendants, Cleopatra herself is unable to perceive it. However, Murry maintains, when Antony dies Cleopatra undergoes a transfiguration, eventually discerning her lover's "royal spirit" and faithfully taking up—until her own death—her "poetic function . . . to maintain and prolong, to reflect and reverberate, that achieved royalty of Antony's." As the play depicts the changes in the triumvir and his queen, the critic holds, their poetic language becomes richer and more rare, fostering the dramatic illusion that Antony and Cleopatra are superhuman figures. Recalling that boy actors played women's roles on the Elizabethan stage, Murry notes that at the very moment when Cleopatra attains her spiritual royalty Shake-*

speare deliberately shatters the illusion by reminding his audience that what they have been seeing in this performance is precisely what the queen fears will happen in Rome: she has been portrayed by a "squeaking Cleopatra . . . in the posture of a whore" (V. ii. 220-21). Additionally, Murry finds a parallel between Antony and his attendants on the eve of the second decisive battle and Christ with his disciples at the Last Supper, and he also compares Enobarbus's desertion and remorse with the biblical account of Judas's betrayal of Christ.]

We all remember—nobody ever forgets; for, although the words may elude his recollection, the impression, the quality, the music: these remain—Cleopatra's description of the dead Antony:

> His legs bestrid the ocean: his rear'd arm
> Crested the world: his voice was propertied
> As all the tunèd spheres, and that to friends;
> But when he meant to quail and shake the orb,
> He was as rattling thunder. For his bounty,
> There was no winter in't; an autumn 'twas
> That grew the more by reaping: his delights
> Were dolphin-like; they showed his back above
> The element they lived in: in his livery
> Walk'd crowns and crownets; realms and islands were
> As plates dropped from his pocket.
>
> [V. ii. 82-92]

Having thus marvellously pictured her dead lord, Cleopatra drops her voice. For a moment she wakes wistfully out of her dream. She has spoken as one inspired, like a Sybil or a Pythonissa: so that Dolabella, to whom she speaks, can cry only, in dumb astonishment: 'Cleopatra!' Now she comes down to earth: her closed and dreaming eyes are opened; and she asks Dolabella, in a voice of apprehension, Was it only a dream?

> Think you there was, or might be, such a man
> As this I dreamed of?
>
> [V. ii. 93-4]

For a moment, she is all a woman, all a girl, all a child, even. In a little while, she will proclaim and prove that there is no more woman in her.

> I have nothing
> Of woman in me: now from head to foot
> I am marble-constant; now the fleeting moon
> No planet is of mine.
>
> [V. ii. 238-41]

But for this instant, she is a child lost in a dark forest, wavering and timorous: caught between her vision of a world made magnificent by Antony, and her knowledge of a world made dead by his death. She is wistful and afraid. She wakes out of her trance, and reaches for a hand.

> Think you there was, or might be such a man
> As this I dreamed of?

And Dolabella speaks to her condition. He reaches out the hand she gropes for: tenderly, like a true man.

> Gentle madam—no!
>
> [V. ii. 94]

The word, so softly spoken, is only the harsher for its tenderness. Cleopatra starts back, thrusts him away, cries shrilly, like one caught in the toils of reality.

> You lie—up to the hearing of the gods!
>
> [V. ii. 95]

The sudden frenzy dies. She sinks back into her dream—the dream that is not a dream. She speaks to herself again. Dolabella is, as he was before, only an eavesdropper, while she murmurs:

> But if there be, or ever were, one such
> It's past the size of dreaming: nature wants stuff
> To vie strange forms with fancy; yet to imagine
> An Antony, were nature's piece 'gainst fancy,
> Condemning shadows quite.
>
> [V. ii. 96-100]

This dream was real. This man she had loved and known, played false and adored. To him she had been 'a right gipsy' [IV. xii. 28]; and his very voice, propertied like all the tuned spheres, had said to her: 'Where's now my serpent of old Nile?' [I. v. 25].

To her dream that was no dream, to her Antony who was, and is, her 'man of men' [I. v. 72], she henceforward turns. She thrusts away reality; but first she looks upon it for what it is, and what it will be. She will be the brooch to the purple cloak of Caesar's triumph.

> Nay, 'tis most certain, Iras: saucy lictors
> Will catch at us like strumpets; and scald rhymers
> Ballad us out o' tune: the quick comedians
> Extemporally will stage us, and present
> Our Alexandrian revels; Antony
> Shall be brought drunken forth, and I shall see
> Some squeaking Cleopatra boy my greatness
> I' the posture of a whore.
>
> [V. ii. 214-21]

And that, let us remember, was what was actually happening when those lines were first spoken. The reality, which Cleopatra thrusts away, thus becomes doubly real. It is not some imagined or apprehended degradation which she can avoid: it has already overtaken her. (pp. 352-54]

This sudden, deliberate shattering of the dramatic illusion by Cleopatra's words, comes out of the very substance of the character. That is to say, this dramatic device of Shakespeare's is really an antidramatic device; perhaps it would be more exact to say a super-dramatic device. And the word 'device', moreover, begs an important question. 'Device' suggests a very deliberate and conscious technical cunning, which indeed Shakespeare possessed in plenty; but I should say that Shakespeare's method here is quite intuitive.

He challenges the dramatic illusion, because he can, and because he must. First, because he can: he has created the imaginative reality of his Antony and his Cleopatra. For us, they *are*. Second, because he must. In the confidence, in the ecstasy, in the 'intensity' of his own creativeness, he must seize the opportunity that has offered itself naturally of directly confronting the order of reality which he has created with the order of actuality which is.

This triumph of art seems to me so wonderful that I must, at the risk of displaying my own clumsiness, enlarge upon it. Let the magnificent and memorable scene between Cleopatra and Dolabella, with which we began, be our starting point. I have tried to indicate the contrast between the ecstasy of Cleopatra's imaginative dream, and the tenderness of Dolabella's human sympathy, which yet springs from and is rooted in the world of actuality. I am sure that I have not read into Shakespeare's text more than is there. Dolabella stands by the Queen—gentle with a man's gentleness, wondering, anxious, eager to comfort and reassure. But she, in her ecstasy, is beyond his ken. He admits it in so many words. He, too, has loved Antony; he grieves for him and he grieves for her. But the region where her mind and heart are wandering is strange to him. At the nature of her grief he must conjecture; yet the vibration of it strikes him to the heart.

> Hear me, good madame.
> Your loss is as yourself, great; and you bear it
> As answering to the weight: would I might never
> O'ertake pursued success, but I do feel
> By the rebound of yours a grief that smites
> My very heart at root.

> [V. ii. 100-05]

It is the incommensurability of Cleopatra's loss, the incommensurability of her suffering, which Dolabella thus registers. It is, in respect of the world which he inhabits and represents—the real world—superhuman. Shakespeare finds a word for it—a word indeed which, taken from its context in this great play, is nothing: but, in this context, is truly a symbol of the magnificence he communicates to us. It is the word 'royal'. In *Antony and Cleopatra* the word 'royal' is royal because it is made royal. Therefore it crowns the close—twice in a dozen lines.

> Now boast thee, death, in thy possession lies
> A lass unparallel'd. Downy windows, close;
> And golden Phoebus never be beheld
> Of eyes again so royal.

> [V. ii. 315-18]

What lines are these! If poetry ever *played* with the universe, it is here. From the bottom to the top of the gamut, Shakespeare moves infallible. 'A *lass* unparallel'd.' Who dare risk it? Who but the man to whom these things were no risk at all? Every other great poet the world has known, I dare swear, would have written, would have been compelled to write: 'A queen unparallel'd.' But Shakespeare's daimon compels him otherwise: compels him not indeed consciously to remember, but instinctively to body forth in utterance, the Cleopatra who dreams, and is a girl: the Cleopatra who is superhuman and human: the Cleopatra who has already answered to the challenge of this same word—'royal'.

> IRAS.   Royal Egypt!
> Empress! . . .
> CLEO. No more, but e'en a woman, and commanded
> By such poor passion as the maid that milks
> And does the meanest chares.

> [IV. xv. 70, 73-5]

Yet the same Cleopatra who proclaims:

> My resolution's placed, and I have nothing
> Of woman in me: now from head to foot
> I am marble-constant; now the fleeting moon
> No planet is of mine.

> [V. ii. 238-41]

And all this, which is Cleopatra, is (as I say) not remembered, but bodied forth anew in Charmian's words: 'A lass unparallel'd.' There is the harmony between 'Royal Egypt!'—and 'the maid that milks'. These two are blent in one in the phrase.

Then the music rises again. Somehow, by the words 'golden Phoebus' Cleopatra herself is suffused with a sunset glow, and her dignity in death is endued with the majesty of the heavens. The order of the words is magical. It gives point and meaning

to Coleridge's definition of poetry as 'The best words in the best order'.

> Downy windows, close!
> And golden Phoebus never be beheld
> Of eyes again so royal.

This order is such that every significance is gathered up into the one word, 'royal'. Now we know what 'royalty' means—it means all that has gone before—all that was gathered up, before, into the 'lass unparallel'd',—all this, moreover, bathed in the majesty of 'bright Phoebus in his strength'. . . . [The] phrase glances . . . backward to the scene with which we began.

> CLEO. I dreamed there was an Emperor Antony:
> O, such another sleep, that I might see
> But such another man.
> DOL.   If it might please ye,—
> CLEO. His face was as the heavens; and therein stuck
> A sun and moon, which kept their course, and lighted
> The little O, the earth. . . .

> [V. ii. 76-81]

Cleopatra is moon to Antony's sun, while they are alive together. When the sun is set, then Cleopatra leaves the moon—

> the fleeting moon
> No planet is of mine—

to take upon her the strength and majesty of the sun. And so what we have called her final royalty is totally suffused by the glory of 'golden Phoebus'. (pp. 355-59)

Into this word 'royal' . . . Shakespeare crams the sense of the superhuman, standing over against the human, which Dolabella recognizes and salutes in his scene with Cleopatra: what I have called the incommensurability of her experience and his. In that scene the contrast takes the form of dream against actuality, trance against waking, inspiration (almost in the literal sense) against reason. It is the contrast, the contraposition of two orders. They are not set in conflict. Dolabella is gentle towards the Queen's ecstasy; it strikes him with awe and wonder and also with sympathy. With Dolabella and Cleopatra at this moment we may compare Enobarbus and Antony in an earlier scene (IV. ii), when Antony, before his last fight, commands one final feast. When the serving-men come in to set the banquet, he takes them by the hand, one by one.

> Give me thy hand,
> Thou hast been rightly honest;—so has thou—
> Thou—and thou—and thou:—you have served me well
> And kings have been your fellows.

> [IV. ii. 10-13]

There is the double touch, which makes Antony Antony—the simple humanity of his handshake with his servants and the reminder that kings have done him the like office. In comparison with Antony and in his own accustomed sight, servants and kings are one. If kings were his servants, so his servants are now made kings. It is, if I may dare to put it thus, the Last Supper of Antony—sacramental, simple and strange. But Cleopatra does not understand it. 'What means this?' she whispers to Enobarbus; and Enobarbus replies:

> 'Tis one of those odd tricks which sorrow shoots
> Out of the mind.

> [IV. ii. 14-15]

Enobarbus half understands. So might an unknown—or may be a known—disciple have said that the Last Supper itself was 'one of those odd tricks which sorrow shoots out of the mind'. An 'odd trick': the words come from Enobarbus' desire to master by bluntness the emotion within himself. Enobarbus does not understand—Antony himself does not understand—but he feels the meaning of the gesture.

Then Antony returns to the theme again.

> Well, my good fellows, wait on me to-night:
> Scant not my cups; and make as much of me
> As when mine empire was your fellow too,
> And suffered my command.
>
> [IV. ii. 20-3]

It is the same thought as before. They serve him now, where kings served him before; and by the change it is not Antony that is declined, but they who are advanced. They are become kings: fellows of empire. A pathetic illusion, some may call it. But it is something rather different from this. Royalty—it is the great burden of this play—is no external thing; it is a kingdom and conquest of the human spirit, an achieved greatness. . . . It is . . . something which lifts man towards the divine, by driving man to be more than man. And this royal essence is a grace of communion between men. By their recognition of, and devotion to, this essence, they also become royal. Thus Antony, at this moment, when there are no more throned monarchs to serve him, invites his servants into royalty. By serving him now, they become kings of the spirit.

Something of all this is in this tiny and wonderful scene between Antony and his servants. It is not the pathos of it, but the royalty of it that strikes Enobarbus to the heart. . . . He knows what Antony means, but he cannot say. We know what Antony means, but we cannot say. As well ask what Jesus of Nazareth *meant* by his gesture in the upper-room, at the brink of death. So Antony goes on:

> Tend me to-night;
> May be it is the period of your duty;
> Haply you shall not see me more; or if,
> A mangled shadow: perchance to-morrow
> You'll serve another master. I look on you
> As one that takes his leave. Mine honest friends,
> I turn you not away; but like a master
> Married to your good service, stay till death.
>
> [IV. ii. 24-31]

The glance at the great marriage-service—'to have and to hold from this day forward, for better for worse, for richer for poorer, in sickness and in health, to love, cherish, and obey, till death do us part'—is neither accidental nor calculated: it is just natural—the spontaneous expression of the sacramental essence of the scene. Antony is 'inspired'.

In this scene it is Cleopatra herself who does not understand. She plays the part towards Antony which bewildered Dolabella will play towards her afterwards, when she, remembering Antony, is likewise 'inspired'. She has yet, crowned queen though she is, to achieve her 'royalty'; and she will achieve it by her resolution to follow her 'man of men' to death.

Let us see now whether we can enter a little more deeply into the secret of this 'royal' essence. There is a moment when Cleopatra, confronted with this 'royal' essence in the Antony she loves, does not understand it: it is, in the simple and literal sense, beyond her. It is not beyond Enobarbus. To Enobarbus, therefore, we must go. A little time before the scene between Antony and the servants, when Antony has been beaten in the sea-fight to which he was persuaded against his better judg-

ment, and in a fit of passion has challenged Caesar to single combat, Enobarbus is torn within himself. He knows, now—none better—that the itch of Antony's affection has nicked his captainship, and that final defect is certain. What is the use of loyalty, he asks himself?

> Mine honesty and I begin to square.
> The loyalty well held to fools does make
> Our faith mere folly.
>
> [III. xiii. 41-3]

To that it seems there is no answer. Reason declares that it is unanswerable. But Enobarbus has an answer.

> Yet he that can endure
> To follow with allegiance a fall'n lord
> Does conquer him that did his master conquer,
> And earns a place i' the story.
>
> [III. xiii. 43-6]

There, in imperishable phrase, is the proclamation of the two orders. Spiritual victory can be wrung out of bodily defeat. 'He that can endure . . .' Again we are reminded of the New Testament: 'He that can endure to the end' [*Mark,* 13:13]. Loyalty is an essence of itself, that somewhere, somehow, can be triumphant over earthly vicissitude; and exists, not merely unscathed by temporal defeat, but because of it. Yet the question is: To whom shall such loyalty be given? What is the secret point of change, where on the one side faith becomes folly, and on the other folly becomes faith? And to that no answer in words can be given. Here the servant must trust himself, or rather the God within him. Is the man he serves worthy of this final allegiance? That only the heart, not the mind, of the servant can declare. And that inward struggle, between the mind and the heart, we see resolved in Enobarbus. Led by his mind, he does forsake Antony; and the mind of the world applauds him, making question only of why he waited so long.

And what is Antony's reaction? Not, as the mind would expect, one of fury.

> Go, Eros, send his treasure after; do it.
> Detain no jot, I charge thee: write to him—
> I will subscribe—gentle adieus and greetings;
> Say that I wish he never find more cause
> To change a master. O, my fortunes have
> Corrupted honest men!
>
> [IV. v. 12-17]

The speech is of the heart, and of that heart which Enobarbus' own heart knew. In response to it, there is an upsurge in Enobarbus' heart. 'Throw my heart,' he cries to the darkness,

> Against the flint and hardness of my fault;
> Which, being dried with grief, will break to powder,
> And finish all foul thoughts. O Antony,
> Nobler than my revolt is infamous,
> Forgive me in thine own particular;
> But let the world rank me in register
> A master-leaver and a fugitive.
>
> [IV. ix. 15-22]

Is it not, imagination asks, the story of Judas, told as it might have been told had a Shakespeare been there to tell it? Enobarbus lives in our memory not as 'the master-leaver and the fugitive' of which he claimed the reputation for his punishment, but as the thing his heart bade him be,—one that could endure to follow with allegiance a fall'n lord. His loyalty is final and secure: he earned his place i' the story.

What is it that compels this final loyalty? The heart in him responsive to the heart in Antony, the thing which made him weep while Antony bade farewell to his servants. But what was that? That royalty in Antony which made his servants kings: that power which was in Antony to say to them simply: 'I am I', and trust to their love of that; the manhood in him which disdained a compelled allegiance, and when allegiance was withdrawn from him, sought instantly, by a natural motion, to find the cause within himself. . . . Royalty and loyalty, then, go hand in hand; and the man who is loyal, by his loyalty, becomes royal.

That, if I were required to state it in so many words, is the true theme of Shakespeare's *Antony and Cleopatra*. And Shakespeare's prodigious art consists first and foremost in convincing us of Antony's royalty. In the last resort, . . . the great motion of the drama derives from that. That is the *primum mobile*. And it operates in the very first scene. There the conflict and the contrast are posited, between the judgment of the mind and the impulse of the heart, between Reason and Energy (as Blake distinguished them). Reason first:

> PHI. Nay, but this dotage of our generals
> O'erflows the measure: those his goodly eyes,
> That o'er the files and musters of the war
> Have glowed like plated Mars, now bend, now turn,
> The office and devotion of their view
> Upon a tawny front: his captain's heart,
> Which in the scuffles of great fights hath burst
> The buckles on his breast, reneges all temper,
> And is become the bellows and the fan
> To cool a gipsy's lust.
>
>   [I. i. 1-10]

That charge Shakespeare must overcome. We must be convinced, straightway, that this is false, or rather that its truth is of another and a lower order than that to which Antony belongs. And Shakespeare does it. We see Antony ignoring the messengers from Rome: he daffs the world aside:

> Let Rome in Tiber melt, and the wide arch
> Of the ranged empire fall! Here is my space.
> Kingdoms are clay: our dungy earth alike
> Feeds beast as man: the nobleness of life
> Is to do thus: when such a mutual pair
> And such a twain can do't, in which I bind,
> On pain of punishment, the world to weet
> We stand up peerless.
>
>   [I. i. 33-40]

'The nobleness of life is to do thus.' There is the challenge. And the magic of the poetry is that the challenge is won. The potency of language which can cram imperial Rome, its arenas and its aqueducts, its roads and its provinces, into a single phrase and topple it over—'let the wide arch of the ranged empire fall!'—has won the challenge in a dozen words. For the power of the poet becomes the power of Antony. It is he, not the poetic genius of Shakespeare, that can build up Rome and lay it in ruins in a moment of the imagination, which is 'spiritual sensation'.

If you look for a description of what has happened in this initial triumph of Energy over Reason, we shall find no better one than the paragraph of Blake's *Marriage of Heaven and Hell*, where he says:

> The giants who formed this world into its sensual existence and now seem to live in it in

chains, are in truth the causes of its life and the sources of all activity; but the chains are the cunning of weak and tame minds which have power to resist energy; according to the proverb, the weak in courage is strong in cunning.

> Thus one portion of being is the Prolific, the other the Devouring: to the Devourer it seems as if the Producer was in his chains; but it is not so, he only takes portions of existence and fancies that the whole.

In this sense Antony is a Giant, a Prolific: he operates by what Shakespeare elsewhere calls 'sovereignty of nature' [*Coriolanus*, IV. vii. 35]. And we are convinced of this, primarily, by the power of utterance which Shakespeare lends him; next, by the power of utterance which Shakespeare lends to those who describe him; then, by the actions which he does; then, by the effect of those actions upon others. And let us remember that, in this kind, we cannot distinguish between act and utterance. What Antony says to his servants, what he bids Eros write to Enobarbus,—the words are his gesture; just as, in the main, their words are the gesture by which they in turn respond to his.

What I am driving at is the power of poetry, as it was used by Shakespeare in this play. It overrides drama; it overrides psychology. The ultimate and enduring structure of the play is in the poetry. Its life, its inward progression, derive from the response of poetry to poetry. That overpowering dynamic, that impression of cumulative growth, of which, from another angle, we have discerned the law as the creation of royalty by loyalty, can be simply reduced to the response of poetry to poetry. Not that we should gain much by so reducing it; but it would at least serve to remind us that we cannot judge such a play as this as a record of action merely; if we do, its essence escapes our judgment. And by essence here, I do not mean something vague, such as we might call the 'soul of the play'; but its vital inward unity. Thus, Antony must be set before our imaginations as one to whom the final sacrifice of Enobarbus and Eros is a natural duty paid, which he receives 'by sovereignty of nature'; he has to be felt by us as belonging to an order of beings who can declare 'he that loseth his life for my sake, the same shall save it' [Matthew 10:39]. It is true that he becomes what he is in our imaginations partly by reason of those sacrifices. When they have happened, we recognize that he is such a man that he can call them forth. But no less, he must already be such that we feel no misgiving, no tremor of a doubt lest their sacrifice should be wasted on an unworthy object: and this, in spite of all we know and see of the havoc his will is working on his reason. To this end two things are necessary. One is that the passion to which he yields should seem to us overwhelming and elemental, a force of nature and a power of destiny. The other is that we should be convinced of his essential nobility. And of these two the second is more important than the first: for once the latter is established, we are bound to take the former for granted, by that logic of humanity which tells us that if a noble nature acts in a way which is contrary to our reason, it is our reason which is at fault.

This is . . . the secret of Shakespeare's method in the great plays. He builds the character of royal nature. We say to ourselves: 'the man *is* noble!' If then he does monstrous things, as Macbeth and Othello do, we can but ascribe it to his falling into the clutches of some superhuman power. And so it is in

Antony and Cleopatra. Cleopatra, judged by herself alone, as she is presented to us in the earlier acts of the play, is not of power to make Antony 'the ruin of her magic' [III. x. 18]; though Cleopatra, as she is described, might be. It is her effects upon the Antony we know that convince us of her witchcraft: she is, so to speak, only a partial embodiment of the power which has overwhelmed him. And it has often been remarked that the Cleopatra of the last act is a far greater figure than the Cleopatra who has been shown to us before. That immediate impression is true enough; but it is due to the fact that up to the death of Antony it is from him that the life of the play has been derived. She is what she is to the imagination, rather in virtue of the effects we see in Antony, than by virtue of herself. He is magnificent: therefore she must be. But when he dies, her poetic function is to maintain and prolong, to reflect and reverberate, that achieved royalty of Antony's.

We have tried to indicate how subtly, yet how simply Shakespeare suggests the gulf between them, as Antony's life draws to an end. When he is inspired to his royal gesture to his servants, Cleopatra is uncomprehending, where Enobarbus comprehends. The supreme relation of royalty and loyalty has not been established in her. Antony upbraids her:

> I made these wars for Egypt; and the queen,
> Whose heart I thought I had, for she had mine;
> Which whilst it was mine had annex'd unto't
> A million more, now lost,—she, Eros, has
> Pack'd cards with Caesar and false-play'd my glory
> Unto an enemy's triumph.
>
> [IV. xiv. 15-20]

Whether she played him, indeed, as false as this, we cannot tell: but she played with him. She plays, desperately, with him now, when she bids Mardian tell him the false news of her death, to turn aside his anger at her cowardice, or her treachery. She is, as yet, neither royal nor loyal.

But, with his death, straightway her nature and her utterance change. She lifts her voice in an imperishable lament:

> The crown o' the earth doth melt. My lord!
> O, wither'd is the garland of the war,
> The soldier's pole is fall'n: young boys and girls
> Are level now with men: the odds is gone
> And there is nothing left remarkable
> Beneath the visiting moon.
>
> [IV. xv. 63-8]

And that, in the order of poetry and the imagination, is our instant security that Antony, being dead, yet liveth. When he breathed out his soul, it found an abiding place in Cleopatra's body. There it must needs struggle, but it will prevail. She, as it were, picks up the note. Antony's last words had been: 'A Roman by a Roman valiantly vanquished' [IV. xv. 57-8]. Cleopatra echoes them:

> Good sirs, take heart:
> We'll bury him; and then what's brave, what's noble,
> Let's do it after the high Roman fashion
> And make death proud to take us.
>
> [IV. xv. 85-8]

Roman, here, is the same as royal. Cleopatra wavers in her resolution, and steels herself to it by the thought of the indignities that await her in Rome. But more, though less consciously, by the thought that death is as a sleep, in a kindly bosom. Death is 'the beggar's nurse and Caesar's'; at whose

breast the tired child 'sleeps and never palates more the dug' [V. ii. 8, 7]. And again she prolongs the note:

> Where art thou, death?
> Come hither, come! come, come and take a queen,
> Worth many babes and beggars.
>
> [V. ii. 46-8]

And this note, as of a musing dream, is sustained: so that it seems to us as though Cleopatra henceforward moves in a trance, governed by some secret music of the kind that marked the passing of God from Antony. As in a dream she speaks to Dolabella the wonderful words with which we began. They are visionary words. Some would call them rhetorical; but to me the epithet seems quite meaningless. They are, of course, full of hyperbole: but hyperbole is an empty grammatical label. The point, and the only relevant point about them, is that they do body forth, against a mighty background, the nature and the meaning of Antony. He is manifested as the force of nature we knew him to be. . . . Think only of the four lines:

> For his bounty
> There was no winter in't: an autumn 'twas
> That grew the more by reaping: his delights
> Were dolphin-like; they showed his back above
> The element they lived in.
>
> [V. ii. 86-90]

In those lines, simply and strangely, Antony is made incorporate with Nature, with the riches of harvest, and the golden splendour of a stubble-field; but no less than with this quiet opulence, incorporate also with the gleam and flash and strong impetuosity of the dolphin. And all this we feel to be true. This is Antony. It is as though his essence had been made plain, his secret revealed to Cleopatra in her vision. (pp. 361-75)

Now in very deed, Cleopatra loves Antony: now she discerns his royalty, and loyalty surges up in her to meet it. Now we feel that her wrangling with Caesar and her Treasurer which follows is all external to her—as it were a part which she is still condemned to play 'in this vile world': a mere interruption, an alien interlude, while the travail of fusion between the order of imagination and love, and the order of existence and act is being accomplished: till the flame of perfect purpose breaks forth:

> Now Charmian!
> Show me, my women, like a queen: go fetch
> My best attires: I am again for Cydnus,
> To meet Mark Antony.
>
> [V. ii. 226-29]

No, not *again* for Cydnus: but now for the first time, indeed. For that old Cydnus, where the wonder pageant was, was but a symbol and prefiguration of this. That was an event in time; this is an event in eternity. And those royal robes were then only lovely garments of the body, now they are the integument of a soul. They must show her like a queen, now, because she *is* a queen, as she never was before.

It is at this moment, of suspense, while the queenly soul in travail of its own royalty awaits the flash of incandescence, that Shakespeare makes the extreme challenge to reality:

> The quick comedians
> Extemporally will stage us, and present

Our Alexandrian revels; Antony
Shall be brought drunken forth, and I shall see
Some squeaking Cleopatra boy my greatness
I' the posture of a whore.

[V. ii. 216-21]

I am not maintaining that this supreme stroke of art was conscious or deliberate: indeed, I do not believe that art of this
order ever can be conscious or deliberate. It just happens, and
'inspiration' is as good a name for what happens as any other
I know: for at least it excludes the fatal suggestion that the
calculating mentality devises and determines such master-strokes
as this. It is the nature and quality of its effect which is our
concern.

From the beginning of the play we have been gradually raised,
by means such as I have tried to describe, to a height far above
that of ordinary dramatic illusion: we have been lifted from
the human to the superhuman. We have watched Antony ennoble the sacrifice of his friends, and be the more ennobled
by that sacrifice; and we have watched him die royally. Then
we have watched the mysterious transfusion of his royal spirit
into the mind and heart of his fickle queen. And all this we
have watched, not merely with the bodily, but with the spiritual
eye; we have heard it, not merely with the bodily, but with
the spiritual ear. The prime instrument of this sustained and
deepening enchantment has been a peculiar quality of poetry,
of such a kind that it is the reverberation of the noble deeds
which our bodily eyes have seen enacted; and more than the
reverberation of them. This quality of poetry conditions those
acts; gives them a quality of significance, over and above and
distinguishable from the declared intention of the acts: so that
the quality of 'inspiration', which our dividing minds would
attribute to the poetry alone, envelops and suffuses the acts
which it accompanies. The poetic utterance passes, without jolt
or jar, into the dramatic deed, as though utterance and act were
but a single kind of expression.

Indeed, one might say that the inward life and creative process
of such a drama as this is the gradual invasion and pervasion
of the characters by the poetry of their own utterance. Their
acts gradually, and reluctantly, move into harmony with their
utterance; and, as the acts slowly change their nature, so the
quality of the utterance becomes more rich and rare. To this
process of attunement of deed to poetry, there is, it seems, but
one inevitable end. The total suffusion of the character by
poetry is death. The nature of this law is spiritual; it derives
from the strange logic of the imagination, which finds response
in the hearts of all men when it takes the form: 'Greater love
hath no man than this, that he lay down his life for his friend'
[John 15:13]. (pp. 375-78)

Of the same kind is the spiritual law of Shakespeare's drama
here. The total self-surrender of chosen or self-inflicted death
is the only symbol of the complete suffusion of the character
by poetry. Whether or not Shakespeare consciously conceived
it thus, is no matter. It may well be that, as a fact of the history
of his poetic creation, that the deaths were foreordained. They
came first, in Shakespeare's mind, no doubt. His task was to
load the particular act of death with all the significance it could
contain; and poetry is the means by which he does it. This is
Shakespeare's supreme dramatic 'device': he entangles his
characters in the compulsive magic of poetic utterance, and
submits them to that alchemy. They change: they needs must
change. The process of change in Cleopatra we have tried a
little to follow and to understand. It is at the very instant when
she is in travail of her final transfiguration that the impulse

comes to Shakespeare to shatter the dramatic illusion—to compel us to see, if we can, in the great queen in travail of her
own royalty a squeaking boy Cleopatra in the posture of a
whore.

We cannot see it; we should not, even if we were watching
now the actual play. But when those words were first spoken
at the Globe, the audience, if they had been able to use their
bodily eyes alone, would have seen just that. Did they, could
they? I do not know. But if they did, as I can imagine that
they did, I cannot doubt that there were some among them,
who dumbly understood, as I do, why Shakespeare made the
fear of the very catastrophe he compelled them to behold the
final motive in the great queen's mind: why he made that the
spark to set her soul ablaze with perfect purpose:

I am again for Cydnus
To meet Mark Antony.

That sudden break: that sudden flash is in the inrush of the
eternal moment.

The great drama was to be played, not again, not once more,
but for the first time—'all breathing human passion far above'
[John Keats, ''Ode on a Grecian Urn'']—in the fields of Eternity, where there is no more Time. (pp. 378-79)

John Middleton Murry, '' 'Antony and Cleopatra','' in his Shakespeare, *Jonathan Cape, 1936, pp. 352-79.*

D. A. TRAVERSI   (essay date 1938)

[*Traversi, a British scholar, has written a number of books on
Shakespeare's plays, including* An Approach to Shakespeare *(1938),*
Shakespeare: The Last Phase *(1954),* Shakespeare: From ''Richard II'' to ''Henry V'' *(1957), and* Shakespeare: The Roman Plays
*(1963). In the introduction to the first of these studies, Traversi
proposed to focus his interpretation of the plays on ''the word,''
stating that the experience which forms the impetus to each of
Shakespeare's dramas ''will find its most immediate expression
in the language and verse.'' In the following excerpt, he asserts
that Shakespeare has endowed the final scenes of* Antony and
Cleopatra *with an aura of triumphant love that develops organically from all aspects of the dramatic action and is underscored
by the poetic images in the play; the deaths of the lovers, Traversi
argues, represent liberations from triviality and ''all the earthly
elements'' which were the bases of their earlier, febrile infatuation. The dramatist does not ignore the imperfections of the protagonists, the critic maintains, but makes their flaws the foundation for their ultimate ascendancy over earthly faults and
limitations. Traversi holds that this process of growth and assimilation is mirrored in the metaphoric patterns associated with*
Antony and Cleopatra, *wherein ''rottenness becomes the ground
for fertility, opulence becomes royalty, [and] infatuation turns to
transcendent passion.'' The critic also declares that the strong
association of Rome with images of opulence, overripeness, decay, and disorder not only characterizes the ''world of the Triumvirs'' as mean and decadent, but also links the lovers and the
Roman world ''in a single poetic creation.''*]

The poetry of *Antony and Cleopatra*, the most harmonious and
completely realized of [Shakespeare's] last plays, shows [an]
extraordinary range of imagery, and implies an equally extraordinary power of fusing it into a single and continuous
effect. Shakespeare himself could not have written this at any
previous point in his career:

O, see, my women,
The crown o' the earth doth melt. My lord!
O, withered is the garland of the war,

The soldier's pole is fall'n; young boys and girls
Are level now with men; the odds is gone,
And there is nothing left remarkable
Beneath the visiting moon.

[IV. xv. 62-8]

One has only to attempt to separate a few of the images in this 'knot intrinsicate' of poetry to realize the *extent* of Shakespeare's control. 'The crown o' the earth' carries on naturally enough the tone of transcendent royalty with which Cleopatra has emphasized Antony's greatness and the depth of her love and grief. The verb 'melt' is not *factually* related to 'crown'; Shakespeare has chosen it because it removes any sense of harshness from Antony's death by suggesting a natural, gentle dissolution into purest air (there is a similar feeling about Cleopatra's own death—'As sweet as balm, as soft as air, as gentle . . .' [V. ii. 311]) and so prepares for the sense of triumph associated with Cleopatra's grief. 'The soldier's pole' is probably the standard of war; but 'pole', taken together with 'crown' and the following 'boys and girls', bears a complex suggestion of May-day, when love and the renewed life of spring meet in triumph; if we set these joyful associations against the corresponding depths of Cleopatra's desolation, we shall feel something of the tremendous emotional range of the play. The final reference to the 'visiting moon' lends further point to this relation of joy to death and sorrow. The fact that, after Antony's death, there is left nothing 'remarkable' beneath the moon suggests not only the extent of Cleopatra's loss, but also implies that their union, while it lasted, reduced all earthly things to a dull uniformity; whilst they were together, kingdoms *were* indeed clay. The whole passage is built upon a breadth of imagery which does not yield in complexity to the ambiguity of the Sonnets; but, unlike them, its complexity is subdued to a harmony which regards both desolation and triumph as integral parts of a single mood. The poetry of *Antony* no longer turns, like that of even the later tragedies, upon a cleavage between 'good' and 'evil' within the unity of experience. It depends rather upon a perfect continuity between the 'flesh', with its associations of earth and death, and the transcendent justification of passion in terms of emotional value and vitality. This continuity is in no way vague or sentimental, but is splendidly realized in a harmonious scale of related imagery; to reconstruct this scale step by step is the critic's task in dealing with Antony.

The story of Antony and Cleopatra is set against an imperial background. Its course is influenced by events significant for the whole Roman world, and Shakespeare deliberately incorporates into his poetry a sense of vast issues and tremendous dominions. Antony is a 'triple pillar of the world' [I. i. 12], and the attendant who bears off the drunken Lepidus carries upon his shoulders 'the third part of the world' [II. vii. 90]; Octavia, again, tells Antony that a quarrel between him and Caesar would be—

As if the world should cleave, and that slain men
Should solder up the rift.

[III. iv. 31-2]

But the world of the Triumvirs, vast as it is and correspondingly opulent, is none the less mean and decayed. Shakespeare's presentation of it is full of touches which carry us back to *Henry IV;* there is a good deal of Prince Hal in Caesar's self-controlled, ungenerous calculation, and Antony's political folly is continually stressed. The great drunken scene (II. vii.) turns upon a contrast between the witless conviviality of the Triumvirs and the 'quicksands' of sober treachery represented by

Menas and turned aside by Antony less through honesty than through weakness; the mastery of the scene, which lies in the superb counterpointing of the related motives of folly and treachery, is beyond *Henry IV,* but the inspiration is that of the earlier play. Shakespeare's matured experience moves him to present his characters in a world whose imperial pretensions are over-ripe and luxurious. He presents this world . . . in terms of bodily surfeit and disorder; Antony describes 'the present state' as one in which—

quietness grown *sick* of rest would *purge*
By any desperate change.

[I. iii. 52, 53-4]

'Rest' is the stagnation produced by opulence which leads to the purge of revolution. When the Messenger, in the following scene, brings Caesar news that 'flush youth revolt' [I. iv. 52], he is relating imperial disorder further to bodily surfeit; his words are given point by those of Caesar which immediately precede them:

This *common* body,
Like to a vagabond flag upon the stream
Goes to and back, lackeying the varying tide
To *rot* itself with motion.

[I. iv. 44-7]

Even without feeling the Elizabethan association of 'common' with sexual promiscuity, we can appreciate that Shakespeare is using this sense of disorder and decay in the body to relate the universal situation to the particular love of Antony for Cleopatra.

The decadence of the Roman world is balanced by similar elements in Antony. His advancing years are stressed more than once, and Caesar's exposures of his vices are too full of poetic individuality, too closely related to the over-ripeness which is so striking a feature of the play, for us to neglect them:

. . . he fishes, drinks and wastes
The lamps of night in revel.'

[I. iv. 4-5]

Nor does Shakespeare pass over the wanton cruelty of Antony's treatment of Caesar's messenger; he is to be whipped until 'he whine aloud for mercy' [III. xiii. 101]. Most decisive of all, every meeting between Antony and Cleopatra, from the moment of that first scathing comment on his poetic ecstasy:

Excellent falsehood!
Why did he marry Fulvia, and not love her?

[I. i. 40-1]

is the exposure of an ageing libertine; though, needless to say, every one of these meetings is a great deal more than that. Shakespeare did not write a great play by ignoring Antony's weaknesses, but by assimilating these weaknesses into the dominating triumphant mood of the play. Antony's love is justified in terms of its intensity and vitality *in spite of* his continual awareness that Cleopatra is 'a whore of Egypt', a stale 'scrap for Caesar's trencher', in spite of the fact that his passion is the infatuation of a middle-aged soldier for a woman who had already served Julius Caesar's pleasure. The gap between this infatuation and the triumphant feeling of the final scenes, with Cleopatra dying on her throne spurning the lord of the world as an 'ass unpolicied', is bridged by a wonderful modification of connected imagery; rottenness becomes the ground for fertility, opulence becomes royalty, infatuation turns to transcendent passion, all by means of an *organic* process which ignores none of its own earlier stages, but passes through them and integrates them in the unity of its purpose.

The starting-point of this poetic 'redemption', so to speak, of the love of Antony and Cleopatra, is the very rottenness we have discovered in the Roman world. This over-ripeness is a fitting background to the story of mature passion, which is related to it, but it also lends point to Antony's assertion of the supremacy of his personal feeling. Antony undoubtedly gambled away his dignity as a 'triple pillar of the world', but the corruption and treachery of that world went far to redeem his folly and to justify his contempt:

> Let Rome in Tiber melt, and the wide arch
> Of the ranged empire fall; here is my space.
>
> [I. i. 33-4]

To assert, however, that Shakespeare was content to make this contrast after the manner of the seeker after moral axioms ('All for Love: or The World Well Lost') is seriously to underestimate his achievement. Shakespeare relates the rottenness of the Roman world *poetically* to the individual fortunes of Antony and Cleopatra; he makes his love-imagery spring from this over-ripeness, joining the lovers and their world in a single poetic creation. This is seen most clearly in the poetry of Cleopatra, and especially in the manner in which it derives from the idea of Egypt, from the overflowing fertility of the Nile. Her love is, in the words of Antony's promise, 'the *fire* that *quickens* Nilus' *slime*' [I. iii. 68-9], a living fertility, vividly expressed in terms of fire, that grows by a continuous process of nature out of the corruption of 'slime'. The play is full of this magnificent balance between decay and fruitfulness; in her declining fortunes, Cleopatra describes herself as 'the blown rose' [III. xiii. 39], combining beauty and decline in a delicate unity of sensation. So assured is Shakespeare's mastery that he can impart dignity even to Cleopatra's relations with Julius Caesar; in those days, she says, she was 'a morsel for a monarch' [I. v. 31], and the 'monarch' redeems the indignity of 'morsel', of being 'a scrap for Caesar's trencher'. But perhaps the greatest example of Cleopatra's conversion of slime into fertility is her speech to Antony immediately after the whipping and dismissal of Thyreus:

> . . . as it determines, so
> Dissolve my life! The next Caesarion smite!
> Till by degrees the memory of my womb,
> Together with my brave Egyptians all,
> By the discandying of this pelleted storm
> Lie graveless, till the flies and gnats of Nile
> Have buried them for prey.
>
> [III. xiii. 161-67]

By sheer intensity of poetic sensing, life is produced from rotting and decay; Shakespeare even makes the speech look forward to the regal oblivion of Cleopatra's death. 'Discandying' imparts an intense sweetness to corruption, and 'dissolve' gives death an ease and inevitability which relates it to the exaltation of the aspic scene; whilst 'the memory of my womb' suggests the full fertility of her passion, the richness of life which is felt to spring from the corruption implied in the 'flies and gnats of Nile'. Within the subtle variations of this speech is contained the whole range of Cleopatra's poetic development.

These complexities have one aim—to evolve the greatness of Cleopatra's passion out of its very imperfection, out of the very impermanence of the flesh and the corrupt world with

which it is organically connected. As the story proceeds, Shakespeare subjects Antony to a similar development, making him, without evading or sentimentalizing his weaknesses, fit for the magnificence of his end. From the first, his generosity and bravery are brought out by contrast with Caesar's calculating meanness and the treachery of the surrounding world. Even his mad renunciation of practical affairs is balanced by the splendid assertion of his love; 'Kingdoms are clay' [I. i. 35], and the only value of the clay is to be a ground in which the fertility of love may take root. In accordance with this intention, the decline of Antony's fortunes is balanced by a whole series of devices which co-operate to make him stand apart from the increasingly trivial issues of the Roman world; that issues so great, so imperial in their scope should be felt as trivial is in itself a measure of the quality of his passion. His generosity to his followers, and in particular to the deserter, Enobarbus, is set against Caesar's mean attempt (which, by a crowning stroke of irony, Cleopatra humours) to seduce the queen from his side; we feel that Antony's prodigality is always close enough to bounty to add strength to the poetic sensation of fertility in love. Shakespeare never disguises Antony's incompetence: even at the end he fails to stab himself to the heart and recommends Cleopatra to trust only the very man (Proculeius) by whom she is immediately betrayed; but this incompetence becomes subsidiary and irrelevant in the depth and intensity of his poetry. The evolution of his dignity balances a similar greatness in Cleopatra until, after their defeat, they are ready for the great meeting on the monument (IV. xv.), in which irony and criticism are dissolved (the word is representative) into transcendent poetry.

Shakespeare's success becomes clear in the final scenes, in which he deals with the deaths of Antony and Cleopatra. Antony's death is a natural consequence of political folly and personal infatuation. We are not allowed to forget that its immediate cause is a miscarriage of Cleopatra's ingenuity, which leads her to announce falsely her own death and so drives him to despair; to the last, Antony is involved in the subterfuges and deceptions which spring inevitably from the nature of his passion. But, just as 'slime' was converted into fertility, just as the folly of renouncing the 'ranged empire' was balanced by the rottenness of that empire, so does death, which is the consequence of Antony's prodigality, become a liberation from triviality and an opening of the way to the poetic assertion of triumph. We can feel this liberation in the very movement of the blank verse, in which 'labour' and its opposite are marvelously fused in a single intuition of peace:

> now all labour
> Mars what it does; yea, very force entangles
> Itself with strength.
>
> [IV. xiv. 47-9]

A little further on, death is explicitly associated with love:

> I will be
> A *bridegroom* in my death, and run into 't
> As to a *lover's bed*.
>
> [IV. xiv. 99-101]

In this way, Antony's suicide becomes an integral part of the final lyrical assertion of the value and transcendence of passion. It looks forward to the poetry of Cleopatra's death, in which 'baser life' is finally transmuted into imagery of fire, air, and immortality.

Cleopatra's last great speech (V. ii.) opens, significantly, with an assertion of 'immortal longings'. The reference to immortality is in full contrast to the impermanence of 'dungy earth', from which her love sprang and in virtue of which her death and Antony's downfall were both inevitable. Yet the immortality invoked by Cleopatra is not a mere abstraction; being connected with 'longings', it is simply the highest assertion of her love for the dead and infinitely exalted Antony, whom she now calls, for the first time in the play, 'Husband!' In the light of this association of love and immortality, death assumes a fresh poetic function; it becomes a dissolution, a purging of all the earthly elements upon which love had been based:

> I am fire and air; my other elements
> I give to baser life.
>
> [V. ii. 289-90]

On the edge of death, only the purest elements remain in Cleopatra—those which are fully, most intensely alive. From a great distance, as it seems, we are reminded of the other elements of 'baser life', the earth and fertile slime from which love sprang, and in virtue of which defeat and death were necessary; but death and defeat have become subdued to the 'immortal longings' which sprang from them, and the adverse fortunes of the world are dismissed as—

> The luck of Caesar, which the gods give men
> To excuse their after wrath.
>
> [V. ii. 286-87]

Yet, in spite of this note of transcendence, the firm basis of poetic imagery on the senses is essential to Shakespeare's effect. The speech is not an abstract triumph, sentimentally imposed upon the body of the play; the elements of 'fire and air' represent a continual refining process from the comparative earthiness of the opening, and the effect of Cleopatra's longings is reinforced by the keenly sensed reference to 'the juice of Egypt's grape' [V. ii. 282], suggesting all that is most alive and delicate in the activity of the senses. This sense of continuity balanced by infinite remoteness is the key to the whole development of Antony and Cleopatra. Shakespeare has so refined, so intensified his love poetry by a progressive distillation of sensible experience that it is able to assimilate the apparently incompatible fact of death:

> The stroke of death is as a lover's pinch
> Which hurts and is desired.
>
> [V. ii. 295-96]

'Hurts' and 'desired', which seem so contradictory, are made to reinforce one another by a splendid balance of imagery; the pain implied in 'hurts' is felt so delicately, so intensely that it becomes fused with the keenness of the lover's desire. In this way, death becomes merely an untying of 'this knot intrinsicate' [V. ii. 304] of body and soul, of infinite desires hitherto subject to adverse and earthly circumstance. The whole development of the play has been tending to this point. The balancing of Antony's generous folly against Caesar's successful meanness, the gradual ascent of the love-imagery from earth and 'slime' to 'fire and air' are all part of one great process which now needs death to complete it. For death, which had seemed in the Sonnets and early tragedies to be incontrovertible evidence of the subjection of love and human values to Time, now becomes by virtue of Shakespeare's poetic achievement an instrument of release, the necessary condition of an experience which, though dependent upon Time and circumstance, is by virtue of its *value* and intensity incommensurate with them—that is, 'immortal'. The emotions of Antony and Cleopatra are built upon 'dungy earth', upon 'Nilus' slime', and so upon Time which these elements by their

nature imply; but, just as earth and slime are quickened into fire and air, whilst retaining their sensible qualities as constituent parts of the final experience, so Time itself becomes a necessary element in the creation of 'immortality'. To say that *Antony and Cleopatra* is Shakespeare's greatest play would be futile, if only because it depends upon the earlier tragedies for its effect; but it is certainly the play in which Shakespeare came nearest to unifying his experience into a harmonious and related whole. The 'ambiguity' of the Sonnets is fully resolved into an integrated intuition of its various elements, and poetic technique has become a completely adequate medium for a unified experience. (pp. 116-27)

> *D. A. Traversi, "The Single State of Man," in his* Approach to Shakespeare, *Sands: The Paladin Press, 1938, pp. 113-46.*

E. M. W. TILLYARD (essay date 1938)

[*Tillyard is best known for his influential* Shakespeare's History Plays *(1944), considered a leading example of historical criticism. In addition to his historical studies, Tillyard also wrote* Shakespeare's Last Plays *(1938),* Shakespeare's Problem Plays *(1949), and* Shakespeare's Early Comedies *(1965), a book he was working on at the time of his death in 1962. In the excerpt below, he discusses* Antony and Cleopatra *as a transitional play between the late tragedies and the romances. Tillyard argues that although in this work Shakespeare was beginning to move towards the dramas of reconciliation and regeneration, the thematic pattern here is only in its early stages. The negative qualities of the two principal characters, he contends, are not reconciled with the nobler aspects of their natures, but are merely abandoned in Acts IV and V when Antony and Cleopatra become "transfigured in death."*]

[One] of Shakespeare's main concerns in his last plays, whether deliberately taken up or fortuitously drifted into, was to develop the final phase of the tragic pattern, to add, as it were, his *Eumenides* to the already completed *Agamemnon* and *Choephoroe,* a process repeated by Milton when he supplemented *Paradise Lost* with *Samson Agonistes.* (p. 20)

The transitional plays between the full tragic period and the romances are *Antony and Cleopatra* and *Coriolanus.* . . . [In] so far as Shakespeare was beginning in these two plays to concern himself with the final, regenerative phase of the tragic pattern, he was indeed beginning his process of transition to the romances. But in neither play did he portray the regenerative process at all completely or convincingly. On the contrary, the hints of a regeneration in the mind of Othello count for more than all the dying ecstasies of Antony and Cleopatra or Coriolanus's yielding to his mother. The difference is this. Othello recognises his errors and transmutes them into his new state of mind; Antony, Cleopatra, and Coriolanus abandon their errors without transmuting them. Hence reconciliation is not the word to apply to their states of mind. It is a different thing to pass from A to B, and to fuse A and B into an amalgam C. Antony does the first, Othello the second. When St. Paul was converted he may have freed himself from a kind of devil, but the fierce angel that was born in the conversion incorporated, among other things, that very devil from which he had broken free. That is the true reconciliation. The vacillations of Antony and his neglect of duty, the cunning and cruelty of Cleopatra, find no part in the creatures who are transfigured in death; they remain unassimilated, held in tension against the pair's expiring nobilities. The reason why *Antony and Cleopatra* is so baffling a play (and why the rhapsodies it provokes tend to be hysterical) is that the effort to see the two main characters simultaneously in two so different guises taxes our strength beyond our capacities. And yet that effort has to be made. Those who see Antony as the erring hero merely, and his final exaltation as ironic infatuation, are as partial in their judgment as those who think that his final heroics wash out his previous frailties. Both sets are part right, but each needs the other's truth to support it. (pp. 20-2)

E. M. W. Tillyard, "The Tragic Pattern: Introductory," in his Shakespeare's Last Plays, *Chatto and Windus, 1938, pp. 16-25.*

MARK VAN DOREN (essay date 1939)

[*Van Doren was a Pulitzer prize-winning poet, American educator, editor, and novelist. In the introduction to his* Shakespeare *(1939), he states that he "ignored the biography of Shakespeare, the history and character of his time, the conventions of his theater, the works of his contemporaries" to concentrate on the interest of the plays and their relevance to the modern reader or spectator. In the excerpt below, Van Doren proposes that the dramatic world of* Antony and Cleopatra *is uniquely luminous, vast, watery, and mercurial, and thus requires a style that is discontinuous and flexible in the interchange of its mosaic-like parts. "Only a supreme effort at writing keeps the play on its tragic keel," he contends, for by virtue of Antony and Cleopatra's clear-eyed appraisal of each other and their willingness to embrace death, they would appear to be better suited for comedy than tragedy. Van Doren emphasizes the serpentine, changeable, and emotive aspects of Cleopatra's nature, asserting that she exactly embodies "the boundless air of Egypt." Through her, the critic avers, Antony discovers a greater, more expansive world than the Roman one, achieving before his death a peaceful stasis in the immobility and timelessness of "Egypt's air."*]

If "Antony and Cleopatra" was written first among the three tragedies in which Shakespeare returned to Plutarch for his source, the writing of it involved the removal of his imagination to a distance that almost staggers measurement. The poet of "King Lear" and "Macbeth" now works freely under a great dome of lighted sky which knows no clouds except an occasional illusory and indistinct one, and which feels no wind beyond the soft one of its own effortless breathing. The world of "Antony and Cleopatra" is so immense that time yawns in it; and this is not because time is going to die as it did in "Macbeth" but because it luxuriates in a sense of perfect and endless health. The mandragora that Cleopatra wants to drink so that she may "sleep out this great gap of time" [I. v. 5] while Antony is away needs scarcely to be drunk in a universe already drugged with a knowledge of its own size. It is all the world that Plutarch knew or that Shakespeare knows as he writes: the Mediterranean world where opulent Africa lies across a gleaming sea from Spain, Italy, and Greece, and where innumerable kingdoms stretch eastward to the horizon. Nor is there terror in such distances. Men are at home in "the wide arch of the rang'd empire," and call each other naturally the most glorious names: "triple pillar of the world," "demi-Atlas of this earth," "senators alone of this great world," "worldsharers," "universal landlord," "sole sir o' the world" [I. i. 33-4, 12; I. v. 23; II. vii. 70; III. xiii. 72; V. ii. 120]. There is no terror because there is so much light. When Iras says

> the bright day is done,
> And we are for the dark,
>
> [V. ii. 193-94]

she is bidding good-by to an afternoon which has been long with life; and the dark for which she is destined seems somehow to have no blackness in it, for the same reason that when Cleopatra utters her command:

> Darkling stand
> The varying shore o' the world
>
> [IV. xv. 10-11]

we cannot imagine that any cliff or headland has ceased to be luminous even though the sun has burned the great sphere it moves in. Light plays on everything with undiscouraged luxury: on land, on rivers, on islands, and on the sea. We are never far away from the limpid and life-giving element of water, which, rather than forming like dew as it did in "A Midsummer Night's Dream," now spreads a rich iridescent film over the whole of a vast daylight existence. There is of course the sea, and Antony is one who with his sword

> Quarter'd the world, and o'er green Neptune's back
> With ships made cities.
>
> [IV. xiv. 58-9]

But there is also the Nile, whose "slime and ooze," creative of "flies and gnats" as well as crocodiles, we are kept no less conscious of than we are kept conscious of flowing streams wherein "tawny-finn'd fishes" play, where swan's downfeathers float at full of tide, and from which rise swifts and mallards [II. vii. 22; III. xiii. 166; II. v. 12]. It is a world of languid and abundant life which cannot surprise us with news that swallows have built their nests in Cleopatra's sails [IV. xii. 3-4], or that the river of Cydnus fell in love with her barge as it burned on its water.

> The oars were silver,
> Which to the tune of flutes kept stroke, and made
> The water which they beat to follow faster,
> As amorous of their strokes.
>
> [II. ii. 194-97]

At night, since night must be, there is nevertheless the moon, whose fleeting terrene visits keep Italy and Egypt flooded with yellow light. And by day again there is certain to be music—"moody food," says Cleopatra [II. v. 1-2], "of us that trade in love." But it is not music played in a chamber, like the music of "Twelfth Night," or on the lawn of a great lady's estate as in "The Merchant of Venice." It has the dome of the world to fill, so that it plays "far off" while Cleopatra fishes [II. v. 11], and runs both through the air and underground when

> the god Hercules, whom Antony loved,
> Now leaves him.
>
> [IV. iii. 16-17]

Such a world needs a special style, and the play triumphantly provides it. The units of this style, curiously enough, are very brief. Nothing is drawn out as with too little thought we might have expected it to be. The action is broken into as many as forty-two scenes; our attention is constantly shifted from one to another portion of the single scene which is the earth. And so with the speech, the characteristic unit of which is almost breathlessly short. There are no rolls of rhetoric, no attempts to loop the universe with language. This universe is too large to be rendered in anything but fragments, too much alive in its own right to care for extended compliment and discourse. It can be handled only by a process of constantly reassembling its many small parts—moving them about in an always flexible mosaic. For the world of "Antony and Cleopatra" shows its strength in nothing so much as its flexibility. Any part, examined closely, yields the whole, just as any speech, once it is made, escapes into some far altitude of the air without exactly losing itself; in the long run it will count. The action expresses itself in many ripples, like a resting sea. The climate in which Antony and Cleopatra so completely love each other permits them the luxury of little phrases, as if with their breath it panted the tale of its own endless well-being. Accommodating itself to its heroine, it utters itself with a refined sensuousness, opening its lips and pronouncing delicious words in which the light sounds of i, short a, s, st, l, and ing predominate. . . . The speech of any person in the play is likely to spill itself in agreeable gasps, as if it came through gills; and the blank-verse line of the earlier dramas has almost lost its form in the fluid element that surrounds it. . . . Such a style suits lovers who make up as quickly as they have quarreled; the anger of Antony and Cleopatra has a short memory, and pardons succeed curses with little shift of accent.

> Courteous lord, one word.
> Sir, you and I must part, but that's not it;
> Sir, you and I have lov'd, but there's not it;
> That you know well. Something it is I would,—
> O, my oblivion is a very Antony,
> And I am all forgotten.
>
> [I. iii. 86-91]

That will do for Cleopatra's text after any altercation; and Antony, who played with half the bulk of the world as he pleased and had superfluous kings for messengers, can humble himself as briefly:

> Fall not a tear, I say; one of them rates
> All that is won and lost. Give me a kiss.
> Even this repays me.
>
> [III. xi. 69-71]

Their misunderstandings are waves which there are other waves to check, just as the bits of acting they practice on each other are chopped short because they know that neither can be deceived.

> *Cleopatra.*   Good now, play one scene
>   Of excellent dissembling; and let it look
>   Like perfect honour.
> *Antony.*   You'll heat my blood. No more.
> *Cleopatra.*   You can do better yet; but this is meetly.
> *Antony.*   Now, by my sword,—
> *Cleopatra.*   And target.—Still he mends;
>   But this is not the best.
>
> [I. iii. 78-83]

This banter is from a queen who is herself a consummate actress, and she knows Antony knows it. Once she fails to see through him, but that is when he is acting for men only and she does not catch the style. As he opens an old vein of oratory and contrives tremulos for the benefit of certain servitors on the eve of battle (IV, ii) she appeals to Enobarbus who is standing by: "What means this?" [IV. ii. 13]. Enobarbus puts her off by saying that it is an odd trick of sorrow; Antony is affected by thoughts of the next day. But as the instrument plays on she asks again: "What does he mean?" [IV. ii. 23]. And Enobarbus, who knows his master even better than she knows her lover, has to confess: "To make his followers weep" [IV. ii. 24]. It is mere wanton art, an expert's oratory. There is of course a final quarrel and a final attempt at deception, for the play is a tragedy and Cleopatra will not be able to undo her subterfuge of the monument (IV, xiii-xv). Yet even there the established style will prevail, and modify the tragedy. And

long before that it will have subdued every item of the action to the tone of its own unique refinement. The drunkenness of the generals on board Pompey's galley (II, vii) is as little gross as the love of Antony and Cleopatra is voluptuous. As wine makes the world-sharers witty, and steeps their senses at last in "soft and delicate Lethe" [II. vii. 108], so love turns the lead of Antony and Cleopatra into gold. Pompey credits the Queen with sultry powers that keep the brain of her lover fuming, but the love we see is light with jest and mellow with amusement. This is because Cleopatra is really queen of her world. When Enobarbus pays her his famous tribute:

> Age cannot wither her, nor custom stale
> Her infinite variety. . . . She makes hungry
> Where most she satisfies, for vilest things
> Become themselves in her,
>
> [II. ii. 234-35, 236-38]

he is placing her in that world which the style of the play is forever creating: a world which is ancient yet not stale, complacent yet still hungry, and as becoming in its vileness as it is cultivated in its virtues. Its infinite variety is a quality of its air, its land, its water, its animals, its clouds, its language, and its people. All are the creation of a style whose imponderable atoms are ever in graceful dance, no sooner combining to produce forms than separating to dissolve them. The next question is whether action is possible in such an atmosphere, and if so, what kind of action.

In one sense "Antony and Cleopatra" is actionless. A world is lost, but it is so well lost that it seems not to have been lost at all; its immensity was not disturbed. The peculiar greatness of this poetry defeats any conceivable dramatic end. Line for line it is perhaps the richest poetry Shakespeare wrote, but the reward it reaps is paradoxical: it builds a universe in which nothing can happen, or at any rate one in which the conflicts and crises of persons cannot be of the first importance. This explains, if it is granted that the gods ordained some sort of greatness for the play, the nakedness of its verbal intensity. The writing has to be wonderful because it is not supported by anything that Aristotle would have called a plot. And it is wonderful. Merely as expression it has that final force which permits many of its passages to stand alone, without the need of a context to recommend them. If they gain from being read in place, the place is an atmosphere rather than an action. The intensity of Hamlet, Othello, Lear, and Macbeth was derived from their respective predicaments; the intensity of Antony and Cleopatra seems to be generated in themselves, and in the poet who is writing their speeches. (pp. 267-74)

In another sense "Antony and Cleopatra" has all the action it desires and deserves. There is as much drama in the deaths of its hero and heroine as there can be in the deaths of two persons who lived, at least while we knew them, without illusion; or lived, it may be more accurate to say, in the full light of accepted illusion. Change is a fairy toy for Theseus in "A Midsummer Night's Dream," and for Macbeth it is a growing terror. For Antony and Cleopatra it is what must be expected, and they have seen so much of it that more cannot surprise them. The changeableness of life is the only thing that does not change; they know this, and to that extent cannot be touched. Their love has been too thoroughly tested to be shaken now. It is founded on its own fact, and on the humorous knowledge they have of each other. Shakespeare put their case perfectly in his 138th sonnet:

> When my love swears that she is made of truth,
> I do believe her, though I know she lies. . . .
> O, love's best habit is in seeming trust,
> And age in love loves not to have years told.

Yet not quite perfectly, either. Each knows the other to be a liar, and ultimately does not care if this is so; but one of their pastimes is telling their years. Their days are past the best, and they know this as well as Enobarbus knows that Antony is an old lion [III. iii. 94], or as well as Caesar knows, or thinks he knows, that his rival is an old ruffian [IV. i. 4]. Antony's remark that gray in both of them has something mingled with their younger brown [IV. viii. 19-20] is only a courteous reference to the white hairs he elsewhere takes to himself [III. xi. 13]. And Cleopatra is content with the boast:

> Though age from folly could not give me freedom,
> It does from childishness.
>
> [I. iii. 57-8]

As lovers go, then, they are old. That is why they can do without illusion—or, better still, why they know what to do with it. They prefer each other's untruth to any truth that has yet to be tried. This does not make them easy material for tragedy. It makes them indeed the most intractable material of all; for tragedy works with delusions, and they have none. They would seem to have been cut out for comedy, and indeed there is much comedy here. Only a supreme effort at writing keeps the play on its tragic keel. And even then it must do without the sense in any line that death is terrible. Tragedy counts, both in its hero and in us, upon the fear of death for its great effects. But these lovers, far from fearing death, embrace it as a third lover. Enobarbus says of Cleopatra: "I do think there is mettle in Death, which commits some loving act upon her, she hath such a celerity in dying" [I. ii. 142-44]. He is satirical, and refers to the actress who puts on shows of death in order to hold her lord. But his intelligence has penetrated to the symbol which Antony no less than she will employ to express an ultimate passion. "I'll make Death love me," swears Antony as he prepares for battle [III. xiii. 192], and as he falls on his sword he elaborates the image:

> I will be
> A bridegroom in my death, and run into 't
> As to a lover's bed.
>
> [IV. xiv. 99-101]

Cleopatra, however, gives it its most sophisticated form:

> The stroke of death is as a lover's pinch,
> Which hurts, and is desir'd.
>
> [V. ii. 295-96]

Antony is a great man, but his dimensions do not express themselves in drama. The play, such as it is, pauses while his praise is sung by Lepidus, by Euphronius, by Caesar, and again and again by Cleopatra. He deserves that such things should be said of him, but we must not expect to see them exemplified in act. They are often negative things: there are not enough evils to darken his goodness, his death is not a single doom, nothing is left remarkable since he is gone, his bounty had no winter in it. And there is a further negative:

> Who tells me true, though in his tale lie death,
> I hear him as he flatter'd. . . .
> Speak to me home, mince not the general tongue.
>
> [I. ii. 98-9, 105]

He does not trade in untruths. We learn much from such negatives, but we learn it directly, through lyric statement while the action rests. His delights were dolphin-like, they show'd his back above the element they liv'd in—the movement there goes on outside our practical vision, in a remote kingdom by the sea of metaphor. Nothing more interesting was ever said

about any man, but it has to be said, it cannot be shown. Antony is finally ineffable, and Shakespeare has the tact to let him tower alone. Bounty . . . is not a dramatic virtue; nor is there any attempt in this play to make it seem one, though the suicide of Enobarbus (IV, vi) states it powerfully, and Cleopatra's encomium is majestic in its range. The virtues of Antony cannot be dramatized because they are one virtue and its name is magnanimity. Actor though he is and orator though he has been, at his best he shows his back above the element he lives in. He can be moved to anger, jealousy, and pride, he can laugh within a minute after he has raged, he can be a man of forty moods; yet our last vision is of one whose spirit has grown stationary. For all his shrewdness Enobarbus does not see what has happened. He speaks of "a diminution in our captain's brain" [III. xiii. 197], but he is wholly wrong. There has been an expansion, not a contraction. Great as is the world of Roman thoughts, and Caesar reveals the limit of that greatness, Antony has found a greater world—one whose soft sky is of infinite size, and one where thoughts melt into one another as water does in water. A soothsayer warns Antony to keep space between himself and Caesar [II. iii. 24], but the space is already there. The discomfort Antony feels in Caesar's presence is based on more than political rivalry between an old lion and a young fox; it is based on an inability to tell Caesar or any other man why Egypt is so attractive. The reason is Egypt's air, which cannot be felt until it is withdrawn; when it must be found and breathed again, for a full breath cannot be taken in any other. Antony grows until he occupies the whole of Egypt's and Cleopatra's air. And his final act of occupation is his death—which, if it withdraws him from us, leaves us an exact equivalent in the greatness of that air.

Cleopatra's dimensions express themselves on the other hand with an excess of drama—in many little plays rather than in one that is round and single. She comes at us in waves, each of which breaks before it reaches us, but the total number of which is great and beautiful. She is fickle, she is spoiled—

> Pity me, Charmian,
> But do not speak to me—
>
> [II. v. 118-19]

she is vain, she is cowardly, she is incorrigibly unserious; yet she is a queen "whom everything becomes" [I. i. 49]. Antony says that, and he means it even of one who is "cunning past man's thought" [I. ii. 145]; her cunning becomes her too, and the holy priests bless her when she is riggish [II. ii. 238-39]. For her variety is infinite; she perfectly expresses the elasticity of Egypt's air. Antony's immobility measures its amount, but its quality can be fingered only in her. She is mercury, she is changeable silk, she is a serpent of old Nile whose movements are too many to count. The messenger's description of Octavia is nicely calculated for the woman to whom it is delivered:

> She creeps;
> Her motion and her station are as one;
> She shows a body rather than a life,
> A statue than a breather.
>
> [III. iii. 18-21]

Cleopatra is not like that; she is a breather, and her life is still more fascinating than her body. It is her life that makes her love so interesting. "There's beggary in the love that can be reckon'd" [I. i. 15]—Antony has learned this from her, and from the boundless air of Egypt. She teaches him even while she tortures him; that is why he can forgive her the long, ghastly effort to die which her lie about the monument imposes upon him (IV, xiv). His pleasure in her alternates with pain, and in fact the play deals more with the pain than it does with the pleasure. But between the lines we read that he could have endured as much again from one whose behavior has never been what Octavia's is, "holy, cold, and still" [II. vi. 122-23]. Cleopatra is too seldom at rest to be easily understood; we shall never be sure, any more than Antony would have been sure, what her intentions were with respect to the treasure she withheld from Caesar [V. ii. 138-92], and whether her decision to die was inspired by loathing for Roman triumphs or by love for the "husband" to whom death would bring her. When the basket of asps arrives she announces to her people:

> My resolution's plac'd, and I have nothing
> Of woman in me; now from head to foot
> I am marble-constant; now the fleeting moon
> No planet is of mine.
>
> [V. ii. 238-41]

Yet her demeanor in dying has no marble in it. She is still all mercury and lightness, all silk and down. "I have immortal longings in me" [V. ii. 280-81] is said with a smile at the expense of the rural fellow who has just gone out wishing her joy of the worm and insisting that its bite is "immortal"; she must have on her robe and crown before she feels the loving pinch of death; when Iras precedes her in death she pretends to worry lest Antony's first kiss in heaven be wasted on another woman; she saves enough breath to call Caesar "ass unpolicied" [V. ii. 307-08], and spends the last of it in likening the immortal worm to a baby at her breast. Charmian, surviving her a moment, echoes "ass unpolicied" with "lass unparallel'd," and bothers to straighten her mistress's crown before she dies. The scene is great and final, yet nothing in it seems to be serious; and the conversation between Caesar and his train when they come in concerns a spectacle that is pretty rather than painful.

> She looks like sleep,
> As she would catch another Antony
> In her strong toil of grace.
>
> [V. ii. 346-48]

The strength of Cleopatra has never appeared more clearly than in the charm with which she yields herself to death. Her greatness cannot be distinguished from her littleness, as water may not be defined in water. (pp. 275-81)

> *Mark Van Doren, "'Antony and Cleopatra'," in his*
> Shakespeare, *Henry Holt and Company, 1939, pp. 267-81.*

JAMES EMERSON PHILLIPS, JR.   (essay date 1940)

[*Phillips maintains that two important precepts of Renaissance political theory—one, that monarchy is the natural organization of political entities, and two, that a ruler's passion must be governed by his reason—underlie the dramatic action of* Antony and Cleopatra. *Although the political events are of secondary interest in the play, he argues, Antony's downfall clearly follows from "his inability to rule himself" and control his excessive passion with reason. Further, Phillips declares that while Octavius may be "dramatically uninteresting," he evinces the requisite self-control, "a certain magnanimity and nobility of character," perseverance, and the sincere conviction "that he is directed by a divine destiny working for the highest good of Roman political society." In contrast to Octavius, neither Lepidus nor Sextus Pompeius is a viable ruler, the critic contends, because the former is incapable of governance or leadership and the latter "lacks*

the resolution" required to carry out his dream of restoring "aristocratic republicanism" in Rome.]

In *Coriolanus* Shakespeare demonstrated that conformity to those principles of order, degree, and vocation which govern the welfare of all states was requisite to the health of the Roman body politic. He condemns democracy as a violation of these principles and accepts aristocracy as more nearly approaching the form of government naturally ordained for a commonwealth. But the tragedy of the consul and the conduct of the sovereign Senate, with its lack of authoritative vigor and decision, indicated that Rome had not yet achieved the most desirable political organization. For according to universal example, "the specialty of rule" must be exercised by a single authority, not divided among several. The political content of *Julius Caesar* and *Antony and Cleopatra* is to be read, I think, as an illustration of this fundamental principle of Renaissance thinking about the nature and structure of states. In *Julius Caesar* we see, in the successful government of the title figure, the advantages of monarchy, and in the disastrous consequences of his assassination the evils of multiple sovereignty. In *Antony and Cleopatra*, secondary as the political theme is in importance, we witness the inevitable restoration of monarchy in the process of elimination which singles out the one man naturally qualified to exercise supreme authority in a political society. (p. 172)

In *Antony and Cleopatra* the chief interest for Shakespeare, as for everyone since who has encountered the play, is the splendid infatuation which the story presents. But as Professor Boas says, "Shakespeare, even when making an elaborate study of amorous passion, does not isolate it from the wider and more material issues of surrounding civic or national life" [see Additional Bibliography]. In dwelling upon the love affair the dramatist only magnified one link in the chain of political events which runs, consistent and unbroken, through ten acts. For it seems evident that the political thinking of the later play, like the historical narrative, is taken up where *Julius Caesar* ended. MacCallum writes:

> The political setting of *Julius Caesar* had been the struggle between the old Order and the New. The Old goes out with a final and temporary flare of success; the New asserts itself as the necessary solution for the problem of the time, but is deprived of its guiding genius who might best have elicited its possibilities for good and neutralized its possibilities for evil. In *Antony and Cleopatra* we see how its mastery is established and confirmed despite the faults and limitations of the smaller men who now represent it [in his *Shakespeare's Roman Plays and Their Background;* see Additional Bibliography].

But it is not, as MacCallum implies, an order which three men can represent. It is a monarchic order which Caesar established, and until the three are reduced to one, who is least faulty and limited, the struggle will not be over. The process of selection by which monarchy will be restored through the reduction of three men to one had already been suggested in the earlier play, in the dissensions within the ranks of the triumvirate and particularly in Antony's anxiety to oust Lepidus. To the completion of this process the political action of *Antony and Cleopatra* is primarily devoted. Here are displayed the qualities of character and ability which determine the outcome. Leveled to this political plane Antony's infatuation and its effect on his character is merely one phase of the evolution toward unitary sovereignty. He and Lepidus are eliminated because they do not possess, as Octavius clearly does, the special qualities which, according to Renaissance thinking, mark a man for the vocation of government. (pp. 188-89)

Julius Caesar does not, politically speaking, end on that note of tranquility and repose for which Shakespearean tragedy is generally celebrated. At the opening of *Antony and Cleopatra* neither the form of government in Rome nor Shakespeare's condemnation of it has altered. So long as the triumvirate exercises "the specialty of rule" the state suffers the social ill-health of an unnaturally organized body politic. For however autocratic in conduct, the triumvirate is essentially an aristocratic form of government, or more accurately, because of its tyrannical nature, an oligarchy. Thus it displays the faults and inflicts the evils generally associated with divided authority in Renaissance political thinking. Even Lepidus is aware of the principal weakness of such government, internal conflict; he warns his fellow triumvirs: "When we debate Our trivial difference loud, we do commit Murder in healing wounds" [II. ii. 20-2]. The disastrous effect of oligarchic administration on the general welfare of Rome is vividly set forth by Antony, who explicitly links the civil chaos with divided rule:

> Our Italy
> Shines o'er with civil swords; Sextus Pompeius
> Makes his approaches to the port of Rome;
> Equality of two domestic powers
> Breed scrupulous faction; the hated, grown to strength,
> Are newly grown to love; the condemn'd Pompey,
> Rich in his father's honour, creeps apace
> Into the hearts of such as have not thrived
> Upon the present state, whose numbers threaten.
>
> [I. iii. 44-52]

But out of the strife engendered by oligarchy, monarchy is gradually emerging through a process of elimination. It had already been established in *Julius Caesar* that in the struggle for sovereignty Lepidus will play a negative part. In fact, he is clearly portrayed as a man completely out of his degree and vocation even as a triumvir, a man, as MacCallum points out, "attempting a part or role that is too big for him." . . . His credulous acceptance of Antony's stories of the crocodile discredits his wisdom; his incontinence is betrayed by the befuddled stupor in which his drinking leaves him; mercy and justice are denied by his cruelty at the proscriptions, which confirms Octavius' assertion:

> I have told him Lepidus was grown too cruel;
> That he his high authority abus'd,
> And did deserve his change.
>
> [III. vi. 32-4]

But it is the lack of the capacity for government and leadership which principally disqualifies Lepidus and is the character weakness directly responsible for his downfall. Some men are born to rule, the rest to obey, wrote theorists of the Renaissance, and Lepidus is clearly one of the latter. He may indeed, as Octavius says, be "a tried and valiant soldier," but the greater fortitude of will and purpose is not his. . . . Lepidus maintains his spineless role on into *Antony and Cleopatra*. There such diversified characters as Pompey, Enobarus, and Agrippa all recognize him as little more than a fawning sycophant. To the end he is merely a tool in the hands of more masterful men, for as Eros tells Enobarbus:

> Caesar, having made use of him in the wars
> 'gainst Pompey, presently denied him rivality,

would not let him partake in the glory of the action; and not resting here, accuses him of letters he had formerly wrote to Pompey; upon his own appeal, seizes him. So the poor third is up, till death enlarge his confine.

> [III. v. 7-12]

Sextus Pompeius constitutes a threat against the authority of the triumvirate and the monarchic aspirations of the triumvirs, but it is difficult to consider him a candidate for the imperial seat. Neither in what he seeks nor what he accepts is there any suggestion that his thoughts fly so high. As far as his political motivation goes, he seems rather to represent the final recrudescence of aristocratic republicanism. His expressed intent is to halt the course of Roman monarchy by restoring the discredited aristocratic state; this reason he associates with a desire for personal revenge for the death of his father, leader of the senatorial party, at the hands of the Caesarian party:

> What was 't
> That mov'd pale Cassius to conspire; and what
> Made the all-honour'd, honest Roman, Brutus,
> With the arm'd rest, courtiers of beauteous freedom,
> To drench the Capitol, but that they would
> Have one man but a man? And that is it
> Hath made me rig my navy, at whose burden
> The anger'd ocean foams; with which I meant
> To scourge the ingratitude that despiteful Rome
> Cast on my noble father.
>
> [II. vi. 14-23]

These are high-minded and sincere convictions, but Pompeius lacks the resolution necessary to establish them as facts. The treaty to which he agrees ruins the real advantages of power and situation which he possessed and paves the way for his downfall by strengthening further the hand of Octavius. Menas accurately identifies the flaw in the political character of Pompeius: "Who seeks, and will not take when once 'tis offer'd, Shall never find it more" [II. vii. 83-4]. So passes the last aristocratic threat to Roman monarchy, the last conflict of the old order with the new.

The contest for empire has resolved itself into a duel between Antony and Octavius. It cannot be said, of course, that Antony is ambitious for sole authority, but he has little active choice in the matter, for Octavius forces the issue on him. It would be futile to argue which is the greater, richer personality, which is more the master of sympathy and compassion, or which held the greater attraction as a dramatic character for Shakespeare. But it would be equally futile to argue which, from a rational political point of view, is destined to exercise monarchic sovereignty in the Roman state. Each possesses in a high degree those qualities and abilities which the Renaissance considered essential to the governor of a state. But Antony suffered a flaw which the Renaissance considered, with equal conviction, fatal to "the specialty of rule." To an analysis of this weakness itself the bulk of the play is devoted; here it will be considered in its political context alone. (pp. 189-93)

Renaissance thinkers concerned with the welfare of states were particularly insistent that in the head of a body politic reason must always rule over passion. It was argued that a man cannot govern others unless he can govern himself. As Erasmus expressed it:

> But you cannot be a king unless reason controls
> you; that is, unless under all circumstances you
> follow [the course of] advice and judgment.

You cannot rule over others until you yourself have obeyed the course of honor [*The Education of a Christian Prince*].

This doctrine was based in part on the conviction that the character of a people is determined by the character of a ruler. To quote Erasmus again:

The corruption of an evil prince spreads more swiftly and widely than the scourge of any pestilence. In the same proportion a wholesome life on the part of a prince is, without question, the quickest and shortest way to improve public morals. The common people imitate nothing with more pleasure than what they see their prince do. Under a gambler, gambling is rife; under a warrior, everyone is embroiled; under an epicure, all disport is wasteful luxury; under a debauché, license is rampant; under a cruel tyrant, everyone brings accusations and false witness. Go through your ancient history and you will find the life of the prince mirrored in the morals of his people. No comet, no dreadful power affects the progress of human affairs as the life of the prince grips and transforms the morals and character of his subjects.

But not only on these grounds of moral influence was passion condemned and the prince exhorted to exercise reason. Passion, and particularly sexual passion, was considered to have a devastating effect on the governing abilities of the ruler himself. Thus Sir Thomas Elyot, who defines continence as "a vertue whiche kepeth the pleasaunt appetite of man under the yoke of reason," places the quality prominently among those essential to a successful governor [in his *The Boke Named the Governour*]. George More, writing in 1611, thus warns against passion in any form:

A Prince to be too passionate and too cholerike is dangerous, for choller sometimes burneth and dryeth up the veines and taketh life, sometimes it blindeth the understanding, and taketh away sense and reason . . . for the mind doth not easily see the truth . . . where passion and affection beareth sway [in his *Principles for Young Princes*].

Specifically he admonishes "a Prince to bee continent in life," for excess of passion "will make him weak and effeminate, and destroyeth both body and soul, losing thereby also sometime both life and kingdom." He goes on to cite numerous historical examples—Locrine, Numidia, and Sophinisba among them—whose political ruin he can trace directly to the debilitating influence of incontinence.

Antony could well have been included among these instances. "For a life like his," MacCallum remarks, "is hardly compatible even in theory with the arduous functions of the commander, the governor, the administrator; and in practice it inevitably leads to their neglect." Each step in Antony's downward course from political power is explicitly linked with his infatuation for Cleopatra and its effect on his character as a leader of men. His fatal passion leads him to disregard political reason and to commit blunder after blunder; such missteps not only demonstrate his unfitness to govern but eventually accomplish his total ruin. At the very opening of the play his followers describe how infatuation is already destroying those abilities by means of which Antony rose to power; their story

is almost a paraphrase of More's warning to incontinent princes quoted above:

Nay, but this dotage of our general's
O'erflows the measure. Those his goodly eyes,
That o'er the files and musters of the war
Have glow'd like plated Mars, now bend, now turn,
The office and devotion of their view
Upon a tawny front; his captain's heart,
Which in the scuffles of great fights hath burst
The buckles on his breast, reneges all temper,
And is become the bellows and the fan
To cool a gipsy's lust.

[I. i. 1-10]

The same excess of passion which "o'er flows the measure" has driven out all concern for his country and the commonwealth, the first consideration of an acceptable ruler; Antony himself exclaims:

Let Rome in Tiber melt, and the wide arch
Of the rang'd empire fall! Here is my space.
Kingdoms are clay; our dungy earth alike
Feeds beast as man; the nobleness of life
Is to do thus.

[I. i. 33-7]

It is Antony's neglect of office which draws the severest condemnation from Octavius. The latter denounces his co-ruler's voluptuousness and consequent effeminacy principally in terms of their effect on the welfare of the state in time of crisis:

From Alexandria
This is the news: he fishes, drinks, and wastes
The lamps of night in revel; is not more manlike
Than Cleopatra: nor the queen of Ptolemy
More womanly than he; hardly gave audience, or
Vouchsaf'd to think he had partners.

[I. iv. 3-8]

Lepidus, as usual, would mediate, but Octavius continues, with accurate political insight:

You are too indulgent. Let's grant it is not
Amiss to tumble on the bed of Ptolemy;
To give a kingdom for a mirth; to sit
And keep the turn of tippling with a slave;
To reel the streets at noon, and stand the buffet
With knaves that smell of sweat: say this becomes him,—
        . . . yet must Antony
No way excuse his soils, when we do bear
So great weight in his lightness. If he fill'd
His vacancy with his voluptuousness,
Full surfeits and the dryness of his bones
Call on him for 't; but to confound such time
That drums him from his sport and speaks as loud
As his own state and ours, 'tis to be chid
As we rate boys, who, being mature in knowledge,
Pawn their experience to their present pleasure,
And so rebel to judgment.

[I. iv. 16-21, 23-33]

Antony himself is not always unaware of his weakness and of the disaster which it threatens to bring to his position. "These strong Egyptian fetters I must break, Or lose myself in dotage" [I. ii. 120], he exclaims early in the play, and in substance repeats on later occasions. But these moments of realization, while rational, are for the most part retrospective; in crucial action he is governed by his passion.

In dividing his portion of the empire to gratify Cleopatra, he gives Octavius added excuse to assume complete authority. In abandoning Octavia he commits another political blunder at the dictation of his infatuation, for Octavius seizes upon the deed as the immediate justification for overthrowing Antony. In the battles which follow, the military genius which could have saved him is vitiated by the influence of his passion for Cleopatra. Because of his feeling for her he blunders in planning and in execution. As a soldier says of the first phase, the fatal decision to fight by sea, ''our leader's led, And we are women's men'' [III. vii. 69-70]. And of the second phase, the disastrous flight from action, Antony himself laments, ''My sword, made weak by my affection, would Obey it on all cause'' [III. xi. 67-8]. To the end Antony's political failure is consistently described in these terms of Renaissance thinking about passion and reason in princes. Whatever his other qualifications, however brilliant his personality and character, his blunders, the result of his inability to rule himself, demonstrate that he is unfit to rule others. No clearer exposition of the Renaissance political principle involved in his downfall could be desired than that given by Enobarbus when he summarizes the whole situation after the battle of Actium. To Cleopatra's query, ''Is Antony or we in fault for this?'' he replies:

> Antony only, that would make his will
> Lord of his reason. What though you fled
> From that great face of war, whose several ranges
> Frighted each other? Why should he follow?
> The itch of his affection should not then
> Have nick'd his captainship, at such a point,
> When half to half the world oppos'd, he being
> The mered question. 'Twas a shame no less
> Than was his loss, to course your flying flags,
> And leave his navy gazing.
>
> [III. xiii. 2-12]

And so Octavius is left to bear the palm alone. He is perhaps an unappealing figure—if not the ''disagreeable, ugly, repulsive, colourless and passive instrument in the hands of destiny'' that [Paul] Stapfer portrays him to be [in his *Shakespeare and Classical Antiquity*], at least one of those of whom MacCallum says, ''The light from heaven never shines on their eyes either to glorify their path or to lead them astray.'' But political reason is clearly on his side. In critical commentary on both *Julius Caesar* and *Antony and Cleopatra*, inadequate emphasis has been given the significance of the fact that Octavius is the same emperor Augustus who was hailed in the Renaissance not only as the man under whom Roman monarchy was restored and civil tranquility established, but as the paragon of princes. Elyot, for example, cites his achievements to prove the necessity for monarchy, and his magnanimity, nobility, tolerance, frugality, and sobriety to illustrate the qualities of a successful prince. Augustus maintained this position in Renaissance political literature of the monarchic school throughout the century. He and his role in history came to symbolize the inevitability and justice of the monarchic form of the state. Shakespeare tempered the concept with realism, perhaps to set off by contrast the brilliance of his central character, but the essential conception of Octavius and the attitude toward him remain the same. It is evident in both plays that, dramatically uninteresting as he may be, Octavius succeeds over his rivals because he possesses those qualifications which, according to Renaissance political thinkers, make a great ruler.

The very characteristic which deprives him of dramatic appeal is one of his chief virtues as a governor. Unlike his great rival,

he allows his political reason to be swayed by no form of excess or passion. His sobriety is a commonplace in criticism of the plays in which he appears. The bacchanalian revels on shipboard are a source of genuine disgust to him:

> I could well forbear 't.
> It's monstrous labour when I wash my brain
> And it grows fouler. . . .
> But I had rather fast from all, four days,
> Than drink so much in one.
>
> [II. vii. 98-100, 102-03]

To one of his temperament affairs of state must be placed before such personal pleasures: ''Good brother, Let me request you off; our graver business Frowns at this levity'' [II. vii. 119-21]. In a similar way the excesses of Antony's passion, as has been noted, offend not only his private scruples but his political principles. No voluptuousness, no incontinence of this sort ''blindeth the understanding and taketh away sense and reason'' in Octavius.

There is a certain magnanimity and nobility of character which further qualifies Octavius for the exalted position which destiny holds for him. The virtue is particularly manifested in his attitude toward Cleopatra in the closing scenes of the play. He tells the Egyptian:

> Bid her have good heart.
> She soon shall know of us, by some of ours,
> How honourable and how kindly we
> Determine for her; for Caesar cannot live
> To be ungentle.
>
> [V. i. 56-60]

Elyot had cited the case of Augustus as an example of lack of vindictiveness in a ruler; Shakespeare's Octavius no less demonstrates the same compassion in victory. He tells the conquered queen:

> Take to you no hard thoughts.
> The record of what injuries you did us,
> Though written in our flesh, we shall remember
> As things but done by chance.
>
> [V. ii. 117-20]

And later:

> Cleopatra,
> Not what you have reserv'd, nor what acknowledg'd,
> Put we i' the roll of conquest. Still be 't yours,
> Bestow it at your pleasure. . . .
> Our care and pity is so much upon you,
> That we remain your friend; and so, adieu.
>
> [V. ii. 179-82, 188-89]

MacCallum believes Octavius' anxiety to exhibit Cleopatra in his triumph betrays an insincerity of feeling here, but it should be noted that her frustration of his schemes does not alter his admiration or prevent the funeral honors which he pays her in the end. The quality of magnanimity is again evident in his tribute to Antony. Political expediency and political justice alike demand that Antony be destroyed; Octavius is the instrument of this necessity, as he himself realizes, but he is generous enough in spirit to recognize the greatness of his victim; ''The breaking of so great a thing should make a greater crack,'' he exclaims upon hearing of Antony's death [V. i. 14-15]. The most accurate analysis of his attitude is his own:

> O Antony!
> I have followed thee to this; but we do lance
> Diseases in our bodies. I must perforce
> Have shown to thee such a declining day,

Or look on thine; we could not stall together
In the whole world: but yet let me lament,
With tears as sovereign as the blood of hearts,
That thou, my brother, my competitor
In top of all design, my mate in empire,
Friend and companion in the front of war,
The arm of mine own body, and the heart
Where mine his thoughts did kindle,—that our stars,
Unreconciliable, should divide
Our equalness to this.

                                        [V. i. 35-48]

But that which chiefly marks Octavius for "the specialty of rule" is his ability to act consistently with reference to a just and legitimate political cause, the welfare of the state which the restoration of the monarchy will accomplish. Personal ambition on his part cannot, of course, be denied, although explicit reference to selfish motives is significantly slight in both plays. Octavius himself is honestly convinced that his cause is right; he believes that he is directed by a divine destiny working for the highest good of Roman political society, and the political scheme of these plays, demonstrating the inevitability and necessity of monarchy, confirms him in this conception of his role. He describes himself in exactly those terms employed by Renaissance theorists to define the nature and function of the absolute monarch; to the abandoned Octavia he says, "the high gods, To do you justice, make them ministers Of us and those that love you" [III. vi. 87-9]. Each event in his career he interprets in terms of his destiny. Referring to his quarrel with Antony he tells Octavia:

Be you not troubled with the time, which drives
O'er your content these strong necessities;
But let determin'd things to destiny
Hold unbewail'd their way.

                                        [III. vi. 82-5]

When his position is established he asserts that it was never ordained by these higher forces that Rome should be governed by a dual authority; over the corpse of Antony he says, "We could not stall together in the whole world" [V. i. 39-40]. And even while lamenting "that our stars, unreconciliable, should divide our equalness to this" [V. i. 46-8], he clearly suggests that his own success in establishing monarchic sovereignty was dictated by this same destiny. Such an outcome, Octavius is certain, is for the highest good of the Roman commonwealth, for only under a monarchic government can that civil tranquility, the chief symptom of a healthy body politic, be attained. Thus just before the final and decisive victory which will establish his authority and end the disastrous civil wars, he exclaims:

The time of universal peace in near.
Prove this a prosperous day, the three-nook'd world
Shall bear the olive freely.

                                        [IV. vi. 4-6]

Octavius succeeds where others failed not only because he possesses adequate natural qualifications, but because he devotes every energy and subordinates every personal feeling to this political philosophy. His subjection of passion and indulgence to reason in this respect has already been observed. His love for his sister is genuine and profound, but, as he explains to her, her own content must be sacrificed to the higher destiny of Rome. He can break his covenant with Lepidus because the latter has endangered the welfare of the state; "Lepidus was grown too cruel . . . , he his high authority abus'd and did

deserve his change" [III. vi. 32, 33-4]. Similarly for political purposes he suppresses his regard for Antony the man and destroys Antony the political figure. Thus relentlessly he fulfills his own destiny and Rome's, so that in the end Thyreus can truly say that he "performs The bidding of the fullest man, and worthiest to have command obey'd" [III. xiii. 86-8].

It must be emphasized in conclusion that the foregoing analysis, for purposes of revealing more clearly a fundamental but oft-neglected aspect of the play, has been developed purely in the perspective of Renaissance political theory. This is by no means to claim that political action occupies a position of more than incidental importance in the play. But it is to claim that subordinate as it is, the political action is an organic part of this drama of splendid passion. Much has been written of the world which Antony well lost for love; little has been written of the nature of that world, or of the integral structural relationship of that loss to the tragedy as a whole. Certainly the grandeur of Antony's love is enhanced by his forfeit of empire. But the tragedy of his passion for Cleopatra is enhanced because this forfeit was no merely noble gesture, no hollow flaunting of Antony's disregard for worldly power. His loss is the inevitable consequence of his infatuation, whether he willed that loss or not. "Not Caesar's valour hath o'erthrown Antony, But Antony's hath triumph'd on itself" [IV. xv. 14-15]. His tragedy in part represents the inexorable working of fundamental laws of political and social conduct which the Renaissance well understood.

With the accession of Octavius as Augustus at the end of *Antony and Cleopatra* the cycle which began with *Caesar* is complete. . . . Out of the welter of divided and conflicting authorities emerges the one man who, according to the political standards of the Renaissance, is qualified to be the natural head of the Roman body politic. With nothing to indicate that the promise of civil peace and order will not be fulfilled, the political action of *Antony and Cleopatra*, unlike that of the earlier play, can end conclusively and happily, for the normal state-structure has been reestablished. (pp. 194-205)

> *James Emerson Phillips, Jr., "The Monarchic Cycle in 'Julius Caesar' and 'Antony and Cleopatra',' in his* The State in Shakespeare's Greek and Roman Plays, *Columbia University Press, 1940, pp. 172-205.*

DAVID CECIL (lecture date 1943)

[*Cecil was an English critic and biographer. His most significant contributions to literary criticism were his publications on nineteenth-century English novelists. His commentary on* Antony and Cleopatra *excerpted below was first delivered as a lecture at the University of Glasgow in 1943. Cecil believes that the historico-political aspect of the play—specifically the rivalry between Antony and Octavius—is the premier element, but he contends that the love story is integral and "inseparably connected" to the larger picture. The central thematic question, he contends, is what kind of man will succeed in "the struggle for power and happiness"; and he further argues that Shakespeare is profoundly doubtful and ironic about whether "worldly success [is] really worth having." The dramatist is intentionally ambiguous, Cecil claims, as to the "judgment of Antony's conduct," leaving us to decide whether his sacrifice of political power for love of Cleopatra was "right or wrong." Additionally, the critic maintains, Shakespeare has chosen to represent the dramatic action as predestined and the principle figures as "no more than puppets in the fingers of a mysterious and irresistible fate." Just as the Soothsayer accurately predicts what will happen, Cecil asserts, the dramatist himself has made it clear from the beginning that Octavius will triumph over Antony—that the latter will sacrifice his political preeminence for Cleopatra—and thus the structure of the play deliberately lacks dramatic suspense.*]

There is no formula for a Shakespeare play. He does anything he likes, changes the scene, varies the characters, digresses from the main theme, is comic or tragic, or poetic just as it suits his conception of his story. Nor does he mould his plot into any accepted pattern of correct play-making. If we are to appreciate him properly therefore, we must free our minds from any pre-conceived ideas of what drama ought to be. For he observes no laws other than those which his taste dictates to suit each particular subject he chooses. This is true of all his plays. But in none is he so audaciously lawless as in *Antony and Cleopatra*. It is the most virtuosic of all his performances; that in which, arrived as he was at the full maturity of his superb technical accomplishment, he stretches the capacities of his form to the most daring limits. Never was he so dazzlingly original, either in conception or execution. No wonder that orthodox critics have been bewildered; no wonder they are worried that it fails to fit into any of their categories of tragedy or love-story or drama. For it is none of these things. It is the single unique example of its species. (p. 7)

It is all nonsense, I may say in passing, to suggest that [Shakespeare] dramatised the story just as it came, in chronicle fashion. He leaves a lot of Plutarch out, and what he leaves in, he often alters. Clearly, there is a deliberate purpose behind his treatment. What was it? The first thing to be said about it is that it is different from that of any other writer—there are a great many of them—who has tried to make a play out of the same story. These others concentrated exclusively on the love-story. Not so Shakespeare. With him the love-story is seen always in relation to the rivalry between Octavius and Antony. A large part of the play is concerned with this only, and not with the love-story at all. We see Antony with Octavius and Pompey and his soldiers quite as much as we see him with Cleopatra. We also see Pompey, Octavius and the soldiers by themselves, without Antony. Shakespeare conceives his play as a piece of history; its interest is largely political.

In this it is of a piece with his other Roman plays. The Roman tragedies differ from the other tragedies, in that they are concerned, not so much with man's private inner life, as with his life in the theatre of public affairs. . . . The Roman plays deal with human beings; but human beings in their external and political aspect, with the clash of character in action on the public stage. Not which side of the hero's nature will prevail, but which person or group of persons will prevail in the political struggle, is the issue presented for our attention. Coriolanus is pitted against the people of Rome; Julius Caesar's murderers are pitted against Octavius and Antony. In these plays the public nature of the drama is obvious. It is not so obvious in *Antony and Cleopatra*. Here there is more private life. But the private life is, as it were, a consequence of the public life. *Antony and Cleopatra* completes the story begun in *Julius Caesar*. The end of *Julius Caesar* left Octavius and Antony sole rivals for the mastery of the Roman Empire after their victory over Brutus and Cassius. Naturally they come into conflict. This conflict between them dictates the general lines on which Shakespeare's play is designed. But history relates that Antony was defeated in it because of his love for Cleopatra. Now this brings in a new element. Love is an extremely private emotion. If Shakespeare means to do justice to it he must leave the theatre of public life during a large part of his play. All the same the love-story is only one feature in a bigger picture. Always as Shakespeare saw it, it is related to the public drama,

and is inseparably connected with it. Its nature would be essentially altered were it to be transferred to a private setting. If Antony and Cleopatra had been private persons, their story simply could not have happened.

His public character is further emphasised by the fashion in which Shakespeare conceives his characters. They are people of action, not thinkers or philosophers. They never withdraw, like Hamlet, to contemplate their story from a detached point of view; and to draw conclusions from it about human life in general. Octavius may let fall a sentence about the inevitability of fate: "But let determined things to destiny hold unbewailed their way" [III. vi. 84-5]. Having said this, however, he continues his career of crafty political scheming. Neither he nor anyone else questions the value of the sort of life they live. Antony, it is true, sacrifices his power to his love for Cleopatra. But he does not do it deliberately. He is so besotted with Cleopatra he cannot give her up; and he deludes himself into thinking that he can somehow manage to have her and political power at once. The very splendour and spaciousness of his mode of life narrowed his vision as it narrows that of his rival. Set high on the throne of the whole known world, the awe and admiration of mankind, they do not doubt that the world's standards are the right standards.

Further, they do not think it right to disregard the impression that their behaviour makes on others. Always they are influenced by the consciousness that they are public persons. Even in the final catastrophe of the play, Antony feels himself driven to suicide, partly because he believes Cleopatra to have killed herself, and he cannot bear to live without her, but still more because she has shewn him the right way for a great man to conduct himself before the world in disaster. With his last breath he expresses his pride that he has been able to do this.

> The miserable change now at my end
> Lament nor sorrow at; but please your thoughts
> In feeding them with those my former fortunes
> Wherein I liv'd, the greatest prince o' the world,
> The noblest; and do now not basely die,
> Not cowardly put off my helmet to
> My countryman; a Roman by a Roman
> Valiantly vanquish'd. Now my spirit is going;
> I can no more.
>
> [IV. xv. 51-9]

Cleopatra is still more dominated by the thought of the figure she cuts. She resolves to kill herself when Antony dies; but she cannot bring herself to do it till she realises that otherwise she will be led publicly in triumph through the streets of Rome. No doubt this is lamentable evidence of her vanity, as her severely-principled critics have not failed to point out. Antony too is vain. But their regard for their reputations is not due only to ignoble motives. It is the inevitable consequence of the light in which they regarded their own position. They are what the Elizabethan calls "great persons"; it was the duty of great persons to behave as such, to take into consideration when deciding on a course of action the impression it would make on the huge audience before whom their lives were acted out. The play is about Kings and Queens and Emperors. They realise it themselves; and Shakespeare means us to realise it too.

Not that it is a play about kingship or imperialism. Shakespeare, as far as we can tell from his work, was not interested in abstract principles. Politics to him meant politicians. History, as he saw it, was the history of individual human beings. The fact that Cleopatra was a queen interested Shakespeare only in so far as it modified her personal character. The clash between Antony and Octavius stirs his attention not as the clash between two different causes, but as the clash between two different sorts of men. He is always striving to penetrate through his characters' official personalities to find the human being. We see the drama of the great world behind the scenes. And "Look", Shakespeare seems to say to us, "look, I will show you what these famous people, whom you only see from a distance, seem like close at hand; this is the sort of life they lead—this is the sort of motive that actuates them." *Antony and Cleopatra* is a study in the life of the great political world, as it shewed itself to one interested in individual human nature. Incidentally, the story must have seemed far more realistic and topical in Shakespeare's day than now. In a monarchial and courtly age, personality and personal feeling counted for a great deal in politics. . . . There is of course no question of *Antony and Cleopatra* being a play about contemporary events under an historical guise. But it can be taken that Shakespeare's omnivorous curiosity was directed at this time to the great world of public affairs; and that this play is the result of his cogitations on the subject.

The character of his picture is further determined by the interpretation he puts on Plutarch's story. To Shakespeare this story was inevitably predestined. Here again his version is different from that given by other writers. These presented it as turning on an uncertain conflict between Antony's love and his political ambition. Antony could have chosen to give up Cleopatra; if he had, he would then have overcome Octavius. As Shakespeare saw the matter there was no question of this. Antony's character made it impossible. He is presented as a typical Elizabethan "great man", brilliant and confident, audacious and unscrupulous, a brave soldier, a subtle diplomat, and with that personal magnetism that, without effort, compels the hearts of his followers. Even cynical Enobarbus loves him; when he publicly bids farewell to his soldiers, he brings tears to every eye. Was he not the same Antony that had won over the people of Rome, after the murder of Caesar, by a single speech? But the very fact that he could achieve success so easily had stopped him from ever learning self-discipline. He is a profoundly self-indulgent character. Trusting to his natural gifts to carry him through a crisis, he had never taught himself to subdue an immediate desire in order to achieve a further end; with the result that he always evaded making the decision between the claims of his public career and his private feelings. He might leave Cleopatra for a time, when things looked bad. But when they looked better again and he began to grow bored, back he went to her. Surely, he told himself, a man of his personality could keep his power and Cleopatra as well. Gradually this habit of mind grew so strong that he gave in to it even when his wiser self had begun to suspect that the issue was not so certain. He fights at sea against his better judgment just because she wants him to; when she flees from the battle, he follows her. It was not that love blinds him to her true character. He realises only too well that she was so unstable that he could not trust her to be consistently loyal to her love for him, let alone to give a sound impartial political judgment. But he had yielded to her so often that now he was incapable of putting up any resistance, however important the issue. The odds against him were further lengthened by the fact that Octavius, as Shakespeare conceived him, was just the opposite kind of man, far-sighted, cool, self-controlled, and so single-mindedly intent on the achievement of his ambition, that nothing, neither the happiness of his sister nor a genuine feeling of pity for Antony in his fall, can turn him from it. When, at the end, Cleopatra tries her charms on Octavius, he appreciates them—"her strong

toil of grace" he speaks of [V. ii. 348]—but he does not succumb to them for an instant. If such are the elements in the situation, its outcome is clear. Octavius must defeat Antony.

But there are hints that Shakespeare looked on his end as determined by greater forces even than these innate qualities of the actors. Early in the play into the frivolous worldly atmosphere of Court and Council Chamber he introduces the strange figure of the soothsayer. Ostensibly he is only a tame fortune-teller hanging about the Court for the entertainment of idle people. Nobody seems to take his predictions very seriously. They are wrong. When Cleopatra's ladies ask him about their future, in occult terms the soothsayer foretells their dreadful end. And when Antony casually asks him whether he or Octavius is likely to get the better of the other, he replies:

> . . . stay not by his side;
> Thy demon—that's thy spirit which keeps thee,—is
> Noble, courageous, high, unmatchable,
> Where Caesar's is not; but near him thy angel
> Becomes a fear, as being o'erpowered; therefore
> Make space enough between you.
>   ANTHONY.   Speak this no more.
>   SOOTHSAYER. To none but thee; no more but when to
>   thee.
> If thou dost play with him at any game
> Thou art sure to lose, and, of that natural luck,
> He beats thee 'gainst the odds; thy lustre thickens

Act III. Scene xi. Antony, Eros, Charmian, Cleopatra, and Iras. By J. H. F. Bacon.

When he shines by. I say again, thy spirit
Is all afraid to govern thee near him,
But he away, 'tis noble.

[II. iii. 19-31]

Destiny, so Shakespeare suggests, a supernatural destiny is
working behind the visible scene to promote its secret purpose.
These great persons, apparently so powerful, and with the
world at their feet, are in reality no more than puppets in the
fingers of a mysterious and irresistible fate. The personal drama
is seen as part of a huge impersonal historical process.

It is, surely, an unusual subject for a play—a wedge of political
history in which every event is represented as inevitable.
Shakespeare invents a very unusual form to fit it. He takes
every advantage of the freedom allowed to an Elizabethan
dramatist. There is not a rule of conventional play-making he
does not break. For one thing, he begins the story in the middle.
The ordinary dramatist would have started with the meeting of
Antony and Cleopatra, and worked it up to a dramatic crisis,
in which Antony would decide between his love and his ambition. The last section of the play would relate the consequences of this decision. Such a plan does not fit Shakespeare's
interpretation of the story. He therefore begins when Antony,
already caught up in Cleopatra's toils, first suspects that his
political position is endangered. He goes back to Rome, makes
it up with Octavius, and marries Octavia, but decides all the
same to return to Cleopatra. This is the first section of the
play. When the third act begins he is back in Egypt; and Octavius has already broken with him. The rest of the play traces
in detail the gradual process of Octavius's victory. But there
is no rise and fall of the hero's fortunes. The play opens with
Antony poised at the top of a slope as it were. After a little
uncertainty, he begins to slide down, and then proceeds faster
and faster until he reaches the bottom. The play would have
been better entitled *"The Decline and Fall of Antony"*. Shakespeare deliberately renounces the possibilities of dramatic suspense offered by the plot. Moreover, so far from keeping out
in the dark as to what is going to happen, he forewarns us of
it in the second act. When Antony has broken with Cleopatra,
Shakespeare goes out of his way to introduce a scene in which
Enobarbus states that this breach is not likely to be a final one.

MECAENAS. Now Antony must leave her utterly.
ENOBARBUS. Never; he will not:
Age cannot wither her, nor custom stale
Her infinite variety; . . .

[II. ii. 232-35]

The Soothsayer, too, explains that Octavius is fated always to
overcome him. Antony's rivalry with Octavius and his love
for Cleopatra—these are the two questions with which the plot
is concerned; and the answers to both are made clear from the
first. That both Cleopatra and Octavius will prevail is presented
to us as axiomatic: we are meant to start off taking them for
granted. Shakespeare is so little interested in the more obvious
dramatic possibilities of the story, that he does not even make
the most of any crisis that does occur in his version of it. There
are three turning points in the action of the first two acts.
Antony leaves Egypt to go to Rome; he comes back to Cleopatra; Octavius breaks with him. The first of these, his farewell
to Cleopatra, is presented deliberately in a light vein, without
any heightening of the dramatic tension; neither of the other
two takes place on the stage at all. We are told about them,
after they have happened. As Shakespeare sees it, what happened is too obvious to be interesting. He is concerned with
how it happened. He wishes to show the effect of events on

character, to trace in what way their declining fortunes gradually affected Antony, Cleopatra, and their followers. Always
we see the actors close up, before critical events take place,
and afterwards; Antony before he leaves Egypt, and after he
returns to it; Octavius before he breaks with Antony and after
the breach. Only at the last, when events are rising to their
final climax, does decisive action take place on the stage. The
drama of the decline and fall of Antony groups itself into three
sections. In the first two acts the situation is expounded to us,
in the third and part of the fourth we follow the process of
decline, and still more its effect on the actors. The last section
exhibits in detail the incidents of that catastrophe which is the
logical outcome of all that has gone before.

The form of the play is further conditioned by the fact that
Shakespeare envisages it as a piece of history. Since it is a
play about the great world of affairs, this great world must be
kept in view. In order to do this, Shakespeare again makes use
of the Elizabethan freedom. He moves the scene about all over
the Roman world. Now we are in Rome, now we are in Egypt,
now in Sicily; for a moment we are wafted to Parthia. With
diversity of scene goes diversity of character. The stage is
crowded with those humbler persons whose fortunes depend
on those of the principal actors—courtiers, soldiers, council-
lors. Never once do the lovers appear alone with each other.
Round them hover Antony's staff, Cleopatra's ladies and eunuchs. We are constantly kept in mind of the public nature of
the subject; we are never intended to forget that Antony's defeat
will prove a disaster to all who have ranged themselves under
his banner. And we see both him and Cleopatra as they appear
to the world. When the great persons leave the scene, the lesser
ones stay behind and make their cynical or enthusiastic comments on them.

This historical attitude to his subject is also responsible for the
fact that the play is so much more varied in mood than are
Shakespeare's regular tragedies. A convincing picture of the
great world cannot be steeped in the consistently tragic atmosphere which envelops *King Lear*. To a detached observer,
the life of the great world is never consistently tragic; it is an
extraordinary compound of sad and comic, prosaic and poetic.
So is Shakespeare's play. There is a great deal of comedy in
it; ranging from the farcical humour of the clown, who brings
the means of death to Cleopatra—ironically this illustrates how
little the great and their misfortunes mean to the humble—to
the cool satire of the scene on Pompey's galley, when "the
third part of the world" [II. vii. 91] is carried drunk to bed.
For these great people, as Shakespeare sees them, are far from
being as dignified as they wish to appear. Cleopatra herself,
during the first half of the play, is a comedy figure, with her
petty feminine vanity, her childish lack of self-control. Even
at the end, when she is on the point of killing herself, she cuffs
her treasurer in a fit of temper because he gives away the fact
that she has been trying to deceive Octavius as to the real
amount of her treasure. Yet, mingled with all this comedy is
the grave statesman's wisdom of the political drama, the tragic
pathos of Enobarbus' end, the passionate lyrical beauty of the
love scenes, the supernatural mystery of the soothsayer scenes,
or that in which the soldiers hear the fading unearthly music
which betokens the departure of the god Hercules, who had,
up to then, protected Antony's fortunes; while over all glows
the light of Shakespeare's sense of the romance inherent in
grand historic events.

Looked at from the right angle then, those features of Shakespeare's play which have bewildered his critics appear clear

and explicable. They are the logical consequence of the way in which he sees his subject. He envisages it less as a drama than as a panorama. Yet, to recognise this is not to prove the critics wrong in their feeling of dissatisfaction. After all, *Antony and Cleopatra* sets out to be a work of art; and a panorama and a work of art are not the same thing. A work of art must have unity, pattern, significance; a panorama need have none of these things. It is Shakespeare's triumph that he does manage to make his panorama into a work of art. For the incoherent heterogeneous material which is his subject-matter is all made to relate to a single presiding theme. This theme is not love; it is success. This fact is the master-key to the riddle of the play. Shakespeare looks at the chaotic spectacle of the great world convulsed in the struggle for power and happiness; and, he asks "What sort of man is successful in it?" Seen in relation to this steady canon of judgment, all the confused variety of his subject falls into proportion and significance. Shakespeare puts his question from various points of view. First of all, he asks, "Which candidate is likely to gain command of the Roman Empire?" Lepidus? No!—he is a weak fool. Pompey? No!—too scrupulous or too timid, he refuses his one chance of getting rid of his competitors when he has them at his mercy. The real test is between Antony and Octavius, Antony the gifted, instinctive, leader of men, or Octavius, the prudent, far-sighted statesman. There is no doubt about Shakespeare's answer. For good or for ill, it is the Octaviuses who get their way in this world.

But Shakespeare does not stop here. To so profound a mind as his, the achievement of worldly power cannot be a final test of success. He goes on to ask, "Is worldly success really worth having?" Shakespeare's unillusioned examination of the story has made him very doubtful. A profound irony colors the scene. Certainly worldly success is not necessarily a proof of worthy service. This is the lesson taught us by the odd little scene in Parthia. Ventidius it is, who is doing Rome real service by defeating her enemies. But he is not a candidate for the throne. On the contrary, he is only too well aware that his very victories may do his career harm, by arousing the jealousy of his master. Again, to sacrifice all to worldly considerations may involve the loss of happiness. Consider the case of Enobarbus. He serves Antony loyally as long as he thinks Antony has a chance of victory. But when he deliberately throws this away from self-indulgent motives, Enobarbus feels justified in leaving him. He cannot be blamed; but, in the event, it proves a terrible mistake. For he loves Antony. Tortured by what he feels to be his treachery, he dies of a broken heart.

But the crucial issue is, of course, that exhibited by Antony's own story. Was he right or wrong in yielding to love rather than to political ambition? Shakespeare is rigorously impartial on the subject. The world of public life is not shewn to us in an ideal light. On the contrary, it is a seething whirlpool of competition and intrigue in which everyone is more or less unscrupulous and no one is wholly disinterested. Antony and Caesar alike are actuated less by a sense of duty, than by the desire to cut a great figure in the world. Yet Shakespeare's attitude is not wholly unsympathetic. For he shared the Elizabethan belief in personal greatness. He thought it natural to want to cut a figure. Like Tamburlaine, he felt it was brave to be a king and ride in triumph through Persepolis. Moreover Antony and Caesar are superior spirits. Shakespeare believed that a superior spirit rightly desires dominion and magnificence. The love-story is presented in an equally impartial way. Neither Antony nor Cleopatra is an ideal figure. They are both middle-aged. Antony's love is a self-indulgent passion that weakens his will and blinds his judgment. While Cleopatra is, by a strict moral standard, a vain, worthless, capricious coquette who does not care in the least about the true interests of her lover, and who is so dominated by the desire to attract that she cannot be faithful to him for half-an-hour once his back is turned. Yet in spite of all, the figures of both are resplendent with romance. Antony is a true king of men, with his charm and his generosity, his courage and rich vein of poetry. As for Cleopatra, she is simply the sorceress of the world. Who could resist such vitality, such grace, such temperament, such wit, so exquisite and unquenchable a sense of pleasure? And their love—how insipid most passions appear in comparison with this leaping, burning, many-coloured fire, aromatic with all the imperial seductiveness of Shakespeare's mature poetic style. Such a love for such a woman is worth weighing in the balance against the empire of the whole known world. "The nobleness of life is to do thus," says Antony [I. i. 36-7] as he kisses her. Are we so sure he is wrong?

Thus Shakespeare states his problem. But himself he gives no answer. Olympian, and enigmatic, he presents us with the evidence and leaves us to judge. It is this ambiguity, I suspect, which has, in reality, given the critics their feeling of dissatisfaction. People often think themselves displeased with a work of art when, in fact, they are displeased with the man who created it. Critics, most of them, are moralists who judge, first of all, by standards of right and wrong. Artists often are not. Artists seldom are the same sort of people as critics—that is why so much criticism is inept. Shakespeare was not a moralist. He appreciated goodness, and disliked evil; but he did not approach life primarily from the moral point of view. He was an observer, and an aesthete. Life interested him passionately: and what stirred him most in it was its beauty, its delightfulness, its power to appeal to the senses, the heart, the imagination. Observation made him unillusioned; appreciation made him romantic; disillusionment and sense of romance combined in an ironical zest for the spectacle of the world, often incompatible with a decisive moral judgment. Some of his most memorable characters—those in which we feel he is expressing his most fundamental sense of values—leave the reader's moral judgment somehow in suspense. . . . So it is with Antony. . . . [Shakespeare] states all the facts. And his conclusion seems to be that it is impossible to be certain in our judgment of Antony's conduct.

The moralistic critic finds such uncertainty painful. To him, a world in which he cannot be sure whom to praise, whom to blame is a disheartening place, whose apparent glories must be suspect. But Shakespeare is only disheartened by a world without glory, a world which weakens his gusto for living. In his darkest mood, he has shown us such a world. But this is not the mood which informs *Antony and Cleopatra*. On the contrary, in it Shakespeare teaches us that it is possible to face life at its most baffling and imperfect and unideal, and yet to find it inextinguishably enthralling and splendid. It is a lesson well worth learning. (pp. 8-24)

> *David Cecil, " 'Antony and Cleopatra'," in his* Poets and Story-Tellers: A Book of Critical Essays, *Constable, 1949, p. 1-24.*

S. L. BETHELL   (essay date 1944)

[*The excerpt below is taken from* Shakespeare and the Popular Dramatic Tradition, *first published in 1944. Bethell asserts that* Antony and Cleopatra *dramatizes the opposition of such Egyptian values as love, pleasure, indulgence, intuition, "spontaneous af-*

fections,'' ''expansive morality,'' and generosity and such Roman values as duty, restraint, reason, ''worldly wisdom or practical common sense,'' ''restrictive morality,'' and prudence. Antony must choose between these value systems, the critic argues, but Shakespeare is careful to invest the play's ''sharply contrasted'' worlds with equal measures of dignity and grandeur and—by virtue of metaphoric language throughout the drama—endow the theme of love with the same cosmic significance as the theme of empire. Bethell contends that Cleopatra is a crystallization of Egyptian values—''not so much a character as an extended metaphysical conceit''—a paradoxical figure in whom opposites are fused, but, above all, a symbol of immortal love and beauty. Shakespeare affirms Antony's choice of the Egyptian values, Bethell concludes, for these provide the basis for ''the good life''; however, he remarks, the dramatist also shows that it is through such ''better Roman qualities'' as ''deprivation and denial'' that Antony and Cleopatra attain a state of eternal grace.]

Antony and Cleopatra has been treated the least kindly of Shakespeare's great tragedies, with the possible exceptions of *Coriolanus* and *Timon of Athens*. The general outcry has been against its loose construction: Dr. Johnson, admitting the play's 'variety', thought that the events were 'produced without any art of connection or care of disposition' [see excerpt above, 1765]. Professor Schücking also deplores 'a decided falling off' in the handling of the plot [see excerpt above, 1919]. He instances the scene on Pompey's galley, where the drinking song (he believes) 'completely *isolates the scene*, detaching it from the context of the whole in a manner which is unequalled even in Shakespeare'. These charges, both general and particular, have been adequately rebutted in Mr. Granville-Barker's *Preface* [see excerpt above, 1930], where the tight and balanced construction is closely analysed, and the blame transferred from Shakespeare to those editors who, thinking in terms of localised scenes, produced an incredible number of them out of Shakespeare's properly indivisible text. The play is now seen to be a careful pattern of interwoven and contrasting episodes, all duly subordinate to the main design: the presentation of Antony and Cleopatra in the broad context of the Roman Empire.

A more serious problem is presented to the critics by apparent inconsistencies in psychology, and a general failure to adhere to Aristotelian precepts. Even the revolutionary critics are troubled. Professor Schücking feels a sharp discontinuity in the presentation of Cleopatra, between the royal courtezan of the earlier scenes, and the tragic queen who in the end chooses death rather than to be the victim of a Roman triumph. Professor Stoll [see excerpt above, 1928] finds the characters nobler than their deeds, or their love 'greater than their natures', and ascribes this, somewhat vaguely, to poetic and dramatic factors; whilst Mr. Granville-Barker suggests that we are concerned with great action rather than psychology. . . . It remains true that, regarding the play psychologically, one cannot reconcile the vicious, the vulgar, and the commonplace in Antony and Cleopatra, with the sublimity with which they are invested, especially as they face defeat and death. With a naturalistic approach to character, one might well regard Antony as a licentious old ruffian whose political and military talents are forfeited through lust; and Cleopatra as the Egyptian harlot, shameless, selfish, cowardly and sex-obsessed. Their transformation in the end would then appear psychologically inconsistent, an unworthy dramatic trick to dodge the moral issue—implying a sort of conversion without repentance, or perhaps the glorification of splendid vice.

In any event, it is quite clear that we are not intended to think of Antony and Cleopatra as a lecher and a strumpet—or only in a strictly qualified sense. To do justice to Shakespeare, we

must radically alter our critical approach, and begin—and end—with the poetry itself. What everybody has noticed in the verse of *Antony and Cleopatra* is its Brobdingnagian imagery: objects of tremendous size and power are constantly utilised to illustrate some quality of character or situation. The employment of such imagery is not limited to one or two personages in the play, but is characteristic of them all. There is, in fact, no attempt to differentiate characters by the verse they speak, except to some extent with Octavius Caesar, whose verse is normally dull and flat and impersonal, or else staccato as he issues orders. But when he speaks of Antony, or Cleopatra, or the Empire, his verse too takes on the grandeur and dignity met with in the others: e.g. his description of Antony's military asceticism:

> . . . on the Alps
> It is reported thou didst eat strange flesh,
> Which some did die to look on;
>
> [I. iv. 66-8]

and his speech on Antony's death is in the same high strain. This pervading suggestion of size and strength and importance, conveys the imperial theme and the dignity of the persons involved. But it is more precisely informative than this. In the first scene, for example, the Romans watch in disgust as Antony, Cleopatra, and their Egyptian train, pass by. Philo, thinking of the old Antony, remembers

> . . . those his goodly eyes,
> That o'er the files and musters of the war
> Have glow'd like plated Mars . . .
>
> [I. i. 2-4]

Antony has since become false to his position in the Empire:

> Take but good note, and you shall see in him
> The triple pillar of the world transform'd
> Into a strumpet's fool.
>
> [I. i. 1-13]

And then we hear Antony and Cleopatra:

Ant: There's beggary in the love that can be reckon'd.
Cleo: I'll set a bourn how far to be beloved.
Ant: Then must thou needs find out new heaven, new earth.
> [I. i. 15-17]

The lovers speak of their love in the same large way in which Philo speaks of Antony the general, or Antony the triumvir. If he is 'the triple pillar of the world', their love is even greater, for this world cannot contain it: the new heaven and new earth of apocalyptic vision are alone adequate to circumscribe it. This speech in the first minute of the play looks forward to the 'husband, I come' [V. ii. 287] of Cleopatra in her triumphant death—an instance of the close unity of Shakespeare's poetic conception. What I must immediately note, however, is the application, here and throughout the play, of the same colossal imagery—the world, the heavenly bodies, the gods, etc.—to the theme of empire and the theme of love. It is a deliberate equation, for these themes are conjoined too frequently for accident. Even Scarus, after the sea-fight, exclaims:

> The greater cantle of the world is lost
> With very ignorance; we have kiss'd away
> Kingdoms and provinces—
>
> [III. x. 6-8]

'kiss'd' as the verb; 'kingdoms and provinces', the object of the verb: in this way, by purely literary means, we are compelled to feel Cleopatra's love as quite commensurable with the honours of war and statecraft against which it must be weighed. The lovers' ceremoniousness with one another—always 'my queen' and 'my lord'—strengthens the dignity of their love. . . . [The] poetic building-up process is continuous. Even the lovers' oaths bring the theme of world empire into the context of passionate love:

> Let Rome in Tiber melt, and the wide arch
> Of the ranged empire fall!
>
> [I. i. 33-4]

> Melt Egypt into Nile!
>
> [II. v. 78]

> Sink Rome, and their tongues rot
> That speak against us!
>
> [III. vii. 15-16]

While the two themes of love and empire are thus paralleled in power and grandeur, they are at the same time sharply contrasted as conflicting alternatives presented to Antony's choice. The contrast is geographically expressed, as between East and West, or Egypt and Rome. 'Cleopatra' and 'Egypt' are almost synonymous: as 'Egypt' [III. xi. 5-6] she is upbraided for her desertion, and she is addressed as 'Egypt'' in passionate reconciliation later:

> I am dying, Egypt, dying . . .
>
> [IV. xv. 18]

Octavius Caesar stands for the Roman qualities, as Cleopatra does for the Egyptian. Octavia is the translation of Rome into woman: on the level of character as well as plot, she is a projection of the theme of empire into the theme of love:

> Octavia is of a holy, cold, and still conversation.
>
> [II. vi. 122-23]
> (pp. 116-20)

Egypt and Rome are thus opposed throughout the play: they represent contradictory schemes of value, contradictory attitudes to, and interpretations of, the universe. It is difficult to isolate these opposed systems in a brief space without appearing to dogmatise, and the reader must understand that a great many supporting quotations have been omitted in order to reduce the argument into a reasonable compass. The whole play should be read with the opposition of Egyptian and Roman values in mind. First, then, Egypt and Rome stand respectively for love and duty, or for pleasure and duty, or even love-pleasure and duty. Supporting quotations are hardly necessary here: Cleopatra embodies the love-pleasure principle, of which the 'Roman thought' [I. ii. 83], the call to duty, is the negation. Closely related to this is the opposition of indulgence and restraint: in Egypt 'Epicurean cooks' [II. i. 24] provided breakfasts as horrifying to Mecaenas as to the modern mind. Caesar is not at home in carousals:

> . . . our graver business
> Frowns at this levity,
>
> [II. vii. 120-21]

he says. Antony's men must drink deep before the battle:

> . . . to-night I'll force
> The wine peep through their scars—
>
> [III. xiii. 189-90]

but Caesar allows a feast after due consideration of supplies:

> And feast the army; we have store to do't,
> And they have earn'd the waste.
>
> [IV. i. 15-16]

'Waste' is a significant word here, and the contrast is forced home by wedging this brief scene in Caesar's camp between two larger scenes with the forces of Antony.

More generally—and more philosophically—we have in the contrast between Egypt and Rome, the old opposition with which Shakespeare was concerned in the comedies and in *Troilus and Cressida*, between 'intuition' and 'reason'; on the one hand the final authority of the spontaneous affections, on the other the authority of worldly wisdom or practical common sense (Caesar is very like Ulysses in general outline). Antony had made, says Enobarbus,

> . . . his will
> Lord of his reason.
>
> [II. xiii. 3-4]

He clings to Cleopatra against all sober judgment (Act III, Scene xiii); he is familiar and a little sentimental with his faithful followers (Act IV, Scene ii); and heaps coals of fire upon Enobarbus (Act IV, Scenes v and vi); he is prepared to meet Caesar in single combat [III. xiii. 25]. Caesar is cold and calculating: for reasons of state he will give up his apparently beloved sister to the lecherous old Antony, and in full and disapproving knowledge of Antony's mode of life:

> Let us grant, it is not
> Amiss to tumble on the bed of Ptolemy;
> To give a kingdom for a mirth; to sit
> And keep the turn of tippling with a slave;
> To reel the streets at noon, and stand the buffet
> With knaves that smell of sweat.
>
> [I. iv. 16-21]

He has a low opinion of the people:

> This common body,
> Like to a vagabond flag upon the stream,
> Goes to and back, lackeying the varying tide,
> To rot itself with motion.
>
> [I. iv. 44-7]

Caesar would never be betrayed into Antony's abandonment of the solid benefits of the triumvirate. He will not be tempted into bravado by Antony's challenge:

> . . . let the old ruffian know
> I have many other ways to die; meantime
> Laugh at his challenge.
>
> [IV. i. 4-6]

Faced with the dead Cleopatra he is either moved for a moment, or speaks out of character:

> . . . she looks like sleep,
> As she would catch another Antony
> In her strong toil of grace;
>
> [V. ii 346-48]

but he has just become interested medically:

> If they had swallow'd poison, 'twould appear
> By external swelling;
>
> [V. ii. 345-46]

and it is this point that he dwells on:

                    Most probable
That so she died;

                                [V. ii. 353-54]

for his last words are merely a ceremonious close to the play, with little significance for character.

Caesar incarnates the practical reason, or worldly wisdom, with which are closely linked the notions of restrictive morality and political order (Stoicism and the Roman law). Antony has a foot in both worlds. . . . He is a Roman and has his share of Roman fortitude; he has mortified the flesh for military glory; and if Caesar will sacrifice his sister for political ends, Antony will sacrifice her, Cleopatra, and himself in the same cause, at least until the lure of Egypt proves too strong. Antony's position is central, for the choice between Egypt and Rome is for him to make. It is Cleopatra who stands opposite Caesar, incarnating 'intuition', the life of the spontaneous affections, with which are linked the notions of expansive morality and aesthetic order (it is the positive affections which transcend her 'baser life' [V. ii. 290]; while the dignity of sense-experience is vindicated poetically in Enobarbus' great description of the barge incident).

Justice is done to Rome, but the tendency is to depreciate the Roman values. There is a machine-like inevitability in Caesar, accompanied by a certain calculating meanness. When he speaks for himself, his verse is deflated:

            Let our best heads
    Know, that to-morrow the last of many battles
    We mean to fight . . .

                                [IV. i 10-12]

Imperial corruption subdues the note of Roman virtue. The banquet scene, with Menas whispering insidious suggestions into Pompey's ear, attains a political *reductio ad absurdum* when the drunken Lepidus is carried out:

    A' bears the third part of the world, man.

                                [II. vii. 90-1]
                                (pp. 122-24)

The Egyptian qualities crystallised in Cleopatra, are correspondingly raised in our esteem by subtle poetic means. The materials are not very promising. This is the Cleopatra who will

        . . . wander through the streets and note
        The qualities of people,

                                [I. i. 53-4]

or

        Hop forty paces through the public street,

                                [II. ii. 229]

or even play a practical joke with 'a salt-fish on his hook' [II. v. 17], and, as she recalls

                    . . . next morn,
        Ere the ninth hour, I drunk him to his bed;
        Then put my tires and mantles on him, whilst
        I wore his sword Philippan.

                                [II. v. 20-3]

It is easy to remember her as that certain queen who, in her 'salad days' [I. v. 73], was carried 'to Caesar in a mattress' [II. vi. 70]: a mixture of hoyden and strumpet, with a strong flavour of Nell Gwynne. But Shakespeare, taking boldly for thesis that 'everything becomes' her [I. i. 49], transmutes these

qualities by poetic paradox. No wonder Cleopatra's character worries the psychologist; it is not so much a character as an extended metaphysical conceit:

        I saw her once
    Hop forty paces through the public street;
    And having lost her breath, she spoke, and panted,
    That she did make *defect perfection,*
    And, *breathless,* power *breathe* forth.

                                [II. ii. 228-32]

The conceit is brought out by the resemblance of form in words of opposite meaning, the opposites in Cleopatra being resolved as the word-sounds are assimilated. Again:

                    . . . other women cloy
    The appetites they feed; but she makes hungry
    Where most she satisfies: for vilest things
    Become themselves in her; that the holy priests
    Bless her when she is riggish.

                                [II. ii. 235-39]

Here again is paradox, and the fusion of opposites: there is a benediction upon her sensuality. Similarly of the love of Antony and Cleopatra:

    Eternity was in our lips and eyes,
    Bliss in our brows' bent; none our parts so poor,
    But was a race of heaven.

                                [I. iii. 35-7]

Their love being heavenly, Cleopatra is herself a goddess. Enobarbus' description has a ritual flavour; and in the barge Cleopatra was actually dressed as Venus:

        O'er-picturing that Venus where we see
        The fancy outwork nature—

                                [II. ii. 200-01]

a characteristic hyperbole for it is claimed that she excels Apelles' picture, which itself excelled nature. She habitually dressed as a deity:

                . . . she
    In the habiliments of the goddess Isis
    That day appear'd; and oft before gave audience,
    As 'tis reported, so,

                                [III. vi. 16-19]

says Caesar, who seems shocked. She has the mystery of divinity:

        She is cunning past man's thought;

                                [I. ii. 145]

her nod, like Jove's, will be obeyed:

                    Cleopatra
        Hath nodded him to her;

                                [III. vi. 65-6]

she has the same sort of immortality as Keats' nightingale, in virtue of her symbolic function:

        Age cannot wither her, nor custom stale
        Her infinite variety.

                                [II. ii. 234-35]

Her age is insisted on, that we may know her beauty and attraction to be perennial: she remembers her 'salad days' [I. v. 73] when old Julius Caesar was in Egypt, and she is unchanged in beauty when she meets his son. Yet she describes herself as being

> . . . with Phoebus' amorous pinches black,
> And wrinkled deep in time.
>
> [I. v. 28-9]

This is perhaps the most significant phrase applied to Cleopatra. In blunt prose she is described as being sunburnt, old, and wrinkled. Taken literally this would contradict all descriptions of her beauty: wrinkles were no more admired in Shakespeare's day than now; and sunburn, strangely enough, was regarded as a serious blemish:

> The Grecian dames are sunburnt and not worth
> The splinter of a lance.
>
> [*Troilus and Cressida,* I. iii. 282-83]

In Cleopatra's remarkable conceit, however, the common attributes of age and ugliness are taken as the material of immortal beauty. The passage is fully intelligible only if symbolically interpreted—if we allow the poetry to do its work. For poetically the 'deep in time' gives her an infinite age: it does not suggest an old woman, but an immortal; and 'Phoebus' amorous pinches' thus become more than a metonymy for sunburn—she is an immortal lover of the sun-god, of Phoebus-Apollo, the god of poetry and song, the paragon of male beauty, and therefore a worthy mate for such as Cleopatra.

The choice which Antony has to make between Rome and Egypt is thus heavily weighted by Shakespeare on the Egyptian side. Antony is a lordly man, a natural Egyptian. In his Roman days he was prodigal of pains (as an ascetic differs from a careful man):

> . . . thou didst drink
> The stale of horses, and the gilded puddle
> Which beasts would cough at: thy palate then did deign
> The roughest berry on the rudest hedge;
> Yea, like the stag, when snow the pasture sheets,
> The barks of trees thou browsed'st; on the Alps
> It is reported thou didst eat strange flesh,
> Which some did die to look on.
>
> [I. iv. 61-8]

He was as magnificent in his Egyptian pleasures:

> . . . his delights
> Were dolphin-like.
>
> [V. ii. 88-9]

His generosity and *bonhomie* have been mentioned: it was his generosity that killed Enobarbus, a natural Egyptian with a deceptively Roman exterior. For Enobarbus tried time-serving—prudence, Caesar would have called it—and died in consequence. . . . (pp. 125-28)

Antony chose Egypt, intuition, the life of the spontaneous affections, with its moral and aesthetic corollaries; of all which Cleopatra is the focus and symbol. Shakespeare does not satisfy the psychologists with his character of Cleopatra; but he does not attempt a character in the sense of Trollope, or George Eliot, or even Dickens. In Cleopatra he presents the mystery of woman, the mystery of sensuality, an exploration of the hidden energies of life, and a suggestion of its goal. Intuition or spontaneous feeling is opposed to practical wisdom, generosity to prudence, love to duty, the private affections to public service; and the former in each instance is preferred. Not that the Roman values are entirely repudiated: there is a case for Caesar, 'Fortune's knave' [V. ii. 3] though he be. But the

Egyptian values are affirmative; the Roman, negative or restrictive: the good life may be built upon the Egyptian, but not upon the Roman. It is a way of saying that the strong sinner may enter heaven before the prudential legislator. In *Antony and Cleopatra* the strong sinners meet their purgatory here. They do not desire or seek it; it is forced upon them from without—grace which visits them in the guise of defeat. Changes of character inexplicable by psychological determinism are readily explained if we perceive that Shakespeare is applying theological categories. Earthly defeat is the providential instrument of eternal triumph: it comes undesired, but when it comes, is freely accepted, and so converted into a process of necessary cleansing. Antony's purgatory lies in military failure and a bungled suicide prompted by the false report of Cleopatra's death; Cleopatra's in surviving Antony, and in the thought of a Roman triumph. In the end the better Roman qualities are needed to transmute the Egyptian into eternal validity. Antony dies,

> . . . a Roman by a Roman
> Valiantly vanquish'd;
>
> [IV. xv. 57-8]

and Cleopatra, too, would emulate the Roman virtue:

> Let's do it after the high Roman fashion,
> And make death proud to take us.
>
> [IV. xv. 87-8]

Shakespeare nowhere approves suicide outside the Roman plays, but in them he seems to accept it, along with the pantheon, as data. It would be wrong, then, to condemn these suicides as from a Christian point of view. Antony's and Cleopatra's view of the hereafter is hardly Christian either, but their assurance is emphatically not pagan. Antony says:

> Where souls do couch on flowers, we'll hand in hand,
> And with our sprightly port make the ghosts gaze:
> Dido and her Aeneas shall want troops,
> And all the haunt be ours—
>
> [IV. xiv. 51-4]

this is not the shadow world of [Virgil's] *Aeneid VI*. Cleopatra's death is more studied, as she symbolises the affirmation of life. She, too, must go by the Roman way of negation:

> My desolation does begin to make
> A better life.
>
> [V. ii. 1]

In desolation she realises her inalienable possessions, that she is above Fortune, whereas Caesar is 'Fortune's knave'. Deprived of earthly love, she is denuded also of her earthly glory, and sees herself

> No more, but e'en a woman, and commanded
> By such poor passion as the maid that milks
> And does the meanest chares.
>
> [IV. xv. 73-5]

She must realise her common humanity for her symbolic function to be of general validity. It is by deprivation and denial that she attains reaffirmation, on a higher plane, of her essential nature; so that she faces death and the hereafter in the fullest confidence, claiming Antony for the first time by the name of husband:

> . . . husband, I come:
> Now to that name my courage prove my title!
> I am fire and air; my other elements
> I give to baser life.
>
> [V. ii. 287-90]

Her death-speeches are as fully sensual as any before: even

> The stroke of death is as a lover's pinch,
> Which hurts, and is desired;
>
>   [V. ii. 295-96]

and she hastens to meet first her 'curled Antony' [V. ii. 301] in heaven.

In *Lear,* Shakespeare struggled with the problem of evil; in *Macbeth,* with the problem of sin in a Christian universe. In *Antony and Cleopatra,* he returns to the old problem: what are the positive bases of the good life? He finds them in the affections, and the affections as rooted deep in the sensual nature. Of these Cleopatra is the symbol, sensual even in death; for, paradoxically, it is these Egyptian values which must survive death. Caesar, the worldly wise, is 'ass unpolicied!' [V. ii. 307-08]. However shocking to the Nordic man, this position is theologically orthodox. Caesar's sins are deeper-seated and more deliberate than the sins of Antony and Cleopatra, and his heart is entirely set on the passing world. There is significance in Cleopatra's greeting to Antony after his short-lived victory:

> Lord of lords!
> O infinite virtue, comest thou smiling from
> The world's great snare uncaught?
>
>   [IV. viii. 16-18]

She is his good, and not his evil genius, rescuing him from an undue preoccupation with the world, which is a snare and a delusion (cf. the Psalmist's frequent use of the 'snare' metaphor, e.g. Ps. CXLI. 10). Nevertheless the Egyptian values need a Roman purgatory to fit them for survival; they are cleansed, through adversity, of the taint of selfishness. Antony kills himself in order to rejoin Cleopatra whom he believes to be dead; Cleopatra looks forward in the same way to their future reunion. Purged of selfish fear, the element of self-giving inherent in the sensual nature is revealed in its eternal significance, while Caesar, on the other hand, has no such selfless hold upon eternity. This is one way of poetically stating the resurrection of the body:

> . . . she looks like sleep,
> As she would catch another Antony
> In her strong toil of grace.

Perhaps here, as elsewhere, the word 'grace' may have a tinge of theological significance. (pp. 128-31)

> *S. L. Bethell, "Further Ramifications of Multi-Consciousness," in his* Shakespeare and the Popular Dramatic Tradition, *1944. Reprint by Staples Press, 1948, 108-36.*

G. S. GRIFFITHS   (essay date 1945)

[*Griffiths contends that because of its unusually high degree of "ecstatic moments, its pure sensations, [and] its gusts of sheer passion,"* Antony and Cleopatra *belongs to a different order of tragedy than* Hamlet, Othello, King Lear, *and* Macbeth. *Both protagonists in this play, the critic asserts, achieve tragic stature when they willingly embrace death. However, Griffith adds, while Cleopatra attains an understanding of the true significance of love and an "insight into the sweet-bitter irony of existence," Antony— unlike Shakespeare's other tragic heroes—dies without gaining enlightenment, self-discipline, or moral insight as a result of his suffering. The critic also describes Enobarbus as "the censor of Antony's conduct and judge of tragic error," maintaining that his principal function is to direct our attention as well as Antony's to the dangerous implications of Cleopatra's demonic energy.*]

In the last words of his essay on *Antony and Cleopatra* A. C. Bradley virtually admits that its main contentions, that only the last phase of the play is truly tragic, that Cleopatra throughout most of the play is not a tragic figure, that already in the play as a whole the tragic emotion is dissolving into the vesper pageant of the last plays, are not strictly speaking criticism at all, for he confesses that the play does not attempt to satisfy the conditions which he considers applicable to the four great Shakespearian tragedies and has indeed applied in this study to *Antony and Cleopatra* [see excerpt above, 1905]. (p. 34)

In *Antony and Cleopatra* there is relatively much more of the ecstasy of passion while there is less of the life of the practical will than in the four great tragedies, and the tragedy needs therefore a different approach from that of Bradley's study. The play exists much more than any other of Shakespeare's in its ecstatic moments, its pure sensations, its gusts of sheer passion: pride, jealousy, remorse, anger, above all love, absolute sole lord of Life and Death, presented with rapturous lyrical energy. (pp. 38-9)

It is Cleopatra as Shakespeare creates her who contributes most to this effect. Enobarbus, the best guide to Shakespeare's attitude to his creature, does not think of her as a 'person' or a 'character' at all, she is a phenomenon, 'a wonderful piece of work' [I.ii.153-54] (p. 39)

When Enobarbus corrects Antony's commonplace reflection on Cleopatra, 'She's cunning past man's thought', he describes her passions as 'made of nothing but the finest parts of pure love' [I. ii. 145, 146-47]. The significance of this to the Elizabethan is made clear in many a passage in Donne's poems. *Love's Growth* begins:

> I Scarce beleeve my love to be so pure
>   As I had thought it was,
>   Because it doth endure
> Vicissitude, and season, as the grasse;
> Methinkes I lyed all winter, when I swore
> My love was infinite, if spring make it more.
> But if this medicine, love, which cures all sorrow
> With more, not onely bee no quintessence,
> But mixt of all stuffes, painting soule, or sense,
> And of the Sunne his working vigour borrow,
> Love's not so pure and abstract, as they use
> To say, which have no Mistresse but their Muse.

'The finest parts of pure love' are the quintessence of love, complete possession. It is significant, too, that Shakespeare makes Cleopatra's beauty a spirit and a motion. She is represented by Shakespeare as at the extreme limit of the thirty-eight years Plutarch gives her at death, her lip is waned, she is wrinkled deep in time, has a tawny front, is sunburnt, but she is love's medium and can 'make defect perfection, and, breathless, power breathe forth' [I. ii. 231-32].

At each successive crisis in the play's action Enobarbus directs Antony's attention and ours to this demonic force which has to be reckoned with. (pp. 39-40)

[Before] Actium Enobarbus notes emphatically the tragic and moral infatuation of Antony's choice to fight by sea and by Cleopatra's side, and he blames Antony alone for what happens. It is true that Enobarbus is a 'character', a humorist, a *raisonneur* [dialectician], and he is engulfed in Antony's tragedy by following the dictate of his reason, but this does not invalidate, rather vindicates it. Shakespeare clearly intends him as an example of the truth-seer who perishes, the blinded prophet.

Shakespeare no doubt regards Enobarbus's reason as a revealer of truth divorced from charity and the affective will, the lightning-flash into the nature of things—the human heart only excepted—the wisdom of Silenus. His vision has the aloofness of the Lucretian gods, its pure appreciation of life and the human spectacle as an aesthetic phenomenon, an object of wonder and contemplation. But Enobarbus is also a human being, and by passing judgement on Antony in his own person and acting against him by going over to Octavius he attempts to live, to be, to incarnate the vision of reason, and thereby delivers himself into the tragic process. (pp. 40-1)

Now Enobarbus as the censor of Antony's conduct and judge of tragic error appears . . . to insist in the crisis in Act I on the occasion of Fulvia's death on the need for Antony to face the great fact of Cleopatra's demonic power and her vital concern with him. Enobarbus regards all Antony's actions up to Actium as weakness, but it is the weakness of a man afraid to face his inner life, his own emotional nature and its entanglements, and eager to cut his human responsibilities and trust to expediency and the easy way out. He is equally sceptical of the marriage with Octavia and foretells the whole ensuing catastrophe. Both Enobarbus and Cleopatra in the first act insist on Antony's moral cowardice in leaving Egypt for Italy, and Antony's anger with both is an involuntary recognition—the barb has gone home. Enobarbus exposes infallibly Antony's drifting, his split personality, his attempting to centre his life deliberately where it will not rest—away from Cleopatra. As the interest of the first act is the spiritual triumph though the temporary check of Cleopatra, that of the second is the drift of Antony to a dreamlike and unreal matrimony and political appeasement with his enemy and the astounding protest of Cleopatra against this. (pp. 45-6)

In the second act again Bradley's critical perspective is at fault. Cleopatra dominates men's thoughts throughout. In the first scene Pompey and the others turn at once to talk of her in the salt coarse strain of the camp: they are interesting only as another chorus.

> We, ignorant of ourselves,
> Beg often our own harms, which the wise powers
> Deny us for our good; so find we profit
> By losing of our prayers.
>
> [II. i. 5-8]

We apply this to the main theme—to Antony's course in Act II. In the second scene Enobarbus is at once choric: Let Antony stand to his guns in the coming struggle with Caesar. He is virtually against the reconciliation of Antony and Octavius and the passion and beauty of the scene is reserved for the rapturous description of Cleopatra pursing up Antony's heart on the Cydnus—the first meeting of the lovers. Enobarbus is emphatic on the demonic power of Cleopatra and the folly of the marriage now under discussion. The main part of the scene is in its own way curiously beautiful. Antony dominates it as a great gentleman, but he does not put forth his strength, and the meaner man stickles for his word and his point. Antony addresses himself reluctantly to the business, breaks the official chill, makes his apology with good grace, goes to the root of the difference in his large free way. (pp. 47-8)

[In] the next short scene, where Antony receives the hand of his bride, we feel his gracious courtesy, but he strikes a warning note and with a strange irony immediately on his promise given to Octavia 'to keep the square' he turns at once to a soothsayer.

The reaction is already complete, though Antony only half knows it.

> I will to Egypt;
> And though I make this marriage for my peace,
> I' the East my pleasure lies.
>
> [II. iii. 39-41]
> (p. 48)

Then in the middle of the act Shakespeare gives Cleopatra's reaction to the marriage, a scene Bradley grudges her as structurally irrelevant to the play. We have seen Octavia, the pearl of women before the gods, bowing her knee in prayer for Antony, of a holy—not cold, except by comparison with Cleopatra—and still conversation. Now we see the opal, and again there is the amazing transformation from reverie to action and storm when Cleopatra learns of Antony's marriage. First her mortal anxiety for Antony, then the transport of anticipation, and the rush of bounty even to the messenger:

> there is gold . . . and here
> My bluest veins to kiss; a hand that kings
> Have lipp'd, and trembled kissing.
>
> [II. v. 28-30]

The splendour of the emotion, its rapid changes, the possessing completeness of each gust of passion, firing the entire nature, do not completely escape Cleopatra's aesthetic consciousness or indeed her conscience. Yet vanity—Bradley's word taken, but misleadingly applied, from Cleopatra's own lips—is not the word for Cleopatra's self-consciousness in passion. Even when launching the bolt Cleopatra is aware of the 'innocent', is aware of her own excess, but aware . . . as an artist. Alas indeed that it is but pathetic fallacy to treat this messenger as a Mercury or a Ganymede—it is not a world of Antonys and when this realization is complete Cleopatra will renounce it. And Cleopatra apologizes to the cowering wretch for this very blunder of generosity! So, too, vanity is a miscalling of the impulse which makes Cleopatra say abruptly to Charmian, 'I am pale, Charmian' just before the storm bursts [II. v. 59]. The messenger has been jocose and vulgar in circumstances like this in his reply: 'For the best turn i' the bed' [II. v. 59]. Cleopatra cannot speak to him. This low vulgarity asks for physical chastisement, and Cleopatra knows what is coming, yet she does not forget the presence of others. The remark to Charmian is a warning to the Court of what is to come. (pp. 49-50)

The messenger, however, is nothing but the innocent lightning-conductor. The real passion is Cleopatra's flaming and outraged loyalty to Antony and her passionate physical jealousy of Octavia and these are the culminating emotions of the scene. The scene is above all a great outburst of elemental forces. Cleopatra's agony expresses itself in fulminations that recall Lear and the other tragic heroes.

> The most infectious pestilence upon thee! . . .
> Some innocents 'scape not the thunderbolt.
> Melt Egypt into Nile! . . .
>
> [II. v. 61, 77-8]

The words fly in gusty whirls, all in disorder, for chaos has come.

The last two scenes of the act and the first of the next act are all political and are treated with a touch of contempt. Talk veers constantly to Egypt and Cleopatra, Enobarbus croaking his warnings that the new marriage will be a strangler of the amity it is intended to secure. Antony's drunken traveller's tales of Egypt—the flow of the Nile with the foison of its fields fed by the slime and ooze, the crocodile, that strange serpent—bring back the spell, but there is little spirit, and only a mockery of mirth in the loving-cup of the reconciled enemies who despise and suspect each other. . . . It is just a maudlin boozing scene, and Antony, the reveller of Alexandria, cuts a poor figure here. . . . [His] role is a depressing one and he cannot shake off or quell in wine his sense of letting down Pompey and really himself. The blare of drums, trumpets, and flutes drowns the hiccups of farewell:

> Sound and be hang'd, sound out!
>
> [II. vii. 133]

This jaded note of weariness and disillusion with high politics sounds in the Syrian scene which is all Shakespeare gives us of the great Parthian campaigns of Antony so impressively told by Plutarch. The disillusion reflects especially on Antony, the politician, and it overflows into the next episode, the leave-taking of the new brothers-in-law and the later parting of Antony and his bride. Agrippa and Enobarbus mock the hypocritical ceremony of affectionate brotherly valediction:

> Hoo! hearts, tongues, figures, scribes, bards, poets cannot
> Think, speak, cast, write, sing, number; hoo!
> His love to Antony.
>
> [III. ii. 16-18]

The actual leave-taking of brother and sister, Octavius and Octavia, is in a beautiful minor key, rather like the solicitous and tender warning of Laertes to Ophelia in *Hamlet,* and Antony listens to it—is in fact part of its theme—watching it, touched, but only aesthetically and contemplatively like that connoisseur of emotions, Enobarbus. . . . Brother and sister are on the verge of tears, she is whispering to him. Enobarbus affects to despise tears which can be traitors and he catches subtly the very cathartic treachery of Antony's mood.

But it is the central crisis of the play that follows the great disaster of Actium that disturbs and disappoints the Aristotelian critic—it puzzles Bradley, and he is inclined to blame the original material of Plutarch's account here for the anti-climax of this world-battle. Shakespeare even heightens the bathos, rendering the whole catastrophe chorically in soldiers' slang, with its beast-fable metaphors to mark the fall in pitch and scale: 'stallion and mare, the ribaudred nag, the cow in June, tail in air, stung by a gadfly, the doting mallard'.

> I never saw an action of such shame;
> Experience, manhood, honour, ne'er before
> Did violate so itself.
>
> [III. x. 21-3]

This conveys the sense of shame and humiliation of Antony only less forcibly than Antony's own outburst when at last realization comes to him. This is the passional centre of the play, the unqualitying disintegration of humiliation rather than of tragic humility. Bradley regards this purgation of shame as a treading of the valley of humiliation, a beginning of a redeeming process in Antony's character. But Antony is roused from this agony not by his own vitality or virtue but by the magnificent acting of Cleopatra, and it is the acting that we see mainly. She 'becomes' overpowering supplication and contrition: 'Pardon, pardon, pardon.' She has the eye for effect of the superb tragic actress. 'Stand by me'—she controls the whole dignified little group of suppliants of which she is the magnificently drooping central figure, inspiring them with the proper gesture and feeling of intercession—and Antony melts.

> Fall not a tear, I say; one of them rates
> All that is won and lost. Give me a kiss;
> Even this repays me.
>
> [III. xi. 69-71]

At this moment as at his death, Antony is supreme as a lover. It is the true gesture of the Dionysiac votary and martyr, and it is something of which Antony would have been incapable alone.

So too in that later revival or regeneration of Antony to which Bradley refers, that accompanies and inspires the rally early in the fourth act, Cleopatra is once again the inspiration:

> O thou day o' the world,
> Chain mine arm'd neck, leap thou, attire and all,
> Through proof of harness to my heart, and there
> Ride on the pants triumphing!
>
> [IV. viii. 13-16]

which with its echo of the imagery and thought of the opening lines of the play recalls the heroic vigour and vitality of Antony's personality and justifies his sacrifice and reneging of temper. Cleopatra meets it sublimely and tenderly:

> Lord of lords!
> O infinite virtue, com'st thou smiling from
> The world's great snare uncaught.
>
> [IV. viii. 16-18]

This is consummation, 'the nobleness of life' [I. i. 36], not death in battle.

Alone, or out of Cleopatra's company, in this phase of the play Antony frequently strikes a note of despondency and self-pity that is not truly tragic, a note of sentiment, almost of sentimentality, which does not recognize, as Hamlet and Cleopatra do when it occurs, the cathartic nature of the spendthrift sigh. (pp. 50-3)

If we turn to the longer speeches of Antony from the point of the defeat of Actium, their passion will be found to be constantly checked by a reflective, elegiac counter-movement, as though he is able to disengage himself from his own emotion and to contemplate it. It is the effect—a check to, and an escape from, the tragic emotion in its purity—which Eliot notes as fairly common in the moments of high tragic tension, even in Shakespeare's acknowledged tragic masterpieces, and which he calls the 'whistling of the hero to keep his courage up' [in his essay "Shakespeare and the Stoicism of Seneca"], instancing Othello's last speech.

Most of the emotion which Antony's words evoke throughout the scene of reunion after Actium, and those that immediately follow, is retrospective and touched with self-pity, and Iras's comment in the reunion scene is acute:

> He is unqualitied with very shame.
>
> [III. xi. 44]

Antony reverts several times to his glorious past and without any effort to integrate it with the present Antony. He frequently visualizes possible postures, dramatizes past and possible future roles, harps on Fortune. True, there are violent outbursts of temper, against Cleopatra coqueting with Thyreus and again in Act IV on the second desertion of her fleet, but these exhaust themselves in words or on a scape-goat. Antony never rallies, reins, and reorientates his passion as Hamlet and even Lear do as suffering enlightens and disciplines them and deepens their moral insight. (pp. 54-5)

The drama of the fourth act consists of the splendid moment of revival, that false dawn of hope, the fleeting triumph of the final sally, whose defeat brings on the catastrophe, the last and this time fatal quarrel of Antony and Cleopatra, and their reconciliation in death. There is, too, the passing of Antony's genius and the death of Enobarbus and Eros, both closely connected with and precipitating Antony's own. There are, I think, several elements of failure here, of Shakespeare not quite achieving his intended effect, a certain flagging of inspiration, though this is fully recovered in the actual death scene of Antony, not the bungling death-stroke but the dying in Cleopatra's arms. To me the death of Enobarbus just fails of its effect. One can see the perfect dramatic point and the not quite achieved purpose of it. Enobarbus has followed Antony to the end of the third act, well past the disaster of Actium, till Antony has really lost touch (the whole of the fourth act is not war), lost his grip on events, and become 'fey'. Enobarbus fully recognizes the symptoms of the infatuated, fascinated, doomed figure of tragedy and reason sanctions quitting a cause that Antony has himself abandoned. Enobarbus has from the first realized the full force of the irretrievable disaster of Actium, and recognized its finality. He has already told Cleopatra prophetically that all that is left to do is to take thought and die. He is himself now to die of the 'gratitude of man', the bounty of Antony. His death is intended as a minor though significant portent of Antony's own, different from that of Eros but like that serving as an example and a stimulus to Antony. Yet something is wanting here. Shakespeare fails to make this cracking of a noble heart as impressive and moving as he intended, for, like Falstaff, Enobarbus, another military free-thinker, dies of a broken heart. There are bystanders who might like Mrs. Quickly [in *Henry V*] have said the right word, if soliloquy in such a case is foredoomed to failure. The cry of anguish 'O Antony, O Antony' [IV. ix. 24] wrings us, but for the rest Shakespeare's cue of passion is wrong, with its invocation to the melancholy moon and the infectious dews of night in the vein of Kyd's churchyard rhetoric. . . . Enobarbus, like all the other faithful fools of Shakespeare—and . . . he does play the buffoon, the tumbler of Truth—is at bottom Charity posing as cynicism, and the last speech is a clear indication that the cause of death is petrification of feeling, the final fatal error of acting on the cynical profession of uncharitable truth, a part that the wisdom of the heart repudiates. But Shakespeare shrank from a powerful imaginative rendering of such a phenomenon with a minor character at this stage of the play, was content to extract the fragrances of the tribute of such a death to Antony's magnanimity, and so, though interesting and thought-provoking, the episode lacks full imaginative realization.

The ecstasy of the last and illusory triumph on the other hand is one of those intense moments—the marriage of Romeo and Juliet and the reunion of Othello, safe from the storm with Desdemona, are others—which the gods envy and are the destruction of mortals. The irony of it at such a moment might more fittingly have broken Enobarbus's heart—Shakespeare places it significantly just before his death. Shakespeare treats this rally of Antony, quite an insignificant scuffle of his bodyguard in Plutarch, with peculiar power and beauty. It has something of the weird effect of recurrence, of re-enacting the great missed chance of Actium. Antony is not one to learn from reincarnation. This time he feels he has Cleopatra behind him, but history repeats itself. . . . [With] the recurrence of failure, Actium over again—Shakespeare almost repeats the words that describe the desertion of Cleopatra's ships which give themselves up—the spell breaks and this time, for the fatal moment only, Antony is not to be placated. The heat of anger brings him to a realization of Cleopatra's treachery at Actium, for such it seems to him, and this time he resists Cleopatra's appeal. His violence is not to be appeased and Cleopatra's art

for once fails her—this is another flaw in the act. She confronts his fury, alone this time, with this:

> Why is my lord enraged against his love?
>
> [IV. xii. 31]

He sees her as a foul Duessa and with difficulty restrains his hands from physical violence, and she retreats. Yet even in the whirlwind of passion there is in Antony an inhibition stronger than the rage in his veins. He has none of Othello's priest-like lust to sacrifice and violate. In his wrath he curses her and gloats over the desecration of her beauty by Octavia, and the humiliation of a Roman triumph, he hints at death, but when his passion is spent he softens to reproach and regret and the dominant feeling is the loss of his own integrity, the ebbing of his sense of personal identity, the readiness for death. The beautiful visionary passage—a symbolist poem—

> Sometimes we see a cloud that's dragonish . . .
>
> [IV. xiv. 2ff.]

is his swan-song. The whole tone after the dying down of the last great passion of Antony is attuned to the final transmutation of feeling to the tragic emotion itself, but this is still not reached, not even with the false news of Cleopatra's death. It is the death of Eros following immediately on the supposed death of Cleopatra that finally keys Antony to the tension of deliberate suicide. A mood of reverie has preceded it, the contemplation, the immersion in the drifting tide that seems asleep, the tired rhythm of the ebbing life-force. Antony does not, however, dedicate himself to Death without the final spur of emulation. It is with the examples of Enobarbus, Eros, and, as he thinks, of Cleopatra before him that Antony gathers his whole being and devotes himself, in characteristic lover's ritual, a bridegroom, to Death. He accepts at once Diomedes' exculpation of Cleopatra and nothing now stands between them and their love but the narrow strait of death. . . . The witch has been transformed by the sacrifice of love-inspired death to the fairy, and Antony determines deliberately on death:

> Dead then? . . . Dead . . .
> Unarm Eros.
>
> [IV. xiv. 34-5]

But the end is not yet. . . . [He] rages for release, tearing at his armour. His consuming eagerness is for reunion with Cleopatra, to sue his pardon. He is tortured with the dilatoriness of death. The obsessing thought is the glory of reunion with Cleopatra in death. Yet the attempted suicide falters in its execution and it is only when Antony reaches Cleopatra that Shakespeare recovers the tragic note.

The first words charged with tragic emotion in the death scene of Antony are Cleopatra's, which strike the keynote:

> All strange and terrible events are welcome,
> But comforts we despise.
>
> [IV. xv. 3-4]

It is the first time in the play she has spoken like this—now Antony's life is ebbing fast, though characteristically she is even now aware of her role. Her greeting to Antony has two marks of the tragic: the disaster becomes for her a cosmic catastrophe, a great eclipse of Nature, and her sheer cry of personal anguish is wrung from the bowels: 'O Antony, Antony, Antony!' [IV. xv. 11-12]. Antony is still concerned even in his dying agony for his Roman freeman's dignity in death and Cleopatra reassures him. She, too, will not suffer the degradation of the captive in Caesar's triumph. The struggle to lift Antony into the sanctuary, and the workmanlike jest and violent exertion of Cleopatra seem to me spirited not heartless—the place is beset, and Antony wants above all and anyhow to end in her arms, and her eagerness to quicken him with kisses at the last is the answer to Antony's prayer:

> Only
> I here importune Death awhile, until
> Of many thousand kisses the poor last
> I lay upon thy lips.
>
> [IV. xv. 18-21]

Again she reassures him that she is not Caesar's in reversion, for this is Antony's last anxiety—this and his honour in death. As Antony dies comes the realization that all values are gone. Cleopatra faints and when she recovers her senses she too, like Antony, accepts death absolutely. She renounces life and is elated, even cheered, and cheers her companions. Yet she is to do all nobly. Her words are resolute, clear, and filled with a concentrated common sense and illuminated humour which has never before been given by Shakespeare to a tragic hero at bay—it is the inspired language of a woman facing reality, and there is a complete mastery and transcendence of the woman. She has at this moment mastered the fear of death and is beyond attitudes and protests, declamation, and divinity. . . . The moment is one of absolute solemnity as she reaches and passes this realization of the human lot, and her spirit rises at the challenge and like Hamlet's her voice is hushed and husky as she formulates the final question:

> then is it sin
> To rush into the secret house of death,
> Ere death dare come to us?
>
> [IV. xv. 80-2]

And then, again like Hamlet's, the voice breaks. The will has won its peace and relaxes: gleefully, irresponsibly, triumphantly, lightly she turns—and how human this is!—to the girls, her *noble* girls, who are to go down to death with her— she knows it. The inspiration of this ecstasy of spirit is the nobility of Antony.

> Ah, women, women, look!
> Our lamp is spent, it's out! . . .
> This case of that huge spirit now is cold.
>
> [IV. xv. 84-5, 89]

Yet there are critics who have denied Cleopatra 'human feeling warm' or true nobility. Cleopatra has learnt in suffering the full meaning of love and its price, and she turns to greet the *Vita Nuova* [New Life] beyond death. This is the play's moral, its supreme ordeal and meaning.

It has always seemed to me that the last act of *Antony and Cleopatra* is one of the greatest of all Shakespeare's dramatic 'ends', not only unfalteringly achieving all its effects as an individual scene but fulfilling every promise of the earlier parts and lifting the whole play consummately to the highest plane of poetic tragedy. There is a pause in the first scene after the successive deaths, all inspired by love, of Enobarbus, Eros, Antony, and the tribute of Caesar and his lieutenants to Antony is a perfect example of Shakespeare's skill and tact in striking the tragic choric note on death. But Caesar's triumph is still incomplete, and having paid his feeling tribute to Antony, Caesar lays his plans with care for capturing and gaining the confidence of Cleopatra.

The greatest dramatic triumph of the play, however, is the last scene. (pp. 56-61)

Cleopatra opens in soliloquy on the high tragic note she had struck on the death of Antony: resolution for death, the deliverer from the ruined house of Life. She draws her resolution from despair. She has turned her back on Fortune and Hope. She sees Life in the perspective of Shakespeare's sages, Prospero [in *The Tempest*], the Friar-Duke in *Measure for Measure*. The great world has shrunk to nothing and Death seems infinitely beautiful and peaceful. The image she uses, first and last, for it, is 'babe' that has sucked itself asleep, the sleep of Nirvana. Caesar's envoy, Proculeius, recommended by Antony's dying breath, arrives outside Cleopatra's little citadel to parley. Cleopatra is frank, astutely so, and confesses in parenthesis her abysmal indifference to his mission. Still she gives her terms for surrender and her diplomatic courtesy is perfect, and it in no way compromises her full freedom of speech. She admits and accepts her virtually helpless position, exaggerates it with intention, for she holds one card—in Plutarch it is her hidden treasure which has roused the cupidity of Caesar—in Shakespeare it is her power to slay herself: death is her trump. Then, perfectly timed, comes Caesar's coup. The citadel is climbed and entered while the envoy holds her in conversation, Cleopatra seized, disarmed, and held as she tried to stab and afterwards to mutilate herself; but Proculeius in the excitement of the struggle blurts out the truth about Caesar's intentions towards Cleopatra and in all the fury of her wild struggle she catches it. Proculeius feels the failure of his efforts to pacify this fury and Caesar's second and more courtly instrument, Dolabella, arrives at this point to supersede him, and now follows one of those amazing feats of Cleopatra which have earned her alone of Shakespeare's women the designation 'genius'.

Dolabella claims former acquaintance with her, but Cleopatra ignores this and plunges instead into her dream of Antony:

> His face was as the heavens; and therein stuck
> A sun and moon, which kept their course, and lighted
> The little O, the earth. . . .
> His legs bestrid the ocean: his rear'd arm
> Crested the world: his voice was propertied
> As all the tuned spheres, and that to friends;
> But when he meant to quail and shake the orb,
> He was as rattling thunder. For his bounty
> There was no winter in't; an autumn 'twas
> That grew the more by reaping: his delights
> Were dolphin-like; they show'd his back above
> The element they lived in: in his livery
> Walk'd crowns and crownets; realms and islands were
> As plates dropp'd from his pocket.
>
> *Dol.*   Cleopatra!
> *Cleo.*   Think you there was or might be such a man
>   As this I dreamt of? . . .
>
> [V. ii. 79-81, 82-94]

All the images are cosmic and categorical, generic or quintessential: his voice has the harmony of the spheres or the terror of Jove's thunder, his bounty is inexhaustible, his delights are dolphin-like (the Dolphin, the King of Fishes), but Shakespeare's way . . . is that of excess—the note of infinity has already broken in with 'inexhaustible'—and the figure changes to some divine Tumbler of a more apocalyptical mythology than the Greek, dropping realms and islands from his pockets. . . . Cleopatra turns this great engine of poetry on Dolabella, but it remains primarily an apology for suicide and a declaration of faith in a love, a person that has been and is no more in time. While Dolabella listens, plunged in wonder, Cleopatra turns to him:

> I thank you, sir.
> Know you what Caesar means to do with me?
>
> [V. ii. 105-06]

This sort of turn one can parallel in Hamlet and in Falstaff but hardly elsewhere even in Shakespeare. Her appeal is irresistible and Dolabella gives his master away: 'Madam, he will, I know't' [V. ii. 110].

At this moment Caesar enters to the blare of trumpets, but Cleopatra is forearmed. She now plays her last act of excellent dissembling. She kneels and propitiates, confesses past frailty, in short assumes the very mask and role that flatters Caesar's own conceit of his infallible political intuition—this is just the magnificent fribble he is expecting to find, and he proceeds to manage the hysterical weakling, announces his will, scarcely veiling his threat of death to her children if she refuses to yield to his grace. In Plutarch's account it is clear that Caesar's anxiety to secure her person and her good will is mainly mercenary and material—only so can he make sure of the vast treasure she is rumoured to have in her keeping somewhere in the mausoleum whither she has retreated. Shakespeare stresses rather Caesar's political anxiety to secure the prestige value of Cleopatra's presence in his triumph, but he gives next, like Plutarch, the incident of the betrayal by Seleucus of Cleopatra's subterfuge to keep back part of her treasure, a treachery which rouses Cleopatra to her last fit of vehement indignation. It is this last and unexpected tempest of passion at such a moment and for so seemingly trivial a cause and person, for the man is just an ordinary time-server quitting a lost cause, a poor worm turning, that is so typical of the noble excess of Cleopatra. Caesar appreciates it almost like Enobarbus and approves its spirit, and it is the outburst of a generous spirit, the outraged protest of woman against a man without nobility. It parallels in a way Antony's rage against Thyreus, but it is stronger and better grounded, for this is a betrayal of personal loyalty, and what loyalty Cleopatra no less than Antony inspires! and to her it is 'the rare baseness of a soulless villain'. The incident shakes her to the depths even now, and Cleopatra ignores and Caesar approves her ignoring the truth of Seleucus's charge. It is a turning of the tables on self-interest, and Caesar respects his enemy's original caution and her indignation at its betrayal, and dismisses the offender. Cleopatra at once resumes her royal dignity on his departure and Caesar makes the mistake again of misinterpreting her behaviour as something too like what his own would have been in such circumstances. Love of power or, failing that, of security at any price is the motive he imputes, and he dares to reassure her of livelihood: 'Feed and sleep' (a beast, no more!) [V. ii. 187]. Cleopatra, jarred by the touch of parvenu pomp and complacency in Caesar's imperial 'we' and his patronizing congé: 'And so adieu', maintains her pose of royal suppliant to the end: 'My master and my lord' [V. ii. 189, 190]. It was her greeting and it is her final salute. And then she turns to Iras and Charmian:

> He words me, girls, he words me, that I should not
> Be noble to myself.
>
> [V. ii. 191-92]

This last act of excellent dissembling is over and Cleopatra reminds Charmian of her final resource. She has outwitted Caesar at his own high political game. Dolabella too has been won and he confirms Cleopatra's conviction that she is intended for a Roman triumph. It is yet another victory (in defeat) for Cleopatra. She imagines the triumph in all its horrors. What bliss for Caesar! The deliberate encouragement of this dream of triumph over her submission is the very way to fool Caesar's preparation and thwart his purpose, as Cleopatra explains to Iras whom she has mischievously scared—and she is mischievous to the last even with the clown: 'Will it eat me?' [V. ii. 271]—with the imaginary degradation of the triumph and the howling varletry of Rome.

And now Cleopatra gets ready with exultation for the final ritual of death, a triumph of another kind. Her dignity grows and dilates as she welcomes the deliverer, the old peasant who brings the asps in his fig-basket and lectures her on their deadly quality. She jests like Hamlet with the grave-diggers with an ironic double vision of the mystery, the ambiguity of life as it reveals itself to us—even this peasant, the humble instrument of a great destiny, embodies it. Then she turns instantly to the grave business of the moment as the god rises in her veins:

> My resolution's placed, and I have nothing
> Of woman in me.
>
> [V. ii. 238-39]

This invocation . . . marks Cleopatra's achievement of moral courage, of tragic power, but there is still a moment's distraction as she toys with the worm—an ominous symbol in Shakespeare—before the final ordeal of death.

The last ceremony of robing as for a coronation or the sacrament of marriage is again accompanied throughout by imaginative dilation, an enduement with heavenly gifts. Virtue seems to rise from her to meet the majesty of the ritual. There is the longing for immortality, the realization of the moral worth of deliberate action, the greater for her physical shrinking, the purging of the lower physical elements, the glow of passionate marital affection for Antony, and the warm touch of her lips for Iras. Like Antony she sees the image of sacrificial death in a follower first—Iras falls from her embrace, dead, and the stroke of death is gentle. This heartens Cleopatra and she applies the asp. The stab of pain quickens her insight into the sweet-bitter irony of existence, and to the asp she is tender and personal. There is a flash of humorous intuition into the complexity and incongruity of things in her sense of the asp calling great Caesar 'ass unpolicied'. Almost the last words are 'intrinsic peace', a lullaby of baby sounds, but the final thought is of Antony. Charmian lingers only to mend her mistress's crown, and to say the right word on the woman, 'the lass unparalleled' [V. ii. 316]. This is the personal good-bye, the farewell of poetry, but her very last word is one of consummate rhetoric, as the world breaks clamorously in to arrest death itself in the name of Caesar:

> Speak softly, wake her not. . . .
> It is well done, and fitting for a princess
> Descended of so many royal kings.
>
> [V. ii. 320, 326-27]

With her dying breath Charmian rallies to meet the challenge of the world and of history, and Caesar, arriving just too late, bows to Cleopatra's beauty and will. (pp. 62-7)

> *G. S. Griffiths, "'Antony and Cleopatra'," in Essays and Studies, Vol. XXXI, 1945, pp. 34-67.*

JOHN F. DANBY (essay date 1949)

[*Danby maintains that "a peculiarly Shakespearean dialectic"—in which contrary principles are juxtaposed, then merge, but ultimately dissolve—controls the dramatic structure of* Antony and Cleopatra. *Noting that the principal characters are constantly being judged by other dramatic figures, by their own conduct, and by "what they say themselves"—and considering the conflict between these opposing perspectives—the critic argues that the nature of judgment itself is a central concern in the play. Danby contends that Octavius and Cleopatra personify the opposing principles of "the World" and "the Flesh," Rome and Egypt, which alternately possess Antony and eventually destroy him. Further, the critic asserts that although Shakespeare shows that the "flesh has its glory and passion its witchery," the love of Antony and Cleopatra is neither redemptive nor transcendent, and thus is not presented as a "final value."*]

To describe the swiftness of *Antony and Cleopatra* we need to draw on the imagery of the cinema. There is more cinematic movement, more panning, tracking, and playing with the camera, more mixing of shots than in any other of Shakespeare's tragedies. At the same time the technique is always under deliberate, almost cool, control.... The technique is inwardly related to the meaning Shakespeare has to express. What is indicated is not enervation or indifference but rather what Coleridge recognized as 'giant power', an 'angelic strength' [see excerpt above, 1813-34].

The swift traverse of time and space has often been commented upon. There is also the mixing. Egypt is called up vividly in Rome by Enobarbus' descriptions. Rome is always felt as a real presence in Egypt. On the frontiers of Empire Ventidius discusses what repercussions his victories will have on the people at staff-headquarters. Equally the present is interpenetrated by the past.... The hinterland of the quarrels that alternately divide and bring together again the triumvirate is constantly being suggested, troubles, truces, and manoeuvres that go back (like Cleopatra's love affairs) to Julius Caesar's days. In no other of his plays is Shakespeare at such pains to suggest the stream of time past and its steady course through the present. In the public world of Roman affairs this is especially so. In the other world of Cleopatra the same suggestion of perspective always frames what is said and done. Is Antony merely the last of a long succession of such lovers? Or is this affair singular and unique as all love-affairs claim to be? Not enough weight has been given in recent assessments of the play to the ambiguity which invests everything in Egypt equally with all things in Rome. Yet this ambiguity is central to Shakespeare's experience in the play. If it is wrong to see the 'mutual pair' as a strumpet and her fool, it is also wrong to see them as a Phoenix and a Turtle.

In addition to the swiftness and the variety of the impacts, and the interpenetration of the parts of time and space as they mix in the speech of the people immediately before us, there is also the added burden which Shakespeare's 'giant power' of compelling presentation imposes. The effects are at once those of a rapid impressionism and a careful lapidary enrichment. Each figure, however minor, has its moment when it comes up into the brilliant foreground light—the Soothsayer with his 'infinite book of secrecy' [I. ii. 10], the Old Man wishing 'much joy o' the worm' [V. ii. 260], Enobarbus describing the barge on the Nile, Lepidus asking 'What manner o' thing is your crocodile?' [II. vii. 41], Ventidius giving once for all the field-officer's view of the higher-ups, the Eunuch and the game of billiards, Dolabella, Octavia, even Fulvia whom we never see: the canvas seems covered with Constable's snow.

Another feature of Shakespeare's technique which makes for the impression of uniqueness might be pointed to here. Shakespeare seems to be innovating also in methods of character-portrayal. Some of the stage-conventions ... do not seem to apply. Which, for example, are we to believe—what Caesar says about Antony after he is dead, or what he says about him, and his conduct towards him, while he is alive? What was Fulvia's 'character', about whom we have such conflicting reports? Throughout the play we are forced by Shakespeare himself not to take comment at its face value. Judgments are more personal here than elsewhere. Goneril and Regan discussing their father's condition [in *King Lear*] are reliable judges. Caesar, Antony, Enobarbus, the soldiers Demetrius and Philo, are not—or not to the same extent. Judgment knits itself back into character as it might do in Ibsen, and character issues from a mutable and ambiguous flux of things. Antony's momentary *agnorisis* [recognition] can be generalized to cover the whole play:

> Sometimes we see a cloud that's dragonish;
> A vapour sometimes like a bear or lion,
> A tower'd citadel, a pendant rock,
> A forked mountain, or blue promontory,
> With trees upon't, that nod unto the world
> And mock our eyes with air: thou hast seen these signs;
> They are black vespers pageants ...
> That which is now a horse, even with a thought
> The rack dislimns, and makes it indistinct
> As water is in water ...
> My good knave, Eros, now thy captain is
> Even such a body: here I am Antony,
> Yet cannot hold this visible shape, my knave.
> [IV. xiv. 2-8, 9-11, 12-14]

There is something deliquescent in the reality behind the play. It is a deliquescence to the full display of which each judgment, each aspect pointed to, and each character, is necessary, always provided that no single one of these is taken as final. The proportion of comment and judgment on the central characters is higher in *Antony and Cleopatra* than anywhere else in Shakespeare. This further underlines its uniqueness and the difficulties of coming by an adequate final assessment. Antony and Cleopatra are presented in three ways. There is what is said about them; there is what they say themselves; there is what they do. Each of these might correspond to a different 'level' of response. Each is in tension against the others. Each makes its continuous and insistent claim on the spectator for judgment in its own right. The pigments vividly opposed to each other on the canvas have to mix in the spectator's eye.

Underlying, however, the bewildering oscillations of scene, the over-lapping and pleating of different times and places, the co-presence of opposed judgments, the innumerable opportunities for radical choice to intervene, there is, I think, a deliberate logic. It is this which gives the play its compact unity of effect and makes its movement a sign of angelic strength rather than a symptom of febrility. It is the logic of a peculiarly Shakespearean dialect. Opposites are juxtaposed, mingled, married; then from the very union which seems to promise strength dissolution flows. It is the process of this dialectic—the central process of the play—which we must trace if we wish to arrive anywhere near Shakespeare's meaning. (pp. 196-99)

The first scene is only slightly more than sixty lines long. Yet it is sufficient to illustrate all the main features of the play we have pointed to, and extensive enough to set up the swinging ambivalences—the alternatives and ambiguities constantly proposed to choice—which will govern and control our whole reaction to the play. There is the speed and oscillation, the interpenetration of Rome and Egypt and of present and past.

Above all there is the dialectic marriage of the contraries and their dissolution through union. The jealousy of Cleopatra towards Fulvia, the outrage of Caesar to Antony's *amour propre*—these negative repulsions can serve to hold the mutual pair together as firmly as positive attractions. Antony and Cleopatra are opposed to the world that surrounds and isolates them. In this isolation their union seems absolute, infinite, and self-sufficient. Yet the war of the contraries pervades the love too. In coming together they lapse, slide, and fall apart unceasingly.

The outstanding achievement of the first scene is the way in which it begins with the soldiers' condemnation and returns us at the end to the same thing—allowing for this side eighteen lines out of the sixty-two. Yet at the end we are no longer satisfied as to the adequacy of what Demetrius and Philo say. Not that what they say has been disproved by what we have seen of Antony and Cleopatra. They are and they remain a strumpet and her fool. To have any judgment at all is to choose, apparently, either the judgment of the soldiers at the beginning of the scene or the lovers' own self-assessment that immediately follows it. . . . To entertain either judgment, however, is not enough. The deliquescent truth is neither in them nor between them, but contains both. *Antony and Cleopatra* is Shakespeare's critique of judgment.

Scene I played out romantic love and lovers' quarrels on a lofty stage. It also gave the sharp local comment of the soldiery. Scene II takes the theme of love below-stairs and changes key. It also gives the universal comment of the Soothsayer, with its suggestion that everything is already decided, the tragedy is in the nature of things, now is already over, the future past, the present always:

> In nature's infinite book of secrecy
> A little can I read . . .
> I make not but foresee . . .
> You have seen and prov'd a fairer former fortune
> Than that which is to approach.
>
> [I, ii. 10-11, 15, 33-4]

In place of the 'romance' of love, Charmian, Iras, and Alexas give the 'reality'. The reality in this case is a strong succession of rich, powerful, and adequate males:

> Let me be married to three kings in a forenoon,
> and widow them all; let me have a child at fifty
> to whom Herod of Jewry may do homage; find
> me to marry with Octavius Caesar, and com-
> panion me with my mistress.
>
> [I. ii. 26-30]

It reads like a parody of Cleopatra's aspirations, just as the women's bickering and teasing of Alexas mimic Cleopatra's handling of Antony:

> Alexas,—come, his fortune, his fortune. O! let
> him marry a woman that cannot go, sweet Isis,
> I beseech thee; and let her die too, and give
> him a worse; and let worse follow worse, till
> the worst of all follow him laughing to his grave,
> fifty-fold a cuckold!
>
> [I. ii. 62-7]

This seems a nightmare version of Antony's fate—the reflection in a distorting mirror of the thoughts and feelings that course through Antony after Cleopatra's desertion in the disastrous sea-fight.

The group is interrupted in its fortune-telling by the entry of Cleopatra. She is looking for Antony. Her remarks prepare us for the different mood about to establish itself:

> Saw you my lord? . . .
> He was dispos'd to mirth; but on the sudden
> A Roman thought hath struck him.
>
> [I. ii. 80, 82-3]

Antony is heard approaching. Cleopatra immediately goes off. Now that he is coming she will refuse to see him.

When Antony appears he is surrounded by the messengers from Rome and immersed in Roman affairs. He veers savagely to the point of view both of the soldiers in the first scene and 'the common liar' [I. i. 60] in Rome. Throughout the play this is what marks him off from Cleopatra and makes him a more complex meeting-ground for the opposites than even she is herself. He can understand and respond to the appeal of Rome as much as he can understand and respond to Egypt:

> Speak to me home, mince not the general tongue;
> Name Cleopatra as she's called in Rome;
> Rail thou in Fulvia's phrase; and taunt my faults
> With such full licence as both truth and malice
> Have power to utter. O! then we bring forth weeds
> When our quick winds lie still; and our ills told us
> Is as our earing. Fare thee well awhile . . .
> These strong Egyptian fetters I must break,
> Or lose myself in dotage.
>
> [I. ii. 105-11, 116-17]

The second messenger brings news of Fulvia's death. It is characteristic of the play that what is hated during life should find favour once it is dead. Later in this scene that is reported to be the case with Pompey in the popular reaction to him:

> our slippery people—
> Whose love is never linked to the deserver
> Till his deserts are past—begin to throw
> Pompey the great and all his dignities
> Upon his son.
>
> [I. ii. 185-89]

This is what happens too in Antony's case when, once he is dead. Octavius sings his praises. It also happens when Cleopatra is thought to have committed suicide and Antony flings from vituperation to acclamation almost without pausing. It happens now with Fulvia. Antony says:

> There's a great spirit gone! Thus did I desire it:
> What our contempts do often hurl from us
> We wish it ours again; the present pleasure,
> By revolution lowering, does become
> The opposite of itself: she's good being gone.
> The hand could pluck her back that shov'd her on.
> I must from this enchanting queen break off.
>
> [I. ii. 122-28]
> (pp. 201-03)

Antony does go back to Rome—but not in the mood and not with the motives of thorough-going reformation in which he remains at the end of Scene II. In Scene III the alchemy of the Shakespearean process is further at work. It works to make Antony do the thing resolved upon but for reasons the very opposite of those which led him to the resolve. The scene of his departure is chosen for Cleopatra's most sincere avowal.

Having tormented Antony beyond all bearing she suddenly breaks off with:

> Courteous lord, one word.
> Sir, you and I must part, but that's not it;
> Sir, you and I have loved, but there's not it;
> That you know well: something it is I would—
> O my oblivion is a very Antony
> And I am all forgotten.
>
> [I. iii. 86-91]

Antony's final words in the scene almost catch the very idiom of *The Phoenix and the Turtle:*

> Let us go. Come;
> Our separation so abides and flies.
> That thou, residing here, go'st yet with me,
> And I, hence fleeting, here remain with thee.
> Away!
>
> [I. iii. 101-05]

It is, so to speak, the honeymoon of the contraries—only possible while the lovers are apart.

The first three scenes show how pervasive is that quality in technique and vision which we have called the Shakespearean 'dialectic'. It comes out in single images, it can permeate whole speeches, it governs the build-up inside each scene, it explains the way one scene is related to another. The word 'dialectic', of course, is unfortunately post-Hegelian. The thing we wish to point to, however, in using the word, is Shakespearean. In *Antony and Cleopatra* Shakespeare needs the opposites that merge, unite, and fall apart. They enable him to handle the reality he is writing about—the vast containing opposites of Rome and Egypt, the World and the Flesh.

Rome is the sphere of the political. Shakespeare uses the contraries . . . to give some sort of rational account of the irrationals there involved. The common people, for example, is 'the common liar'. Antony has already noted that its love is 'never link'd to the deserver till his deserts are past' [I. ii. 186-87]. Caesar, too, has his own cold knowledge of the same fact:

> It hath been taught us from the primal state
> That he which is was wished until he were;
> And the ebb'd man, ne'er loved till ne'er worth love,
> Comes dear'd by being lack'd. This common body,
> Like to the vagabond flag upon the stream,
> Goes to and back, lackeying the varying tide,
> To rot itself with motion.
>
> [I. iv. 41-7]

The great men, however, behave exactly as they say the commons do, too. With Antony, Fulvia becomes dear'd by being lack'd. In Caesar's case it is the same. The threat of Pompey makes him suddenly appreciate the grandeur of Antony's leadership, courage, and endurance. The magnanimous praise of Antony in Act V is only possible because Antony by then is dead. The law is general: judgment is a kind of accommodation to the irrational on reason's part:

> men's judgments are
> A parcel of their fortunes, and things outward
> Do draw the inward quality after them,
> To suffer all alike.
>
> [III. xiii. 31-4]

Even soldierly 'honour' is rooted in the ambiguous. When Pompey's man mentions his treacherous scheme for disposing of all Pompey's rivals at one blow (the rivals are also Pompey's guests on board ship) Pompey exclaims:

> Ah, this thou should'st have done
> And not have spoke on't. In me 'tis villainy;
> In thee 't had been good service. Thou must know
> 'Tis not my profit that does lead mine honour;
> Mine honour it. Repent that e'er thy tongue
> Hath so betray'd thine act; being done unknown,
> I should have found it afterwards well done,
> But must condemn it now.
>
> [II. vii. 73-80]

The law is general because it reflects the nature of the terrene world—the tidal swing of the opposites on which all things balance on a motion that rots them away.

The self-destruction of things that rot with the motion which their own nature and situation dictate is almost obsessive with Shakespeare throughout the play. The political world is the manipulation of the common body they despise by the great men whom the commons can never love until they are safely rid of them. The pattern which remains constant in all the possible groupings is that of open conflict alternating with diseased truce, neither of them satisfactory:

> Equality of two domestic powers
> Breeds scrupulous faction. The hated, grown to strength,
> Are newly grown to love . . .
> And quietness, grown sick of rest, would purge
> By any desperate change.
>
> [I. iii. 47-9, 53-4]

Compacts between the great men merely represent the temporary sinking of lesser enmities in front of greater:

> lesser enmities give way to greater.
> Were't not that we stand up against them all
> 'Twere pregnant they would square amongst themselves.
>
> [II. i. 43-5]

Pompey's is a correct appreciation. It is because of him that Octavius and Antony are reconciled. They will rivet the alliance by means of Antony's marriage to Caesar's sister. Enobarbus knows automatically that this union is a certain way of making conflict ultimately inevitable:

> you shall find the bond that seems to tie their
> friendship together will be the very strangler of
> their amity.
>
> [II. vi. 120-22]

Octavia is one of Shakespeare's minor triumphs in the play, beautifully placed in relation to the main figures and the tenour of their meaning. Her importance is apt to be overlooked unless her careful positioning is noted. Her presence gives a symmetrical form to the main relations of the play. Octavia is the opposite of Cleopatra as Antony is the opposite of Caesar. She is woman made the submissive tool of Roman policy, whereas Cleopatra always strives to make the political subservient to her. (It is the thought of being led in triumph by Caesar as much as the thought of Antony's death which finally decides Cleopatra for suicide). Where Caesar and Cleopatra are simple and opposite, Octavia—like Antony—is a focal point for the contraries. There is nothing in her as a 'character-study' to account for the effect her presence has. It is rather that she is transparent to the reality behind the play and one of its least mistakable mediators. On the occasions when she appears herself, or when mention is made of her, it is the interfluent life of this reality rather than the personality of its vehicle which fills the scene. (pp. 204-06)

Octavia never escapes from her position midway between the contraries that maintain and split the world. With Antony away in Athens, her brother first falls on Pompey then finds a pretext to destroy Lepidus. He is now ready to mount his attack on the last remaining rival, his 'competitor in top of all design' [V. i. 42-3]. Hearing of it, Octavia cries:

> A more unhappy lady,
> If this division chance, ne'er stood between,
> Praying for both parts . . .
> . . . Husband win, win brother,
> Prays and destroys the prayer; no midway
> 'Twixt these extremes at all.
> [III. iv. 12-14, 18-20]

Octavia's is the alternative plight to Cleopatra's for woman-hood in the play. The choice is merely between alternative methods of destruction—either at one's own hands, or through the agency of the process. The 'swan's down feather' [III. ii. 48], like the 'vagabond flag' [I. iv. 45], can only swing on the tide until it rots with motion.

Rome is the world of politics and policy. Its supreme term is Octavius Caesar himself. He, like Octavia, must be brought into relation with the pattern which he helps in part to define. Half his significance is lost if he is seen only as a 'character'. In Octavius' case we have aids external to the play which help towards a clear focus on what Shakespeare intends by him. He falls recognizably into Shakespeare's studies of the 'politician'—the series that begins with Richard III and continues down through Edmund [in *King Lear*].

Octavius is a notable development in the figure which started as a machiavel pure and simple. Shakespeare now betrays no sign of alarm, no hint of revulsion or rejection, almost no trace of emotion in putting him into a story. He is taken completely for granted. He has arrived and he will stay. He is part of the structure of things. He is 'Rome'. In matters of politics and policy it is obvious that only the politicians count: and politics is one half of life. The politician is a perfectly normal person. Given all his own way he would doubtless bring—as Octavius is certain his triumphs eventually will bring—a 'universal peace'. To be normal like him, of course, and to enjoy the peace he offers, two conditions are necessary. First, one must sacrifice the other half of life; then, one must be prepared to make complete submission. By the time Shakespeare comes to depict Octavius he has refined away all the accidentals from the portrait—the diabolism, the rhetoric, the elaborate hypocrisy, the perverse glamour: everything but the essential deadliness and inescapability. Octavius marks an advance on Goneril and Regan. He shares their impatience with tavern and brothel. He has no share in the lust which entraps even them. We might almost doubt whether Octavius has any personal appetite at all, even the lust for power. His plan to lead Cleopatra in triumph has the appearance of a desire for personal satisfaction, but it is more likely that it fits into an impersonal wish on Caesar's part to subdue all things to Rome. Caesar, of course, is Rome—but a kind of impersonal embodiment. He is more like a cold and universal force than a warm-blooded man. He is the perfect commissar, invulnerable as no human being should be. Egypt has no part in his composition.

Caesar has the deceitfulness of the machiavel, but he plays his cards without any flourish. He can rely on his opponents to

undo themselves: they are more complicated than he. He puts the deserters from Antony in the van of his own battle:

> Plant those that are revolted in the van,
> That Antony may seem to spend his fury
> Upon himself.
> [IV. vi. 8-10]

The strength and weakness of those ranged against him constitute Caesar's fifth column. The opposition will rot away or eat the sword it fights with.

It is in the last act that Egypt and Rome confront each other singly, the duplicity of Caesar pitted against the duplicity of Cleopatra. There is no doubt as to who shall survive the contest. The tension is maintained throughout the fifth act only by the doubt left in spectator's mind right up to the end as to which way Cleopatra will jump: will she accept submission or will she take her own life? The whole play has prepared us for just this doubt. In a sense, whichever way the decision goes, it is immaterial. The point of the play is not the decisions taken but the dubieties and ambivalences from which choice springs—the barren choice that only hastens its own negation. Rome, from the nature of things, can admit no compromise. Egypt, equally, can never submit to its contrary. So Cleopatra kills herself.

Cleopatra has been loved by recent commentators not wisely but too well. As Caesar impersonates the World, she, of course, incarnates the Flesh. Part of Shakespeare's sleight of hand in the play—his trickery with our normal standards and powers of judgment—is to construct an account of the human universe consisting of only these two terms. There is no suggestion that the dichotomy is resolvable: unless we are willing to take the delusions of either party as a resolution, the 'universal peace' of Caesar, the Egypt-beyond-the-grave of Antony and Cleopatra in their autotoxic exaltations before they kill themselves.

Cleopatra is the Flesh, deciduous, opulent, and endlessly renewable:

> she did make defect perfection . . .
> Age cannot wither her, nor custom stale
> Her infinite variety; other women cloy
> The appetites they feed, but she makes hungry
> Where most she satisfies; for vilest things
> Become themselves in her, that the holy priests
> Bless her when she is riggish.
> [II. ii. 231, 234-39]

The Flesh is also the female principle. Cleopatra is Eve, and Woman:

> No more but e'en a woman, and commanded
> By such poor passion as the maid that milks
> And does the meanest chares.
> [IV. xv. 73-5]

She is also Circe:

> Let witchcraft join with beauty, lust with both!
> [II. i. 22]

Shakespeare gives Cleopatra everything of which he is capable except his final and absolute approval. Cleopatra is not an Octavia, much less a Cordelia [in *King Lear*]. The profusion of rich and hectic colour that surrounds her is the colour of the endless cycle of growth and decay, new greenery on old rottenness, the colour of the passions, the wild flaring of life as it burns itself richly away to death so that love of life and greed for death become indistinguishable:

> there is mettle in death which commits some
> loving act upon her, she hath such a celerity in
> dying.
>
> [I. ii. 143-44]

The strength of the case Shakespeare puts against her is undeniable. The soldiers, and Caesar, and Antony when the consciousness of Rome speaks through him, are right, as far as they go. The strength of the case for her is that it is only Rome that condemns her. And Egypt is a force as universal as Rome— as hot as the other is cold, as inevitably self-renewing as the other is inescapably deadly. And the only appeal that can be made in the play is from Egypt to Rome, from Rome to Egypt. And neither of these is final, because between them they have brought down Antony, the 'man of men' [I. v. 72].

For the tragedy of *Antony and Cleopatra* is above all the tragedy of Antony. His human stature is greater than either Cleopatra's or Caesar's. Yet there is no sphere in which he can express himself except either Rome or Egypt, and to bestride both like a colossus and keep his balance is impossible. The opposites play through Antony and play with him, and finally destroy him. To Caesar (while Antony is in Egypt, and alive) he is:

> A man who is the abstract of all faults
> That all men follow.
>
> [I. iv. 9-10]

To Cleopatra he appears instead a 'heavenly mingle';

> Be'st thou sad or merry,
> The violence of either thee becomes,
> So it does no man else.
>
> [I. v. 59-61]

When she sees him returning safe from the battlefield she cries:

> O infinite virtue! Com'st thou smiling from
> The world's great snare uncaught?
>
> [IV. viii. 17-18]

After he is dead she remembers him as a kind of Mars:

> His face was as the heavens, and therein stuck
> A sun and moon, which kept their course, and lighted
> This little O, the earth . . .
>   . . . Nature wants stuff
> To vie strange forms with fancy, yet t'imagine
> An Antony were nature's piece 'gainst fancy,
> Condemning shadows quite.
>
> [V. ii. 79-81, 97-100]

This, of course, is again the past catching fire from the urgent needs of the present, flaring in memory and imagination as it never did in actuality. Antony is nothing so unambiguous as this. The most judicious account of him is that of Lepidus when he is replying to Caesar's strictures:

> I must not think there are
> Evils enow to darken all his goodness:
> His faults in him seem as the spots of heaven,
> More fiery by night's blackness; hereditary
> Rather than purchased, what he cannot change
> Than what he chooses.
>
> [I. iv. 10-15]

Here the ambiguities of the play's moral universe get their completest expression: faults shine like stars, the heaven is black, the stars are spots. Ambivalence need go no further. (pp. 207-10)

The Roman condemnation of the lovers is obviously inadequate. The sentimental reaction in their favour is equally mistaken. There is no so-called 'love-romanticism' in the play. The flesh has its glory and passion its witchery. Love in *Antony and Cleopatra* is both these. The love of Antony and Cleopatra, however, is not asserted as a 'final value'. The whole tenour of the play, in fact, moves in an opposite direction. Egypt is the Egypt of the biblical glosses: exile from the spirit, thraldom to the flesh-pots, diminution of human kindness. To go further still in sentimentality and claim that there is a 'redemption' motif in Antony and Cleopatra's love is an even more violent error. To the Shakespeare who wrote *King Lear* it would surely smack of blasphemy. The fourth and fifth acts of *Antony and Cleopatra* are not epiphanies. They are the ends moved to by that process whereby things rot themselves with motion—unhappy and bedizened and sordid, streaked with the mean, ignoble, the contemptible. Shakespeare may have his plays in which 'redemption' is a theme (and I think he has) but *Antony and Cleopatra* is not one of them.

Antony and Cleopatra is an account of things in terms of the World and the Flesh, Rome and Egypt, the two great contraries that maintain and destroy each other, considered apart from any third sphere which might stand over against them. How is it related to the plays of the 'great period', the period which comes to an end with *King Lear*?

The clue is given, I think, in the missing third term. *Antony and Cleopatra* is the deliberate construction of a world without a Cordelia, Shakespeare's symbol for a reality that transcends the political and the personal and

> redeems nature from the general curse
> Which twain have brought her to.
>
> [*King Lear*, IV. vi. 206-07]
>
> (p. 211)

The theme of 'Nature' runs through the whole of *Macbeth*, *King Lear*, and *Timon*. Its absence from *Antony and Cleopatra* suggests Shakespeare's satisfaction that for him the theme is exhausted. He is inwardly free now to look at a classical story, deliberately excise the Christian core of his thought, and make up his account in terms of what then remains over.

This explains the effect, I think, of *Antony and Cleopatra*. Freedom from the compulsive theme of the Natures, the conscious security gained from having given it final expression, enabled Shakespeare to handle something new and something which was bound to be intrinsically simpler. Part of the energy formerly absorbed in grappling with theme now bestows itself on technique. *Antony and Cleopatra* gives the impression of being a technical *tour de force* which Shakespeare enjoyed for its own sake.

The excision also explains, I think, the tone of the play—the sense of ripe-rottenness and hopelessness, the vision of self-destruction, the feeling of strenuous frustration and fevered futility, that which finds its greatest expression in Antony's speech before he gives himself his death-blow:

> Now
> All length is torture; since the torch is out,
> Lie down and stray no further. Now all labour
> Mars what it does; yea, very force entangles
> Itself with strength; seal then, and all is done.
>
> [IV. xiv. 45-9]

The excision, finally, explains what might be regarded as a diminution of scope in *Antony and Cleopatra*. We are, of course, only comparing Shakespeare with himself. The theme of Rome and Egypt, however, is simpler than the theme of 'Nature', the trick of using the contraries (again, for Shakespeare) relatively an easy way of organizing the universe. It is unusual, at any rate, for Shakespeare to rely on one trick so completely as he seems to do in *Antony and Cleopatra*. At times we are almost tempted to believe he has fallen a victim of habitual mannerism.

One last comment might be made. . . . *Antony and Cleopatra* is not the aftermath of *Lear* in any pejorative sense. There is something in it that is new and exciting and profound. Shakespeare remained still the youngest and the greatest of his contemporaries. In *Antony and Cleopatra* he is making his own adjustments to the new Jacobean tastes. The play is Shakespeare's study of Mars and Venus—the presiding deities of Baroque society, painted for us again and again on the canvasses of his time. It shows us Virtue, the root of the heroic in man, turned merely into *virtù*, the warrior's art, and both of them ensnared in the world, very force entangling itself with strength. It depicts the 'man of men' soldiering for a cynical Rome or whoring on furlough in a reckless Egypt. It is the tragedy of the destruction of man, the creative spirit, in perverse war and insensate love—the two complementary and opposed halves of a dis-creating society. (pp. 212-13)

> *John F. Danby, "The Shakespearean Dialectic: An Aspect of 'Antony & Cleopatra'," in Scrutiny, Vol. XVI, No. 3, September, 1949, pp. 196-213.*

L. C. KNIGHTS (essay date 1949)

[*A renowned English Shakespearean scholar, Knights followed the precepts of I. A. Richards and F. R. Leavis as he attempted to identify an underlying pattern in all of Shakespeare's work. His* How Many Children Had Lady Macbeth? *(1933)—a milestone study in the twentieth-century reaction to the Shakespearean criticism of the previous century—disparages the traditional emphasis on "character" as an approach which inhibits the reader's total response to Shakespeare's plays. In the following excerpt, Knights asserts that John F. Danby (see excerpt above, 1949) supplied a much-needed corrective to prevailing romantic assessments of* Antony and Cleopatra, *for, in Knights's judgment, Shakespeare treats the love of his hero and heroine with clear-eyed realism. In their passion, the critic argues, there is monotony and artifice, as well as variety and vitality, an impulse toward both self-destruction and regeneration. Knights contends that after the second battle Antony discovers that the love he believed was "solid and enduring" is really immaterial and that he has been led to his downfall by "'Egyptian' magic and gipsy-like double-dealing." The critic concludes that the pathos of the final scenes arises from our appreciation of the possibilities that have not been realized, for we learn that Antony is not the figure of Cleopatra's dream speech and the asp held to her breast "is not, after all, a baby— new life; it is simply death."*]

Mr. Danby's essay on *Antony and Cleopatra* [see excerpt above, 1949] . . . was refreshing. I had for a long time felt that most criticism seriously distorts the play: even critics who as a rule are far enough from finding in Shakespeare an exalted reflection of their own notions, who show in fact that they are capable of responding to Shakespeare's clear-sighted moral realism, seem unable to resist the temptation to romanticize this play. Mr. Danby, to my mind, corrected a firmly established misreading. If, following in his footsteps, I offer some further comments, it is not because of any disagreement with the gen-

eral tenour of his essay, so far as I understand it, but because it seems to me that the tragedy is more clearly defined than appears in his account. I cannot in fact make clear to myself what he intends by 'the reality behind the play'; the metaphysical conclusions in terms of a Shakespearean dialectic of contraries elude my grasp; and I find myself wanting to express my sense of the play's sharper and more definite impact on the mind. Anyone who bothers to read both accounts will see that a substantial measure of agreement with Mr. Danby is implied in my own.

The central theme of *The Tragedy of Antony and Cleopatra* is the relationship of Antony and Cleopatra. That relationship is evoked and defined with a variety of resources that has behind it almost the whole of Shakespeare's working lifetime. Different and apparently irreconcilable evaluations are explicit in commentary and implicit in direct speech and action: as we move from point to point in the play our sympathy changes direction, and as a result of recurrent shifts of the emotional current, 'judgment' becomes more complex. No single statement that we are given concerning the central love-relationship or the individual lovers can be taken as summing up what the play as a whole has to offer, and it is a task of no little difficulty (though not, for the reader of Shakespeare, an unfamiliar one) to expose oneself to the whole experience rather than to some selected part of it. Now it is a significant fact that those who most glorify the passion of the lovers draw largely on the great speeches of Cleopatra just before her death. And although it may be argued that these great utterances represent a culmination or transcendence of what has gone before, the impression I always receive is that the part has been taken for the whole, and the total meaning thereby obscured. If we are to understand these last scenes fully, and with them the nature and meaning of the whole tragedy, we must read them with a present consciousness of *all* that has preceded them.

Those who see the play as a triumphant assertion of the positive value of the love of Antony and Cleopatra speak of the energy expressing itself in and through that passion. Middleton Murry [see excerpt above, 1936] . . . sees the play in terms of a conflict between Reason and Energy; and D. A. Traversi speaks of 'the transcendent justification of passion in terms of emotional value and vitality' [see excerpt above, 1938]. 'Vitality,' of course, in dealing with this play, is a word one can hardly avoid. But even though one readily agrees that any kind of vitality in love at once establishes a qualitative difference from the mean and indistinct fantasyings of lust, there are further important distinctions to be made. From the very opening of the play we have been made aware of something practised in the coquetry, the retreats, skirmishes, and encounters. In the great central scenes—with a deliberate avoidance of glamour— the dramatist seems insistently to demand that we question ourselves about the nature and conditions of the energy which the lovers release in each other.

The sequence of scenes between Actium and the final defeat of Antony opens, as Granville Barker remarked, with a suggestion of dry and brittle comedy. In an apparent abeyance of feeling the lovers are more or less pushed into each other's arms by their respective followers; and there is something of inert resignation ('Love, I am full of lead. Some wine, within there . . .' [III. xi. 72-3]) in the reconciliation that follows. Feeling does not well up in Antony until he discovers Cæsar's messenger kissing Cleopatra's hand. It is a perverse violence of cruelty—'Whip him, fellow, Till, like a boy, you see him cringe his face' [III. xiii. 99-100]—that goads him into a semblance of energy; and it is in the backwash of this emotion that Cleopatra can humour him until she is, as it were, again present to him. Shakespeare, however, leaves us in no doubt about the overwrought nature of Antony's feelings. The resolution that issues from the reconciliation

> I will be treble-sinew'd, hearted, breathed,
> And fight maliciously
>
> > [III. xiii. 177-78]

is in much the same key as his earlier angry ranting,—

> > O that I were
> > Upon the hill of Basan, to outroar
> > The horned herd!
> >
> > > [III. xiii. 126-28]

Now, according to Cleopatra, 'my lord is Antony again' [III. xiii. 185-86]; but the very look of him is given us by Eno-barbus—'Now he'll outstare the lightning' [III. xiii. 194].

Antony, in short, is galvanized into feeling; there is no true access of life and energy. And the significance of this is that we know that what we have to do with is an emphatic variation of a familiar pattern. Looking back, we can recall how often this love has seemed to thrive on emotional stimulants. They were necessary for much the same reason as the feasts and wine. For the continued references to feasting—and it is not only Cæsar and his dry Romans who emphasize the Alexandrian consumption of food and drink—are not simply a means of intensifying the imagery of tasting and savouring that is a constant accompaniment of the love theme. They serve to bring out the element of repetition and monotony in a passion which, centring on itself, is self-consuming, leading ultimately to what Antony himself, in a most pregnant phrase, names as 'the heart of loss' [IV. xii. 29]. Indeed, the speech in which this phrase occurs (IV, xii) is one of the pivotal things in the play. In its evocation of an appalled sense of insubstantiality it ranks with Macbeth's,

> My thought, whose murder yet is but fantastical,
> Shakes so my single state of man, that function
> Is smother'd in surmise, and nothing is,
> But what is not.
>
> > [*Macbeth*, I. iii. 139-42]

With this difference: that whereas Macbeth is, as it were, reaching forward to a region 'where nothing is but what is not', Antony is driven to recognize the element of unreality and enchantment in what he had thought was solid and enduring. The speech has a superb sensuous reality that is simultaneously felt as discandying or melting, until the curious flicker of the double vision—both intensified and explained by the recurrent theme of 'Egyptian' magic and gipsy-like double-dealing—is resolved in the naked vision:

> Betray'd I am:
> O this false soul of Egypt! this grave charm,—
> Whose eye beck'd forth my wars, and call'd them home;
> Whose bosom was my crownet, my chief end,—
> Like a right gipsy, hath, at fast and loose,
> Beguiled me to the very heart of loss.
>
> > [IV. xii. 24-9]

Unless we are intoxicated by what is said about Cleopatra by her admirers, notably by Enobarbus, this seems to me a reading that is forced upon us by the play itself. It is a reading in which I am confirmed by Mr. Danby. Yet it is certainly not the whole story. The vitality of the poetry is not *only* the vitality of the

creating mind, disengaged, as it were, from what it evokes with such clear-sighted realism; and the effect on the reader or spectator is not *only* that of watching the inevitable working out of a self-consuming passion. Passages that compel a 'positive' response to the central love relationship may be far fewer than the usual romantic accounts of the play suggest, but they are certainly there,—and not only, as Mr. Danby suggests, when the lovers are separated or about to part:

> > when you sued staying,
> Then was the time for words: no going then;
> Eternity was in our lips and eyes,
> Bliss in our brows' bent; none our parts so poor,
> But was a race of heaven.
>
> > [I. iii. 33-7]

The description of Cleopatra by Enobarbus (to an audience—it is a characteristic touch—a little too eager for news from Egypt) has a freshness and energy counteracting its suggestions of a deliberate sensuousness; and the famous Cydnus passage modulates easily into a racy buoyancy:

> > The city cast
> Her people out upon her; and Antony,
> Enthroned i' the market-place, did sit alone,
> Whistling to the air; which, but for vacancy,
> Had gone to gaze on Cleopatra too
> And made a gap in nature.
>
> > [II. ii. 213-18]

And it is not only a matter of isolated passages or small touches that compel our sympathy or admiration: the whole poetry of 'Egypt'—in marked contrast to the 'Roman' poetry of buildings and substantial *things*—evokes a world of natural forces within which Antony and Cleopatra have their being.

This, then, is what the play asks of us: to be true to both these impressions of the presented relationship. On the one hand, a closed circle of passion, of which the boasted 'variety' is, in the end, entirely dependent on the application of fresh stimulants; on the other hand, natural force and fertility and spontaneous human feeling, all apparently inextricably tied ('this knot intrinsicate' [V. ii. 304]) with passions directed to death. It is this paradox which is expressed in the metaphysical conceit of 'heart of loss'.

Regarded in this way the consummation of the tragedy is seen to be perfect, and perfectly in keeping. As I have said, Cleopatra's lament over the dying Antony, her later evocation of his greatness and bounty, have weighed too heavily in the impression that many people seem to take from the play as a whole. That these things are great poetry goes without saying. But the almost unbearable pathos of the last scenes, as Mr. Danby rightly insists, is for what has *not* in fact been realized.

> *Cleopatra:*   For his bounty,
> There was no winter in't; an autumn 'twas
> That grew the more by reaping: his delights
> Were dolphin-like; they show'd his back
> above
> The element they lived in: in his livery
> Walk'd crowns and crownets; realms and
> islands were
> As plates dropp'd from his pocket.
> *Dolabella:*   Cleopatra!
> *Cleopatra:* Think you there was, or might be, such a
> man
> As this I dreamt of?

Dolabella: Gentle madam, no.
Cleopatra: You lie, up to the hearing of the gods.
               But, if there be, nor ever were, one such,
               It's past the size of dreaming: nature wants
               stuff
               To vie strange forms with fancy; yet, to
               imagine
               An Antony, were nature's piece 'gainst
               fancy,
               Condemning shadows quite.

                                              [V. ii. 86-100]

The figure that Cleopatra evokes may not be fancy,—the poetry invests it with a substantial reality; but it is not the Antony that the play has given us; it is something disengaged from, or glimpsed through, that Antony. Nor should the power and beauty of Cleopatra's last great speech obscure the continued presence of something self-deceiving and unreal. She may speak of the baby at her breast that sucks the nurse asleep; but it is not, after all, a baby—new life; it is simply death.

It is, of course, one of the signs of a great writer that he can *afford* to evoke sympathy or even admiration for what, in his final judgment, is discarded or condemned. In *Antony and Cleopatra* the sense of potentiality in life's untutored energies is pushed to its limit, and Shakespeare gives the maximum weight to an experience that is finally 'placed'. If we do not feel both the vitality and the sham vitality, both the variety and the monotony, both the impulse towards life and the im-

Act IV. Scene iv. Eros, Antony, and Cleopatra. By Frank Dicksee. The Department of Rare Books and Special Collections, The University of Michigan Library.

pulse towards death, we are missing the full experience of the play. It is perhaps this that makes the tragedy so sombre in its realism, so little comforting to the romantic imagination. For Shakespeare has chosen as his tragic theme the impulse that man perhaps most readily associates with a heightened sense of life and fulfilment: fulfilment not only in continued fertility and the perpetuation of life ('the sun that quickens Nilus' slime' [I. iii. 68-9]), but in the living present ('Eternity was in our lips and eyes . . .'). It has not been part of my purpose to explore the range and depth of the poetry in which the theme of vitality twinned with frustration, of force that entangles itself with strength, is expressed; but it is, of course, the range and depth of the poetry that make Antony and Cleopatra into universal figures. At the superb close, Cleopatra—both empress and lass unparalleled—is an incarnation of sexual passion, of those primeval energies that are both necessary and destructive, that insistently demand fulfilment in their own terms, and, by insisting on their own terms, thwart the fulfilment that they seek. The scene is rich in overtones, and I do not think that it is a forced interpretation that hears in the not-so-nonsensical warnings of the rural fellow with his serpent an echo from the traditional Christian myth. But this is only an echo, not a key: and the tragedy is explained—so far as it needs explanation—entirely in terms of directly presented experience. 'There is no evil impulse', says Martin Buber, 'but that which is separated from the whole being'. It is precisely this that *The Tragedy of Antony and Cleopatra* reveals. (pp. 318-23)

L. C. Knights, "On the Tragedy of 'Antony and Cleopatra'," in Scrutiny, *Vol. XVI, No. 4, Winter, 1949, pp. 318-23.*

JOHN DOVER WILSON   (essay date 1950)

[*Dover Wilson was a highly regarded Shakespearean scholar who was involved in several aspects of Shakespeare studies. As an editor of the* New Cambridge Shakespeare, *he made numerous contributions to twentieth-century textual criticism of Shakespeare, applying the scientific bibliography developed by W. W. Greg and Charlton Hinman. As a critic, Dover Wilson combined several contemporary approaches and does not fit easily into any one critical "school." He was concerned with character analysis in the tradition of A. C. Bradley; he delved into Elizabethan culture like the historical critics, but without their usual emphasis on the importance of the concept of hierarchy and the Great Chain of Being; and his interest in visualizing possible dramatic performances of the plays links him with his contemporary, Harley Granville-Barker. In the excerpt below, Dover Wilson describes Antony and Cleopatra as a celebration of the warmth and vigor of human nature—in effect, Shakespeare's "Hymn to Man." Through the triumph of Antony and Cleopatra over those who lack vitality and imagination, the critic argues, Shakespeare dramatizes the theme of "contempt for the world and the kingdoms thereof." Dover Wilson also focuses on the episode with Seleucus, concluding that it demonstrates Cleopatra's firm resolve for death and her successful attempt to mislead Octavius about her intentions. In portions of his essay not reprinted here, the critic also discusses the play's probable date of composition, other English dramatic treatments of the Antony and Cleopatra story, Shakespeare's use of Plutarch, and the authority of the First Folio text.*]

Bradley atones for leaving *Antony and Cleopatra* out of his earlier volume [*Shakespearean Tragedy*] by devoting to it the best of his *Oxford Lectures on Poetry* [see excerpt above, 1905]. He devotes also the best paragraphs therein to what he calls the 'courtesan of genius'. It took some pluck in 1905 for an elderly Victorian gentleman to echo with enthusiasm Dolabella's cry 'Most sovereign creature!' [V. ii. 81] or to write:

'Many unpleasant things can be said of Cleopatra; and the more that are said the more wonderful she appears.' When, therefore, in the freer air of a generation later, Lord David Cecil dismisses the lecture with the remark that Bradley seems to find 'the moral atmosphere unpleasant', he seems a little unfair and more than a little misleading [see excerpt above, 1943]. He refers, no doubt, to Bradley's confession that, although 'we close the book in a triumph which is more than reconciliation, this is mingled with a sadness . . . that the catastrophe saddens us so little', since

> with all our admiration and sympathy for the
> lovers we do not wish them to gain the world.
> It is better for the world's sake, and not less
> for their own, that they should fail and die.

No doubt, too, when in another place Bradley speaks of them coming before us 'in a glory already tarnished, half-ruined by their past', he has moral considerations in mind. But then, so had Shakespeare, or he would not have underlined the facts that give rise to them; while it is a profound mistake to imagine that Shakespeare had not to reckon himself with a Mrs Grundy in Jacobean London. The story of the play needs, indeed, no underlining to secure the disapprobation of moralists, whether in the nineteenth or the seventeenth century.

Yet nothing is more remarkable . . . about this play, in which an imperial courtesan is the central figure, than the sobriety and coolness of its atmosphere. There is plenty of frank speaking, some ribaldry, and not a little sexual imagery, but of sensuality not a note; and Shakespeare could be sensual enough when he chose; he wrote *Venus and Adonis,* for example, and *Sonnet* 151. . . . The two soldiers who introduce the protagonists to us at the opening of the play as a lustful 'gipsy' and 'a strumpet's fool' [I. i. 13], reveal what the prosaic and bawdy world thinks of the love that binds them. Nevertheless, when the lovers enter immediately after, we learn from their lips that this same love is more spacious than 'the wide arch of the ranged empire', more precious than kingdoms or the whole 'dungy earth', and so boundless that it requires 'new heaven, new earth' to contain it [I. i. 33-4, 35, 17]. And the initial contradiction, or antithesis, runs throughout: the comment of *l'homme moyen sensuel* [the average sensual man] is never silent, the amorous side of the passion never exhibited, and its illimitability and cosmic significance ever more strongly stressed. Compare Dryden's *All for Love,* which exalts the passions after the manner of the Cavalier and Restoration poets, and we perceive what *Antony and Cleopatra* is not. Donne and the 'metaphysicals' would seem to bring us nearer since, while treating love and sex realistically, they use them as the occasion, the take-off, for flights through infinities of space, eternities of time. . . . Marvell argues with a 'coy mistress'; and when Donne awakes his love to talk *à la* Hakluyt of 'sea-discoveries', 'maps', and 'hemispheres', he reminds us of Antony's 'new heaven, new earth'. Further, behind both Donne and this play may be felt the sudden lifting of the medieval horizon, revealing continents of unknown limits lying west and south of Europe, and a starry universe which the mathematicians of the early seventeenth century were only beginning to explore. Yet there is a profound difference. Whereas 'metaphysical' love poetry, as Sir Herbert Grierson puts it, is 'sensuality aerated by brilliant wit', in *Antony and Cleopatra* sensuality is not the main theme at all, but merely the medium through which Shakespeare conveys something different.

What this something else may be we shall inquire presently. For the moment, it is enough to point to it as the obvious source

of that sense of 'triumph which is more than reconciliation' which Bradley speaks of. Note too that, while he remained beneath its spell, Bradley was as obviously untroubled by any other reflections. It was only after he had 'closed the book' and begun to 'look back on the story' (i.e. to forget the poetry and recall the 'facts'), that his 'sadness' came over him. And the trouble was, not so much the reassertion of 'moral' considerations as the return to consciousness of the whole political and philosophical apparatus of Victorian thought, in which a rigid standard of sexual decorum was but part. In a word, he began to judge. 'It is better for the world's sake . . . that they should fail and die' reveals the standpoint, words that Dr Arnold might have written, but that would have been quite incomprehensible to Shakespeare, in whose day the notion of 'progress' was unheard of, and to whose generation 'the world', perfect on the sabbath of creation, had been corrupted by the sin of Adam and his descendants; was falling more and more to decay; and would presently, no man could say how soon, like some

> insubstantial pageant faded,
> Leave not a rack behind.
>
>   *[The Tempest,* IV. i. 155-56]

There is no reason to suppose that Shakespeare did not share such views; and whether he did or not, he found it convenient for dramatic purposes to make use in this play of the attitude of mind they represent. Not that the atmosphere is in any way Christian. Antony's infatuation for Cleopatra is condemned by other characters as 'dotage', a grave error of judgement, extreme folly, or even dishonour and abomination in a general or ruler, never as 'sin' in the man. On the other hand, self-slaughter, from which Hamlet shrinks because the Everlasting had fixed his canon against it, and about which even Brutus has scruples, is glorified as the noblest act of both hero and heroine. Finally, death translates the lovers to the timeless Elysian fields where, Antony foretells,

> we'll hand in hand,
> And with our sprightly port make the ghosts gaze:
> Dido and her Aeneas shall want troops,
> And all the haunt be ours.
>
>   [IV. xiv. 51-4]

The religious and ethical tone is in fact pagan; and, though for the classical simplicity and restraint of *Julius Caesar* we have in this sequel a romantic richness of style and exuberance of form greater than are to be found in any other play of Shakespeare's, the universe in which Brutus and Cassius move is still post-medieval, while that of Antony and his mistress has become, with one exception, Roman; the exception being the . . . contempt they both express for this 'little O, the earth' [V. ii. 81], and even that Shakespeare might have explained, had Jonson taxed him with it, as a kind of stoicism. In any case, it constitutes one of the leitmotivs of the play.

> Kingdoms are clay: our dungy earth alike
> Feeds beast as man: the nobleness of life
> Is to do thus.
>
>   [I. i. 35-7]

So Antony announces it in the opening scene; and we hear it stated again in the last, as Cleopatra's prelude to the final catastrophe:

> 'Tis paltry to be Caesar;
> Not being Fortune, he's but Fortune's knave,

A minister of her will: and it is great
To do that thing that ends all other deeds;
Which shackles accidents and bolts up change;
Which sleeps, and never palates more the dung,
The beggar's nurse and Caesar's.

> [V. ii. 2-8]

The two passages, echoing each other in the word 'dung', span the play like an arch and are supported by much that lies between. (pp. xvii-xxii)

[For] all the splendour of this Roman world and the miracle of Shakespeare's presentation, a satirical light plays over it from first to last, as both Bradley and Cecil after him perceive, though neither, I think, has connected it with the theme of contempt for the world and the kingdoms thereof heard in the first and last scene.... *Antony and Cleopatra* is no tragedy of 'hollow men' in a 'waste land', but of a 'peerless pair' who 'stand up' against the widest and most splendid panorama Shakespeare, or I think any poet, ever painted, and are magnified, not dwarfed, by it because it is represented as mere 'clay' or 'dung' in comparison with them.

It is the tragedy of them both equally.... Cecil, intent on his 'political' solution, ignores Act 5, when the political plot is practically over and Cleopatra has the play all to herself. In the first four acts, it is true, we get something like the normal Shakespearian tragedy, with Antony as hero, whose soul is the scene of the inner conflict, with whom 'the passion that ruins' him 'also exalts him', since it is here that 'he touches the infinite' [Bradley, *Shakespearean Tragedy*], and who comes to his catastrophe in the defeat, shame and suicide of the fourth act. Finally, his death in the arms of Cleopatra excites pity in the highest degree; and Aristotle has taught us to regard pity as one of the essentials of tragedy. (pp. xxiii-xxv)

But it is also Cleopatra's tragedy; she too must find her true greatness and be touched to finest issues. This is the theme of Shakespeare's fifth act, which is his response to the challenge of the source; for when the memoirs of the physician Olympus fell into Plutarch's hands he was led to add a postscript to his *Life of Antony* which supplied the dramatist with matter that could not be fitted into the normal tragic scheme, and was yet of such surpassing interest and beauty as to compel incorporation. Thus Shakespeare was driven to compose a *coda* to the tragedy of Antony which many consider the most wonderful movement in any of his great symphonies. Not of course, as this might suggest, that he took the play scene by scene from the source as a child builds his house by picking wooden bricks one by one from the box. The *coda* is the culmination of the whole, every part of which takes tone and colour from it. Nor is the last act merely a second catastrophe with Cleopatra as protagonist. That 'undivided soul' is no hero or heroine of the ordinary Shakespearian type; while her death, which she does not run to 'as to a lover's bed' [IV. xiv. 101] but awaits crowned and in her royal robes, as is

> fitting for a princess
> Descended of so many royal kings,
>
> [V. ii. 326-27]

so far from arousing pity, fills us with exultation and delight. Indeed,

> Nothing is here for tears, nothing to wail
> Or knock the breast,
>
> [John Milton, *Samson Agonistes*]

For even Antony himself is translated to a sphere far above pity by her speech saluting the grandeur of his spirit. And, having crowned him thus, she is ready to ascend the throne at his side—

> Give me my robe, put on my crown, I have
> Immortal longings in me. Now no more
> The juice of Egypt's grape shall moist this lip.
> Yare, yare, good Iras; quick. Methinks I hear
> Antony call; I see him rouse himself
> To praise my noble act; I hear him mock
> The luck of Caesar, which the gods give men
> To excuse their after wrath. Husband, I come:
> Now to that name my courage prove my title!
> I am fire and air; my other elements
> I give to baser life.
>
> [V. ii. 280-90]

Such a word of farewell means, not death, but an undying triumph in the eternal city of the imagination of mankind, and a triumph over Caesar and every other political 'ass unpolicied' who finds in life no purpose but an extension of his own tethered range upon this 'dungy earth'.

The character of Cleopatra has been too often and too well praised for me to attempt to weave her another garland. Let two things only be said. First, a reply to the charge by Bradley and others, including Granville-Barker [see excerpt above, 1930], which now seems generally accepted, that she shrinks from following Antony 'after the high Roman fashion' [IV. xv. 87]. 'Her first thought,' Bradley writes.

> is too great for her. She would live on if she could, and would cheat her victor too of the best part of her fortune. The thing that drives her to die is the certainty that she will be carried to Rome to grace his triumph. That alone decides her.

This view, as Stahr [see Additional Bibliography] and Furness [see excerpt above, 1907] had seen earlier springs from a misinterpretation of the Seleucus episode, which they rightly explain, not in Bradley's terms, but as a cunning and entirely successful device to 'unpolicy' Caesar, to make an 'ass' of him, to put him off the scent by persuading him that she has no intention of committing suicide since she discovers herself busy trying to save the best part of her treasure for life in the future. True, this is not explicit in the text; though Cleopatra seems to me clearly acting the part throughout. But the text shows nothing to contradict it; the episode can readily be played so as to bring it out to the audience; and the interpretation is confirmed, to my mind, not merely by her general attitude towards 'the beggar's nurse and Caesar's', which is quite incompatible with any shift to 'palate more the dung', but more particularly by Plutarch, who concludes his account of Caesar's visit: 'and so he took his leave of her, supposing he had deceived her, but indeed he was deceived himself'—a point which North emphasizes in the following marginal comment, not noticed by Furness: 'Cleopatra finely deceiveth Octavius Caesar as though she desired to live.' Shakespeare never neglects anything in North he can turn to dramatic use; and it is inconceivable that he overlooked a first-rate hint like this, or seeing it put it by. And once realize that Cleopatra is in this scene only pretending to desire to live lest Caesar should thwart her resolution for death, the resolution is left unquestionable. She announces it at the end of 4. 15 immediately after Antony's own death, reiterates it at the opening of 5.2, and is only forced to postpone it by her unexpected capture and the interview with Caesar. The moment Caesar has left, however, she returns to her purpose and dispatches Charmian to fetch the asps, according to the plan already 'provided', no doubt between 4. 15 and 5. 2. Is it stretching a point to suggest that, like a good strategist, she did a little rehearsing with Seleucus during the same interval, in case of accidents? For my own part, however, if anyone asked how she managed this collusion with Seleucus after her arrest, I should reply: 'That is the sort of question we should not put to Shakespeare.'

To remove this obstacle, to show that the death of Antony is no less potent a force with Cleopatra than the news of her death was with Antony himself—a purge, purifying, integrating, exalting—brings us round to the central theme once more, and to our second point about the heroine. . . . [Because] she, 'all fire and air', is also the genius of the play, vitality is its true theme; vitality as glorified in them both, and in the form which Shakespeare most admired: 'the nobleness of life' [I. i. 36], the strength and majesty of human nature, its instincts of generosity, graciousness and large-heartedness; its gaiety of spirit, warmth of blood, 'infinite variety' of mood. The play is, in short, its author's Hymn to Man; a symphony in five acts, elaborating Hamlet's prose canticle:

> What a piece of work is a man! how noble in reason; how infinite in faculties, in form, and moving; how express and admirable in action; how like an angel in apprehension; how like a god!—the beauty of the world, the paragon of animals.
>
> [*Hamlet*, II. ii. 303-07]

At that it stops; there is not a hint anywhere of the 'quintessence of dust' [*Hamlet*, II. ii. 308]. Man is now 'all fire and air'; as the poet who contemplates him is, in this play at least, all full of a 'happy valiancy', in style and in spirit. (pp. xxxii-xxxvi)

> *John Dover Wilson, in an introduction to* Antony and Cleopatra *by William Shakespeare, Cambridge University Press, 1950, pp. vii-xxxvi.*

WILLARD FARNHAM   (essay date 1950)

[*Farnham was an American scholar, editor, and critic who in his* Medieval Heritage of Elizabethan Tragedy *(1936) examined the concept of tragedy in the Middle Ages and traced its evolution into the Renaissance historical narrative. Farnham maintained that this development influenced all of Shakespeare's drama, his histories as well as his tragedies. He continued this type of historical approach in his* Shakespeare's Tragic Frontier: The World of His Final Tragedies *(1950). In the excerpt below from this last-named work, Farnham argues that Shakespeare endowed Antony and Cleopatra with serious flaws as well as "regal natures" and treated them with an unusual combination of detachment and sympathy. Their love for each other, he contends, has a similar "paradoxical nobility," arousing our admiration even while we see Antony become "a pitiful figure" because of his passion for Cleopatra. Farnham maintains that although "Cleopatra never comes to have a love for Antony to match his love for her," she does perceive "what it would be like to achieve such a love." Shakespeare's balanced judgment is also evident in his dramatization of Cleopatra's death, the critic holds, for he provided evidence for both the traditional arguments: that she kills herself because she cannot live without Antony and that she elects suicide to escape public humiliation in Rome.*]

Technically the protagonist of *Antony and Cleopatra* is Antony, but one finds it difficult to think of Cleopatra as the less im-

portant tragic figure of the play, and one finds it impossible, even if one is proof against her spell, to give less attention to her than to her "man of men" [I. v. 72]. Both Antony and Cleopatra are finished studies in paradoxical nobility, and the title of their tragedy, pairing their names as it does, is appropriate. Lady Macbeth, by attraction and repulsion exerted together, arouses in us a mixture of emotions somewhat comparable to that which her husband arouses, but her tragic paradox is definitely subsidiary to his. For a time she shares the center of the stage with him. Later she is withdrawn from this position, and her death has representation only in a cry of women offstage. Cleopatra, on the other hand, is given so much of the stage that as long as Antony is alive she shares the center of it with him, and then, when he is dead, makes the center all her own. (p. 139)

Shakespeare's Antony is born to lead men and to make crowns and crownets wear his livery. It is part of his tragedy that, though he has a luxuriant personal force which seems irresistible, he is not equal to the task of crushing a less opulent great spirit like Octavius and winning the rulership of the entire world. Shakespeare's Cleopatra is born to assume queenly position and to make the world accept her as royally magnificent. Though she is not gifted with anything like Antony's force, she has woman's subtlety to the fullest degree. It is part of her tragedy that with her subtlety she wins control of his force and by winning this control ruins him and herself. (p. 174)

Largely because Shakespeare takes care to give his hero and heroine regal natures that demand expression, *Antony and Cleopatra* is not a drama in which the world is well lost for love. That is, it does not show the world to be, to the losers, as nothing when compared to their love. We certainly do not find Shakespeare implying that the world which is finally lost to Octavius weighs little in the balance against what Antony and Cleopatra find in each other. He lets us know that it weighs very much indeed.

Shakespeare does not organize his tragedy as a drama of the love of Antony and Cleopatra, but as a drama of the rise and fall of Antony in the struggle for world rulership that takes place after he has met Cleopatra. (p. 175)

Yet though Shakespeare organizes his tragedy as Antony's struggle for world rulership and gives it a pyramidal form showing a rise and fall in the hero's fortunes, he develops within it a psychological drama of love with a course of its own. The action of this drama is in general a rising action to the end. It has its falls, but they are minor, even though sometimes sharp. It takes Antony and Cleopatra from a low point in their relationship to the height reached at their death. Beginning with Antony in revulsion from the dotage produced by the meeting at the Cydnus, and with Cleopatra showing all the light-mindedness of which she is possessed, it rises to a point at which the Cleopatra who has scorned Fulvia as "the married woman" [I. iii. 20] exclaims in all simplicity as she dies, "Husband, I come!" [V. i. 287]. But the love of Antony and Cleopatra, like themselves, never ceases to be deeply flawed, however much it becomes capable of arousing admiration. It is like them in having a paradoxical nobility.

We cannot fail to see that Shakespeare has sympathy for Antony and Cleopatra, and especially for Cleopatra. Anyone who does not fall in some degree under the spell of Shakespeare's Cleopatra is resolute in resistance to her and to Shakespeare himself. The danger is that one may fall too far under her spell and give her a sympathy that Shakespeare does not justify. (p. 177)

It was not the tendency of the age in which Shakespeare wrote to wash out the faults of Antony and Cleopatra in romantic sentiment. . . . Elizabethan writers who found cause to mention Antony and Cleopatra in passing were apt to deal harshly with them: Antony was "besotted" upon Cleopatra and lost fame, power, and life through "blind loue" of her [Sir Richard Barckley, *A Discourse of the Felicitie of Man*]; Cleopatra, "Antonius harlotte," was a woman who worked mischiefs "by subtill meanes," and it was known that there were "horrible murthers she had done of manye Princes and noble men of all coūtreyes where she came" [Richard Reynoldes, *A Chronicle of All the Noble Emperours of the Romans*]; Antony and Cleopatra got "that punishment which they both deserued," a punishment that was one of "Gods heauy iudgements" [Thomas Beard, *The Theatre of Gods Iudgements*].

Nor can it be said with truth that the final effect of Shakespeare's play is a romantic washing out of the faults of his hero and heroine. Certainly the spirit in which he deals with their faults is not that of the preaching moralist; but neither is it that of the preaching romanticist who, because of sympathy for Antony and Cleopatra, would free them from the judgment of the moralist. Samuel Johnson's remark, in the preface to his edition of Shakespeare, that Shakespeare "seems to write without any moral purpose," but that from what he writes "a system of social duty may be selected, for he that thinks reasonably must think morally," is peculiarly true of the Shakespeare we find in *Antony and Cleopatra*. Despite the appeal that the matter of the play has to Shakespeare's sympathy and imagination and despite the warmth and "happy valiancy of style" resulting from this appeal [see excerpt above by Samuel Taylor Coleridge, 1813-34], Shakespeare can, and often does, turn upon his subject a cold white light. (pp. 178-80)

[The play's] first lines are a condemnation of Antony by one of his friends for having fallen into a dotage, for having turned his captain's heart into the bellows and the fan to cool a gypsy's lust, for having transformed himself from one of the three pillars of the world into a strumpet's fool. The condemnation of Antony is contemptuous enough, but it involves a condemnation of Cleopatra even more contemptuous. What immediately follows in this first scene is seeming justification for all that has been said there in denigration of the lovers. Antony daffs the world aside in the person of a messenger from Rome and is willing to let the arch of empire fall while he finds the nobleness of life in embracing a Cleopatra who apparently accepts his love only to taunt him, to make a blushing fool of him, and in general to prove her power over him. (pp. 183-84)

Almost at once after the opening scene we know that we are asked to make no such simple judgment concerning the characters of Antony and Cleopatra as that scene seems to demand. Antony breaks the spell cast upon him by Cleopatra—and does so in a masterful manner—when he decides that the world needs him in Rome. Cleopatra, when she finds that her artifice will not serve to keep Antony from leaving her, says farewell to him in a way that makes us wonder whether she may not after all be capable of more than light-mindedness. We cannot be certain that there is depth of feeling in the speech of Cleopatra ending:

> O! my oblivion is a very Antony,
> And I am all forgotten.
>
> [I. iii. 90-1]

But if this speech shows only artifice taking a new course, it is artifice that is successful in speaking like sincerity.

As the play proceeds, we find that to understand Antony and Cleopatra we must understand that they are voluptuaries, but to understand them thus is to understand much that is admirable in them as well as much that is not admirable. In large part their paradox is that by being voluptuaries, for which they may be scorned, they are led to have certain qualities for which they may be respected. (pp. 184-85)

Antony is a man who fights for high place in the world because he has an unlimited desire to gratify his senses. He can waste time with Cleopatra in the most inane amusements, but his sensualism drives him to high endeavor as well as to such wasting of time. He has love for the strongest colors the world can show and the most pompous grandeur it can yield. To win commanding position in the world and the delight that for him goes with it he is capable at times of denying himself and even of undergoing rigorous hardship. He is a great leader because he is a fearless and able general and because, though he can now and then be cruel, as the selfish sensualist tends to be cruel, his love of the world includes love of the human scene. He understands people, craves boon companionship, and wins affection from followers. His love for the human scene can even, at rare intervals, produce the truest humanity in him, as it does when he hears of Fulvia's death. (pp. 185-86)

Antony . . . is at his best as a statesman-like contender for world power when he deals with Octavius in Rome. He says to Octavius that he will play the penitent to him as nearly as he may, but will not let his honesty make poor his greatness. He does play the penitent, and at no cost to his greatness. That he is honest when he speaks penitently to Octavius of "poisoned hours" spent in Alexandria we may doubt. It is very soon after this that to Octavia he confesses an ill-regulated past life and promises reformation, only to declare to himself, when she has left him and he has had an opportunity to talk with the soothsayer, that he will return to Egypt and its pleasures. (p. 187)

From what we see of Cleopatra before Antony returns to her, we know surely that there are depths in her character which the opening scene of the play does not lead us to suspect. We are not surprised when she beats the messenger who brings news that Antony has married Octavia, or when she hales him up and down by the hair, or even when she threatens to take his life with her dagger. These demonstrations of passionate folly amuse us and do not in any way shock us. We are prepared for them. But we are not prepared for the demonstration of something other than folly that is made by Cleopatra when she herself finally is shocked by her mistreatment of the innocent bearer of ill tidings and declares that she has acted ignobly. Even her royal spirit is paradoxical. It can produce both the pettiness shown by her assault upon the messenger and the high-mindedness shown by the following condemnation of that assault:

> These hands do lack nobility, that they strike
> A meaner than myself; since I myself
> Have given myself the cause.
>
> [II. v. 82-4]

While Antony is in Rome, Cleopatra is willing to unpeople Egypt in sending messengers to him. Her thoughts are with him constantly, and she has no zest for her usual round of frivolities. All this does not prove that what she feels for Antony has great depth, but it does prove that what she feels has some depth. At the very least it proves that she is captivated by her demi-Atlas and has for the time being made him the supporter of her world of sensuous pleasure. Shakespeare brings her to this state of captivation on his own authority. From what Plutarch says, one might guess that when Antony left Alexandria for Rome, Cleopatra was heartless enough to go on with her normal life of pleasure, whatever wound her pride may have suffered. Thus we begin to see that Shakespeare is more charitable than Plutarch toward the Cleopatra of that part of the story which precedes the Battle of Actium.

We continue to see this greater charitableness on the part of Shakespeare when he shows Antony and Cleopatra reunited and moving toward the battle. In the period of preparation for the battle there is no devious action by Cleopatra against Antony—no bribing, as there is in Plutarch, of Canidius by Cleopatra in order that she may take care of her own interests at the expense of Antony's. There is nothing to indicate that Cleopatra wants to fight the battle by sea in order to have an easy way to save herself should the action be lost, despite the very plain statement by Plutarch which would justify the giving of that selfish motive to her. Nor does Cleopatra, with a jest, irresponsibly make light of danger when the advance of Octavius becomes known, as she does in Plutarch; instead of suggesting that the advance of Octavius to Toryne means little, she says sharply that it shows a celerity in Octavius which Antony has lacked. As she takes part in the preparations, Cleopatra is a dignified queen, asserting her responsibility as the "president" of a kingdom and declaring firmly that she will appear in the battle "for a man" [III. vii. 18].

Cleopatra flees from the battle because she is unqueened by fear. In Antony a natural physical courage exists in combination with sensualism. In Cleopatra it does not. This is not merely to say that Antony is a man used to the danger of battle, and Cleopatra a woman unused to it. Sensualism, with its appetite for the worldly pleasures to be obtained through rulership, helps to make Cleopatra a queen, as it helps to make Antony a shaper of empire, but it works upon her, as it does not work upon him, to make flight from pain instinctive. When she finally takes her own life, with what she conceives to be queenly courage, it is only after she has made a search for "easy ways to die" [V. ii. 356].

After Antony has followed Cleopatra away from Actium "like a doting mallard" [III. x. 19] and then with a kiss has forgiven her "fearful sails," there is never any real question that he is firmly bound to her by love. His judgment of men and affairs decays as he gives himself more and more completely to her, and Enobarbus draws attention to the decay. As a leader Antony becomes a pitiful figure. Yet he retains nobility. He still shows largeness of heart toward his followers, and still shows bravery. Enobarbus, dying as a conscience-stricken renegade, assesses him finally in these terms:

> O Antony!
> Nobler than my revolt is infamous.
>
> [IV. ix. 18-19]

But after the defeat at Actium we soon find ourselves confronted with a very real question about Cleopatra's feelings toward Antony: we are forced to wonder whether she is bound to him as he is to her. The question rises when Octavius, hoping that Cleopatra will betray Antony, sends Thyreus to talk with her. At this point Shakespeare deals less charitably with Cleopatra than Plutarch, who, without giving us any very definite cause to doubt Cleopatra's faithfulness, says briefly and noncommittally that she did such honor to Thyreus and talked so long with him that Antony in jealous anger had him whipped and sent back to Octavius. Shakespeare gives us much more

definite cause to suspect Cleopatra as he presents her interview with Thyreus. When Thyreus says that Caesar knows she embraced Antony not as she did love but as she feared him, Cleopatra exclaims, "O!" This interesting "O!" certainly does not mean that Cleopatra is shocked to hear the suggestion that she never loved Antony but was merely forced into an alliance with him. What follows makes it quite clear that, as Kittredge says: "Cleopatra's exclamation is meant to convey to Thyreus not only eager acceptance of Caesar's theory of her union with Antony, but also gratified surprise that Caesar should have shown so sympathetic an understanding of the case" [see Additional Bibliography]. It is possible, of course, that Cleopatra eagerly accepts the suggestion of Thyreus because she plans to beguile Caesar in the interests of both Antony and herself. But Enobarbus, without hesitation, interprets Cleopatra's reply to Thyreus in the worst possible way. "Thy dearest quit thee" [III. xiii. 65] is what he thinks Antony must be told. Shakespeare has made Enobarbus a shrewd judge of character, and by making him now suspect the worst of Cleopatra he seems to be leading us to suspect the worst.

It must be added that Cleopatra appears to be dallying with the thought of using her charm to make one more conquest when she says archly, as she allows Thyreus to kiss her hand:

> Your Cæsar's father oft,
> When he hath mus'd of taking kingdoms in,
> Bestow'd his lips on that unworthy place,
> As it rain'd kisses.
>
> [III. xiii. 82-5]

To say the least, the reminiscence is in bad taste. It is one that a Cleopatra faithful to Antony and bound to him by common disaster might well have foregone. Antony's ordering that the hand-kissing Thyreus be whipped and sent back to Octavius is like an action recorded in Plutarch, but his ensuing excoriation of Cleopatra for having been "a boggler ever" [III. xiii. 110], incapable of faithfulness in love, is like nothing in Plutarch. How much or how little are we meant to discount the furious lines in which Antony implies that he has given himself wholly to a woman who cannot give herself wholly to any man, and implies further that his eyes have been seeled by the gods so that he will adore his errors as he goes to his confusion? His instant forgiveness of Cleopatra after he has disposed of Thyreus and after she has sworn with a few working words that her love for him is not cold seems to confirm what he has said about adoration of errors. It rounds out the picture he has given of his subjection to her and does nothing at all to make her words and actions in the interview with Thyreus less suspicious.

This scene shows, as much as any, whatever irony of superiority Shakespeare brings to his handling of Antony and Cleopatra. Here he lays himself out to prove that though he presents these two as worthy of sympathy he is no special pleader for them. The marvel is that his detachment can be so great and yet leave room not merely for some sympathy, but for much sympathy. Shakespeare shows detachment in all the plays that make up his last tragic world, but in no one of the others, perhaps, is his combination of detachment with sympathy so remarkable as in *Antony and Cleopatra*.

Shakespeare gives no reason why Cleopatra should be suspected of playing false when the ships and land troops remaining to Antony refuse to fight, and when Antony, thinking that she has betrayed him, turns once more against her in fury. It adds to the poignancy of Antony's tragedy that at the end he needs little cause to distrust Cleopatra and can all too easily revive the thought of her being a "triple-turn'd whore" [IV. xii. 13], but nevertheless is completely hers. When he hears the false news of her death, he falls on his sword with intent to overtake her in the next world and weep for pardon. When he finds that he is dying because she has practiced one of her artifices and that she is alive and free to deal with Octavius if she will, he is beyond being able to feel resentment. With true unselfishness he even urges her to deal with Octavius and gain safety if she can.

Antony's death brings from Cleopatra an expression of grief that may seem either superbly histrionic or superbly genuine. The question raised at this point is whether Cleopatra has developed a love for Antony that makes it impossible for her to live without him. Will love for him be the actual cause of her suicide and will she, then, die in the odor of sanctity as one of Cupid's saints? In the manner of her suicide will it be plain that, to use Chaucer's words [in his poem, *The Legend of Good Women*], there "was nevere unto hire love a trewer quene"?

An assumption that Cleopatra took her life for no other reason than that she wanted to avoid being led in triumph by Octavius was made often enough in Elizabethan England. Writers who made that assumption saw no reason to think that a woman of her character was capable of being true in love and of dying for love. They were allowed, though certainly not compelled, by what they found in Plutarch, to think that Cleopatra would not have killed herself if Octavius had not taken steps to have her sent to Rome. (pp. 188-94)

In writing the closing scenes of *Antony and Cleopatra* Shakespeare pays his compliments in two directions with marked evenhandedness, now to the tradition that Cleopatra was really moved to end her life by concern for herself and her honor, and now to the tradition that she was really moved to do so by love for Antony. His evenhandedness can be exasperating to anyone bent upon determining whether his Cleopatra does or does not die as one of Cupid's saints; he takes and uses effectively almost everything to be found in either tradition. (p. 196)

Obviously, an advocate who would have Shakespeare's Cleopatra enrolled in the catalogue of Cupid's saints can make a case for canonization. Having many times previously sworn her love for Antony, she dies with that "Husband, I come" and that "O Antony!" upon her lips. It may be argued that these words, spoken at the moment when she would naturally reveal whatever lies deepest in her heart, show that her love for Antony has come to be the center of her being. She seems to think of herself as winning the right to call Antony husband by demonstrating, in the face of defeat and threatened dishonor, the courage to make a Roman exit from life such as he has made. She visualizes Antony as rousing himself in the next world to praise her "noble act" and mock "the luck of Caesar" [V. ii. 286].

But, just as obviously, a Devil's advocate can make a case against canonization. Cleopatra seems to have thought of escaping Caesar's triumph by suicide before Antony gives her his Roman example of suicide. Before Antony dies she seems quite capable of deciding her fate independently. After he dies she prolongs her stay in the world that he has deserted, and she ends that stay only after she is absolutely certain that Caesar plans to lead her in triumph. As she makes her decision to end her life, she says nothing of a desire to rejoin Antony or a desire to do what Antony would approve, but talks only of being noble to herself. It seems that the self to which she is

to be noble means far more to her than her children, and we may therefore all the more readily believe that it means more than Antony. As for the "Husband, I come" and the "O Antony!" of the death scene, it may be effectively argued by the heartless critic that in these words an ever-histrionic Cleopatra is dramatizing her exit from the world with a fine show of sentiment.

Perhaps it is the Devil's advocate who in the way of reason can make the better case. He has an advantage in that he argues from both words and actions of Cleopatra's, not merely from words, as his opponent does.

But by following reason coldly the Devil's advocate may arrive at a condemnation of Cleopatra that Shakespeare will not support. The beauty and sublimity of the poetry given to her upon more than one occasion when she speaks of what Antony means to her must be felt and duly taken into account by the critic if the Cleopatra whom he judges is to remain Shakespeare's. This beauty and this sublimity are parts of a certain splendor lent by Shakespeare to his heroine which persistently refuses to be written off as in every way false. If we are to understand that the love of Cleopatra for Antony, like her character, continues to be deeply flawed to the end of her life, we are nevertheless to understand that, like her character, it has its measure of nobility. If Cleopatra never comes to have a love for Antony to match his love for her, she at least comes to have magnificent visions of what it would be like to achieve such a love, and her climactic vision leads her to call him husband as she dies.

Shakespeare seems to have done his poetic best to make us feel that the full achievement of Cleopatra in love is a dark matter, dark perhaps even to her, but that though she very possibly does not attain to a noble constancy in love, she does attain to a noble aspiration in love. Also, Shakespeare seems to have done his poetic best to make us sense in the "immortal longings" of Cleopatra a paradox to cap the other paradoxes in her character—a paradox which gives her the visions of a daughter of the game at the same time that it gives her those of a constant wife. The waiting woman Iras dies before her mistress submits herself to the asp. Says Cleopatra, in haste to overtake her:

> This proves me base:
> If she first meet the curled Antony,
> He'll make demand of her, and spend that kiss
> Which is my heaven to have.
>
> [V. ii. 300-03]

One may gather that for Cleopatra Elysium is to be an eternity of faithfulness in love and yet somehow it is also to be an eternity of delightful competition for kisses. Competition between the mistress and the maid is not to be excluded. Cleopatra is very much the queen, but even more she is the woman, and merely as a woman she is willing to take her chances with any other woman in this world or the next.

As we pass from *Macbeth* to *Antony and Cleopatra* we see the problem of evil suddenly lose urgency for Shakespeare. In *Antony and Cleopatra* there are no villains. The hero and heroine have nothing of true villainy in them, and their ruin is not brought about, even in part, by villainy in others. Shakespeare might, on the authority of Plutarch, have given them much more strongly marked strains of cruelty than they have, but he chose in the main to make their vices the more amiable ones and to show them as destroyers of themselves rather than destroyers of others. They are in no sense trapped into doing what they do to themselves, either by human or by supernatural opponents. They go their own ways to destruction.

We may even gain the impression that outside forces are often kind to Antony and Cleopatra and in general go so far as to favor them until what the lovers create for themselves becomes too strong for benevolent powers to counteract. Before the Battle of Actium, friends do all they can to save Antony from making false judgments. At the battle, "vantage" appears "like a pair of twins" [III. x. 12], and that of Antony and Cleopatra even seems to be "the elder," until Cleopatra flees and Antony follows. Enobarbus turns renegade only when his leader's fortunes are completely hopeless, and the god Hercules waits even longer to remove his protection from Antony. The fate that works through human character is against Antony when he brings himself into competition with Octavius. Antony accepts without demur the soothsayer's judgment that the guardian spirit of Octavius has a mysterious power to reduce his own spirit to fear, and to dim the luster of it, when he and Octavius come together. But this fate nevertheless is generous to Antony. For his daemon is

> Noble, courageous, high, unmatchable
>
> [II. iii. 21]

when not near Caesar's.

In *Antony and Cleopatra* there is nothing to suggest that the order of life is in a state of decay or that medicine needs to be administered to a sickly weal. There is no one in the play who struggles idealistically against wrong. Octavius puts Antony down and becomes a better lord of the whole world than Antony could ever have been, but though he despises the sensualism of Antony he does not fight against him to free the world from that sensualism and its effects. He fights against him simply to work out his own imperial destiny.

As Shakespeare proceeds with the creation of his last tragic world, he comes logically to that view of the tragic scheme of things which we find in *Antony and Cleopatra*. Seeing tragedy more and more as a product of flaw in character, he sees less and less of mystery in its causation. Then suddenly the mysteries of evil and injustice cease to challenge him. This does not mean that he turns to a presentation of tragedy which has nothing in it of the enigmatic and that he does violence to life by reducing it to the neat form of a solved problem. In the amplitude of *Antony and Cleopatra* there are enigmas in abundance. But all of them that really matter are within the hero and heroine; they are enigmas of personal constitution. At last, Shakespeare's growing interest in the paradox he has discovered in deeply flawed yet noble character becomes very distinctly his sustaining interest in the writing of tragedy. This paradox, which in *Timon* and *Macbeth* has been for him one of the most challenging of tragic mysteries, becomes for him in *Antony and Cleopatra* the all-absorbing tragic mystery. (pp. 200-05)

Willard Farnham, " 'Antony and Cleopatra'," in his Shakespeare's Tragic Frontier: The World of His Final Tragedies, *University of California Press, 1950, pp. 139-206.*

M. R. RIDLEY (essay date 1954)

[*In the following excerpt from his introduction to the 1954 Arden edition of* Antony and Cleopatra, *Ridley asserts that Cleopatra's resolution to die—made at the moment of Antony's death and in a mood of exaltation—subsequently wavers and that the Egyptian queen does, indeed, explore the possibility of preserving her life. Examining in turn the episode with Seleucus, her conversation with Proculeius, and what may have transpired during the interval between the close of Act IV, Scene xv and the beginning of Act V, Scene ii, the critic suggests that Cleopatra would have negotiated "terms with Caesar if she could make her own," but that Dolabella's confession convinces her of Caesar's humiliating intentions. Ridley also states that although the protagonists' passion for each other is not the most laudable form of love, it is idle to attempt to judge its morality or immorality, for in the dramatic world of* Antony and Cleopatra *such disputes are meaningless.*]

Stahr [see Additional Bibliography] pointed out that Plutarch says, at the end of the account of Caesar's interview with Cleopatra, "and so he took his leave of her, supposing he had deceived her, but indeed he was deceived himself" (North's translation); and North underlines this and makes the design explicit, by a marginal comment, "Cleopatra finely deceiveth Octavius Caesar *as though she desired to live*" (italics mine). That is to say, the whole scene with Seleucus is a put-up job, possibly even rehearsed beforehand. The easiest way of convincing Caesar that she desires to live is to be exposed as having retained, and omitted from her declaration, half her fortune, to support not only life, but life in something like her former state.

This interpretation has two dramatic advantages. It prevents Cleopatra's assault on Seleucus being no more than an undignified repetition of the earlier scene with the messenger—a drop in tone which at this point of the play is hardly tolerable. And it gives us the pleasure of watching Caesar out-played, not only walking headlong into the trap but [in V. ii. 184-89] thinking himself clever as he does so, so that Cleopatra's "My master, and my lord!" [V. ii. 190] can carry its full charge of irony, since she knows that he is already the ass, unpolicied. The only trouble about the interpretation is whether it can be made plain to the audience, since if it cannot it is not what Shakespeare the practical playwright intended. But I think it can be done. In the first place, the more quick-witted of the audience will wonder why Cleopatra brings in Seleucus at all— and it is her doing, not Caesar's that he is introduced. If Caesar will not take her own word for her "brief" he is not likely to take that of a subordinate official, presumably under her thumb. "Hullo," says the suspicious spectator, "there is more here than meets the eye." But I think the vital point is the way in which the actress playing Cleopatra delivers the words "Speak the truth, Seleucus" [V. ii. 144]. They are his cue. After that both he and Cleopatra, by slight exaggeration, he of his fears and she of her tantrums and her humiliation, indicate that they are playing a game.

But if the interpretation is right in itself, I think that in the application of it Dover Wilson overplays his hand [see excerpt above, 1950]. He is so anxious to establish Cleopatra's unswerving nobility, to show that her resolution to follow Antony at once never wavered, that he takes this interpretation of the Seleucus scene as proof positive of the unwavering resolution, and he also neglects an awkward interval and the conversation with Proculeius. Now that conversation, though it is possible to get round it, cannot safely be neglected; and the Seleucus scene turns out, on examination, to be irrelevant to the main issue. No one denies that Cleopatra contemplates suicide as at least a possibility. Even if she is only going to be driven to it as a last resort, still she will, when convinced of its necessity, need time for its achievement, and this time, she hopes, the scene with Seleucus will provide. If she finds that she can make satisfactory terms, little will have been lost; if she cannot, everything will have been gained. That is to say, the "put-up job" interpretation of the Seleucus scene fits as neatly and as dramatically into either reading of Cleopatra's state of mind as into the other.

It is perhaps worth while examining for a moment the stages in Cleopatra's progress towards suicide. In the first place, at any time we like anterior to the climax of the play, she has pursued infinite conclusions of easy ways to die. In a crisis, therefore, her thoughts will not be exercised by the mechanics of suicide, but only by its necessity or desirability; and we guess that the compulsion will need to be strong that drives her to it. Under the immediate shock of Antony's death she rises to a mood of exaltation; the odds is gone, the world is a dull place, we have no friend but resolution and the briefest end, so let us act after the high Roman fashion, rush into the secret house of death and make death proud to take us. There is no mistake about that. But is it cynical to suggest that even here she does not exactly "rush" into the house of death, as Antony did or tried to do, but gains time even from her own resolution on the grounds of burying Antony? There is then an interval, during which we have no clue to her thoughts except that she sends the "poor Egyptian" to Caesar to enquire his "intents." When next we see her (v. ii) she is again contemplating suicide, though in more philosophic fashion. She then has an interview with Proculeius, in which she expresses submission, states her terms, and suggests an interview with Caesar. When captured by the guard she attempts suicide, and gives as reason for the attempt the hateful prospect of Caesar's triumph—not a word of Antony. Her last message now to Caesar is "I would die" [V. ii. 70]. Left alone with Dolabella she pays tribute to Antony, and having got Dolabella well-tempered she comes out with the direct question, "Know you what Caesar means to do with me?" [V. ii. 106] and forces an answer from him. She has no time to comment on it before Caesar enters. She plays her scene with Caesar and Seleucus, and after Caesar has gone despatches Charmian, presumably to arrange for the introduction of the asps. While Charmian is away she receives from Dolabella further confirmation of Caesar's intentions and paints for herself and Iras a picture of the degrading circumstances of Caesar's intended triumph. From the moment of Charmian's return not only is her "resolution" indeed "placed" and she "marble-constant" but Antony at last is the expressed motive for the resolution. She is again for Cydnus to meet him, she claims him as her husband, and she will not, if she can help it, let Iras reach him first.

That, I think, is a fair statement of what the text shows us. Nothing can detract from Cleopatra's royal splendour at the end; but we should not allow our eyes to be so dazzled by it that we cannot examine what happens, or does not happen, earlier. There is, first, the short conversation with Proculeius before her capture. This reads to me like an honest attempt at negotiation. I admit that it may be construed as a dishonest playing for time; but if her resolution had been constant the time should not have needed to be played for. Far more crucial than the interview with Proculeius is the interval between the end of iv.xv and the opening of v.ii, an interval from which the supporters of the unwavering purpose resolutely avert their eyes, and do their best to avert the eyes of their readers. Dover Wilson, for example, says "She announces it [the resolution] at the end of 4.15 immediately after Antony's own death, reiterates it at the opening of 5.2, and is only forced to postpone it by her unexpected capture and the interview with Caesar." "Only forced to postpone it" seems to me a piece of clever

but somewhat disingenuous special pleading. It is true *of the moment;* but what has Cleopatra been doing with the interval before this moment? There is as yet, so far as we know, no guard through whom the bearer of the asps has to be brought in, and so nothing in the world to prevent her arranging for his arrival when she chooses. I think that after her first moment of exaltation she would make terms with Caesar if she could make her own, and is brought back to her original resolution only by her later conviction of Caesar's intentions.

I have laboured the point only because I think that Shakespeare's portrayal of Cleopatra at the end of the play is far more subtly penetrating, and more unsparing, than some of his critics would like it to be. (pp. xlv-xlix)

It is easy to miss the cutting and balanced precision of Shakespeare's delineation of Cleopatra. If only we will hear, it is as though we were members of a jury, listening to the summing-up of the most dispassionate and brilliant of judges. When once we have read the play it is hard not to reflect back upon the Cleopatra of the first four acts the light and colour of the Cleopatra of the last. In the last act she is the great queen, and is indeed fire and air; no doubt she would have made terms with Caesar if she could have made her own, but, seeing that she cannot, she will follow Antony, and if she is to die, she will die indeed painlessly, but she will do it after the high Roman fashion; and Death would be a poor creature if he was not proud to take her. But if our eyes are not dazzled by this reflection we shall recognize that it would be hard to find anywhere in literature a more unsparing picture of the professional courtesan than Shakespeare's picture of Cleopatra in the first four acts. Her aim indeed is not ignoble; she is genuinely, and perhaps for the first time in her life, in love; Antony at last realizes her ideal; but the methods by which she achieves her aim and holds him are those of the past-mistress in her ancient art, learnt and perfected to the last finesse of technique in years in which she hung the scalps of Caesar and Pompey, amongst others, at her belt. The bafflement of the critics, or some of them, about her seems to depend on a confusion of complexity with variety. She is infinitely varied, but not in the least complex; she is as single-minded in pursuit of her aim as Lady Macbeth in pursuit of hers, and all the quick shifts of temper are little more than part of her brilliant technique. Perhaps in the end the best description of her is Enobarbus' simple "a wonderful piece of work" [I. ii. 153-54]. That at least avoids any idle questionings as to the morality or immorality of the love of Antony and Cleopatra.

Since, unless we suffer from a kind of moral myopia, we are little troubled as we read, and even less as we see, by questions of worthiness or unworthiness, still less of morality and immorality. We have been transported to a world in which such disputes seem to lose their meaning. Admittedly it is far from the noblest kind of world, as the two main figures are far from human nature at its noblest. But, being what they are, they are by their mutual passion lifted to the highest pitch to which they are capable of soaring. It is the merest fatuity of moralizing to deny the name of "love" to their passion, and write it off as "mere lust." No doubt it is not the highest kind of love; it is completely an *égoisme à deux* [self-centered relationship], and has no power to inspire to anything outside itself; but it has in it something that should be an element in the highest kind of love; and at least it is the passion of human beings and not of animals, of the spirit as well as of the body. It was not by her beauty (of which by all accounts the gods had not been lavish) but by her superb vitality that Cleopatra took Antony captive and held him.

And it is by that same vitality that she takes us captive also. We may attempt to analyse the play, to apply critical criteria to it, to examine the characters, and so on; and no doubt we are right to do so, and by so doing help our appreciation of the play. But in the end these intellectual exercises and their results drift down the wind like the idle thistledown that for this play they are; we know in our hearts that what in this play Shakespeare has to offer us is a thrill, a quickening of the pulses, a brief experience in a region where there is an unimagined vividness of life; and we surrender, with Antony, if anything so vitalizing can be called surrender, to the "strong toil of grace" [V. ii. 348]. (pp. lii-liv)

M. R. Ridley, in an introduction to Antony and Cleopatra *by William Shakespeare, edited by M. R. Ridley, revised edition, 1954. Reprint by Cambridge, Mass.: Harvard University Press, 1956, pp. xlv-lvi.*

NORMAN HOLMES PEARSON   (lecture date 1954)

[*The disparity between words and actions in* Antony and Cleopatra, *Pearson declares, parallels the division of values that have resulted from Rome's rejection or debasement of friendship and loyalty after the death of Julius Caesar. The critic maintains that the play moves toward a triumphant recognition that the values exemplified by Rome and Egypt are complementary rather than mutually exclusive, for harmony is achieved when the principal figures discern the interdependency of seemingly opposing qualities. The redemptive process begins with Enobarbus's suicide, Pearson contends, for with his death Enobarbus returns to Antony the spiritual love and loyalty his master demonstrated toward him, thereby generating a "new nobility" in the triumvir. The critic asserts that before their own deaths, both Antony and Cleopatra comprehend that the essential harmony of marriage springs from the conjunction of love and honor, intuition and reason, two hearts and two minds. Pearson's commentary was first delivered in a lecture at the Yale Shakespeare Festival in 1954.*]

A few weeks ago I asked a friend what he considered the chief difficulty of [*Antony and Cleopatra*]. His thoughtful answer was in terms of the audience. Shakespeare, he said, requires much more of us, and in a different way, from what our usual situation is in regard to the characters of a dramatic work in the theatre. For we normally judge characters, whether in a play or in life, by their actions; here we are asked to assess them finally by their words. We are not used to depending so much on words when we hear them spoken. He was right. *Antony and Cleopatra* is a play on words, as well as a play made from them. The action revolves about words and their justness. We can watch the action of *Antony and Cleopatra* with attention, but we must hear and remember with concentration the words which accompany the action. Only as these spoken words remain firmly with us, fixed but lively in our consciousness, can we fully see the conflict between what the players say and what they do, and feel the progress of the drama through a series of tensions toward the final apocalyptic congruence.

The life as well as the particular quality of *Antony and Cleopatra* come from this interplay. The initial disparity of action and statement on the part of the two chief characters makes the validity of their first declarations seem absurd although beautiful, mere lovers' exaggerations.... On the other hand, it is the suitability of their irresponsible deeds to Philo's opening and choragic disapproval of them, which makes the quasi-anonymous Philo seem, at the beginning, the proper rhetorician and the impartial judge. From this conflict of opening impressions, the progress of the play stems; and it continues in the

achievement of definitions, establishing some and destroying others, until at the end we understand in triumphant awareness, parallel to a tragic awareness though mollified, what neither we nor the chorus nor Antony and Cleopatra themselves could, at the opening, fully grasp in the clarification of character and diction.

If in practise I prefer to read *Antony and Cleopatra* rather than see it performed on the stage, it is because the process of understanding is simplified on the printed page. The words which I can thus see with concentration, take precedence over the action, which I can only fancy. I can linger over the printed words, delaying the action until I have absorbed the words, as I linger over the verbal counters of a poem. Where words become supreme in this way, almost at the expense of action, we approach the realm of the closet drama rather than the theatre. It would be inept to consider *Antony and Cleopatra* simply as a poem rather than a play, but in this instance we are close to that thin line which divides poetic drama from a dramatic poem. Certainly the intensely, almost metaphysically contrived verbal texture of *Antony and Cleopatra*—Shakespeare's sense of words which waver in definition and must be filled with significance established within the play itself—brings the manner of this drama close to the verbal excitement which is the stimulant of much of our contemporary concern with poetry. It is no wonder that Coleridge admired this particular work so much.

But perhaps there is something to be said, after all, for Dryden as man of the theatre. He made no such demands, in his version, as Shakespeare does, either on actors or audience. What the theatre uniquely gives, of course, is visible action as a mode of definition and a way towards understanding. That which is most theatrical is apt to be least wordy.... Dryden knew language, but he simplified its use in verse. Action in his play becomes dominant in a straight though impassioned line; verse follows it. Dryden's play is first-class theatre and good poetry. It is only when we compare it, as an absolute literary achievement, to Shakespeare's ironic and ultimately triumphant interinvolvement of words with action, that *All For Love* diminishes in appeal and we can understand what makes *Antony and Cleopatra* so terrifying to produce and so overwhelmingly a display of the absolute limits of drama. (pp. 127-29)

It is Shakespeare's extraordinary power that makes his ... figures of speech dramatically active and organic rather than merely ornamental or tasty. There is purple in the passages of the play, but it is imperial and not patch. Even Enobarbus's supreme description of Cleopatra, as she approaches on the Cydnus, is not pure display but tactics of language. For *Antony and Cleopatra* is a drama of persuasion, an exercise in rhetoric which will explain and justify the values which a Roman world ignores.

"I will tell you," Enobarbus says [II. ii. 190], but not simply to Agrippa and Maecenas who are with him in his return to a Roman world. Enobarbus speaks also as though to Caesar and to Lepidus who do not hear. He speaks to Pompey, too; for none of these Romans can understand what drew the "demi-Atlas of the world" [I. v. 23] to Egypt. Egypt and Cleopatra are beyond their experience. Enobarbus, reaching for the limits of sensory verse, tries to create experience as a magnet for these two who stand as surrogate for all the rest.

Can't you sense it! he seems to say. Listen to me! It's this way! For poetry describes the quality of things; and Cleopatra's quality is what Enobarbus grasps, in words that spring forth like a vision not before beheld by us, for we have seen too little of her;—until now, that is, since Enobarbus also speaks to us. Sight, sound, smell, touch bombard us; and we learn from these what reason will not tell but "flower-soft hands" [II. ii. 210] can give. "O, rare for Antony!" Agrippa says [II. ii. 205], when Enobarbus finishes his first verse paragraph. Agrippa thinks, as we have thought, of Antony imperially apart from us, and Cleopatra wrought for him alone. But when the verse goes on, and "a strange invisible perfume hits the sense of the adjacent wharfs" [II. ii. 212-13], Agrippa cries out this time, "Rare Egyptian!" His exclamation shifts its referent. Antony is forgotten. Agrippa thinks now only of the queen, for she has conquered him in verse, and he runs "to gaze on Cleopatra too" [II. ii. 217]. We run on with him and the crowd. We have begun to share with Antony.

Such is the persuasion of this single little scene within the play, but it works more. It helps define such early words as these, which Cleopatra spoke to Antony:

> Eternity was in our lips and eyes,
> Bliss in our brows bent; none our parts so poor
> But was a race of heaven. They are so still. . . .
>
> [I. iii. 35-7]

From the first lines of the play, this effort, through language and feeling, to break through the limits of reason to that which cannot be "reckon'd", provides the essential dramatic strain.

> Cleo.   I'll set a bourn how far to be belov'd.
> Ant.   Then must thou needs find out new heaven,
>   new earth.
>
> [I. i. 16-17]

It is such a glimpse of heaven that Enobarbus gives, an apotheosis that lifts Cleopatra up from the rank of queen to that of goddess of Love and finally to an estate of pure sense. Thus, none their "parts so poor" but can become a race (that is, a root) of heaven. More definition is still needed before Cleopatra is again for Cydnus, but Enobarbus has added something to her realization, and the words of the play have progressed in their special manner.

Enobarbus's description of Cleopatra's welcome at Cydnus prepares us also to learn something about the character of Caesar. That is, if Enobarbus's lines are, as they should be, still fresh in mind when we read Caesar's analogous description of the "ideal" approach of his sister, Octavia, to Rome:

> Caes: Sister: The wife of Antony
>   Should have an army for an usher, and
>   The neighs of horse to tell of her approach,
>   Long ere she did appear. The trees by the
>   way
>   Should have borne men, and expectation
>   fainted,
>   Longing for what it had not. Nay, the dust
>   Should have ascended to the roof of Heaven,
>   Raised by your populous troops. But you are
>   come
>   A market-maid to Rome, and have prevented
>   The ostentation of our love; which left
>   unshown
>   Is often left unlov'd. We should have met
>   you
>   By sea, and land, supplying every stage
>   With an augmented greeting.
>
> [III. vi. 43-55]

What sort of expectation faints? One, choked by the dust the horses raised, while "longing" for fresh air "it had not"? Not this, of course, but one to be overcome by a display of pomp or expectation of it. And what is that which "left unshown is often left unlov'd"? It is the "ostentation" of a brother's love, made a show of, exhibited through troops, and not by heart-felt tropes. Is this a brother's love? Will "market-maid" prove in the end to be so foul an epithet, when we find Cleopatra as "the maid that milks and does the meanest chares,"—"a lass unparallel'd" [V. ii. 316]? Octavius stays aloof; he does not share, at best he but bestows. Only what's rank, not ripeness, counts for him.

It is not simply that Caesar's diction differs from that of Enobarbus. Caesar's words should not have been the same as Enobarbus's. A brother's love is different, but it should be love. We know Octavius Caesar through the words he chooses. And though these words are reasonable, he is not capable of that personal emotion which informs words as poetry, any more than he is capable of such felt love for his sister as would have prevented his attempts to hoop the world together through the cold formality of Octavia's Roman marriage to Antony. Caesar is defined for us, not by any direct statements about his character—or at least by comparatively few of them—but dramatically: partly by contrast of his words and deeds, and also by contrast of his words with those which others speak: Enobarbus in this case, and Antony almost everywhere. Caesar's lines are flat. It is not Shakespeare's lack, but Caesar's, in them.

No wonder then that Antony can scorn this beardless boy of 23, who had not wived and could not love, was passionless, had never singly fought in combat but had "worded" men and made his way by tricks of conscience. Caesar spoke eloquently of honor, friendship, unity and love, but never knew each as a fact. So Lepidus, too, slung words about, flabby, with no core in them. This Pompey understood:

> Caesar gets money where
> He loses hearts; Lepidus flatters both,
> Of both is flattered; but he neither loves,
> Nor either cares for him.
>
> [II. i. 13-16]

It is this absence of felt love, even the denial of the capacity for love, which marks the world and the language of the world which Caesar makes.

More than the empire split in bits after the death of Julius Caesar by the swords. Man himself divides, matching the splinters. Man's personal nature is no longer whole, when as a citizen his allegiance must be pledged either to one half or the other of the world. Nothing remains between the poles. One can begin to understand *Antony and Cleopatra* better, as a play, if, as Professor Bethell [see excerpt above, 1944] and others have shown us, we see the ultimate opposition between Rome and Egypt not simply as a political struggle for power, but as a conflict between two ways of life expressed by the extremes. Between them Antony is pulled. Roman values of duty are opposed to Egyptian values of pleasure; reason against intuition; mind against the senses; shrewdness against idealism; and prudence against daring. In a world which is a whole, these values need not be in conflict, for a whole world at peace had contained both Rome and Egypt too. Each way of life is a part of that reduced facsimile of the world which man himself becomes. But let man place too great an emphasis upon one set of values in himself: this set will crowd the other out, as it itself expands in opportunity. Make one extreme: its adversary too becomes extreme, and there are nothing but extremes to choose from.

This was what Rome had done, and Caesar was its icon. Honor became debased. At best it was a word without a soul, though highly polished by much use. Caesar had learned to tongue it late in its career in Roman talk; Antony had learned it young, and mourned its gradual loss of quality. Antony was a man. What had been starved by Roman ways he hungered for. Deprive a man of food for years, and he will gorge when once he has the chance. Antony craved more than power, and could not find the things he sought in Rome.

If hunger is a common urge, and shared by men alike, the goals of hunger must, then, be defined and understood. Caesar, for example, was young and hungered. Caesar hungered for power; but since the world was already conquered, he could only, as Antony would not, prey upon friends. Or rather, Caesar did not feel these people as his friends; nor think of *honor* save as it became a useful word to flaunt; or *order* save as an excuse for seizing power, to be achieved by foment of discord. Nothing stood in his way: not friendship,which is based on love; nor honor, which depends on loyalty. These qualities he lacked, and when he used the words, he tricked with them to cover up the motive underneath. His deeds belied his words,— if when we think of deeds we can forget his dignity of movement on the stage, his toga'd wrap of hollow, polished words, remembering Caesar as he is when he fights Pompey, or tricks Lepidus, or knowingly slights Antony, and breaks the spirit of his word, as others understood the meaning from his speech, and only later knew it was not so from what he did.

For Antony the usual tokens of aspiration were achieved. A man has fame, is conqueror, a triumvir, had done the things he does so well that repetition has no meaning any more. And these are not enough: something is lacking, and he is not whole. Antony felt only partial so he plunged, splashing the past in quest of something more:

> Let Rome in Tiber melt, and the wide arch
> Of the rang'd empire fall! Here is my space.
> Kingdoms are clay; our dungy earth alike
> Feeds beast as man; the *nobleness of life*
> Is to do this; when such a mutual pair
>   (Embracing)
> And such a twain can do't, in which I bind,
> On pain of punishment, the world to weet
> We stand up peerless.
>
>   [I. i. 33-40]

Possibly Antony could only recognize and could not really define the urge which drove him toward Egypt, away from Rome, away from Fulvia and his Roman marriage to her, as later it would send him off from Caesar and Octavia. This was a kind of spiritual and physical restlessness such as a long-starved middle age can feel, when nothing man has won has satisfied. This was the straining, through the surge of feeling and language, to break the limits of reason—to repeat an observation made apropos of Enobarbus's and Cleopatra's speech. Antony now felt the "nobleness of life" and could make poetry of it. He had his intimations of the "heaven" and the "eternity" which Cleopatra felt. (pp. 131-36)

[The] nobility of life comes from a proposition demanding such a doubly coupling phrase as "mutual pair" and such twinned unity as "twain." This way, the path of union is begun again. For Shakespeare, what was partial was but unresolved; with love came harmony. This was the binding and completing force

of love, unknown to Rome. Redemption came when man loved man, was therefore joined to man.

Thus our first view of Antony, save for the words of Philo's speech, is not of him alone, but him and Cleopatra entering as a pair. And their embrace is fixed upon our mind, and kept there through the play. We know the play to be not Antony's alone, but theirs, involving her. If harmony is to return to that which circumstance has split apart, then these two must at last embrace again to form their icon of an ideal world. And Enobarbus cannot die alone, for he and Antony make another kind of pair.

Yet the view, rather than the vision, of Antony and Cleopatra in embrace is not a simple one to comprehend.

>   . . . and our ills told us
>   Is as our earing.
>
>   [I. ii. 110-11]

So Antony tells the messenger who comes to him from Rome. The lines are a kind of warning, or motto. In their implication they are as important for all other characters in the play as for Antony, or for us who listen. What do these lines mean? "Is as salutary to us as ploughing is to weed-grown fields"—so, dictionary-wise, the verb "to ere" becomes "to plough," and so the glosses to the textbooks read. But: "is as our 'earing" (pronounced cockney-like); "is as our *hearing*"; "is as we hear as ills, or hear them otherwise." . . . [What] is in question is not only the consequence and harvests of ill-deeds, or their future prevention, but whether we hear them as ill-deeds at all, and can therefore agree in their definition and hence in their consequence.

Antony later makes this problem clear to Caesar, when Antony says, "I learn you take things ill which are not so" [II. ii. 29]; and though he adds, "or being, concern you not" [II. ii. 30], the second is subordinate to the first. For hearing goes on everywhere within the world, and what sounds one way when man hears in Rome, sounds otherwise when told in Egypt. Thus, understanding sways. Antony's own powers of hearing shift, as when in Egypt he begins a Roman thought, and listens with a Roman ear to his ill-deeds; or when in Rome his spirit wanders toward the Nile. Two sets of values strain the words he hears. Sometimes he hears through one, sometimes the other sets the key; and, each way, words seem different. Antony duplicates the problem the world faces; or vice versa. What is important is that the world and Antony are shown to be alike. If Shakespeare's far-flung, swiftly-shifting scenes need any organic explanation for their prodigality, it can be found in their involvement of the world in a problem of ambiguity which might seem, otherwise, restricted and too personal. (pp. 138-39)

Complexity in *Antony and Cleopatra* becomes, if I am right, the very sense and substance of the play, its strength and not its weakness. We are never permitted to linger very long in one spot or with one point of view; but we are never allowed, either, to forget where we have been before. As we approach some sort of eventual simplicity of understanding, we realize that we have warrant to approach it only because of the experience of complexity and the recognition of inter-dependencies. There are a series of climactic events in the final scenes of *Antony and Cleopatra,* on which to test our judgment. First is the death of Enobarbus, then the death of Antony, and at the end the death of Cleopatra. These are linked. Together they establish the definition and the involvements of love. . . . (p. 141)

I look at Enobarbus's death in this way. ''O Antony!'' he cries; and at the end of this last speech, ''O Antony!'' again, ''O Antony!'' [IV. ix. 18, 23]. This is his masculine pledge of loyalty, and with it re-ties bonds that slipped. Enobarbus's departure had been the culminating symbol of the desertion of old friends and soldiers, moved by discretion rather than by their will. Reason may have shown Enobarbus, after his arrival in Caesar's camp, what happened to others who deserted to Caesar, but prudence would have kept him there, had not his heart leaped up at Antony's ''gentle adieus and greetings'' [IV. v. 14] sent loyally to him. The quality of loyalty which Antony had shown was what the Roman camp had lost, and Enobarbus missed it now. So Enobarbus made an honorable act of heart; his suicide became an act of love. Thus is love Platonized; and what with Antony and Cleopatra has seemed only of the flesh, here becomes spiritual instead. Or, as we later know: a thing of fire and air, not earth and water save as purified.

Antony's own solitary state, alone, had changed by what he did for his departed friend. What he gave Enobarbus, Enobarbus had returned to him. This spark of loyalty had stayed in Antony. It was the opposite from what we call a tragic flaw. It was instead the germ of new nobility. Antony had known the words with which to speak of nobleness of life, but had not known what really stood up peerless in embrace. (pp. 141-42)

[Now] what is false and shallow has been swept away, and Antony [can] settle on the issues thus made clear. Eros has killed himself for Antony, as Enobarbus did; and Antony thinks Cleopatra dead by her own hand. ''My queen and Eros,'' Antony says:

> Have by their brave instruction got upon me
> A nobleness in record; but I will be
> A bridegroom in my death, and run into't
> As to a lover's bed.
>
> [IV. xiv. 97-101]

This is a further definition of nobleness which does not contradict the ''nobleness of life,'' the proposition he had felt at first, but it explains it as he did not know it then. ''Since Cleopatra died,'' he said to Eros, before Eros killed himself, ''I have lived in such dishonor, that the gods detest my baseness'' [IV. xiv. 55-7]. But what Antony felt was base was his disloyalty to her, expressed by reason at the expense of love. Dishonor finds its opposite in honor; heaven is the opposite of base; a race, or root, of heaven should breed gods. So Antony, like a bridegroom, honoring her, unites with her in death. His purgatory of experience is passed. This kind of bridegroom he had never been before, nor had he used the word, nor run to just this kind of married lover's bed. Marriage itself is a symbolic alliance he had never felt, nor had he known what really makes a mutual pair, contracted by their love. His link to Octavia was made, instead, by purely Roman virtues at their best. Reason and practicality made the bond between himself and her, as between him and Fulvia. Cleopatra had not been a wife before, only the mistress of his flesh, a union with no standing in itself. Yet the Egyptian way held in it something which the Roman way had lacked. True marriage sanctifies the senses, but it starts with them. What was now needed was to recognize the vows of loyalty which couples make: to join, that is, with love and fix with honor. This is true wedding; this, Antony now pledged; meaning his word, as bridegroom, as he ran to her.

As Enobarbus's death, and Eros's, joins them in manly love for Antony; so Antony's death in turn joins him to Cleopatra

as a spouse. Thus groups begin to form within the world again, where otherwise man only stood alone. As Enobarbus seemed, dramatically, to point attention toward Antony, that we might test if Antony were worthy of the pledge which Enobarbus made; so Antony's vows direct us on to Cleopatra. She becomes a test for both. For if Antony's love has been pledged to an unworthy object, then he is wholly made the fool, and Enobarbus has been foolish in his turn. How, then, will Cleopatra understand and act, where will she turn when her own moment of decision comes? And will we understand? ''Not know me yet?'' [III. xiii. 157].

''My desolation does begin to make a better life,'' she says [V. ii. 1-2]. For she has had her purgatory, felt her own loneliness. ''What poor an instrument,'' she says, meaning herself, ''may do a noble deed'' [V. ii. 236-37]. Yet ''none our parts so poor,'' she once had said, ''but is a race of heaven.'' So be it now for her, giving new definition to the words. It is a noble deed she seeks; nobility becomes important to her too. She is resolved by Antony's witness what to do; and those who think she later shrewdly toys with shifting of her lot to Caesar's care, forget how shrewdly Roman Cleopatra has become, though she will prove it in a nobler way within herself. They have forgotten too, or did not hear, what she replied when Antony said to her: ''Of Caesar seek your honor with your safety'' [IV. xv. 46]. ''They do not go together,'' Cleopatra cried [IV. xv. 47]. This was a paradox she recognized; for honor at the first had seemed a purely Roman word, but so did prudent safety too. And honor now was only to be found when one pursued with daring, not a Roman trait.

''Then is it sin,'' she said to Charmion, when Antony had died,

> To rush into the secret house of death,
> Ere death dare come to us? . . .
> We'll bury him; and then, what's brave,
>   what's *noble,*
> Let's do it after the high Roman fashion,
> And make death proud to take us.
>
> [IV. xv. 80-2, 86-8]

If she spoke otherwise than this to Caesar later on, she spoke with worn-out Roman words as they had been debased by Caesar's tongue: a *lingua roma* [Roman idiom] not to be believed by either side in such a dialogue. But Cleopatra knew what words and deeds can really mean, and that to link them was a marriage too. ''Now Charmion,'' Cleopatra says,

> Show me, my women, like a queen; go fetch
> My best attires; I am again for Cydnus,
> To meet Mark Antony.
>
> [V. ii. 226-29]

And so she is again for Cydnus in her death. But not as her own final words are proof, for Cydnus to repeat the meaning of the scene as she and others understood it then, but to begin again, to clarify what had been vague at first.

> Give me my robe, put on my crown; I have
> Immortal longings in me; . . .
>
> [V. ii. 280-81]

So she had always had, when she had known

> Eternity was in our lips and eyes,
> Bliss in our brows bent; none our parts so poor
> But was a race of heaven.

Now it was the union which counted; not Antony's kiss nor the embrace of bodies, but the marriage which binds even after death, and which she makes from death. "Husband, I come," she says; "now to that name my courage prove my title!" [V. ii. 287-88]. Now—what significance the adverb has!—when Cleopatra's words and deed unite, Shakespeare has made of suicide what turns it to a proto-Christian sacrament. . . . The words of Cleopatra are what modify the deed, and by her words we know her and her final elements. Not earth and water: these were of the Nile and bred the aspic which brought death; but "fire and air; my other elements I give to baser life" [V. ii. 289-90].

In marriage she embraces all the bourgeois terms and values she had seemed to scorn. And, in her, blossom all the states which woman has as a potential, no matter what her rank. She is in her own words a milkmaid, wife and mother of a babe, although she keeps her status as a queen and Venus ("O eastern star" [V. ii. 308], that morning star), and fire and air, giving up earth and water as mere flesh. It is in this complete and purifying way that Cleopatra catches up all woman in herself. *La donna e mobile* [Woman is changeable] is not relevant at all, though critics sometimes say so. What is all woman in her is her scope and her capacity for love, and this amalgam she binds to her "man of men." [I. v.72].

The marriage is the thing. This Dryden also knew, for when he named his play *All For Love,* he took a phrase that Shakespeare's time and his used for a posy (the inscription) in a marriage or betrothal ring. Marriage requires the giving of a ring; it is the symbol of the binding force, becomes a witness of the pact, when with the ring one weds. Had Cleopatra earlier in the play received a ring from Antony as token of what "twain" meant to him then, its posy might have read, as some rings in Elizabethan times did read:

Pity my passions.

This was what drew them then. Reason they cast aside. But now, the wedding ring she would have worn, ready and suited for it at the end, should be inscribed like this, as some rings read in Shakespeare's day, to show what Antony and Cleopatra learned:

A pledge that binds
Two hearts, two minds.

(pp. 142-46)

It was the amalgamation of seeming contraries of heart and mind that counted in the end to fill the lacks in each alone, and make a mutual pair. This was a twain to make a union firm; and they had learned to read what words contain, and what they spoke. And so, I hope, with Shakespeare's help, can we. For when the play began, this regal pair seemed inaccessible in height to us. Yet as these two were stripped down to our lot, we came to share and were involved with them. Their first words had remained superlatives. But in the end they carried no hyperbole. The pair had proved their right to share nobility, and by their deeds had proved at last these words as suitable. (p. 147)

> *Norman Holmes Pearson, "'Antony and Cleopatra'," in* Shakespeare: Of an Age and for All Time, *edited by Charles Tyler Prouty, The Shoe String Press, 1954, pp. 125-47.*

DANIEL STEMPEL (essay date 1956)

[*Stempel holds that a profound misogyny—reflective of Elizabethan anti-feminism—pervades* Antony and Cleopatra, *determining its structure and characterization, and influencing Shakespeare's*

treatment of a central theme in the play: the restoration of order and health in the body politic. Cleopatra's domination of Antony signals "an unnatural reversal of the roles of man and woman," the critic contends, which is paralleled by the dominance of Antony's will over his reason and by disruptive contention against "the rational Octavius." Examining the frequent association of Cleopatra with images of witchcraft, poison, and serpents, and describing her as motivated by eroticism and a "lust for power," Stempel posits that she chooses death because she has failed to subvert Octavius; with her demise, he concludes, "the morbid disease" that ruined Antony is "removed completely as a source of danger to the state." Discerning many elements of irony in the play and relating these to the characterization of the lovers, the critic also maintains that tragic elements in Antony and Cleopatra *are subsidiary to Shakespeare's satiric presentation of Antony as "a slave of passion" and Cleopatra as, after all, "only a woman."*]

If we are to understand correctly the dramatic structure and characterization of *Antony and Cleopatra,* we cannot substitute our own values for Renaissance values. The theme of the play is *not* "all for love, or, the world well lost". A cursory comparison of the versions of Shakespeare and Dryden will show that Dryden's play turns out to be something totally different, but critics have persisted in treating the drama as an example of the triumph of love. As James E. Phillips has shown in his brilliant study, *The State in Shakespeare's Greek and Roman Plays* [see excerpt above, 1940], the plays on classic themes are all concerned with the restoration of health to the diseased state. Stated in its broadest terms, the fundamental problem in these plays is the problem of order.

For the Renaissance mind, the order of the universe meant something quite different from the cosmological order accepted by the modern mind. This fundamental distinction can be reduced to the following simplification: the Renaissance, following medieval practice, organized its cosmology by reasoning from biological analogies, that is, by organizing phenomena according to the principles governing living organisms, rather than by the use of mechanical analogies or mathematical descriptions, the methods pursued by post-Galilean thinkers. The effect of this approach was to establish a hierarchy of realms of order, all organized on similar principles, so that general correspondences of structure and function could be formed between the different levels. Microcosm and macrocosm—nature, the state, and man—existed and operated according to the same rules of order.

In a cosmology of this sort, where location and value are interdependent, the change of place involves a change of value; not only is this a subversion of order on the level in which the change takes place, but also, through the destruction of the correspondence between that level and all others, it introduces a disturbance that reverberates throughout the cosmos. The most infinitesimal breach of order was an opening through which the floodwaters of chaos could pour.

The spread of chaos on the level of political organization, in particular, was feared by men of the Renaissance. Shakespeare's classical plays reflect this fear; it is the ultimate source of the conflict of values in all of them, including *Antony and Cleopatra.* Antony's domination by Cleopatra is an unnatural reversal of the roles of man and woman, and where there is a change of place, there is an inversion of values. On the psychological level, this change of values corresponds to the similarly unnatural dominance of reason by will in Antony's character, and, on the political level, it is mirrored by the struggle of Antony and Cleopatra against the rational Octavius.

Is this far-reaching disturbance of order merely a background for the portrayal of a great love or is it the dominant theme of the play? This is not an idle question, for it involves the major problem of plot structure and development. Even Phillips, who has carefully analyzed the political significance of the play, feels that this aspect is subordinate to the love story. "In *Antony and Cleopatra*", he writes, "the chief interest for Shakespeare, as for everyone who has encountered the play, is the splendid infatuation which the story presents." . . . If this is true, why does Shakespeare prolong the action beyond the death of Antony by adding scenes depicting Cleopatra's dealing with Octavius and her final suicide? The splendid infatuation, for all practical purposes, ends with the death of Antony, and Cleopatra's death scene might well have been added without the intervening scenes which have distressed some critics because they seem to be an irrelevant postponement of the dénouement. If, however, the major theme is the safety of the state, then the death of Antony does not remove the chief danger to political stability—Cleopatra. She has ensnared Julius Caesar, Pompey, and Antony—how will Octavius fare? The last act shows us that Octavius is proof against the temptress, and the play ends, as it should, with the defeat and death of the rebel against order. The theme is worked out to its logical completion, and the play is an integrated whole, not merely a tragedy with a postscript.

If this is accepted as the dominant theme of the play, then the entire drama, both in general intent and in detailed interpretation, possesses a significance which is not apparent to those who follow the conventional romantic approach. The key to the problem lies in the character of Cleopatra and her relations with the other characters in the play. Here our knowledge of Elizabethan mores can come to our aid. The war between the sexes is perennial, of course, and its historians can be numbered in the thousands between the author of Genesis and James Thurber. The methods of warfare, however, became especially vicious in the sixteenth century. The well-stocked medieval arsenal of arguments against women supplied the weapons, and the old charges were leveled with a new fervor. The most extreme of these misogynic arguments was that, in effect, man was woman's faculty of reason. Woman was a creature of weak reason and strong passions, carnal in nature and governed by lust. She could be trusted only when guided by the wisdom of her natural superior, man. This point of view was fully developed by medieval clerics, to whom women were the slaves of their own insatiable desires, which goaded them to subvert nature by dominating men. The accusation may be traced back to St. Paul and St. Jerome; and Chaucer's Wife of Bath, who was a scholar's wife blessed with a retentive memory, has supplied us with an excellent bibliography of these clerical attacks.

It is against this background that we must place Shakespeare's Cleopatra. If she is measured against the model of unbridled desire rising in revolt against the rule of reason, supplied by the extreme misogynists, her motives and the resulting actions become understandable. She is not so much a tragic slave of passion in herself as a symbol of Antony's slavery to desire. She is the tempter and the temptation; she destroys the balance of Antony's nature by arousing his physical desire to the point where it defeats his reason. And by making it his guide, she makes it the guide of the state. The paramount value in the classical plays is the stability of the state, and the Elizabethan mind would have seen no problem in judging the morality of Cleopatra's conduct. As Lawrence Babb writes, "To the Elizabethan, a conflict between reason and love would necessarily be a conflict between virtue and vice. Romanticism has greatly changed our thinking on this subject" [in his book *The Elizabethan Malady*].

The upheaval in the natural order of things which Cleopatra symbolizes is made amply clear in the direct statements of both protagonists. Both subordinate the welfare of the state to the gratification of their own desires. In the opening scene, Antony declaims:

Let Rome in Tiber melt and the wide arch
Of the rang'd empire fall! Here is my space.
Kingdoms are clay. . . .

[I. i. 33-5]

In the same fashion, Cleopatra rages in her jealousy: "Melt Egypt into Nile!" [II. v. 78], and, farther on, expresses the wish:

O, I would thou didst,
So half my Egypt were submerg'd and made
A cistern for scal'd snakes!

[II. v. 93-5]

This attitude, which seems so natural to the romantic and so perverse to the Elizabethan, has its roots in the destruction of Antony's psychological balance. Enobarbus comments that he "would make his will / Lord of his reason" [III. xiii. 3-4]. Externally, this is indicated by his submission to Cleopatra, and, specifically, by his interchange of roles with her. Octavius contemptuously describes him as

. . . not more manlike
Than Cleopatra, nor the queen of Ptolemy
More womanly than he. . . .

[I. iv. 5-7]

Cleopatra herself boasts that when he was drunk, she ". . . put my tires and mantles on him, whilst / I wore his sword Philippan" [II. v. 22-3].

Disorder is contagious in the Renaissance cosmos, and chaos spreads downward from Antony. Canidius, one of his soldiers, sees clearly where the danger lies: "So our leader's led, / And we are women's men" [III. vii. 69-70]. And later Antony, informed of Enobarbus' defection, recognizes himself as the source of the contagion: "O, my fortunes have / Corrupted honest men!" [IV. v.16-17]. Octavius sums up the case against Antony when he grants that voluptuousness may have its proper occasion for satisfaction, but not when there are great causes at stake:

. . . 'tis to be chid
As we rate boys who, being mature in knowledge,
Pawn their experience to their present pleasure
And so rebel to judgment.

[I. iv. 30-3]

The first step, then, toward clarifying our understanding of the play must be to divest ourselves of that admiration for Cleopatra which comes instinctively, it seems, to the modern mind. With the romantic veil removed, the breadth and pervasiveness of the misogynic bias running through the play is gradually revealed; and it will be evident that it is not merely playful satire, the jesting of a good-natured Mercutio [in *Romeo and Juliet*] or Benedick [in *Much Ado about Nothing*]. It is far more serious and far more deadly. Its influence molds both character and language; more important, it is so fundamental to the structure of the drama that the very genre of *Antony and Cleopatra* is determined by it.

It must not be assumed, of course, that all the characters react to Cleopatra with the open violence of a polemic pamphleteer. On the contrary, there are significant variations in the attitudes of Antony, Octavius, and Enobarbus. Antony's reaction is as extreme as his slavery. When he breaks free of her domination, he heaps on her such epithets as "Triple-turn'd whore!" [IV. xii. 13]. His opinion of her reaches the depths of Philo's contemptuous remarks in the opening scene of the play. But his reaction is not rational; it is one extreme of the swing of passion's pendulum, and Antony dies still subject to her will. In contrast, the misogyny of Octavius is founded on right reason. His one general statement on the nature of woman echoes the sentiments of Shakespeare's contemporaries:

> Women are not
> In their best fortunes strong, but want will perjure
> The ne'er-touch'd Vestal.
>
> [III. xii. 29-31]

Both reactions are touchstones of character and of destiny. When the play ends, it is Octavius, the man who is shielded against temptation by reason, who triumphs. Antony vacillates between love and hate, but his behavior in either case is not rational. By Renaissance standards, the fall of Antony is the inevitable concomitant of the rise of Octavius, as the soothsayer warns Antony [II. iii. 19-24].

Enobarbus' attitude toward Cleopatra is an indication of a third and somewhat different type of motivation. Enobarbus is not an extremist. His position is that of the realist, to use the somewhat ambiguous term coined by David L. Stevenson [in his *The Love-Game Comedy*]. This attitude, according to Stevenson, is found in its purest form in goliardic poetry and in the fabliaux, where "love was presented sometimes grossly and obscenely, sometimes merely joyously and simply, but always with emphasis on the act of coition." . . . An example familiar to the general reader appears in the vulgar (and commonsense) approach of the waterfowl in Chaucer's *Parlement of Foules*:

> "Ye quek!" yit seyde the doke, ful wel and fayre,
> "There been mo sterres, God wot, than a payre."

Thus Enobarbus does not rebuke Antony for his attachment to Cleopatra. When Antony, in his first expression of revulsion, says, "Would I had never seen her!" [I. ii. 152], Enobarbus replies, "O, sir, you had then left unseen a wonderful piece of work, which not to have been blest withal would have discredited your travel" [I. ii. 153-55]. The famous description of Cleopatra by Enobarbus is not a romantic panegyric; it reflects the gross realism of the speaker's attitude. He praises her for her "infinite variety", but the phrase indicates a much narrower meaning than that which romantic interpretation has assigned to it. His praise is for her sexual attractions alone, not for any other qualities, as the following lines clearly show. She is, to use that brief description by Ten Brink which Bradley borrowed, a "courtesan of genius" [see excerpts above, 1893 and 1905], and Enobarbus, with his dispassionate sensuality, bestows on her the appreciation of a connoisseur. . . . In the earlier scenes Enobarbus makes no attempt to recall Antony to reason, but this does not mean that he too is blinded by passion. After Actium he bluntly places the blame for defeat on Antony, who is rebuked for his loss of reason and self-control:

> The itch of his affection should not then
> Have nick'd his captainship, at such a point,
> When half to half the world oppos'd, he being
> The meered question.
>
> [III. xiii. 7-10]

The amused irony of Enobarbus' early comments on his master's infatuation has turned to cynical rejection. He perceives the strength of Cleopatra's domination, which he has previously tolerated, and this is the immediate cause of his treason. Antony's weakness destroys the natural loyalty of this plain soldier and leads him to desert his general in the hour of failure. Antony, as we have seen, is aware of this. The fall of Enobarbus reflects the fall of Antony, but Enobarbus' weakness is not the weakness of Antony. He is not tempted by Cleopatra; he has simply underestimated her power.

Similarly, much of the imagery of the play derives from the misogynic hostility toward Cleopatra. The language is often coarse, not only on the level of the underlings, both Roman and Egyptian, but also in the exchanges of the major figures. Lust and physical gratification are constant themes. This is in keeping with the general premise, familiar to all in Shakespeare's time, that eroticism is the primary motivation of women. There are also, however, more specific and less obvious trends of imagery which stem directly from Renaissance misogyny. These images are all associated with Cleopatra and fall into three classes: references to magic and witchcraft, to poisons, and to serpents. It is clear that these are actually a single group united by the common theme of witchcraft in its broadest (and worst) connotations. (pp. 62-6)

Witch-hunting was the most virulent manifestation of the hatred for women in Renaissance society; the arguments used by the foes of witchcraft have the authentic ring of medieval antifeminism. James I, a notable misogynist, stated the case against women in its simplest terms in his *Daemonologie* (1597):

> Philomathes: . . . What can be the cause that there are twentie women giuen to that craft, where ther is one man?
>
> Epistemon: The reason is easie, for as that sexe is frailer than man is, so is it easier to be intrapped in these grosse snares of the Deuill, as was ouer well proued to be true, by the Serpents deceiuing of *Eua* at the beginning, which makes him the homelier with that sexe sensine. . . .

The most encyclopedic study of witchcraft was the famous *Malleus Maleficarum*. . . . According to this treatise, the "natural reason" for the attraction of women to witchcraft is that "she is more carnal than a man, as is clear from her many carnal abominations". Woman is constantly seeking domination over man, and the result of this is of great consequence. "If we inquire, we find that nearly all the kingdoms of the world have been overthrown by women." Significantly, one of the classic examples is the following: "The kingdom of the Romans endured much evil through Cleopatra, Queen of Egypt, that worst of women." (pp. 66-7)

The references to witchcraft in the play are both general and specific. Egypt itself, since the time of Exodus, has been considered a land of magicians. The term "Egyptian", then, connotes sorcery, as does its derivative form, "Gypsy", both of which are applied freely to Cleopatra. The following specific references form a thread which runs through the play. Philo's speech, which opens the play, condemns Antony for becoming "the bellows and the fan / To cool a gypsy's lust" [I. i. 9-10]. After being summoned back to Rome, Antony resolves, "I must from this enchanting queen break off" [I. ii. 128]. One of the clearest statements is Pompey's adjuration to the absent Cleopatra:

> But all the charms of love,
> Salt Cleopatra, soften thy wan'd lip!
> Let witchcraft join with beauty, lust with both!
>
> [II. i. 20-2]

After Actium, Scarus calls Antony "... The noble ruin of her magic ..." [III. x. 18]. In [IV. ii. 37], Antony swears, "Now the witch take me if I meant it thus", ironically unaware that the witch has already taken him. After his defeat, Antony turns on Cleopatra in revulsion:

> O this false soul of Egypt! This grave charm—
> Whose eye beck'd forth my wars and call'd them home,
> Whose bosom was my crownet, my chief end—
> Like a right gypsy hath at fast and loose
> Beguil'd me to the very heart of loss!
>
> [IV. xii. 25-9]

When Cleopatra enters immediately after this speech, he greets her with the formula of exorcism: "Ah, thou spell! Avaunt!" [IV. xii. 30]. He resolves that "The witch shall die" [IV. xii. 47]. But her spell is renewed and Antony remains her thrall until his death.

The themes of poison and serpents are intertwined throughout the play, culminating in the final scene when the asp, a poisonous serpent, cuts the knot intrinsicate and end Cleopatra's career. One of Cleopatra's speeches, if read correctly, identifies her, by her own words, as a poisonous serpent:

> He's speaking now,
> Or murmuring "Where's my serpent of old Nile?"
> For so he calls me. Now I feed myself
> With most delicious poison.
>
> [I. v. 24-7]

The emphasis should be on *myself*. The implication of these lines in Cleopatra's reverie is that hitherto she has been feeding her delicious poison to Antony. Antony himself refers to his stay in Egypt as "poisoned hours" [II. ii. 90]. Twice Cleopatra curses Egypt with the plague of serpents in her jealous reaction to the news of Antony's marriage. At the meeting of the triumvirate, Lepidus attempts to stir up Antony's anger by impertinent questions on the fauna of Egypt—specifically, the crocodile—which are obvious references to Cleopatra. Antony's evasive answers leave Lepidus with the weak retort: "'Tis a strange serpent" [II. vii. 48]. To which Antony replies, "'Tis so. And the tears of it are wet" [II. vii. 49]. The poison theme also appears independently of the serpent theme in two references. In [III. xiii. 158-161], Cleopatra invokes death by poison for herself if she has been faithless to Antony. And in Antony's rebellion against Cleopatra he compares his rage and pain to the pangs of the shirt of Nessus which poisoned Alcides [IV. xii. 43].

Both characterization and language are meaningful only within the total dramatic situation, and in *Antony and Cleopatra* they reinforce and support the development of the action from beginning to end. There are no violent reversals of intention; the pattern is worked out in full detail through the play, unmarred by the rapid shifting from scene to scene which is characteristic of *Antony and Cleopatra*.

The opening scene is vital to a proper reading of the drama. Philo introduces the protagonists with a bitter and cynical analysis of their relationship. Against this background, Antony and Cleopatra exchange professions and boasts of love. These speeches have been taken as great poetry, but the more finely attuned ear detects the flat note of fustian. Granville-Barker curtly remarks of the opening exchange, "This is convention itself", and of Antony's declamatory rejection of empire, "Pure rhetoric." ... Here we have the setting of tone for the whole play: a tawdry infatuation whose empty boasts are easily penetrated by the cynical jibes of an inferior. There is then, at the very beginning, a lowering of the level of the play to satirical incongruity, rather than a transcendent heightening of emotion. Much has been made of images of spaciousness and regal power in *Antony and Cleopatra,* particularly in the opening scene, but this merely demonstrates the danger of placing the enumeration of images above the dramatic purpose to which they are put in specific speeches. Against the background of worlds and empires, the spectacle of Antony become the bellows to fan a gypsy's lust appears truly ironic, as it is diminished to its proper ignoble proportions. To place lust, the expense of spirit in a waste of shame, in the balance against the destiny of a great empire, as Shakespeare does, is a masterpiece of *saeva indignatio* [fierce indignation] worthy of Swift. The degradation of Antony, the servant of chaos, is profound. The ironic juxtaposition of high rank and ignoble conduct applies not only to Antony, but also to the triumvirate at their carousal, where only Octavius keeps his dignity; and it is, of course, exemplified in Cleopatra's treatment of the messenger from Rome, as well as in other instances.

The first three acts may perhaps be conceded to the *advocatus diaboli* [devil's advocate] by the romantic defenders of Cleopatra; their triumph, traditionally, is the death scene of Cleopatra. Schücking [see excerpt above, 1919] ... could not reconcile the noble end of Cleopatra with her earlier sensuous and wilful nature. Other critics simply swept the seeming inconsistencies into one heap and affixed the label, "Woman," thus neatly avoiding the necessity for judging Cleopatra by any standards, moral or otherwise. Their refuge was the ineffable nature of woman.... But contrast, incongruous contrast, is also the very essence of irony and satire. If this is kept in mind, the final scenes of the play will be seen to demonstrate a thoroughly consistent development of character in accordance with the narrower and more clearly defined Renaissance attitude toward women. The death of Cleopatra grows naturally from the unfolding of the plot and theme; it is foreshadowed in the language and imagery of the earlier acts. It is, in point of fact, the only fitting conclusion to the drama; it is not merely a sudden change of level from scurrility to nobility, nor, as some think, an escape to Elysium.

Cleopatra's outburst of grief for Antony seems to set a new standard of conduct for her, not Egyptian but Roman. It also, however, brings her a moment of insight into her own nature. To Iras' "Royal Egypt! / Empress!" [IV. xv. 70-1], she replies,

> No more but e'en a woman, and commanded
> By such poor passion as the maid that milks
> And does the meanest chares.
>
> [IV. xv. 73-5]
> (pp. 67-9)

This speech concludes with a call for the "briefest end", but that noble resolution wavers as she postpones her death to test her powers on Octavius. She pretends to relinquish her instinctive quest for domination and requests, with assumed humility, a personal interview with Octavius:

> I hourly learn
> A doctrine of obedience, and would gladly
> Look him i' the face.
>
> [V. ii. 30-2]

This is the supreme test for Octavius—and for Cleopatra. She appears penitent, subordinate, and conscious of her frailties as a woman.

> Sole sir o' th' world,
> I cannot project mine own cause so well
> To make it clear; but do confess I have
> Been laden with like frailties which before
> Have often sham'd our sex.
>
> [V. ii. 120-24]

But to her final plea, "My master and my lord!", Octavius counters a decisive refusal of her proffered dominion, "Not so. Adieu" [V. ii. 189-90]. He has successfully rejected her, and now there is indeed only one way out. If she cannot rule, she will die.

Her next lines show where she has been wounded most deeply—in her ambitious pride. "He words me, girls, he words me, that I should not / Be noble to myself!" [V. ii. 191-92]. No word of Antony here. Her deepest allegiance is to her own nature and to the lust for power which that nature enforces on her. This is the fundamental motivation that drives her inexorably to suicide, and Antony becomes the symbol of the height of her power, a reminder of past glories which she uses as a spur to drive her on to death. She torments herself with the thought that this liaison with Antony, the climax of her career, will be mocked and degraded by the Romans in their triumph.

The theme of the nature of woman dominates the death scene. Cleopatra introduces it:

> My resolution's plac'd, and I have nothing
> Of woman in me. Now from head to foot
> I am marble-constant. Now the fleeting moon
> No planet is of mine.
>
> [V. ii. 238-41]

But the theme falls into the hands of the rustic clown, who ironically twists it with jests which might have been taken verbatim from the satires on women:

> You must not think I am so simple but I know the devil himself will not eat a woman. I know that a woman is a dish for the gods, if the devil dress her not. But truly, these same whoreson devils do the gods great harm in their women; for in every ten that they make, the devils mar five.
>
> [V. ii. 272-77]

Cleopatra prepares for death, calling on Antony to witness the nobility of her act and the thwarting of Caesar's purpose. She divests herself of the base elements of nature and assumes the title of wife: "I am fire and air, my other elements / I give to baser life" [V. ii. 289-90]. This is an ironic echo of earlier lines. We recall Lepidus' sly question: "What manner of thing is your crocodile" [II. vii. 41]? Antony replies, "It is shap'd, sir, like itself, and it is as broad as it hath breadth. It is just so high as it is, and moves with its own organs. It lives by that which nourisheth it, and the elements once out of it, transmigrates" [II. vii. 42-5]. This is the transmigration of the crocodile, the death of the serpent of old Nile.

But the transmigration is not quite complete. When Iras faints, a sudden fancy strikes Cleopatra, and her instinctive jealousy revives:

> This proves me base.
> If she first meet the curled Antony,
> He'll make demand of her, and spend that kiss
> Which is my heaven to have....
>
> [V. ii. 300-03]

Cleopatra cannot rise above the level of eroticism; she knows well the passion to which Antony has been enslaved, and its indifference to its objects.

> Peace, peace!
> Dost thou not see my baby at my breast,
> That sucks the nurse asleep?
>
> [V. ii. 308-10]

have been taken as the height of tender pathos, and many romantic souls have been stirred by them. But they are neither pathetic nor tragic. What more fitting end for the serpent who has fed Antony with delicious poison than to die by her own weapon? The asp is indeed her "baby", and she is the proper nurse for an asp. The current of serpent imagery reaches its logical and dramatic conclusion; it is the climax of earlier references, and points the irony of the final scene.

Similarly, there is ironic justice in Charmian's epitaph for Cleopatra. She is truly a "lass unparalleled" [V. ii. 316] as well as a queen. The death of a queen is leveled to the death of a woman, an exceptional woman, but still only a woman, with all that that term implies in the context of the play. She is no more than the meanest milkmaid, although her rank is that of royalty and her stage has been the realms of the earth. Even Octavius, who has a generous word for his enemies in death, cannot withhold a brief reference to the gift for evil domination which this woman possesses above all the rest of her sex:

> ... she looks like sleep,
> As she would catch another Antony
> In her strong toil of grace.
>
> [V. ii. 346-48]

No tragedy can bear the brunt of this pointed satire and remain a tragedy. Even Bradley, who firmly clung to the belief that *Antony and Cleopatra* was a great tragedy, felt that the play did not meet the criteria of tragedy found in Shakespeare's other plays. "It attempts something different", Bradley wrote, "and succeeds as triumphantly as *Othello* itself." ... Bradley did not tell us what this "something different" is, but a modern scholar has given us the key to the mystery.

Professor Oscar J. Campbell has advanced the theory [in his *Shakespeare's Satire*] that *Timon of Athens* and *Coriolanus* represent a mixed genre, tragical satire, which was modeled on Jonson's *Sejanus*. (pp. 70-2)

Professor Campbell describes *Coriolanus* as a "satiric representation of a slave of passion designed to teach an important political lesson." ... A close analysis of *Antony and Cleopatra* shows that this description is completely applicable to this play as well. The degradation of a strong man enslaved by lust to a woman who is the embodiment of physical desire in its most attractive form is traced to its disastrous conclusion. The point of the play, however, is that Antony is one of the contenders for the rule of an empire, and that the morbid disease which has destroyed him must be removed completely as a source of danger to the state. With the death of Cleopatra, the end which Octavius has envisioned is finally reached:

> The time of universal peace is near.
> Prove this a prosperous day, the three nook'd world
> Shall bear the olive freely.
>
> [IV. vi. 4-6].
> (p. 72)

Daniel Stempel, "The Transmigration of the Crocodile," in Shakespeare Quarterly, *Vol. VII, No. 1, Winter, 1956, pp. 59-72.*

BRENTS STIRLING   (essay date 1956)

[*The central issues dramatized in* Antony and Cleopatra, *Stirling argues, are whether the hero and heroine should be viewed as tragic figures and whether their love is a truly tragic passion. He contends that the diversity of responses to these questions provided by the vairous characters is underscored by the way in which the dramatic action repeatedly swings back and forth "between grandeur and ignominy," between assertions of value and challenges to those statements, between triumph and defeat, and between periodic movements of sympathetic affirmation of the protagonists and satirical or realistic presentations of them. Shakespeare depicts "the whole Antony," Stirling maintains—a figure sometimes comical, sometimes absurdly self-conscious, occasionally worldly wise and dignified; but before his death, the critic claims, Antony foregoes his self-defeating tendency to "strain at sublimity" and thereby achieves an elevated stature. The critic also holds that we are given a similarly balanced final view of Cleopatra, for the play's characteristic evenhandedness between satire and seriousness is evident in the juxtaposition of the Seleucus episode and Octavius's final encomium of her.*]

In G. B. Shaw's preface to *Three Plays for Puritans* there is a spirited disposition of *Antony and Cleopatra* which is both well remembered and often misunderstood [see excerpt above, 1900]. . . .

> Shakespear's *Antony and Cleopatra* must needs be as intolerable to the true Puritan as it is vaguely distressing to the ordinary healthy citizen, because, after giving a faithful picture of the soldier broken down by debauchery, and the typical wanton in whose arms such men perish, Shakespear finally strains all his huge command of rhetoric and stage pathos to give a theatrical sublimity to the wretched end of the business, and to persuade foolish spectators that the world was well lost by the twain.
>
> (p. 157)

Shaw continues with "a technical objection to making sexual infatuation a tragic theme." Experience shows that it should be assigned, perhaps not eagerly, to forms other than tragedy:

> Let realism have its demonstration, comedy its criticism, or even bawdry its horselaugh at the expense of sexual infatuation, if it must; but to ask us to subject our souls to its ruinous glamor, to worship it, deify it, and imply that it alone makes our life worth living, is nothing but folly gone mad erotically—a thing compared to which Falstaff's unbeglamored drinking and drabbing is respectable and rightminded.

The rhetoric here may be Victorian but, contrary to most of Shaw's critics, it is not framed to deny sexual infatuation a place in literature; rather, it merely asks that the passion remain "unbeglamored." Allow realism and comedy to treat the subject, but be mature enough to resist the glow which tragedy often casts upon it and other forms of egoistic obsession. (pp. 157-58)

I hope to show that Shakespeare did not "see life truly and think about it romantically" [Shaw], and that there is no meretricious sublimity cast even over the ending of *Antony and Cleopatra*. Instead, it is engagingly satirical throughout, but it remains great tragedy because the satire is combined effectively with other qualities. It is interesting that Shakespeare seems to have anticipated the problem of sexual infatuation as a tragic theme by actually posing the question as a theme within his

play. Conventional "romantic" tragedy, with its concepts of stature-in-degradation, flaw, and soulful catastrophe, becomes an issue among the characters very early in the action. Disposition of the issue occurs, moreover, at the very place in which Shaw thought that satire and realism give way to false sublimity. And the disposition should have pleased him greatly.

Attention to the basic device of exposition will help us; Act I, scene i establishes a theme for the play by pointing clearly to our question. Here, at his moment of self-declaration, Antony claims tragic status for love amidst the ruins of empire:

> Let Rome in Tiber melt, and the wide arch
> Of the rang'd empire fall! Here is my space.
> Kingdoms are clay; our dungy earth alike
> Feeds beast as man; the nobleness of life
> Is to do thus, when such a mutual pair
> And such a twain can do't, in which I bind,
> On pain of punishment, the world to weet
> We stand up peerless.
>
> [I. i. 33-40]

This "nobleness of life," which a falling Rome is called upon to see as peerless, is a notion which Cleopatra will later take very seriously. Here, however, she adds to the satire directed at Antony's claim to nobility by terming it an "excellent falsehood," and by declaring that she will seem the fool she is not—"Antony will be himself" [I. i. 42]. The opening lines of the scene already have invoked "this dotage of our general's," and have pointed to his "captain's heart" which "is become the bellows and the fan / To cool a gipsy's lust" [I. i. 1, 9-10].

> Take but good note, and you shall see in him
> The triple pillar of the world transform'd
> Into a strumpet's fool. Behold and see.
>
> [I. i. 11-13]

And the wry note is consistent; the scene which begins with Philo on the general's dotage ends with Demetrius on his public relations:

>   I am full sorry
> That he approves the common liar, who
> Thus speaks of him at Rome.
>
> [I. i. 59-61]

Scene ii now shifts the theme of dedicated sensuality to lesser though equally explicit characters. Iras and Charmian, open it on a note of bickering with the fortuneteller over their future as whores for the great, and they conclude with some soothsaying of their own which promises sexual misfortune for Alexas. Here Enobarbus establishes his role of amused participant and one-man chorus by remarking in a line which sums up the episode, "Mine, and most of our fortunes tonight shall be— drunk to bed" [I. ii. 45-6]. The protagonists are at last given their entry. Antony, whose new mood is heralded by Cleopatra ("On the sudden / A Roman thought hath struck him" [I. ii. 82-3]), faces first a messenger who bears stiff news of the Parthian wars, and then the man from Sicyon who is to tell of Fulvia's death. In the course of the play Antony will often exhibit self-knowledge and his revelation of it will occasionally be spurious, self-conscious, or even gravely comic. In depicting the whole Antony, however, Shakespeare continually, and always at the apt moment, redeems him from solemnity. After his questionable claim to tragic afflatus in the opening scenes, Antony's behavior with the messenger and Enobarbus promptly restores him. The scene is so central and so expertly rendered that extensive quotation is needed:

> *Enter another* MESSENGER *with a letter*.
> *Antony*.   What are you?
> *Messenger*. Fulvia thy wife is dead.
> *Antony*.   Where died she?
> *Messenger*. In Sicyon:
>   Her length of sickness, with what else more serious
>   Importeth thee to know, this bears.
>   *Gives a letter*.
> *Antony*.   Forbear me.
>   *Exit* MESSENGER.
>   There's a great spirit gone! Thus did I desire it.
>   What our contempt doth often hurl from us,
>   We wish it ours again; the present pleasure,
>   By revolution low'ring, does become
>   The opposite of itself. . . .
>
> *Antony*. Fulvia is dead.
> *Enobarbus*. Sir?
> *Antony*. Fulvia is dead. . . .
>
> *Antony*. The business she hath broached in the state
>   Cannot endure my absence.
> *Enobarbus*. And the business you have broach'd here
>   cannot be without you; especially that of Cleopatra's,
>   which wholly depends on your abode.
> *Antony*. No more light answers. Let our officers
>   Have notice what we purpose.
>   [I. ii. 117-26, 156-58, 171-77]
>   (pp. 159-63)

Antony, the half-maudlin epicure of scene i, who has wanted his wife to die and now admits it with a sorrow which surprises him, emerges with . . . dignity. . . . The reason for this lies not so much in Antony's code of honesty as in his manner, his style, which will govern his really impressive moments throughout the play. His stature will scarcely depend upon his triumviral status, or his peerless grand passion, or his repetitive and almost priggish self-examination in which "Roman thoughts" abound. It will depend upon scenes like the one just quoted which evoke respect for his worldly intelligence, scenes in which his self-understanding is suggeested but never intrusively expressed as it is in his more solemn passages. (p. 163)

After allowing Antony his recovery, Shakespeare quickly revives the satirical tone. When Roman gravity has triumphed over Cleopatra's histrionics ("Cut my lace, Charmian, come!" [I. iii. 71]), I. iv introduces Octavius who recasts Antony in the earlier manner. He "is not more manlike / Than Cleopatra, nor the queen of Ptolemy / More womanly than he" [I. iv. 5-7]. It is now the turn of Lepidus, with his characteristic heaviness, to announce the principle of tragic flaw:

>   I must not think there are
> Evils enow to darken all his goodness.
> His faults in him, seem as the spots of heaven,
> More fiery by night's blackness; hereditary,
> Rather than purchased; what he cannot change,
> Than what he chooses.
>   [I. iv. 10-15]

This suggests Hamlet's "mole of nature" [*Hamlet*, I. iv. 24], but with a sentimentality which Octavius promptly deflates:

Act IV. Scene iv. Cleopatra, Antony, Charmian, and Eros. By Henry Tresham.

> You are too indulgent. Let's grant it is not
> Amiss to tumble on the bed of Ptolemy;
> To give a kingdom for a mirth . . .
>   yet must Antony
> No way excuse his foils, when we do bear
> So great weight in his lightness. . . .
>   [I. iv. 16-18, 23-5]

Octavius is thus given a choric function in which he questions Lepidus' bestowal upon Antony of the flawed hero's role.

Scene v now ends the exposition in a mood of the earlier soothsayer's scene. Its theme is again the sexually grotesque: Cleopatra reflecting that the "unseminar'd" Mardian can have no "freer thoughts" to stray forth from Egypt, as do hers after the absent Antony; Cleopatra threatening, by Isis, to give Charmian bloody teeth for presuming to compare Antony with Julius Caesar.

In the discussion of I.ii it was observed that Antony retains dignity in the face of satire not by virtue of his moral conflict but because of his tact and worldly understanding. The core of Act II enlarges this conception of Antony and exhibits the same unpretentious quality in other characters; their sharing of the trait points up Antony's possession of it, just as the plain-dealing of Kent and the Fool augments Cordelia's frankness in *Lear*. That Shakespeare considers the urbane opportunism of Enobarbus, Pompey, Menas, and Antony to lack ultimate wisdom may be assumed, but he clearly wishes us to admire men who know what they are and, without straining at it, play a role for what it is. (pp. 164-66)

By the end of Act II the satirical and affirmative elements of the play are present in excellent proportion. At this point also, the fortunes of Antony rest in balance. Act III abruptly brings the descent, and in keeping with the satirical and realistic tone previously set, the fall is not "dramatic" like that of Macbeth or Othello; Antony, who has ridden high in *Realpolitik* ending in marriage with Octavia of the "holy, cold, and still conversation" [II. vi. 122-23], simply and surely reverts. In scene vi, reports from Alexandria declare that "Cleopatra and himself," surrounded by Caesarion "and all the unlawful issue that their lust / . . . hath made between them" have been publicly enthroned [III. vi. 4, 7, 8]. "As 'tis reported, so," says Caesar, and Maecenas adds, in one of those beautifully understated lines, "Let Rome be thus inform'd" [III. vi. 19-20]. Conventional "catastrophe" is at a minimum. In scene vii, after Enobarbus has told Cleopatra that Antony has been "traduc'd for levity" and that Romans believe "Photinus an eunuch and your maids / Manage this war" [III. vii. 13, 14-15], the decision of Antony to fight by sea is set down as imbecile by three choric characters in workman-like succession: Enobarbus, Canidius, and the significant common soldier. In scene x, only twenty lines later, comes a report of the naval battle. It is a sight that has "blasted" Enobarbus' eyes; he and Scarus describe it in Shakespeare's full range of satirical eloquence which even lampoons Antony's role as "noble ruin." (pp. 170-71)

[The] degrading of Antony is intensified in IV. i by Octavius:

> He calls me boy, and chides as he had power
> To beat me out of Egypt. My messenger
> He hath whipp'd with rods; dares me to personal
> combat,
> Caesar to Antony. Let the old ruffian know
> I have many other ways to die; meantime
> Laugh at his challenge.
>
> [IV. i. 1-6]

And the diminution in our captain's brain is finally confirmed with Antony's puzzlement over news brought by Domitius that Octavius rejects the absurd challenge.

In a brief but affecting scene, Antony now calls upon his followers to tend him, to scant not his cups, an action which reduces them to tears and evokes comment from Enobarbus which again qualifies sympathy with clear insight: "Look they weep; / And I, an ass, am onion eyed" [IV. ii. 34-5]. There follows the premonitory music "i' th' air" and "under the earth," a sign, the soldiers say, that the god Hercules whom Antony loved "now leaves him" [IV. iii. 13, 17]. Casual, inexorable collapse; scene v brings the abandonment of Antony by Enobarbus, and the succeeding one briefly shows Enobarbus, stricken by Antony's generosity, seeking out "some ditch wherein to die" [IV. vi, 37].

The rhythm of triumph and defeat has begun to quicken: within less than a hundred lines (scenes viii to xii. 15) the narrative takes Antony from sinister victory ("O infinite virtue, com'st thou smiling from / The world's great snare uncaught?" [IV. viii. 17-18]) to the depth of betrayal, at which he names Cleopatra as the "triple turn'd whore" who has "sold" him "to this novice" [IV. xii. 13, 14]. (pp. 174-75)

The play begins with a slow alternation between grandeur and ignominy, and as it advances this tempo increases until the end of Act IV. There, appropriately, it slows and stops.

At this point Shakespeare returns to the note heard in the opening exposition, the theme of high tragedy itself which came close to parody in Antony's vision of the "nobleness of life." In Act I this vision was mocked or rejected by several characters, including Cleopatra, but it is now her turn to claim the amenities of tragedy as the full play of satire is resumed. Antony, however, will no longer strain at sublimity and will grow in stature becuase of his reticence.

Act IV, scene xv arises from the decision of Cleopatra, advised by Charmian in scene xiii, to repossess Antony by withdrawing and sending word that she is dead. "To th' monument! / Mardian, go tell him I have slain myself" [IV. xiii. 6-7]. And with a child's casual effrontery: "Hence, Mardian, / And bring me how he takes my death" [IV. xiii. 9-10]. The monument scene with its frequently sentimentalized lines ("I am dying, Egypt, dying . . ." [IV. xv, 18, 41]) thus stems directly from a desire of Cleopatra to create situation, to write her own tragedy.

As he is brought to his end by the false news of Cleopatra's death, Antony's last words express no spurious sublimity. He seems almost to anticipate Shaw's "wretched end of the business" by speaking of his fate as a "miserable change" which his followers must neither "lament nor sorrow at" [IV. xv. 52]. True, he recalls his role as "the noblest," but here he describes his former status which he plainly distinguishes from the miserable change. He asks only to die "not basely," not "cowardly [to] put off my helmet to / My countryman" [IV. xv. 56-7]. Cleopatra, however, does assert the grand descent, and a familiar egoism colors her statement:

> Noblest of men, woo 't die?
> Hast thou no care of me? Shall I abide
> In this dull world, which in thy absence is
> No better than a sty? O, see, my women.
> The crown o' th' earth doth melt. My lord!
> O, wither'd is the garland of the war,
> The soldier's pole is fall'n! Young boys and girls
> Are level now with men; the odds is gone,
> And there is nothing left remarkable
> Beneath the visiting moon.
>
> [IV. xv. 59-68].

To say that the sentiment of this passage is merely selfish would be as untrue as to say that it amounts to genuine renunciation. Perhaps, as some have believed, we do have a new Cleopatra here, but in a contextual reading of these lines there must still be heard the old one who created the scene, not too unwittingly, for herself. She has become the chorus of conventional tragedy even to the extent of rendering inversely the doctrine of "admiration" or wonder ("there is nothing left remarkable / Beneath the visiting moon"). And after invoking Antony as the "noblest of men" she bestows the same nobility upon her coterie:

> My noble girls! . . .
> Our lamp is spent, it's out!
>
> [IV. xv. 84, 85]

The "girls" are thus endowed by Cleopatra with the stuff of tragedy; had Mardian been on hand there is the off-chance that he might have been translated too.

If this interpretation suggests an irony too modern, the possible anachronism may be tested by referring to V.i and V.ii. Again Shakespeare follows the plan of his early exposition by allowing orthodox notions of fallen grandeur to be stated and then questioned. Act V, scene i presents a galaxy of stock comment upon tragic stature and tragic flaw; it is very nearly a manual of the subject, and it is hard to understand why it has not been emphasized in discussions of Elizabethan critical doctrine. As Dercetas acquaints Octavius, Maecenas, and others with news of Antony's death, dialogue ensues in which each speaker amplifies the convention. First, from Octavius, there is the concept of magnitude, of world-wide convulsion.

> The breaking of so great a thing should make
> A greater crack. The round world
> Should have shook lions into civil streets,
> And citizens to their dens. The death of Antony
> Is not a single doom; in the name lay
> A moiety of the world.
>
> [V. i. 14-19]

Now Agrippa, who seems to be thinking of fate, flaw, and compulsion: "strange it is / That nature must compel us to lament / Our most persisted deeds" [V. i. 28-30]. And Maecenas specifically on the flaw principle: "His taints and honours / Wag'd equal with him" [V. i. 30-1]. Next, Agrippa must show that he understands this:

> A rarer spirit never
> Did steer humanity; but you gods will give us
> Some faults to make us men.
>
> [V. i. 31-3]

Then appears the *de casibus* theory with the mirror for magistrates. As Agrippa declares that "Caesar is touched," Maecenas explains: "When such a spacious mirror's set before him, / He needs must see himself" [V. i. 33, 34-5]. Finally Octavius again, with a summation:

> O Antony!
> I have followed thee to this; but we do lance
> Diseases in our bodies. I must perforce
> Have shown to thee such a declining day,
> Or look on thine; we could not stall together
> In the whole world: but yet let me lament,
> With tears as sovereign as the blood of hearts,
> That thou, my brother, my competitor
> In top of all design, my mate in empire,
> Friend and companion in the front of war,
> The arm of mine own body, and the heart
> Where mine his thoughts did kindle,—that our stars,
> Unreconcilable, should divide
> Our equalness to this. Hear me, good friends,—
> But I will tell you at some meeter season.
>
> [V. i. 35-49]

Dolabella, however, is elsewhere and if we read the next scene in context we may intuit the reason. After the retinue of Octavius has been converted to a chorus and has presented the subject of tragedy in every standard detail, Cleopatra promptly continues the theme in scene ii with a vision of Antony's stature and flaw. Dolabella, however, is apparently assigned the function of reducing her illusion in a single, well-turned line. As he confronts Cleopatra she loses no time in leading to the issue.

> *Cleopatra.* I dream'd there was an Emperor Antony.
> O, such another sleep, that I might see
> But such another man!

> *Dolabella.*   If it might please ye,—
> *Cleopatra.* His face was as the heavens; and therein stuck
> A sun and moon, which kept their course and lighted
> The little O, the earth.
> *Dolabella.*   Most sovereign creature,—
> *Cleopatra.* His legs bestrid the ocean; his rear'd arm
> Crested the world; his voice was propertied
> As all the tuned spheres. . . .
>   His delights
> Were dolphin-like: they show'd his back above
> The element they liv'd in. In his livery
> Walk'd crowns and crownets; realms and islands were
> As plates dropp'd from his pocket.
> *Dolabella.*   Cleopatra!
>
> [V. ii. 76-84, 88-92]

Note Dolabella's interruptions which seem to imply that a public airing of nobility in these terms approaches travesty and destroys a dignity which should be maintained by reticence. Note that the climax of Cleopatra's fantasy dwells upon Antony's sensuality, his "delights." Like the dolphin they rise with Antony above their element in a perfect image of the tragic protagonist who transcends his world of evil. Note finally how the fantasy is rejected. Turning to Dolabella just after her lines on Antony and the dolphin, Cleopatra puts the ultimate question: "Think you there was or might be such a man / As this I dream'd of?" And Dolabella in one line of memorable timing: "Gentle madam, no" [V. ii. 93-4]. Here is one of the shortest dramatic commentaries on record, and its choric nature is warranted. Plot devleopment, narration, calls merely for Dolabella to inform Cleopatra of Caesar's intention to lead her through Rome in triumph. Shakespeare, however, expands the situation into dialogue between a romanticist and a sympathetic realist on the subject of Antony's role as tragic hero.

We should not interpret V.i-V.ii as a simplified denial of tragic dignity. Even Dolabella, after rejecting Cleopatra's vision, qualifies himself: "Your loss is as yourself, great" [V. ii. 101]. And the previous "colloquium" on tragedy is modified, not rejected, by Cleopatra's excesses on the theme it introduced. Of one thing, however, we can be sure; Cleopatra colors the issue with her notions of the sublime, and Dolabella anticipates Shaw in denying the scale of grandeur she finds in her dolphin-protagonist. In Shaw's words, but with a contrary application, realism is allowed to "have its demonstration," and at a key point of the tragedy.

The end is well known—Cleopatra and the asp, wih lines such as "Finish good lady; the bright day is done, / And we are for the dark" [V. ii. 193-94]. It would be foolish and unnecessary to say that Cleopatra's descent is unmoving. But it is unperceptive to see it as the august event she desires. As it runs its final course she is caught concealing a large portion of her goods and money in a statement to Caesar which Seleucus, her treasurer, refuses to verify. Her response is to berate Seleucus in an ignominious scene which is ended by still another assertion of her royal claim to tragedy. This time her pose is unmistakably tinged with the comic for she ascribes all elements of pettiness in her "fall" to Seleucus who, after all, simply told the truth when she called upon him, characteristically, for a dramatic fib. With Seleucus shouldering the pettiness, Cleopatra's inimitable logic can now claim the dignity:

Be it known that we, the greatest, are misthought
For things that others do; and, when we fall,
We answer others' merits [Seleucus's demerits] in our
  name,
Are therefore to be pitied.

[V. ii. 176-79]

Pity for the "fall" of "the greatest"—the traditional vocabulary of tragedy—and Cleopatra uses it to put a solemn face on matters which are far from solemn. In Plutarch's version of the Seleucus incident, Octavius "fell a laughing." Here Octavius may be more decorous, but Shakespeare's major change in the scene points to an ironical purpose. In Plutarch, Seleucus, unasked, eagerly exposes Cleopatra in order to please Caesar; in Shakespeare, Cleopatra calls Seleucus forth, ordering him to corroborate her story, and it is only then that he tells the truth, asserting "peril" to be his motive. Cleopatra's line, "the greatest are misthought / For things that others do," could thus be a moving one in the situation given by Plutarch. In the one Shakespeare provides, her extraction of tragedy from the incident is something less, or more, than moving.

Thus in *Antony and Cleopatra* the quality of tragedy, as an attribute of the protagonists, is an actual issue within the tragedy itself. It is a theme which appears in the exposition and is resumed with great particularity toward the close of the play. When the protagonists self-consciously assume a flawed stature, the role is ironically denied them; when they are simply themselves they achieve a subdued dignity. The dignity, however, is qualified by satire which constantly keeps the tragedy within bounds of moral realism.

At the play's end, however, do Caesar's words pronounced over the "pair so famous" deny the satire and introduce what Shaw called "theatrical sublimity"?

> Take up her bed;
> And bear her women from the monument.
> She shall be buried by her Antony;
> No grave upon the earth shall clip in it
> A pair so famous. High events as these
> Strike those that make them; and their story is
> No less in pity than his glory which
> Brought them to be lamented. Our army shall
> In solemn show attend this funeral;
> And then to Rome. Come, Dolabella, see
> High order in this great solemnity.

[V. ii. 356-66]

The travesty of fallen grandeur in Cleopatra's encounter with Seleucus immediately precedes the episode which these lines conclude. And it is interesting that Octavius bestows upon Cleopatra the same tragic dignity she had assumed for herself in the Seleucus scene. There she had laid dubious claim to pity for the fall of "the greatest," and here Caesar grants her fame, and a pity equal to his own glory. In short, a subject of comedy (see Plutarch) has within two hundred lines become a theme of high seriousness which ends the play.

In most tragedies this would be a reversal of tone and point of view. Had Brutus been given lines toward the end of *Julius Caesar* in which he had described himself, amidst laughter from the audience, as the noblest Roman of them all, the speech of Antony which concludes the play on that note would have suffered, and not mildly. The tragedy, in fact, would have been maimed at the point of Brutus' statement. In *Antony and Cleopatra*, however, just this kind of a situation is successful, and for the obvious reason that *Antony and Cleopatra* is not at all

like *Julius Caesar*. The latter play is "straight" tragedy, the former a tragedy in which satire and seriousness are in continual suspension. The satire, moreover, is directed constantly at claims of tragic stature which the protagonists assert for themselves. Consistently then, the suspension of opposites is carried through to the end: in the Seleucus incident Cleopatra's claim, for herself, of the *de casibus* role is comic; in Caesar's lines her posthumous assumption of the role is not at all comic.

If we are asked which of these concluding notes should prevail, the answer, I believe, is that neither is controlling. Each supplies context for the other and the balanced result agrees perfectly with a tone set throughout; anything other than this blend of satire and tragedy would have destroyed a quality present from the beginning. Caesar's lines ask us, of course, to respect death and the dead, and there is no mockery in them. But if context has meaning, Shakespeare is not asking us to forego smiles when we remember Seleucus. (pp. 175-84)

[A] "satirical tragedy" like *Antony and Cleopatra* is in no sense anomalous. Although spirited it is soberly honest; although astringent it is sympathetic; and although realistic in outlook it contains great art. *It* has the stature, whether or not the hero attains greatness, and it, not Antony or Cleopatra, embodies the ultimate insight intended for an audience. *Antony and Cleopatra* asserts human dignity, value, because it confronts defeat with a superb expression of ironical truth. As the audience joins in the confrontation and expression, it perceives events not in the manner of Antony or Cleopatra but of Shakespeare. (p. 191)

> Brents Stirling, "The Nobleness of Life," in his Unity
> in Shakespearian Tragedy: The Interplay of Theme
> and Character, *Columbia University Press, 1956, pp.*
> *157-92.*

MAURICE CHARNEY (essay date 1957)

[*Charney maintains that Antony's downward movement after the battle of Actium, together with his willing acceptance of his fate, is mirrored in the play's imagery. The frequent allusions to "sword and armor," the critic avers, have dual referents: on one hand, they emphasize Antony's political and military functions as a Roman commander, but—in association with Egypt—they may also have sexual or phallic connotations. Thus, Charney contends, metaphors of powerless swords refer not only to Antony's military losses and his "abandonment of his Roman role of soldier and world conqueror," but also to his emasculation as a result of Cleopatra's domination. Persistent images of "vertical dimension and dissolution" further underscore Antony's downward progress, the critic holds, although these emphasize as well Antony's elevation at his death and the cessation of the conflict between Roman and Egyptian values.*]

Shakespeare's Antony resembles Hamlet in this respect: both have an acute awareness of their moral situation, but they are without the power to change it. Their tragedy does not come from a blindness or error of judgment, but from a deep-seated paralysis of will. Hamlet, however, is catapulted into a tragedy to which he remains alien and unreconciled, whereas Antony seems to choose his fate deliberately and knowingly. He goes through the motions of suicide, for example, only to learn that Cleopatra is "playing" dead in her monument. At this point it is possible for the action to move in an entirely different direction from the one Shakespeare actually takes. This discovery of Cleopatra's trickery could be the final ironic act of the "serpent of old Nile" [I. v. 25]. But instead, the discovery is minimized and Antony says only, "Too late, good Diomed.

Call my guard I prithee'' [IV. xiv. 128]. His dying wish to be carried to Cleopatra is an acknowledgment and acceptance of his fate. In this way the death scene (IV.xv) passes from tragedy to rhapsodic affirmation.

These movements in the fate of Antony grow out of the tragic conflict between the values of Egypt and Rome. Symbolically as well as geographically, they are separate and divided worlds. . . . This symbolic conflict is deeply rooted in the imagery of the play, especially in the themes of sword and armor, vertical dimension, and dissolution. The sword and armor Antony wears are the visible signs of his soldiership and power— he is the "triple pillar of the world . . ." [I. i. 12]. But as the play progresses, the power of Antony's sword is undercut by his association with Cleopatra, and his unarming is a formal dumbshow for his renunciation of Rome. This pattern of Antony's tragedy is also reflected in images of lowness and height and in a very characteristic imagery of dissolution. Out of many possible themes, these three express the fate of Antony with most significance and originality.

Antony is visibly present in sword and armor for a good part of the play. This is a direct presentational image of Antony's role as soldier and triumvir, his "royal occupation" [IV. iv. 17], and the verbal imagery helps to support this impression. We see him in military dress throughout the battle scenes (from II.vii to IV.xii), and probably also in the conferences with Caesar (II.ii) and Pompey (II.vi) in Rome—the formal dress of sword and armor would be in keeping with the gravity of public affairs in these scenes. As a matter of fact, Lepidus very specifically indicates "soldier's dress" [II. iv. 4] for the scene with Pompey (II.vi). Antony is also probably in sword and armor when he first appears in the play. This would give Philo's allusions to "plated Mars" [I. i. 4] and "The buckles on his [captain's] breast" [I. i. 8] an immediate applicability to the Antony we see enter a few lines further. Philo wishes to indicate that the sword and armor are only an appearance, while in actuality the "triple pillar of the world" has been "transform'd / Into a strumpet's fool" [I. i. 12-13].

The basic reference of the sword and armor imagery is to the Roman concerns of war and soldiership. This is part of that Roman world of hard material objects and practical business that stands in sharp contrast to the luxuriousness and indolence of Egypt. Originally, it is the "civil swords" [I. iii. 45], or civil war, in Italy that call Antony back to Rome, so that his return to Egypt is an acceptance of his tragedy. After Antony's shameful flight from battle, his sword becomes an image of his former glory. He recollects that the now triumphant Octavius

> . . . at Philippi kept
> His sword e'en like a dancer, while I struck
> The lean and wrinkled Cassius; and 'twas I
> That the mad Brutus ended. He alone
> Dealt on lieutenantry and no practice had
> In the brave squares of war. Yet now—No matter.
>
> [III. xi. 35-40]

Now Caesar, whose sword served no more function than a dancer's ornament, has defeated Antony, and the extent of Antony's present shame is indicated by that prolonged and emphatic "now." Antony tries to restore the power of his sword by challenging Caesar to single combat:

> . . . I dare him therefore
> To lay his gay comparisons apart
> And answer me declin'd, sword against sword,
> Ourselves alone.
>
> [III. xiii. 25-8]

It is an unreal, histrionic effort, for Caesar is not interested in this public display of bravery; he has, indeed, already refused Antony [III. i. 31-5]. The aside of Enobarbus serves as chorus here:

> Yes, like enough high-battled Caesar will
> Unstate his happiness and be stag'd to th' show
> Against a sworder!
>
> [III. xiii. 29-31]

"Sworder" is a contemptuous word and it signifies that Antony now wears his sword "e'en like a dancer" [III. xi. 36]—the power of war has gone out of it. Enobarbus seems to have a closer affinity for Caesar than for Antony, and it is in this scene that he finally decides to desert his master. His ominous and incisive comment closes the scene:

> . . . When valour preys on reason,
> It eats the sword it fights with. I will seek
> Some way to leave him.
>
> [III. xiii. 198-200]

This Roman virtue of "reason" is valor's sword, and Caesar's conquest of the "three nook'd world" [IV. vi. 5] shows how well he has learned this lesson.

There is an ironic comment on the ineffectiveness of Antony's sword in his suicide scene (IV.xiv). He entreats Eros to draw "thy honest sword" [IV. xiv. 79] and kill him, but Eros takes his own life instead. This gives Antony the courage to fall on his sword, but he is only able to inflict a mortal wound. He prays the Guard, then Diomedes, to make an end of his blundering work: "Draw thy sword and give me / Sufficing strokes for death" [IV. xiv. 116-17]. Antony's sword is powerless even for death, and this is a graphic stage image of Antony's tragedy. The inability of Antony's sword reflects the abandonment of his Roman role of soldier and world conqueror.

Our final image of Antony's sword balances the fall of Antony against the rise of Caesar. Once again, the sword enters significantly into the stage action. As Antony lies dying, Dercetas steals his sword, which "but shown to Caesar, with this tidings, / Shall enter me with him" [IV. xiv. 112-13]. We see Dercetas again at the beginning of Act V, where his portentous entrance with the bloody sword of Antony in his hand gives Caesar a sudden fright—it is a final reflection of the power of Antony. This sword, once the symbol of his Roman virtue and dominion, is handed over to Caesar, who is now indeed "Sole sir o' th' world" [V. ii. 120]. . . . [The] presentation of Antony's sword to Octavius acts out the tragic transfer of power that is a central issue in the play, and the ritual stage business serves as a brusque investiture for Caesar.

In a sense, sword has one set of connotations in Egypt and another in Rome. This difference reflects Antony's tragedy, for his sword in its Roman role is rendered powerless in Egypt, and his association with Cleopatra tends to develop the sexual overtones of the image. Although this theme is directly stated only two or three times in the play, it underlies a good part of the action in Egypt. As Agrippa tells us, Cleopatra has the ability to charm swords to inaction: "She made great Caesar lay his sword to bed. / He plough'd her, and she cropp'd" [II. ii. 227-28]. This utterly un-Shavian Julius Caesar is the model for Antony, and the strong phallic suggestion in "sword" indicates its transformation into an instrument of sensual pleasure. The passage suggests Cleopatra's recollection of the time she drank Antony to his bed, "Then put my tires and mantles on him, whilst / I wore his sword Philippan" [II. v. 22-3]. In both passages Cleopatra's dominance involves control of her lover's sword, the symbol of his manliness and soldiership. There is perhaps an allusion to Hercules' enslavement by Omphale here, for Omphale forced Hercules to wear her clothes, while she dressed in his lion-skin and carried his club. This identification is very specifically indicated in the "Comparison" that follows the "Life of Antony" in North's *Plutarch:*

> . . . we see in painted tables, where Omphale secretlie stealeth away Hercules clubbe, and tooke his Lyons skinne from him. Even so Cleopatra oftentimes unarmed Antonius, and intised him to her, making him lose matters of great importance, and verie needefull jorneys, to come and be dandled with her, about the rivers of Canobus, and Taphosiris.

This is the sort of effemination that Cleopatra has inflicted on Antony, and it is no wonder that when Cleopatra enters in I.ii, Enobarbus says sardonically: "Hush! Here comes Antony" [I. ii. 79].

This reversal of roles between Antony and Cleopatra is illustrated by the battle of Actium: it is to please her and against all reason that Antony accepts Caesar's dare to fight at sea. A Soldier warns him against it, but the Soldier's "sword" and "wounds" [III. vii. 63] cannot persuade Antony above the whims of Cleopatra, who insists on appearing at Actium "for a man" [III. vii. 18]. Antony blames her for his defeat while he acknowledges his own "dotage" in Egypt:

> . . . You did know
> How much you were my conqueror, and that
> My sword, made weak by my affection, would
> Obey it on all cause.
>
> [III. xi. 65-8]

"My sword made weak by my affection" is a key statement for the tragedy of Antony. His power to act, represented by the Roman sense of "sword," has been overwhelmed by his power to feel ("affection"). Enobarbus, too, blames "affection" for the defeat at Actium. When Antony followed Cleopatra from battle, "The itch of his affection should not then / Have nick'd his captainship . . ." [III. xiii. 7-8]. Antony's "captainship" is conceived as the blade of a sword which Cleopatra has damaged and made useless. He is thus being made aware of the price of Egypt, which gives a tragic dimension to what began as frivolity and indulgence of the senses.

There is a final reflection of this theme in the scene of Antony's suicide (IV.xiv). The entrance of Cleopatra's Eunuch, Mardian, sends Antony into a rage: "O, thy vile lady! / She has robb'd me of my sword" [IV. xiv. 22-3]. This is another way of stating the tragedy of Antony. Cleopatra has deprived him of the power to act and conquer that made him "triple pillar of the world" [I. i. 12]. This is the obvious Roman sense of sword, but there is also a play on the sexual connotations of the image. From a Roman point of view, Antony has become as impotent as this Eunuch Mardian: his sword is only an instrument of "affection," the symbol of his dominance by Cleopatra. But in the values of Egypt this is sufficient, and in itself can offer a transcendence. When Antony learns that Cleopatra has not betrayed him to Caesar but has committed suicide in her monument, there is a marvelous change in his attitude. His sword is no longer his concern, nor any temporal thing, as he prepares to follow his lady. This is a final, tragic acceptance of the values of Egypt, and it marks a strong poetic heightening in the dramatic action.

This "turn" in the action begins with Antony's request to Eros: "Unarm me, Eros. The long day's task is done, / And we must sleep" [IV. xiv. 35-6]. Antony by disarming now visibly abandons his Roman role of soldier just as Cleopatra assumes the role of queen by putting on robe and crown; both are the final symbolic acts of the protagonists, and in both the costume properties have strong thematic significance. (pp. 149-54)

Antony's public position of Roman soldier and triumvir has been visibly embodied in the sword and armor images throughout the play, so that his unarming in IV.xiv marks a new—and final—movement in the action. The bitterness and misgivings of tragic conflict in Antony are gone; there is only a desire for haste (cf. Cleopatra and Iras [V. ii. 283ff.]):

> . . . Off, pluck off!
> The sevenfold shield of Ajax cannot keep
> The battery from my heart. O, cleave, my sides!
> Heart, once be stronger than thy continent,
> Crack thy frail case! Apace, Eros, apace.—
> No more a soldier. Bruised pieces, go;
> You have been nobly borne.
>
> [IV. xiv. 37-43]

"No more a soldier" marks the end of the unarming. Antony has explicitly identified armor with the role of soldier, and now, unarmed, he feels himself to be entering a new spiritual state. (pp. 154-55)

In addition to the sword and armor theme, Antony's downward movement is indicated by a persistent imagery of vertical dimension and dissolution. This is a simpler and more literal sort of imagery than the sword and armor, but it serves to keep us vividly aware of the tone and structure of Antony's fall. The simplest pattern here is the contrast in vertical dimension between high and low, up and down. This is best seen in two presentational images. Antony's despair and remorse after Actium are summed up in a significant bit of stage action: *"Sits down"* [s.d., III. xi. 24]. . . . It is not part of the decorum of majesty for Antony to be sitting down, and this action becomes a literal stage image of Antony's lowness at this point: "He is unqualitied with very shame" [III. xi. 44]. One may easily overlook this image in reading the play, but in the theater it is an effective and eloquent expression of Antony's tragic state. The image is supported by verbal references which do not allow us to forget Antony's position. Cleopatra wishes to join him: "Let me sit down. O Juno!" [III. xi. 28], but Antony protests bitterly: "No, no, no, no, no!" [III. xi. 29]—the passage in its intensity recalls the "never's" of King Lear [*King Lear,* V. iii. 309]. And Antony is still seated [at III. xi. 46], when Eros says: "Most noble sir, arise. The Queen approaches." It is not presumably until a few lines further [III. xi. 50] that Antony stands, and this action brings with it a recovery of equilibrium.

Antony achieves a different kind of height from Caesar's in IV.xv, when he is lifted, dying, to Cleopatra's monument. The stage action, *"They heave Antony aloft to Cleopatra"* [s.d., IV. xv, 37], presents a literal stage image of height in the use of the balcony. We see Antony being raised by his Guard to the upper stage, and they are assisted by Cleopatra and her girls from "aloft." The physical theater thus provides us with a metaphor of elevation for Antony's death which is accompanied by a corresponding heightening of style. Cleopatra's speech is full of ironic puns about the stage business:

> Here's sport indeed! How heavy weighs my lord!
> Our strength is all gone into heaviness:

That makes the weight. Had I great Juno's power,
The strong-wing'd Mercury should fetch thee up
And set thee by Jove's side. . . .

[IV. xv. 32-6]

Cleopatra uses the word ''sport'' ironically to fit in with the stage business, as if all the Egyptian pleasures ended in this final sport: the awkward manual labor of lifting a dying captain to his place of death. But this place is an elevated one, and in its own way defies the temporal height of Caesar. The tone of fulfillment and reconciliation in this image places the fate of Antony outside the toils of tragedy.

Antony's fallen state is represented most brilliantly by the imagery of dissolution. The pattern in the play is one of melting, fading, dissolving, discandying, disponging, dislimning, and losing of form that marks Antony's downward course after Actium, ''for indeed I have lost command'' [III. xi. 23]. (pp. 155-57)

The dissolution theme is acted out on a mythological plane in IV.iii, where the god Hercules, Antony's supposed ancestor and tutelary deity, abandons him. Shakespeare develops this scene from a marginal note in Plutarch: *''Strange noyses heard, and nothing seene.''* One company of soldiers is relieving another on the night before the second day of battle, and *''They place themselves in every corner of the stage''* [s.d., IV. iii. 8]. The sense of isolation and dispersal over a large area would be intensified on the bare, projecting Elizabethan platform stage. Suddenly, after the Third Soldier has said, ''Tis a brave army, / And full of purpose'' [IV. iii. 11-12], *''Music of the hautboys is under the stage''* [s.d., IV. iii. 12]. This muffled, distant-sounding oboe music belies the false optimism of the soldiers. It is a striking, portentous effect, and they listen with attentive fear:

2. Sold. Peace! What noise?
1. Sold.   List, list!
2. Sold. Hark!
1. Sold.   Music i' th' air.
3. Sold.   Under the earth.
4. Sold. It signs well, does it not?
3. Sold.   No.
1. Sold.   Peace, I say!
        What should this mean?
2. Sold. 'Tis the god Hercules, whom Antony lov'd
        Now leaves him.

[IV. iii. 12-17]

This scene is in the symbolic tradition of the medieval pageant wagon, where the stage itself represented the world, with heaven above and hell below. As a matter of structure, the departure of Hercules occurs at almost the same time as the desertion of Enobarbus; in some sense Enobarbus has been Antony's Hercules, and IV.iii gives his desertion a mythological compulsion. By the strange voice of oboes from the underworld, we are prepared for Antony's defeat and tragic end—the image is harbinger of the ''discandying'' and ''dislimning'' that is to follow.

After his final defeat (IV.xii), Antony speaks again in the imagery of dissolution:

        All come to this? The hearts
    That spaniel'd me at heels, to whom I gave
    Their wishes, do discandy, melt their sweets
    On blossoming Caesar . . .

[IV. xii. 20-3]

Antony's powers ''discandy'' and ''melt'' onto the ''blossoming Caesar,'' who waxes as Antony wanes. Compare Cleopatra's melting imagery in III.xii; if she be cold-hearted to Antony,

    From my cold heart let heaven engender hail,
    And poison it in the source, and the first stone
    Drop in my neck; as it determines, so
    Dissolve my life! The next Caesarion smite!
    Till by degrees the memory of my womb,
    Together with my brave Egyptians all,
    By the discandying of this pelleted storm,
    Lie graveless, till the flies and gnats of Nile
    Have buried them for prey!

[III. xiii. 159-67]

Like Antony, Cleopatra imagines death as a dissolving and a ''discandying.'' This last word, ''discandying'' (also ''discandy'' [IV. xii. 22]), is a coinage of Shakespeare's to indicate the sweetness and strength going out of life. ''Disponge,'' is used similarly for Enobarbus' death, when he prays that

    The poisonous damp of night disponge upon me,
    That life, a very rebel to my will,
    May hang no longer on me!

[IV. ix, 13-15]

This is the earliest example of ''disponge'' (spelt ''dispunge'') in the *New English Dictionary,* and its status as an unfamiliar word strengthens its poetic effect.

The most extended imagery of dissolution is in the pageant of cloud shapes Antony sees in IV.xiv, which melt and dissolve into each other and cannot hold their form:

    That which is now a horse, even with a thought
    The rack dislimns, and makes it indistinct
    As water is in water.

[IV. xiv. 9-11]

''Dislimns'' is another of those unfamiliar words of dissolution which call attention to themselves and give a characteristic quality to this play (cf. ''discandy'' and ''disponge''—''dissolve'' is also part of this ''dis-'' prefix group). Shakespeare seems to be creating his own vocabulary here to establish the feeling of disintegration of the Roman world. The firm substance of life is being undone, things are losing their form, changing and fading with the indistinctness of water in water— this image is the essence of the dissolution theme. There is no bitterness here but only resignation and a certain aesthetic pleasure. The process of thought obeys this same progress of forms, mingling as water in water. The complexity of the image lies in the fact that ''water'' and ''water'' are the same substance, yet in their being together, or in one's being in the other, subtle differences appear. Perhaps it is the idea of difference approaching similarity, as cloud shapes (''The rack'') soon merge into simple clouds. This whole process of indiscernible change is the essence of ''dislimning.'' Antony sees his own inner state reflected in this insubstantial show:

    My good knave Eros, now thy captain is
    Even such a body. Here I am Antony;
    Yet cannot hold this visible shape, my knave.

[IV. xiv. 12-14]

It is ironic that the name remains—''Here I am Antony''— while the physical reality, ''this visible shape,'' cannot be retained.

Finally, Cleopatra marks the moment of Antony's death with these words: "O, see, my women, / The crown o' th' earth doth melt. My Lord!" [IV. xv. 62-3]. Antony is not only her "lord" but the "crown o' th' earth." This image attempts to objectify, to hyperbolize the personal dimension of the play to a cosmic plane. There is a peace and effortlessness in "melt," as if there were no barrier between life and death, and one could flow easily into the other. It is a fitting close for Antony. His end is not really a "tragic" one in the sense of King Lear, or Othello, or Macbeth. Rather than being resolved, the conflict between Egypt and Rome ceases to exist, and the hard "visible shapes" of Rome are dissolved into an ecstatic, poetic reality.

The themes of sword and armor, vertical dimension, and dissolution show the stresses of Antony's tragedy in clear detail. In the developing course of the action, the images "seed" the mind in the sense that their meanings grow and intertwine. Thus the sword image in any particular context implies either the Roman idea of manliness and conquest or the Egyptian idea of the phallus. But as the play progresses these meanings tend to coalesce, so that the Egyptian and Roman senses of the image reflect each other. In this way the imagery is made to express the tragic theme. The images affect us not only through the language of the play, but also through the presences and properties of the actual stage production. When Antony sits down, we understand the meaning of Actium, and Antony is heightened at his death by the mechanism of being lifted to the upper stage; the stage action here has a metaphoric and symbolic function. These images, both verbal and non-verbal, help to establish the tone and atmosphere of the play—the dissolution theme, for example, permeates the last acts of the play and develops the mood and texture of Antony's fate. In this sense, a study of imagery brings us close to those qualities in the work of art that are unique and characteristic, and this effort is, perhaps, the central concern of criticism. (pp. 158-61)

> *Maurice Charney, "Shakespeare's Antony: A Study of Image Themes," in* Studies in Philology, *Vol. LIV, No. 1, January, 1957, pp. 149-61.*

BENJAMIN T. SPENCER   (essay date 1958)

[*Spencer relates Shakespeare's use of paradox in* Antony and Cleopatra *to his presentation of the conflict between Egyptian and Roman values and to his dramatization of "the contradictions and unpredictability and irrationality of human affection and passion." Instead of providing a resolution that demonstrates a predilection for one value system over another, the critic argues, Shakespeare offers "an undefined synthesis" of the two cultures that is reflected in the discrepancies between appearance and reality, the elements of bafflement and surprise, and the compatibility of "seemingly incompatible terms." Spencer further claims that "apparent contradictions" in the behavior of Antony and Cleopatra should not lead us to judge them as inconsistently drawn. Rather, he holds, the "concentrations of paradoxical metaphor around Cleopatra and Antony" enhance the portrayal of protagonists who "make defect perfection" (II. ii. 231).*]

Even in the first speech of *Antony and Cleopatra* Shakespeare introduces a rhetorical mode which in its reiteration throughout the five acts is peculiar to this play and hence provides a clue to its implications. Antony's heart, remarks the Roman spokesman Philo, is no longer the organ of martial courage but has become rather "the bellows and the fan / To cool a gypsy's lust" [I. i. 9-10]. We should have expected here some such verb as "inflame" instead of "cool"; but the Egyptian atmosphere has sufficiently disturbed the confident order of the

Roman mind and code to beget a kind of discourse which is obliged to take account of the contradictions and unpredictability and irrationality of human affection and passion. Thus the beat of Antony's imperial and militant heart, which should have set the measure to the farther advances of Roman power, has become instead the sighing bellows whose cooling current serves but to revive the latent flame of Cleopatra's lust. For this kind of expression which persists through the play perhaps the phrase "paradoxical metaphor" will serve most inclusively, for it involves the sense of bafflement and surprise, the inherent contradiction, and the unexpected reality beneath appearance which are associated with paradox.

To the rhetoric-conscious Elizabethans of the literate classes paradox was, of course, a familiar device, and many of them may have recognized in this tragedy its recurrent appearance in the form of synoeciosis, a yoking of seemingly incompatible terms. Shakespeare himself occasionally alludes to paradox, and even more frequently he employs it as a rhetorical mode in his poems and plays. In the opening scene of *Macbeth* he has the witches proclaim that "Fair is foul, and foul is fair" [I. i. 11], but this paradoxical thesis he elaborates in that play rather through surprising episodes of reversal than through explicit verbal commentary and discourse. But uniquely in *Antony and Cleopatra* he underscores by reiterated verbal pointers the paradoxical element that pervades and dominates behavior and catastrophe. The play begins and ends on such a note, and attention to this emphasis would do much, I suggest, to dispose of the charge of scholars like Schücking [see excerpt above, 1919] that the play breaks apart in the middle—that the sultry Queen of the first three acts could not become the "lass unparalleled" of the final two, or that the Antony who has been a "strumpet's fool" for most of the play could not deserve Octavius Caesar's tears in the last scene. Through the reiterated paradox Shakespeare would seem to remind his audience that apparent contradictions in behavior are not necessarily ultimate inconsistencies in value and motive; for the paradox serves to hold contradictions in solution, as it were. It is an admission of the unresolved conflict between common sense or current code and a new experience which cannot as yet be explained and therefore can only be reported. In *Antony and Cleopatra* it thus becomes a staple in the utterance of the Roman characters, for they have hitherto been conditioned to a firm, legalistic, and rational world; and now, confronted by the alien culture and mysterious phenomena of Egypt, they can only report and wait.

The most concentrated expression of this sense of the self-contradictory in the Egyptian scene is to be found in the description of Cleopatra and the barge. Like Philo, the rationalistic Enobarbus can express his bafflement only in paradox. A half-dozen times within the course of thirty lines he goes beyond the account in Plutarch, which Shakespeare otherwise so closely paraphrased, to insert paradox or synoeciosis. In Plutarch "the oars of silver . . . kept stroke in rowing after the sound of the music of flutes, hautboys, citherns, viols, and such other instruments as they played upon in the barge." Shakespeare dispenses with all the instruments except the flutes and substitutes Enobarbus' impression that the oars "made / The water which they beat to follow faster, / As amorous of their strokes" [II. ii. 195-97]. By this additional observation on the all but masochistic water Enobarbus would seem to be projecting into his description the paradoxical conduct of love as he has observed it between Antony and Cleopatra. Quite explicitly in the first act [I. iii. 1-10] the Queen has announced to Charmian her technique of captivating Antony by crossing him at every turn—by dancing when he is sad, by feigning illness when he is in mirth. Cleopatra's acts are the strokes of the oars, as Enobarbus has seen, which paradoxically cause the amorous Antony ''to follow faster''. The climactic stroke comes at the height of the battle of Actium when, as Scarus reports, Cleopatra ''like a cow in June'' hoisted sail and fled with her sixty ships and Antony ''like a doting mallard'' followed after [III. x. 14, 19].

To Enobarbus the magic of Cleopatra seemed not to lie so much in sheer sensuous splendor as in the contradictions in which the splendor is wreathed. Even the ''pretty dimpled boys'' in the very act of cooling her with ''divers-colored fans'', he observes, made her cheeks glow and ''what they undid did'' [II. ii. 202, 203, 205]. The paradox of the cooling wind which effects the opposite from that which is expected is entirely absent from Plutarch, who is content with describing the magnificence of the scene in which ''pretty fair boys apparelled'' like Cupid ''fanned wind upon her.'' . . . Just as Philo has already concluded that Antony's sighs have served as a fan to ''cool a gypsy's lust'', so Enobarbus also notes that where Cleopatra is concerned the cooling winds produce an unexpected heat. But not only on the barge, Enobarbus tells Mecaenas and Agrippa, does the Queen mock expectation. Once hopping forty paces through the street she panted breathlessly, only to have her very deficiency become her peculiar glory: ''. . . she did make defect perfection, / And breathless, power breathe forth'' [II. ii. 231-32]. For the conclusion of his tribute Enobarbus, in a typical Shakespearian mode, resorts to multiple allusion in an attempt to fix for his hearers the uniqueness of Cleopatra's paradoxical charm: she defies the withering process of age; she makes her victims hungrier even as she satisfies their appetites; her very wantonness is so becoming that it is blessed by the holy priests [II. ii. 234-39]. (pp. 373-75)

Though Shakespeare makes the Queen the greatest paradox in the play, he again goes beyond Plutarch in developing Antony as a character who is not merely an aggregate of diverse and contrasting traits but rather one who, like Cleopatra, seems to make ''defect perfection''. This view is introduced in the first act when Lepidus declines to accept Octavius' summary condemnation of Antony as ''the abstract of all faults / That all men follow'' [I. iv. 9-10]. In refutation Lepidus, through a startling inversion of the normal identification of the stars with the good and the beautiful, construes Antony's faults as the ''spots of heaven'' which are made ''More fiery by night's blackness'' [I. iv. 12-13]. . . . Thus in effect Lepidus would seem to be saying that out of the vast darkness of Antony's virtues his faults shine like stars—that his very defects involve a bright beauty. But it is Cleopatra herself, of course, who in her final eulogy of Antony hits upon the more memorable figure to express the paradoxical aspect of his character. The generous abandon which Octavius condemned and Lepidus compared to the ''spots of heaven'' becomes for her a ''bounty'' which had ''no winter in't'' but was an ''autumn . . . / That grew the more by reaping'' [V. ii. 87-8]. Here in this final sublimating portion of the tragedy the paradoxical hints at the transcendental; for, though I should find it difficult to accept a recent argument that Cleopatra bespeaks a Christian pattern of values in her last hours, she clearly repudiates the normal secular view in measuring Antony's richness by what he gave away. To both the Roman reason of Octavius and the possessive mind of the earlier Cleopatra the uncalculating generosity of Antony seemed a foolish and inexplicable denial of self-interest. And so it was to Enobarbus, who, unable to square Antony's mag-

nanimous and affectionate nature with Roman imperialism, deserted, only in the end to give back his allegiance to his foolish master to whose overwhelming and perplexing ''bounty'' he must yield, even as did Cleopatra [IV. vi. 32].

In addition to these concentrations of paradoxical metaphor around Cleopatra and Antony, Shakespeare diffuses lighter touches of the same mode throughout the play. Thus Antony observes that the ''slippery people'' never love ''the deserver / Till his deserts are past'' [I. ii. 186-87]—that is, they never love a deserver till he is a non-deserver; and in this judgment Octavius concurs later by finding ''the ebbed man, ne'er loved till ne'er worth love'' [I. iv. 43]. Sometimes the paradox is approached through a pun, as when Octavius complains of the great weight he must bear as a triumvir because of Antony's ''lightness'' [I. iv. 25]. Sometimes it is suggested by incongruous or unlikely associations in epithet and noun, as when Agrippa terms Cleopatra a ''royal wench'' [II. ii. 226], or when Scarus describes Antony as a ''noble ruin'' [III. x. 18]. Or again it may appear with more complex ethical overtones in Ventidius' recognition that a virtue may be an evil—that ''ambition, / The soldier's virtue'', may serve to demote rather than promote its exemplar, and hence that he must more wisely make ''choice of loss / Than gain which darkens him'' [III. i. 22-3, 23-4]. Persistently in the last scenes the tragedy injects its paradoxical stresses through Antony's conclusion, just before his suicide, that ''with a wound'' he ''must be cured'' [IV. xiv. 78] and that, after his slave Eros' exemplary action in killing himself, the master Antony will die ''scholar'' to his bondman [IV. xiv. 102]. In somewhat the same vein Cleopatra welcomes ''the stroke of death'' because, like ''a lover's pinch'', it ''hurts, and is desired'' [V. ii. 295, 296]. And in the last scene even Caesar, to express the contradictions of pride and fear and beauty fused in the deaths of Cleopatra and Charmian, must characterize their suicide as a ''noble weakness'' [V. ii. 344].

From this large incidence of the paradoxical in the lines of the play one can but conclude, I think, that here lay Shakespeare's ultimate construction of the tragedy of Antony and Cleopatra. How much of it was a consciously applied verbal design, how much of it emerged from those uncalculated processes and associations that seem to have been a function of his imagination, one cannot and need not confidently presume to say. But the sense of the paradoxical was surely the matrix from which much of the characterization and the action sprang, and in the more comprehensive sweep of the plot it inevitably passed into the ironic. The line which separates the two elements in the play, indeed, is often hard to fix. Both involve contradiction, surprise, and the variance of the apparent with the real; but paradox inclines toward the static, whereas irony, at least in a dramatic context, looks more explicitly to antecedent expectation and action. A case in point is the role of Octavia. Unlike Cleopatra, she herself is not presented in paradoxical terms, although one feels that Shakespeare might have written of her that ''she makes perfection defect''. Her marriage to Antony is hastily interpreted by Menas as an alliance that will forever knit Antony and Octavius together; but more perceptively Enobarbus sees this ''band that seems to tie their friendship together'' as one which ''will be the very strangler of their amity'' [II. vi. 120-21, 122-23]. Or, as he says a few lines later in transposing the metaphorical into the abstract: ''that which is the strength of their amity shall prove the immediate author of their variance'' [II. vi. 128-30]. Octavius, too, has suspicions that this ''piece of virtue'', Octavia, which should be the ''cement'' of love between Antony and himself may actually prove to "be the ram to batter / The fortress of it" [III. ii. 30-1]. The fact that the "band" is not yet but rather becomes the "strangler" and that time also plays a part in making the "cement" into the "ram" perhaps pushes the figures away from paradox into irony. But whatever distinction one may wish to make between the two modes, they serve here as related media manifesting the mood of paradox which is the imaginative premise from which the major elements of the play are wrought.

In ending the tragedy Shakespeare held to the paradoxical and ironic as a tonic chord. Antony dies a victorious victim, or as he says, "a Roman by a Roman / Valiantly vanquished" [IV. xv. 57-8]—one whose valor "hath triumphed on itself" [IV. xv. 15]. Around Cleopatra the ironies and paradoxes are even more richly sustained. Still egotistically possessive she feeds her pride by anticipating Antony's grief over the false news of her death; but, unprepared for the suicide which followed her irresponsible ruse, she is ironically pushed further by Antony's magnanimity and example toward her own decision to die. Resolved to end her life in the "high Roman fashion" [IV. xv. 87], she yet, as Caesar says, chooses one of the "easy ways to die" in the aspic's bite [V. ii. 356]. Confessing herself to be but "e'en a woman" like "the maid that milks / And does the meanest chares" [IV. xv. 74-5], she nevertheless dies proudly like a queen in royal robes and with a crown that must not be left awry at her death. Supposing herself to be "marble-constant" and to have "nothing / Of woman" in herself [V. ii. 238-39], she yet vainly preserves such beauty in death that Caesar feels that she could "catch another Antony / In her strong toil of grace" [V. ii. 347-48]. Thinking herself all fire and air and purged of the baser elements, she can still jealously fear that Antony will "spend" his first kiss upon Iras after death [V. ii. 300-03]

In the aura of such constant paradox a one-dimensional reading of the tragedy would seem scarcely convincing. Certainly a narrow didacticism, whether moralistic or political, gradually dissolves in the cumulative ironies and contradictions of character, plot, and catastrophe. To suppose that Shakespeare should have simply intended the play as an apology for Christian values through Cleopatra's transformation or as a defense of political order through the triumph of the "rational Octavius", is to wind the tragedy too neatly and tightly around a hypothetical Elizabethan thesis. It is also to ignore much of the text and the prevailing response of varied generations of readers and viewers of the play. What we have in the tragedy, I think, is the mirror held up to the disturbance of values when two large and incompatible cultures come into conflict. As Occidentals we incline at first to suppose that the Romans Philo and Enobarbus bespeak Shakespeare's moral and political views if not, indeed, some eternal verities. But Shakespeare is neither Roman nor Egyptian in his dramatic stance, I believe, but is above and beneath both cultural patterns. Hence there is no clear resolution in behalf of any of the characters, as there tends to be in the other major tragedies. The virtue whose feature the dramatic mirror shows here is an as yet undefined synthesis lying beyond both Rome and Egypt but partaking of the values of both. For this undefined synthesis paradox was the inevitable mode of discourse. Hence at the end of the play we have the paradox of nobility in failure and pettiness in success, of magnanimity in passion and calculation in reason. What Shakespeare precisely intended we can never know. But who is to say that an age which nurtured the art of John Donne would not have found itself even more at home than we with

the cumulative paradox that lies at the very heart of *Antony and Cleopatra*? (pp. 375-78)

Benjamin T. Spencer, "'Antony and Cleopatra' and the Paradoxical Metaphor," in Shakespeare Quarterly, Vol. IX, No. 3, Summer, 1958, pp. 373-78.

MAURICE CHARNEY (essay date 1959)

[*Charney analyzes the poetic style of* Antony and Cleopatra, *particularly Shakespeare's use of hyperbole "to express the spaciousness and scope of the play's themes." Boldness and extravagance are implicit in this form of rhetorical overstatement, the critic contends, and it suggests the effort to convey ideas or experiences conceivable in the imagination but beyond nature or reality. Charney adds that there is also a constant, paradoxical undermining of the play's hyperboles, especially with regard to Cleopatra's "infinite variety"; in his judgment, the dramatist thus draws attention to the elements of "artifice and boredom" in a compulsively sensual life. The critic sees a similar ambiguity in the portrayal of Cleopatra's death, remarking that hints of violence are apparent beneath her regal splendor, so that even at the end she shows herself to be both whore and monarch.*]

[*Julius Caesar and* Antony and Cleopatra] form an interesting pair for discussion since they come from two distinct periods in Shakespeare's development and their style is so radically different. Yet both are "Roman" plays based on North's Plutarch. Actually, the Roman world in *Antony and Cleopatra* is very similar to that of *Julius Caesar*, but this is "overreached" in the play by the world of Empire and the splendors and perils of Egypt. Antony abandons the Roman world and the Roman style of Octavius Caesar—it is public, political, and objective as in *Julius Caesar*—and enters into the Egyptian world and the Egyptian style of Cleopatra. These two plays show the working of Shakespeare's imagination in two different moods: in *Julius Caesar* he seems to be deliberately limiting his imaginative resources, while in *Antony and Cleopatra* he appears to be trying to extend them "past the size of dreaming" [V. ii. 97]. (pp. 355-56)

The sense of order, limitation, and control in the "Roman" style of *Julius Caesar* is expressed in the rhetorical form of close analogy, especially the simile. This form uses explicit and carefully worked-out comparisons, and there is an attempt to indicate just what specific aspects of the vehicle (image proper) are to be applied to the tenor (idea). (p. 360)

By the time of *Antony and Cleopatra*, Shakespeare has abandoned the analogy form of *Julius Caesar*. We may see this contrast in style in the very unorthodox and dramatic way he uses similes. In Cleopatra's final speech, for example, the similes make a slow, rich music of monosyllables: "As sweet as balm, as soft as air, as gentle—" [V. ii. 311]. There is an hypnotic sense of falling asleep, in which it is dramatically just to leave the final figure incomplete—Cleopatra follows the turn of her thought to "O Antony!" [V. ii. 312]. These similes dramatize the effect of the asp-bite as described by Plutarch; it

> causeth only a heauines of the head, without swounding or complaining, and bringeth a great desire also to sleepe, with a litle swet in the face, and so by litle and litle taketh away the senses & vitall powers, no liuing creature perceiuing that the patients feele any paine. For they are so sorie when any bodie awaketh them, and taketh them vp; as those that being taken

out of a sound sleep, are very heauie and desirous to sleepe.

A similar type of simile is used in Antony's speech to Eros in
IV, xiv. The changing shapes of the clouds present a pageant
of Antony's dissolution:

> That which is now a horse, even with a thought
> The rack dislimns, and makes it indistinct
> As water is in water.
>
> [IV. xiv. 9-11]

So Antony himself is ''indistinct / As water is in water'' and
''cannot hold this visible shape'' [IV. xiv. 14]. The strong
Roman sense of reality is slipping away from Antony, and the
paradoxical simile is used to emphasize the process. These
similes push beyond the ordinary limits of the analogy form
to an area of hyperbole and symbol.

This dramatic use of similes in *Antony and Cleopatra* is part
of a larger stylistic purpose very different from the ordered
perfection of *Julius Caesar*. The characteristic figure in *Antony
and Cleopatra* is the hyperbole, or what Puttenham, in his *Arte
of English Poesie* (1589), calls ''for his immoderate ex-
cesse . . . the ouer reacher'' or ''the loud lyer,'' and he defines
it as ''by incredible comparison giuing credit.'' In Greek, ''hyperbole'' is ''*a throwing beyond: an overshooting, superiority,
excess* in anything . . .'' (Lidell-Scott Dictionary). This would
include the ideas of extravagance and boldness as well as exaggeration and overstatement. In essence, hyperbole is the
reaching-out of the imagination for superlatives. This is perhaps
what Coleridge means when he calls the style of *Antony and
Cleopatra* ''*feliciter audax*''—literally, ''felicitously bold or
audacious,'' but which is best translated by Coleridge's own
phrase, ''happy valiancy of style'' [see excerpt above, 1813-34].

This type of style is needed to express the spaciousness and
scope of the play's themes. Perhaps the best example is Cleopatra's dream of Antony:

> His face was as the heav'ns, and therein stuck
> A sun and moon, which kept their course and lighted
> The little O, the earth.
>
> [V. ii. 79-81]

The image of Antony becomes the whole cosmos, and this
earth is only a ''little O'' in comparison—we cannot imagine
in higher terms. Cleopatra continues: ''His legs bestrid the
ocean: his rear'd arm / Crested the world'' [V. ii. 82-3]. This
is the Marlovian strain of invidious comparison, which we may
paraphrase thus: as to the ocean, his legs ''bestrid'' it; as to
the world, his reared arm ''crested'' it. Cleopatra goes so far
as to question the reality of her dream, as if it were beyond
our mortal sense of possibility:

> Think you there was or might be such a man
> As this I dreamt of?
> *Dol.*   Gentle madam, no.
> *Cleo.* You lie, up to the hearing of the gods!
> But if there be or ever were one such,
> It's past the size of dreaming. Nature wants stuff
> To vie strange forms with fancy; yet, t'imagine
> An Antony were nature's piece 'gainst fancy,
> Condemning shadows quite.
>
> [V. ii. 93-100]

This image of Antony is ''past the size of dreaming.'' It is
unrealizable because reality (''Nature'') cannot present all the
forms imagination (''fancy,'' a kind of dreaming) can con-

ceive. But even to think that the forms of imagination may
exist is an argument for ''Nature.'' We may take this statement—''Nature wants stuff / To vie strange forms with fancy''—
as a key to the character of the style. The imagination acts as
hyperbole: it throws beyond, overshoots, is superior to, and in
excess of nature, yet it cannot go past the size of dreaming,
and therefore must remain implicit in the dramatic action and
words. Where *Julius Caesar* limits and defines its figures and
insists on the proper logical application of vehicle to tenor,
Antony and Cleopatra uses a figurative language, the ''strange
forms'' of ''fancy,'' that tries to force itself beyond the bounds
of mere ''Nature.''

We may explore this ''hyperbolical'' style of *Antony and Cleopatra* in a more extended example showing Shakespeare's characteristic fusion of verbal and non-verbal elements. Cleopatra's
''infinite variety'' is a leading hyperbole in the play which
draws its strength as much from the poetic language lavished
on Cleopatra as from the presented image of the character—
the role demands an ''infinite variety'' of gesture and stage
action. In this sense, the ''infinite variety'' is at once a figure
of speech and a figure on the stage.

These notions are best illustrated in Act II, scene v, where
Cleopatra's ''infinite variety'' is seen as roving desire searching for objects. We begin with the consciously poetic and
languorous tone of *Twelfth Night*: ''Give me some music! music, moody food / Of us that trade in love'' [II. v. 1-2]. The
music is called for, but Cleopatra is distracted by the entrance
of Mardian, the Eunuch: ''Let it alone! Let's to billiards'' [II.
v. 3]. Now begins a series of sexual puns in the style of
Shakespeare's early comedies; Cleopatra explores the witty
possibilities of ''play:''

> *Cleo.* As well a woman with an eunuch play'd
> As with a woman. Come, you'll play with me, sir?
> *Mar.* As well as I can, madam.
> *Cleo.* And when good will is show'd, though't come
> too short.
> The actor may plead pardon.
>
> [II. v. 5-9]

But she quickly tires of this sport and has a new impulse:

> Give me mine angle! we'll to th' river. There,
> My music playing far off, I will betray
> Tawny-finn'd fishes. My bended hook shall pierce
> Their slimy jaws; and as I draw them up,
> I'll think them every one an Antony,
> And say, 'Ah, ha! y'are caught!'
>
> [II. v. 10-15]

The suggestion of music at the opening of the scene is taken
up again, but the mood is entirely different. The absent Antony
is ''caught'' or ''hooked'' in the physically violent image of
the slimy-jawed fish.

Once struck, the note of passion is intensified with the appearance of the Messenger:

> O, from Italy!
> Ram thou thy fruitful tidings in mine ears,
> That long time have been barren.
>
> [II. v. 23-5]

It is a sudden sexual fury to have Antony himself in the tidings
about him. When the Messenger tells his news of Antony's
marriage, he is struck down by Cleopatra [s.d., II. v. 61 and
62], haled up and down [s.d., II. v. 64], and threatened with

a knife [s.d., II. v. 73]. The luxuriant poetic tone of the passage has now issued out into the physical violence of the stage action. This is all part of the style of Cleopatra's "infinite variety," which runs the gamut from "music, moody food" [II. v. 1] to "Rogue, thou hast liv'd too long" with the stage direction *"Draw a knife."* [II. v. 73 and s.d.].

This ambivalent tone of "infinite variety" was first established by Enobarbus right after his splendid set speech of Cleopatra in her barge on the Cydnus. Enobarbus assures Maecenas that Antony cannot break off from his "enchanting queen":

> Never! He will not.
> Age cannot wither her nor custom stale
> Her infinite variety. Other women cloy
> The appetites they feed, but she makes hungry
> Where most she satisfies; for vilest things
> Become themselves in her, that the holy priests
> Bless her when she is riggish.
>
> [III. ii. 233-39]

Cleopatra is outside the withering toils of age and custom and cloying appetite, for "vilest things / Become themselves in her," achieve their apotheosis and inner perfection. She is even blessed when she plays the strumpet ("riggish")—this is the strange issue of the "holy palmers' kiss" of *Romeo and Juliet* [I. v. 100].

The rhapsodic and transcendental aspects of "infinite variety" are only too plain. Yet there is a strong sense in which the hyperboles of the play are constantly undercut. This is perhaps what Coleridge meant when he said that Cleopatra's passion "springs out of the habitual craving of a licentious nature, and that it is supported and reinforced by voluntary stimulus and sought-for association, instead of blossoming out of spontaneous emotion." Such terms as "habitual," "voluntary," and "sought-for" convey a sense of the effort and ennui involved. But Coleridge safeguards the balance of his judgment by noting that "the sense of criminality in her passion is lessened by our insight into its depth and energy...." This is precisely the paradox of Cleopatra's "infinite variety," that it not only suggests an unlimited creative vitality, but also artifice and boredom. New pleasures are essential to a life of pleasure, as Antony says in the first scene of the play (where the whole Egypt-Rome conflict is stated in extreme form): "There's not a minute of our lives should stretch / Without some pleasure new" [I. i. 46-7]. This concern for the new pleasure of every "minute" suggests Pater, who proposes "to give nothing but the highest quality to your moments as they pass, and simply for those moments' sake" [in his book, *The Renaissance*]. Thus, behind the appearances of splendor and fulfillment in Egypt lies a burdensome compulsion: the life of the senses must have "infinite variety" or cease to exist.

As a final example, the hyperbole of "infinite variety" in Cleopatra is perhaps most vividly seen in her suicide. It is not quite done in the "high Roman fashion" [IV. xv. 87], but with a priestly deliberateness and an aesthetic enjoyment of robe and crown and the effect of the asp-bite. Shakespeare here takes advantage of all the richness of the Elizabethan staging to enforce the poetic splendor of Cleopatra's final scene. She is to be shown "like a queen" [V. ii. 227] in elaborate stage ritual and costume. Incidently, we know from Henslowe's account books that gorgeous robes were one of the chief expenses of an Elizabethan production.

In her death, Caesar affirms her magnificence:

> she looks like sleep,
> As she would catch another Antony
> In her strong toil of grace.
>
> [V. ii. 346-48]

Part of the effectiveness of this passage rests in the acting of the part. Cleopatra must really look "like sleep," with an indefinable expression of grace—perhaps a smile. In Elizabethan English, "grace" is a complex word whose meanings range from physical attraction and charm of personal manner to preeminence of nobility, moral rightness, and divine blessing. Cleopatra's "strong toil of grace" is a union of the queen who "beggar'd all description" [II. ii. 198] and the "serpent of old Nile" [I. v. 25]—she could "catch another Antony" now as she caught the first one. We recall the Cleopatra of II, v, whose "bended hook shall pierce" the "slimy jaws" [II. v. 12, 13] of fish, and "think them every one an Antony, / And say, 'Ah, ha! y'are caught!'" [II. v. 14-15]. We should not overlook the violence in Cleopatra's "strong toil of grace" and its ability to "catch." The word "toil," for example, refers to a net or trap to snare game. Cleopatra is heightened, but not transcendentalized by her death, and her character and motives remain in a certain ambiguity even at the end. She is always both "queen" (female monarch) and "quean" (wench, whore), and in this covert pun lies the secret of her attraction. (pp. 361-66)

Maurice Charney, "Shakespeare's Style in 'Julius Caesar' and 'Antony and Cleopatra'," in ELH, *Vol. 26, No. 3, September, 1959, pp. 355-67.*

MAYNARD MACK (essay date 1960)

[*Mack is a noted American critic, biographer, and educator, whose areas of scholarship include the Renaissance, the Augustan age, and contemporary literature. He has published a highly respected series of lectures on Shakespeare entitled* King Lear in Our Time *(1965) and several studies on the life and work of Alexander Pope. In the excerpt below drawn from his 1960 introduction to* Antony and Cleopatra, *Mack proposes that Shakespeare's ambivalence toward the lovers may be seen in the pervasive ambiguity not only of their characterization, but of "almost everything in the play" as well. There are no certainties in this dramatic world, he contends, for here "nothing is stable, fixed, or sure; not even ultimate values; all is in motion." Mack asserts that the love of Antony and Cleopatra is clearly unstable and self-destructive throughout most of the play, but he claims that the evidence of the final scenes is indeterminate about whether this passion becomes exalted and whether the lovers themselves become transcendent. We are in no doubt about what Antony and Cleopatra have lost for love, he concludes, but "what . . . if anything, has been won?" Mack's introduction to* Antony and Cleopatra, *from which this excerpt was drawn, has been frequently cited by subsequent critics.*]

Macbeth and *King Lear*, like *Othello* earlier, are dark plays, filled with actions taking place in what can only be called "dramatic" as well as literal night, a dark night of the soul engulfed by evil. *Antony and Cleopatra*, on the other hand, is a bright play. *Macbeth* and *King Lear*, too, are savage—if one fully responds to them, terrifying. There is no savagery in *Antony and Cleopatra*; it is moving, exhilarating, even exalting, but contains nothing that should tear an audience to tatters. The humor of *Macbeth* and *King Lear* is either grim or pitiful: a drunken porter at the gate of hell, a court jester shivering on a stormy heath. The humor of *Antony and Cleopatra* is neither grim nor pitiful, although sometimes acrid enough. Cleopatra is given qualities that make her a very unqueenly queen: she lies, wheedles, sulks, screams, and makes love, all with equal abandon. Antony is given qualities that make him in some senses more like an elderly playboy than a tragic hero. We are encouraged by Shakespeare in this play to disengage ourselves from the protagonists, to feel superior to them, even to laugh at them, as we rarely are with his earlier tragic persons.

Against laughter, however, the playwright poises sympathy and even admiration. Tawdry though he has made these seasoned old campaigners in love and war, he has also magnified and idealized them, to the point at which their mutual passion becomes glorious as well as cheap. Antony, the play tells us, has "infinite virtue," Cleopatra "infinite variety." He is the "triple pillar of the world" [I. i. 12], she is the "day o' th' world" [IV. viii. 13]. He seems a "plated Mars," she more beautiful than Venus. His guardian spirit is called "unmatchable," she is called a "lass unparalleled." He descends from the god Hercules, she from the moon-goddess Isis. She sees him as the sun and moon, lighting this "little O, th' earth" [V. ii. 81]; Charmian sees her as the "Eastern star." When Antony cries Ho! "Like boys unto a muss, kings would start forth" [III. xiii. 91]; Cleopatra has a hand that "kings Have lipped, and trembled kissing" [II. v. 29-30]. When Antony will swear an oath, he cries, "Let Rome in Tiber melt and the wide arch Of the ranged empire fall!" [I. i. 33-4]. When Cleopatra will swear, she cries, "Melt Egypt into Nile! and kindly creatures Turn all to serpents" [II. v. 78-9]. Antony, about to die, thinks of death as a continuing amour with Cleopatra: "Where souls do couch on flowers, we'll hand in hand, And with our sprightly port make the ghosts gaze" [IV. xiv. 51-2]. When Cleopatra is about to die, she sees death in the same transcendent terms: "Go fetch My best attires. I am again for Cydnus, To meet Mark Antony" [V. ii. 227-29].

Traces of Shakespeare's duality of attitude toward his lovers may be found in Plutarch, whose *Lives of the Noble Grecians and Romans Compared Together* he had read in Thomas North's magnificent English rendering (1579) of Jacques Amyot's translation of the original into French (1559). So eloquent was North's prose that in certain instances it could be assumed into blank verse with a minimum of change, as in the . . . well-known description of Cleopatra going to meet Antony in her barge, which should be compared with the lines of Enobarbus [II. ii. 191-239] in Shakespeare's play. (pp. 14-16)

Shakespeare's play owes to Plutarch's life of Antony many of its incidents, and to North's prose the wording of occasional passages like the lines of Enobarbus referred to above. It precipitates, however, an interpretation of these materials that is spectacularly Shakespeare's own. Plutarch's narrative, for all its stress on the baffling blends of vice and virtue in great minds, is at bottom the relatively familiar story of the Great Man and the Temptress. His Antony loses the world for love, not wisely but too well, and his Cleopatra, though possibly she rises to genuine love before the end (Plutarch leaves this point undecided), is rather the instrument of a great man's downfall than a tragic figure in herself. . . . Plutarch's Cleopatra is all siren, every effect calculated to ensnare the senses of the conquering Roman. Shakespeare's Cleopatra is all siren too, but she is more. The repeated paradoxes in Enobarbus' language serve notice on us that everything about her is impossible, mysteriously contradictory. Her page-boys cool her cheeks only to make them burn, "and what they undid did" [II. ii. 205]. Her gentlewomen are seeming mermaids, half human, half sea-creature. The silken tackle swells with a life

of its own at "the touches of those flower-soft hands" [II. ii. 210]. The wharves come alive and have "sense," quickened by her "strange invisible perfume" [II. ii. 212]. The city comes alive, to "cast" its people out upon her. Antony is left sitting in the market place, whistling to the air, and the air itself, except that nature abhors a vacuum, would have "gone to gaze on Cleopatra too" [II. ii. 217] and left a gap behind. She is a creature, says Enobarbus in conclusion, who makes defect perfection, and, when breathless, power breathes forth. Other women cloy the appetites they feed, "but she makes hungry Where most she satisfies" [II. ii. 236-37]. Even the vilest things are so becoming when she does them that "the holy priests Bless her when she is riggish" [II. ii. 238-39].

This is clearly not a portrait of a mere intriguing woman, but a kind of absolute oxymoron: Cleopatra is glimpsed here as a force like the Lucretian Venus, whose vitality resists both definition and regulation. Yet enveloped as she is by Enobarbus' mocking tones, wise and faintly world-weary, calculating amusedly the effect of his words on these uninitiated Romans, she remains the more a trollop for that. His reliable anti-romanticism undercuts the picture he draws of her, and at the same time confirms it, because it comes from him.

The ambiguity of these lines extends to almost everything in the play. In the world the dramatist has given his lovers, nothing is stable, fixed, or sure, not even ultimate values; all is in motion. Seen from one point of view, the motion may be discerned as process, the inexorable march of causes and effects, exemplified in Antony's fall and epitomized by Caesar in commenting to Octavia on the futility of her efforts to preserve the peace: "But let determined things to destiny Hold unbewailed their way." Seen from another angle, the motion reveals itself as flux, the restless waxing and waning of tides, of moons, of human feeling. Especially of human feeling. Antony pursued Brutus to his death, we are reminded by Enobarbus, yet wept when he found him slain. So within the play itself Caesar weeps, having pursued Antony to his death; and Antony, desiring that Fulvia die, finds her "good, being gone" [I. ii. 126]; and Enobarbus, seeking some way to leave his master, is heart-struck when he succeeds; and the Roman populace, always fickle, "Like to a vagabond flag upon the stream, Goes to and back, lackeying the varying tide, To rot itself with motion" [I. iv. 45-7].

In such a context, it is not surprising that the lovers' passion is subject to vicissitudes, going to and back in ever more violent oscillations of attraction and recoil. Shakespeare nowhere disguises the unstable and ultimately destructive character of their relationship, and those who, like Shaw [see excerpt above, 1900], have belabored him for not giving sexual infatuation the satiric treatment it deserves have read too carelessly. It is likewise not surprising that the play's structure should reflect, in its abrupt and numerous shifts of scene, so marked a quality of its leading characters—their emotional and psychological vacillation. Though these shifts have also met with criticism, some finding in them a serious threat to unity, they are easily seen in the theatre to be among the dramatist's means of conveying to us an awareness of the competing values by which the lovers, and particularly Antony, are torn. "Kingdoms are clay," he declares in Egypt: "The nobleness of life Is to do thus," and embraces Cleopatra [I. i. 35, 36-7]. A few hours later, however, he says with equal earnestness, "These strong Egyptian fetters I must break Or lose myself in dotage," and he departs for Rome. Again, he declares to Octavia in Rome, hereafter everything shall "be done by th' rule," yet scarcely thirty lines later, after his interview with the soothsayer, he has added, "I will to Egypt" [II. iii. 7, 39]. From this point on follows a succession of fluctuations in both war and love. In war, confidence of victory shifting to despair at loss, then to new confidence, then to new despair. In love, adorings of Cleopatra changing to recriminations, then to renewed adorings, then to fresh disgust. This aspect of the play's rhythm is vividly summed up in two speeches in the third act (III, xi). "I have offended reputation," Antony says after the first sea defeat, "A most unnoble swerving" [III. xi. 49-50]: there is the voice of Rome and the soldier. A few seconds after, he says to Cleopatra, "Fall not a tear, I say: one of them rates All that is won and lost" [III. xi. 69-70]; this is the voice of Egypt and the lover.

"All that is won *and* lost" is of course the crucial ambiguity of this tragedy. Perhaps it is one about which no two readers are likely finally to agree. Much is obviously lost by the lovers in the course of the play, and Shakespeare underscores this fact, as Plutarch had done, by placing their deaths in Cleopatra's monument—that is to say, a tomb. All those imperial ambitions that once mustered the "kings o' th' earth for war" [III. vi. 68] have shrunk now to this narrow stronghold, which is also a waiting grave. Antony had said as he put his arms about Cleopatra in the opening scene, "Here is my space" [I. i. 34]. Now that challenge has been taken up. This is his space indeed.

But what then, if anything, has been won? The answer to this question depends as much on what one brings to *Antony and Cleopatra* as on what one finds there, for the evidence is mixed. Antony does give his life for his love before the play ends, and we observe that there are no recriminations at his final meeting with Cleopatra; only his quiet hope that she will remember him for what was noblest in him, and her acknowledgment that he was, and is, her man of men. But then, too, his death has been precipitated by her duplicity in the false report of hers; it has among its motives a self-interested desire to evade Caesar's triumph; and the suicide is even bungled in the doing: if this is a hero's death, it is a humiliating one. Likewise, Cleopatra seems to give her life for love. As Antony will be a bridegroom in his death, "and run into't As to a lover's bed" [IV. xiv. 100-01], so Cleopatra will be a bride in hers, calling, "Husband, I come," receiving darkness as if it were "a lover's pinch, Which hurts, and is desired," and breathing out, in words that could equally be describing the union of life with death or the union of lover with lover, "As sweet as balm, as soft as air, as gentle—O Antony!" [V. ii. 287, 295-96, 311-12]. This, however, is the same woman who has long studied "easy ways to die" [V. ii. 356], who ends her life only after becoming convinced that Caesar means to lead her in triumph, and who has cached away with her treasurer Seleucus more than half her valuables in case of need. True, the scene with Seleucus can be so played as to indicate that she is using his confession to dupe Caesar about her intention to die. But that is precisely the point. What the actor or reader makes of her conduct here will be conditioned by what he has made of her elsewhere, by what he makes of the play as a whole, and even, perhaps, by his beliefs about human nature and the depiction of human nature in art.

Are we to take the high-sounding phrases which introduce us to this remarkable love affair in the play's first scene as amorous rant?

CLEOPATRA
If it be love indeed, tell me how much.

ANTONY
There's beggary in the love that can be reckoned.
CLEOPATRA
I'll set a bourn how far to be beloved.
ANTONY
Then must thou needs find out new heaven, new earth.

[I. i. 14-17]

Or is there a prophetic resonance in that reference to "new heaven, new earth," which we are meant to remember when Cleopatra, dreaming of a transcendent Antony—

His face was as the heav'ns, and therein stuck
A sun and moon, which kept their course and lighted
The little O, th' earth. . . .
His legs bestrid the ocean: his reared arm
Crested the world: his voice was propertied
As all the tunèd spheres

[V. ii. 79-81, 82-4]

consigns her baser elements to "baser life"? Does the passion of these two remain a destructive element to the bitter end, doomed like all the feeling in the play to "rot itself with motion" [I. iv. 47]? Or, as the world slips from them, have they a glimmering of something they could not have earlier understood, of another power besides death "Which shackles accidents and bolts up change" [V. ii. 6]? Is it "paltry to be Caesar," as Cleopatra claims, since "Not being Fortune, he's but Fortune's knave" [V. ii. 2, 3]? Or is it more paltry to be Antony, and, as Caesar sees it, "give a kingdom for a mirth" [I. iv. 18], as well as, eventually, the world?

To such questions, *Antony and Cleopatra*, like life itself, gives no clear-cut answers. Shakespeare holds the balance even, and does not decide for us who finally is the strumpet of the play, Antony's Cleopatra, or Caesar's Fortune, and who, therefore, is the "strumpet's fool." Those who would have it otherwise, who are "hot for certainties in this our life," as Meredith phrased it [in his poem "Modern Love"], should turn to other authors than Shakespeare, and should have been born into some other world than this. (pp. 16-21)

Maynard Mack, in an introduction to Antony and Cleopatra *by William Shakespeare, revised edition, Penguin Books, 1970, pp. 14-21.*

WILLLIAM ROSEN (essay date 1960)

[*Antony and Cleopatra, Rosen proposes, is principally concerned with both the struggle between Antony's two personalities—"the illustrious public figure of the past and the decadent private figure of the present"—and with Antony's failure, because of his own weakness and the pernicious influence of Cleopatra, to regain his heroic stature. The critic argues that in his dying moments Antony is consoled by the memory of his former honor and reputation and that, like Cleopatra, he dies with "royal dignity"; but he also insists that neither of the protagonists is altered or transfigured in the final scenes of the play. The perception that they become transcendent figures or that the play exalts the value of love, Rosen asserts, arises from the radical shift in point of view in the last scenes: the realistic or caustic commentary offered earlier by such intermediaries as Caesar and Enobarbus is absent here, and instead we see Antony and Cleopatra directly, view events through their eyes, and forget the significance of previous incidents. The critic maintains that we are also misled by the play's language and imagery which, in its extravagant treatment*] *of Cleopatra, Egypt, and passion itself, is directly at odds with the dramatic action.*]

If all texts of Shakespeare's *Antony and Cleopatra* disappeared and only the criticism remained, we would confront such contradictory opinions about the play and its protagonists that we would wonder whether the critics had discussed the same work, or whether Shakespeare had written at least two different versions. (p. 104)

Critics disagree about the most important features of the play. Some condemn its construction as panoramic and loosely connected; others insist that it is superbly integrated. Critics disagree about the play's meaning, its morality, and the inherent worth of *Antony and Cleopatra*. The most important reason why *Antony and Cleopatra* has been interpreted in so many ways is that we, as audience, are constantly forced to change our point of view. At one moment we are in Egypt; suddenly we are transported to Rome. We see the actions of Antony and Cleopatra through Roman eyes and Roman judgments; we see these same actions from the Egyptian point of view; we hear the lovers' own judgments of their actions. Antony is called "not more manlike / Than Cleopatra" [I. iv. 5-6]; "the abstract of all faults" [I. iv. 9]; "libertine" [II. i. 23]; "amorous surfeiter" [II. i. 33]; "old ruffian" [IV. i. 4]. These are Roman views. Opposing them are Egyptian descriptions of Antony as "the demi-Atlas of this earth" [I. v. 23]; "the crown o' th' earth" [IV. xv. 63]; a being so wondrously magnificent that he was "past the size of dreaming" [V. ii. 97]. Nor do all Roman views denigrate Antony. Lepidus, a Roman, defends him against Caesar's denunciations:

> I must not think there are
> Evils enow to darken all his goodness.
> His faults, in him, seem as the spots of heaven,
> More fiery by night's blackness.
>
> [I. iv. 10-13]

And a Roman soldier, who tells the renegade Enobarbus that Antony has sent Enobarbus' treasures to Caesar's camp, says:

> Your emperor
> Continues still a Jove.
>
> [IV. vi. 27-8]

Whose point of view are we to accept finally?—this becomes a crucial problem in the analysis of the play. (pp. 105-06)

It is possible to resolve such conflicting judgments on character and morality by defining the major concern of the play, the opposing forces that give to the drama its structure. The opening scenes of Shakespeare's mature plays often serve as a kind of overture to the entire work, setting forth the mood and themes that shape its central action. In *King Lear* and *Antony and Cleopatra* the first scenes have significant similarities: both end with recapitulating analyses of the hero. In *Lear,* Goneril and Regan review what has happened and incisively analyze the king. Their concluding speeches point to the dominant action of the play—their future treatment of their father. Through the speeches of Goneril and Regan at the end of the first scene of *Lear,* Shakespeare foreshadows the themes which order the entire drama: an old world of certain values embodied by Lear; the sudden transition to a new world of new values; and the mordant clash between the two.

One might well ask whether the concluding speeches of Demetrius and Philo in the first scene of *Antony and Cleopatra* also point to the major concern of the play:

Demetrius. Is Caesar wth Antonius priz'd so slight?
Philo. Sir, sometimes, when he is not Antony,
   He comes too short of that great property
   Which still should go with Antony.
Demetrius.   I am full sorry
   That he approves the common liar, who
   Thus speaks of him at Rome; but I will hope
   Of better deeds to-morrow. Rest you happy!

> [I. i. 56-62]

Their brief speeches emphasize Antony's heroic past as well as his ignominious present. Antony's life in Egypt is seen as a terrible fall from his heroic life. He is not what he should be. Yet the scene ends with the hopeful expectancy that Antony will belie his present disgrace, that he will soon regain the nobility he once had. While Caroline Spurgeon has noted that the word "world" occurs forty-two times in this play, far more often than in any other Shakespearian drama [see excerpt above, 1935], I suggest that the play is not concerned primarily with the clash between the values of Egypt and Rome but with Antony, his divided allegiance, and most important, his fulfilment as man, which demands that he recapture his heroic past.

In the first scene the introductory speech by Philo and the concluding remarks between Demetrius and Philo point to the forthcoming dramatic conflict as they sound the same questions: will the debauched private life of Antony prevail, or will he again assume his glorious public role? The opening speech prefigures the protagonists unfavorably as Philo invites us to remember the great Antony of the past and compare that memory with the Antony of the present:

> Nay, but this dotage of our general's
> O'erflows the measure. Those his goodly eyes,
> That o'er the files and musters of the war
> Have glow'd like plated Mars, now bend, now turn
> The office and devotion of their view
> Upon a tawny front; his captain's heart,
> Which in the scuffles of great fights hath burst
> The buckles on his breast, reneges all temper,
> And is become the bellows and the fan
> To cool a gipsy's lust.
>
> [I. i. 1-10]

Philo defines for us the soldier's ideal of magnificent action in wars which made Antony the greatest of men. He now sees Antony as ridiculous and corrupt, for Antony has fallen away from that standard which shaped his noble reputation in the public world. Antony's descent from public virtue to private indulgence is abhorrent because it is the abnegation of moral discipline, an escape from duty and honor to a private world whose private values the soldier can neither sympathize with nor understand. "Look, where they come!" Philo points, as to an exhibition or a play to be enacted:

> Take but good note, and you shall see in him
> The triple pillar of the world transform'd
> Into a strumpet's fool. Behold and see.
>
> [I. i. 10-13]

Philo's words constitute a kind of prologue to the forthcoming action. And since his speech is addressed to soldiers and audience alike, we, the audience, are asked to view the ensuing performance in a very particular way: to determine whether Antony and Cleopatra, in their words and actions, either confirm or deny Philo's judgment.

There can be little doubt that Antony proceeds to act out the role Philo has attributed to him. The first words spoken by Cleopatra after Philo's introduction, "If it be love indeed, tell me how much" [I. i. 14], are answered by Antony, "There's beggary in the love that can be reckon'd" [I. i. 15]. The immediate preoccupation with love calls attention to Philo's preview of the two lovers. And upon entering into their private world we find that for Antony it is an escape from the world of honor and duty and public action. "I'll set a bourn how far to be belov'd" [I. i. 16], says Cleopatra, and Antony replies, "Then must thou needs find out new heaven, new earth" [I. i. 17]. His love would transcend mundane reality. He would escape into a world beyond the confines of the here and now, a world he must fashion in language of hyperbole. (pp. 107-09)

"Let Rome in Tiber melt, and the wide arch / Of the rang'd empire fall!" [I. i. 33-4] is his cry of renunciation. Egypt is his refuge, and he turns from the gloomy thought of Roman duty to the glamor of sensual exaltation:

> Here is my space.
> Kingdoms are clay; our dungy earth alike
> Feeds beast as man; the nobleness of life
> Is to do thus, when such a mutual pair
> And such a twain can do't, in which I bind,
> On pain of punishment, the world to weet
> We stand up peerless.
>
> [I. i. 34-40]

As the ideal of the lovers' private morality Antony invokes the "love of Love and her soft hours" [I. i. 44]; he would live in a world free from the entanglements of time, public duty, thought, a world in which not a minute of their lives "should stretch / Without some pleasure now" [I. i. 46-7].

We must view the words of Philo and Antony as part of the dramatic context of the scene. The meaning of the play cannot be said to derive wholly from what the hero says of himself. No matter how grandiose the imagery of Antony's speeches in this scene, to extract an imagery pattern stressing the overwhelming nature of love, to say that Shakespeare here magnifies Antony's figure and presents his love as life's highest value, is to neglect dramatic situation and indulge in romantic delusion. The actions of Antony and Cleopatra are unmistakenly framed in this scene. At the beginning, Philo judges them by the standard of public duty; an audience is prepared to accept this standard. When Antony and Cleopatra come on stage, their words do not alter or contradict this point of view. Finally, the scene ends as it began, with a soldier's condemnation; Demetrius joins Philo in his disapproving Antony's present conduct. The deliberate framing of the lovers cannot be dismissed. No matter how noble Antony and Cleopatra wish to appear, the derogatory judgment of their actions by Philo and Demetrius reduces their stature.

When Philo and Demetrius depict Antony's two opposing personalities, they point to the conflict that will go on throughout the play. Which of Antony's personalities will ultimately prevail? This question arises even in the interplay between Antony and Cleopatra at the middle of the scene. When Antony extols the sensual values of Egypt, calling on Rome to melt in Tiber, asserting that kingdoms are but clay and that he and his beloved stand peerless, Cleopatra dismisses his hyperboles and harshly challenges his honesty:

> Excellent falsehood!
> Why did he marry Fulvia, and not love her?
> I'll seem the fool I am not.—Antony
> Will be himself.
>
> [I. i. 40-3]

There are two Antonys: the illustrious public figure of the past and the decadent private figure of the present, the Antony of Rome and the Antony of Egypt. "Antony will be himself," says Cleopatra, and almost immediately afterwards Philo echoes a similar idea to Demetrius:

> When he is not Antony,
> He comes too short of that great property
> Which still should go with Antony.
>
> [I. i. 57-9]

Part of Antony endorses the soldier's ideal and urges him to return to public life, recapture his reputation as peerless warrior and become the magnificent man he used to be. The other part of Antony yields to private emotion, the all-consuming passion for Cleopatra, and urges him to love in the grand manner, to deny and exclude the outside world and create a romantic paradise. However, to be at once Roman and Egyptian is impossible. If Antony is to return to his public role and regain his manhood, he must throw off Cleopatra and her influence. He can regain his manhood only through self-mastery; if he yields to passion, he is unmanned.

Antony's heroic past is significantly the only unquestioned ideal in the play. When his past is evoked, it serves as contrast to an ignominious present; but, equally important, it presents an image of perfection. By fulfilling the role of peerless soldier, Antony, on this basis alone, became a man of many splendid qualities, held the world's wonder, and earned his place in history. (pp. 110-12)

When *Antony and Cleopatra* begins we see Antony fallen away from that role which gave him nobility; he has abandoned what had been his life's work to build; he has lost his identity. "His taints and honours / Wag'd equal with him" [V. i. 30-1] is the judgment which Maecenas pronounced upon hearing of Antony's death. His honors, it is to be observed, are wholly in the past; his taints, in the present. To gain great stature Antony must plunge back to an old life rather than remain in his present one.

Preventing Antony from fulfilling his soldierly role, from again being the man he once was, is Cleopatra. Now if we view her as cutting Antony off from his goal in the world, which is to fulfill his destiny to be a man above all men, then she takes on the role of temptress, or even sorceress. If perfection is cankered because of her, then no equivocation can possibly save her from being maligned. It is concerning her role in the play that so many critics have put forth so many interpretations. Cleopatra has been called the eternally feminine, the lass unparalleled who is forever baffling, who cannot be reduced and confined by the cavils of criticism. . . . But other commentators, less enraptured, have insisted that moral tests should be applied, and in doing so have sternly pronounced Cleopatra guilty, called her whore and snake of the Nile. Those who treat the Egyptian queen with tart discourtesy are less numerous than her admirers, but no less emphatic. (pp. 115-16)

To indulge in a highly personal reaction to Cleopatra too often results in uncovering not Shakespeare's intent but one's own prejudices or inclinations. We come to a more objective rendering of her character by applying not personal or moral standards but dramatic tests, by analyzing her role as it relates to the play's developing action. What the *dramatis personae* say of Cleopatra's past is as revealing as what they say of Antony's previous life. While no one ever reproaches Antony for his past, no one ever glorifies Cleopatra's. Whether it is Cleopatra remembering her former days, or whether another character in the play recalls the life she led before meeting Antony, in all instances one characteristic is emphasized: her magnetic sensuality which never fails to catch men in her strong toil of grace. (pp. 116-17)

After Enobarbus' celebrated description of the first meeting between Antony and Cleopatra, Agrippa makes this jolting comment:

> Royal wench!
> She made great Caesar lay his sword to bed.
> He plough'd her, and she cropp'd.
>
> [II. ii. 226-28]

What a magnificent earthy wench! is Agrippa's view of the queen. He does not idealize her; he praises her sensuality in a realistic manner, and we have no illusions about her character. The same tone prevails when, in the Roman camp at Misenum, Pompey alludes to her past. Bantering with Antony, he praises Egyptian cookery, says he heard Caesar grew fat with feasting there; and then he says of Cleopatra's past, "And I have heard, Apollodorus carried—" [II. vi. 68] which Enobarbus completes, "A certain queen to Caesar in a mattress" [II. vi. 70].

Antony's own remembrance depicts Cleopatra in an even more uncomplimentary fashion. To be sure, he is speaking in a rage, having caught Cleopatra entertaining Caesar's messenger; moreover, he is incensed that she would allow the messenger to kiss her hand. Nevertheless, this is the only time we receive from Antony a disclosure of how, before succumbing to her charms, he first regarded her:

> I found you as a morsel cold upon
> Dead Caesar's trencher; nay, you were a fragment
> Of Cneius Pompey's; besides what hotter hours,
> Unregist'red in vulgar fame, you have
> Luxuriously pick'd out; for, I am sure,
> Though you can guess what temperance should be,
> You know not what it is.
>
> [III. xiii. 116-22]

Nobody has illusions about the queen's character. In mentioning Cleopatra's past, Agrippa, Pompey and Antony deprive her of all radiance and mystery and reduce her to a morsel for men. Thinking of her own past, Cleopatra reveals the motives which still control her actions: fully aware of her attraction, she is the coquette fascinated with her ability to bend great men. What Agrippa and Pompey and Antony say of her former days in no way contradicts what she says of herself.

There would be little value in presenting isolated references to Antony and Cleopatra's past were these not so consistently formulated. Antony must choose between his past and the temptress who would bind him to the present. This collision of opposites gives the play its structure. (pp. 118-19)

There are three separations of the lovers in the play, three reunions, and as many indecisive moments when Antony inclines now to Rome, duty, and honor, now to Cleopatra and love. In each crisis Antony alternately rejects and embraces Cleopatra; he realizes his need to renounce her, but each time finds this impossible. Leaving Cleopatra, in the first instance to journey to Rome (I. iii), Antony, it is suggested, does so not because of a strong sense of patriotism, but because Sextus Pompeius, in commanding the sea, has become a threat to his personal power, because there is the danger that the slippery Roman people might at any moment shift their favors to Pompey. We have no great illusion about his enterprise; nor have we any illusion about his ability to regain the past by breaking

away from Cleopatra. Shakespeare constructs a succession of scenes culminating in what seems to be Antony's recovery of political power and prestige: reconciliation with Caesar; an expedient marriage with Octavia, its sole purpose to hold the two leaders together; and, finally, a banquet which supposedly celebrates personal amity and political unity. But throughout these events Shakespeare continually exposes to the audience the weakness and imminent collapse of political union, and the inevitability of Antony's return to Egypt. While the scenes range over the world, rapidly shifting from Rome to Egypt to Messina, they are ordered and held to a fixed center. Their unifying function is the uncovering of Roman policy, its demands upon Antony, and the presentation of an opposing claim for Antony's allegiance, Cleopatra's appeal, which we are never allowed to forget or minimize.

The main drama lies in the exposure of vying demands upon Antony; and Shakespeare dispels all illusions about these conflicting interests. Fidelity to Rome involves few ideals. The health of the Roman state, the lives of many depend upon Roman leaders who are shown to be neither good nor just nor heroic. Caesar is grimly politic; he readily agrees to Agrippa's scheme to insure peace with Antony by bartering his dearly beloved sister Octavia. Lepidus is an unthinking fool. Pompey is a man of honor: he would have rewarded Menas for slitting the throats of his three guests and rivals; being done unknown, the deed would have afterwards been found well done, but now Pompey can only condemn such a plan. When Menas determines to quit Pompey's cause, he reveals the hollowness of a world struggle based not on a concern for the state's welfare but personal gain: "Who seeks, and will not take once 'tis offer'd, / Shall never find it more" [II. vii. 83-4].

In the scene aboard Pompey's galley, only Caesar, always resolutely detached from the pressures of the moment, retains a semblance of self-control. Lepidus, a third part of the world, is carried off drunk; Antony calls upon conquering wine to steep them all in soft and delicate Lethe. Finally, the glorious leaders of the world join hands to sing their drunken paean. Around and around go the leaders of the Roman world; and their intemperance, we are made to see, approaches that of the Egyptians. "This is not yet an Alexandrian feast" [II. vii. 96], says Pompey. "It ripens towards it" [II. vii. 97], replies Antony. The destiny of Rome is in the hands of the shrewdly politic, the fool, the self-seeking pirate, the weak. Purportedly signaling harmony, the banquet presages, instead, treachery and disorder.

Shakespeare also presents Antony in such a way that the audience entertains no illusions about his progress away from Cleopatra and back to what he should be. Antony is torn by a dilemma that yields no resolution. With Cleopatra he cannot live as he knows he should; without her, he cannot live at all. The price of love is high; it involves the ruin of strength and the fall of valor. Antony's reason tells him this; but his passions overrule acceptance and he wavers between two worlds, making the worst of both. (pp. 122-24)

In the first episode of separation from Cleopatra and reunion with her, Shakespeare gives Antony the role of impotent observer of his own affairs; he is a man who seems to know what is happening and how his fate is affected, but he does not articulate that awareness fully. Powerless to act in a forthright manner, Antony sways with the demands of different occasions; and when he decides to return to Egypt, that action is really an escape. His point of view does not prevail in these scenes; it is taken over by sentient observers who lend perspective and judgment to his experience; they, instead of Antony, mirror the conflict between East and West, between Cleopatra's charms and the requirements of a soldier's duty. Indeed, before Antony's arrival in Rome we are given two extended appraisals of his current reputation, the first by Caesar, who longs for his return, for he needs his aid, the second by Pompey, who hopes that Antony will remain in Egypt lest he add great strength to Caesar and Lepidus, for "his soldiership," says Pompey, "is twice the other twain" [II. i. 34-5]. (pp. 128-29)

Our view of Antony's life depends, for the most part, on the reflections of others. From Enobarbus, that cynical and realistic commentator who constantly sees through people and events, we get a more detailed and convincing analysis of Antony's impulse to return to Cleopatra than we do from Antony himself. His engrossing accounts of the wonderful abandon of Egyptian life, his celebrated description of the first meeting between Antony and Cleopatra and of her immediate conquests, his breathless description of the queen—all these have an important function: they build a vision of a marvelous life which only the insensate would exchange, and of a woman, magnificent and incomparable, whom no man could possibly desert—for long.... Enobarbus supplies what Antony does not himself unfold, precise motivation for the subsequent return to Egypt. "Octavia," says Enobarbus to Menas, "is of a holy, cold, and still conversation" [II. vi. 122-23]. Antony is not; and Enobarbus accurately anticipates the next scene and its outcome: "He will to his Egyptian dish again" [II. vi. 126]. (pp. 129-30)

Shakespeare so arranges event that Antony's personality is continually distanced in perspective: his interior life, the revelation of inner being through soliloquy, is rarely the focal point of a scene; instead, we have recurring choric, denunciatory analyses of his actions and his personality. Philo, Demetrius, Caesar, Pompey, and Enobarbus are among those who supply an audience with information about Antony which he himself either discounts or does not fully comprehend; they subject the lovers to incessant comment, constantly directing us to guide our emotions away from them, reminding us, at significant moments, of the judgment we should make. Continually seeing the protagonists from the outside, through the eyes of those who describe their lives, reproduce their dilemmas, define the quality of their actions, we are—until the death scenes toward the end of the play—blocked for the most part from being intimately caught up in their personalities. (p. 134)

Shakespeare repeatedly prefigures and analyzes his protagonists; only afterwards do we see them in the flesh. And when they appear, what they do coincides precisely with what has been previously suggested. At the defeat at Actium, for example, first Antony's character is set in perspective because of the caustic remarks of his men. Then the next scene moves to a close-up view and we hear Antony's own recognition of guilt and despair. Remembering the man he once was, he thinks of the now triumphant Caesar who in the past had no practice in "the brave squares of war" [III. xi. 40], who at Philippi kept his sword "e'en like a dancer" [III. xi. 36] while Antony struck down Cassius and ended the mad Brutus. Thoughts of his former valor and decisiveness make his present ignominy all the more humiliating. And while the horror of his subjection to Cleopatra breaks forth as he berates himself for losing command, offending reputation, and ending in shameful dishonor, his recognition brings no resilient, lasting opposition to the woman who has gained full supremacy over his spirit. (p. 138)

When we read Plutarch's account of Antony's life we see how Shakespeare alters incidents in his primary source to build up

Antony's weaknesses in detail, putting more blame on him than on Cleopatra, whom Plutarch continually castigates in the manner of a scourging moralist.... In Shakespeare's play Antony alone decides, in a fit of pique, to battle Caesar on sea rather than on land. In Plutarch's account, the responsibility for this decision is attributed to Cleopatra. And while Shakespeare shows Antony as stubborn and thoughtless in replying to those who rationally argue against his plan to battle on sea, Plutarch has a different version, for he places complete blame on a selfish, insidious Cleopatra.

Shakespeare's departures from Plutarch support a view which the play's developing action makes clear: that Cleopatra's overt influence over Antony is less responsible for determining events than Antony's own deterioriation of willpower and judgment. "Is Antony or we in fault for this?" [III. xiii. 2] Cleopatra asks of Enobarbus after the defeat at Actium, and he replies, "Antony only, that would make his will / Lord of his reason" [III. xiii. 3-4]. The techniques that Shakespeare employs to make Antony's weaknesses transparent explain Arthur Sewell's criticism that the personalities of Antony and Cleopatra "do not lead us beyond themselves" [in his *Character and Society in Shakespeare*]. First, there is the prefiguring of characters. In *Antony and Cleopatra,* as in *Coriolanus,* the device of having *dramatis personae* accurately analyze and predict future actions is extensively used. When, in both plays, the protagonists proceed to act according to predetermined judgments, they lose stature, for they are unchanging; they display little freedom to be different from what we have been led to presume. Whether in literature or in life, the possibility of man's change and growth engages sympathetic attention; the glory of man is his capacity to adapt and develop, to confront entirely new situations and in a trial of strength exhibit maturity which excites admiration. (pp. 140-41)

Antony does confront conflict: to regain his heroic stature he must overcome Cleopatra's debilitating influence. But only in reverie does he recapture the image of the man he once was. (pp. 143-44)

Each conflict is resolved by the collapse of Antony's willpower; and this characteristic also affects an audience's attitude towards him. In confronting his world, Antony undergoes no change or development; no new possibilities are opened to him, and through him, to the community which is the audience. It is significant that Enobarbus, the *raisonneur* [dialectician], not Antony, experiences the only conflict which leads to a definite resolution; his self-recognition is the most poignant; and only his death entails moral judgment.

The language of *Antony and Cleopatra* is a miracle of the imagination. It can sound the complete range of emotions and impart boldness and strength to the turmoil of passion as well as to the profound mysteries of love. But the rich texture of the poetry opposes the dramatic structure; Shakespeare lavishes his imaginative splendors not upon military values and the ideals which Antony must attain, but upon Cleopatra, love, and the Egyptian attractions he is called upon to renounce. Consequently, those who are dazzled by the incomparable language often celebrate its paean of love and minimize or disregard the unfolding events that chronicle a man's fall.

Cleopatra is repeatedly described in the language of magical wonder; she excels, Enobarbus tells us, even the delights of art, "O'er-picturing that Venus where we see / The fancy outwork nature" [II. ii. 200-01]. So it is that the exciting drama inherent in the poetry surrounding Cleopatra competes with the more mundane drama of the play's action: when Cleopatra demonstrates most forcefully the power of her attraction, Antony is at his weakest, he is a woman's man, stripped of the judgment he must have to be his heroic self. (pp. 145-46)

Cleopatra generates enormous excitement, and this accounts for her great appeal. Never passive, her energy is as boundless in grief as in love. Mistress of infinite variety, she commands a tremendous repertoire of emotions and moods to suit all occasions. At one moment her sincerity can be overwhelmingly poignant—as when she faces the inevitability of Antony's departure from Egypt. Trying to find words that will make her tangled emotions felt and understood, she begins with facts— parting and loving—but facts are hopelessly inadequate:

> Sir, you and I must part, but that's not it;
> Sir, you and I have lov'd, but there's not it;
> That you know well. Something it is I would,—
>
> [I. iii. 87-9]

she breaks off; and groping for that which would explain all, she reaches truth that is both poetry and illumination: "O, my oblivion is a very Antony, / And I am all forgotten" [I. iii. 90-1]. Her "oblivion" is the loss of Antony as well as of speech; without him life is a senseless void.

But there are other moments when her sincerity is feigned, when calculation leads her into enacting every kind of pose. Again and again she becomes the incomparable actress, proficient in emotional acrobatics. Shakespeare calls attention to her dominant characteristic in the repetition of "play-acting" images and allusions. Her predilection for dazzling show is made quite explicit at the play's beginning when Antony decides to return to Rome. Enobarbus anticipates the poses that can be expected from Cleopatra, who "catching but the least noise of this, dies instantly; I have seen her die twenty times upon far poorer moment" [I. ii. 140-42]. Nor does her appearance upset his prediction, for we see her direct Charmian to seek Antony and act out a role appropriate to the occasion:

>   If you find him sad,
> Say I am dancing; if in mirth, report
> That I am sudden sick. Quick, and return.
>
> [I. iii. 3-5]

As soon as Antony enters, Cleopatra begins her performance: "I am sick and sullen" [I. iii. 13]; and she continues to dramatize herself and her emotions, passing from despair to joy, or balancing the two extremes ("I am quickly ill and well, / So Antony loves" [I. iii. 72-3]), always with enormous presence, always with poetry that presents the exact curve of feeling.

Sometimes it is difficult to determine whether Cleopatra is merely playing a superb role, or whether she is completely truthful; and perhaps one should not make the distinction, for her personality is such that she always gives the impression of playing at life, of being intensely aware of every stance, as if she cannot help but live and die before a mirror. Acting is so much a part of her that at a time of great crisis, when after the Alexandrian defeat Antony seeks her, raging, "The witch shall die" [IV. xii. 47], she still attends to the staging of dramatic effects. Accepting Charmian's advice to feign death, she instructs her servant in the precise manner of speaking her lines:

>   To th' monument!
> Mardian, go tell him I have slain myself;
> Say that the last I spoke was "Antony,"
> And word it, prithee, piteously.
>
> [IV. xiii. 6-9]

Finally, her act of suicide is at once the consummate escape from the world and her most accomplished self-dramatization. She carries off her last performance wth perfect artistry, robing and crowning for death, speaking magnificent poetry in her farewell address. (pp. 149-51)

So dazzlingly impressive are Cleopatra's final moments in the play that they have always brought forth excited bravos from spectators and panegyrics from critics. Indeed, many commentators have been so overwhelmed by the ending that they read the play backwards, attempting to reconstruct a consistent characterization so that the final glory of Cleopatra may prevail. Such a reading would maintain that Cleopatra recovers full innocence at her death; that she and Antony are transfigured; therefore, Shakespeare's play is not about corruption and human weakness but the exaltation of love and its final triumph over death and the world. To interpret the ending this way, however, is to distort what we have seen to be the developing action of the play, Antony's attempt to regain his heroic past. It is to reconcile the irreconcilable, for we cannot gloss over Cleopatra's role as temptress, nor minimize the consequences of her preventing Antony from regaining his virtue to become again the wonder of the world, ideal man. Nor can we expunge the treachery she contemplated, her resolve to forsake Antony and yield to the triumphant Caesar [III. xiii. 60]. Furthermore, even her conduct at the time of Antony's death is hardly exemplary. Indeed, the events approach the point of being ludicrous. Antony bungles his suicide. He is carried to the queen, who looks down at him from the height of her monument. While she laments the misfortune and calls on the sun to burn itself out and cast the world in darkness, she refuses to come down to her lover, lest she be captured. Hoisted up to her, the dying Antony tries to speak a few words of comfort and advice: "I am dying, Egypt, dying. / Give me some wine, and let me speak a little" [IV. xv. 41-2]. But Cleopatra breaks in forcefully, "No, let me speak"; and what she says is merely the empty and shrill sounding of Senecan hyperbole:

>   and let me rail so high,
> That the false housewife Fortune break her wheel,
> Provok'd by my offence.
>
> [IV. xv. 43-5]

In having Cleopatra enact this stock pose of tearing a passion to shreds, Shakespeare is certainly not intent on glorifying her. He makes the queen appear even more vain and self-determined in the final exchange with her lover. In great pain, gasping his dying words, Antony tries to give advice:

> *Antony.*   One word, sweet queen:
>   Of Caesar seek your honour, with your safety. O!
> *Cleopatra.* They do not go together.
> *Antony.*   Gentle, hear me:
>   None about Caesar trust but Proculeius.
> *Cleopatra.* My resolution and my hands I'll trust;
>   None about Caesar.
>
> [IV. xv. 45-50]

Each time Cleopatra sharply contradicts Antony, a departure from Plutarch's *Life,* for there she is persuaded by his speech: "When he had drunk, he earnestly prayed her, and persuaded her, that she would seek to save her life, if she could possible, without reproach and dishonour: and that chiefly she should trust Proculeius above any man else about Caesar."

When Antony dies, Cleopatra is overcome with genuine grief. Because the language of her lament is so beautiful, no one could possibly be insensitive to her despair:

> Young boys and girls
Are level now with men; the odds is gone,
And there is nothing left remarkable
Beneath the visiting moon.
>
> [IV. xv. 65-8]

She even decides to join Antony in suicide "after the high Roman fashion" [IV. xv. 87]. But in the next act she is still importuning death in beautifully shaped language, falling rather awkwardly from tragic heights when her treasurer reveals to Caesar her deceit in holding back her wealth. Clearly she entertains the possibility of living on, though Antony is dead.

Cleopatra's shifting moods and emotional acrobatics may testify to her infinite variety, but they do not lend great support to the view that her last moment, magnificent as it is, transfigures her and provides the key to the entire play: the assumption that Shakespeare's final vision is of a love which glorifies man and woman and ultimately redeems them. This judgment is based on a consideration of the play's structure and events. While a change seems to come over the protagonists towards the drama's end, does this result from inner transformation, or is it to be explained by the sudden shift in character presentation and an attendant shift in point of view?

When Antony approaches his death, for the first time in the play all *raisonneurs* fall away; there is neither derogatory framing of his deed nor critical analysis. We see Antony directly, not through intermediaries who would alienate an audience by exposing discrepancies between what he says and what he does or should do. The irony, which has continually been directed at Antony's affirmations and aspirations, fades away; judgment, therefore, is held in abeyance. What Antony now says, we accept at face value. Furthermore, there is no ignominy to tarnish his end. He confronts death with stoic honor and dignity; and those who chorus on his imminent death invest it with solemnity and awe. "The star is fallen," the Second Guard intones [IV. xiv. 106]. "And time is at his period," mourns the First Guard [IV. xiv. 107]. "Alas and woe!" is the communal lament [IV. xiv. 107]. Until this scene, choral commentary, whether individual or communal, provided a commonsense norm to measure Antony's actions. Now the chorus grieves the loss of a great public figure and elevates his stature.

There is a significant change in the way an audience sees Antony; there is no transfiguration. Antony's death does not glorify his love nor make of it the play's transcendent value. His final thoughts do not in any way extenuate his decline and fall; nor do they celebrate his love for Cleopatra. He tells her:

> The miserable change now at my end
Lament nor sorrow at; but please your thoughts
In feeding them with those my former fortunes
Wherein I liv'd, the greatest prince o' th' world,
The noblest; and do now not basely die,
Not cowardly put off my helmet to
My countryman,—a Roman by a Roman
Valiantly vanquish'd. Now my spirit is going;
I can no more.
>
> [IV. xv. 51-9]

To have an honourable reputation—this is what matters most. Antony dies with a vision of his best self before him. At the end of his life he does not invoke remembrances of a life with Cleopatra, but a time before, when he was the greatest of men. And he dies with the comforting thought that in taking his own life he shows himself strong and valiant, worthy of the virtue and nobility associated with his former fortunes.

It cannot be said, therefore, that Antony changes. He does not confront an experience that brings about a resettlement of his being. In drawing comfort and dignity from memory, he only repeats what he has previously done on many occasions. What Antony is at his death, he was before. There is this important difference, however: for the first time in the play we are not called upon to judge him; and we are asked to remember his public greatness—but this greatness, we should keep in mind, was of an Antony who flourished before the play began.

Cleopatra also faces death with royal dignity. The fear of a Roman triumph prevails over her fear of death and convinces her to escape the world's great snare. "Know, sir," she tells Proculeius,

> that I
Will not wait pinion'd at your master's court;
Nor once be chastis'd with the sober eye
Of dull Octavia. Shall they hoist me up
And show me to the shouting varletry
Of censuring Rome? Rather a ditch in Egypt
Be gentle grave unto me!
>
> [V. ii. 52-8]

Dolabella confirms her misgivings: Caesar will indeed lead her in triumph, make of her a public spectacle. She thinks of the degrading horror, of mechanic slaves with greasy aprons uplifting her to common view, of being enclouded in the stinking breath of the multitude. And she tells Iras:

> Saucy lictors
Will catch at us like strumpets, and scald rhymers
Ballad us out o' tune. The quick comedians
Extemporally will stage us, and present
Our Alexandrian revels; Antony
Shall be brought drunken forth, and I shall see
Some squeaking Cleopatra boy my greatness
I' th' posture of a whore.
>
> [V. ii. 214-21]

The words describe what we have already witnessed in the play; we have heard Cleopatra called whore, we have seen Alexandrian revels and a drunken Antony. Her words even describe the present moment, for they are being delivered to Shakespeare's audience by a squeaking boy. The Egyptian queen creates a wonderful illusion: all the play, she would persuade us, has been fictional and cheap; what we are witnessing at this heightened occasion is more real than the play-world. In embracing her own illusions, Cleopatra would have us imagine that she transcends the unreality of fiction, just as she would have Dolabella accept her dream of Antony as fact. "I dream'd there was an Emperor Antony" [V. ii. 76], she tells him: his face was as the heavens, his legs bestrid the oceans, in his livery walked crowns and crownets. "Think you there was or might be such a man" she asks him [V. ii. 93-4]; and he replies, "Gentle madam, no" [V. ii. 94].

For Cleopatra illusions are real and the real enactments of the play are but shadows. Dolabella's gentle rebuke has little effect upon her. Nor does it have too great an effect upon an audience because in these final scenes we become one with Cleopatra, seeing events through her eyes. There is no sharp discontinuity between the Cleopatra of the early scenes and the Cleopatra of the play's finale; she has not undergone any great change in vision or personality. But now there are no caustic commentators who stand about her to prefigure action, guide judgment, or tear aside illusions to uncover hypocrisy or self-deception. It is the radical shift in the point of view established towards Cleopatra that brings about audience rapport with her and helps explain why so many critics have insisted that an entirely new Cleopatra emerges in these last scenes. (pp. 152-58)

At the moment before death, Antony seeks what is most noble in his life; once again he is in love with his honor, and he finally achieves integrity not through private love but the remembrance of his public worth. Antony's final commitment is to his reputation and his honor. At her end, Cleopatra strives for a comparable vision. She sees herself as wife. Robing and crowning for death, she embraces, wth complete sincerity, a self-created dream and is overpowered by it. "Methinks I hear / Antony call," she exclaims; and immediately she translates vision into fact: "I see him rouse himself / To praise my noble act" [V. ii. 283, 283-84]. With self-conscious awareness, as if acting before Antony, seeking his approbation, she terms her deed "noble." "Husband, I come!" Cleopatra calls to him, and then, as if realizing the significance of her utterance, she would consciously elevate herself to noble thought and deed that she might be worthy of the name she has just taken: "Now to that name my courage prove my title!" [V. ii. 287, 288]. Whereupon she proceeds to verbalize her determined ascent: "I am fire and air; my other elements / I give to baser life" [V. ii. 289-90].

An audience, awed by spectacle and superb language, can imagine a Cleopatra suddenly changed in personality, though her own words reveal that step by step she is convincing herself of the role she must enact before Antony. But unlike Antony, she cannot sustain the vision; hers is inspired by a dream; Antony's is the recall of an actual past. When Cleopatra forgets that Antony is watching, she breaks her own tragic spell. Seeing that Iras has died, she hastens to apply another asp, lest Antony "spend that kiss / Which is my heaven to have" [V. ii. 302-03]. The spell broken momentarily, she descends even further from tragic heights as she gloats that her action will thwart the great Caesar:

> Poor venomous fool,
> Be angry, and dispatch. O couldst thou speak,
> That I might hear thee call great Caesar ass
> Unpolicied!
>
> 　　　　　　　　　　　　　[V. ii. 305-07]

Her instinct to dominate and rule prevails to the end. She made a fool of the first Caesar; she will do the same to the second.

The energy of Cleopatra's thoughts and actions, her infinite variety, compel admiration, "since things in motion sooner catch the eye / Than what not stirs" [*Troilus and Cressida,* III. iii. 183-84]. . . . [But there] is the danger of confusing energy with moral stature and of so mistaking admiration for approval that Cleopatra's final moments are wrongly interpreted as a redemption and a transfiguration which make all previous conduct of no account. Such a view distorts character and action in this play. Certainly Antony and Cleopatra achieve great nobility in death; but the play, after all, is a chronicle of their lives and an exposure of the illusions they would live. Neither Antony nor Cleopatra changes identity. Even in death Cleopatra looks "As she would catch another Antony / In her strong toil of grace" [V. ii. 347-48]. Caesar makes this observation at the close of the play; and he says further:

> 　　　　　　　　　　　　their story is
> No less in pity than his glory which
> Brought them to be lamented.
>
> 　　　　　　　　　　　　　[V. ii. 361-63]
> 　　　　　　　　　　　　　(pp. 158-60)

William Rosen, "'Antony and Cleopatra','' in his Shakespeare and the Craft of Tragedy, *Cambridge, Mass.: Harvard University Press, 1960, pp. 104-60.*

EUGENE M. WAITH　(essay date 1962)

[*In sections of his* The Herculean Hero in Marlowe, Chapman, Shakespeare, and Dryden *(1962) not reprinted here, Waith analyzes Renaissance treatments of the myth of Hercules and examines variations on this type of tragic hero—usually ''a warrior of great stature who is guilty of striking departures from the morality of the society in which he lives''—in seven dramas of the sixteenth and seventeenth centuries. In the following excerpt, he discusses Antony's affinity to the Herculean hero, contending that the triumvir's furious rages, his struggle against Rome, and his extravagant nature are characteristic of this dramatic type. Like his tutelary deity, Waith maintains, Antony's principal shame is his loss of honor, for it signifies to him a resultant loss of integrity and even selfhood. The critic argues that Antony is also Herculean in his recovery of honor, his rediscovery of himself, and the courage with which he faces death, but concludes that he represents a departure from the traditional pattern in his final assertion of personal integrity and the value of love.*]

Both Marlowe and Chapman place their heroes in the context of history, where the problem of individual worth is debated in an endless dialectic between society and the hero. The hero fights against the representatives of society—emperors, governors, dukes—in a struggle to impose his will upon the world, and yet he is not truly an enemy of society, for he fights against what he sees as corrupt. He is acclaimed as a benefactor like Hercules, who laid waste cities and committed murder, yet saved society from tyrants and monsters. . . . The stories of Antony and Cleopatra and of Coriolanus present just such a contest between a mighty individual and a city, and it is not in the least surprising that this kind of story should occur in Roman history, for Rome, as described by her historians, both encouraged the cultivation of individual valour and exacted the most complete devotion of her heroes. (p. 112)

The first of Shakespeare's plays to be set in the historical Rome, and the first one he drew from Plutarch, contains no Herculean figure. Caesar, who might be so presented, is more important in the play as an idea than as a man, and his hesitations about going to the senate are hardly heroic. Brutus, on the other hand, is far too reasonable (however mistaken) and too self-sacrificing to be called a Herculean hero. However, Antony, as he appears in *Antony and Cleopatra,* is explicitly compared to Hercules, and throughout most of the play is at war with Rome and all that Rome represents. While the importance given to Cleopatra and to Antony's final commitment to her makes the play as a whole something other than the tragedy of a Herculean hero, it nevertheless contains a major treatment of the type. . . . (p. 113)

Two images of Antony dominate *Antony and Cleopatra,* the Roman and the Egyptian, Caesar's Antony and Cleopatra's. Caesar's is the tough soldier who could stand any hardship [I. iv. 56-71]—the "plated Mars" of Philo's opening speech. To the Romans it seems that this Antony has melted under the influence of Cleopatra into an effeminate libertine, whose eyes "now bend, now turn / The office and devotion of their view / Upon a tawny front", and whose "captain's heart" is no more than "the bellows and the fan / To cool a gypsy's lust" [I. i. 4-6, 9-10]. Later we hear from Cleopatra herself how she put her "tires and mantles on him" while she wore his sword [II. v. 22], a prank which seems to symbolize all too exactly the transformation lamented by Caesar. It is Hercules unmanned by Omphale.

The Antony we see in Egypt is not merely the soldier debauched by a woman's influence, however, nor does Cleopatra want him to be anything less than the greatest of soldiers. His being the "demi-Atlas of this earth, the arm / And burgonet of men" [I. v. 23-4] is part of his vast attractiveness as a lover. Her grandiose imagination fashions an ideal for Antony which is not only larger but more complex than Caesar's. Excesses which seem to Caesar repellent and improper she finds becoming (as others find her passions and fits becoming to her), and she goads him into statements of his love which abolish all limits: "There's beggary in the love that can be reckon'd" [I. i. 15]. Thus the characteristics which adulterate the Antony of Caesar's military ideal serve to round out the heroic figure in the mind of Cleopatra, for whom Antony is not merely a soldier but a "man of men" [I. v. 72], and finally a colossus, whose "legs bestrid the ocean"—a man "past the size of dreaming" [V. ii. 82, 97]. In the contrast presented by Shakespeare, Caesar, the emblem of reasonable self-control, shrinks to a Machiavellian schemer as Antony grows to heroic proportions.

Antony's faults, like those of other Herculean heroes, are emphasized rather than glossed over: Maecenas says, "His taints and honours / Wag'd equal wth him" [V. i. 30-1]. But they are not the superb egotism nor the heartless cruelty of a Tamburlaine. The Antony who flees from the battle of Actium has offended not merely against a Roman code of values but against what he and everyone else recognize as a basic concept of his own integrity. He has told Octavia, "If I lose mine honour, / I lose myself" [III. iv. 22-3], and this violation of "experience, manhood, honour," as Scarus sees it [III. x. 22] so shames Antony that he feels he has indeed lost himself. Plutarch comments that this failure to be himself proves the truth of an old man's jest, that "the soul of a lover lived in another body, and not in his own", and Shakespeare has Antony tell Cleopatra, "O'er my spirit / Thy full supremacy thou knew'st" [III. xi. 58-9]. At this moment there appears to be nothing in Antony to answer the expectations of either Caesar or Cleopatra. Shortly afterward she appears to be considering seriously the possibility of coming to terms with Caesar.

Cleopatra's part in this débâcle gives some colour of truth to the Roman view that the transforming power of a woman has destroyed what Antony was by taking possession of his soul, but the remainder of the play shows that destruction is not the end of the process of transformation. Out of the fragments of the Roman image of Antony grows the great image presented in Cleopatra's speeches in the fifth act—an image which owes as much to the ideals of romance as to the older heroic ideal. The hero is re-created and yet . . . not entirely made anew, for the process in which Cleopatra has so important a part is a reassertion of qualities Antony already possesses, a shift of emphasis, a rediscovery of self.

The Antony who commits suicide at the end of the play is no longer a world-conqueror in the obvious sense of the term, yet neither is he the defeated man we have seen after Actium. In his own way he has conquered the world and himself. "So it should be," as Cleopatra says, "that none but Antony / Should conquer Antony" [IV. xv. 16-17]. If in some respects he is no longer Herculean, in others he is more so than ever. This situation seems to be reflected in the allusions to Hercules, for although "the god Hercules, whom Antony lov'd", is said to be leaving him on the eve of one of his last battles [IV. iii. 16] some of the most striking identifications with Hercules are

made shortly before Antony's death. They emphasize certain characteristics which he continues to share with his former protector. Notable among these is Antony's violent rage, the more conspicuous for being allied with an extravagant generosity, shown on occasion to those who have merited rage. Bounty and rage, mingling and interacting, account for a large share of Antony's heroic nature.

Antony displays his remarkable bounty immediately after Actium, when he urges his loyal followers to divide his treasure and go. Shortly afterwards he assures a penitent Cleopatra that one tear is worth "all that is won and lost" [III. xi. 70]. On the eve of his next battle he moves his soldiers to tears by his gifts and good wishes; Enobarbus dies of a broken heart, overcome by a generosity which he can scarcely comprehend. Indeed, from the Roman point of view these examples of Antony's bounty are as patently unreasonable as his debauches. In both cases Antony is spending his substance prodigally—in effect, giving himself away. Looked at in this way, Antony's generosity is closely allied to the self-destructiveness which leads up to Actium, and an analogue to both is found in the melting imagery first applied to the world Antony scorns, and finally to himself, when he finds that he "cannot hold this visible shape" [IV. xiv. 14].

The same imagery of melting and disintegration is one of the means Shakespeare uses to affirm the positive value of Antony's giving. When the flood-waters of the Nile recede, they leave the adjacent land covered with mud and with insects which complete the dissolution of the creatures drowned in the water [III. xiii. 166-67; V. ii. 58-60], yet "upon the slime and ooze" the seedsman scatters his grain, from which comes Egypt's rich harvest [II. vii. 21-3]. When Antony hears the false news of Cleopatra's death, he strips off his armour, aided by Eros, completing by this action the destruction of the warrior image to which he has just alluded in his speech about the "visible shape" which is no more fixed than the cloud-shapes of dragons, bears or citadels. However, the act for which he prepares is an assertion more than a denial, and requires a warrior's courage. It is a final giving, which indicates strength rather than weakness. His words, addressed to Eros and to his own body, present the bursting forth of a greatness which can no longer be contained:

> Off, pluck off!
> The sevenfold shield of Ajax cannot keep
> The battery from my heart. O, cleave, my sides!
> Heart, once be stronger than thy continent,
> Crack thy frail case! Apace, Eros, apace.—
> No more a soldier. Bruised pieces go;
> You have been nobly borne.
>
> [IV. xiv. 37-43]

The situation makes it clear that Antony speaks to a lover's heart as well as to a soldier's. He would end his life not only to recover a soldier's honour but to be worthy of Cleopatra. Once again it might be said that the lover's soul is not entirely his own, but where the pursuit of the beloved led to shameful self-betrayal at Actium, here it is the affirmation of an ideal exalted in romances and in Renaissance love-poetry generally: the lover finds only in the beloved the completing of himself.

To the largeness of Antony's spirit all his excesses testify—his prodigious feasting and lovemaking as well as his generosity and the final extravagance of suicide. Sensual indulgence, magnanimity and self-immolation appear to be manifestations of a single bent. So, too, through its sheer intensity, does Antony's most Herculean trait, his rage.

It is ironical that Cleopatra seems less moved by Antony's generous forgiveness of her after Actium than by his outrageous behaviour in ordering Caesar's messenger whipped for kissing her hand. It is after he has gone on to rebuke her in some of the most violent and memorable language of the play that she makes her most positive declaration of love for him. When he sends a personal challenge to Caesar (as he had already done before Actium) and then makes plans for a battle on land, she speaks like one whose confidence has been restored: "That's my brave lord! . . . since my lord / Is Antony again, I will be Cleopatra" [III. xiii. 176, 185-86]. We cannot suppose that this change is due entirely to fear. Her equivocal answers to the offers from Caesar suggest that she has been bewildered and alarmed by the defeated and forgiving Antony, as if she could not be sure of the meaning of such abject behaviour. The Antony who whips a messenger she can understand, as her own treatment of another messenger shows well. The spectacle of Antony *furens* [frenzied] is one which she admires rather than fears. From this time she never wavers in her commitment.

Antony's anger in this scene is a clear indication to the audience as well as to Cleopatra that he is in the process of rediscovering himself. Aware that "Authority melts from me" [III. xiii. 90], he insists clamorously upon obedience from his servants while he rails at Cleopatra and the messenger. In all his relationships he is reasserting the authority of a leader. The re-emergence of this essential heroic quality is what Cleopatra applauds.

At the same time, the sceptical comments of Enobarbus, who has remained loyal up to this point, remind us that no practical benefits can be expected now from Antony's rage. When the messenger is sent to be whipped, he says, " 'Tis better playing with a lion's whelp / Than with an old one dying" [III. xiii. 94-5], and at the end of the scene:

> I see still
> A diminution in our captain's brain
> Restores his heart. When valour preys on reason,
> It eats the sword it fights with. I will seek
> Some way to leave him.
>
> [III. xiii. 196-200]

The irrational valour of the hero, exposed to the criticism of Roman practicality, is shown to be absurd—a posture which the logic of the situation will easily demolish. Enobarbus is right, of course, for the one battle Antony wins has no great military significance, and is succeeded by the final, crushing defeat. The inevitability of disaster is orchestrated by the unearthly music heard by the soldiers (IV, 3) and interpreted as the departure of Antony's patron, "the god Hercules" [IV. iii. 16].

Antony's reassertion of his heroic self in the latter part of the play is entirely personal. What he asserts is individual integrity, not the integrity of a Roman general. The scene in which Cleopatra and Eros help him to arm (IV, 4) presents a cheerful ritual whose significance is mainly for the lovers themselves. Antony alternately teases Cleopatra about her ineptitude and praises her by way of chiding Eros. He wishes that she could watch him fight and appreciate the fine points of "the royal occupation" [IV. iv. 17]. When he leaves, Cleopatra comments as might a heroine of romance upon her knight's going forth to battle:

> He goes forth gallantly. That he and Caesar might
> Determine this great war in single fight!
>
> [IV. iv. 36-7]

The entire scene (wholly invented by Shakespeare) emphasizes the intimacy of the lovers and the importance to them of Antony's behaving heroically. When he returns victorious it is again the personal significance that is important. The contrast between the "world" and the two lovers is apparent in Cleopatra's greeting to the victor:

> Lord of lords!
> O infinite virtue, com'st thou smiling from
> The world's great snare uncaught?
>
> [IV. viii. 16-18]

The chief joy of the victory is that Antony, having demonstrated his superiority, is not ensnared by the world. Despite Antony's awareness of the continuing peril, he and Cleopatra treat the victory as if it were absolute, but it is absolute only as a demonstration to them of heroic quality. Heroism rather than heroic achievement becomes the important thing in this part of the play. Even Enobarbus recognizes this when his realistic appraisal of Antony's situation gives way to the unbearable perception of Antony's inherent nobility.

As the reward of the momentary victory is Cleopatra's esteem, so the bitterness of the ensuing defeat is the suspicion that she has compounded with Caesar. Here Antony closely resembles Seneca's Oetaean Hercules. . . . Each one feels that his death has been robbed of all honour. And each longs passionately for revenge and then death. Hercules says:

> Would that with lifted club I might crush out
> her wicked life just as I smote down the Ama-
> zonian pest upon the slopes of snowy Caucasus.
> O well-loved Megara, wast thou wife to me
> when madness came upon me? Give me my
> club and bow, let my right hand be defiled, let
> me put stain upon my glory, and let a woman
> be chosen as the last toil of Hercules. (*Hercules
> Oetaeus*, ll. 1449-55)

Antony says, "When I am reveng'd upon my charm, / I have done all" [IV. xii, 16-17], and when Cleopatra appears, he threatens:

> Vanish, or I shall give thee thy deserving
> And blemish Caesar's triumph. Let him take thee
> And hoist thee up to the shouting plebeians.
> Follow his chariot, like the greatest spot
> Of all thy sex. Most monster-like be shown
> For poor'st diminitives, for doits, and let
> Patient Octavia plough thy visage up
> With her prepared nails.
>
> [IV. xii. 32-9]

In the latter part of this speech, made after Cleopatra has been frightened away, Shakespeare makes the comparison to Hercules explicit:

> 'Tis well th'art gone.
> If it be well to live; but better 'twere
> Thou fell'st into my fury, for one death
> Might have prevented many. Eros, ho!
> The shirt of Nessus is upon me. Teach me,
> Alcides, thou mine ancestor, thy rage.
> Let me lodge Lichas on the horns o' th' moon
> And with those hands that grasp'd the heaviest club
> Subdue my worthiest self. The witch shall die.
>
> [IV. xii. 39-47]

Rage is the characteristic response of the Herculean hero to an attack on his honour. Both Hercules and Antony want more than anything to recover some part of their lost honour in order to make themselves worthy of a hero's death. Both of them wish that revenge upon a perfidious woman might atone for their guilt towards an innocent woman, as well as punishing an infamous betrayal.

From the vantage-point of this scene of Antony's Herculean rage one can appreciate the significance of a very early episode, in which this important trait is first established. There Cleopatra goads him, as part of her remarkable technique of seduction, to the verge of an angry outburst, and when he warns her to desist, comments:

> Look, prithee, Charmian,
> How this Herculean Roman does become
> The carriage of his chafe.
>
> [I. iii. 83-5]

The words are mocking, yet they suggest, even here, a certain awe for Antony's heroic fury. Antony's rage at Cleopatra is brought to an abrupt end by the news that she has killed herself for his love, just as Hercules' rage at Deianira ends when Hyllus reveals her innocent intentions, her horror at the outcome, and her suicide. But the difference between Antony and Hercules is brought out by Antony's response to the news. To Hercules the full import of this news is that an old prophecy has been fulfilled, and that he is meeting the heroic death promised him. He is able to reassert his old self and muster the fortitude necessary to face the flames of his funeral pyre because it is clear that Deianira was merely instrumental in his undoing, and of no real importance. He then dismisses her from his thoughts. The news brought by Mardian means to Antony that Cleopatra, instead of betraying him, has given him a model of heroic death, and that life without so wonderful a woman is not worth living. There is Herculean fortitude in his suicide; there is also the final assertion of love. The meaning of Antony's tragedy does not lie entirely in the Herculean pattern.

Cleopatra both accentuates and modifies what is Herculean in Antony. Like Caesar, she admires the man of valour and noble rage, but she also encourages his carousals. To Caesar as Shakespeare portrays him even Hercules might have seemed excessive; every excess can be assimilated into Cleopatra's ideal of warrior and lover. What Caesar wants to see in Antony is less than a Hercules, but what Cleopatra wants is more. When she asks Dolabella if "there was or might be such a man / As this I dreamt of", he replies, "Gentle madam, no" [V. ii. 93-5]. Antony's suicide is in one sense a recognition of the impossibility of achieving Cleopatra's ideal in the world. It is a noble Roman's death, but more than that, it is a dedication of himself to Cleopatra, the final custodian of his heroic image.

The structure of the play does justice to the dimensions of the heroic portrayal. More episodic than any other play of Shakespeare's, *Antony and Cleopatra* ranges like [Marlowe's] *Tamburlaine* over vast areas and achieves the effect of the sort of magnitude which we normally associate with epic. The number of very brief scenes makes the technique seem to us almost cinematic, though it was perfectly adapted to the stage of Shakespeare's day. Mark Van Doren remarks that the units of style are characteristically brief like the units of action. "This universe is too large to be rendered in anything but fragments" [see excerpt above, 1939]. Not only the universe but the hero. The dimensions of the world to which Antony is opposed serve as an analogue of his Herculean magnitude. (pp. 113-21)

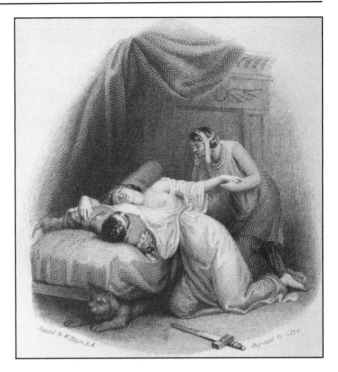

Act IV. Scene xv. Antony, Cleopatra, and Charmian. By William Hilton (1826). The Department of Rare Books and Special Collections, The University of Michigan Library.

Eugene M. Waith, "Shakespeare: 'Antony and Cleopatra'," in his The Herculean Hero in Marlowe, Chapman, Shakespeare and Dryden, *Chatto & Windus, 1962, pp. 112-21.*

ROBERT B. HEILMAN   (essay date 1964)

[*An American scholar and educator, Heilman has written* This Great Stage: Image and Structure in "King Lear" (1948), Magic in the Web: Action and Language in "Othello" (1956), *and commentary on modern and pre-Shakespearean drama; he has also edited the works of several nineteenth-century novelists. Heilman generally employs a pluralistic approach in his criticism, but he is principally concerned with the many dimensions of poetic language and the relation of patterns of imagery to the dramatic action of a play. In the excerpt below, Heilman focuses on Antony's self-knowledge, arguing that in Act I the triumvir realizes he must overcome his weakness and break away from Cleopatra, but that from the time he leaves for Rome until his death his understanding dissolves in delights and passion. After each of the two disastrous military losses to Octavius, the critic contends, Antony is momentarily jolted into consciousness, but he is able to retreat from or find substitutes for these flashes of insight even on these occasions, because "whatever bitter judgment of self there is . . . , it is not deep and final." Heilman further characterizes Antony as a hero of unusual charm and charisma, able to captivate all around him, and he questions whether such a hero is capable of reflection and inner-directedness. Antony's personal attractiveness, the critic concludes, "evokes an aesthetic responsiveness that all but persuades us to forego judgment of character"; indeed, he contends, the prospect that Shakespeare gives us here of a glittering realm "where all vital powers conspire against self-knowledge" allows us, if we are so inclined, to experience for ourselves "the brilliant unconcern of these special creatures."*]

Self-knowledge, in the view of some critics, is an important element in tragic structure: when the hero comes to understand himself—to know what he has done or has been or is—the tragic form has fulfilled its potentialities. Whatever its theoretical merits, this argument is rooted in a sense of the dramatic method of eminent tragedies. The very essence of the story of Oedipus, as it is dramatized by Sophocles, is that Oedipus comes to enlightenment: he learns what man he is and what manner of life he has lived. (p. 17)

Though Shakespeare generally dealt with tragic protagonists of some thoughtfulness, he did not discover in the heroes of his earlier plays a characterizing movement toward self-knowledge. Romeo and Brutus, for instance, are preoccupied with outer antagonists, a dramatic situation not conducive to looking within. We do see Brutus making choices that might lead to a drama of self-questioning, but his serenity remains largely unpunctured. It is rather Cassius's inner turmoil that is the genesis of the later tragic personalities. Such an inner turmoil, though it is differently compounded, first takes the center of the stage in Hamlet. Highly self-conscious he makes a troubled and demanding inspection of motive and meaning; above all he wants to avoid the deed of which self-condemnation may be the consequence.

Three years after *Hamlet* Shakespeare swings into, and in two years completes, his great middle period of tragedies with three heroes who have varying degrees of Hamlet's self-consciousness but who are rasher, more reckless, more driven than he. Othello carries through the vengeance over which Hamlet hesitated; Lear leaps unhesitantly into punishments (and disastrous rewards); Macbeth cannot resist murdering his way to a throne. Here are all-out commitment and action bound up, for Shakespeare, in the drama of self-knowledge. (pp. 17-18)

From *Macbeth* Shakespeare goes on, within two years, to *Antony and Cleopatra* and *Coriolanus*. In all three plays the protagonist is a public figure in the prime of life—not a youngster like Romeo or Hamlet, or an octogenarian like Lear, or a minor official like Othello. In all there is an ample record of public life, with a certain architectonic cumbersomeness; especially in *Antony and Cleopatra* there is so much history of the state and its battles that it might well dispossess all history of the mind and its conflicts.... In both *Macbeth* and *Antony and Cleopatra* the dramatist's sense of social context leads him to expand others' comments on the protagonist. Antony is talked about—praised, pitied, or criticized—by Enobarbus, Lepidus, Caesar, and Pompey, by Demetrius, Philo, Ventidius, Maecenas, Scarus, Dercetas, Agrippa, and Eros, and of course by Cleopatra and her women. More than most Shakespeare heroes, including even Macbeth, he is interpreted by human mirrors. This method, which has a dramatic function to be noted later, is so extensively used that it seems almost a planned surrogate for the drama of self-confrontation; and of course the clarity with which most of the others see Antony is in ironic contrast with his own much fuzzier sense of himself.

Macbeth and *Antony and Cleopatra* have a still closer resemblance in a more important matter: from the start, both Macbeth and Antony possess a kind of knowledge that Othello and Lear must have beaten into them by harsh experience. Macbeth knows that dreams he cannot get rid of are evil. In the opening scene Antony refers to "my faults" [I. ii. 107]; resolves: "These strong Egyptian fetters I must break, / Or lose myself in dotage" [I. ii. 116-17]; repeats: "I must from this enchanting queen break off; / Ten thousand harms, more than the ills I know, / My idleness doth hatch" [I. ii. 129-30]. Both dramas

exist because the protagonists cannot act in terms of the knowledge that haunts them. But the formulations are completely distinct. Macbeth has to suppress the knowledge of what he is up to in order to be up to it, whereas in doing what he does Antony drifts away from knowledge of it. In Macbeth we see the quelling of conscience by action; in Antony, the decay of conscience in passion.

The death of Fulvia, reinforced by the ironies of Enobarbus, who plays Fool to Antony's Lear, provides the occasion when Antony might break from Cleopatra, of whom he says: "Would I had never seen her!" [I. ii. 152]; but the knowledge implied in such a wish is a frail thing before Cleopatra's skills, and he quickly assures her that, part though he must, "my full heart / Remains in use with you" [I. iii. 43-4]. From now on there is no word of the "faults," "fetters," and "harms" which he so unequivocally named at the start. All Antony's subsequent political dealings with Caesar, Lepidus, and Pompey, not to mention his marriage with Octavia, are in the style of a man untroubled by knowledge of weakness or obsession. Within thirty-five lines he can urge Octavia, "Read not my blemishes in the world's report," and then, with no apparent sense of inconsistency, soliloquize: "I will to Egypt; / And though I make this marriage for my peace, / I' th' East my pleasure lies" [II. iii. 5, 39-40]. When Caesar tells him to treat Octavia well, Antony is a little touchy ("Make me not offended / In your distrust"—[III. ii. 33-4]); this may reveal a subliminal awareness that he has earned distrust. We might also infer a sense of guilt in the charges that Antony makes against Caesar during their subsequent split (III. iv), since Shakespeare's heroes cling to a self-absolving blame of others whenever they can. But in the main the long stretch of the play between Antony's departure from Egypt and the battle of Actium makes absolutely nothing of a split in motives in Antony—a split that might be expected when, after his initial resolve to leave Cleopatra for good, Antony begins to drift back to her. It may be that this possibility simply faded away in the large shadow of Plutarch, for there is an inordinate amount of historical detail here. It is more likely that Shakespeare sensed Antony as a man in whom the clear knowing of self and of moral options has been all but deadened by the impulses that determine his direction. Macbeth had a bitter, long-continuing battle with his scruples; Antony's are almost dissolved in delights that are like an erotic dream come true. Early in the play, defending himself against Caesar's charge that he "denied" military help, Antony says that no, he only "neglected" the request—"And then when poisoned hours had bound me up / From mine own knowledge" [II. ii. 90-1]. It is as though he were now unpoisoned and knowing, an irony pointed by the words of Canidius after Antony's flight at Actium: "Had our general / Been what he knew himself" [III. x. 25-6]. Antony assumes, and Canidius assumes, that wrong conduct by Antony represents a collapse of self-knowledge—not an inability to have it, or a struggling, willed rejection of it, but a spontaneous dissolving of it in deep currents of feeling that well up and force life into their channels. This is Shakespeare's new version of the tragic hero in relation to the problem of self-knowledge.

For such a man, only a severe shock can restore perspective, in whole or in part: the unconscious flight at Actium punctures unconsciousness. Antony comes to in something like horror. The land, he says, "is asham'd to bear me" [III. xi. 2]; "I / Have lost my way for ever" [III. xi. 3-4]; "I follow'd that I blush to look upon" [III. xi. 12]; he speaks of "despair" and intimates suicide.... Cleopatra comes in and hears him saying to himself, "No, no, no, no, no" and "O fie, fie, fie!" [III.

xi. 29, 31]. To her he goes on in this vein, yet soon with some subtle alterations, with the first gropings for a shield against the cutting edge of self-understanding. Even severe shocks do not guarantee conversion, especially for severe cases. Shaken as he is, Antony tends to see his disgrace only within limits; his fuzziness shortens horizons. His flight in the wake of Cleopatra's ships is really a symbolic summation of his career, but this fact is what does not come through to him; he does not see into the depths, or undergo an Oedipean response to an enveloping and irremediable truth. What he sees is a specific piece of disgraceful conduct, and hence he is able to nibble at psychological antitoxins. He recalls how much better than Caesar he fought at Philippi [III. xi. 35ff.]. This gives him courage for a relatively strong note of self-condemnation: "I have offended reputation, / A most unnoble swerving" [III. xi. 49-50]. But his sense of "unnoble swerving" is bounded by Actium; and in effect it dissolves in the speaking of the words, for Shakespeare shows Antony replacing the sanction by which the judgment could have become an immitigable sentence. Not the gods judge, but Cleopatra: it is to her that he says, "How I convey my shame out of thine eyes..." [III. xi. 52]. Precisely, not the eyes of heaven, but of the woman who sees no shame at all; for she is in no position to make a judgment, even if she would, and she attempts none. Antony defines her omnipotence as he adds a layer to his protective shield by blaming her:

> O'er my spirit
> Thy full supremacy thou knew'st, and that
> Thy beck might from the bidding of the gods
> Command me.
>
> [III. xi. 58-61]

In effect he acknowledges a new divinity; she has only to shed a tear, and in that he finds a balm for such wounds of self-knowledge as he has felt. "Give me a kiss. / Even this repays me" [III. xi. 70-1]. *Repays* is not far from *redeems*. We have seen almost a parody of the divine mercy that cleanses and restores. Macbeth had to rely on his own toughness; Antony turns to another god.

Yet nursing the wounds of self-knowledge demands, of a warrior, some self-help too. We now recognize the Macbeth mode in a curious diminishment, a dissolute man's version of the hero and then of the ruthless tyrant. First Antony challenges Caesar, and Shakespeare uses Enobarbus to make sure we don't miss the point: "That he should dream / ... the full Caesar will / Answer his emptiness!" [III. xiii. 34-6]. Next Antony has Caesar's messenger, Thyreus, whipped; though the occasion is sexual jealousy, the cause is need of enlargement after the knowledge of meanness. "I am / Antony yet" [III. xiii. 92-3] is an endeavor to affirm that all is as it once was.... The effort at rehabilitation continues in the extended abuse of Cleopatra, now possible because Antony is not, as he was in the Actium affair, also implicated: he has the advantage of catching her off base, and he can enjoy the rare privilege of righteous indignation, one of the most tonic antidotes to self-knowledge. As a matter of fact, she is not very far off base, if at all, that he goes on so volubly on this slight occasion evidences the largeness of his need, one hardly modified, as it might be in another man, by a valuing of restraint and dignity. Even amid all this insulating rodomontade, however, Shakespeare still reads Antony as not quite avoiding momentary shocks of truth. The much admired lines—

> And when we in our viciousness grow hard—
> O misery on't—the wise gods seel our eyes;

> In our own filth drop our clear judgements; make us
> Adore our errors; laugh at's while we strut
> To our confusion.
>
> [III. xiii. 111-15]

are often taken to be Antony's comment on himself, but the situation is not so unambiguous. In the context these lines have to be a part of his arraignment of Cleopatra. That the sardonic images happen to apply also to himself he apparently comes to recognize: that is the suggestion of "O misery on't!" But whatever bitter judgment of self there is in these words, again it is not deep and final. This is not doomsday but a disagreeable episode, and Antony breaks quickly away into the partial comfort of abusing Cleopatra and whipping Thyreus. He complains that Caesar is "Proud and disdainful, harping on what I am, / Not what he knows I was" [III. xiii. 142-43]; the "am" and "was" clearly refer to worldly status, not moral being. He completes his pull-back from the harrowing glimpse of truth by three safety measures. His faith in Cleopatra is re-confirmed ("I am satisfied" [III. xiii. 167]); he now resolves on the full Macbeth way to self-affirmation ("I'll set my teeth / And send to darkness all that stop me" [III. xiii. 180-81]); and climactically he calls, "Let's have one other gaudy night" [III. xiii. 182]. It is a therapy that appears only in this play, and is at its very heart: insulation by intoxication. The next time he appears, Antony again announces, with an increase in emphasis, his second and third measures. He'll "fight", either to "live, / Or bathe my dying honour in the blood / Shall make it live again" [IV. ii. 5-7]; and he calls for "supper, come, / And drown consideration" [IV. ii. 44-5]. "Drown consideration": it is the very mode of the play.

"Reputation" and "honor" are words that may cut deep morally. Yet as Antony uses them they seem to measure less a flaw of spirit than a slip in public decorum, less an inner decay than an error in affairs. Other words show his tendency to look outward, to stress an uncooperativeness in circumstances. His "good stars" have "empty left their orbs" [III. xiii. 146]. When Enobarbus changes sides, Antony explains: "O, my fortunes have / Corrupted honest men!" [IV. v. 16-17]. It is "my fortunes," not "my behavior," though Enobarbus's words show that what he has been worried by is the behavior and the disintegration it testifies to. When the fleet joins Caesar's, Antony concludes, "Fortune and Antony part here" [IV. xii. 19]. What is even more central in his thoughts is the idea that he has been "betrayed," for he uses the word twice [IV. ii. 10, 24]. The point is not his rightness or wrongness in this view, but that he stops at this view; the trouble, as he sees it, is in outer, not inner, events; he is a victim of betrayal by others, not of a prior betrayal by himself. He thinks of himself in heroic terms as a descendant of Hercules [IV. ii. 43ff.], and he addresses his armor: "You have been nobly borne" [IV. xiv. 43]. He continues to blame Cleopatra, and in familiar terms: "false play'd" and "betray'd" [IV. xiv. 19, 26]. When he is told the lie that she is dead, his indignation yields immediately to grief and to a sense of tardiness in honor: this time honor refers to the style of dying and hence, as before, not to the quality of living. He must remedy the "dishonour" of Cleopatra's dying first, and the "penetrative shame" of being prisoner to Caesar. And this is the burden of his final dialogue with Cleopatra, from his intial boast that his "valour... hath triumph'd on itself" [IV. xv. 15] to his last-breath insistence that he does "not basely die, / Nor cowardly put off my helmet to / My countryman" [IV. xv. 55-7]. (pp. 18-24)

To trace Antony's approaches to self-knowledge, and his retreats from it or substitutes for it, may seem like an exercise in disparagement, and to say that he cannot face himself may seem to fall short of justice to a man who usually evokes a good deal of fondness. The subject, however, is not Antony's claim on our hearts but Shakespeare's management of a theme in some way present in all of the tragedies: man's difficulty in knowing himself. The heroes differ in their greater or less knowing of themselves and in the combination of this knowing with other elements. In Antony the other elements encourage antithetical interpretations, from both of which the present one diverges. One, the more traditional one, is that Antony is an exemplar of moral misconduct; the other, in effect a rebuttal, is that in their love Antony and Cleopatra have found another order of morality, a nobler sanction than that of the empire politics of even a great empire. . . . If it is too simple to dismiss Antony as a roué (and Cleopatra as a trollop), it is a contrary excess to see in him only greatness of spirit. Not that Antony is not brave, buoyant, proud in some ways, generous at some times; but it romanticizes him, and actually thins out a complex portrait, to claim for him a largeness of soul which would leave him nothing to know about himself. What is more, to read him thus is to substitute one kind of moral view for another. All readers feel Antony's attractiveness, his ability to captivate, his combination of amiability and strength, his recklessness which vicariously releases their own impulse to burst through limits. . . . Antony's gift is the occasional human one of seeming immune to the rules, to the usual ways of looking at and assessing man; like Falstaff, he evokes an enthusiastic aesthetic responsiveness. One kind of reader acknowledges this and, albeit reluctantly, applies the rules anyway; another kind of reader invents counter-rules by which to convert aesthetic responsiveness into justifiable admiration.

The problem of interpretation is created by Shakespeare's feat of giving us, in Antony, the portrait of an extraordinary, rarely equaled, charismatic personality. Antony has a personal charm that distinguishes him among Shakespeare's tragic heroes. It is difficult to think of Macbeth, in some respects Antony's twin, as having any charm at all. Lear has the devotion of Kent, the Fool, and Cordelia, but in him there is more of a naive, tempestuous power than of winsomeness. Antony, with no witches and no kingship to shore him up, indeed with the nagging sense that his "angel" always quails before Caesar's, draws people to him magically. Of all the tragic heroes, as we have seen, he is most talked about by other characters; though they may attribute weakness and vice to him, and pity him, they are interested in him, excited by him, attracted as if by some mysterious pull, all but enchanted. He has the charisma that is often felt in actor or artist or poet, the gift of inexplicably pleasing or moving or influencing men and women that sometimes accompanies great talent. Caesar is not entirely immune to it; Octavia clearly feels it; Pompey responds to it; Ventidius and many others are moved by it. Antony can be a leader as well as a blind follower, a warrior as well as an infatuate, generous as well as mean-spirited. But above all he is instinctively a "good fellow," a summoner to gaiety, a plucker of heart strings, a creator of a sense of common enterprise, a converter of Auld Lang Syne into fraternal good spirits amid disaster, an evoker of loyalty. Eros kills himself rather than kill Antony, Enobarbus is heartbroken over deserting him, Cleopatra reserves for him alone the tribute of ultimate fidelity.

Personal charm, the mystery of winning attachment, has never been better dramatized. Antony charms all about him, and through them he charms us. The powerful, non-rational suasiveness of being—"personality," as we tend to call it—evokes an aesthetic responsiveness that all but persuades us to forego

judgment of character. On the one hand character seems an irrelevance; on the other we tend to feel uncomfortable with the human being as pure work of art, incomplete in our apprehension of him. Hence our efforts either to distinguish charm and character, or to translate charm into approvableness, and make Antony a spacious repository of human values.

To note the shortcomings of Antony's self-understanding is not the counter-translation of charm into disapprovableness but is, instead, an examination of Shakespeare's new variation upon a theme, and perhaps his most remarkable variation. For Antony poses a question raised by none of the other heroes: can the man of charm look within? *Dare* he? What substance might he find by which to estimate the thing done, the life lived? Or is charm itself a free floating, a rejection of all anchoring fixities that might appear in one character as stabilities, in another as rigidities? Alternatively, is he *able* to look within? The flow of his psychic energy is all outward; he is a kind of mesmerist. It is most difficult to imagine Antony, of all the Shakespeare heroes, pondering the claims of this life or that upon him, the authority of this imperative or that. An instinctive exciter of warm admiration can hardly challenge himself fundamentally, though he may well see that an external and visible act—the flight at Actium—does not provide an image of the admirable. Further, the man of charm is himself charmed, by a woman who is all instinct and who embodies, better than any other heroine, an intuitive sense of how to achieve her ends; instrumental intelligence is in her very pores, and it is all her enlightenment.

In this remarkable union of charm and instinct there is, as it were, an autonomous realm, alien to the reflective, to self-assessment; it simply *is,* asserting itself by energy and magnetism, self-conscious only with respect to its own splendor and to unfriendly fortunes, not at all in the matter of how it may be placed by assay and comparison. Shakespeare is here imagining, as he does in no other tragedy, a world where all vital powers conspire against self-knowledge. To say this may give some clue to a particular charm in the play, to the actual hypnotism of an *is* beyond reflection. The very absence of a self-knowledge that may pass like a current from characters to spectators gives spectators an extra measure of freedom to share in the gay abandonment, the brilliant unconcern of these special creatures who in a chosen, un-ascetic outside surpass the cool and ordered establishment of Caesar and Octavia; to explore all intoxications and discover fulfilment; to command the luxuries of the palace and yet dwell unfettered in bohemia, and in a bohemia expanding into cosmic unlimitedness and infused with a transcendent glory; and thus, floating over the crude evidences of ordinary disaster, to mount to a final gilding in death and to discover, in despair of life, a triumph. Behind the facade of a lost world, sometimes a theme for sermons, flames a glittering life which, undisturbed by self-knowledge in its occupants, is warmly inviting to the romantic sensibility. What is most bewitching perhaps is the brilliant "gypsy," amidst whose exotic splendors is subtly embedded the ultimate creation of the male erotic dream—not the enumerable charms, the intimated skills, the unpredictable vitality, and the infinite variety, but the soul of the promiscuous woman faithful, in the end, to oneself alone. (pp. 24-8)

Robert B. Heilman, "From Mine Own Knowledge: A Theme in the Late Tragedies," in The Centennial Review of Arts & Science, *Vol. VIII, 1964, pp. 17-38.*

NORTHROP FRYE (essay date 1966)

[*Frye is considered one of the most important critics of the twentieth century and a leader of the anthropological or mythic ap-*

proach to literature which gained prominence during the 1950s. As he outlines in his seminal work, An Anatomy of Criticism *(1957), Frye views all literature as ultimately derived from certain myths or archetypes present in all cultures, and he therefore sees literary criticism as an unusual type of science in which the literary critic seeks only to decode the mythic structure inherent in a work of art. Frye's intention was to formulate a method of literary interpretation more universal and exact than that suggested in other critical approaches, such as New Criticism, biographical criticism, or historical criticism—all of which he finds valuable, but also limited in application. In the essay excerpted below, written in 1966 and delivered as a lecture that same year in an abridged form, Frye focuses on the juxtaposition in* Antony and Cleopatra *of the Roman or Western "day world of history" with its emphasis on "order, rule, and measure" and the Egyptian "night world of passion"—Dionysian and overflowing all measure. The critic employs the paradigm of "the wheel of fortune and history" to describe the way in which Antony's disastrous wavering between these two worlds and his eventual "fall out of history" are synchronized with Octavius's rise to supremacy. But even though Octavius attains the chief position in the temporal, historical realm, Frye concludes, Antony achieves an incomparable vision of "a part of nature that can never be ordered, a colossal exuberance of powers." Additionally, the critic notes that through her association not only with such mythic or legendary figures as Venus, Isis, Circe, and Omphale, but with the whore of Babylon as well, Shakespeare's Cleopatra ultimately represents both the legendary and the Biblical views of Egypt.*]

Antony and Cleopatra is the definitive tragedy of passion, and in it the ironic and heroic themes, the day world of history and the night world of passion, expand into natural forces of cosmological proportions. The Western and Roman world is pervaded by order, rule, and measure: when Antony tries to live by its standards he says:

> I have not kept my square; but that to come
> Shall all be done by th' rule.
>
> [II. iii. 6-7]

Its commander is Octavius Caesar, the very incarnation of history and the world's greatest order-figure, a leader who is ruthless yet not really treacherous given the conditions of a ruler's task, who is always provided with all the justifications he needs for destroying Antony. Here, turning the wheel of history appears in its most persuasive form as conquering the world, and conquering the world, being thought of as ultimately the most real activity, is presented as a duty. It has many moral imperatives on its side, but we can hardly say that it is a pattern of virtue, at least so far as it affects Antony. As a Roman soldier, Antony reminds us more of the Antony in *Julius Caesar,* an altogether smaller character. His lieutenant Ventidius, in a highly significant speech, alludes to the danger of a subordinate's doing so well as to affect his superior's "image," as we would say now. Antony is much more calculating, when doing his conquering duty, than he is when he rewards the deserting Enobarbus, or when he turns the conference on Pompey's ship into an epiphany of Dionysus.

The Eastern and Egyptian world is presided over by Cleopatra, queen of the ancient and timeless land which renews its fertility by the overflowing of the Nile each year. The play opens with the remark that Antony's dotage "O'erflows the measure" [I. i. 2], which is a Roman view, and Cleopatra's world is a Dionysian world of gigantic feasting and drunkenness and lovemaking. Both worlds are equally hard on the taxpayer, to use a standard that Plutarch at least is aware of even if Shakespeare ignores it. Each world is a self-evident reality to itself and an illusion to its rival. To the Romans, Antony is "not Antony" in Egypt: to Cleopatra, if he stays there, he "will be himself."

Antony himself, of course, tends to find his identity in his immediate context, and to waver disastrously between the two. But just as Octavius is the incarnation of history, so Cleopatra . . . is a counter-historical figure. Most of what she substitutes for heroic action is idleness and distraction, and there is plenty of textual justification for making her a straight temptress like the other Renaissance sirens who entice the hero from his quest with some Bower of Bliss or lotus land. The Egypt of the play includes the Biblical Egypt, the land of bondage, and the Egypt of legend in which serpents and crocodiles are spawned from the mud of the Nile. Cleopatra, the serpent of the Nile, is a Venus rising from it in Enobarbus' speech; she wears the regalia of Isis; she is a *stella maris* [star of the sea], a goddess of the moon and the sea. She has affinities with the kind of goddess figure that both Hebraic and Classical religions kept trying to subdue by abuse: she is a whore and her children are all bastards; she is a snare to men and destroys their masculinity, making them degenerate slaves like Circe; she is an Omphale dressing her Hercules in women's clothes; she has many characteristics of her sister whore of Babylon. This last gives a curiously apocalyptic tone to the play: just as *Troilus and Cressida* is something of a secular fall, so *Antony and Cleopatra*, with its references to "Herod of Jewry" [I. ii. 28-9], seems a kind of summing up of the old dispensation. The final cadences of the play seem to unite the two Biblical demonic themes, Egypt and the serpent, in a way that makes Cleopatra a central symbol of everything sinister in human history:

> This is an aspic's trail: and these fig-leaves
> Have slime upon them, such as the aspic leaves
> Upon the caves of Nile.
>
> [V. ii. 351-53]

But *Antony and Cleopatra* is not a morality play, and Egypt is not hell: it is rather the night side of nature, passionate, cruel, superstitious, barbaric, dissolute, what you will, but not to be identified with its vices, any more than Rome can be identified with its virtues. Prince Henry finds himself in the same Dionysian night world when he is a youth, and still has the choice of going up the wheel of fortune and history or of plunging downward into a world which becomes with increasing clarity a world of thieves and whores [in *1* and *2 Henry IV*]. But Henry, like Odin in the Eddas, learns a good deal from his descent and escapes from it at the sacrifice of some of his humanity. Antony is on the other side of the wheel: he can only fall out of history and action into the anti-historical and mythical world of passion opposite it, where the dominating figure is female and the hero is her subordinate. The slighter and younger Octavius goes up the wheel and takes command of history: Antony goes on to a hero's destruction, yet even in his death he is upstaged by Cleopatra, who monopolizes the attention of the audience to the end, looking in her death ready to "catch another Antony" [V. ii. 347] and start all over. She is worth the attention, because she is all we can see of a world as big as the Roman world, and not only all we can see of it but that world in herself, a microcosm of passion "whom everything becomes" [I. i. 49]. Her Egypt is able to bring a superhuman vitality out of Antony that Rome cannot equal, not in spite of the fact that it destroys him, but because it destroys him.

At the close of the play the two ends of the wheel confront each other: the Cleopatra who has

> pursued conclusions infinite
> Of easy ways to die
>
> [V. ii. 355-56]

and the Caesar who has been equally busy in pursuing difficult ways to live. Rome with its measure and order has won out over the overflowing Nile: the last line of the play urges us, in Caesar's voice, to see "High order in this great solemnity" [V. ii. 366]. But we can see something else besides high order: we can see that there is a part of nature that can never be ordered, a colossal exuberance of powers, the tailors of the earth as Enobarbus calls them, that weave and unweave the forms of life. Antony has caught a glimpse of these powers at the price of disappearing like a cloud when "the rack dislimns" [IV. xiv. 10], for it is only a self-destroying will that can bring one close to them. In fact Antony may say, with Slender in *The Merry Wives*, "I am freely dissolved, and dissolutely" [*The Merry Wives of Windsor*, I. i. 251-52]. Hercules has deserted him, but we remember how Hercules got rid of the burden of the world by tricking Atlas into re-assuming it: perhaps there is something gullible about Caesar, as Cleopatra suggests when she says she hears Antony

>   mock
> The luck of Caesar, which the gods give men
> To excuse their after wrath.
>
>   [V. ii. 285-87]

However, Caesar is now the master of his world, the secular counterpart to Christ, the off-stage presence in *Cymbeline* who is able to exact tribute from the end of the world in Britain even when defeated there. We say, in Roman terms, that Antony has lost "the world" for love. But his disappearance from that world is also, in a final twist of the tragic paradox, the appearance of another world that endures no master. (pp. 70-4)

> Northrop Frye, "The Tailors of the Earth: The Tragedy of Passion," *in his* Fools of Time: Studies in Shakespearean Tragedy, *University of Toronto Press, 1967, pp. 43-76.*

NORMAN RABKIN   (essay date 1967)

[*Rabkin considers* Antony and Cleopatra *"profoundly dualistic" in both its presentation of the nature of love and its depiction of Rome. As in Shakespeare's earlier works, the critic avers, love is here shown to be deeply paradoxical, for it is simultaneously liberating and demanding, combines spirituality with sensuality, and finds its most complete expression in "the finality of death." Rabkin contends that Antony and Cleopatra are torn between "the love of life and the yearning to renounce it," but once they elect death they pursue it with "joyous abandon, explicitly aware of what they are doing." The critic discovers a similar ambivalence in the play's two views of Rome: on the one hand, Shakespeare emphasizes Rome's honor, fame, and colossal military achievements; on the other, he depicts its viciousness, treachery, and hollowness. But Rabkin concludes that we must take both perceptions into account in evaluating Antony's commitment to the empire.*]

Romeo and Juliet is about youth and age. A young man's play, it stages the internal conflict in love as a tension between the consuming eros of adolescence, which so insists on the complete satisfaction of the ego that it must end in the annihilation of the self, and its polar opposite, that mature social love which insists on the sacrifice of the ego's fulfillment for another kind of good, a world that fosters rather than destroys. The lovers die for the one; recognizing their complicity in the tragedy, their survivors pledge to remake themselves so that they can survive for the other. To speak of both these forms of love is to beg the question as the very word "love" does.

To see love thus as a polarized value because of its generational aspect is to associate it with the problems of libido as *Henry IV* does, where Falstaff tragicomically insists on his perennial youth. But it is a young Hal who must reject the values of his old friend, and at such moments Shakespeare would have us understand that the problem is more than simply generational. More than a decade past *Romeo and Juliet* and within a very few years of his retirement from the theater, an older Shakespeare returns once more, in *Antony and Cleopatra,* to the theme of romantic art. The unanimity of critical applause, the absence of voices to tell us that elements of the play reflect levels of vision not fully liberated from a less mature point in the poet's development, and a plenitude controlled with more obvious success all point to the fullest realization of the theme with which Shakespeare had been concerned since *Venus and Adonis. Antony and Cleopatra* does not negate what *Venus and Adonis* and *Romeo and Juliet* told us; but it separates the question of the role of eros from the problems of adolescence. In pitying Adonis and Romeo and Juliet for leaving life before they have had a chance to learn what it is that they are leaving, we find ourselves disappointed by a world that does not conform to the ideals of the young. But as we watch Antony and Cleopatra choosing between self-destruction for a similar love and all the power that the adult world has to offer, we confront a more disturbing challenge: The world as seen from the point of view of its own maximum achievements may not be worth the keeping. After Romeo and Juliet are gone, a purged and reconciled polity remains to profit by their instruction; with the deaths of Antony and Cleopatra, "the crown o' the earth doth melt. . . . And there is nothing left remarkable / Beneath the visiting moon" [IV. xv. 63, 67-8]. As often happens in the later tragedies, the order restored makes a mockery of our aspirations to a good life that *Romeo and Juliet* could suggest to the end is possible.

This is not to suggest that *Antony and Cleopatra* is simpler or more monistic than the earlier works. If anything, it is more profoundly dualistic. So complementary is its vision that some critics continue to find in it a demonstration, depending on their particular sensibilities, either of the absolute transcendence or of the utter worthlessness of the love it presents, for both views are legitimately occasioned by aspects of the play. Like *Hamlet, Antony and Cleopatra* has emerged in recent years from the clouds of partisan and partial interpretations into the light of an increasingly communal reading which makes one think in optimistic moments that literary study may be a progressive phenomenon, and that the insights of individual critics may be contributions to a body of enduring knowledge. Even to cite all the critics who have argued for a complementary reading of *Antony and Cleopatra* would be an enormous task; and those critics are to be thanked for the fact that about one of the most complex of Shakespeare's plays the least need be said.

One point needs still to be stressed, however: As the last of Shakespeare's studies of romantic love, *Antony and Cleopatra* bases its complementarity as much on its author's late vision of the political world and of tragedy as it does on his previous understanding of love. It may be helpful to recall that the play was written most probably in the same year as *Coriolanus,* Shakespeare's most pessimistic political play. In *Antony and Cleopatra*—as not in *Romeo and Juliet*—the world which love throws away is presented ambivalently. Thus Shakespeare gives us two pictures of Rome. One is of the world that Antony loses in choosing Cleopatra: a world in which honor is the watchword, military men are giants who can survive superhuman trials, and fame is the spur to noble men's ambition. But the other picture is of a vicious political arena where honor is meaningless and comes only to men who do not deserve it; a general atmosphere of treachery and triviality makes Rome seem hardly worth the contemning. Seeing Rome the first way we agree with Antony's friends that he has thrown away a magnificent life in order to waste the lamps of night in futile Alexandrian revelry; seeing Rome the second way we realize that Antony alone among the men of Rome has found a way to escape its pointless way of life and to fulfill himself. Judging Antony's commitment to Cleopatra, we must take both of these pictures into account. Implicated in each of these valuations of Rome is a corresponding valuation of the romantic alliance; but even without reference to political grandeur the play establishes a pair of polarized responses to the affair. Love is ennobling and liberating as nothing else in life can be, yet only at the expense of everything else we ordinarily prize in the world, including honor, for it demands full payment of both Antony and Cleopatra before it gives them what they seek. In other complementary terms present throughout the play love appears, in the play that apotheosizes Shakespeare's vision of it, as preposterously bound to aging flesh, and yet as so far beyond the merely physical that to give it expression the whole world, life itself, must dissolve. As in *Romeo and Juliet,* so in *Antony and Cleopatra:* Love is of the flesh, yet only the liberation from flesh and the finality of death can express its full value.

Romeo and Juliet divest themselves of the world as of a thing of no value; from the moment in which their love is conceived their lives are a pilgrimage toward one inevitable and desired end. But Antony and Cleopatra are more complicated people. They have both the talent and the taste for power, and they fight to keep from surrendering it. True, Antony is willing to "let Rome in Tiber melt" [I. i. 33] in the very first scene; he knows that to find the measure of his love one must "find out new heaven, new earth" [I. i. 17]. And Cleopatra seems to care at the moment of Antony's first departure for Rome only for the "eternity" that "was in our lips and eyes" [I. iii. 35]. But not until they have been defeated by the world, not until Actium has put an end to Antony's last claim to Rome and Caesar to Cleopatra's sway over Egypt, not until life offers no alternative but death and, in the world's terms, complete failure are these world-weary lovers ready to commit themselves to that death so readily embraced by Romeo and Juliet. "My desolation does begin to make / A better life," remarks Cleopatra [V. ii. 1-2]. Having been forced to renounce the ambition to define themselves as pillars of the world—remember the play's insistence on the questions Who is Antony? and Who is Cleopatra?—Antony and Cleopatra are finally free to pledge themselves as sacrifices to it. If they begin to give up their hold on life more reluctantly than Romeo and Juliet, they do so finally with more joyous abandon, more explicitly aware of what they are gaining than Shakespeare's first tragic lovers:

> 'Tis paltry to be Caesar;
> Not being Fortune, he's but Fortune's knave,
> A minister of her will: and it is great
> To do that thing that ends all other deeds;
> Which shackles accidents and bolts up change;
> Which sleeps, and never palates more the du[n]g,
> The beggar's nurse and Caesar's.
>
> [V. ii. 2-8]

> But I will be
> A bridegroom in my death, and run into't

> As to a lover's bed.
>
> [IV. xiv. 99-101]

> Give me my robe, put on my crown; I have
> Immortal longings in me: now no more
> The juice of Egypt's grape shall moist this lip: . . .
>   husband, I come:
> Now to that name my courage prove my title!
> I am fire and air; my other elements
> I give to baser life.
>
> [V. ii. 280-82, 287-90]

Of all of Shakespeare's characters, the lovers demand most of life. Venus and Adonis, Romeo and Juliet, Antony and Cleopatra want, each in his own way, a satisfaction of the ego's desires so complete that no obstruction remains to their commitment. With the exception of Venus, who survives to will her unhappiness to them, this means for all of them the final dissolution of the ego itself: a definition of self gained by the loss of selfhood. In his greatest tragedy of love Shakespeare makes most fully explicit the paradox of love which he recognized already in composing *Venus and Adonis.* Turning the complementary vision toward perhaps the most familiar cautionary legend against love in his tradition, he finds in the myth of the archetypical lovers the supreme model of the paradoxes of love. Cleopatra's defining characteristic is her infinite variety. She embodies the sensuality and spirituality, the intense egotism and the ultimate selflessness, the love of life and the yearning to renounce it, that live side by side in the western myth of romantic love. Attracted by all her qualities, sharing her dichotomized longings, torn even more than she by another notion of his selfhood that struggles for the repudiation of what she represents, Antony is the most powerful image between Gottfried's Tristan and Wagner's of the passion that we regard alternately as the most noble and the most absurd of human engagements. As a play about Rome and love, as the vehicle of some of Shakespeare's most memorable poetry, and as one of the last of his tragedies, *Antony and Cleopatra* is unique. It is not, however, an aberration from his other work; rather, as a simultaneously exultant and despairing dramatization of the unresolvable dialectic between opposed values that claim us equally and of the necessary tragedy of choice, it is a paradigm of Shakespeare's art. (pp. 184-88)

Norman Rabkin, "Eros and Death," in his Shakespeare and the Common Understanding, *The Free Press, 1967, pp. 150-91.*

JULIAN MARKELS   (essay date 1968)

[*Instead of rejecting either Roman or Egyptian values by the choice of one over the other, Markels maintains, Antony reconciles the two systems so that they "gradually become coexistent in his mind and conditional upon each other." The critic asserts that as a consequence of Antony's achieved understanding of the mutual relevance of Rome and Egypt, the triumvir accepts the vacillations of fortune, "transforms endurance into magnanimity," and "brings new dimensions of right conduct into the range of possibility." After the battle of Actium, Markels declares, Cleopatra begins to understand that public values are relevant to her private life, but it is only by reenacting Antony's ultimate suffering and glory in her suicide that she attains an appreciation of his vision; thus, in* Antony and Cleopatra, *Markels avers, death is not a catastrophe, but an apotheosis. In addition, the critic offers an explication of Antony's conduct in Rome in Acts II and III, claiming that while he is there he earns and regains the ideal species of Roman honor that contrasts so vividly with the degraded versions of that public virtue exhibited by Octavius.*]

[*Antony and Cleopatra*] is built upon the opposition of public and private values. However we name them—love or honour, lust or empire—we know from the moment of Philo's opening speech that the issue before us is the form in which this opposition is to be resolved. It is usually said that Mark Antony is confronted by a choice between the values represented by Cleopatra and those represented by Octavius Caesar; and that however inadequate either value might be, he resolves this conflict by choosing Cleopatra and giving up the world. Instead I shall argue . . . that Mark Antony is disciplined in the distinctive vision of the play, wherein he is challenged either to choose between the opposed values represented by Cleopatra and Octavius or not to choose between them; and that instead of choosing, he resolves the conflict by striving equally toward both values and rhythmically making each one a measure and condition of the other. The result of his effort is that instead of becoming more "effeminate," as in North's Plutarch, Shakespeare's Antony grows larger in manhood until he can encompass both Rome and Egypt, affirming the values that both have taught him until both are fulfilled. Then his death comes, as Cleopatra's does later, not as dissolution but as transcendence, a sign of his having approached as close to immortality as a poet may dare to imagine by becoming everything that it was in him to be. That I think is why the lovers' deaths produce a feeling of exaltation that so many critics find unique in Shakespeare. In the concrete detail of the play's rendition, these deaths are not permitted to break the continuity of existence. Antony kills himself with his own world-sharing sword, yet does not complete the work, so that he may be left to die upon a kiss, which in turn is not quite so much to die as to "melt" and "discandy." Cleopatra desires death, like a "lover's pinch," to satisfy her immortal longing. She has found a means of death that will cause neither inward pain nor outward disfigurement; and she succeeds so well that in the embrace of the asp she merely "looks like sleep" [V. ii. 346]. For her and Antony death is not a limitation but a transformation of existence into a state of peace where the energy and the sweetness of life are at last unfettered. Their deaths signify not that one half of life is well lost for another but that both halves are found at last and hinged upon each other, in order that the whole world may be won. (pp. 8-10)

Antony and Cleopatra goes beyond *King Lear*—not above it but beyond it, to break new ground, and to fill out the whole contour of Shakespeare's development. The opposite of self-dramatization, Regan herself tells us in *King Lear,* is self-knowledge. By the time Lear achieves what measure of self-knowledge he is granted, he wants the safety of a "wall'd prison" to protect his personal accomplishment from any further threat of public life. One reason he is denied even this rescue is that Shakespeare has come to see that self-knowledge is not a condition but a process, like life itself, in which public and private values must remain in continuing negotiation with each other and in which not even the old and wise are permitted a separate peace, as Prospero will come to recognize. Meanwhile Shakespeare creates in Antony a character whose earned self-knowledge does not result in a desire to renounce the world for the safety of Lear's prison, but instead a desire to remain in the world, and, since it must continue to suffer his flaws, a magnanimous insistence upon giving freely to his world of his strength, virtue, and treasure as well. By accepting fully his own imperfection along with the world's, Antony is able to remain unprotected, and to let what goodness he has earned perform whatever acts of magnanimity are possible. For Shakespeare in *Antony and Cleopatra*, then, self-knowledge and the virtue it entails become not a place but a pathway, continually

renewed in and through public action; and Shakespeare's progression from *King Lear* to *Antony and Cleopatra* is toward this conception, with its corollary vision of the immortal joining of public and private values. (pp. 14-15)

Antony's Roman duty and his Egyptian appetite are represented as necessary alternatives in the beginning. Though Cleopatra is to be regarded neither as the object of a Wagnerian passion nor as a passing itch, she is placed clearly at the center of Antony's private life, which everywhere in the first act is weighed against his public commitments. (p. 17)

He begins by sharing the general opinion that he must choose between Rome and Egypt and by rejecting one for the other. At first he wants only "some pleasure now" [I. i. 47], and will not hear the news from Rome. Later, having heard the messengers, he decides he must break with Cleopatra "Or lose myself in dotage" [I. ii. 117]. (p. 18)

Antony is not in the condition that post-Freudian thought calls "conflicted." He is not aware all at once of contradictory alternatives, then torn and weakened by the need to decide, and finally rendered impotent or else aloof, and in either case unready for action. Antony's way is precisely not to weigh his alternatives and divide himself against himself, but to live each alternative in turn, and lift his whole self back and forth across the line that divides Rome from Egypt. He devotes himself wholly to each world in turn, at first dismissing the Roman messengers with "There's not a minute of our lives should stretch / Without some pleasure now" [I. i. 46-7]; and later dismissing himself from Egypt with "The strong necessity of time commands / Our services awhile" [I. iii. 42-3]. He lives for the moment, indeed; but he is to give himself just as fully to the Roman moment as to the Egyptian. In each place where he stands is obliterated every connection with another time, place, or value. This discontinuity in thought and action is distinctive of Antony's character, and it is pervasive in the play, where character and conduct, motive and action, cause and effect, are everywhere forced apart and hidden from each other. (p. 20)

From the time Antony leaves Egypt, at the end of I. iii, until the time when his new wife Octavia leaves him at Athens, at the end of III. iv, Antony devotes himself to satisfying both in letter and in spirit his country's claim upon him. Back in Rome, confronted with the embarrassing fact that his wife Fulvia had made war upon his partner Caesar while he was fishing in the Nile, Antony begins by patching up his excuses to Caesar with whatever temporizing and self-deception are necessary. He argues that Fulvia's wars against Caesar were subtly directed against himself as well to get him away from Cleopatra, but that honor and good breeding required that he stay in Egypt and avoid meeting his own wife and brother in battle. . . . Having pleaded first that honor made him stay there, soon Antony finds it convenient to regard his sojourn in Egypt as a lapse. To the charge that he has denied military aid to Caesar in those wars "Which fronted mine own peace," he replies:

> Neglected rather;
> And then when poisoned hours had bound me up
> From mine own knowledge. As nearly as I may,
> I'll play the penitent to you; but mine honesty
> Shall not make poor my greatness, nor my power
> Work without it. Truth is, that Fulvia,
> To have me out of Egypt, made wars here,
> For which myself, the ignorant motive, do
> So far ask pardon as befits mine honour
> To stoop in such a case.
>   [II. ii. 89-98]

The more he attempts to justify himself, the more desperately he fastens upon any argument that lies at hand, no matter how incoherent or debasing to his manhood. He ends by abandoning all pretense of argument, resorting to a compulsive assertion of his honor independently of anything he has done to maintain that honor. For as long as Antony is bent only upon making peace with Octavius and renewing his credentials in the Roman world, he has forfeited his only possible argument: that to him Egypt and Cleopatra represent indispensable human values. What Octavius has called his "lascivious wassails" Antony described earlier as "the nobleness of life" [I. i. 36]. But now while Antony chooses to share Octavius' standards, his life in the East is wholly vulnerable to Octavius' criticism, and he is barred from making a plausible defense of his conduct.

Ironically, Antony's shabby rationalizations brilliantly serve their immediate purpose of restoring his pre-eminence in the Roman world, even to the point of making him an eligible husband for Octavia. The essential Roman issue is not Antony's past conduct but his political reliability in the future. Octavius, who needs Antony's strength and skill in the expected war with Pompey, is not eager to scruple nicely about honor at such a moment. He wants from Antony a quick sign of good intentions, some gesture of willingness that will justify him in binding his sister in marriage to Antony. Thus Antony's empty posturing is exquisitely matched by the ethical shallowness of Octavius' response, for Octavius is willing to respect a mere show of honor if it helps to consolidate his power.

But Antony does not continue merely to put on a show until he can return conveniently to Egypt. The unimproved flimsiness of his patched alliance with Octavius is not enough at best to maintain his restored status among the Romans. Nor can his large spirit have its measure taken by any form of abject timeserving. Once turned back toward Rome, Antony progresses from a mere posture to a committed pursuit of the inner spirit of Roman honor. Immediately after his marriage, he says:

> My Octavia,
> Read not my blemishes in the world's report.
> I have not kept my square; but that to come
> Shall all be done by th' rule. Good night, dear lady.
>
> [II. iii. 4-7]

This candid statement is accurate both about his past and his future. With Octavia he does not temporize as he did with her brother. He makes no excuses for his past; and the sincerity of his promise for the future is to be borne out by events.

Immediately after the speech quoted above, Octavia exits and Antony's Egyptian soothsayer enters. Antony, palpably satisfied by the progress of his affairs in Rome, asks the soothsayer: "Now, sirrah; you do wish yourself in Egypt?" [II. iii. 10]. The soothsayer wishes them both in Egypt, for, as he says, though Antony is a better man than Caesar—"Noble, courageous, high, unmatchable" [II. iii. 21],—Caesar has the better luck. Once near Caesar, Antony's good angel leaves him, so that Caesar invariably beats him against the odds. This reminder overturns Antony's high spirits, and after the soothsayer exits, Antony confesses that what he said is right. Then, less than forty lines after he has promised Octavia to live by the rule, Antony says:

> I will to Egypt;
> And though I make this marriage for my peace,
> I' th' East my pleasure lies.
>
> [II. iii. 39-41]

These lines more than any other provide grounds for the customary interpretation of Antony's activity at Rome: that out of weakness or cynicism, no matter which, Antony is simply mending his political fences and watching hawk-eyed for the earliest opportunity to return to Egypt. There is a discontinuity indeed between Antony's promise to Octavia and his promise to himself; and this one surely lends color to the traditional view of Antony's dissolute character.

But here is just the moment when Antony stops vacillating between two worlds in Drydenesque fashion and begins to make each value, Rome and Egypt, relevant to the other. He means everything he says in both speeches, and neither one supersedes the other. What he calls his "pleasure" surely has its dissolute side; but it is neither dissolute nor contradictory to want to live by the rule and still to take pleasure in life. The soothsayer reminded him, after all, that he is overshadowed even in those pastimes that the austere Octavius allows himself; and it is a fair inference that his pain here lies in fully recognizing the circumscription of Roman values for the first time since his return. Antony's sudden depression of spirits after the soothsayer's speech suggests that his marriage to Octavia was neither desperate nor disingenuous. He took pleasure in his marriage, and his leading question to the soothsayer implies that he for one does *not* wish himself back in Egypt. When the soothsayer reminds him of his fainting luck in Caesar's presence, to be sure, he changes his mind with characteristic abruptness. But this time his newly aroused desire does not lead him to jump for Egypt at the first opportunity, or to break his promise to Octavia and stop living by the rule. Although he is still divided between Rome and Egypt, now for the first time he stops rejecting one for the other. In his remaining conduct throughout the play, the two values gradually become coexistent in his mind and conditional upon each other. Antony comes slowly to realize that he cannot escape Caesar's better luck, but still must put his virtue and his honor in the scales against it. He comes to recognize that the Roman peace upon which his Egyptian pleasure depends can be achieved only by the fact and not the show of honor; that his aspirations must sustain each other rather than compete. If there is little doubt in his mind or in ours that he will return to Egypt, the crucial fact is that he does not take the opportunity until he has fulfilled himself as a Roman, until he has lived conscientiously "by th' rule" and found himself betrayed in that conduct by lucky Caesar himself. Only when he discovers what he could not have anticipated, that Octavius rather than he has acted unconscionably, does Antony turn back toward Cleopatra. By then he has become the best of Romans, and even then he does not permit his conduct back in Egypt to undermine his reinstated Roman honor.

The immediate task of the reunited triumvirs is to settle their business with Pompey. Antony had wished to avoid war with Pompey, if he could also avoid debasing his reputation into the bargain:

> I did not think to draw my sword 'gainst Pompey;
> For he hath laid strange courtesies and great
> Of late upon me. I must thank him only,
> Lest my remembrance suffer ill report;
> At heel of that, defy him.
>
> [II. ii. 153-57]

He had been unwilling to defy Octavius, and thus had lost his honor while protesting it. But now he takes the initiative in negotiating with Pompey an acceptable peace, which manifests simultaneously Antony's desire to avoid bloodshed, his uncertainty over the outcome of a possible battle, his personal regard for Pompey, and yet his readiness to defy Pompey and all these personal considerations for the sake of the public order at stake. Now for the first time we see him masterfully hinge together his public and private interests, and thereby displace Octavius in the seat of leadership. (pp. 23-7)

Antony refuses to threaten or to distort the facts in order to gain a rhetorical advantage over Pompey, and in the process he gains the desired advantage. He does not deny Pompey's naval superiority; and whereas Octavius threatens Pompey with the dangers of refusing their offer, Antony invites him to consider the intrinsic value of that offer. Even his final indirect reference to Cleopatra bears a new significance, through which we see Rome and Egypt becoming simultaneous values for him. To Octavius he had apologized for his ''poisoned hours'' in Egypt and abased himself in the false confession implied by that metaphor. To Octavia he had spoken broadly of not having kept his square, but without embarrassing himself by specific admissions. Now to Pompey he says only that the beds in the East are soft, which sounds less like a confession of guilt than an estimate of value. In suavely thanking Pompey for taking him away from his soft bed, he begins to put his Egyptian idyll beyond the reach of Roman criticism; and then he turns discontinuously to the present and says he has gained by his return to Rome.

What he has gained is Octavia; and the play goes on to demonstrate the sincerity with which he values that gain. . . . When Octavius and Octavia exchange farewells, Antony says of his wife ''The April's in her eyes. It is love's spring, / And these the showers to bring it on. Be cheerful'' [III. ii. 43-4]. The episode is highly complex. On the one hand, Shakespeare has gone out of his way, in an already crowded plot, to conduct this test of Antony's probity. But he offers no immediate evidence, either in the tone of Antony's speeches or in the surrounding context, that Antony is guilty of duplicity. On the contrary, Antony's beautiful description of Octavia, which continues throughout another speech beginning ''Her tongue will not obey her heart'' [III. ii. 47], shows a true and eloquent lover. Yet we all heard Antony say before that he makes this marriage for his peace. If we confine our attention to this episode in context, then I do not see how we can believe that Antony's speech hides a deliberate intention to return to Egypt. If Antony is dissembling here, then his cynicism is even greater than his most severe detractors have claimed, and the play itself becomes an incoherent babble in which we cannot trust what the poetry tells us. Everything in Antony's utterance bespeaks the honor of his motives and the integrity of his love; and we can only conclude that if he said before that he makes this marriage for his peace, that is distinctly not what he is saying now. The two statements are simply discontinuous; and yet the action of the play does not permit either one to supersede the other.

Only in the light of the genuine honor won by his marriage to Octavia and his negotiation with Pompey may we discover the significance of Antony's departure for Egypt when it finally comes. In the scene of his farewell to Octavia, he begins by listing the grievances that have turned him against her brother:

Nay, nay, Octavia; not only that—
That were excusable, that and thousands more
Of semblable import—but he hath wag'd
New wars 'gainst Pompey; made his will, and read it
To public ear;

Spoke scantly of me: when perforce he could not
But pay me terms of honour, cold and sickly
He vented them, most narrow measure lent me;
When the best hint was given him, he not took't,
Or did it from his teeth.

[III. iv. 1-10]

He shows here that same jealous regard for his honor that lay behind his earlier temporizing with Octavius, and this might suggest that he is retreating into the old self-deception and paving the way for his long-intended return to Cleopatra. But this time he is not protesting too much, in view of his conduct since returning from Egypt. (pp. 30-1)

Antony's last words to Octavia, then, are those of a man who latterly has ''kept his square'' while everybody around him has been tracing hyperbolas:

Gentle Octavia,
Let your best love draw to that point which seeks
Best to preserve it. If I lose mine honour,
I lose myself. Better I were not yours
Than yours so branchless. But, as you requested,
Yourself shall go between 's. The mean time, lady,
I'll raise the preparation of a war
Shall stain your brother. Make your soonest haste;
So your desires are yours.

[III. iv. 20-8]

And again:

When it appears to you where this begins,
Turn your displeasure that way, for our faults
Can never be so equal that your love
Can equally move with them. Provide your going;
Choose your own company, and command what cost
Your heart has mind to.

[III. iv. 33-8]

In the personal inflection of these lines there is nothing of the forced declamation that characterized Antony's earlier parting speech to Cleopatra [I. iii. 41-56] or his reconciliation speech to Caesar [II. ii. 89-98]. Here as in those earlier speeches, he is attending to his Roman honor. But this time his voice rings with conviction because this time his honor has been earned; and with the peerless tact, modesty, and confidence of a man who has had to undergo a reformation, who can no longer afford to be righteous unless he is right, he offers Octavia all possible help in making a journey that cannot help being an effrontery to him.

That effrontery, for all its noble motive, frees Antony for Egypt— not because it gives him a convenient excuse but because it measures his inner fulfilment of Roman honor against the external forms enacted by his wife and brother-in-law, and thus challenges him to make viable his Roman honor in an Egyptian life. . . . The play now frees him for Egypt, not to relapse into a familiar luxury, but to achieve on condition of his earned Roman honor that further ripeness which only the Nile generates. He is not left free to exchange one world for another; but by winning one world, he is enabled to reach for the other, to redeem each world through the other and make each one relevant to the other's glory.

Up through the end of Act III, scene v . . . , Shakespeare has located in Rome and its various adjuncts a total of eleven scenes comprising 863 lines, and in Egypt a total of six scenes comprising 606 lines. After Antony's departure from Egypt in I. iii, Shakespeare locates his remaining Egyptian scenes (I. v,

II. vi, and III. iii) in places along the sequence that dramatize the contrast in tone, texture, and values between a Roman world whose ideal of rational, disinterested politics is uniquely capable of degenerating into the cynical bargaining of ward bosses, and an Egypt whose highest values of emotional fulfilment are equally capable of collapsing into mere willfulness and sybaritic vanity. This first half of the play, while presenting Antony's character and conflict, provides us also with a comparative anthropology of these two worlds, a running critique of the criteria of civilization as they are hammered out in the confrontation of the two cultures. Although this geographic polarization of values is rare in Shakespeare, there is nothing unfamiliar in the particular values represented by Rome and Egypt, nor in the fact of their opposition. (pp. 34-7)

The public values of Rome arise from the same source as always in Shakespeare: the ideal of order, harmony, and mutuality in the state. At the beginning of the play Antony's lapsed honor is inseparable from the failure of the Roman peace, like two sides of a coin. To Antony's question on his return to Rome, "My being in Egypt, / Caesar, what was't to you?" [II. ii. 35-6], in effect Caesar had already given an answer:

> If he fill'd
> His vacancy with his voluptuousness,
> Full surfeits and the dryness of his bones
> Call on him for't! But to confound such time
> That drums him from his sport and speaks as loud
> As his own state and ours—'tis to be chid
> As we rate boys who, being mature in knowledge,
> Pawn their experience to their present pleasure
> And so rebel to judgement.
>
> [I. iv. 25-33]
> (p. 37)

Octavius in his speech doesn't mention Rome, doesn't refer even to a single community of which he and Antony both are members. The threat of Pompey is not . . . to an organic political society whose wholeness must be sustained by love, justice, and truth. It is a threat merely to "his own state and ours," to an accidental sum of wealth and power that has passed from the hands of Julius Caesar through those of his assassins, and now has accrued, "Like to a vagabond flag upon the stream" [II. iv. 45] to the present triumvirs. In the design of the play the condition of Rome is subordinated to, and frequently obscured by, the interests and intrigues of persons. Before we pursue the sordid political implications of this fact, we must recognize also that in the design of the play Rome's security is guaranteed, regardless of the conduct and character of her citizens. In *Antony and Cleopatra* as in *Julius Caesar,* no matter how much our attention is focused abstractly upon politics, we are not permitted to fear concretely for the survival of the state. (pp. 38-9)

[In *Antony and Cleopatra*] Rome has achieved a cosmic identity. Her political foundations have become so secure that her imagined destiny transcends the timeserving deeds of men. For Shakespeare's dramatic purpose Rome . . . becomes an idea, an abstract value with an almost allegorical significance. Having certified imaginatively the permanence of Rome as a political institution, Shakespeare is free to scrutinize the idea of Rome and to treat it as only one item in a pluralistic world of values.

Once he can do that, he attributes to Rome—pre-eminently in the person of Octavius Caesar—a political opportunism and a human mediocrity that amply confirm Cleopatra's final judg-

ment, "'Tis paltry to be Caesar" [V.ii. 2]. Octavius, a man essentially unmarked by malice or by love, is full of the cloistered virtue of the letter of the law. He is all but a cipher of the public world, a Roman Henry V, who, as the late Harold Goddard pointed out, is as quick to give up his sister for an empire as man ever was to give an empire for a whore [see Additional Bibliography]. He violates the pact with Pompey, deposes and executes Lepidus, and seeks every means to ruin Antony and insure Cleopatra's public humiliation. (p. 41)

Octavius is only the play's most conspicuous example of Roman opportunism and duplicity. In Menas, Pompey, and in Antony himself, we have further evidence of degradation in the political values of Rome. To Menas' grotesque plan for cutting loose the ship on which the triumvirs are feasting and then cutting their throats, Pompey makes a hypocritical reply that is equally characteristic of Shakespeare's English and his Roman plays:

> Ah, this thou shouldst have done,
> And not have spoken on't! In me 'tis villany;
> In thee 't had been good service. Thou must know,
> 'Tis not my profit that does lead mine honour;
> Mine honour, it. Repent that e'er thy tongue
> Hath so betray'd thine act. Being done unknown,
> I should have found it afterwards well done,
> But must condemn it now. Desist, and drink.
>
> [II. vii. 73-80]

Antony's lieutenant Ventidius shows another facet of debased Roman honor when, after his victory in Parthia, he explains that although he can conquer still more territory for Antony, Antony would become jealous if he did. He makes in advance the necessary adjustment of Antony's profit to Antony's honor: "Better to leave undone, than by our deed / Acquire too high a fame, when him we serve's away" [III. i. 14-15].

This public world is naturally impatient of private feelings. Its calculating politics drain off the passions; and Octavius exemplifies its norm of temperament as well as its public practice. In his political efficiency he rejects everything personal, whether it is Antony's challenge to individual combat, or the reeling camaraderie of Pompey's banquet. Coupled with his devastating exposure of Roman pretensions in the banquet scene on Pompey's galley—both in the drunkenness of the celebrants and in Menas' plan for killing them—Shakespeare gives us a portrait of Octavius as nevertheless the most repellent Roman of them all. His superior restraint only enhances his unloveliness. This impersonality permeates his conduct throughout the play, from his reference to his sister as a "piece of virtue" [III. ii. 28] that will "cement" him to Antony, to his desire to show his love for her publicly, "Which, left unknown, / Is often left unlov'd" [III. vi. 52-3], and finally to his effort to humiliate Cleopatra. Attempting to woo Cleopatra from Antony, Thyreus says of his master:

> But it would warm his spirits
> To hear from me you had left Antony
> And put yourself under his shroud,
> The universal landlord.
>
> [III. xiii. 69-72]

The juxtaposition of "warm . . . spirits," "shroud," and "universal landlord" implies a fundamental inhumanity that is Caesar's private counterpart to his political practice.

In this respect Octavia is unhappily her brother's sister. To all Romans but Enobarbus—to Octavius, Agrippa, Maecenas,

Menas, and Antony himself—she is an ideal woman; and all share Maecenas' hope that her "beauty, wisdom, modesty, can settle / The heart of Antony" [II. ii. 240-41]. We come to perceive and admire these virtues, and so does Antony. But they cannot settle his heart, because Octavia appeals only to that forensic fragment of himself that found its halting voice in the overblown rhetoric of his farewell to Cleopatra. Enobarbus explains with customary accuracy her incompatibility with Antony: "Octavia is of a holy, cold, and still conversation" [II. vi. 122-23]; and her attempt to reconcile Antony and Octavius, although it is nobly aimed at preserving peace in the family and the world, is inadequately grounded in loyalty to Antony and justifies the description.

Shakespeare's image of Rome, then, is variegated and complex, yet coherent. I have spoken of the degradation of Roman values; but behind that lies a high ideal of selfless devotion to the public good, a belief that honor, honesty, and order come before profit and pleasure, and that men must be loyal above all to those public duties that guarantee the human community. This ideal brings Antony back to Rome and prompts his marriage to Octavia. But behind the idealized public values is the suppression of private feeling and the cold impersonality of the political leader. This human inadequacy of the Roman ideal leaves Antony's marriage spiritually unconsummated and frees him for Egypt. At its worst the Roman ideal is perverted into Octavius' systematic spoliation of the world. At its best it produces the holy coldness of Octavia, in whom the breath of life has been diminished almost to nothing.

Cleopatra is set in deliberate contrast to Octavia, and Cleopatra is nothing less than Egypt and human feeling. She is all heat and motion and immoderate overflowing; she can barely be contained in loving, teasing, and then missing Antony, and is overwhelmed into a kind of madness by her jealousy of Octavia. She is truly the incarnation of private life, and she begins by regarding all public loyalties as forms of timeserving. She resists totally Antony's efforts to subject his personal life to public standards: she assumes that his Roman obligations are distracting and irrelevant to his life with her, and she is merely impatient to discover that "A Roman thought hath struck him" [I. ii. 83]. Later she will be schooled to the importance of public values, so that after Antony's death she chooses to kill herself "after the high Roman fashion" [IV. xv. 87]. But at the beginning she balances Octavius and his sister by showing us both the perversion and the human inadequacy of merely private values.

In one sense Cleopatra is committed to the public world from the start, simply as Queen of the Nile. . . . [She] is a public figure whether she likes it or not; and . . . she takes a histrionic satisfaction in her role. But she refuses to honor by word or deed the expectations of the public world. She uses her public status simply as an instrument of her pleasure and an extension of her privacy. She is selfish and spoiled, and she overcomes all obstacles to her desire simply by making the world her oyster. For one thing, she needs the world as a large enough stage to support her Alexandrian revels. Nothing less than the public eye can do justice to the scope and vitality of her private life, and all her pleasures (or almost all) are had in the open. (pp. 42-5)

But however much Cleopatra lives her intimate life in the open air, private and public values do not meet and merge in her. Her beauty and passion vanquish all other considerations, and the public world exists simply to show her off. Cleopatra recognizes as a condition of her grandeur that she must outwit the world and bend it to her purpose. She devotes her intelligence and energy to cultivating those wily arts by which she can impose her interests upon the world and twist its great men around her fingers. The world must either be her plaything, as when she is ready to "unpeople" Egypt and fill the sea with messengers to express her passion for Antony, or it must be her enemy until it can be made her plaything. (pp. 45-6)

Cleopatra dazzles us by her wild effort to personalize all of life and to vivify the world by her beauty and her passions. To our own time, which repeatedly compares itself regretfully to Rome, her celebration of the self, with all its recklessness, seems vastly preferable to all calculated claims to selfless public virtue. But her recklessness is finally self-destructive. It is not simply that in her antipathy to Rome she resorts to deceits and violence that subvert legitimate public values like honesty, loyalty, marriage, and public order, no less than Octavius ignores private values. Just as the ideal of Roman public life, carried far enough, becomes in Octavius the impersonal Machiavellian cynicism that is its opposite, so Cleopatra's persistence merely in private pleasure brings her to an inchoate restlessness where the self has no contour and therefore no substance. At the beginning of the play her quick shifts from mirth to sadness are designed to beguile only Antony. But in the three marvelous scenes where she is busy missing Antony, when she shifts from dreams of mandragora to dreams of former lovers, and from music to billiards to fishing, she is trying to beguile herself; and without the discipline of any commitment to those public values that have separated Antony from her, she is as unsuccessful with herself, as she was with him. Her spirit can find no rest, and finally loses all coherence in venting itself upon the messenger who brings the news of Antony's marriage to Octavia. We find that outburst bewitching, perhaps, but only in the same uncomfortable way that we admire Octavius' sobriety at Pompey's banquet. For Cleopatra is doing violence not only to the messenger but to herself. In Cleopatra as in Octavius there is a surrender of human dignity, in him by an excessive self-control that stifles emotion, and in her by a failure of control that dissipates all emotion and causes Charmian to cry out, "Good madam, keep yourself within yourself, / The man is innocent" [II. v. 75-6]. Rome and Egypt truly require the discipline of each other. As I have suggested, that is the discipline Antony pursues. . . . (pp. 48-9)

From the time of Antony's return from Egypt until the end of the play, Shakespeare elaborates the vision he had achieved in *King Lear* in the climactic action of *Antony and Cleopatra*. There are no villains here, no separate forces of evil in the world. Octavius and Cleopatra are not Antony's enemies in any usual sense but only, in their different ways, his occasions for becoming an enemy to himself. Good and evil are seen as related aspects of his undivided being, and their conflict with each other is endlessly renewed from moment to moment. . . . From moment to moment he gains and loses and regains himself, always wrestling with his own nature, full of unalterable propensities for folly as well as heroism.

Lear, for all his final contrition, cannot change himself; but after what he has suffered, he needs his walled prison to protect him from further incitements of his own nature as well as from the world. Antony takes the next step, and without such protection risks his equally human frailty amidst the uses of the world, where he tries to make good his mistakes from moment to moment by becoming continuously responsible for his own nature. In this process Antony goes beyond contrition to magnanimity. He keeps giving of his treasure and his spirit, not in a grandiose gesture at the end but in repetitive discrete actions, to those who have no claim on him as well as to those whom his folly has hurt. Antony is spiritually elevated to a vision that is incomprehensible to the other characters, even while it continues to inspire, or to restore, their enormous loyalty to him. In the last half of the play we see Shakespeare moving toward that comprehension of life which is characteristic of his last plays; and we might say of the later Antony, changing only the sexual designation, what Florizel says to Perdita in *The Winter's Tale:*

> Each your doing,
> So singular in each particular,
> Crowns what you are doing in the present deed
> That all your acts are queens.
>   [*The Winter's Tale,* IV. iv. 143-46]

To follow Antony here (and Cleopatra later), is to follow the moral process by which one outgrows the politics of order. After his return to Egypt and for the rest of his life, Antony is unable to pursue an outwardly consistent or a politically responsible line of conduct. Although the reason of mankind sits in the wind against him, at Actium he decides to fight Octavius at sea rather than on land where his forces are more experienced. (pp. 123-24)

There is no reason . . . to doubt the accuracy of Antony's own explanation of his decision to fight by sea: "For that he dares us to't" [III. vii. 29]. If he was eager to challenge Octavius to single combat in the knowledge that he is the better swordsman [III. vii. 30], it is only appropriate that he accept Octavius' dare and risk a fight at sea where he has reason to think his opponent the better naval tactician. Antony not only accepts in Egypt his continuing obligation of Roman honor, he enhances that honor by investing it with a final meaning. Shakespeare now develops his most elaborate contrast between the timeserving policy of Octavius, which is "predestinated" to preserve the order of the state because it is aimed carefully at his "vantage," and the timeless honor of Antony, which outstrips the requirements of any possible doctrine of order in the state. Antony, so to speak, platonizes the conflict between himself and Octavius. He projects intact their present balance of power upon a transcendental battleground of moral values: he will endure voluntarily the unpredictable blows of fortune, in the form of Octavius' navy, even if Octavius will not risk his sword. Though it makes no practical difference where their duel is held, Antony proposes to fight Octavius "at Pharsalia / Where Caesar fought with Pompey" [III. vii. 31-2], as if to achieve a symbolic revenge for the young Caesar's betrayal of the young Pompey. In his earlier peace negotiations with Pompey, Antony did not underestimate his opponent's prowess by sea but declared himself nevertheless ready to risk a sea battle. Then he went on to remind Pompey of the triumvirs' strength by land and to conclude a peace negotiated on the basis of each party's recognition of the other's position of superior strength. His effort to make war with Octavius on the same basis constitutes the most scrupulous possible defense of that Roman honor which he earned in the negotiations with Pompey, and which Octavius betrayed by ruining Pompey in his grinding pursuit of power.

In *King Lear* . . . , the ability of the good characters to endure the ravages of fortune even unto death, although it answers Hamlet's question of what it means to really live, still does not comprise for Shakespeare the ultimate power or the human value of life. Now we begin to see why. Although the good characters of *King Lear* are active, not passive, their activity

only goes to prove that life has meaning and is therefore possible. Antony's willingness to risk a sea battle is not merely for the sake of defending the order of the world, his own place in it, and thereby the minimal meaning of life. That kind of action is now seen as only the protection of fortuitous, and hence irrelevant, worldly advantages. Antony's action is more disinterested than that; it is action undertaken for the wholly gratuitous reason that Octavius dares him to it. This voluntary submission to the uncertainties of fortune transforms endurance into magnanimity and infuses all of life with the particular meaning of Antony's new honor. Antony's submission generates new possibilities for life, and then goes on to value these possibilities according to the most rigorous ethical standards. Where Cordelia's necessary endurance was conservative, Antony's voluntary submission is creative. It brings new dimensions of right conduct into the range of possibility and thereby offers men new chances to make his own world. Cleopatra said at the beginning that she would "set a bourn how far to be belov'd" [I. i. 16]; and Antony told her she would then have to find new heaven and new earth. Now, in his insistence on the inmost meaning of Roman honor as the basis for his Egyptian strategy, Antony is beginning the search himself.

He is not only submitting himself to the most disinterested standard of Roman virtue but, at the same time, is reversing the process and painfully incorporating his union with Cleopatra in his affirmation of public values. From the beginning, of course, these public and private considerations have been connected for him: his liaison with Cleopatra has been the proximate cause of the civil war. But during this last residence in Egypt, just as in Rome before, he tries to outstrip the timeserving world of proximate causes. A man of worldly discretion, concerned immediately with his "vantage," would have listened to the choric exponents of reason who warned against Cleopatra's participation in the war. He would have ordered her to her boudoir to await the outcome in the company of a eunuch. But for Antony now, war must be the immediate and complete expression of his love as well as his honor. Just as he needs to risk Octavius' navy, so he is ready to have Cleopatra at his side in the sea battle; and later he will have her perform Eros' function of buckling on his armor for the land battle. (pp. 129-31)

Antony must have both worlds, now, Rome and Egypt. Octavius, in refusing the duel, and Cleopatra, in running from the naval battle, both obstruct him, each one pursuing only the "vantage" of his single meaning and thereby challenging Antony constantly to choose either one or the other. But Antony keeps moving back and forth, even here in Egypt, trying to encompass both; and this oscillating action becomes the locus of his final suffering and glory. One source of his suffering is that Octavius and Cleopatra leave him no room even to articulate his deepening vision. Another is his inability to make good that vision in continuous action, and hence his moment-to-moment maiming of one part or the other of his emergent identity. Nevertheless, his glory arises from that courage to be himself and spend himself which results from this failure, and which produces finally, if impermanently, the dazzling success of the land battle, with its confirming unification of Antony's manifold aspirations.

No major Shakespearean hero is so eloquent and severe in judging himself as the later Antony. Beside Antony's self-recriminations, the lesson of Lear's madness seems partial, and even Macbeth's celebrated conscience looks incomplete. (p. 132)

Amid his self-reproval, Antony keeps reminding himself and us of his former glory as "the greatest prince o' th' world" [IV. xv. 54]. He looks back nostalgically to the old Antony of reputation:

> Look thou say
> He makes me angry with him; for he seems
> Proud and disdainful, harping on what I am,
> Not what he knew I was. He makes me angry;
> And at this time most easy 'tis to do 't,
> When my good stars that were my former guides
> Have empty left their orbs and shot their fires
> Into th' abysm of hell.
>
>   [III. xiii. 140-47]

But in these consolatory references to his past, and there are many others, Antony does not evade the ethical demands of the present through a false image of himself. He knows that the past is indeed past, and he speaks repeatedly of the decline in his present fortunes. But even in the teeth of adverse fortune he tries to earn in the present the reputation of the past. His good stars may have shot their fires into hell, but in so doing they have left empty their orbs, which need to be refilled; he attempts to meet this need by his renewed challenge to Octavius for single combat and by his insistence upon coming back fighting, once Cleopatra has replenished him after the defeat at Actium. His consolatory speeches are not stages in the creation of a false image of himself that will enable him to ignore his debacle, like Richard II's, for example, or Lear's at the beginning; they are rather the final stages of recognition that began with self-reproval and that lead to that bounteous sharing of himself with others, both in strength and weakness, into which self-dramatization has now been transformed. From Actium onward Antony is unable to hide from himself. He has discovered the meeting ground between his two worlds; and if he is thwarted in his effort to occupy that ground, he is nevertheless unable to return to that stage of circumscribed awareness whose sign is self-deception. He cannot cheer himself up, as the earlier protagonists managed to do, because his unfulfilled aspirations have been so much more inclusive than theirs. He has been willing to risk all the selfhood that they tried to protect by self-dramatization, and this now earns him that creative enlargement of selfhood in magnanimity which becomes his final identity.

That identity is achieved in the whole action surrounding Antony's land victory that precedes his final defeat at sea. (pp. 135-36)

Antony announces that victory with a speech in which he regards his soldiers' triumph over the enemy as a result of their inner triumph over themselves, a transcendence of timeserving, in which public and private aspirations have been unified. The army itself has achieved for this moment what Antony aspired to by his challenge to single combat and his submission to a sea fight:

> We have beat him to his camp. Run one before
> And let the queen know of our gests. To-morrow,
> Before the sun shall see's, we'll spill the blood
> That has to-day escap'd. I thank you all;
> For doughty-handed are you, and have fought
> Not as you serv'd the cause, but as't had been
> Each man's like mine. You have shown all Hectors.
> Enter the city, clip your wives, your friends,
> Tell them your feats, whilst they with joyful tears

> Wash the congealment from your wounds and kiss
> The honour'd gashes whole.
>
>   [*To Scarus*] Give me thy hand.—
> To make this great fairy I'll commend thy acts,
> Make her thanks bless thee. [*To Cleo.*] O thou day
>   o'th' world,
> Chain mine arm'd neck! Leap thou, attire and all,
> Through proof of harness to my heart, and there
> Ride on the pants triumphing!
>
>   [IV. viii. 1-16]
>   (p. 138)

For Antony, nobody has served another's cause. Each man has made the public issue personal, and this fusion is projected into the future: a battle in which men have achieved their separate wholeness can leave no scars, and it takes only tears and kisses to restore health all round. Gashes are doubly honored when they are kissed whole. This equation between kisses and gashes, love and honor, culminates in Antony's final lines to Cleopatra. In the morning he had called her the armorer of his heart; now he invites her to achieve by her love what no man could do with a sword, to penetrate his armor and reach his heart, and yet not to displace the armor but to merge with it, and thus "ride on the pants triumphing." In that fabulous image Antony encompasses his whole range of experience and aspiration. Its obscenity reflects accurately one ingredient of his relation with Cleopatra, which must finally justify his approaching ruin. But its obscenity also becomes part of its exuberance, part of that enlargement by which naked privacy becomes a sign of public health and Antony's several parts of life are fused. For this moment Antony has made good in the world his greatest aspirations; he has become God's spy in the battle itself, not looking down from a protected viewpoint. This completes a process by which he has managed not to reject the world in its stale practice but to consume it, to use up and incarnate all its positive values. The seemingly erratic vacillations of conduct by which he moved back and forth from Egypt to Rome without denying either, and the suffering and self-reproval attendant upon that process, have enlarged him to a point where he is able to contain those public and private loyalties that were formerly opposed. He has achieved in his life, though only momentarily, the equation of love and honor, and he is ready to depart from the world leaving nothing wasted. He has earned the right to emerge on a plane of existence where "souls do couch on flowers" [IV. xiv. 51], which does not compensate his loss of the world but reflects his absolute mastery of life. On the morning after his victory on land, Antony himself announces this emergence in a line deeply prophetic of Cleopatra's later symbolic transformation. Going forth to the battle that will end in his defeat and death, he is already no longer a man but a spirit, ready not to give up the world but to fight for it in and through the very elements of which it is made:

> I would they'ld fight i' th' fire or i' th' air;
> We'ld fight there too.
>
>   [IV. x. 3-4]

The grand climax of the whole action is reserved for Cleopatra, who now learns the lesson of Antony's life, gives up her one-sided effort to bend the public world to her narrow purposes, and by her loyalty to him confirms Antony's achieved balance of public and private values. Until Actium, Cleopatra has tried to beguile Antony from his Roman thoughts and, in the process, has devoted her main energy to self-consciously primping herself up into an attractively elusive mistress. But with the defeat at Actium she begins to learn that the Roman honor that Antony now serves can never again be dismissed, evaded, or undermined. She has depended upon Antony either to ignore his public commitments in order to prove the measure of his love, as he was ready to do in the first scene of the play, or else to perform them in the perfunctory fashion of one who keeps his heart uncaught by the world and thus keeps himself worthy of her love. Much to her surprise, her expectations are continuously disappointed: Antony now insists upon a more rigorously defined honor than he had first gone to Rome to renew. That is why he is so violent in railing at himself and her, and Cleopatra is shocked and unprepared for his intensity. She recognizes after Actium that the elaborate stratagems by which she handled him earlier in the play can no longer be effective, but she does not know what alternatives to pursue, and she—Cleopatra!—is left speechless and nonplussed. She resorts to fragmentary, stuttering, disingenuous attempts to placate Antony and fend him off until she can gauge his mood and learn to respond accordingly. . . . It takes Antony's death to make her understand that he has passed as far beyond her Egyptian wiles as beyond . . . Roman reason. . . ; and even then, she only perceives the significance of Antony's final suffering and glory by having to re-enact it herself. Antony must be cleared out of the way, so to speak, before Cleopatra can recover her balance and her voice, for Antony, in his effort to connect his public and private interests, has in fact been protecting Cleopatra from any need to face the problem. Antony has been her buffer, and, in the paradoxical manner characteristic of tragedy, the price of Cleopatra's self-centeredness has been Antony's painful growth. (pp. 138-41)

When it becomes clear that her safety and her honor no longer can go together, when the world proves no more hospitable to her aspirations than it had been to Antony's, it turns out that she has used her cunning to prepare for the event. She has not merely used Dolabella to discover Caesar's plans for her and arranged to have the asps smuggled into her monument. In dealing with Caesar and his factors she has preserved her loyalty to Antony in such a fashion that her suicide can be a morally coherent event, the logical culmination of her life rather than an erratic, impulsive effort merely to rob death of its sting or to avoid embarrassment at Rome. Like Antony's, her suicide becomes a merging of safety and honor, private and public values. She has re-enacted Antony's experience, and thus has earned the right to platonize her aspirations and transform herself from a triple-turned whore into a true wife:

> Husband, I come!
> Now to that name my courage prove my title!
> I am fire and air; my other elements
> I give to baser life.
>
> [V. ii. 287-90]
> (p. 147)

[The] play's symbolic treatment of death as apotheosis, poised against the usual dramatic significance of death as catastrophe, marks an important place in Shakespeare's development. It looks backward to King Lear and Macbeth in that Shakespeare is not yet willing to lighten the weight of suffering and death as the price of human frailty and therefore of life itself. Yet he has outgrown the earlier conception of death as the avenging instrument of a providential order, for he has discovered in life an element of reconciliation that cannot be rendered in a naturalistic treatment of death. His symbolic treatment of that powerful force in the final speeches of Antony and Cleopatra looks forward to Cymbeline, The Winter's Tale, and The Tem-

pest, plays on the theme of reconciliation that are uniformly symbolic in method. But where we may sometimes feel in those last plays that Shakespeare's symbolic technique lightly veils the actual boundaries of life in order to avoid the inescapable significance of death, in Antony and Cleopatra his willingness to face up to death leaves no such evasive impression. Antony and Cleopatra encompasses both the naturalism of death in King Lear and the symbolism of reconciliation in The Tempest. That is why, in this play alone among Shakespeare's works, death itself is exuberant. And that in turn is why Antony and Cleopatra may be placed alongside King Lear and The Tempest as one of Shakespeare's supreme masterpieces. (pp. 150-51)

> Julian Markels, in his The Pillar of the World: "Antony and Cleopatra" in Shakespeare's Development, Ohio State University Press, 1968, 191 p.

A. P. RIEMER (essay date 1968)

[Riemer contends that Antony and Cleopatra is markedly different from Shakespeare's major tragedies, especially because it lacks both a sense of evil and any implicit metaphysical world with which the temporal one may interact. The play exists solely on "the human, social and political level," the critic holds, and "deals with issues intrinsically much less important than those of the great tragedies," so that its applicability to our lives is particular rather than universal or generalized. Riemer argues as well that we are less likely to identify with the protagonists here because, while Shakespeare permits us to understand them, he does not require us to evaluate them, and thus an effect of emotional detachment is established. Language and imagery also heighten this distancing and create ambivalences, the critic asserts, for even passages of swelling verse are frequently characterized by punning and hyperbole—deterring our emotional involvement—and are often surrounded by ironic commentary or action.]

In discussing whether Antony and Cleopatra can be properly seen as tragic, it is important to distinguish between two possible applications of the term. On a strictly formal level, Antony and Cleopatra fulfils the requirements of orthodox tragedy in its depiction of Antony's fall (and, incidentally, Cleopatra's) in reasonably decorous terms, even though a concomitant of traditional tragic theory—a strongly didactic or exemplary purpose—seems much reduced, if not totally absent. But there is no evidence to suggest that either Shakespeare or any major Elizabethan or Jacobean dramatist considered the fulfilment of these requirements sufficient for the production of tragedy, and in all their plays—even the most inept—there is a consistent attempt to present the protagonists and their situations in a significantly 'tragic' light. Inevitably for the English Renaissance, tragedy meant much more than the decorous treatment of certain exalted themes; it was always an attempt to explore the fate of mankind in a manner that recognised an interaction between the human and the metaphysical worlds. (p. 88)

A comment of Farnham's seems relevant at this point:

> As we pass from Macbeth to Antony and Cleopatra we see the problem of evil suddenly lose urgency for Shakespeare. In Antony and Cleopatra there are no villains. The hero and heroine have nothing of true villainy in them, and their ruin is not brought about, even in part, by villainy in others [see excerpt above, 1950].

No one would want to question this assertion seriously. The play is notable for Shakespeare's avoidance of presenting traits of personality as evil, especially when traditional attitudes provided specific grounds for such a presentation. Philo's speech at the opening of the play, which is the expression of an attitude towards Antony's dotage, could have presented the Roman's apostasy from duty as evil or sinful, but it remains merely an expression of personal regrets of anger, not a moral proposition in all but a purely expedient or worldly sense. . . . It is important to ask, however, whether it is possible for tragedy to exist without an awareness of evil in the strict sense of the term. Evil is more than ill-fortune or the self-seeking opportunism of mankind: as it appears in tragic literature, it is an aspect of a metaphysic, and without evil this metaphysical sense cannot exist. In all of Shakespeare's tragic drama written before *Antony and Cleopatra,* evil is predicated in the contravention of some concept of universal harmony or order which exists in these plays either explicitly or as a possibility (it is *Lear* alone of these plays that seriously questions the validity of this concept). Ultimately, the tragedies find their existence and intellectual as well as emotional articulation in this metaphysical world so conspicuously absent from *Antony and Cleopatra* and *Coriolanus.*

The metaphysic of the major tragedies is not easily definable: it does not reside in orthodox religious notions, even though Ribner attempted to endow Shakespeare with an attitude described as 'Christian humanism'. Yet, in the tragedies of the middle period, the actions of humanity are measured against an implied other world, one which cannot be discovered, but whose presence is felt instinctively by the play. When King Lear divides his kingdom and banishes Cordelia for refusing to partake of his love-auction, these are not merely actions of personal and political folly or of wanton cruelty. They contradict the demands of a mysterious order of harmony which, in that play, is other than the world of the human protagonists or their society, though it can be glimpsed only through human actions and institutions. Despite the melodrama of Lear's curse on Cordelia, his invocation is not merely fanciful or eccentric:

> For by the sacred radiance of the sun,
> The mysteries of Hecate and the night,
> By all the operation of the orbs,
> From whom we do exist and cease to be,
> Here I disclaim all my paternal care,
> Propinquity and property of blood,
> And as a stranger to my heart and me
> Hold thee from this forever.
>
> [*King Lear*, I. i. 109-16]

The sacred radiance of the sun, the mysteries of Hecate, the operation of the orbs are imaginative realities in that play, representing that mysterious other world which responds to the actions of humanity, and it is Lear's abuse of them that gives his curse such chilling magnitude.

But in *Antony and Cleopatra* this interrelation between the human and the metaphysical world is entertained only as a possibility, it is never accepted by the play, not even in the only 'metaphysical' scene, Act IV Scene iii. Cleopatra, when she learns of Antony's suicide, is given a speech strikingly similar in imagery to Lear's curse:

> O sun,
> Burn the great sphere thou mov'st in, darkling stand
> The varying shore o' the world.
>
> [IV. xv. 9-11]

but in this instance—one of the few points where such imagery is employed—the notions are pertinent only to Cleopatra and her state of mind at that moment, not at all to the play's view of its world. *Antony and Cleopatra* finds its existence, therefore, on the human, social and political level; it has no religious or metaphysical overtones, and its protagonists are presented only in relation to the temporal world in which they live. In such circumstances, tragedy is impossible. (pp. 95-7)

Neither Antony nor Cleopatra struggles against a world which is mysterious and ineffable, yet responsive to their actions: in this play the external world is merely that of human society, and because of the imaginative daring of the lovers, they seem easily to dominate this world which finally crushes them. In one sense (though clearly not in another), Antony and Cleopatra have much greater magnitude than Lear or Hamlet (despite their own peculiar magnitude) when they are pitted against their austerely tragic universe. It was noted . . . [earlier] that the disappearance of a metaphysical context went hand in hand with the banishment of the sense of evil from the play, and with this the strongest of tragic impulses has also vanished. *Antony and Cleopatra* cannot rise to that universality of application that the major tragedies possess, and this may indirectly account for the marked critical difficulty this work has produced.

The play does not lend itself to the metaphoric statements that abound in discussion of the other tragedies. Unlike *King Lear,* it does not explore the concept of nature; it is not intent on the examination of evil, as *Macbeth* seems to be; and it is not concerned with the nature of identity and self-knowledge which some critics find in *Hamlet. Antony and Cleopatra* is not generalized, but remains on a particular level: it is concerned with Mark Antony, with Cleopatra, with the fortunes of the late Republic, and it is this retention of the play on a particularized level (a result, largely, of the disappearance of the metaphysical context) that seems to bring about its restricted scope, as it does in some senses. But from this apparent restriction, there emerges a unique understanding of human behaviour and human relationships which extends to include the highest and most complex forms of secular activity, the processes of history and of public life. It is not fortuitous that in this play, as in *Coriolanus,* the absence of the metaphysical world is compensated for by an understanding of history and politics unsurpassed even by the overtly political history plays. Having liberated his world from the metaphorical and allegorical generalities of tragedy, Shakespeare was able, in these two plays, to present human life with keen understanding, he could present it with thrilling exuberance, and this is largely brought about by the suspension of specific moral judgements. The chief glory of *Antony and Cleopatra* is that it is capable of expressing these things in terms of superbly buoyant poetry, and, more remarkable still, that it can contain them in a treatment of the most emotional and 'metaphysical' of subjects, the story of great lovers.

The intellectual exuberance of the play is best observed through its poetry and through the characteristic detachment from moral judgements, and these can be seen particularly clearly in the opening scene where Shakespeare was obviously at pains to establish such concepts . . . Philo's speech at the opening of the play is a vivid and magnificent exposition of a Roman and specifically individual proposition: Antony's Egyptian sojourn is a dereliction from the most sacred dictates of patriotism and duty. The speech is strong, unequivocal and dramatic; its exaggerations, its astonishing range of imagery, which can comprehend Antony in the space of a line and a half of verse both as a 'triple pillar of the world' and as 'a strumpet's fool' [I.

i. 12, 13], prepare us for the qualification these views later receive. We are, in a sense, put on our guard against accepting them implicitly. By seventeenth-century standards of dramatic decorum, there is nothing remarkable about Philo's extreme articulateness or about the splendour of the images he employs. His function in this opening scene is apparently choric, and his presentation could have become as impersonal as that of the chorus in *Henry V* with whom he shares a number of characteristics. Yet remarkably, even when taken out of its context and removed from its surrounding qualifications, this speech communicates a deeply personal tone through its commitment to a particular ideal. When Philo speaks of Antony's eyes glowing like 'plated Mars', when he describes the object of their attention as a 'tawny front', and when the splendid, heroic image of Antony is reduced to 'a strumpet's fool', we are presented with a unique view of this world, one which comprehends these extraordinary contradictions. The result is that this intemperate condemnation of intemperance becomes contained within a morally neutral context. The presentation of this world of extremes, of empires, of heroic battles, of dark-skinned temptresses, appeals to our imaginative faculties through the daring and extent of its hyperbole. But the recognition that this is hyperbolic, exaggerated and hence individual, retains our response to the speech in an equipoise between its imaginative splendour and its clearly individual (possibly eccentric) bias.

This balancing of antitheses is perhaps even more remarkable in Antony's speech a few lines later, where once more a similar opposition persists:

> Let Rome in Tiber melt, and the wide arch
> Of the rang'd empire fall! Here is my space,
> Kingdoms are clay: our dungy earth alike
> Feeds beast as man; the nobleness of life
> Is to do thus: when such a mutual pair,
> And such a twain can do't. . . .
>
>   [I. i. 33-8]

These magnificently egoistic images (like Philo's superb contradictions) demand our imaginative endorsement, but this is kept in constant check by the dialectical context of the scene where these extreme attitudes are balanced against each other in a series of constantly shifting emphases. Consequently, our complete abandonment to the splendour of Antony's egoism (or the magnificence of Philo's vituperation) is prohibited, and this is largely the result of the essential detachment of the play from its material, a detachment which forces us to regard Antony's attitudes in this speech (and, more significantly, the expression of these attitudes) as parts of a dialectical process. What the dramatist creates for us is an understanding of a particular and fascinating situation, he does not require an evaluation of it.

Understanding in place of evaluation could almost become a motto for the play, but its application requires some elucidation. In the tragedies composed just before *Antony and Cleopatra*, Shakespeare requires from his audience and readers the adoption of more or less distinct attitudes towards the situations and the characters. This is, naturally, not a matter of simple priorities; the attachment to certain characters or certain attitudes is mostly paradoxical, and this reaches its culmination in *King Lear* where, in its opening scene, our feelings are torn between our endorsement of Cordelia's refusal to partake of her father's game of love-arithmetic, and our illogical sympathy with the magnitude of Lear's irrational and possibly evil passion. The unique effect of that play is achieved through Shake-

speare's constantly demanding from us an evaluation of Lear's world against Cordelia's, though, paradoxically, he prevents its occurrence, and this accounts for much of the nearly unendurable tension of the tragedy. There is a similar hiatus in *Antony and Cleopatra* between Philo's speech at the beginning and Antony's a few lines later; but these problems or propositions are of much less moment than the cosmic claims made at the beginning of *King Lear;* there is not enough universality in this opposition of the Roman ethos with the Egyptian one to engage our full moral and ethical senses. The debate in this play is concerned with questions of social behaviour (in the broadest sense of the term), not with universal concepts, and consequently the confrontation between contradictory attitudes does not proceed to the destructive cataclysm that overtakes *Lear* by its end of its first act. That more orthodox tragedy postulates the evaluation of its contrary worlds through the absoluteness of the terms in which they are presented, and, as already intimated, the agonized tension of the play is produced by the irresolution of a conflict that cries out for resolution. But the predominantly social problem presented in *Antony and Cleopatra* ensures that the urgency of the paradox is much reduced, and it is through this that the dramatist can produce that unique freedom and understanding of the play's situation which results directly from the fact that we remain, to a certain extent, uncommitted to its world and its people. Since the opening scene of *Antony and Cleopatra* deals with issues intrinsically much less important than those of the great tragedies, Shakespeare can afford to sustain in his audience an ambivalence of attitude which the universal, metaphysical and at times supernatural concerns of the other plays cannot allow. Precisely because we are able to remain indifferent to Antony's behaviour in Egypt (as we cannot be indifferent to Hamlet's dilemma or Lear's blind folly), we can participate in Shakespeare's superbly detached, intellectual presentation of this world where the magnificence and daring of the poetry is contained by its surrounding ironies and by our rational awareness of the situation. (pp. 101-05)

In [Enobarbus's] description of Cleopatra's progress on the Cydnus, in Antony's great 'tragic' moments, in Caesar's political maxims, and, above all, in Cleopatra's two splendid speeches in Act V, both the poetry and the play's overall structure preserve a much greater emotional and thematic distance between the characters and the audience than previously encountered in Shakespeare's tragic drama. The contrast is, once more, best provided by *King Lear:* when Lear fulminates on the heath in Act IV Scene vi, when he makes those blinding discoveries about nature and human society, his emotions and attitudes are transferred to the audience to a considerable extent—not completely, because total identification with the protagonist would destroy the play's tragic ambiguity. Nevertheless, when Lear achieves his discoveries, when his emotions rise to fever pitch, the audience participates with him, despite the fact that his madness is constantly emphasized in order to prevent his figure from swamping the meaning and significance of the scene. The power of the tragedy emanates in large part from the sizeable degree of identification between Lear and the audience; but in Cleopatra's great eulogy the identification is prevented by the surrounding ironies, and by Shakespeare's placing the language of this speech in a detached, isolated poetic context. When she discovers her vision of the dolphin-backed Antony, its impact is introverted: it is pertinent to her, to her role and the position she has reached at this point in the narrative, and it is consequently of the foremost importance; but these emotions are not transferred to the audience; we are not required to share either her feelings or the truth of her vision. All that is required of us is to recognize the splendid imagination which could produce this Antony who is 'nature's piece 'gainst fancy' [V. ii. 99], we are forced to admit that we have never met this Antony in the play, that possibly he has never existed, and yet we must recognize that the vision is *right* (supremely so) for Cleopatra herself, but that it is almost completely devoid of larger significance except that it allows us to achieve a unique understanding of the world in which these characters live. . . . [The] way in which Shakespeare surrounds Cleopatra's ecstasy with qualifying ironies partially ensures this, but the effect is further enhanced by the poetry itself which does not communicate an emotional tone, though it deals with one.

It is a contemporary critical *cliché* to liken the poetry of *Antony and Cleopatra* to the works of the metaphysical poets. Though there is considerable danger in overlooking the important differences between a dramatic construct and a lyric utterance, the comparison has some pertinence as long as it does not beguile the reader (and critic) into searching for non-existent parallels. But the language of Cleopatra's vision is strikingly similar to metaphysical poetry in its 'witty' detachment from the considerable emotional experience it generates in the character. Just as Donne's punning sophistications create an incongruous detachment from his emotion-charged ecstasies in such poems as 'The Canonization', in Cleopatra's speech, the light, buoyant rhythms and the Donne-like puns help to create a difference between the character's emotional state and the tone of the poetry. There is a certain metaphysical wit and consequent alienation of emotion in lines such as:

> For his bounty,
> There was no winter in't: an autumn 'twas
> That grew the more by reaping: his delights
> Were dolphin-like, they show'd his back above
> The elements they lived in . . .
>
> [V. ii. 86-90]

In both these statements Cleopatra is given what amounts to a metaphysical conceit, a figure of speech depending on its logical rather than emotive, sensuous or even simply metaphoric significance, and the consequent presence of punning serves the same function as the hyperboles of the metaphysicals: to minimize our emotional attachment to the situation, but to afford us a remarkable insight into and an understanding of the particular emotion and situation which produce it.

It is considerations such as these that give Cleopatra's last speech its telling effect. Here, at the moment of death, she rides on an immense wave of emotion, seeing herself as purified in spirit, now truly royal, courageous in her haste to join Antony. Rationally, we must recognize that this exalted state is the product of delusion; the notion of union in love after death is never entertained even as a 'poetic' possibility. But to insist on this is partly to miss the point of the speech, since our understanding of the situation is kept in check by Cleopatra's magnificent outpouring of emotion, and the result is a neutrality of attitude which can, nevertheless, include our being deeply moved by her experience. We feel pity for her—a pity free of sentimentality and mawkishness—and this also engenders a strong experience of admiration and wonder. But the sense of pity is not accompanied by the other facet of Aristotle's tragic dichotomy, the term usually translated as 'fear', by which he probably meant that emotional identification with the hero that accompanies the pity experienced for his fate. The pity we feel for Cleopatra is a sublime one, and it results directly from the structure of the play and from the nature of its poetry which

depends on intellectual not emotional use of image and rhetoric. The following is an excellent example:

> Come, thou mortal wretch,
> With thy sharp teeth this knot intrinsicate
> Of life at once untie: poor venomous fool,
> Be angry, and despatch. O, could'st thou speak,
> That I might hear thee call great Caesar ass,
> Unpolicied!
>
> [V. ii. 303-08]

Here the wonderful intricacy of life is seen in intellectualized terms in the adjective 'intrinsicate', and in this curious word, devoid of emotional overtones, and with those sharp vowel sounds often noticed in the play, the peculiar quality of the verse is epitomized. It is light and buoyant, keenly intelligent in its use of language, image and rhythm, but not at all communicative of the emotions with which it is concerned. Cleopatra's final words are in marked contrast to this, however. Here Shakespeare produces emotionalism of a sort that comes close to sentimentality:

> Peace, peace!
> Dost thou not see my baby at my breast,
> That sucks the nurse asleep?
>
> [V. ii. 308-10]

It is in this lachrymose vein that Cleopatra dies with the enigmatic words:

> As sweet as balm, as soft as air, as gentle.
>
> [V. ii. 311]

referring perhaps to death, perhaps to Antony or perhaps to the snake's fang. The effect of these lines is striking and daring: at the very end Shakespeare feels free to indulge in a form of sentimentality that could have ruined a play dealing with such overtly emotional material as this one. Yet so well has he established the general principle of detachment, the intellectual contemplation of this world, that these unashamedly emotional images can be absorbed into our understanding of Cleopatra at the moment of her death. There is, mercifully, no attempt to squeeze the last drop of pity from these words: we pity Cleopatra, we are moved by her death, but in a very different sense, and it is our essential lack of commitment that can allow Shakespeare to let her die thus. (pp. 107-10)

A. P. Riemer, in his A Reading of Shakespeare's "Antony and Cleopatra," *Sydney University Press, 1968, 119 p.*

ROY W. BATTENHOUSE (essay date 1969)

[*Battenhouse is well known for his studies on religion and literature and for his theory that Shakespeare's works embody a specifically Christian world view. In the excerpt below, he maintains that primarily through symbolism and diction, Shakespeare provides a deeply ironic perspective on the transcendence of the lovers in* Antony and Cleopatra, *thereby giving us the "true view" of the dramatic events. Antony's and Cleopatra's passion for each other and their deluded view of themselves as deities, Battenhouse argues, are parodied by allusions to the discrepancy between* eros *and* agape *and by "dark analogy to Christian legend." The critic further asserts that the lyricism and "gorgeous spectacle" of the drama are constantly disarmed by comic elements, and he discovers such parodic effects even in the death of Cleopatra, which he believes reveals "an underside of parody" that reflects Shakespeare's "own metaphysical wit." Battenhouse also addresses the issue of tragic anagnorisis, or self-knowledge, contending that although both Antony and Cleopatra achieve a measure of self-*

understanding, in neither instance is this followed by repentance or change of conduct.]

[Romanticists] such as G. Wilson Knight see in [*Antony and Cleopatra*] a metaphysic of "transcendental Humanism," in which life conquers death by a Phoenix-like love that is infinite and divine. At the end of the play, Knight believes, we are left "with a sense of peace and happiness, an apprehension of pure immortality" [see excerpt above, 1931]. Dover Wilson in part echoes this view by reading the play as Shakespeare's "Hymn to Man." [see excerpt above, 1950]. On the other hand, however, M. R. Ridley has characterized the passion of the lovers as "an *égoisme à deux*" [see excerpt above, 1954]; and to William Rosen the play's final events "approach the point of being ludicrous" [see excerpt above, 1960]. In Rosen's view, Cleopatra's suicide is her "consummate escape from the world and her most accomplished self-dramatization."

The romantic estimate, I would say, is little other than a latter-day amplification of the view the lovers assume. It is not ultimately Shakespeare's. As poet he is an adroit master of double perspective.... He knows well how to depict the psychology of self-fashioned dream, but his true view is the covert one which Ridley and Rosen have rightly sensed. The "transcendence" the lovers achieve is surrounded and punctuated therefore with Shakespeare's dramatic irony. The triumph in death which they imagine turns out to be both glamorous and hollow—evidence of a nobility in phosphorescent decay. Step by step the lovers delude themselves, fascinated from the start with their own dissembling and playacting. With soaring language they trick themselves into a world of heroic lie, which becomes for them a compensating eternity for the earthly disasters into which they betray love. Appropriately to tragic art, Shakespeare does not moralize this truth but indirectly reveals it as the reality beneath the grandly pitiful and fearful events of his story. Let us turn to an examination of the play to show how this is so, and to discover with what larger implications it is enriched.

Suppose we put aside for the moment the drama's first half and turn to its anagnorisis.... Do we not find Antony and Cleopatra arriving at a "discovery" which brings self-knowledge in a desperate sense only? A remorse is evident, although more self-critical on his part than on hers, after their flight from Actium has disgraced them and reversed their fortunes. The immediate means of anagnorisis is here the flight itself, by which Antony recognizes in himself a person tied to Egypt's rudder. He then feels an over-whelming shame for having "offended reputation"; and Cleopatra cries out, "Forgive my fearful sails!" [III. xi. 55]. Yet this is not a self-knowledge which brings repentance. Antony does nothing toward giving up the rash doting for which he reproves himself, nor does Cleopatra give up her coquettish angling. His lament that "Now I must . . . dodge / And palter in the shifts of lowness" [III. xi. 61-3] strikes us as an epitome of what both he and Cleopatra have been doing in this scene and will continue to do. With shifts and dodges, they will palter not only with Caesar but with each other. Their actions thus enter on a maze of self-contradiction. Cleopatra has such "full supremacy" over his spirit, says Antony, that she might command him "from the bidding of the gods" [III. xi. 60]; yet two scenes later he is railing at her, himself now playing the role of a jealous god. Raging, he upbraids *her* for intemperance. What Antony's anagnorisis expands into, in these scenes, may be summed up in several phrases: "I / Have lost my way forever"; "Let's mock the midnight bell"; "I'll make death love me" [III. xi. 3-4; III. xiii. 184; III. xiii. 192].

Discovery takes on a second phase when, in a later contest at sea, all of Cleopatra's ships desert, this time to join Caesar's. With fortunes now utterly hopeless, Antony cries out:

> O this false soul of Egypt! This grave charm,
> Whose eye becked forth my wars and called them home,
> Whose bosom was my crownet, my chief end,
> Like a right gypsy hath at fast and loose
> Beguiled me to the very heart of loss.
>
> [IV. xii. 25-9]

Here he recognizes that his "chief end" has been the bosom of a "Triple-turned whore" [IV. xii. 13], and that her eye is indeed a "grave" charm, since it has brought him to a shirt of Nessus, like that which destroyed Hercules. The "witch" shall die for it, he resolves. Yet the revenge to which he now turns is essentially a reverse kind of jealous dotage. And when, a moment later, a report comes that Cleopatra has beaten him to the crownet of a love-death, by having already slain herself, Antony quickly tacks about in order to sail after and emulate her supposed courage. His dream at this point of emulating Aeneas is Shakespearean irony, for it was by sailing away from Dido that the historical Aeneas showed *his* courage. (pp. 161-63)

Even Antony's last labor, his attempt to ennoble death as a lover's bed, is undercut by comic aspects. He bungles his suicide, and lives to learn that Cleopatra has merely faked hers. His dignity is then reduced to being carried, marred of body, to a Cleopatra who is more concerned for her own safety than for his. Unceremoniously he must be hoisted up to her, with what Cleopatra in mock-irony calls "sport indeed." And when at last in her arms, he finds his own efforts to speak interrupted by hers. (This is characteristic: she had interrupted him six times in Act I, scene iii.) The whole scene has a different import from Plutarch's: Shakespeare's Cleopatra wipes away no blood on Antony's face, does not here greet him as husband, or forget her own misery for his. Instead, she upstages him in self-dramatization. The very hyperboles in which she sings his greatness call our attention chiefly to herself. And ironically, the self-discovery she proclaims after his death is that she has "no friend" except her own resolution. The Antony of her imagination, we infer, cannot be thought her friend.

Cleopatra's experience of tragic recognition, until this scene, has been minimal. She has known, earlier, moments of disfavor which always have seemed reparable by shifts of one kind or another. But now Antony's suicide confronts her not only with the loss of an idol of her affections but (more importantly) with imminent danger of public obloquy, since how can she henceforth avoid rebukes from Octavia, or be safe from display as a showpiece by Caesar? It is this fear, only marginally admitted, that makes of Antony's dying such a doomsday event for her. "O sun, / Burn the great sphere thou movest in!" she cries [IV. xv. 9-10]. Let there be a general conflagration of the world. For, otherwise, only by the operation of knife, drugs, and serpents can she keep "safe" her honor!

The size of Cleopatra's sorrow is proportioned to this half-repressed worry. Fear prompts, we can suspect, much of the fervor of her wish that she could quicken Antony with kissing. "Noblest of men, woo't die? / Hast thou no care of *me*?" [IV. xv. 59-60]. Here the note of self-concern (which Shakespeare correlates with a linguistic lapse into the vulgar "woo't"—as in Hamlet's mouthing in the graveyard) hints the real nature of her plight. The absence of Antony makes the world seem for her no better than a sty—not simply because Antony can be imagined as the "crown o' the earth" [IV. xv. 63] and the world's "jewel," but because now she finds melting in her hands, and slipping from them, a crown and gem on which her own glory as Queen-mistress depends. The "garland" that is withering was *her* prize, the trophy to *her* greatness. This fact, not openly confessed, is our clue to why she rails at "the false housewife Fortune" [IV. xv. 44]—as if thereby to hide from her own offense of false housewifery. It can explain, likewise, her impulse to "throw my scepter at the injurious gods" [IV. xv. 76], for now her own status as an earthly goddess is at stake. Her threat brings to focus her resentment of the gods, whom paradoxically she would rival by her own self-deification. Shakespeare allows her the ironic self-recognition of desperation:

> impatience does
> Become a dog that's mad. Then is it sin
> To rush into the secret house of death
> Ere death dare come to us?
>
> [IV. xv. 79-82]

Implicit here is a haunting sense of sin, from which she can be free only by making herself first mad. For then (as a dog in a sty) she will be able to rush "becomingly" to the house of death which hides her secret fear of loss of status.

In this circumstance we see her turning instinctively . . . to a make-believe joy:

> What, what! Good cheer! Why, how now, Charmian!
> My noble girls! Ah, women, women, look,
> Our lamp is spent, it's out!
>
> [IV. xv. 83-5]

The lamp that is "spent," ironically, is here (while overtly that of Antony's life) covertly that of daylight reason and troublesome conscience. And the imagery further suggests the queen of a house of ill fame cheering up her girls. This underside of the truth, the quean or wench within the female monarch, is the secret of Cleopatra's gay self-abandon.

> Let's do it after the high Roman fashion,
> And make death proud to take us.
>
> [IV. xv. 87-8]

Yet such transcendence, of course, is the reverse of John Donne's "Death, be not proud." It accords, rather, with that of the cult which Plutarch mentions as flourishing in Alexandria during the days after Actium—the order called *Synapothanumenon*, of those who agreed to die together and made great feasts to their fraternity, while Cleopatra studied poisons for ease of self-destruction.

But just as there were shifts and delays between Antony's first declaring a love of death and his final suicide, so likewise in Cleopatra's case. Despite her famed "celerity in dying" [I. ii. 144], she must so to speak hop a forty paces first, in order to make defect seem perfection, and thus delusively wind up our breathlessness into blessing what's riggish. (pp. 164-66)

Even when locked in her monument, Cleopatra squirms and wriggles—to probe the possibility of gaining a new earthly status from Caesar. In asking instruction of him

> That she preparedly may frame herself
> To the way she's forced to
>
> [V. i. 55-6]

is she not ambiguously inviting him to "force" her to be his mistress? But Caesar can be equally ambiguous. His reply is that he "cannot live / To be ungentle" [V. i. 59-60]. That tells

her nothing of what he means by "gentle." She desires to learn an "hourly" obedience, she replies, but first would gladly look him in the face. A moment later, when Proculeius breaks in, she stresses her determination never to submit to Octavia's chastising eye or to Rome's varletry. Then, through hymning to Dolabella her dream of Antony's "bounty," she seduces Dolabella to tell her Caesar's secret intentions.

Thus forewarned, Cleopatra tries her most brilliant tactic for melting Caesar's purpose. She turns a defect into perfection, as regards her false account of money matters, by explaining that she has but kept some token for friendly use—for instance to induce Livia and Octavia to mediate on her behalf. Is she not implying that as Caesar's mistress she would know how to mollify his wife and sister? At the same time, through blushes and a tongue-lashing of Seleucus, she is advertizing her femininity and her need for a lordly understanding on Caesar's part, a "mercy" toward her frailties. But Caesar will not be seduced, even though she twice calls him "My master and my lord!" [V. ii. 116, 120]. "Not so. Adieu," he replies [V. ii. 200]; a "friend" only will he be. This is not what she wants. It leaves her with the choice of either living to see her arts disgraced in public parody or being "noble to myself" [V. ii. 192] through suicide. A middle road, that of accepting personal humiliation in order to keep her kingdom for her sons, she never considers. Instead, she now issues orders to put into effect her contingent plan for the aspic trick.

Shakespeare has made the death scene itself a gorgeous spectacle of tragic irony. Every detail has an emblematic quality. The figs and the worm have obvious sexual connotations as well as symbolizing, more generally, an earthy lushness and the poisonous serpent this harbors. When the First Guard remarks afterwards, "And these fig leaves / Have slime upon them" [V. ii. 351-52], we are reminded of the fig leaves of the Genesis story, there used as a cover for shame, or we think of the slime of the Nile, which Cleopatra herself had associated with decay and gnats. "Look you," says the clown, "the worm is not to be trusted but in the keeping of wise people, for indeed there is no goodness in the worm" [V. ii. 265-67]. Yet we see Cleopatra welcoming this "pretty worm of Nilus" [V. ii. 243]; for now nihilism is being imagined as liberty.

We perhaps here recall her earlier curse, "Melt Egypt into Nile. And kindly creatures / Turn all to serpents!" [II. v. 78-9]. She had invoked that curse when venting anger on a supposed "rogue" and "villain" who had brought her unwelcome news. But now she is fulfilling it in herself. Her words are truer than she knows when she resolves:

> I have nothing
> Of woman in me. Now from head to foot
> I am marble-constant. . . .
>
> [V. ii. 238-40]

From head to foot she is in fact making herself marble-hearted—thus negating true womanhood for the stony immortality of an Egyptian mummy. Genuine motherhood (i.e., any care for her living sons) is being neglected, while constantly she dreams of the serpent she can nurse as her "baby." This magnificent parody of love is Shakespeare's invention, not mentioned by Plutarch.

Added also by Shakespeare is the telltale fact . . . that the crown Cleopatra calls for is set on her head "awry," giving her queenship a comic aspect. Further, her very kiss becomes one of death, when Iras falls dead after kissing her. "Have I the aspic in my lips?" she asks [V. ii. 293]—and then speaks of her eagerness to have Antony spend his kiss on her lips. That would be her Heaven. We recall at this point her earlier vow that if ever she were cold-hearted toward Antony, let Heaven dissolve her life by dropping a poisoned hailstone in her neck. Is this not being figuratively fulfilled within a neck, poisoned with jealousy, which now we see Cleopatra dying to offer Antony? Jealous love essentially is a paradoxical fire of cold-heartedness which dissolves life by slaying with its embraces. (Compare the kiss with which Othello killed Desdemona, in the name of a ''marble Heaven.'') In Cleopatra's case we note, as the final spur to her suicide, a jealousy lest her so-called ''husband'' spend his kiss on Iras. The moral irony of this Shakespearean detail is equalled only by what follows, Cleopatra's placing of the asp as a kind of brooch to her royal robe. Triumph can then be made satisfying by scornfully calling Caesar an ''ass''—after which comes the music of a swan song, concluded by Charmian's comment:

> Death, in thy possession lies
> A lass unparalleled. Downy windows, close . . .
> [V. ii. 315-16]

In a double sense, here, Cleopatra's eyes are ''downy'': feathered with a swansdown loveliness, while shuttered down against the light of truth. (pp. 166-68)

Thus while on the surface of Shakespeare's dramatic scene there has been resounding an entrancing lyricism, his symbolism and his canny choice of diction have revealed an underside of parody, reflecting his own metaphysical wit. He has furnished us, moreover, a counterpointing folk wisdom on the part of Egypt's rural clown. This serves much the same purpose as do the remarks of the Gravedigger-clown in Act V of *Hamlet*. Cleopatra's joy, in this witty servant's estimate, is ''joy of the worm'' [V. ii. 279]. Those who die of it, he adds, ''do seldom or never recover'' [V. ii. 247-48]. A woman ''something given to lie'' [V. ii. 252] may make ''good report'' of the worm; yet anyone who will believe all that such reporters claim ''shall never be saved by half that they do'' [V. ii. 256-57]. After this jest, and another on how the devil can ''mar'' five out of every ten women (a parabolic jest which Shakespeare may be adapting from his recollection of the biblical virgins who failed to keep oil in their lamps), surely at least a few of the play's auditors, perhaps five out of ten, should be able to recognize Cleopatra's love-death for what it is, a martyrdom *marred* by vainglory.

Let us pursue further the wit of the play, even at the risk of discovering a Shakespeare cunning past man's thought. . . . [Scenes] of low comedy in a tragedy provide the author a medium through which he can toy with some major motifs in his main theme. With this in mind, let us recall from II. vii. Antony's mock-description of the Egyptian crocodile. This strange serpent, Antony tells Lepidus, moves with its own ''organs,'' and ''the elements once out of it, it transmigrates'' [II. vii. 45]. The figurative relevance of this to Cleopatra, Antony's well-organed ''serpent of Old Nile'' [I. v. 25], can scarcely escape audience notice. Further, part of this lore's amusement depends on its outlandish superstitiousness—which for Elizabethan auditors could evoke their contrasting knowledge of Christian doctrine. That is, they could recognize in Egypt's notion of immortality a fake ''mystery,'' the comic reverse of Christian mystery lore. In this same scene, a remark by Lepidus may have a similar overtone for the audience. ''I have heard the Ptolemies' pyramises,'' he says, ''are very goodly things'' [II. vii. 34-5]. Since Lepidus apparently means to say ''pyramids,'' his slip of the tongue is comic as suggesting

a drunken lisp. But besides this, I think, ''pyramises'' can be taken as a Shakespearean pun on the fiery ''misses'' of Egypt; or it can be heard as an allusion to Pyramus of Babylon, the Asian world's archetypal hero of love-death legend. And since Babylon and Egypt are synonymous in Christian typology, any indirect mention of Pyramus could remind an Elizabethan auditor of the whole catalog of paganism's ''saints''—which in Chaucer's listing was headed by Cleopatra, and next to her, Thisbe. The immediate dramatic irony is that Antony might have recognized in the malapropism of Lepidus a prophecy of his own fate as a ''Pyramus.'' (Just as Pyramus slew himself on mistakenly supposing his beloved dead, so likewise will Antony do.) Yet how many of *us* would be alert enough to catch ''oracle'' in the babblings of a winebibber?

Chaucer was certainly being ironic in his *Legend of Good Women*. There was ''nevere unto hire love a trewer quene'' than Cleopatra, he tells us, but at the same time pictures her as choosing, for the climax of her love, a pit full of serpents. His point, both sly and compassionate, is that she was a martyr to blind Cupid, even to the nth power of Cupid's godhead, a pitiably idiotic worship to which good women are prone—especially in Egypt, which Christians know to be a land of ''fleshpots'' and spiritual darkness, to which Babylon is a next door neighbor, both of them parodies of life's ''promised land.'' Chaucer's reserve in not making this implication explicit is the mark of his ontological, rather than didactic, focus. In this respect he anticipates the genius of Shakespeare's art.

Both poets no doubt shared the estimate of Cleopatra which prevails in Western tradition. (pp. 168-70)

Whereas Roman authors emphasized usually Cleopatra's lustfulness and Antony's intemperance, Christian authors tended to focus on her hellish guile and on Antony's idolatry. This latter stress on the falsely religious attitude of the lovers was a more ultimate dimension in characterizing them. That is, they were understood as parodies of Christian sainthood. . . .

Precisely because pagan flight mimics Christian pilgrimage, and because an exclusive dependence on *eros* can counterfeit the higher version of love which Christians call *agape*, there is analogy between these two which renders the substitute version ironic. (p. 170)

Shakespeare seems to be suggesting a dark analogy to Christian legend in the story of Antony and Cleopatra. Antony's farewell supper in Act IV, for instance, has a tantalizing similarity to Christ's Last Supper. There is a traitor at the table in the person of Enobarbus, who will later kill himself in remorse. Antony is trying to comfort his followers. He does so with phrases such as ''Scant not my cups,'' ''Haply you shall not see me more,'' ''Tend me tonight two hours,'' and ''I hope well of tomorrow, and will lead you / Where rather I'll expect victorious life . . .'' [IV. ii. 21, 26, 32, 42-3]. These words have a ring oddly like Christ's. But there is an underlying contrast to the Christian paradigm. Antony is inviting his men to ''drown consideration'' in drink; his purpose for the morrow is to ''fight maliciously.'' On that next day, indeed, his most loyal follower, Scarrus—who for Shakespeare, let me suggest, may be a kind of parody of Christ's ''beloved'' disciple, John—is so inspired to the ''sport'' of war that he now fights

> As if a god in hate of mankind had
> Destroyed in such a shape.
> [IV. viii. 25-6]

For this, Scarrus is rewarded by being given Cleopatra's hand to kiss (compare Calvary's "Woman, behold thy son!" and "Son, behold thy mother," of John 19:27), while Antony cries out: "Behold this man" [IV. viii. 22] (a parody of the Ecce Homo of John 19:6). Perhaps even the detail of Scarrus' scar has an emblematic significance. It formerly, we are told, had the shape of a "T" (which suggests true sacrifice, prefiguratively that of the cross), whereas now it has the shape of an "H" (which suggests, besides the pun on "ache," an upended and overdone "T," perhaps a "Hades" wound).

Shortly after this, Antony himself becomes an ironic Christ. His side pierced, he is lifted up limp on a stone monument, to commit there his spirit to Cleopatra's arms. Then we see Cleopatra, in turn, dead set against the kind of suffering which Christians associate with Calvary, and which Shakespeare's diction evokes. It would disgrace her if

> Mechanic slaves
> With greasy aprons, rules and hammers, shall
> Uplift us to the view.
>
> [V. ii. 209-11]

Rather than any such submitting to Rome's rule, she resolves to "make / My country's high pyramides my gibbet" [V. ii. 60-1]! Within Egypt's pyramid she then stages a self-immolation which unwittingly parodies a crucifixion.

Some readers may feel that I have been probing excessively the implications of Shakespeare's language. There may be a nettle danger here, I grant; yet if we run from it we risk not grasping the full import of the play. Shakespeare's details of story, it seems to me, serve two purposes simultaneously: the enriching of surface splendor with touches of realistic verisimilitude, while yet so selecting these as to point an underside of irony. And the full dimension of this irony includes some dark analogy to Christian lore by the echoing of a contrast.

Recent support for this way of reading the play comes from a note by Peter Seng [in his essay "Shakespearean Hymn Parody?"] on the "Egyptian Bacchanals" which conclude the galley scene of Act II. Seng has discovered that the song, "Come thou monarch of the vine," which a boy is brought forward to sing while Antony leads the Triumvirs in holding hands, has a stanza form, rhyme scheme, and metrics which duplicate those of the Christian pentecostal hymn *Veni sancte spiritus* [Come holy spirit]. He reasons that Shakespeare is here capping the ironic tensions of the Triumvirs' peace covenant with a parody of Christian pentecostal experience. Marvelous parody it indeed is, especially if we consider its context in the drama—the patched-up nature of the peace these "brothers" are making. For the better sealing of their union, Caesar has approved a marriage of convenience, which Antony accepts; but we overhear the prediction of Enobarbus that "the band that seems to tie their friendship together will be the very strangler of their amity" [II. vi. 120-22]. This will prove true—not only because the friendship bond of a "holy" Octavia will be neglected by Antony, but because the motive for his doing so will be his preference for the spirit of Egyptian bacchanal, which will become a dissolvent, not a bond, of his political friendship with Caesar. And further, there is the irony that this will cause Enobarbus himself to turn traitor to Antony, since Enobarbus' own loyalty, as resting principally on conventional self-advantage, cannot hold up when Egyptian bacchanal takes over Antony.

Contextually we are aware also that the covenant between the Triumvirs is being made aboard a pirate's galley, a fit emblem of Rome's ship of state at this moment. ("Without justice, what are kingdoms but great piracies?" is a question St. Augustine asks in his *City of God*.) It is noteworthy, however, that Caesar, the one man on this ship who remains sober by scanting the wine of the festival, soon afterwards finds occasion to rid himself of the pirate Pompey, and then in a final contest at sea rids himself of Antony. Since Antony's break with Caesar is in the name of Pompey's honor, with which he closely associates his own (see III. iv), Antony is by implication a second Pompey, a greater pirate. And if we recall how in *Measure for Measure* Shakespeare had associated the name Pompey with bawdry, absurd pomp, and piracy, we realize that the moral aura there comically dramatized is serving here in *Antony and Cleopatra* as the subsurface of tragic story.

Another motif in Shakespeare's symbolism is embodied in the character Eros. The name and role of Eros had been briefly mentioned by Plutarch but is much expanded by Shakespeare, who sounds the name a total of twenty-one times. The first mention is when Enobarbus calls out, "How now, friend Eros!" [III. v. 1] at the beginning of Act III, scene v. The immediately preceding scene, let us note, began with Antony's words, "Nay, nay, Octavia . . ." [III. iv. 1]. Through juxtaposing these scenes, Shakespeare may be suggesting that once Octavia is shuffled off by Antony he will turn to Eros for a substitute friendship. When we next see Eros, in III. xi, he is urging Cleopatra to comfort Antony; and by IV. iv. he has become Antony's armorer. But now Cleopatra is virtually identified with him when, arising from bed to give Eros assistance, she is called by Antony "The armorer of my heart" [IV. iv. 7]. "False, false," Antony then mutters—with apparent reference to some misbuckling by Eros and Cleopatra, yet allowing the play's auditors to apply these words also in a moral sense. A few lines later, we hear Antony say: "Thou fumblest, Eros, and my Queen's a squire / More tight at this than thou" [IV. iv. 14-15]. More tight at what? At buckling Antony into what will become, before long, his shirt of Nessus? This implication seems to overarch the literal dialogue. For when Antony in Act IV, scene xii, becomes aware of his Nessus-shirt, his outcry is against a bosom partner who has "at fast and loose / Beguiled me to the very heart of loss" [IV. xii. 28-9]. And at this point, as Leeds Barroll has noted [in his essay "Enobarbus' Description of Cleopatra"], the ambiguity of Eros as Queen becomes the subject of an entrance confusion. Antony calls out, "What, Eros, Eros!" [IV. xii. 30]—but instead of Eros, Cleopatra enters. Antony thereupon shouts: "Ah, thou spell! Avaunt!" [IV. xii. 30]

The whole situation figuratively seems to epitomize Antony's plight: he would call in Eros to solace him, yet Cleopatra herself stands for *eros*. He adds the cry: "Vanish, or I shall give thee thy deserving" [IV. xii. 32]. Ironically, both Eros and Cleopatra will later give themselves their deserving by vanishing into suicide. But, further, Antony's own suicide will be punctuated by the cry: "Eros!—I come, my Queen. Eros!—Stay for me" [IV. xiv. 50]. In this line, the identity of three-in-one (Antony, Eros, and Cleopatra) is complete. . . . [Metaphysically] considered, eros is paganism's dark analogue of agape, its passion parody of Saving Passion. (pp. 173-76)

Our concern in probing the language and structure of *Antony and Cleopatra* has been to demonstrate, through accumulative evidence, how a drama can carry clues to interpretation which are beyond the ken of its protagonists. A Christian author when dramatizing pagan times can punctuate his story with a figurative overplot, and its diction with an underside of meaning.

Thereby he challenges us to grasp the final significance of the action by the light of a Christian *Weltanschauung*. A recent editor's remark that in Shakespeare's day "Western Europe knew very little of Egypt, either ancient or contemporary" [John Dover Wilson, in his introduction to *Antony and Cleopatra*], is only half true. It overlooks the typological knowledge of Egypt which all readers of Scripture had, not merely from the book of Exodus but as a continuing symbolism throughout the Old and New Testaments and especially in the book of Revelation. Egypt, typologically, was a land of fleshpots, sorcerers, and bondage, whose rulers could vacillate between generosity and hardness of heart, and whose unholy civilization God punished by plagues. Would Shakespeare's auditors not have recalled these associations when viewing a play which echoes them in its imagery, and in which the name Egypt is sounded (see Bartlett's *Concordance*) in forty-two separate speeches? Additionally, the word "Egyptian" occurs eleven times. Only a scholar would wonder at these ill-omening numbers. Many an ordinary spectator, however, would sense in Antony's question, "O, whither hast thou led me, Egypt?" [III. xi. 51] and in his twice-repeated final cry, "I am dying, Egypt, dying" [IV. xv. 18, 41], a figurative and thematic summation of his tragedy.

These facts of symbolism can prompt us to modify somewhat the view of critics who would hold, as W. K. Wimsatt does, that *Antony and Cleopatra* is "a great poem, yet immoral" [see Additional Bibliography]. The play "celebrates" or "pleads for" certain evil choices, says Wimsatt, by presenting them "in all their mature interest and capacity to arouse human

Act V. Scene ii. Iras, Cleopatra, and Charmian. By Heinrich Spiess. The Department of Rare Books and Special Collections, The University of Michigan Library.

sympathy." This is partly the case, no doubt. We do see evil choices being celebrated by the play's tragic personages. Yet what about the irony, invisible to these actors but built into the play? When, for instance, Eros hails Antony as "that noble countenance / Wherein the worship of the whole world lies" [IV. xiv. 85-6], is the play merely pleading for us to admire Antony? If we but give the line a double take, do we not recognize that *the world* indeed *lies* in worshipping face? This covert *sententia*, I suggest, is a moral which can mature our estimate of the morals of the tragic actors.

The classic concept of imitation, which ultimately Wimsatt mentions, seems to me our best approach. The play imitates, he suggests, "the reasons for sin, a mature and richly human state of sin." To this I would only add (what Wimsatt omits saying), that sin is richly human in the sense of "all too human"—with a richness which Shakespeare shows as maturing to the ruin of man's essential humanity. The play's artistic imitation of immorality implies an ontology. It shows us the awesomely pitiful glory of actions truly ab-hominable. If it arouses our sympathy for sin, it does so in order that by our witnessing sin's devastations we may be brought to pity the grandeur we have initially admired. (pp. 181-82)

Roy W. Battenhouse, "Toward Clarifying the Term 'Christian Tragedy'," in his Shakespearean Tragedy: Its Art and Its Christian Premises, *Indiana University Press, 1969, pp. 131-203.*

PHYLLIS RACKIN   (essay date 1972)

[*Rackin argues that* Antony and Cleopatra *dramatizes aesthetic questions about "the nature and value of art," the veracity of the poet, and the concept of "the golden world of poetry" and "the brazen world of Nature." The Romans' reliance upon quantitative measurement "as an index of truth" and their skeptical response to the lovers' rhetoric, she contends, echo Plato's assertion that rational principles are required to counter the lies and delusions fostered by the poet. Rackin maintains that the Romans' objection to Cleopatra stems from their distrust of her "seeming" and "showing"—activities that link her directly with her creator. In the final scene of the play, she avers, Shakespeare undermines his earlier comic portrayal of the queen as he depicts her renouncing all her weaknesses, "showing" her greatness, reincarnating her love for Antony in the golden world of the imagination, and at last convincing even Octavius that her vision is reality.*]

> The quick comedians
> Extemporally will stage us, and present
> Our Alexandrian revels: Antony
> Shall be brought drunken forth, and I shall see
> Some squeaking Cleopatra boy my greatness
> I' the posture of a whore.
>
>   [V. ii. 216-21]

In these lines, Shakespeare's Cleopatra describes for her women the treatment they will receive in the theater if they allow themselves to be taken to Rome. . . .

Shakespeare's strategy in this speech is worth exploring, for it is daring to the point of recklessness, and it provides a major clue to his strategy in the play as a whole. The treatment Cleopatra anticipates at the hands of the Roman comedians is perilously close to the treatment she in fact received in Shakespeare's theater, where the word *boy* had an immediate and obvious application to the actor who spoke it. Insisting upon the disparity between dramatic spectacle and reality, implying the inadequacy of the very performance in which it appears, the speech threatens for the moment the audience's acceptance of the dramatic illusion. And the moment when the threat occurs is the beginning of Cleopatra's suicide scene—her and her creator's last chance to establish the tragic worth of the protagonists and their action.

Recklessness, perhaps most apparent here, is in fact the keynote of Shakespeare's *Antony and Cleopatra*: it is the characteristic not only of the love and the lovers the play depicts but also of its dramatic technique. The play seems perfectly calculated to offend the rising tide of neoclassical taste and to disappoint rational expectation. The episodic structure, with its multiplicity of tiny scenes ranging in setting from one end of the known world to the other, directly opposed the growing neoclassical demand for the Unities. . . .

Recklessness is apparent also in the language of the play, with its curious mixture of the most elevated Latinisms and the coarsest contemporary slang, its mixed metaphors, its elliptical constructions, and its exuberant disregard for grammatical convention. (p. 201)

What is perhaps most reckless of all, and most offensive to neoclassical taste, is Shakespeare's presentation of his heroine, for his Egyptian queen repeatedly violates the rules of decorum. If Sir Philip Sidney found the mingling of kings and clowns distasteful [in his *An Apologie for Poetrie*], one can imagine his reaction to a queen who not only consorted with clowns but behaved suspiciously like one herself. "A boggler ever" [III. xiii. 110], Cleopatra repeatedly betrays Antony's trust. Moreover, in many scenes, her behavior is not simply ignoble but comical as well. . . . In the face of the conflicting evidence, some critics have ignored the comedy, and others have denied the nobility, but most today would agree with T. J. B. Spencer [in his essay "The Roman Plays"] that "the behaviour of Cleopatra in the play, at least in the first four acts, does not quite correspond with the way in which some of the others talk about her," although they differ widely in their explanations of the incongruity.

The question of Cleopatra's worth can hardly be answered by reference to Antony's enslavement, for if Cleopatra is an ambiguous character, so is Antony, and his ambiguity is inextricably bound up with hers. In Antony's case, just as in Cleopatra's, the hard facts tend to suggest—and a number of the critics tend to agree—that the unsympathetic view is justified. The mismanagement of his military and political affairs, the repeated vacillations of his allegiance, and the bungling of his suicide provide ample evidence that Antony has diminished from the triple pillar of the world into a strumpet's fool. To the rationally minded this evidence is conclusive. George Bernard Shaw, for instance, was thoroughly convinced: "I always think of what Dr. Johnson said: 'Sir, the long and short of it is, the woman's a whore!' You can't feel any sympathy with Antony after . . . Actium. . . . All Shakespear's rhetoric and pathos cannot reinstate Antony after that, or leave us with a single good word for his woman" [in an interview with a correspondent for the *Liverpool Post*].

It is significant that Shaw quotes the reasonable doctor, for, as Shaw recognized, Shakespeare's play calls the very basis of reason into question. In the tenth book of *The Republic*, Plato argues the inferiority of the imitative arts to those activities that spring from the "rational principle of the soul" by pointing out the unreliability of appearance and the consequent necessity of "the arts of measuring and numbering" to rescue

the human understanding from the delusions imposed by the senses:

> The same object appears straight when looked at out of the water, and crooked when in the water; and the concave becomes convex, owing to the illusion about colours to which the sight is liable. Thus every sort of confusion is revealed within us; and this is that weakness of the human mind on which the art of conjuring and of deceiving by light and shadow and other ingenious devices imposes, having an effect upon us like magic. . . . And the arts of measuring and numbering and weighing come to the rescue of the human understanding—there is the beauty of them—and the apparent greater or less, or more or heavier, no longer have the mastery over us, but give way before calculation and measure and weight. . . . And this, surely, must be the work of the calculating and rational principle in the soul.

Plato's view here is very much like Shaw's and Johnson's and very much like that of the Romans in the play. The play opens with Philo's contemptuous judgment that Cleopatra is a worthless strumpet and Antony her degraded fool. The Romans, like Shaw and Johnson, are contemptuous of Antony's devotion to Cleopatra: to them it represents the enslavement of his reason to his baser passions. They are almost puritanical in their scorn for the sensuous delights of Egypt, and in this too they resemble the great rationalists. But what is perhaps most important is their epistemology. Philo's opening statement—"this dotage of our general's o'erflows the measure" [I. i. 1-2]—demonstrates his rationalistic reliance upon measurement as an index of truth. In direct opposition, Antony's opening statement—"There's beggary in the love that can be reckon'd" [I. i. 15]—asserts the inadequacy of a merely quantitative, reckoning standard and denies that the real is always measurable.

This opposition between the rationalistic view and its antithesis is thus represented within the play as well as among its critics. Philo's opening speech ends with the words "behold and see" [I. i. 13]—an invitation to the audience, but more obviously to Demetrius. Within the play as without, the rationalistic view insists upon the faults of the lovers, relies upon ocular proof, weighs what Antony sacrifices—a third of the Roman world—against what he gains—the illicit love of the notorious Egyptian—and finds his action foolish. The rationalists within the play, like those among its critics, are unmoved by Cleopatra's arts. They pity and scorn Antony's enthrallment because they discount the rhetoric by which the lovers claim for themselves a greatness surpassing the limitations of the Roman world. Antony's and Cleopatra's dialogue in the opening scene implies the inadequacy of a merely reckoning standard because it invokes a transcendent world in which the claims of time and space and measurement are irrelevant. To Demetrius, however, there is only one salient fact to be derived from their performance—Antony's failure to hear Caesar's messengers. When the lovers leave the stage, he speaks one line only—"Is Caesar with Antonius priz'd so slight?" [I. i. 56]. The language here is significant: according to Demetrius, Antony has made an error in measurement. Antony has prized Caesar too "slight" to satisfy Demetrius' rational standard of reckoning. Thus, Antony's performance has corroborated Philo's opening statement—his dotage does "o'erflow the measure." Ignoring the rhetoric, Demetrius has assessed the actions, and although he is sympathetic to Antony and ''will hope of better deeds to-morrow'' [I. i. 61-2], what he has seen today is just what Philo said he would see.

This refusal of the rationalists, inside and outside the play, to be impressed by delusory shows and seductive rhetoric accounts for their low estimate of Cleopatra. For the critics, it also means that the play itself is deficient. When Shaw says, ''after giving a faithful picture of the soldier broken down by debauchery, and the typical wanton in whose arms such men perish, Shakespear finally strains all his huge command of rhetoric and stage pathos to give a theatrical sublimity to the wretched end of the business, and to persuade foolish spectators that the world was well lost by the twain'' [see excerpt above, 1900], he is demonstrating his rationalistic and neoclassical predilection for ''true'' imitations of the ''typical'' and his Platonic distrust for the delusory powers of the imitative arts. Shaw's objection to the play rests on the same premises as the Roman objection to its heroine: in each case what is finally at stake is the nature and value of art.

Cleopatra's incredible parade of shifting moods and strategems, together with Shakespeare's notorious reticence about her motives, has led even her admirers to conclude that her one salient quality is, paradoxically, her lack of one—the magnificent inconstancy that Enobarbus calls ''infinite variety.'' To the unsympathetic, of course, it is inconstancy pure and simple—the moral weakness of her sex, the vice that directly opposes the Roman virtue of steadfastness. Behind all her turnings, however, one motive does remain constant: from beginning to end, Shakespeare's Cleopatra is a dedicated showman. In the opening scene of the play, she tells the audience, ''I'll seem the fool I am not; Antony will be himself'' [I. i. 42-3], a remark that serves as a pithy keynote to her character. Cleopatra's action throughout, like that of the playwright or actor, is seeming: she is a contriver of shows, mostly for Antony's benefit, but he is by no means her only audience. . . . Some of Cleopatra's shows are obviously trivial—''play'' in both senses of the word—as when she changes clothes with Antony or has a salt fish hung on his fishing line or acts as his armorer. Others are more calculated strategems, contrived to insure her hold over Antony:

> See where he is, who's with him, what he does:
> I did not send you. If you find him sad,
> Say I am dancing; if in mirth, report
> That I am sudden sick. Quick, and return.
>
> [I. iii. 2-5]

But at the end of the play they prove the last best weapon in the lovers' arsenal, for it is by means of Cleopatra's trickery that Caesar suffers the only defeat inflicted upon him in the course of the play. For once, the luck of Caesar fails him, the great emperor is ''beguiled,'' and the lovers have their triumph. The death of Cleopatra is in fact a double triumph of show-manship—hers and her creator's. But the two are so entirely related that neither can be seen unless the other is appreciated.

Thus, in a very important sense, the entire play turns on the question of the proper response to a show. To the Romans, and to the critics who follow them in discounting the seductions of rhetoric and the delusions of the senses, the shows are false and their sublimity merely ''theatrical.'' To the sympathetic among her audience, Cleopatra's wiles identify her with her creator as a fellow artist—an identification that is especially easy today, when we have read Joyce and Mann and Gide. In contemporary literature this association between the artist and

the confidence-man has become almost a cliché. But in *Antony and Cleopatra*, the ancient version of the same association—Plato's charge that the poet is a liar—is also relevant. The Romans in Shakespeare's play, like Socrates in Plato's *Republic*, are able to make a good case against the creator of illusions when they appeal to our rational faculty to discount the evidence of the senses in favor of calculation and measurement. (pp. 202-04)

Answering Plato's charge that the poet is a liar, Sidney points out that the golden world of poetry is not amenable to ordinary truth-criteria: the poet ''nothing affirmes, and therefore never lyeth'':

> What childe is there that, comming to a Play, and seeing *Thebes* written in great Letters upon an olde doore, doth beleeve that it is *Thebes*? If then a man can arive, at that childs age, to know that the Poets persons and dooings are but pictures what should be, and not stories what have beene, they will never give the lye to things not affirmatively but allegorically and figurativelie written. And therefore, as in Historie, looking for trueth, they goe away full fraught with falshood, so in Poesie, looking for fiction, they shal use the narration but as an imaginative groundplot of a profitable invention.

However, Sidney contradicts himself in a later portion of the essay and undercuts this defense when he attacks *Gorboduc* for being ''faulty both in place and time, the two necessary companions of all corporall actions'':

> For where the stage should alwaies represent but one place, and the uttermost time presupposed in it should be, both by *Aristotles* precept and common reason, but one day, there is both many dayes, and many places, inartificially imagined. But if it be so in *Gorboduck*, how much more in al the rest? where you shal have *Asia* of the one side, and *Affrick* of the other, and so many other under-kingdoms, that the Player, when he commeth in, must ever begin with telling where he is, or els the tale wil not be conceived. Now ye shal have three Ladies walke to gather flowers, and then we must beleeve the stage to be a Garden. By and by, we heare news of shipwracke in the same place, and then wee are to blame if we accept it not for a Rock.

Sidney here offers a standard argument for the Unities—the need to bring the stage as close as possible to the reality of this world. . . . [However], when Sidney argued for the Unities as necessary for verisimilitude, he implicitly repudiated his own notion of the golden world of poetry. The golden world, he had said, is separate from the brazen world of Nature experienced by ''our degenerate soules, made worse by theyr clayey lodgings'' in ''the dungeon of the body'' since the Fall. The poet, in this view, redeems his audience for the moment, enabling them to recapture that prelapsarian vision of perfection. In contrast, the universals imitated by the neoclassicists are firmly rooted in Reason and Nature. What is to be imitated is the highest truth of this world, and the playwright is therefore answerable to all the rationalistic criteria designed to cope with this world.

Although Sidney's essay seems to imply that the golden world conforms to neoclassical rules of decorum, his claim that the poet of the golden world, "disdayning to be tied to any . . . subjection" to Nature, creates a world which is not amenable to ordinary truth-criteria actually denies the great sanction underlying those rules—the assumption that it is the poet's business to provide just imitations of general Nature. The contradiction in Sidney's essay, like the conflict in Shakespeare's play, is finally a conflict between two theories of poetry and two orders of reality; but while Sidney seems unaware of the contradiction, Shakespeare insists upon it.

Antony and Cleopatra depends for its workings upon a defiance of the rules of decorum, but the defiance is meaningless unless we know the rules and appreciate the arguments by which they were justified. When Shakespeare refuses to be bound by the Unities of Time and Place, he is able to evoke a vision of a transcendent world of the imagination only because we first see that his settings are in fact unreal by the standards of "common reason" that we bring to "all corporall actions." Similarly, his squeaking boy can evoke a greatness that defies the expectations of reason and the possibilities of realistic representation only because we share those expectations and understand the limits of those possibilities. Before the boy can evoke Cleopatra's greatness, he must remind us that he cannot truly represent it. In Egypt—and to the Egyptian imagination—he could become the queen he enacted on Shakespeare's stage, but only after he reminded us that he would appear in Rome—and that he was in fact in Shakespeare's London—a squeaking boy. (pp. 206-07)

When Cleopatra contracts for a moment to the squeaking boy who acted her part, she reminds us that what we have been watching is a deceitful show. The reminder should make us doubt the validity of the conclusions we have reached on the basis of what we have beheld. In effect, she turns Plato's argument against poetry inside out and uses its major premise to refute its conclusion. For if the objects of our perception are delusive and inadequate misrepresentations, then how seriously can we take the calculations we have made on the basis of what we have seen? The audience is thus forced into a kind of "double take" which prepares them to reorganize their disparate and jarring impressions of Cleopatra into a new synthesis.

The squeaking boy speech brings to a head the two major issues of the play—the issue of Cleopatra's character and the issue of the nature of plays. Throughout, Cleopatra has been depicted as a showman: showing has been her great defect and also her consummate virtue. In this speech, and in the scene that follows, the question of her worth is directly associated with the question of the worth of shows. Here she seems to set the two at odds: only if we reject the shows we have seen can we accept the unseen greatness of Cleopatra. But in her suicide she will present a new show that validates both, and even in this speech the validation begins. The very fact that Cleopatra can talk about the show and claim that it is a poor parody implies that she has access to a level of reality beyond what has been presented. By implying the inadequacy of the representation, she implies also that she can transcend it.

That Cleopatra's suicide is a show would be apparent in the theater: she even changes costume for it onstage. "Show me, my women, like a queen," she says, "go fetch my best attires" [V. ii. 227-28]. Much is made of dressing, and Charmian's dying gesture is to straighten her dead queen's crown. Her words, "Your crown's awry, I'll mend it and then play," echo Cleopatra's order for the costume, "when thou hast done this

chare, I'll give thee leave to play till doomsday" [V. ii. 318-19, 231-32]. The word *play* emphasizes both the hedonistic and the theatrical aspects of the very Egyptian death these women are contriving, but the fact that the crown is their central concern unites these aspects with another—the wholly serious matter of royalty. For the crown is the emblem of Cleopatra's royalty, and when she puts it on here, it establishes in a fully theatrical manner the nature of this queen who is so thoroughly involved with the world of art and illusion that she is incomprehensible except within its terms.

Cleopatra commands her women to "show" her "like a queen," but for the characters onstage, as well as the audience, the likeness becomes reality. After Cleopatra dies, Charmian says, "golden Phoebus, never be beheld of eyes again so *royal*!" [V. ii. 317-18]. When Caesar's guard asks, "Is this well done?" she replies, "It is well done, and fitting for a princess descended of so many *royal* kings" [V. ii. 325-27]. Discovering Cleopatra's death, Caesar says, "Bravest at the last, she level'd at our purposes, and being *royal* took her own way" [V. ii. 335-37]. Of these lines, only the interchange with the guard is taken from North, and North's adjective is "noble." All these tributes to Cleopatra's royalty act as refutations to the earlier charge that she violated the decorum of her station. Those charges remained valid only so long as she was content to "seem the fool" [I. i. 42] in a performance susceptible to neoclassical standards of propriety and realism. Once she repudiates that performance, she can invoke a fully theatrical world where she can put on her royalty with its emblems. In this world, the costume we see, the poetry we hear, and the act we see performed are sufficient, for they satisfy the only kind of truth-criteria available within the context of the theater. . . . The stage itself, no less than the audience, is here freed from the demands of rationally plausible neoclassic verisimilitude, and for once in the play we can see before us the greatness that was only boyed in what we beheld earlier.

The interview with Dolabella, which has no real basis in North, indicates the difference. It contrasts not only with the interview with Proculeius, which immediately precedes it, but also with the scene where Enobarbus describes his vision at the Cydnus. . . . Her dream of Antony, like Enobarbus' vision of her, evokes a greatness that is not physically present, and it uses the language of paradox and hyperbole: "For his bounty, there was no winter in 't: an autumn 'twas that grew the more by reaping. . . . In his livery walk'd crowns and crownets: realms and islands were as plates dropp'd from his pocket" [V. ii. 86-8, 90-2]. There are some important differences, however. The cosmic imagery—"His face was as the heavens, and therein stuck a sun and moon, which kept their course, and lighted the little O, the earth. . . . his voice was propertied as all the tuned spheres" [V. ii. 79-81, 83-4]—directly establishes the translunary context of the vision. In Enobarbus' vision, Cleopatra was associated with "that Venus where we see the fancy outwork nature" [II. ii. 200-01]. In Cleopatra's, Antony is "past the size of dreaming: nature wants stuff to vie strange forms with fancy, yet to imagine an Antony were nature's piece, 'gainst fancy, condemning shadows quite" [V. ii. 97-100]. At this point the truth of the imagination has become reality for Cleopatra: her dream is a vision of the golden world from a vantage point within that world rather than outside of it.

Cleopatra's ascent to the golden world is also an ascent from comedy, which shows men worse than they are, to tragedy, which shows them better. When the clown arrives to bring her the means by which she will ascend, she says, "Let him come in. What poor an instrument may do a noble deed!'' [V. ii. 236-37]; and in the scene that follows he serves as her scapegoat, for he attracts the laughter which has become a fairly well-conditioned response to the figure of the queen while she preserves the decorum of her superior station. Similarly, the clown's speeches serve, as Donald C. Baker has remarked [in his essay ''The Purging of Cleopatra''], to purge ''the baser elements of the language of the play as Cleopatra purges herself and leaves her other elements 'to baser life.''' The clown's basket helps to define the transition. Early in the play [I. ii. 32], Charmian says, ''I love long life better than figs.'' Now she and her mistress will choose the deadly figs and by their choice transform themselves from comic characters devoted to the life and sensual pleasures of this world to tragic characters who have the nobility to choose a good higher than mere survival. The asps as well as the figs are the products of the Nile, and the deaths of the Egyptian women demonstrate that their ''o'erflowing'' river breeds material for high tragedy as well as low comedy. Like Cleopatra's description of the asp as a babe that sucks its nurse asleep, the clown's basket unites appetite and death to sublimate both. His jokes make the same point: if ''a woman is a dish for the gods'' [V. ii. 274], appetite is godly.

Cleopatra's death sublimates appetite, but first she rejects it, in both its Roman and its Egyptian manifestations. She rejects the coarse diet available in Rome, where ''mechanic slaves with greasy aprons . . . shall uplift us to the view. In their thick breaths, rank of gross diet, shall we be enclouded, and forc'd to drink their vapour'' [V. ii. 209-10, 210-13]; and she also resolves, ''Now no more the juice of Egypt's grape shall moist this lip'' [V. ii. 281-82]. Similarly, she denies the woman's nature that made her a boggler in the sublunary world—''I have nothing of woman in me: now from head to foot I am marble-constant; now the fleeting moon no planet is of mine'' [V. ii. 238-41]—before she assumes the name of Antony's wife in the world of immortal longings. In each case, and in the case of all the other qualities that have led us to doubt her nobility, the renunciation is only a prelude to redefinition and fulfillment.

During the suicide scene, Cleopatra systematically and explicitly renounces the weaknesses charged against her by the Romans and made credible to the audience by her earlier performance. If she drank Antony under the table, she will now renounce the grape. If she was his strumpet, she will now become his wife. If her vacillation lost him battles, she will now be marble-constant. If his devotion to her made him effeminate, she will now renounce her sex. But she does not renounce her sex in order to collapse into a squeaking boy, any more than her rejection of his shows meant that she was done with showing. Her character, like her showmanship, is not destroyed in the final scene but sublimated. Even her sensuality remains: ''the stroke of death is as a lover's pinch, which hurts, and is desir'd'' [V. ii. 295-96]; and the new heaven and new earth she anticipates with Antony, where he is ''curled'' just as he was ''barber'd ten times o'er'' at the Cydnus [II. ii. 224], will abound in sensuous delights. One way to describe this process of sublimation is to say that we are now made to share the romantic lovers' own vision of their passion; another way is to say that the passion in the world of Nature is destroyed in order to be reborn in a new incarnation in the golden world, which is also the afterlife that Cleopatra envisions with Antony.

In the opening scene, Antony's rhetoric rejected the world for a kiss:

> Let Rome in Tiber melt, and the wide arch
> Of the rang'd empire fall! Here is my space
> Kingdoms are clay: our dungy earth alike
> Feeds beast as man; the nobleness of life
> Is to do thus: when such a mutual pair,
> And such a twain can do't.
>
>   [I. i. 33-8]

In the final scene, Cleopatra's act validates his choice. In the first scene, Antony suggested that to know the limits of their love, Cleopatra ''find out new heaven, new earth'' [I. i. 17]. Here she prepares to find them out. In this final vision of Cleopatra's, Antony at last triumphs over Caesar. ''Methinks,'' she says, ''I hear Antony call. . . . I hear him mock the luck of Caesar, which the gods give men to excuse their after wrath'' [V. ii. 283-84, 285-87]. In the natural world, the soothsayer's warning to Antony holds true: Caesar will win at any game, for ''of that natural luck, he beats thee 'gainst the odds. Thy lustre thickens, when he shines by . . . thy spirit is all afraid to govern thee near him; but he away, 'tis noble'' [II. iii. 27-9, 29-31]. Cleopatra can see Antony triumphing over Caesar because she looks beyond the world of time and change and luck where Caesar is always triumphant to a world where Antony's magnanimity can find its proper milieu. In the brazen world of Nature, where most of the play is set, Caesar is the master politician, but when Cleopatra chooses to leave that world, she can call him ''ass, unpolicied'' and his intents ''most absurd.''

After Cleopatra's death, when she has in act as well as in vision repudiated Caesar's world, her vision becomes reality in Caesar's world as well as her own. Caesar, says the guard who finds her dead, has been ''beguil'd.'' And Caesar is beguiled in two, equally significant, senses. In the first place, he is tricked out of his triumph: Cleopatra outwits the master manipulator at the end. But just as important, he is beguiled in the sense that he responds to Cleopatra's charm. Seeing the dead queen, Caesar says, ''she looks like sleep, as she would catch another Antony in her strong toil of grace'' [V. ii. 346-48]. For the first and only time in the play, Caesar sees what Antony saw in Egypt. He now knows Cleopatra's charm, not as an abstract consideration to be reckoned in Rome, troublesome or useful to him in his political maneuverings, but as a response within himself. Caesar has come to Egypt for his final vision of Cleopatra, and his response, like Enobarbus' memory of the Cydnus, attests the validity of the vision that drew Antony from Rome. (pp. 208-11)

The last speech in the play, like the first one, is spoken by one Roman to another. And, like the first, it ends with an injunction to ''see'';

>   Our army shall
> In solemn show attend this funeral,
> And then to Rome. Come, Dolabella, see
> High order, in this great solemnity.
>
>   [V. ii. 363-66]

If we make the kind of association I have been suggesting and identify the Roman view of the lovers with the perceptions available to fallen man in the brazen world of mundane life, we might say that the audience, about to leave the theater, is about to return to the ''Rome'' from which they entered it. Like Caesar, however, they have been in the interval to Egypt where they have, at first, beheld Cleopatra's deceptive show and, at the end, seen her in another show, of "high order" and "great solemnity."

Before the final scene can be enacted and the sight of Cleopatra's greatness made available to the audience, Shakespeare must establish and then undermine the comic conception of her character that was based on the boy actor's imitation of her appearance in the natural world to which the Roman comedians are limited. Like the Romans, we must accept its verisimilitude before we can appreciate the force of Cleopatra's charge that it is a poor parody of the greatness she possesses in the golden world which is the high product of the tragic poet's making. Thus the ambivalence of our reactions to the first four acts is as important an element of our total experience of the play as is our response to the final scene, which resolves the ambivalence. The golden world of poetry became necessary only after the Fall of man, and the worth of the poet can only be seen when his handiwork is compared to the products of the arts that are bound by the limitations of Nature. (p. 211)

> *Phyllis Rackin, "Shakespeare's Boy Cleopatra, the Decorum of Nature, and the Golden World of Poetry," in* PMLA, *87, Vol. 87, No. 2, March, 1972, pp. 201-12.*

A. L. FRENCH   (essay date 1972)

[*Evaluating* Antony and Cleopatra *in light of opposing interpretations of it as "lyrical tragedy or remorseless exposure," French concludes that the dramatic mode is one of genial detachment, "more amused than censorious." That Shakespeare regarded Antony as "an illusory hero," the critic argues, is evident from the hollowness, sanctimony, indignation, and desperate need for admiration that characterize his speeches throughout the play. French contends that after Antony's death, Cleopatra—up to this time "shrewd, pragmatic, and honest"—adopts both the "Antony language," which she had earlier parodied, and her lover's way of evading reality; and French cautions that while her speeches from that point on are superlative verse, they represent "a truth for her which is poignantly untrue for us." Finally, the critic maintains that unlike Shakespeare's major tragedies,* Antony and Cleopatra *provides no laceration of emotions and no pain that requires mitigation, for the play imposes "no insight . . . which desperately needs to be evaded."*]

Whatever we may finally make of *Hamlet, Othello* and *Lear*, no-one, I imagine, would deny that in them Shakespeare is in deadly earnest: he is completely possessed by his interests; his art is upsetting and frequently unnerving. But does anyone ever leave the theatre, after seeing *Antony*, feeling bruised? I doubt it; and while I wouldn't for a moment imply that *Antony* is no more than a *jeu d'esprit*, I want to suggest that 'seriousness' is a very different thing in *Hamlet* or *Lear* from what it is in *Antony*. The questions we have to ask, then, are about the *mode* of this play.

I think its mode is suggested at the very outset, in the well-known speech of Philo:

> Nay, but this dotage of our general's
> O'erflows the measure . . .
> . . . his captain's heart,
> Which in the scuffles of great fights hath burst
> The buckles on his breast, reneges all temper,
> And is become the bellows and the fan
> To cool a gipsy's lust.
>
> [I. i. 1-2, 6-10]

There is much wit here, but it isn't Philo's: the unknown soldier's hero-worship sounds idolatrous, perhaps only because he has an axe to grind in that he very badly wants to convince Demetrius *quantum mutatus ab illo* [how different he is from his former self]. Perhaps there may be something in Antony which could genuinely have inspired such devotion once upon a time, but Philo is skirting absurdity when he tells us that Antony's heart burst 'the buckles on his breast'. In fact, right at the start we are getting a view of Antony which is shared by most of the characters, including Antony himself—but it is a view to which no human being could possibly conform.

Though we may feel on our own account that Philo's praise is impossibly extreme, we have to wait for Antony's appearance to decide whether the charge of 'dotage' (foolish affection *and* senile folly) is just. Here I take it that the appearance of the eunuchs 'fanning' the 'strumpet' (whose 'fool' Antony is said to be) is pretty decisive, especially since the 'fanning' takes up Philo's word—

> the bellows and the fan
> To cool a gipsy's lust.

As the first scene develops it becomes clear that there is a good deal in what Philo said about his master's decline, and that we therefore can't dismiss his judgment as malicious; so that the opening of this play is very unlike the opening, say, of *Othello*, where it becomes plain very early on that Iago has a grievance which explains his tone about *his* master. In fact I can't think of any other Shakespeare play where the first few lines so completely inhibit our sympathy towards one of the main characters. . . . Our mood is . . . one of detachment, but a detachment that is more amused than censorious: we are not to be continuously involved with these people, so that we can very easily afford to let them entertain us. I think this means that the play isn't a tragedy, but it has its own peculiar sort of desolating clarity about *bovarysme* [the will to see things as they are not; from Flaubert's *Madame Bovary*].

To talk about *bovarysme* runs full tilt into the quite common account of the play which offers us the love between Antony and Cleopatra as something 'transcendental'. Even those critics who are unhappy about claiming anything so large nevertheless feel that there are continual suggestions of something of the kind and that Shakespeare, perhaps, never quite made up his mind what he thought or wanted us to think. Mr Mason, for example, in his recent book [*Shakespeare's Tragedies of Love;* see Additional Bibliography], is puzzled by the lovers' behaviour in I. iii: 'The two characters themselves do not quite know where they stand'. I can see that there is much alternation of tone and mood in this scene, but to say that the lovers don't know where they stand would only be a criticism of Shakespeare if we thought they *should*. I admit that the reason for Antony's decision to go back to Rome remains pretty obscure, though I suspect that on the stage the spectacle of several messengers bringing news of various disasters that make Antony's position insecure would make the decision look reasonable enough. Whatever the reason, Antony does make up his mind to go, and the encounter between him and Cleopatra is superbly comic: Cleopatra tries on everything she knows to stop him, and Antony, even though he has his way in the end, mostly dances to her tune. Of course, there are lines which, out of context, look as though they are claiming something very large; for example:

> Nay, pray you, seek no colour for your going,
> But bid farewell, and go: when you sued staying,

Then was the time for words: no going then;
Eternity was in our lips and eyes,
Bliss in our brows' bent; none our parts so poor
But was a race of heaven . . .

> [I. iii. 32-7]

People's memories stop short there. But Shakespeare's heroine adds:

> . . . they are so still,
> Or thou, the greatest soldier of the world,
> Art turned the greatest liar.

> [I. iii. 37-9]

Antony is furious, but Cleopatra taunts him still further. He can only stand up to her by addressing her as though she were a public meeting:

> Hear me, queen:
> The strong necessity of time commands
> Our services awhile; but my full heart
> Remains in use with you.

> [I. iii. 41-4]

Commentators gloss 'in use' variously, but I don't see that it *means* very much; it is as verbal a protestation as Antony's remark at the end of the scene,

> Our separation so abides and flies,
> That Thou, residing here, goes yet with me,
> And I, hence fleeting, here remain with thee.

> [I. iii. 102-04]

We need only think of Donne to feel the hollowness. It is precisely of this that Cleopatra accuses him when he tells her of Fulvia's death:

> Where be the sacred vials thou shouldst fill
> With sorrowful water? Now I see, I see,
> In Fulvia's death, how mine received shall be.

> [I. iii. 63-5]

She is very skilfully turning Antony's exaltedly platitudinous tone against him (she is a brilliant parodist): 'sacred vials' is pure Wardour Street. Antony doesn't notice he is being made fun of, though it does strike him that he is being told off; and again he speaks with a sublimity so gross as to be impudent:

> Quarrel no more, but be prepared to know
> The purposes I bear; which are, or cease,
> As you shall give th'advice. By the fire
> That quickens Nilus' slime, I go from hence
> Thy soldier, servant, making peace or war
> As thou affects.

> [I. iii. 66-71]

Obviously he himself really believes all this, though it is laughably inconsistent: if Antony's 'purposes' really depend on Cleopatra's 'advice', then he wouldn't be even thinking of going away; and as Cleopatra has no apparent desire to make war, Antony is merely being disingenuous in leaving her the option. Her summary—'So Antony loves' [I. iii. 73]—is both bitter and a simply true summary of what we have been seeing in this scene and also earlier in the play. Again Antony's reply seems remarkable for its unconsciousness:

> My precious queen, forbear;
> And give true evidence to his love, which stands
> An honourable trial.

> [I. iii. 73-5]

What sort of 'trial' is Antony saying that his love can or will sustain? Does he mean that it's very trying to have to go to Rome, or that Cleopatra is putting him through his paces? In fact he could mean several things, but there isn't much sense of his *meaning* any of them; all he offers is verbiage. Cleopatra now makes him look so ridiculous that he threatens to leave, to which Cleopatra answers

> Sir, you and I must part, but that's not it:
> Sir, you and I have loved, but there's not it:
> That you know well: something it is I would:
> O, my oblivion is a very Antony,
> And I am all forgotten.

> [I. iii. 87-91]

Apart from the obvious reproach, the lines make an appeal to which Antony could have responded without loss of face; but he is so annoyed by her earlier resistance that he turns the knife in the wound:

> But that your royalty
> Holds idleness your subject, I should take you
> For idleness itself.

> [I. iii. 91-3]

It seems odd that Antony feels free to accuse her of 'idleness' (frivolity) in view of his own behaviour in I. i. Cleopatra is left with no weapon but her talent for burlesque and, quite unnoticed by Antony, she gives in with a perfect take-off of the noble-Roman pose which he has insisted on assuming:

> Your honour calls you hence;
> Therefore be deaf to my unpitied folly,
> And all the gods go with you! Upon your sword
> Sit laurel victory! and smooth success
> Be strewed before your feet!

> [I. iii. 97-101]

Cleopatra is doing this consciously, of course, but there are plenty of places in this play where people fall into a similarly heightened mode of speech in the effort to dissimulate (or simulate) feelings. (pp. 206-11)

[A] speech of Caesar's, much later, looks on the face of it like a handsome, if conventional, tribute to the dead Antony:

> The breaking of so great a thing should make
> A great crack: the round world
> Should have shook lions into civil streets,
> And citizens to their dens. The death of Antony
> Is not a single doom; in that name lay
> A moiety of the world.

> [V. i. 14-19]

We doubtless feel, on the level of 'character', that with Antony safely out of the way Caesar can afford this verbal generosity, just as Aufidius can afford it when Coriolanus has been disposed of. But the uncomfortable fact remains that what Caesar says is that he is surprised how *little* Antony's death seems to have meant to the world. Again the heightened mode is, paradoxically enough, realising a blankness or hollowness at the heart of things. Doesn't Bradley's striking phrase for our considered response to the play, 'the sadness of disenchantment' [see excerpt above, 1905], have a singular, if unintended, felicity?

Of course the issue raised by Caesar's epitaph is one that confronts us throughout the play and especially when it deals with Antony. Why, one might ask, should Octavius have supposed that Antony's death ought to have caused such disturbances? Here we run straight into the problem raised by Mr Mason:

> We are *told* I don't know how many times that [Antony] was a supreme specimen of humanity, so lofty indeed that to indicate the scale it was necessary to suppose that his nature partook of the divine. The Anthony who is presented dramatically never makes us believe in these reports.

I maintain that this problem solves itself if you think that it was all along Shakespeare's intention to insist on the gap between what Antony is said to be and what he really is. No-one in the play ever quite grasps that the Mark Antony of the olden days—the man who at Philippi

> struck
> The lean and wrinkled Cassius
>
> [III. xi. 36-7]

or who drank

> The stale of horses and the gilded puddle
> Which beasts could cough at
>
> [I. iv. 62-3]

—has long been dead and has been replaced by a man who is much more human and therefore much less dependable. And the play's comedy stems, over and over again, from the fact that everyone (except Enobarbus) is a dupe of Antony's reputation—that is, a dupe of words. That is not, of course, an uncommon situation in Shakespeare; but quite often characters come face to face with their verbal evasions and are shattered by seeing that they are merely verbal; whereas in *Antony* that kind of tragic laceration never happens at all. The characters are so insulated from reality that they can't recognize it even when they stumble over it. . . . [Though] people are the dupes of words, they are equally, when it suits them, masters of words: the trouble is that they keep confusing a mastery over words with a mastery over brute facts. Hence much of the comedy.

Once we have the idea in our heads that amusement is a permissible (and indeed essential) response to large tracts of this play, Antony's fury after Actium, his treatment of Thidias, and his row with Cleopatra, come into sharper focus than hitherto. (pp. 212-15)

The . . . interview between Cleopatra and Thidias is overtly comic. He tells her that Caesar

> knows that you embraced not Antony
> As you did love, but as you feared him.
>
> [III. xiii. 56-7]

Her reply—'O!'—could hardly fail to produce laughter in the audience whatever tone the actress adopted. Thidias goes on:

> The scars upon your honour therefore he
> Does pity as constrainèd blemishes,
> Not as deserved.
>
> [III. xiii. 58-60]

She answers:

> He is a god and knows
> What is most right: mine honour was not yielded,
> But conquered merely. . . .
>
> [III. xiii. 60-2]

It now looks as though Cleopatra . . . is thinking about working her passage home, although it is not quite clear how far she

is just teasing Thidias and how far there is some seriousness underlying the teasing: when she invites him to kiss her hand she sounds parodic—

> Your Caesar's father oft
> (When he hath mused of taking kingdoms in)
> Bestowed his lips on that unworthy place,
> As it rained kisses.
>
> [III. xiii. 82-5]

This sounds ludicrous enough, especially in contrast to her words to another Messenger:

> and here
> My bluest veins to kiss: a hand that kings
> Have lipped, and trembled kissing.
>
> [II. v. 28-30]

Perhaps, as with her farewell speech to Antony (at the end of I. iii), she is both satisfying her intelligence and also saying what the other person wants to hear.

Antony's attitude to her *rapprochement* with Thidias is curious. Earlier in the scene, when the Schoolmaster told him of Caesar's offer of 'courtesy' to her 'so she / Will yield us up', Antony had munificently said 'Let her know't' [III. xiii. 15-16]. But now, when he comes in at [III. xiii. 85] . . . he loses his temper, not with Cleopatra but, on the quite specious pretext of jealousy, with Thidias; and has him whipped. To keep one's dignity while losing one's temper is rather difficult, but Antony tries hard:

> Authority melts from me. Of late when I cried 'Ho!'
> Like boys unto a muss, kings would start forth,
> And cry 'Your will?' Have you no ears?
> I am Antony yet. Take hence this Jack, and whip him.
>
> [III. xiii. 90-3]

Commentators don't seem to notice that in his rage Antony is saying the opposite of what he means: for if a 'muss' is 'a game in which small things are thrown down to be scrambled for' (Dover Wilson from *OED*) then what does that make Antony? He tries to belittle the 'kings' but succeeds in belittling himself even more. And we notice that he is now going to prove his powers undiminished by having Thidias flogged. Enobarbus' comment . . . places Antony's behaviour:

> 'Tis better playing with a lion's whelp
> Than with an old one dying.
>
> [III. xiii. 94-5]

But perhaps even this is too complimentary: an old lion may be spiteful, but we scarcely expect him to be grotesquely sanctimonious, as Antony goes on to be when he rages at Cleopatra:

> You were half blasted ere I knew you . . . Ha!
> Have I my pillow left unpressed in Rome,
> Forborne the getting of a lawful race,
> And by a gem of women, to be abused
> By one that looks on feeders?
>
> [III. xiii. 105-09]

It is a useful debating-point to call Octavia a 'gem of women', but that's all it is; moreover Antony has never shown the slightest sign of wanting children to carry on the family name. As for the charge about being 'half blasted', Antony goes on to expand it a moment later:

> I found you as a morsel cold upon
> Dead Caesar's trencher; nay, you were a fragment

Of Gnaeus Pompey's; besides what hotter hours,
Unregistered in vulgar fame, you have
Luxuriously picked out: for I am sure,
Though you can guess what temperance should be,
You know not what it is.

[III. xiii. 116-22]

It is not merely that Antony has no right to take this kind of tone: it is also that Cleopatra has never set herself up as a moral paragon—she is honest about what she is in a way that Antony never is about himself. During this long outburst Cleopatra has been interjecting brief protests such as 'Wherefore is this?' [III. xiii. 122]; after the flogged Thidias has been dismissed she coolly asks 'Have you done yet?' [III. xiii. 153]— a question that cunningly combines contempt for Antony with the tacit assumption that all will soon be well and that the relationship will continue much as before. Antony's reply is in character:

Ant.   Alack, our terrene moon
          Is now eclipsed, and it portends alone
          The fall of Antony.
Cleo.   I must stay his time.
Ant.   To flatter Caesar, would you mingle eyes
          With one that ties his points?
Cleo.   Not know me yet?
Ant.   Cold-hearted toward me?
Cleo.   Ah, dear, if I be so,
          From my cold heart let heaven engender
               hail . . .

[III. xiii. 153-59]

It is a ludicrous contrast between the eclipsed 'terrene moon' Antony makes of the Queen and the married shrug with which she waits for the storm to blow itself out. But with the swerve into pathos in 'Cold-hearted toward *me?*' Antony is obviously vulnerable again and, once again, Cleopatra judges her tone exquisitely:

From my cold heart let heaven engender hail,
And poison it in the source, and the first stone
Drop in my neck: as it determines, so
Dissolve my life! the next Caesarion smite!
Till by degrees the memory of my womb,
Together with my brave Egyptians all,
By the discandying of this pelleted storm
Lie graveless, till the flies and gnats of Nile
Have buried them for prey!

[III. xiii. 159-67]

Yes, an exquisitely judged tone; and she must be very sure of its effect on Antony to allow herself to call her Egyptians 'brave', a term which, in any of its senses, is about the least appropriate that could be imagined. Yet Antony's reply is 'I am satisfied' [III. xiii. 167]. A good many commentators are also satisfied: they are too busy talking about the profound significance of the imagery of fertility in decay to notice that, as she has done before and will do again, the Queen is talking to her lover in what we have come to recognise as Antony-language—an idiom in which sense counts for little and grandiosity for much. . . . Of course one doesn't want to deny that Cleopatra's speech is good poetry despite its hollowness: it is good because it is funny, but the funniness, though kindly enough (on Shakespeare's part), is ultimately desolating in what it tells us about the engagements the two lovers think they have with each other. Cleopatra knows this is the only way to hold Antony, if indeed she really wants, by this stage, to hold him; while Antony will listen to any nonsense if it

restores his *amour-propre,* although the very fact of his accepting it diminishes him still further in our eyes and, for that matter, in Cleopatra's. He goes on, here, to delude himself that 'There's hope in't yet,' and to prepare himself for the coming day's battle by having 'one other gaudy night' [III. xiii. 176, 182]. There is nothing for it but to agree with Enobarbus when he calls all this a 'diminution in our captain's brain' [III. xiii. 197]; and those who want to make him out to be a nasty cynic, who really can't appreciate the full beauty of the relationship between the lovers, will have to explain why what he says is so often right—not merely intelligent, but accurate too. He usually speaks, in fact, with the voice of the play: which may well make us want to ask what sort of play it is which can afford to have its vision summed up by an Enobarbus—a play to the summing-up of which an Enobarbus is only too adequate. That may seem a harsh thing to say about Antony (and the play); but is there really, in the next scene but one, more to Antony's farewell to his servants than Enobarbus sees?

Well, my good fellows, wait on me to-night:
Scant not my cups, and make as much of me
As when mine empire was your fellow too
And suffered my command.

[IV. ii. 20-3]

He says this, according to Enobarbus, 'to make his followers weep' [IV. ii. 24]; of course Enobarbus has himself just decided to seek some way to leave his master, so his view isn't disinterested; but then Antony's own explanation isn't very convincing:

I spake to you for your comfort, did desire you
To burn this night with torches: know, my hearts,
I hope well of to-morrow, and will lead you
Where rather I'll expect victorious life
Than death and honour.

[IV. ii. 40-4]

But it can't have been very 'comforting' for them to be told

Haply you shall not see me more, or if,
A mangled shadow.

[IV. ii. 26-7]

So that the far from impartial Enobarbus goes straight to the point.

Yet even he dies deceived. Admittedly, Antony has heaped coals of fire on his head by sending all his treasure after him, and it is this that breaks his heart:

O Antony,
Thou mine of bounty, how wouldst thou have paid
My better service, when my turpitude
Thou dost so crown with gold! . . .
. . . I will go and seek
Some ditch wherein to die; the foul'st best fits
My latter part of life.

[IV. vi. 30-3, 36-8]

Yet we should beware of viewing Antony's generosity exactly as Enobarbus does: after all, we have just been seeing him make his servants cry, and if that episode has a point at all it is to suggest that he badly needs to be thought well of. His words when he hears of Enobarbus' desertion are significant:

Go, Eros, send his treasure after; do it;
Detain no jot, I charge thee: write to him—

> I will subscribe—gentle adieus and greetings;
> Say that I wish he never find more cause
> To change a master. O, my fortunes have
> Corrupted honest men!
>
> [IV. v. 12-17]

It all sounds so terribly sweet, but in fact no message could be more calculated to embarrass Enobarbus and make him feel a traitor. (If Antony had been a Christian, he would doubtless have added: 'And tell him I shall pray for him.') The strategy succeeds admirably: Enobarbus hates himself and his heart breaks. The trouble is, as Mr Mason complains, that the Antony we have been seeing is simply not worth this kind of devotion; but then that, it seems to me, is Shakespeare's point. It may also be true that he couldn't afford the dry pragmatism of Enobarbus any longer; he may perhaps have felt that if he was going to make any attempt at all to produce a *tragic* catastrophe, the belittler would have to go. But this would imply that the play is a tragedy *manqué,* and what I've been questioning all along is whether it is anything of the sort. Let us try to test these thoughts against what happens in the final episodes of the play—the defeat and death of Antony in Act IV and the suicide of Cleopatra in Act V.

In a way, the movement of IV. xii and xiii repeats that of III. x and xi (the battle of Actium); but whereas in the earlier battle—also lost through the defection of Egyptian forces—Antony needed little persuasion to return to his mistress, he this time has to hear that she is dead, and himself make a botched attempt at suicide, before they are reconciled. Antony's mood, when he sees the battle is lost, is as usual compounded of self-pity, furious indignation, and other pleasant emotions. . . .

> Betrayed I am.
> O this false soul of Egypt! this grave charm—
> Whose eye becked forth my wars and called them home,
> Whose bosom was my crownet, my chief end—
> Like a right gipsy hath at fast and loose
> Beguiled me to the very heart of loss.
>
> [IV. xii. 24-9]

Antony is fibbing in saying that Cleopatra 'becked forth my wars and called them home', rather as he did much earlier in the play—

> I go from hence
> Thy soldier, servant, making peace or war
> As thou affects.
>
> [I. iii. 69-71]

It is one of Antony's great talents to be able to convince himself that anything he wants to do is absolutely essential to Cleopatra's well-being. We can't leave the commentary there, however; we can't avoid facing the question, Is there something which substantiates that compelling phrase 'the very heart of loss'? I think the answer is best given by quoting another piece of Shakespeare:

> Why should a dog, a horse, a rat have life,
> And thou no breath at all?
>
> [*King Lear,* V. iii. 307-08]

I apologise for the shock. But if this tells us something ultimate about a sense of 'loss', I can only think that Antony's phrase is no more than a phrase, reminding us of that other remark, 'I / Have lost my way for ever' [III. xi. 3-4]. Furthermore, the implications of 'fast and loose' aren't very flattering; Antony may intend the suggestion of laxity in 'loose' (as well as the

whole phrase) to apply only to Cleopatra, but it takes something of a gull to *be* cheated. More generally, I think we are entitled to ask what we are to make of the military genius of a man who, already let down appallingly by the Egyptian navy at Actium, reposes his trust in it again. (pp. 216-24)

Cleopatra enters with the question

> Why is my lord enraged against his love?
>
> [IV. xii. 31]

the artificiality and affectation of which must be intentionally absurd. If it is, how seriously can we take what it prompts, the raging of Antony between line 32 and the end of the scene?

> The shirt of Nessus is upon me: teach me,
> Alcides, thou mine ancestor, thy rage:
> Let me lodge Lichas on the horns o'th'moon,
> And with those hands that grasped the heaviest club
> Subdue my worthiest self.
>
> [IV. xii. 43-7]

We know that Antony claims Hercules as his forbear, but the parallel isn't very exact: Deianira, Hercules' wife, gave him the poisoned tunic thinking that it would simply keep him faithful to her; whereas Cleopatra (or so Antony has been claiming) deliberately betrayed him. And while it was one thing for the legendary hero to throw his page Lichas into the sea, it is quite another for this big fleshy fellow to bluster about throwing him up high—'on the horns o'th' moon' adds a disintegrating touch of pure farce. After adding, twice, that he is going to take his revenge by killing Cleopatra, Antony leaves, but returns after a short scene (IV. xiii) devoted to the Queen's deciding to have him told she is dead. But when he does re-enter, after being offstage for only a couple of minutes, his mood has swung from mindless fury to a sense of inner and outer dissolution:

> Sometime we see a cloud that's dragonish,
> A vapour sometime like a bear or lion,
> A towered citadel, a pendent rock. . . .
> . . . now thy captain is
> Even such a body: here I am Antony,
> Yet cannot hold this visible shape . . .
>
> [IV. xiv. 2-4, 12-14]

The poetry is so marvellous that there is a temptation (which we should resist) to drink it in without thinking about the implications of Antony's comparison. As soon as we do so, we realise that, throughout, he is talking about an optical illusion which, in time, becomes obviously just that. The 'towered citadel', after all, was never more than 'air' together with the fanciful daydreaming of the beholder. Can he be saying that *he* has never been more than an illusory hero—a simulacrum substantiated by the admiring lookers-on? Hardly; but that, I think, is what Shakespeare means, and it is the gap between anything Antony can be supposed to intend and what his creator gives him to say that makes the lines comic in a peculiarly delicate way. (pp. 224-25)

Comedy—of a peculiar kind—is what takes the stress, too, in the scene of Antony's death. And if we want a text by which to test the either/or view of the play—the one that insists it is lyrical tragedy or remorseless exposure—we can do no better than listen to the notes struck here. Isn't it at least disconcerting to hear Cleopatra say this?—

> Here's sport indeed! How heavy weighs my lord!
>
> [IV. xv. 32]

with its echo of

> O happy horse, to bear the weight of Antony!
>
> [I. v. 21]

And what are we to make of this exchange?—

Ant.	Give me some wine, and let me speak a little.
Cleo.	No, let me speak, and let me rail so high, That the false huswife Fortune break her wheel, Provoked by my offence.
Ant.	One word, sweet queen. Of Caesar seek your honour, with your safety. O!
Cleo.	They do not go together.
Ant.	Gentle, hear me: None about Caesar trust but Proculeius.
Cleo.	My resolution and my hands I'll trust; None about Caesar.

[IV. xv. 42-50]

In North's Plutarch, which Shakespeare is sometimes accused of having followed rather lazily, there is nothing corresponding to these repeated attempts by Antony to get Cleopatra to pay attention to what he is saying, and there is nothing either to suggest that Cleopatra, as usual, keeps on interrupting Antony, taking the words out of his mouth, refusing to follow his advice, and in general making him look a trifle foolish. If we didn't know this was meant to be a solemn moment, could we infer it from the quoted passage? I doubt it; and my doubt makes me wonder just how solemn the moment is really meant to be. No doubt a critic who took the either/or view would want, if he were brought to see that there is an element of humour in Antony's death scene, to assimilate it to the 'ruthless exposure'; but then the trouble is that there is nothing in the least ruthless or exposing about this death-bed comedy, which (oddly enough) seems rather genial and kindly, almost indulgent, and most certainly not censorious or indignant. (pp. 227-28)

Before Antony's death, Cleopatra has been the more 'realistic' of the pair—shrewd, pragmatic, and honest. But after it, a change comes over her; and we have to ask whether she too becomes a slave of words. No-one will deny that the verse she speaks is wonderful; and it is very easy to see why 'transcendental' is a term that keeps cropping up in accounts of the play—

> O, see, my women—
> The crown o'th'earth doth melt. . . .
> . . . the odds is gone,
> And there is nothing left remarkable
> Beneath the visiting moon.
>
> [IV. xv. 62-3, 66-8]

We don't have to agree with her to find the speech moving; indeed, one reason why it is so moving is perhaps that she is so completely self-deceived—and what is more, she is self-deceived in a mode she has learnt from Antony. We again recall this exchange:

Ant.	Alack, our terrene moon Is now eclipsed, and it portends alone The fall of Antony.
Cleo.	I must stay his time.

[III. xiii. 153-55]

This is what I earlier called 'Antony-language'; and what happens is that, at the precise moment of Antony's death, this language becomes the staple of *Cleopatra's* speeches. Reality having finally become too unpleasant to face, she takes her dead lover's way of not facing it. (p. 229)

That Cleopatra mostly talks Antony-language in the last episodes of the play is confirmed by that dream-Antony she describes to Dolabella. We cannot write it off as merely, or even mainly, a tactic to bedazzle Dolabella so that he will tell her what Caesar intends to do with her, though that element is certainly present.

> His legs bestrid the ocean, his reared arm
> Crested the world: his voice was propertied
> As all the tunéd spheres, and that to friends;
> But when he meant to quail and shake the orb,
> He was as rattling thunder. For his bounty,
> There was no winter in't; an autumn 'twas
> That grew the more by reaping: his delights
> Were dolphin-like, they showed his back above
> The element they lived in: in his livery
> Walked crowns and crownets; realms and islands were
> As plates dropped from his pocket.
>
> [V. ii. 82-92]

I wonder if we are meant, when hearing about the 'rattling thunder', to repel our memory of Antony's treatment of Thidias:

> Whip him, fellows,
> Till like a boy you see him cringe his face,
> And whine aloud for mercy.
>
> [III. xiii. 99-101]

or the bluster of

> O, that I were
> Upon the hill of Basan, to outroar
> The hornéd herd!
>
> [III. xiii. 126-28]

—to take two examples out of many. Likewise, the Antony we have been seeing did not 'grow the more by reaping', but consistently diminished. And in what 'element' did his delights live? A 'sea of pleasures', suggests Ridley, the Arden editor; is the Queen's suggestion, then, that he emerged from it only occasionally, to draw breath? Yes; but the dolphin's rise and fall also suggests love-making. At the same time we are reminded of other fish:

> Give me mine angle, we'll to th'river: there
> My music playing far off, I will betray
> Tawny-finned fishes; my bended hook shall pierce
> Their slimy jaws, and as I draw them up,
> I'll think them every one an Antony,
> And say 'Ah, ha! you're caught.'
>
> [II. v. 10-15]

When we come to the end of Cleopatra's eulogy, we may perhaps wonder why she is ascribing Antony's loss of 'realms and islands' to mere regal carelessness, when we have the two disastrous sea-battles fresh in our minds. In fact it seems to me that almost everything in this speech refers back to incidents we have seen and heard earlier in the play, and when we make such reference we find that the Queen's words are magnificent fantasy. I nearly said *just* magnificent fantasy, but the privative word is obviously questionable, if only because so many commentators have taken Cleopatra here to be glimpsing through (rather than in) Antony some reality of a transcendent nature. And by glimpsing it in such marvellous verse, Cleopatra creates it not only for herself but also for the play—for us. My rather reductive commentary (it could be argued) is accurate enough in its own way, but its own way isn't good enough. Yet, while no-one can doubt that Cleopatra is laying hold of possibilities that are intensely meaningful to her, we can't help asking, I think, whether these meanings really could emerge without deception from the possibilities that *we* have been allowed to see in Antony. It is understandable at the end of *Lear* that the King should see all value inhering in Cordelia, though, significantly, it is not something he can celebrate. But by the end of this play it seems to me that Antony is too discredited—genially and kindly, no doubt, but still discredited—for us to be able to simply accept what Cleopatra says as anything beyond a truth for her which is poignantly untrue for us. She can only glimpse what she does through Antony by forgetting about the real man altogether—which is precisely the point of my suggesting that much of what she says relates to what we have been seeing *per contra*. Yet Cleopatra herself, we notice a little later in the same scene, is not so convinced by her own vision that she can no longer imagine what other people (in this case the Roman mob) will make of the relationship: and for her to be able to set aside their view is more a tribute to her need than to the authenticity of her transcendental imaginings. The swelling plenitude of the Antony eulogy is surely qualified by the sharp focus and comic vivacity of this:

> saucy lictors
> Will catch at us like strumpets, and scald rhymers
> Ballad us out o'tune: the quick comedians
> Extemporally will stage us and present
> Our Alexandrian revels; Antony
> Shall be brought drunken forth, and I shall see
> Some squeaking Cleopatra boy my greatness
> I'th' posture of a whore.
>
> [V. ii. 214-21]

Very coarse of them, no doubt, but *how* wrong would they be? (pp. 230-32)

Antony and Cleopatra is not, of course, the story of a drunk and a whore: such a tale would be merely tedious. And in any case the play's vision is not simple and moralistic. But neither is it the piece that Wilson Knight [see excerpt above, 1931] and others make of it, a celebration and justification of transcendental love—Shakespeare's *Tristan und Isolde*. Its mocking clearsightedness inhibits that kind of simplicity too. (p. 233)

[What] marks off *Antony* (and *Coriolanus*) from the earlier and less perfectly realised tragedies is not something that is wholly to the advantage of the later pieces. I wonder if there isn't after all something essentially rather reductive about the art of *Antony*. That is what I meant by asking, at the beginning . . . , whether anyone ever left the theatre, after seeing it, feeling unnerved and emotionally bruised. I am not suggesting that the function of Tragedy is merely to upset us; but a full experience of a tragedy does seem to involve a certain laceration of spirit; and in Shakespeare's darkest plays such mitigation of the pain as there is results from the playwright's contrivance—from his not being able to face the consequences of his insights (the last scene of *Hamlet* shows what I have in mind). No such manipulation is needed in *Antony*, because there is no insight in the play which desperately needs to be evaded. Its vision, as I have been arguing, is too genial for that; and what I've called its 'desolating clarity' about *bovarysme* is desolating in the sense of being no more than (if certainly no less than) poignant. And though, in the gross, more hangs on the fate of the lovers than hangs on the fate of Lear or Othello,

there is little sign that the future of the Roman world is something that Shakespeare thought or cared much about. (pp. 233-34)

[The] figures in this play are less important, less significant, than the earlier heroes. The sensibility deployed here, for all its generosity of gesture, is narrower than what we find in *King Lear*. It is not that Shakespeare has ceased to see troubling things, but that they don't trouble him so much. *Antony* isn't, as it were, written in blood; indeed, the hero uses an appropriate counter-metaphor:

> That which is now a horse, even with a thought
> The rack dislimns, and makes it indistinct
> As water is in water.
>
> [IV. xiv. 9-11]

The characters try, not so much to make sense of their experience, as to find any experience stable enough, graspable enough, to look at without its shifting and dissolving into something else, or into nothingness. (pp. 234-35)

> *A. L. French, "'Antony and Cleopatra',' in his* Shakespeare and the Critics, *Cambridge at the University Press, 1972, pp. 206-36.*

ANNE BARTON (lecture date 1973)

[*In portions of her lecture not reprinted here, Barton examines what she terms "the divided catastrophe"—a structural device whereby a tragedy does not end with the death of the seeming protagonist, but instead develops an extended treatment of another character—in three plays of Sophocles; she also discusses versions of the story of Antony and Cleopatra by Cinthio, Chaucer, Spenser, Jodelle, Garnier, and Daniel. In the excerpt below from that lecture, she analyzes the impact of Shakespeare's decision not to end his play with the death of Antony, but to continue it through more than four hundred lines which principally focus on "Cleopatra's hesitation and delay" and, ultimately, her own death. This unusual structure, Barton contends, achieves several effects: 1) it imposes a new perspective on earlier dramatic events so that our response to them is modified; 2) it subdues and transfigures the ambiguities that have persisted throughout the play; 3) it transforms Antony's bungled suicide; and 4) it "makes us understand something about historical process." The critic asserts that by her flawless death as a tragic queen, Cleopatra defeats any attempt by Octavius or the "quick comedians" to cheapen the story of the lovers, and in her dream of Antony she endows him with "an heroic identity so colossal, but also in a sense so true . . . that it will defeat Time."*]

Antony and Cleopatra appeared originally in the Shakespeare First Folio without act and scene divisions. This omission, as A. C. Bradley remarked, is of no particular consequence. In fact, the tragedy divides logically and inevitably into five acts. Within this overall structure, Shakespeare has created a divided catastrophe, split between acts four and five. Antony's crushing defeat at Actium comes in Act III. In Act IV, scenes four through eight, there is for him a moment of respite. Not only does he seem, momentarily, to regain his lost, heroic identity: he moves towards a reconciliation within himself of the warring values of Rome and Egypt. May it not be possible after all to be a soldier, a triumphant workman in 'the royal occupation' [IV. iv. 17] during the day, and still return to feast and sleep with Cleopatra in the night? Scenes seven and eight in particular are scenes in which we delude ourselves into thinking that there will be no tragedy. Caesar is beaten back. Antony discovers that Antony can be 'himself . . . but stirr'd by Cleopatra' [I. i. 43]. That formula for the reconciliation of opposites which, when it appeared in the first scene of the play, so patently rang false, here becomes almost true. And, for reasons buried deep in our own psychology and in that of the play, we want terribly to believe it. After all, beneath the surface of this tragedy lies one of the great Renaissance wish-dreams: the dream not only of harmony but of exchange and union between the masculine and feminine principles.

Shakespeare's use of the Heracles/Omphale myth—Antony tricked out in Cleopatra's tires and mantles whilst she wore his sword Philippan—always seems to be regarded by the play's critics through the cold eyes of Octavius: as an indication of Antony's utter degradation. He 'is not more manlike / Than Cleopatra; nor the queen of Ptolemy / More womanly than he'. The indictment here seems clear-cut. The image of a transvestite Antony is not only comic in itself, it seems to epitomise the destruction of his masculinity at the hands of Cleopatra. Almost nothing in this play, however, up to the point of the final scene, is either simple or easy to judge. (pp. 5-6)

The heroic Antony of past time, the one recollected by Octavius, Pompey, Philo and Demetrius, was intensely male. On one level, it is clearly bad that Cleopatra has made him womanish. On another, his Egyptian bondage asks to be read as an attempt to regain the kind of wholeness, that primal sexual unity, about which Aristophanes is half joking, half deadly serious, in Plato's *Symposium*. Certainly there is something not just unattractive but maimed about the exclusively masculine world of Rome in this play. It emerges in that distasteful all-male party on board Pompey's galley in Act II, a party which ripens towards an Alexandrian revel but never gets there, as it does in the desperately public, chilly ostentation of Caesar's affection for his sister. Octavia, it seems, is the only woman in Rome and . . . she exists only in order to be manoeuvred and pushed about by the men.

Cleopatra is as quintessentially feminine as the younger Antony was male. Left alone among women and eunuchs after Antony's departure, she finds that life is scarcely worth living. This, one would expect. And yet she does try, particularly in the second half of the play, to become a kind of epic, warrior maiden. She is not exactly cut out to be a Britomart [in Spenser's *The Faerie Queen*]. When she tries to act as Antony's male body-servant in Act IV, she merely succeeds in putting his armour on the wrong way round. She must have looked preposterous wearing his sword. At Actium, she announces that she will appear 'for a man' but, when the battle is joined, it is as a fearful woman that she runs away. Nevertheless, it is important that she should at least have tried to participate in Antony's masculine world, that he should feel that one of her rebukes to him for military delay 'might have well becom'd the best of men'. Like Desdemona in Cyprus, she seems for a while to reconcile opposites, to become Antony's 'fair warrior'.

This moment of harmony is brief. As is usual in the fourth acts of Shakespeare's tragedies, a door is left temptingly ajar to reveal the sunlit garden of a possible happy ending, and then slammed shut. What is unique about *Antony and Cleopatra* is that this door closes where it opened, in Act IV, and not—as in the other tragedies—in Act V. In scene twelve of the penultimate act, Antony loses the third and climactic battle. This time, there can be no recovery. He also loses all conviction of his own identity and all faith in his grasp of Cleopatra's, let alone any belief that the values of masculine Rome and feminine Egypt might, after all, be united. Only the false report of her death can restore Cleopatra for him as a person. His own identity, from the very first scene of the play a persistent source of question and debate for the characters who surround

him, now becomes for Antony himself as cloudlike and indistinct 'as water is in water' [IV. xiv. 11]. For him . . . , the way to self-definition, to the recovery of the man that was, seems to lie through heroic suicide. . . . [However], Antony bungles his death. The greatest soldier of the world proves to be less efficient than Eros, a former slave. Antony fails to kill himself cleanly, and no one will respond to his requests for euthanasia. Decretas simply steals his sword and carries it to Caesar in the hope of promotion. Wallowing on the ground in agony, Antony receives the equivocal news that his serpent of old Nile has once again demonstrated what Enobarbus called her remarkable 'celerity in dying' [I. ii. 144]—and in reviving again at a propitious moment. Because Cleopatra is too frightened to leave her monument, Antony must be hauled up to her, slowly and unceremoniously, with ropes. He finds it almost impossible to make the queen listen to his dying words, so obsessed is she with her tirade against fortune and Octavius. The advice he gives her to trust Proculeius is, characteristically, misguided. With a last attempt which, under the circumstances, seems pathetic rather than convincing, to re-establish his heroic identity as 'the greatest prince o' the world . . . a Roman, by a Roman valiantly vanquish'd' [IV. xv. 54, 57-8], he expires in his destroyer's arms. (pp. 6-7)

[This] is not really a glorious or even a very controlled end. But it does feel distinctly like an end, in a sense that goes beyond Antony's individual death. Even at this point, this is already a long play; it positively seems to hanker after conclusion. The whole tragedy, after all, has been focussed on Antony far more than on Cleopatra. He has been the character standing, like Heracles at the cross-roads, with an important choice to make. He has done the journeying, while she stayed put in Egypt, and these journeys have not been simply geographical, but the pilgrimages of a divided mind. Rome or Egypt, virtue or vice, the active life or the life of pleasure, the Antony of the past or the sybarite of the present: these are the great antinomies between which his will has vacillated and swung and the movement has been, to a large extent, the movement of the play. Now that he is dead, the world seems almost as vacant and still as Cleopatra imagines: a 'dull world, which in thy absence is / No better than a sty' [IV. xv. 61-2]. There is room for tragic obsequies—'The crown o' the earth doth melt' [IV. xv. 63]. 'O, wither'd is the garland of the war' [IV. xv. 64]—but not, as one feels, for tragic continuation. It is true that Cleopatra remains to be accounted for, but that conclusion seems to be foregone:

> We'll bury him: and then, what's brave, what's noble,
> Let's do it after the high Roman fashion,
> And make death proud to take us. Come, away,
> This case of that huge spirit now is cold.
> Ah, women, women! come, we have no friend
> But resolution, and the briefest end.
>
>   [IV. xv. 86-91]

No matter how well one knows the play, it is difficult not to be tricked at this point into believing in that 'briefest end.' Surely Cleopatra will send out on the spot for a commodity of asps and follow Antony without delay. What we are emphatically not prepared for is a second catastrophe sharply divided from the first: a catastrophe, moreover, which is going to occupy an entire fifth act and more than four hundred lines of the tragedy. (pp. 7-8)

Like the vagabond flag of Caesar's image, *Antony and Cleopatra*, up to the point of its final scene, 'goes to and back, lackeying the varying tide, / To rot itself with motion' [I. iv.

46-7]. This restlessness is expressed not only in terms of a continual shifting of place, from Alexandria to Rome, to Misenum, to Athens, to Parthia, to Rome again, to Egypt, but also of the vacillation of the perspective picture, Mars dissolving into the Gorgon and then again becoming Mars. By the end of Act IV, we long for stasis, for the movement to stop. But it does not. Most of Act V is taken up with Cleopatra's hesitation and delay. Indeed, all of its dramatic tension derives from our uncertainty as to whether, despite all her protestations, she will keep her word and follow Antony in death. And, oddly enough, in a way for which there is no parallel in any other Shakespearean tragedy, we want Cleopatra to die. The reaction is one that flies in the face of normal tragic convention. After all, most of the suspense generated in the fifth act of *Hamlet* springs from our hope that somehow Hamlet himself will manage both to kill Claudius and to escape alive. In *Othello*, there remains the tantalizing possibility that the Moor will see through Iago and recognize Desdemona's innocence before it is too late, or, in *Romeo and Juliet*, that Juliet will wake before Romeo takes the poison. Only in *Antony and Cleopatra* do we long for a protagonist who has not, like Macbeth, been a villain to decide to die and do so.

Shakespeare's reason for employing the double catastrophe was, I think, precisely to elicit this unconventional reaction from the audience, and then, to gratify our desires in a way that modifies our feelings about the entire previous development of the tragedy. As Cleopatra wavers and procrastinates, we see that there can be only one way of putting doubt and ambiguity to rest. This love story has hovered continually between the sublime and the ridiculous, the tragic and the comic. We have never been able to decide which of the two sets of perspective images was the right one, or to reach any compromise between them. Only if Cleopatra keeps faith with Antony now and dies can the flux of the play be stilled and their love claim value. The act itself is indeed one that 'shackles accident and bolts up change' [V. ii. 6], and not merely in the sense that it will free Cleopatra herself from mutability and time. It will also transform the past. . . . The vagabond flag will come to rest, leaving the triple-turned whore a lass unparallel'd, the Gorgon an immutable if injudicious Mars. It may even be possible to adumbrate a reconciliation between masculine Rome and feminine Egypt more lasting than the one achieved so briefly in Act IV: one which will diminish Caesar forever as half-human by comparison.

Caesar, of course, is the enemy. He wants passionately to get a living Cleopatra back to Italy because, as he says, 'her life in Rome / Would be eternal in our triumph' [V. i. 65-6]. If only he can do this, he will fix the qualities of the story forever in his own terms, which are those of the strumpet and the gorgon, not the lass unparallel'd and the Mars. Cleopatra will fade into a mere parody queen in the epic pageant of his own imperial greatness, and Antony become the brother-in-arms who deserted his superior for a light woman and got what he deserved. This threat makes it imperative not only that Cleopatra should die, but that she should die in the way she does: ostentatiously as a tragedy queen. Shakespeare makes us understand that the achievement was difficult. Cleopatra at last makes up her mind. Despite her apparent duplicity with Seleucus, her anxious enquiries as to Caesar's intentions, and her own fear of physical pain, she does finally recognise and repudiate Octavius' plan: 'He words me, girls, he words me, that I should not be noble to myself' [V. ii. 191-92]. She understands what will happen in Rome:

> the quick comedians
> Extemporally will stage us, and present

> Our Alexandrian revels; Antony
> Shall be brought drunken forth, and I shall see
> Some squeaking Cleopatra boy my greatness
> I' th' posture of a whore.
> [V. ii. 216-21]

If she does not die well, this is the way her story, and Antony's, will be told for all of time that matters. The puppeteers, the ballad-makers and the quick comedians will cheapen and impoverish a love which was flawed at best, but never just absurd.

Appropriately, the last obstacle Cleopatra faces on her way to death is Comedy: personified by that ribald and garrulous countryman who brings her asps concealed in his basket of figs. Patiently, she listens and even responds to the clown's slanders about women, to a kind of sexual innuendo that threatens to diminish the whole basis of love tragedy. When he cautions her that the worm is not worth feeding, she asks humorously: 'Will it eat me?' [V. ii. 271], and one realises that she has brought together and reconciled in death two warring images of herself from earlier in the play: the positive one in which she was 'a morsel for a monarch' [I. v. 31], but also Antony's savage description of her as mere broken meats: 'a morsel cold upon dead Caesar's trencher' [III. xiii. 116-17]. When she finally persuades the clown to depart—and the woman committed to tragedy has to ask comedy to leave no fewer than four times—we feel that precisely because she has walked through the fire of ridicule, the thing she most dreads and potentially the thing most deadly for her, she has earned the right to say, 'Give me my robe, put on my crown, I have / Immortal longings in me' [V. ii. 280-81]. And she does so at once, without a break or a mediating pause. Comedy simply flowers into tragedy.

'Immortal', of course, was one of the words that the clown stumbled over most comically: 'I would not be the party that should desire you to touch [the worm]', he cautioned, 'for his biting is immortal: those that do die of it, do seldom or never recover' [V. ii. 245-48]. It must have taken courage for Cleopatra to use that word 'immortal' again, so differently, within so short a space of time. She succeeds, however, in winning it back as part of the vocabulary of tragedy. Indeed, she even imposes, in retrospect, a truth upon the clown's blunder that he never intended: the biting of this particular asp will indeed be 'immortal', the agent of Cleopatra's, and through her of Antony's, undying fame.

Cleopatra dies perfectly, as a tragedy queen. In doing so, she not only redeems the bungled and clumsy nature of Antony's death in Act IV by catching it up and transforming it within her own, flawless farewell; she crystallises and stills all the earlier and more ambiguous tableaux of the play—Cydnus, her appearance throned in gold as the goddess Isis, even the dubious spectacle presented to the Roman messenger in the opening scene. This is a divided catastrophe of a very special kind. Not only does it alter the way we feel about the previous development of the tragedy, hushing our doubts about Cleopatra's faith, it makes us understand something about historical process. After all, there does seem to have been something about Cleopatra's death as the story was perpetuated in time that made it impossible for Cinthio and Jodelle, Garnier and Daniel, not to mention Chaucer and Spenser, to condemn her, whatever the overall moral pattern of the poem or play in which she appeared. There are no satirical comedies about Antony's infatuation with an Egyptian whore.

Shakespeare's second catastrophe stands as a kind of explanation of this phenomenon. Cleopatra's death, as he presents it, demonstrates how the ending of this story transfigured its earlier, more suspect stages. The modification of feeling which it imposes upon us as an audience is a repetition and re-enactment of what has happened within historical time. In the play itself, we watch as Octavius acquiesces to Cleopatra's tragedy, consents (indeed) to become its Fortinbras [in *Hamlet*]. Here will be no parody queen led in triumph before a hooting mob, no bawdy Roman ballads, no comic puppet-shows presenting and coarsening the revels of Alexandria. Instead,

> She shall be buried by her Antony.
> No grave upon the earth shall clip in it
> A pair so famous. . . . Our army shall
> In solemn show attend this funeral,
> And then to Rome. Come, Dolabella, see
> High order in this great solemnity.
>
> [V. ii. 358-60, 363-66]

Because Cleopatra has left him no real choice, Caesar consents to become an actor in her tragedy. Indeed, his order that the Roman army should, 'in solemn show', attend her funeral merely extends and develops Cleopatra's final pose.

Does it diminish Cleopatra in our eyes that the last scene of her life was just that: a tragic pose? That she assumes costume and a role, gathers Iras and Charmian as minor players around her, ransacks the treasuries of rhetoric, and confronts Caesar and his soldiers when they break in upon her with a contrived and formal tableau of death which they understand as such? I think not. When he remembered Cleopatra at Cydnus, Enobarbus said that the sight 'beggar'd all description' [II. ii. 198]. As she lay in her pavilion, she o'er-pictured 'that Venus where we see / The fancy outwork nature' [II. ii. 200-01]. That is, the living Cleopatra surpassed a picture of Venus in which art itself had outdone reality. Cleopatra herself develops this favorite Renaissance paradox when she tells Dolabella, shortly before her death, about the mythical Antony of her dreams: 'His legs bestrid the ocean, his rear'd arm / Crested the world: his voice was propertied / As all the tuned spheres' [V. ii. 82-4]. Asked if there 'was or might be such a man / As this I dreamt of', Dolabella answers literally: 'Gentle madam, no' [V. ii. 93-4]. And Cleopatra flashes out:

> You lie up to the hearing of the gods.
> But if there be, or ever were one such,
> It's past the size of dreaming: nature wants stuff
> To vie strange forms with fancy, yet to imagine
> An Antony were nature's piece 'gainst fancy,
> Condemning shadows quite.
>
> [V. ii. 95-100]

An Elizabethan cliché, the conceit of an art more realistic than reality itself, acquires in the second catastrophe of *Antony and Cleopatra* a very special meaning. Cleopatra here bestows upon Antony an heroic identity so colossal, but also in a sense so true—after all, those kingdoms dropping like plates, unregarded, from his pockets summon up the careless Antony we have always known—that it will defeat Time. She is also working towards her own death scene, a fictional masterpiece of another kind which is going to out-class the normal fictions of tragedy by also being real. In this death, reality will borrow the techniques of art as a means of fighting back against oblivion. Moreover, it will be victorious. Hitherto, all the images of stasis offered by a tragedy yearning towards rest have been either distasteful, like Caesar himself and his 'universal peace' spread through a silent world from which everything remark-

able has departed, or else obviously fragile: 'the swan's down feather, / That stands upon the swell at the full of tide, / And neither way inclines' [III. ii. 48-50]. We know that, in the next moment, the tide will ebb. It is Cleopatra who finally arrests the eddying of the vagabond flag, who gives to the swan's down feather an immutable poise. She does so by creating a tableau, 'still and contemplative in living art' [*Love's Labour's Lost*, I. i. 14], which transfigures and quiets the events in which it was immanent in a way that Sophocles, surely, would have understood. (pp. 16-20)

> *Anne Barton, in her* "Nature's Piece 'gainst Fancy,"
> the Divided Catastrophe in "Antony and Cleopatra":
> An Inaugural Lecture, *Bedford College, 1973, 20 p.*

JANET ADELMAN   (essay date 1973)

[*Adelman's book on* Antony and Cleopatra *addresses virtually all aspects of the play, and it has been frequently cited and praised by later critics. In the following excerpt from that work, the critic contends that in experiencing this drama we are forced to struggle with the same concern of "right judgment" that so obsesses all the characters and to recognize—as the lovers do—both "the folly of judgment" and the notion that, on occasion, ambiguities may be confronted only by a "leap of faith." Adelman maintains that the gap between poetry and dramatic events is partly the cause of frustrated judgment, but she asserts that this discrepancy is heightened by Shakespeare's use of paradox and hyperbole, which "shape not only the language but also the presentation of character, the structure, and the themes."* Antony and Cleopatra *is also deeply concerned with "immoderate excess," she argues, and while Octavius exemplifies Roman moderation and graceless temperance, Egypt—in its recognition of the contiguity between fertility and corruption—provides a scale against which to measure Antony's Nile-like "mingled abundance." Adelman avers that Antony's propensity to "overflow the measure" is associated with Herculean excess, and she declares that the allusions to the god serve not only to emphasize the triumvir's diminished heroic stature, but, more importantly, to direct us "toward belief in the impossible." The critic concludes that by their hyperbolic assertions of love and union in death and their paradoxical loss of self in order to gain it again,* Antony and Cleopatra *lead us to see "that occasionally truth can be told only in lies."*]

The critical history of *Antony and Cleopatra* can be seen largely as a series of attempts to assess the motives of the protagonists and to arbitrate between the claims of Egypt and Rome. But this search for certainty often encounters the stumbling block of the play itself: at almost every turn, there are significant lapses in our knowledge of the inner state of the principal characters; and we cannot judge what we do not know. The characters themselves continually tell us that they do not know one another, that their judgments are fallible. Nor can we attribute the critics' persistent search for answers merely to their stubbornness: for the play demands that we make judgments even as it frustrates our ability to judge rationally. This frustration is not an end in itself: it forces us to participate in the experience of the play and ultimately to make the same leap of faith that the lovers make. In this sense, our uncertainty is an essential feature of the play. (p. 14)

Throughout the play, the characters themselves question its meaning for us; the questioning is so habitual that it occurs explicitly even in those relatively minor scenes where the meaning does not seem to be at issue. When the soothsayer tells Charmian that she shall be far fairer than she is, the two women debate his meaning:

Char.   He means in flesh.
Iras.   No, you shall paint when you are old.

                                [I. ii. 18-19]

Their debate is poignant because neither can guess the true meaning of his prophecies. The question of meaning is most explicitly raised in the small scene in which Antony bids his servants farewell; there it is raised four times in thirty-five lines. We would expect Cleopatra to know Antony as well as anyone; yet she asks Enobarbus, "What means this?" . . . and, ten lines later, "What does he mean?" [IV. ii. 13, 23]. Enobarbus then asks Antony directly: "What mean you, sir, / To give them this discomfort?" [IV. ii. 33-4]. Antony immediately denies that he meant his words as Enobarbus and the servants have taken them:

> Ho, ho, ho!
> Now the witch take me, if I meant it thus!
> Grace grow where those drops fall, my hearty friends;
> You take me in too dolorous a sense,
> For I spake to you for your comfort.

                                [IV. ii. 36-40]

Antony's attempt to console his followers by rearranging his meaning explicitly raises the issue of interpretation; even here, we are faced with one of the central dilemmas of the play. Virtually the only way out of this dilemma is the way that Antony takes at the end of the scene, when he in effect plays Horatio to his own Hamlet: "Let's to supper, come, / And drown consideration" [IV. ii. 44-5]. (pp. 20-1)

Nothing goes unquestioned in this play. In most literature there is a convention that character is knowable as it rarely is in life, that characters act in accordance with certain constant, recognizable, and explicable principles which we and they can know. This convention does not operate in *Antony and Cleopatra*. There the characters do not know each other, nor can we know them, any more clearly than we know ourselves. In the midst of Antony's rage against Cleopatra and Thidias, Cleopatra asks him, "Not know me yet?" [III. xiii. 157]. Antony can scarcely be blamed for not knowing Cleopatra; the question stands as central to the play. From Cleopatra's "If it be love indeed, tell me how much" [I. i. 14] to the First Guardsman's "Is this well done?" [V. ii. 325], questions of motive, of value, and of the truth of the emotions are insistently raised. . . . Antony thinks Cleopatra's passions are feigned: "She is cunning past man's thought" [I. ii. 145]. But Enobarbus answers that "her passions are made of nothing but the finest parts of pure love" [I. ii. 146-47]; and whatever his tone of voice, his words at least contradict Antony's. Enobarbus and Agrippa mock Lepidus's protestations of love for both Antony and Caesar (3.2). Cleopatra idly asks, "Did I, Charmian, / Ever love Caesar so?" [I. v. 66-7], and is most displeased with Charmian's teasing answer. (pp. 22-3)

The full acknowledgement of all this uncertainty is in Antony's quiet lines, "I made these wars for Egypt, and the queen, / Whose heart I thought I had, for she had mine" [IV. xiv. 15-16]. Does Antony have her heart? . . . In the end, the uncertainty implicates us as well as the characters: we must question Cleopatra's love for Antony as she plans her suicide; Shakespeare's insistence upon her dread of a Roman triumph forces us to question it. But in this play, not even skepticism is a secure position: Enobarbus shows us that. He persistently questions the sincerity of the passions, but when he follows his reason, he dies of a broken heart. At his death, we who have agreed with his rational skepticism are at a loss: skepticism

itself is no more reliable than passion. If we are finally convinced of Cleopatra's love—and I think we are—we have had to develop a faith nearly as difficult as Antony's, a faith in what we cannot know.

> Though he be painted one way like a Gorgon,
> The other way's a Mars.

                                [II. v. 116-17]

If we are forced to participate in this questioning of emotion, with all its consequences, we are also forced to participate in the act of judgment. The desire to judge and be judged correctly is one of the dominant passions of the play; it is no wonder that the critics have spent so long trying to judge between Rome and Egypt when the characters themselves are so concerned with right judgment. "Is Antony, or we, in fault for this?" [III. xiii. 2], Cleopatra asks after Actium: it is another of those questions which seem central to our experience of the play. Enobarbus answers "Antony only" without hesitation; but he can afford to give this partial judgment because he had already condemned Cleopatra before the fact ("Your presence needs must puzzle Antony" [III. vii. 10]. Antony's desire to die nobly, Cleopatra's dread of a Roman triumph: both are part of this overriding concern with judgment. Throughout the play, we see people making images of themselves, rearranging their own story. Cleopatra virtually stage-manages her death; and Caesar tries to arrange for correct judgment of himself with nearly every word he speaks. (pp. 24-5)

Throughout the play, the audience hears characters ask apparently unanswerable questions and watches them discuss one another without reaching any accord. We listen to a series of reports and judgments which are neither true nor false, or are both together, until even the concepts of truth and falsity lose their meanings. Shakespeare is not dallying with us only to confuse us. He is instead deliberately playing with these dramatic techniques in order to draw us into the act of judging. In effect, we are forced to judge and shown the folly of judging at the same time: our double responses are an essential part of the play. (p. 39)

From the first words of the play ("Nay, but"), our reactions have been at issue. We are given judgments that we must simultaneously accept and reject; we are shown the partiality of truth. But finally we are not permitted to stand aside and comment with impunity. . . .: we must choose either to accept or to reject the lovers' versions of themselves and of their death; and our choice will determine the meaning of the play for us. But the choice becomes increasingly impossible to make on the evidence of our reason or our senses. How can we believe in Enobarbus's description of Cleopatra as Venus when we see the boy actor before us? The Antony whom Cleopatra describes in her dream is not the Antony whom we have seen sitting on stage in dejection after Actium or bungling his suicide. Although the lovers die asserting their postmortem reunion, all we see is the dead queen and her women, surrounded by Caesar and his soldiers. The stage action necessarily presents us with one version of the facts, the poetry with another. This is the dilemma inherent in much dramatic poetry; and the more hyperbolical the poetry, the more acute the dilemma. (pp. 102-03)

The poetry of the last two acts is generally acknowledged as the sleight-of-hand by which Shakespeare transforms our sympathies toward the lovers, in despite of the evidence of our reason and our senses. Although even Caesar speaks in blank verse, the language of most richness and power is in the service of the lovers: it is the language in which Enobarbus creates

Cleopatra as Venus and the lovers assert the value of their love and their death. In this play, the nay-sayers may have reason and justice on their side; but as Plato suspected when he banished poetry from his republic, reason and justice are no match for poetry. . . . If it is true that Shakespeare uses the poetry to dazzle our moral sense and undo the structure of criticism in the play, then we may find *Antony and Cleopatra* satisfying as a rhetorical showcase, but we cannot admire the play as a whole. It is refreshing to find this charge made explicit by G. B. Shaw, who clearly enjoys expressing his contempt for a poet who finds it necessary to rescue his lovers from our moral judgment by means of a rhetorical trick.

> Shakespear's Antony and Cleopatra must needs be as intolerable to the true Puritan as it is vaguely distressing to the ordinary healthy citizen, because after giving a faithful picture of the soldier broken down by debauchery, & the typical wanton in whose arms such men perish, Shakespear finally strains all his huge command of rhetoric & stage pathos to give a theatrical sublimity to the wretched end of the business, & to persuade foolish spectators that the world was well lost by the twain. Such falsehood is not to be borne except by the real Cleopatras & Antonys (they are to be found in every public house) who would no doubt be glad enough to be transfigured by some poet as immortal lovers. Woe to the poet who stoops to such folly! . . . When your Shakespears & Thackerays huddle up the matter at the end by killing somebody & covering your eyes with the undertaker's handkerchief, duly onioned with some pathetic phrase . . . I have no respect for them at all: such maudlin tricks may impose on tea-house drunkards, not on me [see excerpt above, 1900].

The final poetry, detached from character and situation, does indeed give us the glorified vision of love that Shaw mistrusted, a vision not wholly consistent with the merely human Antony and Cleopatra, though Antony is far more than a debauchee and Cleopatra anything but typical, no matter how wanton. But the poetry is not [rhetorical]. . . . Its assertions and the problems they present to our skepticism have been inherent throughout: and if the poetry strains our credulity toward the end, the strain itself is a necessary part of our experience. Are the visions asserted by the poetry mere fancies, or are they "nature's piece 'gainst fancy" [V. ii. 99]? Precisely this tension between belief and disbelief has been essential from the start. When the lovers first come on stage, very much in the context of an unfriendly Roman judgment, they announce the validity of their love in a hyperbolical poetry which contrasts sharply with Philo's equally hyperbolical condemnation. Here, at the very beginning, two attitudes are set in juxtaposition by the use of two equally impossible images which appeal to two very different modes of belief. Philo uses hyperbole as *metaphor:* "his captain's heart / . . . is become the bellows and the fan / To cool a gipsy's lust" [I. i. 6, 9-10]. This is the deliberate exaggeration which moral indignation excites; it does not in any sense call for our literal belief. The hyperbolical metaphor is morally apt, and that is all. The Roman metaphor is carefully delineated as metaphor: it never pretends to a validity beyond the metaphoric. But what of the lovers? "Then must thou needs find out new heaven, new earth" [I. i. 17]; "Let Rome in Tiber melt" [I. i. 33]. Strictly speaking, these

hyperboles are not metaphor at all. Antony's words assert his access to a hyperbolical world where such things actually happen, a world beyond the reach of metaphor. They claim, like Cleopatra's dream, to be in the realm of nature, not of fancy. His words do not give us the protection of regarding them merely as apt metaphors: they make their claim as literal action. We may choose to disbelieve their claim; but in doing so, we are rejecting a version of reality, not the validity of a metaphor. And precisely this kind of assertion will become more insistent—and more improbable—as the play progresses. (pp. 103-06)

If we come to believe in the assertions of the poetry, it is, I think, precisely because they are so unbelievable. One of the tricks of the human imagination is that an appeal to the rationally possible is not always the most effective means of insuring belief: occasionally an appeal to the impossible, an appeal to doubt, works wonders. *Antony and Cleopatra* embodies in its structure the paradox of faith: the exercise of faith is necessary only when our reason dictates doubt; we believe only in the things that we know are not true. The central strategy of *Antony and Cleopatra* depends upon this process: we achieve faith by deliberately invoking doubt. And in fact this process dictates not only the broad structure of the play but also its poetic texture. The imaginative vision of the play is based firmly on the two rhetorical figures that are themselves dependent on this strategy: paradox and hyperbole.

The incidence of paradox and hyperbole in *Antony and Cleopatra* is not merely an accident or Shakespeare's sleight-of-hand: these figures inform the shape and the substance of the play. For they posit in their very structure the tension between imaginative assertion and literal fact that is part of the state of love. . . . Shakespeare expresses his sense that love transcends the limits of reason and fact in the overreaching paradoxes of "The Phoenix and the Turtle": here the lovers can transcend number ("Two distincts, division none," line 27), space ("Distance, and no space was seen / 'Twixt this turtle and his queen," lines 30-31), and identity ("Property was thus appalled, / That the self was not the same," lines 37-38). Reason itself is confounded by these paradoxes and cries: "Love hath Reason, Reason none, / If what parts can so remain" (lines 47-48).

Antony and Cleopatra is the exploration of this *if:* it is the working out of these paradoxes in human terms, with all their human contradictions. The paradoxes so easily stated in "The Phoenix and the Turtle" are the hard-won conclusions of the lovers: that one must lose oneself to gain oneself; that the only life is in death, the only union in separation. To regard either paradox or hyperbole as merely rhetorical ornament is to overlook their enormous potency in the play: in a very literal way, they shape not only the language but also the presentation of character, the structure, and the themes. And if the tension between skepticism and belief is resolved for a moment at the end, it is resolved only insofar as we for a moment accept paradox and hyperbole as literally true, despite their logical impossibilities. (pp. 110-13)

The descriptive hyperboles that surround Antony and Cleopatra are essential to our understanding of them: for the lovers and the world they inhabit are themselves hyperbolical. *Antony and Cleopatra* is preeminently about immoderate excess: excess which the Roman world successfully measures and subdues. (p. 121)

[The] first words of the play introduce us to the Roman scale of measurement, on which man is but a man. Antony's dotage overflows the measure: his heart "reneges all temper" [I. i. 8]. Implicit in the word "measure" are two significantly related concepts: *moderation* and *measurement*. Here moderation, temperance, are the measuring rods for man: it is literally by his temperance that a man must be measured. Antony plays on these two concepts when he tells Octavia, "I have not kept my square, but that to come / Shall all be done by the rule" [II. iii. 6-7]: in the Roman world, the rule is that by which one is measured. The same cluster of concepts is implicit in Cleopatra's description of the "mechanic slaves / With greasy aprons, rules, and hammers" [V. ii. 209-10], whose presence she so dreads in the Roman triumph: they will attempt to measure her by their rules and will presumably proclaim her whore. (p. 122)

Octavius is the exemplar of measure in *Antony and Cleopatra:* and his virtue is scarcely heartwarming. His victory promises a civil peace for the world:

> The time of universal peace is near:
> Prove this a prosperous day, the three-nook'd world
> Shall bear the olive freely.
>
> [IV. vi. 4-6]

Peace is of course highly desirable, but we see how freely Caesar's peace will be borne in his treatment of Lepidus and the kings who have revolted from Antony and in his plans for Cleopatra. Octavius's comparative sobriety on Pompey's galley suggests both the negative and the positive aspects of the virtue. There is no question that his measured behavior is more suitable for a world leader than Antony's excess: but at the same time, there is something niggardly in his refusal to be a child of the time, to give himself to the situation. Temperance will keep man under control, but it does not allow room for love or grace. Both love and grace must necessarily overflow: they are inimical to measure. . . . The man of measure is necessarily miserly in his relations with other people; he will commit no excesses, but neither will he give himself. And if he never loses himself, it is at least partly, we suspect, because he has no self to lose. We are never permitted to see Octavius in a private context. We see him always in the light of an insistent publicity; moreover, he seems to determine his own emotions by public and political effect. His love for his sister does not prevent his pawning her for political gain. His grief at Antony's death seems designed to emphasize his own greatness: he mourns for Antony as "the arm of mine own body" [V. i. 45]. And his tears for his great competitor are too public to be entirely convincing; they are easily interrupted as soon as business intervenes [V. i. 48-50].

If Octavius is the exemplar of measure, Antony is the exemplar of that loss of self which intemperance necessitates. His attempt to live by the rule must fail; his dotage will overflow the measure. From the Roman perspective, Antony illustrates precisely the results of sexual intemperance: when feminine passion dominates masculine reason, effeminacy and loss of manhood are necessarily the results. Antony's act of overflow is specifically sexual: and he pays the consequences. Early in the play, Philo finds the symptoms of this loss of self:

> . . . sometimes, when he is not Antony,
> He comes too short of that great property
> Which still should go with Antony.
>
> [I. i. 57-9]

When Antony is under the influence of his Egyptian fetters, Enobarbus cannot tell him from his queen [I. ii. 79]; like Cleopatra's description of the exchange of clothing, Enobar-

bus's error suggests the diminution of Antony's masculine identity. Octavius enters the play condemning Antony's intemperance and his consequent loss of manhood [I. iv. 1-7]. And immediately after Antony's flight at Actium, Scarus says,

> I never saw an action of such shame;
> Experience, manhood, honour, ne'er before
> Did violate so itself.
>
> [III. x. 21-3]

But we learn the value of measure less from Antony's Roman critics than from his own perception of his loss: throughout, he sees his own folly and intemperance with a Roman clarity of moral vision. He knows from the start that he is losing himself: "These strong Egyptian fetters I must break, / Or lose myself in dotage" [I. ii. 116-17]. And after Actium, when he has quite literally lost himself, he perceives his loss more clearly than anyone else. He bids his followers fly to Caesar because his own flight has instructed them in desertion: "I have fled myself, and have instructed cowards / To run, and show their shoulders" [III. xi. 7-8]. As he overflows the measure, he feels himself becoming "indistinct / As water is in water" [IV. xiv. 10-11].

Antony loses himself and feels his boundaries dissolving; and without boundaries, he can contain nothing. As Antony's worldly fortunes worsen, there is an implied contrast between his emptiness and Octavius's fullness: Antony overflows his measure and becomes empty, while Octavius is filled with fortune's gifts. At Antony's death, he is wholly empty: his body is merely "the case of that huge spirit" [IV. xv. 89]. And Octavius has become "full-fortun'd Cæsar" [IV. xv. 24], "the fullest man" [III. xiii. 87]. Enobarbus makes the contrast explicit when he comments on Antony's folly in expecting Octavius to accept his challenge to single combat:

> . . . that he should dream,
> Knowing all measures, the full Cæsar will
> Answer his emptiness.
>
> [III. xiii. 34-6]

But it is part of Antony's folly that he no longer knows all measures; for measure is the necessary virtue in the realm of fortune, the realm of business which Octavius manages so well and Antony so poorly. As Antony overflows his measure and loses himself to Cleopatra, he becomes a strumpet's fool; as Octavius maintains his measure and is filled with fortune's gifts, he becomes fortune's knave. The choice is not attractive: and Rome allows us no other alternatives.

At his most Roman, Antony will accuse Cleopatra of intemperance: "I am sure, / Though you can guess what temperance should be, / You know not what it is" [III. xiii. 120-22]. Despite his tone of disappointed surprise, we can no more imagine a temperate Cleopatra than a Nile which behaves like the Tiber or the Thames. For Egypt is itself hyperbolical: everything there overflows the measure, and excess is the normal state of affairs. However abhorrent to Roman notions of agriculture, the survival of Egypt is dependent on the mingled fertility of the overflowing Nile, breeding both crops and serpents. In Rome, overflow is a human vice; in Egypt, it is a natural necessity. Overflow here is neither moral nor immoral; it breeds good and evil indifferently. The sense of an enormous and mingled fertility is everywhere in the play. Antony swears "By the fire / That quickens Nilus' slime" [I. iii. 68-9]; Lepidus tells us that "Your serpent of Egypt is bred now of your mud by the operation of your sun: so is your crocodile" [II. vii. 26-7]. Cleopatra imagines the water flies on Nile breeding a corrupt vitality in her dead body: ''on Nilus' mud / Lay me stark-nak'd, and let the water-flies / Blow me into abhorring'' [V. ii. 58-60]. But this corruption of the overflowing Nile is essential to its fertility; without serpents, there would be no crops.

Antony, like the Nile, overflows the measure: and that overflow which is purely loss from the perspective of Rome is partly gain in Egypt. The mingled abundance of the Nile serves as an analogy for the mingled abundance of Antony himself, excessive in all he does. (pp. 123-27)

Antony's Jove-like generosity is a central element in Cleopatra's hyperbolical vision of him:

> . . . For his bounty,
> There was no winter in't: an autumn 'twas
> That grew the more by reaping.
>
> [V. ii. 86-8]

To grow by reaping: like the Nile itself, Antony's excess breeds life out of death. In this world the only life comes from loss and death: the autumnal vitality of the lovers, which grows the more by reaping. And if Antony overflows the Roman scale, on which man is but a man, he will find a new scale in Egypt. For Egypt is itself hyperbolical; here, the only adequate scale is one which will measure the overflow. As Antony is telling Lepidus about the mysteries of Egypt on Pompey's galley, he gives us just such a scale:

> Thus do they, sir: they take the flow o' the Nile
> By certain scales i' the pyramid; they know,
> By the height, the lowness, or the mean, if dearth
> Or foison follow. The higher Nilus swells,
> The more it promises.
>
> [II. vii. 17-21]

On this scale, fecundity and corruption are seen as necessarily part of the same process. The pyramid, the tomb of Egypt, becomes the measure of fertility; death quite literally becomes the measure of life. The overflowing Nile and the scale that measures it can stand as the defining image for the tragic experience to which Rome is immune; for the Nile itself, like Antony, grows the more by reaping. And it is only this scale that is adequate to Antony's autumnal bounty. In this fluid world, only the capacity for loss and death can measure the life of man; only by the scales of the pyramid can we measure Antony's fatal and triumphant excess.

In Rome, it is an easy matter to measure a man; and in Rome, Antony loses himself and becomes empty. But in Egypt, loss is the only way to gain. For Antony's enormous bounty is entirely dependent upon his generosity of self, finally upon his loss of himself. He will give himself wholly and without that regard for consequences that reason dictates. He will give himself away. And if Rome (and Antony himself in his Roman mood) will see that loss of self as the result of effeminate intemperance, it can also be seen as evidence of a final and overwhelming generosity. . . . One takes one's choice: either a world of lavish overflow and the attendant risk of serpents; or a world of measure and the attendant risk of sterility. . . . [There] is no middle ground: the only way to fertility is through dissolution. (pp. 128-30)

Cleopatra's Egypt is associated with overflow and Octavius's Rome with measure: but Octavius's is not the only Rome we see. Although Octavius is the spokesman for measure, he is by no means the spokesman for the idea of Rome itself: our sense of ancient Roman virtue comes not from Octavius but

from the descriptions of Antony as he used to be. And in these descriptions, Rome itself is hyperbolical: Antony's excess is associated not only with Egypt and Cleopatra but also with his own past glory as a Roman soldier. Even as a Roman, Antony is consistently opposed to Roman measure: the heroic virtue which Philo, Pompey, and Octavius extol is quite as inconsistent with measure as the love which they deplore. Bursting the buckles of one's breast and drinking the stale of horses are hardly the marks of a temperate man. Philo's portrait of his warrior is as excessive as Cleopatra's of her lover: hyperbole is the mode used to describe him in either arena. The Roman valor associated with Antony's past and the Egypt of overflow are both equally excessive and equally inimical to the measured Rome of the present. For Octavius's moderate world necessarily excludes heroic virtue: just as it allows no room for the overflowing of human emotion, so it allows no room for the outsized individual who may in some respects be more than man. . . . *Antony and Cleopatra* is usually seen as some sort of debate between Egypt and Rome; but if this is the debate, then the debaters are grossly unbalanced. In fact, the opposition is never between the Rome of honor and heroic virtue and the Egypt of the senses: Octavius firmly rejects heroic virtue, and Roman honor has dwindled to Pompey's scrupulous desire for clean hands, for murder by proxy.

The Roman virtues of valor and heroism in the play are distinctly in the past tense: we must look to Antony's own past and to the fathers of our modern Romans. And however much Shakespeare may have challenged the grandeur of Julius Caesar in *Julius Caesar*, he is ''great Caesar'' or ''broad-fronted Caesar'' in this play, an almost mythic figure who towers over the generation of his heir. The play similarly insists on the elder Pompey's greatness. These were the great exemplars of Roman virtue; and they seem to belong to a time when one man was more than a man. Compared to this near-mythic generation, the sons have dwindled in stature. Octavius and Pompey are Cleopatra's harshest critics; but their fathers were her lovers. Shakespeare makes the point abundantly clear:

> . . . Broad-fronted Caesar,
> When thou wast here above the ground, I was
> A morsel for a monarch: and great Pompey
> Would stand and make his eyes grow in my brow,
> There would he anchor his aspect, and die
> With looking on his life. . . .
>
> [I. v. 29-34]

For the fathers, the mighty excesses of heroic virtue and passion can be conjoined; but the sons are so shrunk in grandeur that they can never embrace Egypt. They must ward it off as a curse. The younger Caesar is apparently immune to Cleopatra's charms. He may dally with her for political purposes, but we know that his very dallying is passionless. But in the past, when men were more than men, the greatest Romans themselves overflowed the measure.

Insofar as the greatest exemplars of Roman virtue were also in some sense Egyptians, our critical vision of the play as a balanced debate between Rome and Egypt is seriously befuddled. Side by side with this debate is another of more permanent consequence: that between the past and the present, the heroic excess of the fathers and the moderation of the sons. And standing behind the near-mythic figures of the past is a figure even more remote and more heroic: the gigantic figure of Hercules himself. Hercules is presented here as a god rather than as a human hero: placed firmly in a mythic past, inaccessible to mere mortals. The role of Hercules as moral analogue in the play has often been noted; but it seems to me much less significant than his role as poetic analogue. Eugene Waith [see excerpt above, 1962] suggests the complex of ideas associating Hercules with heroic virtue, the virtue of excess, magnanimity, and all that which overflows ordinary human limits: the labors and loves of Hercules were equally excessive. After Seneca, his gigantic rage and madness became stage properties as commonplace as his gigantic heroism, and inevitably bound up with it. Indeed, *Antony and Cleopatra* consistently emphasizes the hyperbolical proportions of his rage rather than the moral significance of his acts. For Hercules is the type of gigantic excess, a figure whose native region is the impossible and whose native speech is hyperbole; he is a hyperbolical braggart who always makes good his claims. He functions in the play neither as Roman nor Egyptian but rather as a distant and godlike figure of achieved excess: a figure who overflows every human scale. For Antony's hyperboles are Hercules' literal actions: he presumably could lodge Lichas on the horns of the moon in fact, while Antony can lodge him there only in rhetoric. At the allusive center of the play, then, is the shadowy figure of one for whom hyperbole is not in fact hyperbole but rather literal truth.

Antony and Hercules are relatives with the same taste for the excessive, no matter how diminished Antony is in power. Both Antony's folly and his grandeur have their literary roots in Hercules: *miles gloriosus* [braggart soldier] and hero are two sides of the same coin; and Antony inherits both literary traditions from his great ancestor. The allusions to Hercules serve partly to remind us of the discrepancy between Hercules' actions and Antony's pretensions, of the degree to which Antony has dwindled from the heroic stature of his great ancestor. Yet Hercules does not serve merely as a contrast to Antony. Here again Shakespeare disarms skepticism by including its perspective within the play. If the presence of Hercules emphasizes the folly of Antony's ventures into the realm of hyperbole, it also emphasizes their grandeur. Hercules becomes in effect a model for hyperbole which we can take perfectly literally: he shows us the way toward belief in the impossible. And although Antony is not Hercules, at the end of the play the hyperbolical realm has become his as well as his ancestor's. Even as Hercules withdraws from Antony, he in effect asserts their likeness: we need only try to imagine his withdrawing from Octavius to demonstrate the point.

We become fully aware of the god only as he is departing from his descendant, withdrawing in effect from the present world entirely. The withdrawal of the god is a scene of enormous imaginative potency, perhaps because it is so wholly irrelevant to the plot. If Hercules had withdrawn before Actium, then we could find in him a cause or at least a portent of Antony's desertion of himself at Actium. But he withdraws after Actium. The departure may signal Antony's loss of heroic virtue, since he has refused to fight; in this sense, Hercules seems to participate in the Roman judgment about Antony. But if Antony has managed to shame himself in the presence of the god, he manages to redeem himself in the god's absence: Hercules' withdrawal is followed immediately by the victorious land battle. But even as the god withdraws from the world, the possibility for significant heroic action goes with him. Antony momentarily recaptures his heroic valor, but to no avail. We are no longer in a world where individual heroism matters. Despite Cleopatra's pride in the valor of her man of men, she knows how little valor ultimately counts for in this world:

> . . . that he and Caesar might

> Determine this great war in single fight!
> Then Antony—; but now—Well, on.
>   [IV. iv. 36-8]

This is no world for single combat. Antony has promised Cleopatra that he will be "treble-sinew'd, hearted, breath'd" [III. xiii. 178], and he keeps his hyperbolical promise, but it no longer matters. The loss at Actium has put us squarely in the realm of present-day Rome, where a man is but a man, the realm most antithetical to Hercules. Hence the withdrawal of Hercules gives us the sense of heroic virtue, of excess and magnanimity itself, withdrawing from the earth, leaving in preparation for the triumph of measure. Our own sense of loss and betrayal here is extraordinarily complex: though the scene signals Antony's self-betrayal and his loss of grandeur, it simultaneously functions to suggest the consequences of the Roman victory. The gods will depart. And at the same time, the scene anticipates our sense of desolation when Antony himself withdraws from the earth.

No matter how diminished Antony was in grandeur, he was nonetheless the only grandeur we had: at his death, there *is* nothing left remarkable beneath the visiting moon. For Antony's place is midway between the generation of the fathers and the generation of the sons: his own Roman glory is past, but it is the only Roman glory of which there is any hint in the play. (pp. 131-37)

If at the start of the play Antony overflows the measure, by its end he has become the measure: at his death, the odds is gone. But even at the first entrance of the lovers, Antony renounces the concept of ordinary measure as irrelevant to their love:

Cleo.   If it be love indeed, tell me how much.
Ant.   There's beggary in the love that can be
          reckon'd.
Cleo.   I'll set a bourn how far to be belov'd.
Ant.   Then must thou needs find out new heaven, new
          earth.
                                     [I. i. 14-17]
                                     (pp. 139-40)

The lovers are not the only ones who must renounce the concept of ordinary measurement: if we are to participate in the play, we must also renounce it. Cleopatra's outrageously excessive portrait of her Antony is only part of the excess to which the play subjects us: we are asked to accept a play with too many short scenes and too many minor characters, with passions generally in excess of their objects and characters who claim to be larger than life: a play which gives us the whole world and then demands that we exchange it for a kiss. We cannot measure this play by any ordinary scale: it violates every principle of classical decorum and establishes a new decorum of its own. Shakespeare seems deliberately to challenge our sense of what is artistically measured, or fitting, throughout the play; and ultimately we must take it on its own terms. . . . Even within the play, Shakespeare insists that we notice his new decorum, a decorum tolerant of excess. Early in the play, Iras prays to Isis to "keep decorum" [I. ii. 73-4] by cuckolding Alexas; later, Cleopatra will define her own thoroughly unclassical decorum:

> . . . our size of sorrow,
> Proportion'd to our cause, must be as great
> As that which makes it.
>   [IV. xv. 4-6]

Cleopatra asserts her Egyptian decorum to Proculeius:

> . . . If your master
> Would have a queen his beggar, you must tell him,
> That majesty, to keep decorum, must
> No less beg than a kingdom.
>
> [V. ii. 15-18]

And even the Roman Dolabella will respect Cleopatra's decorum: "Your loss is as yourself, great; and you bear it / As answering to the weight" [V. ii. 101-02]. At the end of the play, Charmian insists on the correctness of Cleopatra's decorum of excess: when the first guardsman discovers Cleopatra dead and asks, "Is this well done?" Charmian replies, "It is well done, and fitting for a princess / Descended of so many royal kings" [V. ii. 325-27]. Egyptian decorum is hyperbolical: it overflows the Roman concept of decorum itself. And in the course of the play, we must learn to accept it as our own: in its very form, the play insists that we acknowledge the limitations of measurement.

The process of measurement is at issue in *Antony and Cleopatra* ultimately because identity itself is at issue. In the Roman world, the object retains its visible shape and is measurable; but in Egypt, the very measures dissolve. We are introduced to a world of continual metamorphosis, in which everything seems to become everything else. Nothing maintains its shape for long enough to be measured: the size and shape shifts that occur even in mid-metaphor and so baffle our critical senses are the manifestation of a world in which no scale is adequate. (pp. 141-42)

This shape shifting is characteristic of a world in which nothing stays to scale because everything overflows its own boundaries. It is to this dangerous and vital world that Antony commits himself. And here he will both lose himself and find himself: only here can we find a scale adequate to him. (p. 144)

Identity in *Antony and Cleopatra* is not merely a question of Antony's Romanness or of his manhood: by its merging and blending of all things, the play questions the very concept of identity. And if there is an answer, it is not in the realm of being at all but in the realm of becoming: identity is defined not by static measurement but by flux. As Antony loses his soldiership, his authority, and even his visible shape, he is nonetheless Antony. Both lovers become each other and themselves: and, in their infinite variety, they virtually become all the world besides. Other figures in the play retain their visible shape: they are precisely what they are. Octavius never loses himself: but neither does he become anything. But our lovers lose their boundaries and absorb everything into themselves.

It is no wonder that this world of fluid size and shape in which nothing stays to scale is reflected throughout the play in the water imagery: this watery world must overflow the measure. The Nile itself is, of course, the central image of overflow; but water is associated throughout with all that does not hold its bounds. (p. 145)

In this watery world, Antony loses himself and becomes empty: that the shifts of size and shape throughout the play are insistently associated with water emphasizes the sexual basis of Antony's dissolution. Water in all its ambiguity is the emblem of the world of generation: if melting and dissolving are associated with lust and its consequences, overflowing is associated with all fecundity. The sea is the birthplace of the great generative principle: and if the water leads us to Actium and Antony's desertion of himself, it also leads us to Cydnus, where

Cleopatra reigns as Venus, surrounded by Nereids and mermaids [II. ii. 206-09]. For water is, in a sense, Cleopatra's terrain: and if Cleopatra is a whore, she is also a generative goddess. The emotional and imagistic nexus of the play lies in the sexual process itself, where one must lose oneself in order to form a new union. The Roman horror of that loss and the ecstatic union which the lovers feel as they die are two elements in the same process: for the dissolution of personal boundaries is both our greatest fear and our highest desire. One must become as indistinct as water is in water to enter this world of enormous loss and enormous fecundity: only here, where all measures dissolve, can the frail case of nature be cracked and the hyperbolical be achieved. (pp. 148-49)

As the lovers die, they are united sexually in a vast act of overflow: so that death is simultaneously their means of escaping from the mutability of nature and their means of participating in it. In its emphasis on changes of size and shape and on all that overflows the measure, the play poses the mysteries of the sexual process: Antony grows the more by reaping. Enobarbus makes the paradox explicit in his description of Cleopatra:

> . . . other women cloy
> The appetites they feed, but she makes hungry,
> Where most she satisfies.
>
> [II. ii. 235-37]

The sense of spirit violently bursting through the case of nature is appropriate to the double nature of man as spirit incarnate, literally embodied; and it is also appropriate to human sexuality on the most literal and physiological level. The ultimate paradox of the play is that even its transcendence is part of the natural world of flux: measure and overflow, flux and stasis, time and eternity, life and death, are all inseparable, a knot intrinsicate.

Past the size of dreaming

[V. ii. 97]

When Cleopatra somewhat coyly asks poor Dolabella whether or not there could be such a man as the Antony she dreamed of, Dolabella denies the possibility of her dream. Her answer is immediate: "You lie up to the hearing of the gods" [V. ii. 95]. The entire play has led us to the point where we, as well as Cleopatra, can find Dolabella's denial of the dream at least as suspect as the dream itself. In what sense do we come to believe in the lovers' assertions, and how are we led to this belief?

One of the paths of assent open to us is that which would see the lovers' paradoxical and hyperbolical assertions as accurate metaphors for psychological facts, as descriptions of the world as it appears to the lovers. Antony says, "Fall not a tear, I say, one of them rates / All that is won and lost" [III. xi. 69-70]. If one of Cleopatra's tears is worth the world to Antony, then one tear *is* worth the world—insofar as we agree to see the world from his perspective. What we think of the bargain is, for the moment, irrelevant. In these matters there need be no "objective correlative": if Hamlet's situation drives him to despair, then it is for him a desperate situation. But does "His legs bestrid the ocean" [V. ii. 82] mean only, "As far as Cleopatra was concerned, Antony's legs bestrid the ocean"? Do we accept the lovers' assertions only as evaluative truths, only as we would perforce accept the truth of the statement, "It looks red to me" (even though the object looks very blue to us)? Is Cleopatra's dream only one more judgment in the long series of partial and erroneous judgments in the play? I think not. To believe in these assertions only as psychological metaphors is Philo's Roman way and does not seem adequate to our experience. "Cleopatra dies at one with Antony in her love for him" simply does not do justice to our sense of affirmation when she says, "Husband, I come" [V. ii. 287]; we cannot translate the impossible statement of fact into any possible statement of emotion without losing its force. As Cleopatra's dream of Antony is in the realm of nature, not of fancy, so these assertions leave the realm of fancy and begin to claim our belief as fact.

To the extent that we are engaged with the protagonist, his judgment will be our judgment; and to that extent it will be dramatic fact. Throughout most of *Antony and Cleopatra,* we are not permitted to become wholly engaged with the protagonists. In fact, most of the structural devices of the play prevent our engagement. . . . But toward the end of the play the dramatic technique changes radically. We tend more often to accept the lovers' evaluation of themselves, to take them at their word, because we are more often permitted to identify ourselves with them. The entire structure of framing commentary and of shifts of scene had forced us to remain relatively detached from them; after act 4, scene 12, it tends to disappear. No one intervenes between us and the lovers; there are no radical and disjunctive shifts in perspective. The final scene of the play is almost twice as long as the next longest scene (364 lines as opposed to 201 in act 3, scene 13): and it is Cleopatra's scene virtually from beginning to end. For once, she is allowed to undercut Caesar by her commentary: "He words me, girls, he words me" [V. ii. 191]. The Clown interrupts Cleopatra, but she turns his presence to her own account: his banter serves as an impetus to her immortal longings. Though he qualifies the solemnity of her death, he does not provide the radical shift in perspective that we have come to expect in this play. We can here take her as seriously as she takes herself, participate with her in the tragic perspective. The critical structure drops away from Antony in act 4, scene 14, in much the same manner. And as we are permitted to become involved with the lovers, their evaluations tend to take on the status of emotional fact even in despite of the literal fact.

If the dramatic structure now permits us to become engaged with the lovers, it also works to give us the feeling of assent in spite of all logic. For most of the play, we have been subjected to the wear and tear of numerous short scenes, to the restless shifts of perspective. Now, as the lovers leave the world of business, we are permitted to rest. The scenes become longer and more leisurely; the entire pace of the play slows. In some ways, the rhythm of the play suggests the rhythm of the sexual act itself, especially in the quiescent melting of its end. And as the lovers come together, even the quality of the language changes. The word "come," used so frequently by the lovers as they prepare to die, suggests that death is a reunion, not a separation—a suggestion not at all mitigated by the secondary sexual meaning of the word. But the sound of the word may be as significant as its meaning. We move from the complexity, rapidity, and lightness of "Our separation so abides and flies, / That thou, residing here, goes yet with me; / And I, hence fleeting, here remain with thee" [I. iii. 102-04] to the simple slowness of "I come, my queen" [IV. xiv. 50]. The restless tension in the language seems to be replaced by a new ease. If we participate in the lovers' sense of release from life, it is at least partly because we are ourselves released from the strain which action and language had imposed on us earlier.

At the same time, we are released from the doubts and scruples which have hedged us in throughout the play. Ultimately our

sense of assent probably comes from the fact that the psychological roots of the play are our psychological roots too. Insofar as *Antony and Cleopatra* concerns overflow, the dissolution of boundaries, bisexuality, and the association of both death and sexual love with loss of self and ecstatic union, it touches many of us where we live. One of the most difficult problems in love of any kind is to strike a balance between the desire to give oneself wholly to another and the desire to keep oneself wholly intact. We have had both sides of this conflict exacerbated in us as we watch the play: and most of the time, the spokesmen for the terrors of dissolution and loss of self have had the upper hand. Antony's fear that he is losing his visible shape may come dangerously close to home: for it is to some extent the fear of everyone in love. When this fear at last becomes desire, when mere loss of self is transformed into "I come, my queen," we are bound to feel the release as well as Antony. As the lovers die asserting that death is union, they temporarily resolve the tension for us; and in that sense, their resolution is bound to be ours.

This sense of resolution prepares us, I think, for the leap of faith necessary at the end of the play; and if we are given the feeling of assent, the play supports our feeling with a logic of its own. Antony's assertion that he and Cleopatra will meet in Elysium has sometimes been regarded as evidence of his delusion-unto-death; but if it is a delusion, it must in some sense be our delusion too. (pp. 156-61)

Antony's impossibility is in some sense confirmed by Cleopatra's independent expression of the same impossibility: "I am again for Cydnus, / To meet Mark Antony" [V. ii. 228-29]. These may be shared delusions, but they nonetheless create in us the sense that the lovers have grown together in death. The lovers are apart or acting at cross-purposes during most of the play: despite the verbal assertions of love and union, the sense we get is of their disunity. But after Antony dies, the feeling of union is gradually created, not only through Cleopatra's resolve to join him in death (as everyone has noted, she is not entirely resolute) but also through the dramatic structure. She begins to echo his phrases as though the lovers were in fact becoming one. But the lovers are not the only ones who assert their impossible reunion. Toward the end of the play, the possibility of the impossible is repeatedly confirmed by a striking technique: the assertions are reiterated by the most unexpected allies. In the end, the lovers do not need to rely on each other for support in their assertions: for their hyperbolical assertions are echoed by characters not ordinarily prone to the hyperbolical vision. Cleopatra finds in Antony's death the signs of the great Apocalypse: "darkling stand the varying shore o' the world"; "The soldier's pole is fall'n" [IV. xv. 10-11, 65]. But even the guardsmen greet Antony's suicide as an apocalyptic event:

> *Sec. Guard.*   The star is fall'n.
> *First Guard.* And time is at his period.
>
> [IV. xiv. 106-07]

Both independently see Antony as a fallen star; we need not depend on the testimony of his mistress alone. Their reaction authenticates her hyperbolical vision. The lovers' assertions that death is a sleep in which they will be reunited are authenticated by the same means. Antony senses in Cleopatra's death the coming of night: "Unarm, Eros, the long day's task is done, / And we must sleep" [IV. xiv. 35-6]. While she lived, she was "thou day o' the world" [IV. viii. 13]; at her death, only darkness is left. Iras urges her mistress to sleep in strikingly similar language: "Finish, good lady, the bright day is done, / And we are for the dark'' [V. ii. 193-94]. For Cleopatra, the asp is the baby ''that sucks the nurse asleep'' [V. ii. 310]. Antony's sleep will permit him to meet Cleopatra where souls do couch on flowers; Cleopatra calls for ''such another sleep'' [V. ii. 77] to repossess her dream of Antony. At the last moment in the play, even Octavius hints that perhaps death is a sleep which will permit them to be reunited: ''she looks like sleep, / As she would catch another Antony / In her strong toil of grace'' [V. ii. 346-48]. The repeated assertion from unexpected perspectives forces us to consider that, despite all probability, the impossible may be true.

After Actium, Thidias bestows some excellent Roman advice on Cleopatra:

> Wisdom and fortune combating together,
> If that the former dare but what it can,
> No chance may shake it.
>
>   [III. xiii. 79-81]

Roman wisdom consists in confining oneself to the possible; but Egyptian wisdom always dares more than what it can. Antony may be a strumpet's fool [I. i. 13], but Octavius is after all only fortune's knave [V. ii. 3]. Cleopatra tells us as she lifts Antony into the monument that wishers were ever fools. Perhaps so: but there are many kinds of folly. . . . Wishers and fools may see more deeply than men of reason: the Soothsayer who sees a little into nature's infinite book of secrecy [I. ii. 10] is a fool.

Act V. Scene ii. Charmian, Cleopatra, Iras, and Roman soldier. By Henry Tresham. The Department of Rare Books and Special Collections, The University of Michigan Library.

Char.	. . . prithee, how many boys and wenches must I have?
Sooth.	If every of your wishes had a womb, And fertile every wish, a million.
Char.	Out, fool! I forgive thee for a witch.

                               [I. ii. 36-40]

Cleopatra, like the Soothsayer, is both witch and wisher: and not all her wishes are fertile. But in the end, her folly is the folly of vision; and the whole play moves us toward the acknowledgment of its truth.

Throughout, the play has insisted on the unreliability of all report and the uncertainty of truth itself. . . . The play teaches us that there are different modes of belief for different kinds of statement. It forces us to acknowledge a fundamental paradox of the human imagination: that occasionally truth can be told only in lies. Cleopatra's dream is her lie in the way of honesty; it is the central paradox of the play that we must both deny it and find it true. Like the other assertions of the impossible, it remains in the unverifiable domain of the true lie. And however impervious to logic this domain is, it occasionally comes closer to our experience than the tidy categories of logic can. There are lies and dreams that are more true than truth itself; the hyperbolical version of their story which the lovers present at the end of the play is one of these lies. The poetry in which the lovers create their version of the story may be only true lies; but the paradoxical true lie may be the only sort of truth available to us in this world. (pp. 161-64)

Janet Adelman, in her The Common Liar: An Essay on 'Antony and Cleopatra', *Yale University Press, 1973, 235 p.*

MICHAEL LONG   (essay date 1976)

[*In sections of his essay not reprinted here, Long discusses several Shakespearean plays in terms of Nietzsche's scheme of the opposing but complementary visions of the Apollonian and Dionysian—the former expressing the inclination toward humane and flexible orderliness in society, the latter a kinetic vision of "the breeding and joy-giving powers of the natural world." In the following excerpt, the critic contends that* Antony and Cleopatra *is constructed in terms of a Dionysian vision, with the first half of the play presenting the lyrical, ribald, expansive, and festive aspects of the song of Dionysos and the second half depicting the volatile, chaotic, and tumultuous elements of that vision. Long argues that by setting those Roman scenes prior to Act III, Scene vi in contrast with the playful, emotional, exuberant scenes in Egypt, Shakespeare heightens his portrayal of the Romans—and particularly of Octavius—as stiff, self-important, and posturing, treating them not with a spate of open parody but with a ripple of "disbelieving laughter." The critic maintains that the second half of the drama, however, demonstrates the paradoxical nature of the Dionysian vision, for from the first battle onward, Rome is no longer absurd, but instead a menacing, inexorable machine of conquest. Under "pressure from the dead hand of Rome, but also under the intrinsic pressures of the Dionysiac," Long declares,* Antony and Cleopatra *respond with hysteria and panic, alternating in the final scenes between humiliation and exaltation, grotesquerie and magnificence, dejection and "spiritual triumph."*]

> I have done ill,
> Of which I do accuse myself so sorely
> That I will joy no more . . .
> I am alone the villain of the earth,
> And feel I am so most. O Antony,
> Thou mine of bounty . . .
>
>   [IV. vi. 17-19, 29-31]

The death of Enobarbus is the death of a man who feels that in forsaking Antony he has forsaken life itself. He has forsaken bounty for barrenness, the fire of the sun for the pallor of the moon, the heat of day for the damp and chill of night, companionship for solitude. The betrayal is so complete as to destroy him at once. The fullness of life that he has seen and shared in Egypt has made him incapable of living and breathing in the thin atmosphere of Rome. That atmosphere touches him like a blight and the life of him simply stops. Life itself is 'a very rebel to my will' [IV. xi. 14]. The sap of him has dried and hardened:

> Throw my heart
> Against the flint and hardness of my fault,
> Which, being dried with grief, will break to powder,
> And finish all foul thoughts.
>
> [IV. ix. 15-18]

He leaves the world feeling himself 'infamous', a 'fugitive'—not only from Antony and Egypt but from all joy, daylight and delighted life.

The poignancy of the two scenes in which we see Enobarbus wither like a blighted plant (IV. vi. and IV. ix) depends upon our apprehension of the fiery lyric of life's capacity for joy which the play imparts throughout its duration—so that the quiet, muted hopelessness of Enobarbus' words has a deadweight of loss or unqualified impoverishment in its tone, set off by the contrast with the lyric world. *Antony and Cleopatra* provides this apprehension of the lyrical with fulsome and voluptuous richness, its language impregnated with the festivity of the Dionysiac, its embodiment of life's most creative and fructifying forces being incomparably sure, sweeping and exuberant. It is an expansively lyrical play in which the romanticism of Shakespeare's metaphysic revels in its own life. (pp. 220-21)

Antony and Cleopatra opens with space, leisure and laughter:

> *Phi.* Nay, but this dotage of our general's
> O'erflows the measure. Those his goodly eyes,
> That o'er the files and musters of the war
> Have glow'd like plated Mars, now bend, now turn,
> The office and devotion of their view
> Upon a tawny front. His captain's heart,
> Which in the scuffles of great fights hath burst
> The buckles on his breast, reneges all temper,
> And is become the bellows and the fan
> To cool a gipsy's lust.
>
> *Flourish. Enter* ANTONY, CLEOPATRA, *her Ladies, the Train, with Eunuchs fanning her.*
> Look where they come!
> Take but good note, and you shall see in him
> The triple pillar of the world transform'd
> Into a strumpet's fool. Behold and see.
>
> *Cleo.* If it be love indeed, tell me how much.
> *Ant.* There's beggary in the love that can be reckon'd.
> *Cleo.* I'll set a bourn how far to be belov'd.
> *Ant.* Then must thou needs find out new heaven, new earth.
>
> [I. i. 1-17]

Poor Philo. No sooner has he been the play's first spokesman for the official Roman view than the words and action of the play move on out of his range of vision to suggest orders of lyric intensity quite beyond Roman knowledge. If we follow his advice to 'take but good note' we shall not find our re-

sponses being much in line with his. His Roman words 'measure' and 'temper' seem comically minute as the spacious range of Antony's words is set against them. The impeding hardness of 'plated Mars' and 'the buckles on his breast' is mocked by the sinewy and voluptuous ease of movement which informs Antony and Cleopatra's speeches. The 'scuffles' of Roman imperialism seem like petty brawls in this atmosphere of leisured extravagance. And the Roman, racial jeering contained in 'a tawny front' and 'a gipsy's lust' is belied as a ludicrous insolence by the laughing and delighted civility which, coquetry notwithstanding, lives in Cleopatra's words. It is nothing like 'dotage' that we are seeing and hearing but the modes of a life incomparably richer than the precious Roman rhetoric of solemnizing grandiosity—'office and devotion'—can ever reach. The Roman version of Egypt is at once set against the realities of Egyptian life; and at once that version is seen not only to be far from the truth but—a vital point—*comically* far from the truth. A few lines down and Cleopatra will invite the continuance of that comic comparison, mocking 'the scarce-bearded Caesar' [I. i. 21], and caricaturing the strutting rhetoric of imperial command:

> 'Do this or this;
> Take in that kingdom and enfranchise that;
> Perform't, or else we damn thee'.
>
> [I. i. 22-4]

These are the first notes of Dionysos' song, simultaneously lyrical and ribald, which will dominate the first half of the play and colour our view of Rome and Egypt throughout. (pp. 241-43)

The Rome of the first half of *Antony and Cleopatra* is seen with airy and scurril comedy as absurd. Its great Titans, Caesar and Pompey, are petty and rather ludicrous men, peevish when they are defied, tetchy about rank and status, 'queasy' (as Agrippa happily puts it) at the 'insolence' of one who falls out of line—in Cleopatra's final opinion 'paltry' and 'absurd'. In the Rome of this part of the play we see little ('scarce-bearded') men living solemnly amid antic visions of themselves wherein they pace the world from edge to edge, frown at levity in the name of 'our graver business' [II. vii. 120] and chase such farcical ambitions as that of Pompey who wants to own the sea. Its characteristic language is of a kind for which Pound's *Homage* will provide description—the language of the 'large-mouthed product' designed to 'expound the distentions of empire'. Pound has his Rome see its great imperial destiny in terms of laughable pettiness: 'Tibet shall be full of Roman policemen'. In Shakespeare's play imperial Caesar, in triumph, is no more than 'the universal landlord' [III. xiii. 72].

We must be clear as to this tone, and have ears attuned to it, for though it seems to me extremely pervasive it has also been subtle enough to elude many critics and producers altogether. But subtlety is of its essence, for Shakespeare uses it not to provide the open torrent of spoof and parody of Pound's poem (or indeed to repeat the scurrilous acerbity of his own *Troilus and Cressida*) but, more gently, to ripple with disbelieving laughter and a quiet sense of knowingness beneath the orotundities and gaucheries of Roman rhetoric, politicking, propriety and self-opinion.

In I. i, as we have seen, the tone announces itself—its humour brought into play when Egypt is first made to sound so delightfully different from Philo's Roman severity on the subject, and then pointed to and enjoyed by the Cleopatra who mimics the order-giving Caesar. I. ii and I. iii then give much of their time to creating a mood of playfulness and levity, lived in

Egypt in the bawdy-talk of the soothsayer and Cleopatra's women, inhabiting Enobarbus' 'light answers' of a bawdy kind on Cleopatra's 'celerity in dying' [I. ii. 144] etc., and inhabiting the coquetry and love-play which is interlaced with incandescent lyricism in Cleopatra's farewell to Antony. We note, in I. ii, that the 'Roman thought' which has struck Antony is said by Cleopatra not to have destroyed his 'passion' or his 'love' but his 'mirth'; and we note too that while we have been asked to begin to create the figure of Antony as the 'Herculean Roman' in our minds as part of our conception of him, we have also been asked to see

> How this Herculean Roman does become
> The carriage of his chafe
>
> [I. iii. 84-5]

—a picture of a hero in a pique, whereby delighted levity comes to the rescue of what might have been overly grandiose.

Thus attuned we come to I. iv to find the dead weight of a solemn slab of Caesarism interposing its ludicrous presence in this lightened world. In Caesar's opening declaration we catch the authentic tone of weighty self-opinion which Cleopatra has already mimicked out of court:

> You may see, Lepidus, and henceforth know,
> It is not Caesar's natural vice to hate
> Our great competitor.
>
> [I. iv. 1-3]

And in the ensuing moralistics, which clearly carry the hatred he has just disavowed, the ripples of our amusement are set going at the expense of an ignorant, scarce-bearded man pouting with a sense of moral outrage:

> (Antony) is not more manlike
> Than Cleopatra, nor the queen of Ptolemy
> More womanly than he
>
> [I. iv. 5-7]

He is a slight man talking largely; and talking primly too (on the immaturity of which pleasure-seeking is a sign), and snobbishly (his distaste for Antony's keeping company with 'knaves that smell of sweat' [I. iv. 21]), and parsonically (sermonizing to Lepidus on the man who is 'the abstract of all faults' [I. iv. 9], from the observation of whom moral lessons can be learnt provided the observer is not 'too indulgent'). Throughout the scene Shakespeare's delicate humour, summoned to our minds already by the delighted levity which Egypt has presented, stalks Caesar subtly, making us quietly aware of every trace of stiffness, self-importance and inflatedness with which the universal landlord, chaste spokesman for old father antic the law, is replete.

The opening Act is so structured as to give Caesar little chance against the ripples of mirthful disbelief inspired by the airy lightness of tone in which life in Egypt is conducted. His appearance in this scene, to talk with a pout and a stamp of the imperial foot against Antony's 'lascivious wassails', has much mischief done to it by having to come after we have seen Antony, Cleopatra, Enobarbus, Charmian, Iras and the Soothsayer living a life which in no way prompts our enthusiasm for his judgments of it; and by having to come before the closing scene of the Act wherein Egyptian blood flows again not only in the language of passion

> Be'st thou sad or merry,
> The violence of either thee becomes,
> So does it no man else
>
> [I. v. 59-61]

but also in the language of mirth or gamesomeness, as in Cleopatra's inability to take pleasure in aught an eunuch has or Charmian's baiting her with the memory of her 'salad days'. If we know how to hear the Act's subtly mirthful tone we shall know that we have seen the antics of Caesarism subjected to the *vif* [animation] of an easeful but probing scepticism which is given life and licence by the counter-comedy of Egypt where moments of incandescent lyricism rise repeatedly from a fertile chaos of humour, bawdy and animal vitality, all tangled together in a 'gamesome' vision of Dionysos' powers.

Built upon this basis, Act Two and the first six scenes of Act Three take the comedy of delicate derision and the comedy of festivity and play to exuberant heights. On the Roman side Pompey appears, full of self-importance, with:

> If the great gods be just, they shall assist
> The deeds of justest men
>
> [II. i. 1-2]

and then spends his time in II. i gloating over his watery dominions ('the sea is mine' [II. i. 9]) and rearing the higher his opinion of himself. In II. ii the fop Lepidus, beginning already to look like a figure from Donne's satires, is pushed about by Enobarbus' sharp tongue just as hopelessly as he was by Caesar's moral lessons; and, in the negotiations that follow, Antony (now struck by Roman thoughts) and Caesar (trying to pretend he never spoke 'derogately' about the lascivious wassailer) experience a rough passage at the hands of Shakespeare's wanton laughter, aided as it is by some fine stage-business:

> *Caes.* Sit.
>
>   *Ant.* Sit, sir.
>
>   *Caes.* Nay then. *(They sit.)*
>
> [II. ii. 28]

and by Enobarbus' capacity for an irreverent assessment of the politicking of the 'noble partners' who are in the act of becoming 'brothers':

> Or, if you borrow one another's love for the
> instant, you may, when you hear no more words
> of Pompey, return it again. You shall have time
> to wrangle in when you have nothing else to
> do.
>
> [II. ii. 103-06]

Enobarbus, though told to be quiet and mend his manners, clearly wins his playful skirmish, and celebrates his victory with the famous description of Cleopatra in her barge, which has the Roman Maecenas boggle-eyed with amazement yet still Roman enough to miss the point entirely. 'Now Antony must leave her utterly', he ventures [II. ii. 232-33]. 'Never!', says Enobarbus, with probability enough. Then Maecenas:

> If beauty, wisdom, modesty, can settle
> The heart of Antony, Octavia is
> A blessed lottery to him.
>
> [II. ii. 240-42]

to the extraordinary unlikeliness of which there can be no reply, so the scene ends without Enobarbus bothering to give one.

In II. iii the blessed lottery makes its sad contribution to the proceedings as we first see the frigid formality of the Antony/Octavia marriage; and then, after Egypt has interposed with another sumptuously playful extravagance of unbridled emotionalism and mirth:

> *Cleo.* Give me some music—music, moody food
> Of us that trade in love.
> *All.* The music, ho!
>
> Enter MARDIAN *the Eunuch*
>
> *Cleo.* Let it alone! Let's to billiards,
>
> [II. v. 1-3]

the Act concludes with the delicious hilarity of the scene on Pompey's galley.

The scene stirs one's memories of Gadshill [in *1 Henry IV*], or of the great set-pieces on the Greek and Trojan camps in *Troilus and Cressida*. Lepidus is now clearly a character from Donne—the semi-travelled fop who is quick to believe and pass on reports of the marvels of foreign parts:

> Nay, certainly, I have heard the Ptolemies' pyramises are very goodly things. Without contradiction I have heard that.
>
> [II. vii. 34-6]

And Enobarbus duly makes haste to derive as much amusement as possible from the spectacle of a member of the great triumvirate in his cups:

> *Eno.* There's a strong fellow, Menas.
> *(Pointing to the servant who carries off Lepidus.)*
> *Men.* Why?
> *Eno.* 'A bears the third part of the world, man; see'st not?
>
> [II. vii. 88-91]

But Caesar and Pompey scarcely fare better. The great Pompey responds like a shoddy little gangster (but burdened with a sense of propriety) to the proposal that his guests should have their throats slit:

> In me 'tis villainy:
> In thee 't had been good service.
>
> [II. vii. 74-5]

Caesar, feeling himself befouled by food and drink, 'antick'd' by merriment, and opining solemnly that 'our graver business / Frowns at this levity' [II. vii. 120-21], is no more prepossessing. And when the Egyptian Bacchanals scatter the 'great fellows' and the revelry goes below stairs with Enobarbus and 'Hoo' and 'Hoo' we have watched a scene in which the spirit of the Lord of Misrule has done his traditional comic damage to the stiffnesses, repressions and formalisms of the law.

Egypt in this Act has been represented by the scene which began with Cleopatra calling for 'music, moody food' and went on with her wild rampage of haling the messenger up and down—both of which performances are too gustily alive with emotional turmoil, the creative chaos of Dionysos, for moral point-making to constitute an adequate response to them. And it has also been represented by the description of the barge. Here Dionysos is brought alive as a breeding chaos of self-replenishing energies creating kinds of luxury and magnificence which have nothing to do with mere 'ornament' or 'ostentation'. All is swarming with life; and once again it is all laughter-filled, gamesome. (pp. 244-49)

Shakespeare's lyrical imagination transformed [Plutarch's] pageant of artifice into a picture of richness which seems like

the florescence of nature itself. Inanimate things become animated in this general florescence of the world—the winds 'love-sick', the water 'amorous', the ropes of the barge swelling in (sexual) response to animate touch, the banks of the river having 'sense'. And the whole spectacle, in Shakespeare's version of it, is filled with self-fuelling and self-replenishing fire wherein 'fancy' and 'nature' dance a playful dialectic of their respective powers. As part of this ever-burning energy the fans carried by Cleopatra's boys

> did seem
> To glow the delicate cheeks which they did cool,
> And what they undid did.
>
> [II. ii. 203-05]

As another manifestation of it Cleopatra, hopping through the public street until she is breathless,

> spoke, and panted,
> That she did make defect perfection,
> And, breathless, pow'r breathe forth.
>
> [II. ii. 230-32]

And again:

> she makes hungry
> Where most she satisfies; for vilest things
> Become themselves in her, that the holy priests
> Bless her when she is riggish.
>
> [II. ii. 236-39]

This is the poetry of Shakespeare's lyric-romantic mind at its finest. The innermost power of it is in that phrase 'become themselves', or on the rhythm of 'undid did', 'defect perfection' and 'breathless, pow'r breathe forth'. . . . Egypt's ability to generate such powers, with their attendant human qualities of sexual vitality and laughter, not only mocks the absurd pretension and juvenile insolence of Roman imperialism. It mocks all moralistics too, having in itself as it does the very essence of the Dionysiac which is seen by Shakespeare, here as in festive comedy, as a *sine qua non* of full psychic life.

So in the first Act the interposition of Rome in a predominantly Egyptian world makes Rome look petty and ludicrous. In the second Act, which has an opposite structure, the interposition of Egypt in a predominantly Roman world annihilates Romanness by its fire and colour and demands an absolute of recognition from the audience. In the Third Act the slow and swaying comedy of Dionysos' song continues, revelling through the contrast between the frigidity of Octavia/Antony and the gusty exaggerations of Cleopatra's enthusiasms; through Enobarbus and Agrippa's merriment at the sham courtesies of the politicians (to which language Lepidus then makes a characteristically ludicrous contribution); and through Enobarbus' later comments on the fall from the triumvirate of the 'poor third':

> Then, world, thou hast a pair of chaps—no more;
> And throw between them all the food thou hast,
> They'll grind the one the other.
>
> [III. v. 13-15]

It all leads excellently to III. vi (before the change in the play's tone) where Rome's deflation by laughter is at its best again.

In this scene the ribaldry of Dionysos does its worst with Caesar before the catastrophe of the play becomes imminent in III. vii. It begins with another stamp of the imperial foot—'Contemning Rome, he has done all this'—and another petulant exhibition of his snobbery—'I' th' common show-place' [III. vi. 1, 12]. It sees Agrippa hitting that exact and unfortunate word 'queasy' to describe Rome's feelings about Antony's 'insolence'. It sees Caesar hoarding up bits of the world for himself (like Lepidus' 'Revenue'), and wanting to hoard up more (like 'Armenia'), while sending off messengers with cheap lies to excuse himself. Then, suddenly, it sees the arrival of Octavia: too suddenly for Caesar, who is thereby prevented from laying on 'an augmented greeting' [III. vi. 55, 52] to show 'the ostentation of our love'—though after forty lines or so he has gathered himself and is launched:

> Welcome to Rome;
> Nothing more dear to me. You are abus'd
> Beyond the mark of thought, and the high gods,
> To do you justice, make their ministers
> Of us and those that love you.
>
> [III. vi. 85-9]

On that claim, made by the universal landlord, to some kind of ministerial status in a platonic, celestial empire, the scene's chicane at the expense of Caesarism has reached its climax. It is quickly finished off by Maecenas with his mouth very full of outrage:

> Only th' adulterous Antony, most large
> In his abominations, turns you off,
> And gives his potent regiment to a trull
> That noises it against us.
>
> [III. vi. 93-6]

Rome has been dealt with by comedy. The catastrophic product of its imperial power will now begin to come forth.

We have reached what is almost exactly the mid-point in this tragedy and yet still the comedy of Dionysos dominates the play with its interlinked tones of scurrility and playful lyricism. Rather as in *Romeo and Juliet*, a 'tragedy of love' spends the bulk of its earlier energies in the creation of a dramatic life both festal and ribald. I labour the point about the play's comic vitality because if we do not feel both the festal laughter of Egyptian lyricism and the ribald laughter directed at Rome we shall read the play more solemnly than it requires and miss the very essence of the vision of the Dionysiac which it has to impart. (pp. 250-52)

The ribald comedy of disbelief in Rome is as much a part of Dionysiac life as is the lyricism of Egyptian passion. It carries the playful intelligence of the Dionysiac, its quick-witted vitality and humane freedom from code and law; and in the case of Egyptian passional life itself, interlaced with festive notes of topsy-turvy and misrule, the playfulness of the Dionysiac is again of supreme importance. . . . It has no other-worldly attachments and involves no flesh-despising or flesh-transcending. It lacks the fierce and self-isolating egotism of heroic passion and it lacks that hankering after darkness and dissolution which brings the language of mystery-religions into the romance of love. It does not thrive upon the sublimation of Eros into religious or aesthetic terms, bent as it is neither upon purity nor upon divinization.

In comparison with the passion of [Wagner's] *Tristan and Isolde*, the passional life of Egypt is full of the richness of the commonplace and the mundane. With the fibrous tangle of its roots deep in the slime of the Nile it is bent upon flowering in the light of the sun, not plunging into the darkness of religious mystery to find therein redemption from the false appearances of the daylight world. Being thus commonplace, rooted in the organic and content with the real, it is in essence laughter-filled. The uninhibitedness of laughter is essential to

it, as is laughter's commonplace, social gaiety. The exuberance of laughter is . . . seen as an intrinsic part of the exuberance of sexuality. It is therefore as characteristic of Egyptian passion to be both *playful* and *erotic* as it is for Wagner's image of passion to be *heroic, sublimated* and *unsmiling*. In that difference the greater humanity and greater *vif* of Shakespearean romanticism seem to me to lie.

So we come to the play's imminent catastrophe with such a vision fully realized before us, and the fulness of romantic life which the vision carries determines our response to the catastrophe. It determines our response to Rome's menace, which now takes over in our minds from our earlier sense of its derisoriness; and it also determines our response to the havoc and panic created by the Dionysiac quality of Egypt itself in response to threat. Both factors are important—Rome's destructive power and thrust and Egypt's own propensity for calamity.

Rome's destructive intrusion into the Egyptian world is terribly swift and quite decisive. In four scenes of scarcely 100 lines between them the organized power of Rome will 'cut the Ionian sea' [III. vii. 22] and rout the forces of Antony and Egypt. Canidius says:

> This speed of Caesar's
> Carries beyond belief
>
> [III. vii. 74-5]

and with that we get a chilling sense of the irresistible. For the rest of the play Caesar in Egypt is a colonialist ravager, bearing the armoured and calculating weight of an empire to the destruction of a flamboyantly alive culture. By III. xii he is installed and trading in the ugly 'realities'. Thyreus talks of his protective influence as 'his shroud', aptly thereby catching the tone of his regimen. At the beginning of Act Four more Realpolitik sees him pleased to use Antony's own soldiers to 'fetch him in' [IV. i. 154] like a hunted animal. In IV. vi he is talking of 'universal peace'—an idea which is made hollow and unlovely by its placement in the midst of Enobarbus' desolation and his revelations as to Caesar's way with men who desert to him.

The low realism of Caesar's powers feels deadly and irresistible again in IV. xi:

> To the vales,
> And hold our best advantage. . . .
>
> [IV. xi. 3-4]

Caesar is not savage . . . ; but there can be no doubting the bleakness and lowness of his presence, the humanly impoverished nature of his authority, the mere efficiency of his marshalling of things.

It is important to note that record of a low power and its deadly weight which the latter part of the play gives us. The hysterical note in Antony's response to it and the wild panic of Cleopatra's gyrations cannot fairly be seen for what they are unless we see that they take place in the path of an oncoming and irresistible machine of conquest. . . . That does not fully 'explain' the crazedness of Cleopatra's and Antony's behaviour in the latter part of the play, nor is it intended to. But it gives us some necessary context whereby a part of the truth can be seen.

But the other part of the matter, and the major part, concerns the nature of the Dionysiac itself, and it sends us, as we consider it, back through the long history of Shakespeare's dealings in tragedy and comedy alike with the hazards and dangers which live in the volatile and creative chaos of kinesis. Even in comedy the experience of the dream-wood of Puck and the fairies [in *A Midsummer Night's Dream*] was fraught with hazard and it confronted the adventurer with the fear of the unknowable. The journey through Dionysiac tumult turns out to be liberating, joy-giving; but while the journey lasts that outcome is far from clear and inevitable. (pp. 253-55)

To live in the tumult of Dionysos is to live creatively, but also to live exposed—without the stabilizing certainties of social evaluation and selection which support dwellers in an unmagical, workaday world. And in tragedy a realistic record of what that tumult feels like to one upon whom its forces are unleashed is given in the life of Lear, the 'poor perdu' on the heath. From contact with the wild flows energy, and the greatest imaginative forces of the psyche. But such contact can only be got from being perilously close to destruction and perilously exposed to torment.

In some sense it will therefore always involve the 'shirt of Nessus' [IV. xii. 43] which Antony wears when he is convinced that Cleopatra has betrayed him again. But it will also involve (with characteristic Shakespearean ambiguity) something far less 'elevated' than that—a kind of ludicrousness, exhibited by a mind subject to the mischief of Puck, the idiot bamboo-zlement of a mind tossed hither and thither without dignity, composure or ordonnance by the currents of racing mischief which are an intrinsic part of the high-force world finding their living emblems in Puck and Queen Mab [in *Romeo and Juliet*]. In comedy that mischief is hurly-burly, though it can occasionally hurt people as it hurts Malvolio [in *Twelfth Night*]. In tragedy it is the awful mischief that the world does to Lear, introducing that element of the grotesque into his tragic experience which was recorded when the thunder *laughed* at the folly of an old man venting his rage on the non-existent daughters of Poor Tom.

It is a sense of all this, generated by the laughing vision of a creative Dionysos, which we need for the latter part of *Antony and Cleopatra*. For there, under pressure from the dead hand of Rome, but also under the intrinsic pressure of the Dionysiac itself, Antony and Cleopatra go through a double process which is humiliating and exalting at the same time, grotesque and magnificent, an ebbing and decrescence of the spirit which is at the same time a spiritual triumph. There is no point in trying to sort out the pros and cons of it all to award moral points for and against. There is a certain moralizing tardiness of the imagination in the mind which wishes to conceive of one part existing without the other—the same moralizing tardiness which wants to feel that Lear is 'learning' and 'being redeemed' but which also wants to reserve the right to make a moral point or two about some of the things he says while the terrible process is going on. In *Antony and Cleopatra* the whole tangle of Dionysiac elements can only be taken as being of a piece, the whole chaos of it all taken as it is in the certain knowledge, imparted by this great romanticism, that without these grotesqueries there will be no creative life, without these indignities (painfully there when Antony botches his suicide, for example) there will be no possibility of Egyptian 'fire and air' [V. ii. 289]. . . . [It] is the case that if you banish Plump Jack you will banish all the world: banish the triple-turned whore and the strumpet's fool and you will simply make over the world to the bleak conveniences of Caesarism.

If we have heard the full power and range of Dionysos' song in the first half of the play, and understood both its high lyricism and its low humour, we should have no difficulty with the

double progress of its major creators in the second half. Instead it will come with beautiful inevitability—the absurd bravado of Antony which Caesar summarily snubs, the hysterical and self-indulgent notes that now run through the vitality of his mind, the desperation of his efforts to recreate with his 'sad captains' the old life of supper, carousing and 'rattling ta-bourines', his humiliating failure to bring off the noble death he proposes; and the hideous whimsicality of Cleopatra's feigned death, the vacillating distractedness that runs through all her dealings with Caesar, the hysterical notes that she too sounds at moments in her grief and confusion: all of it will come through as the inevitable, essential, inalienable concomitant of that spirit which produces the contrary movement of the play's great lyric and triumphant end. (pp. 256-58)

That 'lyric and trimphant end' is, of course, what we get in the play's incomparable exhibition of the poetry of wanton, romantic exuberance and charmed flight. . . . It reaches its apex in Cleopatra's speech of 'immortal longings' and 'fire and air', but it has been growing steadily to that peak ever since the 'sad captains' and the eclipse of the 'terrene moon' in III. xiii, where the decrescence of Egypt first began to produce the poignantly continuing autumnal fire which comes from a bounty with 'no winter in't' [V. ii 87]. Shrunk and dispersed almost to extinction, Egypt simply cannot help bringing forth from the strong toil of its grace that succession of wonderful images of exultation which share the last two Acts with the grotesque twists and turns of panic and humiliation. (p. 258)

[In] *Antony and Cleopatra* the fulness of Dionysos involves a price, which . . . has to do with precariousness and vulnerability, and . . . makes it a part of an essentially tragic vision. The life of Egypt gets its exuberant and wanton energy from constant proximity to the tumult of the kinetic. It is thence that it draws into itself the tremendous resources of energy that place the quality of its life so far beyond the reach of Rome. But by virtue of that very proximity its life is lived in constant peril. It is constantly on a brink of self-destruction or self-dissolution; and it is people living on that brink whom we see create the song of Dionysos but also the panic and hysteria of their later life. . . .

[But] in *Antony and Cleopatra* there is no shuddering back into the arms of Caesar. The critics who have had their 'reservations' [about this play] . . . seem to me to have been involved in just such a retreat from the furious but generous energies of Shakespeare's tragic metaphysic. That retreat might have been avoided had the connexions between tragedy and festive comedy been better understood; or had more people known as surely as Nietzsche did that 'one must still have chaos in oneself to be able to give birth to a dancing star'. (p. 259)

*Michael Long, "The Songs of Apollo and Dionysos,"
in his* The Unnatural Scene: A Study in Shakespearean Tragedy, *Methuen & Co. Ltd., 1976, pp. 220-59.*

ANDREW FICHTER   (essay date 1980)

[*Fichter argues that Christian allusions in* Antony and Cleopatra *direct us to see the imperfections and limitations of "tragic vision itself." Although the Christian perspective on dramatic events is a retrospective one, the critic maintains, its promise of redemption offers a bold contrast to the impoverished world we find at the close of the play. Fichter discovers deep irony in the characters' unawareness of the impending birth of Christ and "the magnitude of the change about to occur," but he contends that Antony's tragically unattainable aspiration of "new heaven, new earth" (I. i. 17) prefigures the Christian vision of true transcendence.*]

With his victory at Actium still hanging in the balance, Shakespeare's Octavius speaks prophetically of a new era of peace:

> The time of universal peace is near:
> Prove this a prosperous day, the three-nook'd world
> Shall bear the olive freely.
>
> [IV. vi. 4-6]

That the 'universal peace' Octavius envisions nearly coincides with that proclaimed thirty years later at Christ's nativity (Luke, ii, 14) is, of course, beyond the capacity of Octavius to see; but a tradition of Christian historiography extending from the early Church Fathers through the Renaissance regards the proximity of these two events with a different awareness. Christian historians viewing the advent of the *Pax Romana* [the peace of Rome] retrospectively could see in it an adumbration of the *Pax Christiana* [the peace of Christ], and they could see in the closeness with which one event followed the other the unfolding of a providential plan. (p. 99)

While only the pagan perspective on history is overtly dramatized in *Antony and Cleopatra*, Shakespeare gives us sufficient evidence, I think, to conclude that we are meant to be aware of the Christian perspective as well. As Antony and Cleopatra paradoxically assert for themselves a love transcending death and a triumph emerging from defeat we are meant to recognize an impulse that is completed in Christian miracle; but we are also meant to realize that in the pre-Christian world of Shakespeare's play the transcendence to which the lovers aspire is tragically impossible. Seen in the light of both Plutarch and Scripture, then, the historical setting of *Antony and Cleopatra*, as J. L. Simmons has observed [in his book *Shakespeare's Pagan World: The Roman Tragedies;* see Additional Bibliography], establishes the play's moral and dramatic contingencies. Antony and Cleopatra claim an ideal of love that remains untenable in their pagan world. To romanticize their vision of an eternity in one another's lips [I. iii. 35] is to ignore the play's moral environment (or environments, if we may invoke both Roman and Christian morality); but to condemn the lovers is to condemn 'not only the heroic but the divine urge' [Simmons].

Yet it remains difficult to avoid the conclusion that as we view the play retrospectively from the vantage afforded by Christian historiography we are seeing a world in which even the most heroic aspirations are ironically delimited. While we are not called upon to dismiss Antony and Cleopatra for having failed according to standards not yet revealed to them, we are, I think, entitled to speak more broadly of the limitations of tragic vision itself. *Antony and Cleopatra* evokes a world in transition, but one ironically unaware of the magnitude of the change about to occur offstage. The action of the play is prologue to a greater action that will ultimately reverse tragedy's fundamental laws. Were the hyperbolical and paradoxical rhetoric of Antony and Cleopatra to have been set in a Christian universe it might have been heard as the language of romance rather than that of tragedy. (We have only to look at Shakespeare's other Augustan play, *Cymbeline*, to see the impact of the Incarnation reflected in drama.) As it is, paradox cannot fully sustain itself in the world of *Antony and Cleopatra*; yet this failure is testimony to the significance of the impending miracle of grace. Through its own collapse, that is, the heroic discourse of the play announces the imminence of the Christian era.

Clearly the difference between the Roman and the Christian fulfillments of Octavius's prophecy of a 'time of universal peace' is for Shakespeare a matter of no little irony. One in-

volves the self-deification of Octavius as Augustus Caesar while the other announces the incarnation of a deity in human form. The *Pax Romana* is the result of the manipulations of one of Shakespeare's most self-serving and irreducibly political characters; Christianity, on the other hand, offers a standard of selflessness of which the actions of Octavius are morally an inversion. In *Antony and Cleopatra,* moreover, we witness the emergence of the *Pax Romana* from the point of view of its antagonists, and if we adopt their perspective we take history to be an essentially tragic process. The progress of Roman civilization leaves a world more impoverished than it found:

> the odds is gone,
> And there is nothing left remarkable
> Beneath the visiting moon.
>
> [IV. xv. 66-8]

The Christian narrative, however, reverses the premise of tragic consciousness, and paradoxically asks that a death be taken as a means to greater enrichment. (pp. 99-100)

The first scene of *Antony and Cleopatra* mirrors the play's thematic movement towards Christian revelation. Antony stands accused by one of his Roman followers, Philo, of a 'dotage' that 'O'erflows the measure' [I. i. 2]—words that unmistakably convey the revulsion he feels at the sight of his general's infatuation with Cleopatra. Antony speaks of his love in terms that alter the tone but retain some of the substance of Philo's remarks:

> *Cleopatra.*
>   If it be love indeed, tell me how much.
> *Antony.*
>   There's beggary in the love that can be reckon'd.
> *Cleopatra.*
>   I'll set a bourn how far to be belov'd.
> *Antony.*
>   Then must thou needs find out new heaven,
>   new earth.
>
> [I. i. 14-17]

The 'dotage' which 'O'erflows the measure' becomes a love that cannot be reckoned. Against Philo's Roman sense of propriety and measure Antony asserts a romanticist's impulse to deny limit, finitude and degree, to transgress the boundaries by which a rationalist mind orders its world. He has confounded, Philo complains, the occupation of a soldier with that of a lover. Antony's banter with Cleopatra already indicates the inherently tragic disposition of his energy and will.

But Antony's words have a prophetic resonance; they refer us to a context in which the quest for 'new heaven, new earth' is no longer an expression of will tragically opposed to reality. Antony and Cleopatra are led by their syllogistic dialogue to what God speaks of to Isaiah and John sees directly in his vision of the Day of Judgement:

> For lo, I will create new heavens and a new
> earth: and the former shall not be remembered
> nor come into mind.
>   (From The Geneva Bible, Isaiah, lxv, 17)

And I saw a new heaven, and a new earth: for the first heaven, and the first earth were passed away, and there was no more sea. And I John saw the holy city new Jerusalem come down from God out of heaven, prepared as a bride trimmed for her husband. And I heard a great voice out of heaven, saying, 'Behold, the Tab-

ernacle of God is with men, and he will dwell
with them: and they shall be his people, and
God himself shall be their God with them. And
God shall wipe away all tears from their eyes:
and there shall be no more death, neither sorrow, neither crying, neither shall there be any
more pain: for the first things are passed.'

(Revelation, xxi, 1-4)

There remains an important difference between syllogism and
revelation, between Antony's assertion of unbounded love and
the divine love of which John speaks. Antony and Cleopatra
may pursue the logic of transcendence to the point where it
verges on a new perception of the universe, but the vision John
records depends on divine intercession rather than heroic romanticism. Antony and Cleopatra come to associate love with
eternity, and they approach death as if it were 'a lover's bed'
[IV. xiv. 101]; they speak of one another as bride and husband
in their final moments, and thereby bring new significance to
conventional terms; but the apocalyptic marriage of which John
speaks, the final reconciliation between God and humanity,
remains beyond their imagination. Antony does not have access
to the vision that fully transforms tragic experience. He assumes instead a posture of heroic denial:

> Let Rome in Tiber melt, and the wide arch
> Of the rang'd empire fall!
>
> [I. i. 33-4]

Antony is bounded on one side by the Christian visionary
tradition to which he cannot attain and on the other by the
Roman epic tradition he partly forsakes. His Roman followers
see him making the choice that Roman history denies to its
first hero, Aeneas. Antony, that is, chooses love over empire,
passion over reason, a foreign 'marriage' over a Roman one,
and thus aligns himself with those forces Roman civilization
sees as impediments to its progress. Yet in a sense Antony
does not wholly remove himself from epic tradition. He refers
to love as though it were another *imperium* [empire], 'new
heaven, new earth', and he embraces Cleopatra—'Here is my
space' [I. i. 34]—in the spirit of an Aeneas arriving on Italian
shores—'hic domus, haec patria est' ['Here is our home, here
our country!']. The love Antony speaks of is both an alternative
to empire and an alternative empire.

Antony, as Adelman has observed [in *The Common Liar*], is
in a sense an antitype of Aeneas. Shakespeare seems to have
invited the comparison by simplifying the itinerary of Antony's
travels he finds in Plutarch. Shakespeare's Antony closely imitates the career of Aeneas up to a point—the play's dramatic
and philosophical turning point—before finally reversing its
direction. Virgil's Aeneas is required to extricate himself from
his romantic entanglement with Dido for the sake of his destined marriage to Lavinia, an alliance with more political than
amorous connotations. Similarly, Antony leaves 'Egypt's widow'
for Rome (I, iii) and agrees to a political marriage with Octavia
(II, ii); but thereafter his movements are, from a Roman point
of view, retrogressive. He returns to Egypt, where his pleasure
lies. Even then he continues to assume the stance of a Roman
hero, though increasingly the posture becomes incongruous.
And in his last moments he envisions himself as having surpassed Aeneas:

> Where souls do couch on flowers, we'll hand in hand,
> And with our sprightly port make the ghosts gaze:
> Dido, and her Aeneas, shall want troops,
> And all the haunt be ours.
>
> [IV. xiv. 51-4]

Antony may be thought to surpass Aeneas, however, only if
the *Aeneid* is read from the perspective of love rather than
empire, from Dido's and Antony's point of view rather than
the Roman one. Only in an imaginative arrest of history does
the Dido and Aeneas tragedy suggest an amorous eternity. Still,
Antony does not so much dissociate himself from Roman history as reinterpret it from his own vantage. Whether his return
to Egypt is a moral regression and an act of self-betrayal, as
his Roman followers see it, or a reaction aimed at transcending
a limited and insufficient heroic ideal is the critical issue with
which the play presents us.

Antony and Cleopatra, then, stands chronologically and metaphysically between the quest traditions of Roman epic and
Christianity. On one hand the play looks to Augustan empire
as the culmination of historical processes, and on the other
hand it conveys the feeling that the energies of its principals
are misdirected, that their goals are insufficient to their needs.
(pp. 101-03)

The battle of Actium, a conflict, as Shakespeare presents it,
as much between Antony and himself as between Antony and
Octavius, stands at what is both the structural and metaphysical
center of the play. It marks the point at which Antony reverses
the Virgilian epic itinerary, turning away from Rome and Octavia towards Egypt and Cleopatra. It is also the place where
Roman and Christian perspectives on the play fully intersect.
On one hand we are asked to see Antony's rejection of Roman
values as the sufficient cause of his tragic fall; on the other
hand that fall, in which Antony and Cleopatra paradoxically
envision themselves triumphant and transcendent, ironically
anticipates Christian redemption. We see Antony in part as an
exemplum of moral degradation offered to a Roman audience,
a hero debased by his extravagant love for an exotic woman,
irrationally bound on a course of self-destruction, simultaneously asserting and undermining his own heroic stature. But
Antony may also be judged by the standard of divine love, in
which death is, as he imagines, encompassed by an eternity.
That his passion for Cleopatra falls short of Christian *caritas,*
the movement of the soul towards God, places his tragedy in
a different light, making it less an instance of decadent im-
moderation than one of misdirected love. (pp. 103-04)

The play does not finally decide between the Antony his Roman
critics see, 'a fall'n lord' [III. xiii. 44] whose judgement is
subdued by his fortunes, and the 'Lord of lords' [IV. viii. 16]
Cleopatra imagines—between a didactic and a mythic vision
of Antony. That Shakespeare erects such an ambiguity, however, does not mean that no standard exists against which
Antony may be measured. Where his behavior seems most
disjointed we are referred to Christian myth. Antony's outburst
of jealousy when he encounters Thidias kissing Cleopatra's
hand, for instance, may be both an overreaction and a potentially comic misdirection of anger—

> O that I were
> Upon the hill of Basan, to outroar
> The horned herd, for I have savage cause—
>
> [III. xiii. 126-28]

but the discrepancy disappears when the words are heard in
their original context:

> Be not far from me, because trouble is near: for
> there is none to help me.
> Many young bulls have compassed me: mighty bulls
> of Bashan have closed me about.
>
> (Psalms xxii, 11-12)

This Old Testament outcry against injustice and betrayal in turn provides the material for the moment Christianity holds to be the ultimate reversal of tragic consciousness, the Crucifixion. It is the psalm from whose beginning Christ quotes as he dies, 'My God, my God, why hast thou forsaken me?' transforming despair into hopefulness as he speaks by using these words to confirm himself as the fulfillment of Old Testament messianic prophecies.

In contrast to Christ's deliberate and ultimately redemptive reference to the psalm, Antony's unconscious and contorted allusion confirms him in his tragic posture, outroaring the surrounding herds. Jealousy and grace work radically dissimilar transformations. But at the same time Antony's allusion suggests the frame of reference from which we may finally arrive at more than a morally ambiguous perception of the play.

Two scenes later Antony proposes a final 'gaudy night', his Last Supper, as J. Middleton Murry suggests [see excerpt above, 1936], echoes of which may be found both in Plutarch and in the Passion narrative, as the interplay between the Roman and the Christian senses of an ending continues. As in Plutarch Antony asks his followers to fill his cups and make as much of him as they can, but then disheartens them with his gloom:

> Tend me to-night;
> May be it is the period of your duty,
> Haply you shall not see me more, or if,
> A mangled shadow. Perchance to-morrow
> You'll serve another master. I look on you,
> As one that takes his leave.
>
> [IV. ii. 24-9]

The words can be found in North's translation of Plutarch, but the tone suggests another reference: Antony's strangely prescient mood and his wavering resolve to accept death are also reminiscent of Christ's agony in the garden at Gethsemane. Like Christ, Antony asks three times that his followers tend him in what he senses are his last hours. The appeal for loyalty subtly draws attention to Enobarbus, who, Judas-like, has by now decided to betray his master. The scene requires of the reader a double vision in which the Christian future is superimposed over the Roman narrative.

Plutarch is again Shakespeare's source when Antony tries to reassure his soldiers:

> I hope well of to-morrow, and will lead you
> Where rather I'll expect victorious life,
> Than death, and honor.
>
> [IV. i. 42-4]

But Shakespeare's Antony contributes another version of this speech in which the distinction between life and death becomes blurred:

> To-morrow, soldier,
> By sea and land I'll fight: or I will live,
> Or bathe my dying honour in the blood
> Shall make it live again.
>
> [IV. ii. 4-7]

The language is susceptible equally to Stoic and Eucharistic interpretations. Though it is his own blood, not Christ's, and the resurrection of his honor, not his body, that Antony has in mind, this is Plutarch rewritten in anticipation of Christian ritual.

It becomes evident that we lack a single standard by which to measure the relative failure or success of Antony's rhetoric.

Throughout this scene we are given the disconcerting spectacle of Rome's master orator alienating his audience and evoking tears where he intends to give comfort. He inadvertently distresses his attendants by speaking of a reversal of roles they find unimaginable, but which again touches on the meaning of the Eucharist:

> I wish I could be made so many men,
> And all of you clapp'd up together in
> An Antony; that I might do you service,
> So good as you have done.
>
> [IV. ii. 16-19]

This seems to Enobarbus further proof of Antony's distraction, 'one of those odd tricks which sorrow shoots / Out of the mind' [IV. ii. 14-15]; but at this point Antony's rhetorical failures and Christian thought are in a sense logically continuous. ('So might an unknown—or maybe a known—disciple', Murry suggests, 'have said that the Last Supper itself was "one of those odd tricks which sorrow shoots out of the mind".') Shakespeare's Antony here begins the imaginative revision of Plutarch's narrative that Christianity will eventually complete. Antony's language, that is, contains logical and visual discrepancies that cannot be resolved in the terms accessible to the world of the play, but which become meaningful in the context of a future discourse. The hermeneutic method *Antony and Cleopatra* asks us to adopt is one that implies the inadequacy of the knowledge available in the dramatic present to unlock the enigmas of the text.

Antony's speech is charged with meanings neither he nor his hearers can comprehend. Even his rather awkward attempt to explain himself reinforces our awareness of the central irony:

> Ho, ho, ho!
> Now the witch take me, if I meant it thus!
> Grace grow where those drops fall. . . .
>
> [IV. ii. 36-8]

'Grace' is the crux, for were he conscious of the eventual significance of the term Antony's attempts to console his followers by speaking of 'another master', a revival of 'dying honor' in a mysterious 'To-morrow' would not seem so disjointed. It is precisely because he lacks the concept of grace that he can only communicate fatalism to his audience. In the end he returns to a literal and Roman feast rather than a symbolic and Christian one, ironically distorting the meaning of that which he prefigures:

> Let's to supper, come,
> And drown consideration.
>
> [IV. ii. 44-5]

We can account for the awkwardness of the scene, I think, by seeing in it an implicit juxtaposition of Roman and biblical texts. The co-existence of Christian and Roman perspectives is necessarily unharmonious: Christ's propitiatory self-sacrifice will reverse the fatalistic, Stoic self-conquest Antony envisions. Antony's unmodulated ambivalence is a parody of Christ's agony, a failing show of courage in the face of despair, just as his jealousy of Thidias was a parody of Christ's moment of cupidity on the cross. We see darkly through the surface of the dramatic present to the Christian future because we are seeing the reflection of an essentially comic myth in a tragic medium.

The greatest loss Antony suffers at Actium is the one he speaks of, perhaps somewhat hypocritically, when he frames his excuse to Octavia for breaking with Octavius:

> if I lose mine honour,
> I lose myself. . . .
>
> [III. iv. 22-3]

As it happens he loses both honor and self in the course of the battle that follows. Those who eventually desert him do so in the conviction that he has already betrayed himself, by fighting at sea ('you therein throw away / The absolute soldiership you have by land' [III. vii. 41-2]) and by not gearing his actions to his strengths ('his whole action grows / Not in the power on't [III. vii. 68-9]). Antony, that is, forgets himself: 'Had our general / Been what he knew himself, it had gone well' [III. x. 25-6]. Enobarbus describes what becomes an internal war among the elements of Antony's character:

> and I see still,
> A diminution in our captain's brain
> Restores his heart; when valour preys on reason,
> It eats the sword it fights with. . . .
>
> [III. xiii. 196-99]

Antony is not unaware of his 'diminution'; he perceives authority melting from him [III. xiii. 90], knows he has 'lost command' [III. xi. 23], and even justifies the desertion of his followers on the grounds that he has set the example: 'Let that be left / Which leaves itself' [III. xi. 19-20]. But when he is brought 'to the very heart of loss' [IV. xii. 29] after his second defeat at sea, he begins to experience tragedy's expression of the law of diminishing returns: self-destruction can be a means of self-recovery. Ironically Antony is led to this discovery by the example of his follower, Eros, and by that which Antony supposes Cleopatra has set in killing herself. We find Eros, of course, in Plutarch; but Shakespeare seems to have seen in the name a significance that the rationalist Plutarch did not. Shakespeare's Eros teaches the way to a death that is more than mere loss: 'Thy master dies thy scholar' [IV. xiv. 102]. Cleopatra, whom moments before Antony had thought the cause of his undoing, the 'Triple-turn'd whore' [IV. xii. 13], becomes with Eros the model of nobility and the agent of his redemption:

> Thrice-nobler than myself,
> Thou teachest me, O valiant Eros, what
> I should, and thou couldst not; my queen and Eros
> Have by their brave instruction got upon me
> A nobleness in record.
>
> [IV. xiv. 95-9]

As previously, the Roman leader is led by Cleopatra; but in this moment of vertiginous climax Antony finds honor in the direction of his downfall, a potential for self-affirmation in self-destruction, and triumph in defeat. Antony expresses it in its Stoic formulation: 'With a wound I must be cur'd' [IV. xiv. 78]; but in this rush of reversals we may also recognize one of Christianity's most fundamental precepts: one must first lose oneself in order to find oneself.

We are on the verge of more than one Christian mystery as Antony envisions a romantic afterlife with Cleopatra [IV. xiv. 51-4], and then metaphorically construes his death as an act of love:

> But I will be
> A bridegroom in my death, and run into't
> As to a lover's bed.
>
> [IV. xiv. 99-101]

As in its other manifestations throughout the play this conceit has both sexual and spiritual overtones. It is Cleopatra's lover speaking, but the words are also reminiscent of John's vision of the New Jerusalem, coming down out of heaven from God, 'prepared as a bride trimmed for her husband'. Echoes from Revelation continue to be heard as Antony, having thrown himself on his sword without managing to kill himself, pleads with the guardsmen to dispatch him. But once again the allusion underscores Antony's separation from the promise of Christian redemption, as he is compared to 'those men which have not the seal of God in their foreheads' when the Apocalypse comes:

> Therefore in those days men shall seek death,
> and shall not find it, and shall desire to die,
> and death shall flee from them.
>
> (Revelation, ix, 6)

Antony's death returns us to the beginning of the play where in another mood he unknowingly alluded to John's vision of 'a new heaven and a new earth', and where he first spoke of finding 'the nobleness of life' [I. i. 36] in Cleopatra rather than Rome. That the completion of these gestures confirms the tragic nature of Antony's experience is a measure of the metaphysical distance between his world and the Christian one. (pp. 104-08)

Where Christian apocalypse opens toward a transcendent reality, a revelation of cosmic purpose, Antony's vision is totally reflexive and personal. He is left to console himself with images from the interior space of tragic consciousness—an amorous eternity with Cleopatra, the dignity of self-conquest, the memory of his 'former fortunes':

> The miserable change now at my end
> Lament nor sorrow at: but please your thoughts
> In feeding them with those my former fortunes
> Wherein I liv'd: the greatest prince o' the world,
> The noblest; and do now not basely die,
> Not cowardly put off my helmet to
> My countryman: a Roman, by a Roman
> Valiantly vanquish'd.
>
> [IV. xv. 51-8]

His claim to have regained nobility in death comes from the core of the play's tragic sensibility; but *Antony and Cleopatra* asks that we compare this sensibility to one that reverses its fundamental premise and denies its ultimate reality. (p. 108)

If *Antony and Cleopatra* seems a formally imperfect tragedy, ambiguous in perspective and problematic in tone, it is because from the point of view of Christian thought tragedy itself is an imperfect perception of experience, shadowy, solipsistic, and ultimately self-negating. Christian vision bears a relation to reality to which tragic imagination cannot attain; it is the fulfillment of Cleopatra's dream of Antony, 'nature's piece, 'gainst fancy, / Condemning shadows quite' [V. ii. 99-100]. In a sense Christian vision denies the substance of all tragic consciousness, but there is a particular urgency to this irony in *Antony and Cleopatra*, whose discord so strenuously anticipates its own inversion in the resolving concord of Christian paradox. (p. 110)

Andrew Fichter, " 'Antony and Cleopatra' : The Time of Universal Peace," in Shakespeare Survey: An Annual Survey of Shakespearean Study and Production, *Vol. 33, 1980, pp. 99-112.*

RONALD R. MACDONALD (essay date 1985)

[*MacDonald posits that in* Antony and Cleopatra *Shakespeare is concerned with the ambiguous relation between reality, meaning, and language. Emphasizing that performance or playing offers "a unique opportunity to exercise the imagination," the critic holds that in this drama character is histrionic rather than psychological, allowing possibilities beyond the limits of reason alone. MacDonald argues that through active command of language and imagination, Antony and Cleopatra create identities for themselves and each other that go beyond the bounds of meanings imposed upon them by Rome or "'reality,' whatever that is." Like the lovers, the critic concludes, Shakespeare "refuses to be passive in the face of received representations" of this story, but instead demonstrates that the meaning of the past is indeterminate—"an open possibility, a collection of meanings in competition, a field as radically ambiguous" as* Antony and Cleopatra *itself.*]

The Victorian lady of Shakespearean apocrypha who emerged from a production of *Antony and Cleopatra* with the observation that it was very unlike the homelife of her own dear Queen suggests that the classical theory of mimesis does not provide the most useful approach to Shakespearean drama. If there is any homelife at all in *Antony and Cleopatra,* one supposes that it is quite unlike any other, real or imagined. It seems wrong to say that Shakespeare was attempting to imitate "the manners of the age," whether contemporary or ancient, and any attempt to recuperate the meaning of the play by mapping it onto a world anterior to the text and already in place seems doomed to failure. Not only do we despair—and we very soon do—of using the homelife of Queen Victoria as our model; we ultimately must despair of finding in any model the one "fit" that will somehow yield explanations. (p. 78)

The ambiguities of *Antony and Cleopatra* are notorious precisely because the majority of them are left unresolved. The most interesting work on this play, and perhaps on the approach to Shakespeare's late work as a whole, has stressed the value of unresolved ambiguity. Thus Janet Adelman, certainly one of the ablest critics of the play in the last ten years, has written [in her book *The Common Liar*]: "Although the play continually raises questions about motives, it simply does not give any clear answers to them. Almost every major action in the play is in some degree inexplicable. Why did Antony marry Octavia if he planned to return to Cleopatra? Was Octavius ruthless or merely blind in his plan to marry his sister to Antony? Does Antony return to the East for love of Cleopatra or because his spirit is overpowered when he is near Octavius?" Shakespeare seems willing enough to abide our questions, but he steadfastly refuses to answer them. Adelman's list could be extended almost indefinitely.

Such questions are simply undecidable not because Shakespeare constructed his play ineptly or didn't know what he really meant, but because his concern was not with knowledge—what we can know (or think we can know) about people and events—but with meanings and the way interpretive energy plays over the infinitely ambiguous world, constructing and reconstructing it in imagination. Undecidability is a way of defeating the search for that anterior world we think the play might be imitating. We are left not with a made or definitively made-up world which we can recuperate by mapping it onto our own, but with characters making a world, dreaming, imagining, performing, and acting. As we shall see, the reader is inevitably drawn into this process and becomes a participant with the characters in the effort after meaning. (pp. 79-80)

One way of producing meaning on the stage is the institution of the messenger. From a purely practical point of view, the messenger is simply a convenience. Rather than have Jocasta hang herself or Oedipus blind himself on stage, rather than

have a chariot and team (to say nothing of a bull appearing from the sea) and somehow contrive to have Hippolytus dragged about by his own horses, Sophocles and Euripides have messengers report these events. In these instances from classical drama it really makes no sense to question the veracity of these reports: they constitute these events for us. As competent readers of drama, we have assimilated this convention so thoroughly that it no longer strikes us *as* a convention.

At least so it seems until a deeply playful dramatist like Shakespeare, working directly against our dramatic competence, begins to make the convention once more opaque. No one gets far into *Antony and Cleopatra* without discovering that it is a play swarming with messengers, perhaps forty or fifty of them, depending on how elastic the definition of messenger is. Hardly a scene goes by without someone bringing news or someone reporting news that has just been brought. The point of all this busy transfer of information is not simply a matter of the contents of various messages, for Shakespeare is ultimately questioning not specific messages or messengers, but the dramatic institution of the messenger as a whole. If we have a model of this institution in mind, it may go something like this: the messenger is faceless, without personality, an empty conduit for the flow of information. News flows through him as water flows through a pipe; and just as the water does not affect the pipe, nor the pipe the water, so the messenger does not form his message, nor is he in turn informed by it. Shakespeare may have taken some delight in pondering the infelicities that can develop to plague this model. Something like the ideal model seems to be what the hapless messenger, who brings the unwelcome news of Antony's marriage in 2.5, has in mind. At least by the time Cleopatra is through with him, he has every reason to *wish* the institution still conformed to the purity of the ideal model.

This scene and the one that concludes the business with the messenger (3.3) are normally taken to provide examples of Cleopatra at her most outrageous and unqueenly. Here, if anywhere, we must see her as trifling, spoiled, childish, and vindictive. It must be admitted that the messenger, under pressure of Cleopatra's threats, learns to play the game according to her rules. He will assent to Cleopatra's assessment that Octavia is "dull of tongue, and dwarfish" [III. iii. 16], when he has reported her to be not as tall as Cleopatra and "low-voic'd." He will even take an active part in the game, when, warming to his performance, he will say of Octavia's gait, "She creeps" [III. iii. 18]. Such word-splitting is very funny, but has it any point beyond showing us a side of Cleopatra that is ignoble and silly?

It has, when we consider the profound questioning of value that Shakespeare conducts throughout the play. To call Cleopatra noble or ignoble at any point is to reduce a text that is constantly telling us that the difference is not the simple matter we ordinarily think it is. However exasperating and silly she may be in her exchange with the messenger, Cleopatra is, after all, fully active, transitive toward the language which she speaks and which is spoken to her. She refuses to accept the worn coin of words sanctioned in their meanings by the social order, and there is, despite all her outrageous fuss, something finely regal about that refusal:

Cleopatra.   Is he married?
     I cannot hate thee worser than I do,
     If thou again say yes.
Messenger.   He's married, madam.

Cleopatra. The gods confound thee, dost thou hold there
           still?
Messenger. Should I lie, madam?
Cleopatra.   O, I would thou didst;
    So half my Egypt were submerg'd and made
    A cestern for scal'd snakes! Go get thee
        hence!
    Hadst thou Narcissus in thy face, to me
    Thou wouldst appear most ugly. He is
        married?
Messenger. I crave your Highness' pardon.
Cleopatra.   He is
    married?

                                  [II. v. 89-98]

The refusal to accept plain facts seems a mark of childishness, until we remember that there are no plain facts in this play. What the messenger has to offer, and what he can only keep repeating, is the language of prose, those words whose meanings are guaranteed by a tacit agreement of the social order. We all know what it means to be married: two parties, male and female, have had a ceremony read, a ceremony consisting of words whose meanings are also guaranteed by the social order. This is minimally what "married" means. Why cannot Cleopatra understand that?

Perhaps the answer is partly in the fact that in Egypt, at least, Cleopatra the Queen *is* the social order. What has she to do with the worn coin of words minted in Rome by Romans? In her kingdom words will mean what she wills them to mean. She will discover meanings in excess of the meanings conferred upon them by the Roman social order, and "reality," whatever that is, had better get out of the way. Cleopatra never does "marry" Antony in the sense the messenger intends, so that in one way her line at the end, "Husband, I come" [V. ii. 287], flies in the face of common sense. But we have little to do here with *common* sense, and few would deny that her courage proves her title to the name.

And so here with the messenger the context has an odd way of bearing Cleopatra out and discrediting his account. We have just heard Antony in the last scene but one saying something about marriage: "I will to Egypt; / And though I make this marriage for my peace, / I' th' East my pleasure lies" [II. iii. 39-41]. We must ask along with Cleopatra in what sense Antony is married to Octavia, for again reality proves to have more meanings than language can easily manage. Shakespeare, at least on the evidence of Sonnet 116, knew of a marriage that has little to do with the messenger's "married." This is the "marriage of true minds" to which he will not "admit impediments." And if it seems incongruous to cite the high Platonism of that sonnet in the context of Cleopatra's scandalous behavior, we can still say that the principle is the same. The poet can ill afford to use words just in the senses that society supplies. If that is all he does, he ceases to be a poet. And if all Cleopatra does is to receive messages from Rome, she ceases to be a queen.

Much of the messenger's difficulty lies not with himself, but with the kind of world in which he must function. As he says meekly to Cleopatra, "I have done my duty" [II. v. 88], and doing your duty is hard enough in a world that, to paraphrase Caesar, rots itself with motion. Bringing news of a world that changes from moment to moment can rarely meet with much success. To tell the truth is often a matter of luck, and certainly not a matter of rehearsing the same old message. In 4.15 Decretas pulls the sword from the dying Antony thinking that it

will ingratiate him with Caesar. We see him next in 5.1 presenting Caesar with the sword and announcing Antony's death. From his point of view this is a lie, for he has left Antony alive. But it *is* true by the time he says it, for Antony has indeed expired between Decretas' first and last appearance. When the "half-life" of information is so short and the value of the message decays even as the breathless messenger approaches his goal, when our customary ways of meaning in general seem to go so utterly awry, how do we find stability, ways of assessing value, a place to stand?

Perhaps one answer to this question lies with Cleopatra's regal attitude toward language, examined above. Cleopatra makes an implicit claim to imagine a better Antony than the prose of the messenger's tale can deliver; in effect, she has rejected the voice of Rome in favor of her own imaginative vision, and it is by no means the only instance the play offers of Cleopatra creating Antony according to the dictates of her own will:

               O Charmian!
  Where think'st thou he is now? Stands he, or sits
    he?
  Or does he walk? Or is he on his horse?
  O happy horse, to bear the weight of Antony!
  Do bravely, horse, for wot'st thou whom thou
    mov'st?
  The demi-Atlas of this earth, the arm
  And burgonet of men.

                               [I. v. 18-24]

At this point Alexas enters with a report of Antony which coincides nicely with Cleopatra's imaginative vision of him:

              "Good friend," quoth he,
  "Say the firm Roman to great Egypt sends
  This treasure of an oyster; at whose foot,
  To mend the petty present, I will piece
  Her opulent throne with kingdoms. All the East,
  Say thou, shall call her mistress." So he nodded,
  And soberly did mount an arm-gaunt steed,
  Who neigh'd so high that what I would have spoke
  Was beastly dumb'd by him.

                                [I. v. 42-50]

We have no way of knowing of course whether Alexas' report hits the truth. He is one of Cleopatra's attendants and presumably is far more skilled at guessing her fancies than the messenger who brings the news of Antony's marriage. But whether this scene is a double imagination of Antony or a happy coincidence, it nonetheless points toward a standard in the imaginative faculty that transcends our normal sense of measure and limit and fact. The very correspondence between Cleopatra's name for Antony here ("The demi-Atlas of this earth, the arm / And burgonet of men") and the phrasing of her later, and far greater vision of him ("His legs bestrid the ocean, his rear'd arm / Crested the world" [V. ii. 82-3]), should make us take careful notice. For ultimately what we respond to in the play is not the search for motive and fact, what someone is really doing and why: this sort of search . . . can only result in an endless chase, a kind of back-and-forth of possibilities that never crystallize into hard truths. It is an attempt, like the bewildered Victorian lady's, to find a stable world to which we can pin the text. By contrast the characters in the play and the reader must submit to and accept paradox and contradiction and ambiguity, even as the playwright appears to have done.

We see this submission everywhere in *Antony and Cleopatra*, but perhaps nowhere more clearly than in Antony's acceptance of Cleopatra's perfect inscrutability and utter perversity. What, for instance, is the meaning of Cleopatra's parley with Thidias in 3.13? Does she contemplate going over to Caesar, or is she merely buying time? The scene will not answer such questions, and when Thidias says to Cleopatra of Caesar, ''He knows that you embrace not Antony / As you did love, but as you fear'd him'' [III. xiii. 56-7], Cleopatra's response is a perfectly ambiguous ''O!'' This is the very sign of emptiness, the creator of a place where we can deposit such meaning as we will, but which resolutely refuses to yield up meanings of its own. Even the violent quarrel which ensues between Antony and Cleopatra is not conducted by accusation and rebuttal, as a legal trial might be, and the reconciliation it brings about comes not because Cleopatra proves herself innocent of disloyal intentions (one wonders how she could do that in any case), but because she affirms strong feeling:

Antony.   Cold-hearted toward me?
Cleopatra.   Ah, dear, if I be so,
From my cold heart let heaven engender hail,
And poison it in the source, and the first
        stone
Drop in my neck; as it determines, so
Dissolve my life! The next Caesarion smite,
Till by degrees the memory of my womb,
Together with my brave Egyptians all,
By the discandying of this pelleted storm,
Lie graveless, till the flies and gnats of Nile
Have buried them for prey!
                                                  [III. xiii. 158-67]

To this bizarre and hyperbolic conceit Antony astonishingly responds: ''I am satisfied'' [III. xiii. 167].

Satisfied, we may ask, by what? Cleopatra has offered nothing in the way of proof that she has not been contemplating disloyalty. Indeed, certain phrases in her speech, ''the memory of my womb,'' for instance, actually bring up the matter of her varied history, serve to remind us that the memory of *her* womb is a long one. She has simply made a passionate and overstated assertion which seems for the moment to suffice. But one could argue that she has engineered the occasion for her grand assertion, deliberately provoked Antony to a ''chafe.'' We have actually seen her doing something of the sort from the very outset, in apparently trivial and teasing moods, where far less seems at stake:

Antony.   You'll heat my blood; no more.
Cleopatra.   You can do better yet, but this is meetly.
Antony.   Now, by my sword—
Cleopatra.   And target.—Still he mends.
          But this is not the best. Look, prithee,
               Charmian,
          How this Herculean Roman does become
          The carriage of his chafe.
                                                  [I. iii. 80-5]

Toward the beginning of the present scene Thidias has said of Caesar's message, ''Hear it apart,'' and after a quick appraisal of the company Cleopatra replies, ''None but friends: say boldly'' [III. xiii. 47]. She knows very well that Enobarbus is listening, and one supposes she must know what he will do when she seems to agree to Thidias' offers: ''Mine honor was not yielded, / But conquered merely'' [III. xiii. 61-2]. These lines of course send Enobarbus straight to his master.

While it would be rash to ascribe motives, we may say that the *effect* of Cleopatra's behavior, whatever its unknowable motives, is to provoke a performance in the grand manner, to stir the strong feeling in Antony (even if that strong feeling is anger) that has been conspicuously absent in him on the first day of Actium:

I am so lated in the world, that I
Have lost my way forever.
                                                  [III. xi. 3-4]

                    Egypt, thou knew'st too well
My heart was to thy rudder tied by th' strings,
And thou shouldst tow me after.
                                                  [III. xi. 56-8]

Fall not a tear, I say, one of them rates
All that is won and lost. Give me a kiss.
Even this repays me. We sent out schoolmaster,
Is 'a come back?
                                                  [III. xi. 69-72]

This last is the withered husk of hyperbole. Can one kiss with any degree of savor or passion a general who has just sent his schoolmaster to parley with a man half his age? In such moments we begin to suspect that Antony may really be the ''doting mallard'' that Scarus has called him [III. x. 19]. Perhaps the rhetoric of measure and limit (''Nay, but this dotage of our general's o'erflows the measure'' [I. i. 1-2]) really is the authentic idiom of the play.

The antidote to this rhetorical flaccidity comes when Antony is provoked into something that begins to resemble the grand manner. The intolerable spectacle of Cleopatra offering her hand to Thidias (and again, we will never know the motive behind this gesture) produces in Antony a ''chafe'' that, while not the best, is still an improvement on ''We sent our schoolmaster.'' One of the reasons that Antony's chafe is not the best is simply that what he says in his ranting is unfair:

                    I found you as a morsel, cold upon
Dead Caesar's trencher; nay, you were a fragment
Of Cneius Pompey's—besides what hotter hours,
Unregist'red in vulgar fame, you have
Luxuriously pick'd out; for I am sure,
Though you can guess what temperance should be,
You know not what it is.
                                                  [III. xiii. 116-22]

Cleopatra's response (''Wherefore is this?'' [III. xiii. 122]) is apposite: it ill becomes Antony to read *anyone* a sermon on temperance. And the effect of disappointment is underscored if we compare this speech with an earlier speech of Cleopatra's which it significantly echoes:

                    Broad-fronted Caesar,
When thou wast here above the ground, I was
A morsel for a monarch; and great Pompey
Would stand and make his eyes grow in my brow;
There would he anchor his aspect, and die
With looking on his life.
                                                  [I. v. 29-34]

While Antony's version makes Cleopatra seem a tired camp-follower (and himself the kind of man who has stooped to a camp-follower), Cleopatra's version makes herself seem part of an authentic heroic tradition: to have had Cleopatra as mistress is to enter the ranks of the truly great. Although Pompey and Caesar were mortal enemies in their actual careers, in Cleopatra's vision they are seen as mysteriously united in their admiration of the queen.

We cannot find Cleopatra's or Antony's the better version, for neither is based on evidence. If we choose between them, we choose Cleopatra's because it is the better performance, creates a generous vision of things, and manages to avoid altogether the priggish tone of Antony's moralistic tirade. Cleopatra's words seem wholly hers, sovereign language indeed, while Antony's seem second-hand, an iteration of that image of Cleopatra sanctioned by the Roman social order. What stirs us is the spectacle of Cleopatra as mistress of language and imagination, creating histrionically her own version of events. What disappoints us is the very different spectacle of Antony as the mere locus of an alien voice, not *Antony* speaking but Rome speaking *in* Antony.

What Cleopatra's provocative performance in 3.13 accomplishes is nothing less than a reawakening of feeling in Antony, a rekindling of the will to act up to a high conception of himself. As soon as he declares himself "satisfied" with Cleopatra's hyperbolic speech, we hear him talk of appearing "in blood," of making death love him, of feasting his men and forcing the wine to "peep through their scars" [I. xiii. 190], as if he would fill them so full they would leak. (When Caesar determines to feast his men in the next scene, he says, "They have earned the waste" [IV. i. 16].) A quiet remark of Cleopatra's may sum up the process that has taken place in this scene: "It is my birthday, / I had thought t' have held it poor; but since my lord / Is Antony again, I will be Cleopatra" [III. xiii. 184-86]. Her remark suggests a conception of character that is more theatrical than psychological, more a matter of will than of what one is or has passively become. What we normally designate as character is a performance, and what we ultimately know of others is what they play at being. The conception is far from trivial, for if it allows for the most painful degradation of the self, it also allows for its greatest exaltation, for the free creation of character in the face of rumor and opinion, those collective representations that make up the cultural susurrus which often comes to be regarded as historical fact. With the histrionic view of character we accept the reality of others rather in the way we accept the reality of characters in a play. We submit ourselves to an illusion and cease to worry about what may lie hidden behind that illusion. We are concerned far more with authenticity than with sincerity.

Much in *Antony and Cleopatra* benefits from being viewed as pure theatricality, the kind of speech and action that is judged by its virtuosity in orchestrating a collection of signs, not by the meaner skill of dissembling meanings, which when found out may be taken as keys to motive. We can therefore distinguish between acting (in the theatrical sense) and mere dissembling. Cleopatra and Antony engage preponderantly in the former, Caesar in the latter. Dissembling is ultimately a rather sneaky business associated with Shakespeare's word "policy." It has to do with stratagems and treachery. Acting, on the other hand, has to do with competition in the open, with single combat, and the generous test of mettle.

Cleopatra's great speech, in which she details her dream of Antony, is a paramount example of acting in the theatrical sense. It is closely related to Enobarbus' description of Cleopatra on the Cydnus not only because it contains some important verbal echoes, but because it is declaimed, and in its declamation triumphantly challenges our categories of understanding. And like Enobarbus' speech, it has its effect on listening Romans. After hearing this speech and expressing a good deal of skepticism about it, Dolabella nevertheless betrays Caesar's plan to lead Cleopatra in triumph.

Cleopatra concludes the speech with a flight of paradox:

> It's past the size of dreaming. Nature wants stuff
> To vie strange forms with fancy; yet t' imagine
> An Antony were nature's piece 'gainst fancy,
> Condemning shadows quite.
>
> [V. ii. 97-100]

This is a challenge indeed, a true lie, a declaimed assertion which has no patience with denials. In Cleopatra's vision it is remarkably *nature* that imagines an Antony, not fancy. With this stroke she calls into question yet another of our customary ways of producing meaning. To the normally opposed pair "fancy/nature" Cleopatra sets up a nature which imagines: "yet t' imagine / An Antony were nature's piece 'gainst fancy." What is this nature of hers that nevertheless imagines?

The answer is perhaps made no simpler by pointing out the punning double reference in the phrase "nature's piece." For this must also be "nature's peace," at least to the ear, and in a time of flexible orthography perhaps to the eye as well: the Folio text has "peece." In a complicated and paradoxical sense Cleopatra may be calling a truce to the striving and competition which seem to be a condition of the world of the play. She may also be rendering unto Caesar what is his, although only what is his and nothing more: "nature's peace" must also refer to her death and repose which she is planning and which she here obliquely mentions: "O, such another sleep, that I might see / But such another man" [V. i. 77-8]. In putting before us a nature that imagines, Cleopatra focuses the highly problematic relationship of art and nature, a relationship that the mature Shakespeare increasingly questioned, until in the late romances he could hardly make the distinction without qualifying it and resubmitting it as an identity. This is altogether more interesting than the neoclassical story about the world and its mirror. After we have experienced fancy outworking nature in Enobarbus' speech, and then nature throwing down a challenge to fancy in Cleopatra's, we can never quite be satisfied with an art that passively mirrors nature. All human behavior in the play is artful in some sense, which must mean that ultimately it is natural to be artful. To tell who is *not* acting is impossible. In one way or another everybody is acting, and if we make the absence of acting our criterion for authenticity, no one is authentic. *Antony and Cleopatra* will not allow us the simple pleasure of identifying a stable world that is then copied in the mirror of art and imagination. Every such stable reality proves to be some kind of posture. In 3.13 Enobarbus comments ironically on Antony's plan to challenge Caesar to single combat:

> Yes, like enough! high-battled Caesar will
> Unstate his happiness, and be stag'd to th' show
> Against a sworder!
>   . . . . Caesar, thou hast subdu'd
> His judgment too.
>
> [III. xiii. 29-31, 36-7]

But the reasonableness of this overlooks the suggestion that Caesar may *already* be staging a show of his own, a suggestion implicit in the foregoing lines of Antony concerning Caesar:

> Tell him he wears the rose
> Of youth upon him; from which the world should note
> Something particular. His coin, ships, legions,
> May be a coward's, whose ministers would prevail
> Under the service of a child as soon
> As i' th' command of Caesar.
>
> [III. xiii. 20-5]

How does one find the real man inside a machine so efficient that it can make anybody look good? Caesar only ''wears the rose / Of youth.'' How do we know that Caesar, like an actor, is not simply in costume?

We can not know of course. But if we bear in mind Cleopatra's paradoxical image of a nature possessed of imagination we can at least glimpse Shakespeare's insight. For it is not that in writing of Roman history Shakespeare makes the theater historical: rather, he comes to see, perhaps in mulling the texts of narrative history that were his sources, that history may fairly be called theatrical. What we conveniently designate as the real, the things and people that are nature, turn out to speak their theatrical piece: a piece that very nearly passes understanding.

Perhaps we are never able to be anything without playing at being it. However an existentialist philosopher may feel about this insight, the playwright must greet it as a liberation. As a playwright and actor and man of the theater, Shakespeare seems to have seen in performance, in playing at being something, a unique opportunity to exercise the imagination, to test its claims and limits, to try its capabilities in opening up the self and the world to possibilities unglimpsed by reason alone. (pp. 85-95)

[A] pervasive feeling for what the Greeks called *agon*, competition or creative strife, is closely connected with the idea of performance, with the idea that in playing at something you challenge denial and triumphantly become it. One of Antony's finest performances in the play amply illustrates the enactment of a high sense of the self in the face of denial and the creative struggle this entails. Here is his great soliloquy in 4.14 on learning the (false) news of Cleopatra's death:

> I will o'ertake thee, Cleopatra, and
> Weep for my pardon. So it must be, for now
> All length is torture; since the torch is out,
> Lie down and stray no farther. Now all labor
> Mars what it does; yea, very force entangles
> Itself with strength. Seal then, and all is done.
> Eros!—I come, my queen!—Eros!—Stay for me!
> Where souls do couch on flowers, we'll hand in hand,
> And with our sprightly port make the ghosts gaze.
> Dido and her Aeneas shall want troops,
> And all the haunt be ours. Come, Eros, Eros!
> [IV. xiv. 44-54]

Here we have an anticipation of ''nature's piece 'gainst fancy, / Condemning shadows quite,'' for those gazing ghosts of Antony's vision are surely condemned shadows beside the sprightly port of the triumphant lovers. The two speeches interpenetrate and support one another even at a considerable distance, where ''distance'' designates both a long run of text and the separation of death. It makes remarkably little difference that Antony's lines are elicited by news that is not true. What we respond to is the intensity of his imagination, his address to the absent queen, quite as if she could hear him and respond to him as literally as his living servant whom he summons from offstage.

We are stirred here, as we have already been stirred by Cleopatra's vision of Caesar and Pompey, the historical mortal enemies, united in their fascination with the Egyptian queen. And we are stirred for much the same reason. Again, the historical facts of the matter recede, and the histrionic control of imagination and language assumes primary importance. In spite of our being stirred, however, we may notice that Antony's lines contain an apparent blunder that the strict neoclassicist will want to attribute to Shakespeare's small Latin,

but that we may pursue to the point where it yields authentic meaning. Antony imagines Dido and Aeneas as united in death, although the *Aeneid* says nothing of the kind: both Shakespeare and Antony seem to have forgotten Sychaeus [Dido's husband].

But perhaps Shakespeare has not forgotten Sychaeus so much as remembered something else. Antony speaks his lines on the field of Actium in 31 B.C. He cannot very well be misinterpreting a poem that never saw the light of day until the author's death in 19 B.C. Antony, it would seem, is creating independently a version of a story that, from a strictly chronological point of view, has not yet been fixed in the canonical form we are familiar with from Vergil's *Aeneid*. If we have fallen into the habit of thinking that Vergil's version is the only possible version, Shakespeare's lines remind us that Vergil's version is itself historical, that it had an origin, that there could have been other versions of the story which the immense prestige of the *Aeneid* has since pushed aside. Antony certainly has every right to his version of the story twelve years *before* the competing version appeared. Moreover—and this is the crucial point—Shakespeare has a right to his version of the story more than sixteen-hundred years *after*.

The key to this assertion lies in the view of history implicit in Antony's lines about Dido and Aeneas, and implicit in the play as a whole. We have seen that reality in *Antony and Cleopatra* is at every point the sum of cultural representations, reports, rumors, surmises—all the communicative acts which make up what we earlier called the cultural susurrus. We have at any one time not a stable whole about which everyone agrees (there is hardly an example in the play of two characters agreeing about *anything*), but a series of versions in competition, each making a bid for authoritative status, none quite attaining the permanent enjoyment of that status. But if this is true of contemporary events which are presumably present for inspection, how much more true must it be for the record of those events, which is a collection of different interpretations in competition?

This relativistic view is crucial, for Antony and Cleopatra *are* in a compelling sense free to create themselves, to refuse the cultural representations that would reduce them or rob them of their reality. And Shakespeare is similarly free to imagine them creating themselves, for in so doing he is not blindly or naively resisting an irreducible reality. He is inserting his own version into what has been revealed as a collection of competing interpretations. History and historiography (including the version of Roman history embodied in the *Aeneid*) are, in short, ways of producing meaning, representations of reality, not reality pure and simple. We have seen Shakespeare throughout *Antony and Cleopatra* ceaselessly calling into question ways of producing meaning.

Thus not only do Antony and Cleopatra struggle to speak their own authentic idiom, and refuse to speak with the alien voices of the Roman social order. Their poet struggles as well. He must not allow his sources to speak in him, but must attempt to speak in and through them. In this his activity is of a piece with Cleopatra's when she refuses to accept the messenger's meaning of ''married,'' or with Antony's when he imagines himself and Cleopatra overgoing a Dido and Aeneas united in death. Shakespeare refuses to be passive in the face of received representations, the interpretation of history embodied in the *Aeneid,* the account found in Plutarch, or any other of the versions of history his tradition supplied him. He rather restores these to us *as* interpretations. His refusal to speak passively with the voices of tradition lies at the heart of the histrionic creation of the self in which Antony and Cleopatra, for all they are defeated in the game of politics and driven to suicide, can ultimately be seen as triumphant.

It would be wrong to call Shakespeare's procedure in *Antony and Cleopatra* "revisionist," for it is not as if, in depriving Vergil, or Plutarch, or any other of authority, he were then awarding it to himself. His play does not claim to replace a false version with a true one, for that would be to betray the sense of play and possibility that we have seen him everywhere creating. *Antony and Cleopatra* asks of us something more challenging than an assent to a single interpretation put forward in a work of historiography. It asks us to see the meanings of history as indeterminate. It sees the past as an open possibility, a collection of meanings in competition, a field as radically ambiguous as the play we have witnessed. All the world is not a stage, but, as the late Erving Goffman remarked [in his book *The Presentation of Self in Everyday Life*], it is often difficult to specify the crucial ways in which it is not. Perhaps people, even (or especially) the great of the earth, do not simply exist but play at being. And perhaps this puzzling and fascinating state of affairs will prevail to the end of the world, when final clarity will come not with the *Aeneid* or Plutarch, not even with *Antony and Cleopatra,* but with the *Last* Judgment. Meanwhile, does not Cleopatra give us leave "to play till doomsday"? (pp. 96-9)

> Ronald R. MacDonald, *"Playing till Doomsday: Interpreting 'Antony and Cleopatra',"* in English Literary Renaissance, Vol. 15, No. 1, Winter, 1985, pp. 78-99.

ADDITIONAL BIBLIOGRAPHY

Barroll, J. Leeds. *Shakespearean Tragedy: Genre, Tradition, and Change in "Antony and Cleopatra."* Washington: The Folger Shakespeare Library, 1984, 309 p.

An analysis of many aspects of the play, including Antony, Cleopatra, Octavius, and Rome itself, as well as Antony's association with Hercules, the role of Fortune, and the implications of the soothsayer episode. Barroll emphasizes the way Antony and Cleopatra believe in and seek to vivify private visions of themselves as the supreme warrior and "the most beautiful woman on earth." Unlike the lovers, Barroll contends, Octavius is not characterized as a personality whose traits determine his fate; however, the hypocrisy, acquisitiveness, and literal-mindedness which he displays are representative of the Roman world in this play.

Berek, Peter. "Doing and Undoing: The Value of Action in *Antony and Cleopatra.*" *Shakespeare Quarterly* 32, No. 3 (Autumn 1981): 295-304.

Maintains that the "vocabulary of doing and undoing" in *Antony and Cleopatra* emphasizes the paradoxical quality of the protagonists' relationship and—by serving as euphemisms for both "making love and making war"—underscores the conflicts and continuities between these two actions. Berek contends that the lovers and Octavius come to understand the limited rewards and high cost of "earthly 'doing'''; because we share this perception, too, the critic holds, we are not saddened by the conclusion of the play, for "we cannot value highly the world the lovers have lost."

Blisset, William. "Dramatic Irony in *Antony and Cleopatra.*" *Shakespeare Quarterly* XVIII, No. 2 (Spring 1967): 151-66.

An assessment of "the many senses of irony" in *Antony and Cleopatra,* particularly focusing on the effect that occurs when one character knows more than another and the audience has a fuller understanding of dramatic events than either of these figures. Blisset also contends that although Enobarbus's superior insight

fits him for the roles of choric commentator and comic deflator of other characters, we come to regard him with deeper irony than we do Antony, for Enobarbus is "ultimately . . . more ignorant of his true condition."

Boas, Frederick S. "The Plutarch Series of Plays." In his *Shakspere and His Predecessors,* pp. 454-503. New York: Charles Scribner's Sons, 1896.

Compares Cleopatra to Falstaff, noting that both possess a "paradoxical grandeur compounded out of all that is most morally worthless." Boas also offers a general discussion of such dramatic concerns as the play's composition date, sources, language, and structure, and he complains that *Antony and Cleopatra* fails to provide a unified perspective on dramatic events.

Brandes, George. "*Antony and Cleopatra.*" In his *William Shakespeare,* pp. 461-76. 1898. Reprint. London: William Heinemann, 1920.

Focuses on Cleopatra, describing her as "the woman of women . . . , Eve and the serpent in one," and likening her to the 'dark lady' of the Sonnets—Shakespeare's own "black enchantress."

Brower, Reuben A. "Heroic Tragedy, Heroic Love: *Antony and Cleopatra.*" In his *Hero & Saint: Shakespeare and the Graeco-Roman Heroic Tradition,* pp. 317-53. New York: Oxford University Press, 1971.

Maintains that although Antony's heroic past and future greatness are betrayed by love, the betrayal is mitigated by the alluring splendor of that love, by Antony's achieved recognition of his self-betrayal, and by Shakespeare's suggestion "that contradictory worlds of value . . . may become one in imagination." Brower examines the language and imagery in *Antony and Cleopatra,* demonstrating how the tone, syntax, and rhythm of certain passages deepen the impression of Antony's nobility; he adds that the cumulative effect of the imagery leads us to apprehend "the hero's greatness and decline as a tremendous movement from sunlike brilliance to 'day's end,' darkness, and night."

Bullough, Geoffrey. Introduction to *Antony and Cleopatra,* by William Shakespeare. In *Narrative and Dramatic Sources of Shakespeare, Vol. V,* edited by Geoffrey Bullough, pp. 213-53. London: Routledge and Kegan Paul, 1964.

A thorough analysis of definite and probable sources for *Antony and Cleopatra,* together with a discussion of pre-Shakespearean treatments of "the Cleopatra legend" and Renaissance dramatic versions of the lovers' story. Bullough notes where Shakespeare modified North's translation of Plutarch and where he followed it closely, remarking that the strong influence of North's "splendid prose" is evident in many other passages besides Enobarbus's description of Cleopatra at Cydnus.

Burke, Kenneth. "Shakespearean Persuasion." *The Antioch Review* XXIV, No. 1 (Spring 1964): 19-36.

Analyzes Shakespeare's dramatic pattern of first establishing the grandeur of Antony and Cleopatra's love, then showing the lovers "in something of the non-imperial humbleness they were born with," and finally annihilating the splendid illusion he has erected. In their acting-out of the idea of imperialism-in-love, Burke argues, Antony and Cleopatra present human weaknesses in amplified form; the critic concludes that because the lovers represent us "only too thoroughly," we can sympathetically renounce our association with them and the illusion they have created, but the undoing of the vision "cannot undo the splendor of its having been done."

Caputi, Anthony. "Shakespeare's *Antony and Cleopatra:* Tragedy without Terror." *Shakespeare Quarterly* XVI, No. 2 (Spring 1965): 183-91.

Argues that the most significant opposition in *Antony and Cleopatra* is between "different ways of being alive" and that our apprehension that Antony chooses the vital, imaginative way helps explain why we feel no terror at the play's conclusion. Caputi holds that Shakespeare was more concerned with dramatizing particularized experience than abstract concepts, and he contends that the lovers' ability to harmonize diverse and discordant elements in life is underscored by the metaphysical quality of much of the play's language.

Champion, Larry S. "The Social Dimensions of Tragedy: *Timon of Athens, Coriolanus, Antony and Cleopatra.*" In his *Shakespeare's Tragic Perspective*, pp. 201-65. Athens: University of Georgia Press, 1976.

Traces Antony's development from egocentricity to self-knowledge to awareness of "the sufferings of those around him," and, ultimately, to triumph over his own nature. Champion maintains that Antony's tragedy is compounded of equal parts of his own selfishness, the decadence and enervating nature of Egypt, and the callousness and duplicity of Rome.

Charney, Maurice. "The Imagery of *Antony and Cleopatra.*" In his *Shakespeare's Roman Plays: The Function of Imagery in the Drama*, pp. 79-141. Cambridge: Harvard University Press, 1963.

One of the most frequently cited essays in the criticism of *Antony and Cleopatra*. This is a revised and expanded version of Charney's earlier publications on the play (see excerpts above, 1957 and 1959).

Colie, Rosalie L. "*Antony and Cleopatra*: The Significance of Style." In her *Shakespeare's Living Art*, pp. 168-207. Princeton: Princeton University Press, 1974.

An analysis of language and imagery in *Antony and Cleopatra*, focusing on the opposition of plain and grandiloquent styles, the function of hyperbole, and the fundamental connection between "speech and style of life." In this play, Colie maintains, Shakespeare and the lovers extend language beyond conventional usage in an attempt to express the intensity and indefinable nature of their love; she asserts that the drama both affirms this love and demonstrates "the values of an honestly ostentatious style."

Cunningham, Dolora G. "The Characterization of Shakespeare's Cleopatra." *Shakespeare Quarterly* VI, No. 1 (Winter 1955): 9-17.

Argues that the paramount antithesis in *Antony and Cleopatra* is the traditional Christian opposition between will and reason and that Enobarbus "makes available to us the specifically Christian principles" whose violation leads to Antony's ruin. Cunningham further contends that as Cleopatra prepares "to die better than she has lived," the queen's efforts parallel the progress of a repentant Christian, moving from rejection of sin to contrition, belief in God's forgiveness, and "the firm purpose of amendment of life." Cunningham's assertions were directly challenged by Elizabeth Story Donno (see entry below).

Daiches, David. "Imagery and Meaning in *Antony and Cleopatra.*" *English Studies* 43, Nos. 1-6 (1962): 343-58.

Maintains that *Antony and Cleopatra* is chiefly concerned with the range of roles to be played on the world's stage and with the connection between these roles and "the player's true identity." Antony's suicide provides him with the occasion to unite his different personae as lover and as man of action, Daiches argues, but it is ultimately Cleopatra's dream of Antony that sums up— in its "tremendous images of power, benevolence and sensuality"—the full range of the hero's identity.

Dickey, Franklin M. "The Tragedy of *Antony and Cleopatra,*" "*Antony and Cleopatra* (II)," "*Antony and Cleopatra* (III)." In his *Not Wisely but Too Well: Shakespeare's Love Tragedies*, pp. 144-202. San Marino, Calif.: The Huntington Library, 1957.

Contends that although Shakespeare makes us feel vivid pity and terror at the downfall of Antony and Cleopatra, he presents them as exemplars of "rulers who threw away a kingdom for lust." Dickey offers an extensive overview of classical, medieval, and Renaissance accounts of the lovers that emphasize, almost without exception, their intemperance and portray Cleopatra as "a wanton and a sorceress, who employed all the conscious arts of love to keep Antony ensnared"; the critic concludes that this is how Shakespeare has drawn them, too.

Donno, Elizabeth Story. "Cleopatra Again." *Shakespeare Quarterly* VII, No. 2 (Spring 1956): 227-33.

Disputes the arguments of Dolora G. Cunningham (see entry above), averring that Cunningham has distorted the text of *Antony and Cleopatra* and seriously misread the role of Enobarbus. Donno questions whether any audience would perceive Enobarbus as providing a Christian perspective from which to view dramatic events; she also contends that in Cleopatra's preparation for death there are elements of defiance, nihilism, and resolution, but nothing of "'the penitent Christian'."

Doran, Madeleine. "'High Events as These': The Language of Hyperbole in *Antony and Cleopatra.*" *Queen's Quarterly* LXXII, No. 1 (Spring 1965): 26-51.

Examines the complex function of hyperbole in *Antony and Cleopatra*, contending that it is sometimes used to diminish as well as to heighten and asserting that it is a highly appropriate trope for this drama of "reaching for the idea of excellence." Doran particularly notes the way in which Cleopatra helps create the concept of an Antony "beyond actuality" both in the dream she describes to Dolabella and in the manner of her death itself.

Eagleton, Terence. "*Coriolanus* and *Antony and Cleopatra.*" In his *Shakespeare and Society: Critical Studies in Shakespearean Drama*, pp. 98-129. London: Chatto & Windus, 1967.

Contends that *Antony and Cleopatra* explores "the problem of reconciling authentic and responsible living" and offers one possible response: the intentional decision to pursue personal fulfillment and live it "to the full with tragic affirmation." Eagleton holds that the play demonstrates that while a commitment may mean disaster, "to avoid one is to surrender integrity, to lose that wholeness which comes only from full engagement."

Ellis-Fermor, Una. "The Nature of Plot in Drama." *Essays and Studies* n.s. XIII (1960): 65-81.

Focuses on Shakespeare's method and intent in individualizing the minor characters in *Antony and Cleopatra*. Ellis-Fermor contends that by means of an unusual perspective, comparable to the way an artist gives depth to a painting, Shakespeare evokes at once the sense of "vastness, of coherence and significance."

Fisch, Harold. "'Antony and Cleopatra': The Limits of Mythology." *Shakespeare Survey* 23 (1970): 59-67.

Maintains that in Act V, Scene ii Shakespeare introduces elements of comic deflation to reverse "the myth-ritual pattern" built up throughout *Antony and Cleopatra*, thus setting the apotheosis of the lovers within an ironic, realistic frame. Fisch asserts that the most significant "mythological grouping" in the play is that of Isis-Osiris-Set, "with Cleopatra functioning as Isis, goddess of nature and fertility, Antony as Osiris, the dying Sun-god who is resurrected in eternity," and Octavius as Set, whose attempt to take Osiris's place is thwarted by Isis.

Fitch, Robert E. "No Greater Crack?" *Shakespeare Quarterly* XIX, No. 1 (Winter 1968): 3-17.

Dispraises *Antony and Cleopatra* for presenting a world in which the dominant values of "Pleasure and Power" preclude any religious or metaphysical vision and for its characterization of love as devious, belittling, and essentially soulless. Fitch contends that the centrifugal dramatic movement, the concern with timelessness, and the discrepancy between action and language signal that "the poet is running away with the playwright" and indicate Shakespeare's increasing interest in the perspective he was to develop in the romances that followed *Antony and Cleopatra*.

Fitz, L. T. "Egyptian Queens and Male Reviewers: Sexist Attitudes in *Antony and Cleopatra.*" *Shakespeare Quarterly* 28, No. 3 (Summer 1977): 297-316.

An attack on the perceived sexist bias of nearly all critical approaches to *Antony and Cleopatra*. Fitz asserts that manifestations of sexism in the critical history of the play include: 1) the comparison of Cleopatra only with Juliet or heroines in the comedies rather than with Hamlet, Othello, Lear, or Macbeth; 2) the failure to note the play's *Lear*-like concern with "love and its relationship to public issues . . ., as well as love's place in the individual's hierarchy of values''; 3) assumptions that love is appropriately a central value for a woman, but only of secondary interest for a man; and 4) the view of Antony as the play's single protagonist. Urging a reassessment of Cleopatra as a tragic hero, the critic argues that Shakespeare's alterations of Plutarch's portrayal exonerate and elevate the queen, provide her with a ''fully developed individuality,'' and, most significantly, depict her as experiencing an intense internal struggle, learning and growing ''as Antony does not.''

Goddard, Harold C. ''*Antony and Cleopatra*.'' In his *The Meaning of Shakespeare*, pp. 570-94. Chicago: University of Chicago Press, 1951.
    Contends that *Antony and Cleopatra* dramatizes the superiority and eventual triumph of spiritual power over mere worldly might. Goddard asserts that Antony's military losses are followed by his transubstantiation into a figure of ''true divinity'' whose refracted radiance lights up the world he leaves behind.

Hallett, Charles A. ''Change, Fortune, and Time: Aspects of the Sublunar World in *Antony and Cleopatra*.'' *Journal of English and Germanic Philology* LXXV, Nos. 1 and 2 (January-April 1976): 75-89.
    Argues that there is no spiritual level in the dramatic world of *Antony and Cleopatra* and thus the characters lack ''a fixed point upon which to anchor their lives.'' Hallett maintains that the play's portrayal of destructive mutability, capricious Fortune, and tyrannous Time emphasizes the instability and impermanence of both Rome and Egypt; in this chaotic, sublunary world, he concludes, it is impossible for the characters to make ''final judgments'' or to find fulfillment.

Hamilton, Donna B. ''*Antony and Cleopatra* and the Tradition of Noble Lovers.'' *Shakespeare Quarterly* XXIV, No. 3 (Summer 1973): 245-51.
    Maintains that Shakespeare's linking of Antony and Cleopatra with ''other famous lovers of antiquity'' tempers the play's moral emphasis, thereby providing an intentionally complex conception of the protagonists. Hamilton holds that the comparisons of Antony and Cleopatra with these other noble lovers—most particularly Dido and Aeneas, Venus and Mars—endows Shakespeare's treatment of the story of the triumvir and his Egyptian queen with ''a dimension of unsurpassable glory.''

Harris, Frank. ''Dramas of Lust: Part II: *Antony and Cleopatra*.'' In his *The Man Shakespeare and His Tragic Life Story*, pp. 304-29. London: Frank Palmer, 1909.
    Claims that Shakespeare identified himself with Antony, emphasized the character's nobility, and denigrated Cleopatra ''because he, too, was passion's slave, and had himself experienced with his dark mistress, Mary Fitton, the ultimate degradation of lust.'' Harris proposes that Shakespeare was bound by historical fact to depict Cleopatra nobly confronting death, so that from the conclusion of Act IV until she dies she is an heroic figure.

Holloway, John. ''*Antony and Cleopatra*.'' In his *The Story of the Night: Studies in Shakespeare's Major Tragedies*, pp. 99-187. London: Routledge & Kegan Paul, 1961.
    Discusses, among other dramatic elements, the nature of Antony and Cleopatra's passion, emphasizing its exuberant vitality and evaluating it as beyond mere lust, but something ''less than love.'' Holloway maintains that where in earlier parts of the play the lovers are principally concerned with their stature and nobility, in Acts IV and V their speeches reveal painful personal feelings, suggesting both their connection to humanity and their tragic alienation from the conventional world.

Homan, Sidney R. ''Divided Response and the Imagination in *Antony and Cleopatra*.'' *Philological Quarterly* XLIX, No. 4 (October 1970): 460-68.
    Proposes that by offering a paradoxical perspective on the power of art and imagination, Shakespeare demonstrates in *Antony and Cleopatra* that there is ''no simple dichotomy between Rome and Egypt.'' Not only is Cleopatra's extraordinary ability to transform reality tempered by the linking of her creativity with dangerous

delusion, Homan argues, but the ''graceless, unimaginative'' aspect of Rome is modified by the optimistic vision of a ''time of universal peace'' (IV. vi. 5).

Honigmann, E. A. J. ''Antony versus Cleopatra.'' In his *Shakespeare, Seven Tragedies: The Dramatist's Manipulation of Response*, pp. 150-69. London: Macmillan Press, 1976.
    Contends that after the battle of Actium, Antony changes radically, acquiring—through bitter shame—the ''high seriousness'' he lacked earlier, dominating Cleopatra where previously she had imposed her will upon him, and losing his belief in her integrity. At the same time, Honigmann argues, our earlier admiration for Cleopatra's ''brilliance as a performer'' is undercut by her theatrical straining after a brave and noble death; the play offers her ennoblement as a possibility, he concludes, but it is ''not one that we can fully believe in.''

Jones, Emrys. ''*Antony and Cleopatra*.'' In his *Scenic Form in Shakespeare*, pp. 225-65. Oxford: At the Clarendon Press, 1971.
    Argues that the structure of *Antony and Cleopatra* divides naturally into two parts: one showing ''preliminaries to a war'' and the second depicting ''the war . . . and its immediate consequences.'' Analyzing the unusual number of short scenes in the play, Jones notes that the disjunctive sequence of these episodes in the first half prevents us from becoming ''emotionally engaged to any great depth'' with the characters, but he maintains that in the second half there is more continuity between the scenes, thereby involving our feelings to a far higher degree. The critic also provides a detailed analysis of scenic progression in *Antony and Cleopatra* and examines Enobarbus as a vitalizing agent.

Jorgensen, Paul A. ''Antony and the Protesting Soldiers: A Renaissance Tradition for the Structure of *Antony and Cleopatra*.'' In *Essays on Shakespeare*, edited by Gordon Ross Smith, pp. 163-81. University Park: Pennsylvania State University Press, 1965.
    Contends that in terms of structure, thematic emphasis, and character, *Antony and Cleopatra* comprises two plays, rather than one. Jorgensen maintains that the first half of the drama is closely connected to the Elizabethan dramatic tradition of ''the noble warrior . . . dishonorably diverted from his proper business by amorous dotage'' and is concluded in Act III when it becomes evident that Antony's personal struggle to conquer his disastrous passion for Cleopatra will fail. The second half of the play depicts a wholly different struggle, the critic asserts, with the lovers allied against Octavius; although they suffer a temporal defeat, Jorgensen claims, by virtue of their loyalty to each other they bring this second conflict to a triumphant conclusion.

Kaula, David. ''The Time Sense of *Antony and Cleopatra*.'' *Shakespeare Quarterly* XV, No. 3 (Summer 1964): 211-23.
    Maintains that time in *Antony and Cleopatra*, except for Caesar, is ''an unsalutary force'' thwarting rather than facilitating life's chief aims. Kaula argues that each of the three principals is associated with a different aspect of time—Caesar with the future, Antony with the past, and Cleopatra with the present—and that these associations help to characterize and ''locate them within the moral universe of the play.''

Kirschbaum, Leo. ''Shakspere's Cleopatra.'' *Shakespeare Association Bulletin* XIX, No. 4 (October 1944): 161-71.
    Asserts that although Cleopatra is somewhat transformed in the concluding scenes, she is consistently portrayed as a voluptuary and a courtesan throughout the drama. Even in her death, Kirschbaum holds, Shakespeare continues to surround her with images of harlotry and to demonstrate that she is ''erotic to the quick.''

Kittredge, George Lyman. Introduction to *The Tragedy of Antony and Cleopatra*, by William Shakespeare, edited by George Lyman Kittredge, pp. vii-xii. Boston: Ginn and Co., 1941.
    Emphasizes Cleopatra's role as Eastern enchantress, but also asserts that in her resolution to die she proves herself ''worthy to be a Roman's wife.'' Additionally, Kittredge describes Antony's passion for the queen as ''tragic infatuation,'' for it renders him incapable of self-knowledge or judgment.

Kuriyama, Constance Brown. "The Mother of the World: A Psychoanalytic Interpretation of Shakespeare's *Antony and Cleopatra*." *English Literary Renaissance* 7, No. 3 (Autumn 1977): 324-51.

Evaluates the latent content of *Antony and Cleopatra* as an erotic fantasy of the paradoxical union of love and death. Examining elements in the play that emphasize Cleopatra as a mother figure and maintaining that the concluding scenes present a psychological victory as well as a physical and political defeat for Antony and Cleopatra, Kuriyama maintains that these final scenes may be read as a fulfillment of the sexual fantasy in which "the pre-Oedipal paradise of complete union with the mother" is regained.

Leavis, F. R. "'Antony and Cleopatra' and 'All for Love'." *Scrutiny* V, No. 2 (September 1936): 158-69.

Emphasizes the superiority of *Antony and Cleopatra* over Dryden's *All for Love* in terms of both poetry and tragic effect. Leavis compares Enobarbus's description of Cleopatra's barge (II. ii. 190ff.) with the parallel passage in *All for Love*, and he declares that here, as well as throughout *Antony and Cleopatra*, Shakespeare's verse is vigorous and organic, "whereas Dryden's is merely descriptive eloquence."

Lloyd, Michael. "Cleopatra as Isis." *Shakespeare Survey* 12 (1959): 88-94.

Analyzes the function of Shakespeare's repeated association of Cleopatra with Isis, the goddess of maternal and wifely devotion. Echoes of this legend in *Antony and Cleopatra*, Lloyd contends, heighten the portrayal of the Egyptian queen and establish her love, in comparison with Antony's, as selfless and creative.

———. "The Roman Tongue." *Shakespeare Quarterly* X, No. 4 (Autumn 1969): 461-68.

An examination of the discrepancies between "Egypt as it sounds in the Roman mouth" and Egypt as we experience it in the play, and of "Rome as it declares itself and Rome as it acts." These discrepancies, Lloyd asserts, expose the Romans as guileful, hypocritical, pietistic, motivated principally by self-interest, and indifferent to human affections.

MacCallum, M. W. "*Antony and Cleopatra*." In his *Shakespeare's Roman Plays and Their Background*, pp. 300-453. London: Macmillan and Co., 1925.

An exhaustive treatment of *Antony and Cleopatra*, with detailed discussions of the three principal figures, the political setting, and Shakespeare's use of his sources. MacCallum views the play as an unusual combination of "chronicle history," "personal tragedy," and "love poem." Originally published in 1910, this work continues to hold an estimable position in the literary criticism of *Antony and Cleopatra*.

Mack, Maynard. "*Antony and Cleopatra*: The Stillness and the Dance." In *Shakespeare's Art: Seven Essays*, edited by Milton Crane, pp. 79-113. Chicago: University of Chicago Press, 1973.

Proposes that *Antony and Cleopatra* is "creatively, painstakingly" founded on a type of "defiant pluralism," paradoxically offering two perspectives on whether "an imperium in the embrace of Cleopatra" is "more life-giving than an imperium in Rome" and asserting the truth of both views. Mack holds that, intentionally, none of the polarities presented in the play is resolved, as if one of Shakespeare's chief concerns is to challenge our conventional standards and "logical expectations." In this highly regarded essay, the critic also examines other aspects of the play, including the way Shakespeare develops his portrayal of a volatile and inconstant world through imagery and dramatic construction.

Mason, H. A. "*Antony and Cleopatra*: Angelic Strength—Organic Weakness." *Cambridge Quarterly* 1, No. 3 (Summer 1966): 209-36.

Argues that Shakespeare was unable to carry out his original intention to treat the story of Antony as a tragedy and that he employed "magnificent subterfuges" to conceal this failure. The concept of competing claims presented in the opening scene is not developed, Mason contends, nor do we see Antony struggle

with this challenge in subsequent scenes; this dramatic lapse will be clear, the critic asserts, if we view the lovers dispassionately and "resist the 'spell' of the 'poetry' whenever it turns out that Shakespeare is substituting spell-binding for the manacling power of the drama."

———. "*Antony and Cleopatra*: Telling *versus* Shewing." *Cambridge Quarterly* 1, No. 4 (Autumn 1966): 330-53.

Contends there is a severe discrepancy between Antony's self-assertions and what others report about him, on the one hand, and what the dramatic events show him to be, on the other. That Shakespeare failed to "focus his mind" on the character of Antony, Mason declares, is evident in such dramatic foibles as the dependence on narration for important actions, our growing disinterest in Antony, though we are expected to remain engaged, after his disgrace at Actium, and the perfunctory references to the gods "to throw a classical aura" around the hero. The triumvir's dying speeches and Cleopatra's lament in Act IV, Scene xv bear little relation to what has been dramatized earlier, the critic concludes, and should be regarded as Shakespeare's "commentary on a situation he has imagined but not embodied."

McFarland, Thomas. "Antony and Octavius." *Yale Review* XLVIII, No. 2 (December 1958): 204-28.

Argues that *Antony and Cleopatra* dramatizes the irrevocable opposition of "love and the world" and the struggle to establish the former as the locus of human virtue. The mood of exhilaration at the close of the play, McFarland maintains, reflects Antony's ultimate transcendence of the world through "the attainment of love."

Mills, Lauren J. *The Tragedies of Shakespeare's "Antony and Cleopatra."* Bloomington: Indiana University Press, 1964, 66 p.

Contends that Cleopatra's tragedy is an incomplete one, for although Antony's suicide brings her some appreciation of his worth and of Roman values, she is blind to the part she has played in his defeat and death. Mills argues that Antony's tragic flaw is his failure to be guided by reason rather than passion; the critic believes that Shakespeare intended to present Antony as "a man of great qualities who might have become ruler of the world," but instead lost both the world and himself through love of "a thoroughly unworthy object."

Miola, Robert S. "*Antony and Cleopatra*: Rome and the World." In his *Shakespeare's Rome*, pp. 116-63. Cambridge: Cambridge University Press, 1983.

Finds a "growing venality and ignobleness" in the Rome of *Antony and Cleopatra* and asserts that in his courageous suicide, Antony remains true to Roman ethics and ideals while repudiating their degraded versions. Miola gives close attention to Shakespeare's use of classical mythology in the play, especially remarking on the way the association of Antony and Cleopatra with legendary figures alternately endows them with "supernatural status" and undercuts their pretensions and "swelling rhetoric."

Nelson, C. E. "*Antony and Cleopatra* and the Triumph of Rome." *University Review* XXXII, No. 3 (March 1966): 199-203.

Maintains that the theme of power shapes both the tragic structure of the love story in *Antony and Cleopatra* and the portrayal of the man who—because of love rather than for the sake of it—did not become ruler of the world. Nelson declares that the play "dramatizes the triumph of morality, the achievement of peace, and the rise . . . of the greatest empire the world had ever seen."

Nevo, Ruth. "The Masque of Greatness." *Shakespeare Studies* III (1967): 111-28.

Focuses on Cleopatra "as she moves toward the fulfillment of her resolve" to die, comparing her imaginative progress to Renaissance court masques. Noting the elements of horror and degradation in the several passages that evoke Cleopatra's participation in Caesar's "anti-masque" of Roman triumph, Nevo maintains that the queen replaces this nightmare with a dream of Antony as a pageant king. In this reshaping of their story, the critic concludes, Cleopatra moves from fear and revulsion to "sovereign contempt" for the world, magnificently affirming Antony's manhood, valor, and virtue, as well as their mutual greatness.

Nochimson, Richard L. "The End Crowns All: Shakespeare's Deflation of Tragic Possibility in *Antony and Cleopatra.*" *English* XXVI, No. 125 (Summer 1977): 99-132.

Acknowledges the presence of tragic elements in *Antony and Cleopatra,* but contends that it is essentially an untragic play. Nochimson asserts that since Shakespeare purposely deflates his protagonists throughout the drama, even in the scenes of their deaths, what happens to them should be of very little interest to us. But because "some characters—especially themselves—see them in tragic terms," and because of our familiarity with other historical and literary treatments of their story, the critic declares, we may find ourselves responding to "the myth of Antony and Cleopatra, rather than to Shakespeare's play."

Ornstein, Robert. "The Ethic of the Imagination: Love and Art in *Antony and Cleopatra.*" In *Later Shakespeare,* edited by John Russell Brown and Bernard Harris, Stratford-upon-Avon Studies 8, pp. 31-46. London: Edward Arnold, 1966.

Evaluates the polarities of Rome and Egypt "in matters of the heart and the imagination." Ornstein argues that Antony learns to renounce the "earthbound and philistine" thought of Rome for the "cosmic poetic amplitude" of Egyptian imagination, eventually taking leave of the world in an imaginative vision that demonstrates the fullness of his poetic sensibilities. All that Cleopatra expresses in her leave-taking has been evident in earlier scenes, the critic maintains, and Shakespeare responds to the artist in her by portraying her death with "an immeasurable bounty of his artistic love, which is immortality itself."

Payne, Michael. "Erotic Irony and Polarity in *Antony and Cleopatra.*" *Shakespeare Quarterly* XXIV, No. 3 (Summer 1973): 265-79.

Contends that although the various polarities in *Antony and Cleopatra*—Egypt and Rome, femininity and masculinity, love and death, transcendence and boundary—at first seem to be "mutually exclusive or dualistic concepts," the play demonstrates instead that they represent the poles of a single continuum. Payne argues that Antony eventually rejects the dualistic Roman perspective, and with his death and Cleopatra's all "existential boundaries are transcended just as the geographical, sexual, and space-time boundaries were transcended in earlier scenes."

Platt, Michael. "*Antony and Cleopatra.*" In his *Rome and Romans according to Shakespeare,* pp. 258-76. Lanham, Md.: University Press of America, 1983.

Analyses the implications of *Antony and Cleopatra*'s portrayal of the end of the Roman Republic and the establishment in its place of imperial government. Platt contends that under the impending peace of Augustus, there is no longer any role for Roman ambition, courage, or valor, and he concludes that implicit in Shakespeare's depiction of Rome is a sense of "a world about to fall apart, or held together in an order which stupefies."

Rothschild, Herbert B., Jr. "The Oblique Encounter: Shakespeare's Confrontation of Plutarch with Special Reference to *Antony and Cleopatra.*" *English Literary Renaissance* 6, No. 3 (Autumn 1976): 404-29.

Maintains that the relationship between historiography and drama, together with such collateral questions as "the issue of narrative truth," are central concerns in the dramatic action of *Antony and Cleopatra.* Rothschild contends that the play reveals both Shakespeare's conviction that his historical source offered "a limited presentation of the truth of the life it took for its subject" and his assertion that the poet's vision is superior to the historian's method of perception; even more importantly, the critic concludes, *Antony and Cleopatra* insists that "people, like the rest of great creating nature, have a being prior to all interpretation."

Schanzer, Ernest. "*Antony and Cleopatra.*" In his *The Problem Plays of Shakespeare: A Study of "Julius Caesar," "Measure for Measure," "Antony and Cleopatra,"* pp. 132-86. London: Routledge & Kegan Paul, 1963.

Focuses on the dualistic structure of *Antony and Cleopatra,* noting particularly that the absence of a single moral framework in which to place Antony's decisions makes this drama "Shakespeare's problem play *par excellence.*" The simple opposition between Rome and Egypt, Schanzer contends, is complicated by three factors: 1) the gradual displacement of the question of choosing between two ways of life by "the glorification of the choice which Antony has made"; 2) Cleopatra's achievement before her death of certain Roman qualities; and 3) the presence in both worlds of such negative characteristics as deceit and cruelty. In this important essay, the critic also demonstrates the structural and organizational parallels between *Antony and Cleopatra* and *1* and *2 Henry IV,* discusses the significance of the play's allusions to classical literature and myth, and provides extended comparisons of Shakespeare's treatment of the story with those of Garnier and Daniel.

Seaton, Ethel. "*Antony and Cleopatra* and the *Book of Revelation.*" *Review of English Studies* XXII, No. 87 (July 1946): 219-24.

The earliest explication of the parallels between the Book of Revelation and the imagery of Acts IV and V in *Antony and Cleopatra.* Seaton maintains that the "visions and phrases of the most mystical of the Scriptures" elevate the dramatic style of the concluding scenes and help transform Antony and Cleopatra from "children of luxury and riot" into "children of light."

Shapiro, Michael. "Boying Her Greatness: Shakespeare's Use of Coterie Drama in 'Antony and Cleopatra'." *Modern Language Review* 77, No. 1 (January 1982): 1-15.

Analyzes the influence on *Antony and Cleopatra* of "the pathetic heroine" traditions in Neoclassical and private theater dramas, and, most significantly, of the self-conscious dramaturgical techniques of the latter group. In Act V, Shapiro argues, Shakespeare deals with obstacles to a sympathetic response to Cleopatra, first by discrediting Roman cynicism and silencing its principal spokesmen, and then by turning the "dual consciousness" of the Jacobean audience—the fact that the queen is being played by a boy actor—to advantage. In the "squeaking . . . boy" passage (V. ii. 220-21), the critic asserts, Shakespeare subtly invites the audience to judge Cleopatra's histrionics by aesthetic rather than moral criteria and to determine not whether her enactment is "deceitful or manipulative," but whether it is "artistic and expressive."

Shapiro, Stephen A. "The Varying Shore of the World: Ambivalence in *Antony and Cleopatra.*" *Modern Language Quarterly* XXVII, No. 1 (March 1966): 18-32.

Maintains that ambivalence is not only a principal theme of *Antony and Cleopatra,* but a central factor in the structure, imagery, and audience response to the internal conflicts of the protagonists as well. Shapiro avers that paradox and ambivalence are central to the play's dramatization of the relationship between the self and the world, for "no simple harmony can resolve the antitheses . . . that govern our lives."

Simmons, J. L. "*Antony and Cleopatra*: New Heaven, New Earth." In his *Shakespeare's Pagan World: The Roman Tragedies,* pp. 109-63. Charlottesville: University Press of Virginia, 1973.

Compares Egypt in *Antony and Cleopatra* to the green world of Shakespearean comedy, noting that both offer release from "the sanctions and restrictions of society," a lack of concern with time, an aura of Saturnalian festival, and the "desire for perfect realization of the emotional life." Simmons argues that at the conclusion of the play, Cleopatra—functioning as a comic heroine who manipulates events and arranges "the happy ending of marriage"—reconciles love and honor; the tragic reconciliation, the critic adds, comes with the world's bestowal upon the lovers of "the height of fame."

Simpson, Lucie. "Shakespeare's 'Cleopatra'." *Fortnightly Review* CXXIX, CXXIII n.s., No. DCCXXXV n.s. (March 1, 1928): 332-42.

Asserts that Cleopatra is the preeminent figure in the play and that *Antony and Cleopatra* deserves to be ranked with *Hamlet*, *Othello*, *Lear*, and *Macbeth*. Simpson rejects earlier views of the queen as a mere courtesan or voluptuary, arguing that like Shakespeare's great tragic heroes she is transformed and purified by the play's dramatic action.

Speaight, Robert. "*Antony and Cleopatra*." In his *Nature in Shakespearian Tragedy*, pp. 122-49. London: Hollis & Carter, 1955.
    Argues that *Antony and Cleopatra* is an affirmation of love and "the transcendental view of life." Speaight calls attention to the way in which the aura of transcendence continually alternates with chords of comedy and realism, particularly noting the many instances where a single passage mingles spacious or timeless images with commonplace slang, and he judges that *Antony and Cleopatra* is "suspended somewhere between the tragic and the comic muse."

Stahr, Adolf. "Cleopatra täuscht ihre Betrüger und giebt sich selbst den Tod." In his *Cleopatra*, pp. 266-73. Berlin: J. Guttentag, 1864.
    The earliest assertion that Cleopatra has devised—and rehearsed with Seleucus—the incident of her supposed concealing of assets. Stahr maintains that the queen's ruse is successful, for it leads Octavius to conclude that Cleopatra does not mean to end her life. This essay is written in German.

Stein, Arnold. "The Image of Antony: Lyric and Tragic Imagination." *Kenyon Review* XXI, No. 4 (Autumn 1959): 586-606.
    Claims that *Antony and Cleopatra* emphasizes the authenticity of self-created images and the validity of the imagination. Focusing on Antony's evanescent cloud speech (IV. xiv. 2ff.) and Cleopatra's dream of her lover (V. ii. 76ff.), Stein argues that these passages underscore the play's assertion that realities created by the human mind need not conform to literal truth in order to be legitimate and authentic.

Stewart, J. I. M. "Professor Schücking's Fatal Cleopatra." In his *Character and Motive in Shakespeare: Some Recent Appraisals Examined*, pp. 59-78. London: Longmans, Green and Co., 1949.
    Denies the charge made by Levin L. Schucking (see excerpt above, 1919) that the figure of Cleopatra in the final scenes of the play is an "astonishing contradiction" of her earlier presentation. Stewart argues that the splendor and vitality of her poetry from the very beginning of the play indicate a profound significance beneath Shakespeare's surface portrayal of a wanton. At the conclusion, he asserts, we believe in the verisimilitude of the character not from any illusion created by the poetry, "but from an actual correlation between high dramatic poetry and insight into substantial human nature."

Stirling, Brents. "Cleopatra's Scene with Seleucus: Plutarch, Daniel, and Shakespeare." *Shakespeare Quarterly* XV, No. 2 (Spring 1964): 299-311.
    A significant contribution to the critical debate over the Seleucus episode in Act V, Scene ii, which asserts that Cleopatra is here acting on her own, playing for time until she finds the resolution to carry out her carefully planned suicide. Stirling argues that, as in several previous episodes that follow the death of Antony, this one is "a dialectic of revolution and back-sliding" that ends with a decisive turn towards resolution. In the scene with her treasurer, the critic maintains, it is not the evidence of concealed wealth that leads Caesar to believe that "Cleopatra loves life too well to die," but the queen's furious and bizarre demonstration of "combative pride" in attacking Seleucus.

Stroup, Thomas B. "The Structure of *Antony and Cleopatra*." *Shakespeare Quarterly* XV, No. 2 (Spring 1964): 289-98.
    Contends that in terms of structural unity *Antony and Cleopatra* "takes its shape" directly from the late morality plays and ultimately from the mystery plays and the psychomachia. Stroup argues that the microcosm of Antony's story, as in these medieval dramas, is set within "the great macrocosm of reality" and emphasis is laid upon the concept of the world as a stage; further, the critic holds, in his movement from sin to repentance, Antony

undergoes a testing by the gods that parallels "the soul-warfare of the morality plays."

Traci, Philip J. *The Love Play of "Antony and Cleopatra": A Critical Study of Shakespeare's Play*. Studies in English Literature, LXIV. The Hague: Mouton, 1970, 171 p.
    A comprehensive analysis of the characterization, imagery, structure, and theme of love in *Antony and Cleopatra*. Traci provides a full account of the critical history, evaluates elements of comedy and bawdry in the play, and describes the dramatic movement of *Antony and Cleopatra* "as a sustained metaphor of the love-act."

Traversi, Derek. "*Antony and Cleopatra*." In his *Shakespeare: The Roman Plays*, pp. 19-203. Stanford: Stanford University Press, 1963.
    A scene-by-scene analysis of *Antony and Cleopatra* that expands upon ideas first put forth in the critic's *An Approach to Shakespeare* (see excerpt above, 1938). Traversi's reading of the play is a noteworthy contribution to the critical history of *Antony and Cleopatra*.

Vincent, Barbara C. "Shakespeare's *Antony and Cleopatra* and the Rise of Comedy." *English Literary Renaissance* 12, No. 1 (Winter 1982): 53-86.
    Views *Antony and Cleopatra* as a contest between tragedy and comedy, maintaining that "although the tragic and ironic vision is never invalidated," the comic one is preeminent at the conclusion of the drama. Vincent likens Antony's reconciliation of tragic (Roman) and comic (Egyptian) conceptions of experience to Shakespeare's demonstration that the genres are most fully realized when they are mingled in a unified vision.

Waddington, Raymond B. "*Antony and Cleopatra*: 'What Venus did with Mars'." *Shakespeare Studies* 2 (1966): 210-27.
    Argues that the mythical pairing of Mars and Venus, rather than the one of Hercules and Omphale, is more significant in understanding Shakespeare's portrayal of Antony and Cleopatra. Remarking that Renaissance iconographers regarded the legend of Mars and Venus as embodying the concept of harmony arising from chaos, Waddington contends that in the later stages of the play Antony and Cleopatra discover that neither Rome nor Egypt is sufficient by itself, and they thus move toward "a mode of behavior which mediates between unnatural extremes and incorporates as well the essential nature of the lover."

Whitaker, Virgil K. "The World Opposed: *Antony and Cleopatra* and *Coriolanus*." In his *The Mirror up to Nature: The Technique of Shakespeare's Tragedies*, pp. 276-310. San Marino, Calif.: The Huntington Library, 1965.
    A noted negative appraisal of *Antony and Cleopatra*. Whitaker argues that the play represents "a falling off" in emotional impact and clarity from *Hamlet*, *Othello*, *King Lear*, and *Macbeth*, principally because although Shakespeare started to compose another "tragedy of moral choice" similar to these, he developed this drama according to the pattern of Elizabethan narrative tragedies. Such characteristics of *Antony and Cleopatra* as its episodic structure, its lack of metaphysical elements, a hero who is "the same man at the end of the play as at the beginning," and the absence of soliloquies that might provide insight into the hero's mind, the critic asserts, are typical of narrative tragedies, which are solely concerned—as is *Antony and Cleopatra*—with telling a story.

Williamson, Marilyn L. "The Political Context in *Antony and Cleopatra*." *Shakespeare Quarterly* XXI, No. 3 (Summer 1970): 241-51.
    Argues that "the grandeur of the portraits" of Antony and Cleopatra must not blind us to "the judgment implicit in the political scenes of the play," to the importance of relations between ruler and subjects, and to the lovers' roles as rulers. Williamson traces the theme of loyalty and betrayal in the attitudes and conduct of Enobarbus and other secondary characters, as well as in the behavior of the protagonists, concluding that the internal divisions of Antony and Cleopatra are mirrored in "the divided world in which they play out their story."

Wilson, Elkin Calhoun. "Shakespeare's Enobarbus." In *Joseph Quincy Adams Memorial Studies*, edited by James G. McManaway, Giles E.

Dawson, and Edwin E. Willoughby, pp. 391-408. Washington: The Folger Shakespeare Library, 1948.

A notable discussion of the character and function of Enobarbus in *Antony and Cleopatra*. Wilson maintains that while Enobarbus acts as a choric figure—helping to bridge gaps in dramatic time and space, serving as "a credible reporter of off-stage events," presciently foreshadowing the tragic outcome, and giving direction to audience sympathies—his detached and judicious commentary is infused with intimate revelations of his own nature. As clear-sighted as he is with regard to the conduct of the lovers and others, the critic concludes, Enobarbus errs in barring sentiment from his decision to desert Antony; however, in his repentance and death we see "the man of feeling beneath the ironist."

Wimsatt, W. K., Jr. "Poetry and Morals: A Relation Reargued." *Thought: Fordham University Quarterly* XXIII, No. 89 (June 1948): 281-99.

A brief commentary on *Antony and Cleopatra* as an immoral work, offered within a discussion of the relation between poetry and morals. Wimsatt maintains that "the play pleads for certain evil choices," presenting them in a way calculated to arouse our sympathy, but also portrays "the reasons for sin, a mature and richly human state of sin."

Richard II

DATE: Scholars generally agree that Shakespeare composed *Richard II* sometime during the mid-1590s, the most frequently cited date being 1595. It is unlikely that the history was written before late 1594 or early 1595, since it was not until then that Samuel Daniel's epic poem *The Civil Wars*—now regarded by most scholars as a primary source for *Richard II*—was listed in the STATIONERS' REGISTER and subsequently published; nor could it have been written after August 29, 1597, for that is the date when *Richard II* was itself licensed for printing and listed in the Register, followed a few months later by the publication of the First Quarto (Q1). Literary historians attempting to determine a more definite date for the play frequently point to Sir Edward Hoby's famous letter of December 7, 1595, in which Hoby invited Robert Cecil, a powerful Elizabethan statesman, to dinner and a private viewing of one "K. Richard." Although recent critics, notably I. A. Shapiro (see Additional Bibliography), have cautioned that this might as easily refer to Shakespeare's *Richard III*, to the work of another author, or perhaps even to a portrait of the king rather than a drama, Hoby's mention of *Richard II*—if that is indeed what it is—would not only establish with some precision the drama's place in the Shakespeare canon, but would also indicate its currency among the highest echelons of Queen Elizabeth's government.

This interest is certainly borne out by *Richard II*'s early publication history (see *TEXT* section below) and by its role in the abortive Essex Rebellion of February 7, 1601, when supporters of the popular and ambitious general Robert Devereux, the Earl of Essex, paid forty shillings to Shakespeare's company for a special performance of *Richard II* at the GLOBE THEATRE, evidently hoping to use the play as propaganda for their cause. Although the plan proved a dismal failure—the uprising was quickly and completely suppressed—*Richard II* acquired a certain notoriety from the events and the subsequent trial of Essex and his men. Thereafter many Londoners regarded the play as a possibly dangerous, albeit unintentional, political caricature. Because of her lack of an heir, and what some of her subjects regarded as a penchant for excessive taxation and indulging costly favorites, Queen Elizabeth was repeatedly compared to the spendthrift, autocratic Richard, while Essex was commonly identified with Bolingbroke. The queen herself was aware of the analogy: "I am Richard II, know ye not that?" she remarked in 1601 to the archivist William Lambarde complaining that Shakespeare's "tragedy was played 40tie times in open streets and houses." Despite *Richard II*'s turbulent political history, no specific lines from the play have ever been identified as topical allusions that would further determine its date of composition.

Given this lack of definitive evidence, critics investigating the date of *Richard II* generally do so in terms of its relation to the rest of the canon. It is widely recognized that the play is roughly contemporaneous with the lyrical *A Midsummer Night's Dream* and *Romeo and Juliet*—similarities have been observed in the language of all three—and with the tragical histories *King John, 1, 2,* and *3 Henry VI,* and *Richard III*—all of which are believed to have been written during the first five years of the 1590s. While it is impossible to determine with absolute certainty the sequence in which these works were composed,

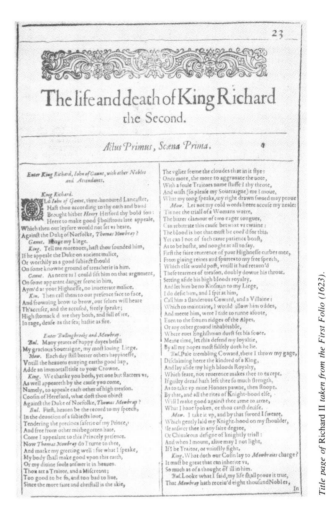

Title page of Richard II taken from the First Folio (1623).

as a group they demonstrate Shakespeare's concern at this point in his career with the themes of kingship and usurpation, with techniques of dramatic exposition and characterization, with language and reality, and with a strong, psychologically complex central protagonist rather than a multiplicity of stock "types." Thus, the consensus of opinion is that *Richard II* is a product of Shakespeare's late apprenticeship, written after *Richard III* and closely followed by its related, but more mature sequel, *1* and *2 Henry IV.*

TEXT: As previously mentioned, *Richard II* was entered in the Stationers' Register in late August of 1597 and first published in QUARTO form shortly thereafter. The title page of Q1 reads: "The tragedie of Richard the second. As it hath been publikely acted by the Right Honourable the Lorde Chamberlaine his Seruants. London Printed by Valentine Simmes for Androw Wise, and are to be sold at his shop in Paules church yard at the signe of the Angel." Since the text of this quarto is generally considered good, it is assumed that Wise, the COMPOSITOR, based his edition on the author's manuscript or a transcription legally acquired from Shakespeare's theatrical troupe. Beyond the typical Elizabethan misspellings and misprints, the only problem with the text of the First Quarto is that it omits

160 lines from Act IV, Scene i—significantly, that portion representing Richard II's abdication. The fact that the controversial dialogue was not reinserted either in the Second or Third Quartos (Q2 and Q3), both published in 1598 when Queen Elizabeth was still on the throne, indicates to most scholars some form of official censorship. Although the noted textual historian A. W. Pollard argued that the episode was excised for artistic reasons, and others, including David M. Bergeron (see Additional Bibliography), claimed that Shakespeare added the so-called deposition scene as an afterthought, writing it sometime between 1601 and 1608, the consensus of opinion is that the episode is part of the original script and was probably acted in all productions, but that the authorities, fearing sedition, suppressed it only in book form. Not until 1608, when the Fourth Quarto (Q4) appeared, was the deposition scene made available to the reading public, and even then in a mutilated and corrupt condition which suggests a MEMORIAL RECONSTRUCTION or a pirated shorthand version.

Textual analysis has shown that Q2 was set from Q1—it repeats most of the errors while adding quite a few of its own—and that each of the successive quartos, five in all, was set from its immediate predecessor. Much speculation surrounds the issue of which of these texts was used in the preparation of the FIRST FOLIO edition of 1623 (F1). Evidently, the Folio printer Isaac Jaggard assembled *Richard II* with some care, introducing act and scene divisions—the quartos are printed without breaks—elaborate punctuation, and expanded stage directions. Nevertheless, F1 is not without errors, only some of which can be traced to the quarto texts. Painstaking collation of variant readings from each of the five quarto editions has led some bibliographers to conclude that Jaggard's assistants probably compiled the Folio version from a copy of Q3 or Q5 containing actors' notes and used as a PROMPT BOOK in the playhouse, in conjunction with some independent version of Act IV, Scene i. The resultant combination of scripts, many scholars maintain, must have then been corrected against Q1 or a very similar manuscript, for some of the first edition's original phrasings—garbled in subsequent quartos—are restored in the Folio.

The 1623 Folio text of the deposition scene is today considered authoritative, being distinctly superior to that of Q4. Textual critics have proposed that Jaggard could have derived it either from Shakespeare's FOUL PAPERS, from a transcript belonging to the theater, or from a copy of Q5 that had been amended for publication or use during rehearsals at the Globe. Concerning the rest of the play, modern scholars customarily regard the Q1 version of 1597 as definitive, and, if crosschecked against divergent readings from the other quartos and the Folio, relatively free from the sort of technical problems that have challenged authorities of some of Shakespeare's other plays. Those "inaccuracies, inconsistencies, and loose ends" that do exist—John Dover Wilson called them "puzzling features of the text" (see Additional Bibliography)—seem to have originated not in the printer's shop, but in Shakespeare's background material (see *SOURCE* section below).

The early textual history of *Richard II* suggests that the play was enormously popular: of all Shakespeare's works, only *1 Henry IV* was as frequently reprinted during his lifetime, and *Pericles* was his only other play to go into two quarto editions in a single year.

SOURCES: "On the basis of what we know at present," literary historian Matthew W. Black once remarked, "Shakespeare prepared himself more thoroughly for the writing of

Richard II than of any other play in the canon'' (see Additional Bibliography). Scholars have identified no fewer than seven sources for the history: RAPHAEL HOLINSHED's *Chronicles of England, Scotlande, and Irelande* (1587); EDWARD HALL's *The vnion of the two noble and illustre famelies of Lancastre & York* (1548); Froissart's *Chroniques,* translated by Sir John Bourchier, Lord Berners (1523-25); Jean Creton's *Histoire du Roy d'Angleterre Richard II; La Chronique de le Traison et Mort de Richart Deux Dengleterre,* possibly by Jean Le Beau; the anonymous history play *Woodstock;* and Samuel Daniel's epic poem *The First Fowre Bookes of the ciuile warres* (1595). Both Creton's history and the *Chronique de la Traison,* though not published until the nineteenth century, were available during Shakespeare's lifetime in manuscript form. Several collateral documents have also been proposed as general models or indirect inspirations for the play.

Undoubtedly, the most important of the sources is Holinshed's *Chronicles.* Shakespeare appropriated much of his information, and even some of his phraseology, from this Renaissance account of Richard II's reign, deposition, and murder. He did, however, depart from the *Chronicles* in a number of significant details, most notably in the area of characterization. Whereas Holinshed's Gloucester, for example, is a dangerous fomenter of civil unrest, Shakespeare makes him a "plain, well-meaning soul" (II. i. 128). Likewise, the John of Gaunt of the *Chronicles* is a greedy, violent, ruthless politician bearing little resemblance to Shakespeare's wise, noble, eloquent, and patriotic elder statesman.

For the general scheme of his play, Shakespeare looked not to Holinshed but to Hall's *The vnion of the two noble and illustre famelies of Lancastre & York.* Ignoring a good deal of the *Chronicle's* background material as well as its descriptions of Richard's Irish campaign and Northumberland's capture of the king, the dramatist chose instead to emulate Hall's sequence of events. Like Hall, Shakespeare begins his account with the challenge of Mowbray by Bolingbroke. Critics are sharply divided, however, on the issue of Hall's effect on the language of *Richard II.*

Scholars also dispute the importance of Shakespeare's French sources, but most agree that for certain colorful incidents in the play, for details of characterization—including what one critic has called his "utterly unhistorical" Gaunt—and for his generally compassionate attitude toward the fallen Richard, Shakespeare was indebted to three medieval accounts: The *Chroniques* of Jean Froissart, *La Traison et Mort de Richart Deux Dengleterre,* and Creton's *Histoire.* The most salient contribution of Froissart's *Chroniques* is its treatment of the illness and death of John of Gaunt. The old knight's wisdom and sternness, his grim assessment of the condition of the kingdom, as well as his nephew's callous dismissal of his warnings—merely noted in Holinshed—are developed at length in Froissart and equally stressed in Shakespeare's play. To the authors of *La Traison et Mort de Richard Deux* and the *Histoire de Roi d'Angleterre* Shakespeare may have owed some verbal echoes as well as whatever anti-Lancastrian sentiments appear in the last three acts of his play. As the Arden editor Peter Ure observed, "Shakespeare's rendering of Richard's character, as he found it in Holinshed, was profoundly modified by the friendly and pitying attitude toward him" that Creton and LeBeau projected (see Additional Bibliography). But commentators on *Richard II* have also often expressed admiration for Shakespeare's balanced and open-minded treatment of the many divergent points of view apparent in his contradictory sources.

Samuel Daniel's *The First Fowre Bookes of the Ciuile Warres between the two houses of Lancaster & Yorke* was published in 1595—a fact frequently mentioned by scholars attempting to assign a date to *Richard II*. That Shakespeare made some use of this epic poem in the course of his researches for his play seems evident; the similarities between the two works are often striking. The king's farewell to his wife, for example, with its poignant exhortation—"In winter's tedious nights sit by the fire . . . [and] tell thou the lamentable tale of me . . ." (V. i. 40, 44)—is only one of several passages with a close parallel in the *Ciuile Warres*. More significantly, Daniel, like Shakespeare, altered the historical facts in making Queen Isabel, Richard's consort, a mature and passionate woman, when in reality her age in the year 1400 was only eleven.

There has been considerable debate over the exact relationship between *Richard II* and the anonymous play known as *Thomas of Woodstock*. This dramatization of the early years of Richard's reign focuses on the murder of the Duke of Gloucester and seems, in the opinion of many scholars, to have served as a kind of prologue to Shakespeare's history. Meticulous comparison of the two works reveals unmistakable borrowings, both verbal and thematic. Moreover, some critics have seen in the saintly character of Duke Thomas a direct model for Shakespeare's cautious, avuncular, and equally ficticious Gaunt. But because the date of *Woodstock* has never been established with certainty, a few literary historians have argued that *Richard II*, not the chronicle play, is the earlier work—a situation which, if true, would discredit *Woodstock* as a source for Shakespeare's history.

An alternative theory on the sources of *Richard II*, advanced by John Dover Wilson, has generated one of the liveliest discussions in the history of Shakespearean study. Dover Wilson was troubled by the many inconsistencies and weaknesses in the play noted by nearly all critics—the fact, for example, that the issue of Gloucester's murder is introduced in Act I but never satisfactorily resolved, and that the character of Bagot, who was one of those "at Bristol [who] lost their heads" [III. ii. 142], suddenly reappears three scenes later. Some experts posited that these and other inconsistencies in the play might be accounted for as present in one of Shakespeare's many sources. Having initially decided to include them in his play, the dramatist later lost track of them in the avalanche of available material and failed either to develop them or to edit them out. Dover Wilson, however, protested that the picture of Shakespeare behaving like a professional historian assiduously laboring amid dusty tomes was implausible and out-of-character. He hypothesized instead that Shakespeare did not systematically consult any of the above-named sources, for the real prototype of *Richard II* was another play entirely, now unfortunately lost. Dover Wilson buttressed his argument with some provocative evidence. He noted the strangely uneven quality of the writing in *Richard II:* how it degenerates from fine poetry in some sections to what more than one commentator has flatly called "doggerel" in others; to Dover Wilson, these inferior couplets, particularly in Act V, seemed different enough to be the work of another author. He also drew attention to the existence of "fossil rhymes" in *Richard II*, claiming that these were the vestiges of an old play that had been in rhyme and was revised by Shakespeare into blank verse. Critics have since objected that no external proof for Dover Wilson's hypothetical source play can be found either in the Stationers' Register or in the form of an extant copy. Nevertheless, experts have looked with great interest at a 1611 diary entry of Simon Forman, who described seeing a drama about Richard II that

was clearly not Shakespeare's, opening the possibility that some such work existed which might have been adapted by Shakespeare as Dover Wilson suggests.

As noted above, scholars have identified a number of works that might have indirectly influenced the composition of *Richard II*. These include, among others, *The Mirror for Magistrates* and Christopher Marlowe's *Edward II*. The former is a collection of stories in verse from the annals of English history. Highly moralistic in tone and rather stilted in diction, these tales are much less sophisticated than *Richard II* and not as psychologically plausible—but "one or two" verbal echoes from them have been detected in Shakespeare's play. *Edward II* is a powerful, violent drama depicting the downfall of a king who, like Richard, was "basely led by flatterers" [I. i. 241-42], and who suffers a particularly grisly death. Marlowe's brilliant poetry, as well as his technique of manipulating audience sympathy so that his protagonist, initially repulsive, in the end commands pity and concern, appear to have been adopted by Shakespeare to good effect in *Richard II*.

CRITICAL HISTORY: Although *Richard II* has never been Shakespeare's most critically acclaimed history—it lacks the powerful villainy of *Richard III* and the human interest of *Henry IV*—it is in some ways his most controversial, inspiring an enormous diversity of critical comment. Scholars of the play have focused primarily on three distinct but by no means unrelated areas of interest: the character of Richard, the significance of his rhetorical language and love of ceremony, and the meaning of his fall. While many critics have dismissed the king as an unsympathetic and inept figure, whose lyrical flights of fancy reflect his immaturity and egotism, others have defended him as the archetypal poet—a sensitive and reflective individual tragically caught up in a changing political world foreign to his nature, and against which he can offer little, if any, resistance. As with all Shakespeare's English histories, there is perennial debate over what political philosophy *Richard II* espouses, but commentators generally agree that the seriousness of the play's underlying themes—the nature of kingship, the relation of language and reality, and the meaning of individual identity—makes it a powerful work despite its technical weaknesses. Other dominant concerns in the critical history of *Richard II* include the characterization or motives of Bolingbroke and the degree to which he controls the outcome of events; Shakespeare's use of formalized rhetoric, ritual, and ceremony and what this language reveals not only about the characters, but also the society in which they live; the importance of the so-called Tudor myth and Tudor theories of kingship; the conflict between appearance and reality; and the significance of family honor or moral inheritance to the rise and fall of the various characters. Scholars have also addressed the problem of *Richard II*'s text and its use of source material, its relation to other works—both by Shakespeare and his contemporaries—and its role in Shakespeare's development as a tragedian.

The earliest reactions to *Richard II* were, for the most part, less critical than political: of those sixteenth- and seventeenth-century references which survive, the majority, including the sworn depositions taken at the trial of the Earl of Essex (see *DATE* section above), are concerned not so much with the play's aesthetic value as with its implicit, and potentially dangerous, commentary on the monarchical system of government. Other than the brief praise of one passage by John Dryden and the comments of Nahum Tate in his adaptation of the drama—both written in the late seventeenth century—few scholars seemed interested in the play beyond its political implications. It was not until the beginning of the eighteenth century that commentators focused on more significant issues, such as Shakespeare's use of his historical sources, the play's structural weaknesses, the question of authorship, and the relevance of Richard's characterization. Writing in 1721, Charles Gildon was the first to disparage Shakespeare's adaptation of historical events in *Richard II* and to question why the dramatist chose to depict "the most despicable character of all our kings" in the first place. Charlotte Lennox likewise pointed out a number of historical inaccuracies in *Richard II*, maintaining that such liberties as Shakespeare took were unpardonable in a work supposedly depicting true events. Over twenty years earlier, Alexander Pope, noting the inferiority of the play's rhymed couplets, suggested that they might be the work of a collaborator. Francis Gentleman also found the lyrical utterances of Richard uncharacteristic and "ill adapted to the serious important situation." Near the end of the century, Charles Dibdin, after studying what he felt was the careless construction of the history, surmised that Shakespeare rushed through its composition, patching together material from earlier chronicles.

The generally negative assessment of Shakespeare's *Richard II* among eighteenth-century scholars is perhaps best exemplified by the comments of George Steevens, who observed that "successive audiences of more than a century have respectively slumbered over [*Richard II*], as often as it has appeared on the stage"; even Samuel Johnson complained that the play afforded little "to effect the passions or enlarge the understanding." Most Augustan critics felt uncomfortable with Shakespeare's defiance of the classical "unities" and his fusion of history and tragedy in *Richard II;* conscious of the need for form in a work of art, they were hard pressed to determine its exact genre and particularly ill at ease with its protagonist, who, they claimed, lacked the tragic stature of a Brutus or a Lear. Indeed, to such moralists as Elizabeth Griffith, the vacillating, sometimes petty Richard was more an "object of contempt than of compassion."

Under the influence of Romanticism, however, nineteenth-century critics offered a more favorable opinion of *Richard II,* especially concerning Shakespeare's presentation of the king himself, but also respecting the structure or unity of his play. In his letter of 1820 to M. Chauvet, the Italian novelist Alessandro Manzoni contended that the classical "rules" for tragedy are irrelevant to *Richard II,* since it is a historical drama in which "characters develop over a [long] period of time." He argued that the appropriate standards for unity in such a work are not the "arbitrary" limits of time or setting, but rather psychological credibility, consistent characterization, and a "lofty and interesting" action. More important to the reevaluation of *Richard II* were the studies of such German critics as August Wilhelm Schlegel, Hermann Ulrici, and G. G. Gervinus. Unlike earlier commentators, Schlegel saw in the king an essentially decent nature obscured by levity and foolishness, but which suffering finally purifies. Although less sympathetic, Ulrici regarded Richard's foibles and inconsistencies not as evidence of Shakespeare's faulty characterization, as Neoclassical critics had done, but as the qualities of an irresponsible ruler. Ulrici attributed the king's tragic downfall to his failure to embody God's grace and justice—what the critic called "the ground-idea of the whole drama"—and to his refusal to recognize that divine right is a solemn vocation, not an unassailable guarantee of kingship. Gervinus was one of the first commentators to notice the importance of the king's language in *Richard II* and to stress that the play is best understood as part

of an epic tetralogy extending through *1* and *2 Henry IV* and *Henry V*. Like Ulrici, Gervinus identified the nature of true kingship as Shakespeare's central concern in the play, and he suggested that the "immortal lesson" which the playwright articulates—primarily through the character of Carlisle, but also allegorically in the Garden scene (Act III, Scene iv)—is that a good ruler must be conscientious, fulfilling his duties to both God and his people. The influence of this German school of thought can be noted in the studies of such English critics as Samuel Taylor Coleridge, Nathan Drake, and William Hazlitt. In his famous lectures of 1811-12, Coleridge described Richard as a mercurial, effeminate man, "not deficient in immediate courage," but overemotional and possessed of feelings which, "amiable in a female, are misplaced in a man, and altogether unfit for a king." In a later essay, however, Coleridge maintained that we sympathize with the character because suffering reveals his noble qualities. It was Coleridge who also first proposed that, in the initial stages of his struggle with Richard, Bolingbroke had not yet consciously determined to overthrow the king and usurp the crown. The question of Bolingbroke's true character and intentions has continued to be an important critical concern to the present day. Drake attributed Richard's weakness to his neglected education and dissipated habits, but contended—like Schlegel and Coleridge—that adversity evokes the monarch's "innate nobility," so much so that we ultimately admire his fortitude and dignity. Hazlitt, also a leading spokesman for the English Romantic movement, was one of the earliest commentators to describe *Richard II* as a brilliant pageant "of the invincible knights of old"; however, he judged that, unlike the knights of romance, Shakespeare's nobles are untruthful, dishonorable, and brutal in the defense of what they consider their rights. Hazlitt added that the king is no match for these ambitious men, concluding that although "we feel neither respect nor love for the deposed monarch," it is impossible not to pity him.

The final decades of the nineteenth century saw increased concentration on Richard's characterization, on the importance of language and ceremony in the play, and on the political repercussions of Bolingbroke's usurpation. Edward Dowden, in his often-cited study of 1881, described Richard as "an amateur in living" whose undisciplined sensibilities isolate him in a world of his own making. Dowden was one of the first commentators to claim that Richard is, in essence, an actor or artist more fascinated with the histrionic effects of his roles as king and martyr than with confronting the reality of his desperate situation. Dowden's insight later inspired numerous essays on Richard's tendency to self-dramatization and his obsession with rhetoric and ceremony. In 1889, Walter Pater conceded that, like many a protagonist in Shakespeare's histories, Richard is no hero, but rather an average human being caught up in great events. The critic also insisted that the play should be appreciated not only as a study of character, but as a beautiful work of art as well, noting what he called its "gay, fresh, variegated flowers of speech." Pater was especially interested in the famous abdication scene (Act IV, Scene i), which he likened to an "inverted" coronation rite, thus becoming one of the earliest critics to stress the importance of ceremony and ritual in *Richard II.* Near the end of the nineteenth century, the American Denton J. Snider offered an Hegelian interpretation of the play, discerning in the struggle between Richard and Bolingbroke a dramatic collision of opposing political forces: Richard's divine right of kingship and "the temporal right of the State." Although the state triumphs in this conflict, Snider emphasized, Bolingbroke's usurpation of the crown generates "a new wrong," for revolution is now sanctified as a legitimate means to kingship; according to the critic, Henry's act also begins the cycle of divine retribution and civil unrest which Shakespeare depicts in such other histories as *Henry VI* and *Richard III.* Thus, Snider was one of the earliest critics to note the relation of the so-called Tudor myth to *Richard II,* an issue taken up by many subsequent scholars.

In the twentieth century, commentary on *Richard II* continued to deal with many of the same issues treated by previous critics: the political implications of the overthrow of a king, including the relation of the Tudor myth and Tudor theories of kingship to Shakespeare's tragic design; the characterizations of Richard and Bolingbroke; and Shakespeare's use of language, rhetoric, and ceremony, especially as related to the conflict between appearance and reality or verbal expression and individual identity. Yet, new questions surfaced as well, including the debate over Shakespeare's attitudes toward his two protagonists; the nature of kingship; the themes of lost identity, family honor, and moral inheritance; the conflict between medieval and Renaissance world views; and the structure of the drama, for modern scholars have paid very close attention to both the play's technical weaknesses and its evident importance to Shakespeare's development as a writer.

One of the liveliest critical debates during the first half of the century involved the question of where, in this contest of wills, Shakespeare's sympathies ultimately lie. In 1901, the renowned poet W. B. Yeats declared that the dramatist preferred Richard to those who depose him, discerning in the character "the defeat that awaits all, whether they be artist or saint, who find themselves where men ask of them a rough energy" and they have nothing to give but "lyrical phantasy, or sweetness of temper, or dreamy dignity." Frank Harris went further and asserted that Shakespeare himself had a temperament very like the king's, that he closely identified with him, and that he felt more affinity "with failure than with success." Like Yeats, E. K. Chambers perceived in the play a conflict between not only two ideals of sovereign kingship, but "even more fundamentally" between two opposing temperaments, the practical and the artistic. Chambers, however, disagreed with Yeats's assessment of the dramatist's supposed sympathies in *Richard II,* stating that Shakespeare "was the last man likely to underrate the hard practical qualities" of a character like Bolingbroke. Later in the century, John Middleton Murry commented on the opinion that "there is much" of Shakespeare in King Richard; he maintained that this assumption is true only to the extent that Richard, as a character, obviously and imperfectly embodies Shakespeare's "dramatic and psychological justification for the operation of [his] own mind, in which the working of fancy is as yet predominant over that of the imagination." Although many subsequent critics demonstrated that Shakespeare's sympathies in *Richard II* are more ambivalent, even contradictory, than such one-sided readings suggest, scholars as late as R. F. Hill offered definitive responses to the question. Writing in 1961, Hill compared the rhetorical styles of the two protagonists and claimed that Shakespeare clearly presents Bolingbroke as the villain, the true dissimulator king, and Richard as the tragic hero of his play.

Modern understanding of *Richard II* has been greatly influenced by historical critics, among them Lily B. Campbell, John Dover Wilson, and E. M. W. Tillyard, who have offered illuminating insights into the effects of Elizabethan culture on Shakespeare's works, especially his histories. In one of the most celebrated of these historical analyses, Campbell asserted that English audiences in the 1590s, being accustomed to think-

ing analogically, would immediately extrapolate from *Richard II*'s lessons a commentary on their own times (see Additional Bibliography). The critic posited that the play's topical relevance would have been obvious to a sixteenth-century Englishman and that the parallels it suggests between Bolingbroke and the disfavored Earl of Essex were more than sufficient to unnerve government officials. In his essay of 1939 and elsewhere, Dover Wilson also insisted that, to be properly understood, *Richard II* must be read in the context of sixteenth-century political attitudes. He maintained that Shakespeare and his contemporaries regarded their monarchs with reverential awe, and that consequently Bolingbroke's assault on the throne would most likely have been viewed, not as the act of a champion of freedom, but as the sacrilege of an ambitious revolutionary who posed a dangerous threat to the divinely established hierarchy of natural and social order. Dover Wilson thus discerned in *Richard II* Shakespeare's endorsement of the Tudor view of English history, stating that Elizabethans anxiously perceived in Richard's dethronement and the subsequent civil disasters a lesson for their own times. Other critics who adopted a historical approach to *Richard II,* or who discerned in it elements of Tudor political philosophy, include George Ian Duthie, Karl F. Thompson, Ernst H. Kantorowicz, and Roy Battenhouse. Duthie (see Additional Bibliography) averred that the principal concern in all of Shakespeare's histories is "the nature of the ideal king" and that the so-called Lancastrian tetralogy, beginning with *Richard II,* dramatizes both the consequent tribulations of "a bad king" and the social chaos initiated by Bolingbroke's usurpation of the throne in an attempt to cure this disorder. Thompson—noting that Richard is frequently referred to as a "martyr," though he dies anything but a martyr's death—suggested the reaction of Shakespeare's contemporaries to this play would undoubtedly have been effected by John Foxe's *Actes and Monuments,* a popular book on religious persecution which held that God's justice would avenge Christian martyrs in this world as well as the next. In his often quoted essay in *The King's Two Bodies,* Kantorowicz explored the medieval and Elizabethan "legal fiction" that a monarch is both an individual and an office. In his view, Richard's tragedy results from a dissolution of the integrity of his paradoxical dual nature—a process that culminates in the king's breaking of the mirror in Act IV, Scene i; according to Kantorowicz, this act symbolizes the destruction "of every possibility of a second or super-body" and provides a final image of the king as "a miserable man . . . void of any metaphysis whatsoever." More recently, Battenhouse contested the idea that *Richard II* essentially endorses Elizabethan policy, asserting instead that Shakespeare was here dramatizing the tragedy inherent in such Tudor doctrines as the *Homilie Against Disobedience and Wilful Rebellion.*

First published in 1944, E. M. W. Tillyard's *Shakespeare's History Plays* opened new vistas to the study of *Richard II.* In this often-cited analysis of the play, Tillyard concluded that the socio-political aspect of *Richard II* was one of its most important features, adding that the struggle between the king and Bolingbroke, far from being a mere clash of personalities, in fact symbolically dramatizes the radical transition in England from medievalism to the modern era. Tillyard drew particular attention to the rigid ceremony that regulates Richard's court and argued that the ritualized protocol and elaborate rhetoric with which the play abounds were Shakespeare's attempt to evoke the ambience of the Middle Ages. According to this view, Richard—being the last English king descended from William the Conqueror—embodies the medieval world view, while Bolingbroke—an ambitious, practical politician—symbolizes the forces of modernism. Tillyard, who held that Eliz- abethans saw the natural and political world as a "great chain of Being" in which hierarchy or "degree" was essential to the maintenance of stability, also contended that in *Richard II* Shakespeare endorses the Tudor interpretation of English his- tory, presenting Bolingbroke's revolt as an attack on the di- vinely established order and the source of the later English civil wars, which are prophesied in this play by both Richard and Carlisle.

Tillyard's seminal study inspired much debate, and many crit- ics—most recently T. McAlindon and Graham Holderness— voiced serious disagreement over those societal values which, according to Tillyard, Richard and Bolingbroke respectively represent. Nearly thirty years after Tillyard's study, McAlindon argued that Richard as well as Bolingbroke "shares in the general failure to be true to himself and others" and that both thus violate the essence of the medieval chivalric code; in fact, McAlindon identified Richard, not his cousin, as "the most blatant offender against ritual propriety." Holderness, on the other hand, regarded Bolingbroke, Mowbray, and even Gaunt and York, as the champions of knighthood and feudal nobility in the play, suggesting that they—not Richard—uphold the time-honored medieval values, while the king, with his ab- solutist policies, attempts to undermine chivalric ideals. Hold- erness also disputed the assumption that in *Richard II* Shake- speare completely supports Tudor political policy and presents the divine right of kings as an unquestionable ideal. Instead, he averred, divine right doctrine is revealed as "a historical myth, emerging . . . in the alienation of Richard's conscious- ness, as it responds to specific conditions of military and po- litical defeat."

Clearly, any verdict on the role of Tudor orthodoxy or on Shakespeare's views of medieval and modern politics in *Rich- ard II* is intimately bound up with one's judgment of the king and Bolingbroke, especially the former. In the present century, critical reaction to Richard has ranged from guarded sympathy to outright contempt. Commentators have long identified the king's dominant personality trait as a passionate love of lan- guage and histrionics that leads him to expound in poetic phrases at moments of crisis or intense emotion, but they continue to debate the effect of this tendency on our judgment of the char- acter. Many have argued that Richard uses words and ceremony as a refuge from reality and a substitute for action, while others have claimed that his sensitivity to the relation between lan- guage and reality provides him with insight into the precar- iousness of monarchical authority and, ultimately, recognition of his true identity. Related to this issue is the question of whether, after his follies and eloquent declamations on the subject of his misery, Richard truly redeems himself morally or spiritually before his death. Despite their disagreement over these important issues, modern critics have generally concurred on one point: Richard's self-dramatization and obsession with ceremony over substance prevent him from fulfilling his role as king. This view can be discerned throughout the twentieth century. In his essay of 1939, Mark Van Doren denied that Richard was in any sense "a great man," but called him instead "a great minor poet" whose infatuation "with the art he so proudly and self-consciously practices" completely under- mines his ability to rule. Richard D. Altick, whose 1947 study of the play's language and imagery is considered seminal, maintained that the king's "complacent enjoyment of the sound of his own tongue" prevents him from dealing effectively with his serious political problems. Likewise, Georges A. Bonnard regarded Richard as a "poseur" whose "absence of character"

and "incompetence as a ruler" make him act a part rather than respond to the realities of his situation. But balancing Richard's shortcomings as a monarch, Bonnard asserted, is his skill as an actor, his ability to adapt his performance to every circum- stance and to control others, such as Bolingbroke, through his play-acting. For other critics, such as James A. S. McPeek, the king's behavior masks a grave personality disorder. Rich- ard's precarious psychological state was noticed as early as 1774, when Francis Gentleman detected "a degree of insanity" in his desperate reaction to Bolingbroke's challenge. Applying a more clinical analysis, McPeek diagnosed Richard as a victim of what he called the "God-complex," characterized by nar- cissism, "fantasies of omnipotence," and an inability to accept personal responsibility. In his study of Shakespeare's use of rhetoric in *Richard II*, R. F. Hill contended that the king's bombast is a mask for his weaknesses as a ruler. Also noting the importance of the play's ceremonial, ritualistic style, James Winny declared that its effect "is evidently calculated to un- derscore a lack of inward reality" in the king, as well as in many members of his court. Most recently, Terence Hawkes maintained that such a "debilitating gulf" between language and reality that Richard endorses in his kingdom is meant to destroy "truly sympathetic communication," concluding that the king's failure results from his attempt to control, rather than converse, through the use of language.

The relation between Richard's experiences and Shakespeare's concern with identity has also been discussed by a number of twentieth-century critics. In his study of 1959, Michael Quinn— noting that many of Richard's difficulties are social in nature— emphasized the king's isolation from those communal "foun- dations on which true personality must apparently be built." According to Quinn, Richard mistakenly views his divine right as a "personal privilege," rather than a solemn duty that binds him to his subjects, and thus cuts himself off from society through his wanton acts. Other critics who discussed the re- lation of identity and Richard's deposition include Herbert B. Rothschild, Jr., Sidney Homan, and Thomas F. Van Laan. Rothschild argued that in *Richard II* Shakespeare is principally concerned with "the existential perplexities of life." He main- tained that Bolingbroke's usurpation of Richard's kingship raises the uncomfortable spectre of "semantic annihilation," for identity itself is here reduced to an arbitrary fiction when one's very name can be rescinded at the whim of society or a powerful enemy. Homan contended that Shakespeare establishes in his play a careful balance between the private world of spiritual awareness and the public sphere of responsible government, observing that, ironically, the king eventually discovers his true self, and gains sympathy as a tragic hero, only by losing his public identity as a king and accepting death. In his 1978 study on the necessity of role-playing to effective leadership, Van Laan averred that Richard's loss of his kingly role anni- hilates him personally, adding that his self-dramatization there- after represents a desperate effort to discover a new self through the creation of a new role.

As mentioned above, a major question confronting commen- tators on Richard's characterization is whether, after all his fluctuations from arrogance to despair to tenderness to mur- derous rage, the king finally achieves moral or spiritual re- demption. Edward Dowden first addressed this issue late in the nineteenth century, concluding that the Richard in Pomfret prison "remains the same person" he was while wearing the crown. Such twentieth-century critics as Bonnard, McPeek, and Winny agreed that the king continues his melodramatic role-playing to the last and never comprehends the extent of his crimes; others, however, disagreed with this assessment. Quinn, for example, asserted that Richard partially redeems himself by his final act of courage in Pomfret prison; in his words, the king "dies as Somebody, a lion over-powered, . . . and not as one who has become nothing." In his 1963 study of the play, Peter G. Phialas compared Richard to King Lear, noting how the deposed monarch, like Lear, achieves a tragic comprehension of his own responsibility for events before his death. And, in his previously mentioned study of Richard's loss of identity, Sidney Homan repeatedly emphasized the king's spiritual awakening as a result of his tribulations.

Interest in the character of Bolingbroke has increased steadily throughout the twentieth century. In addition to the controversy over the morality of Henry's actions, modern critics have also debated the degree to which he consciously plans his usurpation of the crown and the nature of his success in the play. Traditionally, most commentators on *Richard II* viewed Bolingbroke as a practical man of action rather than words, a figure better equipped to rule a nation than the sentimental and indecisive Richard. Such an interpretation of the character is perhaps best reflected in the essays by Yeats and Chambers. Later critics, however, though they generally conceded that Bolingbroke is a more effective administrator than Richard, discerned in his actions and language a more cynical, manipulative intent. Undoubtedly the leading contributor to this assessment of Henry was Irving Ribner, who in his 1948 study, "Bolingbroke, a True Machiavellian," drew a portrait of the future Henry IV as an unscrupulous and calculating politician with a clear sense of his own goals and a ruthless determination to pursue them. Focusing on Bolingbroke's ascent of the throne, both Brents Stirling and Georges A. Bonnard stressed the ambiguous, self-effacing nature of the character's acts. Stirling described Henry as a duplicitous opportunist who operates behind external events and who provides an "oblique admission" of his true purpose only when Richard—in the scene before Flint Castle—"drops his sentimental role and states the truth of his position." Bonnard, too, labelled Bolingbroke an opportunist, though he added, in a more favorable response, that the future king has "a very limited share in shaping the circumstances that lead to his ascending the throne." R. F. Hill examined Bolingbroke's rhetoric and, like Ribner, argued that Henry is a manipulative man, deceptive and ambitious. In an overall discussion of Shakespeare's construction of *Richard II,* A. L. French proposed that the dramatist offers two very different Bolingbrokes: one who neither overtly plans nor solicits support for his usurpation of the crown, and another, in later portions of the play, who ruthlessly topples Richard and ascends the throne. Terence Hawkes maintained that although Richard is the play's true violator of "genuine human communication," Bolingbroke as well manipulates language and contributes to the breakdown between reality and expression in the kingdom. T. McAlindon likewise noted Henry's corruption of language, calling him "the real master of sweet words" in *Richard II,* and Harold F. Folland examined how Richard successfully demonstrates—for both us and Henry— the illegitimacy of the new king's reign, thus seriously tarnishing Bolingbroke's political victory. Like some earlier commentators, Folland also emphasized that Bolingbroke, not Richard, becomes the dissimulating actor after his return from exile, while the king plays the realist, constantly exposing the duplicity behind Henry's actions.

Rather than offer such conclusive assessments of either Richard or Bolingbroke, a handful of critics have stressed Shakespeare's ambivalent presentation of these figures—a fact especially ev-

ident, they claim, in the entire process of the king's deposition. In 1967, Norman Rabkin noted how Shakespeare keeps "our sympathies in suspense" by depicting the two principal characters as "morally ambiguous." Each man has strengths, each weaknesses, Rabkin asserted, adding that "the tragedy of *Richard II* is the complementarity of its protagonists' virtues, which seem . . . incapable of being commingled." A few years later, Sidney Homan echoed this assessment, maintaining that while Richard is "manifestly unfit" to rule, Bolingbroke's efficiency and pragmatism—the qualities that make him a good administrator—undercut his sensitivity as a human being. Thus, according to the critic, our sympathies are divided between these two characters. Homan further averred that inasmuch as Shakespeare recognizes that these two ideal personalities are oftentimes sadly incompatible, he teaches us "the futility of seeking absolutes in our own reality." A related controversy has developed around the question of who—Richard or Bolingbroke—actually influences the transfer of monarchical power in this play. Critics as early as M. M. Mahood, who claimed in her 1957 study that Richard's decision to relinquish the crown occurs long before Bolingbroke openly seeks it, have wondered whether the king himself does not stage his own abdication rather than unwillingly surrender to his more formidable cousin. As previously mentioned, Brents Stirling stressed the ambiguity of those scenes preceding the formal transfer of power, suggesting at one point that Richard "deposes himself in an agony of play-acting before the unsentimental Bolingbroke." Bonnard, too, hinted that it is the king, not Henry, who controls the situation through his play-acting and asserted, again as noted above, that the future monarch has no influence over events as they progress. A. L. French went so far as to contend that there is an authorial confusion in the very structure of the drama over this transfer of power. French postulated that Shakespeare "started to write about a Richard who abdicated rather than being deposed," but then changed his dramatic strategy and attempted, unconvincingly, to generate sympathy for the king, making Bolingbroke appear as a ruthless usurper. Although they have not always offered such focused studies of the ambiguity in *Richard II,* many other modern critics have emphasized the similarities of the two protagonists, especially with regard to their role-playing and their use of language, thus suggesting that Shakespeare was perhaps more interested in the ambivalent nature of kingship itself than in the clash of opposing ideal personalities.

While the nature of Shakespeare's characters and his presentation of historical events in *Richard II* continue to fascinate scholars, another equally significant body of criticism has developed around the play's peculiar use of language, rhetoric, and ceremony, especially as these reflect more pervasive themes. In 1935, Caroline F. E. Spurgeon discussed several different image patterns in the play, including those of gardening, plants, sun or fire, birth, generation, and filial inheritance. In his influential essay of 1947, Richard D. Altick likewise examined certain "leading metaphors and verbal motifs"—such as the references to "earth," "blood," "tongue," "tears," "snakes," and "sun"—and claimed that these images form verbal and visual patterns that unify the action of the play and endow it with symbolic resonance. In 1952, Leonard F. Dean identified the many diverse references to acting and the theater in *Richard II,* maintaining that these images reflect "a picture of a sick state in which appearance and reality are at odds." The critic pointed out that many of the characters in this play are figuratively actors, costumed and masked behind a "glib ritualistic style" and elaborate ceremonies that conceal their true emotions. Dean added that this situation, though seemingly the product of Richard's court, remains the same "despite the change in rulers." Two other important studies of the language in *Richard II,* by J. A. Bryant, Jr., and M. M. Mahood, were written during the 1950s. Bryant focused on Shakespeare's appropriation of Christian and pagan rituals and of Old Testament allusions in the play, noting that these religious metaphors provide a resonance of meaning beyond that of any prosaic historical chronicle. Mahood discussed Shakespeare's manipulation of the meaning of words in *Richard II*—the vast discrepancy between the name and its object—and averred that "the play's verbal ambiguities" contribute "to the rigid symmetry of [its] action," reflecting the tragic and historical themes. Mahood described the tragic action as Richard's loss of his faith in language and his discovery "that words express only desires and not facts . . . , that the name King, despite the sacramental nature of a coronation, does not imbue a man with kingly authority."

Since 1960, a number of other critics have examined Shakespeare's use of language, imagery, and rhetoric or ceremony in *Richard II;* these include, among others, R. F. Hill, Terence Hawkes, Herbert B. Rothschild, Jr., Helmut and Jean Bonheim, and Stanley R. Maveety (see Additional Bibliography). Hill justified the rhetorical, artificial style of *Richard II* and Shakespeare's other early tragedies, especially at moments of intense emotion, claiming that although this formalized mode "may keep us at a distance from the feeling at the back of it, the presence of feeling is unmistakably established." Hawkes emphasized the thematic importance of language in this early history, contending that Richard and Bolingbroke experience "the same debilitating gulf between language on the one hand and reality" on the other. The critic discerned a healthy contrast to either the king's or Henry's abuse of verbal expression in the figure of Gaunt, whose "language not only touches reality, it both shapes and is shaped by it." Similar to Mahood, Rothschild identified as the play's central concern the breakdown between the word or symbol and its corresponding object, initiated by Bolingbroke's usurpation of Richard's legitimate kingship. Rothschild thus disputed those critics, in particular Richard D. Altick, who identified Shakespeare's central concern as the king's downfall from a fatal attraction to formal expressions, asserting instead that *Richard II* is more concerned with "the existential perplexities of life," foremost being the question of whether words actually correspond to "hard reality." Helmut and Jean Bonheim discussed the numerous image-clusters of growth and vegetation in *Richard II,* remarking that throughout the play Richard is consistently identified with sterility and Bolingbroke with fertility. Adopting an anthropological approach, they argued that the king's deposition reenacts an ancient myth—the "passing of the crown" from an old and decrepit ruler to a young and potent one—which in many cultures is associated with the seasonal end of winter and the beginning of spring. Analyzing those dominant image-patterns noted by earlier commentators, Maveety declared that Shakespeare wrote *Richard II* with "the first narratives of Genesis in mind." Like J. A. Bryant, Jr., Maveety identified the parallels in the play with "the stories of Cain and Abel, of Adam, Eve, and the Garden of Eden," concluding that all these allusions and images are "subordinate parts of a single image-complex," the second fall of humankind, reenacted through "the flawed characters of Richard and Bolingbroke."

Shakespeare's use of language, rhetoric, and ceremony, and his interpretation of historical events in *Richard II* have also been analyzed in relation to the theme of kingship in the play. As previously mentioned, George Ian Duthie maintained that

the nature of kingship is a central concern in both of Shakespeare's tetralogies. With respect to *Richard II,* Duthie identified the king as a prototype of the disordered and neglectful ruler who brings chaos to his realm, but he admitted that Bolingbroke's "attempt to cure this disorder" ironically causes yet more conflict for subsequent generations. S. K. Heninger, Jr., focused on the "tension between actual and ideal" kingship in *Richard II,* noting the two ways in which Shakespeare establishes a cosmological and archetypal standard by which to judge the actions of Richard and Bolingbroke: first, "by the addition of fictional scenes to the historical accounts"; and second, by employing cosmological imagery that relates, for example, the king to the sun and the commonwealth to the Garden of Eden. In his often controversial 1964 study of Shakespeare's plays, *Shakespeare, Our Contemporary,* Jan Kott declared that *Richard II* is in fact "a tragedy of dethronement" in which the loss of regal power portends the destruction of "the entire order of the universe." Norman Rabkin, in his analysis of the repercussions of Richard's fall, stated that the principal question the play poses is "what to do about a king whose continuance on the throne is essential to the continued order of a state . . . but who is manifestly unfit personally for what is required of him." Stressing the uncertainty this situation produces in the audience, Rabkin added, however, that the primary source of ambiguity in *Richard II* is something more universal than the circumstances and behavior of the two protagonists, and that is the tragic nature of kingship itself, for the qualities that make a successful ruler like Bolingbroke are the same ones that detract from an individual's humanity. Other critics who discussed the importance of the theme of kingship in Shakespeare's play include Robert B. Pierce, Sidney Homan, and Thomas F. Van Laan. Pierce demonstrated the significance of the theme of inheritance in *Richard II,* though he observed that Shakespeare was not primarily concerned here with "the family as an emblem of disorder in the state"—as he was in *Henry IV*—but instead was "more interested in another subject, the psychology of kingship." Homan, as noted above, emphasized the tension in *Richard II* between the public demands of responsible kingship and the quest for personal or spiritual awareness. Likewise, Van Laan, in his study of 1978, asserted that Shakespeare is here concerned with the public "part" any monarch and successful politician must learn, concluding that Richard fails to some degree because he has only mastered the "external histrionic characteristics" of the role of king, without realizing "the accumulated repertory of moves proper to kingship and obligatory for every occupant of the office." Importantly, Van Laan added that Bolingbroke, once he ascends the throne, repeats the same "discrepant role-playing" that marred Richard's reign.

Twentieth-century commentators have also systematically interpreted *Richard II* from the technical point of view of its plot structure, its consistency of characterization and verse, and—perhaps most importantly—its contribution to Shakespeare's development as a tragic dramatist. Whereas the earliest critics resigned themselves to the play's various weaknesses and seemingly careless construction, modern scholars have attempted to explain its shortcomings, foremost being the missing Gloucester plot, the uncertainty of both Bolingbroke's and Richard's characterizations, and the abrupt juxtaposition of poetic styles. In 1909, Algernon Charles Swinburne postulated that the play's mixture of lyricism and tragic melodrama, which he considered unsuccessful, reflects Shakespeare's experimentation with the styles of two prominent contemporaries: Robert Greene and Christopher Marlowe. Nearly forty years later, H. B. Charlton likewise described *Richard II* as an experiment in dramatic construction. Comparing the play to *Richard III*, Charlton described it as Shakespeare's attempt to develop "his own idea of tragedy," and he noted that although it falls short of its goal, "as portraiture progressing towards the psychological realism which is a part of the great tragedies, *Richard II* is a great step beyond *Richard III*." Bonnard, in his 1951 study cited elsewhere, compared *Richard II*, in its general structure, to *King John* and *Henry IV;* but he pointed out that while these works contain pairs of equally strong and fascinating characters, *Richard II* is a curiously "unbalanced play." Bonnard suggested that although this drama "was certainly planned" as a conflict between two opposing leads, the king and Bolingbroke, in the course of its composition Shakespeare altered his strategy and created "a soul's drama" about one person only: the flawed but attractive Richard. Travis Bogard, like Charlton, compared *Richard II* to *Richard III*—a play which preceded it by some two or three years—and claimed that Shakespeare was here experimenting with techniques of characterization and exposition, learning in the process how to convey the most profound emotions through suggestion and "implicit" expression, rather than "explicit" statement. Bogard admitted that technically *Richard II* is weaker than the melodrama of Richard Crookback, but he noted that without this "second" Richard Shakespeare's greatest tragedies might never have been written as they were. In one of the most frequently cited studies of Shakespeare's construction of *Richard II*, A. P. Rossiter attributed the play's seeming inconsistencies and confusion to the likelihood that Shakespeare relied heavily on the anonymous and evidently successful *Woodstock*, but that in so doing he failed to provide the necessary motives that are so prominent in this earlier work, especially concerning Richard's guilt in the murder of Gloucester. Significantly, Rossiter claimed that without our sure knowledge of the king's part in his uncle's murder the play fails to justify both Richard's behavior in Acts I and II and "Bolingbroke's incredibly easy usurpation" of the crown. Another notable essay on the importance of *Richard II* to Shakespeare's development as a dramatist was offered by Peter G. Phialas in 1963. Phialas demonstrated that in its emphasis on individual responsibility rather than fate, *Richard II* represents Shakespeare's first departure from the medieval *de casibus* tradition, which, according to the critic, he used exclusively in his earlier tragic works. And, as previously mentioned, A. L. French provided a compelling explanation for what many regard as the play's central confusion: whether the king unwillingly renounces the crown or whether, in fact, he initiates his own abdication. Noting evidence for both readings, French concluded that *Richard II* "suffers from [a] . . . double vision," beginning with a king who, for reasons that remain unclear, masochistically invites Bolingbroke to topple him, and ending with the impression that Richard was, indeed, ruthlessly deposed.

Despite its flawed and sometimes confusing organization and its inconsistent, even contradictory, hero, *Richard II* continues to impress modern scholars. Whereas eighteenth- and nineteenth-century commentators either condemned or overly sympathized with its central figure and its interpretation of history, present-day scholars are more concerned with identifying those themes that Shakespeare developed more fully and successfully in his later works; these include the nature of kingship, the relation between language or verbal expression and reality, individual identity, the conflict between medieval and modern forms of government, and the meaning of social responsibility. Richard, moreover, though egotistical and immature, is one of Shakespeare's first protagonists to struggle not only against the circumstances of fate or fortune and the progress of time, but

against his own limitations as a human being. If it is true that this king falls short of becoming a truly tragic hero, as many critics have claimed, it is also true that he seriously challenges the validity of his adversaries' more worldly definitions of success. Perhaps for these reasons *Richard II* remains Shakespeare's most moving history, an unforgettable monument to the pathos, if not the power, of a poet-king.

SIR EDWARD HOBY   (letter date 1595)

[*The earliest extant document which contains a possible reference to* Richard II *is a social invitation. On December 7, 1595, Sir Edward Hoby, a courtier and diplomat, asked his friend Robert Cecil to dinner the following Tuesday, at which time "K. Richard [shall] present himself to your vewe." The early twentieth-century historian and critic E. K. Chambers inferred that Hoby's letter thus fixes a terminal date for the composition of Shakespeare's play (see Additional Bibliography). Recently, however, scholars have challenged Chambers's conclusions.*]

Sir, findinge that you wer not convenientlie to be at London to morrow night I am bold to send to knowe whether Teusdaie [December 9] may be anie more in your grace to visit poore Channon rowe where as late as it shal please you a gate for your supper shal be open: & K. Richard present him self to your vewe. Pardon my boldnes that ever love to be honored with your presence nether do I importune more then your occasions may willingly assent unto, in the meanetime & ever restinge At your command Edw. Hoby.

> *Sir Edward Hoby, in a letter to Sir Robert Cecil on December 7, 1595, in* The Riverside Shakespeare, *Houghton Mifflin Company, 1974, p. 1839.*

AUGUSTINE PHILLIPPS   (essay date 1601)

[*Early in February of 1601, supporters of the Earl of Essex commissioned a special performance of* Richard II *at the Globe theater—in the mistaken belief that it would incite the London populace to rebellion. Essex's plans miscarried completely: few citizens rallied to his cause, and he was eventually beheaded for treason. In the aftermath of the abortive coup, Augustine Phillipps, a member of the Lord Chamberlain's Men, was briefly detained for questioning by the authorities, but his testimony, excerpted below, apparently cleared Shakespeare's theatrical troupe of any complicity in the plot.*]

The *Examination* of Augustyne Phillypps servant vnto the L Chamberlyne and one of hys players taken the [18th] of Februarij [1601] vpon hys oth.

He sayeth that on Fryday last was sennyght or Thursday Sir Charles P*e*rcy Sir Josclyne P*e*rcy and the L. Montegle w*i*th some thre more spak to some of the players in the p*r*esans of thys exam*i*nate to have the play of the deposyng and kyllyng of Kyng Rychard the second to be played the Saterday next p*r*omysyng to gete them xl*s*. [40 shillings] more then their ordynary to play yt. Wher thys Exam*i*nate and hys fellowes were determyned to have played some other play, holdyng that play of Kyng Richard to be so old & so long out of vse as that they shold have small or no Company at yt. But at their request this Exam*i*nate and his fellowes were Content to play yt the Saterday and had their xl*s*. more then their ordynary for yt and so played yt accordyngly. . . .

Augustine Phillipps, in an extract from The Shak-
spere Allusion-Book: A Collection of Allusions to
Shakspere from 1591-1700, Vol. 1, *edited by John
Munro, revised edition, 1932. Reprint by Books for
Libraries Press, 1970; distributed by Arno Press,
Inc., p. 82.*

FRANCIS LORD BACON (essay date 1601)

[*Bacon, the Elizabethan statesman-philosopher who wrote* Novum
Organum *(1620),* The Advancement of Learning *(1605), and Essays (1597), is also well known, through the efforts of anti-
Stratfordians, as the leading alternate author of those works usually attributed to Shakespeare. In his own time, Bacon combined
scientific investigation with an active career in government. As
a member of the queen's counsel, he participated in the 1601 trial
of his former friend the Earl of Essex and helped to prepare the
official report of the ill-fated coup. The following excerpt, taken
from that report, details the plan of Gilly Merricke, one of the
conspirators, to procure a performance of* Richard II *on the afternoon before the rebellion. Merricke was eventually executed
for his role in the plot, but Shakespeare's company, The Lord
Chamberlain's Men, succeeded in establishing their innocence
and avoided prosecution.*]

[The] afternoone before the [Essex] Rebellion, *Merricke*, with
a great company of others, that afterwards were all in the
Action, had procured to bee played before them, the Play of
deposing King *Richard* the second.

Neither was it casuall, but a Play bespoken by *Merrick*.

And not so onely, but when it was told him by one of the
Players, that the Play was olde, and they should haue losse in
playing it, because few would come to it: there was fourty
shillings extraordinarie giuen to play it, and so thereupon playd
it was.

So earnest hee was to satisfie his eyes with the sight of that
Tragedie, which hee thought soone after his Lord should bring
from the Stage to the State, but that GOD turned it vpon their
own heads.

Francis Lord Bacon, in an extract from The Shak-
spere Allusion-Book: A Collection of Allusions to
Shakspere from 1591-1700, Vol. I, *edited by John
Munro, revised edition, 1932. Reprint by Books for
Libraries Press, 1970; distributed by Arno Press,
Inc., p. 92.*

JOHN DRYDEN (essay date 1679)

[*Dryden, the leading poet and playwright of Restoration England,
helped formulate the Neoclassical view of Shakespeare as an
irregular genius whose native talent overcame his ignorance of
the proper "rules" and language for serious drama. He was also
instrumental in establishing Shakespeare's reputation as the foremost English dramatist, and his assessment of Shakespeare influenced critics well into the following century. The extract below
is taken from Dryden's famous preface to his adaptation of* Troilus
and Cressida, *published in 1679. In it, he praises the scene in
which Richard II is paraded through the streets of London behind
his exultant rival, Bolingbroke: "the painting of it is so lively,"
he observes, "and the words so moving, that I have scarcely read
anything comparable to it, in any other language."*]

Bombast is commonly the delight of that Audience, which
loves Poetry, but understands it not: and as commonly has been
the practice of those Writers, who not being able to infuse a
natural passion into the mind, have made it their business to

ply the ears, and to stun their judges by the noise. But *Shakespear* does not often thus; for the passions in his Scene between
Brutus and *Cassius* [in *Julius Caesar*] are extreamly natural,
the thoughts are such as arise from the matter, and the expression of 'em not viciously figurative. I cannot leave this
Subject before I do justice to that Divine Poet, by giving you
one of his passionate descriptions: 'tis of *Richard* the Second
when he was depos'd, and led in Triumph through the Streets
of *London* by *Henry* of *Bullingbrook:* the painting of it is so
lively, and the words so moving, that I have scarce read anything comparable to it, in any other language. Suppose you
have seen already the fortunate Usurper passing through the
croud, and follow'd by the shouts and acclamations of the
people; and now behold King *Richard* entring upon the Scene:
consider the wretchedness of his condition; and his carriage in
it; and refrain from pitty if you can.

> As in a Theatre, the eyes of men
> After a well-grac'd Actor leaves the Stage,
> Are idly bent on him that enters next,
> Thinking his prattle to be tedious:
> Even so, or with much more contempt, mens eyes,
> Did scowl on *Richard:* no man cry'd God save him:
> No joyful tongue gave him his welcom home,
> But dust was thrown upon his Sacred head,
> Which with such gentle sorrow he shook off,
> His face still combating with tears and smiles
> (The badges of his grief and patience)
> That had not God (for some strong purpose) steel'd
> The hearts of men, they must perforce have melted,
> And Barbarism it self have pity'd him.
>   [V. ii. 23-36]

John Dryden, in his Troilus and Cressida; or, Truth
Found Too Late, 1679. *Reprint by Cornmarket Press,
1969, 69 p.*

NAHUM TATE (essay date 1681)

[*An Irish-born playwright of the seventeenth and early eighteenth
centuries, Tate specialized in adaptations of the Elizabethan dramatists, particularly Shakespeare, but also John Webster and Ben
Jonson. He is best known for his adaptation of Shakespeare's*
King Lear, *completed in 1681. For over a century and a half,
Tate's version eclipsed Shakespeare's play and dominated the
English stage. Tate's efforts on behalf of* Richard II *were much
less successful, however, for his 1681 adaptation was banned
after only two performances. Attempting to salvage the production, Tate hastily changed the play's title and its locale, but this
disguise failed to mollify the censors, and "The Sicilian Usurper," as it was then called, was likewise declared too controversial for the stage. The author's preface to the first edition of
this work, which was allowed to go to print and from which the
following excerpt is taken, reveals both Tate's frustration and his
bewilderment—echoed by many critics since—that the story of
Richard should still excite such intense political reactions. His
"epistle in vindication" is interesting to scholars today as a
defense of the Restoration taste for unblemished heroic protagonists; in an effort to correct what he regarded as the king's
unkingly characteristics, Tate explains, his Richard is in every
way "a wise, active, and just Prince."*]

The Buisiness of this Epistle is more Vindication than Complement; and when we are to tell our Grievances 'tis most
natural to betake our selves to a Friend. 'Twas thought perhaps
that this unfortunate Offspring [*Richard II*] having been stifled
on the *Stage*, shou'd have been buried in Oblivion; and so it
might have happened had it drawn its Being from me Alone;

but it still retains the immortal Spirit of its first-Father, and will survive in Print, though forbid to tread the *Stage*. They that have not seen it Acted, by its being silenc't, must suspect me to have Compil'd a Disloyal or Reflecting *Play*. But how far distant this was from my Design and Conduct in the Story will appear to him that reads with half an Eye. To form any Resemblance between the Times here written of, and the Present, had been unpardonable Presumption in Me. If the Prohibiters conceive any such Notion I am not accountable for That. I fell upon the new-modelling of this Tragedy, (as I had just before done on the *History of King Lear*) charm'd with the many Beauties I discover'd in it, which I knew wou'd become the *Stage;* with as little design of Satyr on present Transactions, as *Shakespeare* himself that wrote this Story before this Age began. I am not ignorant of the posture of Affairs in King *Richard* the Second's Reign, how dissolute then the Age, and how corrupt the Court; a Season that beheld *Ignorance* and Infamy preferr'd to *Office* and *Pow'r,* exercis'd in Oppressing Learning and Merit; but why a History of those Times shou'd be supprest as a Libel upon Ours, is past my Understanding....

Our *Shakespeare* in this Tragedy, bated none of his Characters an Ace of the Chronicle; he took care to shew 'em no worse Men than They were, but represents them never a jot better. His *Duke of York* after all his buisy pretended Loyalty, is found false to his Kinsman and Sovereign, and joyn'd with the *Conspirators*. His King *Richard* Himself is painted in the worst Colours of History, Dissolute, Unadviseable, devoted to Ease and Luxury. You find old *Gaunt* speaking of him . . . without the least palliating of his Miscarriages, which I have done in the new Draft, with such words as These.

> Your Sycophants bred from your Child-hood with you,
> Have such Advantage had to work upon you,
> That scarce your Failings can be call'd your Faults.

His Reply in *Shakespeare* to the blunt honest Adviser runs thus.

> And Thou a Lunatick Lean-witted-fool, &c.
> Now by my Seat's right Royal Majesty,
> Wer't thou not Brother to great *Edward*'s Son.
> The Tongue that runs thus roundly in thy Head
> Shou'd run thy Head from thy unreverent Shoulders.
> [II. i. 115, 120-23]

On the contrary (though I have made him express some Resentment) yet he is neither enrag'd with the good Advice, nor deaf to it. He answers Thus—

> ——Gentle Unkle;
> Excuse the Sally's of my Youthfull Blood.
> We shall not be unmindfull to redress
> (However difficult) our States Corruptions,
> And purge the Vanities that crowd our Court.

I have every where given him the Language of an Active, Prudent Prince, Preferring the Good of his Subjects to his own private Pleasure.... Nor cou'd it suffice me to make him speak like a King (who as Mr. *Rymer* says in his *Tragedies of the last Age considered,* are always in Poëtry presum'd Heroes) but to *Act so too,* viz. with *Resolution* and *Justice.* Resolute enough our *Shakespeare* (copying the History) has made him, for concerning his seizing old *Gaunt*'s Revennues, he tells the wise Diswaders,

> Say what ye will, we seize into our Hands
> His Plate, his Goods, his Money and his Lands.
> [II. i. 209-10]

But where was the Justice of this Action? This Passage I confess was so material a Part of the Chronicle (being the very Basis of *Bullingbrook*'s Usurpation) that I cou'd not in this new Model so far transgress Truth as to make no mention of it; yet for the honour of my Heroe I suppose the foresaid Revennues to be *Borrow'd* onely for the present Exigence, not *Extorted.* . . .

My Design was to engage the pitty of the Audience for him in his Distresses, which I cou'd never have compass'd had I not before shewn him a Wise, Active and Just Prince. Detracting Language (if any where) had been excusable in the Mouths of the Conspirators: part of whose Dialogue runs thus in *Shakespeare:*

> *North.* Now, afore God, 'tis shame such wrongs are borne
> In him, a royal prince, and many moe
> Of noble blood in this declining land.
> The King is not himself, but basely led
> By flatterers, and what they will inform,
> Merely in hate, 'gainst any of us all,
> That will the King severely prosecute
> 'Gainst us, our lives, our children, and our heirs.
>   *Ross.* The commons hath he pill'd with grievous taxes,
> And quite lost their hearts; the nobles hath he fin'd
> For ancient quarrels, and quite lost their hearts.
>   *Willo.* And daily new exactions are devis'd,
> As blanks, benevolences, and I wot not what.
> But what a' God's name doth become of this?
>   *North.* Wars hath not wasted it, for warr'd he hath not,
> But basely yielded upon compromise
> That which his noble ancestors achiev'd with blows.
> More hath he spent in peace than they in wars.
> [II. i. 238-42, 246-47, 249-55]

with much more villifying Talk; but I wou'd not allow even Traytors and Conspirators thus to bespatter the Person whom I design'd to place in the Love and Compassion of the Audience. Ev'n this very Scene (as I have manag'd it) though it shew the Confederates to be Villains, yet it flings no Aspersion on my Prince.

Further, to Vindicate ev'n his *Magnanimity* in Regard of his Resigning the Crown, I have on purpose inserted an intirely new Scene between him and his Queen, wherein his Conduct is sufficiently excus'd by the Malignancy of his Fortune, which argues indeed Extremity of Distress, but Nothing of Weakness.

After this account it will be askt why this Play shou'd be supprest, first in its own Name, and after in Disguise? All that I can answer to this, is, That it was *Silenc'd on the Third Day.* I confess, I expected it wou'd have found Protection from whence it receiv'd Prohibition; and so questionless it wou'd, cou'd I have obtain'd my Petition to have it perus'd and dealt with according as the Contents Deserv'd; but a positive Doom of Suppression *without Examination* was all that I cou'd procure....

For the two days in which it was Acted [under the title "The Sicilian Usurper"], the Change of the Scene, Names of Persons, &c. was a great Disadvantage: many things were by this means render'd obscure and incoherent that in their native Dress had appear'd not only proper but gracefull. I call'd my Persons *Sicilians* but might as well have made 'em Inhabitants of the Isle of *Pines,* or, World in the *Moon,* for whom an Audience are like to have small Concern. Yet I took care from the Beginning to adorn my Prince with such heroick Vertues, as afterwards made his distrest Scenes of force to draw Tears from the Spectators; which, how much more touching they would have been had the Scene been laid at Home, let the Reader judge. . . .

> *Nahum Tate, in a preface to his* The History of King Richard the Second, *Richard Tonson and Jacob Tonson, 1681.*

[CHARLES GILDON]   (essay date 1721)

[*Gildon was the first critic to write an extended commentary on the entire Shakespearean dramatic canon. Like many other Neoclassicists, he regarded Shakespeare as an imaginative playwright who, nonetheless, frequently violated the dramatic "rules" necessary for correct writing. One of the earliest scholars to recognize Shakespeare's histories as a distinct genre, Gildon, in the excerpt below, nevertheless objects to their numerous departures from the facts, complaining that plays like* Richard II *include no moral instruction and afford "little or no improvement of the lives and manners of men." He professes not to understand why Shakespeare chose Richard, "the most despicable character of all our kings," as the subject for a drama in the first place.*]

In a conversation betwixt *Shakespear* and *Ben Johnson, Ben* ask'd him the reason "why he wrote those historical Plays." He reply'd, "That finding the people generally very ignorant of history, he writ them in order to instruct them in that particular." A very poor and mean undertaking for a great poet, which not only afforded little or no improvement of the lives and manners of men, but could by no means obtain the very end he propos'd; since the representing of a few events found in history could never make them historians, the writing the histories themselves being only capable of that, which, when obtain'd, would make the general readers or hearers little the wiser, and not at all better men; nay, he has in some particulars, if not falsify'd, yet at least not justly represented the characters he has made use of, as history represents them; particularly in *Richard* the second, who, as we find him in history, was the most abandon'd tyrant that ever sat upon the *English* throne, guilty of the most barbarous oppressions, most servilely fearful in adversity, and most intolerably insolent when the danger was either remov'd, or at some distance; and I see no reason, why he made choice of the most despicable character of all our kings, unless it was for the sake of two or three fine descriptions, and some agreeable topics, or common places, in which some of our modern *Play-wrights* have endeavour'd to imitate him; for having got together two or three descriptions, no matter of what, or whether to any purpose, or not, these they tack together with some odd incoherent scenes, which are directed to no certain end, and can therefore be of no use.

But say the [defenders] of our stage, these pieces give pleasure, which is one considerable end of all poetry. But I must reply, that the pleasure they give is but mean, poor, and lifeless, and infinitely short of that transporting delight which a just and regular *Tragedy*, written according to art, excites in the soul, at the same time that it conveys lessons of the highest importance to human life. (pp. 158-59)

> [*Charles Gildon], in his* The Laws of Poetry, *1721. Reprint by Garland Publishing, Inc., 1970, 351 p.*

ALEXANDER POPE   (essay date 1723)

[*Pope was the foremost English poet of the first half of the eighteenth century, as well as a prolific author of satires written at the expense of his literary contemporaries. Between 1723 and 1725 he published a six-volume edition of the works of Shakespeare which was based upon the text of Nicholas Rowe. Pope was more concerned with poetics than with editorial scholarship, and thus his edition is replete with corruptions, principally interpolations and omissions which he believed would improve the metric patterns of Shakespeare's dramatic verse. In the excerpt below, from his emendations to* Richard II, *Pope argues that the general inferiority of the rhymed passages in the play compared to the blank verse sections may indicate the hand of someone other than Shakespeare. Pope's conclusions have not, however, met with wide acceptance among twentieth-century critics.*]

I must make one remark in general on the *Rhymes* throughout [*Richard II*]: they are so much inferior to the rest of the writing that they appear to me to be of a different hand. What confirms this is that the context does every where exactly (and frequently much better) connect without the inserted Rhymes, except in a very few places; and just there, too, the rhyming verses are of a much better taste than all the others, which rather strengthens my conjecture. . . .

> *Alexander Pope, in an extract from* Shakespeare, the Critical Heritage: 1623-1692, Vol. 2, *edited by Brian Vickers, Routledge & Kegan Paul, 1974, p. 416.*

[CHARLOTTE LENNOX]   (essay date 1754)

[*Lennox was a novelist and Shakespearean scholar who compiled a three-volume edition of translated texts of the sources used by Shakespeare in twenty-two of his works, including some analyses of the manner in which he used these sources. In the following excerpt, from Volume Three of that work, she reviews the reign of the historical Richard II and points out a number of discrepancies in Shakespeare's version of events. Lennox concludes that the dramatist's "inattention" to the actual facts is quite unjustifiable in a work whose principle merits reside in its truth to history.*]

It has been observed, that *Shakespear*, in his Historical Plays, was a close Copier of the Histories from whence he took them; yet, in *Richard* the Second, there are some Deviations and some Omissions that throw different Lights on the Characters of his Persons, and tend greatly to mislead our Judgments in the Opinions we Form of them.

The Murder of the Duke of *Gloucester*, Uncle to the King, is one of the Crimes that *Bolingbroke* charges on the Duke of *Norfolk;* the King, in many Passages of the Play, is said to have commanded it: The old Duke of *Lancaster* upbraids him with having shed the Blood of the great *Edward*, and *Richard*'s Silence to that Accusation is not only a tacit Confession of the Guilt, but a Proof that he had nothing to offer in Vindication of it.

In the History it is not absolutely clear that King *Richard* had any part in the Death of his Uncle; but 'tis certain that the Duke of *Gloucester* was engaged in several Conspiracies against him, and that the King having discovered a dangerous One, in which not only his Crown and Dignity but his Life was aimed at, he found himself under a Necessity of seizing his disloyal Uncle; which he did by a well contrived Stratagem at his own Castle, and sent him to *Calais;* where he confessed all his Treasons, and was assassinated, as some Report, by *Richard*'s Order.

Shakespear's Silence, upon this Head, is very unfavourable to the Character of *Richard*, on whom, by that Means, he draws the Imputation of a Murderer and Paracide; and yet, in his

Misfortunes, he proposes him as an Object of Compassion, and makes Use of all his pathetic Powers to melt the Souls of the Audience in his Favour.

The Historians say that *Bolingbroke,* when in Banishment, was invited by the chief Nobility in *England* to return and force the Crown from *Richard,* whom they judged unworthy to Reign.

Shakespear takes no Notice of this Circumstance, but makes *Bolingbroke,* on his Arrival, declare that he only came to demand a Restitution of the Honours and Estates he had been unjustly deprived of; and the Lords join him upon this Supposition.

In the History we are told, that King *Richard,* finding himself abandoned by many of his Friends, his *Welsh* Army, on whom he had the greatest Confidence, dispersed, and *Bolingbroke* absolute Master of his People's Hearts, retired to *Conway* Castle, which he determined to hold as long as it was possible; thither the Earl of *Northumberland* came from *Bolingbroke* with Offers of Submission, on his Part, provided the King would pardon what was past, repeal his Banishment, and restore him to all his Rights and Dignities.

King *Richard,* being persuaded to accept of these Conditions, and to go to *Rutland* to confer with *Bolingbroke,* falls into an Ambush prepared for him, and is led Prisoner to *London.*

Shakespear drops the Circumstance of the Ambush laid for the King, and represents *Bolingbroke* confering in a submissive Manner with him at *Flint* Castle; and the King, upon his Cousin's solemn Assurance of attempting nothing against his Crown and Dignity, willingly accompanies him to *London,* where, at a meeting of the Parliament, he is deposed and the Crown offered to *Bolingbroke.*

This Play affords several other Instances in which *Shakespear*'s Inattention to the History is plainly proved; and is therefore the less pardonable, as the Subject of it is not one entire Action, wrought up with a Variety of beautiful Incidents, which at once delight and instruct the Mind; but a Dramatick Narration of Historical Facts, and a successive Series of Actions and Events which are only interesting as they are true, and only pleasing as they are gracefully told. (pp. 106-09)

> [*Charlotte Lennox*], *"The Plan of K. Richard the Second," in her* Shakespear Illustrated; or the Novels and Histories, on Which the Plays of Shakespear are Founded, Vol. 3, *1754. Reprint by AMS Press Inc., 1973, pp. 101-21.*

SAMUEL JOHNSON   (essay date 1765)

[*Johnson has long held an important place in the history of Shakespearean criticism. He is considered the foremost representative of moderate English Neoclassicism and is credited by some literary historians with freeing Shakespeare from the strictures of the three unities valued by strict Neoclassicists: that dramas should have a single setting, take place in less than twenty-four hours, and have a causally connected plot. More recent scholars portray him as a critic who was able to synthesize existing critical theory rather than an innovative theoretician. Johnson was a master of Augustan prose style and a personality who dominated the literary world of his epoch. In the following excerpt from his 1765 edition of* The Plays of William Shakespeare, *Johnson briefly discusses certain key passages in* Richard II, *such as Richard's speech on the indefeasible right of kings and his reactions upon returning from Ireland. The excerpt below also includes Johnson's*

famous remark that the play cannot "be said much to affect the passions, or enlarge the understanding."]

> RICHARD. The breath of worldly men cannot depose
> The deputy elected by the Lord.
>
> [III. ii. 56-7]

Here is the doctrine of indefeasible right expressed in the strongest terms, but our poet did not learn it in the reign of King James, to which it is now the practice of all writers, whose opinions are regulated by fashion or interest, to impute the original of every tenet which they have been taught to think false or foolish. (p. 439)

> RICHARD. Mine ear is open, and my heart prepar'd.
> The worst is worldly loss thou canst unfold.
> Say, is my kingdom lost? why, 'twas my care,
> And what loss is it, to be rid of care?
> Strives Bolingbroke to be as great as we?
> Greater he shall not be; if he serve God,
> We'll serve him too, and be his fellow so.
> Revolt our subjects? that we cannot mend;
> They break their faith to God, as well as us.
> Cry, woe, destruction, ruin, loss, decay;
> The worst is death, and death will have his day.
>
> [III. ii. 93-103]

It seems to be the design of the poet [in this play] to raise Richard to esteem in his fall, and consequently to interest the reader in his favour. He gives him only passive fortitude, the virtue of a confessor rather than of a king. In his prosperity we saw him imperious and oppressive, but in his distress he is wise, patient, and pious. (p. 440)

> RICHARD. By heav'n, I'll hate him everlastingly,
> That bids me be of comfort any more.
>
> [III. ii. 207-08]

This sentiment is drawn from nature. Nothing is more offensive to a mind convinced that his distress is without a remedy, and preparing to submit quietly to irresistible calamity, than these petty and conjectured comforts which unskilful officiousness thinks it virtue to administer. (pp. 441-42)

This play is one of those which Shakespeare has apparently revised; but as success in works of invention is not always proportionate to labour, it is not finished at last with the happy force of some other of his tragedies, nor can be said much to affect the passions, or enlarge the understanding. (p. 452)

> *Samuel Johnson, "Notes on Shakespeare's Plays: 'Richard II'" in his* The Yale Edition of the Works of Samuel Johnson: Johnson on Shakespeare, Vol. VII, *edited by Arthur Sherbo, Yale University Press, 1968, pp. 429-52.*

FRANCIS GENTLEMAN   (essay date 1774)

[*Gentleman, an Irish actor and playwright, was the author of* The Dramatic Censor; or Critical Companion *(1770) and contributed the introductions to John Bell's 1774 edition of Shakespeare's plays. In the following textual notes from his introduction to* Richard II *in that edition, Gentleman draws attention to Richard's "fanciful," "romantic" tendencies, observing that "in his mode of resignation, [he] shows some degree of insanity." Gentleman asserts that the character evidences "a most wretched shameful pusillanimity," and he is conspicuously unmoved by the Pomfret*

Castle soliloquy, much of which he claims would "be better omitted than retained."]

[*K. Rich.* Dear earth, I do salute thee with my hand,
Though rebels wound thee with their horses' hoofs.
As a long-parted mother with her child
Plays fondly with her tears and smiles in meeting,
So weeping, smiling, greet I thee, my earth,
And do thee favors with my royal hands. . . .
Mock not my senseless conjuration, lords,
This earth shall have a feeling, and these stones
Prove armed soldiers, ere her native king
Shall falter under foul rebellion's arms.]

                                        [III. ii. 6-11, 23-6]

Richard's address to the earth is pathetic and fanciful, but rather romantic and ill adapted to the serious important situation of his affairs: the author appears sensible of this by calling it a senseless conjuration.

[*K. Rich.* What say you now? What comfort have we now?
By heaven, I'll hate him everlastingly
That bids me be of comfort any more.
Go to Flint castle, there I'll pine away—
A king, woe's slave, shall kingly woe obey.
That power I have, discharge, and let them go
To ear the land that have some hope to grow,
For I have none. Let no man speak again
To alter this, for counsel is but vain.]

                                        [III. ii. 206-14]

Richard here discovers his true character, a most wretched shameful pusillanimity, a cowardice and despondency that would stigmatize a private man, much more a monarch, who from birth, education, and station, ought to think with more magnanimity and act with more resolution.

[*K. Rich.* With mine own tears I wash away my balm,
With mine own hands I give away my crown,
With mine own tongue deny my sacred state,. . .
Make me, that nothing have, with nothing griev'd,
And thou with all pleas'd, that hast all achiev'd!
Long mayest thou live in Richard's seat to sit,
And soon lie Richard in an earthly pit!
God save King Henry, unking'd Richard says,
And send him many years of sunshine days!
What more remains?]

                                        [IV. i. 207-09, 216-22]

Richard, in his mode of resignation, shows some degree of insanity, for which his distressful situation may, as he all through shows a feeble mind, apologize. . . . The thirty nine . . . lines [at V. v. 3-41] would, for recitation particularly, be better omitted than retained, as they tend more to puzzle conception, than to inform judgment. The author seems to have indulged his own fancy, without consulting either the stage or closet.

Francis Gentleman, in notes to "Richard II," in
Shakespeare, the Critical Heritage: 1774-1801, Vol.
6, *edited by Brian Vickers, Routledge & Kegan Paul,
1981, p. 103.*

ELIZABETH GRIFFITH   (essay date 1775)

[*Griffith exemplifies the seventeenth- and eighteenth-century preoccupation with searching through Shakespeare's plays for set speeches and passages that could be read out of dramatic context for their own sake. Griffith, however, avoided the more usual practice of collecting and commenting on poetic "beauties" and*

concentrated instead on the "moral" subjects treated in the text. In the following excerpt, Griffith discerns in Richard II a character devoid of any "true heroism," who "alternately rises to a vain confidence in his indefeasible right, and then sinks again under a despondency about his fortunes. . . ." She finds the king's behavior disgusting, stating that "the representation of a great man suffering misfortunes meanly, is rather an object of contempt than of compassion."]

[In Act III, Scene ii of *Richard II,* the] bishop of Carlisle, endeavouring to awaken the king to a manly exertion of his spirit against the rebellion, and neither to trust to the weak defence of right against might, nor expect that Providence shall, out of respect to his *divine right,* fight his battles for him, while he looks idly on, says,

The means that Heaven yields must be embraced,
And not neglected; else, if Heaven would
And we would not Heaven's offer, we refuse
The proffered means of succour and redress.

                                        [III. ii. 29-32]

To which the king, after expressing a contempt for Bolinbroke and his adherents, makes a reply agreeable to the vain notion and political superstition of those times, with regard to the absurd doctrine of *indefeasible right.*

King. Not all the water in the rough rude sea
    Can wash the balm from an anointed king;
    The breath of worldly men cannot depose
    The deputy elected by the Lord.

                                        [III. ii. 54-7]
                                        (p. 199)

However, he afterwards begins to speak more rationally upon this subject; for though he appears a little cast down at first, yet, on hearing some further ill news, he rouzes himself again, in the following speech:

King. I had forgot myself. Am I not king?
    Awake, thou coward majesty, thou sleep'st;
    Is not the king's name forty-thousand names?
    Arm, arm, my name; a puny subject strikes
    At thy great glory. Look not to the ground,
    Ye favourites of a king, are we not high?
    High be our thoughts.

                                        [III. ii. 83-9]

But this poor abdicating king had no true heroism in his soul; for, upon the intelligence of some more cross events arriving to him just after, he suddenly drops the character of a fighting prince, and immediately sinks into that of a preaching priest. . . .

Say, is my kingdom left? Why, 'twas my care;
And what loss is it, to be rid of care?
Strives Bolinbroke to be as great as we?
*Greater he shall not be; if he serve God,
We'll serve him too, and be his fellow so.*
Revolt our subjects, that we cannot mend;
They break their faith to God, as well as us.
Cry woe, destruction, ruin, loss, decay;
The worst is death, and death will have his day.

                                        [III. ii. 95-103]

This kind of homily he continues afterwards, in the same Scene; including, however, some good reflections on the unstable and unsatisfactory state of mortality, even in the highest spheres of life; which would have become his confessor better than they did himself, as the spirited Bishop, a true son of *the church militant,* tells him. . . . (pp. 199-200)

There are several other passages of the same kind, in this and the subsequent Act, where Richard alternately rises to a vain confidence in his *indefeasible right,* and then sinks again under a despondency about his fortunes; which I shall not disgust the Reader with here, as the representation of a great man suffering misfortunes meanly, is rather an object of contempt than of compassion. (pp. 201-02)

> *Elizabeth Griffith, "'Richard the Second'," in her* The Morality of Shakespeare's Drama Illustrated, *1775. Reprint by Frank Cass & Co. Ltd., 1971, pp. 189-204.*

CHARLES DIBDIN (essay date 1797-1800)

[*Didbin was a colorful eighteenth-century actor and dramatist, whose fame during his own lifetime was based primarily on a collection of some 1200 popular maritime verses titled* A Collection of Songs *(1790). He was also the author of forty-seven plays— none of which achieved great commercial or critical success— and of a five-volume anecdotal history of the English stage, the value of which today rests more on its lively vignettes of theatrical figures than on its scholarly insights. In the following excerpt from the critical study, Dibdin considers* Richard II *weak and carelessly constructed, speculating that Shakespeare rushed through its composition and merely patched together accounts from earlier chronicles.*]

[*Richard II*] is suspected to have been only revised by SHAKE-SPEAR. Certainly we cannot trace in it his usual force, either as to the characters or the language. The probability is that it was written in a hurry, which by the way is no excuse, and, as the circumstances are wholly taken from the historians and chroniclers of that day, many passages may have been literally transplanted from the history to the play. This having been done, the subject was found so unproductive that the author never thought it worth his while to finish it; and then the utmost we can say is that SHAKESPEAR was to blame for letting a play come forward unworthy of his reputation. (p. 68)

> *Charles Dibdin, in his* A Complete History of the Stage, *Vol. III, N. p., 1797-1800, 392 p.*

AUGUST WILHELM SCHLEGEL (essay date 1811)

[*A prominent German Romantic critic, Schlegel holds a key place in the history of Shakespeare's reputation in European criticism. His translations of sixteen of the plays are still considered the best German editions of Shakespeare. Schlegel was also a leading spokesman for the Romantic movement, which permanently over-threw the Neoclassical contention that Shakespeare was a child of nature whose plays lacked artistic form. The following analysis of* Richard II *comes from an English translation of his* Über dramatische Kunst und Literatur *(1811), a popular series of lectures which Schlegel delivered in 1808 then collected and revised into book form three years later. The critic offers one of the first Romantic reappraisals of Richard's character, maintaining that the king has an essentially noble nature, initially obscured by levity and foolishness but afterwards purified by suffering. The issue of whether Richard's character is static or dynamic has sharply divided critics ever since.*]

In *Richard the Second,* Shakespeare exhibits a noble kingly nature, at first obscured by levity and the errors of an unbridled youth, and afterwards purified by misfortune, and rendered by it more highly and splendidly illustrious. When he has lost the love and reverence of his subjects, and is on the point of losing also his throne, he then feels with a bitter enthusiasm the high vocation of the kingly dignity and its transcendental rights, independent of personal merit or changable institutions. When the earthly crown is fallen from his head, he first appears a king whose innate nobility no humiliation can annihilate. This is felt by a poor groom: he is shocked that his master's favourite horse should have carried the proud Bolingbroke to his coronation; he visits the captive king in prison, and shames the desertion of the great. The political incident of the deposition is sketched with extraordinary knowledge of the world;—the ebb of fortune, on the one hand, and on the other, the swelling tide, which carries every thing along with it. While Boling-broke acts as a king, and his adherents behave towards him as if he really were so, he still continues to give out that he has come with an armed band merely to demand his birthright and the removal of abuses. The usurpation has been long com-pleted, before the word is pronounced and the thing publicly avowed. The old John of Gaunt is a model of chivalrous honour: he stands there like a pillar of the olden time which he has outlived. His son, Henry IV, was altogether unlike him: his character is admirably sustained throughout the three pieces in which he appears. We see in it that mixture of hardness, mod-eration, and prudence, which, in fact, enabled him to secure the possession of the throne which he had violently usurped; but without openness, without true cordiality, and incapable of noble ebullitions, he was so little able to render his gov-ernment beloved, that the deposed Richard was even wished back again. (p. 424)

> *August Wilhelm Schlegel, "Criticisms on Shake-speare's Historical Dramas," in his* A Course of Lectures on Dramatic Art and Literature, *edited by Rev. A. J. W. Morrison, translated by John Black, revised edition, 1846. Reprint by AMS Press, Inc., 1973, pp. 414-45.*

SAMUEL TAYLOR COLERIDGE [as reported by J. P. COLLIER] (lecture date 1811-12)

[*Coleridge's lectures and writings on Shakespeare form a major chapter in the history of English Shakespearean criticism. As a channel for the critical ideas of the German Romantics and as an original interpreter of Shakespeare in the new spirit of Ro-manticism, Coleridge played a strategic role in overthrowing the last remains of the Neoclassical approach to Shakespeare's works and in establishing the modern view of the dramatist as a con-scious artist and masterful portrayer of human character. The excerpt below is taken from a shorthand report by J. P. Collier of one of Coleridge's lectures delivered between 1811 and 1812. While not verbatim, Collier's text is closely corroborated by other accounts and apparently reproduces with what one scholar called a "fine precision" many of Coleridge's original phrases. The critic briefly compares* Richard II *with* Richard III, *stating that both are, in a sense, studies of ambition, and he lauds the mag-nificent patriotic exhortation of John of Gaunt in Act II, Scene i. Coleridge then makes a point which he later amended (see excerpt below, 1834): that Richard, despite his radical mood shifts, does not substantially change in the course of the history. The critic also maintains that, in the early stages of his conflict with the king, Bolingbroke had not yet fully determined to usurp the crown— an interpretation that has evoked much commentary from twentieth-century scholars.*]

I will now proceed to offer some remarks upon the tragedy of 'Richard II.,' on account of its not very apparent, but still intimate, connection with 'Richard III.' As, in the last, Shake-speare has painted a man where ambition is the channel in

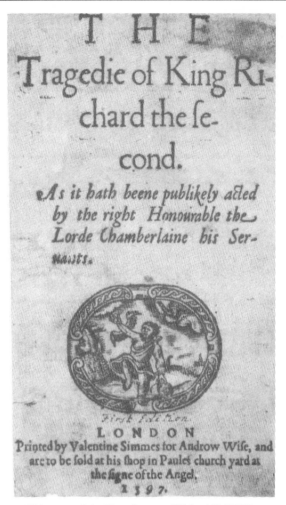

Title page of the First Quarto of Richard II *(1597).*

which the ruling impulse runs, so, in the first, he has given us a character, under the name of Bolingbroke, or Henry IV., where ambition itself, conjoined unquestionably with great talents, is the ruling impulse. In Richard III. the pride of intellect makes use of ambition as its means; in Bolingbroke the gratification of ambition is the end, and talents are the means. (p. 141)

The principal personages in this tragedy are Richard II., Bolingbroke, and York. I will speak of the last first, although it is the least important; but the keeping of all is most admirable. York is a man of no strong powers of mind, but of earnest wishes to do right, contented in himself alone, if he have acted well: he points out to Richard the effects of his thoughtless extravagance, and the dangers by which he is encompassed, but having done so, he is satisfied; there is no after action on his part; he does nothing; he remains passive. When old Gaunt is dying, York takes care to give his own opinion to the King, and that done he retires, as it were, into himself. (p. 143)

I will now advert to the character of the King. He is represented as a man not deficient in immediate courage, which displays itself at his assassination; or in powers of mind, as appears by the foresight he exhibits throughout the play: still, he is weak, variable, and womanish, and possesses feelings, which, amiable in a female, are misplaced in a man, and altogether unfit for a king. In prosperity he is insolent and presumptuous, and

in adversity, if we are to believe Dr. Johnson, he is humane and pious [see excerpt above, 1765]. I cannot admit the latter epithet, because I perceive the utmost consistency of character in Richard: what he was at first, he is at last, excepting as far as he yields to circumstances: what he shewed himself at the commencement of the play, he shews himself at the end of it. Dr. Johnson assigns to him rather the virtue of a confessor than that of a king.

True it is, that he may be said to be overwhelmed by the earliest misfortune that befalls him; but, so far from his feelings or disposition being changed or subdued, the very first glimpse of the returning sunshine of hope reanimates his spirits, and exalts him to as strange and unbecoming a degree of elevation, as he was before sunk in mental depression: the mention of those in his misfortunes, who had contributed to his downfall, but had before been his nearest friends and favourites, calls forth from him expressions of the bitterest hatred and revenge. Thus, where Richard asks:

> Where is the Earl of Wiltshire? Where is Bagot?
> What is become of Bushy? Where is Green?
> That they have let the dangerous enemy
> Measure our confines with such peaceful steps?
> If we prevail, their heads shall pay for it.
> I warrant they have made peace with Bolingbroke.
>   [III. ii. 122-27]

Scroop answers:

> Peace have they made with him, indeed, my lord.
>   [III. ii. 128]

Upon which Richard, without hearing more, breaks out:

> O villains! vipers, damn'd without redemption!
> Dogs, easily won to fawn on any man!
> Snakes, in my heart-blood warm'd, that sting my heart!
> Three Judases, each one thrice worse than Judas!
> Would they make peace? terrible hell make war
> Upon their spotted souls for this offense!
>   [III. ii. 129-34]

Scroop observes upon this change, and tells the King how they had made their peace:

> Sweet love, I see, changing his property
> Turns to the sourest and most deadly hate.
> Again uncurse their souls: their peace is made
> With heads and not with hands: those whom you curse
> Have felt the worst of death's destroying wound,
> And lie full low, grav'd in the hollow ground.
>   [III. ii. 135-40]

Richard receiving at first an equivocal answer,—'Peace have they made with him, indeed, my lord,'—takes it in the worst sense: his promptness to suspect those who had been his friends turns his love to hate, and calls forth the most tremendous execrations.

From the beginning to the end of the play he pours out all the peculiarities and powers of his mind: he catches at new hope, and seeks new friends, is disappointed, despairs, and at length makes a merit of his resignation. He scatters himself into a multitude of images, and in conclusion endeavours to shelter himself from that which is around him by a cloud of his own thoughts. Throughout his whole career may be noticed the most rapid transitions—from the highest insolence to the lowest humility—from hope to despair, from the extravagance of love to the agonies of resentment, and from pretended resignation to the bitterest reproaches. The whole is joined with the utmost richness and copiousness of thought, and were there an actor capable of representing Richard, the part would delight us more than any other of Shakespeare's master-pieces,—with, perhaps, the single exception of King Lear. I know of no character drawn by our great poet with such unequalled skill as that of Richard II.

Next we come to Henry Bolingbroke, the rival of Richard II. He appears as a man of dauntless courage, and of ambition equal to that of Richard III.; but, as I have stated, the difference between the two is most admirably conceived and preserved. In Richard III. all that surrounds him is only dear as it feeds his inward sense of superiority: he is no vulgar tyrant—no Nero or Caligula: he has always an end in view, and vast fertility of means to accomplish that end. On the other hand, in Bolingbroke we find a man who in the outset has been sorely injured: then, we see him encouraged by the grievances of his country, and by the strange mismanagement of the government, yet at the same time scarcely daring to look at his own views, or to acknowledge them as designs. He comes home under the pretence of claiming his dukedom, and he professes that to be his object almost to the last; but, at the last, he avows his purpose to its full extent, of which he was himself unconscious in the earlier stages.

This is proved by so many passages, that I will only select one of them; and I take it the rather, because out of the many octavo volumes of text and notes, the page on which it occurs is, I believe, the only one left naked by the commentators. It is where Bolingbroke approaches the castle in which the unfortunate King had taken shelter: York is in Bolingbroke's company—the same York who is still contented with speaking the truth, but doing nothing for the sake of the truth,—drawing back after he has spoken, and becoming merely passive when he ought to display activity. Northumberland says,

> The news is very fair and good, my lord:
> Richard not far from hence hath hid his head.
>
> [III. iii. 5-6]

York rebukes him thus:

> It would beseem the Lord Northumberland
> To say King Richard:—Alack, the heavy day,
> When such a sacred king should hide his head!
>
> [III. iii. 7-9]

Northumberland replies:

> Your grace mistakes me: only to be brief
> Left I his title out.
>
> [III. iii. 10-11]

To which York rejoins:

> The time hath been,
> Would you have been so brief with him, he would
> Have been so brief with you, to shorten you,
> For taking so the head, your whole head's length.
>
> [III. iii. 11-14]

Bolingbroke observes,

> Mistake not, uncle, farther than you should;
>
> [III. iii. 15]

And York answers, with a play upon the words 'take' and 'mistake':

> Take not, good cousin, farther than you should,
> Lest you mistake. The heavens are o'er our heads.
>
> [III. iii. 16-17]

Here, give me leave to remark in passing, that the play upon words is perfectly natural, and quite in character: the answer is in unison with the tone of passion, and seems connected with some phrase then in popular use. Bolingbroke tells York:

> I know it, uncle, and oppose not myself
> Against their will.
>
> [III. iii. 18-19]

Just afterwards, Bolingbroke thus addresses himself to Northumberland:

> Noble lord,
> Go to the rude ribs of that ancient castle;
> Through brazen trumpet send the breath of parle
> Into his ruin'd ears, and thus deliver.
>
> [III. iii. 31-4]

Here, in the phrase 'into his ruin'd ears,' I have no doubt that Shakespeare purposely used the personal pronoun, 'his,' to shew, that although Bolingbroke was only speaking of the castle, his thoughts dwelt on the king. In Milton the pronoun, 'her' is employed, in relation to 'form,' in a manner somewhat similar. Bolingbroke had an equivocation in his mind, and was thinking of the king, while speaking of the castle. He goes on to tell Northumberland what to say, beginning,

> 'Henry Bolingbroke,

which is almost the only instance in which a name forms the whole line; Shakespeare meant it to convey Bolingbroke's opinion of his own importance:—

> Henry Bolingbroke
> On both his knees doth kiss King Richard's hand,
> And sends allegiance and true faith of heart
> To his most royal person; hither come
> Even at his feet to lay my arms and power,
> Provided that, my banishment repealed,
> And lands restor'd again, be freely granted.
> If not, I'll use th' advantage of my power,
> And lay the summer's dust with showers of blood,
> Rain'd from the wounds of slaughter'd Englishmen.
>
> [III. iii. 35-44]

At this point Bolingbroke seems to have been checked by the eye of York, and thus proceeds in consequence:

> The which, how far off from the mind of Bolingbroke
> It is, such crimson tempest should bedrench
> The fresh green lap of fair King Richard's land,
> My stooping duty tenderly shall show.
>
> [III. iii. 45-8]

He passes suddenly from insolence to humility, owing to the silent reproof he received from his uncle. This change of tone would not have taken place, had Bolingbroke been allowed to proceed according to the natural bent of his own mind, and the flow of the subject. Let me direct attention to the subsequent lines, for the same reason; they are part of the same speech:

> Let's march without the noise of threat'ning drum,
> That from the castle's tatter'd battlements
> Our fair appointments may be well perused.

Methinks, King Richard and myself should meet
With no less terror than the elements
Of fire and water, when their thundering shock
At meeting tears the cloudy cheeks of heaven.

                                         [III. iii. 51-7]

Having proceeded thus far with the exaggeration of his own importance, York again checks him, and Bolingbroke adds, in a very different strain,

         He be the fire, I'll be the yielding water:
         The rage be his, while on the earth I rain
         My waters; on the earth, and not on him.

                                         [III. iii. 58-60]

I have thus adverted to the three great personages in this drama, Richard, Bolingbroke, and York; and of the whole play it may be asserted, that with the exception of some of the last scenes (though they have exquisite beauty) Shakespeare seems to have risen to the summit of excellence in the delineation and preservation of character. (pp. 145-50)

> *Samuel Taylor Coleridge [as reported by J. P. Collier], "Lectures on Shakespeare and Milton: The Twelfth Lecture," in* Shakespearean Criticism, Vol. II, *edited by Thomas Middleton Raysor, second edition, Dent, 1960, pp. 141-55.*

WILLIAM HAZLITT   (essay date 1817)

[*Hazlitt is considered a leading Shakespearean critic of the English Romantic movement. A prolific essayist and commentator on a wide range of subjects, Hazlitt remarked in the preface to his* Characters of Shakespear's Plays, *first published in 1817, that he was inspired by the German critic August Wilhelm Schlegel and was determined to supplant what he considered the pernicious influence of Samuel Johnson's Shakespearean criticism. Hazlitt's commentary is typically Romantic in its emphasis on character studies. His experience as a drama critic was an important factor in shaping his descriptive, as opposed to analytical, interpretations of Shakespeare. Hazlitt's study of* Richard II, *taken from his 1817 book and excerpted below, is among the first to emphasize the importance of the king's enemies at court: "there is neither truth nor honour in all these noble persons," he declares, but in their "accomplished barbarism" they provide a marvellously colorful background to the action. Hazlitt's main interest, however, lies with Richard himself, a protagonist who, he states, inspires pity but not love or respect: "The sufferings of the man make us forget that he was ever a king." Hazlitt compares Richard II's personality and circumstances with those of another Shakespearean monarch, Henry VI, and contrasts their respective reactions to adversity.*]

Richard II. is a play little known compared with *Richard III.* which last is a play that every unfledged candidate for theatrical fame chuses to strut and fret his hour upon the stage in; yet we confess that we prefer the nature and feeling of the one to the noise and bustle of the other; at least, as we are so often forced to see it acted. In *Richard II.* the weakness of the king leaves us leisure to take a greater interest in the misfortunes of the man. After the first act, in which the arbitrariness of his behaviour only proves his want of resolution, we see him staggering under the unlooked-for blows of fortune, bewailing his loss of kingly power, not preventing it, sinking under the aspiring genius of Bolingbroke, his authority trampled on, his hopes failing him, and his pride crushed and broken down under insults and injuries, which his own misconduct had provoked, but which he has not courage or manliness to resent. The change of tone and behaviour in the two competitors for

the throne according to their change of fortune, from the capricious sentence of banishment passed by Richard upon Bolingbroke, the suppliant offers and modest pretensions of the latter on his return to the high and haughty tone with which he accepts Richard's resignation of the crown after the loss of all his power, the use which he makes of the deposed king to grace his triumphal progress through the streets of London, and the final intimation of his wish for his death, which immediately finds a servile executioner, is marked throughout with complete effect and without the slightest appearance of effort. The steps by which Bolingbroke mounts the throne are those by which Richard sinks into the grave. We feel neither respect nor love for the deposed monarch, for he is as wanting in energy as in principle: but we pity him, for he pities himself. His heart is by no means hardened against himself, but bleeds afresh at every new stroke of mischance, and his sensibility, absorbed in his own person, and unused to misfortune, is not only tenderly alive to its own sufferings, but without the fortitude to bear them. He is, however, human in his distresses; for to feel pain, and sorrow, weakness, disappointment, remorse and anguish, is the lot of humanity, and we sympathize with him accordingly. The sufferings of the man make us forget that he ever was a king. (pp. 110-11)

Richard II. may be considered as the first of that series of English historical plays, in which 'is hung armour of the invincible knights of old" [William Wordsworth, Sonnet XVI], in which their hearts seem to strike against their coats of mail, where their blood tingles for the fight, and words are but the harbinger of blows. Of this state of accomplished barbarism the appeal of Bolingbroke and Mowbray is an admirable specimen. Another of these "keen encounters of their wits," which serve to whet the talkers' swords, is where Aumerle answers in the presence of Bolingbroke to the charge which Bagot brings against him of being an accessory in Gloster's death. (p. 112)

[But the] truth is, that there is neither truth nor honour in all these noble persons: they answer words with words, as they do blows with blows, in mere self defence: nor have they any principle whatever but that of courage in maintaining any wrong they dare commit, or any falsehood which they find it useful to assert. How different were these noble knights and "barons bold" from their more refined descendants in the present day, who, instead of deciding questions of right by brute force, refer every thing to convenience, fashion, and good breeding! (p. 113)

The character of Bolingbroke, afterwards Henry IV. is drawn with a masterly hand:—patient for occasion, and then steadily availing himself of it, seeing his advantage afar off, but only seizing on it when he has it within his reach, humble, crafty, bold, and aspiring, encroaching by regular but slow degrees, building power on opinion, and cementing opinion by power. His disposition is first unfolded by Richard himself, who however is too self-willed and secure to make a proper use of his knowledge. (pp. 114-15)

[Bolingbroke's] bold assertion of his own rights, his pretended submission to the king, and the ascendancy which he tacitly assumes over him without openly claiming it, as soon as he has him in his power, are characteristic traits of this ambitious and politic usurper. But the part of Richard himself gives the chief interest to the play. His folly, his vices, his misfortunes, his reluctance to part with the crown, his fear to keep it, his weak and womanish regrets, his starting tears, his fits of hectic passion, his smothered majesty, pass in succession before us, and make a picture as natural as it is affecting. Among the most striking touches of pathos are his wish "O that I were a mockery king of snow to melt away before the sun of Boling-broke'' [IV. i. 260-61], and the incident of the poor groom who comes to visit him in prison, and tells him how ''it yearned his heart that Bolingbroke upon his coronation-day rode on Roan Barbary'' [V. v. 76-8]. (pp. 115-16)

Shakespear was scarcely more remarkable for the force and marked contrasts of his characters than for the truth and subtlety with which he has distinguished those which approached the nearest to each other. For instance, the soul of Othello is hardly more distinct from that of Iago than that of Desdemona is shewn to be from Æmilia's; the ambition of Macbeth is as distinct from the ambition of Richard III. as it is from the meekness of Duncan; the real madness of Lear is as different from the feigned madness of Edgar as from the babbling of the fool. . . .

All these several personages were as different in Shakespear as they would have been in themselves: his imagination borrowed from the life, and every circumstance, object, motive, passion, operated there as it would in reality, and produced a world of men and women as distinct, as true and as various as those that exist in nature. The peculiar property of Shakespear's imagination was this truth, accompanied with the unconsciousness of nature: indeed, imagination to be perfect must be unconscious, at least in production; for nature is so.—We shall attempt one example more in the characters of Richard II. and Henry VI.

The characters and situations of both these persons were so nearly alike, that they would have been completely confounded by a common-place poet. Yet they are kept quite distinct in Shakespear. Both were kings, and both unfortunate. Both lost their crowns owing to their mismanagement and imbecility; the one from a thoughtless, wilful abuse of power, the other from an indifference to it. The manner in which they bear their misfortunes corresponds exactly to the causes which led to them. The one is always lamenting the loss of his power which he has not the spirit to regain; the other seems only to regret that he had ever been king, and is glad to be rid of the power, with the trouble; the effeminacy of the one is that of a voluptuary, proud, revengeful, impatient of contradiction, and inconsolable in his misfortunes; the effeminacy of the other is that of an indolent, good-natured mind, naturally averse to the turmoils of ambition and the cares of greatness, and who wishes to pass his time in monkish indolence and contemplation.— Richard bewails the loss of the kingly power only as it was the means of gratifying his pride and luxury; Henry regards it only as a means of doing right, and is less desirous of the advantages to be derived from possessing it than afraid of exercising it wrong. (pp. 135-36)

When Richard first hears of the death of his favourites, Bushy, Bagot, and the rest, he indignantly rejects all idea of any further efforts, and only indulges in the extravagant impatience of his grief and his despair, in that fine speech which has been so often quoted:—

Aumerle. Where is the duke my father, with his power?
K. Richard. No matter where: of comfort no man
    speak:
Let's talk of graves, of worms, and epitaphs,
Make dust our paper, and with rainy eyes
Write sorrow in the bosom of the earth!. . .
For heaven's sake let us sit upon the ground,
And tell sad stories of the death of Kings:

How some have been depos'd, some slain in war;
Some haunted by the ghosts they dispossess'd;
Some poison'd by their wives, some sleeping kill'd;
All murder'd:—for within the hollow crown,
That rounds the mortal temples of a king,
Keeps death his court: and there the antic sits,
Scoffing his state, and grinning at his pomp!. . .
Cover your heads, and mock not flesh and blood
With solemn reverence; throw away respect,
Tradition, form, and ceremonious duty,
For you have but mistook me all this while:
I live on bread like you, feel want, taste grief,
Need friends, like you;—subjected thus,
How can you say to me—I am a king?
                [III. ii. 143-47, 155-63, 171-77]

There is as little sincerity afterwards in his affected resignation to his fate, as there is fortitude in this exaggerated picture of his misfortunes before they have happened.

When Northumberland comes back with the message from Bolingbroke, he exclaims, anticipating the result,—

What must the king do now? Must he submit?
The king shall do it: must he be depos'd?
The king shall be contented: must he lose
The name of king? O' God's name let it go.
I'll give my jewels for a set of beads . . . ,
And my large kingdom for a little grave—
A little, little grave, an obscure grave.
                        [III. iii. 143-47, 153-54]

How differently is all this expressed in King Henry's soliloquy, during the battle with Edward's party:—

This battle fares like to the morning's war,
When dying clouds contend with growing light,
What time the shepherd blowing of his nails,
Can neither call it perfect day or night.
Here on this mole-hill will I sit me down;
To whom God will, there be the victory!
                        [*3 Henry VI*, II. v. 1-6]
                        (pp. 137-38)

This is a true and beautiful description of a naturally quiet and contented disposition, and not, like the former, the splenetic effusion of disappointed ambition. (p. 139)

> *William Hazlitt, ''Richard II'' and ''Henry VI, in*
> *Three Parts,'' in his* Characters of Shakespear's Plays
> & Lectures on the English Poets, *The Macmillan*
> *Company, 1903, pp. 110-16, 133-40.*

NATHAN DRAKE   (essay date 1817)

[Nathan Drake was a physician who, like many gifted amateurs of his day, made useful contributions to criticism and, as his biographer wrote, did ''much to stimulate a taste for useful and elegant literature.'' Drake's poems and essays, which appeared regularly from 1790 to 1828, were chiefly fashionable, pre-Romantic pieces with titles like Evenings in Autumn *and* Mornings in Spring, *but in 1817 he produced* Shakspeare and His Times, *a two-volume study of the dramatist's life as well as a history of the ''Manners, Customs, and Amusements, Superstitions, Poetry, and Elegant Literature of His Age.'' In the following excerpt from this work, Drake is one of the earliest commentators to identify the source of Richard's maladjustments as his ''neglected . . . education.'' A childhood and youth given over to idleness, dissipation, and spoiled self-indulgence, in Drake's view, ultimately leads the king to destruction. The critic adds, however, that ad-*

versity calls forth from Richard the "innate nobility of his heart,"
so that his courage and dignity finally win our admiration.]

Of the character of [the] unfortunate young prince [Richard the Second], Shakspeare has given us a delineation in conformity with the general tone of history, but heightened by many exquisite and pathetic touches. Richard was beautiful in his person, and elegant in his manners; affectionate, generous, and faithful in his attachments, and though intentionally neglected in his education, not defective in understanding. Accustomed, by his designing uncles, to the company of the idle and the dissipated, and to the unrestrained indulgence of his passions, we need not wonder that levity, ostentation, and prodigality, should mark his subsequent career, and should ultimately lead him to destruction.

Though the errors of his misguided youth are forcibly depicted in the drama, yet the poet has reserved his strength for the period of adversity. Richard, descending from his throne, discovers the unexpected virtues of humility, fortitude, and resignation, and becomes not only an object of love and pity, but of admiration; and there is nothing in the whole compass of our author's plays better calculated to produce, with full effect, these mingled emotions of compassion and esteem, than the passages which paint the sentiments and deportment of the fallen monarch. Patience, submission, and misery, were never more feelingly expressed than in the following lines:

> *K. Rich.* What must the king do now? Must he
> submit?
> The king shall do it. Must he be depos'd?
> The king shall be contented: Must he lose
> The name of king? o'God's name, let it go:
> I'll give my jewels, for a set of beads;
> My gorgeous palace, for a hermitage; . . .
> [III. iii. 143-48]

and with what an innate nobility of heart does he repress the homage of his attendants!

> Cover your heads, and mock not flesh and blood
> With solemn reverence; throw away respect,
> Tradition, form, and ceremonious duty,
> For you have but mistook me all this while:
> I live with bread like you, feel want, taste grief,
> Need friends:—Subjected thus,
> How can you say to me—I am a king?
> [III. ii. 171-77]

Nor does his conduct, in the hour of suffering and extreme humiliation, derogate from the philosophy of his sentiments. In that admirable opening of the second scene of the fifth act, where the Duke of York relates to his Duchess the entrance of Bolingbroke and Richard into London, the demeanour of the latter is thus pourtrayed:—

> Men's eyes
> Did scowl on Richard; no man cried, God save him;
> No joyful tongue gave him his welcome home:
> But dust was thrown upon his sacred head;
> Which with such gentle sorrow he shook off,—
> His face still combating with tears and smiles,
> The badges of his grief and patience,—
> [V. ii. 27-33]
> (pp. 376-78)

Of the secondary characters of this play, "Old John of Gaunt, time-honour'd Lancaster" [I. i. 1], and his son Henry Bolingbroke, are brought forward with strict attention to the evidence

of history; the chivalric spirit, and zealous integrity of the first, and the cold, artificial features of the second, being struck off with great sharpness of outline, and strength of discrimination. (p. 378)

> *Nathan Drake, "Chapter X: 'King Richard the Second'," in his* Shakspeare and His Times, Vol. I, *T. Cadell and W. Davies, 1817, pp. 375-78.*

ALESSANDRO MANZONI   (letter date 1820)

[*Best known for his masterpiece* I Promessi Sposi—*held by many to be the greatest Italian novel ever written—Manzoni combined lyrical intensity, psychological penetration, patriotism, and a deep religious fervor to become one of Europe's most prominent spokesmen for Romanticism in the early nineteenth century. In his 1820 "Letter to Monsieur Chauvet concerning the unities of time and place in tragedy," excerpted below, Manzoni takes issue with those Neoclassical theorists who had traditionally disparaged* Richard II *and other plays for their failure to follow certain strict rules governing setting and duration of action. Manzoni cites* Richard II *as a work that "requires more latitude than the rule of the two unities accords," adding that "all the great monuments of poetry have as their basis events given by history," not invented facts.*]

The action of [*Richard II*] is the overthrow of Richard from the throne of England and the elevation of Bolingbroke in his place. The play begins at the moment when the designs of these two characters appear in open opposition; when the king, having conceived a genuine uneasiness concerning the ambitious projects of his cousin, in order to thwart these ambitions, throws himself into measures which end by bringing on their execution. He banishes Bolingbroke: the Duke of Lancaster, the latter's father, being dead, the king seizes his properties and leaves for Ireland, Bolingbroke infringes the order of exile and returns to England on the pretext of claiming the inheritance which has been taken away from him by an illegal act. His partisans flock to him in crowds: as their number increases, he changes his language, passes by degrees from claims to threats; and soon the subject who has come to demand justice is a potent rebel who lays down laws. The uncle and lieutenant of the king, the Duke of York, who goes to meet Bolingbroke in order to oppose him, ends by treating with him. The character of this figure unfolds with the action in which he is engaged: the duke speaks successively, first to the rebellious subject, then to the chief of a numerous faction, finally to the new king; and this progress is so natural, so exactly parallel to events that the spectator is not surprised to find at the end of the play a good servant of Henry IV in the same character who had learned with the greatest indignation of Bolingbroke's landing. As the first successes of the latter become known, it is naturally toward Richard that interest and curiosity turn. One is eager to know the effect of so great a blow on the soul of this irascible and haughty king. Thus, Richard is summoned to the scene by the expectation of the audience at the same time as by the course of the action.

He has been warned of the disobedience of Bolingbroke and of his attempt: he hurriedly leaves Ireland and lands in England at the moment when his adversary is seizing the county of Gloucester; but certainly, the king ought not to march straight against the bold aggressor without having prepared to resist him. Here plausibility denied, as expressly as history itself, the unity of place, and Shakespeare has not followed the latter more rigorously than the former. He shows us Richard in the land of Wales: he could without difficulty have arranged his subject so as to produce the two rivals successively on the same terrain; but what would he not have had to sacrifice for that? and what would his tragedy have gained thereby? Unity of action? By no means; for where would one find a tragedy in which the action is more strictly unified than in this one? Richard deliberates, with his remaining friends, as to what he ought to do; and it is here that the character of this king begins to assume a development so natural and so unexpected. The spectator had already made the acquaintance of this astounding personality and flattered himself that he had fathomed it; but there was in it something secret and profound which had not appeared at all in prosperity and which adversity alone could elicit. The foundation of the character is still the same; it is still pride, it is still the highest ideal of its own dignity: but this same pride which, when it was accompanied by power, showed itself by levity, by impatience with every obstacle, by a thoughtlessness which did not permit it even to suspect that all human power has its judges and its limits: this pride, once deprived of force, has become grave and serious, solemn and measured. What supports Richard is an unalterable consciousness of his own greatness, it is the certainty that no human event has been able to destroy, since nothing can cancel his birth and his kingship. The enjoyments of power have escaped him; but the idea of his calling to the highest rank remains: in what he is, he persists in honoring what he was; and this obstinate respect for a title which no one any longer acknowledges to be his removes from the sense of his misfortune everything which could humiliate or dishearten him. The ideas, the emotions through which this revolution in Richard's character is manifested have great originality, are expressed in the most exalted poetry, and are even very touching.

But this historical tableau of Richard's soul and of the events which modify it necessarily embraces more than twenty hours, and the same is true for the progress of the other deeds, passions, and characters developed in the rest of the action. The clash of the two factions, the ardor and increasing activity of the king's enemies, the tergiversations [equivocations] of those who are waiting for victory in order to know positively to which cause respectable people ought to be attached, the courageous loyalty of one single man, loyalty which the poet has described just as history has sanctioned it, with all the ideas true and false that determined this man to render homage to adversity in spite of force: all these are admirably depicted in this tragedy. A few improprieties, which one could remove without altering its order, could not impose upon the grandeur and beauty of the whole.

I am almost ashamed to give so fleshless a sketch of so majestic a tableau. But I flatter myself that I have said enough about it to show at least that what is characteristic in this subject requires more latitude than the rule of the two unities accords. Let us now suppose that Shakespeare, having composed his *Richard II,* had shown it to a critic convinced of the necessity of this rule. The latter would probably have said to him: "There are in your play some very fine situations, and above all some admirable sentiments; but plausibility is deplorable offended. You transport your public from London to Coventry, from the county of Gloucester to the land of Wales, from parliament to Flint Castle; it is impossible for the spectator to create for himself the illusion necessary to follow you. There is a contradiction between the various situations in which you wish to place the spectator and the real situation he is in. He is too certain of not having changed position to be able to imagine that he has made all these journeys which you demand of him."

I don't know, but it seems to me that Shakespeare would have been quite astonished by such objections. "Oh Good Heavens!" he might have replied, "how you talk of displacements and journeys. There is no question of that here; I never dreamed of it, nor did my spectators, either. I place before their eyes an action which is unfolded by degrees, which is composed of events that arise successively from one another and that occur in different places; it is the mind of the spectator which follows them—he has no traveling to do except to imagine to himself that he is traveling. Do you think that he has come to the theater to see real events? and has it ever entered my mind to create for him such an illusion? to make him believe that what he knows has already happened several hundred years ago is happening now once more? that these actors are men really engrossed in the passions and concerns which they are speaking of, and speaking of in verse?"

But I have too much forgotten, sir, that it is not on the objection drawn from plausibility that you base the maintenance of the rules, but rather on the impossibility of preserving without them unity of action and stability of character. Let us see, then, whether this objection can be applied to the tragedy of *Richard II.* Well! How would one set about proving, I ask you with some curiosity, that the action is not unified, that the characters are not constant, and this, because the poet has remained in the places and times given by history, instead of shutting himself up in the space and length of time which the critics have measured out on their own authority for all tragedies? What more would Shakespeare have replied to a critic who had come to oppose to him the law of twenty-four hours! "Twenty-four hours!" he would have said, "but why? Reading the chronicles of Holinshed supplied my mind with the idea of an action simple and great, unified and varied, full of interest and of lessons; and this action—I should have had to distort, to mutilate from pure caprice! The impression which a chronicler has produced on me—I should not have sought to render, after my fashion, to spectators who asked nothing better! I should have been less a poet than he (Holinshed)! I see an event of which each incident relates to all the others and serves to motivate them; I see fixed characters develop in a certain time and in certain places; and in order to give the idea of this event, in order to depict these characters, it will be absolutely necessary for me to mutilate both the one and the others to the point where the duration of twenty-four hours and the precincts of a palace might suffice for their development!"

There would be in your system, sir, I admit, another reply to make to Shakespeare: one could tell him that these pains he has taken to reproduce the facts in their natural order with their most authenticated principal circumstances makes him like a historian rather than like a poet. One could add that it is the rule of the two unities which would have rendered him a poet, in forcing him to create one action, a nexus, of the peripaties; for "it is thus," you say, "that the limits of art give impetus to the artist's imagination and force him to become a creator." That is precisely, I agree, the true consequence of this rule; and the slightest acquaintance with the drama which has accepted it proves, moreover, that it has not failed in its effect. That is a great advantage, according to you: I dare not to be of this opinion and on the contrary to regard the effect which is involved as the gravest disadvantage of this rule from which it results; yes, this necessity to create, imposed arbitrarily on art, separates it from truth and mars it, both in its results and in its means.

I don't know whether I am going to say something contrary to received ideas: but I believe that I am merely stating a very simple truth, in advancing the idea that the essence of poetry does not consist in inventing facts: that invention is what is most easy and most vulgar in the work of the mind, what requires the least reflection and even the least imagination. Thus there is nothing more prevalent than creations of this kind; whereas all the great monuments of poetry have as their basis events given by history, or, what comes down to the same thing, by what has once been regarded as history.

As for dramatic poets in particular, the greatest ones in each country have avoided, with all the more care as they have had more genius, putting into drama facts of their own creation; and in some cases substantially altered—by his nephew H. N.and on each occasion that has occurred of telling them that they have substituted, on essential points, invention for history—far from accepting this judgment as praise, they have rejected it as blame. If I did not know how much temerity there is in too general historical assertions, I should dare to assert that there is not, in all that remains to us of the tragic drama of the Greeks, nor even in all their poetry, a single example of this sort of creation, which consists in substituting for the principal known causes of a great action, causes wantonly invented. The Greek poets took their subjects, with all their important circumstances, from the national traditions. They did not invent the facts; they received them just as their contemporaries had transmitted them: they accepted, they respected history just as individuals, peoples, and time had made it. (pp. 130-35)

> *Alessandro Manzoni, in a letter to M. Chauvet, translated by Françoise Rosen, in* Shakespeare in Europe, *edited by Oswald LeWinter, World Publishing Company, 1963, pp. 129-35.*

SAMUEL TAYLOR COLERIDGE (essay date 1834?)

[*Coleridge's remarks on Shakespeare come down to posterity largely as fragmentary notes, marginalia, and reports by auditors on the lectures, rather than in polished essays. After Coleridge's death in 1834, these fragments were prepared for publication— and in some cases substantially altered—by his nephew H. N. Coleridge. The following excerpt comes from one such edition, entitled* Shakespeare, Ben Jonson, Beaumont and Fletcher: Notes and Lectures (1881); *since it is unknown when Coleridge penned the following commentary, its date is based on the year of his death. Coleridge considers* Richard II *ill-suited for the stage because of its long poetic speeches and the fact that, excepting Richard's murder, violence is reported, not depicted; but he held that as closet drama it is the "most admirable of all Shakespeare's purely historical plays." He also maintains that the king is no "vulgar debauchee" but simply weak and incapable of controlling his emotions. Revising an opinion he had expressed in his lecture on the play (see excerpt above, 1811-12), Coleridge observes in the king, despite his moral weakness, "gradually emergent good qualities" that ultimately arouse our sympathy. The real drama of* Richard II *is psychological, Coleridge argues, "a history of the human mind when reduced to ease its anguish with words instead of action, and the necessary feeling of weakness which such a state produces."*]

From the length of the speeches, and the circumstance that, with one exception, the events are all historical, and presented in their results, not produced by acts seen by, or taking place before, the audience, [*Richard II*] is ill suited to our present large theatres. But in itself, and for the closet, I feel no hesitation in placing it as the first and most admirable of all Shakespeare's purely historical plays. For the two parts of *Henry IV.* form a species of themselves, which may be named the mixed drama. The distinction does not depend on the mere

quantity of historical events in the play compared with the fictions; for there is as much history in *Macbeth* as in *Richard,* but in the relation of the history to the plot. In the purely historical plays, the history forms the plot; in the mixed, it directs it; in the rest, as *Macbeth, Hamlet, Cymbeline, Lear,* it subserves it. But, however unsuited to the stage this drama may be, God forbid that even there it should fall dead on the hearts of jacobinised Englishmen! Then, indeed, we might say—*præteriit gloria mundi* [the bygone glory of the world]! For the spirit of patriotic reminiscence is all-permeating soul of this noble work. It is, perhaps, the most purely historical of Shakespeare's dramas. There are not in it, as in the others, characters introduced merely for the purpose of giving a greater individuality and realness, as in the comic parts of *Henry IV.,* by presenting as it were our very selves. Shakespeare avails himself of every opportunity to effect the great object of the historic drama,—that, namely, of familiarising the people to the great names of their country, and thereby of exciting a steady patriotism, a love of just liberty, and a respect for all those fundamental institutions of social life, which bind men together. . . . (pp. 161-62)

Admirable is the judgment with which Shakespeare always in the first scenes prepares, yet how naturally, and with what concealment of art, for the catastrophe. Observe how he here presents the germ of all the after events in Richard's insincerity, partiality, arbitrariness, and favouritism, and in the proud, tempestuous, temperament of his barons. In the very beginning, also, is displayed that feature in Richard's character, which is never forgotten throughout the play—his attention to decorum, and high feeling of the kingly dignity. These anticipations show with what judgment Shakespeare wrote, and illustrate his care to connect the past and the future, and unify them with the present by forecast and reminiscence. (p. 163)

[The] scene of the quarrel between Mowbray and Bolingbroke seems introduced for the purpose of showing by anticipation the characters of Richard and Bolingbroke. In the latter there is observable a decorous and courtly checking of his anger in subservience to a predetermined plan, especially in his calm speech after receiving sentence of banishment compared with Mowbray's unaffected lamentation. In the one, all is ambitious hope of something yet to come; in the other it is desolation and a looking backward of the heart. (p. 165)

[In Act I, Scene iv] a new light is thrown on Richard's character. Until now he has appeared in all the beauty of royalty; but here, as soon as he is left to himself, the inherent weakness of his character is immediately shown. It is a weakness, however, of a peculiar kind, not arising from want of personal courage, or any specific defect of faculty, but rather an intellectual feminineness, which feels a necessity of ever leaning on the breasts of others, and of reclining on those who are all the while known to be inferiors. To this must be attributed as its consequences all Richard's vices, his tendency to concealment, and his cunning, the whole operation of which is directed to the getting rid of present difficulties. Richard is not meant to be a debauchee; but we see in him that sophistry which is common to man, by which we can deceive our own hearts, and at one and the same time apologize for, and yet commit, the error. Shakespeare has represented this character in a very peculiar manner. He has not made him amiable with counterbalancing faults; but has openly and broadly drawn those faults without reserve, relying on Richard's disproportionate sufferings and gradually emergent good qualities for our sympathy; and this was possible, because his faults are not positive vices, but spring entirely from defect of character. (p. 167)

The amiable part of Richard's character is brought full upon us by his queen's few words—

> So sweet a guest
> As my sweet Richard.—
>
> [II. ii. 8-9]

and Shakespeare has carefully shown in him an intense love of his country, well-knowing how that feeling would, in a pure historic drama, redeem him in the hearts of the audience. Yet even in this love there is something feminine and personal:—

> Dear earth, I do salute thee with my hand,—
> As a long parted mother with her child
> Plays fondly with her tears, and smiles in meeting;
> So weeping, smiling, greet I thee, my earth,
> And do thee favour with my royal hands.
>
> [III. ii. 6, 8-11]

With this is combined a constant overflow of emotions from a total incapability of controlling them, and thence a waste of that energy, which should have been reserved for actions, in the passion and effort of mere resolves and menaces. The consequence is moral exhaustion; and rapid alternations of unmanly despair and ungrounded hope,—every feeling being abandoned for its direct opposite upon the pressure of external accident. And yet when Richard's inward weakness appears to seek refuge in his despair, and his exhaustion counterfeits repose, the old habit of kingliness, the effect of flatterers from his infancy, is ever and anon producing in him a sort of wordy courage which only serves to betray more clearly his internal impotence. (pp. 170-71)

I would once more remark upon the exalted idea of the only true loyalty developed in this noble and impressive play. We have neither the rants of Beaumont and Fletcher, nor the sneers of Massinger;—the vast importance of the personal character of the sovereign is distinctly enounced, whilst, at the same time, the genuine sanctity which surrounds him is attributed to, and grounded on, the position in which he stands as the convergence and exponent of the life and power of the state. (p. 172)

> *Samuel Taylor Coleridge, "Richard II," in his* Shakespeare, Ben Jonson, Beaumont and Fletcher: Notes and Lectures, *Edward Howell, 1881, pp. 161-73.*

HERMANN ULRICI (essay date 1839)

[*A German scholar, Ulrici was a professor of philosophy and the author of works on Greek poetry and Shakespeare. The following excerpt is from an English version of his* Über Shakespeares dramatische Kunst, und sein Verhaltniss zu Calderon und Göthe, *a work first published in 1839. This study exemplifies the "philosophical criticism" developed in Germany during the nineteenth century. The immediate sources for Ulrici's critical approach appear to be August Wilhelm Schlegel's conception of the play as an organic, interconnected whole and Georg Wilhelm Friedrich Hegel's view of drama as an embodiment of the conflict of historical forces and ideas. Unlike his fellow German critic G. G. Gervinus, Ulrici sought to develop a specifically Christian aesthetics, but one which, as he carefully points out in the introduction to the work mentioned above, in no way intrudes on "that unity of idea, which preeminently constitutes a work of art a living creation in the world of beauty." Ulrici considers Richard II a "noble, but spoiled and corrupted" character, whose unbridled folly left England near chaos, and he regards the ascendancy of the prudent, moderate Bolingbroke as providential for the nation. The critic further notes that Richard's fatal flaw is his inability*

to recognize the solemnity of his kingly vocation, maintaining that "the ground-idea of the whole drama" is the priority of the monarch's responsibility to God's grace and justice over claims of legality and heredity.]

"Richard the Second" may for many reasons be regarded as the companion of "King John." While John employs every evil means to maintain his usurped dignity, Richard forfeits his just right by a weak use of it. The vitality of history endures no abstract, dead notion. The fixed formula of an outward, legal, and conventional right, is as nothing in the sight of history, for which nothing is right but what is truly so, as having its foundation in *morality*. This Richard has forfeited before the eyes of men, by treading it himself under foot. The highest earthly power is not exempt from the eternal laws of the universe; the majesty which is by the *grace of God* loses its title as soon as it abandons its only foundation in the grace of God, whose justice acknowledges no jurisprudence, no rights of family and inheritance, as against the immutable rights of truth and reason. Richard urges in vain his legal title and the sacred name of majesty; to no purpose does he invoke the angels of Him who set him on the throne; the rights and title of a king avail not to move a straw, because they are devoid of the mighty force of inward rectitude; God will send no angel to protect him who has rejected His grace. The people, too, in turn abandon him who had first abandoned them. The injustice of rebellion prevails. The truly noble, but spoiled and corrupted nature of Richard, wanes before the prudence and moderation of Bolingbroke. However little of true moral power Henry the Fourth subsequently exhibits, nevertheless, as contrasted with the unworthy and most unkingly conduct of Richard, he looks a model of virtue, and designed by nature for a throne. In the doubtful scale a grain of sand turns the balance.

Under such an unkingly sovereign the people are of necessity plunged in dissension and misery. . . . Caprice follows upon caprice, accumulating infamy upon infamy. [Richard] lets out his kingdom to farm, and rapaciously confiscates the property of the House of Lancaster to furnish the expenses necessary for putting down the rebellion in Ireland. While he trusts to his hereditary claims and to the divine right of kings, he nevertheless violates all the right of family and inheritance, and, by putting his own divine office out to hire, he becomes, with suicidal inconsistency, the first rebel, and with his own hand sows the seed of the revolution which eventually robs him of his life and crown. By disregarding in his own person the rights of the historical past—which is the true meaning of the so-called principle of stability—he places himself on an unsubstantial future. None but the more aged of his subjects—those who live on in a better past, who still see in him his heroic and noble-minded father, such as the old York and his sons, the Bishop of Carlisle, and the old Salisbury—remain faithful to him; all the vigour of youth and manhood, on the other hand, that from its very nature is engrossed by the present and future, which, however undermined by Richard, totters and threatens to fall, hesitates also, and at last goes over to the rebel Bolingbroke. Here, too, the guiding hand of God is discernible. Had Richard returned *one* day sooner from Ireland, he would have found an army ready equipped for battle; but deceived by the accidental delay, and a rumour of the death of the king, it had dispersed or gone over to Henry. His resources being thus cut off, lost to himself, and powerless, he yields himself into the hands of his enemy; his spirit, like a rotten stem, is broken by the storm which he himself had raised. (pp. 365-67)

A single idea, it is plain, runs through the whole piece and its several parts. The poet has here laboured to illustrate the high historical significance of the kingly dignity in the light that it appears to the christian view of things, as the most exalted, but at the same time the most responsible vocation, that Heaven imposes upon man. Absolutely speaking, every man has no doubt his vocation from God; but whereas the duties and office of every individual member of the state are more or less modified by the governing power, the dignity of the sovereign stands in an immediate relation to God and his all-ruling grace. It pre-eminently is "by the grace of God." And, both on this account, and because, as Shakspeare shews, the happiness of the whole people depends on the sovereign, he ought to be only the more mindful of divine grace, and the greater is his guilt, whenever, forgetting his true dignity, he acts unkingly, and contrary to justice and to grace. When he contradicts his high vocation he will call in vain upon its divinity to protect him. In being called to it, he was *called* to do justice; and it is only by obeying its call that he can maintain his own right. While, then, the poet has thus attempted to elucidate the true relation both of man to his own historical position, and of his vocation in life to God, and while he thus places the essence of the kingly dignity in its observance of its relation to God and the world, he has successfully illustrated modern political history under one of its most essential aspects, and in one of its principal ideas. This is the ground-idea of the whole drama. (pp. 367-68)

> Hermann Ulrici, "Histories: 'Richard II'," in his Shakespeare's Dramatic Art: And His Relation to Calderon and Goethe, *translated by A. J. W. Morrison, Chapman, Brothers, 1846, pp. 365-68.*

G. G. GERVINUS (essay date 1849-50)

[*One of the most widely read Shakespearean critics of the latter half of the nineteenth century, the German critic Gervinus was praised by such eminent contemporaries as Edward Dowden, F. J. Furnivall, and James Russell Lowell; however, he is little known in the English-speaking world today. Like his predecessor Hermann Ulrici, Gervinus wrote in the tradition of the "philosophical criticism" developed in Germany in the mid-nineteenth century. Under the influence of August Wilhelm Schlegel's literary theory and Georg Wilhelm Friedrich Hegel's philosophy, such German critics as Gervinus tended to focus their analyses around a search for the literary work's organic unity and ethical import. Gervinus believed that Shakespeare's works contained a rational ethical system independent of any religion—in contrast to Ulrici, for whom Shakespeare's morality was basically Christian. In his* Shakespeare Commentaries, *originally published in German in 1849-50 and excerpted below, Gervinus identifies the central conflict of* Richard II *as that of a weak but legitimate monarch opposed by a competent, statesmanlike usurper, and he stresses the momentous political implications of this struggle. For him,* Richard II *teaches an "immortal lesson" about true kingship, articulated chiefly by the Bishop of Carlisle but presented allegorically in the Garden Scene as well: namely, that the doctrine of Divine Right Monarchy cannot legitimize a ruler who fails to fulfill his responsibilities to both God and his people. Gervinus was also one of the first critics to stress Richard's obsession with language and his growing need throughout the play for self-dramatization. He further argued that* Richard II *is best understood as part of an epic tetralogy that extends through* 1 *and* 2 Henry IV *and* Henry V.]

Richard II. must be read in a series with *Henry IV*. and *V*. in order thoroughly to understand it. The finest touches for the explanation of characters and actions in the first play of the series are to be met with in passages of the third and fourth plays of the series, and we might almost say are intentionally

concealed in them. The principal character of the fourth piece, *Henry V.*, is already mentioned in the first, that is in *Richard II.*, and his wild youth is pointed out at a period when he was only twelve years old. The character of the Duke of Aumerle, who plays no brilliant part in *Richard II.* after his mother has saved him from the punishment of high treason, and has prayed to God to make 'her old son new' [V. iii. 146], is again silently brought forward by the poet in *Henry V.*, a new man indeed, who has become great with the heroic age, and dies the death of a hero at Agincourt. Thus the most delicate threads entwine around the four plays, uniting them together; other allusions equally delicate place this Lancastrian tetralogy in an opposite relation to that of York. The similarity of the historical events in the rise and fall of the two houses did not escape the poet; had he handled the history of the House of York, later in point of time, *after* instead of *before* the history of that of Lancaster, he would have had the opportunity of marking these similarities and relations even more sharply in both cases. Richard II. appears in this tetralogy, as Henry VI. did in the York. A young prince, not without fine human talents, surrounded by uncles and arrogant protectors, by favourites and protégés, in both cases brings the kingdom to ruin; both lose their hereditary throne through usurpers, and die by violence in prison. Bolingbroke undermines Richard's throne in a similar manner to that in which York attacks that of Henry VI.; the one falls perjured before he has obtained the last object of his ambitious path; the other reaches his aim through fortune and merit, and maintains it by estimable administration and repentant compensation. But retribution threatens the one usurping house as well as the other; domestic discord reigns in the family of Henry IV. as among the sons of York under Edward IV. From this moment, however, the destinies of the two houses are sundered by a rigorous contrast . . . ; from the ill-starred family circumstances under the Lancastrians rose Henry V., who in the midst of his wild youthful excesses took the grand resolution to restore to the English throne the splendour of the Edwards, whilst from the York house rose Richard III., who, in the midst of a career of warlike fame, forms the project of clearing for himself a way to the throne by a series of base actions. A great ruler in the one makes us forget by his virtues for a brief glorious period the misdeeds of the Lancastrians, in the other a bloody tyrant brings by his wickedness the utmost dishonour upon the house of York, and hurries it to ruin. (pp. 280-81)

Richard II. was the son of the Black Prince, Edward III.'s brave eldest son. According to historical tradition he was most beautiful; and Shakespeare also, in contrasting him with Richard III., who is urged by his deformity to avenge himself on nature, has not unintentionally invested him with a beautiful form, which, according to Bacon, renders 'him generally lightminded whom it adorns, and whom it moves;' he calls him in the lips of Percy 'a sweet lovely rose' [*1 Henry IV*, I. iii. 175]. He gives him the outward features of his father, and allows us occasionally to perceive a mental likeness also: the mild nature of the lamb and the violence of the lion, which the poet speaks of as combined in the Black Prince, are both exhibited in him. The first is scarcely to be mistaken; it becomes visible even at the last moment in the many tokens of attachment which he receives at a time when it is dangerous to manifest it, and it is apparent after his death in the longing for him which is aroused in the adversaries who had conspired against him. The other quality is more hidden in single scattered traits. He appears throughout like a 'young hot colt' [II. i. 70] easily provoked, like a violent flame consuming itself quickly; he compares himself to the brilliant Phaeton, who, incapable and daring, tries to manage his refractory steeds; in the moment of misfortune the defiance of an innate nobility is aroused in the midst of his sorrow, and in his death he appears as 'full of valour as of royal blood' [V. vi. 113]. But this fine disposition is wholly obliterated; in the early season of his life and reign he has lost his reputation; he is surrounded by a troop of creatures and favourites, parasites and men who preyed on the kingdom, who stop his ear with flatteries, and poison it with wanton imaginations; who make him tyrannical and imperious, incapable of hearing a word of blame and admonition even from the lips of his dying uncle; men who made him shallow with Italian fashions, who surrounded him with every low vanity, and enticed him into ostentation and extravagance.... The poet has left this merry frivolous society in the back ground, which perhaps, considering the play of *Richard II.* by itself, would be a defect; but he had matter of too similar a character to depict in *Henry IV.*, and he was obliged to avoid repetition; he gave the jovial picture to the cheerful play, and left it out of the tragic one. In its stead, most wisely, that he might not make the tragedy of the national history laughable, he placed the serious and tragic side of this conduct. (pp. 281-83)

Beyond the scattered touches and the insinuations which denote the inability of the king, and his wavering between unseasonable power and weakness, the poet has chosen only one event for greater dramatic prominence, and with this the catastrophe of Richard's fate is united, namely, the knightly quarrel between Bolingbroke and Norfolk with which the play begins. (p. 284)

[The scene] serves essentially to place in opposition to each other, in their first decisive collision, the two main characters, Richard and Bolingbroke, the declining king yet in his power and glory, and the rising one in his misfortune and banishment. In his accusation of Norfolk, Bolingbroke besets the king remotely with hostile designs. The guilt of Gloster's death rests in the public opinion upon the king and his associates; subsequently Aumerle emerges as the immediate instrument; the guilt of having known it and concealed it falls upon Norfolk alone, a guilt of which he accuses himself; but the popular hatred turns upon him as upon the king. Bolingbroke, as we learn expressly in the second part of *Henry IV.* (Act. IV. sc. 1), uses this circumstance to nourish the hatred and to draw upon himself the favour of the people, whilst he exhibits the Lancastrians honourably solicitous about a sacred family matter.... The survivors of the murdered Gloster spur on the Lancastrians to revenge, their own security being concerned; the old Gaunt indeed commits vengeance to God, but his son Bolingbroke holds it far more certain if it is in his own human hand. The venerable old man, whom Shakespeare invests with riper years than history does, has transmitted to his son the elements which are blended together in his deeply reserved character. The hoary hero has borne in his heart the welfare of his fatherland, and his patriotic feelings obtain so much in his dying hour over his fidelity as a subject, that in words of the greatest enthusiasm for his glorious country he cuttingly reproaches the sinful Richard with what he has done with this 'demi-Paradise' [II. i. 42]. Sorrow for the country, and sorrow for his banished son, hurried him to the grave. Mingled with his patriotic feeling we see family feeling and self-love; both are also strong in the son. The son's far-stretching domestic policy accompanies and determines his whole life; his patriotic feeling breaks forth in the touching lament on his banishment, which justly has been called not only very beautiful, but very English. To both these traits is joined that diplomatic cunning which lies in the very recesses of his nature, and is therefore concealed without difficulty. This, too, the son appears to have

inherited from his father; for shrewdness of purpose cannot be more delicately coupled with magnanimity than in the old Gaunt, who, in the council of state, gives his vote for the banishment of his son, which subsequently breaks his heart, in the idea of moving the rest to a milder judgment by his own too severe sentence. Similar in the deep reserve of his character is the delineation which Shakespeare has given of the son, who in one touch alone, in *Richard II.*, appears without a mask, and who in all others, throughout the three plays, remains a riddle even to the attentive reader, until at length the last hour of life elicits a confession to his son. The same mysterious obscurity marks even the commencement scene between Bolingbroke and Norfolk. We have just intimated the designs and motives which actuate the former, but we have gathered them from subsequent disclosures; in the moment of action it is not clear at what he is aiming, and Norfolk's bearing increases the obscurity. The voice of innocence and honour speaks in him mostly in his voluntary confessions, and no less so in his strong appeal to his fidelity towards the king. It goes so far that he does not attempt to raise the veil from the misdeed of which he is accused, not even after the king's sentence of a dateless banishment has fallen on him 'all unlooked for' [I. iii. 155], when he hoped for other reward than this disgrace. The king, too, condemns him, we likewise learn at the end of *Henry IV.* (Part II. Act IV. sc. 1), against his will, because of the general feeling against him, but the enthusiasm of popular favour was already directed to Bolingbroke, who at his departure behaves to the multitude as a condescending prince. The weak Richard, who Norfolk predicts will rue this deed, ignobly banishes for a lifetime the man whom he loves, and who would have been his most faithful support, and for a few years the other whom he hates, whose ambitious thoughts he fears, and whose banishment he has in his heart faithlessly resolved as limitless. He disturbs the combat between the two, whose peace he fears still more: he strikes his enemy and provokes him without making him harmless, and displays the helplessness of a man of a troubled conscience, who knows not the right occasion for mildness or severity. The chronicle sums up the faults of his government in these words: he showed too great kindness to his friends, too great favour to his enemies. Both are just. But in this case he shows in his severity towards his friend that he is inconsistent moreover, and he allows himself to be influenced by the power of opinion in an unessential point, when he neglected to attend to it in an essential one.

Fully in the sense of the sentence quoted from the chronicle Shakespeare draws the political moral from Richard's rule in the garden scene (Act III. sc. 4) with its simple allegory. The wise gardener cares to give 'supportance to the bending twigs, which like unruly children make their sire stoop with oppression of their prodigal weight' [III. iv. 30-2]; he cuts off the heads of too fast-growing sprays, that look too lofty on the commonwealth; he roots up the noisome weed. Richard, who had not observed the first of these rules in his jealousy of Gloster, who had neglected the second in his too great favour to Bolingbroke, and the third in his too great kindness to his parasites, Bagot and Bushy, now sees the fall of the leaves.... Had he cherished and nurtured his kingdom as the gardeners did their garden, he would have treated the great as they did their trees, wounding the bark at times to prevent the too luxuriant growth; he would have lopped away the superfluous branches, and thus he might have tasted and enjoyed their fruits and retained his crown.

Instead of this he did everything which could forfeit his crown. We have seen the king's unadvised conduct in the quarrel between Bolingbroke and Norfolk. Hardly is this dispute settled than the old Gaunt dies: the Irish revolt demands a remedy; the extravagant prince has no money; he now seizes the Lancastrian property, which kindles even the good-natured York, indolent and rest-loving as he is. Richard goes in person to Ireland, and leaves behind him the irritated York, the weakest whom he could choose, as governor of England. Instantly the banished Bolingbroke seizes the occasion to return to the kingdom thus vacated, under the pretext of taking possession of his lawful inheritance. The apprehensive nobles, the Percys, join themselves to him; the miserable friends of the king give up their cause at once as lost; the helpless York goes over. When Richard returns from Ireland he possesses no more of the kingdom than his right to it. He persuades himself, though he is far from convinced of it, that with this right he has everything. He comes back from Ireland conscience-stricken, foreboding, paralysed, and inactive. With his wonted enthusiasm, when he again sets foot on English ground, he hopes that the 'earth shall have a feeling, and the stones prove armed soldiers, ere her native king shall falter under foul rebellious arms' [III. ii. 24-6]. He buries himself in poetical and religious consolation, and intrenches himself behind his divine right and authority. . . . Then suddenly his confidence in his good right forsakes him. He calls upon his name and his majesty, but on a new message of misfortune his courage breaks down even to abdication. Once more subsequently he asserts to Northumberland his divine right, and declares that no human hand can seize his sacred sceptre without robbery and violence. But the blessing of Heaven is now visibly on the side of power; he whom the people uphold stands more surely than the anointed of God.

Shakespeare writes here an immortal lesson upon the royalty of God's grace and the law of inviolability. His ground is here also that two-sided one of entire impartiality and candour to which we unweariedly point, as to the greatest characteristic of his extraordinary mental superiority. He places his opinion chiefly in the mouth of the Bishop of Carlisle, the grand type of genuine loyalty, who stands faithfully by the side of the lawful king, without concealing from him the stern voice of truth; who defies the unlawful usurper in the public assembly, but still who elicits, even from the latter, true honour, favour, and esteem. Absorbed in his meditations upon show and reality, upon which we see Shakespeare brooding throughout this period of his life, he cannot regard the halo of divine right as the characteristic of royalty. No inviolability can protect the anointed head if it render itself unworthy of the divine possession; no legitimacy and no balm can absolve the ruler from his duties to the land of his care! Every vocation would appear to our poet of God, and with the vocation every duty. The fulfilment of duty is even the king's first condition of stability; by his neglect of it he forfeits possession and right; by this he loses himself, his inner dignity, his consecration, and his power. Thus Henry IV. distinctly tells his son that, unbridled and self-forgetful as he then was, he was only 'the shadow of succession' [*I Henry IV*, III. ii. 99]; that the honourable Percy, though a rebel, deserved rather to be the heir. Dutiful illegality is compared with duty-forgetting legitimacy, and is placed above it by the man who had once elevated himself by it, and who would now secure his legality by the fulfilment of duty. . . . The peculiar right of the king is not esteemed by Shakespeare more sacred than any other; these views took deeper root in England from the period of Shakespeare and the Dutch Republic, till Milton, in his 'Defensio pro Populo,' enforced them with marked emphasis. As soon as Richard had touched the inheritance of Lancaster, he had placed in his hands, as it were,

the right of retaliation. The indolent York thus speaks to him immediately:—

> Take from time his rights; . . .
> Let not *to-morrow* then ensue to-day;
> Be not thyself, for how art thou a king,
> But by fair sequence and succession?
> [II. i. 195, 197-99]

He tells him that he 'plucks a thousand dangers on his head,' that he loses 'a thousand well-disposed hearts,' and that he 'pricks his tender patience to those thoughts, which honour and allegiance cannot think' [II. i. 205-08]. (pp. 284-89).

The poet, who has not allowed us fully to know the young king in his prosperity, unfolds his character the more fascinatingly and minutely in his misfortune. As soon as with Bolingbroke's landing the turning point in his fortune arrived, at the very conjuncture at which we should have wished to see the powerful ruler, there stands conspicuously before us the kindly human nature, which was before obscured in prosperity and mirth, but which even now is accompanied by weakness and want of stability, the distinguishing feature of his character. He has always needed props, and strong props he has not endured; he had sought them in climbing plants, which had pulled himself to the ground; Gaunt and Norfolk he had alienated. For this reason at the first moment of misfortune he falls past recovery. As soon as the first intelligence of the defection of his people arrives he is pale and disheartened; at the second message, which threatens him with a new evil, he is submissive, and ready for abdication and death. When Aumerle reminds him of his father York he rouses himself once more, but as soon as he hears that even this last prop is broken, he curses his cousin for having led him forth 'of that sweet way he was in to despair' [III. ii. 205]; he renounces every comfort, every act; he orders his troops to be discharged; capable of no further effort he will be reminded of none, and himself removes every temptation to it. A highly poetic brilliancy is cast upon the scenes of the humiliation and ruin of the romantic youth, whose fancy rises in sorrow and misfortune to a height which allows us to infer the strength of the intoxication with which he had before plunged into pleasure. The power which at that time had carried him beyond himself, turns now with fearful force within, and the pleasure-loving man now finds enjoyment in suffering and sorrow, and a sweetness in despair. . . . At the very first, in the beginning of his sufferings, he broods upon thoughts of graves and death; he wishes to let the fate of all fallen kings pass before his mind, and then (as if the words of the dying Gaunt were in his thoughts, when he said to him that a 'thousand flatterers' [II. i. 100] sit within the small compass of his crown, wasting the land) he pictures to himself the image of the crown in sad contrast to his present position, as if within its hollow temples the antic Death kept his court, allowing the wearer of the crown 'a breath, a little scene to monarchise' [III. ii. 164-65]. When he afterwards appears before his enemies (Act III. sc. 3), a paroxysm of his kingly fancy exhibits him to the sneaking Northumberland with a show of power; indeed, this was now the moment for arresting with dignity and courage the yet undefined plot. But before Bolingbroke had declared his intentions—at a time when, even in the presence of the weak York, no one might omit the royal title before Richard's name without apology—suddenly and without any cause his wings hang wearied, and he himself speaks of the subjection of the king; and, as he sees Aumerle weep, his lively fancy at once runs away with him to the borders of insanity: his words remind us in these scenes of the passionate melancholy of Lear which is the prelude to his madness. He asks whether they shall 'play the wantons with their woes, and make some pretty match with shedding tears? as thus;— to drop them still upon one place, till they have fretted a pair of graves' [III. iii. 164-68]. Even here, it seems, we cannot help looking back shudderingly from all this wretchedness and misery to that vain intercourse and waste of time in which Richard formerly lived with his companions. The play on words and the conceits in these scenes have been censured as inappropriate, but nowhere are they inserted with so deep and true a purpose; those whose whole intercourse consisted formerly in raillery and quibbling, naturally speculate immoderately in such a position, and delight in exhausting an idea aroused by the force of circumstances. Richard remembers that he is talking but idly, and remarks that they mock at him; the worst is that Northumberland has heard his foolish words, and designates him to Bolingbroke as a frantic man. That which the rebels would not have ventured to demand, the childish man, whom the feeling of being forsaken has quite cast down, offers of himself to them; he himself first designates the danger which surrounds him, when in his half-insane words he calls Northumberland prince and Bolingbroke king; in the ears of all he gives himself and his inheritance into Bolingbroke's hands, even before any one had asked it. In the scene also of the deposition, which accords excellently with the nature of the king and is the crowning point of the characterisation, we hear him giving vent to beautiful poetic images upon his misfortune, and we see him burying himself in his sorrow with a kind of pleasure. He pictures to himself, as in a drama, the scene over which another would have passed quickly. Only when he is subjected to the indignity of reading his own indictment does his proud nature once again break out, and he perceives too late how miserably he had become a traitor to himself. Later too, when we see Richard on the way to prison and in prison, even in his resignation he is ever employed in picturing his painful condition to himself as still more painful; revelling, as it were, in his sorrow, and emptying the cup to the very dregs. He peoples the little space of his prison with his wild fancy, he studies how he may compare it to the world. An air of music drives him to reflect how he has here 'the daintiness of ear to check time broke in a disordered string,' whilst 'for the concord of his state and time he had no ear to hear his true time broke' [V. v. 45-8]. He wasted time, which now wastes him; and thus again in another melancholy simile he pictures himself as a clock, which time had made out of himself. It is wise of the poet that out of the different stories of Richard's death he chose that which exhibits him to us at the end in honourable strength, after having allowed us also to perceive the attractive power of his amiability; it is therefore not without esteem that we take our leave of the commiserated man. (pp. 290-93)

The group of characters in *Richard II*. is arranged very simply. . . . In contrast to the incapable legitimate king and his helpless inactive followers stands the rising star of the thorough statesman-like and royal usurper and his over-active adherents. In the midst of the struggle between right and merit stands Carlisle, as a man of genuine loyalty, knowing no motive but fidelity and duty, not concealing the truth from the lawful king, and ruining himself in opposing unsparingly the shield of right against the usurper who raises himself to power. Contrasted with him is the old York. . . . The true picture of such an agitated age would be wanting if this character were absent. He is the type of political faintheartedness and neutrality, at a time when partisanship is a duty, and that of cowardly loyalty which turns to the strong and powerful. When Richard is still in his full power, he considers he has gone too far in extolling

to the young king the virtues of his father. When Richard seizes the Lancastrian lands, his natural sense of right, and his anxiety respecting his own property, urge him to utter impressive warnings, but when the king makes him as a 'just' man his governor in England, he allows himself to be appeased. Bolingbroke lands, and York sees through his project, and warns him not to take what he should not; his integrity even here shows him the path which his weakness suffers him not to follow. He would like to serve the king and to discharge his duty to his lord, but he thinks he has also a duty of kinship and conscience respecting Bolingbroke's lawful claims to his inheritance. That he stood for the moment in the place of the king he heeds not. Helpless as to action, he loses his head in unutterable perplexity, but not his character. He resolves to remain neutral. He sees the finger of God in the desertion of the people, and lets it be; for Richard he has tears, few words, and no deeds. With loyalty such as this countries go to ruin, while they prosper at usurpations such as Bolingbroke's. But that this weakness of the weak can amount to a degree in which it becomes the most unnatural obduracy, and in which the cruelty of the usurper is guiltless when compared with it, has been displayed by Shakespeare in a truly masterly manner when he suffers York to accuse his own son of high treason and to urge his death with pertinacity. He goes so far as to wish that the king may 'ill thrive, if he grant any grace' [V. iii. 99]. In this trait conscientiousness and fidelity are mingled indistinguishably with the fear of exposure and suspicion. Such is servile loyalty; under the rule of the weak it is weak, and affords but a frail support; under that of the strong it is strong, and is an efficient and trustworthy power. (pp. 296-97)

G. G. Gervinus, "'Richard II'," in his Shakespeare Commentaries, *translated by F. E. Bunnètt, revised edition, 1877. Reprint by AMS Press, Inc., 1971, pp. 279-97.*

EDWARD DOWDEN   (essay date 1881)

[*Dowden was an Irish critic and biographer whose* Shakspere: A Critical Study of His Mind and Art, *first published in 1875 and revised in 1881, was the leading example of the biographical criticism popular in the English-speaking world near the end of the nineteenth century. Biographical critics sought in the plays and poems a record of Shakespeare's personal development. As that approach gave way in the twentieth century to aesthetic theories with greater emphasis on the constructed, formal nature of literary works, the biographical analysis of Dowden and other critics came to be regarded as limited and often misleading. The following excerpt is taken from one of the seminal studies of* Richard II *written in the nineteenth century. In it, Dowden describes the king as a stunted, disengaged individual, "an amateur in living"—who dissipates his vital energies in fruitless fantasizing and who affects the appropriate image rather than acts in critical situations. According to Dowden, this "boyish" Richard, abandoned to self-indulgence and trapped in a world of his own making, having "a kind of artistic relation to life, without being an artist," essentially never grows up. The critic also questions whether Richard "earnestly" repents and morally redeems himself after "his humiliation as a king," concluding that the man "in prison remains the same person as [that] on the throne." Critics regard Dowden's recognition of Richard's histrionic tendencies—his habit of play-acting even in moments of peril or crisis—as a major contribution to our understanding of his character.*]

The play of *King Richard II*. possesses none of the titanic stormy force which breathes through *King Richard III*., but in delicate cunning in the rendering of character it excels the more popular play. The two principal figures in *King Richard II.*, that of the king who fell, and that of the king who rose—the usurping Bolingbroke—grow before us insensibly through a series of fine and characteristic strokes. They do not, like the figures in *King Richard III.*, forcibly possess themselves of our imagination, but engage it before it is aware, and by degrees advance stronger claims upon us, and make good those claims. It will be worth while to try to ascertain what Shakspere looked upon as most significant in the characters of these two royal persons—the weak king who could not rule, and the strong king who pressed him from his place.

There is a condition of the intellect which we describe by the word "boyishness." The mind in the boyish stage of growth "has no discriminating convictions and no grasp of consequences." It has not as yet got hold of realities; it is "merely dazzled by phenomena, instead of perceiving things as they are." The talk of a person who remains in this sense boyish is often clever, but it is unreal; now he will say brilliant things upon this side of a question, and now upon the opposite side. He has no consistency of view. He is wanting as yet in seriousness of intellect, in the adult mind [as stated by John Henry Newman in his *The Idea of a University*]. Now, if we extend this characteristic of boyishness from the intellect to the entire character, we may understand much of what Shakspere meant to represent in the person of Richard II. Not alone his intellect, but his feelings, live in the world of phenomena, and altogether fail to lay hold of things as they are; they have no consistency and no continuity. His will is entirely unformed; it possesses no authority and no executive power; he is at the mercy of every chance impulse and transitory mood. He has a kind of artistic relation to life, without being an artist. An artist in life seizes upon the stuff of circumstance, and, with strenuous will and strong creative power, shapes some new and noble form of human existence.

Richard, to whom all things are unreal, has a fine feeling for "situations." Without true kingly strength or dignity, he has a fine feeling for the royal situation. Without any making real to himself what God or what death is, he can put himself, if need be, in the appropriate attitude towards God and towards death. Instead of comprehending things as they are, and achieving heroic deeds, he satiates his heart with the grace, the tenderness, the beauty, or the pathos of situations. Life is to Richard a show, a succession of images; and to put himself into accord with the aesthetic requirements of his position is Richard's first necessity. He is equal to playing any part gracefully which he is called upon by circumstances to enact. But when he has exhausted the aesthetic satisfaction to be derived from the situations of his life, he is left with nothing further to do. He is an amateur in living; not an artist.

Nothing had disturbed the graceful dream of Richard's adolescence. The son of the Black Prince, beautiful in face and form, though now past his youth, a king since boyhood, he has known no antagonism of men or circumstance which might arouse the will. He has an indescribable charm of person and presence; Hotspur remembers him as "Richard, that sweet, lovely rose" [*1 Henry IV*, I. iii. 175]. But a king who rules discontented people and turbulent nobles needs to be something more than a beautiful blossoming flower. Richard has abandoned his nature to self-indulgence, and therefore the world becomes to him more unreal than ever. He has been surrounded by flatterers, who helped to make his atmosphere a luminous mist, through which the facts of life appeared with all their ragged outlines smoothed away. In the first scene of the play

he enacts the part of a king with a fine show of dignity; his bearing is splendid and irreproachable. Mowbray is obstinate, and will not throw down the gage of Bolingbroke; Richard exclaims,

> Rage must be withstood.
> Give me his gage: lions make leopards tame.
> [I. i. 173-74]

But Mowbray retains the gage. "We were not born to sue, but to command" [I. i. 196], declares Richard, with royal majesty; yet he admits that to command exceeds his power. What of that? Has not Richard borne himself splendidly, and uttered himself in a royal metaphor—"Lions make leopards tame?"

At this very moment Bolingbroke, with eye set upon his purpose afar off, has resolutely taken the first step towards attaining it. The challenge of Mowbray conceals a deeper purpose. So little does Bolingbroke really feel of hostility to his antagonist that one of his first acts, as soon as he is in a position to act with authority, is to declare Mowbray's repeal. But to stand forward as champion of the wrongs of England, to make himself the eminent justiciary by right of nature, this is the initial step towards future kingship; and Bolingbroke perceives clearly that the fact of Gloster's death may serve as fulcrum for the lever which is to shake the throne of England. Nor is the King quite insensible of the tendency of his cousin's action. Already he begins to quail before his bold antagonist:

> How high a pitch his resolution soars!
> [I. i. 109]

Richard tries gracefully to conceal his discomposure, and to deceive Bolingbroke; but he is not, like Richard the hunchback, a daring and efficient hypocrite. He betrays his weakness and his distrust, administering to the two men decreed to exile an oath which pledges them never to reconcile themselves in their banishment, and never to plot against the King.

Bolingbroke accepts his exile, parts from the English crowd with an air of gracious, condescending familiarity which flatters (whereas Richard's undignified familiarity only displeases), and bids farewell to his country as a son bids farewell to the mother with whom his natural loyalty remains, and whom, in due time, he will see again. John of Gaunt is lying on his death-bed. The last of the great race of the time of Edward III., no English spirit will breathe such patriotism as his until the days of Agincourt. With the prophetic inspiration of a dying man, he dares to warn his grand-nephew, and to rebuke him for his treason against the ancient honor of England. Richard, who, with his characteristic sensibility of a superficial kind, turns pale as he listens, recovers himself by a transition from overawed alarm to boyish insolence. The white-haired warrior, now a prophet, who lies dying before him, is

> A lunatic, lean-witted fool,
> Presuming on an ague's privilege,
> [II. i. 115-16]

who dares, with a frozen admonition, to make pale the royal cheek of Richard. The facts are very disagreeable, and why should a king admit into his consciousness an ugly or disagreeable fact?

By-and-by, being informed that John of Gaunt is dead, Richard has the most graceful and appropriate word ready for so solemn an occasion:

> The ripest fruit first falls, and so doth he;
> His time is spent, our pilgrimage must be.
> [II. i. 153-54]

In which pilgrimage the first step is to seize upon

> The plate, coin, revenues, and movables,
> Whereof our uncle Gaunt did stand possess'd.
>
> [II. i. 161-62]

Even York, the temporizing York, who would fain be all things to all men if by any means he might save himself, is amazed, and ventures to remonstrate against the criminal folly of this act. But Richard, like all self-indulgent natures, has only a half-belief in any possible future. He chooses to make the present time easy, and let the future provide for itself; he has been living upon chances too long; he has too long been mortgaging the health of to-morrow for the pleasure of to-day:

> Think what you will, we seize into our hands
> His plate, his goods, his money, and his lands.
>
> [II. i. 209-10]

But now the tempest begins to sing. Bolingbroke (before he can possibly have heard of his father's death and the seizure by Richard of his own rights and royalties) has equipped an expedition, and is about to land upon the English coast. The King makes a hasty return from his "military promenade" in Ireland. The first words of each, as he touches his native soil, are characteristic, and were doubtless placed by Shakspere in designed contrast. *"How far is it, my lord, to Berkeley now?"* [II. iii. 1]. The banished man has no tender phrases to bestow upon English earth, now that he sets foot upon it once more. All his faculties are firm-set, and bent upon achievement. But Richard, who has been absent for a few days in Ireland, enters with all possible zeal into the sentiment of his situation:

> I weep for joy
> To stand upon my kingdom once again.
> Dear earth, I do salute thee with my hand,
> Though rebels wound thee with their horses's hoofs;
> As a long-parted mother with her child
> Plays fondly with her tears and smiles in meeting,
> So weeping, smiling, greet I thee, my earth,
> And do thee favors with my royal hands.
>
> [III. ii. 4-11]

Which sentimental favors form a graceful incident in the play of Richard's life, but can hardly compensate the want of true and manly patriotism. This same earth which Richard caressed with extravagant sensibility was the England which John of Gaunt, with strong enthusiasm, had apostrophized:

> This blessed plot, this earth, this realm, this England,
> This nurse, this teeming womb of royal kings,
> Fear'd by their breed, and famous for their birth,
> Renowned for their deeds.
>
> [II. i. 50-3]

It was the England which Richard had alienated from himself and leased out "like to a tenement or pelting farm" [II. i. 60]. What of that, however? Did not Richard address his England with phrases full of tender sensibility, and render her mockery favors with his royal hands?

Bolingbroke has already gained the support of the Welsh. Richard has upon his side powers higher than natural flesh and blood. Shall he not rise like the sun in the eastern sky, and with the majesty of his royal apparition scare away the treasons of the night? Is he not the anointed deputy of God?

> Not all the water in the rough rude sea
> Can wash the balm from an anointed king:
> The breath of worldly men cannot depose
> The deputy elected by the Lord.
>
> [III. ii. 54-7]

Yes; he will rely on God; it is devout; it is not laborious. For every armed man who fights for Bolingbroke,

> God for his Richard hath in heavenly pay
> A glorious angel.
>
> [III. i. 60-1]

And at this moment Salisbury enters to announce the revolt of Wales. Richard has been slack in action, and arrived a day too late. Remorseless comment upon the rhetorical piety of the King! A company of angels fight upon his side; true, but the sturdy Welshmen stand for Bolingbroke! He is the deputy elected by the Lord; but the Lord's deputy has arrived a day too late!

And now Richard alternates between abject despondency (relieved by accepting all the aesthetic satisfaction derivable from the situation of vanquished king) and an airy, unreal confidence. There is in Richard, as Coleridge has finely observed, "a constant overflow of emotions from a total incapability of controlling them, and thence a waste of that energy, which should have been reserved for actions, in the passion and effort of mere resolves and menaces. The consequence is moral exhaustion and rapid alternations of unmanly despair and ungrounded hope, every feeling being abandoned for its direct opposite upon the pressure of external accident" [see excerpt above, 1834]. A certain unreality infects every motion of Richard; his feelings are but the shadows of true feeling. Now he will be great and a king; now what matters it to lose a kingdom? If Bolingbroke and he alike serve God, Bolingbroke can be no more than his fellow-servant. Now he plays the wanton with his pride, and now with his misery:

> Of comfort no man speak:
> Let's talk of graves, of worms and epitaphs; . . .
> For God's sake, let us sit upon the ground
> And tell sad stories of the death of kings.
>
> [III. ii. 144-45, 155-56]

At one moment he pictures God mustering armies of pestilence in his clouds to strike the usurper and his descendants; in the next he yields to Bolingbroke's demands, and welcomes his "right noble cousin" [III. iii. 122]. He is proud, and he is pious; he is courageous and cowardly; and pride and piety, cowardice and courage, are all the passions of a dream.

Yet Shakspere has thrown over the figure of Richard a certain atmosphere of charm. If only the world were not a real world, to which serious hearts are due, we could find in Richard some wavering, vague attraction. There is a certain wistfulness about him; without any genuine kingly power, he has a feeling for what kingly power must be; without any veritable religion, he has a pale shadow of religiosity. And few of us have ourselves wholly escaped from unreality. "It takes a long time really to feel and understand things as they are; we learn to do so only gradually" [Newman]. Into what glimmering limbo will such a soul as that of Richard pass when the breath leaves the body? The pains of hell and the joys of heaven belong to those who have serious hearts. Richard has been a graceful phantom. Is there some tenuous, unsubstantial world of spirits reserved for the sentimentalist, the dreamer, and the dilettante? Richard is, as it were, fading out of existence. Bolingbroke seems not only to have robbed him of his authority, but to have encroached upon his very personality, and to have usurped his understanding and his will. Richard is discovering that he is no more than a shadow; but the discovery itself has something unreal and shadowy about it. Is not some such fact as this symbolized by the incident of the mirror? Before he quite ceases to be king, Richard, with his taste for "pseudo-poetic pathos," would once

RICHARD II   *SHAKESPEAREAN CRITICISM, Vol. 6*

more look upon the image of his face, and see what wrinkles have been traced upon it by sorrow. And Bolingbroke, suppressing his inward feeling of disdain, directs that the mirror be brought. Richard gazes against it, and finds that sorrow has wrought no change upon the beautiful lips and forehead. And then, exclaiming,

> A brittle glory shineth in this face,
> As brittle as the glory is the face,
>
> [IV. i. 287-88]

he dashes the glass against the ground.

> For there it is crack'd in a hundred shivers,
> Mark, silent king, the moral of this sport,
> How soon my sorrow hath destroy'd my face.
>   *Boling.* The shadow of your sorrow hath destroy'd
> The shadow of your face.
>   *K. Rich.*   Say that again.
> The shadow of my sorrow! ha! let's see.
>
> [IV. i. 289-94]

Does Richard . . . rise morally from his humiliation as a king? Is he heartily sorry for his misdoings? While drinking the wine and eating the bread of sorrow, does he truly and earnestly repent, and intend to lead a new life? The habit of his nature

Act V. Scene v. Richard II, Exton, the Keeper, and servants. Frontispiece to the Rowe edition (1709). By permission of the Folger Shakespeare Library.

is not so quickly unlearned. Richard in prison remains the same person as Richard on the throne. Calamity is no more real to him now than prosperity had been in brighter days. The soliloquy of Richard in Pomfret Castle (act v., sc. 5) might almost be transferred, as far as tone and manner are concerned, to one other personage in Shakspere's plays—to Jaques [in *As You Like It*]. The curious intellect of Jaques gives him his distinction. He plays his parts for the sake of understanding the world in his way of superficial fool's-wisdom. Richard plays his parts to possess himself of the aesthetic satisfaction of an amateur in life, with a fine feeling for situations. But each lives in the world of shadow, in the world of mockery wisdom or the world of mockery passion. (pp. 171-81)

Yet to the last a little of real love is reserved by one heart or two for the shadowy, attractive Richard: the love of a wife who is filled with a piteous sense of her husband's mental and moral effacement, seeing her "fair rose wither," [V. i. 8], and the love of a groom whose loyalty to his master is associated with loyalty to his master's horse, roan Barbary. This incident of roan Barbary is an invention of the poet. Did Shakspere intend only a little bit of helpless pathos? Or is there a touch of hidden irony here? A poor spark of affection remains for Richard, but it has been kindled half by Richard, and half by Richard's horse. The fancy of the fallen king disports itself for the last time, and hangs its latest wreath around this incident. Then suddenly comes the darkness. Suddenly the hectic passion of Richard flares; he snatches an axe from a servant, and deals about him deadly blows. In another moment he is extinct; the graceful, futile existence has ceased. (p. 181)

>   Edward Dowden, "The English Historical Plays,"
>   in his Shakspere: A Critical Study of His Mind and
>   Art, third edition, Harper & Brothers Publishers,
>   1881, pp. 144-97.

WALTER PATER   (essay date 1889)

[*A nineteenth-century essayist, novelist, and fictional portrait writer, Pater is one of the most famous proponents of aestheticism in English literature. Distinguished as the first major English writer to formulate an explicitly aesthetic philosophy, he advocated the "love of art for art's sake" as life's greatest offering—an artistic creed discernible in the essays collected in his* Studies in the History of the Renaissance *(1873) and* Appreciations *(1889). Pater is also recognized as a master prose stylist and a leading exemplar of impressionist criticism. In his discussion of* Richard II *excerpted below, Pater discusses Richard's "eloquence"—his "exquisite," lyrical verse—claiming that its cumulative effect is like a musical composition, contributing a sense of unity to the play. Nevertheless, Pater admits, Richard's eloquence is merely a facet of his "fatal beauty" and cannot save him from catastrophe. In the critic's view, irony saturates* Richard II, *as it does all Shakespeare's English histories, for the king is not heroic, but rather an average human being caught up in great events. The irony of Richard's plight is most strikingly presented in the abdication scene (IV. i.), which—as Pater writes in a celebrated passage—takes the form of an "inverted" coronation rite.*]

> A brittle glory shineth in this face:
> As brittle as the glory is the face.
>
> [IV. i. 287-88]

The English plays of Shakespeare needed but the completion of one unimportant interval to possess the unity of a popular chronicle from Richard the Second to Henry the Eighth, and possess, as they actually stand, the unity of a common motive in the handling of the various events and persons which they bring before us. Certain of his historic dramas, not English, display Shakespeare's mastery in the development of the heroic nature amid heroic circumstances; and had he chosen, from English history, to deal with Cœur-de-Lion or Edward the First, the innate quality of his subject would doubtless have called into play something of that profound and sombre power which in *Julius Cæsar* and *Macbeth* has sounded the depths of mighty character. True, on the whole, to fact, it is another side of kingship which he has made prominent in his English histories. The irony of kingship—average human nature, flung with a wonderfully pathetic effect into the vortex of great events; tragedy of everyday quality heightened in degree only by the conspicuous scene which does but make those who play their parts there conspicuously unfortunate; the utterance of common humanity straight from the heart, but refined like other common things for kingly uses by Shakespeare's unfailing eloquence: such, unconsciously for the most part, though palpably enough to the careful reader, is the conception under which Shakespeare has arranged the lights and shadows of the story of the English kings, emphasising merely the light and shadow inherent in it, and keeping very close to the original authorities, not simply in the general outline of these dramatic histories but sometimes in their very expression. (pp. 185-86)

One gracious prerogative, certainly, Shakespeare's English kings possess: they are a very eloquent company, and Richard is the most sweet-tongued of them all. In no other play perhaps is there such a flush of those gay, fresh, variegated flowers of speech—colour and figure, not lightly attached to, but fused into, the very phrase itself—which Shakespeare cannot help dispensing to his characters, as in this "play of the Deposing of King Richard the Second," an exquisite poet if he is nothing else, from first to last, in light and gloom alike, able to see all things poetically, to give a poetic turn to his conduct of them, and refreshing with his golden language the tritest aspects of that ironic contrast between the pretensions of a king and the actual necessities of his destiny. What a garden of words! With him, blank verse, infinitely graceful, deliberate, musical in inflexion, becomes indeed a true "verse royal," that rhyming lapse, which to the Shakespearian ear, at least in youth, came as the last touch of refinement on it, being here doubly appropriate. His eloquence blends with that fatal beauty, of which he was so frankly aware, so amiable to his friends, to his wife, of the effects of which on the people his enemies were so much afraid, on which Shakespeare himself dwells so attentively as the "royal blood" [II. i. 118] comes and goes in the face with his rapid changes of temper. . . . [It] blends with his merely youthful hopefulness and high spirits, his sympathetic love for gay people, things, apparel—"his cote of gold and stone, valued at thirty thousand marks," the novel Italian fashions he preferred, as also with those real amiabilities that made people forget the darker touches of his character, but never tire of the pathetic rehearsal of his fall, the meekness of which would have seemed merely abject in a less graceful performer. (pp. 193-95)

Strangely enough, Shakespeare supposes [Richard] an overconfident believer in that divine right of kings, of which people in Shakespeare's time were coming to hear so much; a general right, sealed to him (so Richard is made to think) as an ineradicable personal gift by the touch—stream rather, over head and breast and shoulders—of the "holy oil" of his consecration at Westminster; not, however, through some oversight, the genuine balm used at the coronation of his successor, given, according to legend, by the Blessed Virgin to Saint Thomas of Canterbury. Richard himself found that, it was said, among other forgotten treasures, at the crisis of his changing fortunes,

and vainly sought reconsecration therewith—understood, wistfully, that it was reserved for his happier rival. And yet his coronation, by the pageantry, the amplitude, the learned care, of its order, so lengthy that the king, then only eleven years of age, and fasting, as a communicant at the ceremony, was carried away in a faint, fixed the type under which it has ever since continued. And nowhere is there so emphatic a reiteration as in *Richard the Second* of the sentiment which those singular rites were calculated to produce.

> Not all the water in the rough rude sea
> Can wash the balm from an anointed king,—
>
> [III. ii. 54-5]

as supplementing another, almost supernatural, right.—"Edward's seven sons," of whom Richard's father was one,

> Were as seven phials of his sacred blood.
>
> [I. ii. 12]

But this, too, in the hands of Shakespeare, becomes for him, like any other of those fantastic, ineffectual, easily discredited, personal graces, as capricious in its operation on men's wills as merely physical beauty, kindling himself to eloquence indeed, but only giving double pathos to insults which "barbarism itself" [V. ii. 36] might have pitied—the dust in his face, as he returns, through the streets of London, a prisoner in the train of his victorious enemy.

> How soon my sorrow hath destroyed my face!
>
> [IV. i. 291]

he cries, in that most poetic invention of the mirror scene, which does but reinforce again that physical charm which all confessed. The sense of "divine right" in kings is found to act not so much as a secret of power over others, as of infatuation to themselves. And of all those personal gifts the one which alone never altogether fails him is just that royal utterance, his appreciation of the poetry of his own hapless lot, an eloquent self-pity, infecting others in spite of themselves, till they too become irresistibly eloquent about him.

In the Roman Pontifical, of which the order of Coronation is really a part, there is no form for the inverse process, no rite of "degradation," such as that by which an offending priest or bishop may be deprived, if not of the essential quality of "orders," yet, one by one, of its outward dignities. It is as if Shakespeare had had in mind some such inverted rite, like those old ecclesiastical or military ones, by which human hardness, or human justice, adds the last touch of unkindness to the execution of its sentences, in the scene where Richard "deposes" himself, as in some long, agonising ceremony, reflectively drawn out, with an extraordinary refinement of intelligence and variety of piteous appeal, but also with a felicity of poetic invention, which puts these pages into a very select class, with the finest "vermeil and ivory" work of Chatterton or Keats.

> Fetch hither Richard that in common view
> He may surrender!—
>
> [IV. i. 155-56]

And Richard more than concurs: he throws himself into the part, realises a type, falls gracefully as on the world's stage.— Why is he sent for?

> To do that office of thine own good will
> Which tired majesty did make thee offer. . . .
> Now mark me! how I will undo myself.
>
> [IV. i. 177-78, 203]
>
> (pp. 196-98)

Yet at least within the poetic bounds of Shakespeare's play, through Shakespeare's bountiful gifts, his desire seems fulfilled.—

>   O! that I were as great
>   As is my grief.
>
>   [III. iii. 136-37]

And his grief becomes nothing less than a central expression of all that in the revolutions of Fortune's wheel goes *down* in the world.

No! Shakespeare's kings are not, nor are meant to be, great men: rather, little or quite ordinary humanity, thrust upon greatness, with those pathetic results, the natural self-pity of the weak heightened in them into irresistible appeal to others as the net result of their royal prerogative. One after another, they seem to lie composed in Shakespeare's embalming pages, with just that touch of nature about them, making the whole world akin, which has infused into their tombs at Westminster a rare poetic grace. It is that irony of kingship, the sense that it is in its happiness child's play, in its sorrows, after all, but children's grief, which gives its finer accent to all the changeful feeling of these wonderful speeches:—the great meekness of the graceful, wild creature, tamed at last.—

>   Give Richard leave to live till Richard die
>
>   [III. iii. 174]

his somewhat abject fear of death, turning to acquiescence at moments of extreme weariness:—

>   My large kingdom for a little grave!
>   A little little grave, an obscure grave!—
>
>   [III. iii. 153-54]

his religious appeal in the last reserve, with its bold reference to the judgment of Pilate, as he thinks once more of his "anointing."

And as happens with children he attains contentment finally in the merely passive recognition of superior strength, in the naturalness of the result of the great battle as a matter of course, and experiences something of the royal prerogative of poetry to obscure, or at least to attune and soften men's griefs. As in some sweet anthem of Handel, the sufferer, who put finger to the organ under the utmost pressure of mental conflict, extracts a kind of peace at last from the mere skill with which he sets his distress to music.—

>   Beshrew thee, Cousin, that didst lead me forth
>   Of that sweet way I was in to despair!
>
>   [III. ii. 204-05]
>   (pp. 199-200)

[In] fact, the play of *Richard the Second* does, like a musical composition, possess a certain concentration of all its parts, a simple continuity, an evenness in execution, which are rare in the great dramatist. With *Romeo and Juliet . . .* , it belongs to a small group of plays, where, by happy birth and consistent evolution, dramatic form approaches to something like the unity of a lyrical ballad, a lyric, a song, a single strain of music. Which sort of poetry we are to account the highest, is perhaps a barren question. Yet if, in art generally, unity of impression is a note of what is perfect, then lyric poetry, which in spite of complex structure often preserves the unity of a single passionate ejaculation, would rank higher than dramatic poetry, where, especially to the reader, as distinguished from the spectator assisting at a theatrical performance, there must always be a sense of the effort necessary to keep the various parts

from flying asunder, a sense of imperfect continuity, such as the older criticism vainly sought to obviate by the rule of the dramatic "unities." It follows that a play attains artistic perfection just in proportion as it approaches that unity of lyrical effect, as if a song or ballad were still lying at the root of it, all the various expression of the conflict of character and circumstance falling at last into the compass of a single melody, or musical theme. As, historically, the earliest classic drama arose out of the chorus, from which this or that person, this or that episode, detached itself, so, into the unity of a choric song the perfect drama ever tends to return, its intellectual scope deepened, complicated, enlarged, but still with an unmistakable singleness, or identity, in its impression on the mind. Just there, in that vivid single impression left on the mind when all is over, not in any mechanical limitation of time and place, is the secret of the "unities"—the true imaginative unity—of the drama. (pp. 202-04)

Walter Pater, "Shakespeare's English Kings," in his Appreciations: With an Essay on Style, *1889. Reprint by Macmillan and Co., Limited, 1910, pp. 185-204.*

DENTON J. SNIDER   (essay date 1890)

[*Snider was an American scholar, philosopher, and poet who closely followed the precepts of the German philosopher Georg Wilhelm Friedrich Hegel and contributed greatly to the dissemination of his dialectical philosophy in America. Snider's critical writings include studies on Homer, Dante, and Goethe, as well as Shakespeare. Like Hermann Ulrici and G. G. Gervinus, Snider sought the dramatic unity and ethical import in Shakespeare's plays, but he adopted a more rigorous Hegelian approach than either of these philosophical critics. In the introduction to his three-volume work,* The Shakespearean Drama: A Commentary *(1887-90), Snider states that Shakespeare's plays present various ethical principles which, in their differences, come into "Dramatic Collision," but are ultimately resolved and brought into harmony. He claims that these collisions can be traced in the plays' various "Dramatic Threads" of action and thought, which together form a "Dramatic Movement," and that the analysis of these threads and movements—"the structural elements of the drama"—reveals the organic unity of Shakespeare's art. Snider observes two basic movements in the tragedies—guilt and retribution—and three in the comedies—separation, mediation, and return. Guilt and retribution are clearly traceable elements in Snider's analysis of* Richard II, *but for him the play's "fundamental theme is the right of revolution." Although crediting Shakespeare with a balanced presentation of each side of the argument, depicting the dangers in both the king's failure to govern and Bolingbroke's usurpation, Snider focuses primarily on Richard, concluding that the monarch's downfall is the necessary consequence of his political naïveté and disregard for law. Snider further contrasts the king and his chief adversary: Richard, poisoned by flattery and a false education, which has instilled in him grandiose notions of his supposed "rights," is an "immense puff-ball" with no internal vigor, while Bolingbroke is an instinctive politician, strong-willed, dispassionate, and quietly efficient. According to the critic, the one inevitably declines as the other inexorably rises. Equally relentless, however, is the dialectic of history; any usurpation, according to Snider's Hegelian perspective, being aimed against stability cannot be very stable in itself. Thus Bolingbroke, guilty of new crimes, necessarily invites new retributions.*]

In *Richard the Second* the fundamental theme is the right of revolution. We behold a king deposed, and the grounds of his deposition declared in the most explicit manner. It is manifest that the Poet intended to justify the change of rulers, and thus to show when revolution may be necessary for the welfare—perhaps for the existence—of the nation. The whole action is the story of a king who loses the essential attribute of kingship, and, hence, loses his crown. In English History the royal authority has been often claimed to be of God; Shakespeare boldly puts this religious element also into the conflict, and makes it subordinate to the national principle. Though Richard asserts the divinity of his office and its superiority to any human control, he is still hurled from his throne by the people of England. There is no disguise, no softening of the collision—it is the divine right of Kings against the temporal right of the State. The latter is supreme—is, indeed, the most divine of all things. (p. 311)

In *King John* we see the monarch making good his defective title by his determined support of nationality. He maintains the independence and honor of England against her stalwart enemies—France and the See of Rome. Thus he is the true ruler, and receives the unquestioned loyalty of the people. But he loses his lofty principle of action, namely, the defense of nationality; he submits abjectly to the Church, and the country suffers the ignominy of a French invasion. . . . The main point to be noticed is that John failed to support nationality against the external powers which sought to subject it; he could not, therefore, remain the representative of the free nation.

In *Richard the Second* it is not a combat without, but a struggle within; it is not the attitude of the king toward foreign States, but his attitude toward his own subjects. The issue is wholly internal, and now the right of the individual becomes the paramount object of interest. (pp. 311-12)

Here lies the violation of King Richard—he assailed the truest principle of nationality by committing wrongs upon the subject. He refused to be controlled by the law; the institution of which he was the head, and whose end is to secure to every man his rights, was perverted by him into an instrument of the most arbitrary extortion. The very ruler was thus destroying the State, was assailing in its most tender germ the principle of nationality. From being the means of protecting person and property, government in his hands had become the most potent engine of their destruction. Such a king must be put out of the way; the struggle cannot be avoided. The question is: Shall the nation or the sovereign endure? The answer is given in this drama by the deposition and death of King Richard the Second.

But the conflict cannot end here. There are two sides—both have their validity; each party has committed a violation. The title of Richard is unquestioned; his right to the crown is asserted by that same law for the defense of which he has been deprived of the throne. The wrong of Richard has been punished by the loss of his kingdom, but his punishment has begotten a new wrong, which by the same inexorable logic, must call forth a new retribution. (pp. 313-14)

King Richard is deposed—in undermining the law he has undermined his own throne, which rested upon the law; the consequence of his deed has been visited upon him. But who is to succeed him? Here it is naturally the man who has been most deeply wronged—who, in his own person, most adequately represents the majesty of violated justice. Thus, a subject has revolted from the king and made himself king; he has obtained the crown by acknowledging and maintaining in arms the right of revolution. The new king has, therefore, called into existence the principle of his own dethronement, and has enforced it as a basis of action for the entire nation. For the conviction of the people must go along with their deed; that

deed has been dethronement, and, hence, their conviction is now grounded upon the right of deposing the legal sovereign.

This is the difficulty of all revolutions; they are aimed at the stability of institutions—hence they cannot be very stable of themselves. A revolutionary government is logically a contradiction in terms, for its purpose is to upset government—to destroy that which is established; hence its success depends entirely upon the speed with which it abandons its own principle. Having seen the right of revolution, we now behold the wrong of revolution—a wrong which will be brought home to every country that attempts revolutionizing, even from the most justifiable causes. A nation has to endure the penalty of violation, although that violation may be absolutely necessary to preserve a higher element of national existence. (pp. 314-15)

The deposition of Richard, therefore, will not end the conflict; revolution has been let loose in the country, and must, in its turn, be put down. It was stated that the act of Bolingbroke is in its nature contradictory of itself; that the dethronement of the king, applied as a general principle, must mean his own dethronement. The logic of the situation at once begins to disclose itself; the very men who aided him in acquiring the crown are just as ready to take it away again. Indeed, they must claim this to be a right of the subject. Thus the government of Bolingbroke inherits rebellion and revolution, which must be put down by force of arms—that is, he is compelled to turn around and undo his own work, counteract his own principle, stamp out the doctrine of revolt by which he ascended the throne. If he is successful, he will restore the nation to harmony, confirm the succession in his family, and solidify the shattered institutions of the land. This is the great work whose accomplishment is portrayed in the First and Second Parts of *Henry the Fourth,* a truly national poem, whose theme is the restoration of England to internal peace and greatness. Therefore, if *Richard the Second* showed the right of revolution and its success, *Henry the Fourth* shows the wrong of revolution and its defeat. Still, there is one deep, underlying principle to both these works—it is the right of nationality, which at one time hurls the monarch from his throne and at another time tramples into dust the standard of rebellion. (pp. 316-17)

The play of *Henry the Fifth* is the last of this group; it exhibits the spirit of nationality bursting its limits and going forth to subjugate other peoples. It is an epoch of national glory; England has become the proud conqueress; she seems poised on the very pinnacle of fame and prosperity. Thus ends the great Lancastrian Tetralogy, passing off the stage in a blaze of success and patriotic fervor. But at the same time it must not be forgotten that just here can be traced the source of the unutterable calamities which followed, and which brought on the overthrow of the Lancastrian dynasty. For England, through foreign conquest, is really destroying herself; she is assailing the independence of other nations, and therein is undermining her own principle of nationality, as well as opposing the world-historical movement of modern times, which is to maintain the autonomy of the individual State. She, therefore, is guilty of the deepest wrong against the spirit of the age and against the family of European nations, as well as of a crime against herself; hence bitter will be her retribution. (pp. 317-18)

The drama of *Richard the Second* may now be unfolded in its details. Its purely poetic merits are of the highest order; in radiant glow of imagery and in fiery intensity of expression it is unsurpassed. It possesses also the national exaltation of the English Historical Drama generally; it lightens with passages of combined patriotic and poetic enthusiasm. Indeed, the leading character may be justly called a poet, whose own misfortunes inspire utterances of deep passion, mingled with the most brilliant hues of fancy. There is a lyrical coloring diffused over the entire work, and as a drama exhibiting action and characterization, it can by no means be esteemed as highly as when it is considered simply as a beautiful poem.

The action exhibits a double change; it is a stream with two currents sweeping alongside of each other in opposite directions. It shows how to lose a realm and how to acquire a realm; it passes on the one hand from kingship to deprivation, and on the other hand from deprivation to kingship. It will, therefore, be manifest that the drama moves on two threads, having as their respective centers of interest the monarch dethroned and the monarch enthroned. (pp. 318-19)

There are also two movements in the play—the first of which shows the guilt of the king, the second his retribution. Each movement carries along within itself the two threads above mentioned—that of Richard and that of Bolingbroke. The one falls, the other rises; at the point of crossing, in their descent and ascent, lies in general the dramatic transition. First we are made acquainted with the crimes and follies of Richard—the murder of his uncle, the supremacy of favorites, the banishment of Bolingbroke, the expedition to Ireland. The counter-thread unfolds the scheme of Bolingbroke, his banishment and his return, together with the disaffection of the nobles and commons. The second movement exhibits the downward career of Richard to dethronement and death, as well as the execution of his favorites, while at the same time Bolingbroke ascends the throne with the general consent of the realm. Thus the guilt of Richard is punished by that person upon whom he has inflicted a most wanton injury; hence wrong and its retribution make up the whole action.

At the beginning of the play the two threads run together for a while, and then separate. The duel shows the opposing sides, though Richard seems to be playing the part of the mediator. . . . Bolingbroke, who is the son of Gaunt and cousin of Richard, makes a number of charges, which seem to be in the nature of indefinite surmises, and which he himself did not seriously entertain; but there is one most emphatic accusation which manifestly embraces the whole ground of the challenge—his uncle, Gloster, was murdered by Mowbray. . . . Mowbray easily answers the other charges, but the death of Gloster he hurries over with an ambiguous expression, in striking contrast with his general candor and plainness of statement. Something is the matter, and we shall watch sharply for the true explanation in the future course of the drama.

Richard tries to conciliate the fiery duelists by a little humorous banter, and then by an exercise of royal authority. But both refuse obedience in the most unequivocal manner. Herein we catch a slight glimpse of a principle which was supreme among the feudal nobility. Honor was above everything; if it collided with authority, the latter must yield; the king had no right of command in its realm. The individual alone is the monarch there, and is responsible for both word and deed. Life belongs to the sovereign and would be readily given at his bidding, but not honor; hence arose the duel, which was a trial above the law. Richard cannot reconcile the combatants, and so appoints a day for the fight.

But, before we proceed to the final result of the contest, we are fully initiated into the motives of all the prime actors. The truth comes out plainly; Richard is himself the cause of Gloster's murder, and Mowbray was at most only his instrument.

The entire situation clears up at once; Bolingbroke is striking at Richard through Mowbray; already the wily politician snuffs the future revolution in the air. Hence throughout this duel the real combatants are the King and Bolingbroke. (pp. 319-22)

The preparations for the duel are made in magnificent style; the two combatants leap forth with an eager delight for the fray, and utter mutual defiance. But, just as they are about to engage, the King stops the encounter and declares against both the sentence of banishment. Here Richard appears in his best light; he says that he will not suffer civil strife in his dominions, and that he will remove all cause for internal war. In such combats he beholds the "grating shock of wrathful iron arms" [I. iii. 136], and he darkly forbodes the bloodshed which will hereafter result from feudal turbulence. The young monarch—for he always appears as a youth—does not lack intellectual vision; he will repeatedly manifest the clearest insight into his surroundings, and foresee results far in the future with the inspiration of a prophet. But there is no action corresponding to his intuition; he can neither control himself, nor does he know how to employ instrumentalities to control others. His attempt to subordinate the principle of honor to authority is worthy of success, but his means are utterly inadequate. When we reflect, too, that he was well aware of the ambition and character of Bolingbroke, we fully comprehend how unable such puny hands were to wield the massive tools of government. (p. 323)

With this duel begins the strife which only ends with the Wars of the Roses. It is the prelude which opens a great epoch of internal struggle—a struggle which lasts nearly three generations, and forms in Shakespeare the theme of two dramatic cycles. Its intensity shows the strength of the disease; the baleful virus of personal animosity and insubordination had permeated the entire body politic. Long will be the fever, deep and oft-recurring the throes of the malady, until the poison is eliminated from the system, and the strong arm of the Tudors, in suppressing individual license, will assail individual liberty, whence will arise a new and almost as lengthy a conflict. But this period lies beyond the work of the Poet. At present we are to witness the transition from feudalism, in which the quarrel of two noblemen could involve the peace of the whole realm, to the modern world, in which the State has brought into subordination the turbulent, though powerful and high-born, subject. (pp. 324-25)

The two threads of Richard and Bolingbroke, which have hitherto run together, here separate, and will not unite again till the situations of the two men are reversed. We can now take up the part of Richard and follow it through to the end of the first movement. Bolingbroke has departed, but his designs are not unknown to the King, who has "observed his courtship of the common people" [I. iv. 24], and noted with just suspicion his great popularity. "Off goes his bonnet to an oyster-wench" [I. iv. 31]—an act of condescension whose motive can easily be discerned. Richard draws the conclusion with absolute precision; Bolingbroke acts "as were our England in reversion his, and he our subjects' next degree in hope" [I. iv. 35-6]. The monarch has unquestioned power of insight—here he states the whole difficulty of the future. But what does he do? He furnishes an opportunity to his enemy by banishment; certainly he takes no steps to act in accordance with his knowledge. Indeed, he appears to defy his own judgment by resorting to the most odious abuses of which government is capable, namely, favoritism and extortion. (p. 326)

[Richard] proceeds to his crowning act of wrong towards the subject—he confiscates the property of the banished Boling-broke. This deed . . . is not accomplished without a warning; even the weak-spirited York utters a protest:—

Take Hereford's rights away, and take from time
His charters and customary rights;
Let not to-morrow, then, ensue to-day;
Be not thyself; for how art thou a king,
But by fair sequence and succession?

[II. i. 195-99]

This passage states in the most direct manner the logical nature of Richard's deed. The same law which secures to Hereford his property secures to the King his crown. If the King, there-fore, disregard that law, he is destroying his own authority. Here we have the thought of the whole play—sovereign and subject have the same fundamental right; if the former tries to ruin the latter, he is really trying to ruin himself, and will succeed in the attempt. Richard thus is strangling his own authority, and—when we consider that the person who is in this manner elevated by his wrongs into being the representative of the cause of right is the powerful and popular Bolingbroke—there can be only one result.

Such is the crowning deed of wrong done by Richard; now follows his crowning deed of folly. He quits England at the critical nick of time, and makes an expedition to Ireland, leav-ing as governor during his absence the Duke of York—aged, imbecile, and not firmly attached to his interests. The strong outlines of the King's character are now before us. There is a divorce between his intellect and will of a peculiar kind; he possesses foresight, he comprehends results, but he seems to think that a monarch's conduct is above all guidance through the judgment. What he knows need not direct what he does; his action is quite the contrary of his thought. Ordinary mortals may be controlled by their intelligence—but is he not sovereign and above all control? Sunk in pleasure, poisoned by flattery, he has come to believe that in his case there is no responsibility for the deed. This is the Richard of prosperity; adversity will soon show a new phase of his character.

Going back and taking up the thread of Bolingbroke after his banishment, we may observe all the tendencies which conspire to bring him to the throne. In the first place, the circumstances are favorable—events which he did not control catch him up and carry him forward in their current. But, in the second place, the greater part of the governing influences he did set in motion; though the time was ripe for a change, he caused himself to be chosen as its leader. This deep political purpose is every-where manifest, and still deeper is his political instinct, which sets him on the right course without his knowing why. (pp. 327-29)

He hastens to make the issue; he intends to reap every possible advantage of the murder of Gloster, for whom he appears as the avenger, knowing all the while who is the guilty man. Profound, too, is his dissimulation; profounder, indeed, than he wills it to be, since it is the very marrow of his nature. To conceal, and at the same time to carry out, his design are the two conflicting objects which must be united in his action. His courtship of the people has partially revealed him, though with-out any evil result, owing to the character of his adversary. But we are mostly left to hover between his instinct and his intention, in seeking to explore the dark depths of his spiritual being. He never soliloquizes, thus manifesting, to a certain

extent, an absence of reflection and of self-conscious purpose. (pp. 329-30)

Bolingbroke, in the most unequivocal manner, places himself at the head of the national movement and centers it in him-self. . . . But towards the men around him he keeps up his dissimulation; he declares that he has come only for his rights. To the King also he professes the most devoted loyalty, yet at the same time prescribes the conditions of his submission. So profound is his concealment that even his most trusted and active supporter, Northumberland, is not fully assured of his future action. Bolingbroke, therefore, has secured the favor of the nation by maintaining that the king is to guard, and not to violate, what is legally established, and that the king himself is not above the law, but its creature. Such is the deepest political principle of the English nationality, and with it the subtle Bolingbroke is careful to place himself in harmony.

A subordinate thread is the reflection of the whole struggle in an unconscious form—in the dim, nebulous forebodings of the soul. First is the Queen; she feels that something is out of joint, yet she does not know what it is. She only knows that there is a dull presentiment of evil weighing down her spirits. . . . In like manner the Welsh, the superstitious men of the moun-tains, have been thrilled with the premonition of impending disaster, and read it in blazing letters inscribed on the face of heaven. So, too, the gardener has felt the throbbing pulse of the time, and, as he looks upon the sprays, weeds, and flowers of his own little commonwealth, he beholds the various man-ifestations of the political world. Each has thus a special way of expressing that which is wildly rocking and heaving in the soul of the nation.

Such is the first general movement of the play. The threads of Richard and Bolingbroke again strike together, and cross at this point; the one man is mounting towards kingship, the other descending to death. In the second movement, which will now be unfolded, both their characters will develop latent phases. Richard is to be stripped of his infatuation, and is to be brought to see that even a monarch is held accountable for his deeds at the bar of eternal justice. Bolingbroke will gradually work out of his ambiguous position, and assume both the title and the authority of ruler.

Taking up the thread of Richard and following it through the second movement, we shall hear poetic strains of enchanting melody, as one wave of misfortune after another rolls the young King towards the final goal of his destiny. He truly becomes a poet now—like the fabled swan, singing his own death-song. It is a new and unexpected phase of his character, yet by no means inconsistent with what we already know of him. Ca-lamity has opened the sluices of the soul; that sensuous nature of his, which was before sunk in self-indulgence, now comes upon the grim reality of life and is stricken into throes of passionate despair. (pp. 331-35)

But before he begins to descend he is to be placed on the very pinnacle of kingly infatuation; this is his belief in divine right—a dangerous doctrine for English monarchs, as English history abundantly shows. He imagines that his presence will be suf-ficient to put down rebellion, that his will is God's will, and that he simply cannot lose his throne by any deed:—

Not all the water in the rough rude sea
Can wash the balm from an anointed king;
The breath of worldly men cannot depose
The deputy elected by the Lord.

[III. ii. 54-7]

The outcome of this doctrine is manifest: The king is not responsible for his action; he is above the great law of retribution. Moreover, his energy is sapped by such a faith; against every soldier on the side of Bolingbroke he imagines that "God for his Richard hath in heavenly pay a glorious angel" [III. ii. 60-1]. The justice of a thing, the moral quality of an act, do not concern the sovereign who rules over eternal right as over the meanest subject. Early authority, false education, and, above all, poisonous flattery, have inflated him into an immense puff-ball, to be blown off his throne by the first rude wind of adversity. Even the Bishop of Carlisle reproves his extreme reliance on a power external to man, declares that "the means that Heaven yields must be embraced" [III. ii. 29]. The good Bishop, though a dignitary of the Church, believes that fate is not religion, and that self-determination in man is the true faith in God. The imagination of Richard has, however, a picture for the situation; he, like the sun, need only appear, when the clouds of revolt will of themselves disperse before his majestic presence. Such is the summit of his delusion.

Reports of misfortune come in rapidly from every side. . . . Finally, when it is announced that York has joined the rebels, the last prop is taken away; universal revolt has wrested England from the scepter of Richard. What now will be his conduct? His intellect will fully comprehend the situation—his imagination will dress it up in all the brilliant colors of poetry; but his will, his power of action, his ability to recover himself, lies paralyzed within him, smothered in the delicious fragrance of his own soul.

A man who relies entirely on external power must fall into despair when everything goes against him—when that external power shows itself hostile. In express contrast to the religious resignation of Richard stands the prelate, Carlisle, who reproves this very element in him and tries to spur him forward to an energetic defense of his cause. Alongside of the worthy Bishop is the secular man of action, Aumerle, who also seeks to rouse the King from his supineness. But Richard can only fluctuate between the two extremes of his nature—between fatuitous reliance and unmanly despair; there is no internal vigor to buoy up his sinking soul. (pp. 335-37)

But the deeper he sinks in despair the brighter becomes his song; from the ashes of action glows the intense fire of poetry. His fancy has the profusion and brilliancy of a tropical garden; it blooms almost to bewilderment and exhaustion. Still, the spiritual necessity is obvious; he must find relief from his sorrow by casting it out of himself into images—into a long and somewhat labyrinthine gallery of pictures. Such of old has been the need of the bard—in fact, of man; suffering makes the poet and the reader of poetry. Nor must we pass over the prophetic insight which Richard here shows; he, too, knows the consequences of revolution; his intellect is unclouded by misfortune. Rebellion is a monster which eternally begets itself, and whose sweetest food is the blood of its warmest supporters. Tell Bolingbroke, says the inspired King:—

> He is come to ope
> The purple testament of bleeding war;
> But ere the crown he looks for live in peace,
> Ten thousand bloody crowns of mothers' sons
> Shall ill become the flower of England's face;
> Change the complexion of her maid-pale peace
> To scarlet indignation, and bedew
> Her pastures' grass with faithful English blood.
>   [III. iii. 93-100]

The crown is next brought, and Richard hands it over to Bolingbroke in person, uttering himself the salutation of the new monarch: "God save King Harry!" [IV. i. 220]. Thus he crowns with his own hand the usurper, and, as he truly observes, has become a traitor to himself with the rest, for he has given his "soul's consent to undeck the pompous body of a king" [IV. i. 250]. But this is not all; he must acknowledge the justice of his deposition—confess his guilt and its merited punishment. "His weaved-up folly" [IV. i. 229] is to be raveled out to the last thread; the believer in divine right is now brought face to face with the opposite right—that of dethronement. He has lost his dignity; he will not keep his name; he is no longer himself. A looking-glass is brought which shows his former face. Its image is flattery; he is not King Richard, and he dashes it to pieces. He has come to see his follies as they are; he has atoned for his wrongs. Deprived of every kingly honor, he is brought to behold his deed in all its nakedness. The world of illusion in which he before lived has vanished, and the world of reality dawns upon his wondering eyes. Responsibility for the deed crushes into his soul, and a new consciousness has arisen; "I see the very book indeed where all my sins are writ, and that's myself" [IV. i. 274-75]. (pp. 338-39)

Bolingbroke accepts the crown; the only voice heard in protest is that of the brave, clear-headed Bishop of Carlisle, who here presents the side of the wrong done by dethroning Richard. A subject can not pass sentence on his king; it is a violation of human law, and still more of divine law. The noble prelate also utters a prophecy of the terrible consequences of the usurpation; the blood of England shall manure the ground; kindred shall war with kindred;

> Disorder, horror, fear, and mutiny
> Shall here inhabit, and this land be called
> The field of Golgotha and dead men's skulls.
>   [IV. i. 142-44]

Thus Bolingbroke has his wrong and its retribution held up before him, and the Poet gives the motive for the plays which are to follow.

A slight reaction begins; a conspiracy in which both clergy and laity are represented is formed to get rid of the new king. The plot is discovered through the carelessness of Aumerle by his father, the Duke of York, who at once sets out to inform the monarch. The interest of this little scene lies in the conflict between father and mother—their son is a traitor. . . . This form of the domestic collision might be made the basis of a whole tragedy, but it seems not to have been touched upon by Shakespeare in any other play.

The conspiracy is broken up; the lords, spiritual and temporal, who were engaged in it lose their heads, except the bold Bishop of Carlisle; Henry Bolingbroke is firmly seated on the throne of England. But the death of Richard he did not purpose; though he wished him dead, he loves him murdered—the fear of retribution is stronger than the hate of the royal person. The wrong of Bolingbroke is now complete, and he has become fully conscious of it. He declares in deep contrition at the end of the play his own guilt, whose stain he intends to wash off by a voyage to the Holy Land. (pp. 342-44)

Denton J. Snider, "'King Richard II'," in his The Shakespearian Drama, a Commentary: The Histories, 1890. Reprint by Indiana Publishing Co., 1894, pp. 311-44.

W. B. YEATS (essay date 1901)

[The leading figure of the Irish Renaissance and a major poet in twentieth-century literature, Yeats was also an active critic of his contemporaries' works. As a critic, he judged the writings of others according to his own poetic values of sincerity, passion, and vital imagination. In his 1901 essay "At Stratford-on-Avon," excerpted below, Yeats initiated a critical controversy with his interpretation of Richard II. *He contends that although Richard might indeed be the sort of languid, inefficient soul whom Edward Dowden dispraised in the previous century (see excerpt above, 1881), Shakespeare clearly sympathized with the king. According to Yeats, the dramatist preferred Richard to those who deposed him, adding that he saw in the character "the defeat that awaits all, whether they be artist or saint, who find themselves where men ask of them a rough energy and have nothing to give but some contemplative virtue."]*

[The nineteenth century was] a century of utilitarianism, when nothing about a man seemed important except his utility to the State, and nothing so useful to the State as the actions whose effect can be weighed by reason. The deeds of Coriolanus, Hamlet, Timon, Richard II had no obvious use, were, indeed, no more than the expression of their personalities, and so it was thought Shakespeare was accusing them, and telling us to be careful lest we deserve the like accusations. . . . Because reason can only discover completely the use of those obvious actions which everybody admires, and because every character was to be judged by efficiency in action, Shakespearian criticism became a vulgar worshipper of success. I have turned over many books in the library at Stratford-on-Avon, and I have found in nearly all an antithesis, which grew in clearness and violence as the century grew older, between two types, whose representatives were Richard II, 'sentimental,' 'weak,' 'selfish,' 'insincere,' and Henry V, 'Shakespeare's only hero.' These books took the same delight in abasing Richard II that schoolboys do in persecuting some boy of fine temperament, who has weak muscles and a distaste for school games. And they had the admiration for Henry V that schoolboys have for the sailor or soldier hero of a romance in some boys' paper. I cannot claim any minute knowledge of these books, but I think that these emotions began among the German critics, who perhaps saw something French and Latin in Richard II, and I know that Professor Dowden, whose book I once read carefully, first made these emotions eloquent and plausible. He lived in Ireland, where everything has failed, and he meditated frequently upon the perfection of character which had, he thought, made England successful, for, as we say, 'cows beyond the water have long horns.' He forgot that England, as Gordon has said, was made by her adventurers, by her people of wildness and imagination and eccentricity; and thought that Henry V, who only seemed to be these things because he had some commonplace vices, was not only the typical Anglo-Saxon, but the model Shakespeare held up before England; and he even thought it worth while pointing out that Shakespeare himself was making a large fortune while he was writing about Henry's victories. In Professor Dowden's successors this apotheosis went further; and it reached its height at a moment of imperialistic enthusiasm, of ever-deepening conviction that the commonplace shall inherit the earth, when somebody of reputation, whose name I cannot remember, wrote that Shakespeare admired this one character alone out of all his characters. The Accusation of Sin produced its necessary fruit, hatred of all that was abundant, extravagant, exuberant, of all that sets a sail for shipwreck, and flattery of the commonplace emotions and conventional ideals of the mob, the chief Paymaster of accusation.

I cannot believe that Shakespeare looked on his Richard II with any but sympathetic eyes, understanding indeed how ill-fitted he was to be king, at a certain moment of history, but understanding that he was lovable and full of capricious fancy, 'a wild creature' as Pater has called him [see excerpt above, 1889]. The man on whom Shakespeare modelled him had been full of French elegances as he knew from Holinshed, and had given life a new luxury, a new splendour, and been 'too friendly' to his friends, 'too favourable' to his enemies. And certainly Shakespeare had these things in his head when he made his king fail, a little because he lacked some qualities that were doubtless common among his scullions, but more because he had certain qualities that are uncommon in all ages. To suppose that Shakespeare preferred the men who deposed his king is to suppose that Shakespeare judged men with the eyes of a Municipal Councillor weighing the merits of a Town Clerk; and that had he been by when Verlaine cried out from his bed, 'Sir, you have been made by the stroke of a pen, but I have been made by the breath of God,' he would have thought the Hospital Superintendent the better man. He saw indeed, as I think, in Richard II the defeat that awaits all, whether they be artist or saint, who find themselves where men ask of them a rough energy and have nothing to give but some contemplative virtue, whether lyrical fantasy, or sweetness of temper, or dreamy dignity, or love of God, or love of His creatures. He saw that such a man through sheer bewilderment and impatience can become as unjust or as violent as any common man, any Bolingbroke or Prince John, and yet remain 'that sweet lovely rose' [*1 Henry IV*, I. iii. 175]. The courtly and saintly ideals of the Middle Ages were fading, and the practical ideals of the modern age had begun to threaten the unuseful dome of the sky; Merry England was fading, and yet it was not so faded that the poets could not watch the procession of the world with that untroubled sympathy for men as they are, as apart from all they do and seem, which is the substance of tragic irony. (pp. 102-06)

W. B. Yeats, "At Stratford-On-Avon," in his Essays and Introductions, *The Macmillan Company, 1961, pp. 96-110.*

E. K. CHAMBERS (essay date 1905)

[Chambers occupies a transitional position in Shakespearean criticism, one which connects the biographical sketches and character analyses of the nineteenth century with the historical, technical, and textual criticism of the twentieth century. While a member of the education department at Oxford University, Chambers earned his reputation as a scholar with his multivolume works, The Medieval Stage *(1903) and* The Elizabethan Stage *(1923); he also edited* The Red Letter Shakespeare *from 1904 to 1908. Chambers investigated both the purpose and limitations of each dramatic genre as Shakespeare presented it and speculated on how the dramatist's work was influenced by contemporary historical issues and his own frame of mind. In the following excerpt, originally published in his introduction to the 1905* Red Letter *edition of* Richard II, *Chambers notes the experimental nature of the history and discusses its central conflict, that between Richard and Bolingbroke. He maintains that their struggle is not only between two ideals of sovereign kingship, but also between two archetypal human personalities: "the practical and artistic temperaments, the men of deeds and the men of dreams and fancies." In addition, Chambers disputes W. B. Yeats's assessment of Shakespeare's apparent sympathies in* Richard II *(see excerpt above, 1901), claiming that the verifiably practical, conservative aspects of the dramatist's personality would make him respond far more warmly to Bolingbroke than Yeats admitted.]*

Richard the Second has, beyond its actual dramatic quality, a singular interest for those who care to study the development of Shakespeare's dramatic methods. With *Romeo and Juliet* and *A Midsummer Night's Dream,* it belongs to the period of a deliberate literary experiment. For the space of a tragedy, a comedy, and a history, Shakespeare essayed to write drama in the lyrical vein, with his singing robes on, with an abundance of passionate and highly coloured speech, and with the aid of rhyme and other devices of lyrical utterance. Afterwards he desisted from this way and sought another manner, more varied and flexible, and therefore more sensitive to the rise and fall of emotion which necessarily underlies dramatic expression. I do not know whether *Richard the Second* has ever been set to music and furnished forth the book of an opera; but it would lend itself to such treatment, and even as it stands it calls less for acting in the naturalistic sense, than for a rhetorical and measured declamation. Richard's own part, in particular, at least after the wheel of fortune has begun to carry him downwards, is one long and elaborated recitative of profound and subtle pathos.

To say that the play is lyric is by no means to say that it is not dramatic also. On the contrary, every element in it is carefully subordinated to the strictly dramatic end of throwing into powerful relief the strong contrast and conflict between the two principal characters, Richard and his cousin and supplanter, Henry of Bolingbroke. This conflict has its political aspect, since the play is, primarily, a study in kingship, and, beyond that, it has its personal aspect, since, even more fundamentally, the play is a study in human nature, and sets in opposition the two types of personality between which, from the beginning, the inheritance of this world has been divided. *Richard the Second* is, of course, the first act in the trilogy which leads up to the portrait of Shakespeare's ideal and heroic king, in *Henry the Fifth.* [This] Henry has every right to sovereignty, the right divine of birth, and the human rights of efficiency and of that sympathy with the instincts and emotions of his folk, the attaining to which is the real explanation of his unprincelike and wayward youth. Like the summer grass, he has grown to kingship—

> Unseen, yet crescive in his faculty.
>
> [*Henry V,* I. i. 66]

Neither Richard the Second nor Henry the Fourth realizes more than a fraction of this tripartite ideal; and therefore each, politically, is a tragic failure. Richard, indeed, has nothing but the irony of the right divine; he is neither efficient nor sympathetic. Bolingbroke is efficient enough, but a self-seeker, and to the end the stain of disloyalty and usurpation mars his kingship. This is the outline of Shakespeare's political philosophy as it finds expression in the trilogy.

It need hardly be said that the antithesis between Richard and Bolingbroke goes much further than politics; it rests upon one of the ultimate distinctions amongst mankind, that of the practical and artistic temperaments, the men of deeds and the men of dreams and fancies. The personal beauty of Richard, on which much stress is laid in the play, is but the map of his delicate intellect and flower-like imagination. He delights in music, in a spectacle, in the pomp and circumstance of his state. He is an orator, with a wonderful flow of eloquent words which runs like a river through scene after scene. He has his intuitions, and can read the hearts of men, although he cannot control them. Like so many of the personages whom Shakespeare the actor made, he is himself a born actor. He loves a dramatic effect. He is in his element, sitting in the high seat

at Coventry and throwing his warder down just at the critical moment when the champions are levelling their spears in the lists. Even in his downfall, it gives him a thrill to take the stage in Westminster Hall and slowly to disembarrass himself of his crown with speeches of studied pathos, while the lookers-on are divided between admiration for the artist, pity for the man, and irritation at the *poseur.* He has no morals and no real feeling for anyone but himself; yet his sensitiveness of soul enables him to hold the hearts of those with whom he enters into personal relations, the queen whose bed he has wronged, the young nobles who plot in his cause, the menial who with much ado gets leave to see his face in prison. In return he has a fund of ready sentiment, which goes out not only to human beings, but also to 'roan Barbary' and to the literal earth of his native land. And when action is called for, it is always sentiment that he succeeds in substituting. The shocks of misfortune stimulate him only to a more and more subtle exercise of his incomparable imagination. He becomes an interested spectator of his own ruin, dressing it out with illuminating phrases and exquisite images, and so turning it into a thing of beauty and of sorrow for himself and the audience; but he makes no effort to avert it, and falls back upon a mystical consciousness of his divine right, and a half-belief in the probability of some incredible divine intervention in his favour. Never at any time does he come face to face with facts; but always sees them through the beautiful and distorting medium of his own dramatic fancy. . . . [In] Shakespeare's psychology, he stands for the type of the artist.

Against Richard, Bolingbroke presents the incarnation of efficiency. He has no gifts or graces; the courtesy which wins him popularity is a matter of deliberate attitude, not of instinct. He speaks few words; none unconsidered or without a definite practical end. You recognize in him 'the still strong man in a noisy land'; one who knows how to bide his time, and moves irresistibly, with something of the terrible precision of a machine, towards his predetermined end. The antagonism between him and Richard declares itself from the beginning, and both are conscious of it. His attitude towards the king during the early part of the play conceals a covert threat; at the end, though the less effective rôle is his, he keeps his temper, and treats the tirades of the victim, whose days he has already numbered, with a contemptuous and studied brevity. Of course *Richard the Second* does not give us by any means the whole of Bolingbroke. Within its limits he is thoroughly successful. In the conflict with Richard, efficiency has its full triumph over imagination. The completion of the picture is left for the second part of the trilogy, discovering his weakness in the want of sympathy which leads him to offend the hot-blooded nobles and to misjudge the finely-tempered nature of his own son. (pp. 88-92)

This, however, is to anticipate. The dramatic intention of *Richard the Second* as a single play must be distinguished from the dramatic intention of the total trilogy of which it forms only one stage. And within *Richard the Second* the issue between Richard the dreamer and Bolingbroke the 'crown-grasper' is a clear one. The sympathies of the audience, naturally enough, swing and sway with the progress of the action. The design of the dramatist requires that they shall be against Richard during the period of his tyranny, and shall gradually be won to his side from the moment when his fortunes begin to decline. This is almost inevitable, since it is of the essence of tragedy that the tragic fate should be intelligible and should none the less awake pity and awe. It is a little more difficult to say whether any ultimate judgment upon the puppets by their interpreter is involved. Mr W. B. Yeats, in his book called *Ideas of Good and Evil* [see excerpt above, 1901], seems to have no doubts about the matter, and decides without hesitation that Shakespeare, as an artist, put the children of light before the children of this world, and was personally in touch with the ineffectual dreamer Richard, rather than with his 'efficient' rival. . . . I am quite sure that Mr Yeats himself, in judging kings or ploughmen, would always give the palm to imagination over efficiency; and for all I know, if human characteristics are reducible to ultimate standards of value, he may be perfectly right. . . . But after all it is not Mr Yeats's vision of life, or mine, that is in question, but Shakespeare's. And I do not for a moment believe that in reading Shakespeare he has succeeded in keeping his eye upon the object. Shakespeare, if I am not mistaken, was the last man likely to underrate the hard practical qualities which go towards efficiency. For a poet, he had the firmest grasp upon the central facts of life. After all, he was not a Celtic idealist, but an honest burgess of Saxon Stratford. . . . I do believe that Shakespeare, who saw all round life, saw it on the whole very normally, and that he weighed his men and women just a little more in relation to the central purposes of the world than Mr Yeats does or is inclined to admit that he did. Naturally he understood his Richard the Second and his Falstaff, as well as his Henry the Fifth, and understanding must always imply some measure of sympathy. Yet I find it difficult to think that his ultimate judgment upon them differed essentially from that of any clear-sighted and broad-minded Elizabethan student of history who did not happen to be a poet. (pp. 92-6)

> E. K. Chambers, "Richard the Second," in his Shakespeare: A Survey, *Hill and Wang, 1958, pp. 88-96.*

FRANK HARRIS (essay date 1909)

[*Harris was a British-American journalist, editor, playwright, and short story writer whose most significant achievement was serving as editor of several London journals, including the* Saturday Review *from 1894 to 1898, and employing such writers as Bernard Shaw, H. G. Wells, and Max Beerbohm. In* The Man Shakespeare and His Tragic Life Story *(1909) and* The Women of Shakespeare *(1911), Harris offered a psychological study of the dramatist, searching through the plays for evidence of Shakespeare's biography. The first of these received high praise from several of his contemporaries, but his Shakespearean criticism has received no commendation and little attention from modern scholars. In his commentary on* Richard II, *Harris notes that Shakespeare's depiction of the king differs radically from that of the earlier historians. According to the critic, the Richard of tradition was little more than "a vile creature in whom weakness nourished crime," but though Shakespeare's hero seems detestable enough at first, he soon becomes more lovable and sympathetic. A possible explanation for this, Harris proposes, is that Shakespeare recognized himself in certain aspects of his fictional creation; and perhaps the remembrance of his own youthful follies, or simply a constitutional tendency toward "gentle sorrow," prompted the dramatist to excuse the shortcomings of his melancholy monarch. Harris discerns in this play and others an indication that Shakespeare "preferred to picture irresolution and weakness rather than strength, and felt more sympathy with failure than with success."*]

[Shakespeare's "King Richard II."] in some respects is his most important historical creation. Coleridge says: "I know of no character drawn by our great poet with such unequalled skill as that of Richard II" [see excerpt above, 1811-12]. Such praise is extravagant; but it would have been true to say that up to

1593 or 1594, when Shakespeare wrote "King Richard II.," he had given us no character so complex and so interesting as this Richard. Coleridge overpraised the character-drawing probably because the study of Richard's weakness and irresolution, and the pathos resulting from such helplessness, must have seemed very like an analysis of his own nature.

Let us now examine "Richard II.," and see what light it casts on Shakespeare's qualities. There was an old play of the same title, a play which is now lost, but we can form some idea of what it was like from the description in Forman's Diary. Like most of the old history-plays it ranged over twenty years of Richard's reign, whereas Shakespeare's tragedy is confined to the last year of Richard's life. It is probable that the old play presented King Richard as more wicked and more deceitful than Shakespeare imagines him. . . . [Tradition] pictured Richard as a vile creature in whom weakness nourished crime. Shakespeare took his story partly from Holinshed's narrative, and partly either from the old play or from the traditional view of Richard's character. When he began to write the play he evidently intended to portray Richard as even more detestable than history and tradition had presented him. In Holinshed Richard is not accused of the murder of Gloster, whereas Shakespeare directly charges him with it, or rather makes Gaunt do so, and the accusation is not denied, much less disproved. At the close of the first act we are astonished by the revelation of Richard's devilish heartlessness. The King hearing that his uncle, John of Gaunt, is "grievous sick," cries out:

> Now put it, God, in his physician's mind,
> To help him to his grave immediately!
> The lining of his coffers shall make coats
> To deck our soldiers for these Irish wars.
> Come, gentlemen, let's all go visit him:
> Pray God we may make haste and come too late.
> [I. iv. 59-64]

This mixture of greed and cold cruelty decked out with blasphemous phrase is viler, I think, than anything attributed by Shakespeare to the worst of his villains. But surely some hint of Richard's incredible vileness should have come earlier in the play, should have preceded at least his banishment of Bolingbroke, if Shakespeare had really meant to present him to us in this light.

In the first scene of the second act, when Gaunt reproves him, Richard turns on him in a rage, threatening. In the very same scene York reproves Richard for seizing Gaunt's money and land, and Richard retorts:

> Think what you will: we seize into our hands
> His plate, his goods, his money, and his lands.
> [II. i. 209-10]

But when York blames him to his face and predicts that evil will befall him and leaves him, Richard in spite of this at once creates:

> Our uncle York, Lord Governor of England;
> For he is just, and always loved us well.
> [II. i. 220-21]

This Richard of Shakespeare is so far, I submit, almost incomprehensible. When reproved by Gaunt and warned, Richard rages and threatens; when blamed by York much more severely, Richard rewards York: the two scenes contradict each other. Moreover, though his callous selfishness, greed and cruelty are apparently established, in the very next scene of this act our sympathy with Richard is called forth by the praise his queen gives him. . . . And from this scene to the end of the play Shakespeare enlists all our sympathy for Richard. Now, what is the reason of this right-about-face on the part of the poet?

It appears to me that Shakespeare began the play intending to present the vile and cruel Richard of tradition. But midway in the play he saw that there was no emotion, no pathos, to be got out of the traditional view. If Richard were a vile, scheming, heartless murderer, the loss of his crown and life would merely satisfy our sense of justice, but this outcome did not satisfy Shakespeare's desire for emotion, and particularly his desire for pathos, and accordingly he veers round, says nothing more of Richard's vileness, lays stress upon his weakness and sufferings, discovers, too, all manner of amiable qualities in him, and so draws pity from us for his dethronement and murder.

The curious thing is that while Shakespeare is depicting Richard's heartlessness, he does his work badly; the traits, as I have shown, are crudely extravagant and even contradictory; but when he paints Richard's gentleness and amiability, he works like a master, every touch is infallible: he is painting himself.

It was natural for Shakespeare to sympathize deeply with Richard; he was still young when he wrote the play, young enough to remember vividly how he himself had been led astray by loose companions, and this formed a bond between them. At this time of his life this was Shakespeare's favourite subject: he treated it again in "Henry IV.," which is at once the epilogue to "Richard II." and a companion picture to it; for the theme of both plays is the same—youth yielding to unworthy companions. . . . Shakespeare identified himself peculiarly with Richard; and his painting of Richard is more intimate, more subtle, more self-revealing and pathetic than anything in "Henry IV."

As I have already said, from the time when Richard appoints York as Regent, and leaves England, Shakespeare begins to think of himself as Richard, and from this moment to the end no one can help sympathizing with the unhappy King. At this point, too, the character-drawing becomes, of a sudden, excellent. When Richard lands in England, he is given speech after speech, and all he says and does afterwards throws light, it seems to me, on Shakespeare's own nature. Let us mark each trait. First of all Richard is intensely, frankly emotional: he "weeps for joy" to be in England again; "weeping, smiling" [III. ii. 2, 10], he greets the earth of England, and is full of hope. . . . A moment later he hears from Salisbury that the Welshmen whom he had relied upon as allies are dispersed and fled. At once he becomes "pale and dead" [III. ii. 79]. From the height of pride and confidence he falls to utter hopelessness. . . . Aumerle asks him to remember who he is, and at once he springs from dejection to confidence again. He cries:

> Awake, thou sluggard majesty! thou sleepest.
> Is not the king's name forty thousand names?
> [III. ii. 84-5]

The next moment Scroop speaks of cares, and forthwith fitful Richard is in the dumps once more. But this time his weakness is turned to resignation and sadness, and the pathos of this is brought out by the poet:

> Strives Bolingbroke to be as great as we?
> Greater he shall not be; if he serve God
> We'll serve him, too, and be his fellow so.

> Revolt our subjects? that we cannot mend;
> They break their faith to God, as well as us.
> Cry woe, destruction, ruin, loss, decay;
> The worst is death, and death will have his day.
> [III. ii. 97-103]

Who does not hear Hamlet speaking in this memorable last line? Like Hamlet, too, this Richard is quick to suspect even his friends' loyalty. (pp. 64-9)

But as soon as he learns that his friends are dead he breaks out in a long lament for them which ranges over everything from worms to kings, and in its melancholy pessimism is the prototype of those meditations which Shakespeare has put in the mouth of nearly all his favourite characters. Who is not reminded of Hamlet's great monologue when he reads:

> For within the hollow crown,
> That rounds the mortal temples of a king,
> Keeps Death his court: and there the antic sits
> Scoffing his state, and grinning at his pomp. . . .
> [III. ii. 160-63]
> (pp. 69-70)

Let us take another two lines of this soliloquy:

> For God's sake, let us sit upon the ground
> And tell sad stories of the death of kings.
> [III. ii. 155-56]

In the second scene of the third act of "Titus Andronicus" we find Titus saying to his daughter:

> I'll to thy closet; and go read with thee
> Sad stories chancèd in the times of old.
> [*Titus Andronicus*, III. ii. 82-3]

Again, in the "Comedy of Errors," Aegeon tells us that his life was prolonged:

> To tell sad stories of my own mishaps.
> [*The Comedy of Errors*, I. i. 120]

The similarity of these passages shows that in the very spring of life and heyday of the blood Shakespeare had in him a certain romantic melancholy which was developed later by the disappointments of life into the despairing of Macbeth and Lear.

When the Bishop calls upon Richard to act, the King's weathercock mind veers round again, and he cries:

> This ague fit of fear is over-blown,
> An easy task it is to win our own.
> [III. ii. 190-91]

But when Scroop tells him that York has joined with Bolingbroke, he believes him at once, gives up hope finally, and turns as if for comfort to his own melancholy fate:

> Beshrew thee, cousin, which didst lead me forth
> Of that sweet way I was in to despair!
> [III. ii. 204-05]

That "sweet way" of despair is Romeo's way, Hamlet's, Macbeth's and Shakespeare's way. (pp. 70-1)

[Then] comes the great speech in which the poet reveals himself so ingenuously that at the end of it the King he pretends to be, has to admit that he has talked but idly. . . . [It] shows how easily Shakespeare falls out of this King's character into his own:

> What must the King do now? Must he submit?
> The King shall do it. Must he be depos'd?
> The King shall be contented: must he lose
> The name of king? O! God's name, let it go:
> I'll give my jewels for a set of beads;
> My gorgeous palace for a hermitage;
> My gay apparel for an alms-man's gown;
> My figur'd goblets for a dish of wood;
> My sceptre for a palmer's walking staff;
> My subjects for a pair of carved saints;
> And my large kingdom for a little grave,
> A little, little grave, an obscure grave. . . .
>   Well, well, I see
> I talk but idly, and you mock at me.—
> Most mighty prince, my lord Northumberland,
> What says King Bolingbroke? will his majesty
> Give Richard leave to live till Richard die?
> You make a leg, and Bolingbroke says ay.
>   [III. ii. 143-54, 170-75]

Every one will admit that the poet himself speaks here. . . . But the melancholy mood, the pathetic acceptance of the inevitable, the tender poetic embroidery now suit the King who is fashioned in the poet's likeness. (pp. 71-2)

In the fifth act, the scene between the Queen and Richard is used simply to move our pity. She says he is "most beauteous" [V. i. 13], but all too mild, and he answers her:

> I am sworn brother, sweet,
> To grim necessity; and he and I
> Will keep a league till death.
>   [V. i. 20-2]

He bids her take,

> As from my death-bed, my last living leave,
>   [V. i. 39]

and for her consolation he turns again to the telling of romantic melancholy stories:

> In winter's tedious nights, sit by the fire
> With good old folks; and let them tell thee tales
> Of woeful ages long ago betid:
> And, ere thou bid good night, to quit their grief,
> Tell thou the lamentable fall of me,
> And send the hearers weeping to their beds,
> For why; the senseless brands will sympathize
> The heavy accent of thy moving tongue.
>   [V. i. 40-7]

I cannot copy this passage without drawing attention to the haunting music of the third line.

The scene in which York betrays his son to Bolingbroke and prays the king not to pardon but "cut off" the offending member, is merely a proof, if proof were wanted, of Shakespeare's admiration of kingship and loyalty, which in youth, at least, often led him to silliest extravagance.

The dungeon scene and Richard's monologue in it are as characteristic of Shakespeare as the similar scene in "Cymbeline" and the soliloquy of Posthumus:

> *K. Rich.* I have been studying how I may compare
> This prison where I live unto the world:
> And for because the world is populous,
> And here is not a creature but myself,
> I cannot do it. . . .
>   [V. v. 1-5]

Here we have the philosopher playing with his own thoughts; but soon the Hamlet-melancholy comes to tune the meditation to sadness, and Shakespeare speaks to us directly:

> Thus play I in one person many people,
> And none contented: sometimes am I king;
> Then treasons make me wish myself a beggar,
> And so I am: then crushing penury
> Persuades me I was better when a king;
> Then am I king'd again. . . .
>   [V. v. 31-6]
>   (pp. 74-6)

In the last three lines of this monologue which I am now about to quote, I can hear Shakespeare speaking as plainly as he spoke in Arthur's appeals [in *King John*]; the feminine longing for love is the unmistakable note:

> Yet blessing on his heart that gives it me!
> For 'tis a sign of love; and love to Richard
> Is a strange brooch in this all-hating world.
>   [V. v. 64-6]

And at the last, by killing the servant who assaults him, this Richard shows that he has the "something desperate" in him of which Hamlet boasted.

The murderer's praise that this irresolute-weak and loving Richard is "as full of valour as of royal blood" [V. v. 113] is nothing more than an excellent instance of Shakespeare's self-illusion. . . . If a hasty blow were proof of valour then Walter Scott's Eachin in "The Fair Maid of Perth" would be called brave. But courage to be worth the name must be founded on stubborn resolution, and all Shakespeare's incarnations, and in especial this Richard, are as unstable as water.

The whole play is summed up in York's pathetic description of Richard's entrance into London:

>   No man cried, God save him;
> No joyful tongue gave him his welcome home:
> But dust was thrown upon his sacred head;
> Which with such gentle sorrow he shook off—
> His face still combating with tears and smiles,
> The badges of his grief and patience—
> That had not God, for some strong purpose, steel'd
> The hearts of men, they must perforce have melted,
> And barbarism itself have pitied him.
>   [V. ii. 28-36]

This passage it seems to me both in manner and matter is as truly characteristic of Shakespeare as any that can be found in all his works: his loving pity for the fallen, his passionate sympathy with "gentle sorrow" [V. ii. 31] were never more perfectly expressed. (pp. 77-8)

In "Richard II.," the weakness Shakespeare pities is not physical weakness, but mental irresolution and incapacity for action, and these Hamlet-weaknesses are accompanied by a habit of philosophic thought, and are enlivened by a nimble wit and great lyrical power. . . . (p. 78)

It appears then that Shakespeare's nature even in hot, reckless youth was most feminine and affectionate, and that even when dealing with histories and men of action he preferred to picture irresolution and weakness rather than strength, and felt more sympathy with failure than with success. (pp. 78-9)

*Frank Harris, "Shakespeare's Men of Action: The
Bastard, Arthur, and King Richard II," in his The*

Man Shakespeare and His Tragic Life Story, *Frank Palmer, 1909, pp. 56-79.*

ALGERNON CHARLES SWINBURNE   (essay date 1909)

[*Swinburne was an English poet, dramatist, and critic who devoted much of his literary career to the study of Shakespeare and other Elizabethan writers. His three books on Shakespeare—*A Study of Shakespeare *(1880),* Shakespeare *(1909), and* Three Plays of Shakespeare *(1909)—all demonstrate his keen interest in Shakespeare's poetic talents and, especially, his major tragedies. Swinburne's literary commentary is frequently conveyed in a style that is markedly intense and effusive, as the following excerpt from* Three Plays of Shakespeare *demonstrates. He detects in* Richard II *the collision of two literary styles that influenced Shakespeare's early career: the lyrical pastoralism of Robert Greene (to whom Swinburne ascribes the authorship of* Titus Andronicus*), and the impassioned dramatic eloquence of Christopher Marlowe. The result in* Richard II, *according to Swinburne, is uneven and immature, with uncertain characterization, vague plot development, and lapses into verse which, though magnificent, are not dramatically justifiable. Swinburne also sees little to admire in Shakespeare's "semi-virile" protagonist; even Richard's famous Act III, Scene ii speech on the coast of Wales Swinburne dismisses as "effeminate."*]

It is a truth more curious than difficult to verify that there was a time when the greatest genius ever known among the sons of men was uncertain of the future and unsure of the task before it; when the one unequalled and unapproachable master . . . stood hesitating between the impulsive instinct for dramatic poetry, the crown and consummation of all philosophies, the living incarnation of creative and intelligent godhead, and the facile seduction of elegiac and idyllic verse, of meditative and uncreative song: between the music of Orpheus and the music of Tibullus. The legendary choice of Hercules was of less moment than the actual choice of Shakespeare between the influence of Robert Greene and the influence of Christopher Marlowe.

The point of most interest in the tragedy or history of *King Richard II* is the obvious evidence which it gives of the struggle between the worse and the better genius of its author. . . . The author of *Selimus* and *Andronicus* [Greene] is visibly contending with the author of *Faustus* and *Edward II* [Marlowe] for the mastery of Shakespeare's poetic and dramatic adolescence. (pp. 59-60)

[*King Richard II*] is not glaringly out of place among the *sottes monstrosités* [foolish monstrosities]—if I may borrow a phrase applied by Michelet to a more recent literary creation—of [*Titus Andronicus*]. . . . Greene, in his best works of prose fiction and in his lyric and elegiac idyls, is as surely the purest and gentlest of writers as he was the most reckless and disreputable of men. And when ambition or hunger lured or lashed him into the alien field of tragic poetry, his first and last notion of the work in hand was simply to revel and wallow in horrors after the fashion, by no means of a wild boar, but merely of a wether gone distracted.

Nevertheless, the influence of this unlucky trespasser on tragedy is too obvious in too much of the text of *King Richard II* to be either questioned or overlooked. . . . The grasp of character is uncertain: the exposition of event is inadequate. The reader or spectator unversed in the byways of history has to guess at what has already happened—how, why, when, where, and by whom the prince whose murder is the matter in debate at the opening of the play [Act I, Scene i] has been murdered.

He gets so little help or light from the poet that he can only guess at random, with blind assumption or purblind hesitation, what may be the right or wrong of the case which is not even set before him. The scolding-match between Bolingbroke and Mowbray, fine in their primitive way as are the last two speeches of the latter declaimer, is liker the work of a pre-Marlowite than the work of Marlowe's discipline. The whole scene is merely literary, if not purely academic: and the seemingly casual interchange of rhyme and blank verse is more wayward and fitful than even in *Romeo and Juliet*. That the finest passage is in rhyme, and is given to a character [Mowbray] about to vanish from the action of the play, is another sign of poetical and intellectual immaturity. The second scene has in it a breath of true passion and a touch of true pathos: but even if the subject had been more duly and definitely explained, it would still have been comparatively wanting in depth of natural passion and pungency of natural pathos. The third scene, full of beautifully fluent and plentifully inefficient writing, reveals the protagonist of the play as so pitifully mean and cruel a weakling that no future action or suffering can lift him above the level which divides and purifies pity from contempt. . . . If we can ever be sorry for anything that befalls so vile a sample of royalty, our sorrow must be so diluted and adulterated by recollection of his wickedness and baseness that its tribute could hardly be acceptable to any but the most pitiable example or exception of mankind. (pp. 62-7)

With the passing of John of Gaunt the moral grandeur of the poem passes finally away. Whatever of interest we may feel in any of the surviving figures is transitory, intermittent, and always qualified by a sense of ethical inconsistency and intellectual inferiority. There is not a man among them: unless it be the Bishop of Carlisle: and he does but flash across the action for an ineffectual instant. There is often something attractive in Aumerle: indeed, his dauntless and devoted affection for the king makes us sometimes feel as though there must be something not unpitiable or unlovable in the kinsman who could inspire and retain such constancy of regard in a spirit so much manlier than his own. But the figure is too roughly and too thinly sketched to be thoroughly memorable as a man's: and his father's is an incomparable, an incredible, an unintelligible and a monstrous nullity. (pp. 70-1)

In the scene at Windsor Castle between the Queen and her husband's minions [Act II, scene ii] the idyllic or elegiac style again supplants and supersedes the comparatively terse and dramatic manner of dialogue between the noblemen whom we have just seen lashed into disgust and goaded into revolt by the villainy and brutality of the rascal king. The dialogue is beautiful and fanciful: it makes a very pretty eclogue: none other among the countless writers of Elizabethan eclogues could have equalled it. But if we look for anything more or for anything higher than this, we must look elsewhere: and we shall not look in vain if we turn to the author of *Edward the Second*. When the wretched York creeps in, we have undoubtedly such a living and drivelling picture of hysterical impotence on the downward grade to dotage and distraction as none but Shakespeare could have painted. When Bolingbroke reappears and Harry Percy appears on the stage of the poet who has bestowed on him a generous portion from the inexhaustible treasure of his own immortal life, we find ourselves again among men, and are comforted and refreshed by the change. (pp. 71-3)

The inspired effeminacy and the fanciful puerility which dunces attribute to the typical character of a representative poet never found such graceful utterance as the greatest of poets has given to the unmanliest of his creatures when Richard lands in Wales [Act II, scene ii]. Coleridge credits the poor wretch with "an intense love of his country" [see excerpt above, 1834], intended to "redeem him in the hearts of the audience" in spite of the fact that "even in this love there is something feminine and personal." There is nothing else in it: as anybody but Coleridge would have seen. It is exquisitely pretty and utterly unimaginable as the utterance of a man. The two men who support him on either side, the loyal priest and the gallant kinsman, offer him words of manly counsel and manful cheer. He answers them with an outbreak of such magnificent poetry as might almost have been uttered by the divine and unknown and unimaginable poet who gave to eternity the Book of Job: but in this case also the futility of intelligence is as perfect as the sublimity of speech. . . . And the utter collapse of heart and spirit which follows on the final stroke of bad tidings at once completes the picture of the man, and concludes in equal harmony the finest passage of the poem and the most memorable scene in the play.

The effect of the impression made by it is so elaborately sustained in the following scene as almost to make a young student wonder at the interest taken by the young Shakespeare in the development or evolution of such a womanish or semivirile character. The style is . . . exuberant and effusive, elegiac and Ovidian, in a degree which might well have made his admirers doubt, and gravely doubt, whether the future author of *Othello* would ever be competent to take and hold his place beside the actual author of *Faustus.* (pp. 73-7)

The fourth act opens upon a morally chaotic introduction of incongruous causes, inexplicable plaintiffs, and incomprehensible defendants. Whether Aumerle or Fitzwater or Surrey or Bagot is right or wrong, honourable or villainous, no reader or spectator is given a chance of guessing: it is a mere cockpit squabble. And the scene of deposition which follows, full as it is of graceful and beautiful writing, need only be set against the scene of deposition in *Edward the Second* to show the difference between rhetorical and dramatic poetry, emotion and passion, eloquence and tragedy, literature and life. The young Shakespeare's scene is full to superfluity of fine verses and fine passages: his young compeer's or master's is from end to end one magnificent model of tragedy, "simple, sensuous, and passionate" as Milton himself could have desired: Milton, the second as Shakespeare was the first of the great English poets who were pupils and debtors of Christopher Marlowe. It is pure poetry and perfect drama: the fancy is finer and the action more lifelike than here. Only once or twice do we come upon such a line as this in the pathetic but exuberant garrulity of Richard: "While that my wretchedness doth bait myself" [IV. i. 238]. That is worthy of Marlowe. And what follows is certainly pathetic: though certainly there is a good deal of it.

The last act might rather severely than unfairly be described as a series of six tragic or tragicomic eclogues. The first scene is so lovely that no reader worthy to enjoy it will care to ask whether it is or is not so lifelike as to convey no less of conviction than all readers must feel of fascination in the continuous and faultless melody of utterance and tenderness of fancy which make it in its way an incomparable idyl. From the dramatic point of view it might certainly be objected that we know nothing of the wife, and that what we know of the husband does not by any means tend to explain the sudden pathos and sentimental sympathy of their parting speeches. The first part of the next scene is as beautiful and blameless an

example of dramatic narrative as even a Greek poet could have given at such length: but in the latter part of it we cannot but see and acknowledge again the dramatic immaturity of the poet who in a very few years was to reveal himself as beyond all question, except from the most abject and impudent of dunces, the greatest imaginable dramatist or creator ever born into immortality. Style and metre are rough, loose, and weak: the dotage of York becomes lunacy. *Sa folie en furie est tournee* [His folly becomes madness]. The scene in which he clamours for the blood of his son is not in any proper sense tragic or dramatic: it is a very ugly eclogue, artificial in manner and unnatural in substance. (pp. 78-81)

The better nature of the young Shakespeare revives in the closing scenes: though Exton is a rather insufficient ruffian for the part of so important an assassin. We might at least have seen or heard of him before he suddenly chips the shell as a full-fledged murderer. The last soliloquy of the king is wonderful in its way, and beautiful from any point of view: it shows once more the influence of Marlowe's example in the curious trick of selection and transcription of texts for sceptic meditation and analytic dissection. But we see rather more of the poet and less of his creature the man than Marlowe might have given us. The interlude of the groom, on the other hand, gives promise of something different in power and pathos from the poetry of Marlowe: but the scene of slaughter which follows is not quite satisfactory: it is almost boyish in its impetuosity of buffeting and bloodshed. The last scene, with its final reversion to rhyme, may be described in Richard's own previous words as good, "and yet not greatly good" [IV. i. 263].

Of the three lines on which . . . [Shakespeare] chose alternately or successively to work, the line of tragedy was that on which its promise or assurance of future supremacy was first made manifest. The earliest comedies of Shakespeare, overflowing with fancies and exuberant in beauties as they are, gave no sign of inimitable power: their joyous humour and their sunbright poetry were charming rather than promising qualities. The imperfections of his first historic play, on which I trust I have not touched with any semblance of even the most unwilling or unconscious irreverence, are surely more serious, more obvious, more obtrusive, than the doubtless undeniable and indisputable imperfections of *Romeo and Juliet.* . . . In the work of a young poet this difference would or should be enough to establish and explain the fact that though he might be greater than all other men in history and comedy, he was still greater in tragedy. (pp. 82-5)

Algernon Charles Swinburne, "'King Richard II',"
in his Three Plays of Shakespeare, *Harper & Brothers, 1909, pp. 59-85.*

CAROLINE F. E. SPURGEON   (essay date 1935)

[Spurgeon's Shakespeare's Imagery and What It Tells Us *(1935) inaugurated the "image-pattern analysis" method of studying Shakespeare's plays, one of the most widely used methods of the mid-twentieth century. In this work, she interprets the thematic structure of the plays through an examination of patterns in the imagery. Spurgeon also sought to learn about Shakespeare's personality from a study of his images, a course which few of her disciples followed. Since the publication of her book, earlier works on image patterns in Shakespeare have been discovered, but none was so important in the history of Shakespearean criticism as hers. In the excerpt below, Spurgeon traces a "constant running metaphor . . . in the early historical plays": the decayed and untended garden that symbolizes withering dynasties and anarchic society. Spurgeon also specifically relates the use of imagery to*

Shakespeare's characterization of Richard. She notes that the "weak, vacillating king" nevertheless possesses a certain charm and dignity, and so, appropriately, the metaphors used to describe him are also contradictory; at some points he is referred to as a "stricken tree" and a falling star, elsewhere as a "fair rose" and a glorious sun. The critic further analyzes recurring references to birth and generation, music, jewels, and sickness, concluding that while the imagery of Richard II *"sometimes emphasises a leading idea," it does not yet function as a central illumination as it would in the later tragedies.]*

The most constant running metaphor and picture in Shakespeare's mind in the early historical plays as a whole (from *1 Henry VI* to *Richard II* inclusive) is that of growth as seen in a garden and orchard, with the deterioration, decay and destruction brought about by ignorance and carelessness on the part of the gardener, as shown by untended weeds, pests, lack of pruning and manuring, or on the other hand by the rash and untimely cutting or lopping of fine trees.

We find it first in the scene in the Temple Gardens in *1 Henry VI* [Act II, Scene iv], with its continuous play, in true Shakespearian style, on white and red roses, thorns, blossoms, canker, plucking, cropping, rooting, withering, growing and ripening, which is carried over into the following scene, where we have the vivid picture of Mortimer as a withered vine, pithless and strengthless, drooping 'his sapless branches to the ground', detained during his 'flowering youth' in a loathsome dungeon, in consequence of an attempt to 'plant' him as the rightful heir; while Richard Plantagenet is described as 'sweet stem from York's great stock' [*1 Henry VI*, II. v. 12, 56, 80, 41].

The metaphor—which probably takes its rise very simply from the badges of York and Lancaster, together with the meaning of the name Plantagenet—clearly pleases Shakespeare, and, having started it in the first part of *Henry VI*, he carries it on in the second and third parts, developing it considerably in *Richard III*. . . . (pp. 216-17)

In *Richard II* this [garden imagery] becomes still more marked. The Duchess of Gloucester pictures Edward III's sons as 'seven fair branches springing from one root' [I. ii. 13]. Some of these have been cut 'by the Destinies', but one flourishing branch (her husband)

> Is hack'd down, and his summer leaves all faded,
> By envy's hand and murder's bloody axe.
>
> [I. ii. 20-1]

Later, Gaunt cries bitterly to Richard not to spare him, nor to hesitate with his unkindness 'To crop at once a too long withered flower' [II. i. 134]; and Richard, when he hears of Gaunt's death, comments complacently,

> The ripest fruit first falls, and so doth he.
>
> [II. i. 153]

The repeated use of the verbs plant, pluck, crop, wither, as applied to kings and members of the commonwealth, shows how continually the picture of a garden is in Shakespeare's mind. Richard himself is a 'fair rose', and as he passes his queen on his way to the Tower, she cries to her ladies,

> But soft, but see, or rather do not see,
> My fair rose wither: yet look up, behold,
> That you in pity may dissolve to dew,
> And wash him fresh again with true-love tears.
>
> [V. i. 7-10]

Act I. Scene iii. The Lists at Coventry. Frontispiece to the Hanmer edition by Francis Hayman (1744). By permission of the Folger Shakespeare Library.

It is interesting to note how, at the thought of Richard, this metaphor recurs to Hotspur when later he reproaches Northumberland for his share in the fate of the unhappy king:

> To put down Richard, that sweet lovely rose,
> And plant this thorn, this canker, Bolingbroke.
>
> [*1 Henry IV*, I. iii. 175-76]

The Bishop of Carlisle warns the nobles that if they depose Richard—the king who has been 'planted many years'—and crown Bolingbroke,

> The blood of English shall manure the ground.
>
> [IV. i. 127, 137]

When Aumerle—Richard's friend—comes after the deposition to see his mother, she asks him who are those now in favour with Bolingbroke, and words her query thus:

> Who are the violets now
> That strew the green lap of the new come spring?
>
> [V. ii. 46-7]

He answers, showing where his sympathies lie,

> Madam, I know not, nor I greatly care not:
> God knows I had as lief be none as one.
>
> [V. ii. 48-9]

Whereupon his father, deeply pledged to the new king, sharply reproves him, carrying on the metaphor:

> Well, bear you well in this new spring of time
> Lest you be cropp'd before you come to prime.
>
> [V. ii. 50-1]

And so what has been but an undertone—at first faint, later clear and definite—in the earlier historical plays, here in *Richard II* gathers strength and volume, until it becomes the leading theme, which is, as it were, gathered up, focussed and pictorially presented near the middle of the play in the curious garden scene [Act III, Scene iv], a kind of allegory, unlike anything else in Shakespeare, deliberately inserted at the cost of any likeness to nature, for no human gardeners ever discoursed like these.

They explain the whole position in detail with a heaviness of touch rare in Shakespeare, and we see that all the horrors suffered by England under the civil wars, shaken and frightened as she was by murders and battles, scheming and treachery, by the putting up and putting down of kings, by waste and misrule, have translated themselves into the pictorial imagination of the young country playwright as the despoiling of a fair 'sea-walled garden' [III. iv. 43], full of fruit, flowers and healing herbs, which ignorance and lack of care have allowed to go to seed, to rot and decay; so that now in spring time, instead of all being in order and full of promise, the whole land is, as the under gardener says,

> full of weeds; her fairest flowers choked up,
> Her fruit-trees all unpruned, her hedges ruin'd,
> Her knots disorder'd, and her wholesome herbs
> Swarming with caterpillars.
> [III. iv. 44-7]

To the real gardener no picture could be more distressing, because he knows that this condition, which is a cumulative result of long-continued neglect, can be set right only by hard years of toil and expense, and the terrible mischief wrought seems out of all proportion to the small amount of skilled attention which would have prevented this deterioration.

The careless gardener, who has 'suffer'd this disorder'd spring', is in turn pictured as a tree, who

> Hath now himself met with the fall of leaf;
> [III. iv. 48-9]

and the parasites of the realm—Richard's false friends—

> The weeds which his broad-spreading leaves did shelter,
> That seem'd in eating him to hold him up,
> Are plucked up root and all by Bolingbroke.
> [III. iv. 50-2]

'What pity is it', cries the head gardener, that Richard had 'not so trimm'd and dress'd his land as we this garden', keeping in check unruly members of the state who are apt to be 'overproud in sap and blood', pruning them as fruit trees are pruned, of which the superfluous branches have to be lopped away so that 'bearing boughs may live' [III. iv. 55-6, 59, 64].

So Shakespeare likens the land he loves to that corner of it he knows and loves best, an orchard and garden, and he pictures its desolation in the homely terms which make the most poignant appeal to him and are the most completely understood, not only by him, but also by the great majority of his countrymen then and now. (pp. 220-24)

In *Richard II*, though the metaphor of the fruit and flower garden is the most continuous, it is by no means the only recurrent one. One of many noticeable things about the play is the way in which our sympathy is called out for the weak, vacillating king, who in action is so selfish and indolent, but in speech is so eloquent. We are made to feel to the full his charm of person and his kingly dignity, and if we look closely,

we see this is done partly through metaphor. If he is the careless gardener and the stricken tree, he is also the 'fair rose' and the rising sun; and the loss of his glory is 'like a shooting star' falling 'to the base earth from the firmament' [II. iv. 19-20].

Shakespeare clearly conceived of Richard as good to look at, probably following Holinshed's remark, 'he was seemelie of shape and favor'; and he is depicted as fair and of a high colour, easily yielding to pallor [II. i. 118; III. ii. 75-9], a characteristic which may have been the reason for his being likened both to a rose and—in the English climate—to the sun. His dramatic entrance on the walls of Flint Castle is prepared for by Bolingbroke's rhetorical assertion that he and the king should meet

> With no less terror than the elements
> Of fire and water, when their thundering shock
> At meeting tears the cloudy cheeks of heaven.
> [III. iii. 55-7]
> (p. 233)

Richard himself earlier, in a long and most elaborate simile, compares himself to the 'searching eye of heaven', who, when

> He fires the proud tops of the eastern pines,

lays bare murders and treasons. So, he argues,

> when this thief, this traitor, Bolingbroke, . . .
> Shall see us rising in our throne, the east,
> His treasons will sit blushing in his face,
> Not able to endure the sight of day.
> [III. ii. 37, 42, 47, 50-2]

This is his own constant idea of himself, and the beauty and grandeur of it impress us; so that when he finally comes down from the walls of Flint to meet his adversary in the base court, the characteristically rhetorical picture he draws of that apparently simple descent seems in keeping with the royal splendour of his appearance earlier,

> Down, down I come; like glistering Phaeton,
> Wanting the manage of unruly jades.
> [III. iii. 178-79]

And when the deposition is an accomplished fact, and he scans his face in the glass he has sent for, it is this dazzling brilliance which is the quality he most prizes and most regretfully loses— 'Was this the face', he asks, 'That, like the sun, did make beholders wink?'

> A brittle glory shineth in this face:
> As brittle as the glory is the face;
> [IV. i. 283-84, 287-88]

and he dashes the glass to the ground.

So that there is deep and poignant meaning in what are his real words of abdication, when the actual power and kingship have passed to Bolingbroke, and he transfers to his successor also the royal qualities of the sun, crying in his bitterness and anguish,

> O that I were a mockery king of snow,
> Standing before the sun of Bolingbroke,
> To melt myself away in water-drops!
> [IV. i. 260-62]

This conception of the king as sun is fairly constant with Shakespeare. Touches of it are to be found in many of the historical plays, both earlier and later than *Richard II*, where it is so fully developed. (pp. 234-35)

[Concerning other] images in *Richard II,* we find that the ideas of birth and generation, also of inheritance from father to son, are a good deal in Shakespeare's mind in this play, and the recurrence of these images undoubtedly increases the effect of Nemesis, of cause and effect, of tragedy as the inevitable result of deeds done and in no way to be avoided.

Gaunt, in his dying speech, first touches on this idea, as he does on various themes which recur during the play, such as music, jewels, sickness, and the 'setting sun' [II. i. 12]—which symbolises, as regards Richard, the end of the whole tragedy. England herself is thought of by Gaunt as

> This nurse, this teeming womb of royal kings,
> Fear'd by their breed and famous by their birth;
>
> > [II. i. 51-2]

and when the queen, after Richard's departure for Ireland, betrays her fear and anxiety to Bushy and Green, she expresses it almost wholly in this particular metaphor. She is depressed naturally in parting with the king, but this sensation, she declares, is something greater than that. She feels within her an unaccountable heaviness, the working of anguish which she believes is about to bring a great grief to birth:

> methinks,
> Some unborn sorrow, ripe in fortune's womb,
> Is coming towards me.
>
> > [II. ii. 9-11]

Bushy assures her it is nothing but conceit (fancy, imagination). Even so, she answers, in one of those passages of involved word play dear to the young Shakespeare, there must be some foundation for it; either her real grief is born of nothing, or her imaginary grief takes its rise in reality; and she clothes the whole in the same metaphor which is still running in her mind:

> conceit is still derived
> From some forefather grief; mine is not so,
> For nothing hath begot my something grief;
> Or something hath the nothing that I grieve:
> 'Tis in reversion that I do possess.
>
> > [II. ii. 34-8]

So that, when she stops speaking, and Green bursts in upon them, bearing the bad news she has been dreading to hear, she naturally cries,

> So, Green, thou art the midwife to my woe,
> And Bolingbroke my sorrow's dismal heir:
> Now hath my soul brought forth her prodigy,
> And I, a gasping new-deliver'd mother,
> Have woe to woe, sorrow to sorrow join'd.
>
> > [II. ii. 62-6]

The whole framework of Richard's last great monologue is built up on birth and generation. He is thinking how he may compare his prison to the world, which is so full of people,

> And here is not a creature but myself.
>
> > [V. v. 4]

So he conceives of his brain and his soul as the mother and father,

> and these two beget
> A generation of still-breeding thoughts,
> And these same thoughts people this little world,
> In humours like the people of this world,
> For no thought is contented.
>
> > [V. v. 7-11]

The idea of inheritance from father to son, constantly debated in the play . . . , and repeated in the imagery, increases the feeling of the inevitable and fore-ordained, as also of the unlimited consequences of action. Repeated emphasis is laid on the unborn children doomed to suffer for their fathers' sins. 'God', says Richard to Northumberland,

> Is mustering in his clouds on our behalf
> Armies of pestilence; and they shall strike
> Your children yet unborn and unbegot,
>
> > [III. iii. 86-8]

and goes on to declare that Bolingbroke

> > > is come to open
> The purple testament of bleeding war,
>
> > [III. iii. 93-4]

that is, the inheritance he has taken on himself. And the deposition scene closes with the chant of the clergy as in chorus:

> A woeful pageant have we here beheld.
> The woe's to come; the children yet unborn
> Shall feel this day as sharp to them as thorn.
>
> > [IV. i. 321-23]

Later, Bolingbroke, in speaking of Aumerle's treason, sees the silver stream of York's loyalty defiled and muddied through his son, but the overflow of York's goodness is so abundant that it washes away this deadly blot. York, taking up the metaphor, answers bitterly,

> he shall spend mine honour with his shame,
> As thriftless sons their scraping fathers' gold.
>
> > [V. iii. 68-9]

There is no question but that the whole brings out with unmistakable emphasis and repetition the idea which dominates not only *Richard II* but the entire series of early histories (*Henry VI* to *Richard II*)—of the terrible heritage of blood and strife, of *evil,* in character and in deeds, which is generated and bequeathed by civil war and all that it brings with it:

> What stratagems, how fell, how butcherly,
> Erroneous, mutinous and unnatural,
> This deadly quarrel daily doth beget!
>
> > [*3 Henry VI,* II. v. 89-91]

The touches of jewel imagery in *Richard II* should also be noticed, for they add beauty to the conception of the value of love, especially of love of country—a leading note in the play—and of the honour and devotion of her sons. Thus Mowbray assures the king that a spotless reputation is the purest treasure he can have:

> A jewel in a ten-times-barr'd-up chest
> Is a bold spirit in a loyal breast.
>
> > [I. i. 180-81]

Richard, when he is alone in prison and hears the sound of music, blesses the heart that gives it him, for it is a sign of love, and love to Richard, he says,

> Is a strange brooch in this all-hating world.
>
> > [V. v. 66]

He means it is a most precious but unfashionable thing; for the brooch, which was a large valuable ornament, seems to have been out of fashion in Shakespeare's time. . . . (pp. 238-42)

The setting of jewels interests Shakespeare, and he draws several well-known images from the way in which the beauty of a precious stone is enhanced by its background or foil, as when Prince Hal declares his earlier irresponsible behaviour will actually add value to his change of conduct later:

> like bright metal on a sullen ground,
> My reformation, glittering o'er my fault,
> Shall show more goodly and attract more eyes
> Than that which hath no foil to set it off.
>
> [*1 Henry IV*, I. ii. 212-15]

The reverse process is illustrated when Richmond denounces Richard III as

> A base foul stone, made precious by the foil
> Of England's chair, where he is falsely set.
>
> [*Richard III*, V. iii. 250-51]

There are two such images in *Richard II*. One is when Gaunt, trying to reconcile his son to the thought of the weariness and pain of his long exile, bids him esteem it

> as foil wherein thou art to set
> The precious jewel of thy home return.
>
> [I. iii. 266-67]

To which Bolingbroke replies,

> Nay, rather, every tedious stride I make
> Will but remember me what a deal of world
> I wander from the jewels that I love.
>
> [I. iii. 268-70]

And one of the best-known lines in all Shakespeare is Gaunt's picture of England herself as a rare and loved jewel, enhanced in beauty and strength by the happy fortune of her setting:

> This precious stone set in the silver sea.
>
> [II. i. 46]
> (pp. 242-43)

[On] the whole this running imagery in the histories fulfils a somewhat different function from what it does in either tragedy or comedy. It is . . . , simpler and more obvious in kind, and although, as in *Richard II*, it sometimes emphasises a leading idea, it does not, as in *Hamlet* or *Macbeth*, shed definite light on the central problem, because, with the exception perhaps of Falstaff, there are in the histories no problems of character. (pp. 257-58)

> *Caroline F. E. Spurgeon, "Leading Motives in the Histories," in her* Shakespeare's Imagery and What It Tells Us, *Cambridge at the University Press, 1935, pp. 213-58.*

JOHN MIDDLETON MURRY   (essay date 1936)

[*A twentieth-century editor and critic, Murry has been called the most "level-headed" of Shakespeare's major biographical critics. Unlike such other biographical scholars as Frank Harris and Edward Dowden, Murry refused to attribute to Shakespeare a definite personality or creative neurosis which determined all his work, but regarded the poet as a man of powerful insights rather than character, an individual possessing Keat's negative capability, in the sense that he was able to withstand "uncertainties, mysteries, doubts, without any irritable reaching after fact and reason." What Murry saw as Shakespeare's greatest gift was his ability to uncover the true spirit of Elizabethan England, to fuse "not merely the poet and dramatist in himself," but to establish "a unique creative relation between himself, his dramatic material, his audience, and his actors." In the following excerpt, Murry comments on the opinion that "there is much" of Shakespeare in King Richard; he maintains that this assumption is true*]

only to the extent that Richard, as a character, obviously and imperfectly embodies Shakespeare's "dramatic and psychological justification for the operation of [his] own mind, in which the working of fancy is as yet predominant over that of the imagination." The critic also contends that the play "utters a unique moment in the growth of Shakespeare's poetic consciousness" and signals a new "historical awareness"; but Murry again emphasizes Shakespeare's freedom from dogmatic single-mindedness, claiming that for all his political sensitivity, the dramatist "has no single solution" to the complex problems posed by Richard II. The characters of Gaunt and York are also examined by Murry, as is the relevance of Elizabethan politics to a complete understanding of Shakespeare's play.]

Richard II falls exactly in the middle of the sequence of Shakespeare's histories. Four historical plays were written before it; four after it. Its content corresponds to its significant chronological position. . . . [It] is marked by an infusion of 'lyricism' and creative spontaneity into the substance of history, and shows traces of a new awareness of the problem of reconciling Shakespeare's needs with those of his audience. There is an approach to self-identification with the character of the king that is new in Shakespeare's histories. It has often been said that there is much of the poet in Shakespeare's Richard II; and in a sense this is true. But that characteristic springs rather from an incompleteness in Shakespeare's self-identification than from deliberate purpose. It comes from the transference of a technical trick of Shakespeare's own mind to his character—a transference of which Shakespeare is partly conscious. 'Can sick men play so nicely with their names?' Richard asks John of Gaunt; and Gaunt replies:

> No, misery makes sport to mock itself.
>
> [II. i. 84-5]

That is an attempt to find a dramatic and psychological justification for the operations of Shakespeare's own mind, in which the working of fancy is as yet predominant over that of the imagination. Richard 'plays the wanton with his woes' [III. iii. 164], ringing the changes of verbal conceit upon them, primarily because that was the way Shakespeare's own creative mind still worked; and the trick, for that very reason, is only half-transmuted into a trait of individual character. But the discrepancy is conscious.

The peculiar charm of *Richard II* lies, to my mind, in the nascent self-awareness with which it is pervaded. It exists on every level. The play is full of verse-experiments. (pp. 141-42)

This technical experimenting is as conscious as the effort to find a psychological justification for the licence given to the fancy. 'Nice playing' with rhythms and words and thoughts is everywhere; but with it, too, an awareness that it is superficial, that

> Grief lies all within
> And these external manners of laments
> Are merely shadows to the unseen grief
> That swells with silence in the tortured soul;
> There lies the substance.
>
> [IV. i. 295-99]

The same thought recurs in the conversation between the Queen and Bushy; and there it, too, is 'nicely played' with.

> BUSHY. Each substance of a grief hath twenty shadows,
>   Which shows like grief itself, but is not so;
>   For sorrow's eye, glazèd with blinding tears,
>   Divides one thing entire to many objects . . .
>
> [II. ii. 14-17]
> (pp. 142-43)

This consciousness of discrepancy between experience and expression belongs to the heart of *Richard II*. The budding of creative spontaneity which was so marked in *The Two Gentlemen of Verona* is graced and disturbed by an awareness of itself, to such a degree that the hiatus between experience and expression may almost be called the submerged theme of the play.

Richard II utters a unique moment in the growth of Shakespeare's poetic consciousness; and it is natural that this poetic self-awareness should be accompanied by a new advent of historical awareness. As the poet looks at his work, so does the patient chronicler of 'York's and Lancaster's long jar's' look at his. (pp. 143-44)

Richard II was, I think, partly conceived as a dramatic exposition of Shakespeare's speculations upon the cause and significance of the events with which he had been dealing hitherto with a detached and 'professional' unconcern. And Shakespeare, being Shakespeare, has no single solution: his mind, like Richard's, is a channel for various and conflicting thoughts. But, again, being Shakespeare, he does not suffer conflict to become confusion.

Richard II is the embodiment of the belief in the divine right for a king; he is its spokesman also. But with less explicitness and more idiosyncrasy than the Bishop of Carlisle.

> My Lord of Hereford here, whom you call king,
> Is a foul traitor to proud Hereford's king:
> And if you crown him, let me prophesy:
> The blood of English shall manure the ground
> And future ages groan for this foul act; . . .
> Prevent it, resist it, let it not be so,
> Lest child, child's children, cry against you 'Woe!'
> [IV. i. 134-38, 148-49]

The deposition of an anointed king is an offence against Heaven, to be visited on the third and fourth generation. That *Richard II* is simply a vindication of this ancient theory is, indeed, a commonplace of criticism; which has to contort itself round the fact that Shakespeare's company got into trouble with the authorities for reviving the play. The mistake of such criticism is the usual one, namely, to conceive Shakespeare as having a 'one-way' mind. Undoubtedly he did put forward, with all the eloquence of which he was then capable, the belief in the divine right of a king. (pp. 144-46)

But Shakespeare does not leave the matter there. The long history of bloodshed on which he had been engaged was not simply the history of a crime against Heaven and its subsequent punishment. Shakespeare was too much the imaginative realist to think thus of these things. Richard *was* deposed. The thing happened; and with a king like Richard, the thing was bound to happen. In the king's uncle, York, Shakespeare depicts the attitude of the good man, distraught between ideal loyalties and practical necessities. Not Richard's eloquence, but the odd dramatic emphasis upon York's behaviour, is the element in the play on which curiosity should be focused.

York defends Richard to the utmost bound of possibility: he is extreme in his loyalty, even to supplying the king's wasted revenues from his private purse. But, Richard once deposed, he is equally extreme in his loyalty to Bolingbroke, even to insisting, against Bolingbroke's own inclination to mercy, on the execution of his son Rutland for treason. This striking contrast is Shakespeare's invention. He had, indeed, historical warrant for York's action in denouncing his own son's treach-

ery to the new king; but Holinshed makes the action wholly due to the fact that York had personally gone bail for Rutland's good behaviour. This was an honourable, but purely personal, motive. Shakespeare deliberately lifted it to the plane of impersonal principle. Carlisle is loyal to the divine right of a king; York is loyal to the divine principle of order.

York's loyalty (perfect in kind) is to royalty as the fount of Order. When royalty ceases to be the fount of order, loyalty is necessarily dissolved. For York, no less than Carlisle, there is a divinity to hedge a king, but for him royalty is divine, only so long as it fulfils the divine purpose. It is not a divine principle in itself, but only a manifestation of the divine principle of Order. Order is God's will; and York's sense of the divine—much more nearly Shakespeare's own, I think—stands against Carlisle's and Richard's.

> Had not God, *for some strong purpose,* steeled
> The hearts of men, they must perforce have melted
> And barbarism itself have pitied him.
> But heaven hath a hand in these events,
> To whose high will we bound our calm contents.
> To Bolingbroke are we sworn subjects now,
> Whose state and honour I for aye allow.
> [V. ii. 34-40]
> (pp. 146-47)

Between the collapse of an old Order and the creation of a new one, there is a hiatus. Of this hiatus in *Richard II*, York is the dramatic embodiment. As far as his conscious expression goes, he is colourless and negative:

> Well, well, I see the issue of these arms:
> I cannot mend it, I must needs confess,
> Because my power is weak and all ill left:
> But if I could, by Him that gave me life,
> I would attach you all and make you stoop
> Unto the sovereign mercy of the king;
> But since I cannot, be it known to you
> I do remain as neuter. So, fare you well;
> Unless you please to enter in the castle
> And there repose you for this night.
> [II. iii. 152-61]

It sounds lame and ineffectual. But it is the expression, in the realm of history, of that discrepancy between experience and expression which pervades the play. The unborn woe which haunts the Queen's mind, the unseen grief that swells in silence in the King's tortured soul, is in York translated from the personal to the impersonal. The dumb pain in him is the pang of a new order: and he, unlike the King and the Queen, cannot escape it by the play of fancy. Not only is he in this unlike the King and Queen; but more markedly still he is unlike John of Gaunt, a figure of age and responsibility like his own. He has none of Gaunt's eloquence, or his wit. Gaunt can afford to be witty, for he is dying. York has to live; and he lives to *experience* the revolution as none of the other characters do. He embodies, in the concrete and impersonal process of history, the discrepancy between experience and expression, which is a merely individual pang to Richard and his queen. His embarrassed, tongue-tied speech is the comment of reality on Richard's self-absorbed facility. (pp. 148-49)

Richard II, as Queen Elizabeth seems to have felt, is somewhat of a prophetic play. True, the great historical happening of which it was premonitory—namely, the English Civil War—was much vaster in scope and upheaved profounder depths than Shakespeare's drama. But the most evident discrepancy between the prophetic poetry and the historical event is that Richard's opponent, in Shakespeare, is a mere stage-figure. Bolingbroke is a noisy and unpleasant non-entity, compared to his king. We are made to see clearly enough that Richard was an impossible monarch; but we certainly are not made to feel that Bolingbroke has any right, human or divine, to supplant him. He is no Cromwell, nor even the semblance of one.

It is partly because of this absence of any worthy antagonist to the deposed king that York takes on so much significance. Whereas Bolingbroke is the mere negation of Richard, as it were nothing more than the naked fact of successful rebellion, York seems to belong to a different world altogether. He is the bewildered and loyal middle-class Englishman, essentially no relation at all to the poetically idealized King, and still less to the stage-figure of the instrument of his overthrow. York is, indeed, a prefiguration of the country gentleman of fifty years on: not the Cavalier of romantic tradition, but the man who was to be the backbone of the Country party, the Church and King man, for whom Laud was too much of a high-flier, but who disliked the idea of a rigid Presbyterianism almost as much as he did that of Popery. In short, in York is the solid substance that would fight for King Charles, and yet at last lose heart, feeling that he was an impossible king; and eventually become, in another generation, the more humdrum country squire with whom Charles II knew better how to deal. (pp. 149-50)

In the acutal Civil War, the future drama of concrete events was to be far more complex than it was in Shakespeare's foreshortened record of the past. In Shakespeare's play the issue is merely a change of kings; for all their difference in personal qualities, Richard and Bolingbroke, when crowned, are royalties of the same order. Once the king is deposed, his sanctity as the divinely appointed source of Order passes to Bolingbroke. For a York the sequence was relatively simple: the old order, a moment of conflict and chaos, then an order of the same kind as the old. But in the Civil War there was a slow and grievous interregnum while the partial creation of a new order was being massively accomplished.

Of such a drama Shakespeare tells us, and could tell us, nothing. But there is no reason to doubt that Shakespeare was capable of imagining a dramatic opposition such as that which emerged in England, to the awe and wonder of the world, forty years after his death. That the clash of King Charles and Cromwell was a nobler and more pregnant historical happening than any on which Shakespeare spent his powers is true; but that was because it was a path forbidden to his creative imagination. When *Richard II* itself was near to treason, a drama of revolution (not mere rebellion) was unthinkable. (pp. 153-54)

John Middleton Murry, "Shakespeare and History,"
in his Shakespeare, *Jonathan Cape, 1936, pp. 141-54.*

JOHN DOVER WILSON   (lecture date 1939)

[*Dover Wilson was a highly regarded Shakespearean scholar who was involved in several aspects of Shakespeare studies. As an editor of the* New Cambridge Shakespeare, *he made numerous contributions to twentieth-century textual criticism of Shakespeare, making use of the scientific bibliography developed by W. W. Greg and Charlton Hinman. As a critic, Dover Wilson combined several contemporary approaches and does not fit easily into any one critical "school." He was concerned with character analysis in the tradition of A. C. Bradley; he delved into Elizabethan culture like the historical critics, but without their usual emphasis on hierarchy and the Great Chain of Being; and his*

interest in visualizing possible dramatic performances of the plays links him with his contemporary, Harley Granville-Barker. In the following excerpt from his 1939 lecture "The Political Background of Shakespeare's Richard II *and* Henry IV," *Dover Wilson reconstructs Elizabethan attitudes and concerns in order to assess the contemporary reaction to Shakespeare's* Richard II *and his other history plays. An audience of 1595, the critic contends, would bring to the theater certain "points of tacit cultural understanding" in many ways alien to ours. Among these was a vivid memory of the anarchy wreaked by the Wars of the Roses, which made stable government and order strong priorities with sixteenth-century Englishmen; the horrors of civil war also engendered a mystical conception of kingship that led Elizabethans to glamorize Richard while they regarded Bolingbroke as a criminal and the source of the disasters. Dover Wilson also stresses the importance of fortune in* Richard II; *he claims that critics err in viewing Bolingbroke as "a deep plotter" and Richard as a "weak-willed, rather contemptible creature," for such assessments ignore the role fortune played in the rise and fall of these two leaders.*]

It is, of course, a truism that every generation possesses the history it desires, refashions the past in its own image, reads into it its own prejudices and looks at it from its own peculiar angle of vision. I speak nationally; for, despite our European history-books and the more pretentious histories of civilisation, what we mean by history is usually the account of our own, national development in a warring world. Employing the term history, then, in this sense, we say that our historical perspective changes from age to age. And this implies not merely that each age interprets the past in the light of its own preoccupations; it signifies something more definite. If you think of it, is it not generally true that the historical vision of most persons is more or less bounded by a particular horizon, beyond which if we see at all we see but little, and which is defined by the main limits of our contemporary interests? . . . In England our watershed . . . lies in the 17th century. There are to be found the origins of the epoch in which we still live. Then took place the changes, which beginning with the Puritan Rebellion and the execution of Charles I and culminating in the Revolution of 1688 gave us the constitutional, social and legal conditions which determine our lives to-day; and of which the great reforms of the xixth century are seen to be merely an extension and a fulfillment. . . . Thus for xixth century and xxth century Englishmen, undoubtedly the most interesting field of historical study was that which began with the struggle between Charles I and his Long Parliament and ended with the Whig victory under William and Mary. Not, let us note, that this victory meant the triumph of one of the two contending parties or principles over the other. It represents a *compromise* which brings the quarrel to an end and ushers in a new age. (pp. 38-9)

If the Civil Wars of the 17th century and the constitutional settlement of 1688 form the watershed of history for modern Englishmen, what was the corresponding watershed for English people who lived before these events took place? What, in a word, was the historical perspective of the Elizabethans? With superficial points of similarity it was profoundly different from that of their successors to-day. They like us (or our fathers) looked back to a great deliverance, a deliverance from a terrible national evil, from a time of chaos, insecurity and bloodshed. They too rejoiced in special institutions, constitutional, legal and social, which though mostly swept away by the Puritan Revolution, were themselves the product of a previous revolution, or rather of the compromise and national consolidation which followed that revolution. The time of trouble to which they looked back was the Wars of the Roses, the English "thirty years war'', in which rival claimants to the throne ravaged the country from 1455 to 1485. The agency of their deliverance, the saviour of England, was the House of Tudor. And so the constitution in which they rejoiced was not a democracy, with a party system and the paraphernalia of parliamentary government, but a monarchy, ruling through its own chosen bureaucracy, a monarchy divinely ordained, strong, absolute, unchallenged, and entirely popular. To them the blessings of the Tudor government were so patent, so unquestionable that their only fear was lest something should arise to theaten its permanence or supremacy.

The most sensitive political spot in the modern Englishman's soul is personal liberty. Let the government, the executive, touch that and in a few hours a storm may spring up which will shake the firmest ministry from its seat. To the Elizabethans the most sensitive spot was Order, together with its external aspect, national Security. The Tudor absolutism made modern liberty possible; for order first, liberty afterwards, is the law of political growth. But liberty was a notion hardly comprehensible to Shakespeare, and only to some—very few— of his contemporaries in the form of religious liberty. Read *Julius Caesar* through, the play which above all others would seem to imply modern conceptions of liberty, and you will not, I think, be able to discover anywhere in the play even a glance at political liberty, as we now understand it. Order, or Degree, is the basis of his political philosophy, as it is of all thinking Elizabethans. (pp. 39-40)

There is no need to insist upon the importance of the monarchy in such a scheme of things. The King or Governor is the sun in the political heavens, that is to say not merely the largest but, in those astrological days, the most potent for good or ill of all stellar bodies. Shakespeare . . . speaks of him as "the glorious planet Sol" [*Troilus and Cressida*, I. iii. 89], and it is often overlooked that sun-symbolism for the majesty of kingship is one of Shakespeare's leading ideas. Indeed, it was the mystical conception of his position and the vital importance of preserving it unimpaired, as the sole defence against anarchy, that accounts for the semi-divine honours which their subjects accorded to Henry VIII and his great daughter Elizabeth. (p. 42)

The historical and political thought, then, of Shakespeare and his contemporaries was determined by their fears of chaos and their gratitude to the royal house which had saved England from it. But what *had* been might happen again. Looking back in horror to the terrible disorders of the Wars of the Roses they asked themselves how such chaos can have come about; and they fixed upon the reign of King Richard II as the crucial turning point, finding the true cause of all that followed in the events that brought Richard to his death and his cousin Henry of Lancaster to the throne. And they were indisputably right. To the men of the late middle ages and the 16th century, the deposition of Richard II was as significant as the execution of Charles I was to Englishmen of the 18th and 19th centuries. Thus they viewed Richard and Henry Bolingbroke in a light quite different from that in which our historians see them today. (p. 43)

The weakness of Bolingbroke's title is what interests our modern historians, because weakness in the executive foreshadows the birth of constitutional and political liberty. But what is almost a virtue in [the historians'] eyes was a crime in that of Tudor Englishmen. Henry of Lancaster was not to them the morning star of the Whig Revolution, but the man at whose door the disorders of the 15th century must be laid. He was in fact a usurper and his usurpation so weakened the executive

that it took over eighty years of struggle to restore the nation to sanity and health, unity and order. (p. 44)

[It] is remarkable that [Edward Hall's *Chronicle* of 1548] begins with the death of the Duke of Gloucester at King Richard's orders and the subsequent quarrel between Mowbray and Bolingbroke; in other words, at exactly the same point where Shakespeare begins his *Richard II*. Indeed, we have three elaborate accounts of the period of the Wars of the Roses, all written in the 16th century, viz. Hall's *Chronicle,* Shakespeare's cycle of historical plays, *Richard II* to *Richard III*, and a long poem by Samuel Daniel entitled *The Civil Wars between the two houses of Lancaster and York*—and they all begin at the same point! Furthermore, this point was selected not only by a sound historical instinct but also because it possessed a very special meaning for England at the time of Elizabeth. The political horizon was for Shakespeare and his contemporaries peculiarly uncertain. Henry VIII, building upon the foundations laid by the first of the Tudors, his father, had rehabilitated the monarchy, and restored unity and order to the nation. And he had been succeeded by three children in turn, the last of them being his most worthy heir. But when Elizabeth died, what then? Was England to relapse once more into dynastic strife? For the Tudor stock was exhausted; Elizabeth had no heirs. Writing in 1600, a lawyer enumerates no fewer than twelve different "competitors that gape for the death of that good old Princess, the now Queen". No wonder that many identified her with Richard II, and looked forward with dread to usurpation and a period of anarchy once again.

Daniel left his poem on the Civil Wars unfinished; and Shakespeare never rounded off his dramatic cycle. Why were these two great literary undertakings to remain uncompleted? The death of Elizabeth in 1603 provides at least one answer to the question. With the peaceful accession of James VI of Scotland and James I of England the problem of the succession was solved. A new dynasty was established upon the throne, a dynasty founded not upon civil war and the rise of a noble house, but upon legal right so strong that it was recognized in a foreign branch of the royal line. (p. 45)

[With the accession of James] the taste for poems and dramas on the troublous times of the fifteenth century disappeared with the political anxieties which had stimulated it. When Shakespeare desired to write history in future, he turned to Plutarch, in whose pages he found dimly reflected, as in some magic glass, a new and hitherto hardly suspected political problem, which was after his death to bring civil war of a new kind to the land. I mean of course, the conflict between the Crown and the Commons, the Governor and his people, an issue already felt in *Julius Caesar* and evident in *Coriolanus*.

But while Elizabeth lived, the older anxieties governed men's thoughts, and in their fears that her reign might be the prelude to yet another period of anarchy, they naturally bent eagerly enquiring eyes upon the events of the reign of Richard II, which had led up to the earlier time of trouble, and particularly upon the actions of the usurper Henry IV. . . . (p. 46)

[That] Shakespeare and his audience regarded Bolingbroke as a usurper is incontestable. This is evident . . . from the whole tone and emphasis of *Richard II*. It is confirmed also by its sequel, *Henry IV,* out of the mouth of the King himself, in the confession he makes to Prince Hal in the Second Part:

> God knows, my son,
> By what by-paths and indirect crook'd ways
> I met this crown; and I myself know well
> How troublesome it sat upon my head.

To thee it shall descend with better quiet,
Better opinion, better confirmation;
For all the soil of the achievement goes
With me into the earth.
[2 Henry IV, IV. v. 183-90]

A sense of guilt, indeed, weighs heavy upon Henry from the very outset of his reign. His first words in *1 Henry IV* are

So shaken as we are, so wan with care;
[1 Henry IV, I. i. 1]

the hand of Death is upon him throughout; and his repeatedly expressed intention to go on a crusade is itself a token of contrition.

Yet he is a tragic figure, not a criminal. Looking back on the events that led up to his accession, he declares solemnly from the sick-bed that he had originally "no intent" to depose his cousin,

But that necessity so bowed the state
That I and greatness were compelled to kiss
[2 Henry IV, III. ii. 73-4]

words which we must accept as the truth in view of the circumstances in which they are uttered. Those critics, therefore . . . , who make him out to be in *Richard II* nothing but a deep plotter are very wide of the mark. One of the dominant conceptions of that play is the notion of the part which Fortune, a very real force in the medieval and Elizabethan universe, played in the affairs of this world; and the unaccountable action of her influence contributes much to the atmosphere of mystery which is so evident a characteristic of the play. Fortune's wheel, indeed, seems to have suggested the very shape and structure of the drama, which gives us a complete inversion. The first act opens immediately after the death of the Duke of Gloucester, when as Froissart notes Richard is "high upon the wheel", exhibiting all the hybris and tyranny expected of persons in that position, while his opponent, Bolingbroke, is shown at the lowest point of his fortunes. But from the beginning of act II, the wheel starts turning mysteriously of itself, or rather by the action of the goddess. The will of the King seems paralysed; he becomes an almost passive agent. Bolingbroke acts, and acts forcibly; yet he too appears to be borne upwards by a power beyond his volition. Circumstance drives him on from point to point; he takes what Fortune and Fortune's puppet, Richard, throw in his path. He is an opportunist, not a schemer. (pp. 47-9)

And if we miss much that Shakespeare intended when we regard Bolingbroke as a mere crafty villain, we miss still more if we write Richard off as the weak-willed, rather contemptible creature that Coleridge makes of him. One of the great attractions of the story of Richard of Bordeaux and Henry Bolingbroke, Duke of Lancaster, for the men of the 15th and 16th centuries was that it afforded, in its spectacle of what Hall calls the "dejecting of the one and the advancing of the other" a perfect example of the mysterious action of Fortune, under Providence. And Shakespeare's play was a mirror, not only for magistrates, but for every son of woman; for when the "dejected" king gazed (on Shakespeare's stage) into the glass, he saw the brittleness not only of his own glory but of all earthly happiness.

Yet Richard stood for much more than a man broken on Fortune's wheel. He was a king, and more even than that too. In the eyes of the later middle ages, he represented the type and exemplar of royal martyrdom, of a king not slain in battle, not

defeated and killed by a foreign adversary, not even like Edward II deposed owing to weakness or tyranny in favour of his legal heir, but thrust from the throne in his may of youth, by a mere usurper, under colour of a process of law utterly illegal, and then foully murdered. By the anti-Lancastrians of his time, and France was full of them, he was almost canonized, as Charles I became later. Men dwelt upon his agony and death; compared his sufferings with those of Christ, and his judges with Pilate; and attributed his fall and capture to treachery as base as that of Judas. He became the centre of a legend, the legend of the hero and gracious monarch, betrayed into the hands of cruel and ambitious men. No fewer than four chronicles, one in Latin and three in French, embodying this legend, have come down to us from the 15th century; and of some versions there exist a large number of manuscript copies on the continent.

On the other hand, the followers of Henry of Lancaster had, of course, their own story, which is still to all intents that of history . . . ; the story of a feckless, moody, tyrannical young man, who surrounded himself with base favourites, surrendered of his own accord, out of cowardice, and abdicated of his own free will.

The two legends are, and were intended to be, contradictory; but under the Tudor monarchy, which united the two houses of York and Lancaster and healed the breach for which Bolingbroke had originally been responsible, the legends became, so to speak, conflated. Both are found (ill-reconciled) in the pages of Holinshed, that Elizabethan tank into which the streams from various chronicle sources flowed, without mingling. Holinshed lacked the imagination to fuse the diverse, and orginally contradictory, elements. Shakespeare succeeded, and his Richard is a convincing portrait, compounded from the two legends, the portrait of a king who seems to us one of the most living of his characters.

It was chance that early in his career, in 1595 to be precise, Shakespeare stumbled in the pages of Holinshed upon these twin but contrary conceptions of Richard's character, and was forced to do what he could to unify them. But it is in my belief that the effort taught him a great lesson which he never forgot, and which is one of the secrets of his dramatic power. It taught him, for example, that he could challenge his audience with an unsympathetic character at the beginning of a play, and win them round to sympathize with the same character in the second half. He accomplished this with great success again in *King Lear*, a play which, as it always seems to me, possesses much closer connexions with *Richard II* than *Hamlet* does. It taught him also something without which the Prince of Denmark, as we know him, could never have come into existence, viz. the tremendous value of apparent contradictions in character for the creation of dramatic versimilitude. It is largely because Hamlet is logically and psychologically inconsistent and, as all the critics have found, beyond the possibility of analysis, that he appears so life-like in action on the stage. King Richard II presents though in simpler form, a similar bundle of contradictions. In this case, however, Shakespeare found the contradictions in his history-book, he did not invent them. It is odd to think that the lying propaganda of Henry Bolingbroke and his partisans at the beginnings of the 15th century may have assisted Shakespeare thus materially in the creation not only of his Richard but also of his Hamlet. (pp. 49-51)

John Dover Wilson, "The Political Background of Shakespeare's 'Richard II' and 'Henry IV'," in Shakespeare-Jahrbuch, *Vol. 75, 1939, pp. 36-51.*

MARK VAN DOREN (essay date 1939)

[*Van Doren was a Pulitzer prize-winning poet, American educator, editor, and novelist. In the introduction to his* Shakespeare *(1939), he states that he "ignored the biography of Shakespeare, the history and character of his time, the conventions of his theater, the works of his contemporaries" to concentrate on the interest of the plays and their relevance to the modern reader or spectator. Concerning Shakespeare's characterization of Richard II, Van Doren writes, ". . . he has not made a great man of him. He has made a poet, a great minor poet." This king—like the dramatist himself at the time, according to Van Doren—"luxuriates" in words, infatuated "with the art he so proudly and self-consciously practices." Van Doren adds, however, that although Shakespeare could channel his creative instincts productively, Richard cannot; his gifts are totally unsuited to his position as king. Still, the critic maintains, Richard is "Shakespeare's finest poet thus far, and in spite of everything he is a touching person."*]

The histories of Shakespeare that deal with later reigns than Richard II's will be eloquent with sympathy for the king whom Bolingbroke deposed. Hotspur will rage whenever he remembers "that sweet lovely rose" [*1 Henry IV*, I. iii. 175] in whom the canker of another man's ambition grew. When Bolingbroke is dying as Henry IV he will confess to his son

> By what by-paths and indirect crook'd ways
> I met this crown.
>
> [*2 Henry IV*, IV. v. 184-85]

And the son as Henry V will do all he can, through prayers, tears, charity, and the building of chantries, to atone for his father's fault. The Bishop of Carlisle, rising in "Richard II" itself to prophesy what things shall follow the triumph of Bolingbroke, speaks with the accent usually reserved by Shakespeare for righteous men:

> Disorder, horror, fear, and mutiny
> Shall here inhabit, and this land be call'd
> The field of Golgotha and dead men's skulls.
>
> [IV. i. 142-44]

There can be no question as to Shakespeare's affection for the hero of his new historical play.

But he has not made a great man of him. He has made a poet, a great minor poet. The author of "Richard II" is perhaps more interested in poetry than he will ever be again. He is still learning to write at a fabulous rate, he is still making the most remarkable discoveries of powers within his pen which he could not have guessed were there before, let alone measured. And the particular power he is now discovering is one that makes him conscious of himself as a poet. It is the power to write the English language musically—with a continuous melody and with unfailing reserves of harmony. His king will be similarly self-conscious; that will explain the sympathy between the author and his creation, as well as provide the author an opportunity to criticize his own excesses in an extension of himself. For Richard will not become a great poet. Merely "musical" poets seldom do. And Shakespeare will understand the limitations of the poetry with which he endows his hero. At the same time he will be as much in love with it as he dares. Nor does any reader of Shakespeare, coming upon this play in the order of its composition, fail to fall in love with the music of its poetry. It is the work of an awakening genius who has fallen in love with the language he writes; who realizes the full possibilities of its idiom and scale; and who lets himself go. The subject of "Richard II" is the reign and deposition of an English king. It is also the beauty of the English language considered as an instrument upon which music can be made. (pp. 84-5)

The play swarms with poets who practice their several styles and upon occasion copy one another. They are sensitive like their author to the call of a cadence; music that one of them hears from another's tongue is likely to linger in his own words later. (p. 88)

[The] great poet of the play, of course, is Richard. And if he has to content himself with being a minor poet, that circumstance is consistent with the character of the man and of the action built around him. The play is organized about a hero who, more indeed than contenting himself with the role of minor poet, luxuriates in it. His theme is himself. He dramatizes his grief. He spends himself in poetry—which is something he loves more than power and more than any other person. His self-love is grounded upon an infatuation with the art he so proudly and self-consciously practices. That is what "Richard II" is about, and what even its plot expresses. Its unity therefore is distinct and impressive.

Its first half shows us a king accomplished in the rhetoric of his office. . . . His talk is big, his rhythms are tremendous. So we might expect him to put traitors quickly down; or, if a rival appeared for his throne, we might be certain that mighty measures, along with mighty phrases, would leave him soon again solitary in unassailable grandeur. What explains his failure to oppose Bolingbroke at all, his sudden collapse, as soon as the threat of deposition becomes real, into a state of sheer elegy, of pure poetry? The answer is simple. Richard is a poet, not a king. Surrounded by favorites and deceived by dreams of his utter safety he can strut in the high style awhile. But an acute ear detects the strut even at the brave beginning; and soon enough there are signs of the precious, conceited musician who hides under the robe. . . . The Duke of York warns Gaunt that the young king will not listen to the wisdom of any old man because his ears are too much in love with the "venom sound" of "lascivious metres" [II. i. 19]. He is too much, York means, the mere poet. York is a foolish old fellow, and may be prejudiced. Yet there is a suspicious excess in the kiss of words bestowed by Richard upon the soil of Wales when he lands from Ireland:

> As a long-parted mother with her child
> Plays fondly with her tears and smiles in meeting,
> So, weeping, smiling, greet I thee, my earth,
> And do thee favours with my royal hands.
>
> [III. ii. 8-11]

And within a few minutes the secret is entirely out; Richard drops his pretense of being a major poet simultaneously with the surrender of his power, with the crumpling of his front. The break is sudden, and poetically, not to say dramatically, it is brilliant. Richard's last speech in the old style is the best he has made in that style; he never spoke with more appearance of strength than he does now when he hears Scroop say that Wiltshire, Bagot, Bushy, and Green have made peace with Bolingbroke:

> O villains, vipers, damn'd without redemption!
> Dogs, easily won to fawn on any man!
> Snakes, in my heart-blood warm'd, that sting my heart!
> Three Judases, each one thrice worse than Judas!
> Would they make peace? Terrible hell make war
> Upon their spotted souls for this offense!
>
> [III. ii. 129-34]

But these words are the last hard and heavy ones he uses. For Scroop explains that Richard's friends have made peace with heads, not hands; and to Aumerle's question concerning the whereabouts of York a new kind of answer comes, in a new style which gives us all at once the man we have been waiting for. The new style is exquisite, high-pitched, limpid, lyrical, and boneless; its phrases run sweetly, easily, without the effort of argument or disguise; its music listens to itself, pleased with the high-born whine of a matchless, inimitable melody; and the diction is literary, the imagery is of books, of writing, of story-telling:

> No matter where; of comfort no man speak.
> Let's talk of graves, of worms, and epitaphs;
> Make dust our paper and with rainy eyes
> Write sorrow on the bosom of the earth.
> Let's choose executors and talk of wills;
> And yet not so; for what can we bequeath
> Save our deposed bodies to the ground?. . .
>
> [III. ii. 144-50]

All this while Richard had been a poet, not a king; a minor poet, waiting for the cues of sorrow and disaster. Now that he has them he will honor nothing else; he will do nothing but compose fine, tender, heart-breaking lines, nothing but improvise endless variations on the rich, resonant theme of his personal woe. (pp. 89-91)

The new poet in Richard will develop at a giddy rate, so that in the great deposition scene (IV, i) he will stand full confessed and wail in perfect glory. In this scene, far from concealing his art, he calls attention to it with every gesture, he wantonly loses himself in its mazes. He enters, talking to himself in the role of Christ—a role he fancies now—betrayed by Judas. Upon York's reminding him that he is here to hand over his crown he dramatically seizes one side of the golden object, offers the other side to Bolingbroke, and begins a long poem about buckets in wells. Bolinbroke interrupts him with the prosaic protest:

> I thought you had been willing to resign
>
> [IV. i. 190]

Richard's rhyming answer is perhaps his honestest speech:

> My crown I am; but still my griefs are mine.
> You may my glories and my state depose,
> But not my griefs; still am I king of those.
>
> [IV. i. 191-93]

But he is not done. For in his next long speech he must pull out the stops of pity and if possible break other hearts than his own; and after that he must keep the parliament waiting while he wonders what name to call himself, now that he is nothing. Poets must have names to call things, and minor poets must have names to call themselves. The thought of his nothingness moves him to request that a mirror be brought so that he can gaze upon his bankrupt self. It is brought, and it turns out to be a wonderful source of further poetic ideas. When they are exhausted he dashes it down and breaks it, remarking to Bolingbroke as he does so:

> Mark, silent king, the moral of this sport,
> How soon my sorrow hath destroy'd my face.
>
> [IV. i. 290-91]

The bewildered Bolingbroke, thus far reduced like everyone else to silence and embarrassed awe, makes the mistake of presenting Richard with a metaphor that he can go on with. "The shadow of your sorrow," says the new king, "hath destroy'd the shadow of your face." He has not bothered to search for a fresh image; this one is already stale in Elizabethan poetry; but it is good enough for Richard, who pounces upon it gratefully:

> Say that again.
> The shadow of my sorrow! Ha! let's see.
> 'Tis very true, my grief lies all within;
> And these external manners of laments
> Are merely shadows to the unseen grief
> That swells with silence in the tortur'd soul.
> There lies the substance; and I thank thee, King,
> For thy great bounty, that not only giv'st
> Me cause to wail but teachest me the way
> How to lament the cause.
>
> [IV. i. 293-302]

There is irony in Richard's thanks, but there is also simple truth; he is happy with his sorrow, he is functioning through grief.

The farewell to his Queen gives him a particularly audible cue, and we should note that it is not her sorrow but his that he embroiders with such beautiful harmonies:

> Good sometimes queen, prepare thee hence for France.
> Think I am dead, and that even here thou tak'st,
> As from my death-bed, thy last living leave.
> In winter's tedious nights sit by the fire
> With good old folks and let them tell thee tales
> Of woeful ages long ago betid;
> And ere thou bid good night, to quit their griefs
> Tell thou the lamentable tale of me
> And send the hearers weeping to their beds.
>
> [V. i. 37-45]

The thought of his own death is delicious pleasure; the alliteration in the third line is something of which he is conscious and sadly proud; the good old folks in France are already weeping for him as he sings. (pp. 92-4)

Richard is Shakespeare's finest poet thus far, and in spite of everything he is a touching person. He is not a great man, nor is the play in consequence a considerable tragedy. But as a performer on the lyre Richard has no match among Shakespeare's many people. And as dramatizer of himself he will be tutor to a long posterity, though none of his pupils—Hamlet is the best known—will be exactly like him. . . . Other persons in the play know grief and taste it: Gaunt, the Duchess of Gloucester, and the Duchess of York when her son Aumerle is in danger of death as a traitor, and the Queen when she overhears the gardener and cannot refrain from coming forward. But they have nothing like Richard's perfection in poetry. And the Duke of York . . . is not so much a sorrower as a worrier; he is perhaps a parody, in the decrepit key, of Richard's full-noted grief. At any rate he is the one clearly comic personage in a play otherwise given over to tragic sentiment. Richard himself would have his comic side if there were a perspective here from which to view it. Shakespeare has the perspective; Bolingbroke, crowned Henry IV, has still one worry, the behavior of his son amongst the taverns of London where Falstaff is king [V. iii. 1-22]; and Falstaff will throw a new light on everything. But "Richard II" admits no such light. It sings in its own darkness, listening sweetly to itself. (p. 95)

Mark Van Doren, "Richard II," in his Shakespeare, *Henry Holt and Company, 1939, pp. 84-95.*

E. M. W. TILLYARD (essay date 1944)

[*Tillyard's* Shakespeare's History Plays *(1944) is regarded by many scholars as one of the most influential twentieth-century works in Shakespearean studies and a leading example of historical criticism. Tillyard's thesis, which is shared, with variations, by other historical critics, discerns a systematic world-view in Shakespeare's plays—and one common to educated Elizabethans—in which reality is understood to be structured in a hierarchical Great Chain of Being. On a social level such a philosophy valued order, hierarchy, and civil peace as the chief political goals. Further, Tillyard notes a basic acceptance in Shakespeare's histories of "the Tudor myth," the critic's term for an interpretation of English history from* Richard II *to* Henry VIII. *According to this "myth," Henry IV was a usurper, and his usurpation set into motion the disastrous chain of events which culminated in the Wars of the Roses between 1455 and 1485. Even Henry V, "the perfect ruler," was unable to prevent the inevitable conflict. Tillyard's remarks on* Richard II *are among the most celebrated in the play's critical history, and even those who disagree with him or would modify his conclusions admit that* Shakespeare's History Plays *opened new vistas for analysis of this drama. Tillyard draws attention to the rigid formality— the ceremonial and ritual expression—that regulates Richard's court and reflects that monarch's response to life. The critic maintains that this emphasis on ritual is Shakespeare's attempt to evoke the ambience of the Middle Ages, a period for which, according to Tillyard, the dramatist and his contemporaries felt an enormous nostalgia. Richard, the last king of the old order to reign by hereditary right of his descent from William the Conqueror, represents the world of Chaucer and Gower, of medieval tapestries, of tournaments and heraldry and knights; Bolingbroke, on the other hand, is an unpoetical, hard-nosed politician who stands for the forces of Modernism; thus the conflict between them concerns more than a clash of personalities—it signals the transition from one historical era to another. Tillyard's interpretation not only helped later scholars appreciate Richard's peculiar psychological position, but it also inspired numerous essays on the larger social repercussions of his fall.*]

However large the apparent differences in style between *Richard II* and *Henry IV,* these plays are connected with a network of cross-references. On the other hand, although *Richard II* may have been written not long after *King John,* the connections are fitful and unimportant. *Richard II* looks forward; and Shakespeare conceived his second tetralogy as one great unit.

The matter is important and calls for substantiation.

First and most important, Richard and Prince Hal are deliberately contrasted characters; Richard being the prince in appearance rather than in reality, Hal being the prince in reality whose appearance at first obscures the truth. Richard's emblem was the sun of royalty emerging from a cloud, a piece of symbolism to which Bolingbroke refers when Richard appears on the walls of Flint Castle:

> See, see, King Richard doth himself appear
> As doth the blushing discontented sun
> From out the fiery portal of the east,
> When he perceives the envious clouds are bent
> To dim his glory and to stain the track
> Of his bright passage to the occident.
>
> [III. iii. 62-7]

But Richard did not live up to his emblem, for he allowed the clouds, his evil advisers, to obscure his proper glory. It is Prince Hal who adopts and justifies in himself the emblem, according to his own declaration at the end of the second scene of *I Henry IV:*

> Yet herein will I imitate the sun,
> Who doth permit the base contagious clouds
> To smother up his beauty from the world,

> That, when he please again to be himself,
> Being wanted he may be more wonder'd at
> By breaking through the foul and ugly mists
> Of vapours that did seem to strangle him.
>
> [*I Henry IV,* I. ii. 197-203]

If this were the one possible cross-reference between *Richard II* and *I Henry IV* we might doubt its authenticity; being one of many it can hardly not be intentional.

Secondly, the whole theme of insurrection and civil war as developed in the plays is continuous, as if conceived as a whole. Carlisle's speech in Westminster Hall, for instance, prophesying civil war if Bolingbroke is crowned proclaims its sequel in future plays:

> My Lord of Hereford here, whom you call king,
> Is a foul traitor to proud Hereford's king.
> And if you crown him, let me prophesy:
> The blood of English shall manure the ground,
> And future ages groan for this foul act; . . .
>
> [IV. i. 134-38]

If these lines in the first play of the tetralogy look forward, Henry's prayer before Agincourt in the last one, that God should not visit on him the death of Richard, looks right back.

Thirdly, the Percies figure in *Richard II* in a way that suggests that they will figure even more prominently in the future. Northumberland is the main executant of Henry's rise; and Richard, informed by Northumberland that he must go to Pomfret Castle, warns him that one day he will think no reward sufficient for his services:

> Northumberland, thou ladder wherewithal
> The mounting Bolingbroke ascends my throne,
> The time shall not be many hours of age
> More than it is, ere foul sin gathering head
> Shall break into corruption. Thou shalt think,
> Though he divide the realm and give thee half,
> It is too little, helping him to all;
> And he shall think that thou, which know'st the way
> To plant unrightful kings, will know again,
> Being ne'er so little urg'd, another way
> To pluck him headlong from the usurped throne.
>
> [V. i. 55-65]
> (pp. 234-35)

King Henry in *2 Henry IV* actually quotes from *Richard II.* He reminds Warwick of the words Richard spoke to Northumberland when about to be taken to Pomfret, and proceeds to quote some of them:

> 'Northumberland, thou ladder by the which
> My cousin Bolingbroke ascends my throne,'
> (Though then, God knows, I had no such intent,
> But that necessity so bow'd the state
> That I and greatness were compell'd to kiss)
> 'The time shall come' thus did he follow it,
> 'The time will come, that foul sin gathering head
> Shall break into corruption'; so went on,
> Foretelling this same time's condition
> And the division of our amity.
>
> [*2 Henry IV,* III. i. 70-9]

Shakespeare would never have quoted from the History Play before last unless he had thought his sequence an organic whole. That he misquotes (as can be seen by comparing the original passage from *Richard II* just quoted) shows that he was more mindful of big than of little things.

If then the plays of the second tetralogy are so closely connected, we must treat them as a single organism. Confronted with different styles in *Richard II* and *Henry IV*, we shall have to refrain from calling the first archaic and the second suddenly and miraculously mature, but shall be forced to admit that Shakespeare knew what he was doing from the start and deliberately planned this stylistic contrast. Once we accept this compulsion we shall be the gainers, finding that the plays form a great symphonic scheme. The first three at least will become not only easier to understand but finer works of art. (pp. 236-37)

Richard II is imperfectly executed, and yet, that imperfection granted, perfectly planned as part of a great structure. It is sharply contrasted, in its extreme formality of shape and style, with the subtler and more fluid nature of *Henry IV*; but it is a necessary and deliberate contrast; resembling a stiff recitative composed to introduce a varied and flexible *aria*. Coming after *King John* the play would appear the strangest relapse into the official self which Shakespeare had been shedding; taken with *Henry IV* it shows that Shakespeare, while retaining and using this official self, could develop with brilliant success the new qualities of character and style manifested in the Bastard [in *King John*]. *Richard II* therefore betokens no relapse but is an organic part of one of Shakespeare's major achievements.

But the imperfections are undoubted and must be faced. As a separate play *Richard II* lacks the sustained vitality of *Richard III*, being less interesting and less exacting in structure and containing a good deal of verse which by the best Shakespearean standards can only be called indifferent. . . . For illustrating the indifferent verse I need not go beyond the frequent stretches of couplet-writing and the occasional quatrains that make such a contrast to the verse of *Henry IV*. It is not that these have not got their function, which will be dealt with later, but that as poetry they are indifferent stuff. They are as necessary as the stiff lines in *3 Henry VI* spoken by the Father who has killed his Son, and the Son who has killed his Father; but they are little better poetically. For present purposes it does not matter in the least whether they are relics of an old play, by Shakespeare or by someone else, or whether Shakespeare wrote them with the rest. They occur throughout the play and with the exception of perhaps two couplets are not conspicuously worse in the fifth act than anywhere else. There is no need for a theory that in this act, to save time, Shakespeare hurriedly began copying chunks from an old play. Until there is decisive proof of this, it is simplest to think that Shakespeare wrote his couplets along with the rest, intending a deliberate contrast. He had done the same thing with the Talbots' death in *1 Henry VI*, while, to account for the indifferent quality, one may remember that he was never very good at the couplet. The best couplets in *A Midsummer Night's Dream* are weak compared with the best blank verse in that play, while few of the final couplets of the sonnets are more than a competent close to far higher verse.

I turn now to a larger quality of the play, of which the couplets are one of several indications.

Of all Shakespeare's plays *Richard II* is the most formal and ceremonial. It is not only that Richard himself is a true king in appearance, in his command of the trappings of royalty, while being deficient in the solid virtues of the ruler; that is a commonplace: the ceremonial character of the play extends much wider than Richard's own nature or the exquisite patterns of his poetic speech.

First, the very actions tend to be symbolic rather than real. There is all the pomp of a tournament without the physical meeting of the two armed knights. There is a great army of Welshmen assembled to support Richard, but they never fight. Bolingbroke before Flint Castle speaks of the terrible clash there should be when he and Richard meet:

Methinks King Richard and myself should meet
With no less terror than the elements
Of fire and water, when their thundering shock
At meeting tears the cloudy cheeks of heaven.
[III. iii. 54-7]

But instead of a clash there is a highly ceremonious encounter leading to the effortless submission of Richard. There are violent challenges before Henry in Westminster Hall, but the issue is postponed. The climax of the play is the ceremony of Richard's deposition. And finally Richard, imprisoned at Pomfret, erects his own lonely state and his own griefs into a gigantic ceremony. (pp. 244-46)

Second, in places where emotion rises, where there is strong mental action, Shakespeare evades direct or naturalistic presentation and resorts to convention and conceit. . . . Emotionally Richard's parting from his queen could have been a great thing in the play: actually it is an exchange of frigidly ingenious couplets.

Rich. Go, count thy way with sighs; I mine with groans.
Qu. So longest way shall have the longest moans.
Rich. Twice for one step I'll groan, the way being short,
 And piece the way out with a heavy heart.
[V. i. 89-91]

This is indeed the language of ceremony not of passion. . . . The case of Gaunt is different but more complicated. When he has the state of England in mind and reproves Richard, though he can be rhetorical and play on words, he speaks the language of passion. . . . But in the scene of private feeling, when he parts from his banished son, both speakers, ceasing to be specifically themselves, exchange the most exquisitely formal commonplaces traditionally deemed appropriate to such a situation.

Go, say I sent thee for to purchase honour
And not the king exil'd thee; or suppose
Devouring pestilence hangs in our air
And thou art flying to a fresher clime.
Look, what thy soul holds dear, imagine it
To lie that way thou go'st, not whence thou com'st. . . .
[I. iii. 282-87]

Superficially this may be maturer verse than the couplets quoted, but it is just as formal, just as mindful of propriety and as unmindful of nature as Richard and his queen taking leave. Richard's sudden start into action when attacked by his murderers is exceptional, serving to set off by contrast the lack of action that has prevailed and to link the play with the next of the series. His groom, who appears in the same scene, is a realistic character alien to the rest of the play and serves the same function as Richard in action.

Thirdly, there is an elaboration and a formality in the cosmic references, scarcely to be matched in Shakespeare. These are usually brief and incidental, showing indeed how intimate a part they were of the things accepted and familiar in Shakespeare's mind. But in *Richard II* they are positively paraded. The great speech of Richard in Pomfret Castle is a tissue of them: first the peopling of his prison room with his thoughts, making its microcosm correspond with the orders of the body politic; then the doctrine of the universe as a musical harmony; then the fantasy of his own griefs arranged in a pattern like the working of a clock, symbol of regularity opposed to discord; and finally madness as the counterpart in man's mental kingdom of discord or chaos. Throughout the play the great commonplace of the king on earth duplicating the sun in heaven is exploited with a persistence unmatched anywhere else in Shakespeare. Finally (for I omit minor references to cosmic lore) there is the scene (III. 4) of the gardeners, with the elaborate comparison of the state to the botanical microcosm of the garden. (pp. 246-49)

Nothing could illustrate better the different expectations of a modern and of an Elizabethan audience than the way they would take the gardener's opening words:

> Go, bind thou up yon dangling apricocks,
> Which, like unruly children, make their sire
> Stoop with oppression of their prodigal weight.
>
> [III. iv. 29-31]

The first thought of a modern audience is: what a ridiculous way for a gardener to talk. The first thought of an Elizabethan would have been: what is the symbolic meaning of those words, spoken by this king of the garden, and how does it bear on the play? And it would very quickly conclude that the apricots had grown inflated and overweening in the sun of the royal favour; that oppression was used with a political as well as a physical meaning; and that the apricots threatened, unless restrained, to upset the proper relation between parent and offspring, to offend against the great principle of order. In fact the scene turns out to be an elaborate political allegory, with the Earl of Wiltshire, Bushy, and Green standing for the noxious weeds which Richard, the bad gardener, allowed to flourish and which Henry, the new gardener, has rooted up. It ends with the queen coming forward and joining in the talk. She confirms the gardener's regal and moral function by calling him "old Adam's likeness" [III. iv. 73], but curses him for his ill news about Richard and Bolingbroke. The intensively symbolic character of the scene is confirmed when the gardener at the end proposes to plant a bank with rue where the queen let fall her tears, as a memorial:

> Rue, even for ruth, here shortly shall be seen
> In the remembrance of a weeping queen.
>
> [III. iv. 105-06]
> (pp. 249-50)

Why was it that in *Richard II*, when he was so much more mature, when his brilliant realism in *King John* showed him capable of making his gardeners as human and as amusing as the grave-diggers in *Hamlet*, Shakespeare chose to present them with a degree of formality unequalled in any play he wrote? It is, in a different form, the same question as that which was implied by my discussion of the other formal or ceremonial features of the play: namely, why did Shakespeare in *Richard II* make the ceremonial or ritual form of writing, found in differing quantities in the *Henry VI* plays and in *Richard III*, not merely one of the principal means of expression but the very essence of the play?

These are the first questions we must answer if we are to understand the true nature of *Richard II*. And here let me repeat that though Richard himself is a very important part of the play's ceremonial content, that content is larger and more im-

portant than Richard. With that caution, I will try to explain how the ritual or ceremonial element in *Richard II* differs from that in the earlier History Plays, and through such an explanation to conjecture a new interpretation of the play. There is no finer instance of ceremonial writing than the scene of the ghosts at the end of *Richard III*. But it is subservient to a piece of action, to the Battle of Bosworth with the overthrow of a tyrant and the triumph of a righteous prince. Its duty is to make that action a matter of high, mysterious, religious import. We are not invited to dwell on the ritual happenings as on a resting-place, to deduce from them the ideas into which the mind settles when the action of the play is over. But in *Richard II*, with all the emphasis and the point taken out of the action, we are invited, again and again, to dwell on the sheer ceremony of the various situations. The main point of the tournament between Bolingbroke and Mowbray is the way it is conducted; the point of Gaunt's parting with Bolingbroke is the sheer propriety of the sentiments they utter; the portents, put so fittingly into the mouth of a Welshman, are more exciting because they are appropriate than because they precipitate an event; Richard is ever more concerned with how he behaves, with the fitness of his conduct to the occasion, than with what he actually does. . . . We are in fact in a world where means matter more than ends, where it is more important to keep strictly the rules of an elaborate game than either to win or to lose it.

Now though compared with ourselves the Elizabethans put a high value on means as against ends they did not go to the extreme. It was in the Middle Ages that means were so elaborated, that rules of the game of life were so lavishly and so minutely set forth. *Richard II* is Shakespeare's picture of that life.

Of course it would be absurd to suggest that Shakespeare pictured the age of Richard II after the fashion of a modern historian. But there are signs elsewhere in Shakespeare of at least a feeling after historical verity; and there are special reasons why the age of Richard II should have struck the imaginations of the Elizabethans. (pp. 251-52)

Richard was the last king of the old medieval order:

> the last king ruling by hereditary right, direct
> and undisputed, from the Conqueror. The kings
> of the next hundred and ten years . . . were es-
> sentially kings *de facto* not *de jure*, successful
> usurpers recognised after the event, upon con-
> ditions, by their fellow-magnates or by parlia-
> ment [A. B. Steel, in his *Richard II*].

Shakespeare, deeply interested in titles as he had showed himself to be in his early History Plays, must have known this very well; and Gaunt's famous speech on England cannot be fully understood without this knowledge. He calls England

> This nurse, this teeming womb of royal kings,
> Fear'd by their breed and famous by their birth,
> Renowned for their deeds as far from home,
> For Christian service and true chivalry,
> As is the sepulchre in stubborn Jewry
> Of the world's ransom, blessed Mary's son.
>
> [II. i. 51-6]

Richard was no crusader, but he was authentic heir of the crusading Plantagenets. Henry was different, a usurper; and it is with reference to this passage that we must read the lines in *Richard II* and *Henry IV* which recount his desire and his failure to go to Palestine. That honour was reserved for the authentic Plantagenet kings. Richard then had the full sanctity of medieval kingship and the strong pathos of being the last king to possess it. (pp. 253-54)

Not only did Richard in himself hold a position unique among English kings, he maintained a court of excessive splendour. Froissart writes as follows in the last pages of his chronicle:

> This King Richard reigned king of England twenty-two year in great prosperity, holding great estate and signory. There was never before any king of England that spent so much in his house as he did by a hundred thousand florins every year. For I, Sir John Froissart, canon and treasurer of Chinay, knew it well, for I was in his court more than a quarter of a year together and he made me good cheer.... And when I departed from him it was at Windsor; and at my departing the king sent me by a knight of his, Sir John Golofer, a goblet of silver and gilt weighing two mark of silver and within it a hundred nobles, by the which I am as yet the better and shall be as long as I live; wherefore I am bound to pray to God for his soul and with much sorrow I write of his death.

But Shakespeare need not have gone to Froissart for such information. In an age that was both passionately admiring of royal magnificence and far more retentive of tradition than our own the glories of Richard's court must have persisted as a legend.... Then there were the poets. Shakespeare must have associated the beginnings of English poetry with Chaucer and Gower; and they wrote mainly in Richard's reign. There must have been much medieval art, far more than now survives, visible in the great houses of Elizabeth's day, illuminated books and tapestry; and it would be generally associated with the most brilliant reign of the Middle Ages. Finally in Richard's reign there was the glamour of a still intact nobility: a very powerful glamour in an age still devoted to heraldry and yet possessing an aristocracy who, compared with the great men of Richard's day, were upstarts.

All these facts would have a strong, if unconscious, effect on Shakespeare's mind and induce him to present the age of Richard in a brilliant yet remote and unrealistic manner. He was already master of a certain antique lore and of a certain kind of ceremonial writing: it was natural that he should use them, but with a different turn, to do this particular work. Thus he makes more solemn and elaborates the inherited notions of cosmic correspondences and chivalric procedure and he makes his ritual style a central and not a peripheral concern. Hence the portentous solemnity of the moralising gardeners, the powerful emphasis on the isolated symbol of the rue-tree, the elaborate circumstances of the tournament between Bolingbroke and Mowbray, and the unique artifice of Richard's great speeches: speeches which are the true centre of the play but central with a far wider reference than to the mere character of Richard. (pp. 254-56)

It has been the habit to contrast the ''poetry'' of Richard with the practical common sense of Bolingbroke. But the ''poetry'' of Richard is all part of a world of gorgeous tournaments, conventionally mournful queens, and impossibly sententious gardeners, while Bolingbroke's common sense extends to his backers, in particular to that most important character, North-

umberland. We have in fact the contrast not only of two characters but of two ways of life. (pp. 257-58)

Thus *Richard II*, although reputed so simple and homogeneous a play, is built on a contrast. The world of medieval refinement is indeed the main object of presentation but it is threatened and in the end superseded by the more familiar world of the present.

In carrying out his object Shakespeare shows the greatest skill in keeping the emphasis sufficiently on Richard, while hinting that in Bolingbroke's world there is the probability of development. In other words he makes the world of Bolingbroke not so much defective as embryonic. It is not allowed to compete with Richard's but it is ready to grow to its proper fulness in the next plays. This is especially true of the conspirators' characters. Hotspur, for instance, is faintly drawn yet in one place he speaks with a hearty abruptness that shows his creator had conceived the whole character already.... Bolingbroke too is consistent with his later self, though we are shown only certain elements in his character. What marks out the later Bolingbroke and makes him a rather pathetic figure is his bewilderment. For all his political acumen he does not know himself completely or his way about the world. And the reason is that he has relied in large part on fortune. Dover Wilson remarked truly of him in *Richard II* that though he acts forcibly he appears to be borne upward by a power beyond his volition. [see excerpt above, 1939]. He is made the first mover of trouble in the matter of the tournament and he wants to do something about Woodstock's murder. But he has no steady policy and having once set events in motion is the servant of fortune. As such, he is not in control of events, though by his adroitness he may deal with the unpredictable as it occurs.... It is worth anticipating and saying that Prince Hal differs from his father in having perfect knowledge both of himself and of the world around him. Of all types of men he is the least subject to the sway of fortune. (pp. 259-61)

Richard II . . . at once possesses a dominant theme and contains within itself the elements of those different things that are to be the theme of its successors.

It must not be thought, because Shakespeare treated history, as described above, in a way new to him that he has lost interest in his old themes. On the contrary he is interested as much as ever in the theme of civil war, in the kingly type, and in the general fortunes of England. And I will say a little on each of these before trying to sum up the play's meaning in the tetralogy to which it belongs.

Richard II does its work in proclaiming the great theme of the whole cycle of Shakespeare's History Plays: the beginning in prosperity, the distortion of prosperity by a crime, civil war, and ultimate renewal of prosperity. . . . In doctrine the play is entirely orthodox. Shakespeare knows that Richard's crimes never amounted to tyranny and hence that outright rebellion against him was a crime. He leaves uncertain the question of who murdered Woodstock and never says that Richard was personally responsible. The king's uncles hold perfectly correct opinions. Gaunt refuses the Duchess of Gloucester's request for vengeance, the matter being for God's decision alone. Even on his deathbed, when lamenting the state of the realm and calling Richard the landlord and not the king of England, he never preaches rebellion. And he mentions deposition only in the sense that Richard by his own conduct is deposing himself. (p. 261)

As well as being a study of medievalism, Richard takes his place among Shakespeare's many studies of the kingly nature. He is a king by unquestioned title and by his external graces alone. But others have written so well on Richard's character that I need say no more.

Lastly, for political motives, there is the old Morality theme of Respublica. One of Shakespeare's debts in *Richard II* is to *Woodstock;* and this play is constructed very plainly on the Morality pattern, with the king's three uncles led by Woodstock inducing him to virtue, and Tressilian Bushy and Green to vice. There are traces of this motive in Shakespeare's play, but with Woodstock dead before the action begins and Gaunt dying early in it the balance of good and evil influences is destroyed. Bushy, Green, and Bagot, however, remain very plainly Morality figures and were probably marked in some way by their dress as abstract vices. . . . [But once] again, as in the earlier tetralogy, England herself, and not the protagonist, is the main concern. Gaunt speaks her praises, the gardener in describing his own symbolic garden has her in mind. As part of the great cycle of English history covered by Hall's chronicle the events of the reign of Richard II take their proper place. But here something fresh has happened. The early tetralogy had as its concern the fortunes of England in that exciting and instructive stretch of her history. *Richard II* has this concern too, but it also deals with England herself, the nature

and not merely the fortunes of England. In *Richard II* it is the old brilliant medieval England of the last Plantagenet in the authentic succession; in *Henry IV* it will be the England not of the Middle Ages but of Shakespeare himself. We can now see how the epic comes in and how *Richard II* contributes to an epic effect. Those works which we honour by the epic title always, among other things, express the feelings or the habits of a large group of men, often of a nation. However centrally human, however powerful, a work may be, we shall not give it the epic title for these qualities alone. It is not the parting of Hector and Andromache or the ransoming of Hector's body that make the *Iliad* an epic; it is that the *Iliad* expresses a whole way of life. Shakespeare, it seems, as well as exploiting the most central human affairs, as he was to do in his tragedies, was also impelled to fulfil through the drama that peculiarly epic function which is usually fulfilled through the narrative. Inspired partly perhaps by the example of Daniel and certainly by his own genius, he combined with the grim didactic exposition of the fortunes of England during her terrible ordeal of civil war his epic version of what England was. (pp. 262-63)

Of this great new epic attempt *Richard II* is only the prelude. What of England it pictures is not only antique but partial: the confined world of a medieval courtly class. In his next plays Shakespeare was to picture (with much else) the whole land, as he knew it, in his own day, with its multifarious layers of society and manners of living. (p. 263)

> *E. M. W. Tillyard, "The Second Tetralogy," in his* Shakespeare's History Plays, *Chatto & Windus, 1944, pp. 234-303.*

RICHARD D. ALTICK (essay date 1947)

[Altick's "Symphonic Imagery in Richard II*" (1947), from which the following excerpt is taken, is regarded by scholars as a landmark analysis of the history. The critic identifies "the insubstantiality of human language" as a major theme in the play, maintaining that the king's "complacent enjoyment of the sound of his own tongue" entangles him in self-indulgent, self-dramatizing monologues that prevent him from dealing realistically with his serious political problems. Altick avers that certain "leading metaphors and verbal motifs"—including "earth," "blood," "tongue," "tears," "snakes," and "sun"—do more than simply illustrate Richard's "propensity for verbalizing." Rather, he suggests, through their frequent repetition these form verbal and visual patterns that unify the action as it develops and endow it with symbolic resonance. Thus, the play's fundamental ideas are vividly embodied in its imagery. Many scholars have since elaborated on aspects of the imagery in* Richard II, *and virtually all of them acknowledge their indebtedness to Altick.]*

Critics on occasion have remarked the peculiar unity of tone which distinguishes *Richard II* from most of Shakespeare's other plays. (p. 339)

How can we account for that impression of harmony, of oneness, which we receive when we read the play or listen to its lines spoken upon the stage? The secret, it seems to me, lies in an aspect of Shakespeare's genius which has oftener been condemned than praised. Critics and casual readers alike have groaned over the fine-drawn ingenuity of the Shakespearean quibble, which, as Dr. Johnson maintained, was "the fatal Cleopatra for which he lost the world, and was content to lose it." But it is essentially the same habit of the creative imagination—a highly sensitized associational gift—that produces iterative symbolism and imagery. Simple word-play results from the poet's awareness of the diverse meanings of words,

Act V. Scene iii. Henry IV, York, the Duchess, and Aumerle. Frontispiece to the Bell edition by E. Edwards (1774).

of which, however, he makes no better use than to demonstrate his own cleverness and to tickle for a moment the wit of the audience. These exhibitions of verbal agility are simply decorations scattered upon the surface of the poetic fabric; they can be ripped out without loss. But suppose that to the poet's associational sensitivity is added a further awareness of the multitudinous emotional overtones of words. When he puts this faculty to use he is no longer merely playing a game; instead, words have become the shells in which ideas and symbols are enclosed. Suppose furthermore that instead of being the occupation of a few fleeting lines of the text, certain words of multifold meanings are played upon throughout the five acts, recurring time after time like leitmotivs in music. And suppose finally that this process of repetition is applied especially to words of sensuous significance, words that evoke vivid responses in the imagination. When these things happen to certain words—when they cease to be mere vehicles for a brief indulgence of verbal fancy and, taking on a burden of serious meaning, become thematic material—the poet has crossed the borderline that separates word-play from iterative imagery. Language has become the willing servant of structure, and what was on other occasions only a source of exuberant but undisciplined wit now is converted to the higher purpose of poetic unity.

That, briefly, is what happens in *Richard II*. The familiar word-plays of the earlier Shakespearean dramas persist: John of Gaunt puns endlessly upon his own name. But in this drama a word is not commonly taken up, rapidly revolved, so that all its various facets of meaning flash out, and then discarded. Instead, certain words are played upon throughout the drama. Far from being decorations . . . , they are woven deeply into the thought-web of the play. Each word-theme symbolizes one or another of the fundamental ideas of the story, and every time it reappears it perceptibly deepens and enriches those meanings and at the same time charges the atmosphere with emotional significance.

The most remarkable thing about these leitmotivs is the way in which they are constantly mingling and coalescing, two or three of them joining to form a single new figure. . . . And since each image motif represents one of the dominant ideas of the play (heredity, patriotism, sycophancy, etc.) the coalescing of these images again and again emphasizes the complex relationship between the ideas themselves, so that the reader is kept ever aware that all that happens in *Richard II* results inevitably from the interaction of many elements. (pp. 339-40)

[The] symbolism of *Richard II* is dominated by the related words *earth, land,* and *ground.* In no other play of Shakespeare is the complex of ideas represented by these words so tirelessly dwelt upon. The words are but three in number, and superficially they seem roughly synonymous; but they have many intellectual ramifications, which become more and more meaningful as the play progresses and the words are used first for one thing and then for another. (p. 341)

Above all, *earth* is the symbol of the English nation. It is used by Shakespeare to connote those same values which we find in the equivalent synecdoche of *soil,* as in "native soil." It sums up all the feeling inherent in the sense of pride in nation—of jealousy when the country is threatened by foreign incursion, of bitter anger when its health has been destroyed by mismanagement or greed. "This earth of majesty," John of Gaunt calls England in his famous speech, ". . . This blessed plot, this earth, this realm, this England" [II. i. 41, 50]. And a few

lines farther on: "This land of such dear souls, this dear dear land . . ." [II. i. 57]. Having once appeared, so early in the play, in such lustrous context, the words *earth* and *land* forever after have richer significance. Whenever they recur, they are more meaningful, more powerful. Thus Richard's elaborate speech upon his arrival in Wales—

> As a long-parted mother with her child
> Plays fondly with her tears and smiles in meeting,
> So, weeping, smiling, greet I thee, my earth,
> And do thee favours with my royal hands. . . .
> Mock not my senseless conjuration, lords.
> This earth shall have a feeling, and these stones
> Prove armed soldiers, ere her native king
> Shall falter under foul rebellion's arms
>
> [III. ii. 8-11, 23-6]

—undoubtedly gains in emotional splendor (as well as dramatic irony) by its reminiscences of John of Gaunt's earlier language. The two men between them make the English earth the chief verbal theme of the play.

Richard, we have just seen, speaks pridefully or "*my* earth." To him, ownership of the land is the most tangible and positive symbol of his rightful kingship. He bids Northumberland tell Bolingbroke that "every stride he makes upon my land / Is dangerous treason" [III. iii. 92-3], and as he lies dying from the stroke of Exton's sword his last thought is for his land: "Exton, thy fierce hand / Hath with the king's blood stained the king's own land" [V. v. 109-10]. It is only natural, then, that *land* should be the key word in the discussions of England's sorry condition. Symbol of Englishmen's nationalistic pride and of the wealth of kings, it becomes symbol also of Englishmen's shame and king's disgrace:

> Why, cousin, wert thou regent of the world,
> It were a shame to let this land by lease;
> But for thy world enjoying but this land,
> Is it not more than shame to shame it so?
> Landlord of England art thou now, not king.
>
> [II. i. 109-13]

Northumberland's sad allusion to "this declining land" [II. i. 240], York's to "this woeful land" [II. ii. 99] and Richard's to "this revolting land" [III. iii. 163] carry on this motif.

But *earth,* while it emblematizes the foundation of kingly pride and power, is also a familiar symbol of the vanity of human life and of what, in the middle ages, was a fascinating illustration of that vanity—the fall of kings. . . . This earth, Richard knows, is accustomed to receive the knees of courtiers: "Fair cousin," he tells Bolingbroke after he has given away his kingdom for the sheer joy of listening to himself do so, "you debase your princely knee / To make the base earth proud with kissing it" [III. iii. 190-91]. And the idea of the ground as the resting place for suppliant knees, and therefore the antithesis of kingly elevation, is repeated thrice in the two scenes dealing with Aumerle's conspiracy.

The irony of this association of *earth* with both kingly glory and abasement is deepened by another role the word has in this earth-preoccupied play. For after death, earth receives its own; and in *Richard II* the common notion of the grave has new meaning, because the ubiquitous symbol of *earth* embraces it too. (pp. 341-43)

A final theme in the symphonic pattern dominated by the symbol of earth is that of the untended garden. Miss Spurgeon has adequately emphasized the importance of this iterated image in the history plays, and, as she points out, it reaches its climax in *Richard II*, particularly in the allegorical scene of the Queen's garden [see excerpt above, 1935]. In Shakespeare's imagination the misdeeds of Richard and his followers constituted an overwhelming indignity to the precious English earth—to a nation which, in happier days, had been a sea-wall'd garden. And thus the play is filled with references to ripeness and the seasons, to planting and cropping and plucking and reaping, to furrows and plowing, and caterpillars and withered bay trees and thorns and flowers.

Among the host of garden images in the play, one especially is unforgettable because of the insistence with which Shakespeare thrice echoes it. It is the terrible metaphor of the English garden being drenched by showers of blood.

> I'll use the advantage of my power
> And lay the summer's dust with showers of blood
> Rain'd from the wounds of slaughtered Englishmen;
>
> [III. iii. 42-4]

threatens Bolingbroke as he approaches Flint castle; and when the King himself appears upon the walls, he casts the figure back in Bolingbroke's face:

> But ere the crown he looks for live in peace,
> Ten thousand bloody crowns of mothers' sons
> Shall ill become the flower of England's face,
> Change the complexion of her maid-pale peace
> To scarlet indignation, and bedew
> Her pastures' grass with faithful English blood.
>
> [III. iii. 95-100]

The Bishop of Carlisle takes up the theme:

> And if you crown him, let me prophesy,
> The blood of English shall manure the ground,
> And future ages groan for this foul act.
>
> [IV. i. 136-38]

And the new King—amply justifying Professor Van Doren's remark that not only are most of the characters in this play poets, but they copy one another on occasion [see excerpt above, 1939]—echoes it:

> Lords, I protest, my soul is full of woe
> That blood should sprinkle me to make me grow.
>
> [V. vi. 45-6]

This extraordinary series of four images is one of the many examples of the manner in which the principal symbols of *Richard II* so often chime together, bringing the ideas they represent into momentary conjunction and thus compounding those single emotional strains into new and revealing harmonies. In this case the "showers of blood" metaphor provides a recurrent nexus between the pervasive symbol of earth and another, equally pervasive, symbol: that of blood.

Both Professor Bradley and Miss Spurgeon have pointed out the splendid horror which Shakespeare achieves in *Macbeth* by his repeated allusions to blood. Curiously enough, the word *blood,* together with such related words as *bloody* and *bleed,* occurs much less frequently in *Macbeth* than it does in most of the history plays. What gives the word the tremendous force it undoubtedly possesses in *Macbeth* is not the frequency with which it is spoken, but rather the intrinsic magnificence of the passages in which it appears and the fact that in this play it has but one significance—the literal one. In the history plays, however, the word *blood* plays two major roles. Often it has

the same meaning it has in *Macbeth,* for these too are plays in which men's minds often turn toward the sword:

> . . . our kingdom's earth should not be soil'd
> With that dear blood which it hath fostered
>
> [I. iii. 125-26]

says Richard in one more instinctive (and punning!) association of blood and earth. But *blood* in the history plays also stands figuratively for inheritance, descent, familial pride; and this is the chief motivating theme of the play—the right of a monarch of unquestionably legitimate blood to his throne. The two significances constantly interplay, giving the single word a new multiple connotation wherever it appears. . . . Because it has this multiple function, the word *blood* in this play loses much of the concentrated vividness and application it has in *Macbeth,* where it means but one unmistakable thing; but its ambiguity here gives it a new sort of power. If it is less effective as imagery, it does serve to underscore the basic idea of the play, that violation of the laws of blood descent leads but to the spilling of precious English blood. That is the meaning of the word as it pulses from beginning to end, marking the emotional rhythm of the play.

In *Richard II*, furthermore, the word has an additional, unique use, one which involves an especially striking symbol. It has often been remarked how Shakespeare, seizing upon a hint in his sources, plays upon Richard's abnormal tendency to blanch and blush. In the imagery thus called forth, *blood* has a prominent part. How, demands the haughty king of John Gaunt, dare thou

> with thy frozen admonition
> Make pale our cheek, chasing the royal blood
> With fury from his native residence.
>
> [II. i. 117-19]

And when the King hears the news of the Welshmen's defection, Aumerle steadies his quaking body:

> Comfort, my liege; why looks your Grace so
>   pale?
> *Richard:*   But now the blood of twenty thousand men
> Did triumph in my face, and they are fled;
> And, till so much blood thither come again,
> Have I not reason to look pale and dead?
>
> [III. ii. 75-9]
> (pp. 344-47)

The idea of pallor and blushing is linked in turn with what is perhaps the most famous image-motif of the play, that of Richard (or the fact of his kingship) emblematized by the sun. More attention probably has been paid to the sun-king theme than it is worth, for although it occurs in two very familiar passages, it contributes far less to the harmonic unity of the play than do a number of other symbol strains. In any event, the conjunction of the sun image with that of blushing provides one more evidence of the closeness with which the poetic themes of the play are knit together. In the first of the sun-king speeches, Richard compares himself, at the length to which he is addicted, with "the searching eye of heaven" [III. ii. 37]. Finally, after some ten lines of analogy:

> So when this thief, this traitor, Bolingbroke,
> Who all this while hath revell'd in the night
> Whilst we were wand'ring with the antipodes,
> Shall see us rising in our throne, the east,
> His treasons will sit blushing in his face. . . .
>
> [III. ii. 47-51]
> (pp. 347-48)

Another occurrence of the sun image provides a link with the pervasive motif of tears. Salisbury, having envisioned Richard's glory falling to the base earth from the firmament, continues:

> Thy sun sets weeping in the lowly west,
> Witnessing storms to come, woe, and unrest.
>
> [II. iv. 21-2]

In no other history play is the idea of tears and weeping so insistently presented. It is this element which enforces most strongly our impression of Richard as a weakling, a monarch essentially feminine in nature, who has no conception of stoic endurance or resignation but a strong predilection for grief. This is why the play seems so strangely devoid of the heroic; the King and Queen are too much devoted to luxuriating in their misery, and the other characters find a morbid delight in at least alluding to unmanly tears. Characteristically, Richard's first question to Aumerle, when the latter returns from bidding farewell to Bolingbroke, is, ''What store of parting tears were shed?'' [I. iv. 5]. . . . In the garden scene the Queen, rejecting her lady's offer to sing, sadly tells her:

> 'Tis well that thou hast cause;
> But thou shouldst please me better wouldst thou
>   weep.
> *Lady:* I could weep, madam, would it do you good.
> *Queen:* And I could sing, would weeping do me good,
>   And never borrow any tear of thee.
>
> [III. iv. 19-23]

And echoing that dialogue, the gardener, at the close of the scene, looks after her and says:

> Here did she fall a tear; here in this place
> I'll set a bank of rue, sour herb of grace
> Rue, even for ruth, here shortly shall be seen,
> In the remembrance of a weeping queen.
>
> [III. iv. 104-07]

The theme reaches a climax in the deposition scene, in which the agonized King, handing his crown to Bolingbrooke, sees himself as the lower of the two buckets in Fortune's well:

> . . . full of tears am I,
> Drinking my griefs, whilst you mount up on high.
>
> [IV. i. 188-89]

And a few lines later he merges the almost ubiquitous motif of tears with another constant theme of the play: ''With mine own tears I wash away my balm'' [IV. i. 207]. Of the frequent association of the anointing of kings, blood, and the act of washing, I shall speak a little later.

Professor Van Doren, in his sensitive essay on *Richard II*, eloquently stresses the importance of the word *tongue* in the play. *Tongue,* he says, is the key word of the piece. I should prefer to give that distinction to *earth;* but there is no denying the effectiveness of Shakespeare's tireless repetition of the idea of speech, not only by the single word *tongue* but also by such words as *mouth, speech,* and *word.* (pp. 348-49)

This group of associated words heavily underscores two leading ideas in the play. In the first place, it draws constant attention to the propensity for verbalizing (as Shakespeare would not have called it!) which is Richard's fatal weakness. He cannot bring himself to live in a world of hard actuality; the universe to him is real only as it is presented in packages of fine words. Aumerle tries almost roughly to recall him from his weaving of sweet, melancholy sounds to a realization of the crucial situation confronting him, but he rouses himself only momen-

tarily and then relapses into a complacent enjoyment of the sound of his own tongue. It is of this trait that we are constantly reminded as all the characters regularly use periphrases when they must speak of what they or others have said. By making the physical act of speech, the sheer fact of language, so conspicuous, they call attention to its illusory nature. . . . That words are mere conventional sounds moulded by the tongue, and reality is something else again, is constantly on the minds of all the characters. The initial dispute between Mowbray and Bolingbroke is ''the bitter clamour of two eager tongues'' [I. i. 49]; Mowbray threatens to cram his antagonist's lie ''through the false passage of thy throat'' [I. i. 125]; and later, in a fine cadenza, he conceives of his eternal banishment in terms of the engaoling of his tongue, whose ''use is to me no more / Than an unstringed viol or a harp,'' and concludes:

> What is thy sentence [then] but speechless death,
> Which robs my tongue from breathing native breath?
>
> [I. iii. 161-62, 172-73]

Bolingbroke, for his part, marvels over the power of a single word to change the lives of men:

> How long a time lies in one little word!
> Four lagging winters and four wanton springs
> End in a word: such is the breath of kings. . . .
>
> [I. iii. 213-15]

[The] remainder of the play is equally preoccupied with the unsubstantiality of human language.

But the unremitting stress laid upon tongues and words in this play serves another important end: it reminds us that Richard's fall is due not only to his preference for his own words rather than for deeds, but also to his blind predilection for comfortable flattery rather than sound advice. Words not only hypnotize, suspend the sense of reality: they can sting and corrupt. And so the tongues of *Richard II* symbolize also the honeyed but poisonous speech of the sycophants who surround him. ''No,'' replies York to Gaunt's suggestion that his dying words might yet undeaf Richard's ear.

> it is stopp'd with other flattering sounds,
> As praises, of whose taste the wise are fond,
> Lascivious metres, to whose venom sound
> The open ear of youth doth always listen.
>
> [II. i. 17-20]

The venom to which York refers and the snake which produces it form another theme of the imagery of this play. The snake-venom motif closely links the idea of the garden on the one hand (for what grossly untended garden would be without its snakes?) and the idea of the tongue on the other. All three meet in the latter part of Richard's speech in III. ii:

> But let thy spiders, that suck up thy venom,
> And heavy-gaited toads lie in their way,
> Doing annoyance to the treacherous feet
> Which with usurping steps do trample thee.
> Yield stinging nettles to mine enemies;
> And when they from thy bosom pluck a flower,
> Guard it, I pray thee, with a lurking adder
> Whose double tongue may with a mortal touch
> Throw death upon thy sovereign's enemies.
>
> [III. ii. 14-22]

And the double association occurs again in the garden scene, when the Queen demands of the gardener,

Thou, old Adam's likeness, set to dress this garden,
How dares thy harsh rude tongue sound this unpleasing
   news?
What Eve, what serpent, hath suggested thee
To make a second fall of cursed man?
                                                  [III. iv. 73-6]

Mowbray elsewhere speaks of "slander's venom'd spear" [I.
i. 171], and to Richard, the flatterers who have deserted him
are, naturally enough, "villains, vipers, damn'd without redemption! / . . . Snakes, in my heart blood warm'd, that sting
my heart!" [III. ii. 129-31].

Although England's sorry state is most often figured in the
references to the untended garden and the snakes that infest it,
the situation is emphasized time and again by at least four other
recurrent themes, some of which refer as well to the personal
guilt of Richard. One such theme—anticipating a similar motif
in *Hamlet*—involves repeated references to physical illness and
injury. . . . *Plague, pestilence,* and *infection* are words frequently in the mouths of the characters of this play. Aumerle,
during the furious gage-casting of IV. i, cries, "May my hands
rot off" if he does not seize Percy's gage [IV. i. 49]; and
elsewhere York, speaking to the unhappy Queen, says of the
King,

         Now comes the sick hour that his surfeit made;
         Now shall he try his friends that flatter'd him
                                                  [II. ii. 84-5]
                                                  (pp. 349-52)

[Secondly] the evil that besets England is frequently symbolized as a dark blot upon fair parchment—an image which occurs
oftener in this play than in any other. The suggestion for the
image undoubtedly came from contemplation of the deeds and
leases by which the king had farmed out the royal demesnes;
as John of Gaunt said, England "is now bound in with shame, /
With inky blots and rotten parchment bonds" [II. i. 63-4]. The
image recurs several times. "No, Bolingbroke," says Mowbray in I. iii, "if ever I were traitor, / My name be blotted
from the book of life" [I. iii. 201-02]. Richard sighs through
blanched lips, "Time hath set a blot upon my pride" [III. ii.
81] and later speaks of the record of Northumberland's offenses
as including

                  one heinous article,
         Containing the deposing of a king
         And cracking the strong warrant of an oath,
         Mark'd with a blot, damn'd in the book of heaven.
                                                  [IV. i. 233-36]
                                                  (p. 353)

The blot image has a very direct relationship with another class
of figures by which Shakespeare symbolizes guilt or evil: that
of a stain which must be washed away. This image is most
commonly associated with *Macbeth,* because of the extraordinary vividness with which it is used there. But the theme is
much more insistent in *Richard II.* Twice it is associated, as
in *Macbeth,* with blood:

              Yet, to wash your blood
         From off my hands, here in the view of men
         I will unfold some causes of your deaths.
                                                  [III. i. 5-7]

      I'll make a voyage to the Holy Land,
      To wash this blood off from my guilty hand. . . .
                                                  [V. vi. 49-50]

But in this play the absolution of guilt requires not merely the
symbolic cleansing of bloody hands; it entails the washing-off
of the sacred ointment of royalty—the ultimate expiation of
kingly sin. The full measure of Richard's fall is epitomized in
two further occurrences of the metaphor, the first spoken when
he is in the full flush of arrogant confidence, the second when
nemesis has overtaken him:

         Not all the water in the rough rude sea
         Can wash the balm off from an anointed king.
                                                  [III. ii. 54-5]

      With mine own tears I wash away my balm,
      With mine own hands I give away my crown.
                                                  [IV. i. 207-08]

Whatever the exact context of the image of washing, one suggestion certainly is present whenever it appears: a suggestion
of momentous change—the deposition of a monarch, the
cleansing of a guilt-laden soul. (pp. 354-55)

Keeping in mind the leading metaphors and verbal motifs which
I have reviewed—*earth-ground-land, blood,* pallor, garden,
sun, tears, *tongue-speech-word, snake-venom,* physical injury
and illness, *blot,* washing [and so on] . . .—it is profitable to
re-read the whole play, noting expecially how widely the various themes are distributed, and how frequently their strands
cross to form new images. There is no extended passage of
the text which is not tied in with the rest of the play by the
occurrence of one or more of the familiar symbols. However,
the images are not scattered with uniform evenness. As in *The
Merchant of Venice,* metaphorical language tends to be concentrated at the emotional climaxes of *Richard II.* At certain
crucial points in the action, a large number of the unifying
image-threads appear almost simultaneously, so that our minds
are virtually flooded with many diverse yet closely related
ideas. (p. 359)

[An] example of the close arraying of image patterns . . . occurs
in [Act III, Scene iii]:

Yet know, my master, God omnipotent,	
Is mustering in his clouds on our behalf	
Armies of pestilence; and they shall	(illness)
strike	
Your children yet unborn and unbegot,	(generation)
That lift your vassal hands against my	
head	
And threat the glory of my precious	(crown)
crown.	
Tell Bolingbroke—for yon methinks he	
stands—	
That every stride he makes upon my land	(earth)
Is dangerous treason. He is come to open	
The purple testament of bleeding war;	(books, blood)
But ere the crown he looks for live in	(crown)
peace,	
Ten thousand bloody crowns of mothers'	(blood, crown,
sons	generation)
Shall ill become the flower of England's	(garden)
face,	
Change the complexion of her maid-pale	(pallor)
peace	
To scarlet indignation, and bedew	
Her pastures' grass with faithful	(blood)
English blood.	

                                                  [III. iii. 85-100]
                                                  (p. 361)

A final aspect of the use of iterative imagery in *Richard II* is the manner in which a particularly important passage is prepared for by the interweaving into the poetry, long in advance, of inconspicuous but repeated hints of the imagery which is to dominate that passage. The method is exactly analogous to that by which in a symphony a melody appears, at first tentatively, indeed almost unnoticed, first in one choir of the orchestra, then another, until ultimately it comes to its reward as the theme of a climactic section. In such a manner is the audience prepared, although unconsciously, for Richard's last grandiose speech. One takes little note of the first timid appearance of a reference to beggary or bankruptcy in Bolingbroke's "Or with pale beggar-fear impeach my height" [I. i. 189]. But in the second act the motif recurs:

> Be York the next that must be bankrupt so!
> Though death be poor, it ends a mortal woe,
>
> [II. i. 151-52]

and a hundred lines later the idea is repeated: "The king's grown bankrupt, like a broken man" [II. i. 257]. The haunting dread of destitution, then, however obliquely alluded to, is a recurrent theme, and adds its small but perceptible share to the whole atmosphere of impending disaster. It forms the burden of two plaints by Richard midway in the play:

> Let's choose executors and talk of wills;
> And yet not so; for what can we bequeath
> Save our deposed bodies to the ground?
> Our lands, our lives and all are Bolingbroke's.
>
> [III. ii. 148-51]

> I'll give my jewels for a set of beads,
> My gorgeous palace for a hermitage,
> My gay apparel for an almsman's gown,
> My figur'd goblets for a dish of wood,
> My sceptre for a palmer's walking-staff,
> My subjects for a pair of carved saints,
> And my large kingdom for a little grave.
>
> [III. iii. 147-53]

But the time is not ripe for the climactic utterance of this motif. It disappears, to return for a moment in a verbal hint in the deposition scene:

> Let it command a mirror hither straight,
> That it may show me what a face I have
> Since it is bankrupt of his majesty.
>
> [IV. i. 265-67]

> Being so great, I have no need to beg.
>
> [IV. i. 309]

The Duchess of York momentarily takes up the motif: "A beggar begs that never begg'd before" [V. iii. 78], and Bolingbroke replies:

> Our scene is alt'red from a serious thing,
> And now chang'd to "The Beggar and the King."
>
> [V. iii. 79-80]

And now finally comes the climax toward which these fleeting references have been pointing: a climax which illuminates the purpose and direction of the earlier talk about beggary and bankruptcy:

> Thoughts tending to content flatter themselves
> That they are not the first of fortune's slaves,
> Nor shall not be the last; like silly beggars
> Who, sitting in the stocks, refuge their shame,

> That many have and others must sit there;
> And in this thought they find a kind of ease,
> Bearing their own misfortunes on the back
> Of such as have before endur'd the like.
> Thus play I in one person many people,
> And none contented. Sometimes am I king;
> Then treasons make me wish myself a beggar;
> And so I am. Then crushing penury
> Persuades me I was better when a king.
>
> [V. v. 23-35]
> (pp. 361-63)

And thus from beginning to end *Richard II* is, in a double sense of which Shakespeare would have approved, a play on words. As countless writers have affirmed, it is entirely fitting that this should be so. King Richard, a poet *manqué* [a would-be poet], loved words more dearly than he did his kingdom, and his tragedy is made the more moving by the style, half rhetorical, half lyrical, in which it is told. Splendid words, colorful metaphors, pregnant poetic symbols in this drama possess their own peculiar irony.

But the language of *Richard II,* regarded from the viewpoint I have adopted in this paper, has another significance, entirely apart from its appropriateness to theme. It suggests the existence of a vital relationship between two leading characteristics of Shakespeare's poetic style: the uncontrolled indulgence of verbal wit in the earlier plays and the use of great image-themes in the plays of his maturity. As I suggested in the beginning, word-play and iterative imagery are but two different manifestations of a single faculty in the creative imagination—an exceedingly well developed sense of association. In *Richard II* we see the crucial intermediate stage in the development, or perhaps more accurately the utilization, of Shakespeare's singular associative gift. In such passages as John of Gaunt's speech upon his name, we are reminded of the plays which preceded this from Shakespeare's pen. But, except on certain occasions when they contribute to the characterization of the poet-king, the brief coruscations of verbal wit which marked the earlier plays are less evident than formerly. On the other hand, when we stand back and view the play as a whole, its separate movements bound so closely together by image themes, we are enabled to anticipate the future development of Shakespeare's art. The technique that is emerging in *Richard II* is the technique that eventually will have its part in producing the poetry of *Lear* and *Macbeth* and *Othello*. Here we have the method: the tricks of repetition, of cumulative emotional effect, of interweaving and reciprocal coloration. What is yet to come is the full mastery of the artistic possibilities of such a technique. True, thanks to its tightly interwoven imagery *Richard II* has a poetic unity that is unsurpassed in any of the great tragedies; so far as structure is concerned, Shakespeare has levied from iterative language about all the aid that it will give. The great improvement will come in another region. Taken individually, in *Richard II* Shakespeare's images lack the qualities which they will possess in the later plays. They are, many of them, too conventional for our tastes; they are marred by diffuseness; they bear too many lingering traces of Shakespeare's affection for words for words' sake. The ultimate condensation, the compression of a universe of meaning into a single bold metaphor, remains to be achieved. But in the best imagery of *Richard II*, especially in those passages which combine several themes into a richly complex pattern of meaning, we receive abundant assurance that Shakespeare will be equal to his task. The process of welding language and thought into a single entity is well begun. (pp. 364-65)

Richard D. Altick, ''Symphonic Imagery in 'Richard II','' in PMLA, 62, Vol. LXII, No. 2, June, 1947, pp. 339-65.

H. B. CHARLTON (essay date 1948)

[*An English scholar, Charlton is best known for his* Shakespearean Tragedy *and* Shakespearean Comedy—*two important studies in which he argues that the proponents of New Criticism, particularly T. S. Eliot and I. A. Richards, were reducing Shakespeare's drama to its poetic elements and in the process losing sight of his characters. In his introduction to* Shakespearean Tragedy, *Charlton describes himself as a ''devout'' follower of A. C. Bradley, and like his mentor he adopted a psychological, character-oriented approach to Shakespeare's work. In an unexcerpted portion of that book, Charlton contrasts* Richard II *with* Richard III *in terms of its effectiveness as a tragedy. The earliest critics of this play were much concerned with the question of its genre—whether it is correctly called a history or a tragedy, and whether, if the latter, it successfully meets Aristotle's requirements for ''genuine'' tragedy. Charlton argues that in the earlier* Richard III, *Shakespeare had mastered the necessary technique of creating a dynamic, larger-than-life protagonist, but that the villainous Richard in effect engineers his own destruction rather than succumbing to fate as a real tragic hero should. In the excerpt below, the critic describes* Richard II *as an experiment designed to bring Shakespeare closer to ''his own idea of tragedy,'' and though Charlton concludes that it falls short, mainly because Richard himself lacks the ''momentousness'' of a true tragic hero, he concedes that ''as portraiture progressing towards the psychological realism which is a part of the great tragedies,* Richard II *is a great step beyond* Richard III.*''*]

[After he wrote *Richard III*], Shakespeare looked for a different kind of character in the traditional repositories of tragic heroes. The chroniclers offered him Richard II. Richard III had been rich in promise of tragic terror or fear; but he was lacking in capacity to excite the no less requisite pity or sympathy—the emotion comprised in the terminology of Aristotle's description of the tragic appeal, pity and fear, and the *to philanthropon* which is compassion, the instinctive sympathy with other men in distress. The Richard II of the chroniclers, however, seems a person eminently fitted to supply this want. Indeed, in Holinshed's portraiture, he seems in all ways a striking contrast to Richard III; he proves his quality, in fact, by capturing Holinshed's own sympathy. 'He was of a gentle nature.' In him, 'if there were anie offense, it ought rather to be imputed to the frailtie of wanton youth, than to the malice of his hart'. (p. 40)

The figure of Richard II which Shakespeare took from Holinshed provided him with ampler opportunity than did Richard III for filling in the intimacies and the simpler subtleties of the finished portrait, for Richard II was so much more the ordinary normal human being, *l'homme moyen sensuel*, than was Richard III. He was a person who could be characterised as an individual rather than a type, a creature stirred, as men are stirred, variously by various moods, and fluctuating at the impulses of his own mingled and wayward instincts. As portraiture progressing towards the psychological realism which is part of the great tragedies, Richard II is a great step beyond Richard III. But since our argument is primarily occupied with progress towards the realisation by Shakespeare of his own idea of tragedy, these many aspects of Richard II's characterisation which mark other features of Shakespeare's growth as a dramatic poet may be passed over. Our main concern is with the play of *Richard II* as an approach to Shakespeare's great tragedies; and our present interest in the character of Richard

II himself is confined to those aspects of it which relate to its efficiency in the scheme of tragedy.

Though the characterisation is Shakespeare's, the character is in Holinshed, as also are occasional hints which Shakespeare developed in his more intimate realisation of the temperament, mind and sentiment of Richard as it expressed itself in the habitual circumstances of his life. Holinshed's Richard was not naturally an evil person; in the chronicler's phrase, he was without 'malice in his hart', 'of nature good enough'. He was prodigal in a kingly way, and delighted in a luxurious display of the bounties which in royal bonhomie he dispensed to all within his circle, intimates and servitors alike.... [He] surrounded himself with the superficial friendliness of many and the real affection of the nameless and meaner few, 'the king's servants'. But it was, in these few, a genuine affection; when Richard was fallen on evil days it was these more lowly folk, 'diverse of the king's servants which by licence had accesse to his person', who sought to comfort him. Inevitably, however, these temperamental habits, 'though otherwise [he was] a right noble and woorthie prince', exposed Richard to the guile of flatterers; 'he was given to follow evill counsell'. He never grew up to a sense of moral responsibility, to a settled judgement, a 'grounded wisdome and ripe discretion', qualities which the Archbishop in his 'breef collation' at Bolingbroke's coronation named as the new king's in express contrast with Richard's. (pp. 41-2)

In the chronicler's story there were hints sufficient to prompt Shakespeare to his portrait of the sensuous, sentimental, poetic king; inclined generally to goodness rather than to evil, but unstable, the sport of his own whims, moods, fancies, and 'rash fierce blazes of riot' [II. i. 33]; morally not so much wicked as frail; a man without backbone, a man who is really a child and suffers the nadir of desolation in the breaking of a doll.

But how could such a figure play effectively his appropriate part in a scheme of tragedy? He is essentially a weak, but not an evil man. Weakness, however, is fragility, and fragility is a liability to break. To be tragic, Richard must be broken; as a man whose prevailing characteristic is fragility, he has within himself the instrument of his own destruction. Ultimately his tragic collapse is inevitable. As his end is thus inevitable, he provides that sense of inevitability which is the main source of tragic conviction. Richard II will not impose on Shakespeare, as did Richard III, an overt complicity in his hero's death; to that extent, he is more suited to the tragic hero's rôle. But his weakness has other dramatic implications. In some of its forms, weakness is a trait capable of stirring compassion, though a compassion which runs to pathos rather than to that pity which is a component of Aristotle's 'pity and fear'. As pathos, it is a potential spring of sympathy; but can it excite a sensation of momentousness, an impression of cosmic significance? This is a query which, on the whole, it is not unfair to submit to a box-office test. *Richard III* has been far more successful in the theatres of the last three hundred years than has *Richard II*. It has gripped the public; and the groundlings, the heterogeneous and representative crowd of average men, the *moltitudine rozza* [the uncouth masses], as an Italian Renaissance critic, Castelvetro, called it, are not only the catcallers of theatrical success, they are, as Castelvetro claimed, the final arbiters, under available guidance, of permanent dramatic values. *Richard III* has proved a better play than *Richard II*. *Richard II* has failed to create a wide and deep sense of its significance for mankind. Though its hero is a king, as a man he is without distinction, too ordinary, of a kind commonly and frequently encountered in the familiar walks of life. Though his lot is formally of great moment, his fate is like that of a multitude of average human beings, men in their weakness overcome by circumstance. His fall . . . presents a general social problem rather than a moral tragic dilemma. Indeed, as mere man, shorn of his regal commitments, Richard might have dallied on with life much longer until at length his weakness should claim its final toll. It is in fact a real dramatic problem for Shakespeare in the latter part of the play to prevent the pathetic weakness of Richard from forfeiting the sympathetic interest of the audience: his hero is in danger of becoming too maudlinly insignificant to excite compassionate lookers-on to a deep concern in his fate. To prevent this, Shakespeare has to exploit many resources of his dramatic technique.

In *Richard II* the dramatist relies extensively on his own poetic as well as on his dramatic powers. Having given to Richard the distinctive moral weakness to which a highly sensuous and sentimental nature is liable, he can give him the exquisite luxuries of sentiment which he, Shakespeare, as a poet is peculiarly gifted to utter. He can lend to sentimentality the momentary might of passion; he can drain the well of pathos dry. But he has more strictly dramatic devices. For the second part of the play, he invents new people whose main function is to restore the fallen king's hold on the audience. There is the groom and the talk of roan Barbary, kindling at once a sense of Richard's gentleness, his power to arouse affection, and his human kindliness for his horse. There is also the queen, a mere child-wife in history, but in Shakespeare a woman grown to the full love of devoted wifeliness. The most audacious dramatic stroke, audacious because it breaks one dramatic law to achieve a larger dramatic purpose, is the arbitrary change of character forced on the Bolingbroke of the later scenes. In earlier stages of the play he has appeared an upright honest man suffering from a despot's injustice to him. But in later scenes, and without substantial warrant from Holinshed, he becomes the cunning political schemer who plots Richard's murder. The murder done, he turns the hired assassins off with a callous phrase, and in the same abrupt tone of mingled commodity and sanctimony, he makes summary plans for the funeral, and for his own journey to the Holy Land there to wash the blood from off his guilty hand. As Bolingbroke thus drops in our regard, his victim Richard inevitably rises. At length, as a final decisive stroke, restoring to Richard the full involuntary esteem of the audience, Shakespeare allows him the traditional heroism of a tragic hero's death. Assailed in his prison by Exton and the armed accomplices, Richard snatches an axe from one of them and kills him and another before he himself is overcome and murdered.

Though these devices are sufficient to counterbalance one shortcoming of Richard's weakness, namely, his danger of forfeiting the sympathy of the audience, they are of no avail to outweigh its major dramatic defect. They do not invest his weakness with the weight of momentousness. (pp. 44-7)

Summarily, then, *Richard II* does not carry Shakespeare appreciably nearer to his tragic pattern. He has hit on a means of securing a sense of inevitability in his tragic plot, and he has found a somewhat limited substitute for universality in its significance. But gaining these, he has sacrificed something which *Richard III* had, the indispensable impression of momentousness; and the generality of implication, which in *Richard II* is a kind of universality, is not the universality of significance which moves to a momentousness more imaginatively

impressive than the momentousness produced merely by such gigantic massiveness as was *Richard III*'s. (p. 48)

H. B. Charlton, "Apprentice Pieces: 'Titus Andronicus', 'Richard III' and 'Richard II'," in his Shakespearian Tragedy, *1948. Reprint by Cambridge at the University Press, 1949, pp. 18-48.*

IRVING RIBNER (essay date 1948)

[*In the folowing excerpt, Ribner holds that Elizabethan Englishmen were quite familiar with the notorious political philosophy of Niccolo Machiavelli, that they frequently burlesqued it in the theater, and that the future Henry IV would have been recognized by them as reflecting a number of precepts advanced in Machiavelli's famous work* The Prince. *The critic cites Bolingbroke's usurpation of the throne through the use of deception, covert attack, calculated manipulation of public sentiment, and even political murder as evidence of his unscrupulous, sophisticated, and ambitious nature. Ribner's study initiated much scholarly debate on the character and motives of Richard's chief antagonist.*]

The wide influence of the "Machiavelli legend" in England may be seen in the traditional "Machiavels" of the Elizabethan stage—the Iagos, Aarons, Gloucesters, and Edmunds of Shakespeare's plays. . . . [An] English translation of *The Prince*, which must have been in existence as early as 1585, though it be in manuscript form, reminds us that the text of Machiavelli's own work was known . . . and that it exerted an influence [on Elizabethan drama]. . . . (p. 177)

A manifestation upon the Elizabethan stage of the actual machiavellian philosophy in *The Prince* may perhaps be seen in Shakespeare's Bolingbroke, both in *Richard II* and in the Henry IV plays. Henry IV's political career, as Shakespeare presents it, coincides strongly with what Machiavelli saw as necessary for the new prince who would unify and strengthen Italy at a time when the Florentine republic had fallen and Medici despotism seemed inevitable.

When we think of Bolingbroke and Machiavelli, we are immediately struck by the similarity between the chaotic England of the one and the chaotic Italy of the other. (p. 178)

Machiavelli, writing *The Prince* in a time of political chaos and corruption, is calling for a governor who will lead Italy out of bondage and restore it to prosperity, and in his book, he sets down the formula by which such a leader may accomplish that end.

> So Italy remains without life and awaits the man, whoever he may be, who is to heal her wounds, put an end to the plundering of Lombardy and the tribute laid on Tuscany and the kingdom of Naples, and cure her of those sores that have long been suppurating. She may be seen praying God to send some one to redeem her from these cruel and barbarous insults.

Shakespeare's Bolinbroke appears to be just such a leader. Coming into power at a similar moment in the history of England, his handling of that power, when it is his, follows closely the formula set down by Machiavelli.

As the curtain rises on *Richard II*, we find Bolingbroke in a typical application of that philosophy. Bolingbroke, in his accusation of Mowbray, is covertly attacking the government of Richard, of which Mowbray is a part. Bolingbroke knows that Richard is as responsible for the murder of Gloucester as is

Mowbray, and all of his passionate speeches are merely the rhetoric of a politician assuming a pose.

This deception for political purposes is completely in line with Machiavellli's words on dissimulation and the keeping of faith, contained in Chapter 18 of *The Prince.* "To those who see and hear him," he writes, "he should seem all compassion, all faith, all honesty, all humanity, all religion." Bolingbroke, to his hearers, seems all of that, but he need only seem, for as Machiavelli says, "It is not necessary, then, for a prince really to have all the virtues mentioned above, but it is very necessary to seem to have them." Bolingbroke is the "prudent" man who "cannot and should not observe faith when such observance is to his disadvantage." The solemn oath he takes to Richard when he is banished, he breaks with ease. Honesty and trust mean nothing to Bolingbroke when his own advantage is involved.

In Chapter 4 of *The Prince,* Machiavelli says that in the type of principality to which England belongs, where "there are a prince and barons, and the latter hold their positions not through the grace of their lord but through the antiquity of their blood," a usurping prince must have a tool among the barons. "You can enter them easily, if you win to your side some baron of the kingdom, because there are always some lords who are discontented and desire revolution; these, for the reasons given, can open you the way to control of the country and make victory easy for you." Such a tool Bolingbroke finds in Northumberland. Note his courtship of the young Percy:

> I thank thee, Gentle Percy; and be sure
> I count myself in nothing else so happy
> As in a soul remembering my good friends;
> And as my fortune ripens with thy love,
> It shall be still my true love's recompense.
> My heart this covenant makes, my hand thus seals it.
>
> [II. iii. 45-50]

Here we have a statement of sworn friendship, but it is a lying and a deceitful statement. . . . Bolingbroke knows that he will have to get rid of the "ladder wherewithal he mounts the throne" [V. i. 55-6] as soon as he is king, and this he does in *Henry IV, Part 1.* This pledge of friendship to the Percys is an excellent example of calculated Machiavellian deceit.

Bolingbroke from the very beginning enlists the good will of the common people upon his side, and here also he is following to the letter a basic precept of Machiavelli. In *The Prince,* we find: . . .

> He who becomes ruler with the aid of the great maintains himself with more difficulty than he who becomes ruler with the aid of the people, because the first is in the position of a prince with a good many subjects whom he regards as his equals, and for this reason cannot direct them as he wishes to. But he who becomes prince with popular favor stands alone, and has no subjects, or at most only a few, who are not ready to obey him. . . . Besides, when the people are unfriendly the prince never can make himself secure, for he has too many against him. . . .
>
> (p. 180)

This is a strongly emphasized point in Machiavelli's philosophy, and it is strongly emphasized in Shakespeare's depiction of Bolingbroke. In the first act of *Richard II,* the king says of him:

> Ourself and Bushy, Bagot here, and Green
> Observ'd his courtship to the common people;
> How he did seem to dive into their hearts
> With humble and familiar courtesy;
> What reverence he did throw away on slaves,
> Wooing poor craftsmen with the craft of smiles
> And patient underbearing of his fortune,
> As 'twere to banish their affects with him.
> Off goes his bonnet to an oyster-wench;
> A brace of draymen bid God speed him well
> And had the tribute of his supple knee,
> With 'Thanks, my countrymen, my loving friends';
> As were our England in reversion his,
> And he our subjects' next degree in hope.
>
> [I. iv. 23-36]

How successful Bolingbroke's wooing of the people is, can be seen in the Duke of York's description of his triumphal march through London:

> Then, as I said, the Duke, great Bolingbroke,
> Mounted upon a hot and fiery steed
> Which his aspiring rider seem'd to know,
> With slow and stately pace kept on his course,
> Whilst all tongues cried 'God save thee,
> Bolingbroke.' . . .
>
> [V. ii. 7-11]

Contrast this with the crowd's reception of Richard, whom he has supplanted. Bolingbroke, in true Machiavellian fashion, had wooed the common people and won them to his side.

In the magnificent deposition scene in *Richard II,* Henry is as Machiavellian as ever. To the crowd, he paints himself as a man of virtue, coming in submission to kingly authority, merely to plead a just cause:

> Henry Bolingbroke
> On both his knees does kiss King Richard's hand
> And sends allegiance and true faith of heart
> To his most royal person; hither come
> Even at his feet to lay my arms and power. . . .
>
> [III. iii. 35-9]

But at the end of the scene, Richard is in Henry's power, and is conveyed to London by him, as a king only in name. Here again Bolingbroke is accomplishing his own unjust ends and, at the same time, giving his act the appearance of justice for the sake of the crowd. "He should strive in all his actions," says Machiavelli, giving his formula for the efficient ruler, "to give evident signs of greatness, spirit, gravity, and fortitude." Bolingbroke is here giving the appearance of having those virtues which Machiavelli says he should pretend to, but need not have.

The first act which Bolingbroke performs upon coming into power is to destroy Bushy, Bagot, Green, and the Earl of Wilshire, the faithful supporters of Richard. Now, one of the most important of Machiavelli's principles, contained in Chapter 3 of *The Prince,* is that when a new prince has come into power, all those who supported the old prince must be destroyed. There is a "natural and normal necessity," he writes, "which makes it always necessary for a new ruler to harm those over whom he places himself," even to the extent of wiping out the race of the old prince. Further confirmation comes from Bolinbroke's immediate arrest of the Bishop of

Carlisle, although he is a member of the clergy, when he speaks against the dethronement of Richard.

Another of the basic principles in the philosophy of Machiavelli is that of legality in the maintenance of a kingdom, and particularly of hereditary legality. . . . (pp. 181-82)

Throughout the plays, Bolingbroke is concerned with the legality of his title. He knows that he has no hereditary right to the throne, and it is to him a constant source of anxiety. In Act IV of *Richard II*, when Richard sends in word that he is ready to give up the crown, Henry says:

> Fetch hither Richard, that in common view
> He may surrender. So we shall proceed
> Without suspicion.
>
>   [IV. i. 155-57]

He wants no doubt cast upon the legality of the transaction. . . . This preoccupation with the importance of title makes necessary the murder of Richard II. While Richard lives, Henry's title to the throne is open to question; so Richard must not live.

According to another principle of Machiavelli, the deposed ruler must always be destroyed.

> But afterwards if you wish to maintain your conquest, these conditions will cause you innumerable difficulties, both with those who have aided you and with those you have overcome. Nor is it enough for you to exterminate the family of the prince, because the nobles will still be left to take the lead in new rebellions. . . .

Bolingbroke, therefore, must destroy both Richard and Northumberland. Richard is destroyed immediately and Northumberland at the first opportunity that arises. That the murder of Richard is an act of extreme cruelty does not dismay Bolingbroke in the least. If his title is to be made secure, and the nation strengthened and united, Richard must be murdered. (pp. 182-83)

As a disciple of the Machiavellian philosophy, Bolingbroke cannot do the killing himself. "Princes should have things that will bring them hatred done by their agents," says Machiavelli, and Bolingbroke accordingly employs Pierce of Exton.

Bolingbroke's last statement in *Richard II* is one in the Machiavellian vein. "I'll make a voyage to the Holy Land," he says [V. vi. 49]. Machiavelli maintains throughout that the good ruler must appear pious in the eyes of his people.

The political activity of Bolingbroke in Shakespeare's *Richard II* closely adheres to Machiavelli's political philosophy as contained in *The Prince*. There are a few incidents where Bolingbroke does not follow Machiavelli to the letter, the most noteworthy of these being his failure to destroy Aumerle; but these incidents, in relation to the whole, are minor. In almost every important act, from his quarrel with Mowbray in the opening scene, to his projected pilgrimage to Jerusalem in the closing, the underlying philosophy of Machiavelli can be seen. (p. 183)

> *Irving Ribner, "Bolingbroke, a True Machiavellian," in* Modern Language Quarterly, *Vol. 9, No. 2, June, 1948, pp. 177-84.*

BRENTS STIRLING (essay date 1951)

[*Focusing on the issue of Bolingbroke's character and the point at which he conceives a plan for usurping the throne, Stirling*

argues that, in fact, Henry makes no conscious "decision" to overthrow the king; through what the critic describes as Shakespeare's "skillful fusion of plot unfoldment, disclosure of political 'moral', and characterization," the reality of Bolingbroke's usurpation is determined by external events and Richard himself, to which Henry offers only "terse" consent. Buttressing his argument with a close examination of the Flint Castle episode and the abdication scene, Stirling maintains that Richard, indulging in his martyr's role, "deposes himself in an agony of play-acting before the unsentimental Bolingbroke"; he adds that Henry remains an ambiguous figure throughout, feigning loyalty to the king and providing an "oblique admission" of his true intents only when Richard suddenly "drops his sentimental role and states the truth of his position." Stirling stresses the irony in this shift in characterization, noting that it is Richard who becomes the realist in these crucial scenes, while Bolingbroke, "who had offered his demands with such consistency and seeming honesty," becomes a duplicitous opportunist.]

When interpreting *Richard II* we are aware, of course, that the king's dethronement was a symbol of challenge to royal authority during Elizabeth's reign, that the deposition scene was censored in certain editions, and that because of its connotations, the play was used by the Essex conspirators to set off their abortive rising. It is not that *Richard II* contained unorthodox political doctrine; on the contrary, in the deposition scene itself Carlisle proclaims that no subject may judge a king and that, should Bolingbroke be crowned, "The blood of English shall manure the ground, / And future ages groan for this foul act" [IV. i. 137-38]. (p. 27)

The doctrine of *Richard II* and the succeeding plays is [indeed] wholly conventional, and the uneasiness which led to banning of the deposition scene must have been evoked, not by any avowed point of view in the play, but by the fact that its theme of usurpation was an issue too critical even to be presented with conservative commentary.

It is well understood that this attitude of concern could have been derived from the characterization which accompanies Shakespeare's presentation of history. Without authority from the established sources, Shakespeare's Richard becomes a royal sentimentalist, a defeatist who resigns the throne as though he preferred acting a rôle of tragedy to one of governing men. With warrant from these sources, Shakespeare's Bolingbroke becomes a victim of extortion who takes over a kingship already bankrupt from abuse and incompetency, and in the play both the extortion and the defunct kingship are dramatically magnified. Carlisle's castigation of Bolingbroke for the "foul act" [IV. i. 138] of revolution is thus easy to interpret as a concession to authority, as a piece of stiff morality almost intrusive in Shakespeare's active world of mixed right and wrong where characters are not to be measured by rigid moral standards.

The only difficulty with such an interpretation is that it is too simple. Granted, it rejects a form of criticism which disregards the tangle of events in which Bolingbroke acted, and would find Shakespeare's moral in Carlisle's prophecy alone. But while rejecting one form of simplicity it substitutes another in introducing the principle that men are too complex to be judged strictly, a point of view long useful in Shakespeare study, but unfortunately misused by those who consider complexity of character to be incompatible, at least in drama, with clear moral judgement.

There will be an assumption in this essay that the political moral of *Richard II* can be described adequately only in terms of the play itself, that the structure of the idea and the structure of the play are inseparable, as they need to be in all good dramatic art. But this uncontroversial premise does not imply that Shakespeare's meaning lacks precision. If we postpone conclusions until we have traced his idea in terms of dramatic action and characterization, it is possible that it will emerge not only as more mature than Carlisle's absolutism, but as less confused than the moral tangle which results if Carlisle's judgment is minimized. It is possible, moreover, that the dramatic structure and motivation of *Richard II* will likewise be found clearer and more mature than before, and the play may thus emerge in several new ways as a landmark in Shakespeare's early development as a dramatist.

In II. i, as resistance against Richard takes form, Northumberland first tells us of the purpose entertained by Bolingbroke's faction:

> If then we shall shake off our slavish yoke,
> Imp out our drooping country's broken wing,
> Redeem from broking pawn the blemished crown,
> Wipe off the dust that hides our sceptre's gilt
> And make high majesty look like itself.
>
> [II. i. 291-95]

So far, nothing of deposition; Northumberland's statement is the first of many which stress a goal modestly short of the throne. Two scenes later Bolingbroke's suit is pressed again; the place is Gloucestershire where the insurgent forces encounter old York, regent in Richard's absence. To York's charge of treason ''in braving arms against thy sovereign'' [II. iii. 112] the reply by Bolingbroke is that he ''was banish'd Hereford'' but returns ''for Lancaster,'' that he remains a subject of the king, and that having been denied ''attorneys'' [II. iii. 113-14, 134] for lawful redress, he has appeared in person. Before Bolingbroke's assembled power which belies his peaceful aims, and before the claim for Henry's inheritance rights, York stands as the absolutist, the strict constructionist:

> My lords of England, let me tell you this;
> I have had feeling of my cousin's wrongs
> And labour'd all I could to do him right;
> But in this kind to come, in braving arms,
> Be his own carver and cut out his way,
> To find out right with wrong, it may not be.
>
> [II. iii. 140-45]

Thus in a scene of unusual strength are the rebels confronted with clear disposition of their pragmatic notions of morality and justice. Ironically, however, in the lines which follow, York collapses pathetically and almost absurdly:

> But if I could, by Him that gave me life,
> I would attach you all and make you stoop
> Unto the sovereign mercy of the king;
> But since I cannot, be it known to you
> I do remain as neuter.
>
> [II. iii. 155-59]
> (pp. 27-8)

In the first two scenes of Act III Shakespeare now presents Bolingbroke and Richard in characterization which emphasizes the utter difference in temperament between them; then, having shown each individually in parallel scenes, he brings them together for an episode in which the issue of deposition is determined, an issue which arises naturally and dramatically as a direct result of character clash. Dramatic structure, characterization, and presentation of idea (the deposition theme) are thus fused to the extent that none of these qualities can properly be discussed without reference to the others.

Scene i presents Bolingbroke, and in keeping with the character it is short and concentrated. It opens in the midst of events with Henry's terse ''Bring forth these men'' [III. i. 1]; Bushy and Green are then presented for his brief but unhurried recitation of the counts against them. . . . These deeds condemn them to death. ''My Lord Northumberland, see them dispatch'd'' [III. i. 35]. Next, the queen must be remembered; to York: ''Fairly let her be entreated'' [III. i. 37]. And lastly Owen Glendower and his forces must be met; unhurried orders are so given. In a little over forty lines Bolingbroke has passed a death sentence, attended to the amenities of courtesy, and has set a campaign in motion.

Scene ii presents Richard and his retinue in a parallel situation, and the contrast of this episode with Bolingbroke's scene lies in its portrayal of the king, initially by soliloquies of self regard, then by wordy defiance which collapses as Richard learns of the Welsh defection, and finally by near hysteria as Aumerle cautions, ''Comfort my liege; remember who you are'' [III. ii. 82]. As Scroop enters with worse news, Richard proceeds from the false stoicism of anticipated defeat into insults directed at his absent favorites, and back again into sentimental despair:

> Let's choose executors and talk of wills;
> And yet not so; for what can we bequeath
> Save our deposed bodies to the ground?
> Our lands, our lives, and all are Bolingbroke's.
>
> [III. ii. 147-51]

The word ''deposed'' is repeated three times as a kind of refrain in the next few lines as Richard offers to ''sit upon the ground / And tell sad stories of the death of kings'' [III. ii. 155-56]. A short speech of defiance as Carlisle warns against this sitting and wailing of woes, and a final descent into sentimental resignation as Scroop reports the joining of York with Bolingbroke, these acts complete Richard's performance in the scene. Lest our account of it end by being merely descriptive, two factors of Shakespeare's inventiveness should be set forth; to Holinshed's version of Richard's misfortune he adds the king's embracing of deposition far in advance of demand or suggestion, and this external behavior he shows to be derived from motives of playing the martyr's role. The scene to come is thus inevitable; Richard in effect will depose himself in an agony of play-acting before the unsentimental Bolingbroke. But Shakespeare reserves a surprise; not the realist but the sentimentalist will call the turn.

The dramatic situation created for this event in the episode before Flint Castle is thus one of encounter between a self-contained realist who has come but ''for his own'' and an emotional defeatist who has determined to give him everything. And at the end of the Flint scene Shakespeare will answer with clear irony our question: *when* did Bolingbroke, after all his protests to the contrary, decide to seize the crown? For one point of the play, it will appear, is that this question has no point.

In a literal reading, Bolingbroke makes no decision prior to Act IV, and there he is scarcely more than at hand to take the throne. Now this set of facts is subject to several interpretations. First, we may assume that prior to the deposition scene there is no stage of the play at which the deviousness of Bolingbroke becomes clear, that there are obvious *lacunae* [gaps] between his disclaimers of ambition in the first three acts and his sudden coronation in Act IV. In that event *Richard II* is just a bad play, and the fact that Henry's coronation is also sudden in the chronicles does not make it better. Or, secondly, we may assume that the historical reputation of Bolingbroke would have led an Elizabethan audience to recognize that his denials of royal ambition were insincere, and that he intended from the beginning to be king. This could be the case, but the play, at least to us, would still be the worse for it. Nor is it Shakespeare's custom to allow major characterization to rest upon undramatized historical background, this in spite of occasional statements to the contrary. Finally, a third explanation of our "indecisive" Bolingbroke is that opportunism, of which he becomes the living symbol, is essentially a tacit vice: that although the opportunist is aware in a sense of the ends to which his means commit him, he relies upon events, not upon declarations, to clarify his purposes. On the basis of the scene before Flint Castle (III. iii) and two prominent episodes which follow it, I believe that the interpretation just expressed is one which fits the dramatic facts.

By the time the Flint scene opens we are aware of Richard's impulses toward virtual abdication, but Bolingbroke has never exceeded his demands for simple restitution of rank and estate. Nor have his followers done so. True, we have heard York tell him that his very appearance in arms is treason, but Bolingbroke's rejoinder to this was both disarming and apparently genuine. At Flint, however, dramatic suggestion begins to take shape. As Henry's followers parley before the castle, Northumberland lets slip the name "Richard" unaccompanied by its title of king. York reproves him with a remark that such brevity once would have seen Northumberland shortened by a head's length. Bolingbroke intercedes: "Mistake not, uncle, further than you should." To which York: "Take not, cousin, further than you should" [III. iii. 15-16].This suggestive colloquy is followed by Bolingbroke's characteristic statement of honest intention: "Go to ... the castle ... and this deliver: Henry Bolingbroke / On both his knees does kiss King Richard's hand / And sends allegiance and true faith of heart / To his most royal person"[III. iii. 32-8]. He will lay down his arms provided only that his lands are restored and his banishment repealed. If not, war is the alternative. With dramatic significance, however, Northumberland, who bears this message from a Bolingbroke "on both his knes," fails himself to kneel before Richard and thus becomes again the medium of "unconscious" disclosure. Richard, in a rage, sends word back to Henry that "ere the crown he looks for live in peace, / Ten thousand bloody crowns of mothers' sons"[III. iii. 95-6] shall be the price in slaughter. Northumberland's rejoinder is a yet more pious assertion of Bolingbroke's limited aims: "The King of heaven forbid our lord the king / Should so with civil and uncivil arms / Be rush'd upon! Thy thrice noble cousin / Harry Bolingbroke ... swears ... his coming hath no further scope / Than for his lineal royalties" [III. iii. 101-13].

Richard's response is to grant the demands, to render a wish in soliloquy that he be buried where his subjects "may hourly trample on their sovereign's head" [III. iii. 157], and, when summoned to the "base court," to cry out symbolically that down, down he comes "like glist'ring phaeton, / Wanting the manage of unruly jades" [III. iii. 178-79]. He enters the base court, and the scene concludes with a priceless mummery of sovereignty, each participant speaking as a subject to his king.

> *Boling.* Stand all apart,
> And show fair duty to His majesty. [*He kneels down.*]
> My gracious lord—
>   *K. Rich.* Fair Cousin, you debase your princely knee
> To make the base earth proud with kissing it.
> Me rather had my heart might feel your love
> Than my unpleased eye see your courtesy.

> Up, Cousin, up. Your heart is up, I know,
> Thus high at least, although your knee be low.
>   *Boling.* My gracious lord, I come but for mine own.
>   *K. Rich.* Your own is yours, and I am yours, and all.
>   *Boling.* So far be mine, my most redoubted lord,
> As my true service shall deserve your love.
>   *K. Rich.* Well you deserve. They well deserve to have
> That know the strong'st and surest way to get....
> Cousin, I am too young to be your father,
> Though you are old enough to be my heir.
> What you will have, I'll give, and willing too,
> For do we must what force will have us do.
> Set on toward London, Cousin, is it so?
>   *Boling.* Yea, my good lord.
>   *K. Rich.* Then I must not say no.
>   [III. iii. 187-201, 204-10]

There is no question of what "London" means. It is dethronement for Richard and coronation for Bolingbroke, an implication which is plain enough here but which Shakespeare underscores in the very next scene where the Gardener, asked by the Queen ..., "Why dost thou say King Richard is deposed?" concludes his explanation with "Post you to London, and you will find it so" [III. iv. 77, 90]. Bolingbroke's answer to Richard, "Yea, my good lord," is the aptly timed climax of the Flint episode, and of the play. With this oblique admission, coming with great effect immediately after his statement of loyalty and subjection, Henry's purposes become clear, and the significant fact is that not he but Richard has phrased his intent. The king's single line, "Set on towards London, cousin, is it so?" is the ironic instrument for exposing a long line of equivocation which the rebels seem to have concealed even from themselves. And in dramatic fact, Bolingbroke is still trying to conceal it; his short answer is the minimum articulation of his conduct, an opportunist's falling back upon "what must be" in order to evade a statement of purpose.

The quality of this turn in the play rests upon a skillful fusion of plot unfoldment, disclosure of political "moral," and characterization, all of which present parallel irony. In plotting, first among these ingredients, the end of the Flint scene is the point at which conflicting forces reach their determination in a climactic disclosure of Henry's true purpose. But this climax is also a studied anticlimax, for the rebels advance upon Flint Castle only, as it were, to find it abandoned with the words, "Come to London," written upon the walls. They, and the audience, had expected not quiet exposure of their aims (the actual climax) but dramatic opportunity for "constitutional" manifestoes.

As for disclosure of political meaning, the second element here, it is during the encounter at Flint that the rebels achieve their most eloquent statement of legality in seeking only a subject's claim to justice from his king. But the luxury of that statement collapses at the end of the scene, again with the word "London." It becomes suddenly apparent that York's previous judgment was sound, that Bolingbroke's use of force to gain just concessions from his sovereign has committed him to the destruction of sovereignty.

The third component at the end of the Flint scene is characterization, a quality which is the basis for all the drama and irony in the direction the play has taken. Shakespeare's prior establishment of Bolingbroke's realism, self-containment, and resourcefulness, along with Richard's romantic defeatism, near-hysteria, and pathetic reliance upon others, has furnished a decided pattern for the meeting of the two at Flint. Bolingbroke and Northumberland thus fulfill their previously set traits of stability and restraint; Richard repeats the performance he had enacted before his own followers in the preceding scene, a performance which richly justifies the description of him by one critic as an inveterate spectator at his own tragedy. Full characterization of Bolingbroke and Richard, both before and during the Flint Castle episode, thus provides all of the expansiveness which is so deliberately deflated in the last lines. There, with Richard's knowing reference to London and Bolingbroke's one-line reply, the ironic shift in characterization materializes. The unstable Richard, who had fled from facts through every form of emotional exaggeration, now drops his sentimental role and states the truth of his position with quiet wit and candor; the plain-dealing Bolingbroke who had offered his demands with such consistency and seeming honesty, now admits his sham of rebellion which was to stop short of rebellion.

The end of Act III, scene iii, is thus a pivotal stage of *Richard II*. Here, upon a question asked by the king and an answer given by Henry, the trend of the play becomes dramatically apparent in plot, in political meaning, and in ultimate characterization. We have also observed that perhaps the main achievement at this point of multiple effect has been a disclosure of ambiguity in Henry Bolingbroke. In concluding this essay I hope to show that, by the time Shakespeare's portrait of Bolingbroke is completed, this ambiguity is presented twice again by means of the same dramatic method.

The first of these repetitions occurs in IV. i (the deposition) which runs directly parallel to the Flint Castle scene. Here again we have Richard confronted by the rebels, and here also he is in turn both defiant and submissive; his sentimental display is likewise in dramatic contrast with Henry's simplicity, forbearance, and directness. But again in the closing lines the paradox comes.

> *K. Rich.* I'll beg one boon,
> And then be gone and trouble you no more.
> Shall I obtain it?
> *Boling.* Name it, fair Cousin.
> *K. Rich.* "Fair Cousin"? I am greater than a king.
> For when I was a king, my flatterers
> Were then but subjects. Being now a subject,
> I have a King here to my flatterer.
> Being so great, I have no need to beg.
> *Boling.* Yet ask.
> *K. Rich.* And shall I have?
> *Boling.* You shall.
> *K. Rich.* Then give me leave to go.
> *Boling.* Whither?
> *K. Rich.* Whither you will, so I were from your
> sights.
> *Boling.* Go, some of you convey him to the Tower.
> [IV. i. 302-16]

Just as at the end of III. iii, "London" meant deposition, so here the Tower means imprisonment and ultimate death. This colloquy between the king and his adversary is exactly parallel in technique to the one which concluded the scene at Flint. In it Richard, who has again run his course of theatrical emotion, now becomes pointedly realistic; in it Bolingbroke, who has again exhibited every sign of gracious honesty, reveals duplicity in a concluding line.

There remains a third and final step in the portrayal of Henry which is analogous in all essentials to the two scenes we have examined. The fact that Shakespeare here drew upon the chronicles might imply that he found in them a suggestion of Bolingbroke's taciturnity marked by sudden revelations of shifting purpose. Piers of Exton, in the short fourth scene of Act V, ponders something he has heard. "Have I no friend will rid me of this living fear?" [V. iv. 2]. Was not that what the new king said? And did he not repeat it? Exton satisfies himself that Bolingbroke did so and convinces himself that in the saying of it Henry "wistly look'd on me" [V. iv. 7]. It is enough, for Exton promptly murders Richard and returns with the body. Henry's lines which conclude the play are well known; he admits desiring Richard's death but disowns Exton's act and pledges expiation in a voyage to the Holy Land.

Three times—at the end of the Flint Castle scene, at the end of the deposition scene, and in the Exton scenes at the end of the play—Henry has taken, if it may be so called, a decisive step. Each time the move he has made has been embodied in a terse statement, and each time another has either evoked it from him or stated its implications for him. Never, in an age of drama marked by discursive self-revelation, has a character disclosed his traits with such economy and understatement. The Elizabethan character with a moral contradiction usually explains his flaw before, during, and after the event. And at length. Until the short choral "confession" at the very end of the play, Bolingbroke, however, exhibits his deviousness in one-line admissions spaced at intervals which are aptly arranged in parallel series for cumulative effect. And while each of these admissions marks a step in characterization, it indicates at the same time a critical stage of plot development. The conflict of forces is resolved, with the line on London concluding the Flint Castle scene, for there Richard and Henry reach mutual understanding on the dethronement issue which the king alone has previously entertained. The falling action becomes defined with the line near the end of the deposition scene which sends Richard to the Tower. The catastrophe is precipitated by the line to Exton which sends him to death.

Finally, at each of these three points of characterization and plot unfoldment the doctrine implicit in the play evolves to a new clarity. At Henry's line on London at Flint Castle it becomes apparent that a "constitutional" show of force against sovereignty leads inevitably to the deposition of sovereignty; at Henry's line in the dethronement scene it appears that deposition of sovereignty requires imprisonment and degradation of the sovereign; and at Henry's line to Exton it becomes plain that murder of sovereignty must be the final outcome. (pp. 29-34)

In passages such as Ulysses' lines on degree in *Troilus and Cressida* Shakespeare excels in a poet's expression of Tudor political dogma. In *Richard II*, however, and early in his career, he shows control of a much more difficult art, that of revealing doctrine integrally with progressive growth of plot and of characterization. With our debt to the English and American revolutions we cannot admire the doctrine as such, but we can recognize in *Richard II* a stage of Shakespeare's development at which, so far as fundamentals are concerned, political morality and artistry become inseparable. (p. 34)

> *Brents Stirling, "Bolingbroke's 'Decision'," in*
> Shakespeare Quarterly, *Vol. II, No. 1, January, 1951,*
> *pp. 27-34.*

GEORGES A. BONNARD   (lecture date 1951)

[*According to Bonnard,* Richard II *in its general structure has similarities to Shakespeare's* King John *and* Henry IV: *each play presents two main characters, one of whom falls from power while the other ascends. But while King John and his nemesis Falconbridge and Prince Hal and his counterpoint Falstaff form pairs of equally strong and fascinating individuals, this is not so in* Richard II, *for the antagonist Bolingbroke is strangely "passive," muted and upstaged by the flamboyant, self-dramatizing monarch. Bonnard suggests that although this drama "was certainly planned" as a conflict between two opposing leads, Shakespeare, in the course of its composition, altered his strategy and created "a soul's drama" about one person only: Richard, a flawed but attractive hero in whom the dramatist found something in common with his own nature. Bonnard describes the king as a "poseur" whose "absence of character" and "incompetence as a ruler" lead him to act a part rather than respond to the realities of his situation. But balancing Richard's shortcomings as a monarch, Bonnard asserts, is his skill as an actor; the critic especially notes the king's ability to adapt his performance to every situation and to control others, such as Bolingbroke, through his play-acting. Bonnard's commentary, excerpted below, was originally presented in a lecture delivered at the Shakespeare Conference at Stratford-upon-Avon in 1951.]*

If the general structure of [*Richard II*] is examined, it appears that Shakespeare planned it on the same lines as *King John* and *Henry* IV, namely as a play with two main figures, one of which rises whilst the other declines. In *King John* the King's failure is balanced by the ascent of Falconbridge to the position of his country's saviour. In *Henry* IV, taking of course the two parts as forming a single play, Prince Hal grows at the expense of Falstaff. Similarly, in *Richard* II, the downfall of the king is the triumph of the rebellion and its head, Bolingbroke. This general structure is excellently illustrated in the image used by Richard himself in the scene of his deposition when he compares his crown to a well and his cousin and himself to two buckets, filling one another,

> The emptier ever dancing in the air,
> The other down, unseen, and full of water:
> That bucket down, and full of tears, am I.
> Drinking my griefs, whilst you mount up on high.
>   [IV. i. 186-89]

For such a plan to be successfully carried out, the two main figures, the two heroes should be of more or less equal interest to the audience. From the beginning to the end of the play, they should both excite our sympathy. Our reasons for liking them would not be the same, of course, and they would probably change in the course of the performance. But the intensity of our sympathy should remain pretty much at the same level. This might be said in other terms: our two protagonists should be more or less equally alive, or again, about the same amount of creative energy should have gone to the making of both. That condition is certainly filled in *Henry* IV. Falstaff and Prince Hal, from Gadshill to the dismissal of the fat old man, are both equally and continuously interesting. (pp. 87-8)

[However], in *Richard* II, the balance is upset. Richard and Bolingbroke, as the play was planned, were surely to be of equal importance. The man who rises should not be less important than the man whose fall allows him to rise. But in Bolingbroke we remain uninterested. This is no doubt partly due to what may be called his passivity. Critics formerly used to lend him the character of the crafty man of action, the hypocrite who carefully hides his game the better to achieve his ends; they maintained that from the beginning of the play he is shown as intent on securing the throne and that, throughout, nothing is done but he does it. . . . Why they ascribed to him a character in such glaring contradiction with the facts as Shakespeare gives them, is hard to say. Did they do so, per-

haps, in obedience to the obscure feeling that the play lacked a proper balance unless Richard's antagonist was the very opposite of the King, a man of strong purpose, bent on achieving it, a usurper by pre-dilection? . . . However that may be, Bolingbroke, according to the text of the play, if not according to what critics used to read into it, is not represented by Shakespeare as planning a usurpation of the throne and wresting it from Richard by craft. Mowbray, his enemy, and Richard himself alone suspect him of entertaining such a design. But there is nothing in what he does or says that could justify us in sharing those suspicions. In fact, as is now widely recognized, he allows himself to be led by circumstances. And he does not create those circumstances. They all result from Richard's own conduct. Urged to it by nobles and commons, as well as by his awareness of England's need for a firm ruler, he merely seizes each opportunity as it arises until he ascends the throne which is offered him. Thus he is but partly responsible for his usurping the power that by right belongs to his cousin. (pp. 88-9)

In Shakespeare's eyes, as is evident from the whole context of his Histories, the deposition of Richard was a calamity: it was the immediate cause of the rebellions that broke out again and again in the usurper's reign, and one of the main causes of the War of the Roses, but it was also a necessity. That it was a necessity had to be made clear. And this could only be done by representing Bolingbroke as almost compelled by circumstances to assume the crown. Had Shakespeare made of him a deliberate usurper, resolved to fight his way to the throne under the flimsy pretence of coming to claim his inheritance, his play could never have conveyed the sense of the inevitability of Richard's deposition, which would have appeared as the successful outcome of Bolingbroke's plans. It might even have impressed its spectators as a justification of the crime of usurpation. And that was certainly the last thing Shakespeare wanted his play to suggest.

But to represent Bolingbroke as having but a very limited share in shaping the circumstances that led to his ascending the throne had a serious drawback. It is difficult to take an interest in a mere opportunist. And apparently Shakespeare did not take much interest in him. Towards him he maintained what Middleton Murry calls a "wholly external attitude" [see excerpt above, 1936]. He could only see him from the outside. He could not, or would not, in any case did not, see him from the inside. We know nothing of Bolingbroke's secret thoughts, of his real feelings, until we come to the very end of the play. Although a highly important person whenever on the stage, he is so constantly silent, so sparing of his words that little attention is perforce given him. The eyes of the spectators are constantly wandering away from him. Although he is not the wholly insignificant figure that some have pronounced him to be—Murry for instance calls him "a shadow", "a mere stage-figure", an "unpleasant non-entity"—he does not appeal to our hearts or imaginations. What of him is indelibly impressed on our memories is his leave-taking of humble citizens as seen and described by Richard himself with the graphic power proper to Richard, and his coming into London as described by York. But we find it extremely difficult to form a distinct idea of his attitude and behaviour before Flint Castle or even in Westminster Hall. As a dramatic character he only comes to life for a brief moment in the Aumerle scenes of the fifth Act. Clearly Bolingbroke is the child of Shakespeare's mind only, of his craftsmanship, of his labours when he was planning his play, but in no respect of his creative imagination. Whereas that is just what Richard is, and is to the fullest extent.

The reason therefore why *Richard* II is an unbalanced play, why, instead of having for its centre, as its structure demanded, two heroes in opposition, in spiritual conflict, it really is a drama about one person only, is probably that, in the actual process of writing it, the poet's imagination was quickened by one of the heroes and not by the other. To such an accident great imaginative writers are perhaps particularly liable. Did it not happen more than once in Shakespeare's career? in *The Merchant of Venice* and in *Hamlet,* for instance? Shylock and the Prince of Denmark may be the children of an activity of their creator's genius which the mere craftsman in him was unable to curb and control so as to make them fit into his preconceived scheme. *Richard* II was certainly planned as a drama of conflict, possibly between two political conceptions—the sacred character of the sovereign whose power rests on divine right, and the right of a people to get rid of a legitimate king if he proved a tyrant—, certainly between two men, the weak incompetent monarch whose sole support is his title and the strong nobleman whom all his fellow-citizens, in their sore need for a firm and just ruler, want to place on the throne, and who accepts to lead their rebellion. But under Shakespeare's pen it became a soul's drama, the sad and moving story of a king who, finding himself unable to face and conquer a revolt of which he is the single cause, divests himself of all his rights. And so are justified the many critics who have felt that Richard is the true, the only centre of the play. (pp. 89-91)

In his study of *Richard* II, Swinburne confessed to his aversion for the king, in his eyes an utterly contemptible figure. From early in the play, "the protagonist", he writes, is revealed "as so pitifully mean and cruel a weakling that no future action of suffering can lift him above the level which divides . . . pity from contempt", and again "the callous cruelty and the heartless hypocrisy of the . . . young tyrant is enough to remove him once for all beyond the reach of . . . sympathy or compassion unqualified by scorn" [see excerpt above, 1909]. And Swinburne declared he could not understand how Shakespeare had the patience to persist in the development of his hero's character. One or two critics have echoed Swinburne's vilification of Richard. . . . But those remained isolated voices. And the great majority recognize that Shakespeare has fully succeeded in turning his hero into a sympathetic character, one for whom we feel the deepest compassion, who casts an irresistible spell upon us, at least from the moment of his return from Ireland, when we know that he is already doomed, since his friends have been executed, his Welsh army has disbanded itself, and York, the regent, feeling powerless to oppose the rebellion, has declared his neutrality.

Two poets, even, Yeats [see excerpt above, 1901] and the present Laureate [John Masefield], have been so "intoxicated" by the exquisite poetry Shakespeare has lent his hero that, forgetting the murder of Gloucester, Mowbray's exile, the illegal seizure of Gaunt's estate, the farming of the realm and the blank charters, they have seen Richard as a man who fails because of his qualities, of those qualities that unfit the artist and the saint for the rough work of this world, but must have endeared him to the poet Shakespeare. For such a mistaken reading of the king's character, interesting for the light it sheds on two young poets—they were young at the time—and their period, Yeats and Masefield were severely and rightly taken to task by John Bailey, and Yeats again by Sir Edmund Chambers [see excerpt above, 1905]. But these two gentlemen went perhaps too far when, though admitting that the dramatist felt some measure of sympathy for the central figure of his play,

they ascribed to him the judgment that they themselves would have passed on such a man as Richard.

The two extreme positions of Swinburne on the one hand and Yeats on the other have remained to this day quite exceptional. Richard has inspired most critics with neither adoration nor repulsion, but with infinite pity for his tragic fate, with admiration for his gifts as an impassioned orator, as a poet in his own right, with some affection too for what they call his charm. Several attempts have been made to try and find out how, by what means, Shakespeare has managed to make of him, despite the first two acts, a sympathetic character. Professor Charlton, for instance, believes that to prevent Richard from forfeiting the sympathetic interest of the audience, his creator turned him into a poet, invented the Queen and the groom, "whose main function", so Charlton says, "is to restore the fallen king's hold on the audience", and changed Bolingbroke from "an honest upright gentleman" into "a cunning political schemer who plots Richard's murder" [see excerpt above, 1948]. Such explanations appear rather inadequate. The main fact is that Richard does not for a moment forfeit our sympathy in the last three acts, though he may very well not conquer it in the first two. But from his return from Ireland, his hold on the audience is continuous, at least until he leaves Westminster Hall, and if this is partly due to the poetry of his speeches, it cannot at any rate be explained by what happens in the fifth act. In this act the interest of the audience in Richard may flag, probably

Act III. Scene ii. Aumerle, Richard II, the Bishop of Carlisle, Salisbury, and soldiers. By William Hamilton. The Department of Rare Books and Special Collections, The University of Michigan Library.

does usually flag, despite his last meeting with the Queen, and the visit of the groom to his royal master in prison, but not its sympathy. The spectators have been too deeply moved to cease feeling pity and compassion for the fallen king. And if their interest does not remain at the same pitch, it is not due to their suddenly realizing what a poor weak man the hero is, for his weakness has been brought home to them all along the third and fourth acts, if they have not guessed it already in the first and the second, but to the creative energy of the poet subsiding after its tremendous display or, as Dover Wilson has suggested [see Additional Bibliography] to his being in a hurry to complete the play.

No, to look for tricks cleverly used by Shakespeare in order to enlist the sympathy of his audience for his weak man of a hero, is to look in the wrong direction. We feel sympathy for Richard because, from the moment he lands on the Welsh coast, we can feel with him. Sympathy in human beings is elicited by self-forgetfulness and the intuitive realization of what others feel. But a dramatist can only enlist our sympathy for his imagined characters if he endows them with such an illusion of reality that, for the time being, they are to us real human beings, and if he makes it easy for us to apprehend their inward life. . . . But when a playwright or a novelist creates such a character in such a way, he does not create them out of nothing. They arise out of the depths of his own being. They necessarily are his children, parts or aspects of his own self. Richard's very weakness was most probably latent in Shakespeare. If so, he certainly overcame it. But that is not a point which I mean to discuss here. Nor am I going to speak of the relations between the poet in Shakespeare and the poet in Richard. But Shakespeare was an actor too, an actor by instinct, though he may not have been a first-rate one. And Richard is instinctively an actor. It is to that aspect of his character that I wish to draw your attention.

But before I can do so, a question of real importance must be settled. Did Shakespeare mean us to believe that, towards the end of his play, his hero experienced a real change of heart, that he truly repented his misdeeds, his misspent life, that he ended as a sincere penitent? The idea that he did so was first put into print—it may of course have occurred to others before—by Dr. Johnson who, in one of his notes to the play, writes: "In his prosperity we saw him imperious and oppressive, but in his distress he is wise, patient and pious" [see excerpt above, 1765]. Such a notion does not appear to have found much favour with English critics. . . . There is only one brief moment in the play that can lend support to the view that Richard turns penitent under the impact of his fall. Meeting the Queen on his way to prison, Richard bids her go to France and cloister herself in some religious house, for, he adds,

> Our holy lives must win a new world's crown
> Which our profane hours here have thrown down.
> [V. i. 24-5]

But in all his conversation with the Queen that follows, there is not the slightest suggestion that he really means to atone for his wasted youth by leading a life of contrition and penitence. Nor is there a trace of humility in the haughty words he addresses to Northumberland, or a hint of repentance. He speaks like one who is assured of his innocence. Others only are guilty. Theirs the sin, not his. . . . [In] his dying exclamation, in his persuasion that his murderers, those he has killed as well as Exton who kills him, are doomed to hell, while he is destined to heaven

> Mount, mount, my soul! thy seat is up on high
> [V. v. 111]

what else can be felt but his kingly pride? . . . So it is not surprizing that to the great majority of critics Richard should appear the same man after his deposition as he was before, that they should all side with Coleridge who perceived "the utmost consistency of character" in him [see excerpt above, 1811-12] and with Hazlitt who said "There is as little sincerity . . . in his affected resignation to his fate" as there is in "the extravagant impatience of his grief and despair" [see excerpt above, 1817]. In fact when he sees his wife for the last time and takes his leave from her, he thinks it fit to act the penitent, as on former occasions he had acted "the king of beasts".

The idea that in Richard there is an actor is by no means a new one. But it only became explicit within the last twenty or twenty-five years. Earlier critics, discussing the hero's character, occasionally used images borrowed from the theatre, but as images merely. Dowden, for instance, says that "he is equal to playing any part gracefully which he is called upon by circumstances to enact" and, in reference to the first scene, that "he enacts the part of a king with a fine show of dignity" [see excerpt above, 1881]. For Pater, Richard, in the scene of his deposition, "throws himself into the part" and "falls gracefully as on the world's stage" [see excerpt above, 1889]. Swinburne sees in the king a "histrionic young tyrant". Stopford Brooke regrets the episode of the mirror as lowering "our pity for Richard because it exhibits his theatrical folly in public" [see Additional Bibliography]. (pp. 91-5)

To call Richard a born actor is both a reflection on the man and a compliment to the artist in him. A man who goes through life acting instead of living, turning into drama, with himself in the chief part, whatever he has to live through, is essentially one that either is wholly lacking in character, in a real personality, who therefore feels insecure, uncertain of himself,—or, because chance has placed him in a position to which he is unfit by nature, cannot afford to be or to appear what he really is, and feels bound to assume attitudes which he imagines will suit the circumstances, to "pose" as the French say. In Richard's case, absence of character combines with incompetence as a ruler to make a "poseur" of him. He is all sensibility and imagination, but he has no strength of mind, no common sense, no grasp of reality, no real understanding of men, in spite of some flashes of insight, no moral convictions, no sense of right and wrong, in short none of the qualities that constitute character. Imagine him in any walk of life, even the humblest one, and he would surely prove a dead failure. His is, to some extent at least, an artist's nature. But . . . an artist he could never have been, for an artist requires self-discipline, concentration on the work in hand, steadiness of purpose, a highly critical mind, and Richard is wilful, capricious, and blinded by self conceit. Ordinary life would quickly have devoured him. From that doom he has been protected by his position. But that position could only shelter him so long as he had nothing to do with its responsibilities. As soon as, ill-advised, he assumed them, he found himself faced with situations with which he knew not how to cope, difficulties he had no idea how to solve. Insecure, deprived of any inward guidance, he cannot possibly let others see him as he really is, and, debarred from appearing his weak, uncertain, vacillating self, what can he do but pretend to be what he is not, but live as an actor on the stage?

To be acting instead of living, besides, is a perpetual temptation to him, for it is easy, natural to him. The very fact that he has no real personality enables him to enter into any part he chooses to play, playing each in turn with conviction, with the illusion, for the time being, of really being the character he impersonates. And he is helped by his gifts, his handsome presence and lovely face, the natural nobility of his deportment, his charm of manners, his sensitiveness, the imagination which provides him with a constant flow of wonderful eloquence. So that, compelled to act, he can act splendidly. But he goes further than the ordinary actor, for he acts in plays of his own composition. Indeed that is his most remarkable gift, the facility with which he can create, sometimes deliberately, sometimes on the spur of the moment, striking situations, a series of striking situations, in which he then plays his part with consummate art, even compelling others to co-operate. So long as he can keep the scene under his control, he is superb, enchanting as a great actor can be, capable of moving his audience—for of course an audience he must have . . .—of forcing them to admire or pity him. Inevitably, moments will come when something happens which he has not foreseen, prepared for, and then at once his inner weakness stands fully revealed; but as a rule his histrionic instinct, served by his lively imagination, quickly comes to his rescue and, out of his very predicament, he can strike a new attitude.

See him in the opening scene. He had ordered Bolingbroke and Mowbray to appear before him in the fond persuasion that, after he had heard their mutual accusations, he could easily, by an assertion of his authority, bring them to reconciliation. He would thus play the noble part, first of a judge, of an impartial sovereign, then of a peacemaker. But he had reckoned without Mowbray's sense of honour and Bolingbroke's resolution. . . . He feebly tries to make them obey him, loses for a while all control of the situation, until, hiding his defeat under a show of majesty—"We were not born to sue, but to command" [I. i. 196]—he bids them meet in single combat at Coventry, as though that decision were his, when it is merely what the irate knights had demanded.

At Coventry, he will not repeat his mistake, allow the situation to get out of hand. The whole elaborate pageant has been carefully thought out; he has decided to have all the stately preliminaries duly performed, but to prevent the ordeal by battle from taking place and have both Bolingbroke and Mowbray exiled by a decision of the Council. . . . [By] returning to the lists at the head of the Council with his prearranged sentence of banishment, he could act the great monarch, whose will is law, to the end of the scene and, after Mowbray's departure, add to this successful performance another scene in which he would appear as the magnanimous sovereign, accessible to pity, and ready to shorten Bolingbroke's term of exile in deference to his old father's grief. Throughout, his single preoccupation has been to act his part to his own satisfaction. He does not give a moment's thought to the realities with which in fact, he is dealing.

At Ely House, on the opposite, he is taken by surprise and can only be his irresponsible self. We know with what sentiments he goes to visit dying Gaunt. But he is ready to play the part of the king who is full of solicitude for the sick old man, his uncle and subject: "What comfort, man? How is't with aged Gaunt?" [II. i. 72]. But Gaunt's passionate outburst, his bitter reproach—"Thou hast made me gaunt" [II. i. 81]—throws him off his guard. His gift of speech deserts him and when, at last, he can interrupt the awful indictment of the dying man, it is with the undignified petulance of an angry child.

Richard's resourcefulness in imaginatively meeting unforeseen situations, his capacity for dramatizing them as they arise, turning them into plays of which he can again and again be the centre, are nowhere seen to greater advantage than in the scene of his return from Ireland. We may take it that his theatrical greeting of his kingdom on disembarking near Barkloughly Castle, his elaborate attitudes, first standing with tears streaming down his handsome face—"I weep for joy to stand upon my kingdom once again" [III. ii. 4-5]—, then kneeling and gently stroking the sand—"Dear earth, I do salute thee with my hand" [III. ii. 6]—, whilst imploring it to destroy his enemies, are, like his gesture at Coventry, premeditated actions. But when Aumerle bluntly tells him he had better get down to work, how wonderfully he can play the offended sovereign rebuking his followers for doubting the power and the will of Heaven to protect "the anointed king"! That such protestations are insubstantial, merely assumed for the moment, is vividly brought home to all by his turning pale at the news of the dispersal of Salisbury's Welshmen and confessing his helplessness, but a word of Aumerle suffices to remind him of his part as the bearer of a name that cannot but awe and defeat his enemies. Thereupon Scroop approaches, with more bad news, and Richard now enters as eagerly into the part of the man who is prepared for the worst, who is ready to bow to fate in perfect resignation. But this new attitude is no less insincere, no less merely acted than the previous one, as we realize almost at once when, by telling him that his favourites have made their peace with Bolingbroke, Scroop causes him to flare up into a brief orgy of invectives, and thus betray his true self, before he can understand that they have been executed. His histrionic nature, however, quickly reasserts itself. He sees, and catches at, the opportunity of acting the moralist, the philosopher, the king who refuses to be honoured as a king because he knows he is no better, no safer, no more immune against hunger, want, grief, and death than his fellow-men.

From Barkloughly Castle, Richard has gone to Flint, resolved there to "pine away". He has accepted his defeat, resigned himself to the loss of his crown, dismissed what forces he still had, forgone all hope, entered his night. But when Bolingbroke arrives, merely to claim his inheritance, Richard, who has resolved to let him ascend his throne, stages a magnificent, a most impressive symbolical scene. He appears in all his majesty on the battlements from which he will come down, king unking'd, looks down long in silence on Northumberland who stands below in cold disdain, refusing to bend his knee, and addresses him at last in his favourite part of God's anointed, as though he was still fully resolved to maintain and defend his rights. The total discrepancy between what he had clearly expected to hear and the simple request of Bolingbroke disconcerts him at first, but he goes on through the pre-arranged scene, as though he had been asked to surrender his crown. From the part of the king whom God alone can dismiss from his stewardship, he passes on to the part of the king who, sick of power and of life, willingly accepts to be deprived of both:

> What must the king do now? must he submit?
> The king shall do it; must he be deposed?
> The king shall be contented; must he lose
> The name of a king? a God's name let it go.
> I'll give my jewels for a set of beads, . . .
> And my large kingdom for a little grave,
> A little little grave, an obscure grave. . . .
> [III. iii. 143-47, 153-54]

On that last line Dr. Johnson commented: "Shakespeare is very apt to deviate from the pathetic to the ridiculous. Had the speech of Richard ended at this line it had exhibited the natural language of submissive misery'' [see excerpt above, 1765]. The rest of the speech certainly borders on the ridiculous. But on purpose. Richard himself is made aware of its growing absurdity: ''Well, well, I see I talk but idly and you laugh at me'' [III. iii. 170-71]. He who plays a part because he cannot, or will not, let himself merely be what he naturally is, is liable to overdoing it and easily falls into the ridiculous when he means to be pathetic. Such is the nemesis that dogs the steps of the actor in real life, of the ''poseur''

The scene of the deposition is one long elaborate piece of acting again, and to be understood as largely premeditated too, which may be the reason why it has impressed and still impresses some as being ritualistic in character, earlier scenes of course, for the same reason, producing the same, or at least a similar, effect.... Richard behaves like a great actor who holds his audience spellbound by his art, so perfect that one forgets it is art, and not nature. It is he who is in comand of the situation, and not Bolingbroke who must do as Richard bids him, nor Northumberland who vainly urges on him the reading of the list of his offenses. Whatever happens is his doing. And the weak man can thus, throughout the long scene, impose his will on the strong men that surround him, because he is playing to perfection the part he has chosen to act. He himself creates the drama of which he is the central figure by virtue of the great dramatic and poetical powers that Shakespeare has lent him.

My purpose . . . was not to offer one more analysis or interpretation of Richard's character, but simply to lay some emphasis on one aspect of it which had not yet received all the attention it deserves. It was inevitable that in so doing I should leave out more than one question that ought to be examined in a full discussion of his character, that for instance of the reality of his grief and suffering. But the complexities and intricacies of our hero's nature have been dealt with by a long line of excellent critics. There is no need to go into them again. But if henceforth, when thinking of Richard, of Shakespeare's Richard, you can give a little more importance than you may have done so far to the actor in him, I shall have gained my point. (pp. 96-100)

Georges A. Bonnard, ''The Actor in Richard II,'' in Shakespeare-Jahrbuch, Vol. 87/88, 1952, pp. 87-101.

LEONARD F. DEAN (essay date 1952)

[*In his well-known 1952 study* ''Richard II: *The State and the Image of the Theater,''* Dean identifies the diverse references in this drama to acting and the theater, ''explicit or implied,'' and demonstrates that they reflect ''a picture of a sick state in which appearance and reality are at odds.'' Many of the characters in this play, he points out, are figuratively actors, costumed and masked behind a ''glib ritualistic style'' and elaborate ceremonies that effectively conceal their true emotions. Artificial posturing and diplomatic maneuvering reduce life at Richard's court to a mere pageant, Dean states; he emphasizes that this situation remains the same ''despite the change in rulers,'' adding that death represents ''the only successful end'' to this dilemma—a fact Richard, but not Bolingbroke, realizes during his abdication of the crown.]

One way to describe the passage from *Richard II* to *Henry V* is to say that the first play is a picture of a sick state in which appearance and reality are at odds and that the last play is a picture of a healthy state in which political appearance and reality are unified in terms of the Elizabethan ideal of monarchy. This essay suggests that one sign of the political sickness in *Richard II* is the presence, explicit or implied, of the Renaissance comparison between the state and the theater. As the suggestion is developed, the reader will be asked to grant that political problems are also philosophical problems, and that plot and character may be controlled expressions of a general moral theme as well as dramatic accounts of typical personalities or recurrent historical situations. (p. 211)

[The] first important point for the present discussion, and one that has not been emphasized, is that Shakespeare's practical decision to follow Halle in beginning *Richard II* and the Henriad with the ordeal by combat between Bolingbroke and Mowbray not only provided him with a spectacular opening scene but also immediately involved him in the theatricalism of politics, and this presumably opened the way for the use of such an established motif as the state-stage comparison. The ordeal by combat was a social institution, like the courtroom process which developed from it, that was deliberately designed to impose a stereotyped or unnatural character upon the participants. The real feelings of Richard, Bolingbroke, Mowbray, and even Gaunt are necessarily masked to a large extent by the calculated neutrality of the ceremony. We sense at once that the king and the nobles are reading lines, that their social behavior is play-acting. Our subsequent judgment that the ceremony is a hypocritical disguise, that it will not cure the disorder which it is momentarily suppressing, is the product both of the glib ritualistic style and of those few lines in which contrary emotions come to the surface and announce themselves through a complication of the normally neutral and ceremonial tone. (pp. 213-14)

The last scene of the first act makes all of this explicit. The historical or social purpose of the ordeal by combat was well enough understood, and it had been stated by the king in his farewell to Bolingbroke: ''Farewell, my blood; which if today thou shed, / lament we may, but not revenge thee dead'' [I. iii. 57-8]. By sublimating the issue and the participants, by purifying their motives, the ceremony was meant through its deliberate impersonality to end the call of blood for blood. But when the king and his followers are finally alone, they remove their masks, and we see that the ritual has left the actuality untouched. Their cynical scorn is emphasized by the manner in which they mock the elaborately formal language of the ceremony: ''How far brought you high Herford on his way? / I brought high Herford, if you call him so, / But to the next highway, and there I left him. / And say, what store of parting tears were shed . . .'' [I. iv. 2-5]. Aumerle exclaims that he was so revolted by the part he was expected to play that he saved himself by a kind of double hypocrisy, pretending that he was too choked with emotion to say farewell. And on the other side, Bolingbroke is also described as busy play-acting, paying ''courtship to the common people; . . . wooing poor craftsmen with the craft of smiles'' [I. iv. 24, 8]. Richard accepts such behavior as a matter of course; it is simply a fact that must be faced and answered with force or guile.

In this theatrical state of England, well-meaning ''on-lookers'' like Gaunt and York are stultified. It is useless or dangerous for them to call things by their right names. Gaunt is obliged to mock his name, the thing he stands for, and to accept from Richard the insinuation that his very dying words are merely unbecoming play-acting. Gaunt's comparison of Eden and England emphasizes the distance this society has fallen from the state in which man and his function or role are indivisible and naturally good. . . . York attempts to withdraw (''I'll not be by the while'' [II. i. 211]), but Richard assigns him a surrogate role, "lord governor of England [II. i. 220]. He does not "Know how or which way to order these affairs / Thus thrust disorderly into my hands," but "somewhat we must do" [II. ii. 109-10, 116].

In this dilemma York is confronted by Bolingbroke, who is presented in a series of tableaux which define him as a man of policy adjusting his appearance to changing audiences. To the opportunistic elder nobles his "discourse hath been as sugar" [II. iii. 6], to the honorable young Percy he offers a gentleman's "covenant" sealing "heart" and "hand" [II. iii. 50]; to the lawful York he presents a humble knee and challenges law for his proper "rights and royalties" [II. iii. 120]; to unnamed "on-lookers" he recites reasons for the execution of Bushy and Green, to wash their "blood / From off my hands here in the view of men . . ." [III. i. 5-6]. Faced with this situation, in which illegalities are compounded and the distance from the ideal doubled, York is as stultified by the behavior of Bolingbroke as Gaunt was by that of Richard. His only recourse is to "remain as neuter" [II. iii. 159].

At this point Shakespeare returns to Richard, and in the interest of theme gives him a character that has scarcely been prepared for in the first act. He now becomes the eloquent spokesman for the ideal. In traditional imagery (garden, sun, time, Christ, etc.), he identifies himself with perfect majesty and that absolute value which has contempt for the world and its ceremonies. But since Richard has been discredited from the start as a Christian king and since he has now failed as a politician, we read this in terms of personality as sentimentalizing and in terms of theme as another way of emphasizing the emptiness of the name without the thing. It is this Richard of course who has been called histrionic, but there is no reason to think of him as being any more so than the politic Bolingbroke. Neither is allowed to exist outside of the theater of the state. Changes and developments which seem to be in the interest of characterization are more basically another view of the general moral sickness, in which "Each substance of a grief," to borrow Bushy's words, "hath twenty shadows . . ." [II. ii. 14]. The Bolingbroke "who never clogs his impulse to action with play-acting" must still do everything for "the manner sake." Richard would welcome a forthright and quicker end: "they well deserve to have," he urges, "That know the strong'st and surest way to get . . . For do we must what force will have us do" [III. iii. 200-01]. But before he can obtain the release of unconsciousness, he must mount the "scaffold" and play out the scene which Bolingbroke is equally obliged to help enact. "What must the King do now?" [III. iii. 143] asks Richard approaching the "stage," and he wishes now for roles from *contemptus mundi* that he has not earned. Then with a self-consciousness that Bolingbroke cannot afford to show and that must be stultified in himself, Richard concludes: "Well, well, I see / I talk but idly, and you laugh at me"[III. iii. 170-71]. But presumably Bolingbroke does not and can not laugh. He is in fact out of earshot, on the edge of the "stage." He confers sharply about tactics with the stage manager Northumberland: "What says his Majesty?" [III. iii. 184]. The answer is crudely psychological and practical: "Sorrow and grief of heart / Makes him speak fondly, like a frantic man; / Yet he is come." Then Richard enters and Bolingbroke advances, kneels, and begins to speak his lines in the mummery: "Stand all apart, / And show fair duty to his Majesty" [III. iii. 184-88].

The garden scene (III. iv), which follows, and which is set off by its allegorical mode from the rest of the play, re-asserts the ideal of the state as Eden and the possibility of its approximation

by an Adam-like king through keeping "law and form and due proportion" in the "sea-walled garden" [III. iv. 41-3]—a possibility perverted by both Richard and Bolingbroke. The next scene (IV. i), the appellants before Bolingbroke, parallels the opening action of the play and shows that the political mode has not been really altered despite the change in rulers. This is attested by Bolingbroke's command: "Fetch hither Richard, that in common view / He may surrender; so we shall proceed / Without suspicion" [IV. i. 155-57]. Once more the care for the "common view" may be read as an extension of the theatrical trope rather than as simply fear of popular uprising. Much of the deposition scene, as many have observed, is an exchange of "stage directions"; "Here, cousin, seize the crown—now mark me—Read o'er this paper—Urge it no more—mark, silent king—Say that again" [IV. i. 181, 203, 269, 271, 290, 293]. Richard must go through the mockery of legal confession, but Bolinbroke too must suit his pace and words to Richard's, or "The commons will not then be satisfi'd" [IV. i. 272]. When Bolingbroke is "silent" it is not for lack of histrionic ability, as has often been suggested, but because his politic role will not let him speak his true thoughts. When Richard sees in the mirror that the "silence in the tortured soul" [IV. i. 298] is the final "substance," we may understand, as the blindly patronizing Bolingbroke and Northumberland cannot, that the discovery applies not exclusively to the personality of Richard but also to the moral situation, that extinction of consciousness is the only successful end to this play. Again the mode has not been changed, but merely the principals, as York observes: "As in a theatre, the eyes of men, / After a well-grac'd actor leaves the stage, / Are idly bent on him that enters next . . ." [V. ii. 23-5]. The Abbot of Westminster likewise describes the scene as a "woeful pageant"; his solution, however, serves only to continue the theatrical events: "a plot / to rid the realm of this pernicious blot . . . shall show us all a merry day" [IV. i. 321, 324-25, 334]. That day is another scene stage-managed by Bolingbroke as he adjusts his policy to circumstances. He is, first, "smooth as oil" [*1 Henry IV*, I. iii. 7] (to borrow his words from *1 Henry IV*) with the deluded Duchess and her son: "Our scene is alter'd from a serious thing, / And now chang'd to 'The Beggar and the King' " [V. iii. 79-80]; then he is "Mighty and to be feared" [*1 Henry IV*, I. iii. 6] as he orders "for our trusty brother-in-law and the abbot . . . Destruction straight . . ." [V. iii. 137-39]. The politic actor is exposed by the Duchess' unwitting irony: "A god on earth thou art" [V. iii. 136], and by the murderous Exton's closing quotation from this "god": "Have I no friend will rid me of this living fear?" [V. iv. 2]. And the exposure is completed at the end of the play when Bolingbroke is faced with Exton and his own doubleness: "The guilt of conscience take thou for thy labour, / But neither my good work nor princely favour" [V. iv. 41-2].

Richard's famous prison speech in the next to the last scene is often read as the climax of his ineffectual attitudinizing; it is also . . . a dramatic analysis of the moral dilemma in the theater-like state. Richard's thoughts are "like the people of this world. For no thought is contented" [V. v. 10-11]. His acting "in one person many persons" leads to the same judgement: "And none contented" [V. v. 31-2]. The source of the discontent is the dualism at the basis of the stage play. . . . Time therefore cannot be redeemed, concludes Richard, and "any man that but man is / With nothing shall be pleased, till he be eas'd / With being nothing" [V. v. 39-41]. But of course one who will succeed in "Redeeming time when men think least [he] will" [*1 Henry IV*, I. ii. 217] has already been introduced. Bolingbroke's "unthrifty son" [V. iii. 1] will miraculously resolve the dualism of the theatrical state. It is not surprising that the dying father is made to describe the coming change in terms of the state-stage comparison:

> God knows, my son,
> By what by-paths and indirect crook'd ways
> I met this crown; and I myself know well
> How troublesome it sat upon my head . . .
> For all my reign hath been but as a scene
> Acting that argument; and now my death
> Changes the mode. . . .
> [2 *Henry IV*, IV. v. 183-86, 197-99]
> (pp. 214-18)

Leonard F. Dean, '' 'Richard II': The State and the Image of the Theater,'' in PMLA, 67, Vol. LXVII, No. 2, March, 1952, pp. 211-18.

TRAVIS BOGARD (essay date 1955)

[*In the following excerpt, Bogard argues that* Richard II *represents a significant milestone in the development of Shakespeare's tragic dramaturgy. By contrasting this history with* Richard III—*a play that preceded it by some two or three years—the critic claims that Shakespeare was here experimenting with techniques of characterization and exposition, learning in the process how to convey the most profound emotions through suggestion and ''implicit'' expression, rather than ''explicit'' statement. Bogard admits that technically* Richard II *is weaker than the melodrama of Richard Crookback, but notes that without this ''second'' Richard, Shakespeare's greatest tragedies might never have been written as they were. According to Bogard, Shakespeare's shift to this new mode of dramaturgy is evident in the deposition scene—or, more specifically, in Richard's few speeches with the mirror. At this point, he adds, Shakespeare became more interested in the private sufferings of the man behind the king than in the histrionic tribulations of a deposed monarch, and he willingly risked the integrity of his tragic characterization in order to express this deeper, more personal subject.*]

A writer is moulded out of faults, and the greatest become much more the better for having had the courage to be a little bad. All writers experiment in some degree with technique, but not many, after their apprenticeship has been served, appear willing to desert the manner in which one achievement has been attained for another, untried, yet potentially permitting fuller and more complex expressiveness. Even less frequently does an established writer change the manner of expression midway in the work, destroying the unity of effect by radical alterations in technique while the work is in progress. In a novel or poem, at least, the new manner is not likely to emerge unexpectedly; a work written for publication can be withheld until its parts are integrated. A dramatist, however—especially one working in close conjunction with a voracious theatre—may not have such an opportunity. Deadlines render revisions luxuries and make beneficial experimentation a catch-as-catch-can matter. Under such circumstances, discoveries that cannot be ignored are likely to be dangerous to both the art and the commerce of the theatre.

In the Elizabethan and Jacobean drama, there is ample evidence of this experiment-on-the-run, and very little of it is important. Marston, for instance, tried everything on for size, and none of it fit. All of his experimentation led him to nothing better than (in Alfred Harbage's memorable phrase) ''a five-act lapse in taste.'' With Shakespeare, however, the case is altered, and to the student of his work, particularly the student of his dramatic technique, the imperfect pieces can be in some ways

more instructive than those secure in their achievement. . . . [They] help to illuminate, first, the masterpieces whose dramatic technique can be more completely understood because of the slight imperfections occasioned by the experiments and, second, the dramatist, who, because of a momentary lack of complete assurance, stands revealed off guard, caught in an act of hesitant choice of an untried way, which in Shakespeare's case led toward a country altogether new.

It is, probably, an ultimately dissatisfying view of the two plays that holds *Richard III* to be almost without qualification successful and *Richard II* ''imperfect,'' even in the relative and limited sense suggested here. It makes matters worse to say that the difference between the plays is most notably to be attributed to the characterization of the two Richards, *Richard III* again being a skilful artistic achievement, *Richard II* being an unsynthesized portrait almost always inadequate to the demands that the play potentially makes upon him. Yet a study of Shakespeare's development of characters fit for tragedy may at least consider as a probability that, had Shakespeare contented himself with the techniques of *Richard III*, and had his impulses not overruled his sense of artistic propriety, *Richard II* would have been a better play, but the great tragedies would have been at a farther remove. It is doubtless extravagant to hold that except for the sudden surprising experimentation of *Richard II*, Shakespeare's tragedies would have been no more remarkable than Chapman's or Webster's. Nevertheless, in *Richard II* Shakespeare began to move in a way that none of the Jacobeans followed; it is here, in fact, that Shakespeare first became himself.

What matter, then, if *Richard II* is an artistic imperfection, if its preliminary assurance is destroyed midway by an unexpected problem of character and is shaken by the excitement of a new solution? It is a heady play for all that, a stageworthy play, and a valuable play to study, for in it—specifically in the ''Deposition Scene''—the maturing Shakespeare first explored the ground leading to the achievement of tragedy in the fullest, most unqualified sense of the term that must be reserved for perhaps a dozen plays in the world's history.

In writing *Richard III*, Shakespeare demonstrated his complete mastery of the known world of drama which from the first provided the solid base of his explorations. (pp. 192-93)

Compared to the miscellany of *Henry VI* and the partially controlled narrative of *Titus Andronicus, Richard III* attains structural unity unusual for a play of the period. (pp. 193-94)

The chief problem of character in *Richard III* was, presumably, to create an imitation of a human being who reasonably could be the agent of the evil episodes which history recorded. It is here precisely that the histories fail; they give no inkling of what kind of man it was who committed the deeds attributed to Richard. To find a man in the raw materials of the histories seems an impossible task. The apparent optional courses for a dramatist both lead to monsters: on the one hand a monster of melodrama, on the other a monster of unintentional farce.

Shakespeare's Richard, however, is neither of these, but a restrained creation, credible at least in context. It skirts the coasts of melodrama and farce, braving both, wrecking itself on neither. No merely primitive response, no jeers, no hisses will suffice to do Richard justice. His energy and his intelligence are worthy of respect; his humorous bravado woos his hearers; his fellowship with evil is so commendably frank as, almost, to clear him of the stigma of hypocrisy. He has in his misshapen way a dark charm that makes him tolerable, if nothing more, and that suggests the restraint with which Shakespeare treated him.

Yet such subtilizing characteristics as he possesses are not in themselves enough to save Richard from the melodramatic or the unintentionally farcical. Tragic drama lapses into melodrama, as comedy into farce, at the moment when the characters cease to be entirely credible as the perpetrators of their deeds. For a play of high dramatic intention on a serious historical theme, the creation of a credible king was an indispensable condition. Here, one would assume, Shakespeare's materials failed him by not providing the clues to Richard's essential nature. Here also, his technical achievement would be most unlikely to support him, for the carefully motivated, full-length portrait of the historical Richard was a different matter from an imaginary (and melodramatic) Titus and from the minor images of historical persons who scurry through the three parts of *Henry VI*. Here, finally, and perhaps most importantly, to the creation of a deeply human creature, the drama of his time provided no entirely competent guide.

Harley Granville-Barker's distinction between "explicit" and "implicit" drama is serviceable in indicating why this was so. Implicit drama carries within its design the totality of its meaning; explicit makes its points *as points,* setting forth its meaning less by its design than by explanations that accrue during the course of the play. (pp. 194-95)

To the time of *Richard III,* Shakespeare's possible models and Shakespeare himself had written almost entirely explicit drama. There are moments in Marlowe when the verse seems about to do more than decorate or explain the action. . . . [Perhaps] the signal example is Faustus' final soliloquy, where emotion is suggested connotatively as well as described by the imagery. But even this scene is "explained," its significance explicitly set forth by the closing chorus which instantly follows. At best, Faustus' soliloquy was only a suggestion of the way language could implicitly present the vivid reality of a man's inner being.

The dialogue of *Richard III* is almost completely explicit in its formulations. Richard, like Tamburlaine, is part orator, and in that capacity—in which he, like Tamburlaine, takes pride— he continually descants on his own deformity, describes and explains his actions, and states his motivation. . . . "I am determined to be a villain" [*Richard III,* I. i. 30], Richard says at the outset, and explains succinctly why this is so. His later motivation is reduced to simple statements of rudimentary fact, serving in the main to clarify possible obscurities and to explain transitions. Continually, in short, the dialogue points to the visual image which the actor will of necessity create and to little, if anything, deeper. It is, though eloquent and elaborate, basically a kind of dramatized stage-direction.

Where in all this is the human being? Where, at least, is his stage equivalent? Where is the misguided and suffering mortal responding with pain to his circumstances? It is doubtful in this play that he exists at all. The explicit method of treating character cannot penetrate deeply into the realities of a human spirit, for such realities, if they are to be received by an audience as real, are not merely grasped by the conscious mind but felt by the total being. (pp. 195-96)

Richard, in short, though he has all the vitality a stage figure may need, is not conceived in terms that enable him to claim an audience as Hamlet or Lear claims it. The techniques of character representation are insufficient to establish him as humanly real. (p. 196)

Richard II is unquestionably an exciting play in the theatre and the study, but it does not represent a technical achievement comparable in perfection to that of *Richard III.* It overreaches itself, goes beyond its anticipated limits, and is therefore less than perfect.

To speak of "imperfections" is not to deny that the play has its unity. Indeed most critics and actors of the title role have been able to see consistency in it. . . . [Richard] is a divided being, a king, the anointed of God, but also a man, frail and doomed in his frailty. Indeed the opinion is repeatedly advanced that Richard is his own Judas, the man betraying the king. (pp. 198-99)

To see Richard as a unified character is undoubtedly best, but an alternate view is possible. It can be maintained that the character of Richard is only to be synthesized by the actor's (or critic's) contribution to the role, which in this instance amounts to sleight-of-hand. Shakespeare is unquestionably concerned with Richard as both a public and a private figure, but the question may be raised whether he is entirely successful in presenting both aspects of Richard simultaneously. Does he perhaps rather present now the king, now the man, allowing the two to alternate so that a tension develops which prohibits the fusion of man and king into a single portrait? Further, a comparison of Richard's consecutive appearances might well suggest that there are three, possibly four Richards in the play, no one of them brought fully into conformity with any other. His first appearance as God's delegate, the symbol of kingliness, is not notably reaffirmed by his appearance as the petulant prince of the scene with Gaunt. Upon his return from Ireland, he and his situation claim sympathy as they have not done before, and again may well cause an audience to revaluate its earlier impression. Finally, although lines of circumstantial and psychological development are drawn, an audience may sense that the philosopher of Pomfret Castle was not really anticipated by the *poseur* on the battlements at Flint.

The present intention is not to dispute the prevailing view of Richard directly, beyond inquiring whether the actor must not labor diligently in the tournament scenes to create a subtle portrait of frivolity where Shakespeare has—in allowing Richard not only to claim but to assert a king's power—provided a portrait of arbitrary, even despotic force. A synthesizing core of character can certainly be found, as the success of the play onstage adequately attests, but it is perhaps worth noting that each of Richard's appearances must in some degree be reinterpreted by later disclosures, and that, in this necessity, the portrait of Richard is different from the unvarying consistency of Richard III or from the portrait of Hamlet which builds itself smoothly from scene to scene, amplifying, complicating, but withal confirming the initial impression presented.

That there is the possibility of disunity in Richard's character is at least suggestive of some slight uncertainty on Shakespeare's part as to the effect he wanted in the character or the means by which the effect was to be achieved. This is admittedly speculative, but setting impressionistic considerations of unity or disunity aside, it would appear that having chosen the story of Richard II, Shakespeare would be faced with two unusual and perhaps unexpected technical problems.

For one thing, the career of Richard centers unavoidably on the opposition between Richard and Bolingbroke, with the result that, however fortuitously, *Richard II* is the first play in English which is developed around a major and continuing conflict of two individuals. . . . Not Fortune's design but his own character puts Bolingbroke on the throne, as Richard's character causes his dethronement and death. What is important is the character of each as it is revealed in the crucial, central struggle, and, consequently, the demands on the playwright's skill at imaging character become much greater. Motivation, action, reaction, consistency—all elements which can be slighted under the conditions of a play like *Richard III* become vital to a narrative developed in terms of focal conflict.

The second unusual demand, again perhaps an accident of Shakespeare's choice of materials, resulted from Richard's being a gentle prince. His gentleness meant that the language of his story had to be refined from what had sufficed for the stories of *Richard III* and *Titus Andronicus*. Coarse-graind rhetoric was quite adequate to project the brutal passion of those stories. Richard III, it will be remembered, is part orator. In *Richard II*, however, though Shakespeare retained the obvious rhetorical character of the verse of *Richard III*, he made it not quite so starkly the language of the orator. There is evident a much greater attempt to adapt the language to the human situation here than in the earlier play, with the result that the rhetoric becomes less trenchant, more subtly aureate. Yet, as it becomes an increasingly subtle vehicle for the projection of emotion, of necessity it will reveal more about the character who speaks it. It follows readily enough that as an audience is permitted more complex and subtle insights behind the façade of character, mere trickery—the creation of an actor king, for instance—will not entirely suffice. There must be something at the character's core which can be seen; a spiritual reality must be projected at all costs.

Both the structure and the language of *Richard II*, therefore, suggest that the techniques for imaging character so successfully mastered in *Richard III* could not entirely have sufficed Shakespeare in his present need. Yet as he begins *Richard II*, he falls back on the identical device that he used in *Richard III*. He makes, or forces his actor to make, Richard an actor king. E. M. W. Tillyard has accurately noted the pervasiveness of the "formal and ceremonial nature" of *Richard II* [see excerpt above, 1944]. His instances include not only the character of Richard, but the language, the action, the emotion and the cosmic references of the entire play. In all its aspects, it is a highly stylized play, going far beyond *Richard III* in its concentration on ritual emotion in ritual event. Richard, as he is first presented, is in perfect accord with this pageant-like ritual. (pp. 199-202)

Unhappily for the actor playing Richard, there is not enough here to anticipate firmly the shallowness of his character as it is reavealed in the second act. Gaunt's comment on him [I. ii. 37-41] suggests that there may be less in Richard than meets the eye, but the point is not decisively made there or elsewhere in Richard's early scenes. All the actor can do to coordinate the early appearances of Richard with those following is to play Richard as one who obviously enjoys the formalities, and who enacts his role therein to the full. Only by this means can he achieve an effective acting point from the stopping of the tournament and prepare for the Richard of the scenes with the dying Gaunt. The possibility of synthesis is there, no doubt, but the playwright has not helped the process by giving the king any of the self-awareness which produced the explanatory ironies of character in *Richard III*.

The absence of explicit clarification of the precise nature of the character is unusual, but it is little more than a straw in the prevailing wind, perhaps the result of accident rather than experiment. The difficulty with Richard in the first two acts

is that he is not "determined" to be anything. When a character has a positive course of action, when what he holds most desirable is strongly evident, the techniques of explicit characterization are serviceable enough. They are less effective in delineating the quiescent, somewhat passive characters whose part is more to suffer than to act. A villain in a tragedy is easier to depict than a suffering hero. When a character does little, it is difficult to show what he is. When his spiritual greatness is revealed by his assertion of his integrity of spirit, a way must be found to represent the substance of that spirit, or the character will not emerge as more than a curiosity, a kind of psychological object-lesson, soulless as a case history. Explicit techniques alone ultimately will not serve. Only with the aid of implicit suggestion can a playwright represent the inner reality of spirit essential to the tragic sufferers.

In the scene at the death of Gaunt, Richard is presented totally by explicit means. He does nothing beyond his avowed course; he is nothing other than what Gaunt explicitly states him to be. The problem here, of course, was to dramatize the misguided and therefore unworthy king with discretion, for reasons political as well as dramatic. This much Shakespeare accomplishes, but very little more. Richard has not, as a person, entered the action in any vital way, nor has the play achieved force and point. There have been great speeches, but the listless action has not embraced them in a truly dramatic design. They remain a little outside, supererogatory, more the poetry of rhetoric than the poetry of drama.

On Richard's return from Ireland, the essential drama begins, for it is at this point that Richard enters on his way of suffering, and it is here that the conflict between Richard and Bolingbroke emerges. Now action begins to generate, but by what means, as the play develops, is Richard characterized?

The most an audience can know of Richard at the time he appears on the Welsh coast is that he is a shallow, gracefully histrionic person. He does not cheat expectation. Once again, the explicit characterization gives him something of an actor's quality. "Dear earth, I do salute thee with my hand" [III. ii. 6] is the musical accompaniment to a ritual gesture. Richard acts and tells why; his words explain his ceremony; his emotion is revealed entirely by his description of it.

Yet shall it be said of this Richard that he is no more than the pageant king of the first two acts, that this is merely an actor's "business," deliberately, somewhat self-consciously pathetic? This indeed has repeatedly been the judgment of his behavior, and certainly there is no clear cause to believe more in Richard's pathos than his pomp. He has not staked any claim to genuine dignity.

This view, however, seems inexact, despite the advantage of its consistency with the precedent action. Richard's ceremony in Act III seems to be meaningful and moving where before it was empty formality. His expression of his devotion to England is not far removed from Gaunt's eulogy of the blessed isle or Mowbray's lament for his lost language. No one, of course, would claim that Richard's patriotism is equal to Gaunt's, but his expression of it draws on the lyric energies which inform the patriotic utterances throughout the play. The verse at least puts him on the side of the angels. Suddenly, unexpectedly, Richard begins to claim sympathy, and, as he does, the demands on the techniques of characterization become more severe than they have been so far. The ceremonial king of the first act could be easily revealed by his outward show. Similarly, Richard's action toward Gaunt reveals an unworthy mortal without difficulty. In the third act, however, as king and mortal are brought into close conjunction, no presentation of externals will entirely suffice to do justice to the sympathetic Richard—to the suffering king entering the world of the dispossessed.

The third act is the first crucial test of Shakespeare's dramaturgy, and he passes it superbly, using the technical resources he had mastered in *Richard III*. The stylized alternation of courage and despair as Richard receives the news of his losses, the sorrowful splendor of his appearance at Flint Castle—explicit characterization can do no more than this. Richard II is a masker by necessity as Richard III is a masker by choice. To protect himself from the cold eyes of Bolingbroke, he must cling desperately to the mask of the ceremonial ruler. Wavering and faint-hearted, he must force himself to maintain the dignity of a king. The effect is poignant, a moving, if somewhat artificial portrait which presents the idea of anointed majesty, but which at the same time suggests the presence of a suffering human being.

Richard's behavior is the focal center of the action and everyone, including Richard, is concerned with it. Inevitably, therefore, his manner will be felt to be part pose. To be sure, the sense of the *poseur* is dramatically justified. His acting is motivated by circumstances and by his character which shapes itself into an entity in these scenes. The artifice which attends the descriptions of falling majesty seems equally appropriate: it is the actor's mask, the formalized image of woe, reminiscent of the lamenting queens of *Richard III*. Furthermore, the lengthy set pieces by whose means Richard holds attention are sufficiently thoughtful to suggest that he is maturing toward some philosophical acceptance of his mortal world. Finally, the silent skepticism of Bolingbroke casts his action into an ironic dimension and provides the scene with an immediacy, a sense of living presence which the stylized lamenting of Richard by itself can not achieve.

It is just here, however, in effectively creating the living presence of Richard, the sufferer—of making Richard an object of pity rather than of wonder—that the explicit manner reaches its limit. Richard is characterized by his artifices, by his mask which can be described by himself and his watchers without awkwardness. But of the man, the best the ironic perspective can show is that he is not what he pretends to be. His sorrow and his weakness are suggested by a kind of negative characterization. Richard points out that kings are mortal, but this is different from showing what mortals are when they suffer. Despite the rhetoric which describes his suffering, despite the attempts of the set pieces to suggest growth, Richard's words for all their handsome lyricism do not quite break through to present tragic suffering as a thing felt rather than as a thing discussed.

To a less rhetorical, more oblique, and paradoxically more direct method of revealing suffering, however, Shakespeare was coming as he wrote. As the play stood in relation to the second tetralogy, Richard did not need to be more than the anointed king, a vital link in the world order. He existed primarily to be unkinged, his deposition serving as the cause of all that followed. It is chiefly as the king—passingly unworthy, yet a king—that Shakespeare presented him through three acts. In doing so, he kept well within his proven technical range. Yet as he wrote, his interest appears to have been more compellingly caught by Richard as human being than as king, and the incoordination of the elements of Richard's portrait is the result of the divided view. The pathetic figure huddling in the

robes of ceremony is of another order of being than the ceremonial ruler whose principal function is to point out the consequences of rebellion against his holy state. His complete emergence in the deposition scene—the spot can be almost precisely fixed—is the final indication that for Shakespeare the known limits of technique were insufficient, and that the farther ranges of revelation must be explored, whatever the cost to the unity of effect of the present enterprise.

The opening episode of Act IV harks back to the dramaturgy of *Henry VI*. The stately donnybrook begun by Bagot's charges is muddled and at this point perilously near irrelevance. The tone of the scene rises at the Bishop of Carlisle's prophecy, which has some of the structural function of Margaret's curses in its delineation of the course of destiny. Yet both episodes are little more than curtain raisers to Richard's sacrificial moment.

At his entrance, he speaks again as an actor, this time as the tragedian caught removing make-up and costume:

> Alack, why am I sent for to a king
> Before I have shook off the regal thoughts
> Wherewith I reign'd?
>
> [IV. i. 162-64]

The new role occupies his mind, and gesture suggests itself:

> I hardly yet have learn'd
> To insinuate, flatter, bow, and bend my knee.
>
> [IV. i. 164-65]

And he must learn his part more perfectly:

> Give sorrow leave a while to tutor me
> To this submission.
>
> [IV. i. 166-67]

The explicit characterization of the earlier sections is still the technical means. Richard is describing himself in literal terms, being somewhat methodically pathetic, and his sorrow, though expressed, is not completely self-expressive. Yet Shakespeare appears instinctively to be seeking a more satisfactory method of projecting the reality of suffering than by describing its appearance, a method that will remove completely from his character the sense of the histrionic which falsifies the suffering. He must show not Richard's vision of his own suffering, but the suffering itself, and he reaches next for an image that will suggest the agony of a man betrayed. A natural, if audacious comparison comes to hand:

> Yet I well remember
> The favours of these men. Were they not mine?
> Did they not sometime cry, "All hail!" to me?
> So Judas did to Christ; but He, in twelve,
> Found truth in all but one; I, in twelve thousand, none.
>
> [IV. i. 167-71]

It is a satisfactory moment on many counts. The image has unexpected propriety, for Richard—as the play reiterates—is God's deputy, and, ruling by God's leave, is touched with divinity. It is startling too in its power to eradicate the callow Richard and to give him, almost for the first time in the play, a true dignity. Finally, it serves to lift his personal sorrow from the commonplace, to generalize it by allowing it to touch an archetypal instance of the suffering of the betrayed. It strikes a chord to which all hearers must respond, for it reaches to common roots, and as it does so, the emotion seems unexpectedly more credible and more noble than before. (pp. 202-06)

It is when he causes Richard to call for the mirror that Shakespeare begins fully to suggest the reality of suffering in his hero. In Shakespeare's dramatic development, the incident is significant. Richard calls for the glass to learn the truth about his sorrow, and what he sees gives him pause:

> No deeper wrinkles yet? Hath sorrow struck
> So many blows upon this face of mine,
> And made no deeper wounds?
>
> [IV. i. 277-79]

The appearance, the gesture, the descriptive language do not tell the truth of the inner suffering. At best, they are a distorted, unfocused revelation. It is a strange moment. There comes a surge of rhetoric reminiscent of Marlowe, and then Richard breaks the glass. As he does so, it is almost as if Shakespeare himself broke the glass by which he had to this moment mirrored suffering.

Bolingbroke says with some irony at what he takes to be mere petulance:

> The shadow of your sorrow hath destroy'd
> The shadow of your face.
>
> [IV. i. 292-93]

Richard, however, understands a deeper irony in the image than does Bolingbroke:

> The shadow of my sorrow! Ha! let's see.
> 'Tis very true, my grief lies all within;
> And these external manners of laments
> Are merely shadows to the unseen grief
> That swells with silence in the tortur'd soul.
> There lies the substance.
>
> [IV. i. 294-99]

Shakespeare is not far now from the revealing irony of

> But I have that within which passeth show,
> These but the trappings and the suits of woe.
>
> [*Hamlet*, I. ii. 85-6]

In *Richard III*, Shakespeare acknowledged no difference between the outer and the inner man. "External manners of laments" were the entire substance, two degrees of appearance the only subtlety. Now—almost with a sense of startled discovery—the dramatist's perception takes him close to what will be a truth of his craftsmanship: that the external manner of lamenting is a shadow only, that true grief can only be imaged as it is, in silence and unseen. Amazingly enough, then, Shakespeare finds the means to project the "substance":

Richard:	I'll beg one boon;
	And then be gone and trouble you no
	more.
	Shall I obtain it?
Bolingbroke:	Name it, fair cousin.
Richard:	"Fair cousin?" I am greater than a king;
	For when I was a king my flatterers
	Were then but subjects; being now a
	subject,
	I have a king here to my flatterer.
	Being so great, I have no need to beg.
Bolingbroke:	Yet ask.
Richard:	And shall I have?
Bolingbroke:	You shall.
Richard:	Then give me leave to go.
	[IV. i. 302-13]

After the ceremony, the symbolic gesture, all the rhetoric of passion, the short lines and their silences are doubly eloquent, and they project matured character with a reality that Shakespeare has not before been able to achieve.

Thus, for a moment, the man emerges from the ritual pageant and, for that moment, his audience is unconcerned with stories of the death of kings. The mask and the man have been brought into revealing opposition, and in consequence, human suffering, the raw material of tragedy, has moved full sympathy in a way the merely royal story can never do again. The tale of dispossession and its sequent national disturbance was originally the focal matter of the drama, but in Act IV, when Richard's character moves into a new, sharp perspective, tragedy, as it were, finally upstages history, and from this last imbalance the play never entirely recovers.

What follows in this play is not of especial importance. Even the sequence in which the "discovery" was made concludes with a flatly explicit couplet. Richard's parting with his queen is in the older manner, and the affairs of the York family are reminiscent of the dramaturgy that found no fault with the miscellaneous episodes of *Henry VI*.

The technical mastery of so difficult a matter is not instantly achieved. The soliloquy in Pomfret Castle seems to be trying without conspicuous success to find a way of imaging the frenzied boredom of imprisonment. . . . [The] soliloquy only partially succeeds in showing finally and in combination the king figure and the suffering man. Its formality is a little self-conscious, and it contrasts perhaps too sharply with the simpler pathos of the scene with the groom. In neither episode is Richard the man revealed in more than half light. He is something less than the king of "Dear earth, I do salute thee with my hand," and far removed from the simple sufferer revealed in "Then give me leave to go."

Discovery—if discovery it be—did not lead in *Richard II* to full exploration. But there was Brutus coming [in *Julius Caesar*] and the story of Hal and Hotspur [in *Henry IV*], where Shakespeare perfected the implicit techniques that enabled him to approach tragedy greatly. Indeed, it is worth noting in passing that so completely implicit is the characterization of *Henry IV* that Hal's explanatory soliloquy at the end of I. ii appears a blot, difficult for a present-day reader to accept without some sophisticating perception detrimental to Hal's character. Yet the soliloquy is only a momentary reversion to the technique of *Richard III*. Hal says, in effect, "I am determined to be a hero," and his words would not give a moment's pause, had the play been cast in the mold of *Richard III*. The older manner, however, is no longer sufficient to his purposes, for Shakespeare has already travelled far down the road to tragedy he came upon, unsuspecting and unready, during the writing of *Richard II*. (pp. 207-09)

*Travis Bogard, "Shakespeare's Second Richard,"
in PMLA, 70, Vol. LXX, No. 1, March, 1955, pp.
192-209.*

KARL F. THOMPSON (essay date 1957)

[Richard II's habit of identifying himself with the suffering Christ and his playing a martyr at crucial moments in Shakespeare's history have been variously interpreted as evidence of sanctity, egotism, admirable courage, and despicable self-pity. In the following excerpt, Thompson judges the validity of the king's pretensions to this saintly title. How much Richard deserves to be called a "martyr," the critic suggests, depends on our definition

of the term; Thompson emphasizes that for an Elizabethan audience raised on the famous Acts and Monuments *of John Foxe— a book about the heroic deaths of victims of religious persecution—the word carried connotations of retribution and resistance not evident in the orthodox view of martyrdom as a passive acceptance of God's will. Thus, according to the critic, Richard's retributive actions before his death should not undercut our view of him as "the martyr-king" as presented in both this play and Shakespeare's sources.*]

[Every] writer on Shakespeare's Richard or on the historical Richard, every interpreter of the unhappy king, all of his "lasting friends"—as every viewer of the play must call himself—agree that Richard was not ignoble. We know this because Richard perished nobly. Shakespeare depends upon this seemingly instinctive recognition of Richard's final nobility in order to effect a unity of character in his protagonist.

This sympathy and admiration is reminiscent of the late Middle Ages when Richard, the last English king to possess the full sanctity of medieval kingship, became an exemplar of royal martyrdom. Shakespeare encountered this attitude in his sources, which drew in turn upon anti-Lancastrian treatises that made Richard a martyr and compared him to Christ and his accusers to Pilate. In his characterization Shakespeare does not, to be sure, use the words martyr-king, but he does employ certain of their connotations.

In presenting the religious and political issues at stake in Richard's history, however, Shakespeare could not, at the risk of creating a superficial account, commit himself to one interpretation only. He could not profitably adopt an unqualified view of Richard as a martyr, using martyr in the orthodox sense of the term, for to Shakespeare's audience Richard was a bad king whose deposition was perhaps inevitable but whose murder was avenged only by a half-century of civil war. The complexities of history, as viewed by the Elizabethan mind, had to be reflected in the complexities of character and drama. There still remained, nonetheless, the task of drawing from these complexities the impression of a whole personality. And in this, so it seems at first, Shakespeare falls somewhat short of success. What appears to be Richard's double nature, man and martyr, is a dilemma, running the course of the play, that has been variously explained. These explanations have a common reference, for in attempting to summarize Richard's character they deal in one way or another, directly or indirectly, with the interpretations of martyrdom implicit in the play, and they all center eventually on the manner of Richard's death. (pp. 159-60)

[In] the response of audiences and critics to Richard's last action, the almost universal sympathy and pity for the murdered king, there may be some unifying solution. Instinctively, it seems, we all realize that here is the heart of the play; here Shakespeare speaks to us most profoundly, eliciting some sort of reaction to the personality of Richard as it shows in its completion.

The question that now attracts is whence does this general approval of Richard spring? Exactly what happens in us to make us render final judgment for Richard? If we can state this, we can see that Shakespeare has developed a complex character from the superficial treatment of Richard as a martyr apparent in his sources, yet has avoided abandoning his protagonist to the dramatic schizophrenia, as it were, that would result from endowing him with two characters, man and martyr. Here it may be worth while to refer again to the term martyr-king to see if in its connotations there may be some answer.

Martyr denotes for the orthodox Christian a person who has testified to his faith in Christ to the point of death and perishes in the sure knowledge that death of the body has freed the soul for immediate entrance into heaven. The true martyr, then, cannot fight back, cannot seek to escape. He must yield in order to be saved, in order to avoid committing evil himself. This is the ultimate Christian gesture, and it is perfectly illustrated by Dostoyevsky's story of Christ's encounter with the Spanish Grand Inquisitor. The Inquisitor defiantly explains to Christ the necessity of burning heretics for the sake of the good health of the Church which he and his fellow churchmen have deliberately reconstituted as the force of anti-Christ; whereupon Christ, far from condemning the Inquisitor, forgives him with the kiss of peace. What other actions could be taken by Christ? What other action is possible for the martyr, witnessing his faith in Christ?

In this severe view of martyrdom God alone is the judge, but His judgment is postponed to a time beyond the knowledge of men when those who have sinned, knowing not what they do, will be judged. Although we may feel that God will judge the persecutors severely, we ourselves cannot condition His judgment by our confident prediction of His vengeance. In this view, furthermore, actions such as the seeking of vengeance, applauded as good in the earthly city, may not insure entrance into the heavenly city. Obviously, then, Shakespeare's Richard of Bordeaux is not a true martyr in the orthodox sense of the term, for his final action, which elicits our praise and admiration, is definitely of the earthly city.

Earlier in the play, however, Richard affects, at least, the pose of the true martyr and repeatedly turns away from the kind of action that might gain him the admiration of men of this world. He does this not so much in the ceremony of deposition, which is his conscious playing to an audience, as in his earlier, more genuine despair. Kierkegaard refers to Richard on this very point when in his *The Sickness unto Death* he writes of man, encountering the unendurable, despairing and resisting all comfort save the possibility of relief which turning to God can bring. This is what Richard attempts to do, and curiously, it is this that forfeits the audience's sympathy for a time. Richard in thus attempting to turn away from this world seems weak, vacillating, morally unkempt.... But when Richard acts on the plane of this world and strikes back, he regains the sympathy of the audience.

In order to ascertain what Shakespeare's purpose was here and at what effect he was aiming, we can profitably consider what might have influenced his handling of the theme of martyrdom inherent in his sources. It must have been a matter of primary concern to him when he came to the writing of *Richard II* to determine the dramatic feasibility of depicting the true martyr.... In *Henry VI,* we see Shakespeare following a set pattern: his Henry VI dies in the odor of sanctity, but ends, in the audience's esteem, a pitiably weak, insignificant man. It would not do, of course, to repeat this, for Shakespeare, like the modern historian, felt that Richard II was not ignoble, and noble figures cannot be dramatically created without conflict.

The question remains, then, of how to reconcile with the theme of martyrdom the conflict that confers nobility. That reconciliation is made possible by the notions of martyrdom entertained by Shakespeare's contemporaries and expressed, better than anywhere else, in Foxe's *Acts and Monuments*. The popular title of Foxe's work, *Book of Martyrs,* shows well that in the popular imagination the term martyrdom had certain meanings and a definite pattern of events. Here, if anywhere, we can see what the term meant for Shakespeare's audience and, consequently, realize that to describe Richard as a martyr-king would not be an inconsistency either in Shakespeare's time or in ours.

It may at first seem contradictory to my thesis to say that Shakespeare's martyrology is like Foxe's, for I have suggested that Shakespeare creates the character of Richard from conflict, from resistance and strife and heroic death. This seems not at all like Foxe's heart-shaking accounts of poor and humble men and women who went quietly rejoicing to the stake: Agnes Bongeor, who gives her infant child to the care of friends and goes joyfully to be burned, or the blind woman Joan Waste, made to sit before the pulpit to hear a sermon on the fate of the souls of heretics, and then taken to be burned, holding her brother's hand on the way. Such accounts induce in the modern reader a desolation of the spirit. But John Foxe and his reader saw these things differently, for Foxe sees to it that the score is righted, that cruelty is avenged, that outrage is undone. The perpetrators of these crimes are, every one, punished not in the hereafter but in the here and now. Foxe dwells with moral satisfaction upon the instructive death and burial, "stinkingly and blindly", of the wicked Romish Bishop Bonner, and the final agonies of Romish officials who had burned God's witnesses. He entitles the accounts of such retributions "The Severe Punishment of God upon the Persecutors of his People", and in these accounts the wheel is made to come full circle.

We see in all this perhaps a less exalted attitude toward martyrdom than that implicit in Dostoyevsky's narrative, but the natural thirst of the human spirit for justice is satisfied at once. The voice of *to philanthropon* [moral sense], to use Aristotle's phrase, requires in its definition of martyrdom an action that is an observable demonstration of the reality, in space and time, of the moral order. In this view, he who dies unavenged dies in vain; the perpetrator of evil must suffer in the here and now, by God's will. God has assumed the martyr's soul into heaven, but God's will is not fulfilled until the martyr's death is avenged. And God's will is always done. In an important way, this attitude is more comforting, more reassuring, and, therefore, more consequential than Dostoyevsky's, for it allows the generality of mankind to live more courageously in this world. There is, moreover, in the finality, in the conclusive nature of the pattern that ends with vengeance for the martyr's death according to God's plan, a scheme ideally suited to drama. The equilibrium that every good drama must attain in its closing scene is also achieved in Foxe's narratives. There is a dramatic and a moral pattern here, and Shakespeare uses the full force of that combination.

That force is brought fully to bear in the scene of Richard's death. The suggestion of Richard's martyrdom is made in Richard's last lines:

> Exton, thy fierce hand
> Hath with the king's blood stain'd the king's own land.
> Mount, mount, my soul! thy seat is up on high,
> Whilst my gross flesh sinks downward, here to die.
>
> [V. v. 109-12]

But his death is avenged in its very occurrence by his destroying two of his assailants. That vengeance will continue is intimated by Bolingbroke's acceptance of the burden of guilt and his casting about for a way to pay the debt as expeditiously as possible:

> I'll make a voyage to the Holy Land
> To wash this blood off from my guilty hand.
>
> [V. vi. 49-50]

That Shakespeare was aware of the connotations of martyrdom which Richard's history had for his audience seems further demonstrated by his repeatedly and openly soliciting the audience's consideration of the implications of martyrdom. Not only is there the deposition scene (IV. i.) and Richard's despairing resolution for a hermit's life [III. iii. 143-75], but Carlisle's warnings of God-inspired vengeance for Richard's dethronement [IV. i. 114-49]. . . . [This] popular view of martyrdom is Shakespeare's deliberate choice, for he was not bound by source or legend or history to one received version of Richard's end. Holinshed, for instance, recites three versions: Richard was starved, he escaped to Scotland and lived a holy hermit there, or he was murdered by Sir Pierce of Exton. The liveliest account is the last, for Holinshed has it that Richard, beset in his prison in Pomfret Castle by Sir Pierce of Exton and eight men-at-arms, dashed back and forth across the cell until Sir Pierce, standing on a chair, felled him with a blow of an axe. Of course Shakespeare had to tame this action in order to render it plausible and effective on the stage.

Shakespeare's choice of this presentation of the manner of Richard's death allowed him, moreover, to make the incident dramatically operative in two ways. On the one hand, Richard's noble end brings the action of the play to a close acceptable to the audience. The play can stand independently. On the other hand, the manner of Richard's death simultaneously provides motive and introduction for the succeeding plays of the tetralogy and sets the tragic tone of the accounts of Richard and the two Henrys on the high moral level that Shakespeare deemed appropriate to the history of England. If, as he was composing *Richard II*, Shakespeare was meditating the plays that were to follow, he must have seen the necessity of ennobling Richard in order to make him at last a man whose fate would sustain the weight of the theme of tragedy he contemplated basing upon it. (pp. 161-65)

The mind of the audience for which Shakespeare wrote demanded a hero who fought: the mind of man generally speaking requires resistance to evil and seeks for the visible defeat of evil. Most of us would incline (if there must be martyrs in our time) to sympathy for the kind of martyrdom that follows a stout resistance and is followed in turn by instant retribution so that we can say that man can end nobly. For better or worse we feel a certain suspicion of the man who yields because, he says, it is the better, more Christian thing to do. (p. 165)

No need, then, to shift the focus of the play, to divide Richard into martyr and man. . . . For all things are drawn together and ordered in Richard's last scene. This world and the moral order, the degrees of men and their duties are defined. All this is shown in the fate of one man, the microcosm in its experience reflecting the macrocosm. Is this not what Richard is about as in his prison he imaginatively builds his state? But the state of man is not complete until Richard does more than weep for it. It is finished when Richard acts for it positively and in his not ignoble death puts in place for us the keystone of an affirmed moral order. Because of this, it seems important to distinguish between the two different ideas of martyrdom that are suggested by the play and to show that there is a unity of character in Richard. (pp. 165-66)

Karl F. Thompson, "'Richard II', Martyr," in Shakespeare Quarterly, *Vol. VIII, No. 2, Spring, 1957, pp. 159-66.*

J. A. BRYANT, JR.   (essay date 1957)

[*Bryant argues that in* Richard II, *Shakespeare first reveals his metaphysical turn of mind, his ability to see "the particular event both as something unique and as something participating in a universal web of analogy.'' The critic suggests that through Shakespeare's appropriation—conscious or otherwise—of Christian and pagan rituals, and above all of Biblical allusions, Richard II assumes a resonance of meaning beyond that of any prosaic historical chronicle. Bryant focuses in particular on the numerous references to Adam, Cain and Abel, and Judas and Christ in the play, and on the dimension of universal significance these contribute to the story of Richard and Bolingbroke; he cautions, however, that strict correspondences between these figures tend to be elusive, for the king is cumulatively Christ, anti-Christ, Adam, and Cain, and his cousin is both the avenger of Abel's murder and, through his endorsed killing of Richard, the descendant of Cain. Bryant concludes that by thus combining these opposing analogies, Shakespeare shows that ''good and evil, innocence and guilt,'' are ''inextricably mixed'' in the human soul.]*

However one looks at it now, *Richard II* seems to mark a kind of transition in Shakespeare's development as a dramatic poet. To his contemporaries it may very well have seemed a relatively tame performance after the exciting combination of historical material and Senecan villainy in *Richard III* and the lyrical movement of his sophisticated *Romeo and Juliet*. For us, it is perhaps easier to see that Shakespeare had reached a terminus of sorts in both of these early plays. . . . Shakespeare, by the time he came to write *Richard II,* had proved that he was capable of achieving as much perfection as was desirable in several of the more important dramatic forms that his predecessors had sketched out for him. It remained for him to show that he had something new to offer, either by producing a startling innovation in form or by offering a new idea of drama. . . . What really sets [*Richard II*] sharply apart from Shakespeare's own earlier work and the work of all his contemporaries is an approach—demonstrable in most of his later work quite without regard to formal classification—which reveals Shakespeare clearly as a poet with a metaphysical turn of mind, capable of seeing the particular event both as something unique and as something participating in a universal web of analogy. We find next to nothing of this in the *Henry VI* plays, in *Comedy of Errors,* in *Love's Labour's Lost,* in *Romeo and Juliet,* or in *Richard III,* which, for all its slick dramaturgy, remains a play about Richard III, at its farthest conceivable extension a warning to would-be usurpers and tyrants. It is in *Richard II,* a play popularly and rightly famous for one passage in glorification of England, that Shakespeare manages for the first time to extend his field of reference to include everybody. . . . If we may believe some of the critics who have written about it, *Richard II* contains much that is unassimilated, contradictory, and without especial significance. That is, if we look at the play ''rightly,'' in Bushy's sense, we see in it at least a partial failure to achieve complete control over the historical materials. Perhaps this is so. Nevertheless, if we take a hint from Richard's Queen and eye the play awry (as, for example, in our recollection of it), it has a way of subtly distinguishing a form that tends to pull all the seemingly irrelevant parts together and make the whole meaningful as no chronicle before it, dramatic or nondramatic, had ever been.

Some writers have attributed this ''informed quality'' of *Richard II* to Shakespeare's conscious or unconscious dependence upon an analogy with ritual. Among those who have acknowledged the importance of ceremony and ritual in the play is E. M. W. Tillyard, who devotes several illuminating pages of his *Shakespeare's History Plays . . .* to the matter [see excerpt above, 1944]; but Tillyard sees ceremony only as part of the data of the play, an attribute of Richard and his medieval kingship, which Bolingbroke is about to destroy. . . . J. Dover

Wilson, on the other hand, following some remarks by Walter Pater, has observed in his edition that *Richard II* stands so remarkably close to the Catholic service of the Mass that it ought to be played throughout as ritual [see Additional Bibliography]. Hardier critics than Wilson have gone still further and made out cases for relating the play to ancient fertility rites, some of which, like their Christian counterparts, present remarkably close analogies with this play. (pp. 420-22)

Suggestive as all these examples of ritual are, however, they have only the most doubtful kind of connection with plays of the Elizabethan theater; for as far as responsible investigators have been able to tell, the theater which Shakespeare inherited was a lineal descendant of neither folk rite nor Christian ritual. It is much more sensible to explain whatever ritual movement we find in *Richard II* as something Shakespeare himself achieved—partly by analogy with existing ritual perhaps, but achieved by himself—in the process of shaping a particular event from chronicle history into a living poetic symbol. In that sense, it may be said that he imported into English drama something that it had not inherited legitimately—or . . . , he rediscovered for drama an almost forgotten path, impossible for most but vastly rewarding for those few capable of using it. The question to be asked and answered is, how did he happen to stumble upon it? One cannot answer such a question with finality. Shakespeare's own profound sense of analogy must, of course, provide nine tenths of any answer anyone might suggest; and the presence in England of a powerful Christian ritual, revitalized by half a century of intermittently vigorous opposition, certainly had something to do with it. But in addition to these aspects of Shakespeare's achievement, one other, related to both and yet isolable in its own right, commands attention; and that is his persistent use of Biblical story as analogue for his secular fable. In *Richard II* this aspect confronts us from beginning to end.

The most obvious manifestation of it is the identification of Richard with Christ, which happens to be an historical one. Shakespeare makes explicit use of it first in Act III, when he makes Richard refer to Bushy, Bagot, and Green as ''Three Judases, each one thrice worse than Judas!'' [III. ii. 132]. In Act IV, of course, there is considerably more of this sort of thing. There the Bishop of Carlisle warns that if Bolingbroke ascends the throne, England shall be called ''The field of Golgotha and dead men's skulls'' [IV. i. 144]. And Richard observes of Bolingbroke's supporters:

> . . . I well remember
> The favours of these men. Were they not mine?
> Did they not sometime cry, ''All hail!'' to me?
> So Judas did to Christ; but He, in twelve,
> Found truth in all but one; I, in twelve thousand, none.
> [IV. i. 167-71]

A bit farther on he calls his enemies by another name:

> . . . some of you with Pilate wash your hands
> Showing an outward pity; yet you Pilates
> Have here deliver'd me to my sour cross,
> And water cannot wash away your sin.
> [IV. i. 239-42]

This set of allusions, familiar even to casual students of the play, serves admirably to point up Richard's own view of the situation and also to underline effectively the official Elizabethan view that (in the language of the *Homilies*) ''The violence and injury that is committed against aucthoritie is committed against God. . . .'' A second set of allusions, equally familiar, begins with Gaunt's reference to "This other Eden, demi-paradise" [II. i. 42], which gets its proper qualification somewhat later in the Garden scene of Act III, when the Gardener's man describes England as a "sea-walled garden" choked with weeds and the Gardener himself receives the Queen's rebuke for presuming to accuse Richard of negligence:

> Thou, old Adam's likeness, set to dress this garden,
> How dares thy harsh rude tongue sound this unpleasing
>   news?
> What Eve, what serpent, hath suggested thee
> To make a second fall of cursed man?
>
> [III. iv. 73-6]

Here with these allusions a second attitude, not exclusively Elizabethan, is underscored: viz., that the king, as himself man, is responsible to God for the right use of sovereignty, both by defending true religion and the honest subject and by punishing the wicked.

Taken together these two sets of allusions give us a double image of Richard—Richard *microchristus* and Richard *microcosmos*, Richard the Lord's Anointed and Richard Everyman. This, of course, is simply the conventional Elizabethan double image of kingship and would not of itself be particularly startling were it not for the additional suggestion of a pattern that unfolds as the play proceeds. The Golgotha of which Carlisle speaks does indeed come to pass. Richard rides to London with many to throw dust upon his head but none to cry, "God save him!" Despised and rejected, he languishes at Pomfret, only to face his executioners with such a manifestation of regality in death that Exton, like the centurion at the foot of the cross (who said of Jesus, "Truly this man was the Son of God" . . .), is compelled to acknowledge it:

> As full of valour as of royal blood!
> Both have I spill'd; O would the deed were good!
> For now the devil, that told me I did well,
> Says that this deed is chronicled in hell.
>
> [V. v. 113-16]
> (pp. 423-25)

Perhaps some Elizabethans, long accustomed to hearing and seeing typological interpretations of Scripture, saw in this combination of allusion and historical fable a kind of significance that we are likely to overlook. What Shakespeare was giving them in this presentation of Richard as a sort of Adam-Christ was nothing less than a typological interpretation of history. In Scripture the fall and death of the First Adam is corrected and atoned for by the sacrificial death of the Second (see *Romans* 5:12-21). That is, Adam's disobedience and death is an anticipatory realization of a pattern that achieved its complete historical realization only in the perfect obedience and death of Jesus of Nazareth, with those resurrection a way was cleared for Adam (and all those who had sinned in Adam) to escape the full consequences of death. From the typologists's point of view this pattern, perfectly symbolized by one Adam's atonement for the other's sin, is the eternal principle of which all history is in one way or another but the spelling out. Whether he realized it or not at the time, Shakespeare, in laying the outlines of such a complex and richly suggestive symbol against the surface of his chronicle material, had given to secular fable a significance that it had achieved only rarely in drama since the days of Aeschylus and Sophocles. To paraphrase Dryden, he had affected the metaphysical in his treatment of it. Moreover, having underscored that revolutionary affectation by utilizing ceremonial in his play, by presenting ceremonially much

that was not strictly ceremony, and by frequently alluding to the symbolic substance of analogous pagan ritual (sun and ice, summer and winter, etc.), he had also produced a work which "eyed awry" strongly suggests an analogy with ritual.

Seeing a ritualistic aspect in a play, however, is not the same as identifying it with ritual or attempting to play it as ritual. To see Richard as a ritual type of Adam-Christ is certainly warranted by Shakespeare's text, but to see him exclusively as that is to see Bolingbroke exclusively as Satan-Judas; and this is certainly *not* warranted by the text. The leading question of the play is not simply "What is true kingship?" but "What is the true king? What is the Lord's Anointed?" Mere ritual is powerless to answer this question, and history and the *Homilies* do little better. Shakespeare could expect his audience to know the report of history that both Richard and the Lancastrian usurper in their turns possessed the title of "Lord's Anointed" and could expect them accordingly to stand with Gaunt when he says ruefully near the beginning of the play:

> God's is the quarrel; for God's substitute,
> His deputy anointed in His sight,
> Hath caus'd his death; the which if wrongfully,
> Let Heaven revenge. . . .
>
> [I. ii. 37-40]

Similarly, he could let York's pained acquiescence in Bolingbroke's accession to the throne serve as as appropriate public moral for the play as a whole: ". . . Heaven hath a hand in these events, / To whose high will we bow our calm contents" [V. ii. 37-8]. Yet there is something less than a martyr's acquiescence in Richard's famous metaphor for the historic turnabout:

> Now is this golden crown like a deep well
> That owes two buckets, filling one another,
> The emptier ever dancing in the air,
> The other down, unseen, and full of water.
> That bucket down and full of tears am I,
> Drinking my griefs, whilst you mount up on high.
>
> [IV. i. 184-89]

The conclusion startles Bolingbroke into saying, "I thought you had been willing to resign." And Richard replies with three lines that would be uncomfortably out of place in a play reduced to the level of ritual:

> My crown I am; but still my griefs are mine.
> You may my glories and my state depose,
> But not my griefs; still am I king of those.
>
> [IV. i. 190-93]

Here Richard is undoubtedly already thinking of himself as a betrayed and repudiated Christ, moving ahead to a sour cross while the Pilates stand about washing their hands. The role evidently delights him, and he plays it well. Nevertheless, we should notice that the role is one he has himself discovered, not one that has come looking for him. We should also notice that Shakespeare cast Richard initially in quite another role, which he plays equally well, in spite of himself, and which temporarily at least disqualifies him as a spotless victim.

The Richard that Shakespeare sets before us at the beginning of the play is not only God's Anointed but a man guilty, ultimately if not directly, of his uncle's death. He knows that no one has proved his guilt, and he thinks that no one, except Aumerle of course, knows exactly what the details of Woodstock's death were. Yet Bolingbroke, in the very first scene, pronounces the murdered man Abel and his murderer by im-

Act IV. Scene i. Richard II, Bolingbroke, the Abbot of Westminster, York, Northumberland, Aumerle, Percy, Fitzwater, Surrey, the Bishop of Carlisle, lords, and officers. By M. Browne.

plication Cain. . . . What Bolingbroke does not realize is that his condemnation and threat of revenge, hurled at the innocent Mowbray, are applicable only to Richard. The Cain he really seeks, however unwittingly, sits on the throne before him and wears the robes of the Lord's Anointed. And ironic as this situation is, it becomes even more ironic when we think of the ancient identification of Abel with Christ and of Cain with the disbelieving Jews who slew him. In Shakespeare's time there was nothing particularly esoteric about such an identification. The New Testament provides ample authority for it (*Matt.* 23:25 and *Heb.* 11:4; 12:-24); there is a reference to it in the Canon of the Mass; and frequent use of it is made in the writings of the Church Fathers. Among Shakespeare's audience there must have been at least a few who had encountered it in contemporary exegetical works and a great many who knew about it from pictorial representations in the familiar *Biblia Pauperum*. Yet even if the identification of Richard-Christ with Richard-Cain escaped the audience entirely, the primary application of Bolingbroke's allusion to the story of Cain and Abel could hardly have escaped them. They all knew well enough what had happened to Woodstock and who was directly responsible for it, and they could not have missed the implication that Richard secretly bore the curse of Cain. A second allusion to the murder of Woodstock, however, completes the identification. It is Gaunt who makes this one:

> O, spare me not, my brother Edward's son,
> For that I was his father Edward's son.
> That blood already, like the pelican,
> Hast thou tapp'd out and drunkenly carous'd.
> [II. i. 124-27]

Here we have one of our oldest symbols for the Savior, the pelican mother who feeds the young with her own blood, inverted by Gaunt to make an accusation against the young king. That is, Richard, who should have been the parent pelican of the figure, prepared to nourish his brood with his own life if need be, is here accused of having caroused on the blood of another (Woodstock), leaving his young to fare for themselves. Perhaps Shakespeare's audience missed this allusion too. No one can say for sure about that. The important point is that Shakespeare put it there; and with it the chain of analogies, as Shakespeare conceived it, seems complete: Richard-Christ-antichrist-Cain, all are linked as one.

But what of Bolingbroke, who also assumes the role of the Lord's Anointed before the play is complete? After Cain had killed his brother, God put his mark on the fugitive murderer and decreed that no vengeance be taken upon him. . . . Bolingbroke, in proclaiming himself the avenger of a murdered Abel, was using a figure of speech, to be sure, but he was nevertheless presuming to make right in his own way something that mere man can never make right. In other words, he was presuming to do something that even as *microchristus* he could not expect to accomplish without committing the same sin he would avenge.

The place of Bolingbroke in the action of the play is perhaps clear enough without the use of Biblical allusion, but such allusion can help us state it: Bolingbroke's story is that of a man who sets out to slay the murderer Cain and does so, only to find that he has the blood of Abel on his hands.

Richard II, then, if it is to be compared to ritual, must be compared to some of the pagan rituals we know, and not to any Christian ritual. The allusions point to a clear, unambiguous analogy with Christ for neither of the principals. Each is a *microchristus* with a specifically human blind spot, a failure to see that kingship, like human nature generally, involves both a crown and a potential Cain who wears the crown. Each discovers, among other things, that the crown is never enough to make the wearer immune to the consequences of being human, but each finds in his turn that the crown can be an eloquent teacher. The crown is a well of instruction, and Richard gets his in the process of descending. From the moment he sets foot on English soil after his return from Ireland, he alternately gropes for and rejects the knowledge which he fully possesses only in the hour of his death at Pomfret. . . . [Bolingbroke] receives a similar enlightenment on the way up. Up to the moment of his coronation Bolingbroke has never once thought of the terrifying efficacy that regal power confers upon human impulses. As Bolingbroke he could wish Richard dead and bury the guilt of the wish in his own soul. As Henry he must learn that even a whispered wish is a powerful command. That he wished Richard dead is now enough to make Richard dead, and the blood of Richard is upon him. Turning upon Pierce of Exton, who held the actual dagger, he condemns him in the words of innocent Mowbray:

> With Cain go wander through the shades of night,
> And never show thy head by day nor light.
>
> [V. vi. 43-4]

But the Mowbray who once left England "To dwell in solemn shades of endless night" [I. iii. 177] now rests in Abraham's bosom and was never Cain. The two lines that follow are at once sober and plaintive:

> Lords, I protest, my soul is full of woe
> That blood should sprinkle me to make me grow.
>
> [V. vi. 45-6]

And with these lines we come full circle. The great Biblical-metaphysical framework of allusion that began with Bolingbroke's reference to the murder of Abel has encompassed the fable and returned to its starting point. We can now state the questions of the play in terms of the analogies that define them: Who is the Cain? Who, the Christ? Can one avenge Abel with becoming Cain? Can Cain dwell with Christ in the same golden well?

Such questions as these inevitably arise whenever a great dramatic poet lays the relatively clear-cut distinctions of mythic pattern against the disorderly flux of human affairs. It makes little difference whether the poet particularizes his myth and so brings it to the status of history (as the Greeks frequently did) or brings to the particularity of chronicle history the outlines of a more ancient imitation. The result is the same. In either case we find good and evil, innocence and guilt, so inextricably mixed that human ingenuity cannot say for sure

where the dividing line is. As in the ancient fertility rites and in the Christian mass, we tend to find slayer and slain, old king and new king, Cain and Christ, united in one human frame. There is no other solution in purely human terms. And the bewildered protagonist who suddenly sees the unresolvable paradox in his human situation can only cry out, as Bolingbroke does:

> Lords, I protest my soul is full of woe
> That blood should sprinkle me to make me grow.
>
> (pp. 426-33)

J. A. Bryant, Jr., "The Linked Analogies of 'Richard II'," in The Sewanee Review, *Vol. LXV, No. 3, July-September, 1957, pp. 420-33.*

ERNST H. KANTOROWICZ (essay date 1957)

[*Kantorowicz's classic study* The King's Two Bodies *(1957), from which the following excerpt is taken, is an exploration of the medieval "legal fiction" that a monarch is simultaneously an individual and, in effect, a corporation. Although this paradoxical theory has all but vanished from modern thought, the critic maintains, it is central to our understanding of* Richard II, *for that king's tragedy results from a dissolution of the integrity of his dual nature. Kantorowicz traces the disintegration of Richard's doubleness in three scenes—III. ii., III. iii., and IV. i.—claiming that each episode culminates in an image of "Man's wretchedness." He adds that "the mirror scene is the climax of that tragedy of dual personality," for Richard's breaking of the mirror symbolizes the destruction "of every possibility of a second or superbody" and provides a final image of the king as "a miserable man . . . void of any metaphysis whatsoever."*]

> Twin-born with greatness, subject to the breath
> Of every fool, whose sense no more can feel
> But his own wringing. What infinite heart's ease
> Must kings neglect that private men enjoy!. . . .
> What kind of god art thou, that suffer'st more
> Of mortal griefs than do thy worshippers?
>
> [Henry V, IV. i. 234-37, 241-42]

Such are, in Shakespeare's play, the meditations of King Henry V on the godhead and manhood of a king. The king is "twin-born" not only with greatness but also with human nature, hence "subject to the breath of every fool."

It was the humanly tragic aspect of royal "gemination" which Shakespeare outlined and not the legal capacities which English lawyers assembled in the fiction of the King's Two Bodies. However, the legal jargon of the "two Bodies" scarcely belonged to the arcana of the legal guild alone. That the king "is a Corporation in himself that liveth ever," was a commonplace [during Shakespeare's lifetime]. . . . Besides, it would have been very strange if Shakespeare, who mastered the lingo of almost every human trade, had been ignorant of the constitutional and judicial talk which went on around him and which the jurists of his days applied so lavishly in court. Shakespeare's familiarity with legal cases of general interest cannot be doubted, and we have other evidence of his association with the students at the Inns and his knowledge of court procedure.

Admittedly, it would make little difference whether or not Shakespeare was familiar with the subtleties of legal speech. The poet's vision of the twin nature of a king is not dependent on constitutional support, since such vision would arise very naturally from a purely human stratum. It therefore may appear futile even to pose the question whether Shakespeare applied any professional idiom of the jurists of his time, or try to determine the die of Shakespeare's coinage. It seems all very trivial and irrelevant, since the image of the twinned nature of a king, or even of man in general, was most genuinely Shakespeare's own and proper vision. Nevertheless, should the poet have chanced upon the legal definitions of kingship, as probably he could not have failed to do when conversing with his friends at the Inns, it will be easily imagined how apropos the simile of the King's Two Bodies would have seemed to him. It was anyhow the live essence of his art to reveal the numerous planes active in any human being, to play them off against each other, to confuse them, or to preserve their equilibrium, depending all upon the pattern of life he bore in mind and wished to create anew. How convenient then to find those ever contending planes, as it were, legalised by the jurists' royal "christology" and readily served to him!

The legal concept of the King's Two Bodies cannot, for other reasons, be separated from Shakespeare. For if that curious image, which from modern constitutional thought has vanished all but completely, still has a very real and human meaning today, this is largely due to Shakespeare. It is he who has eternalized that metaphor. He has made it not only the symbol, but indeed the very substance and essence of one of his greatest plays: *The Tragedy of King Richard II* is the tragedy of the King's Two Bodies. (pp. 24-6)

It appears relevant to the general subject of this study, and also otherwise worth our while, to inspect more closely the varieties of royal "duplications" which Shakespeare has unfolded in the three bewildering central scenes of *Richard II*. The duplications, all one, and all simultaneously active, in Richard—"Thus play I in one person many people" [V. v. 31]—are those potentially present in the King, the Fool, and the God. They dissolve, perforce, in the Mirror. Those three prototypes of "twin-birth" intersect and overlap and interfere with each other continuously. Yet, it may be felt that the "King" dominates in the scene on the Coast of Wales (III. ii), the "Fool" at Flint Castle (III. iii), and the "God" in the Westminster scene (IV. i), with Man's wretchedness as a perpetual companion and antithesis at every stage. Moreover, in each one of those three scenes we encounter the same cascading: from divine kingship to kingship's "Name," and from the name to the naked misery of man.

Gradually, and only step by step, does the tragedy proper of the King's Two Bodies develop in the scene on the Welsh coast. There is as yet no split in Richard when, on his return from Ireland, he kisses the soil of his kingdom and renders that famous, almost too often quoted, account of the loftiness of his royal estate. What he expounds is, in fact, the indelible character of the king's body politic, god-like or angel-like. The balm of consecration resists the power of the elements, the "rough rude sea," since

> The breath of worldly man cannot depose
> The deputy elected by the Lord.
>
> [III. ii. 56-7]

Man's breath appears to Richard as something inconsistent with kingship. Carlisle, in the Westminster scene, will emphasize once more that God's Anointed cannot be judged "by inferior breath" [IV. i. 128]. It will be Richard himself who "with his own breath" releases at once kingship and subjects [IV. i. 210] so that finally King Henry V, after the destruction of Richard's divine kingship, could rightly complain that the king is "subject to the breath of every fool."

When the scene (III. ii) begins, Richard is, in the most exalted fashion, the "deputy elected by the Lord" and "God's substitute . . . anointed in his sight" [III. ii. 57; I. ii. 37-8]. . . . He still is sure of himself, of his dignity, and even of the help of the celestial hosts, which are at his disposal.

> For every man that Bolingbroke hath press'd . . . ,
> God for his Richard hath in heavenly pay
> A glorious angel.
>
> [III. ii. 58, 60-1]

This glorious image of kingship "By the Grace of God" does not last. It slowly fades, as the bad tidings trickle in. A curious change in Richard's attitude—as it were, a metamorphosis from "Realism" to "Nominalism"—now takes place. The Universal called "Kingship" begins to disintegrate; its transcendental "Reality," its objective truth and god-like existence, so brilliant shortly before, pales into a nothing, a *nomen*. And the remaining half-reality resembles a state of amnesia or of sleep.

> I had forgot myself, am I not king?
> Awake thou coward majesty! thou sleepest,
> Is not the king's name twenty thousand names?
> *Arm, arm, my name!* A puny subject strikes
> At thy great glory.
>
> [III. ii. 83-7]

This state of half-reality, of royal oblivion and slumber, adumbrates the royal "Fool" of Flint Castle. And similarly the divine prototype of gemination, the God-man, begins to announce its presence, as Richard alludes to Judas' treason:

> Snakes, in my heart-blood warm'd, that sting my heart!
> Three Judases, each one thrice worse than Judas!
>
> [III. ii. 131-32]
> (pp. 26-9)

However, neither the twin-born Fool nor the twin-born God are dominant in [III. ii.]. Only their nearness is forecast, while to the fore there steps the body natural and mortal of the king:

> Let's talk of graves, of worms and epitaphs. . . .
>
> [III. ii. 145]

Not only does the king's manhood prevail over the godhead of the Crown, and mortality over immortality; but, worse than that, kingship itself seems to have changed its essence. Instead of being unaffected "by Nonage or Old Age and other natural Defects and Imbecilities," kingship itself comes to mean Death, and nothing but Death. And the long procession of tortured kings passing in review before Richard's eyes is proof of that change:

> For God's sake let us sit upon the ground,
> And tell sad stories of the death of kings—
> How some have been deposed, some slain in war,
> Some haunted by the ghosts they have deposed,
> Some poisoned by their wives, some sleeping killed;
> *All murdered*—for within the hollow crown
> That rounds the mortal temples of a king,
> Keeps Death his court, and there the antic sits
> Scoffing his state and grinning at his pomp,
> Allowing him a breath, a little scene,
> To monarchize, be feared, and kill with looks,
> Infusing him with self and vain conceit,
> As if the flesh which walls about our life,

Were brass impregnable: and humoured thus,
Comes at the last, and with a little pin
Bores through his castle wall, and farewell king!

[III. ii. 155-70]

The king that "never dies" here has been replaced by the king that always dies and suffers death more cruelly than other mortals. Gone is the oneness of the body natural with the immortal body politic, "this double Body, to which no Body is equal". . . . Gone also is the fiction of royal prerogatives of any kind, and all that remains is the feeble human nature of a king:

> mock not flesh and blood
> With solemn reverence, throw away respect,
> Tradition, form, and ceremonious duty,
> For you have but mistook me all this while:
> I live with bread like you, feel want,
> Taste grief, need friends—subjected thus,
> How can you say to me, I am a king?

[III. ii. 171-77]

The fiction of the oneness of the double body breaks apart. Godhead and manhood of the King's Two Bodies, both clearly outlined with a few strokes, stand in contrast to each other. A first low is reached. The scene now shifts to Flint Castle.

The structure of the second great scene (III. iii) resembles the first. Richard's kingship, his body politic, has been hopelessly shaken, it is true; but still there remains, though hollowed out, the semblance of kingship. At least this might be saved. "Yet looks he like a king," states York at Flint Castle [III. iii. 68]; and in Richard's temper there dominates, at first, the consciousness of his royal dignity. . . . [But the] "cascades" then begin to fall as they did in the first scene. The celestial hosts are called upon once more, this time avenging angels and "armies of pestilence," which God is said to muster in his clouds—"on our behalf" [III. iii. 87, 86]. Again the "Name" of kingship plays its part:

> O, that I were as great
> As is my grief, or lesser than my *name*!

[III. iii. 136-37]

> Must (the king) lose
> The *name* of king? a God's *name*, let it go.

[III. iii. 145-46]

From the shadowy name of kingship there leads, once more, the path to new disintegration. No longer does Richard impersonate the mystic body of his subjects and the nation. It is a lonely man's miserable and mortal nature that replaces the king as King:

> I'll give my jewels for a set of beads:
> My gorgeous palace for a hermitage:
> My gay apparel for an almsman's gown:
> My figured goblets for a dish of wood:
> My sceptre for a palmer's walking staff:
> My subjects for a pair of carved saints,
> And my large kingdom for a little grave,
> A little little grave, an obscure grave. . . .

[III. iii. 147-54]

However, the second scene—different from the first—does not end in [these] outbursts of self-pity which recall, not a Dance of Death, but a dance around one's own grave. There follows a state of even greater abjectness. (pp. 30-2)

Shakespeare, in [III. iii.], conjures up the image of another human being, the Fool, who is two-in-one and whom the poet otherwise introduces so often as counter-type of lords and kings. Richard II plays now the rôles of both: fool of his royal self and fool of kingship. Therewith, he becomes somewhat less than merely "man" or (as on the Beach) "king body natural." However, only in that new rôle of Fool—a fool playing king, and a king playing fool—is Richard capable of greeting his victorious cousin and of playing to the end, with Bolingbroke in genuflection before him, the comedy of his brittle and dubious kingship. (p. 33)

The jurists had claimed that the king's body politic is utterly void of "natural Defects and Imbecilities." Here, however, "Imbecility" seems to hold sway. And yet, the very bottom has not been reached. Each scene, progressively, designates a new low. "King body natural" in the first scene, and "Kingly Fool" in the second: with those two twin-born beings there is associated, in the half-sacramental abdication scene, the twin-born deity as an ever lower estate. For the "Fool" marks the transition from "King" to "God," and nothing could be more miserable, it seems, than the God in the wretchedness of man.

As the third scene (IV. i) opens, there prevails again—now for the third time—the image of sacramental kingship. On the Beach of Wales, Richard himself had been the herald of the loftiness of kingship by right divine; at Flint Castle, he had made it his "program" to save at least the face of a king and to justify the "Name," although the title no longer fitted his condition; at Westminster, he is incapable of expounding his kingship himself. Another person will speak for him and interpret the image of God-established royalty; and very fittingly, a bishop. The Bishop of Carlisle now plays the *logothetes* [spokesman of God]; he constrains, once more, the *rex imago Dei* [king in the image of God] to appear:

> What subject can give sentence on his king?
> And who sits here that is not Richard's subject? . . .
> And shall the figure of God's majesty,
> His captain, steward, deputy-elect,
> Anointed, crowned, planted many years,
> Be judged by subject and inferior breath,
> And he himself not present? O, forfend it, God,
> That in a Christian climate souls refined
> Should show so heinous, black, obscene a deed! . . .

[IV. i. 121-22, 125-31]

[It] is the bishop who, as it were, prepares the Biblical climate by prophesying future horrors and foretelling England's Golgotha:

> Disorder, horror, fear, and mutiny
> Shall here inhabit, and this land be called
> The field of Golgotha and dead men's skulls.

[IV. i. 142-44]

The bishop, for his bold speech, was promptly arrested; but into the atmosphere prepared by him there enters King Richard.

When led into Westminster Hall, he strikes the same chords as the bishop, those of Biblicism. He points to the hostile assembly, to the lords surrounding Bolingbroke:

> Did they not sometimes cry 'all hail' to me?
> So Judas did to Christ: But He, in twelve,
> Found truth in all, but one: I in twelve thousand, none.

[IV. i. 169-71]

For the third time the name of Judas is cited to stigmatize the foes of Richard. Soon the name of Pilate will follow and make the implied parallel unequivocal. But before being delivered up to his judges and his cross, King Richard has to "un-king" himself.

The scene in which Richard "undoes his kingship" and releases his body politic into thin air, leaves the spectator breathless. It is a scene of sacramental solemnity, since the ecclesiastical ritual of undoing the effects of consecration is no less solemn or of less weight than the ritual which has built up the sacramental dignity. . . . Walter Pater has called it very correctly an inverted rite, a rite of degradation and a long agonizing ceremony in which the order of coronation is reversed [see excerpt above, 1889]. Since none is entitled to lay finger on the Anointed of God and royal bearer of a *character indelibilis,* King Richard, when defrocking himself, appears as his own celebrant:

> Am I both priest and clerk? well then, amen.
>
> [IV. i. 173]

Bit by bit he deprives his body politic of the symbols of its dignity and exposes his poor body natural to the eyes of the spectators:

> Now mark me how I will undo myself:
> I give this heavy weight from off my head,
> And this unwieldy sceptre from my hand,
> The pride of kingly sway from out my heart;
> With mine own tears I wash away my balm,
> With mine own hands I give away my crown,
> With mine own tongue deny my sacred state,
> With mine own breath release all dutious oaths:
> All pomp and majesty do I foreswear. . . .
>
> [IV. i. 203-11]

Self-deprived of all his former glories, Richard seems to fly back to his old trick of Flint Castle, to the rôle of Fool, as he renders to his "successor" some double-edged acclamations. This time, however, the fool's cap is of no avail. Richard declines to "ravel out his weaved-up follies," which his cold-efficient foe Northumberland demands him to read aloud. Nor can he shield himself behind his "Name." This, too, is gone irrevocably:

> I have no name. . . .
> And know not now what name to call myself.
>
> [IV. i. 255, 259]

In a new flash of inventiveness, he tries to hide behind another screen. He creates a new split, a chink for his former glory through which to escape and thus to survive. Over against his lost outward kingship he sets an inner kingship, makes his true kingship to retire to inner man, to soul and mind and "regal thoughts":

> You may my glories and my state depose,
> But not my griefs, still am I king of those.
>
> [IV. i. 192-93]

Invisible his kingship, and relegated to within: visible his flesh, and exposed to contempt and derision or to pity and mockery—there remains but one parallel to his miserable self: the derided Son of man. Not only Northumberland, so Richard exclaims, will be found "damned in the book of heaven," but others as well:

> Nay, all of you, that stand and look upon me,
> Whilst that my wretchedness doth bait myself,
> Though some of you, with Pilate, wash your hands,

> Showing an outward pity; yet you Pilates
> Have here delivered me to my sour cross,
> And water cannot wash away your sin.
>
> IV. i. 237-42]

It is not at random that Shakespeare introduces here, as antitype of Richard, the image of Christ before Pilate, mocked as King of the Jews and delivered to the cross. . . . The parallel of Bolingbroke-Richard and Pilate-Christ reflects a widespread feeling among the anti-Lancastrian groups. Such feeling was revived, to some extent, in Tudor times. But this is not important here; for Shakespeare, when using the biblical comparison, integrates it into the entire development of Richard's misery, of which the nadir has as yet not been reached. The Son of man, despite his humiliation and the mocking, remained the *deus absconditus,* remained the "concealed God" with regard to inner man, just as Shakespeare's Richard would trust for a moment's length in his concealed inner kingship. This inner kingship, however, dissolved too. For of a sudden Richard realizes that he, when facing his Lancastrian Pilate, is not at all like Christ, but that he himself, Richard, has his place among the Pilates and Judases, because he is no less a traitor than the others, or is even worse than they are: he is a traitor to his own immortal body politic and to kingship such as it had been to his day:

> Mine eyes are full of tears, I cannot see. . . .
> But they can see a sort of traitors here.
> Nay, if I turn mine eyes upon myself,
> I find myself a traitor with the rest:
> For I have given here my soul's consent
> T'undeck the pompous body of a king. . . .
>
> [IV. i. 244, 246-50]

That is, the king body natural becomes a traitor to the king body politic, to the "pompous body of a king." (pp. 34-9)

The mirror scene is the climax of that tragedy of dual personality. The looking-glass has the effects of a magic mirror, and Richard himself is the wizard who, comparable to the trapped and cornered wizard in the fairy tales, is forced to set his magic art to work against himself. The physical face which the mirror reflects, no longer is one with Richard's inner experience, his outer appearance, no longer identical with inner man. "Was this the face?" The treble question and the answers to it reflect once more the three main facets of the double nature—King, God (Sun), and Fool:

> Was this the face
> That every day under his household roof
> Did keep ten thousand men?
> Was this the face
> That, like the sun, did make beholders wink?
> Was this the face, that faced so many follies,
> And was at last outfaced by Bolingbroke?
>
> [IV. i. 281-86]

When finally, at the "brittle glory" of his face, Richard dashes the mirror to the ground, there shatters not only Richard's past and present, but every aspect of a super-world. His catoptromancy [divination by means of a mirror] has ended. The features as reflected by the looking-glass betray that he is stripped of every possibility of a second or super-body—of the pompous body politic of king, of the God-likeness of the Lord's deputy elect, of the follies of the fool, and even of the most human griefs residing in inner man. The splintering mirror means, or is, the breaking apart of any possible duality. All those facets are reduced to one: to the banal face and insignificant *physis* [physical nature] of a miserable man, a *physis* now void of any metaphysis whatsoever. It is both less and more than Death. It is the *demise* of Richard, and the rise of a new body natural. (pp. 39-40)

> Ernst H. Kantorowicz, "Shakespeare: 'King Richard II'," in his The King's Two Bodies: A Study in Mediaeval Political Theology, *Princeton University Press, 1957, pp. 24-41.*

M. M. MAHOOD (essay date 1957)

[*Mahood discusses Shakespeare's manipulation of the meaning of words in* Richard II—*the vast discrepancy between the name and its object—noting how "the play's verbal ambiguities" contribute "to the rigid symmetry of [its] action" and reflect the tragic and historical themes. The critic describes the tragic action as Richard's loss of his faith in words "and his consequent self-discovery that for all the wordy flattery of others he is not ague-proof"; this action also encompasses Bolingbroke's recognition that "words have no inherent potency of meaning"—a knowledge that for Richard undermines the very essence of his life, but for Bolingbroke is the key to his deception of others. Mahood identifies the historical action or theme as "Bolingbroke's perilous contravention of the divine decree which made Richard king." Interestingly, the critic claims that Richard's abdication of the crown is essentially complete by the end of Act III, Scene ii, for here the king already recognizes the falsity of language, "that words express only desires and not facts . . . , that the name King, despite the sacramental nature of a coronation, does not imbue a man with kingly authority."*]

Richard II is a play about the efficacy of a king's words. Shakespeare here sets 'the word against the word' [V. v. 13-14]: the words of a poet against the words of a politician. Richard is a poet, but not, of course, for the reason that as a character in a poetic drama he speaks verse which is magnificent in its imagery and cadence. If the whole play were in prose, he would still be a poet by virtue of his faith in words; his loss of this faith and his consequent self-discovery that for all the wordy flattery of others he is not agueproof, constitute Richard's tragedy. Bolingbroke, on the other hand, knows words have no inherent potency of meaning, but by strength of character and force of arms he is able to make them mean what he wants them to mean. The historical, as distinct from the tragic, action of the play lies in Bolingbroke's perilous contravention of the divine decree which made Richard king; and this historical action is not self-contained but belongs to the whole sequence of the mature Histories.

These two themes are supported and often impelled by the play's verbal ambiguities which nearly all have to do with language. The words most often played upon include *breath* in the meaning of 'respiration', 'life', 'time for breathing', 'utterance' and 'will expressed in words'; *title* in meanings ranging from 'legal right', through 'appellation of honour' to 'a label'; *name* either as a superficial labelling or as inherent reputation; *honour* in a range of meanings to be further developed when Falstaff answers his own question: 'What is honour? a word!' [*1 Henry IV*, V. i. 133-34]; *tongue* as the mere organ that makes sounds or as the whole complex organisation of a language; *sentence* meaning 'a unit of speech', 'judgment', 'an apophthegm' or 'significance'; and the word *word* itself, signifying on the one hand 'an element of speech' and on the other, 'contention', 'command', 'promise', 'apophthegm' or 'divine utterance'. The almost polar extremes of meaning in many of these words contribute to the rigid symmetry of the play's action, the descent of Richard and rise

of Bolingbroke like buckets in a well. At the same time, the most delicate nuances of meaning between these extremes are used to give a poetic subtlety which can only be suggested here in a brief survey of the play's development.

Shakespeare uses his favorite device of a play-within-a-play at the very beginning of *Richard II*. As soon as the playhouse trumpet has sounded and the actors are entered Richard, with his own triple blast of resonant language, stages a miniature drama between Bolingbroke and Mowbray, which he promises himself shall be a good show:

> Then call them to our presence face to face,
> And frowning brow to brow our selues will heare,
> The accuser and the accused freely speake.
>
> [I. i. 15-17]

The poet is never more a maker than when he enacts the very semblance of life in a play; and the poet Richard combines the work of producer and chief actor when he attempts to stage, by royal command, a drama of quarrel and reconciliation in which he himself will play the controlling part of *deus ex machina*. But Bolingbroke and Mowbray, for all the splendour of their rhetoric, are not content with words. They are in such haste to make their accusations good by their deeds, that the words themselves take on the nature of action: Bolingbroke stuffs the name of traitor down Mowbray's throat; Mowbray, as he spits out his counter-challenge, retaliates by cramming these terms of abuse *doubled* down Bolingbroke's. Each detail of Bolingbroke's charge is prefaced by his resolve to verify his words with deeds. . . . (pp. 73-5)

The king has no wish to see Mowbray's guilt exposed by a trial of arms, and he attempts to end this scene of quarrel by his own trite epilogue on the theme of 'Forget, forgive'. But neither contestant will swallow his words. Mowbray's 'fair *name*' is more to him than an appellation: it is his reputation, the dearest part of him—'Mine honour is my life, both grow in one' [I. i. 182]. Bolingbroke will not be *crestfallen:* unless he can prove his words in battle, he has no right to the armorial bearings which signify his nobility. The words of both are pitted against the king's words, and by force of character they carry the day. The king who was 'not borne to sue, but to commaund' [I. i. 196] must wait until the meeting at Coventry for his decree in Council to carry the authority which his own words lack.

A dancing tattoo of language accompanies the flourishes and fanfares of trumpets at the Coventry lists. There is a gaiety of rhythm and image in the farewell speeches of Mowbray and Bolingbroke; both speak of the approaching fight as a feast, both are savouring this chance to prove by action the truth of their words. But the king asserts the authority of his word in Council, the fight is called off and the champions banished the kingdom. At this point Mowbray, not an important character in the plot, is given a significant speech full of puns upon *breath, sentence* and *tongue*—words which shuttle back and forth to weave the elaborate verbal fabric of the play. In contrast to the 'golden vncontrould enfranchisment' [I. iii. 90] promised by the contest, he now faces an enforced inactivity among people whose language he cannot speak. The irony of this becomes clear in the fourth act, when a noisy and abortive war of words between the nobles is silenced by Carlisle's account of how Mowbray in fact led a life of honourable action after his banishment:

> Manie a time hath banisht Norffolke fought,
> For Iesu Christ in glorious Christian feild,
> Streaming the ensigne of the Christian Crosse,

Against black Pagans, Turkes, and Saracens,
And toild with workes of warre, retird him selfe
To Italie, and there at Venice gaue
His bodie to that pleasant Countries earth,
And his pure soule vnto his Captaine Christ,
Vnder whose coulours he had fought so long.

[IV. i. 92-100]

Placed as they are in the play, these lines strengthen its symmetry of action. As Bolingbroke's star rises, he himself declines in our estimation; as the fortunes of Richard and his friends deteriorate they win new regard and sympathy from the audience. When this praise of Mowbray's 'pure soul' is spoken, Bolingbroke is king, and this gives the words a further ironic value. Throughout his reign Bolingbroke will long to expiate his usurpation in a crusade, but that hope is destroyed when he fulfils a quibbling prophecy by dying in 'Jerusalem'—the Jerusalem Chamber at Westminster.

The first climax of the play is reached at Coventry. The king plays with the power of the royal word by changing the years of Bolingbroke's banishment from ten to six. It is a dramatic instant, the moment when, with Richard at the height of his power and Bolingbroke at the lowest reach of his fortunes, the buckets begin to move; for Bolingbroke seems suddenly to comprehend and covet the efficacy of a king's words:

How long a time lies in one little *word*,
Foure lagging winters and foure wanton springes,
End in a *word*, such is the *breath* of Kinges.

[I. iii. 213-15]

By Elizabethan analogy the breath of the king should be a life-giving force, a human imitation of the Divine Spirit; but whereas Bolingbroke's reaction to the king's words is the envious acknowledgment of their god-like power, Gaunt sees only the king's human limitations and speaks of them in words which echo Bolingbroke's, but with subtle differences of meaning:

Thou canst helpe time to furrow me with age,
But stoppe no wrinckle in his pilgrimage:
Thy *word* is currant with him for my death,
But dead, thy kingdome cannot buy my *breath*.

[I. iii. 229-32]

The court leaves. Gaunt tries to console Bolingbroke with empty words that bear no relation to his real thoughts, while his son cannot find words that are adequate to his grief. . . . At the end of the scene, the contrast between the outlooks of father and son is formalised into two rhetorical speeches. Gaunt sententiously proclaims that there is no virtue but necessity, and Bolingbroke, who knows the real meaning of Richard's sentence, cries out against such deceptive verbiage:

Oh who can hold a fier in his hand,
By thinking on the frosty Caucasus?

[I. iii. 294-95]

This is just what Richard, who has always been deceived by the seeming power of words, will strive to do when his fortunes turn. Bolingbroke, although he is not to be so deceived, uses the conceptual power of words to snare others; and Richard implies this when he describes his cousin's departure after his banishment:

Our self and Bushie,
Obserued his *courtship* to the common people,
How he did seeme to diue into their harts,
With humble and familiar *courtesie*,

What *reuerence* he did throw away on slaues,
Wooing poore craftsmen with the *craft* of smiles
And patient *under-bearing* of his fortune
As twere to *banish their affects* with him.

[I. iv. 23-30]

Bolingbroke's double-dealing is implicit in the choice of words here. *Courtship* may be a serious attempt to gain affection, or mere bowing and scraping; *courtesy* can be an innate virtue, *la politesse du coeur,* or a formal curtsey ('Me rather had my hart might feele your loue, Then my vnpleased eie see your curtesie' Richard says to Bolingbroke at Flint Castle [III. iii. 192-93]); *reverence* is likewise either the deepest regard or the outward sign of a respect which may or may not exist; and *craft* can be either the craftsman's admirable skill or a deplorable cunning. The last two lines can be interpreted in two ways. Either they mean 'making so light of his troubles that he seemed not to want people to worry about him'—the superficial appearance of Bolingbroke's behaviour—or they mean 'supporting great sorrow so bravely that he has taken their love into exile with him'—the actuality of the scene for both Bolingbroke and the populace. All the dangerous power of Bolingbroke's 'candied courtesy' [*1 Henry IV,* I. iii. 251] is here made vivid in a few words.

At Coventry, Gaunt protested that the king's words which should, in the nature of things, give life to their country, could deal only death; and at the beginning of Act II Gaunt himself dies, uttering with his last breath words which would be life to both king and kingdom if only Richard would heed them. We are made aware of the depth and weight of the language in this scene by the way Shakespeare has framed it between two pieces of dialogue in which words are identified with life: the opening quibbles on *breath* and *breathe:*

Gaunt. Wil the King come that I may *breathe* my last?
          In holsome counsell to his vnstaied youth.
Yorke. Vex not your selfe, nor striue not with your
          breath,
          For all in vaine comes counsell to his eare.
Gaunt. Oh but they say, the tongues of dying men,
          Inforce attention like deepe harmony:
          Where words are scarce they are seldome spent
          in vaine,
          For they breathe truth that breathe their wordes
          in paine,

[II. i. 1-8]

and the announcement of Gaunt's death:

North. My liege, old Gaunt commends him to your
          Maiestie.
King. What saies he?
North. Nay nothing, all is said:
          His tongue is now a stringlesse instrument,
          Words, life, and al, old Lancaster hath spent.

[II. i. 147-50]

The Sceptred Isle speech has a much richer meaning within this sharply-defined context than when it is extracted for a patriotic set piece, and it is worth seeing what are the elements that go to its composition. 'This earth of maiestie, this seate of Mars' [II. i. 41] fits in with the garden theme which is a *motif* of the play from its first hints in the opening scenes (Gaunt's pun about 'unstaied youth'—giddy, or unpropped—at the beginning of the present scene being one) to its full statement in Act III, scene iv. Here the garden is that of Eden symbolic of security ('this fortresse built by Nature' [II. i. 43]) and of fertility ('this happy breede . . . this teeming wombe of royall Kings' [II. i. 45-51]). But we do not expect to find Mars in Eden; and this same line—'This earth of maiestie, this seate of Mars' operates in another way by introducing a string of paradoxes and oxymora. *Earth* can be mere soil or the great globe itself, *seat* is any stool till Mars makes it a throne, *stone* would be any pebble if the restrictive adjective did not make it a jewel. The effect is of something which might appear without value but is in fact of untold value, and 'this *dear dear* land' sharpens the paradox: what is dear in the sense that it is loved cannot be dear in the sense that it is priced for sale. . . .

This land of such deare soules, this deere deere land,
Deare for her reputation through the world,
Is now leasde out; I dye pronouncing it,
Like to a tenement or pelting Farme.

[II. i. 57-60]

What is beyond all value has been valued and leased. The king, whose relation to his kingdom should be that of God to Paradise, who ought to 'regain the happy seat' has, instead of redeeming it . . . , jeopardised its security and fertility by farming it out. The God-King analogy is a real one to Gaunt who has already been shown, in the second scene of the play, to have such belief in the divine right of kings that he 'may neuer lift An angry arme against his minister' [I. ii. 40-1]. Yet he knows how little there is of the godlike in Richard's nature, and his bitter awareness of this gap between the ideal and the actual passes to the audience and later conditions our response to Richard's 'dear earth' speech over the land he has farmed out, or to his identification of himself with the betrayed and condemned Christ at a further stage of the drama.

From the profound wordplay of this speech to Gaunt's quibbles on his own name may seem a sharp descent; but the 'Gaunt as a grave' puns have a force which the king acknowledges when he asks 'Can sicke men play so *nicely* with their names?' [II. i. 84]. *Nicely* means 'subtly' as well as 'trivially'. Gaunt's pun is not only true to the trivial preoccupations of the dying; it also reminds us of the play's dominant theme, the relationship between names and their bearers. Gaunt is saying in effect: 'I am true to my name, Gaunt, but you are not true to the name you bear of King'. (pp. 76-82)

This by no means exhausts the puns with which Gaunt endeavours to pack the most meaning into the few words left for him to utter. But his efforts are in vain. Richard seizes Bolingbroke's estates and leaves for Ireland. Northumberland, Ross and Willoughby remain to sound each other's feelings from behind the cover of verbal ambiguities: 'My heart is *great* but it must *breake* with silence' [II. i. 228] says Ross, and the other lords take this in its oblique sense that his courage is high and he needs must speak his thoughts. Soon they are sure enough of each other to appreciate Northumberland's

We see the wind sit sore vpon our sailes,
And yet we *strike* not, but securely perish,

[II. i. 265-66]

and the scene ends with their resolve to

Wipe off the dust that hides our Scepters *guilt*,
And make high Maiestie looke like it selfe,

[II. i. 294-95]

which could be either a promise to reclaim Richard or a threat to overthrow him. It depends how we read *gilt*—and it is a pun which Shakespeare is seldom able to resist.

The scenes of Bolingbroke's progress through Gloucestershire and of Richard's landing in Wales balance each other in the play's symmetrical action. This is the point at which the two buckets in a well pass each other. From Northumberland's fulsome praise, we gather that Bolingbroke has beguiled the tedium of their journey by the same charm of tongue that he exercised upon the citizens at his departure. His reply to this flattery is, however, short and meaningful: 'Of much lesse value is my company, Then your good wordes' [II. iii. 19-20]. Unlike Richard, who believes in the extensional power of words and that the bearer of them will really be paid on demand, Bolingbroke knows his words of promise to his supporters to be pure speculation. . . . York's wordy rejection of his nephew's courtesies—

grace me no grace, nor vnckle me no vnckle,
I am no traitors Vnckle, and that word Grace
In an vngratious mouth is but prophane

[II. iii. 87-9]

—implies what *Henry IV* confirms: that Bolingbroke's words are in fact as blank as Richard's charters. Bolingbroke has however, enough military strength to carry York along with him on the tide of rebellion; and by the time Bristol Castle is taken, Bolingbroke's fair words have won him the power to speak with regal authority in his sentence upon Bushy and Green. His words, unlike those of Richard, are no sooner said than done. The terse 'See them *dispatcht*' [III. i. 35] means 'Send them away, see they are executed and hurry up about it'. Such is the breath of kings—but such death-dealing is not the breath of a true king; and the Pilate image with which Bolingbroke washes his hands of the two minions' blood shifts our sympathy towards Richard even while our admiration mounts for Bolingbroke.

Meanwhile Richard has landed on the Welsh coast, unconscious of the fact that his glory is falling 'like a shooting star' [II. iv. 19] and confident in the belief that

Not all the water in the rough rude sea,
Can wash the balme off from an annointed King,
The breath of *worldly* men cannot depose,
The deputy elected by the Lord,
For euery man that Bullingbrooke hath *prest*,
To lifte shrewd steele against our golden *crowne*,
God for his Ric: hath in heauenly pay,
A glorious *Angell*; then if *Angels* fight
Weake men must fall, for heauen still gardes the right.

[III. ii. 54-62]

The secondary meaning of *worldly*—'mercenary'—provokes a shock of dissent with Richard's trust in his divine right. Worldly men like Bolingbroke, who offer rewards, and worldly men like Northumberland, who are hungry to be rewarded, can easily depose the Lord's anointed. The monetary senses of *crown* and *angel*, which are prompted by the sub-meaning of 'minted' for *pressed*, sustain this threat that might, bought by the promise to pay, is going to make short work of even divine right.

As the king's real power melts away in the disastrous news brought by Salisbury and Scroop, he clings hard to the illusory power of words: first to the power of his name:

Is not the Kings name twenty thousand names?
Arme arme, my name a puny subject strikes,
At thy great glorie;

[III. ii. 85-7]

then to the worn consolations of philosophy, the trite 'sentences' so fiercely rejected by Bolingbroke in his misfortunes:

> Say, is my kingdome lost? why twas my care,
> And what losse is it to be rid of care?
>
> [III. ii. 95-6]

and then to the power of curses against those who have deserted him:

> Would they make peace? terrible hel,
> Make war vpon their spotted soules for this.
>
> [III. ii. 133-34]

Even these words are as futile as the Queen's vain curse upon the gardener's plants, for Bushy and Green were not traitors. Words cannot blow out facts, and finally, in a great speech, Richard acknowledges this. When he sits to tell sad stories of the deaths of kings he is no longer camouflaging hard truths with verbal fictions. He is admitting the discovery that the word and its referent are two things, the self-discovery that he is not all he has been called; although like the self-discovery of most of Shakespeare's tragic heroes this comes too late for disaster to be averted. This is Richard's real abdication. It is also in a sense his coronation, for he is made a king of griefs by a vision of human insignificance which carries him far beyond the discovery that the king is a man as other men are. (pp. 82-5)

Wordplay and imagery here combine to give a poetic depth, rivalled only by the verse of *Macbeth*, to Richard's discovery that life has lost its meaning. The cliché implies, if we pause to ask what meaning here means, a philosophical experience of the first importance. Richard has discovered that words express only desires and not facts, that to call a man friend does not ensure the reality of friendship, that the name King, despite the sacramental nature of a coronation, does not imbue a man with kingly authority. If Richard were of the stature of Hamlet or Lear this tragic insight would remain clear even at the expense of his sanity, but his temperament cannot bear the sight of such bleak reality for long. He soon begins to draw round it the rags and shreds of appearance, to act the regal role once more—with this difference, that now he knows himself to be acting and that his words carry no effective weight. The king is playing a part throughout the scene at Flint Castle, whether the role is that of offended majesty calling down vengeance upon those who dare to question his sovereignty or the role of a man disillusioned with pomp and power, willing to be buried in the king's highway. The elaborate verbal fancies—'I talke but idlely, and you laugh at me' [III. iii. 171]—reveal that these speeches are not the real humility of Lear. They represent rather Richard's efforts to conceal his revelation from himself as well as others. His true feelings are exposed only for an instant in his cry to Aumerle:

> Oh that I were as *great*
> As is my griefe, or lesser than my name!
>
> [III. iii. 136-37]

A greater character could bear the reality he has glimpsed and now tries to obscure with words; a character less great in the material sense, in authority and reputation, would never have suffered from the illusion that Richard has lost.

The deposition scene, for all its brilliance, adds very little to the total effect of the play. If *Richard II* was ever acted in the mutilated text represented by the first and second Quartos—and the long and rather irrelevant 'gage' scene which precedes the deposition reads like the padding to an abbreviated text—

the loss, though serious, cannot have been structural, for the deposition only repeats the contrast, made in the scene at Flint Castle, between the reality of Richard's inward grief and its sham appearance in a profusion of words. . . . [The] ritual of abdication invented by Richard, his rhetorical outbursts to Northumberland, the pantomime of the mirror, are all the shadows of his sorrow. In these speeches, Richard behaves as if words had value and effective meaning; whereas the substance of his sorrow is the unseen grief—unseen because undemonstrable—that no meaning is left in words. Bolingbroke has acted upon this knowledge ever since his banishment; and Richard's quibbles before the mirror weigh his own disastrous self-deception against Bolingbroke's politic deception of others:

> Is this the Face, which *fac'd* so many follyes,
> That was at last *out-fac'd* by Bullingbroke?
>
> [IV. i. 285-86]

The long duel ends here in a curious sort of truce; both king and usurper now know there is no way of crossing the gulf between the world of words and the world of things. The knowledge has won the throne for Bolingbroke. It has also gained for Richard a kingly dignity he did not possess as king:

> You may my Glories and my State depose,
> But not my Griefes; still am I King of those.
>
> [IV. i. 192-93]

Richard retains this crown till the end of the play. The Elizabethan belief in the sanctity of kingship is not the only reason why the callow and capricious figure of the first acts is shown to die with the dignity of a martyr. Disaster has held up a mirror to Richard and in it he has glimpsed 'the truth of what we are'. He himself goes on playing with words, even alone at Pomfret; but at the motionless centre of this coloured wheel of language is the still and inescapable knowledge that it is all a play:

> Thus play I in one person many people,
> And none contented; sometimes am I King,
> Then treasons make me wish my selfe a beggar,
> And so I am: then crushing penurie
> Perswades me I was better when a king,
> Then am I kingd againe, and by and by,
> Thinke that I am vnkingd by Bullingbrooke,
> And strait am nothing. But what ere I be,
> Nor I, nor any man, that but man is,
> With nothing shall be pleasde, till he be easde,
> With being nothing.
>
> [V. v. 31-41]
> (pp. 86-8)

M. M. Mahood, "Richard the Second," in her Shakespeare's Wordplay, *Methuen & Co. Ltd., 1957, pp. 73-88.*

JAMES A. S. McPEEK (essay date 1958)

[*Richard II's precarious psychological state has long been evident to commentators on Shakespeare's history play. In the following excerpt, McPeek brings modern clinical techniques to an analysis of the king's personality. Borrowing the terminology of the psychoanalyst Ernest Jones, McPeek argues that Richard evidences a pattern of behavior known as the "God complex" and that he consistently substitutes fantasy for realistic action. The critic identifies and discusses the principal traits of this complex as it is manifested in the king, citing, among others, narcissism, self-dramatization, "fantasies of omnipotence," love of rhetoric and ceremony, and an inability to accept personal responsibility.*]

The appeal of *Richard II* to modern audiences may be attributed in part to Shakespeare's constant portrayal of Richard as a character dominated by a set of fantasies which manifest themselves regularly in his actions and speech and which compose a pattern of behavior that Dr. Ernest Jones has named the God-complex. Since these fantasies occur to some extent in every man (as Shakespeare appears to realize in that he has Richard identify himself with every man), everyone finds some affinity with Richard as the action develops, and this feeling helps to build the fascination that the antic king arouses. But whereas with normal people the sense of reality controls these fantasies and modifies their expression, with Richard a failing sense of reality weakens his inhibitions and his fantasies tend to become real to him. Just how far Richard's feeling for reality is weakened it is not easy to say, but the evidence suggests that it is feeble. People of this sort who are thus dominated by illusions but who still maintain enough contact with reality to give otherwise a general impression of being normal are today recognized by psychiatrists as having some characteristics of schizophrenia and are known as schizoids or ambulatory schizophrenics.

Was Shakespeare aware of this consistent pattern in Richard or did he simply assemble the pattern without realizing that he was describing a special state of mental disintegration? Shakespeare first of all devises conduct. Though he does not probe deeply into the causes for Richard's condition (as he does later for Coriolanus), he does have him exhibit his symptoms in full before our eyes. The portrait is without contradictions, and it is probable that Shakespeare (as always) knew what he was about. As Horace recommends for new and strange characters, the pattern of Richard's strange behavior is sustained from beginning to end. (pp. 195-96)

The most striking feature of Richard's character is, as is well known, a strong narcissism, which manifests itself in many ways and which is also the outstanding and controlling feature of the God-complex. In person resplendent, Richard is extremely self-conscious, oddly preoccupied with his appearance. Even in the most serious situations, instead of immediately considering possible plans of action, Richard is first intent upon his emotional responses. . . . (pp. 196-97)

This narcissism so deeply controls Richard that all his other attributes stem from it, as is characteristic of the complex. It manifests itself in self-love, marked by a love for personal adornment, self-pity, and related self-dramatization (defined by Jones as narcissistic-exhibitionistic tendency). Thus at Flint Castle, as Richard contemplates the imminence of his deposition, his thought, conditioned by his nature, turns first to his jewels and robes which weigh as importantly as his subjects; even his subjects are to be traded for a pair of carved saints, sensed here as objects of personal adornment rather than true symbols of felt religion, and he develops the idea fittingly in a long distributive figure:

> I'll give my jewels for a set of beads,
> My gorgeous palace for a hermitage,
> My gay apparel for an almsman's gown,
> My figur'd goblets for a dish of wood,
> My sceptre for a palmer's walking staff,
> My subjects for a pair of carved saints,
> And my large kingdom for a little grave,
> A little little grave, an obscure grave. . . .
> [III. iii. 147-54]

It may be argued that in using these symbols, Richard is not just playing the poet, but shows a tendency to regress to the primitive or archaic thinking symptomatic of his condition: with him the symbol is a substitute for the reality behind it— that is, the symbol has become the reality. For him kingship has come to mean no more than its trappings.

At the same moment his ever-present self-pity reaches a masochistic pitch in which he relishes the grief that would make a normal man speechless. He will yield his kingdom "for a little grave, A little little grave, an obscure grave''; or they can bury him in the highway, where his subjects, now trampling on his heart, can trample on his head. . . . He is brought back to reality by the pained embarrassment of his nobles:

> Would not this ill do well? Well, well, I see
> I talk but idly and you laugh at me.
> [III. iii. 170-71]

Richard's exhibitionistic tendency manifests itself in all his appearances: he delights in attention and self-display. At the trial by combat when the attention is focused on the contesting nobles, he dramatically draws it to himself by throwing down his warder. At Flint Castle his manner suggests that he expects to overawe Bolingbroke and the rebel lords by his mere appearance [III. iii. 61-76]. That Bolingbroke and York play up the splendor of Richard's appearance emphasizes his love for display. In the deposition scene, though subdued in fact, he dominates the action. The surrender of his crown is a glittering opportunity for his self-dramatization. With his tears, his hands, his tongue, his breath he relinquishes sovereignty. And though this behavior is seemingly renounced with the breaking of the mirror, the gesture itself indicates his disturbed condition, and Richard's vanity, his love for display, is undiminished by grief, as is apparent from his later curiosity about how roan Barbary went under Bollingbroke.

Yet another aspect of Richard's extreme narcissism is his tendency toward fantasies of omnipotence as seen in his special interpretation of his role as vicegerent of God on earth. The merest hint for this development of his character is provided by Holinshed:

> Sir John Bushy in all his talks when hee proponed any matter unto the King, did not attribute to him titles of honour, due and accustomed, but invented unused terms, and such strange names as were rather agreable to the divine majestic of God, than to any earthly potentate. The Prince, being desirous inough of all honour, and more ambitious than was requisite, seemed to like well of his speech, and gave good eare to his talke.

In *Richard II* this hint is amplified enormously through two images, both symptomatic of the God-complex, those of the sun-king and the Son of God or Christ. In presenting Richard as a sun-king, Shakespeare is obviously drawing on familiar lore, and in particular on the knowledge that Richard's emblem was the sun emerging from clouds; further, he was to use the same image effectively for Hal. But whereas with Hal the image is felt as simple metaphor, with Richard it becomes a near-obsession. In the scene presenting his return from Ireland he identifies in splendor with the sun. Now that he has returned from the Antipodes, treason and conspiracy will be dissolved by his mere appearance:

> So when this thief, this traitor, Bolingbroke,
> Who all this while hath revell'd in the night,
> Whilst we were wand'ring with the Antipodes,

Shall see us rising in our throne, the East,
His treasons will sit blushing in his face,
Not able to endure the sight of day,
But self-affrighted tremble at his sin.

[III. ii. 47-53]

Faced with unpleasant reality, Richard has no plan of action. His ego instead regresses to primitive or archaic thinking, the method of magic as opposed to a normal response which would try to meet this situation and control it with real measures. Here and elsewhere Richard substitutes a more agreeable world of fantasy for distasteful reality. Properly played, the scene makes one aware of the king's resort to fantasy as a release. The other actors stand ill at ease, and little gestures indicate their barely polite tolerance of Richard's fancies. At one moment he exults in the thought that God's angels are his invisible defense against Bolingbroke [III. ii. 58-61], in the next his spirits plummet at the news of the dispersed Welsh army [III. ii. 64-74]. (pp. 197-200)

This cycle of alternate confidence in his omnipotence ("An easy task it is to win our own" [III. ii. 191]) and instant, unreasoning despair as reality breaks the illusion is repeated in a vivid pattern throughout the scene. So far is Richard subject to the illusion of his power as God's representative that he apparently believes that forces of nature (storms and pestilence) will destroy those who offend him [III. iii. 82-9]. In the grasp of this illusion he fancies that he does the earth favor by touching it with his royal hands [III. ii. 6-11]. Weeping, smiling, like a mother (and matriarchal features are not uncommon in delusions of this sort) he greets *his* earth, and he even conjures small creatures of his earth, spiders, toads, nettles, and snakes to oppose and thwart Bolingbroke [III. ii. 14-26]. (p. 200)

But Richard is not only a sun-king whose presence he hopes will dazzle and disperse his enemies. As the representative of Christ on earth, he shows a tendency to identify with Christ in his trials and sorrows, and Shakespeare develops the theme at greater length than appears to be commonly realized, and with pointed irony. The image is not necessarily meant to arouse sympathy for Richard, but rather to record the historic view of the Richard faction and at the same time to develop further Richard's complex. Patently the ironic contrast between Richard's true nature and that of Christ, so obvious to us, would be appreciated by the Elizabethan audience. We are prepared for the identification through certain aspects of Richard's view of himself as a sun-king. At his coming, as when Christ comes to judge the sinners, the guilty will "stand bare and naked, trembling at themselves" [III. ii. 41-6]. It is almost to be expected that in the next breath he would assume that God's deputy has supernatural protection: to every soldier that Bolingbroke has conscripted, a glorious angel will be opposed [III. ii. 56-61] in Richard's defense. Some in the audience would perhaps remember that Christ rejected the temptation of claiming supernatural protection: Richard in claiming such aid inverts, as his conduct does throughout the play, the Christ symbol. In the same scene, when Richard mistakes Scroop's ironic report that Bushy, Green and Wiltshire have made peace with Bolingbroke, he condemns them as Judases:

Three Judases, each one thrice worse than Judas!
Would they make peace? Terrible hell make war
Upon their spotted souls for this offense!

[III. ii. 132-34]

The inversion of Christ's attitude is recognized by Scroop, who responds:

Sweet love, I see, changing his property
Turns to the sourest and most deadly hate.
Again uncurse their souls. Their peace is made
With heads and not with hands.

[III. ii. 135-38]

In the deposition scene his identification with Christ and its ironic implications become yet more apparent. We are prepared for Richard's assumption of the pose of the martyred Christ by the Bishop of Carlisle's ardent but specious defense of Richard in which he predicts that if the deposition occurs, England will be called the field of Golgotha [IV. i. 136-44]. Richard does not hear and does not need such prompting. Scanning the assembled parliament and the courtiers of Bolingbroke, he finds that while Christ had but one Judas, all are Judases to him:

Yet I well remember
The favors of these men. Were they not mine?
Did they not sometime cry "All hail"! to me?
So Judas did to Christ; but he in twelve,
Found truth in all but one; I in twelve thousand, none.

[IV. i. 167-71]

They are not only Judases, but those who are passively accepting his deposition are Pilates, washing their hands and delivering him to crucifixion:

Nay, all of you that stand and look upon
Whilst that my wretchedness doth bait myself,
Though some of you, with Pilate, wash your hands,
Showing an outward pity, yet you Pilates
Have here delivered me to my sour cross,
And water cannot wash away your sin.

[IV. i. 237-42]

As Richard's sweet love turns to sourest hate, as is characteristic of victims of the complex when they are offended, so the redeeming cross becomes a sour cross for him.

At least by strong suggestion, if not by direct allusion, Shakespeare sustains the image with its negative implications in the rest of the action. In Act V, after Richard has been sent to Pomfret, York recounts for his duchess the story of Richard's coming to London (his Jerusalem):

. . . dust was thrown upon his sacred head;
Which with such gentle sorrow he shook off,
His face still combating with tears and smiles
(The badges of his grief and patience),
That had not God for some strange purpose steel'd
The hearts of men, they must perforce have melted,
And barbarism itself have pitied him.
But heaven hath a hand in these events,
To whose high will we bound our calm contents.

[V. ii. 30-8]

Richard's patience here, together with his strange inability to resort to action against his enemies, might appear to be modelled on the exemplary patience of Jesus. The king of griefs is perhaps meant to imitate the Man of Sorrows in his patient endurance of affliction. But Richard does not maintain this pose. In the closing scene he renounces his patience for despairing violence ("Patience is stale, and I am weary of it" [V. v. 103], beats the keeper, and presently kills two servants (Holinshed has four tall men), consigning their souls to Hell, all in marked contrast to the man who died between two thieves with forgiveness for his tormentors. That Piers of Exton interprets Richard's desperation as valiancy only heightens the irony, as likewise does Richard's own certainty of his salvation ("Mount, mount, my soul! thy seat is up on high" [V. v. 111]). (pp. 201-03)

Another aspect of the complex (as observed by Dr. Jones) is Richard's interest in psychology, his love for interpreting situations and examining his own thought-processes and those of others. People of this sort, in whom the unconscious has come to dominate the ego may be acutely perceptive in some directions of the unconscious urges of others. Hence Richard's intuitive sensing of the motives of Bolingbroke is characteristic, a perception that is counterbalanced by his complete insensibility to the serious obligations of kingship and a consequent inability to devise any plan of action to oppose the enemy. He is aware of the menace of Bolingbroke from the start:

> How high a pitch his resolution soars!
>
> [I. i. 109]

> A brace of draymen bid God speed him well
> And had the tribute of his supple knee,
> With 'thanks, my countrymen, my loving friends';
> As were our England in reversion his,
> And he our subjects' next degree in hope.
>
> [I. iv. 32-6]

Instead of being intent, as his counselors belatedly are, on how to meet this threat, he helplessly divines Bolingbroke's nebulous purpose and perhaps even shapes that purpose by expressing his willingness to surrender his crown before Bolingbroke, so far as we can see, has consciously entertained the idea of taking it.

His love for examining his thought processes leads him to interpret in detail each situation, as is illustrated by his speeches in the deposition scene and, better still, by the extensive exposition of his thoughts in prison. Associated with this interest in observation of self and situation is Richard's love for language, shown in his habit of interpreting every situation in terms of rhetorical display (Shakespeare probably did not mean us to admire Richard's rhetorical extravagance any more than his courtiers do). This interest in language for its own sake is a noteworthy trait of the complex.

With Richard's love for rhetoric may be associated his extreme tendency toward ritual, his habit of reducing every situation to ceremony. This use of ceremony, when controlled by reason, is normal, a stabilizing social influence, and most of the characters in the play resort to its devices at times, as Tillyard indicates [see excerpt above, 1944]. But the tendency becomes abnormal when carried to excess, as it is with Richard, who converts every situation to ceremony. With him his devotion to ritual appears to mark a continuing regression to conceptual thinking, an attempt to reconstitute the world of the past as an escape from an oppressive reality. This tendency in Richard is well illustrated in the ceremony of his farewell to his wife, in which the form of love is projected as a substitute for reality (careful analysis of the scene, together with other evidence in the play, suggests that Richard loves only himself).

It is but natural that anyone with these propensities should never seriously question the rightness of his conduct and that he should justify his proceedings simply by virtue of his inherent right. Richard's behavior neatly fits the pattern here. He does not claim infallibility or righteousness, but why should

he? As God's deputy, he is a "rightful" king. Criticism arouses anger in him, as when he resents Gaunt's sharp criticism:

> A lunatic lean-witted fool,
> Presuming on an ague's privilege,
> Dar'st with thy frozen admonition
> Make pale our cheek, chasing the royal blood
> With fury from his native residence.
>
> [II. i. 115-19]

But he does not attempt to meet or refute Gaunt's charges, nor will he alter his ways. The sense of Gaunt's serious accusations makes no impression, save for his resentment: those who have age and sullens like Gaunt should die [II. i. 139-40].

When York in turn reproaches Richard with his faults (some of them crimes), Richard, who has ignored the charges or only idly attended them as matters of no consequence, exclaims, "Why, uncle, what's the matter?" [II. i. 186]. Moved by Richard's imperviousness, York makes the charge more specific: if Richard seizes Bolingbroke's estates, he violates the laws of succession by which he himself is king. But Richard is above human law; his will is sufficient reason for his action: "Think what you will, we seize into our hands His goods, his money, and his lands" [II. i. 209-10]. York punctuates his open disapproval by leaving, and in the next moment, after sending Bushy to expedite the plundering of Bolingbroke's estates, this strange king appoints York lord governor of England for the period of his absence in Ireland ("For he is just and always lov'd us well" [II. i. 221]). Later, in a parallel pattern of behavior, when he reflects on the dispersal of his forces and the death of his favorites, he does not connect his plight with his misdemeanors, but muses instead on the fortunes of kings: kings, he asserts, die in prison or from violence, and none peacefully. His fortunes are the universal lot [III. ii. 155-60]. It does not occur to him to consider that his lot might be the result of his conduct.

It is manifest that Richard, true to the conditions of his complex, is incapable of really conceiving his guilt or suffering remorse for his sins. Once or twice he seems to recognize his misconduct, but the recognition is superficial and quickly put aside for the vanities that obsess his mind. Thus for a moment he senses reality in the deposition scene as he scans his features (unworn by the cares that would line the face of a good ruler) in the mirror: his glory is a brittle glory; the face in whose glory he believed is a shadow, not a reality. Even his external shows of grief are (he realizes for a moment, with Bolingbroke's help) but shadows of the true grief. . . . Though Richard's disease has not progressed to the point that he has lost all contact with reality, his behavior, as recorded in this great key passage, is suggestive of the schizophrenic who attempts to regain contact with the objective world, but who succeeds only in recapturing the shadows of that world, namely the word representations. Richard has a moment of normal insight here as he perceives that he has been deluding himself with shadows. But in the next moment, as earlier with Northumberland [IV. i. 229-36], he transfers the blame:

> O, good! Convey! conveyors are you all,
> That rise thus nimbly by a true king's fall
>
> [IV. i. 317-18]

And in the prison scene, a discord in the music reminds him that he has wasted time and that time wastes him [V. v. 42-9]; but his reflections turn from this seeming realization of personal guilt to his habitual solace in rhetorical self-pity. His time, he says, "Runs posting on in Bolingbroke's proud joy" [V. v.

59]. He has already analyzed the situation to suit his condition: he suffers from discontent, yes; every man is discontented until he becomes nothing (and one must recall Macbeth's soured conclusion that life is vanity). No matter what sort of life I might have led, he rationalizes, I should have still been discontent. His consideration of the lives he might have led is a characteristic evasion of the facts about the life he has led. (pp. 203-07)

And in prison he is not concerned with his kingdom sick with civil disorder (as Henry IV is at the end of his reign), but with the vanity, as we have seen, that roan Barbary went so proudly under Bolingbroke. He can implore the forgiveness of the absent Barbary for his railing at him, but he has none for Henry of Lancaster.

Richard's fantasy in prison is in itself a special symptom of his disorder. It takes the shape of a rebirth fantasy, which is similar in nature to those experienced by schizophrenics, a fantasy which is based on the patient's unconscious desire to reconstruct his disordered universe. Richard's still-breeding thoughts seek refuge in theology, but find contradictions of his own making [V. v. 11-17]; yet other thoughts bearing on possible escape from imprisonment and on the vicissitudes in the lives of kings and beggars, all in themselves barely suppressed queries as to what has gone wrong in his management of his life, end in futility:

> But whate'er I be,
> Nor I, nor any man that but man is,
> With nothing shall be pleased till he be eased
> By being nothing.
>
> [V. v. 38-41]

In this negative way Richard wins reassurance: his search for a solution to his dilemma leads him to the conclusion that all men are discontent till they sink back into nothingness—a conclusion which, since it excuses himself, is obviously not one leading to a better mental health.

Seen from this perspective, all the behavior and the utterances of Richard fall into one large unified pattern, forming one of Shakespeare's earliest studies of diseased mentality, acutely observed and unerringly integrated. Dominated by his complex, Richard continually substitutes his fancies for action. Lost in the dream of his glory, remote from reality, he is equally incapable of either well-considered civil policy or military strategy, and natural prey for flatterers like Bushy and Green. That some people of the time, including Elizabeth herself, should be disturbed by so clinical a portrait and suspect its topical reference is not surprising. Whatever Shakespeare intended, he created in Richard II a haunting character whose case is hopeless from the start. (pp. 207-08)

> *James A. S. McPeek, "Richard and His Shadow World," in* American Imago, *Vol. 15, No. 2, Summer, 1958, pp. 195-212.*

MICHAEL QUINN (essay date 1959)

[*In the following excerpt, Quinn examines the concepts of divine right kingship, family honor, and patience "to demonstrate Richard's increasing isolation from the social foundations on which true personality must apparently be built." According to the critic, Richard "cuts himself off from the community" and, in fact, undermines his own identity as king in three ways. First, he mistakenly views divine right as "a personal privilege, a right without corresponding duties, a special preference of God for one man. . . ." Second, he transgresses against family honor by both*

confiscating Bolingbroke's legitimate inheritance and failing to sustain the honor of his own father, The Black Prince. Third, he refuses to act, to assert his kingly authority, instead demonstrating an excessive patience and a fascination with his own grief. Quinn adds, however, that Shakespeare allows Richard a truly tragic death in Pomfret prison, stating that, through his final act, the king "dies as Somebody, a lion overpowered, . . . and not as one who has become nothing."]

Is Shakespeare's *Richard II* a tragedy or a history play? Nineteenth-century critics generally regarded it as a tragedy, and a not very satisfactory one; the tendency in the twentieth century has been to make rather more of the political aspects of the play and especially to see it as the first part of a Lancastrian tetralogy. The question involves more than an academic wrangle about the definition of *genres,* for it sums up a certain ambiguity in our reaction to the play. If we regard the play as primarily a history play and consequently as concerned more with public than with private virtues, then King Richard makes a poor showing and probably deserves the retribution that comes to him. On the other hand, to conceive Richard as the tragic hero would seem to drive us towards the position of W. B. Yeats who saw Richard as one of Shakespeare's "children of light," facing a "rough world" with only an admirable but inadequate "contemplative virtue" [see excerpt above, 1901]. It may well be that our need for a "double plane of vision" when we look at Richard derives from a modern separation of politics and ethics that would have been largely incomprehensible to an Elizabethan, and particularly unreal in a discussion of kingship. In this essay I want to explore some features of the intricate relationship between public and private values as they are revealed in this play; the exploration will, I hope, demonstrate that the historical and tragic aspects of *Richard II* are strictly inseparable and may possibly throw some light on the kind of reaction we should have to Shakespeare's version of the story of the life and death of Richard Plantagenet.

The method that I shall use is to abstract three ideas—divine right, honor, and patience—and to examine the political and ethical judgments that they seem to require us to make on the main characters in the play. I do not wish to suggest that these ideas are the only important ideas or even that they are the most important; least of all, that such abstractions can, in any sense, sum up the whole meaning of Shakespeare's *Richard II.* I use each simply as a convenient lens to focus in a single issue the complex interaction of tragedy and history, politics and ethics. None of the ideas considered calls forth from the spectator or reader an absolute moral judgment. There are other ideas in the play, the idea of tyranny or of rebellion, for instance, which define clearly enough contrasting extremes of judgment; but these ideas remain abstract—in no sense do the leading characters embody them like virtues and vices in a morality play. Richard and Bolingbroke take up their stations, not at the opposite ends of the lists, but at varying points in the no god's land between. One finds, indeed, that these characters are required to appear on more than one battlefield simultaneously, that the audience is required to assess them according to several different standards, and that the consequent judgments do not entirely agree; the final verdict must be ambiguous and in the mist of moral indecision the characters spring to life. Yet one may expect even life to be intelligible, and it is in the explanation of the character of King Richard himself that I find these three ideas most helpful: divine right focuses the complex and often ambiguous thoughts of an Elizabethan about the mystery of kingship; honor highlights, without exactly clarifying, some of the problems of the individual's relations with society; and patience tells us something about the debt that a man owes to himself. Divine right is primarily a political concept, patience mainly a matter of ethics, but each has implications extending to the opposite pole and their interaction is mainly in the field of honor.

In the first two acts of *Richard II* Shakespeare lays down the general political principles within which his more subtle enquiries are to be conducted. He states, in fairly explicit terms, the familiar tension of Elizabethan political thought: that between tyranny and rebellion. King Richard heeds flattery rather than wise counsel, bleeds the commonwealth for his private pleasures, and is in some measure guilty of the murder of his uncle Gloucester. He is condemned as a tyrant by a very unhistorical Gaunt and by York and others (I. ii; II. i). But Gaunt and York make it equally plain that tyranny can never justify rebellion (I. ii; II. iii). By the end of the second act the dilemma is established: Richard is true king and false tyrant; Bolingbroke has right on his side but his means are wrong. Judgment balances between them and, as if to insist that the balance be maintained, Shakespeare realizes the dilemma on the stage in the person of old York: bound to the one by "oath and duty," to the other by "conscience and kindred," he does not know how "to order these affairs" but recognizes that, no matter how impossible the moral situation may seem to be, "somewhat we must do" [II. ii. 108-15].

The dramatic effectiveness of this balance of judgment between Richard and Bolingbroke is put to the test when they first face each other on the stage as opponents. The contrast between the two characters partly depends, however, on their respective relations to the concept of divine right. To say that Richard is true king and false tyrant would not, for an orthodox Elizabethan, stand as a simple statement of fact; it involves a difficult paradox, for to be truly a king meant to be the opposite of a tyrant. Kingship was conceived as a sacrament, but it differed from priesthood in that the efficacy of the political sacrament could not be dissociated from the minister in the same way as could the sacrament of the Eucharist: a bad priest may consecrate validly but by definition a bad king rules badly. Nevertheless, Tudor propagandists vehemently insisted that, though the king be corrupt, kingship remained of divine ordination and institution, and rebellion against the crown was sacrilege. Shakespeare resolved the seeming *impasse*, not by modifying the principle, but simply by observing history, seeing what happened in practice in a particular instance; and this observation seems to have focused mainly on the question of the relationship between the idea of kingship and the person of the king.

Before the dramatic meeting of Richard and Bolingbroke, Shakespeare devotes to this question a static "mirror-scene" (III. ii) that does little to advance the action but much to clarify the issues. Richard is presented struggling not with an antagonist but with an idea; the progress of the struggle tells us much about the king's character and its outcome determines a good deal of the following action. Richard has returned from Ireland to face Bolingbroke, who is sweeping all before him; like York he must face a demand for action. The king's advisers, eminently practical men, are anxious that he should not refuse "The proffered means of succour and redress"; but they never make clear in what way they consider Richard to be "too remiss" [III. ii. 32, 33]. The practical issue—is it possible for Richard to defeat or in any way outwit Bolingbroke?—is apparently not faced at all. Richard rests confident in his divine right and the Bishop of Carlisle agrees that God "Hath power to keep you king in spite of all" [III. ii. 28]. But if God is to

act against these rebels, how will He do it, by miraculous intervention or through the ordinary processes of cause and effect? Shakespeare's earlier histories show that he conceived the world as "Made to run even upon even ground" [*King John,* II. i. 576]. . . . In time God will make evil work to His own ends, make one evil cancel out another, and so leave good triumphant; it is "Time's glory" to untie the knots, "To unmask falsehood, and bring truth to light" [*Lucrece,* II. 939-40], and this is as true of sins against divine right as of other sins.

But this is not how Richard conceives his position as a divinely ordained king. Despite the scepticism of his companions, who mock at his "senseless conjuration," Richard is confident that divine right carries with it the assurance of immediate and direct assistance from heaven:

> This earth shall have a feeling, and these stones
> Prove armed soldiers, ere her native King
> Shall falter under foul rebellion's arms.
>
> [III. ii. 24-6]

Bolingbroke has been successful only because the King was absent; "His treasons will sit blushing in his face" and he will be unable "to endure the sight of day" now that the Sun-King has returned from "the Antipodes." For every rebel "God for his Richard hath in heavenly pay A glorious angel"; victory is certain "for heaven still guards the right" [III. ii. 51, 49, 60-1, 62]. Richard, ready enough at a later stage to compare himself to Christ, has forgotten that Christ could have asked His Father for ten legions of angels but instead submitted Himself to the natural process of cause and effect and consequently suffered. If this could happen to the Son of God, it can also happen to "God's deputy" [III. ii. 57]. Richard's confidence, founded on the expectation of a miracle or other false premises—"the King's name" is worth "twenty thousand names," "An easy task it is to win our own,"—quickly collapses and, after his third fall, he settles finally into the "sweet way" that leads to "despair" [III. ii. 85, 191, 205]. These rapid oscillations between hope and despair serve as an effective way of presenting dramatically the instability of Richard's character, but the movement of the scene depends at least as much on intellectual distinctions as on aesthetic feelings about the nature of character. Here is a king who believes divine right to be a personal privilege, a right without corresponding duties, a special preference of God for one man. . . . Because he fails to realize [that he is bound by circumstances], Richard proves unstable in a crisis and lacks the motive power necessary to adapt himself to the new situation. Thus circumscribed, opportunism is the politician's most useful virtue and, in direct contrast to Richard, the "vile politician" Bolingbroke has it in abundance: he is always aware of the limitations imposed by circumstances and so can shape his behavior to the occasion, can seize fortune by the forelock, and so is "Fortune's minion."

An answer to the question—what could Richard have done to defeat or outwit Bolingbroke?—now begins to emerge. He might have faced Bolingbroke as Claudius faces Laertes in *Hamlet,* or as he himself faces the rebellious mob in the play of *Iacke Straw.* This may be speculation, but it helps explanation: Richard might have remained a king if he had behaved like a king. Unlike York, he did not understand that, no matter how insoluble the dilemma, "somewhat we must do" [II. ii. 116]. From this point in the story onwards, divine right has much to do with Henry Bolingbroke, but little with Richard Plantagenet; its relevance to Richard's personal tragedy diminishes as the breach between Richard as man and as king widens, for the concept belongs primarily to the realm of po-

Act IV. Scene i. Richard II and Bolingbroke. By H. C. Selous. The Department of Rare Books and Special Collections, The University of Michigan Library.

litical judgments and large-scale historical movements. Richard's inadequacies cut him off increasingly from this world of political history and isolate him in a world where the only relevant judgments are ethical. Yet this political idea has been used to point an ethical judgment and, as we shall see, the later ethical judgments never lose contact with the realities of political society.

Richard's deficiencies may be further illuminated by a consideration of the idea of honor. . . . [We] may perhaps define honor, in the vaguest terms, as that principle of integrity that should govern a person's relations with society, his family, and himself. Each of these three aspects is considered by Shakespeare in a series of studies that contrast pointedly with the career of Richard, and the whole discussion is extended in scope and complexity in the *Henry IV* plays. It is, as we shall see, intimately related to the problems posed by the conflict of tyranny and rebellion.

The theme is introduced in the first scene. In the opening clash between Bolingbroke and Mowbray, the behavior of both prosecution and defence hardly lives up to their protestations of humble submission to the crown; both strictly limit their obedience according to their conception of honor. Mowbray's sense of "duty" (the individual's obligation to the community or state, here a personal obligation to King Richard) makes him willing to give up his life for Richard, but he will not surrender

his "fair name" to "dark dishonour's use," for his name will survive death, will live "upon (his) grave":

> The purest treasure mortal times afford
> Is spotless reputation; that away,
> Men are but gilded loam or painted clay.
> A jewel in a ten-times barr'd-up chest
> Is a bold spirit in a loyal breast.
> Mine honour is my life; both grow in one;
> Take honour from me, and my life is done.
> [I. i. 168-69, 177-83]

Mowbray, like Hotspur [in *Henry IV*] and Cassio [in *Othello*], holds that "name" or "reputation" is a man's mark of identity, that which makes him himself, distinguishes him as a unique and hence valuable individual. Honor, as Mowbray understands it, must override all claims, even those of duty.

The discussion between Gaunt and the Duchess of Gloucester in the second scene of the play extends and complicates the tension between duty and honor by drawing attention to another important obligation. Introduced here by the Duchess, but running through the whole play, is a conception of the family as a sort of mystical communion: the phrase is justified, I think, by the strongly theological overtones of Shakespeare's own language on the subject. The seven sons of Edward III

> Were as seven vials of his sacred blood,
> Or seven fair branches springing from one root.
> [I. ii. 12-13]

Gaunt's blood is Gloucester's blood and, coming from the same womb, he is "slain in him." In refusing to act against Gloucester's murderers, Gaunt is consenting "In some large measure to (his) father's death," for Gloucester "was the model of (his) father's life" [I. i. 25, 26-8]. (pp. 169-75)

The difficult decision involved in the choice between personal and family honor and political allegiance is realized on the stage in the persons of Gaunt and York. Gaunt recognizes the force of the Duchess of Gloucester's arguments:

> Alas, the part I had in Woodstock's blood
> Doth more solicit me than your exclaims
> To stir against the butchers of his life!
> [I. ii. 1-3]

Nor does he seem to deny the right of private vengeance generally; but he does insist that a subject's obligations to his king limit and, when necessary, override all other claims. The decision is not an easy one for Gaunt to make, for it obliges him to vote for the banishment of his own son. . . . The same dilemma recurs, in the different context of the reign of Henry IV, in the Aumerle scenes in the fifth act, scenes which to some critics and most producers have seemed a distraction from the main themes of the play. In this brief 'interlude,' varying in tone from "a serious thing" to the near-farce of "The Beggar and the King" [V. iii. 79-80], the public and private aspects of honor are again brought into direct conflict. The Duchess of York's plea for her son is based on a conception of honor similar to that held by the Duchess of Gloucester and Bolingbroke; she pleads on the grounds, first, of maternal affection, and, secondly, of family continuity: Aumerle is York's "own," "as like (him) as a man may be" [V. ii. 89, 108]. And Bolingbroke, with politic consistency and no doubt with his own "unthrifty son" and his "sparks of better hope" [V. iii. 1, 21] in mind, sees it in the same way: he is prepared to forgive the "treacherous son" because of the "loyal father" [V. iii. 60]. York, however, cannot dissociate personal and family honor from the duty of loyalty to the reigning sovereign. . . . [He] shares Mowbray's conviction that man truly 'lives' only in his honor but denies his distinction between honor and duty; and with Gaunt he shares the misery of living in two worlds, of filial affection and political obligation, that pull in opposite directions, for, when he demands the execution of his son, it is the judge that speaks, not the father:

> His eyes do drop no tears, his prayers are in jest;
> His words come from his mouth, ours from our breast.
> He prays but faintly and would be denied. . . .
>
> [V. iii. 101-03]

In these two instances Shakespeare has focused the conflict of the two allegiances in the sharpest way possible: a father, whose "honor" or "name" depends on his son, is obliged to condemn that son in the interest of duty and yet, paradoxically, only by doing so may he truly preserve his "honor." The audience is not, I think, expected to feel complete sympathy with either Gaunt or York in their determination to perform their duty; it may well feel as uncertain as to how it should judge between York and Aumerle in the last act as it did in the earlier conflicts between Bolingbroke and Mowbray and between Richard and Bolingbroke.

But no such uncertainty need affect the audience's judgment on Richard. In him alone duty and honor are one; he has one loyalty only, to himself as king, and in this he fails. His failure may be focused through the concept of family honor, against which he offends in two striking instances. In the first place he is in some major sense guilty of the murder of his uncle of Gloucester and so has shed one of the vials of Edward's "sacred blood" [I. ii. 12]. But he goes further and strikes at the whole legal basis of family inheritance when he confiscates Bolingbroke's lands and refuses him the name of Lancaster. As York points out to him, "just" Gaunt deserved and had a "true" and "well-deserving son" [II. i. 192, 193] to carry on his name, and to deny that son's right to sustain his father's name is to undermine the whole social order and Richard's own position as well:

> Take Hereford's rights away, and take from Time
> His charters and his customary rights;
> Let not to-morrow then ensue to-day;
> Be not thyself—for how art thou a king
> But by fair sequence and succession?
>
> [II. i. 195-99]

And York precedes this protest with a telling contrast between Richard and his father, the Black Prince, whose "hands were guilty of no kindred blood" [II. i. 182], who won what he spent and who frowned, not on his friends, but on the French. Richard is the undeserving son who fails to sustain his father's "name"; moreover, he fails to recognize that his identity, that which makes him himself, a king, depends on this handing-on in time of his father's honor.

Shakespeare presses his analysis of the conflict between duty and honor further into the realm of ethics and personal motives. An offence to a man's honor may provoke him to some positive reaction or it may be borne passively: the two possible attitudes are continually opposed to each other throughout *Richard II*. The Duchess of Gloucester tells Gaunt that his determination to "let heaven revenge" is not "patience" but "despair":

> That which in mean men we entitle patience
> Is pale cold cowardice in noble breasts.
>
> [I. ii. 33-4]

In the opening scene Mowbray insists that, though his words may seem "cold," he cannot "of such tame patience boast" [I. i. 47, 52] that it will allow him to stomach dishonor; Bolingbroke accuses his adversary of "pale" cowardice and is determined that his honor shall not be impeached by "pale beggar-fear" [I. i. 189]. York finds that Richard's sequestration of Bolingbroke's estates pricks his "tender patience" to thoughts "Which honor and allegiance cannot think" [II. i. 207-08]. The implications seem clear: the degree to which one should be patient is determined by one's place in the social hierarchy, which defines the quality of one's honor: the greater one's honor, the less the claim of patience.

This idea of patience seems to be so important in the structure of the play that, although essentially an undramatic quality, it must have a dramatic correlative, and this is supplied by the passion of grief; and the natural expression of grief is in speech:

> the tongue's office should be prodigal
> To breathe the abundant dolour of the heart.
>
> [I. iii. 256-57]

The expression of grief is the subject of several sketches, the first occurring in the second scene when the Duchess of Gloucester, disappointed of her hopes of revenge, reverts to grief, which she images as a deserted, derelict house [I. ii. 58 ff.]. This is followed by the grief of Gaunt and Bolingbroke at parting, Aumerle's mock-grief at bidding farewell to Bolingbroke, the grief that makes Gaunt gaunt, the two scenes portraying the Queen's grief, and, finally and most important, Richard's grief at the loss of his crown. . . . Being a thing of the mind, grief breeds only in the mind; as Bushy explains to the Queen,

> Each substance of a grief hath twenty shadows,
> Which shows like grief itself, but is not so;
> For sorrow's eye, glazed with blinding tears,
> Divides one thing entire to many objects,
> Like perspectives which, rightly gaz'd upon,
> Show nothing but confusion—ey'd awry,
> Distinguish form.
>
> [II. ii. 14-20]

To escape this mental world of shadows, grief must be concerted into a motive for action.

Richard, who as king should be more honorable and less patient than his subjects, is described by Gaunt as "too careless patient" [II. i. 97]. And his excessive patience springs from the same root as his misconception of the nature of divine right. When, in Act III scene ii, Richard first begins to lose faith in the likelihood of immediate divine assistance and to recognize the possibility of a distinction between himself as king and as man, he turns to grief in the form of a meditation *de contemptu mundi* [of contempt of the world], a meditation described as "that sweet way . . . to despair" [III. ii. 205], the epithet suggesting an indulgence that is almost sensual. Richard indulges again in sweet despair when, having descended "like glist'ring Phaethon" from the ramparts of Flint Castle, he surrenders, not his crown (that is the matter of the formal abdication scene that follows), but his royal nature: he debases himself in looking "so poorly" and speaking "so fair" and in descending to the "Base court, where kings grow base" [III. iii. 178, 128, 180]. Each abdication, of the power to act and of his royal nature, is thus associated with a denial of the values of this life and a resort to a faith in another world that rights the wrongs of this. The implication of Richard's attitude would seem to be that, if God will not act positively for Richard in this world, then God lives only in heaven; the absolute sovereignty of "antic" Death, that keeps his court "within the hollow crown" of a mortal king, reduces to meaninglessness all "solemn reverence" and "respect," all "Tradition, form, and ceremonious duty" [III. ii. 160, 172, 173]. Such a faith destroys the foundations of social order as effectively as Richard's earlier assault upon the legal basis of hereditary honor.

From Skelton's *Magnyfycence* to Marlowe's *Edward II*, dramatists, and others, used the *contemptus mundi* as an excuse or evasion for the fallen man, claiming from their audience or readers a sympathy that forgot the victim's crimes. Shakespeare, however, goes out of his way to stress that this fall of Richard is not the work of an irrational and fickle goddess, though it may seem so to the victim himself. This "second fall of cursed man" [III. iv. 76] occurs because the king has not 'trim'd and dress'd his land" [III. iv. 56] as a good gardener should, so that in the balance against "great Bolingbroke" he has "nothing but himself, And some few vanities that make him light" [III. iv. 86-7]: the image of the balance brings out specifically, not the capriciousness of fortune, but the element of moral responsibility. . . . Having fallen short of the requirements of his office, Richard is indeed no more than a pilgrim who may well despise the world, but had he maintained that identification of himself as King his status would have warranted a more positive approach to life. That the judgment on his easy adoption of contempt of the world should be condemnatory is evident from two pointed comments. When Richard first indulges this luxury, the Bishop of Carlisle, echoing Queen Margaret in *3 Henry IV* [V. iv. 1] warns him of the dangers:

> My lord, wise men ne'er sit and wail their woes,
> But presently prevent the ways to wail.
> To fear the foe, since fear oppresseth strength,
> Gives, in your weakness, strength unto your foe,
> And so your follies fight against yourself.
> Fear and be slain—no worse can come but fight;
> And fight and die is death destroying death,
> Where fearing dying pays death servile breath.
>
> [III. ii. 178-85]

Carlisle's "wise men," of whom Mowbray is undoubtedly one, set little value on life because they are convinced that death can be conquered by a brave assertion of individual honor. And in the last act, when Richard urges the quest for "a new world's crown" [V. i. 24] on his queen, she rejects the attitude angrily:

> What, is my Richard both in shape and mind
> Transform'd and weak'ned? Hath Bolingbroke depos'd
> Thine intellect? Hath he been in thy heart?
> The lion dying thrusteth forth his paw
> And wounds the earth, if nothing else, with rage
> To be o'erpow'r'd; and wilt thou, pupil-like,
> Take correction mildly, kiss the rod,
> And fawn on rage with base humility,
> Which art a lion and the king of beasts?
>
> [V. i. 26-34]

Even Richard himself recognizes that he is a traitor among "a sort of traitors":

> For I have given here my soul's consent
> T'undeck the pompous body of a king;
> Made glory base, and sovereignty a slave,
> Proud majesty a subject, state a peasant.
>
> [IV. i. 249-52]

From the first impact of misfortune the king has submitted too patiently (one is tempted to say, too piously) and has, as a consequence, suffered a gradual loss of his royal nature.

Shakespeare displays dramatically this pitiful abdication of selfhood by insisting on Richard's habit of conceiving himself in terms of grief rather than of action or the externals that are the symbols of action. "A king, woe's slave, shall kingly woe obey" [III. ii. 210]:

> You may my glories and my state depose,
> But not my griefs; still am I king of those.
>
> [IV. i. 192-93]

But true identity cannot be founded on a purely mental process: no exercise of "bare imagination" can "cloy the hungry edge of appetite" [I. iii. 296-97]. Richard has been fascinated by the idea of divinely-ordained kingship but blind to the need to realize that blessedness in blessed action. He believes that he, the Sun-King, will dissolve Bolingbroke's rebellion by his mere appearance. Bolingbroke, however, has a reality that Richard lacks: he has not been content to be a mere "journeyman to grief" [I. iii. 274] but has transformed his grief into a motive for action; his honor is real in that it is a true continuation of the honor of his father; in life he looks for opportunities, not miracles. Consequently, he proves indissoluble before Richard's heatless sun. . . . All that is left [Richard] is the shadow of his face, too easily cracked into a hundred shivers. In surrendering his kingship Richard has lost his honor and hence his identity as a person.

This study of the dissolution of a personality is carried a stage further in Richard's last scene (V. v), when we find him struggling to come to terms with his world, now a bare prison dungeon. . . . Grief has reduced him to a welter of tears, a mirror of indecision reflecting successive and contradictory ideals of character, a clock that does no more than count the passage of time without realizing its significance or making anything of it. Patience, expressed in grief, degenerates into "despair," an utter carelessness about the things of this world, something very different from theological despair. For Richard, a man at odds with an "all-hating world" [V. v. 66], one in whom the music of life has kept no proportion and who has wasted time so that now time wastes him, for such a man there is no pleasure or ease but in being "nothing."

Richard's identification of himself as "nothing" might be described as a profession of faith in Hell, a seeking for peace by the way of negation: the personality becoming so ingrown that it is not personality in the sense that it has no outward manifestation in action. And this nihilism is presented as the logical consequence of Richard's isolation of himself from his social context. By his own acts he cuts himself off from the community of the family; by his refusal to act in his own defence he has destroyed his own identity. In a play in which the father-son relationship is prominent, Richard has no child; he alone can perform no "breeding act," that is, an act that will perpetuate the glory of his family and his name. In his last hour he is reduced to making his brain and soul parody the sex-act, so as to breed, instead of children, "A generation of still-breeding thoughts" [V. v. 8]. Others may look to their sons to maintain their "immortality," but Richard can look only to thoughts and images. And this inclination to believe that ideas carry more weight than actions, that imagination has the power to change the nature of reality, expresses itself in a submergence in the passion of grief and derives from his isolation of himself from his social context. Richard has been made a coward by his particular kind of "conscience" and so has lost "the name of action" [*Hamlet*, III. i. 83, 87].

This is not, of course, the end of Richard's story. The three concepts of divine right, honor, and patience may help to illuminate the causes of the King's failure to act, but the last episode of Richard's life suggests that for Shakespeare there remains at the heart of action the mystery of the human will. In the last minutes of Richard's life three agents combine to effect a sudden and radical change in his character, so that he regains "the name of action" by one violent exercise of will. The musician who plays to him and the groom who visits him disprove that it is an "all-hating world" and Richard begins to learn the value of gratitude; in particular, the groom, who apparently wears Richard's livery ("What my tongue dares not, that my heart shall say" [V. v. 97-8]), reminds the ex-king of what he once was. But the third agent is the most important. Roan Barbary was proud to carry a king on his back even if that king was Bolingbroke; his concern was with the office, not the man. For a moment Richard reverts to his old faith in an arbitrary providence that should have intervened on his behalf: could not Barbary have stumbled and broken Bolingbroke's neck, "Since pride must have a fall" [V. v. 88]? But the horse was only doing its duty, performing its proper part in the hierarchy of functions: he was created to be awed by man, was born to bear. Richard, the sun-king, bears his burden like an ass, "Spurr'd, gall'd, and tir'd, by jauncing Bolingbroke" [V. v. 94]. This image, a thought that is not a fantastic elaboration but no more than an image of the truth, is one that moves Richard to the realization that "Patience is stale" [V. v. 103]. He seizes a weapon and kills two of the murderers before Exton stabs him:

> The lion dying thrusteth forth his paw
> And wounds the earth, if nothing else, with rage
> To be o'erpow'r'd. . . .
>
> [V. i. 29-31]

Richard dies "As full of valour as of royal blood" [V. v. 113]: the required equation between personal honor and office is made, too late to win success in this world, but in time to make Richard's end truly tragic, for he dies as Somebody, a lion overpowered, a king deposed, and not as one who has become nothing.

That Richard's last redeeming act of will springs from three experiences, each of which is related to the hierarchical view of man's social life, can hardly be accidental. Each of the three ideas we have examined serve, in the complex organic development of the play, to demonstrate Richard's increasing isolation from the social foundations on which true personality must apparently be built. The idea of divine right sets forth, in a form susceptible of powerful imagistic expression, one of the essential elements of historical reality as Shakespeare understood it: that the requirements of justice are always satisfied but not necessarily within the narrow time-view of an idividual man; Richard, however, sees divine right as a personal privilege, a special endowment of himself as an individual, and not as a guarantee of the moral status of his personal office, and this presumption lies near the core of his personal tragedy. In the idea of honor is focused most of the complexities of the individual's relations with society; and again Richard is presented as cutting himself off from the various obligations that membership of a social unit implies. And finally, Richard's isolation of himself from society permits him to be "too careless patient" and to indulge in the creation of a dream-world of tears that has no experiential reality: life in such a dream-

world can be no more than play-acting, a succession of illusory roles that have no common basis in the reality of a 'social personality' that expresses itself in action. So, in the last analysis, the spectator's ethical judgment on Richard's failure to be a true man finds its ground in the easier and more obvious judgment on his political failure. Ethics and politics cannot be separated.

To offer this analysis as a complete account of the play would, of course, be to fall a victim to the attraction of orderly ideas and to blind oneself to the complexity that necessarily follows the dramatic realization of concepts. There is not space to suggest even a few of the modifications that would be needed to make this examination something like a complete account. One must be mentioned, however, if only as an example of the kind of modification that would be needed. Richard's turning away from the cares of social responsibility and his taking refuge in contempt of the world may be unworthy of a king; but the attitude still calls up the traditional medieval condemnations of temporal ambition and consequently throws a sombre light on the apparent success of Bolingbroke. Moreover, it suggests a more complete awareness of man's predicament and a greater sensitivity to the experience of suffering than the politic opportunism of Bolingbroke and his friends; such an awareness is explicit in Richard's great speeches and does much to justify Richard's indulgence in grief. On several occasions in the play, what might be called an aesthetic judgment cuts across the strictly moral verdict. Perhaps the best instance is in the last act when the Duchess of York pleads for Aumerle on the grounds of affection, against the strictly legal plea of York; when Bolingbroke accepts her plea in preference to that of York, the Duchess names him "a god on earth" [V. iii. 136]. With this widening of his sympathy, this addition of mercy to justice, Bolingbroke becomes truly king. And he remains king because he never waits too patiently on God but transforms grief into a motive for action and so preserves his honor. (pp. 176-86)

Michael Quinn, "'The King Is Not Himself': The Personal Tragedy of Richard II," in Studies in Philology, *Vol. LVI, No. 2, April, 1959, pp. 169-86.*

A. P. ROSSITER   (essay date 1961)

[*Many scholars have noted the presence in* Richard II *of dramatic "loose ends"—elements of plot development that are introduced then apparently forgotten, a discontinuity in characterization, and inconsistencies in tone or the style of verse. In the following excerpt, Rossiter attributes these seeming inconsistencies to the likelihood that Shakespeare relied heavily on an existing play in writing* Richard II—*the anonymous and evidently successful* Woodstock—*but that in so doing he failed to provide the necessary motives that are so prominent in this earlier work, especially as concerns Richard's guilt in the murder of Gloucester, taking it for granted that his audience would be familiar with the background history. Significantly, Rossiter claims that without our sure knowledge of Richard's guilt in the murder of his uncle,* Richard II *fails to establish the tragic source of the process of divine retribution that continues through the subsequent histories. Lacking this information, he adds, the play also fails to explain the king's behavior in Acts I and II and "Bolingbroke's incredibly easy usurpation." Rossiter is also the editor of the definitive critical text of* Woodstock *(see Additional Bibliography).*]

The ancients had a thrifty habit of scrubbing parchments and using them again: these written-over documents are called palimpsests. It is a pity that frugal Elizabethan dramatists did not use parchments for play-books: we should not then need to rely on the hazardous ultra-violet of interpretative criticism or the infra-red of critical bibliography, to decide whether to treat a play as a palimpsest or some other kind of problem, such as lack of coherence in its author's mind, divided aims, and the like. We only want to know things like this where immediate or considered subjective reaction makes us feel some kind of discontinuity, or inconsistency, in the *stuff* (a vague term, used deliberately: ultimately, the arrangements of words and their effects).

Over *Richard II* most critics have felt this. Pater is an exception: for him it does possess 'like a musical composition . . . a certain concentration of all its parts, a simple continuity, an evenness in execution, which are rare in the great dramatist' [see excerpt above, 1889]. . . . Other commentators are bothered by inconsistencies or discontinuities; and I share their view. Whether you approach *Richard II* from the angle of the texture of the verse, the verse-styles, character, plot or theme, you encounter what geologists call 'unconformities'. . . . (p. 23)

If ours is the character-approach, we find a lack of continuity between the Richard of Acts I and II and the melancholy introvert re-imported from Ireland. Those who praise the play as character-piece most highly, seem to *begin* their reading with Act III; and to 'explain' the autocratic, capricious Richard of the first two acts as an imperious adolescent play-acting. This does not cover up the *lack of inside* in the early Richard; and when Coleridge remarks on 'a constant flow of emotions from a total incapability of controlling them . . . a waste of that energy which should have been reserved for action' [see excerpt above, 1834], he as clearly labels the *second* Richard as he misses the *first,* who shows uncontrolled *action* and a lack of *feeling.* He makes him a Hamlet of the sentiments: i.e. what Coleridge thought 'thought' was to Hamlet, he made emotion to Richard.

Dowden [see excerpt above, 1881], in a study mainly very sound in what it points to, leaves him as sentimentalist, dreamer and dilettante; with a wistful charm, but condemned morally for want of what Newman called 'seriousness of the intellect: the adult mind'. That at any rate gives a firm line. There is something in Richard which calls out the latent homosexuality of critics; and I am gratified to find Dowden resisting it. Pater is all the other way: Richard is 'an exquisite poet . . . from first to last, in light and gloom alike, able to see all things poetically, to give a poetic turn to his conduct of them'. . . . Others take the diametrically opposite view of exactly the same matter: plainly more from moral than dramatic reasons. And for all but the stern moralists, Richard's physical beauty is almost a main characteristic. You can dodge all contradictions by taking Aristotle's [theory of consistently inconsistent characterization], but, despite Aristotle, I think that such a character cannot be tragic: it surely lacks the perspicuity which makes logic of the tragic action.

About the other characters the critics are fairly agreed. Bolingbroke is an outline—a strong one; Gaunt is made rather too much of, considering he is gone by Act III; the Favourites are zeros; York 'an incomparable, an incredible, an unintelligible and a monstrous nullity' (Swinburne [see excerpt above, 1909]) or (G. M. Young) 'the first civil servant in our literature'. (I do not offer these as synonyms.) In short, they are mainly orchestra: Gaunt, the wood-wind Queen, Messengers, marches and noises-off.

If we consider the play's themes, we find that although political approaches—making the play historical-epical-moral—do

something to smooth-in the Duchess of Gloucester (I, ii.), the omens, the Gardener and the substance of Gaunt, they cannot make the beginning unragged, nor the rumpus in Westminster Hall (the second Quarrel-scene) clearly relevant; nor do anything to put the York-Aumerle scenes into any sort of order or 'degree'. To generalize, most commentators direct attention to parts of the play which they *can* manage, and tacitly divert it from 'misfits' they cannot; and in this there is no great critical difference between 'character' and 'thematic' approaches. Both do vaguely agree in taking measures to smooth over a kind of 'fold' between Acts II and III; and both, in different ways, have difficulties over Shakespeare's not very pellucid method of presenting some of the essentials of the story, over the awkward way in which he leaves us to guess here and there, mainly in, or as a result of, Acts I and II. This also applies to his artistic intentions. The view of the play as 'ceremonial'; Dover Wilson's contention that 'it ought to be played throughout as ritual . . . it stands far closer to the Catholic service of the Mass than to Ibsen's *Brand* or . . . *St. Joan*' [see excerpt above, 1939]; the lyrical-tragedy view; the poet-king view: all show a similar smoothing-over of unconformities, once taken back to the text.

If we look at the verse, it is a crude discrimination to say there are three styles: rhyme (mainly couplets) and two sorts of blank verse—that of the Deposition, say, and an 'earlier' kind. The 'early' type in fact ranges from a flattish competence (Act I, or Bolingbroke [at V. iii. 1-12], 'Can no man tell me of my unthrifty son? . . .') to a jumbled incompetence, aptly described by York's comment on the state of England . . . :

> All is uneven,
> And everything is left at six and seven.
>   [II. ii. 121-22]

The couplets vary as much, although this is less striking, as Shakespeare wrote within a convention that did not *hear* bad couplets as we hear them; and in Acts I and II especially they pop in and out most disconcertingly. The worst in both kinds, rhyme and blank verse, is distressingly or comically bad. As a *formal* type of play in what Dover Wilson calls 'deliberately patterned speech', it contrasts strikingly with the operatic consistency of *Richard III.* (pp. 23-6)

It is not only that there is more wit in the word-connections than in the thought (and the 'wit', even when called 'metaphysical', is always rather shallow); it is that these 'formal' tricks, like the eruptions of couplets, upset and confuse the *tone* both for reader and actor. Take, for instance, Bolingbroke's lines in III. i., 'Bring forth these men . . .' [III. i. 1ff.]: blank verse in neither the 'early' nor the 'more mature' style, but extremely fluent, very competent, totally without flourish. He has a statement of a heart-felt grievance to make, and he makes it: with force, clarity and cool dignity. Look back at Bolingbroke's lines in Act I, and you see at once how difficult two such disparate manners are for the best of actors.

The result tends to be recitation in a pageant, where dress and décor are everything (bar, of course, Richard). Once again, there is a kind of fold (or 'fault') in the play: Acts I and II are on one side of it, III and IV on the other; and in Act V something comes up to the surface which one is very strongly tempted to call 'half-revised Old Play'. I cannot pretend that the division in verse-texture is as sharp as all that; but the view of the play as 'ceremonial' rests heavily on the Quarrel, the Lists and the 'patriotic' oration of Gaunt; and in Act III there does come a marked change. Richard's

> Well you deserve. They well deserve to have
> That know the strong'st and surest way to get
> [III. iii. 200-01]

has, for example, in context, a sinewy force, an essential *unobtrusive* poetry, which is totally absent in Acts I and II (say what you will of Gaunt's melodious lamentation on England gone to the dogs).

It is on the assumption of that unconformity of Acts I and II that I shall rest my further examination of the play: accepting, that is, a discontinuity in character; some marked incoherences and dubieties in the story; a related uncertainty in the theme (tragic or political); and more than one kind of inconsistency in the texture of the verse. In so doing, I shall seem to be quarrelling with the 'political' view of the play: that here we have the fall of a rightful king, brought about by wilful rebellion, the lifting of 'an angry arm against God's minister', his Deputy; and that the curse that this brings on Lancaster and England is the uniting theme of an English dramatic-epic, in Shakespeare's peculiar double tetralogy. I am not really refuting the political pattern, although it has been given too much emphasis, and also, I think, made too *simple*. What I really question is the *unity*, the integral quality of the sequence.

Richard II, as the first play, seems to me to have no real beginning; a coherent middle; and a ragged, muddled end, only some of which can be explained as a Shakespearian parallel to the famous 'end-links' of Chaucer. Taken by itself, if we stand back far enough, it does look like the Aristotelean 'simple' tragedy: the sort he thought inferior, having neither *peripeteia* [reversal of fortune] nor any real *anagnorisis* [discovery or recognition]. Richard seems to slip steadily into calamity, mainly through 'force of circumstances'; and his *hamartia . . .* is a fatal step, a *blunder,* the mishandling of a quarrel between two violent noblemen. But go near enough to grasp the *action,* sticking tight to the text, and you will find that this alleged first term in a coherently planned series is thoroughly uncertain about its own start, and uncertain at the simplest level of the story, as well as on the major matter of essential (or political) rights and wrongs.

From now on, I shall dogmatize: state my case, and leave it to your verdicts.

Richard II's value as first term in an epic-historical series is seriously flawed by its peculiar dependence on *Woodstock:* peculiar since Shakespeare not only took items from it, but also *left behind* in it explanations badly needed in his play, items taken for granted, or as read, which produce puzzles that cannot be cleared up without reference to the earlier play. To some extent, then, *Richard II* as a play does not contain within itself the reason why it is thus and not otherwise. If so, the alleged epic scheme is faulty, since the 'beginning' is not a beginning.

Richard II is about the fall and deposition of a King. The fall results from two events: *(a)* the quarrel of Bolingbroke and Mowbray, which Shakespeare invites us to focus down to the pin-point *hamartia* of throwing down the warder in the lists . . . ; and *(b)* the falling-away of York, and all England, on Bolingbroke's landing. This second event has to do with Richard's failings as monarch: with 'the state of England', which some critics make a main theme, although (Gaunt's reproaches apart) there is very little about it in the text. Ross . . . says, 'The

commons hath he pill'd with grievous taxes' [II. i. 246]; but that, as it happens, is a direct echo from *Woodstock . . .* , where 'Plain Thomas', being mocked about his homespun frieze, says: 'did some here wear that fashion, / They would not tax and pill the commons so.' In short, the connection between favourites and extravagance, extravagance and exaction, exactions and Richard's loss of power, is crystal-clear in *Woodstock* and nowhere else. In *Richard II* Willoughby takes up Ross with a mention of 'daily new exactions', 'As blanks, benevolences, and I wot not what' [II. i. 249-50]; and we wot not what neither. *Editors* tell us; but the fact is, there is precious little in Holinshed about 'blanks'; nothing about 'benevolences' (devised by Edward IV!); and one sentence about a *rumour* 'that the King had set to farme the realme of England unto sir Wm. Scroope earle of Wiltshire . . . to Sir Jno. Bushie, sir Jno. Bagot, and sir Hy. Greene knights'. . . . If we look at *Richard II,* taking it as it comes (as an audience *must*), we find: (1) *Before* Gaunt's accusations, only one inexplicit line by Richard, 'We are enforc'd to farm our royal realm' [I. iv. 45]; a bit more on blank charters following it, but no connecting of either with the evil influence of favourites. (2) It is only 190 lines *after* Gaunt's 'Bound in with . . . inky blots and rotten parchment bonds' [II. i. 63-4], that Ross growls, 'The Earl of Wiltshire hath the realm in farm' [II. i. 256]. (3) *Between* these references lie Gaunt's two nearly-unintelligible charges: 'rotten parchment bonds' and 'Thy state of law is bond-slave to the law' [II. i. 64, 114]. The Arden edition notes show these *are* obscurities: both notes are nonsense.

Now these things are perfectly clear and straightforward to anyone who reads *Woodstock,* Acts II, III and IV of which are concerned with the rise to power of the favourites, headed by the villainous Lord Chief Justice Tresilian; their financial iniquities when *in* power (III and IV); and what 'blanks' meant to the Commons (IV. iii.). I can make but one point: the author of *Woodstock* scrambles and hashes history to make Richard's extortions a matter of *legal* iniquity: slavery to bonds, regal servitude to the law of contract. And he therefore *stages* Richard presented with a legal instrument (a bond or lease), giving the favourites full command of the Exchequer and all the royal estates etc. in exchange for a monthly stipend of £7,000. That is what Gaunt is alluding to; and the whole difficulty of the financial wickedness of both Richard and the favourites in *Richard II* is simply that Shakespeare *alludes* and never explains. . . . This is not simply a source-hunter's game: it affects the whole moral complexion of Richard in Acts I and II, and alters both the colour of the theme and Shakespeare's reading of history.

It also bears on what we make of the *personae,* as 'characters' or as 'symbols': especially the favourites, but, by repercussion, Gaunt too. In *Richard II* the blank-charter iniquity is less skimped; but only in *Woodstock* does the wickedness of income-tax returns signed 'blank' (leaving the collector to invent the income) receive the emphasis we can call 'normal'. Nor, in Richard, is the dressy extravagance of favourites and Court made a clear cause. Shakespeare's Bushy, Greene and Bagot are nearly 'blank-charters' themselves: once again because they are taken as *seen* (in their bad habits as they lived—on the stage); and 'recognised' as shadows of vanity, flattery and contempt of good counsel, opposed symbolically and morally to what Gaunt stands for (which is identical with what he and York and Thomas of Woodstock stood for in *Woodstock*: in flat defiance of Chronicle and truth). Shakespeare's play leaves us wondering what vices they had. . . . (pp. 27-33)

Their real evil, which Shakespeare presents only by allusion, is that they *were* the political and moral opposites to Richard's 'good old uncles', all of whom, in both plays, are economy, retrenchment, conservatism, public service and plain-Englishry. A phrase here points incontrovertibly to *Woodstock*. Gaunt's 'My brother Gloucester, plain well-meaning soul' [II. i. 128], refers solely to the other play. 'Plain homespun Thomas', who wears frieze at Court and is comically mistaken for a groom by an overdressed popinjay (III. ii.). . . . In Chronicle there is no such person: he is purely a *dramatis persona*, partly modelled on the good Duke Humphrey of *2 Henry VI* and with comparable moral functions. Against Dover Wilson's attempt to extract a 'good' Gaunt from Froissart, I find that Shakespeare's Gaunt is the same 'form' (or 'shadow' in an allegory of State) as Thomas. By this I do not mean that either lacks 'character': only that moral function, not history, determines their forms.

The most unquestionably historical thing that Woodstock does is to get murdered; and here the events of *Woodstock,* assumed to be known, have their most important bearing on the moral structure of Shakespeare's play: on the character of Richard, the mechanism of his fall, and the essential rights and wrongs behind the quarrel. No one can read *Richard II* and not encounter the problem, 'Who killed Woodstock?' Bolingbroke accuses Mowbray of it; Gaunt tells the Duchess of Gloucester that Richard was responsible; Bagot and Fitzwater say it was Aumerle: they imply, moreover, that the murder took place *after* Bolingbroke was banished, and add that Mowbray said so [IV. i. 80]. To say they are all liars is no more than they all say to one another. The whole thing makes sense, and makes the plot of Acts I and II far more coherent, as soon as we know that Woodstock was (1) kidnapped in a masque, with Richard and his favourites present; (2) conveyed to Calais, the Governor of which is called Lapoole in the play, but *was* Thomas Mowbray; and (3) there put to death (in a stirring scene) not by the Governor, but rather against his will, and by two experts in tidy murder sent from England.

Thus in the quarrel, Mowbray knows that Richard knows the truth, and that Bolingbroke knows most of it. Hence Richard's desire to quiet the pair, and his saying *he* will calm Norfolk, while Gaunt calms Bolingbroke. . . . Hence, too, the riddling lines where Mowbray says:

> . . . For Gloucester's death—
> I slew him not, but to my own disgrace
> Neglected my sworn duty in that case.
>   [I. i. 132-34]

Reference to *Woodstock* suggests at once that the allusion is to Act V. i. where Woodstock appeals to Lapoole 'by virtue of nobility' and 'on that allegiance / Thou ow'st the offspring of King Edward's house' . . . , when he fears murder. The lines in Shakespeare mean, then, that Mowbray admits he was Governor (which is known to everyone), and that he failed in his sworn duty to protect the blood royal (which again is obvious). But simultaneously he reminds Richard of *why* he failed (Richard threatened his life if Woodstock was not killed), while giving nothing away. For 'I slew him not' is perfectly true of Lapoole himself: Woodstock was killed by agents, and all Lapoole-Mowbray did was not to prevent them.

This criminal collusion with Mowbray *could* supply the motive for the stopping of the single-combat at Coventry. The principle of trial-by-arms is that it gives 'the judgement of God'; and we may plausibly make the induction that Richard is afraid

that God will give the right verdict. But it is only a reasonable *induction,* for Shakespeare gives no hint of Richard's motives. Character-critics are content to see here only an exhibition of Richard's exhibitionism: his self-regarding theatricality in the kingly role—even, perhaps, the actor-manager's vanity, in dramatically focusing all eyes on himself and dragging them away from the combatants (like a film-star at a prize-fight). (pp. 33-5)

But this act of throwing down the warder is of fatal consequence: fatal and fateful. From that one act a strict logic of events throws down Plantagenet and, inside ninety years, throws up Tudor. The logic of the eight-play series *and* the exact apprehension of the 'tragedy' demand that we should know if it was *guilt* (and guilt of royal blood) which started this momentous sequence. If not, where is the beginning of the epic-drama? Further back. Then it has no unity. And in this case we cannot delve into *Woodstock* for the answer and come out certain.

We must be satisfied with a fair degree of probability and the absence of final certainty. The explanation of the King's desertion by England is writ large in *Woodstock:* favourites, vanities, extravagances, taxation, extortion, antipathy to sound counsel: all these are kingly vices. The explanation of the quarrel is there too: briefly, 'Woodstock's blood', the wanton murder of a royal prince, epitome of the right-mindedness and political and social responsibility which are expressed in Gaunt. Integrate the causes of Richard's fall, and his confused actions throughout Acts I and II derive from a guilt, or guilts, out of which there is no clear path. Shakespeare knows this—indeed too well: he slips into the lecturer's commonest fault, of assuming that everybody must know what, as it happens, many do *not*. But this applies mainly to the first two acts alone. It explains Richard as he there appears, and explains too why a different Richard arrives from Ireland in Act III. It also suggests why Bolingbroke's intentions about the crown are left rather obscure. I believe that the *historic* fact is that there was a well-contrived conspiracy, leading to a well-timed landing. But Shakespeare took Halle's hint that Bolingbroke had no glimmer of what fate had in store for him: that chance would have him King (as we should say), and so chance crowned him. It is, after all, what he tells Warwick before his death:

> . . . God knows, I had no such intent,
> But that necessity so bow'd the state
> That I and greatness were compell'd to kiss.
>   [*2 Henry IV*, III. i. 72-4]

If, though, we accept the many hints in *Richard II* that Richard was a guilty *King*—and it is the guilt of the King, much rather than the innate wickedness of the man, that *Woodstock* emphasizes—then Bolingbroke's walk-in to kingship is itself one more instance of that process of retributive reaction which is the really *tragic* element in the History plays (the judgement of God in the process of history . . .). This retributive reaction, as a divinity that shapes the ends of England, is a principle which makes sense and logic of Bolingbroke's incredibly easy usurpation. Richard is *wrong*, but Bolingbroke's coronation is *not right*; and Richard's murder converts it to the blackest wrong. This greatly reduces the possibility of regarding Richard as a 'royal martyr' or 'sacrificial-king'. It should also prevent our making Shakespeare a kind of sentimental conservative, looking nostalgically back, like Walter Scott, to the 'great age' of Chivalry and showing us 'the waning of the Middle Ages'. (pp. 35-7)

The central experience in *Richard II* is its *middle,* the substance of Acts III and IV. The ceremonial or ritual scenes and styles do matter: although only six scenes out of nineteen can be called 'ritualistic' or formalized. They matter because of what they *contrast* with; for in that contrast there is a tonal and visual rendering of the contrast of Richard and his group and Bolingbroke and his, but more as *Weltanschauungen* [world views] or aspects of human experience than as just 'characters'.

However and whenever *Richard II* is played, the pageant-element is important (as much for 1955 as for 1595). But this element is double, not single. After the lists, etc., a new tone begins to emerge at the end of II. i, in the huddle of sullen earls plotting together after the fops have gone. Northumberland emerges there; and a grim meaning is given him at once in:

> Not so; even through the hollow eyes of death
> I spy life peering . . .
>   [II. i. 270-71]

That is more than 'character'. When Bolingbroke lands, Northumberland is there beside him; and in III. i. and III. iii. I am sure that the *visual* contrast between these armed campaigners and the toy warfare of the lists, the brilliant and vapid refinement of the Court, are part of the play as images. Elizabethan eyes saw iron as we see khaki battle-dress and camouflage. And, significantly, Richard's words in banishing Bolingbroke foreshadow this very change: he would *avoid* the

> . . . harsh-resounding trumpets' dreadful bray,
> And grating shock of wrathful iron arms. . . .
>   [I. iii. 135-36]

But the iron comes; and with it a touch of iron in the verse: as witness Bolingbroke's opening lines in the scenes before and after Richard's speech on landing in Wales, 'Dear earth, I do salute thee with my hand . . .' [III. ii. 6]. The answer to that is the efficient staff-officer's: 'So that by this intelligence we learn / The Welshmen are dispers'd' [III. iii. 1]. It is more than character-contrast: the verse, backed by the hardening of the human exteriors, the steel-framed faces, jars two worlds together. The same jar is in the Deposition-scene. It gives the play its meaning and experience, as a kind of tragic drama: the obscure tragedy, unclear, interesting, rather disheartening, of 'Shakespearian history'.

The nature of the jar—the nature of those two worlds—makes Richard less than the fully tragic hero. One is the half-fantasy world of the Court, where Richard's half-dream kingship reigns, with angels at his beck and serpents for his foes; the other is that other dream, of action, will and curt-worded decision, in which he is nothing, or a passive sufferer, a king of woes (or merely a king of words). In the mirror-episode the two dreams doubly confront each other. This it is that makes the Arden editor, following Pater, tell us Richard's nature is 'that of the poet who has unfortunately had kingship thrust upon him'. One need not reply, 'If so, surely a very *bad* poet'; for the answer is in Dowden, or in what Dowden quotes from Kreyssig: '. . . he affords us the shocking spectacle of an absolute bankruptcy, mental and spiritual no less than in the world of outward affairs, caused by one condition only: that nature has given him the character of a Dilettante, and called him to a position which, more than any other, demands the Artist.' (pp. 38-9)

A. P. Rossiter, "'Richard II'," in his Angel with Horns and Other Shakespeare Lectures, *edited by Graham Storey, Longmans, 1961, pp. 23-39.*

R. F. HILL   (essay date 1961)

[*In the following excerpt, Hill justifies Shakespeare's use of the rhetorical, artificial style in* Richard II *and his other early tragedies, especially at moments of intense emotion. He claims that although the rhetorical mode "may keep us at a distance from the feeling at the back of it, the presence of feeling is unmistakably established." He also states that in such plays of elevated poetry as* Richard II, *the further heightening of language at crucial moments of tension and "emotional distress" is necessary to indicate "some degress of heightened response." Hill then examines the respective rhetorical styles of Richard and Bolingbroke. He describes the king's bombast as a mask for his weakness, while Bolingbroke, he maintains, is purely manipulative, adapted to deceive others and to serve as "an instrument for the execution of power."*]

Richard II is not the model of dramatic excellence that Coleridge would have us believe [see excerpt above, 1834], but it achieves much within the limits of its artifice. It is necessary, as I have argued elsewhere, to accept the artifice, to see it as a projection of life in terms of a highly conventionalized art. Such a view is most helpful to an understanding of the passages of involved word-play in *Richard II*. The plays on 'down/base-court' [III. iii. 178-83], 'care' [IV. i. 195-99], 'face' [IV. i. 281-88] are artificial and obtrusive. Worse, they issue from the lips of Richard at his moments of deepest suffering when, in terms of natural psychology, one would expect a distraction which prohibits orderly discourse, expressing itself, if at all, in broken, simple language. Has Shakespeare falsified here through his delight in quibbling? Must Richard's grief be shallow since he can so file his phrases? Any answer must recognize that it is not only Richard who vents distress in this mannered way. His wife plays nicely upon the words 'joy' and 'sorrow' in her mood of anxious foreboding [III. iv. 10-16] and John of Gaunt, in greater torment, is even more dexterous in his quibble on 'Gaunt' [II. i. 74-83]. Furthermore an examination of the style of the early tragedies and tragical histories shows that mental and emotional distress is always accompanied by a heightening of language in the direction of patterning and contrivance. . . . [This] can hardly be the result of chance. Shakespeare is deliberately at his most artificial where one would expect him, in terms of natural psychology, to aim at spontaneity. Hence one's impression of bad taste in the early word-play, its alienation rather than enlistment of sympathetic response.

But if Shakespeare is not attempting naturalistic representation the error may lie in our approach. Representation in *Richard II* is consistently rhetorical, in the sense of its being unashamedly aware and proud of its linguistic means. At this level one should expect intensification of feeling to be matched by an intensification of the characteristic means. Such moments are the cue for an added virtuosity which will distinguish them from what is throughout a high pitch of elaboration. Shakespeare certainly succeeds in this. Further, whilst the artifice may keep us at a distance from the feeling at the back of it, the presence of feeling is unmistakably established, for any heightening of language, however unusual in kind or unexpected in particular contexts, creates some degree of heightened response. John of Gaunt and Richard establish that they *are* distressed though we may wonder at their clever play of thought and word. Granted a taste for such cleverness it may be admired at some expense to the tragic feeling it is expressing. Viewed absolutely such a cleavage between art and matter is a failure of Art. But the absolute view is not the best way to an understanding of *Richard II*. Viewed relatively, as rhetorical tragedy, a place must be allowed to language for its own sake; Shakespeare wanted to be admired for his words. (pp. 101-03)

It has been argued that in the presentation of heightened emotional states *Richard II* consistently observes a convention. How successful is the rhetoric in characterization? The simple view of Richard as a verbal trifler, as one acting out his life rather than living it, must already be qualified by the recognition that in the early tragic style high feeling is always accompanied by high and often patterned rhetoric. The apparently self-conscious control of language does not, of itself, indicate dispassion and triviality in character. Having regard to this I shall examine the language of the play particularly in its definition of Richard and Bolingbroke.

The prevailing elevated diction of *Richard II* is immediately apparent in Richard's summoning of Bolingbroke and Mowbray:

> Then call them to our presence; face to face,
> And frowning brow to brow, ourselves will hear
> The accuser and the accused freely speak:
> High-stomach'd are they both, and full of ire,
> In rage deaf as the sea, hasty as fire.
>
> [I. i. 15-19]

The elaborate repetitions, the tautology of the last two lines with their high-pitched similes, suggest a relish for ceremony, a determination to make the utmost of a public appearance which will demonstrate the irresistible authority of the crown in subduing headstrong subjects. His comment on Bolingbroke's passionate accusation of Mowbray—

> How high a pitch his resolution soars!—
>
> [I. i. 109]

furthers one's impression of his irresponsible enjoyment of a serious situation. Having enjoyed the spectacle of their mutual hatred he expects to dispose of it lightly:

> Wrath-kindled gentlemen, be ruled by me;
> Let's purge this choler without letting blood:
> This we prescribe, though no physician;
> Deep malice makes too deep incision;
> Forget, forgive; conclude and be agreed;
> Our doctors say this is no month to bleed.
>
> [I. i. 152-57]

The jingle of the rhymes, the skipping rhythms, compel one to see the punning physician image as hovering on the verge of levity. If Richard is playing a game the antagonists are in deadly earnest; neither is to be daunted by mere words. Richard tries the power of words again, this time rhetorical commonplaces—'Rage must be withstood', 'lions make leopards tame' [I. i. 173-74]—but Mowbray neatly turns the second of these into an argument for his continued defiance. Richard is forced to concede to a settlement of the quarrel in the lists at Coventry.

In essentials Richard is already 'placed' for us; an immature delight in the ceremony of power coupled with a fatal tendency to equate the word of authority with authority indeed. Yet, although he speaks with a conscious distinction, he is no more eloquent and ornate than Bolingbroke or Mowbray.... It is Bolingbroke who tells us that his exile is to be 'a long apprenticehood To foreign passages' which will end in no greater boast than that he was 'a journeyman to grief' [I. iii. 271-72, 274]. His answer to his father's speech of consolation is a cluster of synonymous illustrations all enforcing the same point [I. iii. 294-303]. The studied rhetoric conveys the vehemence of grief but overlays distinction of character.

However, more may be revealed than is at first apparent. Richard's speech beginning 'Draw near And list what with our council we have done' [I. iii. 123-43] looks like a self-indulgent display of royal authority blown to its fullest with repetitions, personifications and double epithets. Second thoughts suggest that the bombast is self-protective, evidence both of an inner insecurity and discomfort in an unpleasant situation. He must convince himself and his auditors that the doom of banishment justly fits the crime. But the quarrel itself is scarcely a crime; exile is necessary for Bolingbroke and Mowbray because Richard himself is involved in the murder of Thomas of Woodstock which lies at the back of the quarrel. Hence Richard's refuge in pretty periphrases to pronounce the judgment which a guilty conscience at once desires and abhors:

> You, cousin Hereford, upon pain of life,
> Till twice five summers have enrich'd our fields
> Shall not regreet our fair dominions . . .
> Norfolk, for thee remains a heavier doom,
> Which I with some unwillingness pronounce:
> The sly slow hours shall not determinate
> The dateless limit of thy dear exile . . .
>
> [I. iii. 140-42, 148-51]

As soon as Mowbray has gone Richard, ostensibly moved by John of Gaunt's sadness, reduces Bolingbroke's sentence by four years. This magnanimity is hard to understand since Richard has already referred to 'sky-aspiring and ambitious thoughts' [I. iii. 130] while Mowbray's last words are a clear warning that Bolingbroke must be closely watched:

> But what thou art, God, thou, and I do know;
> And all too soon, I fear, the king shall rue.
>
> [I. iii. 204-05]

And the tone of Bolingbroke's comment on Richard's gesture is ominous:

> How long a time lies in one little word!
> Four lagging winters and four wanton springs
> End in a word: such is the breath of kings.
>
> [I. iii. 213-15]

Periphrasis, which for Richard was self-protective, is for Bolingbroke a means of subtle antagonism, since 'Four lagging winters and four wanton springs' draws out his bitter realization of Richard's capricious power. Further, 'such is the breath of kings' is a veiled perception and threat; an envious gibe at the king's authority and a recognition that the breath of a king may be cut off with a word. The perspicacity and daring of this speech, its indication of the power to use language effectively rather than take refuge behind it, are marks of the emerging usurper.

The direction of this criticism is furthered in I. iv where his ability to act a chosen role is suggested by Richard, who observed

> his courtship to the common people;
> How he did seem to dive into their hearts
> With humble and familiar courtesy,
> What reverence he did throw away on slaves,
> Wooing poor craftsmen with the craft of smiles . . .
>
> [I. iv. 24-8]

Now Richard's account presumably shows the exaggeration of bias but its underlying truth is confirmed in the scene which records Bolingbroke's return to England (II. iii.). Northum-

berland is sycophantic in his tribute to the delights of Bolingbroke's companionship, yet his comment is still suggestive:

> . . . your fair discourse hath been as sugar,
> Making the hard way sweet and delectable.
>
> [II. iii. 6-7]

It is a meed of sugared words that Henry Percy receives when
he pledges his service to Bolingbroke:

> I thank thee, gentle Percy; and be sure
> I count myself in nothing else so happy
> As in a soul remembering my good friends.
>
> [II. iii. 45-7]

Ross and Willoughby, too, are greeted fulsomely:

> Welcome, my lords. I wot your love pursues
> A banish'd traitor: all my treasury
> Is yet but unfelt thanks, which, more enrich'd,
> Shall be your love and labour's recompense.
>
> [II. iii. 59-62]

Bolingbroke is apparently humble, artless, frank. But for all
the simplicity of his speeches here do they not betray calculation in their over-humility, over-sweetness? Is he not exercising that 'craft of smiles' that he had employed on the populace? Time would show. The Percys were to find to their cost
what an accomplished politician they had to deal with.

Richard's comments on Bolingbroke's courtship of the people
do not appear to be occasioned by apprehension of his motives.
Perhaps it was an instinctive distaste, for Richard himself shows
in this play little power of successful dissimulation. Even when
John of Gaunt was dying he made no attempt to conceal his
levity and wounded pride. Throughout it is evident that his
countenance and words freely registered the truth of inner
experience.

During Richard's absence in Ireland Bolingbroke returns from
exile. Whether his return in arms masked from the outset a
usurping design behind the ostensible demand for restitution
of his rights is a much debated question. . . . The chroniclers
Froissart and Holinshed unequivocally state that Bolingbroke
was recalled by the enemies of Richard to seize the throne,
and Samuel Daniel's account only differs in working by insinuation. If Shakespeare wished to alter this important detail
from his sources why did he run the risk of misinterpretation
by merely suppressing it instead of directly exonerating Bolingbroke? . . . Was Shakespeare trying to show Bolingbroke,
as Dover Wilson puts it, as 'borne upward by a power beyond
his volition' [see excerpt above, 1939], or was the suppression
designed to achieve the ambiguity of a politic usurper? All the
clues point to the second alternative. Bolingbroke is as subtle
here as in the *Henry IV* plays, and he would not have risked
alienating the waverers in his faction by admitting the full truth
about his aims. He had to move warily; his usurpation must
appear inevitable, but undesigned.

Bolingbroke's control of his destiny is mirrored in his careful
manipulation of language after his return to England. He exercises an easy art of persuasion on the simple Duke of York
[II. iii. 113-36]. With winning casuistry he argues that he was
banished as Duke of Hereford but returns as Duke of Lancaster.
Then follows an emotional appeal, the orator's most powerful
weapon:

> You are my father, for methinks in you
> I see old Gaunt alive: O, then, my father,
> Will you permit that I shall stand condemn'd
> A wandering vagabond . . .
>
> [II. iii. 117-20]

A short logical statement is then succeeded by more emotional
play, with a new twist given to the father idea:

> You have a son, Aumerle, my noble cousin;
> Had you first died, and he been thus trod down,
> He should have found his uncle Gaunt a father,
> To rouse his wrongs . . .
>
> [II. iii. 125-28]

After a citation of his wrongs he concludes with the trump
argument that he is compelled to resort to force because, although his claim is lawful, law will not help him. All is delivered with disarming plausibility and frankness. It is significant that Bolingbroke had no need to bandy words with York
since the power lay in his hands to do exactly as he wished;
but he was astute enough to see the value of always proceeding
with an appearance of justice and injured innocence.

The growing purposiveness of the rhetoric is apparent in the
scene of Richard's arrival in Wales (III. ii). Carlisle's quibbling
and sententious platitudes characterize the well-meaning but
ineffectual Bishop; his manner is neatly off-set by the incisive
speeches of Aumerle. But the importance of this scene is its
delineation of Richard's emotional unbalance and predisposition to despair which unfit him for the throne. At one extreme
he is the creature of passion, but the sensuous imagination
which ministers to active pleasure ministers equally to mor-
bidity, issuing in images of death and decay. The vein of
contemptus mundi [contempt for the world], whether real or a
perverse imaginative pleasure, ill sorts with the demands of a
material kingdom. Richard's fall was as inevitable as Bolingbroke's rise—character is destiny. This pattern of rise and fall,
symbolized in the 'well' image of the deposition scene, can
be traced in this scene as Richard's emotions fluctuate between
elation and despair. He begins with a long apostrophe to his
'Dear earth' [III. ii. 6] and although the sentiments express
defiance the dominant impression is of weakness, partly on
account of the slow movement of the verse and partly because
the pathetic fallacy, by which the earth becomes an active
sympathizer, is mere extravagance. To defend his throne his
impulse is to look to the miraculous assistance of the world of
nature, just as he relies upon the power of the mere name of
king.

When he is reminded that his divine appointment must be
guarded by determined action he simply reiterates his reliance
on the terror and divinity that encompass a king. The mood is
now of intransigent assertion, expressed in an elaborate allegory of the sun-king image sweeping through a verse paragraph. The conclusion is characteristically a triumph of words,
drumming with alliteration:

> Not all the water in the rough rude sea
> Can wash the balm off from an annointed king;
> The breath of worldly men cannot depose
> The deputy elected by the Lord.
>
> [III. ii. 54-7]

After further marked fluctuations of spirit Scroop arrives with
the threat of more bad news whereupon Richard sinks into
piteous resignation, a strange blend of stoicism and Christian
contempt for the world. The parallel rhythms of the question
and answer rhetorical device, and the strong-paused, slow-
paced verse finely convey the mood:

> Say, is my kingdom lost? why, 'twas my care;
> And what loss is it to be rid of care?
> Strives Bolingbroke to be as great as we?

Greater he shall not be: if he serve God,
We'll serve Him too, and be his fellow so:
Revolt our subjects? that we cannot mend;
They break their faith to God as well as us.

[III. ii. 95-101]
(pp. 103-09)

The last blow falls with the news of York's defection. When Richard addresses Aumerle,

Beshrew thee, cousin, which didst lead me forth
Of that sweet way I was in to despair!

[III. ii. 204-05]

he supplies the key to his unfitness for rule. The sweetness of the way of despair indicates both a morbid imagination and a real penchant for a rejection of the world with its active pressures and responsibilities. He was not a religious hermit *manqué* [a would-be hermit] as was Shakespeare's Henry VI, yet his indolent, pleasure-loving nature would instinctively conjure up, in moments of worldly trouble, the attractiveness of an obscure religious life. Further, there was interwoven a deeper sense of the vanity of the world, certain to be present in a reflective mind. So it is that in this scene and the next he associates himself with a succession of religious images which reaches its climax in his projection of himself into a hermit's life, as he sees his deposition imminent. However, just as Richard would evade the responsibilities of the throne, so also he evades all but the superficies of the religious life. His picturesque selection of detail—a set of beads, a dish of wood, a pair of carved saints, a little grave—is a characteristic retreat behind words.

The meeting between Richard and Bolingbroke at Flint castle (III. iii) is couched in rhetoric of considerable subtlety. In the opening dialogue between Bolingbroke, Northumberland and York devices of repetition and pun generate tension, characterize, and underline leading ideas. Bolingbroke tries to defend Northumberland to York:

Mistake not, uncle, further than you should.

[III. iii. 15]

The quibbling of York's reply emphasizes an important theme:

Take not, good cousin, further than you should,
Lest you mistake the heavens are o'er our heads.

[III. iii. 16-17]

Bolingbroke is too good an actor in his part of injured innocence to 'take' undisguisedly what York is implying, and the heavens are far enough away to be left for later propitiation. So he pursues his deposition of a divinely appointed king, masking his intent behind pious sentiment and blown rhetoric:

Noble lords,
Go to the rude ribs of that ancient castle;
Through brazen trumpet send the breath of parley
Into his ruin'd ears, and thus deliver:
Henry Bolingbroke
On both his knees doth kiss King Richard's hand
And sends allegiance and true faith of heart
To his most royal person.

[III. iii. 31-8]

The loyalty of the last lines is denied by the personification of the ruined castle through which Bolingbroke insinuates the ruin of Richard himself ('Into his ruin'd ears'). Moreover, by means of this circumlocution and the succeeding long metaphor of the 'crimson tempest' [III. iii. 46] he generates a sense of

occasion which blunts one's perception of his underlying purpose. When Richard appears on the walls Henry Percy furthers the pretence by likening Richard to the sun, but however vaunting the language the whole image is suggestive of fading glory [III. iii. 62]. Richard counters with equal magnificence of language, but whereas his rhetoric masks weakness (or rather is the only strength he ever shows) Bolingbroke's rhetoric is an instrument for the execution of power. . . . The whole [scene] shows the subtlety possible to the artificial linguistic mode.

At the end of this scene Bolingbroke is still making a leg and professing allegiance when it is quite clear to everyone that he is toppling over the throne. If Bolingbroke owes fealty to Richard why must Richard take orders from him?

RICHARD.   Set on towards London, cousin, is it so?
BOLING.   Yea, my good lord.

[III. iii. 208-09]

The tactical value of denying the crime one is evidently committing is as clearly recognized by Police State rule as it was by Machievellan politicians.

In the deposition scene the lone voice of the Bishop of Carlisle, asserting the iniquity of Bolingbroke's action, is quickly silenced. Richard must endure his misery in isolation. As he reflects upon this isolation the image of the betrayed Christ presents itself to him [IV. i. 167-71] as it does a little later when he sees those about him showing an outward pity like Pilate, but delivering him to his 'sour cross' [IV. i. 241]. This religious imagery signifies not only protective self-dramatization but also a predisposition to despair leading on to a rejection of the world. Willing to relinquish the struggle for the crown he cannot, however, so easily shed the attendant grief, and the word-play which follows is the inevitable rhetorical expression of his anguish. Just as his grief hammers upon 'care' [IV. i. 195-99] so later, as he gazes in the mirror, he reiterates the word 'face' [IV. i. 277-91] which reminds him of his departed glory. This quibbling is not merely indicative of Richard's love of words and effect. The supreme flowering of the mannered style at emotional peaks may not sound natural but its intensity is the rhetorical projection of psychological intensity. The limitation of the method is that the surface brilliance tends to obscure by distraction at the same time as it strives to articulate feeling.

We have seen that Bolingbroke knows how to use words; in this scene he demonstrates his policy in not using them. He has proceeded so far behind a mask. The actual deposition is the point of dramatic unmasking and discretion bids that he should keep in the background as far as possible. Thus the ruthless and officious Northumberland is allowed prominence in the unpleasant aspects of the deposition, consequently attracting to himself some of its obloquy. When Bolingbroke does speak he is terse and carefully polite; he knows when to restrain Northumberland—'Urge it no more, my Lord Northumberland' [IV. i. 271]—whose importunity threatens the desired quiet course of the deposition. He knows how to curb Richard's extravagances and in so doing gives the supreme contrast between the realist and the dreamer. When Richard smashes the mirror he admonishes Bolingbroke,

Mark, silent king, the moral of this sport,
How soon my sorrow hath destroy'd my face.

[IV. i. 290-91]

Bolingbroke at once turns the argument back on Richard with an unerring eye for the reality of the situation:

> The shadow of your sorrow hath destroy'd
> The shadow of your face.
>   [IV. i. 292-93]
>   (pp. 110-13)

Bolingbroke has it all. He must now exercise his politic art in consolidating his position. Sir Pierce of Exton was the first of the accomplices to suffer from his calculated hypocrisy.

York's detailed description of the arrival of King Richard and Bolingbroke in London [V. ii. 7-36] inevitably brings to mind Richard's earlier account of ostentatious humility:

> Whilst he, from the one side to the other turning,
> Bare-headed, lower than his proud steed's neck,
> Bespake them thus: 'I thank you, countrymen'.
>   [V. ii. 18-20]

York then uses a simile from the theatre in which Bolingbroke is likened to a 'well-graced actor' [V. ii. 24]. Certainly a decorative simile but remarkably appropriate to both the immediate situation and an underlying truth. It is, indeed, the 'well-graced actor' in Bolingbroke which ensures his rise to power and subsequent strength. Can anyone who has observed him closely as pretender and king accept at its face value his self-righteous rebuke of Exton?

> The love not poison that do poison need,
> Nor do I thee: though I did wish him dead,
> I hate the murderer, love him murdered.
>   [V. vi. 38-40]

No one better than Bolingbroke can act the part that policy requires and in this special sense I call him the actor-king. His command of language issues in effective action whereas Richard's stagnates in reflection. Richard is only an actor in that he is prone to the weakness of self-dramatization.

Bolingbroke apparently justifies his usurpation in that he shows himself admirably fitted for rule. Yet morally he is an equivocal figure. Indeed, *Richard II* is curiously ambiguous in its ethical attitude towards both Bolingbroke and Richard. Neither is presented as an evil figure so that it is difficult to adjust oneself to the moral and religious issues involved in the conflict. Perhaps one should not ask what was Shakespeare's attitude since he was dramatizing historical events with an intractable dilemma at their core—political expediency versus divine right. Yet speculation may throw some oblique light.

Shakespeare's tragic heroes, heroines, villains, clowns, wits, form groups with distinct characteristics. My impulse is to place Bolingbroke with the villains and Richard with the heroes. Rationalization of this impulse discerns that Bolingbroke shares with Richard III, Cassius [in *Julius Caesar*], Claudius [in *Hamlet*], Lady Macbeth, Edmund, Goneril, Regan [in *King Lear*], Iago [in *Othello*], the Tribunes in *Coriolanus*, an essentially practical nature, combined with powers of dissimulation employed in the attainment of selfish ends. There is usually great self-control itself related to a coldness of nature which may interest itself in lust but knows nothing of the generosities of love. The imaginative and reflective part of man is in abeyance, together with a freedom from moral and religious impulses, so that the numinous quality is entirely lacking. This 'villainous' generalization stands whatever qualifications apply in individual cases.

Richard, on the other hand, whilst lacking the moral fibre of Shakespeare's tragic heroes and good characters, is like them in the general tendencies of his nature. In morals he is an absolutist; he may do wrong things wilfully or irresponsibly but he does not confound right and wrong with sophistry and expediency. Being of an impractical, contemplative bent he is an easy prey of the worldly wise; the more so in that he is little skilled in the hypocritical arts essential in some degree to any worldly success. Imaginative, reflective, he soon loses grip of the actuality and demands of an immediate situation. He has a warm, impulsive nature though he faults in his over-indulgence of feeling. Above all things he has an open rather than a close personality. In thus characterizing Richard, I have sketched the essential common nature of Shakespeare's tragic heroes and good men—with the reservation that in Richard potential worth is vitiated by weakness. (pp. 113-14)

It is consistent with the closeness of Bolingbroke that he never soliloquizes in this play, while Richard lays bare his thoughts in soliloquy and quasi-soliloquy. And Bolingbroke's one soliloquy in the *Henry IV* plays, the apostrophe to sleep, merely confirms what one suspects of his troubled conscience; he does not admit the cause. Now, whether or not one is prepared to see Bolingbroke as a villain in his usurpation, it is certain that he is a schemer. As a schemer who does not soliloquize he stands alone among the villains and schemers of the early plays. One effect of such soliloquies, in which the audience is taken into the villain's confidence, is the creation of dramatic irony. Another effect is that the intrigue, however clever in fact, appears simple, even naïve; this impression envelopes the intriguer so that he appears transparent, a simple villain. Because he has allowed us to see into his mind we know its depth exactly. Richard III, for all his brilliance, is deep only to his enemies not to us.

We cannot chart Bolingbroke's mind. Its silent workings are never glimpsed in soliloquy and little is revealed in public for Bolingbroke never discusses his affairs with his associates. That Shakespeare should thus eschew soliloquy for a special portraiture is a particular instance of the general control of soliloquy in this play. *Richard II* is unusual in having only one soliloquy, for in the other early plays, and indeed in plays up to *Hamlet* at least, Shakespeare makes free with this handy convention. Apart from its obvious use in conveying to the audience secret thoughts and intentions, the soliloquy is also given choric, prophetic, thematic functions. In addition it is a simple means of conveying information about character and action; it may be effective for heightening suspense, as in the soliloquies of Juliet; it may be used as a comic setpiece; it may provide a shorthand method of relating changes of heart, as in *The Two Gentlemen of Verona*. Since the soliloquy is an accepted convention, one among others in Elizabethan drama, one cannot quarrel with Shakespeare's frequent resort to the convenience. Provided that it attunes us to the essentials of the action, or clears the way for their bold presentation, there is no cause for complaint. Nevertheless, with the exception of the soliloquies of Juliet, its various functions as detailed above may be described as dramatically convenient rather than as inevitable. They are functions which could be performed by other dramatic means, without recourse to soliloquy.

Now there is another kind of soliloquizing which is not talking to the audience but a kind of talking to oneself. And one normally talks to oneself alone. Hence such soliloquies may be called inevitable or 'natural'. (pp. 115-16)

The 'natural' soliloquy is ill-nourished in the *Henry VI* plays and in *Richard III* where a variety of surface excitement engages one's attention. *Richard II*, too, has its surface excitement of language and its public question of the ethics of kingship. None the less, it concentrates its action closely about the fall of a king, a man presented with sufficient inner life to engage interest in the agonizing pressures which attend his fall. Add to this his reflective nature, and the 'natural' soliloquy becomes inevitable; Shakespeare gives us the soliloquy in Pomfret castle.

However, if the dungeon soliloquy looks forward to *Hamlet* in its reflectiveness and release of inner pressures it betrays early composition in its obtrusive rhetoric. Zest for the artifices of language here imperils the successful communication of tragic experience. . . . [The] submission of the audience to tragic experience will only occur when the dramatist himself appears to be lost in that experience, and when the tragic character is lost in his tragic situation, to the exclusion of other interests. If the dramatist can sidetrack into self-conscious verbal display, if the tragic character can speculate upon his situation with calculated eloquence, then the audience senses an emotional failure, detachment, and remains detached also. It is significant that Shakespeare's early mannered style is more successful in comedy than in tragedy. (pp. 116-17)

As a piece of consciously beautiful writing to mark a climax of feeling [Richard's final] soliloquy is in accord with the manner of rhetorical tragedy. Functionally it is successful to the extent that it furthers the characterization of a man who is prone to self-dramatization, one who endeavours to elude the immediate experience by enclosing it in a cage of words. It fails, however, in tragic impact. It has the content of a tragic meditation, for Richard speaks of his past folly and present misery. But he does not make us feel them. The necessary urgency of language is smoothed away in the controlled patterns of statement. Richard has made such an intricate cage of words that we look at that instead of at the sorrow it encloses. Further, the surface control is such that Richard appears detached and with his detachment comes ours.

That Shakespeare intended us to remain detached from Richard in his last hour is unlikely. Richard's soliloquy was the opportunity for the soul-searchings of a tragic figure; it was also, unfortunately, the opportunity for a virtuoso set-piece of which an Elizabethan wit might be proud. And Shakespeare had his rhetoric ready at his tongue's end. (pp. 117-18)

In indicating the limitations of the decorative manner I am not suggesting that Shakespeare experienced . . . Richard as he experienced Hamlet and Lear, failing only in articulation because of his linguistic means. It is possible that over-excitement about means may have checked an early development of that inwardness of experience felt in the plays of Shakespeare's maturity; it is equally likely that attention to language for its own sake was itself symptomatic of a thinness of tragic experience. This much is certain. Where Shakespeare transmits intense feeling his means are not obtrusive. Not only are the means refined but, as Longinus has taught, passion validates the splendours of the elevated style. (p. 119)

In the early high style the language asked to be admired to a degree detrimental to the primary functions of meaning. As Shakespeare matured this balance of emphasis was not entirely reversed, for our wonder at the language of *Hamlet* is not restricted to a recognition of its justness as a plain vehicle of meaning. It is a very beautiful thing whose colours and mod-

ulations can excite admiration for their own sakes; wonder at the language remains part of the pleasure of Shakespeare's great tragedies. The difference is that as we experience these plays the wonder blends with the total apprehension of human nobility and degradation.

Although Shakespeare smiled at the much art and little matter of Polonius he had been similarly at fault in his early writing. A study of *Richard II* can find only a qualified achievement in the consciously artificial manner. The qualification vanishes as the rhetoric is transmuted in the process of a deepening experience of life. The eloquence of Hamlet's soliloquies is a schooling of the old copiousness, and their distinction reaches back to the figures of rhetoric. (pp. 120-21)

> R. F. Hill, ''Dramatic Techniques and Interpretation in 'Richard II','' in *Early Shakespeare, Edward Arnold (Publishers) Ltd.*, 1961, pp. 101-21.

PETER G. PHIALAS   (essay date 1963)

[*Phialas is a well-known editor and critic whose works include* Shakespeare's Romantic Comedies (1966) *and a number of articles on the histories. In the following excerpt, he examines the importance of* Richard II *to Shakespeare's development as a dramatist, observing that the play represents a departure from the medieval* de casibus *tradition upon which Shakespeare had previously relied, in that here the emphasis for the first time is on individual responsibility rather than fate. As part of this pattern of responsibility, Phialas stresses the king's eventual recognition of his own accountability, thus becoming one of the relatively few commentators who maintain that Richard does indeed grow to a new self-understanding by the end of his life.*]

A few years ago Professor Travis Bogard published an essay in which he proposed the theory that in writing *Richard II* Shakespeare ''first became himself'' and that therefore the play marked a turning point in his career as dramatist [see excerpt above, 1955]. It was Professor Bogard's notion that midway in the composition of that play Shakespeare discovered the need to project human suffering implicitly, in spare, nonrhetorical style, if he was to create great tragedy, that he employed such style in one or two passages, and that as the discovery was sudden and unprovided for, the result is a divided play and three or four Richards instead of one. I am concerned here chiefly with the view that *Richard II* takes an important step towards Shakespeare's tragic masterpieces, a view I share with Professor Bogard, although my reasons are quite different from his. My own conclusion is that what distinguishes the play from its predecessors and anticipates the later and greater tragedies is not the style of a few passages but the nature of the tragic process itself: *Richard II* is the first Shakespearean play which not only makes a transition from *de casibus* tragedy to one of individual responsibility but also records that transition in the development of the King's character. For the first time Shakespeare creates a hero who achieves what has been called tragic illumination, who experiences a demonstrable change in his attitude towards the cause and meaning of his tragedy. (p. 344)

It is probable that Shakespeare ''first became himself'' in the mid-1590's, the years of *Romeo and Juliet, A Midsummer Night's Dream,* and *Richard II,* three very different plays posing closely related problems of dramaturgy. It is fairly certain that in their composition Shakespeare made discoveries concerning dramatic modes which he was to follow throughout his career. For instance, what he could and could not do with love as a tragic theme he may have discovered in the writing of *Romeo and Juliet*. . . It may be true that Shakespeare was not altogether happy with his treatment of love in that play and that *A Midsummer Night's Dream* records, as many believe, a reaction to that treatment. But *A Midsummer Night's Dream* does more than that, for it initiates an important type of Shakespearean comedy. . . . Such plays as *The Merchant of Venice, As You Like It,* and *The Tempest* will follow its symbolic structure: lovers will be taken from the workaday world to an idealized one where love finds fruition, and after union of lovers and general reconciliation the characters are returned to their earlier world, now made better.

As *A Midsummer Night's Dream* is thus related to *Romeo and Juliet* on the side of theme, *Richard II* is related to it on the side of genre, for like *Romeo and Juliet, Richard II* is an experimental play treating a political theme in the tragic mode, but with greater success, at least in so far as an important aspect of later Shakespearean tragedy is concerned. In both plays the dramatist attempts the difficult problem of assigning relative functions to Fate and to individual responsibility, but in *Richard II* he succeeds for the first time in establishing a new and more complex relationship between the two tragic themes, and he furthermore dramatizes that relationship in the development of Richard's character. And this in part is precisely what Shakespeare went on to do in the later and greater tragedies. (pp. 346-47)

[Whatever] inevitability attaches to the tragic process in [*Romeo and Juliet*] is not explicitly related to the deliberate choices and actions of the lovers. Instead, the dramatist attempts to create the impression of impending doom by means of certain devices, such as the premonitions of the lovers, allusions to dreams, and compression of time. But the attempt is not altogether successful, for instead of demonstrating inevitability, it merely hints at a vague fear that trouble is in store for Romeo and Juliet. Their falling in love, however, need not precipitate their death; there are too many accidents, too much ill luck, far too much mistaking of purposes leading to the lovers' downfall. Their universe may be called tragic, but it is tragic in a limited sense; and that is the chief reason why the play fails to move in the manner of Shakespeare's later tragedies.

The difference in tragic effect between *Romeo and Juliet* and a later tragedy like *King Lear* is due not to the difference in their means of projecting suffering but in the quality of suffering itself. The suffering in *Romeo and Juliet*, as in all *de casibus* tragedy, is the sort occasioned by sudden and apparently undeserved loss, some accident or profound disappointment; and although such suffering may be called tragic, when dramatized alone it fails to produce and communicate that emotional experience which is the characteristic mark of Shakespeare's great tragedies. It is very different, for instance, from the suffering of Lear and Gloucester late in their play, the suffering which flows out of or accompanies their hard-won awareness that they are in great part responsible for their tragedy. But this awareness and the attendant suffering are achieved by a tragic process quite different from that of *Romeo and Juliet*. *Romeo and Juliet* is a *de casibus* tragedy; *King Lear* is a tragedy of retribution in which the *de casibus* motif is presented . . . in a special relationship to the more prominent theme of individual responsibility. (pp. 348-49)

At some point in his career Shakespeare discovered or accepted two very old and very simple but important features which must have seemed indispensable to him for the creation of great tragedy: first, the tragic hero must be in great part responsible for his suffering and death; and second, he must discover and

accept that responsibility before the play's end. The dramatist may have made the discovery during the writing of *Richard II;* or he may have done so earlier, but it is clear that if the discovery antedates *Romeo and Juliet* it is not reflected in that play. Instead, *Richard II* is not only a tragedy whose action proceeds wholly from character but also, and far more important, it is the first Shakespearean play in which the hero's attitude towards his tragic predicament changes significantly in the course of that action: from a *de casibus* concept of his fall Richard advances to full awareness and acceptance of his own moral involvement.

Early in the play Richard is warned by both York and Gaunt that if he continues his irresponsible governance he will most certainly lose the crown. When the king visits Ely House to bid a last farewell to the dying Gaunt, he is told by him that it is he, Richard, who is ill and about to die, that the whole island is his death-bed, and that if Edward III had foreseen Richard's evil reign,

> From forth thy reach he would have laid thy shame,
> Deposing thee before thou wert possess'd
> Which art possess'd now to depose thyself.
>
> [II. i. 106-08].

Later when the King seizes Bolingbroke's inheritance, York speaks of the same direct connection between the King's acts and his future deposition and death. . . . But to these warnings Richard pays no heed, believing that he is exempt from the obligations which bind him to his subjects, and placing himself outside the principle of inheritance to which he owes the crown. At this point in the play Richard is convinced that not only can there be no conflict between his acts and the divine power from which he derives the crown but that the very responsibility for those acts—the responsibility for the crown itself—rests with that power rather than with himself. And thus when upon his return from Ireland he is informed of Bolingbroke's advance against him, Richard most readily agrees with Carlisle's estimate of the royal position.

> . . . that power that made you king
> Hath power to keep you king in spite of all. . . .
>
> [III. ii. 27-8]

It is no wonder that later, when he reflects upon his fall, Richard sees it as unavoidable, as a change due to the operations of a power outside himself, as a necessary element in the scheme of things. Upon being told that the Welsh army has defected and that Bushy, Greene, and the Earl of Wiltshire are dead, he is convinced that his own death is imminent, for he believes that a King's crown carries within it the certainty of his fall and death:

> . . . for within the hollow crown
> That rounds the mortal temples of a king
> Keeps death his court and there the antic sits,
> Scoffing his state and grinning at his pomp,
> Allowing him a breath, a little scene,
> To monarchise, be fear'd and kill with looks,
> As if this flesh which walls about our life
> Were brass impregnable, and humor'd thus
> Comes at the last and with a little pin
> Bores through his castle wall, and farewell king! . . .
>
> [III. ii. 160-70]

[The] emphasis is upon death's absolute control of the events in the royal destiny. The lines clearly echo the so-called medieval view of tragedy. . . . It is a concept from which Richard at this point in the play excludes all personal responsibility; it is the *de casibus* notion of tragedy which informs *Romeo and Juliet* and is utilized in the early scenes of *King Lear*.

But before the play's end Shakespeare carries Richard beyond this commonplace concept by incorporating into the King's thoughts the overriding theme of personal folly and moral responsibility; and by so doing he takes a most significant step towards the great tragedies, for he is now able to introduce complexity not only into the thought of a play but also into the delineation of the chief characters. Without dismissing Bolingbroke's guilt, Richard gradually yields to the admission that he is no less culpable than his rival. And thus while he thinks of himself as another Christ betrayed by Pilates who have delivered him to his "sour cross," Richard simultaneously likens himself to Phaethon, like whom he falls "wanting the manage of unruly jades!" [IV. i. 241; III. iii. 179]. But he goes further still, for although he has been betrayed he knows that he has also betrayed himself:

> Mine eyes are full of tears, I cannot see,
> And yet salt water blinds them not so much
> But they can see a sort of traitors here.
> Nay, if I turn mine eyes upon myself,
> I find myself a traitor with the rest.
>
> [IV. i. 244-48]

Shortly before this passage Richard makes another equally significant admission. When Northumberland insists that the King read "these accusations and grievous crimes," Richard responds with the question:

> Must I do so? and must I ravel out
> My weav'd-up follies?
>
> [IV. i. 228-29]

In the famous "mirror" passage a few lines later he further admits his own folly but again without excusing Bolingbroke's guilt:

> Was this the face that fac'd so many follies
> And was at last outfac'd by Bolingbroke?
>
> [V. i. 285-86]

Finally Richard makes the fullest and clearest statement of his awareness in the soliloquy at Pomfret Castle. . . . [Here] the gradual change in Richard's attitude is complete; and the full recognition of his own moral responsibility is stated with particular force in the lines employing imagery which is suggested by the music played beneath the prison window:

> Music do I hear?
> Ha! ha! keep time—how sour sweet music is
> When time is broke and no proportion kept!
> So is it in the music of men's lives.
> And here have I the daintiness of ear
> To check time broke in a disordered string;
> But for the concord of my state and time,
> Had not an ear to hear my true time broke:
> I wasted time, and now time wastes me;
> For now hath time made me his numb'ring clock.
>
> [V. v. 41-50]

With this awareness Richard takes a step towards the tragic hero's partial rehabilitation which Shakespeare was to dramatize in the concluding episodes of the later tragedies. (pp. 349-54)

This gradual but sure movement towards awareness and acceptance by the tragic hero of his own moral involvement in

his tragedy becomes the pattern of action for the tragedies which follow, and, as we have seen, it is most clearly in evidence in *King Lear*, a play *Richard II* prefigures in many important aspects. *Richard II* is indeed a milepost in Shakespeare's progress towards the great tragedies of his later years; for in composing that play the dramatist attempted something new by making human causality the chief tragic force in the structure of the tragedy, and instead of dismissing the old *de casibus* theme of the earlier plays he worked it into the hero's initial notion of his tragic experience, a notion he slowly abandons as he advances to a new awareness of moral responsibility. This relationship of the two tragic themes appears with varying prominence in Shakespeare's later tragedies: in play after play the self-comforting thought that "As flies to wanton boys are we to the gods" [*King Lear*, IV. i. 36] is countered by the conviction that "the fault . . . is not in our stars but in ourselves" [*Julius Caesar*, I. ii. 140]. Beginning with Shakespeare's second Richard his tragic heroes ultimately see themselves as men more sinning than sinned against, and, as we have seen, the suffering which accompanies this awareness is of a different order from that of the heroes of the earlier tragedies. This is the special quality of *Richard II*, the feature which distinguishes it from *Romeo and Juliet* and anticipates the tragic masterpieces which followed. It is in this sense that in writing *Richard II* Shakespeare "first became himself." (pp. 354-55)

> *Peter G. Phialas, " 'Richard II' and Shakespeare's Tragic Mode," in* Texas Studies in Literature and Language, *Vol. V, No. 3, Autumn, 1963, pp. 344-55.*

JAN KOTT (essay date 1964)

[Kott is a Polish-born critic and professor of English and comparative literature now residing in the United States. In his well-known study Shakespeare, Our Contemporary, *originally published in Polish as* Szkice o Szekspirze *in 1964, he interprets several of the plays as presenting a tragic vision of history. Kott calls this historical pattern the Grand Mechanism. The influence of Marxist theory is clearly evident in Kott's interpretation of* Richard II. *Kott sees Shakespeare's tetralogies as the bloody chronicle of an endless, grim cycle of Edwards, Richards, and Henrys—an eternal, irrational struggle characterized by relentless violence and ultimate futility. The critic compares medieval English politics to a great staircase up which ambitious men ascend, dethroning those above them, only to plunge themselves into the abyss below as others take their place. Kott's contention that in Shakespeare's works history is never just enacted—it is itself a protagonist in tragedy—aroused opposition from both anti-Marxist scholars and from those who objected that Shakespeare is not as nihilistic as Kott supposes. Concerning* Richard II, *Kott argues that it is not only "a tragedy of dethronement," but a tragedy of the loss of "regal power" and the destruction of "the entire order of the universe."]*

Shakespeare is like the world, or life itself. Every historical period finds in him what it is looking for and what it wants to see. A reader or spectator in the mid-twentieth century interprets *Richard III* through his own experiences. He cannot do otherwise. . . . By discovering in Shakespeare's plays problems that are relevant to our own time, modern audiences often, unexpectedly, find themselves near to the Elizabethans; or at least are in the position to understand them well. This is particularly true of the Histories.

Shakespeare's History plays take their titles from the names of kings: *King John, King Richard II, Henry IV, Henry V, Henry VI, Richard III*. . . . They constitute an historical epic covering over a hundred years and divided into long chapters corresponding to reigns. But when we read these chapters chronologically, following the sequence of reigns, we are struck by the thought that for Shakespeare history stands still. Every chapter opens and closes at the same point. In every one of these plays history turns full circle, returning to the point of departure. These recurring and unchanging circles described by history are the successive kings' reigns.

Each of these great historical tragedies begins with a struggle for the throne, or for its consolidation. Each ends with the monarch's death and a new coronation. In each of the Histories the legitimate ruler drags behind him a long chain of crimes. He has rejected the feudal lords who helped him to reach for the crown; he murders, first, his enemies, then his former allies; he executes possible successors and pretenders to the crown. But he has not been able to execute them all. From banishment a young prince returns—the son, grandson, or brother of those murdered—to defend the violated law. The rejected lords gather round him, he personifies the hope for a new order and justice. But every step to power continues to be marked by murder, violence, treachery. And so, when the new prince finds himself near the throne, he drags behind him a chain of crimes as long as that of the until now legitimate ruler. When he assumes the crown, he will be just as hated as his predecessor. He has killed enemies, now he will kill former allies. And a new pretender appears in the name of violated justice. The wheel has turned full circle. A new chapter opens. A new historical tragedy. . . . (pp. 5-7)

This scheme of things is not, of course, marked with equally clear-cut outline in all Shakespeare's Histories. It is clearest in *King John* and in the two masterpieces of historical tragedy, *Richard II* and *Richard III*. It is least clear in *Henry V,* an idealized and patriotic play which depicts a struggle with an enemy from without. But in Shakespeare's plays the struggle for power is always stripped of all mythology, shown in its "pure state". It is a struggle for the crown, between people who have a name, a title and power.

In the Middle Ages the clearest image of wealth was a bag full of golden pieces. Each of them could be weighed in hand. For many centuries wealth meant fields, meadows and woods, flocks of sheep, a castle and villages. Later a ship loaded with pepper, or cloves, or big granaries filled with sacks of wheat, cellars full of wines, stores along the Thames emitting a sour smell of leather and the choking dust of cotton. Riches could be seen, handled and smelt. It was only later that they dematerialized, became a symbol, something abstract. Wealth ceased to be a concrete thing and became a slip of paper with writing on it. Those changes were described by Karl Marx in *Das Kapital*.

In a similar fashion power was dematerialized, or rather, disembodied. It ceased to have a name. It became something abstract and mythological, almost a pure idea. But for Shakespeare power has names, eyes, mouth and hands. It is a relentless struggle of living people who sit together at one table.

> For God's sake let us sit upon the ground
> And tell sad stories of the death of kings!
> How some have been depos'd, some slain in war,
> Some haunted by the ghosts they have depos'd,
> Some poisoned by their wives, some sleeping kill'd—
> All murthered; . . .
>
> [III. iii. 155-60]

For Shakespeare the crown is the image of power. It is heavy. It can be handled, torn off a dying king's head, and put on

one's own. Then one becomes a king. Only then. But one must wait till the king is dead, or else precipitate his death. (pp. 8-9)

In each of the Histories there are four or five men who look into the eyes of the dying monarch, watch his trembling hands. They have already laid a plot, brought their loyal troops to the capital, communicated with their vassals. They have given orders to hired assassins; the stony Tower awaits new prisoners. There are four or five men, but only one of them may remain alive. Each of them has a different name and title. Each has a different face. One is cunning, another brave; the third is cruel, the fourth—a cynic. They are living people, for Shakespeare was a great writer. We remember their faces. But when we finish reading one chapter and begin to read the next one, when we read the Histories in their entirety, the faces of kings and usurpers become blurred, one after the other.

Even their names are the same. There is always a Richard, an Edward and a Henry. They have the same titles. There is a Duke of York, a Prince of Wales, a Duke of Clarence. In the different plays different people are brave, or cruel, or cunning. But the drama that is being played out between them is always the same (p. 9)

Emanating from the features of individual kings and usurpers in Shakespeare's History plays, there gradually emerges the image of history itself. The image of the Grand Mechanism. Every successive chapter, every great Shakespearean act is merely a repetition:

> The flattering index of a direful pageant,
> One heav'd a-high to be hurl'd down below, . . .
>
> [*Richard III*, IV. iv. 85-6]

It is this image of history, repeated many times by Shakespeare, that forces itself on us in a most powerful manner. Feudal history is like a great staircase on which there treads a constant procession of kings. Every step upwards is marked by murder, perfidy, treachery. Every step brings the throne nearer. Another step and the crown will fall. One will soon be able to snatch it.

> . . . That is a step
> On which I must fall down, or else o'erleap, . . .
>
> [*Macbeth*, I. iv. 48-9]

From the highest step there is only a leap into the abyss. The monarchs change. But all of them—good and bad, brave and cowardly, vile and noble, naive and cynical—tread on the steps that are always the same. (pp. 10-11)

Let us begin by tracing the working of the Grand Mechanism as Shakespeare shows it in his theatre. On the proscenium two armies fight each other. The tiny inner stage is turned into the House of Commons, or the King's chamber. On the balcony the King appears, surrounded by bishops. Trumpets are blown: the proscenium is now the Tower courtyard where the imprisoned princes are being led under guard. The inner stage has been turned into a cell. The successor to the throne cannot sleep, tormented by thoughts of violence. Now the door opens, and hired assassins enter with daggers in their hands. A moment later the proscenium is a London street at night: frightened townsmen hurry past talking politics. Trumpets again: the new monarch has made his appearance on the balcony.

Let us begin with the great abdication scene in *Richard II*, the scene omitted in all editions published in Queen Elizabeth's lifetime. It revealed the working of the Grand Mechanism too brutally: the very moment when power was changing hands.

Act V. Scene i. Northumberland, Richard II, the Queen, soldiers, and attendants. By J. McL. Ralston.
The Department of Rare Books and Special Collections, The University of Michigan Library.

Authority comes either from God, or from the people. A flash of the sword, the tramping of the guards; applause of intimidated noblemen; a shout from the forcibly gathered crowd; and behold: the new authority, too, comes from God, or from the will of the people.

Henry Bolingbroke, late King Henry IV, has returned from exile, landed with an army and captured Richard II, deserted by his vassals. The coup d'état has been accomplished. It has yet to be legalized. The former King still lives.

> Fetch hither Richard, that in common view
> He may surrender. So we shall proceed
>   Without suspicion.
>
> [IV. i. 155-57]

Richard enters under guard, deprived of his royal robes. Following him are noblemen carrying royal insignia. The scene takes place in the House of Lords. The proscenium represents Westminster Hall, which has been reconstructed by Richard and given its famous oak ceiling. He has been brought beneath it only once, in order to abdicate.

Says the King, deprived of his crown:

> Alack, why am I sent for to a king
> Before I have shook off the regal thoughts
> Wherewith I reign'd? I hardly yet have learn'd
> To insinuate, flatter, bow, and bend my limbs.

> Give sorrow leave awhile to tutor me
> To this submission. Yet I well remember
> The favours of these men. Were they not mine?
> Did they not sometime cry 'All hail!' to me?
>
> [IV. i. 162-69]

But he is not allowed to speak for long. He is handed the crown to hold it for a moment and give it to Henry. Give it of his own free will. He has already renounced his power, rents and revenues. He has cancelled his decrees and statutes. What else can they want of him? ''What more remains?'' Shakespeare knew:

> . . . No more, but that you read
> These accusations and these grievous crimes
> Committed by your person and your followers
> Against the state and profit of this land,
> That, by confessing them, the souls of men
> May deem that you are worthily depos'd.
>
> [IV. i. 222-27]

Says the King, deprived of his crown:

> Must I do so? and must I ravel out
> My weav'd-up folly? Gentle Northumberland,
> If thy offences were upon record,

Would it not shame thee in so fair a troop
To read a lecture of them?

[IV. i. 228-32]

But again he is not allowed to speak for long. The act of dethronement has to be completed quickly and absolutely. The King's royal majesty must be extinguished. The new King is waiting. If the former King is not a traitor, then the new one is a usurper. One can well understand Queen Elizabeth's censors:

NORTHUMBERLAND

My lord, dispatch. Read o'er these articles.

KING RICHARD

Mine eyes are full of tears; I cannot see.
And yet salt water blinds them not so much
But they can see a sort of traitors here.
Nay, if I turn mine eyes upon myself,
I find myself a traitor with the rest;
For I have given here my soul's consent
To undeck the pompous body of a king; . . .

[IV. i. 243-50]

When dramatizing history, Shakespeare first and foremost condenses it. For history itself is more dramatic than the particular dramas of John, the Henrys and the Richards. The greatest drama consists in the working of the Grand Mechanism. Shakespeare can contain years in a month, months in a day, in one great scene, in three or four speeches which comprise the very essence of history.

Here is the grand finale of any dethronement:

KING RICHARD

Then give me leave to go.

BOLINGBROKE

Whither?

KING RICHARD

Whither you will, so I were from your sights.

BOLINGBROKE

Go some of you, convey him to the Tower. . . .
On Wednesday next we solemnly set down
Our coronation. Lords, prepare yourselves.

[IV. i. 313-16, 319-20]

It is nearly the end. There is just one more act to come. The last one. But this act will at the same time be the first act of a new tragedy. It will have a new title, of course: *Henry IV*. In *Richard II* Bolingbroke was a "positive hero"; an avenger. He defended violated law and justice. But in his own tragedy he can only play the part of Richard II. The cycle has been completed. The cycle is beginning again. Bolingbroke has mounted half way up the grand staircase of history. He has been crowned; he is reigning. Dressed in the royal robes, he is awaiting the dignitaries of the realm at Windsor Castle. They duly arrive.

NORTHUMBERLAND

First, to thy sacred state wish I all happiness.
The next news is, I have to London sent
The heads of Oxford, Salisbury, Blunt, and Kent. . . .

BOLINGBROKE

We thank thee, gentle Percy, for thy pains
And to thy worth will add right worthy gains.
(*Enter* FITZWATER)

FITZWATER

My lord, I have from Oxford sent to London
The heads of Brocas and Sir Bennet Seely,
Two of the dangerous consorted traitors
That sought at Oxford thy dire overthrow.

BOLINGBROKE

Thy pains, Fitzwater, shall not be forgot.
Right noble is thy merit, well I wot.

[V. vi. 6-8, 11-18]

The most terrifying thing about this scene is its natural matter-of-factness. As if nothing has happened. As if everything went according to the natural order of things. A new reign has begun: six heads are being sent to the capital for the new King. But Shakespeare cannot end a tragedy in this way. A shock is needed. The working of the Grand Mechanism has to be highlighted by a flash of awareness. Just one; but it is a flash of genius. The new King is waiting for one more head; the most important one. He has commanded his most trusted follower to commit the murder. Commanded—this is too simple a word. Kings do not order assassination; they only allow it, in such a way that they shall not know about it themselves. But let us go back to Shakespeare's own words. For this is one of those great scenes that history will repeat; scenes that have been written once and for all. There is everything in them: the mechanism of the human heart, and the mechanism of power; there is fear, flattery, and "the system." In this scene the King does not take part, and no name is mentioned. There are only the King's words, and their double echo. This is one of the scenes in which Shakespeare is truer to life than life itself.

EXTON

Didst thou not mark the King, what words he spake?
'Have I no friend will rid me of this living fear?'
Was it not so?

SERVANT

These were his very words.

EXTON

'Have I no friend?' quoth he. He spake it twice
And urg'd it twice together, did he not?

SERVANT

He did.

[V. iv. 1-6]

And now, in the very last scene of *Richard II*, this most faithful of loyal subjects enters, with servants carrying a coffin:

Great King, within this coffin I present
Thy buried fear. Herein all breathless lies
The mightiest of thy greatest enemies,
Richard of Bordeaux, by me hither brought.

[V. vi. 30-3]

It is now that a flash of genius manifests itself. Let us omit the King's reply: it is pedestrian. He will banish Exton, order a state funeral for Richard with himself as the chief mourner. All this is still within the bounds of the Grand Mechanism, described drily, as in a medieval chronicle. But the King lets slip a sentence that foreshadows the problems of *Hamlet*. And, indeed, *Hamlet* must only be interpreted in the light of the two *Richard* plays. This sentence expresses a sudden fear of the world and its cruel mechanism, from which there is no escape, but which one cannot accept. For there are no bad kings, or good kings; kings are only kings. Or let us put it in modern terms: there is only the king's situation, and the system. This situation leaves no room for freedom of choice. At the end of the tragedy the King speaks a sentence that might be spoken by Hamlet:

> They love not poison that do poison need, . . .
>
> > [V. vi. 38]

In Shakespeare's world there is a contradiction between the order of action and the moral order. This contradiction is human fate. One cannot get away from it. (pp. 11-17)

[But what] world did Shakespeare write about, what times did he want to depict? Was it the world of feudal barons, slaughtering one another in the middle of the fifteenth century, or perhaps the world of the reign of the good, wise and devout Queen Elizabeth? That same Elizabeth who cut off Mary Stuart's head when Shakespeare was twenty-three years old, and sent to the scaffold some fifteen hundred Englishmen, among them her own lovers, ministers of the realm, doctors of theology and doctors of law, generals, bishops, great judges. . . . Or did Shakespeare consider history to be one continuous chain of violence, an unending stormy week, with the sun only very infrequently breaking through the thick clouds at noon, with an occasional quiet, peaceful morning, or a calm evening when lovers embrace and go to sleep under the trees of a Forest of Arden? (p. 30)

[What] fact the Grand Mechanism mean for Shakespeare? A succession of kings climbing and pushing one another off the grand staircase of history, or a wave of hot blood rising up to one's head and blinding the eyes? A natural order that has been violated, so that evil produces evil, every injury calls for revenge, every crime causes another? Or a cruel social order in which the vassals and superiors are in conflict with each other, the kingdom is ruled like a farm and falls prey to the strongest? A naked struggle for power, or a violent beat of the human heart that reason cannot accelerate or stop, but a dead piece of sharp iron breaks once and for all? A dense and impenetrable night of history where dawn does not break, or a darkness that fills the human soul? (pp. 30-1)

History in the theatre is mostly just a grand setting; a background against which the characters love, suffer, or hate; experience their personal dramas. Sometimes they are involved in history, which complicates their lives, but even then does not cease to be a more or less uncomfortable costume: a wig, a crinoline, a sword knocking about their feet. Of course, such plays are only superficially historical. But there are plays in which history is not just a background or a setting, in which it is played, or rather repeated on the stage, by actors disguised as historical personalities. They know history, have learned it by heart, and do not often go wrong. Schiller was a classic author of this kind of historical drama. Marx used to call his characters speaking trumpets of modern ideas. They interpret history because they know the solutions it offers. They can even sometimes express real trends and conflicts of social forces. But even this does not mean that the dramatization of history has been effected. It is only a historical textbook that has been dramatized. The textbook can be idealistic, as in Schiller and

Romain Rolland, or materialistic, as in some dramas of Büchner and Brecht; but it does not cease to be a textbook.

Shakespeare's concept of history is of a different kind from the two mentioned above. History unfolds on the stage, but is never merely enacted. It is not a background or a setting. It is itself the protagonist of tragedy. But what tragedy?

There are two fundamental types of historical tragedy. The first is based on the conviction that history has a meaning, fulfils its objective tasks and leads in a definite direction. It is rational, or at least can be made intelligible. Tragedy consists here in the price of history, the price of progress that has to be paid by humanity. A precursor, one who pushes forward the relentless roller of history, but must himself be crushed by it for the very reason of his coming ahead of his time, is also tragic. This is the concept of historical tragedy proclaimed by Hegel. It was near to the views of the young Marx, even though he substituted the objective development of ideas. He compared history to a mole who unceasingly digs in the earth.

> Well said, old mole! Canst work i' th' earth so fast?
> A worthy pioneer!
>
> > [*Hamlet*, I. v. 162-63]

A mole lacks awareness, but digs in a definite direction. It has its dreams but they only dimly express its feeling for the sun and sky. It is not the dreams that set the direction of its march, but the movement of its claws and snout, constantly digging up the earth. A mole will be tragic if it happens to be buried by the earth before it emerges to the surface.

There is another kind of historical tragedy, originating in the conviction that history has no meaning and stands still, or constantly repeats its cruel cycle; that it is an elemental force, like hail, storm, or hurricane, birth and death. A mole digs in the earth but will never come to its surface. New generations of moles are being born all the time, scatter the earth in all directions, but are themselves constantly buried by the earth. A mole has its dreams. For a long time it fancied itself the lord of creation, thinking that earth, sky and stars had been created for moles, that there is a mole's God, who had made moles and promised them a mole-like immortality. But suddenly the mole has realized that it is just a mole, that the earth, sky and stars had not been created for it. A mole suffers, feels and thinks, but its sufferings, feelings and thoughts cannot alter its mole's fate. It will go on digging in the earth, and the earth will go on burying it. It is at this point that the mole has realized that it is a tragic mole.

It seems to me that the latter concept of historical tragedy was nearer to Shakespeare, not only in the period when he was writing *Hamlet* and *King Lear*, but in all his writings, from the early Histories up to the *Tempest*.

> > > . . . for within the hollow crown
> That rounds the mortal temples of a king
> Keeps Death his court; and there the antic sits,
> Scoffing his state, and grinning at his pomp;
> Allowing him a breath, a little scene,
> To monarchize, be fear'd, and kill with looks;
> > . . . and humour'd thus,
> Comes at the last, and with a little pin
> Bores through his castle wall, and farewell king!
>
> > [III. ii. 160-65, 168-70]
> >
> > (pp. 35-7)

The names of the kings may change, but it is always a Henry who pushes a Richard down, or the other way round. Shakespeare's Histories are *dramatis personae* of the Grand Mechanism. But what is this Grand Mechanism which starts operating at the foot of the throne and to which the whole kingdom is subjected? A mechanism whose cogs are both great lords and hired assassins; a mechanism which forces people to violence, cruelty and treason; which constantly claims new victims? A mechanism according to whose laws the road to power is at the same time the way to death? This Grand Mechanism is for Shakespeare the order of history, in which the king is the Lord's Anointed.

> Not all the water in the rough rude sea
> Can wash the balm off from an anointed king.
> The breath of worldly men cannot depose
> The deputy elected by the Lord.
>
> [III. ii. 54-7]

The sun circles round the earth, and with it the spheres, planets and stars, all arranged in a hierarchic order. There is in the universe an order of the elements, an order of angelic choirs, and a corresponding order of rank on earth. There are superiors and vassals of the vassals. Royal power comes from God, and all power on earth is merely a reflection of the power wielded by the King. (p. 38)

Richard II is a tragedy of dethronement. It is, however, not just Richard's dethronement, but that of the King. Dethronement, in fact, of the idea of regal power. . . . In *Richard II*, the Lord's Anointed, the King deprived of his crown, becomes a mere mortal. In the first acts of the tragedy the King was compared to the sun: others had to lower their eyes when faced with his dazzling Majesty. Now the sun has been hurled down from its orbit, and with it the entire order of the universe.

> . . . what can we bequeath,
> Save our deposed bodies to the ground?
> Our lands, our lives, and all are Bolingbroke's,
> And nothing can we call our own but death
> And that small model of the barren earth
> Which serves as paste and cover to our bones.
> . . . Throw away respect,
> Tradition, form, and ceremonious duty;
> For you have but mistook me all this while.
> I live with bread like you, feel want, taste grief,
> Need friends. Subjected thus,
> How can you say to me I am a king?
>
> [III. ii. 149-54, 172-77]

"E pur si muove!" [Galileo] These words can be read with different intonations. "And still it moves . . ." There is also a bitter sort of laughter in those words. There is no heaven and hell, no order of the spheres. The earth moves round the sun, and the history of the Renaissance is just a grand staircase, from the top of which ever new kings fall into the abyss. There exists only the Grand Mechanism. But the Grand Mechanism is not just cruel. There is another side to it: it is a tragic farce. (pp. 39-40)

Richard II is a tragedy of knowledge gained through experience. Just before being hurled into the abyss, the deposed King reaches the greatness of Lear. For *King Lear*, like *Hamlet*, is also a tragedy of man contemporary with Shakespeare; a political tragedy of Renaissance humanism. A tragedy of the world stripped of illusions. Slowly, step by step, King Lear walks down the grand staircase, to learn the whole cruelty of the world over which he had once ruled, but which he did not know; and to drain the bitter cup to the dregs. Richard II is brutally and suddenly pushed into the abyss. But with him will

founder the structure of the feudal world. It is not only Richard who has been deposed. It is the sun that has ceased to move round the earth.

> Give me the glass, and therein will I read.
> No deeper wrinkles yet? Hath sorrow struck
> So many blows upon this face of mine
> And made no deeper wounds? O flattering glass,
> Like to my followers in prosperity,
> Thou dost beguile me! Was this face the face
> That every day under his household roof
> Did keep ten thousand men? Was this the face
> That like the sun did make beholders wink?
> Was this the face that fac'd so many follies
> And was at last outfac'd by Bolingbroke?
> A brittle glory shineth in this face.
> As brittle as the glory is the face,
>   *(Dashes the glass to the floor.)*
> For there it is, crack'd in a hundred shivers.
> Mark, silent king, the moral of this sport, . . .
>
> [IV. i. 276-90]
> (pp. 40-1)

There is no tragedy of history without awareness. Tragedy begins at the point when the king becomes aware of the working of the Grand Mechanism. This can happen when he falls victim to it, or when he acts as executioner. These are the points at which Shakespeare carries out his great confrontations, contrasting the moral order with the order of history. (p. 41)

In *Richard II* Shakespeare deposed not only the king, but the idea of kingly power. . . . After the great abdication scene Richard II calls for a mirror, and when he finds his face unchanged, breaks it. The King has become a man, the crown has been torn off the head of the Lord's Anointed. But the world has not been shaken in its foundations, and nothing has changed, not even his own face. So the crown was no more than sham. (p. 47)

Shakespeare views the implacable mechanism without medieval awe, and without the illusions of the early Renaissance. The sun does not circle round the earth, there is no order of the spheres, or of nature. The king is no Lord's Anointed, and politics is only an art aiming at capturing and securing power. The world offers a spectacle similar to a storm or hurricane. Weak bushes are bowed down to the earth, while tall trees fall uprooted. The order of history and the order of nature are both cruel; terrifying are the passions that breed in the human heart. (pp. 47-8)

> *Jan Kott, "The Kings," in his* Shakespeare, Our
> Contemporary, *translated by Boleslaw Taborski, new*
> *edition, Anchor Books, 1966, pp. 3-55.*

A. L. FRENCH (essay date 1967)

[In the following excerpt, A. L. French discusses what he calls a "blur" in Richard II—*that is, a confusion over whether the king is compelled to renounce the crown, or if he in fact initiates his own abdication. French contends that although many scholars suppose that Bolingbroke usurped the throne by force, such an interpretation is not justified by the text of the play. After pointing out a number of passages which clearly indicate that Bolingbroke neither overtly discusses nor solicits support for a* coup d'etat—*at least before Act IV, Scene i—French postulates that Shakespeare "started to write about a Richard who abdicated rather than being deposed," but then changed his dramatic strategy and attempted, unconvincingly, to generate a sympathetic response to*

the unhappy king, making Bolingbroke usurp his crown. The result, according to French, is that Richard II *"suffers from . . . double vision," beginning with a king who, for reasons that remain unclear, masochistically invites Bolingbroke to topple him, and ending with an approach more congenial to Tudor orthodoxy. The critic also argues that any interpretation of the tetralogy as a whole which assumes that Richard was deposed unwillingly should be reevaluated in light of this discovery.*]

A couple of years ago I saw a competent amateur performance of *Richard II*. As it happened I had not read the play for some time, and I naturally approached it with certain assumptions in mind—assumptions derived ultimately, no doubt, from scholars such as Tillyard [see excerpt above, 1944]. But as I watched, I first felt puzzled, then irritated, and finally astonished. The play was not making sense in the only way in which (I had thought) it *could* make sense; nor did it seem to be making sense in any other way. Afterwards I re-read the piece, to see where I or the actors had been stupid; but to my further surprise I found that the puzzlement I had felt was quite justified. The blur was not in the performance and not in my mind, but in Shakespeare's play. The present article is an attempt to describe this blur.

The assumptions we take to *Richard II* are, I have said, derived from Tillyard and others. The most important one is that Richard was deposed by Henry Bolingbroke, who by his action involved England in a century of unrest and civil war which was only brought to an end at last by Henry VII. This is in fact the interpretation not only of *Richard II* but also of the eight main Histories that Tillyard proposed over twenty years ago; and it has dominated scholars' and critics' thinking ever since. (p. 411)

Now, there is no particular reason why this account of Histories should be wrong: if Tillyard found it in Edward Hall's Chronicle, Shakespeare could have found it there too; and since it is a nice neat account, he may well have made use of it. Indeed, in History plays apart from *Richard II*, Shakespeare more than once refers to Richard's deposition. In *2 Henry VI*, for example, Richard Duke of York tries to convince Salisbury and Warwick of his title to the throne, and in the course of his argument refers to Richard II

> Who, after Edward the Third's death, reigned as king
> Till Henry Bolingbroke, Duke of Lancaster,
> The eldest son and heir of John of Gaunt,
> Crowned by the name of Henry the Fourth,
> Seized on the realm, deposed the rightful king,
> Sent his poor queen to France, from whence she came,
> And him to Pomfret, where as all you know,
> Harmless Richard was murdered traitorously.
>
> [*2 Henry VI*, II. ii. 20-7]

Here it is assumed as a fact that Richard was deposed; though whether it is as *important* an assumption as E.M.W. Tillyard made out is another question entirely. The Henry VI plays were written before *Richard II;* but in *1 Henry IV,* written after it, the charge that Richard was 'deposed' is repeated—by the very Northumberland who, in *Richard II,* helped to procure the crown for Bolingbroke. He talks of the time when

> the unhappy King—
> Whose wrongs in us God pardon!—did set forth
> Upon his Irish expedition;
> From whence he intercepted did return
> To be deposed, and shortly murdered.
>
> [*1 Henry IV*, I. iii. 148-52]

And in *Richard II* itself, Richard makes the same accusation. When in the 'deposition scene' Northumberland tries to make him sign a confession of his 'grievous crimes' Richard retorts that if Northumberland's own crimes were 'upon record', he would

> find one heinous article,
> Containing the deposing of a king.
>
> [IV. i. 233-34]

When Richard bids farewell to his queen, he asks her to 'tell the lamentable tale of me', the result of which will be that

> some will mourn in ashes, some coal-black,
> For the deposing of a rightful king.
>
> [V. i. 49-50]

Nevertheless, the assumption that, in *Richard II,* the King is deposed by Henry Bolingbroke is, in my view, not wholly borne out by the text of the play. You may ask: if that is the case, how comes it that almost everyone takes away from the piece the impression that this is what in fact happens? The answer to this question will (I hope) emerge from my critical scrutiny of the text; and we shall be led right into the imaginative blur in the play—a blur that seems to me far more crucial than the oddities which commonly worry critics (e.g. Woodstock's murder, or Richard's blanks and benevolences). The business of the deposition is of course connected with the puzzle about Bolingbroke's motivation: so I shall discuss both issues, and shall proceed more or less chronologically.

Our difficulties begin towards the end of II. i. After Richard has departed for Ireland, Northumberland, Ross and Willoughby are left by themselves, and begin a diatribe against Richard's rule (he has just confiscated Gaunt's estates). England is going to the dogs, and they wonder what they can do to save her. Total wreck is unavoidable, says Ross. Not so, says Northumberland, arrestingly if obscurely—

> Not so, even through the hollow eyes of death
> I spy life peering; but I dare not say
> How near the tidings of our comfort is.
>
> [II. i. 270-72]

Ross and Willoughby understandably ask what he means, and he replies that he has just heard that Bolingbroke and many others have set sail from Brittany and mean to land in the north. He goes on:

> If then we shall shake off our slavish yoke,
> Imp out our drooping country's broken wing,
> Redeem from broking pawn the blemished crown,
> Wipe off the dust that hides our sceptre's gilt,
> And make high majesty look like itself,
> Away with me in post to Ravenspurgh.
>
> [II. i. 291-96]

Asked to comment on the kind of metaphors we find here, we would probably say, disparagingly, that they are simple, conventional, emblematic—typical, in short, of the young Shakespeare and the early 1590s. True enough, as long as we add that, in the given context, the metaphors are very obscure indeed. The phrase 'shake *off* our slavish yoke' suggests getting rid of the king, but it is not clear whether 'imp out' means '*engraft* new feathers' (i.e. strengthen England by removing the people who are misleading Richard), or 'engraft *new* feathers' (i.e. substitute someone else for Richard). The same sort of difficulty arises over 'redeem' and 'wipe off'—nor are we sure in the latter case whether the gilt/guilt pun is a hit at

Richard's (? assumed) complicity in Woodstock's murder. The penultimate line could mean either that they must make Richard 'look' more kingly, or else that they must put another, more kingly, monarch in his place. Northumberland, in fact, is talking in riddles so far as the audience is concerned, though his fellow lords seem to be quite satisfied with his meaning. We do not know whether he means to seat Bolingbroke on the throne, or whether he only wants to use him to force Richard to reform—and, as a matter of historical fact (which Shakespeare could have found in Holinshed) Richard had been restrained in this way before, by the so-called 'appellants' between 1387 and 1389.

The difficulties continue in the next scene, which brings the news of Bolingbroke's arrival and the desertion of the people to him. At [II. ii. 40] Greene comes in and tells the Queen, Bushy and Bagot what has happened; he refers to Bolingbroke as an 'enemy', says he comes 'with uplifted arms', and reveals that many powerful lords have 'fled to him'. When York enters [II. ii. 72] he says that Bolingbroke and his followers have come to make Richard 'lose at home' [II. ii. 81], repeats that many nobles have deserted, and adds that 'the commons [are] cold' [II. ii. 88] and may revolt. At [II. ii. 104] he is wondering how he can get 'money for these wars', and a moment later asks the favourites to go and muster men. Thus the impression we have at this point is that Bolingbroke has come back to get, by force of arms if need be, something—but what? The favourites, too, towards the end of the scene . . . , are full of foreboding, and clearly expect a conflict; but at no juncture do we gather *what* they think Bolingbroke is after.

The opening of the next scene looks as though it might be going to give us an answer, but our expectations are raised only to be disappointed. We see Bolingbroke come in with Northumberland, and we probably expect—reasonably enough—that their words will reveal something of their plans and intentions. Not a bit of it: they pass the first few moments of the scene in mutual compliment, Northumberland spending seventeen lines congratulating Bolingbroke on the excellence of his conversation. We never learn what this 'fair discourse' was about. Vital information is withheld in a way that seems capricious; and as a result when Bolingbroke and Northumberland confront Richard in the third Act, we remain ignorant whether they have concerted their plans, or even whether they have any plans. It is curious that, if Shakespeare was the Tudor propagandist he is alleged to be, he should have missed this very easy opportunity of showing his Tudor audience how wicked Bolingbroke was. It is odder still that, as a competent dramatist, he should have missed his chance to suggest at least *something* about the working of Bolingbroke's mind.

At [II. iii. 70] Bolingbroke says for the first time why he has come back: when Berkeley addresses him as 'My Lord of Hereford', he retorts that his name is Lancaster,

And I am come to seek that name in England.
[II. iii. 71]

This is his story, and he sticks to it with dogged pertinacity right up to the point in Act IV where, *after* York has told him that Richard has adopted him heir 'with willing soul', he exclaims 'In God's name, I'll ascend the regal throne' [IV. i. 113]. At no point before this does Bolingbroke give the least hint that he is aiming at the crown. We may conjecture that this was what was 'really' in his mind all along, but that is a kind of guesswork irrelevant to the highly conventional art of which Shakespeare was a master; such speculations would

probably never have crossed an Elizabethan's mind. But the fact that in *Richard II,* forewarned though we are, some such questions do persistently occur to us, suggests that Shakespeare may be misusing his conventions rather than using them. (pp. 412-16)

I pass now to the first of the three crucial scenes which bring together my two themes—Bolingbroke's motives and the nature of Richard's fall. The scenes are III. ii, III. iii and IV. i.

Returning from Ireland, where he has heard from Bagot of Bolingbroke's expedition, Richard talks about 'rebels', 'treacherous feet', 'usurping steps' and 'foul rebellion' [III. ii. 4ff.], referring to Bolingbroke as the 'sovereign's foe'. In his second long speech [III. ii. 36-63] he says that when the sun is hidden

Then thieves and robbers range abroad unseen
In murthers and in outrage boldly here,
[III. ii. 39-40]

but when the sun comes out,

Then murthers, treasons, and detested sins . . .
Stand bare and naked, trembling at themselves.
[III. ii. 44, 46]

He goes on to identify Bolingbroke as 'this thief, this traitor'. It is not clear at first how far we are meant to identify the emblematic robbers and murderers with Bolingbroke; but the last phrase clinches the matter. Richard is suggesting—the first time anyone definitely does so—that Bolingbroke is after the crown. This interpretation of his admittedly oblique words is confirmed by his explicit use, a few lines later, of the verb 'depose':

The breath of worldly men cannot depose
The deputy elected by the Lord.
[III. ii. 56-7]

The idea has now entered his head, and we note that it has done so *before* he hears the disastrous tidings brought by Salisbury and Scroope—that is, he does not yet know that his own forces are weak. When he learns that the Welshmen have dispersed, he asks 'is my kingdom lost?' [III. ii. 95] and, a moment later, 'strives Bolingbroke to be as great as we?' [III. ii. 97]. In the long speech provoked by the news of the favourites' death, he says:

Let's choose executors and talk of wills.
And yet not so—for what can we bequeath
Save our deposéd bodies to the ground?
[III. ii. 148-50]

This use of 'deposed' . . . links up with the 'sad stories of the death of kings', because some kings 'have been deposed' [III. ii. 156-57]. By the end of the scene Richard has convinced himself that he is about to be supplanted by Bolingbroke. He goes so far as to discharge his remaining followers, and with these words:

let them hence away,
From Richard's night, to Bolingbroke's fair day.
[III. ii. 217-18]

Thus, so far as the audience are concerned, it is Richard himself who first expresses the idea that his crown is at stake. (pp. 418-19)

[There] is little evidence to suggest that the Bolingbroke faction have ever given a thought to deposing Richard: Shakespeare puts all the talk about deposition into Richard's own mouth. Indeed, it would not be fantastic to wonder whether Shakespeare did not intend us to see Richard as suggesting the idea to Bolingbroke. At all events, that is a more tenable theory than that Bolingbroke forces it on Richard.

When the King finally meets his cousin face to face, it is still Richard who keeps harping on the crown. Bolingbroke kneels to him, but Richard, pointing to his crown, says

> Up, cousin, up; your heart is up, I know,
> Thus high at least, although your knee be low.
>
> [III. iii. 194-95]

He twists Bolingbroke's protestation that 'I come but for mine own', retorting 'Your own is yours, and I am yours, and all' [III. iii. 196-97]. Bolingbroke again protests:

> So far be mine, my most redoubted lord,
> As my true service shall deserve your love,
>
> [III. iii. 198-99]

and again Richard plays on the words:

> Well you deserve. They well deserve to have
> That know the strong'st and surest way to get.
>
> [III. iii. 200-01]

Finally Richard acknowledges, or half-acknowledges, Bolingbroke as his 'heir', and adds

> What you will have, I'll give, and willing too,
> For do we must what force will have us do.
>
> [III. iii. 206-07]

He has capitulated; capitulated not to force (as he says) nor to persuasion, not to York or Northumberland or Bolingbroke, but to himself. No 'force' is necessary. This is not the case in Holinshed, where Northumberland, solemnly promising Richard safe-conduct, ambushes him and takes him prisoner.... For Shakespeare's Richard the mere *show* of force, mounted (so far as the audience know) to gain a strictly limited objective, is more than enough. Thus he has precisely fulfilled the prophecy made by the dying John of Gaunt:

> O, had thy grandsire with a prophet's eye
> Seen how his son's son should destroy his sons,
> From forth thy reach he would have laid thy shame,
> Deposing thee before thou wert possessed,
> Which art possessed now *to depose thyself.*
>
> [II. i. 104-08]

Richard has done just that: at no-one's prompting but his own, he has deposed himself.

The reason why people have accepted without question the view that Richard was deposed by Bolingbroke is, perhaps, that it is Richard's own view.... [His] view of himself is the one which, elsewhere, Shakespeare apparently accepts. Moreover in *2 Henry IV,* Henry—the former Bolingbroke—says to his son:

> God knows, my son,
> By what by-paths and indirect crook'd ways
> I met this crown....
>
> [*2 Henry IV,* IV. v. 183-85]

It is easy enough, armed with Richard's remarks about himself and with references to him in other Histories, to read back into *Richard II* the notion that Bolingbroke was the guilty party and that Richard, though not blameless (over favourites, finances, and Woodstock), was deprived of his office by force. This is in fact the assumption that critics have habitually started from. What I question is whether it represents a true and accurate

response to Shakespeare's play—never mind about the other Histories, the Tudor Myth, and the National Epic. Bearing in mind such doubts, let us go on to look at the 'deposition scene'.

After the bitter quarrel in which four men accuse Aumerle of having caused Woodstock's death (an episode which adds a further touch of confusion to the already vague attitude the play has taken to Richard's complicity therein), York enters with news from Richard:

> Great Duke of Lancaster, I come to thee
> From plume-plucked Richard, who with willing soul
> Adopts thee heir, and his high sceptre yields
> To the possession of thy royal hand.
> Ascend his throne, descending now from him,
> And long live Henry, fourth of that name!
>
> [IV. i. 107-12]

One incidental detail of the message is intriguing: how are we supposed to take 'with *willing* soul'? Those who want to share Richard's view of things must turn York into a sycophant, which he is surely too honest to be. If, on the other hand, my reading is correct, we must take the phrase quite literally, and after all Richard, at the end of III. iii, *was* 'willing'. (pp. 424-26)

When Richard comes in he starts play-acting, and in response to one of his fantasies Bolingbroke, with some impatience, says

> I thought you had been willing to resign.
>
> [IV. i. 190]

('Willing' picks up York's use of the word at [IV. i. 108]). Richard replies:

> My crown I am, but still my griefs are mine.
> You may my glories and my state depose,
> But not my griefs; still am I king of those.
>
> [IV. i. 191-93]

Perhaps it is the familiarity of this dying fall that blinds us to the fact that Richard is engaging in double-think: he admits he is 'willing' to resign his 'crown', but at once charges Bolingbroke with having 'deposed' him! And, as we saw earlier, he charges Northumberland too with 'deposing' him [IV. i. 234]. In reply to another reminder from Bolingbroke, Richard equivocates:

> Ay, no; no, ay; for I must nothing be.
> Therefore no 'no', for I resign to thee.
>
> [IV. i. 201-02]

He is having his cake and eating it: extracting the maximum pleasure from seeing himself in the role of a deposed king, and also from protesting that he should never have been deposed in the first place. And it is in this self-regarding role that he throws out the account of what has happened which has become the official version. He now resigns the office of king with deliberate and knife-twisting formality.... Northumberland asks him to read and sign the list of his crimes,

> That, by confessing them, the souls of men
> May deem that you are worthily deposed.
>
> [IV. i. 226-27]

The surprising thing here is that Northumberland has fallen into Richard's own terminology and view of the situation—a view which Northumberland has not held before, which only Richard has ever put forward (but see my comment on the Garden scene, below). I do not think that Shakespeare is being subtle, though it would be attractive to argue that Richard has hypnotised the tough Earl as well as many willing critics. Two other explanations are possible. One is that Shakespeare simply nodded—which is not an explanation at all. The other is that he suddenly realised, at this late stage, that he could not write the sort of play he had set out to write, that it was a practical impossibility for him to present on the Elizabethan stage a Richard so much at odds with the official one (who was political dynamite anyway). He therefore started to make the play's 'truth' correspond with Richard's personal 'truth', and scattered hints of the Ricardian view throughout the play. Unfortunately he did not go back and remove the non-Ricardian view which holds good till nearly the end of Act III. I do not pretend to know why he started to write about a Richard who abdicated rather than being deposed. Perhaps he was genuinely confused about the deposition business—and it *is* terribly confusing, whether you go to Holinshed or to modern historians. . . . If professional historians who have access to all surviving documents dealing with the events of 1399 make heavy weather of them, we shall not perhaps be surprised if Shakespeare did too.

At all events Shakespeare's change of mind comes out almost disarmingly in the Garden scene (III. iv). It intervenes between the Flint Castle scene and the 'deposition scene', and prepares the way for the latter in a manner that has apparently gone unnoticed. The gardener, his 'man' and the Queen all refer to deposition. The gardener's mate asks

> What, think you the king shall be deposed?
>
> [III. iv. 67]

and the gardener answers

> Depressed he is already, and deposed
> 'Tis doubt he will be.
>
> [III. iv. 68-9]

The Queen breaks in and demands

> Why dost thou say King Richard is deposed?
>
> [III. iv. 77]

This exchange follows on from the long analogy between the commonwealth and a garden—an analogy which it is reasonable to call choric and conventional. The trouble is that the personae are then used to give an apparently disinterested (because choric) account of Richard's fall in terms of his *being* deposed—the gardener's use of the passive voice very subtly slips in the Ricardian view where we might expect such a commentator to take the play's view. This is not dramatic craftsmanship, it is dramatic craft—sleight of hand. And it is this legerdemain which has ensured that readers take away from *Richard II* a view which is largely confined to the latter part of the play and which is completely inconsistent with what has gone before. Shakespeare has to work increasingly hard as the play progresses to attract the audience's emotional regard to Richard and repel it from Bolingbroke; readers have proved curiously eager to sentimentalise Richard in the way that Richard sentimentalises himself. . . . Self-dramatising self-pity can always attract sympathy, of course; but . . . in *Richard II* Shakespeare, having left so late his effort to put Richard in a favourable light, simply cannot afford to qualify our sympathy. Hence, no doubt, the sugared poignancies of the exchanges between Richard and his Queen (V. i.), the words of York to his wife [V. ii. 23 ff.], and the grotesque elaboration of Richard's soliloquy in prison (V. v).

Now there were, even for the most orthodox Elizabethan, two quite different ways of looking at Richard's fall. As it happens

Shakespeare dramatised them elsewhere. In *3 Henry VI* there is a bitter debate between the Yorkist and Lancastrian factions about Henry VI's title to the throne. Part of it runs as follows:

> *Henry* Tell me, may not a king adopt an heir?
> *York*   What then?
> *Henry* An if he may, then am I lawful King;
>   For Richard, in the view of many lords,
>   Resigned the crown to Henry the Fourth,
>   Whose heir my father was, and I am his.
> *York*   He rose against him, being his sovereign,
>   And made him to resign his crown perforce.
>
> [*3 Henry VI*, I. i. 135-42]

Each man here naturally takes the line that serves his own interests: Henry wants to prove his title good, York the reverse. Nevertheless the episode does suggest that there could be genuine doubt in an Elizabethan mind about Richard's fall. (It further suggests, incidentally, that long before *Richard II* Shakespeare could and did stage a deposition scene in which the participants thrashed out the complex issues thoroughly—the debate goes on for about 140 lines.)

But the fact that there *could* be genuine doubt does not, I think, exculpate Shakespeare in *Richard II*. The trouble is not that he merely dramatises the doubt, for this could imply that however many subjective 'truths' there are, the play as a whole comprehends them, organises them, sees them from a coherent point of view. This happens in *Othello* where, although there are as many 'truths' as there are personae, the play gives us a truth which transcends any single character's truth. No, the trouble with *Richard II* is that it suffers from what we might call double vision, giving us one truth in one place, and another in another, with apparently equal weight and conviction. It leaves us to settle matters, but does not contain within itself the evidence by which alone we could do so.

Some critics have found *Richard II* unsatisfactory in this general way, but for other reasons: A. P. Rossiter, for example [see excerpt above, 1961], thinks that Richard's financial misdemeanours and his hinted complicity in Woodstock's murder are left very obscure, and that the York-Aumerle scenes in Act V are incoherent. With some reservations I agree; but Rossiter still does not seem to me to put his finger on the play's central weakness, for the shortcomings he lists do not, perhaps, amount to a very formidable indictment; and they certainly do not in themselves explain why the overall impression produced by an attentive reading or witnessing of the piece is one of bafflement and irritation at the way our sympathies are tampered with. If we concentrate on the question which forms the title of this essay, we can at least give a more cogent account of this impression—an account which ties in, as we have seen, with Shakespeare's uncertain handling of Bolingbroke, and indeed with the worries that Rossiter felt without being able to organise fully.

But such an account calls into question more than the merits or demerits of *Richard II*. It also casts the gravest possible doubt on the orthodox reading of the eight main Histories as demonstrating God's punishment for England's sin of deposing her lawful King. I have elsewhere shown that in the earlier tetralogy (i.e. *1, 2* and *3 Henry VI* and *Richard III*) Shakespeare makes only passing reference to the fate of Richard II, and that the 'sin' which England is expiating is no single or simple thing. We can now add that the later tetralogy (*Richard II* to *Henry V*) presents what is historically the first term in the whole series, *Richard II*, in a fundamentally confused way. So we are perhaps entitled to ask whether Shakespeare really is the Celebrator of the Tudor Myth. Surely, at least in the best Histories—*Richard III* and *Henry IV*—he is a very great deal more than that; so much so that to talk in terms of the Tudor Myth is merely reductive. In any case, it is about time that we started to read the plays Shakespeare actually wrote, rather than the ones written for him by historical critics. To read *Richard II* is, at all events, what I have been attempting to do. If it has turned out to be a lesser thing than orthodox taste has made it (examining bodies never tire of setting it), the blame will, I hope, be laid where it belongs: on the capable shoulders of William Shakespeare. (pp. 428-32)

    A. L. French, "Who Deposed Richard the Second?" in Essays in Criticism, *Vol. XVII, No. 4, October, 1967, pp. 411-33.*

NORMAN RABKIN (essay date 1967)

[*For Norman Rabkin, "the question that* Richard II *poses is the question of what to do about a king whose continuance on the throne is essential to the continued order of a state . . . but who is manifestly unfit personally for what is required of him." The critic contends that Shakespeare never answers this question, but rather keeps "our sympathies in suspense" by depicting both Richard and Bolingbroke as "morally ambiguous." Each man has strengths, each weaknesses, and, as Rabkin asserts, "The tragedy of* Richard II *is the complementarity of its protagonists' virtues, which seem . . . incapable of being commingled." He adds, however, that the primary source of ambiguity in* Richard II *is something more universal than the circumstances and behavior of these two characters, namely, the tragic nature of kingship itself, in that the qualities that make a successful ruler like Bolingbroke are the same qualities that detract from one's humanity.*]

It is a truism in certain schools that Shakespeare's plays are the defining embodiment of Elizabethan ideals of order and degree, the Tudor myth of the polity as beehive and history as the working out of a providence that sanctions kings as divine agents and condemns regicide or anything that might lead in its direction as sacrilege. For this view, promulgated with eloquence, learning, and insight by E. M. W. Tillyard and others, there is much to be said, and innumerable passages and incidents from the plays leap to mind in support of it. There can be no doubt that with the possible exception of Dante no great western writer has so dearly loved the ideal of hierarchical social order as Shakespeare, whose vision of it helped England through its severest trials in the twentieth century and has given to English-speaking peoples a local habitation and a name for much that we hope for in the state. On the other hand, many readers have realized for a long time that this reading of Shakespeare's politics is too simple. One need not go so far as Jan Kott [see excerpt above, 1964], who sees the history plays as embodying "the image of the Grand Mechanism," an image in which the precepts of Machiavelli and the blind movement of the wheel of fortune are fused to reflect a cruel and meaningless process in which only power counts, to recognize that against ideal and wishful dramatic images of Tudor political ideals Shakespeare poses a powerful sense of *Realpolitik*. In politics as in everything else Shakespeare incites contradictory readings in men of different natures, showing to the modern British patriot, with his nostalgia for good old days that may never have existed, the vision with which he would shore up the last days of England, and to the east European participant in the revolutions of our century a vision of the morbid police state cast up on the tides of brutal historical process. Both

images are in the work; taken together they suggest a complementary approach to the problems of history.

I am not going to suggest that politics is any more one substance for Shakespeare, one set of givens toward which he expresses one attitude, than love. Apart from the fact that we can find, as we would expect, cultural sources for all the attitudes on which Shakespeare bases his political plays, that he appeals to a certain stock of political ideas of various kinds—just as he appeals to demonstrably traditional ideas of love—there is only one constant in Shakespeare's political plays: the view of politics as problematic. Every political play that he wrote, without exception, shows the state in crisis—crisis of the sort that calls all into question, forces us to examine all our political assumptions and ideals, and leaves us finally with a resolution that does not allow for simplistic adherence to particular political ideals. And because politics is the art of managing the social world in which we live and attempting to solve its insoluble problems, Shakespeare's politics is tragic. As I hope to make clear, this is not to say that Shakespeare leaves us with the comfortable conclusion that because action is necessarily simplistic and therefore inevitably wrong, we may simply avoid action. Shakespeare's politics is tragic precisely because he will not allow us the luxury of evading action, because he shows us why we must act in history, and err. (pp. 80-1)

Had [Shakespeare] attempted to design a situation more nearly embodying the moral ambiguities he develops in *Richard II*, [he] could scarcely have equaled the opportunities he finds ready-made in his material. Here as in *Julius Caesar* he seizes on a historical event whose meaning was a matter of dispute and of inescapable concern to the unstable moment of history in which he composed his plays. *Richard II* is all problem. (p. 82)

As always, the problem shapes the structure of the play. The question that *Richard II* poses is the question of what to do about a king whose continuance on the throne is essential to the continued order of a state governed by hereditary monarchy, but who is manifestly unfit personally for what is required of him. Shakespeare plunges us immediately into the problem by setting it up in the opening scene in a debate—its circumstances and issues veiled both because they are too dangerous even to be discussed in public in the play's fictional world and because they are familiar to an audience which knows the history and has recently seen it performed on the stage. Richard has secretly employed Thomas Mowbray, Duke of Norfolk, to murder the Duke of Gloucester, uncle to the King and possibly dangerous to his control of England; and Richard's cousin Henry Bolingbroke, obviously unable to suggest the King's complicity even if he is aware of it, has challenged Richard's position by attempting to expose Mowbray. It might serve the purpose of immediate stability in the realm for Bolingbroke to keep silent, but he is an irascible and ambitious man, who can only profit by Richard's capitulation, and moreover—as ever in Shakespeare and the world, the elements are mixed in him—he is a patriotic and righteous man whose own father, brother to the murdered Duke, is implicitly threatened by the King's ruthless act. Though it is not often in Bolingbroke's nature to be deeply disturbed by the moral implications of the actions he contemplates, he has a problem, and he shares it with the audience.

The problem is explicitly stated, and one traditional answer to it given, by John of Gaunt, Duke of Lancaster and father to

Bolingbroke, as he responds to the plea of his widowed sister-in-law that he avenge the crime:

> God's is the quarrel; for God's substitute,
> His deputy anointed in His sight,
> Hath caused his death: the which if wrongfully,
> Let heaven revenge; for I may never lift
> An angry arm against His minister.
>
> [I. ii. 37-41]

In a sense Gaunt shares the view of Mowbray, who is not presented as a blackguard, yet has served the wishes of a monarch who felt the murder necessary to uphold his own position as king. If the unthreatened rule of the King is the principle of the state's survival, there may be some justification for what he has caused to be done. At any rate, to take arms against God's minister is to Gaunt an even more egregious crime than Richard's. And if history is providentially governed, then to oppose its course is sacrilegious. What happens in history is what heaven wants.

An obvious answer to Gaunt's position underlies all the action; ironically Shakespeare puts it into advice delivered to Richard himself as in the deposition scene the King helplessly falls back on the idea that God controls history and will protect his minister: "Fear not," the Bishop of Carlisle instructs the King, now mournfully yielding to passive anticipation of impending disaster;

> Fear not, my Lord: that Power that made you king
> Hath power to keep you king in spite of all.
> The means that heaven yields must be embraced,
> And not neglected; else if heaven would,
> And we will not, heaven's offer we refuse,
>
> [III. ii. 27-32]

And Aumerle, son of the Duke of York and loyal to Richard, immediately translates Carlisle's meditative statement into practical power politics: Bolingbroke is growing strong while we hold ourselves back. Richard's advisors, then, share Gaunt's belief in providence's stake in history, but they oppose to his and Richard's passive fatalism the notion that providence depends on the actions it makes available to individuals who know how to use power.

To their advice Richard responds with a deeply felt statement of his belief that heaven will take care of him:

> Not all the water in the rough rude sea
> Can wash the balm off from an anointed king;
> The breath of worldly men cannot depose
> The deputy elected by the Lord.
>
> [III. ii. 54-7]

The statement is clearly presumptuous and ultimately wrong in terms of the plot, yet difficult to refute, since Bolingbroke and England will have to pay dearly for what happens to prove it wrong. No matter how much Shakespeare makes us understand that Richard is here whistling in the dark, playing at being kingly instead of defending his threatened crown, he will not allow us to think of the problem entirely in terms of power politics. Again, simply on the level of plot, the play's world reacts precisely as Richard believes it will to the deposition of a king whose legitimacy is a matter as much of religion as of politics. At the moment that Richard officially yields all to Bolingbroke, the same Bishop of Carlisle pronounces a curse against those who strike out against "the figure of God's majesty, / His captain, steward, deputy-elect, / Anointed, crowned, planted many years" / [IV. i. 125-27] and predicts, as Richard

will do shortly again [V. i. 55-68] in language which his successor will ruefully remember later [*2 Henry IV*, III. i. 67-79], the bloody civil wars that all the audience is fully aware of. If Richard argues in surrendering his throne that "With mine own tears I wash away my balm" [IV. i. 207], we know that he cannot. Divinity does seem to hedge the seat of royal power and to punish those who oppose it with power no matter for how good a reason. Yet it allows Richard himself to be destroyed; and to make the paradox even more unsettling, providence will, in the fullness of time, place on the throne a son of the usurping Bolingbroke who will save England from its enemies, within and without, as the sacrilegiously deposed Richard could not.

Thus Gaunt's "God's is the quarrel" states the question of the play and the tetralogy but does not answer it. The question is inevitable in a state whose political stability is defined in the light of a benevolent providence that places absolute sanctions on the power of fallible rulers. It is no wonder that, given such postulates, historiography and political theory should find themselves caught in almost insuperable contradictions and conflicts in the age that most explicitly defines the royal prerogatives and puts them to the test; the problem is built into the European idea of kingship. The same contradictions are implicit in the version of the myth that first defines that idea, and explicit in Samuel's advice to the Hebrews not to demand a king. As the authors of the books of Samuel are fully aware, men are simply incapable of creating the kind of political stability that the Tudor myth envisions. The very first King of Israel was a tragically bad one, and if his mistakes can be explained in large part by the fact that he had not learned how to make the transition from the statecraft of a judge to that of a monarch, the fact remains that David confronting Saul was faced with a problem identical to Bolingbroke's. Like Bolingbroke he was motivated both by the drive to power and by love of country; like him he discovered that regicide must follow deposition in order to bring about a new legitimacy, and like him he had to spend a tragic life trying to atone for an inexpiable sin. Like Richard, Saul recognized immediately that to yield an inch to his challenger, even to let him cut off a corner of his garment, was to have given up all his power. And like Israel, England discovers that the new and benign order brought about by the creation of monarchical stability has legitimized in the process of its creation a kind of permanent challenge to the crown that will ultimately destroy kingship itself.

This is the insoluble problem of history as the chronicle plays make us see it. Shakespeare poses it brilliantly in little in the scene (III. iv) in which the gardeners, employing a familiar analogy, discuss the state as garden and Richard II as incompetent caretaker. The well-tended garden, in which natural process properly controlled brings forth flower and fruit in their appointed season and the community of the whole lives in wholesome balance, is the ideal to which we must contrast the disorder and disease rampant in the England of *Richard II*. . . . Through the myth of the garden Shakespeare suggests the King's providential function, his sacred place in the natural order, and the inevitable ruin of those who attack it, but he does not allow us to share Gaunt's momentary and Richard's perennial sense that with the aid of providence the garden will somehow take care of itself as long as the King retains his power. The problem of *Richard II* is the problem of England; it is not accidental that the most moving hymn to England ever composed occurs here in the passionate words of the dying Gaunt. Shakespeare does not solve the problem—only history and a new set of assumptions unimaginable in the sixteenth century were to do that; rather, he understands it as few of his contemporaries did, and he makes us fully and painfully aware of it.

The primary technique of *Richard II* is that of keeping our sympathies in suspense. The structure of the play demands that we choose: Is our allegiance to Richard or to Bolingbroke? If to the former, then we have resolved the play's problems along the lines set out by conservative Tudor thinkers like Thomas Elyot and Richard Hooker, who consistently evade the issue of the problems created by a bad monarch by wishing he were better and by refusing to countenance the legitimacy of usurpation. If we feel final allegiance to Bolingbroke and what he represents, no matter how much feeling for the great tradition we may have, we find we have opted for the new men who see the polity as a contract in which bad kings must be replaced and who see politics as an arena of perpetual conflict where only power counts. But Shakespeare does not let us make the choice. A good index to the play's intentions is the role played by Gaunt's brother, the Duke of York, perhaps the first of Shakespeare's "reflector" characters, who . . . epitomizes and directs our shifting sympathies. Like us York begins with a poignant sense of loyalty to the crown; like us he soon finds his sympathy virtually exhausted and declares an end to his former approval. When Richard rejects his advice, we come quickly to question the King's legitimacy (II. i). In the next scene York finds himself wavering between the conflicting principles represented by Richard and Bolingbroke:

> If I know how or which way to order these affairs
> Thus thrust disorderly into my hands,
> Never believe me. Both are my kinsmen:
> The one is my sovereign, whom both my oath
> And duty bids defend; the other again
> Is my kinsman, whom the king hath wrong'd,
> Whom conscience and my kindred bids to right.
> Well, somewhat we must do.
>
> [II. ii. 109-16]

York is still undecided when Bolingbroke, illegally violating the terms of his exile, arrives at Berkeley castle; he denounces him but nevertheless puts him up for the night. In the deposition scene which ensues almost immediately, York's sympathies have become more defined. Horrified by what is happening, he declares his fealty to the King, and by the beginning of the fourth act he is Richard's ambassador to Bolingbroke, unhappily assisting his nephew's abdication. The sequence of events has fully awakened and crystallized York's allegiance to the principle of sacred kingship. In the last act it is his account, to his wife, of Richard's disgrace at Bolingbroke's hands that turns us most against the usurper, and when he denounces the ruthless new King, we find it hard to disagree with him. Torn morally as at the outset, York decides to pledge fealty to the new King. But now comes a final turn: York discovers that his son Aumerle is part of a conspiracy against Henry IV, acting out his father's sympathies. With all the anger of a father who has reluctantly made his decision against a large part of his own moral feeling to support a principle in which he only half believes, and now finds his son actively engaged in supporting the position he has reluctantly ruled out for himself, York turns on Aumerle and rushes off to Windsor to denounce him before the King. At this final juncture Shakespeare is able to use York in order to make us admire and respect the usurper who throughout has so offended the conscience of this indecisive epitome of our own feelings; for after hearing out the opposed pleas of the Duke and Duchess of York and Aumerle's

contrite petition for pardon, the usurper about to have Richard murdered in the Tower becomes the wise, humane ruler, aware like David of his own limitations, that his predecessor could not be, and at the play's close York is loyal servant to the new King.

York thus calls to our attention the ambivalence upon which the play is structured. That ambivalence arises immediately from the fact that Bolingbroke is embarked on an action simultaneously good and evil and must in the course of time be regarded both as patriotic citizen righteously avenging the dual outrage to his country and himself and as regicide, both as the savior of the English polity and as plotter against its crown. But ultimately, and this is why *Richard II* is more than simply a sensitive account of a peculiar and local political problem, the play's ambivalence originates in a tragic understanding of man as political animal which expresses our gravest doubts about the possibility of human virtue in the public world.

I have indicated that the ambivalence of *Richard II* is built into its structure. But that structure, even as I have thus far described it, depends entirely on character, for our response to the politics of the play is a response not to theory but to the men whose lives and actions make theory necessary in the world. Bolingbroke's situation as Shakespeare dramatizes it almost necessitates an ambivalent response, but it is his character that makes it difficult for us to reach conclusions about him easily. At once patriotic and ambitious, manly and ruthless, he is above all always mysterious. We simply do not know for sure what his motives are at any point in the play. Interestingly, Shakespeare denies him soliloquies, so that we never see him from within. What we see is what the world sees: a powerful man who says and does the right thing at the right moment to reach the throne, and who—whether out of virtue or of a tough political astuteness we cannot know—has always the most convincing reasons for what he does. (pp. 82-9)

One characteristic device will show how Shakespeare creates a sense of moral uneasiness about Bolingbroke. Immediately upon hearing of the death of John of Gaunt, one of the play's most affecting moments, Richard dismisses his dead uncle with a heartlessness for which the audience will never fully forgive him, and to York's horror and ours seizes all of Gaunt's possessions, now rightfully Bolingbroke's. There is no doubt in our minds that Bolingbroke is being robbed, or that in simple justice he has a right to reclaim what Richard thus cynically takes from him. As the royal party leaves the stage, however, a small party remains behind, a knot of malcontent lords whom the Earl of Northumberland quickly binds into a conspiracy against the King. Shakespeare elicits our sympathies for their mission by showing us Richard at his worst, and by putting in their mouths worried speeches about the mistakes of more national import that the King is committing, to England's disaster. Now, if ever, we are ready and eager to have Bolingbroke return to England and save it. But at this point, in the very scene in which Gaunt has died and Richard stolen his property, Northumberland reveals to the patriots whose confidence he has tested that Bolingbroke, already sailing with confederates and three thousand men, has virtually reached the northern shores of England. In Holinshed's chronicle account of these events, most immediate source for Shakespeare's version, time is not so telescoped: Gaunt dies, England suffers under Richard's rule, messages are sent abroad to Bolingbroke, and finally the Duke undertakes his voyage. Shakespeare's strategy makes Bolingbroke's return morally ambiguous. To our outraged sense of justice it is an appropriate response to

Richard's highhandedness, while it is simultaneously apparent from the chronology that the voyage must have other purposes than the regaining of what Bolingbroke does not know he has lost. By not showing us the mobilizing of forces and the making of the decision to come back to England, Shakespeare leaves us in doubt as to what Bolingbroke is really up to, and we retain that doubt to the end. If Bolingbroke's motives are thus obscured, the play's conclusion, on the other hand, shows us a king able to deal, as Richard was not, honorably and wisely with the assassin he has employed. By the end we know that—for whatever reasons—Bolingbroke is going to be a good king.

The presentation of Richard is similarly ambiguous, but as the play's tragic center he is a far more complex character, and the extremes of our response to him are farther apart. Where Bolingbroke is adequately competent and strong, Richard is appallingly incompetent. Where Bolingbroke earns our rational admiration and at times our moral approval, Richard commands our deepest emotions. It is a notorious fact that productions of *Richard II* which stress the King's faults while playing down his virtues make the play fail; for the real power of this historical tragedy lies in its ability to elicit our increasing sympathies for the King whose fall we recognize as inevitable and even desirable. Richard begins the play as a man unwilling to stand behind the immoral commitments his power struggle has necessitated, and his dismissal of Mowbray, whose only hint of complaint is the tactful suggestion that he had expected better treatment than banishment, puts him in a bad light. Moreover, he uses his power to make a humiliating charade of a conflict he would do better to settle amicably and out of the public eye. . . . Followed by the disgraceful dishonoring of the dead Gaunt, whose whole concern was the preservation of England, Richard's behavior at the beginning of the play makes it clear that he is unfit to be king, and his never self-possessed and sometimes hysterical response to Bolingbroke's successive challenges confirms our sense of his unfitness. On the other hand, Shakespeare begins early to work on our sympathies, not only by making us suspicious of Bolingbroke and by engaging us in York's problems, but more poignantly by showing us the loyalty of the Queen. And simultaneously with the movement of the play toward an awareness of the horror of Bolingbroke's action, climactically conveyed in the curse the Bishop of Carlisle utters at the moment Richard surrenders all to Bolingbroke, we begin to see the richness of sensibility, language, and imagination in the King that leads some to see in him the prototype of Hamlet. His helpless struggles in the machine in which he is caught do not make us wish a different end to the play, but they do make him the most sympathetic character in the play. In the last act, where we finally come to admire the newly crowned Henry IV, we also come to admire Richard, for entirely different reasons. At the beginning of the act he is a new man, strong and able to bear his adversity with a manliness not apparent before: he has been instructed by his suffering. . . . [Richard] reaches by the point of his death a full acceptance of his responsibility for his demise that requires a moral courage more impressive than anything demanded of Bolingbroke in *Richard II*.

So much is built into the political problem with which Shakespeare is dealing, and into the dynamics of chronicle plays. Similarly in Marlowe's more schematically structured *Edward II* we come to admire a disastrous king only as the woes he brings down on his head and his country overwhelm him, and finally to disdain the forces that necessarily replace him. But, unlike Marlowe, Shakespeare uses the tragic situation as a platform on which to stage a greater tragedy, and this is the

genius of *Richard II*. The complementarity of the play does not rest in its opposition of ideas of the commonwealth, but makes us understand the perennial tragedy of politics, a tragedy not of systems but of men. From Aeschylus to Ibsen and Camus, great dramatists have found in politics the kind of problem which enables them to examine the human condition as only art can examine it, but always when their art is great it is so because it uses politics not to tell us about the polity what the historian and the political scientist can tell us with greater precision and knowledge, but to make us understand man in politics and therefore in the world. A historian might rest content with the knowledge that Henry IV saved England and managed to pass on his crown to his more successful son. Shakespeare recognizes all this and would not have us underestimate its importance, but he is more concerned with the human loss involved. For the fact, as Shakespeare constructs it in *Richard II* and the history plays that follow it, is that the man who succeeds is, though better constituted for success, farther from our deepest ideals as a man than the failure he must displace. On one level *Richard II* is a play about political success and the ideal of the commonwealth, and on that level Bolingbroke is admirable; on another it is about what it is to be a fully sentient human being, and on that level only Richard commands our respect. Shakespeare perennially distrusts success and the men who achieve it. Mark Antony is Brutus' inferior, Fortinbras Hamlet's, Aufidius Coriolanus'.

What Bolingbroke lacks, and the lack accounts in good part for his success, is inwardness, the capacities to suffer and to dream. At the play's first crisis we become aware of the lack, and we recognize it as a source of his strength and a concomitant of his political resoluteness. Banished by his high-handed cousin, Bolingbroke is advised by his sensitive father to ignore the conditions under which he will have to live abroad, to ''Think not the king did banish thee, / but thou the king'' [I. iii. 279-80], and to imagine wherever he is that that is where he should be, ''For gnarling sorrow hath less power to bite / The man that mocks at it and sets it light [I. iii. 292-93]. To this stoic commonplace, the advice that a man's mind is his kingdom, Bolingbroke responds with a scornful rejection of the poetic imagination that transforms the world for its possessor:

> O, who can hold a fire in his hand
> By thinking on the frosty Caucasus?
> Or cloy the hungry edge of appetite
> By bare imagination of a feast?
> Or wallow naked in December snow
> By thinking on fantastic summer's heat?
> O, no! the apprehension of the good
> Gives but the greater feeling to the worse:
> Fell sorrow's tooth doth never rankle more
> Than when he bites, but lanceth not the sore.
> [I. iii. 294-303]

Of course he is right, and his literalistic insistence on what he is and what is his keeps his will focused on the goal he finally achieves. But in his answer to Gaunt Bolingbroke dissociates himself from those ''wrong'' characters in Shakespeare—Troilus and the unfallen Othello are their tragic, the lovers in *A Midsummer Night's Dream* their comic archetypes—whose vision points higher than material fact. In declaring his fidelity to realistic clarity of vision Bolingbroke gives us his first insight into the stuff he has to bring him power, but ironically he suggests to us at the same time what makes us care more at the end for Richard.

Now there can be no denying that imagination is Richard's disease, or that in politics it is for him, as shortly we shall see that it is also for Brutus, a fatal one. His famous meditation, "Let's talk of graves, of worms and epitaphs" [III. ii. 144-77], is a perfect example. It is a mortifying piece of self-dramatization and self-pity, and as an answer to Aumerle's simple question, "Where is the duke my father with his power?" [III. ii. 143] it is, as the Bishop of Carlisle remarks, totally inappropriate. On the other hand, it is one of the most moving and memorable speeches in the play, and for good reason. For Richard's response to adversity is simultaneously a retreat within and probing outward, a questioning of the meaning of all things in the face of the fact of mortality. His medieval *ubi sunt* [search for truth] leads him to a contemplation of the dance of death. Such a meditation is inappropriate to his political responsibilities, but it deals with issues fundamental to the growth and understanding of man.... If the burden of the history plays is the tragedy of history, it is Richard who comes closest to our understanding, to what the plays would have us think of as wisdom. But that wisdom seems in *Richard II* incompatible with the other kind of human greatness by which a man can function as he must.... The tragedy of *Richard II* is the complementarity of its protagonists' virtues, which seem there incapable of being commingled. (pp. 89-95)

Norman Rabkin, "The Polity," in his Shakespeare and the Common Understanding, *The Free Press, 1967, pp. 80-149.*

JAMES WINNY   (essay date 1968)

[*The importance of the ceremonial or rhetorical mode in* Richard II *and Richard's love of self-dramatization have been leading issues in twentieth-century commentary on the play. In the following excerpt, Winny examines both of these concerns and applies them to Shakespeare's characterization. He claims that Richard is a king who lacks inner substance or reality, who fails to confront personal and political facts, and who "repeatedly takes refuge from reality in verbal fantasy." He asserts that the king never seriously acknowledges this weakness in himself, and therefore "never acquires tragic force," adding that the few times he does recognize his essential nothingness he lapses into "pathetic conceits" and self-pity, rather than affirm tragic self-awareness. Winny also examines how Shakespeare provides "a mode of ironic commentary" through the various father-son relationships presented in* Richard II, *revealing "moral contradictions not recognized by the [characters] themselves." The critic contends that this pattern—"in which a noble father is disgraced by a morally degenerate son"—is especially apparent in the behavior of both York and Bolingbroke.*]

Richard II begins by declaring a concern with formal titles and modes of address which characterises the play. Its opening words, spoken to 'old John of Gaunt, time-honoured Lancaster' [I. i. 1], identify an important figure and also establish the curiously impersonal idiom of Richard's kingdom, where even gardeners speak in set rhetorical terms. This stilted mode of address suggests the addiction to ceremonial form which Richard seems to find natural whatever the circumstances: an appropriate concomitant of the personal majesty which he never allows himself to forget. As his subjects follow his example, little of the action of *Richard II* escapes from the formal atmosphere of public ceremony or kingly ritual. The range of emotions through which the King runs, from elation to tragic despair, is expressed in set terms which inhibit any show of spontaneous feeling: the dialogue is recited within a frame of predetermined response. Even when Richard bids farewell to

the Queen there is a strange lack of *rapport* between the two, who speak as though listening to themselves; uttering declarations rather than conversing. This effect is evidently calculated. Richard lives on the surface of experience, denied contact with the inward reality of the self by his complete absorption in the identity of king, which he mistakes for it. The other characters of *Richard II* exist by virtue of their names and titles rather than as individual beings; and like him express themselves in prescribed forms and set rhetorical figures which mask direct personal response. The being of the man resides in his name.

The ritual of self-identification before the lists at Coventry, where appellant and defendant are required to declare themselves, has thus a wider significance within the play. The marshal's command, 'In God's name and the King's, say who thou art' [I. iii. 11], suggests that the anonymous armed figures will give sufficient proof of their true identity simply by naming themselves.... This public declaration of title is echoed several times by the heralds as both sides prepare for the combat that will test the 'foul traitor's name' [I. i. 44] applied to Mowbray. The formality of ancestral title covers more than disloyalty towards Richard in one of the combatants. The ceremony might have been devised to suppress all the personal traits which make up human character, and to oblige the participants to represent themselves by a bare name. Apart from their formal titles they are nothing.

Not only naming but the speaking of words assumes a significance in the opening scenes of *Richard II* which is justified by later developments, when the King repeatedly takes refuge from reality in verbal fantasy.... As Richard lives inside the illusion of majestic authority which his own speeches create, so the disputants are forced to accept angry speeches as a substitute for physical action. Bolingbroke is not allowed to prove 'what my tongue speaks' [I. i. 46] on the spot; and when later his accusation is about to be put to the test of combat, the King's intervention again frustrates his wish to give his words substance. The sentence of banishment passed upon Mowbray provides the motive for elaborations on the theme of speech—pronounce, word, breathe, mouth, language, tongue, teeth, lips, sentence, speechless—which make its utterance seem more momentous than the judgement itself. Mowbray's complaint implies that by preventing him from speaking his native language, Richard has condemned him to death. In terms of character this objection is hardly plausible, and the remark that

> Within my mouth you have engaoled my tongue
> Doubly portcullised with my teeth and lips.
>
> [I. iii. 166-67]

reveals an absorption in courtly conceit which any strong emotion would suppress. To account for the seeming triviality of Mowbray's reaction we must look beyond character to the purpose indicated by this concentration of interest on words and speech. Deprived of language, Mowbray will cease to exist. Fanciful in itself, his protest suggests the vital importance of words to the sense of actuality which they induce in a speaker who mistakes them for the objects they name.

Bolingbroke is quick to take advantage of the fact that man is not merely identified but represented by his name. At the death of Gaunt he returns from banishment with a new title, insisting that he must now be acknowledged as Lancaster, and that in this person he cannot be charged with Bolingbroke's act of treason.... [But the] title of Lancaster is only part of the inheritance which he comes for. Bolingbroke assures both the King and his own supporters that he has returned 'but for mine own' [III. iii. 196], but the phrase is calmly equivocal, and includes what he can make his own as well as his legal inheritance. As a banished man, he has been dispossessed by Richard—or in Ross's vigorous expression, gelded of his patrimony—and he may now seize Richard's inherited rights and title. During one of his phases of unrealistic confidence, Richard assures Aumerle that it will be simple to reassert his collapsed authority: 'An easy task it is to win our own' [III. ii. 191]. What he assumes to be his unalienable property has already passed out of his hands. The name of king which he prizes will be won by the man who knows 'the strong'st and surest way to get' [III. iii. 201], and who makes Richard's crown his own.

Richard's conception of his royal title and office is too lofty to admit the possibility that a rival might take over his function. He knows himself King by right of due succession and divine will, and is convinced that no earthly power can depose him. His belief that

> no hand of blood and bone
> Can gripe the sacred handle of our sceptre,
> Unless he do profane, steal, or usurp,
>
> [III. iii. 79-81]

encourages him to ignore the approach of political disaster. His supporters watch him talking himself into a state of self-hypnotic assurance in which mere insistence upon his divinely protected authority becomes an acceptable substitute for purposeful action. Because he cannot divorce himself from the idea of kingly magnificence and sanctity, he habitually speaks of himself as an unearthly being whose trivial acts demand respectful attention. Himself the awed spectator of the royal performance, he is also the ecstatic commentator whose description clothes every action in the majesty which Richard claims for himself. His greeting to his kingdom when he returns from Ireland is characteristic of this self-admiring commentary, which supplies stage directions to his acting-out of royal condescension:

> So weeping, smiling, greet I thee, my earth,
> And do thee favours with my royal hands.
>
> [III. ii. 10-11]

To describe Richard as a poet would discount the importance of critical self-awareness in good writing, but in one sense the description is justified. He has the power of using words creatively, to produce impressions of reality strong enough to overpower his perception of material actuality. His misfortune is that he alone is deluded by these shadows of reality. He cannot realise that the splendid role with which he identifies himself has no more substance than an actor's part, and is not the basis of his individuality. The effortless majesty and power which he continually tries to project has no more actuality than his creative eloquence can give, and Richard does not recognise that his words make no impression upon political facts. How badly he deludes himself becomes evident when he is confronted by the direct challenge of Bolingbroke's insurrection. The danger will dissolve without exertion on Richard's part: stones will be transformed into armed warriors, the rebels will be overthrown by angelic intervention, or shamed into surrender by the mere appearance of their true sovereign:

> So when this thief, this traitor Bolingbroke . . .
> Shall see us rising in our throne, the east,
> His treasons will sit blushing in his face,
> Not able to endure the sight of day.
>
> [III. ii. 47, 50-2]

This fantasy of himself as *le roi soleil* [the sun-king] is fathered by Richard's belief that as crowned monarch he must possess the irresistible powers which he associates with the name of king. The scene with Gaunt at Ely House suggests how far the title itself represents the personal majesty which Richard assumes his own. He appears to shrug off Gaunt's rebuke of his prodigality until it reaches the denial of his royal title:

> Landlord of England art thou now, not king.
>
> [I. i. 113]

At this his rage boils over. Gaunt has committed the unpardonable crime of disputing Richard's right to the name on which his whole identity depends, and must feel the weight of the King's uncontrolled fury. Later, when Bolingbroke's rapid exploitation of success strikes away Richard's supports one after another, the King is momentarily dislodged from his royal *persona* and has to be prompted to recall who he is. 'I had forgot myself,' he admits;

> Am I not king? . . .
> Is not the king's name twenty thousand names?
> Arm, arm, my name; a puny subject strikes
> At they great glory.
>
> [III. ii. 83, 85-7]

Richard could not show more explicitly how far he has sunk his individual self in his royal title. He has indeed forgotten himself. Mesmerised by the bare name of king, he makes over to it all the authority which he should command by force of character, attributing to it supernatural powers of multiplying itself and of acting with irresistible energy. The full shock of political disaster compels Richard to acknowledge the emptiness of his grand identity, and to fall back towards the simply human character whose development he has ignored. . . . As Richard senses that he is losing grasp of his kingly name, he attempts to fit himself into another role, as pathetic as the first had been splendid; but again without means of becoming the part. When he fails to bluff Bolingbroke into submission, 'because we thought ourselves thy lawful king' [III. iii. 74], he has no reserves of personality to fill up the gap left by his dwindling title. The exchange between York and Northumberland before the meeting at Flint indicates how rapidly Richard is losing the respect due to his royal name. Northumberland remarks that Richard is close at hand, and is rebuked for speaking so unceremoniously:

> It would beseem the Lord Northumberland
> To say, 'King Richard': alack, the heavy day,
> When such a sacred king should hide his head!
>
> [III. iii. 7-9]

Northumberland defends his neglect of protocol: 'only to be brief Left I his title out' [III. iii. 10-11]; but this political realist knows that Richard's claim to be king is now more than ever a form of words. The awesome figure of majesty and the negligible human being who has tried to fill the role are about to be separated. As Richard sees himself about to be humiliated by Bolingbroke's political triumph, he wishes he might be as great as his grief 'or lesser than my name' [III. iii. 137], unconscious that he has always fallen short of its magnificence. The prospect of losing his title is a threat of becoming personally nameless, and the most painful form of deprivation that he can suffer:

> What must the king do now? must he submit?
> The king shall do it. Must he be deposed?
> The king shall be contented. Must he lose
> The name of king? . . .
>
> [III. iii. 143-46]

The formal act of deposition follows. Invited to resign the crown, Richard swings between contradictory impulses, 'Ay, no; no, ay:' [IV. i. 201] and then resolves his indecision by an answer which allows him to play on the sense of the words he has just used: 'for I must nothing be' [IV. i. 201]. So far from offering resistance, he himself carries out the sentence which strips him of majesty, rights and possessions, and reduces him to an anonymous cypher. . . . By the end of the ceremony and his final exercise of kingly rights, Richard has effectively ceased to exist; and although Northumberland is eager to press charges against the human nonentity whom he has become, Richard's question, 'What more remains?' [IV. i. 222] invites his audience to recognise how completely he has destroyed himself. As Northumberland persists, he goads Richard into an outburst of self-pitying indignation, and an acknowledgement of the nameless being which is his new character:

> No lord of thine, thou haught insulting man,
> Nor no man's lord: I have no name, no title;
> No, not that name was given me at the font,
> But 'tis usurped. Alack the heavy day,
> That I have worn so many winters out,
> And know not now what name to call myself!
>   [IV. i. 254-59]

This consciousness is not tragic, for Richard finds in being nobody a distinction which compensates for his ignominious loss of majesty. From this point his behaviour leaves the impression of a man wilfully bent upon destroying himself. Earlier, Gaunt has diagnosed such an impulse in Richard by describing him as 'possessed now to depose thyself' [II. i. 108]; a warning not much weakened by the play on words. Richard surrenders himself to Bolingbroke as though he wished to ensure his political abasement, hinting broadly at Bolingbroke's larger ambition before there has been any show of an attempt on the crown. His deliberateness of manner at his deposition, when he ceremoniously takes the king to pieces, deepens the impression that Richard is set upon self-obliteration. . . . He moves towards the state of nothingness as towards the satisfaction of a perverse desire. Although he has insisted that his rights and title are inviolable, he is not prepared to undertake the simplest physical measures to defend them. If the stones will not rise against Bolingbroke, and no angelic host fight the King's battles for him, then Richard must contract out of the political system which has refused to substantiate his idea of the king. He retires into a world of private fantasy, where hard facts cannot impinge disrespectfully upon the royal performance of which he is now sole spectator.

In banishing Bolingbroke at Coventry, Richard had been impelled less by political motives than by a wish to be rid of a rival whose solid substantiality stood as a mock to his own pretensions to kingly power. Bolingbroke's popularity with the common people piques Richard, as though depriving him of adulation that he should receive by right; but he is more deeply irked by his inability to impose his royal will upon Bolingbroke's tougher spirit. When he tries to force the quarrelling nobles to make peace, his comment,

> We were not born to sue, but to command;
>   [I. i. 196]

reminds Richard as well as his two angry subjects of the royal authority which should prove itself in their obedience. Put to the test, this notion of kingly power collides with the defiant will of the disputants and collapses ignominiously: a rebuff

whose humiliation Richard repays at Coventry. By interrupting the combat he is making a purely wilful manifestation of power, designed to reinstate his damaged self-esteem at the expense of ordered ritual. Instead of allowing the combat to run its course he takes judgement into his own hands, making it the instrument of private malice, and ridding himself of the figure whose innate sovereignty tacitly discredits Richard's efforts to fill the role of king. His savage treatment of Mowbray suggests that Richard lacks the nerve to impose a drastic sentence on the man whom he is most anxious to put out of his kingdom. By reducing Bolingbroke's term of banishment he hopes to induce his rival to go quietly into exile without suspecting—as Richard hints to Aumerle—that he will not be allowed to return.

Resentment of Bolingbroke's natural authority is the motive of Richard's behaviour after the death of Gaunt, when he seizes Lancaster's estates, denies Bolingbroke access to his inheritance, and allows his favourites to erase all marks of ancestral right from the banished man's properties. The sober truth behind Gaunt's remark, 'Thou dost seek to kill my name in me' [II. i. 86], is now revealed. Richard is trying to put a stop to the house of Lancaster, whose heir discredits Richard's royal performance merely by showing the authentic personal authority of a king. Banishment, dispossession and outlawry are intended to reduce Bolingbroke to a penniless nobody; the shadow of a man deprived of name and legal rights, and permanently excluded from the kingdom to which he seems naturally entitled. Ironically, it is Richard who suffers the personal obliteration which he designs for Bolingbroke. The attempt to starve Bolingbroke of substance recoils upon Richard as the banished man springs back upon him in the assurance of superior power. It is not Richard whose dazzling sovereignty puts the shamefaced pretender to flight. The contest between the two claimants is quickly resolved, Richard's authority proving a sham as the pressure of Bolingbroke's substance is brought to bear. Where a political interpretation of the play sees a lawful king deposed by a sacrilegious usurper, the imaginative purposes of *Richard II* centre upon a confrontation of a majestic imposture by the robust reality it has attempted to evade. Despite its lack of legality, Bolingbroke's claim to the crown has a natural cogency which discredits Richard's title without recourse to argument. When he speaks after his deposition of having been 'outfaced by Bolingbroke' [IV. i. 286], Richard acknowledges that his royal bluff has been called. (pp. 48-61)

As a prisoner in Pomfret Castle, Richard is cut off from all relationship with the outside world and denied communication with other beings. His physical circumstances as a prisoner, caged-up inside granite walls with 'not a creature but myself' [V. v. 4], represent the psychological state to which Richard has always tended. His immature habit of thrusting disconcerting facts out of sight, and of substituting fantasy for unpalatable truth to protect his self-esteem, has now hardened into a condition which he has no power to cast off. Because he has refused to come to terms with personal and political realities, he is now confined within the state of being which he has always preferred, beyond contact with actuality and obliged to act as audience to himself. His only society is a company of phantasmal creatures, begotten upon himself:

> My brain I'll prove the female to my soul,
> My soul the father; and these two beget
> A generation of still-breeding thoughts;
> And these same thoughts people this little world.
>   [V. v. 6-9]

This bodiless offspring, multiplying like a cloud of gnats, is the only progeny which Richard could produce. He has played with words, treating them as though they embodied reality and gave the speaker possession of their substance. Now he tries to generate forms through the sterile commerce of words alone, enacting male and female roles in his single self, much as he sought relationship with the mirror-self reflected in a glass. The paradoxes and doublings of verbal sense which have delighted Richard now turn against him as he struggles to establish some unequivocal truth. Thoughts of things divine, he discovers,

> are intermixed
> With scruples, and do set the word itself
> Against the word.
>
> [V. v. 12-14]

His soliloquy becomes an attempt to hammer out some analogy between the world at large and Richard's cell, where the eddies of his unstable purpose will duplicate the wide range of human temperament in society. In fact, his comparisons illuminate only Richard's capacity for assuming character-parts, none of them realised in any depth, and leave no impression of a more substantial identity beneath. Eventually he abandons the performance, admitting its shallowness:

> Thus play I in one person many people,
> And none contented.
>
> [V. v. 31-2]

The instability of character which he has always shown dominates him as he swings in thought between extremes of personal circumstance, passing from sovereignty to beggary and back again as conflicting impulses pluck at him, and ending in nothing. . . . His mind works without real purpose, best pleased when it can admire the effect of what he enacts in the mixed role of king and nobody. In his last scene Richard describes himself perceptively as an actor who runs perfunctorily through a variety of parts without discovering any character in which he can sink himself. He can bring nothing substantial to the part he plays. When he is robbed of his leading role as king, he turns towards nothingness as the only state which promises him satisfaction:

> Whate'er I be,
> Nor I, nor any man that but man is,
> With nothing shall be pleased, till he be eased
> With being nothing.
>
> [V. v. 38-41]

The seriousness of the remark is sacrificed for the trivial pleasure of word-play, and the part is denied importance. In his taste for frivolity Richard has always been pleased with nothing, and it is poetically just that he should become a completely anonymous being. As the central character of the deposition scene he tries to present himself as a tragic figure; but although deeply moved by his own performance he can give the part no weight, and his audience remains stonily unmoved. As later his attempt to populate his cell with 'still-breeding thoughts' [V. v. 8] suggests his inability to invest his ideas with vital substance, so generally Richard's acting proves the insubstantiality of the private self behind the being who tries to exist in the role he plays. (pp. 65-8)

Like other Shakespearean characters who become absorbed in the pathos of their own situation, Richard has no creative energy to spend on the world about him, for his narcissism starves him of substance. He recognises only at the end of his life that self-admiration has drained him of vitality to no purpose: 'I

wasted time, and now doth time waste me' [V. v. 49]. Yet even here Richard cannot break himself of the trivial habit of playing with words, and the hard truth of his comment is turned aside into frivolity.

If Richard ever becomes critically aware of his weakness, his discovery never acquires tragic force. He diagnoses his personal condition accidentally, in the course of developing a pathetic conceit as he faces the humiliation of losing his crown:

> O that I were a mockery king of snow
> Standing before the sun of Bolingbroke,
> To melt myself away in water-drops!
>
> [IV. i. 260-62]

The image appeals to Richard by suggesting a tearful dissolution, where tears are unfailingly moving, but his conceit acknowledges the want of substance which exposure to Bolingbroke has found out. As sovereign he is, in effect, melting away as he speaks before the vital energy of the authentic king-figure whose splendour he had claimed for himself. His wish to be a mockery king, dissolving at the touch of Bolingbroke's solid reality, is expressed as a momentary whim; but it describes the actual relationship of the two men more accurately than Richard is able to realise.

Bolingbroke has shown his force of character much earlier. When he is banished, his father tries to palliate the distress of exile by offering fanciful consolations. . . . [Gaunt] advises Bolingbroke to imagine himself moving towards, and not away from whatever he most loves:

> Suppose the singing birds musicians,
> The grass whereon thou tread'st the presence strew'd,
> The flowers fair ladies, and thy steps no more
> Than a delightful measure or a dance.
>
> [I. iii. 288-91]

Such make-believe consolation protects Richard against unwelcome facts, but Bolingbroke has no inclination to delude himself by charming fantasy. However painful, the sensations of reality form a currency which he refuses to debase. 'Who can hold a fire in his hand,' he objects,

> By thinking on the frosty Caucasus?
> Or cloy the hungry edge of appetite
> By bare imagination of a feast?
>
> [I. iii. 295-97]

His speech gives further proof of the unsentimental outlook which Bolingbroke has already shown by making no protest against the sentence of banishment. His reticence puzzles Gaunt, but Richard's extravagant lamentations later in the play point the significance of Bolingbroke's sparing use of words. . . . His restraint in misfortune and his rejection of imaginary comfort prove before the end of Act I how wide a disparity of outlook separates him from Richard. He has no faith in the magic power of words to achieve political ends, and no disposition to waste himself upon fantasies of personal magnificence. During the deposition scene this economy of speech irritates Richard, as though he realised that Bolingbroke's silence was a sign of mastery, and of contempt for Richard's squandering of potential upon a charade. When Bolingbroke has been publicly acclaimed king, and Richard is walled up inside Pomfret Castle with his aimless ruminations, both men have reached a natural culmination of growth. Bolingbroke has taken control of the political organism through which he will extend his domination of material events. Richard, ruined by his addiction to fantasy, is now irrevocably lost in the mirror-

York's description of the arrival of Bolingbroke and Richard II in London, Act V, Scene ii. By James Northcote. The Department of Rare Books and Special Collections, The University of Michigan Library.

world of his own mind, unable to exert any influence on the current of political affairs or to answer the challenge of external reality which it represents.

Two such challenges confront Bolingbroke as soon as he begins to rule, each the counterpart of a threat which Richard had been unable to dominate. Bagot's accusation of Aumerle, supported and denied by an increasing number of witnesses, places Bolingbroke in the same predicament as Richard had faced when Mowbray was indicted. Both accusations are violent and contradictory, as before, and the task of arbitrating between so many conflicting statements is appreciably more difficult. Bolingbroke takes firm hold of the situation. His order, 'Bring forth Bagot' [IV. i. 1], has a businesslike brevity altogether lacking in the flowery elegance of Richard's address. Where Richard tries to patch a deadly quarrel with a trivial joke, Bolingbroke does not intervene in the conflict; and he concludes the hearing with a cold assertion of authority:

> Lords, you that here are under our arrest,
> Procure your sureties for your days of answer.
>   [IV. i. 158-59]

A more serious challenge comes from the Abbot of Westminster's plot to assassinate Bolingbroke and reinstate the deposed king. This conspiracy is much more dangerous than Bolingbroke's exploitation of Richard's weakness. The new king is opposed by an organised faction who can claim it their moral duty to conspire against the usurper, who has no legal title to the crown. But where Richard surrendered to an unspoken ultimatum, Bolingbroke moves instantly to defend his questionable authority. The fact that his own brother-in-law is among the conspirators does not weaken his determination to crush the plot at once and without mercy. . . . Richard had felt a more sentimental concern for the blood-relationship between himself and the man who deposed him.

To this actual blood-tie Richard adds a fanciful relationship, that of father to his youthful inheritor. The prospect of deposition offers him the agreeable paradox of handing down his possessions to an heir the same age as himself. The conceit contains a dangerous hint that Richard will not resist Bolingbroke's growing ambition, but the attraction of the idea is too much for Richard's sense of discretion, even when he has just surrendered to his enemy:

> Cousin, I am too young to be your father,
> Though you are old enough to be my heir.
> What you will have, I'll give, and willing too.
>   [III. iii. 204-06]

The point recurs in York's report that Richard has agreed to abdicate, and to adopt Bolingbroke as his heir. These hints of a father-son relationship between the two cousins contribute to the working-out of a theme which involves most of the chief characters of *Richard II*. Many of the references to family relationship are put in a form which allows son and fathers to be mentioned, although the kinship is less direct. Gaunt addresses his nephew Richard as 'my brother Edward's son', and then describes himself as 'his father Edward's son' [II. i. 124, 125], making his point at the expense of clarity. When Richard sets aside his relationship with the appellant Bolingbroke, he confuses their actual kinship in a similar way, choosing to be roundabout for the sake of referring to another family tie:

> Were he my brother, nay, my kingdom's heir,
> As he is but my father's brother's son.
>
> [I. i. 116-17]

Instead of describing the relationships between descendants of Edward III directly, Shakespeare makes the speaker trace the son's line of descent back to the father, and to the ancestor whom he shares with the second character. York does not describe himself simply as uncle to Richard, but as

> the last of noble Edward's sons,
> Of whom thy father, Prince of Wales, was first.
>
> [II. i. 171-72]
> (pp. 69-74)

The father-son relationships of *Richard II* are developed in part as a form of conceit with no more imaginative consequence than the verbal quibbles which characterise the play. But in the parallels which they set up between different pairs of characters, they constitute a mode of ironic commentary by which Shakespeare reveals moral contradictions not recognised by the speakers themselves. The fact that York, like Bolingbroke, is the father of a troublesome son invites this form of unspoken commentary by parallel. When his son's part in the conspiracy is disclosed, York is thrown into a frenzy of anxiety to prove his own loyalty, and insists that Aumerle should not be pardoned. His behaviour contrasts sharply with Gaunt's attitude towards the banishing of his son:

> You urged me as a judge, but I had rather
> You would have bid me argue like a father . . .
> A partial slander sought I to avoid,
> And in the sentence my own life destroyed.
>
> [I. iii. 237-38, 241-42]

York's argument against clemency involves a denial of the natural bond between father and son. It also exactly reverses Gaunt's position by asserting that the course of strict justice that destroys the son will regenerate the father:

> Mine honour lives when his dishonour dies,
> Or my shamed life in his dishonour lies:
> Thou kill'st me in his life; giving him breath
> The traitor lives, the true man's put to death.
>
> [V. iii. 70-3]

Both situation and argument are deeply ironic. York is pleading for strict justice from a king without legal right to his judicial authority. He is also demanding that the man who adopted him as father shall pass sentence of death upon his proper son, Aumerle. These ironies are compounded in the personal dishonour which York has brought upon himself by surrendering Richard's power to Bolingbroke. As regent, he has acted as treacherously to his king as Aumerle to the usurper, and deserves the punishment he is demanding for his son. (pp. 75-6)

The ironies of the scene go further. Bolingbroke turns in horror from the 'heinous, strong and bold conspiracy' [V. iii. 59]

which York has uncovered, to praise the integrity of the father who has just betrayed his own child:

> O loyal father of a treacherous son!
> Thou sheer, immaculate and silver fountain
> From whence this stream, through muddy passages
> Hath held his current, and defiled himself!
> Thy overflow of good converts to bad.
>
> [V. iii. 60-4]

In fact Aumerle has followed the example of his father's disloyalty to the reigning king. Addressed to York, Bolingbroke's remarks are badly misapplied, and become fully—and ironically—appropriate only when they are associated with Bolingbroke's own father, whom its terms immediately suggest. Quite unconsciously, Bolingbroke is supplying a double moral commentary upon himself, by admiring the integrity of a confederate who shares his own dishonour, and by lamenting the disgrace which a dissolute son has brought upon the noble reputation of his father; by implication, upon Gaunt. The complex ironies of the scene are finally wound up by the disclosure that Bolingbroke is himself the father of a riotous son. . . . Allusions to Hal's life among the London stews and taverns with 'unrestrained loose companions' [V. iii. 7] build up the picture of an unruly wastrel. The sudden appearance of Aumerle interrupts the discussion without shifting the subject very far; one dishonourable son replacing another, and York taking over Bolingbroke's character of virtuous father outraged by the moral degeneracy of his heir. Bolingbroke overlooks the parallel between himself and York, and neither parent recognises that his son's ignoble behaviour acts as mirror to the father's unacknowledged guilt.

The accumulated ironies of this scene show that Shakespeare is now imaginatively involved in the moral aspects of Bolingbroke's actions. The contest between Bolingbroke and Richard interests him mainly as a struggle between the substance and the shadow of kingship, in which the moral implications of usurped rule are very lightly treated. In the latter part of *Richard II* Shakespeare becomes concerned with the contradictions of Bolingbroke's position as usurper. No moral judgement is offered. Carlisle's warning of the disasters which must follow usurpation—

> The blood of English shall manure the ground,
> And future ages groan for this foul act
>
> [IV. i. 137-38]

—seems a true prophesy, but is too simple an explanation of the disorder and violence represented in *Henry VI* to be mistaken for an editorial comment. Like Richard's claim to be 'the deputy elected by the Lord' [III. ii. 57] whom no mortal power can depose, Carlisle's warning characterises the speaker without illuminating Shakespeare's private opinion. We can feel more certain of Shakespeare's editorial presence where the ironies of a speech reveal a dangerous want of self-awareness in the speaker. By using irony in this way, Shakespeare provides an oblique commentary on moral character without appearing to intervene. Such commentary upon York and Bolingbroke is made through the unrecognised sense of their discussion over Aumerle. Although their valuation of personal honour and family reputation exposes the instinctive duplicity of both men, it leaves these standards intact as a basis of moral judgement by which all three speakers are condemned. For the ironies to be effective, the standards must be consciously implanted in the play by its author. His characters are to be judged only by the moral standards which the play itself proposes.

By this oblique means Bolingbroke is made to provide a moral commentary upon himself, not in the general terms which Carlisle might use but within a particular context of ideas which are developed steadily from the earliest scenes of *Richard II.* The remark, 'O loyal father of a treacherous son!' with its covert application to Bolingbroke and to Gaunt, reaches back further and spreads into the body of the play from a more distant historical source. Gaunt, York, and Bolingbroke are overshadowed by the legendary figure of the great warrior-king to whom they are all related. For Richard, the reputation of a famous grandfather is joined with the nobility and heroism of his father, the Black Prince; but he fails ignominiously to match his great ancestors. Gaunt does not spare Richard when he describes his debasing of a noble reputation:

> O had thy grandsire, with a prophet's eye,
> Seen how his son's son should destroy his sons,
> From forth thy reach he would have laid thy shame,
> Deposing thee before thou wert possessed. . . .
>
> [II. i. 104-07]

Gaunt's rebuke is seconded by York later in the same scene, when Richard resolves to seize Lancaster's estates to redeem his own bankruptcy. Speaking of the Black Prince, York protests:

> His noble hand
> Did win what he did spend, and spent not that
> Which his triumphant father's hand had won.
>
> [II. i. 179-81]

The contrast between thrift and prodigality provides a moral positive by which other characters than Richard are judged. As king, Richard has ignored his illustrious father's example, emptying his treasury and squandering his noble heritage to the point where crippling taxes and enforced levies cannot restore his credit. This is the disgrace, Gaunt argues, which Edward III might have avoided by denying Richard's right of succession after the death of his father. When York discovers Aumerle's part in the conspiracy against Bolingbroke he shows a similar eagerness to obstruct his son's inheritance, using the same images of prodigality and wastefulness to enforce his argument. . . . But York himself has squandered a noble patrimony by betraying Richard, and the character of a prodigal son who has wasted a rich inheritance fits him better than Aumerle. The usurper who has flung away another golden estate, the time-honoured name of Lancaster, is another prodigal. (pp. 76-80)

The human field of *Richard II* includes four fathers, all noble in rank if not in behaviour: Edward the Black Prince, Gaunt, York, and Bolingbroke. Each has a son—Richard, Bolingbroke, Aumerle, Hal—who disappoints expectation by proving morally degenerate; a prodigal who dissipates his inherited wealth and good name by an ignoble course in life. Hal is not yet the enigmatic figure of *Henry IV*, pursuing a hidden purpose under cover of dissolute character, but the 'unthrifty son' [V. iii. 1] who has been lost among taverns and brothels for three months. In York's judgement at least, Aumerle is another prodigal son. Each of the four stands indicted by York's commendation of the noblest of sons, Edward the Black Prince, who 'spent not that which his triumphant father's hand had won', whether knightly honour or revenue. The theme of the prodigal who wastes his patrimony, dishonours a respected name, and burdens his father with disgrace, is repeated in these central characters of *Richard II*, and in the relationships they assume with one another. Gaunt admonishes Richard's wastefulness in the figure of a father, the traitor Bolingbroke asks

to be recognised as adopted son to York, and Richard gives the idea some further currency by acknowledging himself too young to be Bolingbroke's father. The royal gardeners reinforce the theme in speaking of the apricots

> Which, like unruly children, make their sire
> Stoop with oppression of their prodigal weight.
>
> [III. iv. 30-1]

This persistent knot of ideas, firmly attached to the historical framework of *Richard II*, is quickened by new interest when Shakespeare returns to the adjoining field of events in *Henry IV*. (pp. 81-2)

[These imaginative figures in *Richard II*] trace out a pattern of events in which a noble father is disgraced by a morally degenerate son who flings away the fortune earned by his great ancestors. In deposing Richard, himself such a prodigal son, seizing his title and finally allowing his kinsman to be murdered, Bolingbroke outrages the tradition of loyalty and probity invested in his family name and brings lasting infamy upon himself. Once established as king, he finds himself occupying the position of noble father, troubled by a son in whom his own wild prodigality is renewed. The ancestral circle has come about, and its ironic design waits to be traced out afresh from this starting-point in the two parts of *Henry IV*. (p. 85)

> *James Winny, "The Name of King," in his* The Player King: A Theme of Shakespeare's Histories, *Chatto & Windus, 1968, pp. 48-85.*

TERENCE HAWKES (essay date 1969)

[*In the following excerpt, Hawkes emphasizes the fundamental importance of language in* Richard II. *He contends that the play depicts Richard as a monarch "ruling over a society in which truly sympathetic communication between the people has deteriorated beyond repair," claiming that the king's attempts to manipulate the outside world by royal pronouncement rather than "genuine human communication" undermine both his own legitimacy as a ruler and the very fabric of his kingdom. Hawkes maintains, however, that Bolingbroke experiences "the same debilitating gulf between language on the one hand and reality" on the other as Richard does, though unlike Richard—who fails by believing he can control the world through language alone—Bolingbroke fails by considering reality unrelated to language whatsoever. A healthy contrast to either course, the critic proposes, may be found in the attitude of Gaunt, whose "language not only touches reality, it both shapes and is shaped by it."*]

"Literature" is the creature of writing. The term presupposes the use of "letters" and the transmission of verbal works of art by those means. This is the region where "literary" style occurs and is identifiable by means of the visual collation of turns of phrase and forms of words.

But Shakespeare's audience . . . was at the very least residually oral in character, effectively nonliterate by our standards, committed far more to speech than to writing. Indeed, its speech, the result like all speech of a gigantic collaborative enterprise over the centuries, had created the language Shakespeare found. So any inquiry into the style of the plays must begin by remarking the large oral elements they embody, as well as the general extent of oral residue in the prosaic style of the period. In any case, drama is not literature, and Shakespeare's "writing,"—by definition, dramatic—is directed in principle away from the printed page and towards the *spoken* language. The words thus manifest the opposite of a "literary" bearing, and their style has ultimately to do with the qualities of the human voice engaged in speech. It is identifiable aurally, rather than visually.

The argument which follows develops a particular aspect of a larger case; that, to a considerable extent, this is also what the plays are *about*; that their subject, of vital concern to an oral-aural society, is the nature, condition, and role of the spoken language itself; and that they thus in an important sense *enact* the style their words exhibit. (pp. 296-97)

[In] a nonliterate society, words would have been a virtually all-embracing feature of life, inhabiting an acoustic and involving, rather than a visual and distancing space for the majority. When that language, that way of life, and the drama which comes out of these are those of an island people, circumscribed, self-sufficient, and hardly susceptible to outside influence for reasons of state and of religion as well as those of geography, then the interaction between these elements must prove correspondingly more fundamental. Language, way of life, and drama will be more closely knit, the influence of each on the other more radically formative.

That the way of life of Elizabethan Britain was insular and self-sustaining, like its little-known language of English, needs no demonstration. What is of interest is the extent to which these factors act significantly as determinants in the plays, making not merely their use of English, but their attitude towards the language, and the social and political implications of its role, a major feature of their relationship with the society from which their first audiences were drawn.

As a play which focuses on a crucial turning-point in British social and political history, *Richard II* invites examination in these terms. And what immediately becomes clear is that the play's central idea of opposition, embodied in its most extreme form as a civil strife, is quite literally made manifest through the language. In fact the social activity of language itself, which obviously always depends on an intrinsic and defining notion of reciprocity, of talking on the one hand and of responsive listening on the other, seems to take on almost opposite qualities in the play. Instead of reciprocity, antagonism; instead of talking and listening, ranting and deafness; in place of the warmth of human colloquy, the play coldly sets, in its own terms, "the word against the word."

Such a conflict (a fundamental infraction, after all, of man's natural role as communicator) appropriately symbolizes the dehumanizing effects of civil war, in which the natural structure of the family, including the larger political family of society, is riven by the unnatural pitting of brother against brother, father against son. In Shakespeare's view, such a situation clearly violates rudimentary moral, political, and social tenets. The destruction of reciprocal talking and listening reduces man to the level of the beast.

From the first, the play depicts Richard as a king ruling over a society in which truly sympathetic communication between the people has deteriorated beyond repair. He brings conflicting Bolingbroke and Mowbray together with the notion that, in his kingly presence, the loss will in some way be restored. They will "freely speak" [I. i. 17] whilst he will "hear" them. Yet in spite of this confident assertion of his traditional social role, certain qualities of Richard's own speech ironically point in an opposite direction. For whilst Bolingbroke and Mowbray are said to have abandoned the very bases of reciprocal communication—despite attempts at reconciliation they remain "In rage, deaf as the sea" [I. i. 19]—Richard's assessment of the situation and of his own part in it itself exhibits a stultifying

quality of rigidity, and suggests certain prevalent habits of conceptualization which seem happiest at the farthest remove from the complexities of actuality.... Richard's method of dealing with reality is to abstract it from its human context and to reduce it to a simplified structure that can be dealt with at a safe distance. His design so controls the situation that the participants can hardly be expected to "freely speak" as human beings; instead they are forced simply to act out the roles he imposes on them. Richard's own involvement, with Mowbray, in the murder of Thomas of Woodstock (a factor known to the audience) supplies a reasonable motive for such an attitude on the level of the plot, but a good deal of support for it comes nevertheless from his interpretation of his own role as king in the matter, and responsive human contact plays no large part in that. As Mowbray comments, doubtless bitterly in the circumstances, Richard's kingship encourages not freedom of expression, but the reverse:

> ... the fair reverence of your Highness curbs me
> From giving reins and spurs to my free speech.
>
> [I. i. 54-5]

In the sense that Mowbray has acted as Richard's tool, the quarrel between him and Bolingbroke becomes a precursor of the later clash between Bolingbroke and Richard, and it helps to characterize that more momentous conflict in that the "bitter clamour of two eager tongues" [I. i. 49] aptly describes a major aspect of both. Indeed, absence of the warmth of human communication receives specific stress, and acquires symbolic force, in the fliting which ensues. Both Bolingbroke and Mowbray use language as a weapon; their words become increasingly pugnacious, accusatory, alarming, and essentially uncommunicative. Neither really *listens* to the other. (pp. 297-99)

The formality of the occasion, inspired by Richard and signalled from time to time by the rhyme which creeps into the combatant's speech [I. i. 41-6, 150-51], of course further militates against any humanity that might have prevailed, even on the level of this becoming a "woman's war" of mere words [I. i. 48]. It does not do so, partly because more serious issues underly it, and to a greater extent because Richard seems determined to settle the matter by inappropriate methods—that is, by removing from it as many human elements as possible. The ludicrous formality of the verse underlines such an approach:

> This we prescribe, though no physician;
> Deep malice makes too deep incision;
> Forget, forgive, conclude, and be agreed;
> Our doctors say this is no month to bleed.
>
> [I. i. 154-57]

Little human contact can be expected from this, and of course none comes.... Words from now on act merely as the sheaths of swords. Animal violence lies beneath them, and becomes the real test of their truth. Each contestant "will in battle prove" his utterances and, as Bolingbroke says, "make good against thee, arm to arm / What I have spoke" [I. i. 76-7]. The "chivalrous design of knightly trial" [I. i. 81] thus serves to embody and abstract the conflict in terms which, from Richard's point of view, satisfactorily simplify it.... (p. 300)

Such unwillingness really to become involved in the complexities of human communication, and such pathetic abandonment of what Shakespeare would regard as his true role as king in favour of a simple assignment of justice to the strong (compare the opposite in the hero-King, Henry V, who talks with humanity to the common soldier), indicates the root of Richard's tragedy. Genuine human communication with his subjects—

and so genuine human reality—eludes him and, whilst he is King, remains absent from his kingdom. Within it, his subjects' lives come to depend on physical strength, not human contact. However much the formality of the lists attempts to conceal this, the combatants there fight like animals. However much the formality of rhyme attempts to conceal it, they snarl and roar at each other like beasts. Indeed, such formalities, representing as they do a considerable degree of abstraction from ordinary human life, perhaps suggest a peculiarly human form of self-debasement, and so of bestiality. For when talking and listening break down, when communication fails, man becomes less than man. (p. 301)

[When] the actual meeting of Bolingbroke and Mowbray takes place at the lists (I, iii), its larger significance as an instance of Richard's failure lies behind the confrontation of the antagonists, and the nature of that failure and its cause overshadows the ensuing action. In fact, the confrontation merely produces so much verbal noise . . . , itself paralleled by the communication-defeating din of physical conflict that, as Richard himself notices, denies any chance of men's peaceful communion, with its

> . . . boistrous untuned drums
> With harsh resounding trumpets' dreadful bray
> And grating shock of wrathful iron arms.
>
> [I. iii. 134-36]

Richard's throwing down of his warder—the ultimate in wordless formality—of course solves nothing, and only serves to make the rift between Bolingbroke and Mowbray permanent, as well as, in the light of the effect of Bolingbroke's banishment, sowing the seeds of the gigantic rift of civil war. A kingly act which, in underwriting division, physical violence, and dehumanizing strife, betrays the institution's unifying function, it momentarily symbolizes Richard's rule and its social effects.

Typically, Richard proceeds to "reduce" the situation one degree further. Confronted by estrangement of a fundamental sort, he deals with it by means of additional and more literal estrangement. Unable to bring the contenders together, he formally separates them from each other, and from himself, and from his and their own country, by banishment.

The degree to which banishment, far from curing lack of communication, serves only to increase it, of course undergoes examination in political terms throughout the rest of the play, and indeed the cycle of plays which succeeds it. For the banishment of the disaffected Bolingbroke not only precipitates the Wars of the Roses, it also initiates a social, moral, and economic disorder without parallel in the Elizabethan mind.

Appropriately, then, on another level, the banishment becomes symbolically relevant to the nature of Richard's failure as a king. That consists, as has been pointed out, in a failure of communication, and accordingly it takes the particular manifestation, at this point in the play, of a prohibition against the communicative faculties themselves. In fact a number of the metaphors in which that prohibition finds expression exhibit a common concern with language and the human voice. Thus Richard "breathes" the "hopeless word" of "never to return" [I. iii. 152] which Mowbray punningly calls a "heavy sentence," one "all unlooked for from your Highness' mouth" [I. iii. 154-55]. He elaborates the complaint that to cut him off from the English language (in Shakespeare's time, as has been said, one of the little-known European tongues) in effect condemns him to social and cultural isolation, and so to virtual

death. His speech vividly suggests the full extent of Richard's crime against man's communicative nature, and thus against the society over which he rules:

> The language I have learnt these forty years,
> My native English, now I must forgo,
> And now my tongue's use is to me no more
> Than an unstringed viol or a harp,
> Or like a cunning instrument cased up,
> Or being open, put into his hands
> That knows no touch to tune the harmony.
> Within my mouth you have enjailed my tongue,
> Doubly portcullised with my teeth and lips,
> And dull unfeeling barren ignorance
> Is made my jailer to attend on me.
> I am too old to fawn upon a nurse,
> Too far in years to be a pupil now;
> What is thy sentence then but speechless death,
> Which robs my tongue from breathing native breath?
>
> [I. iii. 159-73]

Of course, the sentence mirrors Richard's own condition. He is tragically unable to communicate through language, however much he talks.

Ironically, the play depicts him as no less tragically unable to listen, and his metaphorical deafness receives frequent comment. Even when Gaunt lies on his deathbed, about to speak those "inspired" dying prophecies that tradition insists should be attentively heard, York says of Richard that "all in vain comes counsel to his ear" [II. i. 4]. Gaunt protests, expressing the hope that "my death's sad tale may yet undeaf his ear" [II. i. 16], but that hope is never realized. Richard's ears remain "stopped with other flattering sounds" [II. i. 17]. Inhumanly "deaf" to worthwhile human communication, despite protestations to the contrary [III. ii. 93], his final account of himself in prison admits exactly this charge:

> . . . here have I the daintiness of ear
> To check time broke in a disordered string;
> But for the concord of my state and time,
> Had not an ear to hear my true time broke.
>
> [V. v. 45-8]

Indeed, before Flint castle, Bolingbroke's sending of his emissary,

> . . . to the rude ribs of that ancient castle
> Through brazen trumpet send the breath of parley
> Into his ruined ears . . .
>
> [III. iii. 32-4]

implicitly suggests the extent to which the civil war has maimed oral-aural communication in the kingdom at large. (pp. 301-03)

Richard D. Altick has argued that Richard's most obvious characteristic, his inability to cope with the world of brute fact, manifests itself in his use of language [see excerpt above, 1947]. Altick goes on to suggest that the play is "preoccupied with the unsubstantiality of human language," and that its characters "By making the physical act of speech, the sheer fact of language, so conspicuous . . . call attention to its illusory nature. . . . That words are mere conventional sounds molded by the tongue, and reality is something else again, is constantly on the minds of all the characters."

Clearly, Richard's use of language does indicate a specific sort of response to the harsh world in which he finds himself, but perhaps it has a more complex quality than Mr. Altick's view allows. To refer to Richard's "complacent enjoyment of the sound of his own tongue" surely oversimplifies the issue, for he is no self-satisfied blowhard. Also, words may be mere conventional sounds, but they are not that easily separable from reality. The notion that language is one thing and reality "something else again," certainly is a view held by the play's main characters. But the play itself seems to argue the reverse case: that language and reality are indivisible, coextensive, and that communication by means of talking and listening embodies man's nature and constitutes his genuine reality. Indeed *Richard II* could be said, ultimately, to document the sort of tragic situation which comes about when that fact ceases to be taken into account.

Thus, when Queen Isabel encounters the Duke of York bringing news of war and social upheaval, she timidly tries to deflect his report, urging ". . . for God's sake, speak comfortable words" [II. ii. 76]. The sense, of course, is that of "comforting" in the way that the Anglican communion service uses the word. The notion that certain words can alter reality, modify it to the design of the speaker, is a very old one, with its roots in pagan thought, and it depends, obviously, on the notion of a relationship between language and reality which conceives the former capable of significantly affecting the latter. It is a notion which presupposes that language is one thing, reality "something else again," that "comfortable" words exist whose efficacy can change harsh fact into a more pleasing shape.

In all its superstitious crudity, this may be said to contain the key to Richard's view of the world for, far from accepting the necessity of man's having to use language in order to communicate with man, and so create the only reality, that of the talking-listening community, Richard acts on the principle that language serves as a "comfortable" moulding device by whose means he *alone* can create his own kingly version of existence which can be imposed on everyone. Life, he believes, will become what his "language," as King, makes it. His downfall springs from his inability to recognize any *communal* reality beyond that painted by his own "comfortable words."

So, when Aumerle tries to draw his attention to Bolingbroke's imminent rebellion, Richard dismisses him as "discomfortable cousin" [III. ii. 36]. Later, when Salisbury, bringing bad news, affirms that "Discomfort guides my tongue" [III. ii. 65], Richard, urged by Aumerle to remember the "comfort" that lies in his kingship—"Comfort, my liege, remember who you are" [III. ii. 82]—does so by asserting the power that "comfortable" words, such as his own title, have for him:

> I had forgot myself: am I not king?
> Awake, thou coward majesty! Thou sleepest.
> Is not the king's name twenty thousand names?
> Arm, arm, my name!
>
> [III. ii. 83-6]

Bolingbroke perhaps most aptly recognizes the relationship between language and "real life" entailed in this when he wryly comments on Richard's somewhat arbitrary reduction of his sentence of banishment from ten years to six:

> How long a time lies in one little word.
> Four lagging winters and four wanton springs
> End in a word—such is the breath of kings.
>
> [I. iii. 213-15]

He sees that the "breath of kings," Richard's "language," has power, not over reality, but over that part of it which society, by its structure and its laws, cedes to him. Richard

can "end in a word" four years of banishment in that sense, and indeed, he has power of life and death. But his words have no real power over the reality of time—a point made by Gaunt only a few lines later:

> *Richard.*   Why! uncle, thou hast many years to live.
> *Gaunt.*   But not a minute, king, that thou canst give;
>   Shorten my days thou canst with sullen sorrow,
>   And pluck nights from me, but not lend a morrow;
>   Thou canst help time to furrow me with age,
>   But stop no wrinkle in his pilgrimage:
>   Thy word is current with him for my death,
>   But dead, thy kingdom cannot buy my breath!
>
> [I. iii. 225-32]

It might be said that Richard's very existence traditionally depends on language and reality being indivisible in him: that he only exists as king in so far as he communicates as one. This is to say that the monarchy's existence depends on the king's tacit acceptance of social contexts and sanctions which determine his role, and thus limit the range of actions which can properly be termed kingly. The king, in other words, must behave *like* a king or he will lose that identity.

In so far as man is essentially a social creature, personal identity depends to a certain extent on social interaction, on social identity. It is a matter of reciprocal communication with other people. Richard's notion that he can mould reality (and so society) as *he* wants to, simply by the use of "comfortable" words, ignores a reality larger than himself: that of a society which creates the communicative fabric that, in turn, creates him. A king, after all, has no reality outside the society that accepts him as king, and in overriding the laws and customs of that society, Richard violates the mechanisms which permit its fundamental interaction, the "language" which permits its living together as human beings, which constitutes its reality and his own. As a result, he puts himself outside society's boundary and context, and so loses his identity as king. And, of course, he has no other. Kingship is a totally involving social role and the king has no private or personal life. Richard was, in fact, the last king of the medieval order, ruling by hereditary right. He did not hold an office that could be arbitrarily taken up or relinquished. Nobody could be an ex-king in Elizabethan England.

Accordingly, York sees Richard's appropriation of Bolingbroke's social rights as a violation of something far more fundamental than civil law: it strikes at the very basis of social "language," of reality, and so of Richard's identity:

> Take Hereford's rights away, and take from time
> His charters and his customary rights,
> Let not tomorrow then ensue today;
> Be not thyself. For how art thou a king
> But by fair sequence and succession?
>
> [II. i. 195-99]

Richard's attempt to impose his own order of things on the communicative structure of "fair sequence and succession" causes that structure to cast him out. When he ceases to communicate like a king, he ceases to be a king; and as we learn later, when "fair sequence and succession" has been replaced by its opposite, then "The King is not himself" [II. i. 241].

The misuse of language thus constitutes a major element in the crimes for which Richard loses his crown. For instance, the play insists over and again that his presence actually inhibits oral-aural interaction. Thus, in II, i, only when Richard leaves the stage do the disaffected nobles feel free to speak, a point which is almost laboured:

Ross.	My heart is great but it must break with silence Ere't be disburdened with a liberal tongue.
Northumberland.	Nay, speak thy mind, and let him ne'er speak more That speaks thy words again to do thee harm.
Willoughby.	Tends that that thou wouldst speak to the Duke of Herefore? If it be so, out with it boldly, man; Quick is mine ear to hear of good towards him.

[II. i. 228-34]

Northumberland is urged "be confident to speak" [II. i. 274] amongst the conspirators, whose purpose seems to them to be the restoration of the reality of communication to society, and to the institution of kingship:

> Redeem from broking pawn the blemished crown,
> Wipe off the dust that hides our sceptre's gilt,
> And make high majesty look like itself.

[II. i. 293-95]

Meanwhile, Richard's efforts to change reality by means of language extend to the physical environment, the very earth of Britain itself. He personifies it, "Dear earth, I do salute thee with my hand" [III. ii. 6], urges it to help his cause, "Feed not thy sovereign's foe, my gentle earth" [III. ii. 12], and this not merely with the degree of license to be expected in a verse play, for his own nobles clearly think that something odd prevails in this attitude. Richard feels constrained to abjure them:

> Mock not my senseless conjuration, lords;
> This earth shall have a feeling, and these stones
> Prove armed soldiers . . .

[III. ii. 23-5]

Such verbal "conjuration" suggests nevertheless a degree of fantasy almost certainly fatal for a man confronted with an adversary such as Bolingbroke, and indeed his advisers do try to bring him literally "down to earth," to make him cope with reality. But Richard's tendency simply asserts itself against all advice. He continues to try to impose the "realities" of language on those of harsh fact, to make metaphors "real" in a concrete sense. Thus the metaphor of king as "Sun" takes on, as he uses it of himself, a note of delusion; he becomes "the searching eye of heaven" [III. ii. 37] who has divine power that only needs to be asserted:

> So when this thief, this traitor, Bolingbroke,
> Who all this while hath revelled in the night
> Whilst we were wand'ring with the Antipodes,
> Shall see us rising in our throne, the east,
> His treasons will sit blushing on his face,
> Not able to endure the sight of day
> But self-affrighted tremble at his sin.

[III. ii. 47-53]

This is the "breath of kings," the words which, Richard imagines, by saying a situation is so, *make* it so. By contrast,

> The breath of worldly men cannot depose
> The deputy elected by the Lord.

[III. ii. 56-7]

But that can only be metaphorically true: the harsh reality lies in the fact that "the breath of worldly men" can depose, and does.

When reality breaks through, Richard typically thinks of his plight in terms of language. Where talking about victory has failed to produce it, he now talks about defeat in an attempt to make that over into something more attractive. His images are those of the means of communication, speaking, writing, reading, which best fit the situation as he sees it:

> . . . of comfort no man speak.
> Let's talk of graves, of worms, and epitaphs,
> Make dust our paper, and with rainy eyes
> Write sorrow on the bosom of the earth.

[III. ii. 144-47]

The world presents itself almost entirely in terms of those communicative instruments with which drab reality may be coloured. England becomes a page written by his tears; his life a "story" told by his own voice:

> For God's sake let us sit upon the ground
> And tell sad stories of the death of Kings.

[III. ii. 155-56]

The "sad stories," inevitably self-dramatisations, lead far away, in the opposite direction from reality. (pp. 304-09)

What follows in the play constitutes a complete dissolution of language in Richard, to the extent that he becomes unable to confront reality at all. Language for him speedily takes the form of a screen behind which he hides, posturing as Christ [IV. i. 169ff., 239-41], and thus desperately trying (and failing) to impose some mythic as well as linguistic order on the facts of his deposition. His words, predictably by now, turn in on themselves, away from reality:

> Here, cousin, seize the crown. Here cousin,
> On this side my hand and on that side yours.
> Now is this golden crown like a deep well
> That owes two buckets, filling one another,
> The emptier ever dancing in the air,
> The other down, unseen, and full of water.
> That bucket down and full of tears am I,
> Drinking my griefs, whilst you mount up on high.

[IV. i. 181-89]

Richard's discovery that reality has eluded him, and will no longer shape itself to "the breath of Kings" leads at last to his recognition that the rights attaching to the crown have a considerable linguistic dimension which must be discarded with it:

> With mine own hands I give away my crown,
> With mine own tongue deny my sacred state,
> With mine own breath release all duteous oaths. . . .

[IV. i. 208-10]

Standing before "the sun of Bolingbroke," "bankrupt of his majesty," his "word" no longer "sterling" in England [IV. i. 261-64], he commands a mirror to be brought so that, as ever, he can look inward, not outward, not communicating directly with the world, with reality, but with himself alone, as King, like a reader who studies alone, without communicating outside the realm of the printed page, abstracted from the warmth of oral-aural contact. Thus abstracted, dehumanized, he finds himself literally reduced to the merely visual level, becoming

> . . . the very book indeed
> Where all my sins are writ, and that's myself.
> [IV. i. 274-75]

Indeed, a glance at his own face in the mirror reveals the absence of a real and communicable identity: "How soon my sorrow hath destroyed my face" [IV. i. 291]. But, as Bolingbroke comments, the situation has a grimmer aspect even than that. Richard has become so far removed from reality that his world even now is one of mere shadows, and

> The shadow of your sorrow hath destroyed
> The shadow of your face.
> [IV. i. 292-93]

The spectacle of Richard staring at his reflection in the mirror perfectly symbolizes his inability to communicate as a human being. When he talks it is to himself; when he listens it is to himself. Thus it seems appropriate that when he ultimately speaks of himself as an actor, he stands in fact for the ultimate perversion of that art: the actor who has no audience but himself, an irony of which Shakespeare would be fully aware.

This, after all, provides the basis for the full irony of his earlier account of the "hollow crown" [III. ii. 160-70]. Literally a "Globe-like" theatre, the golden circle within whose walls Death allows

> . . . a little scene
> To monarchize, be feared, and kill with looks,
> [III. ii. 164-65]

contains no audience, and the kings are merely actors whose acting fails to communicate with anybody. We are not surprised, later, to hear Richard's ride through London described in theatrical terms:

> As in a theatre the eyes of men,
> After a well-graced actor leaves the stage
> Are idly bent on him that enters next,
> Thinking his prattle to be tedious.
> [V. ii. 23-6]

The "well-graced actor" is of course Bolingbroke. Richard, as ever uncommunicative, utters only tedious "prattle."

The final sight we have of Richard confirms and restates all these points. His failure is a failure of humanity, because it involves a failure of human communication. His final soliloquy suggests exactly this. Alone, unable to communicate, unable to face reality still, and still attempting to force external circumstances into a shape which his words have predetermined, he utters the final exhalation of the "breath of kings":

> I have been studying how I may compare
> This prison where I live unto the world:
> And for because the world is populous,
> And here is not a creature but myself,
> I cannot do it.
> [V. v. 1-5]

He finds it difficult to produce words as "comfortable" as he feels the situation demands. Yet he forces the language to this task:

> . . . Yet I'll hammer it out:
> My brain I'll prove the female to my soul,
> My soul the father, and these two beget
> A generation of still-breeding thoughts;
> And these same thoughts people this little world,
> In humours like the people of this world.
> [V. v. 5-10]

The metaphor finally, and ironically, betrays him, for he finds that, mirroring the events of his own kingdom, the thoughts, the people he has created, cannot live happily as a community but fight amongst themselves in a civil war which usurps the principle of order lying at the very basis of human existence, in language itself:

> For no thought is contented. The better sort,
> As thoughts of things divine are intermixed
> With scruples, and do set the word itself
> Against the word. . . .
> [V. v. 11-14]

From the very first, a distinction clearly emerges between Richard and Bolingbroke in the matter of language. As Gaunt points out, Bolingbroke "hoards" his words [I. iii. 253] where Richard, by implication, "spends" them. Where Richard's "breath of kings" acts as an instrument for changing reality, a means of colouring it, Bolingbroke's view of the world seems to rest on the notion of a static reality which remains stable, unchanging, whatever may be said about it. The same debilitating gulf between language on the one hand and reality as "something else again" that was noticed in Richard clearly also operates in his usurper.

To Bolingbroke language thus consists "merely" of words, and so words have no special value for him. He does not scatter them with Richard's profusion, for he has not Richard's ends in view. When, in the deposition scene, Richard says "And if my word be sterling yet in England / Let it command a mirror hither straight" [IV. i. 264-65], Bolingbroke's words prove to be the ones which genuinely command, nevertheless: "Go some of you, and fetch a looking glass" [IV. i. 268]. The contrast between these two ways of speaking, the one formal and, in the circumstances, slightly ornate, pretentious, and ultimately ineffectual, the other direct, homely, and effective, is ironic and sharp.

An earlier illustration of the same principle occurs in the scene (I, iii) in which Gaunt attempts to persuade Bolingbroke that his fate, the sentence of banishment, can be made to seem other than it is by means of the language in which one clothes it. He urges "Call it a travel that thou taks't for pleasure" [I. iii. 262]. Bolingbroke replies that this would be to "miscall it," and in response to Gaunt's further suggestion,

> Think not the King did banish thee,
> But thou the King. Woe doth the heavier sit
> Where it perceives it is but faintly borne.
> Go, say I sent thee forth to purchase honour
> And not the King exiled thee; or suppose
> Devouring pestilence hangs in our air,
> And thou art flying to a fresher clime.
> [I. iii. 279-85]

one which perhaps embodies a notion of language's true role in society as we shall see later, Bolingbroke typically rejects such counsel on the grounds that reality cannot be changed by language. As he says,

> O who can hold a fire in his hand
> By thinking on the frosty Caucasus
> Or cloy the hungry edge of appetite
> By bare imagination of a feast?
>
> [I. iii. 294-97]

Insofar as their attitudes to reality so fundamentally affect one another, Richard and Bolingbroke seem set on a "collision course" very early in the play, and nothing can stop the outcome, civil war. The war could thus be said in one dimension to be about the nature of reality, and the relationship of men and men's language to it, with the play focusing attention on the function of the institution of kingship in the matter. Both Richard and Bolingbroke ultimately realize that the whole truth of the situation has eluded them. Richard finds actuality much firmer, harsher, and more unchangeable than his belief in non-material, transcendental, and perhaps ultimately unknowable reality would allow. However much "the breath of kings" attempts to reorder the things of this world, however Richard "words" life, his deposition remains undeniable.

On the other hand, Bolingbroke discovers that reality is not firm, tangible, solid, and unmoving: it shifts as one alters one's point of view and one's way of talking about it. The clash between Bolingbroke and Richard, therefore, is oversimplified if stated as a clash between an idealistic king and a worldly usurper. In fact, the clash occurs between two opposed views of language. And the centrality of that issue to Shakespeare's culture emerges more positively when it is realized what is at stake. As M. M. Mahood puts it, "Verbal authority passed to the king at his coronation. . . . The king's word was immediately effective and so were the words spoken by those to whom he deputed legal authority. . . . In Shakespeare's lifetime the old hierarchy of delegated verbal authority was breaking up, and many words which had once seemed to hold magical efficacy were losing their connotative power" [see excerpt above, 1957]. In such an atmosphere, "To doubt the real relationship between name and nominee, between a word and the thing it signified, was to shake the whole structure of Elizabethan thought and society." This, in essence, is exactly what Bolingbroke does. (pp. 310-15)

Bolingbroke's . . . accession to the throne provides the play with its deepest irony on the level of language and communication. It has earlier been noticeable that for all his original bluntness, for all his interest in the unchanging nature of reality, Bolingbroke nevertheless becomes extremely concerned about names and titles when deprived of these by Richard. When Berkeley comes bringing a message, Bolingbroke will not reply to it unless addressed in what he considers a fitting manner:

> *Berkeley.*   My lord of Hereford, my message is to
>   you.
> *Bolingbroke.* My lord, my answer is,—to Lancaster;
>   And I am come to seek that name in
>   England,
>   And I must find that title in your tongue
>   Before I make reply to aught you say.
>
> [II. iii. 69-73]

and, as he later declares to York,

> As I was banished, I was banished Hereford,
> But as I come, I come for Lancaster.
>
> [II. iii. 112-13]

Such interest in names seems almost worthy of his antagonist, and in fact Bolingbroke in his own way quickly begins to exhibit Richard's worst faults. This point neatly emerges in a scene which echoes the play's first. Where, earlier, we had encountered an uncommunicating Richard ruling over a society in which truly sympathetic communication had decayed and all but vanished, now we find that, under a new king, the situation has not improved: the first scene of Act IV directly balances the first scene of Act I. Where Richard proclaimed that men might "freely speak" [I. i. 17] in front of him, Bolingbroke now urges Bagot to "freely speak thy mind" [IV. i. 2]. The clash of nobles which follows exactly parallels the earlier clash between Bolingbroke himself and Mowbray. Accusations are made, loyalties denied, ears are said to be "treacherous" [IV. i. 54], gages are hurled down as the prelude to combat, and true communication ceases. . . . Bolingbroke's later bald interjections between Richard's ornate abdication speeches cannot thus pass, as they often do, as the blurtings of a plain, blunt man. In context they suffer from the same fault as the words of Richard: a debilitating gap yawns between them and the reality of kingship.

Words dominate Bolingbroke's "new world" then, as much as they did Richard's old one. And it may be noticed that, where Richard's world ends in silence (parting from his Queen he urges that they "dumbly part" [V. i. 95], and resolves "the rest let sorrow say" [V. i. 102]), we hear, moments later, the clamour of words which greets Bolingbroke's accession. As York puts it,

> . . . all tongues cried "God save thee Bolingbroke!"
> You would have thought the very windows spake.
>
> [V. ii. 11-12]

Richard's deposition puts him in Bolingbroke's former position; Bolingbroke's accession makes him another Richard, and he assumes Richard's linguistic mantle with his crown. Almost literally, he becomes the "Richard the second" of the title. Under him, the communicative units of society begin to break up. Families divide as the great gulf between York and Lancaster begins to yawn. Aumerle literally cannot communicate with his parents (V, ii), and Bolingbroke's own son, Hal, proves notably disaffected from his father [V. iii. 1 ff.]. The atmosphere swirls with plot and counterplot, and the scene in which Aumerle begs for pardon from Bolingbroke, only to have his father urge the new King to deny it (V, iii), seems to symbolize the dissension's intensity. Much is made of locked doors which keep people from contact with each other, and a climax of alienation occurs when York impeaches his own son, callously suggesting that Bolingbroke speak the promised pardon only in French, ". . . say Pardonne moy" [V. iii. 119]—that is, "excuse me, I cannot pardon you." The Duchess's comment on this aptly suggests the whole scene's atmosphere; it is a mother speaking to a father about their son:

> Dost thou teach pardon pardon to destroy?
> Ah, my sour husband, my hardhearted lord!
> That sets the word itself against the word.
>
> [V. iii. 120-22]

The mutual incomprehensibility, as of French word against English word described here, takes us back to Richard's England of dissent, quarrels, absence of communication, that, as he himself put it, "do set the word itself / Against the word" [V. v. 13-14]. (pp. 316-18)

The irony of the situation finally inheres in the fact that both for Richard and Bolingbroke, the institution of kingship seems to contain a self-destructive principle which makes one monarch hardly distinguishable from his successor. To place an immortal mantle on the shoulders of a mortal man seems in itself to cause that gap between words and actuality which, in both old and new king, impairs the sanctity of the office. The gap between words and things in the outlook of both Richard and Bolingbroke mirrors, and perhaps mocks, that between the *name* of king, which suggests harmonious social ordering, and the *nature* of man which causes the discordancy of civil war.

Where, then, does true reality lie? How can word and object, king and man, name and nature be reconciled? The play seems to argue that such a division can only be overcome by a refusal to recognize the terms in which it is cast; and it locates this ''right'' attitude primarily in the character of Gaunt.

In Gaunt's view of the world, words and actuality prove not only inseparable, but coextensive: they contain and condition each other. His language not only touches reality, it both shapes and is shaped by it. In fact, words and things, names and nature, literally unite in his person:

> O how that name befits my composition!
> Old Gaunt indeed, and gaunt in being old!
> Within me Grief hath kept a tedious fast;
> And who abstains from meat that is not gaunt?
> For sleeping England long time have I watched:
> Watching breeds leanness, leanness is all gaunt.
> [II. i. 73-8]

The language goes beyond mere punning to the truth, a point which notably escapes Richard, who regards this as merely ''playing'' with names [II. i. 84]. . . . This quality of Gaunt's language of course makes his long speech on England central to the play's linguistic as well as political themes. He speaks it as ''a prophet new inspired'' [II. i. 31], and, significantly, its central concern is the relation of England to her kings, of the self-sufficient, circumscribed, tightly-knit island culture to its own little-known native language, of nature to name. Thus the main line of the argument claims that, under Richard, the ''royal throne of kings,'' the ''sceptred isle,'' the ''other Eden, demi-paradise,'' the England of numinous ineffable qualities, this ''fortress . . . Against infection,'' has been ''leased out . . . Like to a tenement or pelting farm'' [II. i. 40ff.]. The supernatural, the immeasurable, the non-negotiable, the cherished, has been assessed like a piece of mere earth, measured, weighed, negotiated, rented out. The true communicative role of kingship, involving a liberating life-giving interaction between crown and people, has been violated. Gaunt's final metaphor of this seems to come directly and poignantly from the heart of a self-contained oral community. Instead of being characterized as a place of warm human colloquy, a resonant world of ''language,'' the ''little world'' of England is pictured as a stale, blotted, and badly-bound book, full of coldly uncommunicative printed words: a silent world of writing. Once ''bound in with the triumphant sea'' she

> . . . is now bound in with shame,
> With inky blots, and rotten parchment bonds.
> [II. i. 61-2]

The vivid island language has been grossly reduced. Gaunt quite rightly expects words such as these to become Richard's ''tormentors'' [II. i. 136], and they linger in the mind as standards against which the later speeches of both kings will be measured. Like the words of the Gardeners, they draw on and generate central life expanding metaphors about England—and

make these part of the only reality; that which language and experience, names and nature, create by their fruitful interaction.

As a result of considerations such as these, *Richard II* ceases to be a play concerned merely with politics in the modern restricted sense of the word, and takes on the implications of a play closely concerned with the structures of society on a much deeper level: with the fundamentals of human interrelationships, and in particular the role of that social institution which once seemed most positively to embody them. For above all others, the institution of kingship had, ideally for the Elizabethans, a communicative function. The purpose of what has been called unitary monarchy was to act as a focal, and so unifying medium through which men could symbolically ''speak'' to one another, and also to God. (pp. 319-21)

Indeed, if, as the play seems to suggest, communication at all levels has a paramount status in human life as the essential element on which the entire moral, political, and social fabric depends, then the setting of ''word'' against ''word'' becomes an appropriate symbol for a literal tearing apart of communal existence, and thus a striking at the very basis of human nature, which renders it unutterably evil. When the perpetrators of that evil are themselves kings, the spectacle becomes a fit one for tragedy. (p. 322)

> Terence Hawkes, ''The Word against the Word: The Role of Language in 'Richard II','' in Language and Style, *Vol. II, No. 1, Spring, 1969, pp. 296-322.*

HERBERT B. ROTHSCHILD, JR. (essay date 1970)

[*Taking issue with such critics as Richard D. Altick (see excerpt above, 1947), who attribute King Richard's downfall to his fatal attraction to language, Rothschild maintains that* Richard II *is more concerned with ''the existential perplexities of life,'' foremost being the question of whether words actually correspond to ''hard reality.'' He argues that by assailing Richard II's title, Bolingbroke places the meaning of all words in theoretical jeopardy. Traditionally, the critic explains, there was felt to be a real and necessary connection between the ''signum'' (word or symbol) and the ''res'' (object or person signified), but Bolingbroke's usurpation of Richard's kingship raises the uncomfortable spectre of ''semantic annihilation'': identity itself is reduced to an arbitrary fiction if one's very name can be rescinded at the whim of society or a powerful enemy. Such an analysis goes far, Rothschild suggests, to explain Richard's sense of desperation and alienation as he gives up his crown; it further lends a coherence to his otherwise apparently bizarre actions, such as his smashing the mirror during the abdication scene. In Rothschild's view, this last action epitomizes the king's efforts to reestablish the weakened link between what is mental and what is concrete, a ''pitiable attempt to maintain the validity of images as he understands them.''*]

No reader of *Richard II* can fail to be impressed with its sheer verbosity—words in excess of matter, language that exists only to call attention to itself. . . . C. L. Barber accounts for this special feature of the play . . . when he writes that *Richard II* ''is a pioneering exploration of the semantics of royalty, shot through with talk about the potency and impotence of language.''

Others who have noticed the concentration on words themselves interpret it as an underscoring of the king's ''propensity for verbalizing'' which they, with Richard Altick, would contend is ''Richard's fatal weakness'' [see excerpt above, 1947]. There are two reasons for rejecting such an interpretation. The first is that many other characters besides Richard seem similarly concerned about language. Even Bolingbroke, whose silence during the deposition scene is frequently and erroneously contrasted with Richard's theatricality to prove that he is a ruler in deed, not in word, exhibits this concern elsewhere. Secondly . . . , the protagonist's political defeat is already assured when he returns from Ireland in III. ii. There are no ''proffer'd means of succors and redress'' [III. ii. 32], as the Bishop Carlisle and Aumerle understand them, for him to embrace. Alienated by their king's past misdeeds, the nobles and commoners have defected to Bolingbroke. To attribute Richard's downfall to a propensity to verbalize instead of act (something that becomes apparent only at this juncture) is to overlook the facts.

Richard, then, is quicker to grasp his situation than are his counsellors, though his knowledge deepens only with his sufferings. For the question before him is not, what should he do, but who can he be; and his concentration on language does not bear on what constitutes a good king, but what constitutes a king. When the play is viewed from this perspective, it becomes clear that Shakespeare has here transcended the vision of *A Mirror for Magistrates* and those dramatists, including himself, who had hitherto written of troublesome reigns. In a way that is often cumbrous and ineffectual, but nevertheless prophetic of the great tragedies, he reaches out with his verse to involve his protagonist's agony in the existential perplexities of life—the problems of conceptual reality and identity.

In addition to the verbosity of *Richard II*, and closely related to it, is the ceremonial quality of its action. Taken seriously, ceremony proceeds on the premise that there is no discrepancy between *signum* and *res*, between the symbol (be it a name, an emblem, a gesture, etc.) for a thing and the thing itself. When Richard swears ''by my scepter's awe'' [I. i. 118] or ''by my seat's right royal majesty'' [II. i. 120], no one in Shakespeare's audience would think that his emphasis on the symbols of kingship evidences his lack of kingly substance. They would assume that to wield the scepter is to be king. The force of the play derives from the revelation that their assumption is not necessarily true, that *signum* is not equivalent to *res*. As Barber says, ''the Elizabethan mind . . . generally assumed that one played one's part in a divinely ordained pageant where each man *was* his name and the role his name implied. The expression of this faith, and the outrage of it, is particularly drastic in the Elizabethan drama, which can be regarded, from this vantage, as an art form developed to express the shock and exhilaration of the discovery that life is not pageantry.''

In *Richard II*, I. i, iii. there is a heavy concentration of imagery related to language—*tongue, mouth, throat, word, speech, name*. Van Doren, the first to notice the recurrence of the word *tongue*, merely related it to the characters' capacity to ''tune the harmonies of English'' [see excerpt above, 1939]. Altick took the matter much further: ''By making the physical fact of speech, the sheer fact of language so conspicuous, they [the images] call attention to its illusory nature—to the vast difference between what the semanticists call the intensional and extensional universes. That words are merely conventional sounds molded by the tongue, and reality is something else again is constantly on the minds of all the characters.'' Altick has identified the issues, but, in his haste to discuss all the imagery of the play, has oversimplified, and therefore distorted, Shakespeare's treatment of them. Perhaps because he believes that Richard's propensity to verbalize instead of act destroys him, Altick refuses to consider that the ''intensional universe'' has its own powerful reality.

Indeed, the examples Altick cites do not bear out his generalization, because in these opening two scenes it is the potency of language that is stressed. Mowbray says of his quarrel with Bolingbroke that

> 'Tis not the trial of a woman's war,
> The bitter clamor of two eager tongues,
> Can arbitrate this cause betwixt us twain.
>
> [I. i. 48-50]

But he cannot remain silent.

> Yet can I not of such tame patience boast
> As to be hush'd and naught at all to say.
> First, the fair reverence of your highness curbs me
> From giving reins and spurs to my free speech,
> Which else would post until it had return'd
> These terms of treason doubled down his throat.
>
> [I. i. 52-7]

Words take on the quality of action in these lines. From Mowbray's metaphor it can be seen how the verbal jousting has the same character and force as the physical joust it is supposed to prelude. It has this quality because it effectively embodies the total energy and substance of the antagonism. Bolingbroke swears,

>   for what I speak
> My body shall make good upon this earth
> Or my divine soul answer it in heaven.
>
> [I. i. 36-8]

And his opponent says,

> I do defy him, and spit at him,
> Call him a slanderous coward and a villain;
> Which to maintain I would allow him odds
> And meet him, were I tied to run afoot
> Even to the frozen ridges of the Alps.
>
> [I. i. 60-4]

There is nothing unsubstantial about these words, then, nothing hollow about the ceremonial confrontation. Not to participate would be equivalent to not entering the lists.

When Mowbray turns down Richard's request to end the quarrel without first vindicating his honor, he introduces other considerations about the substance and potency of language.

>   My fair name,
> Despite of death that lives upon my grave,
> To dark dishonor's use thou shalt not have.
> I am disgrac'd, impeach'd, and baffled here;
> Pierc'd to the soul with Slander's venom'd spear,
> The which no balm can cure but his heart-blood
> Which breath'd this poison.
>
> [I. i. 167-73]

Here a verbal attack assumes the nature of a physical assault, but ''Slander's venom'd spear'' strikes at the very soul. At this point, then, name is equated with a man's essence. What his name comes to mean is what the man is. His substance (*res*) is not matter, but that which only language (*signum*) is able to convey. Precisely this distinction is made in some further lines that Mowbray speaks.

> The purest treasure mortal times afford
> Is spotless reputation. That away,
> Men are but gilded loam or painted clay.
>
> [I. i. 177-79]

Without his name, a man can have no meaning in a social context. He is imprisoned in his own body. (pp. 56-60)

It is only through the conceptual process, especially speech, that entities besides man come to have meaning apart from and beyond their material existence. This is what takes place in Gaunt's famous speech about England in II. i. "This royal throne of kings," he begins, and it is not until he has set seventeen more names in apposition that he concludes, "is now leas'd out—I die pronouncing it— / Like to a tenement or pelting farm" [II. i. 40-60]. The force of the passage derives from the feeling of reduction at its close. To think that all this could be treated as if it existed in no more than its basest form—matter, dirt. Yet, for Richard to farm out his realm may not be the offense against God, Nature, and history that Gaunt's rhetoric persuades his hearers that it is. All the meanings he attributes to England may only be the products of his inflated language. Ontologically, England is a large piece of real estate, and Gaunt may have made this materialistic point of view disreputable by conceiving of the fact of England in terms to which it ultimately may not correspond.

During the scene, of course, it is impossible to criticize in this fashion the generation of meaning and values, and it comes to mind only later when the full implications of Richard's predicament are realized. Nonetheless, there is a foreshadowing of what is to come in Gaunt's parting with his banished son. To lighten his burden, the old man advises him to think of his exile in other terms. "Call it a travel that thou tak'st for pleasure," he suggests [I. iii. 262]. Or again, "Go, say I sent thee forth to purchase honor, / And not the king exil'd thee" [I. iii. 282-83]. Gaunt is suggesting that different, more comfortable meanings can be derived from the situation if Bolingbroke would only exercise his conceptual powers. "Call," "esteem," "think," "say," "suppose," "imagine" are the terms he uses. But this advice will not do.

> O, who can hold a fire in his hand
> By thinking on the frosty Caucasus?
> Or cloy the hungry edge of appetite
> By bare imagination of a feast?
> Or wallow naked in December snow
> By thinking on fantastic summer's heat?
> [I. iii. 294-99]

A hard material reality exists which will not yield up such meanings. Because of the extremity of the situation, the effect is just to indicate a limitation to the process of conceptual thinking, a boundary to the intensional universe. Yet it is the first hint that there may be no *res* to correspond to *signum* except in the mind of man.

A similar limitation, which affords the same kind of hint, is introduced in regard to the power of Richard's words. When he reduces Bolingbroke's sentence by four years, they seem coextensive with his vast authority, and Henry exclaims,

> How long a time lies in one little word!
> Four lagging winters and four wanton springs
> End in a word. Such is the breath of kings.
> [I. iii. 213-15]

Then Gaunt says that Richard's act of mercy will do him little good, since a death which Richard can do nothing to delay will claim the father before his son's return.

> Thou canst help time to furrow me with age,
> But stop no wrinkle in his pilgrimage.
> Thy word is current with him for my death,
> But dead, thy kingdom cannot buy my breath.
> [I. iii. 229-32]

Here again are the intractable facts of material life. When faced with these same facts later, Richard will have no power, by virtue of being king, to banish them from consideration. Salisbury tells him, upon his return from Ireland,

> O, call back yesterday, bid time return,
> And thou shalt have twelve thousand fighting men!
> Today, today, unhappy day, too late,
> Overthrows thy joys, friends, fortune, and thy state.
> [III. ii. 69-72]

For the most part, though, these inklings of what is to come do not disturb the ceremony, and the conception of reality that ceremony implies, in the beginning of the play. They do not because the substance with which ceremony deals, it cannot be emphasized enough, is not the material facts of life. A man is not king because he has more power than anyone else; he has more power than anyone else because he is king. If a man calls himself by the right name, presumably that name will be accepted at face value. (pp. 61-3)

When Bolingbroke lands at Ravenspurgh to discover that the English nobles and commoners flock to his banner, and when Richard lands at Barkloughly Castle to find that all his power is dispersed, there begins a contrapuntal movement in the play. This is not the rise of one fortune at the expense of another, since Shakespeare has removed all doubt about the power struggle by III. ii. The character of the movement can best be conveyed by examining two parallel incidents. An emissary sent by York to Bolingbroke on his march from Ravenspurgh says, "My Lord of Herford, my message is to you," to which Henry replies,

> My lord, my answer is—to Lancaster,
> And I am come to seek that name in England,
> And I must find that title in your tongue
> Before I make reply to aught you say.
>   *Barkly.* Mistake me not, my lord. 'Tis not my meaning
> To raise one title of your honor out.
> To you, my lord, I come, what lord you will.
> [II. iii. 70-6]

Later, when the report is received that the king's men have fled and he is hiding, Northumberland says to Bolingbroke,

> The news is very fair and good, my lord.
> Richard not far from hence hath hid his head.
>   *York.* It would beseem the Lord Northumberland
> To say 'King Richard.' . . .
>   *Northumberland.* Your grace mistakes. Only to be
> brief
> Left I his title out.
>   *York.*   The time hath been,
> Would you have been so brief with him, he would
> Have bin so brief with you to shorten you,
> For taking so the head, your whole head's length.
> [III. iii. 5-8, 10-14]

Bolingbroke, who has the force to become what lord he wills, and who soon chooses to become king, must seek verification in the tongues of men of the roles he will assume, even though they are powerless at the moment to prevent his adopting them. If he is king *de facto,* yet fails to convince the world to give him a name that acknowledges a different kind of royal substance (i.e. "king" instead of "usurper"), then his power is confined to his own person and those people whom he can directly impress with it. . . . While Bolingbroke tries to gain through force a name that will be recognized as legitimate,

Richard is testing what force there is in a legitimate name. He now has no power to make people give him his title. York's reminder to Northumberland of what was merely calls attention to what no longer is. But if they call him king voluntarily—and even the rebels do until he resigns the crown, though Northumberland's verbal "mistake" is ominous—then may he not logically presume that he has the authority of a king? Surely there must be something substantial in his name.

Temporarily roused from his despair over the loss of his twelve thousand Welsh soldiers, Richard says,

> I had forgot myself. Am I not king?
> Awake, thou coward majesty. Thou sleep'st.
> Is not the king's name twenty thousand names?
> Arm, arm, my name!
>
> [III. ii. 83-6]

Despite the absurdity of the final line, there is a logic behind it. Discounting the second line, the speech has the form of a syllogism. If there is something radically wrong with the conclusion, the fault must lie with the premises. So it does, but pinpointing it requires a radical shift in Elizabethan thought and raises vexing questions which we ourselves cannot claim to have put to rest. Is Richard not king? If the answer is no, the next question is the one Richard asks later:

> If we be not, show us the hand of God
> That hath dismissed us from our stewardship?
>
> [III. iii. 77-8]

Here is a special belief about kingship which Elizabethans cherished, and a great deal has been written about the way it is violated in *Richard II*. Undoubtedly, Shakespeare brings it to the fore, but it involves far more than itself. Suppose it is acknowledged as a fiction that the king has divine protection, that he cannot be deposed by men even if he does not live up to his role as king; suppose society can take away his name when it believes that he is not deserving of it, as indeed Richard is not; does it not then follow that each man's identity is to an uncomfortable extent in the hands of other people? Even Bolingbroke is not satisfied to have only "men's opinions and my living blood" [III. i. 26] to testify to his true being. If Richard cannot presume that society will judge him to be the man his name, bestowed on him in a public ceremony, stands for, then who can be sure that the names he gives himself will be accepted as the right ones? Barber puts it this way: "Whatever your assumptions about semantics, when you have to act, to be somebody or become somebody, there is a moment when you have to have faith that the unknown world beyond will respond to the names you commit yourself to as right names." Without assurance that his name will have an absolute content in a social context, man is always in danger of being reduced, in his social nature, to mere physical presence, "the gilded loam and painted clay" [I. i. 179] of which Mowbray spoke. This is exactly what happens to Richard. His doom bears an existential similarity to that of Mowbray. The latter, though free to wander, was imprisoned in his own body because he had no way of communicating the reality of his being to an alien society. Richard is imprisoned in a cell, though free to talk all he wishes, because the words in which he communicates his meaning are not accepted as valid.

If the first premise ("Am I not king?") of Richard's syllogism is correct and the second is wrong ("Is not the king's name twenty thousand names"), the same kind of considerations are raised. The authority that his name embodies remains as it was, yet it cannot now command twenty thousand troops. Then what

was the nature of that authority in the first place if it has no unchanging value? The answer must be that it has no meaning other than that which society accords it. From this point on, all concepts, all words must lose their fixed reference points and depend wholly upon the way people choose to receive them. The world of meanings and values becomes dangerously relative.

Richard is quick to sense that he cannot depend on men to uphold his authority, and if he turns for aid more and more to powers of a conceptually absolute realm, be it heaven or his own language, it is no more than his situation compels him to do. As he does so, symbols that were thought by the whole society to have ontological content become emptied of it. Words, names, the signs of office ring hollow. Simultaneously, one begins to feel—and with trepidation—that there is no ontological reality except what may be measured by its physical properties. . . . Because Richard cannot extend his physical presence beyond his own dimensions, the king's domain is his body and the space it occupies.

> And nothing can we call our own but death
> And that small model of the barren earth
> Which serves as paste and cover to our bones.
>
> [III. ii. 152-54]

When the deposed Richard appears before Bolingbroke and Parliament in IV. i., he goes through a ceremony that is a travesty and which relates by contrast, not comparison, to the ceremony of Act I. He gives away all his signs of power—his throne, his scepter, his oaths of fealty—none of which corresponds to any level of reality. Yet as long as Richard can think of himself in terms of the symbols of what he was, he does not have to face the reality of what he is. He can hardly be prepared to face it, because he cannot comprehend himself without a name to give him his meaning.

> I have no name, no title;
> No, not that name was given me at the font,
> But 'tis usurped. Alack the heavy day,
> That I have worn so many winters out
> And know not now what name to call myself!
>
> [IV. i. 255-59]

So he calls for a mirror to see if he has any substance whatsoever. When he discovers that he has a face that means no more than itself, that is not a symbol of his past glory or even his present self-styled crucifixion, he tries to destroy it by destroying its reflection. Smashing the mirror is Richard's last and most pitiable attempt to maintain the validity of images as he understands them. Bolingbroke tells him, "The shadow of your sorrow hath destroyed / The shadow of your face" [IV. i. 292-93], the truth of which he acknowledges: "'Tis very true, my grief lies all within" [IV. i. 295].

Bolingbroke's behavior is characterized by silence throughout the deposition scene, but not because he is the "real" king who does not need to flourish the symbols of his power. The fact is that he has none. If there is any legitimate value in them, they legitimately are Richard's until he gives them away. Nor can Bolingbroke afford to mock Richard's futile ceremony. As it has been pointed out, he knows how important it is that men accept names and titles as meaningful, that symbols have a potency beyond the force that backs them up. He must acquire Richard's and restore to them the legitimacy they once seemed to possess, or he will have attained a throne that will be regarded as the prize of the strongest.

Act V. Scene v. Exton, Richard II, and servant. By Abraham Cooper (1826). The Department of Rare Books and Special Collections, The University of Michigan Library.

As early as *Richard II,* then, Shakespeare had been led to think about the nature of identity and social order by exploring the reality of language. By allowing his protagonist to depend on a conceptually absolute understanding of himself and society, by equating Richard's validity with its validity, Shakespeare could discover through Richard's inevitable failure that life would not yield to such an understanding. However, given such an irresponsible protagonist, he could discover no further than that identity and social order were problems in the drama of human life. His insights remain on a rather speculative level, unrooted in man's irreducible experience. Like the language of his characters, which tends to isolate and reflect upon itself, Shakespeare's thought here seems to be divorced from his feeling about how life must be acted out. We do not draw back from shouldering Richard's burden because we lack the courage. It was not until Shakespeare could create protagonists who shouldered the necessary burdens, who accepted full responsibility for what we cannot dispense with in our effort to lead a human existence, that his earlier insights could reveal their fullest implications. It was not until he had men like Lear and Coriolanus to confront with problems like those Richard faced that Shakespeare discovered the human drama itself to be problematical. (pp. 63-8)

> *Herbert B. Rothschild, Jr., "Language and Social Reality in 'Richard II'," in* Essays in Honor of Esmond Linworth Marilla, *edited by Thomas Austin Kirby and William John Olive, Louisiana State University Press, 1970, pp. 56-68.*

HELMUT BONHEIM AND JEAN BONHEIM (essay date 1971)

[*Adopting an anthropological approach to* Richard II, *Helmut and Jean Bonheim argue that the play is not only a political drama depicting the dangers of usurpation and the Tudor view of Richard*

as a martyred king, but is also a historical-mythical reenactment of the "passing of the crown"—the ancient ritual of the killing of the old, sterile king and a coronation of the new. The critics note the association of this myth in many cultures with the changing of the seasons, and they identify numerous image-patterns surrounding both Richard and Bolingbroke that lend credence to their assessment.]

Richard II is normally thought to argue against the usurpation of royal power, to be "patently loyalist in tone" [see essay by John Dover Wilson cited in the Additional Bibliography]. And there is no denying that such a doctrinal content—supporting the divine-right theory and the so-called "Tudor myth"—does appear in Shakespeare's history plays. But we overstress the doctrinal bias of *Richard II* if we try to see Bolingbroke as a villainous usurper and Richard as a royal martyr, at the very least this view underrates the dramatic subtlety achieved in this relatively early play. It is true that Holinshed shows Bolingbroke deceitful and Richard noble. But Shakespeare has altered his sources to the point where readers cannot agree whether his Bolingbroke is admirable or sly and opportunistic, whether his Richard is heroic or despicable. It has been claimed that both of them change in character as well as political power in the course of the play.

Some of Richard's and Bolingbroke's traits of character are established not so much by what they do or say as by the patterns of imagery associated with them. The most important of these patterns associates Bolingbroke with fertility and Richard with impotence and sterility. This pattern is related to another: a pattern of cyclical progress in nature, in fortune, in man and in time. Finally the pattern of fertility and sterility and the positions of Richard and Bolingbroke on the political wheel of fortune suggests that in the central action of the play, and the ritual of the deposition scene in particular, Shakespeare is presenting a reenactment of the ancient rite of the new king displacing the old.

Although a few of the images and conceits dealing with infertility and impotence apply to old or dying people such as the Duchess of Gloucester and John of Gaunt, most such rhetorical figures concern Richard and his Queen. . . . (pp. 169-70)

Richard and his Queen have no children of their own, and Richard professes little respect for lawful progression from father to son. Nevertheless they are always metaphorically involved in the process of procreation. But to what do they give birth? To woes, to thoughts, nothing more.

Consider the scene in which Richard, on his way to the tower, meets the Queen. Richard is the first to present a metaphor on the theme of procreation: "So two, together weeping, make one woe" [V. i. 86]. An infertile union, at best. (p. 170)

In the tower Richard, all alone, desired to populate his little world:

> And, for because the world is populous
> And here ist not a creature but myself,
> I cannot do it.
>
> [V. v. 3-5]

He cannot do it, for here as elsewhere he is essentially "barren and bereft of friends" [III. iii. 84]. And so Richard can only give birth to thoughts begot of brain and soul—a poor substitute for real children. The Queen too talks metaphorically about her own sterility when, at Windsor Castle, she complains of her anxieties. She imagines "Some unborn sorrow ripe in Fortune's womb" [II. ii. 10] and, when she is confronted by

Bushy, who tells her that her griefs are "nought but shadows" [II. ii. 23], she picks up, like Ophelia at the dumb-show, the sexual implication implicit in his "nought" and develops it:

> I cannot but be sad; so heavy sad,
> As, though on thinking on no thought I think,
> Makes me with heavy nothing faint and shrink.
>
> [II. ii. 30-2]

Bushy answers: "'Tis nothing but conceit, my gracious lady" [II. ii. 33]. But the Queen is wiser:

> 'Tis nothing less: conceit is still deriv'd
> From some forefather grief; mine is not so,
> For nothing hath begot my something grief,
> Or something hath the nothing that I grieve—
> 'Tis in reversion that I do possess—
> But what it is that is not yet known what,
> I cannot name: 'tis nameless woe, I wot.
>
> [II. ii. 34-40]

The Queen develops "nothing" into a three-fold pun. "Nothing" applies, literally, to the fact that there is no definable cause for the oppression she feels. Secondly, it refers to the actual woe that she bears within her. But the Queen is also talking about her infertility, for here, as in other plays, Shakespeare uses the yonic (sexual) symbols of O, nought, nothing, ball, and hollowness. The Queen bears a woman's burden, yet it has not been naturally conceived. (And indeed the only living thing to proceed from her is the rue tree, a symbol of sorrow, which will spring from her tears.) And because she bears a burden which is not a child she repeatedly reminds herself of the unnaturalness and the essential barrenness of her position. (pp. 171-72)

Like the Queen . . . , John of Gaunt also plays with the idea of hollowness, although he applies it to death rather than to sorrow. He, like the other two, speaks in terms of unfulfilled fecundity, despite the fact that he has a son: "Gaunt am I for the grave, gaunt as a grave, / Whose hollow womb inherits nought but bones" [II. i. 82-3]. Richard speaks of his "hollow" crown: ". . . for within the *hollow* crown / That *rounds* the mortal temples of a king / Keeps Death his court . . ." [III. ii. 160-62].

Of the five places where "hollow" is used in this play, four refer to the life-death opposition (as, for example: "Even through the hollow eyes of death I spy life peering . . ." [II. i. 270-71]). Nowhere else in Shakespeare is "hollow" used in this way.

Just as Richard is shown to be infertile, so the ideal England and Bolingbroke are fertile and thriving.

England, in John of Gaunt's famous speech [II. i. 31 ff.] is a "nurse," a "teeming womb of royal kings"; she is compared to a farm, her children are "this happy *breed* of men." England has fostered Bolingbroke's and Mowbray's blood [I. iii. 126]: England, says Bolingbroke, is "My mother and my nurse that bears me yet!" [I. iii. 307] (Richard, on the other hand, in feminine fashion thinks of himself as the mother of England [III. ii. 8]. This is the only place where Richard is considered as the parent of anything tangible.) England as a mother is emphasized by references to her "green lap" [III. iii. 47; V. ii. 46-7] and to her bosom [III. ii. 19].

Bolingbroke, like the ideal England, is connected with fertility. The sun, as critics have noted, pictures Richard's position as king on fortune's wheel—he rises, falls (like Phaethon) or sets; when King Richard is powerful his glory (the sun) lights up

"every guilty hole" and detects "murthers, treasons, and detested sins" [III. ii. 44]. Richard in his glory made people wink, as does the sun [IV. i. 284]. But the sun is also connected with Bolingbroke, and here the sun has quite different functions. Bolingbroke's is the sun which warms, which causes growth, which makes fertile, which gives light. Bolingbroke himself described his sun:

> . . . this must my comfort be,
> That sun that warms you here, shall shine on me,
> And those his golden beams to you here lent
> Shall point on me and gild my banishment.
>
> [I. iii. 144-47]

King Richard, in the deposition scene, wishes the new king "many years of sunshine days!" [IV. i. 221] And Richard recognizes the contrast between himself and Bolingbroke:

> O that I were a mockery king of snow,
> Standing before the sun of Bolingbroke,
> To melt myself away in water-drops!
>
> [IV. i. 260-62]

In the earlier scene at Flint Castle Bolingbroke had pictured himself as water to Richard's fire, but water which would not rain down on Richard, but on the earth, so that things might grow.

> Be he the fire, I'll be the yielding water;
> The rage be his, whilst on the earth I rain
> My waters—on the earth, and not on him.
>
> [III. iii. 58-60]

Whether Bolingbroke is sun or rain, always *he* is the fertile one; Richard, the other partner in the image, is futile snow or fire. Even the Gardener recognizes this fertility in Bolingbroke, comparing him, not to weeds and monstrous things, but to a great tree full, too full, of sap [III. iv. 55-63].

In the final lines of the play Bolingbroke calls attention to his own growth: "My soul is full of woe / That blood should sprinkle me to make me grow" [V. vi. 45-6]. While Bolingbroke's "woe" serves to remind us that he too is subject to fortune, that he cannot stay young for ever, still this woe is not the woe of which Richard and the Queen complain. Their woe is central to them; it is their creation: but Bolingbroke's woe, although it is a burden, is only an additional strain, for the central theme, emphasized in the last word of the sentence, is that he does indeed grow and flourish. Contrast this with Richard's own indictment of himself when, having fallen into despair on the coast of Wales, he tells Aumerle to dismiss his men:

> That power I have, discharge, and let them go
> To ear the land that hath some hope to grow,
> For I have none.
>
> [III. ii. 211-13]

It is appropriate that Richard be called pale, be compared to ice, depart for the north on bidding a final farewell to his Queen; for as the moon is barren, as John of Gaunt, that "lunatic lean-witted fool" [II. i. 115] is barren because of age and sickness, so Richard is essentially barren. (pp. 173-75)

Our discussion thus far has centered on particular images. But in Act V, scenes ii and iii, some of the concerns of the imagery, fecundity and parenthood, rise to the surface. In scene ii the Duke of York discovers that his son is a traitor to Bolingbroke; his wife pleads with him to act as a father, but York, a loyal subject, is prepared to sacrifice his son.

The next scene begins with Bolingbroke's enquiries about *his* son. This is not simply Shakespeare's way of introducing a character who is to appear in an important role in a later play. The interlude ties in with the concern of the last scene—a father's relation to his son—and it throws light on the scene to come. For Bolingbroke is shown as a father who loves his son in spite of serious flaws in the boy's character:

> As dissolute as desperate! But yet
> Through both I see some sparks of better hope,
> Which elder years may happily bring forth.
>
> [V. iii. 20-2]

Later in the same scene York appears at Windsor Castle to argue against his son, Aumerle, while the Duchess prays as a mother that Bolingbroke pardon that son. Bolingbroke commends York as the "loyal father of a treacherous son!" [V. iii. 60]; yet he forgives Aumerle because, as he says, "Your mother well hath pray'd . . ." [V. iii. 145]. Bolingbroke allows the plea of the mother to triumph over considerations of state.

This scene recalls the earlier one where Richard hears Gaunt complain of the banishment of *his* son, Bolingbroke, and Richard points out that Gaunt himself helped decide the sentence. Says Gaunt: "You urg'd me as a judge, but I had rather / You would have bid me argue like a father" [I. iii. 237-38]. But Richard, unlike Bolingbroke, has not the mercy of a father: "Cousin, farewell—and uncle, bid him so, / Six years we banish him and he shall go" [I. iii. 247-48].

In contrast to Bolingbroke, Richard's fatherhood is suggested only to be denied. At Flint Castle he says: "Cousin, I am too young to be your father, / Though you are old enough to be my heir" [III. iii. 204-05]. Richard imagines Bolingbroke in the role of close kinsman, and then proceeds to reject the obligations of this relationship: "Where he my brother, nay, my kingdom's heir, . . . Such neighbour nearness to our sacred blood / Should nothing privilege him . . . [I. i. 116, 119-20]. In the context this rejection of the ties of blood seems reasonable, yet Richard's disrespect for such ties is made explicit; in the next scene we hear that Richard had had his Uncle Gloucester murdered and we note how lightly Richard treats Gaunt's illness and death, and how he then usurps Gaunt's property—his own cousin's patrimony. Richard may be contrasted with Bolingbroke in this respect, who makes a point of claiming his uncle, York, as his father: "You are my father, for methinks in you / I see old Gaunt alive" [I. iii. 117-18].

We have tried to show the division between Bolingbroke and Richard, stressed both by imagery and event, whereby the old king is shown to be infertile, and the new king fruitful. This contrast may remind us of the ancient connection between a ruler's infertility and the troubles of his country. Fundamental to *Richard II* are the assumptions that the health of the land depends on the fertility of the king, and that the natural cycle of growth which commences in spring is intimately connected with the king's fruitfulness. In *Richard II* we see a version of these old beliefs—the due cycle of nature replaces an incompetent king with one more fit. At a number of points the play stresses this connection between Richard's infertility and the troubles of England: The Gardener, who acts as commentator, charges Richard with political failure. Richard has impeded natural growth and fecundity; he has permitted the weeds to flourish and has failed to encourage and tend the fruit [III. iv. 55-66]. Although Richard wishes "to farm our royal realm" [I. iv. 45] he only means that to support his own extravagances he is willing to lease his lands. Later he himself fancies that

his sorrow will kill the crops: "Our sighs and they [our tears] shall lodge the summer corn, / And make a dearth in this revolting land" [II. iii. 162-63]. The Gardener stresses the relation of King Richard's political fortunes to the seasons of the year in lines which pun on the words "spring" and "fall": "He that hath suffered this disordered spring / Hath now himself met with the fall of leaf" [III. iv. 48-9]. Not only is Richard portrayed as waxing and waning with the seasons (just as elsewhere he waxes and wanes with the sun), but the reign of Richard's Queen is also shown to be allied with the natural cycle: "She came adorned hither like sweet May, / Sent back like Hallowmas or short'st of day" [V. i. 79-80].

Bolingbroke become king is, as we should expect, the spring. The Duchess of York, referring to the new order, says: "Who are the violets now / That strew the green lap of the new-come spring?" [V. ii. 46-7]. And the Duke of York says to his son: "Well, bear you well in this new spring of time, / Lest you be cropp'd before you come to prime" [V. ii. 50-1]. Bolingbroke is the spring sun who will melt Richard, the winter snow, as Richard himself suggests [IV. i. 260-62].

The passing of the crown from the old king to the new (Exton bears the "dead king to the living king" [V. v. 117]) is part of a larger pattern of cyclical movement in *Richard II*; the pattern is also apparent in time, fortune, the weather, the seasons, man himself. Time has a spring. For instance, York says: ". . . bear you well in this new spring of time . . ." [V. ii. 50]. (pp. 175-78)

Fortune waxes and wanes, night follows day, sunshine alternates with storm, wanton spring follows frozen winter; "the sweet infant breath of gentle sleep" [I. iii. 133] is followed by "hot youth" [II. iii. 99] and by death. (p. 178)

The rôle of God in *Richard II* is ambiguous. On the one hand Richard and Carlisle claim that God will *in future ages* revenge the crime of Bolingbroke; these statements of Tudor myth (the view of Richard's deposition as a "secular fall of man") work powerfully on the political level, for history had emphasized their validity to the Elizabethans. God resents Richard's fall. On the other hand, *Richard II* is also a play about the working out of God's justice on Richard. . . . York, describing Richard's march through London, implies that Bolingbroke is an instrument of God:

> . . . had not God for some strong purpose steel'd
> The hearts of men, they must perforce have melted,
> And barbarism itself have pitied him.
> But heaven hath a hand in these events,
> To whose high will we bound our calm contens.
>
> [V. ii. 34-8]

This play presents a political ideal on the one hand—that kings must not be deposed—and on the other shows us the historical fact that kings are deposed, and that their deposition may be inevitable; the deposition itself is shown to be part of the universal and divine pattern of nature. Indeed not an ideal, the divine right of kings, and its violation, but two contrary ideals are contained in this play. The presence of these two ideals accounts for an ambiguity in *Richard II* which we are more accustomed to asssociate with Shakespeare's later plays. (pp. 178-79)

Helmut Bonheim and Jean Bonheim, "The Two Kings in Shakespeare's 'Richard II'," in Shakespeare Jahrbuch, *1971, pp. 169-79.*

ROBERT B. PIERCE　(essay date 1971)

[*Arguing that* Richard II *is in part "a drama of fathers and sons," Pierce examines the conflicting obligations that the code of chivalry, family honor, and loyalty to one's sovereign place upon such characters as Gaunt, York, and Bolingbroke. In such an analysis, the critic contends, "the theme of inheritance is a major one," for Richard's isolation from his kin and his violation of his cousin's rights to the Lancastrian estate, threatening as they do the very foundations of the social order, set in motion his own downfall and Bolingbroke's revolt. Pierce adds, however, that in* Richard II *Shakespeare was not primarily concerned with "the family as an emblem of disorder in the state"—as he was in* Henry IV—*but instead was "more interested in another subject, the psychology of kingship."*]

Richard II is in part a drama of fathers and sons, not only in its emphasis on orderly succession, but also in its study of moral inheritance. The opening two scenes establish the theme in two different keys. In the first it appears in a setting of splendid pageantry and public utterance, but the second scene is a deeply emotional private discussion. The immediate impression of the opening scene is of chivalric heroism with two knights defying each other in the finest oratorical vein. Mowbray and Bolingbroke repeatedly call on the traditional association of heroic courage and honor with noble birth, the great Renaissance tradition of aristocratic idealism. Bolingbroke touches on this idea in his first defiance:

> Thou art a traitor and a miscreant,
> Too good to be so, and too bad to live,
> Since the more fair and crystal is the sky,
> The uglier seem the clouds that in it fly.
>
> 　　　　　　　　　　　　　　[I. i. 39-42]

That is, Mowbray is "too good," too wellborn, to be a traitor; a base nobleman is so unnatural as to have forfeited his right to live. Mowbray shows proper respect for the king's blood in his enemy, but with Richard's permission returns the charges of "this slander of his blood" [I. i. 113]. When Bolingbroke refuses to withdraw his challenge, he suggests the son's duty to emulate his father in courage: "Shall I seem crest-fallen in my father's sight?" [I. i. 188].

The most serious charge that Bolingbroke brings against Mowbray is the murder of Gloucester, Bolingbroke's paternal uncle. Hence his challenge is an act of filial piety, vengeance for his injured family. He refers to his uncle's blood:

> Which blood, like sacrificing Abel's, cries
> Even from the tongueless caverns of the earth
> To me for justice and rough chastisement;
> And, by the glorious worth of my descent,
> This arm shall do it, or this life be spent.
>
> 　　　　　　　　　　　　　　[I. i. 104-08]

He sees his pursuit of revenge as a sign of his noble birth. But his comparison of Gloucester and Abel suggests that there is another side to all this splendid pageantry, since Abel was killed by one of his own family. Clearly the reference is a veiled attack on the king himself, who is ultimately responsible for his uncle's death. For all his public stance of impartiality and feudal correctness, Richard has shed the blood of his own family; the judge is an unnamed defendant.

Just as Richard's position is equivocal, so is Bolingbroke's. His arrogation to himself of the duty to dispense justice is presumptuous in the presence of his king, however guilty that king may be; Gaunt's declaration of Tudor orthodoxy in the next scene makes that clear. Richard is moved to a veiled

reproof of his cousin's boldness even while proclaiming his impartiality:

> Were he my brother, nay, my kingdom's heir,
> As he is but my father's brother's son,
> Now by my sceptre's awe I make a vow,
> Such neighbour nearness to our sacred blood
> Should nothing privilege him nor partialize
> The unstooping firmness of my upright soul.
>
> 　　　　　　　　　　　　　　[I. i. 116-21]

On the surface this speech is a fine public display of impartiality, but behind it is a double irony. Richard dwells with conscious sarcasm on the names of kinship that locate Bolingbroke, a mere cousin of the king in spite of his presumption. He is denying the significance of Edward III's blood in Bolingbroke and hence the basis of his own royalty, whereas in a later scene Northumberland affirms "the royalties of both your bloods" [III. iii. 107] even while plotting against Richard. Neither man accepts the full implications of the orthodox values he evokes.

Hence it is already clear that Richard is not impartial and cannot afford to be in the face of an attack on his sovereignty. But there is a second, unconscious, irony in the words, for this upstart is soon to prove "my kingdom's heir" indeed. The lines foreshadow Richard's bitter play on the same relationships as he surrenders to Bolingbroke's power:

> Cousin, I am too young to be your father,
> Though you are old enough to be my heir.
>
> 　　　　　　　　　　　　　　[III. iii. 204-05]

It is significant that Bolingbroke defies his father's command to throw down Mowbray's gage. He visibly rebels against his duty as a son just as he later will against his duty as a subject. All the spectacle and rhetoric in the first scene only partly cover a grave disorder in the state, and the theme of inheritance is closely involved with both spectacle and disorder.

If on the surface this scene illustrates proper inheritance of courage and loyalty, the second reveals a dilemma of conscience typical of a disordered state. John of Gaunt and his brother's widow debate whether his duty to Gloucester, his brother, outweighs his duty to the king. The duchess defends the family in a set piece on the sons of Edward III . . . , which alternates metaphors of blood and a growing tree, the standard images of the family. She sees the claim of family unity as absolute. . . . In the ordered universe of orthodox vision, the family is a union of supernatural power, part of the whole order of being. In a magical sense the son is indeed the father reincarnate. Gloucester's spilt blood is a physical sign of the noble inheritance in the House of Lancaster. For Gaunt to omit vengeance is to deny his birth, to commit the sin of despair in the name of patience. . . . Gaunt does not deny the validity of her arguments. His words acknowledge "the part I had in Woodstock's blood" [I. ii. 1], but appeal to what he considers an even more basic principle than family loyalty, the sanctity of the king. Gaunt argues that in a deeper sense he lives up to his birth by his submission. He shows that Edward III's sons have not forgotten their prime duty of loyalty to the English monarch, the head of their family. Brother of one great warrior and son of another, he is the last full inheritor of their heroic virtue. (pp. 150-55)

[The] main function of the scene is to establish John of Gaunt's role of aged wisdom. In a demonstration of the noblest orthodoxy, he is prepared to sacrifice the dearest ties of kinship and love to the ideal of political order, which both his son and his nephew violate.

The first two scenes of *Richard II* have several important functions. They establish the theme of inheritance as a major one. They make clear that behind the ceremonial pomp of the state is a disorder that creates painful conflicts of duty. They begin a contrast between what seems to be happening and what really is, between proclaimed purpose and hidden motive, between word and deed. Finally, they make John of Gaunt a standard against which his son and nephew are measured. As the play develops, the family theme centers on three figures—the Duke of York, Bolingbroke, and Richard himself. Analysis of these three in their family relationships should indicate the direction that Shakespeare's art is taking.

For most of the play the Duke of York has a straightforward role. He is a weaker John of Gaunt, one who voices all the right sentiments, but lacks the will to carry out his good intentions. When Richard confiscates Gaunt's estates, York protests in words that predict the whole course of events:

> Take Herford's rights away, and take from time
> His charters, and his customary rights;
> Let not to-morrow then ensue to-day:
> Be not thyself. For how art thou a king
> But by fair sequence and succession?
>
> [II. i. 195-99]

To violate succession, the outward equivalent of moral inheritance, is to deprive a man of his place in society and hence of his very identity, as Richard is to discover. But York cannot act on this wisdom, nor can he oppose the rebel Bolingbroke despite his bold "I am no traitor's uncle" [II. iii. 87]. York is the last of Edward III's seven sons, a fading remnant of the old order. In this new order in which there is no simple duty, no clear object of loyalty, he is an anachronism. Like Humphrey, Duke of Gloucester, and that other Gloucester in the anonymous play *Woodstock,* he fails as a statesman through a too-innocent goodness, one that cannot cope with the power politics of a degenerate age.

At the end of the play York transfers his loyalty to the new Henry IV as king *de facto,* having convinced himself that Richard's voluntary deposition is valid. However, since his son Aumerle is Richard's zealous supporter, York is caught in another dilemma of loyalty. When he discovers that Aumerle has joined a plot against the king, he threatens to denounce his son and does so. If York's determination here seems to contradict the established impression of his vacillating character, perhaps it is because Shakespeare indulges in rather frivolous self-parody. . . . Often before he has created scenes of stylized emotion using couplets, stichomythy, and abstract language. Even in this play Gaunt expresses just such a dilemma of loyalty as York's in stiffly formal couplets [I. iii. 236-46]. But nowhere else has the dignity of the technique been so undermined by comic bathos. While York rages at his son's treachery, he calls angrily for his boots. The duchess caps a noble appeal to the pains of childbirth with a housewifely proof of her son's legitimacy:

> He is as like thee as a man may be,
> Not like to me, or any of my kin.
>
> [V. ii. 108-09]

Finally, so that Aumerle may hasten to get the king's pardon, his mother proposes that he steal York's horse.

The confrontation before the new king at first seems serious enough. In nobly metaphorical language Henry expresses the traditional shock at vice descended from virtue, a muddy stream sprung from a silver fountain [V. iii. 60-3]. But with the arrival of the duchess he comments, "Our scene is alt'red from a serious thing" [V. iii. 79], as he drops into the prevailing couplets. From now until the speech with which he closes the episode, Henry is almost as taciturn as in the deposition scene; but his countenance, varying between anger and amusement, governs the tone. The old-fashioned style of this dispute is as out of place in the usuper's court as is York's anachronistic virtue. Both are objects of laughter to the generous but pragmatic king. It is as though Shakespeare were bored with the easy success of a stylized dilemma-scene. The Duke of York amuses him too much to be taken seriously in a tragic conflict of loyalty between son and king.

The shadowy figure of Bolingbroke is shown both as son and as father, the latter only briefly in this play. He is a somewhat colorless figure so as not to compete with Richard in dramatic interest, but Shakespeare turns this technical necessity into a point of characterization. At moments of crisis he is taciturn, Richard's "silent king" [IV. i. 290]. Although he is not without eloquence, there is always an element of calculation to his rhetoric, as though the reality were something colder and harder that lay behind his words. Shakespeare makes this quality clear by contrast with his father, that magnificently conventional figure. His virtue established in the first two scenes, John of Gaunt acts as another of the idealized old counselors of the king. . . . On his deathbed he expresses the political ideal of the play in the accents of public rhetoric. "Like a prophet new inspir'd" [II. i. 31], he denounces his nephew's crimes:

> O, had thy grandsire with a prophet's eye
> Seen how his son's son should destroy his sons,
> From forth thy reach he would have laid thy shame,
> Deposing thee before thou wert possess'd,
> Which art possess'd now to depose thyself.
>
> [II. i. 104-08]

Behind the elaborate wordplay is Gaunt's sense of Richard's unnatural and self-destructive attack on his family, the roots of his being. The clearest dramatic representation of Richard's guilt and the act that ensures his deposition is the betrayal of this old man's loyalty by seizing his estates. As he appeals to the traditional sanctions of family and state, Gaunt's poetry is laden with the abstract eloquence characteristic of virtue in the first tetralogy.

As Richard relies on his inherited right against the usurper's threat, so Bolingbroke with scrupulous piety cites his inheritance from this great father:

> O thou, the earthly author of my blood,
> Whose youthful spirit in me regenerate
> Doth with a twofold vigour lift me up
> To reach at victory above my head,
> Add proof unto mine armour with thy prayers.
>
> [I. iii. 69-73]

But both members of the new generation have lost touch with the meaning behind their words. Although Gaunt gives Bolingbroke his blessing, his son has defied both him and their king in pressing the quarrel with Mowbray. Still Shakespeare is careful not to turn his future king into an unredeemed rebel or a pure Machiavel. Bolingbroke is a chastened figure when Richard announces his banishment, and the grief of his parting from father and homeland seems real enough. But later, when his uncle York chastises his rebellious return to England, he shows his glib mastery of the language of filial piety. With sincere feeling he argues his right of inheritance, which is legitimate, but he also plays on York's emotions:

> You are my father, for methinks in you
> I see old Gaunt alive.
>
> [II. iii. 117-18]

York is able to sort out the valid from the specious in his nephew's plea, though he lacks the power and will to act on his knowledge. No doubt Bolingbroke's pride in his inheritance is real, but most of his public appeals to the bonds of family are mere rhetoric at the service of practical ends.

At least in *Richard II* Bolingbroke is the master of this contrast between verbal tribute to family ideals and the reality of power politics. Deprived of his proper inheritance from the noble John of Gaunt, he makes himself seem to be moral inheritor of the Black Prince and true bearer of England's royalty. Only at the end of the play does his son's alienation give a hint of the nemesis that threatens him. He complains of the wastrel Prince of Wales just before facing York's rebellious son. Bolingbroke seems unconscious of any parallel, but the suggestion is that disorder in the state growing out of his usurpation has put an unnatural strain on the bonds of father and son. The isolation characteristic of Shakespeare's kings, and especially of his usurpers, has enveloped the new ruler. At the end of the play, the only member of his family who appears with him in un-shaken loyalty is his ineffectual old uncle York. Tainted with his cousin's blood, Bolingbroke suffers from a guilt and loneliness that run deeper than pragmatic politics.

It is in Richard, however, that Shakespeare first develops with full power the tragic effects of isolation. Richard III freely chooses to alienate himself from his family, and the early Richard II does much the same thing. His counselors are not his wise uncles, but the favorites Bushy, Bagot, and Greene. He has had one uncle killed and confiscates the estate of another. His flippant cynicism with his coterie about his kinsmen Bolingbroke and Gaunt (I. iv) is less evil than Richard III's ironic scorn at family bonds only because Richard II is weaker. He is an amateur playing at professional villainy. In the scene (II. i) that most clearly establishes his guilt, both Gaunt and York suggest that he has repudiated his heroic father's example. The cavalier way in which he names his uncle York to govern in his absence suggests, not only his folly in appointing a weak man, but also his bland confidence in an affectionate loyalty that he has just come near to shattering. He exploits the family bond that he is not willing to support himself.

But if this Richard willfully chooses his isolation, the later Richard feels the weight of loneliness. Stripped of the realities of power and of any meaningful personal contact, he tries to generate these things verbally. Over and over again he creates ceremonies to replace the lost ceremonial pomp of his office. Because he knows that he has lost the reality of power, the ceremonies are aimless and perverse. Since the ideals of succession and kingly right that he appeals to are real ones, his voice every now and then catches a note of prophetic insight, but it soon dwindles into petulance and self-pity. (pp. 155-62)

Having forfeited his place in the state and in his own family, Richard can only play with the remnants of his glory. When he confronts Bolingbroke at Flint Castle, his first speech is an impressive declaration of divine right, ending in a prophecy that foresees the whole course of the Wars of the Roses:

> But ere the crown he looks for live in peace,
> Ten thousand bloody crowns of mothers' sons
> Shall ill become the flower of England's face,

> Change the complexion of her maid-pale peace
> To scarlet indignation and bedew
> Her pastures' grass with faithful English blood.
>
> [III. iii. 95-100]

Here in passing is the familiar use of a general family reference in order to intensify a broad view of disaster. Even the cold-blooded Northumberland seems taken aback by this speech, but he is soon moved to scorn as Richard's voice rises to hysteria. By the time that the waning king descends to the base court, self-consciously pointing out the symbolism of the act, his language has become shrill and maudlin. His next appeal to the family is the petulant irony of calling Bolingbroke his heir. In the deposition scene he turns the renunciation of his inherited crown into a loss even of "that name was given me at the font" [IV. i. 256]. (The speech is more naturally read as the embroidery of Richard's despair than as an obscure reference to the legend of his bastardy recounted by Froissart.) To break the unity of the king's two bodies, his office and his private self, is to destroy his personal identity, which is as much based on inheritance as his crown.

One might have expected Shakespeare to make considerable use of the queen, whose continued loyalty to her husband counterpoints the nobles' treachery, but he does not. Only once does Richard talk to her on stage, when she intercepts him on the way to the Tower. The result is a conventionally lyric expression of joint sorrow, given a touch of irony by the presence of the cynical Northumberland through most of it. (pp. 163-64)

To Richard the family is little more than a useful figure of speech. Having forfeited the loyalty of his own kin, he can find little consolation in his wife's love. In his prison cell he makes only one reference to the family, a strained conceit that describes the working of his imagination [V. v. 6-10]. Even this late he shows only the most general consciousness of his guilt and none at all of his crimes against the right of succession, on which he bases his own sense of injustice. Alone, self-destroyed, even now self-deceived, he achieves only the lesser triumph of fighting bravely against his assassins. In his world nothing is real enough to make his isolation from the ties of family love tragically painful. (p. 165)

[Shakespeare's Elizabethan audience] were accustomed to see the family as an emblem of disorder in the state, and they must have noticed this device in *Richard II*. All the familiar pattern of violated order and inherited guilt is sketched out there. Richard's crime against his uncles begins the cycle, and Bolingbroke's crime against his king and cousin extends it.

Nevertheless, this technique is less obtrusive in *Richard II* than in the first tetralogy once the ceremonial use in the early scenes fades away. Shakespeare is now more interested in another subject, the psychology of kingship. He shows, not only the qualities that make Richard lose his crown, but also what happens to his vision of himself when he is deprived of the position that gives him identity. Richard imaginatively projects himself into a simpler world where right and power are the same, though in flashes he is bitterly conscious of the self-deception. But for him there is no bearable alternative. Because he lives in an unreal world, he cannot have a truly intimate relationship. That is why the parting between him and Isabel has to be conventional. Though his suffering is real enough, it is almost entirely egocentric.

Consequently the family in *Richard II* hangs in a kind of limbo. As an emblem for political morality, it suffers the fate of all ideals in this play. The moral voice of Richard's wise uncle, John of Gaunt, is real enough, but Gaunt dies. Transferred to Richard's emotional tirades, the old code becomes illusory, unsupported by real physical power. On the other hand, Shakespeare cannot explore family bonds in a more psychological way because of his tragic hero's special character. The great dramatic power of *Richard II* lies in its study of a ruler whose weakness betrays him as a king and isolates him as a man. . . . (pp. 166-67)

Robert B. Pierce, "Richard II," in his Shakespeare's History Plays: The Family and the State, *Ohio State University Press, 1971, pp. 149-70.*

SIDNEY HOMAN   (essay date 1972)

[*One of the critical facts surrounding* Richard II *is the great variety of reactions it has elicited: while some regard Richard as a "sweet lovely rose"* (1 Henry IV, *I. iii. 175) and Bolingbroke as a Machiavellian usurper, others consider the king a weak, effeminate ruler and Henry the precursor of the ideal Prince Hal. Homan reconciles these divergent interpretations by pointing out the abundant evidence in the text for either reading. The play is deliberately constructed, he maintains, in such a way that audience sympathy remains divided between Richard and Bolingbroke, between the private world of tragedy and spiritual awareness and the public world of responsible governance. Inasmuch as he recognizes that these two ideals are sometimes sadly incompatible, the critic adds, Shakespeare teaches us "the futility of seeking absolutes in our own reality." Importantly, Homan also examines Richard's spiritual development throughout the play, stating that the king discovers his true self only by losing his public identity and accepting death.*]

I believe that Shakespeare consciously invests both Richard and Bolingbroke with paradoxical qualities and, by doing so, elicits a divided response from the play's audience. It is precisely this response which makes the play "dramatic" and which defines the art of the theater: we witness a complete aesthetic world which calls forth a wider variety of emotions than would be possible in real life, thereby offering us, to use T. S. Eliot's terms, by this "concentration, of a very great number of experiences" something of a "new art emotion" [in his essay "Tradition and the Individual Talent"]. In life we are compelled to take sides, to commit ourselves or not; and characters within a play, unaware of their theatrical status, are likewise compelled. But our omniscience as audience allows us to see the world as an artifice, albeit an artifice taking up a theme relevant to the real world encompassing the theater; and by this omniscience in *Richard II* we suspend judgment, holding within us contradictory responses to the characters, with no ultimate need to assign them places in some moral hierarchy.

I trust I am talking here about something more than what normally is meant by terms such as "complex characterization" or a "relative reading" of the play. For when I speak of paradoxical characters I mean just that: the character, as he exists in the play and in the eye of the spectator, is at once aesthetically complete (Richard has no dimensions as a character outside his play) and yet morally unresolved. A play thus offers no mere "dramatization" of a story, in the sense that television commercials are labeled as a "dramatization" of some crisis and its resolution. Rather, our witness to unresolved tensions may indeed mirror, as a recent critic suggests, "the unresolvable tensions that are the fundamental conditions of human life" [see excerpt above by Norman Rabkin, 1967]. In the midst of World War II, for example, it was fairly easy to

give way to . . . the ultimate melodrama of war, to see Hitler as incarnate evil, the allies as Virtue figures—in effect, to convert the war into a morality play. However, our own recent venture, knowledge about the involvement of American industry in pre-war Germany, reassessment of our collective crimes—all these suggest that while Hitler may well remain just what we have always thought him to be, the rest of us may have fallen short of perfection as we participated in the general guilt that war invokes, that our human condition is by nature paradoxical, for, to echo Hamlet, what should such fellows as we do "crawling between earth and heaven?" [*Hamlet*, III. i. 127-28].

This principle of divided response is, I also suggest, only one function of the drama. A great deal of time has already been spent taking sides with regard to the play at hand: Richard as a sweet lovely rose or the deserving victim of Bolingbroke, the usurper as a precursor of Prince Hal or a crude upstart and blasphemer. But taking sides is not a bad thing, and to sow contention among spectators seems a legitimate function of the drama. I do think that this principle functions at a very high and consistent level in Shakespeare, however. Surely our response toward Hamlet is a divided one, for while we very much see Denmark through his eyes and delight in his philosophic overview of that very world in which Claudius and Gertrude so unthinkingly confide, it is also true that Hamlet is something of a mass murderer. He should rank no higher on a scale of social acceptability than his step-father, but the case for Claudius is not that interesting. As he dies with a faithful kiss on the lips of his dead wife, does Othello in that final speech achieve a victory over Iago and what he represents, or is he merely "cheering himself up," hoodwinking the audience by trying to balance a recent and obscene butchery with memories of earlier battles? Or may we be allowed both responses at the death scene? (pp. 65-6)

[Recognizing] that what one man calls divided response may be for someone else mere evidence of critical confusion or a playwright's muddled purpose, I would contend that *Richard II* does offer us a valid example of this dramatic principle in operation. Clearly it is difficult to have a singular response to the king. Unlike Marlowe's Edward II, Richard remains at all times a faithful husband; nor is he ever totally indifferent to the responsibilities of the throne. Indeed, he seems a wellmeaning sovereign, though incompetent and tragically shortsighted—and, most important, stained because of his own part in the usurpation of the crown. If the world demands qualities lacking in Richard, it is equally true that Richard possesses qualities lacking in that world. The formalized duel he arranges between Bolingbroke and Mowbray may seem too ornamental, a mere stop-gap in place of a more realistic confrontation of the basic issues dividing the men. From another perspective, however, the duel is a civilized method, however ineffective, of preventing raw violence, far preferable to Bolingbroke's own more practical stratagems by which he will assert what he considers his own "rights." Effeminate, unbecomingly poetic as Richard may appear, he also harks back to a decorum which more modern men like Bolingbroke have long since lost. Richard's judgment against the combatants may seem onesided, but then this is his royal prerogative. Morally, administratively defective, Richard is not alone in his guilt. He is also part of an inexorable pattern which cannot be broken until the emergence of the first untainted king in *Henry V*. Add up the defenses and counter-charges that can be made in his name and we can only conclude that Richard embodies that complex of appealing traits and appalling vices defining most men who fall below sainthood but above unmitigated villainy. (pp. 66-7)

Bolingbroke may be seen as representing the successful man as defined by [the] "modern" world which has passed Richard by. Clearly a man of the time, Bolingbroke is one who moves with the events of the world, one who will not "stand condemn'd / A wandering vagabond" [II. iii. 119-20]. With his keen sense of history he is well aware of the "charters and . . . customary rights" of "Time" [II. i. 195-96]. Of such qualities are made the leaders of men. In contrast Richard is one who has "wasted time" [V. v. 49], failing in the larger decisions that time forces upon a man in power. Salisbury's wish that he could "call back yesterday, bid time return" [III. ii. 69] underlines the king's own dilemma; awareness *in* time is the polar opposite of hindsight. That Bolingbroke's character will be continued in both parts of *Henry IV* and will lead to the unqualified hero of *Henry V* argues Shakespeare's great interest in him, and in the world he typifies. His character is perfectly explicit within the confines of the present play, and this is how it should be; yet in serving as part of the context in which Richard moves he is still a representative man, not merely limited by his utility in Richard's delineation.

The price Bolingbroke pays, however, for being a man of the present world is the loss of his soul, for imprisoned within his resplendent body is a soul "full of woe," lamenting that "blood should sprinkle [him] to make [him] grow" [V. vi. 45-6]. His victory is charged with a moral defeat, and he exits to the strains of a dirge rather than the triumphant music of war. The contradiction inherent in his existence equals that of Richard; at the end of the play the two antagonists merge slowly into a single symbolic figure. The irony of the world in *Richard II* is that it destroys both those men who succeed and those who fail in holding the power it offers. The personality of its king, whether deposed or emerging, has a certain sameness, for at the end Bolingbroke assumes Richard's role as the bloody, guilt-ridden usurper.

It has frequently been argued that, whatever his faults as a magistrate, Richard achieves at last a spiritual victory. But the notion that he ends as a completely heroic figure, a "sweet lovely rose," exonerated from his earlier failures, is strangely at odds with his own self-condemnation. And Richard's "achievement," it should be remembered, comes at great cost, for his profligacy has disrupted a kingdom and brought to the surface the worst aspects of Bolingbroke. It is an extremely charitable view which would make Richard that martyr who dies "in order to avoid committing evil himself" [see excerpt above by Karl F. Thompson, 1957]. Clearly the play is no argument for martyrdom as a way of life, or of death; Richard's self-awareness comes tragically after the fact, and his death is a necessary act of purgation for a sick state.

Still, Richard's status as a tragic figure, however qualified, may also appear, from another perspective, as a victory of sorts. As he fails in the public world and is forced into the exile's private world, he moves from that earlier imagery attending the throne—the sun, Phaethon, light, fire—to its antithesis in imagery of the ocean, water, shadows, darkness, and death. But the transition to this new world is a slow, awkward one as Richard gropes for the right images only to find them in a simple poetry which contrasts strongly with the inflated metaphors of his earlier speeches:

> Make me, that nothing have, with nothing griev'd,
> And thou with all pleas'd, that hast all achiev'd!
> Long mayst thou live in Richard's seat to sit,
> And poor lie Richard in an earthly pit!
>
> [IV. i. 216-19]

As he moves toward his tragic fulfillment each adjustment of his initial character is plagued with doubts, for as an earlier identity is cast aside he finds himself unsure of "what name to call himself" [IV. i. 259]. The final adjustment will demand the obliteration of his former self. Yet this voyage into potential nothingness will, paradoxically, offer him his one sure role as the king of tears, not men, finding his world in the infinite space of a nutshell.

Appropriately, Richard's fulfillment as a tragic character is marked by the most complex poetry in the play, that of his prison soliloquy, "I have been studying how I may compare / This prison where I live unto the world" [V. v. 1-2]. We see here an extraordinary mind at work as he peoples a mental world without a woman's help and converts his isolated cell into a microcosm of the real world. This intellectual complexity underlies the change of values Richard himself undergoes, the movement from the tangible world to that of the mind, from the body to the soul, from things temporal to things spiritual. His retreat to this world nourished with thought rather than action is also an achievement. As much as Shakespeare is concerned in *Richard II* with reordering the kingdom, he is also concerned with a man's finding of his true self, however incompatible that true self be with the affairs of the public world.

It is significant that as he dies Richard, like Lear, performs an act of valor in slaying two of the hired assassins. Death holds no fear for him; at his end he assumes a gaiety, transfiguring dread, acting boldly in this world because to lose, *to die*, would be no loss but a victory. With his new perspective he can reduce, as Hamlet will do, one's course in life to an unconscious role which invariably corrupts the soul's purity. The cure for his misery is to cast off the body; Gaunt speaks prophetically when he says the "correction" lies in Richard's own hands. Banishment earlier seems a punishment to Bolingbroke, and Gaunt argues with him in vain to convert an injury into a blessing. But Richard proves the argument true in finding an individual happiness in a world not within the kingdom but away from the kingdom.

Again, this new individual world comes at great cost to the state, for Richard's failure in the public world has serious consequences for his kingdom. Moreover, we see Richard in a variety of poses throughout the play, and thus for some critics his most detestable—and persistent—flaw is this posturing as king, as victor, as victim, and conceivably even as a tragic figure. Thus a question of sincerity complicates our response to him at almost every moment. Yet I think that like his predecessor Gaunt he speaks from his cell with a mature and honest voice. Gaunt accurately observes, for himself and for Richard, that the "tongues of dying men / Enforce attention like deep harmony" [II. i. 5-6]. The king who so lacked perspective now sees the world through a clear tragic glass. Bolingbroke detects only the outward sorrow of shadows when he comments that the shadow of Richard's sorrow has destroyed the shadow of his face. Like Hamlet, Richard knows that real sorrow, the inability to delight in the world, goes deeper, for real sorrow passes show. Once he possesses this tragic glass Richard can feel himself waking from a "happy" but untrue dream into the "truth of what we are" [V. i. 18-19]. The truth is bitter, yet his earlier ignorance is not bliss. Nor does it absolve Richard from his necessary pilgrimage, here the path leading to suffering and a tragic fall. (pp. 67-70)

Shakespeare's concern here remains divided between two worlds, that private world close to death, the domain of the tragic hero, and that public world moving toward a new order in *Henry V*. The representatives of these two antithetical worlds, Richard and Bolingbroke, are both incomplete as men. Bolingbroke's addiction to the world robs him of the larger perspective gracing Richard's tragic vision. Yet Richard stands indicted as a failure in history whose sole concern must be how one performs in the here and now. As a result we cannot fully admire him since his fall threatens a kingdom. We see his "untimely bier" [V. vi. 52], yet he does not pass before our eyes in glory as Hamlet does with the full rites of war bestowed by Fortinbras. Richard exists in a play that is both a history and a tragedy. His death therefore has national as well as individual dimensions: "O, that I were as great / As is my grief, or lesser than my name" [III. iii. 136-37]. One cannot be at once a king and a tragic hero; paradoxically, Richard's obligation was to remain as king. He can find himself only by failing that first obligation.

This impossible equipose between achievement in the public world and self-realization in a private world thus runs deep in Shakespeare. Moreover, the present tragedy spills over its own confines, looking back, as Richard's own guilty conscience forces him to do, to events preceding his coronation. For this purpose Gaunt stands as chronicle. And it looks forward to Henry's troubled reign, the seeds of which are even now being sown. As one tragedy ends another begins, and Richard remains Henry's "buried fear" [V. vi. 31] even after his death. Richard will stay lodged in Bolingbroke's conscience until he too is relieved by death. Our divided response thus becomes, I believe, a metaphor for the contradictory world of the play. Our immunity from ultimate judgment here suggests the futility of seeking absolutes in our own reality. (pp. 70-1)

Sidney Homan, "'Richard II': The Aesthetics of Judgment," in Studies in the Literary Imagination, *Vol. V, No. 1, April, 1972, pp. 65-71.*

HAROLD F. FOLLAND   (essay date 1973)

[*The rivalry between Richard and Bolingbroke is recognized by critics as a major source of interest in* Richard II, *and a debate continues over which man ultimately emerges as the more admirable. In the following excerpt, Folland focuses on the decisive abdication scene to argue that although Richard indeed loses his throne, his insistence that Bolingbroke acts immorally, that he is a usurper whose reign can never be accepted as legitimate, ruins the new king's hopes for a smooth transition of power. The critic thus maintains that despite his political victory, Bolingbroke becomes "king of a disaffected kingdom, . . . a defeated man, in his mouth the sour taste of self-disapproval and guilt." Significantly, like some earlier commentators, Folland notes that Bolingbroke—not Richard—becomes the dissimulating actor after his return from exile, while the king plays the realist, constantly pointing out the reality behind Henry's actions.*]

Shakespeare's Richard II, charming, feckless, poetic, given to dramatization of his self-pity, and apparently incapable of forthright heroic resistance, refuses to fight for his kingdom and surrenders before he is attacked. Yet, in the climactic scene of his public abdication in which he loses all, by a tenacious stubbornness in yielding he wrests from a hopeless situation a kind of victory by nonresistance. Since Richard's abdication is a foregone conclusion of which the scene presents only a public verification, it has been regarded as merely lyrical, a showcase for Richard's virtuoso performance as a man of sorrows acquainted with grief. But the scene is dramatically powerful, and much of its power comes not only from its poetic and emotional intensity, but also from the way Richard, behind

and through his apparently helpless self-dramatization, continues to fight his case against Bolingbroke so as to achieve a moral victory which has enduring political consequences. And in passing the royal power on to Henry, Richard subtly alters its character by dimming its numinous light.

The scene is the culmination of a conflict between Richard and Bolingbroke which, after being quietly established, is long sustained and often indirect as the antagonists move in relation to each other but never seem quite to come to grips. The crucial scenes are ceremonial rather than personal and violent; rituals replace battles. But beneath the surface of ceremonies mortal engagements play themselves out, while one or the other of the antagonists behaves as if there were no real conflict. This fight, then, not always in the open, is neither simple nor one-sided: both victory and defeat are qualified in ways that dramatize the ambiguous nature of power and some ways of wielding it.

The antagonism between Richard and his cousin is only hinted at in the opening scenes, in which ostensibly Richard is simply trying to reconcile Bolingbroke with Mowbray; the question of Richard's complicity in the death of Thomas of Gloucester, which might be exposed in the dispute, lurks uneasily in the background. But Richard is defined at once as a king whose commands may be ignored, and he attempts to recover ascendancy by a kind of wry joke, saying in effect, "Since you will not obey this order I will change it, and command you to do what you insist on doing." And when, with the concurrence of his council, he stops the trial by combat and exiles both contestants, he seems to have recovered his fumble and taken an effective initiative which reassures his power. That he does all this histrionically is proper both to his own style and to the occasion: a public defiance must be dealt with publicly, and with the authority of ceremony.

But one pattern of Richard's behavior has been established. He places high value on the ceremonies and symbols of power as if the power were inherent in the forms, and he tends to use them instead of swords and armies. Nor is this an illogical attitude to God's vicegerent, for they are the visible manifestations of divine sanction. Symbols and images do indeed exert political force, and Richard eventually learns not to hide behind them but to use them as means of understanding reality and coping with it, even as weapons. As he learns that forms and symbols are futile when they are empty, his opponent will learn that power without formal sanctions is not enough either. And Richard's wry victory will take place in a competition of ceremony, which he respects and handles with more skill than his antagonist perhaps because he understands better both its weakness as an idol and its strength as a shadowing forth.

When Bolingbroke has departed into exile, Richard's affairs appear to be in equilibrium. But this prologue concludes with anticipatory hints, in Richard's description of Bolingbroke's successful courtship of the crowds watching his departure, that Richard uneasily feels the threat of competition in his bold cousin. And immediately Richard initiates the conflict by his fatal decision to confiscate Bolingbroke's patrimony. As York warns Richard, in this one act he shatters the very forms and principles of succession whereby he holds his own royal power, and ignoring the implications of his act, sets in motion the causal series that brings about his fall. In direct response, Bolingbroke is impelled to a firm and unconsidered decision to violate his sentence, return to England with military forces, and demand restitution of his rights.

Like Richard, Bolingbroke fails at first to realize the drastic implications of his act, and Shakespeare has not indicated just when he realizes how little distinction there is between his forcible demand for right and rebellion, and how inevitably successful rebellion must lead him to the throne. Meanwhile, it is he who tries to maintain the forms and ceremonies of feudal fealty even while he is pressing upon his sovereign with raw military force. With elegant courtesy he moves ruthlessly on, apparently not at first conscious that his retaliatory action, though morally justified as Richard's was not, nevertheless shatters the very principles of loyalty which his language invokes and which might have made his rule secure.

Richard and Henry are set in a collision course, but their confrontation is delayed. As we learn that the King's forces have melted away and Bolingbroke's correspondingly swelled, each antagonist is shown as he takes cognizance of the rapid shift of power. (pp. 390-91)

[When] Richard sets foot again on his kingdom, saluting the earth with his hand in filial love, his cause is, as we have been told, already lost: his forces, believing him dead, have dispersed and his glory, which ought to be stable and radiant as the sun, is falling like a shooting star. In this scene, which dwells at length on Richard's step-by-step realization and acceptance of the completeness of his disaster, he suffers a succession of cruel jolts, and his mood progresses by extreme reversals. From faith and valor, forlorn hope, and desperate determination, he falls each time to intense despair until he comes to rest in flat resignation to the truth of his nothingness.

He begins in full confidence that the very stones will rise to aid the right, and dismisses the Bishop of Carlisle's wise admonition to stir himself to use what means God has given him with the blithe assurance that the very presence of the King will, like the sun, drive thieves to cover while angels take arms on his side. But reality counters in the news that it is too late, "For all the Welshmen, hearing thou wert dead, / Art gone to Bolingbroke, dispersed and fled" [III. ii. 73-4].

For a moment he sets his hopes on the powers of the magic name of King, only to be told that all his people are in revolt, and that Bushy and Bagot have been executed. The name is proved a mere powerless word, and defeat has become personal bereavement. Then, as he sits upon the ground to contemplate the sad tales of the deaths of kings, he is not merely indulging himself. As he does throughout the scene, he is trying to work out some formulation, some order, some rational or symbolic way of looking at a piece of shocking news so that he can comprehend it and come to terms with it, a process that becomes complete only just before his death in prison when he painfully works out the relation of his inner world to the even more intractable outer one that destroys him. . . . The Bishop of Carlisle urges him to leave lamenting and fight to the death, for such a valorous death is a kind of conquest, at least of fear. But as Richard once more rouses himself to valor, the final blow strikes him down. On learning that York and all his men have joined Bolingbroke, he dismisses his forces and quietly accepts the cold truth: pragmatically, the man who has the power is king. Richard sees that he is not a king, not even a simple subject—he is a name, and a name is nothing.

In this mood of extreme disillusion, wearing the royal symbols and making the royal gestures which he knows to be meaningless and futile, Richard then moves to the first of his two crucial confrontations with his antagonist. When at Flint Castle the man who is really ruler but is not ready to say so publicly

meets face to face the titular King who knows that he is nothing, it is Bolingbroke, the hard realist, who insists on maintaining the gracious formalities and Richard the disabused formalist who punctures the pretenses and bares the unacknowledged truth. The real situation is revealed at once by a slip of Northumberland's tongue when he refers to the King simply as "Richard." York once more reminds the rebels that they have no legal status. The exchange is significant. Northumberland casually explains, "Only to be brief / Left I his title out" [III. iii. 10-11], as if titles were meaningless. York points out that when Richard was powerful such casualness about a title might have been a mortal matter. And Bolingbroke's uneasiness about York's plain speaking is reflected in his attempt to stop the interchange: "Mistake not, Uncle, further than you should" [III. iii. 15].

The message he sends to Richard is altogether double-tongued.

> Henry Bolingbroke
> On both his knees doth kiss King Richard's hand
> And sends allegiance and true faith of heart
> To his most royal person, hither come
> Even at his feet to lay my arms and power,
> Provided that. . . .
>
> [III. iii. 35-40]

But what kind of humble submission includes a proviso? "If not, I'll use the advantage of my power / And lay the summer's dust with showers of blood . . ." [III. iii. 42-3].

That this message, with all its empty formality of loyalty, is a threat, is made plain by Bolingbroke's instructions that during the parley his powerful army should be visible marching on the plain, though "without the noise of threatening drum" [III. iii. 51]. Bolingbroke is well aware that this is the crucial meeting of opposites. But at first it is a meeting of two role-players, Bolingbroke playing the wronged man begging justice, Richard playing the benevolent monarch granting it. But Northumberland, Henry's hatchet man, almost gives away the show: neglecting to kneel, he gives Richard an opportunity to rebuke him and define the situation: if I am King, why are you not kneeling?

> If we be not, show us the hand of God
> That hath dismiss'd us from our stewardship;
> For well we know, no hand of blood and bone
> Can gripe the sacred handle of our sceptre,
> Unless he do profane, steal, or usurp.
>
> [III. iii. 77-81]

Here, then, is the one point Richard can and must establish: either Richard is King, or his successor is a rebel and usurper. And though he gives up all else, on this one point he will not yield. Meanwhile, Richard plays the comedy on by answering the message in the mode in which it is given: "And all the number of his fair demands / Shall be accomplish'd without contradiction" [III. iii. 123-24].

While Northumberland returns to report to Henry, Richard gives full voice to his pain and humiliation; and though his conduct is hardly heroic, his grasp on fact and reality can hardly be faulted; it is Bolingbroke who thinks he can eat his cake and have it too. But he cannot both be King and be rightly King, and Richard persists in demonstrating this fact publicly. His bitter speech to Northumberland is couched in the kind of irony that cannot be successfully answered.

> What must the King do now? must he submit?
> The king shall do it: must he be deposed?
> The King shall be contented. . . .

Most mighty prince, My Lord Northumberland,
What says King Bolingbroke? will His Majesty
Give Richard leave to live till Richard die?

> [III. iii. 143-45, 172-74]

The only answer, Northumberland's motion of obeisance, leaves Richard free to clinch his point in a final sarcasm; "You make a leg, and Bolingbroke says ay" [III. iii. 175].

The order that Richard should descend to parley in the base court is couched in language of almost excessive courtesy ("May it please you to come down" [III. iii. 177]), but by comparing his descent to Phaeton's, Richard expresses both his awareness of his misconduct and the unfittingness of the sun-king's coming down to the level of his vassal instead of scattering thieves by his glory. And when the two antagonists confront each other, it is Bolingbroke who stands on ceremony and Richard who strips it away to show the truth. To Henry's kneeling, he responds,

> Up, cousin, up; your heart is up, I know,
> Thus high at least, although your knee be
>   low,
> Boling. My gracious lord, I come but for mine own.
> K. Rich. Your own is yours, and I am yours, and all.
>
> [III. iii. 194-97]

Bolingbroke's answer keeps the parley in terms of propriety and courtesy: "So far be mine, my most redoubted lord, / As my true service shall deserve your love" [III. iii. 198-99]. But Richard again returns the dialogue to hard fact, in a tone of bitter irony.

> Well you deserve: they well deserve to have,
> That know the strong'st and surest way to
>   get. . . .
> What you will have, I'll give, and willing
>   too;
> For do we must what force will have us do.
> So on towards London, Cousin, is it so?
> Boling. Yea, my good lord.
> K. Rich.   Then I must not say no.
>
> [III. iii. 200-01, 206-09]

Though Bolingbroke, with his "my good lord" has maintained his fiction to the last of the scene, Richard has made a point, and made it in public: Bolingbroke and his army have in fact taken Richard prisoner, and though Richard was not taken by violence, he was most surely taken by force. And although Bolingbroke is in power, he is not altogether in the right.

In this scene, then, Richard, emotional and self-dramatizing though he is, exhibits the strength to face up to his own failures as well as to the realities of the military and political situation. He knows a lost cause when he sees it, and accepts the loss. But in his indirect way, he is fighting at least to have the record set right. For in the long run the public record does matter, as Henry will painfully know when he himself faces rebellion. There are, indeed, other things than physical force to be reckoned with in political power, such as the sanction of right, and the reputation for integrity, and the force that emanates from the mystical body of kingship.

This is the issue of the final and crucial conflict—too tacit and concealed to be called a clash—between Richard and Henry in the Deposition Scene in Westminster Hall. The question of power was settled when Bolingbroke landed, before Richard even got back; the question of right is still wide open. At the beginning of the scene (IV. i), Bolingbroke's clearheaded, decisive, and effective dealing with the fierce mutual accu-

sations of his nobles demonstrates how much more fitted he is than Richard to control fractious nobles. And when York brings word that Richard has abdicated and adopted Bolingbroke as his heir, he is ready to "ascend the regal throne" [IV. i. 113] then and there, and so take over publicly without further formality. But the faithful Bishop of Carlisle, who had failed to rouse Richard to his own defense and prevent his surrender, speaks up courageously to protest this highhanded judgment and arrogant disposal of King Richard, "himself not present" [IV. i. 129]. He point-blank accuses Bolingbroke of treason, and like a prophet of old warns him of the catastrophic civil war that must follow from his treasonous usurpation. Northumberland, loud, tactless, and ruthless as usual, promptly arrests Carlisle for treason, and moves on to the next matter of business. But Bolingbroke has understood the message; his future security depends on the clear rightness of his act in the public record. "Fetch hither Richard," he orders,

> . . . that in common view
> He may surrender; so shall we proceed
> Without suspicion.
>
> [IV. i. 155-57]

For only so may he proceed without opposition. But this is asking one more thing of Richard than he will grant.

What follows, then, is a planned public performance, with Richard as star performer. But Bolingbroke is the producer of it and has planned the script; Richard is to play the role of a king weary of rule, willing and even glad to relinquish his power, position, and cares to the younger, stronger man, who will accede to Richard's wish and accept the burden. So will his position as King be publicly stamped as valid. Instead, Richard improvises a script of his own in which he does, to be sure, abdicate in favor of Bolingbroke, but in such a way as to put Bolingbroke and his supporters in the wrong and establish himself as a victim forced by superior power to abdicate after being betrayed by those who owed him allegiance. Without denying his own unarguable failings and errors as King, he succeeds in showing Bolingbroke as a ruthless grasper of power and the nobles as betrayers who follow their own interests to the winning side. Richard takes command of the scene—the scene planned by Bolingbroke as well as that written by Shakespeare—from his first lines to the very end, and conducts it in such a way that it would be more dangerous for Bolingbroke to stop him than to let him continue. Bolingbroke, indeed, had made a miscalculation less than but similar in kind to the one Brutus made when he permitted Antony to speak at Caesar's funeral.

Richard's skill in using style and rhetoric as weapons appears in his first speech, in which he disposes of the fiction that he is still King much as he had by addressing "King Bolingbroke" [III. iii. 173] at Flint Castle. Why, he asks, is he "sent for to a king?" [IV. i. 162]. But before there can be an answer, as he passes by the nobles he brands them as Judases, without implying that he is himself Christlike except in being betrayed. And when he cries "God save the King!" [IV. i. 172] and waits in silence for a responsory amen, he throws into their midst the embarrassing question of just who, at this moment, is their rightful King. And asking "To what service [an aptly menial word for a King obeying orders] am I sent for hither?" [IV. i. 176] he elicits from York a statement of the official scenario:

> To do that office of thine own goodwill
> Which tired majesty did make thee offer,
> The resignation of thy state and crown
> To Henry Bolingbroke.
>
> [IV. i. 177-80]

Then, in the first of two symbolic pantomimes whereby Richard dramatizes his situation visually, he takes the crown and holding it in his hands, says "Here, Cousin, seize the crown" [IV. i. 181]. But the last thing Bolingbroke now wants is to be obliged to seize the crown, even in a symbolic action; he stands reluctant, and must be coached by Richard—"here, Cousin" [IV. i. 182]—to take hold of it. And in the moments when both men are holding the golden circle symbolizing the absolute, the divine power of rule, the whole moral ambiguity of the positions of the two men is diagrammed to the spectators. As Bolingbroke stands, holding the crown that has not yet been relinquished to him, he is forced into the embarrassed remark, "I thought you had been willing to resign" [IV. i. 190], which Richard deftly turns to a consideration of the griefs and cares that accompany power. And to Bolingbroke's perfunctory words of philosophic comfort, he responds, much as Bolingbroke had responded to his father's attempts to mitigate the pain of exile by wise saws, with hard realism: "Your cares set up do not pluck my cares down" [IV. i. 195].

Bolingbroke keeps trying to bring Richard back from his paradoxical but awkwardly suggestive wordplays to the intended script: "Are you contented to resign the crown?" [IV. i. 200]. Then Richard does at last make the abdication, but not simply. Contented? Both yes and no: he must perforce be contented to do what he is forced to do, but can a man be content to deny his very identity? For what of the man is left, his function denied?

In the formal parallel rhetoric of the abdication he turns over everything to Bolingbroke and cancels out himself and his reign. Yet the lines are full of suggestions that this act is not only painful but almost blasphemous. Earlier he had said, "Not all the water in the rough rude sea / Can wash the balm off from an anointed king" [III. ii. 54-5]. But now, "With mine own tears I wash away my balm." He holds back nothing, not even generosity: "God pardon all oaths that are broke to me! / God keep all vows unbroke are made to thee!" [IV. i. 207, 214-15].

Richard, then, has finally done what he was brought in to do. But it is not enough that he openly resign his state; he must read aloud a full statement of his crimes. Bolingbroke wants not only a clear title, but also public acknowledgement that what he has done is an act of justice, so that "the souls of men / May deem that you are worthily deposed" [IV. i. 226-27]. The scene, which had almost come to rest, moves into a second and intenser stage of tacit conflict.

There is a nice irony in the fact that Bolingbroke does not himself make this humiliating demand, but lets Northumberland enact his ruthlessness for him—Northumberland who will later rebel against him. Irony, too, in the invitation this order offers Richard to open up publicly the whole question of guilt, and to make plain that his guilt for past actions does not hide or mitigate that of the men who are deposing him or those who are standing embarrassed, trying to be neutral, pitying but inactive and uncommitted like Pilate. As Northumberland presses him, Richard's inner grief and shame—shame not only for the deeds he cannot bring himself to read out but also for the weakness of what he is doing here—define the feckless but sensitive man within the King. Even in this flow of emotion, however, he remembers to check Northumberland's specious use of the humble address "My lord—"

> No lord of thine, thou haught insulting man,
> Nor no man's lord; I have no name, no title . . .
> But 'tis usurped.
>
> [IV. i. 254-55, 257]

And in this crisis of lost identity, Richard hits upon his second device of pantomimic parable, this one a demonstration of the ambiguity of the relations between appearances and reality. He asks that a mirror be brought—and even in the request stigmatizes Bolingbroke: "Good King, great King, and yet not greatly good" [IV. i. 263]. Bolingbroke humors his request, and when Northumberland presses once again for the public confession and Richard lashes out in anguish, Bolingbroke must recognize that Richard is not only carrying the scene, but winning sympathy; he quietly instructs Northumberland to "Urge it no more" [IV. i. 271].

The precise import of Richard's play with the mirror is difficult to formulate for he plays subtly upon the two contradictory symbolic significances of mirrors, both familiar even to commonplace. First, a mirror is not a complete truthteller, for it shows only a surface, though without some kind of mirror man cannot see the truth about himself. Besides, since man can read in it selectively and see only what he wants to see, the mirror can be a flatterer. And so Richard, regarding himself in the glass, realizes that he sees truth, but only a partial truth and a flattering truth at that: he sees the appearances that belong to public show, ceremony, glory. By breaking the mirror he enacts the suddenness with which glory and power may be shattered, leaving the man, the human truth, unchanged and unrevealed. And Bolingbroke's attempt to turn Richard's tantalizing and somehow minatory formulations of this parable into a simpler and more commonsensical proposition only gives Richard a stepping stone to a still subtler and more disturbing statement about the durability of grief among transiencies.

And when Richard, near the breaking point, begs a final boon, he turns Bolingbroke's unctuously gracious phrase, "Name it, fair Cousin," against him: "I have a king here to my flatterer. / Being so great, I have no need to beg" [IV. i. 304, 308-09]. His boon, simply to be relieved of this painful scene, he asks in a simple anguished cry: "Then give me leave to go." Bolingbroke asks, as if Richard had a choice, "Whither?" "Whither you will," cries Richard, "so I were from your sights" [IV. i. 313-15].

And now, without any more pretense of reverence or courtesy, Bolingbroke springs the trap shut: "Go, some of you convey him to the Tower." But even from the wording of that openly ruthless command Richard takes opportunity to score unequivocally a final time: "Oh, good! convey? conveyers are you all, / That rise thus nimbly by a true king's fall" [IV. i. 316-18]. And as Richard goes, the new King sets the date for his coronation, and brusquely orders the lords to prepare themselves for it. Stripped of its velvet glove, Henry's hand shows forth iron, and Richard's moral victory is sure.

It was not much of a victory, for Richard lost a kingdom, but for Henry it was a considerable defeat. As Shakespeare shows, he spent most of his reign trying to quell rebellions, to justify his title to the throne, and to regain the confidence of his nobles. Even his son Henry V, as he approached the battle of Agincourt, feared that his father's debts were not paid. It was Richard's performance at Westminster which showed to all that, however inevitable and even desirable was Henry's rise to power, his deed itself was not good, nor would all of its results be. That this was the turning point of Henry's success is made evident by a dramatic juxtaposition: no sooner has Henry left the stage than, without any break in continuity of scene, the Abbot of Westminster, the Bishop of Carlisle, and Aumerle respond to this "woeful pageant" by laying the first of the plots against the new king, "To rid the realm of this pernicious blot'' [IV. i. 321, 325]. Carlisle helps to initiate fulfillment of his prophecy.

Two two antagonists will not be seen to meet again, but there is still a final stage in their conflict. We hear a report of their performances in their new roles in the procession into London, Henry playing the gracious—and demagogic—victor, and Richard, with his new humility and self-confidence in sorrow, enduring quietly and patiently the contempt and violence of the fickle mob. Yet the underlying conflict continues. Though Richard is imprisoned and powerless, his sympathizers plot against Henry's life. The Duke of York accuses his own son of treason and with almost grotesque determination demands that he be punished, as if he would make up for failing Richard by last-ditch loyalty to the new king, but Henry, realizing that in his precarious reign he cannot afford to lose more friends, grants pardon in order to gain a supporter. But he still feels that Richard's very existence is a threat even though he is helplessly enduring solitude, humiliation, and filth in prison.

There, even while Bolingbroke is fearing him, Richard comes to terms with himself, his past, and his fate without hatred or impulse to vengeance. In his final long performance with only himself as audience, he asserts a kind of spiritual valor when he hammers out the stubborn analogy of the prison to the world. He is, indeed, finding out what inner resources he has when he is deprived of all else. . . . And when murderers invade the solitude where unaccommodated man stands stripped of the dignity of forms and ceremonies, Richard finds valor to attack his attackers and, after the one burst of physical violence in the whole play, escapes out of life as out of a prison.

But even in his death, in his final loss of all, Richard indirectly scores once more against his antagonist, as the final moments of the play make plain. For just as Henry, impulsively rising to action in order to regain his rights, found himself on a tide that swept him at once to the triumph of kingship and the guilt of usurpation, so by inadvertence—or was it deviousness? We cannot surely know—he finds that his spoken wish for some friend to rid him of "this living fear" [V. iv. 2] of Richard has led not only to Richard's death, but to Henry's becoming, in his own conscience at least, a murderer. I see no reason to regard his final speech as cynical or hypocritical, or anything less than expression of an appalled realization of the exorbitant price in guilt that political success may exact. He wanted to be King, but not usurper; he wanted to have Richard dead, but not to be a murderer. The wheel has almost come full circle. As behind Richard's public actions at the beginning the play lurked the question of who was responsible for the death of Thomas of Gloucester, so Henry is beginning a reign haunted by Richard's death. He is pursued by uninvited guilt, and hamstrung by the precedent of rebellion he has set. Though Richard's victory is a pallid one, neither overt nor heroic, it leaves his opponent king of a disaffected kingdom, but a defeated man, in his mouth the sour taste of self-approval and guilt. (pp. 392-99)

> Harold F. Folland, "King Richard's Pallid Victory," in Shakespeare Quarterly, Vol. XXIV, No. 4, Autumn, 1973, pp. 390-99.

T. McALINDON   (essay date 1973)

[McAlindon's point of departure in the following excerpt is the "air of Medievalism" that pervades Richard II. Unlike such earlier critics as W. B. Yeats (1901) and E. M. W. Tillyard (1944), whom he directly disputes, McAlindon denies that Richard is presented as "the last of an old race of kings compelled by historical necessity to give way to a new breed of efficient and prosaic rulers." Rather, he argues that Richard, along with Bolingbroke and nearly all the other characters, "shares in the general failure to be true to himself and others" that constitutes the essence of the feudal chivalric code and its ideals. McAlindon focuses especially on Shakespeare's use of language, ritual, and ceremony in Richard II to dramatize the breakdown of medieval order, labelling Bolingbroke "the real master of sweet words" in the play, but identifying Richard as "the most blatant offender against ritual propriety."]

One of the most distinctive features of Richard II is its air of medievalism. In giving this character to the play, however, Shakespeare was not aiming chiefly at historical accuracy or the delights of period flavour; nor was he seeking to show that Richard is the last of an old race of kings compelled by historical necessity to give way to a new breed of efficient and prosaic rulers.

To understand the artistic purpose of the play's medievalism we have to bear in mind that it is conveyed to us entirely through the use of chivalric rites, ideals, and manners. The nobles who surround King Richard are knights rather than courtiers—men whose models are found in Malory and Froissart rather than in Castiglione and Guazzo. They are, nonetheless, the obvious progenitors of Renaissance gentlemen, and their declared values are an integral part of their descendants' view of life. They accept that a knight should be 'true'—should not lie, should keep his word, should be loyal. They believe that the proper end of military skill is to enable one to fight in the service of a noble cause. And they would agree that no man could win a finer eulogy than that accorded by the Bishop of Carlisle to Thomas Mowbray, Duke of Norfolk, who spent the last years of his life in the service of Christ and in the defence of truth itself against error and barbarism—'black pagans, Turks, and Saracens' [IV. i. 92-100]. But the whole point of Carlisle's beautifully evocative panegyric is that true knighthood has vanished from England. For although they give many impressive signs to the contrary, Richard and his divided followers are a collection of talkers, flatterers, liars, slanderers, and 'recreant traitors' [I. i. 144]. The only war for which they become famous is not fought against the enemies of England, much less against black pagans and Turks: it is an unnatural conflict between Englishman and Englishman, cousin and cousin, father and son. (p. 19)

Throughout Richard II, Shakespeare represents the actions which lead to or constitute civil war as departures from what is natural and customary and therefore becoming. Thus in one passage Bolingbroke is seen as an overflowing river which ignores natural bounds and as a leader who forces people to adopt attire and accoutrement, and modes of speech and behaviour, which are quite inappropriate to their age, profession or sex [III. ii. 106-19]. Elsewhere attention focuses more narrowly on the unfitness of Englishmen fighting their compatriots instead of Frenchmen and Saracens, and committing atrocities which would move 'barbarism itself' to tears [V. ii. 36]: 'Ten thousand bloody crowns of mothers' sons / Shall ill become the flower of England's face' [III. iii. 96-7]. . . . But this in turn is narrowed down to a form of indecorum with which 'civil and uncivil arms' [III. iii. 102] are most continuously identified throughout the play: the spectacle of knights whose every word and deed is a betrayal of knighthood. The glorious England of John of Gaunt and the Black Prince 'hath made a shameful conquest of itself' [II. i. 66]. It has done so because its knights have betrayed what they stand for, and because in so doing they have proved treacherous to one another. No one, admittedly, would even begin to think of Richard as 'the prince of chivalry' (to borrow a phrase from *Troilus and Cressida* [I. ii. 229]). But that itself is a point of dramatic significance; and it must be related to the larger truth that, although Richard suffers most from betrayal, he shares in the general failure to be true to himself and to others. His volatile shifting from confidence to despair and from arrogance to self-abasement, his painful self-consciousness, and his pathetic inability to keep a firm hold on his own identity, make him, like Hamlet and Lear, the kind of character from whom no spectator can ever really dissociate himself—thoroughly credible and human. Part of Shakespeare's considerable achievement in this play, therefore, is that the commonest moral blemish in the nation becomes a psychological reality in Richard and even accounts for his remarkable immediacy as a character creation. Coleridge has suggested that what individualises Richard is the consistent inconsistency of his behaviour [see excerpt above, 1811-12]. But the Elizabethans would probably have used the term inconstancy. This can imply not just an unwillingness to act in an orderly and consistent fashion, but disloyalty to others, disloyalty to self, and (cognate with this) an inability to confront the vicissitudes of Fortune without loss of dignity and self-control. All these forms of changefulness are present in Richard and account in large measure for his downfall.

Richard's errors and failures are all accompanied by pointed reminders of the role or identity to which he should be faithful. While he is succumbing to the flat refusal of Bolingbroke and Mowbray to make peace at his request, he recalls almost wistfully that he was 'not born to sue, but to command' [I. i. 196]. The dissident lords do not ascribe his wretched management of national affairs to any ingrained incompetence but to the fact that he has surrendered his will to others: 'The King is not himself, but basely led / By flatterers' [II. i. 241-42]. And it seems that their intention in siding with Bolingbroke is not to unseat Richard but to 'make high majesty look like itself' [II. i. 295] by eliminating his flatterers. What turns them into usurping rebels is the way in which Richard disintegrates at the approach of merely seeming disaster. When he hears of Bolingbroke's return from banishment, he fluctuates repeatedly from excessive confidence to unwarranted pessimism, and finally subsides in total despair; his whole emotional condition is an image of absolute subjection to the inconstancies of Fortune's wheel. He is, of course, reminded that his gloom is both base and unjustified: 'Comfort, my liege; remember who you are' [III. ii. 82]; but this simply provokes in him an absurdly bombastic strut which leaves him all the more vulnerable to the next piece of bad news: 'I had forgot myself; am I not King? / Awake thou coward majesty! thou sleepest' [III. ii. 83-4].

In the upshot Richard throws away his crown in what he considers to be a royal gesture of resignation to Fortune's cruelty: 'A king, woe's slave, shall kingly woe obey' [III. ii. 210]. But the queen takes a different view of his abject submissiveness. For her it means that he has been transformed and deposed 'both in shape and mind' [V. i. 26-8], having forgotten that 'the king of beasts' paws in rage against its enemy and never fawns with 'base humility' [V. i. 29-34]. Richard does, in fact, die like a lion, and with perhaps the most magnificent cry of rage in all Shakespeare: 'Go thou and fill another room in hell' [V. v. 107]. It is an almost invariable rule in Shakespeare's history plays that nothing in the life of a fallen prince or nobleman becomes him like the leaving of it.

Richard is right in recalling that the self to which he should be true is located in the name of king—in what he has inherited 'by fair sequence and succession' [II. i. 199]. But he makes the classic aristocratic error of assuming that a name or title has virtue irrespective of the behaviour of the person who carries it. (pp. 20-2)

Names function with exceptional prominence in *Richard II* as an index of value and order. This is partly because an anxious concern for rank, rights and responsibilities is proper in times of political and social upheaval, but partly too because the hallmark of a knight is an almost mystical obsession with honour and reputation. The play opens with Mowbray protesting that he is 'a loyal gentleman' and angrily rejecting the charge—which almost everyone else of importance will face sooner or later—that he deserves 'a foul traitor's name' [I. i. 148, 44]. In pleading with the king for trial by combat, he explains that 'spotless reputation' is 'the purest treasure mortal times afford' and that without it 'men are but gilded loam or painted clay'—remove it from a man and he will cease to exist [I. i. 177-83]. One of the ironies of this fervent speech is that it is addressed to someone who in effect has done far more than Bolingbroke to disgrace Mowbray's 'fair name' [I. i. 167]—for the murder of which Mowbray is accused is mainly Richard's crime. From the outset, therefore, it is apparent that Richard abuses not only the name of king but the names of other men as well. He finds it improper that the dying Gaunt should 'play so nicely' with his name; but Gaunt defends himself by presenting this as a bitter reaction to the banishment of his son and heir—an act which implies an attempt to destroy his family name: 'Since thou dost seek to kill my name in me, / I mock my name, great king, to flatter thee' [II. i. 86-7]. Richard's subsequent seizure of all Gaunt's possessions completes the effect of banishment on Bolingbroke, reducing him to a bare, unaccommodated man without a single sign of his noble identity [III. i. 24-7]. And as York warned Richard, the unnaming of Bolingbroke is a fatal error, since it attacks the principle of temporal order and hereditary succession on which his own identity depends: 'Be not thyself' [II. i. 198]. In the short term, it provides Bolingbroke with a good excuse for returning from exile and so initiates the chain of events which ends in Richard's deposition and death.

With the return of the banished man in search of a title, there is a rapid decline in social order marked by impropriety and confusion in the use of names and forms of address. Richard's emissary addresses Bolingbroke by his old title of Hereford and is told in effect that he must be talking to the wrong man [II. iii. 70-3]. Later, Northumberland's communication with Bolingbroke is sharply interrupted when York rebukes him for omitting Richard's title: 'It would beseem the Lord Northumberland / To say "King Richard"'—such impropriety would once have cost him his head, adds York [III. iii. 6-14]. Yet Richard himself will soon be heard conniving at this very form of indecorum, for he addresses Northumberland with the half-mocking, half-defeatist question: 'Most mighty prince, my Lord Northumberland, / What says King Bolingbroke?' [III. iii. 172-73]. This kind of speech prepares for the moment when Richard will volunteer to 'submit . . . and lose the name of king'—and will even call himself 'a traitor with the rest' [III. iii. 143, 145-46; IV. i. 248].

The renaming of Bolingbroke merely increases uncertainty and discord. When he offers to ascend the throne 'in God's name', and York cries, 'And long live Henry, fourth of that name!' [IV. i. 112], the Bishop of Carlisle protests: 'My Lord of

Act V. Scene ii. The Duchess, Aumerle, and York. By William Hamilton. The Department of Rare Books and Special Collections, The University of Michigan Library.

Hereford here, whom you call king, / Is a foul traitor to proud Hereford's king' [IV. i. 134-35]. But Carlisle himself is deemed to be the traitor and is arrested for 'capital treason' on the spot [IV. i. 151]. This kind of stark disorder in the placing of names and words dominates the last scenes of the play—or the first phase of Bolingbroke's reign. It is caused mainly by reactions to the discovery that Aumerle and others are conspiring to kill the new king; but it begins just before the actual discovery when York corrects his wife for referring to their son by his customary titles: 'Aumerle that was / But that is lost for being Richard's friend, / And madam, you must call him Rutland now' [V. ii. 42-4]. This sounds like a courteous correction, yet it is as unbeseeming in York as the rude brevity which he once condemned in Northumberland. And it is not the only remark of its kind which he makes here. Not long ago he referred to Richard as 'my sovereign, whom both my oath and duty bids defend' [II. ii. 112-13]; but now he is telling his wife that he is one of Bolingbroke's 'sworn subjects' and that he has pledged in parliament for his son's 'truth and lasting fealty to the new-made king' [V. ii. 39, 44-5]. Not long ago, too, he rebuked the ingratiating Bolingbroke for addressing him as 'My gracious uncle!' [II. iii. 85]: 'I am no traitor's uncle; and *that word grace* in an ungracious mouth is but profane' [II. iii. 88-9]. Yet when he finds that his son has sworn himself to a conspiracy against the usurper, he explodes with: 'Treason, foul treason! Villain! traitor! slave!' [V. ii. 72]. The wild impropriety of these words in his mouth is greatly increased

by the hysterical show of physical energy and moral enthusiasm which follows. Loftily brushing aside his wife's appeals ('Peace, foolish woman . . . Thou fond mad woman'), he calls out repeatedly for his riding boots and then, although 'weak with age' and 'prisoner to the palsy' [II. ii. 83; II. iii. 104], gallops off to the new-made king to demand the instant execution of his 'disloyal' son. The climax of all this unseemliness occurs in the unctuous and bombastic outburst of the usurper:

> O heinous, strong, and bold conspiracy!
> O loyal father of a treacherous son!
> Thou sheer, immaculate, and silver fountain,
> From whence this stream through muddy passages
> Hath held his current and defil'd himself!
> Thy overflow of good converts to bad;
> And thy abundant goodness shall excuse
> This deadly blot in thy disgressing son.
>
> [V. iii. 59-66]

Himself the treacherous son of a loyal father, Bolingbroke (like York) can never again rebuke anyone of treachery or disobedience without his words turning instantly against himself. This is an irony of which superb use is made in *Henry IV.*

Too much emphasis, I believe, has been placed on Bolingbroke's pardoning of Aumerle and Carlisle. The remark of Aumerle's pleading mother that there is 'no word like "pardon" for kings' mouths so meet' [V. iii. 119] is perfectly correct. But it forces us to reflect that all the other words used by Bolingbroke and his associates after he becomes king are very unmeet. While news flows in about the businesslike beheadings of the other 'dangerous consorted traitors' who sought his 'dire overthrow' [V. vi. 15-16], and while King Richard is being brutally murdered in his prison-cell ('What means death in this rude assault?' [V. v. 105]), Bolingbroke ('Great King') and his supporters ('Kind uncle York', 'gentle Percy', etc.) courteously greet one another with gracious words and titles which do not match their conduct. (pp. 23-6)

It should be apparent from what I have said so far that although the misuse of names is of great importance in the design of *Richard II,* it is only one part of a large and complex pattern of linguistic disorders—moral, semantic and stylistic—which signal the decline of this other Eden and demi-paradise into an unweeded garden. It has, of course, been observed many years ago that Shakespeare was much concerned with language in *Richard II*—that 'tongue' is its key word. . . . There is in the play an unremitting concern for 'the tongue's office' [I. iii. 256], for the relationship between tongue and heart, word and deed; and the verse itself seems most harmonious when—as in Gaunt's eulogy on the lost paradise, or Carlisle's on the redeemed Mowbray—the understanding tells the ear that the music in the words is an echo of the profound harmony of natural and moral order. (pp. 26-7)

Since justice is the basis of social harmony, the words spoken by the king in his capacity of supreme judge and arbiter are the words which matter most in any realm. Accordingly, Richard's first failure in justice—his handling of the dispute between Bolingbroke and Mowbray—is continuously represented as part of his disrespect for and deficiency in good words. Unable at first to settle the quarrel by oral arbitration, he gives in to the two men's demand for the rougher method of trial by combat. But in the middle of this second trial he reverts abruptly to oral judgement, imposes a sentence of exile on both men, and offers no explanation whatever for the enormous disparity between the sentences: ten years for Bolingbroke, life for Mowbray. Mowbray's anguished response to 'the hopeless word of ''never to return''' [I. iii. 152] simultaneously suggests that Richard delivers the gravest of sentences in a light and thoughtless fashion and that in so doing he is bent on the destruction of speech itself—the quibble on 'sentence' neatly associates judicial and rhetorical disorder:

> A heavy sentence, my most sovereign liege,
> And all unlook'd for from your Highness' mouth.
> A dearer merit, not so deep a maim
> As to be cast forth in the common air,
> Have I deserved at your Highness' hands.
> The language I have learnt these forty years,
> My native English, now I must forgo;
> And now my tongue's use is to me no more
> Than an unstringed viol or a harp; ...
> What is thy sentence, then, but speechless death,
> Which robs my tongue from breathing native
>   breath?
>
>   [I. iii. 154-62, 172-73]

The hint that Richard utters grave sentences lightly is confirmed by his curt and unfeeling reply to Mowbray, and by his sudden reduction of Bolingbroke's sentence from ten to six years (on seeing Gaunt in tears). Even Bolingbroke comments on the disorders in Richard's sentencing . . . :

> How long a time lies in one little word!
> Four lagging winters and four wanton springs
> End in a word: such is the breath of Kings.
>
>   [I. iii. 213-15]
>   (pp. 27-8)

Richard's essential opposition to well-ordered speech, and his notable facility for delivering light and callous words at grave and painful moments, are exhibited again at the death of Gaunt. . . . Since Gaunt is his uncle and the most respected of his counsellors, Richard should receive his dying words with reverence and humility. To emphasise this, Shakespeare makes use of the traditional belief that God endows the last words of good men with special wisdom. . . . But after mustering a few light-hearted queries, the young king is enraged by Gaunt's solemn warnings and reacts by calling him 'a lunatic lean-witted fool' who deserves to be beheaded for speaking so disrespectfully to his king: 'This tongue that runs so roundly in thy head / Should run thy head from thy unreverent shoulders' [II. i. 115, 122-23]. A few moments after he leaves Gaunt, Richard is told by Northumberland that the 'prophet' has died, and the phrasing of the announcement is such as to suggest that Richard's unreverent words, added to his reckless sentence, have finally destroyed an antique and sacred instrument. . . . (pp. 29-30)

Gaunt's character has indeed been of verbal significance from the start. In the opening lines of the play we learn that he has kept his oath and bond but that he has been unable to do more than 'sift' his son on his motives for bringing the charge of treachery against Mowbray. Implicit in this introductory exchange between the young king and his time-honoured uncle are a number of ideas about verbal behaviour which are of fundamental importance for the two trial scenes which follow, and indeed for the rest of the play. Oaths are important, and it is necessary for men to reveal their thoughts candidly at the right time—to 'be even and direct', as Hamlet puts it [*Hamlet*, II. ii. 287]. But as soon as we pass from men like Gaunt—one of the last representatives of a noble age—we have no guarantee that men speak freely and truly and keep their word,

or that they will allow others to do so. At first impressed by the vigour and solemnity with which the many oaths are uttered, one soon becomes uneasy and eventually concludes (if one reflects on them at all) that their principal effect is to make lies, slander, disloyalty and 'indirect crook'd ways' [*2 Henry IV*, IV. v. 184] all the more reprehensible. Largely through them, language is built up into an ostentatious covering for 'empty hollowness' [I. ii. 59]: 'hollow' is another one of the play's key words. (p. 30)

An important part of Shakespeare's strategy in [the first] two scenes is to put on stage a man known to have brought two centuries of chaos to England through his breach of the oath of fealty—and to have him do nothing else but proclaim that his word is sacred and that it betokens love and loyalty for his king. In subsequent scenes, too, the unreliable nature of Bolinbroke's oaths and promises continues to be exposed. On returning to England he makes humble and flattering expressions of gratitude to those who support him and, quite unnecessarily, enforces these with a promise—uttered five times—of material reward. One has no need of prophetic powers (or a knowledge of *Henry IV*) to evaluate this promise: its unsolicited, repetitious and essentially ignoble nature is sufficient to indicate that it will not be kept. But there is another reason why Bolingbroke's followers might well treat this promise with some scepticism: and it is ultimately connected with the oath of fealty. 'Trust not him that hath once broken faith,' said Elizabeth in *III Henry VI* [IV. iv. 30]; and in this play Bolingbroke makes an oath before his new friends which they are soon to see him break. It is his oath assuring York (as the king's deputy), and later the king himself, that although he has returned prematurely from banishment, he has no rebellious intentions whatever—indeed his love and loyalty are undiminished. All Bolingbroke's assurances are either repetitious or inflated; this one is both, and in the highest degree. (pp. 31-2)

It is left to Richard to condemn Bolingbroke, and all Englishmen who side with him, for 'cracking the strong warrant of an oath' and so breaking faith with God as well as man [IV. i. 235; III. i. 101]. And he lives long enough to see that disharmony between tongue and heart will afflict even good men when Bolingbroke is king: 'What my tongue dares not, that my heart shall say', promises the faithful groom [V. v. 97]. But such is Shakespeare's impartial distribution of responsibility that even Richard himself is seen as a perjurer. In reducing Bolingbroke's sentence from ten years to six, he breaks the vow of impartiality which he made to Mowbray [I. i. 115-21]. And by surrendering his kingship without a struggle, he openly supports and participates in the sin of his forsworn subjects: 'With mine own breath [I] release all duteous oaths, / All pomp and majesty I do forswear' [IV. i. 210-11]. Richard's previous remark that 'the breath of worldly men cannot depose / The deputy elected by the Lord' [III. ii. 56-7] offers the best comment on this suggestion that with his own breath he can undo promises made by others and himself to God. (pp. 32-3)

There is in Richard's court the appearance of a highly developed sense of propriety, expressed in gracious and ceremonious manners. It is so prominent and so skilfully expressed that it has led many to look on Richard as a king of old-world courtesy—a 'sweet lovely rose' [*1 Henry IV*, I. iii. 175]—whose refined and touchingly fragile world is rudely shattered by a no-nonsense politician and his train of brazen upstarts. Support for this view can be found in some incidents which mark the rise of Bolingbroke: 'Rude misgoverned hands from windows' top / Threw dust and rubbish on King Richard's head' [V. ii.

5-6]; while news of his downfall is conveyed to the gentle queen not by some well-born and suitably eloquent ambassador but by 'the harsh rude tongue' of an old gardener [III. iv. 74]. Yet this sort of social behaviour represents only one of two objectionable extremes, and it is as untypical of Bolingbroke as it is of Richard. The other extreme is the kind of courtesy or 'courtship' which, instead of revealing a gentle mind and a desire to cement human relations, is really the instrument of self-interest, narcissism or ambition. This is the sin against courtesy—the profaning of civil conversation—which characterises Richard's court; and it is by no means confined to the king and his favourites.

The most elaborately courteous speeches delivered or reported in the play are all reinforced by formal gestures: by kissing and embracing, by handshaking and removing the hat, and, above all, by bowing and kneeling. In a technical sense, therefore, they are 'ceremonies' and so have some of the sanctity of oaths—a point emphasised by the fact that they are often explicitly offered as expressions of reverence and duty and with the idea of degree in mind. This prevailing ceremoniousness of manner—this search for grace or graciousness—is an extension of the ritual character of the great scenes; and with them it combines to give the play a ceremonial quality which some critics, with considerable justification, have treated as a fundamental clue in the interpretation of its principal characters. Influenced in part by Walter Pater, W. B. Yeats argued that Richard has a deep and genuine love of ceremony [see excerpts above, 1889 and 1901]; he thought that this reflects the imaginative richness of Richard's mind and the elegance of a medieval and aristocratic way of life which he personifies. E. M. W. Tillyard also saw Richard as a man in love with ceremony, and he, too, construed this as a sign that Richard stands for a medieval and unpractical view of life to which Bolingbroke's modern spirit is naturally antagonistic [see excerpt above 1944]. Quite unlike Yeats, however, Tillyard believed that Shakespeare intended Richard's regard for ceremony to be taken as a fatal defect. The trouble with Richard, said Tillyard, is that he is always 'more concerned with how he behaves, with the fitness of his conduct to the occasion, than with what he actually does.' He and his friends are interested only in 'the sheer propriety' of what they say and do; they are 'mindful of propriety and . . . unmindful of nature', and so their behaviour always betokens 'ceremony, not . . . passion'.

These remarks offer good material for a lesson on semantics and the history of ideas. That an Elizabethan scholar so knowledgeable and so intelligent as Tillyard could adopt this conception of decorum in the interpretation of a Shakespearian play—a modern conception, and one so debased and so unsubtle as to be virtually opposite in meaning to the original—makes it in no way surprising that Shakespeare's interest in decorum should have escaped notice for so long. Tillyard, of course, was right in relating ceremony to propriety; and Yeats, too, was right in assuming that for Shakespeare and his contemporaries ceremony was the ethical and aesthetic manifestation of life lived at its best. But both critics were quite wrong in assuming that Richard is identifiable with ceremony and propriety and that Bolingbroke is a pragmatic, modern spirit indifferent to it. The text makes it perfectly clear that Bolingbroke and Northumberland are at least as addicted to ceremonious courtesies as Richard and Aumerle, and that Bolingbroke can throw himself into ritual performances with histrionic zeal; while a knowledge of Renaissance ethical and aesthetic

theory, together with the text, shows that the king and the usurper are alike corrupters of ceremony.

One kind of debased and apparent courtesy commonly referred to or represented in the play is flattery, the evil which traditionally threatens every king. Richard seems to show the right attitude towards it when he exclaims: 'He does me double wrong / That wounds me with the flatteries of his tongue' [III. ii. 215-16]. But these words are simply one more instance of Richard's distressing habit of saying the right thing at the wrong time or in the wrong way, for they serve as a petulant response to sound and encouraging advice. (pp. 33-5)

It must be added, however, that although Shakespeare reproduces the chroniclers' conception of Richard as a king misled by flatterers, he does little to make this a dramatic reality: not once in the play is Richard flattered by any of his favourites. The real master of sweet words is Bolingbroke, the smooth politician who knows, like Claudius of Elsinore, that the way to control events is to flatter this man and slander that one— in general to pour poison in at the ear. His gracious protestations of respect and affectionate good-will towards Richard (dead and alive), towards the common people, towards his closest associates, towards the deposed queen, and towards the dead enemy whom he once described as 'the first head and spring' of 'all the treasons for these eighteen years / Complotted and contrived' in England [I. i. 95-7]—all these add up to a ceremonious manner which does not fit. York's tart criticism applies to every one of Bolingbroke's gracious speeches: 'That word grace in an ungracious mouth is but profane' [II. iii. 88-9]. (p. 35)

Before the trial by combat begins, Bolingbroke announces that he must 'take a ceremonious leave / And loving farewell' of his friends [I. iii. 50-1]; and begins by kneeling to his king and cousin, kissing his hand, and embracing him. It might be too much to describe this as the kiss of Judas rather than a ceremony performed out of love and 'in all duty' [I. iii. 52]. But it certainly has the ignoble distinction of being the first of a series of superficially graceful and essentially hollow farewells. Coming after this exhibition of overdone eloquence, Aumerle's purportedly eloquent speechlessness is merely tit-for-tat.

Moreover, Aumerle's account of his hollow parting from his cousin is followed immediately by Richard's account of their cousin's farewell to the common people. And in this we are given a graphic picture—later confirmed by York [V. ii. 8-21]— of Bolingbroke as a crafty politician who not only employs ceremonious behaviour for his own ends and reduces it to an empty show, but also breaks some of its most elementary rules as a result of his tendency to protest too much. Richard, Bushy, Bagot and Green all observed that in 'his courtship of the common people' he did 'seem to dive into their hearts / With humble and familiar courtesy': he 'threw away' [my italics] reverence and smiles on slaves and poor craftsmen, offered a brace of draymen 'the tribute of his supple knee', and doffed his bonnet to an oyster-wench [I. iv. 24-8, 31-3]. Such behaviour offends not merely by its insincerity and affectation: it completely obscures distinctions of rank or degree, which ceremony should always uphold. This is a fine dramatic point and fits in well with the conception of Bolingbroke as a man whose courteous humility is an essential part of a plan—conscious or unconscious—to get to the pinnacle of pride [I. iv. 35-6].

As the action proceeds, Bolingbroke's ceremoniousness becomes more conspicuous and more patently false. Although he has disobeyed the sentence of exile, he is quick to show the suppleness of his knee when he encounters the king's deputy. But York acidly remarks: 'Show me thy humble heart and not thy knee, / Whose duty is deceivable and false' [II. iii. 83-4]. When he later confronts Richard himself, he makes a great fuss to the effect that he and his followers should kneel and 'show fair duty to his Majesty'—and, as with York, he uses the word 'gracious' as if it were his alone [III. iii. 188, 196]. Richard reacts to this performance with a cunningly ironic comment on the difference between his cousin's visible courtesy and his invisible feelings, between his low knee and his 'high' heart.

Characteristically, however, Richard is critical of disorder and disorderly himself at one and the same moment, for he encourages Bolingbroke to ignore the ceremonious gestures which every subject owes his king [III. iii. 194]. Earlier, when he heard that Bolingbroke had returned in arms, he showed in much more emphatic form, and untouched by irony, this defeatist inclination to make others treat him as an equal. Then he advised his remaining followers to cover their heads in his presence, to forget about 'solemn reverence', and to '*throw away* respect, / Tradition, form, and ceremonious duty' [III. ii. 171-73]. Nevertheless, it is not in the sphere of manners but rather in the great ritual actions, or at essentially ritual and solemn moments, that Richard contributes most to the destruction of ceremony. These provoking invitations to others to 'throw away' reverence and traditional form in his presence are important only as echoes of his own public violations of ritual order and as premonitions of the moment when he will throw away his kingship and profane the coronation rite.

Although Bolingbroke is just as falsely ceremonious in the trial scenes as Richard, and although he participates in the sacrilege of the abdication, Richard comes off as the most blatant offender against ritual propriety. The trials by arbitration and by combat are judicial rites of a different kind; but in both of them, Richard—enthroned on his chair of state and surrounded by his counsellors—is at once the supreme judge and the embodiment of formal order. Both rites are irremediably disordered from the start, since Richard, being guilty of the crime of which the defendant is accused, is utterly unfitted for the role of judge—a point which is very deliberately brought to our notice by the dialogue between Gaunt and the Duchess of Gloucester in the intervening scene. Yet the fact that Richard cannot even qualify for the role of judge does not have nearly so powerful an effect on an audience as the inconstancy of purpose which prevents him from allowing either rite to reach its proper conclusion. In the trial by combat—most revered perhaps of the traditional 'rites of knighthood' [I. i. 75]—his capricious reversal to the procedure which was proper in the first trial constitutes a most unsettling breach of decorum. And it is rendered all the more noticeable by his own solemn injunctions that the rite should be conducted in an 'orderly' fashion, 'formally, according to our law' [I. iii. 9, 29], by the sense of hieratic correctness which prevails until the knights are about to charge, and by the incomparably perverse timing of his decision to settle matters in a different way.

So the impression in these scenes (and it is quite a strong one) that Richard likes things to be done in an orderly, traditional, and formal fashion—that he will uphold ceremony at all costs—is utterly misleading: as misleading as his physical resemblance to the Black Prince. But perhaps it is the abdication scene which offers the most plausible evidence for the view of Pater and Yeats that Richard is deeply and nobly in love with cer-

emony: there he could be said to supply a great ceremonial need and to invent a rite for the solemn act of abdication when none already existed. Yet, although Richard's performance at this point of his career might well seem creative and imaginative to minds imbued with *fin de siècle* aestheticism, it can only have seemed perverse and destructive to Shakespeare's audience. This, after all, is where Richard throws away his duties, and for that very reason his behaviour could not be deemed ceremonious or ceremonial in the true sense. What Richard produces here for his own narcissistic pleasure (hence the mirror) is a parody and undoing of the coronation rite—a degrading and disgracing in which he 'undeck[s] the pompous body of a king' [IV. i. 250], denies his 'sacred state' [IV. i. 209], crowns a usurper, plays the part of 'both priest and clerk' [IV. i. 173]; and confirms his sacrilege by resorting to mock ritual language [IV. i. 204-21]. (pp. 36-9)

T. McAlindon, "Richard II," in his Shakespeare and Decorum, *Macmillan, 1973, pp. 19-43.*

ROY BATTENHOUSE (essay date 1974)

[*Battenhouse offers an assessment of Shakespeare's political orientation in* Richard II. *Contesting the often expounded idea that the play essentially supports Elizabethan governmental policy, he reviews the famous* Homilie Against Disobedience and wilful Rebellion—*a series of carefully prepared and widely preached sermons that became the administration's most influential piece of propaganda—and avers that Shakespeare was here dramatizing the tragedy inherent in the various teachings of this doctrine. Battenhouse focuses on four principal characters—Richard, Carlisle, York, and Gaunt—and demonstrates how Shakespeare ironically underscores the inadequacies of the Tudor theories adopted by each, especially the fundamental teaching of "nonresistance."*]

Scholars are increasingly aware that Shakespeare was a critic of ideas and not merely their mouthpiece. The ideas his characters voice are always aspects of some human purpose, whose validity then becomes exposed in its fruits. A typically Tudor doctrine of political duty, for example, is voiced by several of the characters in *Richard II*. But few scholars nowadays argue, as did Tillyard thirty years ago, that the play essentially supports Tudor orthodoxy [see excerpt above, 1944], or that, as Miss Campbell supposed, Shakespeare was restating the Tudor political ethic simply in order to raise the problem of whether a king might for any cause be deposed [see Additional Bibliography]. Rather, the play sets forth the tragedy of how Richard came to be deposed by Henry Bolingbroke, and includes as causes of this outcome the reasonings and tactics of both these men and others. The story, tragic for England as a whole, is an occasion for audience pity and fear. But what is pitiable and fearful is not merely Bolingbroke's ambition and crime of usurpation, which the chronicler Holinshed emphasizes, or on the other hand Richard's wanton acts, which Holinshed laments. Shakespeare reveals, behind the reciprocal injustices, what John Elliott has termed "the weakness of Richard's philosophy of kingship" [see Additional Bibliography]. Richard's dethroning comes about less through the strength of Bolingbroke's arms than through Richard's own misunderstanding of his office. (p. 31)

We know from modern studies of Richard that his era was one in which continental publicists and some English theologians were emphasizing the divine sanctions of monarchy, and that Richard himself, as one scholar tells us, "grasped at theoretical bucklers for royal power wherever he found them," and developed without logical consistency more extreme claims for royal absolutism than any of his predecessors had done, pro-claiming himself immune from interference by anyone either in the realm or outside it, and magnifying the importance of symbols and ceremonies "as a means of retaining prestige which had formerly been based upon tacit recognition of func-tion" [Richard H. Jones, in his *The Royal Policy of Richard II: Absolutism in the Later Middle Ages*]. In this respect, Rich-ard's stance foreshadows that of the Tudors, and Shakespeare must have been aware of this fact either through wide reading or through oral tradition. (pp. 31-2)

But in Shakespeare's play the actions taken by proponents of these doctrines turn out to be tragic and beset by strange con-tradictions. The Richard who declares in Act III that "the breath of worldly men cannot depose / The deputy elected of the Lord" [III. ii. 56-7] later cooperates in his own deposition. While regarding his opponents as rebels and traitors, he never-theless gives his "soul's consent" to be "a traitor with the rest" [IV. i. 249, 248] and do whatever Bolingbroke wishes. "What you will have, I'll give, and willing too, / For we must do what force will have us do" [III. iii. 206-07]. Thus Richard accepts spinelessly and fatalistically what he believes to be wrong. His doctrine that subjects are unconditionally bound to obey royal authority turns into his own abject obedience to a usurper, making Richard in effect the usurper's accomplice. Is Shakespeare suggesting that this outcome is an all-too-likely consequence of the Tudor theory of non-resistance to the pow-ers that be? The play shows us also, in the careers of other spokesmen of Divine Right doctrine, other forms of conse-quence, equally ironic. It seems likely, therefore, that the dra-matist is testing and exposing latent deficiencies in the premises of Tudor thinking.

Many critics of the drama have complained that Richard is too much a poet who plays with words, or too much an actor engaging in histrionics. But do we not find a similar penchant for self-dramatization in other characters as well, though their less prominent roles give this penchant lesser scope? England's whole ethos in this play is elaborately ceremonious. Tillyard attributes the highly formalistic quality of the play's language and action to Shakespeare's characterizing of the Middle Ages as an era in which men valued "means more than ends." More accurately, P. G. Phialas sees Richard's love of ceremony as a shocking change from earlier medieval attitudes, and hence as Shakespeare's portrayal of a "declining" England [see ex-cerpt above, 1963]. And D. A. Traversi, without generalizing regarding the Middle Ages, finds in the high formality of the play's action "a sense of pose" and of "majesty in decay," and in its ending a mood of "fatalism rather than of acceptance of subjection to events rather than a true concordance with them" [see Additional Bibliography]. Wilbur Sanders [in his *The Dramatist and the Received Idea*], more boldly and I think rightly sees this quality of behavior and outcome as the con-sequence of a "sadly gelded version" of the medieval concept of the sacredness of kings. Whereas older Divine Right theory, Sanders remarks, rested on a concept of the mutuality of king and people in a *corpus mysticum* [mystical body], of which the king was protector, the Tudor version divorced right from responsibility and neglected the prince's traditional role as fa-ther and shepherd to his people.

It is this aspect of the play's meaning which I wish to amplify and illustrate. Richard and others, by substituting a ceremonial interpretation of duty for the more traditional sacramental the-ory, reduce kingship to a hollow parade in which high preten-sions mask a subsurface of intrigue and evasive practice. The

whole community thus becomes ripe for the virtually Machia-vellian tactics of Henry Bolingbroke. He merely wedges him-self into the vacuum created by a breakdown of concern for community welfare. And this breakdown is related to an ide-ology of political duty which has all the half-truths and con-fusions of understanding one can find, for instance, in the Elizabethan *Homilie Against Disobedience and wilful Rebel-lion,* first published in 1571 and ordered to be preached reg-ularly in the pulpit, its six parts on six Sundays. Let me begin, therefore, by examining the potentialities for tragedy latent in this homily, and then show how Shakespeare exhibits in four of the characters in his play variant forms of tragic outcome to which the homily's premises might lead.

The clerical authors of this *Homilie* are curiously feeble as theologians. They make no mention of charity as being the first of the theological virtues, or of justice as being chief of the natural virtues. Rather, we are told in the homily's first paragraph that "obedience is the principall vertue of all vertues, and indeed the very root of all vertues, and the cause of all felicitie." Man's pre-fallen state is held up as a model. But then we are told that after Adam and Eve had breached this obedience by rebellion, "the very root of all other sins," God forthwith "repaired again the rule and order of obedience" by giving man laws ordaining due obedience to his majesty and, when mankind increased, obedience to special governors and rulers. The impression this statement gives is that the "re-paired" order has the same absolute validity as the pre-fallen one. The homilist grants that there may sometimes be evil princes, but he insists that subjects are by Scripture's teaching "bounden to obey them," the evil ones as well as the good ones—and, indeed, that the authority of the Prince is such that "the subject that provoketh him *to displeasure* sinneth against his own soule." One wonders, in that case, how the homilist would regard, for instance, John the Baptist's incurring the displeasure of Herod or Paul's incurring the displeasure of the magistrates at Philippi.

A carefully selective use of proof-texts runs through the hom-ily. Much is made, of course, of Romans 13 and of 1 Peter 2, but there is no mention of Acts 5:29, "We ought to obey God rather than men." Likewise, much is made of David's twice refusing an opportunity to slay King Saul although Saul was seeking David's destruction. But no mention is made of the people's resisting Saul when he purposed to slay Jonathan (1 Sam. 14); or of the fact that David would have resisted Saul at Keilah if he could have counted on citizen support (1 Sam. 23); or of David's offering his services to the Philistine enemy; or of the fact that, once David had a base of citizen support in Hebron after Saul's death, "there was long war between the house of Saul and the house of David" (2 Sam. 3:1), with David eventually supplanting Saul's heir. Those episodes, in-convenient for Tudor propaganda, are silently avoided. (pp. 32-4)

Even murmuring against a prince is declared to be displeasing to God. The punishment of those who murmured against Moses, says the homilist, is an example to stay us from "speaking once an evil word against our Prince," even secretly. And see how God punished rebels such as Absalom and Sheba. Here the homilist is apparently presupposing that Elizabeth is a sec-ond Moses or a second David, although he offers no evidence to support this premise other than his reference to Elizabeth as "our gracious sovereign." The supporters of the Northern re-bellion of 1569 he characterizes as "most rash and hairebrained men, the greatest unthrifts, that have most lewdly wasted their owne goods and lands." What they falsely call reformation, he declares, is only a defacing or deformation; and though they parade banners painted with ''God speed the plough,'' or flags picturing the five wounds of Christ, they neither plough nor suffer others to do so, and they little know what the Cross of Christ means, which ought to be in the heart and not on flags. But in saying this, is not the homilist begging the whole question of whether Elizabeth's own government has at heart the Cross of Christ, and whether it itself has not wasted church goods and lands? (pp. 34-5)

The philosophical crunch in any doctrine of unconditional nonresistance comes at the point when its theorist must face the question of what a citizen's duty is in the case of an evil king. The homilist answers this question simplisticly. A rebel, he says (Part I), is worse than the worst prince, and rebellion is worse than the worst government of the worst prince. Then, shifting his ground cagily, he contends that rebellion is ''an unfit and unwholesome medicine to reform any small lackes in a prince,'' for if all subjects who mislike their prince should rebel, no realm would ever be without rebellion. But what if a prince be evil indeed, and evidently so to all men's eyes? To this question the homilist answers by placing the whole matter beyond human judgment. God forbid, he says, that subjects should judge which prince is wise and godly and his government good, and which prince is otherwise; that would be ''as though the foot must judge of the head: an enterprise very heinous.'' (pp. 35-6)

The homilist argues simply that people must be content with whatever kind of king God chooses to give them. Since kings are called gods in Psalm 82:6, they rule or should rule like God their king. But here a curious distinction between resembling God's mercy and resembling his justice is propounded. The nearer an earthly prince comes to following heavenly example, says the homilist, the greater ''blessing of God's mercy'' he is to the people; but, on the other hand, the further he swerves from heavenly example, the greater ''plague of God's wrath'' he is, as a just punishment on the people's sins. Might we infer, then, that Pharaoh's plaguing of the Israelites was a just punishment for sins of theirs? That is a case the homilist does not raise. He merely generalizes that the most subjects can do is to amend their own lives by obeying the king's rule and praying for him. When St. Paul exhorted Christians to pray for kings, says the homilist, he was including kings such as Caligula, Claudius, and Nero, cruel tyrants; and what he meant was that we are bound to obey even a heathen tyrant if God gives us such a one because of our wickedness. Note how this logic seems to imply that the early Christians deserved to have Nero as a ruler. One infers that the political status quo is ordained to be what it is, whatever it is.

We have noted how the focus of the entire homily is on the duty of Englishmen to their ruler, with virtually nothing said of his duty to them. The relationship envisaged is solely hierarchical, the king being pictured as one of the gods of Psalm 82, while the people are pictured simply as subjects. This interpretation does not accord well with the traditional medieval view, as incorporated for instance in English rites of coronation. Those rites, whether in the fourteenth century or the sixteenth, had three well marked divisions: 1) the ''recognition'' of the king, a mode of election by the people; 2) the oath taken by the king to rule in accordance with law and justice by maintaining customary rights and liberties; and 3) the benediction super-added to the covenant so made between king and people, the benediction's holy oil being regarded as a sacramental, a means by which grace might be obtained.

Traditional coronation implied a king's duty to public covenant, and his acceptance of dependence on divine grace, matters which the homily bypasses.

Now Shakespeare's Richard, as we have noted, interprets his office as that of ''deputy elected by the Lord.'' In the opening scene he emphasizes his ''sacred blood,'' his ''upright soul'' and his impartiality. But we soon sense, from the way in which Richard treats Mowbray and Bolingbroke, that his claim to impartiality is masking a self-protective motive. The two dukes are asking that the truth of Bolingbroke's charge be settled by trial by combat, a long-established medieval custom for seeking Heaven's judgment. Richard seeks to prevent this, because the charge that Mowbray plotted the Duke of Gloucester's death is one that indirectly glances at Richard. To keep hidden this delicate matter (in which the orderer of the murder was really Richard, as we later learn) Richard describes the quarrel as one of choler merely, and prescribes ''forget and forgive'' [I. i. 156]. But when the accused Mowbray throws himself at the King's feet to protest that he cannot sacrifice his honor, Richard consents to let justice have its opportunity at Coventry—though he says also, ominously, ''We were not born to sue but to command'' [I. i. 196].

At Coventry itself, two scenes later, he halts the contest, and in the name of ''our Council'' pronounces banishment—on Bolingbroke for ten years and on Mowbray for life. His explanation is that he cannot allow ''civil wounds'' which ''we think'' are motivated by ''rival-hating envy'' [I. iii. 124, 128-29, 131]. But note that Richard is here using his authority to override appeal to Divine judgment, thus himself causing, as Shakespeare lets Mowbray's son say in *2 Henry IV* [IV. i. 123-27], all England's subsequent woes. And note also the inequality of the sentences handed down. It suggests a bargain worked out in the ''Council'' meeting, which Shakespeare refrains from dramatizing in order to prompt our guessing at the backstage intrigue which underlies the elegant surface-show of kingly authority. Perhaps Bolingbroke's father, a member of the Council, would give his consent only on condition of terms which implied his son's lesser fault; and perhaps Richard consented to scuttle the loyal Mowbray, not only to let the public infer great guilt in Mowbray (and hence innocence in Richard), but also to ensure that Mowbray would never return to England to reveal what he knew of the Gloucester murder. Shakespeare has indicated adroitly the double-talk of outward uprightness and inner shadiness that characterizes Richard's ceremonious kingship, and his Council's dealings also.

In Act II we see a second instance of irresponsibility on Richard's part. When the dying John of Gaunt laments malpractices by Richard, the King retaliates by confiscating the dead man's estates. When York protests this violation of feudal custom, Richard replies merely, ''Think what you will, we seize unto our hands . . . his lands'' [II. i. 209-10]. Then he appoints York himself to govern during Richard's absence in Ireland, and York accepts the assignment, although in a self-divided mood that makes him ineffective as a protector of Richard's interests. York soon buckles before a Bolingbroke who breaks banishment and returns to England to demand his family inheritance.

Richard on returning to meet this situation salutes the ''dear earth'' [III. ii. 6] of England, terming it a child wounded by rebels. But he shows no concern for the welfare of Englishmen. His sole concern is to be an ''eye of Heaven,'' rising like the sun from the East, to light up the fact of Bolingbroke's treason and make him ''tremble for his sin'' [III. ii. 37, 53]. God has angels to fight for Richard, he says, and Heaven will guard the right. But when he hears that his Welsh supporters have dispersed, he turns pale; and on hearing that Bushy and Green are gone, he accuses them of being Judases. His attitude now becomes one of fatalistic submission:

> Revolt our subjects? That we cannot mend.
> They break their faith to God as well as us.
> Cry woe, destruction, ruin and decay.
>
> [III. ii. 100-02]

All he has learned from this crisis is the mortality of monarchizing. He must now be "woe's slave" [III. ii. 210], he reasons, since he cannot be a king when subjected to a need of friends. He regards himself not as one who has betrayed his obligation to England, but rather as a Phaeton who has failed to manage "unruly jades" [III. iii. 179] and therefore must debasingly yield to them. (pp. 36-8)

Resigning the crown in Act IV, Richard likens himself to Christ betrayed by Judases:

> Did they not sometime cry "All hail!" to me?
> So Judas did to Christ. But He in twelve
> Found truth in all but one, I in twelve thousand, none.
>
> [IV. i. 169-71]

He will give up his "glories" and his "state," he says, but his deposers must answer for their sin, a "blot damned in the book of Heaven" [IV. i. 236]. He will choose non-resistance because "we must do what force will have us do" [III. iii. 207], and because kingship has proved to be a brittle glory, in which a usurper such as Bolingbroke can outface him. He calls for a mirror to look at his own face, Narcissus-like, that he may study what must now be shattered. The only sin he finds in himself is in his giving his soul's consent to "undeck the pompous body of a king," thus being "traitor with the rest" in making "glory base and sovereignty a slave" [IV. i. 250, 248, 251].

Meanwhile, he refuses to read the list of accusations drawn up against him. And it never occurs to him to propose redresses of injustice, by which he might continue as ruler. He prefers to focus attention instead on his own willing-yet-unwilling resigning of all "pomp and majesty" [IV. i. 211]—as if he equated kingship not with its function but with its symbols of privilege. "Now mark how I will undo myself," he says:

> With mine own tears I wash away my balm,
> With mine own hands I give away my crown,
> With mine own tongue deny my sacred state,
> With mine own breath release all duty's rites.
>
> [IV. i. 203, 207-10]

We notice here that he regards even the sacramental balm and the "rites" which marked his installation in office as somehow properties belonging to him, natural possessions supernaturally guaranteed, but which worldlings are now sacrilegiously asking him to give up. His implication is that he must consent to dispossess himself because a martyr must yield to the powers that be, must make himself a "nothing" when betrayed by an evil world. As if to demonstrate his Christ-like piety, he adds:

> God pardon all oaths that are broke to me!
> God keep all vows unbroke that swear to thee!
>
> [IV. i. 214-15]

But notice that those whom he here prays God to pardon are the very ones he upbraids, twenty-two lines later, as "damned" for breaking their oath to him. Such piety is hopelessly con-

tradictory. Richard's non-resistance to the "sour cross" [IV. i. 241] to which he says Pilates are delivering him is certainly understood by Shakespeare as a histrionic pseudo-piety. (pp. 38-9)

In [the Pomfret] prison scene, however, we see [Richard] wrestling with what he calls "thoughts of things divine . . . intermixed with scruples" which "set the word itself against the word" [V. v. 12-14]. What he cannot reconcile are two scriptural texts:

> "Come, little ones," and then again,
> "It is as hard to come as for a camel
> To thread the postern of a small needle's eye."
>
> [V. v. 15-17]

He finds himself divided between, on the one hand, ambitiously desiring to "tear a passage through the flinty ribs / Of this hard world" [V. v. 20-1], and on the other hand, seeking contentment by a stoic resignation to misfortune. It should be evident to readers of this scene that he understands neither one of the biblical texts he has cited. Finally, when armed men enter his prison he beats them to the draw by suspecting their intent of murder and attacking them with an axe, killing two, before being himself struck down—whereupon he cries out:

> Mount, mount, my soul! Thy seat is up on high,
> Whilst my gross flesh sinks downward, here to die.
>
> [V. v. 111-12]

Here we can see the gnosticism of Richard's piety, his notion of heaven as a high station which rewards the soul which has extricated itself from the body, in effect through denying charity and mounting above what the Bible means by flesh, namely, man's native humanity. This ending accords with the philosophy of kingship we have seen in Richard throughout the play, his idea that kings are not bound by ties to ordinary human beings and their needs.

Other outworkings of divine right theory, less extreme than Richard's but nevertheless tragic, can be seen in other characters of Shakespeare's drama. Suppose we trace, for instance, the role of the Bishop of Carlisle. He first appears as Richard's counsellor, in Act III, when Richard on returning from Ireland is lamenting the treachery of "foul rebellion's arms." Carlisle speaks up to advise against grief:

> Fear not, my lord. That Power that made you King
> Hath power to keep you King in spite of all.
> The means that Heaven yields must be embraced,
> And not neglected; else, if Heaven would
> And we will not, Heaven's offer we refuse,
> The proffered means of succor and redress.
>
> [III. ii. 26-32]

It is evident that the Bishop regards Richard's kingship as of Heaven's making. But it is less clear what "means" he thinks Heaven would have Richard embrace. He makes no mention of succor through Confession or Holy Communion, the means which a clergyman might himself offer. Having made his grand generalization, he is simply silent for the next 140 lines while Richard first rouses himself to boast of being "the eye of heaven" [III. ii. 37], then despairs on hearing his troops have fled, then curses his deserters as "vipers, damned beyond redemption" [III. ii. 129], then sits on the ground for further wailing. No attempt is made by the Bishop to correct these attitudes.

He speaks only after Richard's wail has wound down into the bitter comment:

> Throw away respect,
> Tradition, form, and ceremonious duty,
> For you have mistook me all this while.
> I live with bread like you, feel want,
> Taste grief, need friends. Subjected thus,
> How can you say I am a king?
>
> [III. ii. 172-77]

Since this question invites an answer, the Bishop offers one, but scarcely such as we might expect of a cleric and pastor. He says nothing about how Richard might acquire friends; nor does he explain, as he ought, that Richard's need for bread makes him only human, no detriment to kingship. Here is the Bishop's opportunity, one might think, to offer Richard an equivalent of heaven's bread, some charitable counsel on how Richard might seek a reconciliation with the English people by initiating moves for the redress of their grievances. Is not *that* the bread really needed? But instead the Bishop offers a comfort which, in effect, amounts to an unwitting throwing away of tradition and duty on *his* part. He counsels:

> My lord, wise men ne'er sit and wail their woes,
> But presently prevent the ways to wail.
> To fear the foe, since fear oppresseth strength,
> Gives in your weakness strength unto your foe,
> And so your follies fight against yourself.
> Fear, and be slain. No worse can come to fight
> And fight and die is death destroying death.
>
> [III. ii. 178-84]

What this means is: Use what troops you still have to sally forth to battle and go down fighting, thus proving you can overcome fear. It is a counsel as empty as the modern slogan, "There is nothing to fear but fear itself." One could say, ironically, that the Bishop's own folly here fights against himself, against at least what heaven ordained *him* to do—mediate a word of *life,* not death. And has such counsel *prevented* ways to wail? Richard's reaction, understandably, is to lapse into a deeper despair: "Let no man speak again," he says, "for counsel is but vain. . . . Discharge my followers" [III. ii. 213-14, 217].

Carlisle's third speech in the play is the well-known one preceding Richard's deposition. York has just entered to announce to the nobles Richard's agreement to make Bolingbroke his heir, and has added an appeal to Bolingbroke to "ascend the throne" [IV. i. 111]. Bolingbroke at once says he will do so "In God's name" [IV. i. 113]. The Bishop here breaks in with a thirty-five-line speech, beginning with "God forbid!" Richard, he reminds the assembly, is "the figure of God's majesty, His captain, steward, deputy elect" [IV. i. 125-26], anointed and crowned. Shakespeare is thus letting Carlisle voice the high theory of the Elizabethan homily. Its central contention is stated in the lines:

> What subject can give sentence on his king?
> And who sits here that is not Richard's subject?
>
> [IV. i. 121-22]

We should note that this question is being asked by a bishop, who ought to know, one might think, that there are at least some areas, notably those of faith and morals, in which he himself is by his own ordination subject to an authority other than Richard's. Carlisle's monolithic premise ignores traditional Christian theory regarding the relation of church and

state, theory as ancient as that of the fifth-century Gelasius. Did not Samuel, in the days of King Saul, judge and give sentence on the monarch?

Had not the Bishop been neglecting all along his own pastoral obligation to teach Christian morals, we might expect him now to use his breath to call attention to principles higher than merely political ones for proceeding in the present situation. Why not offer some alternative to the polarized stances of the two parties? Yes, the nobles are Richard's subjects, but are they not all also God's subjects? Are they not responsible to two overlapping but not identical authorities? And even in the political realm solely, are not ruler and subjects alike bound by the king's coronation oath to act justly and in accord with customary law? A churchman might raise, furthermore, a third question: whether the legal terms, ruler and subject, might not better be subordinated to a concept such as that of father and children. All these considerations, however, the Bishop ignores and thereby misses his opportunity to act as a mediator. By his partisan and merely negative stance, he does nothing to illuminate the issue, and thus nothing capable of preventing the outcome he deplores. He is reduced to a helpless pronouncing of dire predictions:

> And if you crown him, let me prophesy,
> The blood of English shall manure the ground
> And future ages groan for this foul act.
>
> [IV. i. 136-38]

Although this prediction was to prove true in England's subsequent history, can we not say that the "foul act" was reciprocally committed? Polarized forms of fault are interdependent in a decadent society or individual: to leave undone that which ought to be done interlocks with doing that which ought not to be done.

The irony of the situation is that the Bishop of Carlisle helps make his own doleful prophecy self-fulfilling. Not simply by his defective counseling, but afterwards by joining a conspiracy to unseat Bolingbroke by military means, he himself sets flowing the bloodshed which his speech has warned against. By Shakespeare's dramatic irony, the final lines of that speech could be turned against the speaker's own subsequent action:

> Oh, if you raise this house against this house,
> It will the woefulest division prove
> That ever fell upon this cursed earth.
> Prevent it, resist it, let it not be so,
> Lest child, child's children, cry *against you* "Woe"!
>
> [IV. i. 145-49]

At the very end of the play, when the conspiracy has been crushed by executions, we see Carlisle brought in as a captive and sentenced by Bolingbroke to the mild penalty of sequestration for the rest of his life. It suits the usurping king's public relations to display by this mildness his own generosity, especially to an incompetent cleric whom he need no longer fear. Thus the final irony is that a bishop who throughout the play has been of no help really to anybody is now assigned to "Choose out some secret place, some reverend room" [V. vi. 25], in which he may enjoy the peace of beholding the world go by oblivious of him, except perhaps to point him out as instance of the new king's magnanimity. To *that* he has made himself subject.

Carlisle's stance as we have traced it differs from King Richard's in not being passively non-resistant to usurpation. One reason for this we can detect in his referring to the king's office as that of God's "captain," which implies some militancy; whereas Richard omits this designation and emphasizes instead his transcendent role as "eye of heaven," which permits him to be (except at his death) non-resistant in outward behavior, sentimentalizing a Christ-role into that of grieving martyr bowing to Necessity. Both Richard and Carlisle, however, end up alienated from the world—one in an imaginary Heaven, the other in an empty "reverend room" on earth. Richard's stance is perhaps more consistent with the specific doctrine of the *Homilie Against Disobedience,* while Carlisle's is more like the actual practice of those who promulgated the *Homilie*—they *did* resist rebels, and had done so when countering the Northern lords in 1569. And it is likely, I think, that had those lords succeeded and gone on further to depose Elizabeth, the proponents of the *Homilie* might conceivably have acted as Carlisle did in joining a conspiracy against the new government. Richard's tack and Carlisle's are scarcely more than two variant possibilities within Tudor theory. In fact, explicit sanction for armed resistance against a usurper is given in the typically Elizabethan *Mirror for Magistrates,* which presents the Establishment view in saying that the Earl of Salisbury was right in joining the plot to restore Richard II after Bolingbroke's usurpation.

But if Carlisle represents the option of urging resistance against a usurper king, there is also an opposite variant shown us by Shakespeare in his portrait of the Duke of York, Richard's uncle. Richard's own emphasis on *not* resisting "Necessity" is exemplified pragmatically by the "Lord Governor" who accepts the usurper on grounds of political expediency. Some readers of the play have inclined to regard York as a spokesman for Shakespeare's own judgment, but I would agree with Sen Gupta's comment [in his *Shakespeare's Historical Plays*]: "Since Shakespeare makes such a spineless, vacillating old man an exponent of the philosophy of order, his own attitude to that philosophy can not be without an element of irony."

It is no doubt symbolic that in the play York refers to his *palsied* arm. His acts have a haphazard quality. One moment we find him protesting Richard's seizure of Gaunt's estates, both verbally by pointing out that this violation of customary rights undermines the "fair sequence" on which Richard's own kingship is based, and then by walking out of Richard's presence. But the next moment we learn that York has accepted the honor of being appointed Governor, and without instituting any reforms. . . . York is a divided man paralyzed by, on the one hand, his sense of duty to defend Richard's sovereignty, and on the other hand, a conscience that he says bids him right wrongs. The first of these, in the form of code duty, predominates when he denounces Bolingbroke's armed return to England as "gross rebellion and detested treason" [II. iii. 109] and boasts:

> Comest thou because the anointed king is hence?
> Why, foolish boy, the king is left behind,
> And in my loyal bosom lies his power.
>
> [II. iii. 96-8]

Yet this loyalty has more rhetoric than substance. To Bolingbroke's plea of grievance York is sympathetic, and in self-defense he says to Bolingbroke's followers: "I labored all I could to do him right" [II. iii. 142]. Those labors, as we have seen, were as weak as his resistance now is. York's chief concern, we can infer, is the safety of his own estates and of his public reputation. . . . [A] claim of neutrality masks (as comparably in Richard's case) a slide into capitulation—and then cooperation with what has been denounced. When Bol-

ingbroke, a moment later, requests York's company for a march against Richard's accomplices, York replies: "It may be I will go with you. . . . Things past redress are now with me past care" [II. iii. 168, 171].

Two scenes later the cooperation becomes commitment. York watches without protest while Bolingbroke orders to execution two of Richard's officers, without trial and simply on the basis of Bolingbroke's denunciation of them. Here York is allowing Bolingbroke to assume kingly prerogatives as arbitrary as those of Richard. And a moment later, when Bolingbroke asks York's help in entreating Richard's Queen, York says he has already dispatched a messenger on that errand. Yet he seems to wish to avoid letting himself realize that Bolingbroke's secret aim is not simply "law" but Richard's deposition. When Northumberland reports, a scene later, that "Richard not far from hence hath hid his head" [III. iii. 6] at Flint Castle, York rebukes such language:

> It would beseem the Lord Northumberland
> To say "King Richard." Alack the heavy day
> When such a sacred king should hide his head!
>
> [III. iii. 7-9]

But those words are York's last in lip-service to Richard's sacred kingship. He stands silent during the long confrontation at Flint Castle, during which Bolingbroke approaches Richard with a ceremonious humility gloving a hard fist of threats, and Richard responds with cynical denunciation while at the same time dramatizing his own readiness to give up all. When next we see York, he is Richard's emissary to the lords at Westminster, announcing to them Richard's agreement to yield the scepter, and adding his own cry to Bolingbroke, "Ascend the throne" [IV. i. 111]. York has now become the advocate of an act that contravenes customary right, the principle he had espoused in Act II.

Such a turnabout is to us both pitiful and comic in its evident opportunism. But York (by Shakespeare's irony) manages to look back on the whole business as the work of God. In Act V he reports to his Duchess on the London crowd's treatment of Richard: they threw dust on his "sacred head," he recounts, which Richard bore with such grief and patience,

> That had not God, for some strong purpose, steeled
> The hearts of men, they must perforce have melted,
> And barbarism itself have pitied him.
> But Heaven hath a hand in these events,
> To whose high will we bound our calm contents.
> To Bolingbroke are we sworn subjects now,
> Whose state and honor I for aye allow.
>
> [V. ii. 30, 34-40]

What York has allowed, though he does not know it, is a steeling of his own heart, and a fatalism which excuses all. (pp. 40-5)

In John of Gaunt, Duke of Lancaster, we have another of Richard's uncles who is committed to a doctrine of non-resistance. Early in the play, when the widow of the Duke of Gloucester begs him to avenge her husband's death, he replies:

> God's is the quarrel; for God's substitute,
> His deputy anointed in His sight,
> Hath caused his death: the which if wrongfully
> Let heaven revenge; for I may never lift
> An angry arm against His minister.
>
> [I. ii. 37-41]

And this view, precisely that of the Tudor *Homilie,* is elaborated by his saying that since "we cannot correct" the fault,

> Put we our quarrel to the will of heaven;
> Who, when they see the hours ripe on earth,
> Will rain hot vengeance on offenders' heads.
>
> [I. ii. 6-8]

The Duchess regards such a stance as not patience but despair. "Where then, alas," she asks, "may I complain myself?" To which he replies: "To God, the widow's champion and defense" [I. ii. 42-3].

We may observe here that God's championing is being thought of solely in terms of punishing wrongdoers, rather than as rescuing or reestablishing family and community welfare. Rather than considering the injustice a problem, it is a "quarrel," which God will settle by raining vengeance. Meanwhile, man must avoid raising an arm against the king. The whole outlook differs from, say, that of the Old Testament book of Judges; and it implies a concept of kingship which itself lacks a promise of deliverance such as characterized David's kingship. Moreover, both Gaunt and the Duchess are failing to consider the kind of positive alternative to anger which David found possible when he was not a king but simply a citizen. Is man's only option either rebellion or passivity? That outlook seems all too characteristic of this society as a whole. (pp. 46-7)

Shakespeare has set Gaunt's theorizing within a paradoxical background. At this very moment Gaunt is on his way to Coventry, where his son Henry is to engage Mowbray in a trial by combat. The drama's first scene has shown us the son's raising of a murder charge against Mowbray, and also Richard's suspicion of this move as masking malice and treachery. Gaunt has replied that "As near as I could sift him" [I. i. 12] no malice is involved, but a concern to protect the King from a danger. On the face of the matter this may be so; but are not hidden motives involved? A charge against Mowbray, the King's closest servant, is indirectly an attack on the King's integrity, and if Gaunt is unaware of this, we can only infer that he is suppressing awareness under a narrowly legal view of the matter. In any case by condoning his son's action, Gaunt is allowing an angry arm to be raised, although within the formal bounds of convention, that could imperil Richard's position. Gaunt's neutrality is not quite what it seems—any more than is the stance of "impartiality" which Richard advertises in his dealing with the threat. As in York's neutrality of Act II, unacknowledged motives are guiding choices. The maintaining of outward propriety is a surface loyalty. But we may note that what Gaunt prays for at Coventry is neither Richard's welfare nor God's judgment, but rather that God may prosper the "good cause" Henry has purposed, namely, to "furbish new the name of John of Gaunt" [I. iii. 78, 76].

A trial by combat implies a genuine concern for justice. But when Gaunt connives with Richard to abort this ancient rite, we can only infer that Gaunt is at heart an opportunist and in tactics no less a vacillator than Richard or (later) York. By agreeing to the banishments worked out in secret council to substitute for the combat, Gaunt implicates himself in compromise and unjust dealing. He has made himself party, in fact, to the punishment of his own son, and to the greater punishment of Mowbray, for no evident crime. Then when Richard, to appear magnanimous in public, announces a shortening of the son's banishment from ten years to six, Gaunt, in order to cover over what the public might think of him for betraying a son, stresses the grief the sentence imposes on his own old age

(termed, by Shakespeare's dramatic irony, "My oil-dried lamp" [I. iii. 221]). No heavenly oil in this lamp, we may say—though there is, paradoxically, much oily rhetoric. Richard to prevent being downstaged interposes:

> Thy son is banished upon good advice.
> Whereto thy tongue a party verdict gave.
>
> [I. iii. 233-34]

And Gaunt to parry this replies:

> You urged me as a judge, but I had rather
> You would have bid me argue like a father.
>
> [I. iii. 237-38]

But if we are alert we can see in this disjoining of the duties of judge and father a symptom of England's times and ethos—perhaps, indeed, the central defect which is making tragedy not merely of kingship but of the office of lesser magistrates. Gaunt's rhymed couplets of serpentine logic as he dwells on the tug within himself between the judge and the father are evidence of a duplicity masking guilt.

Is not the speech also masking something else—a dim awareness that the pose of martyr on his part can aid his son's future ambitions? In a later conversation with his son before Henry's departure from England, Gaunt speaks adages which have a cryptic quality:

> Think not the king did banish thee,
> But thou the king. . . .
> Go, say I sent thee forth to purchase honor
> And not the king exiled thee. . . .
> Look, *what thy soul holds dear, imagine it
> To lie that way thou go'st.* . . .
>
> [I. iii. 279-80, 282-83, 286-87]

Such language has a double-sidedness. On the one hand, it is a formal stoicism, advocating that miseries can be conquered by a contentment which the wise man achieves through taking refuge in an inviolate kingdom of the mind, constructed by his own imagination. But on the underside the words suggest also that banishment can be used as a means for forwarding ulterior aims, and even that it may "purchase honor" for Henry in the public eye. And all this is being said in elaboration of the adage:

> Teach thy necessity to reason thus—
> There is no virtue like necessity.
>
> [I. iii. 277-78]

This is a doctrine, as I have earlier noted, to which other characters in the play (notably Richard and York) likewise turn. Here I sense in it the overtones of a Stoic-Machiavellian version of salvation. It states perhaps the subsurface reality of Tudor political attitudes. For if we recall the ups and downs of ecclesiastical-political fortunes in the sixteenth century, during the course of which many Englishmen bowed to one "settlement" while plotting another, the adage comes near to being the "virtue" of that century. (pp. 47-9)

[Gaunt] in Holinshed's account is characterized, although only glancingly, as a turbulent and self-seeking noble—this by way of Holinshed's mitigating Richard's "hard dealing" with Gaunt's property. On the other hand, Shakespeare could have read in the chronicler Froissart that Gaunt did not attempt to avenge the murder of Gloucester but "wisely and amiably he appeased all these matters." In Shakespeare's dramatization we see an overtly non-revenging Gaunt who at the same time is covertly self-seeking. His amiability is suspect. When his jeremiad ends with the thrust,

> Live in thy shame, but die not shame with thee!
> These words hereafter thy tormenters be!
>
> [II. i. 135-36]

Richard characterizes Gaunt as sullen or sulking, and York has to step in to beg Richard to "impute his words / To wayward sickliness and age in him" [II. i. 141-42]. Sickliness indeed! When, as further soothing, York adds:

> He loves you, on my life, and holds you dear
> As Harry Duke of Hereford, were he here
>
> [II. i. 143-44]

Richard shrewdly but sardonically replies:

> Right, you say true. As Hereford's love, so his.
> As theirs, so mine, and all be as it is.
>
> [II. i. 145-46]

This is: each would love to see the other dispossessed or deposed. The critic John Palmer has commented that Richard's response is not altogether unjustified: "Richard saw in this Galahad of the sceptred isle a political enemy masquerading as a patriot, a cantankerous nobleman whose son had already made mischief in the land and was to make more" [see Additional Bibliography]. Suspicious earlier of Bolingbroke's "craft of smiles" [I. iv. 27], Richard is here suspicious of Gaunt's craft of woeful lament, and with considerable justification, I would say.

For we can scarcely avoid noting that Gaunt's prophesying is all doleful, nothing hopeful, and all critical of Richard, while advertising Gaunt's own pious nobility. It is difficult for me to imagine how the realm of England could have come to the sorry pass Gaunt protests, without his own consent to various of Richard's unwise policies, or without a silent allowing of them by other nobles who lacked a genuinely patriotic statesmanship of their own. Gaunt's complaint exaggerates Richard's deficiencies, and it certainly proposes no program for the future. Its effect, and perhaps its hidden motive, is to undermine Richard through harassment, thus setting the stage for Henry's return as a reformer. A great many of Gaunt's pronouncements could be turned against himself (by a dramatic irony of which I believe Shakespeare was conscious when he carefully phrased them)—for instance:

> Thy deathbed is no lesser than thy land,
> In which thou liest in reputation sick.
> And then, too careless patient as thou art,
> Commit'st thy anointed body to the cure
> Of those physicians that first wounded thee.
>
> [II. i. 95-9]

Gaunt's vision is myopically an adversary one, unconcerned to examine his own shortcomings. And all this comes from a man whose code has been not to raise an angry arm against the king, God's minister. The latent contradictions stick out.

Many literary critics have supposed that Gaunt is Shakespeare's spokesman in the play. But a consideration of Gaunt's entire career in the play, and in particular of his wordplay on his own name in the deathbed scene, convinces me otherwise. His apology that "I watched, / Watching breeds leanness, leanness is all gaunt" [II. i. 77-8] strikes me as a pitiful confession of the quality of his watching. Has it been that of a shepherd? England is indeed declining into disorder; but in part because he himself has done nothing to initiate remedy.

The play as a whole seems to me a remarkable exposé of the tragedy to which various deficient reasonings can lead. The exposure, however, is through ironies which undercut the didacticisms voiced by speakers in the story—and in this respect is not at all like the method of *The Mirror for Magistrates*. The characters' root-defects are left by Shakespeare implicit rather than explicitly labeled, and thus the dramatization arouses our pity and fear over blindnesses of understanding that might be our own in similar circumstances. Yet the result of our seeing the plights of contradiction and disaster which stem from shallow codes is an insight on our part regarding the need to rethink questions of political duty. Tudor theory's outcome in variant forms of fatalism can prompt in us a concern to reinvigorate more traditional concepts. For in retrospect, for instance, Gaunt's "other Eden" [II. i. 42] can be recognized as a realm concerned for "reputation," rather than for the blessedness of the Bible's Eden. And through our perceiving how piety can be counterfeited, by Gaunt and others, the nature of authentic duty becomes reunderstood. The tragedy, through its dramatization of duties distorted and hence self-defeating, invites us to reconceive and return to a wholesome reality which these distortions have forfeited. (pp. 49-51)

Roy Battenhouse, "Tudor Doctrine and the Tragedy of 'Richard II'," in Rice University Studies, *Vol. 60, No. 2, Spring, 1974, pp. 31-53.*

THOMAS F. VAN LAAN   (essay date 1978)

[*Many critics have noted that the atmosphere of* Richard II *is theatrical and "show-like"—not only because of its emphasis on spectacle and pageantry, but also because of the king's disastrous tendency to evade reality through rhetorical flights of fancy and self-dramatization. In the following excerpt, however, Van Laan maintains that Shakespeare is also concerned with the public "part" that any monarch and successful politician must learn—much as a* commedia del arte *actor acquires skills of diction and movement for the stage—and he suggests that Richard II fails to some degree because he has only mastered the "external histrionic characteristics" of the role of king, without realizing "the accumulated repertory of moves proper to kingship and obligatory for every occupant of the office." Van Laan contends that after the abdication Richard attempts to select a new "role" for himself: his self-dramatization represents a groping for self-discovery, for the loss of his kingly role is tantamount to personal annihilation; indeed, the critic asserts, one of the facts Richard confronts in his Pomfret Castle soliloquy is that without a role to give him identity, man is nothing. Importantly, Van Laan notes that Bolingbroke, once he ascends the throne, repeats the same "discrepant role-playing" that marred Richard's reign.*]

The opening scene of *Richard II* quickly establishes a highly distinctive language. One senses it from the very first words, and within a few lines its ring has become unmistakable. Here, for example, is Richard's third speech:

> Then call them to our presence: face to face
> And frowning brow to brow, ourselves will hear
> The accuser and the accused freely speak.
> High-stomach'd are they both and full of ire,
> In rage, deaf as the sea, hasty as fire.
>
> [I. i. 15-19]

The royal plural does not ordinarily call attention to itself, but it does here—partly because of the rare 'ourselves,' more so because it is accompanied by such clearly rhetorical devices as the balanced phrasing and the rhyme. The comparisons, abrupt and conventional, have come not from the heart but from a handbook, and there can be no doubt that it is Richard rather than Shakespeare who has looked them up. The speech as a whole has a decidedly studied effect. Bolingbroke and Mowbray easily sustain this effect, because, contrary to Richard's claim, they do not 'freely speak.' They may very well get said what they wish to say, or at least what can safely be said under the circumstances, but the words they use nearly all form themselves into obvious formulas as they pronounce the required speeches of royal flattery and cast their accusations and counter-accusations in quasi-legal terminology. Soon, as they throw down their gages, ritualistic speech finds a counterpart in ritualistic action. No one in the scene can unequivocally be convicted of play-acting—even though Mowbray and Bolingbroke charge each other with lying—but the established milieu is undeniably histrionic and theatrical.

The next scene reveals that Richard is primarily guilty of the major crime with which Bolingbroke has charged Mowbray, and this reinforces the effect of the opening scene by implying that Richard, at least, *was* play-acting. Scene iii increases the theatrical aura of Richard's milieu by more direct means, by multiplying the effects that suggest the theatre. The trial-by-combat in the lists at Coventry occasions an abundance of spectacle and pageantry. Trumpets sound frequently. A large number of splendidly costumed figures fill the stage. Patterned, ritual-like movements and the careful assumption of precise stations—visually attesting to the long tradition behind the trial—provide a recognizable choreography. Whole speeches echo each other nearly verbatim, as not just the Marshal and the Heralds but all the characters involved employ a purely formulaic language. It is all a grand show, and it is suddenly made to seem even more show-like when Richard cuts it short just as the main event is about to begin, the event that would make the ritual newly meaningful by suffusing it with fresh action. Richard himself becomes the centre of attraction as he substitutes for this event his pronouncing of the sentences on Bolingbroke and Mowbray which, it soon becomes clear, he and his council have decided on *ahead of time*. This renders the preceding ritual entirely purposeless; it has been nothing but empty show, and one can explain its existence only by surmising that Richard has let things go thus far for the sake of the show itself. Evidently he enjoys a good show—especially one in which he can take a leading and impressive part.

Richard II stands at the midpoint, numerically as well as chronologically, of the sequence of nine history plays that Shakespeare devoted so much effort to during the 1590s. The central focus of these histories is a specific role, the social office of king, and these details from the first three scenes of *Richard II* constitute Shakespeare's first concerted attempt to bring out the role-like qualities of the kingly office by emphasizing its ritualistic, spectacular, and showy attributes, and by trying to associate with it a distinctive language (with its own vocabulary, rhetorical characteristics, and store of ready-made sentences and phrases), which can sound to some extent like a permanent attribute of the office, something that every occupant of the office must learn as the commedia dell'arte actor learns the language belonging to his role. Occasional moments in the *Henry VI* plays and *Richard III* anticipate in a minor way this direct dramatization of the gestures—the external histrionic attributes—of the kingly office, but by and large in the earlier plays Shakespeare works more by implication to define kingship as a role. He stresses the current king's inadequacy, his failure to be a *good* king, and this necessarily indicates that the office which he holds and which so many others aspire to consists of more than just a title, a crown, and an undefined amount of power.

Richard II also carries over this technique. Scene iv gives the spectators their first glimpse of Richard out of the public eye, in company with only those he trusts, and it becomes apparent at once that Richard is no more 'aptly fitted' for the kingship than the kings Shakespeare has previously created. . . . He has squandered the wealth of his country and now intends to lease it out for profiteers to exploit. He prays for the immediate death of John of Gaunt, his wise, loyal councillor and his uncle, so that he can plunder the wealth that by law and custom should pass on to Bolingbroke. Richard's misbehaviour as king is also the principal theme of the scene that follows (II. i.), in which it is developed through the accusations that his uncles, Gaunt and York, direct at him. Richard may look like a king—he does, as York points out, physically resemble his father, the Black Prince, who would have made a perfect king [II. i. 176-83]—but in no other respect can he be said to qualify for the office he holds, which, according to Gaunt, he has so abused that he has transformed it into a base parody of itself: 'Landlord of England art thou now, not King' [II. i. 113]. The insistent implication of these two scenes is that Richard's behaviour is wrong not only because it is evil but also because it violates his office. The stress on his misbehaviour thus keeps in focus a role-like quality of this office that is far more important, though less conspicuous, than its gestures. This quality is the accumulated repertory of moves proper to kingship and obligatory for every occupant of the office. The string of crimes and other failings accruing to Richard helps provide through contrast some sense of what this repertory consists of.

In using Richard's bad performance to define kingship as a role, these scenes also, of course, simultaneously establish a far more significant dramatic fact: Richard's own situation. The relation between Richard and the role his birth has assigned him, which perfectly exemplifies the theme of the discrepancy between the actor and his part, has more than one dimension. Richard's actions violate his role by conflicting with, and often inverting, the moves proper to it, but at the same time Richard publicly pretends to play what James I called 'the wise King's part.' Scene iv also establishes this dimension of Richard's discrepant role-playing, because the wrongs this scene attributes to him not only brand him as unkingly, they also expose the falsity of specific public representations of himself he has projected in preceding scenes. (pp. 117-19)

These two dimensions of Richard's tenure as player-king liken him to the immediately preceding king from Shakespeare's histories, Richard III. But in the case of Richard II, 'player-king' has also a third dimension, which makes Richard II unique among Shakespeare's kings and gives him much of his dramatic interest. He cannot play his role by fulfilling its proper moves, but he can play to perfection its external histrionic characteristics. He not only, as York observes, looks the way a king should look, but he can stand, move, wear his costume, and speak in the best kingly manner. He loves the showy attributes of his role, as his handling of the trial-by-combat demonstrates, and he has completely mastered them—too well, perhaps, for this mastery also contributes to the impression of discrepancy. It does so partly because it emphasizes Richard's simultaneous failure to master the proper moves of his role, but mostly it is a matter of the same kind of overacting to which Claudio in *Much Ado About Nothing* and the King and his Lords in *Love's Labour's Lost* subject the role of lover. Like them, Richard theatricalizes his role, turns it into nothing but a part.

In III. ii, the scene of the return from Ireland, the tendency to theatricalize has become the dominant element in Shakespeare's presentation of Richard. It manifests itself in the ex-aggeration and excessive self-dramatization of individual moments, such as Richard's regreeting of his kingdom's earth. And it manifests itself in the ease and rapidity with which he shifts from one mood to another on cue, as if he were proving his ability to represent in proper rhetorical style each of the various passions. There is almost an impression of fakery in Richard's performance during this scene, but of course he is not faking. It is simply that his world is so completely a stage that only outward show truly exists for him. His feelings are genuine, but if he is to experience them fully, they must find expression in appropriate speech and mime. Richard, this scene implies, fails to be a good king because . . . he devotes all his energies to a fictitious role of his own devising. It may be that he cannot properly fulfil the kingly office because he is already entirely taken up with the role of King Richard.

The performance of III. ii should in no way surprise a spectator who has seen the show at Coventry in I. iii, but Richard has never before seemed quite this histrionic, nor has his prior role-playing involved displays so likely to detract from the image of a strong and self-sufficient king. Performances like the one at Coventry may lead to suspicion or doubt, but it is clear that Richard intends them as a means of enhancing himself in the eyes of his audience: he has always before sought admiration or awe rather than, as now, pity. The performance of III. ii is noticeably different, then, and one is tempted to ask why this should be the case. The answer lies, I believe, in a further effect recorded by the scene, Richard's discovery that he can no longer feel secure about the role he has been playing so flamboyantly. (pp. 119-20)

Richard has been deeply affected by news of Bolingbroke's successes, and he continues to be shocked by further reports—almost as much so as his extreme reactions indicate. He tries to mislead himself as well as others, but he can evidently see with perfect clarity that he stands in jeopardy of having his power and position violently wrenched from him. At least he has unquestionably come to a related realization, one that he expresses in the central speech of the scene [III. ii. 144-77]. His self-dramatization of every mood and every reaction has led him from an exclusive awareness of himself as *the* king to a consideration of 'the death of *kings*' [III. ii. 156]. He has discovered that it is Death who actually 'Keeps . . . his court . . . within the hollow crown / That rounds the mortal temples of a king' [III. ii. 162, 160-61]. It is Death that does the ruling, mockingly allowing the king 'a little scene, / To monarchize' [III. ii. 164-65].

The theatrical image epitomizes Richard's new perception of himself. He can die and someone else can become king in his place, and since this is so, he cannot really regard himself as king. The kingship is not, as he seems to have assumed, a dimension of himself, but an external role that he as actor has been allowed to perform for a certain (short) length of time. And now, he suggests to his followers, the performance has come to an end:

> Cover your heads, and mock not flesh and blood
> With solemn reverence; throw away respect,
> Tradition, form, and ceremonious duty;
> For you have but mistook me all this while.
> I live with bread like you, feel want,
> Taste grief, need friends; subjected thus,
> How can you say to me I am a king?
>
> [III. ii. 171-77]

Richard here suggests that his followers should stop playing their subordinate roles because he, the leading actor, has already abandoned his part. His discovery that he, like all monarchs, is merely a player-king in one crucial respect is evidently *by itself* sufficient to bring about his deposition.

The following scene, at Flint Castle, where Richard has gone to 'pine away' [III. ii. 209], certainly bears out this implication. Bolingbroke, Northumberland, and York are surprised to learn that Flint Castle contains a king, but once they know it, they act accordingly. Bolingbroke's charge to Northumberland about what he shall say to Richard vigorously indicates that Bolingbroke will not yield one inch with regard to what he considers his just demands, but otherwise his speech thoroughly reflects a sense of Richard's royalty and of the proper ceremony due him as king. . . . Richard responds to the occasion with a splendid speech in which he expresses with unusual force a sense of both the reality and the invulnerability of his kingship [III. iii. 72-100]. It is, however, a farewell performance. He must accept Bolingbroke's demands, and, as he reveals to Aumerle, this necessity painfully convinces him that despite the single splendid speech he now sadly misperforms his role:

> We do debase ourselves, cousin, do we not,
> To look so poorly and to speak so fair?
> Shall we call back Northumberland, and send
> Defiance to the traitor, and so die?
>
> [III. iii. 127-30]

He can no longer play his role, and so he surrenders it. It is Richard that suggests deposition [III. iii. 143-46], and, after having come down from the castle walls to the 'base court' at Bolingbroke's request, it is Richard that makes Bolingbroke—'King Bolingbroke,' as Richard already calls him [III. iii. 173]—stop showing him the ceremony due a king. The deposition in London will merely embody formally an event that has already taken place.

Richard's abdication occasions several new moments of self-dramatization as Richard recites speeches far more studied than any he has yet pronounced. Two of these occur before he has left Flint Castle. 'What must the King do now?' he asks [III. iii. 143], like an actor seeking guidance for a role he does not know how to play, and then answers his own question by verbally divesting himself, one by one, of all the trappings accompanying his role, until all he has left for himself is 'A little little grave, an obscure grave' [III. iii. 154]. He sees his descent to the courtyard as a fall like that of 'glist'ring Phaethon' [III. iii. 178], and through repetition and other rhetorical devices tries to make his listeners also see it that way.

At London, Richard is the central figure in what the Abbott of Westminster will ultimately call 'a woeful pageant' [IV. i. 321]. . . . He repeats and improves upon one of his moments at Flint Castle, for this time in verbally divesting himself of his kingly attributes he actually removes and surrenders his crown and sceptre. And he provides a brilliant climax for the whole performance by calling for the looking-glass, which he then smashes. Bolingbroke may object when Richard defines the smashed mirror as his own face, which his sorrow has destroyed, but Richard could scarcely have selected a better symbol to summarize his experience. He has existed, as it were, only at some removes from himself. Richard has been, first of all, a series of gestures; either those belonging to his social office or, as now, those arising from his own dramatization of losing that office. And he has also been a series of responses by others, who—like mirrors—have let him see reflected by them the success of his performance.

More than once the self-dramatization of Richard's abdication scenes involves an attempt to select and play a new role as a replacement for the one that has been lost. Already in III. ii, even before he had fully articulated—and thus really experienced—his awareness of himself as player-king, Richard's misunderstanding about the fate of Bushy, Green, and the Earl of Wiltshire had prompted him to call them 'Three Judases, each one thrice worse than Judas!' [III. ii. 132], but it is not until the scene at London that he fully assumes the role of another Christ [IV. i. 169-71, 239-42]. Other roles with which he associates himself include the hermit, 'almsman,' or 'palmer' whose circumstances he will, he says, exchange his kingly trappings for [III. iii. 147-54], 'glist'ring Phaethon,' whose fall he imitates [III. iii. 178], both the priest who intones 'God save the King!' and the clerk required for the response of 'amen' [IV. i. 172-74], 'a mockery king of snow' [IV. i. 260], and a damned soul, crying out to Northumberland, 'Fiend, thou torments me ere I come to hell' [IV. i. 270].

All these roles, as well as the excessive overdramatizations, constitute attempts by Richard to lend substance to the nebulous condition he has entered into in losing his role as king and to provide gestures for what he perceives as a new role, the role he designates when he opposes to Bolingbroke's title of 'King Henry' his own new one of 'unking'd Richard' [IV. i. 220]. He describes some characteristics of his new role when he tells Bolingbroke, 'I hardly yet have learn'd / To insinuate, flatter, bow, and bend my knee. / Give sorrow leave awhile to tutor me / To this submission' [IV. i. 164-67]. But most of the gestures of this new role cannot be so easily acquired because they are far less clearly known. They must first be discovered, and Richard's self-dramatizations represent his attempt to make this discovery, to shape the experience of losing the kingship in such a way that it can seem to be, for himself and others, a role as traditional and familiar as the kingship itself.

Richard's efforts to shape a new role for himself have a desperate quality about them which suggests that they spring from profound need. There can, moreover, be no doubt about the source of this need. . . . When Bolingbroke asks him if he is contented to resign the crown, Richard seems to reply that he is not because if he does he then 'must nothing be' [IV. i. 201], but his words here are too cryptic to paraphrase with any certainty. There is, however, no doubt at all about his sense of what he has become once he finally does resign the crown:

> I have no name, no title—
> No, not that name was given me at the font—
> But 'tis usurp'd. Alack the heavy day,
> That I have worn so many winters out,
> And know not now what name to call myself!
> O that I were a mockery king of snow,
> Standing before the sun of Bolingbroke
> To melt myself away in water drops!
>
> [IV. i. 255-62]

The first half of this speech apparently derives from the attempts by contemporaries of the historical Richard to brand him a bastard, but the background has certainly not been dramatized. What the lines do dramatize is the agonized feeling of Shakespeare's character that he has indeed become nothing, that in losing his role of king he has wholly lost his identity. And thus, in the lines that follow, he expresses his desire for a new role to replace the old, in this case a role especially

suited to the actor who will play it. The speech explains and sums up a great deal. Richard's constant self-dramatizations and frequent attempts to cast himself in new roles have sprung from the awareness recorded here. His identity has consisted wholly of his role as king, and therefore losing the kingship also means losing everything. It leaves him without identity, without any bearings, without any structure by means of which he can relate himself to the rest of reality. He must find or create some kind of role to play, any kind at all, in order to stave off the alternative of sheer emptiness, and in keeping with the peculiar nature of Richard's histrionic sensibility, the new role, like the old, must incorporate a high degree of conspicuous theatricality.

Richard's prison soliloquy of V. v. re-enacts the experience he has gone through, while giving it further clarification. His effort to 'beget / A generation of still-breeding thoughts' with which to 'people this little world' of his prison [V. v. 7-9] involves him, as he realizes, in further role-playing, and because he realizes it, he is able to provide an explicit statement that pertains not only to the present moment but also, at least in its opening words and its basic drift, to his whole career:

> Thus play I in one person many people,
> And none contented. Sometimes am I king;
> Then treasons make me wish myself a beggar,
> And so I am. Then crushing penury
> Persuades me I was better when a king;
> Then am I king'd again; and by and by
> Think that I am unking'd by Bolingbroke,
> And straight am nothing.
>
> [V. v. 31-8]

He also realizes *why* his role-playing is and has been necessary to him:

> But whate'er I be,
> Nor I, nor any man that but man is,
> With nothing shall be pleas'd till he be eas'd
> With being nothing.
>
> [V. v. 38-41]

Without a role or roles to give him identity man is nothing; yet nothingness is a state that can be borne only by the dead. The man who lives must attain an identity of some kind, even if he has to 'hammer it out' [V. v. 5] from his own imagination. (pp. 121-25)

Richard's association of himself with 'any man that but man is' [V. v. 39] argues that in the need he has shown for some kind of role he is typical rather than unique, and the action of the play helps confirm this implication by centring in part on another career with important parallels to Richard's. This other career, of course, is that of Bolingbroke, whose role loss has two phases, the one occasioned by his exile, the other by Richard's decision to seize the dead Gaunt's valuables and property and prevent Bolingbroke's inheritance of his father's title. Gaunt's death should make Bolingbroke the Duke of Lancaster but he gains this position 'Barely in title, not in revenues' [II. i. 226]. Having lost one role and being prevented from playing another he knows to be his due, Bolingbroke has ample reason to feel the sense of deprivation and outrage he expresses to York in II. iii:

> I . . . stand condemn'd
> A wandering vagabond; my rights and royalties
> Pluck'd from my arms perforce, and given away
> To upstart unthrifts.
>
> [II. iii. 119-22]

Bolingbroke gives no more decisive expression of how the loss he has experienced actually feels to him, because although he parallels Richard in suffering the loss of role that threatens loss of identity, he by no means resembles Richard in other respects. He is, in contrast to Richard, a man of action. He acts while Richard plays, or, better, he acts while Richard *merely* acts. And, as he insists when saying farewell to his father, he lacks completely the kind of imagination Richard possesses in such abundance, for he cannot find any satisfaction in substituting mental images for concrete actuality, cannot, for example, 'cloy the hungry edge of appetite / By bare imagination of a feast' [I. iii. 296-97]. Both Bolingbroke's obvious affinity for action and his lack of Richard's verbal imagination are thoroughly reflected in the language he speaks when he is most himself. His language, in sharp contrast to Richard's, is without noticeable rhetorical flourishes; it is sparse in images, terse, conditioned to the needs of argument. . . . Bolingbroke, one is tempted to say, speaks a totally different language from Richard's, and nowhere is the contrast-conflict between the two more effectively epitomized than in the speeches they exchange during the formal deposition at London.

Bolingbroke's nature prevents him from responding to his loss of role in Richard's manner: he cannot and would not try to cling to an identity by dramatizing his situation or by acting out imaginary self-reassuring roles. But he does, obviously, feel the loss as acutely as Richard and experience a similar need to secure a substitute role, because he also emulates Richard in satisfying this need. He does it, however, in his own manner—by seizing a role that already exists. . . . [When] Richard's role as king becomes available through its present occupant's own willing abdication, Bolingbroke, who fits the part admirably, makes it his own.

Richard claims at the time of Bolingbroke's exile that Bolingbroke has been wooing the common people, 'As were our England in reversion his, / And he our subjects' next degree in hope' [I. iv. 35-6], but prior to the deposition Bolingbroke himself never directly reveals even the slightest aspiration towards the role he eventually seizes, and this extreme reticence means that a spectator tends to experience him simply as the actions he performs. There is no self-dramatization to call undue attention to the performer, and the gestures of the performance are too inconspicuous, too thoroughly untheatrical to suggest that a part of any kind is being played. One cannot even acquire an impression of the performer as an autonomous agent by thinking about what he does, by contemplating, for example, its morality; he acts too rapidly and, if not without forethought, at least without foretalk. This perfect equivalence between the performer and his performance suggests that Bolingbroke will readily become the ideal king Richard failed to be. But this promise is not fulfilled, and Bolingbroke's performance *as king* is accompanied by almost as many images of discrepant role-playing as was Richard's.

To the extent that Bolingbroke's assumption of the kingship can be pinpointed in time, it occurs when York proclaims, 'long live Henry, fourth of that name!' and Bolingbroke replies, 'In God's name, I'll ascend the regal throne' [IV. i. 112-13]. The next words, however, come from the Bishop of Carlisle, who sounds the first strong note of discrepancy: 'My Lord of Hereford here, whom you call king, / Is a foul traitor to proud Hereford's king' [IV. i. 134-35]. York's attitude towards the new king, whom he intends to serve loyally, differs sharply from Carlisle's, yet he too contributes to the sense of discrep-

ancy when, in a later scene, he describes the impression Richard made while following Bolingbroke into London:

> As in a theatre the eyes of men
> After a well-grac'd actor leaves the stage
> Are idly bent on him that enters next,
> Thinking his prattle to be tedious;
> Even so, or with much more contempt, men's eyes
> Did scowl on gentle Richard
>
> [V. ii. 23-8]

There is no criticism here of the better-grac'd Bolingbroke, and no insinuation—even in the preceding account of Bolingbroke's behaviour during the entry—that he, as Richard had done, exaggerates his performance of the more conspicuously histrionic attributes of kingship. There is nothing more than the image of Bolingbroke as an actor on the stage and the parallel in this respect between him and Richard. But this is in itself quite sufficient to evoke the notion of discrepancy and associate it with the new king as well as the old.

In assuming the kingship, Bolingbroke has, moreover, become involved in something much like a play. The first half of IV. i. occurs before York's proclamation, but Bolingbroke has in effect become king already, and here he is confronted by a situation paralleling the one Richard found himself facing in the opening scene. The public quarrel between Aumerle and his opponents, with its charges and counter-charges, is actually far more serious a conflict than the one Richard had to cope with, because this new quarrel involves more nobles: it seems to imply an even greater breach in the fabric of the kingdom's order than did the conflict that has already brought about a change in kings through something approximating civil war. Bolingbroke avoids duplicating Richard's performance (he does not use the occasion for self-dramatization and self-glorification) but he can do no more than Richard did to resolve things on the spot; he too must simply postpone final action until a later date. The occasion is thus not one that Bolingbroke controls but one that controls him. And because it is virtually the same sort of occasion as Richard had experienced, it assigns to the kingship a further role-like attribute. The kingship, this scene implies, resembles a role not only because of its gestures and moves but also because of the characteristic episodes it requires each of its occupants to act out.

It is, nevertheless, a later scene that most fully defines Bolingbroke's new life as unusually play-like, the scene in which York tries to persuade King Henry to kill his treasonous son, Aumerle, while Aumerle and his mother plead for his life. The basic situation is theatrical in itself, as King Henry notes when the Duchess arrives: 'Our scene is alt'red from a serious thing, / And now chang'd to "The Beggar and the King"' [V. iii. 79-80]. Shakespeare has, moreover, greatly exaggerated the theatrical effect with all the locking and unlocking of doors, the kneeling, and above all the extremely artificial language. In the strained rhetorical effects and the constant rhyme of this scene, the language of the beginning of the play is heard once more. It is as if nothing has happened, as if someone with a new way of speaking had not taken over the kingship. The point is, of course, that it is the kingship that has done the taking over. Bolingbroke speaks as he does here not because it is his kind of language but because he is trying to achieve the speech of kingship. Bolingbroke sounds neither like himself nor like Richard when he was king; he merely sounds strained and uncomfortable. He is quite obviously playing something quite other than himself, a part that does not wholly suit him.

Richard II thus ends as it had begun, by stressing that kingship is a kind of role. Once again, however, the more significant dramatic consequence of this emphasis pertains to the actor possessing this role, for the emphasis necessarily occurs at his expense: it insists on his failure, his inability to fulfil the role well enough to deflect attention away from the notion of a player playing a part. *Richard II* rightly closes with Bolingbroke's feelings of guilt for the murder of Richard—and for whatever else has contributed to the feelings—because the action as a whole has dramatized a change-over not from a bad king to a good one but from one player-king to another. Richard's birth and blood entitle him to play the role, but (in the terminology of *The Taming of the Shrew*) he is not aptly fitted for it, and therefore he is incapable of natural performance, of properly observing the gestures and moves of kingship and acting out its characteristic episodes in the best manner possible. Bolingbroke seems quite aptly fitted, seems entirely capable of giving a natural performance, but he can never achieve it because he lacks the one qualification Richard has possessed. His failure to achieve the role in the proper manner means at the very least that he must devote most of his energy simply to holding on to it. If Richard has reduced the role to a parody of its gestures, Bolingbroke looks as if he will reduce it to a vehicle for intrigue. (pp. 125-29)

> *Thomas F. Van Laan, ''The Pattern of the Histories,'' in his* Role-Playing in Shakespeare, *University of Toronto Press, 1978, pp. 117-51.*

Act V. Scene vi. Exton, Henry IV, the Bishop of Carlisle, and the body of Richard II. By Friedrich Pecht. The Department of Rare Books and Special Collections, The University of Michigan Library.

GRAHAM HOLDERNESS   (essay date 1981)

[*Drawing a vivid picture of the medieval political events that preceded Shakespeare's* Richard II, *Holderness disputes such critics as E. M. W. Tillyard (1944) and D. A. Traversi (see Additional Bibliography) that this play reflects the conflict between medieval monarchy, ritual, and ceremony, as embodied in Richard, and ''new Machiavellian power-politics,'' as exemplified by Bolingbroke and his revolutionary nobles. Instead, he contends, it dramatizes the struggle between the king's sovereignty and absolutist policies ''and the ancient code of chivalry,'' championed by such characters as Bolingbroke, Mowbray, and even to a large extent by Gaunt and York. Holderness thus overturns traditional assumptions and identifies the play's ceremonial, medieval nature— not with Richard—but with the feudal barons and nobles. The critic discerns the tragic source of* Richard II *as well not in ''the overturning of a traditional order by new, ruthless political forces,'' but in Richard's attempt ''to impose on feudal power an absolutist solution.'' Interestingly, Holderness further contends—again, specifically against those critics who have noted in* Richard II *a sincere vision of Tudor and Elizabethan political policy—that the Divine Right of Kings theory is not presented in the play as an unquestionable ideal of Richard's kingdom; instead, it is revealed as ''a historical myth, emerging . . . in the alienation of Richard's consciousness, as it responds to specific conditions of military and political defeat.''*]

Richard II is perhaps the most difficult of Shakespeare's history plays, not excluding the earlier *Henry [VI]—Richard III* cycle. It is distinguished sharply from the other histories by its peculiar *style*—what Tillyard called the 'extreme formality' of its shape and pattern, the elaborately ceremonial and ritualistic character of its action, and the very heightened and overtly lyrical style of Richard's tragedy [see excerpt above, 1944]. These peculiarities make the play in some ways a self-contained and self-referential dramatic poem: even though it is clearly incorporated into a series by the *Henry IV* plays, its individual treatment of history remains distinctive. And yet no other historical drama of Shakespeare's has proved more difficult to understand and interpret without the aid of external authorities. (p. 2)

The conventional understanding of the 'history' dramatized by this play is well known: it is thought to portray a mediaeval society (that which John of Gaunt looks back on), which was a harmonious, organic community, dominated by kings, bound together by order, hierarchy, degree; an order which is mismanaged by Richard, and therefore falls prey to the civil conflict which deposes him. But the nature of that old society guaranteed that Richard's deposition could not be a mere change of régime; Bolingbroke's usurpation destroyed a traditional, divinely-ordained and divinely-sanctioned monarchy, and thereby destroyed the old mediaeval 'order' irrevocably. The break ushers in civil war, which divides the realm until the Tudor reconciliation.

If, as I am proposing, Shakespeare developed his own understanding of history from his historical sources—rather than simply interpreting the past by the concepts and images of Tudor political and historical philosophy—then he would have known the Middle Ages, *not* as a period dominated by order and legitimacy, the undisputed sovereignty of a monarchy sanctioned by Divine Right; but as a turbulent period dominated by a great and fundamental conflict, fought out again and again and rarely suppressed, between the power of the Crown, and the power of the feudal barons.

Holinshed relates in considerable detail the constitutional struggles between monarchy and nobility which led ultimately to Richard's deposition, and which modern historians regard as the decisive political developments of this transitional late-mediaeval reign. We can enter Holinshed's narrative conveniently in 1386. In that year Richard advanced two close friends, Aubrey de Vere and Michael de la Pole, to high office—they became respectively Duke of Ireland and Lord Chancellor. These men did not have the approval of the powerful group known variously as the Magnates, the Lancastrian party, the Baronial Opposition; and these nobles secured the support of the Commons in a bid to accuse de la Pole of treason. That tactic, that pattern, will become a familiar one, up to its final and conclusive appearance in Bolingbroke's challenge to Mowbray. The baronial opposition engage in a power-struggle against the King and his policies, using the 'favourites' as pawns; at this point the nobility strengthened their grasp over the reins of power. . . . The opposition faction has here taken shape: the five opposition leaders who came to be known as the appelants (or Lords Appelant) are here identified as a group: their leader, Thomas of Woodstock, Duke of Gloucester (brother to Lancaster and York); Thomas Earl of Arundel; the Earl of Warwick; and the other two, here obscured by their titles, but easily recognisable by their policy—Henry Bolingbroke, son to the Duke of Lancaster, here Earl of Derby, later Earl of Hereford; and Thomas Mowbray, here Earl of Nottingham, later Earl of Norfolk. (pp. 3-4)

The struggle [between the king and the barons] continued until 1396. In 1397 Gloucester, Arundel, Warwick and Derby plotted to murder Richard; Mowbray, who was initially privy to this conspiracy, informed the King. Warwick and Arundel were arrested and indicted, Mowbray being one of the accusers. Arundel was beheaded. Warwick was exiled. Gloucester was murdered at Calais, because Richard feared to risk a public trial and execution. The gang of five was thus reduced to one: Bolingbroke.

In 1397, Richard consolidated his power by means of a Parliament which taxed heavily, disinherited estates, made huge borrowings and devised the 'blank charters'; and sought new oaths of allegiance from those alleged to have supported the Appelants. Richard, says Holinshed, had become a tyrant. 'He began to rule by will more than by reason, threatening death to each that obeid not his inordinate desires.' The Crown became increasingly unpopular. Bolingbroke, the only surviving Appelant, became the focal point and leader of popular discontent. Re-enacting the Appelant policy for the last time, in 1398 he accused Thomas Mowbray of treason.

This is the point where Shakespeare chose to begin his play: the appeal of treason by Bolingbroke against Mowbray.

The choice of incident testifies to his dramatic skill *and* to the depth and complexity of his historical sense. The quarrel between the Earls is an appropriate inception for the action of *Richard II,* as all the succeeding events can be seen to flow from it. But this incident also links the play indissolubly to precedent history, as Shakespeare read it in Holinshed: the appeal is the climax of that conflict between monarchy and feudalism which had been actively fought out throughout Richard's reign. The last remaining Appelant accuses the King's favourite of treason, ostensibly in defence of King and realm; the central accusation concerns the murder of the King's greatest enemy, leader of the Baronial opposition, Thomas of Woodstock, Duke of Gloucester. The appeal is the latest and last in a long succession of similar bids for power by the opposition faction of powerful feudal lords.

It is important to see the characters in this kind of context, and forming this kind of pattern: Mowbray the erstwhile Appelant turned King's favourite; Bolingbroke the last surviving representative of the Appelant faction, now the leader of popular discontent with the policies of the Crown; Richard recognizing instinctively the full implicit significance of Bolingbroke's challenge.

Critics such as Tillyard and Traversi [see Additional Bibliography] have spoken of the 'high formality' and 'courtly ceremony' of these proceedings; recognizing that the elaborate formal style is Shakespeare's attempt to create a specifically 'mediaeval' atmosphere and tone. . . . The King himself is regarded as the source of this specifically 'mediaeval' culture, which is dramatized here to show what mediaeval society was at the moment of its undermining by the more 'modern' forces of political ambition, power-politics and Machiavellianism. To these critics feudal law and chivalry mean, quite simply, 'order' and 'Kings.'

It is advisable to be exact about this 'formality', these 'ceremonies', and to define precisely what they are. Neither Tillyard nor Traversi seems particularly conscious of the fact that the appeal of treason and the consequent trial by battle are stages of a legal process, conducted in the Court of Chivalry, according to definite procedures which Shakespeare appears to have known and understood. The sense of legal procedures being followed in this initial meeting of the Earls is absent from any of the sources: it is Shakespeare's invention, and it shows the King adhering to procedures which (though odd indeed from the point of view of modern law, and clearly enough distinguishable from Elizabethan justice) according to feudal law are conducted throughout with perfect propriety.

The King, the fount of justice, presides over this legal process: legally his authority is absolute; in practice (in the drama as in actual history), his control is somewhat tenuous. In the first scene he restricts himself carefully to the role of mediating authority, 'chairman'. But the scene resolves itself into an assertion by the Barons of a code of values which is actually antagonistic to royal power, *hostile* to Richard's authority as sovereign; and the ceremony and pagentry of the proceedings are *connected more closely* with *that* code of values, than with the courtly culture of the Crown. It is in recognition of this fact that Richard seeks to remain ostensibly neutral (a position which symbolizes very precisely the predicament of a King in a still largely feudal society). The conflict which ultimately leads to the King's deposition is not a conflict between old and new, between absolute mediaeval monarchy and new Machiavellian power-politics. It is a conflict between the King's sovereignty and the ancient code of chivalry; which is here firmly located in the older and more primitive tribal and family code of blood-vengeance. Richard initially acquiesces in this code (as mediaeval Kings tended perforce to do); although it is actually independent of royal authority. But like the later mediaeval European Kings who tried to stamp out trial by battle (by the introduction of Roman law codes in the 13th century) Richard subsequently attempts to affirm a policy of royal absolutism, which insists on the King's prerogative overriding the procedures of chivalric law. Richard's political response to this constant clamouring for power on the part of the feudal lords, is to impose a policy of *absolutism*.

Throughout the first scene Richard's behavior is absolutely proper, formal, legal, impartial: a sense of order does actually flow from his presence. . . . He is there to see that justice is observed, and to counsel agreement; but he doesn't seek—at this stage—to intervene or suppress the rights enjoyed by the lords under feudal law; even though his own position (as we see later) is very remote from the feudal conception of justice.

Bolingbroke and Mowbray both offer formal expressions of allegiance, which Richard accepts with prudent reservation. Bolingbroke's speech of appeal [I. i. 30-46] can be recognised clearly as a continuation of the policy of Baronial Opposition: he *is* attacking the King, but is very careful to establish (as the Baronial Opposition always had) that his challenge is not to the King's authority, which is above reproach, but against the 'evil counsellor':

> In the devotion of a subject's love
> Tend'ring the precious safety of my prince . . .
> . . . Since the more fair and crystal is the sky
> The uglier seem the clouds that in it fly.
>
> [I. i. 31-2, 41-2]

Under the mediaeval law the appeal of treason (gradually replaced by the procedure of impeachment in Parliament) was an individual accusation, which did not have to be proved or defended—if the accused denied the charges, the appeal went straight to trial by battle. As Bolingbroke implies, the only 'proof' necessary is that of his 'right drawn sword' [I. i. 46]. Mowbray further clarifies this antiquated legal process by setting aside discussion and reason, and offering in their place a central image around which the play's first Act could be said to revolve—that of *blood*. The quarrel is one of 'blood's', hot, angry, impatient. But the hot blood is also knightly blood, the honourable blood of noble men; the quarrel can therefore be properly resolved by chivalric blood-battle [I. i. 47-60].

Bolingbroke snatches at the blood-image as quickly as he throws down his gage; and in a striking declaration *disclaims* the King's kinship [I. i. 70-1], rejects his royal connection, and invokes 'the rites of knighthood' . . .—he is therefore the first to suggest that the obligations of chivalry and those of royal allegiance can enter into conflict. Mowbray replies in the same chivalric language—

> I'll answer thee in any fair degree
> Or chivalrous design of knightly trial . . .
>
> [I. i. 80-1]

—all reference to the King has disappeared.

Bolingbroke then makes his accusations against Mowbray. The charges of embezzlement and conspiracy are vague and uninteresting: but they would actually have more place in a charge of treason than the third accusation—the real substance of Bolingbroke's attack on Mowbray—that Mowbray was instrumental in the clandestine execution of the King's greatest and most ambitious enemy, Thomas of Woodstock, Duke of Gloucester:

> . . . That he did plot the Duke of Gloster's death
> suggest his soon-believing adversaries
> And consequently, like a traitor coward
> Sluic'd out his innocent soul through streams of blood
> Which blood, like sacrificing Abel's, cries
> Even from the tongueless caverns of the earth
> To me for justice and rough chastisement.
>
> [I. i. 100-06]

The glittering veil of the Baron's chivalric language trembles a little here, and behind it we perceive the shape of something more primitive—the motive of blood-vengeance for a slaughtered kinsman. For Bolingbroke there is no disparity at all between chivalry and blood-vengeance—the one is the means to the other; justice can be 'proved' by force of arms. But a different texture of language encourages the reader to separate the two different concepts: Bolingbroke's 'rough chastisement' is surely a cruder, more primitive thing than the abstract concept of 'Justice'.

The code of chivalry enables Bolingbroke to regard *himself* as a responsible administrator of justice, because blood-vengeance of kin and justice are for him synonymous; he is speaking the language of an ancient code of feudal values. He believes that his 'glorious descent' [I. i. 107] (which is exactly the same as Richard's) gives *him* greater responsibility for prosecuting the law than the king himself. With Holinshed's history as context, we can appreciate the full seriousness of this assertion, which is a direct baronial challenge to the power of the throne; and appreciate also the justice of Richard's sarcastic remarks, which put Bolingbroke firmly in his place:

> How high a pitch his resolution soars! . . .
> . . . Were he my brother, nay my kingdom's heir
> As he is *but my father's brother's son* . . .
>
> [I. i. 109, 116-17]
> (pp. 5-9)

Richard asserts that the ties of blood and kin don't have the same significance to him as they do to Bolingbroke: his 'sacred blood' [I. i. 119] is absolved from such partialities; all are equal before his 'sceptre's awe' [I. i. 118], the dignity of his sovereign authority. Royal absolutism and feudal kinship are placed in sharp opposition. (p. 9)

Throughout Richard remains inactive: but it would be wrong to interpret this inactivity as weakness. The King is confronted with a powerful baronial offensive, articulating itself in chivalric terms. The power struggle is fought out within the ideology of chivalry, which gives the King a tenuous control, but is actually based more firmly on feudal power and values than on the sovereignty of the Crown. Richard tries initially to reason with them, to secure agreement and compromise—a solution which, like the subsequent affirmation of absolutism, cuts across the structure of feudal values.

Such compromise, however, is impossible. A spirit of reason and compromise, acceptable also to the royalist baron Gaunt, who co-operates in the attempt at reconciliation, meets the stubborn, intractable values of chivalry which now break away completely from the structure of monarchic authority which had striven to control and contain them, subdue them to a royalist social pattern:

> Bolingbroke: Myself I throw, dread sovereign, at thy
> foot
> My life thou shalt command, but not my
> shame:
> The one my duty owes, by my fair name
> Despite of death, that lives upon my
> grave,
> To dark dishonour'd use thou shalt not
> have. . . .
> Mowbray: Mine honour is my life, both grow in one,
> Take honour from me, and my life is
> done . . .

Bolingbroke: O God defend my soul from such deep
                   sin!
          Shall I seem crest-falled in my father's
              sight?
          Or with pale beggar-fear impeach my
              height
          Before this out-dared dastard? Ere my
              tongue
          Shall wound my honour with such feeble
              wrong
          Or sound so base a parle, my teeth shall
              tear
          The slavish motive of recanting fear . . .
              [I. i. 165-69, 182-83, 187-93]

The piling-up of chivalric language here is remarkable, and it is virtually all Shakespeare's invention. It is used to show that in this conflict King's man and opposition baron have both broken away from royal authority, into the realm of knighthood. Honour has become more absolute than allegiance; loyalty to kin has superseded duty to sovereign; chivalric personal dignity has exceeded civil obligation. Monarchy has failed to control the power of feudalism.

The second scene continues to develop the main themes of the first, and establishes clearly the centrality and significance of Gloucester's death. Gaunt continues his son's use of the 'blood' image, in a similar way: his blood-kinship to Gloucester places the obligation of blood-vengeance upon him also—the 'murdered' kinsman's blood cries out to the brother as it had to the nephew. But Gaunt's instinct of blood-vengeance is subdued to a clear conception of loyalty to a divinely-ordained sovereign. (It is perhaps worth mentioning that this is the first mention of such an idea; Richard himself does not invoke it until half-way through Act III).

The Duchess, Woodstock's widow, speaks—as her nephew speaks—an older, more primitive language: sovereignty has no hold over her imagination, which is possessed by the imagery of blood-kin and blood-vengeance. The highly personal utterance of the widow (Woodstock's 'next of kin') places the strongest of personal pressures on Gaunt: to revenge your own blood is a form of personal survival; to decline it a form of personal self-destruction. The old woman, like Bolingbroke, identifies justice with chivalric law, synthesizes the language of blood-vengeance with that of chivalric justice:

    O sit my husband's wrongs on Herford's spear
    That it may enter butcher Mowbray's breast
    . . . And throw the rider headlong in the lists
    A caitive recreant to my cousin Herford!
              [I. ii. 47-8, 52-3]

Gaunt makes no concession here: he stands by his concept of Divine Right and royal prerogative—'God's is the quarrel' [I. ii. 37]—and even suggests that the murder of Gloucester may not have been 'wrongful':

    . . . for God's substitute,
    His deputy anointed in His sight,
    Hath caused his death; the which *if wrongfully*,
    Let heaven revenge . . .
              [I. ii. 37-40]

Gaunt believes firmly in the necessary subjugation of feudal rights to royal prerogative. In the next scene however (the Combat) we find Gaunt using the widow's language; and it becomes apparent that one of the purposes of Act I, sc. ii, is

to dramatize the conflicting pressures operating on Gaunt, just as strongly as they operate on his brother York. Bolingbroke again invokes his noble lineage, this time as 'blood':

    Oh thou, the earthly author of my blood,
    Whose youthful spirit in me regenerate
    Doth with a twofold vigour lift me up
    To reach at victory above my head . . .
              [I. iii. 69-72]

Stirred by this appeal, Gaunt's loyalism is shaken:

    God in thy good cause make thee prosperous
    Be swift like lightning in the execution,
    And let thy blows, doubly redoubled,
    Fall like amazing thunder on the casque
    Of thy adverse pernicious enemy!
    Rouse up thy youthful blood, be valiant and live.
              [I. iii. 78-83]

Gaunt encourages the 'youthful blood' of the chivalric spirit, and identifies it with justice. The imagery of thunder and lightning confers on Bolingbroke extraordinary powers as the instrument of divine and natural justice. Gaunt has here adopted the language of chivalry, blood, kin and justice which we have learned from his son and his deceased brother's wife. He remains, of course, divided: his ambivalence is made clear later when he agrees in Council with Richard's decision to banish the Earls, but distinguishes between his *personal* and his *political* allegiances.

Richard's decision to stop the combat is another open question for which various explanations have been offered, and various motives supplied. If we presuppose the stated historical context, listen carefully to Richard's speech at [I. iii. 124-38], and understand his behaviour in I, iv, the implications of the decision become clearer.

The speech itself is an impressive homily against civil war, and the disorganizing militaristic feudalism which has precipitated that danger. It also gives us a sense of Richard's own image of his kingdom. Running through the speech is an underlying pattern of images creating a strong positive sense of the realm as it should be:

    Our kingdom's earth . . . : plough'd up . . . our peace,
    sweet infant, . . . till twice five summers
    have enrich'd our fields.
              [I. iii. 125-41]

The pastoral imagery of rural peace, fecundity, new life, is violated by the language of bloodshed, civil wounds, swords; the assertive arrogance of feudal pride; 'the grating shock of wrathful iron arms' [I. iii. 136]. If feudalism has become a real threat to the stability and harmony of the realm, then Richard is clearly attempting not just to banish two quarrelling Earls, but to dismantle the very structures of feudal power. (pp. 9-12)

Gaunt's famous speech [at II. i. 31-68] . . . is clearly one of the strongest incentives to accept the conventional ideas of 'mediaeval kingship'. His language is uncompromisingly royalist: the realm is (or rather has been—the speech is an elegy) properly defined in terms of its monarchy, its history distinguished by the quality of its kings. Gaunt, unlike Bolingbroke, identifies kingship and chivalry, and looks back nostalgically to a time when England united the two. That identification, and the rôle Gaunt adopts towards Richard (that of sage counsellor) imply a kingdom in which a careful and diplomatic balancing of forces synthesized Crown and nobility into a united 'Happy breed of men'—a situation which prevailed in the reign of Edward III. The appropriate image for this marriage of Crown and aristocracy, of Christian monarchy and 'true chivalry', is that of the crusade. Though Gaunt's language is that of royalism and Divine Right, he is certainly no absolutist: his Golden Age is that of a feudalism given cohesion and structure by the central authority of a king, bound to his subjects by the reciprocal bonds of fealty.

The climax of Gaunt's speech draws the attack on Richard's economic policies into a powerful image of the dissolution of traditional social bonds: England, formerly united in itself and against other nations, is now bound together by economic contracts:

> England, bound in with the triumphant sea
> . . . is now bound in with shame
> With inky blots and rotten parchment bonds.
>   [II. i. 61, 63-4]

Gaunt's elegy is no panegyric of absolutism: it is a lament for the dissolution of a society in which King and nobility were organically bound together into a strong and unified nation: the King is now a mere 'Landlord' [II. i. 113]. The unnatural quality (from the baronial point of view) of these developments is focussed by a reiteration of the charge about Gloucester's murder: an offence against kin, a stain of dishonour on the family of Edward III; a cause of division within the patrician order. (p. 13)

The Duke of York presents a different point of view: and I think it is important to understand and to acknowledge the seriousness of his position. York's ideas are usually compromised by attention to his very obvious self-division—on stage the rôle is usually played as that of a fussy and indecisive senior civil servant. But we have seen the same self-division in Gaunt as well, resolved only by his death; York has to live with the difficulty of carrying his divided allegiance into the new conditions:

> Oh my liege
> Pardon me, if you please; if not, I pleas'd
> Not to be pardoned, am content withal.
> Seek you to seize and gripe into your hands,
> The royalties and rights of banished Herford?
> Is not Gaunt dead? and doth not Herford live?
> Take Herford's rights away, and take from time
> His charters, and his customary rights;
> Let not tomorrow then exceed today:
> Be not thyself. For how art thou a King
> But by fair sequence and succession?
>   [II. i. 186-91, 195-99]

The spirit underlying this speech is that of Magna Carta. Richard is demanding *obedience* rather than *fealty:* fealty being a reciprocal relationship which guarantees the lord certain constitutional rights in exchange for his service and loyalty. Fealty binds subject *and* ruler: Bolingbroke's homage to Richard is no mere subjection but the entry into a reciprocal social bond. York's image of society is that of a social contract: the king, by violating the contract, inevitably raises the spectre of rebellion even in the most 'well-disposed' hearts [II. i. 206]. There is even a touch in York's speech of the early mediaeval view that rebellion could be justified against a monarch who

violated his own side of the 'fealty' contract. York's self-division is clearly expressed again at II, ii.

> . . . Both are my Kinsmen:
> Th'one is my sovereign, whom both my truth
> And duty bids defend; th'other again
> Is my kinsman, whom the King hath wrong'd,
> Whom conscience and my kindred bids to right.
>   [II. ii. 111-15]

York recognises here two equally valid but conflicting conceptions of justice and duty: a historical contradiction. Richard, who has made it plain that he regards the Lancastrians in general as enemies,—('Right, you say true; as Herford's love, so his; As theirs, so mine; and all be as it is' [II. i. 145-46].)—deals with York's sliding loyalty by a characteristic political gamble: appointing him Protector in his absence.

By the end of this scene rebellion is a reality. Northumberland (Shakespeare's classic Machiavellian) makes it plain here, despite his covert and non-committal speech, that he is proposing to rescue the Crown from its present incumbent: to reclaim the throne on behalf of the nobility. The barons are preparing to replace the dynastically legitimate King with one of their own choice and approval.

The loyalist and baronial ideologies are brought into direct collision, in the meeting between York and the newly-returned Bolingbroke. (II, iii). Within the language of royalism . . . Bolingbroke's actions receive their automatic valuation as 'gross rebellion and detested treason' [II. iii. 109]. Bolingbroke's case however is also reasonable and valid, within its limits—he restricts his thinking to feudal terms, and does not imagine or conceptualize the consequences of his pushing at the balance of power. (pp. 13-15)

York cannot deny the justice of [Bolingbroke's] case, although he cannot see rebellion as an appropriate means of securing justice; and he also detects a larger purpose underlying the conspiracy:

> Well, well, I see the issue of these arms.
>   [II. iii. 152]

This is perhaps confirmed by Bolingbroke's decision to seek out the 'caterpillars' [II. iii. 166]; though that too is compatible with traditional baronial policy. . . . York wavers into neutrality, but is already half-way to joining the revolution. He is 'loath to break our Country's laws' [II. iii. 169], but is unable to resolve the historical contradiction—the paradox of *two* laws, each in its way valid and absolute, but incompatible and mutually exclusive.

By this stage the political and military battles are really over: and in the speech of Salisbury at II, iv, we hear the first stirrings of the language and imagery of royal tragedy, divine right and apocalyptic prophecy which will dominate the rest of the play.

Act III opens with Bolingbroke in a commanding position— (though not necessarily any nearer to the throne than the Barons had been in 1388, when the King's supporters were executed by Parliament). His speech defines very precisely his specific relationship with England: it is the solid, proprietary language of a nobleman talking about his estate: it contrasts with Gaunt's impersonal conception of the realm as a feudal nation; and even more sharply with Richard's image of England, as it is revealed in the next scene. Like the charges against Mowbray, those against the favourites are no more than a gesture towards public justice: and just as those charges collapsed into the fundamental accusation of Gloucester's murder, so the allegations of treason carry very little weight by comparison with the *personal* injury sustained by Bolingbroke himself—*that* part of the speech carries an accent of personal grudge and recrimination, the response to an offence against the aristocratic class:

> Myself—a prince by fortune of my birth,
> Near to the King in blood, and near in love,
> Till you did make him misinterpret me—
> Have stooped my neck under your injuries,
> And sigh'd my English breath in foreign clouds,
> Eating the bitter bread of banishment,
> Whilst you have fed upon my signories,
> Dispark'd my parks and fell'd my forest woods,
> From my own windows torn my household coat,
> Rac'd out my imprese, leaving me no sign,
> Save men's opinions and my living blood,
> To show the world I am a gentleman.
>
> [III. i. 16-27]

("Signories" = Estates; "imprese" = a heraldic device).

The 'caterpillars' have fed on Bolingbroke's *property,* his *estates,* concepts defined very precisely by his clear, concrete images of parks, forests, emblazoned windows, coats-of-arms, personal heraldic symbols—the concrete social identity of a 'gentleman'. Bolingbroke's consciousness is still that of a rebellious baron rather than the incipient King: although in fact he has already pushed the policy of opposition beyond the point of balance; the whole realm of England is about to become the baron's property.

That solid, possessive sense of England as private property contrasts sharply with Richard's feelings about his kingdom on his return from Ireland, in the next scene. (III, ii). For the first time, Richard's speech moves towards the language and imagery of Divine Right—though there is no explicit affirmation of this doctrine for almost forty lines. In the preceding lines we see a fantastic reduction of Divine Right to a kind of childish superstition: the strong and bitter masculinity of Bolingbroke's relation to his estate, gives way to Richard's intimate, sentimental, physical cherishing of 'my Kingdom' [III. ii. 5]. The conjuration is that of a child, who invokes the supernatural to combat the apparent omnipotence of parents: it is the voice of an imagination already beginning to experience defeat.

A sentimental poetic fancy peoples the realm with 'familiars', sympathetic creatures who will resist Bolingbroke's assault. Having failed in his ruling of society, Richard seeks to imagine a kingdom of nature, in which everything is subject to his will, everything naturally loyal to his sovereignty. We hardly need the Bishop of Carlisle to inform us that the 'power' of Divine Right, and the kind of power that can rule a state, have become separated from one another.

For it is here, at the point where his defeat is imminent, that Richard's mind begins to split king and man, divine power and practical authority. 'Divine Right' is not seriously offered by the play as an unquestionably valid understanding of Plantagenet England: it is shown as a historical myth, emerging with its full imaginative force and splendour in the alienation of Richard's consciousness, as it responds to specific conditions of military and political defeat.

If we listen sympathetically to the practical, common-sense advice of his followers, it is easy to assume that Richard is experiencing a simple failure of the will, an indication of his personal weakness and unfitness for royal office. But he is no longer interested in the practical 'means of succour and redress' [III. ii. 32]. His kingship has been faced with a situation which could be resolved only by conciliation or absolutism. Choosing the latter course, Richard has appeared throughout as the absolutist monarch in the legal, economic and political spheres. The baronial rebellion makes conciliation impossible, and absolutism impracticable: so Richard's imagination begins to seek out new kingdoms to dominate with the absolute power of his will. The kingdom of nature succumbs to his fantasy; the whole cosmos is subdued to his power in the imagery of Divine Right.

The state itself ready to fall into Bolingbroke's hands, Richard's imagination is released to a vivid realization of the difference between effective power and 'mere' legitimacy; between the power of the man and the authority of the royal office; between the man who can rule a state and the King who has only the charisma of 'Divine Right'. He feels that he has reached death, and has nothing to bequeath to his heirs, no property in the realm. The only substance of his kingship is now the experience of royal tragedy: the only thing he can bequeath is his own tragic myth: 'sad stories of the deaths of Kings' [III. ii. 156]. This speech is a penetrating tragic insight into the hollowness of 'Power' without power—the imagery of hollowness runs from the hollow grave, to the hollow crown, to the 'wall of flesh' encircling the mortal life, which seems as impregnable as a castle, but contains only a vulnerable, isolated life. . . . (pp. 15-17)

The final culmination of Richard's absolutism is his isolation in prison. (V, v). The prison is a world without people, a kingdom without subjects, which he can fill with his own personality: he can be both ruler and ruled. At last Richard's imagination and will are supreme—now his kingdom has been reduced to the confines of his own mind.

It should be clear by now that *Richard II* is far from being a simple redaction of some 'official' Elizabethan ideology; a play designed to support and confirm that ideology by reducing the complexities of mediaeval history to a dogmatic orthodoxy—substantiating the Divine Right of Kings, condemning the deposition of a King as a crime against God, nature and humanity, and demonstrating the inevitable providential consequences of deposition, in discord, rebellion and civil war. On the contrary the play *challenges* that ideology of Divine Kingship: showing that society is a social contract which can easily be broken, and that the historical myth of Divine Right, for all its power, can never effectively heal the breach from which it is generated. The play *exposes* Shakespeare's contemporary ideology by showing that a monarch rules not by the will of God but by social contract; that a sovereign *can* be deposed (the very act of *showing* such a possibility was regarded as a challenge by Elizabeth's censors); that a powerful aristocracy *can* topple the monarch and rule the kingdom. Nevertheless, the play's *demystification* of the theory of Divine Kingship, its effort to return the mythology of Richard's reign to real history, takes place within the framework of Shakespeare's contemporary 'general ideology'. The *unmasking* of ideology re-inserts itself into the general ideology, with the ultimate aim of revivifying and reconstructing, but nevertheless re-producing, that ideology as a whole. So despite its 'anti-ideological' character, the play insists that the deposition and murder of a King *are* productive of civil war, a legacy of bloodshed and strife. But—as the *Henry IV* plays show even more clearly—these consequences follow not because of the wrath of God or providential visitations; but by a process closer to what we would call 'laws of historical development'. (pp. 18-19)

At the beginning of Act IV we learn that the action we have seen taking place within the microcosmic kingdom of Richard's imagination, is almost separable from the action taking place in the realm itself. The distance is measured by Act IV, sc. i, Bolingbroke's 'parliament' in Westminster Hall, which demonstrates not simply that those who subvert 'order' inevitably create discord within and amongst themselves; but the specific consequences of a power-group of feudal lords becoming a ruling caste. The occasion is Bolingbroke's attempt to 'purge' elements likely to be sympathetic to Richard: Aumerle is accused, on the evidence of Bagot, of Gloucester's murder. Bolingbroke's peremptory manner, and his anticipation of the outcome [IV. i. 2-4], suggest that he expects a straightforward show trial. The result, perhaps, surprises him.

What happens is a complex and comically-presented collision of individual feudal 'honours'. Legal accusations and counter-accusations fly across the hall, each accompanied by a gage, the emblem of chivalric challenge. The exchange is studded with chivalric language:

> Dishonour . . . honour soil'd . . . to stain the
> temper of my knightly sword . . . valour . . .
> vauntingly . . . appeal . . . brandish more
> revengeful steel / O'er the glittering helmet
> of my foe . . . my honour's pawn . . . , etc.
>
> [IV. i. 21-55]

Clearly there can be no resolution of this deadlock of conflicting interests. The multiplying of accusations becomes almost farcical, until Aumerle, by asking to borrow another gage to challenge yet another rival, comes close to betraying the absurdity of the whole procedure. At this point Henry simply stops it:

> Lords appelants
> Your differences shall all rest under gage
> Till we assign you to your days of trial.
>
> [IV. i. 104-06]

As Henry IV, Bolingbroke will never resolve the contradictions between his feudal and his monarchical ideologies. But his imposition here of such peremptory authority indicates that from now on chivalry will be subordinated to *Real politik*. *This* King will not tolerate feudal challenges to his power—even though (or perhaps because) it was through such a challenge that he reached the throne. (pp. 20-1)

One more scene requires commentary, Act V. sc. ii, which turns again to the central question of family honour. What has happened to the noble family, central institution of feudal values? It is now split and divided: the Duke of York, who completed the transition from loyal retainer to rebel baron, is now uncompromisingly loyal to the new King, and has guaranteed the 'truth' (loyalty, allegiance) of his son Aumerle:

> I am in parliament pledge for his truth
> And lasting fealty to the new-made King.
>
> [V. ii. 44-5]

Aumerle, former ally of Richard, is now involved in a plot to kill Henry. York informs the King of his son's treason, subordinating paternal love to family honour:

> He shall spend mine honour with his shame
> Mine honour lives when his dishonour dies
> Or my sham'd life in his dishonour lies. . . .
>
> [V. iii. 68-70]

Henry, apparently unshaken in his composure by these revelations, hints that this collision of conflicting values, like the chivalric chaos of IV, i, has its ridiculous side:

> Our scene is altered from a serious thing
> And now changed to 'The Beggar and the King'.
>
> [V. iii. 79-80]

He appears to be unmoved by the discovery; he rejects York's appeal to family honour; and he unhesitatingly pardons Aumerle.

Henry is displaying here a complete break with the values and conventions which he had formerly espoused, and which led him to seek and achieve the throne. Although the challenges and appeals of Act IV, sc. i, are a precise repetition of his challenge to Mowbray, Henry shows little concern for the principles and procedures of feudal justice. Although York's assertions of family honour are echoes of his own baronial sense of family dignity, he does not accede to them and overrules them just as absolutely as Richard did in his turn.

It is clear, then, that the 'history' of the play is much more complex than the conventional accounts allow. Shakespeare grasps very firmly and clearly the central contradiction of early mediaeval society: the struggle between royal authority and feudal power. He sees the deposition of Richard II, not as the overturning of a traditional order by new, ruthless political forces: but as the consequences of an attempt by a later mediaeval monarch to impose on feudal power an absolutist solution. The victorious forces are not new but old: feudal reaction rather than political revolution. The society we see dissolving had been an effective unity and balance of royal prerogative and feudal rights: both parties in the conflict have pushed their interests to the point of inevitable rupture.

This argument does not seek to invalidate the concept of divinely-sanctioned kingship, which is clearly central to the play; but to suggest a different view of its *status*. The play does not tell us that this conception represents Shakespeare's understanding of the structure and quality of mediaeval society before the deposition of Richard II. On the contrary, the precedent past, the 'pre-history of the present' is dramatized as a social contract held together by the mutual agreement of powerful forces. The older generation of barons, sons of Edward III, *are* committed (though in different ways) to the concept of monarchy; but they see this operating *only* within a conception of commonwealth, a union of Crown and nobility, and independence or absolutism on the part of the King distresses them deeply. Richard himself does not describe his rule as sanctioned by Divine Right until his defeat is well under way.

The idea of Divine Right is actually presented in the play as a historical myth (not a mystifying fiction, but a real and powerful form of human consciousness) which develops and emerges from the defeat of the monarchy. Richard dramatizes that myth as the monarchy itself dissolves; he affirms it most powerfully as his power disappears; and as his effective rule declines, his tragic myth exerts ever more powerful pressures on the imaginations of those responsible for his defeat. It is a matter of critical commonplace that Richard is not only a tragic role on the stage, but a 'tragic actor' . . . , conscious of the role he is playing; and that he is not only a mouthpiece for tragic poetry, but a poet, composing his own 'lamentable tale' [V. i. 44]. We can now add to these a third role: Richard is also a historian, constructing and creating the myth of his own tragic history.

Once created, that myth becomes a powerful ideology: and the play reveals it to be precisely that. Like the ideology of monarchic feudalism, which was both organic order *and* battle-ground of historical forces, the myth of Richard's tragedy (in its twin form of martyr king and deposed tyrant) continues to haunt the civil conflicts of his successors, who are thus, in T. S. Eliot's words, 'united in the strife which divided them'; *and* determines the shape and form of the ultimate reconciliation. When Richmond at the end of *Richard III* unites the red rose and the white, his action is subsumed into the powerful mythology created by his predecessor, 'that sweet lovely rose' Richard II. (pp. 21-3)

Graham Holderness, "Shakespeare's History: 'Richard II'," in Literature and History, *Vol. 7, No. 1, Spring, 1981, pp. 2-24.*

ADDITIONAL BIBLIOGRAPHY

Albright, Evelyn May. "Shakespeare's *Richard II* and the Essex Conspiracy." *PMLA* XLII, No. 3 (September 1927): 686-720.

Surveys the events of February 7, 1601, when supporters of the Earl of Essex commissioned a performance of *Richard II* at the Globe theatre in an attempt to incite the London populace to rebel against Queen Elizabeth's government. Albright also considers the reasons why the play was regarded by Elizabethans as such an explosive political work.

Allman, Eileen Jorge. "History Enacted: The Emergence of a Player-King." In her *Player-King and Adversary,* pp. 19-53. Baton Rouge and London: Louisiana State University Press, 1980.

Employs modern psychological theories of role-playing as a means of exploring and manipulating behavior to analyze the personality differences between Richard II and Bolingbroke. Allman contends that Richard, having lost his identity as king, is forced to create a new definition of self and learn through his struggles how to interact with the world. Bolingbroke, on the other hand, merely seeks to impose his self-image on those around him; thus, he does not finally achieve the degree of growth and development which Richard experiences.

Berger, Harry, Jr. "Psychoanalyzing the Shakespeare Text: The First Three Scenes of the Henriad." In *Shakespeare: The Question of Theory,* edited by Patricia Parker and Geoffrey Hartman, pp. 210-29. New York and London: Methuen, 1985.

Defends the premise that "patriarchal ideology is shown in the Henriad to create deep tensions which are not dispelled, are often exacerbated, by its mechanisms of repression...." Berger concentrates on the relationship between Gaunt and his son Bolingbroke in *Richard II,* declaring that "the fury, splendor, frustration, and politics" in the play "can only be understood and evaluated by the excavation that psychoanalyzes the text."

Bergeron, David M. "The Deposition Scene in *Richard II.*" In *Renaissance Papers 1974,* edited by Dennis G. Donovan and A. Leigh Deneef, pp. 31-7. Durham, N.C.: The Southern Renaissance Conference, 1975.

Suggests that the episode in Act IV, Scene I depicting King Richard's abdication was not written until sometime between 1601 and 1608. Bergeron briefly examines the Elizabethan political climate, with particular emphasis on the Essex Rebellion of 1601, and concludes that it is unlikely that this scene was censored by government officials.

Black, Matthew W. "The Sources of Shakespeare's *Richard II.*" In *Joseph Quincy Adams Memorial Studies,* edited by James G. McManaway, Giles E. Dawson, and Edwin E. Willoughby, pp. 199-216. Washington: The Folger Shakespeare Library, 1948.

Challenges John Dover Wilson's assumption that Shakespeare's *Richard II* is based on a "lost play" (see entry below). Presuming that "it was Shakespeare's custom to prepare himself, whether for the writing of a new play or the revising of an old one, by

consulting more sources than the one he chiefly followed," Black reviews Holinshed, Daniel, *Woodstock,* Hall, Froissart, and the French chronicles, noting the possible influences each may have had on the composition of *Richard II.*

———. ed. *A New Variorum Edition of Shakespeare: "The Life and Death of King Richard the Second."* Philadelphia: J. B. Lippincott Co., 1955, 655 p.

Includes important information on the text, dating, and sources of *Richard II.* Black also offers discussions of the play's critical and stage history and its political significance in the age of Elizabeth.

Blanpied, John W. "Sacrificial Energy in *Richard II.*" In his *Time and the Artist in Shakespeare's English Histories,* pp. 120-41. London and Toronto: Associated University Presses, 1983.

Adopts a metadramatic approach to the play, contending that Shakespeare, in his historical tetralogies, both generated "a vision of the past" and developed "the means of ordering its complexities onstage." Blanpied suggests that on one level *Richard II* represents the dramatist's struggle to understand his own art, adding that in the character of the king, "Shakespeare parodies himself."

Bloom, Allan. "*Richard II.*" In *Shakespeare as Political Thinker,* edited by John Alvis and Thomas G. West, pp. 51-61. Durham, N.C.: Carolina Academic Press, 1981.

Holds that *Richard II* is a highly political play which explores the problem of kingly "legitimacy." Bloom contends that if Richard II's court does represent medieval order, as many critics have claimed, that order is already moribund and exhausted. He also maintains that Richard fails as a ruler because, given his Christian vision, the world of politics has no significance for him, whereas Bolingbroke of necessity embraces a form of practical Machiavellianism.

Boas, Frederick S. "The Chief Group of Chronicle History Plays." In his *Shakspere and His Predecessors,* pp. 249-59. London: J. Murray, 1896.

Discusses *Richard II*'s relationship to other plays in Shakespeare's canon. Boas offers a synopsis of the plot based on the premise that "the sentimentalist, in Shakespeare's view, is always a dangerous factor in society; in *Richard II* we see him enthroned, and the result is national disaster, till a deliverer arises in Bolingbroke, the iron-willed man of affairs."

Booth, Stephen. "Syntax as Rhetoric in *Richard II.*" *Mosaic: A Journal for the Comparative Study of Literature and Ideas* X, No. 3 (Spring 1977): 87-103.

Offers a linguistic interpretation of why audiences find Richard a frustrating, negative character in the opening scenes of *Richard II* and why we feel ambivalent about the characters in general, even those who are obviously meant to be sympathetic figures, such as Gaunt. Examining the first act, Booth contends that Shakespeare purposely garbles Richard's speech to emphasize an important theme: "Not getting to the point, not letting actions and situations finish so that new ones can follow, is of the essence in this play." More significantly, the critic adds, this wordiness of Richard and the other characters serves as a metaphor for the wastefulness, the weakness, and the failure to wield power effectively evident throughout Richard's kingdom. Booth links audience reaction to the various characters to the presence of such "syntactical mushiness," suggesting that one factor which contributes to our favorable change in attitude toward Richard is the king's clearer, more straightforward phraseology after his return from Ireland.

Bornstein, Diane. "Trial by Combat and Official Irresponsibility in *Richard II.*" *Shakespeare Studies* 8 (1975): 131-41.

Examines both sides of the Renaissance debate over the legality and morality of duels or jousts. Bornstein notes that Italian tradition held that such defenses of one's honor were legitimate, while Christian humanists countered that they were irreligious and illogical.

Bradbrook, M. C. "Tragical-Historical: *Henry VI, Richard III, Richard II.*" In her *Shakespeare and Elizabethan Poetry: A Study of His*

Earlier Work in Relation to the Poetry of the Time, pp. 135-40. London: Chatto and Windus, 1951.

> Maintains that the "image of the trampled garden" embodies *Richard II's* dominant theme. Bradbrook also explores Shakespeare's development in this history of sophisticated expository techniques, in-depth characterizations, and a "multiplicity of points of view" which contribute a sense of tragedy to the play.

Bromley, John C. "The Allegory of the Garden in *King John* and *Richard II*." In his *The Shakespearean Kings*, pp. 41-60. Boulder: Colorado Associated University Press, 1971.

> Investigates examples of growth and vegetation imagery in two Shakespearean history plays in order to identify the dramatist's vision of the ideal king.

Brooke, Nicholas. "*Richard II*." In his *Shakespeare's Early Tragedies*, pp. 107-37. London: Methuen and Co., 1968.

> Takes issue with "the conception of Richard as a wilting poet," identifying those passages which establish the king's "criminality" rather than his supposed weaknesses. Brooke argues that *Richard II* is too often misinterpreted as a poignant character-study, when in fact "the main structure of the play is rhetorical," indicating Shakespeare's interest not only in personal problems but in public, political themes as well.

Brooke, Stopford A. "*Richard II*." In his *On Ten Plays of Shakespeare*, pp. 71-99. London: Constable and Co., 1925.

> Scrutinizes *Richard II* and *Richard III* for indications of the political mood in England during the 1590s. Brooke relates Shakespeare's two tetralogies to the vast panorama of the Wars of the Roses, but also stresses their artistic and ethical dimensions, declaring that while Greek tragedy is dominated by "Destiny working out her moral will," the unifying theme in Shakespeare's histories is Divine justice. On other matters, Brooke finds the abdication scene melodramatic and indelicate and states that the Aumerle episode "offends the natural instinct of the heart." He admires, however, the complete spiritual regeneration of Richard II during the fifth act.

Bullough, Geoffrey, ed. "*Richard II*," by William Shakespeare. In his *Narrative and Dramatic Sources of Shakespeare, Vol. III, Earlier English History Plays: "Henry VI," "Richard III," "Richard II,"* pp. 353-491. London: Routledge and Kegan Paul, 1966.

> Includes a detailed discussion of the possible sources for Shakespeare's play and provides excerpts from the source texts themselves.

Calderwood, James L. "*Richard II* to *Henry IV*: Variations on the Fall." In his *Metadrama in Shakespeare's Henriad: "Richard II" to "Henry V,"* pp. 10-29. Berkeley and Los Angeles: University of California Press, 1979.

> Maintains that a major concern in *Richard II* is "the fall of speech." The critic finds in the breakdown of traditional symbolism, particularly as it applies to language, a parallel to the cataclysmic political upheaval set in motion by Bolingbroke's coup. He further implies that Shakespeare, as a poet and dramatist himself, experienced the sort of confusion regarding metaphor and its relation to reality that he depicts in the character of Richard.

Campbell, Lily B. "An Introduction into the Division Between Lancaster and York." In her *Shakespeare's "Histories": Mirrors of Elizabethan Policy*, pp. 168-212. Los Angeles: The Ward Ritchie Press, 1947.

> Maintains that sixteenth-century Englishmen regarded history in general as a kind of political mirror, offering relevant lessons for their own times. Campbell notes that Elizabethans would have recognized many similarities between the reigns of Richard II and Queen Elizabeth. In support of this assumption, the critic examines several highly controversial pamphlets and plays on the subject of the deposed Richard and traces their influence on the ill-starred career of the Earl of Essex.

Cauthen, I. B., Jr. "*Richard II* and the Image of the Betrayed Christ." In *Renaissance Papers: A Selection of Papers Presented at the Renaissance Meeting in the Southeastern States, Duke University, April 23-4, 1954*, edited by Allan H. Gilbert, pp. 45-8. Columbia, S.C.: University of South Carolina Press, 1954.

> Examines Richard's references to Jesus, Judas, and Pilate throughout Shakespeare's play. While admitting that the king's identifying himself with Christ "is not a completely just comparison," Cauthen writes that it "invests the play with a sombre aura" and leads the audience "to think of Richard not simply as a bad king but also as a king whose deposition parallels an event of far greater significance to mankind."

Chambers, E. K. "*Richard the Second*." In his *William Shakespeare: A Study of Facts and Problems*, pp. 348-56. Oxford: Clarendon Press, 1930.

> Presents verbatim titles of the early editions of the play, with information about its sources, date, and textual difficulties. Chambers also briefly discusses a number of possible contemporary references to *Richard II*, including the Hoby letter of 1595 (see excerpt above).

Champion, Larry S. "History as Tragedy: *Richard III, Richard II*." In his *Perspectives on Shakespeare's English Histories*, pp. 54-91. Athens: The University of Georgia Press, 1980.

> Identifies the various literary models which might have helped Shakespeare develop the form of his historical tragedies. Champion also discerns evidence in *Richard II* of a movement in the dramatist's art toward greater focus on character, and he discusses how the expository techniques in this play differ from those of *Richard III*.

Clemen, Wolfgang. "*Richard II*." In his *The Development of Shakespeare's Imagery*, pp. 53-62. London: Methuen and Co., 1951.

> Argues that imagery must be related to elements in *Richard II*, such as character, situation, and setting, rather than examined in isolation. Clemen maintains that the tenor of the imagery in this history enhances its thoughtful mood, that the king's peculiar use of visual language helps to vitalize his character, and that symbolism frequently underlies the imagery in the play, particularly in the allegorical garden scene of Act III.

————. "Shakespeare's Art of Preparation: *Richard II*." In his *Shakespeare's Dramatic Art: Collected Essays*, pp. 31-7. London: Methuen and Co., 1972.

> Demonstrates how *Richard II* contributed to Shakespeare's development as a dramatist. Clemen compares this play with earlier Shakespearean works and argues that it reveals its author's more sophisticated handling of plot development and characterization. He further observes that by the time *Richard II* was written, Shakespeare's skill as a dramatist had "become altogether more subtle and indirect, being more than in the previous histories linked up with imaginative vision, subjective foreboding and poetic anticipation."

Cowan, Louise. "God Will Save the King: Shakespeare's *Richard II*." In *Shakespeare as Political Thinker*, edited by John Alvis and Thomas G. West, pp. 63-81. Durham, N.C.: Carolina Academic Press, 1981.

> Focuses on individuals rather than the political issues in *Richard II*, suggesting that the play's universal appeal derives from Richard's experiences in "that realm where humanity confronts the mystery of the divine order." Cowan argues that although the subject matter of the play "is the politics of statecraft ..., its central concern seems to lie with human destiny itself, touching upon metaphysical and spiritual regions that far transcend the political."

Craig, Hardin. "*Richard II*." In his *An Interpretation of Shakespeare*, pp. 124-36. New York: The Citadel Press, 1948.

> Contends that Shakespeare wrote *Richard II* in part as a response to Marlowe's *Edward II*. Craig points out certain passages in Shakespeare's text which, though obscure for modern audiences, would have been common literary material for Elizabethans familiar with the works of Marlowe. On other matters, Craig develops a view of the king and Bolingbroke as "opposite and irreconcilable forces."

Cutts, John P. *"Richard II."* In his *The Shattered Glass: A Dramatic Pattern in Shakespeare's Early Plays*, pp. 135-53. Detroit: Wayne State University Press, 1968.

Focuses on the mirror incident during Richard's abdication in Act IV, Scene i and suggests that in breaking the glass, the king recognizes the fragmentation of his own personality.

Davies, Thomas. *"King Richard II."* In his *Dramatic Miscellanies*. 1784. Reprint. New York: Benjamin Blom, 1971, 310 p.

Disparages *Richard II* as an inferior, apprentice piece in Shakespeare's canon. Davies expresses annoyance with the dramatist's "predilection" for "quibble and conceit," though he concedes that the plot contains elements of greatness. Davies's chapter also contains a disquisition upon the nature of tragedy and the critic's claim that *Richard II* was still regarded as dangerously seditious some two-hundred years after it was written.

Dillon, Janette. *"'This Prison Where I Live': Richard II."* In her *Shakespeare and the Solitary Man*. pp. 61-76. Totowa, N.J.: Rowman and Littlefield, 1981.

Proposes that Shakespeare's attitude toward solitary individuals gradually changed during his career, from a basically medieval stance that isolation, being "a separation of the self from the wider human context," is undesirable, to an increasing sympathy with individuality and introspection. According to Dillon, however, Richard II's "preoccupation with his own private world results in his political downfall," and Shakespeare, "despite his increased sympathy for ... solitude," shows in this early play that "disengagement from social concerns and devotion to the self" lead "inexorably towards death."

Doran, Madeleine. "Imagery in 'Richard II' and 'Henry IV'." *The Modern Language Review* XXXVII, No. 2 (April 1942): 113-22.

Assesses the development of Shakespeare's imagery by comparing its function in two history plays. Doran contends that in *Richard II* images "tend to be direct or explicit, complete, correspondent, point by point, to the idea symbolized, and separate from one another; whereas the images in *1 Henry IV* tend to be richer in implicit suggestion and in ambiguity, not fully developed, fluid in outline and fused with one another."

Dorius, R. J. "A Little More than a Little." *Shakespeare Quarterly* XI, No. 1 (Winter 1960): 13-26.

Examines *Richard II*'s connection to the other plays in the Lancastrian tetralogy. Focusing on the recurring allusions to "carelessness, excess, waste, and disease"—an image-pattern common to each play in this tetralogy—Dorius contends that *Richard II* illustrates "a kind of Aristotelean norm" between extravagance and barrenness, "an ideal of moderation or equilibrium among opposing forces." Especially apropos is the allegorical garden scene (Act III, Scene iv) in which the careful cultivator of the flower beds contrasts his methods of husbandry with the negligent political practices of King Richard.

Draper, John W. "The Character of Richard II." *Philological Quarterly* XXI, No. 2 (April 1942): 228-36.

Illuminates certain apparent inconsistencies and contradictions in Richard's personality by reference to the sixteenth-century physiological theory of "humours." According to this system, a person's moods and temperament are determined by the presence of various fluids—blood, phlegm, yellow bile, and black bile—in the body; an excess of one or the other makes a man joyful, angry, lethargic, or melancholy by nature. Draper suggests that while modern readers are sometimes confused by Richard's unpredictable, volatile behavior, an Elizabethan audience, familiar with the concept of humours, would immediately diagnose him as an example of the "mercurial" type—that is, an individual in whom the balance of humours is in a constant state of flux.

Duthie, George Ian. "History." In his *Shakespeare*, pp. 115-56. London: Hutchinson's University Library, 1951.

Examines *Richard II* in light of the Elizabethan political climate. Duthie argues that the principal theme in all Shakespeare's histories is "the nature of the ideal king," adding that the two tetralogies dramatize both the disorder brought about by a ne-

glectful ruler and the subsequent civil strife caused by Bolingbroke's usurpation of the throne in "an attempt to cure this disorder." Duthie also discusses the numerous prophesies of disaster in *Richard II* consequent to Bolingbroke's usurpation, noting how these foreshadowings link this history to the later plays in the series.

Elliott, John R., Jr. "History and Tragedy in *Richard II*." *Studies in English Literature 1500-1900* VIII, No. 2 (Spring 1968): 253-71.

Explores Shakespeare's departures from his sources in order to define the differences between historical drama and tragedy. Elliott classifies *Richard II* as a "political play" but notes elements of tragedy in the protagonist's failure to understand properly the role and function of king.

Ellis-Fermor, Una. "Shakespeare's Political Plays." In her *The Frontiers of Drama*, pp. 34-55. London: Methuen and Co., 1964.

Stresses the importance of viewing *Richard II* as part of a monumental tetralogy extending through *1* and *2 Henry IV* and *Henry V*. Ellis-Fermor contends that one of Shakespeare's primary aims in writing his historical epic was to formulate a definition of the ideal statesman-king, a "composite-figure" which he "builds up gradually through the series of political plays. . . ." Clearly, she maintains, Richard II falls far short of such an ideal, but his very limitations contribute to the refinement of Shakespeare's final image of what qualities an English monarch should possess.

Farnham, Willard. "The Establishment of Tragedy upon the Elizabethan Stage (Continued)." In his *The Medieval Heritage of Elizabethan Tragedy*, pp. 368-421. Oxford: Basil Blackwell, 1956.

Relates *Richard II* to the literary sources of sixteenth-century historical drama, such as *The Fall of Princes* and *The Mirror for Magistrates*, with special reference to Shakespeare's dependence upon, and occasional departures from, the *de casibus* tradition. Farnham also notes that the brand of *contemptus mundi* displayed by Richard in the extremity of his crisis is merely "the hopeless bitterness of a broken man," and not the spiritual resignation and trust advocated by medieval mystics and theologians.

French, A. L. *"Richard II* and the Woodstock Murder." *Shakespeare Quarterly* XXII, No. 4 (Autumn 1971): 337-44.

Supports the idea that "the murder of Thomas of Woodstock, Duke of Gloucester, is a central issue in Shakespeare's play." French pursues this thread through the quarrel between Bolingbroke and Mowbray, Richard's confiscation of the Lancastrian estates, Bolingbroke's return from exile, and the king's subsequent fall from power, agreeing in conclusion with A. P. Rossiter that *Richard II* is largely unintelligible without reference to the anonymous play *Woodstock* (see excerpt above, 1961).

Friedman, Donald M. "John of Gaunt and the Rhetoric of Frustration." *ELH* 43, No. 3 (Fall 1976): 279-99.

A revisionist evaluation of John of Gaunt's famous "sceptr'd isle" paean to England (II. i. 40-60)—a speech, according to the critic, that is often uncritically accepted as an expression of conservative orthodoxy. Friedman questions the extent to which Shakespeare's histories "were intended as dramatic illustrations of . . . Tudor political doctrine," suggesting that the dramatist seldom presents "a spokesman for a political or moral viewpoint without asking us to evaluate the spokesman as well as the viewpoint." He maintains that Gaunt in this speech is not a disinterested patriot, but a spokesman for the feudal nobility, more concerned with his own property rights and family honor than with nationalistic ideals.

Frye, Northrop. "The Bolingbroke Plays (*Richard II, Henry IV*)." In his *Northrop Frye on Shakespeare*, edited by Robert Sandler, pp. 51-81. New Haven and London: Yale University Press, 1986.

Detects in Shakespeare's histories some degree of fidelity to their medieval sources and loyalty, with reservations, to the Tudor "mystique of royalty." Frye assesses the role of the noble barons during the Middle Ages but holds that the dramatist's real interest in *Richard II* lies with the office and character of the king. He defends Bolingbroke's Machiavellian tendencies, stating that "a successful leader doesn't get hung up on moral principles: the place for moral principles is in what we'd call now the PR job."

Nevertheless, Frye maintains, *Richard II* ends on a morally ambiguous note which emphasizes the fragility of "the world of history."

Gaudet, Paul. "The 'Parasitical' Counselors in Shakespeare's *Richard II*: A Problem in Dramatic Interpretation." *Shakespeare Quarterly* XXXIII, No. 2 (Summer 1982): 142-54.

Reexamines the knights Bushy, Bagot, and Greene, referred to by Bolingbroke as "caterpillars of the commonwealth" (II. iii. 166) and generally regarded by critics as villainous characters who corrupt and exploit Richard. Gaudet argues that such definitive condemnation is not justified by a close reading of the play's actual text. He reviews the "commonly accepted view" of the favorites which Raphael Holinshed and the anonymous drama *Woodstock* disseminated, then contrasts Shakespeare's treatment of them in his history, concluding that the far more complex and less vicious portraits one finds in *Richard II* indicate the dramatist's "ambivalent" response to the historical situation.

Goddard, Harold C. "*Richard II.*" In his *The Meaning of Shakespeare*, pp. 148-60. Chicago: University of Chicago Press, 1951.

Combines critical commentary with a brief plot synopsis. Goddard regards Richard II as an immature, poetic man who is "hopelessly miscast for the role of king," but who—unlike Henry IV—does not have "the sense to realize his limitations," and hence "makes a mess of the kingdom and himself."

Harris, Kathryn Montgomery. "Sun and Water Imagery in *Richard II*: Its Dramatic Function." *Shakespeare Quarterly* XXI, No. 2 (Spring 1970): 157-65.

Demonstrates how the references to "sun" and "water" in *Richard II* help to enrich the characterizations of the king and Bolingbroke. Harris adds that these images also convey a sense of Richard and Bolingbroke's mutual opposition, their falling and rising fortunes, and transmute "political events into personal tragedy."

Hasker, Richard E. "The Copy for the First Folio of *Richard II.*" In *Studies in Bibliography*, edited by Fredson Bowers, pp. 53-72. Charlottesville: Bibliographical Society of the University of Virginia, 1952.

Argues "that the copy for the Folio was an exemplum of Q3 containing some leaves from a copy of Q5." Hasker addresses a number of textual problems in *Richard II* and presents information about sixteenth-century publishing procedures, the practices of Elizabethan compositors, and the probable use by Shakespeare's theatrical company of annotated quartos for prompt-books at the Globe.

Heninger, S. K., Jr. "The Sun-King Analogy in *Richard II.*" *Shakespeare Quarterly* XI, No. 3 (Summer 1960): 319-27.

Focuses on the "tension between actual and ideal" in Shakespeare's depiction of kingship in *Richard II*, arguing that the dramatist establishes a cosmological, ideal context with which to judge the actions of both Richard and Bolingbroke in the play. Heninger examines in detail the two ways in which this context is created: first, "by the addition of fictional scenes to the historical accounts" Shakespeare found in his sources; and second, by "cosmological imagery," which, for example, relates the king to the sun and the commonwealth to the Garden of Eden.

Hexter, J. H. "Property, Monopoly, and Shakespeare's *Richard II.*" In *Culture and Politics from Puritanism to the Enlightenment*, edited by Perez Zagorin, pp. 1-23. Berkeley and Los Angeles: University of California Press, 1980.

Hypothesizes that Bolingbroke's motivation in *Richard II* is intimately related to the idea that a subject's worldly goods are protected by law against the encroachments of even a monarch. Hexter argues that an Elizabethan audience would not respond favorably to Bolingbroke "as an armed Paladin for justice to all Englishmen," but would sympathize with him and support him "as a man seeking to vindicate his property rights."

Hockey, Dorothy C. "A World of Rhetoric in *Richard II.*" *Shakespeare Quarterly* XV, No. 3 (Summer 1964): 179-91.

Offers a technical analysis of medieval and Renaissance oratory to dispute the claim that Richard's characteristic speech patterns are significantly different from those of the other characters in the play.

Hunter, Edwin R. "Shakspere's Intentions Regarding King Richard II." In his *Shakspere and Common Sense*, pp. 31-48. Boston: The Christopher Publishing House, 1954.

Emphasizes the grotesque, embarrassing quality of Richard's self-dramatization. Hunter maintains that even the king's final soliloquy is "simply" an exercise in "the old rhetorical flair," and he concludes that Shakespeare "does not expect [Richard] to be taken as contemptible or vulgar, but as ineffectual." He adds that "in developing this complexity of character Shakespeare projects situations which come dangerously close to the ridiculous."

Kastan, David Scott. "Proud Majesty Made a Subject: Shakespeare and the Spectacle of Rule." *Shakespeare Quarterly* 37, No. 4 (Winter 1986): 459-75.

Demonstrates why *Richard II* was regarded as seditious and dangerous by Elizabethan authorities. According to Kastan, the censors felt that the spectacle of monarchs in the theater resulted in a demystification of the ruling powers, effectively making the audience "the ultimate source of authority in its willingness to credit and approve the representation of rule."

Kelly, Henry Ansgar. "Shakespeare's Double Tetralogy: *Richard II.*" In his *Divine Providence in the England of Shakespeare's Histories*, pp. 203-14. Cambridge: Harvard University Press, 1970.

Observes that Shakespeare provides implicit points of view in his histories, although he abstains from the sort of editorial commentary which characterized the medieval chronicles, except when an occasional choric figure speaks. One issue treated thus by the dramatist, according to Kelly, is the role of Providence in the affairs of men; he concludes that, in spite of *Richard II*'s many references to guilt, dire prophesies, and retribution, Shakespeare minimizes the importance of divine will, instead placing responsibility for human action squarely on the shoulders of the concerned individuals themselves.

Kelly, Michael F. "The Function of York in *Richard II.*" *Southern Humanities Review* 6, No. 3 (Summer 1972): 257-67.

Postulates that the role of York is far more important to the plot of *Richard II* than is generally realized. Kelly underscores the Duke's pivotal position in the transfer of power from Richard to Bolingbroke and emphasizes his importance as a guide to audience response, in that he articulates and directs increased sympathy toward the deposed monarch. He claims that York provides significant insights into the history's complexities and into Shakespeare's dramatic techniques as well.

Kliger, Samuel. "The Sun Imagery in *Richard II.*" *Studies in Philology* XLV, No. 2 (April 1948): 196-202.

Provides "a sustained analysis" of the imagery in *Richard II*—the many references to "golden beams," "light," "summer's heat," "the searching eye of heaven," and so forth—and demonstrates that metaphorical language is "different in tragedy from that found in comedy, and both different from that in lyric, non-dramatic poetry." Kliger, in other words, explains these "images and their function within the organic scheme of the play."

Knight, G. Wilson. "The Prophetic Soul: A Note on *Richard II*, V. v. 1-66." In his *The Imperial Theme: Further Interpretations of Shakespeare's Tragedies, Including the Roman Plays*, pp. 351-67. London: Oxford University Press, 1931.

Discerns in Richard's Pomfret Castle soliloquy a state of mind analogous to that associated with lyric impulses by Wordsworth and Keats, a "creative consciousness which gives birth to poetry." Knight, however, claims that "in *Richard II* we find the usual Shakespearean dualism of the individual soul's quest . . . and the ambitions or calls of world-glory, empire, [and] state-order," suggesting that although Richard, in his solitary musings, has experienced the consciousness of "beauty and truth," he is fit only "for tragedy and death, . . . not for the duties of life."

Thus, according to Knight, "the fallacy of a purely individualistic mysticism is exposed."

Knights, L. C. "Shakespeare: Four Histories." In his *Explorations 3*, pp. 157-86. Pittsburgh: University of Pittsburgh Press, 1976.

Asserts that *Richard II* "is a political play with a difference," the point of which is to show "how power—hardly conscious of its own intentions until the event fulfils them—must necessarily fill a vacuum caused by the withdrawal of power." Knights's focus is on the character of Richard, "an egotist who, like egotists in humbler spheres, constructs an unreal world that finally collapses about him." He suggests that the king's behavior when confronted by his assassins is not, as some critics have maintained, a sign of new-found, uncharacteristic valor, but rather Richard's final expression of frustration that the life he had imagined to be heroic and glorious ends in a thoroughly "brutal," prosaic fashion.

LaGuardia, Eric. "Ceremony and History: The Problem of Symbol from *Richard II* to *Henry V*." In *Pacific Coast Studies in Shakespeare*, edited by Waldo F. McNeir and Thelma N. Greenfield, pp. 68-88. Eugene: University of Oregon Books, 1966.

Discerns in *Richard II* a conflict between the ritualistic, ceremonious world of the king and the existential, political world of Bolingbroke, noting Shakespeare's irony in simultaneously presenting both the good and unfortunate aspects of the transition from one world to the other. LaGuardia also explains the significance of words in the play as the primary illuminators of symbol, adding that Richard's tragedy arises from his confusion about the differences between literal and symbolic kingship.

Logan, George M. "Lucan—Daniel—Shakespeare: New Light on the Relation Between *The Civil Wars* and *Richard II*." *Shakespeare Studies* IX (1976): 121-40.

Examines the relationship between Samuel Daniel's epic poem *The Civil Wars* and Shakespeare's history play. Logan contends that the dramatist was endebted to the poet—not vice versa, as some critics have claimed—and that Daniel derived some passages in his poem from the *Pharsalia* by Lucan—a work which, presumably, was not read in the original Latin by Shakespeare, but which was translated in Daniel's work and then revised by Shakespeare for inclusion in his own *Richard II*.

MacIsaac, Warren J. "The Three Cousins in *Richard II*." *Shakespeare Quarterly* XXII, No. 2 (Spring 1971): 137-46.

States that the complex, shifting interrelationships between Richard and his cousins Bolingbroke and Aumerle embody several important themes in the play and propel the dramatic action forward.

Mack, Maynard, Jr. "This Royal Throne Unkinged." In his *Killing the King: Three Studies in Shakespeare's Tragic Structure*, pp. 15-74. New Haven and London: York University Press, 1973.

Interprets *Richard II* as a struggle between political philosophies: the "old order" articulated by Gaunt and represented by the king, even though he abuses it, and Bolingbroke's order, based on self-interest, realism, expediency, and efficiency. Although Mack stresses the enormity of any act of usurpation which would defy a divinely ordered hierarchical structure, he observes that Shakespeare presents both the good and the bad aspects of each of the warring antagonists, thus endowing the play with a richness of irony and ambiguity.

MacKenzie, Clayton G. "Paradise and Paradise Lost in *Richard II*." *Shakespeare Quarterly* 37, No. 3 (Autumn 1986): 318-39.

Inquires into the significance of the frequent references in *Richard II* to Pardise, Eden, and the garden. MacKenzie details "the ways in which *Richard II* develops and expands" the linguistic figures of "a central mythology of an English transgression and a paradise lost" that was current in Elizabethan times and presumably a factor in the response of Shakespeare's audiences to the events depicted in this history.

Manheim, Michael. "Of Strong Kings and Weak" and "The Wanton King." In his *The Weak King Dilemma in the Shakespearean History Play*, pp. 1-14, 15-75. Syracuse, N.Y.: Syracuse University Press, 1973.

Suggests that *Richard II* and other English chronicle dramas of the same period may be seen as attempts to explore, if not to resolve, certain crucial Elizabethan questions about the nature of good government and the art of politics. Comparing *Richard II* with *Woodstock* and Marlowe's *Edward II*, Manheim notes that all three works wrestle with the "inevitable frustrations and contradictions associated with the royal image." Richard, according to the critic, is a ruler who excites both antagonism and sympathy; "frivolous, whimsical, and lazy" at first, he is nevertheless not without sensitivity and intelligence, and finally reveals "some signs of new self-awareness."

Marriott, J.A.R. "Richard the 'Redeless'—The Amateur in Politics." In his *English History in Shakespeare*, pp. 59-94. New York: E. P. Dutton and Co., 1918.

Presents material on the historical background of *Richard II*, concentrating in particular on the character of the king. Marriott also discusses the date of the play and its place in the Shakespeare canon, describing it as "very unequal in quality," a work which displays both "matchless beauty but also immaturity."

Maveety, Stanley R. "A Second Fall of Cursed Man: The Bold Metaphor in *Richard II*." *Journal of English and Germanic Philology* LXXII, No. 2 (April 1973): 175-93.

Examines the dominant image-patterns in *Richard II*—those of exile, blood, false speech, the serpent, and "a large sprawling, complex image" of gardening, earth, fertility, birth, and inheritance. Maveety contends that Shakespeare wrote his history "with the first narratives of Genesis in mind." Noting the parallels in *Richard II* with "the stories of Cain and Abel, of Adam, Eve, and the Garden of Eden," the critic asserts that all of these allusions and images are "subordinate parts of a single image-complex"—namely, the second fall of humankind, reenacted through the "flawed characters of Richard and Bolingbroke." Maveety thus takes issue with Richard D. Altick (see excerpt above, 1947), who maintained that although *Richard II* is rich in complex, interrelated images, it lacks just such a "single bold" unifying metaphor.

Montgomery, Robert L., Jr. "The Dimensions of Time in *Richard II*." *Shakespeare Studies* IV (1968): 73-85.

Argues that in *Richard II* time does more than "indicate mere duration." Montgomery concentrates on the surprisingly numerous references to days, weeks, seasons, years, and so on, to demonstrate that "the imagery of time . . . is expressive of subjective feeling; it involves the broad theme of natural rhythm; and it provides the terms for Richard's assessment of himself as well as for our assessment of him." The critic adds that "it expresses finally, for Richard and the audience, a way of distinguishing timeliness . . . from opportunism, a principle evident in Richard's failure to achieve it." Montgomery thus maintains that the king, before his death, achieves "a state approaching repentance and resolution," to the extent that he passes beyond self-pity and recognizes his failure to uphold "natural and political order."

Ornstein, Robert. "*Richard II*." In his *A Kingdom for a Stage: The Achievement of Shakespeare's History Plays*, pp. 102-24. Cambridge: Harvard University Press, 1972.

Examines the medieval elements in *Richard II* to challenge the notion that Shakespeare depicts "England under Richard as a prelapsarian paradise, a world of order and harmony that was to be destroyed by a primal sin of disobedience." Ornstein describes the king as a being more pathetic than tragic, whose folly—as well as the hypocrisy of his enemies—brought disorder to the realm. He further suggests that, in this history, Shakespeare provides no solutions to the issues raised, but only shows the enormous difficulty of the problems inherent in a complex political situation.

Palmer, John. "Richard of Bordeaux." In his *Political Characters of Shakespeare*, pp. 118-79. London: Macmillan and Co., 1945.

Declares that for all Shakespeare's concern with public issues, his primary interest as a dramatist was with private passions and personal convictions. Palmer contends that Richard II, like Hamlet, is in a situation ill-suited to his "wayward and introspective" temperament, and he adds that although Shakespeare is to a remarkable degree immune to political bias, he often seems to display more empathy for failed people than successful ones—a predilection which may have contributed to his sympathetic portrayal of the fallen Richard.

Phialas, Peter G. "The Medieval in *Richard II.*" *Shakespeare Quarterly* XII, No. 3 (Summer 1961): 305-10.

> Rebuts E.M.W. Tillyard's theory that *Richard II* is Shakespeare's nostalgic recreation of the Middle Ages, with the king and his court representing chivalry and medieval ceremony (see excerpt above, 1944). Instead, Phialas contends that "the contrast established in the play is not between life during Richard's reign and that of the Tudors; the contrast is between Richard's enfeebled and devitalized England on the one hand and, on the other, England's national strength and international prestige during the reign of Richard's ancestors."

Pollard, Alfred. Introduction to *King Richard II: A New Quarto,* pp. 5-102. London: Bernard Quaritch, 1916.

> Addresses, in an introduction which precedes a facsimile of the 1598 edition of *Richard II,* the play's textual problems and its history in print, by comparing variant readings from the early quartos and the Folio. Pollard discusses the challenges that Shakespearean bibliographical scholars in general face, as he hypothesizes "what happened" to the scripts of the plays "from the moment when Shakespeare handed over his copy to the Players."

Potter, Lois. "The Antic Disposition of Richard II." *Shakespeare Survey* 27 (1974): 33-41.

> Postulates that the king is far more disingenuous than is often suspected, observing in his behavior during the abdication scene a deliberately orchestrated scenario designed to cast a pall over the entirety of Bolingbroke's reign.

Prior, Moody E. *The Drama of Power.* Evanston, Ill.: Northwestern University Press, 1973, 410 p.

> In three separate chapters, Prior reviews the criteria used to divide the tetralogies into various groups: chronological sequence of events, order of composition, theme, treatment of the protagonist, and so forth. He then follows the thread of the *de casibus* tradition through *Richard II* and contrasts medieval mysticism with Shakespeare's commonsense attitude toward human nature and the realities of politics. Unlike many critics, Prior concludes that Richard's growing self-knowledge nearly brings him to the point of heroism.

Provost, Foster. "The Sorrows of Shakespeare's Richard II." In *Studies in English Renaissance Literature,* edited by Waldo F. McNeir, pp. 40-55. Baton Rouge: Louisiana State University Press, 1962.

> Disputes the idea that the character of the king in *Richard II* lacks unity or that Shakespeare never "had a firm concept" of what kind of man he was. Provost finds consistency in Richard's "compulsive desire for mental comfort at any cost"—a weakness that leads him to reject "anything which interferes with his pleasant dreams," blinds him to the demands of justice or good policy, and explains his well-known proclivity for tears and tantrums.

Ranald, Margaret Loftus. "The Degradation of Richard II: An Inquiry into the Ritual Backgrounds." *English Literary Renaissance* 7, No. 2 (Spring 1977): 170-96.

> Surveys elements of traditional chivalric, military, and ecclesiastical degradation ceremonies, chronicle reports, Biblical and homiletic allusions, and famous historical cases of knightly or clerical disgrace which may have influenced the deposition scene in *Richard II.*

Reed, Robert R., Jr. "Richard II: Portrait of a Psychotic." *Journal of General Education* 16, No. 1 (April 1964): 55-67.

> Explains Richard's chronic indecision and hesitancy—behavior not accounted for in the chronicles—through psychoanalysis, diagnosing the king as a masochist suffering from "ungratified libido tension" which ultimately manifests itself as a death wish.

Reese, M. M. "*Richard II.*" In his *The Cease of Majesty: A Study of Shakespeare's History Plays,* pp. 225-60. London: Edward Arnold, 1961.

> Modifies E. M. W. Tillyard's conception of Shakespeare as a defender of Tudor orthodoxy (see excerpt above, 1944). Although Reese detects reservations in *Richard II*'s endorsement of Bolingbroke, the play never underestimates, in his view, the extent of the king's culpable folly and misgovernment. In addition to the above commentary, Reese offers a history of *Richard II* in performance.

Reiman, Donald H. "Appearance, Reality, and Moral Order in *Richard II.*" *Modern Language Quarterly* XXV, No. 1 (March 1964): 34-45.

> Contends that almost all the major characters in *Richard II,* with the exception of York, habitually dissemble, substituting "formal rhetoric and external symbolic action for sincerity." Richard alone, the critic asserts, eventually breaks this pattern and recognizes that words cannot substitute for true feeling; according to Reiman, the king thus learns "his place in the human community and the moral difference between appearance and reality."

Ribner, Irving. "Shakespeare's Second Tetralogy." In his *The English History Play in the Age of Shakespeare,* pp. 151-303. London: Methuen and Co., 1965.

> Places Shakespeare's epic drama of the internecine struggle between the Houses of York and Lancaster in the context of Elizabethan political attitudes and theatrical practice. Ribner detects in *Richard II* elements of medieval morality tradition as well as echoes from several chronicle accounts of Richard's fall and Bolingbroke's rise. He argues that the result of Shakespeare's eclectic researches was not a confident reaffirmation of divine-right monarchy, but an ambivalent response that delineates "various royal types" and indicates the qualities of the perfect English king"— a response marked by irony and a questioning, skeptical tone.

Richmond, H. M. "*Richard II.*" In his *Shakespeare's Political Plays,* pp. 123-40. New York: Random House, 1967.

> Argues that Shakespeare's histories are "calculatedly political" and offers an analysis of *Richard II* that is sympathetic to the king and critical of Bolingbroke, whom Richmond calls "a ruthless manipulator." The critic concludes that the play presents an account of the "decline from the primal innocence of the ideal Medieval society to a Machiavellian pragmatism in the modern vein."

Rossiter, A. P., ed. *Woodstock: A Moral History.* London: Chatto and Windus, 1946, 255 p.

> The definitive edition of the anonymous play that is widely regarded as a source for Shakespeare's *Richard II.* Rossiter has elsewhere argued that Shakespeare assumed familiarity with *Woodstock* among his spectators and hence left much background material unexplained in his own work (see excerpt above, 1961).

Sanders, Wilbur. "Shakespeare's Political Agnosticism: *Richard II.*" In his *The Dramatist and the Received Idea: Studies in the Plays of Marlowe and Shakespeare,* pp. 158-93. Cambridge: At the University Press, 1968.

> Asserts that justice in *Richard II* is elusive and mystifying and that Shakespeare's obfuscation of the Gloucester affair was a deliberate attempt to "establish . . . the moral impenetrability of the political order." Sanders maintains that the "tasks of balancing Richard II's kingly rights against Bolingbroke's neglected duty become extremely problematical," and he quotes D. H. Lawrence's remark that "it takes two people to make a murder: a murderer and a murderee"—that is, "a man who in a profound if hidden lust desires to be murdered." In this light, Sanders suggests, Richard, in many ways is an accomplice in his own destruction.

Schoenbaum, S. "*Richard II* and the Realities of Power." *Shakespeare Survey* 28 (1975): 1-13.

> Demonstrates that in *Richard II* "Shakespeare treats in a most sophisticated way the manipulation of power in a poker game where the stakes are exceedingly high." Schoenbaum reviews the

early history of the play in performance and print to underscore its controversial topicality for Elizabethans. He suggests that *Richard II* reveals Shakespeare's intense interest in politics but scorns the idea that the dramatist was regarded by Queen Elizabeth and her court as "a sort of minister without portfolio."

Scott-Giles, C. W. "*King Richard II.*" In his *Shakespeare's Heraldry*, pp. 56-83. London: J. M. Dent and Sons, 1950.

Offers illustrations of various shields, helmets, and coats of arms used by Richard II and suggests that Shakespeare's familiarity with such heraldic devices can be inferred from certain lines in his play. Thus, according to Scott-Giles, when the groom at V. v. 99 declares, "What my tongue dares not, that my heart shall say," he might be construed to be making a pun in reference to the deer ("hart") embroidered on the livery of Richard's servants.

Shapiro, I. A. "*Richard II* or *Richard III* or . . .?" *Shakespeare Quarterly* IX, No. 2 (Spring 1958): 204-06.

Disputes E. K. Chambers's claim that Sir Edward Hoby's letter of 1595 necessarily alludes to the private performance of a Shakespearean play (see entry above). Shapiro avers that dating *Richard II* on the basis of this "reference" is accordingly unjustified.

Simpson, Richard. "The Politics of Shakspere's Historical Plays." *The New Shakspere Society Transactions*, Series 1, No. 1 (1874): 396-441.

Speculates whether *Richard II* contains topical allusions and general political commentary and whether Shakespeare's position on such matters as the church and the nobility may be inferred from his characterizations in this play.

Smidt, Kristian. "King Richard's Guilt and the Poetry of Kingship." In her *Unconformities in Shakespeare's History Plays*, pp. 86-102. Atlantic Highlands, N.J.: Humanities Press, 1982.

Discusses a number of apparent technical weaknesses in *Richard II*, including "extensive passages of rhymed couplets . . . which on the whole are inferior in style to the blank verse" sections; "substantial contradictions" in scenes involving Bolingbroke, Gaunt, and Aumerle; "confusions and omissions," such as the strange itinerary of Bagot; and "a major problem of composition," namely, Shakespeare's handling of the Gloucester murder, a plot element that is introduced and then allowed to atrophy. Smidt concludes that the dramatist "began to write an historical revenge tragedy based on a murder" in rhymed verse, then changed his plan in the course of composition to concentrate on the rivalry of Richard and Bolingbroke. She suggests that the text as it exists today includes many revisions and apparently few authorial deletions.

Smith, Hallett. "The Poetry of the Lyric Group: *Richard II, Romeo and Juliet, A Midsummer Night's Dream*." In *Shakespeare's Craft/Eight Lectures*, edited by Philip H. Highfill, Jr., pp. 69-93. Carbondale and Edwardsville: Southern Illinois University Press, 1982.

Draws attention to the similarities in style between *Richard II* and other early Shakespearean comedies and tragedies, on the one hand, and with the works of Christopher Marlowe, on the other. Smith also reminds us that Richard II, as a poet, is not unique: all the characters in the play, he asserts, expound in lyric phrases.

Soellner, Rolf. "*Richard II:* Looking into the Mirror of Grief." In his *Shakespeare's Patterns of Self-Knowledge*, pp. 97-112. Columbus: Ohio State University Press, 1972.

Elucidates Richard's moral development in terms of various medieval and Renaissance traditions, including those of *de casibus* and *specula principis*. Soellner further discusses a number of writers—among them Thomas Elyot, Pope Innocent, and Levinus Lemnius—who may have indirectly influenced Shakespeare's thought.

Speaight, Robert. "Shakespeare and the Political Spectrum: As Illustrated by *Richard II*." In *Stratford Papers on Shakespeare*, edited by B. W. Jackson, pp. 135-54. Toronto: W. J. Gage, 1965.

Discerns in *Richard II* an opposition of two kinds of authority—that of a legitimately invested divine-right monarch, on the one hand, and of a capable, popularly supported usurper, on the other—

to contend that this, "Shakespeare's picture of how politics work," reveals its author's attitudes on such issues as kingship, practical administration, and the fickleness of the mob.

Suzman, Arthur. "Imagery and Symbolism in *Richard II*." *Shakespeare Quarterly* VII, No. 4 (Autumn 1956): 355-70.

Concentrates on the "rising and falling" pattern of images in *Richard II*. Suzman offers evidence that these images reinforce the theme of Richard's decline and Bolingbroke's ascendancy.

Talbert, Ernest William. "*King John, Romeo and Juliet, Richard II*." In his *Elizabethan Drama and Shakespeare's Early Plays: An Essay in Historical Criticism*, pp. 262-322. New York: Gordian Press, 1973.

Examines the narrative structure of *Richard II*, discovering three distinct points of view in the play: "an anti-Richard one" from Act I, Scene i through Act II, Scene i; "an equivocal one" from Act III, Scene ii through Act IV; and "a pro-Richard one" in Act V. Although Talbert emphasizes the ambiguity which arises from these conflicting perspectives, he notes that certain themes do emerge unequivocally out of the action, among them "that the gravest disorder occurs when a ruler does not act like a king, when he forgets his duty and the love that should exist between ruler and ruled."

——. "Shakespeare's Deposition of Richard II." In his *The Problem of Order: Elizabethan Political Commonplaces and an Example of Shakespeare's Art*, pp. 146-200. Chapel Hill: The University of North Carolina Press, 1962.

Investigates the early quartos of *Richard II* and speculates on why the abdication scene was suppressed in these editions. Talbert then carefully examines this episode and the Flint Castle confrontation for evidence of Elizabethan attitudes toward politics, psychology, and history, concluding that Shakespeare intentionally maintains a highly equivocal stance with regard to the play's political and philosophical issues—so much so, according to the critic, that *Richard II* could justifiably be called a "problem play."

Thayer, C. G. "The Death of Divine Kingship: *Richard II*." In his *Shakespearean Politics: Government and Misgovernment in the Great Histories*, pp. 1-61. Athens: Ohio University Press, 1983.

Asserts that in *Richard II* Shakespeare is not a spokesman for Tudor orthodoxy, contending instead that he presents a humane, man-centered form of kingship over the divine-right monarchy and passive obedience defended by John of Gaunt. The action of the play, according to Thayer, consistently undercuts its pro-absolutist ideology and even discredits the doctrine of the King's Two Bodies, a medieval theory which assumed that a sovereign was sacred and his position as ruler unassailable.

Traversi, Derek. "*Richard the Second*." In his *Shakespeare from "Richard II" to "Henry V*," pp. 12-48. Stanford, Calif.: Stanford University Press, 1957.

Establishes the connection between matter and manner in *Richard II*, proposing that one of the most original features of the play is its "effort to diversify artificial forms, to make the elaboration of contrasted styles respond to the tensions which constitute the true tragic theme." Traversi stresses as well the clash of personalities between Richard and Bolingbroke. He describes the king as a fatalistic, self-indulgent man, not without insight, but possessed of a "morbid, febrile imagination" and a willingness "to live with a certain complacency at the center of a tragic situation which his own weakness, practical incompetence, and a kind of unconscious cynicism have brought into being." Bolingbroke, less glamorous, is nevertheless more capable; yet his administrative skill, Traversi adds, does not mitigate the "guilt" of his usurpation.

Ure, Peter. "The Looking-Glass of *Richard II*." *Philological Quarterly* XXXIV, No. 2 (April 1955): 219-24.

Notes that two traditional symbols—a diadem and a looking-glass—are used in the abdication scene of *Richard II* and reads "the movement from Crown to mirror as part of a climbing sequence, which gradually modulates from the 'external manners' to the tortured soul within." Ure emphasizes that while a conventional understanding of the mirror as a metaphor for vanity or truth certainly enriches the episode, Shakespeare's use of it in this drama conveys a highly original insight into the nature of Richard's self-recognition.

———. Introduction to *King Richard II,* by William Shakespeare, edited by Peter Ure, pp. xiii-lxxxiii. The Arden Edition of the Works of William Shakespeare, edited by Harold F. Brooks and Harold Jenkins. London: Methuen and Co., 1961.

A comprehensive review of textual problems, date and source information, and the turbulent political history of *Richard II.* Ure also addresses several controversies surrounding the character of the king, Bolingbroke's role in precipitating the crisis, the causes of Richard's fall, and Shakespeare's position on the issues involved, but maintains that the fundamental question posed by the play concerns the effect on Richard himself when "unarmed and deficient majesty" is confronted by "armed and able usurpation."

Watson, Robert N. "Kinship and Kingship: Ambition in Shakespeare's Major Histories." In his *Shakespeare and the Hazards of Ambition,* pp. 14-82. Cambridge and London: Harvard University Press, 1984.

Studies Shakespeare's treatment of the moral implications of rebellion and usurpation, with particular reference to subliminal Oedipal conflicts in the characters of *Richard II* and to Elizabethan political attitudes.

Wickham, Glynne. "Shakespeare's *King Richard II* and Marlowe's *King Edward II.*" In *Christopher Marlowe's "Edward II": Text and Major Criticism,* edited by Irving Ribner, pp. 199-212. New York: The Odyssey Press, 1970.

Compares the two histories and argues that Marlowe's play is "in intention and execution" far closer to genuine tragedy than is Shakespeare's "chronicle." Wickham notes that while Edward II differs greatly from his chief adversary, Mortimer, Richard II and Bolingbroke share many striking characteristics. The critic adds that Shakespeare's structure seems to have been inspired less by ancient Greek models than by Biblical stories and medieval accounts of the Wars of the Roses.

[Wilson, John Dover]. Introduction to *King Richard II,* by William Shakespeare, edited by John Dover Wilson and Sir Arthur Quiller-Couch, pp. vii-lxxvi. Cambridge: Cambridge at the University Press, 1976.

A famous scholarly overview of the available factual material relating to *Richard II.* Dover Wilson discusses what is known about the date, text, and sources of the play, and reviews some highlights of past criticism. This essay also introduces Dover Wilson's widely debated theory that Shakespeare depended upon an earlier, now-lost drama on the subject of Richard for much of the action, and even some of the words, in his own version of the history.

Zitner, Sheldon. "Aumerle's Conspiracy." *Studies in English Literature 1500-1900* XIV, No. 2 (Spring 1974): 239-57.

Examines the Aumerle-York scenes in Act V of *Richard II* to argue that they are more than just expendable, "ill-considered trifles." Zitner maintains that through their use of madcap farce, these episodes of unguarded family life undercut the "illusion that man's existence in history is faithfully rendered in the huge public stylization of historical tragedy."

The Two Gentlemen of Verona

DATE: Most scholars agree that *The Two Gentlemen of Verona* was written and first performed sometime between 1590 and 1595, several years prior to the only known contemporary reference to the play, that of FRANCIS MERES in his *Palladis Tamia* of 1598. Further narrowing this period of composition has proved especially difficult for critics because of the lack of external evidence other than Meres's allusion. Adding to this difficulty is the fact that *The Two Gentlemen* was not published in any QUARTO edition during Shakespeare's lifetime, but initially appeared in the FIRST FOLIO of 1623. Consequently, scholars attempting to date the play have necessarily based their conjectures on such attributes as its style, content, and language in comparison to Shakespeare's other early comedies. Accordingly, most have placed the drama's composition after *The Comedy of Errors* and *The Taming of the Shrew*, claiming that the classic and Italian elements in these two early works suggest the first efforts of a new playwright, while the romantic content of *The Two Gentlemen of Verona* foreshadows Shakespeare's later comedies, for example, *Twelfth Night* and *As You Like It*. Other theories on the play's date of composition include those of S. A. Tannenbaum, James G. McManaway, and the New Arden editor Clifford Leech (see Additional Bibliography). Tannenbaum postulated that Shakespeare revised *The Two Gentlemen* as late as 1598, the year in which the English translation of its main source—Jorge de Montemayor's *Diana Enamorada*—was published. McManaway supported a 1594 dating based on the play's parallels with Arthur Brooke's *Romeus and Juliet* (1562), the source Shakespeare had perhaps recently consulted for his *Romeo and Juliet*, which scholars generally believe was written sometime between 1595 and 1596. Leech suggested that Shakespeare began *The Two Gentlemen* in 1592 but continued to revise the text until its completion in 1593. Although a consensus on a specific date for *The Two Gentlemen of Verona* is yet to be reached, most authorities agree that the play's tone, structure, themes, and language indicate that it is among Shakespeare's earliest works.

TEXT: The First Folio, as mentioned above, is the earliest extant copy of *The Two Gentlemen of Verona;* it is also the sole authoritative text from which all subsequent editions, including the SECOND, THIRD, and FOURTH FOLIOS are derived. However, the peculiar condition of the Folio text—inconsistent and contradictory at many points—has been a major concern of critics throughout the history of the play. Several scholars, in fact, have questioned Shakespeare's sole authorship of the drama, citing such discordant elements as the uncertainty of the main setting, which is variously labeled Milan, Padua, and Verona, and an inconsistency in characterization as evidence of two or more hands in the composition. They also note the presence of meaningless and unmetrical verse in the play, discrepant information regarding several elements of the plot, the brevity of the action, Valentine's oversea voyage from one inland city to another, and several other anomalies, all unusual for a dramatist of Shakespeare's ability. Yet, whether these peculiarities are the contributions of another author or are due to Shakespeare's own neglect of details remains debatable. John Upton, writing in 1748, compared *Love's Labour's Lost* and *The Two Gentlemen of Verona* to Shakespeare's other plays and concluded that both should be removed from the list of the playwright's works because of their inferior manner and

Title page of The Two Gentlemen of Verona *taken from the First Folio (1623).*

style. Several twentieth-century scholars, in particular Sir Arthur Quiller-Couch, attempted to identify those parts of the play that appear to have been written by a second author, though they considered enough of the comedy Shakespeare's to keep it in the canon. Others disagreed with the theory of multiple authorship altogether, contending that the irregularities are the result of Shakespeare's own oversight; they postulated that he wrote the play in several stages over a period of time and, perhaps, hastily concluded it for a specific performance. Such diverse commentators as Edmund Malone, Crompton Rhodes, and J. Dover Wilson have attributed the anomalies in *The Two Gentlemen of Verona* to its transmission, maintaining that the Folio was based on an ASSEMBLED TEXT. This theory gained credence primarily because of the somewhat unusual format of the Folio text, which lists the characters at the start of each scene in the order of their appearance but provides no additional entry information during that scene. E. K. Chambers disputed this theory, countering that a text transcribed in this manner would have more major errors and mislineations than *The Two Gentlemen of Verona* actually has. Clifford Leech also disagreed, stating that although only three texts in the First Folio are presented in this particular format, the technique is typical of many other Elizabethan texts, all of which, he claimed, could not possibly be based on assembled texts. He added that it is also very unlikely that all the separate character parts were still available to complete the assembled text when the First Folio was compiled in 1623. In fact, Dover Wilson himself later refuted his earlier theory. In light of this, most present-day scholars accept Leech's hypothesis that the Folio text was transcribed from Shakespeare's FOUL PAPERS, more than likely by a professional scribe named Ralph Crane, whose distinctive scribal characteristics have since been noted throughout the edition.

SOURCES: The main source of *The Two Gentlemen of Verona* is Jorge de Montemayor's Spanish romance *Diana Enamorada* (1559), which depicts the tale of Felix, an unfaithful lover, and his ardent mistress Felismena. With the notable exception of Silvia's lover Valentine, Shakespeare's play closely follows the storyline of Montemayor's romance, including variations of such significant events as Felismena's feigned disinterest in Felix's love letter, her male disguise donned in order to follow him on his journey, and her inadvertent discovery of his infidelity. Although it is conceivable that Shakespeare's textual source was the Spanish original, most scholars assert that it was probably one of two French translations by Nicolas Collin, published in 1578 and 1587, or an English version by Bartholomew Yonge published in 1598 but available in manuscript form sixteen years earlier. It is perhaps even more likely that Shakespeare encountered the story through the anonymous lost play—*The History of Felix and Philiomena*—based on the *Diana* and performed at court in early 1585 by the Queen's Men. Another often-cited source of *The Two Gentlemen of Verona* is the story of Titus and Gisippus from Book II, Chapter XII of Sir Thomas Elyot's *The Governour* (1531), which contains a scene parallel to the final one in Shakespeare's play, in which Valentine offers his faithful lover to his perfidious friend Proteus. This work—as well as Richard Edward's play *Damon and Pithias* (1571), another possible source—deals with the ideals of true friendship as portrayed in Boccaccio's *Decameron*. The theme was common from the Middle Ages to Shakespeare's time, and, as in *The Two Gentlemen of Verona*, the bond of friendship was often depicted in conflict with that of romantic love. Scholars also regard several of John Lyly's plays, especially his *Euphues, or the Anatomy of Wit* (1578), as a significant influence on Shakespeare's depiction of friendship and love in *The Two Gentlemen*. Perhaps more importantly, Lyly contributed to Shakespeare's use of dramatic techniques and comic wit, evident in the similarities between Lyly's *Endimion* (c. 1588) and *Midas* (1592) and *The Two Gentlemen of Verona*. Other possible analogues of the play include the popular Italianate comedies, Chaucer's *The Knight's Tale*, the anonymous German play *Julius and Hyppolita*, Robert Greene's *James IV*, Sir Philip Sidney's *Arcadia*, Arthur Brooke's poem *Romeus and Juliet*, and the lost play *The Pastoral Comedy of Robin Hood and Little John*.

CRITICAL HISTORY: Critical reaction to *The Two Gentlemen of Verona* has not always reflected the same praise and approval received by many of Shakespeare's other plays. In fact, many of the earliest commentators derided the play for its deficiencies in plot, language, and characterization. These apparent faults naturally led to the question of Shakespeare's authorship of the comedy. Several critics, particularly those in the twentieth century, doubted only certain passages based on their anomalous verse or content; others, however, averred that Shakespeare did not compose the play at all. Additional issues of critical importance during the past three centuries include the

language of the play, its moral or Christian implications, Shakespeare's technique of contrasting characterization, the function of Launce and Speed, the meaning or relevancy of the final scene, and the relationship of love and friendship. In-depth character studies, mainly of Proteus, also appeared in the nineteenth and twentieth centuries, as did discussions of the nature of love, the function of the green world, the play's structure, the mixture of the romantic and comic elements, and Shakespeare's approach—either ironic or sympathetic—to the courtly conventions of romance. Since the mid-twentieth century, the issues of appearance and reality, education, and personal identity have also been explored, as has the significance of both the characters' and the audience's varying levels of awareness in the play. Through their explications, critics have clarified and, in some cases, resolved many of the problems first noted in *The Two Gentlemen of Verona*.

One of the first critical concerns in the history of *The Two Gentlemen of Verona* was the issue of authorship. Writing in 1710, Charles Gildon discerned the distinctive marks of Shakespeare in certain lines, but other critics, such as John Upton, differed, arguing for the removal of the play from the canon. Benjamin Victor and Samuel Johnson both countered such suggestions, maintaining that much in the play is attributable to no one but Shakespeare. For lack of convincing evidence to the contrary, Elizabeth Griffith likewise attributed *The Two Gentlemen* solely to Shakespeare.

Beginning with Gildon's disparagement of the defects in "Plot, Conduct, Manners, and Sentiments" of this play, the eighteenth-century critical response to *The Two Gentlemen of Verona* was for the most part unfavorable. While Alexander Pope commended the drama's "natural and unaffected style," though not its "trifling conceits," other critics, including Charlotte Lennox, Victor, and Griffith, expressed less praise and more complaint. Lennox claimed that the comedy is as "deficient" and "improbable" as its source and labeled Silvia a "Village Coquet." In the advertisement for his adaptation of *The Two Gentlemen of Verona*, Victor derided Shakespeare's play as rank with "weeds," though he also acknowledged its "poetical flowers." Victor was thus the earliest commentator to focus, if only briefly, on the dramatic language of the play, an approach apparent in later essays by Samuel Johnson, Charles Dibdin, William Hazlitt, G. G. Gervinus, and Algernon Charles Swinburne, among others. Griffith was the first to comment on *The Two Gentlemen*'s Christian or moral aspects; she expressed disappointment with the morality of the comedy, describing Proteus's degeneration from initial virtue to "baseness" and "villainy" as abrupt, inconsistent, and unexplainable.

Throughout the nineteenth century, critical interest generally shifted away from the authorship of *The Two Gentlemen of Verona* and the moral or didactic shortcomings of the play to focus on other, more intrinsic concerns, such as its contrasting characterization, the resolution of the drama, its language and poetry, its central themes, and the function of the comic underplot.

In his essay of 1800, Charles Dibdin was the first to note the contrast in Valentine's and Proteus's characters, describing them as respective examples of the "etiquette" and "perfidy" of polite life." He also pointed out how Launce and Speed serve as foils to their masters and praised the play's poetry, which he claimed surpasses that in any of Shakespeare's previous works. Nearly fifty years later, Charles Knight offered one of the earliest in-depth discussions of the pattern of conflicting characterization in the comedy, demonstrating how the opposing natures of the six main figures contribute to Shakespeare's plot and dramatic structure. Likewise, the German critic G. G. Gervinus averred that "the characters and events [in *The Two Gentlemen of Verona*] are so exactly placed in relation and contrast to each other that not only those of a similar nature, but even those of a contrary one, serve mutually to explain each other." William Watkiss Lloyd further defined the complementary nature of the characterization and events in Shakespeare's play, noting one such interesting parallel in Launce's devotion to his dog Crab and Julia's selfless love for Proteus. Lloyd claimed, in fact, that through the comic situation of the clown and his dog Shakespeare was parodying the ideal of self-sacrifice embodied in Julia and Valentine, thus raising the issue of irony in the play which has since dominated modern criticism. In a rather unfavorable assessment, Edward Dowden asserted that the characters are "contrasted with almost too obvious a design." And near the end of the century, Frederick S. Boas described each of Shakespeare's principal characters, noting in particular how Proteus remains the most powerfully conceived figure in the comedy and Launce and Speed complement the main romantic action.

Disparagement of Shakespeare's final scene in *The Two Gentlemen of Verona* began as early as 1710, when Gildon faulted Valentine's easy reconciliation with Proteus. In the nineteenth century, the question of the purpose and success of the closing episode was taken up by a number of critics, including Charles Armitage Brown, Gervinus, Dowden, Grace Latham, and Boas. In his in-depth analysis of Proteus, Brown contended that the villain's repentance in Act V, Scene iv is not implausible, but accurately reflects his sudden awareness of the futility of his lust for Sylvia and the extent of his degeneration. Gervinus acknowledged that although the plot at this point in Shakespeare's comedy is indeed carelessly treated, the ending is not arbitrary, for Valentine's sacrifice of his beloved to Proteus is in harmony with his character throughout. He added that this selfless act echoes the behavior of both Julia and Launce at other points of the play. Dowden questioned Shakespeare's authorship of the final scene as it now exists, declaring that the characters' actions are so "unreal and ill-contrived" that someone must have altered the original text. Dowden's view was further advanced by, among others, the twentieth-century commentators Arthur Quiller-Couch and Thomas Marc Parrott. In her discussion of the heroines in *The Two Gentlemen of Verona*, Latham praised Silvia's constancy and perfect dignity, but asserted that her quiet submission to Valentine's offer and, in effect, betrayal of their love is "a flaw both in the climax and the characterization." Boas, too, disapproved of the final scene, asserting that the actions of both Valentine and Silvia are impossible to justify and that Proteus's repentance remains unconvincing.

Shakespeare's use of language and poetry in *The Two Gentlemen of Verona* was also examined by some of the commentators already mentioned, as well as by William Hazlitt and Algernon Charles Swinburne. Like Dibdin, Hazlitt praised the "quaintness of humour" and "high poetical spirit" of certain passages in the comedy, though he also acknowledged that the narrative was "loosely sketched in" and "dramatized with very little labour or pretension." The critic further defended the low-comic scenes from Alexander Pope's attack and concluded that the play is "undoubtedly Shakespear's," despite its shortcomings. Gervinus compared the love poetry of Silvia's three suitors—Thurio, Valentine, and Proteus—to illustrate each one's capacity for love, while Dowden discussed Shakespeare's developing application of prose and verse in this work. Likewise,

Swinburne sensed a new style for Shakespeare in the comedy, marked by "an even sweetness, a simple equality of grace in thought and language which keeps the whole poem in tune."

Perhaps the most significant issue in nineteenth-century commentary on *The Two Gentlemen of Verona*, from the perspective of the present century, is the question of the play's central theme. In his influential lectures published in 1811, the German romantic critic August Wilhelm Schlegel was the first to contend that the comedy's superficiality is not merely a sign of Shakespeare's immaturity, but is closely related to his exploration of the "transient youthful caprice" of love. Schlegel was also the earliest to link this concern to the theme of friendship in the play, demonstrating how the comedy treats both "the irresolution of love" and love's "infidelity to friendship." Another German critic, Hermann Ulrici, regarded love, in its "diversified forms," as the principal theme in *The Two Gentlemen of Verona*. He examined the love of each character, from Silvia's embodiment of unwavering passion to Launce's "inexhaustible fund of inconsistency," and claimed that Shakespeare depicts all of these manifestations as "equally weak, foolish, perverse, and self-indulgent." Likewise, Gervinus maintained that the central theme of *The Two Gentlemen* is "the essence and power of love"; Gervinus noted as well that the play dramatizes love's "twofold nature": the self-centered and artful passion of Proteus and the self-denying, naive devotion best represented by Silvia and Valentine. Dowden, like Schlegel, identified "love and friendship, with their mutual relations," as Shakespeare's principal concern. In a structural analysis of the play, Denton J. Snider traced the three movements depicting the dissolution and reintegration of the ties of friendship and love, stressing the importance of Shakespeare's idyllic forest in this process of reconciliation. Late in the century, George Brandes offered further evidence in support of "faithful and faithless love" as Shakespeare's major theme.

While several of the eighteenth- and nineteenth-century critical concerns carried over into the twentieth century—most notably the debate over the play's thematics, the purpose and success of Shakespeare's final act, and the comic function of the Launce-Speed subplot—modern critics initiated many new perspectives on *The Two Gentlemen of Verona*. Among these perhaps the most important is the question of Shakespeare's view of the romantic conventions treated in his comedy: is the play a sympathetic portrayal or a comic parody of the courtly love tradition embodied in its heroes? Other prominent concerns include the structure of *The Two Gentlemen*, Shakespeare's adaptation of his sources, the role of the forest or "green world," the comedy's Christian elements, and the significance of themes other than those of love and friendship, including appearance and reality, education, personal identity, and repentance or forgiveness.

During the first decades of the twentieth century, most commentators continued to focus on the comedy's shortcomings, especially as evidenced in the final act. In 1903, W. J. Courthope discussed, among other topics, the tragic potential within *The Two Gentlemen of Verona*, labeling this work "the first of Shakespeare's tragicomedies." The critic, however, also disparaged numerous aspects of the play, including its "tedious" and unrelated comic underplot, Proteus's unnatural treachery and abrupt repentance, and Valentine's unexplainable offer of his beloved to his unworthy friend. Likewise, E. K. Chambers presented as evidence of the comedy's early composition date its excessive "verbal ingenuities," inept characterization, and "sentimental bankruptcy." He especially lamented the "almost cynical brevity and lack of psychology" in the climax of the play and averred that by "putting humanity into the puppets of romance" Shakespeare undermined his romantic conventions. Shortly after Chambers's commentary, R. Warwick Bond, too, recognized several flaws in *The Two Gentlemen*, but he defended the problematic ending from allegations of inconsistency and textual corruption, stating that the line "all that was mine in Silvia I give to thee" (V. iv. 83) is intentionally ambiguous. According to Bond, Valentine's words are understood by everyone but Julia to express his equal affection for both Silvia and Proteus, and are not meant as an offering of the former to the latter. Richard Garnett, like Chambers, attributed the "inferiority" of *The Two Gentlemen* to Shakespeare's youthful inexperience, calling it the dramatist's "simplest and least ambitious" play. He identified as its cardinal fault its subordination of character to action. Martin W. Sampson disputed Bond's interpretation of Valentine's remark to Proteus at V. iv. 83 as an offer of his love, not of Silvia. Instead, he countered that the conclusion of the play is intended to emphasize the superiority of friendship over love, thus expressing a conventional belief undoubtedly accepted, despite its deficiencies, by Shakespeare's original audience. On other matters, Sampson disparaged the dramatist's construction of *The Two Gentlemen of Verona*, claiming that "the action is very slow in getting under way, and the situations . . . are not always worthy of the honor they thereby receive," but he praised its "mood of youthful beauty." As previously mentioned, Arthur Quiller-Couch—in an otherwise favorable assessment—maintained that the language of the comedy's final episode is so "slipshod" and "vicious" that it must be adulterated—in his words, "a piece of theatre botchwork patched upon the original."

Shakespeare's treatment of the theme of love and friendship has frequently been linked with his adaptation of his sources or his adherence to Elizabethan ideals, and the troublesome ending of *The Two Gentlemen* has often been explained in those terms. In 1925, Oscar James Campbell demonstrated the comedy's indebtedness to Italian models at every point, asserting that Shakespeare's resolution is not shocking, but is simply the "expected indisputable proof of the complete victory of friendship in its moral struggle with love," as required by Italian comedy. Alwin Thaler similarly considered *The Two Gentlemen* Shakespeare's "most elaborate essay in the friendship theme" that had been developed by earlier and contemporary writers; he thus regarded the unfavorable reaction to its ending, including arguments suggesting an alternate author, as simple "misconceptions." Thomas Marc Parrott, on the other hand, did discern signs of adulteration in the play's final scene; however, the critic did not include Valentine's renunciation of Silvia among the material revised. Noting a similar renunciation in the sonnets, Parrott concluded that this gesture "seemed to Shakespeare—and to his Elizabethan audience—a heroic example of romantic friendship." Continuing this general view of Shakespeare's sources, Ralph M. Sargent argued that the behavior of both Valentine and Silvia in the final scene is consistent with the ideal of friendship presented in Shakespeare's principal model for the theme, Thomas Elyot's story of "Titus and Gisippus." He added that Silvia's silence is in accord with her rigid adherence to the prescribed ideals of friendship demonstrated throughout the play and that Valentine's offer, though also consistent with standardized conduct and equally sincere, is tendered with the assumption that Proteus will refuse it and, like the other three lovers, endorse the ideals himself by choosing Julia over Silvia. M. C. Bradbrook further explicated the influence of the courtier tradition on the

events and characters of *The Two Gentlemen of Verona*, asserting that the play is "a study of manners rather than sentiments, of behavior rather than emotion." Both Valentine and Proteus exemplify the actions of typical courtly lovers, she maintained, adding that Valentine's generous gift to Proteus is meant to demonstrate the cardinal virtue of Magnanimity, and Silvia's silence regarding this sacrifice is consistent with her role as the "prize" of the opposing lovers. Karl F. Thompson examined the pervasive influence of the courtly love tradition—specifically, the religion of love—on the characterization and structure of *The Two Gentlemen of Verona*, claiming that this convention supports the play's central theme: "that honor is an essential part of love, that the two cannot exist independently." More recently, Inga-Stina Ewbank compared the comedy to Shakespeare's sonnets in its treatment of romantic conventions and its dialectical presentation of language as a medium which can both substantiate human experience and—being conventionalized itself—falsify that experience. Locating the play's "real inconsistency" in "the fulfillments of Act V," Ewbank argues that in the final episode Shakespeare wanted to dramatize an idea frequently explored in his early poetry—namely, the uncertainty of intimate relationships—but he failed because his characters never give more than verbal expression to their passionate experiences.

The question of Shakespeare's relation to his romantic material in *The Two Gentlemen of Verona* was not seriously raised until 1930. In that year, H. B. Charlton examined the mixture of romantic and comic elements in the play and concluded that Shakespeare "unexpectedly and inadvertently made romance comic" by juxtaposing the courtly behavior of his heroes, with which he sympathized, with the incompatible world of his heroines and clowns. Charlton's commentary initiated a debate over Shakespeare's comic intent in the play that has continued to the present day. Nearly twenty years later, E. C. Pettet took issue with Charlton's claim that Shakespeare had unintentionally made romance comic, contending that the parody of romance provided by Speed and Launce clearly reflect the dramatist's ironic design. He added that such romantic characters as Valentine and the band of outlaws also indicate Shakespeare's distance from the conventions of romance. Harold C. Goddard concluded that one may read *The Two Gentlemen of Verona* in one of two ways: as either Shakespeare's "most juvenile work," in which the playwright accepts whole-heartedly the romantic ideals he presents, or as an ironical comedy, in which he subtly mocks "'gentlemanly' manners and morals." Goddard preferred the second reading, identifying Launce and Speed as the vehicles of this ironic humor. Derek Traversi considered *The Two Gentlemen* Shakespeare's earliest attempt to employ a literary convention "to attain, beyond convention itself, a position from which excess, self-ignorance and self-indulgence have been eliminated." He examined such elements as the conventional, artificial behavior of Valentine and Proteus, the comic interludes of the servants, and—especially—the heroines' "firm and clear-eyed view of reality," to demonstrate that Shakespeare undercuts the romantic ideal of love presented in the play.

Other critics who have examined whether Shakespeare adopts an ironic view of his romantic material in *The Two Gentlemen of Verona* include Harold F. Brooks, Stanley Wells, Howard Nemerov, Peter G. Phialas, Ralph Berry, Alexander Leggatt, Ruth Nevo, and Camille Wells Slights. A comprehensive outline of the similarities between the romantic and parodic scenes in *The Two Gentlemen* was provided by Brooks, who concluded that these numerous parallels indicate Shakespeare's ironic distance from romantic, courtly love. Reviewing the superficial, technical, and organic peculiarities that disrupt the romance of Shakespeare's play, Wells modified Charlton's assessment and concluded that *The Two Gentlemen* is a limited success which both intentionally and unintentionally makes romance comic. Nemerov countered the principal interpretations of earlier critics on the relative failure of the comedy, declaring that neither the comic treatment of the romantic lovers nor the parody provided by Launce and Speed destroys the value of courtly love. Phialas commented on Silvia's significance in Shakespeare's presentation of both the romantic and ironic conceptions of love; he regarded the combination of these two viewpoints in her character as one of Shakespeare's "most significant advances towards romantic comedy." In an analysis of the themes of change and illusion in the play, Berry emphasized both Valentine's and Proteus's self-absorbed romantic delusions, asserting that neither of these characters views Silvia as a living individual, but only as the object of a conventionalized pattern of behavior. This adherence to external romantic norms, the critic proclaimed, eventually distorts the heroes' own identities. Leggatt described the "essential gap between different minds" in *The Two Gentlemen of Verona*, focusing on Shakespeare's technique of distancing "the experience of love" presented in the play through the comic parody of his low-characters and the lovers' conventional responses, as well as the placement of their serious speeches in ironic circumstances. In her essay dealing with the theme of identity in the comedy, Nevo focused on Valentine's and Proteus's reversal of roles as lovers and their acceptance of love as a "fashion" or "imitation," rather than a personal experience. Most recently, Slights has opposed this growing consensus and claimed that *The Two Gentlemen* is an "exploration of the nature and function of a gentleman" rather than either a promotion of conventional views of friendship and love or an ironic parody of Elizabethan romantic ideals.

Although the debate between the romantic and parodic readings of *The Two Gentlemen of Verona* has dominated much of the modern critical response to the play, several other significant issues have been discussed as well. The relationship of appearance or illusion to reality is one such topic. Traversi discussed this theme in his study of 1960, as stated above, when he asserted that by contrasting the conventional, false, and superficial behavior of Valentine and Proteus with the more reasonable and realistic attitudes of his female characters, Shakespeare wanted "to free valid human attachments from excess and emptiness, restoring them to a sane and balanced conception of life." A number of critics have addressed this issue in light of Shakespeare's treatment of love in the comedy. John Vyvyan perceived the dichotomy of reality and illusion in the two heroes, asserting that while Valentine—in his quest for true perfection—struggles to control and purify the "rebel powers" in the forest, symbolic of those in his soul, Proteus betrays his true self for "illusion" and "shadow." In his essay on Proteus's purely visual love and Valentine's desire for a more inward, spiritual affection, Norman Sanders emphasized Julia's role in this dialectic pattern, stating that the heroine establishes a mean between the two male lovers and embodies "some special standard of constancy and ultimate test of love's reality." This design, the critic averred, is marred only by Valentine's flawed intellect and inconsistent use of language, which prevent him from commanding the audience's empathy or interest as Proteus does. John Arthos stressed the significance of Silvia's embodiment of knowledge, constancy, and love, especially as it is opposed to Proteus's obsession with appearances or "shadows." Arthos concluded that although

The Two Gentlemen of Verona demonstrates a belief in a divine principle that makes constancy in love possible, its artistic shortcomings indicate that Shakespeare had personal doubts concerning the viability of this philosophy. Ralph Berry approached the theme of appearance and illusion from yet a different perspective, citing Valentine's consistent reliance on conventional norms of behavior and his eventual transformation into the typical lover to emphasize the play's principal concern with illusion and change. The character's self-indulgent renunciation and theatrical forgiveness of his unfaithful friend, Berry asserted, reflect the extent of his egotism, providing as well a "grotesque parody of Julia's quiet and undramatic forgiveness of Proteus." As previously mentioned, Alexander Leggatt also discussed the "essential gap" between the characters' understanding of love in *The Two Gentlemen*, noting Valentine's and Proteus's reliance on "appearances, conventions, and verbal surfaces" as opposed to Julia's complex interplay of language and emotion. Most recently, Ruth Nevo has identified the ideas of "shadow and substance, image and idol" in the comedy, which she maintained are dramatized in both the heroes' acceptance of love as a "fashion" and in Julia's disguise as the male page Sebastian.

Interest in the characters' conventional romantic behavior is important not only to the discussion of appearance and reality in *The Two Gentlemen*, but also to the theme of education. In his essay of 1954, Thomas A. Perry associated Proteus's acquired expertise in poetry and fashion after he arrives in Milan, as well as his sudden "inconstancy and disloyalty," with his efforts to become a sophisticated courtier. Perry thus concluded that *The Two Gentlemen of Verona* is not merely "another tale of friendship and love," but is "primarily the timely story of the Italianated youth in whom false friendship and false love accompany the attempts of the youth to acquire sophistication." John Vyvyan's interest in the theme of education centered on his reading of the play as "a parable of love as a saving power," and he cited Valentine's and Proteus's gradual recognition of the "essence of love" as the foundation of their eventual self-knowledge, identity, and inner peace. In his extensive review of Shakespeare's use of parallel construction in *The Two Gentlemen of Verona*, Harold F. Brooks related Launce's attempt to teach Crab by example to the gradual education of Proteus in the drama. Several years later, William Leigh Godshalk treated the comedy's concern with education in his discussion of its structure, averring that one of the three unifying elements in the drama is the educative process of journeys. He asserted that although the characters' initial movements to Milan all "go awry" and fail to achieve their goals, the final journey to the pastoral world leads to the ultimate success of love. In his essay previously cited for its treatment of appearance and reality, Arthos emphasized the importance of education in the characters' quests for truth, self-knowledge, and constancy, asserting that when Proteus ignores the opportunity for enlightenment he thereby disobeys the guiding force of "divine injunction." Peter Lindenbaum later argued that the themes of education and perfection are more central to *The Two Gentlemen of Verona* than those of friendship and love. He contended that Proteus and Valentine are initially corrupted by Italian society, but added that they grow to recognize the inadequacies of courtly behavior and, in the world of the forest, come to accept God's perfecting influence. In her essay on the "nature and function of a gentleman," Camille Wells Slights maintained that the attempts of Proteus and Valentine to become perfect courtiers initially cause conflict, undermine social cohesion, and threaten each individual's sense of self. The critic added that once they recognize the ultimate brutality of courtly corruption—epitomized in Proteus's attempted rape of Silvia—the heroes return to society with different attitudes and expectations, finding that communal happiness is achievable "when people combine idealism with realistic understanding of human imperfection."

Another important theme in the later half of the twentieth century is individual identity, evident in the criticism of Vyvyan, William O. Scott, Arthos, Berry, Thomas E. Scheye, Ruth Nevo, Maurice Hunt, and Slights. As previously noted, Vyvyan dealt with this theme in relation to the heroes' gradual recognition of the "essence of love," as opposed to "illusion" and "shadow." His analysis of Proteus's initial betrayal of his true identity was echoed by William O. Scott. Tracing Proteus's denial to Shakespeare's sources, Scott averred that the change in this character is linked to his "fundamental changes of loyalty" from friendship to love. The critic also asserted that it is only through Valentine's generosity and Julia's "steady, though despairing, love" that Proteus's true identity is restored. Arthos explored the characters' pursuit of truth, constancy, and love, arguing that these personal objectives are attainable only through self-knowledge and acceptance of that principle of divinity in all human beings. For Berry, the identities of the protagonists are distorted by the conventions of romance they blindly adopt. The critic identified an extreme example of this process in Proteus's and Valentine's relations with Silvia, stating that the heroes undermine their own identities—as well as the heroine's—when they view her not as a living individual, but as the object of a conventionalized pattern of behavior. Citing Thomas Elyot's *The Governor* and Shakespeare's own *The Comedy of Errors* as earlier works in which two characters unite in a single identity, Scheye compared this process to Proteus's usurpation of Valentine's self in Milan. According to the critic, Valentine recovers his identity only when he enters the green world; there he gains conviction as well as self-knowledge and is able to forgive his friend and bring about the play's final multiple reconciliations. Like Scheye, Nevo perceived a complete reversal of roles between the two male lovers in Act V, Scene iv, abruptly halting what she regarded as the giddy movement of the plot through numerous transformations and interchanges of characters. Associating the issue of personal identity with the Christian "paradox of salvation," Hunt contended that Proteus, Valentine, and Julia all experience self-loss before discovering their true selves through contrition, understanding, and charitable love. Lastly, Slights discerned Proteus's and Valentine's self-loss and ultimate self-discovery in their misguided preoccupation with conventional gentlemanly perfection and in their final realization of the "selfishness and shallow hypocrisy of courtly fashion."

Concern for the Christian or moral intent of *The Two Gentlemen of Verona*, first discussed by Elizabeth Griffith in 1775, was revived in the twentieth century by such critics as John F. Danby, John Vyvyan, Robert Grams Hunter, John Arthos, Peter Lindenbaum, and Maurice Hunt. In his 1960 essay, Danby emphasized the "serious moral background" behind the play's "trivial" and unspectacular storyline. The critic described the love of Julia and Valentine as Christian in its redeeming quality and stated that we are not meant to dwell on the villainy of Proteus—or to disparaise him as an immoral figure—but to witness through his experience the power of human compassion to elevate the erring individual "to the quality of the love bestowed." In his essay, of the same year, Vyvyan frequently noted the Platonic and Christian influence on Shakespeare's presentation of the redeeming power of love in *The Two Gentlemen*. Hunter placed the play, along with several other Shake-

speare plays, in the tradition of "the comedy of forgiveness," asserting that Valentine's controversial offer of Silvia to Proteus is a "summation of the Christian attitude toward repentance which . . . underlies the denouement in forgiveness." As previously discussed, Arthos regarded Silvia as the embodiment of the play's principle of divinity and traced Proteus's wayward, selfish love to his willful disobedience of "divine injunction." In his assessment of the drama's educative elements, Lindenbaum also noted Shakespeare's belief, exemplified by Valentine and Julia, that ideal human conduct must be "in harmony with and modeled after divine precept." And in his essay concerning the relationship of identity and Christian love in *The Two Gentlemen of Verona*, Hunt described Julia—who loses herself in charitable, rather than romantic, love and discovers her true spiritual self through sacrifice to another human being—as the play's leading example of "the original meaning of the paradox of salvation."

In their essays examining the principal critical topics in *The Two Gentlemen of Verona*, several modern commentators also addressed the significance of the forest, or "green world," in this play. Although Denton J. Snider and George Brandes had raised this issue at the end of the nineteenth century, Danby, in 1960, was one of the earliest twentieth-century critics to comment on the forest, identifying it as a "timely shelter to natural values" and a place where love and friendship are restored. William E. Stephenson emphasized the importance of this sylvan setting to Shakespeare's depiction of his immature protagonists, explaining that the "incredible forest scenes," as well as the troublesome final episode, are best understood not as realistic drama, but as enactments of typical adolescent fantasies about love and heroism. He concluded that the contrast of these youthful "dreams" and "life's actualities" provides a "coherence and credibility" to the drama as a whole. Scheye saw the green world as the reverse of Milan—"the house of mirrors"—and the place where Valentine and Proteus recover their identities lost in the city. Peter Lindenbaum also described the forest as the place where identities are secured, where the two friends learn to "define themselves accurately by their own actions rather than words." Maurice Hunt pointed out that Valentine's discovery of his "noble identity" takes place only in the green world, while Camille Wells Slights regarded the attempted rape of Sylvia in the forest as the shocking event that motivates the heroes' final recognition of both their own wayward identities and the corruption of courtly society.

The dramatic structure of *The Two Gentlemen of Verona* is also an important issue in twentieth-century commentary on the play. Early in the century, R. Warwick Bond praised Shakespeare's structure of contrasting characterization and incident in *The Two Gentlemen of Verona*. Later, however, George Pierce Baker (see Additional Bibliography) disparaged Shakespeare's inefficient scene management in the work, asserting that it took the playwright ten scenes, instead of an acceptable three, simply to establish the relationships of his characters. In 1963, Harold F. Brooks analyzed the play's pervasive comic parallelism, citing, for example, Launce's parody of love and friendship and the images of defection, near-loss, and seeking which occur in both the comic subplot and the romantic story of the lovers. As previously mentioned, Stanley Wells analyzed the superficial, technical, and organic peculiarities of Shakespeare's plot and discerned several basic flaws in the playwright's method of construction, including an inability "to manipulate more than a few characters at once," a limited use of dramatic devices, and numerous discrepancies between the demands of characterization and those of his romantic conventions. On the other hand, in 1969 William Leigh Godshalk affirmed the play's structural unity by tracing the interaction of three recurring elements: the allusions to tragic classical myths at crucial moments, the patterned use of love letters which go awry and thus suggest the inadequacies of verbal communication in the realm of love, and the motif of journeying as an educative process. Shakespeare, the critic proclaimed, "builds an almost subliminal sense of crisis, suspense, and tension" through his use of these elements.

Several modern commentators on *The Two Gentlemen of Verona* have probed the relationship between audience and character perception. This concern was introduced by Bertrand Evans in 1960. Evans outlined the shifting advantages and disadvantages in awareness among the characters of the comedy, discerning at least six "notable secrets" and four levels of perception. Although nearly all the characters are alternately aware and ignorant of the intentions of the others and of the circumstances of the plot, the critic averred, Julia gains the "highest vantage-point" next to that of the audience, allowing her to pity her unfaithful lover. Evans's essay was followed several years later by Norman Sanders's treatment of the play. Examining Valentine's and Proteus's dialectically opposed "attitudes to love," Sanders linked this dualistic pattern with Shakespeare's unsuccessful attempt to balance "two standards of reality"—that of the audience and that of the play. He noted ways in which Shakespeare both moves his play into the world of the audience and draws his audience into the world of the play, adding that the effectiveness of this interaction makes it impossible to accept "the stilted characteristics and idiom of the Romance convention" when the playwright resorts to this method, as he does in the final scene. In his essay on "laughing with the audience," Robert Weimann demonstrated how this comic technique provides "a mutual extension of awareness" or a "comic concurrence" between an audience and an actor-character. He discerned three instances of this shared awareness in *The Two Gentlemen of Verona:* in Act II, Scene i, where Speed comments in asides on Silvia's and Valentine's "high-flown compliments"; in Act II, Scene iii, where Launce directly addresses the audience on his departure from his family; and in those scenes where Julia appears disguised as the male servant Sebastian.

Although many different issues have been addressed in the critical history of *The Two Gentlemen of Verona,* nearly all of the commentaries have reflected a concern with the flaws or oddities of the play. Whether concerned with love and friendship, appearance and reality, education, identity, morality or Christianity, the role of the forest, the structure, or the discrepant awarenesses in the comedy, critics have consistently tried to explain its anomalies and unexpected turns of events, particularly Valentine's surprising gift of his lover Silvia to his perfidious friend Proteus. It even remains debatable whether the play's faults are Shakespeare's, and, more importantly, whether they are truly faults at all, or simply part of Shakespeare's design. In either case, the anomalies seem to echo the pattern of contraries within the plot of the play—the serious and comic, treacherous and loyal, loving and indifferent, and ideal and real—encouraging us, in the words of Inga-Stina Ewbank, to be in "two minds at once: to accept and criticize the life presented to us."

[CHARLES GILDON] (essay date 1710)

[*Gildon was the first critic to write an extended commentary on the entire Shakespearean dramatic canon. Like many other Neo-classicists, he regarded Shakespeare as an imaginative playwright who nevertheless frequently violated the dramatic "rules" necessary for correct writing. In the following excerpt, Gildon cites numerous "Faults" and "Absurdities" in* The Two Gentlemen of Verona *which, he asserts, verify the play's early date. Despite these defects of "Plot, Conduct, Manners and Sentiments," Gildon detects lines which, he states, prove the play to be Shakespeare's, thus raising the issue of authorship which several later critics have considered in greater detail. He also disapproves of Valentine's easy reconciliation with Proteus in the final act.*]

['Tis] evident from the Writing, and the Faults and even Absurdities, that [*The Two Gentlemen of Verona*] was writ long before [*The Tempest*], for I can by no means think that *Shakespear* wrote worse and worse; for if his Fire may be suppos'd to abate in his Age, yet certainly his Judgment increas'd, but most of the Faults of this Play are Faults of Judgment more than Fancy. (p. 274)

Besides the Defect of the Plot which is too visible to criticise upon the Manners are no where agreeable, or convenient. *Silvia* and the rest not behaving themselves like Princes, Noblemen or the Sons and Daughters of such. The Place where the Scene is, by the original Error of the Press not yet corrected, for to be sure the Author cou'd not make the Blunder sometimes the Emperour's Court, sometimes *Millan,* and sometimes *Padua,* as is plain, is from the running the Eye over it.

But how defective soever this Interlude may be in the Plot, Conduct, Manners and Sentiments, . . . it is not destitute of Lines, that discover the Author to be *Shakespear.* (pp. 275-76)

The fifth Act of the Play is much the best, but *Valentine* is too easily reconciled to a Man, whose Treachery and Villany deserv'd the Stab especially when it is discovered at the very Time, that he goes to ravish his Friend's Betrothed. (p. 278)

> [*Charles Gildon*], "Remarks on the Plays of Shakespear: The Argument of 'The Two Gentlemen of Verona'," *in* The Works of Mr. William Shakespear, *Vol. 7, 1710. Reprint by AMS Press, Inc., 1967, pp. 274-78.*

[ALEXANDER POPE] (essay date 1723)

[*Pope was the foremost English poet of the first half of the eighteenth century, as well as a prolific author of satires written at the expense of his literary contemporaries. Between 1723 and 1725 he published a six-volume edition of the works of Shakespeare which was based upon the text of Nicholas Rowe. Pope was more concerned with poetics than with editorial scholarship, and thus his edition is replete with corruptions, principally interpolations and omissions which he believed would improve the metric patterns of Shakespeare's dramatic verse. In the following excerpt, Pope notes that the style of* The Two Gentlemen of Verona *is "more natural and unaffected" than that of the majority of Shakespeare's plays. He also states that the whole of Act I, Scene ii is "compos'd of the lowest and most trifling conceits," justifiable only by the "gross taste" of Shakespeare's Elizabethan public, a criticism which has incited varied responses from later critics.*]

It is observable (I know not from what cause) that the Style of [*The Two Gentlemen of Verona*] is less figurative, and more natural and unaffected, than the greater Part of [Shakespeare's], though suppos'd to be one of the first he wrote. (p. 153)

[Act I, Scene ii of *The Two Gentlemen of Verona*] is compos'd of the lowest and most trifling conceits, to be accounted for only from the gross taste of the age [Shakespeare] liv'd in; *Populo ut placerent* [that they should please the people]. (p. 157)

> [Alexander Pope], " 'The Two Gentlemen of Verona'," in The Works of Mr. William Shakespear: Consisting of the Comedies, Vol. I *by William Shakespeare, edited by Alexander Pope, 1723. Reprint by AMS, 1969, pp. 153-229.*

JOHN UPTON   (essay date 1748)

[*Upton suggests that on the basis of "manner and style" both* Love's Labour's Lost *and* The Two Gentlemen of Verona *should be stricken from the canon of Shakespeare's works "and seek for their parent elsewhere." He was among the earliest critics to discredit not just individual passages or scenes, but the entire play as a Shakespearean composition.*]

There are [no] strong external reasons for rejecting [from the list of Shakespeare's works] *Love's Labour's Lost,* and the *Two Gentlemen of Verona:* but if any proof can be formed from manner and style, then should these be sent packing, and seek for their parent elsewhere. How otherwise does the painter distinguish copies from originals? And have not authors their peculiar style and manner, from which a true critic can form as unerring a judgment as a painter? (p. 289)

> John Upton, "Book II, Sect. xvi," in his Critical Observations on Shakespeare, *second edition, G. Hawkins, 1748, pp. 284-93.*

[CHARLOTTE LENNOX]   (essay date 1754)

[*Lennox was a novelist and Shakespearean scholar who compiled* Shakespear Illustrated *(1754), a three-volume edition of translated texts of the sources used by Shakespeare in twenty-two of his plays, including some analyses of the ways in which he used these sources. In the excerpt below, taken from the third volume of this work, Lennox faults* The Two Gentlemen of Verona *for its "Absurdities" and "Improprieties" in both characterization and plot throughout. Like other critics, she disapproves of Valentine's offer of Silvia in the final scene. Furthermore, Lennox regards Silvia's behavior as "the rustic Smartness, and awkward Gaiety of a Village Coquet," not the virtuous decency expected of a gentlewoman, and she finds the heroine's acceptance of Valentine implausible "after so striking a Proof of his Indifference and Ingratitude."*]

Part of the Plot of [*The Two Gentlemen of Verona*] is taken from the Story of *Felismena,* in the Second Book of the *Diana* of *George Mantemayor,* a Pastoral Romance, translated from the *Spanish* in *Shakespear*'s time; the Loves of *Protheus* and *Julia,* in the Play their Characters and Adventures are the same, with those of *Felix* and *Felismena* in this Romance (p. 4)

The Story, indeed, is highly romantic and improbable, and *Shakespear*'s Judgment in rejecting many of the Circumstances [in his source] might be praised, if those he has invented were not equally absurd: 'tis generally allowed, that the Plot, Conduct, Manners, and Sentiments of this Play are extreamly deficient.

The Court and Palace of the Duke of *Milan,* to which first Sir *Valentine,* and then Sir *Protheus,* are sent to improve their Politeness in, has less Dignity and Decorum in it, than the House of a private Gentleman. *Silvia,* the Duke's Daughter, notwithstanding we are told with wonderful Simplicity, in different Passages of the Play, that she is *a virtuous civil Gentlewoman,* yet behaves with all the rustic Smartness, and awkward Gaiety of a Village Coquet.

She is introduced flirting from Room to Room, followed by two of her Lovers, and laughing equally at the Man she favours, and him she rejects, slyly inciting them to quarrel, and when she has set them together by the Ears, enjoys the Jest, 'till the good Prince, her Father, comes in to part them.

Sir *Valentine*'s Courtship of this Princess, it must be confessed, is extreamly singular, and the Appearance of his dirty Footman, *Speed,* in the *Presence-Chamber,* breaking Jests upon his Master and her Highness, while they are discoursing, has something in it very new and uncommon. (pp. 24-5)

Silvia, notwithstanding [her] seeming Indifference, is so violently in Love with *Valentine,* that being prevented in her Design of marrying him privately, and in Consequence of her refusing to marry Sir *Thurio* (a foolish Knight whom the Duke thinks a fit Match for the Princess, his Daughter, because he has a great deal of Money) being confined in a high Tower, resolves to forsake her Father's Court, and follow the banished *Valentine* to *Mantua.*

The poor Princess being in such a perplexing Situation, confined, guarded, and not suffered to have any Correspondence with any Person, but her destined Husband *Thurio,* and her Lover's false Friend *Protheus,* one would imagine some great Degree of Invention must be exerted to contrive a probable Stratagem to release her.

The Poet gets over this Difficulty with wonderful Ease: *Silvia* is shewn talking from her Chamber-window in the Tower in broad Day, to Sir *Eglamour,* her Confidant, below, settling with him, whom she desires to accompany her, the Method of her Escape, which is to be effected by his meeting her with Horses at Friar *Patrick*'s Cell, whither she intends to go to Confession.

To make all this probable, 'tis necessary that the Spies and Guards set over this Princess, must be all blind, otherwise she and Sir *Eglamour* must unavoidably be seen by them.—Tis also necessary that they should be deaf, or else they could not fail to hear the whole Contrivance; for her Chamber, we are informed, is in a high Tower, at a great Distance from the Ground, which made it impossible for Sir *Eglamour* and her to settle their Schemes in Whispers: and lastly, 'tis absolutely necessary, that this confined Princess should have the Liberty of rambling alone out of her Tower to Confession, or she could not so confidently make an Assignation with *Eglamour* at Friar *Patrick*'s Cell, nor so securely keep it.

Nothing can be more inconsistent than the Character of *Valentine;* nothing more improper than the Manners attributed to him as a Lover.

Passionately enamoured as he is with *Silvia,* he recommends a new Lover to her with the utmost Earnestness, and will not be satisfied 'till she promises to entertain him.

When he is banished to *Milan,* and in the extreamest Despair for the Loss of his Mistress, the Fear of Death prevails upon him to become the Head of a Gang of Banditti, and having in this Situation fortunately rescued his beloved *Silvia,* from the Violence of his treacherous Friend, who was going to ravish her, a few repentant Words uttered by that Friend, makes him resolve to resign her to him, notwithstanding the generous

Proof she had given him of her Tenderness, in running so many Hazards to be with him. (pp. 30-2)

This Part of the Intrigue of the Play, such as it is, that relates to the Loves of *Silvia* and *Valentine,* is probably the Poet's own Invention; but the Adventure of *Julia* and *Protheus* are copied closely from the Pastoral Romance.

The Poet drops the Story at the Flight of *Silvia,* and adds all the remaining Circumstances.

He also paints *Protheus* in much more disadvantageous Colours, than he is represented in the Original; there we find him indeed inconstant to his Mistress, who loves him passionately, and forsaking her for one that treats him with the utmost Disdain.

But *Shakespear* shews him treacherous in the highest Degree to his Friend, base and ungrateful to the Duke his Benefactor, and guilty of intended Violence towards the Woman he professes to love; yet, wicked as he is, he escapes not only without Punishment, but is made as happy as the renewed Tenderness of his injured Friend, and the inviolable Fidelity of his once loved *Julia* can make him.

The Character of *Julia* is much nearer the Original than that of *Protheus;* but in the Romance we find her, when she is in the Quality of a Page to Don *Felix,* exerting a very extraordinary kind of Generosity, in solliciting her Rival's Favour for her Lover.

Shakespear very judiciously makes her act a quite contrary Part, instead of endeavouring to move her Rival's Compassion for *Protheus,* she tries to engage it for the unhappy Object of his former Affection, representing her Love, her Constancy, her Grief at being abandoned, in the most pathetic Terms, and by artfully intermixing some Praises of her Beauty, insinuates the little Reliance she ought to have upon the prostituted Vows of a Man so prone to change. (pp. 33-4)

This Play every where abounds with the most ridiculous Absurdities in the Plot and Conduct of the Incidents, as well as with the greatest Improprieties in the Manners and Sentiments of the Persons.

The Princess, because it is necessary she should meet with her Lover in the Wood, without having the Power of making herself invisible, gets away from her Guards, and out of her high Tower, and gallops like an Amazon, attended only by one Squire to *Mantua.*

'Tis no Wonder therefore, that in such an Equipage, and engaged in such a romantic Design, she should fall into the Hands of the Banditti; nor that she should meet with her Lover amongst them, since the Poet had prepared us for this wonderful Incident, by a preceding one, full as astonishing, in making the noble Youth the Captain of this Band of Villains.

It seeming necessary also to the Poet's Design, that the Duke of *Milan* should fall into the same Danger, we find the good old Prince, upon the News of his Daughter's Flight, instead of dispatching several Parties of his Guards different Ways to overtake and bring her back, mounting his Horse himself, and with no other Attendants than *Protheus,* who is a Stranger in his Dominions, and *Thurio,* the foolish Knight he designed for his Son-in-law, riding away in Search of her.

'Tis easy to see, that by this Management he must fall into the Hands of the Banditti, and accordingly there we meet with him next. The Duke's bestowing his Daughter upon *Valentine,* whom he finds at the Head of this desperate Gang of Ruffians, after

refusing her to him, when he lived in his Court with an unblemished Reputation, is indeed a little incomprehensible, as is also *Valentine*'s Willingness to resign his beloved Mistress to his false Friend, who had offered Violence to her Chastity, and *Silvia*'s giving her Hand to him, after so striking a Proof of his Indifference and Ingratitude. (pp. 44-5)

> [*Charlotte Lennox*], ''The Fable of the 'Two Gentlemen of Verona','' in her Shakespear Illustrated; or, The Novels and Histories, on Which the Plays of Shakespear Are Founded, Vol. III, *1754. Reprint by AMS Press, Inc., 1973, pp. 1-53.*

BENJAMIN VICTOR   (essay date 1762)

[*Benjamin Victor wrote an adaptation of* The Two Gentlemen of Verona *which was performed at Drury Lane on December 22, 1762. In the following excerpt from the author's advertisement for that production, Victor derides his source as rank with ''weeds'' but acknowledges its ''poetical flowers'' as well; touching on the question of the play's authorship, he contends that Shakespeare alone could have created the comedy's better parts.*]

It is the general opinion that [*The Two Gentlemen of Verona*] abounds with weeds, and there is no one, I think, will deny, who peruses it with attention, that it is adorned with several poetical flowers such as the hand of a Shakespeare alone could raise. The rankest of those weeds I have endeavoured to remove; but was not a little solicitous lest I should go too far and, while I fancy'd myself grubbing up a weed, should heedlessly cut the threads of a flower.

The other part of my design, which was to give a greater uniformity to the scenery and a connection and consistency to the fable (which in many places is visibly wanted), will be deemed of more importance if it should be found to be executed with success. (p. 525)

> *Benjamin Victor, in an extract from* Shakespeare, the Critical Heritage: 1753-1765, Vol. 4, *edited by Brian Vickers, Routledge & Kegan Paul, 1976, pp. 525-33.*

SAMUEL JOHNSON   (essay date 1765)

[*Johnson has long held an important place in the history of Shakespearean criticism. He is considered the foremost representative of moderate English Neoclassicism and is credited by some literary historians with freeing Shakespeare from the strictures of the three unities valued by strict Neoclassicists: that dramas should have a single setting, take place in less than twenty-four hours, and have a causally connected plot. More recent scholars portray him as a critic who was able to synthesize existing critical theory rather than as an innovative theoretician. Johnson was a master of Augustan prose style and a personality who dominated the literary world of his epoch. In the following excerpt from comments first published in his 1765 edition of Shakespeare's plays, Johnson identifies certain lapses in coherence and faults of characterization in* The Two Gentlemen of Verona, *but also emphasizes its poetic beauty. He concludes that the comedy is ''a strange mixture of knowledge and ignorance, of care and negligence'' which is undoubtedly Shakespeare's, for no other dramatist, Johnson asserts, could ''rise up to his lowest'' flights of imagination.*]

When I read [*The Two Gentlemen of Verona*] I cannot but think that I discover both in the serious and ludicrous scenes, the language and sentiments of Shakespeare. It is not indeed one of his most powerful effusions, it has neither many diversities of character, nor striking delineations of life, but it abounds in [maxims] beyond most of his plays, and few have more lines or passages which, singly considered, are eminently beautiful. I am yet inclined to believe that it was not very successful, and suspect that it has escaped corruption, only because being seldom played it was less exposed to the hazards of transcription. (p. 162)

In this play there is a strange mixture of knowledge and ignorance, of care and negligence. The versification is often excellent, the allusions are learned and just; but the authour conveys his heroes by sea from one inland town to another in the same country; he places the Emperour at Milan and sends his young men to attend him, but never mentions him more; he makes Protheus, after an interview with Silvia, say he has only seen her picture, and, if we may credit the old copies, he has by mistaking places, left his scenery inextricable. The reason of all this confusion seems to be, that he took his story from a novel which he sometimes followed, and sometimes forsook, sometimes remembred, and sometimes forgot.

That this play is rightly attributed to Shakespeare, I have little doubt. If it be taken from him, to whom shall it be given? This question may be asked of all the disputed plays, except *Titus Andronicus;* and it will be found more credible, that Shakespeare might sometimes sink below his highest flights, than that any other should rise up to his lowest. (p. 173)

> *Samuel Johnson, "Notes on Shakespeare's Plays: 'The Two Gentlemen of Verona'," in his* The Yale Edition of The Works of Samuel Johnson: Johnson on Shakespeare, *Vol. I, edited by Arthur Sherbo, Yale University Press, 1968, pp. 161-73.*

ELIZABETH GRIFFITH   (essay date 1775)

[*Griffith exemplifies the seventeenth- and eighteenth-century preoccupation with searching through Shakespeare's plays for set speeches and passages that could be read out of dramatic context for their own sake. Griffith, however, avoided the more usual practice of collecting and commenting on poetic "beauties" and concentrated instead on the "moral" subjects treated in the text. In her commentary below, she briefly notes her disappointment in the morality of* The Two Gentlemen of Verona; *more importantly, Griffith touches on the issue of the play's authorship, claiming that were she "to offer any doubt upon this point," it would be because of the character of Proteus, whose degeneration from initial virtue to "baseness" and "villainy" she describes as abrupt, inconsistent, and unexplainable. Despite these charges, Griffith refrains from attributing the flawed work to an author other than Shakespeare, asserting that the proffered reasons for deleting it from the Shakespearean canon remain unconvincing.*]

The Fable of [*The Two Gentlemen of Verona*] has no more moral in it, than [*A Midsummer Night's Dream*], nor does it make us much amends, either by the number, or variety of its documents. I would, therefore, have passed it by, as some of the editors have done, on the supposition of its not being one of Shakespeare's; but that I thought any thing which had ever been imputed to that author, had a right to claim a place in this Work; unless the rejection of it were established upon better grounds, than the diversity of opinions about its authenticity, among the Commentators.

And, indeed, were I to offer any doubt upon this point, myself, it should not be so much from the objections adduced by the editors, as on account of the unnatural inconsistency of character, in the person of Protheus; who, in the first Act, and during above half the second, appears to stand in the most amiable and virtuous lights, both of morals and manhood, as a fond lover, and a faithful friend; and yet suddenly belies his

fair seemings, by an infidelity toward the first object, and a treachery with regard to the second. 'Tis true, indeed, that in the latter end he expresses a sort of contrition for his crimes; but yet this still seems to remain equivocal; as it does not appear to have arisen from any remorse of conscience, or abhorrence of his baseness, but rather from a disappointment in his pursuit, and an open detection of his villainy.

There are but few instances of this kind, that I remember to have met with, throughout the drama of Shakespeare; for however he may sport, as he often does, with the three *unities* of Aristotle, *time, place,* and *action,* he seldom sins against a fourth, which I am surprised the Critics have not added, as being worth them all—namely, that of *character;* the tenor of which is generally preserved, from first to last, in all his works. This consistency is required in the epic, and why not insisted on in the dramatic poem, I cannot conceive. (pp. 25-6)

> *Elizabeth Griffith, "'The Two Gentlemen of Verona'," in her* The Morality of Shakespeare's Drama Illustrated, *1775. Reprint by Frank Cass & Co. Ltd., 1971, pp. 25-32.*

CHARLES DIBDIN   (essay date 1800)

[*Dibdin is one of the first critics to contrast Valentine and Proteus as respective examples of the "etiquette" and "perfidy of polite life" depicted in* The Two Gentlemen of Verona. *He also denotes Launce and Speed as foils of their masters, an observation which has been discussed by several later critics in greater detail. He concludes his remarks on* The Two Gentlemen of Verona *by asserting that the "sublime heights" of its poetry exceed those reached by any of Shakespeare's previous works.*]

[*The Two Gentlemen of Verona*] displays a prodigious variety of those beauties which belonged only to SHAKESPEAR. The plot, which is taken from a novel, as far as it relates to the management of the scenery is certainly very intricate and almost inexplicable, but considered merely as a story, it has great simplicity and nature. The characters are drawn with strength and truth, and it is remarkable that in this play we have the first idea of what has been since called genteel comedy. The elegance, yet the contrast in VALENTINE and PROTHEUS, is a very striking picture, not only of the etiquette, but the perfidy of polite life; for PROTHEUS, is more corrupted by education than nature, of which his remorse and his contrition are proofs, while VALENTINE has a mind so correctly inclined to rectitude that fashion and folly cannot corrupt it.

But this is not all. The two servants, LAUNCE and SPEED, who are the foils of their masters, make the whole a complete resemblance of that sort of play which is the foundation of almost all the comedies of both the Spaniards and the French; and as these plays did not obtain with them, at least in this perfect form, till CALDERON, who was cotemporary with CORNEILLE, SHAKESPEAR may be said to have been the founder of this species of comedy. We must admit at the same time that the germ was in the Spaniards, but his mind was the only soil which could expand and bring it to perfection. (pp. 38-9)

The Two Gentlemen of Verona abounds with poetical beauties such as we have not before been able to discover even in SHAKESPEAR. His towering fancy in this particular piece playfully ascends to those sublime heights, dangerous to others but always familiar to him; sometimes hazardous, but never alarming; often trackless, yet always astonishing. (pp. 39-40)

> *Charles Dibdin, "'The Two Gentlemen of Verona'," in his* A Complete History of the English Stage, *Vol.*

III, *1800. Reprint by Garland Publishing, Inc., 1970, pp. 38-40.*

AUGUST WILHELM SCHLEGEL (essay date 1811)

[*A prominent German Romantic critic, Schlegel holds a key place in the history of Shakespeare's reputation in European criticism. His translations of sixteen of the plays are still considered the best German editions of Shakespeare. Schlegel was also a leading spokesman for the Romantic movement, which permanently overthrew the Neoclassical contention that Shakespeare was a child of nature whose plays lacked artistic form. In the following excerpt, taken from an English translation of his* Über dramatische Kunst und Literatur *(1811), Schlegel is the first to relate the lightness and superficiality of* The Two Gentlemen of Verona *to its treatment of the "transient youthful caprice" of love. Furthermore, in noting "the irresolution of love" and "its infidelity to friendship," Schlegel is the earliest to identify the themes of friendship and love and to record their conflict within the play.*]

The Two Gentlemen of Verona paints the irresolution of love, and its infidelity to friendship, pleasantly enough, but in some degree superficially, we might almost say with the levity of mind which a passion suddenly entertained, and as suddenly given up, presupposes. The faithless lover is at last, on account of a very ambiguous repentance, forgiven without much difficulty by his first mistress; for the more serious part, the premeditated flight of the daughter of a Prince, the capture of her father along with herself by a band of robbers, of which one of the Two Gentlemen, the betrayed and banished friend, has been against his will elected captain: for all this a peaceful solution is soon found. It is as if the course of the world was obliged to accommodate itself to a transient youthful caprice, called love. Julia, who accompanies her faithless lover in the disguise of a page, is, as it were, a light sketch of the tender female figures of a Viola [in *Twelfth Night*] and an Imogen [in *Cymbeline*], who, in the latter pieces of Shakspeare, leave their home in similar disguises on love adventures, and to whom a peculiar charm is communicated by the display of the most virginly modesty in their hazardous and problematical situation. (p. 380)

> *August Wilhelm Schlegel, "Criticisms on Shakespeare's Comedies," in his* A Course of Lectures on Dramatic Art and Literature, *edited by Rev. A. J. W. Morrison, translated by John Black, revised edition, 1846. Reprint by AMS Press, Inc., 1965, pp. 379-99.*

WILLIAM HAZLITT (essay date 1817)

[*Hazlitt is considered a leading Shakespearean critic of the English Romantic movement. A prolific essayist and critic on a wide range of subjects, Hazlitt remarked in the preface to his* Characters of Shakespear's Plays, *first published in 1817, that he was inspired by the German critic August Wilhelm Schlegel and was determined to supplant what he considered the pernicious influence of Samuel Johnson's Shakespearean criticism. Hazlitt's criticism is typically Romantic in its emphasis on character studies. His experience as a drama critic was an important factor in shaping his descriptive, as opposed to analytical, interpretations of Shakespeare. In the following excerpt from the work mentioned above, Hazlitt initially calls* The Two Gentlemen of Verona *"little more than the first outlines of a comedy loosely sketched in," a story "dramatised with very little labour or pretension." However, he defends the low-comic scenes from Alexander Pope's attack (see excerpt above, 1723), praising their "farcical drollery and invention." Touching on the question of authorship, Hazlitt asserts that the "quaintness of humour" and the "high poetical spirit" of certain scenes are "undoubtedly Shakespear's".*]

[*The Two Gentlemen of Verona*] is little more than the first outlines of a comedy loosely sketched in. It is the story of a novel dramatised with very little labour or pretension; yet there are passages of high poetical spirit, and of inimitable quaintness of humour, which are undoubtedly Shakespear's, and there is throughout the conduct of the fable a careless grace and felicity which marks it for his. One of the editors (we believe Mr. Pope) remarks in a marginal note to the *Two Gentlemen of Verona*—"It is observable (I know not for what cause) that the style of this comedy is less figurative, and more natural and unaffected than the greater part of this author's, though supposed to be one of the first he wrote" [see excerpt above, 1723]. Yet so little does the editor appear to have made up his mind upon this subject, that we find the following note to the very next (the second) scene. "This whole scene, like many others in these plays (some of which I believe were written by Shakespear, and others interpolated by the players) is composed of the lowest and most trifling conceits, to be accounted for only by the gross taste of the age he lived in: *Populo ut placerent* [That they should please the people]. . . ." It is strange that our fastidious critic should fall so soon from praising to reprobating. The style of the familiar parts of this comedy is indeed made up of conceits—low they may be for what we know, but then they are not poor, but rich ones. The scene of Launce with his dog (not that in the second, but that in the fourth act) is a perfect treat in the way of farcical drollery and invention; nor do we think Speed's manner of proving his master to be in love deficient in wit or sense, though the style may be criticised as not simple enough for the modern taste. (pp. 163-64)

The tender scenes in this play, though not so highly wrought as in some others, have often much sweetness of sentiment and expression. There is something pretty and playful in the conversation of Julia with her maid, when she shews such a disposition to coquetry about receiving the letter from Protheus; and her behaviour afterwards and her disappointment, when she finds him faithless to his vows, remind us at a distance of Imogen's tender constancy. Her answer to Lucetta, who advises her against following her lover in disguise, is a beautiful piece of poetry. (pp. 164-65)

If Shakespear indeed had written only this and other passages in the *Two Gentlemen of Verona*, he would *almost* have deserved Milton's praise of him—

> And sweetest Shakespear, Fancy's child,
> Warbles his native wood-notes wild.

But as it is, he deserves rather more praise than this. (p. 165)

> *William Hazlitt, "'The Two Gentlemen of Verona'," in his* Characters of Shakespear's Plays & Lectures on the English Poets, *The Macmillan Company, 1903, pp. 163-65.*

CHARLES ARMITAGE BROWN (essay date 1838)

[*In the excerpt below, Brown is the first critic to examine the character of Proteus in detail. He contends that Proteus has been misunderstood, that he is not evil, but merely a "wavering and confused" youth, innocent until his first temptation. Brown admits that Proteus's self-interest contrasts unfavorably with Valentine's virtue, but states that his vice is "consonant to nature"; he also argues that Proteus's "sudden conversion" is not improbable, but naturally follows his awareness of the futility of his crime and the depth of his degeneration.*]

[*The Two Gentlemen of Verona*] appears to me enriched with all the freshness of youth; with strong indications of [Shakespeare's] future matured poetical power and dramatic effect. It is the day-spring of genius, full of promise, beauty, and quietude, before the sun has arisen to its splendour. I can likewise discern in it his peculiar gradual developement of character, his minute touches, each tending to complete a portrait: and if these are not executed by the master-hand as shown in his later plays, they are by the same apprentice-hand,—each touch of strength sufficient to harmonize with the whole. We dwell with pleasure on Valentine, the two ladies, and the two servants, especially Launce; whose whimsical drollery is acknowledged by every one to be the most irresistible of all his clowns; but Proteus has been declared unworthy of the poet,— a compound of contradictions; a being, either infamous or honourable, either criminal or penitent, according to the exigences of the scene. Proteus has been neglected and misunderstood; and, regarding his conduct as natural and admirably delineated, I crave permission, at some length, to introduce him, as a creation of Shakespeare, to more favourable notice.

There appear to be three principal objections against the consistency and propriety of his character: one is inconstancy and guilt, without apparent cause, in a man praised and beloved by the other persons of the drama; the second is the improbability of his sudden repentance, and of his return to Julia's arms, with all his former love, uninjured by the treachery of broken faith; and the last is, the immoral conclusion that may be drawn from his remaining not only unpunished, but rewarded, and that at the sacrifice of a lovely and interesting girl. These seeming incongruities vanish when we attend to the impression made on us by the character, and carefully examine the text.

From his being the associate of Valentine, and the favourite of Julia, we are apt to conceive a higher opinion of his qualities than he can justly claim. When we bring him nearer to our view, and scrutinize his character by the assistance of Shakespeare's pen, developing the secrets of the heart, we shall find him a youth who, on the first temptation, was likely to become false and treacherous. He is deficient in kindly affections; he is a stranger to every warm and generous sensation; he is wrapped up in self, keenly alive to the effects of public disgrace, but little affected by the consciousness of dishonour; a proficient in learning, but wanting natural ability. His reputation has been obtained, among the old, by his studies, and by his being free from the excesses of a wild and thoughtless disposition; and these properties, together with a handsome person, and the accomplishments of a gentleman, gain applause among the young. His presumptive goodness is founded on his not having committed evil; he is not addicted to the follies of his age; he is neither quarrelsome nor vindictive; he offends nobody. (pp. 231-33)

After this description of him, it may be asked, how could Valentine bind to his bosom, in the closest ties of friendship, one so bereaved of every amiable qualification? Shakespeare tells us, and the information is enough, that

> From their infancy
> They had conversed, and spent their hours together.
> [II. iv. 62-3]

It was an early attachment,—therefore strong; not connected by a congeniality of disposition, but by habit, and a continuance of mutual kindness. Had they not been schoolfellows, and their friendship matured before their judgment, it is scarcely possible

they would have been common acquaintances. These two friends form one of Shakespeare's happy contrasts. There is a life, a gaiety about Valentine, in every thing he says and does, and his raillery is as elegant as it is inoffensive. He never opens his lips but he speaks the language of his soul, and wins at once our admiration and esteem. By the strength of his natural talents he has overleapt mere scholarship; and, unconscious of superiority, bestows unmerited applause on Proteus, who knows no more than what is told him by his tutor. In short, Valentine is a man from whom a woman derives a higher dignity, and is ennobled among her sex, the instant he declares his passion.

Perhaps it is difficult entirely to excuse Julia for having made choice of Proteus. He was handsome, and had not betrayed a single fault; which are much to an unsuspicious girl. Julia, though exquisitely portrayed, is inferior to most of Shakespeare's women; she has beauty, constancy, and tenderness, but no other brilliant attributes. Compare her with Viola [in *Twelfth Night*], in a similar situation with herself, and she will appear to great disadvantage. To define the love in the breast of Proteus, I should say it was not in the slightest degree mental, but corporeal; it neither had its source from the intellect, nor was it fed from it; but it proceeded from mere changeable nature. Like an idolater in religion, he must have his deity continually before him, or his adoration ceases. (pp. 233-34)

The comedy opens with the separation of the two friends, when Proteus displays no ardour of attachment,—although his conduct is wholly blameless. . . . When left alone, not a word falls from him expressive of regret. Instantly he talks of self, of his passion for Julia, and laments her cruelty in a strain ridiculous in any but a young pedant.

> Thou, Julia, thou hast metamorphosed me,
> *Made me neglect my studies, lose my time.*
> [I. i. 66-7]

At length Julia promises to be his! Never having dwelt with enthusiasm on the perfections of his mistress, feeling no more than a partiality and the warmth of youth, it ought not to be expected that the news should madden him into rapture; it is quite enough that he is highly pleased. (pp. 234-35)

Proteus bids adieu to Julia, coolly advises patience, declares he will return as soon as possible, and promises constancy in a set speech.

One of the maxims of Rochefoucault is, "absence diminishes the weak passions, and augments the strong, as the wind blows out a candle, and increases a fire." This is proved by Proteus, who no sooner arrives at Milan than "his candle is blown out," and

> The remembrance of his former love
> Is by a newer object quite forgotten.
> [II. iv. 194-95]

In his passion for Silvia he is conscious of his "false transgression," and seems startled at the self-knowledge he has just obtained. How naturally he confesses the immediate effects of his perfidy!

> Methinks, my zeal to Valentine is cold;
> And that I love him not, as I was wont.
> [II. iv. 203-04]

He strives to summon up the powers of his mind, and hopes to "check his erring love" [II. iv. 213]; but, in the same sentence, perplexed in irresolution, and fearfully looking forward to the doubtful contest, determines, should he chance to fail in his endeavours, to employ his abilities in the attainment of his desire. For a while we behold him wavering and confused; on the utmost boundary of innocence, but shuddering to make the fatal step beyond it. Hitherto the absence of temptation had withheld him from the commission of an unworthy action, and the first deviation from virtue alarms him. His conscience is wounded to the quick, and he can do nothing till the pain has ceased. He stands in need of a "flattering unction," seeks for it in the sophistries of his perverted brain, and at last, by their assistance, becomes a mean disgraceful villain, boasting that he has brought over reason to his side. His arguments are selfishly ingenious. Like Hudibras [in Samuel Butler's "Hudibras"], he discovers not only a palliative, but an excuse for his perjury.

> To leave my Julia shall I be forsworn;
> To love fair Silvia shall I be forsworn;
> To wrong my friend, I shall be much forsworn. . . .
> Unheedful vows may heedfully be broken;
> And he wants wit, that wants resolved will
> To learn his wit to exchange the bad for better.
>
> [II. vi. 1-3, 11-13]

Then, for his own interest, what he says is incontrovertible:—

> Julia I lose, and Valentine I lose:
> If I keep them, I needs must lose myself;
> If I lose them, this find I by my loss,
> For Valentine, myself; for Julia, Silvia:
> I to myself am dearer than a friend.
>
> [II. vi. 19-23]

Having proceeded thus far, the inevitable conclusion is,—

> I cannot now prove constant to myself,
> Without some treachery used to Valentine.
>
> [II. vi. 31-2]

From this moment his crimes increase in number and magnitude. No sooner has he placed his foot on the empire of guilt, than, according to the ancient custom of the country, he receives a passport to travel into any part of it without interruption. We need not follow his steps.

At length, wearied out by his fruitless villainies, and exasperated at Sylvia's reproaches, he attempts to violate her person; and it is here, at the very height of his depravity, and at the overthrow of all his schemes, that he becomes a penitent. All this is consonant to nature, and particularly so with Proteus. Had he been stopped in the midst of his career, his sudden conversion would be less probable; a man is more sincere in his detestation of crime, when, after having tried it in every possible way, he is convinced of its inefficacy. The disgrace endured by Proteus was so overwhelming, so insupportable, that he was ready to adopt any means to deliver himself from the dreadful punishment; and as nothing but absolute contrition could be of service, he flew to it with more ardour than he ever displayed in any action of his life. . . . I look upon him, at the end, as on a child, who had committed a heinous fault, and was effectually reformed by timely chastisement.

Let those blame Shakespeare for the immoral tendency of this comedy, who have not charity, like Valentine, to forgive; and who imagine that a few lines of solemn admonishment, just as the curtain drops, are of service to mankind. Shakespeare's morality is less in his fables, than in his characters; where the good are incitements to virtue, and the erring are dissuasives from vice. There are very few among us who are not compelled tacitly to acknowledge their similarity of Proteus, and to blush

Act V. Scene iv. Julia disguised as Sebastian, Silvia, Proteus, Valentine, the Duke, Thurio, and outlaws. Frontispiece to the Rowe edition (1709). By permission of the Folger Shakespeare Library.

at the resemblance,—who are not aware of their having, at times, and in a degree, clothed their justification in the same wretched subtleties, when prompted by self-interest or passion. Proteus is our brother.

The disputed difficulty towards the end of the play I would solve by abolishing it, as an interpolation by some one capable only of counting a line on his ten fingers, in order to give Julia's fainting another direct cause, but at the expense of Valentine's character, who is compelled preposterously to say,

> And, that my love may appear plain and free,
> All that was mine in Silvia, I give thee.
>
> [V. iv. 82-3]

Julia faints at the sight of Proteus, overcome by remorse and shame; then, as she recovers, seeing that moment the most propitious for the discovery of herself, she has recourse to the artifice of the two rings.

Against the opinion of others, mine is that this play does not conclude too abruptly. (pp. 236-40)

> *Charles Armitage Brown, "His Dramas: 'The Two Gentlemen of Verona'," in his* Shakespeare's Autobiographical Poems: Being His Sonnets Clearly

Developed, with His Character Drawn Chiefly from His Works, *James Bohn, 1838, pp. 230-40.*

HERMANN ULRICI   (essay date 1839)

[*A German scholar, Ulrici was a professor of philosophy and the author of works on Greek poetry and Shakespeare. The following excerpt is from an English translation of his* Über Shakespeares dramatische Kunst, und sein Verhältniss zu Calderon und Göthe, *a work first published in 1839. This study exemplifies the "philosophical criticism" developed in Germany during the nineteenth century. The immediate sources for Ulrici's critical approach appear to be August Wilhelm Schlegel's conception of the play as an organic, interconnected whole and Georg Wilhelm Friedrich Hegel's view of drama as an embodiment of the conflict of historical forces and ideas. Unlike his fellow German Shakespearean critic G. G. Gervinus, Ulrici sought to develop a specifically Christian aesthetics, but one which, as he carefully points out in the introduction to the work mentioned above, in no way intrudes on "that unity of idea, which preeminently constitutes a work of art a living creation in the world of beauty." In the commentary excerpted below, Ulrici examines the nature of love in* The Two Gentlemen of Verona, *noting that Shakespeare depicts the various aspects of this passion as "equally weak, foolish, perverse, and self-indulgent." He explores the love of each character, from Silvia's unswerving love, to Launce's "inexhaustible fund of inconsistency." Stressing the comic design of Shakespeare's play, Ulrici concludes that chance and the "changing and fickle humours of the lovers" create and resolve all complications, resulting in a "true picture of human life in general."*]

In parts, no doubt, the "Two Gentlemen of Verona" is sparkling with beauties, but as a whole it betrays a certain youthful awkwardness, and in execution a want of sustained power and depth. The composition is distinguished by the easy and harmonious flow of its language, by a peculiar freshness of view, by the *naïveté* of the particular thoughts, an unrestrained burst of wit and humour (*e. g.* in Speed and Launce), and by the delineation of the dramatic characters, which although but sketchily executed, is nevertheless striking, and invariably truthful. On the other hand, both the general view and the particular thought are deficient in depth; the parts do not readily round themselves off and combine into a whole; much is merely indicated which ought to have been more fully developed, and the conclusion especially is brought about too rapidly and without due preparation. Still it is ever Shakspeare, even though we here meet him at the outset of his career. Even at this early date he has shown rare judgment in the management of the comic materials—chance, humour, error, and intrigue, with human folly and perversity; the element of intrigue is predominant, but yet ably supported by the fantastic one of objective and subjective contingency. Love is regarded as the foundation and ruling spring of life; and it is manifestly the design of the piece to exhibit the instability and rottenness of this basis, and, as it appears within the comic view of things, in its infinite disporportion to the true idea of life. Accordingly, love is presented under the most diversified forms, but is in all equally weak, foolish, perverse, and self-indulgent. The centre of interest is in the love of Proteus for Julia; his twofold faithlessness, and his rapid repentance. A look from Silvia is enough to make him forget his affection for one for whom but a moment before he was passionately sighing, and for whose absence the tear-drops were still hanging on his eyelashes. For her love, he is content to be false to the dear friend of his youth, and to betray the confidence of the Duke her father, and of Thurio, whose suit he pretends to favour. Proteus is the impersonation of fickle inconstant love. In contrast with him, Julia appears

at first in the fitful humour of a coy maiden; she refuses to receive the letter of her lover, and yet chides her maid for not forcing her to read it; unopened she tears it in pieces before her, in order to gather the fragments afterwards, and read the contents in secret. Soon, however, this coyness is all forgotten, and she passes into the other extreme; disregarding all maidenly fears and decorum, she dresses herself in man's attire, and runs after her faithless lover to bear his messages to Silvia, and to throw herself, after the endurance of much contumely and mortification, into his arms. The other pair of lovers, Valentine and Silvia, are more constant; spite of all obstacles, troubles, and sufferings, they are faithful to each other. And, yet, Valentine is ready to resign the hand of his beloved, for whom he had done and suffered so much, and whom he was ready to carry off from her father, in favour of his treacherous and only half-repentant friend; although Silvia's aversion to Proteus would have prevented him from reaping any benefit from the sacrifice. Thurio, lastly, is a lover of a very ordinary character. He is a wealthy blockhead, who knows his own mind as little as he understands his more talented rival; he continues to woo, *although* his suit has been rejected with contumely and scorn, and then withdraws it, *because* it has been so treated. This fickle, inconstant, and inconsistent love and friendship, is worthily associated with the old Duke's parental fondness for his daughter, which also is in the highest degree blind and capricious. After purposing to force his daughter's inclination in favour of a captious old noodle, he at last consents to her union with a captain of outlaws, whose suit as an honourable knight he had rejected. The perversity, however, and inconsistency of love, reaches its consummation in the inimitable Launce, one of those delightfully amusing characters which we meet nowhere else but in Shakspeare. He who for wailing and grief can scarcely leave his father's roof, whose tears might fill the dry river, and whose sighs might drive the boat that is to bear him from his home; . . . he who has so tender a heart for his dog, rejoiced nevertheless in the correction of his friend Speed, for a fault into which he himself had led him. He is in fact an inexhaustible fund of inconsistency—of foolish sentimentality, and sentimental folly.

Thus, then, is love—that primary and fundamental motive of life and history, here depicted under different aspects in all its weakness and frailty, finiteness and nothingness. Chance, and the changing and fickle humours of the lovers, bring on the complication which is again untied by chance, fickleness, and necessity: all ultimately returns into the right track, and leads to a happy result. A true picture of human life in general! (pp. 285-87)

Hermann Ulrici, "Criticisms of Shakspeare's Drama: 'Love's Labour's Lost'—'Two Gentlemen of Verona'—'All's Well That Ends Well'," in his Shakspeare's Dramatic Art: And His Relation to Calderon and Goethe, *translated by A. J. W. Morrison, Chapman, Brothers, 1846, pp. 280-88.*

CHARLES KNIGHT   (essay date 1849)

[*Knight, an English educator and publisher, wrote numerous books and periodicals intended to educate the Victorian working class. Among these were his highly popular illustrated edition of Shakespeare's plays and a complementary illustrated biography of Shakespeare. In addition, Knight also produced a book of critical commentary on the plays,* Studies in Shakspere *(1849), and was a founder of the first Shakespeare Society. Citing comments by Samuel Johnson (1765) and William Hazlitt (1817) on* The Two Gentlemen of Verona, *Knight states that although the play may lack power, it evidences "elaboration" and "elegance." In support of this assessment, he offers one of the earliest in-depth discussions of the pattern of conflicting characterization in the comedy, emphasizing the importance of the opposing natures of the three main character-pairs: Proteus and Valentine, Julia and Silvia, and Launce and Speed.]*

Coleridge, the best of critics on Shakspere, has no remark on ['The Two Gentlemen of Verona'] beyond calling it "a sketch." Hazlitt, in a more elaborate criticism, follows out the same idea: "This is little more than the first outlines of a comedy loosely sketched in. It is the story of a novel dramatised with very little labour or pretension; yet there are passages of high poetical spirit, and of inimitable quaintness of humour, which are undoubtedly Shakspere's; and there is throughout the conduct of the fable a careless grace and felicity which marks it for his" [see excerpt above, 1817]. We scarcely think that Coleridge and Hazlitt are correct in considering this play "a sketch," if it be taken as a whole. In the fifth act, unquestionably, the outlines are "loosely sketched in." The unusual shortness of that act would indicate that it is, in some degree, hurried and unfinished. If the text be correct which makes Valentine offer to give up Silvia to Proteus, there cannot be a doubt that the poet intended to have worked out this idea, and to have exhibited a struggle of self-denial, and a sacrifice to friendship, which very young persons are inclined to consider possible. Friendship has its romance as well as love. In the other parts of the comedy there is certainly extremely little that can be called sketchy. They appear to us to be very carefully finished. There may be a deficiency of power, but not of elaboration. (pp. 101-02)

There are in this play the germ of several incidents and situations which occur in the poet's maturer works—the germ of some others of his most admired characters—the germ of one or two of his most beautiful descriptions. When Julia is deputed by Proteus to bear a letter to Silvia, urging the love which he ought to have kept sacred for herself, we are reminded of Viola, in 'Twelfth Night,' being sent to plead the Duke's passion for Olivia, although the other circumstances are widely different;—when we see Julia wearing her boy's disguise, with a modest archness and spirit, our thoughts involuntarily turn not only to Viola, but to Rosalind [in 'As You Like It'], and to Imogen [in 'Cymbeline'], three of the most exquisite of Shakspere's exquisite creations of female character. . . . When Valentine exclaims,

> And why not death, rather than living torment?
>
> [III. i. 170]

we recollect the grand passage in 'Macbeth,' where the same thought is exalted, and rendered terrible, by the peculiar circumstances of the speaker's guilt:—

> Better be with the dead,
> Whom we, to gain our place, have sent to peace,
> Than on the torture of the mind to lie
> In restless ecstacy.
>
> [*Macbeth*, III. ii. 19-22]

There are, generally speaking, resemblances throughout the works of Shakspere, which his genius alone could have preserved from being imitations. But, taking the particular instance before us, when with matured powers he came to deal with somewhat similar incidents and characters in other plays, and to repeat the leading idea of a particular sentiment, we can, without difficulty, perceive how vast a difference had been produced by a few years of reflection and experience;—

how he had made to himself an entirely new school of art, whose practice was as superior to his own conceptions as embodied in his first works, as it was beyond the mastery of his contemporaries, or of any who have succeeded him. It was for this reason that Pope called the style of 'The Two Gentlemen of Verona' "simple and unaffected" [see excerpt above, 1723]. It was opposed to Shakspere's later style, which is teeming with allusion upon allusion, dropped out of the exceeding riches of his glorious imagination. With the exception of the few obsolete words, and the unfamiliar application of words still in use, this comedy has, to our minds, a very modern air. The thoughts are natural and obvious, the images familiar and general. The most celebrated passages have a character of grace rather than of beauty; the elegance of a youthful poet aiming to be correct, instead of the splendour of the perfect artist, subjecting every crude and apparently unmanageable thought to the wonderful alchymy of his all-penetrating genius. (p. 103)

Johnson . . . considered this comedy to be wanting in "diversity of character" [see excerpt above, 1765]. The action, it must be observed, is mainly sustained by Proteus and Valentine, and by Julia and Silvia; and the conduct of the plot is relieved by the familiar scenes in which Speed and Launce appear. The other actors are very subordinate, and we scarcely demand any great diversity of character amongst them; but it seems to us, with regard to Proteus and Valentine, Julia and Silvia, Speed and Launce, that the characters are exhibited, as it were, in pairs, upon a principle of very defined though delicate contrast. We will endeavour to point out these somewhat nice distinctions. (p. 104)

Valentine and Proteus are the "two gentlemen"—Julia and Silvia the two ladies "beloved"—Speed and Launce the two "clownish" servants. And yet how different is the one from the other of the same class! Proteus, who is first presented to us as a lover, is evidently a very cold and calculating one. He is "a votary to fond desire" [I. i. 52]; but he *complains* of his mistress that she has metamorphosed him—

> Made me neglect my studies—lose my time.
>
> [I. i. 67]

He ventures, however, to write to Julia; and when he has her answer, "her oath for love, her honour's pawn" [II. i. 47]: he immediately takes the most prudent view of their position:—

> Oh that our fathers would applaud our loves!
>
> [II. i. 48]

But he has not decision enough to demand this approbation:—

> I fear'd to show my father Julia's letter,
> Lest he should take exceptions to my love.
>
> [II. i. 80-1]

He parts with his mistress in a very formal and well-behaved style;—they exchange rings, but Julia has first offered "this remembrance" [II. ii. 5] for her sake;—he makes a commonplace vow of constancy, whilst Julia rushes away in tears;—he quits Verona for Milan, and has a new love at first sight the instant he sees Silvia. The mode in which he sets about betraying his friend, and wooing his new mistress, is eminently characteristic of the calculating selfishness of his nature:—

> If I can check my erring love, I will;
> If not, to compass her I'll use my skill.
>
> [II. iv. 213-14]

He is of that very numerous class of men who would always be virtuous, if virtue would accomplish their object as well as vice;—who prefer truth to lying, when lying is unnecessary;—and who have a law of justice in their own minds, which if they can observe they "will;" but "if not,"—if they find themselves poor erring mortals, which they infallibly do, they think

> Their stars are more in fault than they.

This Proteus is a very contemptible fellow, who finally exhibits himself as a ruffian and a coward, and is punished by the heaviest infliction that the generous Valentine could bestow—his forgiveness. Generous, indeed, and most confiding, is our Valentine—a perfect contrast to Proteus. In the first scene he laughs at the passion of Proteus, as if he knew that it was alien to his nature; but, when he has become enamoured himself, with what enthusiasm he proclaims his devotion!—

> Why, man, she is mine own;
> And I as rich in having such a jewel
> As twenty seas, if all their sand were pearl. . . .
>   [II. iv. 168-70]

[After his banishment, Valentine] is compelled to join the outlaws, but he makes conditions with them that exhibit the goodness of his nature; and we hear no more of him till the catastrophe, when his traitorous friend is forgiven with the same confiding generosity that has governed all his intercourse with him. We have little doubt of the incorrect sense in which the passage is usually received, in which he is supposed to give up Silvia to his false friend—or, at any rate, of its unfinished nature. But it is perfectly natural and probable that he should receive Proteus again into his confidence, upon his declaration of "hearty sorrow" [V. iv. 74], and that he should do so upon principle:—

> Who by repentance is not satisfied,
> Is nor of heaven, nor earth.
>   [V. iv. 79-80]

It is, to our minds, quite delightful to find in this, which we consider amongst the earliest of Shakspere's plays, that exhibition of the real Christian spirit of charity which, more or less, pervades all his writings. (pp. 104-05)

The generous, confiding, courageous, and forgiving spirit of Valentine are well appreciated by the Duke—"Thou art a gentleman" [V. iv. 146]. In this praise are included all the virtues which Shakspere desired to represent in the character of Valentine;—the absence of which virtues he has also indicated in the selfish Proteus. The Duke adds, "and well derived." "Thou art a gentleman," in "thy spirit" [V. iv. 140]—a gentleman in "thy unrivalled merit" [V. iv. 144]; and thou hast the honours of ancestry—the further advantage of honourable progenitors.

We have dwelt so long upon the contrasts in the characters of the "two gentlemen," Proteus and Valentine, that we may appear to have forgotten our purpose of also tracing the distinctive peculiarities of the two ladies "beloved." Julia, in the sweetest feminine tenderness, is entirely worthy of the poet of Juliet and Imogen. Amidst her deep and sustaining love she has all the playfulness that belongs to the true woman. When she receives the letter of Proteus, the struggle between her affected indifference and her real disposition to cherish a deep affection is exceedingly pretty. Then comes, and very quickly, the development of the change which real love works,—the plighting her troth with Proteus,—the sorrow for his absence,—the flight to him,—the grief for his perjury,—the forgiveness. How full of heart and gentleness is all her conduct after she

has discovered the inconstancy of Proteus! How beautiful an absence is there of all upbraiding either of her faithless lover or of his new mistress! Of the one she says,

> Because I love him, I must pity him;
>   [IV. iv. 96]

the other she describes, without a touch of envy, as

> A virtuous gentlewoman, mild, and beautiful.
>   [IV., iv. 180]

Silvia is a character of much less intensity of feeling. She plays with her accepted lover as with a toy given to her for her amusement; she delights in a contest of words between him and his rival Thurio; she avows she is betrothed to Valentine, when she reproves Proteus for his perfidy, but she allows Proteus to send for her picture, which is, at least, not the act of one who strongly felt and resented his treachery to his friend. When she resolves to escape from her prison, she does not go forth to danger and difficulty with the spirit of Julia,—"a true-devoted pilgrim" [II. vii. 9]—but she places herself under the protection of Eglamour ("a very perfect gentle knight," as Chaucer would have called him)—

> For the ways are dangerous to pass.
>   [IV. iii. 24]

She goes to her banished lover, but she flies from her father—

> To keep me from a most unholy match.
>   [IV. iii. 30]

When she encounters Proteus in the forest, she, indeed, spiritedly avows her love for Valentine and her hatred for himself; nor is there, in any of the slight distinctions which we have pointed out, any real inferiority in her character to that of Julia. She is only more under the influence of circumstances. Julia, by her decision, subdues the circumstances of her situation to her own will.

Turn we now to Speed and Launce, the two "clownish" servants of Valentine and Proteus. (pp. 106-07)

Speed and Launce are both punsters; but Speed is by far the more inveterate one. He begins with a pun—my master "is shipp'd already, and I have play'd the sheep (ship) in losing him" [I. i. 72-3]. The same play upon words which the ship originates runs through the scene; and we are by no means sure that, if Shakspere made Verona a seaport in ignorance (which we very much doubt),—if, like his own Hotspur, he had "forgot the map" [*1 Henry IV*, III. i. 6],—whether he would, at any time, have converted Valentine into a land-traveller, and have lost his pun upon a better knowledge. In the scene before us, Speed establishes his character for "a quick wit" [I. i. 125]; Launce, on the contrary, very soon earns the reputation of "a mad-cap" and "an ass." And yet Launce can pun as perseveringly as Speed. But he can do something more. He can throw in the most natural touches of humour amongst his quibbles; and, indeed, he altogether forgets his quibbles when he is indulging his own peculiar vein. That vein is unquestionably drollery,—as Hazlitt has well described it,—the richest farcical drollery. His descriptions of his leave-taking, while "the dog all this while sheds not a tear" [II. iii. 30-1], and of the dog's misbehaviour when he thrust "himself into the company of three of four gentlemanlike dogs" [IV. iv. 16-17], are perfectly irresistible. We must leave thee, Launce; but we leave thee with less regret, for thou hast worthy successors. Thou wert among the first fruits, we think, of the creations of the greatest comic genius that the world has seen. . . . Thou wert conceived, perhaps, under that humble roof at Stratford, to gaze upon which all nations have since sent forth their pilgrims! Or, perhaps, when the young poet was, for the first time, left alone in the solitude of London, he looked back upon that shelter of his boyhood, and shadowed out his own parting in thine, Launce! (p. 108)

Charles Knight, '''The Two Gentlemen of Verona','' in his Studies of Shakspere, Charles Knight, 1849, pp. 95-108.

G. G. GERVINUS   (essay date 1849-50)

[*One of the most widely read Shakespearean critics of the latter half of the nineteenth century, the German critic Gervinus was praised by such eminent contemporaries as Edward Dowden, F. J. Furnivall, and James Russell Lowell; however, he is little known in the English-speaking world today. Like his predecessor Hermann Ulrici, Gervinus wrote in the tradition of the "philosophical criticism" developed in Germany in the mid-nineteenth century. Under the influence of August Wilhelm Schlegel's literary theory and Georg Wilhelm Friedrich Hegel's philosophy, such German critics as Gervinus tended to focus their analyses on a search for the literary work's organic unity and ethical import. Gervinus believed that Shakespeare's works contained a rational ethical system independent of any religion—in contrast to Ulrici, for whom Shakespeare's morality was basically Christian. In the following excerpt from comments originally published in German in 1849-50, Gervinus explores the "strict parallelism" of structure in* The Two Gentlemen of Verona, *stating that "the characters and events are so exactly placed in relation and contrast to each other that not only those of a similar nature, but even those of a contrary one, serve mutually to explain each other." Maintaining that the central theme remains the "essence and power of love," he compares the poetry of Silvia's three suitors to illustrate each one's capacity for love. The critic also justifies the ending of the comedy as appropriate to the characters' contrasting behavior, arguing that Valentine's sacrifice of his beloved to Proteus is not "unjustifiable," but illustrates his selfless nobility.*]

[*The Two Gentlemen of Verona*] treats of the essence and the power of love, and especially of its influence upon judgment and habit generally, and it is not well to impute to it a more defined idea. The twofold nature of love is here at the outset exhibited with that equal emphasis and that perfect impartiality which struck Goethe so powerfully in Shakespeare's writings. The poet facilitated the solving of this double problem by an æsthetic aritifice peculiar to himself, which we find especially evident in this youthful work, and which we see repeated in almost all his dramas. The structure and design of the play are carried out in a strict parallelism; the characters and events are so exactly placed in relation and contrast to each other that not only those of a similar nature, but even those of a contrary one, serve mutually to explain each other. Upon this point we shall lay the chief stress in our discussions.

Two friends, Valentine and Proteus, are separating in the first scene. The names have already a significance, which hints at their opposite characters. Valentine, a good honest nature, is a man of action; urged by honour to go out into the world and into military and courtly service, he is travelling to Milan; he belongs to the simple and plain kind of country gentlemen, with no finely-sifted speech; with him heart and lips are one; his generosity knows no doubt; himself good, he deems the bad good also; his nature is not soon affected by any emotion, his acts are not disturbed by reflections. A golden friend, ready for every great sacrifice, he has yet never known affection for the other sex; on the contrary, his derision is provoked by the absorbing passion of his more excitable friend. Proteus, on the

other hand, is a man of reflection, full of attractive virtues and faults, and of great mental capability. It is said of him that 'of many good he is the best' [I. ii. 21]; this goodness is exhibited throughout the piece (and this is a decided error) not in deeds, but only in the superiority of his talents. Entirely given up to love, completely filled with its desires and aspirations, he accuses himself of spending his days in 'shapeless idleness;' thirsting for love as he is, he is in danger through selfishness and self-pleasing of renouncing his manly character; he appears as a youth of that young and tender wit, which, like 'the most forward bud, is eaten by the canker ere it blow' [I. i. 45-6]. The one-sidedness of each character is now to find its complement, as it were, as a corrective. Proteus in the midst of his successful suit, is, to his despair, sent by his father to Valentine in Milan, in order like him to be 'tutored in the world' [I. iii. 21]; on the other hand Valentine's original bent for 'active deeds' meets with penance, as he himself calls it in Act II., sc. 4, from the fact that in Milan, Silvia, the duke's daughter, falls in love with him. In the case of Valentine this new condition brings an increase of experience and refinement, which he appropriates after his own fashion; in that of Proteus the change causes a restraint, against which his self-loving nature struggles. The way in which both behave in this change of situation is developed in the finest manner from the original disposition of their characters. The honest, unsuspecting Valentine, occupied with manly dealings, must be sought after by love, if love is to touch him; the daughter of the duke, above all others, is able to fascinate him as an object which at the same time excites his aspiring ambition. But, as we should expect from him, he acts like a novice in the work of love; he betrays his increasing inclination by open 'gazing' noticeable by all, and by imperious offensive treatment of his rival Thurio. When she meets his modesty half way and woos him in her letter, he understands her not, and his servant Speed is obliged to explain her intention. His wont when he laughed to crow like a cock, when he walked to walk like one of the lions, is now passed away; his friend Proteus might now find matter for ridicule in the metamorphosis which love has effected. Since difference of position places obstacles to a union, with his peculiar want of consideration and readiness for action he enters on a plan for eloping with Silvia; instead of guarding himself from the snares of the duke, unsuspicious and confident he proceeds to entangle himself still further. When his plan of elopement has been punished with banishment, he surrenders himself passively and unhesitatingly to a band of outlaws; desperation urges him, the active life suits him, and the man who invites his company touches his heart by the similar fate which he too has suffered. Such is the extremity to which the treachery of his friend has driven him. For Proteus, as soon as he had arrived at Milan, had at once forgotten his Julia. His love is, first and foremost, self-love. Completely absorbed in this one affection, arrived at Milan, and separated from Julia, his weak, love-seeking nature cannot endure for a moment the unusual void and desolation. Just as Romeo, rejected by his beloved, falls all the more violently in love with a new object, so does Proteus, when separated from Julia; he casts his eye on the beloved of his friend, and giving way to this one error, he falls from sin to sin, and runs the gauntlet of crime. Once befooled by the intoxication of the senses, he uses the finest sophistry to justify and to excuse his misdeeds. False and wavering, he forgets his oath to Julia, he ensnares the duke, he betrays his friend, he goes so far in baseness that he proposes slander as a means for making Silvia forget Valentine, and he himself undertakes the office of slanderer. His behaviour towards his rival Thurio shows what a judge he is of love, with what power he practices the arts of love, and how secure and victorious he knows himself compared to such an adversary. He teaches him the secrets of love, well knowing that he understands them not; he, a poet himself, enjoins him to woo Silvia by 'wailful sonnets,' when he knows that he can only fashion miserable rhymes. In the amorous style of the three lovers, the poet has given us an excellent insight into their capacity for love. In the verses of Thurio we see a few paltry insipid rhymes, which German translators have too confidently received as a specimen of the genuine Shakespearian lyric. The poet possesses true poetry enough not to fear putting silly verses in the lips of the silly wooer, and thus, whilst he intentionally inserts a poem of no merit, he acquires the further merit of characterization. The poem which Valentine addresses to Silvia (Act III. sc. 1) is of the same characteristic kind; composed in the usual conceit-style of love, it evidences tolerable awkwardness of rhyming talent, and is rather the work of the brain than the outpouring of excited feeling. Of Proteus' poem, we have only fragments and scattered words, which Julia imparts to us from his torn letter: 'kind Julia—love-wounded Proteus—poor, forlorn Proteus, passionate Proteus, to the sweet Julia' [I. ii. 106, 110, 121-22]—words sufficient to tell us that among the three this is the man who understands the true rhetoric of love. With this letter he had taken by storm the free heart of the unguarded, unsuspecting Julia; but so well does he understand the strategy of love, that towards Silvia, whose heart was given to Valentine, he needed more studied tactics; and for this reason he seizes every opening, procures himself helpers and allies in the father and the rival, and endeavours to insinuate himself by the cunning of slander. He has reckoned every point but that of a woman's character, which has as much masculine power about it as his own has feminine weakness.

The two loved ones stand in reversed contrast to the two lovers. The fair Julia, the friend of Proteus, is just as much a pure womanly nature as Valentine is a pure manly one. Chaste, reserved, observing the strictest modesty, she must be sought by Proteus, and will hardly allow him to seek her; she will not believe her Lucetta, that 'fire that is closest kept burns most of all' [I. ii. 30], for she has not yet gained the experience, which she subsequently expresses in almost the same words. When Proteus' love first finds a hearing, she remains in her quiet thoughtful life the same sweet being: at the moment of farewell her full heart finds not a word. But separated from Proteus, she experiences like Valentine the change in her whole being; the energy and vehemence of his passion are kindled in herself, just as Silvia's giddy desire for flight is in Valentine. She undertakes a journey after the man of her heart, she dreams of Elysium at the end of it, at that point at which she is to be awakened from her dream by the faithlessness of Proteus. She is not to be restrained by the consideration that the step may 'make her scandalized' [II. vii. 61]. She feels in herself that the purest and most guiltless love endures most heavily the hindrances in its path. The beloved of Valentine is exhibited in as great a contrast to this gentle creature, as Proteus is to Valentine. The auburn-haired Silvia, rash and reckless, steps somewhat beyond the sphere of a woman's nature; she is less tender than Valentine and Julia, and more intellectual and clever, like the scheming Proteus; teazingly she delights in putting off Thurio and in deriding him; she possesses that ready wit, with which Shakespeare has invested all his bolder prominent female characters. She herself makes advances to Valentine, she perceives the hopelessness of their love, and contrives a plan for flight; she sees through Proteus and his tissue of faithlessness; she abandons at last her position and her father to follow Valentine, and, observant of human nature and certain of success,

she chooses in Eglamour a companion in whose faith and honour she can repose, who himself has loved and has lost his beloved.

The plot is unravelled at length by a romantic meeting of all, in a conclusion which appears to all critics sudden, abrupt, and inartistic. It is undeniable that here the form of the plot is carelessly treated. We must, however, be cautious not to criticise rashly. For, in a pathological point of view, the catastrophe has been most attacked just where it is most to be defended. It is, namely, essentially brought about by the offer of Valentine to sacrifice his beloved one to his faithless friend. This . . . [has been] considered an unjustifiable act of heroic friendship. But this trait essentially belongs to Valentine's character. That it was not unintentionally introduced may also be traced from the mere parallelism observed throughout the composition. For Julia also is exhibited to us in the same aspect of resignation and self-renunciation springing from pure good-nature, which in her as in Valentine stands out in contrast to the self-love of Proteus. She enters Proteus' service as a page, she delivers his messages to Silvia with the intention of playing the fox as 'shepherd of his lambs' [IV. iv. 92], but Silvia so attracts her, that her hostile intention is at once disarmed. Valentine, subjected to the most violent alternation of feeling, with a nature quick to perceive and quicker to act, is in this scene of the catastrophe wrought up to the highest pitch of excitement. Longer and more united to his friend than to Silvia, and according to his nature not comprehending the base in one whom he had believed to be noble, this same man, who immediately afterwards in the presence of the duke threatens the hated Thurio with death, has no wrath, no revengeful feeling against his friend, even when he learns his treachery and sees him place 'rude uncivil touch' [V. iv. 60] upon Silvia. Nothing but the bitter sigh of disappointment escapes him: 'I am sorry, I must never trust thee more, but count the world a stranger for thy sake' [V. iv. 69-70]. Of the possession of Silvia, the outlaw may not think; to win back his repentant friend, the noble-minded man offers his greatest sacrifice. His feelings, according to his nature, overcome him at the outset; Proteus, on the contrary, sees a way out of his errors from a remark of Julia's, which speaks rather to his head than to his heart, and goads with cutting reproof his sense of honour far more than his feeling.

All this indeed is finely designed, full of striking traits of character, and all from one fount. Compared to Shakespeare's later works, it is nevertheless of a lighter kind; it is, however, important enough to outweigh whole opera omnia of our Romanticists, who ventured to blame their hero-poet in this play, imagining that the love-phrases were intended to represent love, and the heroic-phrases heroism. . . . [It has also been] considered that the low comic scenes, the heroes of which are the servants Speed and Launce, are not connected with the subject, but are intended only to excite laughter. In this manner, as we have before seen, the poets previous to Shakespeare worked at the burlesque parts of their dramas, in order to meet the taste of the vulgar. The case is similar also to Shakespeare's early attempts, such as the *Comedy of Errors* and the *Taming of the Shrew,* where the Dromios and Grumios, with their coarse jests, form an outwork of no importance, in so far as they have no influence as active characters upon the intricacies of the plot. This, however, is altered in the *Two Gentlemen of Verona;* and ever after Shakespeare, obeying the necessity in which he saw himself placed of satisfying in some measure the rough taste of a laughter-loving public, seized that skilful expedient to which we have also before alluded: he gave henceforth to his lower comic parts a close reference to the main actions of the piece. Not alone are the servants Speed and Launce placed in characteristic opposition to their masters, the witty Speed to the simple Valentine, the awkward Launce to the clever Proteus; not alone are they stationed by the side of their masters as disinterested observers, to whose extreme simplicity that is apparent which in the infatuation of passion escapes the understanding of the wise; so that Speed perceives the love of Silvia before his master, and even the simple Launce sees through the knavish tricks of his lord; but they are also by actions of their own placed as a parody by the side of the main action, in a manner which invests even the commonest incidents with a high moral value. Launce's account of his farewell may be regarded as a parody of Julia's silent parting from Proteus; the scene in which Speed 'thrusts himself' into Launce's love affairs and 'will be swinged for it' [III. i. 382], caricatures the false intrusion of Proteus into Valentine's love; but a deeper sense still lies in the stories of the rough Launce and his dog Crab, the very scenes which undoubtedly occur to the gentler reader as the most offensive. To the silly semi-brute fellow, who sympathizes with his beast almost more than with men, his dog is his best friend. He has suffered stripes for him, he has taken his faults upon himself, and has been willing to sacrifice everything to him. At last, self-sacrificing like Valentine and Julia, he is willing to resign even this friend; he is ready to abandon his best possession to do a service to his master. With this capacity for sacrifice, this simple child of nature is placed by the side of Proteus—that splendid model of manly endowments, who, self-seeking, betrayed friend and lover. This fine relation of the lower to the higher parts of the piece is moreover so skilfully concealed by the removal of all moralizing from the action, that the cultivated spectator of the play finds the objective effect of the action in no wise disturbed, while the groundling of the pit tastes unimpeded his pure delight in common nature. (pp. 157-63)

> G. G. Gervinus, "Second Period of Shakespeare's Dramatic Poetry: 'The Two Gentlemen of Verona'," in his Shakespeare Commentaries, translated by F. E. Bunnètt, revised edition, 1877. Reprint by AMS Press, 1971, pp. 157-63.

WILLIAM WATKISS LLOYD (essay date 1856)

[In the excerpt below, Lloyd traces the error of "misjudging confidence" throughout The Two Gentlemen of Verona, stating that Proteus, Valentine, and Silvia all at some point choose the wrong person to deliver their important messages of love, which are consequently misguided or lost completely. Lloyd also emphasizes the complementary nature of the characterization and events in the play; the critic discerns one such interesting parallel in Launce's devotion to his dog Crab and Julia's selfless love for Proteus, claiming that in the former situation Shakespeare is parodying the ideal of "self-sacrifice of the better for the baser." In contrast to many later critics who have admired Silvia's quiet devotion, Lloyd chastises her "dangerous coquetry towards Proteus" and her lack of gratitude for Valentine's rescue. Lloyd's commentary on The Two Gentlemen of Verona was originally published in S. W. Singer's 1856 edition of Shakespeare's plays.]

Sir Proteus and Sir Valentine, gentlemen twain and friends, of Verona, are enamoured respectively of Julia and Silvia: parallel in their loves,—for both find favour, and the lady of either is prepared to quit sire and home for their sakes without leave or leavetaking; they are as nearly parallel in their attendance,—Speed is the boy-page of Sir Valentine, and Launce waits after a genius and fashion of his own, upon Sir Proteus.

It is the inconstancy of Sir Proteus—a name suggested by his character, that chiefly gives movement to the story. Separated from his own love, he becomes enamoured of his friend's, whom his friend only too incautiously brings him near; and incited by his new passion he betrays Valentine to procure his banishment; makes a catspaw of another rival to gain opportunity for pressing his own suit; receives even encouragement enough to excuse some loss of head: is repentant, pardoned, and again loyal to Julia, when Valentine upbraids him, and when—O potent mystery of love! the first object is again present to vindicate her power.

The excuse that renders the falsehood of Proteus tolerable, is the foolish "braggardism" of Valentine in setting forth his mistress; the fault of the boy in Much Ado about Nothing, "who found a bird's nest and told his comrade, and he stole it" [Much Ado about Nothing, II. i. 223-24]. The little consideration he shows or admits for the prepossessions of Proteus in favour of another, is great apology for reciprocation on the part of his confidant, who practically rebukes him by adopting his opinion to his cost. Valentine's love has no slightest savour of jealousy,—he despises the pretensions of Thurio, and thence of all others. He heralds and proclaims the perfection of Proteus beforehand, and urges Silvia to "confirm his welcome with some special favour."—"Sweet lady entertain him for your servant" [II. iv. 101, 104-05]. He certainly professes that he must follow Silvia as Thurio is with her, and "love thou knowest is full of jealousy" [II. iv. 177]; but the next minute he forgets that errand, and is off to his chamber, and forgets his yet warm maxim too, for he invites Proteus to full confidence in all his schemes and counsel for elopement, and when he is banished he apparently falls entirely in with the offer of Proteus to "confer at large of all that may concern his love affairs" [III. i. 255-56], and to be the medium of clandestine correspondence. Valentine was wrong—he ought to have known better the tendencies of a susceptible nature, whose lady love is at a distance, and for a long time likely to be so.

Valentine is imprudent, but Thurio is ridiculous; the mistake of the romantic lover is with the sordid rival distorted into a blunder. Assuredly we feel no indignation against Proteus in this second faithless attorneyship, and his impunity in the second somewhat carries off the feeling of heinousness associated with the first, which it seems like casuistry to construe very differently. Proteus is too near akin to his fellow gentleman quite to escape his error of misjudging confidence, though with less serious consequences. He sends his love-letter to Julia by his friend's page who delivers it to Julia's waiting-woman, as if to herself. He sends his present of a pet dog to Silvia by Launce, who loses "the squirrel" and substitutes his own brute Crab, unmannerly cur; messengers undeft enough, but at least they were not rivals. As a last resource, he falls into the last absurdity of engaging his old love to promote his suit with his new one. The art of delegation is at fault throughout the play, and Valentine is vain to hope for love-making by proxy in his exile, when he cannot get the commonest message delivered as it should be; Launce, who has charge of it, . . . simply improves the opportunity to get Speed a whipping by delaying him for half an hour. Silvia, after all, has best judgment in choice of both secretary and messenger, when she makes Valentine write a letter in her name to himself, and to himself deliver it—yet strange to say, even in this case, it hardly comes to hand. But what exception can be taken to her choice as convoy and conductor to Mantua, of the loyal Sir Eglamour?

> And for the ways are dangerous to pass,

I do desire thy worthy company,
Upon whose faith and honour I repose.

[IV. iii. 24-6]

For faith and honour let Sir Eglamour pass; but where was he
when most needed in "the dangerous ways?"—"Where is the
gentleman that was with her? Being nimble-footed he hath
outrun us, answers one outlaw to another; but Moyses and
Valerius follow him" [V. iii. 6-8], and it is my sincere hope
that he was caught. (pp. 1-2)

By usual fatality the fickle lover [Proteus] has gained a truly
constant heart—for such is Julia's; and Julia is the most charming character in the play, and more than rudimentary of more
than one of Shakspeare's most charming heroines. From her
lips fall the lines of sweetest poetry in the play, expressive of
the behaviour of true affection in all circumstances; in difficulty, excited and lively; in prosperity and ease, availing itself
only of such happiness to pursue its course—untarrying, un-
divergent, a beauty and a blessing; and varied in this manner
by contingent fortunes, but ever in itself the same, is the affection of Julia and the history of its course.

Silvia, "hard beset" with lovers in her father's court, though
she gives proof not to be excepted against that she loves Valentine, betrays not the less a tinge of the temper of her wooer
Proteus. It must be said without disguise, that it was not absolutely necessary for her to give her picture to Proteus while
she was upbraiding him with falsehood to his friend and to a
former love; and if the act was not falsehood on her part towards
Valentine, it was dangerous coquetry towards Proteus, and goes
far to account for the interpretation he evidently put upon her
coyness, when he had added the service of rescue from the
robbers to former fervent protestations. Her bitter upbraidings
are phenomena that Homer and Paris Alexander knew, and
Proteus may therefore not unnaturally have thought, to be far
less sincere than they may sometimes have sounded; and Valentine himself who unseen was looking on and listening at the
scene, may have had his own apprehensions too, and interfered,
it may be, to rescue Silvia scarcely more from Proteus than
from herself. Thus may be, but only thus can be accounted
for, the remainder of the scene; thus the more than Christian
eagerness of pardon with which Valentine overwhelms the
abashed Proteus, and the alacrity of his renunciation of all
previous rights in the blushing damsel who has no word of
recognition or gratitude to greet him with, but is tongue-tied
to the end.

And that my love may appear plain and free,
All that was mine in Silvia I give thee.

[V. iv. 82-3]

The distress and revelation of Julia set all to rights. Proteus is
recalled to his first attachment and his better nature; Valentine
recalls his gift of Silvia by heartily joining the hands of Julia
and her recovered knight; and the arrival of Thurio, and the
graciousness of the duke, give hint for the revival of his own
passion—the recovery of his confidence, at least to a point that
will not prevent his being more circumspect in future.

One may be tempted to think, as Valentine draws the Duke's
attention gracefully to the blushing page, that he and Julia
would have been the more fitting match. But love manages not
these matters on this wise, and it is quite in the order of his
dispensations, that the two most constant and sincerest lovers
should each be mated with a husband and a wife who had
hitherto at least had neither steadfastness nor sincerity to spare.

Launce and Speed are complementary to each other like their
masters, but in lower grade, mortals still more inferior to the
heroes than the heroes are to the gods. Personally Speed is
contrasted with Launce whose age is undefined, by constant
indications of youthfulness yet unescaped from boyhood. He
is equally matched with Launce in the wit of word-catching,
but appropriately, as the servant of the more refined Valentine,
he wants the humour of the servant of Proteus, humour that
smacks so strongly of worldly wisdom, that consorts in easy
familiarity with whatever coarseness may come in the way or
even lie a little beside it, and that is as little checked in its
indulgence by theoretical delicacy as by mischievous consequence to master or fellow. It is quite intelligible that Launce
should relish the misbehaviour of the substituted Crab,—he
waited, of course, in expectation of such reward; and when he
believes he has got Speed into trouble, he looks forward to "a
sight of the boy's correction" [III. i. 384] while he shall stand
by in the character of moralist, as the completion of the fun.

Both Speed and Launce surpass their masters in the quality of
mind denoted by the term shrewdness—the epithet "clownish," in the original list of actors refers not to rusticity, but to
the stage clown of the day—Speed interprets Silvia to his puzzled master, and Launce discerns the knavery of Proteus with
perspicacity enough. Proteus, in his excuse to his father, only
over-reaches himself, and Valentine gives himself up to the
inartificial discovery of the duke with an aptitude for being
bewildered, that is delightful.

There is sufficient indication in the play that when it was
written, Shakspeare had already conceived the principle by
which in his more perfect works he so wonderfully harmonizes
the farcical and the comic; thus, the parting of Julia and Proteus,
when kiss and token are interchanged, but poor Julia, more
moved than her swain, is fain to break away, is "gone without
a word" and leaves Proteus to reflect—

Ay, so true love should do: it cannot speak;
For truth hath better deeds than words to grace it.—

And,

Alas! this parting strikes poor lovers dumb,—

[II. ii. 16-18, 20]

a scene in which the comparative coldness of the lover is
certainly palpable, introduces the still more ominous monologue of Launce descriptive of the passionate domestic scene
at his own leavetaking, and the cruelhearted indifference of
the dog Crab, "that all this while sheds not a tear nor speaks
a word" [II. iii. 30-1].

Launce's communication of his love-texts to Speed, and the
punishment of prying incurred by the latter, give pale reflex
of the too confidential Valentine and Thurio and the little prof-
iting of Proteus the eager confidant, thereby. It may be sin to
say so, but I verily believe that the account given by Launce
of his self-devotion to rescue Crab from the results of his
transgression once and again, presents designedly the farcical
aspect of the self-sacrifice of the better for the baser, that in
the aspect of loftier comedy is presented in the end of the scene
by the disguised Julia. (pp. 3-5)

For a judgment on the play at large we may in this case appeal
to Shakspeare himself, whose appreciation is discernible in the
remarkable fact, that its scenes, incidents, images and situations, are met with in others of his later plays—always extended, developed, and refined—and we may infer that the
poet considered that in this work he had recorded ideas of great

poetical worth, but still with a certain crudeness that made him feel no scruple in making other appliance of them. (p. 5)

[One] fundamental coincidence directs attention to what is really the weak point in the structure and elaboration of the play. *The Two Gentlemen of Verona* has the imperfection that perplexes us in *All's Well that Ends Well;*—the motive incident of the intrigue is prolonged and tightened, until, by the necessity of a close, a greater strain is put upon our faith in the sincerity of conversions taken up suddenly and when no further evasion is available, than that faith when most charitably disposed, very willingly bears. In dramas, therefore, that we may confidently consider of later date, Shakspeare avoids making such a demand in the case of any of the chief characters of the play; and in the case of subordinates, as Jacques de Bois and the usurping Duke, in *As You Like It,* he accords a variety of preparatory incident, and either does not re-introduce the penitent in presence again, or at least avoids exhibiting the very moment of conversion. But, in the *Midsummer Night's Dream,* he recurred to his early theme of the volatility of love, and heightened the dilemmas it induces, of interchanging fancy and sudden revolutions and vagaries of affection, by double complexities and cross purposes, that outvie the transformations of Proteus, the dallying uncertainty of Silvia, the impulse of Valentine; but here he is still more bold, because he is at the same time more indulgent; and he is able to achieve the full interest of all the situations because he entirely relieves the agents of responsibility for their fickleness, by the intertwining with the course of their action and the very origin of their imaginations, the influence of faery charms and the finest of all fantastic supernatural influences. (p. 6)

> *William Watkiss Lloyd, "Critical Essay on 'The Two Gentlemen of Verona'," in Essays on the Life and Plays of Shakespeare, C. Whittingham, 1858, pp. 1-6.*

EDWARD DOWDEN (essay date 1877)

[*Dowden was an Irish critic and biographer whose* Shakspere: A Critical Study of His Mind and Art, *first published in 1875 and revised in 1881, was the leading example of the biographical criticism popular in the English-speaking world near the end of the nineteenth century. Biographical critics sought in the plays and poems a record of Shakespeare's personal development. As that approach gave way in the twentieth century to aesthetic theories with greater emphasis on the constructed, formal nature of literary works, the biographical analysis of Dowden and other critics came to be regarded as limited and often misleading. In the following excerpt, Dowden stresses the significance of* The Two Gentlemen of Verona *as the first play in which Shakespeare told a "romantic love-story" in dramatic form. He also asserts that the characters in the comedy are "contrasted with almost too obvious a design." Furthermore, touching on the issue of authorship, the critic considers the characters' interactions so "unreal and ill-contrived" in the fifth act of the play that he suspects some alterations or omissions from Shakespeare's original text. On other matters, Dowden describes the comedy's central theme as "love and friendship, with their mutual relations," and he concludes his brief remarks with a discussion of the play's language.*]

The Two Gentlemen of Verona, though in parts slightly worked out, exhibits an advance on the preceding comedies. The *Errors* was a clever tangle of diverting incidents, with a few passages of lyric beauty, and one of almost tragic pathos; *Love's Labour's Lost* was a play of glittering and elaborate dialogue. In *The Two Gentlemen of Verona* Shakspere struck into a new

path, which he was to pursue with admirable results; it is his earliest comedy in which a romantic love-story is told in dramatic form. Here first Shakspere records the tender and passionate history of a woman's heart, and the adventures to which love may prompt her. Julia (who is like a crayon sketch of Juliet, conceived in a way suitable to comedy instead of tragedy) is the first of that charming group of children of Shakspere's imagination which includes Viola [in *Twelfth Night*], Portia [in *The Merchant of Venice*], Rosalind [in *As You Like It*], and Imogen [in *Cymbeline*]—women who assume, under some constraint of fortune, the disguise of male attire, and who, while submitting to their transformation, forfeit none of the grace, the modesty, the sensitive delicacy, or the pretty wilfulness of their sex. Launce, accompanied by his immortal dog, leads the train of Shakspere's humorous clowns [with] his rich, grotesque humanity. . . . The play contains a number of sketches, from which Shakspere afterwards worked out finished pictures. . . . The characters are clearly conceived, and contrasted with almost too obvious a design: the faithful Valentine is set over against the faithless Proteus; the bright and clever Silvia is set over against the tender and ardent Julia; the clown Speed, notable as a verbal wit and quibbler, is set over against the humorous Launce. The general theme of the play we may define as love and friendship, with their mutual relations. The *dénouement* in Act V., if written by Shakspere in the form we now have it, is a very crude piece of work. Proteus' sudden repentance, Valentine's sudden abandonment to him of Silvia, under an impulse of extravagant friendship ("all that was mine in Silvia I give thee;" [V. iv. 83]), and Silvia's silence and passiveness whilst disposed of from lover to lover, are, even for the fifth act of a comedy, strangely unreal and ill-contrived. Can it be that this fifth act has reached us in an imperfect form, and that some speeches between Silvia and Valentine have dropped out? The date of the play cannot be definitely fixed; but its place among the comedies is probably after *Love's Labour's Lost,* and before *A Midsummer Night's Dream.* The language and verse are characterised by an even sweetness; rhymed lines and doggerel verses are lessening in number; the blank verse is written with careful regularity. It is as if Shakspere were giving up his early licences of versification, were aiming at a more refined style (which occasionally became a little tame), but being still a novice in the art of writing blank verse, were timid, and failed to write it with the freedom and "happy valiancy" which distinguish his later manner. (pp. 68-9)

> *Edward Dowden, "Introductions to the Plays and Poems: 'The Two Gentlemen of Verona'," in his Shakspere, Macmillan and Co., 1877, pp. 68-70.*

ALGERNON CHARLES SWINBURNE (essay date 1880)

[*Swinburne was an English poet, dramatist, and critic who devoted much of his literary career to the study of Shakespeare and other Elizabethan writers. His three books on Shakespeare—A Study of Shakespeare (1880), Shakespeare (1909), and Three Plays of Shakespeare (1909)—all demonstrate his keen interest in Shakespeare's poetic talents and, especially, his major tragedies. Swinburne's literary commentary is frequently conveyed in a style that is markedly intense and effusive. In the following excerpt, a comparison of the language in* The Comedy of Errors, Love's Labour's Lost, *and* The Two Gentlemen of Verona, *Swinburne praises the last of these works for "an even sweetness, a simple equality of grace in thought and language which keeps the whole poem in tune." He considers Shakespeare's style in* The Two Gentlemen "a sensible change of manner, signalised by increased firmness of hand and clearness of outline."*]

What was highest as poetry in the *Comedy of Errors* was mainly in rhyme; all indeed, we might say, between the prelude spoken by Ægeon and the appearance in the last scene of his wife: in *Love's Labour's Lost* what was highest was couched wholly in blank verse; in the *Two Gentlemen of Verona* rhyme has fallen seemingly into abeyance, and there are no passages of such elegiac beauty as in the former, of such exalted eloquence as in the latter of these plays; there is an even sweetness, a simple equality of grace in thought and language which keeps the whole poem in tune, written as it is in a subdued key of unambitious harmony. In perfect unity and keeping the composition of this beautiful sketch may perhaps be said to mark a stage of advance, a new point of work attained, a faint but sensible change of manner, signalised by increased firmness of hand and clearness of outline. Slight and swift in execution as it is, few and simple as are the chords here struck of character and emotion, every shade of drawing and every note of sound is at one with the whole scheme of form and music. Here too is the first dawn of that higher and more tender humour which was never given in such perfection to any man as ultimately to Shakespeare; one touch of the by-play of Launce and his immortal dog is worth all the bright fantastic interludes of Boyet and Adriano, Costard and Holofernes [in *Love's Labour's Lost*]; worth even half the sallies of Mercutio [in *Romeo and Juliet*], and half the dancing doggrel or broad-witted prose of either Dromio [in *The Comedy of Errors*]. (pp. 48-9)

> Algernon Charles Swinburne, "First Period: Lyric and Fantastic," in his A Study of Shakespeare, R. Worthington, 1880, pp. 1-65.

DENTON J. SNIDER (essay date 1890?)

[*Snider was an American scholar, philosopher, and poet who closely followed the precepts of the German philosopher Georg Wilhelm Friedrich Hegel and contributed greatly to the dissemination of his dialectical philosophy in America. Snider's critical writings include studies on Homer, Dante, and Goethe, as well as Shakespeare. Like Hermann Ulrici and G. G. Gervinus, Snider sought for the dramatic unity and ethical import in Shakespeare's plays, but he presented a more rigorous Hegelian interpretation than those two German philosophical critics. In the introduction to his three-volume work* The Shakespearian Drama: A Commentary *(1887-90), Snider states that Shakespeare's plays present various ethical principles which, in their differences, come into "Dramatic Collision," but are ultimately resolved and brought into harmony. He claims that these collisions can be traced in the plays' various "Dramatic Threads" of action and thought, which together form a "Dramatic Movement," and that the analysis of these threads and movements—"the structural elements of the drama"—reveal the organic unity of Shakespeare's art. Snider observes two basic movements in the tragedies—guilt and retribution—and three in the comedies—separation, mediation, and return. In the second volume of the series mentioned above, Snider discusses the three movements in* The Two Gentlemen of Verona *which depict the dissolution and the reintegration of the ties of friendship and love. He considers Proteus's "emotion without the permanent, rational element" the impetus to the action, noting how such emotion "drives man into a violation of all honor and virtue." Snider asserts that when Proteus and the other characters meet in the idyllic "World of Outlaws," a forest free from civil authority, a return to the forsaken institutions of the Family and the State is mediated, and a reconciliation of friendship and love takes place.*]

[*The Two Gentlemen of Verona*] is, doubtless, one of the youthful plays of Shakespeare. Its theme is the passion of youth; fullness and warmth characterize its descriptions, and, at the same time, there is a feeling of resignation to the power of

love which amounts to weakness. The coloring is peculiar and uniform throughout; there is felt the lassitude of the stricken shepherd; there is seen the complete absorption of the individual in the fancy and emotions. The mood of the Poet is diffused through the entire work, giving it the fragrance as well as the languor of early Spring—the season which in so many ways represents youth. The tone often resembles that of the pastoral romances of Spain and Italy; it is the feeling of the lorn lover, who has lost himself and wanders round in a dreamy quest like a shadow. Such is the artistic hue which colors this drama, and gives its distinctive characteristic; it is the true poetic element, which no analysis can reach, and which can only be felt. (p. 320)

In the present drama the thought is not so profound, the organic structure is not so perfect, the characterization is not so rich, as they are seen in later works; but the germs of many of the most beautiful parts of Shakespeare are to be found here. The reader is continually reminded of scenes, incidents, and motives which occur in other plays. But the peculiar and striking fact is that the Poet gives in this play the outlines of his most notable literary form, namely, the Mediated Drama, together with the introduction of the idyllic realm to harmonize the conflicts of life. Here it is, though in an incipient stage; the outlaws in the forest form a world of their own, which becomes the great instrumentality for doing justice to the wronged, for inflicting retribution upon the guilty, and for restoring to society its banished members.

We may now pass to consider the organization of the drama. There are three movements, though they are are not marked with such precision as in some other plays, nor have they quite the same order and signification. The first movement exhibits the two chief male characters as devoted friends on the one hand, and as devoted lovers on the other. The emotional unity which cements one individual to another, and makes both, as it were, a single person, is here shown in its two most important phases. Friendship and love, therefore, constitute the theme—the former existing, in its highest and truest manifestation, mainly between people of the same sex, the latter mainly between people of different sexes. The second movement shows the disruption of this unity in both directions; through the faithlessness of one person the friends are separated and the lovers torn asunder. Here occur the struggles and conflicts which give to the drama its serious tone, though it still remain in the realm of Pure Comedy. The third movement portrays the return out of this state of disruption, the restoration of friendship and love, and the harmonious solution of all the conflicts. The instrumentality is the world of outlaws.

The two friends are first introduced, who, however, at once separate—the one, Valentine, is eager to set out on his travels; the other, Proteus, remains at home because he is inthralled by love. Valentine derides the condition of his friend, who is so utterly absorbed by his passion, and then departs. The thread of which Proteus is the center may now be followed to its conclusion, in the first movement. Julia is the name of the loved one; through her shrewd waiting-woman she has received a letter from Proteus containing a declaration of his affection. After a pretended resistance and various strange caprices she yields to the influence of the winged god—the sufficient reason being because she is loved, and must requite the affection unless there is some good ground for not doing so. Nor is any motive given for the love of Proteus, except that he loves. Man and woman belong together, and will come together unless there is some excellent reason for their remaining asunder; the burden of proof lies on the side of separation—not of union, which can always be taken for granted. . . . Proteus and Julia thus, in a rapid whirl, love, declare, pledge.

But now comes the painful separation. The father of Proteus is not yet satisfied with his son's education; he is determined to send him abroad to see the world and to gain its experience. . . . There ensues the parting scene between the lovers, with the oaths of eternal fidelity—soon to be broken—and the customary accompaniment of tears and sighs. Such is the external separation. The destination of Proteus is the court of Milan, where he will meet his old friend, Valentine.

We shall now go back and pick up Valentine's thread, and see what he has been doing. We beheld him setting out upon his travels with many a jibe and derisive taunt against love and its thralls; but retribution has come, and the mighty traveler has been stopped in his journey, at Milan, by the eyes of Silvia, the Duke's beautiful daughter. But the most gratifying news comes through his knowing servant, Speed—his affection is reciprocated. . . . [However, an] old wealthy suitor, that goblin of youthful lovers and favorite of parents, puts in his appearance, and is, of course, supported by the father. Thurio is his name. The conflict is inevitable. . . . The principles which collide are the right of choice on the part of the daughter against the will of the parent. The outcome of the struggle is indicated in the mere statement—the daughter must triumph, her right must be maintained, even at the expense of disobeying and deceiving her father. If he demands conditions which render the Family impossible, the Family must set him aside; such, at least, is Shakespeare's solution.

Just at this most interesting point of the struggle Proteus arrives at court, and by his conduct changes the whole attitude of affairs. Instead of the ordinary two-sided combat, it becomes an intricate triple fight, with abundance of stratagem and treachery. This part will be developed in the next movement. We have had brought before us the double relation of friendship and love; there has also been an external separation in each. Still, the internal bond has not been destroyed by absence; fidelity to both principles remains as yet in the hearts of all. (pp. 321-25)

The second movement, which portrays the conflict and dissolution of the ties just mentioned, is next in the order of explanation. Proteus has come to the court of Milan; is immediately admitted into the Duke's confidence upon the recommendation of his friend, who also receives him with affection and joy. But, he faithless to Julia, at once falls in love with Silvia, the chosen one of his friend. This sudden change rests in his susceptible disposition; it requires the presence of the fair object to keep up his fidelity. He is unable to subordinate emotion to reason; in his soliloquies he states the true principle of his action—love is above duty. The result is, he commits a deed of triple treachery—he is faithless to friendship, to love, to hospitality. He is truly the victim of passion, the thrall of love, which drags him from one object to another in hopeless bonds. Such is emotion without the permanent, rational element; it drives man into a violation of all honor and virtue. (p. 327)

The second thread of this movement is the actions and adventures of the two women, Julia and Silvia. The Poet has not made the separation here implied by these threads except in a few scenes, but for the convenience of the analysis, some such division may be permitted. Both these characters have the fundamental type which is seen in all of Shakespeare's women—

Act V. Scene iv. Silvia, Proteus, Julia disguised as Sebastian, and Valentine. Frontispiece to the Hanmer edition by Francis Hayman (1744). By permission of the Folger Shakespeare Library.

devotion to the Family. Those whom he wishes to portray as good are endowed with this one highest purpose, to which all their other qualities are subservient. They are depicted with various degrees of intellectual ability, and with various degrees of power of will; but they are all women, and ultimately unite in the single trait of supreme womanhood. Julia, here so modest and gentle in her nature, assumes the garments of a page in order to go to Proteus; her devotion supplies the courage to accomplish such a bold act, though its audacity in no sense taints her innate modesty. She discovers the faithlessness of her lover; the premonition of her waiting-maid has turned out true. With her own eyes she beholds Proteus wooing Silvia; indeed, she, in her disguised habit, carries to the latter a missive of love and her own token of betrothal from the perfidious gallant. What will she now do? Not revenge, nor even jealousy, fires her bosom—she remains true to her principle; her feeling with Proteus is so intimate that she even pities his unrequited love for Silvia. His case is also her own; her affection blends with his suffering and partakes of it, though her success depends just upon his want of success. Love has here reached quite the point of self-contradiction; it hugs the object which destroys the end of its being. Essentially the same character and essentially the same incidents will be repeated by the Poet in at least four of his later plays.

Silvia has also the characteristic trait of devotion, and manifests it in its full intensity. Her struggle is different from that of

Julia—it lies with the will of her father. She has also to with-stand the importunate suits of Thurio and Proteus, but this does not cost her much trouble. She has been separated from her lover by the violent mandate of her parent, but the separation is only external; both are still one in emotion, though asunder in space. Julia's case is more difficult, for the separation is internal, since Proteus has proved faithless. Silvia thus has only to get rid of the intervening distance in order to reach her purpose, which requirement she at once proceeds to carry out; for the true existence of the Family is her highest end; her courage and daring will rise to the emergency; she will even defy an otherwise valid ethical principle, namely, parental au-thority. (pp. 329-31)

At this point we observe one of Shakespeare's most peculiar and effective dramatic means. It is the transition to a primitive or idyllic state in order to cure the wrongs of society. The latter falls into strife and injustice; it becomes destructive of insti-tutions which lie at its own foundation; man no longer finds his abode in it, but must leave it in order to get rid of its oppression. Valentine and Silvia desire to form a family, plac-ing it upon its true and only possible basis; the parent, who is also the ruler of the State, interferes to disrupt the union. The Family must flee unless it cease to exist, since its very essence is assailed by the supreme authority of the country. It must find a spot where there is no such authority; hence it betakes itself to the woods—to an idyllic life, in which it is free from the conflicts of society. The lovers thus have gone to a forest, whose sole inhabitants are outlaws—that is, those who have renounced the civil authority of the land.

The third movement, which now follows, will portray this World of Outlaws, and that which it brings about through its influence. Already in the first scene of the Fourth Act is a description of its nature and origin. The outlaws tell what they have done—it is some offense against the laws of the country which they have committed, and which compelled them to flee from society; yet the Poet has shaded lightly their deeds, for, though they were guilty, they were not mean in their crimes. The allusion to Robin Hood, the English ideal of chivalric brigandage, gives the true tinge to their character. The superior breeding and learning of Valentine, who happens to pass through their abode, conquers at once their esteem; he consents to become their chieftain on the honorable condition that they "do no outrages on silly women and poor passengers" [IV. i. 69-70]. But they have never done this, and strongly asseverate that they "detest such vile practices" [IV. i. 71]. Robin Hood is clearly the model of these Knights of the Forest. They have violated and deserted the institutions of men, but they still seek to preserve personal honor.

Silvia also flies in order to avoid the conflict with the mandates of society. She must, therefore, go where she will find no oppressive social order standing in the way of her purpose; there she will find Valentine, who has been forced to depart for the same realm. Union is now possible, since all restriction is removed; the Family can be built up from the foundation. But this new world has thus become antagonistic both to the authority of the parent and to the authority of the ruler; it has also deprived the two unrequited lovers of their prey. The result is that, when the flight of Silvia becomes known, the Duke, Thurio, and Proteus—the latter attended now by the faithful Julia—follow at once the runaway to the forest. Society thus attempts to assert itself against this other world which has sprung up at its side; its representatives try to restore by force what it has lost. It will be seen in the end how they succeed.

Silvia is at first captured by some of the outlaws, but is retaken by Proteus, who seizes the opportunity to press his suit anew. She rejects his advances with her old reproaches of his infidelity to Julia; then he dares to essay violence. At this moment Val-entine, who has heard the whole conversation in his hiding-place, comes forward; he has discovered the treachery—his supposed friend has been the cause of all his misfortunes. But now follows the sudden change. Proteus repents of his conduct and expresses the deepest contrition. Surprise awaits us again. Valentine just as suddenly forgives him, which alacrity may be tolerated on account of the previous friendship; but when Valentine offers to surrender to him the devoted Silvia—to subordinate true love to treacherous friendship—both feeling and reason protest to Heaven. It is almost impossible to think that Shakespeare is the author of the passage. But Julia is here to settle the difficulty. She now throws off her disguise; her presence restores the affection of her inconstant lover; the two pairs are thus free from both the internal and the external conflict; friendship and love have passed through their struggle into complete harmony and reconciliation. Such is the result of the love-collision.

Now comes the final act—the restoration to parent and to so-ciety. The Duke and Thurio are brought in by the outlaws; Thurio cowardly resigns his claim to the hand of Silvia in the presence of Valentine; the latter has the true element of union, namely, requited love, whose right can now in this realm be enforced. The father then relents and is reconciled; this obstacle is thus swept away. Finally, the Duke, as ruler, pardons the bandits at the intercession of Valentine, and they all go back to the place whence they had fled. Thus the World of Outlaws is dissolved, and no longer stands in hostility to legal authority; the internal disruption of society is also healed, and the conflict in the Family has received its solution. This is the return to the world of institutions; the reconciliation with Family and State is complete; and the personal relations of friendship and love, which were so disturbed, are restored to their pristine energy.

The elaboration here presented is, no doubt, fuller than the mere text of this play warrants. But, for the sake of the light which is thrown upon a whole series of the Poet's works, and for the sake of illustrating his most peculiar and original dra-matic form, the present play is worthy of the most careful study and analysis. It is, however, only a germ, which has not yet unfolded, but which shows the future flower in all its details. A comparison with his later procedure in the ideal class of mediated dramas will demonstrate the immense advance in depth and completeness of treatment, but will also prove that every essential element is to be found embryonically in *Two Gentlemen of Verona*. Hereafter he will free his idyllic realm from its present taint of illegality and crime, for now he almost seems through its use to excuse the wicked deed; he will also portray it with far greater fullness and beauty, and give to it a more definite place in the action. Hereafter, too, he will assign supreme validity to repentance, which is now so lightly and so unsatisfactorily dismissed. The restoration also will be more strongly emphasized, and, indeed, will be of itself ele-vated to an entire movement of a play. Finally, the divisions of the action will be changed to their true logical order: The Disruption, the Mediation through an idyllic world, the Res-toration. It will be seen that this play belongs to the class of mediated dramas, whose form and instrumentalities it has throughout; also it leans toward the purely comic treatment.

Such is unquestionably the species to which *Two Gentlemen of Verona* belongs, but its other relations to the works of the

Poet are worthy of notice. Julia, with her disguise and her situation, is reproduced in *Twelfth Night* in the person of Viola, though the latter is in every way more complete. In fact, no comparison can better show the difference between the youthful possibility and the mature realization of a great artist than a comparison of these two characters. A less distinct adumbration of the traits will be found in Portia [in *The Merchant of Venice*], Imogen [in *Cymbeline*], Helena [in *All's Well That Ends Well*], and others. Then, again, the reflections of Valentine in the forest recalls vividly the soliloquy of the gentle Duke in *As You Like It*. But the resemblance to *Romeo and Juliet* is the most intimate of all. The two stories of the dramas often seem to run together; there is the same collision with the parent and with the rejected suitor; there are often noticed the same incidents and the same instrumentalities, even down to the ladder of ropes; there is the same style of imagery, language, and versification; we observe a like extravagance of the emotions, particularly of love; there are the same general outlines of characterization. But the quality which links these two dramas together most closely is the tone which runs through each, the indescribable coloring which leaves all its hues in the feelings and fancy, so that the mind is strongly impressed with the conclusion that both plays must have been written in the same mood and about the same time.

In the play there is much beautiful expression, but it seems to be uttered for its own sake often; that is, it does not spring from the character or the situation. We feel the idyllic beauty of many passages, but we also feel the Poet enjoying himself in his own poetry, in the exercise of his sweet gift. Part of the story seems to have been derived from a romance written in Spanish, called *Diana enamorada*, by a Portuguese poet, Jorge de Montemayor, and the drama is filled with the soft romantic air of the South. Like other comedies of the poet there is the tendency to the employment of characters by pairs—a pair of gentlemen, a pair of ladies, a pair of fathers, a pair of clowns. Of course all dialogue demands two speakers at least.

It is clear that in this early drama Shakespeare sees the necessity of repentance for the mediation of the guilty man. Valentine says:—

> Who by repentance is not satisfied,
> Is nor of heaven nor earth, for these are pleased,
> By penitence the Eternal's wrath's appeased.
>
> [V. iv. 79-81]

Proteus, whose name suggests his many transformations though love, declares his "hearty sorrow" as his "ransom for offense" [V. iv. 75]; and we hope his fickleness has been repented of when he says: "I do truly suffer, as e'er I did commit" [V. iv. 76-7]. Still the poet's idea of repentance is to deepen until it becomes, in the last period of his life, the great mediatorial axis of the dramatic movement. If, in this respect, we compare the present play with *Winter's Tale*, we may see on what path and to what point he advanced in his spiritual development.

Still the main fact which links this play with the grand Shakespearian series is the beginning we trace in it of the idyllic world. Particularly the allusion to Robin Hood connects it with a phase of old English life and poetry, and joins it to the following play *As You Like It*, in which a similar allusion occurs, though the two dramas lie eight or ten years apart in time. (pp. 328-38)

> *Denton J. Snider, "'Two Gentlemen of Verona',"*
> *in his* The Shakespearian Drama, a Commentary: The
> Comedies, *Sigma Publishing Co., 1890? pp. 320-38.*

GRACE LATHAM   (lecture date 1891)

[*In the following excerpt from a lecture delivered February 18, 1891, Latham contrasts the "faithful, loving" Julia and the "wise and holy" Silvia of* The Two Gentlemen of Verona. *Here, for the first time, she declares, Shakespeare develops his female characters; and Julia, in particular, is his first "subtly conceived" portrait of a woman. According to the critic, however, Shakespeare "has not learnt to blend characteristics," and thus Julia often appears contradictory and inconsistent. Latham is also one of the first commentators to praise Silvia's constancy and perfect dignity, even though her quiet submission to Valentine's betrayal is a "flaw, both in the climax and the characterization."*]

[Julia] is the first of Shakspere's female characters which he has given us with any fulness of detail. The ladies of *Love's Labour's Lost* are mere pegs on which to hang sharp speeches; Adriana and Luciana of the *Comedy of Errors* are slight if faithful sketches of a jealous and a commonplace woman. Julia, of *The Two Gentlemen of Verona*, on the contrary, though the various developments of her character are not led up to or sustained as in his great comedy period, though she lacks the logical perfection of his later studies of women, is yet as subtly conceived, and possesses as much individuality as they do.

Although in the main true to itself, the part is written as it were in pieces, each scene giving us a different side of the character, to the exclusion, and sometimes to the apparent contradiction of the rest. Shakspere has not yet learnt to blend characteristics, so as to make us feel that we have one and the same woman in each scene, heralding by earlier hints and touches the qualities which each new situation brings into play. It is almost as though, while he perceived the component parts of her nature, he did not grasp it as a whole, and still believed that women's characters are contradictory, whereas they are as consistent to themselves as those of men, but are moved and influenced by different, and differently-proportioned motives and feelings.

There is, however, one point in Julia's nature which would be likely to lead a young dramatist astray in his pourtrayal of it. She is so fully possessed by the mood of the moment, as to leave little room for any other feeling; at one time soaring into the seventh heaven of happiness, at another struck down to earth at an unexpected reverse; to-day a triumphant beauty, wayward and coquettish, to-morrow a tender, sighing lover. But even in people of this description the dominant traits of character, the habitual modes of thought and action, which form the groundwork of individuality, influence their moods, and mould the fashion in which they are expressed; this is the point which the young Shakspere missed here, and here only. (pp. 319-20)

Much *apparent* inconsistency in the character of Julia is also due to the fact that it is written in several styles, each well fitted to give the comic or pathetic touch needed by the play, but which, taken together, do not harmonize, and give us the impression of different persons under one name. The task, therefore, of welding this part into a consistent whole falls upon the student-critic, or on the actress, who has more to do for the Julia than for any other of Shakspere's heroines.

Her first scene is written in lightest comedy. Julia is a spoilt beauty, a freakish heiress, surrounded by suitors, and delighting in the sway she bears over them. In her vanity she accepts it all as her due, and would like to hold the same rule in her home-life; she enacts pretty little scenes to charm her gentlewoman Lucetta, as though what would please a gentleman must needs delight her; while Lucetta, poor thing, wears an iron yoke, bows to her mistress's caprices, and yet has an underhand, unexpressed influence over her. This is very important as a clue to Julia's nature: the violence of her moods deceives her into the belief that she is strong; but she is really weak, and at the bottom of her heart is half conscious of it; her tyrannous humours being that protest of the independence of will and judgment, commonly made by those who seek support, and need an external force to propel them even into the course they wish to take. There is too a touch of causeless, instinctive jealousy that any one, even Lucetta, should admire the man on whom she has set her mind.

Julia plays with her love as though Proteus himself were before her: she will, and she will not; she would be led to talk of him, would be advised to love him, and yet when his letter is offered her, the little coquette hangs back, puts on a grand air of virtue, and will not commit herself by touching what she is longing to read. (pp. 320-21)

Now all this, though most dramatic, belongs to an artificial nature, and is treated in the spirit of an artificial school of comedy.... [This] first scene of Julia's seems to have been modelled on a comedy of intrigue rather than one of feeling, and, so far as the passionate, realistic sixteenth century can be said to be like the artificial eighteenth century, is more in the style of Sheridan, in the sense that, though founded on accurate observation and knowledge of human nature, the dramatic effects are exaggerated to obtain greater brilliancy. It is also a mistake in the dramatic composition of the play, showing the author to be as yet inexperienced, to begin a principal part, intended to be one of passion and romance, with such marked comedy; a first scene stamps a character to the audience, and this one raises expectations that are never fulfilled.

Julia's vanity and affectation, her bursts of petulance, her love of mystery and intrigue, the comedy husk of the part, are now left on one side as sufficiently expressed; but Shakspere retains for further working out the romance, the impulse and passion, the imperative persistent will, with the underlying strain of weakness. As is usual with him, he struck the keynote of the character in the first scene, but its full import is obscured by the style in which it is written.

It is necessary to add that Julia here impresses us as making too many and too open claims for admiration to be quite well-bred or accustomed to society; she is a girl out of the nursery, not a woman of the world, as she would fain have us believe. This characteristic also runs through other scenes. It is in the answer she sends to Proteus; she pours out her love at his feet, never pausing to think if such frankness be wise.

Proteus is one of those who cease to value the good they have grasped; secure of Julia, he can leave her to start on his travels with pleasant anticipations and mitigated pain. At their parting Julia gives way entirely; she neither rages against circumstances, nor plans to overcome them; too weak to withstand the shock, she droops in enforced patience, and cannot say farewell for tears. The romantic little scene shows us this side only of her nature, the one which was then most fully in action.

The separation over, Julia's native obstinacy and persistence reassert themselves; the spoilt girl cannot endure contradiction, even from circumstances; her love is passionate and impatient like herself, and her lover's absence not to be borne. Again we see the touch of weakness; she extorts the advice to do what she wishes from Lucetta, hoping to shift or divide the responsibility of her actions—an impossibility, for we must

each bear the outcome of our deeds, no matter who counselled us to do them.

Julia has really made up her mind down to the very details of her flight; she will not listen to the objections, at which Lucetta hints in her reluctant answers. We are not shown why the idea of the faithlessness of Proteus had entered her mind, for the only ground she brings forward is the general one of the deceitfulness of man. The comedy in this scene is chiefly sustained by Lucetta's dry replies; Julia's part in it is unconscious, and there is nothing artificial in it. Her chief fear is the gossip which will be aroused by her departure.... All this is in keeping with her character, as it is shown us in the opening scene; but the better to depict her love, her tone, as well as the style of writing, is again changed; her petulance, and the self-consciousness which belonged to it, are alike gone. Now, if there is an instinct which, once well developed, is quite ineradicable, it is self-consciousness. A great shock, a supreme moment of intense feeling may dispel it for a time, as in her parting from Proteus, but it always returns; and here, where she is in her usual state of mind, it should be present—but it is not. She has become a heroine of romantic passion, speaking, as befits her, in smooth numbers, at great expense of simile and metaphor; and we feel the jar of an incongruous development of the character, or rather of one side of it at the expense of the rest. The original Julia would have loved as romantically, but there would have been the sense that she was speaking for effect, as well as to express her feelings, and this the actress must divine and indicate.... Here, if the wording be somewhat far-fetched, it follows the style of early Shaksperian love-making, which goes out of its way to introduce ornament; but the speaker has entirely forgotten herself. Now Rosalind, in *As You Like It,* is less self-conscious than Julia is shown to be in her first scene; but the quality runs right through her part.

It is, however, when we next see Julia that her character is, as it were, broken across. She reaches Milan, and is brought by the host of her inn where she may see Proteus and hear him speak. She does not yet know of his faithlessness; for when she sees the troop of serenaders, she asks in surprise: "Is he among these?" [IV. ii. 37] but notwithstanding the fire and energy, which have been among her chief characteristics, have suddenly deserted her. Even when she hears him celebrate the beauty of her rival, there is no anger, none of the bitterness of a proud and passionate woman forced to acquiesce in her wrongs; instead we find a patient submission to inevitable suffering, appropriate enough to an Ophelia or a Hero, but scarcely to Julia. The host says, "The music likes you not" [IV. ii. 55-6]; and she answers in hopeless misery, "You mistake; the musician likes me not" [IV. ii. 57]. Not that Julia has *no* patience; she sees its necessity: "where is no remedy" [II. ii. 2]. And this scene is only the working out in an exaggerated fashion of Act II. sc. ii., where she parts from Proteus. It is the *quality* of her present patience, its lack of all fire, even of active grief, which is so new and so astonishing. The loss of Proteus must certainly have been a numbing shock, but it is before she is aware of it, that the change takes place. Fresh circumstances often alter outward behaviour; and it may have been intended to show, that out of her home nest, away from Lucetta's guardianship, Julia felt lost, and unable to cope with events; but if this is so, it is not expressed, and we give it merely as a possible solution of a difficulty.... In Julia we have a subordinate characteristic suddenly overpowering and blotting out others hitherto prominent and active; and although an immature girl like Juliet may develop in a night, under pressure of circumstances, it takes time to modify qualities that are already formed, and, what is more important, traces of them always remain. It is, however, to be remembered, that, true to the system on which he wrote this part, of devoting a scene to each of its aspects, Shakspere probably gave Act IV. scene ii. to pathos; and, being inexperienced, allowed the quality to over-weight the character. Julia's next step is to inquire where Proteus lodges, and to profit by her disguise to become his page, the country-bred Launce proving too loutish and unknowing for courtly employments. It is quite in Shakspere's manner thus carefully to account for how and why she was able to enter her faithless lover's service. It is significant too of her persistent will, that even in the midst of her deep depression she thought out a plan, and began to put it in execution. (pp. 321-26)

Julia hopes to detach Proteus from Silvia, but the very first commission entrusted to her is to deliver the ring she had given him to her rival. It is handed to her with a boast of the love she bore him, and when she tries to discover if he really believes her dead, she finds that it is only the way he takes to quiet Silvia's scruples in accepting his love. She hears it with patience, and without resentment, striving to wake his pity and remorse by reminding him that Julia suffers for love of him, even as he does for Silvia. He turns a deaf ear to her plea; it was not likely that he would allow interference from his new page, though he might brag of his conquest to him; he bids him go do his message, and leaves him.

Julia stands undecided. A touch of the old self-consciousness peeps out, as well as recoil from her task, when she says: "How many women would do such a message" [IV. iv. 90]. We catch a glimpse of her intention in taking service with him in the words—"Alas, poor Proteus, thou hast entertained a fox to be the shepherd of thy lambs" [IV. iv. 91-2]. Still she has a deep pity for the love-pain, she thinks she understands so well; her faithful affection bids her sacrifice her desires to his, but she is too irresolute for either love or selfishness to gain a victory; she temporizes, the usual refuge of weak minds: "Yet will I woo for him; but yet so coldly as, heaven it knows, I would not have him speed" [IV. iv. 106-07]. Therefore as soon as she receives an impulse in the desired direction, on hearing Silvia condemn her master's infidelity, she forgets her self-denying intentions, and uses all her eloquence, by a beautiful and pathetic description of her own sufferings, to deepen that lady's generous pity. (pp. 326-27)

As the interview goes on, Julia's courage increases, and with it her admiration for the gracious, sympathizing woman who usurps her lover's heart. It shows Julia in a nobler light than we have yet seen her—that she should feel so justly and generously towards the lady whose very virtues were drawing Proteus to her. Then follows a soliloquy, full of that unconscious comedy in which Shakspere excels, mixed with an exquisite touch of pathos. The grave comparison of Julia's own charms, one by one, with those of her rival; the comment: "And yet the painter flattered her a little, unless I flatter with myself too much" [IV. iv. 187-88]; the jealousy that will not be suppressed; the envy of the treatment the very canvass will receive from Proteus: "Thou shalt be worshipped, kissed, loved and adored" [IV. iv. 199]; the longing for revenge, kept in check by the remembrance of Silvia's kindness, make up a scene in the very best vein of naturalistic comedy. It is a great opportunity for the actress, and differs entirely in style, though not in psychology, from the rest of the part.

In the next scene Julia rather helps the dramatic effect, than develops her own character; an amused and scornful spectator

of Thurio's foolish conceit, exposing Proteus's deceitful flattery to the audience by her comments. She follows him into the forest, to cross him in his love, not to betray kind Silvia, and witnesses his dastardly attempt to coerce her into accepting his affection. Again Julia is unequal to the crisis. Instead of declaring herself at once, she keeps silence; when Valentine hands Silvia over to his reconciled friend, Julia can only swoon, and it needs the kind encouragement of both, before she will produce the ring given her by Proteus, and discover herself. Then, however, she reproaches him with all the fire and energy which is to be expected from the original Julia; and he, now repentant, has the grace to feel how much he has wronged her, and to return to his old allegiance.

The second great female character in The Two Gentlemen of Verona is worked out far more perfectly and consistently than the first, probably because it is much simpler; there are no puzzling contradictions in it, and but few gradations. Silvia's mind and birth are alike dignified; she is full of self-control, and has an innate strength which makes her quite capable of taking her own part in life.

Until the last scene we only see her in public, and under that social restraint which suppresses our inequalities of manner and temper, the scene in which she pleads for Valentine being described, not represented. This it is which makes the style in which her scenes are written so much alike; Julia we see at all times and seasons, in every variety and phase of feeling; Silvia, whether in her jesting or her serious moments, can never lose control over herself, and never touches her strongest power of expression. They are examples of two of Shakspere's chief types of the female character; the strong, which is self-sustained, and the weak, which needs support, and they are designed to contrast with each other at every point.

Julia's attraction must have lain in her beauty, her brilliancy, and her ever-shifting moods; even while we criticize, we delight in her. If we are to believe the unprejudiced Speed, Silvia is not really beautiful, owing her complexion to paint, which then was not held to be shameful. It is her tact and refinement, her grace and sweet discourse, her gentle kindness, which give her the great charm she undoubtedly possesses, and, blinding the eyes of her adorers, make them hold her fair. Her real attraction is a moral and intellectual one; the serenade in her honour is almost severe in tone, it celebrates her as wise and holy, and this is the impression she makes on us. Neither epithet would apply to Julia, faithful, loving soul though she be.

Like her, Silvia's first scene belongs to comedy of intrigue, but where by comparison it loses in brilliancy, it gains in delicacy; allowing for the manners of the time, it is free from exaggeration, for Silvia's evenly-balanced nature is foreign to it.

Brought up at the court of which she is chief, Silvia is too worldly-wise to have her head turned by her many suitors. She despises Thurio, rates his admiration, probably inspired by her high position, at what it is worth, and, untempted by his wealth, fixes her affections on the unknown Valentine. But how to tell him she returns his love, and that from being her "servant," or recognized formal adorer and follower, he may aspire to her hand? It is obvious that to do so in plain words would be, from one in her exalted position to a simple gentleman, too like a command, and she is evidently not quite sure of his feelings. Accordingly, she has recourse to the graceful device of bidding him write a letter in her name to a "secret nameless friend" [II. i. 105] of hers, intending to deliver it again to him, that, should he desire it, he may make himself a loophole of escape by feigning not to understand her meaning, and avoid what would have been an awkward situation for both of them. She possesses the real power of intrigue which Julia aims at; but honest, open-hearted Valentine has not the most elementary knowledge of it. (pp. 327-30)

We next find her keeping the peace between Sir Thurio and Valentine, who is striving to shine in her presence at the expense of his rival. With ready tact she averts a quarrel, and praises both; she dares not do otherwise, Thurio being favoured by her father; but her gracious reception of Proteus, the humility with which she accepts him as her servant, are all really addressed to his friend. She has no fear lest she may thereby catch a heart, which she believes to be occupied, for it is made clear to us before the entrance of Proteus that she has been told all about his love for Julia. A doubt of his fidelity does cross her mind when she hears he has left his lady to travel abroad, but she is too full of her own affairs for it to remain there; her elopement is planned, and she is busy blinding her father's eyes by a show of courtesy to Sir Thurio, while she enjoys the delicious, stolen bliss of secretly communicating with Valentine, and covertly assuring him of her affection in the very hearing and presence of his rival.

The great difference between Julia and Silvia is shown when Valentine is banished through the treachery of Proteus. This sudden reverse does not crush Silvia, she wastes no time in lamentation; prompt and decided in action, she throws herself at her father's feet, pleading for the culprit with all the energy of her strong will, and bringing into play her woman's weapons of "sad sighs, deep groans, and silver-shedding tears" [III. i. 232], so increasing her father's anger that he commits her to close prison, "with many bitter threats of biding there" [III. i. 238]. Though she has failed, she does not give up the struggle; she ask neither help, advice, nor sympathy; fearless of consequences, she throws off all concealment. She no longer shows Thurio even courteous tolerance, avoiding him when she can, railing at him when he is brought into her presence, and taking no pains to conceal her grief at the loss of Valentine. With the blindness of many elders, the Duke hopes she may soon forget her lover, and accept this wealthy and eligible candidate for her hand; but his stupidity has to be combated, as well as her firm determination, and with a total misjudgment of the character of Proteus, the Duke makes him his advocate.

True as steel herself, treachery in another excites Silvia's utmost abhorrence; Proteus may outwit the Duke, Thurio, and Valentine; he cannot hoodwink her keen eyes, and she has no vanity to be flattered by crime undertaken for her sake. She hates him, and almost loathes herself for being the object of his affection; that he should dare to woo her is an insult to her understanding and her moral nature, and she tells him so with the utmost plainness:

> Think'st thou, I am so shallow, so conceitless,
> To be seduced by thy flattery.
>
> [IV. ii. 96-7]
> (pp. 330-32)

No fear of her father's confidential agent and favourite restrains her tongue; his announcement that Valentine is dead does not distress her in the least, for she does not believe one word Sir Proteus says, and shows it, though she avoids the discourtesy of saying so. That after all this she should give him her picture has been objected to, but she doubtless intended to throw dust in the eyes of this subtle man, the most dangerous of all her

enemies; yet she will not seem false to Valentine, even for his sake, and the words with which she promises the gift cut like a whip:

> I am very loth to be your idol, sir;
> But, since your falsehood shall become you well
> To worship shadows and adore false shapes,
> Send to me in the morning and I'll send it:
> And so, good rest.
>
> [IV. ii. 128-32]

Her last words are intended as a dismissal, for her trysting time with Eglamour is close at hand.

Silvia has determined to fly to Valentine; alone if need be, but she is very desirous to have a safe protector during her journey, and she chooses Eglamour for this purpose; a man of high character, set apart from all love-making by his sad story and vow. She confides in him no farther than she must, for she says no word of Proteus, showing herself to be a worldly-wise woman, who knows the golden value of silence, but she appeals to the things and principles Sir Eglamour holds most dear; his own untarnished reputation, his love for his dear dead lady, and speaks strong and touchingly of her own grief, and of the sin of marriage with one "whom her very soul abhors" [IV. iii. 17], and easily wins the help of the kind, romantic man.

How different is this discreet elopement, only undertaken as a last resource, to poor Julia's headlong flight, into a world of which she knows nothing, in a disguise which she never considers how to support; as Portia, Rosalind, and Viola all do; Julia will not even sacrifice her pretty locks to her safety. (pp. 332-33)

Silvia manages her escape in the simplest fashion possible; under the pretext of intended confession she evades her attendants, meets Eglamour at the abbey, and gets away to the forest, merely disguised by the "sun-expelling mask" then worn by ladies out of doors. A more complicated plan would have involved other confidants, and would have been far less likely to succeed. They are attacked by robbers, and Sir Eglamour, alas, belies his reputation, and flies instead of defending his ward. Quiet and self-controlled as ever, Silvia is being taken to the captain of the band, when she is rescued by Proteus, and now at last her calm gives way. She might possibly have prevailed on the robber chief with "an honourable mind," to forward her on her journey. To be saved by Proteus means a return to captivity; and when he profits by her isolation to press his suit, she scolds him roundly, unmindful of the fact that she is absolutely in his power.

The play is about the *Two Gentlemen*, and when they meet again, their ladies have to take the second place. We must feel it as a flaw, both in the climax and the characterization, that Silvia should tamely submit to be handed over by Valentine to his false friend; but it is satisfactory to leave her happy in her father's consent to her marriage, and finally delivered from the two disturbers of her peace, Thurio and Proteus. (p. 333)

> *Grace Latham, "Julia, Silvia, Hero and Viola," in*
> The New Shakspere Society's Transactions, *1887-92,*
> *pp. 319-50.*

GEORGE BRANDES (essay date 1895-96)

[*Brandes was a prominent Danish scholar and literary critic. His* William Shakespeare *(1895-96) was translated into English in 1898 and widely read in both Germany and England. In the excerpt below from that work, Brandes stresses Shakespeare's careful exploration and portrayal of his female characters, whom the critic views as superior to those in the playwright's earlier comedies, and he praises "the careless gaiety which makes its first triumphant appearance" in the figures of Speed and Launce. Brandes also defines the play's central theme as "faithful and faithless love," and he mentions Shakespeare's earliest presentation, in this comedy, of his love of nature.]*

[*The Two Gentlemen of Verona*] surpasses the earlier comedies in two respects: first, in the beauty and clearness with which the two young women are outlined, and then in the careless gaiety which makes its first triumphant appearance in the parts of the servants. Only now and then, in one or two detached scenes, do Speed and Launce bore us with euphuistic word-torturings; as a rule they are quite entertaining fellows, who seem to announce, as with a flourish of trumpets, that, unlike either Lyly or Marlowe, Shakespeare possesses the inborn gaiety, the keen sense of humour, the sparkling playfulness, which are to enable him, without any strain on his invention, to kindle the laughter of his audiences, and send it flashing round the theatre from the groundlings to the gods. He does not as yet display any particular talent for individualising his clowns. Nevertheless we notice that, while Speed impresses us chiefly by his astonishing volubility, the true English humour makes its entrance upon the Shakespearian stage when Launce appears, dragging his dog by a string.

Note the torrent of eloquence in this speech of Speed's, enumerating the symptoms from which he concludes that his master is in love:—

> First, you have learn'd, like Sir Proteus, to wreath your arms, like a malcontent; to relish a love-song, like a robin-redbreast; to walk alone, like one that had the pestilence; to sigh, like a school-boy that had lost his A B C; to weep, like a young wrench that had buried her grandam; to fast, like one that takes diet; to watch, like one that fears robbing; to speak puling, like a beggar at Hallowmas.
>
> [II. i. 18-26]
> (pp. 51-2)

All these similes of Speed's are apt and accurate; it is only the way in which he piles them up that makes us laugh. But when Launce opens his mouth, unbridled whimsicality at once takes the upper hand. He comes upon the scene with his dog:—

> Nay, 'twill be this hour ere I have done weeping; all the kind of the Launces have this very fault.... I think Crab, my dog, be the sourest-natured dog that lives: my mother weeping, my father wailing, my sister crying, our maid howling, our cat wringing her hands, and all our house in a great perplexity, yet did not this cruel-hearted cur shed one tear. He is a stone, a very pebble-stone, and has no more pity in him than a dog....
>
> [II. iii. 1-11]
> (p. 52)

Here we have nothing but joyous nonsense, and yet nonsense of a higly dramatic nature. That is to say, here reigns that youthful exuberance of spirit which laughs with a childlike grace, even where it condescends to the petty and low; exuberance as of one who glories in the very fact of existence, and rejoices to feel life pulsing and seething in his veins; exuberance such as belongs of right, in some degree, to every

well-constituted man in the light-hearted days of his youth—how much more, then, to one who possesses the double youth of years and genius among a people which is itself young, and more than young: liberated, emancipated, enfranchised, like a colt which has broken its tether and scampers at large through the luxuriant pastures.

The Two Gentlemen of Verona—which, by the way, is Shakespeare's first declaration of love to Italy—is a graceful, entertaining, weakly constructed comedy, dealing with faithful and faithless love, with the treachery of man and the devotion of woman. Its hero, a noble and wrongfully-banished youth, comes to live the life of a robber captain, like Schiller's Karl von Moor two centuries later, but without a spark of his spirit of rebellion. The solution of the imbroglio, by means of the instant and unconditional forgiveness of the villain, is so naïve, so senselessly conciliatory, that we feel it to be the outcome of a joyous, untried, and unwounded spirit. (pp. 52-3)

One or two points in the play remind us of *Love's Labour Won*, which Shakespeare had just completed in its original form; for example, the journey in male attire in pursuit of the scornful loved one. Many things, on the other hand, point forward to Shakespeare's later work. The inconstancy of the two men in *A Midsummer Night's Dream* is a variation and parody of Proteus's fickleness in this play. The beginning of the second scene of the first act, where Julia makes Lucetta pass judgment on her different suitors, is the first faint outline of the masterly scene to the same effect between Portia and Nerissa in *The Merchant of Venice*. The conversation between Sylvia and Julia, which brings the fourth act to a close, answers exactly to that between Olivia and Viola in the first act of *Twelfth Night*. Finally, the fact that Valentine, after learning the full extent of his false friend's treachery, offers to resign to him his beautiful betrothed, Sylvia, in order to prove by this sacrifice the strength of his friendship, however foolish and meaningless it may appear in the play, is yet an anticipation of the humble renunciation of the beloved for the sake of the friend and of friendship, which impresses us so painfully in Shakespeare's Sonnets.

In almost every utterance of the young women in this comedy we see nobility of soul, and in the lyric passages a certain pre-Raphaelite grace. (pp. 53-4)

And although the men are here of inferior interest to the women, we yet find in the mouth of Valentine outbursts of great lyric beauty. (p. 54)

Besides the strains of passion and of gaiety in this light acting play, a third note is clearly struck, the note of nature. There is fresh air in it, a first breath of those fragrant midland memories which prove that this child of the country must many a time have said to himself with Valentine ... :

> How use doth breed a habit in a man!
> This shadowy desert, unfrequented woods,
> I better brook than flourishing peopled towns.
>
> [V. iv. 1-3]

In many passages of this play we are conscious for the first time of that keen love of nature which never afterwards deserts Shakespeare, and which gives to some of the most mannered of his early efforts, as, for example, to his short narrative poems, their chief interest and value. (p. 54)

George Brandes, "Love's Labour's Won," translated by William Archer, in his William Shakespeare, *William Heinemann, 1920, pp. 47-54.*

FREDERICK S. BOAS (essay date 1896)

[*Boas was a specialist in Elizabethan and Tudor drama who combined the biographical interest prevalent in the late nineteenth-century with the historical approach that developed in the first decades of the twentieth century. His commentary thus reflects the important transition that occurred in Shakespearean criticism during this period. In the following excerpt, he discusses the contrasting characterization of the four protagonists in* The Two Gentlemen of Verona, *describing Valentine as "somewhat obtuse," Silvia as pure and of "keen intellect and resolute will," and Julia as of a "pensive, dependent nature." The critic considers Proteus the most powerfully conceived character in the play; he refers to him as an individual who lacks the morals necessary to control his self-interest and is thus "swept along in pure abandonment of feeling." Boas also notes how both Speed and Launce—especially the latter in the episodes with his dog—complement the main action. On other matters, the critic disapproves of the final scene, asserting that the actions of Valentine and Silvia are impossible to justify and that Proteus's repentance remains unconvincing. Like many earlier critics, he also defines the play's central interest as the workings of "love and friendship in a variety of shifting relations."*]

The plot of *The Two Gentlemen of Verona* corresponds in its main features with the story of the Shepherdess Felismena in the Spanish prose pastoral *Diana* by Montemayor. Shakspere may have had access to a manuscript copy of Yonge's translation of the tale, not printed before 1598; or he may have drawn upon an earlier dramatic handling of the subject, *Felix and Philomena*, mentioned in 1584. In favour, perhaps, of the more second-hand source of inspiration, is the fact that the play makes no attempt to reproduce Italian surroundings. What little there is of scenic detail is English, and Verona and Milan, like Navarre, Ephesus, and Athens are merely dramatic spellings of Stratford. Thence are drawn the allusions to the 'uncertain glory of an April day' [I. iii. 85], to the current that 'gives a gentle kiss to every sedge' [II. vii. 29], to the schoolboy sighing at the loss of his 'A, B, C,' to the robin red-breast that relishes a love-song, to the 'pageants of delight' [IV. iv. 159] played at Pentecost.

But this frank absence of local colour is the more venial in that the theme of the story, love and friendship in a variety of shifting relations, is not of local but of universal significance. It is in effect a stock subject of the novelist and dramatist in every age, and it cannot but be embodied in certain stock characters. The lover and friend who is faithless in both capacities, the man of the world who mocks at passion, but who, when subdued to its sway, is true as steel, the brainless and repulsive but wealthy suitor, as odious in the eyes of the lady as he is acceptable in those of her father, the tender-hearted maiden, loyal to her fickle wooer and forgiving to a fault, the high-spirited girl, single-hearted in her affection and yet with a trace of coquettish pride in the spectacle of rival swains at her feet—all these are familiar types, and they are grouped with the somewhat obtrusive parallelism of Shakspere's early method. But the touch of the master-hand, though yet in its noviciate, makes itself felt in the delicacy with which these types are developed up to a certain point, in the tender grace of the sentiment which steeps the main story, and in the dexterous comic relief.

Decidely foremost in interest among the characters is Proteus, whose name, in accordance with a device which Shakspere now first used and which he affected till the last, betokens the fickleness of his nature. He is eminently the product of the new age of culture: as described by his friend,

> He is complete in feature and in mind,
> With all good grace to grace a gentleman.
>
> [II. iv. 73-4]

But it is a culture which in his case has developed the sensibilities while relaxing the moral fibre, and has made of him a Renaissance Werther [in Johann Wolfgang von Goethe's *The Sorrows of Young Werther*], swept along in pure abandonment of feeling. Whilst uncertain of Julia's answer to his suit, he is plunged in a self-pitying melancholy, 'Poor forlorn Proteus: passionate Proteus' [I. ii. 121]; her message of affection draws from his lips ecstatic invocations, 'Sweet love, sweet lines, sweet life' [I. iii. 45], but he conceals its contents from his father with a faint-hearted piece of duplicity which only lends itself to Antonio's scheme for sending him to join Valentine at Milan. Even the sentence of separation from his mistress draws from him no manly protest, though he is not at a loss for graceful images to describe his change of state, and though he takes farewell of Julia with exaggerated vows of constancy.

But the moment that he reaches Milan and beholds Silvia, who has taken the heart of Valentine captive, a more novel and intense sensation drives out the sensation that has hitherto been true love's counterfeit within his breast. He is not whirled along by a headlong current of passion which sweeps away the distinctions of right and wrong, nor does he defiantly trample upon moral law. He knows, and indeed with a certain *naïveté* confesses, that he is playing the traitor, and he would shun temptation, could it be done without effort. But it is just from the needful effort that sentimentalism recoils; it is so much pleasanter to drift with the stream.

> If I can check my erring love, I will:
> If not, to compass her I'll use my skill.
>
> [II. iv. 213-14]

And thus he is found shortly afterwards arguing with sophistical dialectic that his treachery is justifiable, for Love, in whose name he has sworn, prompts his perjury, and there is, moreover, a sacrifice of self which friendship cannot claim: 'I to myself am dearer than a friend' [II. vi. 23]. So the soft outer husk of the sentimental nature is peeled away, and only the hard, bitter kernel is left, and in the spirit of this declaration Proteus pursues his course. He reveals to the Duke Valentine's plan of elopement with Silvia, and thus procures his banishment, while by engaging to slander his friend in the interest of Thurio he dexterously gains a vantage-ground for pressing his own suit. But his schemes are shattered against the true-hearted constancy of Silvia, who, loyal to her own love, scorns unfaithfulness in others. The utmost that his abject entreaties can wring from her is her picture, the shadow of herself, and at last she seeks relief from persecution in flight after Valentine. Chance, however, places her for a moment in Proteus' power, and the selfish passion of the sentimentalist is unmasked in its naked hideousness, when he seeks by force to make her his victim. The scene is crude in execution, but it is not wanting in psychological truth. This cannot, however, be said of Proteus' sudden and forced repentance, and his reconversion to love of Julia. The concluding act of the play bears throughout marks of imperfect workmanship, and thus, whether through haste or through incapacity as yet for absolutely finished portraiture, the dramatist blurs in his closing touches the most powerfully conceived character, outside the historical field, that he had hitherto attempted.

Morally and intellectually Valentine is the strongest contrast to his friend. His is the plain, soldier nature that 'hunts after honour'[I. i. 63], and sees in love only 'shapeless idleness,' and waste of good days. Youth, with its intoxicating vitality, thrills through his every nerve and limb, as Speed reminds him later, in his mournful glance backwards over this happy time:

'You were wont, when you laughed, to crow like a cock: when you walked to walk like one of the lions: when you fasted it was presently after dinner, when you looked sadly it was for want of money'[II. i. 26-30]. It is, however, precisely such a buoyant and self-confident nature that falls in most headlong defeat before some unexpected assault of love, and thus Valentine, when transplanted to the novel surroundings of the Milanese Court, is 'metamorphosed' by the first glance of Silvia's eyes. But he retains the simplicity of his character and the somewhat obtuse perception that goes with it. His own servant Speed has to interpret to him the transparent device by which Silvia volunteers a confession of her love for him, and he falls readily into the trap which the Duke sets for exposing his scheme of elopement. It never crosses his mind that Proteus, his confidant, has broken faith, for when banished from Milan he accepts his offer to be the letter-carrier to his mistress. It is only when, as captain of a band of peculiarly high-toned outlaws, he is a witness of the dastardly attempt on Silvia's honour that he realizes that Proteus is a 'common friend, that's without faith or love' [V. iv. 63], and renounces all trust in him for ever in words of manly and sorrowful indignation. But a few words of penitence on the part of the wrongdoer disarm his wrath, and with an incredibly quixotic sacrifice of the claims of love to those of friendship, and with airy indifference to the feelings of Silvia, he hands her over to the man who has just offered her the grossest outrage.

The crudity of the situation is heightened by the character of Silvia, which is as far as possible from lending itself to such a summary disposal. 'Holy, fair, and wise is she' [IV. ii. 41]: so sing the company of serenaders at her window, and her bearing throughout the drama testifies that it is no idle praise. She is the first and most lightly sketched member of a favourite Shakesperean order of womanhood, which unites outward fairness and transparent purity of soul to keen intellect and resolute will. With good reason do 'all our swains commend her' [IV. ii. 40], and her treatment of the rivals for her hand illustrates her tact and firmness of purpose. To Valentine, the man of her choice, she tenders a proof of her favour which, without compromising her maidenly dignity may give him a hint whereon to speak: Thurio she skilfully keeps at a distance, though she offers him no direct incivility, and listens with seeming impartiality to the volleys of wit between Valentine and him: Proteus, in spite of his outward gallantry and skill in the game of love, she sees in his true colours, and repulses with cutting words of scorn. Difficulties are with her only a spur to action, and as she assents to the elopement with Valentine, in order to checkmate her father's scheme for thrusting her into the arms of Thurio, so she afterwards conceives the plan of following her lover in his banishment, and with discriminating eye picks out Sir Eglamour as her fittest companion and helper. That a woman of such high spirit should, in the closing scene, stand by in dumb resignation, while the man whom she has risked all to find turns her over to the traitor from whom she has fled, is the crowning absurdity in a tangle of psychological impossibilities.

The threatened wholesale catastrophe is averted by Julia's self-revelation. She too has braved danger to follow her beloved, but otherwise she is a complete contrast to Silvia, and belongs to a class of women which occupies a relatively subordinate place in Shakspere's gallery of the sex. The fact that in pursuit of Proteus she dons masculine disguise—a device here used by the dramatist for the first time—suggests a likeness between her and Portia [in *The Merchant of Venice*] or Rosalind [in *As You Like It*]. But the resemblance is superficial, for she entirely

lacks the commanding spirit and gaiety of heart of these heroines, and with her pensive, dependent nature is akin in certain aspects to Viola [in *Twelfth Night*], but finds her true sister in the Euphrasia of Beaumont and Fletcher, who, like her, takes service as a page with the man whom she loves. Self-sacrifice is the law of her being, as self-love is that of Proteus, and though cut to the very core by his perfidy she can endure, in the strength of her devotion, to be his messenger to her rival, and even to bear between them the ring that had been the pledge of her own troth. The spectacle of such humiliation awakens in us a pity not untouched with contempt, and it is a relief to find that she has yet enough womanly instinct left to draw comparisons, by no means to her own disadvantage, between Silvia's face and hers. Truly feminine, too, is her analysis of her rival's picture, and the consoling reflection that 'the painter flattered' her a little [IV. iv. 87], while even her instinct to 'scratch out the unseeing eyes' [IV. iv. 204] on the canvas is natural under the circumstances. But she refrains from such an outrage, for Silvia's loyalty and sweetness have won her tender heart, and buoyed her up with the belief that Proteus' perfidious suit must fail. Thus the crowning blow comes when she sees Valentine himself surrender his betrothed to this perjured wooer, and she sinks fainting to the ground. Then follows the confession that she is Julia in the habit of a page, and Proteus' sudden relapse to his original attachment; and if he wins her pardon on far too easy terms, this is a dramatic flaw which marks not only the hurried close of *The Two Gentlemen of Verona*, but which clung, as will be seen, to Shakspere's method even in the most matured period of his art.

Parallel to the romantic interest, but not so interwoven with it as in *The Comedy of Errors*, runs a humorous underplot, which introduces for the first time the Shaksperean Clown in the stricter sense. The class has here two representatives. Speed and Launce, akin and yet contrasted, as each is contrasted further with the master whom he serves. To the slow-witted Valentine is attached the nimble-tongued Speed, whose plays upon words, repartees, and snatches of doggrel sparkle upon the surface of the main action without stirring its current. Of greater significance is Launce, the attendant on Proteus. His is a richer, more pensive humour, which discharges itself mainly in soliloquies, with his dog Crab as auditor. Round this dumb companion, 'one that I brought up of a puppy' [IV. iv. 2-3], the thoughts of Launce steadily revolve: we hear, indeed, of a 'milkmaid' who has won his heart, and whose 'items' he discusses with Speed, but her highest praise is, 'She hath more qualities than a water-spaniel, which is much in a bare Christian' [III. i. 271-73], and this does not imply an equality to so unique an animal as Crab. It is only grief over any imperfection in one who is beloved that leads to the assertion, 'I think Crab, my dog, to be the sourest dog that lives,' because 'he sheds not a tear nor speaks a word' [II. iii. 5-6, 31], while Launce's household is plunged in lamentation at his departure for Milan. And Launce's affection is ready to stand the severest test, that of suffering on behalf of its object: 'I have sat in the stocks for puddings he hath stolen: otherwise he had been executed: I have stood on the pillory for geese he hath killed, otherwise he had suffered for 't' [IV. iv. 30-3]. Yet even this friend, for whom he has endured so much, Launce offers to sacrifice in order to do Proteus a service, though he has an instinct that things are not what they should be, 'I am but a fool, look you, and yet I have the wit to think my master is a kind of knave' [III. i. 263-64]. And this knavery of the highly-gifted Proteus finds an emphatic though unobtrusive condemnation in the fidelity of his simple servant to the poor cur that has shared his life of hard words and still harder knocks. Thus here, again, the main plot and the underplot, without dovetailing in an elaborate manner, play round the same theme, and embrace, in an unbroken network of relationships, the entire *dramatis personae* from 'the two gentlemen' down to poor dog Crab. (pp. 190-96)

> Frederick S. Boas, ''Shakspere's Poems: The Early Period of Comedy,'' in his Shakspere and His Predecessors, Charles Scribner's Sons, 1896, pp. 158-96.

W. J. COURTHOPE (essay date 1903)

[*In the following excerpt, Courthope touches upon several important topics in the criticism of* The Two Gentlemen of Verona, *including its sources, structure, comic elements, and its tragic potential, a possibility which the critic discerns in Julia's ''pathetic situation'' and in Proteus's ''selfish passion.'' Courthope is the earliest commentator to note this tragic element in the play, and because of its presence he labels* The Two Gentlemen of Verona ''the first of Shakespeare's tragicomedies.'' *The critic also identifies certain weak aspects of the play, such as the ''tedious'' repartee of the servants, the flimsy structure, and the inconsistent, unnatural behavior of Proteus and Valentine.*]

[*The Two Gentlemen of Verona* is] the first of Shakespeare's tragicomedies, and also the first in which he reflects deeply on the nature of a passion which, above all others, discloses the frailties of the human will. On the one hand, *The Two Gentlemen of Verona* touches the tragedy of *Romeo and Juliet*, which it also resembles in the poetical euphuism of its style; on the other, it is the precursor of that series of dramatic romances with a happy ending, comprising *The Merchant of Venice, As You Like It, Much Ado About Nothing, All's Well that Ends Well, Measure for Measure,* and *The Winter's Tale.* The tragic element appears in the corrupting influence of selfish passion on the character of Proteus, and in the pathetic situation of the injured Julia. In this character the romance of the play centres. The story is suggested by the *Diana Enamorada;* but, when Julia is compared with Viola in *Twelfth Night,* we see how gradually Shakespeare arrived at his final conception of the self-devotion which is the crowning beauty of woman. What seems mainly to have impressed him in the idea of *The Two Gentlemen of Verona,* as afterwards in *A Midsummer-Night's Dream,* is the contrariety in the fortunes of true love. This is made apparent in the speech of Julia, when she has undertaken to fetch Silvia's picture for Proteus—the climax of the romance:—

> How many women would do such a message?
> Alas, poor Proteus! thou hast entertained
> A fox to be the shepherd of thy lambs.
> Alas, poor fool! why do I pity him
> That with his very heart despiseth me?
> Because he loves her, he despiseth me;
> Because I love him, I must pity him. . . .
> I am my master's true-confirmed love;
> But cannot be true servant to my master,
> *Unless I prove false traitor to myself.*
> Yet will I woo for him, but yet so coldly
> As, heaven it knows, I would not have him speed.
>   [IV. iv. 90-6, 103-07]

The dramatic interest, therefore, lies in the external complexity of the situation, not, as in *Twelfth Night,* in the complete self-surrender of the will, illustrated by the impassioned pleading of Viola to Olivia on behalf of the Duke.

The comic element in the play is developed, in the underplot, by means of the characters of the two servants Launce and Speed. These are modelled on the characters of Licio and Petulus, in Lyly's *Mydas;* and one scene is imitated directly from that play, as may be seen from a comparison between the soliloquy of Launce, beginning, ''I am but a fool, look you'' [III. i. 263], and followed by the dialogue between himself and Speed (in which there is a catalogue of his mistress's qualities) and the conversation between Licio and Petulus. . . . [These two characters] entertain the audience with a display of verbal repartee in the—it must be confessed—eminently tedious vein of Shakespeare's two servants. The wit of Launce in *The Two Gentlemen of Verona* is grounded on what Speed calls ''your old vice still: mistake the word'' [III. i. 284]: Speed's talent lies in bringing his logic to absurd conclusions: both are dramatic inventions of the author of *Euphues.*

In other respects the play exhibits, germinally, many of the characteristics of Shakespeare's finest work. The poet's power of bringing together materials from different quarters is conspicuously displayed. Besides his obligations to the *Diana Enamorada*, Sidney's *Arcadia* furnishes him with two suggestions: the close friendship between Valentine and Proteus, imitated from the friendship between Pyrochles and Musidorus; and the election of Valentine to be captain of the outlaws, as Pyrochles in the *Arcadia* is chosen leader of the Helots. With this romantic atmosphere are also very happily blended allusions to actual life, as in the description Panthino gives of the habits of modern travel among the English aristocracy:—

> Men of slender reputation
> Put forth their sons to seek preferment out:
> Some to the wars, to try their fortune there;
> Some to discover islands far away;
> Some to the studious universities.
>
>   [I. iii. 6-10]

The humours of the servants afford a pleasant contrast to the misfortunes of the leading personages. On the other hand, the structure of the play is somewhat feeble. The underplot—if the conversations between Launce and Speed can be so called—is connected very slenderly with the main plot; and the principal action itself is not developed in such a manner as to explain the extraordinary inconsistencies of character; there is, for example, nothing to render probable the depths of baseness and treachery to which Proteus suddenly sinks in his passion for Silvia; still more unnatural in his abrupt reconversion to virtue; most incredible of all, the offer of Valentine to resign the love of his mistress in favour of his mean-spirited friend. (pp. 88-91)

> W. J. Courthope, ''Shakespeare's Early Comedies: Influence of Lyly,'' in his A History of English Poetry: Development and Decline of the Poetic Drama, Influence of the Court and the People, Vol. IV, The Macmillan Company, 1903, pp. 70-103.

E. K. CHAMBERS (essay date 1905)

[*Chambers occupies a transitional position in Shakespearean criticism, one which connects the biographical sketches and character analyses of the nineteenth century with the historical, technical, and textual criticism of the twentieth century. While a member of the education department at Oxford University, Chambers earned his reputation as a scholar with his multivolume works,* The Medieval Stage *(1903) and* The Elizabethan Stage *(1923); he also edited* The Red Letter Shakespeare *from 1904 to 1908. Chambers investigated both the purpose and limitations of each dramatic genre as Shakespeare presented it and speculated on how the dramatist's work was influenced by contemporary historical issues and his own frame of mind. In the following excerpt from his introduction to the 1905 Red Letter edition of* The Two Gentlemen of Verona, *Chambers presents evidence supporting the comedy's early composition date, such as its unconvincing ending, excessive "verbal ingenuities," faults in characterization, and "sentimental bankruptcy." The critic especially laments the "almost cynical brevity and lack of psychology" in the climax of the play and avers that by "putting humanity into the puppets of romance" Shakespeare undermined his romantic conventions. Offering an autobiographical assessment, Chambers also discusses the similarities between this comedy and Shakespeare's sonnets in terms of the feelings they reveal about love and friendship. Indeed, Chambers attributes the failure of the play's climax to Shakespeare's injection of his own "humanity" into the requirements of his romantic, tragicomic convention.*]

No play of Shakespeare, to my thinking, bears upon it such obvious marks of immaturity as *The Two Gentlemen of Verona*. . . . [The play] really declares itself as immature because it is Shakespeare's first essay at originality, at fashioning for himself the outlines of that romantic or tragicomic formula in which so many of his most characteristic dramas were afterwards to be cast. Something which is neither quite tragedy nor quite comedy, something which touches the heights and depths of sentiment and reveals the dark places of the human heart without lingering long enough there to crystallize the painful impression, a love story broken for a moment into passionate chords by absence and inconstancy and intrigue, and then reunited to the music of wedding-bells; such is the kind of dramatic scheme which floated before him, when he first set pen to paper in making a play of his very own. And the difficulties which the conception entails, in bringing about a happy ending that may find acceptance without proving demonstrably untrue to the facts of human nature, were perhaps greater than he had dreamed. Certainly, neither in *The Two Gentlemen of Verona*, nor in some later plays, whose handling is in the main surer and more masterly, did he altogether overcome them. Consider the last scene in the greenwood near Milan. Since the end of the second act, Proteus has earned our gathering detestation. He has been successively false to Julia, to Valentine, to the duke, to Thurio. The wanton attempt to force the unprotected girl who has repelled his dishonourable advances puts a climax on his iniquities. No audience can help wanting to see him punished; he must needs be wholly unsympathetic. And suddenly the natural development of the situation stops. The uplifted hand of poetic justice fails to strike. Within the space of not more than sixty lines, Proteus is converted by Valentine's reproaches; Valentine not merely forgives him, but makes the impossible offer to resign to him his own claim on Silvia's affections; and apparently the gift is only averted by the revelation of Julia and the discovery by Proteus that after all there is nothing in Silvia's face that he cannot spy more fresh in that of Julia. One recognizes that tragicomedy must have its reconciliation; but surely this is a reconciliation, in its almost cynical brevity and lack of psychology, to leave one gasping. Yet I do not know that it is really more amazing than the reconciliation of *Much Ado About Nothing*, in which the despicable Claudio is first offered a cousin in substitution for Hero, and finally recovers the very bride whom his disloyal acceptance of an incredible slander has well-nigh done to death; or than the reconciliation of *Measure for Measure*, in which the lechery and the hypocrisy of Angelo are rewarded with the hand of the much-wronged Mariana. Intent, as it would seem, on putting humanity into the puppets of romance, Shakespeare failed to observe that, as one result of the process, the conclusions of romance would cease to convince.

The sentimental bankruptcy, then, of *The Two Gentlemen of Verona*, although doubtless a more practised hand might have palliated it, is not by itself an infallible sign of an early play. But there are other signs to be noted. One is to be found in the abuse of verbal ingenuities. Shakespeare never quite lost his taste for these, but in *The Two Gentlemen of Verona* they are at once excessive in number, and of a puerility which may be exampled by the astounding puns upon 'ships' and 'sheep,' 'laced muttons' and 'lost muttons,' the 'tide' and the 'tied,' and other gems of speech which bedeck the conversation of the pages, to whom, after the fashion of Lyly's recently published comedies, the play looks for its comic relief. There is another in the lack of adroitness which allows the characters, as in *The Comedy of Errors*, and even, a little later, in *A Midsummer Night's Dream*, to fall into pairs. A Proteus and a Valentine, a Julia and a Silvia, a Launce and a Speed, do not provide a grouping of sufficiently varied interest. And there is a third in the constant appearance of motives which recur in later plays, with the suggestion that Shakespeare regarded the introduction of them into *The Two Gentlemen of Verona* as having been of the nature of a tentative experiment, that did not disqualify him from making further use of their tested capabilities when designing more mature and considered work. . . . Apart alike from what is merely anticipatory and what is merely colourless in the play stands the figure of Sir Eglamour, the knight vowed to chastity, and the chivalrous aider of distressed women. He is slightly sketched enough, but is romantic in a sense in which Shakespeare does not normally read romance. I do not recognize a character of quite the same type in any later play.

After all, *The Two Gentlemen of Verona* is interesting, not so much for its strictly dramatic content as for what it implies, for the evidence it affords of what Shakespeare was preoccupied with when he wrote it. One is commonly told that Shakespeare is the most objective of writers, and that is of course true in the sense that, beyond most other men, he had the gift of dispassionate observation and the power of projecting himself into all kinds of personalities most alien to his own. But I will never admit it to be true if by it is meant that he is not also subjective, that no reflex of his own personality is to be found among the creatures of his fashioning, and no shadow there of the experiences and ambitions which swayed and moulded the life of their creator. After all, even the most objective of writers cannot build cast-iron doors across the chambers and galleries of his brain. A poet will write of what interests him, whether within or without; nor is there any reason to suppose that Shakespeare was less interested in himself than in other people. Personally I find it impossible to read *The Two Gentlemen of Verona* except in the light of the *Sonnets,* some of which at least must be almost exactly contemporary with the play, and which portray clearly enough the temper of mind in which Shakespeare came to its composition. I do not claim to have any special key to the mysteries of the *Sonnets.* I do not know to whom or of whom they were written, or how far they are an actual record and how far an imaginative transcript of the facts that underlie them. I only know that there is heart's blood in them, and that to treat their passion as a mere literary exercise is to betray a more than average insensibility to the nature of poetic utterance. That, when no longer quite a young man, Shakespeare fell seriously into love; that love brought him little satisfaction and much disturbance in other relations of life, especially in that of friendship; that he came away with an experience behind him and the bitter taste of disillusion in his mouth; I do not see that you can infer much less than this. . . . One can hardly be surprised, however, that the first play written by Shakespeare after so disconcerting an adventure should bear some traces of his discomfiture. In *The Two Gentlemen of Verona* it is clear that he has been given furiously to think about love. Love, indeed, viewed professedly in the abstract, but pursued with a commentary not wholly free from personal bias, is the central theme of the play, the staple of conversation not only for the principal personages, who are lovers, but also for their apes and echoes, and occasionally shrewd critics, the page-boys. And if the maxims and reflections which the contemplation of love inspires at every turn and corner of the dialogue are not wholly free from a suspicion of commonplace, perhaps that is precisely because they are of the class which is suggested afresh to men in every generation by the common yet eternally new experience. Ordinarily, indeed, the references to love in *The Two Gentlemen of Verona* reproduce pretty faithfully the familiar range of ideas and even the traditional phrases of Elizabethan sonnetting. There is the same insistence upon the inevitable and abitrary character of the passion, the same tendency to make—

> A couplement of proud compare
> With sun and moon, with earth and sea's rich gems,
> With April's first-born flowers and all things rare,
> That heaven's air in this huge rondure hems;
>
> [Sonnet 21]

the same extravagance of hyperbole, as when Valentine fears for his mistress—

> Lest the base earth
> Should from her vesture chance to steal a kiss,
> And, of so great a favour growing proud,
> Disdain to root the summer-swelling flower,
> And make rough winter everlastingly.
>
> [II. iv. 159-63]

As a rule you will not take it all too seriously. But from time to time the mask of lightness is withdrawn and a haggard face looks out. A profoundly convinced, even bitter, personal note sounds through. To this Shakespeare, Love has in reality proved a mighty lord; he has actually known what hell it is—

> To be in love, where scorn is brought with groans;
> Coy looks with heart-sore sighs; one fading moment's mirth
> With twenty watchful, weary, tedious nights. . . .
>
> [I. i. 29-31]

Above all, one may fairly recognize in Proteus, Proteus the passionate and the perjured, not perhaps a 'portrait' of the false friend and supplanting lover, whoever he may be, of the *Sonnets,* but at least an image which would not have been drawn, or at any rate not in such deeply bitten lines, had not the friend of the *Sonnets* given Shakespeare cause to drink his potions of siren tears.

And now it may be noted that the presence of this personal element in the play gives a peculiar emphasis to that romantic unreality in the ending which has already been considered. It is because Shakespeare knew his Proteus, and knowing him, painted him as he was, without taking the trouble to keep him within the lines of the romantic convention, that the purely conventional and unconvincing repentance and forgiveness which await him in the Milanese forest appear to us things to be so much resented. Had he been a mere puppet, we should not have grudged him a puppet's reward. But the man is more than the poet; and it were ungrateful to complain that Shakespeare has introduced a bit of Shakespeare's humanity into The Two

Act V. Scene iv. Proteus, Silvia, Julia disguised as Sebastian, and Valentine. Frontispiece to the Bell edition by E. Edwards (1774).

Gentlemen of Verona, even at the cost of destroying the flawless perfection of a work of art. (pp. 49-57)

> E. K. Chambers, "'The Two Gentlemen of Verona'," in his Shakespeare: A Survey, *1925. Reprint by Hill and Wang, 1958? pp. 49-57.*

R. WARWICK BOND (essay date 1906)

[*In the excerpt below, Bond outlines in detail the structure of contrasting characterization and parallel events in* The Two Gentlemen of Verona. *Although he recognizes several faults in the play, Bond defends the ending from allegations of inconsistency and textual corruption, stating that the line "all that was mine in Silvia I give to thee" (V. iv. 83) is intentionally ambiguous—a contention later disputed by Martin W. Sampson (see excerpt below, 1912). Valentine's words are understood by everyone but Julia to express his equal affection for Silvia and Proteus, Bond continues, and are not meant as an offering of the former to the latter.*]

[The influence of John Lyly on Shakespeare's writing of *The Two Gentlemen of Verona*] is seen most, perhaps, in the symmetrical balance of structure, a point noticed by many critics. Lyly was fond of introducing characters in pairs or triplets: here we have two lovers; their two mistresses, each of whom forsakes home in pursuit of the man she loves; their two servants, each of whom, like Lucetta, sees as much or more than his master, Speed translating Silvia's overture to Valentine, Launce fathoming the knavery of Proteus; also two opposing fathers, and two secondary figures at Court, Thurio and Eglamour. But Shakespeare pays far more attention than Lyly to contrast of character and variety of circumstance. The frank and forthright Valentine, a faithful friend and lover, is opposed to the subtle and tortuous Proteus, false in both relations; and in accord with this, Silvia, though a noble honest-hearted girl, is hardly so deep or strong a character as Julia; in her higher position she has both less of maiden scruple, and less power in the face of material dangers—we are not to accept Thurio's epithet of "reckless," nor yet to accuse her of coquetry because, with her flight already planned, she sends Proteus her portrait,—her task is to baffle the importunities of undesirable suitors, Julia's harder one to recover a lost affection: the opposition of Silvia's father is based on Valentine's inferiority of rank; that which Proteus dreads from his may be one of prejudice merely, for if Proteus can secure the best recommendations at Court, yet Julia has goods, lands, and accomplishments: and the servants, while characteristically opposed to their masters, and so to each other, the wit-hunting observant Speed to the somewhat simple Valentine, the honest unconventional Launce to the adroit worldling Proteus, yet reflect something of their masters' relations, for Launce, as the elder, has the better headpiece though he be the less practically efficient. But, to come back to Lyly, we have in these servants, not indeed an underplot, a title to which they have too little independent interest to pretend, yet a kind of comic parallelism or parody of the serious action, first found, I believe, in the play of *Endimion*. . . . Julia's silent tearful farewell to her lover is comically echoed in Crab's stolidity during Launce's lachrymose parting from home: Speed's thrusting himself into Launce's love-affairs parodies Proteus' intrusion into Valentine's, and Valentine's voluntary admission of Proteus to his confidence contrasts with Launce's professed reserve on the point of love: Launce's self-sacrifice for his dog-friend contrasts with Proteus' selfish betrayal of his man-friend, and his willingness to surrender Crab to serve his master has even been thought a reflection of Valentine's (supposed) surrender of Silvia to his friend. Such comic parody in a measure compensates us for the want of essential share by these comic servants in the plot, and for the want of a progressive action of their own, such as is found at least in Lyly's *Midas*. In the kind and tone of the comic relief they afford, in their friendliness tempered by a readiness to take the points off each other on occasion, they present a close general likeness to Lyly's pages; with a specific imitation, in the scene where Launce catalogues his young woman's qualities, of that in *Midas* where Licio recites to Petulus the personal marks of Celia, whose page he is. Lylian, too, as Mr. Courthope points out [see excerpt above, 1903], are Launce's "old vice" of "mistaking the word" [III. i. 284] and Speed's trick of comic logic, of which instances are found in *Sapho and Phao* (1582). Both have the inveterate punning habit, and Launce also a touch of malapropism.

But Launce jets, straight as an American oil-fount, into a heaven of unforced, unageing humour where Lyly could never come; and with him, admitted to that equal sky, the stubborn brute he adores. "When didst thou see *me* heave up my leg—!" [IV. iv. 37]. Somewhat coarse it may be: Shakespeare had to please a taste which still recalled the grossness of *Gammer Gurton* or the long-past interludes of Heywood, and against which Lyly had struggled gallantly. But Launce—this feckless lout with a vein of ideality, whose shrewdness, sententiousness,

and power of description are merely the rueful protest of brain and tongue against a practical inefficiency imposed by temperament—Launce with his kindliness and his cur, and that indefinable lack of the smart touch that so distastes the clever Proteus, is not merely almost the first of the Shakespearean clowns; he is one of the very best. . . . I need waste no more words on a merit so obvious. Speed, clearly the younger of the pair, is much nearer the Lylian convention, a compound of 'cuteness, effrontery, and conviviality. (pp. xxviii-xxxi)

A word must be devoted to that lyrical character which [*The Two Gentlemen of Verona*] shares with *Love's Labour's Lost*, and, especially, *Romeo and Juliet*. Lyrical feeling is unusually present in the diction and sentiment, and often reflected in the form of the verse. Throughout occur passages reflecting on the nature of love, or the conflict between love and friendship. Julia, Valentine, and Proteus are never tired of uttering axioms on the subject . . . and even Speed must reel off the marks of the passion, and Launce discuss the qualities of a wife. Often these utterances take a form of metaphor or elaborate simile, giving us the best poetry of the play. . . . (p. xxxii)

This lyric character of *The Two Gentlemen* is appropriate to it as the first of the romantic comedies, Shakespeare's earliest attempt to transfer romantic temper and subject to the stage: the first—for *Love's Labour's Lost* is too purely a play of wit and polite forms to deserve that title, it has no pretensions to plot and no connection with romance; while the *Errors*, though not without romantic elements, is nearer farce. . . . [Here] Shakespeare first opens the vein he worked so richly afterwards—the vein of crossed love; of flight and exile under the escort of the generous sentiments; of disguised heroines, and sufferings endured and virtues exhibited under their disguise; and of the Providence, kinder than life, that annuls the errors and forgives the sin: and here first he lays his scene in Italy. Naturally, anticipations of later work abound. (pp. xxxiii-xxxv)

The Duke strikes me as a good portrait for this early date, most like Duke Frederick [in *As You Like It*] in his *bonhomie* when unruffled, in the arbitrary or base lengths to which a passionate self-will can carry him, and in the rising of his better nature against Thurio, as Frederick's does against Oliver. Interesting little points are his smile at Valentine's eulogy of his friend, his reluctance to damage his prospects [III. i. 28-31], and his curious probing of his motives [III. i. 68-79]. The meanness of engaging Proteus to slander Valentine may be prompted by some contempt for the traitor. A certain inconsistency in this character, however, may be acknowledged among the defects of the play. Another slight one is the upper tower in which Silvia is said to be lodged at night, certainly too high for her nocturnal interviews of IV. ii., iii., and in odd contrast with her freedom in the daytime in II. iv. . . . [The outlaws'] sudden election of [Valentine] as captain seems improbable, though the poet labours to show grounds for it, and in their clamorous interruption of each other possibly suggests their existing anarchy. The Duke's pardon of them, rash in any case, is also *ultra vires,* as they are not his subjects [IV. i. 45-9]—and we really must not press the "emperor"—and loses something of its grace from the fact that he is in their power.

But these defects, and the hasty winding-up, may well be due to careless revision or abridgment, the most obvious sign of which is the complete silence of Silvia from the moment of Valentine's appearance, notwithstanding a succession of startling events in which she has the liveliest interest. Chief amongst these must be reckoned her lover's apparent renunciation of her to his friend, that renunciation which has caused so much discussion. . . . [We] must not hastily reject this renunciation as quite beyond the pale of Shakespeare's intention; and much has been urged in justification of it. The notion of Valentine suspecting some frailty in Silvia seems untenable in view of her protest of love for him at lines [V. iv. 36-7], and [one critic's] suggestion that he may not have overheard all is inconsistent with his intervention at precisely the right moment. Nor is . . . [a proposed] parallel, found in Valentine's request that Silvia will receive Proteus as his "fellow-servant" [II. iv. 105], at all similar. Better, perhaps, is . . . [the] argument that such a sacrifice made to him by Valentine is a method of showing us that Proteus cannot be quite unworthy of Julia. . . . But in truth all these explanations are but acknowledgments of the difficulty felt at least by moderns; and against any such intention on Shakespeare's part is certainly Silvia's strange silence, and Valentine's emphatic assertion of his interest in her just afterwards [V. iv. 126]. . . . I believe the true solution has been reserved for Dr. Batteson, who holds that the text is right, and the words rightly placed, but that they are *intentionally ambiguous* on the poet's part [a hypothesis suggested at a meeting of the Sunday Shakespeare Society in 1902, but never published]. In Valentine's mouth

> And that my love may appear plain and free,
> All that was mine in Silvia I give thee
>
> [V. iv. 82-3]

means nothing more than "I give you my love as frankly and unreservedly as I gave it to Silvia: you shall have as much interest in my heart as she"—too handsome a concession, doubtless, but a piece of rhetoric at an impassioned moment, well understood by all present—except one. For Julia, anxiously watching in her disguise the progress of affairs, hampered by her modesty yet seeking some opportunity of discovering herself, the poet, studious as ever of stage-effect, has decided on a swoon (a faint that is no feigning) as a means of drawing general attention to her, and bringing on his *dénouement*. He secures his swoon by putting ambiguous words into Valentine's mouth, which in her overwrought mood she misinterprets. I would add that the Duke's repudiation of Thurio at [V. iv. 136-38],

> The more degenerate and base art thou
> To make such means for her as thou hast done
> And leave her on such slight conditions,

argues much unlikelihood that the poet would assign to Valentine a change of front at all like his. (pp. xxxvi-xxxix)

> *R. Warwick Bond, in an introduction to* The Works of Shakespeare: The Two Gentlemen of Verona *by William Shakespeare, edited by R. Warwick Bond, 1906. Reprint by Methuen and Co. Ltd., 1925, pp. ix-xliv.*

RICHARD GARNETT   (essay date 1907)

[*Garnett attributes the "inferiority" of* The Two Gentlemen of Verona *to Shakespeare's youthful inexperience at the time of its composition and calls it the dramatist's "simplest and least ambitious" play. He identifies as a principal fault the comedy's subordination of character to action—a situation, the critic claims, which Shakespeare never repeated in his later works. Garnett praises, however, the "easy and natural" management of the action and asserts that even the "absolutely inconceivable" conclusion is "in harmony with the recklessness and inconsequence of youth" implicit in the play.*]

[In] action as in diction, "The Two Gentlemen of Verona" is one of Shakespeare's simplest and least ambitious productions. It has the charm of the opening bud, the herald of the rose, but not yet the rose itself. . . . [The] most evident testimony to the development of Shakespeare's mind is afforded by the comparison of "The Two Gentlemen of Verona" with "Twelfth Night," where Julia has flowered into Viola. No two of his plays are more nearly related in apparent contrast; and the relation is not wholly that of the undeveloped to the mature, but also that between two contending schools of dramatic authorship.

In almost all Shakespeare's works character takes the lead of action: not that the action is not commonly most absorbing, and in its conception and conduct an example of supreme art, but that it seems to exist for the sake of the characters, while the characters do not exist for it. The primary purpose of "Macbeth" and "Hamlet," for example, is to depict the aspects of human nature revealed in those personages, and the tremendous accompaniments, natural and supernatural, are but adjuncts to this design. In "The Two Gentlemen of Verona," on the other hand, Shakespeare does not greatly concern himself with character painting. He writes such a play as a good Italian dramatist of the age might have written, diversified indeed with strokes of poetry and humour beyond the reach of any contemporary, but which in the main appeals to the reader or spectator not by its character but by its incidents. The special gift in virtue of which he so infinitely transcends all other dramatists is in abeyance: we admire not so much the insight into human nature as the easy grace by which the personages are so nicely discriminated that they can never be confused. Critics have pointed out the delicate antithesis between characters in other respects but faintly individualised by which this object is mainly accomplished. "Proteus, the fickle," says Professor Dowden, "is set against Valentine the faithful: Silvia, the bright and intellectual, against Julia, the ardent and tender; Launce, the humourist, against Speed, the wit" [see excerpt above, 1877]. The personages all belong to the accepted types of the classical drama, but all are living men and women, none mere masks as in Plautus and Terence, the models of the contemporary Italian stage.

The obvious reason of the inferiority of "The Two Gentlemen of Verona" in the pourtrayal of character is the youth of the author. Assuming 1590 as the year of its production, Shakespeare would be twenty-six, in general the commencement of a period of great development of genius on its intellectual side; witness Byron, Shelley, Wordsworth, and Coleridge. A few years later he would have handled the subject differently; in truth, "The Two Gentlemen of Verona" would have become "Twelfth Night." In everything that he did undertake, nevertheless, his mastery is conspicuous. The play which does not attempt character must appeal to action, and here the young author approves himself already a master. The interest created by the first scene goes on growing to the end. Julia gains upon us continually, and the sympathy thus aroused serves to smooth over the great difficulty inherent in the action, the disposal of Proteus. It is shocking to poetical justice that a double traitor to friend and mistress should make his final exit hand in hand with so charming a creature; but if the arrangement is essential to the charming creature's happiness, what can be said? We must fortify ourselves by the reflection that "The Two Gentlemen of Verona" is in every respect the comedy of youth. Except the two "heavy fathers" and the sage Panthino, there is not an elderly person among the *dramatis personæ*. The young people have it all their own way, and elope, assume equivocal disguises, carry off other people's daughters, and become captains of robbers on short notice with all the ease and carelessness befitting the April of life. Hence, to the apprehension of the more mature, the incidents and sentiments sometimes assume a tinge of unreality, which they would not have suggested to the youthful author and his youthful *dramatis personæ*. (pp. xvii-xx)

The dramatic economy of the piece is as praiseworthy as its power of exciting sympathy. The progress of the action is delightfully easy and natural. One scene brings the next inevitably on; or if any appear at first parenthetical, they are indispensable as reliefs to the more serious action, and assume their proper relation with it upon a survey of the drama as a whole. If there is any fault, it is that perhaps Julia's romantic resolution to seek her lover in male attire is insufficiently motived. It would have been easy to justify it by the introduction of some element of jealousy. Rumours might have been supposed to have reached Julia's ears, or she might have been swayed by the insinuations of a gossiping friend, or her extravagant estimate of Proteus' perfection might have suggested to her that her monopoly of such a paragon might be rudely challenged. This might have been expressed in a soliloquy, to avoid the necessity of taking Lucetta entirely into her confidence. We scarcely doubt that at a later period Shakespeare would have devised something of this nature. In the play as we have it he seems to avoid highly pitched emotion and complication of whatever kind. His pen must have travelled fleetly and lightly over his paper. If this prevents him from manifesting his full power, there is some compensation in the unusual transparency of his language, which would hardly be consistent with a weighty burden of thought or passion.

One most palpable fault is not a defect of construction, but a vice inherent in the action, an instance, unique in Shakespeare, of untruth to Nature—Valentine's momentary resignation of his mistress to Proteus in the fifth act. The incident is absolutely inconceivable; its only apology is that Julia's swoon is essential to the dénouement, and that Shakespeare apparently could not find, nor have any of his critics since found for him, a more effectual way of bringing it to pass. "Cæsar did never wrong, but with just cause" [*Julius Cæsar*, III. i. 47-8]. That he was dissatisfied with it may be inferred from the extreme lightness with which it is touched upon; it is no sooner come than it is gone. Here, at all events, we may admire his art. Ere the spectator has had time to take in Valentine's ingratitude to Silvia, or his cool donation of her to another without her consent, he is absorbed in compassion for Julia, around whose helpless form all the *dramatis personæ* are immediately grouped. Silvia herself has no time or opportunity to visit Valentine with the weight of her indignation; and when Julia opens her lips a new situation is unfolded, and the occurrences of the last five minutes belong to ancient history. There can therefore be no foundation for the notion that the scene has been mutilated by the actors, and Shakespeare's avoidance of the expository discourses from leading characters which some have missed stands to the credit of his consummate judgment. It may be added that the incident, impossible and offensive as it is, is quite in harmony with the recklessness and inconsequence of youth which has been noted as a leading element in "The Two Gentlemen of Verona," and that Shakespeare and his contemporaries were much more concerned about the effect of their plays upon spectators than with the judgment of readers in the closet, whose very existence they hardly contemplated. (pp. xxi-xxiii)

"The Two Gentlemen of Verona" is remarkably exempt from one class of faults incident to the early works of men of genius.

It is exceedingly unpretentious. It reveals none of the vague and magnificent aspirations so frequent and natural with gifted youth. The Hamlet in Shakespeare's soul remains unfolded. He announces no startling doctrines, attacks no established institutions, affords no hint of any introspective tendency. Like Goethe, who carried a Werther in him as Shakespeare a Hamlet, he begins his career with a light and lively piece, whose serious episodes are only conjured up to be conjured away. The play, besides, has more practical wisdom than might have been looked for in the work of a young inexperienced writer. It is certainly an overstatement when Johnson says, "It abounds in [maxims] beyond most of his plays" [see excerpt above, 1765], but it would have been no overstatement to have said that many of its sentences have become aphorisms. The chief intellectual token of juvenility is an occasional tendency to hyperbole and fine writing, as when Valentine says:—

> Bear my lady's train, lest the bare earth
> Should from her vesture chance to steal a kiss,
> And of so great a favour growing proud,
> Disdain to root the summer-swelling flower
> And make rude winter everlastingly. . . .
>
> 　　　　　　　　　　　　　　　[II. iv. 159-63]

But such extravagance is exceptional. As a rule, Shakespeare confines himself closely to the development of his action, and does not seek to adorn it with the flowers of poetry. (pp. xxiii-xxiv)

> *Richard Garnett, in an introduction to* The Complete Works of William Shakespeare: The Two Gentlemen of Verona, Vol. II *by William Shakespeare, edited by Sidney Lee, George D. Sproul, 1907, pp. ix-xxvi.*

MARTIN W. SAMPSON　(essay date 1912)

[*In the excerpt below, Sampson refutes R. Warwick Bond's contention that Valentine's infamous line, "All that was mine in Silvia I give to thee" (V. iv. 83), is meant as an offer of love, rather than of Silvia herself (see excerpt above, 1906); instead, he counters that "it is hardly likely that this supersubtle meaning, which has escaped students for three centuries, would be apparent to an audience on first hearing." Like several other critics, Sampson states that the conclusion of the play is intended to emphasize the superiority of friendship over love; he avers that, despite its deficiencies, this was a convention undoubtedly accepted by Shakespeare's audience. On other matters, Sampson disparages the uneven construction of* The Two Gentlemen of Verona, *but he praises its "mood of youthful beauty."*]

Although [*The Two Gentlemen of Verona*] successfully tells a capital story, it cannot be maintained that Shakespeare exhibits here a true mastery of dramatic technique. The action is very slow in getting under way, and the situations which are dramatized are not always worthy of the honor they thereby receive. There are sins of omission, of compression, of diffuseness, of inaction, and of false leading, that accompany the virtues of well conceived and felicitous presentation. Thus the first two acts are largely talk, filling the intervals between unacted incidents; the farewell of Proteus and Julia, and the succeeding lament of Launce, properly belong before the scene in which Sylvia hands back to Valentine the unsatisfactory yet all-sufficient letter; and the wooing of Julia and the winning of Sylvia fail to receive the stage presentation that they deserve. The third act, on the other hand, is excellently constructed, and does precisely what is required of it. The fourth and fifth acts, barring the dénouement, move well. Roughly speaking, then, the play improves as it advances, and this none too common virtue is in itself enough to mark a great improvement over the crude technique of the conclusion of *Love's Labour's Lost*.

The great charm of the play lies in its mood of youthful beauty. Youthful love is seen as a delightful human thing, to be dealt with sympathetically, not as a thing merely affording an author an opportunity to display his wit; grief appears as something to touch the heart, not as a provocation to stylistic lamentation; humor shows as something genial, not merely as a vehicle of verbal cleverness. In short, what the advertisers of contemporary fiction and drama call ''the heart interest''—an overworn name for a good thing—stands out in our play as a reality; gayety, intrigue, misfortune, success, are enveloped in human tenderness that is never mawkish or forced. The poetry of the play, as has been hinted, is neither great nor intense, but it is sincere and truly charming; in quality lyric rather than dramatic: ''The uncertain glory of an April day'' [I. iii. 85] represents the finest felicity it attains.

None of the characters presents a real problem in portrayal. The play is not a ''study'' of human nature; it is a story in which the personages, whose traits are chosen in advance to meet the plot's demands, reveal their qualities as they are needed. Over and above the mere necessities of situation, however, the characters are now and then, by a fine emphasis, rendered strongly individual. Julia's silent farewell to Proteus, for example, is an early indication of Shakespearean insight. The personages themselves are all free of complexity or subtlety. Valentine is a gallant young gentleman and steadfast, Proteus the changeable variety of the same genus; the other men are little more than types, save that Eglamour's courtesy is distinctive. Antonio, the Duke, and Thurio derive their interest wholly from situation. The two charming heroines differ in fortune rather than in nature, although that difference is so marked as to prevent an impression of repetition. Such unlikeness as may be ascribed to them makes Sylvia the forerunner of Portia [in *The Merchant of Venice*] and Beatrice [in *Much Ado about Nothing*]; Julia an earlier Viola [in *Twelfth Night*] or Imogen [in *Cymbeline*]; and both heroines share the honor of foreshadowing Rosalind [in *As You Like It*]. With Julia and Sylvia begins that wonderful group of characters that we call ''Shakespeare's women.''

The flaw in the play is its dénouement. Valentine's instant belief in the contrition of Proteus may pass unchallenged, but his immediate proffer of Sylvia to his friend is unreal in the highest degree. It is little wonder that Sylvia has not another word to say thereafter. Ingenious efforts have been made to explain away the unnaturalness, but their very ingenuity is against their plausibility, for the concluding part of a play must be lucid, and a fresh intricacy is least of all in place. Dr. Batteson's solution, altered for the better by Mr. Bond [see excerpt above, 1906], may be mentioned as the most ingenious explanation of all: Valentine's ''all that was mine in Sylvia I give thee'' [V. iv. 83] is to be regarded as meaning that Valentine gives Proteus his affection, which is all that is truly his own in Sylvia; this figure of speech is thereupon understood by all but Julia, who, taking it literally as Valentine's renunciation, swoons with grief. In other words, Valentine means to offer Proteus his love again, while Julia thinks he is offering Proteus his lady, Sylvia. But it is hardly likely that this supersubtle meaning, which has escaped students for three centuries, would be apparent to an audience on first hearing.

To the present editor it seems that Shakespeare's intention was wholly clear and wholly unconvincing. Valentine is the faithful man who was the friend of Proteus before he was the lover of Sylvia. Unlike Proteus, who was disloyal even to a constant friend, Valentine will be loyal even to an inconstant friend, and the more inconstant the friend the greater Valentine's loyalty. When the clash of obligations comes, the prior loyalty, friendship, takes precedence over the second loyalty, love. Proteus, the fickle, had asked, ''In love who respects friend?'' [V. iv. 53]. Valentine, the steadfast, now supplies the answer. For his friend he will give up his dearest possession, all of Sylvia that he could call his own. However untrue to the human soul this is, it possesses a sort of theoretic validity in making constancy the absolute contrast to changeableness. There is no reason, moreover, to think that the situation seemed novel to Shakespeare or to the well-read Elizabethan. It must be remembered that the story of a man giving up his betrothed to a friend had been repeatedly told since the twelfth century (Petrus Alphonsus) and that it probably dates back to the Greek romances. The artificiality of the issue was doubtless acceptable enough to an age accustomed to a highly antithetic literary interpretation of love and friendship. Shakespeare's own forty-second sonnet shows much the same artificiality, and finds in a mere phrase a reward for renunciation. (pp. xii-xvi)

Yet when all is said, the great fact remains that the play possesses a wholesomeness, a straightforwardness, a charm, that are worthy to herald the approach of Shakespeare's maturity. (p. xvi)

> *Martin W. Sampson, in an introduction to* The Two Gentlemen of Verona *by William Shakespeare, edited by Martin W. Sampson, Macmillan Publishing Company, 1912, pp. vii-xvi.*

[SIR ARTHUR QUILLER-COUCH]   (essay date 1921)

[*Quiller-Couch was editor with J. Dover Wilson of the New Cambridge edition of Shakespeare's works. In his study* Shakespeare's Workmanship *and in his Cambridge lectures on Shakespeare, Quiller-Couch based his interpretations on the assumption that Shakespeare was mainly a craftsman attempting, with the tools and materials at hand, to solve particular problems central to his plays. In the excerpt below from his introduction to the New Cambridge edition of* The Two Gentlemen of Verona, *Quiller-Couch discusses the language of the play, especially in the final scene, where it is so ''slipshod'' and ''vicious'' that he regards the entire episode as another writer's adulteration, ''a piece of theatre botchwork patched upon the original.'' He also asserts that in this comedy Shakespeare broadened his previous concern with construction and began for the first time to ''weld character into his plot.'' Launce and Proteus are two interesting experiments in characterization, the critic suggests, but the women of the play embody the most reality and humanity.*]

[We may] read in *The Two Gentlemen* something more than a graceful story charmingly told. It is that: but it also fixes and holds in arrest for us a fleet youthful and peculiarly fascinating phase or moment in the efflorescence of Shakespeare's art. . . . (p. x)

The diction is melodious, on the whole too mellifluous. 'Fine writing' still engages him, and a butterfly 'conceit' still allures him to pursue and over-run it. Lucetta has already [I. ii. 30] announced of love that

Fire that's closest kept burns most of all—

and Julia elaborates this later [II. vii. 24-32] into

> The more thou damm'st it up, the more it burns:
> The current that with gentle murmur glides,
> Thou know'st, being stopped, impatiently doth rage:
> But when his fair course is not hinderéd
> He makes sweet music with th'enamelled stones,
> Giving a gentle kiss to every sedge
> He overtaketh in his pilgrimage;
> And so by many winding nooks he strays,
> With willing sport, to the wide ocean. . . .

We all remember the passage for its imagery, its cadence, and its delicately chosen words. But it is boyish, inexperienced: it keeps the speaker dallying luxuriously with an image while the dramatic moment slips away; the passion requisite for fusing the two having had time to cool. It is pretty: but it has not the masterly touch of

> And unregarded age in corners thrown
>   [As You Like It, II. iii. 42]

or

> O liméd soul, that struggling to be free
> Art more engaged! Help, angels! make assay. . . .
>   [Hamlet, III. iii. 68-9]

For promise of that, to find it in The Two Gentlemen, we must seek among chance lines:

> Poor wounded name: my bosom, as a bed,
> Shall lodge thee till thy wound be throughly healed.
>   [I. ii. 111-12]

> Wilt thou reach stars, because they shine on thee?
>   [III. i. 156]

> Who should be trusted, when one's own right hand
> Is perjured to the bosom?
>   [V. iv. 67-8]

But the promise is there.

There is notable promise, too, in the characters. The Two Gentlemen would seem to be the earliest play in which Shakespeare turned from 'construction'—that idol of artistic beginners—to weld character into his plot. Again as in The Comedy of Errors he gives us two gentlemen with a servant apiece: but this time he discriminates master from master, servant from servant, to individualise them. To be sure, because he has to follow a ready-made story, we find him experimenting most happily upon the characters—upon Launce, for example—who give him most liberty because they are least tied to obey the exigencies of the intrigue. Proteus has to play the almost incredibly false friend, in order to work the story; and to make it plausible, even to himself, must spend most of his time and ours upon cold sophistries. . . . The plot allows [Valentine and Silvia] high moments of generosity—nay, even works upon these—yet in its motion treats the pair as dupes, almost as dummies. For example, it is not by proof or by prowess that Valentine becomes captain of the outlaws, but simply because they like his looks and accept his bare word for his linguistic attainments.

Nevertheless, and throughout the play, we feel that Shakespeare, though—with the exceptions of Julia and Launce—he cannot, without making them dull, keep any of his dramatis personae steadily consistent, is always keeping them lively and always bringing them to the edge, at least, of startling us by some individuality. We feel, as we read, that these people are impatient of the convention within which they are held: that

any one of them, at any moment, may break out and do something original; and this holds us in an atmosphere of expectancy which, if not the same as reality, curiously resembles it. Yet while individualising these people, he is learning to give them—the women especially—that catholic kinship which communicates to us, as we wander in Shakespeare's great portrait gallery, a delightful sense of intimacy, of recognition. They belong to a family—our family—the Human Family. (pp. x-xii)

We come now to the final scene, and, in particular, to the passage which has offended so many critics of sensibility: the lines in which Valentine 'empties'—as the Germans say—'the baby with the bath,' and, after pardoning his false friend, proceeds to give away (in every sense) his most loyal lady-love to her would-be ravisher. . . . 'All that was mine in Silvia I give thee' [V. iv. 83]—one's impulse, upon this declaration, is to remark that there are, by this time, no gentlemen in Verona.

We must not, without a second thought, pronounce that this and the preceding line are not Shakespeare's—could not have been written by Shakespeare. They are uncouth: but he wrote, first and last, many uncouth lines. . . . (pp. xiii-xiv)

For mediaeval and Renaissance writers had a fashion with Friendship: a literary convention of refining, idealising, exalting it out of all proportion, or at any rate above the proportion it bears, in our modern minds, either to love between man and woman or to parental love. . . . That the convention lay strong upon [Shakespeare] no one can doubt who studies the Sonnets, or weighs the claims of friendship and love in The Merchant of Venice. . . . [May we admit then that Shakespeare was] working on an old play; and that, in the end, after re-furbishing the story and making its characters life-like, he found himself faced with a conventional dénouement and closed the account with a tag of doggerel either contemptuously invented or transferred literally from the corpus vile [worthless matter]?

It is possible: and we will give a devil's advocate yet a little farther scope. There is a tradition (which we are unable to trace to its source) that The Two Gentlemen of Verona proved a failure on the stage. If so, nothing in the play would account for it so easily as this most crucial blunder.

Allowing something—not too much, we think—to this tradition, we offer another hypothesis. . . . [Here] we deal with the most flagrant and vitiating passage, and suggest a possible explanation—there is no possible excuse. It may be, then, that Shakespeare invented a solution which at the first performance was found to be ineffective; that the final scene was partly re-written—not by Shakespeare—and given its crude and conventional coup de théâtre [sudden, striking change]; that in this mutilated form it remained on the play-copy; and that it so reached the printer. We believe, at any rate, that no one can re-read this scene carefully without detecting that pieces of it are Shakespeare's and other pieces have been inserted by a 'faker' who not only was not Shakespeare, but did not possess even a rudimentary ear for blank verse. The opening lines bewray him:

> I Outlaw. Come, come, be patient: we must bring you
>   to our captain.
> Silvia. A thousand more mischances than this one
> Have learned me how to brook this patiently.
> 2 Outlaw. Come, bring her away.
> I Outlaw. Where is the gentleman that was with her?
> 3 Outlaw. Being nimble-footed, he hath outrun us.
> But Moses and Valerius follow him:

Go thou with her to the west end of the wood,
There is our captain: we'll follow him that's fled.

                                        [V. iii. 1-10]

Shakespeare's prosody is often easy-going, and not seldom—
to a pedantic mind—perverse: but to our ear it is never slipshod
or vicious *in that way*. And this faultiness exactly coincides
with a significant, if a minor, fault of dramatic craftsmanship—
the damnation of Sir Eglamour's taking-off. Sir Eglamour—
not to be confused with the knight of that name who figures
among Julia's suitors in Act i, Scene 2—has obviously been
dragged into the plot by no fault of his own. He is just an
honest, simple gentleman on whose chivalry Silvia makes claim
for help in a most difficult adventure.

            O Eglamour, thou art a gentleman . . .
            Upon whose faith and honour I repose.

                                        [IV. iii. 12, 26]

His answer is prompt, as his service is punctual. Without warning or excuse he is reported to have taken to his heels like the
veriest poltroon! At once, helped by muddled versification, we
perceive that this scene is running agley, that same interposing
hand is murdering the verse along with dramatic consistency.
Amid lines that have Shakespeare's trick and cadence are thrust
strange ones that no ear can accept for his. Suddenly, with the
crisis, we come upon the doggerel:

            And that my love may appear plain and free,
            All that was mine in Silvia I give thee.

                                        [V. iv. 82-3]

Having noted the jingle which follows on the rhyme of 'pleased'
and 'appeased,' we note further that there is only one other
instance in this melodiously written play of an unrhymed speech
finished off with two rhymed couplets; and that is the very
speech (uttered by Proteus) which, if it have any meaning at
all, improves in caddishness upon Valentine's offence:

                O heaven, were man
            But constant, he were perfect; that one error
            Fills him with faults . . .

                                        [V. iv. 110-12]

—so far Shakespeare, perhaps: now for cacophony followed
by nonsense:

            makes him run through all th' sins;
            Inconstancy falls off ere it begins:
            What is in Silvia's face, but I may spy
            More fresh in Julia's *with a constant eye*?

                                        [V. iv. 112-15]

Can anyone believe Shakespeare guilty of this pair of tags: the
first lame in scansion and unmeaning, the second balanced for
our choice between nonsense and rascality? And where is Silvia
in all this business? She is merely left. She utters not a word
after Valentine's pseudo-magnificent, pseudo-romantic, renunciation. . . . It would be an ingenious [essay that] could
account for Silvia's silence here save by the alternatives, *either*
of her being sick and tired of both her lovers, *or* of the whole
scene's being (as we submit) a piece of theatre botchwork
patched upon the original. (pp. xv-xviii)

            [*Sir Arthur Quiller-Couch*], *in an introduction to* The
            Two Gentlemen of Verona *by William Shakespeare,
            Cambridge at the University Press, 1921, pp. vii-xix.*

O. J. CAMPBELL   (essay date 1925)

[*An American scholar and critic, Campbell is best known for his*
Comicall Satyre and Shakespeare's "Troilus and Cressida" *(1938),
an influential study in which he posits that Shakespeare was imitating a new dramatic genre invented by Ben Jonson—namely,
satire—when he wrote* Troilus and Cressida. *In his following
publication,* Shakspere's Satire *(1943), Campbell continued his
emphasis on the satiric elements in Shakespeare's plays and established himself as an innovative interpreter of Elizabethan drama,
particularly with his characterization of* Timon of Athens *as a
tragic satire, rather than a tragedy. Campbell was also the editor
of* The Living Shakespeare, *an edition of twenty-one of Shakespeare's most popular plays, and* The Reader's Encyclopedia of
Shakespeare, *an indispensable guide to the poet's life and work.
In the following excerpt, he disputes R. Warwick Bond and
George P. Baker (see excerpt above, 1906, and Additional Bibliography), both of whom attribute to Shakespeare, rather than
his source material, most of the elements in* The Two Gentlemen
of Verona. *Instead, Campbell maintains that nearly everything in
the play—the plot, the characters, and various details—closely
follows its Italian sources, such as Flaminio Scala's* Flavio Tradito
and other works of the Commedia dell'Arte *tradition. The critic
thus concludes that it is misleading to credit Shakespeare in* The
Two Gentlemen of Verona *with inventing Elizabethan romantic
comedy, asserting instead that what he did do was transform
Italian comedy into a sensitive story of the "beauty and poetry
of youthful love." In addition, Campbell asserts that the resolution
of Shakespeare's play is not shocking, but is simply the "expected
indisputable proof of the complete victory of friendship in its
mortal struggle with love," as required by Italian comedy.*]

[The] relations of [*The Two Gentlemen of Verona*] to the continental drama contemporary with it and immediately anterior
to it have, I believe, never been properly understood. (p. 49)

The assumption that the tale of Felix and Felismena, in the
form which it assumes in Montemayor's romance [*Diana Enamorada*], is the sole source for the central story in *The Two
Gentlemen of Verona* has led to two sorts of rather extreme
views about this comedy. The first is that of Bond [see excerpt
above, 1906]. . . . He believes that Shakespeare is practically
the inventor of most of the distinctive comic traits of this play
and therefore of Elizabethan romantic comedy. It is undoubtedly true that the part played by Shakespeare in giving to this
type of play its poetry and imaginative reach cannot be over-
estimated; yet the essential nature of this aspect of his genius
and the interesting course of its development have been partially obscured by the belief that romantic comedy as a type
sprang full-grown from his brain.

Professor George P. Baker's critical opinion of this play [see
Additional Bibliography], which is based on the same notion
of its inception and growth, is quite different from that of Bond.
He assumes that the entire comedy, with the exception of the
Proteus-Julia story, is Shakespeare's invention and so to be
studied as evidence of his power to construct a complicated
plot. Thus regarded *The Two Gentlemen of Verona* proves to
be a weak and tentative effort. Shakespeare now recognizes
the value of a complicated plot, Professor Baker believes, but
he cannot develop with any firmness, the story that he has so
constructed. He also realizes the need of creating suspense in
his audience, but he does not know how to satisfy the suspense
when once he has aroused it. Consequently the critic believes
that the dénouement of the play is a "complete confession of
dramatic ineptitude."

These two somewhat contradictory views of the work, each
one rather extreme, are at least partly the result of a narrow
view of the origin of *The Two Gentlemen of Verona*, and of

its relation to similar drama on the Continent,—particularly to that of Italy. (pp. 51-2)

Resemblances certainly do exist between . . . the Italianate comedies . . . and *The Two Gentlemen of Verona*. However, they occur, without exception, in situations which are commonplaces of Italian comedy as a type, both of the literary and popular sort. This form of drama, it will be remembered, possesses rigid conventionality of both plot and incidental device. Characters and situations recur indefinitely. This fact suggests the difficulty of finding the one Italianate play among those still extant which was the source of *The Two Gentlemen of Verona*. A search for time-worn commonplaces of Italian comedy in this drama, however, has convinced me that practically all its important structural elements are patterned after recurrent features of ''Italian comedy.''

If this be true, certain general truths in regard to the inception of *The Two Gentlemen of Verona* become evident. If, for example, Shakespeare possessed a definite dramatic source for this comedy, such as the lost *Felix and Philiomena*, that must have been a thoroughly Italianate play. If, on the other hand, he had only a slender thread of story, such as that in Montemayor's *Diana*, upon which to build, he must have made all his additions to it from devices chosen from the wide-spread traditions of Italian comedy. In either case we shall have to recognize Shakespeare's contributions to the growth of romantic comedy, not in new forms of dramatic ingenuity, but in the emotional deepening of elements taken bodily from a drama which was at once comedy of intrigue and high complicated farce.

The plot structure of *The Two Gentlemen of Verona* is modelled on that of a typical Italian comedy. Ideally the play is a conflict between love and friendship illustrated by the love of two friends, Proteus and Valentine, for the same girl, Silvia. In the story Proteus, faithless to his friend, supersedes him in the favored position of suitor. Silvia's father prefers a third wooer, the foolish Thurio, a sort of braggart captain. Eventually Proteus finds himself in danger of death, whence he is rescued by Valentine. Whereupon he repents, surrenders his claim to Silvia, and takes for his wife his first love Julia, who has followed him from Verona and served him in the disguise of a page. The various scenes in this double story are interrupted by intermezzi of verbal wit and horseplay carried on by two clowns, one intensely keen-witted and verbally adroit,—Speed; the other loutish and stupid,—Launce.

All of these elements are commonplaces of Italian comedy. Many of them appear in . . . [Flaminio Scala's] *Flavio Tradito.* . . . The intellectual strife between love and friendship was a favorite theme of debate in all the bourgeois academies of Renaissance Italy; and this subject naturally became the intellectual substance of comedies composed by the cultivated members of the Gelosi troupe. . . . [The] contest of the three rivals, two young men and one clown, invariably the father's favorite, for the hand of the *prima donna* is a time-worn convention of Italian comedy. It is one of the commonest variations of the multiform love story which is a constant feature of both sorts of Italian comedy and particularly of the *Commedia dell' Arte*.

Oratio in *Flavio Tradito*, renouncing the obligations of friendship, contrives to make Flavio believe that Silvia has been false to him, with the result that he abandons her. Flavio learns of his friend's falseness through the craftiness of a servant, but bides his time for unmasking Oratio and exposing his treachery. His opportunity comes one day when the false friend is defeated

in a duel and about to be slain. Flavio exhibits his unswerving friendship by rescuing him from this pressing danger. This generous act fills Oratio with so great remorse that he forthwith gives up Isabella to Oratio and consoles himself immediately with the ever willing Flaminia. Friendship thus triumphs, as it should in the soul of a Renaissance gentleman. However, Oratio, by quick thinking and equally quick acting, enables the comedy to close with the rigorously prescribed double marriage.

This dénouement is like that in *The Two Gentleman of Verona*. Valentine arrives in the nick of time to rescue Silvia from the unwelcome embraces of an outlaw, who proves to be the false Proteus. As soon as the mutual recognition takes place, Proteus immediately asks, and as immediately receives, forgiveness. Then follows a generous passing back and forth of the ladies without any regard for their wishes. This naturally seems to a modern critic like Professor Baker ''complete dramatic ineptitude.'' To the author of this sort of Italianate comedy, it was the expected indisputable proof of the complete victory of friendship in its mortal struggle with love. Moreover it precipitated neatly the situation demanded for the proper ending of a *Commedia dell' Arte*. The *prima donna* and the *secunda donna* [second female] had each to be provided with a husband before the final curtain. Consequently when the author's attention had been largely devoted to his intrigue, the husbands were thrust upon the ladies almost *all' improviso*, utterly without psychological preparation for the author's beneficence.

The larger features even of the Julia-Proteus plot are also conventions of the Italian drama. The male disguise of the girl was the authorized solution of a universal problem of stage realism. The scene of all the action in Italian comedy, both learned and professional, was a public place. But Italian customs of the cinquecento forbade the appearance of a respectable citizen's daughter on the street with the men. If the girl, therefore, was to have any sort of extended speech with the men in these comedies, she had either to talk to them from a window or a balcony, or to assume some sort of male disguise. Consequently, all Renaissance comedy is filled with these two situations.

As the writers of the comedies became more skillful in giving their plots unity, they naturally wished the disguised girl to bear some intimate relation to the love intrigue. The disguise of page was hit upon as solving most successfully this problem of unity. A girl could most realistically impersonate a page and in this character she could naturally attach herself to one of the *amorosi*.

In at least three of Scala's collection of scenarios, the heroine is disguised as a page. In two of these, *Il Ritratto* and *La Fortunata Isabella*, she follows her errant lover to a distant city where he has fallen in love with another girl. (pp. 53-7)

The girl who disguises as a page and takes service in that capacity with the lover is an equally common figure in the *commedia crudita*. Parabosco's *Il Viluppo*, 1547, Ceechi's *I Rivali*, the same author's *Le Pellegrine*, 1567, and *Gl'Ingannati*, written by the Intronate of Siena, are some of the best known of a large number of plays in which the heroine assumes some form of masculine disguise. In the two last mentioned she serves as the page of her lover. (p. 57)

These examples should be sufficient to show that all the structural points of similarity between the Proteus-Julia story and that of Felix and Felismena are commonplaces of Italian comedy. Indeed, one might pronounce them the most frequently recurrent features of that drama. Only the circumstances attendant upon the dropping of the love-letter and the conditions under which the disguised page overhears the serenade remain as evidence of a direct relationship between the plot of *The Two Gentlemen of Verona* and the story from the *Diana Enamorada.* (p. 58)

Still other conventions of Italian comedy appear in the play. Critics have remarked the large number of Petrarchan conceits and of the half-lyrical *tirades* on love and on the conflict between love and friendship in which this drama abounds. This curious mixture of sincere emotional exaltation and mere imaginative ingenuity, sometimes called Petrarchism, permeated the lyrical poetry of nearly every nation of Europe during the years of the sonneteering vogue.... Though widely diffused, in no drama of the time did it assume a form so close to that employed, in *The Two Gentlemen of Verona* as in the love tirades contributed by Isabella Andreini to the *Commedia dell' Arte* as played by the Gelosi troupe. Her letters, a series of carefully wrought literary exercises, preserve these tirades in a form very like that which they must have assumed in the plays. Here appear the subtle sentimentalities of the sonneteers expressed in a slightly inflated style. Here are the elaborate puns, the conventional love-laments and the fine-spun debates on the nature of love and on its distracting conflicts with friendship.

The vogue of this intellectual exercise was so wide-spread that verbal parallels between the *tirades* of Isabella, the *amorosa,* and the speeches of characters in *The Two Gentlemen of Verona* would not prove a direct relationship between the two. The significant fact is that the nature of the dramatic conversations about love in this play of Shakespeare's—the very essence of romantic comedy—is of exactly the same sort as the similar dialogue of the most highly developed form of *Commedia dell' Arte* that was composed in Shakespeare's time. The romantic story of *The Two Gentlemen of Verona,* then, and the dramatic form which it assumes are close reflections of the narratives of Italian comedy.

The fun provided by Speed and Launce in their *intermezzi* is of the essence of this comedy, particularly of the *Commedia dell' Arte.* The traditional view is that these clowns bear at least a general likeness to Lyly's pages. Courthope states definitely that they are modelled on the characters of Licio and Petulus in *Mydas* [see excerpt above, 1903]. He also asserts that the dialogue between Launce and Speed, in which the latter gives a catalogue of his mistress's qualities and Launce makes a feebly witty comment upon each item, is founded on a similar conversation between Licio and Petulus. This latter fact seems highly probable, inasmuch as it is certain that Shakespeare when writing these early comedies imitated the dramatic style of Lyly. In these encounters between Launce and Speed, however, Shakespeare develops and emphasizes the amusing contrast between the quick-witted rogue and the slow-minded rustic which he presented only tentatively in *Love's Labour's Lost,* but which Lyly does not suggest. Even in the scene under discussion in which the conventional form of the dialogue obscures a little the firm outlines of Launce's character as established elsewhere in the play, his replies do not ever display the ingenuity of those habitual to Petulus. On the contrary, they are pretty consistently heavy-footed and stupid.

In the *Commedia dell' Arte,* however, by the end of the sixteenth century, this relationship had become one of its firmest traditions. The books of dramaturgy laid down the conventions which had to be observed in conceiving and presenting these characters. Both Moth and Costard, and Speed and Launce

conform closely to the types. The dramatic possibilities of the two contrasted clowns are naturally more thoroughly realized in the later play. There, also, the nationalization of the booby's stupidity has proceeded further, so that Launce seems a typical English country lout whose Italian origin is never obvious.

Launce's immortal dog, who gives occasion to much "unforced unageing humor" seems to be English to the core. Yet even he may have escaped from some Italian scenario. At least live animals of all sorts, particularly dogs, were often introduced upon the stage of the *Commedia dell' Arte* and very seldom elsewhere. I have not forgotten Balaam's ass and the boisterous comedy that he provoked in both French and English Miracle plays. However, other live animals seem not to have found their way upon the English stage in his company; but the farcical atmosphere of the *Commedia dell' Arte* was very congenial to the incalculable improvisation in which animals might indulge. (pp. 58-61)

The rustic or stupid clown in Italian comedy . . . would as often as possible bring his live dog with him. Launce, inheriting the rôle of this Italian figure, inherited his cur also and brought the beast with him into *The Two Gentlemen of Verona,* to the delight of every reader of Shakespeare's comedy.

These parallels between essential situations and mere incidental comic devices of *The Two Gentlemen of Verona* and Italian comedy show with reasonable certainty that Shakespeare's source was some thoroughly Italianate play. If that was by chance the lost *Felix and Philiomena,* we may assume that this drama was a conventional Italian comedy into which some of the details of the Spanish story had been inserted to give the play its distinctive features. (p. 62)

By being thus able to assume that this *Felix and Philiomena,* or whatever the play that served as the source of *The Two Gentlemen of Verona,* supplied Shakespeare with many more elements of his comedy than has hitherto been suspected, we are able to revise the traditional opinion in regard to Shakespeare's contribution to the development of Elizabethan romantic comedy. He can no longer be regarded as having invented the type in all of its distinctive features. Nor can he be regarded as an experimenter attempting to graft foreign material upon a slender romantic story and producing an ill-constructed play.

His method must be conceived, rather, as much more nearly analogous to that which he applied to the development of other types, such as Senecan tragedy and Chronicle history. He found in his source his plot in all its constructive elements, and he found there many of the type-figures needed to animate it ready to his hand. This perfectly conventional material occasionally appears in *The Two Gentlemen of Verona* in its original stiff caricature of reality, as in the hurried dénouement. Usually it is made to assume new forms of authentic life through Shakespeare's creative sympathy with youthful emotion, particularly in the soul of the woman. This interest expressing itself in dramatic form completely changed the spirit of Italian comedy. It released the love story from its bondage to the intrigue and gave it the central point of interest through its revelation of the beauty and the poetry of youthful love. The result was a comedy, new in kind, which was to develop into one of the most characteristic manifestations of Elizabethan art. (pp. 62-3)

O. J. Campbell, "'The Two Gentlemen of Verona' and Italian Comedy," in Studies in Shakespeare, Milton and Donne *by Members of the English De-*

partment of the University of Michigan, The Macmillan Company, 1925, pp. 47-64.

ALWIN THALER (essay date 1927)

[*Thaler considers* The Two Gentlemen of Verona *Shakespeare's "most elaborate essay in the friendship theme" and regards the unfavorable reaction to its ending, including arguments suggesting an alternate author, as "misconceptions." He views the play's conclusion, though "quixotic" and "very silly," as in keeping with Shakespeare's treatment here of friendship and love; Thaler is also the first critic to suggest that Silvia's strange silence after Valentine's proposal is not the result of her grief, but is partly because she recognizes her lover's act as yet another of his "sentimental whimsies." In addition, Thaler cites several other textual problems in the last act, but considers most of these anomalies "merely characteristic instances of Shakespeare's free and easy workmanship in the early plays."*]

It has generally been felt that in *The Two Gentlemen* [Shakspere] achieved a perfect specimen of the unhappy happy ending. To Pope the dénouement of this piece seemed "very odd," and his opinion is about as mildly put as any. That this is the most lame and impotent conclusion of them all . . . is the all but unanimous verdict of outstanding critics and comentators . . . , [several] of whom thought the ending so bad that Shakspere could not have written it. On the other hand, the rationale of the thing has been effectively set forth once or twice, especially by Professor Sampson in the Tudor edition [see excerpt above, 1912]. My reason for returning to it at some length is that the old misconceptions seem to flourish as vigorously as ever. . . . I need hardly say that I am not engaged here or elsewhere in this paper in seeking to whitewash Shakspere. . . . [The ending] is, however, by no means so blind or incomprehensible as it is almost always represented; and much of the criticism lavished upon it is simply beside the point.

Let us recall the difficulties. (1) The fickle Proteus forgets his love for Julia (who follows him, disguised as a page), betrays his faithful friend Valentine, and threatens force to win Silvia—in the forest—after Sir Eglamour, her protector, has run away. Sir Eglamour's unceremonious exit is the first hurdle to stop the critics. (2) Valentine, who has captained the outlaws and has seen and heard Proteus's villainy, charges him with treachery—more especially with falsehood to friendship. Proteus is shamed and asks pardon. This Valentine, the perfect friend, grants, and, to heap coals of fire upon the head of the late offender, resigns the lady to him:

> And that my love may appear plain and free
> All that was mine in Silvia I give thee.
>
>   [V. iv. 82-3]

(3) Julia, present in disguise, speaks up and reveals herself; whereupon Proteus's wandering affections immediately return to her—Silvia remaining silent the while. (4) The Duke, who had exiled Valentine rather than accept him as a son-in-law, changes his mind without winking an eyelash. Of these several difficulties, the second—the "mawkish generosity" of Valentine in offering to surrender Silvia to Proteus—is, of course, the gravest. . . . As recently as 1921 . . . , Quiller-Couch and J. Dover Wilson, in their (Cambridge) edition of the play, have once more insisted that this part of the ending cannot be Shakspere's [see excerpt above]. . . . They conclude that the couplet in question, and most of the other "anomalies" noted, are assignable to an unknown adapter, or to the actors. This conclusion can only be described as a total misunderstanding of what Shakspere was about. His play, as the title indicates,

concerns primarily the friendship of the two gentlemen, who are types of the perfectly faithful and of the absolutely faithless friend. The piece is Shakspere's most elaborate essay in the friendship theme, a theme everywhere alive and active in Elizabethan literature. It appears prominently in *Euphues* [by John Lyly], in the *Arcadia* [by Sir Philip Sidney], and in other romances early and late; in the sonnets (notably in Shakspere's sonnet No. 42) and everywhere in other lyrics; as also in Shakspere's other plays, especially in *The Merchant of Venice* (in which Bassanio tells Antonio that "life itself, *my wife*, and all the world" are not with him "esteemed above" [IV. i. 284-85] Antonio's safety) and in *The Winter's Tale* and *Twelfth Night.* The theme was a commonplace, moreover, in the work of Shakspere's fellow dramatists. Lyly's treatment of it in *Endymion* is close to that of *The Two Gentlemen,* and one aspect or another of it is made much of in plays ranging all the way from Edwards' *Damon and Pythias* to Greene's *Friar Bacon* and Marlowe's *Edward II.*

In *The Two Gentlemen* the keynote is struck at the start. "Sweet Valentine" and his "loving Proteus," we learn, "from their infancy. . . . have conversed and spent their hours together" [II. iv. 62-3]. In the course of his betrayal Proteus in so many words admits his "treachery" to his friend and to his code, "the law of friendship" [III. i. 5], though he dismisses it for the moment: "I to myself am dearer than my friend" [II. vi. 23]. Silvia, of course, forcibly reminds him of his evil-doing—to her he is "subtle, perjured, false, disloyal" [IV. ii. 95], a "counterfeit" to his "true friend." Valentine himself, a youthful sentimentalist who has had much time to feed his fancy while superintending his comic-opera outlaws in the greenwood, drives home the point:

> Thou common friend that's without faith or love. . . . .
>   O time . . . . accurst,
> 'Mongst all foes that a friend should be the worst.
>   [V. iv. 63, 71-2]

Proteus thereupon acknowledges his fault, and Valentine, in the supposed exaltation of the moment, offers the supreme sacrifice to friendship—a Silvia for a Proteus. It is quixotic, of course, and very silly; but not nearly so important or tragic as the critics suggest. Silvia remains silent not, as is universally supposed, because she is struck to the heart. She is merely breathless after her struggle and fright. Moreover, she knows her Valentine and his fine sentimental whimsies—and she will have plenty of time to talk later! For the moment Julia, who has as much at stake as anybody, but hasn't had a chance to say a word, very naturally breaks in and, after a momentary swoon, takes command of the situation. That Proteus relapses so speedily to his first love and that Julia is willing to take him back, may seem incredible. It must suffice here to observe that Shakspere seems not to have taken the fickleness of young blades too seriously—witness the analogous instances of Romeo and Rosaline, and of Demetrius and Helena in *A Midsummer Night's Dream.* Julia, moreover, is very much in love, and she, at least, knows all sides of her bargain. (pp. 743-47)

The remaining anomalies are merely characteristic instances of Shakspere's free and easy workmanship in the early plays. He does not bother to explain why the brave Sir Eglamour ran away. The man had to be gotten out of the way—and out he goes. Sir Eglamour is of little account anyhow, and might well have been left out altogether. The Duke's convenient change of front is explicable on the same general principle—a principle operative also in the later plays. Obviously there is a vast difference between those of Shakspere's kings (or dukes) who are also human beings with large potentiality for good or evil—such as King Claudius, and Richard II, and, in my judgment, the Duke in *Measure for Measure*—and those who are only nonentities in royal robes, such as the three dukes of the early comedies and Duke Frederick, the usurper of *As You Like It*. His royal highness of *The Two Gentlemen* swallows his objections without a gulp. His brothers in *A Midsummer Night's Dream* and in *The Comedy of Errors* politely end by setting aside the law of the land—against undutiful daughters and straying Syracusans, respectively—the sanctity of which they had proclaimed from the housetops at the start. Similarly, Duke Frederick in *As You Like It* begins with an act of violent usurpation and ends with an equally violent conversion and renunciation. . . . It might be argued that they are merely tyrants, above the law of the land and the law of plausibility. It is more to the point to remember that they are lay figures: humanly and dramatically speaking they equal zero, and zero inverted at the happy end is zero still. As regards *The Two Gentlemen*, finally, it is only fair to add that its final disposition of the characters is in keeping with the slightness of characterization throughout, and that its chorus hymeneal is merely an unskillful postlude to the coronation march of the faithful friend. (p. 747)

> Alwin Thaler, "Shakspere and the Unhappy Ending," in PMLA, 42, Vol. XLII, No. 3, September, 1927, pp. 736-61.

H. B. CHARLTON   (lecture date 1930)

[*An English scholar, Charlton is best known for his* Shakespearian Tragedy (1948) *and* Shakespearian Comedy (1938)—*two important studies in which he argues that the proponents of New Criticism, particularly T. S. Eliot and I. A. Richards, were reducing Shakespeare's drama to its poetic elements and in the process losing sight of his characters. In his introduction to* Shakespearian Tragedy, *Charlton described himself as a "devout" follower of A. C. Bradley, and like his mentor he adopted a psychological, character-oriented approach to Shakespeare's work. In the following excerpt, taken from a lecture delivered January 8, 1930, at the John Rylands Library, Charlton is the first commentator to discuss the relationship of the romantic and comic elements in* The Two Gentlemen of Verona. *He states that the play exemplifies the attempts by Elizabethan dramatists to "lift bodily" romantic conventions onto the comic stage, and he describes the resulting incongruities of Shakespeare's effort in this regard. Charlton especially laments the unfavorable effect the synthesis of romance and comedy has on Valentine, who is "so true a son of romance that he can never again be mistaken for a creature of human nature." On the other hand, Charlton adds, neither Julia nor Launce is constrained by the conventions of romance; in fact, the critic asserts, it is through Launce that "the incompatibilities and the unrealities of romantic postulates are laid bare." Charlton concludes that in* The Two Gentlemen of Verona *Shakespeare "unexpectedly and inadvertently made romance comic."*]

In its first intention, Elizabethan romantic comedy was an attempt to adapt the world of romance and all its implications to the service of comedy. *The Two Gentlemen of Verona* shows that intention at its crudest. In the story of it, there are all the main marks of the mediæval tradition as that tradition had been modified, elaborated and extended by the idealism of Petrarch and by the speculations of the Platonists. It is yet the same tradition in its essence, corroborated rather than altered by the modifying factors; as, for instance, at the hands of Ficino, Platonism brought a medico-metaphysical theory to explain the love-laden gleam of a beautiful eye. Shakespeare's play embodies a literary manner and a moral code; its actions are conducted according to a conventional etiquette and are deter-

mined by a particular creed; and every feature of it, in matter and in sentiment, is traceable to the romantic attitude of man to woman. It presents as its setting a world constituted in such fashion that the obligations and the sanctions of its doctrines could best be realised. The course of the whole play is determined by the values such doctrine attaches to the love of man and woman.

A note struck early in the play recalls one of the few passionate love-stories of classical legend—"how young Leander crossed the Hellespont" [I. i. 22],—and at another moment, Ariadne is remembered "passioning for Theseus' perjury" [IV. iv. 168]. But the real colour of the tale is given unmistakably by the presence amongst its characters of Sir Eglamour. By his name is he known and whence he springs. He points straight back to the source of the religious cult of love: "servant and friend" [IV. iii. 4] of Sylvia, he is ready at call to rush to any service to which she may command him. His own lady and his true love died, and on her grave he vowed pure chastity, dedicating himself to the assistance of lovers in affliction, recking nothing what danger should betide him in the venture. His home is in the land of mediæval romance; and his brethren are those consecrated warriors who will undertake all danger, though it stands next to death, for one calm look of Love's approval. He comes to life again in a play where knightly vows are spoken, where errantry is the normal mode of service, where the exercise of tilt and tournament is the traditional recreation, where lovers name themselves habitually the servants of their ladies, where such service may impose as a duty the helping of one's lady to a rival, and where the terms of infamy to which the utmost slander can give voice are "perjured, false, disloyal" [IV. ii. 95]. And that is the world in which Shakespeare makes his Two Gentlemen live.

Throughout the play, "Love's a mighty lord,"

> There is no woe to his correction
> Nor to his service no such joy on earth. . . .
> [II. iv. 136, 138-39]

Heavy penance is visited on unbelievers

> for contemning Love,
> Whose high imperious thoughts will punish him
> With bitter fasts, with penitential groans,
> With nightly tears and daily heart-sore sighs.
> [II. iv. 129-32]

Sleep is chased from such a rebel's now enthralled eyes, to make them watchers of his own heart's sorrow. From true votaries, nothing less than absolute devotion is required. They must hold no discourse except it be of love. Absent from their lady, they must let no single hour o'erslip without its ceremonial sigh for her sake. The more such languishing fidelity appears to be spurned, the more must it grow and fawn upon its recalcitrant object. Apart from love, nothing in life has the least significance . . . :

> Unless I look on Sylvia in the day,
> There is no day for me to look upon.
> She is my essence, and I leave to be,
> If I am not by her fair influence
> Fostered, illumined, cherished, kept alive.
> [III. i. 180-84]

Such is the consecrated desolation of the romantic lover. . . . (pp. 27-9)

When cruel circumstance separates him from his lady, etiquette prescribes the proper behaviour and the right demeanour. He resorts to the congenial solitude of woods or wildernesses. In the earlier days of the cult, his manner on these occasions was more violent than ceremonious. Tristan [in *Morte d'Arthur*], as Malory tells us, exiled and separated from his love, goes mad for grief; he would unlace his armour and go into the wilderness, where he "brast down the trees and bowes, and other-whyle, when he found the harp that the lady sent him, then wold he harpe and playe therupon and wepe togethre." But in the course of time the manners of solitaries became more polite. Chaucer (or the author of the *Romaunt of the Rose*) advises the lover to cultivate a proper solitude. . . . The lover in the French romance *Flamenca* "in the dark of night goes of custom to listen to the nightingale in the wood." Just, in fact, as does Valentine: in the intervals between inspecting the arms or allocating the booty of his bandit-band, he takes his laments for Sylvia into the woods for orchestral effects from the nightingales. . . . Such is the way of lovers in romances, and *The Two Gentlemen of Verona*. Their state of spiritual ecstasy is revealed by the progressive ætherialisation of their sustenance. . . . On occasion, the true lover . . . is like to fade away, and can only eat when his lady serves the dishes to him with her own delicate hands. Our Valentine had been a good trencherman before he became a romantic lover; in those days, when he fasted, it was presently after dinner. But once he becomes a votary, not even ambrosia nor nectar is good enough for his æthereal table: "now can I break my fast, dine, sup, and sleep upon the very naked name of love" [II. iv. 141-42]. How he thrives on this diet will become a primary article of the literary and dramatic criticism of *The Two Gentlemen of Verona*.

So much for the spirit of romance in the play. Now for the world in which it is set,—since, taking its religion thence, it must also take the romantic world in which such religion may reveal itself. Not men living dully sluggardised at home, but those bred and tutored in the wider world, seeking preferment out, trying their fortunes in war or discovering islands far away,—these are they who have scope to put such religion to the proof. So in *The Two Gentlemen of Verona*, the scene is laid in Italy, the country which to Shakespeare's fellows was the hallowed land of romance. But it is an Italy of romance, not of physiographic authenticity. It has inland waterways unknown to geographers; the journey from Verona to Mantua is a sea-voyage; it is indeed a scenario in which all the material trappings of romance may be assembled. Mountain and forest are indispensable, mountains which are brigand-haunted, and forests in the gloom of which are abbeys from whose postern gates friars creep into the encircling woods, so wrapt in penitential mood that lurking lions, prowling hungrily for food, are utterly forgotten. In such a locality, the tale of true love may run its uneven course. The poetically gifted lover meets such obstacles as a rival, at whom he hurls his cartel, and a perverse father whose plans for his daughter are based on such irrelevant considerations as the rivals' bank-balances. The father's castle has its upper tower far from the ground, and built so shelving that to climb it is at apparent hazard of one's life. And here is the angelic daughter's chamber wherein she is nightly lodged, within doors securely locked, so that rescue can only be by a corded ladder to her chamber window. Then unexpected difficulties will be expected to intrude: the best-laid plot to carry her away is foiled by the machinations of a villain out of the least suspected quarter. Banishment naturally follows, and at length, with the flight of the heroine and the pursuit of her by the entire court, all will work out well by a series of surprising coincidences, to which rivals, brigands, friars, and lions are all somehow contributory. In this way, romantic love makes its romantic universe; and this in fact is the setting and the story of *The Two Gentlemen of Verona*.

This, both in matter and in spirit, is the tradition which the Elizabethan dramatists desired to lift bodily on to their comic stage. But something somehow went wrong. The spirit of mediæval romance seemed to shrivel in the presence of comedy. . . . [In] *The Two Gentlemen,* a sheer clod of earth, Launce by name, will, quite unwittingly, expose the unsubstantiality of the romantic hero with whom the play throws him into contact. But we are anticipating. The consequences of Shakespeare's attempt to dramatise romance must be watched in closer detail.

There is little wonder that the Elizabethan dramatists saw the dramatic possibilities of such material, and did not at first perceive its dramatic disadvantages. They felt the dramatic thrill of following these lovers and setting the world at nought. Nor is it very difficult to set the geographical world at nought, at least to the extent of making inland seas in Italy or liberating living lions in its woods. Yet sometimes the distortions of the physical universe necessarily ventured by the romanticist entail violent wrenches of our common consciousness. The dukes of Shakespeare's Italy, for instance, apparently have magic power over the flight of time; for whilst a banished man is speaking but ten lines, the proclamation of his banishment is ratified, promulgated, and has become publicly known throughout the

Act I. Scene i. Proteus and Valentine. By Walter Crane (1894). The Department of Rare Books and Special Collections, The University of Michigan Library.

duchy, and sentinels have already been posted along the frontiers to prevent a surreptitious return of the exile to the land which he has not yet had time to pack his suit-case for leaving. . . . Proteus, engaging the disguised Julia, says that the engagement is specifically on the recommendation of the applicant's face; but he does not recognise, as he gazes into this face, that it was the one he was smothering with kisses a few weeks before when its owner, in her proper dress, was his betrothed. Yet these are really only minor impediments, requiring but a little and a by no means reluctant suspension of our disbelief. They are altogether insignificant compared with the reservations involved when romance displays its peculiar propensity for setting the world of man at nought. To satisfy its own obligations, it perforce demanded super-men; at all events, the heroes it puts forward as its votaries in the play are something either more or less than men.

Romantically speaking, Valentine is the hero, and not alone in the technical sense. In classical comedy the hero is simply the protagonist, the central figure who is the biggest butt of the comic satire. But here the protagonist is the upholder of the faith on which the play is built, the man with whom the audience is called upon to rejoice admiringly, and not the fellow at whom it is derisively to laugh. He is to play the hero in every sense of the word. Yet in the event, the prevailing spirit of romance endows him with sentiments and provides him with occupations which inevitably frustrate the heroic intention. The story renders him a fool. Convention may sanctify his sudden conversion from the mocker to the votary of love, and may even excuse or palliate his fractious braggardism when he insults Proteus with ill-mannered comparisons between Silvia and Julia. But his helplessness and his impenetrable stupidity amount to more than the traditional blindness of a lover. Even the clown Speed can see through Silvia's trick, when she makes Valentine write a letter to himself. But Valentine plays out the excellent motion as an exceeding puppet, unenlightened by the faintest gleam of common insight. And despite his vaunt that he knows Proteus as well as he knows himself, he is blind to villainies so palpable, that Launce, the other clown of the piece, though he be but a fool, has the wits to recognise them for what they plainly are. The incidents are dramatically very significant, for both Launce and Speed come into the play for no reason whatever but to be unmistakable dolts. One begins to feel that it will be extremely difficult to make a hero of a man who is proved to be duller of wit than the patent idiots of the piece. Even when Valentine might have shone by resource in action, he relapses into coventional laments, and throws himself helplessly into the arms of Proteus for advice and consolation. Heroic opportunity stands begging round him when he encounters the brigands. But besides demonstrating that he can tell a lie—witness his tale of cock and bull about having killed a man—the situation only serves to discredit him still more: for the words of his lie, his crocodile tears for the fictitious man he claims to have slain, and his groundless boast that he slew him manfully in fight without false vantage or base treachery, are in fact nothing but an attempt to make moral capital by means of forgery and perjury. . . . But Valentine's utmost reach of ineptitude comes with what, again romantically speaking, is meant to be the heroic climax of the play. When he has just learnt the full tale of the villainy of Proteus, the code permits him neither resentment nor passion. Like a cashier addressing a charwoman who has pilfered a penny stamp, he sums up his rebuke—"I am sorry I must never trust thee more" [V. iv. 69]. And worse follows immediately. With but five lines of formal apology from the villain, Valentine professes himself so completely satisfied that he enthusiastically resigns

his darling Silvia to the traitor. Even Valentine must have seen that the gesture was a little odd, because he quotes the legal sanction. It is the code, a primary article in the romantic faith—"that my love may appear plain and free" [V. iv. 82]. But it makes a man a nincompoop. Nor does it help much that after this preposterous episode, Valentine is allowed to spit a little fire in an encounter with another rival, Thurio. He has already proved himself so true a son of romance that he can never again be mistaken for a creature of human nature.

Proteus is less hampered by romantic obligations; because the plot requires him to have just sufficient of salutary villainy to make him throw over their commandments for his own ends. Yet the villain of romance suffers almost as much from the pressure of romanticism as does the hero. The noble fellows whom he, as villain, is called upon to deceive are such gullible mortals that little positive skill is necessary. Proteus can fool Thurio and Valentine and the Duke without exerting himself. But on the one occasion when he might have shown his wits, he only reveals his lack of them. Making love to Silvia, he meets her protest against his disloyalty to Julia by inventing the easy excuse that Julia is dead. Silvia replies that, even so, he should be ashamed to wrong Valentine. It is, of course, a tight corner: but the best Proteus can do is to say "I likewise hear that Valentine is dead" [IV. ii. 112]. He might at least have displayed a little more ingenuity in invention; he fails in precisely such a situation as would have permitted the clown of classical comedy to triumph. Moreover, the main plot requires Proteus to be guilty of incredible duplicity, and of the most facile rapidity in changing morals and mistresses. . . . The trait becomes intolerably ludicrous when, all his sins forgiven him, and Julia restored to his arms, all he can utter in confession is his own fatuous self-conceit:

> O heaven, were man
> But constant, he were perfect.
>
> [V. iv. 110-11]

It is, of course, a fine sentiment; but the audience, having seen Valentine, simply will not believe it.

Even the brigands of romance will scarcely stand the test of the stage. They enter with metaphorical daggers in mouths bristling with black mustachios and with desperate oaths. Callous and bloodthirsty ruffians, spoiling for a fight, their chief regret is that fate is sending only one defenceless traveller to be rifled instead of ten. But when the destined victim turns out to be two, courage perhaps abates a little: at all events, the travellers are warned to keep their distance, and throw over the booty or otherwise to assume a sitting posture, whilst the rifling is safely done by the desperadoes themselves. Perhaps this, and not his customary ineptitude in speech, is what makes Valentine address the villains as "My friends." But, of course, his assumption is, for the trade of brigandage, economically unsound. And so, with apologies for correcting him, Valentine is informed that he is not playing the game—"that's not so, sir; we are your enemies" [IV. i. 8]. But the outlaws are connoisseurs of masculine beauty, and Valentine's fine figure secures him an opportunity for a hearing. . . . They will take him for a linguist merely "on his own report" [IV. i. 54], and, mainly because he "is beautiful with goodly shape" [IV. i. 53-4], they offer him the leadership, pathetically promising to love him as their commander and their king. Clearly such a thoroughly unbrigandlike procedure as this election has almost put them out of their parts. They must be allowed to recover in a traditional tableau. Daggers are whipped out, threats become fierce, and Valentine, with steel points at his throat, is given the choice of being a king or a corpse. Perhaps his fear is responsible for the odd proviso that "silly women" shall be exempt from the depradations of the gang over which he is to rule; but it is of course too much to expect of better men than Valentine to require them to anticipate a variation in the meaning of a word. Neither before nor after *The Two Gentlemen of Verona* has dramatic literature known a band of outlaws like to these—except once: there are the Pirates of Penzance: but then Gilbert meant his to be funny.

One begins to suspect that everything which is hallowed by the tradition of romance is made thereby of no avail for the purposes of drama. But there are Julia and Launce to reckon with; and these are figures universally accounted the most substantial beings in the play. So indeed they are. But they owe it entirely to the fact that they are under no obligation whatever to the code of romance. The behaviour of Valentine is entirely conditioned by the doctrine of romantic love. But the code allowed to woman no duty but to excite by her beauty the devoted worship of her knight. (pp. 30-40)

When Shakespeare takes over a tradition whose women are like [those of French romance], so long as he preserves the beauty of their faces, he can endow them with whatever character he may please. His Julia is a creation, not a convention. As she is a woman, acting on a woman's instinct—"I have no other but a woman's reason, I think him so because I think him so" [I. ii. 23-4]—she is depicted in moods, whimsies, and vagaries which are in fact the stuff of dramatic characterisation. Like the heroine of romance, she will cover her first love-letter with kisses, and press the precious manuscript to her heart. But like the spirited independent young lady of the world, she will not expose herself to the chuckles of her maid by exhibiting the common symptoms of her affections. Hence the pretended contempt, and the struggle to keep up appearances, even at considerable risk to the sacred document. But for what seriously concerns her love, Julia is too level-headed to over-reach herself. As far as may be, she will avoid the disapproval of opinion: but where there is no remedy, she will defy a scandalised world, and undertake her pilgrimage of love. She knows the hazards of the road and the many weary steps it will involve. But she also knows her own capacities, and has duly taken note of all material things she will stand in need of. And although Proteus is a poor thing on whom to lavish so much love, Julia knows that love is indeed a blinded god; and in her capable hands even a Proteus may be moulded to something worth the having.

Launce is another who insists on remaining in the memory. He has no real right within the play, except that gentlemen must have servants, and Elizabethan audiences must have clowns. But coming in thus by a back-door, he earns an unexpected importance in the play. Seen side by side with Speed, his origin is clear. Whilst Speed belongs to the purely theatrical family of the Dromios [in *The Comedy of Errors*], with their punning and logic-chopping asininities, Launce harks back to the native Costard [in *Love's Labour's Lost*]. And as Costard shows his relationship to Bottom [in *A Midsummer Night's Dream*] by his skill in village theatricals, so Launce reveals by his wooing his family connection with Touchstone, and Touchstone's Audrey [in *As You Like It*], who was a poor thing, but his own. All the kind of the Launces are thus palpably a mighty stock. Their worth, compared with that of the Speeds and the Dromios, is admirably indicated by Launce's consummate use of Speed's curiosity and of his better schooling. Launce gets his letter deciphered; he gets also an opportunity to display his

own superior breeding, and to secure condign punishment for the ill-mannered Speed: "now will he be swinged for reading my letter; an unmannerly slave, that will thrust himself into secrets! I'll after, to rejoice in the boy's correction" [III. i. 382-84].

Launce is happiest with his dog. Clownage can go no farther than the pantomimic representation, with staff and shoe and dog, of the parting from his home-folks. Laughter is hilarious at Launce's bitter grief that his ungrateful cur declined to shed a tear. That Launce should expect it is, of course, the element of preposterous incongruity which makes him a clown. But when he puts his complaint squarely, that his "dog has no more pity in him than a dog" [II. iii. 10-11], the thrust pierces more than it was meant to. Romance itself has expected no less largely of Valentine, of Proteus, and of the rest. It has demanded that man shall be more than man, and has laid upon him requisitions passing the ability of man to fulfil. At the bidding of romance, Valentine and Proteus have become what they are in the play, and the one thing they are not is men like other men. A further incident in which Launce is concerned takes on a similarly unexpected significance. He has made as great a sacrifice as did Valentine himself: he has given up his own cur in place of the one which Proteus entrusted to him to take to Silvia. But the effect hardly suggests that self-sacrifice is worldly-wise. And so once more it seems to bring into question the worldly worth of the code which sanctifies such deeds. Unintentionally, Launce has become the means by which the incompatibilities and the unrealities of romantic postulates are laid bare. And Launce is palpably the stuff of comedy: awakening our comic sense, he inevitably sharpens our appreciation of the particular range of incongruities which are the province of comedy—the incongruity between what a thing really is and what it is taken to be.

Romance, and not comedy, has called the tune of *The Two Gentlemen of Verona*, and governed the direction of the action of the play. That is why its creatures bear so little resemblance to men of flesh and blood. Lacking this, they are scarcely dramatic figures at all; for every form of drama would appear to seek at least so much of human nature in its characters. But perhaps the characters of the Two Gentlemen are comic in a sense which at first had never entered the mind of their maker. Valentine bids for the sympathy, but not for the laughter of the audience: the ideals by which he lives are assumed to have the world's approbation. But in execution they involve him in most ridiculous plight. He turns the world from its compassionate approval to a mood of sceptical questioning. The hero of romantic comedy appears no better than its clowns. And so topsy-turvy is the world of romance that apparently the one obvious way to be reputed in it for a fool, is to show at least a faint sign of discretion and of common sense. Thurio, for instance, was cast for the dotard of the play, and of course he is not without egregious folly. But what was meant in the end to annihilate him with contempt, turns out quite otherwise. Threatened by Valentine's sword, he resigns all claim to Silvia, on the ground that he holds him but a fool that will endanger his body for a girl that loves him not. The audience is invited to call Thurio a fool for thus showing himself to be the one person in the play with a modicum of worldly wisdom, a respect for the limitations of human nature, and a recognition of the conditions under which it may survive. Clearly, Shakespeare's first attempt to make romantic comedy had only succeeded so far that it had unexpectedly and inadvertently made romance comic. The real problem was still to be faced. (pp. 41-3)

H. B. Charlton, "Romanticism in Shakesperian Comedy," in his Shakespearian Comedy, Methuen & Co. Ltd., 1938, pp. 19-43.

THOMAS MARC PARROTT (essay date 1949)

[*In the excerpt below, Parrott postulates that the last scene of* The Two Gentlemen of Verona *was originally much longer, full of contemplations of the nature of friendship and love which were omitted and replaced by the lines of "some playhouse hack." Parrott does not include Valentine's renunciation of Silvia among these emendations, for he notes a similar renunciation in the sonnets, asserting that this gesture "seemed to Shakespeare—and to his Elizabethan audience—a heroic example of romantic friendship." He concludes by calling* The Two Gentlemen of Verona *"a landmark in the development of Shakespeare's art," in that it was the first of his comedies to treat the theme of love, "checked and crossed by misadventure," and to present characters "who control the action by the inner necessity of their being."*]

If *The Comedy of Errors* is a piece of prentice work following a set pattern, *The Two Gentlemen of Verona* may be regarded as an example of work by the same apprentice given a free hand to compose without a model. The result is a pleasant little play, full of promise, but quite as full of faults, particularly in the matter of plot construction. This, it seems, the apprentice had not yet mastered. Faulty construction, vagueness of characterization, except for a few figures, and uncertainty of metrical expression all mark *The Two Gentlemen* as an early play, possibly *c.* 1592. It has never been a popular stage-play, a fact which, after all, is not surprising; the prentice was still far from becoming a master of his craft. (p. 108)

So unhappy, in fact, is [the] conclusion that two recent editors of the play are quite certain that Shakespeare was not guilty of it. One of them, the lamented Quiller-Couch, ventures the strange suggestion that 'Shakespeare invented a solution which at the first performance was found to be ineffective; that the final scene was rewritten—not by Shakespeare—and given its crude and conventional *coup-de-théâtre*' [see excerpt above, 1921]. It would be hard, if not impossible, to imagine a scene from Shakespeare's pen less effective than the present text, yet such a scene is implied in this suggestion. The truth is that Quiller-Couch was no fit judge here; he so resented Valentine's speech that he was, he admits, tempted to exclaim: 'By this time there are *no* gentlemen in Verona.' But what did Shakespeare, who was proud to sign himself 'gentleman,' think of such a renunciation as Valentine's? The answer may be found in his *Sonnets;* in Sonnet XXXIV he shows himself so moved by the repentance of the friend who had robbed him of his mistress that he declares the friend's tears 'ransom all ill deeds'—compare Valentine's words to Proteus:

> Who by repentance is not satisfied
> Is not of heaven nor earth.
>
> [V. iv. 79-80]

Shakespeare goes even further, for in Sonnet XL he cries to his repentant friend: 'Take all my loves,' as complete a renunciation certainly as that of Valentine's. Clearly this renunciation which shocks us so seemed to Shakespeare—and to his Elizabethan audience—a heroic example of romantic friendship.

Yet after all is said in its defense, the business of the renunciation is anything but satisfactory. The main fault, perhaps, is the haste with which it is handled. Within the compass of about twenty lines Proteus tries to force Silvia; Valentine rescues her and denounces him as a 'ruffian'; Proteus begs for-

giveness; Valentine is satisfied and renounces his lady in favor of his friend. This is more than racing speed, especially when compared with the leisurely dialogue between Valentine and the Duke which follows. Perhaps a modified form of Quiller-Couch's suggestion might be tentatively put forward. Shakespeare's first draft of the scene ran, let us suppose, along the lines of the present text, but was far longer and included a debate between the two gentlemen packed with the conceits and metaphors so frequent in the *Sonnets* that deal with the theme of love and friendship. The actors, however, impatient to bring the play to an end and well aware that figures of speech permissible in sonnets were impossible on the stage, may have insisted on heavy cuts. The young playwright, not yet established as a master, would be forced to turn over his script to some playhouse hack. This scribbler then not only cut it to bits, but patched up the holes with jigging rhymes: 'most accurst'—'Be the worst'; 'plain and free'—'I give thee'; 'I may spy'—'constant eye' [V. iv. 71-2, 82-3, 114-15]—rhymes that grate upon the ear. If this hypothesis is too fanciful and the present text must stand as Shakespeare wrote it, we can only suppose that the young playwright invented a situation that he was incapable of handling. There is no such situation in the source which furnished a pattern for earlier scenes, and without such a pattern the prentice playwright made a bad mess of his denouement. (pp. 112-13)

[Besides the problems with the final scene, there] is a constant shifting of place, and the topography of the play is most confusing. Valentine leaves Verona for the Court at Milan, but later the Duke of Milan says he loves 'a lady in Verona here' [III. i. 81], and Valentine tells Thurio, a courtier at Milan, 'Verona shall not hold thee' [V. iv. 129]. Valentine is supposed to live in exile at Mantua, but he turns up in a wood near Milan, and Speed welcomes Launce to Padua, where neither of them has any business to be. Where, after all, is the action taking place? Unless this confusion is due to revision without the author's knowledge, we must find Shakespeare guilty of inexcusable carelessness. The main action, also, is repeatedly interrupted by long stretches of witty word-play and by scenes in which a clown plays up to the audience. Perhaps Shakespeare felt that the plot he had devised was too slight to hold the interest of his hearers, and so proceeded to pad it out with whatever came handy. (pp. 113-14)

Shakespeare's use of language in *The Two Gentlemen* looks at once forward and back. The backward glance is reminiscent of the dialogue in Lyly's plays. The opening scene, for example, presents two of Lyly's gentlemen in debate and runs on into a dialogue between a lover and a page that reads almost like a transcript from one of Lyly's comedies. Valentine and Proteus mock the foolish Thurio in the very style of Lyly's witty gentlemen, and Lylian antithesis, quips, puns, and word-play besprinkle the dialogue throughout. The considerable amount of prose, between a third and a fourth of the whole play, is itself a testimony to Lyly's influence, although the best prose scenes, Launce's soliloquies, are marked by a homely realism that Lyly never knew.

On the other hand we have the forward-looking aspect in the lyric-poetic diction of this play. The vein of poetry that was checked in *The Comedy of Errors* breaks out here in musical flow. And this is right and proper; the *Errors* is a play of action and situation; this is a comedy of sentiment and emotion. The horseplay of beatings, of the rope's end and the crowbar, has vanished along with most of the clownish doggerel, the poet of *Venus and Adonis* and the *Sonnets* gives himself free hand here. He has not yet attained the height of supreme dramatic utterance, but there are already hopeful signs as in Julia's cry when she retrieves her lover's name from the letter she has torn in feigned anger:

> Poor wounded name! My bosom, as a bed
> Shall lodge thee till thy wound be throughly heal'd.
>   [I. ii. 111-12]

For the most part the verse is graceful and easy, rather fanciful than forceful. Such an imperfect quatrain as this might come from a lost sonnet:

> O, how this spring of love resembleth
>   The uncertain glory of an April day,
> Which now shows all the beauty of the sun,
> And by and by a cloud takes all away!
>   [I. iii. 84-7]
>   (pp. 114-15)

In the field of characterization *The Two Gentlemen* at once surpasses the *Errors* and gives promise of better things to come. In the *Errors* the tangled plot depends upon the simultaneous presence in Ephesus of two pairs of identical twins. This is an external fact in no way dependent upon the characters of the actors. In *The Two Gentlemen,* on the contrary, all that happens to the four chief characters happens because they are what they are: Valentine a true lover and a trustful friend; Proteus inconstant both in love and friendship; Silvia a modest, but faithfully loving lady; Julia a reckless and passionate girl. It might be objected, perhaps, that the gentlemen are types rather than fully rounded characters. They have been created to carry out a preconceived action and the action at times is so hurried as to throw a shadow of unreality upon them. This is particularly noticeable in the final scene, but it appears elsewhere as well. It is hard to believe, for instance, that Proteus at the first sight of Silvia should forget, to use his own words, 'the remembrance of my former love' [II. iv. 194]. Romeo, to be sure, does much the same, but his behavior is at least excused by the hardheartedness of Rosaline and the instant response of a Juliet ready to return 'grace for grace, and love for love' [*Romeo and Juliet,* II. iii. 86]. There is no such excuse for Proteus, and it may be that Shakespeare realized this, for in a scene that almost immediately follows this change of affection he puts into the mouth of Proteus a long soliloquy attempting to justify his behavior by a string of sophistical arguments, culminating in the pure egotism of 'I to myself am dearer than a friend' [II. vii. 23]. Silvia is rather a charming sketch than a full-length portrait, but there is something delightfully feminine in her first advances, always within the bounds of courtly etiquette, to a shyly hesitating lover. Julia, on the other hand, the first of Shakespeare's loving girls, has been completely transformed from the conventional heroine of romance in the source. Her struggle between desire and shame before she dons a page's suit to follow her lover, her firm confidence in the welcome she will meet, her disillusion falteringly revealed by her comments on the serenade that betrays the inconstancy of Proteus, the soliloquy in which she compares Silvia's picture with her own forsaken charms, all are original with Shakespeare.... There is, indeed, something almost feline in her instinctive impulse to scratch out the eyes of her rival's portrait. And, if we may trust the text as it stands, it is her quick wit and instant interference at the moment of supreme complication that brings about the happy ending.

The two comic servants play a very small part in the action; yet *The Two Gentlemen* would be a duller play without them.

They are called in 'the names of all the actors' affixed to the Folio text, 'Speed, a clownish servant to Valentine' and 'Launce, the like to Proteus.' Modern editors religiously follow this designation, but to group Speed and Launce together as Clowns is to ignore Shakespeare's plain intention. There is nothing of the Clown in Speed, unless the term is stretched to cover every type of merrymaker. We hear of Speed early in the play as 'Sir Valentine's page' [I. ii. 38], and a sensitive reader will recognize him on his appearance in the first scene of the play as a typical Lylian page, saucy, critical both of his master and of his master's friend, and very wide-awake to what is going on about him. It is he who picks up the glove Silvia has dropped for a love-token, unnoticed by her dreamy lover, and it is he who interprets to his master the significance of the letter that Silvia first bade him write and then returned to him. (pp. 115-17)

Launce, on the other hand, is a true Clown, the first and one of the best of the noble company of Costard, Bottom, and Dogberry. He and his fellows derive from a late development of the Vice, the boorish, stupid butt of the mischief-makers. Shakespeare raised them above this rather clumsy type by giving them a good conceit of themselves, and a homely, hardly self-conscious, gift of humor. Launce, for example, is not aware of the fun in the funny things he says. The actor who plays this role must keep a straight face even when he cracks such a joke as 'when didst thou see me heave up my leg' [IV. iv. 37-8]. We may be sure that the first actor to play this part was Will Kempe, and the part, no doubt, was written with an eye on him, since a play for Shakespeare's Company without a good part for the chief comedian would be quite unthinkable. Launce has even less to do with the plot than Speed; he does not appear till the action is well in progress and he drops out before the last act. But it is a capital role for Kempe.... In his two best scenes Launce has the stage to himself and can talk, as doubtless Kempe did, directly to the audience. In two other scenes he plays over against Speed, and in both his rustic mother-wit gets the better of the smart young page. We can almost hear the chuckle with which he sends the boy off to the whipping he has earned by his delay in prying into Launce's love affair. It is impossible, of course, to think of Launce without thinking of his dog, Crab, and one of Launce's most sympathetic traits is his affection for this ill-mannered cur. We may easily imagine the play that Kempe made on the stage with Crab. Perhaps his play was a bit too far on the side of buffoonery for Shakespeare's taste; certainly Shakespeare wrote other parts for Kempe, but Crab never appears on Shakespeare's stage again.

With all its faults *The Two Gentlemen* is a landmark in the development of Shakespeare's art. It heralds his entrance into the field where he was to win some of his greatest triumphs, that of romantic comedy. It develops the theme of love, checked and crossed by misadventure, but winning at last to its happy goal. To prevent this theme from sinking into sentimentality Shakespeare balances it with scenes of wit and humor. The young poet joins hands with the prentice playwright to throw a gleam of April sunshine on the love story; the humorist allows himself to laugh at times at its extravagance. Most important of all, Shakespeare here creates for the first time characters who control the action by the inner necessity of their being, and two at least of these characters, Launce and Julia, are lasting contributions to Shakespeare's gallery of living men and women. (pp. 117-18)

Thomas Marc Parrott, " 'The Two Gentlemen of Verona'," in his Shakespearean Comedy, *Oxford University Press, 1949, pp. 108-17.*

E. C. PETTET   (essay date 1949)

[*Disputing H. B. Charlton's assertion that Shakespeare had inadvertently made romance comic in* The Two Gentlemen of Verona *(see excerpt above, 1930), Pettet offers evidence of the dramatist's "conscious and amused detachment from the romantic mode and tradition." He contends that the parody of romance provided by Speed's verbal mockery of the cult of love and by Launce's reduction of his mistress to a list of her attributes and defects are Shakespeare's intentional, humorous criticisms of romantic love. Pettet adds that such romantic characters as Valentine and the band of outlaws also reflect the playwright's comic distance from the conventions of romance, concluding that Shakespeare, at this point in his career, "already had a glimpse of their shallowness and falsity."*]

None of Shakespeare's comedies is more deeply infused with romantic elements than *The Two Gentlemen of Verona,* which, if we exclude *The Comedy of Errors,* is probably the first or second of this group in order of composition. By itself it furnishes an almost complete anthology of [the] doctrine of romantic love . . . , while its narrative, wholly concentrated on a serious love-story, is pure romance. As H. B. Charlton comments: 'its actions are conducted to a conventional etiquette and are determined by a particular creed; and every feature of it, in matter and sentiment, is traceable to the romantic attitude of man to woman' [see excerpt above, 1930].

Yet *The Two Gentlemen* is not merely a romance; it is also a comedy. Further, as Charlton clearly perceives, there is a vital connection between the comedy and the romance: the play is not just a serious romantic story with detached or loosely connected scenes of comic relief. The romance element itself generates humour. But, according to Charlton, this humour is largely unconscious, the fumblings of an apprentice hand intent on manipulating the dangerous material of romance into drama: 'Clearly, Shakespeare's first attempt to make romantic comedy had only succeeded so far that it had unexpectedly and inadvertently made romance comic'.

No doubt the serious romantic story of the play does produce such instances of inadvertent humour as Charlton demonstrates—the hero, who ought to be something of a superman, exhibiting himself as a dolt with less wit than the official fool of the play, the impossible forest outlaws with no parallel in literature except the Pirates of Penzance. But Charlton's analysis is deficient, if not mistaken. He fails to notice the abundant signs that even at this early stage in his development Shakespeare was capable of standing in conscious and amused detachment from the romantic mode and tradition. So far from the comedy of the piece being merely a matter of inadvertent humour, Shakespeare deliberately uses Speed and Launce—as he later uses Touchstone [in *As You Like It*]—to guy romantic sentiment through the realistic and occasionally satiric chorus of the clown.

Admittedly this function of Speed is not much in evidence at his first entry, for though he brings the soulful image of the typically dejected Proteus—

> Thou, Julia, thou hast metamorphosed me,
> Made me neglect my studies, lose my time,
> War with good counsel, set the world at nought
>
> [I. i. 66-8]

down to the cruder and (for the gallants in the audience) the more realistic level of laced 'muttons' and bawdy jokes, this note is soon smothered in a riot of punning and back-chat. But when Speed next comes on to the stage his purposes are obvious

enough. In the first place, he is employed to ridicule Valentine, who, having in the meanwhile fallen in love himself, is now as absurdly 'a votary to fond desire' [I. i. 52] as ever Proteus was. The material-minded Speed, in love only with his bed, finds his master easy game and banters him with what is in effect a comic outsider's view of the cult of dejection:

> Val.:   Why, how know you that I am in love?
> Speed: Marry, by these special marks: first, you have
>   learned, like Sir Proteus, to wreathe your arms,
>   like a malcontent; to relish a love-song, like a
>   robin-redbreast; to walk alone, like one that had
>   the pestilence; to sigh, like a schoolboy that
>   had lost his A B C. . . . [You] are metamorphosed
>   with a mistress, that, when I look on you, I
>   can hardly think you my master.
>
> [II. i. 17-23, 30-2]

Secondly, Speed remains on the stage to keep up a mocking commentary that flickers over the encounter of the lovers, which is conducted to the stilted code of romantic courtship, with its 'Mistress' and 'Servant', its lady's absolute commands and knight's unquestioning obedience. His words at his exit have the decisive ring of his own mundane conclusions: 'though the chameleon Love can feed on the air, I am one that am nourished by my victuals and would fain have meat' [II. ii. 172-74].

The meeting between Speed and Launce (Act II, Scene V), coming between Valentine's extravagant tributes to the peerless divinity of his mistress and Proteus' perjured, though equally high-flown, dedication of himself to her, has a similar effect of comic deflation. . . . (pp. 101-03)

However, it is in the coarse, peasant realism of Launce's own love affair that the anti-romantic note is struck most audibly. Not for Launce the rosy spectacles or lyricism of religious devotion; the maid whom he has an eye on can be reduced to the business-like points of a bare catalogue—to a list of practical virtues and defects: 'Item, she brews good ale. . . . Item, she can wash and scour. . . . Item, she is not to be kissed fasting, in respect of her breath. . . . Item, she hath no teeth' [III. i. 303, 311, 323-24, 340]. What makes this episode (which foreshadows Touchstone's pursuit of Audrey) particularly striking is that it occurs immediately after Valentine's banishment—that is to say, precisely at the point in the narrative when we ought to be most concerned with the fate of the lovers of the romance.

Naturally an acute Shakespearean critic like Charlton does not altogether overlook the anti-romantic significance of Launce. 'A sheer clod of earth, Launce by name, will . . . expose the unsubstantiality of the romantic hero with whom the play throws him into contact.' But he mars that perception by slipping in between 'will' and 'expose' the peculiar phrase 'quite unwittingly'. 'Quite unwittingly' to Launce himself, no doubt; but to Shakespeare . . . ? The suggestion is fantastic. Shakespeare had not 'unexpectedly and inadvertently made romance comic' when he created Launce. Launce was one mask of a dramatist who had already learnt to laugh at the romantic conception of love.

But though this burlesque or choric satire of Speed and Launce provides the chief criticism of romance in the play, there are one or two slighter notes of depreciation. For instance, there is a gratingly obvious discord against the dominant romantic harmonies of the play in Act III, Scene i, where Valentine is advising the Duke on courtship. Here we have—the more remarkable in that it is spoken by the hero, and with little dramatic necessity—a description of . . . the cynical, machiavellian tactics of courtship. This sentiment is so rare in Shakespearean comedy that Valentine's speech deserves quoting in full:

> A woman sometimes scorns what best contents her.
> Send her another; never give her o'er;
> For scorn at first makes after-love the more.
> If she do frown, 'tis not in hate of you,
> But rather to beget more love in you:
> If she do chide, 'tis not to have you gone;
> For why, the fools are mad, if left alone.
> Take no repulse, whatever she doth say;
> For 'get you gone', she doth not mean 'away!'
> Flatter and praise, commend, extol their graces;
> Though ne'er so black, say they have angels' faces.
> That man that hath a tongue, I say, is no man,
> If with his tongue he cannot win a woman.
>
> [III. i. 93-105]

We should wantonly distort the meaning of the play if we threw an exaggerated stress on passages of this kind, isolated as they are and few in number. They are momentary variations, undeveloped themes, faint undertones. But, like the prominent chorus of the clowns, they do show us that even in his youthful and most enthusiastic days, when romance was the main inspiration of his work, Shakespeare, with the comprehensiveness of true genius, was capable of smiling at what he cherished, was critical of romantic doctrines (especially of love) and perhaps already had a glimpse of their shallowness and falsity. When the repentant Proteus cries out:

> O heaven! were man
> But constant, he were perfect. That one error
> Fills him with faults; makes him run through all the sins,
>
> [V. iv. 110-12]

he may be merely speaking in part. But if Shakespeare shared those sentiments, he was on his way to question, though not necessarily to reject, one of the basic assumptions of the romantic attitude to love. (pp. 103-05)

E. C. Pettet, "Shakespeare's Detachment from Romance," in his Shakespeare and the Romance Tradition, *1949. Reprint by Haskell House Publishers Ltd., 1976, pp. 101-35.*

DONALD A. STAUFFER (essay date 1949)

[*In the excerpt below, Stauffer describes love's transforming power and generosity in* The Two Gentlemen of Verona, *asserting that it is the "warm and unchanging love" of Julia, Silvia, and Valentine which reforms the aberrant Proteus. Their love, he continues, is not illusory but powerful and real because it has suffered in a world of indifference. Stauffer concludes that even in such an early work as this "Shakespeare was aware that compensation for the frailty of others may lie in the mind's unswerving loyalty to what it cherishes."*]

The typical Renaissance romance makes love into a game of tag, or, if one is ambitious, into a minuet or square-dance. Given two men and two women, the possibilities of entanglement may be mathematically calculated. Shakespeare conscientiously tried out in *The Comedy of Errors* and *The Two Gentlemen of Verona* the permutations and combinations that he handles most brilliantly and exhaustively in *A Midsummer Night's Dream.* Love is a sweet unreason—sweet to the lover, unreasonable to all but him. Through watching its errors, there-

fore, all lookers-on may enjoy its comedy. Within the form of the conventional Italian-French-Spanish romance, this odd passion must lead its devotees through amusing situations and hairbreadth escapes at last to pleasure.

Writing under some such unexpressed assumptions, Shakespeare dramatized a run-of-the-mill story in *The Two Gentlemen of Verona.* Here he first touched the tone of his own characteristic comedy, transmuting the spirit of the romances into a love so true and certain that it can support the catastrophic swervings of the plot and the laughter and bawdry of low characters. Insofar as they have any personality at all, which is not much, Julia and Valentine and Silvia derive theirs from their own warm and unchanging love. One need hardly be reminded that the answer to the famous song, "Who is Silvia?" [IV. ii. 39] proclaims her to be holy, fair, wise, endowed with grace, admirable, kind, beautiful, pitying, and excelling all mortals. Julia is adept at describing "the inly touch of love" [II. vii. 18], and Valentine in two glowing speeches earns himself a place among love's doctors. He says of his lady:

> She is my essence, and I leave to be
> If I be not by her fair influence
> Foster'd, illumin'd, cherishe'd, kept alive.
>
> [III. i. 182-84]

For he has found at last that "Love's a mighty lord" [II. iv. 136].

Shakespeare's secret, learned early, is that such exalted sentiment must be kept sweet by seasoning. Valentine's praise is rendered more convincing because in the first scene he has been railing at Proteus for being "a votary to fond desire" [I. i. 52]. And Julia, aware of her own coyness, knows that love may be wayward and foolish, "like a testy babe" [I. ii. 58]. We accept more willingly Julia's obedient wooing of Silvia for her own Proteus because it occurs in a play where the contemptible Thurio, crawfishing, says with dull common sense:

> I hold him but a fool that will endanger
> His body for a girl that loves him not.
>
> [V. iv. 133-34]

The fine flowerings of the trio of lovers—Julia, Valentine, Silvia—grow in the atmosphere of this ordinary world, in which a tavern-keeper can fall asleep during a scene of betrayal, because it does not concern him, and in which one of the clowns can remind us that "Though the chameleon Love can feed on the air, I am one that am nourish'd by my victuals" [II. i. 172-74].

Such ideal love is real, the argument runs, because it exists in a believable world. Moreover, it is so strong that it can confidently suffer insult and reversal. Shakespeare gives it plenty of chances to prove its quality in opposition to Proteus, who notably furnishes the key to Shakespeare's moral ideas at this early time. Proteus is, in his own eyes, a triple traitor—to leave his Julia, to love fair Silvia, and to wrong his friend Valentine. Yet Shakespeare practically accuses him of "angel-like perfection." To his friend Valentine

> He is complete in feature and in mind
> With all good grace to grace a gentleman.
>
> [II. iv. 73-4]

And to Julia he is of "divine perfection"; his looks are her soul's food.

Shakespeare does not develop the irony far. It is all love's fault. What can even an angel do against love, which is so powerful and so unreasonable? Proteus blames his actions on this errant god:

> And ev'n that pow'r which gave me first my oath
> Provokes me to this threefold perjury.
>
> [II. vi. 4-5]

He has had his moment of self-analysis:

> Is it mine eye, or Valentinus' praise,
> Her true perfection, or my false transgression,
> That makes me reasonless, to reason thus?
>
> [II. iv. 196-98]

But he sweeps such maunderings aside and accepts with alacrity a choice whose end he already knows:

> If I can check my erring love, I will;
> If not, to compass her I'll use my skill.
>
> [II. iv. 213-14]

The three lovers who have been lucky enough not to find desire a disease, help the changeable Proteus in his affliction. They, too, recognize sympathetically that it is not his fault. Love itself is a fool, and all lovers, all, are fond. "'Tis pity love should be so contrary," says Julia. But though 'tis pity, 'tis true, and must be accepted as a fact of nature in which all lovers participate, the bad and the good. And therefore when Julia, fully aware of her lover's perfidy, exclaims: "Alas, poor fool! Why do I pity him?" [IV. iv. 83, 93] the scholiasts might have a merry argument as to whether the poor fool is Proteus or Julia herself. "Were man but constant, he were perfect!" [V. iv. 110-11]. Since he is not constant in fact and act, he must be made so in the level of one's dreams. Even so early, then, Shakespeare was aware that compensation for the frailty of others may lie in the mind's unswerving loyalty to what it cherishes. If the world be false, all the more reason that one should to one's own world be true. Julia makes this clear when she reproaches her maid:

> Now, as thou lov'st *me,* do him not that wrong
> To bear a hard opinion of his truth!
> Only deserve my love by loving him.
>
> [II. vii. 80-2]

Love, then, can afford to be generous because in itself it is so unshakable. And this generosity cannot be carried too far. In one of those surprising scenes where Shakespeare suddenly abandons his characters in his enthusiasm for his thesis, Valentine proves that love is boundless as the sea. Proteus stands revealed in all his baseness before the three lovers. Now he declares himself repentant. And Valentine is so delighted at this quick conversion that he gives away the happiness of three perfect lovers for the benefit of the strayed fourth:

> And, that my love may appear plain and free,
> All that was mine in Silvia I give thee.
>
> [V. iv. 82-3]

This is too much even for Julia, and she swoons. She has little to worry about. In such an atmosphere of generosity, the most changeable penitent would find small joy in returning to his fickleness, and the play ends with "One feast, one house, one mutual happiness" [V. iv. 173].

The Two Gentlemen of Verona is hardly more than a light sketch, its lines hasty and undeveloped. Shakespeare's own inventions, additions to the original story, are the theme of friendship and the prodigality of love in the denouement. In this play, Shakespeare makes his first bold, characteristic, im-

portant moral assumption: that perhaps you can give away your cake and eat it too. Love—is it not conceivable?—can be so confident, so illimitable in its romantic devotion, so generous, that it can dissolve the mistaken world into its own smiling happiness. (pp. 35-8)

> *Donald A. Stauffer, "The Country Mouse," in his* Shakespeare's World of Images: The Development of His Moral Ideas, *W. W. Norton & Company, Inc., 1949, pp. 11-38.*

RALPH M. SARGENT (essay date 1950)

[*Addressing previous critical attacks on* The Two Gentlemen of Verona *and drawing information from the play's sources, Sargent attempts to elucidate the contemporary standards and ideals which Shakespeare endorsed in the characterization and the controversial resolution of his play. He views Proteus, in particular, as the playwright's study of human fallibility in the pursuit of such ideals, claiming that the originality in Shakespeare's treatment of the love-friendship conflict resides in this investigation, rather than in his conventional resolution. Sargent devotes most of his analysis to a demonstration of the numerous parallels between Sir Thomas Elyot's narrative of "Titus and Gisippus," published in his* The Governor (1531), *and the friendship theme in* The Two Gentlemen of Verona, *asserting that both Silvia's silence and Valentine's offer in the final scene are consistent with the ideals presented in the source story. Indeed, Valentine's offer, according to Sargent, is tendered with the assumption that Proteus will refuse it and, like the other three lovers, endorse the ideals himself by choosing Julia over Silvia.*]

Dr. Johnson said of *The Two Gentlemen of Verona:* "When I read this play I cannot but think that I discover both in the serious and ludicrous scenes, the language and sentiments of Shakespear" [see excerpt above, 1765]. But this play has since fared ill with the critics. (p. 1166)

Not content with pointing out that the major characters lack the depth and winning qualities associated with those in Shakespeare's mature plays, the critics have struck at the very psychology and codes of conduct of these early characters. The disparagers have particularly joined in condemning the jam-packed concluding scene. The points of attack there have been three: 1. The sudden conversion of Proteus is psychologically unconvincing; and Valentine's forgiveness even worse. 2. The (in)famous line in which Valentine offers to surrender Silvia to Proteus is both unbelievable and ungallant. 3. The silence of Silvia at this point is untrue to feminine nature, and a major dramatic lapse.

Nor have the critics stopped with mere unfavorable judgment on the play. Representative of the radical approach to *Two Gentlemen* are the editors of the Cambridge New Shakespeare. Since he cannot approve the actions in the final scene, Sir Arthur Quiller-Couch refuses to accept the central passage as Shakespeare's; he asserts it to be a "piece of theatre botchwork patched on the original.... Our hypothesis being ... that Shakespeare had another denouement which possibly proved ineffective on the stage, and that the one we have is a stage-adapter's substitute" [see excerpt above, 1921].... Thus, starting from a preconceived notion of what is "Shakespeare," the Cambridge editors proceed to disintegrate and reconstruct the Shakespearean text.

It is often easy to misread Shakespeare, especially when the critic's own standards of conduct and ideas of psychology differ, without his realizing this fact, from Shakespeare's. Some attention to the literary background of *Two Gentlemen* makes it plain that Shakespeare is simply assuming, without explanation or question, standards and goals the exact nature and force of which may not be readily apparent to the modern reader. The present study, therefore, proposes: 1. To indicate certain standards of conduct and ideals of life with which Shakespeare is working in this play, and to suggest Shakespeare's literary sanction for them. 2. To point out the second of Shakespeare's two major literary sources for the action of the play itself. 3. To review a portion of the play in the light of these sanctions and actions; to note the problems posed and the terms in which Shakespeare achieves his solution. 4. To show that the final scene derives consistently from the play, is thoroughly Shakespearean, and provides a dramatic finish to the comedy; in short, that no omissions, no adapters' hands need be posited.

There is no disposition on the part of the writer to claim *Two Gentlemen* as a masterpiece. But it is believed that such a study will reveal in this play at the start of Shakespeare's career major concerns, convictions, and aims which became fundamental to the peculiarly Shakespearean view of human life and relations.

The Two Gentlemen of Verona was long regarded as primarily a comedy of love, something of an early sketch, for example, of *As You Like It*. It is certain that romantic love is given its just due at the conclusion. But the play contains a disturbing factor, the theme of masculine friendship, involving an ideal which rivals the demands of romantic love. The title, indeed, calls attention to this second theme. Scholars anxious to defend the play have become so conscious of this second theme that they have ranked it above that of love between the sexes. . . . It should be obvious, rather, that Shakespeare consciously introduces both themes (and ideals) on somewhat equal footing: romantic love and masculine friendship. Such a procedure is far from isolated. On the contrary it is a characteristic phenomenon of the Renaissance that in the field of personal relationships literature exalted two ideals: love and friendship. The resulting clash, with its infinite variations, provided comic writers with their opportunity. A commonplace in Italian literature, this love-friendship conflict became in Elizabethan comedy from Peele and Lyly to Fletcher and Massinger almost as popular as did the revenge theme in tragedy. (pp. 1166-68)

The story of the rise of these two ideals is long and impressive, forming a major strand in the development of occidental literature and society. To show the significance of the Shakespearean position, only a few facts need to be recalled. Of rare and late appearance in classical literature, the romanticizing of love between the sexes must be considered mainly a mediæval phenomenon. The all-justifying power of love, the beyond-earthly bonds, could scarcely be carried further than in the great mediæval cycles of romance. In the course of the mediæval period, the theme of romantic love accepted and absorbed the conventions of courtly love and the chivalric code. By the time of Spenser and Shakespeare in the English Renaissance, romantic love, trailing its mediæval clouds of glory, was combined with a Christian ideal of marriage. The strong feminine element in this ideal should be noted: it gives woman, by her very sex, an essential role in ultimate human relations. (p. 1168)

Mediæval literature also exalted a kind of friendship. Among other elements, the mediæval conception included the sworn-brother idea. Two men, often of different rank, swear an oath of loyalty to the death in some undertaking. This notion of friendship excludes consideration of general virtues in the friends,

or even of the merit of the project on which the sworn-brothers may be engaged. Its aim is utility. (pp. 1168-69)

But it was classical literature, from Plato and Aristotle to Cicero and Plutarch, which really apotheosized friendship between men. Greek and Roman moralists regarded friendship as one of the amenities of life, an expression of the good life, an ultimate good in itself, in fact a supreme good. . . . Such friendship was based on equality of status and congeniality of minds; above all, it required virtuous life of both parties. By implication, classic literature found friendship between men superior to love between man and woman. Hence it represented a masculine view of human relations.

It was precisely this classical ideal of friendship which the Renaissance recovered and injected into the literature of its own time. Obviously in the society of the Renaissance, with its recognition of the importance of women, there was bound to be some clash between ideals of love and friendship.

Immediately preceding or contemporary with *Two Gentlemen* appeared, for example, two plays, Lyly's *Endimion* (*c.* 1588) and Peele's *Old Wives' Tale* (*c.* 1591), as well as two prose fictions, Lyly's *Euphues* (1578) and Sidney's *Arcadia* (1590). . . . Each of these exalts both friendship and love, brings them into conflict, and then provides a resolution. All make the same point: if the claims of friendship are first fully lived up to, then, and only then, is it possible also to achieve the rewards of true love. Loyalty in friendship and loyalty in love go, as it were, hand in hand. (p. 1169)

Here, then, is the background against which *Two Gentlemen* must first be seen. It is the literary milieu out of which *Two Gentlemen* arose, a knowledge of which Shakespeare assumed in his audience: four works which presented the contact between love and friendship—and all came to the same conclusion as *Two Gentlemen*. A recent analyst of Shakespeare's moral ideas says of *Two Gentlemen*: "In this play, Shakespeare makes his first bold, characteristic, important moral assumption: that perhaps you can give away your cake and eat it too" [see excerpt above by Donald A. Stauffer, 1949]. In the light of his own day the conclusion to *Two Gentlemen* can scarcely be called bold. That Shakespeare accepted, and tried in his own way to reconcile, the rival claims of love and friendship is, of course, important; but the conventionality of the actual conclusion suggests that Shakespeare's originality lies elsewhere. Shakespeare's contribution to the love-friendship theme in *Two Gentlemen* can be seen, rather, in his scrutiny of the ideals in terms of human beings; a study of what those ideals entail; the human difficulties which thwart them, the cost to men and women, and the conditions on which the goals may be achieved.

For his own treatment of the love-friendship theme, Shakespeare could have got suggestions from Lyly and Peele; for the nature and ideal of true friendship he could have gone to the classics, let us say to Cicero and Plutarch. But it is much more likely that he turned to the *locus classicus* for the exposition of friendship in the English Renaissance, namely to *The Boke of the Gouernour*, by Sir Thomas Elyot (1531). We know that Shakespeare found this a congenial work, drawing upon it for ideas on government and episodes in his plays of the middle period. In Book II, Chapter xi, on *Friendship*, or *Amity*, Shakespeare would have found all the necessary ideas on friendship for the Renaissance ideal. When a study of this chapter reveals that Shakespeare stresses exactly the elements in friendship which Elyot does, the probability that Shakespeare used the book for *Two Gentlemen* is greatly enhanced. (p. 1170)

[The] one essential quality of friendship to which Elyot returns again and again is *constancy*. (He refers to it no less than four times in his short chapter on friendship.) It is worth noting that this is the key quality stressed in Shakespeare's *Two Gentlemen*. Elyot admits that the ideal of friendship is a rare achievement in this world. Nevertheless, trust in friendship forms a very foundation stone in the moral order of man's universe. . . . Here in Elyot, then, may be seen the nature and sanctions of friendship which lie behind *Two Gentlemen*. These are the ideals which Shakespeare proposed to illustrate in drama, and to integrate with the ideals of romantic love. (p. 1171)

It is now suggested that we simply look at the chapter in *The Gouernour* following that on Friendship, namely Book II, Chapter xii, entitled: ''The wonderfull history of Titus and Gisippus, and whereby is fully declared the figure of perfect amitie.'' There follows the tale of an ideal friendship between two aristocratic students in Athens, the one Greek, the other Roman. Gisippus, the Greek, becomes engaged; he makes the mistake of extolling his fiancée to his friend Titus, and then introducing her to him. Titus falls deeply in love with his friend's fiancée. Inner turmoil results for Titus. Finally, upon learning of the situation, and the struggle within Titus, Gisippus in a supreme gesture offers his fiancée to his friend. And the offer is made in almost the exact terms which Shakespeare's Valentine uses in making a similar gesture to Proteus.

This story of Titus and Gisippus proved a ubiquitous favorite of the Renaissance. (pp. 1171-72)

[As] late as 1639, John Fletcher in *Monsieur Thomas* picked up and developed neglected aspects of the story. English poets of the Renaissance, including Spenser, put the non-classical friends, Titus and Gisippus, alongside the classical pairs of Damon and Pithias, and Pylades and Orestes. What made the story of Titus and Gisippus so apt for the Renaissance was the fact that it introduced, as the classical stories of friendship did not, the twin ideals of love and friendship.

There can now be little doubt that it was exactly this story of Titus and Gisippus which Shakespeare used as the second of his major sources for the action of *Two Gentlemen*. It provides the theme of friendship, the two characters, the mental responses of the love-smitten friend, and the denouement of *Two Gentlemen*. And a perusal of all the extant versions reveals that at divergent passages Shakespeare follows the version of Sir Thomas Elyot.

With this summary review of the background, we may turn to a few crucial points in the play itself for a reassessment of its integrity and achievement. In *The Two Gentlemen of Verona* Shakespeare stresses two major characters: Julia, the girl who is left behind—and does something about it—and Proteus, the man who is fickle in both love and friendship. The rôle and character of Julia have been adequately appreciated and need not detain us here. It is the part of Proteus which needs attention. Doubtless the rôle of Proteus (Titus) in Elyot attracted Shakespeare's interest; he had a predilection for the fallible creature caught between impulse and ideal, who finds the ideal too much for him. It should be apparent that Proteus became a central figure for his play; most of the important soliloquies are his. His inner struggle and fall form the heart of the dramatic conflict; these lead to his overt perfidy, which is the mainspring of the dramatic action. Or, to put it the other way round, Shakespeare, taking the outward events produced by Proteus' conduct, traces them to their source in Proteus' inner breakdown.

The play opens with Proteus and Valentine united in Renaissance bonds of friendship. When, in Act II, Proteus follows Valentine to Court, he finds Valentine in love there with Silvia. Valentine makes the mistake of introducing Silvia to Proteus, and praising both his friend and his beloved in front of them both. Just how Shakespeare took over this incident from Elyot's story of friendship may be realized by glancing at the account in *The Gouernour*. There, Gisippus, having become secretly engaged to a maiden, Sophronia, is unable to keep his pleasure to himself. . . . Later, when forced by his friendship to confess his infatuation with Sophronia, Titus reminds Gisippus that it was Gisippus himself who had led him (Titus) into his predicament in the first place. (pp. 1173-74)

Nevertheless, Titus remains perfectly aware of his own obliquity. In his later confession to his friend Gisippus, he complains of what this lapse from the ideal has done to his friendship. . . . (p. 1175)

This whole episode in Elyot was particular grist to Shakespeare. Both the uncontrollable course of such a love, and the consciousness of moral lapse which it brought, were of prime interest to him. Only, Shakespeare doubled the stakes, as it were: for Proteus to give himself up to love of Silvia meant being false to his former love (as in Montemayor) as well as to his friend (as in Elyot).

After Proteus has seen Silvia, and after Valentine has exalted her charms, Proteus comes forward alone. He reveals that he

JULIA. "To Julia,"—Say, from whom?   Act.1
LUCETTA. That the contents will show.   Sc. 2

Act I. Scene ii. Lucetta and Julia. By Walter Crane (1894). The Department of Rare Books and Special Collections, The University of Michigan Library.

has been stricken by Silvia—and is himself disturbed by the event:

> Is it mine eye, or Valentinus' praise,
> Her true perfection, or my false transgression,
> That makes me reasonless to reason thus?
>   [II. iv. 196-98]

But possibly Proteus has not yet wholly succumbed to this sudden love. He concludes the scene:

> If I can check my erring love, I will;
> If not, to compass her I'll use my skill.
>   [II. iv. 213-14]

Thus Shakespeare at the end of this scene leaves a wisp of suspense about Proteus in the minds of the audience. Compared with Elyot's Titus, Shakespeare's Proteus puts up a slightly longer struggle. And he considers the consequences before his full commitment.

In II, vi, we are shown Proteus deciding the issue for himself in a long soliloquy. He clearly announces to himself—and his audience—the nature of the perfidy involved in his contemplated action:

> To leave my Julia, shall I be forsworn;
> To love fair Silvia, shall I be forsworn;
> To wrong my friend, I shall be much forsworn.
>   [II. vi. 1-3]

(Note that treachery to friendship is regarded as the culminating fault.) He blames his predicament on the invincible power of Love: "Love bade me swear, and Love bids me forswear" [II. vi. 6]. In presenting the struggle and downfall of Proteus, therefore, Shakespeare is dramatizing the course of the man who knows in advance perfectly well what the ideal calls for, but when seized by the power of desire cannot summon up the moral will-power to hold to the ideal. (pp. 1175-76)

Proteus is presented, then, as a man who recognizes and admires fidelity in love and friendship. But he is also susceptible to the pressures of the moment. He is, for Shakespeare, the kind of man who is not yet morally lost; he still has the potentialities for reclamation when the pressures are altered, when the right appeals are put to him. But once having let himself succumb to Silvia, Proteus determines to pursue and win her, at all costs. (p. 1176)

The central drama of Two Gentlemen depends on the consequences of the decision made by Proteus. And the action reaches its culmination in the disputed final scene (V, iv). At this late point in the play, although he has broken all rules in the attempt, Proteus has failed to win Silvia; Julia has followed Proteus to Court, disguised as a page boy, and now at last, all—first Valentine, then Silvia, Proteus, and Julia—have taken to the woods. There . . . Shakespeare releases his rapid succession of shocks which bring the play to its speedy denouement.

Proteus overtakes Silvia (alone, he thinks) and attempts to force himself on her. In her defense, Silvia tries to appeal to Proteus' better nature. She proves a spirited and well-informed dialectician. First she insists she does not love Proteus; this appeal does not move him. Then she accuses him of faithlessness to his first love, Julia; and finally, bringing up her weightiest charge, she brands him perfidious in friendship to Valentine: "Thou counterfeit to thy true friend," she proclaims [V. iv. 53]. Proteus, who has long since considered the nature of his own conduct, replies in cynical fashion: "In love, / Who respects friend?" The instant reply of Silvia is fully revealing

of her attitude: "All men but Proteus" [V. iv. 53-4]. These are the last words but two (an exclamation when Proteus lays hands on her) by Silvia in the play. With them, Silvia indicates that she understands the code of masculine friendship.

Exactly at this juncture, Valentine, who has been watching these proceedings of his erstwhile friend with his fiancée, leaps forward and saves Silvia from Proteus. Valentine then turns to Proteus. Not a word to Silvia; Valentine trusts her, and she can now make her own decisions. But the attack on Proteus is bitter. On what grounds is it made? Valentine says nothing of Proteus' love for Silvia, nor of his faithlessness to Julia; it is only the lapse in friendship which Valentine berates in Proteus. This entire passage, culminating in Valentine's startling gesture, is treated wholly within the convention of the friendship ideal. (pp. 1176-77)

Now look at Proteus. However lightly and conventionally the audience and critics may take the sudden appearance of Valentine, it was an intervention to shock Proteus to his depths. He had been caught at the very nadir of his perfidy; and here is Valentine in the flesh, condemning him, by showing Proteus that his own conduct has shaken the foundations of both their worlds, which had been based on the rock-bottom of trust in friendship. Proteus' quick repentance, in such a situation, and upon such an appeal, is neither undramatic nor implausible:

> My shame and guilt confounds me.
> Forgive me, Valentine. . . .
> . . . I do as truly suffer
> As e'er I did commit.
>   [V. iv. 73-4, 76-7]

Valentine's reply, if still consciously self-righteous, rises to the occasion:

> Then I am paid;
> And once again I do receive thee honest.
> Who by repentance is not satisfied
> Is nor of heaven nor earth.
>   [V. iv. 77-80]

Both the act and the sentiments of Valentine occur so frequently in Shakespeare that they have come to be regarded as typically Shakespearean. They can be seen in the Sonnets, and right up to the end of his career in The Tempest. To question the genuineness of repentance and forgiveness in Shakespeare is to deny a fundamental tenet of his drama.

From the vantage of moral elevation, then, Valentine proceeds to his famous gesture of renunciation. Up to this point, be it remembered, it has been Proteus who has had to make all the hard decisions. Everything has worked out automatically to the advantage of Valentine. And Valentine has talked grandly about the claims of friendship. Now, for the first time, Valentine has the chance to make a decision which will prove his willingness to accept the code of friendship by really costing him something: "And," he says to Proteus, "that my love may appear plain and free, / All that was mine in Silvia I give thee" [V. iv. 82-3]. It is the ultimate acknowledgment of the claims of friendship. Not only is the offer conceived wholly within the convention of Elyot on "Amity"; actually, the very gesture is taken directly from Elyot's version of the Titus-Gisippus story. When Gisippus, in Elyot, learns that Titus is pining away for love of Sophronia, Gisippus declares: "Here I renounce to you clerely all my title and interest that I nowe haue or moughte haue in that faire mayden." The offer of fiancée to friend forms a high point, a supreme gesture, of Elyot's story illustrating the noble state of friendship. And as such Shakespeare doubtless took it over from Elyot. In terms of a code which he assumed his audience would recognize, Shakespeare has carefully led his characters up to this position. Yet Valentine's gesture comes as a shock. That was Shakespeare's aim as a dramatist.

But what of Silvia in all this business? exclaim the critics. She is not consulted, nor does she, as things stand, say a word. Here, either Shakespeare has faltered, in presenting human nature or in exemplifying human conduct; or else his original scene has been cut. Now there can be no doubt that Shakespeare did foresee and consider Silvia's position at this juncture. And he has turned a necessity (her silence at this point) into a virtue. Just before Valentine's gesture—as we have noted, a point overlooked by so many critics of Silvia's silence—Shakespeare had taken pains to reveal Silvia as recognizing the ideal of masculine friendship. When, therefore, Valentine reaches the ultimate in that code by his gesture of renunciation, Silvia can scarcely do less than hold her tongue. To add to, or detract from, Valentine's proposal would be equivalent to upsetting her delicate role of ideal feminine conduct at the moment. It is part of Silvia's character, as presented by Shakespeare, to be capable of such rigorous devotion to accepted codes. By her silence—golden in this light—she reaches her peak of propriety. No, there is no secret about Silvia's silence. Nor has anything been subtracted from Shakespeare's scene at this point; nor do we need to call in an "adapter."

In the Elyot story the offer is accepted, and thus devotion to friendship as an ideal is demonstrated. For Shakespeare, however, the gesture at one and the same time carries Valentine to the peak of loyalty in friendship, and opens the way to Proteus' regeneration and restoration to moral dignity. If Proteus is really repentant, if he has really been recalled to his better self, he must be given the chance to demonstrate that reconstruction by being allowed to choose for himself between Silvia and Julia. By the same token, if Julia is actually to be *chosen* by Proteus, not just forced on him because he cannot get Silvia, Proteus must be given a free hand for that choice.

Of course, in offering Proteus that choice, Valentine is taking some risk. It is taken in devotion to friendship, but it is also based on confidence that the friend will now live up to an equal standard. And Valentine is so confident of the outcome that he does not hesitate to let Silvia take the same risk. As presented by Shakespeare, however, does the offer actually involve much of a risk? Valentine has just seen, a few moments before, that Silvia has completely rebuffed Proteus; and Proteus has acknowledged the error of his way.

At this point, Valentine and Silvia have played their parts. Now again Proteus has a decision to make. But immediately Shakespeare brings in the warmth of the feminine touch. Julia, bold but pathetic, lacking the sterner stuff and rigid confidence of Valentine and Silvia, by nature or design, swoons at the offer of Silvia to Proteus. In the discovery which follows, Julia reveals her loyalty to Proteus. It is the final shock for Proteus. Thus confronted with the presence of Julia, and the evidence of the lengths to which she has gone for love of him, he completes his return to his former self and ways, and deliberately chooses Julia. Then, the regenerated Proteus, who has by now earned the right to them, speaks the tag lines of the play: "O heaven! were man / But constant, he were perfect" [V. iv. 110-11].

In the postscript, Shakespeare finishes off all in proper fashion by having Valentine remove Thurio as a suitor (Valentine thus

demonstrating once more his full virility), and then receive formally the hand of Silvia from her father the Duke. So friendship and love triumph together in the play.

Thus, by seeing the material and conventions with which Shakespeare has been working in *Two Gentlemen*, we can realize that he has shown his characters as human beings involved in the problems of loyalty to two ideals. When one character finds himself unable to live up to either, all is upset. But the willingness of the other three characters to live up to the highest demands of their ideals ultimately lifts that fourth character to their level. And at this level, the conflicting claims of friendship and love may be reconciled. In *The Two Gentlemen of Verona* Shakespeare is revealing his theme that human beings are fallible, but when presented with confidence in friendship and love, and allowed sound decisions by deepest convictions, then it may be possible for them to achieve durable human relationships—a fundamental value in his universe. (pp. 1177-80)

Ralph M. Sargent, "Sir Thomas Elyot and the Integrity of 'The Two Gentlemen of Verona'," in PMLA, 65, Vol. LXV, No. 6, December, 1950, pp. 1166-80.

HAROLD C. GODDARD (essay date 1951)

[*In the excerpt below, Goddard asserts that one may read* The Two Gentlemen of Verona *in one of two ways: either as Shakespeare's "most juvenile work," in which the dramatist accepts wholeheartedly the romantic ideals he presents, or as an ironical play, in which he subtly mocks "'gentlemanly' manners and morals." Goddard prefers the second reading, pointing to Launce and Speed as the vehicles of this ironic humor. Adding that the comedy is not a typical satire, the critic asserts that Shakespeare's burlesque of the ideal Renaissance gentleman is "so full of humanity, humor, and poetry that it is easy to miss the cutting edge of his condemnation."*]

At bottom, there seem to be just two ways of taking *The Two Gentlemen of Verona:*

1. We may consider it far and away the most juvenile work among the plays whose authorship has never been seriously questioned. There is much to back up this view. The play does reveal a certain skill in plotting [and] . . . an effective use of disguise, though what is essentially the same situation is so much better exploited in *Twelfth Night* that the handling of it here seems relatively poor and thin. To more than offset its merits, however, the play contains some of the most boring "wit," some of the most amazingly motivated actions, and quite the most incredible ending to be found in Shakespeare. The two heroines, Julia and Silvia, redeem it to a slight extent. Julia especially, who is more individualized than Silvia, is charming in her way, though, even allowing for the wretched specimens of manhood that charming women will fall in love with in real life, it is hard to find any reason except the requirements of the plot for Julia's having considered "divine" such a combined weathercock and cad as Proteus.

But how about Launce? someone will ask. How did such a masterpiece of characterization get into this early play? It is a question that must be confronted, unless we adopt the improbable hypothesis that he is a later interpolation. Launce—or rather Launce-and-his-dog-Crab, for the two are inseparable—is stamped with Shakespeare's genius. He could walk into any play the author ever wrote and not jar us with any sense of immaturity in either conception or execution. Perhaps in this paradox we may find a clue to how Shakespeare wanted his play taken, how so apprentice-like a piece could have been produced so close chronologically to works that so utterly surpass it.

Launce has more sense, humor, and intelligence in his little finger than all the other men in the play have in their so-called brains combined, and it happens that in the course of it he gives his opinion of each of the two gentlemen of Verona. Proteus, his master, he tells us, is "a kind of knave" [III. i. 264], and Valentine, the other gentleman, "a notable lubber" [II. v. 45]. Now it happens that the play confirms these judgments to the hilt. Indeed, Proteus' treatment, in succession, of Julia, Valentine, and Silvia makes the name "knave" quite too good for him, as Silvia recognizes when she calls him a "subtle, perjur'd, false, disloyal man" [IV. ii. 95], or when she declares that she would rather be eaten by a lion than rescued by such an abject creature. We have his own word for it that he is a sly trickster, and the story proves him to have been not only that but a perfidious friend, a liar, a coward, a slanderer, and a ruffian and would-be ravisher of the woman for whom he had deserted his first love. And this, forsooth, is the man whom his friend Valentine describes as having spent his youth in putting on an "angel-like perfection" of judgment and experience, until

> He is complete in feature and in mind
> With all good grace to grace a gentleman.
>
> [II. iv. 73-4]

Valentine, it is true, is a paragon of virtue compared with such a bounder as Proteus, but his estimate of his friend does little credit to his intelligence and is enough in itself to justify the label "lubber" that Launce puts on him. But if Launce's say-so is not enough, proof is afforded to an almost supernatural degree by the "ladder scene." How any man could act more inanely than Valentine does on that occasion it would be hard to imagine, if we did not have the final incredible scene of the play in which the same man outdoes himself.

Now if Launce had reached the same conclusions about these two gentlemen that the action of the play forces on us independently, it is hard to believe that Shakespeare himself was not in the secret. It sets us wondering just what he meant by his title, *The Two Gentlemen of Verona,* and how far he may have written the play with his tongue in his cheek. If there is anything in this suggestion, we may have to revise our opinion of its juvenility and consider whether some of its apparent flaws are not consciously contrived ironical effects. This is the second of the two possible ways of taking the play.

2. No one who knows Shakespeare can doubt for an instant the high regard in which he held genuinely noble and aristocratic character and background, nor the ease with which he detected their counterfeits. He had himself been rebuked by one of his "betters" [Robert Greene] for the effrontery of his own aspirations in histrionic or dramatic art, or both, and had been held up to the public gaze as "an upstart Crow," a "Tyger," "an absolute *Iohannes fac totum*" [Jack of all trades], and one who in his own conceit was "the onely Shake-scene in a countrey." And so it is no strain on the imagination to fancy him saying to himself, as he observed some of the "gentlemen" who frequented the contemporary theaters with their everlasting talk of "love" and "honour": "I will create a compendium of all the fashionable vices, give him a running mate devoid of sense, call the two 'gentlemen,' and palm them off on their English counterparts as the genuine article." What sport!

Make this simple assumption, and most of the crudities and difficulties of the play disappear like mist when the sun comes out. There is much in the piece to support this hypothesis.

Leaving out a minor servant, an innkeeper, and a band of outlaws, there are eight men in the cast. We have taken a look at the two gentlemen themselves and at Launce. The other clown, Speed, though he is intelligence itself compared with the gentlemen of the play, impresses us mainly as a mere trifler and trickster with words. That leaves the two fathers, Antonio and the Duke, and two other gentlemen, Sir Thurio and Sir Eglamour. The fathers are a typical pair of patriarchal tyrants. Proteus' father sums himself up in one line,

> For what I will, I will, and there an end,
>
> [I. iii. 65]

and Silvia's father discloses himself in one practice: he keeps his daughter under lock and key at night. Sir Thurio, "a foolish rival to Valentine" for Silvia's hand,

> Vain Thurio, whom my very soul abhors,
>
> [IV. iii. 17]

as that lady describes him, is a complete nincompoop, a sort of first sketch for Andrew Aguecheek in *Twelfth Night*. In Sir Eglamour, whom Silvia engages to help her escape, we think at first that finally we have come on a truly chivalric figure.

> O Eglamour, thou art a gentleman,
>
> [IV. iii. 11]

she declares, and, even if she doesn't, we are tempted to stress that "thou." But alas! when the two are met by outlaws, Sir Eglamour abandons the lady to them and runs—at top speed, it is implied. Shakespeare was nothing if not thoroughgoing in this play. If there is anything in this ironic way of taking it, he apparently decided that it should live up to its title and that there should be not one genuine gentleman in it—except Launce, who, by a stroke that seems almost to prove the poet's sarcastic purpose, is chivalric to his dog to the point of Quixotism. Catch that thrust, and you see how delightfully the story of the clowns is integrated with the rest of the play. Launce, the gentleman! Or we might, without stretching it too far, include Speed and have the two gentlemen of Verona!

Compared with their crew of attendant gentlemen in the other sense, the two women are epitomes of virtue and intelligence. This, too, is prophetic of the superiority that Shakespeare almost always gives his heroines over his "heroes" in comedy, and often in tragedy.

If one were to seek a passage brief enough to quote that illustrates the inanity of this play if taken at face value, one might choose the moment when the Duke, Silvia's father, seeks Proteus' aid in forwarding the match between Sir Thurio and his daughter:

> DUKE: What might we do to make the girl forget
>   The love of Valentine, and love Sir Thurio?
> PRO.: The best way is to slander Valentine
>   With falsehood, cowardice, and poor descent,
>   Three things that women highly hold in hate.
> DUKE: Ay, but she'll think that it is spoke in hate.
> PRO.: Ay, if his enemy deliver it;
>   Therefore it must with circumstance be spoken
>   By one whom she esteemeth as his friend.
> DUKE: Then you must undertake to slander him.

PRO.: And that, my lord, I shall be loath to do.
       'Tis an ill office for a gentleman,
       Especially against his very friend.
DUKE: Where your good word cannot advantage him,
       Your slander never can endamage him;
       Therefore the office is indifferent,
       Being entreated to it by your friend.
PRO.: You have prevail'd, my lord.

                                        [III. ii. 29-46]

It would seem impossible to go beyond that. But Shakespeare
does go beyond it—far beyond—in the closing scene of the
play. (pp. 42-5)

Some commentators have tried to explain this psychological
hash on the ground that Shakespeare had to have his "happy
ending" at any price. Others have tried to squirm out of the
absurdity by talk about the Renaissance conception of friendship as transcending love. But the notes of disgust or apology
on the part of the critics are too nearly unanimous to escape
the inference that nobody likes the ending. Why, then, try to
make ourselves think that Shakespeare liked it, except in an
ironical sense, any better than we do? The two possibilities are
plain. Either this is excellent burlesque of "gentlemanly" manners and morals, or else the young author fooled himself as
well as the rest of us by swallowing such silliness because it
was sweetened by melodious verse. Take your choice. For
myself, I prefer the alternative implying that one of the greatest
geniuses of the ages was not quite a fool even as a young man.

The play, taken thus, is not satire in the usual sense. The satirist
so hates the custom, institution, or human type he is exposing
or deriding that he ceases, like any man in a passion, to see
truly. In lashing his victim he lashes himself into blindness.
But Shakespeare is like Chaucer. He is so full of humanity,
humor, and poetry that it is easy to miss the cutting edge of
his condemnation.

If we reread the play in the light of this hypothesis, we see
how full it is of hits at the education of the young Renaissance
gentleman.

       Home-keeping youth have ever homely wits,
                                        [I. i. 2]

says Valentine. It is about his wisest remark. In view of Launce's
homely wit and profound humor one wonders whether all the
travel and adventure, the experiences of camp and court, the
university training, the music and sonnet-writing that were
demanded of the cultured young gentlemen of the time were
worth the trouble. One of the best strokes of all is the fact that
the outlaws pick Valentine as their captain because he is a great
linguist!

This interpretation of the play, I believe, both prophesies and
is borne out by what Shakespeare did in the rest of his works.
From *The Two Gentlemen of Verona* to *The Tempest*, without
any deviation, he drew one portrait after another of the fashionable gentleman, either Italian or after the Italian model, and
there is no possible mistaking what he thought of them, no
matter how good their tailors or how "spacious" they themselves "in the possession of dirt" (as Hamlet remarked of
Osric's real estate) [*Hamlet*, V. ii. 87-8]. . . . Let anyone who
doubts trace the word "gentleman" with the help of a concordance in the texts of Shakespeare's works as a whole. He
will be surprised, I think, to find how often the situation or
context shows it to be used with ironical intent.

There is a story that Abraham Lincoln, on being told that in
England no gentleman ever blacks his own boots, asked in his
quiet manner, "Whose boots does he black?" If I am not
mistaken, *The Two Gentlemen of Verona*, even more quietly,
makes the same point. (pp. 46-7)

        *Harold C. Goddard, " 'The Two Gentlemen of Ve-
        rona'," in his* The Meaning of Shakespeare, *The
        University of Chicago Press, 1951, pp. 41-7.*

M. C. BRADBROOK (essay date 1951)

[*Bradbrook is an English scholar noted especially for her commentary on the development of Elizabethan drama and poetry. In
her Shakespearean criticism, she combines both biographical and
historical research, paying particular attention to the stage conventions of Elizabethan and earlier periods. Her* Shakespeare and
Elizabethan Poetry *(1951) is a comprehensive work that relates
Shakespeare's poetry to that of George Chapman, Christopher
Marlowe, Edmund Spenser, and Philip Sydney, and describes the
evolution of Shakespeare's verse. In the following excerpt, Bradbrook explicates the influence of the courtier and the courtly love
tradition on the events and characters of* The Two Gentlemen of
Verona, *asserting that the play is "a study of manners rather
than sentiments, of behavior rather than emotion." Both Proteus
and Valentine, she states, are typical courtly lovers: Valentine
exemplifies the despairing student of romance and Proteus typifies
the self-deluded love poet reciting Petrarchan lines to his beloved.
The resolution of the play also reflects the courtier tradition,
Bradbrook avers, for Valentine's generous gift to Proteus demonstrates the cardinal virtue of Magnanimity, and Silvia's silence
regarding this sacrifice is consistent with her role as the "prize"
of the dueling lovers.*]

The earliest and most colourless of Shakespeare's romantic
comedies, *The Two Gentlemen of Verona*, has been passed
over by critics, except for its textual problems. Yet behind the
prefiguring of so many later characters and the first draft of
so many lines there is a particular germ or 'cause'.

The title indicates the subject, the friendship of two Italian
courtiers. The virtues of a courtier, which were the four cardinal
virtues, included first of all, as a part of Justice, Fidelity or
Constancy. Proteus' name marks him out as a sinner against
this requirement, as Valentine's name marks him the true lover.
But friendship remains here the personal relationship; love, the
courtly one.

The courtier's occupation was largely discourse, at least according to Castiglione, who devotes the whole of his second
book to this important subject; and Platonic love was his religion. *The Two Gentlemen* is a study of manners rather than
of sentiments, of behaviour rather than emotion; there is little
feeling anywhere. Proteus' wooing of Julia is purely Petrarchan: his phrases are all out of the sonnets—'Love-wounded
Proteus', 'poor forlorn Proteus' [I. ii. 110-21]—and Julia's
tearing up of his letter can be paralleled from Spenser's *Amo-
retti.* . . . (p. 147)

Silvia loves Valentine, Valentine Silvia; but they are never left
alone together, and do not exchange one intimate word. It is
Courtly love: Valentine has all the marks which Rosalind failed
to find in Orlando [in *As You Like It*]—he cannot even put on
his hose properly. His wit combats with Thurio, the rival, are
'a fine volley of words quickly shot off' [II. iv. 33-4]: he
cherishes a glove and in all ways 'does penance for condemning
love' [II. iv. 129], though his earlier condemnation has been
also spoken by the book. When he is accosted by the outlaws,
he conceals his love according to the best courtly code and

pretends he is banished for manslaughter; while some of the outlaws, less nice, confess to 'stealing a wife' [IV. i. 46]. At first Proteus is shown as a student, whereas Valentine is more active and looks forward to education at Court;

> to practice tilts and tournaments,
> Hear sweet discourse, converse with noblemen,
> And be in eye of every exercise
> Worthy his youth and nobleness of birth.
>
> [I. iii. 30-3]

He finds however that his chief occupation is in the School of Love, where he proves an apt pupil. Although deep in the study of *Hero and Leander*—

> a deep story of a deeper love
>
> [I. i. 23]

with crossed arms and ungartered hose, Proteus is outdone by Valentine, whose new role of despairing lover is set forth and most robustly mocked at by his servant. When Proteus arrives at the court of Milan and is entertained by Silvia as one of her 'servants'—note that there is so little personal implication about this that Valentine entreats the honour for his friend—he receives so magnificent a panegyric on love from the converted Valentine that he is impelled to call it 'braggardism'. Valentine is himself aware of his own absurdity, and rejoices in it. He is completely identified with his idol.

'Call her divine' he says and when Proteus replies, 'I will not flatter her' his besotted friend retorts, 'O! flatter me, for love delights in praises' [II. iv. 147-49]. Valentine knows he dotes, but his senses, pleased with madness, do give it welcome. In the midst of all this his true human relation to Proteus is not forgotten:

> Forgive me that I do not dream on thee
> Because thou see'st me dote upon my love.
>
> [II. iv. 172-73]

His agreeable madness is unfortunately infectious; Proteus' fancy, bred in his eye, is altogether unstable, and Valentine's praise has been too rhetorically telling. He announces in soliloquy that he is now in love with Silvia. This may be unworthy of *homo rationale* [rational man], but we are not in the presence of *homo rationale*. Had Puck [in *A Midsummer Night's Dream*] been at hand with his little western flower, Proteus would be justified. He does not give much thought to Julia: it is his discourtesy to his friend, his 'dissembling' which makes him culpable in his own eyes: he is most of all foresworn in wronging his friend [II. vi. 3]. Proteus' argument with himself is not so much a revelation of perplexity, as an exercise in self-excuse. It may be contrasted with Shakespeare's own 'salve for perjury' [*Love's Labour's Lost*, IV. iii. 284] which in its ingenuity goes beyond anything Valentine could reach:

> But here's the joy, my friend and I are one,
> Sweete flattery, then she loves but me alone.
>
> [Sonnet 42]

The mind of a lover was by definition changeable, a 'very opal', and the fickleness of Proteus is a more dangerous symptom than the perversity of Julia or Valentine's rapid oscillation between rapture and despair, but not different in kind. Only the divine Silvia remains constant; and like Imogen [in *Cymbeline*] importuned by fool and knave in turn, she can spare pity for the unknown Julia in the midst of her own distress. Valentine is made stupid by love, so that he cannot detect Silvia's courtly trick of making him write a letter to himself, and has

to be enlightened by the clown. Proteus is made treacherous, like Helena of Athens [in *A Midsummer Night's Dream*], and Julia driven to reckless venturing, like Hellen of Narbonne [in *All's Well That Ends Well*].

The play is full of prefigurings, which throw the reader's mind forward to greater works. The Duke's impulsive rejection of his daughter

> Let her beauty be her wedding dower
>
> [III. i. 78]

anticipates Capulet [in *Romeo and Juliet*]: Julia's debate on her suitors, the debate of Portia and Nerissa [in *The Merchant of Venice*]: her embassage to Silvia, Viola's to Olivia [in *Twelfth Night*]; there are frequent echoes of Romeo in Valentine's part, of Moth in Speed's, and of Costard [in *Love's Labour's Lost*] in Launce's. There is even a Friar [in *Romeo and Juliet*] who helps Silvia to escape. The play in its turn furnished hints to other dramatists. In Chapman's *Monsieur d'Olive* (1606) there is a direct recollection of that most abused and universally rejected scene in which Valentine releases his interest in Silvia to the repentent Proteus.

> And that my love may appear plain and free
> All that was mine in Silvia I give thee
>
> [V. iv. 82-3]

he says, although not twenty lines before Proteus was attempting to ravish her.

The schoolboy cries of 'cad' and 'scoundrel' with which Valentine is pelted by critics, the epigrams of Q ('By now there are *no* gentlemen in Verona' [see excerpt above by Arthur Quiller-Couch, 1921]) would have struck Shakespeare's audience as simply a failure in understanding. (pp. 147-50)

In releasing Silvia, Valentine was displaying in transcendent form the courtly virtue of Magnanimity, the first and greatest virtue of a gentleman. . . . The magnanimous man ignored wrongs done to him, so that the question of forgiveness did not even arise. He sought always to confer benefits rather than receive them, and any benefit which he received must at once be repaid with interest. This free spirit constrained Antonio to pledge his life for Bassanio [in *The Merchant of Venice*], impelled Antony to forgive Cleopatra's treachery with a kiss—'even this repays me' [*Antony and Cleopatra*, III. xi. 71]—and to send treasure after the renegade Enobarbus, and did not distinguish between liberality and prodigality. It is his Magnanimity which is the justification of Timon. So when Proteus says simply

> Forgive me, Valentine,

Valentine responds equally simply

> Then I am paid
>
> [V. iv. 74, 77]

The brevity of their exchange—some twenty-four lines in all—should not prevent recognition that it is the germ or core of the play. When he is banished from Silvia, Valentine's despair is philosophical, full of nice respects. It is an exposition of Platonic doctrine in rhetorical terms:

> What light is light if Silvia be not seen?
> What joy is joy if Silvia be not by?
> Unless it be to think that she is by,
> And feed upon the shadow of perfection. . . .
>
> [III. i. 174-77]
>
> (p. 151)

This can be paralleled from the sonnets (cxiii is a variation on the same argument); but Valentine's reproach of Proteus has the accent of direct speech; it is deeply personal and strikes a note to be heard again—incongruously—in Henry V's reproach of the traitor Scroop, in Antonio's reproach of Sebastian in *Twelfth Night* and faintly echoing even in the speech of Prospero to his brother [in *The Tempest*].

> Thou hast beguil'd my hopes: naught but mine eye
> Could have persuaded me: now I dare not say
> I have one friend alive: thou would'st disprove me.
> Who should be trusted, when one's right hand
> Is perjur'd to the bosom? Proteus,
> I am sorry I must never trust thee more,
> But count the world a stranger for thy sake.
>
> [V. iv. 64-70]

Trust is more dangerous than love, for it commits to the keeping of another not only our happiness and affections, but our values and beliefs, of which they are taken as the embodiment.

At this point the two young men may be well down on the forestage, but with Valentine's forgiveness and proffer, Silvia and Julia are brought into the action again. It has been asked how Silvia should be expected to react to this summary disposal of her favour. Clearly she should not react at all. She is the prize, for the purpose of argument, and must not call attention to herself, but stand like the 'mistress' in *Cynthia's Revels* [by Ben Jonson] before whom the courtiers conduct their amorous verbal duels, a lay figure. Leading ladies may not relish this, but leading boys would have been more tractable.

Julia swoons. She has been accused of calculation: a Julia who throws herself on the grass at what she adjudges the critical moment is absolutely unthinkable in Elizabethan terms. It is part of the modern vulgar search for 'personality' at all costs. Her action precipitates the dénouement. Julia contrasts herself quite formally with Proteus—he has changed his mind, she has changed her 'shape' or costume. Proteus matches her with a little panegyric of constancy. Valentine treats the reasonable Thurio with an unmeasured ferocity he had not shown the unreasonable Proteus, for this distinguishes the action proper to a lover where friendship is not involved. Everything ends happily:

> One feast, one house, one mutual happiness.
>
> [V. iv. 173]

The mirror which is here held up to nature reflects your fine gallant. His world is an artificial one, except for the clowns, and they can sometimes make play on the dramatic convention by a direct appeal to the audience. 'I speak this speech in print, for in print I found it' [II. i. 169], says Speed after one of his gems of proverbial wisdom. Launce's 'parting' from his family completely kills Proteus' parting with Julia (which it immediately follows) using even the same puns. Julia's praise of love or Valentine's satiric character of women, given to the Duke, are set speeches; this last is in the quipping vein and aptly describes Julia's coquetry but has nothing in common with his own feelings or practice. It might be anyone's. As for the action, whenever Shakespeare can think of nothing else to do, he puts in a misdirected letter, of which there are a record number in this play. The parody of the clowning acts impartially against all—Launce's dialogue with his dog is in such a powerful contrast with the elegance of the courtier that a modern audience cannot do justice at once to Silvia's divinity and her befouled farthingale; but this indecorum was decorus in the literary if not the social sense, as long as the heroics and

the clowning, the high style and the low were used in contrast, as black and white, and not allowed to blend. It is like the juxtapositions in Chaucer between the Knight and the Miller, or the story of patient Griselda and the prologue of the Wyf of Bath. (pp. 152-53)

On the popular stage there was no compelled decorum. The clowns who popped into tragedy, the fairies who darted into history, and the complete disregard of chronology which could put Ben Jonson into the court of William Rufus and a modern clown in *The Rape of Lucrece* were the fruits of licence and not the consequences of emancipation. Shakespeare, who had practised a regular style in *The Comedy of Errors,* did not continue on those lines. His own recipe was the bold one of blending different species, or 'kinds', to form a balanced and harmonious pattern. In this he even did not scruple to mix figures of the tragic stage, such as Shylock [in *The Merchant of Venice*], with those of romantic comedy. (p. 154)

> *M. C. Bradbrook, "The Fashioning of a Courtier: Sonnets, 'Two Gentlemen of Verona',"' in her* Shakespeare and Elizabethan Poetry: A Study of His Earlier Work in Relation to the Poetry of the Time, *1951. Reprint by Cambridge University Press, 1979, pp. 141-61.*

KARL F. THOMPSON   (essay date 1952)

[*Thompson examines the pervasive influence of the courtly tradition—specifically, the religion of love—on the characterization and structure of* The Two Gentlemen of Verona, *claiming that this convention supports the play's central theme: "that honor is an essential part of love, that the two cannot exist independently." He also maintains that the action of the comedy depends "more on the courtly conventions than on the conventions of friendship." Thompson underscores this point by asserting that the mainspring of the intrigue is Proteus's violation of "his vows made to Julia in accordance with the religion of love," and that the character's subsequent betrayal of Valentine is simply "the deed of one already spotted with sin."*]

[*The Two Gentlemen of Verona*] is, in one view, an earlier play than the revised *Love's Labor's Lost,* but since it follows the original version of *Love's Labor's Lost* it will be regarded here as Shakespeare's second dramatic adaptation of the courtly tradition. In it we find practically all of the conventions employed again. The first and most obviously used is the commandments of love. At the very beginning of the play [I. i. 63-9] Proteus describes himself as a love-sick lover. His lady, remarking his symptoms, felt obliged by custom to reject his advances disdainfully. This is the way Julia behaves publicly. But in private, as the audience is privileged to see, she too is love-sick.

The dramatic problem here is how to show these signs of love. Moping and pining, writing love verse, proclaiming the virtue and beauty of one's lady do not make for very exciting stage presentation. One way out of this dilemma is to show the lover behaving in a manner at variance with the commandments to which he formally subscribes. Thus, Julia, when Lucetta gives her Proteus' letter, is at first a conformist; she is angry. But when she is alone, she pieces together the letter she had torn and utters conventional Petrarchian sentiments about "love-wounded Proteus" [I. ii. 110]. The contrast is nicely done.

Proteus is, of course, an expert on the behavior of lovers and later advises Thurio how to behave, urging that unzestful lover to write complaints to his lady, to sing serenades to her. These actions Proteus turns to his own profit and under guise of assisting Thurio woos Silvia for himself.

Proteus is not the only expert, however. Valentine proves an apt pupil, practitioner, and instructor in applying the lessons of the school of love. When the Duke asks him for advice (III. i), Valentine offers the suggestion that the Duke woo his supposititious lady with gifts. . . . Valentine here draws upon the early medieval code when he suggests secrecy and clandestine meetings: "Resort to her by night" [III. ii. 110], he advises and offers for the Duke's use "an engine," a rope ladder, which he can provide almost at once. This suggestion provides a crisis for the plot, for it proves Valentine's undoing. The Duke, opening Valentine's cloak, discovers the ladder that Valentine is at the very moment carrying toward Silvia's balcony. To have the enthusiastic novice-instructor in love's stratagems thus discomfited by the old, cynical Duke, who believes that love is but "a figure trenched in ice" [III. ii, 6-7], is a masterpiece of irony.

Dramatic apprehension for the fate of the characters is created in this comedy by reference to the tradition in more direct fashion than in *Love's Labor's Lost* with its elaborate court, for here the scoffer at love, who will, the audience knows, be converted, is alone in his defiance of the powers of the god of love. There is no group of youths to lend each other support and encouragement. Valentine scoffs at first as he leaves Verona, but when we next see him he is an ardent devotee. Apparently the god of love finds such scoffers easy converts. And Valentine, subscribing to the religion of love and its commandments, speaks, like Berowne [in *Love's Labour's Lost*], in the passionately enthusiastic accents of the newly converted:

> O, gentle Proteus! Love's a mighty lord,
> And hath so humbled me as I confess
> There is no woe to his correction,
> Nor to his service no such joy on earth
>   [II. iv. 136-39]

How important the religion of love is for purposes other than pleasant badinage is revealed in the action of the last act in which the traitor to love, Proteus, repents his sins, confesses, and at last is given absolution. But the religious metaphor is used throughout the play: Valentine, for instance, has made his *mea culpa* and has become a votary. And Proteus, when he resolves on treachery, hypocritically conceals his true purpose like a notable sinner by invoking the aid of the deity:

> Love, lend me wings to make my purpose swift
> As thou hast lent me wit to plot this drift.
>   [II. vi. 42-3]

The feudal service of love, too, is used for purposes of badinage as well as preparation for the reversal in the last scene. The servant-master relationship, of which the medieval romancers were so fond, is toyed with by Silvia and Valentine in their word-play. Silvia says, "Sir Valentine and servant" [II. i. 100], and almost every time they meet they exchange the terms, "Servant" and "Mistress."

This same relationship enters into the situation of the disguised Julia, who takes service as page to Proteus. She refers to the anomalous position of her who was, and should now be, mistress of him whom she now serves.

> I am my master's true-confirmed love,

> But cannot be true servant to my master,
> Unless I prove false traitor to myself.
>   [IV. iv. 103-05]

The most important use of the feudal convention, however, is as a support, together with the religion of love convention, of the central theme of the play, the theme that honor is an essential part of love, that the two cannot exist independently. This theme was touched upon briefly in *Love's Labor's Lost* where the repentant youths are put on their honor to do penance before they can win their ladies. But in *The Two Gentlemen of Verona* the idea that loyalty and honor must be present before love can rise above lust comes to the fore and becomes for Shakespeare increasingly important in the remaining romances.

In his excellent discussion of the play, Ralph M. Sargent [see excerpt above, 1950] has pointed out the interweaving of the two themes of romantic love and the Renaissance ideal of friendship. The action of the play, however, depends on the whole more on the courtly conventions than on the conventions of friendship. We are warned early, for instance, that one of these young gentlemen is a false reasoner and liable to corruption. It is Proteus who says, after Valentine has departed for Milan, "He after honor hunts, I after love" [I. i. 63]. As if the two were separable. Young Proteus, then, is revealed to the audience as a man suspect because of his quibblings about love and honor. The honorable man will be true to his vows of love and of friendship. But the intrigue has as its impellent Proteus' forswearing of his vows made to Julia in accordance with the religion of love. This violation of the romantic code is the great cause of the play, and Proteus' subsequent violation of the humanistic ideal of the friendship of man for man is the deed of one already spotted with sin. Even in the last act, Proteus is not altogether restored to virtue by his repentance of his treachery to his friend. It is not until he swears fealty to Julia that the play achieves that equilibrium, that necessary releasing of tension, which is the end of any dramatic action.

The action of *The Two Gentlemen of Verona* is consistent, for if we have accepted Valentine's quick conversion to love and Proteus' quick change of mistresses, we can accept the instantaneous changes of the last act. We cannot single out one preposterous incident from the play to object to; we must say either that the whole is preposterous and we will have none of it, or that the whole is consistently preposterous and we accept it. What makes this latter choice possible is the preparation afforded us by the courtly tradition. Love and honor: these were inextricably bound up together in the religious metaphor, and Shakespeare evidently found the union of the two congenial to his dramatic purpose.

But what is the reward of lovers who have learned that love and loyalty are one? In Shakespeare's comedies the reward is marriage. The lovers of *The Two Gentlemen of Verona* think that love and weddings are inevitably consequent, and the play ends on a note of affirmation of the romance of marriage: faith, honor, loyalty, love—all these are comprehended in the sworn contract, the plighting of faith, the pledging of loyalty that gives assurance and strength to that institution. All faithful lovers must come to this decision in comedy, in which the world is well disposed to youths and maidens of good will. (pp. 1085-88)

Karl F. Thompson, "Shakespeare's Romantic Comedies," in PMLA, 67, *Vol. LXVII, No. 7, December, 1952, pp. 1079-93.*

THOMAS A. PERRY (essay date 1954)

[*In the following excerpt, Perry discusses the importance of the Italian courtier tradition and the travel motif in* The Two Gentlemen of Verona. *The critic demonstrates the Italian influence on all of the characters, especially Proteus, in whom he notes an acquired expertise in poetry and fashion after he arrives in Milan, as well as the Italian traits of "inconstancy and disloyalty," stereotypes which the critic attributes to the antiforeign sentiment in England at the time Shakespeare wrote the play. Perry also examines the anomalous ship voyage between the two landlocked cities in the play, contending that this is not an error but one of Shakespeare's many conscious references to water and shipping, indicative of his concern here with the effects of travel on his characters. Indeed, the critic claims that* The Two Gentlemen of Verona *is not merely "another tale of friendship and love," but is "primarily the timely story of the Italianated youth in whom false friendship and false love accompany the attempts of the youth to acquire sophistication."*]

Students of Shakespeare too generally have ignored or minimized the travel motif in *The Two Gentlemen of Verona*. True, it is the story of faithlessness in friend and lover; yet that faithlessness is consequent to an inexperienced youth's traveling abroad and is part of his transformation into an Italianate courtier. To understand Proteus properly one must see him first of all as the wry-transformed traveller.

Hints for this Italianate character of Proteus exist in the principal source—the tale of Felis and Felismena in Montemayor's *Diana*. Felis, not yet out of his "mocedad" [youth], is sent to the far distant court lest he waste his youth at home. . . . The reasoning is typically Renaissance-Humanist and is paraphrased in the opening lines of Shakespeare's play. In sharp contrast to this Felis is the later, sophisticated Felis among the courtiers of the Princess Augusta Cesarina. This Felis is revealed with striking suddenness when the reader, following Felismena, one night hears the unfaithful Felis serenading another lady—with an Italianate sonnet! Then, as Felismena arrives at the court, the reader sees Felis for the first time since his departure from Vandalia—a richly dressed, clothes-conscious Felis. In an unusually detailed passage Montemayor describes the clothes. In this changed Felis two traits stand out, traits commonly attributed to the Italianate: sonneteering and concern with fashionable dress. To these must be added a third, inconstancy.

This, basically, is also the story of Shakespeare's Proteus. In the first act he is yet to be "tried and tutor'd in the world" [I. iii. 21]. He is urged to "see the wonders of the world abroad" lest "living dully sluggardiz'd at home [he] / Wear out [his] youth with shapeless idleness" [I. i. 6-8]. Then, when he is sent to Milan and its new world of "wailful sonnets" and fashionable dress, and amorality, he changes as completely as did Felis. The new Proteus is not only inconstant, but he also becomes increasingly sophisticated and amoral, so that eventually even the Duke turns to him for worldly advice and for instruction in intrigue [III. ii. 16-30].

This basic plot Shakespeare has reinforced with elements not in the *Diana* but contributing to the more complete picture which it suggests of a wry-transformed traveller. For instance, the conventional reason for travel—obviously transplanted from the *Diana*—appears in the opening speech of the play, but is developed further in the third scene, when Antonio and Panthino are discussing Proteus' education. Here Shakespeare obviously draws upon the great mass of didactic literature stress-

ing the role of travel in such education. Proteus' uncle, of the ambitious lesser nobility, conventionally pronounces that it "would be great impeachment to [Proteus'] age, / In having known no travel in his youth" [I. iii. 15-16]. Since the traveller was expected to see and observe foreign courts, Panthino suggests the Milanese court, which he naively idealizes as a place where a youth may "practise tilts and tournaments, / Hear sweet discourse, converse with noblemen, / And be in eye of every exercise / Worthy his youth and nobleness of birth" [I. iii. 30-3]. This is, of course, a piece of Shakespearian irony. Another original touch is the realism of the uncle's jibe about Proteus' spending "his youth at home, / While other men, of slender reputation" are providing the proper education for their sons [I. iii. 5-6]. (pp. 33-4)

Those [critics] who argue Shakespeare's careless disregard of geographical fact [because of the implausible voyage between Verona and Milan] have overlooked his consistent and apparently deliberate placing of puns and water images to emphasize that the young Veronese leave aboard ship. At the same time he has carefully ordered his expository details to make this clear to his audience. For instance, from the very beginning of the play and throughout the first two acts, the primary interest is in the "shipping" of Valentine and Proteus, and later [II. iv. 187] with the disembarkation of Proteus in Milan. Meanwhile, puns on *sheep* and *ship, tied* and *tide* [I. i. 72-4; II. iii. 33-54] are placed strategically at the exact moments of embarkation—as the servants rush to catch the ship. The play on the double meaning of *tide*—"The tide is now:—nay, not thy tide of tears; / That tide will stay me longer than I should"— as Proteus bids Julia farewell, likewise emphasizes the mode of travel [II. ii. 14-15].

The skillful scattering of water images throughout the first half of the play—especially in the first two acts—suggests that Shakespeare was consciously reminding his audience of water travel at the critical moments of departure. For example, Proteus' figure of speech as he reacts to the news that he is being sent to Milan carries double meaning: "Thus have I shunn'd the fire for fear of burning, / And drench'd me in the sea, where I am drown'd" [II. i. 78-9]. . . . Valentine's allusion in the opening scene to young Leander, who "cross'd the Hellespont" [I. i. 22] may presage his crossing the sea to find Sylvia. It also comes as the conversation shifts from the first major topic, sea travel, to the other, love, and within itself contains elements of both topics.

While other water images refer less directly to the action and are apparently introduced for ornament's sake only, yet they too appear at the critical moments when the dramatist is creating an impression of sea travel. Subtly and indirectly they make their contribution, as though they were the natural figures for a people living close to the sea and for the moment intent upon traveling. (pp. 34-5)

Granted Shakespeare's emphasis on water travel, is it not possible, . . . that Shakespeare is only being careful to conform to the geographical fact that sixteenth-century Verona was an important port for large ships navigating the Adige? It is true that two of the water images are unmistakably river images, and that others could refer as well to river as to sea travel. . . . On the other hand, most of the images suggest or unmistakably pertain to sea travel, not river travel. The difficulty is resolved when one remembers that London is on the Thames, and that the Thames, unlike the Adige, soon runs into the sea. Its ships are sea vessels. Down it Julia may follow Proteus "like a current . . . with willing sport to the ocean" [II. vii. 25, 32].

From here Valentine may cross his Hellespont to find a Hero. Likewise, the several allusions to tides, more notably characteristic of the Thames, would suggest London to the English audience. Shakespeare may have chosen Verona for his play because it was a port on a navigable river, but the embarkations of Valentine, Proteus, and Julia are more like departures from London than Verona.

This new world into which Proteus comes, to undergo his metamorphosis into an Italianate courtier, like the court in the *Diana*, is fashion conscious. In choosing Milan as the setting, Shakespeare makes use of its popular reputation, not only as the traditional seat of the imperial court but also as an important fashion center and maker of fashionable clothing. (pp. 35-6)

Shakespeare's periodic allusions to special styles of dress exploit this reputation and keep the audience aware of it. Lucetta, preparing Julia for her journey to Milan, asks, "What fashion, madam, shall I make your breeches?" [II. vii. 49]. . . . Valentine's pun on *doublet* and *double* [II. iv. 20-1] calls attention to the dress of Thurio and especially to an article of dress whose frequently changing style was an important feature of Renaissance fashion. Likewise, the rather lengthy business of the cloak under which the Duke is to hide a ladder [III. i. 130-36] focuses attention on the dress of Valentine and again on a style which attracted considerable comment in the 1590's. The jests about farthingales [II. vii. 51; IV. iv. 38-9] direct similar attention to women's styles.

Other fashions come in for comment, too. That "squirrel," Proteus' dog Jewel, is a tenth the size of Crab [IV. iv. 48-60]. Proteus' expert advice on the "wailful sonnet" and its conceits [III. ii. 67-86] is, of course, of a piece with the discussion of fashions in love-making between the Duke and Valentine [III. i. 84ff.]. (pp. 36-7)

[Proteus] also begins to show other Italianate traits. He is a "complement-munger" and flatterer. "Thus subtle, perjur'd, false, disloyal man! / Think'st thou I am so shallow, so conceitless, / To be seduced by thy flattery" [IV. ii. 95-7], Sylvia angrily answers his smooth words of courtship. His hypocrisy stands without question, so that his advice to Thurio rings ironic: "Frame some feeling line / That may discover such integrity" [III. ii. 75-6]. He is a Machiavellian slanderer and plotter [III. ii. 31ff.], so gifted in intrigue that he can make Thurio and even the Duke his dupes. Finally, he is . . . guilty even of attempted rape. In this patterned description of an Italianated youth one naturally expects inconstancy and disloyalty.

In the background are the other Milanese, echoing these qualities in Proteus, though they are not so extreme nor so intolerable. Even Valentine, admirable as he is throughout most of the play, is not above advising the Duke in his intrigue for possession of the "lady of Verona" and suggesting the use of flattery. The Duke is a willing partner in Proteus' plot to slander Valentine. Thurio, the third partner, in his way proves as inconstant to Sylvia as Proteus to Julia. The shift from court to woods must have been intended as a welcome relief from the insincerity and immorality of the court. One could hardly expect Proteus' repentance in Milan. (p. 37)

Shakespeare's use of the motif of the "wry-transformed traveller" acquires additional importance when one sets *The Two Gentlemen of Verona* within the social framework of the 1590's. To assume that because this was a perennial topic for Renais-

sance writers it did not have particular pertinency around 1590 is to misunderstand the play. While Renaissance England came under the powerful influence of Italy on the one hand, and witnessed with dismay the moral decay of that same Italy and a disturbing revolution in her own youth; on the other hand, certain events around 1590 gave a special timeliness to the issue and put an edge on Elizabethan opinion of the Italianate. (p. 38)

Despite a temporary wave of feeling against the Italianate Earl of Oxford in the 1570's, England had seen hundreds of translations of Italian books, a growing frequency in the visits of traveling Italian actors, a marked increase in the number of Italian grammars and dictionaries, and English books and plays with Italian settings. In this period the vogue of the sonnet and sonnet sequence, with their Petrarchan conceits, was strongest. This influence had reached its peak in the 1580's. But by the time of *The Two Gentlemen of Verona* a reaction had set in, aggravated by the unrest following the execution of Mary Stuart and the defeat of the Armada. These two events, instead of quieting, intensified English fears. The next decade was a period of strong nationalist feeling, marked by hatred of everything foreign. Spaniard, Italian, and Papist were often synonymous, a fact that is not surprising since much of Italy was politically under the Spanish king and thousands of Italians served in the Spanish army. . . . The growing hatred is reflected in the all-inclusive attacks of Hall and Marston on Italian clothes, vice, poisoning, and English imitations of Italian verse. (p. 39)

At such a time Shakespeare wrote his tale of the wry-transformed traveller. To dismiss *The Two Gentlemen of Verona* as only another tale of friendship and love is to misread it. It is primarily the timely story of the Italianated youth in whom false friendship and false love accompany the attempts of the youth to acquire sophistication. Unfortunately the idealized pattern envisioned for the traveling Proteus by Panthino was not realized. Rather, Proteus was to become the Machiavellian plotter, the inconstant. That travel does not always have such drastic effects is illustrated by Valentine, only slightly affected by the lesser vices of the court, who never is at home there so much as Proteus is.

Towards the early Proteus Shakespeare is sympathetic. Towards the repentant Proteus of the Mantuan forest he is forgiving. He is mildly satirical of sonnet fashions (as he is in his own sonnet sequence). He laughs at the fashionable tiny dogs and at foibles in dress. But he has no patience with treachery, intrigue, lust, or inconstancy, whether in Proteus or Thurio—until there is an honest self-appraisal and an honest change of heart. Therefore, one must read this play as comedy. Proteus is no villain in the accepted sense of the word; he is the inexperienced youth being tried and tutored in the world— the Italianate world. This particular youth is finally brought to his senses and is able to profit from his experiences. He is at last neither the untutored youth nor the Machiavel. Like the outlaws, he may be forgiven for "what [he has] committed here." They are all "reformed, civil, full of good, / And fit for great employment" [V. iv. 154, 156-57].

Here the common sense of Shakespeare speaks out again on a topic that too often was treated hysterically or unfairly. He can smile and he can frown at Proteus, but at the last, knowing that the Proteus of Milan is a passing phase, he accepts him— with his more sensible and less susceptible companion—just as he is later to accept the chastened Jaques of *As You Like It*. (pp. 39-40)

Thomas A. Perry, "Proteus, Wry-Transformed Traveller," in Shakespeare Quarterly, *Vol. V, No. 1, January, 1954, pp. 33-40.*

JOHN F. DANBY (essay date 1960)

[*Quoting from the play itself, Danby calls* The Two Gentlemen of Verona *a "shallow story of deep love" (I. i. 21), emphasizing the "serious moral background" beneath its "trivial" plot. He notes a "marked serenity" and "optimism" throughout the comedy, despite the transformations in the characters' fortunes, which he attributes to two sources: one, the fact that the protagonists "are pieces moved by the mechanism of the story," rather than its wellsprings; and two, because the characters themselves and the play's underlying message remain optimistic or comic in a Christian sense. The critic also suggests that we are not meant to dwell on the villainy of Proteus—or to dispraise him as an immoral figure—but to witness through his experience the power of human compassion to elevate the erring individual "to the quality of the love bestowed." In addition, Danby is one of the earliest of modern critics to comment on the significance of the forest in* The Two Gentlemen of Verona, *which he identifies as a "timely shelter to natural values" and a place where love and friendship are restored.*]

[As] a story, [*The Two Gentlemen of Verona*] is merely trivial. Nor can it sustain any serious interest as a study of character. Yet the total impression the play leaves one with is of something neither trivial nor uninteresting. At one point early in the first act Proteus and Valentine have the following exchange:

> *Proteus:* Upon some book of love I'll pray for
>   thee.
> *Valentine:* That's on some shallow story of deep
>   love.
>
> [I. i. 20-1]

Shakespeare was aware of the different ways in which stories could be taken. Without being by any means an allegory the play is still "a shallow story of deep love". There is a serious moral background against which plot and *dramatis personae* define themselves, and to which we are constantly referred. It is this traffic between the levels of story and hinterland that gives *Two Gentlemen* its special tension of lightness and gravity. (p. 314)

No one [can] say *Two Gentlemen* [is] 'a drama'. There is no build-up to an epiphanic crisis, no conflict, no suspense. The technique is linear-narrative. The play is a story with speaking parts. . . . The processes of change in the characters, or in their mutual relations, are never lived through, only announced—often in long, beautifully formal passages of verse. Instead of the enactment of the process of change we have a declaration from prepared stations, as it were, of the play's progress along Love's varied course. Where a bare outline of what happens would suggest that all the time the characters are jerking idiotically from the false to the impossible . . . the movement and tone of the play suggests the opposite of this. Everyone involved in the central situation of the play moves with marked serenity and poise.

This serenity has two sources, one having to do with the external and the other with the internal form of the play. Let us take the external first. The characters, to insist again, do not confront each other at the moments of changing direction. They are either alone, or, so to speak, with their backs turned on each other. They do define themselves, however, against the background, or 'psychic envelope' of the play. The plot of the play . . . rather than the 'characters' is a main vehicle for the meanings the whole play integrates, the plot and the poetry.

The plot (what *people* do in the Ibsen theatre) does not spring (as it does in Ibsen) from what people *are*. It has the independent force of a providence. The people involved in the set-dance of the plot conform to the steps of the dictated and meaningful movement. They remain conspicuously human, except that they are not conceived as originating agents. They are pieces moved by the mechanism of the story, and the story is arranged to exhibit the laws of Love. In Shakespeare's early comedy we have always to remember . . . the comparative disjunction, or free association, of Aristotelian plot, character, and diction. The serenity of the persons involved in the plot partly depends, then, on this: they are buoys marking a course.

The other thing that buoyantly upholds them is the pervasive moral optimism of the play. Everyone moves through a kind of chequered sunlight, in a Spring fore-destined to turn into Summer. Proteus expresses it perfectly when he finds himself forced by his father from Julia's side:

> O, how this spring of love resembleth
> The uncertain glory of an April day,
> Which now shows all the beauty of the Sun,
> And by and by a cloud takes all away.
>
> [II. i. 84-7]

The characters all come to share this central vision. Even Launce and his dog going through the pantomime of home-leaving translate the central seriousness into a comic mode. . . . (pp. 316-17)

Love in *Two Gentlemen* is seen as a discipline, and the lover as an initiate. The object of love may be a woman, but woman as the focus and embodiment of values that impose their own constraint on 'base affection'. By means of love the lover is admitted into the realm of the values and thereby submitted to a life-process the outcome of which he can neither force nor dictate. One outcome may be the ecstasy of union. Another might be ineluctable separation. Either way, however, the initiate achieves (and this is his real reward) an assured stability in the midst of rival complexities,

> an ever-fixed mark
> That looks on tempests and is never shaken.
>
> [Sonnet 116]

He learns to hold together fulfilment and sacrifice and realise both as the two faces of Love. So that fulfilment is never an end and separation not an ultimate deprivation. Something more than what we nowadays call 'sex' is involved in the Sonnets and in *Two Gentlemen,* homo-sex or hetero-sex. . . . The Petrarchan, sometimes thought of as only a fashion of writing, is clearly more than this. It is a mode and manner of experience, and not an eccentric one. In their great sonnet sequences Sidney and Shakespeare are initiated into one of the main mysteries of human experience: meeting and parting, togetherness and separation, union and division; the inescapable paradoxes imposed on man by virtue of his condition as a creature made for his fellows and for himself alone.

It would be superfluous to illustrate all this from the *Sonnets.* "Friendship and love" . . . are the warp and woof of the situation Shakespeare expounds. In approaching *Two Gentlemen* with these considerations in mind there is no danger of us saddling the play with a greater 'system of ideas' than it can carry. *Two Gentlemen* is one of Shakespeare's finest early poems. Even more clearly than the Sonnets themselves it makes explicit the fundamentals of the human condition it is concerned with. Julia, for example, has just had separation imposed upon her, and resolves to overcome it. She is talking to her confidante, Lucetta:

Lucetta: I do not seek to quench your love's hot fire,
               But qualify the fire's extreme rage,
               Lest it should burn above the bounds of
               reason.
Julia: The more thou dam'st it up, the more it
               burns.
               The current that with gentle murmur glides,
               Thou know'st, being stopp'd, impatiently
               doth rage;
               But when his fair course is not hindered,
               He makes sweet music with th'enamelled
               stones,
               Giving a gentle kiss to every sedge
               He overtaketh in his pilgrimage;
               And so by many winding brooks he strays
               With willing sport to the wild ocean. . . .
                                   [II. vii. 21-32]

[Julia's] speech gives the central vision. It brings together, too, some of the basic metaphors of educated Western experience: the forward-moving stream, by indirections finding and holding to its own direction, impatient yet patient, giving a gentle kiss to every sedge overtaken in the pilgrimage, making sweet music with the enamelled stones, urging with willing sport towards the wild ocean, securely confident that "after much turmoil" [II. vii. 37] there will be the blessedness of Elysium. The poetry is magnificent in its synthesis, an unanxious and dynamic assurance maintained in the full knowledge of recognised hazards: ease, courage, modesty, delicacy combined. The measure of the play is the measure of such verse as this, and Julia's speech is not an isolated purple-passage.

Two Gentlemen is in fact more integrated and patterned than has often been supposed. Pattern is one of the more obvious features of the early Shakespearean drama. And the external pattern answers the internal pattern. The universe of *Two Gentlemen,* like that of Davies' *Orchestra,* is one in which discord is resolved into the harmony of the cosmic dance—the basic metaphor for the moral optimism of the Elizabethan golden age. The divine comedy is one of meeting and parting and meeting again at the passionate pilgrim's journey's end.

Thus Julia and Silvia are balanced against one another. Like Helena in *All's Well,* or Imogen in *Cymbeline,* Julia is the symbol of pursuing love. The idea is one I would call essentially Christian (the love of God is not that we loved him but that he first loved us) but one need not invoke Christianity to call it into being, to explain it, or ratify it. Julia's action in the play is an extrapolation from her speech. She must be patient as the gentle stream, she cannot restrain her course whatever the impediments, or even if the wild ocean is its ultimate destination. We are apt to prefer, nowadays, the fiction of love as a compatibility of temperaments. It is not more arbitrary or less wise of Shakespeare to imagine love as being other and maybe more than this. Proteus . . . seems to get more than he deserves: it could be parable, it could also be what happens, and not idly or ironically so: for give every man his deserts and who would escape whipping?—Is Proteus a worthless cad? We are not intended to take him as such. Instead we are to see him on the one hand as Julia's beloved, and on the other as Valentine's friend. . . . He is, of course, also what his name suggests: the shifting, inconstant stuff that gives redemptive love its task, its test, and its chance of triumph. Part of Shakespeare's moral optimism, if we call it that, is the belief that love is efficacious, that the beloved can be converted to the quality of the love bestowed. In the very final scene of the

play—which some have thought squalid, perfunctory, infamous, and maybe by another hand—the inmost meaning of love, as Shakespeare conceived it, is displayed. Proteus' conversion is effected by the shock of self-realisation, and by the realisation of the boundlessness of Valentine's friendship. Valentine's is the achieved 'freedom' of Love:

     And that my love may appear plain and free,
     All that was mine in Silvia I give thee.
                        [V. iv. 82-3]

Finally he sees again his "first best love", Julia, and the turn is completed:

          O heaven, were man,
     But constant, he were perfect. That one error
     Fills him with faults, makes him run through
          all th' sins.
     Inconstancy falls off ere it begins.
                      [V. iv. 110-13]

The forgiveness of Proteus is spontaneous, immediate, and totally effective. But, the moral optimist would say, that is what forgiveness has to be if it is to be at all.

Julia and Proteus, then, are the redeeming and the redeemable. They are balanced against Silvia and Valentine. Who is Silvia? Fortunately the answer is in the play:

     Who is Silvia? What is she,
       That all the swains commend her?
     Holy, fair, and wise is she:
       The heaven such grace did lend her,
     That she might admired be. . . .
                   [IV. ii. 39-43]

The song brings to a climax the fusion of religious and love imagery, which is a persistent feature of the play. Valentine and Silvia are the perfect marriage of true minds, and would be completely secure were it not for the hostility of their environment. But society (in the person of Silvia's father and an ageing suitor) and human protean unreliability admit impediments to their happiness; they are separated from each other, but finally, in the Forest, re-united. The Forest is the same as that Sir Satyrane inhabits in the *Faerie Queene:* it can be hazardous, but it can also give timely shelter to natural values which society, to its own impoverishment, often banishes. It is the Forest of Sherwood, and, of course, a fore-runner of Arden. It is from this Forest that love and friendship emerge restored.

Some maintain that the only interest *Two Gentlemen* retains is historical and accidental. In it Shakespeare assembled the 'props', and sketched the rudimentary form of his so-called 'romantic comedy'. 'Romantic', applied to Shakespeare, is always anachronistic, and 'comedy' too has undergone a semantic change which makes it an unreliable label. However, the opinion holds that *Two Gentlemen* is an imperfect attempt to write a 'mature' *Twelfth Night.* It seems to me that this view gets both plays exactly wrong. *Twelfth Night* borrows its transvestism from *Two Gentlemen,* just as *As You Like It* borrows the forest of exile. But the curious thing is, nothing else is handed over, and much is lost in between the two plays. We can admit that the story of *Two Gentlemen* is reducible to nonsense. . . . The 'characters', too, are incredible, as naturalistic portraits. We have seen, however, that the play has behind it an intrinsically interesting, un-trivial, and integrated world-view. The moral meanings are explicit in the poetry, and time and again given impressive expression. The comedy is devoid of drama and not very interested in fun. It exists to put before us, sometimes schematically, in plot, poetry, and *persona,* the cosmic dance of meeting and parting and meeting again, an optimistic view of things which assumes that every culpability can also be felicitious. At each significant station of the story as it winds or violently changes course there is an expository monologue or dialogue. In *Twelfth Night* we have nothing like this. The story there is not played against an important and charted moral background. Neither Orsino, Viola, Olivia, nor Sebastian, in any of their words or deeds, open windows on to the spiritual landscape of *Two Gentlemen* or the *Sonnets. Twelfth Night,* in fact, an audience can be forgiven for feeling, has to try and save itself by becoming a rather miserable and brutal kick at a major-domo who presumes to think (anachronistically) room at the top is available on the usual terms: the kick is delivered by below-stairs hangers-on of an above-stairs establishment. It seems to me that the internal world of *Two Gentlemen* is infinitely finer than that of *Twelfth Night*—though of course *Twelfth Night* has more 'fun', and, if we empty love of its meaning, more 'romance'. (pp. 317-21)

> John F. Danby, ''Shakespeare Criticism and 'Two
> Gentlemen of Verona','' *in* Critical Quarterly, *Vol.
> 2, No. 4, Winter, 1960, pp. 309-21.*

JOHN VYVYAN (essay date 1960)

[*Discerning Platonic and Christian elements in* The Two Gentlemen of Verona, *Vyvyan asserts that the play is ''a parable of love as a saving power.'' He contends that the comedy traces Valentine's and Proteus's gradual recognition of the ''essence of love,'' embodied in the two heroines, and demonstrates their achievement of self-knowledge, identity, and inner peace. He further avers that Valentine's attempt to control and purify the ''rebel powers'' in the forest, symbolic of those in his soul, is a quest for true perfection, contrasting him with Proteus, who betrays his true self for ''illusion'' and ''shadow.'' Vyvyan also considers the problematic final episode in keeping with Shakespeare's allegorical themes, and he closes his study by stressing the importance of reconciliation in* The Two Gentlemen of Verona, *maintaining that Shakespeare created a commendable but still inadequate illustration of ''the power of love'' to ''change discord into heavenly harmony.''*]

In *Love's Labour's Lost* Shakespeare took two activities, learning and loving; first, he displayed them, in superficial forms, as antagonistic; then, by deepening and expanding the meaning of each, he drew them together: at the end, the characters embark on a fresh course of study, which will be crowned by love. (p. 98)

In *The Two Gentlemen of Verona* he takes two qualities—this time, friendship and love. He exhibits them in opposition:

> —In love
> Who respects friend?
>
> [V. iv. 53]

And then, acting on principles that we will presently discuss, he resolves the conflict into the harmony of a new whole, ending with the climatic line:

> One feast, one house, one mutual happiness.
>
> [V. iv. 173]

Clearly, he is using the same method in both plays, and it is one he will not forget:

Act II. Scene iii. Crab and Launce. By Walter Crane (1894). The Department of Rare Books and Special Collections, The University of Michigan Library.

> —I would by contraries
> Execute all things—
>
> [*The Tempest,* II. i. 148-49]

that is, by bringing the contraries into a creative relationship all problems may be solved. From play to play, we shall watch the sphere of the self, or of self-knowledge, being expanded; and in time we shall be brought, with understanding, to the proposition that to be true to oneself makes all falsity impossible. . . . It is to this state of truth or constancy to the self and to love that Shakespeare is leading his characters. In this play, we have the line:

> O heaven, were man
> But constant, he were perfect!
>
> [V. iv. 110-11]

The idea is reiterated many times; and Shakespeare implies that when this condition is achieved, it will be reflected in the world. Cosmos is emergent from chaos first within and then without.

The play opens with two young men, bosom friends from childhood, who, for the first time in their lives, are about to part. Valentine is to set out for Milan, the purpose of his journey is to see the world: Proteus is to stay in Verona, because he will not leave his sweetheart. . . . Proteus is in love with Julia. It turns out to be an unreliable sort of love—although not irredeemable—that fails at the first temptation. Valentine, who has never been in love, is even more condescending on this, in fact, he is scornful:

> If haply won, perhaps a hapless gain;
> If lost, why then a grievous labour won . . .
> . . . by love the young and tender wit
> Is turn'd to folly . . .
> But wherefore waste I time to counsel thee . . .?
>   [I. i. 32-3, 47-8, 51]

We at once suspect, remembering *Love's Labour's Lost,* that the supercilious Valentine is about to be educated, that love will be the subject of his studies, and that at the end of the play Shakespeare will touch a deeper level than we expect. . . . That these guesses prove correct encourages confidence in the reliability of Shakespearean patterns. Here, once again, the false is to be contrasted with, and stripped from the true; and henceforth we should expect this from Shakespeare. He is always sensitive to the fact that every virtue has a corresponding falsity, masquerading under the same name; and we should constantly remind ourselves that when his characters speak of ''love'', ''honour'', ''nobility'', and so forth, we must measure their conceptions by his standard if we are to discover what he really intends. . . . To rely on habitual reactions will never do. And Shakespeare's own judgments do not rest on the conventional compromises, but on constancy to principles, by no means obvious, that we must try to ascertain.

We will follow the thread of Valentine's character first.

When he and Proteus part, Valentine is of the opinion that love is folly, ''one fading moment'' [I. i. 30] bought at a ridiculous price; and by implication, he rates his love-lorn friend a fool. When they meet again, in the second act, this time at Milan, Valentine's education has begun. He has fallen in love with Silvia. And he now candidly admits that it was he who was the fool. . . . This is progress, these are the proper sentiments. (pp. 98-101)

Valentine, in the second act, is now in the sonnetry and idolatry class, a most promising pupil. ''Call her divine!'' [II. iv. 147] he orders Proteus. And the highest honour he can invent for any other woman is:

> To bear my lady's train, lest the base earth
> Should from her vesture chance to steal a kiss,
> And, of so great a favour growing proud,
> Disdain to root the summer-swelling flower,
> And make rough winter everlastingly.
>   [II. iv. 159-63]

To which Proteus very justly answers:

> Why, Valentine, what braggardism is this?
>   [II. iv. 164]

But by Shakespeare's measure, Valentine is doing well; he is passing through a phase in which truth is compounded with nonsense; this is normal, and what matters is that he is nearer to truth now than he was in the previous act. But Shakespeare brings his characters to self-knowledge by putting them through a number of tests, and Valentine is about to be tested.

The Duke of Milan is Valentine's host and Silvia's father. He is an indispensable figure in their love-affair—but he forbids it: he favours Valentine's rival, Thurio. Sylvia loves Valentine and hates Thurio. We are in no doubt that the duke's attitude is wrong; but is Valentine therefore right to deceive a generous host and attempt to abduct his daughter? We will notice later how frequently in Shakespeare it is the duty of children to

rebel, in the right way, against their parents: quite often, the older generation represents the old law, which must be superseded by the new. But laudable rebellion is a fine art, and it does not extend to elaborate deception and a multitude of lies. (pp. 102-03)

[On his way to elope with Silvia, Valentine] is caught red-handed, rope-ladder and all. He is therefore banished by the duke. . . . [The] shock of it immediately increases Valentine's understanding of the true nature of love. . . . [The] heroine, according to Shakespeare's habitual allegory, is a love-symbol; and being so, she must of necessity coincide with a quality within the hero. More than to anything else, it is to this quality—love, as a standard in his own soul—that the hero must be constant. If he is not . . . he is lost. But he cannot be constant, understandingly, until he has realized love as a divine essence within. And Shakespeare uses his heroines to show us, in allegory the making of this discovery: he does so here, and he is still doing it, to take a single example, in *The Winter's Tale,* where Florizel says:

>   —I cannot be
> Mine own, or anything to any, if
> I be not thine—
>   [*The Winter's Tale,* IV. iv. 43-5]

This is a most important principle in Shakespeare; and in the soliloquy that follows Valentine's sentence of banishment, we see it clearly for the first time. Henceforth, if we bear this idea in mind, it will shed light on many an obscure situation. Valentine exclaims:

> —Silvia is myself: banished from her,
> Is self from self . . .
> She is my essence: and I leave to be,
> If I be not by her fair influence
> Fostered, illumined, cherished, kept alive.
>   [III. i. 172-73, 182-84]

It would seem to be Shakespeare's proposition here that love is the soul's essence, so that when it denies love, it denies its own being. And since his method is to show the hero making a gradual discovery of love and beauty—through the shadows to the reality—it is likely that he is thinking in terms of the Platonic ascent. (pp. 104-06)

That Shakespeare was acquainted with the current forms of Neo-Platonism is indubitable, it is probable that he knew a fair amount of pure Platonism as well, and it is being increasingly recognized that there is allegory in his plays. We must expect, then, that part of the allegory will yield to a Neo-platonic interpretation, although there are many other elements in it as well.

The opening scene of the fourth act is a highway running through a forest. Outlaws are lying in ambush. The banished Valentine, with his servant Speed, comes along the road, and the outlaws spring upon them. There is a brief parley. And it is soon evident that these outlaws are not the common robbers we expect:

> Know, then, that some of us are gentlemen,
> Such as the fury of ungoverned youth
> Thrust from the company of awful men.
>   [IV. i. 42-4]

And after a few more words, they make Valentine—a chance wayfarer entirely unknown to them—an astonishing offer:

>   —be the captain of us all:
> We'll do thee homage and be ruled by thee,
> Love thee as our commander and our king.

But if not:

> —thou diest!
>
> [IV. i. 63-6]

If we have a feeling for Shakespearean allegory, everything about this scene—which is quite unrealistic, but highly symbolic—suggests that there is a meaning below the surface.

Kingship or death: it is the alternative, in respect of the soul's inner kingdom, that Shakespeare unfailingly presents to us in his major plays. What the tragic hero does, as he yields to a series of temptations, is to lose, step by step, the lordship of his own soul:

> —and the state of man,
> Like to a little kingdom, suffers then
> The nature of an insurrection.
>
> [*Julius Caesar*, II. i. 67-9]

In this condition of inner turmoil, self-sovereignty is replaced by the fury of ungoverned passions; and the outcome, as Shakespeare invariably depicts it, is tragedy and death. Conversely, to enter the Shakespearean path of regeneration, the hero must gain command of himself. All Shakespearean drama is concerned with this, to him, fundamental problem of self-sovereignty. Those who achieve it—like the Duke of Vienna [in *Measure for Measure*] and Prospero [in *The Tempest*]—become, for that reason, something more than men. (pp. 107-08)

If this scene is a parable—and I believe Shakespeare put many parables into his plays—then it would seem that the forest is another version of the "naked hermitage" [V. ii. 795] of *Love's Labour's Lost*, or of "the life removed" [I. iii. 8] of *Measure for Measure*, or of the chapel of penitence in which Leontes [in *The Winter's Tale*] . . . learned how the tragic wound may be healed. Shakespeare never ran short of metaphors, but one clear conception is behind all these: a hero who is on the upgoing path must, at some time, spend a period in the wilderness; and the purpose of doing so is to gain self-knowledge, self-sovereignty, and a fuller realization of love. It may come to him as a penance imposed, or as a decision of his own, but come it will. If he presses through it successfully, he will be well on the way to being "a perfect man". (pp. 109-10)

If the forest does stand for the same conception as the "naked hermitage", then what of the outlaws, who spring upon the hero there? We notice, to begin with, that they are really gentlemen, and their background is much like Valentine's own. He assumes command of them, but remains constant in himself to his ideal of love. As a result of this the outlaws are pardoned at the end of the play, and all are restored, but still under Valentine's guidance, to their true estates. If this is a parable, then it is not very difficult to pierce. The outlaws must be the "rebel powers" that "array" the hero's soul. During his sojourn in the wilderness he has to face them, learn to know them for what they are, and control them. If he does not rule them, they will destroy him; but if he does, it will be for their salvation as well as his. For they are not presented to us as evils to be rooted out, but rather as true powers of the self which are either untamed, "as the fury of ungoverned youth" [IV. i. 43], or have run wild. It would seem as if the first purpose of the hero's penance is to control this unregenerate nature, to chasten, purify and restore the "rebel powers". It is not an easy thing to accomplish, as, in soliloquy, Valentine laments:

> These are my mates, that make their wills their law—
> —I have much to do
> To keep them from uncivil outrages.
>
> [V. iv. 14, 16-17]
>
> (pp. 110-11)

In the same soliloquy in which he tells of his struggle to keep his "mates" from uncivil outrage, he murmurs what is virtually a prayer:

> Repair me with thy presence, Silvia!
>
> [V. iv. 11]

And who is Silvia? All through, but particularly in this context, Silvia is a personification of Love or of the Platonic Beauty that is love's eternal goal. Valentine is passing, with success, something very like the test that, we may remember, was set to the King of Navarre:

> If frosts and fasts, hard lodging and thin weeds,
> Nip not the gaudy blossoms of your love,
> But that it bear this trial and last love,
> Then, at the expiration of the year,
> Come, challenge me, challenge me by these deserts,
> And, by this virgin palm now kissing thine,
> I will be thine.
>
> [*Love's Labour's Lost*, V. ii. 801-07]

Valentine is bearing a comparable trial and maintaining his love; and the reward is that his "prayer" is answered—Silvia joins him in the forest. If we may make an inference from the position Shakespeare takes up in later plays—in *Measure for Measure*, for example—then, having passed the test, Valentine ought to be, if not yet a perfect man, at least something above the ordinary. And in particular he ought to possess—on the analogy of the Duke of Vienna and Prospero—the power to make creative mercy effective. Perhaps, that is what Shakespeare is trying to demonstrate in the last scene. This *dénouement* has called forth a torrent of adverse criticism, and I think it likely that Shakespeare was the first person to recognize that it fails. But if our supposition is correct, that would be a minor matter: the significance would lie in the attempt. For the moment, however, we must leave Valentine in the forest. (pp. 112-13)

Proteus is the first sketch of a type of character that is of the highest importance in Shakespeare: the erring hero, who would, if strict justice were done to him, come to a tragic end; but who is, in the event, saved by Shakespearean justice. Shakespearean justice, as it appears in the great plays of healing, where tragedy is resolved, is a quality inseparable from love, of which the purpose is not the punishing, but the saving of the offender. This shines as a steady light throughout Shakespeare, and in this play we watch it being kindled.

At the opening, as we have seen, Proteus and Valentine, lifelong friends, part. Proteus, a "home-keeping youth" [I. i. 2], is held in Verona by an attachment that he supposes to be love. But it is worth noticing a remark that he lets fall, in the first scene:

> I am not Love.
>
> [I. i. 38]

This may be one of those subtle hints that Shakespeare likes to give to the heedful listener, akin to Iago's, "I am not myself" [*Othello*, I. i. 65]. We cannot feel sure that it is so, in such an early play; but when we have once established the special place of love and the self in Shakespeare's philosophy, and also noticed how fond he is of speaking *sotto voce* to those who have conditioned themselves to hear the remarks, then no speech of this kind can slip by unquestioned. And we may think back to it, when Valentine says of Silvia, who is certainly an allegorical figure of Love, "She is my essence" [III. i. 182]. Love is not—or, at least, not yet—of the essence in

Proteus. His is a counterfeit of the real thing. But the love of his sweetheart, Julia, is true: and it is Shakespeare's contention that there is an alchemical power in this that may transmute the counterfeit to gold.

Valentine has hardly left Verona when Proteus, most unwillingly, is also uprooted. His father ordains that he must travel:

> I have consider'd well his loss of time,
> And how he cannot be a perfect man,
> Not being tried and tutor'd in the world.
> > [I. iii. 19-21]

Once again, we have the theme of the "perfect man". And again it is made clear that perfection is not gained by being sheltered from temptation. *Constancy* is a key-word in this connection: we hear much of it in this play; and in *Measure for Measure* it is among the points made by the duke. Ultimately, the triumphing hero is seen to be constant to the highest quality in himself—"to thine own self be true" [*Hamlet*, I. iii. 78]; and correctly understood, that is the only thing that is needful. Shakespeare, as has been said, conceives this highest quality as love, symbolizes it by the heroine, and we may gauge the hero's progress by his relations with her. Inconstancy to the ideal is, therefore, the all-inclusive sin—"were man but constant, he were perfect" [V. iv. 110-11]. (pp. 113-15)

In spite of the disgraceful treachery that is to come, it is evident that we are intended to look on Proteus as kindly as we can. He turns out to be a young knave, but he is not a hardened villain; and his faults are mainly to be attributed to the uncertain weather of spring. That is the mood Shakespeare wishes to evoke. In point of fact, the later behaviour of Proteus is so caddish that it is difficult to feel indulgent. But I am only concerned with trying to establish what Shakespeare aimed at; to estimate the extent of his success in making the audience appreciate these aims is a different matter.

Proteus, then, is shipped off to Milan—"shipped" quite literally, an oddity I will not attempt to explain!—and when he gets there, Valentine introduces him to Silvia. In later work, Shakespeare would have presented this as a temptation scene; but that is a technique he has not yet developed. It is a test, none the less; and Proteus fails it completely. At sight of Silvia, Julia is forgotten; and he is infatuated by the true sweetheart of his best friend. (pp. 115-16)

If Shakespeare had been writing in one of the savage moods of his maturity, he might easily have drawn Proteus as a monster. Proteus betrays Valentine, cheats Thurio, deceives the duke, and does his best to seduce Silvia. How is it that he is not lost? There is a compound answer to this, and the part Valentine plays in it will be discussed when we come to the last scene; but the aspect of it that is shown to us first, exemplifies a principle that is constant to all Shakespearean salvation: the counteraction of Love. Just as, in *Measure for Measure,* the pleading of Mariana, Angelo's discarded sweetheart, is decisive in winning his reprieve from death, so now does Julia, the rejected, come to serve Proteus in disguise. . . . Shakespeare, with his extraordinary gift of weaving diverse threads into a single pattern, presents love-justice as a unity. Julia's constant love, and Valentine's "perfect" justice, work, though in appearance separately, in absolute accord. (pp. 117-18)

[When] Julia steps into the fourth act—always, we may remember, the love-act; and when Shakespeare puts music, two heroines and moonlight on to the stage at once, we may be quite certain that the power of love is about to change discords

into heavenly harmony. It may not succeed immediately, but the transmutation has begun.

> Who is Silvia? What is she,
> > That all our swains commend her?
> Holy, fair, and wise is she;
> > The heaven such grace did lend her—
> > [IV. ii. 39-42]

Perhaps Shakespeare is seeing Silvia as Beauty at this point—the Platonic Beauty in the sense in which the Renaissance had re-interpreted the idea—while Julia is Love. If so, they are essentially one; and certainly, from their first meeting, we find them in accord. (pp. 119-20)

Julia is naturally expecting to be welcomed by her lover: instead, at her first sight of him—herself standing in the shadows—she finds him serenading Silvia. Ostensibly, this is on Thurio's behalf; but the innkeeper, who has brought Julia to the spot, soon informs her of his infatuation. She does not disclose herself, but reveals her bitterness in several asides. It is a hard test of love, and worse will follow.

There is, however, one good portent: Silvia does not wish to be a rival. When Thurio and the musicians have gone, Silvia, from her tower-window, speaks to Proteus:

> —my will is even this:
> That presently you hie you home to bed.
> Thou subtle, perjured, false, disloyal man!
> > [IV. ii. 93-5]
> > (pp. 121-22)

The two heroines, although they do not know each other, are made allies by their constancy to love's ideal. But Proteus is unabashed, and begs Sylvia for her portrait. . . . Sylvia—for no other valid reason than to enable Shakespeare to enrich his allegory—consents:

> I am very loath to be your idol, sir;
> But since your falsehood shall become you well
> To worship shadows and adore false shapes,
> Send to me in the morning, and I'll send it.
> > [IV. ii. 128-31]

The theme of shadow-worship is one that is never done with in Shakespeare. No play is quite without it. He handles it lightly and tragically, in laughter and in despair; it is the foible of Armado [in *Love's Labour's Lost*], and the doom of Macbeth. His tragic heroes pay lip-service to spirit and truth, but they have lost consciousness of both; they adore false shapes, not dreaming that they are false, and that is their disaster. (pp. 122-23)

[In] her soliloquy that closes the [fourth] act, Julia says, as she picks up Silvia's portrait:

> Come, shadow, come, and take this shadow up,
> For 'tis thy rival.
> > [IV. iv. 197-98]

This is a most important clue to the meaning of the last scene of the play. Rivalry exists only between the shadows: unity resides in the reality behind them. In their inner nature, there is no division between Silvia and Julia. And Julia's soliloquy goes on:

> O thou senseless form,
> Thou shalt be worshipp'd, kiss'd, loved and adored!
> And, were there sense in his idolatry,
> My substance should be statue in thy stead.
> > [IV. iv. 198-201]

This is precisely what Silvia has said already. Therefore we shall not end among the dangers of the eternal triangle, but in the stability of an ideal square. (p. 125)

Before turning to the last act, we must give a glance at the minor characters. Proteus and Valentine are each attended by a comic servant—Launce and Speed respectively. And Launce is a servant to his own ungrateful servant, Crab. . . .

When Launce and Speed are discussing their masters, and in particular, whether the projected marriage between Proteus and Julia will take place, we have this dialogue:

> LAUNCE: Ask my dog: if he say ay, it will; if he say no, it will; if he shake his tail and say nothing, it will.
> SPEED: The conclusion is, then, that it will.
> LAUNCE: Thou shalt never get such a secret from me but by a parable.
> SPEED: 'Tis well that I get it so.
>
> [II. v. 35-41]

From this we might risk a guess that the parable is about Proteus and Julia; that there is a dog in it; and that if the secret is not too deep for Speed, we, too, should be able to unearth it. It is also clear that we are being invited to look to the dog. (p. 126)

Crab is little better than "ingrateful man"—and, incidentally, most undoglike. His resemblance to Proteus is remarkable. Proteus, too, in his present phase, is being "a dog in all things" [IV. iv. 13]; he, too, has thrust himself into the company of gentlemanlike dogs around the duke's table, and misbehaved there; and he would have stolen more from Silvia, had he been able, than a capon's leg. "O, 'tis a foul thing when a cur cannot keep himself in all companies!" [IV. ii. 9-10]. But there must be something about Crab and Proteus that is lovable and worth saving; and saved they are, by the "charity that suffereth long and is kind". There can be no further doubt that Launce and Julia both exemplify this quality, and Shakespeare proceeds to give us one of those neat tie-ups that are most satisfying. In [Act IV, Scene iv], where Julia is told to take her own ring and present it to Silvia, she remarks aside:

> How many women would do such a message?
>
> [IV. iv. 90]

It exactly corresponds to what Launce had said a few minutes earlier:

> How many masters would do this for his servant?
>
> [IV. iv. 29-30]

But Shakespeare, in all his work, never falters in the belief that the greatest in the kingdom is the servant of all—provided always that he serve for love. (pp. 129-30)

Critical opinion on the fifth act is nearly unanimous. . . . Certainly, this act, which in the form we have it contains only a hundred and seventy-three lines, must have been rather brutally cut, perhaps for some particular production, and that may account for much, but not for everything to which exception has been taken. But this criticism, however justifiable it may be, is based on the assumption that convincing characterization and a good *coup de théâtre* is Shakespeare's only aim. I hope I have convinced my readers that it is not. Shakespeare is writing an allegory as well as a play, neither is finished, and the conclusion must take account of both. I will not claim that this answers the objections, but only that it has been overlooked.

When drama is also allegory, compromise is inevitable: sometimes the one and sometimes the other will predominate. And when a scene in Shakespeare presents difficulties from the dramatic and psychological standpoints, we may suspect at once that the parable is being given special stress. This may account, in the present play, for Valentine's captaincy of the outlaws; and the last misdeed of which Launce accuses Crab is, as realism, incredible. Perhaps it will help us with the conclusion; but even if it does not, it must still be borne in mind.

At the beginning of the act, Silvia escapes, in the hope of joining Valentine. She is pursued. And after various confusions in the forest, she falls into the hands of Proteus—still attended by his "page". As Silvia is not to be won by fair words, Proteus threatens rape, and at that moment Valentine steps out from the trees:

> Ruffian, let go that rude uncivil touch!
>
> [V. iv. 60]

So far, so good. Weapons glint. The *coup de théâtre* is admirable. But what about the allegory? That requires a perfect ending, and the play has only a hundred and thirteen more lines to run. Shakespeare has undertaken to do a good deal; and before we blame him for failure it is fair to consider his problem. Julia set out for Elysium, and she is not to be disappointed. The saving power of constancy to love is to be demonstrated; and also, perhaps, that of creative mercy. Valentine is at least approaching the condition of being a "perfect man", and he must act accordingly. And hardest of all, love and friendship, in their ideal state, are to be shown as one. To do all of this in the space at his disposal is impossible, but Shakespeare attempts it—and in that lies the fascination of the scene. The first step is the repentance of Proteus:

> Forgive me, Valentine: if hearty sorrow
> Be a sufficient ransom for offence,
> I tender't here. I do as truly suffer
> As e'er I did commit.
>
> [V. iv. 74-7]

As it stands, it is perfunctory and unconvincing; but it is an abiding principle with Shakespeare that sorrow and suffering do ransom an offence, and later he works this out in detail—notably in *The Winter's Tale*. Valentine, being on the ascending path, *must* accept this: again, it is a Shakespearean principle. . . . Valentine does but announce this theme:

> Who by repentance is not satisfied
> Is not of heaven nor earth—
>
> [V. iv. 79-80]

Rejection of it, in Shakespeare, would indicate a hell-ward course. There may, also, be a passage of something more in Valentine's forgiveness—the power of creative mercy, but I will not press this point. So far, whether the act has been tampered with or not, its leading ideas are characteristically Shakespearean. But is this true of the couplet that has caused most of the trouble? Is there any inner necessity for Valentine to continue:

> And, that my love may appear plain and free,
> All that was mine in Silvia I give thee. . . .
>
> [V. iv. 82-3]

I have suggested that it is Shakespeare's intention to present [friendship and love] as a harmony. Of course, in this play, he failed to do so to the conviction of his audience; but the couplet, I believe, is related to the purpose. In later work, it is evident that he is aiming to make division grow together, not as a compromise, but perfectly. And that this thought was now in his mind, before he had the literary experience to make it comprehensible to anyone else, is suggested by the last lines of the play:

> —Our day of marriage shall be yours;
> One feast, one house, one mutual happiness.
>
> [V. iv. 72-3]

Harmony between the two heroines has already been established, and, clearly, we are meant to picture Valentine and Proteus, Silvia and Julia enjoying a happiness quite out of the ordinary. It may be that our reason is confounded by the contemplation of it, and that on the way there our sensibilities have been shocked. But this only proves what we might have expected: Shakespeare, at this stage, was unable to give adequate expression to his immense ideas. It is not his intention merely to endorse a familiar romantic standard: he is seeking a new ethic, one that will be conducive and appropriate to another golden age. In this scene he is not contrasting friendship with love. . . . nor evaluating one in terms of the other: he is uniting them. (pp. 130-34)

[Shakespeare] assumes that love is the essence of the self, and that perfect love is therefore a recognition, in this innermost sphere, of identity. He has already announced this theme in, "She is my essence" [III. i. 182]. He returns to it in future plays; and in *The Phoenix and the Turtle,* carries it as far, perhaps, as language ever will:

> So they love'd, as love in twain
> Had the essence but in one;
> Two distincts, division none:
> Number there in love was slain.
>
> [*The Phoenix and the Turtle*, 25-8]

At this level, obviously, distinctions of sex are less than irrelevant—they do not exist; and some, at least, of the sex ambiguities in Shakespeare may be better understood if we bear this conception in mind.

Perhaps we may yet find an acceptable meaning in the words of Valentine:

> All that was mine in Silvia I give thee.
>
> [V. iv. 83]

But again we must raise the question, Who is Silvia? And again I suggest that, in Shakespeare's mind, she is more than a girl in a play; she is also a symbol of the eternal Beauty. No man possesses that for himself alone. Valentine has won his part in it by merit: on Proteus, it is bestowed as friendship's perfect gift. (pp. 134-35)

*John Vyvyan, " 'The Two Gentlemen of Verona',"
in his* Shakespeare and the Rose of Love: A Study
of the Early Plays in Relation to the Medieval Philosophy of Love, *Chatto & Windus, 1960, pp. 98-135.*

BERTRAND EVANS (essay date 1960)

[*In two studies of Shakespearean drama,* Shakespeare's Comedies
(1960) *and* Shakespeare's Tragic Practice *(1979), Evans examines
what he calls Shakespeare's use of "discrepant awareness." He
claims that Shakespeare's dramatic technique makes extensive
use of "gaps" between the different levels of awareness the characters and audience possess concerning the circumstances of the
plot. In the following excerpt from his* Shakespeare's Comedies,

*Evans outlines the complex structure of shifting advantages and
disadvantages in awareness among the characters of* The Two
Gentlemen of Verona, *discerning at least six "notable secrets"
and four levels of perception. Although nearly all the characters
are alternately aware and ignorant of the intentions of the others
and of the circumstances of the plot, the critic avers, Julia gains
the "highest vantage-point" next to that of the audience.*]

Whereas *The Comedy of Errors* afforded for exploitation only one discrepancy in awareness, all Ephesus being denied and ourselves provided with one all-important fact, *The Two Gentlemen of Verona* exploits multiple gaps that involve no fewer than six notable secrets. The first comedy used no deliberate 'practisers'; the second has almost as many as it has participants. In *The Comedy of Errors* a single, initial expository scene sufficed to establish the single, static situation, open the single gap between awarenesses, and sustain our single advantage over participants for all of five acts; in *The Two Gentlemen of Verona* the first two acts are used to create the principal situation and open the main gaps, and thereafter repeated expository passages, including asides and soliloquies, are added to keep the circle of our vision complete. Whereas in the earlier play the participants remained equally ignorant of the situation, here we share with one participant our advantage over others with respect to one part of the situation, and with another participant our advantage with respect to another part of it. In *The Comedy of Errors* the single exploitable gap lay between all the participants on the one side and ourselves on the other. But in *The Two Gentlemen* Shakespeare makes use of differences in awareness between participant and participant, besides those between participants and ourselves: the fact represents a great step from the earlier comedy toward the mature ones.

All the named persons of *The Two Gentlemen* except the clowns—who here as hereafter, like the heroines of comedy and the villains of tragedy, are commonly immune to the condition of unawareness—stand at one time or another ignorant of some relevant fact. On the other hand, each of these persons except Thurio sometime holds advantage over another participant; each, that is to say, serves either as a secret-holder or as a perpetrator of practices on others. We are provided with advantage over some participant or other during nine of nineteen scenes—a much lower proportion than in *The Comedy of Errors*.

In summary, although alike in that both make large use of exploitable discrepancies in awareness, the two plays contrast markedly in the complexity which characterizes their paraphernalia of exploitation. The first is Roman in this respect, the second Elizabethan, elaborate. *The Two Gentlemen* is clearly on the high road to *Twelfth Night*.

Although Shakespeare does not begin until the third act to exploit the main discrepancies, two scenes in Act II deserve notice as the first in which we hold advantage over participants and also as prophetic of greater scenes in later plays. In II. i. we share with Silvia and Speed an advantage over Valentine. 'Last night', says Valentine to his servant, 'she enjoin'd me to write some lines to one she loves' [II. i. 87-8]. Since we have not yet seen Silvia or otherwise been prepared, we cannot know just yet that her request is in fact a way of hinting her interest in Valentine and of inviting him to woo her. Indeed, it is uncertain at what exact point in the ensuing dialogue the dramatist intends us to catch on. . . . [But by] the time of Silvia's final speech, certainly, we have gained advantage over Valentine; even Speed, by this time, perceives the truth, for he remarks, aside, 'And yet you will; and yet another "yet" '

[II. i. 120]. But Valentine—true prototype of heroes and secondary heroes of comedies to come . . .—does not glimpse it, either here or during the next eighty lines, though Speed exhausts himself with pointing out the truth. . . . With this device Silvia becomes the first practiser in the play, Valentine the first victim whose ignorance is exploited for comic effect.

The second scene in which we hold advantage ends Act II. Here the discrepancy in awareness is exploited not for loud laughter, as in the scene just noted and as throughout *The Comedy of Errors,* but for subtler effect of a kind Shakespeare would seek again and again by means of adroit manipulation of the awarenesses. It will be well, therefore, to examine in detail this first of a frequent kind.

This is a scene of ninety lines between Julia and her waiting woman, Lucetta. It is primarily expository, existing to inform us of Julia's intention to dress in weeds 'As may beseem some well-reputed page' [II. vii. 43] and seek out Proteus in Milan. . . . Viewed only in its own light, with nothing before or after, it would be a sparkling scene, its qualities of love, youth, wit, and lyricism rendering it pleasing and dramatic. But it is not to be viewed only in its own light.

Shakespeare has equipped our minds with special knowledge just before he shows this scene. The scene just preceding it, set in Milan, is all composed of a sharply pointed soliloquy uttered by Proteus, in which he expresses determination to commit 'three fold perjury' [II. vii. 5], by leaving Julia, loving Silvia, and betraying Valentine. The lines of this soliloquy are emphatic, as though the dramatist meant their impression to be indelible:

> I to myself am dearer than a friend,
> For love is still most precious in itself;
> And Silvia—witness Heaven, that made her fair!—
> Shows Julia but a swarthy Ethiope.
> I will forget that Julia is alive,
> Rememb'ring that my love to her is dead,
> And Valentine I'll hold an enemy,
> Aiming at Silvia as a sweeter friend.
>
> [II. vi. 23-30]

Immediately the scene shifts to Verona, where we here Julia asking Lucetta to tell her 'How, with my honour, I may undertake / A journey to my loving Proteus' [II. vii. 6-7]. Proteus's soliloquy inevitably casts a special light over what follows—a light which is surely as much a part of the total scene as the dialogue itself. Julia's expression of devotion to Proteus, the merriment as the girls plan her costume, Lucetta's doubts and Julia's certainties—our view of all this is conditioned by Proteus's soliloquy; seen by a double light, its own and that from Proteus's soliloquy, the whole takes on a richness which, through inferior to that of the great scenes of later comedies, is yet precious enough. It is not merely for the bold flashes of irony that starkly outline the gap between Julia's awareness and ours—

> But truer stars did govern Proteus' birth;
> His words are bonds, his oaths are oracles,
> His love sincere, his thoughts immaculate,
> His tears pure messengers sent from his heart,
> His heart as far from fraud as heaven from earth.
>
> [II. vii. 74-8]

—that the dramatic effect is notable; flashes of irony are the most spectacular but not always the richest effects produced by exploitation of discrepant awarenesses. In the fuller scenes of mature comedies it will be appropriate to distinguish the subtler, pervasive effects from the flashier surface manifestations. It may suffice to say here only that the Julia–Lucetta scene, exhibited under the special light of Proteus's soliloquy, anticipates these finer effects of later scenes.

In the scene just reviewed our advantage owes simply to the device of scene-placement, the dramatist having immediately preceded the particular action by a speech calculated to cast a transforming light on it. The deliberateness of this placement is itself noteworthy. The soliloquy spoken by Proteus could easily have been placed not to precede but to follow the Julia-Lucetta scene. . . . Again, the soliloquy could readily have been incorporated in Proteus's earlier soliloquy which closes II. iv, where it would have joined on smoothly. Either of these placements would have been less awkward than that which in fact Shakespeare chose. But had he placed the soliloquy after rather than before the Julia-Lucetta scene, we should have lacked its special light as we watched that scene; coming afterward, it would of course have cast some light back upon the scene already played, and in retrospect we might have caught a little of the irony of Julia's lines. *But almost invariably Shakespeare preferred to project light forward upon a scene to be played rather than to cast it backward on action already past.* On the other hand, he regularly avoided setting his light-casting scene too far in advance of the action it should illuminate, lest intervening action blur the effect. . . . Since, thus, Julia was to say 'tell me some good means / How, with my honour, I may undertake / A journey to my loving Proteus', Shakespeare's method required that we hear Proteus say—neither afterwards, nor several scenes before, but immediately before—'I will forget that Julia is alive'.

Dramatically the most significant speech in the play, Proteus's light-casting second soliloquy is indispensable both to our view of the Julia-Lucetta scene and to our view of the three subsequent acts. It contributes greatly to the disposition of awarenesses with which Act III opens—the first truly complex disposition that Shakespeare had attempted in comedy. Excepting the clowns, all persons who take part in Act III are ignorant of one or another crucial fact of the situation. Moreover, the participants are stationed on different levels of awareness, some higher, some lower, rising from Thurio at the bottom to Proteus at the top. Excepting Thurio, every principal person attempts deception, with Proteus as the out-topping practiser. It is the Duke who stands on the lowest level when the act opens, as Proteus, feighing reluctance, exposes Valentine's elopement plan. . . . Proteus speaks truthfully in that Valentine does intend to carry off Silvia—but the Duke is nevertheless deceived because he knows nothing of the motives which Proteus exhibited to us in that same indispensable soliloquy which earlier gave us advantage over Julia. So the Duke thanks Proteus, and, himself unwitting, lays a trap for the unsuspecting Valentine, who, being practised on by one who is himself ignorant, accordingly replaces the Duke on the lowest level of awareness. Yet Valentine, entering immediately after Proteus has exposed the elopement plan, supposes himself to occupy a vantage point above the Duke's, and, knowing nothing of Proteus's practices, supposes that no point higher than his own exists. Hiding beneath his coat the corded ladder he expects to use, he is privileged, as he imagines, to relish his advantage. With Silvia's image in his mind and the ladder under his cloak, being asked how one may woo, win, and wed 'a lady of Verona here' [III. i. 81] whom the Duke pretends to affect, he replies boldly, describing the details of reaching her chamber 'aloft, far from the ground, / And built so shelving that one cannot climb it / Without apparent hazard of his life'—

> Why then, a ladder, quaintly made of cords,
> To cast up, with a pair of anchoring hooks,
> Would serve to scale another Hero's tower.
>
> [III. i. 114-19]

Such a ladder, he brazenly suggests, might be hidden under just such a cloak as his own. The cat-and-mouse game here played between Proteus's two mice, each supposing himself the cat, extends through eighty-five lines, until the Duke snatches off Valentine's cloak and exposes the ladder and a sonnet to Silvia. With that act, of course, which equalizes the awarenesses of the two, the main exploitable discrepancy on which depend the effects of the scene vanishes, leaving only Proteus's unsuspected vantage-point above them, and above all others.

Or so Proteus supposes. Throughout Act III, like a minor Iago [in *Othello*], he overpeers, deceives, and manipulates Valentine, the Duke, and Thurio. In the dialogue that follows the Duke's banishment of Valentine, Proteus consoles his friend, brings him the latest news, advises him, seems solicitous for his safety, offers to escort him to the city-gate, and, with Valentine gone, he turns his attention to stealing Silvia under the very auspices of the Duke and Thurio. As though reluctant, he promises to slander Valentine, and, as he 'unwinds' Silvia's former love, promises 'to bottom it' on Thurio. The Duke and Thurio urge him on in perfect confidence, for, as the Duke says,

> . . . we know, on Valentine's report,
> You are alredy Love's firm votary
> And cannot soon revolt and change your mind.
>
> [III. ii. 57-9]

Thus throughout Act III Proteus rides high over the others, exulting in his position, practising on them all. But even as the Julia-Lucetta scene which ends Act II is changed by Proteus's soliloquy which immediately precedes it, so the effect of Act III is transformed by the Julia-Lucetta scene. For while we watch Proteus's confident manipulation of Valentine, the Duke, and Thurio, we hold an advantage that makes his villainy laughable rather than dangerous: we know that as he is making his triply treacherous play for Silvia, Julia, habited like 'some well-reputed page' [II. vii. 43], is on the road to Milan. Though still ignorant of Proteus's duplicity, she must surely discover it before Proteus learns that all his passes are observed. *The heroines of Shakespeare's comedies either hold from the outset, or very shortly gain, the highest vantage-point in their worlds.* Julia is the first of these heroines, and Proteus, from our point of view, can appear only a somewhat taller mouse than his own dupes, Valentine, the Duke, and Thurio.

In Act IV, still working his imagined advantage, Proteus continues his successful practice on the dull Thurio, but fails miserably in his attempts to deceive the heroines. From any point of view, perhaps, but certainly from that of the management of awareness, the finest scene of this act is the serenade of Silvia, ostensibly for Thurio's but in reality for Porteus's own purposes. . . . [With] great shrewdness, Shakespeare has made it virtually impossible for us to lay aside our awareness of the total situation while we hear the song, for he has opened the scene with a new soliloquy which prods our recollection of Proteus's perfidy. We are thus prompted to hear the song not in itself alone, but in its special meanings for the participants who hear it, and particularly we are kept mindful of Valentine, who, though absent, has with Julia the keenest interest in any

wooing of Silvia by Proteus. To Thurio, quite oblivious, nothing is apparent in the situation or the song itself except what is obvious—and quite wrong: it seems to him that his own suit to Silvia is being forwarded. To Proteus, gloating in his sense that he alone comprehends all that is happening, the song is a device for betraying everyone and winning Silvia for himself. To the Host, to whom the details of the situation are quite irrelevant, it is only a lovely song in the night. To Silvia, while the music plays, it is hardly more than a flattering serenade for which she thanks the unknown musicians. But when she hears Proteus speak, her quick wit catches the full import:

> Thou subtle, perjur'd, false, disloyal man!
> Think'st thou I am so shallow, so conceitless,
> To be seduced by thy flattery,
> That hast deceiv'd so many with thy vows?
>
> [IV. ii. 95-8]

But what, now, is it to Julia? It is her presence, 'unobserved, in boy's clothes', that most transforms the scene. Like Silvia, she catches the significance of the song, which advises her of Proteus's treachery with jolting abruptness. . . . Her discovery raises her abruptly to our level of awareness. Unobserved, she has observed Proteus's passes, heard his lies, recognized Silvia's integrity, and at the end of the scene is quite ready—like her very capable heroinely successors—to use her advantage for victory: 'Pray you, where lies Sir Proteus?' [IV. ii. 136]. It is not she, but Proteus, suddenly the hunted rather than the hunter, who is now to be pitied. Fallen from top place in the scheme of awarenesses, he is lost and does not know it.

The inferiority of his position is conspicuous in IV. ii, when, oblivious, he dispatches his disguised and watchful mistress to woo Silvia for him—sending a ring that Julia had once given him. If Julia's situation is hardly a happy one, yet neither is it desperate. Her vision has full sweep; she is perfect mistress of her situation, and knows it. So absolute is her advantage that she can pity her prodigal lover, who, in confident obliviousness, has chosen an inappropriate love-emissary.

In his relation to Julia, then, Proteus the practiser has become the practisee, she the practiser: he is under her eye, his waywardness observed, his duplicity exposed. In relation to Silvia he is not better off. She has recognized and castigated his hypocrisy from the first. And now, immediately before the scene in which Proteus sends Julia to woo Silvia, Shakespeare has set a scene which lights the latter and displays a further depth in Proteus's unawareness. For in the preceding scene Silvia tells us that she will go to find Valentine in Mantua, 'where I hear he makes abode' [IV. iii. 23]. The true position of Proteus, then, is hardly enviable: supposing himself the master practiser with all strings in hand, he sends as love-envoy his own mistress, who can cross him at need; and she to whom the messenger is sent has already arranged to leave the city. The case of Proteus, hero bent on making a villain of himself, is typical: in the comedies, villainy can but peep at what it would, for it is circumscribed and rendered impotent, if not ridiculous, by the bright-eyed heroines who with their superior awareness control everything in this woman's world.

The gap between Proteus's awareness and ours continues as the principal exploitable condition during Act V. Here not only is Julia constantly at his elbow, her disguised presence reminding us of the true state of things, but, within this situation, Shakespeare contrives to set him at a further disadvantage in relation to both Silvia and Valentine. Act V, ii, when Proteus and Thurio discuss Silvia while Julia speaks 'asides', is noteworthy as showing Shakespeare's first use of four simultaneous levels of awareness. At the top is our own awareness, packed with all the facts of the situation: that Silvia has fled the court (as the dramatist, taking no chances with our forgetfulness, has just reminded us in the preceding scene); that Proteus's page, 'Sebastian', is in fact his betrothed Julia; that Proteus supposes himself to have deceived Julia, the Duke, Valentine, and Thurio in his wooing of Silvia and that he is now in the act of deceiving Thurio by reporting his progress with Thurio's love suit. On the level just below ours stands Julia, possessed of all our facts but one: that Silvia had fled the court. Below Julia is Proteus, who is ignorant that Silvia has gone, ignorant that Julia is beside him, and aware only that Thurio is deceived. And at the bottom is Thurio, who here as before and after is wrong about everything. The dialogue which exploits the gaps between these levels is itself not so remarkable as is this first appearance of the stair-stepped structure of awarenesses which becomes a fixture in the climactic scenes of subsequent comedies.

In the final scene of the play the disposition and uses of awareness again significantly mark the direction of Shakespeare's development. The preparation of our minds for this scene was begun far, far back—when Julia first took up her boy's masquerade. It continued through to Act IV, when Valentine became the outlaws' captain on his own terms:

> I take your offer and will live with you,
> Provided that you do no outrages
> On silly women or poor passengers.
>
>   [IV. i. 68-70]

When in IV. iii, therefore, fleeing the court to seek Valentine in Mantua, Silvia fears for her safety—'And, for the ways are dangerous to pass, / I do desire thy worthy company' [IV. iii. 245]—we have had reason enough to know that this forest is safe for her. Even so, in the third scene of Act V, when she is caught by outlaws, the dramatist—making doubly sure that we shall feel no alarm for Silvia's safety—again reminds us that no harm can befall her; for in the first line of the scene the First Outlaw, struggling with his captive, commands her, 'Be patient; we must bring you to our captain' [V. iii. 2]—who, of course, can be none but Valentine. When Proteus snatches Silvia from the outlaws, it is noteworthy that Shakespeare neither shows her in his company—more dangerous to her than the outlaws—nor even lets us know that he has taken her, until we have again been assured that all is well. The final scene opens with Valentine's brief soliloquy which ends abruptly at the approach of Proteus, Silvia, and Julia: 'Withdraw thee, Valentine; who's this comes here?' [V. iv. 18]. And thereafter, lest the excitement of threatened violence to Silvia make us forget Valentine's comforting presence, Shakespeare has him speak an 'aside' to remind us that he is at hand, hearing, observing, armed, and ready to act.

Once more, then, in this final moment, it is this comedy's eager but thwarted representative of villainy who stands in the inferior place, unwittingly circumscribed and impotent. Proteus is doubly, pitifully unaware: for not only is Valentine, Silvia's betrothed, hidden within a sword's length of him, but also, at his side, disguised, is his own betrothed. When, therefore, rebuffed, he turns savage and seizes Silvia with 'I'll force thee yield to my desire' [V. iv. 59], we perceive that any real peril in the situation is his, not hers. For Silvia, knowing no more than Proteus of the presence of Julia and Valentine and accordingly in mortal terror, the truth apparent to us is much better than she imagines; for Proteus it is far worse. Hemmed in, he can only expose himself to humiliation. Such is always

the plight of the villain in the comedies: as Proteus in *The Two Gentlemen of Verona*, so also Shylock in *The Merchant of Venice*, Don John in *Much Ado about Nothing*, and Angelo in *Measure for Measure*. Not only cannot villainy harm innocence; it is even prevented from doing irreparable harm to itself. (pp. 9-19)

Bertrand Evans, "Here Sit I in the Sky: First Explorations," in his Shakespeare's Comedies, *Oxford at the Clarendon Press, Oxford, 1960, pp. 1-32.*

DEREK TRAVERSI   (essay date 1960)

[*Traversi, a British scholar, has written a number of books on Shakespeare's plays, including* An Approach to Shakespeare *(1938),* Shakespeare: The Last Phase *(1954),* Shakespeare: From "Richard II" to "Henry V" *(1957),* Shakespeare: The Early Comedies *(1960), and* Shakespeare: The Roman Plays *(1963). In the introduction to the first of these studies, Traversi proposed to focus his interpretation of the plays on "the word," stating that the experience which forms the impetus to each of Shakespeare's dramas "will find its most immediate expression in the language and verse." In the following excerpt, Traversi places* The Two Gentlemen of Verona *in its relation to Shakespeare's later comedies, claiming that it is the first of many works to explore the theme of appearance and reality; he adds that it is also Shakespeare's earliest attempt to employ a literary convention "to attain, beyond convention itself, a position from which excess, self-ignorance and self-indulgence have been eliminated." The critic examines such elements as the conventional, artificial behavior of Valentine and Proteus, the comic interludes of the servants, and—especially—the female characters' "firm and clear-eyed view of reality," all of which serve to undercut the romantic ideal of love presented in the play. Traversi maintains that* The Two Gentlemen of Verona, *despite its shortcomings, remains an important work in the Shakespearean canon, for like the later comedies it aims to reestablish the bounds of reason in love, "to free valid human attachments from excess and emptiness, restoring them to a sane and balanced conception of life."*]

The Two Gentlemen of Verona, which may have been written after *The Comedy of Errors* and *The Taming of the Shrew*, has some claim to be considered Shakespeare's most tedious play. It is more profitable, however, to see it as standing between these early exercises in comic realism and *A Midsummer Night's Dream*, to think of Shakespeare as finding that he had, for the moment, exhausted the possibilities of realistic comedy and popular farce and turning to romantic convention in a first, and very imperfect, effort to see how far its various themes could be used as a reflection of some aspects of real life. (p. 18)

The central theme of the play is, for the first of many occasions, the difference between appearance and reality, what seems and what is. Anticipations of this subject can be found in *The Taming of the Shrew*, in Sly's transformation and in the behaviour of the contrasted lovers and their equally contrasted mistresses; but here the entire conception is made to rest upon it. Valentine, who begins by repudiating romantic love in the person of his friend Proteus . . ., ends by falling a victim to it; Proteus, who declares himself as the play opens 'a votary to fond desire', whose heart is 'sick with thought' [I. i. 52, 69], ends by deserting the object of his passion and by planning to betray his friend. Thus contrasted, each serves to provide by implication a comment upon the other, and does indeed do so on occasion explicitly. Thus, when Valentine has so far fallen a victim to the ill he affected to despise as to invite Proteus to call Silvia 'divine', the latter answers 'I will not flatter her' [II. iv. 148], and when he falls further into the idealistic excess of 'dignifying' Proteus' own mistress Julia with

> this high honour—
> To bear my lady's train, lest the base earth
> Should from her vesture chance to steal a kiss,
> [II. iv. 158-60]

his friend repudiates these high-flown words as so much empty 'braggartism'. Yet this same realism is in turn exposed when Proteus himself comes to covet the love of that very Silvia whom he formerly upbraided his friend for loving and for whose sake he becomes ready to inflict the deepest of 'private wounds' upon his life-long associate.

The point thus made is developed throughout the action, tediously indeed and often inexpertly, but with some consistency. Valentine, having once fallen a victim to the passion he began by so confidently despising, expresses his new sentiments with characteristic excess:

> why, man, she is mine own;
> And I as rich in having such a jewel
> As twenty seas, if all their sand were pearl,
> The water nectar, and the rocks pure gold.
> [II. iv. 168-71]

Proteus, on the other hand, as he finds out that 'one nail by strength drives out another' [II. iv. 193], shows the beginnings of psychological analysis. 'Love bade me swear, and love bids me forswear': 'Unheedful vows may heedfully be broken' [II. vi. 6, 11] as he puts it in soliloquy; and the speech, as it proceeds, develops into a certain significant complexity:

> I cannot leave to love, and yet I do;
> But there I leave to love where I should love.
> Julia I lose, and Valentine I lose:
> If I keep them, I needs must lose myself;
> If I lose them, thus find I by their loss
> For Valentine, myself, for Julia, Silvia.
> I to myself am dearer than a friend,
> For love is still most precious in itself.
> [II. vi. 17-24]

The effort to make Proteus' transformation credible, to relate it to some dramatically plausible interpretation of his motives, makes itself felt in such lines as these. Working through the artificiality of the literary conceit, it aims at pressing that artifice into the service of a rudimentary analysis. The intention is finally that of the exposure of egoism. Precisely because Proteus can regard it as axiomatic that 'I to myself am dearer than a friend', he can find in love an emotion 'most precious in itself' and is ready to seek self-gratification through betrayal and abasement. Though we shall scarcely find him convincing as a human being, we may feel that the very existence in the play of a character who thus exposes his inner contradictions represents a meaningful irruption of reality into the closed world of literary convention which provided it with its point of departure.

It is significant, in this connection, that this same Proteus, ready as he is to carry egoism to the point of betrayal, has at his fingertips, when occasion demands, the most far-fetched expressions of romantic idealism. These he uses, most typically, to advance his own cause with Silvia under the guise of advising the aged Sir Thurio how to make his own preposterous claim:

> Say that upon the altar of her beauty
> You sacrifice your tears, your sighs, your heart:
> Write till your ink be dry, and with your tears
> Moist it again; and frame some feeling line
> That may discover such integrity; . . .
> [III. ii. 72-6]

It is already characteristic of what will come to be Shakespeare's distinctive comic method that this, which can be read as one of the play's more distinguished expressions of emotion, is at the same time a revelation of the limitations of the romantic attitude to love. Proteus, in recommending the writing of 'some feeling line' which will produce an illusion of 'integrity' in the being to whom it is addressed, reveals by implication the artifice that underlies his 'dire-lamenting elegies', the 'deploring dumps' [III. ii. 81, 84] of his self-conscious melancholy. Similarly, in the immeasurably finer context of *Twelfth Night,* Orsino, using a similar poetic idiom, will at once feel and indulge feeling, combine in his own moody self-awareness the related attractions and shortcomings of romantic love.

Other devices, some of them already familiar from the preceding plays, contribute in a similar way to the complete effect. Just as the behaviour and comments of Valentine and Proteus throw light upon what is partial or false in their respective attitudes, so does the comic prose of the servants provide, much as it had already done in *The Comedy of Errors,* a realistic judgement on the behaviour of their masters. When Speed says to Valentine 'though the chameleon love can feed on the air, I am one that am nourished by my victuals, and would fain have meat' [II. i. 172-74], the crudity with which he states his position may conceal from us a rejection of abstraction and artifice in their relation to what are, after all, solid human realities. A similar effect of contrast can be detected in the comments of the women who come out of this comedy so notably better than the men who respectively idealize or betray them. When Julia speaks of Proteus' 'divine perfection' and of herself as 'a true-devoted pilgrim' [II. vii. 9] in the name of love at the very moment when he is engaged in betraying her, the waiting-woman Lucetta is perfectly aware that she is speaking 'above the bounds of reason' [II. vii. 23]; and it is to re-establish these bounds, to free valid human attachments from excess and emptiness, restoring them to a sane and balanced conception of life, that this play may be said, however clumsily and imperfectly, to aim.

The Two Gentlemen of Verona sets out, in short, to use convention to attain, beyond convention itself, a position from which excess, self-ignorance and self-indulgence have been eliminated. The depths to which these faults may lead human beings can be glimpsed occasionally in the later scenes of the play. When Proteus, knowing his behaviour to be ignoble sinks into the degradation which his unrequited passion implies, he tells us, again in soliloquy, that Silvia

> bids me think how I have been forsworn
> In breaking faith with Julia whom I loved: . . .
> Yet, spaniel-like, the more she spurns my love,
> The more it grows, and fawneth on her still.
> [IV. ii. 10-11, 14-15]

'Spaniel-like': 'fawneth': Proteus could have used no more characteristic Shakespearean images of· abasement and self-disgust to express his predicament. His situation is one which, so the play would seem to suggest, proceeds from a conception of love as empty in content as it is artificial in expression.

It is left to Silvia and Julia, who anticipate in this the heroines of later comedies, to oppose to corrupt convention their own firm and clear-eyed view of reality. Silvia denounces Proteus as a 'subtle, perjured, false, disloyal man' and upbraids him roundly for thinking that she can be

> so shallow, so conceitless
> To be seduced by thy flattery;
> [IV. ii. 96-7]

and Julia, reading into Proteus' devotion to her rival's painted image a reflection of the confused values which have led to her tragedy. turns her meditation into a denunciation of the idolatry which love of this kind implies:

> O thou senseless form,
> Thou shalt be worshipp'd, kiss'd, loved, and adored
> And, were there sense in his idolatry,
> My substance should be statue in thy stead.
> [IV. iv. 198-201]

For this reason the best-known lines in the play, though sung on behalf of Sir Thurio in his vain effort to seduce Silvia from her true devotion, contain a truth which transcends their setting in convention and aristocratic intrigue:

> Who is Silvia? what is she,
>   That all our swains commend her?
> Holy, fair, and wise is she;
>   The heaven such grace did lend her,
>   That she might admired be. . . .
> [IV. ii. 39-43]

'Holy, fair, and wise' we may feel to be terms which surpass in their full meaning anything that the play can offer, which not even the integrity shown by this heroine in her moments of tribulation can fully match. They belong, indeed, to a kind of idealization which is of its essence literary, and partakes of the limitations of mere literature; but such significance as they have lies in the dramatist's effort to give them through Silvia herself a foundation in flesh and blood, to show them as operative in terms of real humanity and normal behaviour. This assertion of feminine common-sense and good faith represents one of the points in which this pale comedy most closely anticipates the future.

The Two Gentlemen of Verona, therefore, needs to be seen, if it is to come to life at all, as an early experiment in the use of convention for positive ends. As such it points to later and more successful developments. Many devices used in later comedies—the disguising of her sex as woman's resourceful response to betrayal, the relation between the intriguing villain and the friend who unwisely trusts him, even (for the brief moment of the bandit episode at the end of the play) the contrast between court artifice and the simple life of the forest—appear here for the first time. We must see in them, beyond such obvious absurdities as Valentine's off-hand renunciation, in the last scene, of his love for the benefit of none other than his betrayer, a first essay in the more meaningful patternings of the later comedies. In these, conventions not altogether dissimilar, though immensely deepened and developed, become instruments for the exploration of human relationships, more especially in love, and for the expression of a true attitude to love itself: an attitude in which poetry and realism, romance and comedy, are variously combined. Although it would be dangerous to read too much into this early piece, it is worth

noting that it ends, like its greater successors, with a reconciliation of conflicting opposites, the uniting of its lovers and the return of its outlaws to civilized and social living: a reconciliation the unreality of which stresses indeed the inadequate use to which its conventions are put, but which has possibilities of development once the dramatic, poetic, and human contents of the action have been simultaneously expanded. (pp. 19-25)

*Derek Traversi, "'The Two Gentlemen of Verona',"
in his* William Shakespeare, the Early Comedies:
"The Comedy of Errors," "The Taming of the
Shrew," "The Two Gentlemen of Verona," "Love's
Labour's Lost," "The Merchant of Venice," *Longmans, Green & Co., 1960, pp. 18-25.*

HAROLD F. BROOKS (essay date 1963)

[*In the excerpt below, Brooks discusses Shakespeare's use of comic parallelism in* The Two Gentlemen of Verona, *claiming that the activities of Launce and Speed are not merely appended to the romantic action, but contribute to the play's thematic development. He cites as evidence Launce's parody of love and friendship, as well as the more subtle recurring images of defection, near-loss, and seeking which appear in both the comic interludes and the romantic main plot. Other dramatic parallels included in Brooks's extensive list are the puns on "tide" and "tied"; the confusions of identity experienced by both Launce and Proteus; the silences of Julia and Crab; the letters of Launce, Proteus, and Silvia; the theme of education; and the servant roles of Crab and Proteus.*]

Despite warm appreciation of Launce as a comic character, it has often been denied that he and Speed have an organic part in the structure of *The Two Gentlemen of Verona*. According to Professor H. B. Charlton, for instance, 'Launce has no real right within the play except that gentlemen must have servants, and Elizabethan audiences must have clowns' [see excerpt above, 1930]. This is to see the dramatic structure too exclusively in terms of plot. There does appear to be only a single place where the behaviour of one of the clowns contributes to the progress of events; the critical moment when Julia, disguised as 'Sebastian', seeks service with her truant Proteus. Here, Proteus is influenced by Launce's recent misconduct: he is the readier to enlist the well-bred Sebastian because Launce has been missing for two days, and by the account he now gives of himself is proved too boorish to be entrusted with further missions to Silvia. Without question, dramatic unity is stronger when, as with Bottom [in *A Midsummer Night's Dream*] or Dogberry [in *Much Ado about Nothing*], the clown impinges upon the romantic plot more obviously and decisively than this. There can be unity however, resulting from development of theme as well as from development of plot: when a play has a plot and themes, the *action* (which is what must have unity) may be regarded as comprising the development of both. Side by side with the causal sequence that carries forward his romantic plot, Shakespeare, in the parts he has given to Speed and Launce, is developing his play by means of comic parallels that illustrate and extend its themes. The parallels, as well as the causal sequence, are part of the organic structure. (pp. 91-2)

The themes in question are those of friendship and love, the first and second subjects of *Two Gentlemen*, which, as in *The Knight's Tale* and some of Shakespeare's own sonnets, are treated in relation to each other. The friendship is that which in Renaissance literature is constantly held up as an exemplar of noble life. The love is courtly. Julia, seeming at first full of 'daunger', soon reveals her 'pité', and later sets out as Love's pilgrim. Valentine, like Troilus in Chaucer, begins as the Love-heretic, but quickly becomes the penitent votary. Proteus, from Love-idolator falls to Love-traitor, until reclaimed and redeemed from his treachery both to love and friendship by the sacrificial fidelity of his lover and the sacrificial magnanimity of his friend. Thurio is Love's Philistine, and the clowns, in this pattern, are Love's plebeians.

From Launce's first entry, each of his scenes refers, by burlesque parallels, to the themes of friendship on the one hand and of love on the other. Speed's scenes earlier, so far as I can see, do not depend on this particular sort of parallelism: Speed is not shown in burlesque roles as lover or friend, except momentarily, when he explains a piece of negligence, comparable to his lovelorn master's, by confessing he was in love with his bed. The scenes for the clowns are mostly built up from comic turns. Together, they play at cross-questions and crooked answers; Launce has his monologue of impersonations with the aid of comic 'props'; and Speed on his first appearance (I. i) has his mock-disputation (like Dromio of Syracuse [in *The Comedy of Errors*]) and his routine of witty begging (like Feste [in *Twelfth Night*]). The episode, all the same, is not irrelevant clownage. It underlines at a single stroke both Proteus' friendship and his love: the friendship with Valentine has allowed him to make Speed, his friend's man not his own, carry his love-letter to Julia. So, at the outset, a clown is linked with both themes. Speed reports Julia 'hard as steel' [I. i. 40-1], thus preparing for the next scene of her metamorphosis to the compassionate lover. Proteus has exclaimed already:

> Thou, Julia, thou hast metamorphis'd me;
>
> [I. i. 66]

the motif is implied in his name, and belongs especially to him: yet Julia and Valentine are each to know metamorphoses, too. In the mock-disputation and its sequel here, this motif (as elsewhere in Shakespeare) is accompanied by imagery of human beings as animals. Speed (or alternatively Valentine) is a 'sheep', and he and Julia are 'muttons'. He is, moreover, a 'lost mutton', and in literal fact is in search of his master: he is in peril of failing to sail with him, a serious defection. The situation, then, and some of the backchat, are in keeping with a drama where defection, near-loss, and seeking are to be important: where Proteus' defection is almost to lose him his true self, and cause him to be lost to Valentine and Julia; where Valentine is almost to lose Silvia, and the heroines must seek their lovers. Among the clown-scenes themselves, two others form a series with this one. Launce at his parting (II. iii) is likewise in danger of missing the ship, and is warned that he would thereby lose his master and his service. And his ultimate dismissal in favour of 'Sebastian' (IV. iv) echoes not only that warning, but Proteus' final comment on Speed here, that he is too unprepossessing a love-messenger and another must be found.

Some of these correspondences an audience will never be consciously aware of, though it will be affected by them. In the next clown-episode, in II. i, everyone sees the relation between Speed's humour and Valentine's high-flown romance. Speed comments directly on his master's love-melancholy. In taking over Valentine's former part as critic of love's absurdities, he helps to mark the metamorphosis: the critic of Proteus' love has become vulnerable to similar criticism himself. The parallels are brought out when Speed quotes him on Proteus and tells him he is blinder now than Proteus was. As critics of love, Speed and Valentine are not, of course, the same. With the eye of yet unconverted scepticism, Valentine had seen its irrationality and its exactions; with the plebeian eye, perma-

Act II. Scene v. Launce and Speed. By C. Green. The Department of Rare Books and Special Collections, The University of Michigan Library.

nently limited though clear, Speed sees its absence of practical common sense. In one respect, his function is that of the Duck and the Goose in Chaucer's Council of Birds, assembled on St. Valentine's Day. Love in the courtly manner, partly because it is so stylized, is very liable, once we entertain an inadequate, everyday view of it, to arouse mere mockery and impatience. Aware of this, both Chaucer and Shakespeare embody the dangerous attitude within the poem or play itself, so as to control and place it; but they place it somewhat differently. In Chaucer, the plebeian view, whatever sympathy he may have with it outside the poem, is introduced chiefly to be rejected. But when Speed protests that while his master may dine on Silvia's favour, he himself needs meat, this is not 'a parfit resoun of a goos': it commands sympathy within the ambit of the play, and partial assent: it is one contribution to the complex dramatic image of courtly love that Shakespeare is building up.

In contrast, there is the admired elegance of the device by which Silvia confesses her love for Valentine. The dullness which prevents his understanding it is a perfectly orthodox effect of love-melancholy; besides, as her true 'servant' he has too much humility to be expecting any such confession. That so ultracourtly a gambit has to be explained to him by the uncourtly Speed is humorous enough. And it is ironical that Speed should do him this office of a good friend in his love, when his courtly friend Proteus is soon to be his false rival.

Diffidently blind here in love, Valentine is to be too rashly and confidingly blind in friendship. The theme of blindness and sight, especially lovesight, is one of the most central in the play. It is because Proteus' fancy is bred only in his eyes, which until the dénouement see no further than outward beauty, that he is altogether unstable. The truest praise of Silvia is that

> Love doth to her eyes repair
> To help him of his blindness.
>
> [IV. ii. 46-7]

The theme continually recurs; and in the present scene the greater part of Speed's cut-and-thrust with Valentine relates to it: 'Love is blind,' 'if you love her you cannot see her,' and the rest, from Valentine's question, on the marks of the lover, 'Are all these things perceived in me?' to Speed's, on Silvia's 'invisible' stratagem, 'But did you perceive her earnest?' [II. i. 70, 68, 33, 157].

From Launce's entry, the relation between the clown episodes and the leading themes, of love and friendship, becomes simpler to describe; for it rests quite evidently throughout on the principle of comic parallelism. One has of course to bear in mind that in Elizabethan as in medieval work, burlesque need not mean belittlement of what is burlesqued.

The scene of Launce's parting (II. iii) is a counterpoise to the high courtly parting of friends, with which Valentine and Proteus open the play. More directly, it is the humorous sequel to the scene of pathos which it follows, the lovers' parting between Proteus and Julia (II. ii). One phrase, on Launce's sister, 'as white as a lily and as small as a wand' [II. iii. 20-1], is in the very idiom of love-romance. Proteus has punned emotionally on the tide or season of his departure, and Julia's 'tide of tears' [II. ii. 14]; Launce puns outrageously on the tide and 'the tied,' namely Crab. At the end of the lovers' scene, Julia, weeping, has made her escape in silence: 'Alas!' cries Proteus in his exit-line, 'this parting strikes poor lovers dumb' [II. ii. 20]. The clown enters in tears, but voluble, and in his monologue re-enacts the weeping of all his kin. Crab's silence is taken otherwise than Julia's; unaccompanied by tears, it is supposed to betoken hardness of heart, and gives his master great offence. Attempting to identify the *dramatis personae* of the reenactment with the 'props' available, Launce confuses himself completely, and in this self-confusion about identities the comic mode of his monologue chimes with . . . the inward self-travesty of Proteus and the outward self-travesty of Julia, soon to be seen, and indeed with the whole theme of true identity and its recognition. The final claim Launce makes for his tears and sighs is likewise in tune with what is to happen. If he did miss the tide, he declares, they would float him and waft him to overtake Proteus. To overtake Proteus is just what Julia's love-sorrow, of which they are the comic counterparts, will shortly impel her to do.

The reunion of Launce and Speed in Milan (II. v) immediately succeeds that of the friends, their masters; and their dialogue comments on the love-theme. It is certain, Launce tells his comrade, that it will be a match between Proteus and Julia. Proteus has just left the stage soliloquizing on his change of allegiance, and is about to return resolving to court Silvia as though Julia were dead. Yet in the end, Launce will prove right after all. Again, he furnishes a comic reminder of the discretion proper in communicating love-secrets even to the bosom-friend. His display of caution ('Thou shalt never get such a secret from me but by parable' [II. v. 39-40]) contrasts with Valentine's indiscreet disclosure to Proteus of the plans

for his elopement, a disclosure made in the previous scene (II. iv). In the next (II. vi) Proteus determines on betraying his friend's confidence to the Duke. His entry alone, meditating this treachery, is set against the amicable exit of Speed and Launce, going off 'in Christian charity' to drink together.

The episode of Launce and his letter (which ends III. i) affords even more striking parallels with both the love and friendship themes. It evokes comparison with the two romantic letter-scenes earlier (I. ii, II. i): Julia receiving Proteus' love-letter, and Silvia giving Valentine the love-letter she has made him write on her behalf. In burlesque contrast with Julia's emotion and Silvia's graceful device, Launce's letter is a step towards a bargain in the marriage-market. It is a report from a go-between on the merits and demerits of his intended; and on the strength of it he makes up his mind to have her, because though toothless she is well-off. This love-transaction, which is not pursued in the courtly way, by courtship of the lady, and which is clinched by mercenary considerations, clean against the canon of true love, casts a light on the next scene (III. ii) and its sequel (IV. ii). Here, by the courtliest kind of courtship—a serenade—but no less against the canon of true love, the assault upon Silvia's loyalty to Valentine is planned on behalf of the foolish Thurio, whom her father prefers for his wealth, and is used by the faithless Proteus as cover for his own pursuit of her. Beside the moral deformity of Proteus' conduct in love, the comic deformity of Launce's is as nothing.

When the letter-episode begins, we have just seen Valentine banished, in consequence of having enlisted Proteus' counsel about the elopement. Launce soliloquizes on Proteus' knavery, and his own secrecy: 'I love . . . but what woman I will not tell myself' [III. i 268-69]—burlesquing at once the code and Valentine's breach of it. Then, like Valentine, he enlists a confidant; and like Proteus, betrays his friend. He cajoles Speed into helping him read the letter, and rejoices that Speed will earn a beating by it. Though the roles are switched (since the confidant, not the confider, is betrayed), the parallel is clear.

Launce's last monologue, just before his dismissal by Proteus and from the play (IV. iv), is of course his tale of Crab's crimes at court, with his own quixotic devotion and fidelity to the ungrateful, ill-conditioned cur. It comes almost straight after Proteus' nocturnal courtship of Silvia, in triple treachery to Julia, Valentine, and Thurio; and between the arrival of Julia in her devotion and fidelity, only to witness this treachery of his (IV. ii), and her taking service with him (in IV. iv), ungrateful and ill-conducted as she has found him. 'When a man's servant shall play the cur' [IV. iv. 1]—so Launce starts his complaint of Crab, and so Proteus might complain of Launce himself, 'who still . . . turns [him] to shame' [IV. iv. 62]. But we have heard this word 'servant' repeated in the sense of 'courtly lover': what when a lady's 'servant' shall play the cur? Yet Julia does not refuse the quixotic task of bearing Proteus' love-plea to her unwilling rival.

I am hinting a comparison of Proteus with Crab; and I do not think it extravagant, provided one is not too serious about it, to see reflected in Crab, comically and a little pathetically, the transgressor in Proteus. The want of sensibility to old ties and to his friend Launce's feelings which Crab is alleged to show at parting from home, is ominous as a parallel to Proteus' parting from Julia and impending reunion with Valentine. As a present for Silvia, Crab resembles the love that Proteus proffers her. He is a sorry changeling for the true love gift Proteus meant to bestow. He is unfit for Silvia (persecuting her with most objectionable attentions!), and offensive where true courtliness should rule. Like Proteus, he gets his friend into trouble. And as Crab is only saved by Launce's quixotic, self-sacrificial affection, so Proteus is only saved by the extremes to which Valentine is ready to carry his friendship and Julia her love. From them Proteus learns his lesson. As in *Love's Labour's Lost,* an opening debate in which love and education were pitted against each other has led into a drama of education in and through love. The theme of education is touched occasionally in the earlier clown-scenes (Speed has been corrected for inordinate love—of his bed), but it appears more plainly when Launce reproaches Crab: 'did I not bid thee still mark me, and do as I do?' [IV. iv. 36-7]. Crab cannot learn; but Proteus learns the value of constancy from the example and reproaches of Julia, Valentine, and Silvia. Whether Crab says ay or no, and whatever the antics of Proteus the transgressor, it is a match between the regenerate Proteus and his Julia. Yet with all this, Crab is the clown's dog, not a symbol or a piece of allegory: I mean simply to suggest that the impression the dog makes on an audience has this various aptness to the main action and its themes. (pp. 93-9)

Harold F. Brooks, "Two Clowns in a Comedy (to Say Nothing of the Dog): Speed, Launce (and Crab) in 'The Two Gentlemen of Verona'," in Essays and Studies, Vol. 16, 1963, pp. 91-100.

STANLEY WELLS (essay date 1963)

[*Responding primarily to H. B. Charlton's assertion that Shakespeare had "inadvertently" made romance comic in* The Two Gentlemen of Verona *(see excerpt above, 1930), Wells carefully analyzes what he terms the superficial, technical, and organic peculiarities of Shakespeare's plot, identifying those flaws which disrupt the romance of the play. Dismissing the superficial flaws as insignificant, he cites Shakespeare's inability "to manipulate more than a few characters at once," his limited use of dramatic devices, and the discrepancies between his characterization and the romantic conventions as several faults which detract from the integrity of the comedy. However, Wells values both the commentary provided by the comic subplot and Shakespeare's preparation of later events through imagery, concluding that the play is a limited success which both intentionally and unintentionally makes romance comic.*]

The Two Gentlemen of Verona has not been a favourite of the critics. Not all have been as damning as that uninhibited lady, Mrs Charlotte Lennox: 'This Play every where abounds with the most ridiculous Absurdities in the Plot and Conduct of the Incidents, as well as with the greatest Improprieties in the Manners and Sentiments of the Persons' [see excerpt above, 1754]. But Coleridge, in making a chronological table of Shakespeare's plays, dismissed it as a 'sketch'; Hazlitt, who was not altogether unappreciative, used similar terms: 'This is little more than the first outlines of a comedy lightly sketched in' [see excerpt above, 1817]; E. K. Chambers considered that no other play of Shakespeare's 'bears upon it such obvious marks of immaturity' [see excerpt above, 1905] and T. M. Parrott found it 'full of faults' [see excerpt above, 1949]. Sketchy though it may be, its inclusion in Francis Meres's list suggests, perhaps that it was acted, and at least that it was regarded as a completed piece of work; so it may fairly come up for critical examination. On the other hand, it is not amenable to those techniques of modern intepretative criticism which are applied to fully developed and highly organised works. There is, perhaps, some danger of under-rating it simply because it is not as good as other plays in which Shakespeare used similar materials. It contains, as has often been remarked, many antici-

pations of later plays, such as *The Merchant of Venice* and *Twelfth Night;* but to consider this too deeply has its dangers. It may lead to a too easy dismissal on the grounds, not that the play is unsuccessful in itself, but that it does not provide the critic with what he wants, and finds elsewhere. It may on the other hand lead to over-interpretation, such as John Vyvyan's theory that the outlaw scenes represent in parable-form Valentine's need to learn control of his baser instincts [see excerpt above, 1960].

A more helpful approach is probably that through earlier literature, such as H. B. Charlton adopts in a chapter of *Shakespearian Comedy* [see excerpt above, 1930] which remains perhaps the most extended critical discussion of this play. Charlton clearly demonstrates Shakespeare's dependence, in the play's more serious aspects, upon the conventions of romantic love as derived from the mediaeval tradition and its modifications by Petrarch and the neo-Platonists; and he adduces some close parallels of idea. In discussing the use Shakespeare made of these conventions, Charlton comes to the conclusion that something went wrong. His thesis is perhaps fairly summed up in his penultimate sentence: 'Clearly, Shakespeare's first attempt to make romantic comedy had only succeeded so far that it had unexpectedly and inadvertently made romance comic.' In order to test the truth of this, it is necessary to look at the methods used by Shakespeare to project and organise his raw material.

The plot—I use the word in a fairly wide sense, to refer both to the actions and to the methods of narrative presentation—seems to me to exhibit a number of peculiarities, limitations and plain faults, which for convenience I divide into the superficial, the technical and the organic. The superficial ones can be passed over with little comment. Dr Johnson drew attention to the play's peculiar geography, and to the fact that it is not even self-consistent [see excerpt above, 1765]; but this might almost be regarded as a normal feature of romance. Johnson's further complaint that, at the end of II, iv, Shakespeare 'makes Protheus, after an interview with Silvia, say he has only seen her picture' is probably answered by the fact that 'picture' could mean 'appearance' (cf. *Hamlet* [IV. v. 86] and *Merchant* [I. ii. 72]) and here implies only superficial acquaintance. In any case, these peculiarities are neither more numerous nor more striking than those to be found in many other, greater plays.

The technical limitations of the plot are, I find, more interesting and revealing. It is a curious fact that Shakespeare's technique in this play is limited almost exclusively to three devices: soliloquy, duologue, and the aside as comment. Thirteen of the twenty scenes go no further than this: they are I, i, ii and iii; II, i, ii, iii, v, vi and vii; IV, ii, iii and iv; and V, i. Moreover, several other scenes, including three of the play's longest (II, iv; III, i; V, iv), escape inclusion in this list only by virtue of a few lines of more complicated dialogue. The climax of this structural method is reached in IV, ii, in many ways the best scene. It begins with a soliloquy from Proteus, followed by a dialogue between him and Thurio, with the musicians in the background; then the Host and Julia enter and speak together unheard by the others; their conversation is broken by the song; it is followed by a brief passage between Proteus and Thurio, after which Sylvia makes her appearance; her conversation with Proteus is commented on in asides by Julia, and the scene ends after Proteus's exit with a few lines between Julia and the Host. The patterning is simple but effective. The silences of the Host and Julia are, of course, explained by their situation; those of Proteus and Thurio offer some difficulty to the producer, but can be partially covered by the preparations for the serenade and by the continuance of instrumental music after it. There is no reason to wish that Shakespeare had attempted anything more complex: the limited technique justifies itself; it could be entirely deliberate.

However, what happens when Shakespeare steps outside these limits may well suggest that they are the consequence of an underdeveloped technique rather than a deliberately restricted one. Several times a character is left in unnatural silence when the dialogue switches from him to someone else. I, iii, for instance, begins with a duologue between Antonio and Panthino. When they have come to a decision, Proteus enters 'in good time' and Panthino stands silently by during the conversation between Antonio and his son until he is haled off by Antonio. In III, i, a feeble effort is made to keep Launce in the picture after he enters with Proteus at [III. i. 188], but he soon drops out and says nothing for 40 lines. In the next scene, where a truly three-cornered dialogue might well have been expected, Thurio speaks only two of the twenty-eight speeches uttered when he is on stage with the Duke and Proteus. (pp. 161-64)

Of the entire play, no scene has given rise to more unfavourable comment than the last; it has been emended, rewritten, reviled and rejected. The difficulties here are complex: both technical and organic. On the latter I reserve comment until later; for the present, it may be worth noticing the inflexibility of technique displayed. Though six important characters as well as a band of outlaws are on-stage, the scene ends with a long duologue between the Duke and Valentine. Thurio has two speeches in the entire scene (admittedly, he enters late), and Sylvia says nothing at all while she is first donated by Valentine to Proteus, then rejected by him in favour of Julia, then claimed by Thurio, only in his next breath to be renounced by him, and finally handed back to Valentine by her father. Was ever woman in this humour won?

The basic technical failure of the play, I suggest, arises from the fact that Shakespeare is still a tyro in dramatic craftsmanship: he has not yet learned how to manipulate more than a few characters at once. This explains the complete failure of that chaste wraith, Sir Eglamour, and of Thurio, since the dramatist did not consider them important enough to be given soliloquies or a foil; and it also goes a long way towards explaining the failure in the last scene to develop a tricky situation in a way that would have achieved a fully articulate emotional resolution. And it is this more than anything else that gives the impression of sketchiness. It does not ruin the play: along with, and partly because of, the sketchiness, there is a wholly charming simplicity and directness: what Hazlitt called 'a careless grace and felicity' 'throughout the conduct of the fable'; but there is not that density and harmonic richness which come where the characters of a play have a subtle complexity of cross-relationships such as we find in *Twelfth Night* and would, to some degree, have been desirable here. (pp. 164-65)

The organic deficiencies of the play are the result of Shakespeare's failure to devise a plot which will enable characters conceived within the conventions of romantic love to behave in a manner compatible with these conventions. We are, for instance, invited to sympathise with Valentine; he is the attractive, intelligent young courtier whose love for Sylvia is seriously and forcefully presented; the man who at the end is capable of the grand romantic gesture of offering to sacrifice

love to friendship. But the exigencies of the plot require this intelligent young man to behave in a manner not merely unrealistic, but downright stupid. Realism, of course, we have no right to expect; the trouble is that Shakespeare cuts across the convention by using his romantic hero as a vehicle for a type of comedy which deprives him of his whole basis of existence. The scene in which Valentine fails to realise that the letter he is writing on Sylvia's behalf is addressed to himself might perhaps have been acceptable as a tenderly absurd illustration of the lover's traditional blindness: the wit made weak with musing; but when the humour of the situation is explicitly pointed for us by Speed, who here shows much more intelligence than his master, the tenderness is in great danger of being lost in the absurdity. A later scene that quite deflates our confidence in the young man is that in which he ingenuously reveals to the Duke his plan for eloping with the Duke's daughter. If the person concerned had been Thurio, all would have been well; but as it is, the situation is at variance with the character.

A somewhat similar difficulty arises with Proteus. Again our first impressions are sympathetic. Before long, not merely is he behaving in the most caddish manner imaginable, but he is inviting our sympathy in what he takes to be a moral dilemma. It must be admitted, I think, that his soliloquy at the beginning of IV, ii comes near to redeeming him as a dramatic character, for he shows quite powerfully his awareness of his falseness to Valentine, his injustice towards Thurio and his worthlessness in comparison with Sylvia; he grows in depth when he tells how, 'spaniel-like, the more she spurns my love, The more it grows and fawneth on her still' [IV. ii. 14-15]. The mature Shakespeare could have done much with this obsessed lover (witness Angelo); but at this stage he has not yet learned to maintain this depth of characterisation, and in a few seconds Proteus goes on to perform with no apparent difficulty the treacheries he has just been deploring. The result is a loss of moral coherence; it is paradoxical that this would have been less evident if Proteus had been more shallowly presented throughout.

In these characters we see the strain imposed by a discrepancy between plot and convention. (pp. 166-67)

These difficulties reach their climax in the passage of the last scene which has become the most notorious literary and dramatic crux of the play: when Valentine, impressed by Proteus's repentance, says:

> And, that my love may appear plain and free,
> All that was mine in Silvia I give thee.
>
> [V. iv. 82-3]

This has provoked many different reactions. (p. 168)

[Doubts] have been cast upon both its authenticity and its textual integrity. . . . Dover Wilson and Quiller-Couch could not stomach it at all [see excerpt above, 1921], and propounded an elaborate theory of play-house interference, tentatively adopted and modified by Parrott [see excerpt above, 1949].

On the other hand, attempts to justify the scene as it stands have been made, for instance, by drawing parallels with the Sonnets. . . . There can be no doubt, I think, that, whatever our opinion of the rest of the scene, its climactic situation in itself would have been perfectly acceptable to an Elizabethan audience. As M. C. Bradbrook has written: 'The schoolboy cries of "cad" and "scoundrel" with which Valentine is pelted by critics, the epigrams of Q ("By now there are *no* gentlemen in Verona'') would have struck Shakespeare's audience as simply a failure in understanding' [see excerpt above, 1951]. . . . The trouble is two-fold: partly that [Shakespeare] had not *enough* interest in the plot to see how it should have been moulded to synthesise with the other elements of the play; and partly sheer inadequacy in the mechanics of his craft, which rendered him incapable of manipulating his characters in a convincing way.

The comic characters . . . at times impinge inappropriately upon the serious ones; but they are more often used to provide a wholly successful comic implied commentary on the romantic agonies of the lovers. When Speed comments on the letter scene between Valentine and Sylvia, he makes Valentine look an ass; he does not simply comment on the romance: he (at least momentarily) destroys it. On the other hand, when he and Launce discuss Launce's requirements of his girl-friend, they provide an attitude that can co-exist with the other: they are not mutually incompatible, but mutually illuminating. The first does, as Charlton says, inadvertently make romance comic; the second provides a perfectly legitimate comic counterpoint to the romance.

In its overall organisation, then, I see this play as a failure. It shows Shakespeare accepting dramatic conventions with one hand and throwing them overboard with the other. He fails, partly because he puts more into the framework than it can hold, and partly because he still has much to learn about the mechanics of his craft. But the play is very far indeed from being a total failure. There are partial successes even in its attempts to be an integrated poetic comedy. Already Shakespeare is making some use of recurrent and significantly placed imagery to prepare us for the turns of the story; we may notice for instance the emphasis on the blindness of love, on the way it 'metamorphoses' a man, so that he wars with good counsel, and his wit is made weak with musing; and the two developed images of the transitoriness of love [II. iv. 200-02; III. ii. 6-10]. These go some way towards preparing us for Valentine's partial blindness and for the shift in Proteus's affections: though they do not make them completely successful, they erode the frontiers of our disbelief. Even the word-play, mechanical as it often is, sometimes takes on anticipatory depths, as in the passage between Julia and the Host [IV. ii. 54-72]. . . . Julia's answers [to the Host's questions] are misunderstandings, but being functional, they are not comic: they stress her isolation and loneliness. There is wit here, but its effect is not one of hilarity; it serves rather to sharpen the poignancy of Julia's situation.

The very tenuousness of the plot, and the shadowiness of some of its characters, help us to accept the situations as it were on a hypothetical basis, and to follow with interest the ways in which they are developed. In this the play resembles the prose romances of the period, in many of which the story exists merely as a machinery to place the characters in interesting situations; then rhetoric takes over, and the emotional ramifications are developed at great length. The parallel does not hold entirely, for there are clear signs that Shakespeare was trying to do more than this; but at least it may help us to see where to look for the play's virtues. And the looseness of action does above all allow Shakespeare to bring in the estimable figure of Launce and the silent Crab, who are much more relevant thematically than structurally, and who show how marvellously creative Shakespeare's imagination already was when given a free rein. Again, though I have stressed the limitations of dramatic technique in this play, it must be repeated that Shakespeare is often wholly successful within the

limits of a single scene. And the most important reason for the play's successes is that, however immature he may be in other ways, he is already completely assured as a writer of comic prose, of lyrical verse, and even sometimes of genuine dramatic verse. When we try to get below the surface of the play, we find that it rests on shaky foundations. In these circumstances the best thing to do seems to be to come up to the surface again and examine that; then we may return to Johnson: 'It is not indeed one of his most powerful effusions, it has neither many diversities of character, nor striking delineations of life, but it abounds in [maxims] beyond most of his plays, and few have more lines or passages which, singly considered, are eminently beautiful.' (pp. 169-73)

> Stanley Wells, *"The Failure of 'The Two Gentlemen of Verona',"* in *Shakespeare Jahrbuch, Vol. 99, 1963, pp. 161-73.*

HOWARD NEMEROV (essay date 1963)

[*In the following excerpt, Nemerov asserts that although Shakespeare's "greatest value" was romantic love, he did not necessarily believe in the seriousness and moral integrity of all lovers. Applying this assumption, the critic counters the two principal interpretations of earlier critics on the relative failure of* The Two Gentlemen of Verona, *contending that neither the comic treatment of the romantic lovers nor the parody provided by Launce and Speed destroys the romance of the play. Nemerov concludes that the resolution of the comedy combines both the humor and the true value of romantic love, for marriage "is both a fulfillment and a comedown for passionate idealism."*]

That [*The Two Gentlemen of Verona*] is one of the earliest of [Shakespeare's plays] is an excuse frequently offered for its admittedly odd behavior: an infant, no more housebroken than Launce's dog: "'Tis a foul thing when a cur cannot keep himself in all companies!" [IV. iv. 9-11]. It is not a well-made play, it contains a number of incidental absurdities, its persons certainly do not behave like real, warm, earthy human beings—these are some of the complaints made by critics, who find the chief interest of *The Two Gentlemen of Verona* in its vague foreshadowing of qualities its author does not yet fully possess. (p. 25)

Much more might be said on this subject, but to little purpose. Though it be true that *The Two Gentlemen of Verona* represents the essentials of Shakespeare's most characteristic action, one which he returned to over and over again, every resemblance we point to is also a difference, and one moreover that in the comparison works to the disadvantage of this play. In the action, for instance, Proteus' role is very like that of Edmund [in *King Lear*], and in its progress shows something of Shakespeare's idea of evil as beginning with reason but proceeding to uncontrollable contagion: thus his initial betrayal of Julia involves him in the attempt to deceive all the others—the Duke, Silvia, Valentine, Thurio—and especially himself; but Proteus is not Edmund, and looks harmlessly inept beside him. Similarly, Valentine's exile and flight into the forest do indeed have the same sense as Edgar's forced flight into the storm of nature and the insane assumptions at the bottom of societies— but those outlaws are pretty silly all the same, aren't they?

Bothers of this sort and others have made the play something of an embarrassment, so that it is not much heard of. Some scholars, those whose theme requires them to discuss all the Plays, or at any rate all the Comedies, have attempted to get round the difficulty in one of two related ways.

The first is to say that what we have here is, after all, apprentice work; that the young Shakespeare has not yet learned to invent a satisfactory plot; that what he has managed to do is marred by inexcusable carelessness; that the characterization, while not much, is at any rate an improvement over that in *The Comedy of Errors*. . . . (pp. 26-7)

The second solution is a specialized development from the first. The play is apprentice work in a particular sense, it shows Shakespeare experimenting with the combination of two genres, Romance and Comedy; he has not yet learned to handle the combination, so that the romantic and the comic parts contradict and corrupt one another, so that the play is, as Valentine says of love, "a folly bought with wit, / Or else a wit by folly vanquished" [I. i. 34-5]. (p. 27)

Now I do not think the scholars were wrong in bringing these matters to attention—somebody had to—nor am I at all certain I can do either other or better. But I do have a difficulty with the mode of attention itself, with a way of regarding works of art which seems peculiarly suited to the study of "development" while somewhat neglecting the specificity of the present example; it tends to see Shakespeare as getting from an earlier play to a later play by means of this one—the hen which is the egg's way of getting to another egg—rather than to see this one as, for the moment, the only object in the world. So I would propose another assumption to begin with, something like this: when a master makes a mistake—let us except the "inexcusable carelessness" (he did write fast, and, as we are told, never blotted)—but when a master makes what looks like a big mistake, look closely and listen, for he may be doing it on purpose, and what you see as incoherence or inconsistency may emerge as his meaning. So it happens, for example, in a greater play than this one, *Troilus & Cressida,* where the way in which things go unpredictably and absurdly wrong with the story turns out to be the story. This view of mine is admittedly based on hero-worship.

The scholarly opinions I have outlined seem to involve some unnecessary and perhaps unwarrantable assumptions as to what plays are, and what poetry is, brought from elsewhere to be applied to this example. If the play is apprentice work, that is surely not because the plot is absurd, for all plots are absurd when considered by themselves; if you don't believe this, say over slowly the plot of *The Tempest*. In fact, the plot of *The Two Gentlemen of Verona* is typically Shakespearean in its outrageously crossing symmetries and improbable manipulations. Were we not so much imposed upon by novelistic ideas of "depth" and "sincerity," we could allow that the apprenticeship of the master poet might show, not a welter of intense emotions and deep thoughts, but just such a brittle and cool charm as this play shows, just such a carelessly brilliant handling of surfaces consistently kept free of the encumbrances of "reality."

Similarly, the idea that the play fails because in it the two separate genres of Romance and Comedy have not been harmonized by the poet seems to substitute a theory for what visibly happens; behind this idea is the old notion, perhaps, of "comic relief." But I do not see that it is necessary to postulate two genres, or that the play fails from any such internal contradiction, or for that matter that the play essentially fails at all—as I shall try to show.

It is perfectly true, and obvious everywhere in the Plays, that Shakespeare believes in romantic love; it is in fact his greatest value, close-allied with a religion of natural sanctions and faith-fulness down to the ending doom. But it is impermissible to identify this belief with a Shakespearean belief in the seriousness, moral worth, intelligence, and fascinating individuality of the persons who embody this belief in the value of romantic love; for these qualities they generally do not have, and in this play as in others the young lovers are such nitwits as to make their poet's belief in love exactly what a proper belief has to be: *quia absurdum, quia impossibile,* &c. [because it is absurd, impossible, and so on]. Here, as in *A Midsummer-Night's Dream,* the characters' belief that they have characters is one of the funniest things in the play, and one of its major points. . . . Such character as the lovers have exists only in relation to love, and is in a remarkable degree conferred upon them by their names (a kind of Platonizing evident throughout the play): Valentine, because he is faithful; Proteus, because he changes. The relation of Julia to "jewel" is a little less obvious, but the price of a virtuous woman is "far above rubies" (Proverbs. XXXI. 10) and her device is the ring. Silvia's name relates her to the wood where she will find Valentine again.

Now it is the essence of love to spiritualize and idealize not only the beloved but the world as well; and to spiritualize and idealize the world is also in a sense to be silly, even if it is upon that silliness that human life, as distinct from the life of beasts, chiefly depends. Shakespeare does not neglect or attempt to conceal this silliness, inseparable from idealism and romance and all impetuous generosity; on the contrary, he is at some pains to emphasize it throughout by constantly asserting the equation of love with idealism (a world whose charm will be its faithfulness to absurdity), with word, image, symbol, and shadow. The four young lovers sigh in a world of poetry and music, a world of no particular stability but what faith in love can give it, where ecstasy and allicholly may in a moment change places; it is not remarkable, then, but perfectly appropriate, that they should concentrate so much of their attention on symbols: letters, rings, a picture, a song; for this is not the real world, and yet, in the moment of their passion, reality itself becomes to a certain extent malleable, even volatile.

This courtly and Platonic strain is the dominant insistence of the play, wherever we are concerned with the lovers; so ideal is the nature of their worship, whether constant or fickle, that it fixes itself repeatedly on word or image rather than on what they represent, on names rather than on things. Thus Julia, after tearing up a love letter from Proteus, puts his "poor wounded name" in her bosom to be healed [I. ii. 111], curses her own name for her unkindness, and finally puts both names together:

> Thus will I fold them one upon another:
> Now kiss, embrace, contend, do what you will.
>
> [I. ii. 125-26]

Proteus, denied by Silvia, begs her picture to love instead:

> For since the substance of your perfect self
> Is else devoted, I am but a shadow;
> And to your shadow will I make true love.
>
> [IV. ii. 123-25]

It is significant that anyone drawn into the sphere of the lovers, whatever his gravity and consequence, at once assumes their silliness for his own: consider the tale the Duke must invent to make Valentine reveal himself as Silvia's lover:

> There is a lady in Milano here
> Whom I affect; but she is nice and coy
> And naught esteems my aged eloquence.
> Now therefore would I have thee to my tutor—
>
> [III. i. 81-4]

leading on to a design of climbing up on the lady's roof by rope ladder. True, this tale is a ruse; but the climate of opinion, so to say, in which Valentine could believe it of the Duke and the Duke could believe it capable of imposing on Valentine, has to be one of an exceptionally weightless kind.

The most outrageous example, appropriately, forms the climax of the play. Fifteen lines after trying to rape Silvia, Proteus repents, whereupon in five or six lines more Valentine's forgiveness reaches the point of offering him Silvia:

> And, that my love may appear plain and free,
> All that was mine in Silvia I give thee,
>
> [V. iv. 82-3]

causing Julia to faint—and one scholar to exclaim that by this time there are *no* gentlemen of Verona [see excerpt above by Arthur Quiller-Couch, 1921]. But this character of extreme lightness and rapid mobility of feeling is undoubtedly intentional, and has been built up throughout the play with remarkable consistency.

For the world of love is also the world of music and poetry, idealizing and spiritualizing, yet having, like love, a power to transform real experience. The theory of all three in their relations is with an odd propriety entrusted to Proteus, in a speech of grand and subtle brilliance, where truth and deceit, technique and effect, are finely fused, as he tells Thurio how to win Silvia "By wailful sonnets, whose composed rhymes / Should be full-fraught with serviceable vows" [III. ii. 69-70]. (pp. 28-31)

Now we may be able to see that the comic parts given to the "low people" do not in the least destroy the romance, but act formally as a balancing countersubject, emotionally as the guarantee of a fine, implicit truth of feeling in the play.

To spell out some simple things which the lovers make us for a time forget—what is romance about? It is about getting married, which is both a fulfillment and a comedown for passionate idealism, having to do with the body, with generation, with care for the future, with life in the moderate temperatures of the real world, the sorrowful-funny.

All the servants in the play represent this circumstance to their heedless masters, acting the part of worldliness in relation to spirit, shadowing forth the grotesque countertruths of the flesh to which the last refinements of romantic adoration are nevertheless designed to lead. When Julia decides to dress as a boy, Lucetta's response is typical: "What fashion, madam, shall I make your breeches?" and "You must needs have them with a codpiece, madam" [II. vii. 49, 53].

But it is the wonderful Launce and his marvelous dog, whether visible or invisible, who chiefly develop this carnal wisdom and humility.

Launce is to Proteus his master as body to mind or spirit. The body, being a servant and fool, understands the mind: "I am but a fool, look you; and yet I have the wit to think my master is a kind of knave" [III. i. 263-64]—for, as Launce says to Speed, "stand-under and understand is all one" [II. v. 32-3]. The same relation is duplicated between Launce and his dog, in a brilliantly detailed development of that traditional wisdom which views the body as a beast—Brother Ass, as St. Francis called it.

In the intermission of the lovers' passionate but abstract bewilderments the poet has placed this most marvelous of clowns in his sorrowing humility. And what does Launce talk about? At his first appearance he talks about—and acts out—family

life and the pains of parting, the tears shed by all except the dog:

> My mother weeping, my father wailing, my sister crying, our maid howling, our cat wringing her hands, and all our house in a great perplexity—yet did not this cruel-hearted cur shed one tear.
>
> [II. iii. 6-10]

Later on, he parodies the main action by trying to choose a wife from a catalogue which lists her qualities, e.g. "*Item.* She is not to be kiss'd fasting, in respect of her breath" [III. i. 23-4]. And at his last coming on stage, in a kind of abject sermon addressed to the dog, he tells in a parable how the body embarrasses, disgraces, and punishes the spirit, how the spirit humbly, lovingly, necessarily suffers the body's dumb unruliness, and puts this behavior of the flesh in direct relation with the romantic heroine:

> Nay, I remember the trick you serv'd me when I took my leave of Madam Silvia! Did not I bid thee still mark me and do as I do? When didst thou see me heave up my leg and make water against a gentlewoman's farthingale? Didst thou ever see me do such a trick?
>
> [IV. iv. 34-9]

If the worst that has been said of the play were true, the existence in it of Launce would alone make it beautifully worth attending to. But the existence of Launce is not merely a brilliant solo irrelevantly set against a mediocre background; rather, he is integral to the play, and in a certain sense the key to the truth of its youthful and pale but spirited charm. (pp. 31-3)

> *Howard Nemerov, "'The Two Gentlemen of Verona'," in his* Poetry and Fiction: Essays, *Rutgers University Press, 1963, pp. 25-33.*

WILLIAM O. SCOTT   (essay date 1965)

[*According to Scott, identity—more than friendship or love—is the controlling force in* The Two Gentlemen of Verona. *Comparing Proteus's transformations with those of mythic figures in Ovid's* Metamorphoses *and Spenser's* Faerie Queene, *the critic examines Shakespeare's use of this tradition to dramatize the lovers' inconsistent behavior that "sacrifices all integrity to the self." He traces Proteus's disguises and changes throughout the story until Valentine's loyalty and Julia's faithful love "remind [him] what he has been"; at this point, Scott adds, Proteus returns "from illusion back to his true form, and marriage will fix him there."*]

Whatever we decide about its intrinsic value, *The Two Gentlemen of Verona* at least shows the nascent form and qualities of Shakespeare's comic art. And for either intrinsic or comparative purposes, the character and function of Proteus, and the themes suggested by his role, deserve more scrutiny. His name has a thematic aptness that would scarcely seem to need mentioning—except that the obvious may put us off further questioning and we may conclude that Shakespeare's intent was shallow before we have sounded it. (p. 283)

One of its Renaissance connotations has been used to build a hypothesis of character development. According to Thomas A. Perry [see excerpt above, 1954], the mythical Proteus, called "god of shapes" by Marlowe, in part suggested to Renaissance authors the changes worked in men by fashion, perhaps through travel. This idea does add to our impression of Proteus' triviality; it seems less valid as an explanation of how he became so. Shakespeare's character is indeed something of a dandy in his wooing of Silvia, but these outward matters are not emphasized, nor is any cause given except Proteus' infatuation. His courtly posturing simply images, without explaining causally, how superficial this infatuation is. Proteus the man of fashion illustrates Proteus the false lover.

But there are other possibilities in the myth. As we might expect, Proteus was a type of lust, or of the variability of passions in the lover. The relevant story is not of Proteus himself, but of another shape-changer sometimes identified with him, Vertumnus, who wooed Pomona by changing his shape [in Ovid's *Metamorphoses*]. Some commentators on Ovid read this as an allegory of trickery or Satanic temptation; and the *Cinque Canti* printed in many editions of *Orlando Furioso* borrowed the name of Vertunno for a deceitful spirit. Or this variable state may figure weakness of soul: in cupidity the human soul changes itself into various forms.

These ideas are implied, along with others, in the remarkable Proteus in Book III of *The Faerie Queene* [by Spenser]. After saving Florimell from the lecherous fisherman by carrying her beneath the sea, he in turn forces his intentions on her. . . . This flatterer pushes his temptations further: when she avows that she loves "none, but a Faerie knight," he obligingly changes into that shape, and others. . . . He tries stronger means: urging "sharpe threates," appearing to her in "dreadfull shapes," and finally casting her in prison.

Several points are important in this passage. The Vertumnus myth is the closest analogue to the tale, which is one of lust and temptation. Proteus appears first as a flatterer; this too is part of the tradition around Vertumnus. Even more significant is the implication, in Proteus' flattery and in his first transformations, that this type of love sacrifices all integrity of the self. (pp. 283-84)

A myth of the lover who changes form might end in various ways. Vertumnus threatens to force his lady, but she yields willingly instead. . . . Harington, translating Ariosto, gives a similar outcome in Proteus' affair with the King of Ebuda's daughter: "With her consent he forst the princely wench. . . ." In Spenser rape becomes imprisonment and the lady fails to cooperate, but the source is still the Proteus and Vertumnus myths combined, perhaps through Ariosto. Shakespeare's character would resort to rape, but through a troubling series of events he discovers that he really loves someone else. Both Spenser and Shakespeare vary the outcome of the myth to fit particular ideas.

According to the myth of Proteus, he should be held fast until he resumes his own shape and tells the truth. . . . In Spenser Proteus remains on the level of appearances, as a rival of Florimell's true love, Marinell. . . . He passes through a variety of moods but can really have no hold on Florimell except force: his phantasms do not interest sensible women.

Though defective as plausible action, the ending of *The Two Gentlemen of Verona* also uses a variant of the Proteus and Vertumnus myths to work out a dialectic of appearance and reality. The mutable Proteus, having perhaps changed somewhat in mood and manner but much more in loyalty, is made to appreciate Valentine's friendship and Julia's love; he returns to his true relations with other people. One might even say that he resumes his true status because Julia has kept him bound fast all the time.

Shakespeare's Proteus shows many of the qualities attributed to the mythic figures. He lies whenever he chooses, and he certainly tries to tempt Silvia, though without success. More important, his change in love is a change of identity, a falling-off from his real self. Just as Valentine defines himself by his love, proclaiming that "Silvia is myself" [III. i. 172], so does Proteus. His chop logic satisfies him that pursuit of his new love, regardless of earlier ties to Valentine and Julia, is really self-fulfilment . . . :

> I to myself am dearer than a friend,
> For love is still most precious in itself. . . .
> I cannot now prove constant to myself,
> Without some treachery us'd to Valentine.
> [II. vi. 23-4, 31-2]

One overriding interest makes up his whole being, and for it he will cancel all else. But, as he almost seems to recall at first, one cannot discard one's past self that easily; the obligations remain, and he is eventually drawn back to his first state. The transformations of this Proteus are not, as in Spenser and the Vertumnus myth, the stratagems of an insecure lover framing his identity to advance his suit, but an attempt at fundamental changes of loyalty.

Proteus failed to predict a consequence of his altering of identity; Julia changes too. Her new status is shown physically by her disguise, adopted in loneliness before she knew of Proteus' treachery. Her discovery of his behavior prompts the feeling that his choice of a false and shallow self has reduced her to a false existence too. On Proteus' request for Silvia's picture, "to your shadow will I make true love," Julia comments to herself, "If 'twere a substance, you would, sure, deceive it, / And make it but a shadow, as I am" [IV. ii. 125-27]. Silvia is quite aware that Proteus has departed alike from his better self and from the real world: "your falsehood shall become you well / To worship shadows and adore false shapes" [IV. ii. 129-30].

By taking service as Proteus' page, Julia plunges more actively into the world of illusion. She gains an ironic distance from her plight and contemplates it as an outsider, with dignified pathos. She is not Ariadne but someone who remembers having played the role of Ariadne. The irony of describing herself in the third person leads her to think of her disguise as made up of grief:

> since she did neglect her looking-glass
> And threw her sun-expelling mask away,
> The air hath starv'd the roses in her cheeks
> And pinch'd the lily-tincture of her face,
> That now she is become as black as I.
> [IV. iv. 152-56]

Her appearance itself shows that outside forces divert her from her true identity. Proteus must become himself before she can.

Her disguise has a practical value too; by purporting to be another she can catch Proteus off guard, prove her love by service to him, and eventually appeal to his better self. Meanwhile she uses her supposedly objective viewpoint to give an outsider's pronouncement on his change of love: "It seems you lov'd not her, to leave her token" [IV. iv. 74]. Earlier [IV. ii. 105-06] Proteus had pretended to Silvia that Julia was dead; now Julia tempts him to falsehood again: "She is dead, belike?" [IV. iv. 75]. He is more honest this time, but he still sends Julia out to woo for him. The tasks she assumes with her disguise contradict her true identity: she cannot be her master's "true servant" unless she is "false traitor" to herself [IV. iv. 104-05].

The chameleon, . . . an emblem of the lover's moods along with the Proteus myth, figures in the play. Sir Thurio is one in his anger [II. iv. 25-7]. In another sense the chameleon resembles lovers since it can live on air, promise-crammed. For Speed this idea is a touchstone of unreality: "though the chameleon Love can feed on the air, I am one that am nourish'd by my victuals and would fain have meat" [II. i. 172-74]. Lucetta is equally matter-of-fact in her punning complaint against Julia's moodiness in love: "I would it were [near dinner-time], / That you might kill your stomach on your meat, / And not upon your maid" [I. ii. 67-9]. Here is the self-mockery of Shakespeare's comedies, servants putting us at an ironic distance from the whole action. (pp. 284-86)

In the final scene of the play Proteus makes his last, most grotesque transformation. It should seem far from his true nature (at least he must admit it is "'gainst the nature of love" [V. iv. 58]), and Valentine promptly recalls him. Two major forces redeem Proteus, both important thematically; he is brought to himself by his friend's generosity and by his lady Julia's steady, though despairing, love. She reveals herself through the ring—that is, through a token of Proteus' former self. . . . The ring as a sign of Julia's identity is more significant than, say, a strawberry birthmark; it reminds Proteus of his obligations to the past, in contrast to his later intentions toward Silvia (represented by the other ring). But Julia holds both rings, and with them she intercepts Proteus' love. She returns Proteus to his true self by comparing her change of identity with his:

> It is the lesser blot, modesty finds,
> Women to change their shapes than men their minds.
>   [V. iv. 108-09]

Once he learns constancy, no more disguises will be needed. (p. 286)

For Shakespeare the theme of identity is the controlling force in [The Two Gentlemen of Verona]—even the concepts of love and friendship are subordinate to it. The basic distinction is between Proteus' true self, defined by his commitment to Julia, and his false one, which arises from his attempt to force his attentions on Silvia. True love corresponds to true self, and false love to false self. Shakespeare plays very heavily on the audience's sense of the happy resolution and their desire for everything to come out well: Julia is around to remind us which love is the true one, and if the ending is to work at all it must rely on the feeling that Proteus has gone momentarily wrong and if something drastic is done in a hurry he may be retrieved. The memory of Proteus' true self is emphasized for the audience through Julia, who loves him.

It is only in Proteus' false self that the conflict of love and friendship arises. The love that puts him in rivalry with his friend is his desire for the wrong woman, Silvia, and for this he betrays his friendship to procure Valentine's banishment and lies about Valentine's death in hopes of winning Silvia. The ending is symmetrical if nothing else, for it unwinds the tangle in reverse order. Valentine reproaches Proteus for his falsehood as a friend, and Proteus is shamed into repentance. When Valentine offers Silvia to Proteus, it would seem that for Valentine friendship has won out over love, just the reverse of Proteus' decision when put in the dilemma. Silvia may have been right when she answered Proteus' question "In love / Who respects friend?" with "All men but Proteus" [V. iv.

53-4]—though Valentine's demonstration of sacrifice is extreme. But Julia's response spares us this calamitous generosity, for her love toward Proteus, and the ring she bears which reminds him of his old obligation, convince him that his genuine love is for her and not Silvia. His ungallant question "What is in Silvia's face, but I may spy / More fresh in Julia's with a constant eye?" [V. iv. 114-15] is meant as a recognition of what is best for him, not as a slur on Silvia—though it is best spoken to Julia, out of Silvia's hearing. Thus he is brought to recall his original self (before "Inconstancy" had made him "run through all the sins" [V. iv. 112]) and the conflict of love and friendship is dissolved. Proteus has made his last change, from illusion back to his true form, and marriage will fix him there.

Early in the play Proteus states a formula that seems to anticipate Restoration drama when he says of Valentine, "He after honour hunts, I after love" [I. i. 63]. Matters are soon changed as Valentine falls in love and Proteus abandons his first love for another, but the description is still valid for later events. When his false love for Silvia conflicts with what had been friendship, Proteus chooses love. But when Valentine is forced into a decision between the claims of love and friendship, both of which he feels sincerely, he prefers the honor of yielding to his friend. Though plausibility is sacrificed, the schematization holds.

Luckily Valentine's sacrifice of love for friendship is avoided, and really his friend should not accept it: Proteus must return to Julia. . . . [In] the audience's experience Julia has been made too real to be ignored; her claim to Proteus is valid, and he will not be fully himself again until he acknowledges her. For this reason, even if Valentine's offer of Silvia were credible and were fair to Silvia, it would be no better than a well-intentioned mistake. We expect Proteus to return to both his true friendship and his original love, and Valentine's offer would have left the movement incomplete. But once our expectations have been fulfilled by Proteus' return to Julia, love and honor are seen to be in harmony; Valentine's loyal friendship and Julia's true love both remind Proteus what he has been. The right love and sincere friendship are compatible, and both belong to Proteus' better self.

In this portrayal of a fickle man the myth of Proteus adds meaning by helping to suggest an underlying reality of character which will remain after the fickleness, and its resultant treacheries, have been purged away. The myth does not appear directly in other comedies in which the heroes are changeable, but the contrast between the real self and its illusory variations is implicit in the characters and sometimes in the very structure of the plays. This is true in A Midsummer Night's Dream, where all the changes of loyalty (except Titania's) take place in the men, and appear as merely "the fierce vexation of a dream" [IV. i. 69]. . . . The audience can laugh from a vantage-point that gives them knowledge superior to the deluded lovers; and the changes cancel out to yield a better result that is confirmed as reality by daybreak and Theseus' horns. (pp. 288-90)

The theme of identity, with its contrast between the real and the false self, gives a meaning and a fittingness to the reform of the erring heroes in some of Shakespeare's comedies. This is the serious subject of The Two Gentlemen of Verona, implied in the myth of Proteus. And Shakespeare has added a significant force which continues in later comedies, the redeeming heroine who brings her man to a true concept of himself. If Proteus can be bound firmly, he holds his true shape. (p. 291)

William O. Scott, "Proteus in Spenser and Shakespeare: The Lover's Identity," in Shakespeare Studies: An Annual Gathering of Research, Criticism, and Reviews, Vol. I, 1965, pp. 283-93.

ROBERT GRAMS HUNTER (essay date 1965)

[In his book-length study Shakespeare and the Comedy of Forgiveness (1965), Hunter places many of the plays in the tradition of "the comedy of forgiveness." In the following excerpt, he disputes H. B. Charlton's claim that the final scene of The Two Gentlemen of Verona fails in its recourse to "a primary article in the romantic faith" (see excerpt above, 1930); instead, Hunter asserts that Valentine's sudden offer of Silvia to Proteus is not a chivalric gesture, but a "summation of the Christian attitude toward repentance which . . . underlies the denouement in forgiveness." Shakespeare's audience, he contends, certainly accepted the conclusion on this basis.]

Geoffrey Bullough has described The Two Gentlemen of Verona as "a dramatic laboratory in which Shakespeare experimented with many of the ideas and devices which were to be his stock-in-trade and delight for years to come" [see Additional Bibliography]. This is certainly true of the play's denouement in forgiveness. That climax in pardon comes at the end of the comedy when Valentine's unexpected appearance on the scene prevents his best friend, Proteus, from raping Silvia, Valentine's sweetheart. Nothing is more conducive to contrition than getting caught, and Proteus immediately repents of his evil ways:

> Prot.: My shame and guilt confounds me:
> Forgiue me Valentine: if hearty sorrow
> Be a sufficient Ransome for offence,
> I tender't heere: I doe as truly suffer,
> As ere I did commit.
>
> [V. iv. 73-7]

Valentine's reply is a summation of the Christian attitude toward repentance which . . . underlies the denouement in forgiveness and gives it its emotional force:

> Val.: Then I am paid:
> And once againe, I doe receiue thee honest;
> Who by Repentance is not satisfied,
> Is nor of heauen, nor earth; for these are pleas'd:
> By Penitence th'Eternalls wrath's appeas'd:
> And that my loue may appeare plaine and free,
> All that was mine, in Silvia, I giue thee.
>
> [V. iv. 77-83]

H. B. Charlton's reaction to "this preposterous episode" [see excerpt above, 1930], is a fair sample of how the scene strikes a modern sensibility . . . :

> Even Valentine must have seen that the gesture was a little odd, because he quotes the legal sanction. It is the code, a primary article in the romantic faith—"that my love may appear plain and free." But it makes a man a nincompoop.

Perhaps. But Mr. Charlton seems not to realize that Valentine's gesture makes him a Christian nincompoop, for it is surely not a "romantic faith" (whatever that may be) or a chivalric code that Shakespeare is invoking here. It is a central tenet of Christianity—the religion which Shakespeare shared with his audience. Proteus informs Valentine that he has experienced "hearty sorrow"—contrition—for his sin. Valentine replies, with complete orthodoxy, that contrition alone makes satisfaction for

sin, and that the wrath of the God of Judgment is appeased by repentance. Sinful man must prove worthy of his own ultimate forgiveness by pardoning those who trespass against him. Such considerations would not, I imagine, make this episode any more palatable to Mr. Charlton. They do, however, make its acceptance by Shakespeare's audience more comprehensible and more interesting, and it is a clear testimony to the power of the concept of forgiveness that Shakespeare could depend upon the invocation of it for the success of so arbitrary a dramatic moment as Valentine's forgiveness of Proteus.

Furthermore, Shakespeare has gone out of his way to include this moment of forgiveness in the comedy. . . . There is a model for the forgiveness of Proteus in the play's source, however. Felix, the Proteus figure, is forgiven in the Diana Enamorada, but his forgiveness is granted, not by a friend, but by the woman he has wronged. One, at least, of Shakespeare's experiments in The Two Gentlemen of Verona was misguided, and he did not repeat it. By setting up the theme of friendship alongside that of romantic love and by making his humanum genus [mankind] figure an offender against both ideals, Shakespeare has dissipated the emotional force of his climax. In the four comedies which I shall label the romantic comedies of forgiveness (Much Ado, All's Well, Cymbeline, and The Winter's Tale) the humanum genus figure offends the woman who loves him and is forgiven by her.

The Two Gentlemen of Verona demonstrates that, from the beginning, Shakespeare associated romantic comedy with the denouement of forgiveness. (pp. 85-7)

Robert Grams Hunter, "Much Ado about Nothing," in his Shakespeare and the Comedy of Forgiveness, Columbia University Press, 1965, pp. 85-105.

WILLIAM E. STEPHENSON (essay date 1966)

[In the following excerpt, Stephenson attributes the absurdities and incongruities of The Two Gentlemen of Verona to the immaturity of Shakespeare's two naive male protagonists. He especially regards the "incredible forest scenes" of Acts IV and V and the inexplicable final scene as indicative of Shakespeare's treatment of youth in this play, contending that these episodes are best understood not as realistic drama, but as enactments of typical adolescent fantasies about love and heroism, depicted "in the guise" of actual events. Stephenson concludes that the contrast of these youthful "dreams" and "life's actualities" gives "coherence and credibility" to The Two Gentlemen of Verona.]

In reading The Two Gentlemen of Verona, it is a help to remember that the heroes Valentine and Proteus are two very, very young gentlemen. The play is often dismissed as an early, inexpert handling of some typical elements of romantic comedy that Shakespeare handled again, masterfully, in later plays. But in this one respect the play is unique: no other work by Shakespeare shows us protagonists quite so immature. They are sixteenth-century adolescents, still of an age to be treated firmly by their fathers as they go through the training that will at last make them polished courtiers. A number of things which otherwise seem incredible or unattractive in Valentine and Proteus take on a meaning and pattern when their extreme youth is stressed. The wild erratic swings of emotion, the naive tentativeness of behavior, the tame submission to elders, all become more understandable when we remember that they occur in youths just past the first changes of puberty.

The dreams and hallucinations of love, which figure importantly in Shakespeare's comedies of the 1590's, are considered in *The Two Gentlemen of Verona* as they affect the very young. The actions and speeches of Valentine and Proteus show them walking the uncertain ground of youthful imaginings, unsecured as yet by any solid experience of the world. They are at an age when dreams are as real as the events of one's life; certainly the dreams of these youths color their love affairs with Julia and Silvia. One may even suggest that Shakespeare in the latter part of the play weaves into the action of his romantic tale some of the timeless, unchanging fantasies of the half-grown—among them dreams of attaining ideal love on one's own terms, and of discovering oneself to have a highly noble character which impresses others mightily, and of being accepted by all elders while still a youth, at one's own valuation, as their equal if not superior.

The young girls of the play, Julia and Silvia, are each mature enough to fix their affections on one boy. But Valentine and Proteus, as Shakespeare shows, are still at the age of being in a dream of generalized romance, vaguely though passionately "in love with love". Their knowledge of the code of love, its traditional niceties and language, is as full as a gentlemanly Renaissance education can make it. But it is an external knowledge only. In Act I, Proteus makes all the proper moves, feels all the traditional feelings, says all the conventional speeches of the lover, in regard to Julia. Act II, however, shows him instantly switching his affection when he hears other proper, traditional, conventional love-language applied (by Valentine) to a second girl. His bewitchment is with the words, Shakespeare makes evident, not with Silvia. Again, Valentine in Act II is quite able to write off a good set example of a love letter, and in Act III shows an alarming rote knowledge of the techniques of successful abduction, in regard to Silvia. Yet he is quite unable to perceive Silvia's interest in him until the older Speed points it out, at which time he promptly succumbs to her, head over heels. Both boys are still "going through the motions", still in the dream of love.

Whether they know the meaning of actual love for the two girls, at least until the end of the play, is left in doubt. Valentine spends his time in the forest mooning over Silvia, while Proteus at court repeatedly refuses to take her clear "no" for an answer. But no sooner are the two reunited in the forest than Proteus gives up Silvia—and Valentine just as promptly says, in effect, "Well, if you really want her, go ahead and take her." How can such disparity between the theory and practise of love, and also such caprice, be explained? We can say unthinkingly, "This is a botched job of playwriting." Or, more discerningly, we can see the trait that Shakespeare is showing: the simultaneous keenness and inexperience and changefulness of youth in its first fancy-laden approach to love between the sexes.

The incredible forest scenes of *The Two Gentlement of Verona* may further be related to the dreaming youthfulness of the heroes. At first reading, the opening scene of Act IV seems simply impossible. Valentine, banished from Milan, enters the forest and is immediately accepted as the leader of a band of outlaws. He is chosen, it appears from the speeches of the scene, because he is young, has little money and no pressing family ties, but has good manners, a decent education, and the ability to speak several languages. The reader may easily think that such traits would better qualify a young man for a traveling scholarship than for the duties of brigandage.

But then on a further look at this scene built around Valentine, a curious resemblance appears to one of the great abiding dreams of adolescence: the dream of acceptance by glamorous strangers immediately after being rejected and scorned by the familiar

authorities of one's life. It is the dream Hans Christian Andersen embodied in his story of the Ugly Duckling. It is at least a possible reading that Shakespeare, following Valentine into the remote, romantic forest setting of the play, presents an adolescent's timeless fantasy of wish-fulfillment in the guise of an actual event of the plot.

If this scene may be read as the dramatic "enactment" of a youthful dream, the other forest scene at the end of Act V can be read as the fulfillment of *several* typical dreams for Valentine. First is the dashing rescue of Silvia from the hands of the ravisher Proteus. Coldly viewed, the details of the assault and rescue are out of character for both boys: impetuous Valentine, earlier a would-be abductor of Silvia, might be expected to assault a girl through sheer force of passion sooner than would Proteus; and Proteus would be more likely to hide and listen, up to the last moment of a scene of rape, than is Valentine. But the rescue itself is a dashing, romantic action— just the sort of thing that thousands of half-grown youths have pictured themselves doing, without any consideration of the realities of their circumstances.

A second dream-situation now follows in the scene: Valentine's high-flown denunciation of Proteus as a wrongdoer, followed by the instant repentance and remorse of the accused. The more ordinary reaction of a young man to a rival's hard words would be utter denial, or a reply having the sense, "All right, if you think you can stop me, go ahead and try." But Proteus is crushed by what Valentine says—thus following the pattern of that evergreen dream whereby one tells an antagonist exactly what one thinks of him, in round terms and with devastating effect.

Valentine's subsequent renunciation of Silvia to Proteus, appalling if viewed as the considered action of a young hero, is better understood as a third classic dream-action. Proteus has, for the moment, cut a noble figure in his speech of repentance. But Valentine can rise above him again by an even greater display of nobility, a towering act of self-sacrifice, of renunciation in unforgettable words. One can hardly estimate how many young people have pictured themselves doing just that sort of thing. Certainly it is a staple scene of romance. To give only one example: by sacrificing himself to the guillotine, while murmuring "It is a far, far better thing that I do . . .", Dickens' Sydney Carton not only rises above his love-rival in *A Tale of Two Cities,* but has become one of the best-remembered figures of nineteenth-century fiction.

After Julia breaks in on this moment of renunciation by fainting and revealing her identity to the others, there is still a fourth dream-situation to follow. The Duke of Milan is hustled onto the stage by Valentine's outlaws, who shout, "A prize, a prize!" [V. iv. 121]. Incredibly, less than fifty lines later, Valentine pleads the reformation of the outlaws and asks for their pardon. No evidence of change whatsoever is offered the Duke, but Valentine's bare word is accepted. Furthermore, the Duke goes on to offer the young outlaw the hand of his daughter—although he had banished Valentine, a young gentleman of good family, simply for aspiring to her in Milan. If this improbable conclusion stood alone in the scene, it might be viewed simply as the forcing down of a necessary happy ending on all the characters. But coming as it does after a number of other "enactments" of fantasy, one can also read it as the last wish-fulfillment of young Valentine, whereby the word and will of the youth are successfully imposed on the hitherto unquestionable authority of a father and elder.

Act IV. Scene iv. Proteus, Julia disguised as Sebastian, Launce, and Crab. By Sir John Gilbert (1858).

In all, a number of the improbabilities of *The Two Gentlemen of Verona*, which have been condemned as the crude romantic writing of an inexperienced Shakespeare, have coherence and credibility as long as the play is read as dealing with two very young, adolescent heroes still more aware of their dreams of life than of life's actualities. Even the implausible, romantic events of the play's ending accord well with the dreams that these youths might be expected to have. We can see that even in such an early play as this Shakespeare knew a great deal about the heart's fantasies of desire, and was beginning to write of them with unusual perception. (pp. 165-68)

> *William E. Stephenson, "The Adolescent Dream-World of 'The Two Gentlemen of Verona'," in* Shakespeare Quarterly, *Vol. XVII, No. 2, Spring, 1966, pp. 165-68.*

PETER G. PHIALAS   (essay date 1966)

[*In the following excerpt, Phialas asserts that* The Two Gentlemen of Verona *is the first of Shakespeare's comedies to demonstrate that "the act of forgiveness lies at the center" of the dramatist's thought, and he outlines the internal and external conflicts that lead to the final reconciliation in the play. While the conflict caused by external circumstances is prominent in* The Two Gentlemen, *he notes, the internal conflict between the characters'*

attitudes to love presages one of Shakespeare's most important comic motifs. Phialas examines these various attitudes to love in the play, describing the servants' parody of their masters and Silvia's slightly ironic view as contrasts to the conventional sentimentality of the other characters. The critic also points out that the presence in Silvia of "antithetical attitudes towards romantic love"—the ironic and sentimental—"is one of the most significant advances toward the Shakespearean comic mode."]

The Two Gentlemen of Verona is Shakespeare's first essay in romantic comedy, and though it is not a successful play, its faults as well as its merits have been somewhat exaggerated. Furthermore, its promise of things to come has been inaccurately identified. The play is promising, the modern argument goes, in that it employs motifs and bits of action which appear in Shakespeare's later comedies, but since the handling of these elements is said to be unsuccessful, it is difficult to see what the play promises in that respect. (p. 44)

Although the love-friendship conflict may have been popular in Shakespeare's age and although it reappears in some of his later plays, it is never again at the center of the action but ancillary to the main theme. In so far as *The Two Gentlemen of Verona* explores the comic handling of the love-friendship conflict, the play anticipates very little in the comedies which followed. On the other hand, *Love's Labour's Lost* deals throughout its action with the conflict of attitudes toward love, the conflict which will dominate the structure of Shakespearean romantic comedy. Nor does *The Two Gentlemen of Verona* contribute significantly to that structure in its use of cord-ladders, a friar's cell, a disguised heroine serving her beloved in his courtship of another woman, motifs which appear in the later comedies. The play's contribution is in terms of other matters. (p. 45)

[If] the conflict between love and friendship is never again given prominence in Shakespeare's romantic comedies, the theme of forgiveness and reconciliation most assuredly is. And in terms of this theme *The Two Gentlemen of Verona* may be said to anticipate an important element in the structure of Shakespearean comedy, romantic or otherwise. And just as the choice of the love-friendship conflict attests to the play's early date and experimental nature, as well as to Shakespeare's immaturity, so does the inexpert handling of forgiveness and reconciliation in the concluding scene. For it is certainly clear that no defense of the play has been able to remove the charge of ineptitude and awkwardness in that final episode. Nor is there any doubt that the same kind of dénouement is handled much more successfully in later comedies. The forgiveness and rehabilitation of Proteus is repeated in such characters as Oliver in *As You Like It,* Angelo in *Measure for Measure,* as well as in other characters in other plays. Indeed, the act of forgiveness lies at the center of Shakespeare's thought; and it is the ultimate measure of human achievement. (p. 53)

[But] Valentine's forgiveness is far too swift and perfunctory. . . . [In] *Measure for Measure* Isabella's forgiveness of Angelo which works his salvation, and in a special sense her own, is agonizingly slow to show itself. At least it is made to seem so to Mariana and to us. And it is precisely this slowness and deliberation which we miss in *The Two Gentlemen of Verona.* Forgiveness is much slower, much more difficult to attain, than repentance. No audience, of course, objects to forgiveness as an ideal of conduct, and no audience would object to it on the stage if it came even to the noblest of men after a recognizable human effort. It may indeed be true that in the final scene of *The Two Gentlemen of Verona* "the inmost meaning of love, as Shakespeare conceived it, is displayed" [see excerpt above by John F. Danby, 1960], but it is a meaning placed upon the incident from the outside so to speak, a meaning displayed indeed, not experienced.

The theme of forgiveness and reconciliation, appearing for the first time in *The Two Gentlemen of Verona,* became a fundamental element in the structure of Shakespearean comedy. In the romantic comedies that theme is an adjunct to the indispensable union of lovers at the conclusion of each play. And since the union of lovers as well as forgiveness and reconciliation imply opposition and strife, it is clear why the action of Shakespearean romantic comedy must express itself in conflict. What matters most here is the kind of conflict or conflicts which serve as the basis of Shakespeare's romantic plots. One of these conflicts is external, the opposition to love and lovers by antagonistic characters or circumstances, such as Proteus' perfidy or the attitude of Silvia's father toward her love of Valentine, or Don John's obstruction of the Claudio-Hero love affair in *Much Ado About Nothing,* or the strife between the two Dukes in *As You Like It.* But in addition there is the far more significant interior opposition proceeding from the lovers' attitudes toward love and each other. In all, Shakespeare dramatizes three such attitudes in his romantic comedies: the idealizing of love and its object, the realistic or matter-of-fact concept of it, and the outright rejection or disdain of love. In *The Two Gentlemen of Verona,* the stress is upon the external conflict between love and friendship, a conflict never again given such prominence in the later comedies. But the play deals also with the internal conflict, that is, with the interplay of attitudes toward love. And it is precisely here where *The Two Gentlemen of Verona* makes its most significant contribution to the emerging form of Shakespearean romantic comedy.

Though the disdain of love, the scoffing at it, is given limited scope in the play, it is nevertheless an important motif, which in such plays as *Love's Labour's Lost* and *Much Ado About Nothing* becomes the basis of most of the comic action. In *The Two Gentlemen of Verona* its role is tentative, as if Shakespeare was trying it out to discover its possibilities. Valentine scoffs at love in the opening scene, and of course upon sight of Silvia later in Milan he falls in love with her at once. And he proceeds to extol her beauty in the fashion of the Petrarchan blazon. In later plays Shakespeare will invent episodes in which the scoffer at love is mocked and will balance these with additional episodes mocking the hyperbolic Petrarchism of the scoffer now transformed into a lover. In the play before us only the latter device is exploited, and this exploitation takes us to the other and larger conflict of these plays, that is the opposition between the conventions or poetics of love and the realistic or matter-of-fact concept of it.

Early in the opening scene Valentine alludes mockingly to one of the archetypal romances which recur throughout Shakespeare's romantic comedies. When Proteus promises to pray for him, Valentine replies that if he does he will pray on

> some shallow story of deep love,
> How young Leander cross'd the Hellespont.
> [I. i. 21-2]

This passage does double duty by not only recording Valentine's mockery of love, his comic hamartia for which he will later do penance, but also by establishing the tone and general atmosphere of the lover's attitude towards his love. For Proteus is indeed in these early scenes the lover of romance, the votary of love, whom the "heavenly Julia" has completely "metamorphosed." But the hyperbolic blazon of the beloved lady is

properly reserved for Valentine, the scoffer who, after seeing Silvia, is himself bitterly suffering the pains of the convention. . . . In the fashion appropriate to romantic lovers he showers conceits upon his lady: she is a "heavenly saint," she is "divine," or

> if not divine,
> Yet let her be a principality,
> Sovereign to all the creatures on the earth.
> [II. iv. 151-3]

She is a "jewel," a "pearl," "pure gold." Even Proteus, himself a lover and therefore adept in the art of hyperbole, is taken aback by Valentine's "braggardism." And later on the letter Valentine intends for Silvia, which the Duke intercepts along with the cord-ladder, is of course a love sonnet, though the Duke reads only eleven lines of it. Finally Valentine's lament for his banishment, anticipating Romeo's, is in the proper self-pitying idiom of the much-suffering romantic lover:

> To die is to be banish'd from myself,
> And Silvia is myself. Banish'd from her,
> Is self from self, a deadly banishment! . . .
> [III. i. 171-73]

Even the foolish Thurio, prompted by Proteus, courts Silvia with a "sonnet," which is presumably the song "Who is Silvia?" [IV. ii. 39] sung to her by his musicians. . . . "Who is Silvia," that "sweet-complaining grievance" [III. ii. 85], though ostensibly offered by Thurio's consort, is used by Proteus to advance his own suit, and a few lines later he takes credit for it. Although "Who is Silvia?" may have been Shakespeare's first attempt to employ song in the comedies, it is clear that the attempt is eminently successful. Not only does the song reproduce and by exaggeration caricature the extravagance of the Petrarchan sonnet, but it also implies a comment upon both Thurio who addresses the song and Proteus who later appropriates it. The incongruousness of the song's spirituality to Thurio's character points up the ridiculousness of his courtship; and the juxtaposition of Proteus' betrayals with that same spirituality vitiates the slightest suggestion of integrity on his part.

Although the two gentlemen of Verona are shown addressing their ladies in the self-satiric conceits of the sonneteers, the ladies themselves offer a striking contrast in their protestations of love. The passionate Julia approaches much closer to the sentiments of the conventional lover, and it is she who, alluding to her intended journey to Milan, speaks of herself as a "true-devoted pilgrim". . . . For Proteus is not like other lovers; he is a paragon of men.

> His words are bonds, his oaths are oracles,
> His love sincere, his thoughts immaculate,
> His tears pure messengers sent from his heart,
> His heart as far from fraud as heaven from earth.
> [II. vii. 75-8]

And it is Julia who later associates her own plight with that of Ariadne, "passioning" for Theseus. But if further evidence is needed that Julia is the true heroine of romance, her conduct in the episode with Proteus' letter early in the play certainly supplies it. More particularly her words to the torn pieces of that letter proclaim her as the romantic lover, a creature of artificial pathos and excessive sentiment.

With Silvia it is not so. In studies of the play she is nearly always dismissed as the representative of convention, as the exemplar of the stilted words and movements imposed by the code of romance. It is true, of course, that she addresses Valentine as her "servant" and that when Proteus is introduced to her she accedes to Valentine's request that she entertain his friend as his "fellow-servant," although she gives her response a slight suggestion of the gentlest irony. And it is also true that her romantic *milieu* is confirmed by the atmospheric function of Sir Eglamour. But Silvia is a much more complex character than that, and the question in the opening line of the song addressed to her has, I believe, a just aptness easy to overlook. The answer given in the song is that she is "holy, fair and wise" [IV. ii. 42], but this is the view of the romantic lover, not her own nor the poet's estimate of her. Much has been made of what Silvia anticipates in the later comedies. She prefigures Juliet in the harsh treatment she receives at the hands of her father, in her flight from a marriage she detests, in her rendezvous at the friar's cell, and so on. In her flight from an angry father she anticipates also Rosalind and Celia of *As You Like It.* Like Imogen she is wooed with a song offered by a detested lover. All this may be true, but of far greater significance is what she anticipates, not in such incidents, but rather in the conception of the chief heroines themselves of the later comedies. And here, it may be said, lies one of the significant innovations of the play.

Silvia differs from Julia not merely in the color of her hair, which the poet, as will be his custom, takes care to indicate, introducing with the gentlest mockery the perverse predilection of both gentlemen of Verona for a brunette, although Julia's own hair is not only Queen Elizabeth's "perfect yellow" but also the indispensable color of the heroine of romance. What further distinguishes Silvia from Julia is that she is possessed of a sturdier nature, greater spirit and directness. And these, though necessary to the most elementary distinction between two characters of the same sex, accompany or perhaps are responsible for a special point of view, a perspective which we shall find in its final perfection in later heroines, in Portia of *The Merchant of Venice* and even better in Rosalind of *As You Like It,* as well as Viola of *Twelfth Night.* Silvia falls in love with Valentine, calls him her servant, she is associated with Sir Eglamour, she is said to be "holy fair and wise"; but she is something else too. She is able to look at romance and its trappings with a gently ironic twinkle. Upon the insipid rivalry of Valentine and Sir Thurio and their protestations she comments directly with the line "A fine volley of words, gentlemen, and quickly shot off" [II. iv. 33-4]. In presenting Proteus to her, Valentine informs her that his friend would have come along with him to Milan

> but that his mistress
> Did hold his eyes lock'd in her crystal
>   looks.
> *Silvia.* Belike that now she hath enfranchis'd them
> Upon some other pawn for fealty.
> *Valentine.* Nay, sure, I think she holds them prisoners
>   still.
> *Silvia.* Nay, then he should be blind; and, being
>   blind,
> How could he see his way to seek out you?
> [II. iv. 88-94]

To Valentine's further protestations, she adds the abrupt "Have done, have done; here comes the gentleman" [II. iv. 99]. What the dramatist attempts to unite in Silvia in this early study of his ideal romantic heroine is sentiment, even passion, with the ability to see both of these as well as one's self in amused perspective. In Rosalind of *As You Like It* . . . , the union of the two seemingly antithetical attitudes towards romantic love

and its concomitants achieves a charming equilibrium. But though that union reaches no such perfection, the attempt is made in earnest for the first time in this play, and that attempt is one of the most significant advances toward the Shakespearean comic mode. For that mode . . . is crystallized in the temperament of Shakespeare's later comic heroines, to whom it gives their very life and being.

But the juxtaposition of two attitudes towards love tentatively expressed in the character of Silvia is supported by the presence of different characters representing the two points of view. In this, Shakespeare is following tradition and his own practice in the earlier comedies where the servants, for instance, parody their masters' romanticism by means of anti-romantic speech or action. . . . The realism of Launce's stage action with his dog, his description of the milkmaid he loves—"She hath more qualities than a water-spaniel . . . she can milk . . . she hath no teeth . . . she hath more hair than wit . . ." [III. i. 272-73, 278, 340, 358]—all these are far too pointedly relevant to the courtship of the aristocratic lovers to be taken as accidental. Launce is indispensable to the conduct and meaning of the story: he is a necessary device in the structure of Shakespeare's emerging comic mode. And where the country lout is absent, his role is assumed by the clown or jester, but the role is the same: to parody through contrasting realistic speech and action the sentimental romanticism of the main story.

In this function Launce is aided by Speed, who is of different ancestry, being an immediate descendant of the classical slave somewhat reduced in both sparkle and stature in the plot. But he does his best to give perspective to the activities of the romantic lovers. It is Speed who delivers himself of a satiric description of Valentine's love symptoms [II. i. 18-32], very like those discovered by Benedick in Claudio and by Rosalind mockingly found wanting in her Orlando. It is Speed who in the midst of his master's soulful concerns with love keeps talking of his belly. When he reminds Valentine that it is dinner time, his master, having just had a meeting with Silvia, sighs that he has dined. To which Speed responds: "Ay, but hearken, sir; though the chameleon Love can feed on the air, I am one that am nourish'd by my victuals and would fain have meat" [II. i. 72-4]. Earlier in the play he informs Proteus that he has carried his letter to Julia. And having exchanged with him some lines of feeble quibbling on ship—sheep and the ubiquitous horn, he says that he, "a lost mutton," gave the letter to "a laced mutton" [I. i. 96-7], and she gave him nothing for his labor. What matters here is not the crudeness of Speed's quibbling but rather the introduction of the phrase "laced mutton." Its function, as the function of bawdry elsewhere in Shakespearean comedy, is simply to oppose and by juxtaposition reduce the excessive sentiment of the romantic action. At least two editors of the play have been scandalized by Speed's apparent liberty, for they assume that he is here referring to Julia. But although that is the apparent meaning of the lines, Speed in fact had given the letter to Lucetta, who in the scene following brings it to her mistress.

But the use of bawdy quibbling for the purpose cited above is not reserved for the servants or even the male characters only. On the contrary, one of the most striking features in the speech of Shakespeare's great comic heroines is its bawdry, although this is not true of the heroines of *The Two Gentlemen of Verona.* Here such speech is given to Lucetta, who insists Julia must have her breeches made with a cod-piece. To which Julia at first objects:

Out, out, Lucetta! that will be ill-favour'd.
Lucetta.   A round hose, madam, now's not worth a
     pin,
     Unless you have a codpiece to stick pins on.
                                        [II. vii. 54-6]

Compared to the bawdry the ladies of *Love's Labour's Lost*
(for instance) bandy about, this is exceedingly feeble, but it
will serve. Like Speed's laced mutton and horns and Launce's
parodies, Lucetta's lines advance the claims of nature by placing them next to the claims and codes of the romantic convention. And the juxtaposition of the two extremes, faintly
here but more forcefully in the later comedies, points to a more
nearly balanced attitude towards the experience of being in
love. It is in this attempt to base part of its comic action upon
the opposition of extreme attitudes and by implication to suggest the mean that *The Two Gentlemen of Verona* can be called
Shakespeare's first romantic comedy. For it is this aspect of
the play's structure which Shakespeare takes up in the later
plays and for which he achieves a near perfect mode in the
"joyous" comedies. (pp. 55-64)

> Peter G. Phialas, "'The Two Gentlemen of Ve-
> rona'," in his Shakespeare's Romantic Comedies:
> The Development of Their Form and Meaning, *The
> University of North Carolina Press, 1966, pp. 44-64.*

NORMAN SANDERS   (essay date 1968)

[*Sanders examines "the dramatic contrast between two divergent
attitudes to love" in* The Two Gentlemen of Verona: *Proteus's
purely visual love of shadow rather than substance and Valentine's
desire for a more inward, spiritual type of affection. He also
emphasizes Julia's role in the dialectic pattern of the play, asserting that the heroine establishes a mean between the two protagonists and embodies "some special standard of constancy and
ultimate test of love's reality." The critic further comments on
the significance of the comic subplot in* The Two Gentlemen *and
concludes by linking Shakespeare's dualistic method with his unsuccessful attempt to balance "two standards of reality"—that
of the audience and that of the play itself—adding that the movements between these two worlds make it impossible to accept "the
stilted characteristics and idiom of the Romance convention."*]

In *The Two Gentlemen of Verona* Shakespeare clearly faced
certain problems in attempting to give dramatic form to the
materials of a literary genre that depended for its effects on
narrative spread, spatial range, a great variety of situations,
largely incredible character motivation, and unspecific geographical location. And, as has often been pointed out, there
are abundant signs in the play of the strain that these problems
imposed.

To begin with, the play's geography is both inaccurate and
inconsistent. Proteus and Valentine go from Verona to Milan
by sea, whereas it is clear that the disguised Julia intends to
make the journey between the two cities by land, as does
Valentine returning after his banishment. The Duke of Milan
in III. i. 81 appears to imagine that the dukedom he rules is
Verona rather than Milan; and [II. v. 2] Speed, in Milan,
welcomes his friend Launce to Padua. . . . (p. 12)

Next, Shakespeare was unable to maintain in his dramatic treatment the necessary balance between the Romance convention
within which he was working and the kind of characterization
demanded by this convention. Valentine is obviously intended
to be the focus of romantic sympathy as an attractive, idealistic
young man whose love for Silvia is credible and whose youthful

responses, first to Proteus's love affair and later to his own
difficulties, are the result of an accurate if not very profound
observation of human nature. Yet he is manipulated like a
puppet by the Duke, and is presented as the risible object of
the wit of both Speed and Silvia. To a lesser degree the character of Proteus suffers also, for the interest generated by his
reactions to his moral dilemma is disproportionate to the stereotyped role he has to enact as a false friend and treacherous
lover. Julia, too, at one moment in the play (V. 2), comments
on Thurio's pretensions as a suitor in a Speed-like manner that
is out of keeping with her character as it has been depicted up
to this point. Among the other figures, Silvia apparently loses
both tongue and intelligence in the final scene, and her would-
be protector and champion, Sir Eglamour, is set up as the ideal
courtly lover and chivalric knight in one scene (IV. 3) only to
be knocked down as a coward at his first testing (V. 3).
(pp. 12-13)

Nevertheless, despite all the acknowledged weaknesses of the
play most students of Shakespeare would underwrite Dr Johnson's over-all impression: 'When I read this play I cannot but
think that I discover both in the serious and ludicrous scenes,
the language and sentiments of Shakespeare' [see excerpt above,
1765]. Many of the playwright's favourite character-types,
themes, situations, and details make their first appearance in
this play in a recognizably Shakespearian form. (p. 14)

The Two Gentlemen of Verona, however, throws far more light
on Shakespeare's later comic vision than any listing of dramatic
situations and character-types would suggest. Simply because
the play reveals a relatively unsure dramatist at work and many
effects managed with a tiro's lack of expertise, it offers us an
opportunity to see more clearly than anywhere else in the canon
what were to become characteristic techniques. It stands as an
'anatomie' or show-through version, as it were, of Shakespeare's comic art and helps us to understand in part the least
appreciated section of the poet's work.

It is obvious from the deployment of the two pairs of lovers
that Shakespeare was aiming at a dramatic contrast between
two divergent attitudes to love, embodied in Valentine and
Proteus respectively; and, further, that Julia was to represent
some special standard of constancy and ultimate test of love's
reality, taking up a position between the two heroes. In a
manner that was to become typical, this contrast was to be
reinforced on the narrative level by the balancing of character
against character and situation against situation. On the poetic
plane, echoing words and iterative imagery were clearly designed to interrelate and develop key ideas or attitudes associated with the different aspects of love presented.

So far as the poetic effects are concerned, it is the verbal
implications of the love-at-first-sight convention that provide
the leading images. Proteus is invariably associated, both in
his honest and dishonourable love affairs, with that kind of
affection which resides in the eyes rather than the mind. In the
first scene of the play, Valentine starts the pattern of imagery
when he says . . . he would desire Proteus's company on his
travels

> Were't not affection chains thy tender days
> To the sweet glances of thy honoured love,
>   [I. i. 3-4]

and Proteus himself maintains the same note, ironically in view
of subsequent events, when he asks his friend . . . to

> Think on thy Proteus, when thou haply seest
> Some rare noteworthy object in thy travel.
>   [I. i. 12-13]
>   (pp. 15-16)

In the later conversation between the two friends [II. iv. 122-91] . . . , their contrasting attitudes to love are projected by a formalized parallelism of phrase. Proteus describes Silvia as an idol to be worshipped, against which Valentine names her a heavenly saint; and to the latter's claim for her divinity, Proteus admits only that she is an earthly paragon. Even allowing for the conventional exaggeration of style in this passage, Shakespeare is clearly showing us one man reaching for a semi-spiritual, Petrarchan definition of his affection while the other is more than content with the earthly limitations of the lady he has but had 'a look of'. After Valentine's exit, these various allusions are drawn together in Proteus's soliloquy, extending the impression thus far created by the introduction of new though related metaphors. Silvia is a 'newer object' which causes the remembrance of his former love to be quite forgotten; her perfections so blind him that his love for his previous mistress is like a waxen image which, when exposed to heat, will lose the 'impression of the thing it' is [II. iv. 202]. (p. 18)

On the other hand, Shakespeare's management of the second element in his opposition of the contrasting types of love is much less sure. Clearly he intended to set against this all too visually receptive Proteus a Valentine who is intellectually blinkered but emotionally clear-sighted. In Valentine's soliloquy after he has been banished by the Duke for aspiring to Silvia's hand, the verbal associations convey an attitude to love in sharp contrast with that of Proteus . . . :

> What light is light, if Silvia be not seen?
> What joy is joy, if Silvia be not by?
> Unless it be to think that she is by,
> And feed upon the shadow of perfection. . . .
> She is my essence, and I leave to be,
> If I be not by her fair influence
> Fostered, illumined, cherished, kept alive.
>   [III. i. 174-77, 182-84]

Here, unlike Proteus, he asserts the value of the substance rather than the shadow, of the tangible reality rather than the appearance; for him, love demands the surrender of self in order to create another 'essence' without which he will 'leave to be', and for which there can be no substitute. In this he is the first of the line of Shakespearian lovers who see truly both the inward as well as the outward beauty of their mistresses.

However, while Shakespeare's intention is clearly to counterbalance the two young men and their ways of seeing and loving, its execution is less happy. Whereas Proteus becomes more interesting as he moves from love of Julia, through a half-regretted fascination with outward show, on to a fond idolatry and violent lust, before making a sudden volte-face in the final scene, Valentine vacillates between lyric utterance and colourless mediocrity, before exhibiting what is perhaps fatal to the romantic hero—namely, sheer stupidity. First, we witness him blundering through the letter scene with Silvia (II. i), where he is unable to perceive the rather graceful courtly gesture by which his mistress declares her love for him, even though, as Speed's commentary on the device assures us . . . , it is a

> jest unseen, inscrutable, invisible
> As a nose on a man's face, or a weathercock on a steeple!
>   [II. i. 128-29]

Later, in III. i, he stands chatting with Silvia's father, with his rope-ladder under his cloak, and is tricked into making known the plans for his projected elopement by means of a ludicrously obvious stratagem on the Duke's part. Next, he is brought into contact with the impossible outlaws, whom one critic has appositely compared to the Pirates of Penzance, and who elect him their captain on the strength of his good looks and his skill in speaking foreign languages. Finally, his adherence to the friendship code obliges him to surrender his mistress to his newly-repentant friend with one of the most impossible lines in the English dramatic repertory [V. iv. 83]. Shakespeare was, of course, to make his audience accept greater incongruities than these later in his career; but here the character of Valentine as created is unable to withstand the strain of incredibility to which these encounters subject it. The result is a hiatus in the dramatic design as Valentine fails to offer any truly effective counterbalance to the figure of Proteus.

In view of this character weakness, one has some sympathy with those critics who have insisted that there is a good deal more allegory in the creation of Valentine than has generally been admitted. In his adventures there has been discerned a pattern similar to that found in the medieval poem and handbook of the Courtly Love code, the *Roman de la Rose* [by Guillaume de Lorris], and Valentine may be seen to pass through the same stages as the Courtly Lover, and to be tested with the same object—that of conquering self and emerging from the shadows into the reality postulated in Platonic theory. Nevertheless, it has to be admitted that, even with this allegorical content, in theatrical terms the character lacks the necessary dramatic interest to share with Proteus the audience's empathetic involvement. For, while Proteus too is in general a flat creation, there are moments in the play at which he enlists our interest, if not our sympathy. . . . [With him] there is a psychological dimension which is totally absent so far as Valentine is concerned; and at certain points later in the play, odd lines carry a conviction of his humanity, as when . . . he laments Silvia's

>   sudden quips,
> The least whereof would quell a lover's hope,
> Yet, spaniel-like, the more she spurns my love
> The more it grows and fawneth on her still.
>   [IV. ii. 12-15]

Interest in Proteus as a dramatic creation is strengthened by his close relationship with Julia and particularly by the role she plays in the later portions of the play. She is much more realistically conceived than either of the two leading male characters. Through a mixture of comic observation and the projection of human inconsistency and genuine feeling, Julia is believably portrayed in the letter scene (I. 2), and emerges as the first of those comic heroines of Shakespeare who are idealized by their lovers, but who impress the audience by their combination of practical good sense and healthy sensuality. It is true that Julia has all the romantic convictions of a young woman in love, and can lyrically transform her projected disguise and journey as a page to Milan into an odyssey of true love. . . . But she can also place the pieces of Proteus's love letter in her bosom in warm contrition, with the words . . . :

> Thus will I fold them one upon another.
> Now kiss, embrace, contend, do what you will.
>   [I. ii. 125-26]

It is, however, during the later parts of the play that Julia acts out her most important role in connexion with the conflict of values represented by Proteus and Valentine. Just before the Duke's banishment of Valentine, it is clear that, by the logical development of the metaphor of sight which has been associated with him, Proteus's attraction to Silvia is no longer merely visual but has become iconolatric. He sees her as an object rather than as a person, as his description of her pleading before her father suggests [III. i. 226-33]. . . . (pp. 18-24)

It is easy to see, in view of this development, what Shakespeare was attempting to do in the episodes leading to the gift of Silvia's portrait in the fourth act. Having been refused possession of Silvia's person, Proteus characteristically settles for ownership of a picture of her. Whereas Valentine in his soliloquy . . . refused to feed upon the 'shadow of perfection' when the substance was not by, this is precisely what Proteus begs to be allowed to do . . . :

> Madam, if your heart be so obdurate,
> Vouchsafe me yet your picture for my love,
> The picture that is hanging in your chamber;
> To that I'll speak, to that I'll sigh and weep,
> For since the substance of your perfect self
> Is else devoted, I am but a shadow;
> And to your shadow will I make true love.
>
> [IV. ii. 119-25]

To this relatively simple dramatic connexion between Proteus's standard of values and consequent action, Shakespeare adds an extra dimension by having Proteus employ the disguised Julia as the agent by which Silvia's portrait is brought to him. In one sense her page's costume makes Julia physically what Proteus is both nominally and morally: that is, a shape-changer, a metamorphosis. However, in her case, the transformation is a proof of constancy of affection rather than of emotional fickleness. (pp. 24-5)

The theme of the shadow-reality dichotomy is still further developed in Julia's meeting with Silvia, although there is no real opposition in the scene because both women are in agreement about Proteus's behaviour and the value of true and faithful love. Thus the exchange between them is pathetic, decorative, and conceited rather than dramatically exciting. Nevertheless, the form which the decoration and conceit takes is interesting in so far as it shows an attempt to develop the ideas of 'shadow' and 'shape-changing' through dramatic rather than poetic metaphor. . . . [We] are called upon to peer through a series of shifting illusions, both invented and actual: the real Julia, the role of the page Sebastian that she is playing now, the imaginary role of Ariadne played at the Pentecost revels. But in doing so we discern that it is the imaginary tears elicited from Julia by the supposed performance that represent the emotional reality of her present situation as she stands before the woman with whom Proteus is infatuated. (pp. 25-6)

[Julia] makes clear the point that Shakespeare has been developing about the true lover's imagination, and adds yet another touch of femininity which rounds out [her] character still further . . . :

> What should it be that he respects in her
> But I can make respective in myself,
> If this fond Love were not a blinded god?
> Come, shadow, come, and take this shadow up,
> For 'tis thy rival. O, thou senseless form,
> Thou shalt be worshipped, kissed, loved, and adored!
> And were there sense in his idolatry,
> My substance should be statue in thy stead.
> I'll use thee kindly for thy mistress' sake,
> That used me so; or else, by Jove I vow,
> I should have scratched out your unseeing eyes,
> To make my master out of love with thee!
>
> [IV. iv. 194-205]

It is in the articulation of what might be called 'the picture theme' that one may find a possible explanation of the most notorious textual crux in the play. At the end of II. 4, during which Proteus has talked with Silvia and Valentine for a space of some eighty lines or so, Proteus assures himself in soliloquy that he has unaccountably begun to love Silvia although, as he says . . . :

> 'Tis but her picture I have yet beheld,
> And that hath dazzlèd my reason's light;
> But when I look on her perfections,
> There is no reason but I shall be blind.
>
> [II. iv. 209-12]

If, as it would appear, Shakespeare designed to have the picture scene closely integrated with the themes of moral change and the deluding imagination associated with the lover, then it seems likely that Silvia's portrait would have made its appearance earlier in the play, possibly during a first meeting of Proteus and Valentine early in the second act, a scene, perhaps, of which the soliloquy at [II. iv. 192-214] might be all that remains.

It was a favourite technique of Shakespeare to have his low comic characters both verbally and conceptually related to the more serious elements in his plays. For example, the mechanicals in *A Midsummer Night's Dream,* Dogberry and the watchmen in *Much Ado About Nothing,* and Malvolio, Sir Toby Belch, and Sir Andrew Aguecheek in *Twelfth Night* are all integrated with the central love plots of their various plays on many different levels and by a multiplicity of poetic and dramatic devices. In fact, when one recalls just how much these character groups are an integral part of the plays in which they appear, and further remembers that a development of this technique of interrelation led ultimately to Prince Hal and Falstaff [in *Henry IV*], then it would perhaps be more accurate to regard it as an essential part of Shakespeare's vision of life as a whole.

In the low comic portions of *The Two Gentlemen of Verona* there is evidence of a similar care and thematic relevance. The two clownish servants, Launce and Speed, are both satirical commentators on their masters' actions and attitudes, particularly where their conventional love posturings are concerned. However, once this common function has been admitted, it is equally clear that their roles are different both in kind and in means of execution.

Speed is the verbal, witty type of clown. He belongs with those clever, prattling schoolboys who inhabit the plays of John Lyly, and with Don Armado's page, Moth, in *Love's Labour's Lost.* His is a brand of cleverness that Shakespeare quickly tired of; he came to prefer more human—and more easily tolerated—clowns. . . . Perhaps also this kind of comedy reminded Shakespeare, the adult actor and manager, too forcibly for him to look on it long with favour, of the popular rival Children's Companies, who are called in *Hamlet* those 'little eyases' crying out against their own succession.

But however this may be, Speed is of this kind. He is conscious of every verbal effect he aims at; every quibble he utters is a calculation; he is overtly satirical; and the deviousness of his puns is unmatched elsewhere in Shakespeare. The humour he provides is that of the patter comedian rather than the true clown, and is a product of the incongruity between his comments and the actual situation on which he is commenting. This being so, his relationship to the themes of love, friendship, and human intercourse generally is tenuous at best. He is a burlesque version of neither lover nor friend, save perhaps momentarily when he explains to Valentine that he is in love with his bed rather than a mistress, or when he urges his master to dinner with the observation that 'though the chameleon Love can feed on the air, I am one that am nourished by my victuals, and would fain have meat' [II. i. 172-74]. More often, his attack is satirically direct, as he criticizes the stupidities of love; it is the clear-eyed view of the emotionally uninvolved which enables him to see through Silvia's courtly device as she tenders Valentine his own letter, while the lover himself stands dulled by love's melancholy. For the rest, however, Speed's role in the play is either purely functional or simply verbally entertaining.

Launce, on the other hand, while certainly able to 'mistake the word' [III. i. 284] as complicatedly as Speed, is not limited in the same way either in his comic effects or in his dramatic relevance. Instead of just making comedy out of an already existing situation, he can create a comic situation out of a deadly serious response to the events of his life. While Speed observes incidents, Launce, out of himself and in his own terms, creates for the audience his ludicrous family leave-taking or the moment of his dog's disgrace, thus making his involvement total and his three monologues (in II. 3, III. 1, and IV. 4) truly comic. It is thus the parallelism and situational inversion of the scenes with Launce and Crab, rather than the straightforward verbal corrective of those involving Speed, which provide the critically humorous dimension of Proteus's fickleness, Julia's faithfulness, and the Romance code of friendship professed by the two men.

Launce makes his first appearance in the second act, and his monologue describing his parting from his family is clearly a parody of the affectionate leave-taking between Proteus and Julia which immediately precedes it on the stage. The relationships between the two situations are numerous and obviously intended. On the one hand, we witness the silent Julia whom Proteus rebukes for weeping and who leaves without a word; and, on the other hand, the clown depicts mock-epically the laments of his father, mother, and sister, and the heartlessness of his recalcitrant cur, who 'all this while sheds not a tear' [II. iii. 30-1]. In ironic contrast also are the talkative and soon-to-be-false Proteus who defines the wordlessness of true affection, and the loquacious and sincere Launce who describes the heartless silence of his dog. (pp. 27-31)

Similarly, the meeting of the two servants in Milan in II. 5 immediately succeeds that of their masters, and their conversation constitutes a commentary on the love theme. Launce's extreme caution about his own master's love affair, as he assures Speed 'Thou shalt never get such a secret from me but by a parable' [II. iv. 39-40], is an implicit reflection on Valentine's freely given confidences about Silvia and himself which puts him in Proteus's power and ultimately brings about his banishment.

The dramatic parallel thus early set up between the comic scenes and the love scenes is further developed in two more episodes. The dialogue in III. 1, in which Launce and Speed read the inventory of the vices and virtues of the former's *inamorata,* echoes both the friendship and the love themes. First, it evokes a contrast with the two earlier letter scenes involving Proteus and Valentine. Secondly, it offers a world far removed from that of romantic idealization: whereas Proteus and Valentine are concerned with the canons of true love and the concept of spiritual oneness with the beloved, Launce is preoccupied with marriage as an economic bargain. In his consideration, halitosis, toothlessness, and a demonstrable lech-

erous nature are of more immediate concern than sparkling eyes which are Cupid's weapons or the feminine graces that are lent by heaven. And it is wealth which overcomes all these deformities for Launce, even as it does for the Duke when he proposes Thurio for his son-in-law. As the scene ends, we realize that, like Valentine with Proteus, Launce has discussed his affair in friendship with Speed; and, as in the main plot Proteus will be punished for his perfidy, so here Speed will be 'swinged' for reading Launce's paper and be corrected like the 'unmannerly slave' he is for thrusting himself into secrets.

In Launce's final monologue in IV. 4, the parallel between master-man and dog-servant on the one hand, and mistress-page and servant-master on the other is developed. The dog Crab is again in disgrace as it enters with Launce, having urinated in Silvia's presence; for this the clown himself has taken the blame and been soundly beaten. In the comic terminology employed, Launce, the master, has been made the whipping-boy for his dog, the servant. . . . As the monologue ends, Proteus enters with the disguised Julia and here again we find a reversal of roles. Proteus, the former lover or 'servant' (to use the Courtly Love terminology employed by the lovers themselves), hires Julia, the former 'mistress', as a servant to fetch and carry for him in an affair which is, according to the play's love ethic, perverted. Launce's sacrifice on behalf of his dog is paralleled by Julia's loyalty, and Proteus's treachery by the behaviour of a wretched mongrel who pesters Silvia with his unwelcome attentions. The man who has betrayed his standards of love and friendship is thus equated dramatically with a dog who is 'a very cur'. And, in case we miss the point, Shakespeare has Launce's question 'How many masters would do this for his servant?' [IV. iv. 29-30] echoed by Julia's line 'How many women would do such a message?' [IV. iv. 90].

It can therefore be argued that the comic scenes do not simply satirize and belittle the love and friendship codes subscribed to in the main plot, but reveal them in a new light. These scenes are the method whereby the characters in the central love situation are shown in terms of a reality which exists even though they ignore it. It is by such methods that Shakespeare makes real and recognizable his Romance world, and, indeed, relates his comic world itself to the actual world of which it is a part.

One scene in the play is particularly successful in performing this essentially Shakespearian feat. It is when the disguised Julia arrives in Milan: she is led by the Host of the Inn to where she may watch her lover as he serenades Silvia under the guise of aiding Thurio's courtship. The song itself is an early example of Shakespeare's lyric skill—a skill later to be exercised extensively in *A Midsummer Night's Dream,* as well as in the other mature comedies. As such its verbal beauty as well as its Petrarchan spiritual values is at odds with both the standards of the singer, Proteus, and the fatuity of Thurio on whose behalf the performance is nominally taking place. This is the first though not the last occasion on which Shakespeare was to link a beautiful song with an unworthy performer; for example, the vicious and foolish Cloten in *Cymbeline* is provided with an equally fine song, 'Hark, hark! The lark at heaven's gate sings' [*Cymbeline,* II. iii. 20], for his adulterous serenading of Imogen. The song in *The Two Gentlemen of Verona* emphasizes musically the distance between Proteus's protestations and the reality of his fickle nature. However, and more important, it is also the means whereby Julia learns of her lover's faithlessness, and by which Shakespeare deepens and widens the issues raised by the central love theme of the play. As the Host and Julia stand watching the musical performance and while the instrumental postlude is being played, they comment in aside to the audience [IV. ii. 54-72]. . . . [Their] exchange contains a fusion of the verbal and the situational which suggests by means of a series of quibbles a contact between what we are watching on the stage and some wider perspective. It is one of the earliest occasions in Shakespeare where a specific personal issue is linked allusively to the universal. In this case, the troubles of a particular love affair are seen to be at odds with the principle of earthly harmony which, to the Elizabethans, was easily visualized as a reflection of that greater divine harmony, known as, and symbolized by, the music of the spheres. As such, this exchange is a simple example of the same magic by which Macbeth's deed of murder is shown as infecting Scotland and the very well-springs of life itself, and by which Goneril's and Regan's inhumanity to King Lear both reflects and becomes Nature's own indifference to suffering mankind.

As this short scene plays itself out, the Host and Julia are the last remaining characters on the stage. Julia turns to her companion and with a heavy heart says, 'Host, will you go?' to which he replies, rousing himself, 'By my halidom, I was fast asleep' [IV. ii. 134-35]. This two-line exchange contains within it one important aspect of the whole spirit of Shakespeare's comic vision. For here is suggested fleetingly what was to be conveyed much more complexly and centrally in the later plays: namely, a human viewpoint other than that which is at the focus of the play's action. At this point, the audience is reminded that while to Julia the music can have one set of implications—that is, the infidelity of her lover and the disharmony possible in the human heart—to the Host it is simply a concord of sweet sounds. Similarly, even as the overheard Proteus-Silvia dialogue is personally central to Julia's life and dramatically central to the audience's theatrical concern, so to the Host it has been merely a sleep-inducing episode. (pp. 32-6)

In all his comedies, Shakespeare conveys this dual vision, and reveals his awareness of two standards of reality: that of the audience and that of the play. Repeatedly, he stresses the one or the other, and, by oscillating between them, effectively destroys the audience-actor division. By a variety of devices—songs, asides, soliloquies, direct address—characters . . . cross the stage front, as it were, and join the audience's world. Conversely, by techniques like the overhearing trick, parallel sympathy, or reflective dramatic situations, the audience is drawn into the world of the play. With the fundamental division in the theatre, represented by the stage-front, thus broken or at least blurred, Shakespeare is able to create a new reality which includes and transcends the other two. Two observations of interest may be made perhaps about this reality. First, it provides both the audience and the play with the opportunity of being both committed and detached, of possessing longsight and nearsight, of belonging and witnessing. Second, it is the result, not so much of the fact that Shakespeare draws some of the materials of his comic art from the theatre or merely makes use of a knowledge of the theatrical experience, as of the fact that his vision's very being is located in the stage world. Shakespeare's comedies are truly theatre as well as drama.

However, it is only in comic masterpieces like *Twelfth Night* or *As You Like It* that we find this vision perfectly and completely articulated and embodied. In *The Two Gentlemen of Verona* it can be detected only from time to time. Yet, the fact that it does appear in scenes like the one discussed above or in the relationship that some of the comic scenes have to the main plot is one reason for the failure of the play as a whole. These small triumphs prevent the audience accepting those longer sections of the play in which Shakespeare falls back into the stilted characteristics and idiom of the Romance convention.

Nowhere in the piece is this more obvious than in the much-criticized final scene. From the text as we have it in the Folio of 1623, Shakespeare appears to be adhering to the conventional development of the 'brotherhood' stories exemplified by the Titus-Gisippus story in Sir Thomas Elyot's *The Book of the Governor*. Thus Valentine hears Proteus's brief repentance and forgives him his transgressions. Furthermore, as a proof of his sincerity he offers him Silvia . . . :

> Then I am paid;
> And once again I do receive thee honest.
> Who by repentance is not satisfied
> Is nor of heaven nor earth, for these are pleased;
> By penitence th'Eternal's wrath's appeased.
> And, that my love may appear plain and free,
> All that was mine in Silvia I give thee.
>
>   [V. iv. 77-83]

Whether these lines represent an abridgement of a much fuller 'repentance episode', as some scholars have argued, cannot be determined with any certainty. What is undeniable, however, is the authentic Shakespearian ring and sentiment of lines 79-80, and that, therefore, the speech, even if it is the result of cutting, must contain within it at least an indication of the direction which the action originally took.

What is important in the whole episode, however, is not the strange silence of Silvia while her fate is being decided, nor the rapidity of Proteus's repentance, nor the 'caddishness' of Valentine's action by twentieth-century standards, nor the unsatisfactory nature of some of the verse. Rather, it is that the playwright is expecting too great a shift of receptivity in his audience. As has been pointed out earlier, for brief moments during the play he has managed to lift some of his creations out of the original Romance framework he adopted; and at this point his success in having done so will not allow them to be fitted back again into the two-dimensional mould. The Proteus we have followed through a half-credible struggle with self and a deluded degeneration into lustfulness, and the Julia who has been for substantial stretches of the play's action a convincing figure both psychologically and symbolically, are simply out of place in what is little more than a Romance tableau.

More important still is that the serious issues raised by the play, such as the double definition of love or the dichotomy between half-realized ideals and a testing reality, find neither their dramatic nor their aesthetic climax in this recourse to an unqualified presentation of a rigid narrative convention. It is a case of Shakespeare's emerging skill as a dramatist causing him to fail in the management of this essentially undramatic convention, even as John Lyly's more limited dramatic gifts enabled him to succeed in approximately the same mode. It was only much later, after a great deal of experience and further experimentation, that the playwright was able to use the Romance and Pastoral conventions (in plays like *The Tempest* or *The Winter's Tale*) in such a way as both to make their theatrical acceptance possible and to widen their boundaries enough to embrace his very personal vision of life.

In *The Two Gentlemen of Verona,* then, Shakespeare was unable to reconcile successfully the many oppositions in his dramatic material—oppositions between his desire to use Romance conventions to enlarge his range of dramatic reference in a way neo-Classical comedy did not allow and the consequent need credibly to juxtapose impossible ideals and observed reality; between the world of Petrarchan love rituals and values and his instinctive perception of the dangers inherent in these for the natural man; between the great goods of mercy, forgiveness, and truth and the difficulty of making these things appear attainable in dramatic terms by none-too-perfect individuals; and between a knowledge of the importance of concepts like true identity, clear vision, constancy, and right relationships, and the necessity of a dramatic projection, in an arranged pattern of experience, of the transformation that such values can work in men. But, although in no general sense successful, Shakespeare came near to achieving his aims in certain details, which is perhaps what makes the play a fascination to anyone interested in his comic achievement as a whole. (pp. 37-40)

> *Norman Sanders, in an introduction to* The Two Gentlemen of Verona *by William Shakespeare, edited by Norman Sanders, 1968. Reprint by Penguin Books, 1981, pp. 7-40.*

ROBERT WEIMANN (essay date 1969)

[*Weimann discusses the technique of "laughing with the audience" as a comic mode in* The Two Gentlemen of Verona *that provides an awareness "through which the main theme of friendship and courtly love . . . is dramatically controlled and comically evaluated." He describes this comic technique as one in which the audience and the actor-character share "a mutual extension of awareness" or a "comic concurrence," as opposed to that in New Comedy, where the comic characters are the objects—and not the subjects—of the humor because they demonstrate "unconventional standards" of behavior. Weimann discerns three instances of this comic concurrence between audience and actor in* The Two Gentlemen of Verona: *in II. i., where Speed comments in asides on Silvia's and Valentine's "high-flown compliments"; in II. iii., where Launce directly addresses the audience on his leave-taking from his family; and in those scenes where Julia appears disguised as the male servant Sebastian.*]

[Laughing with the audience] on the comic stage has both a history and a theory, and from a comparative point of view it may perhaps be desirable to try and link up the historical (or theatrical), and the theoretical (or typological) aspects. Quite to integrate them must in the last resort involve both a historical view of theory and a theoretical view of history, and it would of course call for a vast amount of documentation. It seems therefore more fruitful just to raise the problem (without necessarily suggesting all the answers) and to do so within the limited context of one Shakespearian play. I shall take as my text *The Two Gentlemen of Verona,* where laughing with the audience can be studied in its dramatic functioning and where it serves, perhaps for the first time in Shakespeare's work, as an essential means of organizing, controlling and evaluating experience through a larger comic vision. Here, then, it assumes something of a structural significance, in the light of which some problems as to the reading of this early and experimental, but seminal, comedy can perhaps be viewed from a fresh angle. (p. 35)

If the comedy of laughing with the audience were to be fitted into a typological scheme, or into a system of types, it would certainly not be classed among what has traditionally been called 'New Comedy'. In the largely neoclassical tradition of

Menander, Jonson, Molière, Lessing, Ostrowski and Ibsen, the audience, if indeed it laughs at all, definitely laughs *at* but never *with* the comic figure. The comic figure so laughed at, usually is the comic *character* of dramatic illusion, but hardly ever the comic *actor.* The resulting laughter is inspired not by a more or less traditional feeling of social unity between audiences and *actors* but by a critical view of the contradictions between the norms of society and the unconventional standards of comic *characters,* be they the dupes or intriguers, the cheats or butts of society. The informing comic vision is essentially critical (or satirical, ironical, etc.) because the resolutions it offers are so many ways of exposing the human inadequacy of the antisocial attitudes of hypocrisy, vanity, snobbery, bureaucracy, as well as all kinds of mechanical or inorganic ways of isolation from the given norms of living. (pp. 35-6)

[We] have to go as far back as Hegel to find a more relevant, though still very general, theory of what I (for the sake of brevity) call laughing with the audience. Hegel in his *Aesthetics* draws attention to the fundamental distinction in comedy, 'whether the acting characters are for themselves comic or whether they appear so only to the audience'. While the latter appear—to Hegel—as merely ridiculous, the former are more truly comic in the sense that they enjoy the 'blessed ease of a subjectivity which, as it is sure of itself, can bear the dissolution of its own ends and means'. . . . Such a comic figure is truly comic, when 'the seriousness of his will and purpose is not to himself serious', and when his own mode of existence is free from any *Entzweiung,* any disunion or disruption of self and society. Now this theoretical or comparative approach to comedy, which my summary very much oversimplifies, suffers, in our present context, from several weaknesses which result from the highly speculative nature of these theories but especially from the fact that they completely ignore the practical and historical experience of the theatre as a social and technical institution. As recent research into Shakespeare's platform stage has made clearer than ever before, his theatre is, historically speaking, a highly complex and transitional institution in which there was room for (in Lyly's words) the most astonishing 'mingle mangle', for a true 'gallimaufray' of medieval and traditional as well as Renaissance and classical conventions, from which no single formula of comedy can be abstracted. Consequently, laughter in Shakespearian comedy cannot be reduced to any one comic pattern, or structure, or mood, and to realize this is to realize the limitations of any typological system, and the limited extent to which Shakespeare's comedy can be fitted into the categories of such a system.

If, then, we understand the various types of Shakespearian comedy and laughter against the historical background and the various social traditions of Shakespeare's theatre, we hardly have to remind ourselves that, in *The Two Gentlemen of Verona,* laughing with the audience is part of a larger whole: it is limited and defined by its context of speech, character and plot. To study the traditional popular mode in comedy, then, is first of all to be aware of this dramatic context which, in *The Two Gentlemen,* is largely built up by several conventions of speech and disguise, and various degrees and ways of audience awareness, such as are mainly associated with the characters of Speed, Launce and Julia.

To suggest the significance of this context, I can look at only two such conventions. First of all there is the series of *comic asides* by Speed in the first scene of the second act; Valentine, addressing Silvia in the style of courtly romance, greets her as 'Madam and mistress' with 'a thousand good morrows'—which

Speed, turning aside, echoes as 'a million of manners' [II. i. 96-9]. While Silvia and Valentine are exchanging their high-flown compliments and Silvia is wooing her Valentine, in Speed's words, 'by a figure' [II. i. 148] (the figure of his self-written love-letter), the clown continues to comment aside. These comments are definitely not overheard by Silvia and Valentine: they form no part of their dialogue, nor are they in the nature of any monologue or self-expression. Rather, they address the audience as from the angle of some kind of comic chorus; and it is through the comic chorus quality of Speed's comments that a dramatic interplay between the wit of the audience and the wittiness of the clown is achieved. The resulting laughter, both in the yard and on the scaffolds, shares the same perspective towards its object. The object (Silvia's and Valentine's high-flown addresses) is part of the play world, but the perspective of his comic asides links the clown with the real world of everyday experience. This involves some contact not simply between the audience and the character Speed, but between the audience and the actor of Speed's part who, as comic chorus with his asides, enjoys a perspective of awareness which is not strictly limited by the play world. The resulting unity of mirth, between the audience and the actor-character, cannot be dismissed as a clowning concession to the groundlings or as to so much genial atmosphere; for it turns out to be highly functional and quite relevant to any reading of the play as a whole. Its functional achievement can be measured by the degree to which it succeeds in the building up of a wider comic vision through which the main theme of friendship and courtly love (so underlined, in this scene, by words such as 'mistress' and 'servant') is dramatically controlled and comically evaluated.

Another and different kind of context in which the audience laughs with, rather than at, a comic person, is marked by Launce's famous leave-taking speech (II. iii.). Again, this is in the tradition of direct address, and, as it is spoken on Launce's first entrance, still harkens back to the extended self-introduction of the older comic figure in Tudor drama. But the way in which this speech achieves a comic concurrence of actor and audience is quite different from Speed's asides which, while they provoke laughter on the stage, direct this laughter at others. Launce, however, enters by himself, and while he and his family experience are the objects of his own mirth, he is also its free and willing subject—subject in the sense of *Subjekt* or ego, or self. His, indeed, is (in Hegel's words) the 'blessed ease of a subjectivity which, as it is sure of itself, can bear the dissolution of its own ends'. For the comic tension between the ridiculousness of the object and the hilarity of the subject (the *Subjekt*) of this speech is altogether remarkable, and it points to the dramatic quality of its comic achievement. This achievement, I suggest, can be measured by the degree to which the given tension between the fictitious object and the actual medium of this speech is solved in terms of the unity (and the contradiction) between the illusory character Launce and the real actor behind this character. For Launce to become the clowning object and the laughing subject of his own mirth and that of the audience, reveals an astonishing stability in his relations to the social whole. These relations connect the character and the actor, illusion and reality, so that the imaginative flexibility of his relation to the play world has much to do with the social security of his relation to the real world. And it is one of Shakespeare's supreme achievements in *The Two Gentlemen* to make these two relations not simply co-exist, but so interact that the resulting phenomenon attains a dramatic coherence and artistic integrity which, I think, is hardly surpassed in any of the mature comedies.

To suggest the comic effects of such laughing with the audience, one can say that Launce, much like Falstaff, is not merely witty in himself but the reason that others have and enjoy their own wit. The audience, or at least a certain section of it, is made to share the implicitly burlesque approach to the experience of leave-taking, but the actor, in performing this, shares the audience's hilarious experience over the scene so enacted. The clowning actor has, as it were, a public capacity for distancing the dramatic illusion and for undermining the social prestige of the main theme of courtly love and friendship; he is, at any rate, still very close to the social attitudes of a popular audience, but the audience in their turn, are no passive spectators, but share in the post-ritual community of theatrical mirth. (pp. 36-8)

[The] joint audience-actor perspective of the play world involves a mutual extension of awareness, if I may here use Bertrand Evans's fruitful term in a somewhat wider and perhaps slightly different sense [see excerpt above, 1960]. Such awareness, one would suggest, reflects and interconnects both the social security of the *actor's* relation to the real world and the imaginative and spatial flexibility of the *character's* relation to the play world, his implicit insight into and criticism of, the action of the play.

This extension of mutual awareness, or what I have called the comic concurrence of actors and audiences, is of course not restricted to Speed's asides or Launce's direct address. A more exhaustive treatment of the subject would have to consider Julia and the problem of disguise—a vast problem, almost too huge to be mentioned here, although like the clowns, the disguised person (such as Julia) is the character who is usually laughed with, but rarely laughed at, by the audience. Julia's disguise, just like Speed's asides and Launce's direct address, form perhaps the most sustained context in which the comic character is comic for himself, that is to say, in which that character himself enjoys the comic situation that he is either watching (as Speed does) or creating by himself (as in the case of Launce).

In *The Two Gentlemen*, as in the mature comedies, this awareness is as characteristic of the disguised person as it is of the clown or fool. In our examples it is shared by Speed who alone can interpret the figure of the self-written love letter by which his master is wooed; but it is also, if more indirectly, shared by Launce whose privileged perspective is implicit in the burlesque quality of his parallel action so that, in a later scene, again in direct address, he can say, quite explicitly:

> I am but a fool, look you, and yet I have the
> wit to think my master is a kind of knave: but
> that's all one, if he be but one knave. . . .
>   [III. i. 263-65]

Here, Launce is utterly secure in the actor's awareness of his own comic function ('I am but a fool', he says . . .). But at the same time he is and remains a character, and as a character he is equally secure in his awareness of other characters: he is aware—as Valentine is not—of the true significance of Proteus's doing.

To express this awareness, he (much as the old Vice does) uses two very revealing figures, a proverb together with a pun. The proverb, as the New Cambridge editor notes [John Dover Wilson], says 'Two false knaves need no broker', but Proteus, being but one knave, does need his broker, that is his go-between.

In using the proverb in this quibbling or perhaps riddling fashion, Launce renews and emphasizes his comic concurrence with the audience and he again appeals, from within the romantic comedy, to the Elizabethan world of everyday experience. But, by using the proverb incomplete, almost in the way of a riddle, he does more than simply express his privileged awareness: he uses this awareness so as to make the audience, as it were, participate in the playing of the game or the solution of the riddle. Basically, this invites the same kind of participation that the gravediggers in *Hamlet* provoke by their quibbling riddling question as to who was the first gentleman, or that the porter in *Macbeth* so ostensibly challenges ('and drink, sir, is a great provoker of three things' [II. iii. 25-6]). Through these riddling jests, of which of course Tarlton was the supreme master, the audience in their turn, being still very keen on sports and mirth, are imaginatively invited to join in the building-up of the comic perspective of the play. It is on the basis of the popular tradition that the clown achieves his comic concurrence with the audience. It is a concurrence which, in Shakespeare's comedy, does not merely relate the play world to the real world but which makes the representatives of the real world, through the associations of proverb, pun and riddle, and disguise, form an implicit element in the dramaturgy, the judgement, and hence the larger comic vision of the play. (pp. 40-2)

> *Robert Weimann, "Laughing with the Audience: 'The Two Gentlemen of Verona' and the Popular Tradition of Comedy," in* Shakespeare Survey: An Annual Survey of Shakespearian Study and Production, *Vol. 22, 1969, pp. 35-42.*

WILLIAM LEIGH GODSHALK (essay date 1969)

[*In the following excerpt, Godshalk substantiates the structural unity of* The Two Gentlemen of Verona *by examining three recurring elements: the allusions to certain tragic classical myths at crucial points in the play; the patterned use of love letters which go awry and thus suggest the inadequacies of communication in the realm of love; and the motif of journeying as an educative process. Shakespeare, the critic states, "builds an almost subliminal sense of crisis, suspense, and tension" through the use of mythic allusions to tragic lovers like Hero and Leander, and further through the ineffectual and misguided love letters which fall into the wrong hands and actually separate, rather than unite, the lovers. The characters' initial journeys to Milan also "go awry", Godshalk contends, adding that only the final journey to the pastoral world of the forest concludes the play with a "comic resolution" and the success of love.*]

Although Shakespeare's early characterization may be, and indeed has been, challenged and adversely criticized, even from the beginning of his career as playwright his sense of structure and his ability to unite the diverse elements of a play into a well-knit whole is unique. Using methods of structural recurrence, he underlines the continuity of action and through similarity and contrast builds the scheme of dramatic irony and suggests the total dramatic significance of the individual incident. (p. 168)

The masterful structure of *The Two Gentlemen of Verona*, however, has been almost completely neglected. In the past thirty years little has been written about the play, and of that little, the most stimulating individual study has been on the theme of identity [see excerpt above by William O. Scott, 1965]. This theme, of course, helps to unify the action: as the names suggest, Proteus is unable to find his identity, and Val-

entine finds his in love. But the recurring structural elements have received scant attention and comment.

Perhaps the least obvious of these is the structure of mythic allusion. The allusions to classical myth are not plentiful, but their distribution is strategic; and they have an especially prominent place in the first scene of Act III, the turning point of the play. Throughout the play, the use of classical myth suggests and even implies a tragic outcome for the action, as the characters become partially or wholly identified with figures in the myths. In this subtle manner, Shakespeare builds an almost subliminal sense of crisis, suspense, and tension. This tragic innuendo is the chief function of the structure of mythological allusion.

The first allusion, to the myth of Hero and Leander, appears in the opening banter of Valentine and Proteus. Proteus promises Valentine:

> Upon some book I love I'll pray for thee.
>
> [I. i. 20]

In jest, Valentine replies:

> That's on some shallow story of deep love:
> How young Leander cross'd the Hellespont!
>
> [I. i. 21-2]

In the myth, of course, both lovers ultimately die, Leander drowning, Hero committing suicide. Thus, even before the action of the play begins to develop, the allusion suggests that true love does not always run smoothly; and, perhaps, the use of the myth gains more suggestiveness—and cogency—when we learn that Valentine is going *by water* to Milan. Nevertheless, the full force of the tragic story is held in abeyance until Act III. Preparing to foil Valentine's intrigue with his daughter, the Duke requests his advice in wooing a fictitious lady of Verona. Blind to the Duke's true intentions, Valentine unhesitatingly explains how the Duke may climb to the lady's window:

> a ladder quaintly made of cords,
> To cast up, with a pair of anchoring hooks,
> Would serve to scale another Hero's tower,
> So bold Leander would adventure it.
>
> [III. i. 117-20]

Although overtly hinting that the Duke himself may play Leander, he obviously thinks of his own plans to take Silvia from her window and thus identifies himself with the young lover of the myth. Consciously he alludes to success in love, but the playgoer, aware how close he is to apprehension, remembers the double tragedy which follows Leander's initial success. The tension inherent in the cat-and-mouse action is increased by the allusion. (pp. 169-70)

[Another] allusion to classical myth is, on the surface, indicative of success in love, but the total effect is fully ambiguous. The perjured Proteus is explaining the uses of "heaven-bred poesy" to the namby-pamby Thurio:

> Write till your ink be dry, and with your tears
> Moist it again, and frame some feeling line
> That may discover such integrity:
> For Orpheus' lute was strung with poets' sinews,
> Whose golden touch could soften steel and stones,
> Make tigers tame and hugh leviathans
> Forsake unsounded deeps to dance on sands.
>
> [III. ii. 74-80]

The situation is in itself openly ironic, and Proteus's emphasis on "integrity" after his betrayal of Valentine and Julia forces us to search out the complete irony of the lines. Orpheus's joy in love was singularly short-lived, his bride Eurydice having been killed by a snake immediately after their marriage. His scheme of retrieving her from Hades failed in the final moments; and, though his music could soften rocks and tame beasts, it was not powerful enough to stop a frenzied group of Maenads from tearing him to pieces in the forest. The allusion to Orpheus may, on Proteus's part, be a conscious irony, suggesting that Thurio's fortune in love will be poor and his songs unable in the end to help him; the very idea of Thurio imitating Orpheus is comic. Nevertheless, conscious irony is laced with unconscious irony, for Proteus's overtures to "holy, fair and wise" Silvia will meet with as little success as Thurio's. Again the ultimate suggestion in the myth is that love will end in tragedy.

Appropriately, Julia (disguised as Proteus's page Sebastian) informs Silvia that in a Pentecostal pageant she played "Ariadne passioning / for Theseus' perjury and unjust flight" [IV. iv. 67-8]. . . . Ariadne, having given Theseus both the clue to the Cretan labyrinth and her love, was abandoned by him on the island of Naxos, where, according to one version of the myth, she died. Julia, by her allusion to and her complex identification with the mythic desertion, underlines her own bleak outlook and suggests the possible resolution of the problem: death.

The total implication of the structure of classical myth, then, is that of tragic resolution. In part, this implication is reenforced by the next structure we will consider, the structure of love letters. In the main plot there are five important love letters, forming an intricate scheme of balance, contrast, and comparison; and they, in turn, are mirrored in the sub-plot by Launce's strange "love-letter." Unfortunately for the *dramatis personae*, however, the letters always miss their mark, are involved in some confusion, or fail in their communication. The final effect of this structure is to raise the question of the efficacy of verbal communication.

The first letter is sent, via Speed, by Proteus to Julia. After a long conversation with Speed about the letter's delivery, Proteus concludes:

> I fear my Julia would not deign my lines,
> Receiving them from such a worthless post.
>
> [I. i. 152-53]

Speed with his usual aplomb has delivered the letter not to Julia but to her maid Lucetta. Finally receiving the letter from her, Julia in maidenly modesty tears it and is kept from piecing the fragments together by Lucetta's reentry. Proteus's initial letter goes awry and fails in its communication. Nevertheless, Julia's return letter seemingly reaches Proteus without hindrance:

> Here is her hand, the agent of her heart;
> Here is her oath for love, her honour's pawn.
>
> [I. iii. 46-7]

And for an instant the letter appears to be successful. However, Proteus's father, Antonio, sees the letter and forces Proteus to lie that the letter is indeed from Valentine, a letter expressing the wish that he, Proteus, join him in Milan. Antonio concurs wholeheartedly with Valentine's supposed wish and insists that Proteus leave the next day. Proteus himself makes the point:

> I fear'd to show my father Julia's letter,
> Lest he should take exceptions to my love;
> And with the vantage of mine own excuse
> Hath he excepted most against my love.
>
> [I. iii. 80-3]

Designed to bring the lovers together, Julia's letter has succeeded only in keeping them apart, in forcing them further asunder.

In Milan where Valentine has fallen in love with Silvia, the exchange of love letters is structurally repeated. Here, the initial love letter fails in its communication because, as Speed explains, "Love is blind" [II. i. 70]. With maidenly modesty, Silvia declines to write directly to Valentine, but, using a "figure," bids him write to one she loves and then asks him to take the letter for his labor. Speed comments:

> O jest unseen, inscrutable, invisible,
> As a nose on a man's face,
>
> [II. i. 135-36]

and tries to explain that "Herself hath taught her love himself to write unto her lover" [II. i. 168]. But with the blindness of a lover, Valentine does not quite comprehend. He remains in a muse. Later, to Julia he ironically insists that "Love hath twenty pair of eyes" [II. iv. 95], although his insensibility and the failure of the love letters up to this point in the action render that judgment extremely doubtful. Thurio has a much better right to believe "that Love hath not an eye at all" [II. iv. 96].

The love letter which structurally complements Julia's letter to Proteus is Valentine's to Silvia, announcing, "this night I will enfranchise thee" [III. i. 151], the elopement. Like Julia's it is meant to bring the lovers together, and like Julia's it succeeds

Act IV. Scene iv. Ursula, Silvia, and Julia disguised as Sebastian. By Walter Crane (1894). The Department of Rare Books and Special Collections, The University of Michigan Library.

in accomplishing the opposite. Having been informed of the planned elopement by Valentine, Proteus, under the guise of duty to the ruler, informs the Duke, who in turn waits to expose the young kidnapper. As we have seen, the ensuing cat-and-mouse game ends with the Duke's finding the rope ladder and the incriminating letter under Valentine's cloak. As Proteus's letter from Julia leads to his being sent from Verona, so Valentine's to Silvia leads to his banishment from Milan. The structural parallels and contrasts between the four letters are fully evident. Ironically, the love letters which should ideally reveal the lovers' deepest emotions have resulted in non-communication and ultimately in the isolation of the lovers one from the other; the letters have thus far propelled the action of the play toward a very possible tragic outcome. (pp. 171-74)

Thematically, this structural device in the main plot is reenforced by Launce's so-called "love-letter" which seems rather to be a parody of the literary blazon, glancing ironically back at Valentine's inflated praise of Silvia to Proteus. Launce and Speed read the letter at the end of the same scene in which Valentine's letter falls into the Duke's hands; and, in a sense, Launce's falls into Speed's hands. Speed reads aloud, while Launce supplies a running commentary, a commentary which is at once on the letter itself and obliquely on the artificial love conventions in which Valentine and Proteus labor. The conventional praise of conventional beauty is replaced by a down-to-earth realism. "Item: She is slow in words." "O villain, that set this down among her vices! To be slow in words is a woman's only virtue" [III. i. 332 ff.]. Indirectly the earthy letter and comments question the validity of the courtly language of love and stand out against meaningless verbiage. Perhaps in the end, actions will speak much more to the point than words; and though love letters may fail in their communication and purpose, deeds of love will not.

In the action of the play, the failure of words leads directly to the success of Valentine's acts in the final scene. By his magnanimity and self-sacrifice in giving up his claim to Silvia in Proteus's favor, he consequently brings about the complete regeneration of Proteus and his return to Julia. As a character, Valentine has been widely criticized for his magnanimity at this point, "Q" commenting that there seem to be no gentlemen in Verona [see excerpt above by Arthur Quiller-Couch, 1921]; but two facts should be remembered: (1) Valentine is still a banished outlaw and has no prospects of marrying Silvia; (2) he has not yet been told that Silvia has fled the court and come to the forest only to be with him. Valentine is, of course, willing to sacrifice himself for the love of a friend, but the proposed sacrifice is in a way merely a selfless yielding to reality. In the world of hard facts, outlaws do not marry Duke's daughters. When the Duke arrives, Valentine immediately and generously frees him from the captivity of his outlaw band. When Thurio claims Silvia, he valiantly replies:

> Thurio, give back, or else embrace thy death;
> Come not within the measure of my wrath;
> Do not name Silvia thine,
>
> [V. iv. 126-28]

offering to fight him. Thurio quickly backs down; his earlier words of courtly love remain unimplemented by deeds. He serves as a significant contrast to Valentine, whose friendship for Proteus, duty to the ruler and love of Silvia have been confirmed by his noble acts, which, in turn, reap their reward. The structure of letters with its attendant theme of the failure of verbal communication and its tragic overtone of human isolation is resolved by right action. The final unity is emphasized in Valentine's last line: "One feast, one house, one mutual happiness" [V. iv. 173].

Although the resolution of the play is comic unity, the major implications in the structures of classical myth and love letters are tragic. However, the last recurring structure to be considered, the structure of journeys, viewed out of context immediately suggests a "happy" outcome. The journey or quest is one of the stock situations of romance and epic—and latterly of Jungian psychology and myth and symbol criticism. In quest of some precious object or person, the hero, embodying the proper traits of character, makes a journey into the unknown. Having passed a series of tests and overcome the guardians of the object or person, he either obtains the precious object or rescues the captive person, which may also entail marrying a fair princess. In pastoral romance, such as Sidney's *Arcadia* or Spenser's Legend of Courtesy, the basic quest story is somewhat modified. The pastoral hero does not travel in search of an external object or person, but journeys to the pastoral world because of unresolved problems in the urban world. In the pastoral world, these problems are, after an educative process, resolved, and the hero returns, readjusted, to the outer world. The pastoral journey obviously provides the basic situation for the denouement of the play.

But Shakespeare's use of the journey structure must be examined in context. (pp. 174-76)

The first complicating action of the play is Antonio's decision to force Proteus on a journey to Milan. . . . [The] main purpose of the journey is educative; it should be a quest after knowledge and wisdom. As we have seen in our consideration of the structure of love letters, this journey is analogous to Valentine's banishment from Milan; it is an enforced departure, and its function in the plot is to isolate Julia from Proteus. Although the guiding purpose and the ultimate outcome may be noble, the initial effect of the journey is not.

In the meantime, Valentine's journey becomes an education in love. Speed, who has the clear sight which seems to be a trait of the menials in the play, tells Valentine what he has learned: "You have learned, like Sir Proteus, to wreathe your arms, like a malecontent; to relish a love-song, like a robin-redbreast; to walk alone, like one that had the pestilence" [II. i. 18 ff.], and so on. Like Chaucer's Troilus, Valentine has been a mocker of [love]. In the first scene, he rather bitingly tells Proteus:

> Love is your master, for he masters you:
> And he that is so yoked by a fool,
> Methinks, should not be chronicled for wise.
>
> [I. i. 39-41]

But in Milan, the mocker has been caught in the toils of love: the mocker mocked. Nevertheless, Valentine has found himself in love. . . . Through his journey and his education in love, Valentine is able to establish a stable identity in his love for Silvia.

Not so with Proteus. Ironically, his journey undermines his stability. From faithful friend and lover, he loses his initial firmness "like a waxen image 'gainst a fire" [II. iv. 201]. Reason bows to passion, and Proteus immediately, perhaps too quickly for verisimilitude, falls in love with Silvia. He completely misinterprets the situation; for he believes that by remaining faithful to Valentine and Julia and thus losing Silvia, he "needs must lose" himself [II. vi. 20]. His observation is ironically significant; for the outcome of his travels, ostensibly in quest of wisdom, has resulted in the complete loss of his true self. However, as we have noticed, even from the opening scene he has but slenderly known himself. Ultimately, on his journey he must come to learn that love is not a disembodied spirit; love is truly an unselfish relationship between two people. His lack of this essential knowledge leads to the central crisis of the play, the banishment of Valentine.

As Proteus, praying love to "lend" him "wings to make" his "purpose swift" [II. vi. 42], intrigues to have Valentine banished from Milan, Julia plans her journey of love to Proteus, thinking to fly to him on "Love's wings" [II. vii. 11]. (pp. 177-79)

Before Julia's arrival in Milan, Valentine, because of certain "unresolved problems in the urban world," is forced to journey into the pastoral forest where he is quickly accepted as the leader of a band of outlaws. He tells them what seems on the surface a palpable lie: "I kill'd a man, whose death I much repent" [IV. i. 27], until we realize that he means himself. His separation from Silvia has left him in a state of nothingness . . . ; with a significant malapropism, Launce tells him, "there is a proclamation that you are vanished" [III. i. 217-18]. Valentine, apostrophizing Silvia in pastoral accents, descants on the theme:

> O thou that dost inhabit in my breast,
> Leave not the mansion so long tenantless,
> Lest, growing ruinous, the building fall
> And leave no memory of what it was!
> Repair me with thy presence, Silvia;
> Thou gentle nymph, cherish thy forlorn swain!
>
> [V. iv. 7-12]

He fears that his absence from his beloved may prove to be the end of love, rather ironically fearing that this journey from Milan may have the same outcome as Proteus's enforced journey from Verona.

Completing her simultaneous journey, ostensibly toward love rather than away from it, Julia pathetically listens to Proteus declaim his love for Silvia, who stands at the window from which Valentine was to have taken her in his planned elopement. Julia's journey, like all the journeys so far, goes awry, does not reach its hoped-for conclusion. In despair and disguised as Sebastian, she becomes Proteus's page and is commissioned to be the go-between in his love relations with Silvia. The irony of the situation is multiple, and twice-compounded when Julia and Silvia become friends, replacing the lost friendship of Valentine and Proteus. After her traumatic conference with Silvia, Julia calls herself a mere "shadow"; by her journey, she has, in effect, lost her "self." She has become Sebastian, no more than Proteus's page; and, as Proteus tells Silvia, "she is dead" [IV. ii. 105].

The near-tragedy of the plot is comically resolved by Silvia's quest in search of Valentine. Paralleling Julia's journey to Milan, Silvia's quest leads, she believes, to Mantua, but actually ends in the pastoral world. Her guide, Sir Eglamour, is less a character than a symbol of undying love [IV. iii. 18-21]; and, when he has brought her to the forest, he conveniently disappears—exit comically chased by Valentine's band. As we have seen, through Valentine's deeds of friendship and love, Silvia's quest is successful. Her name, of course, suggests that the forest will be the place of her good fortune.

However, she is followed to the pastoral world by both Proteus and Julia, whose several journeys also must reach their culmination here. Proteus finally understands that love is not an abstraction to be sought in every beautiful woman, but only to be found in a permanent commitment to one:

> O heaven! were man
> But constant, he were perfect. That one error
> Fills him with faults; makes him run through all the sins.
> Inconstancy falls off ere it begins.
>
> [V. iv. 110-13]

With this basic truth his educative journey ends, and Julia's quest in search of love is consequently successful. The Duke's arrival merely confirms the arrangements decided on by the lovers. Only the dastardly Thurio, the true "chameleon" and the symbolic opposite of Eglamour, leaves the stage in disappointment.

Thus Shakespeare unifies the action of his play. The Hero and Leander of the drama, Valentine and Silvia, of course, do not suffer a double tragedy. Theseus-Proteus returns to Ariadne; and only Thurio-Orpheus loses his Eurydice. The tragic undertones of the classical myths are silenced by the promised wedding-song. In their parallel educative journeys, both Valentine and Proteus learn the basic pieces of knowledge which concern them most: Valentine, to love; Proteus, to be faithful in love. With wisdom attained, their original friendship is restored. And with this restoration, the parallel quests of Julia and Silvia in search of love are successful. The love letters which have caused so much misunderstanding, isolation, and heart-ache are forgotten, pushed into the background by the true deeds of love and the unity of the oncoming double marriage.

The unity of the play as a whole, then, is in large measure a product of the recurring structural elements. As we have seen, these elements function in various ways. The mythic structure is basically ironic, suggesting a possible tragic outcome to the comic plot. Since a tension is thus set up between the mythic structure and the plot, the playgoer becomes aware of what we have called the tragic innuendo. The structures of letters and journeys operate somewhat differently. Acting as a complicating factor in the plot, the letters unite with the theme of noncommunication. The letters, again, suggest a possible tragic resolution. The journeys, united with the theme of education, stand as a counter-balance to the letters. Although the initial journeys lead to complications in the plot, the final pastoral journey ends in comic resolution and unity. Both Valentine and Proteus have received their necessary education. The recurring elements provide a series of mirrors, reflecting and refracting. The Hero and Leander myth reflects the love of Silvia and Valentine; but the image is distorted. Silvia's receiving Proteus' final letter mirrors Julia's receiving his first; but the images are inverted. Valentine's initial journey is mirrored by Silvia's journey to the forest. Both find love at the end of their travels. With these mirrors Shakespeare accomplishes two important things. He underlines the significance and the continuity of action, and builds a scheme of dramatic irony. And thus he demonstrates a mastery of structural unity. (pp. 179-81)

William Leigh Godshalk, "The Structural Unity of 'Two Gentlemen of Verona'," in Studies in Philology, *Vol. LXVI, No. 2, April, 1969, pp. 168-81.*

RALPH BERRY (essay date 1972)

[*In the following excerpt, Berry explores the themes of metamorphosis or change and illusion in* The Two Gentlemen of Verona. *He cites Valentine's consistent reliance on conventional norms of behavior and his eventual transformation into the typical lover to emphasize his self-absorbed romantic delusions. The critic also discerns the central images of illusion and change in such recurring terms as "chameleon," "idol," and "figure," asserting that both Proteus and Valentine view Silvia not as a living individual, but as the object of a conventional pattern of behavior, thus distorting their own identities with the aid of these romantic images. Even in the conclusion of the drama, he contends, Valentine's self-indulgent renunciation and theatrical forgiveness of his unfaithful friend demonstrate "the magnitude" of his egotism, providing as well a "grotesque parody of Julia's quiet and undramatic forgiveness of Proteus."*]

The Two Gentlemen of Verona is an experiment, but a controlled experiment. Shakespeare does not "inadvertently" stumble into his design, which is to make comedy out of romance. That design is plain from the opening speech of the play; it does not merely evolve later. The notion emerges, from the critical consensus, of the Romantic conventions controlling Shakespeare. On the contrary, *Two Gentlemen* reveals Shakespeare depicting people as deeply under the spell of conventions. Conventions, in other words, are not simply a code of writing plays, but of behavior in life. To understand *Two Gentlemen* it is necessary to see Valentine and Proteus as two role-playing young men (Valentine especially) who adhere to a fantastic code of conventional behavior. Thus the climax of the final scene in no way impairs the psychological credibility of the action. It is merely Shakespeare's mode of synthesizing the requirements of the conventions, and of life. In the climax of *Two Gentlemen* can be seen one of the earliest examples of the inexorable organic logic of a Shakespeare play, achieving a conclusion that is astonishing, but inevitable. It is like the coup of a chess master whose final combination crowns the approach-work of many moves. And nowadays one awards the *prix de beauté* [beauty prize] not to the startling conclusion, but to the preparation that has made it logical.

To our analysis of the play, then. As is usual in a Shakespeare play, the opening lines merit the closest attention:

> *Valentine:* Cease to persuade, my loving Proteus;
> Home-keeping youth have ever homely wits.
> Were't not affection chains thy tender days
> To the sweet glances of thy honored love,
> I rather would entreat thy company
> To see the wonders of the world abroad
> Than, living dully sluggardis'd at home,
> Wear out thy youth with shapeless idleness.
> But since thou lov'st, love still, and thrive
>   therein,
> Even as I would when I to love begin.
>
>   [I. i. 1-10]

Valentine is praising conventional behavior. It is proper for young men to travel, hence he intends to travel. The generalization of line 2 is an index to his mind; the general conditions his specific behavior. The point, though, lies in the tail of his speech. Proteus is a lover, hence a quite different set of values applies to him; and Valentine quite approves of this, too. Hence the give-away final line, "Even as I would, when I to love begin." That line affords the essence of Valentine. It recognizes that when the time comes for Valentine to play the role of lover, he will do so with an entire acceptance of its requirements. Behavior is governed by convention.

Hence Valentine, friend but not (as yet) lover, does the conventional thing in mocking the situation of his friend. His raillery of Proteus [I. i. 29-35] reveals him entering wholeheartedly into the spirit of the role. And the essential immaturity

of both young men is well implied in the repeated "writers say" [I. i. 42, 45]. Each needs an authority of sorts to govern his behavior. It is worth adding that in this play as in *Love's Labour's Lost* the opening contains an unrealistic vow. The effect of this comparison is to suggest that Shakespeare looks upon the whole transaction much more skeptically than is at first apparent, for in *Love's Labour's Lost* the matter is very much sharpened. The young men of *Two Gentlemen*, as in *Love's Labour's Lost*, are early seen to be fixed in a strong vein of attitudinizing.

This becomes fully apparent in II, 1, as Valentine enters upon his next role, that of lover. (A role, significantly, that he has "learned," as Speed sardonically notes [II. i. 19]). His language, figuring the whole play, is a send-up of the Romantic conventions: "Sweet ornament, that decks a thing divine!" he gasps, over Silvia's glove [II. i. 4]. In this, Valentine is being perfectly consistent with himself—the conventions require one to ring the changes of behavior as the role changes; but it is nonetheless true, as Speed points out, that the changes involved are ridiculous. A key image motif is initiated to make this point. Valentine is "metamorphosed with a mistress," according to Speed [II. i. 30-1]; the word repeats Proteus' "Thou, Julia, thou hast metamorphosed me" [I. i. 66]. Moreover, the idea extends to "chameleon," for the "chameleon Love" jest of Speed [II. i. 172] alludes to that animal's capacity for instant change of color—according to its situation—as well as its feeding on air. "Chameleon," in fact, is a witty symbol for the young lovers, and Thurio too has to endure its application [II. iv. 26].

Speed develops his critical appreciation of his master's folly in the remarkable "figure" passage that follows Valentine's presentation of the letter to Silvia. It is an early instance of Shakespeare presenting the symbolic through a literal passage rich in significance. For, as Speed points out, "O excellent device—was there ever heard a better? / That my master being scribe, to himself should write the letter!" [II. i. 139-40]. That is it, exactly; for the letter, nominally directed at Silvia's "friend," really, to Silvia, is most aptly redirected to Valentine. For it is, in a sense, written to himself, to his personal idol, not a real woman, Silvia. The letter is a noncommunication, a monument to his role playing, that precisely foreshadows the play's climax in which Silvia ceases altogether to *be*. Self-absorption, at all times, is the clue to Valentine's conduct.

The inherent anomalies in the relations between the two egotists of Verona become apparent in II, 4. The roles are reversed from the opening scene; Proteus is now the skeptical friend, Valentine the despairful lover, whose description of his pangs leaves little to the imagination: "Ay, Proteus, but that life is altered now," and so on through a catalogue of woes [II. iv. 128-42]. To which Proteus, gazing on the miniature of Silvia, affixes the right term: "Was this the idol that you worship so?" [II. iv. 141]. The "idol" image is the central one hereabouts. It is extended into Proteus'

> For now my love is thawed,
> Which, like a waxen image 'gainst a fire
> Bears no impression of the thing it was.
>
>   [II. iv. 200-02]

The metaphor is strengthened by the Duke's repetition of it later:

> This weak impress of love is as a figure
> Trenchèd in ice, which with an hour's heat
> Dissolves to water and doth lose his form.
>
>   [III. ii. 6-8]

As, in these two instances, the love/image/figure-analogy is associated with change, it links with the "chameleon" idea. And the visual implications of "idol" are elaborated into Proteus' "'Tis but her picture I have yet beheld, / And that hath dazzlèd my reason's light" [II. iv. 209-10]. A nice inversion, this; Valentine makes an "idol" out of a reality, a living woman; Proteus a reality out of an "idol," a picture. It is another passage of transparent symbolism. "Idol" is the satiric reduction of Antipholus of Syracuse's "mine own self's better part" [*The Comedy of Errors*, III. ii. 61]. In brief, the image-cluster that comprises "chameleon," "idol," "image," "figure" is the central one of the play. It projects the ideas of illusion and change that are associated with love, and is later to be absorbed in the implications of "shadow" and "picture." These latter terms refer to a concrete object, hence the course of the play effortlessly dramatizes ideas originally introduced as metaphors.

The ironies of II, 4, then, contain the key to this comedy. They are pleasantly enough handled by Shakespeare; particularly disarming is Valentine's departure to keep an eye on Thurio, coupled with his explanation: "... and I must after, / For love, thou know'st, is full of jealousy" [II. iv. 176-77]. The "thou know'st" is especially revealing; Valentine, half-apologetically, is explaining that he *has* to do this, it is the done thing for lovers. The ironies are plain enough in III, 1, when Valentine, left to himself, laments the failure of his plans for elopement. He observes, quite truthfully—in a sense he cannot comprehend—

> To die is to be banished from myself.
> And Silvia is myself; banished from her
> Is self from self.
>
> [III. i. 171-73]

And, in a line of finality, "She is my essence" [III. i. 182]. True: she has no external life from himself. Silvia as a stage being may lead an autonomous life, but in Valentine's mind she has largely the status of anima. Hence there is a frosty irony underlying the song title for which the play is best known. Who, indeed, *is* Silvia? And what is she?

For Proteus, as for Valentine, she is essentially another variety of idol. The point is again hammered in, through the dialogue of IV, 2 that repeats the motif:

> *Proteus:* Madame, if your heart be so obdurate,
> Vouchsafe me yet your picture for my love,
> The picture that is hanging in your chamber:
> To that I'll speak, to that I'll sigh and weep;
> For, since the substance of your perfect self
> Is else devoted, I am but a shadow,
> And to your shadow will I make true love.
> *Julia:* [Aside] If 'twere a substance, you would,
> sure, deceive it
> And make it but a shadow, as I am.
> *Silvia:* I am very loath to be your idol, sir.
> But, since your falsehood shall become you
> well
> To worship shadows and adore false
> shapes ...
>
> [IV. ii. 119-30]

It is an analysis of the situation that covers Valentine just as much as Proteus. And the scene that extends the promise (IV, 4) clinches the matter. Julia's reactions to the painting of Silvia are interesting [IV. iv. 184-201]. She sees clearly that the differences between her looks, and Silvia's, do not account for

the "idolatry" [IV. iv. 200]. Julia's meditation foreshadows the idea of the interchangeability of the love object, that plays so large a part in *A Midsummer Night's Dream* and *Twelfth Night*. And her conclusion

> What should it be that he respects in her
> But I can make respective in myself
> If this fond Love were not a blinded god?
> Come, shadow, come and take this shadow up,
> For 'tis thy rival. O thou senseless form,
> Thou shalt be worshipped, kissed, loved, and adored!
> And, were there sense in his idolatry,
> My substance should be statue in thy stead.
>
> [IV. iv. 194-201]

rounds off the image motif that dominates the play for—typically for a heroine in the comedies—love involves no illusion whatsoever. She sees very clearly the self-delusion and inconstancy of the male, yet takes Proteus for what he is. The contrast between the male and female roles is exact, and merciless.

The climax to the action is the reductio ad absurdum of the role playing that has characterized the conduct of the male lead. Valentine, intervening in the intended rape, disposes of Silvia to the rapist upon a vow of repentance. It is pure drama of sensibility. The twenty-four lines of the Valentine-Proteus exchange compose as Miss Bradbrook remarks, "the germ or core of the play" [see excerpt above, 1951]. With the essential sense of this I agree, but I think the metaphor may be misleading. The "germ" of a Shakespeare play is found, organically, in the opening passages; the conclusion is the inexorable manifestation of growth tendencies that have driven the action of the play. Shakespeare does not contrive a conclusion; he reveals that a given outcome must necessarily be so. And it is so here. The magnanimous/fatuous/ungentlemanly action of Valentine in disposing of Silvia, a stage prop in the drama of Valentine, has excited the horror of critics on moral or aesthetic grounds. But this act, theatrical and compelling as it is, is merely the consequence and embodiment of the speech that precedes it.

> *Valentine:* Thou common friend, that's without faith
> or love,
> For such is a friend now. Treacherous
> man,
> Thou hast beguiled my hopes. Naught but
> mine eye
> Could have persuaded me. Now I dare not
> say
> I have one friend alive; thou wouldst
> disprove me....
>   O time most accurst,
> 'Mongst all foes that a friend should be
> the worst!
>
> [V. iv. 62-6, 71-2]

Not a single expression of concern for Silvia escapes his lips. She does not exist. *He,* Valentine, is the injured one. It is a sublime, a Balzacian expression of the ego. And his gesture of renunciation forms, if you like, a grotesque parody of Julia's quiet and undramatic forgiveness of Proteus. On the plane of romantic comedy, the magnitude of Valentine's ego demands comparison with Milton's Satan. The infallible good taste of Shakespeare renders silent the unfortunate Silvia, a word from whom would have sufficed to blow away the pretensions of the Big Production staged by Valentine and Proteus for their own benefit, and abetted by the Duke. The only reality-figure who is allowed a voice at the end—Thurio—very sensibly refuses to get hurt in the affair, and walks off to the hoots of the groundlings and the derision of those notable judges of human conduct, the Duke and Valentine. But Shakespeare's predilection for locating the common-sense viewpoint among clowns, boobies, and servants is already marked; and we should take, as the final internal criticism of the action, the words of Thurio: ''I hold him but a fool that will endanger / His body for a girl that loves him not'' [V. iv. 132-34].

I have concentrated in this analysis upon Valentine, because he embodies the central idea of the play—that is, the romantic conventions foundering, like capitalism in Marxist mythology, of inner contradictions. The ending of *Two Gentlemen* is self-evidently a refutation of the postures adopted by both young men in scene one. Strictly, no further refutation is required. But the romantic ideal, or illusion, is of course under fire from other quarters as well. It is attacked explicitly, by Speed; it is derided analogously, through the Launce-Crab infatuation. As everyone agrees, this relationship parodies (if rather heavy-handedly) the friendship and self-sacrifice of the male leads. And the Outlaws, too, supply their quota of satire. This mob of junior role players is sufficiently identified by the leader of their choice, Valentine. They are sketched in most economically. Valentine wins their hearts by his claim to have killed his man; whereupon they, anxious not to lose face, insist that they *too* have done desperate deeds. The point is that we know Valentine to be a liar, and therefore infer that the Outlaws are his mental siblings. Leader and led parallel, and implicitly criticize the other.

Nor is it necessary for the final page of the comedy to set the record straight. Critics frequently talk as if the attainment of self-knowledge is the major criterion of high-quality drama. Not at all. A perfectly legitimate alternative method, proper to comedy, is to allow a fair run to certain viewpoints, and then to suppress or gloss over them in the conclusion. It is sufficient for the audience—and not necessarily the principals—to have arrived at a proper view of the matter. Moreover, for all the principals to attain self-knowledge is surely to strain the bounds of comedy; the process is too painful. And so the self-satisfaction of the hero is in this play allowed to remain unpunctured. It is provocative, but it is legitimate. And the insufferable Valentine, as he departs patronizing everyone from the Duke downwards, is simply dramatizing a tautology of life: conventional behavior is applauded by the conventional.

To conclude, the fundamental critical error with *Two Gentlemen* is to take Valentine at his own evaluation as an attractive, appealing male lead. He is nothing of the sort. He is (and I gladly accept Charlton's term) a ''nincompoop'' [see excerpt above, 1930]; and this is the germ of the play, not an unsightly development forced on a tyro playwright by the exigencies of the conventions. I add that any reputable production of *Two Gentlemen* makes this clear. It can hardly be played in any other way; this comedy needs to be seen to be believed. For the rest, the play's center of sanity is placed unequivocally with the women. Silvia is necessarily a sketch only, but Julia is of the line that produces Portia [in *The Merchant of Venice*] and Viola [in *Twelfth Night*]. The play as a whole, which has very justly been termed Shakespeare's ''laboratory,'' contains all the *parts* of a Shakespeare comedy; technically it is all there, and Shakespeare needed only to adjust the relation of the parts to the whole. That is, the idea of romance countered by realism, of folly raked by wisdom, achieves a more satisfying synthesis in the later plays. The Shakespearean system

of internal checks and balances, developed to perfection in *As You Like It* and *Twelfth Night,* is essentially only a refinement of *Two Gentlemen*. And this play, finally, stakes out an area of concern that its author remains with throughout the comedies. It is illusion. The ironic coup of Valentine's renunciation is a masterly revelation of self-infatuation; the ending is illusion condoned. *Two Gentlemen,* like all the subsequent comedies, may make use of disguise; but the true focus is that for which disguise is but a figure, the world of illusion. (pp. 42-53)

> *Ralph Berry, ''Love and Friendship,'' in his* Shakespeare's Comedies: Explorations in Form, *Princeton University Press, 1972, pp. 40-53.*

JOHN ARTHOS (essay date 1972)

[*In one of the most comprehensive examinations of the thematic issues in* The Two Gentlemen of Verona, *Arthos discusses the philosophical nature of constancy as presented by Shakespeare, which he claims is achieved through truth and knowledge of oneself. He also discerns in the play a principle of divinity—of which Silvia is the living example—that leads the characters toward perfection in love and life; this divine principle also constitutes the essence or ''substance'' of the self that promotes identity and nourishes constancy in a world where change and conflict are unavoidable. Arthos further stresses the importance of the individual's freedom to choose the pursuit of knowledge, love, and constancy, citing Silvia's positive example in this regard and, on the other hand, Proteus's willful disobedience of ''divine injunction'' in his obsession with ''shadows'' and his sacrifice of self-knowledge to wayward love. Considering the final scene of* The Two Gentlemen of Verona *a dramatic failure, Arthos concludes his study by questioning Shakespeare's philosophical convictions; he suggests that although the play demonstrates a belief in real and divine love, its artistic shortcomings indicate that Shakespeare had personal doubts as to the viability of this philosophy.*]

In the first part of [*The Two Gentlemen of Verona*] there is a succession of scenes in which we see the chief persons in their happiness, happy at least in their prospects, and then we soon see them in distress. They become separated from each other and at odds. One after another is driven to flight, one or another becomes a pursuer. Because the scenes present us with these manifold effects of one young man's transferral of his affections and because so much attention is given to representing states of feeling, our interest in the events is for some time relatively subdued. The drama thus comes to centre on the pain and disruption in the betrayed and the betrayer in their immediacy.

Love's Labour's Lost also tells about perjuries, lightly of course but seriously enough, too, to require seriousness in the winding-up that will put an end to the separations. *The Two Gentlemen of Verona* tells of wrongs that follow upon inconstancy and a breach of faith not in so high-spirited a way, although there is enough of the fanciful and enough humour to lighten its more troubled seriousness. The audience will not be led to respond with the fullest sympathy to the depth of pain these wrongs point to, partly because there is so much that is fanciful but partly, too, because so much of the expression of feeling is instantly translated into analysis and into philosophizing. So many of the scenes in the first acts are given to acquaint us with what it is that Julia feels for Proteus, that Silvia feels for Valentine, and also what the significances of these feelings are—Valentine uses quite philosophical language in speaking of Silvia, and Julia expresses her devotion for Proteus half religiously. Even Launce takes to speculation in speaking with his dog. Quite differently than in *All's Well that Ends Well,* say, the depths of pain at the centre of the action are sounded more in the development of thought than in the representation of anguish.

The character of the wrongs and the pain is defined by the largeness of the hopes for happiness. . . . [When] it seems [the lovers] will be disappointed they take to desperate, however conventional, devices—Julia masking as a page, Valentine joining outlaws, Silvia in flight to the country, Proteus to outrage. All is sufficiently preposterous and sometimes picturesque and amusing enough to conceal the force of the distress that has brought about the flights and the threats, but the terms which all of them use in thinking of their joys and troubles are the terms of absolute good and evil, of life and death, of constancy and falseness. . . . (pp. 105-06)

But just as the romantic exaggerations allay the intensity of feeling inherent in the separations and the wrongs, a certain attention to the details of common life tempers the exposition of philosophy that is required to explain the reconciliations at the end. Ultimately it is made clear that the issues in the play are conceived of in the most far-reaching of meanings, but the solutions that are provided, humans must settle for as humans. The particular problems before us have to do with engagements, marriage contracts, preparations for life in the world of affairs. The lovers are the wards of parents, fathers send their sons to court to enlarge experience, and so we see these young romantic lovers in circumstances that we all recognize as belonging to social life and maturing. At the end Valentine, educated as his father had intended, acts as a true prince and not as the fanciful ruler of good-hearted brigands in an idyll, but in the society they have all inherited, governing, dispensing justice, even pardoning. The wayward Proteus is brought to his senses and forgiven, the lovers and friends are united as they should be, and Valentine in his new authority points to a happy prospect for them all. Even in this there is the obvious recognition of the nature of the world as it is—where there is the necessity for compromise, and where reconciliation must go forward even when all the issues in the quarrel have not been settled. In this ending that looks towards the restoration of ideal loves the compacts are those all men must make.

This counter-balancing of the philosophic and the circumstantial, the ideal and the real, poetry and prose, is of course characteristic of Shakespeare, and he is able in quite different works to mingle these emphases to a variety of effects. In this play the romantic exaggerations and a series of scenes in which there is little dramatic development permit him to play down the depth of passion and anguish inherent in the betrayals and disappointments and to give fuller play to commentary. At other times, in *A Midsummer Night's Dream* and *As You Like It,* the fantasy and the poetry open up into the loveliest of visions. Here they lead more into the vistas of philosophy and religion.

And in the reverse, the real and the circumstantial, even with Launce and Speed, tempering the lyric and the fantastic, set significant limits upon the philosophic, above all in establishing the humanity of these young persons who call to mind ideas of the immanent and transcendent. As Valentine sees it, grace is a function of the sovereign. When he is merciful to the penitent they escape the eternal wrath [V. iv. 81]. As it was in *Love's Labour's Lost,* the guilty follow the precise, traditional procedures that ensure forgiveness.

It is even the earthly and the spiritual that balance each other, although in the conclusion there is doubt for once that Shakespeare has brought this off. The lovers and friends who have been separated are rejoined and reconciled and they are to live together now in untroubled happiness. This should be a conclusion the audience would be happy to accept, as it is in fairy tales or when a *deus ex machina* intervenes as our sympathies require. Such a satisfaction is evidently aimed at here, but in this play it is not only the requirements of probability that must be met or else disposed of, the resolution of the issues must be in accord with the reasoning that has been so complexly presented hitherto. Valentine pardons as a governor, but he also blesses. It is almost as a priest absolving Proteus that he attests to the allaying of the eternal wrath, and Proteus is expected to follow just such directions as a priest would set. And finally, in the language of the reconciliations there opens up the prospect of the harmony for which the prior philosophizing was an introduction.

With such ends in view the play is accordingly managed in complex ways. At the beginning there is a certain obviousness inherent in the oppositions that are laid before us, of whole-hearted love and none at all, of undying friendship and betrayal. The themes, too, are explicit but as always with Shakespeare the issues inherent in the oppositions are being presented indirectly, for the initial confusions and deceptions are but preparations for more far-reaching ones whose consequences are all but unimaginable. (pp. 107-08)

At first glance it might also seem curious that the sense of the moment, concentration upon the immediate state of being, should be so stressed in a work in which ideas of the eternal are to be so seriously invoked, when *Love's Labour's Lost,* which has so much to do with the processes of time, should follow another course. I think, however, this is in harmony with the ending celebration of the play, with the words—

> One feast, one house, one mutual happiness,
>
> [V. iv. 173]

which not only signify the conclusion to strife, they speak of a state of happiness and peace. The reasoning in the play as well as the turn of events have prepared for this, but it is the attention given from the very beginning to the representation of states of feeling that prepares us for the sense these words give of a life of ever-continuing love.

The success of the ending—and it is far from being what we need—must be founded in all that has been presented in showing the forms life takes in suffering certain wrongs, founded in the representation of the growth of understanding in these friends and lovers of what suffering as well as reason teaches about friendship and love. (p. 109)

[The] governing movement of the play arises from the exploitation of opposites, in which opposition in the nature of the dynamism of life gives rise to a disposition or an act which in coming into being meets with its own opposition. The Petrarchan conventions and psychology offer much in enabling the playwright to develop such a movement and rhythm, but still other antitheses than these provide are also at work. (p. 111)

In the course of events one after another of the four chief persons in the play moves from one state to its opposite—Proteus from complacency to furious pursuit; Julia from tremulous happiness to fear and another kind of pursuit; Valentine from a hopeful life of study, first, to love, and then to exile; Silvia from love and security into great danger. These reversals affect us less as misfortunes leading into disaster than for what they signify as the corruption of peace and joy. It is certain that no mere quasi-divine revelation, as in *The Comedy of*

Errors and *L'Ammalata,* can set things right, more is involved than bringing people together and removing misunderstandings. Change of circumstance in itself cannot allay the trouble, restore trust, and allow love once more to prosper. Proteus must cease to love Silvia and return to loving Julia. He must make peace with Valentine, and Valentine must know how to forgive him. Silvia and Julia are also called upon to forgive. With them all there must be complex and profound changes, although these are not to be shown to us in a brief final scene, but merely indicated. Yet even here the same pattern remains clear—forgiveness is the means proposed of reconciling the oppositions of love and rivalry, and of love and honour, and of nature itself, where love does not inevitably obtain the return it hopes for.

At the end of *Love's Labour's Lost* everyone is asked to wait to see if a year spent in holy discipline can make the men better disposed to be true. In *The Two Gentlemen of Verona* forgiveness is offered as if more profound betrayals could be absolved and deeper disturbances erased in no time—through an instant's remorse on Proteus' part and through a simple blessing from Valentine. In the one play nature is given its due, and the processes of reformation and absolution are known to require time. In the other, miracle-working means, if not sacramental power, effect the changes, and so abrupt is the appeal to these that the sense remains of conflicts continuing in the very nature of things.

Dramatically and poetically it may appear that the reconciliation has not come off, but putting that matter aside for the moment, one may observe this, that we have here at the end the continuance and indeed the climax of the oppositions set up in the chaffing with which the play began, in the Petrarchan antitheses, in the dilemmas of those for whom love is not requited, in the dialectics of love worked out in philosophy, and in the disharmonies of nature itself. And as the pattern of opposition became more and more comprehensive, taking in more and more of the issues of existence, there was concurrently developed a more and more comprehensive formulation of what could contain change, what could guide lovers who were only human, what could hold friends together. The question became increasingly how could even the best of men, and all who aimed for the best of ends, perfection, justify trust. The answer was, hopefully, through knowing truth.

Constancy, evidently, that composition of the affections that allows for unwavering behaviour, is impossible under the conditions in which mortals find themselves. Proteus is only the extreme example of the state of men in nature, at once entertaining hope and fear, knowing calm only as a respite from storms, in peace prepared for danger, love itself being fire and ice, or master and slave—in one of its worst tyrannies, making its postulants servile:

> Yet, spaniel-like, the more she spurns my love,
> The more it grows, and fawneth on her still.
>
> [IV. ii. 14-15]
> (pp. 113-14)

But although mortals are inconstant, the idea of constancy persists. From within every mortal, and most splendidly in the 'angel-like' [II. iv. 66], there shines all-ruling truth, the authority for the marriage of minds, invincibly redeeming. (p. 115)

Through the changes all the persons in the play come to know there persists the idea of attachments that are not the playthings of time, of resolutions that are not mere truces. In Valentine's praise of Silvia, in Julia's praise of Proteus, in the doctrine of

forgiveness at the end, there are allusions to a transcendent world of truth. There are many suggestions of some other sovereignty than that of the passions or of nature, and while the elaborations of argument are indispensable in the presentation of the idea of truths that do not mislead, the power of the play will ultimately depend on the degree to which the characters in their life-likeness will substantiate the doctrines. So much has to do with the condition of mortals, rooted in change, and yet we are to discover in the beauty and charm and strength of Valentine and Silvia and Julia and even of Proteus the qualities that are to justify reason and faith both. The benediction with which the play ends is to provide more than the culmination of an argument, it is to represent the condition nature in humans aspires to and on occasion attains.

The patterns of parallel and opposition are the initially formative elements of the first scenes, but they are soon assimilated within other developments as the relations between the various persons take form in the expression of more complex feelings. In the juxtaposition of scenes in which the interests of the different ones are seen to bear upon each other there begins to form the sense of a single power at work in bringing these lives together and in complicating them, and a theme as well, or several themes, arise out of ideas and words and out of conflicts in which there seem to be clear issues. There are times when the assimilation of the various interests is less than perfect, in which one or another comes forth in such a way as to unbalance the movement of the work, but generally all is managed with success and the parts lose their identity in the life of the whole. (pp. 116-17)

[As] these scenes succeed each other, as sometimes the same idea appears in different manifestations, or as situations are contrasted, a theme begins to become known. As the ramifications of this become clearer we begin to see how the theme is throwing light upon the situations in which the persons find themselves, as their circumstances in turn extend the references of the theme. When a certain kind of suspense does grow, we become interested in discovering the fuller import of certain suggestions. Above all, we are being held by the hope of discovering the principle that it seems enables individuals to perfect themselves, to establish constancy in their relationships, a principle that has a directing power over the life of any individual who consults with it. And in the contrary, as we see Proteus taking to troubled ways, we become anxious to discover what he might have done differently, what the error was that misled him, and how the principle that directs men to grow towards perfection, in the misguided destroys them. At the end of *Love's Labour's Lost* we were told that men must accommodate themselves to a salutary principle in the rhythm of nature. Here, we are not so much being told, as we are being shown, how a quite other principle is setting the terms for happiness and unhappiness. . . . [We] are being inducted into the ways of growth in the consciousness of those who in loving follow, or fall off from, the knowledge that alone sustains love. (p. 123)

[At] the beginning of the play, by the very charm of the language, we see that we are being brought into accord with the simplicity of the young in their happiness, their air of perfect trust. The warmth of their words is such we have no choice but to accept them as they are uttered, and as unselfconsciously as Valentine we are attracted to this apparently untried innocence. The words reveal no tension to strain our sympathy, and as the play proceeds we come to understand as well as to feel that what we are recognizing here is a sound that will persist through the entire work:

> from our infancy
> We have conversed and spent our hours together;
> And though myself have been an idle truant
> Omitting the sweet benefit of time
> To clothe mine age with angel-like perfection,
> Yet hath Sir Proteus, for that's his name,
> Made use and fair advantage of his days;
> His years but young, but his experience old;
> His head unmellowed, but his judgment ripe.
>
> [II. iv. 62-70]

This simplicity, this air of gentleness and idealism, is carried forward into the view of a kind of perfection in life, as if perfection were attainable and the barriers in its way not insurmountable. Valentine has suggested that love may be too demanding, that it may get in the way of men's proper ambitions, encouraging 'shapeless idleness' [I. i. 8], and the father of Proteus goes further:

> I have considered well his loss of time,
> And how he cannot be a perfect man,
> Not being tried and tutored in the world.
> Experience is by industry achieved,
> And perfected by the swift course of time.
>
> [I. iii. 19-23]

But most striking of all is the character of Silvia—

> She excels each mortal thing
> Upon the dull earth dwelling.
>
> [IV. ii. 51-2]

What is in one view a delightful simplicity, in another is affectation and exaggeration, and the Petrarchan and Platonic conventions in the mouths of the untried may simply be foretelling the disasters the innocents are thereby asking for. It is charming to joke about love in the language of religion, to talk of replacing the holy book of Christendom with the holy book of love, but the fashionable exaggerations may signify that neither the claims of religion nor of love are taken seriously enough, and that there may be a deep misunderstanding of the demands that love can make as well as of the requirements for perfection of any kind. The virtues of simplicity and affection are real enough, and these young people are far more genuine than false and they are right in recognizing the all but supernal charm of Silvia. But even in loving her, Proteus certainly and Valentine pretty certainly, are seeing through a glass darkly. Their virtues by their limitations become faults. (pp. 125-27)

They themselves of course recognize the other side of the ambition for perfection, the completeness of failure. Almost every move that is being made is a wager on the absolute value of every undertaking and every attachment; every disappointment threatens to be fatally discouraging. As the play develops, the idea of becoming a perfect man in the world is displaced by the idea of perfection in love, although at the end something of that first concern will return in Valentine's demonstration of sovereign power. But in the interim the claims of love, both justified and exaggerated, will be asserted many times, and it will come to seem that the roots of the claim for perfection in this are much as they are in the exaggerations of generosity and ambition generally. (p. 128)

Valentine, Proteus, and Julia all admit excess [in love], even Silvia is fearful of it, all are enthralled, but only Proteus knows of another fault in what he has to offer:

> But Silvia is too fair, too true, too holy
> To be corrupted with my worthless gifts.
>
> [IV. ii. 5-6]

Before it has run its course, he was carried by the passion 'to so foule an extreme, as with violent hands, and such unseemly force to sease upon his beloved' [Jorge de Montemayor, in his *Diana Enamorada*]. Unlike the savages in *Diana* he knew he was corrupted and he knew the very character of the act he contemplated—

> [I shall] love you 'gainst the nature
> of love—force ye.
>
> [V. iv. 58]

Throughout the play it is not an idea of nature but an idea of reason at work in the very whirlwind of the passions that will be known to be the counter to excess, but more even than that, a principle with a life of its own. Excess is a manifestation of the disposition to unreason, it unbalances and it unmoors, whereas the prosperity of life as of love depends on constancy, a still and unwavering obedience to reason. What reason is and what it holds to will be the key business of the play to unfold. It will do this not as [Giordano Bruno's] *Il Candelaio* does in making its point about the unity of vice, nor as *Love's Labour's Lost,* with argument and emblem. Rather, the philosophic reasoning of this play will be carried as a burden making itself known to us sometimes in metaphysical and theological statement, sometimes indirectly as in the song to Silvia, but mostly through the sense the play is able to communicate that these young people in their encounters with each other and in their thoughts reveal what we all know to be the stuff of consciousness and that this itself is the demonstration of whatever principles may be said to be real.

As the play begins, two friends are taking leave of each other talking about love and honour, but already they are being carried along by more than talk. Soon their affairs become complicated and troubled, and love and the problems it brings are at the heart of it. Distress follows upon distress until finally nothing can compose the dismay and confusion except something very like a miracle. And so it goes, the tangled problems of these young people holding us as many another comedy does about love and beauty and mischief. But all the while a certain intellectuality is making itself known, a certain idea is seen to comprehend vast implications, and the issues of the plot come to be known as the pieces of a game, the game being the life of love and the rules that govern it. When it is over, someone or something will have won, and we shall want to know what that is to be, but our chief content will be in seeing that what is presented to us as a play and an imitation of persons in life is in its very form and being a manifestation of an intelligible principle at work in guiding human affairs.

All comes to centre about what is true and what is false, and it is Proteus at every point who leads the reasoning into the complexities of the issue. He does not appear to doubt that his new love, for Silvia, is lasting, and the audience is given no sign to the contrary, yet Proteus is struck by the change that has come over him and he is puzzled—

> Is it mine eye, or Valentine's praise,
> Her true perfection, or my false transgression,
> That makes me reasonless to reason thus?
>
> [II. iv. 196-98]
> (pp. 128-30)

The difficulty, he sees, goes deeper than that of finding excuses, the power of love is too much for reason:

> I cannot leave to love, and yet I do;
> But there I leave to love where I should love.
> Julia I lose, and Valentine I lose.
> If I keep them, I needs must lose myself; . . .
> I cannot now prove constant to myself,
> Without some treachery used to Valentine.
>
> [II. vi. 17-20, 31-2]

In some ways this hodge-podge of distinctions is no more confused, and cherishing of confusion, than that Petrarchan-Platonic language with which he and Valentine were playing in the first scene of the play, and if this is 'reasonless', it is a fine-spun substitute for reason. Nevertheless, it does express some truths, and this above all, that he still loves Julia and Valentine. He has as vivid a sense of their worth as ever, but the new feeling that has swept over him is so powerful he comes to speak of them as if they were either his enemies or else dead to him. To be 'reasonless' now means to submit himself to mere power, to submit in mere subjection, and Proteus will even become forgetful of Silvia as someone good and holy and to be honoured:

> For love is still most precious in itself.
>
> [II. vi. 24]

He thinks he has no choice but to conspire with this force and he finds authority for his state and his behaviour in interpreting his subjection to love as obedience to himself and to truth. Even perfidy becomes the witness of his faith. If he remains by the side of Julia and Valentine he is 'constant'. He must value 'himself' above all else, and to secure that he will abandon all friends and all other claims. He turns the words about as if contradictions were irrelevant. The more the reasoning becomes obscure the more he returns to the assertion he must be 'constant' to himself. All he is really saying is that the wind may bear him where it will and he will call his compliance constancy.

Proteus speaks more of the power of love than of Silvia. One may think that it was something in her that effected the change, a loveliness that would have won anyone over, that it was her 'true perfection', not his 'false transgression' that was to be held to account. But in an important sense this is not true, for neither now nor later does Proteus give any indication that he thinks of Silvia as Valentine does and as the lovely song causes us to think of her. For him her 'true perfection' means something he can ignore in entertaining the thought of a good deal less:

> For since the substance of your perfect self
> Is else devoted, I am but a shadow,
> And to your shadow will I make true love.
>
> [IV. ii. 123-25]

He knows the language of philosophy and he can speak and think of her as of the transcendental, he can think of himself as but the semblance of an equal excellence, and with the same kind of fooling with paradoxes as in speaking of his constancy to himself he can use equivocations to justify the betrayal of all he appears to be honouring.

As we shall see, the conceits are pointing to the traditional oppositions of body and soul and they will turn out to be central to the themes that are developing in the play. Julia, for example, will be using the same language in reflecting upon the 'falsehood' in Proteus' love, and although here, and elsewhere, we

shall be struck by the interest of these young persons in developing conceits, we must also recognize the depth of the thought the language is preparing us for. . . . (pp. 131-33)

In this play as in other of the early writings there appears from time to time the idea that truth harbours in the soul, or in the self. We have seen how both Valentine and Proteus ring many changes, on the need to be true to the self and the danger of losing touch with the self. In the simplest interpretation the idea seems to be that an individual, when neither observation nor argument offers answers to vital questions, may have recourse to an inner sense, a sort of oracular authority that provides answers. Or it may mean that an individual, reflecting on the relationships of love, for example, will suppose that he is responding to another with all that he values most in himself, and he may call this his very identity, his inmost being, some constant and most precious consciousness. He will suppose he is sharing with another all he values most in himself and what he would share only with that one who could be trusted to value this as he does.

These paraphrases are vague partly because the idea is difficult to fix, and partly because in its simplest sense the self is a concept pointing to what is anything but a clearly designated faculty in men. The concept refers in fact to what ought not to be defined except in the most general way, perhaps only as the power in an individual that treats with truth as nothing else does.

In *The Two Gentlemen of Verona* the various persons appeal to the self with some such meaning as often as they do because the play has so much to do with constancy, in love and in friendship. Constancy can only exist between what is conceivably unchanging in individuals, and this always comes down to what can be thought of as truth, to what by nature and definition would be unchanging.

So much might be said and the matter left at that if it were not that Valentine, for one, at several places uses the world *self* in conjunction with terms of necessarily metaphysical significance. . . .

> To die is to be banished from myself;
> And Silvia is myself. Banished from her
> Is self from self.
>
> [III. i. 171-73]
> (pp. 133-34)

When Valentine says of Silvia, 'She is my essence' [III. i. 182], elaborating on 'Silvia is myself' . . . , he is including this sense of the invaluable, what is to be cherished at all costs, but in introducing the philosophical term he is extending the reference to include a conception of reality, a conception both Proteus and Julia also have in mind in using the philosophical term *substance* in speaking of the self. . . . 'Substance' is what is real and good, the reality underlying the self, and as Julia takes up the term this comes to signify divinity:

> And, were there sense in his idolatry,
> My substance should be statue in thy [Silvia's] stead.
>
> [IV. iv. 200-01]

Thus with the words *self, substance, essence,* we are being inducted into a view of the reality underlying appearances, divine in nature and of absorbing interest to humans. (p. 135)

[In] this conception the self, the repository of truth and participant in reality and in divinity, is not static or passive, but is, rather, a form of perfection, sharing in the character of life.

The self is an unfolding, perfection is a process of growth in the truth. In a rudimentary way this was in Antonio's mind in sending Proteus abroad:

> he cannot be a perfect man,
> Not being tried and tutored in the world.
>
> [I. iii. 21-2]

Valentine, under Silvia's influence, is 'kept alive'. Proteus himself emphasizes the apparent paradox:

> O heaven, were man
> But constant, he were perfect!
>
> [V. iv. 110-11]
> (p. 137)

If one pursued the matter abstractly it would follow that a failure in the knowledge of oneself, or a failure to permit that self to flourish in the only way it can, in growing towards perfection, would be inconstancy. In the terms of the play, this would be the state of one who followed shadow instead of substance, either mistaking or preferring it. This might be a failure of knowledge, or of reason—that is, either in ignorance of the truth or through permitting reason to be overruled. And it is here that, as so often elsewhere, it is love in one or another of its infinite forms that overpowers reason. In these early writings all those whom love endangers believe themselves to be moving towards perfection, none of them lacks that fundamental faith, in his truth, in the power of knowing it, and in the proper inviolability of the self. The failures are always the failures of reason. (p. 138)

It is a short step from relating the idea of obeying the principle within oneself that is leading one to perfection to submitting oneself to another in love when that other embodies just such perfection as one's self. The conventions of the lover suing to his sovereign mistress are at hand for Valentine, he becomes such a servant, yet he may do it proudly, for in taking over the language of philosophy and theology—'she is my essence, myself'—there is no subjection and no loss of identity, she comes to share in that which makes him perfect. Constancy therefore is one and the same in being true to oneself and to that other who is true to herself, constancy is the relation to substance or essence by that in an individual which alone knows essence, participating in it and knowing himself in his primary being and worth.

Deceptions arise from the very character of the thought which speaks of love and knowledge as of like nature, the love and knowledge of persons as of truth. Valentine says of Silvia, 'speak the truth by her' [II. iv. 151], but he also said of Proteus, before the betrayal, 'I knew him as myself' [II. iv. 62]. Such a use of words and the union of love with knowledge may be in the nature of things but here there is the extension of the belief in identifying truth with reality and essence, and in identifying love and knowledge of a person with the love of perfection and the divine. Neo-Platonism and Christian belief and perhaps Scholasticism as well are therefore being drawn on to support the ambitiousness in the love of these courtiers and ladies and to help account for the fallings off as well.

The inconstancy of Proteus is all but spelled out as the errant conduct of a man mistaking shadow for substance, knowing he is thereby untrue to himself, wasting his life, deliberately doing wrong. Love, leading him to embrace shadows, confuses the power in him that seeks perfection. He knows he is no longer himself, or so he thinks of it, he knows he is using reason foolishly—which is to say, in treating shadow as sub-

stance, in dishonouring the divine which is alone reality. (pp. 139-40)

As long as he is 'banished from himself', 'alienated' from himself, Proteus cannot in the nature of things be constant. In that long casuistical speech in which he acknowledged that he had become 'reasonless', that he had 'lost' himself, he took the responsibility for it all, not in the usual way saying merely that love had overcome reason. He has turned to [Silvia] not because she means more to him than [Julia] or Valentine or himself, all of whom he must betray, knowing it is betrayal, but because love has persuaded him that love in itself counts for more than that to which it is given—

> For love is still most precious in itself.
>
> [II. vi. 24]

Love replaces truth and substance and self as his lord, and being itself unruly, even though the child of reason, forces its subject to reason in defence of all that is unruly. Proteus has fallen into the trap the Neo-Platonists argued against unceasingly, turning away from the source and foundation of truth within himself. . . . (pp. 140-41)

Proteus understands and agrees with all that Valentine or anyone would say about self and truth and perfection, and his obsession with the word *constancy* reveals his understanding that constancy is determined by the nature of that to which the individual is devoted. It is love as love, the wayward, not Julia or Silvia or truth Proteus is serving—constrained 'to make a profession of it'. Once a lover is unfaithful, until he returns to that faith, if he still loves he must love shadow instead of substance. Proteus knew this well as he juggled his contradictions, justifying treachery, and Silvia knew it quite as well, putting it accurately when she agreed to give him her portrait:

> I am very loath to be your idol, sir;
> But since your falsehood shall become you well
> To worship shadows and adore false shapes,
> Send to me in the morning, and I'll send it.
>
> [IV. ii. 128-31]

Proteus has given himself to love, and love is making him over into such an ever-changing thing as itself:

> This weak impress of love is as a figure
> Trenchèd in ice, which with an hour's heat
> Dissolves to water, and doth lose his form.
>
> [III. ii. 6-8]

Proteus demonstrates the truth of the doctrine of Plato and Petrarch and so many Neo-Platonists, that the lover becomes what he loves. (pp. 141-42)

I believe one must always resist the interpretation of individual characters in the Shakespeare plays as either allegorical or symbolic representations, just as no single play can be usefully thought of as an allegory. . . . But in *The Two Gentlemen of Verona* there are weavings of ideas that bring forth a . . . view of Silvia where it may be permitted to believe that she is to be likened to a certain part of that complex weaving. As I think the glorious song in her praise attests sufficiently, she is such a person as life can produce, but the emphasis also on her more-than-mortal fineness obliges us to discover as clearly as we may what that more-than-mortal character is. We do this in part by relating those epithets of holy, wise and fair to what else is said of her, relating them as abstractions to the ideas developed in the praise of constancy and truth. The meanings in the song more than conform to the central Platonic and

Christian affirmations that are made so much of in the play, they contribute a certain authority to them. (pp. 142-43)

Almost her last words in the play, as Proteus is assaulting her, are as much a plea for his good as they are a repulse:

> Read over Julia's heart, thy first, best love,
> For whose dear sake thou didst then rend thy faith
> Into a thousand oaths; and all those oaths
> Descended into perjury, to love me.
> Thou hast no faith left now, unless thou'dst two,
> And that's far worse than none; better have none
> Than plural faith, which is too much by one.
> Thou counterfeit to thy true friend!
>
> [V. iv. 46-53]

These are remarkable words, at once tender, strong, and just, although curiously scholastic-like in making distinctions. But in their tone there is not only the assurance of steadfastness, there is something queenly and noble, a sense, even in rebuke, of an untroubled peace.

In the rest of the play she says little, and when we put it all together we are not able to have as clear an image of her and of her quality as we have, say, of Kate, in *The Taming of the Shrew,* or the heroines of the middle comedies. The characterization is not filled out, one is tempted to say, enough—it is more as it is with Helena and Hermione in *A Midsummer Night's Dream.* Although we know her in the essentials, the character of a living being as that can be created in drama is missing.

We do, of course, relate the impression she makes upon us to what is said of her because in the matter of verisimilitude is the crux of the play. A question is put forward—is this superlative being the proof that the right honouring of the truth within an individual is the key to constancy and serenity and the requital of love? The characterization itself does not give a clear answer, although in a certain remoteness as well as strength and clarity, Silvia gives us something to go on. On the other hand, when we examine her function in the play, it is evident that she is serving as a model for the philosophizing, and if it is not accurate to speak of her as an embodiment of the truths the Neo-Platonists suppose to be at issue in the relationship between God and humans, she yet possesses the quality that alone would lead anyone to respect the doctrines, the serenity that lends assurance to admiration.

She is said to be perfection, and in the text we take this to mean that she is conversant with the divine. As remark follows upon remark we learn how much the play and her role in it are developing ideas about the nature of love that derive from Plato and Plotinus. The reasoning in the play is so much of a piece that we find ourselves taking a song, which is from one point of view of incomparable simplicity, as an expression infinitely rich with thought.

The song is saying that Silvia is in the midst of the world and yet apart from it, content as those are whose thoughts are with God—

> [her] worth makes other worthies nothing;
> She is alone.
>
> [II. iv. 66-7]

The singer speaks of her as if he too were seeking recourse with the divine. . . .

> Is she kind as she is fair?
> For beauty lives with kindness.
> Love doth to her eyes repair,
> To help him of his blindness,
> And, being helped, inhabits there.
>
> [IV. ii. 44-8]
> (pp. 144-45)

I believe we are to refer the sense here to the meanings in Valentine's words about Silvia, that she is the very sustenance of his life, the light by which he sees, what gives wonder and beauty to the world. Holy, fair, and wise, in her presence he is repaired. The language, which expresses the idea of the closest union one can conceive of—'she is myself'—never gives the sense of that phrase from *Diana,* that the lover lives 'in the body of the beloved'. Loving is not only embracing, it is seeing and knowing and above all being, the being that is shared through the knowledge of reality. The doctrine from the Neo-Platonists, that 'true Love doth spring of reason', that *Diana* emphasizes is, I think, being illustrated in the love this play tells of. Silvia gives light to see by—in her presence music, the creatures of the earth, all life become themselves. Whatever this suggests of some more than earthly influence is reinforced by the idea that love 'inhabits' with her, for in this word is just such a meaning as the Neo-Platonists used in speaking of the relationship of the soul to the One. The suggestion is that in loving Silvia one exists in that very relationship that hers is with the source of light and music and life. (pp. 146-47)

So much of what we take to be Platonism in this play comes from explicit statements, what amount to expressions of doctrine. Putting these together we observe coherence and in effect

Act IV. Scene iv. Ursula, Silvia, and Julia disguised as Sebastian. By James Stephanoff (1826). The Department of Rare Books and Special Collections, The University of Michigan Library.

the accumulations of argument. The play itself we continue to accept as a certain kind of romantic comedy, in which the central business is the loves of some young aristocrats taken up with all sorts of courtly concerns and conventions. There are also fantastic adventures as well as reminders of life lived in the light of common day. But we are not allowed to remain only with drama of that order, the drift of the ideas that come forward is causing us to be intent on another kind of action simultaneously, the processes of existence in humans. We are being held by two matters at once but differently than in allegory, although as there the two interests frequently coincide not only in the characterization but in the plot—for example, the thwarting of Proteus' attack upon Silvia is accompanied by the revelation of the manner in which good may overcome evil. Yet even though no character has such vividness as to threaten, as Shakespeare's characters so generally do, to walk off the stage into life, neither does any one perform simply as an abstraction in an argument.

The play centres upon the character and situation of Silvia and Proteus. In a manner of speaking Silvia is put upon a pedestal to show us all what perfection is like. Proteus, the chief instigator of the trouble, is similarly always before us, and it is from him that we learn most about the ways of love and what happens to those who in loving fail to honour truth. Again, we need to make a distinction between what the characterization communicates to us and what Proteus' function is in the unfolding of the argument. (pp. 149-50)

[There] are one or two remarks early in the play that suggest [Proteus] has some sense of the ways of his nature. Julia, he says, has 'metamorphized' him [I. i. 66], reminding us of the ancient Proteus and transformations as complete as his, the demon-like god turning into fire or fleeting water. . . . His mind grows darker and in his perversity he reasons about the loss of reason, or its misdirection. He is evidently as committed to ideas of transcendence and immanence as Valentine and so in judging his own behaviour he does not hold back from calling it mad and corrupt. He remains courtly almost to the end but I think there is cynicism in what he says as he asks for Silvia's portrait.

His skill in reasoning never leaves him, and at the end he will still be twisting words even in straightening his course:

What is in Silvia's face, but I may spy
More fresh in Julia's with a constant eye?
[V. iv. 114-15]

The duplicity in that use of the word 'constant' is so consistent with his usual turning of words inside out that it may divert us from recognizing what must be a more important point that is being made. The mind intent on that which makes constancy possible will indeed discover that essence in Julia, it is the very truth Proteus was on the way to knowing earlier, and it is everywhere the same. But he would spy it more freshly now in her for in renewed faithfulness to her he would be repairing the faith he owed to himself that he had weakened in leaving her. He would be 'returning to himself' as he could not otherwise.

The reasoning in the play requires us to extricate such a meaning from these words although as elsewhere in this scene we are not well enough prepared either for the sudden turn of events or for the reversals of purpose and changes of mind. But we do need to hold on to the thought that in times past Proteus had won golden opinions for himself, and he always showed he knew wherein honour lay. (pp. 150-52)

We are to understand that he knows the cost as well as the nature of his transgression, we guess that he knows what he needs to regain:

My shame and guilt confounds me.
[V. iv. 73]

Pursuing his confession, he makes the statement that, had the context been fuller, we should accept as reasoning developing the full meaning of the play:

O heaven, were man
But constant, he were perfect! That one error
Fills him with faults, makes him run through all th' sins:
Inconstancy falls off ere it begins.
[V. iv. 110-13]

Again he is being too clever with words but the thought could only have arisen in one who had a just perception of the wrong:

If hearty sorrow
Be a sufficient ransom for offense,
I tender 't here; I do as truly suffer
As e'er I did commit.
[V. iv. 74-7]

Unfortunately the scene does not express the depth of the suffering and a quality to the contrition that would justify Valentine in words so serious that they seem to be speaking of the ransoming of sinners by divinity:

Then I am paid;
And once again I do receive thee honest.
Who by repentance is not satisfied
Is nor of heaven nor earth, for these are pleased,
By penitence th' Eternal Wrath's appeased.
[V. iv. 77-81]

The meaning is clear enough but the play has not prepared us for the full weight of the contrast—if the love of the angel-like be light and life, transgression is the way of everlasting death.

Consequently, we may not think of Proteus as a true embodiment of the fires running in the veins of his namesake although Shakespeare will show us well enough what that is like, in Hamlet and Leontes and many another. In *The Two Gentlemen of Verona,* as generally in the early writing, Shakespeare has less to do with the passions than with the love of God. (pp. 152-54)

[In] all such loves as Shakespeare tells about in these early plays the idea of a loving union is always being illustrated by the traditional idea of the love becoming the very person of the beloved—as Petrarch puts it, of being transformed into the other. There will be ideally—Valentine says it clearly—a union of such sympathy that one might think of it as a sharing of identity—'She is my essence'—although it will not be exactly that. To be lost in the body of the beloved is neither what Petrarch had in mind nor Valentine:

O thou that dost inhabit in my breast,
Leave not the mansion so long tenantless,
Lest, growing ruinous, the building fall,
And leave no memory of what it was!
Repair me with thy presence, Silvia.
[V. iv. 7-11]

It appears that love, surrendered to as love, as it is with Proteus, displaces the self as the power does that transformed the god into beast and monster, reasonless and unconfinable. That power is tyrannic, and it is reasonless because it seeks its forms only within bodies, themselves by nature mortal and ever changing. The god could not escape change ever, but Proteus the man, we discover, may, for there remains with him the knowledge of that which allows for constancy.

In these early works certainly, and I think always, Shakespeare was enraptured with the idea of an inherent purity men know to be such. In crises, particularly, they would appeal to this as the justification of their being. When we examine the idea carefully we discover, I think, a foundation in Platonic and Christian beliefs, and we also discover something about the nature of the evil that comes about in the loss of that central integrity.

As the reasoning that sustains this notion is reconstructed, the clear meaning that is, however perfection is to be defined, in striving for it, whether in maturing or in love, an individual must make the right choices freely. (pp. 154-55)

The plots in the plays and poems have much to do with what endangers such fulfilments, and in them it is often love in one form or another that misleads or destroys men. Antipholus of Syracuse [in *The Comedy of Errors*], Adonis [in *Venus and Adonis*], Lucrece [in *The Rape of Lucrece*], Silvia, all must resist the unwanted offering of love or the attacks of lust. All make their resistance in the name of freedom, not condemning love itself, but insisting on the need to receive it freely and in season, receiving freely when able to give it freely. All contemplate with horror the damage done when love is not returned as love and the damage of violation of any kind. It must be that all these lords and ladies believe themselves stewards of a precious treasure whose safety is in part within the keeping of the will. This precious possession they will speak of as 'self' or 'truth' or 'troth'—the words may be interchangeable. Proteus could be using any of them when he said—

> I leave my self, my friends, and all for love.
>
> [I. i. 65]

Or the terms could be kept distinct, as with Berowne—

> We to ourselves prove false,
> By being once false forever to be true
> To those that make us both.
>
> [*Love's Labour's Lost*, V. ii. 772-74]

But whatever the discriminations, this self, this truth, whether the knower or the known, must avoid expropriation, must exist on its own terms in order to confer and to receive. In so doing it does not live to itself alone but in its relation to a sovereign power:

> were man
> But constant, he were perfect!
>
> [V. iv. 110-11]

Through the relationship of cognition, constant to substance, to essence, to that perfection which sustains and forms the reason that perceives it, perfection is a sovereign who is not a tyrant to the freely serving subject. (pp. 156-57)

In these early writings, in all the ways of flourishing—in the service of the fair and holy, in the pursuit of wisdom, in the contemplation of being—the individual retains his identity. If he loses freedom he loses himself, and he may be irretrievably lost, as it is in death, when the boar kills Adonis or when Lucrece kills herself or when Suffolk surrenders to Margaret [in *2 Henry VI*]. But the self can allow no expropriation other than death's, it cannot permit a wrong against it that would

oblige the individual to an act he has not freely chosen, and is not free to reverse. Silvia's defiance is a sufficient example of the definitive doctrine:

> Had I been seizèd by a hungry lion,
> I would have been a breakfast to the beast,
> Rather than have false Proteus rescue me.
>
> [V. iv. 33-5]

The root of the matter seems to be that wrong—breaking or violating trust—harms through depriving the individual of the freedom to choose to serve that to which it is necessary to be constant—truth, being, good. (pp. 157-58)

This is why the word sin comes into frequent use—the wrong is disobedience to divine injunction. The violation of another is the betrayal of the self, whose life as light exists in order to serve perfectly that which gave it being—

> that pow'r which gave me first my oath.
>
> [II. vi. 4]

Proteus is referring to love and also, I think, to the power behind love. (p. 159)

The expropriation of the person in defiance of his wishes and will touches upon that individual's very being in what he judges to be a sacrilegious way. From the examples of Lucrece, Adonis, Julia, Silvia, it is clear that it is not physical union itself that does the harm. The corruption of the soul's pure truth is in the complicity with the overthrow of reason:

> O sweet-suggesting Love, if thou hast sinned,
> Teach me, thy tempted subject, to excuse it!
>
> [II. vi. 7-8]

The sticking point in the last scene, more even than the haste with which the denouement is effected, the instant changes of feeling, the instant transfers of love, the immediate removal of resentment, is Valentine's act in surrendering Silvia and as it were consigning her to Proteus.

It seems to be fair to put it this way, and, if it is, one would be saying this is as foolish and offensive a trick-ending as one would find in the crudest of writers. Since it is Shakespeare's, with all the faults there must be something more to it than this. For whatever it is worth, the ending, following upon the preposterous adventures in the forest, need not meet all the requirements of verisimilitude. There is this, too, that following the initial concern with engagements, elopements, plans for education, the practical interests were increasingly swallowed up in fantasies and in the speculations of philosophy, so much so that a conclusion was required in which there would be marvellous rescues in company with the triumph of idealism. If enough is to be made of the theme that constancy shares in the character of divinity, it would be right for a sovereign to illustrate the very power of divinity, even in apotheosis to come down and manifest his efficacy in this troubled world.

Valentine has indeed taken on the manner of sovereignty, he has evidently attained that poise his father sent him abroad to attain, and his first act is king-like and even god-like, for he not only proposes that hereafter all shall be

> One house, one feast, one mutual happiness,
>
> [V. iv. 173]

he proclaims it. He is enjoining not a domestic accommodation but a state of harmony and joy in which the requirements of friendship as well as the demands of love are fulfilled. The demands of constancy in the terms in which the play has presented them are being met. . . . For all those truly intent upon reality and divinity there can be no rivalries, lovers and friends all share in the one good and there are no exclusions of any true loving, 'all their minds transfigured so together' [*A Midsummer Night's Dream*, V. i. 24].

Having said this, one wonders how a scene could have been devised that would bring the idea off. The few lines allowed to carry such a heavy burden, the brief time to dispose of all the questions the characters in their life-likeness are asking, are not enough. But the failure may be as much in the philosophy as in the art. The difficulty the problem of evil poses for Neo-Platonism is notorious, and the dilemma that faces Valentine may be showing itself to be insuperable. I think there is some sense of this we get through his use of words that remind us of Christian belief and the authority of a priest to absolve sin. It is as if Shakespeare in defeat fell back upon the thought of sacraments and true miracles. But this too was not enough, for Valentine, after all, was but a young courtier, handsomely come into manhood and power, but neither priest nor divinity.

The final question then becomes—is the failure of the ending evidence that Shakespeare realized that the philosophy he was exploiting was inadequate in the face of the issues? The works that follow would lead us to answer that question affirmatively. (pp. 159-61)

> *John Arthos, " 'The Two Gentlemen of Verona'," in his* Shakespeare: The Early Writings, *Bowes & Bowes, 1972, pp. 104-73.*

INGA-STINA EWBANK   (essay date 1972)

[*Ewbank compares* The Two Gentlemen of Verona *to Shakespeare's sonnets in its treatment of romantic conventions and its dialectical presentation of language as a medium which can both substantiate human experience and—being conventionalized itself—falsify that experience. Stressing the play's undramatic quality, its dependency on language as opposed to the development of character in action, Ewbank discerns three successive stages in the comedy's exploration of this dialectic in light of the themes of love and friendship. It is in the last of these three stages—what she describes as "the fulfillments in Act V"—that the critic locates the play's "real inconsistency"; Ewbank claims that in the last scene of* The Two Gentlemen *Shakespeare wanted to dramatize an idea frequently explored in his sonnets—namely, the element of uncertainty in intimate relationships—but he failed because his characters never give more than verbal expression to their passionate experiences. Ewbank concludes by echoing her original assessment of language: that in* The Two Gentlemen of Verona *we are led both "to accept and criticize" the romantic, conventional world as presented to us.*]

Whatever the exact chronology of either [*The Two Gentlemen of Verona*] or [the] sonnets, a kinship between them has long been a recognized fact. It consists both of verbal echoes—similar, often Petrarchan, topics and conceits being developed through similar vocabulary—and of a kind of plot similarity. Whatever the true story behind either play or sonnets, in both cases Shakespeare is creating a fiction to explore the joys and agonies, the betrayals and fulfilments, of interconnecting love relationships. Proteus, the betrayer of both love and friendship, is most like the Youth of the sonnets, with an element of the Dark Lady; Valentine and the two girls all share features of the sonnets' 'I': adoration of the beloved, faithfulness, constancy; and Valentine in the end takes up the all-forgiving and renouncing position of, for example, Sonnet 40. Obviously I

am not concerned here with 'plot' similarities as indicating any autobiographical truths behind these works: the 'truth' of the sonnets lies in Shakespeare's dramatic ability—unique among Elizabethan sonneteers—to create a sense of 'what it feels like' in a given human situation. Paradoxically, that dramatic ability is less evident in the combinations and permutations of love and friendship (with, it should be noted, the friendship theme being given much less scope than the love theme) which make up the pattern of the play. Nor am I suggesting that a single sonnet, like 40, *justifies* the final scene of the play, but that it may help to illuminate its dramatic inconsistencies.

For, in the end, the really important relationship between *The Two Gentlemen of Verona* and the sonnets seems to me to have to do with Shakespeare's attitude to his own poetry and to the traditions of love poetry in which he finds himself writing. More important than any local similarities is the fact that the sonnets, like the play, show us Shakespeare working within a well-established convention, both using it and criticizing it—writing, as it were, through and around it. Apart from a handful of simply conventional Petrarchan exercises, his aim (explicit and implicit) in the sonnets is to subordinate his style to his subject matter, to use the convention only insofar as it helps him to render the true image of the person he is writing to and of. Thus, to take an extreme example, what he wants to say about the Dark Lady in Sonnet 130 only makes sense through an evaluation of the Petrarchan convention; yet the real point of the poem remains the 'rareness' of the Lady, not the dig at the convention. Related to this feature of the sonnets is Shakespeare's attitude to language: an apparently paradoxical combination of a tremendous belief in the powers of his own poetry (again both implicit in the writing itself and explicitly stated) with an equally insistent sense that language is inadequate to express the beloved's identity—the quintessential statement being 'that you alone are you' [Sonnet 84]. It is in the sonnets that Shakespeare most clearly faces the problem which, of course, he shares with any love poet: that he needs language to define the uniqueness of the beloved and his feelings about him or her, but that, at the same time, language itself is conventional and conventionalizes experience.

When love poetry is transferred to the stage, when the inner-drama of a sonnet's 'I' and 'thou' has to be translated into the flesh-and-blood interaction of two lovers and probably also their conflicts with several others 'I's and 'thou's, then the problem is further confounded. In *Romeo and Juliet* Shakespeare partly solved it by contrasting the empty attitudinizing of Romeo's love for Rosaline with the beauty of the formality which surrounds and expresses his love for Juliet, from their first meeting on a shared sonnet. . . . [The] lovers in *The Two Gentlemen of Verona* can liken each other to the sun, or the moon, or the stars, can be blinded by love or weep floods of tears, or generally draw on the stock-in-trade of Petrarchan love poetry. But, as in the sonnets, Shakespeare in this play also shows an awareness that conventionalized language, like conventionalized behaviour, may be false. In this self-consciousness about conventional language and situations lie many of the play's inconsistencies, but also much of its sense of life.

We do not have to read or listen to *The Two Gentlemen of Verona* for very long before we discover a tendency in its main characters to be self-conscious about the language they use, to veer between exuberance and deflation, indulgence in Lyly-like wit games and sudden dismissals of them. In I. i Valentine deflates Proteus' love rhetoric even before he has had time to utter any of it; in II. iv the positions are reversed, as Valentine takes up exactly the role he ascribed to Proteus in the first scene and, in his turn, has his hyperboles punctured:

Pro. Why, Valentine, what braggardism is this?
Val. Pardon me, Proteus; all I can is nothing
To her, whose worth makes other worthies nothing;
She is alone.
Pro. Then let her alone. . . .
[II. iv. 164-67]

This effect of contrast and deflation does not seem to be tied to character as much as to the needs of the situation or scene. In II. iv Silvia initially has something of the same function of commonsense critic as, at other times, is given to Speed or Launce. She undercuts the sparring between Valentine and Thurio, and she exposes the absurdity of Valentine's conceits to the cold light of reason. . . . [A] few lines later, as Proteus has arrived and entered upon a courtesy duologue with Silvia, the function of commentator has also passed from her to Valentine:

Leave off discourse of disability.
[II. iv. 109]

Related to this tendency in the play, and also tied to scene rather than to character, is a reminder, which tends to crop up at key moments, of the impotency of words. Proteus' motivation of the brevity of the parting scene between him and Julia—'For truth hath better deeds than words to grace it' [II. ii. 17]—may in itself be merely conventional, but Julia on her next appearance makes an ironically genuine-sounding statement of the reality of love being beyond the power of words. 'Didst thou but know', she says to Lucetta, 'the inly touch of love',

Thou wouldst as soon go kindle fire with snow
As seek to quench the fire of love with words.
[II. vii. 19-20]

The irony is double here, for not only does Julia's paean to her and Proteus' love come just after we have witnessed his decision to abandon her, but the very questioning of the power of words is put in such an exuberant form as to question the question. Ironically, too, Julia's argument is inverted and perverted by Proteus as he threatens to rape Silvia:

Nay, if the gentle spirit of moving words
Can no way change you to a milder form,
I'll woo you like a soldier, at arms' end,
And love you 'gainst the nature of love—force ye.
[V. iv. 55-8]

And significantly it is, at this point, visual and not verbal evidence that brings about Valentine's recognition: 'nought but mine eye / Could have persuaded me' [V. iv. 64-5]. The questioning of language does not loom as large, nor occupy as thematically central a place, in *The Two Gentlemen of Verona* as it does in *Love's Labour's Lost,* but it is in some ways still more disturbing. In *Love's Labour's Lost* reliance on fine words and clever patterns indicates an empty idealism, an ivory tower knowledge of life, which collapses before real experience—be it of love or death. The collapse can be funny, but it can also be poignant, as when the Princess holds up the irrelevancy of the King's diction in the final scene: 'I understand you not; my griefs are double' [V. ii. 752]. Berowne—for it takes the wittiest mind to see the limits of wit—is the one to take the point: 'Honest plain words best pierce the ear of grief' [V. ii. 753]. And so we are prepared for the play's final resting point,

on good deeds versus words. In *The Two Gentlemen of Verona,* 'honest plain words' play little part, and the alternatives to wit are, on the one hand, silence and, on the other, force and brutality.

It would be tempting to suggest that in Valentine's passage of *peripeteia* [sudden reversal] and *anagnorisis* [self-recognition] Shakespeare anticipated those moments in his later plays where the reliance on eyes rather than ears is an essential part of his technique as a theatre poet. But it is probably closer to the truth to say that it is one of the moments in a play heavily dependent on its language where we are yet reminded that experience may outrun language. For the technique of this play is almost entirely verbal. Ingenious producers have to add to *The Two Gentlemen of Verona* those scenes of 'pure theatre' which are so important in the structure of other Shakespearian comedies. The social ritual, with the exception of Proteus' serenade, consists (even for the clowns) exclusively of talk; the text provides for no banquet, no masked ball, no concluding dance but just a verbal promise of social harmony—

One feast, one house, one mutual happiness— . . .
[V. iv. 173]

So love as courtship, and love and friendship as social forces, are handled through language alone—to the point where we feel that characters are used as an excuse for speeches and the plot as a device to bring about situations where characters can make speeches or engage in duologues. In this respect the play is still close to the descriptive-contemplative mode of non-dramatic poetry. Shakespeare's technique is still limited almost exclusively to three devices: soliloquy, duologue and the asides as comment. Clearly the debate structure of Lyly's plays underlies the pattern. And yet, as I have already suggested, there is also an action *in* the language itself which makes it uniquely Shakespearian (and relates it to the sonnets)—a sort of dialectic between a sense that 'much is the force of heaven-bred poesy' [III. ii. 71], on the one hand, and a doubt and undercutting of that force (even as that *credo* by the Duke is undercut by the ironical situation in which it is uttered). Delight in wit, in verbal conceits and Petrarchan diction, co-exists not only with the conventional regret that love, in Berowne's words, 'sings heaven's praise with such an earthly tongue' [IV. ii. 118], but also with a critical awareness that words may substitute for or falsify experience.

Because of this dialectic there is more to the real form—by which I mean that which relates the parts of the play to each other—of *The Two Gentlemen of Verona* than a 'structure-ridden' narrative, opening on a parting in which the themes of love and friendship are introduced and closing on a double reunion and an exaltation of love-through-friendship. That structure is obviously there, but it is questioned and explored so that only rarely may we take it at its face value. Longitudinally, the exploration seems to move through three stages. In the first of these—I. i through to the beginnings of Proteus' defection at [II. iv. 192]—a perspective is established for us in which the play's world of witty artifice, in action as in language, is both celebrated and criticized. The opening scene between Valentine and Proteus moves rapidly through a duologue which, in Lyly's manner, sets up two antithetical attitudes, leaving Proteus alone on stage to clinch the antithesis in a soliloquy:

He after honour hunts, I after love;
He leaves his friends to dignify them more:
I leave myself, my friends, and all for love.
[I. i. 63-5]

At this stage there is no reason to doubt that these lines are a straightforward enunciation of theme, but subsequent action and speeches will question all the key-words: 'honour', 'love', friends'—even 'self'. Indeed the last line ominously looks forward to having its meaning revalued when Proteus, in II. vi, discovers that 'I to myself am dearer than a friend' [II. vi. 23], and so leaves his true self for the selfish gratification of pursuing a new love. The Speed-Proteus duologue which completes I. i casts the light of burlesque on courtly wit, but, with its puns on ship/sheep/shepherd/mutton, it also keeps us in a dramatic world where life is dealt with as a kind of linguistic game. In the next scene this perspective is delightfully maintained by Julia's coquetry over Proteus' letter, both in the duologue with Lucetta and in her one-woman show with the letter as the only prop. In a scene like this we obviously do not regard language and action from Launce's unsophisticated point of view: 'to be slow in words is a woman's only virtue' [III. i. 334]; but, on the other hand, a sense is developing that sophistication may be mere padding. As one of my students recently said, when Julia rips up her letter from Proteus and then changes her mind and from the torn pieces picks out simple phrases like 'kind Julia', or 'passionate Proteus', or just 'Proteus', then we feel that she probably has the essence of the letter and has not lost much by losing the conventional decorations. It is notable—and in the context not just an inherited plot-trick—that so much of the intercourse between characters in this play is carried out by way of letters, a medium even further conventionalized than formal speech. Typically Proteus comes on reading a letter from Julia:

> Sweet love! sweet lines! sweet life!
> Here is her hand, the agent of her heart;
>
> [I. iii. 45-6]

and this, apart from their brief parting scene, is the only dramatic statement of their mutual love—just as later Launce's lady-love exists only through her 'conditions' set down in writing. 'Lines' are made the vehicle, indeed the essence, of 'love' and 'life' in this world, even as the 'hand' that writes is the chief agent and evidence of the 'heart' that feels.

The first scene between Valentine and Silvia (and the only one in which they have any kind of privacy, though even here Speed is present) develops this perspective further: in their relationship at this instance, love is the stuff for words; and the words are delightful and wittily patterned, but at the same time curiously depersonalized. It is absurdly apt that Valentine should have been asked to, *and* been able to, write a letter on behalf of somebody else to an unknown recipient. The separation of word and feeling could not go much further than this, and, unlike the love-blinded Valentine, we do not really need Speed to see how deliberate the absurdity is. . . . The deliberateness goes outside even Speed's superior awareness (it is significant that the letter-carriers are basically so much wittier than the letter-writers and receivers in the play), to a comment from the dramatist on how in this kind of courtship one situation is interchangeable for another, how relationships are as formalized and as dependent on verbal elaboration as conceits. Indeed, in this part of the play Shakespeare delights in constructing scenes which are, as it were, verbal conceits (and often standard Petrarchan conceits) turned into stage-tableaux—such as Julia's game with names in I. ii and the two parting scenes in II. ii-iii.

The clown scenes are obviously used to puncture by parody this tendency to formalization—without, therefore, demolishing the inherent truth in a conceit. Launce's one-man show

with Crab has, by now, probably received more critical attention than all the other scenes of the play put together, and deservedly so. It draws together several other scenes: in technique it echoes Julia's speaking tableau in I. ii; in his delicious confusion over which prop represents which member of his grieving family, Launce recalls the gay confusion over the identities of letter-writers and receivers in II. i but also anticipates the serious confounding of identities involved in Proteus' betrayal; in theme, of course, the scene parodies the excessive emotion of the parting between Proteus and Julia which has just taken place. But it is interesting that, in his rebuking of the silent Crab (hard-hearted as Proteus is soon going to be), Launce is so much wordier than the lovers themselves, and also that, within the comic frame of the scene, the diction and patterning of courtly love poetry came so eaily to Launce. . . . [There] is a mixture of genuine feeling and mockery in his elaboration on Proteus' image:

> Why, man, if the river were dry, I am able to
> fill it with my tears; if the wind were down, I
> could drive the boat with my sighs.
>
> [II. iii. 51-3]

So Launce makes comically explicit a critical perspective on the absorption in the conventional attitudes and language of love—a perspective which the 'serious' scenes have implicitly demonstrated—without in any way denying, as might happen in a satire, the holiness of the heart's affections or the need to put them into words.

In the second stage of its dialectic—from the end of II. iv through the rest of Act II and the whole of Acts III and IV—the play seems to take us into two new directions, on the one hand putting the patterned and apparently conventional language to serious uses and, on the other, establishing scenes which are, as it were, counter-conceits and in which the language and attitudes of courtly convention are found altogether invalid.

Under the pressure of the serious complications in the plot, those involving tension of mind and suffering and heartbreak, verbal ingenuity itself becomes a vehicle for a sense of life. The first sign of this is Proteus' soliloquy in II. vi:

> To leave my Julia, shall I be forsworn;
> To love fair Silvia, shall I be forsworn;
> To wrong my friend, I shall be much forsworn.
> And ev'n that power which gave me first my oath
> Provokes me to this threefold perjury:
> Love bade me swear, and Love bids me forswear. . . .
> I cannot leave to love, and yet I do;
> But there I leave to love where I should love.
> Julia I lose, and Valentine I lose;
> If I keep them, I needs must lose myself;
> If I lose them, thus find I by their loss:
> For Valentine, myself; for Julia, Silvia.
> I to myself am dearer than a friend;
> For love is still most precious in itself.
>
> [II. vi. 1-6, 17-24]

In this speech many of the stylistic features of the play are concentrated: the end-stopped lines: the antitheses or paradoxes pivoted on the caesura or brought out by the perfect symmetry of two consecutive lines; the patterning of repetitions towards a climax; the argument through conceits (mainly in such lines as the following pair: 'At first I did adore a twinkling star, / But now I worship a celestial sun' [II. vi. 9-10]). But here, instead of drawing attention to itself as it would have done earlier in the play, and unlike the careful patterning in the apparently similar weighing of love against friendship in *Endimion,* the verbal scheme truly suggests the staccato movements, the to-and-froing, the see-saw of impulses within a mind which, while it believes itself divided, is already set on its course. Compared to Euphues in a similar conflict situation, Proteus is much less self-conscious or concerned with looking before and after, much less aware of the appearance of the situation from every viewpoint; indeed the most impressive feature of this speech is its enactment of gradual self-absorption, until Proteus gives us the first hint of the Iago figure whose limited self—''tis in ourselves that we are thus and thus' [*Othello,* I. iii. 319-20]—is the centre of any argument. The casuistical argument against vows . . . is not merely, or mainly, an exhibition of clever wit; it produces a dizzy sense of the precariousness of language. When Lyly's debaters weigh up 'love', in a much more intellectualized fashion than Proteus, the word remains an entity with a permanent reference; here it means what Proteus' heedless emotion wants it to mean: 'I cannot leave to love, and yet I do' [II. vi. 17]. In the mouth of the unscrupulous, language changes its meaning, and—like Iago—Proteus can pretend to change actuality through words:

> I will forget that Julia is alive,
> Rememb'ring that my love to her is dead.
>
> [II. vi. 27-8]

On the other hand, of course, a metamorphosed actuality can give a new human content and poignancy to an old game of words, as when Julia speaks of her heavy task of wooing Silvia on Proteus' behalf:

> I am my master's true confirmed love,
> But cannot be true servant to my master,
> Unless I prove false traitor to myself.
>
> [IV. iv. 103-05]

The same is true for Valentine's banishment speech which, one might almost say, bears the same relation to the partial sonnet which the Duke discovers on him as Romeo's love for Rosaline does to that for Juliet. Valentine's discovery that he has so 'garner'd up his heart' [*Othello,* IV. ii. 57] in another person that his own identity can only be defined through her,

> To die is to be banish'd from myself,
> And Silvia is myself; banish'd from her
> Is self from self, a deadly banishment.
> What light is light, if Silvia be not seen?
> What joy is joy, if Silvia be not by?
>
> [III. i. 171-75]

passes beyond conventional attitudinizing to an attitude in which verbal patterning is functional and central. (pp. 42-6)

The echoes here of themes and images from several sonnets may help us to see that, as in the sonnets, Shakespeare is working *through* the convention. At least one of the finest moments in the play is arrived at—much like Sonnet 130, 'My mistress' eyes are nothing like the sun'—through a kind of anti-sonnet technique. When Silvia questions the supposed Sebastian about Julia, 'Is she not passing fair?', and Julia replies by fictionalizing herself,

> She hath been fairer, madam, than she is.
> When she did think my master lov'd her well,
> She, in my judgment, was as fair as you;
> But since she did neglect her looking-glass,

> And threw her sun-expelling mask away,
> The air hath starv'd the roses in her cheeks,
> And pinch'd the lily-tincture of her face,
> That now she is become as black as I,
>
> [IV. iv. 149-56]

then her nouns—the looking-glass, the sun, the roses, the lily-tincture—are those of the Petrarchan convention; but her verbs—neglect, throw away, starve, pinch—enact the reality behind the convention, the vulnerability of the roses and the lilies. We are . . . made to sense 'what it feels like' in the particular dramatic situation. As fiction and reality in Julia's narrative meet in 'That now she is become as black as I', language has become truly dramatic, indeed hardly more than a stage-direction.

If Shakespeare's handling of convention and language at this stage of the play suggests a new seriousness and critical alertness, then we might in this context re-view two scenes which are often criticized for the wrong reasons and which, it seems to me, are in fact carefully controlled counter-conceits. The first is the one where Valentine with unbelievable stupidity gives away to the Duke his love for Silvia and his plan for elopement with her. The Duke's ruse of asking Valentine to 'tutor' him in how to court 'a lady in Verona here / Whom I affect' [III. i. 81-2] provides the scaffold for a duologue (especially [III. i. 89-105]) which is a take-off on conventions of courtship in the rest of the play. The main comic point lies not just in Valentine's stupidity but in the freewheeling, or in terms of Valentine's consciousness almost mesmeric, effect which the convention has once the duologue is under way, so that the right key-word planted by the Duke will provoke the right (in terms of convention *and* of the Duke's intentions) response from Valentine:

> *Duke.* That no man hath access by day to her.
> *Val.* Why, then I would resort to her by night.
> *Duke.* Ay, but the doors be lock'd and keys kept safe,
> That no man hath recourse to her by night . . .
> *Val.* Why then a ladder quaintly made of cords,
>
> [III. i. 109-12, 117]

and so on. Shakespeare is, by the structure of the dialogue and by a slight quaintness of syntax, exaggerating the mechanical effect of patterned speech. . . . In the Shakespearian situation, love behaviour and language is seen to have become a mechanized gesture, the lover a puppet who can be manipulated at will by a detached outsider. Valentine is not just stupid but a comic character in the Bergsonian sense. Not only is the love convention, in attitudes and speech, tested and found absurd but, in a microcosm of the whole play's pattern, it is seen to explode in violence. The image with which the Duke starts his dismissal of Valentine may, in its magnitude, seem to ameliorate the situation by exalting it:

> Why, Phaethon—for thou art Merops' son—
> Wilt thou aspire to guide the heavenly car,
> And with thy daring folly burn the world?
> Wilt thou reach stars because they shine on thee?

But that, too, explodes in ugly, unvarnished brutality:

> Go, base intruder, over-weening slave,
> Bestow thy fawning smiles on equal mates.
>
> [III. i. 153-58]

If this situation is artificial, there is yet a sense of life in its implicit comment on artificiality and its effects.

The second scene to be set in this context is that in which Proteus, the most wickedly clever character in the play, in response to Silvia's reproaches can only produce two identical, and identically feeble, excuses:

> I grant, sweet love, that I did love a lady;
> But she is dead. . . .
> I likewise hear that Valentine is dead. . . .
>   [IV. ii. 104-05, 112]

Much like Valentine in the scene just discussed, Proteus is moving as a puppet of the courtly love code, which for a situation like this prescribes, in Valentine's words to the Duke:

> If she do chide, 'tis not to have you gone,
> For why the fools are mad if left alone.
> Take no repulse, whatever she doth say;
> For 'Get you gone' she doth not mean 'Away!'
>   [III. i. 98-101]

The trouble is that Silvia does not go by the courtesy book but by genuine human reactions. Proteus, who was so voluble a letter-writer to Julia and so articulate in sacrificing an old love to a new, is inventive enough as long as he can play with conceits in the wooing-the-reluctant-mistress game. . . . But he cannot cope with a woman who persists in taking a severely practical view of his wit . . . and in being ruthlessly literal about the conceit of his 'pure heart's truth' [IV. ii. 88]. So, as she gives him the wrong cues (as against the all-too-right ones in the case of the Duke vis-à-vis Valentine), he has no language to reply with but a cry of 'dead'. Once, indeed, he thinks he has picked up a cue, as Silvia assures him that in Valentine's grave (if he is dead) 'my love is buried':

> Sweet lady, let me rake it from the earth.
>   [IV. ii. 114-15]

But Silvia quickly disabuses him of the idea that he has found an idiom through which he can advance his interests:

> Go to thy lady's grave, and call hers thence;
> Or, at the least, in hers sepulchre thine.
>   [IV. ii. 116-17]

From this deadlock—'he heard not that' [IV. ii. 118], the listening Julia significantly comments—the only way forward is via a totally new conceit, that of Silvia's picture, which leads to a sonnet game on 'shadow' and 'substance' [IV. ii. 123-30]. The presence of Julia and the sleeping Host throughout this scene enables Shakespeare not only to puncture Proteus' conceits and inanities with Julia's sharp asides but also to construct a situation which consists of several layers of non-communication. And the scene closes on Julia's words, as directly in contact with human reality as Desdemona's 'Faith, half asleep' [*Othello*, IV. ii. 97]:

> it hath been the longest night
> That e'er I watch'd, and the most heaviest.
>   [IV. ii. 135-36]

So, in exploring its world of romantic courtship, *The Two Gentlemen of Verona* repeatedly and in various ways reminds us that there is a world elsewhere. We are made to delight in the beauty and wit of the romance world, but we are also made to sense that it is fragile and vulnerable, ready to topple over into absurdity on the one side and brutality on the other. The sense of life that informs the play is something like a tightrope walk, and the scene which I have just discussed is an epitome of the tightrope pattern.

But IV. ii (which is generally regarded as the best scene in the play) is also an indication of where the play's radical dramatic weakness lies: in the tendency for each scene to form, much as each Shakespearian sonnet does, a kind of 'still' from a play, a virtually self-contained picture of human relationships. Shakespeare has obviously had difficulties in translating the 'I' and the 'thou' (and occasionally 'she') of the sonnets into the multiple voices and interactions of a dramatic structure. The lovers hardly ever meet: apart from the last scene, each twosome comes together in two scenes, but even then their contacts are often perfunctory. There is nothing like Romeo's and Juliet's minds meshing in a sonnet, nor like the formalized intimacy of the couples and cross-pairings in *Love's Labour's Lost* and *A Midsummer Night's Dream*. Lovers appear apart, talking about their love; and paradoxically Valentine and Silvia 'meet' more in his banishment speech than in any actual co-presence on stage. The same is true for the two friends: their relationship is most alive and meaningful in Proteus' soliloquy in II. vi. All this means that the fulfilments in Act V—which forms what I have here called the third stage in the structure of the play—operate in something of a vacuum. When Valentine, faced with Proteus' perfidy, speaks of his friend as physically and morally a part of himself—'one's own right hand / Is perjured to the bosom' [V. iv. 67-8]—and voices an almost Cleopatra-like sense that the whole world has turned a stranger, then these words do not have tentacles which reach back into the play.

The real inconsistency, then, of this play, and the one which becomes most apparent when he tries to dramatize constancy, is that Shakespeare is trying to use as his raw material what characters say (attitudes) rather than what they are (people). Plot is forever crystallizing into attitudes, and the structural pattern is one of scenes, each demonstrating one or more attitudes to love (or friendship). Some scenes are entirely contained in a single emblematic stance, like the two versions of parting with dear ones in II. ii and II. iii; some, like II. iv, move through a whole gamut of attitudes—more by adding one tableau to another than by causally linking each with the other. The longest scene of all—III. i (374 lines)—is the longest not because more happens (the final scene in which so much happens is less than half as long) but because we move through a particularly wide range of stances: through moments deeply moving, moments which implicitly reveal their own absurdity, and moments which explicitly deflate the love code (Launce's and Speed's duologue on Launce's mistress). And what applies within the longer scenes also holds true for the relationship between scenes in the play as a whole. Their interconnection is determined not by growing and changing personalities but by their evaluation of the word and concept of 'love'. In other words, Shakespeare is trying to handle dramatic structure as if it were the verbal structure of a sonnet. To show what I mean, I should like at this point to return to Sonnet 40, which not only is very close in idea to Valentine's renunciation but also helps us to see why in *The Two Gentlemen of Verona* Shakespeare produced a work which is ultimately less dramatic than many of his sonnets. (pp. 46-52)

In the sonnet, through the verbal action of devices like pun, paradox, antithesis and oxymoron, the pattern becomes an enactment of the poet's feelings for his friend; and the meaning of this 'love' grows both more specific and more evocative, until it is defined—or, rather, held in suspension—in the contrary pulls of the couplet. Verbal ingenuity is entirely in the service of the dramatic evocation of 'what it feels like'. This is, of course, exactly what happens to the word-patterns and images in Shakespeare's mature plays; to a key-word like 'see' in *King Lear,* which changes and grows in human meaning, from Lear's first to his last 'see' and right through to Edgar's closing 'never see so much' [*King Lear,* V. iii. 327]. The sonnet is dramatic, too, in its dynamic form: what may look like a static attitude in the opening line develops through the fourteen lines into a live and complex relationship. The final 'yet we must not be foes' is both a desperate appeal and an affirmation—a far more troubled statement than the apparent nonchalance of the first line. It reveals the quality which perhaps most definitely bespeaks the dramatist in the sonnet: the dual voice (or viewpoint), which asserts and yet also questions, affirms an utter self-effacement in devotion and is yet also aware of the absurdity of such an attitude—the ability, in other words, to be both inside and outside an experience.

The play is less dramatic on all these counts. The character interaction and development which *should* translate the verbal action of the sonnet is lacking, and so the sense of 'what it feels like' is fitful and there is no overall dynamism. In the structural climax marked by Valentine's couplet,

> And, that my love may appear plain and free,
> All that was mine in Silvia I give thee,
>
> [V. iv. 82-3]

'my love' *should* be a more meaningful dramatic reality than the 'love' bandied about in the opening debate of the play. (The dénouement of *Twelfth Night,* for example, shows how the word 'love' has been through just this dynamic process.) But in fact it is not. Nor is the ending sustained by that complex viewpoint which we find in the sonnet (and again in the final scene of *Twelfth Night*). Involvement and detachment have alternated during the first four acts, sometimes (as in IV. ii) coalescing; but in the last scene, and particularly in Valentine's lines, the drama seems to fall between the two.

If, with due care, we continue the sonnet analogy, it would appear that Shakespeare conceived this last scene in much the same way as in several of his sonnets he used a surprise couplet—one which, after twelve lines of argument in one direction, leaps to a sudden reversal with an antithetical 'Yet' or 'But' or 'Ah, but'. In the sonnets where this happens, the break in the logic and the frequent introduction of a new simplicity (not to be mistaken for facility) suggests that the couplet records more of a desperate wish-fulfilment than a real conclusion, a willed belief rather than a state of emotional conviction. The same seems to me to be true for the last scene of *The Two Gentlemen of Verona.* The trouble (the ultimate inconsistency) is that there is a theoretical pressure on the scene which is not practically realized. The connections, both thematic and verbal, between Valentine's situation and other instances of inconstancy and betrayed trust in Shakespeare—not least, of course, in the sonnets—indicate that pressure. The sonnets which contain a reversal in the couplet are all in one way or another concerned with . . . the fear that one's love and trust may be betrayed—and this fear, it seems to me, is what Shakespeare tries and fails to instil as an undertone in the scene. The central episode is dealt with in an extraordinary shorthand fashion. There are 24 lines between Proteus' attempted rape and Julia's swoon, and in these we are bounced from one extreme attitude to another: disillusionment and reproach, penitence, forgiveness and demonstration of magnanimity. The shock to Valentine's consciousness is hauntingly expressed:

> Proteus,
> I am sorry I must never trust thee more,
> But count the world a stranger for thy sake.
>
> [V. iv. 68-70]

But thereafter the experience does not seem to pass through either character's mind. We are asked to accept it through general truths and universal statements, like Valentine's motivation of his forgiveness:

> Who by repentance is not satisfied,
> Is nor of heaven, nor earth; for these are pleas'd
> By Penitence th'Eternal's wrath's appeas'd.
>
> [V. iv. 79-81]

In a sonnet like 'Why didst thou promise such a beauteous day' [Sonnet 34], which also turns from reproach to sudden forgiveness, the reversal in the couplet is organically part of the whole, for it embodies the very point of the poem: the irrationality, recognized as such and yet treasured, of a deep commitment. Nor is the couplet a simple reversal, for there is a strong undertone of irony in the way its imagery relates to the rest of the sonnet and contradicts the assurance it is supposed to state:

> Ah! but those tears are pearl which thy love sheds,
> And they are rich, and ransom all ill deeds.

How can the artificiality of pearl be commensurate with, still less compensate for, the unnatural hurts which the friend has inflicted? The irrationality of Valentine's argument is not placed in a saving perspective—Speed and Launce have disappeared at this stage of the play, and the women are mute. Nor is there any room for irony in the interchange between sinner and forgiver: Proteus' plea that 'hearty sorrow / Be a sufficient ransom for offence' is taken with the simplest 'Then I am paid' [V. iv. 74-5, 77] from Valentine. Nor do Valentine's lines have any of the interpenetration of grief and the desire to forgive which dominates Sonnet 34. (pp. 53-6)

The reason why I have paid so much attention to what is *not* there in *The Two Gentlemen of Verona* is that it is the combination of what *is* there with what is not that makes it a disturbing play. Certain aspects of its structure and language, as I hope to have shown, enable us to be in two minds at once: to accept and criticize the life presented to us. We are aware of the beauty *and* precariousness of the romance world. But individual characters' speeches cannot reach to the kind of *felt* uncertainty which is there in Helena's inability to settle for complete trust—'And I have found Demetrius like a jewel, / Mine own, and not mine own' [*A Midsummer Night's Dream,* IV. i. 191-92]—and which rankles in many of the sonnets:

> Thee have I not lock'd up in any chest,
> Save where thou art not, though I feel thou art,
> Within the gentle closure of my breast.
>
> [Sonnet 48]

It is that uncertainty within the closest relationships ('where thou art not, though I feel thou art') which I think Shakespeare has wanted to render in *The Two Gentlemen of Verona,* and which gives a peculiar poignancy to Proteus' outcry: 'O heaven, were man / But constant, he were perfect' [V. iv. 110-11]. If the ending is an example of ineptitude in early Shakespeare, then the very ineptitude suggests the troubled vision of a man who cares immensely about love and friendship, what they do to people and make people do to each other. (pp. 56-7)

Inga-Stina Ewbank, '' 'Were Man but Constant He Were Perfect': Constancy and Consistency in 'The Two Gentlemen of Verona','' in Shakespearian Comedy, Stratford-upon-Avon Studies, No. 14, *Crane, Russak & Company, Inc., 1972, pp. 31-57.*

THOMAS E. SCHEYE (essay date 1974)

[*Scheye explores Valentine's loss of identity in* The Two Gentlemen of Verona, *suggesting that the character unconsciously changes from a self-declared skeptic of love into the "mirror image of Proteus," his false ideal of the perfect gentleman. The critic points to Shakespeare's source, Thomas Elyot's* The Governor, *and the dramatist's own* The Comedy of Errors *as earlier works in which two people unite in a single identity, comparing this process to Proteus's usurpation of Valentine's self in Milan, the "house of mirrors." Scheye further argues that in Milan's opposite, the green world, this loss of self is reversed, stating that Valentine gains conviction as well as self-knowledge in the forest, enabling him to forgive his friend and bring about the play's final multiple reconciliations. However, Scheye concludes that Valentine's "process of self-discovery is almost external to the character" and is due largely to the Duke's interference, rather than his own actions.*]

[*The Two Gentlemen of Verona*] is Shakespeare's first story of true love, whose course never did run smooth until the happy ending. It is also the play where Shakespeare maps out his comic territory. In Northrop Frye's familiar formula, "the action of the comedy begins in a world represented as a normal world, moves into the green world, goes into a metamorphosis there in which the comic resolution is achieved, and returns to the normal world" [see Additional Bibliography]. The forest which provides the scene for the resolution of *Two Gentlemen* is Shakespeare's earliest venture into the green world: it is the place where Valentine is reunited with Silvia and Proteus reconciled to Julia, as a reconstructed society, which even includes the outlaws, forms up around the young couples. But before it moves into the forest, this comedy of Verona stops for nearly three acts in another setting, the city of Milan, where all the preparations for a quick and easy denouement are laid. Milan is no green world; Valentine falls in love there and is almost ready to elope with Silvia, but his plans are foiled. He is slandered and betrayed by his best friend, and condemned and banished by the duke; then he can describe being in Milan as "living torment" [III. i. 170].

The action in Milan is clearly played for comedy, but the fact remains that the second world of the play is not idyllic; it is an unpleasant and even somewhat dangerous place for the protagonist. Of course, there is usually a place like this in Shakespeare's romantic comedies; in the phase when the fortunes of the hero run down, the cross-wooing threatens to get out of control, and games of disguise and mistaken identity take unexpected, unhappy turns. This phase can be more conveniently isolated for examination in *The Two Gentlemen of Verona* because of the changes of scene; and perhaps by attention to what happens to the two gentlemen in Milan we can approach a paradigm to describe what happens in the green world.

The paradigm I want to propose has to do with the search for identity since that would seem to be Valentine's motive for coming to Milan in the first place. In the opening scene he has told Proteus that he is making a journey "To see the wonders of the world abroad" [I. i. 6], possibly because he has considered, as Proteus's father has, "how he cannot be a perfect man, / Not being tried and tutor'd in the world" [I. iii. 20-1]. The journey is part of his education, a way of making himself a perfect or complete man, or of growing up; Proteus says it is a search after "honor" [I. i. 63]. In *Two Gentlemen* Valentine comes to Milan in search of "honor" or experience so that he can realize himself to the fullest. But as soon as he arrives, he forgets about honor and education and the rest; he

sets eyes on Silvia and falls in love. Now love will be seen as learning: in love in Milan Valentine will learn about himself.

At first, though, love makes Valentine lose his old self. In Verona he was someone who scorned Proteus's love as "shapeless idleness" and "folly bought with wit" [I. i. 8, 34]; in Milan he is love's abject servant, the fool who goes ungartered. And the effect of this radical change in Valentine, "from the mocker to the votary of love" [see excerpt above by H. B. Charlton, 1930], is apparent even to Speed: "when I look on you, I can hardly think you my master" [II. i. 31-2]. Valentine has lost himself in love so that now he is the mirror image of Proteus instead of his opposite. Speed says,

> . . . you have learned, like Sir Proteus, to wreathe your arms like a malcontent, to relish a love-song like a robin-red-breast, to walk alone like one that had the pestilence, to sigh like a schoolboy that had lost his A B C. . . .
>
> [II. i. 18-23]

And he concludes, "You are metamorphosed with a mistress" [II. i. 30-1], recalling to us Proteus's apostrophe, "Thou, Julia, thou hast metamorphosed me" [I. i. 66]. By love's metamorphosis Valentine has lost his identity until he no longer even looks like himself; he looks like Proteus instead.

Valentine's resemblance to his best friend is not too surprising since it was traditional during the Renaissance to describe friendship in terms of identity, or one soul in two bodies. This resemblance is especially acute in Milan where Valentine executes his protean about-face and turns lover like his friend, and both men for a time are in love with the same woman. . . . Valentine claims to know Proteus as he knows himself (Julia, disguised as the page, will tell Silvia she knows Julia "Almost as well as I do know myself" [IV. iv. 143]); for the two friends have grown up in identical circumstances. . . . Valentine has been temporarily separated from his friend so that experience can do the work of time and bring his character closer to angel-like perfection. And Proteus is the image of that perfection, "complete in feature and in mind" [II. iv. 73] as Valentine would like to be, his ideal and his model.

Their friendship is strained when Proteus too falls in love with Silvia, the competition in love causing the conflict in Milan. Such competition belongs to the conventions of the literature of friendship which Shakespeare reflects in *The Two Gentlemen of Verona,* with the most apposite source, apparently, being the story of Titus and Gisippus as told by Sir Thomas Elyot in *The Governor.* (pp. 11-13)

When he comes to borrow from this version of Titus and Gisippus for *The Two Gentlemen of Verona,* Shakespeare carries over the competition in love along with the notion of spiritual kinship and similitude of appetite [in his characterizations of Valentine and Proteus]. On the other hand, he does not include any suggestion of physical identity between the two friends, possibly because he had just written, or was about to write, a play about a pair of actual twins in *The Comedy of Errors.* Even so, twinship might provide a model for the relationship between Valentine and Proteus as it does for the two Antipholi. And perhaps from this perspective *The Comedy of Errors* can also help to explain the paradigm for *Two Gentlemen.*

The Comedy of Errors is set on the day when Antipholus of Syracuse arrives in Ephesus in search of his twin brother and the rest of his family; he has made the voyage because he believes that without relations his identity will be incomplete.

And though he tells a friendly merchant he meets there that he will spend the day in Ephesus sight-seeing ("I will go lose myself, / And wander up and down to view the city" [I. ii. 30-1]), he later elaborates the figure of losing himself:

> I to the world am like a drop of water
> That in the ocean seeks another drop,
> Who, falling there to find his fellow forth,
> Unseen, inquisitive, confounds himself.
> So I, to find a mother and a brother,
> In quest of them, unhappy, lose myself.
>
> [I. ii. 35-40]

Antipholus loses himself in Ephesus hoping that, like the drop of water, he can make sense not as a single body, but in the world's body. He loses himself in order to find himself through his twin. At first, though, the fact that Antipholus of Syracuse looks exactly like his brother and is called by his name only heightens his sense of self-loss; since he is continually taken for someone else by the citizens of Ephesus, he is almost convinced that he is "Known unto these, and to myself disguised" [II. ii. 214]. Until they are reunited, the twins will seem to share a single identity in Ephesus, that of the native brother, since the existence of another Antipholus is unknown. And in a continual interchange of roles one brother gains identity as the other loses it.... At the denouement the native Antipholus can be seen to have acted, unwittingly, as genius to his brother, who gains not only his family but also his individual identity once the confusion is sorted out.

On the day of errors, then, Antipholus of Syracuse has lost himself and found himself through the mirror image which is provided by his twin brother. And something like this happens to Valentine in *The Two Gentlemen of Verona*. The process begins when Valentine comes to Milan and falls under Silvia's spell; he is "metamorphosed with a mistress" and he begins to lose his old identity. At first Valentine's appearance changes so that he no longer resembles his former self. Then Love deprives him of his senses.... In love-blindness Valentine cannot see himself or see how much he looks like Proteus. And love has not only blinded Valentine; it has also struck him dumb. As he cannot know himself yet, he cannot express himself either. Though he is eloquent to Proteus in praise of his beloved, Valentine cannot tell Silvia of his devotion directly. And so he has resorted to letters, to which she has not replied. Letters are normally an unsuccessful means of communication, as Act I has shown with the letter Proteus has written to Julia. He has sent it to her by Valentine's servant, Speed, but when Speed returns he brings no answer and tells Proteus,

> Sir, I could perceive nothing at all from her:
> no, not so much as a ducat for delivering your
> letter. And being so hard to me that brought
> your mind, I fear she'll prove as hard to you
> in telling your mind.
>
> [I. i. 136-40]

The resemblance between the letters is more obvious after Speed interprets them. (Is this a reason for having Valentine's servant deliver Proteus's letter?) When Silvia bids Valentine write a letter to a "secret, nameless friend" [II. i. 105]—Valentine himself at this point—and then tells him to keep it, Speed asks, "do you not perceive the jest?" [II. i. 153-54]. Valentine does not perceive it, and yet the jest is so transparent that the foolish servant has caught it immediately.... Silvia's device is as plain as the nose on your face, Speed says. Val-

entine can see it only as well as he can see himself, as he will only understand his love after he understands himself.

The letter Silvia returns to Valentine is meant to teach a lesson: that he must love himself, and know himself, before he can love another. But for that lesson Proteus, the mirror image, will be a better teacher. When he arrives in Milan and falls in love with Silvia at first sight, Proteus understands immediately that the selfless devotion of friendship must give way before self-interest in love:

> Methinks my zeal to Valentine is cold,
> And that I love him not as I was wont.
> O, but I love his lady too too much,
> And that's the reason I love him so little.
>
> [II. iv. 203-06]

Proteus hesitates for a moment—his soliloquy is broken into two parts by an intervening comic scene between Launce and Speed—but when he resolves to move against his friend he knows that Valentine must lose himself if he (Proteus) is going to find himself:

> I cannot leave to love, and yet I do:
> But there I leave to love where I should love.
> Julia I lose and Valentine I lose.
> If I keep them, I needs must lose myself;
> If I lose them, thus find I by their loss:
> For Valentine, myself;
>
> [II. vi. 17-22]

Proteus imagines that he will gain his selfhood at the price of Valentine's self-loss, and the situation may recall that of the Antipholus twins in *The Comedy of Errors* sharing a single identity between them: when one of the brothers had identity, the other was selfless. Antipholus of Syracuse had taken over his twin's identity without meaning to, but Proteus consciously wishes to usurp Valentine's identity, to displace him in Silvia's affections and to replace him at the court of Milan. So he discloses Valentine's planned elopement, and Valentine is banished; banishment confirms Valentine's loss of identity. When he pronounces sentence the duke not only exiles Valentine but damns him for aspiring beyond himself to Silvia, calling him "base intruder" and "overweening slave" [III. i. 157]. The duke is denying Valentine his status, his position at Milan and his state as a nobleman, two essential props to his identity at this point. When he threatens Valentine, "as thou lov'st thy life, make speed from hence" [III. i. 169], Valentine says he is as good as dead already, in a state of nonexistence:

> To die is to be banished from myself.
> And Silvia is myself; banished from her
> Is self from self, a deadly banishment....
> She is my essence, and I leave to be,
> If I be not by her fair influence
> Fostered, illumined, cherished, kept alive.
>
> [III. i. 171-73, 182-84]

Death is nothing more than absolute selflessness; and since his fulfillment depends on Silvia—his "essence," or self-image—without her Valentine is so lacking in selfhood that he says he is no longer Valentine.

His situation is tragic in its implication, and the parallel with Romeo has often been pointed out. Now as if to distance us from a potentially tragic reaction, Proteus and Launce are brought on for comic relief. Launce makes a significant malapropism about exile: "Sir, there is a proclamation that you are vanished'' [III. i. 217-18]. Then Valentine and Proteus have their cross-talk on the subject:

> *Proteus.*   Valentine?
> *Valentine.*   No.
> *Proteus.*   Who then? His spirit?
> *Valentine.*   Neither.
> *Proteus.*   What then?
> *Valentine.*   Nothing.
> [III. i. 193-98]
> (pp. 14-18)

The point has been made then, at considerable length, both seriously and humorously, that Valentine without Silvia is dead or nonexistent, utterly without identity. If his fate were tragic, like Romeo's, the play might end here, or go on to show the death of the hero. But Valentine has only come two-thirds of the way along the comic curve. He has lost himself now that Proteus has displaced him in Milan; but he will find himself. He has been told by the duke to ''Bestow thy fawning smiles on equal mates'' [III. i. 158], and, though the duke was talking about other women, Valentine will find his equal mates when he moves into the green world of the forest.

Valentine is accosted by the outlaws as he is going ''to Verona'' [IV. i. 17]. He is headed home, but he will find a new home with the outlaws as he had hoped to do with Silvia in Milan; in the forest it is the outlaws who offer a mirror image of his condition. Valentine has been banished for trying to elope with the duke's daughter, though he tells the outlaws that his offense was murder. The second of the outlaws too has been exiled as a murderer, while the third one says,

> Myself was from Verona banished,
> For practicing to steal away a lady,
> An heir, and near allied unto the Duke.
> [IV. i. 45-7]

This duplication—in which one outlaw has committed Valentine's pretended crime and another his actual crime—is strange, and yet it enforces the parallel between Valentine and the outlaws who are already allied as fellow exiles. One of them refers to Valentine as ''a man of such perfection / As we do in our quality much want—'' [IV. i. 55-6], recalling Valentine's praise of Proteus to the duke. The outlaws offer Valentine to be their king, and instead of robbing him of what little he has been left after banishment, they lead him to their treasure which they put ''at thy dispose'' [IV. i. 74]. In the forest the process of self-loss will be reversed and the scene laid for Valentine to find himself.

In this green world Valentine regains all the friends he has lost in Milan, and though he has one more moment of selflessness when he hands Silvia over to Proteus, he gains by this too. Valentine's proof of friendship, along with the sudden discovery of Julia, brings pressure on inconstant Proteus to execute a second about-face—mercurial changes come as easily to Proteus as to his namesake—which puts him back where he started. . . . So Valentine and Proteus are reconciled while Valentine is reunited with his ''essence,'' Silvia, and Proteus with Julia; the symmetry of the scene further enforces the parallel between the two gentlemen. In this moment Proteus has come to some kind of self-realization in part through the efforts of Valentine; in the same moment Valentine is reunited with his sworn brother and his beloved. Proteus and Silvia are the two people who have provided the mirror images in which Valentine might see himself, and the scene in which they are reconciled also demonstrates their effect on Valentine. When

his rival Thurio makes a claim on Silvia, Valentine shows how much he has recovered his identity, since for the first time he stands up for himself:

> Thurio, give back, or else embrace thy death.
> Come not within the measure of my wrath.
> Do not name Silvia thine; if once again,
> Verona shall not hold thee. Here she stands;
> Take but possession of her with a touch—
> I dare thee but to breathe upon my love.
> [V. iv. 126-31]

The duke applauds this show of spirit and self-interest, pardons Valentine, and approves the marriage. . . . The duke had once confirmed Valentine's loss of identity by exiling him and condemning him as ''base'' and ''overweening.'' Now he confirms Valentine's true identity by subscribing to his ''new state,'' inviting him ''home'' to Milan, and attesting to his nobility as ''Sir Valentine.'' The search for identity will come to an end when Sir Valentine returns to his new home and marries Silvia.

And so Milan will be the state where Valentine loses himself to find himself. The conceit is fairly familiar in Shakespeare, with the most famous statement of it coming in *The Tempest* and Gonzalo's description of the action:

> in one voyage
> Did Claribel her husband find at Tunis,
> And Ferdinand her brother found a wife
> Where he himself was lost; Prospero his dukedom
> In a poor isle; and all of us ourselves
> When no man was his own.
> [*The Tempest*, V. i. 208-13]

Gonzalo describes the effect of the voyage toward the green world with more vision and eloquence than anyone in *Two Gentlemen* can muster. But the earlier play can show more clearly how things are managed.

The Two Gentlemen of Verona is such a thin play that one can almost see through it, and the process of self-discovery is almost external to the character of the hero. Valentine has identity thrust upon him rather than achieving it for himself. There is no evidence that the mirror images Valentine confronts act like the glass Hamlet sets up before his mother, ''Where you may see the inmost part of you'' [*Hamlet*, III. iv. 20]. It is his status—what other people think of him rather than what he thinks of himself—which is seen to change. But this very lack of interest and definition in the character of Valentine leads away from theories of personality to a consideration of the scene in which the action is played out, and the second world, of this play at least, emerges as a house of mirrors, in Spenser's phrase ''a world of glass.'' Before he sets about the creation of full-blooded characters the playwright must construct a place for them to live. And for Shakespeare's comic world *The Two Gentlemen of Verona* may be a slightly smudged blueprint. (pp. 19-21)

> *Thomas E. Scheye, ''Two Gentlemen of Milan,'' in* Shakespeare Studies: An Annual Gathering of Research, Criticism, and Reviews, *Vol. VII, 1974, pp. 11-23.*

ALEXANDER LEGGATT   (essay date 1974)

[In the following excerpt, Leggatt describes the ''essential gap between different minds'' in The Two Gentlemen of Verona, *focusing on Shakespeare's technique of distancing ''the experience of love'' presented in the play. He maintains that Shakespeare*

achieves this distancing effect through both the comic parody of his servants and, more importantly, the lovers' conventional responses and the placement of their serious speeches in ironic circumstances, a device Leggatt refers to as "comic dislocation." The critic further describes each character's relation to love, from Proteus's reliance on "appearances, conventions, and verbal surfaces" to Julia's "wider range of feeling" and complex interplay of language and emotion. Leggatt concludes that although in Act V Shakespeare "still does not provide a positive assertion of the rightness of love," for the comic perspective remains at work, we are meant "to be content with the somewhat narrower satisfaction of seeing the lovers get what they want." Thus he adds that The Two Gentlemen of Verona *is "counseling us, if it counsels anything, not to expect too much."*]

The dating of Shakespeare's earliest comedies is uncertain, and it may be that *The Two Gentlemen of Verona,* rather than *The Comedy of Errors,* was his first venture in the genre. It would be difficult to argue that either play developed out of the other; rather, they seem to lie side by side. Certainly *The Two Gentlemen* shows quite a different use of the technique [of dislocation than that in *The Comedy of Errors*]. Instead of setting a variety of different kinds of experience against each other in a swift and flashing interplay, Shakespeare takes one particular experience—that of being in love—and sets it against a background that varies between hostility and indifference. The technique of dislocation is the same, but the concentration is steadier, and we are allowed more time to examine and explore the central experience. Being in love dominates the mind of the victim; it is a private, enclosed and very special state, and our awareness of how special it is is sharpened when we see the lovers against the indifference, or the sardonic detachment, of an outside world full of people who are not in love. The breakdown of understanding between the Syracusans and the Ephesians in *The Comedy of Errors* depended partly on the external situation of mistaken identity; here, we are more aware of an essential gap between different minds: there is less bustle on the stage, more attention to the interplay of personalities. It is worth remarking that this play has the smallest cast in Shakespeare, and consists to an unusual degree of scenes involving only two or three speakers.

The most obvious device, and the one that (properly enough) has received the most thorough critical attention, is the use of the clowns to provide a satiric perspective on the lovers. While it would be forcing the issue to claim that the parallels between the lovers and the clowns are sustained and systematic, there are many touches here and there to show the clowns mirroring, in a comic way, the events of the love plot. Proteus's farewell to Julia is followed by Launce's account of his parting with his family, and small touches tighten the connection: Julia cannot speak, Crab will not weep; there are plays on the word 'tide' in both scenes [II. ii. 14-15; II. iii. 37-40]. The reunion of the friends in Milan is followed by the reunion of the servants. Proteus's trick on Valentine, leading to his banishment, is followed by a scene in which Launce (Proteus's servant) tricks Speed (Valentine's servant) into delaying an errand, and the scene concludes with Launce's boast, 'I'll after, to rejoice in the boy's correction' [III. i. 384]. With the leisure provided by reading, as opposed to watching, the play, one could go on accumulating such parallels for a long time, and it would be easy to exaggerate their importance. In the theatre, one is sufficiently aware of them to keep the lovers in mind while watching the clowns, and this is what matters. To watch similar events causing emotional crises in one case, and casual laughter in the other, trivializes the events by removing their uniqueness. It also reminds us how far apart the characters really are.

But there are many moments which do that more sharply and directly. We see Proteus worrying about the reception of his love letter, and Speed simply concerned with being paid for delivering it [I. i. 96-147]. Valentine, satisfied in love, declares, 'I have din'd', but Speed insists, 'though the chameleon Love can feed on the air, I am one that am nourish'd by my victuals, and would fain have meat' [II. i. 171-74]. Launce speaks less directly to the lovers, but his own courtship, in which wealth becomes the deciding factor [III. i. 301-70], reminds us of the practical side of marriage, hardly touched on by the lovers; and he reminds us too, as they do not, of the practical side of love: 'when it stands well with him, it stands well with her' [II. v. 22-3].

For Speed, especially, the lovers have become strange creatures, hardly recognizable as normal human beings. From his point of view—as for Dromio of Syracuse—the transformations wrought by love are comically degrading. . . . Not only is the lover [Valentine] 'metamorphis'd', but his view of his lady is a vision the ordinary eye cannot recognize:

> SPEED: You never saw her since she was deform'd.
> VALENTINE: How long hath she been deform'd?
> SPEED: Ever since you lov'd her.
>
> [II. i. 63-5]

Love is a chameleon in more than its capacity to feed on air. At moments like this, the clowns have something like a choric function, a special authority to comment. And this authority is increased by their special relationship with the audience: they are partly characters in the story, but partly also Elizabethan stage clowns, half outside the borders of the play, belonging to a world not only larger than that of the lovers, but larger than the play itself. Launce addresses the audience directly, even intimately; and the business with his shoes may perhaps remind us that he is also Will Kemp, famous for his comic footwear. Speed not only speaks in rhyme but *knows* he is speaking in rhyme:

> VALENTINE: How now, sir! What are you reasoning with yourself?
> SPEED: Nay, I was rhyming: 'tis you that have the reason.
>
> [II. i. 141-44]

And a few lines later, when he remarks 'All this I speak in print, for in print I found it' [II. i. 169], we see him stepping back from one of his own speeches. At moments like this the clowns put us at a distance not only from the lovers, but from the play itself.

But Shakespeare is not content simply to set lovers against clowns, amusing though that exercise may be; within the play, there are other devices to make us see the lovers' experience as special and limited. The outside world is constantly impinging on them, interrupting their private contemplations, jarring them loose from their absorption in love. The play opens with a dialogue between a man who is in love and a man who is not, and the outside world has an awkward habit of breaking in, even on the lovers' soliloquies. Julia, reassembling Proteus's letter, indulges in a romantic fantasy of coupling their names together:

> Thus will I fold them one upon another;
> Now kiss, embrace, contend, do what you will.
>
> [*Re-enter* Lucetta.
> LUCETTA: Madam,
> Dinner is ready, and your father stays.
>
> [I. ii. 125-28]

As the fantasy reaches its climax, mundane reality breaks in, and Julia suddenly looks as foolish as someone caught delivering a speech to the bathroom mirror. The effect is echoed, and the challenge to love is sharper, in the following scene. We have just heard of Antonio's plans to send his son away when Proteus enters rapt in the contemplation of a letter from Julia:

> Sweet love! sweet lines! sweet life!
> Here is her hand, the agent of her heart;
> Here is her oath for love, her honour's pawn.
> O that our fathers would applaud our loves,
> To seal our happiness with their consents!
> O heavenly Julia!
> ANTONIO: How now! What letter are you reading there?
>
> [I. iii. 45-51]

Again, a private fantasy of love is broken, and with more damaging results: far from applauding their love, Antonio is about to separate the lovers. And while Proteus is left alone to contemplate the insubstantiality of love, the scene ends not with his soliloquy but with the entrance of the servant Panthino: 'Sir Proteus, your father calls for you; / He is in haste; therefore, I pray you, go' [I. iii. 88-9]. Jolted out of the narrow, enclosed world of love, Proteus is being sent away—significantly—to broaden his education.

Even when there are no direct interruptions, the lovers' statements about love are often placed in a context that dislocates them. Seen in isolation, Proteus's speech on the power of music is serious and eloquent:

> For Orpheus' lute was strung with poets' sinews,
> Whose golden touch would soften steel and stones,
> Make tigers tame, and huge leviathans
> Forsake unsounded deeps to dance on sands.
>
> [III. ii. 77-80]

But Proteus is advising the clownish Thurio on the winning of a woman whom he fully intends to court for himself; at least in part, the eloquence is the eloquence of a confidence trickster dazzling his victim. And for all the beauty of the serenade, no Orphean magic hypnotizes Silvia, who remains stubbornly hostile to both men. 'Who is Silvia?' [IV. ii. 39] is, like Proteus's celebration of Orpheus, easy to quote out of context as a gem from Shakespeare, a rare touch of beauty in an otherwise unsatisfying play. But seen against its proper background the beauty is edged with irony. Nor is romantic beauty the only effect to be dislocated in this way: Valentine's advice to the Duke on courting a lady makes him sound like a very clever, worldly wise young man; but gradually, as the Duke turns the conversation towards the subject of rope ladders, we realize how much the glib-sounding lecture is actually being manipulated by its listener; however blasé Valentine may sound, he is really playing into the hands of a man more clever and worldly wise than he is. Proteus as a romantic, and Valentine as a cynic, both sound like confident and experienced spokesmen of love. But each is comically out of his depth. The realization of this strikes us more slowly, with less explosive laughter, than when Adriana addresses a serious and eloquent appeal to the wrong Antipholus—but the basic comic technique is the same.

With the later comedies in mind, we might expect these devices to be counterbalanced by a defiant acceptance of love, like Orlando's 'I would not be cured, youth' [*As You Like It*, III.

ii. 425]. But when we look for this counterbalance here, it is curiously difficult to find.... [For] the most part, love is embraced with a rueful awareness of the burdens it imposes, and of how insubstantial its satisfactions are:

> O, how this spring of love resembleth
> The uncertain glory of an April day,
> Which now shows all the beauty of the sun,
> And by and by a cloud takes all away.
>
> [I. iii. 84-7]

The idea of lovers as victims is conventional enough, and is present throughout Shakespeare's comedies; but normally it is played off against other views of them. Here, to an unusual degree, it is the dominant impression. Scenes are juxtaposed in such a way as to show the lovers ironically trapped in situations they do not understand. As Proteus celebrates his success with Julia, the audience knows he is about to be sent away from her; as Julia prepares to journey to Proteus, looking forward eagerly to their reunion, the audience knows he has already betrayed her. Pushed hither and thither by awkward parents, dependent on cheeky and unreliable servants, victimized by the workings of the plot, the lovers appear helpless and vulnerable. They have the pains of love, but few opportunities to indulge in its satisfactions. Thus the comic distancing of love, instead of contributing to a doubleness of vision, seems to be in itself the play's main function.

But a comic interplay of perspectives is maintained through the presentation of the lovers themselves. They may not struggle against the indifferent outside world with any great conviction or success; but there are struggles within their own natures that give them tension, life and dramatic interest. Much of this tension is centred on the way they feel and express their love. Since love has been established as such a special, peculiar experience, it is natural that its expression should also be special and peculiar. The play is full of formal set pieces on love.... Valentine and Proteus are revealed in their first dialogue as two bookish young men:

> PROTEUS: Yet writers say, as in the sweetest bud
> The eating canker dwells, so eating love
> Inhabits in the finest wits of all.
> VALENTINE: And writers say, as the most forward bud
> Is eaten by the canker ere it blow ...
>
> [I. i. 42-6]

—and so forth. Throughout the dialogue Proteus seems at least as concerned with matching Valentine's puns as with defending love ([I. i. 19-27], for example). The whole passage is something between a formal debate and a verbal game.... Passages like this, in which love is not so much an experience as an announced subject of debate, show the lovers as having a detachment from their feelings, and consequently a self-control, that contrast interestingly with the more emotional absorption in love they express at other times, especially when they are alone. One of the play's fundamental patterns, in fact, is an alternation between dialogues on love, which are clever, detached and frequently satiric, and soliloquies in which love is expressed in a straightforward, serious way. In Proteus's altercation with Speed over his letter to Julia, for example, the lover is distracted from his concern with the letter by the temptation to play verbal games with the servant. He becomes fully serious about it only at the end of the scene, when he is alone. It is as though the very privateness of love makes it difficult, even for a lover, to be fully serious about it in company.

But love cannot remain private if it is to communicate to the

Act V. Scene iv. Julia disguised as Sebastian, Silvia, Valentine, and Proteus. By W. Holman Hunt.

beloved. Despite what Proteus says of Julia's silence at their parting—'so true love should do: it cannot speak; / For truth hath better deeds than words to grace it' [II. ii. 16-17]—words are vitally important to the lovers of this play. Major declarations are made by letter, and the men especially display their love by displaying their verbal wit: Valentine and Thurio fight for Silvia, not with sword or lance, but with (to quote Silvia herself) 'a fine volley of words' [II. iv. 33]; in applauding the skill of the players, she underlines the artificial, set-piece quality of their dialogue. But the clowns also engage in wit matches, in which puns are prominent: as Speed remarks, 'Well, your old vice still: mistake the word' [III. i. 284]. This points to a central problem. The fact that verbal cleverness comes so easily to lovers and clowns alike shows how far it is from the essence of love; anybody can play with words. Yet even when love is seriously expressed, the expression is likely to be formal, literary, self-consciously eloquent:

> And I as rich in having such a jewel
> As twenty seas, if all their sand were pearl,
> The water nectar, and the rocks pure gold.
> [II. iv. 169-71]

John F. Danby has remarked that in this play the lovers' feelings 'are never lived through, only announced—often in long, beautifully formal passages of verse' [see excerpt above, 1960], and for Howard Nemerov 'so ideal is the nature of their worship, that it fixes itself repeatedly on word or image rather than

on what they represent, on names rather than on things' [see excerpt above, 1963]. Love depends for its expression, in fact, on the sort of verbal cleverness that can actually detach the speaker from his feelings. It depends on words, and words are (like Launce and Speed) unreliable servants.

With this in mind, it seems appropriate that the character most thoroughly dependent on appearances, conventions and verbal surfaces is Proteus. He thinks cleverly, and he thinks in images, describing his change of heart: 'Even as one heat another heat expels / Or as one nail by strength drives out another' [II. iv. 192-93]. From description he goes to justification, invoking the power of love to provide him with some convenient rationalizations. . . . The fact that he can talk cleverly about his betrayal seems to make it acceptable to him; he literally talks himself into it. The air of self-conscious calculation with which he does this begins to affect all his relations with the others. He treats affections as commodities to be weighed and measured:

> Methinks my zeal to Valentine is cold,
> And that I love him not as I was wont.
> O! but I love his lady too too much,
> And that's the reason I love him so little.
> [II. iv. 203-06]

There is a touch here of the cold legalism of Ephesus. And as he calculates gain and loss, the logic of his argument slowly reveals his essential selfishness:

Julia I lose, and Valentine I lose;
If I keep them, I needs must lose myself;
If I lose them, thus find I by their loss:
For Valentine, myself; for Julia, Silvia.
I to myself am dearer than a friend;
For love is still most precious in itself.

[II. vi. 19-24]

The clever rhetorical balancing reveals a coldness at the heart. We are firmly prepared for the ironic distancing of his eloquence in the later scenes. Even in his later role as a spurned lover there is an element of pose, of calculation. He says to Julia, 'Your message done, hie home unto my chamber, / Where you shall find me sad and solitary' [IV. iv. 88-9]. His feelings may be real enough, but he cannot express them without striking attitudes. Proteus seems at first glance the most introspective and self-aware of the lovers; yet he is the one with the smallest mind, and the narrowest sense of the possibilities of love.

Valentine, in conversation, can be as glib and clever as Proteus, and seemingly as cold. There is a cynical detachment in his advice to the Duke, with its calculating assessment of female behaviour and its jingling, artificial style:

If she do frown, 'tis not in hate of you,
But rather to beget more love in you;
If she do chide, 'tis not to have you gone,
For why the fools are mad, if left alone.
Take no repulse, whatever she doth say;
For 'Get you gone' she doth not mean 'Away!'

[III. i. 96-101]

But, as I have argued, this attempt at worldliness (like Proteus's attempt at romantic eloquence) is comically dislocated. And shortly afterwards, when he is banished, he speaks in a different voice, revealing what we may take to be private feeling, wrung from him by grief, rather than social pose:

To die is to be banish'd from myself,
And Silvia is myself; banish'd from her
Is self from self, a deadly banishment. . . .
She is my essence, and I leave to be
If I be not by her fair influence
Foster'd, illumin'd, cherish'd, kept alive.

[III. i. 171-73, 182-84]

The rhetorical balance is still there; it is the only language he has; but the contrast in tone and content is striking. Like Antipholus of Syracuse—and unlike Proteus—he is willing to lose himself in love: so much so that when Proteus calls him, he refuses the name 'Valentine' and calls himself 'nothing' [III. i. 193-98]. Launce makes a joke of it, offering to strike at 'nothing' [III. i. 199-201]; and the rhetorical balancing of Valentine's speech still keeps us somewhat detached from it; but we may feel that for once an ideal has been expressed that can fight against the distancing devices, and restore some of the balance between serious assertion and mockery. Yet Valentine's innocence can also cause laughter, as when he fails to understand Silvia's transparent device for declaring her love, or when he seems astonished that Speed has noticed he is in love [II. i. 42-4]. He seems curiously inept at defending or protecting himself, and he himself describes Proteus as more experienced and sophisticated [II. iv. 62-74]. Like Proteus, he is comically limited and subject to irony, though his helpless innocence and his capacity for self-surrender rouse a more indulgent kind of laughter.

Silvia's function in the play is comparatively simple: to receive adoration, accepting or rejecting it as the case may be. She shows a modicum of calculation in her first appearance, and a certain degree of initiative towards the end. She can display both wit and feeling, but in the last analysis her role is a passive one, dependent on the actions of the men, as her curious silence in the final stages of the denouement may indicate. But Julia is another matter. She has generally been regarded as the most fully realized character in the play, and one reason for this may be that she presents the most complex interplay of form and feeling, of engagement and detachment. In her first scene she veers back and forth between treating love as a game of flirtation (in which her role is to pretend indifference) and being angry with herself for doing so. In conversation with Lucetta, she rejects Proteus's letter, and then in soliloquy admits ruefully that she is simply playing a game:

What fool is she, that knows I am a maid
And would not force the letter to my view!
Since maids, in modesty, say 'No' to that
Which they would have the profferer construe 'Ay.'
Fie, fie, how wayward is this foolish love,
That like a testy babe will scratch the nurse,
And presently, all humbled, kiss the rod!

[I. ii. 53-9]

In displaying her feelings, she also displays a refreshing capacity for wry, satiric self-criticism. And yet the pretence of which she accuses herself is not so easily thrown away, for despite her intention of playing straight, as soon as Lucetta returns Julia puts the mask back on:

My penance is to call Lucetta back
And ask remission for my folly past.
What ho! Lucetta!

[Re-enter Lucetta.
LUCETTA: What would your ladyship?
JULIA: Is't near dinner time?

[I. ii. 64-7]

—and once more she pretends indifference to the letter, to the point of tearing it up. But even this apparently final gesture is not so final as it looks, for once Lucetta is offstage again, Julia quickly reassembles the fragments. In doing so, she reveals how much even the frank expression of love depends on forms. She now plays another and more earnest game, in which the words on a sheet of paper acquire a special reality in the eyes of love: . . .

And here is writ 'love-wounded Proteus.'
Poor wounded name! my bosom, as a bed,
Shall lodge thee till thy wound be throughly heal'd;
And thus I search it with a sovereign kiss.

[I. ii. 110-13]

—until once again the appearance of Lucetta (in a passage quoted earlier) jolts Julia from her fantasy, and restores the pose of indifference. Throughout this sequence Lucetta—like Speed and Launce—provides a sardonic background commentary, knowing perfectly well that Julia's indifference is pretence; but the effect is different from, say, the dialogues of Valentine and Speed, in which the master's innocence and the servant's shrewdness are placed in simple opposition. Here the contrast is between the rapid, volatile shifting of Julia's mind and the steady honesty of Lucetta's—and Julia, once Lucetta is offstage, can express Lucetta's point of view. In the interplay between social pose and private feeling, Julia can be both a player in the game and a looker-on, commenting on her own play. And even in her frankest expressions of feeling there is still a certain playful irony.

At this point, Julia is to a great extent immune from the irony that affects Valentine and Proteus, since she is capable of being ironic about herself in a way that they are not. But after Proteus's betrayal, she is placed by the plot in an ironic state of ignorance, and this is reflected in her behaviour in the scene where she decides to journey to Proteus, disguised as a boy. She has lost some of her balance, expressing her devotion to Proteus—and her misplaced faith in his constancy—with passionate extravagance. . . . But once Julia has arrived in Milan and realized the truth about Proteus, not only is her balance restored but (as happens to other disguised characters in the comedies) her capacities are extended. Her disguise is a pretence, but unlike the falsehood of Proteus it is a pretence that reveals truth: her disguised role as a servant to Proteus reflects her genuine dependence on his favour. The same idea is reflected in a more complex way in the much discussed account of how she, dressed in Julia's gown, depicted the forsaken Ariadne and moved Julia to tears with the truth of her performance [IV. iv. 158-72]. . . . Like Valentine she is now one of the victims of love; but unlike Valentine she can look after herself, and the disguise suggests that too. It gives her the masculine freedom of action that Silvia lacks (and that results in her dependence on the unreliable Sir Eglamour). In serving as the messenger of Proteus's love, she decides—like Proteus—to keep her own interests first. But her feelings are more complex, less calculated, and she comes to her declaration of practical self-interest with some of the shifting and hesitation that marked her earlier behaviour:

> How many women would do such a message?
> Alas, poor Proteus, thou hast entertained
> A fox to be the shepherd of thy lambs.
> Alas, poor fool, why do I pity him
> That with his very heart despiseth me?
> Because he loves her, he despiseth me;
> Because I love him, I must pity him . . .
> I am my master's true confirmed love,
> But cannot be true servant to my master
> Unless I prove false traitor to myself.
> Yet will I woo for him, but yet so coldly
> As, heaven it knows, I would not have him speed.
>
> [IV. iv. 90-6, 103-07]

The different styles and points of view present throughout the play begin to come together in the figure of Julia, a woman in male attire, a lover disguised as a servant. We now hear from her the sort of sardonic, joking asides that we heard from Speed, Launce and Lucetta earlier in the play—as in V. ii, when she heckles Thurio from the sidelines, exposing his own worthlessness and Proteus's hypocritical flattery of him. She is even capable of wry jokes about her own situation, as when Proteus claims his former love is dead: ''Twere false, if I should speak it; / For I am sure she is not buried' [IV. ii. 106-07]. In the first shock of seeing Proteus courting Silvia, she expresses her grief in a series of rueful puns on musical terms: the reticence and detachment enforced by her conversation with the host forbid a passionate soliloquy, and there is something touching in the way the play's characteristic verbal juggling is adapted to an expression of feeling. She appreciates Silvia's rejection of Proteus's courtship, and her sympathy for his first love; even across the barrier imposed by the disguise, a bond of sympathy is established between the two women. Yet when she is given Silvia's picture to take to Proteus, this

sympathy is combined with an awareness of her own injuries, a certain natural resentment and, at the end, a brief, refreshing touch of vulgarity. . . . Julia's position in these later scenes could have called forth nothing more than a self-indulgent display of grief; but she is given a wider range of feeling, and consequently of style—the widest range, in fact, displayed by any character in the play—including tart exasperation and sardonic detachment. (pp. 21-37)

By this time she has taken the dramatic focus away from the two gentlemen, who dominated the early scenes, but who in the process were revealed as inadequate spokesmen for love—Proteus being too calculating, Valentine too helpless, and both of them too vulnerable to mockery. The growing dominance of Julia, capable of both suffering and action, prepares us for the fulfilment of love in the final scenes. We are also prepared for it in other ways. Little has been said in the play of the positive value of love but, towards the end, the persistent playing on the idea of 'shadows' suggests that without fulfilment in love, the lovers are incomplete beings, worshipping only the images of one another. As Proteus says, begging Silvia's picture:

> For since the substance of your perfect
>   self
> Is else devoted, I am but a shadow;
> And to your shadow will I make true
>   love.
> JULIA *(aside)*:   If 'twere a substance, you would, sure,
>   deceive it,
> And make it but a shadow, as I am.
>
> [IV. ii. 123-27]

There are several such passages, and they carry the implication that only fulfilment in love can restore the lovers to wholeness of being. It is characteristic of the play, however, that the positive side of the idea is implied, not directly stated, and we are more aware of the hunger than the satisfaction. Equally characteristic, and more striking, is the way the triumph of love is prepared by the comic dislocation of another value. I refer, of course, to the most hotly debated moment of the play. The speaker is Valentine:

> Who by repentance is not satisfied
> Is nor of heaven nor of earth, for these are
>   pleas'd;
> By penitence th' Eternal's wrath's appeas'd;
> And, that my love may appear plain and free,
> All that was mine in Silvia I give thee.
> JULIA: O me unhappy!
>
> [V. iv. 79-84]

The ideals of friendship and forgiveness, bound together in this passage, are initially quite serious, but Valentine's expression of them quickly becomes overblown, as he identifies himself with the Almighty, grandly dispensing forgiveness and handing over Silvia as though she had no say in the matter. More important, he treats what is happening as a private affair between the two men, and Julia's swoon (real or pretended) is a sharp, comic theatrical reminder that there are other interests at stake. The value of friendship is subjected to the dislocating technique that was used on love in the earlier scenes—the sudden intrusion of a new perspective.

But this still does not provide a positive assertion of the rightness of love; rather, we are made to feel that other ideals are just as vulnerable to mockery (this may apply not only to friendship but to the virginal chivalry of Sir Eglamour, whose response to a real crisis is to run away). We have to be content with the somewhat narrower satisfaction of seeing the lovers get what they want. Even the positive side of Julia's nature is directed more towards winning Proteus than understanding why the effort is worthwhile. And in the final scene, love's dependence on surfaces, on forms and appearances, is as great as ever: 'What is in Silvia's face but I may spy / More fresh in Julia's with a constant eye?' [V. iv. 114-15]. This dependence, whatever we think of it, has finally to be accepted; in later plays the issue will get a fuller airing. In watching the two couples join hands, there is the technical satisfaction of seeing a dance pattern completed. In one's theatrical experience of the play, this satisfaction runs very deep, and its importance should not be underestimated. But one cannot help noticing that the final image of harmony includes the glib forgiveness of those comic-opera outlaws, banished for such 'petty crimes' as murder [IV. i. 50], but forgivable, it appears, because they have attempted to raise the tone of their profession [IV. i. 53-74; V. iv. 152-57]. (H. B. Charlton's witty and accurate analysis of the outlaws, comparing them with the Pirates of Penzance, falls short only in denying that Shakespeare, like Gilbert, means to be funny [see excerpt above, 1930].) Even the final harmony of the comic ending is shown to have its laughable side, and is thus placed at a slight distance, recognized as a matter of literary artifice.

This is quite different from the ending of *The Comedy of Errors*, where the positive value of the family reunion is explored at length, and allowed to affect us quite seriously. The ending of *The Two Gentlemen* is, by comparison, rushed and somewhat apologetic, and the satisfactions it offers are more fragile. When we come to the ending of the other play we realize that behind its comic dislocation of various experiences is a solid centre, one experience that is not mocked. *The Two Gentlemen of Verona* is a play without such a centre: the experience of love is distanced and exposed by techniques similar to those of the other play, but this time there is nothing to put in its place. Love, for all its frailties and limitations, is all that the central characters have. And that limited (though real) defence is the only defence it can put up. The comic strategy of the play is formidable, but one feels the play would give more satisfaction if this strategy were exercised against a more resilient object. That, however, is to ask for a different play. *The Two Gentlemen of Verona* is not so easy to like as the later comedies, but it has a quality of its own—cool, reticent and somewhat rueful, counselling us, if it counsels anything, not to expect too much. On the occasions—still comparatively rare—when the play is defended, it is usually defended as a testing ground for ideas that Shakespeare will develop more fully in later work. Such a defence is valid as far as it goes, but takes too little account of the play's own unique qualities—though ironically, in counselling the acceptance of small satisfactions, it shares in the play's essential spirit. (pp. 37-40)

Alexander Leggatt, "'The Two Gentlemen of Verona',' in his Shakespeare's Comedy of Love, *Methuen, 1974, pp. 21-40.*

PETER LINDENBAUM (essay date 1975)

[*Lindenbaum considers the themes of education and perfection more central to* The Two Gentlemen of Verona *than those of friendship and love. He asserts that Proteus and Valentine are originally sent to Milan to become perfect Italian gentlemen, but that gradually their ideal of perfection changes, until they recognize the inadequacies of courtly behavior and come to accept* their own fallen natures as needing divine guidance. Lindenbaum demonstrates how Proteus and Valentine are first corrupted to different degrees by Italian society, contending that once they reach the forest, however, they learn to "define themselves accurately by their own actions rather than words." According to Lindenbaum, both Valentine's and Julia's examples prompt Proteus's recognition of his own imperfect nature, underscoring the idea that ideal human conduct must be "in harmony with and modeled after divine precept."]

Few confess to have been charmed by *The Two Gentlemen of Verona*, and praise of the play is usually confined to discussion of its clowns or of those elements in it Shakespeare was to use more effectively in his later romantic comedies—a girl disguised as a page attempting to test or win her beloved's affection, or the very focus, probably for the first time in Shakespeare's career, on romantic love as a subject for comedy. The play is by no means one of Shakespeare's best, but the generally low estimation of it is in large part a function of the way it is most often interpreted, and that is as a clash between the ideals of love and friendship in which friendship gains the upper hand in a dramatically disastrous final scene. Yet at only one point in the play do the claims of ideal love and ideal friendship come into possible conflict with one another—the almost universally deplored moment at which Valentine, apparently adhering to the code of ideal friendship, gives up to the repentant Proteus all claim to Silvia. And even in this instance, Shakespeare is making a point not about friendship's precedence over love or man's inability to satisfy the demands of both love and friendship, but rather about the importance of penitence for past sins in any attempt to lead a good life. Elsewhere in the play, the two codes are not even in apparent conflict. Proteus, when being a traitor to his friend Valentine, is simultaneously violating his promises to Julia and thus the dictates of romantic love. And it is Silvia, the object of his misplaced affections through much of the play, who repeatedly points out to Proteus that he is violating both codes at once:

> *Sil.*   Read over Julia's heart, thy first best love,
>   For whose dear sake thou didst then rend thy faith
>   Into a thousand oaths; and all those oaths
>   Descended into perjury, to love me.
>   Thou hast no faith left now, unless thou'dst two,
>   And that's far worse than none: better have none
>   Than plural faith, which is too much by one.
>   Thou counterfeit to thy true friend!
> *Pro.*   In love,
>   Who respects friend?
> *Sil.*   All men but Proteus.
>   [V. iv. 46-54]

It is notable that both here and in Act IV, in her other extended denunciation of Proteus [IV. ii. 93-111], Silvia does not immediately present what would have been her most obvious, direct, and personal reason for rejecting Proteus' suit, that her heart is already given to Valentine; instead, she dwells primarily on Proteus' unfaithfulness to Julia and to his friend, Valentine.... Silvia is putting Proteus through the same education that Valentine is later, when he serves as an object lesson for Proteus and shows him what it is like to act in an ideal manner. The fact that Silvia clearly recognizes Proteus' manifest faults and is trying to bring Proteus himself to a fuller and more meaningful recognition of them provides an answer to another of the frequent objections to the final scene: that Silvia's silence throughout the period in which she is handed back and forth between Valentine and Proteus is unrealistic, unreasonable, and particularly unfeminine. Silvia is silent when Valentine gives up his claim to her because she fully understands what he is doing. She has been insisting throughout on Proteus' departure from the ideals of love and friendship and thus recognizes that Valentine's gesture is part of the education of Proteus in which she too has been taking an active part. It is, in fact, this education, and not any intent to exalt the ideals of friendship or romantic love, which provides the central organizing principle of *The Two Gentlemen of Verona*.

There is some question, though, as to what form that education takes, what precisely it is that Proteus is to learn, for there are several different educational goals postulated in the play. The play begins with Valentine taking his leave of Proteus and Verona and setting out for the emperor's court in Milan, an enterprise Valentine describes simply as seeing "the wonders of the world abroad" [I. i. 6]; two scenes later, when Proteus' guardians decide that Proteus should join his friend at the royal court, they provide a more detailed and explicit statement of the advantages they expect a young gentleman to gain from his travels:

> 'Twere good, I think, your lordship sent him thither:
> There shall he practise tilts and tournaments,
> Hear sweet discourse, converse with noblemen,
> And be in eye of every exercise
> Worthy his youth and nobleness of birth.
>
> [I. iii. 29-33]
> (pp. 229-31)

The course of action Valentine devotes himself to at the beginning of the play and the one which Antonio wants his son Proteus also to follow is designed, Antonio tells us, to make a young gentleman "perfect":

> I have consider'd well his loss of time,
> And how he cannot be a perfect man,
> Not being tried and tutor'd in the world:
> Experience is by industry achiev'd,
> And perfected by the swift course of time.
>
> [I. iii. 19-23]

At this point in the play the "perfect man" envisioned by Proteus' guardians, and presumably by those of Valentine as well, is merely a gentleman adept in the social arts, or a courtier, that relatively pale Elizabethan reflection of the early Humanists' ideal moral and political advisor to a prince. The words "perfect" and "perfection" appear at several important junctures in the play; by the time that the adjective "perfect" is used in the final scene, it will have a far more serious and significant meaning than is denoted by this initial reference to a "perfect man" as one who is experienced in the ways of the world and thoroughly at ease at court. A full education for Proteus will take him not simply to the court but to the country as well, where he will learn what being perfect actually would involve and thus how he is—and, because he is human, cannot fail to be—very imperfect. And the change in the definition of a "perfect man" will mean that it is not only Proteus who is to be educated in the course of the play, but also Valentine, and through him the play's society as a whole.

The court does not achieve even the relatively superficial educational goals that Antonio intends. The Milan of this play is not the vicious Italian court of the type Marston and Webster were later to portray, but the effect of court life on Proteus is to make him "Italianate" in the worst sense of that word's meaning for an Elizabethan. While in Verona Proteus was

guilty only of idling away his time, neglecting his studies, and lying to his father about the contents of a letter. Proteus himself lamented that his love for Julia had already "metamorphos'd" him [I. i. 66]; and in order to accept his conversion at the end of the play we may be obligated to believe him, but it is at the Milanese court that we actually see Proteus *transformed*— from a love-smitten, idle, and perhaps shapeless youth into an out-and-out villain. When he sees Silvia, he immediately and consciously puts his promises to Julia out of his mind and just as easily casts aside his feelings for Valentine [II. iv. 192-214]. He gives himself over completely to self-interest, and recognizing that "I cannot now prove constant to myself, / Without some treachery us'd to Valentine" [II. vi. 31-2], he proceeds to betray his friend by telling the Duke of Valentine's plan to elope with Silvia. When first stricken with love in Verona, Proteus complained that his love made his wit weak with musing [I. i. 69]; here in Milan and with his second bout with love, his wit appears to make a recovery of sorts, as is seen when he first suggests to the Duke that only a friend of Valentine could succeed in changing the "form" of Silvia's love, initially refuses to carry out the slander he himself advises, and then graciously allows himself to be convinced to take on the task:

> *Duke.* Then you must undertake to slander him.
> *Pro.* And that, my lord, I shall be loath to do:
> 　　'Tis an ill office for a gentleman,
> 　　Especially against his very friend.
> *Duke.* Where your good word cannot advantage him,
> 　　Your slander never can endamage him;
> 　　Therefore the office is indifferent,
> 　　Being entreated to it by your friend.
> *Pro.* You have prevail'd, my lord.
>
> [III. ii. 38-46]

The Duke's logic is patently inadequate: that Proteus' slander can never harm Valentine because good words cannot help him is simply untrue, and the Duke's "therefore" by no means makes his conclusion as incontrovertible as the use of a word of such great rhetorical weight implies. "You have prevail'd" ought probably, then, to arouse our laughter, and with conspirators such as these we are, no doubt, not meant to worry overmuch about the outcome of their plot. But even with the detachment that such humor provides, we can still see that Proteus is not making much progress towards any kind of perfection.

It is Speed's belief that Valentine too, once he has fallen in love, has been "metamorphosed with a mistress" [II. i. 30-1]. Valentine's own phrase describing his new state, that his life is "alter'd" now [II. iv. 128], is probably more apt since it does not suggest as complete and drastic a change as a metamorphosis. For, though love does have an initial detrimental effect on Valentine, as it did on Proteus, it never prompts Valentine to acts equivalent to Proteus' villainy. While his vision and powers of perception are certainly hindered by his love, Valentine never loses his initial nobility of character. He is incapable of seeing through Silvia's ruse of courting him through letters he himself writes for her, a trick so obvious that Speed can recognize it as a "jest unseen, inscrutable, invisible, / As a nose on a man's face" [II. i. 135-36]. But the closest Valentine comes to being guilty of a moral fault as a result of his new-found love, is simply his egocentric insensitivity while singing the praises of Silvia to Proteus. He insists that Proteus flatter him by acknowledging his beloved Silvia as divine, sovereign to all creatures on earth. When Proteus objects that he too has a love and thus has good reason to prefer his own mistress as the most sovereign of beings, Valentine ignores completely what might be his friend's feelings, and goes on to suggest that Proteus' beloved shall be dignified with the honor of bearing Silvia's train,

> lest the base earth
> Should from her vesture chance to steal a kiss,
> And of so great a favour growing proud,
> Disdain to root the summer-swelling flower,
> And make rough winter everlastingly.
>
> [II. iv. 159-63]

In resorting to such hyperbolic phrases, Valentine is of course slipping into the role of the conventional courtly lover—but without realizing that he is taking part in a convention. As far as he is concerned, he is the first man ever to utter the trite and exaggerated formulas he comes up with when talking to and about Silvia. His exaggeration and conventionality, however, do not escape the observation of others who are aware of how far Valentine's expression exceeds and departs from an objective description of what he and they see. Speed prefaces the first conversation we witness between Valentine and Silvia with the deprecatory aside that we are about to observe a puppet show [II. i. 94-5]. Silvia herself joins the servant in mocking, though more gently, Valentine's exuberant but naive use of extremely conventional expression. When Valentine greets her with a flamboyant ''Madam and mistress, a thousand good-morrows,'' she counters with the slightly more outlandish ''Sir Valentine, and servant, to you two thousand'' [II. i. 96-7, 100-01]. And when a moment later he breaks off his thought in mid-sentence with a hesitant ''and yet,'' she implies that she has heard such talk before and that he need not therefore bother to finish his sentence:

> A pretty period. Well, I guess the sequel;
> And yet I will not name it; and yet I care not.
> And yet take this again; and yet I thank you,
> Meaning henceforth to trouble you no more.
>
> [II. i. 116-19]

With her four ''and yet's'' in two lines, she has again carried his banal lover's rhetoric to absurdity.

Valentine's failure in perception, his inability to see Silvia's ruse of wooing him by his own letters, arises directly from the stance he assumes as a courtly lover. He is so humble before the woman he idolizes that he could not at first even dare to imagine that she might care for him. But his blindness and his penchant for exaggerated expression, in fact his whole love affair, are only part of a larger pattern in Valentine's conduct, of what we can call his overall reaction to his whole court experience. When Antonio and Panthino were discussing the reasons for sending Proteus to court, Panthino suggested that at court a young gentleman could ''Hear sweet discourse'' and ''be in eye of every exercise / Worthy his youth and nobleness of birth'' [I. iii. 31-3]. That Valentine means his Petrarchan hyperboles seriously while others see them as thoroughly conventional and even expected of a lover, suggests that he has been watching others but has not quite made what he has seen fully his own. Certainly he has not achieved that ironic distance or vision which would enable him as a sophisticated courtier not to lose sight of the real nature of what he sees around him while he is describing it in the expected, artificial courtly formulas. At the one point he does perhaps manage to assume and master a tone appropriate to the particular court in which he finds himself—when wittily advising the Duke on how to

woo a young lady [III. i. 93-105]—this achievement works against him. While indulging in courtly wit, Valentine in fact talks himself straight into the Duke's trap and is discovered hiding a rope-ladder under his cloak.

A more striking example of the confusion or difficulty Valentine experiences in living at court is to be found in his exaggerated and highly rhetorical praise of Proteus to the Duke when he learns that his friend is also coming to Milan. He speaks of Proteus as if he already were the perfect gentleman Antonio hoped he would become in the future:

> I knew him as myself; for from our infancy
> We have convers'd, and spent our hours together,
> And though myself have been an idle truant,
> Omitting the sweet benefit of time
> To clothe mine age with angel-like perfection,
> Yet hath Sir Proteus (for that's his name)
> Made use and fair advantage of his days:
> His years but young, but his experience old;
> His head unmellow'd, but his judgment ripe;
> And in a word (for far behind his worth
> Comes all the praises that I now bestow)
> He is complete in feature and in mind,
> With all good grace to grace a gentleman.
>
> [II. iv. 62-74]

In the play's opening scene Valentine was worried lest Proteus, ''living dully sluggardis'd at home,'' wear out his youth with ''shapeless idleness'' [I. i. 7-8]. Here, in an urbane and self-deprecatory manner—that very tone is itself a type of formal convention for a courtier—Valentine takes upon himself the charge of idleness so as to build up by contrast the picture of Proteus. Valentine's enthusiasm and extravagance at this point arise not simply from the warmth of his feelings for Proteus, but also from a self-conscious desire to impress his audience, a desire betrayed in the deliberate balance and verbal antithesis in lines like: ''His years but young, but his experience old; / His head unmellow'd, but his judgment ripe.'' In the speech in which Valentine, as a courtier, advises the Duke on how to overcome a woman's coyness, he is to state ''That man that hath a tongue, I say is no man, / If with his tongue he cannot win a woman'' [III. i. 104-05]; being a courtier is plainly connected, in Valentine's mind, with rhetorical skill. The desire to impress in his praise of Proteus, and particularly to impress by the manipulation of words, rather than to report the truth in a direct, unadorned, and unimpassioned manner, can also be viewed, then, as part of Valentine's response to living at court. But once again, his stance as a courtier is complicated by the fact that he is apparently convinced by his own rhetoric; again he takes the conventional formula very seriously and literally. He fully believes what he says about Proteus here; for when later in the forest he discovers the villainy Proteus is capable of, he is as profoundly shocked as Proteus is in being discovered. The overly elaborate and largely unjustified praise Valentine heaps on Proteus here points to the way in which Valentine also needs to be educated. He is perhaps capable of exemplary conduct and he has done much of what Proteus' guardians might ask of a young gentleman, but he has become so addicted to courtly formulas and flattery that he no longer can see the real man beneath the courtly dress of words with which he has clothed him.

It is to bring Valentine and Proteus to a proper recognition of unaccommodated man, and specifically of Proteus as unaccommodated man, that Shakespeare moves both of his young gentlemen from the court to the country. At court, Valentine has become confused, and Proteus' experience there has only prompted the bad side of his character to show itself. The country is customarily in pastoral literature the place where courtier or king can talk with a shepherd on equal terms, where courtly definitions and formulas do not apply and hence cannot limit or confuse men. And in this play, the green world is the place where various characters define themselves accurately by their own actions rather than words so that they can be recognized by themselves and by others for what they truly are. Valentine in the country displays his true nobility, instead of a mere courtly wit, to the point that the Duke after having earlier banished him and called him a peasant [V. ii. 35] now recognizes him as a fitting match for his daughter. Thurio reveals himself as totally selfish and unfeeling, caring not for Silvia but only for his own honor and reputation. Julia, having posed as a male page, reveals her true sex and the extent of her love for Proteus. And Proteus, having posed as a friend and lover, plumbs the full depth of his villainy, is exposed, and is finally brought to a true and meaningful understanding of his own character.

The most important of these unmaskings or revaluations of character is, of course, that of Proteus: it is his exposure and reform which provides the climactic turning point of the play and it is towards this turn that the other three main characters—Valentine, Silvia, and Julia—direct their efforts for much of the play. Proteus has since his arrival in Milan been conscious of his own treachery and has at least acknowledged the existence of codes of behavior which he is violating. But in dedicating himself solely to self-interest and remaining constant only to himself, he denies the relevance of those codes to his own actions. It will take the combined work of Valentine and Julia, both displaying ideal conduct in their respective realms of friendship and love, to bring Proteus to recognize the full significance of his own bad actions. Only then can Proteus be said to be educated in the largest sense that the play suggests.

In the forest, Proteus assumes his final pose, that of protector of distressed young maidens. He enters the play's final scene talking to Silvia of the attack from which he claims just to have saved her:

> Madam, this service I have done for you
> (Though you respect not aught your servant doth)
> To hazard life, and rescue you from him
> That would have forc'd your honour and your love.
>
> [V. iv. 19-22]

We have seen no attempt to force Silvia's honor and love, and it is reasonable to assume that Proteus, in order to help his own suit, is overstating the danger Silvia was in. When the outlaws captured Silvia, they assured her that they intended no harm, and one of them was in the process of taking her to their captain who "bears an honourable mind, / And will not use a woman lawlessly" [V. iii. 13-14], when Proteus evidently arrived and accomplished what he calls his rescue. While Valentine has just admitted in his soliloquy that he has much to do to keep the outlaws from "uncivil outrages" [V. iv. 16-17], these outlaws have from their first entrance been presented as comic figures we, Silvia, or anyone, should have little reason to fear. Proteus' pose as a protector, in any case, is very short-lived, as he proceeds almost immediately to launch his own attack on Silvia's honor and her love—only to have Silvia be rescued once again, this time in earnest.

Or indeed, in too much earnestness; Valentine, perhaps stunned by Proteus' villainy, comes up with two rather dreadful lines

in saving Silvia: "Ruffian! Let go that rude uncivil touch, / Thou friend of an ill fashion" [V. iv. 60-1]. We have some cause to consider the possibility that such lines, like those of Bonario when he rescues Celia in [Ben Jonson's] *Volpone,* were intended by Shakespeare as burlesque. Valentine has had trouble finding precisely the right expression and tone through much of the play, and hence mockery of him and of the ideals he adheres to has never been far off. His bombastic outburst here is probably best viewed as another of his attempts to encompass too much with words. But despite the extravagance of his language, we must be prepared to accept Valentine's words and actions, at least in part, on the heroic level he himself perceives them. For if we consider these lines and the subsequent denunciation of Proteus as a "common friend" and "treacherous man" [V. iv. 62-3] as designed by Shakespeare solely to make Valentine look silly in his adherence to a ridiculous convention or ideal, we would be unable to account for the obvious sincerity and seriousness of the remorse Proteus exhibits when the particularly imperfect nature of his conduct has been discovered by his friend:

> My shame and guilt confounds me.
> Forgive me, Valentine: if hearty sorrow
> Be a sufficient ransom for offence,
> I tender 't here; I do as truly suffer,
> As e'er I did commit.
>
> [V. iv. 73-7]

As far as Valentine is concerned, hearty sorrow *is* sufficient ransom for Proteus' offenses, and he responds with lines that have been the subject of even greater critical dispute:

> Then I am paid;
> And once again I do receive thee honest.
> Who by repentance is not satisfied,
> Is nor of heaven, nor earth; for these are pleas'd:
> By penitence th' Eternal's wrath's appeas'd.
> And that my love may appear plain and free,
> All that was mine in Silvia I give thee.
>
> [V. iv. 77-83]

The speech may not be dramatically successful. We may not have seen Proteus repentant long enough for us to be fully prepared to accept such a complete pardon and offer from Valentine. But it can be reasonably argued that Shakespeare is intentionally trying to overwhelm us as well as Proteus, so as deliberately to point out the ideal and extraordinary nature of Valentine's action. By the patent artificiality of rhymed verse, then, Shakespeare momentarily dispenses with any claim to be presenting everyday experience; he sets the last four lines of this speech and the action they embody off from the rest of the play, so as to suggest an order of experience different from that which has been presented thus far. And it is thus no accident that the speech should look to more than human standards of conduct. Valentine and Proteus have referred to heaven earlier, but these references were wholly within the confines of the courtly love convention: Proteus had appealed to heaven to witness the beauty of Silvia [II. vi. 25], and Valentine had in Petrarchan manner referred to his mistress as a heavenly saint and a divine being [II. iv. 145, 147]. Here the reference is specifically religious. Valentine in forgiving Proteus is consciously modeling his action after what he takes to be God's own practice, and in doing so suggests a frame of reference for judging human acts which is totally opposed to Proteus' earlier refusal to look any higher than mere self-interest.

We are to see Proteus' acknowledgment of this new standard for judging his acts, but not immediately. For right after Valentine's display of ideal conduct, Julia puts in her claim for Proteus with what is in effect a well-timed swoon. Julia also has had to be educated in the course of the play in order to arrive at a just view of Proteus as a man. When she started on her journey from Verona to Milan, she, like Valentine, was convinced that the young gentleman she knew and loved was already perfect:

> A true-devoted pilgrim is not weary
> To measure kingdoms with his feeble steps,
> Much less shall she that hath Love's wings to fly,
> And when the flight is made to one so dear,
> Of such divine perfection as Sir Proteus.
>
> [II. vii. 9-13]

Like the Petrarchan lover, Valentine, she also uses religious imagery in her expressions of love. The "divine perfection" she cites certainly does not refer to the state of Proteus' soul judged theologically, but simply to Proteus' general attractiveness as a suitor. Yet, while Julia starts out merely on a lover's pilgrimage in search of her beloved, her trip turns out to be a type of religious pilgrimage after all as she too becomes intimately involved in the spiritual regeneration of Proteus. Despite her new awareness in Milan that Proteus is not a loyal and trustworthy lover, she determines to remain in the struggle for his love [IV. iv. 180-205], and by her swoon, be it intentional or not, she is preventing any possibility of Proteus accepting Valentine's offer of Silvia. The revelation of her continued love provides Proteus with a living example of how he should have acted and prompts the completion of the conversion that Valentine's forgiveness and act of friendship began.

It is immediately after Julia reveals the extent of her suffering and sacrifice for Proteus that he finally acknowledges what it means to be perfect and how far his own actions have departed from standards of ideal conduct. In speaking of perfection here, though, he refers not simply to faithfulness as a lover but beyond that to the more general and exalted standard suggested by Valentine a moment earlier, the standard which views ideal human conduct as in harmony with and modeled after divine precept and example:

> O heaven, were man
> But constant, he were perfect. That one error
> Fills him with faults; makes him run through all th' sins;
> Inconstancy falls off, ere it begins.
> What is in Silvia's face but I may spy
> More fresh in Julia's, with a constant eye?
>
> [V. iv. 110-15]

In the last couplet here, Proteus refers specifically to his violation of the code of romantic love and his foolishness in neglecting Julia, but clearly he sees this one error as a sign or token of man's sins in general: his inconstancy involves him in all human sins, and the final recognition that he is not perfect stands as an acknowledgment of his very flawed, his fallen, nature. The phrase "were man / But constant, he were perfect" is the final correction of the earlier statements about Proteus' supposed perfection by Valentine and Julia. But the line stands for more than that. For Proteus speaks not in personal terms simply of his own offenses, but of a generalized "man." This use of the generalized noun along with the fact that this speech also falls into couplets—suggestive this time of aphoristic *sententiae* or general truths which hold for all men—points to the fact that Shakespeare wished us to view Proteus at this stage, not as a particular case, but as a representative of all mankind. A proper and realistic view of Proteus, or of any man, would

have to take into account the ways in which he is not perfect; and anyone who seeks to improve the quality of man's life would have to grant as his first premise that man is human and fallen.

There is, then, in the course of *The Two Gentlemen of Verona* a radical change in the definition of a "perfect man" from a mere courtier to, in effect, an unfallen being, and in this process of redefinition, Proteus, Julia, Valentine, and by extension Proteus' guardians back in Verona, have all been educated to see man, and particularly Proteus, for what he is as imperfect and fallen. Each change of locality in the action—from Verona to the Milanese court, and from the court to the forest—marks a crucial step in this education, bringing the play's characters and ourselves closer to a full understanding of the true nobility that man is at times capable of and of human limitation. We might note in passing that the play's two "clownish servants," as the Folio calls them, also function indirectly in the education I have outlined: Speed, with his mocking of Valentine's love-induced blindness (II. i), and Launce, with his parody of a lovers' parting (II. iii) and his burlesque of a Renaissance lover's blazon poem in his "love letter" (III. i), both remind us that despite Valentine's high aspirations and Proteus' pretension to nobility these young gentlemen are vulnerable to mockery and, hence, are very human. The detachment from the main action that the servants help us to achieve serves to prepare us for the final and much more serious assertion of Proteus and all men as quite imperfect beings. All of this argues, it seems to me, for a very sure hand on Shakespeare's part in the overall construction of his play. In this obviously early and much criticized work, Shakespeare knew very well how to organize his material around a central structure or progress—an education—which would lead to and constitute a coherent and clear statement about the world he was portraying and the men in it.

That is not to say, however, that there still are not serious flaws in the play, and flaws we might call structural. There is, for instance, a remarkable disharmony between the realistic vision of man that the play as a whole moves towards and the unrealistic setting in which this vision is finally achieved. The forest of the last two acts is typified by the outlaws living in it, and these pasteboard figures who equate an outright murder with an attempt to elope with a Duke's daughter, calling both "petty crimes" [IV. i. 45-50], are handled with a humor by Shakespeare which, while delightful enough in itself, detracts from the serious intent of the rest of the play. The whole sequence of events from the moment that the exiled Valentine in effect applies for membership in the outlaw band by inventing an offense far more serious than the intended elopement of which he was guilty [IV. i. 26-9] to his final request that the Duke pardon those companions "full of good, / And fit for great employment" [V. iv. 156-57], is simply wish-fulfilling fantasy. The conception of human perfection the outlaws hold to is no better, if not worse, than that of Antonio or of Valentine when he was at court; they consider Valentine a "man of such perfection" [IV. i. 55] that they elect him their leader, having based their judgment simply upon his lie that he has killed a man, his "goodly shape," and his own claim that he is a "linguist" (here too, the mere mastery of language alone is viewed as a distinguished achievement in itself). There is plainly little reason why Proteus' final recognition of himself and all men as imperfect and fallen must take place in this particular forest. While using the Renaissance pastoral romance's retreat to the green world in order to resolve difficulties arising at court, Shakespeare fails to take full advantage of a natural setting which might better have served as a reflection of the fallen men going into it and thereby have enhanced the education which was the main focus of the play.

But placed against the very sure overall structure of an education in this play, such a failure—representing primarily a missed opportunity for Shakespeare, and one he would not miss in a later pastoral play such as *As You Like It*—appears relatively minor. This central structure of an education in one's own nature was, it hardly needs be said, one Shakespeare was to rely upon again and again in his later comedies. In *Much Ado About Nothing*, for instance, Beatrice and Benedick will be brought to know themselves and hence to know that they are capable of, and can even delight in, love. In *Twelfth Night*, Orsino and Olivia will come to recognize the need to abandon their respective self-imposed cloisters and to commit themselves to love and to active participation in the human community. Here in *The Two Gentlemen of Verona*, the education in one's own nature is also in part, but only in part, a preparation for love. A Proteus who has been brought to concentrate upon and be penitent for his own inconstancy will presumably be able to devote himself more steadily and with greater dedication to Julia in the future. But because the play combines material from two different sources and has Proteus violate both the romantic love and friendship codes, Proteus' inconstancy is compounded to the point that he becomes an outright

villain, and his education takes on a more overtly moral cast than do those of the later romantic comedies. In any case, it is the use of an education as the central structure of a play's whole action which constitutes *The Two Gentlemen*'s importance for and legacy to Shakespeare's later comedies. In *The Two Gentlemen of Verona*, Shakespeare can be said to have found his congenial comic form. (pp. 231-44)

Peter Lindenbaum, "Education in 'The Two Gentlemen of Verona'," in Studies in English Literature, 1500-1900, *Vol. XV, No. 2, Spring, 1975, pp. 229-44.*

RUTH NEVO (essay date 1980)

[Noting the absence of a central comic device or trickster in The Two Gentlemen of Verona, *Nevo states that the trouble with the play "is that the farcical, exorcist principle has got lost in the elaboration of the sentimental reversals." Ideally, she suggests, the comedy would "generate its own panaceas by virtue of its own absurdity"; instead, she states, it focuses mainly on character transformations, on "the interchange of partners and rivals," until it eventually deadlocks in Proteus's and Valentine's culminating reversal of roles in Act V, Scene iv. Nevo also notes the play's anticipation of qualities essential to Shakespeare's later works, including the ideas of "shadow and substance, image and idol"—demonstrated by the male lovers in their acceptance of*

Act V. Scene iv. Valentine, Proteus, Silvia, and Julia disguised as Sebastian. By Angelica Kauffman.
The Department of Rare Books and Special Collections, The University of Michigan Library.

love as a "fashion" or "imitation"—and "the density and vivacity of characterization by impersonation."]

In *The Two Gentlemen*, the doubling structure of *The Comedy of Errors* is repeated with some elaboration, but the scene of operations, so to speak, is thoroughly interiorized. The issue of mistaken identities is now predominantly within, a question of psychic identity rather than optic identification, a question of the self that the self chooses, or is driven, to be. Much has been written on the 'friendship literature', the cult of friendship and its conflict with the cult of love, from which *The Two Gentlemen* is said to derive. But it may be profitable to consider these themes from the point of view of a deeper structure. For the purpose of examining the choice of selves and self-images, twins are conveniently replaced by friends, and by that aspect of the friendship of young men which is a matter of likeness and liking, of imitation and rivalry.

In *The Comedy of Errors* there were two identical twin servants; here, there are two antithetical servants, one artless and one witty, chiastically arranged to match their masters, one witty, one foolish. Speed, the pert servant, a witty beggar who is later to reappear in Feste, in point of character would have been better matched with Proteus, and indeed at the beginning, in one of the play's notorious inconsistencies, he does carry letters from Proteus to Julia. Possibly Shakespeare changed his mind at some stage of his ruminations when he saw the advantages of cross-matching his servants. In *The Comedy of Errors* there were two ladies (sisters), one married and betrayed, one unwed and available. Here the two ladies are spiritual sisters, both in fact unwed, but one is betrothed and betrayed. Both young men are transformed and metamorphozed—truly, not apparently—but Valentine is the equivalent of the travelling Antipholus who discovers love; Proteus of the (apparently) shape-shifting resident twin, who despises the love he possesses. The freeing of the relationships from the strictly determining family roles and the raising of affairs of the heart to the level of courtly ardour and artifice gives the play an added interest and resonance, while it advances the critique of Petrarchanism; but the trouble with *The Two Gentlemen* is that the farcical, exorcist principle has got lost in the elaboration of the sentimental reversals.

The usual complaint against farce is that it is too 'situational'; but in *The Two Gentlemen* there is not enough comedy of situation to render the reversals theatrically ludicrous however susceptible of interpretation as mockery or satire they may be. Partly this is because there is no central comic device—no trick or stratagem to breed deceptions, and evoke or exacerbate follies. Julia's disguise comes too late for this and is the effect rather than the cause of Proteus' treacheries. As a consequence, there is no central comic protagonist-trickster—a Petruchio or an Oberon—to engineer and exhibit absurdities. And the result is that the deracination of folly is not mediated by means of mockery, but is merely announced. *The Two Gentlemen* is rich in comic potentiality, as its implied contrasts between *amour propre* and love proper, and its reversals, suggest; but for this particular collection of ills and follies Shakespeare has not yet found the right form of remedial exposure, though . . . he is within a stone's throw of his own best discovery.

Briefly, the story which *The Two Gentlemen* recounts concerns the replacing of one triangular relationship in a group of four by another, and the eventual emergence of two couples. Valentine is odd man out at the start. Symmetry reigns briefly when he falls in love with Sylvia, and each Jack has his Jill,

as Puck would have said. Then, when Proteus abandons his Julia to pursue Valentine's Sylvia, Julia, now odd man out, sets off in disguise in pursuit of her love. Sylvia defiantly follows her now banished lover as well, and in the wood relations, already criss-crossed, are dizzily disrupted: Proteus is about to violate romantic propriety and Sylvia's honour by raping her; Valentine, rescuing her, repudiates his false friend. The latter repents, and Valentine's response to the challenge of that friend's repentance is the magnanimous renunciation of Sylvia. This pleases no one, neither the renouncer nor the renounced nor the recipient of the renunciation, since repentant Proteus will presumably no longer be content with a virtual rape victim in place of an adored mistress, nor the onlooker—the disguised and rejected Julia.

In Act V of *The Two Gentlemen* there is an intensified accumulation of the kind of switchback reversal which has structured the plot all along in the interchange of partners and rivals; the possibilities of further reversal are fairly exhausted or deadlocked by Proteus' bid for violence and Valentine's total renunciation. The only possible further move is for Proteus to refuse to accept the renunciation, thus outdoing his friend in magnanimity. And then? Either Valentine gets the girl, and Proteus is left forlorn, himself now odd man out, or both continue to vie with each other in magnanimity with poor Sylvia as pawn between them. Julia's unmasking following her swoon (which has been read as deliberate), her appearance in her own presence to be recognized and to bring about resolution and reconciliation, is clearly what the plot demands for its remedy, and the initial deficiency for its correction. It is the logically satisfying closure for the initial asymmetrical situation. Proteus is disabused of 'delusions' as was Antipholus of Ephesus, and the ecstatic pair are free to continue to find themselves in each other. Yet there is little comic profit in this remedy because the accumulation of errors and ills, the 'increase and progression of perturbations' has not been shown to generate its own panaceas by virtue of its own absurdity and so, in effect, to exorcise itself as it progresses cumulatively and giddily towards exhaustion. Towards the accomplishment of this secret of his craft Shakespeare's early comedies make uncertain and erratic progress. And *The Two Gentlemen*, though richer and more diversified in surface features than *The Comedy of Errors*, manages its comic structure less surely. (pp. 53-6)

The Two Gentlemen is properly named, as are the two gentlemen themselves. For this is still a play in which the masculine view and the masculine initiative dominates. The differentiation between these two—friends and rivals,—is, it turns out, a standard antithetical contrast between foolish virtue and cunning knavery transposed into the key of romantic love. Valentine is the credulous simpleton (witness the letter scene) and Proteus guilefully deceitful (witness his exploitation of Valentine's banishment). But this is itself a reversal of what appeared to be their original posture, when Valentine preached worldly wisdom to Proteus' 'homely wits'. Speed openly mocks the slower wits of Valentine, while Launce, the dunce, who serves the too-quick-witted Proteus, graphically depicts for us situations which point parodically to the moral deficiencies of his master by way of remonstrances and complaints over the faithless Crab:

> my mother weeping, my father wailing, my
> sister crying, our maid howling, our cat wring-
> ing her hands, and all our house in a great
> perplexity, yet did not this cruel-hearted cur

shed one tear. He is a stone, a very pibble stone,
and has no more pity in him than a dog.

                                        [II. iii. 6-11]

In the matter of love one is votary and one is heretic—the
interest will be in the comic reversal of a notable lover into,
as Launce would have it, 'a notable lubber' [II. v. 42-6], and
of an anti-lover into an emblem of love. The play is going to
examine the effects of love, the folly of love. So it says. But
this is not exactly what it does. It examines the remedial and
beneficent power of the ladies' love, and the uncertain, image-
dependent, wavering, volatile nature of the gentlemen's. And
as a result of this shift of the centre of gravity, so to speak, it
examines the way two gentlemen become themselves when
possessed of quite mistaken initial notions of what becomes
them. This is a fascinating theme and a truly Shakespearean
outcome, but it is as if this early comedy does not quite know
what it is about, and therefore does not quite realize its own
inherent possibilities.

Folly in *The Two Gentlemen* is identified by fancy-free Valentine. It is to be in love, he says, interpreting the signs:

        where scorn is bought with groans;
   Coy looks with heart-sore sighs; one fading moment's
      mirth
   With twenty watchful, weary, tedious nights:
   If happ'ly won, perhaps a hapless gain;
   If lost, why then a grievous labor won;
   However—but a folly bought with wit,
   Or else a wit by folly vanquished.

                                        [I. i. 29-35]

So, by your circumstance, you call me a fool, says Proteus,
getting, not surprisingly, the point. And against the folly of
love Valentine proposes the wisdom of foreign travel. Seeing
the wonders of the world broadens the mind—shapes the mind,
he says. Proteus will wear out his youth dully sluggardized at
home, for 'Home-keeping youth have ever homely wits' [I. i.
2]. Thus is romantic love, the finest flower of Renaissance
courtship, nominated sluggardry by Valentine. Proteus, replying to Valentine, is curiously ambiguous:

        Yet writers say: as in the sweetest bud
        The eating canker dwells, so eating love
        Inhabits in the finest wits of all.

                                        [I. i. 42-4]

Proteus grants Valentine's point at the very moment when he
defends his condition by appeal to the good company he keeps.
The very finest wits are affected—so he defends himself. But
by what? By an eating canker!

Proteus, left alone on the stage, entirely reflects his friend's
view. 'He after honour hunts, I after love' [I. i. 63]. Proteus
is a chameleon, a colour- and shape-shifter, as his name tells
us. His desires are reflections of what he believes others desire.
Therefore self-improvement, Valentine's aim, at once appears
to him infinitely desirable. Thus, too, it is Valentine's denigration of love which is at once reflected in Proteus' change
of mood:

   I [leave] myself, my friends, and all, for love.
   Thou, Julia, thou has metamorphis'd me,
   Made me neglect my studies, lose my time,
   War with good counsel, set the world at nought;
   Made wit with musing weak, heart sick with thought.

                                        [I. i. 65-9]

He is a perfect example of what René Girard has called 'triangular desire'—the desire of an object because it is desired
by another—and interestingly enough, he is fully conscious of
this when he finds himself in love with Valentine's chosen
mistress:

   Even as one heat another heat expels,
   Or as one nail by strength drives out another,
   So the remembrance of my former love
   Is by a newer object quite forgotten.
   [Is it] mine [eye], or Valentinus' praise,
   Her true perfection, or my false transgression,
   That make me reasonless, to reason thus?

                                        [II. iv. 192-98]
                                        (pp. 56-8)

Proteus' desire for what the envied other desires is set off
against Valentine's total self-absorption in his own newly-dis-
covered raptures:

             why, man, she is mine own,
   And I as rich in having such a jewel
   As twenty seas, if all their sand were pearl,
   The water nectar, and the rocks pure gold.
   Forgive me, that I do not dream on thee,
   Because thou seest me dote upon my love.

                                        [II. iv. 168-73]

The two gentlemen are each other's doubles, or mirror images,
as Speed points out, obligingly explaining to Valentine how
he knows the latter is in love:

   Marry, by these special marks: first, you have
   learn'd, like Sir Proteus, to wreathe your arms,
   like a malecontent; to relish a love-song, like
   a robin-redbreast; to walk alone, like one that
   had the pestilence; to sigh, like a schoolboy
   that had lost his ABC. . . .

                                        [II. i. 18-23]
                                        (pp. 59-60)

For Valentine only Sylvia, his *alter ego,* can illuminate and
enliven the world. He has lost himself in her:

   Except I be by Silvia in the night,
   There is no music in the nightingale;
   Unless I look on Silvia in the day,
   There is no day for me to look upon.

                                        [III. i. 178-81]

And when he gives her up to Proteus the reversal of roles is
complete.

For Proteus, the world is well worth losing for self-gratification:

   I cannot leave to love, and yet I do;
   But there I leave to love where I should love.
   Julia I lose, and Valentine I lose:
   If I keep them, I needs must lose myself;
   If I lose them, thus find I by their loss—
   For Valentine, myself; for Julia, Silvia. . . .

                                        [II. vi. 17-22]

But the self Proteus thus gains becomes a perverse masochism
of monstrous proportions, filling his world: . . .

   When to her beauty I commend my vows,
   She bids me think how I have been forsworn
   In breaking faith with Julia whom I lov'd;

> And notwithstanding all her sudden quips,
> The least whereof would quell a lover's hope,
> Yet, spaniel-like, the more she spurns my love,
> The more it grows, and fawneth on her still.
>
> [IV. ii. 9-15]

Valentine's loss of the worldly world on the other hand gains him 'this shadowy desert, unfrequented woods' which he 'better brook[s]' than 'flourishing peopled towns' [V. iv. 2-3]. Both are thus contrarily isolated: Valentine in the forest deprived of the 'thou that dost inhabit in [his] breast' (though he does at least gain the brotherhood of the bandits), and Proteus within his obsession.

It is the cause of this sorry state and one possible remedy which is parodied by Launce's clown pantomime of canine faithlessness and dogged devotion [at IV. iv. 1-39]. . . . (pp. 60-1)

Structurally, this comic remonstrance is crucially placed: the faithlessness of Proteus has been laid bare; that of both Thurio and Sir Eglamour (Love's Philistines, as Harold Brooks has called them [see excerpt above, 1963]) to the doctrine and discipline of courtly love is still to come; the faithful devotion of Valentine (and both Silvia and Julia) are in the process of trial and testing. It is an excellent example of what [has been] . . . described as simultaneously foil and parody. If an ungrateful cur is parodic proxy for Proteus, the rustic buffoon his owner is foil for Julia, his unconquerable good nature acting not to undercut but to underwrite Julia's 'folly'. It is the play's richest comic counterpoint, and its foolishness casts an exquisitely ludicrous light upon the courtly company. (p. 62)

Act IV of *Two Gentlemen* excellently exemplifies certain Shakespearean ways of reflecting, and reflecting upon, that which his play presents as remedial in the situation which it depicts. Act IV, scene i introduces the outlaws, opening a window upon a world antithetical to the cultivated, spurious, accommodating and deceptive court. Nearer, as Charlton pointed out [see excerpt above, 1930], to the Pirates of Penzance than to any seriously-entertained image of natural simplicities, nevertheless their Spenserian and Italian pastoral antecedents are evident and their intended connotations plain enough. This presence is the informing spirit of Act IV. The specifically Shakespearean therapy of the forest is no more than germinal in this early play, but it is to be noticed that events in the forest do bring the absolutism of excluded middles in which the gentlemen are deadlocked to a crisis and an exhaustion. Proteus' threat of rape is a maximization of egoism, Valentine's renunciation—of Silvia, who is his essence—an ultimate in absolute altruism. The logic of either/or has by then run the play into a logical *cul-de-sac*, from which only the devoted presence of Julia can save it.

Once Valentine has been accepted into the outlaws' company (on the rather odd grounds of his linguistic accomplishments) we move to Silvia's window, where the devious Proteus serenades his friend's beloved, ostensibly for Thurio's sake. This double betrayal is rejected by Silvia with the contempt it deserves and witnessed by the abandoned Julia herself, in disguise.

The unknowing encounter between Julia and Silvia is the high point of the Act. And in it is realized the beneficent, saving irrationality which in blithe defiance of the law of excluded middles plunges toward solutions. Julia's speech sets out her dilemmas:

> Because he loves her, he despiseth me;
> Because I love him, I must pity him.
> This ring I gave him when he parted from me,

> To bind him to remember my good will;
> And now am I (unhappy messenger)
> To plead for that which I would not obtain,
> To carry that which I would have refus'd,
> To praise his faith which I would have disprais'd.
> I am my master's true confirmed love;
> But cannot be true servant to my master,
> Unless I prove false traitor to myself.
>
> [IV. iv. 95-105]

The antitheses echo Proteus:

> I cannot now prove constant to myself,
> Without some treachery used to Valentine.
>
> [II. vi. 31-2]

and Valentine's despairing

> To die is to be banished from myself,
> And Silvia is myself: banish'd from her
> Is self from self, a deadly banishment!
>
> [III. i. 171-73]

But it ends with the illogic of compromise:

> Yet will I woo for him, but yet so coldly
> As heaven it knows, I would not have him speed.
>
> [IV. iv. 106-07]

This is consonant with Julia's vividly-rendered vacillations over the letter from Proteus in Act I, scene ii. And there, too, the character is built up by the need to play a part. She is pretending to Lucetta that she has no interest in the letter. Carried away by the playing of the part she goes so far as to tear it up, only to fall frantically to trying to put it together again the moment her mocking maid is out of the room. Not consistency but inconsistency is the secret of dramatic character, and that of Julia deserves a more accomplished play.

In Act IV, scene iv, Julia, telling Silvia of Proteus' abandoned lady and inspired by the playing of her page's part, improvizes the story of the pageant ostensibly to justify her assessment of the lady's height—'about my stature', but actually, we are invited to infer, to cloak her own scarcely controllable tears:

> About my stature; for at Pentecost,
> When all our pageants of delight were play'd,
> Our youth got me to play the woman's part,
> And I was trimm'd in Madam Julia's gown,
> Which served me as fit, by all men's judgments,
> As if the garment had been made for me;
> Therefore I know she is about my height.
> And at that time I made her weep agood,
> For I did play a lamentable part.
> Madam, 'twas Ariadne passioning
> For Theseus' perjury and unjust flight;
> Which I so lively acted with my tears
> That my poor mistress, moved therewithal,
> Wept bitterly; and would I might be dead
> If I in thought felt not her very sorrow.
>
> [IV. iv. 158-72]

This, for the first time, is the density and vivacity of characterization by impersonation to which later comedies will accustom us. It is, paradoxically, out of the rendering of dissimulation that the impression of a genuine personality emerges. The gap between the ostensible (the story of the pageant) and the inferred (what we know of the speaker and her possible motives) is such as to provoke and exercise the imagination of the audience, and it is this exercise of the imagination which creates the mimetic illusion. The effect, of course, is foregrounded by the disguise, but the page disguise is not indispensable, as the first scene shows.

The girl-boy disguise device of the *novelle* may well have represented itself to the dramatist as an invaluable bonus in the development of a sophisticated character portrayal, but it also precipitates the imagining of a complex and double point of view. So, in Julia's soliloquy upon the portrait of Silvia—that 'virtuous gentlewoman, mild and beautiful' [IV. iv 180]—she promises herself an auburn wig to take the place of her own 'pefect yellow' (if that is what is required) and concludes with lines of resonant and reflective maturity almost sufficient to persuade us that she might make a reality even of Proteus' cardboard love if she should ever regain it:

> Come, shadow, come, and take this shadow up,
> For 'tis thy rival. O thou senseless form,
> Thou shalt be worshipp'd, kiss'd, lov'd, and ador'd;
> And were there sense in his idolatry,
> My substance should be statue in thy stead.
>
> [IV. iv. 197-201]

Shadow and substance, image and idol: these recurrences point to a preoccupation which later comedies will explore and immensely deepen. *The Two Gentlemen* moves on the threshold only of these later concerns; but in its song to Silvia gives lyric expression to what the discovery of Julia dramatizes. In this context 'Who is Silvia, what is she / That all our swains commend her?' is a key question; and 'Love doth to her eyes repair / To help him of his blindness' [IV. ii. 39-40, 46-7], a key remedy which later comedies will wonderfully explore.

Though *The Two Gentlemen* does not live up to its comic potentialities, its resolution is an interesting foreshadowing. The scandal of Act V (Quiller-Couch says, with Victorian primness, 'there are by this time *no* gentlemen in Verona' [see excerpt above, 1921]) has distracted attention from the real significance of the play's resolution. The intended rape, however, is no more than the moment of incipient danger and harm which is statutory in Shakespearean comedy to demarcate its frontiers and mark its remedy. It might even be argued, since human deficiencies generate tragedy as readily as comedy, that the remedies of comedy require no less than a deliberate, perilous skirting of harm and danger. The real trouble is the absence, in their speech, of nuance, of an expressive self-awareness.

However, when Julia defends her disguise on the grounds that modesty finds women's shape-changing a 'lesser blot' than men's mind-changing, Proteus exclaims:

> 'Than men their minds?' 'tis true. O heaven, were man
> But constant, he were perfect; that one error
> Fills him with faults; makes him run through all th' sins:
> Inconstancy falls off ere it begins.
> What is in Silvia's face, but I may spy
> More fresh in Julia's with a constant eye?
>
> [V. iv. 110-15]

The speech has been faulted for lack of eloquence but there is a certain disingenuous, uncouth vehemence in its exclamatory confirmation of the primacy of 'mind' over 'eye' that does carry conviction. Proteus blames his 'inconstancy', but audience hindsight, collating all it has seen, comprehends at a higher level of generality the nature of the folly or comic disposition of Verona's young men. To neither gentlemen at the start of the play was love anything but a fashion, or an imitation. They use the language of metamorphosis, but their adolescent attachment to each other is largely unchanged. As Nietzsche said, everything absolute belongs in the realm of pathology; and their compulsive vacillations between disjunctive alternatives: either be him or kill him, either all or nothing, is certainly that.

When Julia faints, however, at the climax of Act V and then produces her ring and is recognized, she is the living proof that exclusive-alternative catastrophe can be eluded, given a certain feminine capacity for waiting upon the event, nourishing and fostering it, till it ripen in its own good time. In Julia craft and constancy, spontaneity and morality, are no longer irremediably sundered as they have been for the two gentlemen, nor self and other doomed to a polarity of identity or nonentity. Julia *is*, it appears, the excluded middle it was their folly not to perceive, and an admirable remedy for the gentlemen's ills. But she lacks, as yet, the Shakespearean trickster-heroine's freedom and élan. (pp. 63-7)

> *Ruth Nevo, "'The Two Gentlemen of Verona'," in her* Comic Transformations in Shakespeare, *Methuen & Co. Ltd., 1980, pp. 53-68.*

MAURICE HUNT (essay date 1982)

[*Hunt contends that* The Two Gentlemen of Verona *dramatizes the Christian "paradox of salvation" in the self-discoveries through self-loss experienced by Proteus, Valentine, and Julia. Proteus's initial loss of identity is the result of his "unethical egoism" and is resolved only by contrition and understanding, the critic states, while Valentine's loss stems from the pursuit of gentlemanly perfection and is repaired when he discovers his "noble identity" in the green world. Julia, Hunt continues, most closely dramatizes "the original meaning of the paradox of salvation" by losing herself in charitable, rather than romantic, love and by discovering her true spiritual self through sacrifice to another human being.*]

"The note of banishment, banishment from the heart, banishment from home," Stephen Dedalus pronounces in *Ulysses*, "sounds uninterruptedly from *The Two Gentlemen* onward till Prospero breaks his staff, buries it certain fathoms in the earth and drowns his book." While the theme of banishment does pervade Shakespearean drama, redemption is often coupled with it—in fact made possible by loss—as the play that Stephen mentions makes quite clear. Banished from the court of Milan, Valentine finds his true nobility in the forest; banished from Proteus's heart Julia finds her love again in the guise of the page Sebastian. By losing themselves, these romantic lovers somehow find the joys for which they have been searching—the better life which Fortune seems to have denied them. This paradox of salvation, a hallmark of the New Testament, helps give *The Two Gentlemen of Verona* a degree of dramatic cohesion and depth. As expressed in the Gospels, the paradox suggests that whosoever shall save his life shall lose it, and whosoever shall lose his life for Christ's sake shall find it (Matthew 16:25). Rephrased in a secular form, the paradox implies that a superior spirituality is found through the loss of the established self. "But tell me true," Speed asks the whimsical Launce concerning the affair of Julia and Proteus, "will't be a match?"

> *Lau.* Ask my dog: if he say "ay," it will; if he say "no," it will; if he shake his tail, and say nothing, it will.
> *Spe.* The conclusion is, then, that it will.
> *Lau.* Thou shalt never get such a secret from me but by a parable.
>
> [II. v. 34-40]

Shakespeare might have been amused by the serious interpretation of a dramatic word that is perhaps no more profound than the wag of a dog's tail. The Parable of the Prodigal Son, if we judge from the plays, does appear to be one of his favorite stories, however, and the chameleonlike Proteus is a good example of the romantic prodigal. Proteus strays from his friend and lover, wasting his virtue and losing himself in a labyrinth of treachery, until he finds a new identity in contrition and self-understanding. We shall see that Proteus's major insight in Act Five takes the form of Elizabethan self-knowledge. "Know thyself"—*nosce teipsum*—was a sixteenth-century admonition which obviously encouraged self-discovery. . . . Proteus's "clarity of mind" at the conclusion of the play certainly is not a dramatic event worthy of the mature Shakespeare. It does result, nevertheless, from a type of self-knowledge made possible by a loss of identity. Proteus's loss of self and spiritual discovery are different in kind from Julia's. Because of her great capacity for charitable love, Julia comes closest to dramatizing the original meaning of the paradox of salvation. Her staging of it in fact creates an ideal by which motives and deeds in *The Two Gentlemen* can be measured.

From the beginning, the passion that shatters the friendships in this play also threatens the lovers with losses of identity. "Sluggardis'd at home," Proteus, in Valentine's opinion, wears out his youth "with shapeless idleness" [I. i. 7-8]. Valentine's statement concerns not only the amorphous nature of idleness; it also suggests a certain lack of identity—a shapelessness—occasioned by love. Proteus, to Valentine's mind, will never become the perfect courtier because he is a lover. By naming the lover "Proteus," Shakespeare evokes the image of the Classical being who could assume all shapes and no shape, who could become everything and nothing, and so encourages his viewer to wonder from the play's outset if this Proteus will lack integrity. While Valentine, who seeks to perfect the Renaissance self by travel, proposes to pursue honor in the Emperor's court—leaving his friends to dignify them—Proteus laments that

I leave myself, my friends, and all, for love:
Thou, Julia, thou hast metamorphos'd me;
Made me neglect my studies, lose my time,
War with good counsel, set the world at nought;
Made wit with musing weak, heart sick with thought.
                                        [I. i. 65-9]

These complaints reflect more than the standard melancholy brought on by love; they point toward a radical, and degenerative, change of character—a metamorphosis downward which is more fully explored in the love relationships of *A Midsummer Night's Dream*. Love, in the form of his sudden passion for Silvia, will undermine Proteus in a manner unimaginable when he recites the above Petrarchan commonplaces. . . . Nonetheless, in one sense Proteus never "leaves" himself because of his "love" for Silvia. Strictly speaking, it is Proteus's *self*-ishness that brings about his ruin. In his shallow practices, aimed at winning Silvia mainly by discrediting Valentine, his self-interest is manifest. Coveting Silvia gratifies Proteus's narrow and firmly grasped ego. He seems unaware of how, through his self-aggrandizing deceits, he truly loses his identity as gentleman by forfeiting Valentine's and Silvia's—to say nothing of the viewer's—respect and affection. When Valentine confronts him in the forest with the image of his brutal self, Proteus's loss of self-respect completes the radical crumbling of identity that has silently but steadily occurred throughout the play. An unethical egoism rather than passion, primarily

erodes Proteus's character. Passion, especially as it relates to Proteus, is more clearly destructive for Julia.

The obliterating force of passion is foreshadowed when Julia, in the play's second scene, tears up Proteus's love letter, only to wish a moment later that she had preserved it. She comically punishes herself by tearing her name out of the shredded letter wherever it appears:

                    unkind Julia!
As in revenge of thy ingratitude,
I throw thy name against the bruising stones,
Trampling contemptuously on thy disdain. . . .
But twice, or thrice, was "Proteus" written down:
Be calm, good wind, blow not a word away,
Till I have found each letter, in the letter,
Except mine own name: that some whirlwind bear
Unto a ragged, fearful, hanging rock
And throw it thence into the raging sea.
                                        [I. ii. 106-09, 114-19]

The love letter, which Lucetta has called "nothing" [I. ii. 70-5], ironically makes Julia wish herself a nonentity. Name, after all, is the symbol for identity, and its annihilation can portend the loss of self. In the letter scene, Julia rehearses—actually wills—her later loss of identity when she adopts a male disguise to journey to Proteus. She becomes Sebastian so that she may safely travel to the man whom she believes loves her. Proteus, however, has deserted her for Silvia, and her defacing costume suggests passion's depersonalizing power once she arrives and learns of the great betrayal. Sebastian's hair is knit up "in silken strings, / With twenty odd-conceited true-love knots" [II. vii. 45-6], and "he" wears round hose and a codpiece stuck with pins—the fashion then most faddish according to Lucetta. Sebastian thus is the reductive stereotype of the fancy-struck lover in whom individuality is obscured. In the case of both the letter and the disguise, romantic passion is the force behind self-effacement. In reference to Silvia's portrait, the "shadow" to which Proteus devotes his changed love, Julia bitterly jests:

If 'twere a substance, you would sure deceive it,
And make it but a shadow, as I am.
                                        [IV. ii. 126-27]

"Shadow" was an Elizabethan term for "actor"—the empty and false role that Julia plays as a page. But the word also poignantly conveys the despairing woman's compromised being—that ephemeral creature, neither man nor maid, who is Sebastian. Julia's persona becomes a prison once Proteus proves unfaithful; since Proteus's love made her womanhood valuable, the loss of his affection makes a return to it unmeaningful. Thus she suffers in her ambiguous role.

The loss of identity associated with love also occurs in the comic action of *The Two Gentlemen*. That is the necessary question that Launce's foolery poses in Act Two, scene three. Launce claims that, in going with Proteus to the Emperor's court, he has received his proportion "like the prodigious son" [II. iii. 3-4]. The phrase of course is a malapropism for the Prodigal Son, and the reference to the Parable evokes the theme of losing and finding. Launce then absurdly stages the manner in which the members of his family wept upon his leave-taking. . . . [He] literally loses himself in personifying his shoes, hat, staff, and dog. . . . Launce's comic disintegration amazes the viewer. But the strange self-divisions somehow remain clear to the clown, and he triumphantly concludes the scenario in a bath of tears. The paradox of salvation is ridiculously caught in this scene. After losing himself in his little play, Launce spiritually finds himself in the love that he bountifully portrays. His imagination, like Bottom's at times [in *A Mid-summer Night's Dream*], is wonderfully humanized; even the family cat, in his unique view, wrings her hands. Like Bottom again, Launce voices a charitable love that the play's main characters, if they would prosper, must embrace. Launce's empathy, however misplaced, converts his malapropism into the truth; with his compassionate heart, he has received his proportion ''like the prodigious son.''

Weighting Shakespeare's lighter scenes with serious critical freight can be a risky business. Still, Launce's comedy reveals a lesser version of the unselfish love that Valentine and especially Julia express at key moments. Measured against charitable feeling, romantic love appears a paltry thing. Proteus, the lover who most closely quotes from the book of courtship, best demonstrates this fact. Troubled by conflicting loyalties to Julia, Valentine, and Silvia, Proteus obscures the question of his ethical duty by seeking refuge in a courtly maxim, whose vagueness allows him to justify his base impulses. He coldly reckons his ''losses,'' including his imagined self-loss, in loving his friend's mistress:

> To leave my Julia, shall I be forsworn;
> To love fair Silvia, shall I be forsworn;
> To wrong my friend, I shall be much forsworn. . . .
> I cannot leave to love; and yet I do;
> But there I leave to love, where I should love.
> Julia I lose, and Valentine I lose;
> If I keep them, I needs must lose myself;
> If I lose them, thus find I by their loss:
> For Valentine, myself; for Julia, Silvia.
> I to myself am dearer than a friend,
> For love is still most precious in itself.
>   [II. vi. 1-3, 17-24]

Romantic love, in the conclusion of the above speech, circles barrenly within the self. Proteus's statement—''For love is still most precious in itself''—is a noble-sounding idea that hides the crudest desires for self-aggrandizement. Because Proteus does not lose himself in an act of charitable love, at this point he makes no spiritual discovery. Romantic love is repeatedly contrasted with charity throughout *The Two Gentlemen,* and the former quality is basically retentive in Shakespeare's view. Silvia's witty method of wooing Valentine by having him write a love letter for her to an unknown friend, who proves to be himself, hints at romantic love's closed, unliberating nature. Julia voices romantic love's self-containment when, as Sebastian, she tells Proteus that, in regard to the ring he gave her,

> Julia herself did give it me,
> And Julia herself hath brought it hither.
>   [V. iv. 98-9]

It is through her role as Sebastian, however, that Julia dramatizes the paradox of salvation, and initiates the sequence of events that assures a happy ending to *The Two Gentlemen.*

Many commentators have noted that Julia's dilemma resembles Viola's in *Twelfth Night*. The man whom each woman loves takes her into his service, thinking she is a male page, and employs her as his messenger to his mistress. Both Julia and Viola experience the hardship of courting another woman on behalf of the man beloved. Julia's predicament in fact is worse than Viola's: her master has betrayed her faithful love and she carries the very ring she gave him as a love token to the new

mistress. Viola never suffers these indignities. Given her plight, Julia understandably seems to think of herself first:

> I am my master's true confirmed love,
> But cannot be true servant to my master,
> Unless I prove false traitor to myself.
>   [IV. iv. 103-05]

Julia feels as though she is juggling one person, or relationship, too many. Proteus had the same impression in his similarly phrased struggle with the demands of love and friendship. Julia, however, does not sacrifice her loyalties to her self-interest; for her, love is not most precious in itself. A finer feeling, which sets her apart from the other lovers, generally softens her passions and overrules potential selfishness. The religious quality of her affection is stressed when, about to journey to the Emperor's court, she refers to herself as ''a true-devoted pilgrim'' who, ''patient as a gentle stream,'' will make a ''pilgrimage'' to her beloved, with whom she will rest as ''a blessed soul doth in Elysium'' [II. vii. 9-38]. The pilgrimage of desire is not simply a witty conceit; the phrase once signified an inner spiritual journey by which men and women were tested and either damned or saved. Charitable love, rather than self-love, was the key to a successful pilgrimage of desire. Julia's elaborate conceit thus provokes the viewer to recollect and consider a kind of love central to the paradox of salvation. In this respect her image is aesthetically appropriate to the play. After Julia learns of Proteus's falling away she is forgiving. ''Because I love him,'' she confesses, ''I must pity him'' [IV. iv. 96]. Perhaps for this reason Julia agrees to carry out Proteus's commands regardless of how humiliating they might be. Her martyr-like loss of self in her role as her betrayer's faithful servant illustrates her charity. Appropriately, this loss of self leads to an important spiritual discovery.

Paradoxically, the absorption of Julia's self in playing a part makes possible her self-fulfillment. When Sebastian appears to plead Proteus's suit, Silvia, thoughtful of the wronged Julia, questions the messenger about Proteus's original mistress. Julia courageously does not reveal her identity, but invents an elaborate fiction through which she can vent her overcharged feelings. . . . In the tale of Theseus's desertion of Ariadne, Julia finds an objective correlative for her misfortune. Art is a creative mirror of reality, a great illusion reflecting the recurring truths of the human condition. In Julia's account, the actor's immersion in his part—his acting a role tearfully and realistically—causes him to feel a fictional sorrow. Moved by such lively art, the spectator weeps, driving the actor to greater passion and a more empathetic portrayal. The ''very sorrow'' that the actor finally feels ''in thought'' is both the fictional character's and the spectator's, which blend together during mimesis. (pp. 6-15)

Valentine's mistress weeps upon hearing Sebastian's words, as though Ariadne's passion were actually played before her. The tears are for Julia, however:

> Alas, poor lady, desolate, and left;
> I weep myself to think upon thy words.
>   [IV. iv. 174-75]

Having found compassion in her heart, Silvia gives Sebastian her purse for the sake of Julia. Because of Silvia's kindness, Julia will bear no malice toward her rival. Concerning Silvia's portrait, which Proteus has commanded his messenger to bring to him, she says:

> I'll use thee kindly, for thy mistress's sake
> That us'd me so; or else, by Jove I vow,
> I should have scratch'd out your unseeing eyes,
> To make my master out of love with thee.
>
> [IV. iv. 202-05]

Thus the play averts a crisis and proceeds to its providential ending. Julia's losing herself in a player's role has been redemptive.

Does Valentine also find himself spiritually once he is exiled and seemingly lost? As in the case of Proteus, the answer is complex: Valentine does discover one aspect of his character in the green world while never actually relinquishing another. When the Duke of Milan banishes him for planning to steal away with his daughter, Valentine anticipates a loss of self:

> And why not death, rather than living torment?
> To die is to be banish'd from myself,
> And Silvia is myself: banish'd from her
> Is self from self. A deadly banishment.
>
> [III. i. 170-73]

When Proteus, aware of the banishment, calls Valentine by name in an effort to rouse the despairing lover, the latter explains that he is not even Valentine's spirit but "nothing"— a status that the verbally inept Launce ironically stresses when he says, "There is a proclamation that you are vanished" [III. i. 217-18]. Deprived of Silvia, Valentine imagines that he will become extinct: . . .

> She is my essence, and I leave to be,
> If I be not by her fair influence
> Foster'd, illumin'd, cherish'd, kept alive.
>
> [III. i. 182-84]

As Valentine's "essence," Silvia resembles his soul. Without her, he imagines that he will disintegrate because he lacks his spirit. The break up of Valentine's character, however, does not occur in the forest in which he loses himself. The green world into which Valentine wanders contains a group of Gilbert-and-Sullivan outlaws who capture him and give him the odd choice of becoming their captain or facing death. They instinctively, and rather comically, defer to his civility and to his mastery of languages (as though learning were important for their rough trade). Valentine commands the quaint rebels much as the reason does the unruly passions; he magnanimously prevents them from harming women and poor travelers. Valentine thus proves himself a civil governor, and finds a viable nobility rather than a textbook gentility. His discovery of his capacity for rule does not appear likely in the courts that Shakespeare slightly depicts in the play. Valentine's realization of the self while an outcast in the wilderness gives a wry twist to the conventional theme of the Renaissance youth's well regulated education. The green world in Shakespearean comedy and romance is often an experimental realm, and Valentine in the forest does have the opportunity to test and prove his ability to rule himself and others. Additionally, he discovers ideas obscured by courtly values:

> How use doth breed a habit in a man!
> This shadowy desert, unfrequented woods,
> I better brook than flourishing peopled towns:

> Here can I sit alone, unseen of any,
> And to the nightingale's complaining notes
> Tune my distresses, and record my woes.
>
> [V. iv. 1-6]

The speech presents a happy blend of Duke Senior's and Jacques's attitudes [in *As You Like It*]; Valentine gains a special understanding of the relativity of custom and the value of the solitary life.

From one perspective, Valentine never loses Silvia, even though they are physically separated. Her name has obvious relevance for the sylvan realm. In the forest where her lover wanders, she, like Petrarch's Laura, becomes a vital source:

> O thou that does inhabit in my breast,
> Leave not the mansion so long tenantless,
> Lest growing ruinous, the building fall,
> And leave no memory of what it was.
> Repair me, with thy presence, Silvia:
> Thou gentle nymph, cherish thy forlorn swain.
>
> [V. iv. 7-12]

Despite feeling overwhelmed by misfortune, Valentine in the forest does not cease being. In his heart remains Silvia's essence (her Idea, if you will), which Valentine regards as his spirit. Unlike Petrarch, who depended upon Laura's absence for his imaginative life (poetically recreating her image in the stones and streams about him), Valentine possesses Silvia's Idea at all times. Never having in one sense lost his mistress, Valentine is never constrained to rediscover her essence. That he does actually rescue her from his outlaws and lustful Proteus is evidence again of the virtues of the green world, where wishes fall out as they are willed. His noble recovery appears to be a final instance of the reasonable man's victory over the illicit will, represented chiefly in this instance by Proteus.

Realizing that Valentine never spiritually loses Silvia helps clarify a notorious misinterpretation—his seeming gift of Silvia to Proteus as testimony of their renewed friendship. Satisfied with Proteus's repentance for his treachery, Valentine states:

> And that my love may appear plain and free,
> All that was mine in Silvia I give thee.
>
> [V. iv. 82-3]

Countless spectators, including Julia, have understood Valentine to mean that he would crudely hand over Silvia to Proteus, simply to cement a male friendship. Julia faints, revealing her identity, and generations of critics have shaken their heads at the swiftness of the action and its doubtful morality. Valentine's selfishness appears worse than Bertram's [in *All's Well That Ends Well*]. Valentine, however, is merely extending his infinite affection to his friend. The words—"All that was mine in Silvia"—do not refer to any rights of ownership, but to his love. Valentine is not an early draft of Cordelia, who gives the impression of being unable to love two persons deeply at the same time. Rather, at this moment, he is like Juliet, whose love, mysteriously increasing as it is given, is as boundless as the sea [*Romeo and Juliet*, II. ii. 133-35]. Valentine's love for Silvia does not abate one jot, even though he pours his bounty upon Proteus. If the case were otherwise, he would not so fiercely oppose Thurio when the Duke's favorite tries to claim Silvia. Valentine's manly challenge [V. iv. 126-31] indicates that he has no intention of forsaking his mistress. Shakespeare's addition of this incident involving Thurio to the lovers' reunions seems designed to assure the viewer that Valentine would never abandon Silvia.

Both Valentine and Proteus have naively endorsed the theoretical perfection of the sixteenth-century gentleman refined by travel and learning. . . . [By the end of the play] Proteus understands not only that the perfection that he formerly sought is a vain ideal but also that inconstancy insures self-defeat.While inconstancy may be Everyman's inheritance, it eventually must be transcended. Constancy in love, Proteus concludes, is more precious than a mistress's outward beauty:

> What is in Silvia's face but I may spy
> More fresh in Julia's, with a constant eye?
>
> [V. iv. 114-15]

Proteus finds that beauty lies in the constantly loving mind of the beholder. That is his discovery, which the complete loss of his self-image makes possible. (pp. 15-20)

The emotional stages in the Protestant ''paradigm of salvation'' are relevant here. It was the Reformation, Barbara Kiefer Lewalski asserts, that stressed ''the application of all scripture to the self, the discovery of scriptural paradigms . . . in one's own life'' [in her *Protestant Poetics and the Seventeenth-Century Religious Lyric*]. The affective phases of the Protestant paradigm consisted of a plunge into depravity and ignorance, a great spiritual crisis, conversion, heart's sorrow and repentance, and receptive faith. Proteus's passage through these stages is recognizable, even though several are given sketchy treatment. The New Testament paradox of self-loss and self-dis-

Act V. Scene iv. Silvia, Valentine, Proteus, and Julia disguised as Sebastian. By Thomas Stothard. The Department of Rare Books and Special Collections, The University of Michigan Library.

covery expressed for Shakespeare the significance of the stages within the Protestant paradigm of salvation. In *The Two Gentlemen*, one of the dramatist's favorite, provocative ideas thus provides a commentary upon the spiritual life as a whole.

That Valentine receives his mistress at last is partly due to the noble identity that he finds while lost in the green world. Because of Valentine's deeds in the forest, the Duke recognizes that he is Sir Valentine, a gentleman [V. iv. 139-47]. In his mind, Valentine is now worthy of Silvia. That Julia and Proteus find themselves, and each other, is mainly due to the paradox described in this essay, a paradox so central to Shakespeare's thought that we find it providing a conclusion for *The Tempest* many years later. The strange happenings on Prospero's isle demonstrate a marvelous truth for old Gonzalo:

> Was Milan thrust from Milan, that his issue
> Should become kings of Naples? O, rejoice
> Beyond a common joy, and set it down
> With gold on lasting pillars: in one voyage
> Did Claribel her husband find at Tunis,
> And Ferdinand, her brother, found a wife
> Where he himself was lost; Prospero, his dukedom
> In a poor isle; and all of us, ourselves,
> When no man was his own.
>
> [*The Tempest*, V. i. 205-13]

This sentiment, composed of different names, relationships, and places, could be uttered as an artistic ending for *The Two Gentlemen of Verona*. The paradox of salvation would be summed up, although the profundity and wonder of the later, greater play would be missing. (pp. 21-2)

> Maurice Hunt, '' 'The Two Gentlemen of Verona' and the Paradox of Salvation,'' in Rocky Mountain Review of Language and Literature, *Vol. 36, No. 1, 1982, pp. 5-22.*

CAMILLE WELLS SLIGHTS   (essay date 1983)

[*Disagreeing with previous criticism concerning the focus of* The Two Gentlemen of Verona, *Slights asserts that the play is* ''*a comic exploration of the nature and function of a gentleman*'' *rather than either a promotion of conventional views of friendship or love or an ironic parody of Elizabethan romantic ideals. She suggests that youthful efforts to become perfect gentlemen, such as those of Proteus and Valentine, can be positive when properly understood and adopted for the betterment of society, but they can also cause conflict, undermine social cohesion, and threaten an individual's sense of self. Indeed, she claims, Proteus's attempted rape of Silvia in the forest exemplifies* ''*the point at which the selfishness and shallow hypocrisy of courtly fashion is indistinguishable from uncivilized savagery.*'' *Once they recognize this shocking brutality as the epitome of courtly corruption, Slights argues, Proteus and Valentine return to society willingly, but with different attitudes and expectations, finding that communal happiness is achievable* ''*when people combine idealism with realistic understanding of human imperfection.*'']

Although commentary on Shakespeare's comedies contains little enthusiasm for *The Two Gentlemen of Verona*, in recent years critics have found a great deal to admire in the comic byplay provided by Speed and Launce, in the character of Julia—the first of the spirited heroines to don male clothing and take to the road in pursuit of love—and in the delicate beauty of some of the poetry. While some critics stress the satiric elements and others the celebratory, on the whole they agree that by combining mockery of artificial conventions with lyric evocation of romantic love, *The Two Gentlemen of Verona* prepared the way for the great romantic comedies to follow. Only the climactic final scene has presented an interpretative crux and provoked almost universal condemnation.

In the last scene, immediately after saving his beloved Silvia from being raped by his treacherous friend Sir Proteus, Valentine accepts without question Proteus' protestations of remorse and offers to withdraw his own suit in favour of Proteus', saying:

> And that my love may appear plain and free,
> All that was mine in Silvia I give thee.
>
> [V. iv. 82-3]

Critics who see the play primarily as a celebration of romantic love are understandably perplexed when the romantic hero suddenly offers the heroine to his rival. From this point of view, Shakespeare has violently contradicted the premises of his own romantic comedy, transforming his young lover into an insensitive brute. Another standard approach places the play in the Renaissance tradition that exalts friendship over love. From this perspective, the scene, far from undermining the basic conventions of its own fictional world, is "the germ or core of the play" [see excerpt above by M. C. Bradbrook, 1951] and Valentine's offer to give up Silvia to Proteus is not boorish but generous, the magnanimous sacrifice of love to friendship.

From either point of view, the exchange between Proteus and Valentine is an artistic failure. If *The Two Gentlemen of Verona* is a celebration of the experience of falling in love—the absurdities and joys of youthful passion—the hero's cheerful offer of his mistress to the man who has just tried to rape her is certainly a blunder. On the other hand, if Valentine is intended as a model of selfless generosity according to Renaissance conceptions of ideal friendship, he is a remarkably weak exemplar of the tradition. (pp. 13-14)

Without denying weaknesses and confusions in the early comedies, I think we should be suspicious of any critical position that convicts Shakespeare of inept bungling. It is not unthinking bardolatry to assume that even as an apprentice playwright Shakespeare would not construct a dramatic climax that signally fails to resolve and clarify any of the emotional or intellectual issues at stake. If the resolution of *The Two Gentlemen of Verona* does not illuminate the relationship of love to friendship, it is probable that interpretations emphasizing the triumph of one or the other are slightly askew. (p. 14)

The Two Gentlemen of Verona is less an evocation of what it feels like to fall in love or an analysis of the relative significance of love and friendship than a comic exploration of the nature and function of a gentleman. (p. 15)

The opening scene introduces us to the play's unifying theme—the question of the proper behavior for a young gentleman—and to its dominant verbal mode—the indirections of polite discourse. Valentine, excited by his imminent departure "To see the wonders of the world abroad" [I. i. 6], and Proteus, "over boots in love" [I. i. 25] with Julia, are engaged in conventional activities for two young gentlemen of Verona, or of London. They debate the merits of their respective choices—foreign travel and love—with the verbal wit of the young gallant.... Although the form of their speech, nipping and pricking at each other, implies opposition, Valentine and Proteus are actually in total agreement. For all his scorn at love's folly, Valentine does not seriously attempt to dissuade Proteus from

loving; he wishes his friend well in love, acknowledging that in time he too expects to fall in love:

> But since thou lov'st, love still, and thrive therein,
> Even as I would, when I to love begin.
>
> [I. i. 9-10]

And Proteus expects a friend's feelings of vicarious pleasure and protective concern from Valentine's travels:

> Wish me partaker in thy happiness,
> When thou dost meet good hap; and in thy danger
> (If ever danger do environ thee)
> Commend thy grievance to my holy prayers.
>
> [I. i. 14-17]

Privately he concedes Valentine's point: love has made his "wit with musing weak" [I. i. 69]. Ostensibly denoting rivalry, their wit actually expresses affectionate concord.

The word-play that signals the young men's pretensions to courtly elegance also indicates their youth and inexperience. Valentine and Proteus, like Romeo and Mercutio or Beatrice and Benedick [in *Much Ado about Nothing*], use puns and ripostes and ironies to impress others with their mental and verbal agility and to give themselves a sense of control over their world as well as to express their high-spirited exuberance and to exercise their developing powers for sheer enjoyment. Their linguistic ingenuity is not the effortless command of language that expresses unselfconscious ease and assurance in a social situation but rather the ostentatious display of wit that indicates vulnerability and insecurity. When Valentine and Proteus are together, like-minded friends who understand and respect each other, mocking repartee is subsumed within the context of frank and open talk, and their conversation has some claim to grace as well as to vitality. In other situations, they are less able to balance the indirections of rhetoric with straightforward communication and consequently appear noticeably more awkward.

In the dialogue between Proteus and Speed that follows Valentine's exit, for example, repeated quibbles on "ship," "sheep," and "mutton" grow tiresome. Since Proteus fails to get a clear report of the delivery of his message to Julia, while Speed does succeed in exacting his tip, Proteus emerges as loser in this contest of wits with his friend's servant. In his next appearance Proteus' language is even more completely at variance from literal truth, and his ingenuity is used to more disastrous—and comic—effect. In scene three, Proteus is exulting in a letter from Julia—"her oath for love" [I. iii. 47]—when his father interrupts to ask what he is reading. Proteus replies that his letter is from Valentine:

> he writes
> How happily he lives, how well-belov'd,
> How daily graced by the Emperor;
> Wishing me with him, partner of his fortune.
>
> [I. iii. 59]

Ironically, the lie designed to hide and protect his relationship with Julia precipitates his separation from her by reinforcing his father's decision that Proteus should join Valentine to complete his education. The adolescent's instinctive impulse to hide his love letter from his all-too-solicitous parent should not be interpreted as evidence of a basically duplicitous character, but the spectacle of Proteus blundering into a trap he has set for himself certainly provokes amusement at his expense.

The same type of youthful gaucherie is the source of humor in both the preceding and following scenes. In the preceding scene Julia indignantly scolds her maid Lucetta first for delivering Proteus' letter and then for interpreting her angry words literally instead of understanding them as conventional expressions of maidenly modesty:

> What fool is she, that knows I am a maid,
> And would not force the letter to my view!
> Since maids, in modesty, say "no" to that
> Which they would have the profferer construe "ay."
>
> [I. iii. 53-6]

After another round of verbal sparring with Lucetta, Julia histrionically tears the letter in pieces and finally is reduced to searching the ground for the precious fragments to piece together. Although subsequently Proteus' fickleness contrasts with Julia's constancy, in Act I it is their similarity that is most striking. Both feel the need to protect the privacy of their new, tender emotions, and both are comically inept in their attempts at dissimulation.

Valentine too finds himself out of his depth in the emotional subtleties and linguistic indirections of polite society. While Proteus and Julia betray their naiveté through their bungling attempts at dissimulation, Valentine displays his through his literal-minded incomprehension. When the scene shifts to Milan we discover that Valentine, the scoffer at love, has fallen in love with Silvia, the Duke's daughter, and is suffering all the paradoxical pain and ecstasy, exaltation and humiliation of the conventional courtly lover. He has even complied with Silvia's request that he write a letter for her to "one she loves" [II. i. 87]. Silvia then feigns anger at Valentine's reluctance to send her love to another and tells him to keep the lines of love he has written for himself:

> I will none of them: they are for you.
> I would have had them writ more movingly.
>
> [II. i. 127-28]

And, to Valentine's offer to repeat his effort:

> And when it's writ, for my sake read it over,
> And if it please you, so; if not, why, so.
>
> [II. i. 130-31]

Although Silvia's jest, as Speed says, is as "unseen, inscrutable, invisible, / As a nose on a man's face" [II. i. 135-36], Valentine fails to understand that she is teaching him to court her in earnest.

Silvia, in fact, is instructing Valentine in just the kind of courtly wit and elegant discourse the young gentlemen from Verona have come to Milan to learn. When Proteus' father and uncle worry that he is wasting his time at home, they canvas the alternatives open to a well-born young man:

> Some to the wars, to try their fortunes there;
> Some, to discover islands far away;
> Some, to the studious universities.
>
> [I. iii. 8-10]

Apparently on the basis of the paramount importance of acquiring the social graces, they decide to send Proteus to court where he will be able to

> practise tilts and tournaments,
> Hear sweet discourse, converse with noblemen,
> And be in eye of every exercise
> Worthy his youth and nobleness of birth.
>
> [I. iii. 30-3]

Several critics have condemned this courtly behavior as trivial or even corrupt, an unworthy goal that Valentine and Proteus must discard before real education can take place. J. A. Mazzeo's defense of Castiglione's *The Courtier* [in his *Renaissance and Revolution*] from similar criticism illuminates, I think, the attitude to courtly sophistication in Shakespeare's play. . . . [Mazzeo asserts that] Castiglione's emphasis on style and gesture, on jokes and games, is essential to his subject, "the creation of the self as a work of art through education," and to his concept of individual perfection as a balance and harmony of all important human capacities without excessive development or suppression of any. This attempt to delineate human perfection in an ideal courtier links *The Courtier* to the important cultural impulse in the Renaissance that produced so much utopian literature and so many books outlining ideal social forms of various kinds. In addition, the popularity of *The Courtier* and other courtesy books reflects concern with social cohesion as well as with individual development. The courtesy books all agree that public service is the gentleman's primary function and that the end of his education in the ways of society is his ability to advise his ruler effectively. The qualities of behavior that characterize the gentleman are those that bind people together in social harmony. (pp. 15-20)

In this context, we can see that when Antonio worries that his son Proteus "cannot be a perfect man" [I. iii. 20] without more experience in the world, he is not identifying himself as a Neoplatonic philosopher striving toward perfection, but neither is he betraying hopelessly superficial values. He endorses an educational program similar to Castiglione's when he chooses life at court as most suitable to his son's "youth and nobleness of birth." The play's early scenes have demonstrated clearly that young gentlemen need social tact, verbal dexterity, even some adeptness at polite dissimulation in order to get along harmoniously with servants, fathers, and women. In the first court scene, Silvia uses the letter as an "excellent device" [II. i. 139] to express her own desires and to help Valentine overcome his timidity without violating social decorum. By calling on the "clerkly" skills of her "gentle servant" [II. i. 108] she utilizes Valentine's gentlemanly accomplishments of the most artificial and conventional kind—courtly love conventions and literary skills—in order to liberate real feeling. The grace and wit with which she employs the artifices of sophisticated society in order to circumvent the obstacles erected by conventions of rank and sex role are no mean accomplishments.

While *The Two Gentlemen of Verona* presents courtly elegance as a positive value, it also shows how fragile and easily corrupted this ideal is. Superficially trivial manners are the necessary texture of a humane society that encourages people to develop their full human potential and that fosters a variety of subtle feelings and relationships among people, yet these same manners may degenerate into hypocrisy or cynical intrigue. The courtly ideal is a precarious balance of self-enhancement and social responsibility. The aristocratic code blends strict devotion to truth (so that proverbially a gentleman's word is his bond) with an elegant grace of manner that involves artifice and pretense, the art of concealing art. . . . *Sprezzatura,* the graceful nonchalance that Castiglione recommends for the ideal courtier, may degenerate into the disdain and contempt that, according to Mazzeo, are "vaguely present" in the concept. Gentlemanly dignity may degenerate into cold arrogance or ostentatious self-display, and playful wit into either irresponsible frivolity or malicious deceit.

The plot of *The Two Gentlemen of Verona* unfolds out of Valentine's and Proteus' acquisition of courtly values and style.

Not surprisingly, superficial manners prove to be more easily learned than the ability to use them to develop well-rounded individuality and social harmony. Valentine, who initially cannot distinguish between what Silvia says and what she means, readily picks up the art of courtly circuitousness and dissimulation. The next time he appears he courts Silvia indirectly by bandying insults with another suitor. His language in this scene demonstrates both the social utility and the danger of courtly linguistic conventions. By rejecting Speed's advice that his hated rival Sir Thurio should be "knocked" [II. iv. 7] and instead expressing his hostility in what Silvia commends as "A fine volley of words" [II. iv. 33], Valentine acts out sexual rivalry with wit and gaiety rather than brutality. But when he adopts the language of courtly love without Silvia's ironic detachment from it, his perceptions are blunted rather than refined by the conventions. By acknowledging that "Love's a mighty lord" [II. iv. 136] and by confessing the sorrow and joy of love's service, Valentine joins in civilized humanity's transformation of sexual appetite into love. But he betrays self-deceit and insensitivity when he insists that Proteus acknowledge Silvia as "divine," not earthly, and when he refers to Julia, Proteus' beloved, with gratuitous contempt:

> She shall be dignified with this high honour,
> To bear my lady's train.
>
> [II. iv. 158-59]

The contradictory tensions inherent in the sixteenth-century idea of gentlemanly behavior become even more evident in Valentine's scheme to elope with Silvia. By planning to release Silvia from the tower where her father locks her and from marriage to the wealthy but doltish Sir Thurio, Valentine is rescuing a damsel in distress in the best chivalric tradition and insisting on the dignity and delicacy of love and marriage. Yet he is also violating the Duke's parental right and abusing his hospitality. When Valentine first confides his plan to Proteus, considerations of the first sort combine with the conventional comic endorsement of youth and love against age and law to direct audience sympathy toward the lovers. The irresponsibility of the plot comes more forcibly to mind later when the Duke, under the guise of seeking love-advice himself, tricks Valentine into revealing his plan. In this scene, Valentine hypocritically praises Thurio as a match for Silvia, cynically explains that women reject men's advances only in order to egg them on and that any woman can be won with gifts and flattery, and proposes a rope ladder to gain access to a woman whose friends have promised her to someone else. The Duke's reply,

> Now, as thou art a gentleman of blood,
> Advise me where I may have such a ladder,
>
> [III. i. 121-22]

reminds us that Valentine is fulfilling his gentleman's duty to advise and serve his ruler in a particularly tawdry way. In this context, we watch with amusement rather than anxiety as the Duke outwits Valentine, discovering the ladder and the incriminating letter to Silvia hidden under his cloak.

In Valentine, then, we can discern the danger of aristocratic self-assurance becoming pride and of delicacy and subtlety becoming duplicity. Proteus perverts the gentlemanly ideal even more radically. As we have seen, his family encourages him to strive to perfect himself. Valentine, who gracefully apologizes for his own failure to achieve "angel-like perfection" [II. iv. 66], praises his friend as a model gentleman:

> He is complete in feature and in mind,
> With all good grace to grace a gentleman.
>
> [II. iv. 73-4]

When Proteus joins Valentine at the court of Milan, this exemplar of the art of self-cultivation becomes the apologist for sheer selfishness. No sooner does he learn of Valentine's love than he determines to win Silvia himself, consoling himself for the loss of Valentine's friendship with the thought, "I to myself am dearer than a friend" [II. vi. 23], and justifying the plot he immediately formulates to betray Valentine to the Duke and subsequently to slander him to Silvia:

> I cannot now prove constant to myself,
> Without some treachery us'd to Valentine.
>
> [II. vi. 31-2]

While Valentine becomes guilty of disdain and deceit, it remains for Proteus to stoop to the even more contemptible practice of detraction and slander. His attempts at self-justification are so absurdly sophistical, however, and his machinations to win Silvia so obviously self-defeating that the audience is again not so much morally outraged by his perfidy as amused by the mess he is getting himself into.

In a sense, aristocratic values seem to contain the seeds of their own destruction. In the process of developing the qualities of a gentleman both Valentine and Proteus lose their status as gentlemen: the Duke denounces Valentine for aspiring to his daughter as a "base intruder, overweening slave" [III. i. 157] and Proteus, even as he undertakes to destroy Silvia's love for Valentine by accusing him of "falsehood, cowardice, and poor descent" [III. ii. 32] admits that slandering his friend is "an ill office for a gentleman" [III. ii. 40]. This breakdown of civilized manners extends even to Launce's dog Crab, who "thrusts . . . himself into the company of three or four gentleman-like dogs, under the Duke's table" and there disgraces himself [IV. iv. 16-18].

The elegant, courtly society that draws all the young people to it through the first two acts begins, in Act III, to self-destruct, literally and physically as well as figuratively and spiritually. Valentine's introduction to courtly love and dissimulation culminates in his banishment from court. His exile precipitates Silvia's flight, which in turn causes the Duke, Proteus, and Thurio to pursue her, while Julia, disguised as a page boy, follows Proteus. By the end of Act IV, all the major characters have abandoned the court of Milan with its dangers and frustrations and have fled to the lawless and dangerous forest.

This contrary motion toward and away from the court suggests that the very qualities that bind people together in civilized society also threaten to fragment and dissolve those bonds. The aristocratic insistence on excellence as a standard and on perfection as a goal encourages individual fulfillment in a complex and humane society, but it is also inherently competitive. This paradox underlies the pattern of imitative desire producing increasing violence that René Girard discerns in Shakespeare's portrayal of love [in *Textual Strategies: Perspectives in Post-Structuralist Criticism*]. (pp. 20-3)

As Girard suggests . . . , throughout the canon Shakespeare dramatizes the conflicts arising from [a] kind of romantic passion that is not a spontaneous response to a desirable and desired other but primarily an imitation of a model. So, in *The Two Gentlemen of Verona* when Valentine insists that Silvia is the ideal woman "whose worth makes other worthies nothing" [II. iv. 167], he teaches Proteus to forsake Julia and make Silvia the object of his desire. Even Proteus admits that "Valentinus' praise" has as much to do with his passion as his own perception of Silvia's perfections [II. iv. 196-97]. And we realize that for him Silvia *"excels each mortal thing"* [IV. ii.

51] primarily *because "all our swains commend her"* [IV. ii. 40]. Proteus' sudden desire for Silvia destroys the social group through betrayal and banishment and also undermines his sense of his own identity. As Girard explains, a metaphysical, mimetic passion is necessarily self-destructive: it is "destructive not only because of its sterile rivalries but because it dissolves reality: it tends to the abstract, the merely representational".... It feeds on rejection and failure: "The impossible is always preferred to the possible, the unreal to the real, the hostile and unwilling to the willing and available".... Although the aspiration to an erotic ideal is basically self-elevating, the worship of an unattainable idol results in the lover's self-abasement expressed in animal images: "Far from raising himself to the state of the superman, a god, as he seeks to do, the subject of mimetic desire sinks to the level of animality. The animal images are the price the self has to pay for its idolatrous worship of otherness".... (pp. 24-5)

Thus Proteus complains that

> spaniel-like, the more she spurns my love,
> The more it grows, and fawneth on her still.
>
> [IV. ii. 14-15]

He begs for a picture of Silvia, announcing that since he cannot possess "the substance of [her] perfect self,"

> I am but a shadow;
> And to your shadow will I make true love.
>
> [IV. ii. 124-25]

And Silvia agrees that it is entirely appropriate for false Proteus "To worship shadows, and adore false shapes" [IV. ii. 130].

Sending Valentine and Proteus to court to learn to act like perfect gentlemen by observing the best models ironically results in loss of self-respect and destruction of social cohesion, but the play also makes clear that refusal to emulate models of decorum can have equally disastrous consequences, as Launce complains to Crab:

> I remember the trick you served me, when I took my leave of Madam Silvia: did not I bid thee still mark me, and do as I do? When didst thou see me heave up my leg, and make water against a gentlewoman's farthingale? Didst thou ever see me do such a trick?
>
> [IV. iv. 34-9]

The genteel lovers experience the disadvantages of life without the restraints of civilization when they flee from court to the lawless wilderness. By escaping from the capricious dangers of courtly hypocrisy and ducal tyranny, they become vulnerable to physical brutality, threatened with robbery, murder, and rape. In the woods outside Milan they learn the worth and the limitations of their conception of gentility.

In this first example in Shakespearean comedy of a rural retreat where courtly lovers overcome their difficulties and adjust their values before returning to civilization, the sylvan setting is far from being a pastoral world of innocence and peace. The woods are inhabited by society's outcasts, outlaws banished for murder and "such like petty crimes" [IV. i. 50], who live by terrorizing and robbing hapless travelers. In this setting, Proteus' frustrations erupt in violence. When Silvia continues to reject him and to condemn him after he rescues her from the outlaws, he tries to rape her.

But if the woods are a setting for violence and uncontrolled passion, they do not represent a state of nature free from social

distinctions and hierarchy. The outlaws are absurdly proud that some of them are gentlemen by birth and feel acutely the need for a leader to command them. Rather than the possibility of an egalitarian society they embody an alternate and older idea of the gentleman, that is, the aristocrat as armed warrior. Fiercely loyal to their own band, sensitive to slights on their honor, they recognize no authority or social obligation beyond the immediate group. Their recognition of Valentine as their natural leader on the basis of his general deportment and linguistic ability is Shakespeare's comic rendition of actual historical process. The chivalric armed warrior, though romantically appealing, must inevitably make way for the educated, accomplished courtier. Given the choice of joining the outlaws as their leader or of being killed for insulting them with his refusal, Valentine accepts an offer he cannot very well refuse, but he soon understands the undesirability of living with men who "make their wills their law" [V. iv. 14]. He finds the "unfrequented woods" a better place to lament his loss of Silvia than "flourishing peopled towns" [V. iv. 2-3], but he knows that total isolation is not possible. He must perforce relate to other people in some kind of social structure, if not as a lawful subject in a civilized community, then as a member of a faction of outlaws whose "uncivil outrages" [V. iv. 17] he can restrain only with difficulty.

In this situation, when Valentine witnesses Proteus' solicitation and attack on Silvia, his response reflects his developed understanding of the individual's relation to society as well as his personal hurt:

> Ruffian! Let go that rude uncivil touch,
> Thou friend of an ill fashion.
> Thou common friend, that's without faith or love,
> For such is a friend now.
>
> [V. iv. 60-3]

Proteus' treachery epitomizes the point at which the selfishness and shallow hypocrisy of courtly fashion is indistinguishable from uncivilized savagery, a paradox expressed in the ambiguous epithet "common": by adopting the debased manners of the fashionable world, Proteus forfeits his claim to being a true gentleman. Betrayal by his most trusted friend forces Valentine to see feelingly that total disillusionment both with the manners of society and with their rejection, instead of allowing him a superior position of intellectual detachment, leads to the terrifying isolation of complete alienation:

> Who should be trusted now, when one's right hand
> Is perjured to the bosom? Proteus,
> I am sorry I must never trust thee more,
> But count the world a stranger for thy sake.
>
> [V. iv. 67-70]

Shocked into realizing what he has become, Proteus repents. Valentine accepts his apology both because forgiveness is at once naturally human and imitative of divinity and because for him the alternative to trusting Proteus is to trust no one. Valentine and Proteus have glimpsed a world of sheer brutality and total cynicism, and together they draw back from the abyss. Their reconciliation fills personal emotional needs and indicates their renewed acceptance of their place in civilized society where men are bound together by mutual trust as well as by civil authority. Valentine's speech accepting Proteus' repentance marks his return to a world where a gentleman's word is his bond but where gentlemen characteristically communicate through indirection. It modulates from the plain statement of the terms of their relationship:

> Then I am paid;
> And once again I do receive thee honest,
> [V. iv. 77-8]

to the elegant indirection of offering to give up Silvia. Because he accepts Proteus as honestly repentant, he has faith that his friend will not renew his pursuit of Silvia. His offer is a courteous gesture that will give Proteus a chance to be his best self.

At this point Shakespeare averts the threatened bathos of repeated, elaborate gestures of repentance and forgiveness and reestablishes the prevailing comic tone by having Valentine's attempt at sophisticated indirection miscarry once again. Although his gesture demonstrates love and trust in Proteus with considerable tact and subtlety, he has no way of considering its effect on the disguised Julia. For her it is the last straw: she faints, revives, and immediately reveals her identity and her claim to Proteus' love and fidelity. Indeed, the happy ending is possible not only because Valentine and Proteus have gained a more complex understanding of themselves and their relation to other people, but because Julia and Sylvia have always had a more balanced view. Both women defy convention and abandon society's protection in pursuit of love, but they struggle to preserve whatever decorum is possible. They do not choose love by others' eyes. Silvia is impervious to slander against Valentine and to praise of Proteus and Thurio. Julia justly resents Proteus' eulogizing of Silvia without learning to despise herself. Because they are confident of their own worth and their own judgment of the men they love, without claiming perfection for either, they can meet the situation that pushes them toward rivalry and conflict with mutual sympathy.

The reestablishment of the bonds of civilization begun with the reconciliation of the friends and lovers is completed by the entry of the Duke and by Valentine's deference to him. The Duke confirms the "new state" [V. iv. 144] of things, announcing, "Sir Valentine, / Thou art a gentleman, and well deriv'd" [V. iv. 145-46] and blessing his union with Silvia.

The play has not, however, merely come full circle back to a celebration of courtliness and conventionality. If the outlaws and Proteus have discredited the image of the noble brigand, the gentleman simply as courtier and courtly lover has also proved inadequate. Silvia has trusted to the protection of Sir Eglamour on the grounds that he is a gentleman [IV. iii. 11-13] and suffered for her folly when he is unable to save her from the outlaws. Thurio, the Duke's choice for son-in-law, proves to be a coward. Valentine no longer relies on indirection and subterfuge to win Silvia but directly warns off Thurio with violent threats. He wins the Duke's favor and reappraisal of his social rank, not by his obedience, but by his high spirit. And for the first time Valentine explicitly mentions serving the state as the gentleman's natural vocation, urging the Duke to pardon the outlaws for they are "fit for great employment" [V. iv. 157]. Indeed, perhaps the secret of Valentine's success is his flexibility—witty and courtly with Silvia, respectful to the Duke, stern but helpful to the outlaws, fierce and violent with Thurio, contemptuous and then trustful of Proteus.

The Two Gentlemen of Verona ridicules the inadequacies of the elegant courtly lover, reckless adventurer, and sycophantic courtier, but the ideas of the gentleman current in the sixteenth century—as polished courtier, scholar, soldier, and statesman—all contribute to the unattainable ideal it suggests. By the end of the play, we feel that Valentine has proved himself

a gentleman through an elusive combination of courtliness, high-spirited courage, social responsibility, and faithful love and friendship. If the play hints darkly that pursuit of an external standard of perfection and lawless self-will both destroy social cohesion and civilized life, it also celebrates the communal happiness possible when people combine idealism with realistic understanding of human imperfection and join self-cultivation and self-assertion with respect for other people. (pp. 25-9)

> *Camille Wells Slights, "'The Two Gentlemen of Verona' and the Courtesy Book Tradition," in* Shakespeare Studies: An Annual Gathering of Research, Criticism, and Reviews, *Vol. 16, 1983, pp. 13-31.*

ADDITIONAL BIBLIOGRAPHY

Atkinson, Dorothy F. "The Source of *Two Gentlemen of Verona.*" *Studies in Philology* XLI, No. 2 (April 1944): 223-34.
  Details the structural and contextual parallels between *The Two Gentlemen of Verona* and Jacques d'Yver's story of Claribel and Floradine as translated by Henry Wotton in his *Cupids Cautels* (1578). Atkinson asserts that d'Yver's tale of friendship and love, not Montemayor's *Diana Enamorada*, was Shakespeare's principal source for *The Two Gentlemen of Verona.*

Bailey, John. "The Earlier Plays." In his *Shakespeare,* pp. 66-138. London: Longmans, Green and Co., 1929.
  Briefly discusses the poetic beauty of *The Two Gentlemen of Verona* as well as its "unattractive absurdities." Bailey suggests that we "cling to the hope" that the "horror of ugliness" manifest in Act V, Scene iv is not Shakespeare's, but the interpolation of a later writer.

Baker, George Pierce. "Early Experimentation in Plotting and Adaptation." In his *The Development of Shakespeare as a Dramatist,* pp. 100-41. New York: The Macmillan Company, 1920.
  Cites as inefficient Shakespeare's employment of ten whole scenes to establish the characters' relationships in *The Two Gentlemen of Verona.* Baker asserts that despite its commendable use of characterization, language, and suspense, the play remains a poorly proportioned and developed story with an unsatisfactory resolution.

Baldwin, T. W. "*Two Gentlemen of Verona*" and "Structural and Chronological Relations between *Two Gentlemen of Verona* and *Romeo and Juliet.*" In his *Shakspere's Five-Act Structure,* pp. 719-41, 749-75. Urbana: The University of Illinois Press, 1947.
  Outlines, in the first essay cited, Shakespeare's successful integration of the love-friendship narrative and the expository machinery of Terence's five-act formula in *The Two Gentlemen of Verona,* and establishes the chronology of Shakespeare's early plays based on their adherence to this structural pattern as well as to their own individual sources. Baldwin's second essay notes several similar passages in *Romeo and Juliet* and *The Two Gentlemen of Verona,* which, the critic asserts, are derived from Brooke's *Romeus and Juliet* and Shakespeare's own *Lucrece.* Baldwin employs these borrowings to establish *Romeo and Juliet's* composition date as closely succeeding that of *The Two Gentlemen of Verona.*

Barton, Anne. Introduction to *The Two Gentlemen of Verona,* by William Shakespeare. In *The Riverside Shakespeare,* edited by G. Blakemore Evans, pp. 143-46. Boston: Houghton Mifflin Co., 1974.
  Contains an overview of the date, text, and sources of *The Two Gentlemen of Verona.* Barton considers Valentine's gift of Silvia to Proteus Shakespeare's "nervous recourse to tradition" which completely negates the previous development of the comedy away from false conventions and toward a supreme love respectful of friendship.

Beckerman, Bernard. "Shakespeare's Dramaturgy and Binary Form." *Theatre Journal* 33, No. 1 (March 1981): 5-17.

Examines the dramatic function of the duet in *The Two Gentlemen of Verona*, defining the term by the number of characters conversing on stage rather than the total number of people present, and including soliloquys in this group as duets between a single player and the audience. Beckerman contends that this structure of functional duets in the comedy is effective because "presentational intensity depends on concentrated interchange," adding that the two contrasting energies on stage enhance audience involvement and interest.

Bennett, Kenneth C. "Stage Action and the Interpretation of *The Two Gentlemen of Verona*." *Shakespeare Jahrbuch* 116 (1980): 93-100.

Discusses both the romantic and the parodic elements in *The Two Gentlemen of Verona*, concluding that in Launce Shakespeare establishes "a solid ground of reality" upon which the contrasting modes of the drama are based and against which the romantic characters themselves may be judged. Bennett asserts that in the final scene there is no further need for the irony of Launce and Speed, for the two "sensible young women" bring their lovers "to their right minds," making obvious the distinction between what is real and what is artificial.

Bonazza, Blaze Odell. "*The Two Gentlemen of Verona*." In his *Shakespeare's Comedies: A Structural Analysis*, pp. 76-104. The Hague, The Netherlands: Mouton & Co., 1966.

Analysis of *The Two Gentlemen of Verona* based on Bonazza's outline of Shakespeare's developing A-B-C-D comic structure, dispraising its utilization of the four parts: the enveloping action, the "romantic love story," the "parodying subplot," and the "atmosphere providing plot" of internal conflict. Bonazza then examines Shakespeare's comic treatment of friendship, love, and matchmaking, reflected in the play's structure, describing the three major movements and their resulting intrigues and ironic reversals; he concludes that although this construction of interlocking actions provides "a neat and balanced pattern," it "fails abysmally" in the resolution of the drama.

Bullough, Geoffrey, ed. "*The Two Gentlemen of Verona*." In his *Narrative and Dramatic Sources of Shakespeare, Vol. I: Early Comedies, Poems, Romeo and Juliet*, pp. 203-68. London: Routledge and Kegan Paul, 1957.

Discusses Shakespeare's stylistic debt to John Lyly as well as his adaptation of the common friendship-love theme found in such sources as Montemayor's *Diana* and Sir Thomas Elyot's *The Governour*, and in several analogues, including Flamino Scala's *Flavio Tradito* and Sir Philip Sidney's *The Countess of Pembroke's Arcadia*, all of which are partially reprinted in this volume.

Campbell, Oscar James. "The Clown." In his *Shakespeare's Satire*, pp. 3-23. New York: Gordian Press, 1971.

Traces in numerous plays the role of Shakespeare's clowns, in particular those portrayed by Will Kemp, and cites Launce of *The Two Gentlemen of Verona* as the first "tiny seed of satire" whose comic techniques would be developed in later dramas.

Chambers, E. K. "Plays of the First Folio: *The Two Gentlemen of Verona*." In his *William Shakespeare: A Study of Facts and Problems*, pp. 329-31. Oxford: At the Clarendon Press, 1930.

Summarizes several critical opinions of *The Two Gentlemen of Verona* and lists possible sources and analogues of the play.

Cunningham, J. V. "'Essence' and the *Phoenix and Turtle*." *ELH: A Journal of English Literary History* 19, No. 4 (December 1952): 265-76.

Compares the theme of courtly love in Shakespeare's *Phoenix and Turtle* with passages from *The Two Gentlemen of Verona*, concluding that the concept of lovers with one "essence" comes from the Trinity and that only this kind of love, based on "true Reason," can triumph in a world of ideas.

Dickey, Franklin M. "The Comical Tragedy of *Romeo and Juliet*." In his *Not Wisely but Too Well: Shakespeare's Love Tragedies*, pp. 63-88. San Marino, Calif.: The Huntington Library, 1966.

Outlines briefly several parallels between *The Two Gentlemen of Verona* and *Romeo and Juliet*, including Speed and Mercutio's critical commentaries, the "wonderfully inflated rhetoric," and the tragedy inherent in "doting love." Dickey claims that tragedy is averted in the comedy by the repentance and generosity of the characters.

Evans, B. Ifor. "From Words to Action and from Words to People: *The Comedy of Errors; The Two Gentlemen of Verona; The Taming of the Shrew*." In his *The Language of Shakespeare's Plays*, pp. 17-30. London: Methuen & Co., 1952.

Notes the association of holiness and love in *The Two Gentlemen of Verona* within a general discussion of the movement from language to action in Shakespeare's early plays.

Frye, Northrop. "The Argument of Comedy." In *English Institute Essays 1948*, edited by D. A. Robertson, Jr., pp. 58-73. New York: Columbia University Press, 1949.

Discusses the cathartic "ritual of death and revival" in Shakespeare's tragedies and dramas of the green world, including *The Two Gentlemen of Verona*. Frye suggests that the combination of both the "other" world and the "normal" world in Shakespeare's comedies results in a "detachment of the spirit born of this reciprocal reflection of two illusory realities."

Gabler, Hans Walter. "Experiment and Parody in Shakespeare's Early Plays." *Studia Neophilologica* XLVI, No. 1 (1974): 159-71.

Assesses the significance of Shakespeare's early dramatic parodies, including Launce's parody of romantic love in *The Two Gentlemen of Verona*, to the development of the dramatist's structure and language. Gabler asserts that in Shakespeare's more complex plays the "styles and modes of expression which were originally adopted in the playful mood of parody become submerged as facets of his own art."

Guinn, John A. "The Letter Device in the First Act of *The Two Gentlemen of Verona*." *Studies in English 1940*, No. 4026 (July 8, 1940): 72-81.

Contends that Aeneas Sylvius Piccolomini's *De Duobus Amantibus* is the source for the letter scene in Act I of *The Two Gentlemen of Verona*, since both contain the unusual episode of the heroine tearing the love letter, then remorsefully kissing the pieces. Guinn further supports *Amantibus* as the source of this episode because, according to the critic, it was more readily accessible to Shakespeare than Montemayor's *Diana*.

Hamilton, A. C. "The Early Comedies: *The Two Gentlemen of Verona*." In his *The Early Shakespeare*, pp. 109-27. San Marino, Calif.: The Huntington Library, 1976.

Discusses several critical issues in *The Two Gentlemen of Verona*, including the conflict of friendship and love and the play's parody of romantic conventions "even while it upholds them." Comparing supreme friendship in Elyot's *Titus and Gisippus* to Shakespeare's treatment of the theme, Hamilton asserts that "love will triumph" in the conclusion of the latter work once Proteus and Valentine fulfill the requirements of both friendship and love.

Harrison, T. P., Jr. "Concerning *Two Gentlemen of Verona* and Montemayor's *Diana*." *Modern Language Notes* XLI, No. 4 (April 1926): 251-52.

Disputes Oscar James Campbell's claim that *The Two Gentlemen of Verona* is based on the lost adaptation of Montemayor's *Diana* called *Felix and Philomena* (see excerpt above, 1925), asserting that the *Diana* itself was available to Shakespeare both in the original Spanish and in translation, and that this text was superior to any other version. Harrison also notes several important parallels of incident that he contends prove the *Diana* to be the playwright's main source.

——. "Shakespeare and Montemayor's *Diana*." *University of Texas Bulletin*, No. 2648 (December 22, 1926): 72-120.

Studies in detail the relationship of Montemayor's *Diana* to Shakespeare's *The Two Gentlemen of Verona, A Midsummer Night's Dream*, and *Twelfth Night*, noting not only the playwright's indebtedness to Montemayor's plot, but his developing attitude towards the pastoral genre as well.

Hunter, G. K. "Lyly and Shakespeare." In his *John Lyly: The Humanist as Courtier*, pp. 298-349. Cambridge, Mass.: Harvard University Press, 1962.

Demonstrates Shakespeare's adaptations of Lylian motifs to explore and develop the emotions of his characters and to enlist the sympathies of his audience. Hunter notes, however, that in such plays as *The Two Gentlemen of Verona* the resulting conflict of in-depth characterization with the simple structural debate of love and honour, or of villain and hero, creates a mixture that is "unbalanced from either point of view."

Jaarsma, Richard J. "The 'Lear Complex' in *The Two Gentlemen of Verona*." *Literature and Psychology* XXII, No. 4 (1972): 199-202.

Evidences King Lear's unconscious sexual desire for his daughter Cordelia and parallels this situation with the desire of the Duke of Milan and his daugher Silvia in *The Two Gentlemen of Verona*. Jaarsma draws several situational and verbal parallels between the two father-daughter relationships.

Kenny, Thomas, "The Plays of Shakespeare: *The Two Gentlemen of Verona*." In his *The Life and Genius of Shakespeare*, pp. 163-65. London: Longman, Green, Longman, Roberts, and Green, 1864.

Discerns little "variety of incident" or "breadth of character" in *The Two Gentlemen of Verona*, but considers it one of the "most lightly and gracefully executed" of Shakespeare's early plays because of its natural youthful simplicity.

Leech, Clifford. Introduction to *The Two Gentlemen of Verona*, by William Shakespeare, edited by Clifford Leech, pp. xiii-lxxv. The Arden Edition of the Works of William Shakespeare, edited by Harold F. Brooks and Harold Jenkins. London: Methuen & Co., 1969.

Contains detailed information on the text, date, sources, and stage history of the play, as well as a brief summary of its critical history. Leech praises Shakespeare's ability to portray several points of view in *The Two Gentlemen of Verona*, encouraging his audience to impartially judge each character and relationship, and to form an "interpretation of Shakespeare's writing as a whole."

Mares, F. H. "Viola and Other Transvestist Heroines in Shakespeare's Comedies." In *Stratford Papers: 1965-67*, edited by B. A. W. Jackson, pp. 96-109. Ontario, Canada: McMaster University Press, 1969.

Compares Shakespeare's use of the disguise convention in several of the playwright's comedies, contending that in *The Two Gentlemen of Verona* Julia's disguise "provides good scenes but is not integral to the plot . . . , nor essential to the statement of the theme," as the motif would be in several later comedies.

Morse, Ruth. "*Two Gentlemen* and the Cult of Friendship." *Neuphilologische Mitteilungen* LXXXIV, No. 2 (1983): 214-24.

Confronts the issues of identity and latent homosexuality in *The Two Gentlemen of Verona*, stating that "it is conceivable that [Proteus] might transfer his love for Valentine to a passion for Valentine's beloved," thereby losing his own identity to the object of another man's desire. Morse claims that it is only after the repugnant nature of Proteus's "possessive passion" is revealed that the "healing balm" of love can resolve the problems of the youthful heroes.

Munro, John. Introduction to *The Two Gentlemen of Verona*, by William Shakespeare, edited by John Munro. In his *The London Shakespeare, Vol. I: The Comedies*, pp. 263-66. New York: Simon and Schuster, 1957.

Discusses the Folio text and the date of *The Two Gentlemen of Verona*, as well as certain plot elements and their sources, including the love triangle, the friendship theme, the outlaws, and the play's similarities to *Romeo and Juliet*.

Parks, George B. "The Development of *The Two Gentlemen of Verona*." *The Huntington Library Bulletin*, No. 11 (April 1937): 1-11.

Explores several theories regarding the contradictions of place in *The Two Gentlemen of Verona* and concludes that the original play, whose action took place in the city of Verona only, was altered to accommodate the female-page story, thus necessitating

a second location. Parks describes Shakespeare's possible construction of the drama before and after the addition of the five episodes featuring the disguised Julia, citing metrical tests to prove that these travel scenes exhibit Shakespeare's later style; he concedes, however, that his theory does not fully explain the unlikely travel routes and the added problem of the sea voyage between the two landlocked cities of Verona and Milan.

Ridley, M. R. "Commentary on the Plays: *The Two Gentlemen of Verona*." In his *Shakespeare's Plays*, pp. 61-4. New York: E. P. Dutton & Co., 1938.

Regards *The Two Gentlemen of Verona* as a failure compared to the plays that immediately precede and follow it in Shakespeare's canon. Ridley especially condemns the artificiality of the characterization, but excludes Launce from this charge, stating that he "does his best to redeem the play from complete mediocrity and artificiality."

Righter, Anne. "Shakespeare's Early Comedies: Shadows, Dreams and Plays." In her *Shakespeare and the Idea of the Play*, pp. 100-12. London: Chatto & Windus, 1962.

Examines the term "counterfeit" as it is used in *The Two Gentlemen of Verona* to express both the disguise motif and Proteus's duplicity and betrayal. Righter also discusses the realms of "illusion and reality" in the play, citing Sebastian's role as the betrayed Ariadne as the ultimate overlapping of actualities, for the sincerity of "the tears wrung from Julia by the stage presentation of a lover's perfidy, in fact represents reality."

Rossky, William. "*The Two Gentlemen of Verona* as Burlesque." *English Literary Renaissance* 12, No. 2 (Spring 1982): 210-19.

Counters the notion that *The Two Gentlemen of Verona* is a "serious dramatization of conventional Renaissance thought" by citing contrary evidence from Shakespeare's sources and other contemporary works. Rossky argues that the burlesquing of the friendship tradition was not uncommon in Shakespeare's time and was indeed the playwright's intention, given the extremely romantic material of this play.

Sider, John W. "The Serious Elements of Shakespeare's Comedies." *Shakespeare Quarterly* XXIV, No. 1 (Winter 1973): 1-11.

Traces the interaction of serious and comic elements throughout Shakespeare's comedies and notes in particular the combination of "the ridiculous and the sentimental" in *The Two Gentlemen of Verona*, best evidenced in Launce's parody of the main characters' romance. Sider concludes, however, that the later comedies do far more with the "emotional potential of grave incidents."

Small, Samuel Asa. "The Ending of *The Two Gentlemen of Verona*." *PMLA* 48, No. 3 (September 1933): 767-76.

Argues that the ending of *The Two Gentlemen of Verona* does not conform to the resolution of friendship and love as prescribed by most sixteenth-century friendship dramas, but contrasts the two values. Small adds that Proteus is consistently false to both precepts and that Valentine's neglect of Silvia is not mere fidelity to friendship, but a sign of his inferior romantic character.

Thomas, Paul R. "The Marriage of True Minds—Ideal Friendship in *Two Gentlemen of Verona*." *Iowa State Journal of Research* 57, No. 2 (November 1982): 187-92.

Parallels the dominance of friendship over love in several early tales of camaraderie, such as Elyot's *Titus and Gisippus*, with Shakespeare's *The Two Gentlemen of Verona*. Thomas regards Silvia as "the impediment preventing the marriage of the minds of Proteus and Valentine" and attributes her fortuitous union with Valentine to Shakespeare's "merciful" nature.

Turner, Robert Y. "Neo-classical Stipulations" and "Comic Characterization." In his *Shakespeare's Apprenticeship*, pp. 146-73, 174-200. Chicago: The University of Chicago Press, 1974.

Asserts in two chapters of his book that *The Two Gentlemen of Verona* is more than a mere farce because its parodic episodes evoke a laughter ''of kinship'' or ''acceptance'' rather than of ''scorn.'' Turner states that in this comedy the audience is meant to understand that ''the standards of rationality and control are ideals which human nature cannot quite fulfill.''

Van Doren, Mark. ''*The Two Gentlemen of Verona.*'' In his *Shakespeare*, pp. 53-7. New York: Henry Holt and Co., 1939.

Briefly discusses *The Two Gentlemen of Verona* as Shakespeare's early and imperfect attempt to weld ''wit and emotion.'' Van Doren identifies several passages of poetic beauty, but criticizes the abundance of ''dry and curiously spiritless'' wit, which, he asserts, adds no ''gaiety'' to any character but Launce.

Vyvyan, John. ''An Introduction to the Heroine as the Heavenly Venus.'' In his *Shakespeare and Platonic Beauty,* pp. 62-76. New York: Barnes & Noble, 1961.

Links the constancy of Valentine and Julia to ''the theme of love as self-sacrifice, which because it is willing to carry its cross, becomes a redemptive power.'' Vyvyan further asserts that together these two characters lead Proteus to experience a revelation of ''true Beauty,'' concluding that a ''parallel with Christ's love'' is Shakespeare's specific intention in this play.

Wales, Julia Grace. ''Shakespeare's Use of English and Foreign Elements in the Setting of *The Two Gentlemen of Verona.*'' *Transactions of the Wisconsin Academy of Sciences, Arts & Letters* XXVII (1932): 85-125.

Discusses the dramatic significance of the English and Italian elements in the setting of *The Two Gentlemen of Verona* and relates them to the contrasts of near and far, particular and universal, and actual and imaginary also evident in the play. These associations, combined with a detailed romantic atmosphere, Wales contends, ''deepen the dramatic and poetic appeal of the whole [play].''

Wilson, John Dover. ''The Happy Comedies: Their Origin and Special Quality.'' In his *Shakespeare's Happy Comedies*, pp. 34-54. Evanston, Ill.: Northwestern University Press, 1962.

Defines Shakespeare's first ten comedies as the ''happy comedies'' and discerns certain elements common to most of them, including a foreign setting, the use of fools or clowns, a class structure, and a happy ending. Dover Wilson briefly compares *The Two Gentlemen of Verona* to the friendship tradition prescribed by its sources and asserts that the characterization of Proteus and Valentine is broader than that of their precursors.

Appendix

The following is a listing of all books used in Volume 6 of *Shakespearean Criticism*. Included in this list are all reprint rights and acknowledgments for those essays for which permission was obtained. Every effort has been made to trace copyright, but if omissions have been made, please let us know.

THE EXCERPTS IN SC, VOLUME 6, WERE REPRINTED FROM THE FOLLOWING PERIODICALS:

American Imago, v. 15, Summer, 1958.

The Bulletin of the John Rylands Library, v. 14, July, 1930.

The Centennial Review of Arts & Science, v. VIII, 1964 for "From Mine Own Knowledge: A Theme in the Late Tragedies" by Robert B. Heilman. Copyright 1964 by *The Centennial Review of Arts & Science*. Reprinted by permission of the publisher and the author.

Critical Quarterly, v. 2, Winter, 1960 for "Shakespeare Criticism and 'Two Gentlemen of Verona'" by John F. Danby. Reprinted by permission of the author.

ELH, v. 26, September, 1959. Reprinted by permission of the publisher.

English Literary Renaissance, v. 15, Winter, 1985. Copyright 1985 © by *English Literary Renaissance*. Reprinted by permission of the publisher.

Essays and Studies, v. XXXI, 1945./ n.s. v. 16, 1963. © The English Association 1963. All rights reserved. Reprinted by permission of the publisher.

Essays in Criticism, v. XVII, October, 1967 for "Who Deposed Richard the Second?" by A. L. French. Reprinted by permission of the Editor of *Essays in Criticism* and the author.

Language and Style, v. II, Spring, 1969 for "The Word Against the Word: The Role of Language in 'Richard II'" by Terence Hawkes. Copyright © 1969 by the Board of Trustees Southern Illinois University. Reprinted by permission of the author.

Literature and History, v. 7, Spring, 1981 for "Shakespeare's History: 'Richard II'" by Graham Holderness. © 1981. Reprinted by permission of the publisher and the author.

Modern Language Quarterly, v. 9, June, 1948.

The Modern Language Review, v. XXIII, April, 1928.

The New Shakspere Society's Transactions, 1887-92.

THE EXCERPTS IN SC, VOLUME 6, WERE REPRINTED FROM THE FOLLOWING BOOKS:

Adelman, Janet. From *The Common Liar: An Essay on 'Antony and Cleopatra'*. Yale University Press, 1973. Copyright © 1973 by Yale University. All rights reserved. Reprinted by permission of the publisher.

Arthos, John. From *Shakespeare: The Early Writings*. Bowes & Bowes, 1972. © John Arthos 1972. Reprinted by permission of The Bodley Head Ltd. for Bowes & Bowes and the author.

Bacon, Lord Francis. From *A Declaration of the Practices & Treasons Attempted and Committed by Robert Late Earle of Essex*. Robert Barker, 1601.

Barton, Anne. From *Nature's Piece 'gainst Fancy,'' the Divided Catastrophe in ''Antony and Cleopatra'': An Inaugural Lecture*. Bedford College, 1973. Reprinted by permission of the author.

Battenhouse, Roy W. From *Shakespearean Tragedy: Its Art and Its Christian Premises*. Indiana University Press, 1969. Copyright © 1969 by Indiana University Press. All rights reserved. Reprinted by permission of the author.

Berry, Ralph. From *Shakespeare's Comedies: Explorations in Form*. Princeton University Press, 1972. Copyright © 1972 by Princeton University Press. Reprinted with permission of the publisher.

Bethell, S. L. From *Shakespeare and the Popular Dramatic Tradition*. Duke University Press, 1944.

Boas, Frederick S. From *Shakspere and His Predecessors*. Charles Scribner's Sons, 1896.

Bond, R. Warwick. From an introduction to *The Works of Shakespeare: The Two Gentlemen of Verona*. By William Shakespeare, edited by R. Warwick Bond. Methuen and Co. Ltd., 1906.

Bradbrook, M. C. From *Shakespeare and Elizabethan Poetry: A Study of His Earlier Work in Relation to the Poetry of the Time*. Chatto & Windus, 1951.

Brandes, George. From *William Shakespeare: A Critical Study, Vol. I*. Translated by William Archer. William Heinemann, 1898.

Brink, Bernhard Ten. From *Five Lectures on Shakespeare*. Translated by Julia Franklin. Henry Holt and Company, 1895.

Brown, Charles Armitage. From *Shakespeare's Autobiographical Poems: Being His Sonnets Clearly Developed, with His Character Drawn Chiefly from His Works*. James Bohn, 1838.

Campbell, O. J. From *Studies in Shakespeare, Milton and Donne*. By Members of the English Department of the University of Michigan. The Macmillan Company, 1925.

Case, R. H. From an introduction to *Antony and Cleopatra*. By William Shakespeare, edited by W. J. Craig. Methuen & Co., 1906.

Cecil, David. From *Poets and Story-Tellers: A Book of Critical Essays*. Constable & Company Ltd, 1949.

Chambers, E. K. From *Shakespeare: A Survey*. Sidgwick & Jackson, Ltd., 1925.

Chambers, E. K. From *The Works of William Shakespeare: Richard II*. The Gresham Publishing Company Limited, 1905.

Charlton, H. B. From *Shakespearian Tragedy*. Cambridge at the University Press, 1948.

Coleridge, Hartley. From *Essays and Marginalia, Vol. II*. Edited by Derwent Coleridge. Edward Moxon, 1851.

Coleridge, Samuel Taylor. From *Shakespeare, Ben Jonson, Beaumont and Fletcher: Notes and Lectures*. Edward Howell, 1881.

Coleridge, Samuel Taylor. From *Coleridge's Essays & Lectures on Shakspeare & Some Other Old Poets & Dramatists*. J. M. Dent & Co., 1907.

Coleridge, Samuel Taylor. From *Shakespearean Criticism, Vol. I*. Edited by Thomas Middleton Raysor. Cambridge, Mass.: Harvard University Press, 1930.

Courthope, W. J. From *A History of English Poetry: Development and Decline of the Poetic Drama, Influence of the Court and the People, Vol. IV*. The Macmillan Company, 1903.

Davies, Thomas. From *Dramatic Miscellanies: Consisting of Critical Observations on Several Plays of Shakespeare*. N.p., 1784.

Dibdin, Charles. From *A Complete History of the Stage, Vol. III*. Charles Dibdin, 1800.

Dowden, Edward. From *Shakspere*. Macmillan and Co., 1877.

Dowden, Edward. From *Shakspere: A Critical Study of His Mind and Art*. Third edition. Harper & Brothers Publishers, 1881.

Drake, Nathan. From *Shakespeare and His Times, Vol. I*. T. Cadell and W. Davies, 1817.

Dryden, John. From *Troilus and Cressida; or, Truth Found Too Late*. Abel Swall, Jacob Tonson, 1679.

Evans, Bertrand. From *Shakespeare's Comedies*. Oxford at the Clarendon Press, Oxford, 1960. © Oxford University Press 1960. Reprinted by permission of the publisher.

Ewbank, Inga-Stina. From " 'Were Man but Constant, He Were Perfect': Constancy and Consistency in 'The Two Gentlemen of Verona'," in *Shakespearian Comedy*. Stratford-Upon-Avon Studies, No. 14. Edited by John Russell Brown and Bernard Harris. Arnold, 1972. © Edward Arnold (Publishers) Ltd 1972. Reprinted by permission of the publisher.

Farnham, Willard. From *Shakespeare's Tragic Frontier: The World of His Final Tragedies*. University of California Press, 1950.

French, A. L. From *Shakespeare and the Critics*. Cambridge at the University Press, 1972. © Cambridge University Press 1972. Reprinted by permission of the publisher and the author.

Frenzel, Karl. From an essay in *A New Variorum Edition of Shakespeare: The Tragedie of Anthonie, and Cleopatra, Vol. 15*. Edited by Horace Howard Furness. J. B. Lippincott Company, 1907.

Frye, Northrop. From *Fools of Time: Studies in Shakespearean Tragedy*. University of Toronto Press, 1967. © University of Toronto Press 1967. Reprinted by permission of the publisher.

Furness, Horace Howard. From a preface to *A New Variorum Edition of Shakespeare: The Tragedie of Anthonie, and Cleopatra, Vol. 15*. Edited by Horace Howard Furness. J. B. Lippincott Company, 1907.

Garnett, Richard. From an introduction to *The Complete Works of William Shakespeare: The Two Gentlemen of Verona, Vol. II*. By William Shakespeare, edited by Sidney Lee. George D. Sproul, 1907.

Gentleman, Francis. From *Bell's Edition of Shakespeare's Plays, Vol. VI*. John Bell, 1774.

Gentleman, Francis. From *Bell's Edition of Shakespeare's Plays, Vol. VII*. John Bell, 1774.

Gervinus, G. G. From *Shakespeare Commentaries*. Translated by F. E. Bunnètt. Revised edition. Smith Elder, & Co., 1877.

Gildon, Charles. From *The Works of Mr. William Shakespear, Vol. 7*. E. Curll and E. Sanger, 1710.

Gildon, Charles. From *The Laws of Poetry*. W. Hinchliffe and J. Walthoe, 1721.

Goddard, Harold C. From *The Meaning of Shakespeare*. University of Chicago Press, 1951. Copyright 1951 by The University of Chicago. Renewed 1979 by Margaret G. Holt and Eleanor G. Worthen. All rights reserved. Reprinted by permission of the publisher.

Granville-Barker, Harley. From *Prefaces to Shakespeare, second series*. Sidgwick & Jackson, Ltd., 1930.

Griffith, Elizabeth. From *The Morality of Shakespeare's Drama Illustrated*. T. Cadell, 1775.

Harris, Frank. From *The Man Shakespeare and His Tragic Life Story*. Frank Palmer, 1909.

Hazlitt, William. From *Characters of Shakespear's Plays*. C. H. Reynell, 1817.

Heraud, J. A. From *Shakspere: His Inner Life as Intimated in His Works*. N.p., 1865.

Herford, C. H. From *A Sketch of Recent Shakesperean Investigation: 1893-1923*. Blackie & Son Limited, 1923.

Heyse, Paul. From an essay in *A New Variorum Edition of Shakespeare: The Tragedie of Anthonie, and Cleopatra.* Edited by Horace Howard Furness. J. B. Lippincott, 1907.

Hill, R. F. From "Dramatic Techniques and Interpretation in 'Richard II'," in *Early Shakespeare.* Edward Arnold, 1961. © Edward Arnold (Publishers) Ltd. 1961. Reprinted by permission of the publisher.

Hill, Sir John. From *A Letter to the Hon. Author of the New Farce, Called "The Rout."* N.p., 1759.

Hugo, Victor. From an essay in *A New Variorum Edition of Shakespeare: The Tragedie of Anthonie, and Cleopatra.* Edited by Horace Howard Furness. J. B. Lippincott Company, 1907.

Hunter, Robert Grams. From *Shakespeare and the Comedy of Forgiveness.* Columbia University Press, 1965. Copyright © 1965 Robert Grams Hunter. Reprinted by permission of the author.

Jameson, Anna Brownell. From *Characteristics of Women: Moral, Poetical, and Historical.* Second edition. N.p., 1833.

Johnson, Samuel. From notes in *The Plays of William Shakespeare, 8 Vols.* Edited by Samuel Johnson. J. & R. Tonson, 1765.

Kantorowicz, Ernst H. From *The King's Two Bodies: A Study in Mediaeval Political Theology.* Princeton University Press, 1957. Copyright © 1957, renewed 1985, by Princeton University Press. Reprinted with permission of the publisher.

Knight, Charles. From *Studies of Shakspere.* Charles Knight, 1849.

Knight, G. Wilson. From *The Imperial Theme: Further Interpretations of Shakespeare's Tragedies Including the Roman Plays.* Oxford University Press, London, 1931.

Kott, Jan. From *Shakespeare, Our Contemporary.* Translated by Boleslaw Taborski. Doubleday, 1964. Originally published as *Szkice o Szekspirze.* Państwowy Instytut Wydawniczy, 1961. Copyright © 1964 Panstwowe Wydawnictwo Naukowe. Reprinted by permission of Doubleday & Company, Inc. In Canada by Jan Kott.

Langbaine, Gerard. From *An Account of the English Dramatick Poets.* G. West and H. Clements, 1691.

Leggatt, Alexander. From *Shakespeare's Comedy of Love.* Methuen, 1974. © 1973 Alexander Leggatt. All rights reserved. Reprinted by permission of Methuen & Co. Ltd.

Lennox, Charlotte. From *Shakespear Illustrated; or, The Novels and Histories, on Which the Plays of Shakespear Are Founded, Vol. III.* A. Millar, 1754.

Lloyd, William Watkiss. From "Critical Essay on 'The Two Gentlemen of Verona'," in *The Dramatic Works of William Shakespeare.* Edited by S. W. Singer. Bell & Daldy, 1856.

Long, Michael. From *The Unnatural Scene: A Study in Shakespearean Tragedy.* Methuen, 1976. © 1976 Michael Long. Reprinted by permission of Methuen & Co. Ltd.

Mabie, Hamilton Wright. From *William Shakespeare: Poet, Dramatist, and Man.* Third edition. The Macmillan Company, 1901.

Mack, Maynard. From an introduction to *Antony and Cleopatra.* By William Shakespeare. Revised edition. Penguin Books, 1970. Copyright © 1960 and 1970 by Penguin Books, Inc. Reprinted by permission of Viking Penguin Inc.

Mahood, M. M. From *Shakespeare's Wordplay.* Methuen & Co. Ltd., 1957.

Manzoni, Alessandro. From a letter, translated by Françoise Rosen, in *Shakespeare in Europe.* Edited by Oswald LeWinter. World, 1963. Copyright © 1963 by The World Publishing Company. Reprinted by permission of Harper & Row, Publishers, Inc.

Markels, Julian. From *The Pillar of the World: "Antony and Cleopatra" in Shakespeare's Development.* Ohio State University Press, 1968. Copyright © 1968 by the Ohio State University Press. All rights reserved. Reprinted by permission of the publisher.

McAlindon, T. From *Shakespeare and Decorum.* Macmillan, 1973. © T. McAlindon 1973. All rights reserved. Reprinted by permission of Macmillan, London and Basingstoke.

Murry, John Middleton. From *Shakespeare.* Jonathan Cape, 1936. Copyright 1936 by Harcourt Brace & Co., Inc. Renewed 1963 by Mary Middleton Murry. Reprinted by permission of The Society of Authors as the literary representative of the Estate of John Middleton Murry.

Nemerov, Howard. From a commentary in *The Two Gentlemen of Verona.* By William Shakespeare. Edited by Charles Jasper Sisson. Dell, 1964. Copyright © 1964 by Dell Publishing Company, Inc. Reprinted by permission of Dell Publishing Company, Inc.

Nevo, Ruth. From *Comic Transformations in Shakespeare*. Methuen, 1980. © 1980 Ruth Nevo. All rights reserved. Reprinted by permission of Methuen & Co. Ltd.

Parrott, Thomas Marc. From *Shakespearean Comedy*. Oxford University Press, 1949. Copyright 1949 by Thomas Marc Parrott. Renewed 1976 by Frances M. Walters. Reprinted by permission of the Literary Estate of Thomas Marc Parrott.

Pater, Walter. From *Appreciations: With an Essay on Style*. Macmillan & Co., 1889.

Pearson, Norman Holmes. From "'Antony and Cleopatra'," in *Shakespeare: Of an Age and for All Time*. Edited by Charles Tyler Prouty. Shoe String Press, 1954.

Pettet, E. C. From *Shakespeare and the Romance Tradition*. Staples Press, 1949.

Phialas, Peter G. From *Shakespeare's Romantic Comedies: The Development of Their Form and Meaning*. University of North Carolina Press, 1966. Copyright © 1966 by The University of North Carolina Press. Reprinted by permission of the publisher and the author.

Phillipps, Augustine. From an extract in *The Shakspere Allusion-Book: A Collection of Allusions to Shakspere from 1591-1700, Vol. 1*. Edited by John Munro. N.p., 1909.

Phillips, James Emerson, Jr. From *The State in Shakespeare's Greek and Roman Plays*. Columbia University Press, 1940.

Pierce, Robert B. From *Shakespeare's History Plays: The Family and the State*. Ohio State University Press, 1971. Copyright © 1971 by the Ohio State University Press. All rights reserved. Reprinted by permission of the publisher.

Pope, Alexander. From *The Works of Mr. William Shakespear, Vol. 1*. Edited by Alexander Pope. Jacob Tonson, 1723.

Pope, Alexander. From *The Works of Mr. William Shakespear, Vol. 3*. Edited by Alexander Pope. Jacob Tonson, 1723.

Quiller-Couch, Sir Arthur. From an introduction to *The Two Gentlemen of Verona*. By William Shakespeare. Cambridge University Press, 1921.

Quiller-Couch, Sir Arthur. From *Studies in Literature, second series*. G. P. Putnam's Sons, 1922.

Rabkin, Norman. From *Shakespeare and the Common Understanding*. Free Press, 1967. Copyright © 1967 by The Free Press, a division of Macmillan Publishing Company. All rights reserved. Reprinted by permission of the author.

Ridley, M. R. From an introduction to *Antony and Cleopatra*. By William Shakespeare, edited by M. R. Ridley. Methuen & Co. Ltd., 1954.

Riemer, A. P. From *A Reading of Shakespeare's "Antony and Cleopatra."* Sydney University Press, 1968.

Rosen, William. From *Shakespeare and the Craft of Tragedy*. Cambridge, Mass.: Harvard University Press, 1960. Copyright © 1960 by the President and Fellows of Harvard College. Excerpted by permission of the publisher.

Rossiter, A. P. From "'Richard II'," in *Angel with Horns and Other Shakespeare Lectures*. Edited by Graham Storey. Longmans, 1961. © Longmans, Green & Co. Ltd., 1961. Reprinted by permission of the publisher.

Rothschild, Herbert B., Jr. From "Language and Social Reality in 'Richard II'," in *Essays in Honor of Esmond Linworth Marilla*. Edited by Thomas Austin Kirby and William John Olive. Louisiana State University Press, 1970. Copyright © 1970 by Louisiana State University Press. Reprinted by permission of the publisher.

Sampson, Martin W. From an introduction to *The Two Gentlemen of Verona*. By William Shakespeare, edited by Martin W. Sampson. Tudor Shakespeare Series, edited by W. A. Neilson and A. H. Thorndike. Macmillan, 1912. Copyright, 1912 by Macmillan Publishing Company. Renewed 1940 by Julia D. Sampson. All rights reserved. Reprinted with permission of Macmillan Publishing Company.

Sanders, Norman. From an introduction to *The Two Gentlemen of Verona*. By William Shakespeare, edited by Norman Sanders. Penguin Books, 1968. All rights reserved. Reproduced by permission of Penguin Books Ltd.

Schlegel, August Wilhelm. From *A Course of Lectures on Dramatic Art and Literature*. Edited by Rev. A. J. W. Morrison, translated by John Black. Revised edition. Henry G. Bohn, 1846.

Schucking, Levin L. From *Character Problems in Shakespeare's Plays: A Guide to the Better Understanding of the Dramatist*. George G. Harrap & Co., 1922.

Seward, Thomas. From a preface to *The Works of Mr. F. Beaumont and Mr. J. Fletcher, 10 Vols.* By Mr. F. Beaumont and Mr. J. Fletcher. J. & R. Tonson & S. Draper, 1750.

Shaw, Bernard. From *Three Plays for Puritans, Vol. 3*. Grant Richards, 1901.

Snider, Denton J. From *The Shakespearian Drama, a Commentary: The Comedies*. Sigma Publishing Co., 1890?

Snider, Denton J. From *The Shakespearian Drama, a Commentary: The Histories*. Sigma Publishing Co., 1890.

Spurgeon, Caroline F. E. From *Shakespeare's Imagery and What It Tells Us*. Cambridge at the University Press, 1935.

Stauffer, Donald A. From *Shakespeare's World of Images: The Development of His Moral Ideas,* Norton, 1949. Copyright 1949 by W. W. Norton & Company, Inc. Copyright renewed 1977 by Ruth M. Stauffer. Reprinted by permission of W. W. Norton & Company, Inc.

Steevens, George. From *The Plays of William Shakspeare, Vol. XII*. Edited by Samuel Johnson and George Steevens. Revised edition. T. Longman, 1793.

Stirling, Brents. From *Unity in Shakespearian Tragedy: The Interplay of Theme and Character*. Columbia University Press, 1956. Copyright © 1956 Columbia University Press, New York. Renewed 1984 by Brents Stirling. Reprinted by permission of the publisher.

Swinburne, Algernon Charles. From *A Study of Shakespeare*. R. Worthington, 1880.

Swinburne, Algernon Charles. From *Three Plays of Shakespeare*. Harper & Brothers, 1909.

Symons, Arthur. From an introduction to "Antony and Cleopatra," in *The Works of William Shakespeare, Vol. VI*. Edited by Henry Irving and Frank A. Marshall. Blackie & Son, Limited, 1892.

Tate, Nahum. From *The History of King Richard the Second*. Richard Tonson and Jacob Tonson, 1681.

Tillyard, E. M. W. From *Shakespeare's Last Plays*. Chatto and Windus, 1938.

Tillyard, E. M. W. From *Shakespeare's History Plays*. Chatto & Windus, 1964. Humanities Press, 1964. Copyright 1944 by Chatto & Windus. Renewed 1971 by Stephen Tillyard, Mrs. V. Sankaran and Mrs. A. Ahlers. Reprinted by permission of Humanities Press International, Inc., Atlantic Highlands, NJ. In Canada by the Literary Estate of E. M. W. Tillyard and Chatto & Windus.

Traversi, D. A. From *Approach to Shakespeare*. Sands: The Paladin Press, 1938.

Traversi, Derek. From *William Shakespeare, the Early Comedies: The Comedy of Errors, The Taming of the Shrew, The Two Gentlemen of Verona, Love's Labour's Lost, The Merchant of Venice*. Longmans, Green & Co., 1960. © Derek Traversi 1960, 1964. Reprinted by permission of the author.

Trench, Richard Chenevix. From *Plutarch: His Life, His Lives and His Morals*. Macmillan and Co., 1873.

Ulrici, Hermann. From *Shakspeare's Dramatic Art: And His Relation to Calderon and Goethe*. Translated by A. J. W. Morrison. Chapman, Brothers, 1846.

Upton, John. From *Critical Observations on Shakespeare*. Second edition. G. Hawkins, 1748.

Van Doren, Mark. From *Shakespeare*. Henry Holt and Company, 1939.

Van Laan, Thomas F. From *Role-Playing in Shakespeare*. University of Toronto Press, 1978. © University of Toronto Press, 1978. Reprinted by permission of the publisher.

Victor, Benjamin. From an advertisement to *The Two Gentlemen of Verona*. By William Shakespeare, edited by Benjamin Victor. N.p. 1762.

Vyvyan, John. From *Shakespeare and the Rose of Love: A Study of the Early Plays in Relation to the Medieval Philosophy of Love*. Chatto & Windus, 1960. © John Vyvyan 1960. Reprinted by permission of the Tessa Sayle Agency.

Waith, Eugene M. From *The Herculean Hero in Marlowe, Chapman, Shakespeare and Dryden*. Chatto & Windus, 1962. © Eugene M. Waith 1962. Reprinted by permission of the author and Chatto & Windus.

Wesley, Samuel. From *Maggots: Or Poems on Several Subjects Never Before Handled*. John Dunton, 1685.

Wilson, John Dover. From an introduction to *Antony and Cleopatra*. By William Shakespeare. Cambridge University Press, 1950.

Winny, James. From *The Player King: A Theme of Shakespeare's Histories*. Chatto & Windus, 1968. © James Winny 1968. Reprinted by permission of the author.

Winter, William. From *Old Shrines and Ivy*. Macmillan and Company, 1892.

Yeats, W. B. From *Essays and Introductions*. Macmillan, 1961. © Mrs. W. B. Yeats, 1961. All rights reserved. Reprinted with permission of Macmillan Publishing Company. In Canada by Michael B. Yeats, Anne Yeats and Macmillan, London, Ltd.

From *An Examen of the New Comedy, Call'd ''The Suspicious Husband'' with Some Observations Upon our Dramatick Poetry and Authors*. N.p., 1747.

Glossary

APOCRYPHA: A term applied to those plays which have, at one time or another, been ascribed to Shakespeare, but which are outside the canon of the thirty-seven dramas generally accepted as authentic. The second issue of the THIRD FOLIO included seven plays not among the other thirty-six of the FIRST FOLIO: *Pericles, The London Prodigal, Thomas Lord Cromwell, Sir John Oldcastle, The Puritan, A Yorkshire Tragedy,* and *Locrine*. These seven were also included in the FOURTH FOLIO, but of them only *Pericles* is judged to be the work of Shakespeare. Four other plays that were entered in the STATIONERS' REGISTER in the seventeenth century listed Shakespeare as either an author or coauthor: *The Two Noble Kinsmen* (1634), *Cardenio* (1653), *Henry I* and *Henry II* (1653), and *The Birth of Merlin* (1662); only *The Two Noble Kinsmen* is thought to be, at least in part, written by Shakespeare, although *Cardenio*—whose text is lost—may also have been by him. Scholars have judged that there is strong internal evidence indicating Shakespeare's hand in two other works, *Sir Thomas More* and *Edward III*. Among other titles that have been ascribed to Shakespeare but are generally regarded as spurious are: *The Troublesome Reign of King John, Arden of Feversham, Fair Em, The Merry Devil of Edmonton, Mucedorus, The Second Maiden's Tragedy,* and *Edmund Ironside*.

ASSEMBLED TEXTS: The theory of assembled texts, first proposed by Edmond Malone in the eighteenth century and later popularized by John Dover Wilson, maintains that some of the plays in the FIRST FOLIO were reconstructed for the COMPOSITOR by integrating each actor's part with the plot or abstract of the play. According to Dover Wilson, this reconstruction was done only for those plays which had not been previously published in QUARTO editions and which had no company PROMPT-BOOKS in existence, a list he limits to three of Shakespeare's works: *The Two Gentlemen of Verona, The Merry Wives of Windsor,* and *The Winter's Tale*.

BAD QUARTOS: A name attributed to a group of early editions of Shakespeare's plays which, because of irregularities, omissions, misspellings, and interpolations not found in later QUARTO or FOLIO versions of the same plays, are considered unauthorized publications of Shakespeare's work. The term was first used by the twentieth-century bibliographical scholar A. W. Pollard and has been applied to as many as ten plays: The First Quartos of *Romeo and Juliet, Hamlet, Henry V,* and *The Merry Wives of Windsor; The First Part of the Contention betwixt the two famous Houses of Yorke and Lancaster* and *The True Tragedy of Richard Duke of Yorke,* originally thought to have been sources for Shakespeare's *2* and *3 Henry VI,* but now generally regarded as bad quartos of those plays; the so-called ''Pied Bull'' quarto of *King Lear;* the 1609 edition of *Pericles; The Troublesome Reign of King John,* believed to be a bad quarto of *King John,* and *The Taming of a Shrew,* which some critics contend is a bad quarto of Shakespeare's Shrew drama. The primary distinction of the bad quartos is the high degree of TEXTUAL CORRUPTION apparent in the texts, a fact scholars have attributed to either one of two theories: some have argued that each quarto was composed from a stenographer's report, in which an agent for the printer was employed to surreptitiously transcribe the play during a performance; others have held the more popular explanation that the questionable texts were based on MEMORIAL RECONSTRUCTIONS by one or more actors who had performed in the plays.

BANDELLO, MATTEO: (b. 1480? - d. 1561) Italian novelist and poet who was also a churchman, diplomat, and soldier. His literary reputation is principally based on the *Novelle,* a collection of 214 tragic, romantic, and historical tales derived from a variety of material from antiquity to the Renaissance. Many of the stories in the *Novelle* are coarse and lewd in their presentation of love, reflecting Bandello's secular interests rather than his clerical role. Together with the dedications to friends and patrons that accompany the individual stories, the *Novelle* conveys a vivid sense of historical events and personalities of the Renaissance. Several translations and adaptations appeared in the third quarter of the sixteenth century, most notably in French by Francois Belleforest and Pierre Boaistuau and in English by William Painter and Geoffrey Fenton.

BLACKFRIARS THEATRE: The Blackfriars Theatre, so named because it was located in the London precinct of Blackfriars, was originally part of a large monastary leased to Richard Farrant, Master of the Children of Windsor, in 1576 for the purpose of staging children's plays. It was acquired in 1596 by James Burbage, who tried to convert the property into a professional theater, but was thwarted in his attempt by surrounding residents. After Burbage died, the Blackfriars was taken over by his son, Richard, who circumvented the objections of his neighbors and, emulating the tactics of Farrant's children's company, staged both children's and adult plays under the guise of a private house, rather than a public theater. This arrangement lasted for five years until, in 1605, the adult company was suspended by King James I for its performance of the satire *Eastward Ho!* Shortly thereafter, the children's company was also suppressed for performing George Chapman's *Conspiracy and Tragedy of Charles Duke of Byron.* In 1608, Burbage organized a new group of directors consisting of his brother Cuthbert and several leading players of the KING'S MEN, including Shakespeare, John Heminge, Henry Condell, and William Sly. These ''housekeepers,'' as they were called, for they shared no profits accruing to the actors, arranged to have the Blackfriars used by the King's Men alternately with the GLOBE THEATRE, an arrangement that lasted from the autumn of 1609 to 1642. Because it was a private house, and therefore smaller than the public theaters of London at that time, the Blackfriars set a higher price for tickets and, as such, attracted a sophisticated and aristocratic audience. Also, through its years of operation as a children's theater, the Blackfriars developed a certain taste in its patrons—one which appreciated music, dance, and masque in a dramatic piece, as well as elements of suspense, reconciliation, and rebirth. Many critics attribute the nature of Shakespeare's final romances to the possibility that he wrote the plays with this new audience foremost in mind.

BOOKKEEPER: Also considered the bookholder or prompter, the bookkeeper was a member of an Elizabethan acting company who maintained custody of the PROMPT-BOOKS, or texts of the plays. Many scholars believe that the bookkeeper also acted as the prompter during any performances, much as a stage manager would do today; however, other literary historians claim that another official satisfied this function. In addition to the above duties, the bookkeeper obtained a license for each play, deleted from the dramatist's manuscript anything offensive before it was submitted to the government censor, assembled copies of the players' individual parts from the company prompt-book, and drew up the "plot" of each work, that is, an abstract of the action of the play emphasizing stage directions.

COMPOSITOR: The name given to the typesetter in a printing shop. Since the growth of textual criticism in modern Shakespearean scholarship, the habits and idiosyncrasies of the individual compositors of Shakespeare's plays have attracted extensive study, particularly with respect to those works that demonstrate substantial evidence of TEXTUAL CORRUPTION. Elizabethan compositors set their type by hand, one letter at a time, a practice that made it difficult to sustain a sense of the text and which often resulted in a number of meaningless passages in books. Also, the lack of uniform spelling rules prior to the eighteenth century meant that each compositor was free to spell a given word according to his personal predilection. Because of this, scholars have been able to identify an individual compositor's share of a printed text by isolating his spelling habits and idiosyncrasies.

EMENDATION: A term often used in textual criticism, emendation is a conjectural correction of a word or phrase in a Shakespearean text proposed by an editor in an effort to restore a line's original meaning. Because many of Shakespeare's plays were carelessly printed, there exist a large number of errors in the early editions which textual scholars through the centuries have tried to correct. Some of the errors—those based on obvious misprints—have been easily emended, but other more formidable TEXTUAL CORRUPTIONS remain open to dispute and have solicited a variety of corrections. Perhaps the two most famous of these are the lines in *Henry V* (II. iii. 16-17) and *Hamlet* (I. ii. 129).

FAIR COPY: A term often applied by Elizabethan writers and theater professionals to describe the corrected copy of an author's manuscript submitted to an acting company. According to available evidence, a dramatist would presumably produce a rough copy of a play, also known as the author's FOUL PAPERS, which would be corrected and revised either by himself or by a professional scribe at a later date. Eventually, the fair copy of a play would be modified by a BOOKKEEPER or prompter to include notes for properties, stage directions, and so on, and then be transcribed into the company's PROMPT-BOOK.

FIRST FOLIO: The earliest collected edition of Shakespeare's plays, edited by his fellow-actors John Heminge and Henry Condell and published near the end of 1623. The First Folio contains thirty-six plays, exactly half of which had never been previously published. Although this edition is considered authoritative for a number of Shakespeare's plays, recent textual scholarship tends to undermine this authority in calling for a broader consideration of all previous versions of a Shakespearean drama in conjunction with the Folio text.

FOLIO: The name given to a book made up of sheets folded once to form two leaves of equal size, or four pages, typically 11 to 16 inches in height and 8 to 11 inches in width.

FOUL PAPERS: The term given to an author's original, uncorrected manuscript, containing the primary text of a play with the author's insertions and deletions. Presumably, the foul papers would be transcribed onto clean sheets for the use of the acting company which had purchased the play; this transcribed and corrected manuscript was called a FAIR COPY. Available evidence indicates that some of Shakespeare's early QUARTOS were printed directly from his foul papers, a circumstance which would, if true, explain the frequent errors and inconsistencies in these texts. Among the quartos alleged to be derived from Shakespeare's foul papers are the First Quartos of *Much Ado about Nothing, A Midsummer Night's Dream, Love's Labour's Lost, Richard II,* and *1* and *2 Henry IV;* among the FIRST FOLIO editions are *The Comedy of Errors, The Taming of the Shrew,* and *Coriolanus.*

FOURTH FOLIO: The fourth collected edition of Shakespeare's plays, published in 1685. This, the last of the FOLIO editions of Shakespeare's dramas, included a notable amount of TEXTUAL CORRUPTION and modernization—751 editorial changes in all, most designed to make the text easier to read.

GLOBE THEATRE: Constructed in 1599 on Bankside across the Thames from the City of London, the Globe was destroyed by fire in 1613, rebuilt the following year, and finally razed in 1644. Accounts of the fire indicate that it was built of timber with a thatched roof, and sixteenth-century maps of Bankside show it was a polygonal building, but no other evidence exists describing its structure and design. From what is known of similar public theaters of the day, such as the Fortune and the Swan, it is conjectured that the Globe contained a three-tiered gallery along its interior perimeter, that a roof extended over a portion of the three-storied stage and galleries, and that the lowest level of the stage was in the form of an apron extending out among the audience in the yard. Further, there is speculation that the Globe probably included a tiring room or backstage space, that the first two stories contained inner stages that were curtained and recessed, that the third story sometimes served as a musicians' gallery, and that beneath the flat roof, which was also known as "the heavens," machinery was stored for raising and lowering theatrical apparatus. It is generally believed that the interior of the Globe was circular and that it could accommodate an audience of approximately two thousand people, both in its three galleries and the yard. The theater was used solely by the LORD CHAMBERLAIN'S MEN, later known as the KING'S MEN, who performed there throughout the year until 1609, when the company alternated performances at the fully-enclosed BLACKFRIARS THEATRE in months of inclement weather.

HALL (or HALLE), EDWARD: (b. 1498? - d. 1547) English historian whose *The Union of the Noble and Illustre Famelies of Lancastre and York* (1542; enlarged in 1548 and 1550) chronicles the period from the death of Richard II through the reign of Henry VIII. Morally didactic in his approach, Hall shaped his material to demonstrate the disasters that ensue from civil wars and insurrection against monarchs. He traced through the dynastic conflicts during the reigns of Henry VI and Richard III a pattern of cause and effect in which a long chain of crimes and divine retribution was ended by the accession of Henry VII to the English throne. Hall's eye-witness account of the pageantry and festivities of the court of Henry VIII is remarkable for its vivacity and embellished language. His heavy bias on the side of Protestantism and defense of Henry VIII's actions against the Roman Church led to the prohibition of his work by Queen Mary in 1555, but his interpretation of the War of the Roses was adopted by all subsequent Tudor historians. Hall's influence on Shakespeare is most evident in the English history plays.

HOLINSHED, RAPHAEL: (d. 1580?) English writer and editor whose *Chronicles of England, Scotlande, and Irelande* (1577; enlarged in 1587) traced the legends and history of Britain from Noah and the flood to the mid-sixteenth century. The *Chronicles* reveal a Protestant bias and depict the history of the British monarchy in terms of the "Tudor myth," which claimed that Henry

IV's usurpation of the crown from Richard II set off a chain of disasters and civil strife which culminated in the reign of Henry VI and continued until the accession to the throne of Henry VII, who, through his marriage to Elizabeth of York, united the two feuding houses of Lancaster and York and brought harmony and peace to England. Holinshed was the principal author of the *Chronicles,* being responsible for the "Historie of England," but he collaborated with William Harrison—who wrote the "Description of England," a vivid account of sixteenth-century customs and daily life—and Richard Stanyhurst and Edward Campion, who together wrote the "Description of Ireland." "The History and Description of Scotland" and the "History of Ireland" were translations or adaptations of the work of earlier historians and writers. The *Chronicles* were immediately successful, in part because of the easily accessible style in which they were composed and because their patriotic celebration of British history was compatible with the rise of nationalistic fervor in Elizabethan England. As in the case of EDWARD HALL, Holinshed's influence on Shakespeare is most evident in the English history plays.

INNS OF COURT: Four colleges of law located in the City of London—Gray's Inn, the Middle Temple, the Inner Temple, and Lincoln's Inn. In the sixteenth and seventeenth centuries, the Inns were not only academic institutions, but were also regarded as finishing schools for gentlemen, providing their students with instruction in music, dance, and other social accomplishments. Interest in the drama ran high in these communities; in addition to producing their own plays, masques, and revels, members would occasionally employ professional acting companies, such as the LORD CHAMBERLAIN'S MEN and the KING'S MEN, for private performances at the Inns. Existing evidence indicates that at least two of Shakespeare's plays were first performed at the Inns: *The Comedy of Errors* and *Twelfth Night.*

KING'S MEN: An acting company formerly known as the LORD CHAMBERLAIN'S MEN. On May 19, 1603, shortly after his accession to the English throne, James I granted the company a royal patent, and its name was altered to reflect the King's direct patronage. At that date, members who shared in the profits of the company included Shakespeare, Richard Burbage, John Heminge, Henry Condell, Augustine Phillips, William Sly, and Robert Armin. Records of the Court indicate that this was the most favored acting company in the Jacobean era, averaging a dozen performances there each year during that period. In addition to public performances at the GLOBE THEATRE in the spring and autumn, the King's Men played at the private BLACKFRIARS THEATRE in winter and for evening performances. Because of the recurring plague in London from 1603 onward, theatrical companies like the King's Men spent the summer months touring and giving performances in the provinces. Besides the work of Shakespeare, the King's Men's repertoire included plays by Ben Jonson, Francis Beaumont and John Fletcher, Thomas Dekker, and Cyril Tourneur. The company continued to flourish until 1642, when by Act of Parliament all dramatic performances were suppressed.

LORD ADMIRAL'S MEN: An acting company formed in 1576-77 under the patronage of Charles Howard, Earl of Nottingham. From its inception to 1585 the company was known as the Lord Howard's Men, from 1585 to 1603 as the Lord Admiral's Men, from 1604 to 1612 as Prince Henry's Men, and from 1613 to 1625 as the Palsgrave's Men. They were the principal rivals of the LORD CHAMBERLAIN'S MEN; occasionally, from 1594 to 1612, these two troupes were the only companies authorized to perform in London. The company's chief player was Edward Alleyn, an actor of comparable distinction with Richard Burbage of the Lord Chamberlain's Men. From 1591 the company performed at the ROSE THEATRE, moving to the Fortune Theatre in 1600. The detailed financial records of Philip Henslowe, who acted as the company's landlord and financier from 1594 until his death in 1616, indicate that an extensive list of dramatists wrote for the troupe throughout its existence, including Christopher Marlowe, Ben Jonson,

George Chapman, Anthony Munday, Henry Chettle, Michael Drayton, Thomas Dekker, and William Rowley.

LORD CHAMBERLAIN'S MEN: An acting company formed in 1594 under the patronage of Henry Carey, Lord Hunsdon, who was the Queen's Chamberlain from 1585 until his death in 1596. From 1596 to 1597, the company's benefactor was Lord Hunsdon's son, George Carey, and they were known as Hunsdon's Men until the younger Carey was appointed to his late father's office, when the troupe once again became officially the Lord Chamberlain's Men. The members of the company included Shakespeare, Will Kempe—the famous 'clown' and the most popular actor of his time—, Richard Burbage—the renowned tragedian—, and John Heminge, who served as business manager for the company. In 1594 they began performing at the Theatre and the Cross Key's Inn, moving to the Swan on Bankside in 1596 when the City Corporation banned the public presentation of plays within the limits of the City of London. In 1599 some members of the company financed the building of the GLOBE THEATRE and thus the majority became "sharers," not only in the actors' portion of the profits, but in the theatre owners' allotment as well. This economic independence was an important element in the unusual stability of their association. They became the foremost London company, performing at Court on thirty-two occasions between 1594 and 1603, whereas their chief rivals, the LORD ADMIRAL'S MEN, made twenty appearances at Court during that period. No detailed records exist of the plays that were in their repertoire. Ben Jonson wrote several of his dramas for the Lord Chamberlain's Men, but the company's success is largely attributable to the fact that, after joining them in 1594, Shakespeare wrote for no other company.

MEMORIAL RECONSTRUCTION: One hypothesis used to explain the texts of the so-called BAD-QUARTOS. Scholars have theorized that one or more actors who had appeared in a Shakespearean play attempted to reconstruct from personal memory the text of that drama. Inevitably, there would be lapses of recall with resultant errors and deviations from the original play. Characteristics of these corrupt "reported texts" include the transposition of phrases or entire speeches, the substitution of new language, omission of dramatically significant material, and abridgements of extended passages. It has been speculated that memorial reconstructions were produced by companies touring the provinces whose PROMPT-BOOKS remained in London, or by actors who sold the pirated versions to printers. W. W. Greg, in his examination of the bad quarto of *The Merry Wives of Windsor,* was the first scholar to employ the term.

MERES, FRANCIS: (b. 1565 - d. 1647) English cleric and schoolmaster whose *Palladis Tamia, Wit's Treasury* (1598) has played a valuable role in determining the dates of several of Shakespeare's plays and poems. The work is a collection of observations and commentary on a wide range of subjects, including religion, moral philosophy, and the arts. In a section entitled "A Comparative discourse on our English Poets with the Greeke, Latine, and Italian Poets," Meres compared Shakespeare's work favorably with that of OVID, PLAUTUS, and SENECA and listed the titles of six of his tragedies, six comedies, and two poems, thus establishing that these works were composed no later than 1598. Meres also praised Shakespeare as "the most excellent" of contemporary writers for the stage and remarked that, in addition to his published poetry, he had written some "sugred sonnets" which were circulated among a group of his "private friends."

MIRROR FOR MAGISTRATES, A: A collection of dramatic monologues in which the ghosts of eminent historical figures lament the sins or fatal flaws that led to their downfalls. Individually and collectively, the stories depict the evils of rebellion against divinely constituted authority, the obligation of rulers to God and their subjects, and the inconstancy of Fortune's favor. William

Baldwin edited the first edition (1559) and wrote many of the tales, with the collaboration of George Ferrers and six other authors. Subsequently, six editions appeared by 1610, in which a score of contributors presented the first-person narrative complaints of some one hundred heroic personages, from King Albanact of Scotland to Cardinal Wolsey and Queen Elizabeth. The first edition to include Thomas Sackville's *Induction* (1563) is the most notable; Sackville's description of the poet's descent into hell and his encounters with allegorical figures, such as Remorse, Revenge, Famine, and War, is generally considered the most poetically meritorious work in the collection. With respect to Shakespeare, scholars claim that elements from *A Mirror for Magistrates* are most apparent in the history plays on the two Richards and on Henry IV and Henry VI.

OCTAVO: The term applied to a book made up of sheets of paper folded three times to form eight leaves of equal size, or sixteen pages. The dimensions of a folded octavo page may range from 6 to 11 inches in height and 4 to 7½ inches in width.

OVID [PUBLIUS OVIDIUS NASO]: (b. 43 B.C. - d. 18 A.D.) Roman poet who was extremely popular during his lifetime and who greatly affected the subsequent development of Latin poetry; he also deeply influenced European art and literature. Ovid's erotic poetry is molded in elegaic couplets, a highly artificial form which he reshaped by means of a graceful and fluent style. These erotic poems—*Amores, Heroides, Ars amatoria*, and *Remedia amoris*—are concerned with love and amorous intrigue, depicting these themes in an amoral fashion that some critics have considered licentious. Ovid's *Metamorphoses*, written in rapidly flowing hexameters, presents some 250 stories from Greek and Roman legends that depict various kinds of transformations, from the tale of primeval chaos to the apotheosis of Julius Caesar into a celestial body. *Metamorphoses* is a superbly unified work, demonstrating Ovid's supreme skills in narration and description and his ingenuity in linking a wide variety of sources into a masterly presentation of classical myth. His brilliance of invention, fluency of style, and vivid descriptions were highly praised in the Renaissance, and familiarity with his work was considered an essential part of a formal education. Ovid has been cited as a source for many of Shakespeare's plays, including *The Merry Wives of Windsor, A Midsummer Night's Dream, The Tempest, Titus Andronicus, Troilus and Cressida*, and *The Winter's Tale*.

PLAUTUS, TITUS MACCIUS: (b. 254? - d. 184 B.C.) The most prominent Roman dramatist of the Republic and early Empire. The esteem and unrivaled popularity he earned from his contemporaries have been ratified by scholars and dramatists of the past five hundred years. Many playwrights from the sixteenth to the twentieth century have chosen his works, particularly *Amphitruo, Aulularia, Captivi, Menaechmi, Miles Gloriosus, Mostellaria*, and *Trinummus*, as models for their own. Plautus adapted characters, plots, and settings from Greek drama, combined these with elements from Roman farce and satire, and introduced into his plays incongruous contemporary allusions, plays upon words, and colloquial and newly coined language. His dramatic style is further characterized by extensive use of song and music, alliteration and assonance, and variations in metrical language to emphasize differences in character and mood. His employment of stock character types, the intrigues and confusions of his plots, and the exuberance and vigor of his comic spirit were especially celebrated by his English Renaissance audience. The plays of Shakespeare that are most indebted to Plautus include *The Comedy of Errors, The Taming of the Shrew, The Merry Wives of Windsor, The Two Gentlemen of Verona, Romeo and Juliet*, and *All's Well That Ends Well*. His influence can also be noted in such Shakespearean characters as Don Armado (*Love's Labour's Lost*), Parolles (*All's Well That Ends Well*), and Falstaff (*Henry IV* and *The Merry Wives of Windsor*).

PLUTARCH: (b. 46? - d. 120? A.D.) Greek biographer and essayist whose work constitutes a faithful record of the historical tradition, moral views, and ethical judgments of second century A.C.

Graeco-Roman culture. His *Parallel Lives*—translated into English by Sir Thomas North and published in 1579 as *The Lives of the Noble Grecianes and Romans compared together*—was one of the most widely read works of antiquity from the sixteenth to the nineteenth century. In this work, Plutarch was principally concerned with portraying the personal character and individual actions of the statesmen, soldiers, legislators, and orators who were his subjects, and through his warm and lively style with instructing as well as entertaining his readers. His portrayal of these classical figures as exemplars of virtue or vice and his emphasis on the successive turns of Fortune's wheel in the lives of great men were in close harmony with the Elizabethan worldview. His miscellaneous writings on religion, ethics, literature, science, and politics, collected under the general title of *Moralia,* were important models for sixteenth- and seventeenth-century essayists. Plutarch is considered a major source for Shakespeare's *Julius Caesar, Antony and Cleopatra,* and *Coriolanus,* and a minor source for *A Midsummer Night's Dream* and *Timon of Athens.*

PRINTER'S COPY: The manuscript or printed text of a work which the compositor uses to set type pages. The nature of the copy available to the early printers of Shakespeare's plays is important in assessing how closely these editions adhere to the original writings. Bibliographical scholars have identified a number of forms available to printers in Shakespeare's time: the author's FOUL PAPERS; a FAIR COPY prepared either by the author or a scribe; partially annotated foul papers or a fair copy that included prompt notes; private copies, prepared by a scribe for an individual outside the acting company; the company's PROMPT-BOOK; scribal transcripts of a prompt-book; a stenographer's report made by someone who had attended an actual performance; earlier printed editions of the work, with or without additional insertions provided by the author, a scribe, or the preparer of a prompt-book; a transcript of a MEMORIAL RECONSTRUCTION of the work; and an ASSEMBLED TEXT.

PROMPT-BOOK: Acting version of a play, usually transcribed from the playwright's FOUL PAPERS by a scribe or the dramatist himself. This copy, or "book," was then presented to the Master of the Revels, the official censor and authorizer of plays. Upon approving its contents, he would license the play for performance and endorse the text as the "allowed book" of the play. A prompt-book represents an alteration or modification of the dramatist's original manuscript. It generally contains detailed stage directions, including cues for music, off-stage noises, and the entries and exits of principal characters, indications of stage properties to be used, and other annotations to assist the prompter during an actual performance. The prompt-book version was frequently shorter than the original manuscript, for cuts would be made in terms of minor characters or dramatic incidents to suit the resources of the acting company. Printed editions of plays were sometimes based on prompt-books.

QUARTO: The term applies to a book made up of sheets of paper folded twice to form four leaves of equal size, or eight pages. A quarto page may range in size from 8½ inches to 12½ inches in height and 6¾ to 10 inches in width.

ROSE THEATRE: Built in 1587 by Philip Henslowe, the Rose was constructed of timber on a brick foundation, with exterior walls of lath and plaster and a roof of thatch. Its location on Bankside—across the Thames River from the City of London—established this area as a new site for public theaters. Its circular design included a yard, galleries, a tiring house, and "heavens." A half-dozen acting companies played there, the most important being the LORD ADMIRAL'S MEN, the chief rival to the LORD CHAMBERLAIN'S MEN, who performed at the Rose from 1594 to 1600, when they moved to the new Fortune Theatre constructed by Henslowe in Finsbury, north of the City of London. Among the dramatists employed by Henslowe at the Rose were Thomas Kyd, Christopher Marlowe, Shakespeare, Robert Greene, Ben Jonson, Michael Drayton, George Chapman, Thomas Dekker, and John Webster. The building was razed in 1606.

SECOND FOLIO: The second collected edition of Shakespeare's plays, published in 1632. While it is essentially a reprint of the FIRST FOLIO, more than fifteen hundred changes were made to modernize spelling and to correct stage directions and proper names.

SENECA, LUCIUS ANNAEUS: (b. 4? B.C. - d. 65 A.D.) Roman philosopher, statesman, dramatist, and orator who was one of the major writers of the first century A.D. and who had a profound influence on Latin and European literature. His philosophical essays castigating vice and teaching Stoic resignation were esteemed by the medieval Latin Church, whose members regarded him as a great moral teacher. His nine tragedies—*Hercules Furens, Thyestes, Phoenissae, Phaedra, Oedipus, Troades, Medea, Agamemnon,* and *Hercules Oetaeus*—were translated into English in 1581 and exerted a strong influence over sixteenth-century English dramatists. Seneca's plays were composed for reading or reciting rather than for performing on the stage, and they evince little attention to character or motive. Written in a declamatory rhetorical style, their function was to instruct on the disastrous consequences of uncontrolled passion and political tyranny. Distinctive features of Senecan tragedy include sensationalism and intense emotionalism, the depiction of wicked acts and retribution, adultery and unnatural sexuality, murder and revenge, and the representation of supernatural beings. Shakespeare's use of Seneca can be discerned most readily in such plays as *King John,* the histories from *Henry VI* to *Richard III, Antony and Cleopatra, Titus Andronicus, Julius Caesar, Hamlet,* and *Macbeth.*

STATIONERS' REGISTER: A ledger book in which were entered the titles of works to be printed and published. The Register was maintained by the Stationers' Company, an association of those who manufactured and those who sold books. In Tudor England, the Company had a virtual monopoly—aside from the university presses—on printing works written throughout the country. Having obtained a license authorizing the printing of a work, a member of the Company would pay a fee to enter the book in the Register, thereby securing the sole right to print or sell that book. Many registered texts were acquired by questionable means and many plays were published whose titles were not entered in the records of the Company. However, the Stationers' Register is one of the most important documents for scholars investigating the literature of that period.

TEXTUAL CORRUPTION: A phrase signifying the alterations that may occur as an author's original text is transmitted through the subsequent stages of preparation for performance and printing. In cases where the PRINTER'S COPY was not an author's FAIR COPY, the text may contain unintelligible language, mislineations, omissions, repetitious lines, transposed verse and prose speeches, inaccurate speech headings, and defective rhymes. Through their investigation of the nature of the copy from which a COMPOSITOR set his type, textual scholars attempt to restore the text and construct a version that is closest to the author's original manuscript.

THIRD FOLIO: The third collected edition of Shakespeare's plays, published in 1663. Essentially a reprint of the SECOND FOLIO, it contains some corrections to that text and some errors not found in earlier editions. The Third Folio was reprinted in 1664 and included ''seven Playes, never before Printed in Folio.'' One of these seven—*Pericles*—has been accepted as Shakespeare's work, but the other six are considered apocryphal (see APOCRYPHA).

VARIORUM: An edition of a literary work which includes notes and commentary by previous editors and scholars. The First Variorum of Shakespeare's works was published in 1803. Edited by Isaac Reed, it was based on George Steevens's four eighteenth-century editions and includes extensive material from Samuel Johnson's edition of 1765, together with essays by Edmund Malone, George Chalmers, and Richard Farmer. The Second Variorum is a reprint of the First, and it was published in 1813. The Third Variorum is frequently referred to as the Boswell-Malone edition. Containing prefaces from most of the eighteenth-century editions of Shakespeare's work, as well as the poems and sonnets, which Steevens and Reed omitted, the Third Variorum was published in 1821. Edited by James Boswell the younger and based on the scholarship of Malone, it includes such a wealth of material that it is generally regarded as the most important complete edition of the works of Shakespeare. The Fourth Variorum, known as the "New Variorum," was begun by Horace Howard Furness in 1871. Upon his death, his son, Horace Howard Furness, Jr., assumed the editorship, and subsequently—in 1936—a committee of the Modern Language Association of America took on the editorship. The Fourth Variorum is a vast work, containing annotations, textual notes, and excerpts from eminent commentators throughout the history of Shakespearean criticism.

Cumulative Index to Topics

[The Cumulative Index to Topics identifies the principal topics of debate in the criticism of each play. The topics are arranged alphabetically; page references indicate the beginning page number of those excerpts offering substantial commentary on that topic.]

Antony and Cleopatra   (Vol. 6)

ambiguity or ambivalence, role of: pp. 53, 111, 161, 163, 180, 189, 208, 211, 228
Antony
    dotage or sensuality: pp. 22, 23, 38, 41, 48, 52, 62, 107, 136, 146, 175
    Hercules, compared with: pp. 41, 172, 211
    magnanimity or generosity: pp. 22, 23, 24, 38
    mixture of Roman and Egyptian traits: pp. 31, 181
    nature of love for Cleopatra: pp. 25, 27, 37, 39, 48, 52, 53, 62, 67, 71, 76, 85, 100, 125, 131, 133, 136, 142, 151, 161, 163, 165, 180, 192
    nobility, question of: pp. 22, 24, 33, 48, 94, 103, 136, 142, 159, 172, 202
    political conduct: pp. 33, 38, 53, 107, 111, 146, 181
    public and private personae, conflict between: p. 165
    as a superhuman figure: pp. 37, 51, 71, 92, 94, 178, 192
    as a tragic hero: pp. 38, 39, 52, 53, 60, 104, 120, 151, 155, 165, 178, 192, 202, 211
    tragic self-knowledge, question of: pp. 120, 131, 175, 181, 192
Cleopatra
    contradictory or inconsistent nature: pp. 23, 24, 27, 67, 76, 100, 104, 115, 136, 151, 159, 202
    creativity: p. 197
    her death: pp. 23, 25, 27, 41, 43, 52, 60, 64, 76, 94, 100, 103, 120, 131, 133, 136, 140, 146, 161, 165, 180, 181, 192, 197, 208

nature of love for Antony: pp. 25, 27, 37, 39, 48, 52, 53, 62, 67, 71, 76, 85, 100, 125, 131, 133, 136, 142, 151, 161, 163, 165, 180, 192
    as a subverter of social order: pp. 146, 165
    as a superhuman figure: pp. 37, 51, 71, 92, 94, 178, 192
    as a tragic heroine: pp. 53, 120, 151, 192, 208
    as a voluptuary or courtesan: pp. 21, 22, 25, 41, 43, 52, 53, 62, 64, 67, 76, 146, 161
    variety and/or magnetism: pp. 24, 38, 40, 43, 48, 53, 76, 104, 115, 155
comic or realistic elements: pp. 52, 85, 104, 125, 131, 151, 192, 202, 219
contemptus mundi, theme of: pp. 85, 133
Dryden's *All for Love,* compared with: pp. 20, 21
Egyptian and Roman values, conflict between: pp. 31, 33, 43, 53, 104, 111, 115, 125, 142, 155, 159, 178, 181, 211, 219
Enobarbus: pp. 22, 23, 27, 43, 94, 120, 142
irony or paradox: pp. 53, 136, 146, 151, 159, 161, 189, 192, 211, 224
language and imagery: pp. 21, 25, 39, 64, 80, 85, 92, 94, 100, 104, 142, 146, 155, 159, 161, 165, 189, 192, 202, 211
love or passion, theme of: pp. 51, 64, 71, 80, 85, 100, 115, 159, 165, 180
Octavius: pp. 22, 24, 31, 38, 43, 53, 62, 107, 125, 146, 178, 181, 219
political and social disintegration, theme of: pp. 31, 80, 146
reason and imagination or passion, theme of: pp. 107, 115, 142, 197, 228

reconciliation or regeneration, theme of: pp. 100, 103, 125, 131, 159, 181
religious or supernatural elements: pp. 53, 94, 111, 115, 178, 192, 224
Roman imperialism and political conflict: pp. 43, 53, 60, 71, 80, 100, 107, 111, 180, 197, 219
royalty, theme of: p. 94
Seleucus episode (Act V, Scene ii): pp. 39, 41, 62, 133, 140, 151
Shakespeare's major tragedies, compared with: pp. 25, 53, 60, 71, 120, 181, 189, 202
Shakespeare's moral judgment of the protagonists, question of: pp. 33, 37, 38, 41, 48, 51, 64, 76, 111, 125, 136, 140, 146, 163, 175, 189, 202, 211, 228
sources: pp. 20, 39
unity and/or structure: pp. 20, 21, 22, 24, 25, 32, 33, 39, 43, 53, 60, 67, 111, 125, 146, 151, 165, 208, 211, 219
wheel of fortune, motif of: pp. 25, 178

As You Like It   (Vol. 5)

autobiographical elements: pp. 25, 35, 43, 50, 55, 61
characterization: pp. 19, 24, 25, 36, 39, 54, 82, 86, 116, 148
Christian elements: pp. 39, 98, 162
dramatic shortcomings: pp. 19, 42, 52, 61, 65
duration of time: pp. 44, 45
Forest of Arden
    as a "bitter" Arcadia: pp. 98, 118, 162
    contrast with Duke Frederick's court: pp. 46, 102, 103, 112, 130, 156

Topic Index

Topic Index

Cumulative Index to Critics

Critic Index

Critic Index

Critic Index